A BIOGRAPHICAL DICTIONARY OF
BRITISH
ARCHITECTS
1600–1840

★   ★   ★

Howard Colvin
Fellow of St John's College
Oxford

John Murray
FIFTY ALBEMARLE STREET LONDON
1978

Printed in Great Britain by
Butler & Tanner Ltd.,
Frome and London
0 7195 3328 7

Contents

PREFACE   7

ACKNOWLEDGEMENTS   10

ADVERTISEMENT   14

ABBREVIATIONS   16

INTRODUCTION   17

BIOGRAPHICAL DICTIONARY   43

APPENDICES

   A   Some Buildings erected before 1840 to the designs of Victorian Architects not included in this Dictionary   969

   B   Names included in *A Biographical Dictionary of English Architects 1660–1840,* but excluded from the present work   973

   C   Public Offices held by Architects 1600–1840   976

ADDENDA   986

INDEX OF PERSONS   987

INDEX OF PLACES

   I   BRITISH ISLES   1015

   II   OTHER COUNTRIES   1079

Preface

AFTER TWENTY YEARS in print, *A Biographical Dictionary of English Architects 1660–1840* needed a new lease of life if it were to serve another generation of architectural historians. For those twenty years have seen a sustained activity in extending our knowledge of British architecture equalled only by the collaborative enterprise which between 1852 and 1892 produced the Architectural Publication Society's *Dictionary*. In this activity *A Biographical Dictionary of English Architects 1660–1840* has played its part by attempting to provide that hard foundation of ascertainable fact without which no historical edifice can safely be erected. But by 1974 scarcely a page that was printed in 1954 could stand without amplification or correction. Not only did many bald and inadequate notices need expansion, but many new ones called for inclusion, and some old ones for exclusion.

This is, however, rather more than merely a revised edition of the 1954 Dictionary. Its scope has been extended both in time and in space. Chronologically the starting date is now 1600 instead of 1660, and biographies of Scottish and Welsh as well as of English architects have been included for the first time. The name of Inigo Jones is perhaps enough in itself to justify the extra sixty years, and the careers of Campbell, Gibbs, Adam, Mylne and Burn serve to demonstrate the close links which existed between English and Scottish architectural practice from the Union onwards, if not before. For the continued exclusion of Irish architects no excuse is needed, since a comprehensive Dictionary of Irish Architects is in active preparation by a consortium of Irish architectural historians. As for the years after 1840, my determination to stray no further into the reign of Victoria will be fully justified by the publication of a companion *Dictionary of Victorian Architects* by Dr J. Mordaunt Crook and Mr Paul Joyce.

Apart from these chronological and topographical extensions, in what ways does this book differ from its predecessor? In principle very little, but the intervening twenty years have made it possible to investigate many new sources and to exploit some old ones in a much more systematic manner than could be attempted in the 1950s. Many documents that then had to be arduously sought out in the muniment rooms of remote country houses are now readily accessible in County Record Offices. Many drawings that were once hidden in the recesses of the R.I.B.A. Library have now been made the subject of an admirable catalogue. Twenty years travelling about the British Isles has also enabled me to see many buildings whose architectural character was at best imperfectly known to me in 1954, and thus to form a clearer idea of the stylistic personality of many individual architects. Too marked an expression of personal opinion would be out of place in a work of reference, but I hope that the attempt to indicate (however briefly and inadequately) the character and quality of the work of at least the more notable architects in this book will meet with the approval of its readers. In forming these brief assessments I have often had recourse to Sir Nikolaus Pevsner's *Buildings of England*, and the photographic archives of the two National Monuments Records in London and Edinburgh have been of great value.

Although more comprehensive in coverage and more consistent in treatment than its predecessor, this Dictionary is of course far from being definitive. Anyone who is familiar with the processes of historical research will be aware that a work of this kind can be no more than a stopping-place on a road that has no end. The more one knows, the more possibilities for further research open before one, and no one is more conscious than myself that the sources for the biography of British architects between 1600 and 1840 have not been exhausted by this book. This is particularly true of the many provincial architects whose careers can only be investigated on a local basis. J. D. Bennett's *Leicestershire Architects 1700–1850* (1968), David Walker's article on the Stirlings of Dunblane, and the catalogue (by Angus Taylor and Jeffrey Haworth) of the recent Webster Exhibition at Kendal show in different ways what can be achieved by painstaking local research to reconstruct the careers of those provincial architects who did so much to shape our towns and villages. Much more work of this sort remains to be done. And there are many individual buildings of importance whose architects have yet to be identified. If the designers of, say, Lees Court, Kent, the Castle Ashby screen, Tredegar House, Barnsley Park, or Shobdon Church could be established, some of the biographies in this Dictionary might read very differently. Here it may be appropriate to say that in this book, as in its predecessor, I have been cautious in admitting attributions based solely on stylistic criteria. In general, such attributions have been included only when they have seemed to me to be so compelling as to amount almost to certainty, and only when documentary evidence appears to be lacking. To clear away the undergrowth of irresponsible attribution that impeded British architectural scholarship earlier in this century was one of the main objectives of *A Biographical Dictionary of English Architects 1660–1840*, and (without of course denying that stylistic attribution has its place in architectural research) a book such as this is no place for speculative guess-work.

In *A Biographical Dictionary of English Architects* it was stated that my aim had been to include everyone 'who habitually made, or may be presumed to have made, architectural designs'. Broadly speaking that still remains true of the present work. But in the state of knowledge prevailing in 1954 it was necessary to include the names of many men for whose architectural activity there was no more evidence than a single exhibit at the Royal Academy, or an ambiguous reference in some document where the distinction between 'architect' and 'builder' was far from clear. Their *bona fides* as architects was in many cases uncertain, and their inclusion in the Dictionary was provisional. After the lapse of twenty years, some of them have emerged as authentic architectural personalities. Others, however, can now be presumed to have died young, to have abandoned architecture for some other career, or to have been in reality no more

8

than executant craftsmen. As such they have now been excluded together with many more of their kind whose names have come to light since 1954. To have included all these architectural nonentities would have encumbered the pages of this Dictionary to little purpose. They have accordingly been omitted, but for convenience of reference their names have been printed in Appendix B, together with a codified indication of the reason for their exclusion. Their places have been more than filled by the names of some 400 English and 250 Scottish and Welsh architects who did not find a place in the 1954 Dictionary.

Many mistakes in *A Biographical Dictionary of English Architects* have been corrected, but in a work of this size new errors will inevitably have arisen, and I can only beg the indulgence of those who may detect inaccuracies that have escaped my vigilance.

OXFORD
December 1975

Acknowledgements

So MANY PEOPLE have, in one way or another, contributed to the writing of this Dictionary that it has assumed almost the character of a cooperative work. My debt to those who have answered my queries or volunteered information is correspondingly great. In 1975, as in 1954, I have benefited greatly from the help and advice of Sir John Summerson. To the late Rupert Gunnis, my genial ally in many joint expeditions in search of architectural records, I also owe much. But no one has contributed more information – or imparted it with more generosity – than Mr. John Harris, the Curator of the R.I.B.A. Drawings Collection.

In England and Wales I have been fortunate in a number of local correspondents who have sent me news of architectural discoveries and answered innumerable queries: in Derbyshire Mr. Edward Saunders, in Devonshire Professor W. G. Hoskins, in Essex Miss Nancy Briggs, in Gloucestershire Mr. David Verey, in Lancashire Mr. Peter Fleetwood-Hesketh and Mr. S. A. Harris, in Lincolnshire Mrs. Joan Varley, in Norfolk Mr. A. Paget Baggs and Mr. David Young, in Northamptonshire Mr. Bruce Bailey, the late Sir Gyles Isham and Mr. P. I. King, in Shropshire Miss M. C. Hill and Mr. James Lawson, in Suffolk Mr. J. Bensusan-Butt, in Yorkshire Dr. Eric Gee, in Wales Mr. Peter Howell and Mr. J. D. K. Lloyd.

In Scotland the late Ian Lindsay formed a small committee to assist me, and but for the unstinted help of its members the Scottish biographies could scarcely have been written. Miss Catherine Cruft and Mr. David Walker not only initiated me into the mysteries of *sasines* and *sederunts*, but freely imparted their immense knowledge of Scottish architects and architecture. No less great is my debt to Dr. and Mrs. Alistair Rowan for the generous hospitality which for five successive summers enabled me to work in Edinburgh in ideal conditions. Other Scottish architectural historians to whom I owe much are Mr. J. G. Dunbar, Mr. Colin McWilliam, Mr. Basil Skinner and Dr. A. A. Tait.

For help in specialised fields I have to thank Canon B. F. L. Clarke (Anglican churches), Mr. Denis Evinson (Catholic churches), Mr. Brinsley Ford (English architects in Italy), Dr. Eileen Harris (architectural books of the eighteenth century), Mr. Paul Quarrie (architectural bibliography), Mr. Peter Reid (destroyed country houses) and Professor A. W. Skempton (engineer-architects).

For information about individual architects I am indebted to Miss Juliet Allan (Henry Flitcroft), Mr. A. Atkinson (John Shaw), Mr. John Baily (Thomas Rickman), Mr. T. Benton (William Dickinson), Mr. Marcus Binney (Sir Robert Taylor), Mr. D. E. Chaffin (Charles Humfrey), Dr. J. Mordaunt Crook (Sir Robert Smirke), Mrs. J. Crosby (Ignatius Bonomi), Mr. P. Denney (Charles Fowler), Mr. J. E. Dimacopoulos (Sir George Whitmore), Mr. Kerry Downes

10

(Sir John Vanbrugh), Mr. Ian Fisher (Thomas Hamilton), Dr. J. M. Frew (James Wyatt), Dr. Andor Gomme (Francis Smith), Mr. C. Gotch (Robert Mylne), Miss Hilda Grieve (James Fenton), Dr. Eileen Harris (Thomas Wright), Mr. William Hawkes (Sanderson Millar), Dr. T. P. Hudson (G. Leoni), Mr. E. H. Jamilly (John Davies), Mr. D. W. Johnson (David Stephenson), Mr. I. Wyn Jones (John Nash), Mr. James Lawson (T. F. Pritchard), Dr. Peter Leach (James Paine), Mr. Paul F. Norton (S. P. Cockerell), Mr. J. O'Callaghan (Daniel Robertson), Mr. R. M. O'Donnell (W. J. Donthorn), Mr. J. D. Potts (John Platt), Miss M. A. Powel (W. F. Pocock), Mr. Tony Preedy and Mr. Ian Stewart (T. E. Owen), Mr. Hugh Roberts (Joseph Bonomi), Mr. P. A. Robb (John Johnson), Dr. J. M. Robinson (the Wyatts), Mr. T. Scott (William Newton of Newcastle), Mrs. Ann Simpson (John Baxter), Mr. James Simpson (William Adam), Miss Dorothy Stroud (Lancelot Brown, Henry Holland and Sir John Soane), Mr. R. Stanley-Morgan (B. D. Wyatt), Mr. Angus Taylor (George Webster), Mr. Nigel Temple (John Nash), Mr. John Titterton (Joseph Badger), Mr. B. G. Ward (the Wyatts), Dr. David Watkin (C. R. Cockerell and Charles Kelsall), Mr. P. Wenham (John Foss), Mr. Roger White (Isaac Ware), Mr. Laurence Whistler (Sir John Vanbrugh), Mr. L. M. Wodehouse (Henry Bell), Mr. Anthony Wood (Sanderson Miller) and Mr. R. B. Wragg (John Carr).

Others whose help I wish particularly to acknowledge are Mr. John Addy, Miss Patricia Allderidge, Mr. Hollis C. Baker, Professor M. W. Barley, Mr. Stephen Bayley, Mr. G. W. Beard, Mr. F. Beckwith, Dr. Robert Beddard, Mr. Alan Bell, Mr. Noel Blakiston, Mr. J. A. Booth, Dr. L. O. Boynton, Mr. Paul Breman, Mr. C. E. B. Brett, Mr. B. Brotherton, Mr. L. D. Butler, Mr. Donald Buttress, Mr. R. G. Cant, Mr. A. G. Chamberlain, Mr. V. C. Chamberlain, Mr. Martin Chapman, Mrs. Bridget Cherry, Professor M. L. Clarke, Mr. Alec Clifton-Taylor, Mr. T. H. Cocke, Mrs. J. C. Cole, Mr. T. P. Connor, Mr. John Cornforth, Miss Mary Cosh, Dr. M. J. Craig, Mr. O. E. Craster, Mr. Edward Croft-Murray, Mr. J. Stevens Curl, Mr. Antony Dale, Mr. Michael Darly, Mr. J. H. V. Davies, Mr. David Dean, Mr. A. C. S. Dixon, Mr. Hugh Dixon, Mr. T. M. Doust, Mr. A. I. Doyle, Mr. William Drummond, Mrs. M. P. G. Draper, Professor P. de la R. du Pré, Mr. Peter Eden, Mr. Richard Emerson, Mr. Edmund Esdaile, Mr. R. R. Fedden, Mr. Peter Ferriday, Mr. John Fleming, Fr. James Forbes, O.S.B., Mr. James Frank, Dr. T. F. Friedman, Mr. John Gifford, Mr. Raymond Gill, Mr. John Gloag, Mr. I. H. Goodall, the Duke of Grafton, Mr. Irvine E. Gray, Mr. David Green, Mr. D. N. Griffiths, Mr. D. B. Hague, Dr. Ivan Hall, Mr. Robert Harling, Mr. J. H. Harvey, Mr. V. A. Hatley, Mr. Jeffrey Haworth, Mr. G. Heelis, Mr. N. M. Herbert, Mr. Richard Hewlings, Mr. M. Hildyard, Mr. N. Hirsman, Mr. Hugh Honour, Mr. Peter Howell, Mr. Edward Hubbard, Miss Margaret Hudson, Mr. E. P. Hyslop, Major J. L. Ingram, Mr. M. E. Ingram, Mr. A. S. Ireson, Mr. Walter Ison, Mr. Gervase Jackson-Stops, Miss Ann James, Mr. C. B. Jensen, Mr. Francis Johnson, Professor E. M. Jope, Mr. Paul Joyce, Mr. J. Kegie, Mr. Frank Kelsall, Mr. J. Knight, Mr. J. Lees-Milne, Mr. W. S. Lewis, Mrs. Jill Lever, Dr. Derek Linstrum, Mr. Bryan Little, Miss K. Longley, Mr. H. J. Louw, Mr. B. Mason,

Miss Mary Mauchline, Mr. A. G. Meecham, Mr. B. R. S. Megaw, Miss Priscilla Metcalf, Mrs. Sandra Milliken, Mr. K. S. Mills, Mr. A. Mitchell, Mr. M. C. Morgan, Mr. Nicholas Moore, Mr. Michael McCarthy, Mr. Ian MacIvor, Mr. Edward McParland, Mr. John Newman, Mr. Julian Orbach, Mr. Arthur Oswald, Mr. B. F. J. Pardoe, the Rev. G. H. Parks, Mr. H. Parris, Sir Nikolaus Pevsner, Mr. Claud Phillimore, Professor Stuart Piggott, Mr. M. H. Port, Dr. A. Quiney, Dr. D. R. Ransome, Mr. J. R. Redmill, Mr. V. Rendel, Miss Anne Riches, Mr. G. W. O. Rickword, Mr. T. Ritchie, Mr. M. J. Rix, Mr. R. Michael Robbins, Mr. H. V. Molesworth Roberts, Mr. T. Robinson, Mr. Andrew Saint, Mr. Norman Scarfe, Mr. I. J. Scott, Mr. Derek Sherborne, Miss M. C. Shoubridge, Professor J. Simmons, Mr. G. E. Smith, Mr. W. J. Smith, Sir Robert Somerville, Mr. G. A. Spain, Mr. G. D. Squibb, Mr. Douglas Stewart, Mr. I. H. Stewart, Professor Lawrence Stone, Dr. Norman Summers, Mr. A. C. Taylor, Mr. R. F. Taylor, Mr. Robert Taylor, Mr. Nicholas Thompson, Mr. Robert Thorne, the Rev. Henry Thorold, Dr. Eric Till, Mr. G. E. M. Trinick, Mr. W. A. A. Walls, Mr. Peter Walne, Mr. Andrew Webb, Mr. Ben Weinreb, Mr. Marcus Whiffen, Mr. David Whitehead, Mr. L. H. H. Whitehead, Mrs. Gweneth Whitteridge, Dr. Peter Willis and the Hon. Mrs. Wayland Young.

It is a pleasant duty to acknowledge the kindness (and often the hospitality) of those who have so kindly allowed me to examine documents or drawings in their possession. They include the late Duke of Argyll, the Duke of Beaufort, the late Duke of Buccleuch, the Duke of Devonshire, the Duke of Northumberland, the Duke of Roxburgh, the Duke of Rutland, the Duke of Somerset, the Marquess of Ailesbury, the Marquess of Anglesey, the Marquess of Bath, the Marquess of Lothian, the Marquess of Northampton, the late Marquess of Salisbury, the Marquess of Zetland, the Earl of Ancaster, the Earl of Bradford, the Earl of Coventry, the Earl of Carnarvon, the late Earl Ferrers, Earl Fitzwilliam, the Earl of Harewood, the Earl of Harrowby, the Earl of Lonsdale, the Earl of Oxford and Asquith, the late Earl of Pembroke, the Earl of Shaftesbury, the late Earl Spencer, the Earl of Stamford, the late Earl of Strathmore, Viscount Camrose, Viscount Scarsdale, Lord Braye, Lord Brownlow, the late Lord Camoys, Lord Hotham, Lord Leigh, the late Lord Monson, Lord St Oswald, the late Lord Vernon, the late Lady Catherine Ashburnham, Sir John Clerk of Penicuik, Bart., the late Sir Francis Colchester-Wemyss, Bart., Sir Ivar Colquhoun of Luss, Bart., Sir Richard Graham, Bart., the late Sir Gyles Isham, Bart., Sir John Molesworth-St. Aubyn, Bart., Sir Richard Proby, Bart., Sir John Pole-Carew, Bart., Sir Ralph Verney, Bart., Sir Marcus Worsley, Bart., Sir Francis Hill, Lady Labouchere, Lady Meade-Fetherstonhaugh, Col. Sir Joseph Weld, Miss I. M. Allen, the late Mrs I. Alston-Roberts-West, Mr. A. Andrews, Mr. R. J. R. Arundell, Miss A. C. Baker, the late Mr. J. Bellyse Baker, Mrs. Humphrey Brand, Mrs. H. M. Budgett, the late Mr. R. F. Cartwright, Col. J. Chandos-Pole, Major J. G. B. Chester, Major E. R. F. Compton, Mrs. B. J. Crichton, Mr. T. Cottrell-Dormer, the late Mr. T. L. Cundy, Mrs. J. Curzon-Howe-Herrick, Mrs. P. R. Davies-Cooke, Col. W. M. E. Denison, Mrs. Glynn, Capt. A. Hammond, Major P. Holderness-Roddam, the late Mr. R. H. A. Holbech, Mrs. Eric Houfe, Mr. Simon Houfe, Mr. Henry Jenney, the late

Major F. H. T. Jervoise, Miss E. Johnstone, Mr. M. W. Kelly, the late Mr. R. W. Ketton-Cremer, the Hon. Christopher Lennox-Boyd, Mr. Bernard Levin, Col. A. B. Lloyd-Baker, Mr. A. P. Lyons, Mr. Paul Mellon, the late Mrs. Godfrey Meynell, Mr. Jasper More, Capt. R. W. Morgan-Grenville, Mr. R. A. Morritt, Miss J. M. H. Mylne, Mr. J. Noble, Capt. Richard Orlebar, Mr. N. F. A. Page-Turner, Capt. J. L. Puxley, Mr. A. W. Richmond, Miss E. Sawbridge, Mrs. W. Calcott Stokes, the late Col. N. V. Stopford Sackville, the late Rev. H. W. G. Thursby, the Hon. Mrs. Trollope-Bellew, Mr. Gladwyn Turbutt and the late Mr. George Wyndham.

The officers of the Surveyors' Club have kindly permitted me to examine their records; so have those of the Royal Academy of Arts and the Incorporated Church Building Society. The Church Commissioners have also allowed me to make use of certain of their archives, and I have received much help from the custodians of those public, county, city and diocesan archives which I have had occasion to consult, many of whom have, with characteristic kindness, gone out of their way to find the information of which I was in search. Finally, I have to express my thanks to the many clergymen who have so patiently endured my investigations into their parochial records.

The Arts Council of Great Britain has kindly provided some financial assistance towards the cost of publication.

Advertisement

THE PURPOSE of this book is sufficiently indicated by its title, but there are certain matters of method which require explanation, notably the chronological and topographical scope of the work and the principles upon which individual architects have qualified for inclusion.

My aim has been to include every architect – and by 'architect' I mean anyone, whether amateur, tradesman or professional, who habitually made architectural designs – the major part of whose career falls within the limiting dates. Thus Decimus Burton (1800–1881) has been included because most of his work was done before he was 40, whereas George Edmund Street, who died in the same year, has not because he was active chiefly in the 1850s and 1860s. Inevitably there have been 'borderline' cases, in some of which no doubt another writer would have made different decisions. But I hope that in this as in other respects the element of personal preference has not been sufficiently great to impair the value of this book as a comprehensive record of British architects who practised between 1600 and 1840.

For the purposes of this Dictionary a 'British' architect is one who, irrespective of national origin, practised in England, Scotland or Wales. Architects domiciled in Ireland have been excluded, but many buildings erected in Ireland to the designs of English or Scottish architects have been noted. No attempt has been made to provide full biographies of architects of British origin practising overseas, but a brief survey of their careers has been given together with references to the relevant literature. Many amateur architects have been given a place, but a man whose architectural activity was limited to designing his own house has not normally qualified for inclusion.

So far as possible the works of each architect have been placed in chronological order. When this has not been practicable they have been listed alphabetically. Whenever it has seemed desirable public and private buildings have been listed separately. The dates printed are normally those of construction (rather than of the whole process of design and construction), but in many cases only an approximate date can be given. No attempt has been made to list unexecuted designs on the same basis as executed ones, but attention has often been drawn to important unexecuted designs either in the body of the biography or in a separate section of the list of works. Dates of demolition and alteration have been stated so far as it has been possible to ascertain them, and an attempt has been made to indicate the employment of Gothic and other non-classical styles, though in neither case is it claimed that the information given is complete. The county boundaries referred to are those in force before the Local Government Act of 1972 and therefore correspond closely to those in use during the historical period covered by this Dictionary.

The authority for each entry in the lists of works will be found either at the head of the list or (more often) within *square brackets* immediately after it. References given within *round brackets* are to books and articles (usually illustrated) which describe the building in question but which are not cited as authorities.

Abbreviations

A.P.S.D.	*The Dictionary of Architecture*, ed. Wyatt Papworth for the Architectural Publication Society, 8 vols., 1852-92.
Arch. Rev.	*The Architectural Review.*
Architectural Mag.	*The Architectural Magazine*, ed. J. C. Loudon, 5 vols., 1834–8.
B.M.	British Museum or British Library.
C. Life	*Country Life.*
D.N.B.	*The Dictionary of National Biography.*
dem.	demolished.
exhib.	exhibited.
Gent's Mag.	*The Gentleman's Magazine*, 1731–1868.
G.R.	The card-index of nineteenth-century churches and their architects compiled by the late H. S. Goodhart-Rendel (R.I.B.A. Library and National Monuments Record).
Hist. MSS. Comm.	Historical Manuscripts Commission.
History of the King's Works	*The History of the King's Works*, ed. H. M. Colvin, 6 vols., 1963–
I.C.B.S.	Records of the Incorporated Church Building Society (Lambeth Palace Library).
Jnl.	*Journal.*
N.L.W.	National Library of Wales, Aberystwyth.
N.M.R.S.	The National Monuments Record of Scotland.
N. and Q.	*Notes and Queries.*
N.S.A.	*The New Statistical Account of Scotland*, 15 vols., 1845.
P.C.C.	Prerogative Court of Canterbury (wills in Public Record Office).
P.R.O.	Public Record Office, London.
Port	M. H. Port, *Six Hundred New Churches*, 1961.
R.A.	The Royal Academy of Arts.
R.C.A.M.	The Royal Commission on the Ancient and Historical Monuments of Scotland or The Royal Commission on Ancient Monuments in Wales.
R.C.H.M.	The Royal Commission on Historical Monuments (England).
R.I.B.A.	The Royal Institute of British Architects.
R.I.B.A.D.	The Royal Institute of British Architects Drawings Collection.
S.R.O.	The Scottish Record Office, Register House, Edinburgh.
V.C.H.	*The Victoria County History of England.*
Vitruvius Britannicus	*Vitruvius Britannicus, or the British Architect*, by Colen Campbell, 3 vols., 1715, 1717 and 1725; continued by J. Woolfe & J. Gandon, vol. iv, 1767, vol. v, 1771.
W.A.M.	Westminster Abbey Muniments.
Willis & Clark	R. Willis & J. W. Clark, *The Architectural History of the University of Cambridge*, 3 vols., 1886.
Wren Soc.	*The Wren Society*, 20 vols., 1924–43.

[   ] a reference in square brackets gives the source or authority for the preceding statement or statements.

(   ) a reference in round brackets is to a book or article which describes the building in question but is not cited as an authority.

Introduction

THE PRACTICE OF ARCHITECTURE, 1600–1840

THE ESSAY that follows, prefaced to *A Biographical Dictionary of English Architects 1660–1840*, was a first attempt to trace the origins of the architectural profession in Britain. Since then two valuable studies have appeared, one historical,[1] the other sociological.[2] But it is still appropriate to begin a biographical dictionary of professional men by giving some account of the history of their profession. Indeed, the history of British architecture is bound up with its own practice, and the careers of those architects and master workmen who figure in this dictionary would scarcely be intelligible without some idea of the conditions under which they designed and built. For many of them architecture was a craft rather than an art: it is therefore with the building trades that the first part of this introduction is concerned. The second attempts to trace the rise of the architectural profession in Britain, a process that falls within–indeed very nearly coincides with–the chronological limits of this book. For in 1600 there were no architects in the sense in which we understand the term today. By 1840 there was an established architectural profession, based on a regular system of pupilage and held together by the newly founded Institute of British Architects. This new profession had come into being through the labours and aspirations of those whose names appear in this volume, and a revised account of its history may not inappropriately serve to introduce their careers.

[1] Frank Jenkins, *Architect and Patron*, 1961.
[2] Barrington Kaye, *The Development of the Architectural Profession in Britain*, 1960.

I

The Building Trades

'As to the Masters, most of them live handsomely; and some, who employ many Hands, and undertake large works, commonly called Master-builders, *obtain good Estates; but then they are such who not only have Money at Command, but take great Pains to qualify themselves for Projecting, drawing Plans, surveying and Estimating Buildings'* (A General Description of all Trades, 1747).

IN ITS BUILDING ORGANIZATION, as in so much else, Britain in the seventeenth century was still dependent on the methods of the medieval past. Today, building is managed by a 'contractor' who makes himself responsible for the engagement of workmen skilled in bricklaying, carpentry, masonry and so forth; then, it was in the hands of the individual master workman, for there were as many masters as there were trades, and the bricklayer, the mason, the carpenter, the joiner, the plumber, the glazier, the painter, the smith and the pavior was each the proprietor of a separate yard or workshop, in which he carried on his appropriate craft. These men served an apprenticeship of seven years, then worked as journeymen, and eventually achieved the status of independent master craftsmen. In London at least, the masters of the principal building trades were members of City Companies which still discharged functions which they had inherited from the medieval craft guilds. The Masons' Company, for instance, still carried out searches for 'false' – that is, defective – workmanship, and endeavoured to restrain 'foreign' masons who were not freemen of the City from carrying on their trade in London. But the Great Fire of 1666 did much to break down this always precarious monopoly, for in order to attract labour Parliament enacted that 'foreigners' should be permitted to work in the City, and that if they remained for seven years, they should enjoy the same liberty as freemen for the rest of their lives. The Companies' control, once lost, was never effectively restored, and by the middle of the eighteenth century they had degenerated into societies whose activities were chiefly sociable and charitable.[1]

In any case, the mason's craft was never centred wholly upon the towns. In the seventeenth and early eighteenth centuries it was still closely connected with the quarries from which the stone was derived. Quarrying villages, like Ketton in Rutland and Painswick in Gloucestershire, were nurseries of masons

[1] For the masons, see E. Conder, *The Hole Craft and Fellowship of Masons*, 1894, and D. Knoop & G. P. Jones, *The London Mason in the Seventeenth Century*, 1935: for the carpenters, E. B. Jupp & W. W. Pocock, *Historical Account of the Company of Carpenters*, 2nd ed., 1887, and B. W. E. Alford & T. C. Barker, *A History of the Carpenters Company*, 1968. For the incorporation of building tradesmen in other towns, see D. Knoop & G. P. Jones, *The Mediaeval Mason*, 1933, pp. 229–33.

throughout the period, and many of the best-known master builders traced their origins to some small place of this sort. It was from Raunds in Northampton-shire that the Grumbolds came to work on the Cambridge colleges in the seventeenth century, and it was only the proximity of the Headington quarries that gave Oxford its flourishing school of masons in that and the following century.[2] The Strongs of Taynton, the Platts of Rotherham, and the Wood-wards of Chipping Campden are further examples of masons whose fortunes were laid in the freestone quarries of the Midlands and north of England. The most successful firms were generally those whose capital and experience was handed on from one generation to another, as was the case with the Smiths of Warwick and the Mylnes of Edinburgh: but even within a single lifetime it was possible for a master mason to make a substantial fortune. Samuel Fulkes, for instance, who worked as a mason in London at 2s. 6d. a day in 1664, took small contracts of £9, £14, £117 and £613 in the 1670s, then much larger ones of £1888, £1946, £3204 and £3335 in the 1680s, and ended as one of the prin-cipal masonry contractors for St Paul's Cathedral.[3] Andrews Jelfe, who was one of the builders of Westminster Bridge, left a country house, a flourishing business, considerable London property, and over £30,000 when he died in 1759. Like most of his type, he combined sculpture with building, and the elaborate monu-ments with which it was the custom to commemorate the dead were a profitable source of income to the eighteenth-century master mason. Their production occupied his yard during the three or four months of the year when building in the open was at a standstill,[4] and they gave him scope to exercise his inventive-ness as a designer. For some ability as a draughtsman was essential to his craft: 'he must learn Designing, and to draw all the five Orders of Architecture, according to their several Proportions', wrote Campbell in his *London Trades-man*; 'his skill in Drawing is likewise employed in taking down with his Chalk upon the Block of Stone, from the Architect's Plan, the Out-lines of any Figure, Moulding, or Scroll, that is to be cut; In a word, without Drawing and Figures he cannot make a Stone-Mason, unless he is to be employed only in cutting and squaring Flag-Stones. It is an ingenious genteel Craft, and not unprofitable. The Master may be ranked among the first Rank of Tradesmen; and the Jour-neyman, when employed, makes Three Shillings a Day, or at least Half a Crown.'[5]

Equally profitable were the trades of the bricklayer and the carpenter – the latter being in many cases combined with that of the joiner.[6] The former, in 1600, was chiefly to be found in the neighbourhood of London, and in counties

[2] For the Headington quarries, see W. J. Arkell, *Oxford Stone*, 1947.

[3] D. Knoop & G. P. Jones, 'The Rise of the Mason Contractor', *R.I.B.A. Jnl.*, ser. 3, vol. 43, No. 20, 1936, 1063.

[4] 'They are idle about four Months of the Year, unless they have some skill in sculpture, in which they may be employed all the Year', says Campbell in *The London Tradesman*, 1747, 159.

[5] R. Campbell, *The London Tradesman*, 1747, 158–9.

[6] 'Carpentry and Joinery ... are often performed by the same Persons though the work of these is much lighter and generally reckoned more curious than that of the Carpenters, for a good Joiner can often do both well, but every Carpenter cannot work at Joinery, especially the nicer Parts of it' (*A General Description of all Trades*, 1747, 124). The plumbing and glazing trades were also fre-quently combined.

such as Norfolk and Suffolk, where stone was not readily accessible: but his influence was to spread rapidly as the use of his material became general in the eighteenth century, and the London Rebuilding Act of 1667 set a standard in domestic brickwork which soon affected building practice throughout the country.[7] The extension of the bricklayer's trade to districts such as Herefordshire and Cheshire was to some extent achieved at the expense of the master carpenter, whose 'black-and-white' architecture had hitherto been the rule in those counties. Certainly there is no example in the eighteenth century of a master carpenter such as John Abel of Hereford (d. 1675), whose timber-framed market-houses are among the outstanding monuments of his craft. But the bricklayer could not dispense with the services of the carpenter altogether. He could and did undertake to 'build by the great' – that is, 'to make an estimate of the total expence of a House . . . and contract for the execution of the whole for the amount of (his) estimate'.[8] But it must be remembered that the training and equipment of an eighteenth-century master workman were confined to his own craft: 'if he was a bricklayer, he would have to sublet the carpentry: if he was a carpenter he must sublet the bricklaying; and in either case he must put all the minor trades into other hands'.[9]

This subcontracting was often accomplished by a species of barter whereby one tradesman aided another in the performance of his appropriate task, thus reducing cash payments to the minimum and making it possible for a group of tradesmen to undertake considerable enterprises with much less capital than would otherwise be necessary. Thus, in speculative building, it was not uncommon for the chief promoter or 'undertaker' to offer his associates a share in the new development in return for work performed or materials delivered. Richard Frith, the builder of the London street which bears his name, adopted this expedient in 1687–8 in connection with a project for laying out a new street of houses on the site of the Royal Mews in St. James's Park. The list of his associates, which has been preserved, includes a mason, a brickmaker, a bricklayer, a carver, and two joiners, each of whom was to receive a plot in the 'new intended streete' in proportion to the amount of 'worke [by him] wrought, or goods sold and delivered'.[10] Speculative building brought great rewards, but it was also attended with great risks, and the names of its victims figure prominently in eighteenth-century bankruptcy lists. 'Both Carpenters and Joiners' – to quote Campbell once more – 'are Undertakers in Building as well as the Master-Bricklayers; and are liable to split upon the same Rock of Building-Projects: But a Gentleman who wants to build with Security as well as Beauty, would do well not to trust entirely to their Skill.'[11] There was, in fact, general agreement among seventeenth- and eighteenth-century architectural writers

---

[7] On this subject, cf. G. F. Webb in *R.I.B.A. Jnl.*, 27 May 1933, 580, and *The Journeys of Celia Fiennes*, ed. C. Morris, 1949, 179 (a new brick house 'in the exact forme of the London architecture'), 183 (houses at Liverpool 'new built of brick and stone after the London fashion').

[8] Thos. Mortimer, *The Universal Director*, 1763.

[9] John Summerson, *Georgian London*, 1945, 60.

[10] B.M., Add. MS. 16370, f. 115. It was by similar methods that in 1819–20 John Nash built the Regent Street Quadrant as a personal speculation (John Summerson, *John Nash*, 1935, 220).

[11] *The London Tradesman*, 1747, 161.

that to put all the work into the hands of a single 'undertaker' was to court disaster.[12] Sir Roger Pratt warned his readers against it,[13] and so did Sir Christopher Wren.

> There are 3 ways of working [he wrote to the Bishop of Oxford in 1681]: by the Day, by Measure, by Great; if by the Day it tells me when they are Lazy. If by measure it gives me light on every particular, and tells me what I am to provide. If by the Great I can make a sure bargain neither to be overreached nor to hurt the undertaker: for in things they are not every day used to, they doe often injure themselves, and when they begin to find it, they shuffle and slight the worke to save themselves. I think the best way in this business is to worke by measure: according to the prices in the Estimate or lower if you can, and measure the work at 3 or 4 measurements as it rises. But you must have an understanding trusty Measurer, there are few that are skilled in measuring stone worke, I have bred up 2 or 3.[14]

The first method advocated by Wren was the direct labour system, which can be traced back to early medieval practice. Thus when the churchwardens of Marlow rebuilt their Church House in 1717 they found the materials (which cost them £48 : 16 : 2½) themselves, and paid the workmen employed by the day. Thomas Gray, bricklayer, received £4 : 4 : 2 for 50 days' work at 20d. a day, and the other men employed were engaged on a similar basis.[15] Building 'by measure' was probably less troublesome, but involved the expense of employing a measurer or surveyor. Most architects were prepared to act as measuring surveyors and although the engagement of a surveyor did not necessarily mean going to him for the design,[16] the two functions were so intimately associated that the terms 'architect' and 'surveyor' were almost synonymous in eighteenth-century parlance.[17] Master builders too were not infrequently employed in this capacity, and according to *A General Description of all Trades* (1747) many of

[12] The practice was forbidden by the Carpenters' Company in 1607 on the ground that 'the King's majesty's subjects being owners of the building are very much and often deceived of true and substantial stuff and workmanship' thereby (Jupp & Pocock, *Historical Account of the Company of Carpenters*, 2nd ed., 1887, 149). The Fellows of St. John's College, Cambridge, found too late that it was a 'way of building not so allowable in works intended for posterity' when they entrusted the erection of their Second Court to two undertakers in 1598–1602 (Willis and Clark, ii, 249), and it was bitter experience of the ways of a contractor (the architect-builder Thomas Johnson) which led the Justices of Warwick to resolve in 1790 'that no contract for building the whole Gaol shall be made with one person' (Warwickshire County Records, Q.S. Class 24 (h)).

[13] 'We shall not only do great prejudice to our building but also in putting out our work by the great, be most exceedingly abused, and overreached by our workmen' (*The Architecture of Sir Roger Pratt*, ed. Gunther, 1928, 48).

[14] *Wren Soc.* v, 20. See also Pratt, *op. cit.*, 141.

[15] *Records of Bucks.* xv, 1947, 6.

[16] Thus William Baker (*q.v.*) frequently acted as surveyor of churches and other buildings which he did not design.

[17] 'A good surveyor of Building, or such as wee call Architects' (Roger North, *Of Building*, f. 7ᵛ); 'architects and surveyors (the terms are now synonymous)' (J. Noble, *The Professional Practice of Architects*, 1836, 19). Johnstone's *Commercial Street Directory* of 1817 gives 108 men who called themselves 'Architect and Surveyor', or 'Surveyor and Architect', but only one who called himself simply 'Architect'. He was Sir John Soane, whose views on the subject were printed in *The Artist* xiv, 13 July 1807.

them made it their 'chief business' to 'survey and estimate other Men's Works'.[18]

That they made designs, both for themselves and for one another, there is abundant evidence, and the author of *The City and Countrey Purchaser and Builder's Dictionary* (1703) was of the opinion that 'there be many Master-workmen that will contrive a Building and draw a Draught, or Design thereof, as well as most (and better than some) Surveyors'. But in the seventeenth century it was still not uncommon – especially in country circles – for the builder to be told to take an existing building as his model. When the tower of Crondall Church in Hampshire was rebuilt in 1659, the churchwardens 'went about looking at other towers, and eventually fixed upon the tower of Battersea Church as the best pattern to go by'. They then sent their workmen to measure it up and build their own in similar fashion.[19] And contracts not infrequently specify that a chimney-stack or an ornamental feature shall be 'like unto or better than' some chosen example of its kind.[20]

It was in this way that the ideas of the London architect percolated slowly into the consciousness of the local master builder. Reminiscences of the Banqueting House in Whitehall, for instance, can be seen in buildings erected in many parts of the country during the seventeenth century. But Inigo Jones's carefully composed façade did not lend itself easily to the rule-of-thumb methods of the country builder, and at Brympton D'Evercy in Somerset (*c.* 1680) the mason has managed his fenestration so clumsily that the terminal pediment at one end is segmental in form while that at the other is triangular. The more empirical, less uncompromisingly Italianate architecture of Wren and his contemporaries adapted itself more readily to imitation by the master builder, and the employment of large numbers of country workmen in the rebuilding of London did much to impress the salient features of the new style upon their minds.[21]

But the degree of control even in the case of works erected under the immediate supervision of the Surveyor-General or one of his colleagues was often far from complete, and it is necessary to distinguish carefully between those few buildings for which he made working drawings and those many others for which he merely 'gave a model' to be interpreted 'in the ordinary language of the London builders'.[22] Wren's City churches, in particular, were the result

---

[18] Venterus Mandey (*q.v.*), for instance, acted as 'measurer' at the building of a house at Barn Elms in 1694–5 (accounts formerly at Aynho Park, Northants.).

[19] C. D. Stokes, *A History of Crondall and Yateley*, 1905, 8.

[20] 'The workmanship of the ffront next the Street not to be inferior to Mr. Honylove's building in ornament' (contract, dated 1668, to build a house in Gracechurch Street, London, among archives of St. John's College, Oxford); 'The Frontespeice and Lucron windowes [and other details] to be like them at Battlesdon' (contract, dated Feb. 1673/4, to build Holme Lacy House, Herefordshire: P.R.O., Chancery Masters' Exhibits, Duchess of Norfolk deeds, Box M, Bundle 24, No. 7789); the water-table, stools of windows of upper stories to be of Portland stone, 'moulded as the Earl of Ranelagh's at Chelsea', the 'severall stackes of chimneys shall be headed with Portland stone as they are at Arlington House' (contract, dated Nov. 1692, to build a house at Petersham for the Earl of Rochester: Surrey County Record Office, S.C. 13/26/102).

[21] For a striking example of this, see the account of the rebuilding of Newent Church, below, p. 811. See also *Wren Soc.* vii, 72.

[22] The quotation is from an unpublished paper by Sir John Summerson on the architecture of the London Temple, which he has kindly allowed me to read in MS.

of cooperation between the Surveyor-General and the highly competent craftsmen whom he employed – men who were quite capable of designing and building a church without the supervision of a member of the Royal Society. And to a great extent they actually did so: the ceilings, altar-pieces, pulpits and other furnishings were usually designed by those who executed them. Sometimes they submitted a drawing or a model to Wren or one of his colleagues: but more often they did not, and it is a tribute to the high standard of contemporary craftsmanship that the resultant interiors were so rarely disharmonious.

It was doubtless inevitable that an architect with so many churches in course of erection at the same time should exercise but a loose control over the details of their execution, especially as the interior fittings were the financial responsibility of the parishes concerned. But that precisely the same methods were followed by a fashionable country-house architect of the period is shown by the papers of Captain William Winde, the architect of Hampstead Marshall (1663 onwards), Combe Abbey (1682–5) and Castle Bromwich (1685–90). Having determined the architectural features of the building in consultation with his client, he assembled a team of craftsmen who submitted designs for the decorative features – ceilings, pediments and gateways – which they were prepared to execute. Their 'draughts' were then signed and dated by the architect to show that they had been 'allowed'.[23] Pierce the carver and Goudge the plasterer both designed their own work in this way and their draughtsmanship is, if anything, more accomplished than that of Winde himself.[24]

Buildings of the period between 1660 and 1720 represent one of the high-water marks of English architectural craftsmanship. How long it was capable of maintaining itself at this level it is impossible to conjecture, for once more the skill of the master workman had to adjust itself to a change of taste – one which was in the long run to prove fatal to his artistic self-sufficiency. There was no room in the Palladian dictatorship initiated by Lord Burlington for the individualism of a Pierce or a Goudge: Vitruvian precedent took the place of personal inventiveness, and although the craftsmanship remains of the highest quality, from about 1730 it is doing the will of the architect to an extent which it had never done before. The pressure of this new architectural discipline was to increase until, by the end of the eighteenth century, the craftsman had sunk to the level of a mere executant, dependent for every detail upon the working drawings supplied by the architect.

The loss of status suffered by the individual craftsman was grievous: instead of being, like Grinling Gibbons or Edward Goudge, 'looked on as the beste master in England in his profession', he was in danger of being classed with what Robert Adam called 'those reptile artisans who have crawled about and infested this country for many years'.[25] But the master builder was not without

[23] Bodleian Library, MS. Gough Drawings a.2; MS. Gough Warwicks. 1.

[24] In 1688 Winde told Lady Bridgeman of Castle Bromwich that Goudge had 'bine employed by mee this 6 or 7 yeares, is an excelent draufftsman and mackes all his desines himeselfe' (letter quoted by G. W. Beard in *Decorative Plasterwork in Great Britain*, 1975, 48). For Pierce, see below, pp. 635–7.

[25] A. T. Bolton, *The Architecture of R. and J. Adam* i, 54. Chambers writes contemptuously of 'the mechanics who assume the profession and arrogate the title of architects', and similar outbursts

his resources: he was neither illiterate nor penurious, and he hastened to buy and to read the folios by means of which Lord Burlington and his circle sought to make converts to their architectural ideals. Leoni's edition of *Palladio*, Campbell's *Vitruvius Britannicus* and Kent's *Designs of Inigo Jones* were the text-books of the new Palladianism, and the printed lists of subscribers include the names of a number of masons, carpenters and joiners. James Gibbs followed suit with his *Rules for Drawing the Several Parts of Architecture*, in which he taught a simplified method of measurement calculated to appeal to the practical builder, who could scarcely be expected to grasp the mysteries of modular proportion. Within a few years, the building craftsman had at his disposal an astonishing number of these manuals, many of them written by men of his own class, like William Halfpenny and Batty Langley, who seem to have found their production more profitable even than building. The bibliography of the architectural pattern-books is, indeed, enormous, and their diffusion does more than anything else to explain the high standard of provincial building in the mid-eighteenth century. Most of them are nowadays exceedingly rare, and the condition of surviving copies suggests that in many cases they were literally thumbed to pieces in the builders' yards.

The pattern-book made it possible for the builder-architect to survive well into the second half of the eighteenth century. But with the reign of George III the tides of British taste began to ebb and flow with ever-increasing rapidity, and as the neo-classical challenged the Palladian, and the Grecian confronted the Gothic, it became yearly more difficult for the builder-architect to hold his own against the professional. While his artistic self-sufficiency was thus being imperilled, his status as an independent craftsman was being jeopardized by economic causes beyond his control. How he reacted to the economic crises of the late eighteenth century has yet to be determined.[26] Nor is it clear how far the Napoleonic wars, by curtailing both public and private building, may have affected the fortunes of the smaller building businesses. What is certain is that the extensive architectural activity of the early nineteenth century – the era of 'metropolitan improvement' in London, of the 'second New Town' in Edinburgh, and of much building and rebuilding of churches and country houses throughout the two kingdoms – brought opportunities for a new type of builder who was more of an entrepreneur than a craftsman. For these were the years which saw the rise of the building contractor, who without being the master of any specific trade himself, engaged a full staff of workmen on a permanent wage basis, and was able to take on contracts which before would have been divided between two or three independent master builders. When contracts were not forthcoming, he developed land in order to keep his men

---

against the builder-architect occur in the prefaces to Leoni's *Palladio* (1715) and Gibbs's *Book of Architecture* (1728). See also J. Gwynn, *London and Westminster Improved*, 1766, 31, 67; Soane in *The Artist* xiv, 1807, 2; J. A. Bell, *A Letter to Lord Farnborough on the expediency of having a Chartered Society for the Advancement and Protection of Architecture*, 1834, 8; and J. Noble. *The Professional Practice of Architects*, 1836, 40.

[26] The effect of these crises on the volume of building (though not on the structure of the building trades) has been studied by T. S. Ashton, *Economic Fluctuations in England 1700–1800*, 1959, 84–105.

employed. The first of this new type of general builder was Thomas Cubitt, whose methods became the model for the great Victorian contractors.[27] Many who a generation earlier would have set up as independent master builders were now content to accept the position of employees and shelter themselves under the wing of a Cubitt or a Peto. Thus economic change, combined with the growing eclecticism of nineteenth-century taste, brought about the extinction of the independent master builder, leaving the field to the building contractor on the one hand, and to the architect on the other. The old type of builder persisted longer in the country than he did in the towns, but by 1840 it would have been difficult to discover a worthy representative of a class which had once stood for so much that was admirable in the history of British architecture.

[27] For these developments see E. W. Cooney, 'The Origins of the Victorian Master Builders', *Economic History Review*, 2nd ser., viii, 1955, and M. H. Port, 'The Office of Works and Early 19th-century Building Contracts', *ibid.* xx, 1967. For Cubitt himself see below, pp. 243–4.

The Architectural Profession

'You must be aware that Architecture is the profession of a Gentleman, and that none is more lucrative when it is properly attended to': Mrs James Wyatt to her son Philip, 1808 (B.M., Egerton MS. 3515).

THE ARCHITECT as we know him today is a product of the Renaissance. This does not mean that the architect, in the sense of 'one who both furnishes the designs and superintends the erection of buildings',[1] had been unknown in the Middle Ages. But the medieval architect was a master craftsman (usually a mason or a carpenter by trade), one who could build as well as design, or at least 'one trained in that craft even if he had ceased to ply his axe and chisel'.[2] He was a master workman whose skill was based on a technical experience of building rather than on a theoretical knowledge of architecture as an art. The word 'architect' itself, used by the ancients in much the same sense as it is by ourselves, came in the Middle Ages to be regarded as the equivalent of 'master mason' or 'master carpenter'.[3]

It was, then, the mason and the carpenter who were the architects of the Middle Ages. That some of them were men of genius cannot be denied, and even if architecture did not rank as a 'liberal art', there is evidence that those who practised it as masters enjoyed a certain status in the society of their time. The recognition that there were able men in the medieval building world, and that those men deserve the name of 'architect', does not, however, imply that their functions were identical with those of architects in modern times. Architectural practice has evolved together with the society which it serves. A modern architect is a professional man set aside from the building trade by education and specialized training. His architectural expertise is acquired by academic instruction rather than by practical experience, and his approach to design is theoretical rather than empirical. When he designs a building he envisages it as a whole and works it out in detail on paper before transmitting the drawings to the executant builder. The medieval architect, on the other hand, was normally a craftsman by training, and frequently acted as one of the executants of the buildings he himself designed. That he was capable of envisaging a building as a whole we cannot doubt, and there is abundant evidence that he could express his ideas on the drawing-board. But in the Middle Ages the processes of design and construction were much more closely linked than is the case today. Much

[1] *A.P.S.D., s.v.* 'ARCHITECT'.
[2] D. Knoop & G. P. Jones, *The Mediaeval Mason*, 1933, 197.
[3] N. Pevsner, 'The Term Architect in the Middle Ages', *Speculum* xvii, 1942, 549–62.

more was left to be worked out on the spot than is normal in modern architectural practice, and even major churches were sometimes begun without any clear idea how they were to be completed. That the technical achievement of the great Gothic churches was possible at all was due partly to the accumulated experience of the Romanesque age, and partly to the rediscovery of Greek science in the thirteenth century. The science of most utility to architecture was of course geometry, and it was above all a knowledge of geometry that distinguished the medieval master mason or master carpenter from his subordinates. That knowledge might find expression in drawn 'patrons' and 'patterns', of which many examples survive on the continent, though few have been preserved in British archives. But it was also more widely disseminated in the form of simple geometrical formulae which made it possible to develop many of the elevational features of a building from a given plan in accordance with predetermined rules of proportion, without the intervention of working drawings.[4]

Another difference between medieval and modern architectural practice must be emphasized. All that we know of the medieval craftsman suggests that it was very rare for a master mason, however eminent, to dictate to a master carpenter, or *vice versa*. Each was supreme in his own sphere, and solved his own problems in accordance with the traditions of his own craft. Each trade was a distinct 'mistery', understood only by its own practitioners, and applied independently to each new commission. Common patronage, common experience and common artistic conventions enabled one trade to work harmoniously beside another, but it was rare for any one individual to exercise that technical and aesthetic control over every component of a building which modern architects have come to take for granted. In studying the careers of medieval architects it is therefore necessary to think of them as members of a team working in collaboration rather than as architects in the sense in which the term has been understood in modern times.

In Italy – and to a lesser extent in France – the authority of the architect was already asserting itself in the sixteenth and early seventeenth centuries. But in Tudor and Stuart Britain medieval practice was still the norm in architectural matters. The great Elizabethan houses were assembled piecemeal rather than designed as artistically coherent entities. 'The plan might come from one source, the details from a number of others. Designs could be supplied by one or more of the craftsmen actually employed on the building; or by an outside craftsman; or by the employer; or by a friend of the employer; or by a professional with an intellectual rather than a craft background.'[5] Though Renaissance detailing might be one ingredient of the whole it was seen as a decorative dressing rather than as a discipline which pervaded the entire design of the building. So those (often of foreign birth) who purveyed it had not yet usurped the functions of the craftsmen architects who still dominated the British architectural scene at the beginning of the seventeenth century. The way was not yet clear for the

---

[4] See P. Frankl, 'The Secret of the Mediaeval Masons', *The Art Bulletin* xxvii, 1945, and Lon R. Shelby, 'The Geometrical Knowledge of Mediaeval Master Masons', *Speculum* xlvii, 1972.

[5] Mark Girouard, *Robert Smythson and the Architecture of the Elizabethan Era*, 1966, 22–3. See also E. Mercer, *English Art 1553–1625*, 1962, 53–9.

genius of a Wren or for the dictatorship of taste of an Earl of Burlington to impose itself on the architecture of an age.

The change, when it came, was the doing, not so much of the builder-architects, as of their patrons. The modern architect did not evolve, as if by an involuntary process, out of the traditional master workman. It is true that changing economic conditions were having their effect on the building trades, notably in releasing them gradually from the restrictions of medieval craft-regulation and in encouraging the growth of the contract system that had made its appearance long before.[6] But neither of these developments did anything to modify their functions in the matter of architectural design. The emergence of the modern architect was therefore due less to changing economic conditions than it was to changing tastes, and in Britain it was the more sophisticated taste of the Stuart court that first allowed a man of genius to exercise the full functions of an architect in the modern sense. That man was Inigo Jones, and it was he who first imposed Italian discipline on English architecture, taking his ideas direct from the Italian masters instead of through the indirect medium of French buildings and German and Flemish pattern-books. For the Palladian architecture which Inigo Jones introduced into England was based on a highly sophisticated theory of design which could not well be studied outside Italy, and was beyond the intellectual grasp of the average master builder. Moreover, its execution demanded that the craftsman should subordinate himself to a single controlling mind in a way which he had never been required to do before. It demanded, in fact, the employment of someone whose education had included the conscious study of design, and whose functions were to be supervisory rather than executive: in other words, the architect.

As Surveyor-General of the Royal Works Inigo Jones was paramount for over twenty years. But he was essentially a court architect, and the extinction of court life during the Civil War and Commonwealth meant a serious set-back for his personal influence. Nevertheless, the taste for Italian culture had taken firm root even in the minds of those who were of the parliamentary persuasion, and after the Restoration there was a general demand among the English aristocracy for houses in what Roger North called 'the Grand maniere of Jones'. Although there were one or two master builders who were tolerably well versed in the new style of architecture,[7] they were in a minority, and a person who wished his house to be in a correct taste had either to educate his workmen himself,[8] or, as Sir Roger Pratt advised, to

> get some ingenious gentleman who has seen much of that kind abroad and been somewhat versed in the best authors of Architecture: viz. Palladio, Scamozzi, Serlio, etc. to do it for you, and to give you a design of it in paper, though but roughly drawn, (which will generally fall out better than one which

[6] D. Knoop & G. P. Jones, 'The Rise of the Mason Contractor', R.I.B.A. Journal xliii, 1936.
[7] E.g. Peter Mills and the sons of Nicholas Stone.
[8] As Sir James Pytts had done in 1618 when he lent his mason 'one booke of Architecture ... which he hath promissed to redeliver unto me' ('The Building of the Manor-House of Kyre Park, Worcestershire', in The Antiquary xxii, 1890, 53), and as Sir Roger Townshend did in 1620 when he took his master mason abroad before setting him to build Raynham Hall (below, p. 281).

shall be given you by a home-bred Architect for want of his better experience, as is daily seen) . . .[9]

The demand thus created was sufficiently general to give employment to a small number of men who specialized in architectural design and supervision. Hugh May, William Samwell and Captain Winde were architects of the type described by Pratt, gentlemen by birth who supplemented their inadequate private incomes by acting as architects and artistic advisers. In a sense they were the founders of the English architectural profession, but in their lifetimes the conception of such a profession was still in the future: for there was no form of architectural education other than apprenticeship to a building trade, and those who called themselves architects had usually been grounded in some other art or discipline. Inigo Jones himself may have begun life as a painter; so, perhaps, did Hugh May;[10] Balthazar Gerbier was a diplomatist and teacher of aristocratic exercises who merely counted the arts of design among his manifold accomplishments, William Winde a military engineer, and Wren a Professor of Astronomy. Only Webb, who had been 'brought up by his Unckle Mr. Inigo Jones upon his late Maiestyes command in the study of Architecture, as well that wch relates to building as for masques, Tryumphs and the like', could claim to have received a specifically architectural training, and he himself had no disciple. It was the accident of the Great Fire which made Robert Hooke a practising architect, and there must have been others who, like John Evelyn and Roger North, were equally well versed in architectural matters, but who did not 'pretend either to great publick designes, nor new models of great houses'. Even in the eighteenth century it was still possible for a soldier like Vanbrugh or a painter like Kent to achieve celebrity as an architect, and the century was to be well advanced before the system of apprenticeship to a practising architect provided the established basis of a professional training comparable to that offered by the Law or even the Church.[11]

Most people, indeed, still thought it unnecessary to consult anyone but a master workman when undertaking building operations, and some, like Roger North, preferred to make the designs themselves without professional assistance. 'For a profest architect is proud, opiniative and troublesome, seldome at hand, and a head workman pretending to the designing part, is full of paultry vulgar contrivances; therefore be your owne architect, or sitt still', was his advice.[12] It is not surprising, therefore, that very few seventeenth-century architects lived exclusively upon their earnings. Some, like Samwell and Pratt, had small private incomes; others, like Wren and Hooke, enjoyed academic posts; while for Ryder and Webb (and later for Wren) it was the Office of His Majesty's Works which gave them a basic income in return for official duties which left them ample time for private practice.

The importance of the Office of Works in the history of the English architec-

[9] *The Architecture of Sir Roger Pratt*, ed. R. T. Gunther, 1928, p. 60.
[10] His early connection with Lely at least suggests such a possibility: see p. 543.
[11] R. Campbell, in his *London Tradesman* (1747), says of architects that 'I scarce know of any in England who have had an Education regularly designed for the Profession'.
[12] *Of Building* (B.M., Add. MS. 32540), f. 23.

tural profession cannot easily be over-emphasized. In the seventeenth and eighteenth centuries it provided by far the greatest number of posts open to architects in the form of surveyorships and clerkships of the works.[13] The most famous architects of the day sat on its Board, and it was through the agency of the King's Works that so many skilled master craftsmen became acquainted with the latest ideas in design and decoration – ideas which in due course they incorporated in buildings for their own private clients. The Office of Works was, in fact, a kind of unacknowledged substitute for a royal academy of architecture such as Colbert established in France, and it retained its importance as the focus of English architectural activity well into the latter part of the eighteenth century. So long, moreover, as the clerkships of the Works remained in the gift of the Surveyor-General (which they did at least until 1782), the latter was able to find places for his chosen subordinates, and it is in the exercise of this patronage that the 'school' of Wren or Chambers must be sought, rather than in the idea of private pupilage.[14] It was by capturing the Office of Works in the 1730s that Lord Burlington was able to impose his Palladian formula upon the public buildings of London, and so create a tradition of official architecture which lasted to the Second World War.

The importance of the Office of Works in maintaining the tenuous thread of architectural experience is shown by the number of eighteenth-century architects who were either 'bred up in the King's Works', or who held office under the Surveyor-General. But outside the royal palaces there was no body of persons trained in architectural drawing and supervision as there is today, and it was not until about the middle of the century that it became possible for a young man to take up architecture as a career, to enter the office of a practising architect, and to learn to design without previously having learned to build. Fortunes were nevertheless to be made by those who had somehow acquired the requisite knowledge and skill to practise the art. 'Few men who have gained any reputation [as architects] but have made good estates', declared Campbell in 1747,[15] and George Vertue, writing in 1749, placed architecture at the head of the artistic professions. 'I must own', he said, '[that] the branch of the art of building in Architecture is much improved and many men of that profession has made greater fortunes ... than any other branch of Art whatever – their manner of undertakings is so profitable, by their agreements at so much per cent for drawings and direction of works of building. ... Indeed this profession of building has many profitable advantages which makes it worth while to study, travel and labour.'[16]

The first architect who was in the habit of taking pupils appears to have been Sir Robert Taylor, of whom it was said that he and James Paine 'nearly divided the practice of the profession between them' until the advent of the

[13] See Appendix C.
[14] Thus James Elmes observes that Chambers 'educated no pupils – that is to say, as the word is now understood. ... His only followers or pupils were bred in the office of the Board of Works, in which he held the situation of surveyor-general' ('History of Architecture in Great Britain', in *Civil Engineer and Architect's Jnl.* x, 1847, 300).
[15] *The London Tradesman*, 1747, 157.
[16] Walpole Society, *Vertue Note Books* iii, 146, 150.

brothers Adam.[17] His rival followed his example, and by the third quarter of the eighteenth century it was usual for the London architect to have in his office one or more young men who were at once his pupils and his assistants. Their status was that of articled clerks, unless they had sufficient experience to rank as 'improvers', in which case they would receive a small weekly wage in addition to board and lodging. Such an apprenticeship, commencing at the age of 16, lasted for five or six years,[18] and in the course of it the intelligent pupil had ample opportunity to learn the essentials of architectural draughtsmanship and professional practice. He would, at the same time, seek to attend the lectures of the Professor of Architecture at the Royal Academy, and would show the best of his own essays in design at the annual exhibition under the address of his tutor and master. He might even gain one of the medals (two Silver and one Gold)[19] offered annually by the Academy for students' work, or gain a 'premium' from the Society of Arts. At the end of his apprenticeship, he aspired to travel – certainly to Rome and northern Italy, if possible to Sicily and Greece, perhaps even to Asia Minor and the Levant. There, for two or three never-to-be-forgotten years, he measured, drew and sometimes excavated the monuments of antiquity, forming a collection of sketches and measured drawings upon which he could draw for inspiration in the future, and some of which he would later work up for future Royal Academy Exhibitions. Thus at the age of 25 or 26 the young architect was fully equipped for professional practice. If he was lucky, he obtained a post as surveyor to a corporation, a charity, a fire insurance office or a Board of Guardians until such time as, through friends, influence, or success in a public competition, he laid the foundations of a successful private practice and began to take pupils of his own. If he was unlucky – and the indications are that by the beginning of the nineteenth century architecture was attracting more aspirants than it could gainfully employ – he spent his life as an assistant in another architect's office, combined architecture with some other occupation, or gave it up altogether. A good many casualties of this sort will be found in the pages of this Dictionary (especially among the names in Appendix B), but successful careers were open to those in whom creative skill was matched by business ability. The worldly wealth of Sir Robert Taylor, Sir William Chambers or Henry Holland was not derived exclusively from professional fees, but in the next generation Sir John Soane made a fortune strictly by professional activity, and the Probate records show that by the reign of Victoria a leading London architect could expect to leave a substantial estate to

[17] Hardwick's 'Memoir of Sir William Chambers', prefaced to Gwilt's edition of *A Treatise on the Decorative Part of Civil Architecture*, 1825.

[18] See the terms of apprenticeship to Sir John Soane, given by A. T. Bolton, *Architectural Education a Century Ago* (Soane Museum Publication No. 12): see also R.I.B.A. *Sessional Papers*, 1855–6, p. 1, for Sir William Tite's statement that a six years' apprenticeship was normal in the early nineteenth century.

[19] For a list of the gold medallists, see J. E. Hodgson & F. A. Eaton, *History of the Royal Academy*, 1905, Appendix VII. A travelling studentship was also offered, but as it was tenable for several years, and awarded alternately from those attending the Schools of Painting, Sculpture and Architecture, the chances of obtaining it were small. The architects who held it during the period 1769–1840 were John Soane (1777), George Hadfield (1790), Lewis Vulliamy (1818), Samuel Loat (1828) and John Johnson (1837).

31

his heirs.[20] Architecture had, in fact, become a reputable and remunerative occupation which an ambitious parent could contemplate with favour for his son–one which no longer depended upon the uncertainties of aristocratic patronage or the doubtful devices of speculative building. The architect had at last taken his place alongside the doctor and the lawyer, and it would not be long before he began to formulate his own standards of professional conduct and to create an organization through which they could be enforced.

By the accession of George III, there was in Britain the nucleus of an architectural profession. But the implications of professional status had hardly begun to make themselves felt in the minds of the architects themselves, still less in those of their patrons. Most architects supplemented their incomes by building speculations, and were thought none the worse of for doing so;[21] nearly all were prepared to contract for the erection of the buildings which they designed;[22] and some acted in the additional capacity of house- and estate-agents.[23] Moreover, there was still no provision for the academic study of design, no place for the exhibition of drawings and models, no forum in which architects could exchange ideas and enjoy one another's society. A few architects had, it is true, been admitted to artists' clubs, like the *Society of Virtuosi of St. Luke*, which counted William Talman, James Gibbs, Christopher Wren, junior, and William Kent among its members; but the activities of such societies were chiefly convivial and their existence was often brief.[24] The 'Society for the improvement of knowledge in Arts and Sciences' to which Robert Morris read his *Lectures on Architecture* in about 1730 was presumably a more serious affair, but seems to have been equally short-lived. Some architects were Fellows of the Royal Society, and the profession has always been well represented in the Society of Antiquaries, but neither body took more than an indirect interest in architectural matters and none in contemporary architectural practice.

In France, architecture was catered for by its own Academy, founded by Colbert in 1671, but in spite of frequent pleas for an artistic academy in this country,[25] it was not until 1768 that the idea came to fruition in the Royal Academy of Arts. The truth is, that in the early eighteenth century England was still too dependent upon foreign artists to justify the creation of a national academy, while the political atmosphere was not favourable to the establishment

[20] Sir Robert Smirke's estate was valued for probate at £90,000. Barry and Blore both left £80,000, Decimus Burton and Lewis Vulliamy £60,000, Burn £40,000 and C. R. Cockerell £35,000.
[21] Wren's Bridgewater Square, Barbican, Paine's Salisbury Street, Strand, Holland's Hans Town, Chelsea, and the Adams' Adelphi Buildings are major examples of speculative building by architects.
[22] 'The Architect either undertakes the whole work for a certain Sum, or is paid for superintending the work only' (R. Campbell, *The London Tradesman*, 1747, 155).
[23] *E.g.* Robert Brettingham, J. J. Cooper and J. Eveleigh.
[24] Whitley, *Artists and Their Friends in England, 1700–1799* i, 1928, 68–70, 74–7; ii, 241–4.
[25] Cf. Stephen Switzer, *The Nobleman, Gentleman and Gardener's Recreation*, 1715, 237; George Vertue, *Note Books* (Walpole Society) ii, 150–5; iii, 74; John Gwynn, *An Essay on Design including Proposals for Erecting a Public Academy to be supplied by Voluntary Subscription (until a Royal Foundation can be obtain'd) for Educating British Youth in Drawing*, 1749; Nesbitt, *Essay on the Necessity of a Royal Academy*, 1755. Matthew Brettingham junior's scheme for a British Academy is outlined in a letter, dated 27 May 1753, in Holkham MS. 744, ff. 136–9.

of an institution elsewhere so closely associated with royal absolutism.[26] It was, characteristically, through the agency of a private but highly aristocratic body that England nearly achieved her academy of the arts in the middle of the century. The *Society of Dilettanti* acquired a site in Cavendish Square for the purpose, and in 1755 entered into negotiations with a committee of artists who submitted a detailed plan for the management of the proposed academy. As no less than six of them were architects,[27] it may be presumed that architecture would have been adequately represented in an academy established under the patronage of the Society which sponsored the publication of the *Antiquities of Athens*. But the project came to nothing, partly (as the younger Matthew Brettingham reported[28]) because of the difficulty of raising money, and partly because the Dilettanti demanded a dominant share in the government of the Academy which the artists were not prepared to concede.[29]

In 1754 architecture received encouragement from a somewhat different quarter. This was the foundation of the *Society for the Encouragement of Arts, Manufactures, and Commerce*, now known as the Royal Society of Arts.[30] Although its primary concern was the encouragement of industrial art, it also sought to promote the 'polite arts' (which included architecture), on the ground that 'the Art of Drawing is absolutely necessary in many employments, trades and manufactures'. So far as architecture was concerned, it did this chiefly by offering small monetary awards for promising designs by student architects. A considerable number of young men received encouragement in this way, and the 'Register of Premiums' includes the names of Edward Stevens, James Gandon, John Plaw, Robert Baldwin and George Richardson.[31]

The Society also provided wall-space for the first public exhibition of paintings in this country, held in April 1760. It was intended to make this an annual event, and to maintain with the proceeds a fund for old and infirm artists. But as the Society would not permit any charge to be made for admission, and also interfered with the hanging of the pictures, the majority of the artists soon seceded and founded their own Society of Artists (incorporated in 1765), which held exhibitions in a room at Spring Gardens from 1761 onwards. Both the *Incorporated Society of Artists* and the rival *Free Society of Artists* (as those who continued to hold exhibitions with the Society of Arts called themselves) had architects among their members, and both admitted architectural drawings to their exhibitions.[32] Architects were, moreover, prominent in the management of the Incorporated Society, and Chambers and Paine both played a leading part in the internal dissensions which led to its eventual dissolution. Paine was one of those who did his best to keep it in being, while Chambers took the initia-

[26] N. Pevsner, *Academies of Art*, 1940, 126.
[27] John Gwynn, Robert Taylor, James Stuart, Isaac Ware, Nicholas Revett and Thomas Sandby.
[28] Holkham MS. 744, f. 136.
[29] Whitley, *Artists and Their Friends* i, 157–8; L. Cust, *History of The Society of Dilettanti*, ed. Colvin, 1898, 53–5.
[30] H. T. Wood, *A History of the Royal Society of Arts*, 1913. Its early members included George Dance, senior, Robert Mylne, James Paine, Sir William Chambers and the three Adam brothers.
[31] See the *Register of Premiums* awarded between 1754 and 1776, printed in 1778.
[32] See A. Graves, *The Society of Artists of Great Britain and the Free Society of Artists*, 1907, and Horace Walpole's notes printed by H. Gatty in *Walpole Society* xxvii, 1938–9.

tive in founding a new body to take its place.[33] This was the Royal Academy of Arts (founded in 1768), which in due course rendered both the older societies redundant, the Free Society holding its last exhibition in 1783, the Incorporated Society in 1791.

The *Royal Academy*, with its royal charter and its rooms in Somerset House alongside the Royal and Antiquarian Societies, represented the first official recognition of the place which native artists and architects had created for themselves in the life of the nation. Five of the thirty-six original Academicians were architects,[34] and the post of Treasurer was given to Sir William Chambers, whose successors in office were, for over a hundred years, members of his profession.[35] Architectural drawings were hung at the annual exhibitions, and the designs for almost every building of importance erected during the latter part of the period covered by this book were shown at the Royal Academy.[36] Moreover, the Instrument by which the Academy was established provided for the appointment of a Professor of Architecture, 'who shall read annually six public lectures, calculated to form the taste of the Students, to instruct them in the laws and principles of composition, to point out to them the beauties or faults of celebrated productions, to fit them for an unprejudiced study of books, and for a critical examination of structures'.[37] Although these professorial lectures could hardly be said to create a school of architecture, admission to the 'Royal Academy Schools' was eagerly sought by young men serving their time in an architect's office, and for more than fifty years formed a regular part of almost every architect's education. So far as his seniors were concerned, election as A.R.A. or R.A. was the acknowledged recognition of professional eminence.

But the handful of architect R.A.s was inevitably in a permanent minority in a body composed mainly of painters, and even Sir William Chambers, dominant though he was in its counsels for nearly thirty years, showed no wish to increase their number, or in any way to associate the Academy with the interests of the architectural profession as such.[38] It was inevitable, therefore, that the first steps towards a professional association should have come from outside the Academy, though it was not until nearly twenty-five years after its foundation that the leading architects practising in London became sufficiently conscious of their mutual interests to form a society composed exclusively of members of their own profession. *The Architects' Club*, as it was called, was founded in 1791 by James Wyatt, George Dance, Henry Holland and S. P. Cockerell, and met at the Thatched House Tavern on the first Thursday in every month.[39] Its composition was highly select, for no one could be a member

[33] Whitley, *Artists and their Friends in England* i, 1928, 248, where the degree of personal rivalry between Chambers and Paine is, however, greatly exaggerated.

[34] Sir William Chambers, John Gwynn, Thomas Sandby, W. Tyler and George Dance, junior.

[35] His immediate successors were John Yenn (1796–1820), Sir Robert Smirke (1820–50), Philip Hardwick (1850–61) and Sydney Smirke (1861–74).

[36] See A. Graves, *The Royal Academy of Arts, 1769–1804*, 8 vols., 1907.

[37] For holders of the Professorship, see Appendix C.

[38] Cf. Dr H. M. Martienssen's unpublished thesis on *The Architectural Theory and Practice of Sir William Chambers*, 1949, 143–6.

[39] The original members, in addition to the four founders, were Sir William Chambers, Robert Adam, Robert Mylne, Richard Jupp, James Lewis, Richard Norris, John Soane, John Yenn, Thomas

who was not an R.A., A.R.A. or Gold Medallist, or a member of the Academies of Rome, Parma, Florence or Paris.[40] Moreover, a single blackball was sufficient to exclude a candidate from admission.[41] Honorary membership was reserved for those whose place of residence was outside London.[42]

Although primarily a dining club, the Architects' Club was not without a sense of its responsibilities as an association of professional men.[43] In 1792 some of its members met in order 'to define the profession and qualifications of an architect',[44] and in 1796 Mylne laid before it a resolution forbidding one architect from interfering in another's commission.[45] In the previous year it had appointed a committee to go into the question of architects' charges. This was a matter upon which Soane held strong views, and his refusal to accept the majority decision to make a measuring charge of $2\frac{1}{2}$ per cent, in addition to the customary 5 per cent for designs and supervision, led to his estrangement from the other members of the Club.[46] This was by no means the only matter over which the Club was divided, and Soane told Farington early in 1796 that he did not think it would last long, 'the members consisting only of persons who are too much in a state of rivalship and frequently crossing each other'.[47] In fact, it survived for at least thirty years.[48] But little more is heard of its activities, and it is clear that so exclusive a body could never adequately represent the interests of a rapidly growing profession.[49]

It is not surprising, therefore, that attempts were made to establish other associations of a more representative character. The first of these was the *Surveyors' Club*, founded in 1792 by sixteen surveyors who met at the Shakespeare Tavern to discuss 'the propriety of forming a meeting of Surveyors on some general and beneficial principles'. But its objects were chiefly of a social and charitable nature, and only three or four of its twenty-four original members were in practice as architects.[50] The rest were District Surveyors appointed under the Act of 1774, or men of the type described in contemporary directories

---

Hardwick, Robert Brettingham and James Paine, junior (T. Mulvany, *Life of James Gandon*, 1846, 295–7).

[40] The insistence upon foreign travel was abandoned in 1803 owing to the Napoleonic War (*The Farington Diary*, ed. J. Greig, ii, 123).

[41] George Hadfield, a Gold Medallist of the Royal Academy, was so excluded in 1795, much to the annoyance of James Wyatt, who was one of his proposers (*The Farington Diary*, ed. J. Greig, i, 85).

[42] John Carr, Nicholas Revett and Thomas Sandby were the first Honorary Members. James Gandon was elected in Dec. 1791.

[43] W. L. Spiers, 'The Architects' Club', *R.I.B.A. Jnl.*, 3rd ser., xviii, 1911, 240.

[44] A. T. Bolton, *Portrait of Sir John Soane*, 67.

[45] Barrington Kaye, *The Development of the Architectural Profession in Britain*, 1960, 59.

[46] A. T. Bolton, *Portrait of Sir John Soane*, 76–7. A skit by Soane on the members of the Club and their pretensions is preserved in MS. in the Soane Museum (Envelope F. Div. 14, No. 40). It is in the form of a dialogue between a representative of the Club and a candidate for membership.

[47] *The Farington Diary*, ed. J. Greig, i, 137.

[48] See the lists of members published in the *British Imperial Kalendar* between 1812 and 1824.

[49] In 1834 its members were invited to participate in the foundation of an architectural institute, but declined 'altering the character or extending the views of the club' (*A Plain Statement of Facts connected with the Coalition between the Society for the Promotion of Architecture and Architectural Topography and the Society of British Architects*, 1834, 11).

[50] E.g. William Purser, Edward Mawley and Peter Upsdell. Other members were James Burton, the builder, and Henry Hurle, a carpenter who founded the 'Ancient Order of Druids'.

as 'Surveyor and Builder'.[51] More important for the history of the architectural profession was the *London Architectural Society*, founded in 1806. The reason given for its establishment was that 'among the Institutions so liberally established in this city there is not one calculated for the encouragement of Architecture. The feeble protection afforded by the Royal Academy can hardly be deemed an exception.[52] The lectures have long ceased,[53] and medals privately distributed, and the use of a library for a few hours one day in the week, and at a time when it is hardly possible for the student in architecture to attend ... cannot be deemed of much value', while the 'few clubs which have been formed by persons in the profession, are rather to enjoy the pleasures of good fellowship among men engaged in the same pursuit, than for the advancement of the art'.[54] The method proposed for the advancement of the art was to require every member to produce annually an original architectural design, under forfeiture of two guineas, and an essay, under forfeiture of half a guinea. The Society met once a fortnight in order to discuss these productions, and anyone who was absent from two successive meetings was fined 5s. The designs and essays were to remain the property of the Society, which undertook to publish such as were considered worthy of the honour. The Society attracted some of the more literary members of the profession, such as Joseph Woods, its president, James Elmes and James Peacock, and it published at least two volumes of its Essays.[55] But rules of such severity were hardly calculated to attract a large membership, and the life of the Society was earnest but short.

A somewhat more genial association was the *Architects' and Antiquaries' Club*, which was founded in December 1819 by ten gentlemen who, having observed the value of foreign academies of architecture, 'could not resist the mortifying contrast which was presented, in comparing the state of Architecture in those cities with that of this kingdom'. The society was to consist of twenty members, and there were to be six dinners annually at the Freemasons' Tavern. Each member was expected 'occasionally to furnish the Society with an Essay on a Subject of Antient Architecture, or some branch of Antiquity connected with domestic economy or the fine Arts'. The members included Edward Cresy, Joseph Gwilt, Augustus Pugin, J. Sanders (its first president) and G. L. Taylor (his successor). The antiquary John Britton acted as Treasurer and Honorary Secretary, and there were two Honorary and Corresponding Members, John Foster of Liverpool and S. T. Whitwell of Leamington.[56]

But, however profitable this intercourse between the architects and the ama-

---

[51] I am indebted to the officers of the Surveyors' Club for their courtesy in allowing me to examine its records.

[52] The Academy's attitude towards its architectural responsibilities is strongly criticized in *The Library of the Fine Arts* iv, 1832, 213-19; see also John Britton's complaint in *Portrait of Sir John Soane*, 317.

[53] Dance, who held the Chair of Architecture from 1798 to 1805, delivered no lectures.

[54] From the preface to *Essays of the London Architectural Society*, 1808.

[55] For some account of the Society, see *The Builder* xxi, 1863, 86, 112–13, 140. Other members were James Savage (Vice-president), C. A. Busby (secretary), Edmund Aikin, W. H. Ashpitel, Samuel Beazley, J. G. Bubb, the sculptor, Coade, the artificial stone manufacturer, and Josiah Taylor, the architectural publisher.

[56] Records of the Society are preserved in the Bodleian Library, Gough Adds. London 8° 405.

teurs may have been, it was no substitute for a professional association, the lack of which continued to be deplored both by those in practice, who needed its protection against inadequate remuneration and unfair competitions, and by their pupils, who compared the meagre ration of instruction which they received at the Royal Academy with the life-classes and other facilities enjoyed by the more favoured students of painting and sculpture.[57] Three figures stand out in this period of uncertainty during which the architectural profession was slowly feeling its way towards that Institute of British Architects which all realized was the ultimate goal: Sir John Soane, who by his personal example set a standard of professional conduct which all respected and some emulated; James Elmes, better known as a writer than as a practising architect, who in either capacity lost no opportunity of impressing the need for association both upon his fellow-architects and upon the general public; and Thomas Leverton Donaldson, the leader of the younger generation, who was to live to become President of the Institute of British Architects, and to hear himself hailed as 'father of his profession' by the Prince of Wales.[58]

It was on Elmes's initiative that the first serious attempt to create a professional organization took place in 1810. A meeting of architects was held in his house, in order to take steps to establish a Royal Academy of Architecture, with a Library and a Museum of Models. Details of the scheme were sent to all the leading architects in London, and favourable replies were received from 'Messrs. Nash, Jeffry and Lewis Wyatt, Ware, Gwilt, Hardwick, Porden, Gandy, Tatham, Bond, Beazley, Lewis and other eminent professors'. Elmes afterwards 'drew it out in the shape of a letter' to Thomas Hope, which he published in *The Pamphleteer*.[59] But, as he afterwards confessed, 'little was done, except in private compliments to me, and one Review which noticed it'.[60]

Much the same happened in 1819 when a fresh series of meetings was held in order to discuss a 'Proposed Institution for the Cultivation and Encouragement of Architecture'. Elmes was appointed secretary, and a number of resolutions were passed which were published in *Annals of the Fine Arts*[61] – a periodical which (under Elmes's editorship) consistently championed the cause of architecture.

There, it would seem, the matter rested until 1831, when a renewed attempt

[57] See an article 'On the Condition of the Architectural Students in the Royal Academy of London compared with those of other Nations' in *Annals of the Fine Arts* ii, 1817, 19, and cf. *Monthly Magazine*, July 1809.

[58] Donaldson was the founder of the *Architectural Students' Society*, whose members were in the habit of meeting together 'to make a design or a sketch from a given subject, or to discuss a paper'. In 1817, as a young man of 26, he organized a meeting of architectural students in Pall Mall to petition the Royal Academy 'to form a School of Architecture and allow them a further extension of the use of their Library'. The Academicians received this demonstration 'in good part', and agreed to open the Library twice a week in term-time instead of only once. But nothing was done to meet the more important demand that Architecture should be placed on the same footing as Sculpture and Painting in the Royal Academy Schools. (*Annals of the Fine Arts* ii, 1817, 124, 258, 340; *The Farington Diary*, ed. J. Greig, viii, 114, 115; R.I.B.A. *Sessional Papers*, 1855–6, 2; R.I.B.A. Library, Pam. Q.11, No. 2.)

[59] 'A Letter to Thomas Hope Esq. on the insufficiency of the existing establishments for promoting the Fine Arts towards that of Architecture and its Professors', *The Pamphleteer* iii, 1814, 330.

[60] *Annals of the Fine Arts* ii, 1817, 261–2.

[61] Vol. iv, 1819, 348–51.

to unite the profession resulted in the formation of the *Architectural Society*, whose ultimate ambition was 'to form a British School of Architecture, affording the advantages of a Library, Museum, Professorships and periodical exhibitions'.[62] It began with a membership of over forty, and attracted some eminent Victorian architects.[63] The Duke of Sussex agreed to become its patron, and in 1835 Sir John Soane signified his approval of its aspirations by the gift of £250.[64] But in spite of all that it did to provide improved facilities for architectural students, the Architectural Society did not satisfy the urgent need for an association which would seek to define the obligations of an architect towards his client, and at the same time to gain for its members a status in business and society comparable to that enjoyed by other professional men. It was with these objects that, in 1834, a committee was formed which included the names of P. F. Robinson (its chairman), T. L. Donaldson (its chief organizer), Charles Fowler, J. Goldicutt, H. E. Kendall, James Savage and James Noble.[65] Its purpose was to draw up a scheme for the formation of an institute 'to uphold the character and improve the attainments of Architects'. The result of its deliberations was a Prospectus explaining the need for such an institute, defining its objects, and setting out its proposed constitution. There was to be a 'Library of works of every kind connected with Architecture' and a 'Museum of Antiquities, Models and Casts'; there were to be 'periodical meetings of the members for the purpose of discussion and improvement by lecture, essay, or illustration', and provision was to be made for the instruction of students in 'the various branches of Science connected with Architecture in addition to those attainable in an Architect's Office, and not provided by any existing Institution'. Membership was to be divided into two classes – Fellows, who were to be elected from architects who had been established in practice for not less than five years, and Associates, who were to be admitted by examination.[66]

This Prospectus was sent to a number of leading architects, who agreed to become original members, and Sir John Soane, the lifelong advocate of professional standards in architecture and the most distinguished member of his profession, was offered the Presidency. This he was obliged to decline owing to a rule prohibiting Royal Academicians from becoming members of any other society of artists, but he indicated his approval of the Institute's programme by a gift of £750. At the same time he presented the sum of £250 already mentioned to the Architectural Society, expressing a hope that the two bodies might before long be united – an event which eventually took place in 1842, largely through the efforts of Sir William Tite.

[62] A copy of its printed *Laws and Regulations* is in Sir John Soane's Museum. Its first president was W. B. Clarke, and the members of the committee were T. H. Wyatt, Benjamin Ferrey, A. W. and J. H. Hakewill, T. M. Nelson, Thomas Walker, George Moore and George Mair. Reports of its meetings were published in Loudon's *Architectural Magazine* and in the *Gent's Mag.*
[63] Including David Brandon, G. E. Street, Ewan Christian and Sir William Tite (President, 1838–42).
[64] A. T. Bolton, *Portrait of Sir John Soane*, 514.
[65] Author of a work on *The Professional Practice of Architects*, 1836.
[66] The Prospectus is printed by Bolton, *Portrait of Sir John Soane*, 509–12. See also the 'Address and Regulations of the Institute of British Architects, explanatory of their Views and Objects', printed in the *Architectural Magazine* ii, 1835, 305–6.

Meanwhile, Earl de Grey had consented to give the Institute the benefit of his social and political influence, and it was under his presidency that the first meeting was held on 3 June 1835. T. L. Donaldson, now Honorary Secretary, was able to announce that the Institute already counted eighty members, that contacts had been established with several foreign academies, and that the nucleus of a library had been formed. In 1836 the Institute began the publication of its *Transactions*, and in 1837 it received the final recognition of a royal charter of incorporation.[67]

With the foundation of the *Institute of British Architects*, architecture had at last achieved its acknowledged place among the professions, and although much remained to be done -- both from within the Institute and from without – to work out all the implications of that status, its attainment marks the end of the process which it has been the object of this Introduction to trace. No Victorian barrister would have dared to question a Fellow of the Institute of British Architects in the terms in which counsel is reported[68] to have addressed himself to Daniel Asher Alexander:

'You are a builder, I believe?'

'No, sir; I am not a builder; I am an architect.'

'Ah well, builder or architect, architect or builder – they are pretty much the same, I suppose?'

'I beg your pardon; they are totally different.'

'Oh, indeed! Perhaps you will state wherein this difference consists.'

'An architect, sir, conceives the design, prepares the plan, draws out the specification – in short, supplies the mind. The builder is merely the machine; the architect the power that puts the machine together and sets it going.'

'Oh, very well, Mr. Architect, that will do. A very ingenious distinction without a difference. Do you happen to know who was the architect of the Tower of Babel?'

'There was no architect, sir. Hence the confusion.'

In fact, the Victorian architect, if he were a man of any ability or enterprise, was well able to make a living without maintaining that connection with the building trade which had been the chief resource of so many of his Georgian predecessors. Churches, prisons, town halls, bridges, warehouses and factories were going up apace in the industrial towns of the Midlands and the north, while country houses and suburban villas continued to provide rich commissions for the domestic architect. The improvement in communications meant that the new professional architect, while retaining his London office, could personally supervise the erection of half a dozen buildings at once, in a way which

[67] It was not until 1866 that the Institute added the epithet 'Royal' to its title. The Royal Gold Medal had been instituted by Queen Victoria in 1848. For the Institute's subsequent history see *The Growth and Work of the R.I.B.A. 1834–1934*, ed. J. A. Gotch, 1934. An *Institute of the Architects of Scotland* was founded in 1840 under the Presidency of the 5th Duke of Buccleuch, but collapsed almost immediately owing to a dispute over the eligibility for membership of David Bryce, who was not yet in independent practice. It was refounded in 1850 as the *Architectural Institute of Scotland*, again with the Duke of Buccleuch as President.

[68] *Builder* xx, 795. The interrogator is said to have been Sir James Scarlett (1769–1844), and the case was probably that of Chapman, Gardiner and Upward *v.* De Tastet (1817), reported in *Annals of the Fine Arts* iii, 1818, 560–65, in which Scarlett appeared for the defendant.

had been quite impossible for his eighteenth-century predecessor, who supplied a plan and elevation, answered queries by letter, and relied on the experience and discretion of his master craftsmen to give satisfaction to his client and observe the established rules of sound building. The Industrial Revolution, which provided the professional architect with so many new opportunities, also provided him with the means to exploit them, and his triumph came in the 1840s and 1850s with the railways, which enabled a Gilbert Scott to rebuild half the parish churches of England in accordance with his own conception of Gothic architecture, and finally destroyed the autonomy and self-respect of the local builder.

With the fruits of these developments this Introduction is not concerned: for they are part of the history of Victorian architecture, and as such lie outside the chronological scope of this book. Most of the men whose biographies it contains saw England from the road, not from the rail, and there were few of them who had no connection with the building trade in one or other of its forms. from the Smiths of Warwick, who were builders first and architects last, to Sir Jeffry Wyatville, the 'honourable augmentation' of whose name did not conceal the fact that he was descended from a typical eighteenth-century building family, or that he himself was 'taken into a profitable partnership by John Armstrong, a large builder of Pimlico'.[69] Sir William Chambers was the contractor for, as well as the architect of, the houses which he built at Peper Harow and Roehampton, and most architects of his generation were prepared to submit an estimate upon which they obtained advances of money, making contracts with the tradesmen, and not infrequently taking a discount or percentage from them in addition to whatever remuneration they obtained from their employer.[70] But this was a very different matter from the earlier identity of builder and designer which had survived from the Middle Ages. It opened the way for dishonesty and shoddy building, and it made Sir John Soane's definition of an architect's duties, uncompromising in its rejection of the past, the only possible basis upon which the new profession was to achieve the respect of the public:

> The business of the Architect is to make the designs and estimates, to direct the works, and to measure and value the different parts; he is the intermediate agent between the employer, whose honour and interest he is to study, and the mechanic, whose rights he is to defend. His position implies great trust; he is responsible for the mistakes, negligences, and ignorance of those he employs; and above all, he is to take care that the workmen's bills do not exceed his own estimates. If these are the duties of an Architect, with what propriety can his situation, and that of the builder or the contractor, be united?

[69] *D.N.B.*
[70] *A.P.S.D.*, *s.v.*, 'ARCHITECT' and 'CONTRACTOR'. Such practices were denounced in vain by Robert Morris in *The Qualifications and Duty of a Surveyor, explained in a Letter to the Rt. Hon. the Earl of ——*, 1752, and in *A Second Letter to the Rt. Hon. the Earl of —— concerning the Qualifications and Duty of a Surveyor*, 1752. See also the anonymous article 'On the Present State of the Professions of Architect, Surveyor, and of the Building Trade in England' in Loudon's *Architectural Magazine* i, 1834, 12–16.

When this was first published in 1788[71] Soane's was a voice crying in the wilderness, but by 1835, when it was reprinted in his Memoirs, he was preaching to the converted. Jeffry Wyatville had found to his mortification that, despite his extensive practice, he was allowed to remain a candidate for admission to membership of the Royal Academy for twenty years, because the 'union of the tradesman with the architect was deemed, by the Royal Academicians, a sufficient bar to the advancement of Mr. Jeffry Wyatt to be one of their society'.[72] When the founders of the Institute of British Architects drew up their Prospectus, they had no hestitation in decreeing that divorce between Architecture and Building which subsequent practice has made absolute. No architect was to be eligible for membership who received 'any pecuniary consideration, or emolument, from Tradesmen, or who had any interest or participation in any Trade or Contract connected with Building'. Henceforth no architect would be able to supplement his income by speculative building, nor even by measuring and valuing works on behalf of builders. But whatever he may have lost in financial opportunity, he gained in social status and respectability: for henceforth he would rank as a gentleman, a scholar and an artist, clearly distinguished from the 'mechanic' who called himself a builder. For his client the gain was equally great: for now he could entrust his architectural affairs to his architect with the same confidence with which previously he had been accustomed to place his legal affairs in the hands of his lawyer. No longer would he be subjected to the confusion, the expense, above all the exasperation, which (as anyone who is familiar with the minutes of eighteenth-century building committees will know) so often resulted from the haphazard methods and ill-defined responsibilities of the time when the architectural profession was still in the making.

[71] In his *Plans, Elevations and Sections of Buildings executed in several Counties*, p. 7.
[72] *Gent's Mag.* xiii, 1840, 546.

A

ABEL, JOHN (*c.* 1578–1675), was a master carpenter who was responsible for several notable examples of the ornamental timber-framed architecture characteristic of the West Midlands in the sixteenth and seventeenth centuries. He lived at Sarnesfield near Leominster in Herefordshire, where a table-tomb in the churchyard refers to him as an 'architector' and records his death in 1674 in his 97th year.[1] The parish register shows that he was buried on 31 January 1674/5.

According to the collections for a history of Herefordshire made by Thomas Blount (d. 1679), Abel built the timber-framed houses at BRECON, 1624 (dem.), KINGTON,[2] 1654 (dem. 1820), and LEOMINSTER, 1633 (dismantled 1861 and rebuilt as a house called 'Grange Court'), and distinguished himself during the Civil War by constructing a corn-mill for use by the royalist forces besieged in Hereford in 1645. [Camden's *Britannia*, ed. Gough, ii, 1789, 460, citing Blount MSS.]

In 1625 Abel contracted to build the plain stone GRAMMAR SCHOOL at KINGTON for £240 [*The History of Kington, by a member of the Mechanics Institute*, Kington, 1845, 164–5]. In 1633 he was employed by Lord Scudamore to 'Survay the woorkes for reparing' ABBEY DORE CHURCH, HEREFS., and surviving accounts show that he performed the structural carpentry of the roofs himself. Presumably he also designed the handsome wooden screen [H. M. Colvin, 'The Restoration of Abbey Dore Church in 1633–4', *Trans. of the Woolhope Naturalists' Field Club* xxxii, 1948, 235–7]. In March 1652/3, as 'John Abell of Sarnesfield, carpenter', he contracted to erect a 'new building' at TYBBERTON COURT, HEREFS., for William Greene [Hereford City Library, L. C. Deed 880 and Brydges Papers 3471]. This does not survive. The attribution to Abel of various other buildings, including the very elaborate timber-framed Market Hall at Hereford (late sixteenth century, dem. 1862) cannot be substantiated. [R. A. Ford, 'John Abel, a 17th century Architect', *Trans. of the Woolhope Naturalists' Field Club*, 1963–8, pp. cvii–cix; N. Drinkwater, 'The Old Market Hall, Hereford', *ibid.* xxxiii, 1949–51, 1–13.]

ABRAHAM, ROBERT (1774–1850), was the son of a builder, and became a pupil of the surveyor James Bowen. It was as a London building surveyor that he began his professional life, and

---

[1] The inscription was recut in 1858, when the date 1674 was inadvertently altered to 1694. The tomb itself was repaired in 1886.
[2] Gough prints 'Knighton', but this is almost certainly a mistake for 'Kington'.

it was not until after the Napoleonic War that, in middle age, he developed a successful practice as an architect. He was fortunate enough to be employed by 'some of the chief Roman Catholic families in England', and many of his most important commissions were due to the patronage of the 12th Duke of Norfolk. He was a competent practitioner in the diverse styles expected of an English architect in the early nineteenth century, but his reputation rested on reliability rather than originality as a designer. His best-known work, the County Fire Office at the top of Lower Regent Street, was an effective re-creation of the south front of Old Somerset House, then believed to be the work of Inigo Jones.

Abraham's extensive knowledge of building practice was passed on to a number of pupils, including his son H. R. Abraham (who died in 1877, aged 73), G. Alexander, H. Flower, J. Lockyer, Thomas Little, T. Mackintosh, R. E. Philips, M. J. Stutely, C. Verelst and J. Woolley. His eldest daughter married Richard Bethell, Baron Westbury, Lord Chancellor 1861–5, whose influence procured for H. R. Abraham the commission for the Middle Temple Library. He died on 11 December 1850, and was buried in the extension of Hampstead churchyard. [*Builder* viii, 1850, 598, 602; *A.P.S.D.*; T. A. Nash, *Life of Richard Lord Westbury*, 1888, i, 44, 49, ii, 13.]

LONDON, COUNTY FIRE OFFICE, REGENT STREET, 1819; dem. 1924 [*Builder, ut supra*] (measured drawings in *Arch. Rev.* lvi, 1924, 234–8).

LONDON, NOS. 176–86 REGENT STREET, for J. Carbonell, wine-merchant, 1820; dem. [*Builder, ut supra*; drawing by Abraham reproduced in *C. Life*, 26 Oct. 1961, Supplement, 22].

LONDON, NORFOLK HOUSE, ST. JAMES'S SQUARE, alterations for 12th Duke of Norfolk, 1819–20 [*Builder, ut supra*; *Survey of London* xxix, 193]. According to Wheatley and Cunningham, *London Past and Present* ii, 1891, 600, he was also responsible for the addition of the portico and balcony for the 13th Duke of Norfolk in 1842. Norfolk House was dem. 1938.

FORNHAM HALL, SUFFOLK, works for the 12th Duke of Norfolk (d. 1842); dem. *c.* 1951 [*Builder, ut supra*].

ARUNDEL CASTLE, SUSSEX, works for the 12th Duke of Norfolk (d. 1842) [*Builder, ut supra*].

LONDON, THE CRAVEN CHAPEL, FOUBERT'S PLACE, 1821–2 [*Survey of London* xxxi, 200–1].

MILDENHALL SCHOOL, WILTS., 1823–4, Gothic [J. Britton, *Beauties of Wiltshire* iii, 1825, 268; inscription on building].

ALTON TOWERS, STAFFS., conservatories and garden buildings for the 15th Earl of Shrewsbury (d. 1827) [J. C. Loudon, *Encyclopaedia of Cottage, Farm and Villa Architecture*, 1846, 784–9] (*C. Life*, 2 June 1960). Some of his drawings for Alton were sold by Quaritch, 9

April 1879, lots 688–92, and there is one in R.I.B.A. Drawings Coll.

HAYLING ISLAND, HANTS., building development for William Padwick, who bought the land from the Duke of Norfolk in 1825 [printed handbill offering building leases and naming Abraham as architect in charge].

LONDON, THE WESTERN SYNAGOGUE, ST. ALBAN'S PLACE, off JERMYN STREET, 1827–8; dem. 1914 [Builder, ut supra].

TOOTING, SURREY, rebuilt NATIONAL SCHOOLS, 1829–30 [W. E. Morden, History of Tooting Graveney, 1897, 227, 232–3].

WORKSOP MANOR, NOTTS., works for the Earl of Surrey, afterwards 13th Duke of Norfolk, including a gardener's cottage [Builder, ut supra; Gardener's Magazine vi, 1830, 34–5].

WESTMINSTER BRIDEWELL, TOTHILL FIELDS, 1830–4; dem. 1885 [Builder, ut supra; T. L. Donaldson, Handbook of Specifications, 1860, 68].

HARLOW, ESSEX, THE FAWBERT AND BARNARD SCHOOL, 1836 [Architectural Magazine iii, 1836, 532].

LONDON OXFORD STREET, houses on the Berners estate, 1836 [A.P.S.D.].

THAME PARK, OXON., reconstructed medieval chapel for Baroness Wenman, 1836, Gothic [Building News, 30 March 1888, 457].

attributed: ARUNDEL, SUSSEX, THE TOWN HALL, for the 12th Duke of Norfolk, c. 1836, Romanesque [closely resembles Abraham's documented Congregational Church, and was evidently one of the works at Arundel mentioned in Builder, ut supra].

ARUNDEL, SUSSEX, THE CONGREGATIONAL CHAPEL (now Union Church), TARRANT STREET, 1836–8, Romanesque [church records, ex inf. Mr. R. Hewlings].

LONDON, THE COLLEGE OF HERALDS, QUEEN VICTORIA STREET, designed RECORD ROOM, 1842–4 [W. H. Godfrey and others, The College of Arms, Survey of London Monograph No. 16, 1963, 26 and pl. 11: see p. 24 for Abraham's earlier scheme for rebuilding the College in the West End].

ACTON, SAMUEL (c. 1773–1837), was the nephew and pupil of Nathaniel Wright (q.v.). He entered the Royal Academy Schools in 1790 at the age of 17 and won the Silver Medal in 1794. He exhibited at the Royal Academy from 1791 to 1802. He held the post of Surveyor to the Commissioners of Sewers for the City of London. In 1822 he was President of the Surveyors' Club, and left £500 to found a Charitable Fund for the benefit of its members and their dependants. He died in Jan. 1837 at Hill House, Chalfont St. Peter, Bucks. [records of the Surveyors' Club].

ADAM, JAMES (1732–1794), born in Edinburgh on 21 July 1732, was the third son of

William Adam (q.v.) and the younger brother of Robert Adam (q.v.). Sketch-books at Penicuik House show that he was already making competent architectural drawings in his early twenties. Among these drawings are a design for CUMNOCK CHURCH, AYRSHIRE, dated 1753, and a plan and elevation of GUNSGREEN HOUSE, EYEMOUTH, BERWICKSHIRE, as built c. 1755. His architectural education was completed by a tour of Italy, upon which he set out in 1760 accompanied by the draughtsman George Richardson. In Venice he was joined by Clérisseau, who accompanied him to Rome. He subsequently visited Naples and Paestum, but projects to visit Greece and Sicily came to nothing. The journal which he kept was printed in The Library of the Fine Arts ii, nos. 9–10, 1831, where it was mistakenly attributed to his brother. It shows the critical attitude towards Palladio and the interest in 'grotesque' and Pompeian decoration which was later to find expression in the introduction to The Works of Robert and James Adam. On his return in 1763 he joined the family partnership in London.

Although an elegant draughtsman and a competent architect, James Adam lacked both the drive and the genius of his elder brother, and was content to act as his junior partner rather than attempt to establish himself in independent practice. By 1763, when he returned to England, Robert had already worked out the essentials of the Adam style, and James's contribution to its genesis appears to have been slight. As Robert's partner he does, however, share the credit for the many buildings which they jointly designed and erected, and his achievement must not be judged merely by the few buildings which he seems to have designed independently. Besides the two early works mentioned above, these included the Ionic entrance gateway at CULLEN HOUSE, BANFFSHIRE, for the 3rd Earl of Seafield, 1767 [drawing in private hands, photo at N.M.R.S. and references to designs by James in letters from John Adam to Lord Seafield in S.R.O. GD 248/982/1], HERTFORD SHIRE AND TOWN HALL, 1767–9 [A. T. Bolton, 'The Shire Hall, Hertford', Arch. Rev., 1 April 1918, vol. 43, 68–73], and the façades of PORTLAND PLACE, LONDON, 1776 [Bolton, Architecture of R. and J. Adam ii, 104–5]. James must also have been largely, if not wholly, responsible for four buildings in GLASGOW which were all built after Robert Adam's death in 1792, namely THE ROYAL INFIRMARY, 1792–4, dem. c. 1910, THE TRON CHURCH, 1794, THE BARONY CHURCH, 1798, dem., and THE ASSEMBLY ROOMS, 1796–8, dem. c. 1890. 'Robert and James Adams' were named as architects of the Infirmary on the foundation-stone, but 'the late Mr. James Adams' is alone credited with the design of the Tron Church and the Assembly Rooms in The Picture of Glasgow, 1812, 87, 125. James Adam also signs the drawings for ST. GEORGE'S

EPISCOPAL CHAPEL, EDINBURGH, built in 1792–4.

In 1769 James Adam succeeded his brother as Architect of the King's Works upon the latter's election as M.P. for Kinross, retaining the post until its abolition in 1782. He was the author of *Practical Essays on Agriculture*, 'carefully collected and digested from the most eminent authors', published in 1789 (2nd ed. 1794) – a compilation from previous writers which, according to a notice in the *Monthly Review*, 'could not be ranked in the class of useful performances' – and projected a treatise on Architecture which was never completed. He died in London on 20 October 1794. Portraits by Allan Ramsay, c. 1754, and Pompeo Batoni, painted in Rome in 1763, are illustrated by Fleming, pls. 22 and 88. Prominent in the latter portrait is the 'Britannic Order' which James Adam invented. A sketch by him for a 'Chapiteau Ecossais' also exists.

Three of James Adam's architectural sketchbooks are among the Clerk papers at Penicuik House, Midlothian (photos. at N.M.R.S.), and several early designs by him are in vol. vii of the Adam drawings in Sir John Soane's Museum. His unexecuted designs for an enormous castellated house for the Earl of Lonsdale at Lowther, Westmorland, dated 1767, are in the Cumberland and Westmorland Record Office at Carlisle, together with alternative schemes by Robert Adam dated 1767 and 1771. [*A.P.S.D.*; *Gent's Mag.* 1794 (ii) 1056; A. T. Bolton, *The Architecture of Robert and James Adam*, 2 vols., 1922; John Fleming, *Robert Adam and his Circle*, 1962].

ADAM, JOHN (–1790), is supposed to have been a relative of Robert and James Adam. He appears in the Glasgow Directories as 'mason and architect', and he was Deacon of the Glasgow Masons in 1769. His known buildings are in a plain early eighteenth-century style with details similar to the work of William Adam. In 1768–72 he built the NEW (JAMAICA) BRIDGE at GLASGOW to the designs of Robert and William Mylne. He also built the range of houses facing Argyle Street from St. Enoch's Burn westwards, including ADAM'S COURT (dem.), which was named after him. In about 1767 he designed and built PETERSHILL HOUSE, nr. GLASGOW, for Alexander Williamson. He died at Glasgow on 30 June 1790. [*Scots Mag.* 1790, 311; *Extracts from the Records of the Burgh of Glasgow*, ed. Renwick, vii–viii, *passim*; Jas. Cleland, *Annals of Glasgow* i, 1816, 448; *The Old Country Houses of the Glasgow Gentry*, Glasgow 1870, pl. lxxxi and text; Senex, *Glasgow Past and Present* ii, 1884, 12, 433; information from Mr. David Walker.]

ADAM, JOHN (1721–1792), was the eldest son of William Adam (*q.v.*). He attended Dalkeith Grammar School, but the demands of the family business prevented him from going on to Edinburgh University. During the 1740s he was gradually taking over the control of his father's affairs, and when William Adam died in 1748 John succeeded him as laird of Blair Adam and as Master Mason to the Board of Ordnance. He immediately took his brother Robert into partnership and in the course of the next ten years they completed the very profitable works at Fort George and elsewhere in the Highlands which their father had undertaken after the rebellion of 1745. They also inherited his extensive architectural practice, which, until Robert established himself in London in 1758, continued to be a family partnership. To this partnership John Adam contributed business ability rather than artistic distinction, but he was nevertheless a competent architect who relied on the established formulae of English Palladianism to direct his taste. Of the buildings listed below, those erected before about 1760 must be regarded as the joint work of a firm in which John was the senior partner: when they are illustrated in *Vitruvius Scoticus* they normally appear above the plural signature *Adam's Architects*.

After about 1770 John Adam was eclipsed as an architect by his brilliant brother and appears to have given up practice. In 1772 he even got Robert and James to make designs (never carried out) for rebuilding his own house at Blair Adam (see Bolton, *Architecture of R. and J. Adam* i, 12). He continued, however, to be very much involved in his brothers' affairs. Indeed, it was chiefly to relieve his financial embarrassment after the failure of Fairholme's bank in 1764 that the firm of 'William Adam & Co.' was established in that year, and when the Adelphi speculation ended in disaster in 1772 he was obliged to mortgage the Blair Adam estate in order to avoid bankruptcy. His own business activities included the sale of stone from the Aberdeen quarries and a partnership in the Carron Iron Works. He died on 25 June 1792, leaving Blair to his only surviving son William Adam (1751–1839), barrister and M.P. A portrait by Francis Cotes at Blair Adam is illustrated by Fleming, pl. 21, and a portrait medallion by James Tassie dated 1791 is in the Scottish National Portrait Gallery. A sketchbook containing drawings of buildings seen by John Adam in England in 1748 is in the R.I.B.A. Drawings Collection. In the same collection there is also a drawing by John Adam for a scheme to unite the old and new towns at Edinburgh dated 1752. [John Fleming, *Robert Adam and his Circle*, 1962; T. C. Barker, 'The Aberdeen Quarries', *Arch. Rev.*, Feb. 1958; R. H. Campbell, *Carron Company*, Edinburgh, 1961, *passim*; L. Namier & J. Brooke, *The House of Commons 1754–1790* ii, 1964, 8–10.]

45

EDINBURGH, house in CANONGATE for Andrew Fletcher, Lord Milton, *c.* 1745/50; dem. [*Vit. Scot.*, pl. 45].

BANFF CASTLE, BANFF, rebuilt for Lord Deskford, 1750–2 [S.R.O., GD 248/984/4 and 248/1169–70].

EDINBURGH, TWEEDDALE LODGING, NO. 14 HIGH STREET, alterations for the 4th Marquess of Tweeddale, *c.* 1750–3 [National Library of Scotland, Yester Papers, *ex inf.* Mr. J. G. Dunbar].

HOPETOUN HOUSE, WEST LOTHIAN, completion of pavilions, offices and most of interior for 2nd Earl of Hopetoun, 1750–6 [J. Fleming, *ut supra*, 91–4].

BUCHANAN HOUSE, STIRLINGSHIRE, alterations to house and gardens for 2nd Duke of Montrose, 1751; largely destroyed by fire 1850 [payment to John Adam 'for drawing plans &c A°. 1751' in S.R.O., GD 220/6, vol. 106: cf. *Scots Peerage* vi, 268].

EDINBURGH, GREYFRIARS CEMETERY, Adam family mausoleum, 1753 [inscription: 'erected in 1750 by John eldest son of William Adam Architect', but not in fact begun until 1753: see Fleming, 338].

attributed: ARNISTON, MIDLOTHIAN, dining and drawing rooms on W. side for Robert Dundas, Lord Arniston (d. 1787), *c.* 1753–5 [A. A. Tait in *Burlington Mag.*, March 1969, 135] (*C. Life*, 15–22 Aug. 1925).

EDINBURGH, THE EXCHANGE (NOW CITY CHAMBERS), 1753–61 [W. Forbes Gray, 'The Royal Exchange and the City Improvements', *Book of the Old Edinburgh Club* xxii, 1938, 12–13].

LEITH CUSTOM HOUSE, enlarged existing building 1754; dem. 1812 [Edinburgh University Library, MS. Laing II, 135].

DUMFRIES HOUSE, AYRSHIRE, for the 4th Earl of Dumfries, 1754–9 [*Vit. Scot.*, pls. 19–21].

INVERARAY, ARGYLLSHIRE, THE TOWN or COURT HOUSE, 1755–7 [I. G. Lindsay and Mary Cosh, *Inveraray and the Dukes of Argyll*, 1973, 158–62].

EDINBURGH, conversion of Lord Lovat's house in High Street into an office for the Commissioners for Annexed Estates, 1756 [S.R.O., E 727/3 and E 727/8/1].

HAWKHILL VILLA, SOUTH LEITH, EDINBURGH, for Andrew Pringle, Lord Alemoor, 1757; dem. 1971 [*Vit. Scot.*, pl. 123★, signed 'John Adam, Architect'; James Simpson, 'Lord Alemoor's Villa at Hawkhill', *Bulletin of the Scottish Georgian Soc.* i, 1972].

DOUGLAS CASTLE, LANARKS., for the Duke of Douglas, 1757–61, Gothic; dem. *c.* 1939 [*Vit. Scot.*, pl. 135] (T. Hannam, *Famous Scottish Houses: the Lowlands*, 1928, 90–1).

YESTER HOUSE, E. LOTHIAN, interior of great saloon for the 4th Marquess of Tweeddale, *c.* 1758–61 [J. G. Dunbar, 'The Building of Yester

House 1670–1878', *Trans. of the E. Lothian Antiquarian Soc.* xiii, 1972, 32–4].

INVERARAY, ARGYLLSHIRE, works for the 3rd Duke of Argyll, including the CHERRY PARK offices, 1760–1, and the Gothic bridge over R. Aray, 1758–60; collapsed 1772 [*Vit. Scot.*, pl. 74, signed 'John Adam Architect'; I. G. Lindsay & Mary Cosh, *Inveraray and the Dukes of Argyll*, 1973, 136–7]. John Adam appears also to have designed the elliptical GARDEN or FREW'S BRIDGE, 1759–61, though in *Vitruvius Scoticus* it is ascribed to James Adam [Lindsay & Cosh, *op. cit.*, 372 n. 47].

BALLOCHMYLE HOUSE, AYRSHIRE, for Allan Whitefoord (d. 1767), *c.* 1760; remodelled in Jacobean style 1887–8 [*Vit. Scot.*, pl. 63].

WHIM, PEEBLESSHIRE, added library (forming S. wing) for the 3rd. Duke of Argyll, 1761 [*R.C.A.M. Peeblesshire* ii, 327].

MOFFAT HOUSE, MOFFAT, DUMFRIESSHIRE, for the 2nd Earl of Hopetoun, 1761 [accounts at Hopetoun House in name of 'Mr. Adam': *ex inf.* Mr. Basil Skinner].

EDINBURGH, HERIOT'S HOSPITAL, gateway and porter's lodge on N. side, 1762; dem. [W. Steven, *History of George Heriot's Hospital*, 1872, 123].

KERSE (or ZETLAND HOUSE), STIRLINGSHIRE, designed offices for Sir Lawrence Dundas, Bart., 1763 [estimate among Zetland papers in N. Riding Record Office]. It is not known whether these offices were built. Kerse was dem. *c.* 1958.

MOY HOUSE, MORAYSHIRE, internal alterations for James Grant, 1763–5 [S.R.O., GD 248/49/3/11 & 16 and 248/178/2].

BANFF, THE TOLBOOTH STEEPLE, 1764–7 [by 'Mr. Adam': *Annals of Banff*, ed. W. Cramond, i, 1891, 311].

CASTLE GRANT, MORAYSHIRE, additions for James Grant, 1765 [S.R.O., GD 248/49/3/25].

DUNROBIN CASTLE, SUTHERLAND, designed quadrangular stables for 17th Earl of Sutherland, 1766 [N.M.R.S., photos of drawings signed by John Adam]. It is doubtful whether these stables were built.

BROOMHALL, FIFE, remodelled house for 5th Earl of Elgin, 1766–71; subsequently rebuilt by T. Harrison 1796 [J. Mordaunt Crook in *C. Life*, 29 Jan. 1970].

CULLEN HOUSE, BANFFSHIRE, minor works for the 3rd Earl of Seafield in conjunction with James Adam, 1767–9 [letters in S.R.O. GD 248/982/1].

ADAM, ROBERT (1728–1792), was born at Kirkcaldy in Fife on 3 July 1728. He was the second surviving son of William Adam (*q.v.*), architect, builder and *entrepreneur*. In Edinburgh, where he attended the High School, and in 1743 matriculated at the University, Robert met some of the leading figures in Scottish intellectual life, among them William Robertson, the historian (who was his cousin), Adam Smith, the political economist (himself a native of Kirkcaldy), David Hume, the philosopher, and Adam Ferguson, another philosopher who was to become his 'particular friend'. In 1745 or 1746 he appears to have left the University without a degree in order to enter his father's drawing-office in the Canongate. When William Adam died in 1748, Robert and his elder brother John entered into partnership in order to carry on their father's business as an architect and contractor. So lucrative was this that by 1754 Robert had a capital of £5000 – more than enough to enable him to embark on that extended Grand Tour from which he hoped to return with fresh architectural ideas derived from a systematic study of the principal monuments of antiquity.

Robert left Edinburgh in October 1754. In Brussels he joined his travelling-companion the Hon. Charles Hope (younger brother of the Earl of Hopetoun, for whom John and Robert Adam were then completing Hopetoun House), whose friendship would automatically give him the entrée to aristocratic society wherever they went. In Florence he persuaded the French architectural designer Clérisseau to join him, thus acquiring the services of a brilliant draughtsman with a strong interest in the neo-classical. In Rome, under Clérisseau's guidance, he studied drawing and antiquity assiduously, acquiring the knowledge and expertise that would enable him to set up in practice as a fashionable architect. Among his Italian acquaintances was another pioneer of neo-classical taste, G. B. Piranesi, who later dedicated his account of the Campus Martius to *Roberto Adam Britann. Architecto Celeberrim.* In the summer of 1757 he set sail from Venice with Clérisseau and two other draughtsmen in order to explore and measure the ruins of the great late Roman Palace of Diocletian at Split in Dalmatia. Owing to the difficulties raised by the Venetian governor, it was clear that a prolonged stay was out of the question, and it was only by 'unwearied application' that the task was completed within the space of five weeks. The result was the publication in 1764 of the *Ruins of the Palace of the Emperor Diocletian at Spalatro*, a magnificent volume sumptuously engraved by Bartolozzi and others.

Robert Adam returned to England by way of the Rhineland during the winter of 1757–8, arriving in London in January. He established himself in a house in Lower Grosvenor Street, where he was soon joined by his two sisters and his brothers James and William. The decision to set up practice in London had already been taken while Robert was in Italy. 'Scotland', he wrote in 1755, 'is but a narrow place. [I need] a greater, a more extensive and more honourable scene, I

mean an English life.' It was with the object of equipping himself for English practice that, according to his own reckoning, he had spent between £800 and £900 a year in Italy, and the time had now come to realize his ambition to become the leading architect, not merely in Scotland, but in England as well. Henceforth he was to be the principal director of the family firm.[1] There can be no doubt that it was he who made it famous by his brilliance as a designer and his enormous capacity for work: but the less spectacular abilities of James and the business acumen of William also contributed to its success, while John Adam provided capital from his estate at Blair Adam. In addition to these private resources, Robert Adam could count on support from his fellow-countrymen in London, including the Duke of Argyll and Lord Bute, George III's first minister, who, although unfriendly at first, in 1761 procured for Adam one of the two newly created posts of Architect of the King's Works, with a salary of £300 p.a. The other went to Sir William Chambers, the king's architectural mentor and Adam's principal rival. Adam was already a member of the Society of Arts, to which he had been elected immediately after his return from Italy, and in 1761 he became a Fellow of the Royal Society. Thus established in practice, Adam set out to revolutionize English domestic architecture, which for thirty years had followed the pattern laid down for it by Lord Burlington. In place of the rigid grammar of the orders as described by Vitruvius and interpreted by Palladio, he substituted a new and elegant repertoire of architectural ornament based on a wide variety of classical sources ranging from antiquity to the Cinquecento. The success of the new style was immediate, and within a very few years it had taken the place of the older Palladianism and become the common property of the London builder. Among architects, only Sir William Chambers remained resolute in his refusal to have anything to do with Adam's 'affectations', and there can be no doubt that it was owing to his disapproval that Robert Adam never became a Royal Academician. Adam, for his part, ignored the Academy, sending none of his designs for exhibition at Somerset House. He did not, however, lack advertisement, for his publication of the *Ruins at Spalatro* was in the nature of a manifesto designed to show that the Palladians had not

---

[1] For the firm of 'William Adam & Co.' set up in 1764 see Alistair Rowan in *Journal of the Royal Society of Arts* cxxii, 1974, 659–78. It was a firm of developers and builders' merchants whose operations included the building of the Adelphi, the management of brickworks in London and Essex, and the quarrying of Aberdeen granite. Despite numerous financial vicissitudes it remained in business until 1801. Robert and James Adam kept a separate account for the profits of their joint architectural practice.

pronounced the last word on Roman architecture, and in 1773 there appeared the first
volume of the *Works in Architecture of Robert and
James Adam*.[1] The second volume followed in
1779, the third being published posthumously in
1822. By 1773 the Adam manner had already
been successfully imitated by others, and the preface to the first volume was intended to assert the
brothers' claim 'to have brought about . . . a kind
of revolution in the whole system' of English
architecture. In particular, they claimed to have
brought back the principle of 'movement', which
(in their own words) 'is meant to express the rise
and fall, the advance and recess with other
diversity of form, in the different parts of a building, so as to add greatly to the picturesque of the
composition'. This quality they recognized and
admired in the works of Sir John Vanbrugh,
though at the same time deploring the 'bar-
barisms and absurdities' which made his bold
designs so different from their own refined
and polished compositions. The picturesque
approach to architectural design revealed by this
passage is illustrated by the romantic landscapes
in the spirit of Salvator Rosa, of which Robert
Adam left a large number executed in pen and
wash, and even more by the dramatic massing of
such castellated mansions as Seton and Culzean
Castles, whose picturesque (yet always symmetrical) grouping, assisted by a minimum of
Gothic detail, was to be imitated by a whole
generation of Scottish country-house architects:
but it is also apparent in more orthodox buildings
such as Gosford House or Edinburgh University.
Here the architectural vocabulary remains
strictly classical, but effects of surprise or movement are achieved that in other hands or at other
periods might be classed as baroque.

It was, however, in interior design that the
Adam revolution made its greatest impact. Here
ingenious and imaginative planning ensured a
progression of varied and interesting shapes in
place of the simple rectangular rooms of earlier
Georgian architecture, and walls, ceilings, chimney-pieces, carpets and furniture – down even to
details like doorknobs and candlesticks – were
designed as part of an elegant, varied and highly
sophisticated decorative scheme incorporating
neo-classical and Renaissance motifs such as griffins, sphinxes, altars, urns and putti. Plasterwork
(often embellished with panels painted by artists
such as Cipriani, Zucchi and Rebecca) played a
large part in every Adam interior. Joseph Rose

(1745–99) was the plasterer who gave actuality to
many of Adam's designs with unfailing technical
skill.

The immense output of the Adam office was
made possible only by the employment of a
number of highly skilled draughtsmen. Of these
the most important were the Scottish George
Richardson (*q.v.*), a Liègois who is probably to
be identified as Laurent-Benoît Dewez (1731–
1812, subsequently the leading Belgian architect), and the Italians Agostino Brunias, Joseph
Bonomi, Giuseppe Manocchi and Antonio
Zucchi. Manocchi, who returned to Italy in 1773,
considered that he had been badly treated by the
Adams, but in the introduction to his *Book of
Ceilings* (1776) George Richardson spoke with
gratitude of the eighteen years he had spent
as an assistant in the Adam office.

Although for nearly thirty years Robert Adam
was one of the two or three busiest architects in
England, he was given few opportunities for
monumental design on a large scale. By the time
of his return from Italy, the great country mansions which reflected the ascendancy of the Whig
aristocracy had already been built, and in many
cases it was left to him only to remodel their interiors in accordance with modern taste. Too rarely
was he permitted to design an important house
from the foundation up, and it was not until the
end of his life that major public commissions
were entrusted to him at Cambridge and Edinburgh Universities. The former, however, came
to nothing, while the latter, unfinished at the time
of his death, was subsequently completed in a
very different way from what its architect had intended. Only the Register House remains as the
nearest approach to a monumental building in
the list of Adam's works.

It is to 'the desire to raise a great building of
a semi-public nature in the monumental manner'
that the Adelphi scheme is, in part at least, to be
attributed. In 1768 the brothers took a ninety-
nine-year lease of an extensive area on the north
bank of the river Thames, upon which they proposed to erect twenty-four first-rate houses,
treated as a single architectural composition and
raised on a terrace whose vaulted interior was intended to be let as warehouses. As a development
it was admirable, but as a speculation it was unprecedented, and in June 1772 work was halted
by a national credit crisis. On 27 June David
Hume wrote to Adam Smith:

> Of all the sufferers I am most concern'd for the
> Adams. . . . But their undertakings were so vast
> that nothing cou'd support them: they must
> dismiss 3000 workmen, who, comprehending
> the materials must have expended above
> 100,000 a year. They have great funds; but if
> these must be dispos'd of, in a hurry and to
> disadvantage, I am afraid the remainder will

---

[1] There are reprints by Thezard 1902, by Tiranti 1939
and 1959, with an introductory essay by John Swarbrick, and by Academy Editions 1975, with an introduction by R. Oresko. In 1821 a small quarto volume
was published, entitled *Designs for Vases and Foliage,
composed from the Antique, by Robert Adam* and consisting of fourteen engravings without any letterpress.

amount to little or nothing.... To me, the scheme of the Adelphi always appeared so imprudent, that my wonder is, how they cou'd have gone on so long.

Having failed to raise sufficient funds by a loan raised on the security of the Blair Adam estate, and by the sale of many of the works of art that they had brought back from Italy,[1] the brothers retrieved themselves from financial disaster by disposing of the whole property by means of a lottery (1774). Meanwhile in 1773 they had become involved (though not as principals) in another great town-planning venture in Marylebone, where they proposed to build a series of detached private palaces on either side of Portland Place. This time the outbreak of the War of American Independence led to the abandonment of the project in its original form, and blocks of houses took the place of the independent mansions originally proposed. The façades were designed by James Adam, but each house was built as an independent speculation.

A prominent feature of the Portland Place houses was the use of stucco for the central features on either side. Having acquired the patents in two stucco compositions – one invented by a Mr. David Wark of Haddington, the other by a Swiss clergyman named Liardet – the brothers obtained in 1776 an Act of Parliament vesting in the patentees the exclusive right to manufacture what they called 'Adam's new invented patent stucco'. A rival composition was put on the market by John Johnson, who maintained that it was based on a stucco invented before either Wark or Liardet had come on the scene. The Adams, however, claimed that Johnson had infringed their patent, and went to law (1778). The case was heard before Lord Chief Justice Mansfield, who, as a client and fellow-countryman of the plaintiffs, laid himself open to the charge of partiality when he gave judgement in favour of the Messrs. Adam. The case attracted considerable publicity, and was the subject of two pamphlets.

From about 1760 to 1780 Robert Adam was the most fashionable architect in England, but in the 1780s he began to be eclipsed by James Wyatt, and during the last ten years of his life his practice was almost confined to his native Scotland, where Wyatt found no patrons. He died suddenly on 3 March 1792, and was buried in the south transept of Westminster Abbey. The funeral was 'private', but the pall-bearers were the Duke of Buccleuch, the Earl of Coventry, the Earl of Lauderdale, Viscount Stormont, Lord Frederick Campbell and William Pulteney of Westerhall. The only official position which Robert Adam held at the time of his death was the Surveyorship of Chelsea Hospital, to which he had been appointed in 1765. He had relinquished the post of Architect of the King's Works in 1769, when he entered parliament as M.P. for Kinross-shire. The death of his brother James in 1794 meant the end of the firm, though William Adam survived to submit designs for the completion of Edinburgh University in 1815. He died in 1822 at the age of 84. He had gone bankrupt in 1801, and in 1818 and 1821 sold all his brothers' pictures, books, furniture, antiques and other possessions.[1]

In 1833 the bulk of the architectural drawings made by Robert and James Adam, nearly 9000 in number, were purchased from the family by Sir John Soane, and now form one of the principal treasures of the Museum which bears his name. Bolton's *Architecture of R. and J. Adam* contains a useful but not infallible index to the collection. Other drawings are in the collections of the Victoria and Albert Museum, the National Gallery of Scotland and the R.I.B.A., while some remain at Blair Adam and Penicuik houses in Scotland. For those in American collections see John Harris, *A Catalogue of British Drawings for Architecture ... in American Collections*, 1971.

The only certainly authentic portraits of Robert Adam known to be in existence are an ivory plaque at Blair Adam and the portrait attributed to Zoffany in the National Portrait Gallery in London. Three medallions in paste-relief by James Tassie are in the Scottish National Portrait Gallery, but two at least are posthumous.

[*Gent's Mag.* 1792 (i), 282–3; John Swarbrick, *Robert Adam and his Brothers: their Lives, Work and Influence on English Architecture*, 1915; A. T. Bolton, 'Robert Adam as a Bibliographer, Publisher and Designer of Libraries', *Trans. Bibliographical Soc.* xiv, 1915–17; A. T. Bolton, *The Architecture of Robert and James Adam*, 2 vols., 1922; A. T. Bolton, 'The Classical and Romantic Compositions of Robert Adam', *Arch. Rev.* lvii, Jan.–May 1925; Paul Oppé, 'Robert Adam's Picturesque Compositions', *Burlington Mag.* lxxx, 1942; J. Steegman & C. K. Adams, 'The Iconography of Robert Adam', *Arch. Rev.* xci, 1942; J. Lees-Milne, *The Age of Adam*, 1947; John Fleming, *Robert Adam and his Circle*, 1962; Eileen Harris, *The Furniture of Robert Adam*, 1963; Namier & Brooke, *The House of Commons 1754–1790* ii, 1964, 7–8; Damie Stillman, *The Decorative Work of Robert Adam*, 1966; Clifford Musgrave, *Adam and Hepplewhite Furniture*, 1966; Damie Stillman, 'Robert Adam and Piranesi', *Essays in the History of Architecture presented to Rudolf Wittkower*, ed. D. Fraser,

---

[1] They were sold at Christie's 25–27 Feb. and 1–2 March 1773.

[1] The catalogue of the 1818 sale is printed in *Sale Catalogues of Libraries of Eminent Persons* iv, ed. Watkin, 1972, 135–92.

1967; John Fleming, 'Robert Adam's Castle Style', *C. Life*, 23–30 May, 1968; John Fleming, 'A Retrospective View by John Clerk of Eldin, with some comments on Adam's Castle Style', in *Concerning Architecture*, ed. J. Summerson, 1968; A. J. Youngson, *The Making of Classical Edinburgh*, Edinburgh 1968, 289–91; A. A. Tait, 'The Picturesque Drawings of Robert Adam', *Master Drawings* ix, 1971, 161–71; *Robert Adam and Scotland, the Picturesque Drawings*, with introduction by A. A. Tait (Scottish Arts Council Exhibition Catalogue, 1972); Alistair Rowan, 'After the Adelphi: forgotten years in the Adam brothers' practice', *Journal of the Royal Society of Arts* cxxii, 1974, 659–710; James Macaulay, *The Gothic Revival*, 1975, chap. vi ('Robert Adam's Northern Castles').]

The basis of the following list of the executed works of Robert and James Adam is Bolton's *Architecture of R. and J. Adam*, which contains a catalogue of the drawings in Sir John Soane's Museum, arranged under names as well as places. A reference has been given to an original drawing only when it cannot readily be found in Bolton's list. The authorities for other additional works are given in square brackets in the usual way.

PUBLIC BUILDINGS, ETC.

LONDON, screen-wall to THE ADMIRALTY, WHITE-HALL, 1760; mutilated by G. L. Taylor 1827–8, restored 1923 (*Works* i, iii).

HIGH WYCOMBE, BUCKS., rebuilt the SHAMBLES AND BUTTER MARKET, 1761. The present lantern was added in *c*. 1900.

LONDON, BUCKINGHAM HOUSE, transparency in honour of King George III's birthday, 1762 (*Works* i).

CROOME CHURCH, WORCS., the Gothic interior decoration for the 6th Earl of Coventry, 1763. The architecture of the church was designed by L. Brown.

EDINBURGH, THE RIDING SCHOOL, YORK STREET,[1] 1764; dem. *c*. 1870.

HERTFORD, THE SHIRE AND TOWN HALL, 1767–9 [A. T. Bolton, 'The Shire Hall, Hertford', *Arch. Rev.*, 1 April 1918, vol. 43, 68–73].

STRATFORD-ON-AVON, WARWICKS., timber rotunda for Shakespeare Jubilee, 1769.

GUNTON CHURCH, NORFOLK, for Sir William Harbord, Bart., completed 1769 (faculty 1765); choir formed 1894.

BATH, SOMERSET, PULTENEY BRIDGE for William Pulteney, 1769–74. The shops have been much altered at various times (W. Ison, *The Georgian Buildings of Bath*, 1948, 65–9).

LONDON, WHITEHALL, remodelled house in SCOT-

LAND YARD as Board Room for Paymaster-General and Commissioners of Chelsea Hospital, 1771 [*Works* i].

KINROSS COUNTY BUILDINGS, architectural embellishment of south front, 1771 [inscription: 'This County House was repaired by the Crown. A.D. 1771. Robert Adam, Knight of this Shire, decorated this front at his own expense'].

LONDON, THE ROYAL SOCIETY OF ARTS, JOHN STREET, 1772–4 [John Summerson, 'The Society's House: an Architectural Study', *Jnl. of the Royal Soc. of Arts* cii, 1954, 920–33] (*Works* i).

DERBY, THE ASSEMBLY ROOMS, designed interior, completed 1774; destroyed by fire 1963 [correspondence with Adam brothers in Muniment Room at Kedleston Hall].

EDINBURGH, THE REGISTER HOUSE, 1774–92; rear portion completed by Robert Reid 1822–30 [A. A. Tait, 'The Register House: the Adam building', *Scottish Historical Review* liii, 1974, 115–123] (*Works* i).

BURY ST. EDMUNDS, SUFFOLK, THEATRE AND MARKET HALL (now TOWN HALL), 1775–80.

LONDON, DRURY LANE THEATRE, altered and refronted, 1775–6; rebuilt by H. Holland 1791–4 (*Works* ii).

PONTEFRACT, YORKS., remodelled THE RED LION INN for Sir Rowland Winn, 1776.

MISTLEY CHURCH, ESSEX, remodelled church of 1735 for Richard Rigby, 1776; dem., except for the twin towers, 1870 (*Works* ii).

CHELSEA HOSPITAL, redecorated Council Chamber, 1776, and other minor works.

EDINBURGH, THE UNIVERSITY, commenced to Adam's designs, 1789–93; completed to modified designs by W. H. Playfair 1817–26; dome added by Sir Rowand Anderson 1887 (*Works* iii).

EDINBURGH, THE BRIDEWELL PRISON, CALTON HILL, 1791–5; dem. *c*. 1884.

GLASGOW, THE TRADES HOUSE, GLASSFORD STREET, 1791–4; enlarged 1808 and 1828; interior reb. 1887.

GLASGOW, THE ROYAL INFIRMARY, CATHEDRAL SQUARE, 1792–4; dem. *c*. 1907.

EDINBURGH, ST. GEORGE'S EPISCOPAL CHAPEL AND MANSE, YORK PLACE, 1792–4, Gothic, now a warehouse [J. Stark, *Picture of Edinburgh*, 1823, 220; R.C.A.M., *City of Edinburgh*, 187].

GLASGOW, rebuilt THE TRON KIRK, 1793–4; now a warehouse.

GLASGOW, THE ASSEMBLY ROOMS, INGRAM STREET, erected 1796–8 to designs made before 1794; terminal pavilions added by H. Holland, 1807; dem. *c*. 1889. Part of the Adam façade was reerected as the McLellan Arch on the Green at the end of Charlotte Street (G. Richardson, *New Vitruvius Britannicus* i, 1802, pls. 8–9).

---

[1] It is not certain that this was built in accordance with Adam's design.

LONDON: DOMESTIC ARCHITECTURE

LANSDOWNE HOUSE, BERKELEY SQUARE, begun probably in 1762 for the 3rd Earl of Bute, who sold it unfinished to John Shelburne, 1st Marquis Lansdowne, a condition of the sale being the completion of the house by Adam at Lord Bute's expense. It was completed in 1768, except for the gallery, which was subsequently fitted up as a library by Joseph Bonomi, but altered by G. Dance, junior, and Robert Smirke. The façade was mutilated in 1936, and the interior of the drawing-room is now in the Museum of Arts at Philadelphia, U.S.A. (*Vitruvius Britannicus* v, 1771, pls. 9–10; *Works* ii, iii).

BUCKINGHAM HOUSE, ceiling and chimney-piece for Queen Charlotte, *c.* 1762; since destroyed [*Works* i].

ARLINGTON STREET, NO. 19, alterations and decorations for Sir Lawrence Dundas, Bart., 1763–6 (*C. Life*, 17 Sept. 1921).

GROSVENOR SQUARE, NO. 18 (later 19), alterations for the 8th Earl of Thanet, 1764–5; dem. (*C. Life*, 1–8 March 1919).

PICCADILLY, COVENTRY HOUSE, NO. 29 (now 106, ST. JAMES'S CLUB), interiors for the 6th Earl of Coventry, 1765–6.

PALL MALL, NO. 25, for Andrew Millar, 1765–6; dem. [*Survey of London* xxix, 325–6].

HILL STREET, alterations to interior of house for Mrs. Montagu, 1766 [*Mrs. Montagu's Letters*, ed. R. Blunt, i [1923], 152–3].

FIFE HOUSE, WHITEHALL, alterations for the 2nd Earl of Fife, 1766–7; dem.

HANOVER SQUARE, NO. 18, added library for Lord Le Despenser, 1766–8;[1] dem.

GREEN PARK, DEPUTY RANGER'S LODGE, 1768; dem. 1841 (*Works* iii).

DUCHESS STREET, PORTLAND PLACE, house for General Robert Clerk, 1768–71 (and 1779?); remodelled by Thomas Hope *c.* 1800; dem. 1851 [David Watkin, *Thomas Hope*, 1968, 93–4].

THE ADELPHI BUILDINGS, STRAND, with JOHN, ROBERT, WILLIAM and JAMES STREETS, 1768–72; dem. 1936, except No. 7 Adam Street.

PICCADILLY, NO. 79 (NO. 1, STRATTON ST.), ceiling for the 11th Earl of Eglinton, 1769; dem. 1929.

HERTFORD STREET, NO. 10, for General John Burgoyne, 1769–71.

SACKVILLE STREET, NO. 29, ceiling in drawing-room for John Parker, cr. Lord Boringdon, 1770 (*Survey of London* xxxii, pl. 146a).

NORTHUMBERLAND HOUSE, STRAND, interior decorations, including the Glass Drawing Room, for the 1st Duke of Northumberland,

1770–5; dem. 1874, but parts reassembled in Victoria and Albert Museum [D. Owsley & W. Rieder, *The Glass Drawing Room*, Victoria and Albert Museum, 1974].

MANSFIELD STREET, 1770–5.

CHANDOS HOUSE, CHANDOS STREET, PORTLAND PLACE, for 3rd Duke of Chandos, 1770–1.

BRITISH COFFEE HOUSE, COCKSPUR STREET, *c.* 1770; dem. 1886 (*Works*, ii; *C. Life*, 25 Aug. 1917).

ST. JAMES'S SQUARE, NO. 33, for Hon. George Hobart, later 3rd Earl of Buckinghamshire, 1770–72 [*Survey of London* xxix, 206–10].

SOHO SQUARE, NO. 20, interior for Baron Grant, 1771–2 (*C. Life*, 7 July 1917).

CURZON STREET, NO. 30, internal alterations, etc., for the Hon. H. F. Thynne, 1771–2.

ST. JAMES'S SQUARE, NO. 20, for Sir Watkin Williams-Wynn, 1771–4; extended by Mewès and Davis, 1936, to incorporate NO. 21, which was given an identical façade [*Survey of London* xxix, 164–74] (*Works* i, ii, iii).

APSLEY HOUSE, PICCADILLY, for 2nd Earl Bathurst, *c.* 1772–8; enlarged and refaced by B. and P. Wyatt 1828–9.

DERBY HOUSE, NO. 23 (later 26) GROSVENOR SQUARE, for Lord Stanley, later 12th Earl of Derby, 1773–4; dem. 1862 (*Works* ii).

ASHBURNHAM HOUSE, NO. 19 (now 30) DOVER STREET, alterations for 2nd Earl of Ashburnham, 1773–6 (*Works* ii).

HOME HOUSE, NO. 20 PORTMAN SQUARE, for Elizabeth, Countess of Home, 1773–6 [Margaret Whinney, *Home House*, 1969].

ST. JAMES'S SQUARE, NO. 11, refronted and some redecoration for Sir Rowland Winn, Bart., 1774–6; portico and balcony added 1877 [*Survey of London*, xxix, 123–4].

FREDERICK'S PLACE, OLD JEWRY (a square containing 'eight capital Dwelling houses'), 1775–6 [M. J. Chandler, 'Frederick's Place', *Arch. Rev.*, Feb. 1958; *R.I.B.A. Drawings Catalogue, A*, 15].

ROXBURGHE (afterwards HAREWOOD) HOUSE, HANOVER SQUARE, remodelled for 3rd Duke of Roxburghe, 1776; dem. 1908 (W. H. Godfrey, 'Harewood House', *Arch. Rev.* xxxvii–xxxviii, 1915).

PORTLAND PLACE, 1776–c. 1780; largely rebuilt.

DRUMMOND'S BANK, CHARING CROSS, alterations for Messrs. Drummond, 1777–8; dem.

NEW BURLINGTON STREET, NO. 10, remodelled interior for Sir John Griffin Griffin, 1778–9; dem. *c.* 1920 [*Survey of London* xxxii, 493–4].

HILL STREET, NO. 17, drawing-room for Sir Abraham Hume, Bart., 1779; since altered.

CUMBERLAND (formerly YORK) HOUSE, 86 PALL MALL, alterations for Henry Frederick, Duke of Cumberland, 1780–1; dem. 1908–12 [*Survey of London* xxix, 367].

HANOVER SQUARE, internal alterations and addition of balconies to house of Sir John Hussey

---

[1] The plumber's bill passed by Robert Adam on 25 July 1768 is in the R.I.B.A. Collection, and the smith's bill is in the Bodleian Library, MS. D. D. Dashwood (Bucks.) B. 12/6/14.

Delaval, Bart., 1781–2 [Newcastle Public Library, Hussey-Delaval Papers, Box 19 (i); Northumberland Record Office, 2 DE/23/1].
FITZROY SQUARE, south and east sides, 1790–4.

EDINBURGH: DOMESTIC ARCHITECTURE

CHARLOTTE SQUARE, designed by Robert Adam in 1791, and executed, with modifications (especially to the east and west sides), between 1792 and 1807.
QUEEN STREET, NO. 8, for Chief Baron Robert Orde, 1770–1.

GLASGOW: DOMESTIC ARCHITECTURE

COLLEGE HOUSES, NOS. 169–77 and 179–85 HIGH STREET, 1793; mutilated.

DUBLIN: DOMESTIC ARCHITECTURE

LANGFORD HOUSE, MARY STREET, ceiling of drawing-room, etc., for Hercules Rowley, 1765; dem. [*Georgian Soc. Records of Eighteenth-Century Architecture in Dublin* v, 1913, 58; drawings in Soane Museum].

COUNTRY HOUSES

GORDON HOUSE (later Seaton House and now Marion Grey Training College), ST. MARGARET'S ROAD, ISLEWORTH, MIDDLESEX, enlarged for General Humphry Bland, 1758–9.
HATCHLANDS, SURREY, interiors for Admiral Edward Boscawen, 1758–61 (*C. Life*, 17 Sept., 1 Oct. 1953).
SHARDELOES, nr. AMERSHAM, BUCKS., portico, interior decorations and stables for William Drake, 1759–63.
HAREWOOD HOUSE, YORKS. (W.R.), modified John Carr's designs and designed the interiors for Edwin Lascelles, cr. Lord Harewood, 1759–71. The house was much altered by C. Barry 1843–50. For further details see under CARR, JOHN.
CROOME COURT, WORCS., designed interiors of house, also orangery, rotunda and garden building called 'the Owl's Nest', for the 6th Earl of Coventry, 1760 onwards [G. W. Beard, 'Robert Adam and Croome Court', *Connoisseur*, Oct. 1953].
KEDLESTON HALL, DERBYSHIRE, completed house for the 1st Lord Scarsdale after Matthew Brettingham and James Paine had begun the central block and quadrants. The Adam brothers were responsible for the south front, the saloon, the interior decoration, the bridge, fishing house, Gothic temple and other buildings on the estate, *c.* 1760–70 (*Vitruvius Britannicus* iv, 1767, pls. 45–51).
BOWOOD HOUSE, WILTS., added portico, designed interiors of house, and remodelled office-block

for 2nd Earl of Shelburne, 1761–4: also designed the mausoleum in the grounds, completed 1764. The main body of the house was dem. 1956.
COMPTON VERNEY, WARWICKS., prolonged north and south wings, added portico, formed great hall, and designed orangery for 6th Lord Willoughby de Broke, *c.* 1761–7 (*Vitruvius Britannicus* v, 1771, pl. 43).
WITHAM PARK, SOMERSET, new house for William Beckford, begun *c.* 1762 (date of drawings) but abandoned after Beckford's death in 1770 [J. Collinson, *History of Somersetshire* ii, 1791, 235; *Vitruvius Britannicus* v, 1771, pls. 38–42].
MERSHAM HATCH, KENT, for Sir Wyndham Knatchbull, 1762–5 (*C. Life*, 26 March 1921).
SYON HOUSE, ISLEWORTH, MIDDLESEX, remodelled interior for the 1st Duke of Northumberland, 1762–9, and designed entrance-screen erected 1773 (*Works* i, ii, iii).
UGBROOKE PARK, DEVONSHIRE, rebuilt for 4th Lord Clifford, 1763–71, castle style [Alistair Rowan in *C. Life*, 20–27 July, 3 Aug., 5 Oct. 1967].[1]
OSTERLEY PARK, MIDDLESEX, remodelled for Robert Child, 1763–80.[2] The brothers Adam also designed the entrance lodges, bridge and garden houses.
MOOR PARK, HERTS., gateway and tea-pavilion for Sir Lawrence Dundas, 1763–5 (J. Harris, 'The Dundas Empire', *Apollo*, Sept. 1967, 176).
AUDLEY END, ESSEX, interior decoration for Sir John Griffin Griffin, later 4th Lord Howard de Walden, 1763–5; three-arched bridge 1764; Temple of Victory on Ring Hill 1772; Palladian bridge and tea-house 1782–3 [J. D. Williams, *Audley End: the Restoration of 1762–97*, Chelmsford 1966] (*C. Life*, 24 July 1926).
KIMBOLTON CASTLE, HUNTS., gatehouse and entrance-screen for 4th Duke of Manchester, 1764–5.
NOSTELL PRIORY, YORKS. (W.R.), remodelled hall and decorated principal rooms for Sir Rowland Winn, 1765–75. The Adams designed new wings, the northern of which was built between 1776 and 1785, when work was suspended: it was finally completed in 1875. The southern wing was never begun. They also designed the Featherstone, Foulby and Wragby Gates 1776–7, and the south and west sides of the stable block *c.* 1776. The north and east sides are by Pritchett and Watson, 1829, but making use of Adam's design for the

---

[1] L. Brown is known to have made a design for this house, but does not appear to have been responsible for the building as executed.
[2] The north side of the house, including the Gallery, had already been remodelled for Francis Child before his death in 1761. His architect was probably Chambers (see John Harris, *Sir William Chambers*, 1970, 240).

cupola [drawings and accounts at Nostell and Soane Museum].

STRAWBERRY HILL, MIDDLESEX, Gothic ceiling and chimney-piece in Beauclerk Room for Horace Walpole, 1766–7 [D. Stillman, *The Decorative Work of R. Adam*, 1966, 111, pls. 169–70].

WIMBLEDON HOUSE, SURREY, interior decoration for Sir Ellis Cunliffe, 1766–7.

AUCHENCRUIVE HOUSE, AYRSHIRE, interiors for Richard Oswald, 1766–7; castellated tower 1778 (*C. Life*, 17 Dec. 1935).

LUTON HOO, BEDS., for 3rd Earl of Bute, 1766–74; left unfinished; altered by R. Smirke *c.* 1815 onwards; reconstructed by S. Smirke after a fire in 1843; upper storey by Mewès and Davis 1903 (*Works* i).

HALSWELL PARK, SOMERSET, Ionic temple for Sir Charles Tynte, Bart., 1767.

LEYTON, ESSEX, THE GREAT HOUSE, remodelled principal rooms for Thomas Oliver, *c.* 1767–9; dem. 1905 [*V.C.H. Essex* vi, 191].

KENWOOD HOUSE, HAMPSTEAD, MIDDLESEX, remodelled existing house and added library and portico for 1st Earl of Mansfield, 1767–9 (*Works* i).

SALTRAM HOUSE, DEVONSHIRE, remodelled interior for John Parker, cr. Lord Boringdon, 1768–79 (*C. Life*, 4–11 May, 14 Sept. 1967).

WHITEHAVEN CASTLE (formerly Flatt Hall, now a Hospital), CUMBERLAND, enlarged and remodelled for Sir James Lowther, *c.* 1768–9, castle style.[1]

LOWTHER VILLAGE, WESTMORLAND, layout of model village for Sir James Lowther, carried out *c.* 1770–5 on the basis of plans made by Adam in 1766 [R. W. Brunskill, 'Lowther Village and Robert Adam', *Trans. Ancient Monuments Society* N.S. xiii, 1967].

MAMHEAD HOUSE, DEVONSHIRE, alterations for 4th Viscount, afterwards 1st Earl of Lisburne, *c.* 1770; rebuilt by A. Salvin 1828–38.[2]

KILDUFF, near ATHELSTANEFORD, EAST LOTHIAN, addition of wings for John Home, 1770; since rebuilt [letter quoted by Bolton, i, 116].

MELLERSTAIN, BERWICKSHIRE, for the Hon. George Baillie, *c.* 1770–8, castle style (*C. Life*, 28 Aug., 4 Sept. 1958).

NEWBY HALL, YORKS. (W.R.), added porch and wings (containing sculpture gallery and offices) and remodelled library for William Weddell, *c.* 1770–*c.* 1780 (Hugh Honour, 'Newby Hall, Yorkshire', *Connoisseur* cxxxiv, 1954; *C. Life*, 19–26 June 1937).

ALNWICK CASTLE, NORTHUMBERLAND, interior decoration of keep in the Gothic style for the 1st Duke of Northumberland, *c.* 1770–80; destroyed *c.* 1854. Adam succeeded James Paine (*q.v.*) as the Duke's architect. The principal rooms for which he was responsible were the saloon, drawing-room and library (for plans of the castle in the eighteenth century see *Castles of Alnwick & Warkworth etc.* from sketches by C. F. Duchess of Northumberland, privately printed 1823 and *R.I.B.A. Sessional Papers 1856–7*, 14). The Adam brothers also designed ALNWICK BRIDGE for the Duke in 1773 [Alnwick archives, U.I. 46], the Gothic BRIZLEE TOWER in Hulne Park 1777–83 [*ibid.* and drawings in Soane Museum], the Gothic interior of HULNE ABBEY, ALNWICK, 1778 [John Fleming, 'Adam Gothic', *Connoisseur* cxliii, 1958], and the gazebo on RATCHEUGH CRAG, *c.* 1780 [drawing at Alnwick].

CASTLE HOUSE, CALNE, WILTS., rebuilt garden front for David Bull, 1770.

HITCHIN PRIORY, HERTS., south front for John Radcliffe, 1770–3. Adam drawings exist in the Soane Museum both for a new house on a different site and for a remodelling of the old house. Neither was carried out, but a new south front was built in 1770–3 by Richard Dixon, carpenter, and Joseph Dixon, mason, both of London. In Sept. 1772 Radcliffe paid 'Messrs. Adams' £140, and in December he paid £26 16s. to 'Mr. Nasmith Foreman to Messrs. Adams for plans' [Herts. R.O., DE 4422/2]. It would therefore appear that the new front with the Drawing and Music Rooms was designed by the Adams (*C. Life*, 17–24 Oct. 1925).

WEDDERBURN CASTLE, DUNS, BERWICKSHIRE, for Patrick Home, 1771–5, castle style [Alistair Rowan, 'Wedderburn Castle', in *The Country Seat*, ed. Colvin and Harris, 1970, and in *C. Life*, 8 Aug. 1974].

STOWE HOUSE, BUCKS., designs for rebuilding south front for 1st Earl Temple, 1771, executed with modifications by Thomas Pitt (*q.v.*), 1772–7.

HEADFORT HOUSE, CO. MEATH, IRELAND, interiors for the 1st Earl of Bective, 1772–5 [John Harris, *Headfort House and Robert Adam*, R.I.B.A. 1973] (*C. Life*, 21–28 March 1936).

HIGHCLIFFE HOUSE, HANTS., for the 3rd Earl of Bute, 1773; dem. 1794 (W. Watts, *Seats of the Nobility and Gentry*, pl. lxv, 1784).

CALDWELL HOUSE, AYRSHIRE, for William Mure, 1773–4, castle style (A. H. Millar, *Castles and Mansions of Renfrewshire*, 1890).

ST. EDMUND'S HILL (now MORETON HALL), BURY ST. EDMUNDS, SUFFOLK, for John Symonds, 1773–6 [*The Beauties of England and Wales* xiv, *Suffolk* by F. Shoberl, 1813, 90; drawings in Soane Museum, xxxiii, 73–5].

THE OAKS, CARSHALTON, SURREY, temporary

---

[1] Bolton's statement (ii, 31) that 'nothing important appears to have been done' is incorrect.

[2] In the Victoria and Albert Museum there is a collection of eighteenth-century drawings connected with Mamhead, including a number of designs by the Adam brothers (2165–2186: 1896).

pavilion in garden for Lord Stanley, afterwards 12 Earl of Derby, for *fête-champêtre* held on 9 June 1774 (cf. *Gent's Mag.* 1774, 264–5). The Adams made designs for rebuilding the house (dem. 1957–60) and may have been responsible for the castellated additions illustrated by D. Hughson, *London* v, 1808, and J. P. Neale, *Views of Seats* ii, 1819.

GREAT SAXHAM HALL, SUFFOLK, alterations for Hutchison Mure, 1774; destroyed by fire 1779 [A. Rowan in *Journal of the Royal Society of Arts* cxxii, 1974, 699].

WOOLTON HALL, LANCS., greatly enlarged for Nicholas Ashton, *c.* 1775 [S. A. Harris, 'Robert Adam and Woolton Hall', *Trans. Historic Soc. of Lancs and Cheshire* cii, 1950].

HAMPTON, MIDDLESEX, alterations to David Garrick's villa, including the addition of the portico, 1775 [cf. letter from Mrs. Garrick to Peter Garrick, n.d., in Victoria and Albert Museum, L. 4631–1970, 86 NN (vii)].

WENVOE CASTLE, GLAMORGANSHIRE, for Peter Birt, 1776–7, castle style; dem. (except the stables) after a fire in 1910. Adam's plans and elevations in the Soane Museum were carried out with modifications. There are, however, no Adam drawings for the interiors. The statement in *Gent's Mag.* 1785 (ii), 937, that Wenvoe was 'rebuilt a few years ago in a grand old castle taste, by Mr. Holland, the celebrated architect', appears to be erroneous. A letter to Birt from Thomas Roberts (apparently the builder) in the National Library of Wales (MS. 20656 B) confirms the date of erection, but throws no light on the identity of the architect employed.

WORMLEYBURY, HERTS., interior decoration for Sir Abraham Hume, Bart., 1777–9 [A. T. Bolton in *C. Life*, 30 Jan. 1915; D. Stillman, *The Decorative Work of Robert Adam*, 1966, 77, 104, 107].

CULZEAN CASTLE, AYRSHIRE, for the 10th Earl of Cassilis, 1777–92, castle style (*C. Life*, 4–11 Sept. 1915).

WEALD HALL, ESSEX, decoration of dining-room for Christopher Tower, 1778; dem. 1950–1 (*C. Life*, 3 Oct. 1914).

LANGSIDE, RENFREWSHIRE, for Thomas Brown, 1778; dem. [drawings in Soane Museum, xlii, 20–5, inscribed 'Aikenhead'] (*The Old Country Houses of the Old Glasgow Gentry*, Glasgow 1870, pl. lxvi).

WYKE HOUSE, SYON HILL, ISLEWORTH, MIDDLESEX, added drawing-room for John Robinson, 1778–9.

BYRAM HALL, YORKS. (W.R.), decoration of library, etc., for Sir John Ramsden, Bart., 1780; dem.

MISTLEY HALL, ESSEX, alterations for Richard Rigby, *c.* 1780; dem. 1835.

LETTERFOURIE HOUSE, BANFFSHIRE, for one of its Gordon owners, probably *c.* 1780 [drawings in Soane Museum, xlv, 90–3: 'design of a House for — Gordon, Esq.'].

OXENFOORD CASTLE, MIDLOTHIAN, remodelled for Sir John Dalrymple, Bart., 1780–2, castle style; altered and enlarged by W. Burn 1842 (view in W. Angus, *Seats of the Nobility and Gentry*, pl. xiv, 1788, 'from a drawing by Robert Adam'; *C. Life*, 15 Aug. 1974).

JERVISTON HOUSE, HOLYTOWN, LANARKSHIRE, for James Cannison, 1782; dem. *c.* 1965.

attributed: PITFOUR CASTLE, PERTHSHIRE, for John Richardson, *c.* 1785, castle style; enlarged by W. Burn 1825 [stylistic attribution: no drawings in Soane Museum].

CASTLE UPTON, CO. ANTRIM, IRELAND, designs for alterations for 1st Lord Templetown, made in 1783 and probably not completed at the time of Lord Templetown's death in 1785; further alterations for 2nd Lord Templetown 1788–9, including castellated stables. The house was altered by Blore *c.* 1830 [A. Rowan, 'Georgian Castles in Ireland', *Irish Georgian Society's Trans.*, Jan.–March 1964, 15].

BRASTED PLACE, KENT, for Dr John Turton, 1784–5; roof heightened, etc., 1871.

ASHBURNHAM PLACE, SUSSEX, lodges at entrance to main drive for the 2nd Earl of Ashburnham, 1785 [accounts formerly at Ashburnham Place].

SUNNYSIDE HOUSE (later KINGSTON GRANGE, now Liberton Golf Club), LIBERTON, MIDLOTHIAN, for Sir Patrick Inglis, 1785–7: south side rebuilt in nineteenth century.

MILBURN, CLAREMONT LANE, SURREY, for 1st Lord Delaval, 1787–90, since considerably altered [drawings in Soane Museum, xlvi, 1–4; Northumberland Record Office, 2 DE/23/1 and 3].

GLASSERTON HOUSE, WIGTOWNSHIRE, for Admiral Keith Stewart, 1787; porch added by W. Elliot *c.* 1820; dem. *c.* 1950 (J. P. Neale, *Views of Seats*, 2nd ser., v, 1829).

KIRKDALE HOUSE, KIRKCUDBRIGHTSHIRE, for Sir Samuel Hannay, Bart., 1787–8; central block reconstructed internally after fire: the octagonal farmstead may well be also by Adam.

BARHOLM (or BALHAZY), nr. CREETOWN, KIRKCUDBRIGHTSHIRE, for John McCulloch, 1788; dem. 1960. The earlier design illustrated in *Vitruvius Scoticus*, pl. 94, was not carried out.

YESTER HOUSE, EAST LOTHIAN, remodelled centre of north front for the 7th Marquess of Tweeddale, 1788–90 [J. G. Dunbar, 'The Building of Yester House 1670–1878', *Trans. of the E. Lothian Antiquarian Soc.* xiii, 1972, 35–6] (*C. Life*, 23–30 July 1932, 9, 16 and 23 Aug. 1973).

ALVA HOUSE, CLACKMANNANSHIRE, alterations and addition for John Johnstone, 1789; dem.

RUSCOMBE HOUSE, HARE HATCH, BERKS., remodelled for Sir James Eyre, 1789; dem. 1830.

NEWLISTON HOUSE, WEST LOTHIAN, for Thomas

Hogg, 1789–90; wings added by D. Bryce 1845 (*C. Life*, 26 Feb. 1916).

DALQUHARRAN CASTLE, AYRSHIRE, for Thomas Kennedy, built 1790 to designs made 1782–5; enlarged 1881; castle style (A. H. Millar, *Castles and Mansions of Ayrshire*, 1885; *C. Life*, 22 Aug. 1974, 494–5).

UDNY HOUSE, TEDDINGTON, MIDDLESEX, added picture gallery for Robert Fullarton Udny (d. 1802), probably *c.* 1790; dem. *c.* 1825 (W. Niven, 'Robert Udny's Villa at Teddington', *Home Counties Magazine*, 1899).

WYRESIDE, nr. GARSTANG, LANCS., alterations, including addition of portico, for J. F. Cawthorne, 1790; rebuilt in nineteenth century (engraving in *The Lonsdale Magazine or Provincial Repository* ii, 1821, 201; Twycross, *The Mansions of England: Lancashire*, 1847–50, ii). The complete scheme of remodelling shown in the Soane Museum drawings and V. & A. 3328–3330 was not carried out.

attributed: FULLARTON CASTLE, AYRSHIRE, castellated stables for Col. William Fullarton, 1790; dem. 1966 [no drawings for the stables exist, but the Adam brothers made unexecuted designs for a new house which are dated 1790].

SETON CASTLE, EAST LOTHIAN, for Alexander Mackenzie, 1790–1, castle style.

AIRTHREY CASTLE, STIRLINGSHIRE, for Robert Haldane, 1790–1, castle style; enlarged 1891 (R.C.A.M., *Stirlingshire*, pl. 201).

ARCHERFIELD HOUSE, EAST LOTHIAN, remodelled interior for William Nisbet, 1790–1 [drawings in Soane Museum; accounts in S.R.O., GD6/1644].

DUNBAR CASTLE (later Castle Park Barracks), EAST LOTHIAN, for the 8th Earl of Lauderdale, 1790–2.

BELLEVILLE (or BALAVIL) HOUSE, ALVIE, INVERNESS-SHIRE, for James Macpherson, 1790–6 (John Fleming, 'Balavil House', in *The Country Seat*, ed. Colvin & Harris, 1970, 178–80).

GLENCARSE HOUSE, PERTHSHIRE, for Thomas Hunter, 1790– ; additions 1889.

GOSFORD HOUSE, EAST LOTHIAN, for the 7th Earl of Wemyss, 1790–*c.* 1800; wings dem. *c.* 1810; house remodelled and new wings built 1883–91 to designs of W. Young; centre block gutted 1940; north wing unroofed *c.* 1950; south wing rehabilitated 1951 (G. Richardson, *New Vitruvius Britannicus* i, 1802, pls. 43–50; *C. Life*, 21 Oct., 4 Nov. 1971).

WALKINSHAW HOUSE, nr. PAISLEY, RENFREWSHIRE, for D. Macdowall, 1791; dem. *c.* 1927 (A. H. Millar, *Castles and Mansions of Renfrewshire*, 1890).

DALKEITH HOUSE, MIDLOTHIAN, bridge ('Montagu Bridge') over R. Esk in grounds for the 3rd Duke of Buccleuch, 1792 [drawing in Scottish National Gallery Print Room signed by R.

Adam and dated 1791; set of drawings at Drumlanrig Castle].

STOBS CASTLE, ROXBURGHSHIRE, for Sir William Elliott, Bart., 1792–3, castle style (*C. Life*, 22 Aug. 1974, 497).

MAULDSLEY CASTLE, LANARKSHIRE, for the 5th Earl of Hyndford, 1792–6, castle style; altered by David Bryce 1860; dem. 1959 (*Scots Magazine*, Sept. 1808; J. M. Leighton, *Select Views on the River Clyde*, 1830, opp. p. 31; *C. Life*, 22 Aug. 1974, 497).

BALBARDIE HOUSE, BATHGATE, WEST LOTHIAN, for Alexander Marjoribanks, 1793; dem. *c.* 1960 except one wing [T. P. Marwick, 'Balbardie House and Robert Adam', *Arch. Rev.* xlviii, 1920, 81–5].

BARNTON CASTLE, MIDLOTHIAN, remodelled for George Ramsay, *c.* 1794, castle style; enlarged by D. Hamilton *c.* 1810; dem. *c.* 1920 [Soane Museum, xlvi, 39–41] (J. Small, *Castles and Mansions of the Lothians* i, 1883).

MAUSOLEA AND MONUMENTS See p. 986

BOWOOD, WILTSHIRE, mausoleum in memory of 1st Earl of Shelburne for his widow, 1761–4.

ST. MICHAEL PENKEVIL CHURCH, CORNWALL, monument to Admiral Edward Boscawen (d. 1761), erected 1763, J. M. Rysbrack, sculptor [signed].

KEDLESTON CHURCH, DERBYSHIRE, monument to Sir Nathaniel Curzon (d. 1758), erected 1763, J. M. Rysbrack, sculptor [signed].

WORCESTER CATHEDRAL, monument to Bishop James Johnson (d. 1774), Joseph Nollekens, sculptor.

MILTON ABBEY CHURCH, DORSET, table-tomb to Lady Milton, 1775, A. Carlini, sculptor [M. I. Webb in *Arch. Rev.*, May 1958, 331].

EDINBURGH, OLD CALTON BURYING GROUND, monument to David Hume (d. 1776), erected 1778.

EDINBURGH, BOTANICAL GARDENS, urn to memory of Sir Charles Linnaeus, 1778.

DUMFRIES, column in memory of the 3rd Duke of Queensberry (d. 1778), erected in Queensberry Square 1780, moved to County Buildings 1934.

HESTON CHURCH, MIDDLESEX, monument to Robert Child (d. 1782), P. M. Van Gelder, sculptor.

CASTLE UPTON, CO. ANTRIM, IRELAND, mausoleum in memory of the Hon. Arthur Upton (d. 1768), erected 1789.

ALVA CHURCHYARD, CLACKMANNANSHIRE, Johnstone family mausoleum for John Johnstone, *c.* 1789 [drawing in Soane Museum, x. 45].

WESTERKIRK CHURCHYARD, DUMFRIESSHIRE, Johnstone family mausoleum for Sir James Johnstone, 1790.

ADAM, WILLIAM (1689–1748), was the leading Scottish architect of his day. Though his forbears, as hereditary proprietors of a small estate near Forfar, had long ranked as minor gentry, William's father John Adam made a living as a builder in Kirkcaldy, where William was born on 30 October 1689. Of his early life nothing certain is known, but he was probably educated locally. By the 1730s he had made himself 'the universal architect' of a country whose belated emergence from a backward and impoverished past offered great opportunities to an enterprising man. In the words of John Clerk of Eldin, William Adam was 'a man of distinguished genius, inventive enterprise and engaging address' who was on excellent terms both with the Scottish aristocracy and with some of the leading figures of the 'Scottish enlightenment'. Unlike Sir William Bruce and James Smith, the two leading architects of the previous generation, whose sympathies had been Jacobite, Adam was a presbyterian Whig and therefore acceptable both to the government and to men of influence such as the 2nd Earl of Stair (who was his particular patron).

Although he always styled himself 'Architect', William Adam was not only a building contractor on a large scale, but also an entrepreneur who engaged in a variety of business enterprises. In 1728 Sir John Clerk of Penicuik 'could not enough admire the enterprising temper of the proprietor who had at that time under his own care near to twenty general projects – Barley Mills, Timber Mills, Coal Works, Salt Pans, Marble Works, Highways, Farms, houses of his own a-building and houses belonging to others not a few'. Although there were times when his friends thought that he had overreached himself ('As for Adams', wrote the Marquis of Annandale in 1724, 'he has so many Real, and so many imaginary projects, that he minds no body nor no thing to purpose'), he made a substantial fortune which he invested partly in house property in Edinburgh and partly in the estate of Blair Crambeth in Kinross-shire, the nucleus of which he bought in 1731 for £8010 Scots and renamed Blair Adam. In 1728 he took up residence in Edinburgh, when he was made a burgess gratis in recognition of the 'good services' which he had rendered to the city. During the previous year Lord Stair had almost succeeded in persuading Walpole to revive for Adam the post of Surveyor of the King's Works in Scotland previously held by James Smith in the reign of Queen Anne, but the proposal fell through because of the king's death. However, in 1728 Adam became Clerk and Storekeeper of the Works in Scotland, and in 1730 he was appointed Mason to the Board of Ordnance in North Britain, a post which brought him large contracts for military fortifications after the '45.

The extent of William Adam's architectural practice can be judged from the buildings listed below. In addition he often acted as a landscape gardener, *e.g.* at Newliston (1731), Taymouth (*c.* 1732), Craigston (1733) and Buchanan House (1745). The formation of his architectural style awaits further investigation. It is, however, evident that (despite his friendship with Sir John Clerk, the Scottish Lord Burlington, in whose company he visited London in 1727) he had 'little taste for the severities of the English neo-Palladian School'. On the contrary he deployed architectural forms from a variety of sources with a freedom of invention which is sometimes bizarre but never dull. Arched windows, channelled masonry, richly carved tympana, prominent swags and other such features give a vigorous and sometimes slightly over-dressed character to his elevations which contrasts strongly with the restraint of most contemporary English architecture. Gibbs and Vanbrugh were undoubtedly influential in the formation of Adam's style, but there is evidence of an early visit to Holland (whence, according to John Clerk of Eldin, he introduced the manufacture of pantiles into Scotland) which may have given him first-hand experience of continental baroque.

In 1727 Adam began to solicit subscriptions for a volume of engravings illustrating the works of himself and other contemporary Scottish architects, but he never brought the project to fruition and, although the drawings and engravings were made, the book was still unpublished at the time of his death.[1] John Adam issued proposals for printing the book by subscription in 1766, but nothing came of his efforts, and it was not until about 1812 that *Vitruvius Scoticus* was at last published by John Adam's son William. It contains 160 plates, of which over 100 illustrate Adam's own designs, but there is no text or introduction.

In 1716 William Adam married Mary Robertson, daughter of William Robertson of Gladney, by whom he had four sons and six daughters. The eldest son John (*q.v.*) succeeded his father as the laird of Blair Adam, and carried on the various family businesses in Edinburgh. Robert and James (*q.v.*), born in 1728 and 1732, left Scotland to go into partnership in London, whither they were followed by the fourth son William (1738–1822), who had a chequered business career in the City.

William Adam died on 24 June 1748, and is commemorated by a bust (illustrated by J. Swar-

[1] In 1733 the English antiquary James West, when in Edinburgh, 'went to see Mr Cowper Engraver who with Mr Adams the Architect is about publishing & engraving all the fine buildings in Scotland to make a *Vitruvius Scoticus*' (MS. Journal of a Tour to Scotland at Alscot Park, Warwicks.).

brick, *Robert Adam*, 1915, 35) in the family mausoleum in Greyfriars Churchyard, erected by John Adam in 1753. Another bust probably of William Adam is in the Scottish National Portrait Gallery, and there is a duplicate in the collection of Mr. John Harris. A portrait by William Aikman at Blair Adam is reproduced by Fleming, pl. 1.

[John Fleming, *Robert Adam and his Circle*, 1962; J. G. Dunbar, *The Historic Architecture of Scotland*, 1966, 107–112; James Simpson, *Vitruvius Scoticus*, unpublished thesis, Edinburgh 1970; biographical notes by John Clerk of Eldin in S.R.O., GD 18/4981. In 1743 there was a lawsuit between William Adam and Lord Braco over his remuneration for designing and building Duff House, Banffshire. The printed *Depositions* incidental to this case throw considerable light on Adam's architectural practice.]

PUBLIC BUILDINGS, ETC.

ABERDEEN, enlarged THE TOWN-HOUSE, 1729–30; dem. 1865 [*Aberdeen Fifty Years Ago*, Aberdeen 1868, 65].

ABERDEEN, ROBERT GORDON'S HOSPITAL, 1730–2; altered and enlarged by John Smith 1830–3, now part of Robert Gordon's School [*Vit. Scot.*, pls. 107–8].

DUNDEE, THE TOWN HOUSE, 1732–4; dem. 1932 [*Vit. Scot.*, pl. 104].

GLASGOW, THE UNIVERSITY LIBRARY, 1732–45; enlarged 1782; dem. *c.* 1887 [*Vit. Scot.*, pls. 155–7].

ABERFELDY, PERTHSHIRE, THE TAY BRIDGE, 1733 [*Vit. Scot.*, pl. 122].

HAMILTON CHURCH, LANARKSHIRE, *c.* 1733; interior remodelled 1926 [*Vit. Scot.*, pls. 12–13].

EDINBURGH, THE ORPHANS' HOSPITAL, 1734–5; dem. 1845 [*Vit. Scot.*, pls. 139–40].

EDINBURGH, GEORGE WATSON'S HOSPITAL, 1738–41; rebuilt by D. Bryce as The Royal Infirmary 1870–9 [*Vit. Scot.*, pl. 151].

EDINBURGH, THE ROYAL INFIRMARY, 1738–48; partly dem. 1884 [*Vit. Scot.*, pls. 149–50; R. Thin, 'The Old Infirmary', *Book of the Old Edinburgh Club* xv, 1927].

ABERUTHVEN, PERTHSHIRE, mausoleum or burial-place for 1st Duke of Montrose, 1741–2 [S.R.O., GD 220/6, vol. 4, p. 192; vol. 12, 18 Feb. 1737; vol. 13, pp. 14, 11].

HADDINGTON, EAST LOTHIAN, THE TOWN HOUSE, 1742–5; Assembly Rooms added 1788, spire 1830–1 [Town Council Minutes in S.R.O., 10 June 1742].

EDINBURGH, ROYAL BANK OF SCOTLAND, OLD BANK CLOSE, HIGH STREET, plans accepted 1744, but carried out 1750–4 by S. Neilson to a revised plan; dem. [J. Fleming, *op. cit.*, 336].

DOMESTIC

FLOORS CASTLE, ROXBURGHSHIRE, for 1st Duke of Roxburghe, 1721–6; remodelled by W. H. Playfair 1837–45 [*Vit. Scot.*, pls. 48–9; Fleming, *op. cit.*, 330; building accounts in Charter Room at Floors].

MAVISBANK HOUSE, LOANHEAD, MIDLOTHIAN, for Sir John Clerk, 1723–7; gutted by fire 1973 [*Vit. Scot.*, pls. 46–7; *Braco Case Depositions*, 1743, 46].

HOPETOUN HOUSE, MIDLOTHIAN, enlarged and remodelled for 1st and 2nd Earls of Hopetoun, 1723–48 [*Vit. Scot.*, pls. 14–21; *Braco Case Depositions*, 1743, 47–9].

LAWERS HOUSE, PERTHSHIRE, reconstructed 1724–6 for Col. Sir James Campbell [*Vit. Scot.*, pls. 158–9; bills attested by Adam in S.R.O., GD 237/99]. Further works in 1737–44, for which bills survive *ibid.*, were probably also by Adam. The south front was altered by R. Crichton *c.* 1810 (*C. Life*, 10 Oct. 1925).

DALMAHOY (formerly BELVIDERE) HOUSE, RATHO, MIDLOTHIAN, for George Dalrymple, 1725–8 [*Vit. Scot.*, pl. 72].

MELLERSTAIN, BERWICKSHIRE, wings for George Baillie, 1725–6: part of a design for a complete new house, for which drawings attributable to William Adam are preserved at Mellerstain (*C. Life*, 28 Aug., 4 Sept. 1958).

NEWLISTON HOUSE, WEST LOTHIAN, stables, offices and garden layout for 2nd Earl of Stair, *c.* 1725–35 [*Braco Case Depositions*, 1743, 22, 24–5; plan for gardens by Wm. Adam in Muniment Room at Blenheim Palace, Oxon.] The design for a new house illustrated in *Vit. Scot.* was not carried out.

CRAIGDARROCH, DUMFRIESSHIRE, for Alexander Ferguson, *c.* 1726–9 [*Vit. Scot.*, pls. 77–8; estimate dated 1726 in S.R.O., GD 77/204/1].

THE DRUM, LIBERTON, MIDLOTHIAN, for James Lord Somerville, 1726–30 [*Vit. Scot.*, pls. 37–8] (*C. Life*, 9 Oct. 1915).

ARNISTON, MIDLOTHIAN, for Robert Dundas, later Lord Arniston, 1726–32 [*Vit. Scot.*, pls. 39–44; A. A. Tait, 'William Adam and Sir John Clerk: Arniston and *The Country Seat*', *Burlington Mag.*, March 1969] (*C. Life*, 15–22 Aug. 1925).

DUN HOUSE, ANGUS, for David Erskine, Lord Dun, 1730 [*Vit. Scot.*, pls. 69–70]. *Vit. Scot.*, pls. 57–8, represents an earlier scheme: the design of 1723 illustrated by J. Fleming, *op. cit.*, pl. 8, is by the Earl of Mar (*q.v.*).

RED BRAES, BONNINGTON, MIDLOTHIAN, for Hew Crawfurd, Clerk to the Signet, *c.* 1730; dem. 1927 [S.R.O., GD 1/51/37, a sketch-plan by R. Mylne 1781 of 'A House designed by old Adam for Mr. Crawford, for Red Brae near Poutherhall': cf. James Grant, *Old and New Edinburgh* iii, *c.* 1880, 93, for view of rear elevation and cf. *Book of the Old Edinburgh Club* xix, 170–1].

BALGREGAN HOUSE, STONEYKIRK, WIGTOWNSHIRE, for John McDowall, *c.* 1730; dem. 1966 [*Vit. Scot.*, pls. 127–8].

YESTER HOUSE, EAST LOTHIAN, alterations including new roof and addition of pilasters and attic to centre of north front for the 4th Marquess of Tweeddale, 1730. The centre of the north front was again altered to its present form by Robert Adam in 1788 [*Vit. Scot.*, pls. 27, 30; *Braco Case Depositions*, 1743, 19; J. G. Dunbar, 'The Building of Yester House 1670–1878', *Trans. of the East Lothian Antiquarian Soc.* xiii, 1972, 26–7] (*C. Life*, 23–30 July, 1932, 9, 16 and 23 Aug. 1973).

CUMBERNAULD HOUSE, DUNBARTONSHIRE, for the Earl of Wigtown, 1731; reconstructed internally after fire in 1877 [*Vit. Scot.*, pls. 125–6].

CHATELHERAULT, LANARKSHIRE, for 5th Duke of Hamilton, 1731–43 [*Vit. Scot.*, pl. 160; S.R.O., GD 31/554 for accounts; A. A. Tait, 'William Adam at Chatelherault', *Burlington Mag.*, June 1968].

HADDO HOUSE, ABERDEENSHIRE, for 2nd Earl of Aberdeen, 1732–5; redecorated internally 1880 [*Vit. Scot.*, pls. 54–6] (*C. Life*, 18–25 Aug. 1966).

HOLYROODHOUSE, EDINBURGH, repairs, 1733–4 [Edinburgh University Library, MS. Laing II, 88].

FALA HOUSE (or HAMILTON HALL), MIDLOTHIAN, for Thomas Hamilton, *c.* 1735; dem. *c.* 1830 [*Vit. Scot.*, pl. 121; *Braco Case Depositions*, 1743, 10, 19, 25–6] (Sir Hew Hamilton Dalrymple, *A Short Account of the Hamiltons of Fala, and of Fala House*, 1907, with plate).

NIDDRIE HOUSE, MIDLOTHIAN, additions for Andrew Wauchope, *c.* 1735; enlarged by W. Burn 1823; dem. after fire in 1959 [*Braco Case Depositions*, 1743, 27, where Andrew Wauchope states that 'Mr. Adams built a Pavilion and Colonnades, and Office-houses for the Deponent, as also a Family Burial-Place, and Court before it of cut Stone']. The design by Adam given in *Vit. Scot.*, pls. 114–15, was not carried out.

DUFF HOUSE, BANFFSHIRE, for William Lord Braco, afterwards 1st Earl of Fife, 1735–9 [*Vit. Scot.*, pls. 146–8; *Vitruvius Britannicus* v, 1771, pls. 58–60]. For Adam's lawsuit with Lord Braco in 1743 see the printed *Petitions* and *Depositions*, from which it appears that he also designed a temple on Downhill, and a temple and a triumphal arch on an island in the river Deveron.

EDINBURGH, TWEEDDALE LODGING, NO. 14 HIGH STREET, stables and coach-house for the 4th Marquess of Tweeddale, 1737–8 [National Library of Scotland, Yester Papers, *ex inf.* Mr. J. G. Dunbar].

TINWALD, DUMFRIESSHIRE, for Charles Erskine, 1738–40; interior destroyed by fire 1946 and reconstructed to a different design 1948 [*Vit. Scot.*, pls. 152–3; *Braco Case Depositions*, 1743, 23, 24, 28–9; letters from W. Adam in National Library of Scotland, MS. 5074, ff. 153, 195].

BALVENY HOUSE, BANFFSHIRE, repaired roof for William Lord Braco, 1739; dem. 1929 [*Petition for William Lord Braco against Mr. William Adams Architect*, 1743, 4–5].

MINTO HOUSE, ROXBURGHSHIRE, for Sir Gilbert Elliot, Lord Minto, *c.* 1738–43; porch, offices, etc., added by A. Elliott *c.* 1810; further alterations by M. Wardrop 1859; dem. 1973 [plan, drawings, accounts, etc., in National Library of Scotland] (plan and elevation dated 1766 in Bodleian, Gough Maps 39, f. 28).

EDINBURGH, MINTO HOUSE, CHAMBERS STREET, for Sir Gilbert Elliot, Lord Minto, *c.* 1739–40; dem. *c.* 1845 [*Vit. Scot.*, pls. 59–60].[1]

MURDOSTOUN CASTLE, LANARKSHIRE, for Alexander Inglis, *c.* 1735/40; heightened and partly rebuilt *c.* 1800 [*Braco Case Depositions*, 1743, 10, 23, 46].

CARNOUSIE, BANFFSHIRE, addition for Arthur Gordon, 1740 [*Braco Case Depositions*, 1743, 32; *An Exact Copy of the Depositions of the witnesses adduced by William Lord Braco*, 1743, 1] (W. D. Simpson in *Trans. Banffshire Field Club*, 1936).

HOLYROODHOUSE, EDINBURGH, decoration of apartment for 5th Duke of Hamilton, 1740 [S.R.O., GD 31/554, John Adam *v.* Duke of Hamilton, 1770].

ELIE HOUSE, FIFE, work including carved pediment for Sir John Anstruther, *c.* 1740 [*Braco Case Depositions*, 1743, 19, 20, 22]. The design for a new house illustrated in *Vit. Scot.*, pls. 88–9, was not carried out.

MOUNT STUART, ISLE OF BUTE, apparently rebuilt main block of house as shown in *Vit. Scot.*, pl. 31, *c.* 1740; destroyed by fire 1877.

CAROLINE PARK, MIDLOTHIAN, offices for John, 2nd Duke of Argyll, 1740–2 [Mary Cosh in *C. Life*, 13 July 1972, 81].

LONMAY, ABERDEENSHIRE, for James Frazer, *c.* 1740/5. Only the pavilions shown in *Vit. Scot.*, pl. 95, appear to have been built, and one of these has since been demolished.

---

[1] According to Henry Mackenzie (1795–1841) 'three houses reckoned the best in Edinburgh – Ross-house, Fife-house and Minto House – [were] all built by the same architect, Mr. John Adam, a man of great sagacity as well as genius' (*The Anecdotes and Egotisms of Henry Mackenzie*, ed. H. W. Thompson, 1927, 50). It is clear from another passage (pp. 120–1) that by 'John Adam' Mackenzie meant William Adam, and as Minto House was certainly built by Adam, he may probably be credited with the other two. Fife House was in Potterow, Ross House occupied the site of George Square and was demolished in 1761.

GARTMORE HOUSE, PERTHSHIRE, for Nicol Graham, *c.* 1740/5; altered by J. Baxter 1779–80; remodelled 1901–2 [*Vit. Scot.*, pl. 83].

DALKEITH HOUSE, MIDLOTHIAN, stables, coachhouses, gardener's cottage and bridge over South Esk for 2nd Duke of Buccleuch, 1741–2 [accounts formerly in Dalkeith Charter Room, Press 6/2/6, now S.R.O., unsorted].

TAYMOUTH CASTLE, PERTHSHIRE, addition of wings and other alterations for the 3rd Earl of Breadalbane, *c.* 1742; rebuilt in nineteenth century [*Vit. Scot.*, pl. 51; *Braco Case Depositions*, 13].

CULLEN HOUSE, BANFFSHIRE, bridge over ravine adjoining house, for 2nd Earl of Seafield, 1743 [letter from Adam to Lord Tweeddale 4 June 1743 in National Library of Scotland, Tweeddale papers, Box 98.F.2] (*C. Life*, 15 Sept. 1906).

CASTLE DOUNIE, INVERNESS-SHIRE, begun for 12th Lord Lovat, 1745, but abandoned after the rebellion of 1745 [J. Fleming, *Robert Adam and his Circle*, 1962, 63–4].

INVERARAY CASTLE, ARGYLLSHIRE, supervised construction to designs of Roger Morris for the 3rd Duke of Argyll, 1745–8 [I. G. Lindsay & Mary Cosh, *Inveraray and the Dukes of Argyll*, 1973, 32, 46, etc.].

attributed: POLLOK HOUSE, RENFREWSHIRE, for Sir John Maxwell, 1747–52; wings added *c.* 1900 [a memorandum among the Maxwell papers in the Glasgow City Record Office (T-PM 106/243) refers (3 June 1734) to the promise of 'Mr. Adams Architect' to 'finish the plan of a house for me', and, W. Fraser, *Memoirs of the Maxwells of Pollok*, 1863, i, 98, states that Adam made a design for the house in 1737. But nothing was done for ten years, and there is no evidence that the design adopted in 1747 was the one made in 1737. However, the house has many features characteristic of Adam's work, and the elevation has affinities with an unexecuted design by Adam for Mellerstain. As William Adam died in 1748 the work was no doubt supervised by his sons] (*C. Life*, 25 Jan. 1913).

The dates of the following houses are uncertain:

AIRDRIE, FIFE, works, probably including the addition of wings (since dem.), for Col. Sir Philip Anstruther [*Braco Case Depositions*, 1743, 2].

BARNTON CASTLE, CRAMOND, MIDLOTHIAN, 'repairs and other works' for William Hamilton, Lord Daer (d. 1742); remodelled by R. Adam *c.* 1794; dem. *c.* 1927 [*Braco Case Depositions*, 1743, 24, 27].

BROXMOUTH, EAST LOTHIAN, a bridge, cascades and repairs to the house for 1st Duke of Roxburghe [*Braco Case Depositions*, 1743, 2].

EGLINTON CASTLE, AYRSHIRE, rebuilt east side and built kitchen and back court for 9th Earl of

Eglinton (d. 1729); rebuilt 1798–1800; dem. 1925 [*Braco Case Depositions*, 1743, 16, 22].

THE HIRSEL, BERWICKSHIRE, work for 8th Earl of Home [*Braco Case Depositions*, 1743, 23].

MAKERSTOUN HOUSE, ROXBURGHSHIRE, probably altered house for — Makdougal in accordance with drawings now belonging to Mr. C. Scott of Gala House, Selkirkshire; remodelled *c.* 1800; restored 1973.

NEWHALL HOUSE, GIFFORD, EAST LOTHIAN, for Lord William Hay (d. 1723); dem. 1909 [*Vit. Scot.*, pls. 73–4; *Braco Case Depositions*, 1743, 2].

The following designs by William Adam do not appear to have been carried out:

AIRTH HOUSE, STIRLINGSHIRE, for James Graham, *c.* 1720 [*Vit. Scot.*, pls. 64–5]; BELHAVEN HOUSE, EAST LOTHIAN, for Lord Belhaven [*Vit Scot.*, pl. 154]; BUCHANAN HOUSE, STIRLINGSHIRE, for the 1st Duke of Montrose [*Vit. Scot.*, pls. 135–6], presumably the 'plan and estimate of the intended buildings at Buchanan A⁰. 1741' for which Adam was paid £315[1] [S.R.O., GD 220/6, vol. 4]; CALLY, KIRKCUDBRIGHTSHIRE, for Alexander Murray [*Vit. Scot.* pls. 111–13]; a garden temple at CASTLE KENNEDY, WIGTOWNSHIRE, for 2nd Earl of Stair [*Vit. Scot.*, pls. 120–1]; FASQUE CASTLE, KINCARDINESHIRE, for Sir Alex. Ramsay [*Vit. Scot.*, pl. 100]; the enlargement of HAMILTON PALACE, LANARKSHIRE, for the 5th Duke of Hamilton [*Vit. Scot.*, pls. 9–11]; KENMURE CASTLE, KIRKCUDBRIGHTSHIRE [*Vit. Scot.*, pls. 51–3]; PRESTON HALL, MIDLOTHIAN, for the Duchess of Gordon [*Vit. Scot.*, pls., 107–8]; SAUGHTON HOUSE, MIDLOTHIAN, for James Watson [*Vit. Scot.*, pls. 116–17]; TORRANCE HOUSE, LANARKSHIRE, for Col. James Stewart [*Vit. Scot.*, pls. 139–40], with the possible exception of the wings.

ADAMS, JAMES (1785–), son of James Adams, a Plymouth surveyor, was a pupil of Sir John Soane from 1806 to 1809. He entered the Royal Academy Schools in 1808, winning the Gold Medal in 1809. By 1818 he was established in Portsmouth, where he appears to have practised for the rest of his life. His recorded works are: some additions to MOUNT EDGCUMBE HOUSE, CORNWALL, for the 2nd Earl of Mount Edgcumbe [exhib. R.A. 1818]; the GENERAL DISPENSARY at DEVONPORT, 1815 [exhib. R.A. 1818]; a transeptal addition to SHEDFIELD CHURCH, HANTS., 1834, dem. *c.* 1875 [I.C.B.S.]; and ST. THOMAS'S CHURCH, ELSON, nr. GOSPORT, HANTS., 1845, in the Early English style [G.R.]. A. F. Livesay of Portsmouth was his pupil.

---

[1] See also S.R.O., RHP 6150, a 'General Plan of the House, Gardens and Parks at Buchanan as proposed for His Grace the Duke of Montrose', signed 'William Adam 1745'.

ADAMS, JOHN EASTRIDGE, of Plymouth, is described in local directories (*c.* 1830–45) as a builder, surveyor and hydraulic engineer. He designed the Greek Revival FREEMASONS' HALL in CORNWALL STREET, PLYMOUTH, 1828, illustrated as his work in J. Britton & E. W. Brayley's *Devonshire Illustrated*, 1829, 43.

ADDISON, EDWARD (1656–   ), was born at Kirkby Thore in Westmorland, where he was baptized on 2 October 1656. He became one of the leading master masons in Cumberland and Westmorland, and in 1693–4 executed the masonry of LOWTHER HALL, WESTMORLAND, for Sir John Lowther [accounts in Cumbria Record Office]. It is not clear who designed the house (which was burned in 1718 and finally demolished in the early nineteenth century),[1] but according to the antiquary Thomas Machell (*q.v.*), who held the living of Kirkby Thore from 1677 to 1698, he (Machell) and Addison were 'the first introducers of Regular building into these Parts'. Machell adds that 'Hutton Hall in the County of Cumberland was Altered by Addison' [Machell MSS., Cathedral Library, Carlisle, vol. I, p. 538]. HUTTON-IN-THE-FOREST, CUMBERLAND, has a classical frontispiece which is evidently the work for which Addison was responsible. This part of the house was built by Sir George Fletcher (d. 1700), and is in a style somewhat similar to the work of Addison's contemporary Robert Trollop of Newcastle. Its exact date is not known, but it was probably built *c.* 1685 (*Archaeological Jnl.* cxv, 1958, pl. 26; *Country Life*, 4–18 Feb. 1965). Other houses of the same style and period for which Addison may have been responsible are MORESBY HALL, nr. Workington, the seat of another branch of the Fletcher family (Belcher & Macartney, *Later Renaissance Architecture in England* ii, 1901, pl. clvii); RIBTON HALL, nr. Camerton, formerly the seat of the Lamplughs (dem., illustrated in M. W. Taylor, *Old Manorial Halls of Westmorland and Cumberland*, 1892, p. 334), and the MANSION HOUSE at EAMOND BRIDGE, nr. Penrith, dated 1686.

The place and the date of Addison's death have not been ascertained, but his surname was a common one in the villages between Appleby and Penrith, and a freemason of King's Meaburn named Robert Addison, reputed to be one of 'the best workmen' in the county of Westmorland, made a font for Bampton Church in 1726 [M. E. Noble, *The History of Bampton*, 1901, chap. xi]. John Addison, of Marwood Park, near Barnard Castle, Co. Durham, mason, who in 1684 contracted to build (or rather enlarge) Ewan Christian's tower-house at UNERIGG or EWANRIGG, nr. Maryport in CUMBERLAND, 'according to a

draught or modell thereof by the said John Addison to the [said] Ewan now delivered' (and still attached to the document), was no doubt a member of the same family [Cumbria Record Office, D/Cu/compt. 11].

AIKIN, EDMUND (1780–1820), was the youngest son of Dr. John Aikin, physician and author. He was articled to James Carr (*q.v.*) and entered the Royal Academy Schools in 1801. Shy, nervous and physically delicate, he hardly had the constitution for independent architectural practice, and a good deal of his time was devoted to literary projects. Together with the artist George Dawe he was employed by Thomas Hope (*q.v.*) to prepare the finished drawings for the latter's *Household Furniture* (1807), and in 1808 he published *Designs for Villas and other Rural Buildings*, with a dedication to Hope, and an *Essay on Modern Architecture* (in the *Essays* of the London Architectural Society, of which he became secretary). His *Essay on the Doric Order*, 1810, was the first work to provide comparative plates of the various exemplars of the Greek Doric orders drawn to the same scale. He also wrote the account of St. Paul's Cathedral for Britton's *Fine Arts of the English School* (1809–12), and an essay on Elizabethan architecture appended to his sister Lucy Aikin's *Memoirs of the Court of Queen Elizabeth* (1818). During this period Aikin's only architectural work appears to have been the PRESBYTERIAN CHAPEL in JEWIN STREET, LONDON, which he designed for Dr. A. Rees, 1808–9, dem. *c.* 1890 [J. Britton, *Original Picture of London*, 27th ed. *c.* 1832, 122, with engraving].

For two or three years (*c.* 1810–13) Aikin assisted General Sir Samuel Bentham, the naval engineer and architect, in his designs for works at Sheerness, Portsmouth, and other dockyards. His success in winning the competition[1] for the WELLINGTON ASSEMBLY ROOMS (now the Irish Centre) at LIVERPOOL (1815–16) induced him to settle there in 1814. He was subsequently employed to adapt an existing house in Colquitt Street for the premises of the LIVERPOOL ROYAL INSTITUTION (opened 1817; dem.; see illustration in *The Stranger in Liverpool*, 1837, 22), and designed various other buildings in Liverpool, including some 'elegant villas'. His only other recorded work appears to have been a villa at TOTTERIDGE, HERTS., illustrated in his *Designs for Villas*, pls. 24–5. In 1819 his health broke down and he died at his father's house at Stoke Newington on 11 March 1820.

As the Wellington Rooms at Liverpool show, Aikin was a fastidious and scholarly Greek Revival architect. Although, under pressure from a

---

[1] For the problem of its authorship see under 'Talman, William'.

[1] The other competitors were Eyes, Gandy, Gwilt, Jay, Lugar and Rickman.

client, he designed a row of Gothic shop fronts in Bold Street, Liverpool, which are said to have 'exhibited great originality and picturesque effect', he regarded the Gothic Revival with disapproval, and rather perversely attempted in his *Designs for Villas* to advocate the merits of Mohammedan architecture as a possible alternative. [Memoir prefaced to 1835 edition of *Designs for Villas*; Lucy Aikin, *Memoir of John Aikin, M.D.*, i, 1823, 267–72; *A.P.S.D.*; W. J. Pinks, *History of Clerkenwell*, ed. Wood, 1851, 268; J. A. Picton, *Memorials of Liverpool* ii, 1875, 212; numerous references in Thomas Rickman's diary].

AINGER, ALFRED (1797–1859), was the son of Samuel Ainger, a carpenter and surveyor of London. He entered the Royal Academy Schools in 1816 and took up the freedom of the City of London in 1826. He was Surveyor to the Trustees of the Charities of the parish of St. Augustine and St. Faith in the City, and in 1830–1 he and J. H. Taylor repaired the church of ST. AUGUSTINE, OLD CHANGE and rebuilt the upper part of the spire [Guildhall Library, MSS. 8881, 8898]. His practice was not extensive as he possessed private means, and his only major work was the NORTH LONDON (later UNIVERSITY COLLEGE) HOSPITAL, 1833, rebuilt 1897–1906 to the designs of Alfred Waterhouse. He also designed a large conservatory in the Royal Horticultural Society's Gardens at Chiswick, Middlesex, in 1838 [*A New Survey of London*, published by John Weale 1853, ii, 484]. Ainger was the author of *Suggestions towards an Amendment of the Building Act*, 1825, and of *The Building and other Acts relating to Building*, 1836. He was the father of Canon Alfred Ainger (1837–1904), Master of the Temple. [*Builder* xvii, 1859, 765; Guildhall Library, MSS. 2738/1 and 2; E. Sichel, *The Life and Letters of Alfred Ainger*, 1906, in which a portrait of the architect is reproduced.]

AIRD, —, described as 'Master of Works', designed the INFIRMARY, DUNCAN STREET, GREENOCK, RENFREWSHIRE, 1808–9, enlarged 1869 [D. Weir, *History of the Town of Greenock*, Greenock 1829, 32].

AITCHISON, GEORGE (1792–1861), was the son of a carpenter and builder at Leyton in Essex. He was first (1808) apprenticed to his father, and then became (1813) a pupil of H. H. Seward, with whom he remained until 1823, when he became principal clerk to Thomas Hardwick. In 1826 he moved to the office of Thomas Lee, but in the following year obtained the appointment of architect or clerk of works to the St. Katherine's

Dock Company. He was also architect to the Founders' Company and to the London and Birmingham Railway Company, for whom he designed TRING STATION, HERTS., in 1838 [exhib. at R.A. 1840]. For the Union Bank of London he enlarged their premises in Pall Mall and designed a branch office in Fleet Street. He is said to have been equally competent as architect, engineer and surveyor, and to have been 'not only excellent at arrangement and construction, but one of the most beautiful draughtsmen of his day'. Both sides of his professional activity were represented in the drawings that he exhibited at the Royal Academy. He was a member of the Society called 'Freemasons of the Church' (for which see p. 93) and in 1842 was given the title of 'Professor of Concreting and Opus Incertum' [*Builder* i, 1843, 24]. He died on 12 June 1861. His son George Aitchison, R.A. (1825–1910), was President of the R.I.B.A. in the years 1896–9. [*Minutes of Proceedings of the Institution of Civil Engineers* xxi, 1861–2, 569–71.]

AITKINS, JOHN, was the architect (otherwise unknown) who was employed by Thomas Stonor to carry out alterations in the Gothic style to the interior of the hall of STONOR PARK, OXON., in 1758–9 [*V.C.H. Oxon.* viii, 142] (*C. Life*, 11 Oct. 1950).

AKROYD, JOHN (1556–1613), was a Yorkshire master mason who achieved celebrity as the builder of the Schools Quadrangle at Oxford University. John Akroyd was the eldest son of William Akroyd, a mason living at Warley in the parish of Halifax, where he was born in November 1556. His only documented work in Yorkshire is the GRAMMAR SCHOOL at HEATH (1598–1601, dem.), but the chairman of the governors at the time was Sir John Savile (d. 1607) of Bradley and Methley Halls, and circumstantial evidence suggests that Akroyd designed or altered both these houses, and that he may also have been employed at Howley Hall by another member of the Savile family: Sir John, afterwards Lord Savile (d. 1630). It was Sir Henry Savile (younger brother of Sir John Savile of Methley) who, as Warden of Merton College, first brought Akroyd to Oxford at a time when there was a dispute between the university and the newly incorporated Company of Freemasons, Carpenters, Joiners and Slaters of Oxford. At Merton, Akroyd and his partner John Bentley (a freemason from Elland, nr. Halifax) undertook the masonry of the GREAT OR FELLOWS' QUADRANGLE in January 1608/9 for £570 and completed it in 1610. The carpenter was another Yorkshireman, Thomas Holt. In August 1611 the College gave Akroyd a gratuity of £20, 'because he had faithfully carried out the work of erecting the new quadrangle'.[1]

In 1610–11 Akroyd was employed by Sir Thomas Bodley to build the ARTS END of THE BODLEIAN LIBRARY, and in March 1613 he and his partner John Bentley undertook to build the adjoining SCHOOLS QUADRANGLE (not completed until c. 1620). Akroyd, however, died in September 1613, long before the building was finished. In the register of St. Mary's Church, where he was buried, he is commemorated as 'Mr. John Acroid, chief builder of the Schools', His partner Bentley died only three months later at the age of 40 (December 1613), and was buried at St. Peter's in the East, where a monument (now destroyed) described him as *Johannes Bentleius Eboracensis novae partis bibliothecae novarumque scholarum architectus peritissimus*.[2] The direction of the works seems then to have passed to John Bentley's brother Michael, who died at Oxford in June 1618, and was also buried at St. Peter's in the East. Thomas Holt, the carpenter, survived until 1624, and (having settled in Oxford) was buried in Holywell churchyard, where Anthony Wood records an inscription *in memorian Thomae Holt Eborac. Scholarum publicarum architecti*.

In the absence of any regular series of accounts for the building of the Schools Quadrangle it is impossible to cite any evidence which demonstrates conclusively that Akroyd (or anyone else) was responsible either for the design of the building as a whole or for that of its most ambitious feature, the Tower of the Five Orders. Undoubtedly Sir Henry Savile, whose judgement was to Bodley 'as the judgement of a mason', must have been closely involved in the general conception. But in England the idea of towers ornamented with superimposed orders, though deriving ultimately from French architecture of the mid-sixteenth century, seems to have found particular favour in the northern counties, notably at Howley Hall, Yorks. (c. 1590), Stonyhurst, Lancs. (c. 1592–5), and Browsholme Hall, Yorks. (c. 1605–10). It is therefore possible to see the Merton tower and its successor in the Schools Quadrangle as a Yorkshire idea which Sir Henry Savile imported to Oxford together with his masons, and if so John Akroyd no doubt made

the necessary drawings from which they were built. Badly integrated into the traditional Gothic quadrangles in which they are set, they certainly show the limited comprehension of classical architecture that might be expected of a Yorkshire master mason.

[T. W. Hanson, 'Halifax Builders in Oxford', *Transactions of the Halifax Antiquarian Soc.*, 1929, 253–317; Rachel Poole, 'The Architect of the Schools and the Tower of the Five Orders', *Bodleian Quarterly Record* iii, 1922, 263–4; I. G. Philip, 'The Building of the Schools Quadrangle', *Oxoniensia* xiii, 1948; Catherine Cole, 'The Building of the Tower of Five Orders', *Oxoniensia* xxxiii, 1968; *V.C.H. Oxon.* iii, 45–7, 102.]

ALBON, WILLIAM (c. 1797–1870), was admitted to the Royal Academy Schools in 1822 at the age of 25, and exhibited architectural drawings at the Academy from various London addresses from 1817 to 1852. Some of his exhibits were of a topographical character, and his career as an architect remains obscure. He died in South Molton Street on 19 May 1870 [Principal Probate Registry, Calendar of Probates].

ALDERSON, MOSES ATHA (1801–1869), was born at Holbeck, nr. Leeds, and appears subsequently to have practised as an architect and engineer at Birmingham, where he died in 1869. He was a member of the Royal Society of Arts and of the London Mechanics' Institution. In 1834 he published *An Essay on the Nature and Application of Steam*. He competed for the Houses of Parliament in 1835. His design is described in the *Catalogue of the Designs for the New Houses of Parliament*, 6th ed. 1836, 65. The two Houses were each to be octagonal, surmounted by a Gothic lantern.

ALDERSON, WILLIAM (–c. 1835), of Chelsea, appears to have been a member of the Society of Friends. When Thomas Rickman called on him in October 1828, Alderson showed him his drawings for the Middlesex County Lunatic Asylum and for Quaker meeting-houses which he had designed at Hoddesden and Stoke Newington [Rickman's diary, 31 Oct. 1828]. He is referred to as 'the late Mr. Alderson' in Loudon's *Architectural Magazine* for July 1835, and his will was proved in June 1836 [P.C.C. 333 STO-WELL].

HODDESDEN, HERTS., FRIENDS' MEETING HOUSE, before 1828 [see above].

STOKE NEWINGTON, MIDDLESEX, FRIENDS' MEETING HOUSE, 1827–8 [see above] (*Arch. Rev.*, April 1946, 113).

THE MIDDLESEX COUNTY LUNATIC ASYLUM (now ST. BERNARD'S HOSPITAL), HANWELL, MIDDLESEX,

---

[1] 'Eodem tempore allocavimus Johanni Acroide architecto viginti libras preter alias 20 li. quas antea accepit quod fidelem operam lavaverat in constructione novi aedificii quadrangularis' (Merton College *Registrum Annalium*, 1567–1731, p. 236).

[2] In 1611 Sir Edward Pytts of Kyre Park, Worcs., 'brought John Bentley ffreemason from Oxford (where he wrought the newe addition to Sir Thomas Bodleigh his famous library) with me as I came from London to Kyer to take instructions from me by veuinge the place to draw me a newe platte...' (Mrs. Baldwyn-Childe, 'The Building of Kyre Park', *The Antiquary* xxi, 1890).

1829–31 [Middlesex Record Office, MA/AJ/1] (description in Weale's *New Survey of London* ii, 1853, 601–7).

ALDHOUSE, FRANCIS, was a surveyor practising in Little Titchfield Street, London, in the early nineteenth century. He was concerned in the remodelling of BAYFORDBURY, HERTS., for William Baker in 1809–12. Plans made by him in 1809 are referred to in correspondence among the Baker family papers in the Hertfordshire Record Office (nos. 401, 402, 405, 407), and no record of any other architect has been found. The elegant Greek Doric additions of 1809–12 are illustrated in *C. Life*, 17, 23 Jan. 1925.

ALDRICH, HENRY (1648–1710), the son of Henry Aldrich (d. 1683), later auditor to the Duke of York, was born in January 1647/8. He was educated at Westminster School and at Christ Church, Oxford, taking his B.A. in 1666 and his M.A. in 1669. In 1682 he became a Canon of Christ Church and received his B.D. and D.D. Finally in 1689 he succeeded to the office of Dean. From 1692 to 1695 he served as Vice-Chancellor.

Aldrich had a reputation for learning in many fields, and his writings included editions of Greek and Latin texts, ecclesiastical tracts, and books on logic, mathematics, heraldry, music and architecture. His library contained many books on antiquities and a large collection of architectural and other engravings. He left his books to Christ Church Library, but all his personal papers were destroyed in accordance with his will, so that little is known about his architectural activities. There is, however, reason to think that he had visited France and Italy, and according to Dallaway's edition of Walpole's *Anecdotes* he had spent 'a considerable time' in the latter country, where he associated with 'the eminent in architecture'. He was certainly regarded as an 'able judge in architecture' by his contemporaries, as is shown by the direction of Sir Edward Hannes, who in 1710 left £1000 for the building of the Westminster School dormitory, 'in contriving whereof he desired Sir Christoper Wren and Dr. Aldrich should be consulted'. At the time of his death he was engaged in compiling an *Elementa Architecturae*, 'intended to have been divided into two parts treating respectively of Civil and Military Architecture'. Each part was to consist of three books, but only Book 1 and part of Book 2 of the Civil section were completed. A few copies of the first 44 pages of the text were printed during the author's lifetime, but the first edition (in Latin and English) was not published until 1789 as *Elementa Architecturae Civilis*[1] (2nd ed. 1818). 'It is

a scholarly rather than a practical work, and contains many quotations from Vitruvius and Palladio, the authors whom he accepted as his chief authorities.' Aldrich was buried in Christ Church Cathedral, where a monument was erected twenty years later by Dr. George Clarke (*q.v.*), his former friend and colleague. His portrait by Kneller is in Christ Church Hall and there is a marble bust in the library. Other portraits at Christ Church and in the Bodleian are listed by Mrs. Poole, *Catalogue of Oxford Portraits* (Oxford Historical Society) i, 78, and iii, 40–2.

Architecture was only one of Aldrich's attainments, and even in Oxford very few buildings can be attributed to him. Indeed, the only building which he is known definitely to have designed is the PECKWATER QUADRANGLE at his own college of CHRIST CHURCH, built by William Townesend between 1707 and 1714. On the foundation-stone laid by the Earl of Shaftesbury, Aldrich was formally described as its 'architect' [Bodleian, Tanner MS. 338, f. 315]. The fourth side of the quadrangle, intended by Aldrich to contain further sets of rooms, was eventually completed as a library in 1717–38 to the designs of Dr. George Clarke [Hist. MSS. Comm., *Portland* vii, 217, and cf. the engravings showing Aldrich's original scheme reproduced by Hiscock, *Henry Aldrich*, pls. 30–1]. Peshall's statement, in his edition of Wood's *City of Oxford*, 1773, 41, that Aldrich was the architect of ALL SAINTS CHURCH, OXFORD, 1701–10, has generally been accepted, and he was certainly concerned in its erection, for his name appears among the list of trustees on the design engraved by M. Burghers which was circulated to appeal for funds after the fall of the tower of the old church in March 1700. The steeple of the new church was not, however, completed until 1718–20, and its design as executed represents a compromise between Aldrich's original proposal and an alternative one submitted by Nicholas Hawksmoor after the Dean's death [H. M. Colvin, 'The Architects of All Saints Church, Oxford', *Oxoniensia* xix, 1954]. In 1675–6 Aldrich had supervised the repair of ST. MARY'S CHURCH, OXFORD, in conjunction with Maurice Wheeler, rector of St. Ebbe's [*Letters of H. Prideaux*, Camden Soc. 1875, 50].

Three other Oxford buildings have been attributed to Aldrich with less certainty. In the case of TRINITY COLLEGE CHAPEL (1691–4) all that is definitely known is that he was one of the 'able

---

[1] The original drawings for 39 of the plates are in Worcester College Library (B.n.8). They were given to

Dr. George Clarke by Aldrich in 1708, and a MS. note by Clarke in his copy (B.n.9) of the printed text states that the drawings were from the Dean's own hand. There is another copy of the early printing in the Bodleian (8° Rawl. 1068). According to a note in the sale catalogue of James West's library (1773) only 10 copies were printed, 'and those never perfected, the author's death preventing' (*ex inf.* Mr. Paul Quarrie).

judges in architecture' whose advice the College took before deciding to rebuild 'wholly upon new foundations'. There is no contemporary evidence to support the conjecture that he was the author of the design submitted to Wren's criticism by the President, Dr. Bathurst [*Wren Soc.* v, 15], but the possibility cannot be dismissed. According to Dallaway's edition of Walpole's *Anecdotes of Painting* iv, 1827, 75, Aldrich designed the FELLOWS' BUILDING at CORPUS CHRISTI COLLEGE, 1706–12. Here the design may have been due to William Townesend, the contracting mason, but the façade bears sufficient resemblance to Peckwater to suggest that Aldrich may have had some influence on it. On the strength of an otherwise unknown engraved design for its elevation in his collection, it has been suggested that Aldrich may have been the architect of QUEEN'S COLLEGE LIBRARY (1693–4), but engraved designs were commonly circulated to attract subscriptions and the survival of one in Aldrich's extensive collection proves nothing.

What is remarkable about Aldrich's one authenticated work is its conscious classicism. The façades of Peckwater Quadrangle (though awkwardly juxtaposed) anticipate those of Queen Square, Bath, by some twenty years, and entitle Aldrich to be regarded as one of the forerunners of the Palladian movement which he did not live to see. In this connection it is worth drawing attention to the fact that it was Aldrich who persuaded C. Fairfax to undertake the Latin translation of Palladio's *Antichità di Roma* that was published by the Clarendon Press in 1709 (cf. *Hearne's Collections*, ed. Dobie, viii, 103) and that in the preface Fairfax states that Aldrich acknowledged Palladio as his professed master in architecture. Further evidence of Aldrich's Palladian interests is afforded by a drawing in Worcester College Library. This is a copy in Aldrich's hand of Webb's drawing of Palladio's Teatro Olimpico at Vicenza.

That Aldrich was a skilled draughtsman is shown by two volumes of his drawings preserved at Christ Church. These are mostly copies of engravings, and many of them are derived from published illustrations of churches and other buildings in the Holy Land. At the Clarendon Press there is a volume of designs for initial letters and decorations which have been attributed to Aldrich by Miss H. M. Petter. The original drawings at Christ Church for the Oxford Almanacs of 1676 and 1689 appear to be in his hand. The latter has an architectural setting, but the only strictly architectural designs by Aldrich that have so far been identified are the drawings for his *Elementa Architecturae Civilis* in Worcester College Library (see p. 63, n. 1), a plan and elevation for All Saints Church that is presumably by him (reproduced in *Oxoniensia* xix, 1954, pl. v), and four drawings among the unexe-

cuted projects for enlarging All Souls College that also appear to be in his hand (see H. M. Colvin, *Catalogue of Architectural Drawings in the Library of Worcester College, Oxford*, 2nd. ed. forthcoming).

[*D.N.B.*; *Hearne's Collections*, ed. Dobie, iii, Oxford Historical Soc. 1889, 89–90; E. F. A. Suttle, 'Henry Aldrich, Dean of Christ Church', *Oxoniensia* v, 1940; W. G. Hiscock, 'Henry Aldrich, Book Collector, Musician, Architect', in *A Christ Church Miscellany*, 1946; W. G. Hiscock, *Henry Aldrich*, 1960.]

ALEFOUNDER, JOHN (1732–1787), was the son of John Alefounder (d. 1763), a well-to-do carpenter and builder of Colchester. He practised as an architect and surveyor in London, where in 1774 he was appointed District Surveyor of the parish of St. Luke, Old Street [Middlesex County Records]. His son John, born 1758, entered the Royal Academy Schools in 1776 as an architectural student, but became a portrait and miniature painter, and died at Calcutta in 1795 [information from Mr. J. Bensusan-Butt; *Gent's Mag.* 1795 (ii), 880].

ALEXANDER, SIR ANTHONY (–1637), was second son of William Alexander, 1st Earl of Stirling (d. 1640). He was educated at Glasgow University, and in July 1626 had licence to travel abroad for three years. On his return he was appointed (1 April 1629) Master of Work to the King in Scotland jointly with James Murray (*q.v.*). Anthony must have owed the appointment to his father, at that time Secretary of State for Scotland, but in the warrant he is stated to have acquired 'eruditione et peregrinando sufficientam peritiam in architectura'. The office was confirmed after Murray's death in 1634, but Alexander himself died at London on 17 September 1637. He had been knighted in 1635. [J. Balfour Paul, *The Scots Peerage* viii, 178.]

ALEXANDER, DANIEL ASHER (1768–1846), a native of London, was educated at St. Paul's School, and became a pupil of Samuel Robinson. He entered the Royal Academy Schools in 1782, and won the Silver Medal the same year. In 1796 he was appointed surveyor to the London Dock Company, for whom he designed very extensive ranges of warehouses at Wapping, 'capacious in size, convenient in arrangement, and magnificent in design and execution'. From 1796 to 1822 he was also Surveyor to the Fishmongers' Company. In 1807 he became surveyor to Trinity House, and designed a number of lighthouses for the Brethren.

Alexander specialized in the designing of large utilitarian buildings such as prisons and warehouses. He was an able and resourceful engineer, and handled large expanses of stone- or brickwork with a sense of drama which reflected his admiration for Piranesi's engravings. The interiors of Maidstone Gaol, in particular, are said to remind the architectural visitor forcibly of the *Invenzioni di Carceri*. His practice was extensive, but his reputation suffered from the revelation of frauds perpetrated by the clerk of works and tradesmen employed at Maidsone Gaol, which he failed to detect, and for which he was obliged to accept responsibility.

In London, Alexander moved in artistic as well as professional circles. Flaxman and Chantrey were his intimate friends, and in their company he made annual visits to France from 1815 onwards. Edward I'Anson was at first his assistant and afterwards his partner. His eldest son, Daniel Alexander (*c.* 1796–1843), had an architectural training in his father's office, but in 1820 gave up architecture for the Church.[1] His pupils included W. H. Ashpitel, James Beek, C. A. Busby, J. P. Pritchett, James Savage, Richard Suter, John Wallen, John Walters, John Whichcord and Joseph Woods. He died at Exeter, where he lived for the last ten years of his life, but was buried at Yarmouth in the Isle of Wight, where he had gratuitously designed the church tower as a memorial to his third son Henry, who died in 1829 aged 19. There is a portrait by John Partridge in the Port of London Authority's Building, and one by Chantrey in the Victoria and Albert Museum. [*Gent's Mag.* 1846 (ii), 210; *Builder* xx, 1862, 795; *A.P.S.D.*; *D.N.B.*; A. E. Richardson, 'The Architect of Dartmoor', *Arch. Rev.*, April 1918.]

LONDON, house at HIGHBURY HILL for Dr. Saunders, *c.* 1790 [*A.P.S.D.*].
SOUTHWARK, SCOTT'S WAREHOUSES, BANKSIDE, *c.* 1790 [*A.P.S.D.*].
LONDON, PURDAY'S WAREHOUSES, NO. 48 MARK LANE [*A.P.S.D.*].
THE MOTE, nr. MAIDSTONE, KENT, for the 1st Earl of Romney, 1793–1801 [MS. accounts in Maidstone Museum].
LONDON DOCK BUILDINGS AND WAREHOUSES, WAPPING, 1796–1820 [*A.P.S.D.*].
ROCHESTER BRIDGE, widened and formed two centre arches into one, 1798 [Nichols, *Literary Illustrations* vi, 736–7; exhib. at R.A. 1799].
ROCHESTER CATHEDRAL, made plans for improving the Close, 1801 [B.M., *King's Maps* xvii, 8].
CAMER COURT, MEOPHAM, KENT, proposed alterations to offices for William Smith, 1801 [Kent Record Office, drawings in U 1127/P23/1–2].
LONGFORD CASTLE, WILTS., alterations and exten-

sive additions (including three new towers) for the 2nd Earl of Radnor, 1802-17, closely following a scheme made by J. Wyatt in 1796 [*A.P.S.D.*].
DARTMOOR PRISON OF WAR, PRINCETOWN, DEVONSHIRE, 1806–9; since much altered [*A.P.S.D.*].
GREENWICH, QUEEN'S HOUSE, addition of flanking blocks and colonnades for Royal Naval Asylum, 1807–10 [P.R.O., Adm. 80/111].
BRISTOL, BAPTIST COLLEGE, STOKES CROFT, *c.* 1810–12; dem. *c.* 1970 [*A.P.S.D.*, *s.v.* 'Bristol'].
MAIDSTONE, COUNTY GAOL, 1811–19 [*Gent's Mag.* 1813 (ii), 32–4, 68, 134–5, 329–32, 645–8].
DOWNTON CHURCH, WILTS., alterations for the 2nd Earl of Radnor, 1812–15 [*A.P.S.D.*].
LONDON, ALL HALLOWS CHURCH, BARKING, repaired 1813 [*Gent's Mag.* 1813 (i), 526–7].
TONBRIDGE, KENT, THE LOWER BRIDGE, plans dated 1814 [Kent County Records, Q.S., Sundry Plans, S.1.].
OLD LONDON BRIDGE, survey and report with Dance and Chapman, 1814 [*A.P.S.D.*].
COLESHILL HOUSE, BERKS., repairs for the 2nd Earl of Radnor, 1814–16; destroyed by fire 1952 [*A.P.S.D.*].
BEDDINGTON HOUSE, SURREY, alterations to south wing (including library) for Mrs. A. P. Gee (with his son), 1818; dem. *c.* 1865 [*A.P.S.D.*].
COMBE BANK, nr. SUNDRIDGE, KENT, alterations [*A.P.S.D.*].
YARMOUTH, ISLE OF WIGHT, designed upper part of church tower, 1831, Gothic (executed by Joseph Squire) [I.C.B.S.; inscription in church].
Lighthouses at ANGLESEY (SOUTH STACK, 1809), FARNE ISLANDS (*c.* 1810), HELIGOLAND (1811), HURST (1812), HARWICH (1818), LUNDY (1820).

ALEXANDER, GEORGE, was described as 'Master of the City's Works and Architect in Perth' in 1820, when he inspected the buildings of Kilspindie School, Perthshire [S.R.O., HR 417/1]. In the Perth Art Gallery there is a survey plan by him of Perth Tolbooth and Council Chamber (dem. 1839), dated 1810.

ALFRAY, ROBERT, appears to claim the authorship of SOMERSBY HALL, LINCS., a small house built in 1722 in the style of Sir John Vanbrugh. Among the Nattes Drawings in Lincoln City Library there is (vol. III, 309) a wash drawing of 'SUMMERSBY HALL in the County of Lincoln the seat of Robert Burton Esq[r]. built 1722. Rob[t]. Alfray Inv[t].: delin.' Robert Burton was a Londoner who had married Katherine Langhorne of Somersby in 1706 [John Harris in *Archaeological Jnl.* cxxxi, 1974, 314]. Alfray is otherwise known only as one of the subscribers to West & Toms' *Views of All the Ancient Churches etc in the Cities of London and Westminster*, 1736–9, where he is described as 'Surveyor'. He may have been a

---

[1] His only independent works were the library at Beddington House, Surrey (dem.), and rebuilding the tower and nave of Walton-on-the-Hill Church, Surrey (Gothic, again rebuilt 1895), both for Mrs. A. P. Gee, 1818 [*A.P.S.D.*].

member of the armigerous family of Alfrey seated at Westdean in Sussex (cf. W. Berry, *County Genealogies: Sussex*, 1830, 244–5).

ALLASON, THOMAS (1790–1852), was a pupil of William Atkinson. He entered the Royal Academy Schools in 1808, and won the Silver Medal in 1809. In 1810 he was awarded a gold palette by the Society of Arts for a design for an Academy of Arts. He travelled in Greece in 1814 as draughtsman to Messrs. John and Edward Spencer Stanhope, for their publications on *The Battle of Platœa*, 1817, and *The Actual State of the Plain of Olympia, and of the Ruins of the City of Elis*, 1824. On his return, he published *Picturesque Views of the Antiquities of Pola in Istria*, 1817, and an etching of Milan Cathedral. He claimed to be the first to observe the entasis of columns in Greek architecture, a discovery for which the credit was in fact due equally to Haller and C. R. Cockerell, with whom Allason discussed the problem on the spot in Athens, and to whom he was indebted for accurate drawings: see his paper 'On the Columns of the Athenian Temples' in *Quarterly Jnl. of Science and Arts* x, 1821, 204–6. He was surveyor to the Stock Exchange, to the Alliance Fire Office, whose building in Bartholomew Lane, London, 1841, was his chief public work, to the Pollen estate, London, the Ladbroke estate, Notting Hill, the Pitt estate, Kensington, and the d'Este estate, Ramsgate. He designed many villas and houses, and is almost certainly the 'eminent villa architect' named 'Thomas A——' whose own house near London is illustrated in Loudon's *Encyclopaedia of Cottage, Farm and Villa Architecture*, 1846, pp. 826–34 (cf. pp. 999–1001). In 1827 he designed a studio at NO. 1 LINDEN GROVE, BAYSWATER, for the artist William Mulready [R. &. S. Redgrave, *A Century of British Painters*, 1947 ed., 327–8]. At ALTON ABBEY (later TOWERS), STAFFS., he designed additions to the house and garden buildings for the 15th Earl of Shrewsbury, and was afterwards much employed as a landscape gardener. In 1841 he carried out extensive repairs to BLENHEIM PALACE, OXON., for the 6th Duke of Marlborough. His last works were PYRGO PARK, nr. ROMFORD, ESSEX for Robert Field, 1851–2 (Messrs. Cubitt, builders; enlarged by E. M. Barry, 1862), and SULHAMSTEAD PARK, BERKS., for M. G. Thoyte, M.P. His only pupil was Charles Day. One of his three sons, Thomas (d. 1868), succeeded to most of his appointments, and rebuilt the Stock Exchange in Capel Court in 1853–4. [*A.P.S.D.*; obituary in *Builder* x, 1852, 241.]

ALLEN, GEORGE (1798–1847), F.I.B.A., was a native of Brentford. He became a pupil of James Elmes, entered the Royal Academy Schools in 1818, and won the Silver Medal in 1820. His practice was largely commercial, consisting of warehouses and the like. He was much employed in making valuations for railway, gas and dock companies, and was surveyor to the Haberdashers' Company, the Deptford Creek Bridge Company, the district of Rotherhithe and Hatcham, and the parishes of St. Olave, Southwark, and St. Nicholas, Deptford. In 1827–8 he prepared and published *Plans and Designs for the Future Approaches to the New London Bridge*, making several suggestions that were adopted by the Bridge Committee. He exhibited at the Royal Academy from 1820 to 1840. His office was in Tooley Street, Southwark. [*A.P.S.D.*]

PENSHURST, KENT, restoration of HARDEN COTTAGE 'in the ancient English style', exhib. at Royal Academy, 1826.
BERMONDSEY, ST. JAMES'S CHURCH, in conjunction with James Savage, who was responsible for the design, 1827–8 [*A.P.S.D.*].
SOUTHWARK, THE NEW LONDON BRIDGE TAVERN, for John Humphery, M.P., 1834 [exhib. at Royal Academy, 1835].
SOUTHWARK, UNION WORKHOUSE, for the parishes of St. Olave and St. John, *c.* 1835 [*A.P.S.D.*].
BRENTFORD, MIDDLESEX, THE INFANT SCHOOL, 1837 [*A.P.S.D.*].
EALING, MIDDLESEX, villa for J. T. Sleap, *c.* 1840 [exhib. at Royal Academy].
SOUTHWARK, ST. OLAVE'S CHURCH, restoration after the fire of 1843; dem. 1926 [*A.P.S.D.*].
SOUTHWARK, ST. JOHN'S GIRLS' SCHOOL, 1845 [*A.P.S.D.*].
BERMONDSEY, CHRISTCHURCH, with W. B. Hays, 1847, Romanesque; dem. *c.* 1966 [*A.P.S.D.*].
Several wharfs, warehouses, etc., in Southwark, including Fenning's Wharf, 1836; those on the north side of Southwark Cathedral, for Mr. Aldis Humphery, 1838; Colton's Wharf, for Messrs. Scovell; Topping's Wharf (after 1843); and Davis's Wharf [Brayley, *Topographical History of Surrey* v, 356, 373].

ALLEN, JAMES, statuary and architect of Bristol, was the son of John Allen, a joiner. In 1752 he was apprenticed to the mason and sculptor James Paty [P.R.O. Apprenticeship Register], and in 1780 was admitted to the freedom of the city as a carver. He was one of the three City Surveyors appointed under the Act of 1788, but resigned in 1792. In the following year he became bankrupt and his house and yard were sold. He subsequently practised as an architect and drawing master [W. Ison, *The Georgian Buildings of Bristol*, 1952, 30–1].

In 1787 Allen submitted a design for St. Paul's Church, Bristol, which was not accepted. Subsequently he designed ST. THOMAS'S CHURCH, BRISTOL, incorporating the medieval tower, 1790–3 [Ison, *op. cit.*, 84–5] and WINFORD

CHURCH, SOMERSET, incorporating the medieval tower, 1796 [parish records, *ex inf.* Mr. B. Little]. A drawing by him of gate-piers at HINTON ST. GEORGE, SOMERSET, is in the collection of Mr. Paul Mellon.

ANDERSON, JAMES (−c. 1856), 'engineer and architect', was admitted a burgess of Edinburgh in 1825 [*Roll of Edinburgh Burgesses,* Scottish Record Soc. 1933, 10]. Thereafter he appears in the directories as 'civil engineer and architect' or 'surveyor' until 1856/7. In 1826 he submitted a design for St. Andrew's Place U.P. Church, Leith [*St. Andrew's Place United Presbyterian Church, Leith,* 1888, 38].

ANDERSON, JOHN, designed two churches in County Durham for the Church Building Commissioners, one at WEST RAINTON, 1825,[1] the other at HETTON-LE-HOLE, 1832 [Port, 177]. The former was rebuilt in 1864, the latter in 1898.

ANDERSON, WILLIAM, *see* HENDERSON

ANDERTON, THOMAS, made designs in 1817 for rebuilding CARLTON-IN-CRAVEN REC-TORY, YORKS. (W.R.) [Borthwick Institute, MGA 1817/4]. In 1819 he made the designs (in a Georgian Gothic style) for rebuilding KETTLEWELL CHURCH, YORKS. (W.R.) [I.C.B.S.; Borthwick Institute, Fac. 1819/2]. The church was again rebuilt in 1882–5. In 1842 the church of ST. JAMES, BARNOLDSWICK, YORKS. (W.R.), was built in the lancet style to the designs of William Anderton, architect and mason of Gargrave, nr. Skipton [I.C.B.S.]. It was dem. 1960.

ANGELL, SAMUEL (1800–1866), F.I.B.A., was the son of William Sandell Angell, deputy alderman of Cornhill Ward, London. He became a pupil of Thomas Hardwick, and entered the Royal Academy Schools in 1816. In 1821–3 he travelled in Italy and Sicily with William Harris (*q.v.*), discovering at Selinus a series of metopes from the Greek temples there. Harris died of malaria in Palermo, but Angell returned to England to publish, in conjunction with Harris's brother-in-law Thomas Evans (*q.v.*), *Sculptured Metopes discovered amongst the Ruins of the Temples of the Ancient City of Selinus in Sicily* (1826).

In 1824 Angell became surveyor to the Clothworkers' Company. He was also surveyor to the Saddlers' Company, and from 1831 was one of the London District Surveyors. He exhibited at the Royal Academy from 1817 to 1850. George Judge and Herbert Williams were his pupils. He

died at Abbey Lodge, Chertsey, on 28 November 1866. F. W. Porter appears to have taken over his practice. [F. Boase, *Modern English Biography* iv, 1908, 135; *Gent's Mag.* 1847 (i), 180–1, 1867 (i), 250.]

LONDON, LAMB'S CHAPEL AND ALMSHOUSES, MONK-WELL STREET, for the Clothworkers' Company, 1825, Elizabethan style; dem. 1872 [J. Timbs. *Curiosities of London,* 1867, 212].

TOTTENHAM, MIDDLESEX, schools on SCOTLAND GREEN, 1836 [*Architectural Mag.* iii, 1836, 190].

ST. THOMAS'S CHURCH, OLD KENT ROAD, 1837–8; dem. 1868 [*Companion to the Almanac,* 1838, 220].

ST. VEDAST'S CHURCH, FOSTER LANE, LONDON, repairs to steeple, 1837 [see DAVY, CHRISTOPHER].

ST. JAMES'S CHURCH, MUSWELL HILL, MIDDLESEX, 1842, Gothic; enlarged 1874–5; dem. 1902 [G. Watson & L. C. Kent, *The Church on the Hill,* 1951].

LONDON, CLOTHWORKERS' HALL, MINCING LANE, 1856–60, Italianate; destroyed by bombing 1940 [T. L. Donaldson, *Handbook of Specifications,* 1860, 481].

ANGUS, GEORGE (*c.* 1792–1845), practised in Edinburgh. He was a competent but eclectic architect, who adapted his style to circumstances. His Dundee High School is in a Greek Revival style similar to Hamilton's Edinburgh High School, but all his churches are Gothic. In Dundee he was responsible for an important piece of town-planning – the formation of Reform Street, with the portico of his High School as the terminal feature. In 1833 he won the competition for the new gaols, police office and sheriff courthouse at Dundee. Owing to financial difficulties the court-house, whose Tuscan portico was to have formed the principal architectural feature, had to be dropped, but it was eventually built in the 1860s with a façade based on Angus's original design. After the advent of James Black (*q.v.*) as Town's Architect of Dundee in 1833 the corporation ceased to employ Angus, but he also designed the Watt Institution and prepared feu-plans for a large layout of villas on the lands of Dudhope which proved largely abortive because of depression in the 1840s. A stone in the Warriston Cemetery in Edinburgh records his death on 8 June 1845 at the age of 53.

EDINBURGH, THE SUBSCRIPTION BATHS AND DRAW-ING ACADEMY (now Masonic Lodge), 17–19a HILL STREET, 1825–8 [Edinburgh Dean of Guild Plans, 10 May 1825].

DUNDEE, THE PUBLIC SEMINARIES or HIGH SCHOOL, 1832–4 [C. Mackie, *Historical Description of Dundee,* 1836, 142].

---

[1] The I.C.B.S. Certificate for this church is, however, signed by Thomas Nicholson, a surveyor and builder at Hexham.

KINROSS CHURCH, KINROSS-SHIRE, 1832, Gothic [*N.S.A.* ix, *Kinross-shire*, 21].

TULLIALLAN CHURCH, FIFE, 1833, Gothic [*N.S.A. ibid.*].

DUNDEE, REFORM STREET, all elevations, and also interiors of the three S.E. blocks, 1833 [David Walker, *Architects and Architecture in Dundee 1770–1914*, Abertay Historical Soc.'s Publication No. 3, 1955, 9–10].

DUNDEE, THE GAOLS AND BRIDEWELL, 1833–6, enlarged 1843–4; dem. [James Thomson, *History of Dundee*, 1847, 152; David Walker, *op. cit.*, 10–11].

ALLOA HOUSE, CLACKMANNANSHIRE, rebuilt for 9th Earl of Mar, 1834–8, in Greek Revival style; remodelled in Tudor style *c.* 1865; dem. *c.* 1954 [S.R.O., GD 17/423/2, 3, 4, 8, 9].

DUNDEE, THE WATT INSTITUTION (now Y.M.C.A.), 1838–9 [Dundee Public Library, minutes of Watt Institution, *ex inf.* Mr. David Walker].

ALLOA EPISCOPAL (subsequently R.C.) CHURCH, CLACKMANNANSHIRE, 1839–40, Gothic [*N.S.A.* viii, *Clackmannanshire*, 43].

KIRRIEMUIR, ANGUS, THE BRITISH LINEN BANK, 45–47 HIGH STREET, 1841–3 [plans at Bank of Scotland dated 16 July 1839, *ex inf.* Mr. David Walker].

TAIN, ROSS-SHIRE, THE BRITISH LINEN BANK, 1845 [contracts advertised in *Aberdeen Jnl.* 30 April 1845, *ex inf.* Mr. David Walker].

APPLETON, ROBERT, appears on the evidence of the I.C.B.S. records to have designed ST. JAMES'S CHURCH, DUNWICH, SUFFOLK, in a plain classical style, 1827–30.

ARCHER, JOHN LEE (1791–1852), was the son of a civil engineer practising in Ireland. In 1812 he obtained employment as a draughtsman in the London office of John Rennie, but left in 1818 in order to set up practice on his own as an architect and engineer. He exhibited at the Royal Academy from time to time, but does not appear to have secured any important commission. In 1826 he obtained the post of Civil Engineer to the government of Van Diemen's Land (now Tasmania), where he designed a number of public buildings of considerable merit, including the Customs House in Hobart, now the Parliament House. In 1838 his department was abolished, and he was given alternative employment as a Police Magistrate. He served in this capacity for fourteen years, dying at Stanley in December 1852. [Roy Smith, *John Lee Archer*, Tasmanian Historical Research Association, 1962; information from Mr. E. R. Pretyman.]

ARCHER, THOMAS (*c.* 1668–1743), was the youngest son of Thomas Archer of Umberslade in Warwickshire, a country gentleman who represented his county in parliament in 1660. He

was educated at Trinity College, Oxford, from 1686 to 1689, and subsequently (1691–5) travelled abroad for four years. Of his itinerary nothing is known beyond the fact that he had a pass to go to Holland in January 1690/1 and was in Padua in December of that year. It may, however, be surmised that he visited Germany and Austria on his way to Italy [*Architectural Review*, August 1957, 88, Sept. 1957, 344]. In 1705 he obtained the court post of Groom Porter, which gave him control of gaming tables in the royal palaces, and was reputed to be worth £1000 a year: this he probably owed to the Duke of Devonshire, then Lord Steward of the Household. In 1715 he was in addition given the sinecure comptrollership of customs at Newcastle. Archer was one of the Commissioners for building Fifty New Churches under the Act of 1711, and in 1713 he sought unsuccessfully to obtain the post of Comptroller of the Works after Vanbrugh's dismissal. No appointment was made as Harley was contemplating a reform of the Office of Works in which the comptrollership would have been abolished, and on the change of government in 1714 Vanbrugh was reinstated.

In 1715 Archer purchased an estate at Hale in Hampshire, where he proceeded to rebuild the house and enlarge the church, and at the time of his death he owned considerable property in Warwickshire, Worcestershire and Dorset as well as in London. His first wife, Eleanor, daughter of a distant relative, John Archer of Welford, Berks., died of smallpox within a year of her marriage. His second wife was Anne, daughter of John Chaplin of Tathwell, Lincs., who survived him. They had no children. Archer died at his house in Whitehall on 22 or 23 May 1743, aged 74, and was buried at Hale in a vault under the north transept of the church, and opposite the monument which he had erected, probably to his own design, in 1739. A portrait attributed to Kneller hangs in the church of St. John, Smith Square.

Archer was an amateur architect in the sense that he did not depend upon architectural practice for his livelihood, and worked chiefly for fellow-members of the English aristocracy. He was, however, an able and active designer and a competent (if hardly an elegant) draughtsman. Nothing is known of his architectural training, but it is evident that his foreign tour must have been crucial in the development of his architectural style. The influence of Bernini and Borromini is obvious in many of his designs, and Archer's work has more in common with continental baroque than that of any other English architect. This is apparent not only in his use of standard baroque motifs such as eared architraves and broken pediments, but in his handling of space and above all in his fondness for convex and concave planes. Whereas Vanbrugh and Hawksmoor created an insular baroque which had few immediate continental precedents, Archer brought a direct experience of European baroque to England. It is this that gives his work a unique place in English architectural history. Among his most accomplished and characteristic works are St. Paul's Church, Deptford, Heythrop House, and the domed garden pavilion at Wrest Park in Bedfordshire. [Marcus Whiffen, *Thomas Archer*, 1950.]

HOUSES

CHATSWORTH HOUSE, DERBYSHIRE, north front for the 1st Duke of Devonshire, 1704–5. The Cascade House (1702) can also be attributed to Archer [Francis Thompson, *A History of Chatsworth*, 1949, 77–8] (*C. Life*, 2 May 1968).

CLIVEDEN HOUSE, BUCKS., addition of wings and quadrant colonnades for the 1st Earl of Orkney, before 1717, perhaps *c.* 1705; colonnades dem. 1849, wings altered in nineteenth century [*Vitruvius Britannicus* ii, 1717, pls. 70–4; G. Jackson-Stops, 'The Cliveden Album: drawings by Archer, Leoni and Gibbs', *Architectural History* xix, 1976].

HEYTHROP HOUSE, OXON., for the Duke of Shrewsbury, 1707–10. The interior was destroyed by fire 1831 and rebuilt 1870 by Alfred Waterhouse, who demolished Archer's wings [letters from Duke of Shrewsbury in B.M., Add. MS. 40776, ff. 55, 61, 63; H. Walpole, *Anecdotes of Painting*, ed. Dallaway & Wornum, ii, 1862, 687] (*Vitruvius Britannicus* v, 1771, pls. 82–5].

attributed: remodelling of AYNHO PARK, NORTHANTS., for Thomas Cartwright, 1707–11, including addition of library, conservatory, stables and coach-house [stylistic attribution]. The library and conservatory were altered by Sir J. Soane in 1800–1 (*C. Life*, 2–16 July 1953).

WREST PARK, BEDS., domed garden pavilion for the Duke of Kent, 1709–11 [*Vitruvius Britannicus* i, 1715, pl. 33] (*C. Life*, 4 Aug. 1917). The demolished Cain Hill House, another garden building erected *c.* 1715–17, can also be attributed to Archer.

ROEHAMPTON HOUSE, WANDSWORTH, SURREY, for Thomas Cary, 1710–12, now part of Queen Mary's Hospital; wings added by Lutyens 1910 [*Vitruvius Britannicus* i, 1715, pls. 80, 81].

HALE HOUSE, HANTS., for himself soon after 1715; much altered by Henry Holland 1770 (*C. Life*, 8 Aug. 1941; *Wren Soc.* xvii, pls. xliv, xlv).

attributed: LONDON, RUSSELL HOUSE, NO. 43 KING STREET, COVENT GARDEN, for Admiral Edward Russell, Earl of Orford, 1716–17 [*Survey of London* xxxvi, 166–178].

attributed: LONDON, MONMOUTH HOUSE, SOHO SQUARE, new façade and other alterations for Sir James Bateman, *c.* 1717–18; dem. 1773 [*Survey of London* xxiii, 109–12].

attributed: MARLOW PLACE, BUCKS., probably for John Wallop, Viscount Lymington, afterwards 1st Earl of Portsmouth, *c.* 1720 [H. M. Colvin in *Records of Bucks.* xv, 1947, 8] (measured drawings in *Arch. Rev.* xxvii, 170–5, xxviii, 282–4, 1910).

HARCOURT HOUSE, NO. 1 CAVENDISH SQUARE, LONDON,[1] for the 1st Visct. Harcourt, *c.* 1725; dem. J. Rocque's engraving of 'The Original Design of Ye Rt. Hon[ble] ye L[d] Harcourt's House in Cavendish Square, as it was drawn by Mr. Archer, but Built and Altered to what it now is by Edward Wilcox Esqr. *Ex Autographis Architecti*' is in B.M., *King's Maps* xxvii, 6.

attributed: CHETTLE HOUSE, DORSET, for George Chafin, after 1711 [G. F. Webb in *C. Life*, 6 Oct. 1928; Arthur Oswald, 'A Plan of Chettle', in *The Country Seat*, ed. H. M. Colvin & John Harris, 1970, 85–7].

Note: there is no reason to think that Archer designed Umberslade Hall, Warwicks., built by his brother Andrew *c.* 1695, as suggested in *A.P.S.D.* and *Wren Soc.* xvii, p. xlii. It is doubtful whether any of his designs for rebuilding Hurstbourne Park, Hants., for the 1st Earl of Portsmouth, were carried out (cf. Whiffen, pp. 28 and 62). For substantial payments to him from Robert Benson (*q.v.*) in 1699–1700, perhaps for architectural work, see G. W. Beard in *C. Life*, 11 Dec. 1958, 1421.

CHURCHES

BIRMINGHAM, ST. PHILIP, 1710–15; tower 1725 (Joseph Pedley, mason); chancel enlarged by J. A. Chatwin 1883–4, and the exterior refaced 1864 and 1911 [MS. Minutes of Commissioners for Rebuilding the Church, preserved in the vestry; *Vitruvius Britannicus* i, 1715, pls. 10–11].

DEPTFORD, ST. PAUL, 1713–30 (Edward Tuffnell and Edward Strong, masons, Thomas Lucas, bricklayer, James Grove and John Meard, carpenters, James Ellis and James Hands, plasterers, John Gilliam, joiner) [original plans in B.M., *King's Maps* xvii, 18 e–i; P.R.O. Declared Accounts, Audit Office, Bdles. 437–9, 572] (G. Pinkerton, 'The Parish Church of St. Paul Deptford', *Arch. Rev.* li, 1922). The rectory designed by Archer was dem. *c.* 1885.

WESTMINSTER, ST. JOHN, SMITH SQUARE, 1713–28 (Edward Tufnell and Edward Strong, masons, Thomas Hues and William Tufnell,

---

[1] Not to be confused with the house on the opposite (west) side of the square built by Lord Bingley, which was known as Harcourt House from 1773, when it was acquired by the 1st Earl Harcourt, until its demolition in 1906.

bricklayers, Robert Jelfes and John James, carpenters); interior gutted 1742, and re-constructed 1744–45 by James Horne, who removed the internal columns; interior re-arranged 1824–5 by W. Inwood; again gutted 1941 and rebuilt to original design by Marshall Sisson 1965–8 [J. E. Smith, *Parochial Memorials of St. John's Westminster*, 1892; *Wren Soc.* xvii, pl. xl, showing Archer's origi-nal design for the towers; W. A. Eden in *C. Life*, 1 March 1962].

HALE, HANTS., rebuilt chancel and added tran-septs at his own expense, 1717 [inscription on monument and memo. in Parish Register]. A central bell-cupola was removed in 1895, when the roof was rebuilt and the modillioned cor-nice added (*Wren Soc.* xvii, pl. xlv).

MONUMENTS

Archer designed the monument in ROUS LENCH CHURCH, WORCS., to Sir Francis Rous (d. 1687). It was erected in 1719 in accordance with the will of Lady Frances Rous (d. 1715), who was Archer's sister [E. A. B. Barnard, 'The Rouses of Rous Lench', *Trans. Worcs. Arch. Soc.*, N.S., viii, 1931, 55–8].

Archer probably designed the monument at HAMPTON, MIDDLESEX, to Susannah Thomas, died 1731, whose will directs him to erect it as her executor [P.C.C. 105 Isham]. It is signed 'W. Powell F[t].'

He no doubt designed his own monument at HALE, which he erected in 1739 during his life-time (*Wren Soc.* xvii, pl. xlvi[1]), and he may have designed that at TANWORTH, WARWICKS., to his father, Thomas Archer, and his mother, Eliza-beth (d. 1703), which was erected by his brother Andrew (*Wren Soc.* xvii, pl. xliii).

ARMSTRONG, WILLIAM (–1858), was an architect and civil engineer of Bristol. He was one of the building surveyors for that city from 1836 until his death in October 1858. He had the reputation of being a practical man whose abili-ties lay in sound construction rather than in the art of design. In 1829 he was one of the un-successful competitors for the bridge over the Avon Gorge at Clifton. He enlarged RADSTOCK CHURCH, SOMERSET, in 1832 [I.C.B.S.], altered ST. PHILIP AND ST. JACOB'S CHURCH, BRISTOL, in 1839–41 [I.C.B.S.], and designed THE INDEPENDENT CHAPEL, GLENDOWER STREET, MONMOUTH, in 1844 [*Monmouthshire Merlin*, 7 June 1844]. E. W.

See p. 986

[1] The supposed 'design for monument to Thomas Archer' by P. Scheemakers in the Soane Museum, illu-strated on the same plate, is, in fact, for the monument to Sir Christopher Powell at Boughton Monchelsea, which is signed by that sculptor. There is no evidence to connect Scheemakers with Archer's monument.

Godwin was his pupil [Dudley Harbron, *The Conscious Stone: the Life of E. W. Godwin*, 1949, 8].

ARNOLD, WILLIAM (–1637?), was an im-portant master mason in Somerset in the early seventeenth century. In 1617 he was living at Charlton Musgrove, nr. Wincanton, and he appears to have been identical with William Arnold, *alias* Goverson, who was a church-warden of Charlton Musgrove in 1600, 1601 and 1622, and who died there in March 1636/7. The name Arnold was associated in the seventeenth century with the freestone quarries at Ketton in Rutland, and in 1621 Arnold Goverson supplied large quantities of Ketton stone for the building of Raynham Hall in Norfolk. It is probable, therefore, that William Arnold was a member of the Ketton family who had moved to Somerset.

William Arnold's first recorded work was the remodelling of CRANBORNE HOUSE, DORSET, for Robert Cecil, 1st Earl of Salisbury, between 1608 and 1612. In December 1609 he was paid £5 for 'drawing a plott for Cranborne house', and in November 1610 'Arnold the freemason' received £40 'in part of £250 agreed upon to build a tar-ryce & a kitchen'. What is almost certainly this 'plot', showing the 'tarris', the new kitchen and other proposed additions, is preserved at Hatfield House (Oswald, *Country Houses of Dorset*, pl. 149). Among the additions made to the house at this time (and shown on the plan) are the two porches, which are treated as *loggie*, with Tuscan columns supporting open arches. The very similar porch at WAYFORD MANOR, DORSET, can confidently be attributed to Arnold, and similari-ties between Cranborne and Wayford on the one hand, and MONTACUTE HOUSE, SOMERSET, on the other, make it very probable that Arnold was also the designer of the last-named house, built by Sir Edward Phelips during the last decade of the six-teenth century.

In 1609 Arnold received an important commission from the executors of Nicholas Wad-ham, whose will provided for the building of the Oxford college which bears his name. As there were difficulties about obtaining masons in Oxford it was decided to send a team of masons from Somerset, with William Arnold at their head. Wadham's widow, writing to her half-brother Lord Petre, praised Arnold as 'an honest man, a perfectt workman, and my neere neigh-boure'. He had, she said, been 'commended' to her by Sir Edward Phelips – further evidence that he had been employed at Montacute. Phelips' good opinion of Arnold was shared by Sir Edward Hext of Low Ham, another Somerset landowner, who considered him 'the absolutest and honestest workeman in England'. Arnold was accordingly engaged to 'be imployed in the provysyon of tymber & stones for Wadham Colledge as also for drawyng of a plott & for the byl-dyng of yt'. His 'plott' was shown to the King, the Archbishop of Canterbury, the Lord Chancellor and the Lord Treasurer (Robert Cecil), and was carried out under his direction between 1610 and 1612 [T. G. Jackson, *Wadham College, Oxford*, 1893, 29–51; Nancy Briggs, 'The Foundation of Wadham College', *Oxoniensia* xxi, 1957, 63, 67–8].

One other documented work of Arnold's is recorded. In 1617 he agreed to supply George Luttrell with a 'plott' and an 'upright' for remodelling the south side of DUNSTER CASTLE, SOMERSET, and to oversee the work. Despite Arnold's 'great experience in architecture', Luttrell was dissatisfied with the result, and a lawsuit ensued in the Court of Chancery. Arnold's work at Dunster was much altered by Salvin in 1869 [H. C. Maxwell Lyte, *History of Dunster* ii, 1909, 366].

Several other houses in Somerset and Dorset have features which suggest that they may have been designed or altered by Arnold, and a Jacobean garden-seat set in a wall at Edington Priory, Wiltshire, is also in his style. Though essentially traditional in character, his architecture is enlivened by the introduction of classical ornaments with a strong mannerist flavour.

[Arthur Oswald, *Country Houses of Dorset*, 2nd. ed. 1959, 25–30.]

ARROW, JAMES (–1791), of Westminster, was a carpenter and joiner by trade. He held the post of Surveyor to the Victualling Office and Inspector of Repairs to the Admiralty from 1774 to 1785, and in 1783 designed extensive new buildings at the ROYAL VICTUALLING YARD, DEPT-FORD [P.R.O., Adm. 111/93, 17 Feb. 1783; drawings in R.I.B.A. Collection dated 1786 and 1788]. In 1768 he was one of the unsuccessful applicants for the surveyorship of the East India Company. Designs for a fireproof arch, submitted by Arrow to the Society of Arts in 1772, are in the R.I.B.A. Drawings Collection. A monument to Ann Littlejohn (d. 1771) in the church of St. Andrew, Halfway Tree, Jamaica, bears the signature of *Jas. Arrow, Archt. and Sefn. Alken, Sculpt.* [*C. Life*, 25 Jan. 1968, correspondence]. James Hunter was his pupil, exhibiting a 'Design for a temple dedicated to the Cardinal Virtues' at the Royal Academy in 1776 from 'Mr. Arrow's, Tothill Fields, Westminster'. Arrow died at his house in Tothill Fields on 28 August 1791 [*Gent's Mag.* 1791 (ii), 874].

ARUNDALE, FRANCIS VYVYAN JAGO (1807–1853), was a pupil of the elder Pugin. He accompanied Pugin on his tour of Normandy, and, in conjunction with G. B. Moore, Benjamin Ferrey and Talbot Bury, made the drawings published in *Specimens of the Architec-*

tural Antiquities of Normandy, 1826–8. In 1829 he was admitted to the Royal Academy Schools on Pugin's recommendation. In 1831 he went out to Egypt in order to assist Robert Hay in his archaeological investigations. Later he joined Catherwood and Bonomi, and in 1833 visited Palestine. After nine years in the East, he returned to England by way of Asia Minor, Greece and Italy, bringing with him a large collection of drawings, many of which he exhibited at the Royal Academy in subsequent years. In 1837 he published *Illustrations of Jerusalem and Mount Sinai*, and in 1842 he contributed to Birch's *Gallery of Antiquities selected from the British Museum* (1842). He was also the author of a folio volume entitled *The Edifices of Andrea Palladio, forming a selection from his most admired buildings* (n.d.), based on measurements made by himself and J. B. Atkinson of York, and of *Examples and Designs of Verandahs* (1851).

Arundale never practised as an architect, and the only building he is known to have designed was a boat-house at HAMS HALL, WARWICKS., for Charles Bowyer Adderley, the design for which he exhibited at the Royal Academy in 1839. While in Egypt 'he inhabited one of the excavated tombs', and as a result was believed to have contracted the maladies which caused his early death. He married the daughter of H. W. Pickersgill, R.A. His portrait by William Brockedon is in the National Portrait Gallery. [*Builder* xii, 1854, 83.]

ASHPITEL, WILLIAM HURST (1776–1852), was a pupil of D. A. Alexander, whom he assisted in his works in the London Docks. He was also for some time an assistant of John Rennie, under whom he was concerned in the construction of the Kennet and Avon Canal. He afterwards entered into partnership with James Savage, and later practised for some time alone. Ashpitel was elected a member of the Surveyors' Club in 1806. He quitted practice early and thereafter 'gave his attention chiefly to improvements upon his own property' at Clapton. He was the father of the architect Arthur Ashpitel (1807–69). He died on 20 April 1852, aged 75.

Memorandum books in the Royal West of England Academy at Bristol and the Avery Architectural Library of Columbia University, New York, throw considerable light on Ashpitel's practice as a London surveyor. His principal architectural works were ST. JOHN'S CHURCH, S. HACKNEY, LONDON (with J. Savage), 1806–10, dem. 1845 (illustrated in W. Robinson, *History of Hackney* ii, 1843, 171); Sir Charles Talbot's house at CHART PARK, nr. DORKING, SURREY, demolished in 1819 by Thomas Hope in order to enlarge his park at Deepdene; THE GROVE, WORTH, SUSSEX; SHENLEY RECTORY, HERTS.; and alterations to NORTH MIMMS CHURCH and NORTH

MIMMS HOUSE, HERTS. A fantastic design by him for a Gothic 'Belle Vue', exhibited at the Royal Academy in 1800, is illustrated in the 3rd Catalogue of Paul Grinke of London, 1971, item 14. [*A.P.S.D.*; John Harris, *A Catalogue of British Drawings for Architecture etc. in American Collections*, 1971, 16–18.]

ASHWELL, THOMAS, was a carpenter and builder of Tottenham in Middlesex. In 1835 he designed and built JESUS CHURCH, FORTY HILL, ENFIELD, MIDDLESEX, imitating (at the patron's request), James Savage's Holy Trinity, Tottenham [E. H. A. Koch, *Forty Hill Church and Parish*, 1935; W. Robinson, *History and Antiquities of Tottenham*, 2nd ed. 1840, i, 155, ii, 134, 355].

ASTLEY, JOHN (?1730–1787), was a spendthrift portrait-painter who is said to have had some ability as an architect. In 1759 he married a rich widow, Lady Duckenfield Daniell, who first settled on him the estate of Over Tabley in Cheshire, and then died (1762), leaving him, on the death of her daughter (which occurred soon after), the Duckinfield estate near Stockport, worth some £5000 a year. Tabley he soon sold (though not before he had 'decorated' and 'built' there), but Duckinfield he retained, building there DUKINFIELD LODGE (dem.), 'two stone bridges over the Tame for the accommodation of the village, and a handsome circus of brick houses, divided into semi-circles by the road'. In 1769 he acquired the lease of SCHOMBERG HOUSE, PALL MALL, LONDON, which he divided into three, occupying the central house himself. He also had a house overlooking the river in the Terrace at Barnes in Surrey, afterwards occupied by Lady Archer.

In the structure and decoration of small buildings..., Astley's architecture was pre-eminent; Pall Mall is one instance; Lady Archer's saloon and conservatory, at Barnes, is another; Duckenfield is yet finer than either. The saloon, the loggio in front, the chambers on each side, and the great octagon, are all as exquisite as original, from the first idea to the last. (W. Betham, *Baronetage of England* ii, 1802, 378–9.)

As (with the possible exception of some plasterwork at Schomberg House, illustrated in *London Survey* xxx, pl. 208) nothing now remains of any of 'Beau Astley's' architectural works, it is difficult to judge his skill as a designer. He died at Dukinfield Lodge on 14 November 1787, leaving the estate to his son (by a later marriage) Francis Duckenfield Astley. [S. Redgrave, *Dictionary of Artists*, 1878, 14–15; *D.N.B.*; *Gent's Mag.* 1759, 606; J. Dugdale, *The New British Traveller* i, 1819, 325.]

ATKINSON, JOHN, of Clutton in Cheshire, designed CODDINGTON CHURCH, CHESHIRE, as rebuilt in 1833, Gothic [I.C.B.S.].

ATKINSON, PETER (1735–1805), born at or near Ripon, was brought up as a carpenter, but became an assistant to John Carr of York, by whom he was employed at Buxton, Harewood and elsewhere. In 1786 he was appointed receiver or steward to the City of York, with responsibility for the maintenance of corporation property, and on Carr's retirement soon afterwards he succeeded to his extensive practice in Yorkshire and the north of England. He died on 19 June 1805, aged 70, and was buried in the churchyard on the north side of the church of St. Mary Bishophill Senior. He was a competent practitioner in the conservative Georgian manner that he had learned from Carr. [*A.P.S.D.*; York Reference Library, MS. Notes on York artists by W. A. Knowles, i, 9.]

YORK, MONK BRIDGE, 1794; widened 1924–6 [*V.C.H. York*, 519].

HACKNESS HALL, YORKS. (N.R.), for Sir R. V. B. Johnstone, Bart., 1797 [*A.P.S.D.*]. The interior was gutted by fire in 1910 and reinstated by W. H. Brierley (*C. Life*, 19 March 1921, where Carr is wrongly described as the architect).

HAINTON HALL, LINCS., rebuilt west front for George Heneage, 1800 [signed drawings preserved in house].

WORTLEY HALL, YORKS. (W.R.), stable-block for James Archibald Stuart Wortley (afterwards 1st Lord Wharncliffe), c. 1800 [Wortley papers in Sheffield City Library, Wh. M. 58/45–6, *ex inf.* Mr. Richard Hewlings].

ORMSBY HALL, SOUTH ORMSBY, LINCS., additions at rear for Charles Burrell Massingberd, 1803 [drawings in Lincs. Record Office signed *Peter Atkinson & Son, 1803*].

YORK, BOOTHAM HOUSE (now SCHOOL), NO. 51 BOOTHAM, for Sir R. V. B. Johnstone, Bart., 1803–4 [R.C.H.M., *York* iv, 60].

HAREWOOD HOUSE, YORKS. (W.R.), gateway for the 1st Earl of Harewood, c. 1803 [R. B. Wragg in *Archaeological Jnl.* cxxv, 1968, 342, n. 4].

ATKINSON, PETER, junior (c. 1776–1843), son and pupil of the above, became his father's partner in 1801, and succeeded to his practice in 1805. He was surveyor and steward to the York Corporation for many years. At first Atkinson was in partnership with Matthew Phillips (*q.v.*), but the partnership was dissolved in 1819, and from that year until 1827 he was in partnership with his former pupil, Richard Hey Sharp (*q.v.*). He was afterwards assisted by his sons John Bownas Atkinson (1797–1874) and William Atkinson (1811–86). He retired in 1836, and lived abroad during the last years of his life, dying in Calcutta on 13 January 1843. A portrait of him, attributed to Martin Archer Shee, hangs in the City Art Gallery at York. It shows him holding a view of the Ouse Bridge, a work for which his design was accepted as a result of an open competition judged by Thomas Harrison of Chester. [*A.P.S.D.*]

Atkinson designed some stylish Greek Revival buildings, but the numerous Commissioners' churches for which he was responsible are somewhat dreary buildings with wide, bleak naves usually lighted by lancet windows. His unexecuted designs for a Rectory at Foston in Yorkshire for the Rev. Sydney Smith are in the Borthwick Institute of Historical Research at York (MGA 1813/1).

PUBLIC BUILDINGS, ETC.

YORK, THE CITY GAOL, 1802–7; dem. 1880 [*A.P.S.D.*].

YORK, enlarged the FEMALE PRISON (now the CASTLE MUSEUM) in the CASTLE, adding the end bays to match Carr's Assize Courts, 1802 [W. Hargrove, *History of York* ii, 1818, 241–2; R.C.H.M., *City of York* ii, 85].

YORK, THE OUSE BRIDGE, 1810–20 [W. Hargrove, *History of York* ii, 1818, 198–200].

YORK, THE FOSS BRIDGE, 1811–12 [W. Hargrove, *History of York* ii, 1818, 288–9].

YORK, THE COUNCIL CHAMBER at THE GUILDHALL, 1811 [W. Hargrove, *History of York* ii, 1818, 436].

YORK, THE SUBSCRIPTION LIBRARY, ST. HELEN'S SQUARE, 1811–12 [W. Hargrove, *History of York* ii, 1818, 443].

YORK, THE HOUSE OF CORRECTION, 1814; dem. *c.* 1840 [W. Hargrove, *History of York* ii, 1818, 179].

BRADFORD, THE GRAMMAR SCHOOL, 1818-20; dem. 1871 [School accounts, *ex inf.* Mr. D. N. Griffiths] (T. Allen, *History of the County of York* iii, 1831, plate at p. 258).

*YORK, THE CONCERT ROOM adjoining the Assembly Rooms, 1824 [*A.P.S.D.*, *s.v.* 'York'].

NABURN, YORKS. (E.R.), THE LOCK OF BANQUETING HOUSE, 1824–5 [York City Archives, Ouse Navigation Trustees Account Book, Jan. 1824, July 1826, *ex inf.* Mr. I. H. Gordon].

*YORK, THE NEW RESIDENCE, DEAN'S PARK, 1824–7 [Hargrove's *Guide to York*, 1838, 96].

*BRADFORD, THE DISPENSARY, DARLEY STREET (now the Bradford Subscription Library), 1826–7; altered 1903 [W. Cudworth, *The Bradford Infirmary*, 1880, 5].

YORK, THE LAYERTHORPE BRIDGE, 1829; widened 1926 [*V.C.H. York*, 519].

CHURCHES

SPROATLEY, YORKS. (E.R.), reconstructed 1819–20, Gothic; altered 1886 [I.C.B.S.: 'we have the same architect as the Wainfleet people, Lincolnshire', but William Hutchinson acted as 'surveyor' and responsibility for the design is not clear].

WAINFLEET ALL SAINTS CHURCH, LINCS., 1820–1, Gothic [I.C.B.S.; B.M., Add. MS. 36,369, no. 139].

†*STANLEY, YORKS. (W.R.), 1821–4, Gothic; largely rebuilt by W. D. Caröe 1912–13 after a fire [Port, 138].

†*ALVERTHORPE, YORKS. (W.R.), 1823–5, Gothic [Port, 138].

†*WOODHOUSE MOOR, nr. LEEDS., YORKS. (W.R.), ST. MARK, 1823–5, Gothic [Port, 138].

*ROTHWELL, YORKS. (W.R.), repaired and enlarged 1824–6 [I.C.B.S.].

†*SCARBOROUGH, YORKS. (N.R.), CHRIST CHURCH, 1826–8, Gothic; chancel added 1873 [Port, 164].

†*LINTHWAITE, YORKS, (W.R.), 1827–8, Gothic; chancel added 1895 [Port, 168].

†SOUTH CROSLAND, YORKS. (W.R.), 1827–9, Gothic [Port, 166].

†GOLCAR, YORKS. (W.R.), 1828–9, Gothic; roof rebuilt by R. D. Chantrell 1844 [Port, 166].

†NEW MILL, YORKS. (W.R.), 1829–30, Gothic; remodelled 1882 [Port, 168].

†BIRKENSHAW, YORKS. (W.R.), 1829–30, Gothic; chancel added 1892–3 [Port, 166].

†MANCHESTER, ST. ANDREW, TRAVIS STREET, 1829–31, Gothic; dem. [Port, 132].

†HECKMONDWIKE, YORKS. (W.R.), 1830–1, Gothic; chancel added 1916 [Port, 166].

†CLECKHEATON, YORKS. (W.R.), 1830–1, Gothic; chancel added 1864 [Port, 166].

STAVELEY, YORKS. (W.R.), 1831, Gothic; rebuilt 1864 [I.C.B.S.].

ATKINSON, THOMAS (?1729–1798), was one of the leading architects in Yorkshire during the reign of George III. Nothing is known of his early life or of his architectural training, but he was probably the Thomas, son of Thomas Atkinson, mason, who was baptized at Holy Trinity, King's Court, York, on 22 June 1729 [*Yorks. Parish Record Soc.* lxxxv, 1928, 65]. His father may have been connected with a family of bricklayers of the same name with interests in both York and Selby. Thomas Atkinson himself has been identified with Thomas Atkinson of Selby, bricklayer, who became a freeman of York in 1758, but as he was a statuary mason by trade, he is more likely to have been the Thomas

---

* Designed in partnership with R. H. Sharp.
† Built for the Commissioners for Building New Churches.

Atkinson, 'stonecutter', who took up his freedom in 1760 [R. Davies, *The Freeman's Roll*, York 1835, 3]. About the same time he appears to have become a convert to Catholicism, and found a number of patrons among the Catholic gentry of Yorkshire. Plans in Sheffield City Library (E. BV.263(11) and 266(1–2)) show that in 1766 he was employed by the 9th Duke of Norfolk to lay out part of his Sheffield estate for building.

Thomas Atkinson had four sons, James, Joseph, John and Thomas, the first three of whom were all masons by trade. Atkinson 'dropped down dead near his own door' in St. Andrewgate, York, on 4 May 1798, aged 70. He died insolvent, but his business was continued by his son John, who erected a tablet to his memory in St. Saviour's Church, York (J. B. Morrell, *York Monuments*, pl. lxxv c).

Atkinson was an able architect in both Gothic and classical styles. Bishopthorpe Palace and the chancel of Coxwold Church are elegant and effective essays in the rococo Gothic of the 1760s, and at Brandsby Church and the chapel of the Bar Convent at York he used the classical orders to achieve interesting and original spatial effects. For his work as a monumental sculptor see Rupert Gunnis, *Dictionary of British Sculptors*, 2nd ed. 1968, 22. A design by him for an Ionic greenhouse will be found in Richard Steele, *An Essay upon Gardening*, York 1793, at end. [*A.P.S.D.*; J. C. H. Aveling, *Catholic Recusancy in the City of York 1558–1791*, Catholic Record Soc. 1970, 150, 371–2; information from Dr. E. A. Gee.]

BISHOPTHORPE PALACE, YORKS. (W.R.), designed stables and other offices 1763, Gothic gatehouse 1763–5, and remodelled house in Gothic style for Archbishop Robert Hay Drummond 1766–9 [Anon., *Eboracum: or the History of the City of York* ii, 1788, 169 note; *Beauties of England and Wales* xvi, 1812, 247] (J. P. Neale, *Views of Seats*, 1st ser., v, 1822; *C. Life*, 12 Jan. 1929).

attributed: BISHOPTHORPE CHURCH for Archbishop Robert Hay Drummond, 1766, Gothic; altered 1842 and dem. 1899 except west front.

?HOUGHTON HALL, YORKS. (E.R.), for Philip Langdale, *c*. 1765 [cf. letter from Beaumont Hotham to Thomas Atkinson printed in A. M. W. Stirling, *The Hothams* i, 1918, 310, and referring to his engagement with 'Mr. Langdale' 1769] (*C. Life*, 23–30 Dec. 1965).

YORK, THE BAR CONVENT AND CHAPEL, BLOSSOM STREET, Chapel 1766–9, first block complete 1775, street front 1786 [Bar Convent archives, *ex inf.* Dr. E. A. Gee].

BRANDSBY CHURCH, YORKS. (N.R.), mainly at the expense of Francis Cholmeley [*V.C.H. Yorks. N.R.* ii, 104, 106].

WARTER HALL, YORKS. (E.R.), alterations for Sir Joseph Pennington, 1768 [correspondence in Pennington–Ramsden papers, Hull University Library].

TIXALL HALL, STAFFS., designs, perhaps not executed, for alterations for the Hon. Thomas Clifford, *c*. 1770 [G. F. Webb in *C. Life*, 3 Sept. 1932, 270]. The house was dem. *c*. 1925.

BROUGH HALL, YORKS. (N.R.), addition of wings and other alterations for Sir John Lawson, Bart., 1772–5 [W. Angus, *Select Views of Seats*, pl. xxii, 1790] (*C. Life*, 12–19 Oct. 1967).

CARLTON HALL (now TOWERS), YORKS. (W.R.), work, probably including new east wing (1774) and interior of library, for Thomas Stapleton [Mark Girouard in *C. Life*, 26 Jan. 1967].

SHEFFIELD, SHREWSBURY HOSPITAL, octagonal chapel, 1776–7; dem. 1825 [reference to Atkinson as architect in the journal of John Platt, the mason who built the chapel: J. D. Potts, *Platt of Rotherham*, Sheffield 1959, 14] (engraving in Joseph Hunter, *History of Hallamshire*, 1868, 179; description in John Wesley's *Journal*, 15 Aug. 1781).

BURTON CONSTABLE, YORKS. (E.R.), bow window of drawing-room, and other designs not executed, for William Constable, *c*. 1776 [G. F. Webb in *C. Life*, 3 Sept. 1932].

COXWOLD CHURCH, YORKS. (N.R.), rebuilt chancel for the 2nd Earl of Fauconberg, 1777, Gothic [B.M., Add. MS. 41,135, f. 17].

SHEFFIELD, ST. PETER'S CHURCH (now Cathedral), added N.E. chapel (converted into an organ chamber 1878-80), 1777 [R. E. Leader, *Surveyors and Architects of Sheffield*, 1903].

SHEFFIELD, surveying new streets and drawing plans and elevations for them, 1779 [Sheffield City Library, R. E. Leader's notes, 141, p. 38].

YORK, NO. 20 ST. ANDREWGATE, for himself, *c*. 1780–90.

TERREGLES HOUSE, KIRKCUDBRIGHTSHIRE, for W. H. Maxwell Constable (of Everingham, Yorks.), 1788; enlarged 1831; dem. 1964 [Hull University Library: letters in Constable Maxwell papers, EV 60/20].

YORK, THE WORKHOUSE, MARYGATE, 1792 [*York Herald*, 7 April 1792].

THE MAUSOLEUM at HALSHAM, YORKS. (E.R.), for Edward Constable of Burton Constable, 1794–1802 [N. Higson, 'The Building of the Halsham Mausoleum', *Trans. of the E. Yorkshire Georgian Soc.* v (2), 1961–3].

ATKINSON, THOMAS WITLAM (1799–1861), was born at Cawthorne, Yorks., of humble parents. After earning his living as a bricklayer's labourer and quarryman he became a stonecarver, and was responsible for sculpture on churches at Barnsley and Ashton-under-Lyne. Then for a period he taught drawing at the latter town, and acted as clerk of the works for Basevi at St. Thomas's, Stockport, and for H. E. Kendall at St. George's, Ramsgate. At the same time he was making a close study of Gothic detail, particularly in the churches of Lincolnshire, and in 1829 published *Gothic Ornaments selected from the different Cathedrals and Churches in England*, with plates drawn and lithographed by himself and Charles Atkinson (who is said to have been his brother, and was certainly in partnership with him about this time – see *The Literary Blue Book*, 1830, 88).

In 1827 Atkinson settled in London, and began to practise as an architect. HYDE CHURCH, CHESHIRE, 1831–2, Gothic, was designed in partnership with Charles Atkinson [Port, 140, 177]. ST. NICHOLAS, LOWER TOOTING, SURREY, consecrated 1833, was another early work in the Gothic style. Several commissions in Manchester induced him to move there in about 1835. In Manchester his principal work was the MANCHESTER AND LIVERPOOL DISTRICT BANK in SPRING GARDENS, 1834, an astylar building (now demolished) whose erection, according to Atkinson's obituary notice in the *Builder*, 'was as important in the architectural history of Manchester, as that of the Travellers' Club was in London'. In ST. LUKE'S, CHEETHAM HILL, MANCHESTER, 1836–9, he made use of his Gothic studies to produce a church that was exceptionally scholarly for its date. Other works were ST. BARNABAS, OPENSHAW, LANCS., 1838–40; THE DISTRICT BANK, HANLEY, STAFFS., 1833, Gothic; dem. 1881 [signed lithograph in William Salt Library, Stafford, iv, 266]; Italianate villas in the neighbourhood of Manchester for Messrs. Heelis, Slater, Bradshaw and others; houses at ASHTON and STALYBRIDGE for Messrs. Swire, Lea and Harrison[1]; HOUGH HILL PRIORY, STALYBRIDGE, for David Cheetham, 1832, and a house at STOCKPORT for a Mr. Walmsley. Atkinson exhibited at the Royal Academy between 1830 and 1842. F. T. Bellhouse and Edward Hall were in his office as pupils, and J. E. Gregan (1813–55) was his assistant until 1840.

'After some reverses, owing perhaps to a too liberal expenditure on works of art', Atkinson returned to London, and in 1844 went to Hamburg to compete unsuccessfully for the church of St. Nicholas, which was awarded to Gilbert Scott. After this he abandoned architecture for the pursuits of an explorer and topographical artist, in which he achieved some celebrity. His best-known works of travel were *Oriental and Western Siberia: a Narrative of Seven Years' Explorations and Adventures* (1858), and *Travels in the Upper and Lower Amoor and the Russian Acquisitions on the Confines of India and China* (1860). He died in Kent on 13 August 1861.

---

[1] Probably William Harrison (d. 1853), of West Hill, Stalybridge.

[Obituary in *Builder* xix, 1861, 590; *A.P.S.D.*; *D.N.B.* (Supplement).]

ATKINSON, WILLIAM (*c.* 1773–1839), was born at Bishop Auckland, Durham, and began life as a carpenter. He was probably a son of another William Atkinson who was employed as a builder at Auckland Castle in the 1760s, and is doubtless the 'Atkinson, Junr.' who signs drawings connected with James Wyatt's works at the Castle for Bishop Barrington in the 1790s [John Cornforth in *C. Life*, 3 Feb. 1972]. Through Bishop Barrington's good offices he became a pupil of Wyatt and moved to London, where he entered the Royal Academy Schools in 1796, winning the Gold Medal in 1797. He subsequently exhibited regularly at the Academy until 1811. In 1805 he published a volume of *Views of Picturesque Cottages*. The Roman cement known as 'Atkinson's cement' was introduced by him to the London market, the raw material being shipped to his own wharf in Westminster from Lord Mulgrave's estates near Whitby. The cement could be used both as an external rendering and as a form of stucco. It was through the favour of Lord Mulgrave, then Master General of the Ordnance, that in 1813 Atkinson succeeded James Wyatt as architect to the Board of Ordnance, a post which he retained until the abolition of his department in 1829.

In 1812–16 Atkinson appears to have had an office in Manchester: it was from Manchester that in February 1812 he wrote to the Duke of Devonshire's London agent about projected works at Burlington House [letter at Chatsworth, *ex inf.* Mr. P. A. Bezodis]; it was also from Manchester that in 1813 and 1814 he exhibited at the Liverpool Academy, and his name appears in the Manchester directories for 1815 and 1816.

Atkinson was primarily a country-house architect, and he specialized in the design of picturesque Gothic houses, usually based on an irregular, asymmetrical plan, with a profusion of battlemented towers and pinnacled gables. He was not a very sensitive architect, and his Gothic detail has lost the elegant charm of the eighteenth century without achieving the scholarship of the nineteenth. Of his few classical works, the interiors of Broughton Hall are the most successful, and show that he could rival some of the best Regency designers.

Atkinson was a keen geologist and botanist. The gardens of his villa at Grove End, Paddington, were planted with rare trees and embellished with 'specimens of the varieties of English stone'. In about 1830 he bought an estate of 170 acres at Silvermere, nr. Cobham in Surrey, where he built himself a house, and was able to indulge in his 'favourite pursuits of horticulture and planting' on a large scale. Here he died on 22 May 1839, and was buried at Walton-on-

Thames. He left two sons, William and Henry
George Atkinson, the younger of whom was also
an architect. His pupils included T. Allason, R.
R. Banks, P. H. Desvignes, M. Habershon and
J. B. Watson, while Thomas Tredgold, C.E.,
spent ten years in his office between 1813 and
1824. [*A.P.S.D.*; *Farington Diary*, ed. J. Greig,
vii, 205; J. T. Smith, *A Book for a Rainy Day*,
1905, 312–3; E. W. Brayley, *Topographical History of Surrey* ii, 1841, 368; letter about planting
at Silvermere in National Library of Scotland,
MS. 587, no. 1202; will, P.C.C. 339 VAUGHAN.]

HOUSES

CASTLE EDEN, DURHAM, castellated lodge and gateway for Rowland Burdon, *c.* 1800 [exhib. at
R.A. 1800].

SCONE PALACE, PERTHSHIRE, reconstructed for the
3rd Earl of Mansfield, 1803–12, Gothic [exhib.
at R.A. 1808, 1811; J. P. Neale, *Views of Seats*,
1st ser., v, 1822]. Atkinson also designed the
stables (1810), and the mausoleum (1807) may
be attributed to him.

BROADWELL GROVE, nr. BURFORD, OXON., for
William Hervey, 1804, Gothic [exhib. at R.A.
1810].[1]

FOOTS CRAY, KENT, house for J. Olive, *c.* 1804
[exhib. at R.A. 1804].

MULGRAVE CASTLE, YORKS. (N.R.), remodelled for
the 1st Earl of Mulgrave, *c.* 1804–11, castle
style [exhib. at R.A. 1804; J. P. Neale, *Views
of Seats*, 2nd ser., ii, 1825].

CHIDDINGSTONE CASTLE, KENT, remodelled for
Henry Streatfield, *c.* 1805–10, Gothic; additions by H. E. Kendall 1836–8 [exhib. at R.A.
1805].

BRETTON HALL, YORKS. (W.R.), Doric lodge and
gateway for Col. T. R. Beaumont, 1807 [exhib.
at R.A. 1807].

TWYFORD ABBEY, WEST TWYFORD, MIDDLESEX, for
Thomas Willan, 1807–9, Gothic [*Beauties of
England and Wales* x (2), 1816, 353; *A.P.S.D.*].

ROSSIE PRIORY, PERTHSHIRE, for the 8th Lord Kinnaird, 1807–15, Gothic; partly dem. [J. P.
Neale, *Views of Seats*, 2nd ser., ii, 1825].

PANSHANGER, HERTS., for the 5th Earl Cowper,
1807–20, Gothic (succeeding Samuel Wyatt);
dem. 1953–4 [*A.P.S.D.*] (*C. Life*, 11–18 Jan.
1936).

BROUGHTON HALL, YORKS. (W.R.), added pedimented wings and made other alterations for
Stephen Tempest, 1809–11 [C. Hussey in *C.
Life*, 31 March, 7, 14 April 1950].

LISMORE CASTLE, CO. WATERFORD, IRELAND,
repairs and alterations for the 6th Duke of
Devonshire, 1811 [Mark Girouard in *C. Life*,
6–13 Aug. 1964].

ROSEBERY, MIDLOTHIAN, for — Hepburn, 1812–

16; since much enlarged [*A.P.S.D.*; cf.
N.S.A. i, 51 note].

BOWHILL, SELKIRKSHIRE, additions for the 5th
Duke of Buccleuch, 1812–17 [*A.P.S.D.*; John
Cornforth in *C. Life*, 5 June 1975] (R.C.A.M.,
Selkirkshire, 65–6).

DITTON PARK, BUCKS., for Lord Montagu, 1813–
17, Gothic [Neale, *Views of Seats*, 1st ser., i,
1818].

CLAPHAM LODGE (afterwards INGLEBOROUGH
HALL), CLAPHAM, nr. SETTLE, YORKS. (W.R.), for
James Farrer, *c.* 1814 [exhib. at Liverpool Academy, 1814].

BIEL, EAST LOTHIAN, additions (since demolished)
for W. H. Nisbet, 1814–18, Gothic [*N.S.A.* ii,
57] (J. Small, *Castles and Mansions of the Lothians* i, 1883; *C. Life*, 30 Aug. 1902).

GARNONS, HEREFORDSHIRE, enlarged and remodelled for Sir J. G. Cotterell, Bart., 1815–*c.*
1830, Gothic [J. P. Neale, *Views of Seats*, 2nd
ser., iv, 1828]. Much of Atkinson's work has
since been removed.

GORHAMBURY, HERTS., rebuilt north wing 1816–
17, demolished south wing and made other
alterations 1826–8 for the 1st Earl of Verulam
[J. C. Rogers in *C. Life*, 25 Nov. 1933].

ABBOTSFORD, ROXBURGHSHIRE, for Sir Walter
Scott, Bart., 1816–23, Gothic, incorporating
suggestions by Edward Blore [National
Library of Scotland, MS. 3889, f. 17; *The Letters of Sir Walter Scott*, ed. H. J. C. Grierson,
1934, iv, 333–6, 526–7, vii, 208].

TULLIALLAN CASTLE, FIFE, for Viscount Keith,
1817–20, Gothic [*A.P.S.D.*] (A. H. Millar,
Fife: Pictorial and Historical ii, 1895, 262).

THE DEEPDENE, nr. DORKING, SURREY, remodelled
for Thomas Hope, 1818–19 and 1823 [David
Watkin, *Thomas Hope*, 1968, 166, 288].

TAYMOUTH CASTLE, PERTHSHIRE, extensive Gothic
additions for the 4th Earl of Breadalbane,
1818–21 and 1827–8 [*A.P.S.D.*; Alistair
Rowan in *C. Life*, 8–15 Oct. 1964].

LONDON, BREADALBANE HOUSE, PARK LANE, work
for the 4th Earl of Breadalbane, 1818–24
[*A.P.S.D.*].

HYLANDS, nr. CHELMSFORD, ESSEX, added portico
and wings for P. C. Labouchère, 1819–25
[*A.P.S.D.*] (J. P. Neale, *Views of Seats*, ser. 1,
ii, 1819).

LONDON, GROVE END, PADDINGTON, for himself, *c.*
1818; dem. [J. T. Smith, *A Book for a Rainy
Day*, 1905, 312–13].

LONDON, added FLEMISH PICTURE GALLERY to
house in DUCHESS STREET, PORTLAND PLACE, to
designs of Thomas Hope, 1819–20; dem. 1851
[D. Watkin, *Thomas Hope*, 1968, 122] (Britton
& Pugin, *Public Buildings of London* i, 1825,
310–12].

SWALLOWFIELD HOUSE, BERKS., alterations for Sir
Henry Russell, Bart., 1820 [Lady Constance
Russell, *Swallowfield and its Owners*, 1901].

---

[1] See also under PACE, p. 605.

CHEQUERS, BUCKS., alterations (removed 1909) for R. Greenhill Russell, 1823, Tudor style [*A.P.S.D.*] (J. G. Jenkins, *Chequers*, 1967).

LONDON, enlarged NO. 34 BURLINGTON GARDENS for Hon. Col. H. F. C. Cavendish, 1823 [*A.P.S.D.*].

LONDON, DUDLEY HOUSE, NO. 100 PARK LANE, for the 4th Viscount Dudley and Ward, 1824 [*A.P.S.D.*].

HIMLEY HALL, STAFFS., enlarged for the 4th Viscount Dudley and Ward, 1824-7 [*A.P.S.D.*] (*C. Life*, 1 Dec. 1934, 570).

MONTREAL, RIVERHEAD, KENT, added extensions on each side of house for the 1st Earl Amherst, 1829; dem. [drawings in Kent Record Office, U 1350, P.21].

SILVERMERE, nr. COBHAM, SURREY, for himself, *c.* 1830 [E. W. Brayley, *Topographical History of Surrey* ii, 1841, 368].

BECKETT PARK, nr. SHRIVENHAM, BERKS., for the 6th Viscount Barrington, built *c.* 1831-4 by the Hon. Thomas Liddell (*q.v.*), apparently in accordance with designs made by Atkinson *c.* 1805; Gothic [see reference under LIDDELL, THOMAS].

HAMPTON COURT, HEREFS., advice about reconstruction of house by Charles Hanbury Tracy (*q.v.*) for John Arkwright, 1832-9 [John Cornforth in *C. Life*, 8 March 1973].

CHURCHES

BISHOP AUCKLAND, DURHAM, ST. ANNE'S CHAPEL in Market Place, added Gothic west tower *c.* 1800, probably based on a design made by James Wyatt in 1796 and preserved in Auckland Castle; dem. 1847 [Brayley & Britton, *Beauties of England and Wales* v, 1803, 219].

TWYFORD CHURCH, MIDDLESEX, reconstructed for Thomas Willan, 1808, Gothic [*A.P.S.D.*].

DURHAM CATHEDRAL, repaired central tower, 1809-12 [*A.P.S.D.*, *s.v.* 'Durham'].

NEWTON HEATH, nr. MANCHESTER, rebuilt ALL SAINTS CHURCH, 1814-16, Gothic; enlarged at east end, 1844; chancel 1880 [by 'Atkinson': Thomas Rickman's Diary, 24 Aug. 1817].

CANONBIE CHURCH, DUMFRIESSHIRE, 1822, Gothic [S.R.O., Buccleuch Muniments, Chamberlains' accounts 1824-5, p. 42].

DITTON CHAPEL, BUCKS., repairs for the 5th Duke of Buccleuch [Dalkeith House, archives VI, 1].

RICKMANSWORTH CHURCH, HERTS., rebuilt except tower, 1826; Gothic; rebuilt 1890 [I.C.B.S.].

PUBLIC BUILDINGS, ETC.

As architect to the Board of Ordnance (1813-29) Atkinson is said to have been responsible for works (probably minor) at THE ORDNANCE OFFICE, PALL MALL, LONDON (dem. *c.* 1910), THE TOWER OF LONDON, and WOOLWICH ARSENAL. In 1823 he designed RANSOM & CO'S BANK, 1 PALL MALL, EAST, and in 1822-3 erected some buildings in the HORTICULTURAL SOCIETY'S GARDENS at CHISWICK [*A.P.S.D.*].

ATTERBURY, LUFFMAN (-1796), was a carpenter by trade, but was also prepared to act as an architect or surveyor. Music was, however, his great interest, and as a composer he gained a degree of celebrity which he never attained as a designer of buildings. Lord Le Despenser appears to have been one of his principal patrons, for it was an oratorio composed by Atterbury that was performed in West Wycombe church in 1775, when Paul Whitehead's heart was buried in the adjoining mausoleum, and in 1780 Atterbury was employed by Lord Le Despenser to supervise the building of a house on the estate at Mereworth in Kent in accordance with designs made by Nicholas Revett. A letter from Atterbury to Lord Le Despenser, complaining, *inter alia*, of the inadequacy of Revett's drawings, is among the Dashwood papers in the Bodleian Library (MS. D. D. Dashwood (Bucks.) B.15.1). For further details of his career see *D.N.B.*

ATWOOD, THOMAS WARR (*c.* 1733-1775), was a prosperous plumber and glazier of Bath. He was a member of a family that was prominent in local affairs, and was himself a member of the Common Council from 1760 onwards. Although there appears to be no evidence that he ever held any formal appointment as city architect or surveyor, he played a leading part in directing the Corporation's building policy and on 3 July 1775 was formally thanked 'for his attention ... in the management of the business relative to the Public improvements in this City'. Public service and private profit went hand in hand, for Atwood himself contracted for much of the ensuing work, and was also in a position to obtain leases of Corporation property upon which he built the PARAGON CRESCENT (1768) and OXFORD ROW (1773). For the city he designed the PRISON in GROVE STREET (1772-3), and the GUILDHALL was being rebuilt to his designs when he was accidentally killed on 15 November 1775 'by the sudden falling of a decayed floor' in an old house that he was examining on the site of his new building. It was decided not to proceed with his plans and the Guildhall as built was designed by Thomas Baldwin, who is also believed to have designed the very elegant monument to Atwood in the churchyard at Weston, nr. Bath. Atwood was a competent though conservative architect whose elevations are excellent examples of the English Palladian tradition as applied to street architecture. A miniature portrait by Van Diest is in the City Art Gallery. [Bath City Council Minutes 1760–1775; W. Ison, *The Georgian Buildings of Bath*, 1948, 35–7.]

AUDUS, JAMES (1781–1867), was the son of John Audus (1752–1809), a wealthy merchant who came to live at Selby in Yorkshire in 1771. After a visit to Bath the father determined to erect a crescent in Selby similar to John Palmer's Lansdown Crescent in that city, and obtained a 99-year lease of a site on the south side of the abbey church from Lord Petre. His death in 1809 prevented the full accomplishment of his plan, but THE CRESCENT was completed by his son James, who was an amateur architect, and designed several buildings in Selby, including the AUDUS ALMSHOUSES which he founded and endowed in Gowthorp in 1833, the COURT HOUSE, 1855, the WESLEYAN CHAPEL in JAMES STREET, and ST. JAMES'S CHURCH, 1866. In 1824 SELBY ABBEY CHURCH was repewed under his direction. Having held 'every office of honour and responsibility in the town of Selby', Audus died there on 14 May 1867. [E. Parsons, *The Tourist's Companion from Leeds and Selby to Hull*, 1835, 107, 108, 109–10, 132–3; W. B. Morrell, *History of Selby*, 1867, 230, 254–8.]

AUSTIN, GEORGE (1787–1848), born at Woodstock, was the son of George Austin, a surveyor of that place, who was employed in connection with the rebuilding of the tower of Woodstock Church in 1784, and by the Duke of Marlborough at Blenheim Palace. In c. 1820 he became surveyor to CANTERBURY CATHEDRAL, which he found in a dangerous condition. In order to save it, he carried out extensive repairs, including the rebuilding of the vault and gable of the south-east transept, resetting the groining of the choir, and restoring the north nave aisle to the perpendicular. After consultation with Thomas Rickman (*q.v.*), he took down the decayed north-west tower, and between 1832 and 1841 erected the present tower to correspond with that at the south-west angle. He designed a new altar screen and the archiepiscopal throne (illustrated in *Builder* vi, 1848, 139). He was buried in a vault under the north-west tower, where a bronze tablet and a stained-glass window were erected to his memory. His son, H. G. Austin (1823–92), succeeded him as surveyor to the cathedral fabric. [Obituary in *Builder*, vii, 1849, 205; *A.P.S.D.*; Bodleian Library: Bishop's Transcripts of Woodstock Parish Register.]

AXTELL, FRANCIS, was the surveyor employed to supervise the repair of LUDLOW CASTLE, SHROPSHIRE, after twenty years of neglect during the Interregnum. Between 1662 and 1667 over £2000 was spent under his direction in reha-

bilitating the castle as the headquarters of the Council in the Marches of Wales [P.R.O., AO 1/2520/611].

AYERS, CHARLES ROBERT (c. 1788–1845), practised from Lower Grosvenor Street and John Street (Berkeley Square), London, during the early nineteenth century. From the drawings which he exhibited at the Royal Academy it appears that he designed the mansion at TREHILL, nr. EXETER, for J. H. Ley, 1827, a Gothic house at PETWORTH, SUSSEX, for J. J. King, 1828, CANONTEIGN HOUSE, DEVON, for the Hon. Capt. P. B. Pellew, M.P. (afterwards 2nd Viscount Exmouth), 1828, and alterations and additions to COLEBROOK PARK, nr. TUNBRIDGE WELLS, KENT, for Sir Edward Colebrooke, Bart., 1829, dem. c. 1870. Trehill and Canonteign are stuccoed houses with Greek Revival detail. Ayers died at Brighton in October 1845, aged 57 [*Gent's Mag.* 1845 (ii), 662].

AYTON, WILLIAM (–1643?), belonged to a family of masons to whom there are numerous references in the minute book of a masons' lodge meeting at Aitchison's Haven, nr. Musselburgh in Midlothian, extracts from which were printed in *Ars Quatuor Coronatorum* xxiv, 1911, 34–41. William Ayton, senior and junior, were prominent members of the lodge in 1598, but the man who is the subject of this entry was probably the William, son of John Ayton, mason in Musselburgh, who was apprenticed to John Brown, mason of Edinburgh, in January 1598/9. He subsequently became the foreman or assistant of William Wallace (*q.v.*). On Wallace's death in 1631 Ayton succeeded him as master mason of HERIOT'S HOSPITAL, EDINBURGH, begun in 1628 and still incomplete. He undertook 'to prosecute and follow forth the Modell, Frame, and Building of the said wark, as the same is alredy begun, and to devyse, plott, and set down what he shall think meittest for the decorement of the said wark'. It was he who brought the building to a state of near completion in the 1640s. In 1633 he was working at Holyroodhouse, and in about 1640 he designed INNES HOUSE, MORAYSHIRE, for the laird of Innes, whose accounts include a payment of £26 13s. 4d. 'to Wm. Aitoun, Maister Maissoun at Herriott his work, for drawing the form of the House on paper'. Innes is a house on the traditional Scottish L-plan with Anglo-Flemish detail similar to that of Heriot's Hospital. Ayton did not become a burgess of Edinburgh until August 1640. He appears to have died three years later, when John Mylne succeeded him as master mason of Heriot's Hospital. His portrait, inscribed 'Measter Meason to Heriot's Vorke', belongs to the Hospital. [*A.P.S.D.*; D. Macgibbon & T. Ross, *The Castellated and Domestic Architecture of Scotland*,

1887–92, ii, 203, iv, 144, v, 560–1; H. Carr, *The Mason and the Burgh*, 1954, 38; *Register of Edinburgh Apprentices 1583–1666*, Scottish Historical Soc. 1906, 9; Alistair Rowan, 'George Heriot's Hospital, Edinburgh', *C. Life*, 6 March 1975.]

B

BACHOP, BAUCHOP, or **BAAK,** TOBIAS (–1710), was the most prominent member of a family of masons working in the neighbourhood of Alloa in Clackmannanshire in the late seventeenth and early eighteenth centuries. Tobias appears to have been the son of Thomas Bachup of Alloa, and was probably apprenticed to his father. In 1680 he was concerned in extensive repairs to ALLOA CHURCH [D. Macgibbon & T. Ross, *The Castellated and Domestic Architecture of Scotland* v, 1892, 378–9], and in 1684 he contracted to reconstruct LOGIE CHURCH, STIRLING-SHIRE, 'conforme to ane draught drawn be the said Tobias himself' [S.R.O., Deeds, Mack, Warrant No. 356 (1687), *ex inf.* Mr. J. G. Dunbar]. These two churches (both now in ruins) were buildings of traditional character, but soon afterwards Bachop came into contact with Sir William Bruce, the pioneer of Scottish classicism, who employed him first at KINROSS HOUSE (1686–90) [S.R.O., Bruce of Kinross papers, GD 29/1982, and Mylne papers, GD1/51/62], and subsequently at HOPETOUN (1698 onwards), CRAIGIEHALL (1699) and MERTOUN (now HARDEN) HOUSE, BERWICKSHIRE (1703) [J. G. Dunbar, *Sir William Bruce*, exhibition catalogue 1970, nos. 154, 165; S.R.O., Register of Deeds, Durie, vol. 124, pp. 213–15]. Bruce evidently thought highly of Bachop and in 1692 recommended him to the 3rd Duke of Hamilton when the latter was about to build Hamilton Palace, though in the event the house was built not by Bachop but by James Smith [Rosalind K. Marshall, *In the Days of Duchess Anne*, 1973, 193].

In about 1690 Bachop built (and probably designed) THE OLD CROSS, ALLOA, and in 1705 he undertook to build the TOWN HALL and STEEPLE at DUMFRIES after an architect or builder from Liverpool called John Moffat had furnished 'a modall' but declined to execute it. The committee accordingly 'resolved to send for one Tobias Bachup, a master builder now at Abercorn' (where he was then building a house), 'who is said to be of good skill'. Bachop is subsequently referred to as 'our architect' and as 'architect and builder of the steeple and council house', but appears to have followed Moffat's design, which was itself based on the steeple of the College at Glasgow [W. McDowall, *History of Dumfries*, Edinburgh 1867, 539–42].

The house which Bachop built for himself in Kirkgate, Alloa, still exists, and bears the date 1695, with the initials of himself and his wife Margaret Lapsley. The well-designed symmetrical façade with classical detailing shows an intelligent understanding of the new architectural principles which Bachop would have learned from Bruce.

[J. Crawford, *Memorials of the Parish of Alloa*, 1874, 61; D. Macgibbon & T. Ross, *The Castellated and Domestic Architecture of Scotland* v, 1892, 127–8, 377–8.]

BACKHOUSE, R— WILLIAM, of London, exhibited designs for a dock at COVE, nr. CORK, IRELAND, at the Society of Artists in 1791, and for 'the Custom-house and Exchange to be built on the new pier' there, at the Royal Academy in 1806. In 1818 he exhibited a design for alterations to SANDBECK HOUSE, YORKS. (W.R.), for the 6th Earl of Scarbrough, and in 1826, when he applied unsuccessfully for the position of surveyor to the Commissioners for Building New Churches, he named the Earl of Scarbrough as a referee, others being the Earl of Coventry, General Isaac Gascoyne, and Messrs. Jolliffe and Banks, the building contractors [Church Commissioners records, file 21744, pt. 5]. In his will, William Jolliffe, M.P. (d. 1802), directed that he was to be buried in Merstham Church, Surrey, in a vault 'to be prepared according to a plan by — Backhouse, architect' [P.C.C. 465 KENYON]. Among Jolliffe papers in the P.R.O. [C 107/93], there is a plan showing alterations to the DOLPHIN INN, PETERSFIELD, HANTS., signed 'R.W.B. architect, London, 1819'. An elevation of BALLS PARK, HERTS., in the R.I.B.A. Drawings Collection, signed by R. W. Backhouse and dated 1786, may indicate that he was employed to alter that house for the Dowager Viscountess Townesend.

R. W. Backhouse should not be confused with Benjamin Backhouse of Ipswich, who designed the CORN EXCHANGE (afterwards the Provisions Market) at BURY ST. EDMUNDS, SUFFOLK, in 1836 [S. Tymms, *Handbook to Bury St. Edmunds*, 1871, 83], nor with Elisha Backhouse, who practised in Leeds in the 1840s and 1850s in partnership with William Perkin. The family may have originated in Yorkshire, for in 1824 designs for rebuilding GARFORTH RECTORY were made by 'William Backhouse and Sons', one of whom, John Backhouse, was described as 'of Whitkirk, surveyor' [Borthwick Institute, MGA 1824/1].

BACON, CHARLES (*c.* 1784–1818), younger son of the sculptor John Bacon, R.A., was a pupil of J. T. Groves of the Office of Works, with whom he remained for some years after the expiration of his articles. In 1811 he succeeded Groves as Clerk of the Works at Whitehall, Westminster and St. James's, and in 1815 he also became responsible for the Mews at Charing

Cross. In 1816 he became architect to Ely Cathedral, and in July of the same year was appointed architect to Princess Charlotte. He also held the post of surveyor to the county of Middlesex from September 1816 until his death on 10 June 1818, at the age of 34 [*Gent's Mag.* 1818 (i), 574]. His diary for 1816–17 is in the Essex Record Office [D/DQ 14/42].

As a private architect, Bacon's principal works appear to have been the Gothic entrance gateway to WOODFORD HALL, ESSEX, for J. Maitland, M.P., 1810 [exhib. at R.A.], and a library at the same house 1816 [Diary]; the rebuilding of WOODFORD CHURCH, ESSEX, 1816, altered 1889 [*V.C.H. Essex* vi, 354; drawing in R.I.B.A. Drawings Collection]; alterations to WALTHAMSTOW CHURCH, ESSEX, 1817–18 [*V.C.H. Essex* vi, 290]; the enlargement of WOODFORD LODGE (now HALL), NORTHANTS., for Charles Arbuthnot, M.P., *c.* 1813 [*A.P.S.D.*; Diary]; and OAKLANDS, nr. OKEHAMPTON, DEVON, for Albany Savile, M.P., a Greek Revival house begun *c.* 1816 and completed after Bacon's death by his pupil Charles Vokins [R. Ackermann, *Respository of Arts*, 3rd ser., viii, 1826, 249–50; J. C. Loudon, *Encyclopaedia of Rural Architecture*, 1846, 915]. In 1809 he shared with J. A. and G. S. Repton the first prize for the design of public buildings then intended to be erected in Westminster [P.R.O., Works 8/10B, 24].

BADGER, JOSEPH (1738–1817), was born at Hathersage in Derbyshire, but established himself in Sheffield, where he conducted a successful business as a carpenter, joiner, builder and architect from his yard in Orchard Street.

In 1776 he was employed by Francis Hurt Sitwell to superintend the conversion of the Great Chamber in the Jacobean RENISHAW HALL, DERBYSHIRE, into a drawing-room in the Adam style, and between 1793 and 1808 he enlarged and remodelled the house for Sir Sitwell Sitwell, Bart., with interiors in the same style. He almost certainly designed the stables built in 1794 [C. Hussey in *C. Life*, 7–14 May 1938]. The dining-room and staircase at THE OAKS, NORTON, nr. SHEFFIELD, bear a marked resemblance to his work at Renishaw, and were probably designed by him for Sir William Chambers Bagshawe early in the nineteenth century.

In 1784 Badger surveyed ECCLESALL BIERLOW CHURCH, YORKS. (W.R.), with John Bishop, mason, preparatory to its rebuilding [*Yorks. Arch. Jnl.* xvii, 68], and in 1788 he measured work done by John Platt (*q.v.*) at WORTLEY HALL, YORKS, (W.R.) [Wortley papers in Sheffield City Library, WhM. 58/26]. In 1801 he was employed to lay out the new MARKET PLACE at ROTHERHAM, YORKS. (W.R.), and to design elevations for the buildings [J. Guest, *Historic Notices of Rotherham*, 1879, 542]. He was presumably the 'Thomas Badger'

who, according to W. Odom, *Memorials of Sheffield, its Cathedral and Churches*, 1922, 86, designed and built ST. JAMES'S CHAPEL, SHEFFIELD, in 1786–9, dem. 1940. His designs for a Sessions House, with adjoining Bailiff's and Gaoler's houses, made for the Duke of Norfolk, are in Sheffield City Library [No. 15263], where there is also a plan by him for proposed additions to a house at Wards End dated 1796 [Wheat Collection 1791], and an agreement to build a coffee house dated 1793 [No. Wil. D.260]. Badger was active as a speculative builder in and around Sheffield, and among the houses he is known to have built were WESTBOURNE HOUSE, CROOKESMOOR, described as 'lately erected' in 1807, and TAPTON GROVE, RANMOOR, both demolished.

Badger died on 15 July 1817, aged 79. His son Joseph Badger, junior, was in James Wyatt's office in 1793, when he exhibited a design for a villa at the Royal Academy, but did not survive his father, dying in 1807 at the age of 33.

In the 1820s the family was represented by another Joseph Badger, a carpenter, and by Jonathan Badger, a carpenter and joiner who died on 18 March 1834, aged 63. These were probably the sons of Joseph Badger's younger brother Jonathan.

[Sheffield City Library, Arthur Jackson's MS. copy of the inscriptions in Sheffield Parish Churchyard, 1894, nos. 518, 2826; R. E. Leader, *Surveyors and Architects of the Past in Sheffield*, 1903; information from Mr. John Titterton.]

BAILEY, CHARLES, of Haywood in Nynehead, Somerset, was a land surveyor and agent to the Sanford family [P. Eden, *Dictionary of Land Surveyors and Cartographers*, 1975, 26]. He appears also to have acted as an architect, for he signs the designs for rebuilding SIR JOHN POPHAM'S ALMSHOUSES (now R.C. Church) at WELLINGTON, SOMERSET, 1833 [P.R.O., C 108/322].

BAILEY, GEORGE (1792–1860), entered Sir John Soane's office as a pupil in 1806, and remained as an assistant until Soane's death in 1837. He was admitted to the Royal Academy Schools in 1813 and exhibited at the Royal Academy in 1811, 1822 and 1823. In 1837 he became the first curator of Sir John Soane's Museum, in accordance with Soane's will, and remained in charge of the museum until his death. He was one of the two Hon. Secretaries of the Institute of British Architects. [Obituary in *Builder*, xviii, 1860, 842; A. T. Bolton, *Architectural Education a Century Ago* (Soane Museum Publication no. 12), 16.]

BAILEY, JAMES (*c.* 1771–1850), was primarily a surveyor. He lived and practised in Lambeth, at first in partnership with Charles Middleton (*q.v.*) and afterwards with his former pupil R. Willshire. In Lambeth he acted as local surveyor to the Duchy of Cornwall, and designed ST. MARK'S SCHOOL, HARLEYFORD ROAD, KENNINGTON, 1824 [*Survey of London* xxvi, 25–7]. In conjunction with Willshire he built the TRINITY HOMES, ACRE LANE, STOCKWELL, for Thomas Bailey in 1822 [*ibid.*, 98–9]. He is perhaps to be identified with the 'Mr. Bailey, an architect of London', who designed COCK'S SAUCE ESTABLISHMENT, DUKE STREET, READING, *c.* 1820, and who at the same time was 'engaged with extensive alterations at Caversham Park Mansion' for Col. Marsac [*Reminiscences of Reading, by an Octogenarian*, 1888, 95], and may have been the J. Bailey who signs a perspective drawing of William Wilkins's design for Downing College, Cambridge, that is preserved at Downing [G. Walkley in *R.I.B.A. Jnl.*, 17 Oct. 1938, 1014]. Bailey was President of the Surveyors' Club in 1812 and 1848, and died on 24 Sept. 1850, aged 79 [*Gent's Mag.* 1850 (ii), 558]. The practice was continued by R. Willshire in partnership with R. Parris. Charles Barry was a pupil of Middleton and Bailey from 1810 to 1816.

BAINE, JOHN, was the author of a scheme for the development of the area to the north of the New Town at Edinburgh, which he submitted to the city authorities in 1801. It was rejected in favour of a layout designed by Robert Reid and William Sibbald, but the 'explanatory memoir' is preserved in Edinburgh University Library (MS. Laing II, 415). It shows that Bain was familiar with town-planning in England and abroad, but throws no light on his origins or occupation. He must, however, be the 'Bain' mentioned in Alexander Campbell's *Journey from Edinburgh through parts of North Britain* ii, 1802, 278, as one of the architects Scotland could boast of.

BAIRD, JAMES, was a master mason of Govan, nr. Glasgow. In 1724 he rebuilt KILBARCHAN CHURCH, RENFREWSHIRE [R. D. Mackenzie, *Kilbarchan*, Paisley 1902, 152–3], and in 1736–8 THE LOW CHURCH at PAISLEY [R. Brown, *History of Paisley* i, 1886, 404].

BAIRD, JOHN (1798–1859), was born at Dalmuir in Dunbartonshire. He was apprenticed to an architect or builder of Glasgow called Shepherd, to whom he was related. When Shepherd died in 1818 Baird, barely 20 and not yet out of his apprenticeship, took over the office and by hard work built up a practice second only to that of David Hamilton. Refusing to take part in public competitions, he acquired a reputation for shrewdness and probity which in later life earned him many commissions as a valuer of property and as an arbitrator in building disputes.

Baird's architecture is marked by a classical reserve from which he rarely deviated. His buildings are always logical and business-like. His style matured early, and, once established, it never changed. Although he lived well into the reign of Victoria he made few concessions to changing fashions. Romanesque, Gothic and Italian were little to his taste, but he did produce one or two churches in the perfunctory Gothic of the 1820s, and his design for the new University buildings at Woodlands, commissioned in 1846, but never carried out, was 'chiefly in the style of Heriot's Hospital'. Even in his later Gothic work he clung tenaciously to the style of the 1820s, his mansion at Urie (1855) being in the late Tudor idiom evolved by Wilkins and Burn forty years earlier. On the other hand the possibilities of iron made a strong appeal to his essentially practical mind. As early as 1827 he designed an iron hammer-beam roof for the Argyle Arcade, and in 1855–6 built in Jamaica Street one of the outstanding iron warehouses of the nineteenth century.

Baird died in December 1859. He had a younger brother Anthony who practised independently until 1834/5, when he took up accountancy. For some years before his death Baird was assisted by James Thomson (1835–1905), who ultimately became his partner and continued his practice under the name of 'Baird and Thomson'. Alexander ('Greek') Thomson (1817–1875) was in Baird's office from 1836 to 1849, when he left to form a partnership with another John Baird (1816–93), who was Thomson's brother-in-law, but apparently no relation of his namesake. Baird's portrait by Daniel Macnee (1857) hangs in Glasgow Art Gallery. Gildard describes him as 'a large and well-built man' who 'had a presence as of one that ought to be in authority'.

[James Maclehose, *One Hundred Eminent Glasgow Men*, Glasgow 1886, i, 21–4; Thomas Gildard, 'An Old Glasgow Architect on some Older Ones', *Trans. Royal Philosophical Soc. of Glasgow* xxvi, 1895; A. Gomme & D. Walker, *The Architecture of Glasgow*, 1968, 265; information from Mr. David Walker.]

GLASGOW; COMMERCIAL AND DOMESTIC BUILDINGS

THE ARGYLE ARCADE, 98–102 ARGYLE STREET, 1827–8 [*A.P.S.D.*, *s.v.* 'Glasgow'].

THE WELLINGTON ARCADE, SAUCHIEHALL STREET, *c.* 1830; new entrance 1861; dem. [*A.P.S.D.*].

SOMERSET PLACE, SAUCHIEHALL STREET, 1840; end block rebuilt 1962 [A. Gomme & D. Walker, *The Architecture of Glasgow*, 1968, 265].

PRINCE OF WALES' BUILDINGS, 34–8 BUCHANAN STREET and PRINCES SQUARE, for Sir James Campbell, 1840 [Maclehose, 22].

CLAREMONT HOUSE (Nos. 7–8) and TERRACE, WOODLANDS, 1842–7 [Maclehose, 21–2].

WOODLANDS TERRACE, WOODLANDS, 1849–50 [Gomme & Walker, 265].

WEST NILE STREET, premises of Messrs. Wilson, Kay & Co., 1851 [Senex, *Glasgow Past and Present* i, 1884, 232].

MACDONALD'S MUSLIN WAREHOUSE, INGRAM, HANOVER and QUEEN STREETS, for Messrs. J. & D. MacDonald, 1854; dem. [*A.P.S.D.*].

SIR JAMES CAMPBELL'S WAREHOUSE, 115–137 INGRAM STREET and 111–128 BRUNSWICK STREET, 1854; planned by Baird, but on Sir James Campbell desiring baronial elevations, they were, at Baird's suggestion, designed by R. W. Billings [Maclehose, 23].

GARDNER'S WAREHOUSE, 36 JAMAICA STREET, 1855–6 [*A.P.S.D.*].

SMITH & SONS' WAREHOUSE, 208–16 ARGYLE STREET, 1856; dem. [*A.P.S.D.*].

CHURCHES

GLASGOW, GREYFRIARS UNITED PRESBYTERIAN CHURCH, 182 ALBION STREET, 1821; dem. [Maclehose, 22; J. Pagan, *Sketch of the History of Glasgow*, 1847, 186].

GLASGOW, WELLINGTON STREET, U.P. CHURCH, 1825; dem. [*A.P.S.D.*].

BONHILL, DUNBARTONSHIRE, 1835–6 [contract drawings in S.R.O., RHP 8164–8171].

GLASGOW, CAMBRIDGE STREET CHURCH, 1834; altered 1846 and 1868; dem. [Church Records *ex. inf.* Mr. David Walker].

GREENOCK, GEORGE SQUARE CONGREGATIONAL CHURCH, 1839–40, Gothic [W. M. Brownlie, *History of the George Square Congregational Church*, 1956, 33].

GLASGOW, ERSKINE U.P. (now BRISBY MEMORIAL) CHURCH, 45 SOUTH PORTLAND STREET, 1842, Gothic [Senex, *Glasgow Past and Present* i, 1884, 148].

KIRKCALDY, FIFE, ST. PETER'S EPISCOPAL CHURCH, TOWNSEND PLACE, 1844 [*The Scottish Episcopal Church Year Book*, 1973–4, 280].

GLASGOW, SHAMROCK STREET U.P. CHURCH, *c.* 1850, Gothic [Senex, *Glasgow Past and Present*, i, 1884, 148].

COUNTRY HOUSES

CLOBER HOUSE, NEW KILPATRICK, DUNBARTONSHIRE, enlarged for Alexander Dunlop in Tudor style, 1833 [*N.S.A.* viii, 49].

CAIRNHILL HOUSE, AIRDRIE, LANARKS., for G. M. Nisbett, 1841, Jacobethan [H. M. Nisbett & S. C. Agnew, *Cairnhill*, Edinburgh 1949, 201].

CARBETH GUTHRIE, STIRLINGSHIRE, additions for William Smith, 1855 [*The Old Country Houses of the Glasgow Gentry*, 1870, pl. xviii].

URIE HOUSE, FETTERESSO, KINCARDINESHIRE, reb. 1855 for Alexander Baird in Tudor style; enlarged 1883–4; gutted [Maclehose, 23].

STONEBYRES HOUSE, LESMAHAGOW, LANARKS., extensive additions for James Monteath; altered *c.* 1900; dem. 1934 [J. B. Greenshields, *Annals of the Parish of Lesmahagow*, 1864, 83].

VIEWPARK HOUSE, UDDINGSTON, LANARKS., probably for William Robertson [Maclehose, 23].

BIRKWOOD HOUSE, LESMAHAGOW, LANARKS., for J. G. McKirdy, castellated [Maclehose, 23] (J. B. Greenshields, *Annals of the Parish of Lesmahagow*, 1864, plate at p. 101).

MONUMENT

GLASGOW NECROPOLIS, monument to James Ewing (d. 1853) [G. Baird, *Sketches of Glasgow Necropolis*, 1857, 182].

BAKER, —, of St. Michael's Mount, described as 'the Superintendent of Sir J. St. Aubyn's late improvements at his castle there', surveyed Crowan Church, Cornwall, in 1831 [I.C.B.S.]. He was doubtless the 'John Baker Esq.' listed as a resident at St. Michael's Mount in Pigot's *Directory* of 1830.

BAKER, CHARLES, of Painswick, Glos., described in Pigot's *Directory* as 'architect, civil engineer and land-surveyor', and on his tradecard [Gloucester Public Library, R.229.56] as 'Land and Timber Surveyor, Land Agent & Civil Engineer', designed Gothic churches at THE SLAD, 1831–4 [I.C.B.S.] and CAINSCROSS, 1835–7 [*Gent's Mag.* 1837 (i), 311], both illustrated in A. Smith, *Ecclesiastical Edifices in the Borough of Stroud*, 1838. He also designed THE BEDFORD STREET CONGREGATIONAL CHURCH, STROUD, 1835–7 [R. Nott, *The Bedford Street Congregational Church 1837–1937*, 1937, 18–19], and WHITESHILL VICARAGE, GLOS., 1841, Gothic [Gloucester Diocesan Records, F4/1]. Baker lived at CASTLE HALE, PAINSWICK, whose front he rebuilt *c.* 1835 [W. St. C. Baddeley, *A Cotteswold Manor, being the History of Painswick*, 1907, 221].

BAKER, H—, exhibited at the Royal Academy from No. 46 Berners Street in 1822 and 1824. W. Baker, who exhibited from the same address in 1823, showed in 1830 a 'Design for a church now about to be erected at Inverness'.

BAKER, RICHARD (1743–1803), son of William Baker of Highfields, Cheshire (*q.v.*), was educated at Repton School. His father's will indicates that at the time of his death in 1771 Richard was helping him in his 'architectural affairs'. Richard lived for a number of years at Leominster, where, however, he used his wife's surname of Hassall 'for the sake of peace and quietness'. He subsequently moved to Stratford-on-Avon, where he died in 1803 [P.C.C.

757 MARRIOTT]. As owner of Highfields he was succeeded by his son Richard Dod Baker (d. 1843).

The Shropshire Quarter Sessions Records show that Richard Baker was frequently employed to survey churches for the purpose of obtaining Briefs, but the only church that is known to have been rebuilt to his designs is ADDERLEY, SALOP., 1801 [MS. churchwardens' accounts and vestry minutes]. It is a cruciform Gothic building with traceried windows of cast iron.

BAKER, WILLIAM (1705–1771), of Highfields, nr. Audlem in Cheshire, was an architect and surveyor much employed in Shropshire, Staffordshire and the adjoining counties in the middle of the eighteenth century. He was the son of Richard Baker of London and Leominster, and was born in London in 1705. In January 1736/7 he married Jane Dod, only daughter and heiress of George Dod of Highfields, a direct descendant of William Dod, who built the house in 1567. For some years after their marriage William Baker and his wife appear to have lived at Bridgnorth, where all their four children were baptized, but by 1748 he was established at Highfields, where he combined the profession of an architect with that of a farmer and small country squire. The survival of his account-book and diary for the years 1748–59 sheds considerable light on the practice of a minor Georgian provincial architect, and shows that in the course of the twelve years which it covers he designed or altered a number of country houses, surveyed or reported on churches in need of repair or rebuilding, and also designed several funeral monuments. His most important work was probably the Market Cross or Butter Market at Ludlow, a robust but unpolished classical building whose façade forms an effective termination to the main street. Like other works of Baker's (*e.g.* Patshull House and St. John's, Wolverhampton), it is strongly influenced by Gibbs. A plan and elevation of the Butter Market are shown in Baker's hands in his portrait (attributed to Hudson), reproduced in *C. Life,* 8 March 1946, 448. Unexecuted designs by Baker for a Town Hall at Bishops Castle, Salop., made in 1745, are among the Powis papers in the Shropshire Record Office [552/14/box 465]. He is also known to have made unexecuted designs for the Shropshire Infirmary, 1745 [minute books of the Infirmary, *ex inf.* Mr. James Lawson], for Hosyer's Almshouses at Ludlow, 1756 [*V.C.H. Salop.* ii, 109], and for the English Bridge at Shrewsbury in 1767 [minute book of the bridge trustees in Shropshire Record Office, *ex inf.* Mr. James Lawson].

William Baker died on 29 November 1771, aged 66, and was buried at Audlem, where there is a tablet to his memory in the south aisle of the church. His elder son Richard (*q.v.*) followed his father's profession. [Arthur Oswald, 'William Baker of Audlem, Architect', in *Collections for a History of Staffordshire* (Staffordshire Record Society), vol. for 1950–1 (1954).]

PUBLIC BUILDINGS

LUDLOW, SALOP., THE BUTTER CROSS, 1743–4 [signed plan and elevation in the Ludlow Museum].

MONTGOMERY, THE MARKET HALL, 1748; upper part rebuilt 1828 [J. D. K. Lloyd, 'Montgomery Town Hall and its Architect', *Montgomeryshire Collections* iv, 1958].

HEREFORD, COLLEGE OF THE VICARS CHORAL, repairs and alterations, 1750.

HOUSES

Baker's account-book shows that he was constantly employed in surveying and altering houses, though it is not always clear exactly what was done. The following are the principal domestic works with which he was concerned during the years 1748–59:

PENN HALL, nr. WOLVERHAMPTON, STAFFS., drawing and surveying for Thomas Bradney, 1748–54.

'BEVERLEY' (probably BEVERÉ) nr. WORCESTER, drawing and surveying for Mr. Brodribb, 1748–9.

MORVILLE HALL, SALOP., surveying etc. for Arthur Weaver, 1748. Baker was probably responsible for the addition of the two office wings and for alterations to the house itself (*C. Life*, 15–22 Aug. 1952). The house was again altered *c.* 1770, when earlier features attributable to Baker were removed. A painting showing these features was sold at Christie's in December 1971.

LIVERPOOL, houses in HANOVER STREET for Messrs. Pardoe, Fletcher and Cunliffe, 1748; dem.

MAWLEY HALL, SALOP., unspecified work for Sir Edward Blount, Bart., 1748.

RANTON ABBEY, STAFFS., surveying for Sir Jonathan Cope, Bart., 1748–9 and 1752–3; dem. *c.* 1940.

POWIS CASTLE, MONTGOMERYSHIRE, unspecified work (probably general repairs) for the 1st Earl of Powis, 1748–54.

OAKLY PARK, SALOP., alterations for the 1st Earl of Powis, 1748–58; remodelled by C. R. Cockerell, 1819–36.

ENVILLE HALL, STAFFS., unspecified plans for the 4th Earl of Stamford, 1748–50.

ALDENHAM HOUSE, MORVILLE, SALOP., drawings for Sir Richard Acton, Bart., 1750–1.

SWYNNERTON HALL, STAFFS., an outbuilding for Thomas Fitzherbert, 1750–6.

TIXALL HALL, STAFFS., rebuilt quadrangle for the 5th Lord Aston, 1750–1; dem. *c.* 1925.

DARLASTON HALL, STAFFS., plans of a house for John Jervis, 1751, perhaps not built; dem. 1953.

ACTON BURNELL HALL, SALOP., enlarged for Sir Edward Smythe, Bart., 1753–8.

WOOD EATON, STAFFS., THE HALL FARMHOUSE for the Rev. William Astley, headmaster of Repton School, 1753–6.

PATTINGHAM, STAFFS., house for Sir John Astley, Bart.

WINGERWORTH HALL, DERBYSHIRE, work for Sir Henry Hunloke, Bart., 1753–4; dem. *c.* 1930.

WOODHOUSE FARM, PEPLOW, nr. HODNET, SALOP., for Charles Pigot, 1754–6.

PATSHULL HOUSE, STAFFS., completion of house for Sir John Astley, Bart., 1754–8. Baker evidently succeeded James Gibbs (d. 1754) as Sir John Astley's architect, and references in his diary to the parlour, library, stables and chapel show that he designed the flanking towers and forecourt which contain these buildings. The entrance gateway is also his work.

HANKELOW HALL, CHESHIRE, alterations, including dining-room, for Mr. Wettenhall, 1755–7.

EGGINTON HALL, DERBYSHIRE, plans for the Rev. Sir John Every, Bart., 1756; probably not carried out (cf. B. Wyatt, p. 936). The house was dem. 1955.

TERRICK HALL, WHITCHURCH, SALOP., plan for Mr. Watson, 1756.

WHITMORE HALL, STAFFS., surveying for Edward Mainwaring, 1756. For possible alterations to this house by Baker see G. Nares in *C. Life,* 6 June 1957.

BRAND HALL, NORTON-IN-HALES, SALOP., minor alterations to interior for Robert Davison, 1756.

HANMER HALL, FLINTSHIRE, additional building for Humphrey Hanmer, 1756.

ASTBURY RECTORY, CHESHIRE, repairs for the Rev. Joseph Crewe, 1757–9.

TEDDESLEY HALL, nr. PENKRIDGE, STAFFS., for Sir Edward Littleton, Bart., 1757–*c.* 1765; dem. 1954.

KEELE HALL, STAFFS., alterations to south front for Ralph Sneyd, 1757–9; rebuilt by A. Salvin, 1855.

DORFOLD HALL, CHESHIRE, repairs for James Tomkinson, 1757–9 (*C. Life,* 31 Oct. 1908).

WOODHOUSE, or WODEHOUSE, nr. WOMBOURNE, STAFFS., plans for Samuel Hellier, 1758–9.

SIDWAY HALL, nr. MAER, STAFFS., for — Eld, 1758–9; since much altered.

CHURCHES

Baker was employed as surveyor in connection with the repair or rebuilding of several churches. STONE CHURCH, STAFFS., of which he 'Lay'd the first stone' in 1754, was designed by William Robinson, Clerk of the Works at Greenwich Hospital, and Baker merely supervised the execution of his plans [W. H. Bowers & J. W. Clough, *Researches into the History of the Parish of Stone,* 1929, 58–61]. Between 1754 and 1756 he was employed as 'Inspector of the work' by the churchwardens of SEIGHFORD, STAFFS., the tower and part of the nave of whose church were rebuilt in the Gothic style [churchwardens' accounts in William Salt Library, Stafford, and his own diary, which records the laying of the foundation stone]. From 1756 to 1759 he was receiving payments as surveyor of ST. JOHN'S CHAPEL, WOLVERHAMPTON, STAFFS., a classical church in the style of Gibbs, for whose design he was no doubt responsible (see illustration in S. Shaw, *History of Staffordshire* ii, 1801, 155). In January 1757 he surveyed ELLENHALL CHURCH, STAFFS., and made a plan and estimate (£1053) for its repair to support the parishioners' application for a Brief. On 26 March 1757, after the upper part of the tower of ACTON CHURCH, nr. NANTWICH, CHESHIRE, had been blown down into the nave, Baker agreed 'to Inspect ye repair of ye church' for £42. The top of the tower was then rebuilt: the clerestory, rebuilt at this time, was again rebuilt in 1879 (cf. R. Richards, *Old Cheshire Churches,* 1947, pl. 15). In 1758 he surveyed the leaning tower of WYBUNBURY CHURCH, CHESHIRE, finding its inclination nearly three feet, and reported that the 'chancel should be new rooft, the timber and lead being much decay'd'. In January 1759 he received 6 guineas from the 3rd Earl of Breadalbane (whose wife came from a Staffordshire family) 'for plans of a Kirk' – probably that of KENMORE, PERTHSHIRE, which was built by the Earl in 1760 and is in the Gothic style.

In addition to these church commissions recorded in the account-book, Baker is said to have been the 'undertaker' employed in 1765 to case in brick the tower of UPPER PENN CHURCH, nr. WOLVERHAMPTON, STAFFS.

MONUMENTS

ACTON SCOTT, nr. CHURCH STRETTON, SALOP., monument to Edward Acton (d. 1747), executed by 'Mr. Hiorn' in 1751.

LEIGHTON CHURCH, SALOP., monument to Elizabeth Leighton (d. 1754).

NORTON IN HALES, SALOP., monument to Samuel and Barbara Davison, erected 1757.

BALDWIN, ROBERT, was a pupil of Robert Brettingham. In February 1763 he was engaged by Robert Mylne at £50 p.a., and remained in his office as the clerk responsible for Blackfriars Bridge until 1766 [Robert Mylne's diaries, 28 Feb. 1763 and 13 Sept. 1766]. From 1762 onwards he exhibited numerous designs at the Society of Artists and the Free Society of Artists, and in 1764 and 1765 he was awarded premiums for architectural drawings by the Society of Arts. In 1768 he became an assistant of George Dance, the City Surveyor, but subsequently caused trouble by claiming to be Dance's partner [Dorothy Stroud, *George Dance*, 1971, 89–90]. Nothing further has been discovered about his career, nor is any building known to have been erected to his designs. Several unexecuted designs by him are, however, recorded. They include an engraved design for a Record Office in Edinburgh made in collaboration with the Earl of Morton, then Lord Clerk Register, and published in 1767 (S.R.O., RHP 6082, and Bodleian, Gough Maps 38, f. 62ᵇ), a set of drawings for a new house at Wardour in Wiltshire among the Arundell family papers, 1768, and an engraved design for a gaol for the county of Essex, n.d. ?1773 (B.M. *King's Maps*, xiii, 11f). In 1769 he published *The Chimney-Piece Maker's Daily Assistant*, vol. ii, in continuation of vol. i of the same title published by John Crunden & others in 1766, and [in 1787] *Plans, Elevations and Sections of the Machines and Centering used in erecting Black-Friars Bridge*, consisting of 7 double-page plates and a large folding plan.

BALDWIN, THOMAS (1568–1641), Comptroller of the King's Works from 1606 until his death in 1641, came from a family of Hertfordshire gentry with property at Watford (where he was born) and Berkhamsted (where he was buried). Nothing is known of his career before his appointment as Comptroller in 1606, and in office he appears to have been more of an administrator than an architect. Nevertheless there is some evidence that on occasion he designed and supervised buildings for private clients. In 1623 he provided the Fishmongers' Company with a 'devise' for the JESUS HOSPITAL at BRAY, BERKSHIRE. This is a quadrangular brick building in the vernacular style, 'devoid of Jonesian influence'. It was completed in 1628 [*History of the King's Works* iii, 131]. In 1632–3 Baldwin was consulted by Oxford University about the building of the SELDEN END of the BODLEIAN LIBRARY. The Vice-Chancellor's accounts record a payment of £9 'to the king's controllour for his coach-hire and in other expences in coming hither to give directions about the staircase', but it may be noted that there was a separate payment of £12 to an unnamed 'surveyor' 'for drawing of modells and three severall journeys about the same business' [*Wood's Life and Times*, ed. A. Clark, Oxford Historical Soc., iv, 1895, 53]. Another building for which the nature of Baldwin's responsibility is ill-defined was a large addition to the west side of HOLLAND HOUSE, KENSINGTON, built in 1638–40 by Henry

Rich, Earl of Holland. The accounts [Leeds City Library, Archives Dept. TN/EA/13/74, ff. 34–5] show that over £5000 were 'Received by the forsaid workmen of Mr. Baldwin'. This addition was demolished in 1704 and no representation of it appears to be known.

Baldwin is commemorated by a monument in Berkhamsted Church carved by Nicholas Stone [*Walpole Soc.* vii, 136 and pl. 42]. As Comptroller he was succeeded by his nephew Francis Wetherid.

BALDWIN, THOMAS (1750–1820), began his career as a speculative builder in Bath. From 1776 onwards he held the post of City Surveyor, for which he received £70 p.a. This appointment followed the death of Thomas Warr Atwood (*q.v.*), who had for some time been in effective control of the city's building activities. In 1779 Baldwin was in addition appointed Deputy Chamberlain at £140 p.a. In 1787 he was appointed Inspector of the Baths, and in 1789 his plans for their development were authorized by the 'Bath Improvement Act'. He was also responsible for planning Bathwick New Town for the Pulteney family, and undertook much of the building himself. In 1791 he was dismissed from his position as Deputy Chamberlain, and in the following year, having failed to deliver up his accounts, from that of City Surveyor. In 1793 the failure of the Bath City Bank resulted in his bankruptcy. Although finished as a town-planner and speculative builder, he continued to practise as an architect until his death on 7 March 1820.

Baldwin was one of the principal creators of Georgian Bath, and designed several of its most celebrated buildings. His best work is in an elegant and accomplished late Georgian style which owes a good deal to the example of the Adam brothers. [Bath City Council Minutes, 1776–1792; W. Ison, *The Georgian Buildings of Bath*, 1948, 37–40.]

The following were Baldwin's principal works in BATH:

THE GUILDHALL, 1776.
NORTHUMBERLAND BUILDINGS, *c.* 1780.
SOMERSETSHIRE BUILDINGS, MILSOM STREET, 1781–3.
THE CROSS BATH PUMP ROOM, *c.* 1784 (altered by J. Palmer *c.* 1798).
Reconstructed the CROSS BATH, *c.* 1786 (converted into a swimming bath *c.* 1880 by C. E. Davis).
COLONNADE on north side of PUMP ROOM, 1786.
PAVILION over KING'S BATH SPRING, *c.* 1788 (dem. early in nineteenth century).
THE NEW PRIVATE BATHS, 1788–9.
ARGYLE BUILDINGS (now STREET), *c.* 1789.
LAURA PLACE, *c.* 1789.
GREAT PULTENEY STREET, *c.* 1789.
SYDNEY PLACE, NOS. 1–14 and houses in BATHWICK STREET, 1788–92.

THE ARGYLE CHAPEL, BATHWICK, 1789 (reconstructed by H. E. Goodridge, 1821).
UNION STREET, c. 1790.
CHEAP STREET, refronted c. 1790.
STALL STREET, refronted c. 1790.
BATH STREET, 1791.
THE GREAT PUMP ROOM, 1791–2 (completed by J. Palmer, 1793–6).
LAURA CHAPEL, BATHWICK, 1795 (dem.).

Outside Bath, Baldwin designed:

HAFOD HOUSE, CARDIGANSHIRE, for Thomas Johnes, 1786–8 [James E. Smith, *A Tour to Hafod*, 1810, 11]. Hafod was gutted by fire in 1807 and rebuilt by Baldwin, with some alterations. It was subsequently altered and enlarged, and was finally dem. c. 1960. An engraving in S. R. Meyrick, *History of Cardiganshire*, 1810, 351, probably shows the building as originally erected.
DEVIZES, WILTS., THE TOWN HALL, 1806–8 [J. Waylen, *Chronicles of the Devizes*, 1839, 316].
RAINSCOMBE HOUSE, nr. OARE, WILTS., remodelled for the Rev. James Rogers, c. 1816 [account for professional services in Wilts. Record Office 754/141; *V.C.H. Wilts*. x, 130 and plate].

BALFOUR, ROBERT (c. 1770–1867), was the son of a farmer at Kilmany in Fife. He is said to have worked as a mason in Edinburgh for the Adam brothers before establishing himself at St. Andrews, where the Town Council minutes show that in August 1799 he petitioned for a piece of ground near Shore Bridge for a workshop and yard. He lived in BALFOUR HOUSE, THE SHORE, which he built for himself, and was probably responsible for several other houses in St. Andrews which show marked Adam influence. He appears to have retired from practice in the 1830s, but lived on until 1867, when he died, almost completely blind, at the age of 97.

Balfour's principal works were the reconstruction of THE TOWN KIRK (HOLY TRINITY), ST. ANDREWS, 1798–1800, again rebuilt 1907–9 [S.R.O., HR 73/1, p. 137]; the addition of the new front wing to STRATHTYRUM HOUSE, nr. ST. ANDREWS, for the Cheape family, c. 1805 [Paterson of Carpow papers, St. Andrews University Library MS. 36220]; CARPOW HOUSE, ABERNETHY, PERTHSHIRE, for the Paterson family, c. 1807; dem. [*ibid*.]; the repair and enlargement of KINGSBARNS CHURCH, FIFE, 1811 [S.R.O., HR 184/1]; alterations to LEUCHARS CHURCH, FIFE, 1812–14 [S.R.O., HR 154/1]; alterations to CRAIL CHURCH, FIFE, 1815 [S.R.O., HR 242/1]; and the refronting of PITMILLY, KINGSBARNS, FIFE, for David Monypenny, Lord Pitmilly, 1818, dem. [St. Andrews Univ. Muniments UC 400, an application by Balfour to quarry stone for the house] (A. H. Millar, *Fife: Pictorial and Historical* i, 1895, 362–3).

[R. G. Cant, 'St. Andrews Architects', *St. Andrews Preservation Trust Year Book* for 1966, 16–17; information from Mr. R. G. Cant and Mr. David Walker.]

BALL, JAMES HOWELL (1790–1857), practised in Plymouth during the first half of the nineteenth century. In 1828–9 he refitted the interior of the CHARLES CHURCH there, gutted 1941 [G. Wightwick, *Nettleton's Guide to Plymouth etc.*, 1836, 24]. He also designed the ELDAD CHAPEL, PLYMOUTH, 1829, in a 'mixed Gothic' style [Wightwick, 25], ST. LUKE'S CHURCH, TAVISTOCK PLACE, PLYMOUTH, 1828–9 [R. N. Worth, *History of Plymouth*, 2nd ed. 1890, 245], and SALCOMBE CHURCH, DEVON, 1843, in a coarse 'Early English' style [I.C.B.S.]. He died on 21 August 1857, aged 60 [monumental inscription in Plymouth cemetery].

BAMPFYLDE, COPLESTONE WARRE (1719–1791), of Hestercombe House, nr. Taunton in Somerset, was a talented country gentleman of whom it was said *nihil tetigit quod non ornavit*. Best known as a landscape-painter, he was also on occasion an amateur architect. His principal achievement in this capacity was the TOWN HALL at TAUNTON, which was built to his designs in 1770–2. He presumably designed the Doric temple which he erected in his own grounds at Hestercombe in 1786, and among the Arundell family papers there is a set of designs for a Palladian mansion at Wardour in Wiltshire 'drawn by Mr. Bampfylde'. [*D.N.B.*; *Proceedings of the Somerset Archaeological Soc.* xviii, 1872, 163–6, lxxxv, 1939, 97; J. Savage, *History of Taunton*, 1822, 581; Kenneth Woodbridge, *Landscape and Antiquity*, 1970, 60.]

BANCKES, MATTHEW (–1706), was an eminent master carpenter of the age of Wren. Probably a son of Matthew Banckes, Master of the Carpenters' Company in 1637,[1] he was apprenticed to John Scott, carpenter to the Ordnance Office, and married a daughter of John Grove, Master Plasterer in the Office of Works. In 1683 he became Master Carpenter in the Office of Works and in 1698 he was Master of the Carpenters' Company. He died in 1706, having previously resigned his official post in favour of his son-in-law John Churchill [*Cal. Treasury Books* xx, 108, 285, 646; xxi, 64]. John James (*q.v.*) was his pupil or apprentice, receiving from

---

[1] In 1633 the elder Banckes was, with Edmund Kinsman (*q.v.*), concerned in the rebuilding of the City Church of ST. ALBAN, WOOD STREET, subsequently destroyed in the Great Fire. In Jan. 1633–4 he was paid £3 'for his drawing of plotts measuringe ye church & comming several tymes' (Churchwardens' Accounts in Guildhall Library, MS. 7673/1).

him 'ten years' instruction in all the practical parts of building' [Hist. MSS. Comm., *Portland* x, 120–1].

In addition to his official work at the royal palaces, Banckes carried out the carpenter's work at six of the City churches, and was employed as surveyor in connection with several buildings designed by Wren, notably the LIBRARY of TRINITY COLLEGE, CAMBRIDGE, when it was built in 1676, and again in 1685–6, when the floor was strengthened under his direction (for the construction see *R.I.B.A. Jnl.*, 3rd ser., xxx, 1923, 388). In the case of the UPPER SCHOOL at ETON COLLEGE, built in 1689–91, the evidence suggests that it may have been Banckes, rather than Wren, who provided the design [Willis & Clark, i. 421, ii, 540; *Wren Soc.* v, 40, 42–3, xix, 108–10], and in 1699 the Provost and Fellows resolved to refit the choir of ETON COLLEGE CHAPEL 'according to the modell designed by Mr. Banks their Surveyor' [Willis & Clark, i, 447]. The reredos and screen which he designed were removed in 1847. Banckes's reputation is shown by the fact that in 1693 the 3rd Duke of Hamilton consulted him about the designs for HAMILTON PALACE. 'I am now consulting with one Banks that carries on the buildings at Hampton Court, who is the best at contriving of any in England', he told the Duchess, and in 1694 Banckes was paid £11 'for drawing some draughts of the Palace of Hamilton at several times' [Rosalind K. Marshall, *In the Days of Duchess Anne*, 1973, 193–4].

In 1692–3 Banckes contracted with Laurence, Earl of Rochester, to rebuild the latter's house at PETERSHAM, SURREY, in two stages, according to an unsigned drawing still attached to the contract. Many of the architectural details were to correspond with those at Ranelagh House, Chelsea, and the Earl of Ranelagh was to act as arbitrator in the event of any dispute [Surrey Record Office, S.C. 13/26/102–3]. The house, which is illustrated by J. Kip, *Britannia Illustrata* i, 1714, pl. 33, was destroyed by fire in 1721. In 1700 Banckes performed the carpentry of WINSLOW HALL, BUCKS., a house probably designed by Wren [*Wren Soc.* xvii, 67–70]. His estimate for making a promenade 130 feet long for the 2nd Duke of Beaufort at BEAUFORT HOUSE, CHELSEA (dem. 1739), is in the British Museum [Sloane MS. 4066, f. 260].

Banckes had two sons who were successful master craftsmen. Henry (*c.* 1679–1716), a mason by trade, was in partnership with Edward Strong, junior, and with him had contracts at Blenheim Palace, Marlborough House, London, and Cannons House, Middlesex. Matthew (*c.* 1682–1714), a carpenter like his father, worked at Blenheim from 1706 onwards, and was associated with his partner John Barton, for 'roofing all the grand Pile' and for making the centering for the great bridge.

BARCLAY, THOMAS, was a master mason of Balbirnie, nr. Markinch in Fife, where in 1785–6 he reconstructed the manse [S.R.O., HR 59/6]. He was probably responsible for the rebuilding of MARKINCH CHURCH in 1786, but this cannot be proved as the Heritors' minutes do not begin until 1788. In 1793 he submitted a design for Monimail Church, Fife, at the request of Lord Balgonie, but a proposal by Thomas Faulkner, a Cupar mason, was preferred [S.R.O., HR 432/1]. His most important work was probably the delightful classical TOWN HOUSE at FALKLAND, FIFE, built by him to his own designs in 1801–2 [S.R.O., B 25/5/2, Minutes of Falkland Town Council 28 Nov. 1800 and 9 Feb. 1801]. He appears also to have designed the MANSE at FALKLAND in 1806–7 [S.R.O., HR 416/1, p. 89, and 416/7].

When the Markinch Heritors wanted to enlarge their church in 1806 they wrote to James Barclay of Edinburgh, who designed and built the north aisle. He was evidently related to Thomas Barclay, for the contract was accepted by the Heritors on condition that it was countersigned by Thomas and George Barclay. In 1807 James designed a new termination to the spire which was built by Thomas [S.R.O., HR 59/1]. James Barclay was also employed at BALBIRNIE HOUSE, where in 1815–21 he enlarged the house to the designs of Richard Crichton and himself designed some cottages [Alistair Rowan in *C. Life*, 6 July 1972]. [Information from Mr. David Walker.]

BARDWELL, WILLIAM (1795–1890), born at Southwold in Suffolk, was a pupil of George Wyatt and of George Maddox. In a letter in the Cambridge University Archives (F.M.1) he stated that he 'afterwards studied nearly two years at Paris' and was concerned in the 'building of the chapelle expiatoire' in the crypt of the church of St. Denis, presumably as a pupil of François Debret, who was in charge of the restoration of St. Denis from 1813 to 1846. He began to exhibit at the Royal Academy in 1829, and also exhibited at the Society of British Artists in 1834 and 1837. In 1835 he competed unsuccessfully for the Houses of Parliament and for the Fitzwilliam Museum at Cambridge. His design for the former building was intended to embody all the successive styles of English medieval architecture: the Royal Entrance was under a 'Norman tower', the House of Lords was in the style of Becket's Crown in Canterbury Cathedral, the House of Commons was an elongated octagon 'in the florid style', and other features were Tudor Gothic. In 1832 he had been responsible for an elaborate town-planning scheme for Westminster, inspired by a Select Committee appointed 'to inquire into the most economical and eligible mode of improving the approaches to the Houses of

Parliament, ... and also of improving the immediate neighbourhood of Buckingham Palace'. This proved abortive, but Bardwell's plan anticipated the construction of Victoria Street, planned in 1844 and opened in 1851 [B. Kitchin, 'An 1832 Town-Planning Scheme for Westminster', *Arch. Rev.* xxxii, 1912, 251–2; P.R.O., MPD 87].

In 1868 Bardwell listed his principal executed works as GLENSTAL CASTLE, CO. LIMERICK, IRELAND, a large and ambitious essay in the Norman style designed for Matthew Barrington and built in 1838–9 (*C. Life*, 3 Oct. 1974); the PRIOR'S CHAPEL in LIMERICK CATHEDRAL, presumably about the same date; 'Picture Galleries, Pall Mall', presumably alterations to the British Institution's Galleries at 52 Pall Mall, demolished in 1868; model cottages for the Labourer's Friend Society at SHOOTERS HILL, KENT (illustrated by J. C. Loudon, *Encyclopaedia of Cottage, Farm and Villa Architecture*, 1846, 237–8); 'Healthy Homes' in the district of St. James's Westminster (contract advertised in *Builder* xiv, 1856, 321); 'dwellings at ENFIELD for the Board of Ordnance'; and 'various country houses'. His designs for an Italianate parsonage and a Grecian villa are illustrated by Loudon, *op. cit.*, 853, 877.

Bardwell was the author of *Temples, Ancient and Modern, or Notes on Church Architecture*, 1837, in which he argued that as Gothic was essentially a mason's architecture, modern churches built in brick ought to be classical in style; *Westminster Improvements: a brief account of ancient and modern Westminster ... by one of the architects of the Westminster Improvement Company*, 1839; *A Brief Historical Narrative of the Royal Church and Parish of St. Margaret, Westminster*, n.d.; *Healthy Homes and How to Make Them*, 1858; and *What a House should be* [1875]. He died on 8 July 1890, aged 94, and was buried in the churchyard at Southwold, where there is a monument to his family. [*The Architects, Engineers and Building Trades Directory*, 1868, 99.]

BARKER, JOHN (1668–1727), of Rowsley in Derbyshire, a carpenter and joiner by trade, was active as an architect and builder in the north Midlands during the early years of the eighteenth century. He was the son of Henry Barker (d. 1705), a joiner of Darley, nr. Bakewell in Derbyshire, to whom he was apprenticed in 1681 [Sheffield Public Library, Barker papers, D. 654]. The 'Mr. Barker, joyner' who was employed in the remodelling of THORESBY HOUSE, NOTTS., in 1684–5 was no doubt his father [B.M., Egerton MS. 3539, ff. 153–163]. In 1700/1 a survey plan of CHATSWORTH HOUSE, DERBYSHIRE, was made by John Barker [Francis Thompson, *A History of Chatsworth*, 1949, 160 and pl. 28]. The proximity of Rowsley to Haddon Hall must have brought

Barker into contact with the Manners family, and in 1704–5 he and two masons contracted to build the STABLES at BELVOIR CASTLE, LEICS., for the 1st Duke of Rutland [Belvoir Castle muniments, Misc. MS. 67]. The simple and rather old-fashioned design was probably due to Barker, for among the drawings for HOPTON HALL, DERBYSHIRE, in the Derbyshire Record Office (Chandos Pole archives) there is a design for a similar block of offices and stables 'drawn for Sr. Phillipp Gell [d. 1719] by John Barker'. In 1709–12 Barker contracted to build ST. ANN'S CHURCH, MANCHESTER. He is referred to as 'the undertaker' of the church in a letter dated 16 May 1710, and on 27 February 1709/10 he wrote from Rowsley directing a correspondent to address a letter 'to my Lodging near the New Church in Manchester or to be left with any of my men the Carpenters there' [Cheshire Record Office, Cholmondeley papers, L 31]. The designer of this large classical church is not known, but Barker must be regarded as a possible candidate, for after the collapse of WHITCHURCH CHURCH, SALOP., in 1711 an estimate was made for rebuilding it 'according to a designe drawn by John Barker to be after the doricke Order the church to be 88 ft. long & 62 ft. wide within'. As the existing church built in 1712–13 by William Smith of Tettenhall corresponds to these dimensions and is decorated with Doric pilasters, it would appear that Barker's design was accepted. The churchwardens' accounts show that in 1711 there was a meeting with 'Mr. Smiths and Mr. Barker', and that when the accounts for building the church were finally settled, John Barker was paid for 'additional' carpenter's and joiner's work. As Smith, a mason or bricklayer by trade, had contracted to erect the entire building 'by the great', it is probable that Barker undertook the woodwork as a sub-contractor [MS. churchwardens' accounts; Shropshire Record Office, Bridgewater collection, 212/ 1–6]. In 1711 Barker contracted with the 2nd Duke of Devonshire to rebuilt the BATHS at BUXTON according to drawings made by him and still attached to the articles of agreement [Sheffield Public Library, Barker papers, D 66]. In 1712 Barker made a design for reconstructing the chapel at CHOLMONDELEY, CHESHIRE, for the Earl of Cholmondeley, that was not proceeded with, but the drawing is preserved among the Cholmondeley papers in the Cheshire Record Office (cf. Lord Cholmondeley to Adams, 28 Jan. 1711/ 12].

Besides acting as a carpenter, joiner and architect, Barker lent money and may have had some experience in the management of property. In 1723 the 3rd Duke of Rutland (for whose grandfather he had built the stables at Belvoir) made Barker his steward. He moved from Rowsley to Belvoir, and was buried at Bottesford when he died in 1727. His elder son John was educated at Wadham College, Oxford, and became a physician. His second son Thomas Barker (1709–54) and his grandson John Barker (1731–95) succeeded him as stewards to the Dukes of Rutland, and were the founders of the family which figures in Burke's *Landed Gentry* as 'Barker of Brooklands'.

[Sheffield City Library, Barker papers, especially D.595, 634, 654–5, 684–5, 828, pp. 82–6, 88, etc.; information from Mr. Edward Saunders.]

BARLOW, THOMAS (–1730), was a master carpenter who was active as a speculative builder in London during the reigns of Queen Anne and George I. He is known to have built houses in Albemarle Street (*c.* 1690), Southampton Street (1708) and Bond Street (where he lived), and Barlow Place (formerly Mews) off Bruton Street is named after him. He was involved in the development of the 1st Earl of Scarbrough's estate round Hanover Square (*c.* 1715), and from 1720 until his death he was employed as surveyor of the Grosvenor estate. In that capacity he was responsible for the layout of Grosvenor Square and the adjoining streets, but probably exercised only a general control over the elevations. Barlow, who was a director of the Westminster Fire Office and a vestryman of St. George's Church, Hanover Square, died in January 1730, leaving a substantial estate to his son Richard, who died in 1740, 'having greatly wasted and outrun his fortune' [information from the Survey of London].

BARNARD, JOHN, designed the wooden bridge which was built over the Thames at KEW in 1758–9. It was replaced by a stone bridge designed by J. Paine in 1783. An engraving of the bridge, dedicated to the Prince and Princess of Wales by 'John Barnard Archt.', is in the Bodleian [Gough Maps, 30, ff. 30ᵛ–31]. Barnard was one of the competitors for Blackfriars Bridge in 1760 [J. Chambers, MS. *Collections for a Biography of English Architects*, in R.I.B.A. Library].

BARNES, DAVID, 'Architect and Surveyor' of Broadstairs, and proprietor of a library and reading-room there [*The Watering Places of Great Britain and Fashionable Directory*, 1833, 42], designed HOLY TRINITY CHURCH, BROADSTAIRS, KENT, 1828–30 [I.C.B.S.]. This small church in the lancet style was remodelled in 1914–15. In 1819 Barnes had subscribed to Peter Nicholson's *Architectural Dictionary* from an address in Cornhill, London.

BARNES, PHILIP, practised in Norwich during the period 1785–1835. He was Secretary of the Norwich Society of Artists in 1817 and President in 1825. From 1832 to 1835 he was a member of the Norwich Sewers Commission. In

1820, in collaboration with J. T. Patience, he submitted a design for a Court House for the county of Norfolk which received a premium but was not executed. In 1823, in collaboration with Edward Brown, he submitted three designs for the new City Gaol. None of them was accepted, but Barnes was employed to erect the new Gaol at the end of St. Giles' Street from the winning designs of Richard Brown of London, 1824–7 (dem.). The working drawings are in Norwich City Archives [information from Mr. A. Paget Baggs].

BARRIE, ANDREW, was a mason of Montrose in Angus. He was one of the two 'undertakers' of the NORTH ESK BRIDGE, nr. Montrose, in 1770–5, and is also named with John Smeaton and John Adam(s) as one of the three 'architects' who designed the bridge [inscription]. In the Register House there is a design by him for a house in High Street, Montrose, for Lieut. Strachan dated 1778 [RHP 6006]. Another design for a house in the same town [RHP 6007] is probably by him.

BARROW, R— J—, *see* LONG, F—

BARRY, SIR CHARLES (1795–1860), the fourth son of a prosperous Westminster stationer, was articled at the age of 15 to Messrs. Middleton and Bailey, a firm of surveyors in Lambeth, with whom he remained for six years. From them he learned the practical side of his profession, but in other respects was largely self-taught. On coming of age in 1816, he decided to spend a modest legacy from his father on an architectural tour of the Continent. He left England in 1817, travelling alone through France and Italy, and in Greece and Turkey in company with C. L. Eastlake (d. 1865) and W. Kinnaird, who was collecting material for a supplementary volume of the *Antiquities of Athens*. He was about to return to England when Mr. David Baillie, an archaeological traveller from Cambridge, who had met him in Athens and admired his drawings, offered to take him to Egypt and Syria and to pay him £200 a year for his sketches of the architecture and scenery of those countries.[1] In 1819–20 he returned to England by way of Cyprus, Rhodes, Malta, Sicily and Italy, where he met his lifelong friend J. L. Wolfe (*q.v.*). It was with Wolfe's help that in Rome and Florence he made those studies of Renaissance architecture that were to be so important in the formation of his architectural style.

On his return to London, Barry established himself in Ely Place, Holborn, and, after a rapid

---

[1] Some of these drawings are now in the Griffith Institute, Ashmolean Museum, Oxford. Barry's own travel sketch-books are in the R.I.B.A. Drawings Collection.

study of Gothic, obtained (probably through the good offices of Soane, who knew his fiancée) the job of designing two of the Commissioners' churches then being erected in the neighbourhood of Manchester. Other commissions followed, notably the Royal Institution of Fine Arts at Manchester, which gave him an opportunity to demonstrate his ability as an orthodox Grecian architect. This was fortunate, for, although Barry could appreciate the dramatic possibilities of Gothic, as St. Peter's, Brighton, shows, he was not in sympathy with the more extreme revivalists, considering that 'deep chancels, high roodscreens and (in a less degree) pillared aisles ... belong to the worship and institutions of the past rather than the present'. These were not sentiments which would lead to ecclesiastical commissions in the future, and while his contemporaries were taking advantage of the spate of Victorian church building, Barry applied himself to the more congenial task of designing public buildings and altering country mansions, in which he could make use both of his Italian studies and of his considerable skill in planning. For by now he had renounced the Greek Revival in favour of the Italianate manner that was to make his fortune as an architect. His success in adapting the features of the Italian *palazzo* to English architecture – first displayed in the Travellers' Club in Pall Mall – provided an acceptable alternative to the extremes of Greek and Gothic hitherto offered to prospective builders, and established him as the leading London architect for club-houses and similar institutions. The Italianate style also permitted a greater richness of detail that Barry did not fail to exploit, and that appealed strongly to a generation tired of the 'chaste' (but often arid) simplicity of the Greek Revival. Barry was not, however, wedded to his Italian formula. 'Grandeur of outline' and 'richness of detail' were the two keynotes of his style, and he was equally ready to provide them in Tudor Gothic (as at Canford Manor), in Jacobethan (as at Highclere and Horsley Towers) or even in Scottish Baronial (as at Dunrobin Castle). But it was the Travellers' Club that made him famous, and it was the Italianate style that represented his personal contribution to the repertoire of Victorian architecture. With rich clients – and some of Barry's clients were very rich indeed – it was a style that could easily become overblown and a little vulgar, and Barry cannot be absolved from contributing to the coarsening of architectural taste that is apparent in the 1840s. In gardening, too, he ranks as one of the creators of Victorian taste: surrounding his opulent mansions with elaborate architectural flower-gardens in place of the subtler Georgian conception of the house as an integral part of a carefully composed landscape.

Many of Barry's early commissions were gained in competition, and in 1836 he won the biggest architectural competition of the century by obtaining the first prize for his design for the new Houses of Parliament. The style was, as the authorities demanded, 'Gothic or Elizabethan', but according to his son Barry 'would have preferred the Italian style', and the underlying discipline of the design is classical rather than Gothic. The prominent towers did, however, give the otherwise symmetrical building a picturesque quality that was recognizably medieval in inspiration, and the employment of A. W. N. Pugin to design much of the detail ensured that it was based on authentic Gothic prototypes. The competition design (for which the drawings are lost[1]) was considerably modified both in plan and in elevational treatment before it was carried out, and many drawings survive (in the P.R.O., House of Lords Record Office, R.I.B.A. Drawings Collection and Society of Antiquaries' library) to illustrate the process. They were the work of a team of draughtsmen which, besides A. W. N. Pugin, included Barry's pupils John Gibson and George Somers Clarke and his sons Charles and Edward Middleton Barry. The difficulties of carrying on so vast a building were exacerbated for Barry by the need to satisfy not only committees of both Houses of Parliament, impatient to see their respective Chambers finished, but also the commissioners appointed in 1848 to supervise the whole operation on behalf of the government, and the Royal Fine Arts Commission set up in 1841 to decorate the interior with the works of contemporary artists. In addition Barry found himself fighting a running battle with Dr. Reid, an expert on ventilation whose failure to cooperate with the architect caused serious difficulties as the work proceeded. Drainage, the great clock, and finally Barry's own remuneration led to further controversy and vexation. It is not surprising therefore that the supervision of this great work became a full-time task which almost eliminated Barry's private practice during the latter part of his life. In 1852, after the Royal Entrance had been used for the first time by the Queen, Barry was knighted, but the building as a whole was incomplete at the time of his death, and was finished by his son E. M. Barry.

Barry died suddenly at his home, Elm House, Clapham Common, on 12 May 1860. He was buried in Westminster Abbey. A statue by J. H. Foley was erected to his memory in the Palace of Westminster in 1864. There is a portrait by J. P. Knight in the National Portrait Gallery and a

[1] Professor H. R. Hitchcock is mistaken in describing the drawings reproduced in his *Early Victorian Architecture* ii, 1954, pls. II, 22–25, as the 'original' or (i, p. 48) 'competition' designs. They are revisions dating from April 1836. For the competition plan see *History of the King's Works* vi, 1972, Fig. 26.

bust by P. Park at the Reform Club. Barry was an R.A. and an F.R.S. and a Vice-President of the R.I.B.A., having refused the presidency on the death of Earl de Grey in 1859. He received the Royal Gold Medal of the R.I.B.A., and was a member of many foreign academies, including the American Institute of Architects. Of his four sons two, Charles (1824–1900) and Edward Middleton (1830–1880), followed their father's profession. From 1848 the former was in partnership with R. R. Banks.

[A. Barry, *The Life and Works of Sir Charles Barry*, 1867; obituary in *Builder* xviii, 1860, 305–7; memoir by M. D. Wyatt in *R.I.B.A. Trans*, 1859–60, 118–137, and *Builder* xviii, 1860, 322, 342; *D.N.B.*; A. R. Dent, 'Barry and the Greek Revival', *Architecture*, 5th ser., iii, 1924–5, 225, 320; Marcus Whiffen, *The Architecture of Sir Charles Barry in Manchester* (Royal Manchester Institution, 1950); H.-R. Hitchcock, *Early Victorian Architecture in Britain* i, 1954, chaps. vi-vii; Peter Fleetwood-Hesketh, 'Sir Charles Barry', in *Victorian Architecture*, ed. P. Ferriday, 1963; Mark Girouard, 'Charles Barry: A Centenary Assessment', *C. Life*, 13 Oct. 1960; Marcus Binney, 'The Travels of Sir Charles Barry', *C. Life*, 28 Aug., 4–11 Sept. 1969; *Catalogue of the R.I.B.A. Drawings Collection: B*, 1972, 18–54.]

Unless otherwise stated, the following list of Barry's executed works is based on Appendix A of A. Barry's *Life and Works of Sir Charles Barry*, where a list of unexecuted works will also be found.

CHURCHES

PRESTWICH, LANCS., ALL SAINTS, STAND, 1822–5, Gothic.

MANCHESTER, ST. MATTHEW, CAMPFIELD, 1822–5, Gothic; dem. 1951.

RINGLEY, LANCS., 1824, Gothic; rebuilt 1851–4.

BRIGHTON, ST. PETER, 1824–8, Gothic; Barry subsequently designed a spire that was not built; chancel added by Somers Clarke 1900.

LONDON, HOLY TRINITY, CLOUDESLEY SQUARE, ISLINGTON, 1826–8, Gothic.

LONDON, ST. PAUL, BALLS POND, ISLINGTON, 1826–8, Gothic.

LONDON, ST. JOHN, UPPER HOLLOWAY, ISLINGTON, 1826–8, Gothic.

HOVE, SUSSEX, THE BRUNSWICK CHAPEL (now ST. ANDREW'S CHURCH), for the Rev. E. Everard, 1827–8, Italianate; chancel added by C. Barry, junior, 1882.

PETWORTH, SUSSEX, rebuilt tower, added spire and altered nave for the 4th Earl of Egremont, 1827. The nave was altered again in 1903 and the spire was removed in 1947.

STOKE NEWINGTON, LONDON, ST. MARY, remo-delled church and added spire, 1827–9; damaged by bombing 1940 and restored 1953, when the north side was rebuilt, minus an additional north aisle added by Barry.

LONDON, ST. MARTIN OUTWICH, repaired and altered, 1827; dem. 1874.

LONDON, ST. PETER, SAFFRON HILL, HOLBORN, 1830–2, Gothic; gutted 1940, dem. 1955.

LONDON, ST. PETER, ISLINGTON, 1834–5, Gothic; enlarged by Gough & Roumieu 1842–3 [I.C.B.S.; S. Lewis, *History of Islington*, 1842, 359–60].

MANCHESTER, UNITARIAN (now WELSH BAPTIST) CHAPEL, UPPER BROOK STREET, 1837–9, Gothic.

HURSTPIERPOINT, SUSSEX, rebuilt, 1843–5, Gothic.

TRENTHAM, STAFFS., reconstructed 1844 for the 2nd Duke of Sutherland, Gothic.

WIMBORNE MINSTER, DORSET, restoration, 1846 [*Ecclesiologist* vi, 1846, 183, 195].

PUBLIC BUILDINGS

MANCHESTER, THE ROYAL INSTITUTION OF FINE ARTS (now City Art Gallery), 1824–35.

BRIGHTON, THE SUSSEX COUNTY HOSPITAL, 1826–8; subsequently enlarged.

LONDON, THE TRAVELLERS' CLUB, PALL MALL, 1830–2 (W. H. Leeds, *The Travellers' Club*, 1839; *Survey of London* xxix, 399–408).

ISLINGTON, ST. JOHN'S NATIONAL SCHOOLS, 1830.

DULWICH COLLEGE, alterations and additions, 1831, Gothic; largely destroyed in the reconstruction by C. Barry, junior, 1858 onwards.

BIRMINGHAM, KING EDWARD VI'S GRAMMAR SCHOOL, 1833–7, Gothic; enlarged by E. M. Barry 1860; dem. 1936.

LONDON, ROYAL COLLEGE OF SURGEONS, LINCOLN'S INN FIELDS, remodelled, 1835–7, retaining but altering G. Dance's portico; attic storey added 1888–9.

MANCHESTER, THE ATHENAEUM (now Annexe to Art Gallery), 1837–9.

LONDON, THE REFORM CLUB, PALL MALL, 1838–41 (*Survey of London* xxix, 408–15).

KENMARE, CO. KERRY, IRELAND, MARKET-HOUSE for the 3rd Marquess of Lansdowne, *c.* 1840 [drawings in R.I.B.A. Drawings Collection, Moulton-Barrett volume].

LONDON, TRAFALGAR SQUARE, layout and fountains, 1840; fountains removed 1948 and re-erected at Ottawa, Canada, 1954.

PALACE OF WESTMINSTER AND HOUSES OF PARLIAMENT, 1840–60; completed by E. M. Barry 1860–70 (M. H. Port in *History of the King's Works* vi, 1972, 573–626).

PENTONVILLE PRISON, ISLINGTON, designed architectural features in accordance with plan made by Major Joshua Jebb, surveyor-general of convict prisons, 1841–2 [*History of the King's Works* vi, 1972, 630–1].

DULWICH GRAMMAR SCHOOL, 1841–2, Tudor Gothic.

OXFORD, UNIVERSITY COLLEGE, extension at west end of High Street front, 1842, Tudor Gothic.

WHITEHALL, reconstructed BOARD OF TRADE and PRIVY COUNCIL OFFICES, 1844–5.

GOLSPIE, SUTHERLAND, fountain in memory of Elizabeth, Duchess of Sutherland (d. 1839), *c.* 1845 [*Building Chronicle* i, 74, 16 Sept. 1854].

ISTANBUL, THE BRITISH EMBASSY, 1845–7, built by W. J. Smith following sketches made by Barry [*History of the King's Works* vi, 1972, 634–8].

DEVONPORT, DEVON, ROYAL NAVAL FACTORY at MORICE TOWN, KEYHAM, 1847–8.

DOWLAIS SCHOOLS, GLAMORGANSHIRE, for Sir John Guest, 1851.

HALIFAX, YORKS. (W.R.), TOWN HALL, 1859–62; executed by E. M. Barry, who was responsible for the interior.

DOMESTIC ARCHITECTURE

BUILE HILL, nr. MANCHESTER, house (now Salford Science Museum) for Sir Thomas Potter, 1825–7; enlarged *c.* 1865.

BRIGHTON, SUSSEX, house (later Xaverian College) in QUEEN'S PARK for Thomas Attree, 1829–30; dem. 1971; part of an extensive housing scheme that was never carried out (*C. Life*, 11 Aug. 1917, supplement).

LONDON, 16–17 PALL MALL (shops and living accommodation) for Thomas Ashton, 1833–4; dem. 1913 [*Survey of London* xxix, 325 and pl. 271].

HORSLEY PLACE (now HORSLEY TOWERS), EAST HORSLEY, SURREY, for William Currie, 1834, Tudor Gothic; tower, hall, library, etc., added by the 1st Earl of Lovelace 1847–8.

BOWOOD HOUSE, WILTS., works for the 3rd Marquess Lansdowne, including the Derry Hill Gateway (1834–8) and alterations to the house (*c.* 1848; dem. 1956) and gardens [*Builder*, 6 Oct. 1849, 474; A. T. Bolton, *Architecture of R. and J. Adam* i, 1922, 210–11; John Cornforth in *C. Life*, 22 June 1972].

TRENTHAM HALL, STAFFS., reconstructed for the 2nd Duke of Sutherland, 1834–40 and 1840–9; dem. 1910 (*Companion to the Almanac*, 1837, 247–50; *C. Life*, 25 Jan., 1–8 Feb. 1968).

KINGSTON LACY, DORSET, recased and internally remodelled for W. J. Bankes, M.P., 1835–9 (A. Oswald, *Country Houses of Dorset*, 1959, 144–7).

WALTON HOUSE (later MOUNT FELIX), WALTON-ON-THAMES, SURREY, reconstructed for the 5th Earl of Tankerville, 1835–9; dem. 1973.

LONDON, STAFFORD (now LANCASTER) HOUSE, ST. JAMES'S, altered the lantern and redecorated the staircase for the 2nd Duke of Sutherland, 1838–43 [H. M. Colvin, 'The Architects of Stafford House', *Architectural History* i, 1958, 28–9].

KENSINGTON, alterations to house in ADDISON ROAD for Charles Richard Fox, 1841–2.

HIGHCLERE CASTLE, HANTS., remodelled for the 3rd Earl of Carnarvon, 1842–*c.* 1850 (Mark Girouard, *The Victorian Country House*, 1971, 68–70). Barry also remodelled the circular Ionic temple in the Park [drawings at Highclere dated 1838].

EYNSHAM HALL, nr. WITNEY, OXON., for the 5th Earl of Macclesfield, 1843; dem. 1904 (lithographs of 1862 in Bodleian, G.A. Oxon. b. 85a (30)).

DUNCOMBE PARK, YORKS. (N.R.), added wings and conservatory for the 2nd Lord Feversham, 1843–6.

HAREWOOD HOUSE, YORKS. (W.R.), altered interior and remodelled exterior for the 3rd Earl of Harewood, 1843–50. Barry also laid out the formal gardens.

DUNROBIN CASTLE, SUTHERLAND, reconstructed for the 2nd Duke of Sutherland, 1844–8, in collaboration with W. Leslie of Aberdeen, who executed Barry's designs with modifications. Barry's principal contribution was the north front.

LONDON, NO. 1, CLEVELAND SQUARE, flank wall for Lord Sydney, 1845; dem. 1895 [*Survey of London* xxx, 495].

LONDON, NOS. 12, 18–19 and 20 KENSINGTON PALACE GARDENS, for Messrs. Grissell & Peto, 1845–7 [*Survey of London* xxxvii, 167–70, 179–181].

LONDON, BRIDGEWATER HOUSE, GREEN PARK, for the 1st Earl of Ellesmere, 1846–51 (*Survey of London* xxx, 496–504).

LONDON, ST. JOHN'S LODGE, REGENT'S PARK, added wings containing library and ballroom, entrance hall, etc., and added upper storey for Baron de Goldsmid, 1847 (A. T. Bolton in University of London: Institute of Archaeology's *First Annual Report*, 1937, 15).

CANFORD MANOR, DORSET, enlarged for Sir John Guest, 1848–52, Tudor Gothic.

SHRUBLAND PARK, SUFFOLK, alterations and additions, including formal gardens, for Sir W. F. Middleton, Bart., 1849–54 (*C. Life*, 24 Sept., 19–26 Nov. 1953).

KIDDINGTON HALL, OXON., remodelled for Mortimer Ricardo, *c.* 1850.

GAWTHORPE HALL, LANCS., altered and restored for Sir James Kay-Shuttleworth, Bart., 1850–2 (*C. Life*, 4, 11 Sept. 1975).

CLIVEDEN HOUSE, BUCKS., rebuilt for the 2nd Duke of Sutherland, 1850–1 (*C. Life*, 7, 14 Dec. 1912, with plan).

GORING HOUSE, SUSSEX, for David Lyon, 1852; dem.

EDGBASTON HALL, WARWICKS., alterations for Lord Calthorpe, 1852.

BARTHOLOMEW, ALFRED (1801–1845), was the son of a watchmaker in Clerkenwell. He was intended by his parents for a commercial career, and 'received only the moderate education of a middle-class school'. But a strong aptitude for mathematics led to his being articled to J. H. Good (*q.v.*). He afterwards taught perspective 'to the younger branches of a noble family', before starting practice. Writing and journalism were, however, to be his real *métier*, and his only architectural work of importance was the (classical) FINSBURY SAVINGS BANK in SECKFORD STREET, CLERKENWELL, 1840 [*Civil Engineer* iii, 1840, 217]. His design for rebuilding the KENTISH TOWN EPISCOPAL CHAPEL, described in the *Civil Engineer* for 1842, was not carried out.

Bartholomew was keenly interested in church worship, and his first publication was a translation of the psalms, entitled *Sacred Lyrics, being an attempt to render the psalms of David more applicable to parochial psalmody*, 1831. He was one of the founders of a society called the 'Freemasons of the Church', whose object was 'the recovery, maintenance, and furtherance of the true principles and practice of architecture', and (although not hostile to classical architecture) was an enthusiastic advocate of the structural rationality of Gothic, which he expounded in the *Essay on the Decline of Excellence in the Structure of Modern English Buildings* which he appended to his *Specifications for Practical Architecture*, 1840, 2nd ed. 1846. He was also the author of *Hints relative to the Construction of Fire-Proof Buildings – and on the failure to produce sound and estimable Architecture by the means at present usually adopted*, 1839, and of a *Cyclopaedia of the New Metropolitan Building Act*, 1844, previously published in the *Builder*, of which he had become editor some time after its foundation in 1843. In 1844 he obtained the post of district surveyor of Hornsey, but died of bronchitis in January 1845, aged 44. The flower-painter Valentine Bartholomew was his elder brother. [Obituaries in *Builder* iii, 1845, 29, and *Gent's Mag.* 1845 (i), 320–1; *A.P.S.D.*; *D.N.B.*; G. G. Pace, 'Alfred Bartholomew, a pioneer of functional Gothic', *Arch. Rev.*, Oct. 1942; C. L. Eastlake, *History of the Gothic Revival*, 1872, 214–16.]

BARTLETT, J— E—, was the author of *An Essay on Design, as applied generally to Edifices, both Private and Public, intended as a guide to Persons engaged in the Study of Architecture and containing pleasing information to private Gentlemen*, published at Lymington, Hants., in 1823. The book contains designs for castellated mansions. Bartlett designed the SOLENT SEA BATHS at LYMINGTON, *c.* 1830 [*Views of the Principal Seats and Scenery in the Neighbourhood of Lymington* drawn by L. Haghe and published by R. A. Grove, 1832]. This building, which was surmounted by a hexagonal reading-room overlooking the sea, has been demolished.

BASEVI, GEORGE (1794–1845), was of Jewish birth. His father, George Basevi, senior, was a brother-in-law of Isaac D'Israeli, and was also related to the Ricardos. After attending Dr. Burney's school at Greenwich, Basevi became in 1811 a pupil of Sir John Soane, who thought highly of his ability. In 1816, on the expiry of his articles, he set out on a tour of Italy and Greece which lasted three years, and included a visit to Constantinople. Avidly studying buildings of every age from Ancient Greece to the High Renaissance, Basevi gradually emancipated himself from the influence of Soane, and returned well equipped to serve the increasingly eclectic taste of George IV's England. In 1820 he established himself in practice in the Albany, and in the following year he became surveyor to the newly formed Guardian Assurance Company. Between 1825 and 1840 he was employed by the financiers W. and G. Haldimand to superintend the erection of the houses in Belgrave Square, all of which, with the exception of the large mansions which occupy the angles, were built to his designs. No. 31 bears the signature 'G. BASEVI, Archt. 1827'. In 1829 he was appointed surveyor to the trustees of Smith's Charity estate in Brompton, and laid out Pelham Crescent, Sydney Place, part of Brompton Crescent, and the adjoining streets. He also acted as surveyor to the Thurloe estate in South Kensington, then being developed by its owner, John Alexander, and designed the handsome houses in Thurloe Place, Thurloe Square, etc., built early in the 1840s.

In 1833 Basevi was one of the architects invited to submit plans for rebuilding the House of Commons (see *Parliamentary Papers*, 1833). By 1835, when he won the competition for the Fitzwilliam Museum at Cambridge, he was established as one of the leading English architects. Two important commissions, which he shared with Sydney Smirke, were the Conservative Club in St. James's Street and the Carlton Club in Pall Mall. The former was completed to their joint designs, but Basevi did not live to carry out the latter, for on 16 October 1845, while inspecting the western tower of Ely Cathedral, he fell through the floor of the belfry, and was killed on the spot. He was buried in the cathedral, where there is a brass to his memory in the north choir aisle. A plaster bust by an unknown sculptor is in the Fitzwilliam Museum: there are casts in the Soane Museum and the R.I.B.A. Drawings Collection. Basevi is said to have been 'cold and somewhat haughty in manner', but scrupulously just in his professional activities. He was a Fellow of the R.I.B.A., the Royal Society and of the Society of Antiquaries. Francis Dollman (1812–1900) is said to have been his pupil. His son James

Palladio Basevi (1832–71) was an officer in the Royal Engineers.

Basevi was probably the most successful of Soane's many pupils. Like other architects of his day, he was prepared to design Gothic churches and Tudor almshouses when required, but it was as a classical architect that he made his mark. In the Fitzwilliam Museum he produced one of the major works of the Early Victorian period, offering to a taste tired of the arid grandeur of the British Museum an opulent display of Graeco-Roman detailing. His London houses in Kensington and Belgravia show a similar (but more discreet) desire to liven up the anonymous uniformity of Georgian street architecture. His country houses are a dull lot which add little to his reputation.

[Obituary in *Builder* iii, 1845, 510–11; *A.P.S.D.* (article by Sydney Smirke); *D.N.B.*; A. T. Bolton, *The Portrait of Sir John Soane*, 1927, 271–8; W. H. F. Basevi, 'The Grand Tour of an Architect', *The Architect*, 7 July–1 Sept. 1922.]

PUBLIC BUILDINGS

OXFORD, BALLIOL COLLEGE, building on west side of Garden Quadrangle, 1826–7; upper storey added by E. P. Warren 1926. In 1841 Basevi made designs for rebuilding the main front of the College facing Broad Street, but they were rejected. The original drawings are in the College Library [*V.C.H. Oxon.* iii, 94–5].

STAMFORD, LINCS., DR. FRYER'S ALMSHOUSES, Tudor Gothic, 1832 [signed].

STAMFORD, LINCS., TRUESDALE'S HOSPITAL, Tudor Gothic, 1832 [signed].

STROUD, GLOS., THE SUBSCRIPTION ROOMS, 1833–4. Basevi furnished the designs gratuitously, and they were carried out by Charles Baker of Painswick [P. H. Fisher, *Notes and Recollections of Stroud*, 1871, 161; specification in Glos. Record Office, D. 1347].

LONDON, enlarged THE MIDDLESEX HOSPITAL, MORTIMER STREET, 1834; dem. 1928 [*A.P.S.D.*].

CAMBRIDGE, THE FITZWILLIAM MUSEUM, 1836–45, completed (with some alterations to the design) by C. R. Cockerell, 1845–8, and by E. M. Barry, 1870–5 [Willis & Clark, iii, 198–228].

HOVE, SUSSEX, ST. MARY'S HALL SCHOOL, EASTERN ROAD, for the Rev. H. V. Elliott, 1836, Tudor Gothic [A. Dale, *Fashionable Brighton*, 1947, 139].

TWICKENHAM, MIDDLESEX, THE NATIONAL (ARCHDEACON CAMBRIDGE'S) SCHOOLS, 1840–1; dem. [*A.P.S.D.*].

LONDON, THE CONSERVATIVE CLUB-HOUSE, ST. JAMES'S STREET, in association with S. Smirke, 1843–4. The exterior was the joint design of the two architects: in the interior the decoration of the ground floor is said to have been due to Basevi, that of the first floor to Smirke [*A.P.S.D.*; *Survey of London* xxx, 478–84].

ELY, CAMBS., PARSON'S ALMSHOUSES, ST. MARY STREET, 1844–5, Tudor Gothic [*A.P.S.D.*].

ELY, CAMBS., addition to the GAOL, 1845 [*A.P.S.D.*].

WISBECH, CAMBS., THE NEW GAOL or HOUSE OF CORRECTION, 1845–6; dem. [Gardner's *History, Gazeteer and Directory of Cambridgeshire*, 1851, 613].

CHURCHES

STOCKPORT, CHESHIRE, ST. THOMAS, 1822–5; chancel added 1890 [Port, 132].

GREENWICH, KENT, ST. MARY, 1823–4; dem. *c.* 1935 [Port, 134; *Gent's Mag.* 1829 (ii), 395–7] (*Greenwich and Lewisham Archaeological Soc.'s Trans.*, 1936).

HOVE PARISH CHURCH, SUSSEX, reconstruction in Norman style, 1833–6 [*A.P.S.D.*].

CHELSEA, ST. SAVIOUR, WALTON PLACE, 1839–40, Gothic; north aisle added 1878, chancel 1890 [Port, 152].

TWICKENHAM, MIDDLESEX, HOLY TRINITY, 1840–1, Gothic; chancel and transepts added by F. T. Dollman 1863 [*A.P.S.D.*].

OXFORD, BALLIOL COLLEGE CHAPEL, plaster Gothic ceiling, 1841; dem. 1856 [*V.C.H. Oxon.* iii, 91].

CHELSEA, ST. JUDE, 1843–4, Gothic; dem. 1933 [Port, 152].

EYE, NORTHANTS., 1845–6, Gothic; steeple built posthumously 1857 by F. T. Dollman [*A.P.S.D.*].

MONUMENT

KENSAL GREEN CEMETERY, family tomb of J. A. Hankey, 1838 [A. W. Hakewill, *Modern Tombs gleaned from the Public Cemeteries of London*, 1851, pl. 2].

LONDON HOUSES

BELGRAVE SQUARE, designed the houses (excluding those at the angles) for W. & G. Haldimand, 1825–40 [*A.P.S.D.*]. No. 31 is signed 'G. Basevi, Archt. 1827'.

SOUTH KENSINGTON, laid out the Thurloe estate for John Alexander (d. 1831) and his son H. B. Alexander, designing ALEXANDER SQUARE, etc., 1827–30, and THURLOE SQUARE, etc., *c.* 1839–45 [Dorothy Stroud, *The Thurloe Estate*, 1959].

SOUTH KENSINGTON, designed PELHAM CRESCENT, PELHAM PLACE, BROMPTON (now EGERTON) CRESCENT and WALTON PLACE for the Trustees of Smith's Charity from 1833 onwards [Dorothy Stroud, *The South Kensington Estate of Henry Smith's Charity*, 1975].

PICCADILLY, NO. 144, alterations for T. W. Beau-mont, c. 1836; dem. [*A.P.S.D.*].

COUNTRY HOUSES

According to Sydney Smirke (in *A.P.S.D.*) Basevi was employed 'more or less extensively' on the following houses:

ASH GROVE (now WEST HEATH SCHOOL), nr. SEVENOAKS, KENT, for W. Haldimand.

BITTON GROVE (now Council Offices), nr. TEIGN-MOUTH, DEVON, for W. Mackworth Praed.

BLAKE HALL, ESSEX, remodelled for Capel Cure, 1822 [cf. *V.C.H. Essex* iv, 14].

BRETTON HALL, YORKS. (W.R.), where he designed the stables for T. W. Beaumont in 1842 [archives of Lord Allendale, *ex inf.* Dr. D. Lin-strum] (*C. Life*, 21–28 May 1938).

BUSHEY GROVE, nr. WATFORD, HERTS., for Stewart Marjoribanks; dem.

FOXHILLS, OTTERSHAW, nr. CHERTSEY, SURREY, for J. I. Briscoe, c. 1840, Tudor style; interiors altered 1923.

GATCOMBE PARK, GLOS., alterations (probably in-cluding stables, conservatory and interior of library) for David Ricardo, c. 1820.

LONGHILLS HALL, nr. LINCOLN, for the Rev. P. Curtois, 1838.

NEWBERRIES PARK, RADLETT, HERTS., for Capt. R. W. Phillimore; dem. c. 1950.

PAINSWICK HOUSE, GLOS., alterations, including addition of wings, for W. H. Hyett, M.P., Basevi's brother-in-law, 1827–32 (*C. Life*, 1 Sept. 1917).

SHERE MANOR HOUSE, SURREY, for Reginald Bray (who did not, however, inherit the estate from his brother until 1866).

TAPLOW HOUSE, BUCKS., enlarged for the 2nd Marquess of Thomond, c. 1840.

TITNESS PARK, nr. SUNNINGHILL, BERKS., for Sampson Ricardo, Tudor Gothic; dem. c. 1950.

In addition he no doubt designed BEECHWOOD, HIGHGATE, LONDON, for his brother Nathaniel Basevi, 1834 [C. Hussey in *C. Life*, 7 March 1952], and it may be conjectured that Basevi was the architect employed by Osman (son of David) Ricardo to reconstruct BROMSBERROW PLACE, GLOS., c. 1825.

BASIL, SIMON (–1615), was Surveyor of the King's Works from 1606 to 1615. His recorded career begins in 1590, when he was employed by the surveyor Robert Adams to draw a plan of Ostend. During Adams's brief tenure of office as Surveyor of the Works, Basil was Clerk of Works at Richmond. Just before his death Adams recommended him to Lord Burghley as com-petent to design fortifications, and in 1597 he is mentioned in connection with a 'modell' of

Flushing. After Burghley's death in 1598, Robert Cecil (afterwards Earl of Salisbury) employed him at SALISBURY HOUSE in the Strand (1601), at THE NEW EXCHANGE in the Strand (1608–9) and at HATFIELD HOUSE, HERTS. (1607–12). Although he was in effective control of the operations at all three buildings, it does not necessarily follow that he made the designs. At Hatfield House these were certainly made, not by Basil but by Robert Liminge (*q.v.*). In the case of the other two build-ings the authorship of the designs must be left in doubt, but Basil was no doubt closely involved in working them out even if he did not draw them himself. The only evidence of his activities else-where is a plan at Hatfield of Sir Walter Raleigh's house, SHERBORNE CASTLE, DORSET, made some time between 1600 and 1609.

In 1597 Basil became became Comptroller of the Works, and in April 1606 he succeeded Sir David Cuningham as Surveyor. His surveyor-ship was marked by important administrative reforms, but he does not appear to have been a designer of any distinction, and even before his death the artistic initiative in the royal works was passing to Inigo Jones. Basil died in September 1615 and was buried at St. Martin's-in-the-Fields. His son Simon (1612–63) followed his father's profession and his career as a Clerk of the Works at Greenwich and Eltham before the Civil War and at Hampton Court after the Res-toration was recorded on a memorial tablet for-merly in Isleworth Church. [John Summerson in *History of the King's Works*, iii, 1975, 108–20, etc.; Lawrence Stone, 'The Building of Hatfield House', *Archaeological Jnl.* cxii, 1955; Lawrence Stone, 'Inigo Jones and the New Exchange', *Archaeological Jnl.* cxiv, 1957; Lawrence Stone, *Family and Fortune*, 1973, *passim*.]

BASNETT, CHARLES HENRY (c. 1784–1859), was the only son of John Basnett of Wok-ingham, Berks. He became a pupil of Jeffry Wyatville, from whose office he exhibited at the Royal Academy in 1804–7. He subsequently moved to Bath, whence he sent architectural drawings to the R.A. exhibitions between 1815 and 1821. Nothing further has been ascertained about his career until his death in Brock Street, Bath, on 18 July 1859, at the age of 75 [*Gent's Mag.* 1859 (ii), 314].

BASSETT, HENRY (c. 1803–), entered the Royal Academy Schools in 1822 at the age of 19. In 1823 he won the Gold Medal of the Society of Arts for a design for a British Museum, and in 1825 he was awarded the Gold Medal of the Royal Academy. He subsequently exhibited at the Royal Academy from 15 Norfolk Street, Strand, the address of George Bassett, who exhi-bited at the Academy as a painter in 1829 and 1832, but who figures in Pigot's *Directory* of

1827–8 as a house agent and surveyor, and in the *Literary Blue Book* of 1830 as an architect. By 1939 Henry Bassett was employed on the Southampton estate in Bloomsbury, giving as his address the Southampton Estate Office in Fitzroy Square. His principal recorded work is BURTON PARK, nr. PETWORTH, SUSSEX, for John Biddulph, an assertively Grecian house of which he exhibited a perspective view at the Royal Academy in 1831 (*C. Life*, 11 July 1936; N. Pevsner, *Sussex*, 123–4). In 1833 he designed a villa for Thomas Clark on Lord Southampton's estate at Highgate [*Catalogue of the R.I.B.A. Drawings Collection: B*, 60 and fig. 43]. In 1844 he exhibited a model of a pair of Italianate villas then being built to his designs in GLOUCESTER ROAD, REGENT'S PARK, probably to be identified as 'Gloucester Villas', dem. 1972. He disappears from the London directories between 1845 and 1850.

BASTARD, a family of architects and master builders based on Blandford in Dorset, and active in that county throughout the greater part of the eighteenth century. The founder of the firm was THOMAS BASTARD (d. 1720), a joiner by trade, who is described on his monument in Blandford Church as 'a man useful, and industrious in his generation...and eminent for his skill in Architecture'. Little is known about his architectural work, most of which must have perished in the fire which destroyed Blandford in 1731, but it is likely that he was responsible for the fine woodwork in the church at CHARLTON MARSHALL, nr. BLANDFORD, rebuilt by the rector, Dr. Charles Sloper, in 1713, and perhaps for SPETTISBURY RECTORY, rebuilt by the same Dr. Sloper in 1716. Thomas may also have supervised the reconstruction of the neighbouring churches of WINTERBORNE STICKLAND and ALMER, DORSET, about this time, but there is no documentary evidence to show that he was consulted.

After Thomas Bastard's death in 1720 his business was continued by his three sons, Thomas, John and William. Thomas died in 1731 and it was his younger brothers JOHN (*c.* 1688–1770) and WILLIAM (*c.* 1689–1766) whose partnership produced a number of handsome buildings mostly designed in a vernacular baroque style of considerable charm though of no great sophistication. A favourite motif that recurs often in their work is a capital with inturning volutes derived from Borromini. This had been used by Archer in the 1720s, and its reappearance in the work of the Bastards may well have been due to personal contact with Archer, who lived only twenty miles away at Hale, nr. Fordingbridge. As carvers and joiners the Bastards often employed rococo motifs, and a sketch-book in a private collection contains designs by them for furniture, chimney-pieces, picture-frames, etc., many of

96

which were copied from the first English rococo manual, Brunetti's *Sixty Different Sorts of Ornaments*, 1731.

It was the fire which destroyed Blandford in 1731 that gave the Bastard brothers the opportunity to leave their mark on this small country town. Their principal works were the TOWN HALL of 1734, which is Palladian in style, and the CHURCH of 1735–9, whose plan (with short transeptal projections) reflects the influence of some of the Fifty New Churches in London. The spire which the Bastard brothers designed was not executed, the existing wooden cupola being due to 'other hands', but the sumptuous Mayor's Seat and other woodwork remain to demonstrate the excellence of their joinery. The chancel was extended in 1896. Galleries, inserted in 1836–7, were removed in 1970. According to the inscription on their monument, John and William Bastard were also responsible for 'several other Publick & Private Edifices'. One of these must have been the GREYHOUND INN (1734–5), now a bank, which was their property, and the RED LION INN can confidently be attributed to them on stylistic grounds. A 'survey book' of John Bastard's now in the County Record Office shows that the two houses (forming a single architectural composition) at the junction of East Street and the Market Place were built by him and his brother, and that they themselves occupied the house on the east side of the entrance (No. 75 East Street). In 1760 John Bastard, as 'a considerable sharer in the general Calamity', erected the Doric Pump-house near the church 'in Remembrance of God's dreadful Visitation by Fire...And to prevent, by a timely supply of Water (With God's Blessing) the fatal Consequences of FIRE hereafter'.

Outside Blandford the firm is known to have executed carver's and joiner's work of high quality at HAZLEGROVE HOUSE, SOMERSET, for C. H. Mildmay in 1732 (illustrated in *C. Life*, 18 May 1929) [bill printed in *C. Life*, 18 Jan. 1930, 99], and at LULWORTH CASTLE, DORSET, much of the interior of which they redecorated and refurnished for Edward Weld *c.* 1740–58 [drawings and accounts in Dorset Record Office]. All their work at Lulworth was destroyed by fire in 1929, but some of it is illustrated in *C. Life*, 9 Jan. 1926, figs. 7 and 14. There is also documentary evidence that the Bastard brothers built, and probably designed, a house (now a School of Art) in MARKET STREET, POOLE, for Sir Peter Thompson, in 1746–9. A monument to John Dirdoe (d. 1724) at Gillingham Church, Dorset, is signed 'John Bastard & Co.'

The two Bastard brothers are commemorated by a monument in Blandford Church, and by a stone obelisk in the churchyard, which records their 'Skill in Architecture and Liberal Benefactions to this Town'. Their portraits hang in the

THE BASTARD FAMILY

THOMAS BASTARD = Bridget Creech
–1720

Thomas = Mary Horlock
of Blandford
c. 1686–1731

JOHN
of Blandford
c. 1688–1770

WILLIAM
of Blandford
c. 1689–1766

Samuel
a ship-modeller
of Gosport
=

BENJAMIN = Elizabeth
of Sherborne   Prankerd
c. 1698–1722

JOSEPH =
of Sherborne
St. John
d. 1783
→

Thomas
'the Younger'
of Blandford
and Charlton
Marshall,
1724–91
= Jane Morgan

Thomas
'the elder'
of Blandford
1720–71

Thomas = Rose Plucknett
of Sherborne
1730–72

JOHN = Sarah
of Marylebone
1722–78
→

97

Town Hall. Neither was married, and their partnership was continued by their nephews, Thomas Bastard 'the elder' (1720–71) and Thomas Bastard 'the younger' (1724–91), neither of whom appears to have been responsible for any architectural work of significance.

BENJAMIN BASTARD (c. 1698–1772), fifth son of Thomas Bastard (d. 1720), was apprenticed in 1712 to William Townesend, the Oxford master mason. He subsequently established himself as a mason at Sherborne in Dorset, where in 1745 he set up the dial on the south gable of the old headmaster's house, now part of the abbey church. Soon after 1720 he or another member of his family designed the large stone-built house in St. Swithin's Street, 'erected chiefly by Henry Seymour Portman', which is now the Digby School for Girls [Hutchins, History of Dorset iv, 1861, 282]. A monument in the cloisters of Wells Cathedral, erected in 1749 to the memory of Peter Davis, Recorder of Wells, and signed 'Benj. Bastard, Sherborne, Fecit', proves that he was also a monumental sculptor. In 1753–4 he refronted and refitted the old SHIRE HALL at DORCHESTER (rebuilt 1796–7), and supplied the furniture for the Grand Jury Room [Dorset County Records]. In 1765 the west tower of WEST COKER CHURCH, SOMERSET, was heightened under his direction [M. Nathan, Annals of W. Coker, 1957, 412]. When he died in 1772, he owned two inns and other property in Sherborne. He was buried at Castleton, where a tablet commemorates both him and his son Thomas, who died the same year, aged 42. In 1738 Benjamin Bastard took as an apprentice his nephew JOHN BASTARD (1722–1778), who established himself as a mason in London, and is known to have executed masonry at the DASHWOOD MAUSOLEUM at WEST WYCOMBE, BUCKS., 1764–5 [Bodleian Library, MS. D. D. Dashwood, B. 12/6/1], STONELEIGH ABBEY, WARWICKS., 1764 [W. A. Thorpe in Connoisseur, March 1947, 19], THE MIDDLESEX HOSPITAL [Hospital Records] and GREENWICH HOSPITAL [P.R.O., Adm. 68/876]. On his tomb in Tarrant Keynston churchyard he is described as 'late of the Parish of St. Mary le Bone ..., Mason and Architect'.

JOSEPH BASTARD (d. 1783), sixth and youngest son of Thomas Bastard (d. 1720), is described in Hutchins's History of Dorset as a 'builder and surveyor' of Basingstoke, Hants. In legal documents he is always referred to as of Sherborne St. John, a village a few miles from Basingstoke, where he died in 1783.

[H. M. Colvin, 'The Bastards of Blandford', Archaeological Jnl. civ, 1948; Arthur Oswald, Old Towns Revisited, 1952, 73–96; Arthur Oswald, Country Houses of Dorset, 1959, 30–8; John Adams, 'The Bastards of Blandford', Arch. Rev., June 1968, 445–50; R.C.H.M., Dorset iii (1), 16–40 (for Blandford); Apprenticeship Registers.]

BATEMAN. Several architects and surveyors of this name practised in Birmingham in the nineteenth century. A Joseph Bateman of Duddeston Street died on 24 June 1811.[1] His occupation is not known, but he may have been the father of Thomas and Joseph Bateman, who are described in Wrightson's New Triennial Directory for 1818 as 'architects, surveyors, auctioneers and appraisers', with an office in Duddeston Street. They must not be confused with their contemporary Thomas Joseph Bateman, building surveyor of Waterloo Street, who died on 4 July 1837. Thomas Bateman, 'surveyor of Yardley', died on 9 July 1829, aged 67, and if (as seems probable) this was the senior member of the firm already mentioned, it was presumably his surviving partner who designed two buildings at LEAMINGTON SPA, WARWICKS. which 'J. Bateman' exhibited at the Birmingham Society of Artists in 1834: the WARNEFORD HOSPITAL, 1832–4, and VITTORIA PLACE, 1834. In 1837–8 'Bateman and Drury' of Birmingham rebuilt the north side of CHILVERS COTON CHURCH, WARWICKS. [I.C.B.S.]. They also designed THE LEEK WORKHOUSE (MOORLANDS HOSPITAL), STAFFS., 1838 [North Staffs. Jnl. of Field Studies ii, 1962, 97], THE QUEEN'S HOSPITAL, BATH ROW, BIRMINGHAM, 1840 [Cornish's Guide to Birmingham, 1864, 80] and THE QUEEN'S COLLEGE, PARADISE STREET, BIRMINGHAM, 1843–4, Gothic [Cornish's Guide to Birmingham, 1864, 87].

By the 1850s the firm was represented by John Jones Bateman (d. 1903), whose son C. E. Bateman carried on the practice until the 1930s. For the last two see Bryan Little, Birmingham Buildings, Newton Abbot, 1971, 123.

BATLEY, WILLIAM (c. 1594–1674). A monument now built into the outside wall of the vestry of Wellingborough Church, Northants., commemorates William Batley, 'architect', who died in November 1674, aged 80 [J. G. Nichols, Literary Illustrations of the Eighteenth Century, v, 601]. In February 1654/5 a builder or surveyor called Batley made an estimate for alterations to SYDENHAM HOUSE, DEVON, for Edward Wise [Trans. Devonshire Assoc. xli, 1909, 144–5] (C. Life, 28 June 1956).

BATTLEY, JOHN, is said to have been 'of some local eminence in Leeds, where he erected the theatre and several considerable buildings in the town and neighbourhood'. His principal works were 'executed about 1770–80' [S. Redgrave, Dictionary of Artists of the English School, 1878, 32].

---

[1] The dates of death given in this entry are all derived from the index to the obituary notices in Aris's Birmingham Gazette at the Birmingham Reference Library.

BAUCHOP, TOBIAS, *see* BACHOP

BAUD, BENJAMIN (*c.* 1807–1875), was a pupil of Francis Goodwin. He entered the Royal Academy Schools in 1829 at the age of 22, and exhibited at the Academy from 1826 to 1851. From 1826 to 1840 he assisted Sir Jeffry Wyatville in the rebuilding of Windsor Castle, and in 1842, in conjunction with Michael Gandy (*q.v.*), he published *Architectural Illustrations of Windsor Castle*, with text by John Britton. His portrait forms the frontispiece to this work.

In 1835 Baud was one of the unsuccessful competitors for the new Houses of Parliament, but in 1838 he won the competition for the WEST LONDON CEMETERY at BROMPTON, and during the next few years designed the domed chapel, main entrance lodge and catacombs for the cemetery's proprietors. In 1844 he was dismissed by the company and appears thereafter to have been chiefly engaged in alterations and additions to private houses. After a slight stroke in his sixties he gave up practice and devoted himself to painting. He died at Richmond, Surrey, on 17 April 1875, aged 69 [obituary in *Builder* xxxiii, 1875, 402; J. S. Curl, *The Victorian Celebration of Death*, 1972, 115–129].

BAXTER, JOHN (–*c.* 1770), was an Edinburgh master mason of considerable repute. He enjoyed the confidence and patronage of Sir John Clerk of Penicuik (*q.v.*) through whose influence he was employed to build a number of large country houses in Scotland in the 1730s and '40s. He could draw as well as build, and understood the plain Palladian style favoured by his patron. His earliest recorded contracts were MAVISBANK HOUSE, MIDLOTHIAN, which he began to build for Clerk in 1723 'according to a design concocted between me [Clerk] and Mr. [William] Adams', and HADDO HOUSE, ABERDEENSHIRE, a house designed by William Adam for the 2nd Earl of Aberdeen under Clerk's direction and built by Baxter in 1732–5 [bills in Aberdeen University Library; Christopher Hussey in *C. Life*, 18–25 Aug. 1966]. In 1738–9 he was building a house for the Master of Ross, presumably HAWKHEAD PARK, RENFREWSHIRE [S.R.O., GD 18/5246/6/41], and in 1740 began GALLOWAY HOUSE, WIGTOWNSHIRE, for Lord Garlies, again with advice from Sir John Clerk. Designs for this house had already been submitted both by William Adam and by John Douglas, but although Douglas's drawings were apparently adopted in 1739, they were considerably altered by Baxter, who in August 1740 told Clerk that he had 'given my Lord Garlies a front of his house...and corrected his plans...taking out 24 windows' [S.R.O., GD 18/5011 and 5246/6: cf. RHP 3868]. In 1745–9 Baxter built ORMISTON HALL, EAST LOTHIAN (now a ruin) for George Cockburn

[S.R.O., Register of Deeds, 1751], and in 1756–9 was employed by Francis Charteris, 6th Earl of Wemyss, to build AMISFIELD HOUSE, EAST LOTHIAN (dem. *c.* 1928), to the design of Isaac Ware [see payments to 'John Baxter, Architect' in the building accounts cited by C. Hussey, *C. Life*, 15 July 1965, 184]. Meanwhile at PENICUIK HOUSE, MIDLOTHIAN, he had in 1753 carried out some alterations for Sir John Clerk's son, James Clerk, and after Sir John's death in 1755 the new baronet, himself an amateur architect, completely rebuilt the house (1761–9) with Baxter as executant architect and builder [Alistair Rowan in *C. Life*, 15–22 Aug. 1968].

In 1753 Baxter had built MAYSHADE HOUSE, nr. LOANHEAD, MIDLOTHIAN, for his own occupation [S.R.O., Edinburgh Sasines]. By 1769 he was in poor health and more or less retired, for on 25 Feb. his son John Baxter, junior (*q.v.*), wrote that his father had been so much indisposed that he 'has given up business to me, ever since my return from Italy' [S.R.O., GD 44/49/16]. The date of his death has not been ascertained, but it must have occurred in about 1770.

[Ann M. Simpson, 'The Architectural Work of the Baxter Family in Scotland 1722–98', Edinburgh University, unpublished thesis, 1971.]

BAXTER, JOHN (–1798), was the son and successor of John Baxter (*q.v.*). In 1761 his father sent him and his brother Alexander to Italy to study architecture. Here John 'became a figure of some standing' among the foreign artists resident in Rome. He competed for at least one architectural prize, and in March 1766 he was admitted a full member of St. Luke's Academy. In 1767, very shortly before his return to Scotland, he was joined by the painter Alexander Runciman, another protégé of Sir James Clerk, who was to decorate the ceiling of 'Ossian's Hall' at Penicuik on his return. In the Vatican there is a painting of the two Baxters, with Runciman and another artist (reputedly Fuseli), which must date from this year.[1] While in Rome Baxter had some chimney-pieces made to his designs by Italian sculptors, probably for Penicuik, but they were all 'broke in pieces in carriage for Scotland' [B.M. Print Room Sc. A. 5.9]. Back in Scotland, he almost immediately took over the family business from his ailing father, and continued to combine the functions of architect and contracting mason throughout his life. Like Robert Adam, Baxter undoubtedly acquired a more sophisticated style of draughtsmanship and design in Rome than he could ever have learned in Edinburgh. But lacking Adam's ambition and genius, he was responsible for no spectacular innovation in Scottish architecture.

---

[1] An oil sketch for this painting is in Mr. John Sparrow's collection.

Indeed, both his Town House at Peterhead and his Bellie Church at Fochabers (the centre-piece of a new town which he laid out for the Duke of Gordon) are surmounted by steeples of a traditional Scottish type derived ultimately from Gibbs, while his elegant Merchants' Hall in Hunter Square, Edinburgh, is a competent performance in the style of Adam himself.

The principal source of information about Baxter's architectural works is the catalogue of drawings and other works of art that were sold after his death:[2] it included a large collection of prints, numerous 'Old Master' drawings, some paintings by Alexander and John Runciman, and a quantity of busts, basso relievos, antique plaster figures, etc. There were also many architectural drawings by Baxter himself, including a set of designs for a 'sepulchral chapel' made in Rome. Among the Gordon Cumming papers in the National Library of Scotland there is a set of plans, signed 'John Baxter Architect 1778', for adding wings and a portico to an unidentified Scottish country house (in portfolio catalogued as 'Bound volumes No. 51'). In 1791 he submitted three designs for a new development near Edinburgh to be called 'Picardy Village', but they were not accepted [Book of the Old Edinburgh Club xxv, 29–30]. Baxter died at Edinburgh in July 1798. He left a son John who was in the service of the East India Company. [Ann M. Simpson, 'The Architectural Work of the Baxter Family in Scotland 1722–98', unpublished thesis, Edinburgh University, 1971; Ann & James Simpson, 'John Baxter, Architect, and the Patronage of the Fourth Duke of Gordon', Bulletin of the Scottish Georgian Soc. ii, 1973; D. Stillman, 'British Architects and Italian Architectural Competitions, 1758–1780', Jnl. of the Society of Architectural Historians (of America), xxxii, 1973, 56–7.]

COUNTRY HOUSES

HALLHEAD HOUSE or CASTLE, ABERDEENSHIRE, repairs or alterations for Sir Robert Gordon, Bart., before 1769, probably in connection with its use as a farm-house [S.R.O., GD 44/43/14: 'It was this young man who drew the plan and directed the work at Hallhead Castle'; cf. D. MacGibbon & T. Ross, The Castellated and Domestic Architecture of Scotland iv, 1892, fig. 870].

PENICUIK HOUSE, MIDLOTHIAN, minor alterations for Sir James Clerk, c. 1770–78, including remodelling of three central windows of rear elevation [Alistair Rowan in C. Life, 15 Aug. 1968].

MORTONHALL HOUSE, LIBERTON, MIDLOTHIAN, for

[2] The only known copy is in Edinburgh Public Library (Cowan bequest).

Thomas Trotter, c. 1769 ['plans and elevation of the house of Mortonhall' in Sale Catalogue] (J. Small, Castles and Mansions of the Lothians ii, 1883; R.C.A.M., City of Edinburgh, 1951, 236–7 and fig. 421).

GORDON CASTLE, MORAYSHIRE, remodelled for the 4th Duke of Gordon, 1769–82, castellated; dem. 1961 [S.R.O., drawings (RHP 1056–1071) and accounts (esp. GD 44/49/16) among Gordon papers; 'various designs for Gordon Castle . . . built by Mr. Baxter' in Sale Catalogue] (Neale, Seats, ser. i, vol. i). Baxter also designed some farm-houses on the estate, for which drawings by him survive (S.R.O., RHP).

GORDONSTOUN HOUSE, MORAYSHIRE, probably responsible for alterations (chiefly internal) for Sir Robert Gordon, Bart., 1772–6 ['plans and elevations of Gordonstoun House' in Sale Catalogue]. The date and authorship of the circular office-court have not yet been established.

EGLINTON CASTLE, AYRSHIRE, castellated gateway for the 11th Earl of Eglinton, 1780 [National Library of Scotland, MS. 580, No. 397 (f. 116)]. Baxter's sale included a set of unexecuted designs for rebuilding the Castle itself.

GARTMORE HOUSE, PERTHSHIRE, alterations for Robert Graham, 1779–80; remodelled 1901–2 [payments in account-book among Graham papers in S.R.O. (GD 22/1/468) and 'south and north elevation of Gartmore House' in Sale Catalogue] (Scottish Field, Nov. 1958).

ELLON CASTLE, ABERDEENSHIRE, alterations for the 3rd Earl of Aberdeen, 1781–7; largely dem. 1851 [drawings dated 1781 at N.M.R.S.; accounts at Haddo House, ex inf. Mrs. Simpson; 'Plans and Elevations of Ellon Castle' in Sale Catalogue].

DUNS CASTLE, BERWICKSHIRE, stables (1792–4), Gothic gateway (1791) and proposed alterations to house (1794) for Robert Hay, 1791–4 [N.M.R.S., photos. of drawings at Duns].

AVONTOUN HOUSE, WEST LOTHIAN, for Robert Blair, 1792–4; dem. c. 1970 [papers belonging to Miss Alice Maconochie; designs in Sale Catalogue].

BALMUTO HOUSE, FIFE, additions (dem. 1962) for Claud Boswell, 1797 [S.R.O., GD 66/1/275, account of mason work by John Baxter & Co.].

GLENFIDDICH LODGE, BANFFSHIRE, alterations for the 4th Duke of Gordon, 1798; subsequently rebuilt to designs by J. Plaw [S.R.O., Gordon papers, GD 44/32/10].

OTHER BUILDINGS

KENMORE BRIDGE, PERTHSHIRE, for the Commissioners for Annexed Estates, 1774 [S.R.O., E 732/18/1–2, GD 112/48 and RHP 971/1].

CALLANDER CHURCH, PERTHSHIRE, for the

Commissioners for Annexed Estates, 1771–3; dem. [S.R.O., E 732/18/2; E 777/169/11(2)].

GARTCHONZIE BRIDGE, over R. Teith nr. Callander, PERTHSHIRE, for the Commissioners for Annexed Estates, 1774 [S.R.O., E 732/18/1 and 21/1].

DALNACARDOCH INN, BLAIR ATHOLL, PERTHSHIRE, for the Commissioners for Annexed Estates, 1774 [S.R.O., E 732/18/2].

FOCHABERS NEW TOWN, MORAYSHIRE, for the 4th Duke of Gordon, 1775–90 [S.R.O., GD 44/32/10].

EDINBURGH, houses in GREENSIDE WELL (below Calton Hill), as a personal speculation, 1780–3 [S.R.O., Edinburgh Sasines].

EDINBURGH, TRON CHURCH, alterations 1785–7 for road-widening in connection with the South Bridge and Hunter Square. Baxter shortened the church by one bay to east and west and reduced the south aisle to a slight pedimented projection with detail carefully matched to the original [Edinburgh Town Council Minutes, 3 June 1788] (plan showing Baxter's alterations in G. Hay, *Architecture of Scottish Post-Reformation Churches*, 1957, fig. 15).

EDINBURGH, MERCHANTS' HALL, 3–4 HUNTER SQUARE, 1788. The ground floor was altered 1894 to form premises for the Royal Bank of Scotland [R.C.A.M., *City of Edinburgh*, 101–2, citing Minute Book of the Edinburgh Merchant Co.] (A. T. Bolton, *The Architecture of R. and J. Adam* ii, 1922, 250).

PETERHEAD, ABERDEENSHIRE, THE TOWN HOUSE (with steeple), 1788 [J. T. Findlay, *History of Peterhead*, Aberdeen 1933, 274].

FEARN ABBEY CHURCH, ROSS-SHIRE, monument to Admiral Sir John Lockhart Ross, c. 1792 [design in Sale Catalogue].

INVERESK CHURCHYARD, MIDLOTHIAN, monument to Sir Archibald Hope, 1794 [design in Sale Catalogue].

BELLIE CHURCH, FOCHABERS, MORAYSHIRE, for the 4th Duke of Gordon, 1795–7 [drawings in S.R.O., RHP 8531–4; accounts in S.R.O., GD 44/32/10; L. Shaw, *History of the Province of Moray*, ed. Gordon, i, 1882, 71] (G. Hay, *Architecture of Scottish Post-Reformation Churches*, 1957, fig. 28).

BAXTER, JOHN, usually referred to in contemporary documents as 'John Baxter, junior, Architect', was the son of John Baxter, a builder of Portobello, nr. Edinburgh. So far as is known they were not related to John Baxter of Edinburgh (d. 1798). The father built Nos. 1–8 BAXTER'S PLACE, a block of houses in Leith Walk, Edinburgh, below Calton Hill, on a site feued to him in 1800 [S.R.O., Edinburgh Sasines]. In 1809 the two Baxters were among the trustees for building Portobello Church (designed by W. Sibbald) [W. Baird, *Annals of Duddingston and*

Portobello, 1898, 321], and in 1813 the son was sufficiently highly esteemed to be one of the architects invited to judge the competition for laying out the Calton Grounds [S.R.O., GD 113/322; A. J. Youngson, *The Making of Classical Edinburgh*, 1966, 149]. He subsequently laid out and developed ROSEFIELD PLACE, ROSEFIELD AVENUE, EAST AND WEST BRIGHTON CRESCENT and 3–8 SANDYFORD GARDENS, PORTOBELLO, from 1823 onwards [S.R.O., Edinburgh Sasines]. [Information from Mr. David Walker.]

BEACHCROFT, SAMUEL (c. 1801–1861), entered the Royal Academy Schools in 1823 at the age of 22. He was a pupil of H. H. Seward, and exhibited at the Academy from 1818 to 1822. In 1825 he became District Surveyor for Chelsea. An inscription in MORTLAKE CHURCH, SURREY, records that the church was enlarged to his designs in 1840, but his work was destroyed when the nave was rebuilt in 1906. Beachcroft became a Fellow of the R.I.B.A. in 1835, retired in 1853, and died at Putney in 1861. C. BEACHCROFT, who entered the R.A. Schools in 1835, used Samuel Beachcroft's address when he exhibited at the Academy in 1833. He died in 1866.

BEARD, JOHN BARON, practised in Taunton. In 1833 he reconstructed the nave of ASHCOTT CHURCH, SOMERSET [I.C.B.S.]. He may have been the same as 'Mr. Beard of Somerton', who in 1813 provided the designs for GLASTONBURY TOWN HALL, built in 1818 [H. F. Scott-Stokes, *Annals of Glastonbury Corporation 1705–1834*, 1925, 17]. In 1821 the nave and chancel of NORTHOVER CHURCH, SOMERSET, were rebuilt under the direction of 'Mr. Beard' [*V.C.H. Somerset* iii, 230, n. 67]. Pigot's *Directory* shows that an architect called Joseph Beard was practising in Bath in 1830.

BEARE, R— S—, of Norwich, exhibited architectural designs at the Norwich Society of Artists in 1812–14. They included 'a Cottage for Samuel Parkinson, Esq.' (1812), a house for Mrs. Hook in Chapelfield, Norwich (1812), and a 'Design for a Theatre proposed to be erected at Lynn' (1813).

BEAZLEY, CHARLES (c. 1760–1829), was a pupil of Sir Robert Taylor. He is said to have deputized for the latter as surveyor to the Bank of England during the last seven years of his life, and succeeded him as steward of the Bank's estates when he died in 1788. For nearly fifty years Beazley was district surveyor to the parishes of St. James and St. John, Clerkenwell. As architect to the Goldsmiths' Company he made designs in 1804 for a new Hall, but they were not executed. He exhibited at the Royal Academy between 1787 and 1806. He died at West End, Hampstead, on 6 January 1829, aged

69 according to the *Gentleman's Magazine* (63 according to *A.P.S.D.*). Samuel Beazley, George Draper, George Maliphant, J. Medland, George New, William Rogers and W. F. Pocock were his pupils. Beazley's surviving works suggest that he was a competent but not particularly interesting exponent of the plain English neo-classical style of the early nineteenth century. [*A.P.S.D.*; *Gent's Mag.* 1829 (1), 92; Walpole, *Anecdotes of Painting* v, ed. F. W. Hilles & P. B. Daghlian, 1937, 199.]

FAVERSHAM CHURCH, KENT, Gothic tower and spire similar to that of St. Dunstan's in the East, London, 1799 [exhib. at R. A. 1799].

MAIDSTONE, KENT, triumphal arch in honour of King George III, 1799 [engraving in B.M., *King's Maps* xvii, 2.2, c].

OSPRINGE PLACE, nr. FAVERSHAM, KENT, for Isaac Rutten, *c.* 1799 [exhib. at R.A. 1799].

SHERNFOLD PARK, nr. FRANT, SUSSEX, a pavilion for C. E. Pigou, 1799 [exhib. at R.A. 1799].

HOLLINGBOURNE HOUSE, KENT, for B. D. Duppa, 1799–1800 [exhib. at R.A. 1799 and 1801].

TODDINGTON HOUSE, GLOS., repaired south wing for Charles Hanbury Tracy, later Lord Sudeley, after a fire in 1800 [*A.P.S.D.*].

CRANFORD PARK, MIDDLESEX, bridge for the 5th Earl of Berkeley [original drawings in B.M., *King's Maps* xxix, 8; exhib. at R.A. 1806].

THE GOLDSMITHS' ALMSHOUSES, ACTON, MIDDLESEX, 1811 [*A.P.S.D.*].

Note: The statement in *A.P.S.D.* that Beazley and George Smith jointly designed the Jewin Street Presbyterian Chapel for Dr. A. Rees in 1808 appears to be incorrect (see Aikin, William), but they may have designed a Wesleyan Methodist Chapel that stood in the same street and was demolished in 1878. For the possibility that Beazley designed the Presbyterian Chapel in Little Chapel Street, Soho, 1822–4, dem. 1894, see *Survey of London* xxxiii, 295.

BEAZLEY, SAMUEL (1786–1851), was the son of the army accoutrement maker of Westminster, and received his architectural training in the office of his uncle, Charles Beazley. He served as a volunteer in the Peninsular War, and, among other exploits, claimed to have rescued the Duchesse d'Angloulême from the Napoleonic forces in Bordeaux in 1815. For the remainder of his life he combined the professions of architect and playwright. As a schoolboy he had distinguished himself by writing a comedy and then constructing the stage upon which he and his friends performed it, and in later life he continued both to write plays and to design their architectural setting. He was the author of over a hundred operas, farces and other dramatic performances of a similar character, many of which he staged himself. He also published two novels,

102

The Roué, 1828, and *The Oxonian*, 1840. He was well-known for his lively and witty conversation, and lived a fashionable life at his London house in Soho Square.

Beazley was the leading specialist of his day in the design of theatres, of which he built a considerable number in London and elsewhere. Towards the end of his life he became architect to the South-Eastern Railway Company, for which he designed the stations on the North Kent Railway, the Lord Warden Hotel at Dover, and a new town at Ashford for the employees in the locomotive works. Stylistically, he was an eclectic designer in a variety of styles, from 'Grecian' to 'Norman', from neo-classical to 'Louis Quatorze'. His writings included a paper on 'The Rise and Progress of Gothic Architecture', in the *Essays of the London Architectural Society*, 1808, and a small book entitled *A General View of the System of enclosing Waste Lands; with particular reference to the proposed Enclosure at Epsom in Surrey*, 1812. He exhibited frequently at the Royal Academy. F. R. Beeston was a pupil. Beazley died suddenly on 12 October 1851 at his country house, Tonbridge Castle, Kent, aged 65. [*A.P.S.D.*; *D.N.B.*; obituary in *Builder* ix, 1851, 694; Dudley Harbron, 'Samuel Beazley', *Arch. Rev.* lxxix, 1936, 131; *Gent's Mag.* 1851, 559, 1852, 2.]

THEATRES

LONDON, THE ROYAL LYCEUM THEATRE, 1816 [Britton & Pugin, *Public Buildings of London* i, 1825, 273–8]; this was destroyed by fire in 1830, and rebuilt by Beazley, 1831–4 [*Builder* v, 489, 507; *R.I.B.A. Jnl.*, 3rd ser., i, 1894, 655]; the theatre was subsequently redecorated in an Italianate style, and in 1902 it was reconstructed, with the exception of the portico.

BIRMINGHAM, THE THEATRE ROYAL, NEW STREET, was rebuilt under his direction between 6 Jan. 1820, when the former building was destroyed by fire, and 14 Aug. of the same year: the façade of 1780, by Samuel Wyatt (*q.v.*), was, however, preserved; dem. 1902 [*A.P.S.D.*].

DUBLIN, THE THEATRE ROYAL, HAWKINS STREET, 1821; destroyed by fire 1880 [G. N. Wright, *Historical Guide to Dublin*, 1821, 271].

LEAMINGTON SPA, WARWICKS., THE COUNTY LIBRARY AND READING ROOMS, ETC., BATH STREET, for Mr. Elliston, 1820–1 [Moncrieff's *Guide to Leamington Spa*, 1833, 51].

LEAMINGTON SPA, WARWICKS., THE ROYAL ASSEMBLY ROOMS, BATH STREET, *c.* 1820 [Moncrieff's *Guide to Leamington Spa*, 1833, 57].

LONDON, THE DRURY LANE THEATRE, remodelled interior, 1822; he also added the colonnade in Little Russell Street, 1831 [Britton & Pugin, *Public Buildings of London* i, 1825, 247; *Survey of London* xxxv, 64–5].

LONDON, THE ROYAL SOHO (afterwards ROYALTY) THEATRE, DEAN STREET, for Miss Fanny Kelly, 1834–7; rebuilt 1882; dem. 1954 [*Survey of London* xxxiii, 215–17].

LEICESTER, THE THEATRE, 1836; dem. 1958 [*Architectural Mag.* iii, 1836, 584, correcting a statement on p. 482 that it was designed by William Parsons] (R. Leacroft, 'The Theatre Royal, Leicester', *Trans. Leics. Arch. Soc.* xxxiv, 1958).

LONDON, THE ST. JAMES'S THEATRE, KING STREET, for John Braham, 1835; dem. 1957–8 [*A.P.S.D.*].

LONDON, THE CITY OF LONDON THEATRE, NORTON FOLGATE, BISHOPSGATE, 1837; dem. [*A.P.S.D.*].

LONDON, THE ADELPHI THEATRE, STRAND, rebuilt the façade, 1841; the theatre was rebuilt by T. H. Wyatt in 1858; dem. [*A.P.S.D.*].

Beazley also made the designs for theatres erected in Belgium, South America and India. His unexecuted designs for The Casino in Leicester Square, London, are illustrated in *Survey of London* xxxiv, pl. 33.

OTHER WORKS

CASTLE BERNARD, CO. OFFALY, IRELAND, designs for park entrance and school for Thomas Bernard, M.P., 1811 [exhib. at R.A.].

EAST DENE, BONCHURCH, ISLE OF WIGHT, for — Surman, *c.* 1825, 'Elizabethan' style [W. B. Cooke, *Bonchurch, Shanklin and the Undercliff*, 1849, 29].

BOGNOR, SUSSEX, THE CLARENCE HOTEL and 'NEW CRESCENT', *c.* 1830 [*The Bognor Guide*, Petworth, 1838].

LEYS CASTLE, INVERNESS-SHIRE, for Col. John Baillie, M.P., 1833, Norman style [exhib. at R.A. 1833].

STUDLEY CASTLE, WARWICKS., for Sir Francis L. Holyoake Goodricke, Bart., 1834, Norman style [exhib. R.A. 1835].

BRETBY PARK, DERBYSHIRE, design for a boudoir for the Countess of Chesterfield, exhibited at R.A. 1838, now in R.I.B.A. Drawings Coll.

CAHIR CASTLE, CO. TIPPERARY, IRELAND, alterations for the 2nd Earl of Glengall, *c.* 1838–40 [exhib. at R.A. 1838].

LONDON, D'OYLEY'S WAREHOUSE, 346 STRAND, 1838 [exhib. at R.A. 1838].

BEDFORD, proposed improvements to BARHAM ESTATE, exhibited at R.A. 1840.

LONDON, THE AMICABLE LIFE ASSURANCE OFFICE, 50 FLEET STREET, 1843; dem. 1911 [exhib. at R.A. 1843; cf. *N. and Q.*, 11th ser., vi, 67].

LONDON, THE PARTHENON CLUB'S LIBRARY, 16 REGENT STREET, 1844 [exhib. at R.A. 1844].[1]

DOVER, improvements on CASTLE HILL, 1847 [exhib. at R.A. 1847].

DOVER, THE PILOT HOUSE, 1848; dem. [*Builder* vi, 1848, 414, with illustration].

DOVER, THE LORD WARDEN HOTEL, 1848–53 [*Civil Engineer* xiv, 519; exhib. at R.A. 1846].

BEECH HILL HOUSE, HIGH BEECH, ESSEX, for Richard Arabin, *c.* 1848 [*A.P.S.D.*].

HILLERSDON HOUSE, CULLOMPTON, DEVON, for W. C. Grant, 1848–9 [exhib. at R.A. 1848].

THEDDINGWORTH, LEICS., cottages for the 4th Earl Spencer, 1851 [*Associated Architectural Societies' Reports and Papers*, 1850–1, 32].

ASHFORD, KENT, housing estate for South-Eastern Railway Co., 1851 [*A.P.S.D.*].

BONN, GERMANY, addition to UNIVERSITY BUILDINGS [*A.P.S.D.*].

RAILWAY STATIONS for the South-Eastern Railway Co., including part of the terminus at LONDON BRIDGE, 1850–1; dem. 1969 [*A.P.S.D.*].

BEDFORD, FRANCIS OCTAVIUS (1784–1858), was perhaps related to Francis Bedford, who was employed by Sir John Soane as a clerk from 1797 to 1798. He may have been a pupil of William Porden, of whose will he was an executor. In 1811–13 he and J. P. Gandy were engaged by the Society of Dilettanti to accompany Sir William Gell as architectural draughtsmen on an expedition to Greece and Asia Minor. Their discoveries were published in 1817 as *The Unedited Antiquities of Attica*, and in 1840 as the third volume of the *Antiquities of Ionia* [*Historical Notices of the Society of Dilettanti*, 1855, 46–52]. The publication of a further volume was delayed by the death of William Wilkins, and the plates which had been engraved for this purpose were forgotten until 1912, when their rediscovery led to the publication of part v of the *Antiquities of Ionia* under the editorship of W. R. Lethaby (see *Catalogue of the R.I.B.A. Drawings Collection: B*, 63).

Bedford's recorded architectural works are almost all churches designed for the Parliamentary Commissioners. Four of them were scholarly Greek Revival versions of the St. Martin's-in-the-Fields formula, with effectively composed steeples rising above a Doric or Corinthian portico. The rest are Gothic and characteristic of the pre-ecclesiological period in which they were built.

Bedford exhibited occasionally at the Royal Academy from 1814 onwards. In the 1820s he was living in Camberwell, where he designed some houses in NORTH TERRACE, PECKHAM ROAD, for a Mr. Spence [Church Building Commis-

---

[1] This appears in the R.A. Catalogue as 'The Pantheon Library, erected in Regent Street', but Mr. John

Harris informs me that the original drawing is inscribed 'The Parthenon Club House Library'. The Parthenon Club's premises were John Nash's former house at 16 Regent Street.

sioners, Surveyor's Reports I, 30, *ex inf.* Mr. M. H. Port], but towards the end of his life he moved to Crayland House, nr. Greenhithe, Kent, where he died on 13 March 1858. Many of the drawings which he made in Greece are in the R.I.B.A. Drawings Collection. He was presumably the father of F. Bedford, junior, who exhibited architectural drawings at the Royal Academy from 1833 to 1849.

LONDON, ST. GEORGE, WELLS STREET, CAMBERWELL, 1822–4 [Port, 134].

LONDON, ST. JOHN, WATERLOO ROAD, LAMBETH, 1823–4; damaged by bombing 1940–1 [Port, 134] (*Survey of London* xxiii, 32–6).

LONDON, HOLY TRINITY, NEWINGTON, 1823–4; converted into Henry Wood Concert Hall 1973–5 [Port, 136] (*Survey of London* xxv, 109–12).

LONDON, ST. LUKE, WEST NORWOOD, 1823–5; altered by G. E. Street 1870–9 [Port, 134] (*Survey of London* xxvi, 173–4).

LONDON, ST. MARY THE LESS, LAMBETH, 1827–8; dem. 1967, Gothic [Port, 154] (*Survey of London* xxiii, 144).

NEWCASTLE-UNDER-LYME, STAFFS., ST. GEORGE, 1827–8, Gothic [Port, 160].

LONDON, HOLY TRINITY, LITTLE QUEEN STREET, HOLBORN, 1829–31, Gothic; dem. 1910 [Port, 152].

RIDDINGS, DERBYSHIRE, ST. JAMES, 1830–1, Gothic [Port, 142].

HORWICH, LANCS., HOLY TRINITY, 1830–1, Gothic [Port, 148].

TUNSTALL, STAFFS., CHRIST CHURCH, 1830–1; chancel, etc., added 1885; Gothic [Port, 160].

BEDFORD, J—, of Acton Green, exhibited three drawings (designs for 'a nobleman's seat', 'a country seat', and 'a villa') at the Royal Academy in 1793. In Sir John Soane's Museum there is a volume (AL 5D) of elegantly drawn designs for houses which is probably by the same person. Included in the volume are designs for a hospital at Marylebone signed 'J. Bedford' and dated 1793.

BEGG, JAMES, is known only as the builder and probable designer of Nos. 1–6 GAYFIELD PLACE and 33 GAYFIELD SQUARE, EDINBURGH, 1791 [S.R.O., Edinburgh Sasines, vol. 433, p. 158]. An otherwise unknown architect called William Begg signs some architectural designs in private possession in Edinburgh. They are dated in the 1820s.

BELK, E—, exhibited architectural drawings at the Society of Artists and the Free Society of Artists between 1762 and 1768, and at the Royal Academy between 1772 and 1786. They included an 'Elevation of a tomb for an officer' (1773), an 'Elevation of the principal front designed for the

townhall at Bath' (1776) and an 'Elevation of a small villa, designed for a gentleman in Flanders' (1786).

BELL, HENRY (1647–1711), was the son of Henry Bell, a prosperous merchant of King's Lynn in Norfolk. After attending the local Grammar School, Bell went to Caius College, Cambridge, where he took his B.A. degree in 1665. A period of foreign travel followed, in the course of which he visited 'most of the politer parts of Europe'. In 1686, on his father's death, Bell inherited his property in Lynn, and continued his business as a producer and exporter of linseed oil and other commodities. In 1690 he became an alderman, and in 1692 and 1703 served as mayor. In 1702 he thought of standing for Parliament as M.P. for King's Lynn, but was induced to withdraw in favour of Robert Walpole. Bell died on 11 April 1711, aged 64, leaving an ample endowment of land and property to his wife and family. On his monument, formerly in St. Margaret's Church, he was described as *vir ingenii admodum capacis, variis artibus, Picturâ praesertim et Architecturâ instructissimus.* This is borne out by his will (P.C.C. 99 YOUNG), in which he mentions paintings by Holbein, Rembrandt, Heemskerk senior and junior, Goltzius and others, books on painting, sculpture, architecture, mathematics, perspective and surveying, and copper plates, engravings, prints and maps. A small number of engravings signed by Bell are preserved in the British Museum and the Bodleian Library (Gough Maps 24 and 44 and MS. Gough Norfolk 21). They are all topographical in character and portray scenes and buildings in King's Lynn. At the time of his death his manuscript which was published posthumously in 1728 as *An Historical Essay on the Original of Painting,* 'by Henry Bell, Architect, late of Lynn-Regis, Norfolk, Esq.' To it is prefixed a brief memoir which is one of the principal authorities for his life.

Like his neighbour, Sir Roger Pratt, Bell was an educated gentleman who took up architecture as a serious pastime, and who had had the benefit of a Grand Tour. According to the author of his memoir his travels 'conduced very much to his Improvement in that particular Science'. 'The Town of Northampton' – he continues – 'which was Rebuilt agreeable to his Plan, and pursuant to his own Direction, is a Testimony sufficient to evince his Masterly Hand in that Noble Science to succeeding Ages. The Place of his Nativity may likewise furnish us with Buildings sufficient to demonstrate the skill of the deceased Architect.'

Further evidence of Bell's responsibility for the rebuilding of Northampton after the fire of September 1675 comes from an entry in Robert Hooke's diary which records his meeting in

August 1676 'one Bell from Mr. Francis Morgan, an ingenious architect, ... a witt', for Francis Morgan was one of the commissioners for rebuilding Northampton, and the purpose of the meeting was no doubt for Hook to pass on some of his experience in the reconstruction of London after the Great Fire of 1666. The minutes of the commissioners are lost, but a document in the Northamptonshire Record Office (formerly Phillipps MS. 12165) records a meeting on 18 January 1676/7 at which it was 'Order'd and Agreed that Mr. Henry Bell and Mr. Edward Edwards, two experienc'd Surveyors now residing in the said Town of Northampton', should be employed as 'managers' for the rebuilding of ALL SAINTS CHURCH, NORTHAMPTON (1677–80). The portico was added in 1701 (presumably to Bell's own designs), and the statue of Charles II in 1711–12. Bell may also have been concerned in the design of the adjoining SESSIONS HOUSE, 1676–88,[1] and it is likely that he was responsible at least for the façades of some of the rebuilt houses (*e.g.* one that survives on the south side of the Market Place).

Bell's other documented works are all in KING'S LYNN. They comprise the CUSTOMS HOUSE, built in 1683 as an Exchange at the expense of Sir John Turner, for which Bell's responsibility is established by an engraving in which he gave his name as architect; the MARKET CROSS, 1707–10, dem. 1831, an elaborate domed structure inscribed 'HENRICO BELL ARCHITECTO'; and the altarpieces of ST. MARGARET'S and ST. NICHOLAS'S CHURCHES, set up in 1684 and 1704 respectively, but both since destroyed [Bodleian, MS. Gough Norfolk 21, f. 101]. To these may probably be added THE DUKE'S HEAD INN built by Sir John Turner *c.* 1684; the house of his brother Charles Turner (d. 1711) in the Market Place, destroyed by fire 1768; the conversion of ST. JAMES'S CHAPEL into a Hospital or Children's Home, 1682–3; and NORTH RUNCTON CHURCH, NORFOLK, for whose rebuilding in 1703–13 Bell was one of the trustees. Bell's responsibility for the last building is confirmed by a notebook of the Rev. Thomas Kerrich, an eighteenth-century antiquary who was a native of Norfolk. In a notebook in the Northamptonshire Record Office he lists Bell's works as 'The Market Cross & Shambles, the Custom House, Mr. Baggs's House, Mr. Mayor's House, [and] some other Houses' at King's Lynn, and 'the Church of North Runcton'. Only stylistic evidence suggests that Bell may perhaps have been concerned in the design of EUSTON CHURCH, SUFFOLK, 1676, the interior of the courtyard at KIMBOLTON CASTLE, HUNTS., *c.* 1685 (?), and STANHOE HALL, NORFOLK, built in 1703 by

Thomas Archdale, a relation by marriage of the Turners of King's Lynn.

As an architect neither of the Court (like Wren and May), nor of the landed gentry (like Winde and Pratt), but of the mercantile community from which he sprang, Bell has a distinctive place in English architectural history. His style was a vigorous reflection of that of the capital, perhaps with some direct influence from Holland. Jarman's Royal Exchange appears to have been the prototype of his Customs House (designed as an Exchange), Wren's St. Mary-at-Hill of the Greek Cross plans of All Saints, Northampton, and North Runcton Church.

[E. M. Beloe, *King's Lynn: Our Borough, Our Churches*, 1899; H. L. Bradfer-Lawrence, 'The Merchants of Lynn', in *A Supplement to Blomefield's Norfolk*, ed. C. Ingleby, 1929, 156–60; E. B. Chancellor, *Lives of the British Architects*, 1909, 159–62; G. F. Webb, 'Henry Bell of King's Lynn', *Burlington Magazine* xlvii, July 1925, 24–33; J. F. Howes, 'Bell of Lynn: a Contemporary of Sir C. Wren', *R.I.B.A. Jnl.*, 3rd ser., xxxv, 13 April 1929; H. M. Colvin and L. M. Wodehouse, 'Henry Bell of King's Lynn', *Architectural History* iv, 1961; Martin Archdale, 'Henry Bell as a Country House Architect', *C. Life* 15, 29 Sept. 1966.]

BELL, HENRY (1767–1830), best known as the pioneer of steam navigation, was for some years an architect and builder in Glasgow. He was the son of a millwright living at Torphichen Mill, nr. Linlithgow, and was apprenticed to his father. Subsequently he became a pupil of an engineer called Inglis, and then went to London to work for Rennie. In 1790 he settled in Glasgow, and in the following year entered into partnership with James Paterson to form the firm of Bell and Paterson, builders. This lasted until about 1800, when Bell turned his attention to the problems of steam navigation. The only building known to have been designed by him is CARLUKE CHURCH, LANARKS., for which the designs of Henry Bell, 'Architect in Glasgow', were adopted by the Heritors in 1799 [S.R.O., HR 179/1]. [D.N.B.; Edward Morris, *The Life of Henry Bell*, 1844.]

BELL, JOHN (–c. 1785), was a builder and architect of Durham. In his *Plans, Elevations and Sections of Noblemen and Gentlemen's Houses* (2nd ed. 1783), James Paine states that Axwell Park, Durham, 'and several other of my designs were carried into execution by Mr. John Bell'. In the 1760s Bell was employed at ALNWICK CASTLE, NORTHUMBERLAND, under Paine's direction [Alnwick MSS. 94, f. 31 and 187A, vol. ii], and in the Yorkshire Archaeological Society's Library (MS. 349) there are sketches of Wressell Castle, Yorkshire, 'by Mr. Bell the architect imploy'd in restoring Alnwick Castle 1765'. He was alive in

---

[1] See, however, pages 284 and 214 for payments to Edwards and C. G. Cibber in connection with the Sessions House.

1783, but is referred to as 'the late Mr. Bell of Durham' in W. Hutchinson's *History of Durham* ii, 1787, 65. He must be distinguished from John Bell of Gateshead, Co. Durham, land-surveyor and antiquary (1783–1864).

BELL, SAMUEL (1739–1813), was the son of John Bell, a wright of Dundee, where he was born on 6 May 1739. He followed his father's trade, but also practised as an architect, and designed most of Dundee's public buildings between 1770 and his death on 23 January 1813 [New Register House, Edinburgh, Dundee Register; *Scots. Mag.* lxxv, 1813, 238]. Though 'provincial and not very up-to-date', he provided Dundee with some attractive buildings in a late Georgian style of basically Palladian character with some Adamsian trimmings [David Walker, *Architects and Architecture in Dundee 1770–1914*, Abertay Historical Society's Publication No. 3, 1955, 4–6].

DUNDEE

ST. ANDREW'S CHURCH, 1772–4 [Town Council Minutes 10 Feb. 1772, *ex inf.* Mr. David Walker].
THE TRADES' HALL, 1776–8; dem. [J. Maclaren, *History of Dundee*, 1874; 184].
THE ENGLISH EPISCOPAL CHAPEL (later UNION HALL), HIGH STREET, 1783–4; dem. 1876 [A. C. Lamb, *Dundee, its Quaint and Historic Buildings*, Dundee 1895, pl. xiii].
ST. CLEMENT'S CHURCH, 1786–8, Gothic; damaged by fire 1841 [Town Council Minutes 15 Jan. 1787, *ex inf.* Mr. David Walker].
attributed: THE SAILORS' HALL or TRINITY HOUSE, YEAMAN SHORE, 1790; dem. 1888 [stylistic attribution, see illustration in *Dundee Delineated*, Dundee 1822, 123].
THE THEATRE ROYAL (now offices), CASTLE STREET, 1807–9 [F. Boyd, *Records of the Dundee Stage*, Dundee 1886, 14].

FORFAR OLD KIRK: Bell was closely involved in the building of this church in 1788–91. In Jan. 1788 John Gibson, 'architect of St. Cyrus', was invited to design a church, but in March a plan submitted by James Millar, mason of Bridgeton, was approved, 'and recommended to Mr. Samuel Bell Architect in Dundee to make out the dimensions of every part of the work'. In 1790 Bell was invited to inspect the old steeple and to receive instructions for a new one. Nothing, however, was done until 1813, when the Town Council 'advertised for contractors for the new steeple to be built to the plans of the late Samuel Bell'. Although the existing steeple built in 1813–14 bears the name of 'Patrick Brown Architect', the design is identical with one of Bell's drawings for the steeple of Monifieth Church, and Brown must only

have been the executant [S.R.O., HR 415/3; D. T. Adam, *Review of the Administration of the Town's Affairs by successive Town Councils between 1660 and 1965*, Forfar 1967, 29–30; S.R.O., RHP 7929–32, tracings of drawings of the church made by Bell in 1795].
TANNADICE MANSE, ANGUS, 1797–8 [S.R.O., HR 465/1].
KINNETTLES CHURCH, ANGUS, 1811–12 [advt. in *Dundee Advertiser*, 28 June 1811, *ex inf.* Mr. David Walker].
MONIFIETH CHURCH, ANGUS, 1812, Gothic [drawings in S.R.O., GD 45/25/29].

BELL, THOMAS, was a Lincolnshire builder. The tower of WELTON-BY-LINCOLN CHURCH, LINCS., bears the date 1768 and the name 'Thomas Bell Builder', while the tower of BASSINGHAM CHURCH, LINCS., is inscribed 'Thomas Bell, Architect, 1783'.

BELL, WILLIAM, designed the classical JUNCTION ROAD CHURCH at LEITH in 1824–5 [*Junction Road U.P. Church*, by one of the Elders, 1896, 13]. In 1826 he submitted a design for St. Andrew's Place U.P. Church, Leith [*St. Andrew's Place United Presbyterian Church, Leith*, 1888, 38].

BELLAS, or BELLHOUSE, HENRY (– 1777), a master carpenter of Appleby in Westmorland, probably designed, and certainly supervised the building of, HILLBECK HALL, nr. BROUGH, WESTMORLAND, for John Metcalfe, 1775–7 [accounts, etc., in Cumbria Record Office, D. Lons. C 13/1]. The fenestration is in a Gothic manner derived from Batty Langley, and in the main street of Appleby there is a house with virtually identical features which may therefore be attributed to Bellas. The Carlisle Probate records show that Henry Bellas died intestate at Appleby in 1777.

BELWOOD, WILLIAM (–1790), was an architect and surveyor of York. In 1753 he was apprenticed to John Robinson of York, carpenter, and in 1761 took up his freedom as William Belwood, 'joiner' [P.R.O. Apprenticeship Register; R. Davies, *The Freeman's Roll*, York 1835, 5]. From about 1760 onwards he supervised the building of HAREWOOD HOUSE, YORKS., to the designs of John Carr and Robert Adam. In 1774 he established himself in Lendal, York, and announced that 'having conducted several capital buildings under the great masters in architecture, Robert and James Adam, Esquires', he 'purposes making designs for buildings from the plainest to the most elegant . . . also designs temples and ornamental buildings, greenhouses, bridges, &c. with estimates' [*York Courant*, 18 Aug. 1774, 30 May and 9 June 1775;

Leeds Mercury, 11 July 1775]. Belwood's competence as a designer in the Adam manner is demonstrated by his designs for the stables at NEWBY HALL, YORKS. (W.R.), now among the Pennington-Ramsden papers in the Cumbria Record Office at Carlisle. Although these elegant stables have in the past been attributed to R. and J. Adam, there is in fact no evidence that they designed them, and from the drawings at Carlisle it appears that in about 1780 alternative designs were submitted to William Weddell by John Carr and William Belwood. Belwood's designs were accepted, and the existing stables correspond in every significant particular to his signed drawings. In 1782 Belwood made designs for alterations to NEWBY (now BALDERSBY) PARK, YORKS. (N.R.), for Thomas, 2nd Lord Grantham, that are preserved at Newby Hall, Yorks. (W.R.), and among Lady Lucas's papers in the Bedfordshire Record Office there are some 'Memorandums [about alterations to Newby Park] left with Wm. Belwood & Redgrave 1786' [L 26/1489].

In 1779 Belwood estimated the cost of rebuilding BURTON LEONARD CHURCH, YORKS. (W.R.), as £1038 17s. 4d. [*Yorks. Arch. Jnl.* xvii, 59–60] and in 1786 the 'cross aisle' of the church of ST. MICHAEL LE BELFRY, YORK, was repaired under his direction [*Associated Architectural Societies' Reports and Papers* xxxvii, 113]. In 1778 he made drawings, now at the Borthwick Institute, York [PR.Y/ASP. F.17, 7–8] for rebuilding the east end of the church of ALL SAINTS, PAVEMENT, YORK, and was probably responsible for the similar design adopted when the east end was curtailed in 1782 in order to widen the street [*ex inf.* Mr. K. S. Mills].

Belwood died at York on 21 May 1790 [*Gent's Mag.* 1790 (i), 482].

BENETT, JOHN (1773–1852), a Wiltshire country gentleman, is stated by Sir Richard Colt Hoare to have rebuilt his family seat, PYTHOUSE, nr. TISBURY, WILTS., in 1805 'from his own designs', and also to have erected in the grounds 'an elegant little chapel, copied from the style of a part of Canterbury Cathedral' [R. Colt Hoare, *Modern Wiltshire: Dunworth Hundred*, 1829, 131]. According to some contemporary MS. notes on the 'District round Shaftesbury', 'Mr. Benett... arranged his own plans and supervised the execution of them from the beginning to the completion, rising at 5 o'clock every morning for that purpose'. The house is a handsome building in the Palladian tradition with an Ionic portico. The Gothic chapel is now in ruins. Colt Hoare states that the top stage of the central tower of TISBURY CHURCH, WILTS., was designed by Benett's father Thomas (d. 1797), so two generations of the family would appear to have been amateur architects. An estimate 'of the mason's work to execute the plan of the new Tower for

Tisbury Church' is preserved among the Benett papers in the Wiltshire Record Office (413/474).

BENHAM, SAMUEL HENRY, was practising in Oxford in 1823, when he enlarged WESTON-ON-THE-GREEN VICARAGE, OXON. [*V.C.H. Oxon.* vi, 347], but by 1833 he was established in Brighton [*The Watering Places of Great Britain and Fashionable Directory*, Joseph Robins, London, 1833]. He altered NEW SHOREHAM CHURCH, SUSSEX, *c.* 1829 [I.C.B.S.], and designed THE CLOCK TOWER, SOUTH STREET, WORTHING, SUSSEX, 1834 [*Architectural Mag.* i, 1834, 245]. He competed for the Houses of Parliament in 1835, submitting a design in the 'collegiate style of the 14th., 15th. and 16th. centuries', as seen at 'Christ Church, Magdalen [and] New College, Oxford'. His unexecuted design for remodelling the New Buildings at Magdalen College, Oxford, in the Grecian style, is preserved in the College Library.

BENHAM, THOMAS, of Southampton, designed the churches of SHEDFIELD, HANTS., 1829, rebuilt by J. Colson 1875-80, and COPYTHORNE, or NORTH ELING, HANTS., 1834, altered and enlarged by Butterfield in 1891–2 [I.C.B.S.].

BENNISON, APPLETON (*c.* 1750–1830), was an architect and builder of Hull, where he died on 29 March 1830, aged 80 [*Gent's Mag.* 1830 (i), 381]. From 1792 to 1810 he was engaged in carrying out works at BRIDLINGTON HARBOUR, and in 1804–5 he rebuilt the bridge over the R. Hull at TICKTON, YORKS. (E.R.), to the designs of William Chapman [*ex inf.* Prof. A. W. Skempton]. In 1801 he advertised in the *Hull Advertiser:* 'Plans and Elevations drawn at shortest notice; Marble Chimney Pieces and Monuments executed in the neatest manner'. In 1800 he contracted to build the REGISTER OFFICE at BEVERLEY, and in 1804–14 he erected the COURT HOUSE and GAOL there to the designs of William Watson [G. Poulson, *Beverlac* i, 1829, 426]. In 1815 he made designs for rebuilding the RECTORY at ROUTH, YORKS. (E.R.) [Borthwick Institute, York. MGA 1815/4]. He refitted the interior of SKIRLAUGH CHURCH, YORKS. (E.R.), in 1819, and designed a Dissenting chapel at COTTINGHAM, YORKS. (E.R.), in the same year [*Hull Advertiser*, 6 Aug., 1 Oct. 1819]. A house at the corner of Albion Street and York Street, Hull, 'recently built by Appleton Bennison Archt. deceased', was advertised in the journal *Rockingham*, 28 Feb. 1834 [information from Mr. A. G. Chamberlain]. When the chancel of NORTHALLERTON CHURCH, YORKS. (N.R.), was rebuilt in 1884, a bottle was found containing a slip of parchment recording the fact that the previous chancel had been built in 1778 to the designs of 'Stephen Bennison, Architect'. As the writing was partly illegible, 'Stephen' may have been a misreading of 'Appleton' [J. L. Saywell,

History and Annals of Northallerton, 1885, 221–2].

BENSON, ROBERT, LORD BINGLEY (*c.* 1676–1731), was the son of a successful Yorkshire attorney, who left him a substantial estate. In 1702 he entered parliament as member for Thetford and subsequently represented the city of York from 1705 until 1713, when he was elevated to the peerage. At first a Whig, he became later a moderate Tory. As such he was appointed a lord of the Treasury in Harley's government (1710) and was Chancellor of the Exchequer from 1711 to 1713. During the last year of his life he was Treasurer of the Household to George II.

Benson had the reputation of being an authority on architectural matters. In Edward Oakley's *Magazine of Architecture* (1730) he is bracketed with Lords Burlington and Herbert as noble experts in architecture, and there are many references in contemporary sources to his architectural knowledge. His advice was sought both by Lord Strafford when building Wentworth Castle and by the Duke of Chandos at Cannons. In 1713 it was even rumoured that he was 'to have the care of seeing Whitehall rebuilt'. How far Benson was a practising architect rather than merely a well-informed patron is uncertain, but a drawing exists which is inscribed in an eighteenth-century hand, 'Lord Bingley's plan for finishing Ledstone' (*i.e.* Ledston Hall, Yorks., the property of Lady Elizabeth Hastings). If, as seems likely, Benson himself designed the country house which he built at BRAMHAM PARK, YORKS. (W.R.), *c.* 1705–10, he was an architect of ability. The house is illustrated in *Vitruvius Britannicus* ii, 1717, 81–2, and *C. Life*, 20–27 Feb., 12–19 June 1958.[1] The central block was gutted by fire in 1828 and restored by Detmar Blow *c.* 1910. In 1726–7 Benson built himself a house (dem. 1906) on the west side of Cavendish Square which was described by Ralph in 1734 as 'one of the most singular pieces of architecture about town', and by Timbs as 'having the appearance of a Parisian mansion'. From 1773, when it was bought by Lord Harcourt, it was known as Harcourt House, and must not be confused with the house on the opposite side of the square designed by Archer for an earlier Lord Harcourt in *c.* 1725.

[*D.N.B.*; G.E.C., *Complete Peerage*; *The Westminster Abbey Registers*, ed. Chester, 1876, 331; *The Wentworth Papers 1705–39*, ed. J. Cartwright, 1883, 85, 133, 200, 442; C. H. & M. I. Collins Baker, *James Brydges, Duke of Chandos*, 1949, 140–1, 302; T. R. Collick, 'The Patronage of Robert Benson', *Arch. Rev.*, Dec. 1965; D.

Linstrum, *West Yorkshire Architects and Architecture*, forthcoming.]

BENSON, WILLIAM (1682–1754), was the eldest son of Sir William Benson, a wealthy iron merchant who was Sheriff of London in 1706–7. As a young man he made a continental tour which included Hanover and Stockholm. When in 1707 he married the daughter of a Bristol merchant, the settlement made by his father included the purchase of lands in Wiltshire to the value of £5000. No house was included, and in February 1708 Benson obtained a 21-year lease of Amesbury Abbey from its owner Lord Bruce [Wilts. Record Office, Antrobus Deeds 283/44, *ex inf.* Mr. T. P. Connor]. However he almost immediately began to build a house for himself on a nearby property of his own. Conceived as a villa, and with a façade directly inspired by Amesbury (then believed to be the work of Inigo Jones), WILBURY HOUSE (*C. Life*, 3–10 Dec. 1959) was a remarkably precocious building for its date. According to Colen Campbell, who illustrated it in *Vitruvius Britannicus* i, 1715, pls. 51–2, the house was 'invented and built' by Benson himself. Even if this was polite flattery, Benson was clearly an architectural patron with advanced ideas. He also appears to have been interested in hydraulics. It was the piped water supply with which he provided the inhabitants of Shaftesbury that helped to secure his election as Whig M.P. for that borough in 1715, and in 1716 he ingratiated himself with George I by 'giving directions' for a 'curious waterwork' in the gardens at Herrenhausen in Hanover. As he was 'a favourite of the Germans' at Court, and the author of a well-known anti-Tory pamphlet, Benson was an obvious candidate for preferment by a Whig government, and in 1718 he persuaded the ministry to dismiss the octogenarian Wren from the Surveyorship of the Works and appoint himself to the post. The appointment was not, however, to be permanent, for it was to last only 'until the said William Benson shall be in possession of one of the two offices of Auditor of the Imprests and Foreign Accounts' (of which he had obtained a reversionary grant in the previous year).

Benson's Surveyorship lasted for fifteen months, in the course of which he sacked his ablest subordinates, declared war on his closest colleagues, infuriated the Treasury and finally brought down upon himself the wrath of the House of Lords for falsely insisting that their Chamber was in imminent danger of collapse. Though apparently the result of incompetence, there is evidence that this extraordinary episode was really a plot on the part of Benson and Colen Campbell (whom he had appointed Deputy Surveyor) to pull down the old Houses of Parliament in order to give them the opportunity to design

---

[1] For the possibility that Thomas Archer was involved in the design of Bramham see G. W. Beard in *C. Life*, 11 Dec. 1958, 1421.

a magnificent new Palladian building. As it was, the only architectural fruit of Benson's Surveyorship was the new state rooms at Kensington Palace (1718–20), which were probably designed by Colen Campbell.

In July 1719 Benson was obliged to relinquish his post, having (to quote Hawksmoor) 'got more in one year (for confusing the King's Works) than Sr. Chris. Wren did in 40 years for his honest endeavours'. Financially he was compensated by the assignment of a considerable debt due to the Crown in Ireland, and after Edward Harley's death in 1735 he enjoyed the profits of the Auditorship of the Imprests which he had been promised in 1717. There is some evidence of a continuing interest in architecture. In 1719 Benson was in some way involved in the building of Stourhead House, Wiltshire, by his brother-in-law Henry Hoare to the designs of Colen Campbell, and in 1723 the two men were jointly responsible for the new chancel of the parish church at QUARLEY, HANTS. (a Hoare property), for the Venetian east window is inscribed GUILIELMUS BENSON & HENRICUS HOARE ARM. F[ECERUNT] A.D. 1723. Benson was also an enthusiastic patron of literature, and in 1737, as a 'professed admirer of Milton', he erected in Westminster Abbey a monument to that poet with a bust by Rysbrack. His Whig politics and his blunder over the stability of the House of Lords exposed him to Pope's satire, and his literary pretensions were severely handled in the *Dunciad*.

In 1734 Benson sold Wilbury to his nephew Henry Hoare II, and retired to Wimbledon, where he died on 2 Feb. 1754, aged 72. There is a copy of the sale catalogue of his library in the British Museum (S.CS. 2(4)).

[*D.N.B.*; *The History of the King's Works* v, chap. v; Kenneth Woodbridge, *Landscape and Antiquity, Aspects of English Culture at Stourhead*, 1970, 18–21; *Survey of London* i (Bromley-by-Bow), 8–9.]

BENTLEY, JOHN (*c.* 1573–1613), *see* AKROYD, JOHN.

BENTLEY, RICHARD (1708–1782), son of Dr. Richard Bentley, the celebrated scholar, has a place in architectural history as a member of the 'Committee of Taste' which superintended the erection of Horace Walpole's Gothic villa at STRAWBERRY HILL, TWICKENHAM, MIDDLESEX. The hall and staircase, the screen in the Holbein Chamber, several chimney-pieces and various other details were designed by him between 1751 and 1761, when he quarrelled with Walpole. His drawings for Strawberry Hill are now in the collection of Mr. W. S. Lewis at Farmington, Connecticut, U.S.A. They are bound up in a volume which contains a number of other architectural drawings by Bentley, with annotations by Wal-

pole. Among them are a Gothic gateway (not executed) for Dr. Trevor, Bishop of Durham, at Bishop Auckland; 'a Triangular Chinese Building designed for the Rt. Honble. Henry Fox at Holland House' (not executed); a 'Design of a fictitious steeple for Nic. Hardinge, Esq. at Kingston', showing a Gothic spire superimposed on the roof of an existing building; a 'Design of a Chimney in the style of Architecture in the reign of James the first' (probably the one designed for Lord Strafford mentioned by Walpole in his letter to Bentley of 27 March 1755); a 'Design (not executed) of a Gothic Columbarium at the Vine' (cf. Walpole to Montagu, 25 Aug. 1757); and an unexecuted design for a fancifully Gothic farm-house for Sir Thomas Sebright of Beechwood, Herts.

Several other light-hearted designs of this character, made by Bentley for Walpole's friends, are mentioned in the latter's correspondence. Among those that were executed were a Gothic cloister added to Richard Bateman's villa at OLD WINDSOR, BERKS., subsequently dismantled by Lord Bateman after his uncle's death in 1774 [H.W. to Montagu, 24 Sept. 1762];[1] ST. HUBERT'S PRIORY, a Gothic farm with a steeple for Henrietta, Countess of Suffolk, on her estate at MARBLE HILL, TWICKENHAM, 1758, pulled down after her death in 1767 [drawing at Farmington]; a Gothic monument to Sir Horace Mann's brother Galfridus Mann (d. 1756) in LINTON CHURCH, KENT [H.W. to Mann, 24 Oct. 1758]; a Gothic 'umbrello' in Menagerie Wood, WENTWORTH CASTLE, YORKS., for the 2nd Earl of Strafford, designed 1756, executed 1759, now collapsed, but illustrated in *C. Life*, 25 Oct. 1924, 641, fig. 15 [Walpole to Strafford, 30 Oct. 1759, to Lady Ailesbury, Aug. 1760, and to Montagu, 1 Sept. 1760]; 'a very pretty Gothic room' for the 4th Earl of Holderness, 1760, probably at HORNBY CASTLE, YORKS. (N.R.), but possibly at ASTON HALL, YORKS. (W.R.) [H.W. to Montagu, 4 July, 1760]; and a Gothic stable at CHALFONT HOUSE, BUCKS., for Lady Mary Churchill, *c.* 1760 [H.W. to Montagu, 4 July 1760].

Bentley was a clever draughtsman rather than an architect, a Georgian Rex Whistler whose decorative talents were equally suited to Gothic follies or to book-illustration. In the latter capacity his principal achievement was the set of drawings which he provided to illustrate the first edition of Gray's poems printed at the Strawberry Hill Press in 1753. After his rupture with Walpole, he turned his attention to play-writing, but his tragedy, *Philodamus*, was received with

---

[1] The drawing illustrated by W. S. Lewis in *Metropolitan Museum Studies* v (i), 1934, fig. 18, as a design for the Strawberry Hill cloister is, as Mr. John Harris and Mr. M. J. McCarthy have pointed out, more likely to be a design for the one at Old Windsor.

laughter, and his comedies seldom lasted for more than two or three nights. Bentley was brought up to no profession, and, having no regular source of income, was constantly in financial difficulties. For several years he was compelled to live abroad, partly in France and partly in Jersey, and among the drawings at Farmington is an unexecuted design for the façade of a town hall at St. Helier, dated 1755. He ended his life in retirement at Westminster. An engraved portrait is reproduced in Cunningham's edition of Walpole's letters, ii (1857), 296.

[D.N.B.; The Yale edition of *Horace Walpole's Correspondence*, ed. W. S. Lewis, vol. 35, 1973, 129–272; W. S. Lewis, 'The Genesis of Strawberry Hill', *Metropolitan Museum Studies*, v (i), 1934; John Harris, *A Catalogue of British Drawings for Architecture, Decoration, Sculpture etc. in American Collections*, New Jersey 1971, 19–29 and pls. 15–18.]

BENWELL, SAMUEL, was a nephew of John Plaw, and became a pupil of J. B. Papworth in 1803. His exhibits at the Royal Academy between 1803 and 1817 included 'The lawn front of a cottage, erected for Mr. Vernon, at Crouch End, Hornsey, Middlesex' (1809), a 'Design for a chapel intended to be built in the neighbourhood of Fitzroy Square' (1810) and 'One of a series of designs made for Ombersley Church, Worcestershire, by direction of the Marchioness of Downshire' (1815). Ombersley Church was not in fact built to Benwell's designs, but to those (1825–9) of Rickman and Hutchinson. Benwell's only other recorded work appears to be THE WESLEYAN CHAPEL, BANBURY, OXON., 1811–12 (now a warehouse) [V.C.H. Oxfordshire x, 119]. He died young. [W. Papworth, *J. B. Papworth*, 1879, 14, 96].

BERRY, THOMAS, of Gainsborough, a carpenter by trade, made designs in 1792 for rebuilding GAINSBOROUGH RECTORY, LINCS. [Lincolnshire Record Office, Gilbert's Act Mortgage papers No. 13]. Two or three years later the church of STAINTON-BY-LANGWORTH, LINCS., was rebuilt to his designs [Nottingham University Library, Pierrepont papers, 3337].

BEST, R—H—, exhibited a 'Design for a Police Office and other buildings forming a quadrangle in front of Covent Garden Theatre and opening a view of that structure from a proposed street connecting Waterloo Bridge with Holborn' at the Royal Academy in 1827. He may have been a 'young man' called Best who was in D. A. Alexander's office in 1819 [Guildhall Library MS. 5862 A, *ex inf.* Miss P. Metcalf]. A 'Mr. Best' is mentioned in the minutes of the East India Company in April 1807, when it was agreed that alterations should be made to HERTFORD CASTLE

(then occupied by the East India College) according to his estimate [*ex inf.* Miss Dorothy Stroud].

BEVANS, JAMES, of London, appears to have specialized in the design of prisons and asylums. The *Report of the Committee on Madhouses in England* published by the House of Commons in 1815 (*Parliamentary Papers* 1814–15 (iv)) contains engraved plates drawn by him of a design on the panopticon principle for a proposed London Asylum for the insane, a plan of the Asylum at Guy's Hospital, and a plan of an intended Asylum for Insane Paupers at Wakefield, Yorks. *The Account of all the Gaols, Houses of Correction etc. in England, Wales, Ireland and Scotland (Parliamentary Papers* 1819 (vii)) contains 4 plates illustrating his design for a penitentiary for 600 prisoners. In 1818 he exhibited at the Royal Academy a design for 'an octagonal building 86 feet in diameter, with a cast-iron roof, designed for the Chrestomathic day-school to be erected in the city of Westminster'.

BEVANS, JOHN, a Quaker builder and surveyor of Plaistow, Essex, designed THE FRIENDS' RETREAT, FULFORD, YORK, 1794–6, an asylum for the insane run by Quakers and illustrated in S. Tuke, *Description of the Retreat*, York, 1813 [V.C.H. York, 471; R.C.H.M., York iv, 51], and the QUAKER MEETING HOUSE at GUILDFORD, SURREY, 1805–6 [H. Rowntree, *Early Quakerism in Guildford*, 1952, 28–30].

BICKERTON, FRANCIS, of York, was one of the surveyors who examined GAINSBOROUGH CHURCH, LINCS., in 1734–5, and a report condemning the church, signed by him and Francis Smith, is in the Record Office at Lincoln (Fac. 9/68). See also *Commons' Journals* xxii, 556–7, 619–21; xxiii, 582, 618. In 1732–3 he was paid a total of £20 for 'directing and supervising the finishing of the Great Room in the Lord Mayor's House', *i.e.* the MANSION HOUSE, YORK, built in 1725–7 [York City Archives: Chamberlains' Rolls, *ex inf.* Dr. E. A. Gee]. In March 1737/8 'Mr. Bickerton' paid the carver Henry Watson for work at WENTWORTH WOODHOUSE, YORKS. (W.R.), on behalf of Lord Malton [Bodleian, MS. English Misc. f. 383]. A person of this name was Clerk of the Works at Richmond (New Park Lodge) from 1749 to 1754, and at the Queen's House, Greenwich, from 1754 to 1768.

BIGGS, RICHARD (–1776), held the post of Clerk of the Works at Windsor Castle from 1745 until his death in 1776. As 'Richard Biggs, Architect', he subscribed in 1739 to part 2 of R. West & W. H. Toms's *Views of All the Ancient Churches in the Cities of London and Westminster*. In 1749 he was one of the arbitrators appointed in connection with a dispute over the repair of

Chertsey Bridge [Surrey County Records, Q.S. 5/7, pp. 67–72]. In 1755 Henry Grenville, brother of Lord Temple, sent Sanderson Miller the plans of a building which he intended to erect to the designs of 'Mr. Biggs' at a place called 'Beechly Mount' [Warwickshire Record Office, CR 125 B/378–9]. Designs by Biggs for additions to a house at HARE HATCH, nr. WARGRAVE, BERKS., for Mrs. Pritchard, dated 1757, are in Sir John Soane's Museum (Drawer 43, v), together with others for alterations to a house at BRAY, BERKS., for R. Bidleson, dated 1763. By his will, dated 10 December 1775, he left a gold ring to Thomas Ripley, senior, and a perspective view of Windsor Castle in straw to Horatio Ripley [P.C.C. 6 COLLIER].

BILBY, WILLIAM, a carpenter, builder and surveyor of Melton, Suffolk, designed and built BREDFIELD RECTORY, SUFFOLK, in 1836, and extensively altered the parsonage houses of DALLINGHOO (1833) and MARTLESHAM (1837) in the same county [*Proceedings of the Suffolk Institute of Archaeology* xxviii, 1961, 300].

BILLING, the name of a family of builders and architects of Reading, of which there appear to have been at least three generations. The founder of the business was RICHARD BILLING I (*c.* 1747–1826), who designed ST. MARY'S CHAPEL, CASTLE STREET, READING, 1798–9; portico and chancel added 1840–2 [J. Doran, *History of Reading*, 1835, 170–1]. He was succeeded by his eldest son RICHARD BILLING II (*c.* 1785–1853), who evidently became a pupil of Samuel Robinson and D. R. Roper, for it was from their office in Southwark that he exhibited a design for a town hall at the Royal Academy in 1806. Richard Billing II was a prominent figure in the municipal life of Reading in the early nineteenth century, held office as surveyor to the Corporation of which he was a member, and took advantage of his position to further his own interests and those of his clients. It was, for instance, on Corporation land, leased to himself for ninety-nine years on his own valuation, that he built Albion Place as a speculation [*Reading Mercury*, 14 Oct. 1833]. In about 1851 he went bankrupt, and thereafter practised only as a surveyor and valuer. He was killed in a road accident at Watlington on 25 July 1853, in his 69th year [*Gent's Mag.* 1853 (ii), 324]. He had three sons, all of whom were in the architectural profession: RICHARD BILLING III (*c.* 1815–1884), JOHN BILLING (1816–1863) and ARTHUR BILLING (1824–1896). Richard carried on the family practice in Reading, while John and Arthur both established offices in London. In addition Richard Billing I had a younger son John who died in 1808 aged 20 [*Reading Mercury*, 8 Aug. 1808]. This was the J. Billing of Reading who in 1807 had exhibited at the R.A.

a 'Design for a house built in Berkshire'. [Information from Canon B. F. L. Clarke.]

The following works are by Richard Billing II or III, either independently or in conjunction:

READING, SOUTHAMPTON PLACE, 1813–18 [P. H. Ditchfield, *Reading Seventy Years Ago*, 1887, 6, 81].

READING, ST. GILES'S CHURCH, enlarged and mostly rebuilt by R. Billing and son, 1821–2 [Parish Records].

EAST WOODHAY CHURCH, HANTS., rebuilt, 1823, Gothic; chancel added 1850. A tablet on the tower is inscribed 'Rebuilt 1823 Billing & Son Architects & Builders'.

READING, ALBION PLACE, 1825–35 [*Reading Mercury*, 14 Oct. 1833].

BEENHAM VICARAGE, BERKS., altered or rebuilt, 1826 [Salisbury Diocesan Records].

READING, ST. MARY'S CHURCH. In 1829 R. Billing, junior, received 1 guinea for his 'Plans, Elevation, Section and Estimate for erecting a new gallery' [Parish Records; I.C.B.S.].

READING, house in Horn Street [*Reading Mercury*, 14 Oct. 1833].

READING, house in The Butts for Mr. Higgs, 1831 [*Reading Mercury*, 14 Oct. 1833].

BLEDLOW RIDGE, BUCKS., Chapel of Ease, 1834; dem. 1868 [Lipscomb, *History of Bucks.* ii, 1847, 122].

BILLINGTON, a family of architects and builders at Wakefield, of whom the following appear to have been the principal members.

JOHN BILLINGTON (–1773) was Surveyor of Bridges to the West Riding of Yorkshire from 1771 until his death [W. Riding Quarter Sessions Order Books]. He was presumably the carpenter of the same name who was employed at SERLBY HALL, NOTTS., between 1760 and 1773 [Serlby archives, *ex inf.* Mr. Peter Leach], and was probably the J.B. who initials designs among the Nostell Priory archives [C 3/4/4, 1–3] for building stables and adding wings to THORNTON HALL, THORNTON CURTIS, LINCS., for Sir Rowland Winn of Nostell. Stables more or less corresponding to the drawing were built in 1766, and similar wings were built in 1769. John Billington, described as a carpenter of Fowlby (on the Nostell estate), signs an undated contract 'to execute and finish the inside of the stables' of HICKLETON HALL, YORKS. (W.R.), for Godfrey Wentworth, 'according to the plan that he hath sent' [Yorkshire Archaeological Soc., Wentworth of Woolley MSS., *ex inf.* Mr. Peter Leach].

JOHN BILLINGTON (*c.* 1780–1835), of Wakefield, was a joiner by trade, but in 1812 advertised that he was starting business as a builder and surveyor, and is subsequently described as an architect. He died in February 1835, aged 55 [information from Mr. John Goodchild of Wakefield Library]. He was presumably the architect surnamed Billington who added a portico to the STAFFORD ARMS HOTEL in WAKEFIELD in 1830 [J. W. Walker, *Wakefield* ii, 1939, 530].

WILLIAM BILLINTON may have been the son of John Billington (d. 1835), who had a son William baptized in Sept. 1807, but spelled his name without a 'g'. He practised in Wakefield as an architect and civil engineer from the mid-1830s until the 1850s. In 1834 he exhibited at the Northern Society for the Encouragement of the Fine Arts at Leeds, showing a design for an intended Savings Bank at Wakefield and a 'bird's eye view of the New Cemetery at Leeds' (presumably an unexecuted design for the Woodhouse Cemetery there). He was engineer to the Wakefield Waterworks Company and contractor for a mile of railway through the town [*ex inf.* Mr. John Goodchild]. As an architect he designed the neo-Norman MONK BRETTON CHURCH, YORKS. (W.R.), 1838–9 [I.C.B.S.], the Greek Revival ATHENAEUM in FAWCETT STREET, SUNDERLAND, CO. DURHAM, 1839–41 [W. Fordyce, *History of the County of Durham* ii, 1855, 477], and a row of houses in BOND STREET, WAKEFIELD, called BOND TERRACE, which he built as a personal speculation in 1840 [J. Goodchild, *Wakefield Town Trail*, 1975, 6]. In the extra-illustrated copy of Whitaker's *Loidis and Elmete* in Leeds Public Library there is (vol. ii) a lithograph showing Billinton's unexecuted design for the Proprietary School at Wakefield, submitted in competition in 1833.

BILLINGTON, JOHN, was the author of *The Architectural Director, being an approved guide to architects, draughtsmen, etc. in the study, employment and execution of architecture*, 1829, 2nd ed. 1834, a work of somewhat similar character to Gwilt's *Encyclopaedia of Architecture*. He is described on the title-page as 'of the Royal Academy of Architecture at Paris'. The book received a hostile review in Loudon's *Architectural Magazine* i, 1834, 84, where it is suggested that 'Billington' was a *nom-de-plume*.

BILLOP, WILLIAM, exhibited a 'Design for a garden pavilion' at the Royal Academy in 1794, giving Catherine Place, Greenwich, as his address. He became a member of the Surveyors' Club in 1806.

BINGLEY, LORD, *see* BENSON, ROBERT

BINNING, A— M—, signs a perspective drawing dated 1832 showing a castellated design for rebuilding ARDKINGLASS HOUSE, ARGYLLSHIRE, the seat of Sir James Campbell, after its destruction by fire in 1831. The design was not carried out. The drawing is preserved at Ardkinglass. The author can probably be identified as Alexander Munro Binning, an Edinburgh lawyer who was a member of the Association for the Promotion of the Fine Arts in Scotland.

BIRCH, J—, of London, appears to have designed GNATON HALL, NEWTON FERRERS, DEVON, for in 1826 he exhibited a 'Villa about to be erected at Gnaton, Devon, for H. R. Roe, Esq.' at the Society of British Artists.

BIRD, JOHN (1768–1829), of Liverpool, 'was one of those self-taught scholars who are more indebted to native genius than to early instructions'. He began life as a landscape-artist. As early as 1789 he provided a drawing (of Lleweny Hall, Denbighshire) for Angus's *Views of Seats*. In 1810 he joined the Liverpool Academy, and was its secretary in 1810–11. He subsequently practised as an architect and surveyor, but his only recorded work in this capacity appears to be ST. NICHOLAS (R.C.) CHURCH, LIVERPOOL, *c.* 1810, Gothic; dem. 1972 [J. A. Picton, *Memorials of Liverpool* ii, 1875, 214]. He was concerned in a publication entitled *The Carpenters' and Joiners' Price Book ... containing the prices of wood and work ... with new and useful tables ... by Isaac Harrison, Robert Jackson, Matthew Nelson, William Potts ... and examined and approved by John Bird, Architect and Surveyor* (Liverpool, 1811), of which there is a copy in the National Library of Wales (MS. 4982 c). He died at Whitby on 5 February 1829, aged 61. [*Gent's Mag.* 1829 (i), 190; H. C. Marillier, *The Liverpool School of Painters*, 1904, 63–4; information from Mr. S. A. Harris.]

BIRD, WILLIAM, *see* BYRD.

BIRKHEAD, BENJAMIN (*c.* 1780–1858), exhibited at the Royal Academy in 1805 and 1808. He was elected to the Surveyors' Club in 1807, and was also a member of the London Architectural Society [*Builder* xxi, 1863, 86]. He died in Hans Place, Chelsea, on 7 October 1858, aged 78 [*Gent's Mag.* 1858 (ii), 541].

BISBROWN, CUTHBERT, was an enterprising builder in Liverpool. In Gore's *Directory* of 1766 he is described as 'builder and cabinet maker', but in 1774 as 'surveyor'. In 1766 he borrowed nearly £12,000 to finance building developments in Liverpool, and in 1771–4 he was the promoter of a scheme for a 'new town' on the Earl of Sefton's estate in Toxteth Park. This was to be called 'Harrington' in compliment to the Countess of Sefton, who was a daughter of the 2nd Earl of Harrington. A church (St. James, Toxteth Park) and a few houses were built, but the scheme ended in failure and Bisbrown's bankruptcy (1776). [J. A. Picton, *Memorials of Liverpool* ii, 1875, 459–61; James Boardman, *Liverpool Table Talk*, 1871, 35; C. W. Chalklin,

The Provincial Towns of Georgian England, 1974, 110–111; *Gent's Mag.* 1776, 95.]

BLACK, ALEXANDER (*c.* 1701–1761), 'architect', is said by S. Redgrave in his *Dictionary of Artists*, 1878, 43, to have 'attained eminence by his works in Edinburgh, where he practised', and to have died there on 19 February 1761, aged 60.

BLACK, JAMES (–1841), was Town's Architect of Dundee from 1833 until his death. He stated in 1835 that he had been in practice since 1805, but nothing is known of his career before 1817, when he came to Dundee. In 1833 he succeeded David Neave as Town's Architect, but found that he had a serious rival in George Angus of Edinburgh, who (despite Black's intrigues) won both the Reform Street competition of 1832 and the Prison and Bridewell competition of 1833. Though quite an able designer, Black had to be content with the relatively minor commissions listed below. He died on 24 May 1841. [David Walker, *Architects and Architecture in Dundee 1770–1914*, Abertay Historical Society's Publication No. 3, 1955.]

Some of Black's papers are preserved in the Albert Institute at Dundee. They include a design for a *cottage orné* and a study for Somerville Place. In the Kinfauns Estate Office at Rockdale there is an unexecuted design by him for a Gothic burying place for the Gray family in the churchyard at Fowlis Easter, Angus, dated 1819 (photograph at N.M.R.S.).

DUNDEE

ST. GEORGE'S CHURCH, SCHOOL WYND, 1824–5; dem. [Walker, 9].
ST. AIDAN'S CHURCH, BROUGHTY FERRY, 1824–6, Gothic [Walker, 9].
BUILDINGS in W. DOCK STREET, DOCK STREET, S. UNION STREET and CRAIG STREET, 1824–5; dem. [*Dundee Advertiser, ex. inf.* Mr. David Walker].
CHARLES STREET, tenements for the Dundee Joint Stock Co., 1824–5 [*ibid.*].
SOMERVILLE PLACE, houses in, 1830 [Walker, 9].
THE HOWFF, BARRACK STREET GATEWAY, 1833–4 [Walker, 11].
NOS. 92–6 NETHERGATE, for the Dundee & Newtyle Railway Co., 1836 [*Dundee Advertiser, ex. inf.* Mr. David Walker].
U.P. CHURCH, W. BELL STREET (now Dundee Schools Orchestral Centre), 1840 [Walker, 11].
Black was also responsible for the layout of S. COMMERCIAL STREET, 1828; LINDSAY STREET and PANMURE STREET, 1839.

ABROATH, THE ACADEMY or HIGH SCHOOL, 1821 [G. Hay, *History of Arbroath*, 1876, 365].
FORFAR, THE MANSE, 1828 [S.R.O., HR 415/3/2].

SOUTH GRANGE HOUSE, MONIFIETH, ANGUS, 1829 [Walker, 9].

BLACK, ROBERT (*c.* 1800–1869), practised in Glasgow, where from 1843 to about 1854 he was in partnership with James Salmon (1805–1888). According to *The Architects, Engineers and Building Trades Directory* of 1868 he had designed 'upwards of twenty churches' and several banks and warehouses. His earlier works included THE MECHANICS' INSTITUTION, NORTH HANOVER STREET, GLASGOW, 1831 [J. Pagan, *Sketch of the History of Glasgow*, 1847, 186], THE CITY OF GLASGOW BANK, VIRGINIA STREET, 1838, dem. [J. Pagan, *op. cit.*, 174]; ADELAIDE PLACE, BATH STREET, 1839 [*The Architects . . . Directory*, 1868]; and a Grecian monument to Prof. John Dick (d. 1833) in THE NECROPOLIS, 1838, which has Black's signature [J. Pagan, *op. cit.*, 184; wrongly attributed to Thomas Hamilton in G. Blair, *Sketches of Glasgow Necropolis*, 1857, 98].

BLACKBURN, WILLIAM (1750–1790), was born in Southwark, where his father was a tradesman. His mother was a Spaniard. He was apprenticed to a surveyor, but is said to have 'derived very few advantages' from his instruction. At the age of 19 he competed for the Royal Exchange at Dublin [*Builder* xxvii, 1869, 781]. He became a student at the Royal Academy Schools in 1772, and was awarded the Silver Medal in 1773. In 1775 he exhibited a 'garden seat' and a 'stable building', both 'designed for a gentleman in Surrey'. In 1782 the course of his life was changed by his success in winning the first premium offered by the commissioners appointed to erect prisons under the Penitentiary Act of 1779. In the event these prisons were never built, but Blackburn's success led to numerous commissions to design other prisons. He became intimate with John Howard, the prison reformer, and had the reputation of being the only architect who had Howard's confidence. He was in fact a pioneer of radial planning in prison design, and his prisons incorporated the latest thinking on solitary confinement, segregation, 'useful labour', etc. Their façades were appropriately and effectively designed.

In 1776 Blackburn was appointed Surveyor to the Watermen's Company. He also held the posts of Surveyor to St. Thomas's and Guy's Hospitals, and to the County of Surrey. His career was cut short by his early death, which occurred at Preston in Lancashire in December 1790, while he was on his way to Glasgow to make designs for a new gaol in that city. Some of his commissions were completed by his brother-in-law William Hobson, a Southwark builder with whom he had been most closely associated.

[*D.N.B.*; John Chambers, 'Collections for Biography of English Architects' in R.I.B.A.

113

Library; obituaries in *Gent's Mag.* 1790, p. 1053, and *Caledonian Mercury*, 9 Dec. 1790; J. Howard, *Account of the Principal Lazarettos in Europe*, 1789; *Report from the Committee of Aldermen appointed to visit several gaols in England*, 1816, 72, 91, 106, 117; Gloucestershire County Records, Q/AG 2–5, 7; T. A. Markus, 'Pattern of the Law', *Arch. Rev.*, Oct. 1954; Helen Rosenau, *Social Purpose in Architecture*, 1970, 84.]

PRISONS

OXFORD, THE COUNTY GAOL (in the Castle), begun *c.* 1785, completed by Daniel Harris 1805; enlarged 1850–2 [Howard, *Lazarettos*, 170; R. Gardner, *History, Gazeteer and Directory of Oxfordshire*, 1852, 331].

OXFORD, THE CITY GAOL, GLOUCESTER GREEN, 1786–9; enlarged 1870; dem. 1879 [Howard, *Lazarettos*, 171].

LIVERPOOL, THE NEW BOROUGH GAOL, 1786–7; dem. 1855 [*Report from the Committee of Aldermen*, Appendix A, 106].

IPSWICH, SUFFOLK, THE COUNTY GAOL, 1786–90 [*Report from the Committee of Aldermen*, Appendix A, 91; Howard, *Lazarettos*, 155].

SALFORD, LANCS., THE NEW BAILEY PRISON, 1787–90; enlarged 1816; dem. *c.* 1872 [record of inscription on foundation-stone in Nostell Priory Library; Howard, *Lazarettos*, 206].

NORTHLEACH, GLOS., THE HOUSE OF CORRECTION (now Police Station), 1787–91 [J. R. S. Whiting, *Prison Reform in Gloucestershire*, 1975, chap. 12].

LITTLEDEAN, GLOS., THE HOUSE OF CORRECTION (now Record Office), 1787–91 [Whiting, *op. cit.*, chap. 10].

HORSLEY, GLOS., THE HOUSE OF CORRECTION, 1787–91; dem. 1880 [Whiting, *op. cit.*, chap. 13].

BRISTOL, THE GLOUCESTERSHIRE COUNTY BRIDE-WELL, LAWFORD'S GATE, 1787–91; destroyed by rioters 1831 [Whiting, *op. cit.*, chap. 11].

GLOUCESTER, THE COUNTY GAOL, 1788–91; enlarged 1845–55 [Whiting, *op. cit.*, chap. 3].

MONMOUTH, THE COUNTY GAOL, 1788–90 [Monmouthshire County Records, QS/MB.: 0003 and C. Bu. 1; Howard, *Lazarettos*, 177].

PRESTON, LANCS., THE COUNTY BRIDEWELL, 1789; governor's house rebuilt 1834 [Howard, *Lazarettos*, 205].

LIMERICK GAOL, IRELAND, *c.* 1789 [J. Chambers, *op. cit.*; Howard, *Lazarettos*, 91].

LEWES, SUSSEX, THE HOUSE OF CORRECTION, 1789–93; enlarged 1814; dem. 1967 [E. Sussex Record Office, QAP/2/11 and QAP 12/E12].

DORCHESTER, DORSET, THE COUNTY GAOL, 1789–95 [M. B. Weinstock, 'Dorchester Model Prison 1791–1816', *Procs. of the Dorset Nat. Hist. and Arch. Soc.* lxxviii, 1956].

EXETER, THE DEVON COUNTY GAOL, 1789–95; dem.

1853 [Devon County Record Office, Gaol Committee Book, 1788–95; Howard, *Lazarettos*, 186 n.].

DUBLIN, alterations to the NEWGATE GAOL; dem. *c.* 1880 [*D.N.B.*].

OTHER BUILDINGS

LONDON, WATERMEN'S HALL, ST. MARY AT HILL, 1778–80 [H. Humpherus, *History of the Watermen's Company* ii, n.d., 321 *et seq.*] (*C. Life*, 14 Nov. 1974, 1488).

CAMBERWELL, NO. 154 DENMARK HILL, for Edward Henshaw, 1785–6 [J. Edwards, *A Companion from London to Brightelmston*, 1801, Part I, 17, §xviii] (*Survey of London* xxvi, 146–9, pls. 52–3).

BRISTOL, THE UNITARIAN CHAPEL, LEWIN'S MEAD, 1788–91 [W. Ison, *The Georgian Buildings of Bristol*, 1952, 81–4].

LONDON, GUY'S HOSPITAL, SOUTHWARK, alterations, *c.* 1788 [Howard, *Lazarettos*, 136].

BLECHYNDEN, RICHARD (–1822), belonged to a family with property at Swanscombe in Kent. He spent most of his life in India in the service of the East India Company and was Civil Architect to the Company from 1803 until his death in 1822. His diaries from 1791 to 1822 are in the British Museum (Add. MSS. 45581–45653).

BLOGG, WILLIAM (*c.* 1767–), was the son of Samuel Blogg, a bricklayer of Norwich. In 1791, at the age of 24, he entered the Royal Academy Schools, winning the Silver Medal in 1792. For a short time in 1791 he was a pupil of Sir John Soane, but in 1793 he was in James Wyatt's office. For a few years he practised in London, exhibiting at the Academy a 'Design for improving the front of Heatherton House' (either HEATHERDEN HOUSE, nr. HURST GREEN, SUSSEX, or HEATHERTON PARK, SOMERSET) (1797), a 'Design for the east front of a new street at Brighton' (1797) and 'Designs for cottages for Sir Christopher Hawkins' of Trewithen, Cornwall (1798). In 1802 he went bankrupt [*European Mag.* 1802], and in August 1803 he was back in Norwich advertising his services as an 'Architect and Surveyor' [*Norwich Mercury*, 6 Aug. 1803]. In 1808 he supervised repairs to the town walls and the demolition of several of the medieval gateways [Norwich City Archives, Minutes of the Tonnage Committee, *ex. inf.* Mr. A. P. Baggs].

BLONDEL, GEORGES FRANÇOIS (*c.* 1730–), was the son of Jacques François Blondel (1705–74), best known as the author of several important architectural books, and as the founder of a celebrated *École des Arts* in Paris.

After a training in his father's school Georges spent some time in Rome before returning to Paris to teach architecture and drawing. He arrived in London in about 1764, the year he signs a red chalk view of the interior of St. Paul's Cathedral, now at the Courtauld Institute. He exhibited various works, chiefly mezzotints, at the Society of Artists and the Free Society in 1765–7 and 1774, and in 1772 held an exhibition of his architectural and other designs in Covent Garden. The printed catalogue shows that he hoped to establish a school of design on the lines of his father's Parisian establishment, but nothing came of the project, and Blondel appears to have returned to France in 1774, the date of his father's death. He himself died some time after 1791. During his stay in England Blondel was employed by Lord Temple at STOWE HOUSE, BUCKS., making a number of designs for which he claimed payment in 1774 (B.M., Add. MS. 41136, ff. 6–7). Few of them were executed, but he may have remodelled Gibbs's Lady's (now Queen's) Temple. What appear to be some of Blondel's original drawings for Stowe remain in an extra-illustrated copy of Lysons' *Buckinghamshire* belonging to Capt. R. W. Morgan-Grenville. [Campbell Dodgson, 'The Mezzotints of G. F. Blondel', *Print Collector's Quarterly* ix, 1922, 303–14; Jeanne Lejeaux, 'G. F. Blondel, Engraver and Draughtsman', *ibid.*, 1936, 260–77; John Harris, 'Blondel at Stowe', *Connoisseur*, March 1964; Laurence Whistler & others, *Stowe, a Guide to the Gardens*, 1968; Michael McCarthy, 'The Rebuilding of Stowe House, 1770–1777', *Huntingdon Library Quarterly* xxxvi, 1973.]

BLORE, EDWARD (1787–1879), was the eldest son of Thomas Blore, F.S.A., a lawyer of antiquarian tastes. His early years were spent at Stamford, where he developed the enthusiasm for Gothic architecture and the skill as a topographical artist that remained with him for life. Before he was 20 he had drawn the illustrations for his father's *History of Rutland* (1811), and he was afterwards employed to make the architectural drawings for many other topographical works, such as Surtees' *Durham*, Baker's *Northamptonshire* and Clutterbuck's *Hertfordshire*. He was also employed by John Britton to make the drawings of York and Peterborough for his *Cathedrals* series, and for portions of his *Architectural Antiquities*. Among his early acquaintances were Sir James Hall, whose *Essay on the Origin, History and Principles of Gothic Architecture* (1813) he helped to illustrate, and Thomas Rickman, with whom he corresponded. In 1816 he was introduced to Sir Walter Scott, who was about to rebuild Abbotsford with the help of the architect William Atkinson. Blore made some sketches which pleased Scott 'as being less Gothic & more in the old fashioned Scotch stile' than Atkinson's.

Both plan and execution remained, however, in Atkinson's hands and Blore was only one of several contributors to the final design. He cannot therefore be regarded in any strict sense as the architect of Abbotsford. The principal result of Blore's friendship with Scott was his employment as 'manager' of *The Provincial Antiquities and Picturesque Scenery of Scotland*, a work for which he provided all the architectural drawings. Owing to financial difficulties and Scott's failing health, only two volumes were issued. In 1824 he published his best-known work, *The Monumental Remains of Noble and Eminent Persons*, containing a fine collection of engravings of medieval brasses and effigies.

By the 1820s Blore had made the transition from an antiquarian draughtsman to a practising architect. How he acquired his practical knowledge of building construction is not clear, but he soon gained the reputation of being a thoroughly trustworthy architect whose estimates were to be relied upon. It was his reputation as 'the cheap architect' that led in 1832 to his employment by the government to complete Buckingham Palace after Nash's extravagance had caused his dismissal. Although never a member of the Office of Works, Blore was also employed to carry out various works at Windsor Castle and Hampton Court. From 1827 to 1849 he was surveyor to Westminster Abbey, where he refitted the choir and rescued the thirteenth-century retable from misuse. He was a Fellow of the Society of Antiquaries and of the Royal Society, and was one of the founders of the Royal Archaeological Institute. In 1834 Oxford gave him an honorary D.C.L., but he refused the knighthood which he was offered on the completion of his work at Buckingham Palace.

Energetic and reliable, Blore built up an extensive practice both as a country-house architect and as a designer and restorer of churches. The 'Tudor' and 'Elizabethan' styles were his speciality, and the elevations of nearly all his numerous country houses were based on his studies of fifteenth- and sixteenth-century domestic architecture. As a church architect he experimented with the Romanesque and the Early English, but was more at home with the Decorated and the Perpendicular. He rarely used the Greek or Roman orders, which were then normal for civic or commercial buildings,[1] and most of his public commissions were for buildings such as schools for which the 'Tudor Collegiate' style was appropriate. Although his knowledge of medieval precedent was probably quite as extensive as Pugin's, Blore lacked the genius which might have transformed his antiquarian expertise into living architecture. A dull com-

---

[1] His only considerable classical works were Buckingham Palace and Haveringland Hall, Norfolk.

petence pervades all his work, and none of his churches count for much in the history of the Gothic Revival. Indeed, the *Ecclesiologist* considered him to be 'entirely unacquainted with the true spirit of Pointed Architecture' (vol. iii, 1843, 99, 2nd ed.).

Blore gave up practice in 1849, but lived on in retirement until his death at his house in Manchester Square on 4 September 1879 at the age of 91. He left 48 volumes of antiquarian drawings, now in the British Museum (Add. MSS. 42000–42047), 'the result of more than seventy years' unremitting labour', and including 'almost every example of ancient castellated and domestic architecture remaining in England'. Other drawings are in the Society of Antiquaries' Library and the R.I.B.A. Drawings Collection, but the principal collection of his architectural designs is in the Print Room of the Victoria and Albert Museum. Account books recording most of his commissions as an artist and architect from 1817 onwards are in Cambridge University Library (Add. MSS. 3954–3956), together with separate volumes relating to his principal architectural works (Add. MSS. 3922–3953).

F. C. Penrose (1817–1902), Frederick Marrable (1818–72)), Henry Clutton (1819–93), William Mason (1810–97), George Moore and William Burges (1827–81) were among his pupils.

Portraits of Blore are reproduced in *Illustrated London News* lxxv, 1879, 280, *C. Life*, 14 Dec. 1945, 1058, and *The History of the King's Works* vi, pl. 5. A reputed portrait by William Hilton, R.A., at the University Press, Cambridge, is reproduced by E. A. Crutchley, *History and Description of the Pitt Press*, 1938, 8. A bust by John Ternouth (1845), formerly at the same institution, was transferred to Abbotsford in 1969.

[Obituaries in *Proceedings of the Society of Antiquaries*, 2nd ser., viii, 1879–81, 347–52, and *Builder* xxxvii, 1879, 1019; C. L. Eastlake, *History of the Gothic Revival*, 1872, 138–41; *D.N.B.*; *Three Howard Sisters*, ed. Maud, Lady Leconfield & J. Gore, 1955, 156; *Catalogue of the R.I.B.A. Drawings Collection: B*, 90–93; correspondence with Sir Walter Scott in National Library of Scotland, especially MSS. 3029 and 3134, no. 172.]

PUBLIC BUILDINGS, ETC.

LONDON, THE CHARTERHOUSE, PREACHER'S and PENSIONERS' COURTS, 1825–30 [W. J. D. Roper, *Chronicles of Charter House*, 1847, 168–9].

OXFORD, completed north wing of CLARENDON PRESS, WALTON STREET, 1829–30, classical [*V.C.H. Oxon.* iii, 57].

WOBURN, BEDS., MARKET HOUSE for the 6th Duke of Bedford, 1830 [*Description of Woburn and its Abbey*, Woburn 1845, 108].

WARMINSTER, WILTS., TOWN HALL and buildings on opposite corner, 1830 [*V.C.H. Wilts.* viii, 95].

WILTON, WILTS., ST. MARY MAGDALENE'S HOSPITAL, 1831–2 [drawings at Wilton House; C.U.L., Add. MS. 3954, f. 65ᵛ].

CAMBRIDGE, THE PITT PRESS, 1831–2 [Willis & Clark, iii, 140–44; R.I.B.A. Drawings Coll.].

OXFORD, WADHAM COLLEGE, alterations to Warden's Lodgings, new entrance gates, etc., 1832 [T. G. Jackson, *Wadham College, Oxford*, 1893, 125, 147].

WEST RETFORD, NOTTS., TRINITY HOSPITAL, 1832–3 [A. Jackson, *History of Retford*, Retford 1971, 69; R.I.B.A. Drawings Coll.; C.U.L., Add. MS. 3954, f. 61ᵛ].

BEDFORD, principal front of THE ENGLISH (later the COMMERCIAL, then the MODERN) SCHOOL, HARPUR STREET, 1833–37 [J. Godber, *The Harpur Trust 1552–1973*, 1973, 39; R.I.B.A. Drawings Coll.].

GREENOCK, THE WATT INSTITUTION AND GREENOCK LIBRARY, UNION STREET, 1835–7; completed 1846 [*N.S.A.* vii, 423; R.I.B.A. Drawings Coll.].

TAVISTOCK, DEVON, THE GRAMMAR SCHOOL, for the 6th Duke of Bedford, 1837 [J. C. Loudon, *Gardener's Mag.* xviii, 1842, 550].

OXFORD, MERTON COLLEGE, reconstructed entrance tower, 1837–8 [A. Vallance, *The Old Colleges of Oxford*, 1912, 21, 23].

OXFORD, SHELDONIAN THEATRE, new cupola, 1837–8 [Gardner's *History, Gazeteer and Directory of Oxfordshire*, 1852, 248; C.U.L., Add. MS. 3956, f. 42].

PENN, BUCKS., THE GIRLS' SCHOOL, for the 1st Earl Howe, 1838–9 [C.U.L., Add. MS. 3956, f. 59ᵛ].

MANCHESTER, offices for the Bridgewater Trust, 1840 [C.U.L., Add. MS. 3955, f. 16].

CHELSEA, ST. MARK'S TRAINING COLLEGE, STANLEY GROVE, 1843–7, 'Byzantine' and 'Norman' styles [*Survey of London* iv, 44].

MARLBOROUGH COLLEGE, WILTS., new buildings, including Chapel (dem. 1884), Dining Hall, Master's Lodge, A House and B House, 1845–8 [A. G. Bradley & others, *History of Marlborough College*, 1893, 83, 104].

LONDON, DEAN'S YARD, enlarged offices of Queen Anne's Bounty, 1847–8 [C.U.L., Add. MS. 3955, f. 86].

DOMESTIC ARCHITECTURE

ABBOTSFORD, ROXBURGHSHIRE, for Sir Walter Scott, contributed ideas for external treatment of house designed by W. Atkinson 1816–23 [*The Letters of Sir Walter Scott*, ed. H. J. C. Grierson, iv, 1932, 289, 333–7, 339, etc.; National Library of Scotland, MS. 3029].

COREHOUSE, LANARKSHIRE, for George Cranstoun, Lord Corehouse, 1824–7 [J. M. Leighton, *Select Views on the River Clyde*, 1830, 17; R.I.B.A. Drawings Coll.].

FREELAND HOUSE, PERTHSHIRE, remodelled for the 6th Lord Ruthven, 1825–6 [C.U.L., Add. MS. 3954, ff. 45ᵛ, 53ᵛ–54; perspective in R.I.B.A. Drawings Coll.]. This house is given to W. Burn in *R.I.B.A. Trans.* 1869–70, and drawings at N.M.R.S. indicate that he was concerned in its building, but as Blore made some 50 working drawings for Freeland he must be regarded as its principal architect.[1]

WESTON HOUSE, nr. LONG COMPTON, WARWICKS., for Sir George Philips, Bart., 1826–33; dem. 1932 [Warwicks R.O., Philips papers, Box 25; exhib. at R.A. 1828; R.I.B.A. Drawings Coll.].

CANFORD MANOR, nr. WIMBORNE, DORSET, reconstructed for William Ponsonby, cr. Lord de Mauley, 1826–36; afterwards much altered and enlarged by Sir Charles Barry [Eastlake; C.U.L., Add. MSS. 3922–6; R.I.B.A. Drawings Coll.].

GOODRICH COURT, HEREFS., for Sir Samuel Rush Meyrick, 1828–31; dem. 1950 [Eastlake; C.U.L., Add. MS. 3927; V. and A. 182 r; R.I.B.A. Drawings Coll.].

NORMAN COURT, HANTS., unspecified work for C. B. Wall, 1829 [C.U.L., Add. MS. 3954, f. 72].

LAMBETH PALACE, rebuilt residential wing, converted Great Hall into Library and remodelled the Chapel (to which he added a stone vault), for Archbishop William Howley, 1829–48 [C.U.L., Add. MSS. 3928–34; V. and A. 182 o; R.I.B.A. Drawings Coll.; *Survey of London* xxiii, 81–103].

ST. ASAPH, N. WALES, enlarged BISHOP'S PALACE for Bishop William Carey, 1830–1 [C.U.L., Add. MS. 3935; V. and A. 182 s; R.I.B.A. Drawings Coll.].

KEELE HALL, STAFFS., stables (now Principal's House) and alterations to house for Ralph Sneyd, 1830–33 [C.U.L., Add. MS. 3955, ff. 5–6; C. Hussey in *C. Life*, 14 Jan. 1960].

MOUNTEVIOT, CRAILING, ROXBURGHSHIRE, new house for the 7th Marquess of Lothian, begun *c.* 1830 but never completed [C.U.L., Add. MS. 3954, f. 71ᵛ; drawings in R.I.B.A. Drawings Coll.].

MIDDLETON PARK, MIDDLETON STONEY, OXON., lodge for the 5th Earl of Jersey, *c.* 1830 [C.U.L., Add. MS. 3955, f. 4ᵛ].

BUCKINGHAM PALACE, LONDON, completed palace designed by J. Nash, 1832–7, adding attic on garden front; converted south-east conservatory into Chapel 1842–3; added east wing facing Mall (refronted by Sir Aston Webb 1913),

1847–50 [M. H. Port in *History of the King's Works* vi, 277–92].

ISLEWORTH HOUSE, MIDDLESEX, for Sir W. H. Cowper, 1832 [W. Keane, *Beauties of Middlesex*, 1850, 66; C.U.L., Add. MS. 3939].

CROSBY HALL, BISHOPSGATE, LONDON, repaired Great Hall, *c.* 1832 [H. J. Hammon, *The Architectural Antiquities of Crosby Place, London*, 1844, 12].

MERTON HALL, NORFOLK, repairs for the 4th Lord Walsingham, 1832, and enlarged for the 5th Lord Walsingham, 1846; mostly destroyed by fire 1856 [*Proc. Soc. Antiq.*, obituary; C.U.L., Add. MSS. 3937–8; R.I.B.A. Drawings Coll.].

VALE ROYAL, CHESHIRE, rebuilt south-east wing for the 1st Lord Delamere, 1833–4 [MS. account of alterations at Vale Royal since 1810, formerly at Vale Royal].

HINCHINBROOKE, HUNTS., reconstruction after fire (1830) for the 7th Earl of Sandwich, 1833–6 [C.U.L., Add. MS. 3956, f. 31; *V.C.H. Hunts.* ii, 136] (*C. Life*, 6, 13 April 1929).

LATIMERS, CHESHAM, BUCKS., rebuilt for the Hon. Charles Compton Cavendish, afterwards Lord Chesham, 1834–8 [C.U.L., Add. MS. 3936; R.I.B.A. Drawings Coll.; G. G. Scott, *Recollections*, 1879, 51; B. Burgess, 'Latimer', *Records of Bucks.* vi, 1887, 35].

OTFORD COURT, SHOREHAM, KENT, for H. St. J. Mildmay, 1834–8; dem. *c.* 1955 [C.U.L., Add. MSS. 3940, 3956, f. 32].

PULL (now WELLS) COURT, BUSHLEY, WORCS., for the Rev. E. C. Dowdeswell, 1834–9 [C.U.L., Add. MSS. 3942–3; R.I.B.A. Drawings Coll.].

GOPSALL HALL, LEICS., alterations to offices for the 1st Earl Howe, 1835; dem. 1951 [C.U.L., Add. MSS. 3944, 3956, f. 35].

KIRKLANDS, ANCRUM, ROXBURGHSHIRE, for John Richardson, *c.* 1835; rebuilt 1907–8 [C.U.L., Add. MS. 3956, f. 30; R.I.B.A. Drawings Coll.; *N.S.A.* iii, 1845, 245].

ESCRICK PARK, YORKS. (E.R.), repairs and alterations for Lord Wenlock, *c.* 1835 [C.U.L., Add. MS. 3955, f. 7ᵛ; *Proc. Soc. Antiq.*, obituary]; cf. R.I.B.A. Drawings Coll. for an unexecuted scheme for further alterations *c.* 1839.

CASTLE UPTON, CO. ANTRIM, IRELAND, enlarged for the 1st Lord Templetown, 1836–7 [C.U.L., Add. MS. 3956, f. 41; V. and A. 182 s].

HARLAXTON MANOR, LINCS. Blore's accounts [C.U.L. Add. MS. 3956, f. 47] show that in 1837 he was employed by Gregory de Ligne Gregory 'to examine the state of the house and arrange plans for carrying on the work'. The house had been begun in 1831 to the designs of Anthony Salvin, but he was dismissed in 1837. Blore's association with the house was brief, for in 1838 William Burn (*q.v.*) took over: cf. *Civil Engineer and Architect's Jnl.* ii, 1839, 39 (where Blore's role is stated to have been advisory only), *C. Life*, 11 April 1957, and C.

---

[1] In Sept. 1830 Burn complaiend to Rickman (then in Edinburgh) 'of Blore for supplanting him in some places'. No doubt Freeland was one of them.

Hussey, *English Country Houses: Late Georgian*, 1958, 242, where, however, Gregory Gregory (d. 1860) is confused with his father George (d. 1822).

MALLOW CASTLE, CO. CORK, IRELAND, design for adding a tower for D. Jephson, 1837 [C.U.L., Add. MS. 3956, f. 49].

COMBERMERE ABBEY, CHESHIRE, stables for the 1st Viscount Combermere, 1837 [C.U.L., Add. MS. 3956, f. 19].

DORFOLD HALL, CHESHIRE, chimney-pieces in Drawing and Dining Rooms for Rev. James Tomkinson, 1837–8 and 1843 [C.U.L., Add. MS. 3955, f. 8ᵛ] (*C. Life*, 31 Oct. 1908).

BALLYDRAIN, CO. ANTRIM, for Hugh Montgomery, 1837–8; damaged by I.R.A. *c.* 1972 [C.U.L., Add. MS. 3956, f. 40; V. and A. 182 r].

LODSWORTH HOUSE, SUSSEX, for Hasler Hollist, 1837–9 [C.U.L., Add. MS. 3947; V. and A. 182 r].

CREWE HALL, CHESHIRE, repairs for the 3rd Lord Crewe, 1837–42; interior destroyed by fire 1866 and rebuilt by E. M. Barry [C.U.L., Add. MSS. 3945–6; R.I.B.A. Drawings Coll.; *Proc. Soc. Antiq.*, obituary].

ALOUPKA, CRIMEA, villa for Prince Michael Woronzow, 1837–40 [R.I.B.A. Drawings Coll.; V. and A. 182 q; *Builder* 1850, 354–5; J. Mordaunt Crook in *C. Life*, 2 March 1972].

SYDNEY, NEW SOUTH WALES, AUSTRALIA, GOVERNOR'S HOUSE, 1837–45 [J. M. Herman, *The Early Australian Architects and their Work*, 1954, 202–3, 219–20; R.I.B.A. Drawings Coll.].

ROCKINGHAM CASTLE, NORTHANTS., work, probably including entrance lodge, for the Hon. R. Watson, 1838 [C.U.L., Add. MS. 3955, f. 6ᵛ].

RAMSEY ABBEY, HUNTS., remodelled for Edward Fellowes, 1838–9 [*Proc. Soc. Antiq.*, obituary; C.U.L., Add. MS. 3949] (*V.C.H. Hunts.* ii, 192–3).

CROM, or CRUM, CASTLE, CO. FERMANAGH, IRELAND, for the 3rd Earl of Erne, 1838–41 [*Proc. Soc. Antiq.*, obituary; R.I.B.A. Drawings Coll.].

HAMPTON COURT PALACE, MIDDLESEX, restoration works, 1838–48 [M. H. Port in *History of the King's Works*, vi, 333–5].

CONNINGTON CASTLE, HUNTS., internal alterations for J. M. Heathcote, 1839–40 [C.U.L., Add. MS. 3956, f. 58ᵛ; *V.C.H. Hunts.* iii, 145].

BOTLEYS, nr. CHERTSEY, SURREY, alterations for Robert Gostling, 1839–40 [C.U.L., Add. MS. 3956, f. 60ᵛ].

CAPESTHORNE HALL, CHESHIRE, remodelled 1839–42 for Edward Davies Davenport; damaged by fire 1861 and rebuilt by A. Salvin 1865–8 [*Proc. Soc. Antiq.*, obituary].

HAVERINGLAND HALL, NORFOLK, for Edward Fellowes, 1839–43; dem. 1946, 'Grecian' [*Proc. Soc. Antiq.*, obituary; accounts in Norwich

City Library; V. and A. 182 d] (J. H. Mason, *Norfolk Photographically Illustrated*, 1865).

WISTON PARK, SUSSEX, alterations for Charles Goring, *c.* 1840 [V. and A. 182 i; C.U.L., Add. MS. 3956, f. 70].

SHADWELL PARK, NORFOLK, south wing for Sir Robert John Buxton, *c.* 1840–3 [C.U.L., Add. MS. 3950; V. and A. 182 e; B.M., Add. MS. 42027, ff. 92–3] (*C. Life*, 2–9 July 1964).

MEREVALE HALL, WARWICKS., for W. S. Dugdale, 1840–2 [*Proc. Soc. Antiq.*, obituary; V. and A. 182 f and g] (*C. Life*, 13–20 March 1969).

WORSLEY HALL, LANCS., for Lord Francis Egerton, 1840–5; dem. 1945–6 [C.U.L., Add. MS. 3951; drawings and account in R.I.B.A. Drawings Coll.] (*Builder* viii, 1850, 270–1).

THE GROVE, WATFORD, HERTS., repairs for the 4th Earl of Clarendon, 1841–2 [C.U.L., Add. MS. 3955, f. 12ᵛ; *Proc. Soc. Antiq.*, obituary].

COOLHURST, nr. HORSHAM, SUSSEX, additions for C. S. Dickens, 1841–4 [C.U.L., Add. MS. 3955, f. 26ᵛ].

MORETON HALL, CHESHIRE, for G. H. Ackers, 1841–6 [Ormerod, *History of Cheshire*, ed. Helsby, iii, 1875, 46; V. and A. 182 b].

WINDSOR CASTLE, BERKS., alterations to Upper Ward for Queen Victoria, 1841–7, and reconstructed Lodgings of Military Knights in Lower Ward, 1840–7 [M. H. Port in *History of the King's Works* vi, 392–3; W. H. St. J. Hope, *Architectural History of Windsor Castle*, 1913, 533, 567, etc.].

HATCHFORD, nr. COBHAM, SURREY, remodelled for Lord Francis Egerton, 1842–3; dem. [C.U.L., Add. MS. 3955, ff. 24, 79].

CASTLE HILL, DEVON, additions for the 2nd Earl Fortescue, 1842–4 [*Proc. Soc. Antiq.*, obituary; C.U.L., Add. MS. 3955, f. 27] (*C. Life*, 17–24 March 1934).

WILLERSLEY CASTLE, DERBYSHIRE, alterations for Peter Arkwright, 1843 [C.U.L., Add. MS. 3955, f. 43].

CRAKAIG, SUTHERLAND, alterations for the 2nd Duke of Sutherland, 1843 [Staffs. R. O., Leweson-Gore MSS., K.1. 10–4; C.U.L., Add. MS. 3955, f. 43].

KINGSTON HALL, NOTTS., for the 1st Lord Belper, 1843–5 [C.U.L., Add. MS. 3952].

NORTH MIMMS PARK, HERTS., alterations, including new entrance hall and staircase, for Fulke Greville, 1844–6 [C.U.L., Add. MS. 3955, f. 50].

THICKET PRIORY, YORKS. (E.R.), for the Rev. Joseph Dunnington-Jefferson, 1844–7 [*Proc. Soc. Antiq.*, obituary; drawings in B.M., Add. MS. 47,610; C.U.L., Add. MS. 3955, f. 45].

THE FRYTHE, nr. WELWYN, HERTS., for William Wilshere, 1846 [*Proc. Soc. Antiq.*, obituary].

HOLDENBY HOUSE, NORTHANTS., stables, etc., for the 3rd Viscount Clifden, 1846 [C.U.L., Add. MS. 3955, f. 82].

HECKFIELD PLACE, HANTS., alterations for Charles Shaw Lefevre, 1847; dem. [C.U.L., Add. MS. 3955, f. 75].

CHURCHES

WINCHESTER CATHEDRAL, organ case in choir, 1824 [Eastlake, 140; cf. Blore's printed *Report to the Dean of Winchester on the proposed removal of the organ from the side to the centre of the Cathedral*, 1823].

BATTERSEA, ST. GEORGE, 1827–8; chancel added 1874; dem. [Port, 150–1; V. and A. 182 o].

PLAISTOW, ESSEX, ST. MARY, 1828–9; dem. 1889 [Port, 144–5; R.I.B.A. Drawings Coll.].

WARRINGTON, LANCS., ST. PAUL, 1829–31 [Port, 150–1; V. and A. 182 p; unsigned drawings in R.I.B.A. Drawings Coll.].

RIPON MINSTER, YORKS., restoration of choir, 1829–31 [*Gent's Mag.* 1830 (ii), 355; 1831 (ii), 168; V. and A. 182 p].

WOBURN CHURCH, BEDS., rebuilt tower, 1830 [*History and Description of Woburn and its Abbey*, Woburn 1845, 109].

CANFORD MAGNA CHURCH, DORSET, westward extension of nave, c. 1830; replaced by a new extension 1876–8 [I.C.B.S.; *R.C.H.M. Dorset* ii, 197; C.U.L., Add. MS. 3955, f. 2].

OXFORD, WADHAM COLLEGE CHAPEL, restored roof and erected stone reredos, 1831–3 [T. G. Jackson, *Wadham College, Oxford*, 1893, 156–7; V. and A. 182 p; R.I.B.A. Drawings Coll.].

CAMBRIDGE, TRINITY COLLEGE CHAPEL, alterations, 1831–2 [Willis & Clark, ii, 986].

PETERBOROUGH CATHEDRAL, stone organ screen (since dem.) and new choir fittings, 1832 [*A.P.S.D.*, s.v. 'Peterborough'; R.I.B.A. Drawings Coll.; C.U.L., Add. MS. 3955, ff. 3–4].

GREAT BRINGTON CHURCH, NORTHANTS., south porch for 2nd Earl Spencer, 1832 [*Architectural Notices of the Archdeaconry of Northants.*, 1849, 262].

WALTHAM CROSS, HERTS., HOLY TRINITY, 1831–2 [Port, 146–7].

OTTERY ST. MARY CHURCH, DEVON, restored stone altar screen, c. 1832 [W. Spreat, *Churches of Devon*, Exeter 1842].

LEYTONSTONE, ESSEX, ST. JOHN BAPTIST, 1832–3 [I.C.B.S.; Eastlake, 140; V. and A. 182 p].

CROFT, LANCS., CHRIST CHURCH, 1832–3 [Port, 148–9; V. and A. 182 o].

LONGFLEET CHURCH, DORSET, 1833–5; enlarged 1864; rebuilt 1915 [I.C.B.S.] (ill. J. Sydenham, *History of Poole*, 1839, 462).

STRATFORD LANGTHORNE, ESSEX, ST. JOHN THE EVANGELIST, 1833–4; chancel added 1882 [Port, 144–5; V. and A. 182 p].

EASEBOURNE CHURCH, SUSSEX, monumental chapel at east end of south aisle, for W. S. Poyntz, 1834–6 [C.U.L., Add. MS. 3956, f. 34].

POTTERS BAR, MIDDLESEX, ST. JOHN, 1835, 'Norman'; dem. [C. Mackeson, *Guide to the Churches of London*, 1894–5, 69].

BATH ABBEY CHURCH, stone choir screen, 1835; removed c. 1860 [*A.P.S.D.*, s.v. 'Bath'; V. and A. 182 o].

WESTMINSTER, ST. MARY THE VIRGIN, VINCENT SQUARE, 1836–7; dem. 1923 [Port, 156–7].

STEPNEY, ST. PETER, MILE END ROAD, 1837–8, 'Norman' [C. Mackeson, *Guide to the Churches of London*, 1894–5, 69].

CHELSEA, CHRIST CHURCH, 1838; altered by W. D. Caroe 1900–1 [*Companion to the Almanac*, 1838, 220; V. and A. 182 o].

OXFORD, MERTON COLLEGE CHAPEL, restored roofs of choir and transepts, 1838–43 [*V.C.H. Oxon.* iii, 101; V. and A. 182 p].

LONDON, ST. LUKE, BERWICK STREET, SOHO, 1838–9; dem. 1936 [*Survey of London* xxxi, 226–7].

LAMBETH, HOLY TRINITY, 1838–9; destroyed by bombing c. 1941 [Port, 154–5].

LONDON, CHRIST CHURCH, HOXTON, 1839, 'Norman'; destroyed by bombing 1944 [*Gent's Mag.* 1839 (ii), 303].

BARKINGSIDE, ESSEX, HOLY TRINITY, 1839–40, 'Norman' [Port, 144–5].

ASWARBY CHURCH, LINCS., rebuilt chancel for Sir Thomas Whichcote, Bart., 1839–41 [C.U.L., Add. MS. 3956, f. 61].

NORWICH CATHEDRAL, repaired west front, c. 1840 [*A.P.S.D.*, s.v. 'Norwich'; V. and A. 182 p; C.U.L., Add. MS. 3956, f. 76ᵛ].

OXFORD, ST. MARY MAGDALEN, restored south aisle, c. 1840 [*Companion to the Almanac*, 1842, 201].

THORNEY ABBEY, CAMBS., new east end at expense of 6th Duke of Bedford, 1840–1, 'Norman' [Gardner's *History, Gazeteer and Directory of Cambridgeshire*, 1851, 560; V. and A. 182 p; C.U.L., Add. MS. 3956, f. 69].

CONNINGTON CHURCH, HUNTS., pews, pulpit, etc., 1841 [V. and A. 182 h].

ELY CATHEDRAL, 'improvements partly executed and partly abandoned', 1840–1 and 1844 [C.U.L., Add. MS. 3955, f. 69ᵛ].

LATIMER CHAPEL, BUCKS., at expense of the Hon. C. C. Cavendish, 1841–2; east end by G. Scott 1867 [J. J. Sheahan, *History of Buckinghamshire*, 1862, 842].

LONDON, ST. JAMES THE GREAT, BETHNAL GREEN, 1841–4 [C. Mackeson, *Guide to the Churches of London*, 1894–5, 65; V. and A. 182 a].

LONDON, ST. THOMAS, CHARTERHOUSE GARDENS, GOSWELL STREET ROAD, 1841–2, 'Norman'; dem. 1909 [*Christian Guardian* 1841, 180; V. and A. 182 o].

WINDSOR, BERKS., HOLY TRINITY, 1842–4; altered 1875 [*Ecclesiologist* ii, 1843, 136; V. and A. 182 p; R.I.B.A. Drawings Coll.].

ADDINGTON CHURCH, SURREY, repairs and alterations for William Howley, Archbishop of

119

Canterbury, 1843 [C.U.L., Add. MS. 3955, ff. 32ᵛ, 70ᵛ; V. and A. 182 o].

OXFORD, ST. JOHN'S COLLEGE CHAPEL, reconstructed 1843 [*V.C.H. Oxon.* iii, 263; V. and A. 182 h].

BUSHLEY CHURCH, WORCS., at expense of Rev. E. C. Dowdeswell, 1843 [C.U.L., Add. MS. 3955, f. 32ᵛ; V. and A. 182 a].

GLASGOW CATHEDRAL, restoration, 1843 onwards (executed by William Nixon) [V. and A. 182 o; E. L. G. Stones, 'Notes on Glasgow Cathedral', *Innes Review* xxi (2), 140–52].

CINDERFORD CHURCH, GLOS., 1843–4 [P.R.O., F17/101].

RAMSEY ABBEY CHURCH, HUNTS., restoration, 1843 [*Builder* xxxvii, 1879, 1019; V. and A. 182 h].

WESTMINSTER ABBEY, canons' stalls and choir fittings, 1843–8; restoration of exterior of north side of nave, 1849 [*A.P.S.D.*, *s.v.* 'Westminster Abbey'].

BRANDISTON CHURCH, NORFOLK, restoration, 1844 [*Builder* ii, 1844, 93].

OXFORD, ST. MARY THE VIRGIN, began restoration of steeple, 1848, but was superseded by J. C. & C. Buckler, 1850 [J. G. Jackson, *St. Mary the Virgin*, Oxford, 1897, 144–6].

LONDON, SAVOY CHAPEL, font and font cover, 1865 [H. White, *Memorials of the Savoy*, 1878, 238; V. and A. 182 j].

DUDLEY, WORCS., ST. THOMAS, font and font cover, 1867 [*Builder* xxv, 1867, 679–80].

MONUMENTS

WADHAM COLLEGE, OXFORD, monuments to Wardens John Wills (d. 1806) and William Tournay (d. 1833) [J. Ingram, *Memorials of Oxford* ii, 1837, Wadham section, 15].

CASTLE ASHBY CHURCH, NORTHANTS., monument to 1st Marquess of Northampton (d. 1828), 1843 [V. and A. 182 h; C.U.L., Add. MS. 3955, f. 30ᵛ].

BISHOP MIDDLEHAM CHURCH, DURHAM, monument to Robert Surtees (d. 1834) [F. Whellan & Co.'s *History, Topography and Directory of Durham*, 1894, 244].

BLICKLING CHURCH, NORFOLK, monument to 7th Marquess of Lothian (d. 1841), 1842 [V. and A. 182 h; C.U.L., Add. MS. 3955, f. 32].

LINCOLN CATHEDRAL, monument to William Hilton, R.A., 1864 [*Builder* xxiii, 1865, 227].

KENSAL GREEN CEMETERY, monument to General Foster Walker, 1866 [*Builder* xxiv, 1866, 306].

BLOXHAM, JOHN (–1715), was a carpenter and surveyor of Banbury. At present his only known work is ADDERBURY RECTORY, OXON., which he contracted to rebuild in 1682 in accordance with 'a draught drawn by the sayd John Bloxham' and still attached to the document. Bloxham is described as 'Surveyor' in the entry

of his burial in Banbury parish register [*Cake and Cockhorse*, the journal of the Banbury Historical Society, March 1965, 207–11].

BLYTH, JOHN (1806–1878), entered the Royal Academy Schools in 1827, and in 1833 exhibited a design for a monument to the Rev. Robert Hall, a celebrated Baptist minister at Bristol. He repaired the church of ST. BARTHOLOMEW THE GREAT, SMITHFIELD, after a fire in 1830, and restored the blocked-up triforium [G. Godwin, *The Churches of London* i, 1838, 10]. His only other recorded works appear to be the NORTHAMPTON TABERNACLE, CLERKENWELL, 1836, and the CITY OF LONDON LITERARY AND SCIENTIFIC INSTITUTION, 165 ALDERSGATE STREET, 1838 [*Architectural Magazine* iii, 41; v, 135–6]. Blyth was President of the Surveyors' Club in 1867. R. C. Carpenter was his pupil. He died in Albert Road, Regent's Park, on 17 February 1878, aged 71.

BOAG, JAMES, had an extensive business as a builder and architect in Sutherland and Easter Ross during the reign of George III. He was a carpenter by trade, and came from the Lowlands, but established himself in Sutherland, first at Golspie Tower and later at Dornoch. Among the many churches which he designed and built were those of RESOLIS or KIRKMICHAEL, ROSS-SHIRE, 1767, and KILDONAN, SUTHERLAND, 1788. He also erected the SPINNINGDALE MILL, SUTHERLAND, 1794, destroyed by fire in 1806. He was a rough man, who 'terrified all the school-boys, as well as every inmate of his own house, by the violence of his temper and his readiness to take offence'. His buildings were in the simplest style of eighteenth-century Scottish vernacular. [Donald Sage, *Memorabilia Domestica; or Parish Life in the North of Scotland*, 2nd. ed., Wick 1899, 57, 121–22; *Scotland's Magazine*, July 1965, 24.]

BODT, or **BOTT**, JOHANN VON (1670–1745), was the son of a German father and a French mother. He was born and brought up in Paris, but as a Protestant he was obliged to leave France after the revocation of the Edict of Nantes in 1685. He went to Holland, where he entered the service of the Prince of Orange as a military engineer. In this capacity he came to England and served in William III's army in Ireland in 1690–1 and in Flanders in 1692–5. He held the rank of a captain of artillery in the Royal Engineers until August 1699, when he resigned to enter the service of the King of Prussia. In this employment he designed and erected several important buildings in Potsdam, including the Arsenal and the steeple of the Parochialkirche (which may have been influenced by Wren's St. Vedast, Foster Lane). In 1728 he transferred to Saxony, rose to the rank of general, and died at Dresden in 1745.

While in England Bodt made designs, which have apparently not survived, for rebuilding Whitehall Palace for William III. These were probably made soon after the fire which destroyed the old palace in 1698. Bodt also made designs for a grandiose royal hospital in the style of Bruand's Invalides which were probably intended for Greenwich. Neither of these schemes was, of course, carried out, but in *c.* 1710–20 it was to Bodt's designs that the east wing of WENT-WORTH CASTLE (STAINBOROUGH HALL), YORKS. (W.R.), containing a magnificent gallery, was built by the 1st Earl of Strafford. The Earl was Ambassador to Prussia from 1706 to 1711, and directed the building operations at Wentworth Castle by letter from Berlin. Horace Walpole, who was a friend of the family, refers to Bodt as the architect in a letter to Bentley of August 1756, and in 1770 the 2nd Earl remembered that the front had been designed by the architect of the Arsenal at Potsdam [*The Letters and Journals of Lady Mary Coke*, Edinburgh 1896, iv, 234]. There is an engraving of it dated 1713 (B.M., *King's Maps* xlv, 29c) made from a drawing by Charles Holzendorf, who was then secretary to the Embassy at Berlin, and it is illustrated in *Vitruvius Britannicus* i, 1715, pls. 92–4. What appear to be Bodt's original designs, differing in several respects from the building as executed, are in the Victoria and Albert Museum (D.212, 1890 and E.307–8, 1937).[1] The interior was eventually completed in 1724 to Anglo-Palladian designs by James Gibbs, but the exterior remains as a remarkable and almost unique example of Franco-Prussian architecture in Georgian England.[2]

[Nikolaus Pevsner, 'John Bodt in England', *Arch. Rev.*, July 1961; John Harris, 'Bodt and Stainborough', *ibid.*; E. F. Sekler, *Wren and his Place in European Architecture*, 1956, 191.]

BOND, JOHN LINNELL (1764–1837), received instruction in architectural drawing from James Malton. He entered the Royal Academy Schools in 1783, aged 19, winning the Silver Medal in 1784 and the Gold Medal in 1786. He was an accomplished draughtsman and enjoyed drawing such compositions as 'the Temple of Jupiter at Olympia, with the procession of the conquerors in the games', which he exhibited at the Academy in 1803. Despite his considerable talents he was too modest and retiring to make a name for himself, and preferred 'to confine his labours to the gratification and service of the few

friends who had discernment enough to appreciate his merits'. His chief patron appears to have been Sir Gerard Noel, M.P., for whom he designed the nucleus of EXTON HALL, RUTLAND, 1811, and the imposing neo-classical STAMFORD HOTEL at STAMFORD, LINCS., *c.* 1810–29. His other works, as exhibited at the R.A., were an unidentified villa at Wimbledon (1796), an anatomical theatre and museum in Blenheim (now Ramillies) Street, London, for J. Brooks (1806), the front 'lately erected' to Messrs. Tatham & Bailey's house, Nos. 13–14 Mount Street, Grosvenor Square (1808), 'a room erecting at Southampton Castle for the Marquis of Lansdowne, after the manner of the Moorish architecture of Granada' (1809), and a villa at Bushey, Herts. (1814). He also made designs for the Strand (*i.e.* Waterloo) Bridge for George Dodd, the engineer at first employed by the Bridge Company, but it was eventually built by John Rennie to his own designs.

In 1818–21 Bond travelled in Italy and Greece. He contributed to the *Literary Gazette* articles as architectural subjects, and left in manuscript a translation of Vitruvius that had occupied him for some twenty years. He exhibited regularly at the Royal Academy from 1782 to 1814, and also at the Society of British Artists in 1833. Drawings of details of Henry VII's Chapel, made by him in 1807, are in the British Museum (Add. MS. 15529). [*Literary Gazette* 1837, 724; *Gent's Mag.* 1837, 655; *A.P.S.D.*; *D.N.B.*]

BONNAR, THOMAS (–*c.* 1832), was the son of John Bonnar, a painter of Edinburgh, and was admitted a burgess of the city in June 1795 [*Roll of Edinburgh Burgesses*, Scottish Record Soc. 1933, 20]. He became a Sworn Measurer in 1807 and was appointed Superintendent of Public Works in December 1809, but was dismissed in 1818 [Edinburgh Town Council Minutes]. From 1810 he also acted as surveyor to Heriot's Hospital. He probably died in 1832, when his name disappears from the Edinburgh directories. As an architect he was chiefly engaged in laying out streets in the New Town.

EDINBURGH[1]

DRUMMOND PLACE, partly revised elevations designed by Robert Reid, 1817–18.
HERMITAGE PLACE, LEITH, NOS. 1–14, 1817–25 [*Edinburgh Evening Courant*, 15 Oct. 1825].
BELLEVUE CRESCENT, 1819–32.

---

[1] These drawings came from the Talman Collection. One of them is inscribed 'W.T. del & inv.', but it is not in William Talman's hand, and the inscription appears to have been due to a later owner who was unaware of its real authorship.
[2] Kettlethorpe Hall, nr. Wakefield (dated 1727), is another, but the identity of its architect is unknown.

---

[1] Unless otherwise stated this list is based on the Scottish Development Department's duplicated *List of Buildings of Special Architectural or Historical Interest in Edinburgh*, 1971, where references are given to the relevant Sasines, etc. Several drawings by Bonnar are preserved among the records of the Heriot Trust.

GLOUCESTER PLACE, NOS. 4–15, 1822.

LONDON STREET, NOS. 42–54, 1823.

CLAREMONT STREET EAST, NOS. 1–85, for the Heriot Trust, 1824–30. Nos. 1–11 Bellevue Crescent were built in a uniform style 1834–56.

ATHOLL CRESCENT and PLACE, and NOS. 3–25 TORPHICHEN STREET, for the Heriot Trust, 1824–31.

QUEEN STREET GARDENS, Gardener's house, 1819 [Heriot Trust records, drawing dated 6 August 1819].

BONOMI, IGNATIUS (*c.* 1787–1870), was the eldest son of Joseph Bonomi (*q.v.*). It was presumably through his father's work at Lambton Hall that he came to be employed in County Durham, where he soon built up an extensive practice rivalling that of John Dobson in Newcastle. Not only did he have a considerable clientele among the local aristocracy, and the clergy both Anglican and Catholic, but he also held the post of Surveyor of Bridges for the county. It was 'Mr. Bonomi's experience in building bridges' that led the Stockton & Darlington Railway Company to employ him to design the first railway bridge in England (at Skerne, nr. Darlington) in 1824. In 1842 he took John Augustus Cory (d. 1887), a pupil of J. J. Scoles, as a partner. J. L. Pearson (1817–97) was in his office from 1831 to 1841. Bonomi retired in 1855, leaving Durham to settle near his younger brother Joseph (1796–1878) at Wimbledon, where he lived on until 1870. Cory continued to practise in Durham until about 1860, when he went into partnership with Scott's pupil C. J. Ferguson (d. 1904) at Carlisle. A portrait in oils by Charles Martin, painted in Florence in 1861, belongs to Mr. Anthony de Cosson in Vancouver, B.C.

Ignatius Bonomi was a competent designer in both neo-classical and Gothic styles. His most interesting secular work is probably Burn Hall, whose channelled masonry and mansard roof suggest the influence of recent French architecture. Some of his churches are unexpectedly convincing for their date. Even the neo-Norman Oxenhope is praised by Pevsner for the authenticity of its detailing, and the Catholic chapel at Brough Hall is remarkable as an archaeologically correct reproduction of the thirteenth-century Archbishop's Chapel at York.

[A. F. Sealey & D. Walters, 'The First Railway Architect', *Arch. Rev.*, May 1964; information from Mrs. J. Crosby.]

PUBLIC AND DOMESTIC ARCHITECTURE

DURHAM, THE COUNTY GAOL and COURTHOUSE, 1810–11, superseding F. Sandys (*q.v.*) [W. Fordyce, *History of Durham* i, 1857, 292–3].

RICHMOND, YORKS. (N.R.), ST. NICHOLAS HOSPITAL,

repairs for the 1st Lord Dundas, 1813 [*Gent's Mag.* 1824 (i), 116].

LAMBTON CASTLE, CO. DURHAM, works including park entrances (*c.* 1815), Lamb Bridge over the R. Wear (1819–20) and enlargement and remodelling of house in Gothic style (*c.* 1820–8) for J. G. Lambton, afterwards Earl of Durham; severely damaged by subsidence 1854 and largely rebuilt by J. Dobson and S. Smirke 1860–4; partly dem. 1930 [Neale, *Seats*, ser. i, ii; Christopher Hussey in *C. Life*, 24–31 March 1966].

DURHAM CASTLE, alterations to entrance lodge for Bishop of Durham, 1817–18 [documents in Gateshead Public Library, *ex inf.* Mrs. J. Crosby].

EGGLESTON HALL, CO. DURHAM, for William Hutchinson, *c.* 1820 [*The Early Life of Clement Burlison*, Durham n.d., 4].

STANHOPE RECTORY, CO. DURHAM, for Dr. Phillpotts, 1821 [*The Early Life of Clement Burlison*, Durham n.d., 5].

MIDDLETON-IN-TEESDALE, CO. DURHAM, new cottages in Masterman Place or New Middleton for the London Lead Co., 1823–4 [E. Mackenzie & M. Ross, *History of the County Palatine of Durham* ii, 1834, 252].

SKERNE BRIDGE, nr. DARLINGTON, CO. DURHAM, for the Stockton & Darlington Railway Co., 1824–5 [A. F. Sealey & D. Walters, 'the First Railway Architect', *Arch. Rev.*, May 1964].

SHINCLIFFE BRIDGE, CO. DURHAM, 1824–6 [M. A. Richardson, *The Local Historian's Table-Book* iii, 1843, 292].

BLAGDON, NORTHUMBERLAND, added *porte cochère* to south front for Sir Matthew White Ridley, Bart., 1826; removed 1944 [Hodgson, *History of Northumberland* ii (2), 1832, 328; Christopher Hussey in *C. Life*, 18 July 1952].

LONDON, 10 CARLTON HOUSE TERRACE, extensively revised Nash's designs for the interior for Sir Matthew White Ridley, Bart, 1827 [*Life and Letters of Cecilia Ridley*, ed. Viscountess Ridley, 1958, 47].

NUNWICK, SIMONBURN, NORTHUMBERLAND, alterations, including addition of dining-room, for R. L. Allgood, 1829 [*History of Northumberland* xv, 199; Gordon Nares in *C. Life*, 12, 19 July 1956].

DINSDALE PARK HOTEL (later Retreat for Mental Invalids), CO. DURHAM, for J. G. Lambton, afterwards Earl of Durham, 1829; dem. [W. Fordyce, *History of Durham* i, 1857, 509].

DURHAM, THE DEANERY, alterations, *c.* 1830 [records in Prior's Kitchen, Durham, *ex inf.* Mrs. J. Crosby].

BURN HALL, CO. DURHAM, for B. J. Salvin, 1821–34 [volume of working drawings, including letter referring to Bonomi as the architect, formerly at Burn Hall].

EASINGTON RECTORY, YORKS. (N.R.), design for

alterations, 1832 [Borthwick Institute, MGA 1832/3].

KIRKLEATHAM HALL, YORKS. (N.R.), minor alterations for Henry Vansittart, 1835 [N. Riding Record Office, ZK 11786, *ex inf.* Mrs. J. Crosby].

THE CROFT SPA HOTEL, YORKS. (N.R.), for Sir William Chaytor, Bart., 1835 [Durham County Record Office, D/Ch./E. 252].

*CLERVAUX CASTLE, YORKS. (N.R.), for Sir William Chaytor, Bart., 1842–3; dem. 1951, 'Norman' style [Durham County Record Office, D/Ch./E. 253–4].

*WYNYARD PARK, CO. DURHAM, restored after fire for the 3rd Marquess of Londonderry, 1842–4 [Durham County Record Office, D/Lo/C. 157 and E. 678].

*LOFTHOUSE-IN-CLEVELAND RECTORY, YORKS. (N.R.), 1844–5 [J. W. Ord, *History of Cleveland*, 1846, plate facing p. 277; Borthwick Institute, MGA 1845/5].

*HESLEYSIDE, NORTHUMBERLAND, alterations, including addition of clock-tower, for W. H. Charlton, *c.* 1847 [*Recollections of a Northumbrian Lady*, ed. L. E. O. Charlton, 1949, 178–9].

Note: No printed or documentary evidence has been found for the attribution to Bonomi (N. Pevsner, *The Buildings of England: County Durham*, 1953, 243) of WINDLESTONE HALL, CO. DURHAM, for Sir Robert J. Eden, Bart., *c.* 1834, but it may well be correct.

CHURCHES

(all Gothic unless otherwise stated)

LOFTHOUSE-IN-CLEVELAND CHURCH, YORKS. (N.R.), rebuilt 1811, retaining old tower; rebuilt 1902 [J. W. Ord, *History of Cleveland*, 1846, 277].

DURHAM, ST. CUTHBERT (R.C.), 1826–7 [E. Mackenzie & M. Ross, *History of the County Palatine of Durham* ii, 1834, 402].

DARLINGTON, ST. AUGUSTINE (R.C.), 1826–7 [E. Mackenzie & M. Ross, *op. cit.* ii, 1834, 135].

WINLATON CHURCH, CO. DURHAM, 1827–9 [E. Mackenzie & M. Ross, *op. cit.* i, 1834, 197].

DURHAM CATHEDRAL, repairs to south gable of Chapel of the Nine Altars and gable of south transept, *c.* 1828 [*A.P.S.D., s.v.* 'Durham'; cf. *Catalogue of R.I.B.A. Drawings Coll.: B*, 95].

FERRYHILL, CO. DURHAM, ST. LUKE, 1828–9; dem. *c.* 1853 [E. Mackenzie & M. Ross, *op. cit.* ii, 1834, 310].

REDCAR CHURCH, YORKS. (N.R.), rebuilt 1828–9; altered 1888 [T. Richmond, *Local Records of Stockton and Neighbourhood*, Stockton, 1868, 153].

SUNDERLAND, CO. DURHAM, ST. MARY (R.C.), 1835 [W. Fordyce, *History of Durham* ii, 1857, 444].

DUDDO CHURCH, NORTHUMBERLAND, 1832, neo-Norman [*The British Magazine* iii, 1833, 602].

CHESTER-LE-STREET CHURCH, CO. DURHAM, Lord Durham's pew, *c.* 1832 [E. Mackenzie & M. Ross, *op. cit.* i, 114].

DURHAM, ST. OSWALD, ELVET, reconstructed 1834 [*A.P.S.D., s.v.* 'Durham'].

BROUGH HALL, ST. PAULINUS CHAPEL (R.C.), YORKS. (N.R.), for Sir William Lawson, 1834–7 [John Cornforth in *C. Life*, 19 Oct. 1967].

UPLEATHAM CHURCH, YORKS. (N.R.), 1835, neo-Norman [I.C.B.S.].

DENTON CHURCH, CO. DURHAM, addition of north transept, 1836; rebuilt 1891 [I.C.B.S.].

HOUGHTON-LE-SPRING, CO. DURHAM, ST. MICHAEL (R.C.), 1837 [M. A. Richardson, *The Local Historian's Table-Book* iv, 401].

WIGTON, CUMBERLAND, ST. CUTHBERT (R.C.), 1837 [B. W. Kelly, *Historical Dictionary of the English Catholic Missions*, 1907, 434].

DODDINGTON CHURCH, NORTHUMBERLAND, restoration and new chancel, 1838 [*History of Northumberland* xiv, 1935, 148–9].

BATTYFORD (MIRFIELD), YORKS. (W.R.), CHRIST-CHURCH, 1838–40 [I.C.B.S.].

? LEEMING (EXELBY), YORKS. (N.R.), ST. JOHN, 1839; tower 1911 [I.C.B.S.].[1]

CORNHILL CHURCH, NORTHUMBERLAND, rebuilt 1840; chancel added 1866 [I.C.B.S.].

BARTON CHURCH, YORKS (N.R.), 1840–1; altered 1910 [I.C.B.S.].

*CROOK CHURCH, CO. DURHAM, 1841–3 [I.C.B.S.].

*SCREMERSTON CHURCH and PARSONAGE, NORTHUMBERLAND, 1842–3 [I.C.B.S.; drawings in R.I.B.A. Drawings Coll.].

*INGLETON CHURCH, CO. DURHAM, 1843 [I.C.B.S.].

*NENTHEAD CHURCH, CUMBERLAND, 1845 [I.C.B.S.].

*GILLING CHURCH, YORKS (N.R.), north aisle, etc., 1845 [I.C.B.S.].

*UPPER HOPTON CHURCH, YORKS. (W.R.), 1846 [G.R.].

*PITTINGTON CHURCH, CO. DURHAM, enlarged 1846–7 [I.C.B.S.].

*DEWSBURY, YORKS. (W.R.), ST. MATTHEW, WEST TOWN, 1848 [I.C.B.S.].

*OXENHOPE CHURCH, YORKS, (W.R.), 1849, neo-Norman [I.C.B.S.].

*SOHAM CHURCH, CAMBS., restoration, 1849 [R. Gardner, *History, Gazetteer and Directory of Cambridgeshire*, 1851, 393].

BONOMI, JOSEPH (1739–1808), was born in Rome on 19 January 1739. He was educated in

---

* Designed in partnership with J. A. Cory.

[1] Bonomi was involved in the building of this church, but may not have been responsible for the design.

---

* Designed in partnership with J. A. Cory.

the Collegio Romano, and became a pupil of the Marchese Teodoli, a nobleman who devoted himself to the study and practice of architecture. There is also evidence that he was taught by Clérisseau [Hist. MSS. Comm. *12th Report* ix, 372]. In 1767 he came to England to work for the brothers R. and J. Adam, with whom he remained for several years. He afterwards assisted Thomas Leverton for a time, in particular (according to A. T. Bolton) in connection with 'the very Adam-like house in Lincoln's Inn Fields (N.-W. angle), and also in building Bedford Square.' In 1783 he went to Italy, probably in company with Lord Aylesford, who visited Italy that year, and was 'much his patron'. It was during this visit that he became an associate of the Clementine Academy at Bologna and of the Academy of St. Luke at Rome. He returned to England in 1784, and established himself in practice in London. In 1789 he was elected A.R.A. by the casting vote of Sir Joshua Reynolds. In the following year Reynolds made an unsuccessful attempt to secure his election as a full Academician in order to qualify him for the vacant professorship of Perspective, and it was the opposition to this proposal that led to Reynold's temporary resignation of the presidency in February 1790. In 1803 Bonomi failed to secure the appointment of architect to the King of Naples [Canova archive, Bassano, 2264], but in the following year he was made an honorary architect to St. Peter's, Rome (for which he had in 1776 made a design for a sacristy).

Bonomi exhibited regularly at the Royal Academy from 1783 onwards. He soon achieved a considerable reputation as a designer of country houses, and is alluded to as a fashionable architect in Jane Austen's *Sense and Sensibility*. Externally his houses have a severity that may be neo-classical in intention but is apt to be somewhat arid in effect unless relieved (as it is at Longford, Rosneath, Eastwell and Laverstoke) by a bold portico designed to act as a *porte cochère*. Within Bonomi preferred a chaste simplicity to the elaborate decorative schemes of Robert Adam, but would on occasion introduce unexceptionably neo-classical features such as casts from antique friezes. At Packington the rich decoration of the gallery, based on Ponce's *Description des Bains de Titus* (1786), reflects the personal taste of his patron the Earl of Aylesford, and the remarkable church, with its primitive Greek columns supporting a vault straight from the Roman baths, was undoubtedly due as much to Lord Aylesford's studies of the antique originals as to Bonomi's own neo-classical sympathies, which did not lie in the direction of Greece. In interpreting his patron's wishes Bonomi did, however, produce a building as radical as anything by Gilly or Ledoux, and the circular belvedere on the roof of Rosneath may afford evidence that Bonomi

was not unaware of Ledoux's work. For the Gothic style Bonomi had absolutely no sympathy: writing to the Earl of Buchan in 1807 he denounced it as having caused the 'total corruption' of medieval architecture throughout Europe except at Rome, and lamented 'the revival of such absurdities in this country' [Sotheby's *Catalogue of MSS.* sold 22 Feb. 1972, lot 599].

Bonomi married in 1775 Rosa Florini, a cousin of Angelica Kauffmann. They had three sons, the eldest of whom is noticed above. The second son, Joseph Bonomi, junior (1796–1878), was distinguished as an Egyptologist and became second curator of Sir John Soane's Museum.[1] Joseph Bonomi died on 9 March 1808, aged 69. The Latin inscription on his monument in the Marylebone cemetery is given in Papworth's memoir and in Lysons, *Environs of London* ii, 1811, 547. There is a protrait by George Dance in the R.A. Library. For his professional charges see J. Noble, *The Professional Practice of Architects*, 1836, 174–5.

['The Life and Works of Joseph Bonomi', *Architect, Engineer and Surveyor*, 1843, 70–1; memoir by Wyatt Papworth in *R.I.B.A. Transactions* 1868–9, 123–134; J. E. Hodgson & F. A. Eaton, *The Royal Academy*, 1905, 37 ff; memoir of Joseph Bonomi, junior, in *Transactions of the Society for Biblical Archaeology* for 1879; *The Farington Diary*, ed. J. Greig, vii, 124; *A.P.S.D.*; *D.N.B.*; *Catalogue of the R.I.B.A. Drawings Coll.: B.*, 95–6.]

LONDON, UPPER BROOK STREET, work for William Locke, 1782 [design for a chimney-piece inscribed 'for Wm Lock's Esqr in Upper Brook Street/Joseph Bonomi Archit Febry 1782' in possession of W. A. Brandt, Esq., 1969].

PACKINGTON HALL, WARWICKS., interiors, probably including the Pompeian Gallery (1785–8), for the 4th Earl of Aylesford, 1784 onwards [Marcus Binney in *C. Life*, 16, 23 July 1970; Desmond Fitz-Gerald in *Connoisseur*, Sept. 1972, 8–9].

DALE PARK, MADEHURST, SUSSEX, for Sir George Thomas, Bart., 1784–8; dem. 1959 [Neale, *Seats*, ser. 2, v].

LONDON, UXBRIDGE HOUSE, BURLINGTON GARDENS, assisted John Vardy, junior, 'in the disposition of the south front' for the 1st Earl of Uxbridge, *c.* 1785–9 [Britton & Pugin, *Public Buildings of*

---

[1] It was Joseph Bonomi, junior, not his brother Ignatius, who in 1842 (not 1838) designed the Egyptian façade of the Temple Mills, Leeds, in association with James Combe of Leeds. See *Companion to the Almanac*, 1844, 241–2, and obituary in *Transactions of the Society for Biblical Archaeology* vi, 1879. He also designed an Egyptian building over a spring at Hartwell House, Bucks., in 1851, and the Hartwell and Stone Schools, 1861 [W. H. Smyth, *Aedes Hartwellianae*, 1851, 156, 222; *Addenda to the Aedes Hartwellianae*, 1861, pl. I].

London i, 1825, 82; *Survey of London* xxxii, 461–3].

STANSTEAD HOUSE, SUSSEX, remodelled, with James Wyatt, for Richard Barwell, 1786–91; destroyed by fire 1900 [J. Dallaway, *Western Division of Sussex* ii, 1815, 159].

THE FOREST HALL, MERIDEN, WARWICKS., 1787–8; enlarged 1845 [*Records of the Woodmen of Arden*, privately printed 1885, 7–8].

LONDON, THE BAVARIAN EMBASSY CHAPEL, WARWICK STREET, 1789–90 [J. Britton, *The Original Picture of London*, 27th ed. *c.* 1832, 123] (G. Houghton–Brown, 'The Bavarian Chapel, London', *Arch. Rev.*, Aug. 1947, 67; *Survey of London* xxxi, 170–2).

GREAT PACKINGTON CHURCH, WARWICKS., for the 4th Earl of Aylesford, 1789–90 [Neale, *Seats*, ser. 1, iii; Marcus Binney in *C. Life*, 8 July 1971].

LONGFORD HALL, SALOP., for Ralph Leeke, 1789–94 [exhib. at R.A. 1797; G. Richardson, *New Vitruvius Britannicus* i, 1802, pls. 15–16] (*C. Life*, 16 Aug. 1962).

LANGLEY PARK, nr. BECKENHAM, KENT, additions for Sir Peter Burrell, afterwards Lord Gwydyr, 1790; destroyed by fire 1913 [*A.P.S.D.*].

ASHTEAD PARK, SURREY, for Richard Howard, 1790, executed by Samuel Wyatt [F. E. Paget, *Some Records of the Ashtead Estate*, 1873, 169].

LONDON, PORTMAN HOUSE, PORTMAN SQUARE, ballroom for Mrs. Elizabeth Montagu, 1790; destroyed by bombing 1940 [exhib. at R.A. 1790].

BARRELLS, WARWICKS., for Robert Knight, 1792–3; portico removed 1856; house dem. 1954 [exhib. at R. A. 1795; account in R.I.B.A. Drawings Coll.]

BOSWORTH HALL, HUSBANDS BOSWORTH, LEICS., east block facing park for F. F. Turville, 1792–3 [Turville papers in Leics. Record Office, *ex inf.* Mr. Edward Saunders].

COWICK HALL, YORKS. (W.R.), alterations for the 5th Viscount Downe, including the west staircase and probably the stables, 1792–*c.* 1808 [drawings in N. Riding Record Office, ZDS; John Killeen, *A Short History of Cowick Hall*, 1967].

KING'S LANGLEY CHURCH, HERTS., monument to Mary E. Crawford (d. 1793), executed by R. Westmacott [signed].

LONDON, THE SPANISH CHAPEL, MANCHESTER SQUARE, 1793–6; enlarged 1846; dem. 1880 [exhib. at R.A. 1793; drawing of interior by Bonomi in vestry of St. James's, Spanish Place].

EASTWELL PARK, KENT, for George Finch Hatton, 1793–1800; enlarged by W. Burn 1849; remodelled 1895; dem. 1926 [exhib. at R.A. 1794 and 1799; G. Richardson, *New Vitruvius Britannicus* i, 1802, pls. 39–41].

HORSLEY PLACE (later TOWERS), SURREY, stables

and coach-houses for William Currie, *c.* 1794; dem. [exhib. at R.A. 1794].

BLICKLING PARK, NORFOLK, pyramidal mausoleum to memory of 2nd Earl of Buckinghamshire, 1794 [exhib. at R.A. 1794; drawings at Blickling].

LAMBTON HALL (now CASTLE), CO. DURHAM, rebuilt for W. H. Lambton, *c.* 1796–7; work interrupted by Lambton's death in 1797; enlarged and castellated by I. Bonomi *c.* 1820–8; largely rebuilt 1860–4 [exhib. at R.A. 1798, 1800, 1802] (*C. Life*, 24–31 March 1966).

LAVERSTOKE PARK, HANTS., for Henry Portal, 1796–9 [exhib. at R.A. 1799; G. F. Prosser, *Select Illustrations of Hampshire*, 1833].

PIERCEFIELD, nr. CHEPSTOW, MONMOUTHSHIRE, saloon and staircase (now destroyed) for Sir Mark Wood, Bart., 1797 [Ackermann, *Repository of the Arts*, ser. 3, v, 1825, 313].

HATCHLANDS, nr. GUILDFORD, SURREY, alterations, including new entrance, for W. B. Sumner, 1797 [H. S. Goodhart-Rendel, *Hatchlands*, National Trust guidebook 1948, 5–7] (*C. Life*, 17 Sept., 1 Oct. 1953).

SANDLING HOUSE, nr. HYTHE, KENT, for W. Deedes, 1799; bombed 1943 and dem. 1945–6 [exhib. at R.A. 1799; Hasted, *History of Kent* viii, 1799, 220].

ROSNEATH, DUNBARTONSHIRE, for the 5th Duke of Argyll, 1803–6; gutted by fire 1947, dem. 1961 [exhib. at R.A. 1806; G. Richardson, *New Vitruvius Britannicus* ii, 1808, pls. 15–16; *R.I.B.A. Trans.*, 1868–9, 129–33].

FISHERWICK PARK, STAFFS., furniture for the Marquess of Donegall [*A Companion to the Leasowes, Hagley and Enville*, n.d., 116].

Bonomi's unexecuted designs included a scheme for fitting up the unfinished gallery at LANSDOWNE HOUSE, LONDON, 1786 [drawings at Bowood, see A. T. Bolton, *Architecture of R. and J. Adam* ii, 1922, 17, n. 24]; a sculpture gallery at TOWNELEY HALL, LANCS., for Charles Towneley, 1789 [*A.P.S.D.*]; alterations to SUTTON PLACE, SURREY, for J. Webbe Weston [*R.I.B.A. Trans.*, 1868–9, 126]; a new wing at WOOLBEDING, SUSSEX, 1791 [Arthur Oswald in *C. Life*, 15 Aug. 1947, 330]; and various works at INVERARAY, ARGYLLSHIRE, for the 6th Duke of Argyll, 1806–7 [I. G. Lindsay & Mary Cosh, *Inveraray and the Dukes of Argyll*, 1973, 311]. In 1809–10 'intended improvements' at SKELTON CASTLE, YORKS. (N.R.), for J. Wharton were exhibited at the R.A. as the work of 'J. Bonomi', then, of course, recently dead.

BOORER, JOHN, obtained the second premium in the competition for rebuilding London Bridge in 1823. He exhibited a design for a new hall for the Fishmongers' Company at the Royal Academy in 1834: it was not executed.

125

BOOTH, JAMES, was a master mason at Stony Middleton in Derbyshire. He was employed to build the stables at Chatsworth to the designs of James Paine in 1758–63, and the stables behind the Crescent at Buxton to those of John Carr in 1779–85. In 1767 he was among the subscribers to Paine's *Plans . . . of Noblemen and Gentlemen's Houses.* In his *Churches of Derbyshire* ii, 1877, 247, J. C. Cox records that STONY MIDDLETON CHURCH was believed to have been rebuilt in 1759 by 'the same architect' who 'designed the stables at the back of the Crescent at Buxton, the stables at Chatsworth, the rectory at Eyam, and Stoke Hall'. STOKE HALL, nr. Stony Middleton, was built in 1757 for the Rev. John Simpson, and Booth was probably the architect as well as the builder, though he may have been assisted by Paine. EYAM RECTORY was built for the Rev. E. Seward *c.* 1765. Simpson and Seward were also among the subscribers to Paine's book. Stoke Hall and the octagonal church at Stony Middleton are both buildings of some architectural pretensions which suggest that their designer was a man of ability.

BOOTH, JOHN (*c.* 1760–1843), was an architect and surveyor who practised in Devonshire Street, London, and later in Red Lion Square. He was a member of the Drapers' Company, and was President of the Surveyors' Club in 1802. He died on 23 February 1843, aged 83 [*Gent's Mag.* 1843 (1), 442]. In 1806–7 he altered MARSTON MORETAIN PARSONAGE, BEDS., in association with Thomas Hatchard of Westminster [Lincs. Record Office, MGA 53], and in 1821 the south aisle of ORE CHURCH, SUSSEX, was rebuilt to his designs [I.C.B.S.]. He was the father of W. J. Booth (*q.v.*).

BOOTH, WILLIAM JOSEPH (*c.* 1797–1872), was the younger son of John Booth (*q.v.*). He became a pupil of George Maddox, and entered the Royal Academy Schools in 1819. A tour of Italy and Greece followed, and in 1822 he exhibited at the Academy a 'View of the Temple of Theseus, taken on the spot in the year 1820'. He became surveyor to the Drapers' Company (of which he and his father were members), for whom he designed various buildings on their Irish property at DRAPERSTOWN and MONEYMORE, CO. DERRY [see designs illustrated by John Hendry, *The Role of Conservation*, Ulster Architectural Heritage Soc. 1971]. In 1833 he exhibited a view of the neo-Norman church recently erected by the Company at MONEYMORE. What appears to be his signature (rather than his father's) on a drawing in the Lloyd-Baker Estate Office may indicate that he designed the houses in Lloyd Square, Lloyd-Baker Street and Granville Square, CLERKENWELL, *c.* 1820–40 [information from Mr. J. S. Curl; cf. *C. Life*, 28 Jan. 1939].

126

Booth retired in 1855 to Torquay, dying there in 1872 [*R.I.B.A. Procs.*, 1872–3, 9]. A pencil portrait of him as a boy (1811) by Cornelius Varley was exhibited by Messrs. Spink of London in 1974.

BORLACH, JOHN, was, as James Gibbs (d. 1754) states in his will, 'for many years' his draughtsman. He made the drawing of Sir William Bruce's house at Kinross that was later engraved in Adam's *Vitruvius Scoticus*. The American architect Charles Bulfinch (1763–1844) owned a collection of 20 engraved plates, cut out and mounted on 10 sheets of paper, and entitled 'Designs of Architecture for Arches or Gates . . . by John C. Borlach, Architect'. This (apparently unique) copy now belongs to the Massachusetts Institute of Technology and is on loan to Boston Public Library [H. Kirker, *The Architecture of Charles Bulfinch*, Cambridge, Mass., 1969, 387]. Nothing else is at present known about Borlach's career, most of which was presumably spent in Gibbs's office.

BORRA, GIOVANNI BATTISTA, was an Italian architect who received a number of English commissions in the 1750s. There were two architects of this name: G. B. Borra (1712–86) of Turin, who was a pupil of Vittone and had a successful career as one of the leading Piedmontese architects, and another G. B. Borra of whom nothing is known except that he was a native of Dogliani (between Brà and Mondovi), and was recognized as a civil architect by the University of Turin on 17 November 1741 [C. Brayda, L. Coli & D. Sesia, *Ingegneri e Architetti del Sei e Settecento in Piemonte*, 1963, 20–1]. In 1750–1 Robert Wood and James Dawkins were accompanied on their celebrated tour of Asia Minor and Syria by an architectural draughtsman named Borra who was known as 'il Torquilino'. His sketch-books survive and are discussed by T. H. Clarke in *Arch. Rev.*, March 1947. He returned to England with Wood and Dawkins in the autumn of 1751 and prepared the finished drawings (now in the R.I.B.A. Drawings Collection)[1] for the engraved plates of Wood and Dawkins's two folio volumes on Palmyra and Baalbec, published in 1753 and 1757 respectively. These plates are variously signed 'J.B. (*i.e.* John Baptist) Borra', 'J. P. Borra' (presumably a misprint) and 'Borra'.

In 1755 'Mr. Bora' was employed by the 9th Duke of Norfolk to design the decoration of some of the principal rooms in his new house in St. James's Square, recently built under the direction of Matthew Brettingham. Norfolk House was demolished in 1938, but the interior of the Music Room was re-erected in the Victoria and

---

[1] Further drawings are in the Mellon Collection.

Albert Museum [for a detailed account see Desmond Fitz-Gerald, *The Norfolk House Music Room*, V. and A. Museum 1973]. Borra's work at Norfolk House is highly accomplished and presents an unusual combination of Italianate rococo with motifs derived from Palmyra. Mr. Fitz-Gerald has pointed out that similar decoration is found in Piedmont in buildings designed by G. B. Borra of Turin (notably the interior of the Racconigi Palace of 1756–7), and in England at WOBURN ABBEY, BEDS. (Queen Victoria's Bedroom, *c.* 1751), STRATFIELDSAYE, HANTS. (Drawing and Dining Room ceilings, dates uncertain), and STOWE HOUSE, BUCKS. (State Bedroom and Dressing-room as redecorated for Lord Temple in 1760). No documentary evidence of Borra's responsibility for work at Woburn or Stratfield Saye has so far been forthcoming, but the employment of 'Signor Borra' at Stowe is well attested by papers now in the Huntington Library in California, which include eight letters dated from London in 1752 and 1754. At Stowe he not only redecorated the two rooms for Lord Temple, and designed the double flight of steps on the south front, but was responsible for the neo-classicizing of several of the early Georgian garden buildings. In 1752 he was making drawings, under Lord Temple's direction, for the Temple of Concord and Victory. He altered the Rotondo in 1752, the Boycott Pavilions in 1758, the Oxford Gate *c.* 1760, and the twin Lake Pavilions soon afterwards. By 1765 he appears to have been superseded as Lord Temple's architect by the Frenchman J. F. Blondel (*q.v.*). [Laurence Whistler, 'Signor Borra at Stowe', *C. Life*, 29 Aug. 1957; John Harris, 'Blondel at Stowe', *Connoisseur*, March 1964; Michael McCarthy, 'Eighteenth-Century Amateur Architects and their Gardens', in *The Picturesque Garden and its Influence outside the British Isles*, ed. Pevsner, Dumbarton Oaks, Washington, D.C., 1974; information from Mr. Michael Gibbon.]

Although the close similarities between the interior of Norfolk House and those at Racconigi point to G. B. Borra of Turin as the 'Signor Borra' of the English records, it is difficult to reconcile the former's growing practice in Piedmont in the 1750s and '60s with his presence in England during the same period. Frequent journeys between the two countries seem very unlikely, especially as most of Borra's English commissions were relatively unimportant. Some of the later designs may conceivably have been sent by post from Italy, but the possibility that Borra's younger namesake from Dogliani should not be forgotten.

BOSTOCK, H—, exhibited at the Royal Academy from Kensington between 1833 and 1841. His works included a 'Design for a private chapel

proposed to be erected for a gentleman in Essex' (1833) and 'Alterations and additions lately completed to the villa of H. D. Raincock Esq. of Croydon, Surrey' (1837).

BOTHAM, JOSEPH, appears on the evidence of Pigot's *Directory* (1828–9) to have practised both in Manchester and in Sheffield, where in 1826 he took Samuel Worth (*q.v.*) into partnership. He designed the EASTBROOK WESLEYAN CHAPEL, LEEDS ROAD, BRADFORD, 1825, Gothic; dem. 1902 [*Bradford Observer*, 19 July 1902].

BOTT, JOHANN VON, *see* BODT

BOTTOMLEY, JOSEPH, exhibited architectural drawings at the Royal Academy from 1791 to 1795. They were mostly representations of existing buildings, but the 'Elevation of Denton Court near Canterbury' which he exhibited in 1795 may indicate that he had some responsibility for the recent rebuilding of that house by Sir Samuel Egerton Brydges. As 'Joseph Bottomley, Architect', he was among the subscribers to George Richardson's *New Designs in Architecture*, 1792. He was presumably the same as the Joseph Bottomley who published *Designs for Fanlights, Sashframes etc.*, 1794, and who for the next thirty years ran a manufactory of fanlights, skylights, etc., at 8 Beech Street, Barbican.

BOWEN, JOHN, is described as 'surveyor and land agent' of the Boconnoc estate in Cornwall in Pigot's *Directory* of 1830. In 1829 a builder contracted to build 'an almshouse adjoining the present almshouse at Fowey according to the plan, elevation and specification drawn by John Bowen of Boconnoc, Gentleman' [P.R.O., C 105/39 (50)]. The John Bowen who in 1826 designed the MARKET HALL at BRIDGWATER, SOMERSET, was presumably the same person. In 1819, as 'John Bowen, Esqr.' of Bridgwater, he had subscribed to Peter Nicolson's *Architectural Dictionary*.

BOWIE, ALEXANDER (–*c.* 1829), was a builder-architect of Stirling, where he was responsible for building several elegant and distinctively detailed houses in Allan Park between 1818 and 1827. CRAIGS HOUSE, STIRLING, built before 1820 for Robert Gillies, may also be attributed to him [David Walker in *C. Life*, 28 Aug. 1969]. He was presumably the Alexander Bowie who enlarged the Romanesque DUNNING CHURCH, PERTHSHIRE, in 1810 [S.R.O., HR 560/1]. Bowie made his will in May 1829 and appears to have died soon afterwards.

BOYCE, GIDEON ACLAND (–1861), practised as an architect and surveyor at Tiverton in Devonshire, where he restored the GREENWAY

CHAPEL in the PARISH CHURCH in 1829, as recorded by an inscription, and designed the MASONIC HALL on ANGEL HILL in 1834 [*Exeter Flying Post*, 11 Sept. 1834]. He died at Tiverton in January 1861 [Principal Probate Registry, Calendar of Probates].

BOYD, G—, exhibited a view of 'Shoreham manor-house, the seat of T. Barnett' (a misprint for 'T. Borrett') at the Royal Academy in 1805, and in 1807 'An elevation for a new manor-house at Shoreham, Kent, the seat of Sir W. Stirling, Bart.' Whether Sir Walter Stirling adopted Boyd's design is not known. Boyd's exhibit in 1810 was a 'Design for a country residence in the Gothic style, about to be built in Gloucestershire'.

BOYD, JOHN, of Glasgow, began life as a mason. After attempting unsuccessfully to set himself up as a builder 'he turned architect and inspector, and taught drawing at his house in Jamaica Street'. One of his pupils records that 'more fun than work went on in the school'. This was in the 1830s. [James Cruikshank, *Sketch of the Incorporation of Masons*, Glasgow 1879, 80.]

BOYD, THOMAS (*c.* 1753–1822), practised in Dumfries, where he died on 23 Sept. 1822, aged 69 [W. McDowall, *Memorials of St. Michael's Churchyard, Dumfries*, 1876, 233]. He was a competent provincial designer, usually in a somewhat old-fashioned Palladian manner. His bridge at Dumfries was ornamented with pairs of Ionic columns copied from Mylne's Blackfriars Bridge. In 1801–5 he made designs for a new bridge over the R. Eden nr. Carlisle, but was eventually superseded by Smirke [M. I. M. MacDonald, 'The Building of the New Eden Bridge at Carlisle', *Trans. Cumberland and Westmorland Arch. Soc.* N.S. lxxi, 1971].

GLENAE, DUMFRIESSHIRE, for Robert Dalzell, 1789 [*Scottish Field*, April 1964, 51, citing contract] (J. G. Dunbar, *Historic Architecture of Scotland*, 1966, fig. 55).

DUMFRIES, THE THEATRE, 1790–2 [W. McDowall, *History of Dumfries*, 1867, 703].

DUMFRIES, THE NEW (BUCCLEUCH STREET) BRIDGE (R. Nith), 1791–4; widened 1893 [W. McDowall, *Memorials of St. Michael's Churchyard at Dumfries*, 1876, 233; signed plan and elevation at Drumlanrig Castle dated 1792].

CALLY HOUSE, KIRKCUDBRIGHTSHIRE, raised wings and corridors for James Murray, 1794 [*Catalogue of R.I.B.A. Drawings Coll.: B*, 99, figs. 73–4].

DUMFRIES, THE TRADES' HALL, 1804–6 [W. McDowall, *History of Dumfries*, 1867, 743].

BOYD, WILLIAM (–1795), 'formerly an eminent architect and builder at Gibraltar', died

at his house in Exeter on 9 November 1795 [*Gent's Mag.* 1795 (ii), 1055].

BOYERS, D—, a surveyor, published *The Art of Conducting and Measuring Buildings, by a Simple Method*, Horncastle 1807. The book was reissued by a London publisher in 1831.

BOYLE, RICHARD, 3RD EARL OF BURLINGTON and 4TH EARL OF CORK (1694–1753), was born on 25 April 1694. He succeeded his father, the 2nd Earl, in 1704 at the age of 10, and inherited extensive estates in Yorkshire and Ireland. He had a country house at Londesborough in the East Riding, a town house in Piccadilly, and a suburban seat at Chiswick in Middlesex. Politically he was brought up a Whig. George I appointed him Lord Treasurer of Ireland and Lord Lieutenant of the East and West Ridings of Yorkshire (1715), George II made him a Privy Councillor (1729) and a Knight of the Garter (1730), but in May 1733 he went into opposition over the Excise Bill and resigned all his appointments. For Burlington the sacrifice was probably not very serious, for his real interests were artistic rather than political. By 1733 he was already securely established as the arbiter of English architectural taste, and it was to architecture and music that his wealth and influence were chiefly devoted.

It was not apparently until about 1716, when he was 22, that Burlington became seriously interested in architecture. He visited Italy as a grand tourist in 1714–15, but although he passed through the Veneto, Palladio's buildings did not attract his attention, and it was not until after the publication of Leoni's translation of Palladio's *Quattro Libri* (1715–16) and the first volume of Colen Campbell's *Vitruvius Britannicus* (1715) that he took up the Palladian cause of which he was soon to be the acknowledged leader. In August 1719 he set out again for Italy, and this time he spent some months at Vicenza studying Palladio's works. He returned shortly before Christmas, in company with William Kent, whom he intended to employ as a history-painter. He had also undertaken to support the Italian sculptor Guelfi, and with Colen Campbell as his architect he hoped to restore Palladian architecture to the position which it had held in England in the time of Inigo Jones. Campbell took the place of James Gibbs, who in 1716 had begun to transform the Earl's house in Piccadilly into 'the only town residence really fit for a British nobleman' by rebuilding the forecourt, and Kent was set to work to adorn the interior. But Burlington's dependence on Campbell appears to have become less close in the early 1720s, when he began to act as his own architect without professional advice, assisted only by Henry Flitcroft ('Burlington Harry'), a young man of humble origin whom he had recently taken into his service, Daniel Garrett, and a draughtsman named Samuel Savill. As early as 1717 he had designed a garden pavilion in the grounds of Chiswick House, and it is possible that he was himself responsible for the famous semicircular colonnade at Burlington House. It was in 1724 that he laid the foundation stone of his first public work, the Dormitory of Westminster School. Drawings for this had already been made by Wren and Dickinson, the surveyors of Westminster Abbey, and the adoption in their place of Burlington's Palladian design therefore marked the first victory of his campaign against the empirical classicism of Wren. Burlington's mission was to reinstate in England the canons of Roman architecture as described by Vitruvius, exemplified by its surviving remains, and practised by Palladio, Scamozzi and Jones. As he did not himself investigate the antique remains in Italy he was largely dependent for his knowledge of them on Palladio's drawings and engravings, which provided the sources for many favourite Anglo-Palladian motifs such as the tripartite window from the Baths of Diocletian, the coffered vaults of the Roman temples, and the close-set columns of the 'Egyptian Hall'. Palladio's villas and palaces and the Jones–Webb drawings were Burlington's remaining sources. Neither was used indiscriminately: indeed Burlington and his colleagues set a standard of classical correctitude in which there was no room either for Palladio's occasional excursions into mannerism or for the Jacobean deviations disclosed in some of the Jones–Webb drawings.

During the 1720s and 1730s almost all the characteristic features of English Palladianism appear in buildings erected to Burlington's designs. It was at Tottenham Park that the pavilion towers from Wilton were first decorated with Venetian windows: it was at Chiswick that the same Venetian windows were first placed in arched recesses: and it was at York, in Burlington's Assembly Rooms, that Palladio's Egyptian Hall was reconstructed with doctrinaire exactitude. By the early 1730s the conventions of the new Palladianism had become established as the accepted style for English country houses and public buildings. As for Burlington himself, his authority as 'il Palladio e il Jones de' nostri tempi'[1] was absolute. He was consulted by everyone, from fellow peers like the Duke of Richmond and the Earl of Leicester to the aldermen of London and York. When Wentworth Woodhouse was building, Sir Thomas Robinson reported that 'the whole finishing will be entirely submitted to Lord Burlington'. Even Hawksmoor's designs for the mausoleum at Castle

Howard were subjected to Burlington's censorship, and given, at his behest, a flight of steps like those at Chiswick. By now Burlington's chief architectural ally was William Kent. Kent, who began his career as a history-painter, had, under Burlington's patronage, found his true vocation as an architect, and became the most influential of those who interpreted his ideas. As Horace Walpole put it, Lord Burlington was 'the Apollo of the Arts', and William Kent was his 'proper priest'. By securing posts for his protégés in the Office of Works, Burlington was able to influence public as well as private architecture, and Kent's designs for the Horse Guards, the Royal Mews and the Treasury Buildings were, like his projects for a Royal Palace and for rebuilding the Houses of Parliament,[1] directly inspired by Burlington's ideas.

Burlington's enthusiasm for Palladio was equalled only by his devotion to Inigo Jones, and besides repairing the portico of St. Paul's, Covent Garden, in 1727, and the Barber-Surgeons' Hall in Monkwell Street, because they were the work of Jones, he purchased a gateway designed by the same architect, which he removed from Beaufort House to his grounds at Chiswick (cf. B.M., Add. MS. 4055, f. 349). In 1720–1 he bought from John Talman a large collection of drawings by Inigo Jones and Webb, and arranged for their publication by William Kent as the *Designs of Inigo Jones*, 1727, with the addition of 'Some few Designs of Buildings' by the Earl himself. With them were the drawings by Palladio that Inigo Jones had purchased in Italy in 1614. Burlington had already acquired Palladio's drawings of the Roman Baths and other buildings, some of which he found rolled up in the Villa Maser in 1718, and some of which he appears to have bought from Mgr. Trevisani, Bishop of Verona.[2] Of these drawings a selection was published by Burlington in 1730 as *Fabbriche Antiche disegnate da Andrea Palladio*, with a preface describing the circumstances of their discovery. A second volume of the arches, theatres and temples was contemplated, but never published. Unpublished drawings in Burlington's collection were used by E. Hoppus in his *Palladio* (1735), by Isaac Ware in his *Designs of Inigo Jones and Others* (1743), and by John Vardy in *Some Designs of Mr. Inigo Jones and Mr. William Kent* (1744). Ware also acknowledged his assistance in

---

[1] Burlington's responsibility for this last is expressly stated in *Gent's Mag.* iii, 1733, 156.

[2] Statements that these drawings were acquired from Dr. Richard Mead are due to a misunderstanding of R. Pococke, *Travels through England*, Camden Soc., i, 81, where Mead is mentioned as owning a book of Mgr. Trevisani's prints, but Burlington is stated to have bought 'all the curious original drawings of Palladio' direct from the Bishop.

---

[1] The phrase was inscribed by the Italian poet Scipione Maffei in a copy of Sanmichele's *Five Orders* which he presented to Burlington.

the Preface to his *Palladio* (1738), which he dedicated to Burlington.

The drawings which Burlington collected descended through his only surviving daughter to the Dukes of Devonshire. Some of them remain at Chatsworth, but the greater part are on permanent loan to the R.I.B.A. Drawings Collection in London. Among them are a number of Burlington's own drawings which prove beyond doubt that he 'could draw and design as well as pay the bill', and it is clear that, as Wittkower has said, 'he must be assigned a decisive share in the development of English neo-classicism, not only as a patron of artists but ... as a practising architect'.

Burlington died on 4 December 1753, and was buried in the family vault at Londesborough, Yorks. A photograph of his inscribed coffin-plate is given in *C. Life*, 19 Dec. 1947. His portrait by George Knapton is in the Duke of Devonshire's collection at Chatsworth. An earlier portrait, painted in about 1718, and showing the garden pavilion at Chiswick in the background, is in the National Portrait Gallery. Burlington's will is P.C.C. 333 SEARLE.

[*A.P.S.D.*; *D.N.B.*; G.E.C. *Complete Peerage* ii, 432–3; MS. letters at Chatsworth and Althorp House; *Walpole Soc.* xix, 160–1; *Vertue Note Books* (Walpole Soc.), iii, 55–6, 73, 139–40; H. Walpole, *Anecdotes of Painting*, ed. Dallaway and Wornum, iii, 773–6; Fiske Kimball, 'Burlington Architectus', *R.I.B.A. Jnl.* xxxiv–xxxv, 1927; J. Lees–Milne, 'Lord Burlington in Yorkshire', *Arch. Rev.*, July 1945; R. Wittkower, 'Lord Burlington and William Kent', *Archaeological Jnl.* cii, 1945, reprinted in *Palladio and English Palladianism*, 1974; R. Wittkower, *The Earl of Burlington and William Kent* (York Georgian Society's Occasional Papers No. 5, 1948); R. Wittkower, 'Un libro di Schizzi di Filippo Juvarra a Chatsworth', in *Bollettino Soc. Piemontese d'Archeologia e di Belle Arti*, 1949, reprinted in *Studies in the Italian Baroque*, 1975; J. Lees–Milne, *Earls of Creation*, 1962, 103–156. For Burlington's London estate see *Survey of London* xxxii. For his collections see W. G. Keith, 'Inigo Jones as a Collector', *R.I.B.A. Jnl.* xxxiii, 1925, 95, and *Catalogue of R.I.B.A. Drawings Coll.: B*, 119.]

CHISWICK HOUSE, MIDDLESEX, Casina or Bagnio, 'the first essay of his Lordship's happy invention', 1717; dem. [*Vitruvius Britannicus* iii, 1725, pl. 26].

LONDON, BURLINGTON HOUSE, PICCADILLY. According to Fiske Kimball (*R.I.B.A. Jnl.* xxxiv, 687, note §), Burlington himself designed the semicircular colonnade, dem. 1868 and removed to Battersea Park, but never re-erected. The east side of the forecourt was designed by Gibbs in 1716, and the refronting of the house, carried out in 1719, was entrusted to Campbell, who also designed the gateway to Piccadilly, illustrated in *Vitruvius Britannicus* iii, 1725, pl. 25. Conclusive evidence as to the authorship of the colonnade is lacking, but as Campbell does not claim the credit for it either for his patron or for himself, the possibility that it was designed by Gibbs cannot be excluded [*Survey of London* xxxii, 398].

TOTTENHAM PARK, WILTS., for Charles, Lord Bruce, 1721 onwards; wings added to Burlington's designs *c.* 1730; enlarged and remodelled by T. Cundy 1826. Flitcroft was the executant architect [R. Wittkower in *Archaeological Jnl.* cii, 1945, 154 and pl. I; the Earl of Cardigan in *Wilts. Arch. Mag.* lii, 1948, 176–83]. Burlington also appears to have designed a Banqueting House, 1743; dem. 1824 (recorded in Marquess of Ailesbury's archives, drawing 361).

WESTMINSTER SCHOOL, THE DORMITORY, 1722–30; altered 1895 by T. G. Jackson, who cut windows through alternate niches; gutted by bombing 1940/1, since restored [*Wren Soc.* xi, 35–45, pls. 8–28].

LONDON, GREAT (NOW OLD) BURLINGTON STREET, NO. 30 for the 6th Earl of Mountrath, *c.* 1721; dem. 1935 [R.I.B.A. Drawings Coll., VI/4; *Survey of London* xxxii, 505–8].

LONDON, GREAT (NOW OLD) BURLINGTON STREET, NO. 29 for General George Wade, 1723; dem. 1935 [*Vitruvius Britannicus* iii, 1725, pl. 10; *Survey of London* xxxii, 500–4].

LONDON, QUEENSBERRY HOUSE, NO. 7 BURLINGTON GARDENS, gateway for the 3rd Duke of Queensberry, *c.* 1723; dem. 1785 [W. Kent, *Designs of Inigo Jones* i, 1727, pl. 59, left; *Catalogue of R.I.B.A. Drawings Coll.: B*, 199].

CHISWICK HOUSE, MIDDLESEX, refronted the existing house (later dem.) and designed and built the adjoining Villa, *c.* 1723–9. The wings, added in 1788, were dem. 1952. In addition to the Casina (above), Burlington also designed the Circular Temple, a Pavilion (dem.) and an Orangery (dem.), all of which are shown on Rocque's engraving of 1736 [W. Kent, *The Designs of Inigo Jones* i, 1727, pls. 70–3] (H. A. Tipping, *English Homes*, Period V, i, 1921, 139–54; John Charlton, *A History and Description of Chiswick House and Gardens*, 1962).

WALDERSHARE PARK, KENT, THE BELVEDERE TOWER, for Sir Robert Furnese, 1725–7. A plan from Chatsworth (D.7) appears to establish Burlington's authorship of this tower, which bears a remarkable resemblance to one of the tower mausolea at Palmyra (cf. R. Wood, *The Ruins of Palmyra*, 1753, pl. lvi). Sir Robert Furnese (1687–1733) was a connoisseur who subscribed to all the Palladian publications. His accounts (Kent Record Office, U 471, A.17) show that it cost over £1000 to build.

LONDON, WARWICK HOUSE, ST. JAMES'S, internal

alterations for Charles, Lord Bruce, 1726–7; dem. 1827 [Marquess of Ailesbury's archives, nos. 1827–33].

ROUND COPPICE, IVER HEATH, BUCKS., for Charles, Lord Bruce, 1726–7; dem. 1954 [drawings from Chatsworth, B.21, C.3–4].

CASTLE HILL, DEVONSHIRE, remodelled for Lord Clinton (afterwards 1st Lord Fortescue) by Roger Morris, working under the direction of Lord Burlington and Lord Herbert, 1729–c. 1740. Morris's contract for the Portland stonework of the exterior, dated 22 Feb. 1728/9, specifies that the proportions of the entablature 'shall be made as the Earl of Burlington or the Lord Herbert shall direct' [Devon County Record Office, Fortescue Papers, E1/93], and on 7 June 1730 Lord Clinton wrote to Lord Burlington asking for a promised drawing of the inside of the hall, 'that cannot be begun till your Lordship is so good as to send me the draught' [Chatsworth letters 198.0]. The centre was gutted by fire in 1934, and subsequently restored (*C. Life*, 17, 24 March 1934, 29 Oct. 1938).

LONDON, RICHMOND HOUSE, WHITEHALL, for the 2nd Duke of Richmond, c. 1730; altered by James Wyatt 1782; destroyed by fire 1791 [H. Walpole, *Anecdotes of Painting* v, ed. F. W. Hilles & P. B. Daghlian, 1939, 161; *Walpole Soc.* xix, 160; bound volume of drawings at Goodwood (Small Library A4) on loan to R.I.B.A.; drawings from Chatsworth, D.17, 18, 19 and probably D.6A].

FOXHALL, CHARLTON, SUSSEX, a banqueting house for members of the Charlton Hunt, among whom the 2nd Duke of Richmond was prominent, c. 1730 [Earl of March, *Records of the Old Charlton Hunt*, 1910, 25, quoting contemporary verses; *A New Display of the Beauties of England* i, 1769, 119] (*C. Life*, 31 Oct. 1936, 466).

NORTHWICK PARK, WORCS. (now GLOS.), east front and entrance hall for Sir John Rushout, Bart., 1730 [R. Wittkower, 'Lord Burlington at Northwick Park', in *The Country Seat*, ed. Colvin & Harris, 1970, 121–30].

YORK, THE ASSEMBLY ROOMS, 1731–2; new entrance front by J. P. Pritchett & W. Watson, 1828. In 1735 Burlington provided designs for an additional building, which was completed in 1739 but dem. 1860 [*Vitruvius Britannicus* iv, pls. 78–81; R. Wittkower, *The Earl of Burlington and William Kent*, York Georgian Soc. Occasional Paper No. 5, 1948; R. Wittkower, 'Burlington and his Work in York', York Institute of Architectural Studies, *Studies in Architectural History* i, 1954, 47–66, reprinted in *Palladio and English Palladianism*, 1974; I. H. Goodall, 'Lord Burlington's York Piazza', York Georgian Soc.'s *Annual Report* 1970].

PETERSHAM LODGE, SURREY, for the 1st Earl of Harrington, c. 1733; wings terminating in polygonal pavilions added by E. Shepherd c. 1740; altered by the 1st Lord Camelford c. 1785; dem. c. 1835 [*Walpole Soc.* xix, 160] (engraving by T. Lightoler in B.M., *King's Maps* xl, 29a).

HOLKHAM HALL, NORFOLK. According to Matthew Brettingham, junior, 'the general ideas ... were first struck out by the Earls of Burlington and Leicester, assisted by Mr. William Kent', c. 1734 [*The Plans and Elevations of the late Earl of Leicester's House at Holkham*, 2nd ed. 1773]. Features specifically attributed to Burlington in that book are the ceiling of the portico (pl. 18) and the ceiling of the north dressing-room (pl. 24).

WOBURN FARM, nr. CHERTSEY, SURREY, octagonal temple for Philip Southcote, 1743; dem. [drawing from Chatsworth, B.15].

COLESHILL HOUSE, BERKS. An inscription dated 31 Dec. 1748 recorded that the chimney-stacks at the angles of the house were 'rebuilt for Sr Mark Pleydell Bt. in 1744 by ye Direct^s. of ye Earls of Burlington and Leicester'. Lord Burlington employed Isaac Ware to make drawings of the ceilings here. The house was destroyed by fire 1952.

KIRBY HALL, OUSEBURN, YORKS. (W.R.), elevation for Stephen Thompson,[1] in association with Roger Morris, 1747–c. 1755; dem. 1920 [contemporary engraving by Basire inscribed 'Elevation by R. Morris Arch^t. and the Earl of Burlington: Executed, & the inside finishings, by J. Carr, Architect. Plans by the Owner, S.T.' (B.M., *King's Maps* xlv, 24–1); *Vitruvius Britannicus* v, 1771, pls. 70–1, inscribed 'E. of Burlington and R. Morris Ar.'; letters from Stephen Thompson to Thomas Grimston in Beverley Record Office, DDGR/41].

EUSTON HALL, SUFFOLK, wooden bridge in the park for the 2nd Duke of Grafton; dem. [described by Sir Thomas Robinson in 1731: Hist. MSS. Comm., *Carlisle*, 87; plan and estimate from Chatsworth, B. 22].

BOYNTON HALL, YORKS. (E.R.), designs for alterations to south and west fronts for Sir William Strickland, Bart. (d. 1735), inaccurately carried out by a local builder. In 1768 Sir Thomas Robinson related how 'Ld Burlington gave him a beautiful design, with a Palladian roof, and an Attic Story, instead of the old wretched and ugly roof of our Gothick ancestors – when the house was compleated, Sir W^m. went down ... when alas he found the old fashioned roof, and many other material alterations from the plan' [*Arch. Rev.*, Aug. 1926, 51; Francis Johnson, 'Boynton Hall', *Trans. E.*

---

[1] The house was built by Stephen Thompson during the lifetime of his father Henry Thompson, who did not die until 1760, aged 83.

Yorkshire Georgian Soc. iii (3), 1954; Arthur Oswald in *C. Life*, 22–29 July 1954].

LONDESBOROUGH HOUSE, YORKS, (E.R.), alterations to his own country house, for which the only specific evidence appears to be a design for a garden gateway from Chatsworth dated 1735 (B.13); dem. 1811.

CLIFTON HALL, NOTTS., Beleveldere Summer House for Sir Robert Clifton, Bart.; dem. 1969 ['Travel Journal of Philip Yorke', ed. J. Godber, *Beds. Hist. Rec. Soc.* xlvii, 1968, 126, 11 Aug. 1744, when he saw the 'Summer house designed by Lord Burlington']. Sir Robert Clifton was a guest at Londesborough in Sept. 1735 [Chatsworth Letters, 127.10].

Burlington's unexecuted designs included a house for Col. William Gee at BISHOP BURTON, YORKS. (E.R.) [drawings in R.I.B.A. Drawings Coll., VI/1]; a villa for Lord Lincoln at OATLANDS, WEYBRIDGE, SURREY [*ibid.*, VI/11]; and a house for William Pulteney (created Earl of Bath 1742) [*ibid.*, VI/3], which was published by Kent, *Designs of Inigo Jones* ii, 1727, pl. 12, as 'a House with an Arcade, Design'd by the Earl of Burlington'. THE SCHOOL AND ALMSHOUSES at SEVENOAKS, KENT, as built in 1727, differ too considerably from Burlington's designs [R.I.B.A., VI/8, and Kent, *Designs of Inigo Jones* ii, 1727, pls. 52–3] to be regarded as his, and although the Duke of Richmond was pressing for his drawings for the COUNCIL HOUSE at CHICHESTER in 1730 [Chatsworth letters, 201.0 and 201.2], the building erected in 1731 does not correspond exactly to either of Burlington's alternative designs [R.I.B.A. Drawings Coll.]. Vertue was no doubt correctly informed in attributing it to Roger Morris, who was associated with Burlington at Kirby Hall, Yorks. (above, p. 131) and may well have been concerned in Sevenoaks School too.

BRADBERRY, THOMAS, entered the Royal Academy Schools in 1820. He was awarded the Silver Medal in 1821 and the Gold Medal in 1823. In 1820 he exhibited a 'View of St. John's Church, Westminster' at the Royal Academy. Directories show that he subsequently practised as an architect from 8 Langbourn Chambers, Fenchurch Street. He drew several plates for Britton & Pugin's *Public Buildings of London*, 1826–8, but no architectural work of his has so far been identified.

BRADIE, JOHN, of London, designed a lodge or cottage at STOKE PARK, WILTS., for Joshua Smith in 1800. It survives as the lodge south of the main road, and the original drawing is in the Cooper Union Museum, New York [J. Harris, *Catalogue of British Drawings for Architecture etc. in American Collections*, 1971, 34].

BRADFORD, JOHN, 'Architect of Coventry', was employed to rebuild the north and south aisles of MERIDEN CHURCH, WARWICKS., in 1826–7 [Vestry Minutes in Warwickshire Record Office, DR 182/28]. His workmanship is sufficiently convincing to have been accepted as medieval in *V.C.H. Warwicks.* iv, 153.

BRADLEY, THOMAS, lived at Halifax, where he was surveyor to the Calder and Hebble Navigation. He was probably a son of Thomas Bradley of Halifax, joiner, to whom he was apprenticed in or shortly before 1758 [P.R.O. Apprenticeship Register]. He designed CROWNEST HOUSE, LIGHTCLIFFE, YORKS. (W.R.), for William Walker, 1788, an elegant but conventional late Georgian house now in ruins [G. Richardson, *New Vitruvius Britannicus* i, 1802, pls. 64–5].

BRADLEY, WILLIAM, of Halifax, perhaps a son of the above, appears in Pigot's 1828–9 *Directory* as a joiner, but subscribed as 'Architect' to several early nineteenth-century architectural books. His only recorded work is COLEY CHURCH, YORKS. (W.R.), 1816, Gothic, described by Pevsner as 'a remarkably serious design for its date' [Borthwick Institute of Historical Research, York, Fac. 1816/2; cf. *Yorks. Arch. Jnl.* xvii, 62, xxii, 355].

BRADSHAW, WILLIAM, was a builder and surveyor of Henley-on-Thames, where he was active during the last quarter of the eighteenth century. In 1789 he supervised the rebuilding of GREAT MARLOW BRIDGE to the designs of R. F. Brettingham [Bridge Commissioners' records in Bucks. Record Office, Aylesbury]. In 1795–6 he built, and perhaps designed, HENLEY-ON-THAMES TOWN HALL, pulled down and re-erected as a private house at Crazies Hill in 1899 [J. S. Burn, *History of Henley*, 1861, 68].

BRADWELL, DAVID, was a bricklayer at Cambridge. In 1786 he and a carpenter named Kaye designed and built a lecture-room (since dem.) in the Botanic Garden [Willis & Clark, iii, 153]. He signs drawings of ROPSLEY PARSONAGE, LINCS., dated 1803, in the Lincs. Record Office (Fac. 5/16).

BRAINE, WILLIAM, was a carpenter living at 43 East Street, Manchester Square. In 1813 he exhibited a design for a villa at the Royal Academy. F. E. Braine, of the same address, exhibited 'a Design for a public bath' in 1822.

BRAMBLE, BENJAMIN (*c.* 1789–1857), was an architect and builder of Portsmouth. His principal work was the Greek Revival GUILDHALL, PORTSMOUTH (afterwards the Museum and Art Gallery), 1837–8; dem. after bombing 1940/1 [R.

East, *Extracts from the Portsmouth Records*, 1891, 809] (J. Summerson, *The Bombed Buildings of Britain*, 1942, 99). He also designed HOLY TRINITY CHURCH, WEST COWES, ISLE OF WIGHT, for Mrs. S. Goodwin, 1832, in the lancet Gothic of the period [G.R.]. He died at Southsea on 18 November 1857, aged 68 [*Gent's Mag.* 1857 (ii), 691].

BRASH, JOHN (–1838/9), practised in Glasgow. Very little is known about him, but such of his works as have been identified show that he was an architect of some ability. The elder James Salmon (1805–88) was his pupil. [A. Gomme & D. Walker, *Architecture of Glasgow*, 1968, 75, 266].

STRATHBLANE CHURCH, STIRLINGSHIRE, rebuilt 1803, Gothic [S.R.O., HR 371/1, p. 15].

GLASGOW, TOLCROSS RELIEF (now CENTRAL) CHURCH, 1806; steeple added 1835 [Gomme & Walker, 266].

GALSTON OLD CHURCH, AYRSHIRE, 1808–9 [S.R.O., HR 797/3 and RHP 14293–8].

GLASGOW UNIVERSITY, THE HAMILTON BUILDING, 1811–13, altering earlier design by Peter Nicholson; dem. [J. Coutts, *History of the University of Glasgow*, Glasgow 1909, 357].

GLASGOW, MCMILLAN CALTON CHURCH (originally First Reformed Presbyterian Congregation), CALTON, 1819 [W. J. Couper, *A Century of Congregational Life*, Glasgow 1919, 30].

SHOTTS CHURCH, LANARKS., 1820, modifying a design by J. Gillespie Graham. Brash was asked to produce 'a corrected plan divested of every sort of unnecessary ornament' [S.R.O., HR 739/2].

GLASGOW, BLYTHSWOOD SQUARE, east, west and south sides 1823, north side 1829 [Gomme & Walker, 75, 266, fig. 53].

BRAY, JOEL (*c.* 1787–1846), practised in London. He was President of the Surveyors' Club in 1835, and died on 23 December 1846, aged 59 [records of the Surveyors' Club].

BRAZIER, EDWARD BARDWELL (1753–) was probably a son of Edward Brazier, a London banker (d. 1789) [*Gent's Mag.* 1789 (i), 86]. He was admitted to the Royal Academy Schools in 1778. A Colchester poll-book for 1788 shows that he had a vote there, but in the same year he used E. Brazier's London address to exhibit at the Royal Academy a design for 'entrances to Callendar Park, Scotland, the seat of William Forbes Esqr'.

BREAM, SAMUEL, was an architect of Great Yarmouth, Norfolk. He made a design for a stone bridge of one arch over Yarmouth Haven, of which an engraving was published in the *Gent's*

Mag. for 1771 (p. 104, and see also pp. 487–8). The then existing bridge was not, however, rebuilt until 1786. In 1792 Bream was among those who submitted designs for rebuilding the Theatre at Birmingham [Minutes of the Proprietors in Birmingham Reference Library].

BREES, SAMUEL CHARLES (–1865), won the gold medal of the Society of Arts in 1830 for his design for a village church. In 1835 he competed for the Houses of Parliament in conjunction with Joseph Griffiths. Their joint design was described as 'Gothic, of various periods, embracing the early castellated, palatial, and Tudor styles' [*Catalogue of the Designs for the New Houses of Parliament*, 6th. ed. 1836, 39–40]. Brees exhibited topographical drawings at the Royal Academy from 1833 to 1837. He subsequently practised as a civil engineer in Croydon, and died on board the ship 'La Hogue' in the West India Docks on 3 May 1865 [Principal Probate Registry, Calendar of Probates].

BREREWOOD, FRANCIS (*c.* 1699–*c.* 1781), was the younger son of Thomas Brerewood, a wealthy linen draper descended from a family well known in Chester. His brother Thomas (d. 1748) married a daughter of the 4th Lord Baltimore, and spent most of his life in Maryland. Francis first appears in 1715 as the author of a translation of the Abbé Terracon's *Discourse on the Iliad of Homer*, but subsequently made a somewhat precarious living as a painter and architect. A portrait of Benedict Leonard Calvert, Governor of Maryland, in the Baltimore Museum of Art, is the chief extant evidence of his ability as a painter. All that is at present known of his architectural activities is that he altered PLACE HOUSE, HORTON, nr. COLNBROOK, BUCKS. (dem. 1785), for his father in about 1725, and worked between 1753 and 1758 at WOODCOTE PARK, nr. EPSOM, SURREY, for the 6th Lord Baltimore, where he added a cupola and other embellishments to the house and landscaped the grounds. In 1736 he was sufficiently well established in England to decline a flattering invitation to visit Maryland and design a Governor's House and other buildings, but towards the end of his life he was in poor circumstances. He died in *c.* 1781 at the age of 82. [*Gent's Mag.* 1791 (2), 713–6, with engraving of a view of Place House painted by Brerewood; Mrs. Russell Hastings, 'The Versatile Francis Brerewood', *Antiques*, Jan. 1934, 15–16; John Harris, 'Woodcote Park', *Connoisseur*, May 1961.]

BRETTINGHAM, MATTHEW (1699–1769), was the second son of Launcelot Brettingham (1664–1727), a bricklayer or mason of Norwich. He was apprenticed to his father, and took up his freedom as a bricklayer in 1719, on the same day

133

THE BRETTINGHAM FAMILY

Launcelot Brettingham =
of Norwich
1664–1727

ROBERT = Lydia
1696–1768

MATTHEW = Martha
1699–1769

Deborah = — de Carle

Mary = Michael Savary Furs

ROBERT FURZE BRETTINGHAM
c. 1750–1820

MATTHEW
1725–1803

Henrietta =
Freston

Robert
worsted manufacturer
c. 1729–69

William
merchant
1739–1816

Rev. Anthony, assumed
surname of Freston
1757–1819

George
1760–1841

MATTHEW
1792–1836

Laura = Sir Robert Smirke

as his elder brother Robert (*q.v.*).[1] He built up a considerable business as a surveyor and building contractor in East Anglia. From 1734 onwards he was employed by the Earl of Leicester to supervise the building of Holkham Hall to the designs of William Kent, and received a salary of £50 a year for 'taking care of his Lordship's buildings' there until the Earl's death in 1759. According to a letter written by his son Matthew, he 'considered the building of Holkham as the great work of his life'. In 1761, when he published *The Plans and Elevations of the late Earl of Leicester's House at Holkham*, he inscribed his own name as 'Architect' on the plates, without any reference to Kent, and his portrait by Heins (1749) shows him proudly holding a drawing of Kent's triumphal arch in the park. His son attempted to justify this conduct by saying that the original designs 'were departed from in every shape and he that had conducted the laying of every Brick from the foundation to the Roof thought he had a better claim to the Reputation of the Fabrick than he who only gave the designs, but never once attended the execution of any part of the work'. However true this may have been – and the architectural history of Holkham has not yet been worked out in detail – the fact remains that Brettingham 'had not the modesty to own that it was built after the design of Kent', and it was left to his son, who brought out a second and enlarged edition of the book in 1773, to admit at least that 'the general ideas were first struck out by the Earls of Burlington and Leicester, assisted by Mr. William Kent'.

It is less clear how much importance should be attached to a letter addressed by a certain William Ingram to the Mayor of Lynn in 1745, in which he claimed to be 'the person who has been employed [by Brettingham] to copy Mr. Kent's works at Holkham and other things of that nature; The drawing of ye Church which he has shown to ye gentlemen of Lynn, and to ye Committee of ye House of Commons, was don by me (tho' its a very poor design as much like a Barn as a Church) in short all the drawings he flashes about the country with, are mine, or of some other person's doing, he being entirely ignorant of drawing or measuring....' For Ingram was a man with a grievance against his employer, who owed him money, and his abusive letters were deliberately intended to damage Brettingham's reputation as an architect. There can be no doubt, however, that Brettingham's employment at Holkham led, in the words of his epitaph in St. Augustine's Church at Norwich, 'to the

Patronage and esteem of the Nobility, the most distinguish'd for their love of *Palladian* Architecture', and his son testified that 'So early as the year 1740 he had a numerous Acquaintance with the Gentlemen of the County, Sr. William Harbord, Sr. Beauchamp Proctor, a Colonel Earle, a Squire Doughty, of Hannow, Mrs. Townsend, of Hunningham, all imploy'd him, and this Lord Orford's father invited him to Houghton, but died before anything could be done there'. He was also 'consulted in all Public Works, built several Bridges in the County, employ'd by Bishop Gooch and the Dean, to direct the Repairs of the Cathedral, erected the Shire house on the Castle Hill, and put on the battlements to the Castle, for which business he never got fully paid for his trouble, through the opposition of some of the County Gentlemen, and the ill behaviour of his Brother Robert, who did the flint stone work of the Shire house'. The building of the Shirehouse was in fact an episode from which neither Brettingham nor his brother emerged with credit. Their accounts were unsatisfactory, if not actually fraudulent, and had to be submitted to arbitration. As a result of this affair Matthew lost the confidence of the magistrates, who had hitherto employed him as surveyor of the county bridges.

By this time, however, Brettingham's practice as an architect was extending beyond the bounds of East Anglia. In London he designed in the course of the next few years important houses for members of the aristocracy as exalted as the Dukes of York and Norfolk, the Earl of Strafford and the Earl of March, and his account-book (P.R.O., C 108/362) shows that in the 1750s and '60s he was being consulted by the owners of country houses in counties as far afield as Warwickshire, Westmorland and Sussex. Through Lord Leicester's good offices he even became a member of White's Club, where, 'being a man of mild manners and an excellent player at cards', he soon became popular, and earned the nickname of 'Rectitude'.

In 1761 he published the designs for Holkham, and, as the preface shows, he intended to follow this work with a collection of designs for country houses made by himself in collaboration with the Earl of Leicester. 'This', he says, 'was our joint study and amusement in the country, and the drawings for this work have been made by me near twenty years; but they were not to appear in print, till after the publication of Holkham: if leisure permits they may possibly be engraved next year, together with the Earl of Leicester's intended plans for a new house in town.'[1]

---

[1] The statement in *D.N.B.* that as a young man Brettingham 'travelled on the continent of Europe', and published *Remarks on Several Parts of Europe ... collected upon the spot since the year 1723*, in 4 vols., fol., 1723–38, is incorrect, as the author of this work was really J. D. Breval (d. 1738).

[1] In the R.I.B.A. Drawings Collection there is a set of drawings for a town house for the Earl of Leicester 'near Berkeley Square' which should be attributed to the elder Brettingham (rather than to his son, as in *Catalogue of R.I.B.A. Drawings Coll.: B*, 192–3).

135

Brettingham was an orthodox but unenterprising Palladian whose dull, well-bred façades betray neither the intellect of a Burlington nor the fancy of a Kent. No masterpiece stands out from the list of his works, but in nearly all of them the solid virtues of mid-Georgian architecture are evident.

Brettingham retired to his house outside St. Augustine's Gate at Norwich, where he died on 19 August 1769, aged 70. The epitaph on his monument in St. Augustine's Church is given by Chambers, *Norfolk Tour*, 1829, 1236, and by Wearing, *Georgian Norwich: its Builders*, 1926, 4. His portrait by Heins, dated 1749, is in the R.I.B.A. Drawings Collection. His will (P.C.C. 300 BOGG) mentions property at Weston in Norfolk and a leasehold estate in London held of the Earl of Leicester. He had three sons, the eldest of whom, Matthew, followed his father's profession. The second, Robert, a worsted manufacturer, was the grandfather of another Matthew (1792–1826), who is described as a surveyor of No. 1 South Crescent, Bedford Square, London, in his will (P.C.C. 8 STOWELL). The Matthew who is the subject of this entry had a sister Deborah who married one of the De Carle family of masons, and for many years he maintained 'his sister Decarle, her old husband, and son'. This circumstance no doubt explains why one of his brother-in-law's family was christened Robert Brettingham De Carle (d. 1791), and why the name of Brettingham was likewise borne by three generations of the Sowerby family of botanists after Robert Brettingham De Carle's daughter Anne married its founder James Sowerby (1757–1822).

Robert Baldwin and Richard Edwin are stated to have been Brettingham's pupils in the *Register of Premiums* of the Society of Arts (1778). William Newton was also in his office for a time.

[Family letters in Bodleian, MS. Eng. misc. c. 504; account-book 1747–64 in P.R.O., C 108/362; *Norfolk Chronicle*, 2 Sept. 1769 (deaths of Matthew Brettingham and of his son Robert); will, P.C.C. 300 BOGG; *A.P.S.D.*; *The Farington Diary*, ed. J. Greig, i, 294; T.W.F., 'Matthew Brettingham, the Architect of Holkham', *East Anglian* ii, 1866, 131–2; S. J. Wearing, *Georgian Norwich: its Builders*, Norwich 1926, 2–5; C. W. James, *Chief Justice Coke*, 1929, chap. 36; H. L. Bradfer-Lawrence, 'The Merchants of Lynn', in *A Supplement to Blomefield's Norfolk*, ed. C. Ingleby, 1929, 194–5 (for W. Ingram); D. E. Howell James, 'Matthew Brettingham and the County of Norfolk', *Norfolk Archaeology* xxxiii, 1962–5; Walter Brettingham, 'The Brettingham Family of Norfolk', *Blackmansbury* vi, nos. 3–4, 1969; D. E. Howell James, 'Matthew Brettingham's Account Book', *Norfolk Archaeology* xxxv, 1971.]

COUNTRY HOUSES

HOLKHAM HALL, NORFOLK. Besides acting as executive architect of the house for the 1st Earl of Leicester from 1734 onwards, Brettingham claimed to have designed the North Lodges, the Temple, the Arch Gate to the Gardens, the Seat in the Orangery, the Bridge at the head of the Lake, and the East Lodge [*The Plans and Elevations of the late Earl of Leicester's House at Holkham*, 2nd. ed. 1773, pls. 54–58, 60, 67].

GUNTON HALL, NORFOLK, for Sir William Harbord, after 1742; enlarged by J. Wyatt c. 1785; centre gutted by fire 1882 [see p. 135 for source] (Neale's *Seats*, 1st ser., iii).

HANWORTH HOUSE, NORFOLK, work for — Doughty, c. 1740–50 [see p. 135 for source].

HEYDON HALL, NORFOLK, internal alterations for Col. Earle, c. 1740–50 [see p. 135 for source].

HONINGHAM HALL, NORFOLK, work for Mrs. (Henrietta) Townshend, between 1738 and 1749; dem. 1967 [see p. 135 for source] (J. J. Sambrook, 'Honingham Hall', *Norfolk Archaeology* xxxiv, 1968).

LANGLEY HALL, NORFOLK, work, including addition of wings, for Sir William Beauchamp Proctor, c. 1745 [see p. 135 for source; cf. *East Anglian* ii, 1866, 271, for architectural history of house] (*C. Life*, 2 July 1927).

MARBLE HILL, TWICKENHAM, MIDDLESEX, alterations (chiefly interior of dining-room) for Henrietta Howard, Countess of Suffolk, 1750–1 [Marie P. G. Draper, *Marble Hill House*, 1970, 43–4].

EUSTON HALL, SUFFOLK, remodelled house and added new offices for the 2nd Duke of Grafton, 1750–56 [P.R.O., C 108/362] (*C. Life*, 10, 17, 24 Jan. 1957).

MOOR PARK, HERTS., alterations for George, Lord Anson, 1751–4 [P.R.O., C 108/362].

WORTLEY HALL, YORKS. (W.R.), probably designed the east wing built by John Platt (*q.v.*) for Edward Wortley Montagu in 1757–9; altered c. 1870 [Wortley Montagu's accounts in Sheffield City Library (Wh.M. 142, p. 133) show that in April 1759 he paid 'Mr. Brettingham' (i.e. Matthew Brettingham, junior) 10 guineas 'for his Journey into Yorkshire' and 5 guineas 'for Draughts & other business done by his father'].

KEDLESTON HALL, DERBYSHIRE, designed new house for Sir Nathaniel Curzon, Bart. (cr. Lord Scarsdale), c. 1758, of which only the wings were built as part of a revised design by James Paine [James Paine, *Plans ... of Noblemen's Houses* ii, 1783, pl. 52].

SHORTGROVE HALL, nr. SAFFRON WALDEN, ESSEX, new bridge, lodge, etc., for Percy Wyndham O'Brien, Earl of Thomond, 1758–62 [P.R.O., C 108/362].

WAKEFIELD LODGE, NORTHANTS., repairs and

alterations for the 2nd Duke of Grafton, 1759 [P.R.O., C 108/362].

BENACRE HALL, SUFFOLK, remodelled for Sir Thomas Gooch, Bart., 1763–4; interior damaged by fire 1926 [P.R.O., C 108/362; H. Davy, *Views of the Seats of Noblemen and Gentlemen in Suffolk*, 1827].

PACKINGTON HALL, WARWICKS., remodelled house for 3rd Earl of Aylesford, 1766–72. The clerk of works was Henry Couchman (*q.v.*), whose MS. autobiography describes Brettingham as architect [Marcus Binney in *C. Life*, 9, 16, 23 July 1970].

PUTNEY HEATH, SURREY, house for Sir William Fordyce, M.D., *c.* 1764 [autobiography of Henry Couchman, *q.v.*].

LONDON

ST. JAMES'S SQUARE, NO. 5, for the 2nd Earl of Strafford, 1748–9 [*Survey of London* xxix, 100–2].

NORFOLK HOUSE, ST. JAMES'S SQUARE, for the 9th Duke of Norfolk, 1748–52; portico added 1842; dem. 1938 [*Survey of London* xxix, 192–202].

ST. JAMES'S SQUARE, NO. 13, unspecified work for the 1st Lord Ravensworth, in or before 1753 [*Survey of London* xxix, 136].

LINCOLN'S INN, unspecified work, 1753 [P.R.O., C 108/362].

DOVER STREET, work for Percy Wyndham O'Brien, afterwards Earl of Thomond, 1754 [P.R.O., C 108/362].

EGREMONT HOUSE, NO. 94 PICCADILLY (afterwards Cambridge House, and from 1862 onwards the Naval and Military Club), for the 2nd Earl of Egremont, begun 1756 [P.R.O., C 108/362].

PICCADILLY, house (Nos. 138–9), for William Douglas, 3rd Earl of March and 4th Duke of Queensberry, *c.* 1760–4; dem. [P.R.O., C 108/362; autobiography of Henry Couchman, *q.v.*].

YORK (afterwards CUMBERLAND) HOUSE, NO. 86 PALL MALL, for Edward Augustus, Duke of York, 1761–3; dem. 1908–12 [*Survey of London* xxix, 364–7; *Vitruvius Britannicus* iv, 1767, pls. 5–7].

SPRING GARDENS, house for Thomas Anson, before 1764; dem. [P.R.O., C 108/362].

PICCADILLY, NO. 80, for Sir Richard Lyttelton, 1764–6; dem. [Bridgewater family papers in County Record Office, Hertford].

PRIVY GARDENS, WHITEHALL, alterations to house for the Hon. Hans Stanley, 1765; dem. *c.* 1820 [autobiography of Henry Couchman, *q.v.*; *Survey of London* xiii, 242–3].

OTHER WORKS

LENWADE BRIDGE, WITCHINGHAM, NORFOLK (R. Wensum), 1741 [plan and elevation initialled

MB in Norfolk Record Office, Rye MS. 17, vol. 1, 153].

KING'S LYNN, ST. MARGARET'S CHURCH, rebuilt nave, crossing, and north and south transepts after fall of spire of south-west tower, 1742–6, Gothic [King's Lynn Corporation Archives, Ae 31; *Commons' Jnls.*, 6 Dec. 1744].

NORWICH, THE SHIREHOUSE, 1747–9; dem. 1822; Gothic [D. E. Howell James in *Norfolk Archaeology* xxxiii, 1965, 346–9; Bodleian Library, MS. Eng. Misc. c. 504, f. 2].

NORWICH, repairs to CASTLE, including new battlements, 1747–9 [Bodleian Library, MS. Eng. Misc. c. 504, f. 1].

NORWICH, the following houses are referred to as his work in a letter from his son printed in *East Anglian* ii, 1866, 131–2:

HOUSE in SURREY COURT, SURREY STREET, for James Crowe; dem. *c.* 1901 (*Norfolk Archaeology* xxiv, 1930, pl. facing p. 74).

HOUSE in SURREY STREET for Dr. Peek.

HOUSE in ST. GILES for Mr. Stannard.

Ironmonger's shop at corner of Dove Lane for Mr. Pattison.

UNEXECUTED WORKS

Several apparently unexecuted works are mentioned in Brettingham's account-book in the P.R.O. They include 'intended alterations' at BLICKLING HALL, NORFOLK, for the 1st Earl of Buckinghamshire, 1753–5; plans for a new house at BELMONT, nr. WARNEFORD, HANTS., for the 11th Earl of Clanrickarde, 1754; designs for a large mansion at LOWTHER HALL, WESTMORLAND, for Sir James Lowther (original drawings now in Cumberland and Westmorland Record Office), 1759; a plan and elevation for an 'intended alteration' to BEECHWOOD PARK, HERTS., for Sir Thomas Sebright (drawing still among Sebright papers at Beechwood, 1967); and plans and drawings for John Buxton of SHADWELL LODGE, NORFOLK, 1760. The 'business' which he transacted for the 1st Earl of Egremont at PETWORTH, SUSSEX, for the 2nd Earl Poulett at HINTON ST. GEORGE, SOMERSET, and for the 1st Earl Gower at BILL HILL, BERKS., cannot readily be identified.

BRETTINGHAM, MATTHEW (1725–1803), was the eldest son of the architect Matthew Brettingham (d. 1769). He visited Italy and Greece in 1747, in company with Stuart and Revett, and remained in Rome until June 1754, studying architecture and sculpture and buying statues and pictures for Lord Leicester, Lord Dartmouth and others. A manuscript notebook, containing an 'account of Monies Received on My Lord the Earl of Leicester's account and of my Father's, Beginning from my first setting out of England, August 1747', is preserved at Holkham (MS. 744), and much of the antique sculpture now in the house was collected by him. He returned by way of Germany and Holland, bringing with him a collection of moulds of ancient sculpture, from which he proposed to take casts for sale. He also hoped to find subscribers who would support a project for the establishment of 'an Academy of Design in England', and made plans for a building in which to house it. At the same time, he was 'preparing to enter on the stage of business' as an architect, although, as he admitted in a letter to a former patron, he had so far had little experience 'in the practical part of Building'. In the late 1750s, however, when his father, 'having much business in Town, could not at that period give up so much of his time to a single building' (i.e. Holkham), Matthew junior 'was stationed there frequently to make up deficiencies of attendance'.

He was subsequently employed by Charles, 2nd Earl of Egremont (d. 1763), a member of the Society of Dilettanti, to buy statues for the gallery at Petworth, and in 1761, when Egremont was appointed British Plenipotentiary to the Congress of Augsburg, Brettingham supervised the housing of him and his embassage in that city. He was also patronized by Lord North, who had met him in Rome, and who, according to Joseph Farington, would have appointed him to the Comptrollership of the Works but for the King's determination to give the post to Chambers. Lord North then made him President of the Board of Green Cloth, a sinecure whose value was somewhat reduced as a result of Burke's Act of 1782, whereupon North made him Deputy Collector of the Cinque Port duties, which (according to Farington) gave him an income of between £400 and £500 a year. He lived at Norwich, and became a freeman of the city in 1769.

The income derived from his sinecures seems largely to have relieved Brettingham from the need to develop an extensive architectural practice. Immediately after his return to England he made a 'plan and elevations' (no doubt for a house in Ireland) for Ralph Howard, later Viscount Wicklow, but it does not appear to have been built [letter to Howard in Holkham MS. 744, f. 133ᵛ]. Letters to his sisters in the Bodleian Library [MS. Eng. Misc. c. 504, ff. 8–10] show that in 1767–9 he was working at Packington, Benacre and Shortgrove, evidently on behalf of his father, and the only important independent commission with which he can be credited was for the 12th Earl of Suffolk at CHARLTON HOUSE, WILTS. Here in 1772–6 he rebuilt the north and east fronts and remodelled the interior, filling the central quadrangle with a domed hall in an elegant neo-classical style. Even here the hall was left unfinished at Lord Suffolk's death in 1779, and was still in an incomplete state in the early nineteenth century [C. Life, 14–21 Oct. 1933, and 4 Nov., p. 483, for inscription on roof recording

that 'This edifice was rendered such as it is under the skilful direction of Matthew Brettingham Architect and the careful superintendance of James Darley Clerk of the Works. Begun A.D. 1772. Finished A.D. 1776'].

In 1771 Brettingham was among the architects who were invited to submit designs for rebuilding part of Lincoln's Inn. His drawings, which were not adopted, were formerly preserved in the library of the Inn, but have since been lost [Records of the Society of Lincoln's Inn: the Black Books iii, 407, 410; iv, 5, 7]. His designs (1785) for a new lecture room in the Botanic Garden at Cambridge also came to nothing [Willis & Clark, iii, 74, 153]. A sketch-book dating from c. 1750 is in the R.I.B.A. Drawings Collection. It contains several sketches of buildings in Rome, and a number of designs in the English Palladian tradition. A recurring theme is, however, a domed hall of the kind he was eventually to build at Charlton Park. In Sir John Soane's Museum there are (4D, ff. 36–73) a number of drawings, mostly designs for houses, which are stated to be by 'Mr. M. Brettingham'. Among them is a design for an ornamental building (probably a street fountain) made by him in Rome in 1752. At Trewithen, Cornwall, there are unexecuted designs for remodelling that house c. 1790 endorsed 'Brettingham's plans'.

Brettingham died at Norwich on 18 March 1803, aged 78. His will is P.C.C. 293 MARRIOTT.

[C. W. James, Chief Justice Coke, 1929, 286–9; East Anglian ii, 1866, 131–2; S. J. Wearing, Georgian Norwich: its Builders, Norwich 1926, 4–5; H. A. Wyndham, A Family History 1688–1837, 1950, 141, 169; The Farington Diary, ed. J. Greig, i, 294; J. G. Nichols, Illustrations of Literary History iii, 725; Lesley Lewis, Connoisseurs and Secret Agents in Eighteenth Century Rome, 1961, 151–4; Catalogue of the R.I.B.A. Drawings Coll.: B, 102–6; MS. copy of a letter from Lord Leicester to Brettingham, 10 July 1755, in R.I.B.A. Drawings Coll.]

BRETTINGHAM, ROBERT (1696–1768), was the eldest son of Launcelot Brettingham of Norwich. He took up his freedom in 1719 as a bricklayer and apprentice of his father. He executed the flint stonework of the Shirehouse at Norwich designed by his brother Matthew (q.v.). In August 1753 he advertised in the Norwich Mercury that, as he 'is leaving off his business of Mason, he intends to act in the character of an Architect, in drawing plans and elevations, giving estimates, or putting out work, or measuring up any sort of building, for any Gentleman in the County'. In October 1753 he was appointed architect and surveyor to the committee for building the Octagon Chapel at Norwich, but he was afterwards superseded by Thomas Ivory, who designed the existing Chapel. Advertisements in the *Norwich Mercury* in 1757 and 1760 show that Brettingham was acting as a house and estate agent. He was sheriff of Norwich in 1764, and is buried under an inscribed slab in St. Giles' Church [S. J. Wearing, *Georgian Norwich: its Builders*, Norwich 1926, 6–10].

BRETTINGHAM, ROBERT WILLIAM FURZE (*c.* 1750–1820), was the son of Michael Savary Furs, who married a daughter of the architect Matthew Brettingham, senior. He was therefore grandson of the elder, and nephew of the younger Brettingham, and adopted their surname, 'supposing that professionally it might be of service to him'. He entered the Royal Academy Schools in 1775, and travelled in Italy from 1778 to 1782. The young John Soane was his companion on the outward journey. In 1783 he exhibited at the Royal Academy a drawing of an 'antique fragment' from the garden of the Villa Medici. He began practice soon after, and in 1790, upon the death of William Blackburn, succeeded him as the architect of several prisons. He does not appear ever to have designed a building of major importance, and difficulties with more than one of his clients suggest either an awkward character or some lapses in professional competence. His surviving or recorded works indicate a classical style comparable to that of James Wyatt.

From 1794 until 1805, when he resigned, Brettingham held the post of Resident Clerk in the Office of Works. He was one of the original members of the Architects' Club on its foundation in 1791, but in 1799 he failed to obtain election as A.R.A. In 1800 he married Mrs. Smith, widow of the banker Samuel Smith, thus obtaining 'a good fortune'. He appears to have retired from practice soon afterwards, dying eventually in 1820. He had several pupils, but the only one 'to continue in the profession' was George Smith (*q.v.*), who supplied information for the somewhat inaccurate account of Brettingham's career in the A.P.S. *Dictionary.*[1] There is a portrait by George Dance in the British Museum. [*A.P.S.D.; The Farington Diary*, ed. J. Greig, i, 80, 294, ii, 80; A. T. Bolton, *The Portrait of Sir John Soane*, 1927, 5, 16, 20, 42–3; W. T. Whitley, *Artists and their Friends in England* ii, 1928, 236; Walter Brettingham, 'The Brettingham Family of Norfolk', *Blackmansbury* vi, nos. 3–4, 1969.]

LONDON, NO. 91 PALL MALL, alterations for the 1st Marquess of Buckingham, 1785–6; rebuilt as Buckingham House by Soane in 1792–5 [*A.P.S.D.; Survey of London* xxix, 360].
'Improved elevations to an old house in the West of England' [exhib. at R.A. 1786].

---

[1] T. J. R. Jackson and S. Woolley were pupils who did not persist.

READING, DUKE STREET BRIDGE (R. Kennet), 1787–8 [*Reading Mercury*, 12 March 1787].
FELBRIGG HALL, NORFOLK, minor alterations for William Windham, 1787–9 [*A.P.S.D.*; Windham's *Diary*, ed. Baring, 1866, 117–19, 190].
'Hermitage built in Middlesex' [exhib. at R.A. 1788].
BENHAM PLACE, BERKS., bridge in the park for the 6th Lord Craven, 1789; dem. [exhib. at R.A. 1790].
GREAT MARLOW BRIDGE, BUCKS. (R. Thames), 1789 (a wooden bridge replaced in 1830) [*Reading Mercury*, 4 Sept. 1786].
DOWNPATRICK GAOL, CO. DOWN, IRELAND, 1789 [*A.P.S.D.*].
LONDON, LITTLE DEAN'S YARD, WESTMINSTER, three houses on the south side, 1789. Of these, Grant's and the house of the Master of the King's Scholars survive. The third, Rigaud's, was dem. in 1896 [L. E. Tanner, *Westminster School*, 1923, 56].
LONGLEAT HOUSE, WILTS., unspecified work for the 1st Marquess of Bath, *c.* 1790 [*A.P.S.D.*; Christopher Hussey in *C. Life*, 29 April 1949].
AUDLEY END, ESSEX, TEMPLE OF CONCORD, for the 4th Lord Howard de Walden, 1790 [exhib. at R.A. 1792, 1793 and 1798; J. D. Williams, *Audley End: the Restoration of 1762–97*, Chelmsford 1966, 47–8].
SAFFRON WALDEN CHURCH, ESSEX, repairs and alterations, 1790–2 [exhib. at R.A. 1799; Lord Braybrooke, *History of Audley End and Saffron Walden*, 1836, 205; Essex Record Office, Braybrooke papers, Annual Accounts, 1793].
NORTHAMPTON COUNTY GAOL, 1791–4; rebuilt *c.* 1840 [*A.P.S.D.*; *Gent's Mag.* 1818 (ii), 499].
LONDON, NO. 21 ST. JAMES'S SQUARE (afterwards Winchester House), for the 5th Duke of Leeds, 1791–5; completed by Sir J. Soane after a disagreement between Brettingham and his client; dem. 1934 [*Survey of London*, xxix, 175–80, pl. 191].
LONDON, BAKER STREET, a house, 1792 [contract between R.B. and John Lane, builder, to erect a house in Baker Street, 9 Feb. 1792, advertised in catalogue of Jantzen of East Grinstead, Sussex, 1966, item no. 181; cf *Blackmansbury* vi, 1969, 39].
'A gentleman's house near Southampton' [exhib. at R.A. 1793].
READING COUNTY GAOL, 1793–4; rebuilt 1842 [Berks. Record Office, Q.S. Order Book 1791–5, 317–20, 439].
TAPLOW LODGE, BUCKS., enlarged or rebuilt for John Fryer, *c.* 1795 [Farington's Diary, 6 May 1795].
DOWNPATRICK CATHEDRAL, CO. DOWN, IRELAND, design for refitting choir [exhib. at R.A. 1795, and by Brettingham's pupil S. Woolley in 1798].
HILLSBOROUGH HOUSE, CO. DOWN, IRELAND,

enlarged for the 2nd Marquess of Downshire, c. 1795–7 [exhib. at R.A. 1797; E. R. R. Green & E. M. Jope in *Ulster Journal of Archaeology* xxiv–v, 1961–2, 145–151].

DOWNSHIRE HOUSE, ROEHAMPTON, SURREY, work for the 2nd Marquess of Downshire, presumably c. 1795 [*A.P.S.D.*].

LONDON, CURZON STREET, NO. 19, library for Sir John Sebright, Bart., 1802 [this commission ended in a lawsuit between Brettingham and Sebright: see *The Farington Diary*, ed. Greig, ii, 80, and correspondence in Sir John Soane's Museum, Soane Case, 'Misc. MSS. relating to Architecture', I].

WALDERSHARE PARK, KENT, work for the Earl of Guilford [*A.P.S.D.*]. Brettingham probably designed the single-storey outer wings, containing library and kitchen, for the 3rd Earl of Guilford (d. April 1802), for their parapets carry suitable neo-classical detail, and they are shown on a plan signed 'R.B. Gloucester Place, March 12th 1802' in the possession of Mr. William Drummond. Gloucester Place was Brettingham's London address at that date.

According to *A.P.S.D.* Brettingham built 'a fine room in the rear of his residence, No. 9 Berkeley Square, London, when he parted with it to the Marquis of Buckingham', but 24 Berkeley Square was the address at which Brettingham was living in the 1790s, and the Marquess of Buckingham's town house was in Pall Mall. Towards the end of his life Brettingham moved to 32 Grosvenor Place.

BREWSTER, JAMES (1805–c. 1845), was the son of the Rev. Dr. James Brewster, minister of Craig, nr. Montrose. He came to Dundee in 1832, when his competition designs for the new seminaries were much admired and only narrowly beaten by Angus's. In November of that year he was entrusted with the layout of Euclid Crescent in consultation with Angus. In 1833 he competed for the Gaols and Bridewell, but was again defeated by Angus. He had left Dundee by 1840, and was dead by 1848. In Dundee Public Library there is a ground plan of his design for the seminaries and an unexecuted design for a hearse house for the Constitution Road Cemetery. [Hew Scott, *Fasti Ecclesiae Scoticanae* v, 386; *Builder* vi, 1848, 553; information from Mr. David Walker.]

DUNDEE, WARD CHAPEL, CONSTITUTION ROAD, 1833, Gothic [C. Mackie, *Historical Description of the Town of Dundee*, 1836, 128].

FORFAR, ST. JAMES'S CHURCH, 1835–6, lancet Gothic [contract in *Dundee Advertiser*, 24 April 1835].

KIRRIEMUIR, ANGUS, WEBSTER'S SEMINARY, 1837–8, Jacobethan style [A. Reid, *Regality of Kirriemuir*, 1909, 177].

MONTROSE, DORWARD HOUSE, 1838, Italianate [advt. in *Dundee Advertiser*, 28 June 1838].

BRIANT, HENRY, of Reading, was the author of the winning designs in the competition for the ROYAL BERKSHIRE HOSPITAL, READING, in 1837. He submitted two designs, one in the Gothic, the other in the Grecian style, both of which were among the first three selected by George Basevi, the assessor. The handsome Greek design was executed in 1837–9, but with internal modifications based on the Gothic plan [*Reading Mercury*, 11 Feb. 1837; *Architectural Mag.* iv, 151–3]. The portico of the CASTLE STREET CHAPEL, READING, was designed in 1840 by Messrs. Henry & Nathaniel Briant, of 164 Friar Street, Reading [*Reading Mercury*, 7 and 14 March 1840]. According to N. Pevsner, *Berkshire* (Buildings of England, 1966), they also designed the Italianate BARCLAYS (formerly SIMONDS) BANK in KING STREET, READING, 1838–9. W. N. Briant, of 25 Sydney Terrace, Reading, exhibited architectural designs at the Royal Academy in 1842–3.

Briant is said to have given up architecture for the church, and if so he must have been the Rev. Henry Briant, of Queens' College, Cambridge, who was ordained in 1843, had a living at Macclesfield, and died at Manchester on 20 May 1884, aged 71 [Venn, *Alumni Cantabrigienses 1752–1900* i, 1940, 374].

BRIDEL, W—, exhibited at the Royal Academy from 1795 to 1797. His drawings included 'a villa erecting for Governor Blunt in America' (1796), and 'A view of the British Magazine at St. Petersburg' (1797).

BRIDGENS, RICHARD H—, was a pupil of the sculptor and modeller George Bullock, from whose premises in Liverpool he exhibited drawings at the Liverpool Academy in 1810, 1811 and 1812. They included a design for a monument, a restoration of the screen in Sefton Church, and a chimney-piece in Speke Hall. In 1813 he began to exhibit at the Royal Academy from London addresses, and the two drawings of Joseph Ridgway's house at RIDGMONT, HORWICH, LANCS., which he sent to the Liverpool Academy in 1814 may have represented his first architectural commission. In 1822 he published a folio volume of engravings of the medieval church at Sefton in Lancashire. He may have visited Italy about this time, for in the same year he exhibited at the Royal Academy 'an attempt to improve the restoration of the Barberini candelabrum now erecting in bronze', and a 'View in the Forum in Rome – showing the excavation made at the charge of Her Grace the Duchess of Devonshire'. He subsequently attempted to establish himself in practice in Birmingham, where James Watt of Aston Hall employed him to design some furniture. In 1826 Bridgens exhibited drawings for the restoration of Aston Hall, but it is doubtful whether they were carried out, and in 1825 Watt told C. R. Cockerell that Bridgens had been obliged to leave Birmingham for lack of employment there [Cockerell's diary, *sub anno*]. All that is known about his subsequent career is that in 1838 he published a volume entitled *Furniture with Candelabra and Interior Decoration designed by R. Bridgens*. This contains designs for furniture in both Gothic, classical and Elizabethan styles.

BRIDGES, JAMES, practised in Bristol from 1757 to 1763. Nothing is known of his origins, but he appears to have come to Bristol from the American colonies. In 1757 he submitted three designs to the commissioners for rebuilding Bristol Bridge, describing them in detail in a pamphlet entitled *Four Designs for Rebuilding Bristol Bridge*, which he published two years later. Other designs were submitted, including one by Ferdinando Stratford for a single-arch bridge, and a controversy arose over their respective merits. In 1762 Bridges published a second pamphlet, entitled *Reasons for Building a Bridge of Three Arches on the Old Foundations with his Objections to the Single Arch Plan*, and it was his design for a three-arch bridge that was eventually completed in 1768. It was executed under the direction of Thomas Paty, for Bridges himself had sailed for the West Indies in October 1763, disgruntled at the treatment he had received from the commissioners. The design was inspired by Labelye's Westminster Bridge of 1739–50. Widening in 1861 and 1873 has effectively destroyed it as a work of architecture.

Bridges' best-preserved work in Bristol is the house known as the ROYAL FORT, which he designed for a wealthy merchant named Thomas Tyndall shortly before 1760. He refers to the model (still preserved in the building) which he made for the Royal Fort in an 'advertisement' appended to his earlier pamphlet, and the house is also mentioned as his in a valedictory letter written by one of his supporters and printed in *Felix Farley's Bristol Journal* for 22 Oct. 1763. The exterior is a handsome though not particularly discriminating composition in the Anglo-Palladian style, but the interior is remarkable for exuberant rococo decoration for which Thomas Paty may have been responsible (*C. Life*, 27 May 1916).

During his stay in Bristol Bridges also designed two churches: ST. WERBURGH, whose nave and chancel he rebuilt in the Gothic style in 1758–61, and ST. NICHOLAS, which he offered to rebuild in 1760 on a plan similar to one he had seen executed in Pennsylvania. His designs were eventually accepted in 1762, and the church was completed in 1769 by Thomas Paty, who took

charge when Bridges left Bristol in 1763. St. Nicholas was a large stone box pierced with simplified 'Perpendicular' windows and decorated with rococo plasterwork, but St. Werburgh was a remarkably convincing reconstruction in the style of the fifteenth century. It was taken down in 1878 and rebuilt in Mina Road, Baptist Mills. St. Nicholas was gutted by bombing in 1940 and subsequently reconstructed as a museum.

[W. Ison, *The Georgian Buildings of Bristol*, 1952, 31–2, 65–70, 114–23.]

BRIGDEN, EDWARD, was employed early in the 1820s to superintend the building of Sir Robert Smirke's churches at Chatham and Bristol [Church Building Commissioners, Minute Books, 22 May 1827, *ex inf.* Mr. M. H. Port]. He subsequently practised in Bristol, where his name is found in the local Directories from 1825 to 1834. DR. WHITE'S HOSPITAL, TEMPLE STREET, BRISTOL, was rebuilt to his designs in 1824 [Bristol City Archives, Dr. White's Hospital Accounts, *ex inf.* Miss Joanna Tolmie]. In 1827 he rebuilt EASTON-IN-GORDANO CHURCH, SOMERSET, again rebuilt 1872 [G.R.]. Later he became surveyor to the Dowlais Iron Company in South Wales [P. Eden, *Dictionary of Land Surveyors and Local Cartographers*, 1975, 45].

BRIGGS, JOHN, is described as a 'Surveyor and Land Agent' of Chepstow in Pigot's *Directory* (1830). He designed the crudely detailed but not ineffective Gothic tower of ST. BRIAVEL'S CHURCH, GLOS., 1830 [parish records, *ex. inf.* Canon B. F. L. Clarke], and added an aisle to WOOLASTON CHURCH, GLOS., in 1839; rebuilt 1859 [I.C.B.S.].

BRINE, THOMAS, practised in the Isle of Man in the early nineteenth century. He was responsible for alterations and additions to BISHOPSCOURT for the Hon. George Murray, Bishop of Sodor and Man, 1814, Gothic; for alterations and additions to the Gaol and Rolls Office in CASTLE RUSHEN, *c*. 1815 and 1827 [P.R.O., H.O. 98/75; *Archaeologia* xciv, 1951, 19], and for ST. MARY'S CHURCH, CASTLETOWN, 1826, Gothic. In 1830 he supervised the arrangements for the laying of the foundation-stone of KING WILLIAM'S COLLEGE to the designs of Hansom & Welch [information from Mr. B. R. S. Megaw].

BRISTOW, J—, exhibited architectural drawings at the Royal Academy from Sun Street, Bishopsgate, in 1792 and 1793. His son, J. J. Bristow, junior, was admitted to the R.A. Schools in 1794 at the age of 19. He exhibited at the Academy from 1793 to 1802, including a 'view of a seat designed to be erected in Scotland' (1802).

BROAD, RICHARD, of Worcester, was admitted a freeman of that city in February 1752. In 1766 he submitted designs for the new Worcester Infirmary which were rejected in favour of those of Anthony Keck (*q.v.*) [Worcester County Record Office, Infirmary Book of Orders 1745–1800]. In 1768 he made a plan of Worcester. Two large tablets in coloured marbles to Henry (d. 1738) and Mary Wolstenholme (d. 1749) at STOKE EDITH, HEREFS., bear his signature. [Information from Mr. D. A. Whitehead.]

BROADBENT, JOHN (1803–1842), was the son of George Broadbent of Walton Breck, nr. Liverpool. He became a pupil of Thomas Rickman, but did not get on with his master. He subsequently practised in Liverpool until his early death at the age of 39 on 5 March 1842. He worked chiefly for commercial and mercantile clients in Liverpool, but in 1837 he designed a house in Ireland for a Mr. Cullen. His most important works appear to have been the churches of ST. AUGUSTINE, SHAW STREET, LIVERPOOL, 1829–30, Greek Revival, dem.; ST. ANTHONY (R.C.), SCOTLAND ROAD, 1832–3, a large Gothic building in a lancet style derived from Rickman; and the tower of WALTON-ON-THE-HILL CHURCH, LANCS., 1831–2, Gothic. Working drawings for St. Augustine's and St. Anthony's are in the R.I.B.A. Drawings Collection. Further details of Broadbent's practice are afforded by his business diaries for 1837 and 1840, now in Liverpool Public Library. [J. A. Picton, *Memorials of Liverpool* ii, 1875, 327, 343.]

BROMFIELD, JOSEPH (*c.* 1743–1824), of Shrewsbury, was a plasterer by trade, but frequently acted in the capacity of an architect or surveyor. As Joseph Bromfield, 'Ornamental Plasterer', he was admitted to the Shrewsbury Carpenters' and Bricklayers' Company in 1777, but it was not until 1792 that he became a burgess of the town. He served as Mayor in 1809, and died on 6 June 1824, aged 81. His will [P.C.C. 581 ERSKINE], in which he describes himself as 'architect', shows that he owned a good deal of property in Shrewsbury, including the houses forming the Crescent (on the south side of Town Walls), and a house at Llandrillo in Merionethshire called Brannas Lodge. He lived in St. Julians Friars, probably at No. 37, a Georgian house whose octagonal dining-room has an elaborately decorated plaster ceiling. 'Books, prints, busts, statues and pictures' are mentioned in his will.

Examples of Bromfield's workmanship as a plasterer can be seen at St. Chad's Church in Shrewsbury, at Oakley Park, Salop. (dining-room ceiling), and in Bishop Hurd's Library at Hartlebury Castle, Worcs. (when he was working to designs by James Smith of Shifnal). He was clearly an able craftsman capable of elegant work. As an architect he appears to have been competent but unremarkable.

[Shrewsbury Public Library: records of the Carpenters' and Bricklayers' Co. (13487); *The Shrewsbury Burgess Roll*, ed. H. E. Forrest, 1924, 40; *Salop. Arch. Soc. Trans.*, 4th ser., ix, 1923–4, 9; information from Miss M. C. Hill.]

WALCOT HALL, SALOP., acted as 'superintendent' of alterations and additions (including new portico) for the 1st Earl of Powis, 1784–90 [Salop. Record Office, Powis 552/9/290] (*C. Life*, 14 Oct. 1939).

attributed: SHREWSBURY, THE CRESCENT, TOWN WALLS, *c.* 1790 [three of the four houses forming this crescent were insured by Bromfield with the Salop. Fire Office in 1791 and 1815; all four are described as his property in his will].

APLEY CASTLE, SALOP., for St. John Charlton, 1791–4; dem. 1955, portico re-erected as an eye-catcher at Hodnet Hall [Salop. Record Office, Apley Castle records, Box 19/1–8, including a rejected estimate by J. H. Haycock, and a contract between St. J. Charlton and Joseph Bromfield of Shrewsbury, 'architect'] (S. Leighton, *Shropshire Houses*, 1901, 11).

STYCHE HALL, SALOP., alterations and additions, including canted bays flanking entrance, for the Hon. Robert Clive, 1796–8 [Salop. Record Office, Powis 552/9/50].

ATTINGHAM PARK, SALOP., lodges, marble bath in house, and unexecuted design for picture-gallery for the 2nd Lord Berwick, 1796–9 [Salop. Record Office, 112, Box 45, vouchers, *ex inf.* Mr. James Lawson].

GLANSEVERN, MONTGOMERYSHIRE, for Sir Arthur Davies Owen, *c.* 1801–7 [Owen papers in National Library of Wales, including a signed drawing for a fireplace, *ex. inf.* Mr. J. D. K. Lloyd].

BERRINGTON RECTORY (now HALL), SALOP., for the Hon. and Rev. Richard Noel Hill, 1805 [*V.C.H. Salop.* viii, 25].

NANNAU, MERIONETHSHIRE, additions (dem.) for Sir Robert Vaughan, Bart., *c.* 1805 [Owen papers in National Library of Wales, *ex. inf.* Mr. J. D. K. Lloyd].

CHURCHSTOKE CHURCH, MONTGOMERYSHIRE, 1811; rebuilt 1881 [parish records, *ex. inf.* Miss M. C. Hill].

BROOKES, WILLIAM McINTOSH (– 1849), was a pupil of George Maddox. He entered the Royal Academy Schools in 1822, exhibited at the Academy from 6 Adam Street, Adelphi, between 1829 and 1838, and became a Fellow of the (R.)I.B.A. His works included a dull Tudor Gothic court at Peterhouse, Cambridge, a Romanesque church at Albury, Surrey, the Perpendicular Gothic Irvingite church at the same place, and the formidable Greek Doric octastyle portico of the demolished Shire Hall at Bury St. Edmunds. He died in the Adelphi on 13 December 1849 [*Gent's Mag.* 1850 (i), 222].

CAMBRIDGE, PETERHOUSE, THE GISBORNE COURT, 1825–6, Tudor Gothic [Willis & Clark, i, 39].

CAMBRIDGE, THE TOWN GAOL, PARKER'S PIECE, 1828, castellated; dem. [Willis & Clark, i, 39].

HACKNEY, LONDON, THE CHURCH OF ENGLAND GRAMMAR SCHOOL, 1829, Gothic [exhib. at R.A. 1831].

LONDON, ST. MICHAEL, WOOD STREET, repairs, 1831, when the west tower was 'thrown open to the body of the church'; dem. 1894 [G. Godwin, *The Churches of London* i, 1838; the builder's contract is Guildhall Library MS. 2259].

EAST HAM VICARAGE, ESSEX, rebuilt 1832 [exhib. at R.A. 1834].

DORKING CHURCH, SURREY, rebuilt 1835–7, Gothic; rebuilt by H. Woodyer, 1872 [E. W. Brayley, *History of Surrey* v, 95].

THAMES DITTON CHURCH, SURREY, north aisle was rebuilt 1836 to the design of 'Mr. Brooks' [Vestry Minutes].

IPSWICH, SUFFOLK, THE COUNTY COURTS, 1836–7, Tudor Gothic [J. Wodderspoon, *Memorials of Ipswich*, 1850, 7].

LONDON, ST. ANNE AND ST. AGNES, GRESHAM STREET, alterations and repairs, 1838–9 [W. McMurray, *A City Church Chronicle*, 1914].

ALBURY, SURREY, CATHOLIC APOSTOLIC CHURCH, for Henry Drummond, completed 1840, Gothic [E. W. Brayley, *History of Surrey*, v, 165–6].

ALBURY CHURCH, SURREY, for Henry Drummond, 1840–1, Romanesque style based on church of Thaon, Normandy; chancel added 1869 [E. W. Brayley, *History of Surrey* v, 95].

BURY ST. EDMUNDS, SUFFOLK, THE SHIRE HALL, 1841–2; dem. 1906 [W. Suffolk Record Office, Q.S. Order Books, 17 March 1841] (H. R. Barker, *West Suffolk Illustrated*, 1907, 62).

EPSOM, SURREY, CHRIST CHURCH, EPSOM COMMON, 1844, Gothic; rebuilt 1877 [E. W. Brayley, *History of Surrey* iv, 365].

EPSOM, SURREY, THE VICARAGE, CHURCH STREET, for Rev. B. B. Bockett [E. W. Brayley, *History of Surrey* iv, 369].

BROOKS, JOSEPH (1707–1788) and JONATHAN, of Liverpool, 'were the great builders of the town' in the mid-eighteenth century. They also carried on business as timber merchants, lime-burners, rope-makers, etc., and owned an extensive yard between Wood Street and the present Bold Street, the site of which for its whole length was their rope-walk. There are considerable payments to them for work on

Liverpool Exchange, built to the designs of John Wood, 1749–54 [Liverpool Treasurers' Books, Picton Reference Library]. Joseph was president of the Infirmary in 1771, and took much interest in the welfare of the poor, having been for some time treasurer of the Workhouse on Brownlow Hill (rebuilt 1846), which he had built in 1769–70, and where his portrait by R. Caddick still, in 1875, hung in the board-room. He was a Nonconformist, and there was a tablet in his memory in the Key Street Chapel. His name is preserved in Brooks Street, where for many years stood his brickyard. In 1774–5 the body of ST. NICHOLAS CHURCH, LIVERPOOL, was rebuilt under his direction in a simple Georgian Gothic style: it was gutted in 1940–1 and rebuilt to a different design. His will (P.C.C. 229 CALVERT) shows that Jonathan predeceased him. [J. A. Picton, *Memorials of Liverpool* ii, 38, 39, 59, 135–6, 154; *Liverpool Vestry Books*, ed. H. Peet, i, 1912, 218 and *passim*.]

BROOKS, WILLIAM (1786–1867), was a pupil of D. R. Roper. He entered the Royal Academy Schools in 1808, and exhibited at the Academy from 1803 to 1815. He was a zealous Nonconformist and anti-Papist, a keen supporter of the movement for the abolition of slavery, and a persistent writer of letters to the newspapers on these and other topics. He was a member of the Goldsmiths' Company. Poor health led him to retire early. He died at Headington on 11 December 1867, aged 80. His son, C. W. Shirley Brooks, was a well-known editor of *Punch*. C. Dyer and L. W. Lloyd were his pupils.

Brooks designed at least two buildings of some distinction – the Finsbury Unitarian Chapel and the ingeniously planned and elegantly detailed London Institution. A drawing by him for alterations to Sutton Place, Surrey (probably not executed), is in the R.I.B.A. Drawings Collection. The 'numerous private edifices' mentioned in his obituary have yet to be identified. [*Gent's Mag.* 1868, 254–5; G. S. Layard, *A Great 'Punch' Editor, the Life of Shirley Brooks*, 1907, 2, 7, 90–1.]

GREAT HOLLAND RECTORY, ESSEX, design for the Rev. H. Rice [exhib. at R.A. 1812].

HARROW-ON-THE-HILL, MIDDLESEX, house for the vicar, the Rev. J. M. Cunningham [exhib. at R.A. 1815].

LONDON, THE LONDON INSTITUTION, FINSBURY CIRCUS, 1815–19; dem. 1936 [Britton & Pugin, *The Public Buildings of London* i, 1825, 186–92; contracts and specifications in Guildhall Library, MS. 2751] (*C. Life*, 11 April 1936).

DUDLEY, WORCS., ST. THOMAS, 1816–17, Gothic [*Gent's Mag.* 1868, 254; J. Noake, *The Rambler in Worcestershire* ii, 62].

LONDON, THE UNITARIAN CHAPEL, SOUTH PLACE,

FINSBURY, 1824; dem. [J. Elmes, *Metropolitan Improvements*, 1831, 163 and plate].

BRISTOL, THE FEMALE ORPHAN ASYLUM (now Salvation Army Home), HOOK'S MILLS, ASHLEY HILL (with C. Dyer), 1827–9 [*Gent's Mag.* 1868, 254].

ISLINGTON, COLLEGE OF THE CHURCH MISSIONARY SOCIETY, *c.* 1828; dem. [J. Elmes, *Metropolitan Improvements*, 1831, 145 and plate].

BROUGHTON, JAMES (*c.* 1647–1711), was appointed surveyor to the Dean and Chapter of Westminster on 14 January 1696/7, in succession to Robert Hooke. In March 1699, in accordance with the Act of Parliament for the repair of the Abbey Church, he became under-surveyor of the fabric at a salary of £50 per annum, the chief surveyor being Sir Christopher Wren. He retained both posts until his death on 31 January 1710/11, aged 63. He is buried in the east cloister, where there is a monument to his memory [Westminster Abbey Muniments; Bodleian Library, MS. Gough Westminster 1, p. 50; his will is P.C.C. 19 YOUNG].

BROWN, GEORGE, was a minor Northumbrian architect of the reign of George III. Among the drawings at Wallington Hall is a design by him for a new kitchen wing there dated 1769 (not executed). In 1772–3 he was employed by the County to report on the state of its bridges after the great flood of 1771, and made designs for a new bridge at Alnwick that were not carried out [Northumberland Record Office, Q.S. Order Books 10, p. 567, 11, p. 37].

BROWN, JAMES (*c.* 1729–1807), was an Edinburgh architect-builder and a wright by trade. He is best known as the designer and builder of GEORGE SQUARE, the first large-scale house-building scheme in eighteenth-century Edinburgh, and the first true square. Built in 1766–85, and named after his brother George, laird of Elliestown and Receiver-General of Excise in Scotland, it consisted of sixty-one houses on sites subfeued by him to speculative masons and wrights. Only the west side now remains more or less intact. A few years earlier he had built BROWN SQUARE, a much smaller development now absorbed into Chambers Street, and he subsequently built most of the houses in CHARLES STREET, CRICHTON STREET, WINDMILL STREET (dem. 1963) and BUCCLEUCH PLACE (1780–92) [W. N. Boog Watson, 'George Square, Edinburgh, 1766–1966', *University of Edinburgh Jnl.* 22, 1965–6; *Book of the Old Edinburgh Club* v, 26, and xxvi; A. J. Youngson, *The Making of Classical Edinburgh*, 1966, 68].

In 1770 Brown was consulted by the Heritors of Kelso about the state of their church [S.R.O., HR 651/3]; in 1775 he published anonymously a pamphlet entitled *The Importance of the Cowgate Bridge etc. considered* [Bodleian Library, Gough Scotland 260 (10)]; in 1779 he provided a design for PEEBLES PARISH CHURCH (completed 1784; dem. 1885), but it was not fully adhered to in execution [Gunn, *Parish Church of Peebles*, 1917, 6–7; J. W. Buchan, *History of Peebleshire*, 1864, 268]; in 1793 he was one of several architects who submitted designs for St. Cuthbert's Manse in Edinburgh [S.R.O., HR 152/2], and in 1796 he built a porch (since dem.) at the east end of ST. CUTHBERT'S CHURCH [W. Sime, *History of the Church and Parish of St. Cuthbert*, 1829, 152]. According to the text accompanying John Kay's *Original Portraits* i, 1837, 75, he built the mansion (dem.) in DRUMMOND PLACE, EDINBURGH, that was formerly occupied by General Scott of Balcomie and was subsequently used as the Excise Office (engraving in T. H. Shepherd, *Modern Athens*, 1829).

Brown died at his house in George Square on 8 December 1807, aged 78 [*Scots Mag.* 69, 1807, 960; Burial Register of Buccleuch Relief Church Burial Ground].

BROWN, JOHN, a 'mason and architect' of Inveraray, built CASTLEHILL CHURCH, CAMPBELTOWN, ARGYLLSHIRE, to the designs of George Haswell of Inveraray in 1778–80 [S.R.O., HR 67/1]. He designed the steeple which was added to CAMPBELTOWN TOWN HOUSE in 1778 [R.C.A.M., *Argyll* i, 186]. His survey plan of SOUTHEND CHURCH, KINTYRE, dated 1788, is in the Scottish Record Office (RHP 7177).

BROWN, JOHN (–1876), was the second son of a merchant of the same name at Yarmouth. In 1835 he stated that he had received his training under William Brown of Ipswich (*q.v.*), whom he described as 'a near relative', and had then practised as an architect and surveyor in London for eight years [*Norfolk Chronicle*, 29 Aug. 1835]. He subsequently established himself as an architect in Norwich, becoming in due course County Surveyor (1836) and Surveyor to the Dean and Chapter. He developed an extensive ecclesiastical practice, and in the latter part of his life had an office in London, where he died on 8 September 1876 [Somerset House, Calendar of Probates]. His early churches are of the Commissioners' type, usually with lancet windows and 'Early English' detail, but some of the later ones are more 'correct' by ecclesiological standards. James Wylson (1811–70), afterwards of Glasgow, joined his office as an assistant in 1836, and Ewan Christian (1814–95) and J. K. Colling are both said to have been his pupils. For a time in the 1840s he was in partnership with John Colson. His practice in Norwich was continued by his son John Henry Brown. [Information from Mr. D. C. Young.]

NORWICH, houses on CASTLE MEADOW, c. 1832 [exhib. at Norwich Society of Artists, 1832].

LOWESTOFT, ST. PETER'S CHURCH, 1832-3; chancel added 1903, Gothic [*British Magazine* ii, 1832, 213].

NORWICH, MUSEUM in EXCHANGE STREET, 1833 [exhib. at Norwich Society of Artists, 1833]. In 1839 the collections were removed to a new building in Broad Street.

YARMOUTH, NORFOLK, THE PROPRIETARY SCHOOL, 1834 [print in Todd Collection, Norwich Castle Museum].

NORWICH, NORWICH YARN COMPANY'S FACTORY, 1834-5; subsequently enlarged [*Norfolk Chronicle*, 25 Nov. 1834, 18 July 1835].

NORWICH, ST. ANDREW'S BROAD STREET, house for Mr. Griffin, surgeon, 1835 [*Norfolk Chronicle*, 18 July 1835].

STAMFORD, LINCS., ST. MICHAEL'S CHURCH, 1835-6, Gothic [G. Burton, *Chronology of Stamford*, 1846, 287; drawings formerly preserved in church].

COLCHESTER, ESSEX, THE UNION WORKHOUSE, BAL-KERNE HILL, 1836 [*Architectural Mag.* iii, 532].

BERGH APTON CHURCH, NORFOLK, enlarged 1837-8 [*Norfolk Chronicle*, 10 Sept. 1838].

NORWICH, THE NORFOLK AND NORWICH MUSEUM, BROAD STREET, 1838-9 [*Norfolk Chronicle*, 23 March 1839].

HAINFORD, NORFOLK, ALL SAINTS CHURCH, 1838-40, Gothic [I.C.B.S.].

SWAFFHAM, NORFOLK, THE SHIREHALL, 1839 [C. Mackie, *Norfolk Annals* i, 1901, 375].

LEE, KENT, ST. MARGARET'S CHURCH, 1839-41, Gothic; remodelled 1876 [*Companion to the Almanac*, 1841, 229-31].

SOUTH RUNCTON CHURCH, NORFOLK, rebuilt 1839, neo-Norman [I.C.B.S.].

BEDFORD, HOLY TRINITY CHURCH, 1839-40, Gothic: chancel added 1866 [*Gent's Mag.* 1841 (ii), 194].

NORWICH, POST OFFICE STREET, house and premises for Joseph Gray, 1841 [*Norfolk Chronicle*, 26 April 1841].

THE NORFOLK LUNATIC ASYLUM, THORPE-NEXT-NORWICH, alterations and additions, 1841 and 1847 [*Norfolk Chronicle*, 20 March 1841 and 12 June 1847].

NORWICH, CHRIST CHURCH, NEW CATTON, 1841-2, Gothic [C. Mackie, *Norfolk Annals* i, 1901, 399].

NORWICH CATHEDRAL, restoration of central tower, 1842 [C. Mackie, *Norfolk Annals* i, 1901, 420].

BEDDINGTON RECTORY, SURREY, 1842-3 [exhib. at R.A. 1844; drawing in R.I.B.A. Drawings Coll. dated 1842].

WITHAM, ESSEX, ALL SAINTS CHURCH, 1842-3 [*Gent's Mag.* 1843 (ii), 75].

BRIDGWATER, SOMERSET, ST. JOHN'S CHURCH, 1843-5, Gothic [*Gent's Mag.* 1845 (i), 641].

BEDDINGTON AND WALLINGTON NATIONAL SCHOOLS, SURREY, 1843, Tudor [Brayley, *History of Surrey* iv, 70; drawings in Surrey Record Office, 264/2].

NORWICH, ST MARK'S CHURCH, NEW LAKENHAM, 1843-4; apse 1864 [I.C.B.S.; C. Mackie, *Norfolk Annals* i, 1901, 427].

BAWDESWELL CHURCH, NORFOLK, rebuilt 1844-5, Gothic; rebuilt 1953-5 [C. Mackie, *Norfolk Annals* i, 1901, 445].

MINTING RECTORY, LINCS., 1845-6 [Lincolnshire Record Office, MGA 302].

TROWSE, NORFOLK, GIRLS' SCHOOL, 1846 [*Norfolk Chronicle*, 25 July 1846].

NORWICH, ST. CLEMENT'S CHURCH, restoration, 1846 [*Norfolk Chronicle*, 14 Feb. 1846].

GREENWICH, CHRIST CHURCH, TRAFALGAR ROAD, 1846-8 [H. H. Drake, *Hundred of Blackheath*, 1886, 97].

NORWICH, ST. MARK'S SCHOOL, NEW LAKENHAM, 1847 [C. Mackie, *Norfolk Annals* i, 1901, 463].

ALDBOROUGH CHURCH, NORFOLK, repairs, 1847-8 [T. H. Bryant, *Norfolk Churches, North Erpingham Hundred*, c. 1900, 68].

LONG STRATTON CHURCH, NORFOLK, restoration, 1847-8 [*Ecclesiologist* ix, 1849, 267-8].

NORWICH, ST. MATTHEW'S CHURCH, THORPE HAMLET, 1848-51, neo-Norman [*Builder* ix, 1851, 513, 577].

SHERINGHAM CHURCH, NORFOLK, restoration, 1848-9 [*Norfolk Chronicle*, 22 April 1848].

BROOKE CHURCH, NORFOLK, restoration, 1849 [*Norfolk Chronicle*, 10 Nov. 1849].

NORWICH CATHEDRAL, restoration, begun 1851 [*Builder* x, 1852, 396; *Ecclesiologist* xii, 1851, 359-60].

NORWICH, THE DIOCESAN TRAINING SCHOOL (for schoolmistresses), 1852 [tender in *Builder* x, 1852, 462].

STOW BEDON CHURCH, NORFOLK, extensive alterations, 1852-3 [*Builder* xi, 1853, 117].

FAKENHAM, NORFOLK, THE CORN HALL, 1854-5 [*Builder* xi, 1853, 455; C. Mackie, *Norfolk Annals* ii, 1901, 44].

WORKHOUSES at LINGWOOD, DOCKING and SWAINSTHORPE, NORFOLK, and OULTON, SUDBURY and WICKHAM MARKET, SUFFOLK [*Architectural Mag.* iii, 330; *Norfolk Chronicle*, 12 Dec. 1835, 2 and 30 April, 7 May, 11 June 1836].

BROWN, LANCELOT (1716-1783), was born at Kirkharle in Northumberland, and educated in the village school at Cambo. At the age of 16 he was engaged as a gardener by Sir William Loraine of Kirkharle, where he was later entrusted with laying out an addition to the grounds. After small landscape commissions at Benwell and other nearby places he left Northumberland in 1739. His first design in the South was a lake at Kiddington Park in Oxfordshire but in 1741 he moved to Stowe as head gardener to Lord

Cobham, becoming virtually clerk of the works for building as well as gardening. Here he came into contact with William Kent, the first great exponent of English landscape gardening, in collaboration with whom he 'naturalized' the formal layout of what was already one of the most celebrated of English parks. As Kent's assistant and Lord Cobham's gardener, his advice was in due course asked by other gentlemen anxious to improve their grounds, and when his employer died in 1749 Brown gave up his post at Stowe and began to practise as a consulting landscape gardener. In the course of the next thirty years he was called upon to exercise his art in every part of the country, and by the time of his death in 1783 his characteristic landscapes, with their serpentine lakes and scattered clumps of trees, had become one of the most familiar features of the English countryside. The house, which before had dominated the estate, was now an integral part of a carefully composed landscape intended to be seen through the eye of a painter, and architecture as well as horticulture necessarily formed a part of Brown's professional equipment. In addition to his fame as a gardener, Brown did, in fact, enjoy a considerable reputation as an architect, and in his *Theory and Practice of Landscape Gardening*, Humphry Repton bears witness to the 'comfort, convenience, taste, and propriety of design in the several mansions and other buildings which he planned'. Croome Court, his earliest architectural work, probably owed something to the advice of Sanderson Miller, and closely resembled the house which the latter soon afterwards designed for Lord Lyttelton at Hagley. Newnham Paddox, another of Brown's early works, followed a similar Palladian model, and Fisherwick was in the same tradition. Elsewhere Brown designed stables and other subsidiary buildings in a Gothic style reminiscent of William Kent. Much of his architectural work was executed by Henry Holland, a masterbuilder of Fulham, with whom he became acquainted soon after leaving Stowe. In 1771 Brown took Holland's son Henry into a kind of informal partnership, introducing him to his clients, and gradually handing over to him the architectural side of his practice. In 1773 the younger Holland married Brown's daughter Bridget, and when Brown made his will in 1779 he named his son-in-law as one of his executors.

In 1764 Brown was appointed Master Gardener at Hampton Court, a post which brought him an official residence at Hampton known as Wilderness House. He died on 6 February 1783, at the age of 67, and was buried at Fenstanton in Huntingdonshire, where he had bought a small estate in 1767.

The earliest list of Brown's architectural works was printed by Humphry Repton in his *Theory and Practice of Landscape Gardening* (1803), from

information supplied by Holland. *Capability Brown*, by Dorothy Stroud (1950; new edition 1975), is a comprehensive study of his work as landscape gardener and architect.

Unless otherwise stated, the following list of Brown's architectural works is based on Miss Stroud's book, where full references will be found.

CROOME COURT, WORCS., for the 6th Earl of Coventry, 1751–2, probably following a design by Sanderson Miller (*q.v.*).

WARWICK CASTLE, alterations for the 1st Earl of Warwick, including rebuilding of porch to Great Hall, 1753–5, and wooden bridge over the R. Avon, 1758 [*V.C.H. Warwicks.* viii, 461, 471].

NEWNHAM PADDOX, WARWICKS., largely rebuilt for the 5th and 6th Earls of Denbigh, 1754–68; remodelled by T. H. Wyatt 1876–9; dem. 1952 [Anthony Wood, 'Lancelot Brown and Newnham Paddox', *Warwickshire History* i (1), 1969, with photograph of main front before 1876].

BURGHLEY HOUSE, NORTHANTS, works for the 9th Earl of Exeter, including alterations to south front of house, Gothic stables, greenhouse and bath-house, 1756–78; bridge in park 1774–7, and staircase 1781–2 [E. Till, 'Capability Brown at Burghley', *C. Life*, 16 Oct. 1975] (Stroud, pls. 12–14).

CROOME CHURCH, WORCS., for the 6th Earl of Coventry, 1758–63, Gothic. The interior decoration was designed by Robert Adam.

LONGLEAT HOUSE, WILTS., gateway to flower-garden for the 3rd Viscount Weymouth, 1760.

CHILLINGTON HALL, STAFFS., bridge in park for Thomas Giffard, before 1761.

CASTLE ASHBY, NORTHANTS., bridge, temple and dairy for the 8th Earl of Northampton, *c.* 1765 (Stroud, pl. 18b).

CORSHAM COURT, WILTS., enlarged house for Paul Methuen, 1761–4; altered by Nash and Repton 1797–8 and by Bellamy 1844–9; also designed Gothic Bath House in North Walk (Stroud, pls. 14–16).

SPRING HILL, nr. BROADWAY, WORCS., for the 6th Earl of Coventry, 1763; remodelled in nineteenth century.

BLENHEIM PALACE, OXON., remodelled High Lodge and designed façade to Park Farm for the 4th Duke of Marlborough, 1764–5, Gothic.

PRIOR PARK, nr. BATH, an unidentified 'additional building' for Ralph Allen (d. 1764), said by Repton to have been built in 1765.

BURTON PYNSENT, SOMERSET, THE COLUMN, for the 1st Earl of Chatham, 1765.

REDGRAVE HALL, SUFFOLK, remodelled for Rowland Holt, *c.* 1765; dem. 1946 (Stroud, pl. 22).

BROADLANDS, nr. ROMSEY, HANTS., remodelled for the 2nd Viscount Palmerston, 1766–8; entrance portico, etc., added by Holland 1788–92 (*C. Life*, 31 March, 7 April 1923).

FISHERWICK PARK, STAFFS., for the 5th Earl (later 1st Marquess) of Donegall, 1766–74; dem. 1816 (Stroud, pl. 47).

ASHBURNHAM PLACE, SUSSEX, work for the 1st Earl of Ashburnham, including greenhouse and alterations to offices, c. 1767.

COMPTON VERNEY, WARWICKS., the Bridge, 1770–2, and the Chapel, 1776–8, for the 6th Lord Willoughby de Broke (Stroud, pl. 38).

SLANE CASTLE, CO. MEATH, IRELAND, the stables for the 1st Viscount Conyngham, c. 1770, Gothic [Alistair Rowan, 'Georgian Castles in Ireland', Irish Georgian Society's *Bulletin* vii (i), 1964, 16–17].

WREST PARK, BEDS., hermitage for the 2nd Earl of Hardwicke, before 1771, when Horace Walpole wrote that Brown had 'built a hermitage and cold bath here'. The latter appears, however, to have been designed by Edward Stevens (*q.v.*).

*CLAREMONT HOUSE, nr. ESHER, SURREY, for the 1st Lord Clive, 1771–4 [G. Richardson, *New Vitruvius Britannicus* i, 1802, pls. 61–3; *Surrey Archaeological Colls.*, lxv, 1968, 91–2].

BROCKLESBY PARK, LINCS., alterations for the 1st Lord Yarborough, 1773; damaged by fire 1898 and subsequently reconstructed; partly dem. c. 1955.

BURTON CONSTABLE, YORKS. (E.R.), the south (office) courtyard for William Constable, 1772–3, Gothic.

SCAMPSTON HOUSE, YORKS. (E.R.), bridge for Sir William St. Quintin, Bart., 1773 (Stroud, pl. 49).

MILTON ABBEY, DORSET, model village for the 1st Lord Milton, c. 1774–80. But see below under Sir William Chambers, who also made designs for the village.

*BENHAM PLACE, BERKS., for the 6th Lord Craven, 1774–5; attic storey added and pediment removed c. 1870.

*CADLAND, nr. SOUTHAMPTON, HANTS., for the Hon. Robert Drummond, 1775–8; wing added by Holland 1782; enlarged by Wyatville 1837; dem. c. 1955 (Stroud, pl. 52).

*TRENTHAM HALL, STAFFS., alterations for the 2nd Earl Gower, 1775–8; reconstructed by Barry 1834–40 and 1840–9; dem. 1910 (*C. Life*, 25 Jan. 1968, fig. 8).

CLANDON PARK, SURREY, stables for the 1st Earl of Onslow, c. 1775; dem. c. 1974.

CHILHAM CASTLE, KENT, lodges, etc., for Thomas Heron, 1777; dem. 1862.

*CARDIFF CASTLE, GLAMORGANSHIRE, reconstruction in Gothic style for Lord Mount Stuart, 1777–8; rebuilt 1875 (*C. Life*, 6 April 1961).

STANSTEAD PARK, SUSSEX, alterations for Richard Barwell, 1781–3, perhaps not executed.

* In collaboration with H. Holland.

*NUNEHAM PARK, OXON., alterations including heightening of wings for the 2nd Earl Harcourt, 1781–2 [M. L. Batey, *Nuneham Courtenay, Oxfordshire*, 1970, 11–12].

WYNNSTAY, DENBIGHSHIRE, the Dairy for Sir Watkin Williams-Wynn, Bart., 1782 [P. Howell in *C. Life*, 6 April 1972, 853 and fig. 8].

ASKE HALL, YORKS. (N.R.), bridge in park for Sir Lawrence Dundas, Bart. (d. 1781).

BROWN, RICHARD, practised in London, but appears from his early exhibits at the Royal Academy to have had some connection with Devonshire. In 1804 he showed 'A design for a villa with distant view of the Catwater, Plymouth, Devon', in 1807 'A Cottage designed for Sir M. Lopez, Bart., to be built in Devonshire' (probably at Maristow, Lopez's seat), in 1808 a 'Design for rebuilding Warleigh House, the seat of J. Radcliff, Esq. Devon' (not carried out), and in 1812 a view of 'Oldaport Farm, Modbury, Devon'. Subsequent exhibits included 'A proposed design for the Regency Park' (1812), a 'Military Chapel and Officers' apartments, erecting by the Royal African Society at Cape Castle, on the Gold Coast of Africa' (1818), and 'A Market House, designed for Great Yarmouth, Norfolk' (1827: not built).

In 1823, in collaboration with W. Cubitt of Ipswich, Brown submitted the winning design in the competition for a new GAOL AND HOUSE OF CORRECTION, ST. GILES GATES, NORWICH. However, in 1824 he withdrew from further participation in this work, and most of the building (dem.) was carried out under the direction of Philip Barnes [information from Mr. A. P. Baggs]. In 1831 Brown designed for the 3rd Lord Holland a lodge at the Kensington High Street entrance to HOLLAND HOUSE [Lord Ilchester, *Chronicles of Holland House 1820–1900*, 1937, 368–71]. The only other building that he is known to have designed is the INDEPENDENT CHAPEL, TOPSHAM, DEVON, a feeble Gothic structure signed 'R^D. BROWN Architect 1839'.

Brown evidently taught drawing, for he frequently called himself 'Architect and Professor of Perspective'. He was the author of *The Principles of Practical Perspective or Scenographic Projection*, 1815; *Domestic Architecture, containing a History of the Science and the Principles of Designing Public Edifices, Private Dwelling-Houses, Country Mansions and Suburban Villas* with a section on Landscape Gardening, 1842 (an indiscriminately eclectic work which includes designs for houses in every European style and several oriental ones as well, from the 'Plantagenet' to the 'Egyptian', and from the 'Swiss Cottage' to the 'Pompeian Suburban Villa'); *Sacred Architecture, its Rise, Progress and Present State embracing the Babylonian, Indian, Egyptian,*

Greek, and Roman Temples,—the Byzantine, Saxon, Lombard, Norman and Italian Churches, with an analytical inquiry into the Origin, Progress, and Perfection of the Gothic Churches in England; and practical directions for restoring these dilapidated Christian Edifices to their primitive beauty, 1845, and other works. His travels in France (1822), Switzerland and Italy are mentioned in *Domestic Architecture* (pp. 277, 279, etc.). His London office was at 23 Wells Street, Oxford Street, but he probably retired to Devonshire, for the preface to *Domestic Architecture* is dated from Topsham, and the preface to *Sacred Architecture* from Exeter. M. A. Nicholson, Clark Rampling and J. Tarring were his pupils. An engraved portrait forms the frontispiece to *Domestic Architecture.*

BROWN, ROBERT, practised in Edinburgh, where he was responsible for laying out a number of building estates in the New Town. In 1813 he was one of the architects who submitted designs for the Calton Hill town-planning scheme [A. J. Youngson, *The Making of Classical Edinburgh,* 1966, 149]. Then in 1815 he acted as Robert Reid's assistant at the Signet Library [S.R.O., E 343/2, p. 197; E 343/3, p. 24]. Between 1810 and 1830 he was engaged in laying out the following streets: PITTVILLE (formerly PITT) STREET, PORTOBELLO, on the Marquess of Abercorn's estate, *c.* 1810; MELVILLE (now BELLFIELD) STREET, PORTOBELLO, 1817–18; 1–16 BRANDON STREET, 1–7 EYRE PLACE and 1–8 HUNTLEY STREET, on James Eyre's estate, 1822–5; MELVILLE CRESCENT, MELVILLE STREET, WALKER STREET and MANOR PLACE, for the Walker Trust, 1822–5; 1–22 ANNANDALE STREET, 1–8 and 17–32 HADDINGTON PLACE and 7–8 and 17–18 HOPETOUN CRESCENT, for Major John Hope, 1825–7; 11–22 CIRCUS PLACE N.W. and ST. STEPHEN STREET, 1825–6; 1–32 CLARENCE STREET and 109–119 HENDERSON ROW, for James Peddie, 1829–36; and 70–88 HAMILTON PLACE, 1830 [Scottish Development Department, duplicated *List of Buildings of Special Architectural or Historical Interest in Edinburgh,* 1971, with reference to Sasines, etc.]. He also designed NEWINGTON AND ST. LEONARD'S CHURCH (originally HOPE PARK CHAPEL), CLERK STREET, EDINBURGH, 1823 [J. Stark, *Picture of Edinburgh,* 5th. ed. 1835, 226], and the BURGHER CHURCH in ROSE STREET, EDINBURGH, 1829 [Minutes of the Burgher Congregation, *ex inf.* Mr. W. S. M. Lucas and Mr. David Walker]. In 1827 he designed a new house for General Graham Stirling at REDNOCK HOUSE, PERTHSHIRE [plans at Rednock, photos. at N.M.R.S.].

Brown's son Robert Brown, junior (*c.* 1802–1860), joined his father's practice in 1830, and appears to have taken it over in the course of the next few years. The Robert Brown who rearranged the interior of YESTER HOUSE, EAST LOTH-

148

IAN, for the 8th Marquess of Tweeddale in 1830, and added a *porte-cochère* in 1838–9, may have been either father or son [J. G. Dunbar, 'The Building of Yester House 1670–1878', *Trans. of the E. Lothian Antiquarian Soc.* xiii, 1972, 37–8]. Nor is it certain which of the two was the Robert Brown of Edinburgh who designed KIRK YETHOLM CHURCH, ROXBURGHSHIRE, in a somewhat crude Gothic style in 1835–6 [S.R.O., HR 189/2]. It was, however, presumably the son who in the 1840s enlarged and remodelled DUNVEGAN CASTLE, SKYE, for Norman MacLeod, adding, among other features, the existing castellated porch [*The Book of Dunvegan,* ed. R. C. MacLeod, 3rd Spalding Club 1938, i, p. xxxvii].

The younger Brown died on 4 December 1860, aged 58, and is commemorated by a monument in St. Cuthbert's Churchyard, Edinburgh. He married the daughter of a builder named Henderson, and left a son Robert who became a civil engineer and died at Bombay in 1869 at the age of 36.

BROWN, THOMAS, of Renfrew, directed the building of ROSS-DHU HOUSE, DUNBARTONSHIRE, for Sir James Colquhoun, Bart., in 1773–4. The house is said, probably correctly, to have been designed by Sir James Clerk of Penicuik (*q.v.*) and if so Brown would only have been responsible for supervising its execution. Several payments to 'Mr. Thomas Brown, Architect at Renfrew, for his attendance &c about my Buildings' are found in an account-book preserved at Ross-dhu.

BROWN, THOMAS (–1840), *see* HAYLEY, WILLIAM

BROWN, THOMAS (*c.* 1781–1850), practised in Edinburgh, where he first appears as a surveyor and drawing master in about 1810. He held the post of Superintendent of the City Works from 1819 until 1847, when he retired on a pension of £150. He died on 5 June 1850, aged 69, and is commemorated by a monument in the Greyfriars Cemetery. David Cousin (1809–78) was his principal assistant and succeeded him as City Architect. John Cunningham (*q.v.*) was his pupil. [City Archives; James Brown, *Epitaphs and Monumental Inscriptions in Greyfriars Churchyard,* 1867, 273.]

Brown's son Thomas Brown, junior, became architect to the Prison Board of Scotland in 1837 and designed, *inter alia,* the County Prison at Inverness, 1845, and the Debtors' Prison on Calton Hill, completed 1846, dem. *c.* 1884. In 1848 or 1849 he took James Maitland Wardrop (1824–82) into partnership, thus founding the firm in which Charles Reid, H. M. Wardrop and Rowand Anderson were subsequently partners. There are plans of prisons by him in the Scottish Record

Office (RHP 21327 *et seq.*), and the National Library of Scotland (MS. 354, B. and C.). He was architect to the Hopetoun estate in the 1840s.

LEITH, EXCHANGE BUILDINGS, CONSTITUTION STREET, 1809–10, incorporating Assembly Rooms of 1783 [Edinburgh Dean of Guild plans, elevation initialled 'T B 2nd. October 1809', *ex inf.* Mr. David Walker].

LEITH, TRINITY HOUSE, 1816–17 [John Mason, *History of Trinity House of Leith*, Glasgow 1957, 173–5].

NORTH LEITH ASSOCIATE BURGHER (later N. LEITH U.P. and ultimately ST. NINIAN'S) CHURCH, COBURG STREET, 1818, Gothic; dem. *c.* 1960 [Edinburgh Dean of Guild plans, 1818].

EDINBURGH, INFIRMARY STREET U.P. CHURCH (now University Works Dept.), 1822 [Edinburgh Dean of Guild plans].

EDINBURGH, ST. MARY, BELLEVUE CRESCENT, 1823–6 [*A.P.S.D.*, *s.v.* 'Edinburgh'; Town Council Minutes, 26 March 1823].

LEITH, THE PRISON, 1824; dem. [*The Scotsman*, 12 Aug. 1824].

EDINBURGH, COMELY BANK, 1817–18 [elevation in S.R.O., RHP 4429]; FETTES ROW, 1821; layout of INVERLEITH ROW, 1823; CUMBERLAND STREET, 1823; PRESTON STREET WEST, 1824; NEWINGTON PLACE WEST and 58–68 NEWINGTON ROAD, *c.* 1825; ROYAL CRESCENT, 1825–9; INVERLEITH PLACE, 1826 [all from Sasines].

EDINBURGH, ST. GILES' CATHEDRAL, fitted up nave as a parish church, 1842 [*History of the King's Works* vi, 254].

BROWN, THOMAS (1806–1872), lived at Uphall in Midlothian. He is first referred to (as 'Thomas Brown, architect') in Pigot's *Directory* of 1825–6, and is presumably the same 'Thomas Brown, Architect' whose tombstone in Uphall Churchyard records his birth on 4 December 1806 and his death on 23 August 1872. In 1836 he enlarged and renovated CARRINGTON CHURCH, MIDLOTHIAN [S.R.O., HR 460/1 under date 16 Nov. 1838]. Early in the 1830s he was employed by William Adam (d. 1839) at BLAIR ADAM in KINROSS-SHIRE, where he designed the Memorial (1833) and various gates and gate-lodges on the estate [Blair Adam archives, *ex inf.* Dr. A. A. Tait].

BROWN, WILLIAM, was described as 'architect' when he was admitted to the Incorporation of Wrights at Glasgow in 1813 [*The Incorporation of Wrights in Glasgow*, Glasgow 1880, 48]. He designed THE LYCEUM, SOUTH ALBION STREET, GLASGOW, an establishment containing a subscription library and news room [*The Picture of Glasgow*, Glasgow 1812, 147–8].

BROWN, WILLIAM, practised in Ipswich, where he designed several public and private buildings, often with Greek Revival detailing. John Brown of Norwich (*q.v.*) was related to him and was his pupil.

IPSWICH, THE MARKET PLACE, consisting of an inner and an outer quadrangle, each surrounded by a piazza, the inner having in its centre a fountain surmounted by an obelisk, 1810–11; dem. [*Ipswich Jnl.*, 17 March 1810; J. Dugdale, *The British Traveller* iv, 1819, 301; J. Wodderspoon, *Memorials of Ipswich*, 1850, 11] (J. Glyde, *Illustrations of Old Ipswich*, 1889, 69).

THE NORFOLK LUNATIC ASYLUM, THORPE-NEXT-NORWICH, 1811–14 [C. Mackie, *Norfolk Annals* i, 1901, 89, 116].

IPSWICH, HANDFORD BRIDGE, repairs, *c.* 1814 [J. Glyde, *Illustrations of Old Ipswich*, 1889, 46].

IPSWICH, NEW ASSEMBLY ROOMS, NORTHGATE STREET (now 'NORTHGATE HOUSE'), 1821 [*Ipswich Jnl.*, 15 Jan. 1825, *ex inf.* Mr. J. Bensusan-Butt].

IPSWICH, terrace of houses (Nos. 27–35) in LOWER BROOK STREET, 1825 [*Ipswich Jnl.*, 31 Dec. 1825, *ex inf.* Mr. J. Bensusan-Butt].

BROWNE, ADAM (–1655), held the post of Surveyor to Westminster Abbey from 1639 until his death in 1655. Among the Westminster Abbey Muniments there are surveys of repairs needed at the Abbey drawn up by Browne, and estimates by him for making a gallery and altering the pews during the Commonwealth [W.A.M. 9908, 9909, 5320, 9828, 24852, 24854, 24855, 24857, 42687, etc.]. Browne was a joiner by trade, and in the 1630s he had been much employed by Archbishop Laud. Thus in 1633–4 University College, Oxford, bought 800 old boards from 'Mr. Browne Joyner of London', who is also described as 'Mr. Brown joyner to my Ld. Grace of Cant.' [University College records]. At that time he was being employed by Laud at St. John's College, where in 1632 he made a screen 'to part the upper end of the Chappell' [P.R.O., S.P. Domestic 226, f. 21]. He was also concerned in building the Canterbury Quadrangle at the same College, for the accounts for its erection show that in Feb. 1632/3 he was paid £5 'for his paines in comming downe [from London] & drawing ye Drafts, & making ye Moulds'. Besides providing the drawings and moulds he negotiated with masons on the College's behalf and drew up a contract with the carpenter [St. John's College Muniments, lxxxi, 2, pp. 81–2]. The drawings in question must have been for the classical arcades and frontispieces, which are designed in a mannerist style derived probably from Antwerp. At Arbury Hall, Warwicks., there is a fine cabinet in a similar style which bears Laud's arms as Bishop of London (1628–33) and may well have been made by Browne. At Lambeth Palace he made an altar and other joinery work for Laud

149

in 1633 [P.R.O., S.P. Charles I/246, no. 88], and in Laud's accounts there are payments to him for picture-frames, three 'cedar chests', a press for copes, work in 'Your Grace's study', etc. [P.R.O., E 101/547/5, *passim*]. At Laud's trial in 1644 'Browne, his Joyner', was a reluctant witness, giving evidence about 'Popish' windows ordered by Laud for his houses at Lambeth and Croydon and put up under Browne's direction [Laud's *Works*, ed. Bliss, iv, 1854, 209, 228; W. Prynne, *Canterburies Doome* ..., 1646, 61]. He appears in effect to have been Laud's personal surveyor, and if the Canterbury Quadrangle at St. John's can be attributed to him he must rank as one of the leading English architectural designers of the 1630s. In his will (P.C.C. 201 AYLETT) he is described as 'of Westminster', but asked to be buried at Hammersmith.

BROWNE, ARTHUR, practised in the Close at Norwich. He was a founder member of the Norwich Society of Artists in 1805, and was its President in 1807. He exhibited at the Society from 1805 to 1833. In 1799 the *Gentleman's Magazine* illustrated a design made by him for an octagonal domed mansion 'intended to be erected at Burnham Market, Norfolk, as a residence for Lord Nelson'. A design for a 'Temple of Victory', published in the same magazine in 1800, appears also to have been made by him, and he signs unexecuted designs for a gaol for Bury St. Edmunds, and for an obelisk in honour of Lord Nelson, which appeared in the *Gentleman's Magazine* in August 1801 and August 1807, respectively. All these designs are of a markedly neo-classical character, as is the obelisk with which he ornamented the Pilgrims' Well at Costessy. Intwood Hall and Magdalene Bridge are, however, Gothic, and it was no doubt a Gothic design which the fellows of St. John's College, Cambridge, expected when in 1825 they invited Wilkins, Browne and Rickman to compete for their new buildings [Willis & Clark, ii, 278]. In the list of Browne's works which follows all references to the exhibitions of the Norwich Society of Artists (N.S.A.) have been provided by Mr. A. Paget Baggs.

LITTLE PLUMSTEAD, NORFOLK, Gothic house or *cottage orné* for Francis Gostling, *c.* 1806 [exhib. at N.S.A. 1806; cf. J. Chambers, *Norfolk Tour* i, 1829, 6].
INTWOOD HALL, NORFOLK, for J. S. Muskett, *c.* 1807; Tudor Gothic [exhib. at N.S.A. 1807].
NORWICH, CARROW BRIDGE (cast iron), 1810; dem. [exhib. at N.S.A. 1810].
NORWICH, CARROW HILL, supervised gratuitously laying out of road, as recorded on a plaque fixed to wall of Black Tower.
COSTESSY, NORFOLK, the PILGRIMS' WELL (obelisk, etc.), *c.* 1810 [drawing in Todd Collection, Norwich Castle Museum, Forehoe Hundred].

NORWICH, ST. ANDREW'S PLACE, house for P. J. Knights, *c.* 1811 [exhib. at N.S.A. 1811].
CAMBRIDGE, four houses near Pembroke College, *c.* 1816 [exhib. at N.S.A. 1816].
SWAFFHAM, NORFOLK, design for 'addition to the house of a gentleman', exhib. at N.S.A. 1816.
NORWICH, Triumphal Arch in Market Place to commemorate coronation of King George IV, 1821 [J. Chambers, *Norfolk Tour* iii, 1829, 1104].
NORWICH, ST. STEPHEN'S CHURCH, monument to W. Stevenson, F.S.A., (d. 1821), executed by De Carle [J. Chambers, *Norfolk Tour* iii, 1829, 1094].
CAMBRIDGE, MAGDALENE BRIDGE (cast iron), 1823 [signed 'Arthur Browne Archt. 1823'].
NORWICH, ST. PETER MANCROFT CHURCH, monument to Rev. C. J. Chapman (d. 1826), executed by William Allen [J. Chambers, *Norfolk Tour* iii, 1829, 1097].
CAMBRIDGE, EMMANUEL COLLEGE, enlarged kitchen and remodelled its west elevation in Tudor Gothic style, 1828 [Willis & Clark, ii, 716]. Browne may also have been responsible for the north range of the New Court, built in 1824.
NORWICH CATHEDRAL, fittings of St. Luke's Chapel [J. Chambers, *Norfolk Tour* iii, 1829, 1104].

BROWNE, EDWARD HENRY, of London, exhibited at the Royal Academy between 1831 and 1843, including the 'Facade of the new fire station-house about to be erected for the London Fire-Engine Establishment in Chandos Street, St. Martin's Lane' (1836), the 'St. John's National Schools, now erecting at Walham Green' (1836), 'A cottage, erecting in Upper Harmer Street, Gravesend, for George Kiallmarll, Esq.' (1843), and 'A cottage erecting in Millfield Lane, Highgate, for Albert Walls, Esqr.' (1843). A design by him for an Italianate villa is in the R.I.B.A. Drawings Collection.

BROWNE, J—, of University Street, London, signs two drawings among the Gordon Castle papers in the Scottish Record Office. One is a design for a mausoleum (RHP 2378), the other for a Grecian temple (RHP 2413). Both were probably made for the 5th Duke of Gordon (d. 1836).

BROWNE, ROBERT, submitted designs for a wooden bridge to the Commissioners for building Westminster Bridge in 1737 [Commissioners' Minutes, P.R.O., Works 6/28, vol. i, f. 69].

BROWNE, ROBERT (1756–1827), junior, was the son of Robert Browne, senior, who was one of the joint clerks of works at Somerset House under Chambers from 1776 onwards, and held the post of Clerk of the Works at the Tower,

Newmarket, Winchester and Greenwich from 1790 until his death in 1796. The son entered the Royal Academy Schools in 1776, and exhibited drawings at the Academy from 1778 to 1798. In 1793 he showed 'A pavilion erected at Ampton', Suffolk. In 1789 he obtained a post in the Office of Works at Clerk of the Works at Windsor Castle, and from 1790 to 1815 held a similar post at Richmond and Kew Palaces. In 1805 he carried out alterations to KEW CHURCH, SURREY, for King George III, including the addition of the west portico and the south aisle [plans in Surrey Archdeaconry Records]. In 1811–12 he designed a wooden bridge over the Thames at DATCHET, BUCKS., dem. 1851 [*Oxford Herald*, 9 March 1811]. In 1815 he was promoted to the office of Assistant Surveyor-General and Cashier, from which he retired in 1822. The arrangements for the coronation of George IV in 1820 were under his direction [A. T. Bolton, *The Portrait of Sir John Soane*, 353]. He died on 14 August 1827, aged 72, and is commemorated by a monument in the churchyard at Kew. R. C. Kidd was his pupil.

BROWNING, BRYAN (1773–1856), was a native of Thurlby, Lincs. In 1817 he submitted designs for rebuilding RINGWOOD PARSONAGE, HANTS. [Winchester Diocesan Records], and in 1821 he designed the SESSIONS HOUSE, BOURNE, LINCS., whose small but effective façade ingeniously combines an external staircase and a columnar screen [*The Lincoln, Rutland and Stamford Mercury*, 4 and 11 May and 26 Oct. 1821]. He was then 'of Doughty Street, London', and the records of the Foundling Hospital in the G.L.C. Record Office show that in 1825 he was concerned in building houses on the north side of MECKLENBURGH SQUARE, LONDON. But in 1834 he was living at Northorpe (between Bourne and Thurlby), and by 1838 he was established in Stamford, where in the 1840s he was retained by Lord Exeter at £180 p.a. In Stamford he designed the WORKHOUSE, 1835, the Greek Revival STAMFORD INSTITUTION on ST. PETER'S HILL, 1842 (of which there is a lithograph signed by his son), remodelled BARN HILL HOUSE in 1843, and designed GRANT'S IRON FOUNDRY, 1845, 4–5 RED LION SQUARE and 1 HIGH STREET, 1848, and BYARD HOUSE, ST. PAUL'S STREET, 1851 [R.C.H.M., *Stamford*, forthcoming]. In 1824–5 he designed THE HOUSE OF CORRECTION at FOLKINGHAM, LINCS., with a dramatic façade suggestive both of Vanbrugh and of Ledoux [unsigned drawings in Lincs. R.O., Kesteven Q.S. records, endorsed 'Mr. Browning's first plans']. In 1834 he enlarged WADENHOE PARSONAGE, NORTHANTS., and in 1840 designed STOKE DRY RECTORY, RUTLAND, Tudor Gothic [Northants. R.O., Peterborough Diocesan Records]. In the Lincolnshire Record Office there are plans by him for altering

or rebuilding the parsonages at ALWALTON, HUNTS. (1833), FLETTON, HUNTS. (1835), GREATFORD, LINCS. (1838), and DEEPING ST. JAMES, LINCS. (1839). He died on 1 October 1856, and is commemorated by a monument in the cemetery at Stamford.

Bryan's son Edward Browning (1816–82) appears to have been in partnership with his father towards the end of his life and succeeded to his practice. In 1847–9 STAMFORD BRIDGE was rebuilt by 'Messrs. Browning' together with the adjoining Conservative Club, originally a toll-house [M. E. C. Walcott, *Memorials of Stamford*, 1867, 31]. Edward worked at BURGHLEY HOUSE and APETHORPE, and restored many churches in the dioceses of Lincoln and Peterborough in the 1850s and '60s. [*The Architect's, Engineer's and Building Trades Directory*, 1868, 103]. Bryan had a younger son Henry (1822–c. 1908) who began life in the family office, but in 1851 went to Cambridge, graduated and in 1855 was ordained.

BROWNING, L—, exhibited at the Royal Academy from South Molton Street, London, between 1812 and 1815, showing in 1815 his design for 'the alteration and improvements of Bunny Park, Nottinghamshire, now executing for Lord Rancliffe'.

BRUCE, SIR WILLIAM (c. 1630–1710), was the younger son of Robert Bruce of Blairhall, a Perthshire laird who was closely connected with other and more prominent branches of the Bruce family, including those represented by the Earls of Kincardine and of Elgin and Ailesbury. The date of his birth is not known, but it is likely that he was born in about 1630. A William Bruce was, however, admitted to St. Salvator's College at St. Andrews for the academic year 1637–8, and if this was the future baronet, he must have been born in the 1620s. Nothing certain is known about his early life. Whatever ability he may have shown as a young man, it was primarily to political services that he appears to have owed his subsequent advancement. According to Sir Robert Douglas's *Baronage of Scotland* (1798) Bruce played a part in converting General Monk to the Royalist cause in 1659, and the existence of a passport for Bruce signed by Monk on 7 Sept. 1659 certainly suggests that he may have been involved in the negotiations which preceded the Restoration, for it not only permits him 'to passe about his occasions on this side the Fryth [of Forth] & other parts of Scotland', but also refers to his impending 'returne to Holland', where the royal court was then in exile. The Clarendon State Papers afford further evidence that Bruce was employed as a confidential messenger between the Scottish lords and Charles II in the months immediately preceding the Restoration. Soon after the Restoration he was knighted, and through the patronage of the Earl (later Duke) of Lauderdale obtained various employments, including those of Clerk of the Bills,[1] receiver of fines, and commissioner of excise in Fife. From March 1672 he also enjoyed the farm of the Scottish customs and had various commercial interests, such as a share in the Royal Fishery Company of 1670. By 1665 he was in a position to acquire a small estate at Balcaskie in Fife, and in 1675 a larger one at Kinross on the shores of Loch Leven. In 1668 his new status as a landed gentleman was recognized by the grant of a baronetcy, and subsequently a peerage may even have been talked of. As it was, he was a landowner, a Justice of the Peace (1673), parliamentary commissioner for Kinross-shire, and for a few months (April 1685 to May 1686) a member of the Privy Council for Scotland.

With the death of Charles II (1685) Bruce's good fortune failed him. For the rest of his life he was politically suspect. James II distrusted him and the governments of William III and Queen Anne, believing him (with some justification) to be a Jacobite sympathizer, placed him under confinement on more than one occasion. After 1686 he devoted most of his energies to the management of his estates, and to the completion of a country seat at Kinross. But, deprived of the financial rewards of office, Bruce found that his building operations could be continued only by burdening his estate with debt. By 1700 he reckoned that he had spent upwards of £10,000 on building operations, and even when they were concluded the cost of maintaining the elaborate formal gardens was still heavy. It was, therefore, only with difficulty that Bruce created the magnificent house which he hoped to hand on to his successors in the baronetcy.

Of Bruce's architectural education there is no record, but 'it is reasonable to suppose that an inherent interest in the subject was developed both by theoretical studies and by travel' (Dunbar). His visits to Holland during the Interregnum may well have extended to France, and he is known to have made a 'foreign journey' in 1663. He was also in England on various occasions, and although France may have been the dominant influence in the formation of his architectural style, several of his country houses conform to the 'double-pile' formula popularized by May and Pratt soon after the Restoration.

Bruce's career as an official architect was limited to the years 1671–8, when he held the post of 'Surveyor-general and overseer of the King's Buildings in Scotland'. This was a revival of the ancient office of 'Master of Work' to the Scottish Crown, vacant since 1668, but with a new title

and an enhanced salary (£300 instead of £100). The appointment was specifically for the purpose of rebuilding the palace of Holyroodhouse, and apart from some repairs to Edinburgh and Stirling Castles and to the fortifications on the Bass Rock, there is no evidence that Bruce carried out any other architectural works for the Crown. The whole scheme appears to have originated with the all-powerful Lauderdale, and it may have been due to political differences between Bruce and Lauderdale that in May 1678 his warrant was revoked on the ground that the reconstruction of Holyroodhouse was finished. In 1671 Holyroodhouse had consisted of an irregular cluster of buildings, of which the sixteenth-century north-west tower was the principal architectural feature. Assisted by Robert Mylne, the King's Master Mason, Bruce created a symmetrical front by erecting a duplicate tower to the south and linking the two together by means of a lower balustraded range incorporating a Doric entrance-portico. The whole design, including the incorporation of late Gothic towers into a formal composition, is thoroughly French in character. Within the main courtyard the restrained classicism of the principal elevations is also French in derivation, and 'introduced a completely new idiom into Scottish architecture', hitherto addicted to the mannerist exuberance of buildings like Heriot's Hospital. The interior decoration was, however, carried out in the rich Anglo-Dutch style of Restoration England.

Apart from his brief tenure of the Surveyor's office, Bruce was essentially a gentleman architect, whose designs were nearly all made for fellow members of the Scottish aristocracy. Defoe called him the 'Kit Wren of Scotland', but Hugh May and Sir Roger Pratt were the English architects with whom it is most appropriate to compare him. The number of country houses for which he was directly responsible is not large, but his architectural influence was much more extensive than the short list of his authenticated works might suggest. His advice was often sought by his friends and their relatives even when there was no question of his assuming direct control over their building operations. In this way he was consulted about designs for new houses by the Earl of Tweeddale in 1670 and by the Earl of Cassilis in 1673–4. A few years later when the Duke of Queensberry proposed to remodel Drumlanrig he made a memorandum that the papers were 'to be looked over and advised be Sr. Wm. Bruice', and in 1692 the Duke of Hamilton did not begin work at Hamilton Palace before he had obtained Bruce's advice about the best man to employ. Bruce's influence was further extended by those who worked with him. To call them his pupils would be misleading, but it was undoubtedly from Bruce that the master masons Robert Mylne and Tobias Bachop (q.v.) learned a more classical

[1] In December 1681 he resigned this post in favour of James Anstruther (Sir John Lauder, *Historical Notices of Scottish Affairs* i, 1848, 344).

152

vocabulary. In the case of James Smith (*q.v.*) the exchange of expertise may have been almost as much to Bruce's advantage as to Smith's, but Smith's importance as an exponent of Bruce's style is evident. Alexander Edward, minister of Kemback (*q.v.*), seems to have begun his architectural career as Bruce's draughtsman, before developing a practice of his own.

Bruce rightly ranks as the effective founder of classical architecture in Scotland. Before him Scottish domestic architecture was still dominated by the basic forms of the late medieval castle overlaid with mannerist decoration from France and the Low Countries. Though highly picturesque, the result was an architectural idiom far removed from the classical conventions which by 1660 were generally accepted (if not always understood) in England. It was Bruce's function to design unfortified houses for the first generation of Scottish lords to realize that the tower-house was an anachronism, and to persuade them to abandon corbel and crow-step in favour of cornice and pediment. Not all Bruce's houses were built on new foundations. Often it was a case of adapting an old fabric to modern uses, and here some compromise with the past was inevitable. At his own house of Balcaskie, at Lauderdale's castle of Thirlestane, at his grandson's seat of Craighall, he was obliged to improvise in a manner which hardly suggests the mastery of his later works. At Holyroodhouse he was even prepared, in the interests of symmetry, to duplicate a sixteenth-century tower block complete with its conical roofs and battlements. But at Dunkeld, Moncreiffe and Kinross he adapted the compact formula developed in England by architects like Webb and Pratt and gave it a dignity and a presence that it rarely attained in English hands. At Craigiehall and Mertoun a basically conventional façade is made interesting by subtle variations in fenestration, while Hopetoun shows that he could handle a more complex design with equal assurance. Not only, therefore, was Bruce, in the words of Sir John Clerk of Penicuik, 'the chief introducer of Architecture in this country': as a designer of country houses he was fully the equal of his English contemporaries.

For Bruce house and garden were part of a single conception. At Kinross in particular the nobility of the architecture is enhanced by the magnificent formality of the setting. At the same time the deliberate alignment of the main vista on the ruins of Lochleven Castle suggests that Bruce, like Vanbrugh, has a place in the prehistory of the picturesque. Although architecture was his dominant interest, Bruce's fondness for horticulture, music and painting is shown by numerous surviving accounts of personal expenditure from 1665 onwards. He may also have been something of a linguist, for besides owning books published in French and Italian, as well

as in Latin and Greek, he appears to have had a reading knowledge of German and Dutch.

Bruce was twice married, first in about 1660 to Mary, daughter of Sir James Halket of Pitfirrane, and secondly (in 1700) to Magdalen, the widow of an Edinburgh merchant named Clerk. He died on 1 January 1710, 'at a very advanced age', and was buried in the family vault at Kinross. His property was inherited, first by his son John, and then by his daughter Anne, who married Sir Thomas Hope of Craighall. A portrait by Michael Wright, painted in 1665, is in the Scottish National Portrait Gallery. Another version of the portrait hangs at Kinross House. At Holyroodhouse there is a portrait of Bruce in old age by Sir John Medina. Some of his papers remain at Kinross House. Others are in the Register House at Edinburgh (GD 29).

[S.R.O., Bruce of Kinross papers (GD 29); B. M., Lauderdale papers, especially Add. MSS. 23134, f. 170, and 23135, ff. 32–6; *Cal. S.P. Domestic 1663–4*, 265, *1671*, 295–6, *1678*, 197; *Acts of the Privy Council of Scotland* i–xii, *passim*; *The Acts of Parliament of Scotland* xii (index), 258; *The Clarendon State Papers*, ed. Routledge; Hist. MSS. Comm., *House of Lords*, N.S. viii, 87, 92, 111, 149, 152–3, 182–3, 191, 195, 199, *Laing* i, 349–50; *Journal of the Hon. John Erskine of Carnock 1683–7*, ed. W. MacLeod, Scottish History Soc. 1893, 154 (reference to Bruce as 'Viscount of Kinross'); Joseph Robertson, 'Notice of a Volume of the Accounts of Sir William Bruce', *Proc. Soc. Ant. Scotland* iii, 1862, 113–17; David Marshall, 'Three Contracts for the Reparation of Holyrood Palace, etc.', *Proc. Soc. Ant. Scotland*, N.S. ii, 1880, 324–37; R. S. Mylne, *The Master Masons to the Crown of Scotland*, 1893: Sir Wm. Fraser, *The Earls of Melville and Leven*, 1890, i, 272, iii, 237, 239; T. C. Smout, *Scottish Trade on the Eve of Union*, 1963, 75; H. F. Kerr in *Quarterly of the Royal Incorporation of Architects of Scotland*, 1924; J. G. Dunbar, *The Historic Architecture of Scotland*, 1966, 93–101; Hubert Fenwick, *Architect Royal*, Kineton 1970; J. G. Dunbar, *Sir William Bruce*, exhibition catalogue published by the Scottish Arts Council, 1970. The last is by far the best account of Bruce's work in print.]

HOLYROODHOUSE, EDINBURGH, enlarged and remodelled for King Charles II, 1671–9 [*Cal. S.P. Domestic 1671*, 295–6; R. S. Mylne, *The Master Masons to the Crown of Scotland*, 1893, chaps. 9–10; drawings and contracts in B.M., Egerton MSS. 2870–1; building accounts in S.R.O.].

LAUDER CHURCH, BERWICKSHIRE, for the 1st Duke of Lauderdale, 1673 [letter from Lauderdale in S.R.O., GD 29/1897/9] (G. Hay, *Architecture of Scottish Post-Reformation Churches*, 1957, fig. 21 and pl. 8b).

EDINBURGH, five cisterns or fountains in the city as part of a new system of water-supply, 1674–5 [*Extracts from the Records of the City of Edinburgh 1665–80*, ed. M. Wood, xlii–xliii, 427].

EDINBURGH, THE EXCHANGE, PARLIAMENT CLOSE, for Thomas Robertson, 1680–1; destroyed by fire 1700 [R. Miller, *The Municipal Buildings of Edinburgh*, Edinburgh 1895, 126–7; Marguerite Wood, 'All the Statelie Buildings of Thomas Robertson', *Book of the Old Edinburgh Club* xxiv, 1942, 137].

KINROSS, SOUTH QUEICH BRIDGE, *c.* 1694, since replaced [R. Sibbald, *The History of Fife and Kinross*, 1803 ed., 274].

STIRLING, THE TOWN HOUSE, 1703–5 [R.C.A.M., *Stirlingshire* ii, 293].

attributed: ABERCORN CHURCH, WEST LOTHIAN, THE HOPE AISLE, for the 1st Earl of Hopetoun, 1707–8 (*C. Life*, 20 Oct. 1966).

COUNTRY HOUSES

LESLIE HOUSE, FIFE, supervised enlargement and remodelling by Robert Mylne (*q.v.*) for the 7th Earl (1st Duke) of Rothes, 1667–72; largely destroyed by fire 1763 [J. Dunbar, *Sir William Bruce* (exhibition catalogue), 10, citing Rothes papers in Kirkcaldy Museum; *Vitruvius Scoticus*, pls. 66–8].

BALCASKIE HOUSE, FIFE, enlarged and altered for himself, *c.* 1668–74 [J. Dunbar, *Sir William Bruce* (exhibition catalogue), 10–11, citing S.R.O., Bruce of Kinross papers] (*C. Life*, 2 March 1912).

THIRLESTANE CASTLE, BERWICKSHIRE, supervised remodelling by Robert Mylne (*q.v.*) for the 1st Duke of Lauderdale, *c.* 1670–77; altered 1840–1 [J. G. Dunbar, 'The Building-activities of the Duke and Duchess of Lauderdale, 1670–82', *Archaeological Jnl.* cxxxii, 1975] (D. MacGibbon & T. Ross, *Castellated and Domestic Architecture of Scotland* iv, 1892, 334–9).

HAM HOUSE, SURREY, gateways for Elizabeth, Countess of Dysart (afterwards Duchess of Lauderdale), 1671 and 1675 [J. G. Dunbar, 'The Building-activities of the Duke and Duchess of Lauderdale, 1670–82', *Archaeological Jnl.* cxxxii, 1975].

PANMURE HOUSE, ANGUS, gateway for the 3rd Earl of Panmure, 1672 [S.R.O., GD 45/18/599].

BRUNSTANE HOUSE, MIDLOTHIAN, enlarged and remodelled for the 1st Duke of Lauderdale, *c.* 1672–5 [J. G. Dunbar, 'The Building-activities of the Duke and Duchess of Lauderdale, 1670–82', *Archaeological Jnl.* cxxxii, 1975].

LETHINGTON (now LENNOXLOVE), EAST LOTHIAN, alterations for the 1st Duke of Lauderdale, 1673–4 and 1676–7, including new stable-block [J. G. Dunbar, 'The Building-activities

of the Duke and Duchess of Lauderdale, 1670–82', *Archaeological Jnl.* cxxxii, 1975].

DUNKELD HOUSE, PERTHSHIRE, for the 1st Marquess of Atholl, *c.* 1676–84; dem. 1830 [J. Dunbar, *Sir William Bruce* (exhibition catalogue), 14].

attributed: MONCREIFFE HOUSE, PERTHSHIRE, for Thomas Moncreiffe, 1679; destroyed by fire 1957 [J. Dunbar, *Sir William Bruce* (exhibition catalogue), 14].

KINROSS HOUSE, KINROSS-SHIRE, for himself, 1686–93 [*Vitruvius Scoticus*, pls. 61–2; Mark Girouard in *C. Life*, 25 March, 1 April 1965; J. G. Dunbar, 'Kinross House', in *The Country Seat*, ed. Colvin & Harris, 1970; S.R.O., Bruce of Kinross papers, GD 29/263, and accounts in Mylne papers, GD 1/51/62].

CRAIGIEHALL HOUSE, WEST LOTHIAN, for the 2nd Earl of Annandale, *c.* 1695–99; altered by R. Lorimer 1926–7 [letters in S.R.O., GD 29/1955].

CRAIGHALL, nr. CUPAR, FIFE, alterations and additions for Sir William Hope (then a minor in Bruce's guardianship), 1697–9; long ruinous, finally dem. *c.* 1955 [accounts in S.R.O., Bruce of Arnot papers, GD 242, box 27; J. Dunbar, *Sir William Bruce* (exhibition catalogue), 16].

KINNAIRD CASTLE, ANGUS, unexecuted design for remodelling house for the 4th Earl of Southesk, 1698 [drawings at Kinnaird Castle, *ex inf.* Dr. Alistair Rowan].

HOPETOUN HOUSE, WEST LOTHIAN, for Charles Hope, afterwards 1st Earl of Hopetoun, 1699–1703; enlarged by William, John & Robert Adam, 1723–56 [*Vitruvius Scoticus*, pls. 14–19; *Vitruvius Britannicus* ii, 1717, pl. 75–77; John Fleming in *C. Life*, 5–12 Jan. 1956].

AUCHINDINNY, MIDLOTHIAN, for John Inglis, 1702–7 [attributed to Bruce by Henry Mackenzie (1745–1831), who lived at Auchindinny: see *The Anecdotes and Egotisms of Henry Mackenzie*, ed. H. W. Thompson, 1927, 216].

MERTOUN (or HARDEN) HOUSE, BERWICKSHIRE, for Sir William Scott, begun 1703; wings added by W. Burn 1843, removed by I. G. Lindsay 1953–5 [*Vitruvius Scoticus*, pl. 142] (*C. Life*, 2–9 June 1966).

HOUSE OF NAIRNE, PERTHSHIRE, for the 2nd Lord Nairn, *c.* 1709–12; dem. 1760. Several people were consulted, including the Earl of Mar and Alexander McGill, and the extent of Bruce's responsibility for the building is uncertain: see J. Dunbar, *Sir William Bruce* (exhibition catalogue), 20; S.R.O., GD 112/40/7 and GD 124/15/788; *Chronicles of the Atholl and Tullibardine Families*, compiled by the 7th Duke of Atholl, ii, 1908, 109].

Note: The attribution to Bruce of WEMYSS HALL (or HILL OF TARVIT), nr. CUPAR, FIFE, for John Wemyss, 1696, though not implausible, is not at present supported by any documentary evidence, and is not sufficiently compelling on stylistic grounds to justify inclusion in the list of Bruce's authenticated works.

EDINBURGH AND GLASGOW

EDINBURGH, TWEEDDALE COURT, HIGH STREET, alterations and improvements during Bruce's possession of the property, c. 1664–70. In 1670 he sold it to the Earl of Tweeddale [National Library of Scotland, MS. Acc. 3495 and Acc. 4862, 99/1 and 99/2].

GLASGOW, GIBSON'S LAND, SALTMARKET STREET, for Walter Gibson, c. 1690; collapsed 1823 [John MacUre, *View of the City of Glasgow*, 1736, 149]. Though early enough to deserve respect, this attribution cannot be regarded as authoritative.

BRYAN was a family of masons and carvers whose business was based on the quarries at Painswick in the Cotswolds. In 1766 George Shirley of Ettington in Warwickshire noted that 'Thomas [*sic*] Bryan lives in Painswick & owns the Quarry' [account-book in Warwicks. R.O.]. The principal members of the family were John (1716–87) and Joseph (1718–79), sons of Joseph Bryan of Painswick (1682–1730). John is described as 'late of this town, carver', on his pyramidal monument in Painswick Churchyard. Joseph established himself in Gloucester, where he died in 1779. His son John married his uncle John's daughter and succeeded to the family business.

The firm was responsible for many tablets and churchyard memorials of excellent quality (for further details see R. Gunnis, *Dictionary of British Sculptors 1660–1851*, revised ed. 1968). They were also masonry contractors. In July 1750 John Bryan of Painswick and Joseph Bryan of Gloucester, masons, together with William Clark of Leonard Stanley, carpenter, undertook to rebuild the west tower of GREAT WITCOMBE CHURCH, GLOS., for £80 [contract among Hicks Beach family papers]. The tower is of traditional Gothic design, with battlements and pinnacles. In 1747–8 John Bryan received 10 guineas for a pair of gate-piers for the entrance to Painswick Churchyard [Painswick Parish Records]. In 1776 Joseph and John Bryan made a proposal for rebuilding the spire of ST. NICHOLAS' CHURCH, GLOUCESTER, which was out of alignment, but nothing was done until 1783, when John Bryan contracted to take down the top of the steeple as far as the coronet and to erect a copper ball and pinnacles thereon, thus giving it its present termination [extracts from Vestry Minutes in Gloucester Public Library, MS. NF. 5.3].

BRYCE, JOHN (1805–1851), was a younger brother of David Bryce (1803–1876), the pupil

and assistant of William Burn. They were the sons of William Bryce, a builder of Edinburgh. William Bryce, junior, who was practising as an architect in Edinburgh in the early 1820s, appears to have been an elder son. He died on 5 September 1823 [*Scots Mag.* 1823, 512]. John Bryce practised in Glasgow, where he designed the DUKE STREET REFORMATORY or HOUSE OF REFUGE, c. 1825; dem.; the column, etc., in the JEWS' BURIAL GROUND at THE NECROPOLIS, 1833; a monument (1834) in THE NECROPOLIS to William McGavin (d. 1832); QUEEN'S CRESCENT, ST. GEORGE'S, 1840; 55–71 ASHLEY STREET, ST. GEORGE'S, 1849; 4–26 BOTHWELL STREET, BLYTHSWOOD (with Alexander Kirkland), 1849; and QUEEN'S TERRACE, 61–127 WEST PRINCES STREET, ST. GEORGE'S, 1850. Unlike his younger brother he remained generally faithful to the Scottish classical tradition. [J. Pagan, *Sketch of the History of Glasgow*, 1847, 180, 183; A. Gomme & D. Walker, *Architecture of Glasgow*, 1968, 266.]

BUCKLE, GEORGE, is listed as an architect practising in London in Pigot's *Directory* of 1827–8 and in *The Literary Blue Book* of 1830.

BUCKLER, JOHN (1770–1851), was born at Calbourne in the Isle of Wight. He is said to have been articled to C. T. Cracklow, an architect of Southwark, but according to the obituary in the *Oxford Herald*, he 'commenced life as clerk to Mr. R. B. Fisher, steward of Magdalen College, Oxford, and for many years held the appointment of bailiff or collector of rents to that society'. In 1849, when he retired, it was stated that he had been in the service of the College for sixty years as the bailiff of its London property. As a boy, he was fond of drawing, and he 'employed all his leisure time when engaged at the College in that pursuit'. At the end of his life he calculated that he had made over 13,000 sketches, mainly of topographical subjects, and his careful drawings of ancient buildings form an invaluable record of much that has since been altered or destroyed. Forty-two volumes of original sketches by himself and his sons are preserved in the British Museum (Add. MSS. 36356–97). They include a systematic record of most of the parish churches and other ancient buildings in Buckinghamshire, Hertfordshire, Oxfordshire, Somerset, Staffordshire, Wiltshire and Yorkshire. From these sketches Buckler was commissioned to produce sets of finished drawings for private patrons. Among these were T. L. Parker, of Browsholme Hall, Yorkshire, for whom he drew 'Ancient Castles and Domestic Architecture' (vol. 2 of which is now in the Mellon Collection); Lord Grenville, for whom he prepared an extra-illustrated copy of Lysons' *Buckinghamshire* in 8 vols. (now in the possession of the Hon. R. W. Morgan Grenville); Sir Richard Colt Hoare, for

155

whom he worked in Wiltshire and Wales; H. Smith Pigott and the Bishop of Bath and Wells, for whom he made drawings of Somerset; Dr. T. D. Whitaker and Francis Maude, who employed him in Yorkshire; John Morier and William Knight, for whom he made a large number of drawings in Hertfordshire; and William Salt and Lord Bagot, for whom he did the same in Staffordshire. A number of his drawings of the latter county are in the William Salt Library at Stafford, and 750 Hertfordshire drawings are in the County Record Office at Hertford (for their acquisition see R. L. Hine, *Confessions of an Uncommon Attorney*, 1946, 124–7). Those of Somerset, made for H. Smith Pigott, are now in the Museum at Taunton, and the Wiltshire drawings made for Colt Hoare (sold from Stourhead in 1883) are in the Devizes Museum (see *Wilts. Arch. Mag.* xl, 148–90). There are several volumes of Berkshire and Oxfordshire drawings by the Bucklers in the Bodleian Library (MSS. Top. Berks. c. 49, 50, 51; Top. Oxon. a. 65–9 and don. a. 2, 3 and 7). One volume of Welsh drawings made for Colt Hoare is in the National Library of Wales.

Buckler occasionally practised as an architect. In 1822 he designed a Gothic tablet to Benjamin Tate in MAGDALEN COLLEGE ANTE-CHAPEL [*Gent's Mag.* 1823 (1), 133 and engraving]; in 1825 a similar tablet to George Tate in MITCHAM CHURCH, SURREY [Wimbledon Public Library, extra-illustrated copy of Brayley's *Surrey* iii (3), 314]; and in 1828 TATE'S ALMSHOUSES, MITCHAM, SURREY [B.M., Add. MS. 36388, ff. 259–61]. In 1828 he repaired and repainted Bishop Waynflete's monument in WINCHESTER CATHEDRAL for Magdalen College. His most substantial architectural works appear to have been HALKIN CASTLE, FLINTSHIRE, for the 2nd Earl Grosvenor, 1824–7, Tudor Gothic; enlarged by J. Douglas 1886 [exhib. at R.A. 1827–8; cf. *Views of Eaton Hall* for views of the house by Buckler]; the tower of THEALE CHURCH, BERKS., built in thirteenth-century style in 1827–8 to correspond with the nave designed by Edward Garbett a few years before [drawings in B.M., Add. MS. 36357]; GLASTONBURY PRIORY, SOMERSET, for J. F. Reeves, 1829–30, Tudor Gothic [exhib. at R.A. 1830; drawings in B.M., Add. MS. 36381]; and POOL PARK, DENBIGHSHIRE, an early essay in the half-timbered style for the 2nd Lord Bagot, *c.* 1828 [exhib. at R.A. 1830]. It is also likely that he had some hand in the Gothic remodelling of BLITHFIELD HALL, STAFFS., for Lord Bagot in 1822–3 [Arthur Oswald in *C. Life* 28 Oct., 4–11 Nov. 1954 and cf. drawings by Buckler in B.M., Add. MS. 36385, ff. 126–151]. All these were buildings in which Buckler's antiquarian knowledge was put to good use by like-minded patrons, but for general architectural practice he had little inclination. As he wrote in 1849, 'to

build, repair, or survey warehouses and sash-windowed dwellings, however profitable, was so much less to my taste than perspective drawing with such subjects before me as Cathedrals, Abbeys, and ancient parish churches, that I never made any effort to increase the number of my employers as an architect, and as the engagements of my old patrons ceased, my occupations in that capacity ceased also ...' He finally gave up practice in about 1830, but his eldest son John Chessell Buckler (1793–1894) and his youngest son George (1811–86) both became architects. The former shared his enthusiasm for sketching, and his pencil drawings of ancient buildings are almost indistinguishable in technique from those of his father. In 1822 he published *Views of the Cathedral Churches of England and Wales*, a collection based on a series of large prints previously issued individually by his father between 1799 and 1814, and in 1826 he and his father published *Views of Eaton Hall in Cheshire*.

In the early 1820s the two Bucklers were involved in the controversy over the reconstruction of the Cloister Quadrangle at Magdalen College, Oxford. John Buckler was among the many architects who were consulted, but his advice was not followed and in 1823 his son published an anonymous pamphlet (*Observations on the Original Architecture of St. Mary Magdalen College, Oxford, and on the Innovations anciently or recently attempted*) deploring the unnecessarily destructive manner in which the Quadrangle was rebuilt by J. T. Parkinson [T. S. R. Boase, 'An Oxford College and the Gothic Revival', *Jnl. of the Warburg and Courtauld Institutes* xviii, 1955]. J. C. Buckler's later publications included *Sixty Views of Endowed Grammar Schools*, 1827, *An Historical and Descriptive Account of the Royal Palace at Eltham*, 1828, a *History of the Architecture of the Abbey Church at St. Albans*, 1847, and *A Description and Defence of the Restorations of Lincoln Cathedral*, 1866. In 1835 he obtained the second prize in the competition for rebuilding the Houses of Parliament, and he designed a number of buildings in the Gothic or Elizabethan styles, including COSTESSY HALL, NORFOLK, 1826, dem. 1920, BUTLEIGH COURT, SOMERSET, 1845, THE CHORISTERS' HALL (now the Library) at MAGDALEN COLLEGE, OXFORD, 1849–51, and the Turl Street front of JESUS COLLEGE, 1854–6. His son Charles Alban Buckler (1824–1905) also practised as an architect, chiefly for Catholic clients.

John Buckler exhibited regularly at the Royal Academy from 1796 onwards. He was elected an F.S.A. in 1810. He died on 6 December 1851, aged 81. There is an engraved portrait of him by Sir W. Newton.

[Family papers and drawings in Bodleian Library; letters to Dr. Routh in Magdalen College Library; C. A. Buckler, *Bucleriana: Notices of the Family of Buckler*, privately printed 1886 (the author's own copy, with additions, is B.M., Add. MS. 37123); *D.N.B.*; W. D. Macray, *Registers of Magdalen College*, N.S. vi, 1909, 33, 43; obituaries in *Gent's Mag.* 1852 (1), 103–4, and *Builder* x, 1852, 7; C. Eastlake, *A History of the Gothic Revival*, 1872, 110–11; R. D. Middleton, *Dr. Routh*, 1938, 180–6; obituary of J. C. Buckler in *Jackson's Oxford Jnl.*, 13 Jan. 1894.]

BULL, SIMEON THOMAS (–1847), was a pupil of George Gwilt. He exhibited at the Royal Academy from Gwilt's office in 1809–10 and subsequently practised from Holles Street, Cavendish Square. He was President of the Surveyors' Club in 1824. The evidence of directories and his will (P.R.O. PROB 11/2057, f. 453) combine to show that he died in 1847.

BULLAR, G— F—, of London, exhibited at the Royal Academy from 1803 to 1808, including a 'Design for the Britannia General Country Fire Insurance Office about to be erected in one of the eastern counties' (1804), a 'Perspective of one side of a square, being part of a series of designs (about to be put in execution) for the improvement of a large estate in the vicinity of the metropolis' (1805), the 'Garden front of a villa to be erected on the banks of the river Orwell at Ipswich' (1807), and the 'South elevation of a nobleman's mansion erecting in the vicinity of Southampton' (1808). An architect named G. Thomas Bullar was in practice in London in the 1830s.

BUNCE, SAMUEL (–1802), was a pupil of James Wyatt, from whose office he exhibited at the Royal Academy in 1786–88. Soon afterwards he went to Rome, where he became intimate with Flaxman. He returned to England in the spring of 1790, and established himself in Hatton Garden. One of the fruits of his Italian expedition was a drawing of the Temple of Apollo at Cori which he exhibited at the Academy in 1797. In March 1796 he was appointed to the newly established post of Architect to the Admiralty, which he held until his death in October 1802 [J. C. Sainty, *Admiralty Officials 1660–1870*, 1975, 91, 113]. In 1797 Bunce designed the studio which the painter George Romney added to his newly acquired house on Hollybush Hill, Hampstead, and a small 'marine villa' at Felpham, Sussex, for Romney's friend William Hayley. Both these buildings survive, the former as ROMNEY HOUSE, HAMPSTEAD, the latter as THE TURRET, FELPHAM, described by Pevsner as 'pasteboard stucco Tudor' [*The Farington Diary*, ed. J. Greig, iii, 53; A. B. Chamberlain, *George Romney*, 1910, 207–9, 214–16].

BURCHELL, STEPHEN (1806–), son of Joseph Burchell of Leatherhead, was a pupil of

Sir John Soane from 1823 to 1828 [A. T. Bolton, *The Works of Sir J. Soane*, Appendix C, p. xlvi]. He entered the Royal Academy Schools in 1825, and won the Silver Medal in 1828 with drawings of Smirke's General Post Office that are now in the R.I.B.A. Drawings Collection. In 1835 he competed for the Houses of Parliament in association with J. Thrupp. They submitted a design in the late Gothic style [*Catalogue of Designs for the New Houses of Parliament*, 6th ed. 1836, 29–30]. Burchell made the drawings for the lithographs of Prior Birde's Oratory at Bath published by E. Davis in 1834. The original drawings are in the R.I.B.A. Collection.

BURGESS, WILLIAM, of Exeter, designed ST. SIDWELL'S CHURCH, EXETER, 1812–13, Gothic, dem. 1942 [inscription recorded by B. F. Cresswell, *Exeter Churches*, Exeter 1908, 158]; THE ROYAL PUBLIC ROOMS, EXETER, 1820, dem. [*A.P.S.D.*, *s.v.* 'Exeter']; THE NEW MARKET HALL, TAUNTON, SOMERSET, 1821, dem. [J. Savage, *History of Taunton*, 1822, 582]; CULLOMPTON VICARAGE, DEVON, 1820 [Devon Record Office, Diocesan Records]; and MEETH RECTORY, DEVON, 1825 [*ibid.*]. In 1825 he partly rebuilt the nave of ILMINSTER CHURCH, SOMERSET [I.C.B.S.]. He was presumably the 'Mr. Burges' who designed HAREFIELD HOUSE, LYMPSTONE, DEVON, for — Gattey in a somewhat crude Soaneic style [R. Ackermann, *Views of Seats* i, 1830, 95].

BURLINGTON, EARL OF, *see* BOYLE

BURLISON, GEORGE, of Darlington, designed the Greek Doric CUSTOM HOUSE (originally THE EXCHANGE), NORTH STREET, MIDDLESBROUGH, YORKS. (N.R.), 1836 [W. Lillie, *History of Middlesbrough*, 1968, 67].

BURN, GEORGE, was the brother of James Burn of Haddington (*q.v.*), who in 1804 stood as surety for 'George Burn of Haddington, architect', in connection with a contract to build a bridge at Nairn [National Library of Scotland, Gordonstoun documents, Box 92]. In the Register House at Edinburgh there is a design by him for BILSDEAN BRIDGE, OLDHAMSTOCKS, EAST LOTHIAN, dated 1797 [RHP 5504]. Subsequently he appears to have moved to N.E. Scotland, for RHP 2008/8 is a design by him for a one-arched bridge dated 'Huntly Lodge 16 July 1800', and drawings by him exist for an unexecuted pedimented building, apparently a chapel, on the Gordon Castle estates, dated 1802 [S.R.O., GD 44/48/70], and for a harbour office at PULTENEYTOWN, CAITHNESS, 1817 [S.R.O., RHP 11803]. In 1801–4 he built the SPEY BRIDGE at FOCHABERS, MORAYSHIRE, partially destroyed in the great flood of 1829 [drawings in S.R.O., RHP 2008/1], and in 1813 he built LOVAT BRIDGE over the

R. Beauly in Inverness-shire [A. R. B. Haldane, *New Ways through the Glens*, 1973, 129]. A design by him for an unidentified house is in the National Monuments Record of Scotland. He was in financial difficulties in 1803, when his estate was sequestrated [*Aberdeen Jnl.*, 15 Nov. 1803].

BURN, JAMES, was an architect and builder of Haddington in East Lothian. He was a wright by trade, and became a burgess of Haddington in July 1777. In 1784 he bought Kinloch House in Market Street, where he established his yard [*ex. inf.* Mr. David Walker]. According to John Martine's *Reminiscences of the Royal Burgh of Haddington* (1883) he 'built a great number of excellent family houses in Haddington and throughout the county, among which may be mentioned Mr. Roughead's and the late Mr. Banks's houses in High Street; Mr. Todrick's in Hardgate; as also the Hopes House, and Newbyth House'. At NEW-BYTH, EAST LOTHIAN (1817–18), Burn was rebuilding the house to the designs of Archibald Elliott (*q.v.*). It is possible, however, that he himself designed as well as built Captain Hay's elegant villa at HOPES, nr. CLIFFORD, EAST LOTHIAN, in about 1825. In Haddington, where he was known as 'Old Timmer', Burn designed and built THE FLESHMARKET in 1804 [Martine, 63], and in 1810 altered and refitted the interior of the CHURCH, with James and Archibald Elliott as consultant architects [S.R.O., HR 101/1–2].

During the first decade of the nineteenth century Burn obtained several commissions in ABERDEEN, including THE ABERDEEN BANK on the south side of Castle Street, 1801 (later extended down Marischal Street by William Smith); THE BRIDEWELL, UNION STREET, 1809, dem. 1868; and the balustraded parapet of the UNION BRIDGE, 1805, replaced by another design when the bridge was widened in 1905–8 [W. Thom, *History of Aberdeen* ii, 1804, 59; *Aberdeen Fifty Years Ago*, Aberdeen 1868, 28–9, 57–8; G. M. Fraser, 'Archibald Simpson and his Times', chap. vi, *Aberdeen Weekly Jnl.*, 10 May 1918]. The Bank has a well-composed façade of Doric pilasters, the Bridewell was designed in a bleak but not inappropriate version of Adam's castle style.

Burn also designed the IMAGE BRIDGE in the grounds of BRECHIN CASTLE, ANGUS, for William Maule, cr. Lord Panmure, 1797 (the piers remain but Burn's timber spans were later replaced by iron) [David Walker in *C. Life*, 19 Aug. 1971], a one-arch bridge over the Birns Water at Milton Ford, Saltoun, East Lothian, 1805 [drawings in National Library of Scotland, Saltoun Collection], and the BRIDGE OF DYCE, ABERDEENSHIRE, consisting of a wooden arch of 100 ft. span over the R. Don, *c.* 1805; rebuilt 1850, dem. *c.* 1970 [*N.S.A.* xii, 128].

The date of Burn's death has not been ascer-

tained, but according to Martine his business 'was carried on by his relation Mr. Hay Walker'.

BURN, ROBERT (1752–1815), was a mason by trade. According to a family tree he was born in 1752 and was 'of Jessfield' (Portobello). The earliest reference to him that has so far been noted shows that in 1775 he was acting as overseer of the masonry of St. Cuthbert's Church, Edinburgh, then being completed by the contractor James Weir (*q.v.*) [S.R.O., GD 69/210]. On 4 April 1782 he was admitted a burgess of Edinburgh [*Roll of Edinburgh Burgesses*, Scottish Record Soc. 1933, 28]. His best-known work as an architect is the Nelson Monument on Calton Hill, a castellated tower which has more the character of a private folly than a public monument.

Burn, who was the father of the better-known William Burn (*q.v.*), died on 5 June 1815 and was buried in the Calton Cemetery in a Perpendicular Gothic burial place erected in 1816 'by his widow and twelve surviving children'. At the N.M.R.S. there is a photograph of a portrait of Robert Burn and his son William as a young man. The original was in 1956 in private possession at St. Andrews. [*Scots. Mag.* 1815, 559; *Gent's Mag.* 1815 (i), 647; information from Mr. Colin McWilliam.]

EDINBURGH, THE PUBLIC DISPENSARY, RICHMOND STREET, 1776; dem. [engraving in Bodleian Library, Gough Maps 39, f. 11, signed 'R. Burn invt. et delint'].

CAIRNESS HOUSE, ABERDEENSHIRE, for Charles Gordon of Cairness, 1782–3; dem. 1791 to make way for new house by James Playfair [David Walker & Colin McWilliam in *C. Life*, 28 Feb. 1971].

?THE HERMITAGE OF BRAID, MIDLOTHIAN, for Charles Gordon of Cluny, *c.* 1785, castellated [Burn is described as 'architect to the late Mr. Gordon' in an inventory of papers belonging to Col. John Gordon of Cluny among the Claeson Gordon family papers, *ex inf.* Dr. A. Rowan].

EDINBURGH, NOS. 141–171 LEITH STREET, 1790–1800 [S.R.O., Edinburgh Sasines, vol. 516 under 'Greenside Place'].

TEVIOT BANK (then THE KNOWES), ROXBURGHSHIRE, for David Simpson, *c.* 1791; rebuilt 1833 [drawing at Teviot Bank, *ex inf.* N.M.R.S.].

?NETHERURD, PEEBLESHIRE, for William Lawson, 1791–4. In the building contract it is stipulated that the completed work shall be inspected by Burn and James McLeran, both described as 'architects', and in the event of any dispute Burn is to act as arbitrator [S.R.O., GD 120/415, dated 25 March 1791].

ST. GILES' CATHEDRAL, EDINBURGH, alterations (masons' work), 1796–7 [J. Cameron Lees, *St. Giles'*, *Edinburgh*, 1889, 402].

158

EDINBURGH, PICARDY PLACE, NOS. 1–12 UNION
STREET, FORTH STREET (excluding Nos. 4–10)
and BROUGHTON STREET, designed 1800, built
c. 1804–10 [*Book of the Old Edinburgh Club*
xxv, 30–3].

EDINBURGH, GILLESPIE'S HOSPITAL (THE ROYAL
BLIND ASYLUM), GILLESPIE CRESCENT, 1800–1,
castellated; enlarged by McGibbon & Ross
1883–4 and 1892; dem. 1975 [signed drawings
in N.M.R.S.].

EDINBURGH, THE ROYAL BANK OF SCOTLAND, HIGH
STREET, design for new entrance, 1803
[S.R.O., RHP 5556].

SALTOUN HALL, EAST LOTHIAN, proposed alterations for General John Fletcher Campbell,
1803 [drawings in National Library of Scotland, Saltoun papers].

SALTOUN MANSE, EAST LOTHIAN, court of offices,
1804 [drawings in National Library of Scotland, Saltoun papers].

LEITH, THE GRAMMAR SCHOOL or ACADEMY, 1804–
6; dem. 1896 [Alexander Mackay, *A Sketch of
the History of Leith Academy*, Leith 1934, 21–
2] (J. Grant, *Old and New Edinburgh* iii, 165).

INVERMAY, nr. FORTEVIOT, PERTHSHIRE, for J. H.
Belshes, 1806 [correspondence in Fettercairn
papers, National Library of Scotland, *ex inf.*
Dr. A. A. Tait].

EDINBURGH, THE NELSON MONUMENT, CALTON
HILL, 1807–16, completed by Thomas Bonnar
[*A.P.S.D.*; drawings in City Architect's
Office].

BURN, WILLIAM (1789–1870), was the son of
Robert Burn (*q.v.*), a builder and architect of
Edinburgh, where he was born on 20 December
1789. After an education at the High School he
was sent in 1808 to London to become a pupil
in Robert Smirke's office. In 1811 or 1812 he
returned to Edinburgh and began practice from
the family building yard in Leith Walk. By 1813
he was sufficiently well known to be one of the
architects invited to report on the plans submitted for the layout of the Calton Hill area, and
in 1814 he established an office of his own in
George Street (at first at No. 78, later at No. 131).
In 1816 his narrow defeat in the competition for
the completion of the Edinburgh University
buildings inaugurated a 'long and in time bitter
rivalry' between himself and the successful competitor, W. H. Playfair.

Burn's earliest works were public buildings,
but in 1817–18 he obtained the first commissions
for the country houses which were to be his speciality for the rest of his long working life. He soon
gained a reputation for skill in domestic planning
which secured him the patronage first of the
Scottish, and ultimately of the English, aristocracy. By 1830 he had a bigger practice than any
other Scottish architect, and could count among
his clients the Dukes of Hamilton and Buccleuch,

the Earls of Haddington and Kinnoull, and many
other influential persons. By 1840 he had already
designed or altered over ninety country houses,
besides thirty churches and twenty-five public
buildings of various sorts. Overwork probably
contributed to the serious breakdown in health
which in 1841 induced him to take his pupil and
assistant David Bryce into partnership. In 1844
he moved to London (6 Stratton Street) in order
to take advantage of the numerous commissions
he was now receiving from English clients, leaving Bryce in charge of the Edinburgh office. The
partnership soon began to show signs of strain
and was finally dissolved in 1850. Towards the
end of his life Burn formed a fresh partnership
with his nephew J. MacVicar Anderson (1834–
1915), who continued his practice after his death.
Burn died on 15 February 1870, aged 80, and was
buried in Kensal Green Cemetery. His estate was
valued for probate at 'under £40,000'. He
married Eliza MacVicar, by whom he had several
children.

Burn was a man of vigorous and independent
character, frank and plain spoken, but very
patient in meeting the wishes of his wealthy and
sometimes idiosyncratic clients. Secure in the
patronage of the great, he could afford to shun
the ordinary media of nineteenth-century architectural publicity, the exhibition drawing and the
professional journal. He never exhibited at the
Royal Academy, and after his initial failure in
1816 he waited forty years before entering for
another public competition.[1] He did, however,
join the Institute of British Architects on its
foundation in 1835, and in 1840 he agreed to
become Vice-President of a proposed Institute of
Architects in Scotland, but resigned almost immediately because of a quarrel with the committee over the eligibility for membership of his
assistant Bryce. In the 1850s he acted as Consulting Architect to the Government in Scotland,
and in 1865 he was one of the three assessors of
the controversial competition for the Foreign
Office in Whitehall.

Burn's early public buildings are in the style
of his master Smirke. John Watson's School and
the Merchant Maiden Hospital are representative of this early phase. They are competent but
conventional essays in Greek Doric. North Leith
Church and St. John's, Edinburgh, are well-
designed churches which compare favourably
with the best works of contemporary ecclesiastical architects in London, but most of Burn's
country churches are routine works of slight
architectural merit. At first his country houses
were derivative in character. Saltoun, with its
Gothic lantern lighting a central hall, resembled
Archibald Elliott's Taymouth Castle; Dundas

---

[1] For the Caledonian Railway Station at Glasgow,
1858. None of the plans submitted were carried out.

Castle was 'a weakly detailed essay in Smirke's early Lowther idiom'; while Blairquhan (c. 1820–4), Carstairs (1822–4) and Garscube (1826–7) owed their Tudor Gothic dress to Wilkins's Dalmeny. The Grecian Camperdown House (1824–6) was an Ionic version of Wilkins's Grange Park. But at Carstairs some of the gables were treated in a manner more Jacobean than Tudor, and by about 1825 Burn had made the Jacobethan manor-house his speciality. Riccarton (1823–7) and Strathendry (1824) were the first complete houses in this style which (like the Tudor Gothic) gave ample freedom for Burn to deploy the elaborate internal arrangements for which he was becoming celebrated. By 1830 Burn was experimenting with the Scottish vernacular style which he introduced at Faskally (1829) and Milton Lockhart (1829–36), and in that year corbelled angle turrets made their appearance at Tyninghame. Thereafter the progression to the fully developed 'Scottish Baronial' style was inevitable, though it was Burn's pupil Bryce rather than Burn himself who was to be its most celebrated exponent. Burn himself continued to turn out innumerable houses in Elizabethan, Jacobean or Scottish vernacular dress as the occasion required. If necessary he could also provide very competent designs in a classical, or even a Georgian, manner (Prestwold Hall, 1843, Swanbourne House, 1864), and in his interiors he showed considerable virtuosity in recreating quite different 'period' styles – Italian Renaissance at Prestwold, Flemish Mannerist and Louis XV at Stoke Rochford, High Baroque at Harlaxton and Revesby. For his great patron the 5th Duke of Buccleuch he provided an appropriate forecourt to the seventeenth-century mansion at Drumlanrig, a Jacobean conservatory and two Gothic churches at Dalkeith, an addition to Bowhill in the late Georgian style, and a French Renaissance chateau in Whitehall.

Despite his immense professional success and his remarkable versatility as a designer, Burn cannot be ranked as a great architect. It is tempting to dismiss him (in the words of the younger Charles Barry) as 'more a man of business than an artist'. Although (as Barry recognized) this would not be altogether fair, Burn's output is more remarkable for its quantity than for its quality. Among the long list of his works not a single building stands out as a masterpiece. His early Grecian buildings are orthodox products of their time, undistinguished by the refinements of scholarship. His Gothic churches are the same. As for his Tudor and Jacobethan mansions, their dry, repetitive detailing rarely succeeds in recapturing the charm of their prototypes: what commended them to Burn's clients was the convenience of their planning – above all, the care taken to safeguard the owner's privacy from both servants and guests – rather than what Robert Kerr

called 'the obsolete forms of a barbarous style'. Nevertheless Burn is a remarkable figure in British architectural history, epitomizing in a single career the whole course of nineteenth-century architecture from Greek Revival to Scottish Baronial.

There is a marble bust of Burn by Thomas Campbell dated 1834 at the Royal Incorporation of Architects of Scotland. The R.I.B.A. Drawings Collection has a plaster cast presented by the sculptor in 1836. For Burn's professional charges see a letter to Sir John Forbes of Craigievar in S.R.O., GD 250/41. David Bryce, Norman Shaw and W. E. Nesfield were Burn's most celebrated pupils. Shaw and Nesfield both left in 1853 for Salvin's office. Other pupils and assistants were W. B. Colling, James (son of T. L.) Donaldson, David MacGibbon, W. L. Moffatt and J. W. Penfold.

A large collection of Burn's drawings was acquired by the R.I.B.A. Drawings Collection in 1950. Many Scottish drawings were subsequently transferred to the Scottish National Monuments Record, and some working drawings were distributed to English County Record Offices.

[Obituaries in *Builder*, 1870, 189, 231, and *Building News*, 1870, 245; memoir by T. L. Donaldson in *R.I.B.A. Trans.* 1869–70, 121–9; John MacLachlan, 'Edinburgh Architects', in *Builder*, 1882, 667–8; *D.N.B.*; R. Kerr, *The English Gentleman's House*, 1864, 476–7; Mark Girouard, *The Victorian Country House*, 1971, 22–4, 32; David Walker, 'William Burn: the country house in transition', in *Seven Victorian Architects*, ed. Jane Fawcett, 1976.]

In the following list 'T.L.D.' stands for the list of Burn's principal works compiled by T. L. Donaldson and printed in *R.I.B.A. Trans.* 1870, 125–8. Original drawings in the R.I.B.A. Collection and the Scottish National Monuments Record are indicated by 'R.I.B.A.D.' and 'N.M.R.S.' A dagger (†) indicates works designed in partnership with David Bryce.

PUBLIC BUILDINGS

GREENOCK, RENFREWSHIRE, THE ASSEMBLY ROOMS (EXCHANGE BUILDINGS), 1812–14; dem. [R.I.B.A.D.].

EDINBURGH, THE MERCHANT MAIDEN HOSPITAL, LAURISTON LANE, 1816–19; dem. [T. H. Shepherd, *Modern Athens*, 1829, 61; N.M.R.S.].

GREENOCK, RENFREWSHIRE, THE CUSTOM HOUSE, 1817–18 [Chapman, *Picture of Glasgow*, 1822, 366–7; R.I.B.A.D.; T.L.D.].

PORT GLASGOW, RENFREWSHIRE, CUSTOM HOUSE, 1821; dem. [N.M.R.S.].

TRANENT, EAST LOTHIAN, GEORGE STIELL'S INSTITUTION, 1821–2 [N.M.R.S.; *N.S.A.* ii, 302].

ELGIN, THE TRINITY LODGE OF MASONS, 1821–2; [*Aberdeen Jnl.*, 14 Feb. 1821, *ex inf.* Mr. David Walker].

PERTH, MURRAY'S ROYAL ASYLUM FOR THE INSANE, 1822–7 [D. Peacock, *Perth, its Annals and its Archives*, Perth 1849, 498; T.L.D.].

DUNDEE, THE UNION (now ROYAL) BANK, 53 MUR-RAYGATE, 1823; since altered [T.L.D.; N.M.R.S.].

EDINBURGH, THE ACADEMY, HENDERSON ROW, 1823–36 [T. H. Shepherd, *Modern Athens*, 1829, 75–6; N.M.R.S.].

EDINBURGH, GASWORKS at TANFIELD, CANON-MILLS, 1824, later the Tanfield Hall; largely dem. [K. F. Schinkel's diary of his visit to Britain in 1826: *Arch. Rev.*, May 1945, 134] (James Grant, *Old and New Edinburgh* iii, 89).

LEITH, THE CUSTOM HOUSE, internal alterations, 1825 [drawings at N.M.R.S.].

EDINBURGH, JOHN WATSON'S HOSPITAL (SCHOOL), BELFORD ROAD, 1825–8 [T. H. Shepherd, *Modern Athens*, 1829, 76; T.L.D.; N.M.R.S.].

KIRKCALDY TOWN HOUSE, FIFE, 1826–32, Romanesque; dem. [N.M.R.S.].

EDINBURGH, SIR WILLIAM FORBES' BANK, 2 PARLIA-MENT SQUARE, 1827; converted into Courts 1885 [T.L.D.].

GLASGOW, THE BANK OF SCOTLAND, INGRAM STREET, 1828; since mutilated [T.L.D.; N.M.R.S.].

CURRIE, MIDLOTHIAN, PAROCHIAL SCHOOL, 1829–30, Gothic [*The Scotsman*, 19 Sept. 1829; S.R.O., CH 2/83/6].

DUNDEE, THE LUNATIC ASYLUM, alterations and additions, 1830 and 1839; dem. [J. Maclaren, *History of Dundee*, 1874, 285].

EDINBURGH, THE THEATRE ROYAL, new façade and other alterations, 1830; dem. 1859 [T.L.D.].

SCHAW'S HOSPITAL, PRESTONPANS, EAST LOTHIAN, 1830–1, Jacobethan [T.L.D.; N.M.R.S.].

ST. ANDREWS, FIFE, MADRAS COLLEGE, 1832–4, Jacobethan [T.L.D.; N.M.R.S.].

HADDINGTON, EAST LOTHIAN, THE COUNTY COURT HOUSE, 1833, Jacobethan [Jas. Miller, *History of Haddington*, 1900, 228; N.M.R.S.; T.L.D.].

STIRLING, THE BANK OF SCOTLAND, 22–4 KING STREET, 1833 [T.L.D.; N.M.R.S.] (*C. Life*, 28 Aug. 1969, 504, fig. 6).

KIRKCALDY, FIFE, THE BANK OF SCOTLAND, 226 HIGH STREET, 1833 [T.L.D.].

EDINBURGH, SIGNET LIBRARY, remodelled W. H. Playfair's staircase in order to open communication between Lower and Upper Libraries, 1833. The Ionic columns, the stairs and the ironwork are by Burn [*History of the Society of Writers to the Signet*, 1890, 439].

DUMFRIES, THE CRICHTON ROYAL LUNATIC ASYLUM, 1834–9 [T.L.D.; R.I.B.A.D.].

INVERNESS, THE COUNTY HALL ('THE CASTLE'), 1834–5, castellated [T.L.D.; G. Cameron, *History of Inverness*, Inverness 1847, 69].

EDINBURGH, THE NEW CLUB, 85 PRINCES STREET, 1834; dem. 1967 [T.L.D.; R.I.B.A.D.].

CUPAR, FIFE, COUNTY BUILDINGS, enlarged by internal remodelling of an adjoining building, 1835–6 [T.L.D.; N.M.R.S.].

GREENOCK, RENFREWSHIRE, BANK OF SCOTLAND, 1837; since altered [T.L.D.; N.M.R.S.].

MONTROSE, ANGUS, BANK OF SCOTLAND, at corner of HIGH STREET and JOHN STREET, 1839 [N.M.R.S.].

EDINBURGH, THE LUNATIC ASYLUM (WEST HOUSE), MORNINGSIDE TERRACE, largely rebuilt 1839–40 [T.L.D.; *A.P.S.D.*, *s.v.* 'Edinburgh'].

EDINBURGH, NORTH BRITISH ASSURANCE OFFICE, 64–5 PRINCES STREET, 1841; dem. *c.* 1901 [T.L.D.; N.M.R.S.].

DUNDEE, BANK OF SCOTLAND, REFORM STREET, 1842 [T.L.D.; N.M.R.S.].

†EDINBURGH, THE ASSEMBLY ROOMS, GEORGE STREET, addition of MUSIC HALL, 1843 [T.L.D.; N.M.R.S.].

†EDINBURGH, EDINBURGH LIFE ASSURANCE OFFICE, now ROYAL SOCIETY, 22–4 GEORGE STREET, 1843 [T.L.D.].

†GLASGOW, WESTERN BANK, MILLER STREET, addition, 1845; dem. [T.L.D.; N.M.R.S.].

†EDINBURGH, THE EDINBURGH & GLASGOW BANK, HANOVER STREET, extension to No. 69 (doubling the elevation) and house at No. 71, 1847 [Edinburgh Dean of Guild plans, 1847].

SOUTH STOKE, LINCS., almshouses for Christopher Turner, 1850–1 [R.I.B.A.D.].

GLASGOW, THE POST OFFICE, MANHATTAN BUILD-INGS, GEORGE SQUARE, 1855–6, Italianate; dem. 1875 [*A.P.S.D.*, *s.v.* 'Glasgow'].

CHURCHES

(All Gothic unless otherwise stated)

NORTH LEITH, MIDLOTHIAN, 1814–16; classical [A. Campbell, *The Present State of Leith*, 1827, 294; R.I.B.A.D.; N.M.R.S.] (G. Hay, *The Architecture of Scottish Post-Reformation Churches*, 1957, fig. 49).

EDINBURGH, ST. JOHN (EPISCOPAL), PRINCES STREET, 1816–18; apse added 1879–82 [T. H. Shepherd, *Modern Athens*, 1829, 72].

DUNFERMLINE, FIFE, THE NEW ABBEY CHURCH, 1818–21 [E. Henderson, *Annals of Dunfermline*, 1879, 598; N.M.R.S.].

DUNDEE, alterations to TOWN'S CHURCHES, 1823; destroyed by fire 1841 [N.M.R.S.].

ST. ANDREWS, FIFE, EPISCOPAL CHURCH, NORTH STREET, 1824–5; new front by Sir G. G. Scott 1854; dem. 1870 and re-erected at Buckhaven [N.M.R.S.].

KINGARTH, BUTESHIRE, 1824–6 [N.M.R.S.].

KINNOUL, PERTHSHIRE, 1826 [*N.S.A.* x, 942; N.M.R.S.].

---

† Wholly or partly by D. Bryce.

ABDIE, FIFE, 1827, Italianate, adapting a design by James Milne [*N.S.A.* ix, 54; S.R.O., HR 649/1, pp. 79–84].

ST. MONANS, ABERCROMBIE, FIFE, reconstructed 1827–8 [*N.S.A.* ix, 351; N.M.R.S.; S.R.O., HR 25/1, p. 69].

CORSTORPHINE, MIDLOTHIAN, largely rebuilt 1828; altered 1903–5 [S.R.O., HR 588/1, p. 177; N.M.R.S.].

CRAMOND, MIDLOTHIAN, repairs and alterations, 1828 [S.R.O., HR 713/5].

STENTON, EAST LOTHIAN, 1829 [*N.S.A.* ii, 57; T.L.D.].

EDINBURGH, ST. GILES' CATHEDRAL, reconstructed exterior, 1829–33 [drawings in N.M.R.S. and P.R.O., MPD 193].

†EDINBURGH, LOTHIAN ROAD U.P. CHURCH, 1830, classical; designed by David Bryce as Burn's assistant [*Builder*, 3 June 1882, 668].

PEEBLES, ST. PETER'S EPISCOPAL CHURCH, 1830–3 [N.M.R.S.].

THURSO, CAITHNESS, 1830–3 [S.R.O., E 329/1, ff. 104–5, 130–2; T.L.D.].

ARDNAMURCHAN, ARGYLLSHIRE, 1831 [*N.S.A.* vii, 148].

TYNRON, DUMFRIESSHIRE, 1835–7 [N.M.R.S.].

NEWBURGH, FIFE, 1833; dem. [*N.S.A.* ix, 71; N.M.R.S.].

DORNOCH, SUTHERLAND, reconstructed for the Duchess of Sutherland, 1835–7 [T.L.D.].

ETTRICK BRIDGE, SELKIRKSHIRE, chapel for the 5th Duke of Buccleuch, 1836 [N.M.R.S.].

MINNIGAFF, KIRKCUDBRIGHTSHIRE, 1836 [*N.S.A.* iv, 134].

RESTALRIG, MIDLOTHIAN, restoration, 1836–7 [W. Burnett, 'Restalrig and its Collegiate Church', *Trans. Scottish Ecclesiological Soc.* ii, part 2, 1907–8, 286].

EDINBURGH, ST. LUKE'S FREE CHURCH, YOUNG STREET, 1836; dem. [N.M.R.S.].

KIRKCUDBRIGHT, 1836–8 [N.M.R.S.].

NORTHESK, MUSSELBURGH, MIDLOTHIAN, 1838 [*N.S.A.* i, 285].

GLADSMUIR, EAST LOTHIAN, 1838–9; destroyed by fire 1886 [S.R.O., HR 115/2; N.M.R.S.].

ST. ANDREWS, FIFE, ST. MARY'S (now Victory Memorial Hall), 1839 [N.M.R.S.].

HAWICK, ROXBURGHSHIRE, EAST BANK CHURCH, for the 5th Duke of Buccleuch, 1839 [T.L.D.].

MORTON, DUMFRIESSHIRE, 1839–41, Romanesque [N.M.R.S.].

PENNINGHAME, NEWTON STEWART, WIGTOWN-SHIRE, 1840 [*N.S.A.* iv, 178].

DALKEITH, MIDLOTHIAN, WEST CHURCH, for the 5th Duke of Buccleuch, 1840 [T.L.D.].

PORTPATRICK, WIGTOWNSHIRE, 1840–2 [T.L.D.].

†LANGHOLM, DUMFRIESSHIRE, 1842–3 [T.L.D.; R.I.B.A.D.].

DUNDEE, SOUTH and EAST CHURCHES, 1842–4 and 1846–7, respectively [J. Maclaren, *History of Dundee*, 1874, 218].

162

†DALKEITH, MIDLOTHIAN, ST. MARY'S EPISCOPAL CHURCH, for the 5th Duke of Buccleuch, 1844–6 [N.M.R.S.].

†DALKEITH, MIDLOTHIAN, ST. NICHOLAS (EAST) CHURCH, restoration, 1848–51 [drawings in S.R.O., RHP 7041–4, and at Drumlanrig Castle].

STOKE ROCHFORD or SOUTH STOKE CHURCH, LINCS., restoration, 1847 [*Gent's Mag.* 1847 (i), 527].

COUNTRY HOUSES

GALLANACH HOUSE, ARGYLLSHIRE, for Dugald MacDougall, 1814–17, castellated; enlarged *c.* 1903 [R.C.A.M., *Argyll* ii, 255].

DUNDAS CASTLE, WEST LOTHIAN, rebuilt for James Dundas, 1818, castellated [R.I.B.A.D.; Neale, *Seats*, 2nd ser., ii, 1825; unsigned drawings in Burn's hand in S.R.O., RHP 12672 *et seq.*].

SALTOUN HALL, EAST LOTHIAN, enlarged for Andrew Fletcher, 1818–26, castellated [signed drawings in National Library of Scotland, Saltoun Collection].

BARROGILL CASTLE (now CASTLE OF MEY), CANIS-BAY, CAITHNESS, enlarged for the 12th Earl of Caithness, 1819; altered 1954 [drawings formerly at N.M.R.S., presented to the Queen Mother 1953].

ADDERSTONE HALL, nr. BELFORD, NORTHUMBER-LAND, for Thomas Forster, 1819, Greek Revival [R.I.B.A.D.].

MOUNT STUART, ISLE OF BUTE, lodge for the 2nd Marquess of Bute, *c.* 1820 [Helen Armet, guidebook to Mount Stuart, n.d., 5].

BLAIRQUHAN, STRAITON, AYRSHIRE, for Sir David Hunter Blair, 1820–4, Tudor Gothic [T.L.D.; R.I.B.A.D.; Neale, *Seats*, 2nd ser., iii; Alistair Rowan in *C. Life*, 19–26 April 1973] (A. H. Millar, *Castles and Mansions of Ayrshire*, 1885).

CARSTAIRS HOUSE, LANARKSHIRE, for Henry Monteith, 1822–4, Tudor Gothic [T.L.D.; R.I.B.A.D.; Neale, *Seats*, 2nd ser., i] (plans and elevations in P. Nicholson's *New Practical Builder*, 1823, 566).

CAMPERDOWN HOUSE, nr. DUNDEE, ANGUS, for the 2nd Viscount Duncan, cr. 1st Earl of Camperdown, 1824–6, Greek Revival [T.L.D.; N.M.R.S.].

NIDDRIE HOUSE, MIDLOTHIAN, castellated additions for Col. William Wauchope, 1823; dem. after fire 1959 [T.L.D.; R.I.B.A.D.].

LOCHEND HOUSE, nr. DUNBAR, EAST LOTHIAN, for Sir George Warrender, Bart., 1823, Gothic [T.L.D.; R.I.B.A.D.]; added offices 1851 [T.L.D.].

RICCARTON, MIDLOTHIAN, enlarged for Sir William Gibson Craig, 1823–7, Jacobethan;

---

† Wholly or partly by D. Bryce.

dem. 1956 [T.L.D.] (J. Small, *Castles and Mansions of the Lothians* ii, 1883).

STRATHENDRY, LESLIE, FIFE, for the Hon. Mrs. Douglas, 1824, Jacobethan [T.L.D.; R.I.B.A.D.; N.M.R.S.].

RATHO HALL, MIDLOTHIAN, for John Bonar, 1824, Jacobethan [T.L.D.; R.I.B.A.D.].

BRODIE CASTLE, MORAYSHIRE, new wing for William Brodie, 1824, Jacobethan [T.L.D.; correspondence at Brodie *ex inf.* Mr. David Walker] (*C. Life*, 26 Aug. 1916).

SNAIGOW HOUSE, PERTHSHIRE, for James Keay, 1824–7, Tudor; dem. 1962 [T.L.D.; R.I.B.A.D.; N.M.R.S.].

PINKIE HOUSE, MIDLOTHIAN, alterations and additions for Sir John Hope, Bart., 1825 [T.L.D.].

PITFOUR CASTLE, PERTHSHIRE, additions for Sir J. S. Richardson, 1825 [T.L.D.].

DRUMFINN (later AROS HOUSE), ARGYLLSHIRE, for Hugh Maclean, 1825; Tudor Gothic; dem. [T.L.D.; R.I.B.A.D.].

TEASSES, CERES, FIFE, for Robert Christie, 1825; Jacobethan; remodelled 1879 [R.I.B.A.D.].

BALNAMOON HOUSE, ANGUS, addition for James Carnegy Arbuthnot, 1825 [plan and specification at Balnamoon, *ex inf.* Mr. David Walker].

FREELAND HOUSE, PERTHSHIRE, see under Blore, Edward, 1825–6.

HODDAM CASTLE, DUMFRIESSHIRE, alterations and castellated additions for General Matthew Sharpe, 1826; these additions dem. 19— [T.L.D.; R.I.B.A.D.].

FETTERCAIRN, LAURENCEKIRK, KINCARDINESHIRE, reconstructed for Sir William Forbes, 1826 [T.L.D.; N.M.R.S.].

DUNTRUNE, ANGUS, for William Stirling Graham, 1826, Tudor Gothic [N.M.R.S.].

GARSCUBE, DUNBARTONSHIRE, rebuilt for Sir Archibald Campbell, Bart., 1826–7, Tudor Gothic; dem. 1955 [T.L.D.; *N.S.A.* viii, 49; R.I.B.A.D.; N.M.R.S.] (J. Irving, *The Book of Dumbartonshire* iii, 1874).

DALHOUSIE CASTLE, MIDLOTHIAN, alterations and additions for the 9th Earl of Dalhousie, 1826–8 [T.L.D.; R.I.B.A.D.: cf. accounts in S.R.O., GD 45/19/188] (J. Small, *Castles and Mansions of the Lothians* i, 1883).

LAURISTON CASTLE, MIDLOTHIAN, enlarged for Thomas Allan, 1827 [T.L.D.; R.I.B.A.D.; J. A. Fairley, *Lauriston Castle*, 1925, 173].

PITCAIRNS, DUNNING, PERTHSHIRE, for J. Pitcairn, 1827, Tudor Gothic [R.I.B.A.D.; N.M.R.S.].

BALCASKIE, FIFE, alterations and additions for Sir Ralph Anstruther, including bridge in park, 1827 [T.L.D.; *N.S.A.* ix, 348] (*C. Life*, 2 March 1912).

WHITTINGHAME HOUSE, EAST LOTHIAN, alterations and additions for James Balfour, 1827 [T.L.D.; N.M.R.S.].

CLIVEDEN HOUSE, BUCKS., for Sir George Warrender, Bart., 1827–30, early Georgian style;

destroyed by fire 1849 [T.L.D.; R.I.B.A.D., wrongly catalogued as 'Clifden, Co. Galway'].

PILRIG HOUSE, MIDLOTHIAN, additions for James Balfour, 1828; removed *c.* 1960 [Barbara Balfour-Melville, *The Balfours of Pilrig*, Edinburgh 1907, 214].

DALKEITH PALACE, MIDLOTHIAN, lodge and gateway for the 5th Duke of Buccleuch, 1828 [National Library of Scotland, MS. 3906, f. 141], followed in *c.* 1830 by an unexecuted scheme for remodelling the house, illustrated in *R.I.B.A. Drawings Catalogue: B*, fig. 119, and in 1834 by the Chamberlain's House and the circular Jacobethan conservatory [T.L.D.; R.I.B.A.D.; Buccleuch papers now in S.R.O.].

DUPPLIN CASTLE, PERTHSHIRE, for the 10th Earl of Kinnoul, 1828–32, Jacobethan; dem. 1967 [T.L.D.; *N.S.A.* x, 878; R.I.B.A.D.; N.M.R.S.; A. H. Millar, *Castles and Mansions of Scotland: Perthshire and Forfarshire*, 1890, 125–137].

GILMERTON HOUSE, EAST LOTHIAN, alterations and new stables for Sir David Kinloch, Bart., 1828–9 [N.M.R.S.].

FASKALLY, PERTHSHIRE, for Archibald Butter, 1829, Scottish vernacular style [T.L.D.; N.M.R.S.]; further alterations and additions 1837 [R.I.B.A.D.].

ST. FORT, FORGAN, FIFE, for Capt. Robert Stewart, 1829, Jacobethan; dem. 1952 [T.L.D.; R.I.B.A.D.; N.M.R.S.] (A. H. Millar, *Fife, Historical and Pictorial* ii, 1895, 280).

TYNINGHAME HOUSE, EAST LOTHIAN, remodelled for the 9th Earl of Haddington, 1829–30, Scottish vernacular style [T.L.D.; R.I.B.A.D.; N.M.R.S.] (*C. Life*, 16 Aug. 1902; A. Hannam, *Famous Scottish Houses of the Lowlands*, 1928, 181–4).

MILTON LOCKHART, CARLUKE, LANARKSHIRE, for William Lockhart, 1829–36, Scottish vernacular style; dem. [T.L.D.; *N.S.A.* vi, 582; R.I.B.A.D.; N.M.R.S.] (G. V. Irving & A. Murray, *Upper Ward of Lanarkshire* ii, 1864, 486).

PITCAPLE CASTLE, ABERDEENSHIRE, restoration for Hugh Lumsden, *c.* 1830 [John Davidson, *Inverurie*, 1878, 817].

AYTOUN HOUSE, BRIDGE OF EARN, PERTHSHIRE, for — Murray, 1830 [N.M.R.S.].

DUNSKEY HOUSE, WIGTOWNSHIRE, enlarged or rebuilt for Forbes Hunter Blair, 1830 [R.I.B.A.D.; N.M.R.S.].

BLANERNE, nr. DUNS, BERWICKSHIRE, designs (? executed), *c.* 1830; gutted 1895 [R.I.B.A.D.].

DRUMLANRIG CASTLE, DUMFRIESSHIRE, repairs and alterations for the 5th Duke of Buccleuch, including a new gardener's house and probably including the forecourt wings, *c.* 1830–4 [T.L.D.; *N.S.A.* iv, 506; J. C. Loudon in *Gardener's Mag.* ix, 2, and *Architectural Mag.* i, 94. For Burn's letter to Sir Walter Scott soliciting this job see National Library of Scotland, MS. 3906, f. 141] (*C. Life*, 25 Aug., 1–8 Sept. 1960).

EDMONSTONE HOUSE, MIDLOTHIAN, drawing-room for Col. John Wauchope, 1830; dem. [J. Small, *Castles and Mansions of the Lothians* i, 1883].

SPOTT HOUSE, DUNBAR, EAST LOTHIAN, reconstructed for James Sprot, 1830, Scottish vernacular style [T.L.D.] (J. Small, *Castles and Mansions of the Lothians* ii, 1883).

RAEHILLS, DUMFRIESSHIRE, enlarged for J. J. Hope Johnstone, 1830–4 [drawings at N.M.R.S. dated 1829–30, but Loudon, *Gardener's Mag.* ix, 1833, 5, and *N.S.A.* iv, 158–9, show that the work was in progress in 1833–4].

BOWHILL, SELKIRKSHIRE, enlarged for the 5th Duke of Buccleuch, 1831 onwards [T.L.D.; R.I.B.A.D.; N.M.R.S.; R.C.A.M., *Selkirkshire*, 65–6; John Cornforth in *C. Life*, 5–26 June 1975].

ARDGOWAN HOUSE, RENFREWSHIRE, repairs for Sir Michael Shaw-Stewart, 1831–2 [T.L.D.; N.R.A. Scotland, Source List: Architecture, 0548].

URRARD, nr. BLAIR ATHOLL, PERTHSHIRE, for Alston Stewart, 1831 [Lord Cockburn, *Circuit Journeys*, 1889, 38].

DAWYCK HOUSE, PEEBLESSHIRE, for Sir John Nasmyth of Posso, Bart., 1831–2; enlarged 1898; Scottish vernacular style [T.L.D.; R.I.B.A.D. under 'Posso'; S.R.O., GD 35/196 (4)].

AUCHMACOY HOUSE, LOGIE BUCHAN, ABERDEENSHIRE, rebuilt for James Buchan, 1831–3; Jacobethan [R.I.B.A.D.; N.M.R.S.]; completed by John Smith (*q.v.*).

KILCONQUHAR CASTLE, FIFE, alterations for Sir Henry Bethune, Bart., 1831–9 [T.L.D.; R.I.B.A.D.; N.M.R.S.; A. H. Millar, *Fife, Pictorial and Historical* ii, 1895, 18–19].

ABERDALGIE MANSE, PERTHSHIRE, for the 10th Earl of Kinnoull, 1832 [*N.S.A.* x, 880].

CHARLETON HOUSE, KILCONQUHAR, FIFE, addition for John Anstruther Thomson, 1832; altered 1855 by D. Bryce and later by R. S. Lorimer [drawings in scrap book at Charleton, *ex inf.* Mr. David Walker].

KIRKMICHAEL HOUSE, DUMFRIESSHIRE, for J. S. Lyon, 1832–3, Jacobethan [R.I.B.A.D.; J. C. Loudon in *Gardener's Mag.* ix, 1833, 5].

AUCHTERARDER HOUSE, PERTHSHIRE, for Capt. James Hunter, 1832–3, Jacobethan; remodelled 1886–9 [T.L.D.; R.I.B.A.D.; N.M.R.S.].

SPOTTISWOODE HOUSE, WESTRUTHER, BERWICKSHIRE, for John Spottiswoode, 1832–4, Jacobethan; dem. *c.* 1928 [T.L.D.; R.I.B.A.D.; N.M.R.S.].

GOSFORD, EAST LOTHIAN, remodelled old manorhouse as temporary residence for the 7th Earl of Wemyss, 1832; dem. [T.L.D.; N.M.R.S.]

(J. Small, *Castles and Mansions of the Lothians* i, 1883).

NEW INVERAWE (now ARDANAISEIG HOUSE), GLENURCHY, ARGYLLSHIRE, for James Archibald Campbell, 1833 [N.M.R.S.; R.C.A.M., *Argyll* ii, 247].

TEVIOT BANK (formerly THE KNOWES), HAWICK, ROXBURGHSHIRE, rebuilt for William Scott, 1833 [R.I.B.A.D.; *N.S.A.* iii, 372].

THE GART, CALLENDER, PERTHSHIRE, for Capt. Houston Stewart, 1833 [T.L.D., R.I.B.A.D.].

NETHERBY HALL, CUMBERLAND, additions for Sir James Graham, Bart., 1833 [T.L.D.; R.I.B.A.D.] (*C. Life*, 21–28 Jan. 1949).

HANLEY LODGE, CORSTORPHINE, MIDLOTHIAN, 1834; dem. ? 1948 [N.M.R.S.].

THURSO CASTLE, CAITHNESS, alterations and additions for Sir John Sinclair, Bart., 1834; dem. *c.* 1875 [T.L.D.].

MARCHMONT, BERWICKSHIRE, alterations for Sir H. P. Hume Campbell, Bart., 1834 [T.L.D.] (*C. Life*, 28 Feb., 7 March 1925).

MEIGLE HOUSE, PERTHSHIRE, additions for Patrick Murray, 1834, Tudor [R.I.B.A.D.].

MONKRIGG, nr. HADDINGTON, EAST LOTHIAN, for the Hon. Capt. William Keith, R.N., 1834–5 [T.L.D.; R.I.B.A.D.; N.M.R.S.; S.R.O., GD 35/196 (4)].

? HAVRA, SHETLAND, house for — Hay, 1835 [R.I.B.A.D.]; uncertain whether built.

MACBIEHALL HOUSE, PEEBLESSHIRE, remodelled for the Rev. J. I. Beresford, 1835, Scottish vernacular style; dem. [R.I.B.A.D.; N.M.R.S.] (W. Chambers, *History of Peebleshire*, 1864, 502).

TYNEHOLME HOUSE, EAST LOTHIAN, for Patrick Dudgeon, 1835 [T.L.D.; R.I.B.A.D.].

PARKHILL HOUSE, POLMONT, STIRLINGSHIRE, alterations for — Henderson, 1835 [R.I.B.A.D.].

ABOYNE CASTLE, ABERDEENSHIRE, alterations and additions (since removed) for the 9th Marquess of Huntly, 1835 [T.L.D.; R.I.B.A.D.; N.M.R.S.].

BOWERHOUSE, nr. DUNBAR, EAST LOTHIAN, for Col. J. Carfrae, *c.* 1835–6 [S.R.O., GD 35/196 (4)].

CARMYLE COTTAGE (now HOUSE), CARMYLE, LANARKS., for John Sligo, 1836 [N.M.R.S.].

STENHOUSE, STIRLINGSHIRE, enlarged for Sir Michael Bruce, Bart., 1836; dem. *c.* 1965 [T.L.D.; R.I.B.A.D.].

ANTONS HILL, COLDSTREAM, BERWICKSHIRE, for General Sir Michael Hunter, Bart., 1836 [T.L.D.; N.M.R.S.].

ARTHURSTONE HOUSE, MEIGLE, PERTHSHIRE, new wing for Patrick Murray, 1836, Jacobethan; taken down 1855 and re-erected as a new house at Cardean (since dem.) ['Mr. Burn' noted as architect on survey plan at Arthurstone, *ex inf.* Mr. David Walker; A. Mackay, *Meigle Past and Present*, 1876, 46–7].

KNOWSLEY HALL, LANCS., boat-house, bridges, etc., for the 13th Earl of Derby, 1836–9 [T.L.D.; R.I.B.A.D.].

DUNCRUB PARK, PERTHSHIRE, alterations for the 8th Lord Rollo, 1836–7; rebuilt 1870 [T.L.D.; R.I.B.A.D.].

IRVINE HOUSE, LANGHOLM, DUMFRIESSHIRE, enlarged for the 5th Duke of Buccleuch (A. H. Maxwell, tenant), 1836–7 [Buccleuch papers now in S.R.O.].

BALCARRES HOUSE, FIFE, enlarged for Col. James Lindsay, 1836–8; Scottish vernacular style [T.L.D.; R.I.B.A.D.] (C. Life, 9 Aug. 1902).

BRANXHOLM CASTLE, ROXBURGHSHIRE, alterations for the 5th Duke of Buccleuch, 1837 [R.I.B.A.D.; N.M.R.S.].

INVERGOWRIE HOUSE, ANGUS, additions for Alexander Clayhills, 1837, Scottish vernacular style [N.S.A. xi, 578; R.I.B.A.D.; N.M.R.S.].

LUDE, nr. BLAIR ATHOLL, PERTHSHIRE, for J. P. McInroy, 1837–40, Jacobethan [T.L.D.; R.I.B.A.D.; N.M.R.S.].

HARLAXTON MANOR, LINCS., completion of house for Gregory de Ligne Gregory, 1838 onwards, following A. Salvin (1831–7) and Edward Blore (1837) [T.L.D.; cf. Civil Engineer and Architect's Jnl. ii, 1839, 39] (C. Life, 11 April 1957; C. Hussey, English Country Houses: Late Georgian, 1958, 242, and A. Grogan in Archaeological Jnl. cxxxi, 1974, 324–9).

ARDDARROCH HOUSE, DUNBARTONSHIRE, for John MacVicar, 1838 [N.M.R.S.] (J. Irvine, Book of Dumbartonshire iii, 1879).

JURA HOUSE, ARGYLLSHIRE, additions, including offices, for Colin Campbell, 1838; dem. [N.S.A. vii, 540].

FINNART HOUSE, FORTINGAL, PERTHSHIRE, for Donald McLaren, 1838; Jacobethan [R.I.B.A.D.; N.M.R.S.].

CASTLE MENZIES, PERTHSHIRE, alterations and additions for Sir Niel Menzies, Bart., 1839–40 [T.L.D.; N.M.R.S.] (A. H. Millar, Castles and Mansions of Scotland: Perthshire and Forfarshire, 1890, 43–63).

MUCKROSS ABBEY, CO. KERRY, for H. A. Herbert, 1839–43, Jacobethan style; enlarged by David Bryce 1853 [T.L.D.; R.I.B.A.D.].

NINEWELLS HOUSE, CHIRNSIDE, BERWICKSHIRE, for Elizabeth Hume, 1839–41; dem. 1964 [N.M.R.S.].

FALKLAND HOUSE, FIFE, for O. Tyndall-Bruce, 1839–44, Jacobethan style [T.L.D.; R.I.B.A.D.].

WHITEHILL HOUSE, LASSWADE, MIDLOTHIAN, for R. B. Wardlaw Ramsay, 1839–44, Jacobethan style [T.L.D.; N.S.A. i, 612; R.I.B.A.D.; N.M.R.S.] (J. Small, Castles and Mansions of the Lothians ii, 1883).

CARDRONA HOUSE, TRAQUAIR, PEEBLESSHIRE, for Miss Alison Williamson, 1840 [N.M.R.S.] (W. Chambers, History of Peeblesshire, 1864, 396).

THIRLESTANE CASTLE, BERWICKSHIRE, alterations and additions for the 9th Earl of Lauderdale, 1840 [T.L.D.; R.I.B.A.D.].

REDCASTLE, ROSS-SHIRE, additions for Col. Hugh Duncan Baillie, 1840, Scottish vernacular style; now in ruins [R.I.B.A.D.].

STOKE ROCHFORD HOUSE, LINCS., for Christopher Turner, 1841–3; Jacobethan [T.L.D.; R.I.B.A.D.] (C. Life, 9 Nov. 1901; M. Girouard, The Victorian Country House, 1971, pl. 27).

†SEACLIFFE HOUSE, NORTH BERWICK, EAST LOTHIAN, for George Sligo, 1841; dem. [T.L.D.].

OXENFOORD CASTLE, MIDLOTHIAN, castellated additions for the 8th Earl of Stair, 1842 [T.L.D.; R.I.B.A.D.; N.M.R.S.] (J. Small, Castles and Mansions of the Lothians ii, 1883; C. Life, 15 Aug. 1974).

GALLOWAY HOUSE, WIGTOWNSHIRE, alterations for the 9th Earl of Galloway, 1842 [T.L.D.; N.M.R.S.] (F. O. Morris, Picturesque Views of Seats iv, 35).

SOUTH RAUCEBY HALL, LINCS., for Anthony Willson, 1842, Elizabethan style [T.L.D.; R.I.B.A.D.].

PRESTWOLD HALL, LEICS., remodelled for Charles William Packe, 1843, classical [T.L.D.; R.I.B.A.D.] (C. Life, 16–23 April 1959; Mark Girouard, The Victorian Country House, 1971, 71–2).

CAIRNHILL HOUSE, CRAIGIE, AYRSHIRE, alterations and additions for John Ferrier Hamilton, 1843, Scottish vernacular style [T.L.D.; R.I.B.A.D.; N.M.R.S.].

MERTOUN (now HARDEN) HOUSE, BERWICKSHIRE, addition of south wing (dem. 1953) for Lord Polwarth, 1843 [T.L.D.] (C. Life, 2–9 June 1966).

RABY CASTLE, DURHAM, alterations and additions for the 2nd Duke of Cleveland, 1843–7, castle style [T.L.D.; R.I.B.A.D.; Alistair Rowan in C. Life, 22 Jan. 1970].

BAMFF HOUSE, PERTHSHIRE, alterations and additions for Sir James Ramsay, Bart., 1844, Scottish vernacular style [T.L.D.; contract in S.R.O., GD 83/961; N.M.R.S.].

REVESBY ABBEY, LINCS., for J. Banks Stanhope, 1844, Jacobethan [T.L.D.; R.I.B.A.D.].

†CARRADALE HOUSE, ARGYLLSHIRE, for Richard Campbell, 1844, Scottish vernacular style [T.L.D.].

DARTREY, CO. MONAGHAN, for Lord Cremorne, cr. Earl of Dartrey, 1844–6, Jacobethan; dem. [T.L.D.; R.I.B.A.D.] (F. O. Morris, Picturesque Views of Seats iii, 57).

REDRICE HOUSE, HANTS., remodelled for the Rev. Thomas Best, 1844; altered c. 1911 and c. 1933; classical [T.L.D.].

†INCHDAIRNIE, KINGLASSIE, FIFE, alterations and

---

† Wholly or partly by D. Bryce.

additions for Mrs. M. A. Aytoun, 1845, Scottish vernacular style; destroyed by fire [T.L.D.] (A. H. Millar, *Fife, Pictorial and Historical* ii, 1895, 82).

†LENY HOUSE, CALLENDAR, PERTHSHIRE, alterations and additions for J. B. Hamilton, 1845, Scottish vernacular style [T.L.D.].

†CLATTO, nr. ST. ANDREWS, FIFE, for Col. John Law, 1845, Scottish vernacular style; altered and partly dem. [T.L.D.].

†LADYKIRK HOUSE, BERWICKSHIRE, alterations and additions for David Robertson, 1845; dem. 1966 [T.L.D.].

EATON HALL, CHESHIRE, alterations and additions for the 2nd Marquess of Westminster, 1846–51; rebuilt 1870 by A. Waterhouse; dem. 1963 [T.L.D.; R.I.B.A.D.] (for views of the principal front as altered by Burn see Eastlake, *History of the Gothic Revival*, 1872, 77, and F. O. Morris, *Picturesque Views of Seats* i, 31).

CALWICH ABBEY, STAFFS., for the Hon. and Rev. A. Duncombe, 1846, Jacobethan; dem. 1926 [T.L.D.].

CREEDY PARK, nr. CREDITON, DEVON, for Col. Sir Henry R. Ferguson-Davie, Bart., 1846, classical; destroyed by fire 1915 [T.L.D.] (F. J. Snell, *Devonshire*, Mate's County Series, Bournemouth 1907, 40).

BANGOR CASTLE (now Town Hall), CO. DOWN, for R. E. Ward, 1847, Jacobethan [T.L.D.].

LINCOLN, THE DEANERY (now Cathedral School), 1847 [Lincolnshire Record Office, M.G.A. 315].

GORHAMBURY, HERTS., alterations and additions for the 2nd Earl of Verulam, 1847 onwards [T.L.D.; R.I.B.A.D.].

IDSWORTH HOUSE, HANTS., for Sir J. Clarke-Jervoise, 1848–52, Jacobethan; altered by H. S. Goodhart-Rendel 1912–14 [T.L.D.; R.I.B.A.D.].

MOOR PARK, HERTS., alterations for the 1st Lord Ebury, 1849 [T.L.D.].

ARUNDEL CASTLE, SUSSEX, alterations and new lodges for the 13th Duke of Norfolk, 1849–53 [T.L.D.; R.I.B.A.D.].

EASTWELL PARK, KENT, large addition in Jacobean style for the 9th Earl of Winchilsea, 1849; dem. [T.L.D.] (F. O. Morris, *Picturesque Views of Seats* vi, 45).

BEECHWOOD PARK, HERTS., remodelled Great Hall and other alterations for Sir Thomas Sebright, Bart., *c.* 1850–4 [T.L.D.] (*C. Life*, 12–19 Nov. 1938).

PEPPER ARDEN, SOUTH COWTON, YORKS. (N.R.), alterations and additions for the 3rd Lord Alvanley, 1850 [T.L.D.].

SURRENDEN-DERING, nr. ASHFORD, KENT, alterations and additions for Sir Edward Dering, Bart., *c.* 1850; destroyed by fire except west wing 1952 [T.L.D.].

BABWORTH HALL, NOTTS., alterations and addi-

tions for H. Bridgman Simpson, 1850 [T.L.D.].

POLTALLOCH HOUSE (or CALLTON MOR), ARGYLLSHIRE, for Neill Malcolm, *c.* 1850–2, Jacobethan; gutted [T.L.D.; R.I.B.A.D.; N.M.R.S.].

ROEHAMPTON GROVE, SURREY, added Italianate wing for S. Lyne Stephens, 1851; dem. [T.L.D.].

STONELEIGH ABBEY, WARWICKS., conservatory and other works for the 2nd Lord Leigh, 1851 [T.L.D.].

THE HIRSEL, BERWICKSHIRE, lodges, etc., for the 11th Earl of Home, 1851 [T.L.D.].

DUNIRA, COMRIE, PERTHSHIRE, for Sir David Dundas, Bart., 1851–2, Scottish vernacular style; dem. [T.L.D.; R.I.B.A.D.; N.M.R.S.].

ORWELL PARK, NACTON, SUFFOLK, alterations and additions for George Tomline, 1851–3 [T.L.D.; R.I.B.A.D.].

RAMPTON MANOR, NOTTS., for the Rev. C. W. Eyre, 1851–3, Elizabethan style ['Office Book' in R.I.B.A.D.].

HOLKHAM HALL, NORFOLK, stables, north and south gates, etc., for the 2nd Earl of Leicester, 1851–5 [T.L.D.; R.I.B.A.D.].

SANDON HALL, STAFFS., for the 2nd Earl of Harrowby, 1851–5, Jacobethan style [T.L.D.; R.I.B.A.D.].

KILRUDDERY HOUSE, CO. WICKLOW, conservatory, etc., for the 11th Earl of Meath, 1852 [T.L.D.].

BRANKSOME TOWER (now Hotel), POOLE, DORSET, for C. W. Packe, 1852, Tudor Gothic [T.L.D.].

KINMEL PARK, DENBIGHSHIRE, work for H. R. Hughes, who succeeded 1852 [T.L.D.]. Burn's surviving drawings [Bangor University Library, Hughes papers, 1794] relate to a gate lodge (1858), gamekeeper's house (1862) and agent's house (1865), but the Palladian stable block, apparently built between 1852 and 1854, is attributed to Burn by M. Girouard, *The Victorian Country House*, 1971, 137 and pl. 283. It is mentioned as existing in Burke's *Visitation of Seats*, 2nd ser., i, 1854, 2.

BUCHANAN HOUSE, STIRLINGSHIRE, for the 4th Duke of Montrose, 1852–4, Scottish vernacular style; dem. 1954 [T.L.D.; R.I.B.A.D.] (plan in M. Girouard, *The Victorian Country House*, 1971, 23).

GODMERSHAM PARK, KENT, alterations (removed 1935) for Edward Knight, 1853 [T.L.D.] (*C. Life*, 16–23 Feb. 1945).

ABBOTSFORD, ROXBURGHSHIRE, added south-west wing for J. R. Hope Scott, 1853–5 [T.L.D.; N.M.R.S.].

CASTLEWELLAN, CO. DOWN, for the 4th Earl of Annesley, 1854, castellated [T.L.D.; R.I.B.A.D.].

---

† Wholly or partly by D. Bryce.

PATSHULL HOUSE, STAFFS., alterations for the 5th Earl of Dartmouth, 1855 [T.L.D.].

TAPLOW COURT, BUCKS., refronted for C. Pascoe Grenfell, 1855–6, Tudor Gothic [T.L.D.].

AMPORT HOUSE, HANTS., for the 14th Marquess of Winchester, 1855–7, Elizabethan style [T.L.D.].

BRODICK CASTLE, ARRAN, castellated addition for the 11th Duke of Hamilton, 1856 [T.L.D.].

BRAWL (or BRAAL) CASTLE, HALKIRK, CAITHNESS (a shooting lodge), 1856 [R.I.B.A.D.].

FONTHILL HOUSE, WILTS., for the 2nd Marquess of Westminster, 1856, Scottish baronial style; dem. 1955 [T.L.D.; R.I.B.A.D.] (C. Life, 28 Dec. 1901).

LYNFORD HALL, NORFOLK, for S. Lyne Stephens, 1856–61, Jacobethan [T.L.D.; R.I.B.A.D.].

HAMILTON PALACE, LANARKS., minor alterations for the 11th Duke of Hamilton, 1856–7 [N.M.R.S.].

SANDBECK PARK, YORKS. (W.R.), internal alterations for the 9th Earl of Scarbrough, 1857 [T.L.D.; drawings in Sheffield City Library, AP 49] (C. Life, 7, 14 and 21 Oct. 1965).

CHEVELEY PARK, CAMBS., alterations and additions for the 6th Duke of Rutland, 1858; dem. [T.L.D.].

TUSMORE HOUSE, OXON., alterations for the 2nd Earl of Effingham, 1858; dem. 1961 [T.L.D.] (C. Life, 30 July, 6 Aug. 1938).

WISHAW HOUSE, LANARKSHIRE, alterations and additions for the 8th Lord Belhaven and Stenton, 1858; dem. 1953 [T.L.D.; N.M.R.S.].

BALINTORE CASTLE, ANGUS, for David Lyon, 1859, Scottish baronial style; dismantled [T.L.D.; R.I.B.A.D.] (H. R. Hitchcock, Early Victorian Architecture, 1954, pl. viii, 33).

STANWAY HOUSE, GLOS., additions for the 8th Earl of Wemyss, 1859–60; partly dem. 1948–9 [T.L.D.; C. Hussey in C. Life, 3–17 Dec. 1964].

RYDE, ISLE OF WIGHT, house for Gilbert Smith, 1859–60, picturesque gabled style [R.I.B.A.D.].

BLITHFIELD, STAFFS., minor works for the 3rd Lord Bagot, 1860 [T.L.D.] (C. Life, 28 Oct., 4–11 Nov. 1954).

CLANDEBOYE, CO. DOWN, HELEN'S TOWER, for the 5th Baron (afterwards 1st Earl of) Dufferin, designed 1848, built c. 1860–2, castellated [T.L.D.; R.I.B.A.D.; M. Bence-Jones in C. Life, 1 Oct. 1970].

DOGMERSFIELD PARK, HANTS., alterations and additions for Sir Henry Mildmay, Bart., 1860 [T.L.D.].

TEHIDY PARK, CORNWALL, alterations and additions for J. F. Basset, 1861; dem. 1919 [T.L.D.; drawings in Cornwall County Record Office].

LAMPORT HALL, NORTHANTS., rebuilt north front for Sir Charles Isham, Bart., 1861–2 [Sir Gyles

Isham, 'The Architectural History of Lamport', Northants. Architectural and Archaeological Soc. lvii, 1951, 27].

THE LEYS, GANAREW, HEREFS., for John Bannerman, 1861–2, Jacobethan [R.I.B.A.D.].

EILDON HALL, ROXBURGHSHIRE, alterations for the 5th Duke of Buccleuch, 1861–7 [N.M.R.S.].

PACKINGTON HALL, WARWICKS., conservatory (dem.) and carriage-porch (dem. 1965) for the 6th Earl of Aylesford, 1862 [G. C. Tyack in Archaeological Jnl. cxxviii, 1971, 242].

POLMAISE, STIRLINGSHIRE, for Col. John Murray, 1863, Scottish vernacular style; dem. [T.L.D.].

GANTON HALL, YORKS. (E.R.), for Sir F. D. Legard, Bart., 1863; dem. [T.L.D.].

SHIRBURN CASTLE, OXON., stables for the 6th Earl of Macclesfield, 1863 [T.L.D.].

BLICKLING HALL, NORFOLK, alterations for the 8th Marquess of Lothian, 1864 [T.L.D.].

KIMBOLTON CASTLE, HUNTS., alterations for the 7th Duke of Manchester, 1864 [T.L.D.].

SWANBOURNE HOUSE, BUCKS., for Sir Thomas Fremantle, Bart., 1864–5, Georgian style [T.L.D.; R.I.B.A.D.].

SPYE PARK, WILTS., for J. W. G. Spicer, 1864–8; gutted by fire 1974 [T.L.D.].

POWERSCOURT, CO. WICKLOW, alterations and additions for the 7th Viscount Powerscourt, 1865 [T.L.D.].

WHITTLEBURY LODGE, NORTHANTS., for the 2nd Lord Southampton, 1865–8, Jacobethan; recons. after fire 1871; dem. 1972 [T.L.D.].

WESTON PARK, STAFFS., alterations and additions, including new entrance and orangery, for the 3rd Earl of Bradford, 1866 [T.L.D.] (C. Life, 9, 16 and 23 Nov. 1945).

WICKHAM COURT, WEST WICKHAM, KENT, alterations for Col. Farnaby Lennard, 1866 [T.L.D.].

HIGHWOODS, MORTIMER, BERKS., for Dr. Walter Bryant, 1866, picturesque gabled style [R.I.B.A.D.].

WORTLEY HALL, YORKS. (W.R.), alterations and additions for the 1st Earl of Wharncliffe, 1867–73 [drawings in Sheffield City Library, AP 51].

OAKLANDS PARK (now LOCKERLEY HALL), HANTS., for F. G. Dalgety, 1867–8 [T.L.D.].

OTTERSHAW PARK, SURREY, new wing for Sir Edward Colebrooke, Bart., 1868; dem. 1908 [T.L.D.].

BROCKLESBY PARK, LINCS., alterations and additions for the 3rd Earl of Yarborough, 1868; reconstructed after fire in 1898; partly dem. c. 1955 [T.L.D.].

RENDLESHAM HALL, SUFFOLK, for the 5th Lord Rendlesham, 1868–71, Jacobean style; dem. c. 1950 [T.L.D.].

CRICHEL, DORSET, additions for H. G. Sturt, 1869 [T.L.D.].

SOMERLEY, HANTS., alterations and additions for

the 3rd Earl of Normanton, 1869–70, continued by J. MacVicar Anderson 1870–4; partly dem. *c.* 1955 [T.L.D.; R.I.B.A.D.; C. Hussey in *C. Life*, 16–23 Jan. 1958].

TOWN HOUSES, ETC.

EDINBURGH, NOS. 6–8 and 10–32 MORRISON STREET (originally ST. ANTHONY'S PLACE) and NOS. 112–116 LOTHIAN ROAD, 1821 [S.R.O., Edinburgh Sasines].

EDINBURGH, NOS. 7–22 CLAREMONT CRESCENT, *c.* 1823 [S.R.O., Edinburgh Sasines].

EDINBURGH, NOS. 2–28 and 32–42A HENDERSON ROW, NOS. 162–168 DUNDAS STREET and NOS. 1A, 2–4 PERTH STREET, for the Heriot Trustees, 1825–6 [S.R.O., Edinburgh Sasines].

LONDON, MONTAGU HOUSE, PRIVY GARDENS, WHITEHALL, for the 5th Duke of Buccleuch, 1853–9, French Renaissance style; dem. [*Survey of London* xiii, 218–19; T.L.D.; R.I.B.A.D.].

LONDON, NO. 22 ARLINGTON STREET, alterations and additions (including the neo-Georgian façade) for the 11th Duke of Hamilton, 1854–6 [T.L.D.; R.I.B.A.D.].

LONDON, NO. 18 CARLTON HOUSE TERRACE, for the 5th Duke of Newcastle, 1863–4 [T.L.D.; R.I.B.A.D.].

LONDON, NO. 17 GROSVENOR SQUARE, for the 3rd Earl Fortescue, 1864; dem. [T.L.D.; R.I.B.A.D.].

LONDON, NO. 7 GROSVENOR PLACE, for Lord George Manners, 1866; dem. [T.L.D.; R.I.B.A.D.].

DUNDEE, layout of UNION STREET, 1825 [David Walker, *Architects and Architecture in Dundee*, Abertay Historical Soc.'s Publication No. 3, 1955, 8].

MONUMENTS, MAUSOLEA, ETC.

EDINBURGH, THE MELVILLE MONUMENT, ST. ANDREW SQUARE, 1821 [N.M.R.S.].

HOPETOUN, WEST LOTHIAN, Hope family mausoleum, 1831, Gothic [N.M.R.S.].

ERSKINE HOUSE, RENFREWSHIRE, obelisk in memory of Lord Blantyre, 1831 [N.M.R.S.].

KILLEARNADALE KIRK, ARGYLLSHIRE, mausoleum for Colin Campbell, 1838 [*N.S.A.* vii, 540].

BEN BHRAGIE, GOLSPIE, SUTHERLAND, pedestal for Chantrey's colossal statue of the 1st Duke of Sutherland, 1837 [J. Barron, *The Northern Highlands in the Nineteenth Century* ii, 1907, 203].

STOKE ROCHFORD, LINCS., obelisk in memory of Sir Isaac Newton, for Christopher Turner, *c.* 1840 [R.I.B.A.D.].

GRANTON, MIDLOTHIAN, proposed monument to commemorate construction of harbour by the 5th Duke of Buccleuch, 1848 [R.I.B.A.D.].

ROEHAMPTON, SURREY, mausoleum (in grounds of Roehampton Grove adjoining churchyard) to S. Lyne Stephens, 1864 [J. Thorne, *Handbook to the Environs of London* ii, 1876, 512; drawings in Surrey County Record Office].

VILLAGE

BRIDGE OF EARN VILLAGE, PERTHSHIRE, partly executed 1832 onwards on the basis of designs made by Burn in 1823 and now in Moncreiffe muniments [*ex. inf.* Mr. David Walker].

BURNELL, T—, was probably a member of a family of sculptors and masons, one of whom, Thomas Burnell, had been Master of the Masons' Company in 1783. He was a pupil of Sir Robert Taylor [H. Walpole, *Anecdotes of Painting* v, ed. F. W. Hilles & P. B. Daghlian, 1939, 198], and exhibited at the Royal Academy in 1802 and 1806, including the (Gothick) 'W. front and conservatory to Berrymede Priory, Acton, Middlesex, one of the seats of Col. Clutton', the 'Front next the Thames, on Hammersmith Mall, [of] the seat of W. Lewis, Esq.', 'Walnut Tree Lodge, E. Moulsey [Surrey], the seat of R. Bradstreet, Esq.', and (1806) the 'Elevation of a house intended to be built in Suffolk'.

BURNS, THOMAS, was an architect and builder of Glasgow. He went bankrupt in 1827, but was still active in the 1830s and 1840s. According to Gildard he designed 'several *quoad sacra* churches before the Disruption'. His executed works included KILMUN CHURCH, ARGYLLSHIRE, 1837 [*N.S.A.* vii, 611] and THE FREE NORMAL SEMINARY (now Glasgow College of Weaving), COWCADDENS, GLASGOW, 1846 [*A.P.S.D.*, *s.v.* 'Glasgow']. [Information from Mr. David Walker].

BURRELL, JOHN, practised in Camberwell for over thirty years. He exhibited at the Royal Academy from 1817 to 1854, including a 'Mausoleum to the memory of Sir T. Picton' (1818), 'A castellated mansion to be erected in Ayrshire' (1820), and 'Alterations and additions for W. H. Child, Esq. at Dulwich' (1828). In 1835 he and Robert Lugar entered a joint design for rebuilding the Houses of Parliament [*Catalogue of the Designs for the New Houses of Parliament*, 6th ed. 1836, 12–13]. He designed a BAPTIST CHURCH in COLDHARBOUR LANE, DENMARK HILL, 1823 [*Survey of London* xxvi, 151].

BURROUGH, Sir JAMES (1691–1764), was the son of Dr. James Burrough, a physician of Bury St. Edmunds in Suffolk. He was educated at the Grammar School at Bury, and at Gonville and Caius College, Cambridge, where he took his M.A. in 1716. In 1727 he became one of the Esquire Bedells of the University, and in 1754 was elected Master of his college. As an amateur architect, he may be compared with Dean Aldrich and Dr. George Clarke at Oxford, and, like them, he 'was a great virtuoso in painting, prints and medals, of which he had a very choice and valuable collection'.

One of the earliest architectural works with which Burrough is known to have been associated was the SENATE HOUSE at CAMBRIDGE, which was intended to form part of a larger complex of university buildings. He was a member of the syndicate responsible for its erection, and himself furnished a design which is said to have been not unlike that submitted by James Gibbs, except that it was 'upon Rustick Pillars' [Hist. MSS. Comm., *Portland* v, 630; *Wren Soc.* xvii, 46–7]. On 8 March 1721/2 he was among those who signed an order that Gibbs should 'take with him to London Mr. Burrough's Plan of the Intended publick Buildings and make what improvements he shall think necessary upon it'. It is not clear to what extent the design eventually adopted was based on his, for, although his friend William Cole, writing shortly after his death, implies that he was the architect, Gibbs published the plan and elevation as his own. On the whole, it seems probable that, as Willis concluded, 'Burrough had no other share in the work than that of suggesting the general arrangement, and of taking an active part in the promotion and management of the building'. In 1752 he made a design, based on Gibbs's scheme of 1722, for rebuilding the east front of the University Library adjoining the Senate House, but this was rejected through the influence of the Duke of Newcastle, then Chancellor, who gave £500 towards the cost, and persuaded the Syndics to adopt an elevation made by his own architect, Stephen Wright. This slight to Burrough caused a good deal of ill-feeling in the University, and, according to Cole, it was 'in order to cajole and bring into temper Mr. Burrough' that the Duke 'soon after procured him a Knighthood'. The actual occasion of this honour was, however, the presentation to George II of an Address on the coming of age of the Prince of Wales in 1759. Burrough's design was engraved and published by James Essex in 1775 [Willis & Clark, iii, 43–70, 536–7].

Burrough was much in demand as an architectural adviser in eighteenth-century Cambridge, and most of his executed works were in that university. In 1733, however, he designed an altarpiece for Canterbury Cathedral, and he is stated in a contemporary letter to have designed the 'apartments' in the Assembly Rooms at Norwich, built by Thomas Ivory in 1754. This is confirmed by a note in a sketch-book of Sir William Chambers in the Victoria and Albert Museum. In 1757 he was consulted by the corporation of Wisbech as to the merits of the plans for a new bridge submitted by Messrs. Swaine and Shar-

man [N. Walker & J. Craddock, *History of Wisbech*, 1849, 419].

Although some of his buildings (notably the range at Pembroke College) are Palladian in character, Burrough was not a strict follower of the Anglo-Palladian school. Like Gibbs he often designed in a chastened baroque style that is as sober in effect as most Palladian work, but belongs to the early rather than to the mid eighteenth century. His elaborate internal decoration is also pre-Palladian in character and almost rococo in feeling, though not in motif.

Being, as Cole tells us, 'a very large and corpulent Man, who lived freely and used no Exercise', Burrough's health was poor, and towards the end of his life he suffered from a variety of complaints. He maintained his interest in architecture to the last, and on the very day of his death 'Mr. Essex (the Builder) was with him after Dinner for half an Hour, talking upon that Business'. He was buried in the antechapel at Gonville and Caius College, where there is a ledger-stone in his memory. His portrait by Heins is in the Master's Lodge. He left the College his collection of Greek and Roman coins and 'all such of my books as they have not already in the Library'. Among the College MSS. (No. 620) is a copy of Aldrich's *Elementa Architecturae* presented by him. None of his drawings appear to have survived. [*D.N.B.*; J. Venn, *Biographical History of Gonville and Caius College* iii, 1901, 127; Willis & Clark, iii, 536–40; J. Nichols, *Literary Illustrations of the Eighteenth Century* iv, 91 n.]

STANWICK RECTORY, NORTHANTS., for Dr. Peter Needham, 1717 [Richard Cumberland, *Memoirs* i, 1807, 50].

GONVILLE AND CAIUS COLLEGE, CAMBRIDGE. Burrough probably designed the cupola erected over the Combination Room in 1728, and in 1729 he directed repairs and improvements in the Master's Lodge. He probably directed the ashlaring of the Gonville Court, 1751–4 [Willis & Clark, i, 188, 201–2].

QUEENS' COLLEGE, CAMBRIDGE, remodelled interior of hall in classical style, 1732–1734: Burrough's ceiling was removed 1846, and in 1861 his fireplace was taken down [Willis & Clark, ii, 46].

CANTERBURY CATHEDRAL, designed classical altarpiece, erected 1733, removed 1820 [C. E. Woodruff & W. Danks, *Memorials of Canterbury Cathedral*, 1912, 347–8; *A.P.S.D.*, s.v. 'Canterbury'].

EMMANUEL COLLEGE, CAMBRIDGE. Burrough received 7 guineas in 1735 'for his assistance in beautifying ye Chappell', but the details of the work are not recorded. In 1752 he made designs for rebuilding part of the College which were not executed [Willis & Clark, ii, 709, 713–15].

BURY ST. EDMUNDS, SUFFOLK, THE 'MANOR HOUSE' (now County Education Offices) for the Countess of Bristol, 1736 [*The Letter-Books of John Hervey, First Earl of Bristol*, ed. S.H.A.H., iii, 1894, 151–3].

PETERHOUSE, CAMBRIDGE, the New Building, designed 1736, executed 1738–42; refronted the main quadrangle 1754–6 [Willis & Clark, i, 35–8].

CORPUS CHRISTI COLLEGE, CAMBRIDGE, altar-piece in chapel, 1742; dem. 1823 [Willis & Clark, i, 295].

TRINITY HALL, CAMBRIDGE, remodelled hall and quadrangle, 1742–5, and made unexecuted design for a new Library Court [Willis & Clark, i, 228–9].

SIDNEY SUSSEX COLLEGE, CAMBRIDGE, remodelled interior of hall, 1749–52; designed stone gateway to Hall Court 1761–2, removed to Jesus Lane 1831 [R. C. Smail, 'Sir James Burrough at Sidney', *Cambridge Review*, 30 April 1960; Peter Salway in *C. Life*, 25 Feb. 1960].

CAMBRIDGE, GREAT ST. MARY'S CHURCH, Doctors' Gallery in the chancel, 1754; removed 1863 [Willis & Clark, iii, 538; C. H. Cooper, *Annals of Cambridge* iv, 1852, 291] (*V.C.H. Cambs.* iii, 131).

NORWICH, ASSEMBLY ROOMS, designed interior of building, 1754 [J. Nichols, *Literary Illustrations* vi, 1831, 804; note by Sir W. Chambers in album in Victoria and Albert Museum, 93 B.21, f. 90, no. 382].

CLARE COLLEGE, CAMBRIDGE, designed new chapel, 1763; completed by James Essex 1764–9, after his death [Willis & Clark, i, 115].

BURTON, DECIMUS (1800–1881), was the tenth son of James Burton, the builder. He received practical training in his father's office. George Maddox taught him architectural draughtsmanship, and he also attended the Royal Academy Schools, to which he was admitted in 1817. Thanks to his father's backing and to the influence of his father's friend Nash, under whose supervision he designed Cornwall and Clarence Terraces in Regent's Park, he was able to begin practice at a relatively early age, 'and found himself before he had completed his 24th year, in the full tide of professional work'. His Colosseum, 'a Greek version of the Pantheon', with a dome slightly larger than that of St. Paul's Cathedral, was regarded as a remarkable achievement for a young man of 23, and he soon obtained important commissions in the Royal Parks from the Office of Woods and Forests. These included the Hyde Park screen and the arch on Constitution Hill. The Athenaeum Club, with its sculptured frieze, also dates from this period.

After a brief career as a public architect, Burton turned increasingly to private patronage for his commissions. He enjoyed great success both as a designer of villas and small country houses, and as a town planner specializing in the kind of picturesque layout of which Regent's Park had been the prototype. Of this the Calverley Estate at Tunbridge Wells was a particularly attractive and successful example. He also had a considerable reputation as an expert in the construction of glass and iron conservatories, of which he designed notable examples at Chatsworth, Regent's Park and Kew.

Although he may be classed as a Greek Revivalist, Burton was by no means an archaeological purist. He visited Italy and Greece only in later life, and his knowledge of the principal antique monuments was based on the published works of others rather than on personal investigation and discovery. His use of the orders is always correct, but he showed a lack of pedantry in their application which sets him apart from some of his more doctrinaire contemporaries, such as Hamilton and Smirke. From Nash he had learned to combine the classical and the picturesque, and it is the picturesque that is predominant in much of his later work. For the Gothic Revival he felt no enthusiasm. He did, it is true, design some houses with pointed windows and turrets, and even some Gothic churches, but his lack of sympathy for the style is apparent enough in the arid interiors and coarse detailing of the churches, which are among the least attractive of their period.

Burton travelled in Canada and the U.S.A. as well as in the Mediterranean, but no details are known of his American tour. He was a Fellow of the Royal Society, of the Society of Antiquaries, and of the R.I.B.A., of which he was at one time vice-president. He retired in 1869, and lived partly at St. Leonards-on-Sea, where he built himself a house (The Cottage, Maze Hill), and partly in London, where he died unmarried on 14 December 1881. His practice was continued by his nephew Henry Marley Burton (d. 1880). John Crake, Henry Currey and George Mair were his pupils. E. J. May joined his office shortly before he retired. His portrait is given in *Illustrated London News* lxxix, 1881, 650. A number of his drawings are in the Victoria and Albert Museum (C. J. Richardson Collection), and there are others in the Hastings Museum, the R.I.B.A. Drawings Collection and the Architectural Association's Library.

[Obituaries in *Builder* xli, 1881, 779, and *Jnl. of the Royal Society* xxxiv, 1882–3, pp. viii–ix; *D.N.B.*; R. P. Jones, 'The Life and Works of Decimus Burton', *Arch. Rev.* xvii, 1905.]

Unless otherwise stated the source of the following list of Burton's works is the *Builder* xli, 1881, 779.

PUBLIC BUILDINGS, ETC.

London

THE COLOSSEUM, REGENT'S PARK, for Thomas Hornor, 1823–7; altered by W. Bradwell 1845; dem. 1875 (J. Britton & A. Pugin, *The Public Buildings of London* ii, 1828, 271–5; *C. Life*, 2 Jan. 1953).

HYDE PARK, Ionic screen at Hyde Park Corner, lodges at Stanhope, Grosvenor and Cumberland Gates, 1824–5; lodge at Prince of Wales Gate, 1846.

PARLIAMENTARY MEWS, PRINCE'S STREET, WESTMINSTER, 1825–6; remodelled as Stationery Office 1853–4; dem. 1950 [*History of the King's Works* vi, 1973, 536–7] (J. Elmes, *Metropolitan Improvements*, 1831, plate).

ZOOLOGICAL SOCIETY, REGENT'S PARK, buildings and gardens, 1826–41. Burton's original plan for the layout is P.R.O., MPE 906. See also *A Series of Ten Views of the Southern Portion of the Gardens of the Zoological Society in Regent's Park laid out to the Designs of D. Burton, Esq., drawn on Stone by James Hakewill*, 1831.

BUCKINGHAM PALACE, archway on Constitution Hill, 1827–8; originally intended as a Royal Entrance to the palace from the north, but moved to its present position 1883 (W. H. Leeds, *Supplement* to Britton & Pugin, *Public Buildings of London*, 1838, 124–34); and enclosure of palace forecourt, 1850–1.

THE ATHENAEUM CLUB, WATERLOO PLACE, 1827–30; attic storey added 1899–1900 (*Survey of London* xxix, 386–99).

THE ROYAL NAVAL CLUB, 160 BOND STREET, 1828–31.

BEULAH SPA, UPPER NORWOOD, pump-room, layout of grounds, etc., 1828–31 [E. Walford, *Old and New London* vi, n.d., 315].

THE JUNIOR UNITED SERVICE CLUB, CHARLES STREET, ST. JAMES'S, alterations, 1830; dem. 1855 (*Survey of London* xxix, 291–2).

THE ROYAL SOCIETY OF LITERATURE, ST. MARTIN'S PLACE, 1830–1; dem.

HYDE PARK, remodelled store-house or magazine for the Grenadier Guards, *c.* 1830.

CLIFFORD'S INN, FLEET STREET, alterations, 1830–4.

CHARING CROSS HOSPITAL, 1831–4; enlarged 1877, 1881 and 1904.

CLUB CHAMBERS, LOWER REGENT STREET, 1838–9; dem. (*Companion to the Almanac*, 1840, 246).

ROYAL BOTANIC SOCIETY'S GARDENS, REGENT'S PARK, conservatory (1845–6, dem. 1932) and other buildings, 1840–59 (*A New Survey of London* J. Weale, 1853, ii, 487–94; measured drawings of the conservatory were published in *Architect and Building News*, 1 April 1932 ('Obituaries of Buildings', No. 25)). Burton's report on the layout of the gardens is printed in *Gardeners' Mag.* xvi, 1840, 514–16.

THE UNION CLUB, TRAFALGAR SQUARE, addition of attic storey, etc., 1841–50.

THE ORIENTAL CLUB, HANOVER SQUARE, additions, 1852–4.

THE UNITED SERVICE CLUB, WATERLOO PLACE, enlargement on east side and alterations to principal elevations, including addition of frieze, 1858–9 (*Survey of London* xxix, 392–4).

Elsewhere

ABERYSCHAN IRONWORKS, MONMOUTHSHIRE, 1826; dem.

ABERDEEN, the Ionic screen to St. Nicholas Churchyard in Union Street was built by John Smith (*q.v.*) in 1830, apparently following designs supplied by Burton in 1829 [G. M. Fraser in *Aberdeen Weekly Journal*, 21 June 1918].

BATH, SOMERSET, report on Public Baths, 1829, and designed THE TEPID SWIMMING BATH, executed by G. P. Manners, 1830; dem. 1923 [W. Ison, *The Georgian Buildings of Bath*, 1948, 64].

DUBLIN, PHOENIX PARK, lodges, etc., 1834–49. There are drawings by Burton in National Library of Ireland, Portfolio 26.

PARIS, BRITISH EMBASSY (HÔTEL CHAROST), alterations and repairs, 1841–50 [*History of the King's Works* vi, 1972, 633–4].

KEW, SURREY, ROYAL BOTANIC GARDENS, Palm House, Entrance Gates to Kew Green and 'Campanile' (water-tower and chimney), 1845–8; Museum of Economic Botany, 1855–7; Temperate House, 1859–62 [*History of the King's Works* vi, 442–5] (G. Godwin, *Buildings and Monuments, Modern and Mediaeval*, 1850, 25–8).

EAST RETFORD, NOTTS., FREE GRAMMAR SCHOOLS (in South Retford), 1855–7, Elizabethan style.

CHURCHES

TUNBRIDGE WELLS, KENT, HOLY TRINITY, 1827–9, Gothic.

SOUTHBOROUGH, KENT, for John Deacon, 1830–1, Gothic; steeple by E. Christian 1883.

RIVERHEAD, KENT, 1831, Gothic; chancel by Sir A. W. Blomfield, 1882. There is an elevation by Burton in the Kent Record Office, U1350 P.23.

GORING, SUSSEX, rebuilt for David Lyon, 1836–8, Gothic.

EASTBOURNE, SUSSEX, HOLY TRINITY, 1837–9, Gothic; aisles by B. Ferrey 1855; remodelled 1909.

FLIMWELL, SUSSEX, 1839–40, Gothic; spire added 1873, chancel 1879.

BOBBINGWORTH, ESSEX, tower and porch, 1840, Gothic [*V.C.H. Essex* iv, 15].

FLEETWOOD, LANCS., for Sir Peter Hesketh-

Fleetwood, Bart., 1840, Gothic; chancel added 1880.

LONDON, TEMPLE CHURCH, restoration with Sydney Smirke, 1841–3 [J. Mordaunt Crook, 'The Restoration of the Temple Church', *Architectural History* viii, 1965, 41–3].

BRADFORD PEVERELL, DORSET, rebuilt for H. N. Middleton, 1849–51, Gothic.

LAUNCESTON, CORNWALL, restoration, 1849–53.

BUILDING ESTATES, ETC.

TUNBRIDGE WELLS, KENT, THE CALVERLEY ESTATE, for John Ward, 1828 onwards; Burton's own house, BASTON COTTAGE, was dem. *c.* 1900 (plans and engravings in J. Britton, *Descriptive Sketches of Tunbridge Wells and the Calverley Estate*, 1832, and Colbran's *New Guide to Tunbridge Wells*, ed. J. Phippen, 1840, 53–9).[1]

BRIGHTON, SUSSEX, QUEEN ADELAIDE CRESCENT, for (Sir) Isaac Lyon Goldsmid, 1830–4. Only the east wing was built under Burton's direction [A. Dale, *Fashionable Brighton*, 1947, 151–2].

LIVERPOOL, LANCS., building estate (unidentified) for R. A. Barton, 1834–5.

EASTBOURNE, SUSSEX, planned an estate for the 2nd Earl of Burlington (afterwards 7th Duke of Devonshire), which was not executed, with the exception of a villa for the owner, 1835–40.

GRAVESEND, KENT, layout of 'a large plot adjoining the high road, for building', 1836 [*Gent's Mag.* 1836 (i), 654].

FLEETWOOD, LANCS., new town, including church, North Euston Hotel, Queen's Terrace, Custom House and two lighthouses, for Sir Peter Hesketh-Fleetwood, Bart., 1836–43.

GLASGOW, Kelvinside building estate for Mathew Montgomerie, 1840.

FOLKESTONE, KENT, planned estate for the 3rd Earl of Radnor, 1843; not proceeded with, drawings in Radnor Estate Office, Folkestone.

QUEENSTOWN (now COBH), CO. CORK, IRELAND, improvements and sea-wall for the 5th Viscount Midleton, 1843–50.

HILL OF HOWTH, CO. DUBLIN, IRELAND, unexecuted project for building for the 3rd Earl of Howth, 1845–6.

BOURNEMOUTH, HANTS., succeeded Benjamin Ferrey as architect to the Gervis Estate *c.* 1845, and advised on development until 1859. For further details see C. H. Mate & C. Riddle, *Bournemouth: 1810–1910*, Bournemouth 1910, 90–92, etc.

[1] According to the 1847 edition of Colbran's *Guide* Burton had by then planned an estate at Tunbridge Wells for the Marquess Camden, but Camden Park does not appear to have been laid out until *c.* 1853, and the five Italianate houses built by 1863, when work stopped, were probably designed by another architect.

DOMESTIC ARCHITECTURE
London

THE HOLME, REGENT'S PARK, for James Burton, *c.* 1819 (J. Elmes, *Metropolitan Improvements*, 1831, 28–9 and plate).

GROVE HOUSE (now NUFFIELD LODGE), REGENT'S PARK, for G. B. Greenough, 1822–4 (J. Britton & A. Pugin, *The Public Buildings of London* ii, 1828, 1–4; J. Elmes, *Metropolitan Improvements*, 1831, 30–2 and plate).

PALL MALL EAST, house (No. 8) and warehouse for Messrs. Hibbert & Co., army clothiers, *c.* 1825; dem.

ST. DUNSTAN'S LODGE, REGENT'S PARK, for the 3rd Marquess of Hertford, 1825; dem. 1937 (J. Elmes, *Metropolitan Improvements*, 1831, plate). Burton's original drawings are at the Architectural Assocation.

PALL MALL EAST, house and shops for Sir H. F. Cooke, 1826–7; dem.

attributed: SOUTH VILLA, REGENT'S PARK, for W. H. Cooper, 1827; dem. 1913–30 [Mr. Bernard Pardoe has pointed out that as Burton was employed by W. H. Cooper at Painshill in 1831–2 it is very probable that South Villa was also designed by him].

SPRING GARDENS, Nos. 10, 12, 14, *c.* 1827, occupied chiefly by himself as house and office; dem. [*Survey of London* xx, 68, pl. 48].

CARLTON HOUSE TERRACE, No. 3 for Lord de Clifford, 1829–31; No. 4 (dem. 1929) for Lord Stuart de Rothesay.

PALL MALL, alterations to house (No. 80) for (Sir) John Kirkland, army agent, 1830 (cf. *Survey of London* xxix, 377).

WHITEHALL GARDENS, No. 6, additions for Cuthbert Ellison, 1831–2; dem. (*Survey of London* xiii, pls. 89–92).

HOLFORD HOUSE, REGENT'S PARK, for (Sir) James Holford, 1832–3; afterwards Regent's Park College; destroyed by bombing 194–.

HOLLAND HOUSE, KENSINGTON, restoration for the 3rd Lord Holland, 1833; destroyed by bombing 1940.

GROSVENOR STREET, additions to No. 18 for the dowager Duchess of Roxburghe and her second husband Col. W. F. O'Reilly, 1835–6.

BELGRAVE SQUARE, additions to No. 10 for the 2nd Earl of Burlington (afterwards 7th Duke of Devonshire), 1839–40.

HYDE PARK GARDENS, No. 18 for Mrs. Drummond, 1841–2.

DEVONSHIRE HOUSE, PICCADILLY, portico, hall and staircase for the 6th Duke of Devonshire, 1843; dem. 1924 (*Builder* i, 1843, 5; B.M., Crace Views, Portfolio x, 96).

GREAT STANHOPE STREET, additions to No. 6 for A. Mitchell, 1853–4.

THE FERNS, VICTORIA ROAD, KENSINGTON, alterations and additions for E. W. Cooke, R.A.,

1864 [E. W. Cooke's MS. diaries, *ex inf.* Mr. Andrew Saint].

Country

BRIGHTON, SUSSEX, villa for H. Fauntleroy, 1822–3.

ALDBURY GROVE, CHESHUNT, HERTS., additions for J. S. Jessop, 1822–4.

ELM BANK, LEATHERHEAD, SURREY, addition for Capt. William Stanley Clarke, 1822–5; largely rebuilt since war-damage.

BASTON HOUSE, HAYES, KENT, additions for S. N. Ward, 1823–5.

HOLWOOD HOUSE, KESTON, KENT, for John Ward, 1823–6 (J. P. Neale, *Views of Seats*, 2nd ser., iv, 1828).

LIVERPOOL, LANCS., house at WEST DINGLE for J. B. Yates, 1827; dem. 1959.

MITCHELLS (now HOLMEWOOD), LANGTON GREEN, TUNBRIDGE WELLS, KENT, for C. H. Okey and J. Carruthers, 1827; burned 1837 and rebuilt to a different design.

HARROW, MIDDLESEX, two houses for General A. M. McGregor of Harrow Park, 1827.

THE GROVE, MOLESEY, SURREY, additions for J. W. Croker, after 1828.

THE GROVE, PENSHURST, KENT, for F. Allnutt, 1828–30.

BECKENHAM, KENT, villa for B. Oakley, 1829.

GREAT CULVERDEN HOUSE, TUNBRIDGE WELLS, KENT, for J. J. Fisher, 1829–30; dem. 1956 (C. Greenwood, *Epitome of County History: Kent*, 1838, plate p. 124).

SPRING GROVE, PEMBURY, KENT, for A. B. Belcher, 1829–30; dem. 1871 [plans in Kent R.O., U 1050].

MABLEDON PARK, QUARRY HILL, TONBRIDGE, KENT, addition for John Deacon, 1829–31, Gothic (C. Greenwood, *Epitome of County History: Kent*, 1838, plate p. 125). This was the house originally built by James Burton as his own residence.

PARK HATCH, WITLEY, SURREY, conservatory, etc., for Joseph Goodman, 1830; dem.

GREAT WOOLSTONE, BUCKS., parsonage for the Rev. Dr. Weeden Butler, 1830; rebuilt *c.* 1855.

CHATSWORTH, DERBYSHIRE, works including Home Farm and Great Conservatory (designed in association with Joseph Paxton 1836–40, dem. 1920) for the 6th Duke of Devonshire, 1830–48. For the question of the responsibility for the design see Francis Thompson in *Derbyshire Countryside* xxi, Aug.–Sept. 1956, and G. F. Chadwick, *The Works of Sir Joseph Paxton*, 1961, 78–80.

SEVENOAKS, KENT, THE RECTORY, for the Rev. Thos. Curteis, 1831–2, Tudor Gothic; dem. 1959.

PAINSHILL, SURREY, additions (including a conservatory, since dem.) for W. H. Cooper, 1831–2 (*C. Life*, 2 Jan. 1958).

EAST CLIFFE HOUSE, RAMSGATE, KENT, additions for Sir Moses Montefiore, 1831–2; dem. 1954.

BURY HILL, nr. DORKING, SURREY, addition for C. Barclay, 1831–3; partly dem. *c.* 1950; observatory for A. K. Barclay 1847–8.

COOMBE LODGE, COOMBE, nr. KINGSTON, SURREY, for W. O. Hunt, 1831–4.

BROOM HILL, nr. TONBRIDGE, KENT, for David Salomons, 1831–8.

BURRSWOOD HOUSE, SPELDHURST, KENT, for David Salomons, 1831–8, Elizabethan style.

BENTHAM HILL, nr. TONBRIDGE, KENT, for A. Pott, 1832–3, Elizabethan style.

WORTH PARK, SUSSEX, additions for Joseph Montefiore, 1833; destroyed by fire 1847.

BRIGHTON, SUSSEX, FURZE HILL VILLA, for (Sir) Isaac Lyon Goldsmid, 1833; dem. 1958 [A. Dale, *Fashionable Brighton*, 1947, 152].

STOCKGROVE, GREAT BRICKHILL, BUCKS., rebuilt for Col. Henry Hanmer, *c.* 1834.

GLEVERING HALL, SUFFOLK, addition (including orangery) for A. Arcedekne, 1834–5.

GREAT BRICKHILL, BUCKS., THE RECTORY, for the Rev. H. Foulis, 1834–5.

OAKLANDS, SEDLESCOMBE, SUSSEX, for Hercules Sharpe, 1834–7.

CHISWICK HOUSE, MIDDLESEX, lodges and gates for the 6th Duke of Devonshire, 1835.

CHISWICK, MIDDLESEX, THE GROVE, alterations for the 6th Duke of Devonshire; dem. 1928.

CHISWICK, MIDDLESEX, SUTTON COURT, alterations for the 6th Duke of Devonshire; dem.

HOLLANDS, or HOLLANDS FARM, SPELDHURST, KENT, for the Rev. H. Cholmondeley, 1835–6.

VEN HOUSE, MILBOURNE PORT, SOMERSET, added wings and conservatory and designed new drawing-room for Sir W. Medlycott, 1835–6. A volume of drawings is preserved at Ven.

KENNINGTON PLACE, KENT, additions for Dr. H. W. Carter, 1835–7.

COGHURST, GUESTLING, SUSSEX, for Musgrave Brisco, 1835–40; dem.

BLACKHURST, PEMBURY ROAD, TUNBRIDGE WELLS, KENT, for Ford Wilson, 1836–8 (C. Greenwood, *Epitome of County History: Kent*, 1838, plate p. 124).

PUTNEY PARK, SURREY, additions for R. Hutton, M.P., 1837–8.

HARROW SCHOOL, MIDDLESEX, house for the Rev. J. W. Colenso, 1838–9.

BLACKHEATH, KENT, house for Jas. Traill, 1838–40.

THE HOOKE, CHAILEY, SUSSEX, additions (largely dem. *c.* 1960) for R. W. Blencowe, 1838–44.

GREENSTEAD, ESSEX, parsonage for the Rev. P. W. Ray, 1839–40.

WOODHAYS, SURREY, additions for William Brown, 1839–41.

STANWICK PARK, YORKS. (N.R.), additions for Lord Prudhoe, afterwards 4th Duke of Northumberland, *c.* 1839 onwards; dem. 1923. At Alnwick Castle there are designs by Burton for works at Stanwick in 1840–2, including a greenhouse, an orangery and a domed entrance hall.

HARROW SCHOOL, MIDDLESEX, Headmaster's House, 1840, and enlarged 1845–6.

ALVERBANK, STOKES BAY, nr. GOSPORT, HANTS., for J. W. Croker, c. 1840.

GRIMSTON PARK, YORKS. (W.R.), rebuilt for the 2nd Lord Howden, 1840–50 (C. Life, 9–16 March 1940).

HAYDON HILL, BUSHEY, HERTS., for T. G. Fournereau, 1841–3.

STAPLETON HOUSE, nr. BRISTOL (now COLSTON'S SCHOOL), additions and alterations for the Ecclesiastical Commissioners, 1841–5, to convert it into residence for the Bishop of Gloucester and Bristol.

HEMINGFORD ABBOTS, HUNTS., house for the Rev. J. Linton, 1842–3.

BAY HOUSE, ALVERSTOKE, HANTS. (now GOSPORT GRAMMAR SCHOOL), for the 1st Lord Ashburton, 1844, Tudor Gothic.

BELLEVUE, TUNBRIDGE WELLS, KENT, for Aretas Akers, 1845.

WHIPS CROSS, WALTHAMSTOW, ESSEX, house for John Masterman, junior, 1845–7.

SYON HOUSE, ISLEWORTH, MIDDLESEX, river terrace, ornamental dairy, etc., for the 4th Duke of Northumberland, after 1847.

CALSTOCK, CORNWALL, rectory for the Rev. C. L. Pemberton, 1853–4.

BOLNORE HOUSE, CUCKFIELD, SUSSEX, additions for Miss Dealtry, 1852–5.

BEARWOOD, nr. WOKINGHAM, BERKS., alterations and additions for John Walter, 1853–8; rebuilt to designs of Robert Kerr 1865–74.

SENNOWE HALL, NORFOLK, additions for Trustees under Court of Chancery, 1855–6; largely rebuilt 1908.

HIGHAMS, nr. CHOBHAM, SURREY, additions for the Hon. Seymour Bathurst, 1855–6.

NORTH COURT, FINCHAMPSTEAD, BERKS., for the Rev. T. Mozley, 1857–8; enlarged 1873; dem. 1970.

BINEHAM, CHAILEY, SUSSEX, rebuilt for J. G. Blencowe, 1858–60; dem.

BURTON, alias **HALIBURTON,** JAMES (1761–1837), was the son of William Haliburton, a Scottish builder who had migrated from Roxburghshire to London. In 1776 he was articled to a surveyor named James Dalton, with whom he later entered into a short-lived partnership. In 1785 he began his career as a speculative builder by erecting four 'third-rate' houses on a site in Southwark, and in 1786 he designed and built for James Parkinson the LEVERIAN MUSEUM, afterwards the SURREY INSTITUTION, in Blackfriars Road (dem.). He became the most enterprising and successful London builder of his time, and

was largely responsible for the development of the Foundling, Skinners' and Bedford estates in Bloomsbury, where he built Russell Square (1800–14) and the adjoining streets, the east side of Tavistock Square (dem. 1938), Burton Street and Burton (now Cartwright) Crescent. He also built Waterloo Place and several of Nash's terraces round Regent's Park, besides a large number of houses in Regent Street itself. His readiness to take sites in this way did much to make the Regent Street scheme a financial success, and in return Nash assisted his son Decimus Burton in his architectural career.

During the years 1805–7 Burton was concerned in a housing estate at Tunbridge Wells, and in 1828 he turned his attention to St. Leonards-on-Sea, for whose development as a seaside resort he was largely responsible. Among the buildings which he erected there were the Greek Doric Assembly Rooms (now the Masonic Hall) and the St. Leonards (later the Royal Victoria) Hotel (remodelled 1903). To what extent he relied on his son Decimus for architectural assistance is not clear, but according to a contemporary guide-book he himself designed the Gothic church which he built at St. Leonards in 1831–4, destroyed by bombing 1944. He appears to have designed some of the houses which he built in Bloomsbury, notably those on the south side of Russell Square, of which he exhibited a view at the Royal Academy in 1800, and Elmes states that the RUSSELL INSTITUTION in GREAT CORAM STREET, 1802 (dem.), was erected 'by and from the designs of James Burton, Esq.' [J. Elmes, *Metropolitan Improvements*, 1831, 132 and plate]. His own town house, the Holme in Regent's Park, was designed by his son Decimus, and J. T. Parkinson appears to have been the architect of the country house which he built at Quarry Hill, nr. Tonbridge, in about 1805. The latter is illustrated in Brayley's *Beauties of England and Wales* viii, 1808, 1295, where it is described as 'erected with the appropriate materials of the country, as the fragment of a castle, but replete with modern conveniences'.

Burton was Master of the Tylers' and Bricklayers' Company in 1801–2 and Sheriff of Kent in 1810. He died at St. Leonards on 31 March 1837, and is commemorated both by a monument in the burial-ground and by a later memorial by the side of the roadway at the junction of Marina and Grand Parade. The third of his twelve children, James, became a pupil of Sir John Soane for a few months, but gave up architecture for Egyptology (see *D.N.B.* under 'Haliburton, J.'). The tenth, Decimus, is noticed above. A notebook and diary kept by Burton from 1784 to 1811 is in the Hastings Museum. There is a copy of the sale catalogue of his library in the British Museum (S.C.W. 33 (6)).

[R. Dobie, *The History of the United Parishes*

of *St. Giles in the Fields and St. George Blooms-bury*, 1829, 144–9; John Summerson, *John Nash*, 1935, *passim*; John Summerson, *Georgian London*, 1945, 152–6; *The Watering Places of Great Britain and Fashionable Directory*, Joseph Robins, London 1833, 106; J. Manwaring Baines, *Burton's St. Leonards*, Hastings 1956; D. J. Olsen, *Town Planning in London*, Yale 1964, 52–3; Christopher Monkhouse, 'St. Leonards', *C. Life*, 21–28 Feb. 1974.]

BUSBY, CHARLES AUGUSTUS (1788–1834), was the eldest son of Dr. Thomas Busby (1755–1838), musician and writer. He exhibited his first drawing (a 'Design for a Mansion') at the Royal Academy at the age of only 13, became a pupil of D. A. Alexander, and in 1807 won the Gold Medal in his first year as a student at the R.A. Schools. By 1808 he had published a book entitled *A Series of Designs for Villas and Country Houses adapted with Economy to the Comforts and to the Elegancies of Modern Life, with Plans and Explanations to Each*. In 1809 he was able to exhibit drawings for two villas for which he had received commissions, and in 1810 he designed a public building, the Commercial Rooms at Bristol, a very competent essay in the Greek Revival. This promising and precocious career was interrupted in 1814 by bankruptcy allegedly brought on by the failure of several roofs Busby had designed on a new principle, whereupon he retreated to America to avoid his creditors. Here he studied the State Penitentiaries and made some experiments connected with paddle-boats, the results of which he published in the *American Monthly Magazine* in the form of 'An Essay on the Propulsion of Navigable Bodies' (1818). Soon after his return to England in 1820 he won the second premium of £100 in the competition for the design of a new Penitentiary at Millbank. But lacking the means to establish himself in independent practice, he was obliged to accept employment in the office of Francis Goodwin, then busy designing Commissioners' churches. Goodwin, who had more commissions than he could properly handle, proposed to pass some of these on to his assistant in return for a suitable consideration, and in this way Busby came to submit designs in his own name for churches at Leeds (Quarry Hill) and Oldham. These were rejected by the Commissioners on the advice of Messrs. Smirke and Nash, who declared Busby's iron roofs to be 'extremely weak and insecure'. In vain did the indignant architect retaliate by the publication of a pamphlet, of which he sent a copy to every Member of Parliament and to every architect and engineer in England.[1] Later in the same year, having quarrelled with Good-

---

[1] There is a copy among C. R. Cockerell's drawings in the Victoria and Albert Museum.

win, he left London and established himself at Brighton, where he entered into partnership with the architect and builder Amon Wilds. The principal product of their partnership was the design and layout of the Kemp Town and Brunswick estates, a view of which was exhibited at the Royal Academy in 1825 under their joint names. It is probable, however, that most of the firm's architectural work was designed by Busby, who, unlike Wilds, had had the advantage of a proper professional training. Despite the failure of his career as a London architect, Busby therefore ranks as one of the principal creators of Regency Brighton.

In 1832 Busby succeeded T. W. Clisby as the surveyor in charge of Brunswick Town at a salary of £40 a year. This post he retained until his death on 18 September 1834, aged 46. He was buried at the Old Parish Church, Hove. In the Victoria and Albert Museum there is a miniature portrait of a young man named Busby who may well have been the architect. It is by J. Fruman and is dated 1807 (P.44–1936).

Besides his *Designs for Villas* (of which there was a second edition in 1835), Busby also published *A Collection of Designs for Modern Embellishments, suitable to Parlours and Dining Rooms, Folding Doors, Chimney Pieces, Verandas, Frizes, etc., on 25 Plates*, 1810.

[A. Dale, *Fashionable Brighton*, 1947, 22–33; *Gent's Mag.* 1811 (2), 84 (marriage), 1834 (2), 446 (death); *The Farington Diary*, ed. J. Greig, iv, 234; *Builder*, xxi, 1863, 113; Michael Port, 'Francis Goodwin ... and his Quarrel with C. A. Busby', *Architectural History* i, 1958.]

CLAPHAM COMMON, SURREY, NIGHTINGALE COTTAGE, NIGHTINGALE LANE, for W. Nunn, 1807 [exhib. at R.A. 1809; Dale, 23].

WINDSOR, BERKS., design for a villa to be erected for S. Dixon, Esq., nr. Windsor, exhib. at R.A. 1809.

BRISTOL, COMMERCIAL ROOMS, CORN STREET, 1810–11 [exhib. at R.A. 1810; W. Ison, *The Georgian Buildings of Bristol*, 1952, 134–5].

HERTS., an unidentified villa executed in 1810, exhib. at R.A. 1811.

BETHNAL GREEN, LONDON, EPISCOPAL JEWS' CHAPEL, 1813–14, with G. Maliphant; dem. 1895 [exhib. at R.A. by Maliphant 1814, but Busby's joint responsibility is shown by a reference in his 1822 pamphlet and by Bethnal Green Museum, *Catalogue of Drawings and Prints relating to Hackney and Bethnal Green*, 1925, no. 125].

GWRYCH CASTLE, nr. ABERGELEY, DENBIGHSHIRE, Gothic design for L. B. Hesketh, exhibited at R.A. 1814. This house was designed by Hesketh himself over a period of years, with assistance from several architects, including Busby, Rickman, Welch and Kennedy. Drawings in

the National Library of Wales show that little of Busby's design was executed [J. P. Neale, *Views of Seats*, 2nd ser., ii, 1825; information from Mr. John Baily and Mr. Peter Howell].
MAIDENHEAD, BERKS., ST. MARY'S CHURCH, 1824–5, Gothic; chancel added 1877–8; dem. *c.* 1964 [J. W. Walker, *History of Maidenhead*, 1931, 32; MS. Vestry Minutes].

For the following documented works in Brighton, all designed by Busby in partnership with A. Wilds, see A. Dale, *Fashionable Brighton*, where many other houses attributable to the firm are mentioned:

BRIGHTON, THE GOTHIC HOUSE, WESTERN ROAD, later known as Priory Lodge, No. 1 Western Terrace, and now part of the premises of Plummer Roddis Ltd., *c.* 1823 (A. Dale, *Fashionable Brighton*, 1948, pl. 89)

KEMP TOWN, BRIGHTON (*i.e.* Sussex Square, Lewes Crescent, Arundel Terrace, and Chichester Terrace), for T. R. Kemp, 1823–*c.* 1850.

BRUNSWICK TOWN, HOVE (*i.e.* Brunswick Square, Terrace and Place, Lansdowne Place and Square), for the Rev. T. Scutt, 1824–*c.* 1830.

BRIGHTON, ST. GEORGE'S CHAPEL, for T. R. Kemp, 1824–5. A complete set of drawings of this chapel by Busby is in the P.R.O. (CO 323/144).

BRIGHTON, PORTLAND PLACE, for Major V. Russell, 1824–*c.* 1830.

BUSH, THOMAS, was a London surveyor much employed as a measurer. His chief claim to notice appears to be the fact that Sir Robert Smirke (1780–1867) was his pupil. J. W. Higgins (1783–1854) was also articled to him. The evidence he gave to the Commissioners of Military Enquiry on the measurement of barracks in 1805 will be found in their *Fourth Report*, appendices 39 and 48 (*Parliamentary Papers*, vol. 7, part i, 1807).

BUTTERWORTH, JOSEPH, of Manchester, is at present known only as the architect of OLDHAM TOWN HALL, LANCS., 1840–1, enlarged 1879–80 [*Oldham; Jubilee of its Incorporation*, 1899, *ex inf.* Mr. W. J. Smith]. He does not appear under Manchester in Pigot's *Directory* of 1828–9, but Slater's *Directory of Manchester* of 1843 gives 'Butterworth and Whitaker' (W. W. Whitaker) as architects practising in partnership.

BUXTON, JOHN (1685–1731), was a Norfolk squire who had some ability as an amateur architect. He was the son and heir of Robert Buxton (d. 1691) of Channons Hall, Tibenham (between Norwich and Diss), and Shadwell, nr. Thetford, and also inherited the Earsham estate near Bungay from his mother Elizabeth (*née* Gooch). Buxton's architectural skill is attested both by local

historians and by a quantity of sketches which remain among his papers, now in Cambridge University Library. According to Thomas Harrison, the author of *Postwick and Relatives* (written in the mid eighteenth century, but not published until 1858), Buxton was 'a fine genius very curious in such designs' and designed BIXLEY HALL, NORFOLK (dem. *c.* 1900), for his cousin Sir Edward Ward, Bart., besides rebuilding his own house at EARSHAM. In 1721 he sold Earsham to Col. Windham and moved to Channons, but subsequently (1727–30) built a new house for himself at Shadwell called SHADWELL LODGE (completely rebuilt in the nineteenth century by Blore and Teulon and now known as 'Shadwell Park'). At CHANNONS HALL (largely demolished 1784) he carried out extensive repairs, modernized the interior and built new stables in 1721–4. Earsham, his only surviving house, is a plain redbrick building with recessed centre and hipped roofs. To judge from an engraving of Bixley (B.M., Add. MS. 23025, f. 203) and a watercolour of Shadwell (reproduced in *C. Life*, 2 July 1964), they were of similar architectural character.

[Burke's *Landed Gentry*, *s.v.* 'Buxton of Shadwell'; T. Harrison, *Postwick and Relatives*, 1858; Armstrong, *History of Norfolk*, 1781, 149; R. W. Ketton-Cremer, *Norfolk Portraits*, 1944, 79; Mark Girouard, 'Shadwell Park', *C. Life*, 2–9 July 1964; A. P. Baggs, 'Channons Hall', *Norfolk Archaeology* xxxiv, 1966; Buxton papers in Cambridge University Library, especially Box 29; information from Mr. A. P. Baggs.]

BYFIELD, GEORGE (*c.* 1756–1813), is said to have been a pupil of Sir Robert Taylor [*Civil Engineer and Architect's Jnl.* iii, 1840, 147]. He exhibited regularly at the Royal Academy from 1780 onwards. In 1794, and again in 1799, he stood for election as an A.R.A., but without success. From 1803 onwards he acted as surveyor to the estates of the Dean and Chapter of Westminster. He was in partnership with H. H. Seward from 1810 until his death, which took place at his house in Craven Street on 9 August 1813, in his 58th year. J. Mills and J. Phillips were his pupils and John Coney, the architectural draughtsman, was in his office from 1805 to 1808.

At the time of his death Byfield was described as 'an eminent architect, who has built several Gaols, and for many years has made this branch of his profession his particular study'. In addition to the three prisons listed below, he is known to have made designs in 1801 for the new County Gaol at Worcester, but those of Francis Sandys were ultimately preferred. His plans for Downing College, Cambridge, submitted in 1804 to satisfy an order of the Court of Chancery requiring a second design in addition to those of James Wyatt, were also unsuccessful [Willis & Clark, ii,

760–1; *R.I.B.A. Jnl.*, 3rd ser., xlv, 1938, 973].
His country houses have (or had) elegant inter-
iors in the Adam manner, but Brockhampton
Chapel is Gothick and the Sessions House at
Canterbury shows Greek Revival influence.
[*Gent's Mag.* 1783 (ii), 1064 (marriage); 1813
(ii), 299, 332 (death).]

DOMESTIC ARCHITECTURE

BASSINGBOURNE HALL, TAKELEY, ESSEX, 'a villa now
building' and 'new-built lodges' for Sir Peter
Parker in Essex were exhib. by Byfield at the
R.A. in 1784. Parker had recently bought Bassingbourne Hall (*c.* 1750; dem.), but does not
appear to have rebuilt it. The lodges still exist
on the A120 road.

PERDISWELL PARK, nr. WORCESTER, for Henry
Wakeman, 1787–8; destroyed by fire 1956
[exhib. at R.A. 1787–8].

LONDON, NO. 4 ST. JAMES'S SQUARE, internal alterations for Marchioness de Grey, 1790 [*Survey
of London* xxix, 90–1].

CRAYCOMBE HOUSE, FLADBURY, WORCS., for
George Perrott, 1791 [exhib. at R.A. 1790] (*C.
Life*, 6 July 1940).

KINNERSLEY CASTLE, HEREFS., 'design for the intended alteration' for Thomas Clutton, exhib.
at R.A. 1793.

BOSTON, U.S.A., 'design for a villa to be erected
near', exhib. at R.A. 1795.

SALWARPE PARSONAGE, WORCS., alterations, 1795
[signed plan in Diocesan Records, Worcestershire Record Office].

COFTON HALL, COFTON HACKETT, WORCS., altera-
tions for Robert Biddulph, 1796 [exhib. at
R.A. 1796; signed drawings in Worcestershire
Record Office].

BRIGHTON, SUSSEX, 'Design for a crescent on the
West Cliff', exhib. at R.A. 1797, apparently
not executed.

HURLINGHAM HOUSE (now the Hurlingham Club),
FULHAM, MIDDLESEX, additions, including
façade to river, for John Ellis, 1797–8 [exhib.
at R.A. 1798; G. Richardson, *New Vitruvius
Britannicus* ii, 1808, pls. 23–4].

MADRESFIELD COURT, WORCS., alterations for
William Lygon, cr. Earl Beauchamp, 1799;
remodelled 1864–75 by P. C. Hardwick [Far-
ington's Diary, 20 July 1799].

GAYNES HALL, nr. ST. NEOTS, HUNTS., for J. Duberley, *c.* 1800 [exhib. at R.A. 1800].

MICHEL GROVE, nr. POLING, SUSSEX, alterations
(Gothic) for Richard Walker, 1801; dem. 1832
[exhib. at R.A. 1801; drawings in Estate Office
at Arundel Castle dated 1801].

KENSINGTON, NOEL HOUSE, KENSINGTON GORE, for
George Aust, 1804 [T. Faulkner, *History of
Kensington*, 1820, 392 and plate].

SPETCHLEY PARK, WORCS., improvements for

Robert Berkeley, 1807; rebuilt 1811 [exhib. at
R.A. 1807].

PAPWORTH HALL (now HOSPITAL), CAMBS., for C.
Madryll Cheere, 1809 [exhib. at R.A. 1808,
1809, 1811].

WESTMINSTER, completed houses on south side of
Dean's Yard built by George Hoare in 1758
for Samuel Cox, but left unfinished (with the
exception of that in the centre), 1809 [designs
in Westminster Abbey Muniments, 52408–9
and P.29].

PERRIDGE HOUSE, DEVONSHIRE, for H. L. Toll (d.
1844) [R. Ackermann, *Repository of Arts*, 3rd
ser., x, 1828, 311].

? WICK HOUSE, ST. JOHN IN BEDWARDINE,
WORCESTER, for Thomas Bund (of which 'the
two intended new fronts' were exhibited at
the R.A. by Byfield's pupil John Phillips in
1790).

PUBLIC BUILDINGS, ETC.

WORCESTER, GUILDHALL, alterations to COUNCIL
CHAMBER, 1791 [J. Chambers, *General History
of Worcester*, 1819, 302].

WORCESTER, THE HOUSE OF INDUSTRY, 1793–4 [V.
Green, *History of Worcester* ii, 1796, 13].

BROCKHAMPTON CHAPEL, nr. BROMYARD, HEREFS.,
for J. Barnaby, *c.* 1799, Gothic [exhib. at R.A.
1799].

KNIGHTSBRIDGE, LONDON, a brewery, 1804
[exhib. at R.A. 1804].

BURY ST. EDMUNDS, SUFFOLK, COUNTY GAOL, 1803
[*Report of the Committee of Aldermen appointed
to visit Several Gaols in England*, 1816, 44].

CAMBRIDGE, COUNTY GAOL, 1802–7; dem. 1930
[exhib. at R.A. 1803].

CANTERBURY, KENT, COUNTY GAOL AND SESSIONS
HOUSE, LONGPORT, 1806–10 [exhib. at R.A.
1806].

BYRD, or **BIRD,** WILLIAM (1624–), was
born in Gloucester and served an apprenticeship
of eight years to Walter Nicholls, a mason of that
city. He came to Oxford in or about 1647, for in
1681, when giving evidence in a lawsuit, he stated
that he had worked in Oxford for thirty-four
years. He had a yard in Holywell, and did a considerable business as a monumental sculptor. But
he also took large masonry contracts, and in 1689
he stated that 'he hath often been employed in
drawing of ground plotts, uprights and making
estimates of the same'. On another occasion he
said that 'since he has been a Master workman
[he] hath in diverse Counties work'd at severall
noble buildings too many to be here mentioned
and lately in Oxford he built the Arch at New
College [over New College Lane] and Edmund
Hall Chappell'. The latter was consecrated in
1682, but was not finally completed until 1685–
6. Other works carried out by Byrd in Oxford

were the stone-carving for Wren's Sheldonian Theatre, 1666–9, including the fourteen 'termains', better known as 'the Emperors' heads', and the new doorway into the Divinity School opposite the Theatre, which he made in 1668–9, perhaps under Wren's direction. In 1683 he contracted to erect the south wing of Winchester Palace to Wren's designs, and it is probable that the plan of the palace, with its stepped-back wings, influenced the Garden Quadrangle at New College, of which Bird built the inner portion on a similar plan in 1682–4 (the south-east block was added in 1700, and the north-east block in 1707). He was no doubt the 'Mr. Bird' who repaired William of Wykeham's monument in Winchester Cathedral in 1664, and who was employed to restore a defective pier on the south side of Winchester College Chapel in 1671. In 1672–3 he was paid £16 2s. for work on the east window of Worcester Cathedral [Treasurer's Accounts of the Dean and Chapter of Worcester, *ex inf.* Mr. David Whitehead].

Bird was a prolific and successful monumental sculptor, and in 1658, according to Anthony Wood, he invented a process for painting or staining marble. The date of his death is not known, and it has not been established whether or not the sculptor Francis Bird (1667–1731) was his son. Thomas Wood (*q.v.*) was his apprentice.

[Mrs. J. C. Cole, 'William Byrd, Stonecutter and Mason', *Oxoniensia* xiv, 1949; Mrs. J. C. Cole, 'The Painting or Staining of Marble as practised by William Byrd of Oxford and Others', *Oxoniensia* xvii–xviii, 1952–3; *Oxoniensia* xxiv, 1959, 65; Rupert Gunnis, *Dictionary of British Sculptors*, revised ed. 1968, 55; T. F. Kirby, *Annals of Winchester College*, 1892, 219, 353; *Wren Soc.* vii, 23, 26, 34–6, 61–6; xix, 92–3, 95–6; Oxford University Archives, Vice-Chancellor's Court, 1688/9, Easter Term, 54.]

BYRES, JAMES (1734–1817), was the eldest son of Patrick Byres of Tonley, Aberdeenshire, a Scottish laird of Jacobite principles and Catholic beliefs. Patrick fled to France after the rebellion of 1745, taking with him his son, then twelve years old. James was brought up in France, and served for a time in the French army in Ogilvy's regiment. In 1756 he returned to Britain, but two years later set out for Italy in order to become a painter. In February 1758 Robert Mylne reported that 'a student of painting one Mr. Byers' was on his way from Aberdeen to Rome, and his arrival in May was noted by Hayward. He became a pupil of Raphael Mengs, but did not prove to have sufficient talent to become a successful painter in oils, and after a short period as a miniaturist turned to architecture. This evidently suited him better, for in 1762 he won a prize in the *Concorso Clementino* at the Academy

178

of St. Luke. His design (for a palace) still survives in the Academy's archives. Despite this success (all the more notable because of his foreign nationality) Byres failed to establish an architectural practice, and although he designed buildings for several influential persons, scarcely any of them is known to have been carried out.[1] It is possible that he lacked the temperament to achieve success as a practical architect, but his preference for grandiose compositions in the late Roman baroque tradition of Fuga and Vanvitelli must have put him at a disadvantage in comparison with more up-to-date neo-classical architects such as Mylne and Chambers: certainly the vast columned halls which he designed for his British patrons were unlikely to commend themselves to a generation which was not yet inured to the cold austerities of the Greek Revival.

Instead, Byres became one of the most successful of the cicerones who displayed Rome to English milords on the Grand Tour. It was he who in 1764 spent several weeks showing Edward Gibbon the remains of the Imperial capital, and other celebrated Englishmen who employed him as a guide included Charles Towneley, Lord Clive, and the Dukes of Hamilton, Northumberland and Grafton. Like other 'antiquaries' Byres was an active dealer in antiquities and works of art, and the Portland Vase and Poussin's *Seven Sacraments* both passed through his hands. His explorations were not confined to Rome. In 1766 he toured southern Italy and Sicily in company with one of the Wilbrahams.[2] His journal, now in the National Library of Scotland, shows that they visited Pompei, Paestum and other Greek sites. Byres's special interest was, however, in Etruscan antiquities. In 1767 he attempted unsuccessfully to publish a work on the *Etruscan Antiquities of Corneto*. This pioneer venture failed to gain enough support, but the plates, engraved for Byres by Christopher Norton, were eventually published in 1842 by Frank Howard, as *Hypogaei, or Sepulchral Caverns of Tarquinia, by the late James Byres, Esq. of Tonley*. Although chiefly known as an authority on classical antiquity, Byres was consulted by Sir James Hall in connection with his *Essay on Gothic Architecture* of 1813, and

[1] In a letter from Father Thorpe to Lord Arundell written in June 1769 the writer refers to Byres's 'excellent plans of Architecture', of which he says 'two or three are now executing in different parts of Gt. Britain', but if so they have yet to be identified. In 1786 Lord Clive's accounts refer to the plan of the stone stairs at Walcot Park, Salop., being 'alter'd by Mr. Byers' (Salop. Record Office, Powis 552/9/290). The only executed designs by Byres so far noted are the two monuments listed below.

[2] Probably Roger Wilbraham of Nantwich (1743–1829), afterwards M.P. for Helston and Bodmin, and well known as an authority on Italian literature.

Bishop Percy was indebted to him for information about old Italian romances.

For over thirty years Byres was resident in Rome, where he lived close to the Piazza di Spagna. He is known, however, to have visited England in 1767; and in 1779 and again in 1783 he made the long journey from Rome to Scotland and back. His career as a cicerone was brought to an end by the French occupation of Italy in 1789. In the following year he withdrew to his Aberdeenshire seat of Tonley, where he lived on until his death in September 1817 at the age of 83.

Several portraits of Byres exist: an oil painting at the Accademia di S. Luca dated 1767 (the year before his election to the Academy); a paste medallion by Tassie in the Scottish National Portrait Gallery dated 1779; a group portrait in private possession showing him demonstrating a map of Rome to members of his family, illustrated in *Burlington Mag.* lxxxii (1943), 46; another family group in the collection of Mr. Brinsley Ford; a portrait by David Martin dated 1769, showing him holding a plan with the Colosseum in the background (in a private collection); an engraved portrait by J. Bogle dated 1782; a portrait by Raeburn painted at the age of 77 (see J. Greig, *Sir Henry Raeburn*, 1911, 40); and a sketch by C. H. Tatham *c.* 1810 illustrated in Weinreb & Breman's catalogue, *The Society of Dilettanti* (1968), item 120.

[A. J. M. Gill, *The Families of Moir and Byres*, 1835; Burke's *Landed Gentry*, *s.v.* 'Moir-Byres'; John Fleming, 'Some Roman Cicerones and Artist-Dealers', *Connoisseur Year-Book*, 1959, 24–6; Basil Skinner, *Scots in Italy in the Eighteenth Century* (National Gallery of Scotland, Edinburgh 1966); Damie Stillman, 'British Architects and Italian Architectural Competitions, 1758–1780', *Jnl. of the Society of Architectural Historians* (of America), xxxii, 1973, 51–4; *I disegni di architettura dell'Archivio storico dell'-Accademia di San Luca*, 1974, nos. 605–11; Brinsley Ford, 'James Byres', *Apollo* xcix, 1974, 446–60; W. T. Whitley, *Artists and their Friends in England 1700–1799* ii, 1938, 347–8; letters in National Library of Scotland, deposit 184; numerous references in Father Thorpe's letters to Lord Arundell of Wardour, now in the possession of Mr. R. J. R. Arundell and of Lord Clifford at Ugbrooke Park.]

EXECUTED DESIGNS

SLEAT CHURCH, SKYE, monument to Sir James Macdonald (d. 1766), 1768 [signed: Macdonald died in Rome in 1766, and in his *Tour to the Hebrides* Boswell records that the monument was made in Rome].

CLUNY, ABERDEENSHIRE, FRASER FAMILY MAUSOLEUM, 1808 [in his will dated 13 Aug. 1811,

Byres directs his trustees to erect a mausoleum at Tough, Aberdeenshire, 'exactly similar to the one I erected at Cluny for Miss Fraser'. This direction was cancelled in an eke or codicil dated 9 Sept. 1816].

UNEXECUTED DESIGNS

EDINBURGH, house in St. Andrew's Square for Sir Lawrence Dundas, 1768 (R.I.B.A. Drawings Coll.).

EDINBURGH, LIBRARY for COLLEGE OF PHYSICIANS, 1768 (College of Physicians, Edinburgh).

WYNNSTAY, DENBIGHSHIRE, mansion for Sir Watkin Williams-Wynn, 1770 (Wynn Estate Office, Denbigh: illustrated in *C. Life*, 23 March 1972, 689).

WARDOUR CASTLE, WILTS., designs for an altar for the 8th Lord Arundell, 1771 (Mr. R. J. R. Arundell).

HENHAM HALL, SUFFOLK, for Sir John Rous, cr. Earl of Stradbroke, 1774 (E. Suffolk Record Office) [Hugh Honour, 'James Byres's Designs for rebuilding Henham Hall', in *The Country Seat*, ed. Colvin & Harris, 1970].

CHARLEVILLE FOREST, TULLAMORE, CO. OFFALY, for the Earl of Charleville, 1789 (Belvedere House, Westmeath).

attributed: KING'S COLLEGE, ABERDEEN, undated (King's College Library, *ex inf.* Mr. David Walker).

Designs for two chimney-pieces, engraved as pl. xli of the edition of Vignola published in Rome in 1770 by Spampani and Antonini (see the preface).

BYROM, WILLIAM, was the son-in-law of John Hope of Liverpool (*q.v.*), and succeeded to his practice, which he later handed on to his nephew Samuel Rowland (*q.v.*). He designed the Ionic BRUNSWICK CHAPEL, MOSS STREET, LIVERPOOL, opened 1811, dem.; the UNITARIAN CHAPEL, RENSHAW STREET, LIVERPOOL, 1811, dem.; and a house for himself in PRIORY ROAD, EVERTON, 1812, dem. *c.* 1868. [*Builder* xxvii, 1869, 803–4; J. A. Picton, *Memorials of Liverpool* ii, 1875, 241, 368, 423.]

C

CABANEL, RUDOLPH, junior (*c.* 1763–1839), was a native of Aix-la-Chapelle (according to some accounts of Liège), who lived in England from his boyhood. He designed the stage of DRURY LANE THEATRE, 1793–4, burned 1809; the ROYAL CIRCUS, afterwards the SURREY THEATRE, BLACKFRIARS ROAD, 1805–6, erected under the superintendence of James Donaldson, burned

1865 (plate in J. Elmes, *Metropolitan Improvements*); and the ROYAL COBOURG THEATRE (afterwards the 'Old Vic'), WATERLOO ROAD, LAMBETH, 1816–18, reconstructed 1924. In 1794 he was consulted by George Saunders, the architect of the Theatre at Birmingham, 'respecting the Machinery of the Stage', and in 1814 he was employed to carry out alterations by the Proprietors [Minutes of the Proprietors in Birmingham Reference Library]. He was of 'an ingenious and inventive turn of mind', and invented a form of roof which bore his name, besides various mechanical appliances. [Obituary in *Civil Engineer and Architect's Jnl.* 1839 (ii), 118; *Gent's Mag.* 1839 (i), 329; *A.P.S.D.*; Brayley, *Surrey* iii, 399, v, 323.]

CAINE, Captain JOHN, was Master of the Tylers' and Bricklayers' Company in 1675–6 and 1697–8. In 1670–3 he built BREWERS' HALL, ADDLE LANE, LONDON, to the designs of one Whiting, the Company's surveyor [building accounts in Guildhall Library, MS. 5502]. He himself designed the TALLOW-CHANDLERS' HALL on DOWGATE HILL, which was built in 1671–3 under his direction [Guildhall Library, MS. 6153/4, Minutes of the Tallow-Chandlers Company; *Builder*, 10 Aug. 1917] (R.C.H.M., *London (City)*, 101–3).

CAIRNCROSS, HUGH (–1808) and GEORGE (–1819), practised in Edinburgh during the reign of George III. Their relationship is not certain, but they were probably father and son. Hugh Cairncross was a pupil or assistant of Robert Adam, under whom he acted as clerk of works at Culzean and Dalquharran Castles.[1] In December 1791 Adam appointed him to be clerk of works for the new University Building at Edinburgh in place of John Paterson, and he continued in this employment for at least ten years [Edinburgh City Archives, College Trust Minute Book, 15 Dec. 1791 and *passim*]. In 1797 he designed ARDGOWAN HOUSE, RENFREWSHIRE, for Sir John Shaw-Stewart, Bart., as stated in Neale's *Views of Seats* vi, 1823, and confirmed by the original drawings signed by Cairncross, now in the collection of Mr. Paul Mellon. In 1801 he was paid 'for measuring & valuing the work in the finishing of the English and Gaelic Churches at Inveraray' [I. G. Lindsay & Mary Cosh, *Inveraray and the Dukes of Argyll*, 1973, 394, n. 13], and in 1801 he submitted a design for rebuilding Falkirk Church which was not adopted owing to a dispute among the parishioners [S.R.O., GD 171/122]. In 1807 he designed NOS. 12–32 GAYFIELD SQUARE, EDINBURGH [S.R.O., Edinburgh Sasines]. Hugh

---

[1] At Culzean there is a design for a timber bridge signed 'H. Cairncross 1796'.

Cairncross died at Melrose on 21 July 1808 [*Scots Mag.* lxxi, 1808, 640]. In 1815 'Mr. Cairncross, son of Hugh Cairncross', provided the Lord Provost with a copy of Robert Adam's elevation for the west side of Edinburgh University [D. C. Horn in *University of Edinburgh Jnl.* xxiv, 1969–70, 39], and in the same year 'Mr. Cairncross, an Ordained Surveyor', measured work at the new Signet Library [S.R.O., Minutes of the Trustees for Public Buildings, E 343/2, p. 197]. 'Mr. Cairncross' was presumably George Cairncross, who died in January 1819, and was buried in the Greyfriars Cemetery [Register in New Register House, Edinburgh, f. 292].

CALVERT, JOHN, 'of Swansea, architect', advertised a 'patent slating' in the *Hereford Journal* in 1784. In 1779 a lawsuit between John Symmons of Slebech Hall, Pembrokeshire, and John Calvert over the latter's charges for building SLEBECH HALL was decided in Calvert's favour [*Hereford Jnl.*, 1779]. Drawings of friezes, etc., for this house are in the Shoppee album in the collection of the late Sir Albert Richardson at Ampthill (see Richardson & Eberlin, *Smaller English Houses of the Later Renaissance*, 1925, figs. 237–8). In the same album there are drawings, probably by the same hand, for a house 'intended for Mrs. Williams at Cadoxton near Neath'. As Calvert was evidently a builder as well as an architect, it cannot be regarded as certain that he was the author of these drawings.

CAMELFORD, LORD, *see* PITT, THOMAS

CAMERON, CHARLES (*c.* 1743–1812), was the son of Walter Cameron, a carpenter and builder of Scottish origin established in London. He was apprenticed to his father in 1760, but subsequently became a pupil of the architect Isaac Ware who, like his father, was a member of the London Carpenters' Company. When Ware died in 1766, Cameron decided to carry out a project which Ware had formed for a new edition of Lord Burlington's *Fabbriche Antiche*. Unlike Ware, however, Cameron proposed to go to Rome in person in order to correct and complete the imperfect drawings of the Roman baths by Palladio which Burlington had used in his publication. In 1767 at the Free Society of Artists exhibition he showed six 'proof prints of ancient Thermae, intended for the work which is publishing', and by 1768 he was busy examining and drawing the original structures in Rome. Here he appears to have claimed Jacobite sympathies and connections which had no basis in fact, but were calculated to gain him credit both in the Vatican and among influential exiles such as the Abbé Grant. Here too he appears to have come into contact with a leading figure in the formation of neo-classical taste, Charles Louis Clérisseau.

The drawings which Cameron eventually published in 1772 as *The Baths of the Romans explained and illustrated, with the Restorations of Palladio corrected and improved*, with identical English and French texts, was a careful and scholarly work which served, as it was intended to do, as a text-book of neo-classical ornament and design. It was dedicated to Lord Bute, whose patronage Cameron no doubt hoped to attract. New issues of the book appeared in 1774 and 1775.

Apart from the publication of his book, and the exhibition of some of the original drawings at the Society of Artists (1772), Cameron's activities between his return from Italy (apparently in 1769) and his departure to Russia (probably in 1778) are by no means clear. The authenticity of a portrait painted by Robert Hunter in Dublin in 1771 or 1773 is too doubtful to be taken as proof of a sojourn in Ireland. In 1774, when he applied for one of the new District Surveyorships in Middlesex he was not interviewed, 'being absent'. In 1775 he published two etchings, one of a silver vessel found in Rome, the other of a design for a shell-shaped vessel by Giulio Romano (Mellon Collection). Of his employment as an architect during this period the only evidence relates to a house in Hanover Square built by his father and others in 1770–4 for Jervoise Clarke. One of the bills is signed 'Charles Cameron Architectus' [Hants. Record Office, 6 M 59]. It is an account for marble supplied by the statuary mason Thomas Carter, and in 1774 Carter was one of those who sponsored Cameron's application for the District Surveyorship. Subsequent litigation between Jervoise Clarke and Walter Cameron over property in White Horse Street, Piccadilly, ended to the latter's disadvantage, and in his financial difficulties Walter Cameron sold a large number of books, prints, busts and pictures belonging to his son which the latter valued at £1500. Failing to recover them, Charles took proceedings against his father which resulted in the latter's imprisonment in the Fleet. This affair, and some story of Cameron's misbehaviour with one of Ware's daughters, were to be remembered to his disadvantage when in 1791 he was considered for honorary membership of the newly established Architects' Club, but was rejected by those 'who wished we might have only men of moral character and high reputation'.

By 1779 Cameron had begun a new life as architect to the Empress Catherine of Russia. How he obtained this spectacular preferment is not at present known. The Empress was of course an enthusiastic patron of artists from western Europe, and Cameron's book would have made his name known in architectural circles abroad. But all that is known for certain is that by 1778 the Empress had acquired the services of one whom she subsequently described as 'Mr. Cameron, écossais de nation, Jacobite de profession, grand dessinateur, nourri d'antiquités, connu par un livre sur les bains romains'. For the rest of his life Cameron was a Russian court architect. For the Empress Catherine he worked chiefly at the PALACE OF TSARSKOE SELO, nr. ST. PETERSBURG, to which he made extensive additions from 1779 onwards, including the Cold Baths, the Agate Pavilion, the colonnaded gallery known as the 'Cameron Gallery', the Empress's private apartments and the church of St. Sophia. Tsarskoe Selo occupied him for fifteen years. From 1782 to 1785 he was engaged on building the PALACE OF PAVLOVSK for the Grand Duke Paul, together with various subsidiary buildings, including a theatre, a town hall and some Grecian temples – the first of their kind in Russia. In the Crimea he carried out important alterations to the Empress's palace of BAKHTCHI-SERAI, probably in connection with her visit in 1787. In 1793 J. L. Bond (*q.v.*) exhibited at the Royal Academy a drawing of a triumphal arch 'to be erected in the Crimea by C. Cameron Esq., architect to the Empress of Russia'. This was probably the one at Bakhtchi-serai. In 1795 Cameron designed a gallery and triumphal arch to be erected at Gatchina, but Catherine died before either had been built.

After Catherine's death Cameron was dismissed by the Emperor Paul, who had already quarrelled with him over the cost of the works at Pavlovsk, and was determined to reverse all his mother's policies. Unemployed and deprived even of his house, Cameron was for a time in considerable financial difficulties. He may have found private employment in the provinces, and there is an unauthenticated story that he returned to England for a period. By 1800, however, he appears to have been back at Tsarskoe Selo, where soon afterwards he designed the Pavilion of the Three Graces and the Elizabeth Gallery for the Dowager Empress. In 1802 the new Emperor, Alexander I, gave him the largely honorary post of Architect to the Admiralty, and in 1803 he supervised the restoration of some rooms at Pavlovsk that had been damaged by fire. Exactly what he designed as Admiralty Architect is uncertain, but he appears to have carried out some works at the naval base of Cronstadt, and to have been concerned in the building of the Cathedral there. Early in 1812 he died at St. Petersburg, leaving a widow who later in the year dispersed his library and drawings by sale.

Cameron was an accomplished designer and decorator in a neo-classical style that has affinities with that of Robert Adam. Like Adam he had first-hand knowledge of the Roman sources of neo-classical ornament, and although he may well have seen some of Adam's early works in England, his style is sufficiently individual to exonerate him from the imputation of being merely an imitator. Like Adam he insisted on designing every detail of furniture in the buildings for which he was responsible. At Tsarkoe Selo he produced some of the most exquisitely elegant interiors in eighteenth-century Europe. His use of colour was particularly effective. In the Agate Pavilion he set red agate columns with gilt bronze capitals against green jasper walls to achieve a rich polychromatic effect. Although in some respects still a Palladian, Cameron was a pioneer of the Greek Revival in Russia, notably in the Greek Doric Temple of Friendship at Pavlovsk, designed c. 1780.

The main collection of Cameron's surviving drawings is in the Hermitage State Museum at Leningrad. Other drawings in Russian collections are listed on p. 27 of the Arts Council catalogue (see below). In the British Isles there is a design for a ceiling by Cameron in Sir John Soane's Museum (xliv, set 9, no. 15) and one small sketch in Glasgow University Library. A portrait by A. O. Orlovsky, dated 1809, is reproduced in the supplement to the Arts Council catalogue and in Isobel Rae's book.

[G. Loukomski, *Charles Cameron*, 1943; *Charles Cameron c. 1740–1812*, catalogue of the Arts Council Exhibition, 1967–8, with text by Tamara Talbot-Rice & A. A. Tait; Isobel Rae, *Charles Cameron, Architect to the Court of Russia*, 1971; Dorothy Stroud, *Henry Holland*, 1966, 135–6.]

CAMPBELL, COLEN (1676–1729), began life as a Scottish lawyer. He was the eldest son of Donald Campbell, a younger brother of Sir Hugh Campbell of Cawdor Castle in Nairnshire. Donald Campbell was the laird of Boghole and Urchany, two small Nairnshire estates which had been given to him by his brother. These estates Colen Campbell inherited at the age of four when his father died in 1680. Of his subsequent upbringing there appears to be no record, but he was reputed to have had 'a liberal education' and he may have been the Colin Campbell who graduated from Edinburgh University in July 1695. It is much less likely that he was the person of the same name who signed the Visitors' Book of Padua University in 1697.[1] But he must have been to Italy, for in 1715 or 1716, in a petition to King George I, he stated that he had 'studied Architecture here and abroad for several years'. What is certain is that in 1702 he was admitted to the Faculty of Advocates at Edinburgh, having 'past his tryalls as ane lawier' with the reputation

of being 'the best civilian that past since the Revolutione'. For the next few years he practised as a lawyer in Edinburgh. He was still described as 'Doctor of Laws' when he designed the Rolls House in London in 1717, but by then he was already established as an architectural designer and publicist.

Exactly how Campbell made the transition from law to architecture is not known. There are, however, indications that he was in some way associated with James Smith (c. 1645–1731, q.v.), whom he was to describe in *Vitruvius Britannicus* as 'the most experienced architect' in Scotland. Together with the drawings by Campbell himself formerly at Newby Hall and now in the R.I.B.A. Drawings Collection there are a number of drawings which are almost certainly by Smith (see below, p. 756). Some of these drawings relate to buildings known to have been designed by Smith, others were drawn for, or at least formed the basis of, plates in *Vitruvius Britannicus*, and others are studies on Palladian themes. None are dated, but as Smith was Campbell's senior by thirty years, there is a strong probability that Campbell was in some sense his pupil. Moreover, the presence of the Palladian studies, and the fact that Smith is known to have travelled in Italy, may suggest that he not only instructed Campbell in the practice of architecture, but also directed his attention to the architecture of Palladio. However this may be, it was as the propagandist of the Palladian movement in British architecture that Campbell made his name. Ostensibly *Vitruvius Britannicus* was a representative collection of plates of modern British architecture, both public and private, but it was a book with a message, and that message was the superiority of 'Antique Simplicity' over the 'affected and licentious' forms of the Baroque. The 'renowned Palladio' and the 'famous Inigo Jones' were held up for admiration, and the works (both authentic and reputed) of the latter figured prominently in the three folio volumes, each containing 100 plates, which Campbell published by subscription in 1715, 1717 and 1725. They were reissued in 1731 and an additional plate of Umberslade Hall, Warwickshire, is found in this edition of the third volume. There is a modern reprint by Benjamin Blom, with an index volume by Paul Breman (1972).

Besides asserting the virtues of neo-Palladian architecture precisely at the moment that the long ascendancy of Sir Christopher Wren was beginning to fail, *Vitruvius Britannicus* served to advertise Campbell's own ability as an architect. All his own works were illustrated, together with a number of unsolicited designs, tactfully addressed to prominent Whig magnates. The first volume was dedicated to George I, who acknowledged the compliment with two gifts, one of 30 guineas in 1717, the other of £30 in

---

[1] Mr. J. G. Dunbar kindly informs me that the Colin Campbell in question was probably an illegitimate son of the Earl of Breadalbane. This Colin Campbell was tutor to a gentleman named William Moncreiffe who signed the Visitors' Book at the same time.

1725. It was, however, to private rather than royal patronage that Campbell was chiefly indebted. As early as December 1708 he had made a first bid for architectural office. The post which he then coveted appears to have been the office of Master of Works in Scotland, previously held by Sir William Bruce and after him by James Smith. Nothing came of this attempt, and ten years elapsed before William Benson, having supplanted Wren as Surveyor-general of the Works, made Campbell Chief Clerk and Deputy Surveyor (Sept. 1718). Benson, though scandalously corrupt, had genuine architectural interests, and Campbell may possibly have had something to do with his country house in Wiltshire, an early essay in Jonesian revivalism dating from 1710 and duly illustrated in *Vitruvius Britannicus*. In July 1719 Campbell shared in Benson's disgrace, losing both his offices. His appointment in December 1719 as Architect to the Prince of Wales does not appear to have carried with it any salary and did not lead to any important commission. But in Lord Burlington he soon found a new patron for whom building was a ruling passion. It was probably the publication of *Vitruvius Britannicus* that had first roused Burlington's interest in architecture, and in 1719 he employed Campbell to remodel his town house in the Palladian style. Later Burlington dropped Campbell in favour of Kent and Flitcroft, but Campbell's subsequent patrons included such rich and influential men as Sir Robert Walpole, Henry Hoare, John Aislabie and the Earl of Pembroke. In 1726 he succeeded Vanbrugh as Surveyor of Greenwich Hospital, and in 1728 he published a revised version of Palladio's *First Book of Architecture*. This was reissued the following year as *The Five Orders of Architecture*, with the addition of 5 plates of his own designs at the end.

Campbell was taken ill in Norfolk in the summer of 1729, and died at his house in Brook Street, London, on or about 13 September. He was buried in the south cloister of Westminster Abbey without any memorial. His estate, which included two London houses, was reputed to be worth £12,000. It was disputed between his wife Jane and his sister Henrietta Grant, who claimed that though Jane lived with Campbell as his wife, they were never legally married. A portrait of Campbell is mentioned in Jane Campbell's will (1738), but its present location is unknown. The head of an architect which forms part of the plaster decoration of Compton Place, Sussex, is supposed (probably rightly) to represent Campbell.

Although he came late to architecture and died in middle age, Campbell was one of the oustanding figures in English eighteenth-century architecture. But for Benson's fall, Campbell, as his Deputy, might have led the Palladian revolution in the Office of Works. As it was, the only royal work that can be attributed to him is the new suite of State Apartments at Kensington Palace, and the evidence for this is by no means conclusive (see *History of the King's Works* v, 196). As a country-house architect, however, Campbell was responsible for some of the key buildings of the Palladian movement. At Wanstead he provided the Palladian answer to Blenheim and Castle Howard – a country house of the first rank conceived in strictly classical terms. It was, in Summerson's words, 'to prove a classic statement by which English country houses were influenced, directly or indirectly, for more than a century', and among its more obvious progeny were Wentworth Woodhouse, Prior Park and Nostell Priory. At Houghton he Palladianized the standard English country house of the late seventeenth century, accenting its principal features with a portico, Venetian windows and (in the engraved design) pedimented towers from Wilton, in a manner that was to be imitated at Lydiard Tregoze, Croome Court, Hagley, Newnham Paddox, Fisherwick and elsewhere. At Mereworth he built 'the first and closest of the four English reproductions of Palladio's Villa Capra at Vicenza', and at Newby and Stourhead he designed the first of a new generation of relatively small but highly finished country houses based on the model of the Palladian villa. Thus between 1715 and 1725 Campbell established the prototypes from which English Palladianism was to develop. When he died in 1729 the Palladian revolution was accomplished, and although it had complex origins, it was very largely to Campbell that it owed its most characteristic architectural forms.

In 1966 a large collection of drawings by Campbell was found in two Yorkshire country houses – Newby Hall and Studley Royal. These drawings, which appear to have belonged to Earl De Grey (*q.v.*), were in 1967 presented to the R.I.B.A. Drawings Collection by the Wates Foundation. A further collection of original drawings for *Vitruvius Britannicus*, formerly at Nostell Priory, was given to the same Collection in 1973. Both collections are described in a volume of the *R.I.B.A. Drawings Catalogue*.

[*A.P.S.D.*; H. E. Stutchbury, *The Architecture of Colen Campbell*, Manchester 1967; G. L. M. Goodfellow, 'Colin Campbell', *Arch. Rev.*, Aug. 1966, 145–6; *Arch. Rev.*, Feb. 1967, 94 (correspondence); G. L. M. Goodfellow, 'Colin Campbell's Last Years', *Burl. Mag.* cxi, April 1969, 185–191; H. M. Colvin, 'A Scottish Origin for English Palladianism?', with note by T. P. Connor on 'Colen Campbell Abroad', *Architectural History* xvii, 1974; *The History of the King's Works*, v, *passim*; Letters at Cawdor Castle, *ex inf.* Mr. J. G. Dunbar and Mr. T. P. Connor; Privy Purse Accounts of George I in Worcs. Record Office; Register of Warrants of George, Prince of Wales (B.M., Add. MS. 24387, f. 76);

Bodleian Library, MS. Rawlinson D. 923, f. 34 (dispute over estate); will (P.C.C. 243 ABBOTT).]

GLASGOW, SHAWFIELD MANSION, for Daniel Campbell, M.P., 1711–12; dem. 1792 [*Vitruvius Britannicus* ii, pl. 51; G. L. M. Goodfellow, 'Colin Campbell's Shawfield Mansion in Glasgow', *Jnl. of the Society of Architectural Historians* xxiii, 1964].

WANSTEAD HOUSE, ESSEX, for Sir Richard Child, cr. Earl of Tylney, *c.* 1714–20; dem. 1824 [*Vitruvius Britannicus* i, pls. 21–2 (the first design), 23–6 (the second design, more or less as executed); iii, pls. 39–41 (the third design, showing unexecuted additions)]. For views of the house as built see a sheet of engravings by Rocque dated 1735, Watts's *Seats* (1783) and Angus's *Seats* (1800). For the gardens see I. Dunlop & Fiske Kimball in *C. Life*, 28 July 1950. Some fittings are now at Wanstead House, Cambridge, and there are two chimney-pieces at Chillingham Castle, Northumberland.

CHESTER-LE-STREET, CO. DURHAM, house for John Hedworth, 1716, probably not built [*Vitruvius Britannicus* ii, pl. 88]. A detailed but undated 'Explanation' by Vanbrugh of his design for a house for Mr. Hedworth was sold at Sotheby's on 24–5 Jan. 1955 (lot 459), and may represent a rival scheme. The former seat of the Hedworth family at Harraton Hall, nr. Chester-le-Street, had passed by marriage to the Lambtons in 1688, and John Hedworth's branch of the family lived at the house called Chester Deanery.

BEVERLEY, YORKS. (E.R.), house in Eastgate for Sir Charles Hotham, Bart., 1716–17; dem. *c.* 1760 [*Vitruvius Britannicus* ii, pl. 87; building accounts among Hotham papers in E. Riding Record Office]. A sketch of the house in Bodleian, Gough Maps 229, f. 273, shows that Campbell's design was not exactly followed in execution: in particular the rusticated arches linking the wings to the centre were omitted.

LONDON, THE ROLLS HOUSE, CHANCERY LANE, 1717–24; dem. 1895–6 [*Vitruvius Britannicus* iii, pls. 44–5; *History of the King's Works* v, 358] (chimney-pieces illustrated in *Arch. Rev.*. xlviii, 1920, 23, 76).

EBBERSTON LODGE, nr. SCARBOROUGH, YORKS. (N.R.), for William Thompson (of Humbleton), 1718 [*Vitruvius Britannicus* iii, pl. 47] (S. D. Kitson in *Arch. Rev.* xxvi, 1909, 231; Arthur Oswald in *C. Life*, 7–14 Oct. 1954).

LONDON, BURLINGTON HOUSE, PICCADILLY, remodelled the front and designed the gateway to Piccadilly for the 3rd Earl of Burlington, 1718–19; gateway dem. and front remodelled by E. M. Barry 1868 [*Vitruvius Britannicus* iii, pls. 22–5; *Survey of London* xxxii, 390–429 and illustrations].

LONDON, NOS. 31, 32, 33 and 34 OLD BURLINGTON STREET, 1718–23 [*Survey of London* xxxii, 508–17 and illustrations].

LONDON, CHANCERY LANE, nine houses on the Rolls Estate for Sir Joseph Jekyll, Master of the Rolls, 1719; dem. [*History of the King's Works* v, 358].

LONDON, THE BURLINGTON SCHOOL FOR GIRLS, BOYLE STREET, 1719–21; dem. 1937. Campbell was involved in this building as the representative of Lord Burlington, but how far (if at all) he was responsible for the design is not clear [*Survey of London* xxxii, 541–2].

WIMBLEDON, SURREY. In 1720 Colen Campbell and John Gould received £70 as 'overseers' of a new house here for Sir Theodore Janssen, Bart., which was unfinished at the seizure of his estates and was demolished soon afterwards [*The Particulars and Inventories of the Estates of the Late . . . Directors of the South-Sea Company*, 1721, 43–4; *V.C.H. Surrey* iv, 123].

LONDON, LEICESTER HOUSE, LEICESTER SQUARE, minor alterations for George, Prince of Wales, 1720–4; dem. 1792 [*Survey of London* xxxiv, 447].

NEWBY (now BALDERSBY) PARK, YORKS. (N.R.), for Sir William Robinson, Bart., 1720–8; interior rebuilt after fire in 1902 [*Vitruvius Britannicus* iii, pl. 46; Lindsay Boynton in *The Country Seat*, ed. Colvin & Harris, 1970, 97–105].

STOURHEAD, WILTS., for Henry Hoare, *c.* 1720–4; wings added 1793–5; portico (to Campbell's original design) 1841; centre restored after fire in 1902 [*Vitruvius Britannicus* iii, pls. 41–3; K. Woodbridge, *Landscape and Antiquity*, 1970, chap. 1] (C. Hussey, *English Country Houses, Mid Georgian*, 1956, 234–8).

HOUGHTON HALL, NORFOLK, for Sir Robert Walpole, begun 1722 to Campbell's designs under the supervision of T. Ripley, and completed 1735 with some modifications (*e.g.* to the towers by Gibbs and to the interior by Kent) [*Vitruvius Britannicus* iii, pls. 27–34] (Isaac Ware, *The Plans, Elevations and Sections of Houghton*, 1735; *C. Life*, 1, 8, 15, 22 Jan. 1921; H. A. Tipping, *English Homes, Period V*, vol. i, 1921, 67–110; C. Hussey, *English Country Houses, Early Georgian*, 1955, 72–86).

MEREWORTH CASTLE, KENT, for the Hon. John Fane, afterwards 7th Earl of Westmorland, *c.* 1722–5 [*Vitruvius Britannicus* iii, pls. 35–8]. The detached wings were built *c.* 1740. (*C. Life*, 12, 19, 26 June 1920; H. A. Tipping, *English Homes, Period V*, vol. i, 1921, 39–66; C. Hussey, *English Country Houses, Early Georgian*, 1955, 58–65).

LONDON, PEMBROKE HOUSE, WHITEHALL, for Henry Herbert, afterwards 9th Earl of Pembroke, 1724; rebuilt 1757; dem. 1913 [*Vitruvius Britannicus* iii, pl. 48; *Survey of London* xiii, 167–75]. An original elevation, dated

August 1723, is in the Lister Collection in the Treasury Library, Whitehall, no. 52b. For an alternative design by William Dickinson dated 1723 see *Wren Soc.* xvii, pl. xlviii.

NOTTINGHAM, house in Stoney Street (north side of St. Mary's Churchyard), for John Plumptre, M.P., 1724; dem. 1853 [*Vitruvius Britannicus* iii, pl. 55]. For drawings connected with this house in Nottingham City Library see Stutchbury, *op. cit.*, Appendix vi.

HALL BARN, nr. BEACONSFIELD, BUCKS., the GREAT ROOM (Garden House) for Edmund Waller, 1724; largely destroyed by fire *c.* 1840, but doorway and windows survive reset [*Vitruvius Britannicus* iii, pls. 49–50] (*C. Life*, 27 March 1942). For Waller's relationship to John Aislabie of Studley Royal see R. Sedgwick, *The House of Commons 1715–54* ii, 1970, 505–6.

WAVERLEY ABBEY, SURREY, for John Aislabie, *c.* 1725; wings added by T. O. Hunter *c.* 1750; centre altered or rebuilt by Sir Robert Rich *c.* 1780; further alterations after fire in 1833 [R. Pococke, *Travels through England* (Camden Soc. 1889), ii, 163; *The Torrington Diaries*, ed. C. B. Andrews, i, 1934, 75]. Campbell's building is shown in the background of S. & N. Buck's engraving of the ruins of Waverley Abbey, dated 1737.

COMPTON PLACE, EASTBOURNE, SUSSEX, reconstructed for Sir Spencer Compton, cr. Lord (later Earl of) Wilmington, 1726–7 [H. A. Tipping, *English Homes, Period V*, vol. i, 134–7; C. Hussey, *English Country Houses, Early Georgian*, 1955, 87–96; G. L. M. Goodfellow in *Burl. Mag.* cxi, April 1969, 186–9].

LONDON, NOS. 76 and 78 BROOK STREET, 1726. No. 76, which survives, was Campbell's own house, and the interiors are illustrated in his *Five Orders of Architecture* (1729) [G. L. M. Goodfellow in *Burl. Mag.* cxi, April 1969, 185–6].

HACKNEY, MIDDLESEX, house for Stamp Brooksbank, 1728; dem. *c.* 1790 [plates in Campbell's *Five Orders of Architecture*, 1729] (view in W. Robinson, *History of Hackney*, 1842, 117).

STUDLEY ROYAL, YORKS. (W.R.), designs and architectural advice for John Aislabie, *c.* 1729. Campbell is known to have given advice about the quadrangular Palladian stables just before his death in 1729, and the Banqueting House can probably be attributed to him on stylistic grounds [G. W. Beard in *C. Life* 10 Aug. 1961; G. L. M. Goodfellow in *Burl. Mag.* cxi, April 1969, 187–9].

UNEXECUTED DESIGNS

Included in *Vitruvius Britannicus* are various designs for houses based on Palladian sources identified in Stutchbury, *op. cit.*, Appendix V; a design for a large and monumental domed church in Lincoln's Inn Fields, made 'at the desire of some Persons of Quality and Distinction' in 1712 (i, pls. 8–9); and a design for Westminster Bridge, *c.* 1722 (iii, pl. 56).

In 1712 Campbell is recorded to have submitted designs for churches to the Commissioners for building Fifty New Churches (Minutes of the Commissioners in Lambeth Palace Library, i, pp. 67–8). These may possibly be the church designs now in the R.I.B.A. Collection.

Unexecuted projects for country houses include a pair of plans (based on Palladio's Villa Emo) for ARDKINGLAS HOUSE, ARGYLLSHIRE, preserved at Inveraray Castle, a scheme for rebuilding GOODWOOD HOUSE, SUSSEX, for the 2nd Duke of Richmond, 1724 (*Vitruvius Britannicus* iii, pls. 53–4), and designs for LOWTHER CASTLE, WESTMORLAND, in the Collection of Mr. Paul Mellon and at the R.I.B.A.

An important design for a uniform palatial treatment of 'seven new intended Houses on the East Side of Grosvenor Sqr.' is represented by an engraved plan and elevation, signed and dated 1725, in the volume of prints in the Gibbs Collection at the Ashmolean Museum, Oxford.

CAMPBELL, DUGAL (–1757) was a military engineer by profession. His recorded career begins in 1734, when he became a Sub-Engineer in the Civil Branch of the Ordnance. In 1739 he was appointed clerk of works to the Ordnance establishment in the Tower of London. In 1742 he was promoted to the rank of Engineer Extraordinary, in 1744 to that of Engineer in Ordinary, and in 1757 to that of Major, with the appointment of Chief Engineer in North America. He took part in the campaign against the Jacobites in Scotland in 1745–6, and served in Flanders in 1746–7 and at Louisbourg in Nova Scotia in 1757. He died in October of that year while on passage from Halifax to New York. [T. W. J. Conolly, *Roll of Officers of the Corps of Royal Engineers from 1660 to 1898*, Chatham 1898; P.R.O., WO 54/204, pp. 120, 153; *Scots Mag.* xix, 1757, 614.]

Dugal Campbell's official work for the Ordnance is represented by drawings in the Public Record Office, the Register House at Edinburgh and the National Library of Scotland, including designs for works at EDINBURGH CASTLE 1742, FORT WILLIAM 1744–6 and THE TOWER OF LONDON [P.R.O., Works 31/129–131, etc.; National Library of Scotland, Z2/4a, 6a, 28, 30a]. In 1743 he gave evidence about William Adam's contracts with the Ordnance in the lawsuit between Adam and Lord Braco [*Depositions in Adam v. Braco*, 1743, 26] and in 1752 he made a report on the Irish Barracks in the Tower which is now in the British Museum (*King's Maps* xxiv, 23, m. 2). In the Duke of Argyll's archives there is a set of drawings by him for rebuilding INVERARAY CASTLE 'in the Castle stile', that is as a polygonal fort, complete with fosse and covered way. This remarkable design, one of the earliest of its kind, must have been made before the 3rd Duke began to build the castle to the designs of Roger Morris in 1746 [I. G. Lindsay & Mary Cosh, *Inveraray and the Dukes of Argyll*, 1973, 45 and fig. 19]. In the Public Library at Northampton there is a drawing signed by Dugal Campbell showing LYVEDEN NEW BUILD (one of the eccentric structures built by Sir Thomas Tresham of Rushton *c.* 1600) completed with a cupola as a house for the titular 'Lord Goreing', *i.e.* Sir Charles Goring of Highden, Sussex.

CAMPLING, JAMES (*c.* 1741–), of Marylebone, exhibited at the Free Society of Artists from 1770 to 1774, including 'The principal front of a building now erecting for a gentleman in Russia' (1772), and a design for a church at Marylebone (1774). In 1774 he was an unsuccessful candidate for a district surveyorship. He was then 33 years of age. [Middlesex County Records, General Orders No. 10, f. 15 *et seq.*]

CANTWELL, JOSEPH (*c.* 1750–1828), was apprenticed in 1764 to Robert Palmer, a tiler and bricklayer of London [Guildhall Library, index to Apprenticeship Registers in P.R.O.]. He practised chiefly as a surveyor, and held one of the London District Surveyorships. He 'realised a handsome fortune, and retired from practice many years before his death'. In 1792 he founded the Surveyors' Club, of which he was President in 1797. In 1807–8 he was Master of the Tylers' and Bricklayers' Company. He died at Stanwell on 7 August 1828, in his 79th year, leaving his house in Great Marlborough Street, London, to his son Robert (*q.v.*). [J. W. Penfold, *A Century of Surveyors*, 1892, 17; *Gent's Mag.* 1828 (ii), 189; *Survey of London* xxxvi, 108–110, 157 n.; *Minutes of Proceedings of the Institution of Civil Engineers* xix, 1859–60, 186; will in P.C.C. 576 SUTTON.]

CANTWELL, ROBERT (*c.* 1792–1858), was the son of Joseph Cantwell (*q.v.*), and continued to occupy his father's house at 20 Great Marlborough Street, London, for many years, though he was living in Wimpole Street at the time of his death on 6 October 1858, aged 66 [*Gent's Mag.*, N.S. v, 1858, 541]. Like his father, he had an extensive practice as a surveyor, and was much employed as an arbitrator. According to his obituary in the *Minutes of Proceedings* of the Institution of Civil Engineers (of which he became an Associate Member in 1841) he 'did not hold any public appointments, nor did he execute any important works'. He did, however, design ROYAL CRESCENT on the Norland Estate in KENS-

INGTON, a drawing of which he exhibited at the R.A. in 1839. This large crescent of stuccoed houses with Doric porches and cast-iron balconies is described and illustrated in *Survey of London* xxxvii, where Cantwell's responsibility for houses on the adjoining Ladbroke Estate, notably NOS. 2–6 and 24–28 HOLLAND PARK AVENUE and 1–4 LADBROKE TERRACE, is discussed.

Cantwell appears to have had some connection with J. B. Papworth (*q.v.*), for a drawing for the Ladbroke Terrace houses is among the latter's drawings in the R.I.B.A. Collection, and in 1847 Cantwell was among those who presented a silver inkstand to Papworth on his retirement [Wyatt Papworth, *J. B. Papworth*, 1879, 94]. The Drawings Collection also contains designs by Papworth for alterations to the Marquis Bonneval's château, nr. Rouen in Normandy, marked 'for Mr. Cantwell to build'. Papworth's diary shows that these were made in 1826.

CAPON, WILLIAM (1757–1827), architectural draughtsman, was the son of a portrait-painter at Norwich. At first he studied under his father, but an interest in architecture led to him becoming a pupil of Michael Novosielski (*q.v.*), whom he assisted in the erection of the Italian Opera House in the Haymarket (1790–1). As Novosielski's assistant he learned the art of theatrical scene-painting which was to be his main occupation in life. He also designed the theatre 'and some other buildings' at Ranelagh Gardens. In 1780 he 'erected a small theatre in the court adjoining Wells Street, Oxford Street', and in 1794 he designed a theatre for Lord Aldborough at Belan House, Co. Kildare. On the completion of the Drury Lane Theatre in 1794 he was engaged by Kemble as scene-painter, and produced many elaborate architectural sets in which considerable antiquarian knowledge was displayed. He excelled in medieval scenes, such as an 'Anglo-Norman hall' for *Hamlet*, or (for *Jane Shore*) 'a correct and beautiful restoration of the Council Chamber of Crosby House'. All his Drury Lane sets were destroyed in the fire of 1809, but illustrations of two characteristic scenes, from surviving drawings by Capon now at Stratford, will be found in the *Magazine of Art* xviii (1894–5). He also worked for some of the provincial theatres, notably for the Bath Theatre from 1805 onwards.

In his spare time Capon was an enthusiastic topographical and antiquarian artist. For over thirty years he lived in Westminster, and, like his friend John Carter (*q.v.*), made the antiquities of the Palace and Abbey his special study. All his more important drawings were carefully coloured, and he was one of the first antiquarian draughtsmen to use colour in order to distinguish the work of one period from that of another (cf. the perspective drawing of the half-demolished

Painted Chamber reproduced as the frontispiece to vol. i of the *History of the King's Works*). The key to his work on the Palace of Westminster was his great coloured ground-plan, which formed the basis of an engraved plan published by the Society of Antiquaries in 1828. Many of his drawings are now in the Local History Collection of Westminster City Library. Some of them were reproduced by the London Topographical Society in 1923–4 as *Views of Westminster by William Capon*, and others by H. M. Colvin in 'Views of the Old Palace of Westminster', *Architectural History* ix, 1966.

At one time Capon hoped to become Surveyor to Westminster Abbey, but this ambition was never realized. In June 1804 he was appointed Architectural Draughtsman to the Duke of York. He was a regular exhibitor at the Royal Academy from 1788 onwards, showing chiefly architectural and topographical drawings. He also exhibited at the Society of Artists, the British Institution and the Society of British Artists. Though Gothic architecture was his main interest, his last work of importance is said to have been a design for a Doric church. He died on 26 September 1827, aged 70. His portrait by W. Bone is engraved in *Gent's Mag.* xcviii (i), 1828, 105. It shows in the background his design for a pyramidal building 205 feet high, to be erected on Shooter's Hill, Kent, as a 'national monument'. There is a copy of the sale catalogue of his drawings, etc., in the Bodleian Library (Douce CC. 284).

[*Gent's Mag.* 1827 (ii), 374–7; 1828 (i), 105–7; 1829 (i), 227; *D.N.B.*; W. J. Lawrence, 'Art in the Theatre. The Pioneers of Modern English Stage Mounting: William Capon', *Magazine of Art* xviii, 1894–5, 289–92.]

CARLINE, JOHN (1761–1835), was a mason and architect of Shrewsbury. His father, John Carline I (1730–1793), was a native of Lincoln, where his family is commemorated in Carline Road (formerly Carline Place). His mother was the daughter of John Hayward, another Lincoln mason (see p. 409). John Carline I moved to Shrewsbury, where he became foreman of the masons who built the English Bridge to the designs of John Gwynn between 1769 and 1774.

John Carline II had a flourishing business as an architect, builder and statuary mason. He lived in the Abbey Foregate in a house which he built for himself on the site of the Technical College. For some time he was in partnership with a bricklayer named John Tilley, but Tilley appears to have died in 1796, and in 1797 Carline entered into a new partnership with Tilley's stepson Henry Linell.

In 1790–2 Carline and Tilley built MONTFORD BRIDGE, SALOP., to the designs of Telford, and after the flood of 1795 they were again employed by Telford to rebuild the bridge over the Rea

Brook at COLEHAM HEAD, SHREWSBURY. In 1793–5, however, it was to their own designs that they built the important WELSH BRIDGE at SHREWSBURY.

Many monuments, often in the Gothic style, were executed by John Carline and his sons, and the lions at the base of Lord Hill's Column, erected in 1814–16, were carved by the firm. An order-book, now in the County Record Office (Longueville Collection, Box 20), gives details of a number of tombstones, chimney-pieces and other jobs carried out in the years 1800–2.

John Carline was the father of John Carline III, architect (*q.v.*), Thomas Carline, sculptor (1799–1868), and of Jane Carline, wife of the Shrewsbury artist Philip Corbet. Thomas, after a period of initial success, failed to maintain his early reputation as a sculptor, and ended his life as Surveyor of Bridges to the North Riding of Yorkshire.

[R. Carline, 'Corbet and the Carlines – Shrewsbury Painters, Sculptors and Architects of the Early 19th. Century', *Shropshire Magazine*, March 1958; *Catalogue of an Exhibition of Works of the Corbet and Carline Families* (Shrewsbury Art Gallery, 1958); J. L. Hobbs, 'Carlines – Architects, Builders and Sculptors', *Shropshire Magazine*, March 1960; A. W. Ward, *The Bridges of Shrewsbury*, 1935, 89–90, 144–9; R. Gunnis, *Dictionary of British Sculptors 1660–1851*, revised ed. 1968.]

BORETON FARM-HOUSE, CONDOVER, SALOP., 1782 [*V.C.H. Salop.* viii, 35].

ADDERLEY HALL, SALOP., built portico of new house for Sir Corbet Corbet, Bart., 1787–8; dem. 1877. The evidence [Shropshire Record Office, 327/Box 269, letter of 5 Sept. 1787] does not make it clear by whom the house was designed.

SHREWSBURY, designed and built THE WELSH BRIDGE, 1793–5 [A. W. Ward, *The Bridges of Shrewsbury*, 1935, 144–9].

SHREWSBURY, designed and built ST. ALKMUND'S CHURCH, 1794–5, Gothic [D. H. S. Cranage, *Churches of Shropshire* vi, 895].

WROCKWARDINE CHURCH, SALOP. repairs, etc., 1808 [D. H. S. Cranage, *Churches of Shropshire* ii, 647].

PRADOE, SALOP., designed and built dining-room for the Hon. Thomas Kenyon, 1810 [plan, specification and estimate in scrap-book at Pradoe, *ex inf.* Shropshire Record Office].

SHADWELL HALL, nr. CLUN, SALOP., designed for William Botfield, 1812 [Shropshire Record Office, Garnett-Botfield Collection, 539].

TOTTERTON HALL, SALOP., alterations for the Rev. J. B. Bright, 1814 [Shropshire Record Office, 807–612].

PELLWALL HOUSE, MARKET DRAYTON, STAFFS., built new house for Purney Sillitoe to the designs of Sir John Soane, 1822–8 [D. Stroud, *The Architecture of John Soane*, 1961, 133].

SHREWSBURY, CLAREMONT BUILDINGS (a terrace) and CARLINE'S FIELDS (cottages) [Ward, 90].

CARLINE, JOHN (1792–1862), was the son and successor of John Carline II (*q.v.*). Like his father, he combined the practice of architecture with the business of a builder and monumental mason. He was prominent in municipal life as a Conservative councillor, and was also interested in ecclesiology and archaeology. Although most of his works are in the Romanesque or Gothic styles, he is said to have made copies of the Elgin Marbles which were later in Shrewsbury Museum, and the monument to Sir John Hill (d. 1824) in Prees Church by his brother Thomas is in a style 'much influenced by the Elgin marbles' (Pevsner).

In about 1835 he took a builder named Richard Dodson into partnership, but Dodson withdrew in 1845. About this time Carline lost heavily over the restoration of Hereford Cathedral, which he contracted to carry out under the direction of L. N. Cottingham (*q.v.*), and his financial position was aggravated by a large sum of money owed to him by his brother Thomas. Discouraged by these difficulties he went to Lincoln to live with his brother Richard, a successful solicitor. The business at Shrewsbury was carried on for a time by his clerk, James Hewitt, but was eventually wound up. Carline died at Lincoln in 1862. His unexecuted designs for rebuilding Skellingthorpe Church, Lincs., dated 1853, are in the local collection in Lincoln Public Library. [For sources see J. Carline (1761–1835).]

All the following buildings appear to be by John Carline III, but some uncertainty arises over the authorship of those built during the lifetime of his father (d. 1835).

SHREWSBURY, THE DRAPERS' ALMSHOUSES, 1825, Gothic [H. Pidgeon, *Memorials of Shrewsbury*, 2nd ed. 1851, 187].

SHREWSBURY, ST. MICHAEL'S CHURCH, 1829–30, Gothic; chancel 1873–4 [*Gent's Mag.* 1831 (i), 596].

SHREWSBURY, ST. MARY'S AND ST. MICHAEL'S PAROCHIAL SCHOOLS, ABBEY FOREGATE, 1832; enlarged 1840; Gothic [Pidgeon, *op. cit.*, 194].

SHREWSBURY, ST. MARY'S CHURCH, stone screen at west end of nave, 1834 (destroyed 1894) and large Gothic monument to Rev. J. B. Blakeway (d. 1826) [Pidgeon, *op. cit.*, 72–3, 82].

GRINSHILL CHURCH, SALOP., 1839–40; neo-Norman [I.C.B.S.]

ALBRIGHTON CHURCH, SALOP., 1840–1; neo-Norman [signed drawings in Shrewsbury School archives, Box A, bundle 8, *ex inf.* Mr. J. B. Lawson].

SHREWSBURY ABBEY CHURCH, neo-Norman altar-

screen, *c.* 1840; removed 1886 [Pidgeon, *op. cit.*, 115].

SHREWSBURY, ST. GILES' CHURCH, pulpit, pews, etc., *c.* 1840 [Pidgeon, *op. cit.*, 126].

CARLOW, SAMUEL STEWART, exhibited a 'design for a church' and a 'view of a gatekeeper's lodge' at the R.A. in 1837. He was a member of the Institute of British Architects in 1842. His name ceases to appear in the London Post Office Directory in 1847/8.

CARMICHAEL, MICHAEL, was an Argyllshire builder-architect of the reign of George III. He was employed as a builder at Inveraray Castle in 1799–1800 [Duke of Argyll's archives, General Accounts, etc.], but the only building he is known to have designed is the very simple church at COLONSAY, 1802 [J. de Vere Loder, *Colonsay and Oronsay*, Edinburgh 1935, 166].

CARR, HENRY (*c.* 1772–1828), was the son of James Carr (*q.v.*) and continued his practice in Clerkenwell, where he owned a number of houses in St. James' Street and Walk. He was elected a member of the Surveyors' Club in 1801 and died on 3 March 1828, aged 56. As Surveyor to the Salters' Company Carr designed SALTERS' HALL, ST. SWITHIN'S LANE, LONDON, 1823–7; dem. 1951. A competition was held in 1821, the first three prizes being awarded to J. C. Mead, Francis Pouget and Maximilian Godefroy (*qq.v.*). Carr then incorporated features from all three designs in a final version of his own which was executed in 1823–7. The attribution to George Smith by James Elmes in his *Metropolitan Improvements* appears to be without foundation. [*A.P.S.D.*; R. L. Alexander, *The Architecture of Maximilian Godefroy*, Baltimore 1974, 163–4; will P.C.C. 133 SUTTON.]

CARR, JAMES (*c.* 1742–1821), was an architect and builder of Clerkenwell, where he lived in a house (No. 12) on the north side of Albemarle Street. He was presumably the James Carr who was President of the Surveyors' Club in 1798. His only known architectural works are ST. JAMES'S CHURCH, CLERKENWELL, 1788–92, a competent but old-fashioned design with a steeple in the Gibbs tradition, and NEWCASTLE PLACE, CLERKENWELL, a terrace of brick houses which he built as a speculation *c.* 1793 [W. J. Pinks, *History of Clerkenwell*, ed. Wood, 1881, 51, 97, 268]. In 1803 he repaired the church of ST. MARTIN ORGAR in the City (dem. 1820) [Guildhall Library, MS. 975].

Carr retired to Cheshunt in Hertfordshire, where he is commemorated by a monument which records his death on 12 January 1821, aged 79 [J. E. Cussans, *History of Hertfordshire* ii, 1878, 228]. He was the father of Henry Carr (*q.v.*)

and Edmund Aikin and Samuel Ware were his pupils.

CARR, JOHN (1723–1807), was for more than half a century the principal architect practising in Yorkshire and the north of England. Although largely self-taught, and without the advantages either of a regular architectural education or of foreign travel, Carr became one of the most competent and successful of Georgian architects. His practice was based on the patronage of the Yorkshire gentry, and country houses formed the bulk of his work. 'It was', as T. D. Whitaker wrote, to Carr's 'good taste' that 'so many families in the county of York are indebted for the comforts and elegancies of their dwellings.' Like his rival James Paine he assimilated in early life the conventions of the Palladian style propagated by Lord Burlington, to which he remained more or less faithful throughout his life. As a young man he had come into contact with Lord Burlington himself over the building of Kirby Hall, and favourite features in Carr's repertoire such as octangular bays and Serlian windows can be attributed to Burlington's influence. The basically Palladian character of Carr's architecture was, however, modified in his earlier works by the rich rococo stucco-work which was provided for him by the York plasterers, and in his later ones by highly accomplished imitations of the elegant neo-classical interiors introduced by Robert Adam. Of the earlier style Heath Hall is perhaps the finest example; of the latter, the Assembly Room in the Crescent at Buxton. Carr could also Gothicize when the occasion required – notably at Raby Castle in Durham, where he designed a dramatic Gothic hall, and at Grimston Garth, where he provided his client with a charmingly romantic occasional residence in the form of a triangular tower with a central hexagonal dining-room.

Neither as a provincial representative of the Palladian school, nor as an imitator of Robert Adam, did Carr ever display the inventiveness of genius: but he handled the formulae of both styles with an assurance which rarely fails to please, and his buildings always exemplify the very best in Georgian craftsmanship. It was, no doubt, Carr's proved competence as a designer, and known reliability as a practical architect, that ensured his success with the Yorkshire gentry. But his election to the London Architects' Club (of which he was the only provincial member), and the number of his works that figure both in Woolfe and Gandon's *Vitruvius Britannicus* (vols. iv and v) and in Richardson's *New Vitruvius Britannicus*, shows that he was also known and respected in more sophisticated circles.

John Carr was a stone-mason by training. His father Robert (1697–1760), his grandfather John (1668–1736), and his great-grandfather Robert Carr (1644–1689) all worked as masons at Horbury, nr. Wakefield, where they owned quarries. Robert Carr, John's father, acted as one of the two Surveyors of Bridges to the West Riding. On his monumental inscription he is dignified with the name of 'Architect', and like other master workmen of his day, he was no doubt capable of making simple architectural designs. The fact that his wife, Rose Lascelles, was the daughter of a gentleman[1] indicates a modest degree of social advancement. John (born in May 1723) was the eldest of his six sons. Educated at the village school, he was probably apprenticed to his father, whom he certainly assisted in the quarry, on buildings for whose masonry the elder Carr had contracted, and in making (1752–3) a survey of the county bridges for the West Riding magistrates. He does not appear to have received any more formal instruction in architecture than was afforded by this practical experience, supplemented by standard manuals such as Morris's *Select Architecture*, Carr's own copy of which is now in Sir John Soane's Museum. Until the death of the elder Carr in 1760 John and his father frequently worked together, but by about 1750 John had already begun to develop an architectural practice. Huthwaite Hall was built to his designs in 1748, and several other houses followed during the next few years. In 1752 the Corporation of York voted to pay £88 to Carr for erecting an ornamental building over the Pikeing Wellhead. On its completion he was (1757) admitted a freeman of the city, in which he had by now taken up residence. Meanwhile he had achieved local celebrity by submitting a design for the grandstand on Knavesmire racecourse which was chosen in preference to one made by James Paine, hitherto the leading architect in the north of England. This work, which was much admired, brought Carr to the notice of the gentry attending the York races. Many private commissions followed, and for the next forty years Carr was busy designing country houses and public buildings throughout the northern counties. In 1760 he succeeded his father as one of the two Surveyors of Bridges for the West Riding, but resigned in 1773 soon after his appointment (1772) to the better-paid post of Surveyor of Bridges to the North Riding.

Despite the extent of his business, Carr found time to play a part in the municipal life of York. In 1766 he was appointed one of the city chamberlains, and in the following year he was elected one of the sheriffs of the city, but paid the usual fine to be excused from serving. In 1769

---

[1] Though her father, John Lascelles of Norton-in-the-Clay, was described as 'gentleman', there is apparently no evidence that he was related to the Harewood Lascelles (Mary Mauchline, *Harewood House*, 1974, 175–6, n. 56).

he was elected an alderman, and in 1770 served as Lord Mayor, an office which he is said to have performed 'with becoming dignity and hospitality'. In 1785, on the death in office of the then Lord Mayor, Carr filled the office for the remainder of the year. In the same year he was appointed one of the magistrates for the West Riding. By now his many commissions, added to his profits as a builder, and to the salary of £100 a year which he received from the North Riding magistrates for inspecting their bridges, had made him a wealthy man. In 1791–3 he rebuilt the church in his native village at his own expense, and in 1789 purchased a house there which he renamed Carr Lodge. This was intended for the residence of his nephew John Carr, for he himself had had no children by his wife Sarah Hinchcliffe, whom he married in 1746. Towards the end of his life he retired to Askham Richard, a village near York, where he purchased a mansion and estate. He retained his vivacity to the last, making long tours round the country to show his buildings to his great-nieces. He died on 22 February 1807, at the age of 83, and was buried in the church at Horbury, where there is a monument to his memory. His place as the leading architect in York was taken by his assistant Peter Atkinson (d. 1805), whose practice was continued by his son Peter (d. 1842) and his grandsons J. B. and W. Atkinson. The firm still exists under the name of Brierly, Leckenby, Keighley & Groom.

A portrait of Carr by William Beechey, presented by himself to the Corporation of York in 1803, hangs in the Mansion House. Another portrait by Beechey, dated 1791, formerly at Browsholme Hall,[1] now belongs to the National Portrait Gallery, but is on loan to the museum at Abbot Hall, Kendal. A bust by Nollekens dated 1800 is in the York Art Gallery, together with a pastel by John Russell. A pencil portrait by George Dance made in 1796 is reproduced in W. Daniell, *A Collection of Portraits sketched from the Life* (1808–14). The silver tea-caddy which Carr presented to the City of York in 1796 is illustrated in *Country Life*, 1 July 1954, 44.

There is no surviving corpus of Carr's drawings or papers. A volume containing drawings by Carr for ceilings in the style of Robert Adam and George Richardson is in the Victoria and Albert Museum (93 H.23). Carr's copy of Robert Morris's *Select Architecture* (1755) in Sir John Soane's Museum contains several sketches of his own designs. An illustrated survey of the country bridges built by Carr in the North Riding was presented by him to the magistrates in 1806 and is now in the N. Yorkshire Record Office. Among

unexecuted designs by Carr attention may be drawn to those for enlarging BUSBY HALL, YORKS. (N.R.), in the N. Yorkshire Record Office (*c.* 1760); for a race-stand at KELSO, ROXBURGHSHIRE (1778), in the National Library of Scotland (Minto Papers 5/1); for the addition of castellated offices to GLAMIS CASTLE, ANGUS (drawings at Glamis); and for WETHERBY GRANGE, YORKS. (w.R.), in the Leeds Public Libraries Archives Office (1783). Among the sketches in Carr's copy of Morris's *Select Architecture* in the Soane Museum is the plan for a house 'Designed for Mr. Grive, Northumberland'. This was probably for SWARLAND HALL, nr. FENTON, NORTHUMBERLAND, built by D. R. Grieve 1765 and dem. 1934. The elevation (recorded by Sir John Summerson in *Architect and Building News*, 15 June 1934, 304) does not correspond to this plan, but represents a design that may well have been by Carr.

[*A.P.S.D.*, article based on information supplied by J. B. Atkinson; R. Davies, 'A Memoir of John Carr', *Yorkshire Arch, Jnl.* iv, 1877; S. D. Kitson, 'Carr of York', *R.I.B.A. Jnl.*, 22 Jan. 1910; Anon., 'A Great Yorkshire Architect', *The Yorkshire Post*, 25 June 1919; R. B. Wragg, 'John Carr: Gothic Revivalist', *Studies in Architectural History*, ed. Singleton, ii, 1956; R. B. Wragg, 'John Carr: Bridgemaster', *York Georgian Society's Report*, 1957; R. B. Wragg, 'John Carr of York', *Jnl. of the W. Yorkshire Society of Architects*, Dec. 1957 and March 1958; R. B. Wragg, 'Stables Worthy of Stately Homes', *C. Life*, 1 Nov. 1962; John Ingamells, 'Portraits of John Carr', *City of York Art Gallery Quarterly* xxxiv, 1971; Ivan Hall, 'John Carr: A New Approach', *York Georgian Society's Report*, 1972; *The Works in Architecture of John Carr* (a list prepared by the York Georgian Society, York 1973); *John Carr of York* (duplicated catalogue by John Bradshaw & Ivan Hall of an exhibition at the Ferens Art Gallery, Hull, 1973).]

PUBLIC BUILDINGS

YORK, THE PIKEING WELL-HOUSE, NEW WALK, for the Corporation of York, 1752–6 [York Corporation Records, House Book 43, 318, 417] (R.C.H.M., *York* iv, 53).

YORK, GRANDSTAND on KNAVESMIRE RACECOURSE, 1755–6; dem. but lower storey survives re-erected in The Paddock [R. B. Wragg, 'The Stand House on the Knavesmire', *York Georgian Soc's Report*, 1965–6; R.C.H.M., *York* iii, 50–1 (*C. Life*, 3 Sept. 1910).

PRESTON, LANCS., THE GUILDHALL, 1760–2; dem. 1862 [P. Whittle, *History of Preston* ii, 1837, 59].

BEVERLEY, YORKS. (E.R.), ASSEMBLY ROOMS, 1761–3; dem. *c.* 1938 [County Record Office, Beverley, DDBC/21/92–105].

---

[1] In 1845 Mary Anne Carr, the heiress of the Carr property, married Thomas G. Parker of Browsholme Hall, nr. Whalley.

WAKEFIELD, YORKS. (W.R.), THE HOUSE OF CORREC-
TION, 1766–70, in association with John Wat-
son; dem. [sources cited in *The Works in
Architecture of John Carr*, 1973, 34].

LEEDS, THE INFIRMARY, 1769–71; dem. 1893
[sources cited in *The Works in Architecture of
John Carr*, 1973, 19].

OPORTO, PORTUGAL, THE HOSPITAL OF SAN
ANTONIO (or MISERICORDIA), begun 1770,
opened 1799, work continued intermittently
until 1843, but never fully completed [R. B.
& M. Wragg, 'Carr in Portugal', *Arch. Rev.*,
Feb. 1959; R. Taylor, 'The Architecture of
Port-Wine', *Arch. Rev.*, June 1961].

YORK, COUNTY LUNATIC ASYLUM (now BOOTHAM
PARK HOSPITAL), 1774–7; altered 1814 [sources
cited in *The Works in Architecture of John Carr*,
1973, 36; R.C.H.M., *York* iv, 47–8].

NEWARK, NOTTS., TOWN HALL AND ASSEMBLY
ROOMS, 1773–6 [G. Richardson, *New Vitruvius
Britannicus* ii, 1808, pls. 11–14].

YORK, ASSIZE COURTS IN THE CASTLE, 1773–7 [G.
Richardson, *New Vitruvius Britannicus* ii,
1808, pls. 1–4].

LINCOLN, THE COUNTY HOSPITAL (now BISHOP'S
COLLEGE HOSTEL), 1776–7 [Minute Book in
Lincolnshire Record Office, pp. 43–105,
passim].

NOTTINGHAM RACECOURSE GRANDSTAND, 1777;
dem. 1910 [R. Thoroton, *The Antiquities of
Nottinghamshire*, ed. Throsby, ii, 1790, 68 and
plate (p. 151); *The Stretton Manuscripts*, ed.
G. C. Robertson, 1910, p. ii].

DONCASTER, YORKS. (W.R.), RACECOURSE GRAND-
STAND, 1777–81, altered 1804 and 1824; dem.
1969 [J. Tomlinson, *Doncaster*, 1887, 207–8
(E. Miller, *History of Doncaster*, 1804, 158,
plate).

NOTTINGHAM, ASSEMBLY ROOMS, LOW PAVEMENT,
1778 [J. Orange, *History of Nottingham* ii,
1840, 940–1]; alterations by Carr 1790 [*The
Stretton Manuscripts*, ed. G. C. Robertson,
1910, 181]; further alterations 1807; rebuilt
1836.

YORK, THE FEMALE PRISON (now CASTLE MUSEUM),
1780–3, to match Carr's Assize Courts. The
builders were Messrs. Wilkinson & Prince of
York, who submitted a plan and elevation
which was approved in 1779. It was probably
made for them by Carr, who was subsequently
paid 'for his trouble in designing and conducting the building in the Castle Yard' [North
Riding Q.S. Order Book, *ex inf.* Mr. R. B.
Wragg]. Only the central portion was built
under Carr's direction, the end bays being
added by Peter Atkinson in 1802 [R.C.H.M.,
York ii, 85].

BUXTON, DERBYSHIRE, THE ASSEMBLY ROOMS in the
Crescent, for the 5th Duke of Devonshire, *c.*
1780–90 [see below].

NORTHALLERTON, YORKS. (N.R.), COURT HOUSE AND

HOUSE OF CORRECTION (now H.M. Prison)
for North Riding, 1784–8 [N. Riding Q.S.
Orders 1782–7, pp. 105, 342].

CHESTERFIELD, DERBYSHIRE, TOWN HALL for the
3rd Duke of Portland, 1787–8; dem. [G. Hall,
History of Chesterfield, 1839, 185].

RAVENFIELD, YORKS. (W.R.), for Mrs. Elizabeth
Parkin, 1756, Gothic [J. Hunter, *South Yorkshire* i, 1828, 398].

KIRKLEATHAM, YORKS. (N.R.), rebuilt for William
Turner, *c.* 1760–3, retaining the mausoleum of
1740 by J. Gibbs. Turner's account book for
1758–64 (in private hands) shows that Carr was
paid £24 3s. 0d. 'for a Draft of the Church at
Kirkleatham' in 1759. It was built by Robert
Corney, a local master carpenter, who according to J. W. Ord's *History of Cleveland*, 1846,
374, was 'both architect and builder' of the
church. He may have modified Carr's design.

DEWSBURY, YORKS. (W.R.), rebuilt tower and north
and south aisles, 1765–7, Gothic; altered by
G. E. Street in nineteenth century [church-
wardens' accounts cited by R. B. Wragg, 'John
Carr: Gothic Revivalist', 18–19].

BIERLEY CHAPEL (now CHURCH), YORKS. (W.R.), for
Dr. Richard Richardson, 1766; enlarged 1828
[W. Hiles, *History of the Parish of Bierley*,
1925, 19].

attributed: BOYNTON, YORKS. (E.R.), rebuilt 1768–
70, Gothic [unsigned drawings published by
A. R. Dufty in *Archaeological Jnl.* cv, 1948, 85,
and attributed to Carr by Arthur Oswald in *C.
Life*, 22 July 1954, and by R. B. Wragg, 'John
Carr; Gothic Revivalist', 20–1].

YORK MINSTER, surveyed fabric and repaired
roofs, 1770; repairs to transepts 1794–7 [J.
Wylson, 'York Minster: its Fires and Restorations', *Builder* iii, 1845, 158; Fabric Accounts
cited in *The Works in Architecture of John Carr*,
1973, 37].

SHEFFIELD, ST. PETER (now CATHEDRAL), repairs
and alterations to south and east sides of
chancel, 1773–5, Gothic [R. B. Wragg, 'John
Carr: Gothic Revivalist', 21–2, and further
sources cited in *The Works in Architecture
of John Carr*, 1973, 30].

ROKEBY, YORKS. (N.R.), completed (1777–8)
church begun by Sir Thomas Robinson (d.
1777) for J. S. Morritt [MS. notebook cited in
The Works in Architecture of John Carr, 1973,
29].

attributed: DENTON, YORKS. (W.R.), for Sir James
Ibbetson, Bart., 1776, Gothic [stylistic attribution combined with the fact that Carr was
building Denton Park at the same time].

OSSINGTON, NOTTS., for Robert Denison, 1782–3,
including a domed mausoleum at the east end
since demolished [Denison papers in Notting-

191

ham University Library; drawings seen at Ossington in 1959].

HORBURY, YORKS (W.R.), 1791–3, at his own expense [inscription and sources cited in *The Works in Architecture of John Carr*, 1973, 17].

BRIDGES

As Surveyor of Bridges to the North Riding of Yorkshire from 1772 to 1803 Carr left a detailed survey-book of the county bridges recording those that he had built or repaired (see A. Booth, 'Carr of York and the Book of the Bridges', *Yorkshire Archaeological Jnl.* xxxviii, 1954, and *The Works in Architecture of John Carr*, 1973, on which the following list is based).

In the *North Riding* Carr designed or remodelled bridges at AYTON (R. Derwent), 1775; BAINBRIDGE (YORE BRIDGE, R. Ure), BIRDFORTH, 1798, dem. 1971; BOW BRIDGE, nr. RIEVAULX, 1789; CATTERICK (R. Swale); CRAMBECK, 1785; CROFT (R. Tees), 1795; DANBY WISKE, 1782; DOWNHOLME (R. Swale), 1773; EAST ROW, SANDS-END, nr. WHITBY, 1777; ELLERBECK, nr. OSMOTH-ERLEY, 1790, dem.; GRETA, nr. ROKEBY, 1773; GRINTON (R. Swale), 1797; HAWNBY, 1800; KILV-INGTON, 1774, dem. 1970; LOW BOURN (R. Burn), nr. MASHAM, 1775; MORTON ON SWALE, 1800–3; SOUTH OTTERINGTON (R. Wiske), 1776; REETH (over Arkle Beck), 1772–3; RICCAL, nr. HELMSLEY, 1803; RICHMOND (R. Swale), 1789; RUTHERFORD (R. Greta), south of BARNARD CASTLE, 1773; SKIPTON ON SWALE, 1781; STRENSHALL, 1798; THIRKLEBY, 1799, rebuilt 1931; THIRSK MILL, MILLGATE (over Cod Beck), 1789; YORK, YEARSLEY BRIDGE (R. Foss), 1794–5, since rebuilt.

In the *West Riding* where he was one of the two Surveyors of Bridges from 1761 to 1772, Carr designed bridges at CARLTON FERRY, nr. SNAITH (R. Aire); CONISTON COLD (R. Aire), 1763; FERRY-BRIDGE, 1797–1804; HAREWOOD (R. Wharfe), 1771; MARLE BRIDGE (R. Dearne), nr. DARFIELD, 1766; and was one of the committee responsible for the wooden bridge at SELBY, opened 1795.

Ferrybridge, Richmond, Morton and Rutherford Bridges were among Carr's most notable bridge-works. Greta Bridge was probably the most elegantly designed and was certainly the one most often painted, notably by J. S. Cotman.

For other bridges widened or repaired by Carr see the two works cited above.

DOMESTIC ARCHITECTURE

The following list is confined to documented or otherwise well-authenticated works, supplemented by a small number of stylistic attributions which are regarded by the author as virtually certain. For doubtful and unexecuted works and a few less certain attributions see the list of *Works in Architecture of John Carr* published

by the York Georgian Society in 1973. References to 'Chivers' are to the diary of Miss Elizabeth Chivers, formerly in the possession of the late Wilfred Partrington, who allowed the author to examine it. Miss Chivers was a neighbour of Carr's at Askham and knew him well. In 1803, 1804 and 1805 she made tours with her parents which were recorded in her diary, and carefully noted whenever she saw a building 'designed by our good neighbour Mr. Carr'. 'Davies' refers to the list of Carr's works given by Robert Davies in his memoir of Carr in *Yorkshire Archaeological Jnl.* iv, 1877.

KIRBY HALL, OUSEBURN, YORKS. (W.R.), employed on erection of house designed for Stephen Thompson by Lord Burlington and Roger Morris, 1747– *c.* 1755; dem. 1920 except stables [contemporary engraving by Basire in B.M., *King's Maps* xlv, 24–1, recording that the house was 'Executed, & the inside finishings, by J. Carr, Architect'] (*Vitruvius Britannicus* v, 1771, pls. 70–1).

HUTHWAITE HALL, THURGOLAND, nr. PENISTONE, YORKS. (W.R.), for John Cockshutt, 1748 [*A.P.S.D.*] (*The Works in Architecture of John Carr*, 1973, pl. 1).

ASKHAM HALL, ASKHAM RICHARD, YORKS. (W.R.), additions for W. Garforth, *c.* 1750; rebuilt 1889 (now H.M. Prison) [letter from Carr cited by Davies, 212].

ARNCLIFFE HALL, INGLEBY ARNCLIFFE, YORKS. (N.R.), for Thomas Mauleverer, *c.* 1750–4; east wing 1841 [*A.P.S.D.*; J. Whellan, *History and Topography of York and the North Riding* ii, 1859, 734] (*C. Life*, 25 Dec. 1920).

YORK, NO. 47 BOOTHAM, for Mrs. Mary Thompson, 1752 [*A.P.S.D.*].

CAMPSMOUNT, nr. DONCASTER, YORKS. (W.R.). Payments to Carr indicate that he probably designed the house built for Thomas Yarborough, 1752–5; dem. 1940. Surviving drawings signed by Carr show that he subsequently designed the adjoining castellated farmyard; dem. 1972–3 [T. Connor, 'The Building of Campsmount', *Yorks. Arch. Jnl.* xlvii, 1975].

LEEDS, YORKS. (W.R.), town house, for J. Dixon,[1] 1753 [*A.P.S.D.*].

NORTHALLERTON, YORKS. (N.R.), house, NO. 84 HIGH STREET, for D. Mitford, *c.* 1754 [*A.P.S.D.*].

HEATH HALL, nr. WAKEFIELD, YORKS. (W.R.), remodelled house and designed stable blocks for John Smyth, senior and junior, 1754–80 [W. Watts, *Seats of the Nobility and Gentry*, pl. lxxxiv, 1786] (*C. Life*, 19, 26 Sept., 3 Oct. 1968).

---

[1] This may have been the house said to have been built by Jeremiah Dixon in Bear Lane in 1750 (R. Thoresby, *Ducatus Leodiensis*, ed. Whitaker, 1816, 5), but the identification is not certain.

YORK, PETERGATE, house for J. Mitchell, 1755; dem. c. 1860 [A.P.S.D].

GILLING CASTLE, YORKS. (N.R.), repairs and minor alterations for the 9th Viscount Fairfax, 1755–6 [Fairfax papers in library of Yorkshire Archaeological Soc., Leeds].

PLOMPTON, nr. KNARESBOROUGH, YORKS. (W.R.), new house begun for Daniel Lascelles c. 1755 but not finished except stables (subsequently partially converted into a house) [Steward's correspondence 1754–62 in Harewood archives; drawing of 'Plompton, S. front as it is executed for Daniel Lascelles 11 May 1761. J.C.' in Sir Albert Richardson's Collection at Ampthill]. For the Gothic farmhouse see R. B. Wragg, 'John Carr: Gothic Revivalist', 15.

attributed: YORK, GARFORTH HOUSE, NO. 54 MICKLEGATE, for the Rev. Edmund Garforth, c. 1755–7 [R.C.H.M., York iii, 76–7].

LYTHAM HALL, LANCS., for Thomas Clifton, 1757–64 [A.P.S.D. and accounts in Lancs. Record Office cited in The Works in Architecture of John Carr, 1973, 20] (C. Life, 21, 28 July 1960).

EVERINGHAM PARK, YORKS. (E.R.), for William H. Constable, 1758–64; altered and enlarged in the nineteenth century; restored c. 1965 [R. B. Wragg, 'Everingham Park: Carr's Work Authenticated', Trans. East Yorkshire Georgian Soc. iv. (2), 1955–6; Arthur Oswald in C. Life, 15–22 Feb. 1968].

ABBOT HALL, KENDAL, WESTMORLAND, for Col. George Wilson, 1759 [The Lonsdale Magazine ii, 1821, 3; J. F. Curwen, Kirkbie Kendall, 1900, 125].

HAREWOOD HOUSE, YORKS. (W.R.), for Edwin Lascelles, afterwards Lord Harewood, 1759–71. The plan and exterior were substantially Carr's design, but the interior decoration of the principal rooms was wholly by R. & J. Adam. Both exterior and interior were considerably altered by Sir C. Barry in 1843–50, when the portico was removed. Carr was also responsible for much of Harewood Village, for a Temple of Venus, 1780 (dem.), and for the stables built in 1755–8, for which Chambers had made a rejected design in 1755 [Vitruvius Britannicus v, pls. 25–8; R. B. Wragg in Archaeological Jnl. cxxv, 1968, 342–7; Mary Mauchline, Harewood House, 1974] (A. T. Bolton, Architecture of R. & J. Adam i, 157–77; C. Hussey, English Country Houses: Mid Georgian, 1956, 61–9).

attributed: KIRKLAND HALL, nr. GARSTANG, LANCS., for Alexander Butler, 1760 [stylistic attribution] (P. Fleetwood-Hesketh, Murray's Lancashire Architectural Guide, 1955, 71).

WENTWORTH WOODHOUSE, YORKS. (W.R.), works for the 2nd Marquess of Rockingham (d. 1782) and his successor the 4th Earl Fitzwilliam, c. 1760 onwards, including Stables, 1766–89;

Keppel's Column, 1776–81; Rockingham Mausoleum, 1785–91; North Lodge, 1793; Rainborough Lodge, 1798; Lion Gate (Brampton Lodge), 1804; and various alterations to the house, notably the raising of the wings and the addition to them of the engaged porticos for the 4th Earl [A. Booth, 'The Architects of Wentworth Castle and Wentworth Woodhouse', R.I.B.A. Jnl., 3rd ser., xli, 25 Nov. 1933, 71–2; M. & R. B. Wragg, 'Admiral Keppel's Column', C. Life, 27 Dec. 1958; R. B. Wragg on the stables in C. Life, 1 Nov. 1962; drawings, accounts and correspondence among Wentworth Woodhouse Muniments in Sheffield City Library] (C. Life, 20 Sept.–11 Oct. 1924; C. Hussey, English Country Houses: Early Georgian, 1955, 147–54).

RAVENFIELD HALL, nr. ROTHERHAM, YORKS. (W.R.), alterations for Mrs. Elizabeth Parkin, c. 1760; and further alterations for her cousin and heir Walter Oborne, 1767–74; dem. [A.P.S.D.; Oborne records in Sheffield City Library cited in The Works in Architecture of John Carr, 1973, 27].

TABLEY HOUSE, CHESHIRE, for Sir Peter Leicester, Bart., c. 1760–7 [Vitruvius Britannicus v, pls. 16–19, where it is called Oakland House; C. Hussey in C. Life, 21, 28 July 1923] (C. Hussey, English Country Houses: Mid Georgian, 1956, 55–60).

CLINTS HALL, nr. RICHMOND, YORKS. (N.R.), alterations for Sir Charles Turner of Kirkleatham 1761; dem. c. 1845 [accounts in Kirkleatham records in N. Yorkshire Record Office cited in The Works in Architecture of John Carr, 1973, 7] (W. Angus, Seats of the Nobility and Gentry, pl. xxiv, 1790).

GROVE HALL, nr. RETFORD, NOTTS., remodelled for Anthony Eyre, c. 1762; dem. 1952 [R. Thoroton, Antiquities of Nottinghamshire, ed. J. Throsby, iii, 1790, 264].

CONSTABLE BURTON, YORKS. (N.R.), for Sir Marmaduke Wyvill, Bart., c. 1762–8 [Vitruvius Britannicus v, pls. 36–7; Farington Diary, ed. Greig, v, 168] (C. Life, 28 Nov. 1968).

ESCRICK PARK, YORKS. (E.R.), enlargement of house and new stables for Beilby Thompson, 1763–5 [E. Riding County Record Office, DDFA/37/28; David Neave & Ivan Hall in York Georgian Society's Annual Report, 1971].

YORK, CASTLEGATE HOUSE, CASTLEGATE, for Peter Johnson, 1763–5 [Davies].

WHITE WINDOWS, SOWERBY BRIDGE, YORKS. (W.R.), alterations for John Priestley, 1763–8 [A.P.S.D.].

GOLDSBROUGH HALL, nr. KNARESBURGH, YORKSHIRE (W.R.), interior remodelled for Daniel Lascelles, 1764–5 [Harewood archives, Steward's correspondence and Letter-book 5, pp. 130, 152, 161].

WELBECK ABBEY, NOTTS., alterations for 3rd Duke

of Portland: chapel, 1763; stables, 1774; east front, 1775–7 [A. S. Turbeville, *Welbeck Abbey and its Owners*, ii, 1938–9, 454; Nottingham University Library, Portland papers, PwF2, 540, etc.].

SWINTON PARK, nr. MASHAM, YORKS. (N.R.), alterations for William Danby, 1764–7 [John Cornforth in *C. Life*, 7, 14, 21 April 1966].

KIRKLEATHAM HALL, YORKS. (N.R.), alterations to Jacobean house for Sir Charles Turner, 1764–7, externally Gothic; dem. 1954–6 [Arthur Young, *Six Months Tour through the North of England* ii, 1770, 107; R. B. Wragg, 'John Carr: Gothic Revivalist', 23–5].

YORK, FAIRFAX HOUSE, CASTLEGATE, remodelled or rebuilt for the 9th Viscount Fairfax, *c.* 1765 [Davies; vouchers in Newburgh Priory papers, N. Yorkshire Record Office, *ex inf.* Mr. R. B. Wragg].

ASKE HALL, YORKS. (N.R.), alterations and additions to house and new stables for Sir Lawrence Dundas, Bart., *c.* 1765–9 [accounts, etc., in Zetland archives, N. Yorkshire Record Office] (J. Harris, 'The Dundas Empire', *Apollo*, Sept. 1967, figs. 2 and 8).

YORK, SKELDERGATE, his own house, 1765–9; dem. 1945 [*A.P.S.D.*; Davies; and sources cited in *The Works in Architecture of John Carr*, 1973, 38].

BOYNTON HALL, nr. BRIDLINGTON, YORKS. (E.R.), alterations for Sir George Strickland, Bart., *c.* 1765–80 [Strickland papers cited in *The Works in Architecture of John Carr*, 1973, 4; drawing for service wing in possession of Mr. Francis Johnson, F.R.I.B.A.] (*C. Life*, 22–29 July 1954). The CARNABY TEMPLE built by Sir George Strickland may also be attributed to Carr.

HALIFAX, YORKS. (W.R.), house, bank and warehouse in George Street for John Royds, 1766; later Rawson's Bank and now office of Huddersfield Building Soc., but partly dem. [*A.P.S.D.*; Davies; and references cited in *The Works in Architecture of John Carr*, 1973, 14].

attributed: GLEDHOW HALL, ALLERTON, YORKS. (W.R.), for Jeremiah Dixon, 1766–7 [stylistic attribution, supported by Dixon's possible employment of Carr to design his town house in Leeds] (plan in *R.I.B.A. Jnl.*, 22 Jan. 1910, 253).

PYE NEST, nr. HALIFAX, YORKS (W.R.), for John Edwards, 1767; dem. 1934 [*A.P.S.D.*; *A Series of Picturesque Views of Castles and Country Houses in Yorkshire*, Bradford 1885] (J. B. Burke, *A Visitation of Seats and Arms*, 2nd ser., i, 1854, 210, plate).

THORESBY HOUSE, NOTTS., for the 2nd Duke of Kingston, 1767–71; dem. 1868; and remodelling of stables, etc., for Lord Newark, 1789–1804 [*Vitruvius Britannicus* v, pls. 11–13; J. H.

Hodson, 'The Building and Alteration of the Second Thoresby House, 1767–1804', *Thoroton Society's Record Series* xxi, 1962, 16–20].

attributed: BISHOP AUCKLAND CASTLE, CO. DURHAM, south wing (Gothic) for Bishops Richard Trevor and John Egerton, *c.* 1767–72 [J. Cornforth in *C. Life*, 3 Feb. 1972; J. Macaulay, *The Gothic Revival*, 1975, 139–40].

RABY CASTLE, CO. DURHAM, alterations and additions, including Gothic entrance hall (1781–5), for the 2nd Earl of Darlington, 1768–88 [Alistair Rowan in *C. Life*, 1–8 Jan. 1970; Alistair Rowan, 'Gothick Restoration at Raby Castle', *Architectural History* xv, 1972].

KILNWICK HALL, YORKS. (E.R.), internal alterations for John Grimston, 1769–72; further alterations for Thomas Grimston, 1781; dem. 1951 [M. E. Ingram, *Leaves from a Family Tree* [1951], 67–70, 113, and sources cited in *The Works in Architecture of John Carr*, 1973, 18].

LEEDS, BRIDGE END, house (now a shop) for Mr. Green, before 1769 [letter of 13 Feb. 1769 in Leeds Infirmary Letter-book cited in *The Works in Architecture of John Carr*, 1973, 19].

THE SHAY, nr. HALIFAX, YORKS. (W.R.), probably for John Caygill, *c.* 1770; dem. [*A.P.S.D.*; cf. *The Works in Architecture of John Carr*, 1973, 30].

DENTON PARK, YORKS. (W.R.), for Sir James Ibbetson, Bart., 1770–81 [G. Richardson, *New Vitruvius Britannicus* i, pl. 54–6] (*C. Life*, 4 Nov. 1939).

BYRAM HALL, nr. FERRYBRIDGE, YORKS. (W.R.), extensive additions, including stables, for Sir John Ramsden, Bart., probably *c.* 1770 (interior decoration by R. Adam, 1780); dem. [*A.P.S.D.*].

attributed: GLEDSTONE HALL, nr. SKIPTON, YORKS. (W.R.), begun by Richard Roundell (d. 1772) *c.* 1770 and completed by the Rev. William Roundell; dem. 1928 except stables [stylistic attribution: see S. D. Kitson in *R.I.B.A. Jnl.*, 22 Jan. 1910, and C. Hussey in *C. Life*, 13 April 1935] (plate in T. D. Whitaker, *History of Craven*, 1812, 72, 1878 ed., 94).

SEDBURY PARK, nr. RICHMOND, YORKS. (N.R.), alterations for Robert D'Arcy Hildyard, *c.* 1770; dem. [Grimston papers, letter dated 1770 from Sir Robert Hildyard to John Grimston in which he refers to Carr's recent work at Sedbury for his son, *ex inf.* Mr. R. B. Wragg].

LONDON, BURLINGTON HOUSE, PICCADILLY, alterations to interior, including the dining-room, for the 3rd Duke of Portland, then the tenant of the house, *c.* 1771–5 [letters from Carr in Portland papers in Nottingham University Library, PwF2, 539, 546; for the Duke's tenancy see *Survey of London* xxxii, 406].

CHESTERS, nr. HEXHAM, NORTHUMBERLAND, for John Errington, 1771; altered by J. Dobson

1832 and 1837 and remodelled by Norman Shaw 1893 [sketch-plan of house 'Designed for — Errington Esqr.' in Carr's copy of R. Morris's *Select Architecture* in Sir John Soane's Museum; R. B. Wragg, 'Chesters', *Archaeologia Aeliana*, 4th ser., xxxvi, 1958].

THIRSK HALL, YORKS. (N.R.), addition of wings and attic storey for Ralph Bell, 1771–3 [accounts in N. Riding County Record Office, ZAG 22].

attributed: ORMESBY HALL, nr. MIDDLESBROUGH, YORKS. (N.R.), the stables for Sir James Pennyman, Bart., 1772 [Arthur Oswald in *C. Life*, 26 Feb. 1959].

ASTON HALL (now Aughton Hospital), nr. ROTHERHAM, YORKS. (W.R.), for the 4th Earl of Holderness, 1771–2[1]: new staircase inserted by J. Platt (*q.v.*) *c.* 1776 [T. Allen, *History of the County of York* iii, 1834, 145; sketch-plan of 'Aston House' in Carr's copy of R. Morris's *Select Architecture* in Sir John Soane's Museum; M. & R. B. Wragg in *C. Life*, 12 April 1956].

ASTON RECTORY, nr. ROTHERHAM, YORKS. (N.R.), for the Rev. William Mason, *c.* 1770 [sketch-plan of 'Revd. Mr. Mason's House at Aston' in Carr's copy of R. Morris's *Select Architecture* in Sir John Soane's Museum; M. & R. B. Wragg in *C. Life*, 12 April 1956].

REDBOURNE HALL, LINCS., works (probably including castellated gateway) for the Rev. Robert Carter Thelwall, 1773 [payment to Carr in accounts in Lincolnshire Archives Office, Red. 3/1/4/6].

BLYTH HALL, NOTTS., alterations for William Mellish, 1773–6; dem. [Barclay's Bank Ltd., ledgers of Gosling's Bank, *ex inf.* Mr. R. B. Wragg].

LEVENTHORPE HALL, nr. LEEDS, YORKS. (W.R.), for Richard Green, 1774; wings dem. and interior stripped [inscription giving Carr's name; Chivers].

CASTLE HOWARD, YORKS. (N.R.), the stables for the 5th Earl of Carlisle, 1774–82 [J. H. Jesse, *George Selwyn and his Contemporaries*, 1843–4, iii, 17; account at Castle Howard cited in *The Works in Architecture of John Carr*, 1973, 6] (*C. Life.* 25 June 1927, 1 Nov. 1962).

attributed: RIBSTON HALL, nr. KNARESBURGH, YORKS. (W.R.), interior of saloon and stables for Sir John Goodricke, Bart., *c.* 1775 [Gervase Jackson-Stops in *C. Life*, 18 Oct. 1973].

PANTON HALL, nr. WRAGBY, LINCS., addition of wings for Edmund Turnor, 1775; dem. 1960 [T. Allen, *History of Lincolnshire* ii, 1834, 70; H. M. Colvin in *Lincolnshire Historian* No. 7,

---

[1] The date given in *A.P.S.D.* is 1772, but numerous, though unspecified, payments to Carr in Lord Holderness's accounts (B. M., Egerton MS 3497) suggests that work started soon after 1760.

1951, but note that demolition revealed structural evidence of Carr's additions not visible in 1951].

NORTON PLACE, BISHOP NORTON, LINCS., for John Harrison, M.P., 1776 [J. Britton, *Beauties of England and Wales* ix, 1807, 670].

BILLING HALL, GREAT BILLING, NORTHANTS., for Lord John Cavendish, 1776; dem. *c.* 1955 [G. Baker, *History of Northamptonshire* i, 1822–30, 22].

BASILDON HOUSE, BERKSHIRE, for Sir Francis Sykes, Bart., 1776; alterations to interior by J. B. Papworth, 1839–44 [G. Richardson, *New Vitruvius Britannicus* i, pls. 12–14] (*Arch. Rev.* lxviii, 1930, 113–19).

COLWICK HALL, NOTTS., remodelled for John Musters, 1776 [R. Thoroton, *History of Nottinghamshire*, ed. J. Throsby, iii, 1790, 8].

WORKINGTON HALL, CUMBERLAND, extensive alterations for Henry and John Christian Curwen, *c.* 1777–82. Most of Carr's work here was destroyed *c.* 1972 [D. & S. Lysons, *Magna Britannia* iv, 1816, 173] (plan in J. F. Curwen, *Workington Hall*, *c.* 1910).

MIDDLETON LODGE, MIDDLETON TYAS, YORKS. (N.R.), for George Hartley, 1777–80 [building contract in N. Riding Record Office, ZKU].

CANNON HALL, nr. BARNSLEY, YORKS. (W.R.), addition of wings and other alterations for John Spencer, 1764–8; further works, including stables and heightening of wings, for Walter Spencer-Stanhope, 1778 onwards [A. M. W. Stirling, *Annals of a Yorkshire House*, 1911, i, 146–8, ii, 116–18, 314–15; accounts in Sheffield City Library cited in *The Works in Architecture of John Carr*, 1973, 5] (J. P. Neale, *Views of Seats* iv, 1821).

METHLEY HALL, nr. WAKEFIELD, YORKS. (W.R.), rebuilt south-east front for the 1st Earl of Mexborough, 1778; remodelled by A. Salvin 1830–6; dem. *c.* 1960 [Harrison's *Picturesque Views of Seats*, pl. 54, 1788] (J. P. Neale, *Views of Seats* v, 1822).

CLIFTON HALL, NOTTS., alterations and additions for Sir Gervase Clifton, 1778–97 [accounts, now in Nottingham University Library, cited by C. Hussey in *C. Life*, 25 Aug. 1923]. The octagonal domed hall was built by Sir Robert Clifton *c.* 1750 and did not form part of Carr's works.

THORNES HOUSE, nr. WAKEFIELD, YORKS. (W.R.), for James Milnes, 1779–81; dem. after fire in 1951 [G. Richardson, *New Vitruvius Britannicus* i, pls. 51–3].

BOLLING HALL, nr. BRADFORD, YORKS. (W.R.), restoration of east wing for Capt. Charles Wood, R.N., 1779–80 [Wood papers at Garrowby Hall, *ex inf.* Major T. Ingram, and sources cited in *The Works in Architecture of John Carr*, 1973, 3] (*Picturesque Views of Castles and Country Houses in Yorkshire*, Bradford 1885).

195

LANGFORD HALL, NOTTS., for Charles Duncombe, *c.* 1780 [Chivers].

BADSWORTH HALL, YORKS, (W.R.), alterations for the 2nd Marquess of Rockingham, *c.* 1780; dem. [Fitzwilliam papers at Sheffield City Library, *ex inf.* Mr. R. B. Wragg].

NEW LODGE, WAKEFIELD ROAD, BARNSLEY, YORKS. (W.R.), for occupation of his nephew John Clark, *c.* 1780 [Chivers, and sources cited in *The Works in Architecture of John Carr*, 1973, 23].

BUXTON, DERBYSHIRE, THE CRESCENT and STABLES, for the 5th Duke of Devonshire, *c.* 1780–90 [S. Glover, *History of Derbyshire* ii, 1833, 176, and sources cited in *The Works in Architecture of John Carr*, 1973, 5] (R. B. Wragg, 'John Carr's Crescent', *Derbyshire Countryside* xxi, Oct.–Nov. 1956).

WIGANTHORPE HALL, nr. MALTON, YORKS. (N.R.), for William Garforth, *c.* 1780; dem. 1955 [plans in possession of Mr. R. B. Wragg; designs for ceilings in Victoria and Albert Museum, 93 H.23, nos. 8, 10 and 11].

GRIMSTON GARTH, nr. ALDBOROUGH, YORKS. (E.R.), for Thomas Grimston, 1781–6, castellated Gothic [M. E. Ingram, 'John Carr's Contribution to the Gothic Revival', *Trans. of the E. Riding Georgian Soc.* ii (3), 1949; M. E. Ingram & Francis F. Johnson in *C. Life*, 17 Oct. 1952].

CLIFTON HOUSE, ROTHERHAM, YORKS. (W.R.), for Joshua Walker, 1783 [J. Guest, *Historic Notices of Rotherham*, 1879, 681; *Minutes relating to Messrs. Samuel Walker & Co. 1741–1829*, ed. A. H. John, 1951, 21].

SAND HUTTON PARK, YORKS. (N.R.), for William Read, 1786; much altered in nineteenth century: dem. 1971 [*A.P.S.D.*; Davies].

EASTWOOD HOUSE, ROTHERHAM, YORKS. (W.R.), for Joseph Walker, 1786–7; dem. [J. Guest, *Historic Notices of Rotherham*, 1879, 681; *Minutes relating to Messrs. Samuel Walker & Co. 1741–1829*, ed. A. H. John, 1951, 22].

FARNLEY HALL, nr. OTLEY, YORKS. (W.R.), addition of large new wing for Walter Hawksworth Fawkes, 1786–90 [J. P. Neale, *Views of Seats* v, 1822] (*C. Life*, 20, 27 May 1954).

CASTLE WILLIAM, BUDBY, NOTTS., for Lord Newark, *c.* 1789, a small castellated house on the Thoresby estate [J. H. Hodson in *Thoroton Society's Record Series* xxxi, 1962, 16–20].

BRETTON HALL, YORKS. (W.R.), remodelled Dining Room for Col. T. R. Beaumont, 1793, and designed garden temples, etc. [archives of Lord Allendale, *ex inf.* Dr. D. Linstrum].

FAWLEY COURT, BUCKS., designs for gateway and stucco-work for his friend Strickland Freeman, 1797, perhaps not executed [Gloucestershire Record Office, Strickland Freeman papers, D. 1245, FF 38].

COOLATTIN PARK (MALTON HOUSE), in SHILLE-LAGH, CO. WICKLOW, for the 4th Earl Fitzwilliam, 1799-1808. The former house, then undergoing alteration to designs supplied by Carr, was burnt during the Rebellion of 1798, and work started on the new building in 1800. [Sheffield City Library, Fitzwilliam papers, MP33, plans and elevations; letter of Jan. 1796 to Benjamin Hall referring to his designs 'for the house at Malton in Ireland'; letter of 22 Jan. to Lord Fitzwilliam; accounts in National Library of Ireland, MSS. 6012–6025, *ex inf.* Mr. E. McParland].

MILTON HOUSE, nr. PETERBOROUGH, NORTHANTS., alterations for the 4th Earl Fitzwilliam, including new library (now dining-room), *c.* 1803 [Northants. Record Office, Fitzwilliam papers, plan No. 126 (watermark 1802) in Carr's hand, and cf. letter referred to by C. Hussey in *C. Life*, 1 June 1961, 1273] (*C. Life*, 25 May 1961, fig. 8, and 1 June 1961, figs. 7 and 9).

attributed: BRAMHAM PARK, YORKS. (W.R.), central block of stables for George Fox, Lord Bingley (d. 1773) [stylistic attribution].

UPLEATHAM HALL, YORKS. (N.R.), refronted and enlarged for Sir Thomas Dundas, Bart., cr. Baron Dundas; dem. [Zetland papers in N. Riding Record Office, cited in *The Works in Architecture of John Carr*, 1973, 33].

OBELISKS

Among the drawings in Carr's copy of R. Morris's *Select Architecture* in Sir John Soane's Museum there is a design for an obelisk inscribed 'design'd pr. J.C. and built by the Ld. primate of all Ireland 1782'. The Irish primate in 1782 was Richard Robinson, Archbishop of Armagh, and son of William Robinson of Rokeby, Yorkshire. In 1782–3 he erected an obelisk on KNOX'S HILL, ARMAGH, to commemorate his friendship with the Duke of Northumberland. Elizabeth Chivers records that Carr designed an obelisk in BRAMHAM PARK, YORKS. (W.R.), for George Fox, Lord Bingley (d. 1773).

CARSTAIRS, DAVID (1721–1764), 'wright and architect in Kirkton of Largo', is commemorated by a tombstone in the churchyard of Largo, Fife.

CARTER, CHARLES JOHN (1784–1851), appears to have originated in Staffordshire, for the plan for Louth vicarage which he made in 1832 is by 'Charles John Carter of Brereton, Staffs., surveyor'. Thereafter he was resident in Louth, and his death in 1851 was commemorated by an inscription in the churchyard there [R. W. Goulding, *Epitaphs in St. Mary's Churchyard, Louth*, 1921, 41]. In the Lincolnshire Archives Office there are designs by him for parsonage houses at LOUTH (1832), GAYTON-LE-MARSH (1834), WELTON-LE-WOLD (1834), BURGH-UPON-BAIN (1834) and LITTLE CARLTON (1843), all in

LINCOLNSHIRE, and at MILTON ERNEST in BED-FORDSHIRE (1835). He repaired WELTON CHURCH, LINCS., in 1828 [I.C.B.S.], increased the seating in LOUTH CHURCH in 1837 [I.C.B.S] and is reported to have made designs for a new gate at SCRIVELSBY COURT, LINCS., in 1833 [N. Pevsner & John Harris, *Lincolnshire*, 1964, 355].

CARTER, EDWARD (–1663) was the younger son of Francis Carter, Chief Clerk of the King's Works (*q.v.*). Nothing is known of his early life, but from 1633 to 1641 he was employed as Inigo Jones's deputy in the great repair of ST. PAUL'S CATHEDRAL then in progress [cf. *Documents illustrating the History of St. Paul's*, ed. Simpson, Camden Soc. 1880, 142, and *Nicholas Stone's Note-Book*, ed. Finberg, Walpole Soc. 1919, 128]. He also appears to have been acting as the Earl of Bedford's surveyor in COVENT GARDEN, where he signed the account for the new church built in 1631–2 to Inigo Jones's designs [*Survey of London* xxxvi, 28]. In 1642–9 he was employed to survey extensive alterations to NORTHUMBERLAND HOUSE, STRAND (dem. 1874), for the 10th Earl of Northumberland, who had just acquired the house by his marriage to Lady Elizabeth Howard [Percy archives at Alnwick Castle, U.III.2]. In 1643, in circumstances that are not altogether clear, Carter took the place of the absent Inigo Jones as Surveyor of the King's Works, 'thrusting out' John Webb, whom Jones had nominated as his deputy [*History of the King's Works* iii, 156, 161]. Until 1653, when he was superseded by John Embree, the Sergeant Plumber, Carter was responsible for the maintenance of the royal houses in circumstances that gave him no opportunities for original architectural work. From his dismissal in 1653 until his death in 1663 all that is known of Carter's activities is that in 1656–8 'Carter' (presumably Edward) was paid £20 for surveying a new building erected by the Inner Temple in Temple Lane [*Calendar of Inner Temple Records*, ed. Inderwick, ii, 1898, 325, 328]. The suggestion that he might have designed HIGHNAM COURT, GLOS. (?1658) (*C. Life*, 12, 19 May 1950), has no foundation either in record or in family tradition. It was first made in 1791 in his *History of Gloucestershire* by Bigland, who, finding that Inigo Jones (then the reputed architect of the house) had died in 1652, concluded that it must have been designed by his successor. The only evidence of Carter's architectural ability at present available is a design for a house among the Trumbull papers in the Berkshire Record Office (D/ED P.5), endorsed as a 'Plott for the new building of East Hampsted Lodge by Mr. Edward Carter', and dating apparently from some time after 1626, when William Trumbull acquired the estate. This shows a rectangular house with hipped roof, pedimented dormer windows, restrained classi-

cal detailing and other features (including an Italianate *loggia*) of a kind which would be hard to parallel at this date outside Inigo Jones's office. Edward Carter is, therefore, a figure whose contribution to English seventeenth-century architecture may have been more important than is at present demonstrable.

Nicholas Stone's nephew Charles Stoakes told George Vertue that Carter 'lived in Covent Garden and dyd soon after the Restoration' (*Vertue's Notebooks*, Walpole Soc., ii, 53). This was correct, for in 1633 Carter had built a large house for himself on the Earl of Bedford's estate in King Street, Covent Garden, and was subsequently prominent in parish affairs during the Commonwealth and Protectorate. The fact that in 1645–8 he was one of the 'triers' of candidates for eldership in the Presbyterian organization of London churches is doubtless indicative of his religious sympathies [*Survey of London* xxxvi, 28, 101]. His burial in March 1662/3 is recorded in the register of St. Paul's, Covent Garden [*Harl. Soc.* xxxvi, 1908, 27].

CARTER, FRANCIS (–1630), was a senior officer in the royal works during the surveyorship of Inigo Jones. He began his official carreer in 1610 as a clerk of works to Henry, Prince of Wales. After the prince's death in 1612 he became (22 Feb. 1614) Chief Clerk of the King's Works, a post which he retained until his death. He was a carpenter by training, and his first recorded work is the timber-work, including the screen, of the hall at TRINITY COLLEGE, CAMBRIDGE, which he performed in 1604–5 [Willis & Clark, ii, 491–2]. The screen is an elaborate classical structure with Jacobean mannerist ornament (R.C.H.M., *Cambridge*, pl. 257). In 1612 Sir Edward Pytts of Kyre (Worcs.), paid 40s. 'to Carter of St. Giles' Lane by Charing Cross . . . for drawing the upright of the fore part of my house at London' [Mrs. Baldwyn-Childe, 'The Building of Kyre Park, Worcs.', *The Antiquary* xxii, 1890, 51]. In 1613–14 Francis Carter was responsible as 'Surveyor or Contriver of buildings' for the design of the new aisle, doorway and cloister of the chapel at CHARTERHOUSE, LONDON, another building in the mannerist style, but of a more sophisticated character than the Trinity screen [Arthur Oswald, *C. Life*, 15 Oct. 1959]. It was in his official capacity that in 1618 he made an estimate of the cost of repairing PONTEFRACT CASTLE, YORKS. (W.R.), for King James I [*History of the King's Works* iii, 289–90]. In 1618 he provided the estimate – and therefore probably also the design – for the SALISBURY CHAPEL which the 2nd Earl of Salisbury added to HATFIELD CHURCH, HERTS. This has Gothic windows and a Tuscan arcade [Hatfield House, Cecil papers, vol. 143, f. 142, *ex inf.* Mr. R. Harcourt-Williams]. Salisbury employed him again in 1627 to convert the shops in the upper floor of THE NEW EXCHANGE in THE STRAND into living accommodation [L. Stone, *Family and Fortune*, 1973, 106].

Carter's will shows that at the time of his death in 1630 he was living in St. Martin's Lane and that he owned property and silver plate of considerable value. He had three sons, Samuel (who predeceased him), William and Edward. To William he left 'my Cabinet in my closet with tabell dorins and bookes of Architeckter that belong to me and those above in his chamber and study that belong to him self' [P.C.C. 110 SCROOPE]. No more is known of William Carter, but Edward Carter's career is described above. A family group, formerly at Blenheim Palace, and now in the National Gallery of Ireland, was reported by Vertue to be 'said to be' either 'Carter Architect, deputy to Inigo Jones before Mr. Webb' or 'Lilly the Mathematician' [*Vertue's Note Books*, Walpole Soc., i, 53; iv, 140]. As the principal figure is holding a pair of compasses over a large terrestrial globe, his identification with the architect seems questionable.

Francis Carter is notable as one of the few subordinates of Inigo Jones in the Office of Works who had any ability as an architectural designer. His style, though far from Palladian, nevertheless 'exhibits a new sophistication, somewhere between the Elizabethan mode and the pure classicism of Jones' [John Summerson in *History of the King's Works* iii, 133].

CARTER, FRANCIS (*c.* 1773–1809), is an architect of whom little would be known but for the survival in the Public Record Office of his account-book, covering the years 1789–98 (C 217/82/1). He appears to have been the son of a surveyor of the same name, for in 1798 he wrote to a debtor for payment due to him 'for surveying business done by my late Father', and it was as 'Francis Carter, Junior' that he exhibited at the Royal Academy in 1788, 1791, 1795 and 1800. At that time he was living in Moorfields and Finsbury, but in 1804 his address was given as Mare Street, Hackney. He was presumably the Francis Carter, of Hanover Street, Newington, who died on 1 November 1809, aged 36, and whose tombstone, formerly in the churchyard of St. Mary's Newington, described him as 'architect'.

The account-book shows that Carter had commissions as a surveyor or architect in counties as far distant as Berkshire and Lincolnshire. As an architect his most important work was the country house at MARDEN HILL, TEWIN, HERTS., which he designed for Robert Mackay in 1790–4. This reveals him as a competent designer in the spare late Georgian style of architects such as Leverton and Mylne. It was altered by Sir John Soane in 1819 (*C. Life*, 22 Aug. 1941). In 1791 Carter designed a chapel (since dem.) for

HERTFORD GAOL [plans in Hertfordshire Record Office]. He was presumably responsible for the ROYAL FREEMASONS' CHARITY SCHOOL FOR GIRLS in ST. GEORGE'S FIELDS, SOUTHWARK (dem.), a drawing of which he exhibited at the R.A. in 1795. Other works recorded in the account-book are a house in London for Charles Fricker, 1794–5; two houses in ABINGDON, BERKS., for George Knapp, 1795–6; a gallery in ST. HELEN'S CHURCH, ABINGDON, 1796–7; alterations to WIGTOFT VICARAGE, LINCS., for the Rev. S. Partridge, 1797; alterations to a villa at KIRTON-IN-HOLLAND, LINCS., for Samuel Fydell, 1798–9; and two new houses at SOUTH END, BOSTON, LINCS., for Thomas Fydell, 1798–9.

CARTER, JOHN (1748–1817), was the son of Benjamin Carter, a mason and monumental sculptor in Piccadilly. When his father died in 1766 he became an assistant of Joseph Dixon, a mason in Lambeth, from whom he received some architectural instruction. From 1768 onwards he made drawings for Henry Holland the elder, and according to one of his obituarists he was for a time employed by James Wyatt as clerk of works. In 1774 he undertook to make the drawings for the *Builder's Magazine*, a serial work projected by the bookseller Newbery, and continued to do so until it ceased publication in 1786.[1] The 185 plates constituted a repertoire of architectural designs, mostly in a fanciful neo-classical style, but with some equally fanciful Gothic examples. The *Builder's Magazine* does not suggest that Carter was an architectural designer of much ability, and what makes his few executed works interesting is the antiquarian knowledge that they exhibit. They are nearly all in the Gothic style of which he was a careful student and a passionate admirer, and although he did not often succeed in recreating medieval architectural forms in a convincing manner, the monument which he designed for Lord Frederick Campbell in Sundridge Church is a remarkable anticipation of High Victorian fidelity to medieval prototypes.

Nervous, irascible and eccentric, Carter was ill-suited to regular architectural practice, and he made a living mainly by drawing medieval antiquities for such publications as Gough's *Sepulchral Monuments* (1786), and for private patrons like Horace Walpole and Sir Richard Colt Hoare. For the latter's *Itinerary of Archbishop Baldwin through Wales* (1806) he wrote a supplementary essay on architecture which was published separately in 1830 as *The Progress of Architecture, illustrated in a series of drawings taken from existing remains in South Wales*. He

---

[1] There was a new edition in 1788, and a reprint with additional text by A. G. Cook appeared in 1820.

was also employed by the Society of Antiquaries, of which he became a fellow in 1795, and at whose expense his drawings of Bath Abbey, St. Stephen's Chapel, Westminster, and of Exeter, Durham, St. Albans and Gloucester Cathedrals were published between 1795 and 1813. Between 1780 and 1794 he published his *Specimens of Ancient Sculpture and Painting* (new edition 1838, reprinted 1887), and in 1786–93 six very small volumes of *Views of Ancient Buildings in England*, republished in 4 vols. as *Specimens of Gothic Architecture* in 1824. All the plates for these works were etched by himself. His major work was *The Ancient Architecture of England* (1795–1814), an attempt to set out 'in a regular manner' the 'Orders of architecture during the British, Roman, Saxon and Norman Æras', and, in particular, to demonstrate the English origin of 'the Pointed Arch style of Architecture'. A second edition with notes by John Britton was published in 1845. The original drawings are in the British Museum (Add. MS 30092). He was also the author of *Specimens of English Ecclesiastical Costume . . . selected from Sculptures, Paintings and Brasses* (1817), containing illustrations originally published in Fosbrooke's *British Monachism*.

Although Carter's drawings and engravings have a permanent value as a record of English medieval antiquities, his views on architectural history were frequently vitiated by his ignorance of foreign examples and by his inability to read any language other than his own. In England, however, he had the reputation of being 'Antiquity's most resolute friend', and from 1798 onwards he contributed to the *Gentleman's Magazine* a remarkable series of articles entitled 'Pursuits of Architectural Innovation', in which he inveighed ceaselessly against the thoughtless destruction and misguided restoration of ancient buildings. It was due to Carter's protests that the Galilee and the Neville screen at Durham were saved from destruction in 1796, and both here and elsewhere he persistently opposed the activities of James Wyatt as an 'improver' of ancient buildings.

In 1805 Carter described himself as 'a man lost in two extremes, one for the Antiquities of England, and the other for the Divine Melodies of the immortal Handel'. He was, in fact, passionately fond of music, and composed 'two operas founded upon the History, Ancient Manners and Customs of this Country', entitled *The White Rose* and *The Cell of St. Oswald*, for which he painted the appropriate scenery.

Carter died on 8 September 1817, and was buried at Hampstead. He never married, though as a young man he had an unhappy love-affair of which he published an extraordinary account (illustrated by an engraving of his *inamorata* in the nude) under the pseudonym of 'John Ramble'.[1] In later life he had a young female servant who (according to Britton) 'occasionally accompanied him on his sketching excursions, dressed in boy's clothes'.

Carter's drawings were sold at Sotheby's on 25 February 1818, and fetched £1695 (catalogue in the Bodleian, Douce, CC.284). Twenty volumes of his topographical drawings are in the British Museum (Add. MSS. 29925–44), and there are many at Westminster City Library and in the Gough Collection in the Bodleian Library, including a fine set of Dorchester Abbey (Gough Maps 227). A volume of his drawings of English costumes from the Middle Ages to the eighteenth century is at Stonyhurst College (Hist. MSS. Comm., *2nd Report*, 1872, Appendix, 144). Other drawings are in the R.I.B.A. Collection and the Victoria and Albert Museum (D. 18–1886 is a design for a Gothic reredos in his hand). Designs by Carter for extensive additions to Bywell Hall, Northumberland, made in 1777, are preserved at the house: see also *Builder's Magazine*, pl. lxxx, and lot 176 in the sale catalogue for designs for a large classical villa for J. Fenwick of Bywell.

[Obituaries in *Gent's Mag.* 1817 (ii), 363–6 and 366–8 (the latter by J. C. Buckler); 1818 (i), 273–6, 382; 1822 (i), 102–3; memoir by John Britton in *Builder* viii, 1850, 302–4; C. L. Eastlake, *A History of the Gothic Revival*, 1872, 103–8; *D.N.B.*]

MIDFORD CASTLE, nr. BATH, SOMERSET, was built *c.* 1775 for H. Disney Roebuck after a design for 'a Gothic Mansion' published by Carter in the *Builder's Magazine*, but it is not known whether he was actually concerned in its erection [C. Hussey in *C. Life*, 3–10 March 1944].

PETERBOROUGH CATHEDRAL, Gothic altar-screen and organ-screen, *c.* 1780; removed 1832 [J. Britton, *History and Antiquities of Peterborough Cathedral*, 1828, 73].

ELTON HALL, HUNTS., Gothic additions and alterations for the 1st Earl of Carysfort, *c.* 1790 [J. Britton, *History and Antiquities of Peterborough Cathedral*, 1828, 74; drawings by Carter in B.M., Add. MS. 29930, ff. 76–9] (*V.C.H. Hunts.* iii, 157, for views; also *C. Life*, 21 Feb., 7 March 1957).

CANTERBURY CATHEDRAL, designs for alterations to choir, 1791 [John Britton, *op. cit.*, 73].

WINCHESTER, ST. PETER'S CATHOLIC CHAPEL, for the Rev. John Milner, 1792, Gothic; dem. [J. Milner, *History of Winchester* ii, 1798, 230].

DEBDEN CHURCH, ESSEX, octagonal Gothic chapel and monument designed by Carter for R. M.

---

[1] *The Scotch Parents; or, the Remarkable Case of John Ramble written by himself*, 1773. The B.M. copy has a contemporary inscription identifying the author as 'Mr. Carter, son of a statuary in Piccadilly', and Soane told John Britton that John Ramble was John Carter (*Builder* viii, 303 n.).

T. Chiswell, 1792–3, but 'not executed under his entire direction' [J. P. Neale, *Views of Seats* ii, 1819, under 'Debden Hall'].

OATLANDS HOUSE, SURREY, Gothic detailing for the new front designed by Henry Holland for Frederick, Duke of York, 1794–1800; dem. [J. Carter, *The Ancient Architecture of England*, frontispiece; *Gent's Mag.* 1808 (i), 9; 1817 (ii), 365].

STOURHEAD, WILTS., ornamental cottage for Sir Richard Colt Hoare, Bart., 1806 [K. Woodbridge, *Landscape and Antiquity*, 1970, 146–7].

WROTHAM, KENT, HELEN BETENSON'S ALMSHOUSES, ST. MARY'S ROAD, 1806, Gothic [*Gent's Mag.* 1817 (ii), 365].

SUNDRIDGE CHURCH, KENT, alterations for Lord Frederick Campbell, c. 1810. Nothing survives of Carter's works here except the Gothic monument which he designed for Lord Frederick (d. 1817) and his wife (d. 1807), for which the original designs are in B.M., Add. MS. 29941, f. 45 [J. Britton, *Descriptive Sketches of Tunbridge Wells and the Calverley Estate*, 1832, 10].

EXETER CATHEDRAL: the great west window, executed in Coade stone under the supervision of Sir John Soane c. 1810, 'was from designs made by Mr. Carter' [*Gent's Mag.* 1817 (ii), 365].

LEA CASTLE, WORCS. Carter's designs for a castle in the Norman style, now in the Metropolitan Museum of Art, New York, are illustrated by John Harris, *British Drawings for Architecture etc. in American Collections*, 46–7, and in B.M., Add. MS. 29942, ff. 136–8, there are designs by Carter for a 'Saxon' ice-house here for J. Knight, dated 1816. Lea Castle has been demolished and it is not known how far Carter's designs were carried out.

SEVENOAKS, KENT, a Gothic chapel 'now completing near Sevenoaks', 1817 [*Gent's Mag.* 1817 (ii), 365].

WESTMINSTER, Gothic details for Edward Hussey Delaval's house nr. Parliament Stairs; dem. [J. T. Smith, *A Book for a Rainy Day*, 1905 ed., 173–4].

CARTER, OWEN BROWNE (1806–1859), spent most of his life in Winchester. Nothing is known of his training, but he was a very competent architectural draughtsman, and was one of those employed by Robert Hay on his archaeological survey of Egypt between 1826 and 1838. Some of the drawings which he made are in the Print Room of the British Museum, and many of them were reproduced in the two folio volumes of lithographs entitled *Illustrations of Cairo* which Hay published in 1840. At Winchester Carter was active as an architectural topographer, providing illustrations for P. Hall's *Picturesque*

Memorials of Winchester (1830), and publishing articles on local ecclesiastical antiquities in Weale's *Quarterly Papers on Architecture* (1844–5). He made the drawings for four lithographs published in 1841 as *Picturesque Views in and near Basingstoke*. Only a few numbers were published of a projected series of views of Wiltshire churches, but 63 of Carter's original drawings are in the library of the Wiltshire Archaeological Society. In 1845, when the Archaeological Institute visited Winchester, Carter acted as one of the secretaries, and was thanked for the drawings which he made for the occasion. In 1847, 1849 and 1851 he exhibited at the Royal Academy. Carter's Gothic churches are not remarkable, but his Winchester Corn Exchange is an attractive and effective classical design with a 'Vitruvian Tuscan' portico inspired by Inigo Jones's St. Paul's, Covent Garden. Carter died at Winchester on 30 March 1859, aged 53. G. E. Street was in his office from 1841 to 1844. [*Gent's Mag.* 1859 (i), 550.; *D.N.B.*; L. Binyon, *Catalogue of Drawings by British Artists in ... the British Museum* i, 1898, 199–201; 'Drawings of Churches by O. B. Carter, 1847–50', *Wiltshire Arch. Mag.* xl, 1918–19, 190–1.]

NORK HOUSE, BANSTEAD, SURREY, designs for additions for the 2nd Lord Arden, 1836; dem. c. 1930 [John Harris, *Catalogue of British Drawings for Architecture etc. in American Collections*, 1970, 46–7].

WAREHAM, DORSET, WORKHOUSE (NOW HOSPITAL), CHRISTMAS CLOSE, 1836, with — Hyde [R.C.H.M., *Dorset* ii (2), 317].

WINCHESTER, THE CORN EXCHANGE (NOW PUBLIC LIBRARY), JEWRY STREET, 1836–8 [*Companion to the Almanac*, 1839, 246–7].

OTTERBOURNE CHURCH, HANTS., 1837–9, Gothic, in conjunction with William Yonge, squire of Otterbourne [*Gent's Mag.* 1839 (ii), 304; Georgina Battiscombe, *Charlotte Mary Yonge*, 1943, 50].

AMPFIELD CHURCH, HANTS., 1838–40, Gothic [*Gent's Mag.* 1839 (ii), 304].

WALLOP HOUSE, NETHER WALLOP, HANTS., for the Rev. Walter Blunt, 1838, Tudor style [signed lithograph published by Carter].

OAKLEY CHURCH, HANTS., added north transept, 1840–1; rebuilt 1869 [I.C.B.S. plan in Library of Society of Antiquaries, London].

COLEMORE CHURCH, HANTS., 1845 [I.C.B.S.].

SOUTHAMPTON, ST. PETER'S CHURCH, COMMERCIAL ROAD, 1845–6, Romanesque [P. Brannon, *Picture of Southampton*, 1850, 44].

NUTLEY CHURCH, HANTS., 1846, Gothic; dem. [I.C.B.S.].

SOUTHAMPTON, rebuilt HOLY ROOD CHURCH, except steeple, etc., 1849–50, Gothic; largely destroyed by bombing and reconstructed 1957 [exhib. at R.A. 1847].

CARTWRIGHT, FRANCIS (*c.* 1695–1758), was a master builder living at Bryanston, nr. Blandford in Dorset. He is described as 'carver' in his will, but his monument in Blandford St. Mary Church shows that he also acted as an architect, for on it are carved a T-square, dividers and rule, and the incised elevation of a house. He died on 24 April 1758, aged 63, leaving a newly erected house in Blandford St. Mary, and directing that all his stock of 'Stone, Marble, Timber and Boards . . . with all Tools Engines and Implements belonging to my trade' should be sold for the benefit of his wife and daughter.

In 1738–41 Cartwright was responsible for alterations to CREECH GRANGE, DORSET, for Dennis Bond, including the rebuilding of the south front 'in a modest country version of the current Palladian style' [Arthur Oswald, *The Country Houses of Dorset*, 1959, 86]. What appears to be the original design for this front is in the R.I.B.A. Drawings Collection (K 4/24(1)). In 1746–50 he designed and built KING'S NYMPTON PARK, DEVON, for James Buller [contract and accounts in Cornwall Record Office, Buller papers, bundles 134 and 689]. This house is a Palladian villa whose general form and principal façade are based on Roger Morris's Marble Hill at Twickenham. CAME HOUSE, nr. DORCHESTER, DORSET, can also be attributed to Cartwright, for the north front closely resembles the elevation incised on his monument. The house was built by John Damer in 1754.

These three buildings establish Cartwright as a competent provincial designer in the Palladian manner. His work as a carver needs further investigation, but it was presumably in that capacity that he was working for Henry Hoare at Stourhead in 1749–55. In 1742–3 he received over £20 from the churchwardens of Blandford Forum for unspecified work.

[Arthur Oswald, *Country Houses of Dorset*, 1959, 34–5, 86, 158; R.C.H.M., *Dorset* ii (2), 270–1, 384–6, iii (1), pl. 119 (illustration of monument); Stourhead archives in Wiltshire Record Office, account-book 383/6; Blandford Parish records; P.C.C. 211 HUTTON.]

CARTWRIGHT, THOMAS (–1702), was one of the leading London mason-contractors during the latter part of the seventeenth century. He served his apprenticeship in the 1630s and was by 1663 a Liveryman of the Masons' Company, subsequently serving as Warden (1671) and twice as Master (1673 and 1694). After the Great Fire he was much employed in the City, rebuilding Moorgate, 1672, dem. 1760 (measured drawing in Bodleian Library, MS. Gough Drawings a.1, f. 6) and undertaking masonry at the Weavers' Hall (1667–9); the Haberdashers' Hall (1669–71); the Drapers' Hall completed 1671); the Tallow-Chandlers' Hall (1672–3) and Mercers' Hall (completed 1672). He was the mason-contractor for three of Wren's City churches – St. Benet Fink (1670–8), St. Mary le Bow (1670–80) and St. Antholin (1678–82). He was also the contracting mason for the new Royal Exchange and after Edward Jerman's death in 1668, 'declared himselfe master of the wholle designe intended for that buildinge'. No new surveyor was appointed in place of Jerman, and on 26 March 1670 Cartwright himself 'presented to the committee a draft of the frontispiece to Cornhill and the cupilo as he advised to build it, of which they approved'. The building was completed in 1671, in which year Cartwright dedicated an engraving of it to the Lord Mayor and Corporation (B.M., *King's Maps* xxiv, 11a, 1). It was destroyed by fire in 1838.

From about 1680 to 1702 Cartwright was engaged in building ST. THOMAS'S HOSPITAL, SOUTHWARK, whose 'frontispiece', ornamented with a statue of King Edward VI and four cripples, he designed and carved. He was also the mason employed to build ST. THOMAS'S CHURCH, SOUTHWARK, in 1700–2, but there is no evidence that he made the design.

Though evidently capable of architectural design, Cartwright was primarily a mason and carver. In the latter capacity his most notable works were the monuments to Sir John Langham at Cottesbrooke, Northants. (1676), and to Sir John Lewys at Ledsham, Yorks. (W.R.) (1677). For further details of his work as a sculptor see R. Gunnis's *Dictionary of British Sculptors 1660–1851* (revised ed. 1968), 86–7.

[D. Knoop & G. P. Jones, *The London Mason in the Seventeenth Century*, 1935, 38; *Wren Soc.*, *passim*; *A.P.S.D.*, *s.v.* 'Jerman'; Guildhall Library, MS. 184/4.]

CARVER, JOHN, was a builder-architect who established himself at Meigle in Perthshire, where either he or his successor built the house called 'Carverfield'. He designed BALHARY HOUSE, ALYTH, PERTHSHIRE, for John Smyth in 1817 [drawings preserved in the house, *ex inf.* Mr. David Walker], and a steading at LEGERTLAW, PERTHSHIRE, in 1830 [Seggieden Letter-Book, 1813–30]. He was presumably the father of John Carver (1834–96), an architect who is commemorated by a tombstone in Meigle Churchyard, and the uncle of the latter's cousin David Carver (1803–78), who practised as an architect at Kinloch.

CARVER, RICHARD (*c.* 1792–1862), was presumably the 'R. Carver' who was a pupil of Sir Jeffrey Wyatville, exhibiting architectural designs at the Royal Academy from Wyatville's office in 1811 and 1812. He established himself in practice at Taunton in Somerset, where he held the post of the county surveyor. Carver's numerous churches, though occasionally showing some originality in plan (*e.g.* Theale, and the octagonal Blackford), are poorly detailed, and were despised by serious Gothic Revivalists. Mr. Carver 'has proved himself entirely ignorant of the principles of Ecclesiastical Architecture' declared the *Ecclesiologist* in 1843. Carver retired from the county surveyorship in 1857, and died at Wilton, nr. Taunton, on 1 September 1862, aged 70. [*Ecclesiologist* ii, 1843, 107, iii, 1844, 158; *Builder* xv, 1857, 78; monumental inscription.]

BLACKFORD CHURCH, SOMERSET, 1823, Gothic [I.C.B.S.].

BISHOP'S HULL, CHURCH, SOMERSET, rebuilt nave, 1826, Gothic [I.C.B.S.].

WIVELISCOMBE CHURCH, SOMERSET, 1827–9, Gothic [inscription on west gallery].

THEALE CHURCH, SOMERSET, 1828 [I.C.B.S.].

SUTTON MALLET CHURCH, SOMERSET, rebuilt 1829, except tower, Gothic [I.C.B.S.].

WELLINGTON, SOMERSET, HOLY TRINITY CHURCH, 1831, Gothic (cruciform); dem. [*Gent's Mag.* 1840 (ii), 307].

MILVERTON, SOMERSET, THE SCHOOL-HOUSE, 1835 [accounts of the Trustees of the Mary Lambe Charity, Milverton, *ex inf.* Miss Mary Dunbar].

BURROWBRIDGE CHURCH, SOMERSET, 1836, Gothic [I.C.B.S.].

WILTON CHURCH, nr. TAUNTON, SOMERSET, rebuilt chancel and eastern end of nave, 1837–8, Gothic [I.C.B.S.].

EAST HORRINGTON CHURCH, SOMERSET, 1838, Gothic [I.C.B.S.].

BURTLE CHURCH, SOMERSET, 1838–9, Gothic [I.C.B.S.].

COXLEY CHURCH, nr. WELLS, SOMERSET, 1838, Gothic [G.R.].

SILVERTON RECTORY, DEVON, 1839 [Exeter Faculty papers in Devon County Record Office].

BRIDGWATER, SOMERSET, HOLY TRINITY CHURCH, 1839, Gothic [*Gent's Mag.* 1840 (ii), 307; I.C.B.S.].

CHEDINGTON CHURCH, DORSET, 1840–1, Gothic [I.C.B.S.].

OVER STOWEY CHURCH, SOMERSET, enlarged 1840, Gothic [Church Commissioners, Church Building Commissioners' records, File 21744, pt. 8].

TAUNTON, SOMERSET, HOLY TRINITY CHURCH, 1842, Gothic [I.C.B.S.].

TAUNTON, SOMERSET, ST. MARY MAGDALENE CHURCH, repairs and restoration (with Benjamin Ferrey), 1842–3 [J. Cottle, *St. Mary Magdalene, Taunton*, 1845, 6].

EASTON (ST. PAUL) CHURCH, SOMERSET, 1843, neo-Norman [I.C.B.S.].

CANNINGTON CHURCH, SOMERSET, refurnishing, 1845 [*Ecclesiologist* i, 1845, 292].

WELLINGTON CHURCH, SOMERSET, repaired and enlarged with C. E. Giles, 1849–50 [I.C.B.S.].

BEAMINSTER, DORSET, HOLY TRINITY CHURCH, with C. E. Giles, 1849–51, Gothic [R.C.H.M., *West Dorset*, 21].

CARWITHAM, THOMAS, of Twickenham, was a pupil of Sir James Thornhill and a decorative painter. He appears to have specialized in architectural ornament, for he was the author of a small treatise entitled *The Description and Use of an Architectonick Sector* (1723), and at the end of it there is an advertisement: 'History and Architect Painting done by the Author'. He should not be confused with John Carwitham, an engraver who published *Various Kinds of Floor Decorations represented both in plans and perspective. Being useful designs for ornamenting the floors of halls, rooms, summer houses ... in twenty-four copper plates* [1739], *A New Drawing Book designed on purpose for Beginners* (n.d.) and (*inter alia*) a portrait of the architect Batty Langley (1741). [E. Croft-Murray, *Decorative Painting in England* ii, 1970, 32; Thieme & Becker, *Künstler-Lexikon* vi, 98; J. Harris, *Catalogue of British Drawings for Architecture ... in American Collections*, 1971, 48.]

CASSON, JOHN WHITESIDE, practised in Liverpool in the 1820s and 1830s. MELLING CHURCH, LANCS., 1834, Gothic, appears to be his only recorded work [I.C.B.S.].

CASTELL, ROBERT (–1729), is known only as the author of *The Villas of the Ancients Illustrated*, 1728. This represented the first attempt to reconstruct the ancient Roman villas from the descriptions of classical authors. Castell printed his sources in the original Latin with an English translation, and accompanied them with elaborate plates engraved by Fourdrinier. These purport to show not only the villas but also their surroundings, and the layouts have interesting affinities with the English landscape-gardening of the period. Sumptuously produced for only 116 subscribers, the book was dedicated to Lord Burlington, but does not seem to have been sponsored by him. There was a less elaborate 'trade edition', omitting the Latin texts [B. Weinreb, Catalogue 2: *Books and Drawings before 1800*, 1963, nos. 30–1]. The book was evidently a financial failure, for in 1728 Castell was imprisoned for debt in the Fleet Prison in London, where he died of smallpox. His ill-treatment by Bambridge, the Warden, was described in the House of Commons in 1729. Though 'born to a competent estate', he died 'leaving all his affairs in the greatest confusion, and a numerous family of small children in the utmost distress' (*Journal of the House of Commons* xxi, 277). At the time of his death he was engaged on a translation of *Vitruvius* which was reported to be already 'pretty far advanced' in November 1727 [John Fleming, *Robert Adam and his Circle*, 1962, 28].

In his *Biographical History of Gonville and Caius College* (1897), Venn tentatively identified the subject of this entry with Robert Castell, son of Abraham Castell of Thrigby in Norfolk, Esquire, who was admitted to Caius College, Cambridge, in 1694 at the age of 17, but in his *Alumni Cantabrigienses* (1940) he withdrew this suggestion, stating that the Cambridge man died at Yarmouth in May 1719, ten years before the author of the *Villas of the Ancients*.

CATHERWOOD, FREDERICK (1799–1854), was born in London, and was a pupil from 1815 to 1820 of Michael Meredith. Between 1821 and 1825 he made an extensive tour in Italy, Greece and Egypt. On his return, he began to practise his profession, designing a large glass-house near Westminster Bridge, and some houses at Pentonville. It was, however, as an archaeological draughtsman that he was to make his name, and in this capacity he left England again in 1831 as a member of Robert Hay's expedition to investigate and record the antiquities of the Nile Valley. In company with Francis Arundale and Joseph Bonomi, he also explored Palestine and Arabia, and, disguised as an Egyptian officer, made measured drawings of the Dome of the Rock in Jerusalem. In the course of his travels he obtained the materials for a series of panoramas which he afterwards exhibited in London and New York. In 1836 he set up in practice in New York in partnership with Frederick Diaper, a pupil of Sir Robert Smirke who became a well-known American architect. But three years later he set out to investigate the Maya cities of Central America in company with J. L. Stephens, and it was his pioneer work in this field which gave him a place in the history of American archaeology which he never attained in that of architecture. His principal publication was the *Views of Ancient Monuments in Central America, Chiapas and Yucatán*, 1844. He also superintended the building of railways in Demarara, Panama and California. He returned to England in 1853, but was involved in the loss of the steamer *Arctic* while returning to America in the following year [V. W. Von Hagen, *Frederick Catherwood, Architect*, 1950].

CATLEY, THOMAS, an architect of Hastings, designed ST. CLEMENT'S CHURCH, HALTON, nr. HASTINGS, SUSSEX, 1838, in the 'Early English' style. A chancel was added in 1888 [*V.C.H. Sussex* ix, 25; *The Watering-Places of Great Britain and Fashionable Directory* (Joseph Robins, 1833), 24].

CATT, BENJAMIN BATLEY (–1867), practised in Ipswich, where he designed THE TOWN HALL, 1818–19, dem., as recorded by the inscription on the foundation-stone given by J. Dugdale, *British Traveller* iv, 1819, 298. According to G. R. Clark's *History and Description of Ipswich*, 1830, he was associated with William Brown (*q.v.*) in the design of the Market Place in 1810–11. He died at Ipswich on 10 June 1867 [Principal Probate Registry, Calendar of Probates].

CAUSFIELD, —, was the architect and builder of the tower of GATESHEAD CHURCH, CO. DURHAM, in 1740. He is said to have been 'ruined by the undertaking' [E. Mackenzie, *History of Newcastle* ii, 1827, 751].

CAVELER, WILLIAM, was the author of a collection of measured drawings of details, etc., of medieval English architecture entitled *Select Specimens of Gothic Architecture*, 4 vols. 1835–6, 2nd ed. in 1 vol. 1839. He also published in 1850 *Architectural Illustrations of Warmington Church, Northamptonshire*. In 1837 he entered a Roman Doric design for the Royal Berkshire Hospital competition [*Reading Mercury*, 11 Feb. 1837] and he exhibited at the Royal Academy in 1844 and 1850. From about 1845 onwards he was practising in Margate, Kent, where he restored the parish church [*Builder* iv, 1846, 532].

CHALKLEY, C—, appears to have been a pupil of Jeffry Wyatville, from whose address he exhibited a 'Design for a Lodge' at the R.A. in 1800. In the W. Sussex Record Office there are two elevations of West Dean Park, Sussex, signed by Chalkley and dated 1805. West Dean Park was then in course of erection to the designs of James Wyatt.

CHALMERS, JOHN, practised in Edinburgh early in the nineteenth century. In 1805 he was one of the architects who reported on the state of Inverkeithing Church, Fife [W. Stephen, *History of Inverkeithing and Rosyth*, Aberdeen 1921, 241]. He made in 1821 a very competent set of plans and elevations of St. Giles' Cathedral, Edinburgh [S.R.O., RHP 6512/8–12]. The death at Edinburgh on 20 February 1822 of John Chalmers, surveyor, 'fourth son of the late John Chalmers of Chamberfield, architect, Esqr.', is recorded in *Edinburgh Magazine* x, 1822, 560.

CHAMBERS, ROBERT (*c.* 1710–1784), was a mason by trade and a native of Gloucestershire. Horace Walpole describes him as 'carver, architect and stainer of marble'. Although best known in the first and last capacities, he did exhibit architectural drawings at the Free Society of Artists, *e.g.* 'A design in architecture of a plan and elevation of a grotesque building with its tessel-lated floor' (1763), plans and sections of the royal vault in Westminster Abbey (1769), and plans of the harbour and pier at Dover (1778, 1782). Designs by him for 'a Bone-House, to be built at the North East Corner of St. Mary's Church in Dover' (1773) and for a new window in the south wall of the same church 'near the font' (1772–3) are preserved in the British Museum (*King's Maps*, xvi, 48). For his work as a sculptor and stainer of marble see R. Gunnis's *Dictionary of British Sculptors*, revised ed. 1968, 90–1. Some designs by Chambers for chimney-pieces at CLAYDON HOUSE, BUCKS., are among the Verney papers there.

CHAMBERS, SIR WILLIAM (1723–1796), was the son of John Chambers, a Scottish merchant established at Gothenburg in Sweden, where he was born on 23 February 1723. His father had him educated in England, sending him to Ripon, where he presumably attended the grammar school. At the age of 16 he returned to Sweden to begin a mercantile career in the Swedish East India Company. In 1740–2 he made his first voyage as a cadet on one of the Company's ships bound for Bengal. In 1743–5 a second voyage took him to Canton, and in 1748–9 he again travelled to China in the capacity of a 'supercargo' on the ship *Hoppet*. His commercial duties were not, however, onerous, and in an autobiographical note among the archives of Uppsala University he recalled that on these voyages he found time to study 'modern languages, mathematics and the free arts, but chiefly civil architecture, for which latter I have from my earliest years felt the strongest inclination'. Moreover, between voyages he was able to visit 'England, Scotland, Holland, Flanders and a part of France'. While in Canton, he had made sketches of Chinese buildings, and some of his European excursions appear to have been architectural in character. By 1749 he had enough capital to abandon his mercantile career and make architecture his 'sole study and profession'.

It was in J. F. Blondel's *École des Arts* in Paris that Chambers began his professional training and there he would have met some of the young men who were to be the leaders of French neo-classicism in the 1760s and 1770s. In the autumn of 1750 he set out for Italy, where he was to spend five years, chiefly in Rome, though he 'also visited . . . Naples, Florence, Bologna, Venice, Vicenza, Genoa, Milan, Turin etc., collecting in all these places all that could serve me and increase my knowledge [of] the science I had chosen for my study'. At Rome he appears to have received tuition from the French drawing-masters Clérisseau and Pécheux, and besides studying a wide variety of buildings, ancient and modern, he was strongly influenced by the neo-classical ideas of

French designers such as Le Geay and Le Lorrain. His reputation among the visiting English as 'a prodigy for Genius, for Sense & good taste' was reported by his rival Robert Adam, who thought that he 'in great measure deserves their encomium'.

In 1755 Chambers returned to England to begin practice. He was accompanied by a wife and an infant daughter. Apart from the fact that she was born Catherine More and came from Bromsgrove, nothing certain is known of the origins of the woman Chambers had married in Rome in March 1753. Joseph Wilton (who met them both in Rome) told Farington that she was 'a milliner girl [who] followed him to Paris'. In London they took lodgings next to Tom's Coffee House in Russell Street, Covent Garden. Although at first he had few commissions, Chambers soon had the good fortune to be recommended to Lord Bute as a suitable person to become architectural tutor to the Prince of Wales, afterwards King George III, an appointment which laid the foundations of the royal favour which he was subsequently to enjoy. While at Rome he had made grandiose designs for a mausoleum to the memory of the prince's father, Frederick, Prince of Wales, and in 1757 the Dowager Princess employed him to lay out the grounds of her house at Kew, and to embellish them with a variety of temples and garden buildings, some classical, others oriental in style. In 1763 he advertised this royal patronage by the publication of a handsome folio dedicated to the princess and entitled *Plans, Elevations, Sections and Perspective Views of the Gardens and Buildings at Kew in Surrey*. A collection of the original drawings bound up by Chambers for presentation to Lord Bute is now in the Metropolitan Museum at New York. This was not Chambers's first book, for in 1757 he had published *Designs of Chinese Buildings, Furniture, Dresses, etc.*, and in 1759 he produced the first part of a projected *Treatise on Civil Architecture*, a work in which he set out 'to collect into one volume what is now dispersed in a great many, and to select, from mountains of promiscuous Materials, a Series of Sound Precepts and good Designs'. The result became the standard English treatise on the use of the Orders and their enrichments, largely superseding Isaac Ware's less discriminating *Complete Body of Architecture*. There was a second edition in 1768, and a third, 'considerably augmented', in 1791, when the title was altered to *A Treatise on the Decorative Part of Civil Architecture*, as the 'constructive' part was never written. There were later editions by Joseph Gwilt (1825) and J. B. Papworth (1826). The former was reissued by W. H. Leeds in 1862. A facsimile reprint of the 1791 edition was published in 1968.

By 1760 Chambers was well established in professional practice, and in the following year he joined the Office of Works as one of the two joint Architects appointed by the Crown at a salary of £300 p.a., the other being Robert Adam. By 1769, when he succeeded Flitcroft as Comptroller of the Works, he had become the effective head of the department, and when it was reorganized in 1782 he became the first holder of the new combined office of Surveyor-General and Comptroller. As head of the royal works Chambers proved to be an able and humane administrator as well as a distinguished government architect. Apart from remodelling Buckingham House for George III, and designing the State Coach that is still in use for coronations, his principal achievement as a public architect was Somerset House. Begun in 1776, and not quite finished at the time of his death, Somerset House became the great preoccupation of Chambers's later life, and absorbed nearly all his energies from the date of its commencement until his death twenty years later. In it he exemplified all the precepts that he laid down in the *Treatise*, making it one of the show-pieces of English architectural design and craftsmanship in the reign of George III. In 1770 he was made a Knight of the Polar Star by King Gustav of Sweden, and was later permitted by George III to assume the rank and title of an English knight. In 1766 he was elected a member of the Swedish Academy of Sciences, and he was also a corresponding member of the French Academy of Architecture (1763) and a Fellow of the Royal Society (1776).

Chambers exhibited at the Society of Arts from 1761 to 1768, and in the latter year played a leading part in bringing about the foundation of the Royal Academy of Arts, of which he became the first Treasurer. For nearly thirty years he was the dominant figure in the councils of the Academy, at times overshadowing even the President (Sir Joshua Reynolds), who is said to have declared on one occasion that 'Sir William was Viceroy over him'. He exhibited at the Academy from 1769 to 1777. He was also a member of the Architects' Club, which began its meetings in 1791 at the Thatched House Tavern.

Chambers's architectural style was a sophisticated compound of French neo-classicism and English Palladianism. It was the former that was predominant when he returned from Italy in the 1750s, but it proved to be too novel for his conservative English clients, and for most of his private commissions he found it expedient to substitute a refined Palladianism. However, Chambers kept in touch with French architects such as Le Roy and de Wailly, and a second visit to Paris in 1774 enabled him to resume contact with French neo-classicism at source, with results that are clearly apparent in Somerset House. Despite his fastidious, almost academic, approach to

architectural design, Chambers was far from being a pedant. He studied Michelangelo and Bernini as well as Palladio and Scamozzi, and there is a judicious balance in his advice to a pupil to 'correct that luxuriant, bold, and perhaps licentious style, which you will have acquired at Rome, Florence, Genoa and Bologna, by the simple, chaste, but rather tame manner [of the two latter architects]'. The Grecian innovations of Stuart and Revett were, however, little to his liking, and he signified his distaste for 'Attic Deformity' both in some lectures 'written for the use of the Royal Academy soon after its institution at a time when the indisposition of the Professor of Architecture [Thomas Sandby] rendered him unfit either to compose or deliver lectures', and in the introduction to the third edition of his *Treatise on Civil Architecture* (1791). With the contemporary fashion for Gothic he had equally little sympathy. Milton Abbey, his only experiment in that style, was designed to please its owner, Lord Milton, and more than one reference in his correspondence to 'this vast ugly Gothic house in Dorset' shows that he disliked the commission as much as he did 'this unmannerly imperious Lord, who treats me as he does every body, ill'. In Kew Gardens, however, Chambers showed that he was capable of the fanciful as well as of the grand manner. The Alhambra, the Moorish mosque and the Chinese pagoda were celebrated examples of their kind, and the fact that Chambers was the only English architect who had actually seen a Chinese town seemed to give him an authority in such matters which he himself was anxious not to exaggerate. His *Designs of Chinese Buildings* came when the vogue for such things was almost over, but had some importance as a source-book for authentic illustrations of Chinese architecture. As for the *Dissertation on Oriental Gardening* which he published in 1772, it was primarily an attack on the bare style of landscape-gardening associated with 'Capability' Brown,[1] and the oriental dress was merely a literary camouflage. To Chambers's embarrassment his supposed championship of the Chinese garden as a model for imitation was taken seriously by the public, obliging him in 1773 to publish a second edition with an 'Explanatory Discourse'. Worse still, the *Dissertation* brought down on him the effective ridicule of a well-aimed reply, published anonymously as *An Heroic Epistle to Sir William Chambers* (1773), but now known to have been

---

[1] Chambers is said to have submitted designs for Claremont which were rejected in favour of those of Brown. Personal pique at the loss of Lord Clive's patronage may therefore have embittered (though it cannot be supposed to have inspired) Chambers's attack on a style of gardening of which he disapproved on aesthetic grounds.

written by the poet Mason with the connivance of Horace Walpole.[1]

From 1758 to 1765 Chambers lived in Poland Street, but in the latter year he moved to a house which he had built for himself in Berners Street. In 1765 he also acquired a lease of the Palladian villa at Whitton, nr. Hounslow, which Roger Morris had built for the Duke of Argyll. Towards the end of his life he moved to a small house in Norton (now Bolsover) Street, where he died on 8 March 1796. He was buried in the south transept of Westminster Abbey, under an inscribed slab.

Chambers's pupils and assistants included James Gandon, Edward Stevens, John Yenn, Thomas Hardwick, Robert Browne, Willey Reveley, Thomas Whetten, John Read, John Rudd and Richard Ripley. A list of over a dozen portraits is given by Harris (p. 173). The most important are those by Carl Frederik Von Breda (R.I.B.A.), Francis Cotes (Scottish National Portrait Gallery) and Sir Joshua Reynolds (Royal Academy and National Portrait Gallery). For a complete list of surviving drawings see Harris, p. 397. The most important collections are in the R.I.B.A. Drawings Collection, Sir John Soane's Museum, the Victoria and Albert Museum and the Royal Library at Windsor. A large collection of Chambers's letters is in the R.I.B.A. Library, and four letter-books containing copies of his professional correspondence from November 1769 to 1775 are in the British Museum (Add. MSS. 41133–6).

A full bibliography will be found in John Harris's Sir William Chambers, 1970, which supersedes all previous biographical notices. T. Hardwick's 'Memoir of the Life of Sir William Chambers', prefixed to Gwilt's edition of the Treatise on Civil Architecture (1825), must, however, be mentioned as a basic source, and H. M. Martienssen, 'Chambers as a Professional Man', Arch. Rev., April 1964, supplements Harris. The sale catalogue of Chambers's library is printed in Sale Catalogues of Libraries of Eminent Persons iv, ed. Watkin, 1972, 107–134.

The following list of works is based on the 'Catalogue Raisonné' in Harris's biography, where full references to the relevant letters, drawings and other sources for each commission will be found. References are, as usual, given in round brackets to illustrations or descriptions of the individual buildings, H. indicating an illustration in Harris, C.A. an engraving in Chambers's Treatise on Civil Architecture. Particulars of various doubtful or very minor works omitted from the list below will be found in Harris, op. cit.

---

[1] See Satirical Poems by William Mason, ed. Paget Toynbee, 1926.

PUBLIC BUILDINGS, ETC.

LONDON, LITTLE DENMARK COURT, STRAND, alterations and additions to the premises of the Society of Arts, including the Great Room, 1759–60; dem.

WOODSTOCK, OXON., THE TOWN HALL, for the 4th Duke of Marlborough, 1766 (H.).

LONDON, THE GERMAN LUTHERAN CHURCH in THE SAVOY, the interior, 1766–7; dem. 1875 (H.).

RICHMOND, SURREY, OBSERVATORY in OLD DEER PARK, for King George III, 1768 (H.).

RICHMOND, SURREY, temporary PAVILION for the reception of King Christian IV of Denmark, 1769 (H.).

HULL, YORKS. (E.R.), TRINITY HOUSE CHAPEL, 1772; dem. 1844.

LIVERPOOL, THE THEATRE ROYAL, 1772; dem. 1802 (R. Brooke, Liverpool in the Last Quarter of the Eighteenth Century, 1853).

DUBLIN, TRINITY COLLEGE, designed facing blocks containing Theatre (or Examination School) on south and Chapel on north, 1775. The Theatre was built 1777–86 under the direction of Graham Myers of Dublin, the Chapel in 1787–c. 1800 (H.). These buildings formed part of a more extensive scheme designed by Chambers but not executed (see Harris, pl. 149).

LONDON, SOMERSET HOUSE, STRAND, 1776–96; completed by James Wyatt 1796–1801. The east wing containing King's College was added by R. Smirke in 1830–5, the west wing containing the Inland Revenue offices by J. Pennethorne in 1851–6. [See, in addition to the references given by Harris, The History of the King's Works v, 1976, 363–80, and vi, 1973, 480–4.]

COUNTRY HOUSES

WILTON HOUSE, WILTS., works for the 10th Earl of Pembroke, 1757–9, including Triumphal Arch (originally in park facing south front, removed to forecourt c. 1800), Casina, Rock Bridge (dem.) and interior of library (dem.) (C.A.; H.) In 1772–4 Chambers designed a Tennis Court (dem.).

KEW GARDENS, SURREY, works for Augusta, Dowager Princess of Wales, including Bridge to 'House of Confucius', 1757 (dem.); Gallery of Antiques, 1757 (dem.); Orangery, 1757–61 (royal arms and cartouches with letter 'A' added 1842); Temple of Pan, 1758 (dem.); Temple of Arethusa, 1758 (dem.); Alhambra, 1758 (dem.); Stables, 1758 (dem.); Temple of Victory, commemorating the Battle of Minden, 1759 (dem.); Ruined Arch, 1759; Theatre of Augusta, 1760 (dem.); Temple of Bellona, 1760 (rebuilt on different site); Menagerie, 1760 (dem.); Mosque, 1761 (dem.);

Temple of the Sun, 1761 (dem.); Pagoda, 1761–2; Temple of Peace, 1763 (not completed); Temple of Æolus, before 1763 (rebuilt 1845); Temple of Solitude, before 1763 (dem.); Palladian Bridge, before 1763 (dem.) (W. Chambers, *Plans, Elevations, Sections and Perspective Views of the Gardens and Buildings at Kew in Surrey*, 1763; *C. Life*, 31 May 1930).

GOODWOOD HOUSE, SUSSEX, added south wing, stables and gate-piers (dem.) for the 3rd Duke of Richmond, 1757–60 (H.).

MARINO HOUSE, nr. DUBLIN, alterations, additions and gate-piers for the 1st Earl of Charlemont, *c.* 1758–75; dem. *c.* 1920.

MARINO HOUSE, nr. DUBLIN, THE CASINO, for the 1st Earl of Charlemont, 1758–76 (*C.A.*; H.).

CASTLE HILL (later DUNTISH COURT), DORSET, for Fitz Foy, *c.* 1760; dem. 1965 (*Vitruvius Britannicus* v, pls. 61–3; plan in R.C.H.M., *Dorset* iii (1), 51).

THE HOO, KIMPTON, HERTS., bridge, gateway and internal alterations to house (dem. 1957) for Thomas Brand, *c.* 1760–4 (illustration of bridge in *Vitruvius Britannicus* iv, pl. 18).

CASTLETOWN HOUSE, CO. KILDARE, work for Thomas Conolly, including internal decoration and probably also the gate-piers, *c.* 1760 (*C. Life*, 3 April 1969; *The Georgian Society Records of Eighteenth-Century Domestic Architecture, etc.* v, 1913).

ROEHAMPTON, SURREY, villa known successively as PARKSTED, BESSBOROUGH HOUSE and MANRESA HOUSE, for the 2nd Earl of Bessborough, 1760–8 (*Vitruvius Britannicus* iv, pls. 11–13; H.).

THE HYDE, nr. INGATESTONE, ESSEX, entrance-hall and staircase for Thomas Brand (afterwards Brand-Hollis), 1761 (J. Disney, *Memoirs of Thomas Brand Hollis*, 1805, plates; H.).

COLEBY HALL, LINCS., TEMPLE OF ROMULUS AND REMUS, for Thomas Scrope, 1762 (H.).

STYCHE HALL, SALOP., house and stables for 1st Lord Clive, 1762–6; alterations in 1796–8 included addition of canted bays flanking entrance.

DUDDINGSTON HOUSE, MIDLOTHIAN, for the 8th Earl of Abercorn, including stables and temple, 1763–8 (*Vitruvius Britannicus* iv, pls. 14–17; *C. Life*, 24 Sept. 1959).

WALCOT HALL, SALOP., remodelled for the 1st Lord Clive, 1764–7 (*C. Life*, 14 Oct. 1939).

KIRKLEATHAM HALL, YORKS. (N.R.), gallery for (Sir) Charles Turner, *c.* 1765; dem. 1955. The extent of Chambers's responsibility for this gallery is uncertain. It was probably built under the direction of John Carr, who may have modified Chambers's design.

TEDDINGTON GROVE, MIDDLESEX, for Moses Franks, *c.* 1765; dem. (J. C. Loudon, *The Gardener's Magazine* xv, 1839, 424–6).

NEWBY (now BALDERSBY) PARK, YORKS. (N.R.), Pheasantry, Menagery and internal alterations for Sir Thomas Robinson, 1st Lord Grantham, *c.* 1765. The interior was rebuilt after a fire in 1902.

POSTON COURT, HEREFS., Casino for Sir Edward Boughton, Bart., date uncertain, probably *c.* 1765; wings added *c.* 1882.

WHITTON PLACE, MIDDLESEX, alterations and garden buildings for himself, *c.* 1765 onwards; dem. *c.* 1847.

HOUGHTON HOUSE, nr. AMPTHILL, BEDS., internal alterations for the Marquis of Tavistock, 1765; dismantled 1794, now a ruin, in which nothing remains of Chambers's work.

PEPER HAROW, SURREY, for the 3rd and 4th Viscounts Midleton, *c.* 1765–75. The stables had already been built to Chambers's designs in 1763 as an addition to the old house. The porch was added by C. R. Cockerell in 1843 (*C. Life*, 26 Dec. 1925; C. Hussey, *English Country Houses: Mid Georgian*, 1956, 111–14).

WREST PARK, BEDS., the Chinese Pavilion may have been designed by Chambers for the 2nd Earl of Hardwicke, *c.* 1766. According to D. & S. Lysons, *Magna Britannia* i, 1806, 86, the 'Roman Temple' over the Cold Bath was designed by Chambers, but see Stevens, Edward.

BLENHEIM PALACE, OXON., works for the 4th Duke of Marlborough, including internal decoration, the ornamentation of the East Gate (to the kitchen court), the Bladon Bridge, the Temples of Flora and Diana, the Tuscan gateway to the kitchen garden, and an ornamental tripod carved by Joseph Wilton, *c.* 1766–75 (*C.A.*, 3rd ed. 1791, pl. 52, design for tripod; D. Green, *Blenheim Palace*, 1951).

STANMORE HOUSE or PARK, MIDDLESEX, completion of a new house designed by John Vardy (d. 1765) for Andrew Drummond, 1766–9; further works for John Drummond 1769–70; dem. (H.).

BARTON HALL, GREAT BARTON, SUFFOLK, library for Sir Charles Bunbury, 1767–8; destroyed by fire 1914.

ANSLEY HALL, WARWICKS., Chinese temple for John Ludford, 1767; dem.

COBHAM HALL, KENT, general restoration and alterations including extension of attic storey on west front of Cross Wing, for the 3rd Earl of Darnley, *c.* 1767–70.

WOBURN ABBEY, BEDS., rebuilding of south wing, interiors including Eating Rooms and Library, and Basin Bridge, for the 4th Duke of Bedford, 1767–72. In 1788–9 Holland raised the level of the terrace in front of the south front, set the end windows in arched recesses, and remodelled Chambers's interiors. The bridge has been shorn of its ornaments (H.).

ADDERBURY HOUSE, OXON., alterations for the 3rd Duke of Buccleuch, *c.* 1768; largely dem. 1808. (*V.C.H. Oxon.* ix, 8, for plan).

AMPTHILL PARK, BEDS., added wings and re-decorated principal rooms for the 2nd Earl of Upper Ossory, 1768–72 (H.).

CASTLE HOWARD, YORKS. (N.R.), the Exclamation Gate for the 5th Earl of Carlisle, c. 1770.

PARTILLE SLOT, GOTHENBERG, SWEDEN, for his brother-in-law, David Sandberg, 1770 (H.).

SKELTON CASTLE, YORKS. (N.R.), minor internal work for John Hall Stevenson, c. 1770.

DANSON HILL, KENT, internal alterations, timber Palladian bridge (dem.) and Doric temple for (Sir) John Boyd, c. 1770. The temple was re-moved to Walden Bury House, Herts., in 1961.

RATHFARNHAM CASTLE, CO. DUBLIN, interiors for the 4th Viscount Loftus, afterwards Earl of Ely, 1770–1 (*The Georgian Society Records of Eighteenth-Century Domestic Architecture, etc.* v, 1913).

KNIGHTSBRIDGE, LONDON, house for John Cal-craft, 1770–2; dem. c. 1838.

MILTON HOUSE, nr. PETERBOROUGH, NORTHANTS., alterations and interior decorations (including the Gallery) for the 4th Earl Fitzwilliam, 1771–3; also a Corinthian temple, 1773, since dismantled (*C. Life*, 1 June 1961).

RICHMOND, SURREY, WICK HOUSE, for Sir Joshua Reynolds, 1771–2; since much altered.

MILTON ABBEY HOUSE, DORSET, for 1st Lord Mil-ton, incorporating medieval Great Hall, 1771–6, Gothic (*C. Life*, 16, 23 and 30 June, 21, 28 July 1966; R.C.H.M., *Dorset* iii (2), 191–7). Chambers and L. Brown both made designs for the model village built by Lord Milton c. 1774–80. The evidence does not make it clear to which of them the final result should be ascribed, but the basic layout seems to have been Chambers's work [Arthur Oswald in *C. Life*, 29 Sept. 1966].

INGRESS ABBEY, KENT, work for John Calcraft, in-cluding a Doric temple to house a collection of Roman altars, before 1772; dem. The temple is now at Cobham Hall, Kent, where it was re-erected in 1820.

KEW, SURREY, THE WHITE HOUSE, alterations for King George III, 1772–3; dem. 1802.

AMESBURY HOUSE, WILTS., Chinese temple for the Duchess of Queensberry, 1772 (H.).

LUCAN HOUSE, CO. DUBLIN, designs for Agmon-desham Vesey, who is said to have built the house 'on a plan of his own', 1773–5. The façade at least is likely to be by Chambers (*C. Life*, 31 Jan. 1947; Desmond Guinness & William Ryan, *Irish Houses and Castles*, 1971, 131–8).

TRENT PLACE, ENFIELD, MIDDLESEX, alterations for Sir Richard Jebb, c. 1777; dem. (H.).

HEDSOR LODGE, BUCKS., for the 2nd Lord Boston, 1778; dem. 1865 (H.).

WINDSOR CASTLE, BERKS., THE QUEEN'S LODGE, 1776–9 (dem. 1823), and LOWER LODGE, 1779–82 (remodelled as 'Burford Lodge',

1842), for King George III, both castellated (H.; *History of the King's Works* v).

HOUSES IN LONDON

RICHMOND HOUSE, WHITEHALL, works for the 3rd Duke of Richmond, including gate to Privy Gardens (*C.A.*) and decoration of gallery, 1759–60; destroyed by fire 1891.

PEMBROKE HOUSE, WHITEHALL, internal decora-tions for the 10th Earl of Pembroke, 1759–60, and riding-house, 1773; dem. 1913 (*C. Life*, 19 Sept. 1936, 294; *Survey of London* xiii, 167–75, pls. 67–88).

BUCKINGHAM HOUSE (later PALACE), remodelling of main façade, interior decoration, addition of north and south wings, Great or West Library, South Library, Octagon Library, East Library and Riding House, for King George III and Queen Charlotte, 1762–73; all dem. or remo-delled 1825–36 [*History of the King's Works* v, 134–7]

BERKELEY SQUARE, NO. 45, internal redecoration for the 1st Lord Clive, 1763–7 (*C. Life*, 2 Jan, 1937).

BERNERS STREET, NOS. 13–22, 44, 45(?), 46, 47, 48–53(?), 54–58, built as a speculation in partner-ship with Thomas Collins, 1764–70; dem. Chambers occupied No. 13 himself.

GRANTHAM HOUSE, WHITEHALL, alterations for Sir Thomas Robinson, 1st Lord Grantham, c. 1765(?); dem. c. 1896 (*Survey of London* xiii, 160–1, pl. 47).

GOWER (afterwards CARRINGTON) HOUSE, WHITE-HALL, for the 2nd Earl Gower, 1765–74; dem. 1886 (*Survey of London* xvi, 176, pls. 94–5).

GROSVENOR SQUARE, NO. 20, alterations and inter-ior decoration for the 3rd Duke of Buccleuch, c. 1767; dem.

CHEYNE WALK, NO. 6, bath-house for Dr. Bartho-lomew de Dominiceti, c. 1768; dem.

ARLINGTON STREET, NO. 21, repairs and alterations for the 3rd Viscount Weymouth, 1769 [B.M., Add. MS. 41133, f. 29].

NEWMAN STREET, NO. 85, for Mr. Gray, c. 1769; dem.

MILTON HOUSE, PARK LANE, additions, including entrance gates and screen, for the 1st Lord Milton, 1769–71; dem. (J. Carter, *The Builder's Magazine* ii, 1774, pl. x).

CLEVELAND ROW, house (now Warwick House) for Henry Errington, 1770–1; altered in nine-teenth century (*Survey of London* xxx, 506–7 and pl. 232).

PICCADILLY, NO. 79 (NO. 1 STRATTON STREET), addition of attic storey for the 4th Earl Fitzwil-liam, 1770–1; dem. 1929.

ST. JAMES'S SQUARE, NO. 22, alterations for Thomas Brand, junior, 1771; dem. 1847 (*Survey of London* xxix, 180–1; xxx, pl. 133).

MARLBOROUGH HOUSE, ST. JAMES'S, addition of

attic and internal alterations for the 4th Duke of Marlborough, 1771–4; altered 1865 (*C. Life*, 17 April 1937).

MELBOURNE HOUSE, PICCADILLY, for the 1st Lord Melbourne, 1771–4; enlarged and reconstructed by Henry Holland and A. Copland as Albany Chambers 1803–4 (*Survey of London* xxxii, 367–89 and pls. 111–19; H.).

GEORGE STREET, NO. 15, alterations, including Doric entrance doorway, for the 2nd Earl Fauconberg, 1774.

GROSVENOR SQUARE, NO. 51, alterations for (Sir) Charles Turner, 1774–5; since rebuilt.

HOUSES IN DUBLIN

CHARLEMONT HOUSE, RUTLAND SQUARE (now the Municipal Gallery of Modern Art), for the 1st Earl of Charlemont, 1763–75. The portico is an addition and the interior has been remodelled (*The Georgian Society Records of Eighteenth-Century Domestic Architecture, etc.* iv, 1912, pls. vii–xi).

LEINSTER HOUSE. redecoration of rooms on first floor of garden front, for the 1st Duke of Leinster, 1767 (*The Georgian Society Records of Eighteenth-Century Domestic Architecture, etc.* iv, 1912, 43–61, pls. xviii–xlix).

HOUSES IN EDINBURGH

ST. ANDREW'S SQUARE, NO. 26, for Gilbert Meason, 1769–72; balustraded parapet added *c.* 1840; north elevation 1878.

DUNDAS HOUSE (now Royal Bank of Scotland), ST. ANDREW'S SQUARE, for Sir Lawrence Dundas, 1771–4; porch added 1828; internal alterations 1825 and 1857–9.

MONUMENTS

CHENIES CHURCH, BUCKS., monument to 2nd Duke of Bedford, 1769, Joseph Wilton, sculptor (signed) (H.).

WESTMINSTER ABBEY, monument in St. John's Chapel to the 6th Earl and Countess of Mountrath, 1771, Joseph Wilton, sculptor (H.).

UNEXECUTED

Among many unexecuted designs listed by Harris, attention may be drawn to the following: a mausoleum in memory of Frederick, Prince of Wales, 1751–2 (H.); a new house at HAREWOOD, YORKS. (W.R.), for Edwin Lascelles, afterwards Lord Harewood, 1756 (H.); BLACKFRIARS BRIDGE, LONDON, 1759 (R. S. Mylne, *The Master Masons to the Crown of Scotland*, 1893, 264); YORK HOUSE, PALL MALL, LONDON, for Edward Augustus, Duke of York, 1759 (H.); successive projects for a palace at RICHMOND, SURREY, for King George

III, 1762 onwards [*History of the King's Works* v, 225–7]; a house at HEADFORT, CO. MEATH, for the 1st Earl of Bective, 1765 [*C. Life*, 21 March 1936, 303]; a palace at SVARTSJÖ, SWEDEN, for the Dowager Queen Louisa of Sweden, *c.* 1769–70 (H.); a new house at ENVILLE, STAFFS., for the 5th Earl of Stamford and Warrington, *c.* 1770 [G. W. Beard, 'A New Design by Chambers', *Arch. Rev.*, Sept. 1953]; a church for the parish of ST. MARYLEBONE, LONDON, 1770–4 (H.); stables at CASTLE HOWARD, YORKS. (N.R.), for the 5th Earl of Carlisle, 1771; a steeple for WOODSTOCK CHURCH, OXON., 1776 [H. M. Colvin, 'The Rebuilding of Woodstock Church Tower', *Oxfordshire Archaeological Society's Report* No. 87, 1949]; and a bridge at DALKEITH HOUSE, MIDLOTHIAN, *c.* 1790 [signed drawings in the Duke of Buccleuch's archives].

CHANTRELL, ROBERT DENNIS (1793–1872), was the son of R. Chantrell of Newington (Southwark). From 1807 to 1814 he was a pupil of Sir John Soane. In 1818 he was employed to carry out some repairs to the parish church at Halifax, and in 1819 he settled in Leeds, where he built up a successful practice, particularly as an ecclesiastical architect. His secular works were in the Greek Revival style, and included the ambitious South Market, which cost £22,000, and had as its focus a striking neo-classical feature in the form of a circular Doric temple. But it was as a designer of Gothic (and occasionally of neo-Norman) churches that Chantrell was best known in Yorkshire. Between 1823 and 1850 he designed at least twenty-five new churches, several of them for the Commissioners for Building New Churches. The smaller ones were generally in the lancet style, but in some of the larger ones (notably St. Peter's at Leeds), Chantrell used a 'Decorated' or 'Perpendicular' vocabulary to good effect. His churches show a progressive development from the thin Georgian elegance of Christ Church, Leeds, with its cast-iron piers, to the more scholarly – but still hardly Puginesque – Gothic of St. Peter's, and ultimately to the serious medievalism of his later churches, in which he employed a system of geometrical proportions derived from a careful study of English Gothic churches (see his paper on the subject in *Builder* v, 1847, 300–2).

In 1829 Chantrell became surveyor to York Minster, but in 1846 he returned to London, where he became architect to the Incorporated Church Building Society. The Yorkshire practice was continued by his son John Boham Chantrell. In 1863 he moved to Eastbourne, and in the following year to Rottingdean. His membership of the R.I.B.A. ceased in 1868, and he died on 4 January 1872 at a hotel in Norwood. Thomas Healey was a pupil. Chantrell exhibited at the Royal Academy in 1812–14, and at the Northern

Society for the Encouragement of the Fine Arts in Leeds from about 1820 onwards.

[A. T. Bolton, *The Works of Sir John Soane*, Appendix C, xliv; *Catalogue of the R.I.B.A. Drawings Coll., C–F*, 1972, 21; M. H. Port, *Six Hundred New Churches*, 1961, 179; Somerset House, Principal Probate Registry, calendar of probates (1872); Bodleian Library, MS. Clarendon dep. c. 19, ff. 149–52; *Gent's Mag.* 1847 (ii), 68–9.]

SECULAR BUILDINGS

LEEDS, THE PHILOSOPHICAL HALL, PARK ROW, for the Leeds Philosophical and Literary Society, 1819–20; enlarged 1861–2; dem. [S. Lewis, *Topographical Dictionary* iii, 1831, 46].

LEEDS, THE PUBLIC BATHS, WELLINGTON ROAD, 1819–20; dem. [S. Lewis, *op. cit.*, 47].

LEEDS, THE SOUTH MARKET, 1823–4; dem. [H. Schroeder, *The Annals of Yorkshire*, Leeds 1851, ii, 20].

LEEDS, THE COURT HOUSE, alterations, 1834; dem. 1901 [J. C. Loudon, *Architectural Mag.* i, 1834, 211].

LEEDS, THE CONSERVATIVE PAVILION (temporary), 1838 [*Catalogue of R.I.B.A. Drawings Coll., C–F*, 21].

RUDDING PARK, YORKS. (W.R.), alterations for Sir Joseph Radcliffe, Bart. [drawings formerly at Rudding, *ex inf.* Mr. Claud Phillimore].

BRAMLEY PARSONAGE, nr. LEEDS, designs, 1823 [Borthwick Institute, MGA 1823/3].

CHURCHES

HALIFAX, ST. JOHN, repairs, 1818 [*Builder* v, 1847, 300].

LEEDS, CHRIST CHURCH, MEADOW LANE, 1823–6; Gothic; dem. 1972 [R. V. Taylor, *The Churches of Leeds*, 1875, 503].

HUNSLEY, YORKS. (W.R.), inserted galleries, 1826; dem. 1862 [I.C.B.S.].

KIRKSTALL, YORKS. (W.R.), 1828–9, Gothic; altered 1863 and 1894 [R. V. Taylor, *The Churches of Leeds*, 1875, 443].

LOCKWOOD, YORKS. (W.R.), 1828–9, Gothic [Port, 179].

NETHERTHONG, YORKS. (W.R.), 1828–9, Gothic; remodelled 1877 [Port, 179].

NEW MILLS, DERBYSHIRE, 1829–30, Gothic [Port, 143].

MORLEY, YORKS. (W.R.), 1829–30, Gothic; chancel added 1885 [Port, 179].

HOLBECK, YORKS. (W.R.), 1829–32, Gothic; spire and chancel by J. W. Hill, 1860 [R. V. Taylor, *The Churches of Leeds*, 1875, 373].

GLOSSOP, DERBYSHIRE, reconstructed (except steeple), 1831–2, Gothic; nave rebuilt 1914–15, chancel 1923 [I.C.B.S.].

PONTEFRACT, YORKS. (W.R.), ALL SAINTS, partial

reconstruction of ruined church, 1832–3 [I.C.B.S.].

BRAMLEY CHURCH, YORKS. (W.R.), enlarged 1833; rebuilt by Perkin & Backhouse 1863 [I.C.B.S.].

SKIPTON, YORKS. (W.R.), CHRIST CHURCH, 1836–9, Gothic [*Gent's Mag.* 1839 (2), 532].

HEADINGLEY, YORKS. (W.R.), ST. MICHAEL, 1837–8, Gothic; rebuilt 1884 [plans in Borthwick Institute of Historical Research, York, Fac. 1836/3].

LEEDS, YORKS. (W.R.), ST. PETER, rebuilt 1837–41, Gothic [J. Rusby & J. G. Simpson, *St. Peter's at Leeds*, 1896; plans at Borthwick Institute of Historical Research, York, Fac. 1837/5, and Society of Antiquaries, London].

LOTHERSDALE, YORKS. (W.R.), 1838, Gothic; chancel added 1886 [I.C.B.S.].

POOL, YORKS. (W.R.), 1839, Gothic; altered 1880 [C. L. Eastlake, *History of the Gothic Revival*, 1872, 377].

LEEDS, YORKS. (W.R.), HOLY TRINITY, rebuilt classical steeple after damage by storm, 1839 [R. S. Shapley, 'Holy Trinity Church, Leeds', *Journal of the W. Yorkshire Society of Architects* xiv (4), 1955, 3].

HOLMEBRIDGE, YORKS. (W.R.), 1839–40, Gothic; chancel added 1887 [G.R.].

ADEL, YORKS. (W.R.), addition of bellcote, 1839, and restoration of chancel, 1843 [*Procs. of Yorkshire Architectural Soc.*, 1888, 103 et seq.].

BATLEY CARR, YORKS. (W.R.), 1840–1, Gothic [R. V. Taylor, *The Churches of Leeds*, 1875, 166].

SHADWELL, YORKS. (W.R.), 1841–2, neo-Norman [G. E. Kirk, *A Short History of the Parish Church of Thorner with some notice of the chapel and new parish church of Shadwell*, 1935, 25].

HONLEY, YORKS. (W.R.), 1842–3, Gothic [I.C.B.S.].

LEVEN, YORKS. (E.R.), 1843–5, Gothic [*Gent's Mag.* 1843 (2), 301; *Builder* v, 1847, 301–2].

GOLCAR, YORKS. (W.R.), rebuilt defective roof, 1844 [I.C.B.S.].

ROBERT TOWN, YORKS. (W.R.), 1844–5, with T. Shaw, Gothic [Port, 179].

BRUGES, BELGIUM, ST. SAUVEUR'S CATHEDRAL, rebuilt roof and added two upper storeys to Romanesque tower, with P. Buyck, 1844–6 [*A.P.S.D., s.v.* 'Bruges'; *Ecclesiologist* xi, 1850, 174].

RISE, YORKS. (E.R.), 1845, Gothic [*Builder* iii, 1845, 585; v, 1847, 302].

LUND, YORKS. (E.R.), chancel, 1845–6, Gothic [inscription on underside of altar, *ex inf.* Mr. I. H. Goodall].

HALIFAX, YORKS. (W.R.), ST. PAUL, KING'S CROSS, 1845–7, Gothic; dem. *c.* 1912 except steeple [*Builder* v, 1847, 302].

LEEDS, YORKS. (W.R.), ST. PHILIP, 1845–7, Gothic; dem. [*Builder* v, 1847, 302, 485, 508].

KEIGHLEY, YORKS. (W.R.), rebuilt 1846–8, Gothic

[W. H. Hatton, *The Churches of Yorkshire* i, 1880, 38].

MIDDLETON, YORKS. (W.R.), 1846–52, Gothic [*Builder* v, 1847, 302].

ARMITAGE BRIDGE, YORKS. (W.R.), 1847–8, Gothic [*Builder* v, 1847, 302; vi, 1848, 249].

FANGFOSS, YORKS. (E.R.), rebuilt 1849–50, neo-Norman [*Architect and Building Gazette*, 24 Aug. 1850, 399].

MALTON (NEW), YORKS. (N.R.), ST. MICHAEL, new chancel, *c.* 1858, neo-Norman [T. Whellan, *History and Topography of York and the North Riding* ii, 1859, 218].

PEASENHALL, SUFFOLK, rebuilt nave and chancel, 1860–1, Gothic [*Ipswich Journal*, 13 July 1861, 5].

CHAPLIN, ROBERT, practised as an architect and surveyor at Ashby-de-la-Zouch in Leicestershire from about 1820 to 1850. For many years he occupied a house in RAWDON TERRACE, of which he may have been the architect. His principal works in Ashby were the ambitious Greek Doric IVANHOE BATHS, 1822, dem. 1962 (*C. Life*, 5 March 1959, 451); and the HASTINGS (now ROYAL) HOTEL, 1826 [Wayte's *Descriptive and Historical Guide to Ashby-de-la-Zouch*, Ashby 1831, 120, 135]. Chaplin was probably the architect of MOUNT PAVILION, COLWICH, STAFFS. (now ST. MARY'S ABBEY), a Gothic house begun *c.* 1830 for Viscount Tamworth, but not finished, and converted into a Benedictine nunnery in 1836. A plan signed by Chaplin is preserved at the Abbey [*ex inf.* Mr. Bryan Little]. Chaplin disappears from the local directories after 1850, but no record of his death has been found [J. D. Bennett, *Leicestershire Architects 1700–1850*, Leicester 1968].

CHAPMAN, JOHN, was the mason employed to rebuild HORTON CHURCH, DORSET, 1722–3. There are many payments in the churchwardens' accounts to him 'for Mason work', 'on account of Rebuilding ye Tower', etc. No surveyor is mentioned, and Chapman probably made the design himself. The tower shows the influence of Eastbury House (Sir John Vanbrugh, architect), upon which Chapman may perhaps have been employed [*C. Life*, 18 Feb. 1949, Correspondence].

CHAPMAN, ROBERT (*c.* 1754–1827), was an architect and surveyor practising from 26 Wormwood Street, London. In 1803 the tower and chancel of ST. PETER'S CHURCH, ST. ALBANS, HERTS., were rebuilt to his designs, but they were much altered by Lord Grimthorpe in 1893 [E. W. Brayley, *The Beauties of England and Wales* vii, 1808, 97–8; W. C. Morgan, 'St. Peter's Church, St. Albans', *Trans. of the St. Albans and Herts. Architectural and Archaeological Soc.* i (2),

1897–8]. In 1806 he enlarged OFFCHURCH VICARAGE, WARWICKS. [signed plans in Warwick County Record Office, DR 302]. ST. HELEN'S CHURCH, BISHOPSGATE, LONDON, was repaired under his direction in 1807–9 [J. E. Cox, *Annals of St. Helen's, Bishopsgate*, 1876, 209, 216], and he repaired and rerooted ST. MARY, ALDERMANBURY, in 1808–10 [P. C. Carter, *The History of St. Mary Aldermanbury*, 1913, 23].

In 1811 Chapman entered into partnership with his nephew and pupil J. B. Gardiner (*q.v.*) and a young man named J. W. Upward. Upward gave up practice in 1815 to become a stockbroker, and Chapman retired soon afterwards. He died at Park Cottage, Camberwell Grove, on 30 March 1827, at the age of 73 [*Annals of the Fine Arts* iii, 1818, 560; *Gent's Mag.* 1827 (i), 377].

CHAPMAN, SAMUEL (1799–), was the son of the head gardener at Harewood House, Yorkshire [*ex inf.* Mr. John Harvey]. He practised in Leeds in the 1820s. He designed ST. MARY'S CHURCH, LOW HARROGATE, YORKS. (W.R.), 1822–5, Gothic, dem. [W. Grainge, *History of Harrogate*, 1882, 245], and the Greek Revival CORN EXCHANGE at LEEDS, 1827–8, dem. [J. Allen, *History of the County of York* ii, 1831, 537].

CHAPPLE, CHARLES, practised in Stonehouse, Devon, during the second quarter of the nineteenth century. In Pigot's 1830 *Directory* he is described as 'architect and surveyor, house and land agent, and registrar of marriages'. Plans in the Cornwall County Record Office signed by him include Valletort Terrace, Hotel and Baths, Stonehouse (1825), a design for public rooms in Stonehouse (1833), five houses to be built in Caroline Place, Stonehouse (*c.* 1835), and proposed improvements on the Battery Hill at Stonehouse (1835). He designed the Greek Revival ST. CHARLES' CHAPEL, PLYMOUTH, 1828–9, dem. [Church Building Commissioners, Minute Books, 26 Aug. 1828, *ex inf.* Mr. M. H. Port], a school (Greek Doric, dem.) in PLYMOUTH [G. Wightwick, *Nettleton's Guide to Plymouth, etc.*, 1836, 14], and ST. KEW PARSONAGE, CORNWALL, 1837 [Devon County Record Office, Faculty papers].

CHASSEREAU, PETER, of London, advertised his services as an architect and land surveyor in the *Gentleman's Magazine* for 1741 (p. 336). He was prepared to design buildings, measure artificers' work, survey land, and draw maps and prospects of gentlemen's seats. A map of the city of York drawn by him was engraved and published by J. Rocque in 1750. He was presumably a member of the French Huguenot family of Chassereau whose genealogy is given in *Miscellanea Genealogica et Heraldica*, N.S. iv, 149–50.

CHATTERTON, JOHN, is at present known only as the author of an unexecuted design for the principal front of HANBURY HALL, WORCS., made c. 1700 [J. Lees-Milne in *C. Life*, 4 Jan. 1968, fig. 6].

CHAWNER, THOMAS (1774–1851), was a pupil of Sir John Soane from 1788 to 1794. He entered the Royal Academy Schools in 1797, and exhibited at the Academy from 1791 to 1800. He obtained a post in the Land Revenue Department and when, in 1810, it was amalgamated with the Office of Woods and Forests, he was appointed one of the surveyors to the combined department. In 1832, when the Office of Woods, Forests and Land Revenues was merged with that of Works, Chawner and his colleague Rhodes continued to deal with the Land Revenue side. He retired in 1845, and died on 6 June 1851, aged 76 [*A.P.S.D.*].

As a Civil Servant, Chawner had few opportunities for architectural design. In 1811 he and Leverton (then the other Land Revenue surveyor) were asked to prepare plans for the layout of Marylebone (afterwards Regent's) Park. Their proposals, unimaginative in character, were rejected in favour of those of John Nash [John Summerson, *John Nash*, 106–9]. Their scheme of 1815 for building houses on the site of St. James's Palace also came to nothing [*History of the King's Works* vi, 367]. The attribution to Chawner of the design of Richmond Terrace, Whitehall, is without foundation (see below, p. 394), and his only official works of any consequence appear to have been BRIXTON PRISON, begun in 1819 [*Survey of London* xxvi, 103–5], an entrance (dem.) to St. James's Park at the north end of the former Duke Street (Whitehall), designed in conjunction with Rhodes in 1834 [*Architectural Mag.* i, 1834, 316], and stabling at CLAREMONT HOUSE, SURREY, at a time (1842) when it was occupied by the royal family [*History of the King's Works* vi, 322]. Numerous survey plans drawn by him are among the Land Revenue records in the Public Record Office. In a private capacity Chawner completed (1807–8) the rebuilding of CHERTSEY CHURCH, SURREY, after the original architect, Richard Elsam, had been dismissed [E. W. Brayley, *History of Surrey* ii, 194], and surveyed (1811) KINGSTON CHURCH, SURREY, designing a new window (since removed) at the east end of St. James's Chapel 'to correspond as nearly as possible with that above the altar' [MS. Vestry Minutes]. Designs by him for altering the front of NO. 6 CHEYNE WALK, CHELSEA, for John Gregory, 1817, are in the Cooper Hewitt Museum in New York (see J. Harris, *Catalogue of British Drawings for Architecture etc. in American Collections*, 62–3). In conjunction with Henry Rhodes he designed COX'S HOTEL, NOS. 53–55 JERMYN STREET, 1836–7; dem. 1923–4 [*Survey of*

London xxix, 275], and some stabling at the corner of HAYMARKET and COVENTRY STREET [*A.P.S.D.*, *s.v.* 'Rhodes, Henry'].

Chawner was a member of the Surveyors' Club and acted as its President in 1811. George Porter (*q.v.*) was his pupil. He lived in Guildford Street and had a country residence in Surrey called Addlestone Cottage [Brayley, *op. cit.* ii, 220].

CHEESMAN, GEORGE, was the son of a Brighton builder of the same name who built houses in Brunswick Square c. 1825. In Brighton he designed the churches of CHRIST CHURCH, MONTPELIER ROAD, 1837–8 (Gothic), and ST. JOHN THE EVANGELIST, CARLTON HILL, 1840 (Greek Doric), and in Lewes that of ST. JOHN SUB CASTRO, 1839–40 (Gothic), all provincial works of little merit [*V.C.H. Sussex* vii, 37, 260–1; A. Dale, *Fashionable Brighton*, 1947, 52, 117, 169].

CHEFFINS, CHARLES FREDERICK (1807–1861), was the son of an employee of the New River Company living at Hoddesdon in Hertfordshire. He had a successful career as a civil engineer, but also acted occasionally as a surveyor and architect. His principal recorded work in the last capacity was a house for J. G. Stokes at HODDESDON, exhibited at the R.A. in 1843. In the same exhibition a design for the NATIONAL SCHOOL at Hoddesdon was shown by 'G. and C. Cheffins'. G. A. Cheffins, who may have been an elder brother, had exhibited architectural designs at the R.A. from a Pentonville address in 1827–8, but was practising in Manchester in 1840 [*Gardener's Mag.* xvi, 1840, 321–2]. Another member of the family who also became an architect or surveyor was William Cheffins, who died in London in 1869. A 'Mr. Cheffins' was one of the competitors for the Fitzwilliam Museum at Cambridge in 1835 [Willis & Clark, iii, 204]. C. F. Cheffins died at 15 Gloucester Terrace on 22 October 1861, leaving two sons, Charles Richard and George Alexander, the former of whom continued his practice as a civil engineer [*Minutes of Proceedings of the Institution of Civil Engineers* xxi, 1861–2, 578–80; Principal Probate Registry, Calendar of Probates].

CHENEY, JOHN, signs designs dated 1795 for extensive alterations to the main block of STOKE BRUERN PARK, NORTHANTS. [B.M., Add. MS. 32352, f. 225]. They do not appear to have been carried out (cf. a photograph of the house as it existed before the fire of 1886 in *C. Life*, 9 March 1967, 526). Cheney had been clerk of works to S. P. Cockerell at Daylesford House, Glos., in 1788–93 [B.M., Add. MS. 29231, ff. 59–60], and was among the subscribers to Richardson's *New Vitruvius Britannicus* in 1802.

CHESHIRE, JOHN, a master mason of Over Whitacre, nr. Coleshill in Warwickshire, was well known as a 'steeple-mender'. In 1789 his skill in this kind of work was the subject of a letter to the *Gentleman's Magazine*, in which 'Gothicus' stated that after several conversations with Cheshire he was convinced 'that he is capable to execute any edifice in the Gothic taste', but that so far 'his abilities have been confined to the rebuilding of some ruinated spires, or new modelling ill-proportioned ones. The spires of the old church at Birmingham, St. Mary's at Leicester, and lately the new-erected spire at Hinckley, are standing objects of his performance' [*Gent's Mag.* 1789 (i), 214]. In November 1792 Cheshire was declared a bankrupt [*Monthly Mag.* xxii], but either he or a son of the same name continued to rebuild spires for another thirty years.

The following are churches whose spires are recorded to have been wholly or partially rebuilt by Cheshire: ASTON, WARWICKS., 1776–7 [A. E. Everitt, 'Aston Church', *Trans. Birmingham Archaeological Soc.*, 1872, 24]; WALSALL, STAFFS., 1777 [F. W. Willmore, *History of Walsall*, 1887, 148]; BIRMINGHAM, ST. MARTIN, 1781 [J. T. Bunce, *Old St. Martin's Church, Birmingham*, 1875, 20]; LEICESTER, ST. MARY, 1783 [*Gent's Mag.* 1789 (i), 214]; HINCKLEY, LEICS., 1788 [*ibid*]; SHREWSBURY, ST. ALKMUND, 1788 [H. Owen & J. B. Blakeway, *History of Shrewsbury* i, 1825, 301]; COVENTRY, HOLY TRINITY, 1802 [T. Sharp, *Illustrations of the History of Holy Trinity Church, Coventry*, 1818, 33]; OLD SWINFORD, WORCS., 1809 [parish records, *ex inf.* Mr. H. J. Haden]; ADDERBURY, OXON., 1815 [H. J. Gepp, *Adderbury*, 1924, 92]; THAXTED, ESSEX, 1822 [Neale & Le Keux, *Views of Collegiate and Parish Churches in Great Britain* i, 1824].

CHILD, JOHN (–1868), practised in Leeds, where he designed two Roman Catholic churches: ST. PATRICK, YORK ROAD, 1831–2, Gothic (converted into a school *c.* 1892) [*Catholic Mag.* ii, 1832, 219–20, 574–5], and ST. ANNE, PARK ROW, 1837–8, Gothic (since rebuilt) [lithograph in extra-illustrated copy of *Ducatus Leodiensis* in Leeds City Library, vol. v]. His designs (1830) for a Rectory at PUDSEY, YORKS. (W.R.), are at the Borthwick Institute in York [MGA 1830/2]. By the 1850s he had been joined in practice by his son Henry Paul Child. He died at Knaresburgh on 22 October 1868 [Principal Probate Registry, Calendar of Probates]. He should not be confused with Charles Child (d. 1862), of Eastwood, nr. Todmorden, and later of Halifax, who was in practice from about 1830 onwards, and designed, *inter alia*, churches at BRADSHAW (OVENDEN) and CRAGG, both in the West Riding [Port, 179], and the ODD-FELLOWS HALL at HALIFAX, 1840 [*ex inf.* Dr. D. Linstrum].

CHISHOLME, JOHN (*c.* 1780–1808), was a native of Aberdeen and was educated at that university. As a very young man he submitted a design for the building of Union Street which was not adopted, although he was the first to propose a single arch for the Union Bridge. He subsequently went to London, where he became a pupil and assistant of John Rennie. While in Rennie's office he is said to have designed the western entrance to the East India Docks. In 1803 he began to exhibit at the Royal Academy, showing a project for a wooden bridge over the R. Don in Aberdeenshire, and in 1808 a design for Assembly Rooms at Aberdeen. In 1807 he joined Telford, and he was engaged in superintending the construction of Telford's new Court House at Carlisle when he died suddenly of heart failure on 2 November 1808, aged only 28. [G. M. Fraser, 'Archibald Simpson, Architect, and his Times', *Aberdeen Weekly Jnl.*, 17 May 1918; *Gent's Mag.* 1808 (ii), 1044.]

CHUTE, JOHN (1701–1776), was the fifth and youngest son of Edward Chute of The Vyne, Hants. He was educated at Eton, and spent much of his time abroad until 1754, when he inherited the family property on the death of his brother Anthony. He was an amateur architect of considerable ability, and Horace Walpole, who had met him in Florence in 1740, described him as 'an able Geometrician, and . . . an Exquisite Architect, & of the purest taste both in the Grecian & Gothic Styles'. He played a prominent part in the designing of Walpole's Gothic villa at STRAWBERRY HILL, and when he died in 1776, Walpole wrote that he was 'my oracle in taste, the standard to whom I submitted my trifles, and the genius that presided over poor Strawberry!' The elevation of the house was largely Chute's work, and his surviving drawings show that the design of the 'South Tower' was influenced by one at The Vyne. It was also Chute who helped to design the detached Gothic Chapel built for Walpole in 1772 by the mason Thomas Gayfere [W. S. Lewis, 'The Genesis of Strawberry Hill', *Metropolitan Museum Studies* v (i), 1934].

In 1752 Chute made Italianate designs (based partly on Serlio, book VII, 49) for rebuilding HAGLEY HALL, WORCS., for Sir George (afterwards Lord) Lyttelton, but they were rejected in favour of a more conventionally Palladian design by Sanderson Miller [Michael McCarthy, 'The Building of Hagley Hall', *Burlington Mag.*, April 1976]. A few years later (*c.* 1755) he helped to remodel CHALFONT HOUSE, BUCKS., for Charles and Lady Mary Churchill, in the style of Strawberry Hill [Walpole's *Letters*, ed. Toynbee, iii, 317] (see Angus's *Seats* for a view of the house before successive alterations by Nash and Salvin). His most considerable and successful essay in the Gothic style was DONNINGTON GROVE, nr.

213

NEWBURY, BERKS., designed in 1763 for the antiquary James Pettit Andrews, for which the original designs are in the W. S. Lewis Collection at Farmington (*C. Life*, 18, 25 Sept., 2 Oct. 1958).

At THE VYNE itself Chute made two notable alterations: the construction (1770) of a dramatic new classical staircase and the addition to the chapel of a Gothic Tomb Chamber in order to receive a monument to his ancestor Chaloner Chute (d. 1659), which was eventually erected after his death by his cousin T. L. Chute 'from the Design of his Precedessor'. The recumbent effigy, which is in the style of the seventeenth century, was executed by Thomas Carter [C. W. Chute, *A History of the Vyne*, 1888; Hants. County Record Office, Account of The Vyne by Horace Walpole, 31 M57/652, and 'Inventionary of Alterations to be made at the Vine July 1st. 1755' (633); Sir Charles Chute, 'A Monument by Thomas Carter', *C. Life*, 27 May 1954; Michael McCarthy, 'John Chute's Drawings for The Vyne', *National Trust Year Book 1975–76*, 70–9] (*C. Life*, 14, 21, 28 May 1921).

Both his drawings and his executed works show that Chute was a talented architectural designer. The staircase at The Vyne is a theatrical *tour de force* that has no parallel in English country-house architecture, and at Strawberry Hill Chute played a leading part in the creation of one of the key buildings in the history of the Gothic Revival.

Several portraits of Chute are preserved at The Vyne, including one by Gabriel Mathias showing him holding a Gothic design for the south front. Some of the architectural books in the library have sketches by Chute on the flyleaves, *e.g.* Langley's *Gothic Architecture* (1747) and *The City and Country Builder and Workman's Companion* (1756). Two folders of his drawings in the Hants. Record Office contain numerous sketches for The Vyne. An album of 64 drawings for Donnington Grove, Hagley, Strawberry Hill and The Vyne is in the W. S. Lewis Collection at Farmington, Connecticut, U.S.A. It was once in Walpole's library at Strawberry Hill. See J. Harris, *Catalogue of British Drawings for Architecture, etc., in American Collections*, 65–72.

Chute's correspondence with Horace Walpole is printed in vol. 35 of the Yale edition of *Walpole's Correspondence*, ed. W. S. Lewis. For a biographical sketch see Warren Hunting Smith, *Originals Abroad*, Yale 1952, 157–76.

CIBBER, CAIUS GABRIEL (1630–1700), was the son of a cabinet-maker to the King of Denmark, and was born at Flensborg in Schleswig. He was sent to Italy in order to improve a natural talent for sculpture, and came to England some time before the Restoration to work for John Stone in the yard in Long Acre where he was

214

carrying on the business founded by his father Nicholas. As a sculptor, Cibber's most celebrated works were the relief on the base of the Monument (1673–5) and the two figures of 'Raving' and 'Melancholy Madness' (now in the Victoria and Albert Museum) which flanked the entrance to Bethlehem Hospital (1680). He also executed important work at Thoresby (1685–7), at Chatsworth (1687–91) where he designed the marble altar-piece in the chapel, and at Hampton Court (1694–8) where he carved the pediment of the east front and the enrichments of the south front.

Cibber was employed as surveyor for rebuilding the Steel-Yard after the Great Fire, and the Arms of the Hanseatic League carved by him for this building (dem. 1863) are now in the Museum of London. After Edward Jarman's death in 1668 he was among those who applied to the Gresham Committee for the post of 'surveyor for carrying on the work at the Royal Exchange'. He was not chosen, but was employed as sculptor of several of the statues of kings which stood in niches round the court. At Northampton he was in some way concerned in the building or decoration of the Sessions House (1676–88), for in 1683 it was ordered that £10 should be paid to 'Mr. Caius Gabrell Sibber for his paines in contriveing of the Sessions House' [Northants. County Records, rough Q.S. Order Book]. His chief architectural work was the DANISH CHURCH, WELLCLOSE SQUARE, LONDON, 1694–6; dem. 1869. This was erected for the use of Danish and Norwegian merchants and sailors, mainly at the expense of King Christian V of Denmark. Cibber, who gave his services free, superseded Thomas Woodstock as surveyor of the church, and his name appears as architect on two engravings of it published by Kip in 1697. Four baroque figures of saints in wood, carved by Cibber for the reredos, are now divided between the Danish Church in Ming Street, Poplar, and the Danish Church (formerly St. Katherine's) in Regent's Park. The church also contained a marble monument erected by Cibber to his second wife, Jane Colley, but this has been lost, together with any inscriptions to Cibber himself and to his son Colley, the actor and dramatist, who were both buried here. According to Vertue, 'he was a Gentleman-like man and a man of Good sense but died poor'.

[H. Faber, *Caius Gabriel Cibber*, 1926; R. Gunnis, *Dictionary of British Sculptors 1660–1851*, 101–3; John Physick, *Designs for English Sculpture 1680–1860*,1969, figs. 11,28; Margaret Whinney, *Sculpture in Britain 1530–1830*, 1964, 48–51; Walpole Society, *Vertue Note Books* i, 39, 91, 99, ii, 36, iv, 165; 'An Account of the Buildings, Charges and Finishing, etc. of the Danish Church in Wellclose Square MDCXCVI', *N. and Q.*, 9th ser., v, 1900, 492; Francis Thompson, *A History of Chatsworth*, 1949; Guildhall Library MSS. 337–8.]

CLARK, —, received £740 for rebuilding the detached tower of BERKELEY CHURCH, GLOS., in traditional Gothic style in 1750–2. No architect was employed, and in 1747 there was a payment of £1 7s. 6d. 'To the Masons for giving in a plan for the Tower and Expenses at meeting the same time' [MS. Churchwardens' Accounts]. In 1742 a master builder named William Clark was among those who reported unfavourably on the repairs recently carried out to TETBURY CHURCH, GLOS. [Gloucester Public Library, MS. R.R. 300. 1, p. 13]. This may, however, have been William Clark of Leonard Stanley, Glos., a carpenter who, together with John Bryan of Painswick and Joseph Bryan of Gloucester, masons, contracted in 1750 to rebuild the tower of GREAT WITCOMBE CHURCH, GLOS. [M. M. Cox & E. M. Clifford, A History of the Parish of Great Witcombe, 1954, 12–15]. 'Jo. Clerk' was one of the 'Gloucester masons' employed to rebuild the Perpendicular east window of WORCESTER CATHEDRAL in 1660–2 [Worcester Cathedral Archives, A. lxxiii].

CLARK, or CLARKE, JOHN (c. 1585–1624), was one of the Yorkshire masons who came to Oxford in the reign of James I to work on the Schools Quadrangle, and died there in 1624. In 1617, when he was admitted to the freedom of the Oxford company of building craftsmen, his age was stated to be 32. His wife Prudence was almost certainly the daughter of John Akroyd (q.v.), the master mason in charge of the new Schools building. In Oxford Clark's most important work was the CARFAX CONDUIT, the elaborately carved terminal of the new water-supply provided at the expense of the lawyer Otho Nicholson, erected in 1616–17 and removed to Lord Harcourt's park at Nuneham in c. 1790. In London Clark was the mason responsible for rebuilding LINCOLN'S INN CHAPEL, a work in which Nicholson was also concerned. It may, indeed, have been on Nicholson's recommendation that Clark was employed, for in May 1618 'Mr. Otho Nicholson' was called in to advise on 'what manner of windows are most fit for the chappel' and also 'on the merits of Oxford freestone'. In November John Clark was asked to draw 'the platforme of the . . . modell', and in 1619–23 he built the existing chapel in a traditional Gothic style that was then still normal in Oxford, though soon to be rendered obsolete in London by the example of Inigo Jones's church in Covent Garden. It may have been as a consequence of his employment at Lincoln's Inn that Clark was, by 1620, a member of the London Masons' Company. He was presumably the John Clarke to whom Edward Marshall (d. 1675) was apprenticed. [Catherine Cole in Oxoniensia xxvi–xxvii, 1961–2, 231, 235–6; and on 'Carfax Conduit', Oxoniensia xxix–xxx, 1964–5, 144; John Summerson, 'Lincoln's Inn Chapel and its Designer', Trans. Ecclesiological Soc. N.S. iii, 1953, 39–41.]

CLARK, JOHN (–1857), was a native of Edinburgh. In 1826 he was successful in the competition for the Commercial Buildings at Leeds. This led him to settle in Leeds, where he practised until a few years before his death. His handsome classical buildings 'show the change from the purely Greek to the mixed Greek-Italianate of the late 30s and the 40s'. In 1836 he competed unsuccessfully for the Houses of Parliament with a Gothic design in which 'the earlier and later eras' were 'slightly intermingled . . . so as to form a harmonious combination with the existing palatial buildings'. [Obituary in Building Chronicle, May 1857, 197; Derek Linstrum, Historic Architecture of Leeds, 1969, 31–33.] In the following list B.C. refers to the Building Chronicle.

LEEDS, THE COMMERCIAL BUILDINGS or EXCHANGE, 1826–9; dem. 1872 [B.C.] (Linstrum, op. cit., 35; T. Allen, History of the County of York ii, 1831, 530).

ROUNDHAY PARK (now Mansion Hotel), nr. LEEDS, for Thomas Nicholson, 1826 [Goodall's Illustrated Royal Handbook to Roundhay Park, 1872, 3].

AIREDALE COLLEGE, BRADFORD, YORKS. (W.R.), 1831–4; dem. 1893–4 [B.C.; Congregational Magazine, 1831, 581, with illustration].

HARROGATE, THE VICTORIA BATHS, 1832 [B.C.].

BRADFORD, ST. PETER'S CHURCH (now Cathedral), reconstructed south aisle, south clerestorey and south porch, 1832–3 [John Ayers, Architecture in Bradford, 1973, 28].

LEEDS, THE TRUSTEE SAVINGS BANK, 30 BOND STREET, 1834; dem. 1971–2 [B.C.].

LEEDS, WOODHOUSE CEMETERY CHAPELS and LODGES, 1835 [B.C.].

HARROGATE, THE ROYAL CHALYBEATE SPA, 1835 [B.C.].

LEEDS, THE YORKSHIRE DISTRICT BANK, 1836 [B.C.].

LEEDS, ST. GEORGE'S CHURCH, 1836–8; apse, etc., added 1900–1, Gothic [B.C.].

LEEDS, ST. JOHN'S CHURCH, repairs, 1837 [B.C.].

OULTON HALL, YORKS. (W.R.), stables for John Blayds, 1837 [drawings in Leeds City Library, Archives Dept., ex inf. Mr. Angus Taylor].

LEEDS, WOODHOUSE MOOR, ALMSHOUSES nr. Church, Gothic [B.C.].

LEEDS, Mills for Messrs. Hives & Atkinson, 1833, and for John Wilkinson, 1842 [B.C.].

ST. CATHERINE'S (now Doncaster Infirmary), nr. DONCASTER, YORKS. (W.R.), for George Banks, 1838, Gothic [drawings in private possession, ex inf. Dr. T. F. Friedman].

ROSSINGTON CHURCH, YORKS. (W.R.), rebuilt (except tower), 1843–4, Gothic [Builder ii, 1844, 289].

BATLEY CARR, YORKS. (W.R.), parsonage, 1846
[Nettleton papers in Leeds City Library,
Archives Dept., *ex inf.* Dr. D. Linstrum].

RAWDON, YORKS. (W.R.), farm-house, etc., for
Robert Milligan, 1847 [*ibid.*].

APPERLEY BRIDGE, YORKS. (W.R.), house for J.
Richardson, 1848 [*ibid.*].

GLEDHOW GROVE (now Chapel Allerton Hospital),
nr. LEEDS, for John Hives [*B.C.*].

MEANWOOD HALL (now Meanwood Park Hospital), nr. LEEDS, alterations for Christopher
Beckett [*B.C.*].

CLARKE, —, of London, is recorded as having
designed two churches in BRIGHTON: ST. MAR-
GARET'S (now a Museum of Costume), 1824
(Ionic), and ST. MARY'S CHAPEL, 1827 (Doric),
dem. 1878. The latter was 'completed under the
direction of Mr. Wilds' [*The Watering-Places of
Great Britain and Fashionable Directory,* Joseph
Robins, London 1833, 30; A. Dale, *Fashionable
Brighton,* 1947, 43]. The only architect named
Clarke listed in Pigot's London *Directory* of
1827–8 is Isaac Clarke, who was still in practice
in 1868.

CLARKE, GEORGE (1661–1736), was the son
of Sir William Clarke, Secretary at War to
Charles II, and was educated at Brasenose College and the Inner Temple. In 1680 he was
elected to a fellowship at All Souls, where he
'showed brisk parts in the examination'. He took
his M.A. in 1683, and later obtained the degrees
of B.C.L. and D.C.L. His parliamentary career
began in 1685, when he was elected as Member
for the University of Oxford. He subsequently
represented the University from 1717 until his
death. Politically he was what Hearne called 'a
Hanoverian Tory'. His first office was that of
Judge Advocate-General (1681–1705). Later he
was Secretary at War (1692–1704), secretary to
Prince George of Denmark, and joint Secretary
to the Admiralty (1702–5). In 1705 he was ejected
from all his posts by the Whig government, but
when the Tories returned to power in 1710 he
was made a Lord of the Admiralty. After the
death of Queen Anne he held no further offices
and retired to Oxford, where he had retained his
college fellowship. For the rest of his life he was
a prominent and highly respected figure in academic society. When he died in 1736 he was
buried in All Souls Chapel, where a monument
commemorates his handsome features, his
courtly manners and his 'taste in architecture,
poetry and painting'. There is a bust by Cheere
in the Codrington Library, a portrait after Kneller in the college hall, and another by Kneller in
the Warden's Lodgings which shows him as
Prince George's secretary. At Worcester College
there are four further portraits and a miniature.

Well known in Oxford as a virtuoso and man

of taste, particularly in architectural matters,
Clarke was frequently consulted by those in
charge of building operations at a time when
many important works were in progress in the
university. Unfortunately the short autobiography which he left is almost entirely political,
and as little of his private correspondence has
survived, his architectural activities have to be
reconstructed largely from the numerous drawings which he left to Worcester College Library.
From these, and from other sources, it is, however, clear that he has a place in the architectural
history of Oxford comparable to that of Sir James
Burrough (1691–1764) at Cambridge. At Oxford
Clarke stepped into the shoes of Dean Aldrich
of Christ Church, the leading figure in Oxford
architecture during the first decade of the eighteenth century. It was probably in 1710 – the year
of Aldrich's death – that Clarke was consulted by
the Vice-Chancellor about the design for the
Clarendon Building, and it is among his collections that various alternative designs by Hawksmoor and others are preserved, as well as Thornhill's sketches for the statues of the Muses that
crown the roof. In 1716 he revised Aldrich's project for a monumental building on the south side
of Peckwater Quadrangle at Christ Church,
retaining the giant Corinthian order which the
Dean had envisaged, but reducing the number
of bays from nine to seven, and introducing the
lower order of Doric pilasters derived from
Michelangelo's Capitoline palace. Thus Christ
Church Library, as built between 1717 and 1738,
is largely Clarke's design.

Surviving drawings make it clear that in conjunction with Hawksmoor Clarke also played an
important part in the planning of the Queen's
College (1710–21), and that it was he who provided the master mason Townesend with the basic
design of the New Buildings begun at Magdalen
College in 1733. At All Souls he built (1706) at
his own cost (and evidently to his own designs)
a new house for the Warden, on condition that
he might occupy it during his lifetime;[1] refitted
the chapel (1713–16); and was throughout deeply
involved in the scheme for a new northern quadrangle which was eventually carried out to
Hawksmoor's designs between 1715 and 1740. At
University College too he was concerned in the
building of the Radcliffe Quadrangle (1717–19)
and with an unfulfilled project for a new Master's
Lodging.

The last college to benefit from Clarke's architectural advice was the new foundation of Worcester. In disgust at the quarrels which divided
his own college, it was to Worcester that he eventually left not only his library, but also the bulk
of his fortune, which was to be devoted to the

[1] The present front to High Street is a refacing of 1825
by Daniel Robertson.

endowment of additional fellowships and the completion of its buildings. The new hall, chapel and library had already been begun in his lifetime, and the basic design seems to have been his, though modified and interpreted by Hawksmoor. To complete the college Clarke envisaged wings projecting westwards to north and south of the library with a new Provost's Lodging at the west end of the north wing. This scheme was published in Williams's *Oxonia Depicta* (1732), but in a codicil to his will Clarke left instructions that an alternative plan and elevation should be followed instead. Part of the north range was duly erected by his trustees between 1753 and 1759, but the corresponding range on the south was never built, and the remainder of the north range, including the Provost's Lodging, was built between 1773 and 1776 to modified designs by Henry Keene.[1]

Outside Oxford Dr. Clarke's only known architectural works are the Rectory at KINGSTON BAGPUIZE, BERKS., which he designed for Richard Blechynden, Provost of Worcester, in about 1723, and some alterations to COKETHORPE HOUSE, OXON., for the 1st Visct. Harcourt, *c.* 1710. His architectural activities were thus largely confined to the circle of his Oxford acquaintances. But as the patron and collaborator of Hawksmoor and as the purchaser of that part of the Jones-Webb drawings that did not pass into the hands of Lord Burlington[2] he is a figure of considerable importance in English architectural history. Moreover, like Aldrich, he has some claim to be regarded as a precursor of the English Palladian revival. Though his architectural taste was more catholic than Aldrich's (Kingston Bagpuize Rectory has a doorway in the style of Giulio Romano), some of his unexecuted designs show markedly Palladian tendencies. As a draughtsman he was clumsy and inelegant, but he could convey an architectural idea to paper well enough to make it comprehensible, and when the need arose he could rely on Hawksmoor and Townesend to act as his architectural amanuenses and interpreters. His architectural library was one of the best of his time, and happily remains intact at Worcester College together with his large collection of prints and drawings.

[*D.N.B.*; autobiography printed in Hist. MSS. Comm., *Leybourne-Popham MSS.*, 1899, 259–89; M. Burrows, *The Worthies of All Souls*, 1874; F. A. Inderwick, *Records of The Inner Temple* iii, 107; W. G. Hiscock, *A Christ Church Miscellany*, 1946; Kerry Downes, *Hawksmoor*, 1959; H. M. Colvin, *Catalogue of Architectural Drawings of the 18th. and 19th. Centuries in the Library of Worcester College, Oxford*, 1964, 2nd ed. forthcoming; for Clarke's literary interests see the note by C. H. Wilkinson in Marvell's *Poems and Letters*, ed. H. M. Margoliouth, 3rd ed. 1971, 432–5.]

CLARKE, JAMES, was a carpenter and master builder of Newbury in Berkshire, where he or his firm built the TOWN HALL, 1742, dem. 1908 (ill. *Newbury District Field Club Trans.* v, 1895–1911, 230), the BRIDGE, 1769, the building in the London Road now known as THE DOWER HOUSE (formerly 'the King's Arms'), 'and most of the principal houses in Newbury of that date' [W. Money, *History of Newbury*, 1887, 353]. The Dower House is boldly designed in an almost Vanbrughian style.

CLARKE, THOMAS HUTCHINGS, appears to have been chiefly employed as an illustrator of architectural books. He was the author of *The Domestic Architecture of the Reigns of Elizabeth and James I* (1833) and of a volume of plans, sections and views of Eastbury House, Barking, Essex (1834). In 1839 he contributed a 'descriptive account' of the minster to W. B. Killpack's *History and Antiquities of the Collegiate Church of Southwell* (1839). In 1833 he exhibited at the Royal Academy his unsuccessful design for the new Grammar School at Birmingham. A drawing by him of the interior of the Palace of Madura in India, dated 1830, is in the British Museum (Add. MS. 31343 Q). This appears to have been copied from another artist's work and does not prove that Clarke had visited India himself.

CLARKE, WILLIAM, wrote a detailed and scholarly account of *Pompei* for the Library of Entertaining Knowledge, 1831–2. When a second edition was published in 1846 it was described as being 'chiefly from the MS. journals and drawings of William Clarke, Esq., architect'. He may perhaps have been the William Clarke who was a pupil in C. R. Cockerell's office from 1822 to 1827 [David Watkin, *C. R. Cockerell*, 1974, 42].

CLARKE, WILLIAM BARNARD, of Chapel Street, Bedford Row, London, exhibited a 'design for the proposed botanical garden on Primrose Hill' at the R.A. in 1832. In 1834 he restored

---

[1] Two monuments which Clarke erected in Oxford should also be mentioned, since he presumably designed them, or at least dictated their general form. One, in St. Mary's Church, commemorates his cousin Elizabeth Cary (d. 1723/4) and is signed 'G.C.F.'. It consists of a portrait medallion set against baroque drapery. The other, in the Cathedral, commemorates Dean Aldrich and was set up in 1732. It incorporates a bust by Cheere.

[2] The date when Clarke acquired these drawings is not known, but it was before 1718, when Edward Southwell wrote to Lord Dartmouth to ask if he would lend a design for Whitehall Palace in his possession for comparison with Clarke's (Staffordshire Record Office, D 1778/L/2/529). In a letter in the Kent Record Office dated May 1713, William Emmett says that the Whitehall design had recently been acquired by Clarke.

THE ELEANOR CROSS at WALTHAM, HERTS., in a manner criticized in *Architectural Mag.* iii, 280 (see also *Gent's Mag.* 1832 (ii), 105). According to the *Companion to the Almanac* for 1838 he was the architect employed to design the new watering-place at SOUTH HAYLING on HAYLING ISLAND, HANTS. He was President of the Architectural Society for several years, but resigned in 1839 on going abroad [*Gent's Mag.* 1839 (i), 81].

CLARKSON, JOHN (–1798), 'architect', died at Glasgow on 9 October 1798 [*Gent's Mag.* 1798, 994].

CLAVERING, ROBERT, a builder, published *An essay on the construction and building of chimneys, including an inquiry into the common causes of their smoking*, 3rd ed. 1793 (preface dated 1779). In the preface he states that his thoughts 'first turned to this subject in 1764', when he attempted to provide smoke-free chimneys in some houses that he was then building. He was also the author of *The Carpenter's and Joiner's Vade Mecum, c.* 1800.

CLAYTON, ALFRED BOWYER (1795–1855), intended at first to become a painter, and studied under Etty, who is said to have 'expressed a high opinion of his talents'. He ultimately decided to be an architect, and was for some time in the office of D. R. Roper (*q.v.*). As Roper's assistant he is said to have been the effective architect of the Greek Revival church of St. Mark at Kennington, and of the well-proportioned Lambeth Shot Tower which was one of the landmarks of the South Bank until its demolition after the Second World War. From Roper's office he moved in about 1827 to that of George Smith (*q.v.*). H. C. Barlow, a pupil of Smith's at the time, remembered that his advent marked the introduction of a 'new style'. Of this the principal example was the London Corn Exchange in Mark Lane, an interesting Greek Revival building which Smith built in 1827–8 with Clayton's assistance. Clayton appears to have been in independent practice by 1833. In 1837 he migrated to Manchester, where for a short time he was in partnership with T. W. Atkinson (*q.v.*). In 1842 he gave his address as Ormskirk, and in 1845 as Liverpool. He died at Everton in April 1855, of delayed shock after falling from a building he was examining at West Derby [*Builder* xiii, 1855, 216; xxvii, 1869, 65].

Clayton exhibited regularly at the R.A. from 1814 to 1837, showing pictorial compositions as well as architectural designs. He also exhibited at the Society of British Artists in 1824 and 1828 and at the Liverpool Academy of Arts in 1837, 1842 and 1845. His designs included a 'sketch of a villa, designed for and proposed to be erected on the estate of Tatnal Boone Esq. [at]

Lewisham', 1833; a design for a farm-house 'now erecting for W. Gambier Esq.' at Harrold, Beds., 1833; a design for a church at Herne Bay, 1834, probably CHRIST CHURCH, HERNE BAY, KENT, 1834, Gothic; an unexecuted design for the Town Hall at Penzance, 1835: 'a country residence now in progress near the Reculvers, Kent', 1836, probably BROOK, nr. RECULVER, KENT, for R. Collard; a 'design for a parsonage house to be erected near Whitstable, Kent, for the Rev. C. Plater', 1836; and 'alterations and additions' to NORLEY HALL, CHESHIRE, for Samuel Woodhouse, described as 'now erecting' in 1845. The last building, illustrated in Twycross's *Mansions of England: Cheshire* i, 1850, 127, is in the Tudor Gothic style.

CLEAVE, WILLIAM, is stated in Neale's *Seats* to have been responsible for extensive alterations to STAPLETON PARK, YORKS. (W.R.), dem. *c.* 1930, for the Hon. Edward Petre, and this is confirmed by the fact that in 1820 he exhibited a 'south-east view of improvements made at Stapleton Park' at the R.A., giving his address as 'Brewer's Green, Westminster'. Reference to Pigot's *Directory* shows that William Cleave of this address was listed as a 'timber-merchant' in 1827–8.

CLEGHORN, CLAUD. 'builder', was admitted a burgess of Edinburgh in April 1800 [*Roll of Edinburgh Burgesses*, Scottish Record Soc., 1933, 35]. He was doubtless the author of a set of unexecuted drawings in the Mellon Collection for ARDGOWAN HOUSE, RENFREWSHIRE, signed 'C. Cleghorn. Edin. 1797'. They represent a competent late Georgian design.

CLELAND, JAMES (1770–1840), was one of the outstanding figures in the life of Glasgow during the first three decades of the nineteenth century. He was a native of the city and a wright by trade, and ran a successful business as a builder. What was remarkable about Cleland was his intellectual ability, his public spirit and his activity in promoting schemes for the improvement of the city. For many years he was a prominent member of the Town Council and in 1831 became a J.P. In 1814 he was appointed Superintendent of Public Works, a post which he held until 1834, and whose duties he performed in an exemplary fashion. In 1819 he carried out a classified census of the population of Glasgow, the first of its kind ever taken in the United Kingdom. He subsequently published several historical and statistical works relating to Glasgow, of which the best known were his *Annals of Glasgow* (1816) and *An Historical Account of the Bills of Mortality, and the Probability of Human Life in Glasgow and Other Large Towns* (1836). His statistical achievements earned him an honorary LL.D from Glasgow University in

1826. When he retired in 1834 a building known as 'the Cleland Testimonial' was erected at the south-east corner of Sauchiehall Street and Buchanan Street and presented to him as a token of public esteem.

Cleland gained his celebrity as a public administrator rather than as an architect. But he was responsible for the design of the following buildings, all in Glasgow: THE POST OFFICE, NELSON STREET, 1810, dem. 1840; THE MAGDALEN ASYLUM, 1812; THE BAZAAR adjoining the City Hall, 1817; and the HIGH SCHOOL, UPPER MONTROSE STREET, 1820. In 1812 he purchased the old goal or tolbooth in Trongate and erected in its place 'a handsome building' for commercial purposes designed by David Hamilton.

[*Extracts from the Records of the Burgh of Glasgow*, ed. Renwick, ix and x, *passim*; G. Eyre-Todd, *History of Glasgow* iii, 1934, 424–7; Joseph Irving, *The Book of Scotsmen*, 1881, 72; *D.N.B.*; R. Chapman, *The Picture of Glasgow*, 1812, 170, 190; Senex, *Glasgow Past and Present*, 1884, i, 392, ii, 129, 389; memoir by J. Cleland Burns prefixed to J. Cleland, *The History of the High School of Glasgow*, Glasgow 1878.]

CLEPHAN, JAMES, practised in London in the 1830s. The name Clephan or Clephane is a North Country one, and James may have been related to William Clephan, an architect and builder at Stockton-on-Tees who died in 1868. Between 1834 and 1839 Clephan acted as executant architect at WREST PARK, BEDS., which Earl de Grey (*q.v.*) was building to his own designs in a French *dix-huitième* style (*C. Life*, 25 June, 2 July 1970). In a MS. account of his works at Wrest Earl de Grey recalled that, when he engaged Clephan, the latter had 'just terminated a similar engagement with Lord Barrington, whose house was built by an amateur architect, his brother [-in-law], Tom Liddell. Clephan had been his superintendent, exactly in the sort of way that I required. I engaged him . . . and from that day to this [he] has given me the greatest satisfaction' [Bedfordshire Record Office, CRT 190/45/2, pp. 1–19]. Clephan had in fact been clerk of works at the Liddells' own castle of Ravensworth in Durham as early as 1815 [see the Coade Stone Co.'s letter-book, P.R.O., C111/106], and had evidently fulfilled the same function at Beckett Park, Berks., whose reconstruction Thomas Liddell (*q.v*) completed for his brother-in-law Lord Barrington in 1834. Clephan also designed the WORKHOUSE (NOW THE CEDARS) at AMPTHILL, 1835–6 [Bedfordshire Record Office, Minutes of the Ampthill Poor Law Union, p. 79], and competed unsuccessfully for one at Bideford in 1837 or 1838 [*Trans. Devonshire Assoc.*, 1, 1918, 552]. In 1838 he designed HOLDERNESS HOUSE, YORKS. (E.R.), for B. M. & W. E. Jalland in an Elizabethan style [J. J. Sheahan, *His-*

tory of Hull, 1864, 625] (G. Poulson, *History of Holderness*, 1840–1, 322, 341). He ceased practice soon after 1850.

CLERK, SIR JOHN (1676–1755), of Penicuik in Midlothian, was Scotland's chief arbiter of taste in matters architectural during the second quarter of the eighteenth century. He was the third generation of a family whose wealth had been founded by John Clerk (1611–1674), an enterprising merchant and art-dealer who bought the Penicuik estate in 1654. His father, Sir John Clerk (d. 1722), had been created a baronet in 1679, and gave his son a legal education, first at Glasgow and later at Leyden, followed in 1697–8 by a Grand Tour. He was admitted to the Scottish Bar in 1700 and subsequently achieved some success as an advocate. From 1702 to 1707 he represented Whithorn in the Scottish Parliament. Politically a Whig and an Anglophile, he was in 1706–7 a commissioner for the Union and was returned as a member of the first parliament of Great Britain. In the following year he was made a Baron of the newly constituted Court of the Exchequer of Scotland, which brought him the then substantial salary of £500 p.a. He was a prominent figure in the intellectual society of Edinburgh after the Union and had many friends among the English intelligentsia of the day, including Lord Burlington, Lord Pembroke and the antiquaries Roger Gale and William Stukeley. He was a Fellow of the Society of Antiquaries and of the Royal Society and Vice-President of the Edinburgh Philosophical Society. 'At home, whether in Edinburgh or at his country-house at Penicuik, he gathered round himself a miniature *Accademia dell' Arcadia* of which the poet Allan Ramsay, the antiquarian Alexander Gordon and the architect William Adam were the principal ornaments; and through them and his other protégés he exerted a wide influence on the development of Scottish art and letters' (Fleming).

Among Clerk's many interests, architecture and landscape-gardening were prominent if not paramount. That they were an inherited taste is demonstrated by the survival of drawings made by his father, the 1st baronet, for a house which he thought of building on his property at Mavisbank, nr. Loanhead, in 1696–8, and by letters which show that in 1703–4 both father and son were helping their neighbour (Sir) David Forbes to design and build a country house at NEWHALL, MIDLOTHIAN [S.R.O., GD 18/5188, nos. 17–29].

In 1710 Clerk bought a house and estate at CAMMO, nr. Cramond, which he subsequently sold in 1726. The house was less than twenty years old, and Clerk's only addition to it appears to have been some stabling [S.R.O., GD 18/1679]. In 1722 he inherited his father's estates and began a new house at MAVISBANK, which he designed in collaboration with William Adam. His journal records that he laid the foundations in 1723 'according to a design concocted between me and Mr. Adams'. Adam was not at first employed as the builder, but (as Clerk explained in 1743) 'after the work had been carried on some time, and not to [his] mind, he then employed Mr. Adams to perfect what was undone' [*Depositions in the Cause William Adam v. Lord Braco*, 1743, p. 46]. Mavisbank was conceived as the small but elegant retreat of a man of affairs rather than as a major country seat. As such it had obvious affinities with the Palladian villa, and as such it was an important innovation in Scottish architecture, setting 'a new architectural fashion for Scottish country mansions of the middle rank' (Dunbar). In 1727, the year Mavisbank was finished, Clerk paid a visit to London, where he made contact with the leader of the English Palladian Revival, Lord Burlington, who not only entertained him at Chiswick, but presented him with two drawings by Inigo Jones from his collection. Clerk also saw Wilton, Wanstead and other important Palladian buildings in the south.

Back in Scotland, Clerk assumed something of the role of a Scottish Burlington. In a long manuscript poem entitled *The Country Seat* (1727) he expounded in sadly pedestrian verse much the same principles of design in architecture and landscape gardening as those that were being disseminated in England by Burlington and Kent. In architecture he insisted that 'the antient Greek and Roman structures, or the Designs of them by Palladio and others ought to be standards fit for the imitation of our modern Architects', while his views on landscape-gardening show that he was moving away from formality towards the 'naturalism' that was soon to transform English gardening.

Though hardly a single building can be attributed to Clerk in its entirety, his advice was often decisive in the choice of architect or design. At ARNISTON, MIDLOTHIAN, the house built by William Adam for Lord President Dundas in 1726–38 has been seen as a direct reflection of the precepts of *The Country Seat*. At HADDO HOUSE, ABERDEENSHIRE (1732–5), though William Adam was again the executant architect, the Palladian restraint of the design was undoubtedly due to Clerk's intervention: indeed, he claimed that 'I myself contributed not a little [to this 'modern regular building'] by concerting with the Earl [of Aberdeen] a plan & model for it & afterwards employing men to execute them' [S.R.O., GD 18/2110]. Apart from Adam, the man principally employed at Haddo was the master mason John Baxter (*q.v.*), who became something of a protégé of Clerk and who subsequently, with Clerk's advice, designed and built GALLOWAY HOUSE, WIGTOWNSHIRE (1740–2), for Clerk's friend Lord

Garlies [S.R.O., GD 18/5011]. In 1738 Clerk gave advice to Charles Erskine before the latter built TINWALD HOUSE, DUMFRIESSHIRE [S.R.O., GD 18/5008], and in 1737 he was summoned by the Earl of Morton to ABERDOUR HOUSE, FIFE, where 'his lordship had invited me to advise him about the situation of a house which he intends to build near the old seat', though in the event nothing was done [S.R.O., GD 18/2113]. At DRUMLANRIG CASTLE, DUMFRIESSHIRE, he designed a cascade for the 2nd Duke of Buccleuch in 1732 [Tait, 137, n. 4 and fig. 40], and in the Register House there is an unsigned sketch by him for a 'Town House' or City Hall to be built on a site adjoining the Parliament House at Edinburgh [S.R.O., RHP 3865].

At PENICUIK HOUSE itself, although Clerk carried out extensive 'improvements' in the grounds, his only strictly architectural work seems to have been the circular tower which he built on Knight's Law between 1748 and 1751. It was left to his son SIR JAMES CLERK (1709–82), the 3rd baronet, to build, in 1761–9, a new house with the aid of the faithful Baxter. Like his father, Sir James was a cultivated man and a competent amateur architect. He studied law at Leyden in 1731–2 and visited Rome in 1732–4. Surviving drawings show that at Penicuik he designed not only the house itself (whose Palladian façade, though faithful to his father's principles, was a little old-fashioned for the 1760s), but also the quadrangular stable-block, whose two entrances are marked, one by a Gibbsian steeple,[1] the other by a full-scale reproduction of a domed Roman building called 'Arthur's Oven' that had stood intact in Stirlingshire until the eighteenth century, but, to the chagrin of Scottish antiquaries, had been pulled down in 1743. At Penicuik the replica serves as a dovecote. Other drawings represent a circular 'Pantheon' library that was never built. Penicuik House, enlarged by the addition of wings (designed by David Bryce in 1857), survives only as a ruin, having been gutted by fire in 1899 (*C. Life*, 15– 22 Aug. 1968).

Other buildings designed by Sir James Clerk are PENICUIK KIRK, with a Doric portico, 1771; HAILES HOUSE, COLINTON, MIDLOTHIAN, for which a plan survives inscribed 'To James Carmichael Esqr. of Hils by S^r. Jas. Clerk'; and ROSS-DHU HOUSE, DUNBARTONSHIRE, built for Sir James Colquhoun in 1773–4, which is stated in A. Whyte & D. Macfarlane's *General View of the Agriculture of the County of Dumbarton*, 1811, 26, to have been 'built upwards of 30 years ago, from a design said to have been given by Sir J. Clerk of Pennycuik' (for a view see J. Irving, *Book of*

---

[1] Penicuik is not unique in its steepled stable. Other eighteenth-century examples can be seen at Blackadder Mount, Berwickshire, and at Tarvit House, nr. Cupar, Fife.

Dumbartonshire iii, 1876). Drawings at Penicuik show an unexecuted design by him for rebuilding ELIE HOUSE, FIFE.

Portraits of Sir John Clerk (by Medina and Aikman) and of Sir James (attributed to William Denune) are preserved at Penicuik. [Clerk family papers in S.R.O. (GD 18) and drawings at Penicuik; *Memoirs of the Life of Sir John Clerk, Bart.,* ed. J. M. Gray, Scottish Hist. Soc., xiii, 1892; *D.N.B.*; Stuart Piggott, *William Stukeley,* 1950; Stuart Piggott, 'The Ancestors of Jonathan Oldbuck', *Antiquity* xxix, 1955; John Fleming, *Robert Adam and his Circle,* 1962; Alistair Rowan, 'Penicuik House, Midlothian', *C. Life,* 15–22 Aug. 1968; W. J. Spink, *The Planning of an Environment; with reference to the Penicuik Estates,* unpublished M.Sc. thesis, University of Edinburgh, 1969; A. A. Tait, 'William Adam and Sir John Clerk: Arniston and "The Country Seat"', *Burl. Mag.,* March 1969; Stuart Piggott, 'Sir John Clerk and "The Country Seat"', in *The Country Seat,* ed. Colvin & Harris, 1970; William Spink, 'Sir John Clerk of Penicuik', in *Furor Hortensis,* ed. P. Willis, Edinburgh 1974.]

CLERK, WILLIAM and ANDREW, were described as the 'Architects' of CRATHIE CHURCH, ABERDEENSHIRE, 1804, dem. *c.* 1893–4, in an inscription recorded by John Stinton, *Crathie and Braemar,* Aberdeen 1926, 264. There are very similar churches at ECHT (1804) and SKENE (1801).

CLINTON, GEORGE, was the surveyor responsible for rebuilding EGLWYSFACH CHURCH, CARDIGANSHIRE, in 1833 [I.C.B.S.]. He was presumably the 'Mr. Clinton, architect, formerly of Shrewsbury and now of Cardiff', who is stated to have designed the classical church of HOLY TRINITY, COLEHAM, SHREWSBURY, in 1836–7 [J. C. Loudon, *Architectural Mag.* iv, 1837, 550]. It is illustrated in H. Pidgeon's *Memorials of Shrewsbury,* 1851, 136. George Clinton of Cardiff designed the MARKET HOUSE at LLANDOVERY, CARMARTHENSHIRE, in 1840 [*Civil Engineer and Architect's Jnl.* iii, 1840, 39]. He died at Cardiff on 5 December 1850 [Principal Probate Registry, Calendar of Probates, 1869].

CLISBY, T— W—, was appointed first surveyor of BRUNSWICK TOWN, BRIGHTON, in July 1830. He emigrated to America in October 1832, and was succeeded by C. A. Busby [A. Dale, *Fashionable Brighton,* 1947, 129].

CLOAKE, GEORGE (*c.* 1761–1812), 'architect', died at Kensington on 10 September 1812, in his 52nd year [*Gent's Mag.* 1812 (ii), 302].

COCK, WALTER BROWN, was a mason and builder at Great Torrington in Devon. In 1828 he rebuilt the Gothic west tower and spire of TORRINGTON CHURCH, apparently to his own designs [contract in parish chest, 1960]. In 1841–2 he and William Dunk, a carpenter, designed and built the classical MARKET HOUSE in the same town [corporation minute-books]. Cock was still in business in 1850.

COCKERELL, CHARLES ROBERT (1788–1863), was the second son of S. P. Cockerell (*q.v.*). He was born in London on 27 April 1788 and was educated first at a private school and then at Westminster. At the age of 16 he began his architectural training in his father's office, where he remained for four or five years. In 1809 he moved to the office of his father's friend Robert Smirke, then engaged in rebuilding Covent Garden Theatre, but in the following year his father decided that the time had come for him to complete his education by a period of foreign travel. France and Italy were enemy territory, and it was in the temporary capacity of a King's Messenger with despatches for Constantinople that Cockerell began his Grand Tour. He reached Turkey after an adventurous voyage that included the capture of a prize off the French coast. Three months later, accompanied by another young architect, John Foster of Liverpool, he left for Athens. Here they found congenial company in the German archaeologists Haller and Linckh, together with whom they discovered the famous Ægina Marbles in the spring of 1811. Cockerell hoped to secure these for the British Museum, but much to his disappointment they eventually went to Munich. The Phigaleian Marbles which Cockerell and his friends soon afterwards discovered at Bassae in Arcadia were, however, purchased by the British government in 1813. In 1811–12 Cockerell and Foster joined the Hon. Frederick North on a tour of Hellenistic sites in Asia Minor. At Smyrna he met Captain Francis Beaufort, commanding H.M.S. *Frederickssteen,* who was engaged in surveying the southern shores of Asia Minor, and who invited Cockerell to accompany him. He parted with Beaufort in Malta in order to visit Sicily, where he spent three months measuring the temple of Jupiter Olympius at Girgenti (Agrigento). After a serious illness in Malta he returned to Greece by way of Albania, and, untiring as usual in his search for classical antiquities, proceeded on a tour of the Peloponnesos and the Archipelago. The abdication of Napoleon in April 1814 now made it possible for Cockerell to extend his tour to Italy, and he spent the winter of 1815–16 in Rome. In the spring of 1816 he visited Florence (where he made a clever pedimental restoration of the Niobe group in the Uffizi) and northern Italy before returning home in 1817 to begin architectural practice at the age of 29.

As a classical archaeologist Cockerell now had a considerable reputation. He had shared in some of the major discoveries of antique sculpture, investigated some important Greek temples, and been (with Haller) the first to observe the entasis of Greek columns. Of architectural practice he had, however, had little experience. His attempt, in 1816, to design a palace for the Duke of Wellington had shown how much he had to learn in that direction, and his fastidious nature recoiled from the drudgery of an architect's office: in a moment of depression he even announced his intention of 'living on a crust of bread' as an artist – a proposal from which he was eventually dissuaded by his father. Although he was soon established in independent practice, he continued to devote much of his time to preparing finished drawings of Greek antiquities for exhibition at the Royal Academy, and as illustrations for a projected history of Greek art, planned in conjunction with Haller, and abandoned only after the latter's death in 1818. In 1819 he exhibited the 'Idea of a Restoration of the Capitol and Forum of Rome...from the existing remains, the authorities of ancient writers, and the dissertations of Piranesi, Nardini, Venuti, and others', and in 1824 a companion restoration of Athens, 'as it may have been in the time of the Antonines'. It was, however, not until 1860 that he at last published his *magnum opus*, *The Temples of Jupiter Panhellenius at Ægina and of Apollo Epicurius at Bassae*. For, although 'drawing was to him as natural a mode of expression as speech', he found writing an effort, and the book, so his son tells us, 'was a load on his conscience all his life'.

Meanwhile in 1819 he had taken his father's place as Surveyor of St. Paul's Cathedral, and by 1822 he was well enough known to be chosen by a Scottish committee to design the National Monument in Edinburgh, intended by its sponsors to be a replica of the Parthenon. In 1833 he succeeded Soane as architect to the Bank of England. He was elected A.R.A. in 1829, R.A. in 1836, and Professor of Architecture in 1840. In 1848 he was the first recipient of the Royal Gold Medal of the R.I.B.A., and in 1860 he succeeded Earl de Grey as the Institute's first professional president. He was a Chevalier of the Legion of Honour, a Member of the Institut de France, of the Academy of St. Luke at Rome, and of many other foreign academies, and Oxford gave him an honorary degree in 1844. He retired from his professorship at the Royal Academy in 1857, and from practice in 1859. He died on 17 September 1863, aged 75, and was buried in the crypt of St. Paul's Cathedral, where a monument to his memory was erected by his son and successor, F. P. Cockerell (illustrated in *Wren Soc.* ix, 5). He married in 1828 Anna, daughter of the civil engineer John Rennie, by whom he had ten children. As a young man Cockerell was the subject of a fine drawing by Ingres, and the R.I.B.A. has a convincing portrait of him in old

age by Sir William Boxall. Other portraits will be found in *Illustrated London News* xliii, 1863, 341–2, and on the podium of the Albert Memorial, where he stands between Pugin and Barry as a representative of Victorian architecture.

Cockerell was at once the most fastidious and the least pedantic of English neo-classical architects. For him as a practising architect scholarship was a servant, not a master, and the influence of his archaeological researches is shown in refinement of detail rather than in the literal reproduction of Greek or Roman architectural monuments. Nor did he disdain to learn from the more recent past. In Italy he had looked appreciatively at the buildings of the sixteenth and seventeenth centuries: as Surveyor of St. Paul's he became an enthusiastic student not only of Wren but also of Vanbrugh and Hawksmoor, whose powerful designs he admired long before anyone else.[1] In consequence his own work is a unique synthesis of neo-classical and baroque, of Greek Revival and English 'Renaissance'. The result is a personal style of great beauty and distinction which stands out clearly from the conflicting trends of Victorian architecture. Boldly conceived in scale and recession, enlivened by the introduction of authentic but unhackneyed antique details such as his favourite 'Bassae' order, and planned with the best French neo-classical prototypes in mind, Cockerell's architecture is rich without being vulgar, eclectic without being imitative. One of its characteristic features is a generous but judicious use of sculptural decoration. 'Sculpture', wrote Cockerell, 'is the language of architecture', and his skill in drawing the human figure enabled him to design appropriate sculpture himself. He also made effective use of different-coloured materials, avoiding in this way the drabness of much Greek Revival architecture when seen in the dull light of northern Europe. Cockerell's style was best deployed in public buildings such as the Ashmolean Museum at Oxford and the unfinished University Library at Cambridge (whose interior, had it been completed, would have been his masterpiece) and his monumental banks established an architectural tradition that has lasted almost to the present day. As a country-house architect he was less successful, but the small houses which he built at Hinchwick in Gloucestershire and Enstone in Oxfordshire deserve to be noted as remarkably sensitive essays in the

[1] Cf. Cockerell's designs for the Houses of Parliament (1835), which he described as 'composed in the Italian and Flemish manner of that day [i.e. the sixteenth century], and with reference to Wren, Vanbrugh, and our own great masters, so as to vary and to discover new combinations of the group at every step' (*Catalogue of the Designs offered for the New Houses of Parliament now exhibiting in the National Gallery*, 6th ed. 1836, 6).

vernacular style of their region. Though Gothic architecture interested him as a scholar, it did not inspire him as an artist, and he designed nothing of much importance in that style. Lampeter College and the Seckford Hospital at Woodbridge are no more than competent performances in Tudor Gothic. At Killerton (Devon), Athens (Greece) and Longborough (Glos.), he designed chapels in the Romanesque, 'Early English' and 'Perpendicular' styles, respectively. Though Cockerell was recognized as one of the leading architects of his time, several important commissions eluded him. Among the buildings for which he competed unsuccessfully were the National Gallery (1833), the Houses of Parliament (1835), the Reform Club (1837), the Royal Exchange (1839) and the Carlton Club (1844). The National Monument at Edinburgh was never completed, and only one wing of his Cambridge University Library was built. All his public buildings in London have now been demolished, and his most important surviving works are the Ashmolean Museum at Oxford and the branch Banks of England at Manchester, Liverpool and Bristol.

Though Cockerell chose to take few if any pupils into his office,[1] the authority of his scholarship and the distinction of his personality made him one of the most revered figures in nineteenth-century British architecture. His Royal Academy lectures, illustrated by his views and restorations of Greek and Roman architecture, attracted much attention, and are described by a contemporary as filled with Academicians and students eager to hear him speak of the 'glories of Athens, Syracuse or Rome'. Though he exhibited only intermittently at the Academy, two of the drawings which he showed became famous. One was the 'Tribute to the Memory of Sir Christopher Wren', showing all Wren's works assembled in a single group (1838). The other was entitled 'The Professor's Dream: A Symposium of the principal architectural monuments of Modern and Ancient times, drawn to the same scale', and was exhibited in 1849.

Cockerell's principal publications were *Antiquities of Athens and other Places of Greece, Sicily, etc.*, supplementary to *The Antiquities of Athens* by Stuart & Revett, London 1830 (German translation 1829); *The Temple of Jupiter Olympius at Agrigentum*, 1830; 'The Architectural Works of William of Wykeham', *Proceedings of the Archaeological Institute at Winchester*, 1845; 'Ancient Sculptures in Lincoln Cathedral', 1848, reprinted in *Proceedings of the Archaeological Institute*, 1850; *Iconography of the West Front of Wells Cathedral*, 1851; 'On the Painting of the

Ancients', *Civil Engineer and Architect's Jnl.* xxii, 1859, 42–44, 88–91; *The Temples of Jupiter Panhellenius at Ægina, and of Apollo Epicurius at Bassae*, 1860;[2] 'Architectural Accessories of Monumental Sculpture', *Civil Engineer and Architect's Jnl.* xxiv, 1861, 333–6; and *A Descriptive Account of the Sculptures of the West Front of Wells Cathedral photographed for the Architectural Photographic Association*, 1862. Cockerell's Royal Academy lectures were reported at length in the *Athenaeum* and in the *Builder* from 1843 onwards. The diary of his early travels was published in 1903 as *Travels in Southern Europe and the Levant, 1810–1817*, ed. S. P. Cockerell. A notebook with sketches of English country houses, etc., visited by Cockerell, entitled by him 'Ichnographica Domestica', was published by John Harris in *Architectural History* xiv, 1971.

The principal collections of Cockerell's drawings are at the Victoria and Albert Museum and the R.I.B.A. His MS. diaries for the years 1821–30 and 1832 belong to his descendant Mrs. B. J. Crichton. A MS. scrap-book compiled by his assistant J. E. Goodchild in 1889 and entitled *Reminiscences of twenty-six years association with the late Professor C. R. Cockerell* is in the collection of the late Sir Albert Richardson. For other drawings and MS. sources see David Watkin, *The Life and Work of C. R. Cockerell*, 1974, which includes a full bibliography. The other principal authorities for Cockerell's life are obituaries in *Gent's Mag.* xv, 1863, 785–91, and *Builder* xxi, 1863, 683–5, 705; S. Smirke, 'Some Account of the Professional Life and Character of the Late Prof. C. R. Cockerell', *R.I.B.A. Transactions*, 1863–4; G. Aitchison, 'C. R. Cockerell', *R.I.B.A. Transactions*, N.S. vi, 1890, 255–61; J. M. Brydon, 'The Work of Prof. Cockerell, R.A.', *R.I.B.A. Jnl.*, 3rd ser., vii, 1899–1900, 349–68; R. P. Cockerell, 'The Life and Works of C. R. Cockerell, R.A.', *Arch. Rev.* xii, 1902, 43–7, 129–46; R. P. Spiers, 'Cockerell's Restorations of Ancient Rome', *Arch. Rev.* xxix, 1911, 123–8; *D.N.B.*; and E. M. Dodd, 'Charles Robert Cockerell', in *Victorian Architecture*, ed. P. Ferriday, 1963.

PUBLIC BUILDINGS

SEVENOAKS, KENT, LADY BOSWELL'S CHARITY SCHOOL, 1818; the two flanking entrances were later heightened [R.I.B.A.D.].

BANBURY CHURCH, OXON., completed tower and portico, modifying original design by S. P. Cockerell, 1818–22 [*V.C.H. Oxon.* x, 102–3].

HARROW SCHOOL, MIDDLESEX, new wing containing Speech Room, 1819–20, Tudor style to form symmetrical composition with Old

---

[1] His principal assistants were James Noble (*q.v.*) and J. E. Goodchild. J. L. Clemence of Lowestoft described himself in 1868 as a former pupil of Cockerell.

[2] The original drawings for this book are in the Mellon Collection.

Schools [E. D. Laborde, *Harrow School*, 1948, 69–71] (*C. Life*, 14 July 1934).

LONDON, ST. PAUL'S CATHEDRAL, restoration including replacement of ball and cross on dome, 1821–22 [Diary].

LONDON, NO. 49 PALL MALL, remodelled for the Travellers' Club, 1821–2; dem. *c.* 1895 [Diary, and cf. Watkin, 160 n.].

OLDCASTLE, CO. MEATH, IRELAND, School, 1821–2 [Watkin, 168].

BRISTOL, THE LITERARY AND PHILOSOPHICAL INSTITUTION (later Masonic Hall), PARK STREET, 1821–3; gutted by bombing 1940–1 [exhib. at R.A. 1821; R.I.B.A.D.].

LONGBOROUGH CHURCH, GLOS., north transept, or 'Sezincote aisle', for Sir Charles Cockerell, Bart., 1822–3, Gothic [Diary].

ST. DAVID'S COLLEGE, LAMPETER, CARDIGANSHIRE, 1822–7, Tudor Gothic [exhib. at R.A. 1829; drawings at R.I.B.A., Lampeter and Royal Library, Windsor].

LONDON, THE HANOVER CHAPEL, REGENT STREET, 1823–5; repaired (by Cockerell) 1845–6; dem. 1896 [Britton & Pugin, *The Public Buildings of London* ii, 1828, 276–82; V. and A.] (P. Waterhouse, 'Hanover Chapel', *R.I.B.A. Jnl.*, 3rd ser., iv, 1897, 111–14).

LONDON, ARCHBISHOP TENISON'S CHAPEL (ST. THOMAS), REGENT STREET, rebuilt west front as façade to Regent Street, 1824; Cockerell's façade was remodelled in 1854 and demolished in 1903. The church was demolished in 1973 [*Survey of London* xxxi, 183–4].

EDINBURGH, THE NATIONAL MONUMENT, CALTON HILL, in collaboration with W. H. Playfair, 1824–9 (unfinished) [correspondence with Playfair in National Library of Scotland, MS. 639].

MIDDLE CLAYDON, BUCKS., designed school for Sir Harry Calvert Verney, Bart., 1827, perhaps the building now used as the Post Office [Diary].

BRISTOL, HOLY TRINITY CHURCH, HOTWELLS, 1829–30; interior gutted by bombing 1940–1 and reconstructed to a different design 1958 [W. Ison, *The Georgian Buildings of Bristol*, 1952, 88–9].

LONDON, THE WESTMINSTER LIFE AND BRITISH FIRE OFFICE, STRAND, 1831–2; dem. 1908 [exhib. at R.A. 1832; R.I.B.A.D.; V. and A.].

LONDON, THE BANK OF ENGLAND, reconstructed the Dividend, Warrant and Cheque Offices and Accountant's Drawing Office, 1834–5. In 1848–50 these were remodelled by Cockerell as a new and enlarged Private Drawing Office. After the Chartist Troubles of 1848 he was employed to reconstruct the attic storey of the Bank as a fortified parapet-walk. In 1835 he published a set of 4 plates entitled *Plan and Section of the New Dividend Pay and Warrant Offices*, etc. See also *Architectural Mag.* iii, 1836, 109–12, and H. R. Steele & F. R. Yer-

bury, *The Old Bank of England, London*, 1930, chap. 7.

PLYMOUTH, DEVON, BRANCH BANK OF ENGLAND, 1835; dem. [Watkin, 216].

WOODBRIDGE, SUFFOLK, THE SECKFORD HOSPITAL, 1835–40, Tudor Gothic [*R.I.B.A. Trans.*, N.S. vi, 1890, 259; drawings in Goodchild Album]. The lodge and gates were designed by Cockerell's assistant, J. Noble, in 1841–2 [Seckford Hospital archives, *ex inf.* Mr. Norman Scarfe].

LONDON, THE LONDON AND WESTMINSTER BANK, LOTHBURY, in collaboration with Sir William Tite, who designed the interior, 1837–9; dem. 1928 [see Tite's account of the partnership in *R.I.B.A. Trans.*, 1863–4, 24; drawings at R.I.B.A. and V. and A.] (measured drawings in *Architect and Building News*, 1 March 1935).

CAMBRIDGE, THE UNIVERSITY LIBRARY, north wing only executed, 1837–40 [Willis & Clark, iii, 103–21; drawings in Cambridge University Library, MS. Add. 6603, V. and A. and Goodchild Album].

HARROW SCHOOL, MIDDLESEX, Chapel, 1838–9, Tudor Gothic; dem. 1853 [E. D. Laborde, *Harrow School*, 1948, 92–5].

KILLERTON, DEVON, chapel, 1840–1, see under 'Domestic Architecture' below.

ATHENS, ENGLISH PROTESTANT CHURCH, 1840–3, Gothic (executed in modified form) [*Builder* xxi, 1863, 705].

LONDON, SUN FIRE OFFICE, THREADNEEDLE STREET, 1841–2; remodelled 1895; dem. 1971 [R.I.B.A.D.; V. and A.].

OXFORD, THE ASHMOLEAN MUSEUM AND TAYLORIAN INSTITUTION, 1841–5 [*V.C.H. Oxon* iii, 57; drawings at R.I.B.A., V. and A. and Oxford University Archives].

PLYMOUTH, BRANCH BANK OF ENGLAND, COURTNEY STREET, 1842 [Watkin, 217].

OXFORD, THE QUEEN'S COLLEGE, conversion into library of arcaded space beneath Upper Library, 1843–5 [*V.C.H. Oxon*. iii, 143].

MANCHESTER, BRANCH BANK OF ENGLAND, KING STREET, 1844–5 [R.I.B.A.D.].

BRISTOL, BRANCH BANK OF ENGLAND, BROAD STREET, 1844–6 [R.I.B.A.D.].

LIVERPOOL, BRANCH BANK OF ENGLAND, CASTLE STREET, 1844–7 [V. and A.].

CAMBRIDGE, FITZWILLIAM MUSEUM, completion after death of G. Basevi, 1845–7. Cockerell's principal contribution, the entrance-hall and staircase, were respectively remodelled and replaced by E. M. Barry in 1870–5 [Willis & Clark, iii, 215–7; V. and A.].

LONDON, NATIONAL DEBT REDEMPTION OFFICE, OLD JEWRY, additions, 1846; dem. *c.* 1900 [*R.I.B.A. Trans.*, N.S. vi, 1890, 259].

LONDON, ST. BARTHOLOMEW'S CHURCH, MOOR LANE, 1849–50, incorporating the fittings of

Wren's St. Bartholomew Exchange: dem. 1902 [R.I.B.A.D.: V. and A.].

LONDON, UNIVERSITY COLLEGE, arrangement, in collaboration with T. L. Donaldson, of the Flaxman Gallery to receive the plaster models of Flaxman's sculpture given to the college in 1848, 1849–50 [*Architect and Building Gazette* ii, 1850, 568].

LIVERPOOL, BANK CHAMBERS, COOK STREET, 1849–50; dem. 1959 [Watkin, 219].

LIVERPOOL, ST. GEORGE'S HALL, completion of interiors after death of H. L. Elmes, 1851–4. Cockerell also designed the sculpture in the pediment executed by W. G. Nicholl [R.I.B.A.D.; Goodchild Album; *Builder* xiii, 1855, 126–7].

LIVERPOOL, LIVERPOOL AND LONDON INSURANCE COMPANY'S OFFICES, DALE STREET, assisted by F. P. Cockerell, 1856–7 [Watkin, 229–31].

WESTMINSTER SCHOOL, designed the scenery for the Latin play, 1858 [*A Naval Career: the Life of Admiral John Markham*, 1883, 14, n. 7].

DOMESTIC ARCHITECTURE

LONDON, NORTHUMBERLAND HOUSE, STRAND, survey and report for the 3rd Duke of Northumberland, 1819 [Alnwick Castle MS. 94, f. 6 *et seq.*].

LONDON, NO. 32 ST. JAMES'S SQUARE, for William Howley, Bishop of London, 1819–21, in collaboration with S. P. Cockerell [*Survey of London* xxix, 203–4].

OAKLY PARK, SHROPSHIRE, remodelled for the Hon. R. H. Clive, 1819–36 [C. Hussey in *C. Life*, 1–8 March 1956; C. Hussey, *English Country Houses: Late Georgian*, 1958, 151–60].

LONDON, GLOUCESTER HOUSE, PARK LANE, repairs to roof for William Frederick, Duke of Gloucester, 1821; dem. [Watkin, 249].

LONDON, ALBANY COTTAGE (now NORTH VILLA), REGENT'S PARK, for T. B. Lennard, 1821 [Watkin, 249].

ABERGWILI PALACE, CARMARTHENSHIRE, repairs for the Bishop of St. David's, 1821 [Watkin, 249].

WOOLMERS, HERTINGFORDBURY, HERTS., alterations for Sir Gore Ouseley, Bart., 1821 [Diary].

LOUGH CREW, CO. MEATH, IRELAND, for J. L. Naper, 1821–9; dem. *c.* 1965, but classical lodge and gates survive [Diary; R.I.B.A.D.].

KINTURK, CASTLE POLLARD, CO. MEATH, IRELAND, alterations, including addition of portico, for W. D. Pollard, 1821–5 [Diary].

BOWOOD HOUSE, WILTS., chapel, library and breakfast-room for the 3rd Marquess of Lansdowne, 1822–4 [list of works in R.I.B.A. *Sessional Papers*, 1863–4, 27] (*C. Life*, 15 June 1972).

LONDON, NO. 33 BROOK STREET, GROSVENOR SQUARE, alterations for Henry Trail, 1823–4; dem. [Watkin, 250].

LONDON, NO. 1 UPPER GROSVENOR STREET, alterations for his brother John Cockerell, 1822–3; dem. [Watkin, 250].

GRANGE PARK, HANTS., additions for Alexander Baring (afterwards 1st Lord Ashburton), including dining-room (dem. 1972) and conservatory (rebuilt *c.* 1880 except for the Ionic portico), 1823–5 [J. M. Crook, 'Grange Park Transformed', in *The Country Seat*, ed. Colvin & Harris, 1970, 223–6].

GREENMOUNT, CO. ANTRIM, IRELAND, remodelled for Mrs. Anna Thompson, *c.* 1823–5; now gutted and used as Northern Ireland Agricultural College [Diary].

SEZINCOTE HOUSE, GLOS., two lodges for Sir Charles Cockerell, Bart., one known formerly as Worcester Lodge, now as Beehive Lodge, 1823 [Diary].

DERRY ORMOND, nr. LAMPETER, CARDIGANSHIRE, for John Jones, 1824; enlarged 1860; dem. 1953 [list of works in R.I.B.A. *Sessional Papers*, 1863–4, 27].

PENTRE, BONCATH, PEMBROKESHIRE, alterations for Dr. Davies, 1824–5 [Diary].

CWMCYNFELIN, nr. ABERYSTWYTH, CARDIGANSHIRE, stables (now converted into dwellings) for J. Lloyd Williams, 1825 [Diary].

HINCHWICK FARM (now MANOR), CONDICOTE, GLOS., for Sir Charles Cockerell, Bart., 1826 [Diary].

LONDON, EATON SQUARE, interior of house for Capt. W. A. Clifford, R.N., 1827 [Hermione Hobhouse, *Thomas Cubitt*, 1971, 274 n.; Watkin, 251].

LONDON, EATON SQUARE, interior of house for Mrs. Belli, Cockerell's aunt, 1828 [Diary].

SEZINCOTE HOUSE, GLOS., office wing for Sir Charles Cockerell, Bart., 1827 [Diary].

WYNNSTAY, DENBIGHSHIRE, Great Room (dem. 1858) and lodge for Sir Watkin Williams-Wynn, Bart., 1827–8 [Peter Howell & T. W. Pritchard in *C. Life*, 30 March, 6 April 1972].

LANGTON HOUSE, nr. BLANDFORD, DORSET, for J. J. Farquharson, 1827–33; dem. 1949 except for stables [list of works in R.I.B.A. *Sessional Papers*, 1863–4, 27].

LYNFORD HALL, NORFOLK, alterations and additions for Sir Richard Sutton, Bart., 1828; rebuilt by W. Burn 1863 [Diary].

NORTH WEALD BASSET VICARAGE, ESSEX, for his brother, the Rev. Henry Cockerell, 1828–9, Tudor style [Diary].

LANGLEYS, ESSEX, advised J. J. Tufnell, 1827, perhaps suggesting formation of entrance-hall by bringing forward three central bays [Diary; cf. Watkin, 251] (*C. Life*, 9 Jan. 1942).

ENSTONE VICARAGE, OXON., 1832–3 [Bodleian Library, MS. Oxford Dioc. papers b. 103, no. 2 b].

BLAISE CASTLE, nr. BRISTOL, picture-room (with Ionic portico) for J. S. Harford, 1832–3 [Alice Harford, *Annals of the Harford Family*, 1909, 54] (*C. Life*, 31 March 1900).

KILLERTON, DEVON, private chapel in park for Sir T. D. Acland, Bart., 1840–1, Romanesque style [R.I.B.A.D.].

BUXTON HILL HOUSE, MALMESBURY, WILTS., for his brother John Cockerell, 1842; rebuilt after a fire in 1846, presumably to Cockerell's designs, Tudor Gothic [MS. list of works at R.I.B.A.].

PEPER HAROW, SURREY, addition of porch and balustrade in front of the attics for the 5th Viscount Midleton, 1843 [*R.I.B.A. Trans.*, N.S. vi, 1890, 259] (*C. Life*, 26 Dec. 1925).

CAVERSFIELD HOUSE, OXON., for the Rev. R. B. Marsham, 1842–5; dem. after fire 1976 [*R.I.B.A. Trans.*, N.S. vi, 1890, 259].

MONUMENTS

NEWCASTLE, ST. NICHOLAS CHURCH (now Cathedral), Admiral Lord Collingwood (d. 1810), 1821, executed by J. C. F. Rossi [R. Welford, *Monuments of St. Nicholas Newcastle*, 1880, pl. xiii].

HAMPTON, MIDDLESEX, John Deverell, 1821, executed by J. C. F. Rossi, but apparently now lost or destroyed [Watkin, Appendix B].

PENBURY CHURCH, nr. BRISTOL, Mrs. H. Battersby, 1823, executed by J. C. F. Rossi [Watkin, Appendix B].

PIDDLETRENTHIDE CHURCH, DORSET, John Bridge (d. 1834), Gothic, executed by W. G. Nicholl [signed].

KENSAL GREEN CEMETERY, Lady Pulteney, 1849 [A. W. Hakewill, *Modern Tombs gleaned from the Public Cemeteries of London*, 1851, pl. 23].

ROYAL HOSPITAL, CHELSEA, granite obelisk to commemorate Victory of Chillianwallah, 1849 [Watkin, Appendix B].

ROYAL HOSPITAL, CHELSEA, catafalque for lying-in-state of the Duke of Wellington, 11–17 Nov. 1852 [*R.I.B.A. Trans.*, N.S. vi, 1890, 259].

BRIGHTON CEMETERY, H. J. Prescott, Governor of the Bank of England (d. 1856), 1858 [*R.I.B.A. Trans.*, N.S. vi, 1890, 259].

ROYAL HOSPITAL, CHELSEA, monument in chapel to the officers and men killed in the Indian Mutiny, 1858 [*R.I.B.A. Trans.*, N.S. vi, 1890, 259].

COCKERELL, SAMUEL PEPYS (1753–1827), was the son of John Cockerell of Bishop's Hull, Somerset.[1] Through his mother he was related to the family of the diarist Samuel Pepys.

[1] According to the account of the family in Debrett's *Baronetage*, 1836, 348, S. P. Cockerell was born on 15 Feb. 1754, but in his diary C. R. Cockerell implies that his father was born on 6 Jan. 1753. This is consistent with his death in 1827 at the age of 74.

He began his architectural career as a pupil of Sir Robert Taylor, whose benevolent tutelage he was to acknowledge many years later in his will, where he refers to him as 'the affectionate prop and support of my early steps and to whom . . . I was chiefly indebted for my first advancement in life'. In 1774 Cockerell obtained his first appointment as District Surveyor for the parish of St. George's, Hanover Square. In 1775 he joined the Office of Works as Clerk of Works at the Tower of London, and in 1780 was also given the clerkship at Newmarket. Though regarded as 'very able in his profession' and 'very diligent and regular in His Majesty's service', he lost both posts as a result of the reorganization of the Office of Works in 1782. However, in 1785 he was appointed Inspector of Repairs to the Admiralty, and on Sir Robert Taylor's death in 1788 Cockerell succeeded to the surveyorships of the Foundling and Pulteney estates in London. In 1791 he obtained the surveyorship to the Victualling Office, and in 1806 that of the East India Company. He was also surveyor to the sees of Canterbury and London, and Surveyor of St. Paul's Cathedral from 1811 to 1819.

As surveyor to the governors of the Foundling Hospital, Cockerell was responsible for the development of their Bloomsbury estate, preparing in 1790 a report which summarized 'the cardinal principles of Georgian town-planning'. During the next fifteen years building proceeded under Cockerell's direction, but some of the governors were not satisfied that his supervision was adequate, and attempted to have him dismissed. Although the General Court appears to have been satisfied with his conduct, Cockerell eventually resigned in April 1808, his place being taken by his pupil Joseph Kay (for further details see D. J. Oleson, *Town Planning in London*, Yale 1964, 74–89). As surveyor to the Bishop of London Cockerell prepared plans for developing his Paddington estate, but they had not been implemented at the time of the architect's death, and the area was eventually laid out for building on the basis of a new scheme by his successor George Gutch (see Gordon Toplis, 'The History of Tyburnia', in *C. Life*, 15 Nov. 1973).

Cockerell was an able architect whose work is often interesting and original. Some of his designs show 'very marked French influence of an advanced kind', notably the destroyed church of St. Martin Outwich, the somewhat eccentric tower of St. Anne's, Soho, and the façade of Gore Court, Kent. At Daylesford and Sezincote he skilfully grafted oriental details on to basically English architectural forms for the benefit of Indian 'nabobs'; and at Tickencote in Rutland he made a serious if not very scholarly attempt to restore a twelfth-century church in a Romanesque style.

If Cockerell visited France or Italy the journey

does not appear to have been recorded, but he is known to have gone to Ireland in July 1795, presumably for a professional purpose [P.R.O., CREST 2/918; Farington's Diary, 15 July 1795]. He lived in a house in Old Burlington Street, and latterly at Westbourne House, Paddington, the former residence of Isaac Ware, where he died on 12 July 1827, aged 74. He left a considerable estate, including the manor of Woolley in Huntingdonshire, which he had acquired in 1803. There are portraits of Cockerell and his wife by George Dance in the British Museum, and a half-length portrait by Beechey was engraved by Thomas Hodgetts (1834). His pupils included Joseph Kay, Benjamin Latrobe, Thomas Martyr, James Noble, William Porden, Robert Sibley, C. H. Tatham, and his (second) son C. R. Cockerell, who gave him considerable assistance during his last years. Some of his drawings are in the R.I.B.A. Collection. His unexecuted design for the Connaught Chapel, Paddington (1827), is in the Victoria and Albert Museum (E 2115, 1909). It is reproduced in *C. Life*, 15 Nov. 1973, p. 1527, fig. 3.

[*A.P.S.D.*; *D.N.B.*; *History of the King's Works* vi, 25; P.R.O., Adm. 111/123, 1 Sept. 1791 (surveyorship of Victualling Office); John Summerson, *Architecture in Britain 1530–1830*, 359, n. 5; diaries of C. R. Cockerell; *Gent's Mag.* 1827 (ii), 93; P.C.C. 470 HEBER; *V.C.H. Hunts.* iii, 126; *Architectural History* xiv, 1971, fig. 14b (plan of Cockerell's house at Westbourne Green).]

PUBLIC BUILDINGS

LONDON, SAUNDERS'S CHOCOLATE HOUSE, later the Albion Club House, 85 ST. JAMES'S STREET, 1786; dem. 1862 ['this Club built by my Father 30 years ago': C. R. Cockerell's diary, 10 Sept. 1823; *Survey of London* xxx, 468].

BANBURY CHURCH, OXON., rebuilt 1792–7; tower and portico completed to modified design by C. R. Cockerell 1818–22 [exhib. at R.A. 1792; *V.C.H. Oxon.* x, 102–3, with plan and illustration of S. P. Cockerell's original design for the tower].

BLOXHAM CHURCH, OXON., gratuitously supervised repair of spire, 1792 [Gardner's *History, Gazeteer and Directory of the County of Oxford*, 1852, 618; *V.C.H. Oxon*, ix, 76].

TICKENCOTE CHURCH, RUTLAND, rebuilt in Norman style, incorporating twelfth-century chancel, at expense of Eliza Wingfield, 1792 [*Gent's Mag.* 1806 (i), 34].

NORMANTON CHURCH, RUTLAND, proposed decorations for Sir Gilbert Heathcote, Bart., exhib. at R.A. 1793; rebuilt 1911.

LONDON, ST. MARTIN OUTWICH CHURCH, BISHOPSGATE STREET, rebuilt 1796–8; dem. 1874 [exhib. at R.A. 1797, 1798, 1799; C. W. F. Goss, 'St.

Martin Outwich', *London and Middlesex Arch. Soc.'s Trans.*, N.S. vi, 1929] (external view in G. Godwin & J. Britton, *The Churches of London* ii, 1839; plan in W. Thornbury, *Old and New London* i, n.d., 534).

LONDON, ST. MARGARET'S CHURCH, WESTMINSTER, new roof, ceiling, galleries, and extensive repairs and redecoration, 1799–1802, Gothic [exhib. at R.A. 1799, 1801; MS. Minutes of the Committee for the Repair of the Church, 1798–1803, Westminster City Library, No. 2625] (H. F. Westlake, *St. Margaret's Westminster*, 1914, pls. vi, ix).

LONDON, WORSHIP STREET, SHOREDITCH, entrance to stables of the Light Horse Volunteers, *c.* 1800 [exhib. at R.A. 1801].

LONDON, ST. ANNE'S CHURCH, SOHO, tower, 1802–3 [*Survey of London* xxxiii, 262–3, 270].

LONDON, THE WESTMINSTER GUILDHALL or SESSIONS HOUSE, 1804–5; dem. [J. Elmes, *Metropolitan Improvements*, 1831, 155, with illustration].

SWANSEA, GLAMORGANSHIRE, THE ASSEMBLY ROOMS, CAMBRIAN PLACE, 1804–5 [*Hereford Journal*, 14 April 1806].

CONGLETON, CHESHIRE, THE GUILDHALL, 1804–5 (dem. 1868), may have been the 'Town Hall and Market House in Cheshire' which Cockerell exhibited at the R.A. in 1803: see illustration in R. Head, *Congleton Past and Present*, 1887, 137.

LONDON, ST. GEORGE'S CHURCH, SOUTHWARK, survey in 1806 prior to repair in 1808 [Surrey Archdeaconry Records].

TENBY, PEMBROKESHIRE, PUBLIC BATHS, for Sir William Paxton, 1811 (now known as Laston House and converted into flats) [J. Dugdale, *British Traveller* iv, 1819, 729].

SEVENOAKS CHURCH, KENT, restoration, including clerestory and plaster vault to nave, 1812 [J. Rooker, *Guide to Sevenoaks Church*, 1910].

LONDON, EAST INDIA HOUSE, LEADENHALL STREET, additions, 1822–3 (assisted by C. R. Cockerell); dem. 1861–2 [C. R. Cockerell's diary].

WINCHESTER, HOSPITAL OF ST. CROSS, restoration, 1827, completed by John Nash [John Summerson, *John Nash*, 1935, 286].

PADDINGTON, LONDON, added four dwellings to parish almshouses in Harrow Road; dem. 1860 [W. Robins, *Paddington Past and Present*, 1853, 67].

DOMESTIC ARCHITECTURE

WHITE KNIGHTS, nr. READING, BERKS., entrance gates and bridge for W. Byam Martin, *c.* 1785 [exhib. at R.A. 1785].

LONDON, WHITEHALL, ADMIRALTY HOUSE, as residence for the First Lord of the Admiralty, 1786–8 [*Survey of London* xvi, 35–9 and pls. 46–57].

WATERSTOCK HOUSE, OXON., for Sir W. H. Ashurst, 1787–90; dem. 1956 [Bodleian Library, MS. d.d. Ashurst d.10, where the architect is called 'Sir Richard Cockerell'; J. Dale & P. H. Ditchfield, *Oxfordshire and Berkshire: County Biographies* (*c.* 1900), where he is called 'Sir C. Cockerell'].

DAYLESFORD HOUSE, nr. MORETON-IN-MARSH, GLOS., for Warren Hastings, 1788–93 [payments, etc., to Cockerell in Warren Hastings' papers in B.M., Add MSS. 29231, ff. 59–60, 39902, ff. 26–33; P. F. Norton, 'Daylesford', *Jnl. of the Society of Architectural Historians* (of America), xxii, 1963].

SALISBURY, ST. EDMUND'S COLLEGE (now Council House), addition of north wing for H. P. Wyndham, 1790 [R.C.H.M., *Salisbury*, forthcoming].

PIERREMONT HALL (now Council Offices), nr. BROADSTAIRS, KENT, for (? James) Forsyth, 1792 [*A.P.S.D.*].

LITTLE KINETON, WARWICKS., house for Richard Hill, begun 1792, but never completed [estimate dated 15 March 1792 in Sir John Soane's Museum].

MIDDLETON HALL, CARMARTHENSHIRE, for Sir William Paxton, 1793–5; gutted by fire 1931 and dem. 1951 [G. Richardson, *New Vitruvius Britannicus* ii, 1808, pls. 62–4]; also a tower in the park in memory of Lord Nelson, *c.* 1815 [*The Beauties of England and Wales* xviii, 1815, 332] (S. Barton, *Monumental Follies*, 1972, 254).

LONDON, GREAT PULTENEY STREET, small house for Sir William Pulteney, Bart., *c.* 1794 [C. R. Cockerell's diary, 22 March 1827].

GORE COURT, TUNSTALL, KENT, for G. Harper, 1792–5; dem. *c.* 1925 [G. Richardson, *New Vitruvius Britannicus* i, 1802, pl. 11].

BUXTED PARK, SUSSEX, proposed alterations and additions for Sir George Shuckburgh Evelyn, Bart., 1801, perhaps not carried out; damaged by fire 1810 [letters in B.M., Add. MS. 38480, ff. 141–2] (*C. Life*, 21–28 April 1934).

NUTWELL COURT, nr. EXETER, DEVON, for the 2nd Lord Heathfield, 1802 [exhib. at R.A. 1802].

LONDON, NO. 13 HARLEY STREET, rooms for Sir William Beechey [Farington's Diary, 13 Oct. 1803].

SEZINCOTE HOUSE, nr. MORETON-IN-MARSH, GLOS., for his brother Sir Charles Cockerell, Bart., *c.* 1805, Indian style [B. M., Add. MS. 29231, ff. 59–60; *Catalogue of the R.I.B.A. Drawings Coll.: C–F*, 34 and (for Thomas Daniell's designs for the Indian garden ornaments, etc.) 64–5 (*C. Life*, 13, 20 May 1939; C. Hussey, *English Country Houses: Late Georgian*, 1958, 66–73).

attributed: LONDON, NELSON SQUARE, SOUTHWARK, *c.* 1807–10 [*Survey of London* xxii, 129–30].

FULHAM PALACE, MIDDLESEX, rebuilt east front for William Howley, Bishop of London, 1814–15 [C. J. Fèret, *Fulham Old and New* iii, 1900, 114] (*C. Life*, 9 Feb. 1929).

LONDON, NO. 32 ST. JAMES'S SQUARE, for William Howley, Bishop of London, 1819–21, in collaboration with C. R. Cockerell [*Survey of London* xxix, 203–4].

BROUGHTON RECTORY, OXON., added bow-windowed drawing-room, 1820 [*V.C.H. Oxon.* ix, 86].

LONDON, NOS. 144, 145 PICCADILLY [*A.P.S.D.*].

COKE, THOMAS (1675–1727), was the son of John Coke (d. 1692), from whom he inherited the mansion and estate of Melbourne in Derbyshire. He was educated at New College, Oxford, and subsequently spent some time in the Low Countries. He sat in Parliament as member for Derbyshire from 1698 to 1710, and for the rotten borough of Grampound from 1710 to 1714. Politically he was a Tory and a supporter of Harley, but retained the Court post of Vice-Chamberlain, to which he was appointed in 1707, throughout the reign of George I.

Coke was a connoisseur and man of taste. When his possessions were sold after his death there were 127 lots of pictures, 443 lots of prints and 1068 lots of books (including many architectural works). We have Vanbrugh's testimony that he was 'a great lover of musique and promoter of operas' [*Letters*, ed. Webb, 20], and at Melbourne, with the professional assistance of Henry Wise, he laid out a formal garden which is one of the best surviving examples of its kind in the country. The muniments at Melbourne afford evidence that Coke was also an amateur architect. A notebook survives containing extracts from Vignola, notes about gardening and memoranda about various internal alterations to the house at Melbourne for which he was responsible.[1] There is also a description in Coke's hand of a design, evidently made by himself, of 'a House for the Duke' (presumably of Marlborough, with whom he was 'well acquainted'), and there are drawings and sketches by him for fitting up the interior of the chapel at DRAYTON HOUSE, NORTHANTS., for Lady Betty Germain, and for rebuilding CRANFORD HOUSE, MIDDLESEX, for a fellow-courtier, the 3rd Earl of Berkeley. The designs for Cranford are mostly in a plain

---

[1] Although Thomas Coke made a plan for remodelling the house with a façade facing the church, it remained basically a fabric of the sixteenth and seventeenth centuries until his son G. L. Coke employed William Smith to rebuild the east (garden) front in 1744. In a MS. *Description of Derbyshire* by William Woolley (*c.* 1715) in the College of Arms (Pegge MS. 15), it is stated that although Coke had 'made very curious Gardens, Fishponds etc., ... the House being all or part of it seated on lands that Belong to the Cathedral of Carlisle ... he has not yet thought fit to rebuild it'.

early Georgian style, with a Vignolesque front doorway, but some of the elevations attempt ineffectively to emulate Vanbrugh. Cranford, as rebuilt in 1722 (dem. 1944), resembled (though it did not exactly correspond to any of) Coke's drawings, so it is possible that he should be regarded as its architect. In 1726 Francis Smith of Warwick submitted an estimate for building a gatehouse at Melbourne for Coke 'according to his Honour's Draught'. An accompanying drawing (by Smith) shows that it was designed to be in the form of a simplified triumphal arch. Through work began soon after, the gatehouse does not now exist, and was probably never completed owing to Coke's death the following year.

Coke died on 17 May 1727. His library and pictures were sold by auction in London in February 1728 (sale catalogue in B.M. C 119.h. 3(7)). His portrait by Michael Dahl hangs at Melbourne.

[Archives at Melbourne Hall; Hist. MSS. Comm., *Cowper* iii; J. Talbot Coke, *Coke of Trusley*, privately printed 1880, 72–4; Lindley Scott in *C. Life*, 7 April 1928; David Green, *Gardener to Queen Anne*, 1956, 41–8; *Survey of London* xxx, 514–5.]

COLE, CHARLES (*c.* 1738–1803), was born at Peterborough, and lived for a time at Stamford. It was, however, in London that he established himself as a builder and surveyor. Here he became Assistant or Deputy Surveyor to the Office of Woods and Forests, in which capacity he successfully repaired the breach in the retaining banks of Virginia Water caused by a storm in 1768. He was, however, dismissed in about 1790 because his charges were considered unreasonable. As a builder his principal venture was the laying out of ELY PLACE, HOLBORN, in 1776, on the site of the Bishop of Ely's palace, which had been sold to him in accordance with an Act of Parliament obtained in 1772 (for further details see P.R.O., Works 6/19, p. 127). The 'handsome and uniform' street which he erected in conjunction with the bricklayer John Gorham is the subject of unfavourable comment in Pugin's *Contrasts*. Cole was Master of the Tylers' and Bricklayers' Company in 1801–2, and died on 24 February 1803, aged 65, leaving a considerable estate. [*A.P.S.D.*; J. Chambers, MS. *Collections for a Biography of English Architects* at R.I.B.A.; *Obituary and Records of Lincolnshire, Rutland and Northants 1800–1850*; W. Stevenson, *Supplement to Bentham's Ely*, 1817, 82; *Gent's Mag.* 1803 (i), 199, 1816 (i), 395; P.C.C. 188 MARRIOTT.]

COLE, MATTHEW (–1692), of Clipston, Northants., was a carpenter by trade. In 1668 he designed and built the SCHOOL AND HOSPITAL (or almshouse) at CLIPSTON, a symmetrical gabled

building in the local vernacular style. He died at an advanced age in October 1692 [Sir Gyles Isham, *Clipston School and Hospital*, 1956, 17–18].

COLE, WILLIAM (1800–1892), was the third architect of his name to practise in Chester. His father and his grandfather were primarily builders, and are not known to have designed any building of importance, though in 1784 William Cole I was the runner-up to Thomas Harrison in the competition for the new gaol at Chester. 'William Cole, junior' (as the subject of this entry was generally called) was born in Chester on 19 June 1800, and at the age of 14 became a pupil of Thomas Harrison. In 1829 he succeeded Harrison as county surveyor, and had the responsibility of completing the Grosvenor Bridge to the latter's designs. In 1833 he visited Italy, Greece, Asia Minor, Egypt and Morocco, and on his return published a volume entitled *Select Views of the Remains of Ancient Monuments in Greece, from drawings taken and coloured on the spot* (1835). In 1840 he moved to Birkenhead, an expanding town in whose development he played an important part, both as an architect, as a commissioner under the Improvement Act of 1833, and as a member of the Birkenhead Dock and Warehouse Company. Despite his training under one of the leading members of the Greek Revival and his foreign travels, Cole is chiefly known today as the designer of a castellated country house and two or three undistinguished Gothic churches.

A tall, handsome, man, Cole was twice married and had seventeen children. He died on 8 October 1892, aged 92. [F. Simpson, 'A Few Cheshire Worthies', *Jnl. of the Chester and North Wales Antiquarian Soc.*, N.S. xxviii, 1928, 116–24; *The Architects, Engineers and Building Trades Directory*, 1868, 106.]

TATTON PARK, CHESHIRE, garden feature based on the Choragic Monument of Lysicrates, for Wilbraham Egerton, *c.* 1820 [Arthur Oswald in *C. Life*, 30 July 1964, 295 and fig. 4].

CHESTER, ST. OSWALD'S CHURCH (south transept of the Cathedral), gallery, etc., 1826; removed 1880 [Simpson, *op. cit.*, 118; I.C.B.S.].

CHESTER, ST. BRIDGET'S CHURCH, 1827–8, Greek Doric; dem. 1892 [Simpson, *op. cit.*, 119].

CHESHIRE COUNTY LUNATIC ASYLUM (now Deva Hospital), UPTON, 1827–9 [J. Hemingway, *History of Chester* ii, 1831, 226, with plan and view].

BOLESWORTH CASTLE, CHESHIRE, rebuilt for George Walmsley, 1829, castellated Gothic; remodelled internally by C. Williams-Ellis 1921 [exhib. at R.A. 1831] (Twycross, *Mansions of England and Wales: Cheshire* i, 1850, 45; *Country Heritage*, Liverpool 1951, 15–18).

CHESTER, ST. PAUL'S CHURCH, BOUGHTON, 1829–30; rebuilt 1876 [*A.P.S.D.*, *s.v.* 'Chester'].

CHESTER INFIRMARY, remodelled interior, 1830 [J. Hemingway, *History of Chester* ii, 1831, 208; W. Cole, *Plans and Sections of Chester Infirmary*, 1831].

CHESTER, THE METHODIST NEW CONNEXION CHAPEL, PEPPER STREET, 1835, Corinthian [Simpson, *op. cit.*, 121].

BIRKENHEAD, ST. ANNE'S CHURCH, 1846–50, Gothic [*A.P.S.D.*, *s.v.* 'Birkenhead'].

BIRKENHEAD, OXTON ROAD CONGREGATIONAL CHURCH, 1857–8, Gothic [*The Architects ... Directory*, *loc. cit.*].

BIRKENHEAD, BAPTIST CHAPEL, GRANGE ROAD, 1857–8, Doric [Simpson, *op. cit.*, 123].

COLEBATCH, GEORGE, a pupil in 1805 of W. R. Laxton (*q.v.*), exhibited at the Royal Academy between 1805 and 1809. He appears in the London directories in the 1830s and 1840s as a surveyor and builder in the Minories. G. Santler was his pupil in 1810.

COLEMAN, WILLIAM (–1718), a carpenter and joiner by trade, was the chief master builder employed in the execution of Sir John Vanbrugh's designs for remodelling KIMBOLTON CASTLE, HUNTS., from 1707 onwards. He had previously made plans himself which were set aside in favour of Vanbrugh's, but the latter had a high opinion of him as a builder, and told the Earl of Manchester that 'if we had such a Man at Blenheim he'd save us a Thousand pounds a Year'. Coleman died in 1718, leaving considerable property in Kimbolton, Wellingborough and elsewhere to his sons Joseph and Thomas. [*The Works of Sir John Vanbrugh* iv, *The Letters*, ed. Webb, 1928, 13, 15, 17, 20, 21, 24; Laurence Whistler, *The Imagination of Sir John Vanbrugh*, 1954, 135–7; building accounts in Hunts. County Record Office, especially dd. MIA.]

COLLIE, JAMES, practised in Scotland. In the 1820s he was in Aberdeen, where he appears to have had some connection with John Smith (*q.v.*), one of whose account-books he signs [N.M.R.S., Abstract Book No. ix, 1829]. In the 1830s and 1840s, however, he was practising in Glasgow. In 1835 he published an *Historical Account of the Cathedral of Glasgow*, with plans and elevations (London, folio), and in about 1847 a similar work on *The Royal Palace of Linlithgow*. He designed THE ROYAL INFIRMARY, MONTROSE, a competent Greek Revival design of 1837–9 [*The Imperial Gazeteer of Scotland*, ed. J. M. Wilson, ii, 446]; the BRIDGE STREET terminal of the Glasgow & South-Western Railway, with a handsome Doric portico (demolished) [Gildard's MS. notes, *ex inf.* Mr. David Walker]; and THE BLYTHSWOOD TESTIMONIAL SCHOOL at RENFREW,

1842 [Renfrew Town Council Minutes, *ex inf.* Mr. David Walker]. In 1839 he competed unsuccessfully for the Blind Asylum at Aberdeen [G. M. Fraser in *Aberdeen Weekly Jnl.*, 30 Aug. 1918]. In 1850–1 he made a very competent survey of Dundee. He was still active in 1869, when he was employed to carry out alterations to the eastern part of HOLY RUDE CHURCH, STIRLING [R.C.A.M., *Stirlingshire* i, 130]. At that date he was living at Bridge of Allan, where he had designed BELLMOIR HOUSE for his own occupation [information from Mr. David Walker]. In 1842 he was made an Honorary Fellow of the London Society called the 'Freemasons of the Church' [*Builder* i, 1843, 24].

COLLINGWOOD, JOHN (*c.* 1760–1831), practised first in Worcester and later in Gloucester, where he held the post of county surveyor from about 1820. He died in Gloucester on 14 March 1831, aged 71 [*Monmouthshire Merlin*, 19 March 1831, *ex inf.* Mr. A. G. Chamberlain].

In WORCESTER Collingwood designed THE DEPOT OF ARMS, QUEEN STREET, 1807 [*Worcester Jnl.*, 26 March 1807], and the octagonal BARBOURNE TOLL HOUSES (one of which survives as a shop), 1814 [*Worcester Jnl.*, 6 June 1814]. In 1811 the tower of ST. HELEN'S CHURCH was taken down under his direction, but it was not until 1819 that it was rebuilt [MS. Vestry Minutes]. Surveys of property in the city by him are in the P.R.O. (MPE 466) and the County Record Office (609 : 1). [information from Mr. D. A. Whitehead].

In GLOUCESTER Collingwood designed THE DEBTORS' PRISON, *c.* 1820 [G. W. Counsel, *History of Gloucester*, 1829, 173], and erected THE COUNTY LUNATIC ASYLUM (now Horton Road Hospital) to the designs of William Stark of Edinburgh, who had died in 1813 [Ann Bailey, 'The Founding of the Glos. County Asylum', *Trans. Bristol and Glos. Arch. Soc.*, etc., 1971, 184].

Elsewhere, Collingwood enlarged APPERLEY COURT, GLOS., for Mrs. Strickland, *c.* 1817–18 [Glos. Record Office, D. 1245 E.3], and designed THE TOWN HALL at SWANSEA, GLAMORGANSHIRE, 1825–7, remodelled by Thomas Taylor 1850–2 [agreement, correspondence and accounts at Swansea Guildhall; elevation at Royal Institution of S. Wales], and THE HOUSE OF CORRECTION at the same town, 1826–8 [Glamorgan County Record Office, QGP. 70].

COLLINS, JAMES, of Birmingham, advertised in *Aris's Birmingham Gazette*, on 24 March 1748, that he 'undertakes Building in its whole Study and Practice, according to the most modern Rules of Architecture'. Soon after 1750 he rebuilt THE WHITE LION INN, STRATFORD-ON-AVON (now NOS. 16, 17 and 18 HENLEY STREET) [*V.C.H. Warwicks.* iii, 231].

COLLINS, JOB, was the son of Thomas Collins of Warwick. In *c.* 1726 he was apprenticed to John Dunkley, mason of Warwick [Guildhall Library, index to Apprenticeship Registers in P.R.O.]. He was one of the contractors who rebuilt the Shire Hall, Warwick, in 1754–7 to the designs of Sanderson Miller [accounts in County Record Office]. In 1760 he was employed to rebuild the central tower of WOLSTON CHURCH, WARWICKS., after it had collapsed [R. Norton, *Wolston Church*, 1952, 11]. In 1774 the parishioners of ST. NICHOLAS, WARWICK, employed 'Messrs. Collins and London, Surveyors', to report on the condition of the north aisle of their church [Vestry Minutes in County Record Office]. According to W. Field, *History of Warwick*, 1815, 131, the church was rebuilt in 1779–80 'under the direction of Job Collins, an architect of Warwick', but the Vestry Minutes show that the architect and builder was Thomas Johnson (*q.v.*).

COLLIS, JAMES (–1886), practised in London. He exhibited at the Royal Academy in 1836–9, and designed THE KEMBLE TAVERN at the corner of Bow Street and Long Acre, a handsome but rather florid classical building illustrated in *The Companion to the Almanac*, 1837, 242. He was the author of two, apparently distinct, books on shop fronts, etc., entitled *The Builder's Portfolio of Street Architecture*, 1837, and *Remarks on Street Architecture*, 1838. Neither is to be found either in the British Library or in the Bodleian Library. Collis was District Surveyor of Lee, Charlton and Kidbrooke from 1844 until his death in 1886 [*Builder* li, 1886, 906].

COLUMBANI, PLACIDO (*c.* 1744–), was a Milanese architect who appears to have spent the greater part of his life in England. Although he is not known to have had any connection with the brothers Adam, he was a popularizer of the antique decorative style associated with them and Pergolesi. According to the *Encyclopaedia Britannica*, 11th ed. (*s.v.* 'Columbani'), his engraved designs were much used by English furniture designers of the late eighteenth century. He was presumably in England by 1766, when designs by him appeared in *The Chimney-piece Maker's Daily Assistant ... from the original drawings of Thomas Milton, John Crunden and Placido Columbani*. His first independent publication was *Vases and Tripods* (1770), followed by *A New Book of Ornaments, containing a Variety of Elegant Designs for Modern Panels, commonly executed in Stucco, Wood or Painting, and used in Decorating Principal Rooms* (1775), and *A Variety of Capitals, Friezes and Cornices, and how to increase and decrease them, still retaining their proportions* (1776). In 1775 he exhibited a 'perspective view of a gentleman's villa' at the Society of Artists,

and in 1786, at the age of 42, he obtained admission to the Royal Academy Schools.

As a practising architect, Columbani is known to have had the following commissions: the embellishment of MOUNT CLARE, nr. ROEHAMPTON, SURREY, with a Doric portico 'and many Architectural Ornaments' for Sir John Dick, Bart., soon after 1780 [W. Watts, *Views of Seats*, pl. lxii, 1784] (*C. Life*, 26 Jan., 2 Feb. 1935); making drawings for the interiors of AUDLEY END, ESSEX, for the 4th Lord Howard de Walden from 1781 onwards [accounts in Essex Record Office]; supervising works at DOWNHILL, CO. DERRY, for the 4th Earl of Bristol and Bishop of Derry, 1783–5 [P. Rankin, *Irish Building Ventures of the Earl Bishop of Derry*, Ulster Architectural Heritage Soc. 1972, 14–15]; designing a walled garden 209 feet square at ANTONY HOUSE, CORNWALL, for Reginald Pole-Carew (1793), making (1794) working drawings of Humphry Repton's design for a lodge at the same house, and (in 1801) plans of Pole-Carew's London house at No. 7 New Cavendish Street [letters and accounts at Antony]; designing a villa in PUTNEY LANE, PUTNEY, SURREY, for Godschall Johnson, 1793 [mentioned in letter at Antony, CE/E 25, 26]; and repairing the church of ST. KATHERINE BY THE TOWER, LONDON, 1799–1800, dem. 1825 [C. Jamison, *St. Katherine's Hospital*, 1952, 126].

COOK, ANDREW GEORGE, 'Architect and Builder', was the author of *The New Builder's Magazine*, a work containing an abstract of the Building Act of 1774, a list of prices 'allowed by the most eminent surveyors in London', an alphabetical glossary of architectural terms, and 177 engravings of architectural designs by John Carter. The latter were reprinted from the plates of the original *Builder's Magazine*, published between 1774 and 1786. Cook's edition was published without a date in *c.* 1810, and again in 1819 and 1820.

COOK, T— M—, was a pupil of Henry Hakewill. He entered the Royal Academy Schools in 1801 and exhibited at the Royal Academy from 1799 to 1802. A drawing of the Woodstock Gate to Blenheim Park, Oxon., signed 'T. M. Cook Oct. 4th 1794' is in the Avery Library of Columbia University, U.S.A. [John Harris, *Catalogue of British Drawings for Architecture etc. in American Collections*, 1971, 76].

COOK, THOMAS (–1803), 'of the City of Gloucester, Architect', was employed in 1787 to erect a temporary prison preparatory to the rebuilding of the Gloucester County Gaol to the designs of William Blackburn [Gloucestershire County Records]. According to J. Chambers's MS. *Collections for a Biography of English Architects* in the R.I.B.A. Library he also designed the

COUNTY GAOL at STAFFORD, 1793–4, and died at Swansea in 1803.

COOK, THOMAS (c. 1777–1842), practised in Leicester, where he died on 1 November 1842, aged 65. He was responsible for alterations to WYGGESTON'S HOSPITAL, LEICESTER, 1805, dem. 1875; alterations to LEICESTER INFIRMARY, 1815; enlarging FRIAR LANE BAPTIST CHAPEL, LEICESTER, 1878, dem.; and for several workhouses in Leicestershire and Derbyshire. His most important work appears to have been the GRAMMAR SCHOOL at MARKET BOSWORTH, LEICS., 1827–8, in the Tudor Collegiate style. His unexecuted designs for St. Nicholas Church, Leicester (1824), are in the Record Office at Leicester [J. D. Bennett, *Leicestershire Architects 1700–1850*, Leicester 1968; letter in Warwick County Record Office, H.R. 29].

COOKE, JAMES, was a statuary mason in Gloucester, and signs a number of monumental tablets in the county dated between 1811 and 1836 (see Rupert Gunnis, *Dictionary of British Sculptors*, 1968, 112). In 1826 he rebuilt the nave of the church of ST. MARY DE LODE, GLOUCESTER, in stucco'd Gothic with cast-iron columns [*Gent's Mag.* 1826 (ii), 506]. In the same year he signed a certificate for the I.C.B.S. concerning the erection of a gallery in ST. JOHN'S CHURCH, GLOUCESTER.

COOPER, GEORGE, exhibited at the Royal Academy from various London addresses between 1792 and 1830. His earliest exhibits were architectural designs, but from about 1800 onwards he showed views of buildings in England and on the Continent. In 1807 he published a volume of engravings entitled *Architectural Reliques, or the Present State of Ancient British Architecture and Sculpture*, containing illustrations of Llandaff Cathedral and Tintern Abbey. Some sketches of Llandaff Cathedral made by him in 1805 are in Sir John Soane's Museum (AL 26, 1–5). According to Redgrave's *Dictionary of Artists* (1878) he 'both drew and etched' the principal plates for Wade's *Walks in Oxford* (1817), but they are in fact signed by Storer.

COOPER JOHN (c. 1793–), entered the Royal Academy Schools in 1816 at the age of 23. He exhibited architectural designs at the Academy from 1813 to 1827, but nothing further is known of him.

COOPER, JOHN, was an architect and builder at Canterbury. In 1811 his designs for rebuilding Strood Church, Kent, were set aside in favour of those of Robert Smirke [H. Smetham, *History of Strood*, 1899, 55–75]. In 1827 he enlarged the aisles of ASHFORD CHURCH, KENT, and refitted the

interior [I.C.B.S.]. He was the father of George Cooper, a monumental mason of Canterbury who was responsible (*inter alia*) for the obelisk at BILSINGTON, KENT, in memory of Sir Richard Cosway (d. 1835). For further details of G. Cooper's works see R. Gunnis, *Dictionary of British Sculptors*, 1968, 113.

COOPER, JOHN, appears to have been a builder-architect at Beaumaris in Anglesey. Some drawings by him for works at BODORGAN, ANGLESEY, for the Meyrick family, are in the Library of the University College of N. Wales at Bangor (Bodorgan MS. 1363). In 1783–5 he carried out alterations to PLAS NEWYDD, ANGLESEY, for the 1st Earl of Uxbridge [R.C.A.M., *Anglesey*, 56], and in 1796 Sir Christopher Sykes noted that he was in charge of alterations at CHIRK CASTLE, DENBIGHSHIRE, for Richard Myddelton, including the interior of the Dining Room [National Library of Wales, MS. 2258 C]. The last work is in a simplified Adamsian style reminiscent of Wyatt (*C. Life*, 12 Oct. 1951, fig. 6).

COOPER, JOHN JAMES (–1839), of Reading, combined the functions of architect, surveyor and auctioneer. He designed an Italianate BAPTIST CHAPEL in the KING'S ROAD, READING, 1833–4 [*Reading Mercury*, 15 April 1833], and designed and built the CASTLE HILL CONGREGATIONAL CHAPEL, opened in 1837 [W. Fletcher, *Reading Past and Present*, 1839]. He also designed a Nonconformist Chapel at SINDLESHAM, BERKS., in 1834, rebuilt 1868 [*Reading Mercury*, 22 Feb. 1834], and in 1837 entered an Ionic design in the competition for the Royal Berkshire Infirmary [*Reading Mercury*, 11 Feb. 1837], The QUEEN'S ROAD 'was formed under (his) superintendence' in about 1833 [W. Darter, *Reminiscences of Reading by an Octogenarian*, 1888, 109], so he may possibly have been responsible for designing the elegant Bath stone houses which form QUEEN'S CRESCENT.

COOPER, T—, of 13 Warren Street, designed the BAYSWATER CHAPEL, PETERSBURG PLACE, NOTTING HILL, LONDON, for Edward Orme, 1818, exhibiting the design at the Royal Academy the same year. In 1819 he exhibited a view of the interior of the Royalty Theatre in Wellclose Square.

COOPER, THOMAS, of Brighton, was the son of a local builder who died in 1826 at the age of 70, as a result of falling from a house under construction in Brunswick Square. Cooper designed the following buildings in Brighton: a CHAPEL in Church Street for George Faithful, the dissenting minister, c. 1826; THE BEDFORD HOTEL, 1829; and THE TOWN HALL, 1830–2. The hotel is a striking but unorthodox composition with Greek Revival detailing. [A. Dale, *Fashionable Brighton*, 1947, 61, 118, 179–80; *The Watering-Places of Great Britain and Fashionable Directory* (Joseph Robins, 1833), 33–5.]

COOPER, WILLIAM, was on 29 June 1727 admitted a member of the Company of Carpenters, Tylers and Brickmakers of Shrewsbury [Shrewsbury Public Library, MS. 13486]. He was presumably 'that ingenious Architect, Mr. William Cooper, Jun., of Salop.' who rebuilt MONTFORD CHURCH, SALOP., in 1735–8 [D. H. S. Cranage, *The Churches of Shropshire* ii, 1903, 766], and the William Cooper who rebuilt MYDDLE CHURCH, SALOP., in 1744 [Churchwardens' Accounts]. Both are small country churches of no architectural pretensions.

COOPER, WILLIAM, surveyed the church of ST. KATHERINE COLEMAN, LONDON, in 1739, and submitted drawings and an estimate for rebuilding it [Guildhall Library, MS. 1133, minutes of the Trustees for rebuilding the church]. He may have been the William Cooper who was Bricklayer to the Commissioners of Sewers in 1738 [S. Perks, *History of the Mansion House*, 1922, 178], and in 1741–2 Master of the Tylers' and Bricklayers' Company.

COPLAND, ALEXANDER (*c.* 1774–1834), was the son of a builder and told a parliamentary committee in 1806 that he had been 'educated as a builder under Mr. Richard Holland' [*Fourth Report of the Commissioners of Military Inquiry*, 1806–7, Appendix 47, p. 315]. His training evidently included architectural drawing, for he entered the Royal Academy Schools as a student in 1788 and in 1817 he figures in a list of architects practising in London (*Annals of the Fine Arts* ii, 585). However, he was better known as one of the partners in a flourishing firm of builders and timber merchants of which the other members were the architect Henry Holland (Richard Holland's cousin) and his nephew Henry Rowles. Their yard in Horseferry Road was the centre of a large-scale building enterprise which made a fortune in building barracks during the Napoleonic Wars. With its own brickworks, sawpits and building tradesmen, it to some extent anticipated the better-known firm of Thomas Cubitt (*q.v.*), established in 1815 [E. W. Cooney, 'The Origins of the Victorian Master Builders', *Economic History Review*, 2nd ser., viii, 1955]. As 'Copland, Rowles & Co.' the firm was still in existence in the 1830s, but Copland died on 12 July 1834, aged 61 [*Gent's Mag.* 1834 (ii), 219]. His library was sold at Sotheby's on 6 December 1837 (catalogue in Bodleian Library, Mus. Bibl. III 8° 416). In 1801 he had bought the greater part of the Gunnersbury estate near Brentford, on which

he built himself the existing GUNNERSBURY PARK, subsequently much enlarged by its later Rothschild owners [J. Thorne, *Handbook to the Environs of London* i, 1876, 160] (*C. Life*, 24 Nov. 1900). F. Copland, who was in Sir John Soane's office from 1817 to 1820, was his son. Some of F. Copland's drawings are in the Soane Museum (Drawer 5, 8) [A. T. Bolton, *The Portrait of Sir John Soane*, 268 n., 287–9].

CORFIELD, THOMAS (–1833), 'surveyor and architect' of Park Street, Grosvenor Square, committed suicide in Greenwich Park on 30 June 1833 [*Gent's Mag.* 1833 (ii), 186].

CORNEY, ROBERT (*c.* 1704–1771), of East Cotham, nr. Redcar, Yorks. (N.R.), is said in J. W. Ord's *History of Cleveland*, 1846, 374, to have been 'both architect and builder' of KIRKLEATHAM CHURCH, YORKS. (N.R.), *c.* 1760–3, but the accounts indicate that a design had been made by John Carr (*q.v.*). Corney, who was a carpenter and joiner by trade, was also employed in building KIRKLEATHAM HOSPITAL from 1741 onwards [accounts in N. Riding Record Office]. In 1764–6 he rebuilt BUSBY HALL, YORKS. (N.R.), for Jane Turner in accordance with a drawing apparently made by himself and now in the N. Riding Record Office (ZDU). A chest-tomb in Kirkleatham Churchyard records his death on 19 January 1771, aged 67.

CORNISH, ROBERT (*c.* 1760–1844), held the post of Surveyor to Exeter Cathedral from 1800 until his retirement in 1838. He was then presented with a piece of plate 'as a Token of the Respect of the Chapter and of the high sense they entertain of the value of his Services'. He died on 9 January 1844 in his 84th year [*Flying Post*, 11 Jan. 1844]. As cathedral architect he was succeeded by his eldest son ROBERT STRIBLING CORNISH (1788–1871), whom Gilbert Scott remembered as 'a very kindly and excellent old gentleman, and a thoroughly practical man' [*Recollections*, 1876, 345]. The younger Cornish was a Councillor and Alderman of Exeter, and held the office of Mayor in 1852–3. He married the daughter of John Powning of Exeter (*q.v.*), and died on 10 February 1871 [obituary in *Flying Post*, 15 Feb. 1871]. J. M. Allen (1809–83) and Edward Ashworth (1815–96) were pupils either of the father or of the son.

HOLY TRINITY CHURCH, EXETER, was rebuilt in 1820–1 by 'Cornish & Sons, Architects and builders' [I.C.B.S.]. ST. EDMUND'S CHURCH, EXETER, appears to have been rebuilt by Messrs. Cornish and Julian (*i.e.* G. H. Julian, afterwards City Surveyor) in 1834 [Diocesan Faculty papers]. Both these are in the elementary Perpendicular Gothic of the period. Messrs. Cornish and Julian also designed FREMINGTON VICARAGE,

DEVON, in 1830 [Diocesan Registry, bundle 339], and repewed ST. PANCRAS CHURCH, EXETER, in 1831 [I.C.B.S.]. The younger Cornish designed THE NEW CITY PRISON at EXETER, 1819 [*The Exeter Guide*, 1836, 47] and parsonages at LYNTON, 1834, and HEANTON PUNCHARDON, DEVON, 1836 [Diocesan Registry, bundle 339]. The designs for the latter are in the Greek Revival style, with incised pilasters of the kind which ornament many early nineteenth-century houses in the suburbs of Exeter.

CORSTORPHINE, JOHN (–1826), of Kingsbarns in Fife, is listed in Pigot's *Directory* of 1825–6 among the 'Nobility and Gentry', but appears to have acted as both builder and architect. In 1797 he designed a new school at Kingsbarns, and in 1810–11 he and Robert Balfour (*q.v.*) were jointly responsible for the repair and enlargement of KINGSBARNS CHURCH to the latter's designs [S.R.O., HR 184/1]. It is possible that the initials J.C. over the doorway of CERES CHURCH, FIFE, indicate that it was to John Corstorphine's designs that it was rebuilt in 1806. The spire is an addition of 1852. The date 1794 and a panel of architect's instruments in the frieze record his occupancy and reconstruction of KINGSBARNS HOUSE in THE SQUARE at KINGSBARNS. He died on 23 August 1826, and is commemorated by a wall monument in Kingsbarns Churchyard.

COTES, P— B—, exhibited architectural designs at the Royal Academy from 1798 to 1805. At first he was a pupil of Thomas Malton, and then of Jeffry Wyatt and his partner John Armstrong. Nothing further is known of him.

COTTINGHAM, LEWIS NOCKALLS (1787–1847), born at Laxfield in Suffolk, was the son of a farmer 'of an ancient and respectable family'. He was apprenticed to a builder at Ipswich, and was subsequently an architect's clerk in London until 1814, when he started practice on his own. In 1822 he became surveyor to the Cooks' Company, and in 1825 he was engaged by the dean and chapter of Rochester to carry out repairs to their Cathedral, including the rebuilding of the central tower (see G. H. Palmer, *The Cathedral Church of Rochester*, 1899, for an illustration of Cottingham's tower before its replacement in 1904). He was subsequently much employed in works of this character, and among the churches which he restored were those of THEBERTON, SUFFOLK, 1836; ASHBOURNE, DERBYSHIRE, 1839–40; ST. MARY at BURY ST. EDMUNDS, 1840–3; MILTON BRYANT, BEDS. (to which he added a new tower), 1841–3; GREAT CHESTERFORD, ESSEX, 1842; ROOS, YORKS. (E.R.), 1842; HORRINGER (*alias* HORNINGSHEATH), SUFFOLK, 1845; CLIFTON, NOTTS., 1846; and MARKET WESTON, SUF-

FOLK, 1844 (see *Builder* ii, 1844, 378). He repaired (1844) the spire of LOUTH CHURCH, LINCS., after damage by lightning, and restored the ABBEY CHURCH of ST. ALBANS, 1833 (see details in *British Magazine* ii, 1832, 207–8; iii, 1833, 112), and the NORMAN GATEWAY at BURY ST. EDMUNDS (cf. his report in *Gent's Mag.* 1842 (ii), 302, and in *Architect, Engineer and Surveyor* iv, 1843, 22). He was also employed at ELVASTON CASTLE, DERBYSHIRE, by the Earl of Harrington, at BROUGHAM HALL, WESTMORLAND, by Lord Brougham, at ADARE MANOR, CO. LIMERICK (*C. Life*, 15, 22 and 29 May 1969) by the Earl of Dunraven, and at COMBE ABBEY, WARWICKS., by the Earl of Craven. At the last house he designed a 'Louis XIV drawing room' which he exhibited at the Royal Academy in 1834. He refitted the chapel of MAGDALEN COLLEGE, OXFORD, in 1830–2, and almost rebuilt ARMAGH CATHEDRAL in 1834–7. Among the comparatively few new buildings which he designed were SNELSTON HALL, DERBYSHIRE, for John Harrison, 1828, an elaborate Gothic house demolished in 1951 but illustrated in Burke's *Visitations of Seats and Arms*, series 2, i, 1854, 228, and a Tudor Gothic SAVINGS BANK (now offices) in CROWN STREET, BURY ST. EDMUNDS, 1846. In 1841 he began the restoration of HEREFORD CATHEDRAL, carried out, according to Gilbert Scott, 'with the most scrupulous regard for evidence, and with the least possible displacement of old stone' (see *Gent's Mag.* 1842 (i), 193–6, and J. Merewether, *A Statement of the Condition and Circumstances of the Cathedral Church of Hereford*, 1842, which contains, pp. 36–41 and 87–9, the text of several testimonials in Cottingham's favour). Owing to the long illness which caused his death in 1847, much of the work at Hereford was carried out under the supervision of his son, who designed the reredos. Although somewhat drastic by modern standards, his restorations were inspired by a genuine love of Gothic architecture, and he showed considerable technical ability in dealing with the structural problems with which he was faced at Hereford and elsewhere.

In about 1825 Cottingham was employed by Mr. John Field to lay out the latter's extensive estate on the south side of Waterloo Bridge. Some of his designs for houses on this estate are in the British Museum (Crace Views, xxxv, 65–7). He built a house (No. 43) for himself in Waterloo Bridge Road, with a museum specially designed to receive his collections of medieval woodwork, Gothic carvings, and plaster-casts of capitals, bosses and sculpture. This collection, of which a *Descriptive Memoir* was published in 1850, was dispersed after his death, but part of it formed the nucleus of the Royal Architectural Museum in Tufton Street, which was afterwards absorbed into the South Kensington Museum. Cottingham was a friend of John Carter and William

Capon, and he published several works on medieval architecture, the most important of which were *Plans, etc. of Westminster Hall*, 1822, and *Plans, etc. of King Henry VII's Chapel*, 1822–9 (2 vols.). He also published an influential pattern-book for ornamental ironwork entitled *The Ornamental Metal Worker's Director*, 1823, enlarged and reissued in 1824 as *The Smith and Founder's Director, containing a Series of Designs and Patterns for Ornamental Iron and Brass Work*. A later edition entitled *The Smith's, Founder's and Ornamental Metal Worker's Director* appeared in 1845. Other publications were *Working Drawings of Gothic Ornaments, etc., with a Design for a Gothic Mansion*, 1824, and *Grecian and Roman Architecture, in 24 large folio plates*. Four of Cottingham's sketch-books are in the Avery Library of Columbia University, New York. The designs which he submitted in the competition for the Houses of Parliament in 1835 are in the R.I.B.A. Collection. They are in the style 'which prevailed in the reigns of Edward III and Richard II'.

Cottingham died on 13 October 1847, and was buried at Croydon, where he is commemorated by a brass in the parish church. His practice was continued by his elder son Nockalls Johnson Cottingham (born 1823), who 'after a rather chequered career' perished in 1854 in the wreck of the steamer *Arctic* on his way to New York. [Obituaries in *Builder* v, 1847, 502, and *Gent's Mag.* 1847 (ii), 648–50; *A.P.S.D.*; *D.N.B.*]

COTTON, HENRY CHARLES (*c.* 1805–1873), was admitted to the Royal Academy Schools in 1824 at the age of 19. He practised in London, dying in Highbury Place on 17 May 1873 [Principal Probate Registry]. His son Henry Robert Cotton was also an architect and surveyor. H. C. Cotton was presumably the Henry Cotton who is said to have designed LIVERPOOL TERRACE, WORTHING, SUSSEX, *c.* 1830 [A. Dale, *Fashionable Brighton*, 1948, 35] – a composition praised by Pevsner for its 'powerfully organised unbroken rhythm of bow fronts accented with plain ironwork' [*Sussex*, 1965, 388].

COTTON, ROBERT TURNER (*c.* 1774–1850), is listed in the London directories as an architect and surveyor from the 1820s until his death on 10 March 1850 at the age of 76 [*Gent's Mag.* 1850 (i), 550].

COUCHMAN, HENRY (1738–1803), was the son of a carpenter at Ightham in Kent. After working for some years as a journeyman carpenter in Kent and London he was employed as a foreman by the builder Joseph Dixon, and then as a clerk of works by the architect Matthew Brettingham. In 1766 Brettingham sent him to Packington in Warwickshire to supervise the

reconstruction of the Earl of Aylesford's country house. An inscription on the lead roof records that 'This house ... was cased with stone and enlarged by Heneage Earl of Aylesford in the year 1772. Henry Couchman Surveyor of the Work.' Couchman's diligence made a favourable impression on Lord Aylesford, who used his influence to obtain for him a lease of Temple House, Temple Balsall, together with the appointment (1776) of Bailiff to the Trustees of Balsall Hospital.

For the rest of his life Couchman practised as an architect and surveyor in Warwickshire. In 1775 he designed THE DRAPERS' HALL at COVENTRY, dem. 1830. His design for the Assembly Room in this building, now in the Pierpont Morgan Library, is illustrated by J. Harris, *Catalogue of British Drawings for Architecture, etc. in American Collections*, pl. 55. After the death of Henry Keene in 1776, Couchman was employed by Sir Roger Newdigate to complete the Gothicization of ARBURY HALL, WARWICKS. Sir Roger was to some extent his own architect, and Couchman's function seems to have been to act as surveyor and draughtsman under his employer's supervision [A. C. Wood, 'The Diaries of Sir Roger Newdigate', *Trans. Birmingham Archaeological Soc.*, lxxviii, 1962] (*C. Life*, 15, 29 Oct. 1953). He fulfilled the same function when Sir Roger Newdigate rebuilt HAREFIELD HOUSE, MIDDLESEX, in 1786, the name of 'Henry Couchman Arch.' appearing on the foundation-stone [Warwick County Record Office, Sir Roger Newdigate's diaries, CR 136/A [617], *ex inf.* Mr. A. C. Wood]. In 1782 Couchman reconstructed the octagonal central tower of ATHERSTONE CHURCH, WARWICKS. [*ex inf.* the late P. B. Chatwin], and HIGHAM-ON-THE-HILL CHURCH LEICS., was rebuilt to his designs in 1791 [Leicester Archdeaconry records, Fac. 173]. Couchman's unexecuted designs for a new church at ETTINGTON, WARWICKS., are among the Shirley family papers in the County Record Office. They show a small classical church with an apsidal chancel and cupola'd bell turret.

In 1782 Couchman was employed by the Warwickshire Justices to report on the performance of Thomas Johnson's contract to rebuild the County Gaol at Warwick [Warwickshire County Records, Class 24 (671)]. In 1783 he designed a new House of Correction in Warwick, built under his supervision between 1784 and 1789, and since converted into a police-station. In 1790–3 he enlarged the Gaol towards Barrack Street, taking in the site of the former House of Correction [*ibid.*, Class 24 (672, 677); extracts from Q.S. Records, Class 24 (h)]. His elevation to Barrack Street was retained when the County Gaol was reconstructed as the County Council Offices in 1929–32.

Couchman died at Temple House in 1803, and

is commemorated by a brass tablet in Temple Balsall Church. He left a son, Henry Couchman, junior (1771–1838), who in 1802 succeeded his father as bailiff to Temple Balsall Hospital and also held the post of 'Bridgemaster' to the County of Warwick. A portrait, believed to be that of the elder Couchman, was in 1954 in the possession of Dr. H. J. Couchman of Morland, Ferndown, Dorset. [*Gent's Mag.* 1803 (i), 94; photocopy of autobiographical fragment in Warwick County Record Office; information from the late P. B. Chatwin.]

COULTHART, WILLIAM, was practising in Lancaster in the 1820s [Pigot's *Directory*], but he subsequently established himself in Leamington Spa, Warwicks., where he designed the houses on the north side of WARWICK STREET, and those on the east side of BEAUCHAMP SQUARE [Moncrieff's *Guide to Leamington Spa*, 1833, 75–6]. In the north he was responsible for repairs to LEVENS HALL, WESTMORLAND, in 1823–4, and for designing a school and cottages in the village [Levens Hall accounts, *ex inf.* Mr. Angus Taylor], and for the RECTORY at HALTON, LANCS., in the Elizabethan style [lithograph dated 1832 in album compiled by George Webster of Kendal, *ex inf.* Mr. Angus Taylor].

COUSE, KENTON (1721–1790), 'was bred an Architect under Mr. Flitcroft of the Board of Works, into which he was introduced as soon as a regular vacancy occurred'. He was apprenticed to Flitcroft in 1735 or 1736, and began his official career in 1746 as Labourer in Trust at Whitehall. In 1748 he became a Writing Clerk in the Office in Scotland Yard, and in June 1750 was promoted to the Clerkship of the Works at Newmarket, but in July of the same year changed places with James Paine, becoming Clerk of the Works at Charing Cross, etc. In 1762, on Thomas Kynaston's death, Flitcroft, now Comptroller of the Works, made Couse his personal clerk. He subsequently became Clerk of the Works at Whitehall, Westminster and St. James's (1766), and in 1775 Secretary to the Board, Clerk Itinerant and Clerk of the Works at the Queen's Palace (Buckingham House). In 1782 he lost all his offices as a result of Burke's Act, but became the first holder of the new post of Examining Clerk, which he retained until his death. For some years he was also Surveyor to the Goldsmiths' Company. A competent and conscientious official, Couse spent his life in the public service, and had comparatively little time or opportunity for private practice. The architectural works listed below show him as a faithful disciple of Flitcroft, maintaining in the age of Adam and Chambers the basically Palladian style of the previous generation. He died at his house in Scotland Yard on 10 October 1790, in his 70th year, and was

236

buried at Lambeth. By his wife Sarah Hamilton, a grand-daughter of the 6th Marquess of Abercorn, he had a son and two daughters. His library was sold in 1791 with that of Francis Hiorne (catalogue in B.M. 129.1.19). Written surveys of the Bishop of Durham's houses at Durham and Auckland Castle made in 1750–1 by Couse and Thomas Shirley are in the B.M. (Add. MS. 9815). [*A.P.S.D.*; *D.N.B.*; Guildhall Library, index to Apprenticeship Registers in P.R.O.; Collins's *Peerage*, ed. Brydges, ii, 1812, 532; *Gent's Mag.* 1790 (ii), 959; J. Nichols, *Literary Anecdotes* iii, 1812, 642–3; John Chambers, MS. *Collections for a Biography of English Architects* in R.I.B.A. Library; *History of the King's Works* v and vi, *passim.*]

LONDON, ST. MARGARET'S CHURCH, WESTMINSTER, west gallery, 1757; repairs and reconstruction of east end 1758 in form of a Gothic apse with sedilia, incorporating stained-glass window from Waltham Abbey [Westminster City Library, MSS. 2421 and 135 (Vestry Minutes and Churchwardens' Accounts)].

NORMANTON PARK, RUTLAND, alterations and additions for Sir Gilbert Heathcote, Bart., 1763–7; dem. [Lincolnshire Record Office, Heathcote papers in Ancaster Collection].

NORMANTON CHURCH, RUTLAND, for Sir Gilbert Heathcote, Bart., 1764; tower added by T. Cundy 1826, nave and chancel rebuilt 1911 [Lincolnshire Record Office, *loc. cit.*].

BOTLEYS, nr. CHERTSEY, SURREY, for Sir Joseph Mawbey, Bart., 1765; altered by E. Blore 1839–40 [*Vitruvius Britannicus* v, pls. 56–7; drawings in Minet Library, Camberwell].

LONDON, NO. 10 DOWNING STREET, rebuilt front to street, 1766–75; altered 1959–60 [*History of the King's Works* v, 442] (*Survey of London* xiv, pls. 108–9).

LONDON, HOUSES OF PARLIAMENT, continued the STONE BUILDING southwards, forming new entrance to House of Commons, Committee Rooms, etc., 1766–9; dem. *c.* 1880 [*History of the King's Works* v, 429–30].

COLNEY (CHAPEL) HOUSE, SHENLEY, HERTS., house begun for Mr. Crespigny, *c.* 1770, but abandoned on death of his wife and ultimately completed by Charles Bourchier, Governor of Madras, *c.* 1780; destroyed by fire *c.* 1880 [plan by Couse *c.* 1775 in Bodleian Library, Gough Herts. 13, f. 64] (E. W. Brayley, *Beauties of England and Wales* vii, 1806, 283; Neale's *Views of Seats*, 2nd. ser., ii).

RICHMOND BRIDGE, SURREY (R. Thames), in collaboration with James Paine, 1774–7; widened 1937 [James Paine, *Plans etc.* ii, 1783, pls. lxxii, lxxiii].

CLAPHAM, SURREY, HOLY TRINITY CHURCH, 1774–6; portico altered 1812, chancel added 1902 [Parish records; drawings by Couse in Surrey

Archdeaconry records, Minet Library, Camberwell, R.I.B.A. Drawings Coll., and Avery Library, Columbia University, New York. The last are reproduced by J. Harris, *Catalogue of British Drawings for Architecture etc. in American Collections*, 1971, pls. 57–8].

WIMPOLE HALL, CAMBS., work for the 2nd Earl of Hardwicke, 1777, probably including the apsidal Eating Room, since remodelled [R.C.H.M., *West Cambridgeshire*, 216].

BARNES, SURREY, THE WORKHOUSE (afterwards Manor House Hotel), 1778 [MS. Vestry Minutes].

OXFORD, THE QUEEN'S COLLEGE, internal reconstruction of west wing after fire in December 1778, carried out by George Shakespear of London with John Gwynn as surveyor in charge [*Letters of Radcliffe & James*, ed. Evans, Oxford Historical Soc. 1888, 270–2].

LONDON, DOWNING STREET, house on south side facing St. James's Park; dem. [Northumberland County Record Office, ZBU B5/6 (13): 'Plan of Mr. Sargent's house built by Couse'].

COWAN, GEORGE, held the post of Superintendent of Public Works in Edinburgh from 1747 until 1758, when he was dismissed for non-attendance [Edinburgh Town Council Minutes]. In the Canongate Churchyard there is a monumental inscription to Alexander Cowan, Builder, who died on 8 March 1776 aged 66, and his son George Cowan, Architect, who died on 23 October 1843.

COWLEY, WILLIAM, perhaps an amateur architect, since he is described as 'esquire', designed CROFT HOUSE, ASHTON-UNDER-LYNE, LANCS., for Samuel Heginbottom in 1810. This small seat is illustrated both in Twycross's *Mansions of England* iii, 1847, 89, and in Burke's *Visitation of Seats* i, 1852, 123.

COWPER, JOHN, was a builder at Lewes in Sussex. He designed DANE HILL CHURCH, SUSSEX, 1836, Gothic; rebuilt 1892 [I.C.B.S.].

COX, H—, of Tooley Street, Southwark, exhibited the 'elevation of a villa now building in Hampshire' at the Royal Academy in 1797.

COXEDGE, J—, of Kensington, was an architect or surveyor of Kensington, of whom F. Goodwin (1784–1835) was a pupil [*A.P.S.D., s.v.* 'Goodwin']. He may have been the Joseph Coxedge, of Edwardes Square, Kensington, whose library was sold on 20 March 1820 [catalogue in B.M., S.C.L. 10 (12)].

CRACKLOW, CHARLES THOMAS, was a surveyor of Southwark, to whom John Buckler (1770–1851) was apprenticed. In 1796 he was the author of one of the schemes for the improvement of the Port of London considered by the commissioners. He advocated the construction of new docks at Rotherhithe [Sir Joseph Broodbank, *History of the Port of London* i, 1921, 86]. Cracklow published *Views of the Churches and Chapels of Surrey*. 1827.

CRAIG, CHARLES ALEXANDER (*c.* 1754–1833), spent the greater part of his life in the Office of Works. Born in Rochester, he became a pupil of Sir Robert Taylor, and was appointed Labourer in Trust at the Charing Cross Mews in 1776. In 1786 he became Resident Clerk, and in 1793 Examining Clerk. He retired when the Office was reorganized in 1814 after the death of James Wyatt. An 'industrious mediocrity', Craig had been largely responsible for the day-to-day running of the Office of Works during the surveyorship of the negligent Wyatt. As an architect he designed little or nothing, but occupied himself as Surveyor to the Commissioners of Westminster Bridge (1801–29), Surveyor, Clerk and Treasurer to the Commissioners for Paving Westminster, and District Surveyor of Lambeth and Newington under the Act of 1774. He died on 11 January 1833, in his 80th year. [*Gent's Mag.* 1833 (i), 91; *History of the King's Works* vi, 50–1 and *passim*; Farington's Diary, 12 April 1816.]

CRAIG, JAMES (1744–1795), was born in Edinburgh on 31 October 1744. He was the son of William Craig, a merchant, and his mother was a sister of the poet James Thomson, a relationship of which Craig was inordinately proud. According to Redgrave's *Dictionary of Artists* (1874) he was a pupil of Sir Robert Taylor, but this statement is not supported by other evidence, and is probably due to a confusion with C.A. Craig (*q.v.*) who is known to have been one of Taylor's pupils. In fact nothing whatever is known of Craig's upbringing or architectural career before 1766, when he achieved celebrity as the author of the winning design for the layout of the New Town of Edinburgh. Six plans were received, and Craig's was adjudged the best by the Lord Provost and John Adam. After further discussions with a committee of the Town Council Craig produced the definitive plan which formed the basis of the existing New Town. It was an effective but not particularly enterprising layout of rectilinear streets with a central axis terminated by a square at either end. Two of the three principal streets (Queen Street and Princes Street) were to have buildings on one side only, thus providing magnificent views over the Forth in one direction and across to the Old Town and the Castle in the other. As the successful competitor Craig duly received the gold medal and the freedom of the city that had been promised, and in October 1767 he went to London and presented a copy of his plan to King George III. In 1786 he published a further plan for the layout of the roads leading to the South Bridge in a pamphlet entitled *Plan for improving the City of Edinburgh*. Incorporating both a crescent and an octagon, this showed a more imaginative approach to town-planning than his scheme for the New Town, but it would have involved extensive demolition and was not adopted.

For the architecture, as opposed to the plan, of the New Town Craig had no responsibility. He was, however, the architect as well as the planner of St. James Square, commissioned in 1773 by Walter Ferguson, W.S., as a private speculation. The elevations were treated as a uniform composition, with severe but elegant detailing. He also designed the Physicians' Hall in George Street, with a handsome façade in the Palladian manner.

Despite the éclat which he gained as the planner of the New Town, Craig failed to develop an extensive practice and never became a fashionable architect like Robert Mylne or the Adams. After 1781 he was constantly borrowing money, and he died in debt. This lack of success appears to have been due in large measure to his own arrogant and intractable character. According to the *Scottish Register* of 1795 'he was unfortunate, owing chiefly, perhaps, to some visionary idea of consequence which he fancied he was entitled to indulge on account of his relationship to Thomson the Poet, a connection which he vainly flattered himself was to procure him consideration and employment, and to supersede in him the necessity of prosecuting those sober plans for success in life which prudence requires of other men'.

Craig died in Edinburgh on 23 June 1795. He is commemorated by a modern tombstone in the Greyfriars Cemetery. There is a portrait by David Allan in the Scottish National Portrait Gallery.

[New Register House, Edinburgh Birth Register; *Scots Mag.* 1795, 411; *D.N.B.*; A. J. Youngson, *The Making of Classical Edinburgh*, Edinburgh 1966, 77–9, 98, 117–19, 288–9; M. K. Meade, 'Plans of the New Town of Edinburgh', *Architectural History* xiv, 1971.]

EDINBURGH, ST. JAMES SQUARE, for Walter Ferguson, W.S., 1773; dem. [M. K. Meade, *op. cit.*].

ST. ANDREWS, ST. SALVATOR'S CHURCH, alterations, comprising the replacement of the vault by a timber roof, 1773 [R.G. Cant, 'St. Andrews Architects', *St. Andrews Preservation Trust Year Book*, 1966–7, 16; elevation by Craig at Culzean Castle, no. 75].

EDINBURGH, THE PHYSICIANS' HALL, GEORGE STREET, 1775; dem. c. 1843 [original plans at Coll. of Physicians; elevation shown in David

Allan's portrait of Craig] (T. H. Shepherd, *Modern Athens*, 1829, 61).

EDINBURGH, THE OLD OBSERVATORY (now OBSERVATORY HOUSE), CALTON HILL, 1776–92 [J. Stark, *Picture of Edinburgh*, 1823, 182].

LEITH GUN-BATTERY, NORTH FORT STREET, LEITH, 1780 [Edinburgh City Archives, Letters, vol. viii, nos. 110, 111].

KILLEARN, STIRLINGSHIRE, THE BUCHANAN MONUMENT, an obelisk in memory of George Buchanan, 1788 [R.C.A.M., *Stirlingshire* ii, 323 and pl. 51A].

The following unexecuted or unverified designs have been noted: designs for altering or rebuilding MOUNT STUART HOUSE, ISLE OF BUTE, for the 3rd Earl of Bute, 1768–9 [payment in Mount Stuart archives 'to the boarding of Mr. Craig, architect, during the five weeks he staid at Mountstuart measuring and making plans of the house']; alterations to MOUNTQUHANIE HOUSE, FIFE, 1770 [elevation at Mountquhanie signed 'Jas. Craig 1770']; alterations to ST. LEONARD'S CHURCH, ST. ANDREWS, c. 1770 [R. G. Cant, 'St. Andrews Architects', *St. Andrews Preservation Trust Year Book*, 1966–7, 16]; proposed addition of wings to DALKEITH HOUSE, MIDLOTHIAN, 1775 [in portfolio at Bowhill House]; design for an urn in memory of Provost Kincaid in GREYFRIARS CHURCHYARD, 1777 [Scottish National Gallery, Print Room, D. 384]; design for pulpit, galleries, etc., in ST. GILES' CATHEDRAL, EDINBURGH, for Dr. Hugh Blair, 1777 [National Library of Scotland, MS. 502, and cf. J. Cameron Lees, *St. Giles', Edinburgh*, 1889, 401]; a library for the Writers to the Signet, 1778–9 [*History of the Society of Writers to the Signet*, Edinburgh 1890, 409–11]; internal alterations to CALLENDAR HOUSE, STIRLINGSHIRE, for William Forbes, 1785 [R.C.A.M., *Stirlingshire* ii, 350]; layout of building land in MEADOWFLATT, GLASGOW, for Col. Campbell of Blythswood and the City of Glasgow, 1792 [*Extracts from the Records of the Burgh of Glasgow*, ed. R. Renwick, viii, 475].

CRAIG, JOHN (–c. 1745), was a wright by trade. He lived in Glasgow, where he had a considerable business as a builder. He appears to have had some sort of business relationship with Allan Dreghorn (*q.v.*) [see *Extracts from the Records of the Burgh of Glasgow 1718–38*, ed. Renwick, 414, 423, 494, etc.]. In 1732 they submitted a joint design for Glasgow University Library, but it was not carried out [Glasgow University, Senate Minutes]. In 1735 Craig was appointed 'town's wright' or carpenter to the municipality of Glasgow, but the appointment was rescinded the following year [*Extracts from the Records of the Burgh of Glasgow 1718–38*, ed. Renwick, 435–6, 472]. Craig must have died shortly before 15 January 1745, when his heirs received a belated payment for his library design of 1732 [Glasgow University Faculty Minutes, vol. 36, f. 168].

CRAIG, JOHN, of Glasgow, was the son of William Craig, a prosperous timber-merchant of that city. In the Glasgow directories of 1787 and 1789 he is described as 'architect to his Royal Highness the Prince of Wales', but how he obtained this (presumably honorary) designation is not known. He visited Italy and was well known in Glasgow as a man of taste who could speak Italian and play the fiddle [Senex, *Glasgow Past and Present* ii, 1884, 278, 330]. In 1787 he married Sarah, sister of William Stark (*q.v.*), but she died at Barcelona in 1792 'on her way to Italy for the recovery of her health' [*Scots Mag.* xlix, 1787, 620; lv, 1793, 50]. His daughter Margaret married General Sir George Napier. He should not be confused with a wright named John Craig who built a house (No. 42) in Miller Street in 1775 [Senex, *op. cit.* ii, 415] and appears to have died in 1783 [Glasgow City Archives, Register of the Incorporation of Masons]. He was still alive in 1815, when he wrote a postscript to the text of Stark's report on the Calton Hill development at Edinburgh in the *Scots Magazine* (vol. lxxvii, 582).

In Glasgow Craig designed THE GRAMMAR SCHOOL (later the Andersonian Institution) ST. GEORGE'S STREET, 1788–9, and THE SURGEONS' HALL, ST. ENOCH'S SQUARE, 1791, both demolished, in an elegant Adamsian style [R. Chapman, *Picture of Glasgow*, 1812, 125, 127]. A drawing at Newhailes, Midlothian, shows that he designed a court of offices for Andrew Stirling at DRUMPELLIER HOUSE, LANARKSHIRE, in 1790. An almost identical stable-block was afterwards built at NEWHAILES, probably by Miss Dalrymple (who inherited the estate in 1792), who evidently obtained the drawing in order to copy it in her own building.

CRAKE, JOHN (*c.* 1811–1859), was presumably related to Michael Crake, 'statuary, surveyor and builder', for whose sculpture see Rupert Gunnis's *Dictionary of British Sculptors*, revised ed. 1968, 116. John Crake became a pupil of Decimus Burton. He entered the Royal Academy Schools in 1831, and was awarded the Silver Medal the same year. He afterwards visited Italy, and on his return commenced practice in London. His exhibits at the Royal Academy indicate that he made designs for the terrace of houses in HYDE PARK GARDENS, 1836, and for an entrance lodge to DEENE PARK, NORTHANTS., for the 7th Earl of Cardigan, 1841. The latter may not have been built, as another design for a lodge at Deene was exhibited at the R.A. by T. H. Wyatt and David Brandon in 1850.

From 1842 to 1844 Crake was a member of council of the R.I.B.A. His marriage to a wealthy lady enabled him to retire from practice in 1852, and he took up residence at Datchet, where a churchyard monument records his death on 27 December 1859, in his 49th year. His widow survived until 1900. A student's design for a triumphal arch by him is in the R.I.B.A. Drawings Collection. [Obituary in *Builder* xviii, 1860, 6.]

CRANESON, W—, designed the PUBLIC BATHS, NEWCASTLE, opened in 1781, of which he published an engraved plan and elevation dedicated to the Mayor and Corporation (B.M., *King's Maps* xxxii, 57 (m)). Before taking up architecture, he had been 'an actor belonging to the Newcastle company of comedians' [M. A. Richardson, *The Local Historian's Table Book* ii, 1842, 268].

CRESWELL, or **CRISWELL,** WILLIAM (–1819), was Surveyor to the Armourers' and Brasiers' Company until his death in 1819. He was President of the Surveyors' Club in 1800, and in 1820 William Wickings presented the Club with an engraved portrait of Cresswell, 'an old and respected Member, whose integrity, rectitude, and abilities will always be had in remembrance' [J. W. Penfold, *A Century of Surveyors*, 1892, 13; *A.P.S.D.*, *s.v.* 'Good, J. H.'].

CRESY, EDWARD (1792–1858), was born at Dartford, Kent, and was educated at Rawes's academy at Bromley in the same county. He became a pupil of J. T. Parkinson, and afterwards spent two years in the office of George Smith 'with the object of perfecting himself in the financial branches of his profession'. In 1816, accompanied by his friend and fellow-pupil G. L. Taylor, he made a walking tour through England in order to measure and draw the principal architectural monuments. In 1817 Cresy and Taylor, accompanied from 1818 by John Sanders, undertook a tour of Europe which occupied the next three years. Travelling mainly on foot, they visited France, Switzerland, Italy, Greece, Malta and Sicily before returning home by way of Italy and France in 1819. The results of their researches appeared in 1821–2 as *The Architectural Antiquities of Rome, measured and delineated by G. L. Taylor and E. Cresy*, 2 vols. (there was a later edition in 1874), and in 1829 they published a work on *Architecture of the Middle Ages in Italy illustrated by views ... of the Cathedral, etc. of Pisa*. A third work on the architecture of the Renaissance was intended, but, after the publication of two parts, it was abandoned owing to lack of encouragement.

Partly as a result of this disappointment, Cresy accepted a professional engagement in Paris in 1829–30, and it was some time before he became

239

well established in England. He refused to take part in competitions at a time when they were the usual way of securing important public commissions, and his practice was, in consequence, 'almost entirely of a private character'. Very little is known of his architectural works, but in 1824 he added a library to THE PRIORY, LEATHERHEAD, SURREY, for William Cotton [Brayley, *History of Surrey* iv, 437]. He also designed HULSWOOD VILLA, WILMINGTON, KENT, for John Hayward in the style of a Burgundian chateau, *c.* 1835 [C. Greenwood, *Epitome of the History of Kent*, 1838, 70], added the Gothic porch to DARTFORD CHURCH in 1846 [S. K. Keyes, *Dartford Further Historical Notes*, Dartford 1938, 385], and designed the NATIONAL SCHOOLS at HORTON KIRBY in 1857 [drawings in Kent Record Office].

Cresy lived from 1824 until 1830 at NO. 6 SUFFOLK STREET, LONDON, a house which he designed himself with a façade in imitation of Palladio's house at Vicenza [J. Elmes, *Metropolitan Improvements*, 1831, 123]. In 1828 he began building THE TOWERS at SOUTH DARENTH, nr. DARTFORD, as his own residence. The chimney-pieces were executed in Paris, in accordance with a design 'suggested by fragments I saw in the galley of the Louvre'. It was at South Darent that he died on 12 November 1858.

Cresy held strongly the view that architecture and engineering were a single profession, and he himself became well known as a sanitary engineer. As superintending inspector under the Board of Health, he gave evidence before the Health of Towns and Metropolitan Sanitary Commission, provided information for the 'Appendix to Report on Drainage of Potteries, 1849', and wrote a 'Report as to the Fall of the Extension of the Main Sewer from the Ravensbourne to the Outlet', 1855, both of which were incorporated in the reports of the Metropolitan Commission of Sewers. He also gave evidence in 1844 before the Commissioners for enquiring into the State of Large Towns and Populous Districts (*Parliamentary Papers*, 1844, xvii, 144). He superintended the construction of the Dartford Gasworks in 1826–7. He published *A Practical Treatise on Bridge Building*, 1839, and *An Encyclopaedia of Civil Engineering*, 1847 (2nd ed. 1856). He also published, in conjunction with C. W. Johnson, a work *On the Cottages of Agricultural Labourers, with Economical Working Plans* [1847].

He became an F.S.A. in 1820, and was also a member of the British Archaeological Association, to whose proceedings he contributed several papers. In 1840 the London Topographical Society published his *Illustrations of Stone Church, Kent, with an historical account.* His wife translated into English Milizia's *Memorie degli Architetti antichi e moderni*, with Notes and Additional Lives, 2 vols., 1826. His eldest son,

Edward Cresy (d. 1870), followed his father's profession. A small MS. notebook belonging to Cresy is preserved in the Dartford Borough Museum. It contains notes on the building of his house at South Darenth, and on local antiquities, etc. Extracts from it were published in the *Trans. of the Dartford Antiquarian Soc.* ii.

[Obituary in *Builder* xvi, 793, xvii, 166; G. L. Taylor, *Memoirs of an Octogenarian Architect,* 1870–2; *D.N.B.*]

CREW, JOHN THISTLEWOOD, entered the Royal Academy Schools in 1834. He exhibited at the Royal Academy from 1833 to 1859, including a number of views of Rome, and in 1841 'Caversham, the seat of William Crawshaw, Esq., shewing the additional colonnades now erecting'. It is probable that he was the architect employed by Crawshaw to enlarge CAVERSHAM PARK, OXON., at about this time.

CRICHTON, RICHARD (*c.* 1771–1817), was the son of James Crichton, an Edinburgh mason who died in 1797. In early life he worked as a draughtsman for the Adam brothers in Edinburgh. In May 1797 he was admitted a burgess of Edinburgh. He was a competent and versatile architect who carried on the traditions established by the brothers Adam in their extensive Scottish practice. Thus Gask, Lawers and the Bank of Scotland on the Mound at Edinburgh are in the restrained classical style of Adam's later years; Rossie Castle was an essay in Adam's distinctive castle style. But Abercairny Abbey was an elaborately Gothic house in the manner of Porden, while the classical Dunglass was a remarkably early essay in picturesque asymmetry, and Balbirnie shows the influence of the Greek Revival.

In 1813 Crichton competed for the important town-planning scheme in the neighbourhood of Calton Hill, Edinburgh. He shared the prize with William Reid of Glasgow and Alexander Nasmyth (the landscape-painter), but none of their proposals were in fact carried out, and in 1814–15 the commission for the associated Calton Bridge went to Elliot instead of to himself. His design for the bridge is illustrated in the *Scots Magazine* for June 1814. Other unexecuted designs by Crichton were for the Merchant Maiden Hospital in Edinburgh [*Book of the Old Edinburgh Club* xxix, 24], and for a monument to Nelson at Forres [Robert Douglas, *Annals of Forres,* Elgin 1934, 318].

Crichton's career was cut short by his early death at the age of 46 on 17 August 1817. He is commemorated by an inscription added to the Graeco-Egyptian monument which he had erected to the memory of his father in St. Cuthbert's Churchyard. His practice was continued by his nephews R. & R. Dickson (*q.v.*)

[*A.P.S.D.*; *Roll of Edinburgh Burgesses*, Scottish Record Soc. 1933, 41; A. J. Youngson, *The Making of Classical Edinburgh*, 1966, 142, 307 n. 36.]

ROSSIE CASTLE, ANGUS, for Hercules Ross, *c.* 1800, castle style; dem. 1957 [*Scots Mag.*, Sept. 1807; J. P. Neale, *Views of Seats*, 1st ser., v; Soane Museum, Designs, vol. iv, pp. 48–52, copies made in 1795 of designs by Crichton dated 1793] (F. O. Morris, *Picturesque Views of Seats* v, 1889, 73).

COLINTON HOUSE, MIDLOTHIAN for Sir William Forbes, Bart., 1801 [drawings in Crichton's hand among Fettercairn papers, National Library of Scotland].

GASK HOUSE, PERTHSHIRE, for Laurence Oliphant, 1801– [J. P. Neale, *Views of Seats*, 1st ser., iv, 1821].

EDINBURGH, THE BANK OF SCOTLAND on THE MOUND, jointly with Robert Reid, 1802–6 [Bank of Scotland Minutes, 29 Oct. 1800: 'Resolved to employ Robert Reid and Richard Chrichton, Architects in Edinburgh, jointly']; remodelled by D. Bryce 1865–70 (T. H. Shepherd, *Modern Athens*, 1829, plate at p. 74).

attributed: GELSTON CASTLE, KIRKCUDBRIGHT-SHIRE, for Sir William Douglas, Bart., *c.* 1805, castle style, now gutted [stylistic attribution].

ABERCAIRNY ABBEY, PERTHSHIRE, begun *c.* 1805 for Col. Charles Moray Stirling (d. 1810), completed to an enlarged plan by R. & R. Dickson for James Moray (d. 1840) and William Moray (d. 1850), Gothic; dem. 1960 [J. P. Neale, *Views of Seats*, 1st ser., vi, 1823; Mark Girouard in *C. Life*, 9–16 March 1961; S.R.O., RHP 1017/22, 36 and 41].

STIRLING, COURT HOUSE AND GAOL, 1806–11 [R.C.A.M., *Stirlingshire* ii, 293; S.R.O., RHP 1884/2–5, 7–9].

DUNGLASS, EAST LOTHIAN, for Sir James Hall, Bart., 1807–11; dem. 1947 [J. P. Neale, *Views of Seats*, 1st ser., iv, 1821, where it is stated that the architect was 'greatly assisted by the taste and judgment of the proprietor'; S.R.O., GD 206/2/160; building accounts in Reading University Library, EAS 1/2/57–9] (*C. Life*, 12 Sept. 1925).

BLAIR DRUMMOND, PERTHSHIRE, 'house for a smith or carpenter', now known as Blair Drummond Corner, 1813 [drawings at Blair Drummond Estate Office].

KINCARDINE-IN-MENTEITH CHURCH, PERTHSHIRE, 1814–16, Gothic [*N.S.A.* x, 1265; specification in S.R.O., GD 24; plans in Blair Drummond Estate Office].

LAWERS HOUSE, PERTHSHIRE, added Ionic portico, etc., for D. R. W. Ewart, *c.* 1815 [J. P. Neale, *Views of Seats*, 1st ser., v, 1822] (*C. Life*, 10 Oct. 1925).

BALBIRNIE HOUSE, FIFE, enlarged and remodelled for General Robert Balfour, 1815–19 [J. P.

Neale, *Views of Seats*, 1st ser., v, 1822; Alistair Rowan in *C. Life*, 29 June–6 July 1972].

CRISWELL, WILLIAM, *see* CRESWELL

CROCKER, EDWARD (*c.* 1757–1836), served the Office of Works in different capacities for more than forty years, ending his career as Clerk of the Works at Whitehall from 1818 to 1829, when he retired at the age of 71. He was a measuring surveyor rather than an architect and is best known for the careful coloured drawings, now in the Ashmolean Museum at Oxford, which he made of the medieval wall-paintings in the Painted Chamber at Westminster [*History of the King's Works* i, 499; vi, 59, 115, 116, 119, etc.].

CROMBIE, ALEXANDER (*c.* 1709–1785), was the founder of a family of masons and architects in Dumfries. A native of Haddingtonshire, he came to Dumfries as a young man in order to work at Tinwald House under William Adam, took a lease of the Castledykes Quarry, and soon became one of the leading builders in the locality. In 1752 he and James Harley, Deacon of the Squaremen, built MOORHEAD'S HOSPITAL, and in 1770 he built the BUTCHER MARKET. His son Alexander (*c.* 1757–1828) and grandson Andrew Crombie (*c.* 1799–1855) were also leading builders and monumental masons in the town, and the latter's nephew Alexander (1812–80) and grand-nephew James (1845–1909) were in practice as architects during the second half of the nineteenth century. [W. McDowall, *Memorials of St. Michael's Churchyard, Dumfries*, Edinburgh 1876, 262–4; *The Architects, Engineers and Building Trades Directory*, 1868, 107].

CROSS, RICHARD (–1837), was responsible for alterations to CHILLINGHAM CHURCH, NORTHUMBERLAND, in 1828–9 [drawings in Northumberland County Record Office]. On 3 July 1837, Cross, described as 'architect at Chillingham Castle', was found 'quite dead' on the road between Wooler and Chillingham [J. Latimer, *Local Records, 1832–57*, Newcastle 1857, 73].

CROWE, WILLIAM (1745–1829), Fellow of New College, Oxford, was born at Midgham in Berkshire, where his father was a carpenter. He became Public Orator of the University of Oxford in 1784, and was also known as a poet and preacher. He was interested in architecture, and occasionally lectured on that subject at New College. In 1804 he lectured on Civil Architecture at the Royal Institution [*The Farington Diary*, ed. J. Greig, ii, 262]. He is sometimes said to have designed the Library of Exeter College, erected in 1779 and demolished in 1859. But in fact John Townesend was both architect and builder, and

Crowe did no more than 'suggest a few amendments in the details' [J. Ingram, *Memorials of Oxford* i, 1837, 14]. A full account of Crowe's career will be found in *D.N.B.*

CRUNDEN, JOHN (*c.* 1745–1835), was born in Sussex, and became an architect and surveyor in London. In 1774 he was appointed District Surveyor for the parishes of Paddington, St. Pancras, and St. Luke, Chelsea. Although dismissed in 1807 after a disagreement with the Middlesex magistrates (see John Coggan, *A Letter to the Magistrates of the County of Middlesex*, 1807), he was reinstated, retaining the surveyorship of St. Pancras until 1824, and the other two until his death in 1835. He exhibited at the Society of Artists from 1766 to 1777, and competed for the Royal Exchange at Dublin in 1769. Most of his private commissions dated from before 1774, for after his appointment to the District Surveyorship nearly all his time was devoted to his official duties. His will shows that he was a keen archer, and that he died in 1835.

Crunden is best known as the author of a number of popular architectural pattern-books. He published *Designs for Ceilings*, 1765; *The Chimney-piece Maker's Daily Assistant*, with T. Milton and Placido Columbani, 1766; *Convenient and Ornamental Architecture, consisting of Original Designs for Plans, Elevations and Sections from the Farm House to the Most Grand and Magnificent Villa*, with a dedication to the Duke of Newcastle, 1767 (several later editions, 1785, 1788, 1791, 1797 and 1815); *The Joyner and Cabinet Maker's Darling, or Pocket Director*, 1770; and *The Carpenter's Companion for Chinese Railing and Gates ... from the original designs of J. H. Morris, Carpenter, and J. Crunden*, 1770.

Crunden's pattern-books reveal him as a designer of no great originality working in the Palladian tradition. Two of his surviving buildings, however, show him developing a more elegant style derived from the brothers Adam. Thus Boodle's Club was clearly inspired by Adam's Royal Society of Arts building in the Adelphi, and Belfield is described by Pevsner as 'an Adamesque essay with rooms of contrasted shapes'. The first 8 plates of J. Ch. Krafft's *Plans des plus beaux jardins pittoresques de France, d'Angleterre et d'Allemagne* (Paris 1809) are given to a Gothic garden pavilion built by Crunden 'dans un parc sur la route de Westminster' and believed to have been situated near Fulham.

[*A.P.S.D.*; A. T. Bolton, *The Portrait of Sir John Soane*, 1927, 181–2; Dorothy Stroud, *Henry Holland*, 1966, 24, 26–7; *Builder* xxvii, 1869, 781; will, P.C.C. 471 GLOUCESTER.]

BROOKLANDS, WEYBRIDGE, SURREY, for George Payne, 1767; dem. [*Convenient and Ornamental Architecture*, pl. 36; Dorothy Stroud, *Henry Holland*, 23–4].

HALTON PLACE, nr. HELLIFIELD, YORKS. (W.R.), 1770 [drawings preserved at Halton, *ex inf.* Mr. P. Fleetwood-Hesketh and Mr. P. Leach] (T. D. Whitaker, *History of Craven*, 1812, 439).

SOUTHAMPTON, THE AUDIT HOUSE, 1771–3; dem. [*The Southampton Guide*, 1787, 32] (*Arch. Rev.* xlv, Feb. 1919, 33).

WOOLCOMBE HALL, MELBURY BUBB, DORSET, for Laurence Cox, *c.* 1772; dem. before 1815 [exhib. at R.A. 1772; there is also an engraving signed 'J. Crunden, Architect'].[1]

BUSHBRIDGE, nr. GODALMING, SURREY, improvements for Gen. Sir Robert Barker, 1775; dem. 1906 [W. Angus, *Views of Seats*, 1787, pl. vi].

LONDON, BOODLE'S (originally the Savoir Vivre) CLUB, ST. JAMES'S STREET, 1775–6; ground-floor rooms remodelled by J. B. Papworth, 1821–4 [T. Malton, *A Picturesque Tour of London and Westminster*, 1791] (*C. Life*, 24 Dec. 1932; *Survey of London* xxx, 441–9).

BRIGHTON, SUSSEX, THE ASSEMBLY ROOMS of the CASTLE HOTEL for Mrs. Shergold, *c.* 1776; converted into the Chapel Royal 1821–2; dem. 1851 [H. D. Roberts, *History of the Royal Pavilion, Brighton*, 1939].

BELFIELD, nr. WEYMOUTH, DORSET, for Isaac Buxton, *c.* 1775–80 [G. D. Squibb, *Belfield and the Buxtons*, privately printed 1954, 2; R.C.H.M., *Dorset* ii (2), 340 and plates].

PORTSWOOD HOUSE, nr. SOUTHAMPTON, for — Taylor, *c.* 1775; dem. *c.* 1850 [E. W. Brayley & John Britton, *The Beauties of England and Wales* vi, 1805, 121].

CUBITT, LEWIS (1799–1883), was the youngest of the Cubitt brothers, and according to family tradition, 'the laziest and least satisfactory of the three'. He was, however, much the most talented as an architect. Born in September 1799, he was apprenticed to his eldest brother Thomas (*q.v.*) in 1815, and became a member of the Carpenters' Company in 1822. He also received some architectural training in the office of H. E. Kendall, whose daughter Sophia he married. He was in partnership with his brothers by 1824, when 'Messrs. T. W. and L. Cubitt' repaired LEYTON CHURCH, ESSEX [J. Kennedy, *History of the Parish of Leyton*, 1894]. Thomas and William dissolved their partnership in 1827, and Lewis eventually left the former brother for the latter in 1832. Later in the 1830s he set up as an architect in independent practice at 77 Great Russell Street.

Lewis appears to have designed many of the houses in Bloomsbury and Belgravia which were

---

[1] Plate 25 of *Convenient and Ornamental Architecture* shows a 'House designed for Lawrence Cox, Esq. to be built at Keston in Kent'. This does not appear to have been built.

built by the Cubitts in the 1820s. In 1837–9 he designed and built, as an independent speculation, a block of Italianate houses on the south side of LOWNDES SQUARE (plans and elevation in *The Surveyor, Engineer and Architect*, 1841, 154, 198). In the 1840s he entered on a successful career as a railway architect, designing in particular the BRICKLAYERS' ARMS STATION in BERMONDSEY (dem.) in 1842–4 and in 1851–2 the KING'S CROSS terminal of the Great Northern Railway (*Builder* ix, 1851, 739). The large scale and expressive simplicity of the latter station show that Lewis Cubitt was capable of something more than the genteel façades of Belgravia.[1] Another railway commission was a large Italianate building at COL-CHESTER, begun as THE VICTORIA HOTEL, but eventually completed in 1843 as a Lunatic Asylum (THE ROYAL EASTERN COUNTIES INSTITUTION) [H. E. von Stürmer, *Historical Guide to Colchester*, 1852, 7].

Little appears to be known about Lewis Cubitt's career after 1852. He received a legacy of £10,000 under Thomas Cubitt's will in 1855, and himself lived on to the age of 84, dying at Brighton on 9 June 1883. His estate was valued for probate at £77,900. A portrait is reproduced by Hobhouse, pl. 104. [Sir Stephen Tallents, *Man and Boy*, 1943, 32; Hermione Hobhouse, *Thomas Cubitt, Master Builder*, 1971, 271 and *passim*.]

CUBITT, THOMAS (1788–1855), was the eldest son of Jonathan Cubitt, a native of Norfolk who moved to London at the end of the eighteenth century. Thomas began life as a journeyman carpenter, and as a young man made a voyage to India as a ship's carpenter. Returning to London in about 1809, he used such money as he had been able to save to set up business as a master carpenter. His first work of importance was to rebuild the defective roof of the Russell Institution in Great Coram Street. In 1814 he became a member of the Carpenters' Company, and was joined in business by his younger brother William (1791–1863). It was in the following year that he took the step that was to make him famous in the history of building. Having contracted to build the London Institution in Moorfields, he decided to set up a comprehensive building establishment of his own instead of following the normal practice of performing the carpenter's work himself and sub-contracting the other trades. 'Thomas Cubitt, bound by his contract under penalty to finish the new building by a certain date, was determined not to be left at the

mercy of this complicated and inefficient system.' He accordingly bought some ground in Gray's Inn Road, built himself workshops upon it, 'purchased horses, carts and material, and engaged ... gangs of carpenters, smiths, glaziers, bricklayers and other workers'. Although such arrangements may not have been wholly without precedent, Cubitt's enterprise was a pioneer venture of its kind, and its success gained him the reputation of having established the first modern building firm.

As a builder with a large labour force on a permanent wage basis, Cubitt could not afford to wait for work to be offered to him. In order to keep his men fully employed he took the initiative by engaging in speculative building on a large scale. In 1815 he began to develop the Calthorpe estate on the east side of Gray's Inn Road. In the early 1820s he built several 'genteel and commodious villas' in Highbury Park, and more in Stoke Newington (Albion Road), Islington (Barnsbury Park) and Bloomsbury (south side of Tavistock Square, in association with the stockbroker Benjamin Oakley). In 1824 he began to develop a further tract of ground on the Duke of Bedford's Bloomsbury estate, on which he built the west side of Tavistock Square, Woburn Place, Endsleigh Street, the greater part of Gordon Square, and part of the south side of Euston Square. The workmanship was excellent, and the competent architectural designing was done in Cubitt's own drawing office, for characteristically he preferred to be independent of architects as he was of other building tradesmen. For this side of the firm's activities his youngest brother Lewis (*q.v.*), who had had an architectural training, appears to have been responsible. The family partnership, however, began to break up in 1827, when William Cubitt left the firm in order to carry on the safer contracting side of the business from the Gray's Inn Yard, and Lewis eventually joined him in 1832.

The scene of Cubitt's greatest building enterprise was in the south-west of London, where the conversion of Buckingham House into a royal palace pointed out the Grosvenor estates as an area for development. In 1824 he took a lease from Lord Grosvenor of the district known as the 'Five Fields', and began to convert the swampy ground bordering the Westbourne river into the substantial squares of Belgravia. Belgrave Square itself was built by George and William Haldimand, the financiers, to the designs of George Basevi, but elsewhere Cubitt built for himself, and largely to his own designs, or those of his brother Lewis. The earlier part of Eaton Square (Nos. 103–18) is definitely attributed to 'T. & L. Cubitt' by Britton & Pugin, *The Public Buildings of London* ii, 1828. Further north, Cubitt built the two great houses which stand on either side of Albert Gate, the eastern of which he sold to

[1] For the probable source of Cubitt's design for the screen-wall – a design for a bourse published by J. N. L. Durand in 1802 – see John Summerson, *Victorian Architecture: Four Studies in Evaluation*, 1970, 29–30 and fig. 7.

George Hudson, the railway magnate, for £15,000. After Belgravia, he built Pimlico (where his Thames Bank works were established), while further afield he was responsible for the laying out of Clapham Park, on land sold to him by Major Atkins Bowyer, the lord of the manor, in 1824.

Meanwhile he was already engaged in building houses in Brighton for Thomas Read Kemp, and in 1828 he was one of the Committee of Management elected by the proprietors 'to superintend the general works and improvements to be done at Kemp Town'. He continued to serve on it until his death in 1855, and played a part in the history of the estate second only to that of Kemp himself.

Although mainly engaged in these great schemes of urban development, Cubitt built a few large houses for private clients either to his own designs or to those of his brothers William and Lewis. Conventionally 'Palladian' or Italianate in style, they were well appointed and substantially built, but somewhat undistinguished as works of architecture. They included POLESDEN LACEY HOUSE, GREAT BOOKHAM, SURREY, for the stationer Joseph Bonsor, 1821–3 [Brayley, *History of Surrey* iv, 472; Hobhouse, 50]; the remodelling of LINTON PARK, KENT, for the 5th Earl Cornwallis, *c.* 1825, for which William Cubitt acted as architect [see his evidence in the *Report of the Select Committee on the Office of Works, Parliamentary Papers* 1828, iv, 409] (*C. Life*, 29 March, 5 April 1946); additions to NOTHERWOOD, nr. LYNDHURST, HANTS., for John Pulteney, 1830–1 [G. F. Prosser, *Select Illustrations of Hampshire*, 1834]; alterations to SPRING (WOODCHESTER) PARK, nr. STROUD, GLOS., for the 2nd Earl Ducie, modified by Anthony Salvin, 1840 [Gloucester County Record Office, D 340a, P. 14]; alterations to the interior of NETLEY PLACE, nr. GUILDFORD, SURREY, for J. Fraser, 1847, destroyed by fire 1848 [*Gent's Mag.* 1848 (i), 76]; and NO. 14 KENSINGTON PALACE GARDENS, for Edward Antrobus, 1849–51 [Hobhouse, 464–5]. The rebuilding of NO. 12 ST. JAMES'S SQUARE in 1836 for Lord King, later 1st Earl of Lovelace, is attributed to Cubitt on stylistic grounds [*Survey of London* xxix, 134]. In 1845–8 he designed and built OSBORNE HOUSE, ISLE OF WIGHT, for Queen Victoria under the direction of the Prince Consort (plan in R. Kerr, *The Gentleman's House*, 1864, pl. 17). In 1846–50 he built the new east front of BUCKINGHAM PALACE to the designs of Edward Blore, and in 1852–6 added the Ball-room, etc., on the south side to those of Sir James Pennethorne (plans in *History of the King's Works* vi, 279, 288). In about 1830 he built a large house for himself in Clapham Park, and in 1850–4 a still larger one at DENBIES, nr. DORKING, SURREY (dem. 1953), where he died on 20 December 1855.

Cubitt left over £1,000,000, a will (then the longest on record) covering 30 skins of parchment, and a reputation for enterprise, integrity and public spirit which made him one of the great figures of early Victorian England. For, besides conducting building schemes on a larger scale than any hitherto known, Cubitt found time to take an active interest in such matters as the disposal of London's sewage, the provision of public parks, and the control of smoke. The creation of Battersea Park was due largely to his initiative, and when the success of the Great Exhibition of 1851 was in doubt, he became one of its guarantors. He frequently gave evidence to parliamentary committees investigating the problems of a rapidly expanding metropolis, and played a leading part in the preparation of the Metropolitan Buildings Act of 1855.

[Sir Stephen Tallents, *Man and Boy*, 1943, 30–6; Hermione Hobhouse, *Thomas Cubitt, Master Builder*, 1971, with full references to obituaries and other sources; *Catalogue of the R.I.B.A. Drawings Coll.*, C–F, 54–5.]

CULLEN, —, designed the TOWN HALL at SOUTH MOLTON, DEVONSHIRE, in 1739, as appears by an entry in the building accounts (now in the Town Museum): 'gave Mr. Cullen for drawing the moddell of the Towne Hall £1–1s.' The building is an attractive example of provincial Georgian architecture.

CUMBERLEGE, CHARLES NATHANIEL (*c.* 1807–1859), was admitted to the Royal Academy Schools in 1827 at the age of 20. He was recommended by his uncle Samuel Ware, to whose practice he succeeded on the latter's retirement in about 1840. He became a Fellow of the R.I.B.A. in 1845 and died in 1859. In 1834 he exhibited a design for 'proposed alterations' to WYDDIAL HALL, HERTS., at the R.A. He competed for the Houses of Parliament in 1835, submitting a design whose elevations were 'free from elaborate ornaments, the whole being intended to be faced with Portland stone'.

CUNDY, THOMAS, senior (1765–1825), was the eldest son of Peter Cundy, the owner of a small estate at Restowrick, St. Dennis, Cornwall. He left home early after a disagreement with his father, and, after a period of apprenticeship to a builder in Plymouth, decided to seek his fortune in London. Here he obtained employment as clerk of works to S. P. Cockerell, and educated himself by private study and attending evening lectures. In 1795 and 1796 he exhibited student's exercises at the Royal Academy. Eventually he set up business as an architect and builder in Ranelagh Street, Pimlico. Here he prospered, and in 1821 obtained the important post of surveyor to Lord Grosvenor's estates in Belgravia and Pimlico, then about to be laid out for building. By then he already had a considerable practice, especially as a designer of country houses either in a picturesque Gothic style reminiscent of Nash, or else in a conventional classical manner calculated to appeal to patrons who disliked the deviations of Dance or Soane. He exhibited some of his designs at the Royal Academy, and many of his works are shown in a small sketch-book now in the R.I.B.A. Collection, containing drawings apparently made by his son while in his father's office (see the *Catalogue* for a detailed list of its contents).

In 1816 Cundy visited Rome together with his son Thomas. He died in Ranelagh Street on 28 December 1825, aged 60, and was buried in the churchyard at Richmond in Surrey, where there is a tomb to his memory. His eldest son Thomas (*q.v.*) succeeded to his practice. James Cundy (1793–1826), his second son, was a statuary mason, and had a son named Samuel (d. 1867) who ran a marble-works in Pimlico and was employed by Gilbert Scott as a mason at St. Albans Abbey and elsewhere [obituary in *Builder* xxv, 1867, 464]. Joseph Cundy (1795–1875), third son of Thomas Cundy, senior, was an architect and speculative builder in Belgravia, and was the father of Thomas Syson Cundy, who became agent to the Fountaine-Montagu family of Ingmanthorpe Hall in Yorkshire and Papplewick, Notts, a position in which he was succeeded by his son and grandson. Nicholas Wilcox Cundy, born in 1778, was a younger brother of Thomas Cundy the elder. He practised as a civil engineer, but his works included the reconstruction of the Pantheon in Oxford Street as a theatre in 1811–12.[1]

A portrait of Thomas Cundy was in the possession of the late T. J. Cundy of Brant Broughton, Lincs., together with a MS. account of the family written by Osbert F. Cundy, F.R.C.S., in 1874.

[*D.N.B.*; MS. by Osbert F. Cundy referred to above.]

The following list sets out the works of Thomas Cundy senior and junior up to the time of the former's death in 1825. 'Sketch-book' refers to the sketch-book in the R.I.B.A. Drawings Collection.

NORMANTON, RUTLAND, farmyard for Sir Gilbert Heathcote, Bart., 1795 (? executed) [sketch-book, p. 65].

RICHMOND, SURREY, ice-house and farmyard (? executed) for the 1st Earl of Leicester, 1800 [sketch-book, pp. 15, 67].

BRIXTON LODGE, BRIXTON, SURREY, for J. Pitter,

---

[1] He had some difficulty in doing this to the satisfaction of the Lord Chamberlain, for whom the building was surveyed by James Wyatt as Surveyor-General, assisted by Thomas Hardwick, George Saunders, John Soane and S.P. Cockerell [Blenheim Palace archives, F.I. 38].

1803 [exhib. at R.A. 1803; sketch-book, p. 93, reproduced in *C. Life*, 9 March 1945, 418].

BEECHWOOD PARK, HERTS., interior of library for Sir John Sebright, Bart., 1804 [drawings at Beechwood, together with a rejected design by Soane] (*C. Life*, 12–19 Nov. 1938).

LONDON, NO. 22 (now 37) HILL STREET, BERKELEY SQUARE, interior for Robert Heathcote, before 1805 [*Gent's Mag.* 1805 (i), 275].

LONDON, NO. 24 HILL STREET, BERKELEY SQUARE, probably designed picture gallery for Sir John Leicester (afterwards Lord de Tabley), *c.* 1806; dem. Leicester formed the gallery out of an existing library soon after purchasing the house in 1805. No documents connected with the works of *c.* 1806 appear to survive, but among the Leicester-Warren papers in the Cheshire Record Office [DLT/C3/41–61] there is an estimate by Cundy dated 24 June 1809 for converting the room under the gallery into an eating-room, etc., and it is likely that he had also been employed to design the gallery itself. The gallery is illustrated by W. Carey, *Memoir of the Patronage and Progress of the Fine Arts in England*, 1826, 129 and in *Walpole Soc.* xxxviii, 1960–2, 62.

MIDDLETON PARK, MIDDLETON STONEY, OXON., altered and refaced house with stone, added Ionic portico and designed stables, etc., for the 5th Earl of Jersey, 1806–10; dem. 1938 [exhib. at R.A. 1806–7; sketch-book, pp. 25–7, 63, 113, 115; *V.C.H. Oxon.* vi, 243, with illustration] (Neale's *Views of Seats*, 2nd ser., v).

BESSINGBY HALL, YORKS. (E.R.), for Harrington Hudson, 1807 [exhib. at R.A. 1807].

BETCHWORTH HOUSE, SURREY, alterations for Charles Henry Bouverie, 1808 [sketch-book, p. 17].

WYTHAM ABBEY, BERKS., remodelled for the 5th Earl of Abingdon, 1809–10, Gothic [sketch-book, p. 21; exhib. at R.A. 1808–9].

HAWARDEN CASTLE (formerly Broadlane House), FLINTSHIRE, remodelled for Sir Stephen Glynne, Bart., 1809–10; castellated [Neale's *Views of Seats*, 2nd ser., v, 1829; exhib. at R.A. 1810] (*C. Life*, 15–21 June 1967).

WYCOMBE ABBEY, BUCKS., greenhouses for the 1st Lord Carrington, 1811 [sketch-book, p. 69, reproduced in *Catalogue of R.I.B.A. Drawings Coll.: C–F*, fig. 44].

LONDON, COVENTRY HOUSE, NO. 106 PICCADILLY (now ST. JAMES'S CLUB), alterations for the 7th Earl of Coventry, 1810–11 [papers at Croome Court, Worcs.].

WASSAND HALL, nr. BEVERLEY, YORKS. (E.R.), for the Rev. Charles Constable, 1813–14 [sketch-book, p. 31] (*Trans. E. Yorks. Georgian Soc.* v (i), 1958–61).

HEWELL GRANGE, WORCS., alterations for the 6th Earl of Plymouth, including addition of portico, 1815; reduced to a ruin *c.* 1890 [sketch-book, pp. 3, 5] (Neale's *Views of Seats* vi, 1823).

TARDEBIGGE PARSONAGE, WORCS., alterations for the 6th Earl of Plymouth, including bow-fronted sitting-room, 1815 [sketch-book, p. 12].

COOLMORE, CARRIGALINE, CO. CORK, lodge, etc. for W. H. Newenham, 1815 [sketch-book, pp. 23, 37, 96–99].

FAWSLEY PARK, NORTHANTS., alterations for Sir Charles Knightley, Bart., 1815–16 [sketch-book, p. 7; exhib. at R.A. 1816].

MIDDLETON STONEY RECTORY, OXON., for the 5th Earl of Jersey, 1816–17, Tudor Gothic, based on a design made for Lord Jersey by Henry Hakewill in 1812. The stables were added in 1819 to Cundy's design [sketch-book, pp. 120–3; *V.C.H. Oxon.* vi, 244].

WIMBORNE ST. GILES HOUSE, DORSET, alterations for the 6th Earl of Shaftesbury, 1816–20, probably including roof of the Stone Hall [R.C.H.M., *Dorset*, v, 95–6].

HANWORTH PARK (now Hotel), MIDDLESEX, Gothic lodges, 1817–18 (? executed) [sketch-book, pp. 116–19].

MONTREAL, nr. WESTERHAM, KENT, rustic cottage for the 2nd Lord (afterwards 1st Earl) Amherst, 1818 (? executed).

TOTTENHAM PARK, WILTS., stables for the 1st Marquess of Ailesbury, 1818–20 [sketch-book, pp. 110–11, designs dated 1818].

LONDON, NORTHUMBERLAND HOUSE, STRAND, new staircase and rebuilding of garden front for the 3rd Duke of Northumberland, 1818–24; dem. 1874 [plan by Cundy of new garden front in Evidence Room at Syon House, B. xv 2. g; *Survey of London* xviii, 17 and pls. 3(b) and 7(b); 'Historical Description of Northumberland House' at Alnwick Castle (C. xiii 1. g)].

SYON HOUSE, ISLEWORTH, MIDDLESEX. Cundy is stated in *D.N.B.* to have carried out works at Syon. As he was being employed at Northumberland House by the 3rd Duke of Northumberland in 1818–24, he was probably the architect responsible for casing the exterior of Syon House in Bath stone in 1819–26. This is supported by the existence in the Evidence Room at Syon of an unexecuted design by Cundy dated 1824 for altering the north side of the house (B. xiii 2. u).

ALTHORP HOUSE, NORTHANTS., THE 'GOTHIC LIBRARY', for the 2nd Earl Spencer, 1819–20; dem. 1853 [drawings and correspondence at Althorp].

GARBALLY PARK, BALLINASLOE, CO. GALWAY, for the 2nd Earl of Clancarty, *c.* 1819 [Northumberland County Record Office ZM1 s. 76/27/44: letter from Lord Clancarty dated 7 July 1819: 'I hear from Garbally that my buildings are proceeding apace; indeed some complaints have reached me that their construction goes

on even more rapidly than Mr. Cundy's designs'].

TOTTENHAM PARK, WILTS., enlarged and remodelled for the 1st Marquess of Ailesbury, *c.* 1823–6 [Lord Cardigan, *The Wardens of Savernake Forest*, 1949, 296; drawings in Ailesbury family archives].

HAWSTEAD PLACE, SUFFOLK, alterations and additions (chiefly to offices) for Philip Metcalfe (d. 1818), date unknown; dem. [sketch-book, p. 13].

BAYHAM ABBEY, SUSSEX, lodge for the 1st Marquess Camden, date uncertain [sketch-book, pp. 100–101].

Note: The additions and alterations designed by Cundy for STANLEY HALL, SALOP., and BURTON HALL, LINCS., were not carried out.

CUNDY, THOMAS, junior (1790–1867), was the eldest son of Thomas Cundy, senior (*q.v.*). As a young man he worked in his father's office, and with him visited Rome in 1816. After his father's death in 1825 he succeeded to his practice and to his position as surveyor of the Grosvenor estate in London. He held this position for forty-one years, in the course of which Belgravia and Pimlico were transformed into a fashionable residential area, largely owing to the speculative enterprise of Thomas Cubitt (*q.v.*).

The two Cundys appear to have formed a single architectural firm, so that until the father's death in 1825 it is impossible to distinguish the son's contribution to the partnership. Though it records works carried out by the elder Cundy as early as 1795, the sketch-book in the R.I.B.A. Collection bears the signature of 'Thomas Cundy junior', and was apparently his work. It may be added that views of BESSINGBY HALL (1807), WYTHAM ABBEY (1809–10) and HAWARDEN CASTLE (1809–10) were exhibited at the Royal Academy under his name, though at the time he was still only in his teens. According to the information supplied to the *D.N.B.* by his son Thomas Cundy III, he was responsible for the works at TOTTENHAM PARK (*c.* 1823–6) listed above, and also for alterations to MOOR PARK, HERTS., for his employer the 1st Marquess of Westminster (*c.* 1830), and for the addition to GROSVENOR HOUSE, UPPER GROSVENOR STREET, LONDON (dem. 1927), first of the picture gallery (1825–7) and then of the Doric entrance-screen (1842–3), both for the same nobleman. A number of Cundy's drawings for Grosvenor House are in the collection of Mr. Paul Mellon; see also John Cornforth in *C. Life*, 15 Nov. 1973. Another work for which he rather than his father was presumably responsible, since it was built in 1826, the year after the elder Cundy's death, was the tower of NORMANTON CHURCH, RUTLAND. This unusual and effective design was copied from a baroque source, the towers of Archer's church of St. John, Smith

Square, with which Cundy must have been very familiar [drawings in parish chest in 1947].

From the late 1840s onwards Cundy was assisted by his third son Thomas (1820–95), who eventually succeeded to his practice and surveyorship. The younger Cundy had some share in the design of most of the Gothic churches built by his father, namely ST. PAUL, WILTON PLACE, KNIGHTSBRIDGE, 1840–3; HOLY TRINITY, PADDINGTON, 1844–6, dem. 1972; ST. MICHAEL, CHESTER SQUARE, 1844; ST. MARK, HAMILTON TERRACE (ST. JOHN'S WOOD), 1846–7; ST. BARNABAS, PIMLICO, 1847–50; ST. GABRIEL, WARWICK SQUARE, 1851–3; and ST. SAVIOUR, PIMLICO, 1864. The earlier churches were pre-Puginesque in character: St. Mark's, Hamilton Terrace, was, in Goodhart-Rendel's words, no more than 'a large broad Gothic riding-school'. By 1847, however, the Cundys had produced in St. Barnabas, Pimlico, what the St. Paul's Ecclesiological Society regarded as 'the most sumptuous and correctly fitted church erected in England since the Reformation'.

Towards the end of his life Cundy retired to Bromley in Kent. He died on 15 July 1867, aged 77. [D.N.B.; obituary in Builder xxv, 1867, 607; Building News, 30 Aug. 1867, 598.]

CUNNINGHAM, JOHN (1799–1873), was the son of a builder at Leitholm in Berwickshire. He was at first apprenticed to his father and then became a pupil of Thomas Brown, the Superintendent of City Works at Edinburgh. After practising for a few years in Edinburgh he married in 1833 and emigrated to New York. But the climate did not suit him, and he returned to Britain in 1834. He now settled in Liverpool, where from 1835 to 1840 he was in partnership with A. H. Holme (q.v.). Here he built up an extensive practice as an architect and waterworks engineer. His interest in geology led to his election as a Fellow of the Geological Society, to whose proceedings he contributed several papers. In the summer of 1873 he retired to Edinburgh, where he died on 2 October of that year.

Cunningham's principal works were THE COURT HOUSE, GREENLAW, BERWICKSHIRE, 1829–31; in LIVERPOOL, THE APOTHECARIES' HALL, COLQUITT STREET (with Holme), c. 1837, dem. 1941, ST. PETER'S (SCOTCH) CHURCH, 1842–3, dem. c. 1930, THE ORPHANS' ASYLUM, 1843–54, dem. c. 1936, THE SAILORS' HOME, 1846–8, Jacobethan, dem. 1974, THE PHILHARMONIC HALL, 1846–9, destroyed by fire c. 1930, and the UNION and COMMERCIAL BANKS, the latter demolished, the former now the Halifax Building Society's offices; THE RIPLEY HOSPITAL (ORPHANAGE), nr. LANCASTER, 1856–64, Gothic (now a school); ARROWE HALL, WOODCHURCH, CHESHIRE, for J. R. Shaw, c. 1840, Jacobethan; HAREFIELD HOUSE (now UPTON MANOR), UPTON, nr. BIRKENHEAD, for William In-

man, 1857, Italianate; BACKFORD HALL, CHESHIRE, for E. H. Glegg, 1863, Jacobethan; the original station and other buildings at CREWE, CHESHIRE; THE BURTON AND UTTOXETER BANK, BURTON-ON-TRENT, STAFFS.; and churches at BIRKENHEAD, CHESHIRE, HOLY TRINITY (with Holme), 1837–40, Romanesque, AIGBURTH, LIVERPOOL, ST. ANNE'S (with Holme), 1837, Romanesque, MORETON (WALLASEY), CHESHIRE, 1862–3, Gothic, and UPTON, nr. BIRKENHEAD, CHESHIRE, 1868, Gothic.

Cunningham's first considerable work, the Court House at Greenlaw, is a handsome building in the Scottish Greek Revival tradition. It is less easy to commend his later works. His Romanesque churches were considered 'laughable' by the Ecclesiologist and 'bizarre' by Professor Pevsner. Comments on his Gothic churches and Jacobethan houses are equally unenthusiastic. But his Sailors' Home at Liverpool was a striking if eccentric building of considerable character, and his Philharmonic Hall was regarded by Picton as 'one of the most successful of the kind ever erected'. Cunningham himself considered it 'joost perfect'.

[Obituary in Builder xxxi, 1873, 821; The Architects, Engineers and Building Trades Directory, 1868, 107 (with list of works); J. A. Picton, Memorials of Liverpool ii, 1875, 23, 145, 229, 251, 328; The Architectural Magazine, ed. Loudon, iv, 402, 486; information from Mr. S. A. Harris.]

CUNNINGTON, JOHN, was a builder of Spalding in Lincolnshire. In about 1813 he built five terrace houses in LONDON ROAD, SPALDING, followed by eleven more some years later. These were probably the late Georgian houses in WELLAND TERRACE [R. Harmstone, Notices of Remarkable Events connected with Spalding, 1846, 41]. In 1820 he designed and built a church at WHAPLODE DROVE, LINCS., which proved to be unsafe, and had to be rebuilt the following year by J. Pacey and W. Swansborough [I.C.B.S.].

CUSTANCE, WILLIAM, was a surveyor and builder of Chesterton, nr. Cambridge. He made a plan of Cambridge, based on that of Loggan (1688), but brought up to date, which was engraved in 1798. He probably designed and built two attractive villas in Cambridge named PEMBERTON'S GROVE LODGE and THE GROVE. The latter is dated 1814 and the rainwater heads have the initials W.C. [R.C.H.M., Cambridge, cxxix, 347, 354 and pl. 299].

CUSWORTH, JOSEPH, was a pupil of Thomas Johnson of Leeds. He afterwards had five years' experience in the office of Peter Atkinson & Matthew Phillips at York. [F. Beckwith, Thomas Taylor, Thoresby Society 1949, 89]. He practised in Leeds from about 1815 until after

1840. He enlarged CHAPEL ALLERTON CHURCH, YORKS. (W.R.), in 1819 [Borthwick Institute, York, Fac. 1819/1].

D

DADFORD, THOMAS, was a canal engineer whose address is at different times given as Wordesley, nr. Stourbridge, Worcs. (1776), Cobridge, Staffs. (1780), and Wolverhampton (1800). He was elected to membership of the Smeatonian Society of Civil Engineers in 1783 [*Trans. Newcomen Society* xliv, 1971–2, 36]. He was evidently a Roman Catholic, for in 1780 he contributed towards the cost of building the Catholic ST. PETER'S CHAPEL at COBRIDGE, dem. 1936 [*Catholic Mag.* v, 1834, 429], for which he may have provided the designs, and in 1800–1 he designed a chapel for the R.C. SCHOOL at SEDGLEY PARK, nr. WOLVERHAMPTON, STAFFS. [F. C. Husenbeth, *History of Sedgley Park School*, 1856, 62; Bryan Little, *Catholic Churches since 1623*, 1966, 53].

DANCE, GEORGE, senior (1695–1768), was the son of Giles Dance, a mason of London and a member of the Merchant Taylors' Company. Besides building work, Giles executed monumental sculpture, an example of which can be seen in the church of Wotton-under-Edge, Glos. (monument to Richard Dawes, d. 1712). He died in 1751. In his will he is described as being in partnership with his son, and in the 1720s 'Messrs. Dance & Co.' carried out masonry at South Sea House worth over £700. George Dance was born in London in 1695, and was made free of the Merchant Taylors' Company on 2 June 1725, being described as a 'stonecutter of Moorfields'. In 1719 he had married Elizabeth, daughter of the surveyor James Gould (*q.v.*), and was living in Chiswell Street. In 1725–8 he probably collaborated with his father-in-law in designing and building the church of St. Botolph, Bishopsgate. In 1735 Dance succeeded the negligent George Smith as Clerk of the Works to the City of London and surveyor of the Bridge House estate. The post, though not then salaried, gave its holder a virtual monopoly of the City's architectural work, together with the appropriate fees, and it was Dance's official position, as much as any other qualifications, that in 1737 led to the acceptance of his designs for the Mansion House in preference to those of Gibbs, James and Leoni. To provide a building of sufficient consequence on an awkwardly constricted site was a difficult task, and it cannot be said that Dance was wholly successful in solving the problem. Externally the result was 'cramped and overdressed' (Summerson), but the interior was more successful and the

248

'Egyptian Hall' is not without grandeur. Dance's other buildings are respectable but unremarkable Georgian performances in which the influences of Wren, Gibbs and contemporary Palladianism can all be detected. Of these, the church of St. Leonard's, Shoreditch, with a steeple derived from St. Mary-le-Bow, is the most ambitious.

Dance's 'diligence and integrity' as Clerk of the City's Works was rewarded in 1746 by a regular salary of £50 p.a. in addition to his fees. Early in 1768, within a few days of his death on 11 February, he resigned his office in favour of his youngest son George (*q.v.*). He was buried in the church of St. Luke's Old Street on which he had worked as a mason forty years earlier. His eldest son James (1722–74) proved to be indolent and irresponsible, but eventually had some success as an actor under the name of Love. His third son was Sir Nathaniel Dance (afterwards Dance-Holland), R.A. (1735–1811).

A portrait of Dance in his sixties by Francis Hayman is in the Fitzwilliam Museum at Cambridge (reproduced by Stroud, pl. 1). A later portrait by Nathaniel Dance hangs in the Mansion House, to which it was presented by Viscount Bearsted in 1934 (reproduced by S. Perks, *History of the Mansion House*, frontispiece). A number of his drawings for the Mansion House and other buildings are in Sir John Soane's Museum.

[*A.P.S.D.*; *D.N.B.*; Dorothy Stroud, *George Dance, Architect, 1741–1825*, 1971, chaps. 1–2; *George Dance the elder and younger*, catalogue of exhibition at the Geffrye Museum, Shoreditch, 1972.]

For a list of minor and unexecuted works see Stroud, Appendix ii.

LONDON

THE FLEET MARKET, 1734–7; dem. 1829 [A Stratton, 'Two Forgotten Buildings by the Dances', *Arch. Rev.* xl, 1916, 21].

ST. LEONARD'S CHURCH, SHOREDITCH, 1736–40; galleries removed 1857; altered 1870; restored 1938; damaged 1944 [H. Ellis, *History of the Church of St. Leonard, Shoreditch*, 1798, 9].

SKINNERS' HALL, DOWGATE HILL, decoration of staircase, etc., 1737 [J. F. Wadmore, *Account of the Skinners' Company*, 1902, 133].

THE MANSION HOUSE, 1739–42. For the alterations by George Dance, junior, in 1795–6, including the removal of the attic over the Egyptian Hall, see below, p. 251. The attic over the ballroom was removed in 1842 [*Vitruvius Britannicus* iv, pls. 41–4; S. Perks, *The History of the Mansion House*, 1922].

ST. BOTOLPH'S CHURCH, ALDGATE, 1741–4; altered internally by J. F. Bentley 1888–91 [G. Godwin, *The Churches of London* ii, 1839; drawings in Soane Museum].

ST. MATTHEW'S CHURCH, BETHNAL GREEN, 1743–
6; interior remodelled 1859–61 after a fire,
when upper stage was added to tower; repaired
1953 after war-damage, when upper stage to
tower was removed [drawings in Soane
Museum].

LAMB'S CONDUIT, HOLBORN, rebuilt 1746; dem.
[Stroud, 43–4].

THE CORN MARKET, MARK LANE, 1747–50;
extended 1853; dem. 1881 [Stroud, 42; *Builder*
xi, 1853, 340].

COWPER'S COURT, SMITHFIELD, TOM'S COFFEE-
HOUSE, THE RAINBOW COFFEE-HOUSE, and two
dwelling-houses, for the 2nd Earl Cowper,
1748; dem. [plan and elevation in Herts.
County Record Office, 1/20029].

THE SURGEONS' HALL, OLD BAILEY, *c*. 1748–51;
dem. [Stroud, 41–2].

ST. LUKE'S HOSPITAL, OLD STREET, 1750–1; rebuilt
1782 [Stroud, 49–50].

LONDON BRIDGE, removal of houses, replacement
of two central arches by a single arch, and erection of balustrades and parapets, in collaboration with Sir Robert Taylor, 1756–66; dem.
1831 [Stroud, 52].

THE GREAT SYNAGOGUE, DUKE'S PLACE, ALDGATE,
enlarged 1765–6; dem. 1790 [Stroud, 77–8].

ELSEWHERE

COLERAINE, CO. LONDONDERRY, MARKET HOUSE, *c*.
1740–3; dem. 1857 [R. Smith, *The Irish
Society 1613–1963*, 1966, 82].

CANTERBURY CATHEDRAL, KENT, rebuilt gable of
south-east transept, 1751; again rebuilt *c*. 1825
[C. E. Woodruff & W. Danks, *Memorials of
Canterbury Cathedral*, 1912, 349].

FAVERSHAM CHURCH, KENT, rebuilt nave, 1754–5
[Stroud, 50–1].

DANCE, GEORGE, junior (1741–1825), was
the fifth and youngest son of George Dance,
senior (*q.v.*). At the age of 17 he went to Italy
at his father's expense, sailing from Gravesend
in December 1758, and eventually arriving in
Rome the following May with his elder brother
Nathaniel, whom he had joined in Florence.
When he returned to England in December 1764
George had had six years' architectural training
in Italy in the course of which he had not only
learned to draw very competently but had also
absorbed the principles of the new neo-classicism. These are already evident in the design for
'a Public Gallery for Statues, Pictures, etc.', with
which he won the gold medal at Parma in 1763.
He had also been admitted to the Academy of St.
Luke at Rome and had become a member of the
Society of Arcadia, a fashionable body of Italian
intellectuals.

In England Dance almost immediately obtained a commission for a city church (All Hallows, London Wall) which demonstrated his
ability as a practical architect, and in 1768 he succeeded his father as Clerk of the City Works. This
post brought him a steady flow of routine municipal work, but it also gave him the opportunity
to design his most famous building, Newgate Prison. As city architect he was also actively engaged
in a number of important town-planning
schemes, and for nearly fifty years exercised an
enlightened supervision over the growth and
redevelopment of the City. Besides the schemes
for which he was directly responsible (by no
means all of which came to fruition) he effected
many minor improvements which cumulatively
did much to modify the medieval street plan of
London. The first developments for which he
was personally responsible were America Square,
Minories, and its adjoining Crescent and Circus
(1768), and Finsbury Square (1777) and Finsbury Circus (designed 1802, but not carried out
until *c*. 1814). He also planned Skinner Street,
Holborn (1790), Pickett Street, Strand (1793),
and Alfred Place, off Tottenham Court Road
(1802–10). In 1785 he provided James Hedger,
the lessee of the Bridge House property in St.
George's Field's, Southwark, with a design for
a huge crescent to be built there and named in
honour of John Howard, the prison reformer.
This was published in the *Gentleman's Magazine*
(Sept. 1786), but the development was vetoed by
the landlords, and nothing was done until the
expiration of Hedger's lease in 1810. In anticipation of this Dance was instructed in 1807 to prepare plans for laying out the property for the
Bridge House Committee, and produced two
schemes for a series of crescents, circles and poly-
gons filling the spaces between the roads laid out
by Robert Mylne on the aproaches to Blackfriars
Bridge. For various reasons very little of Dance's
plan materialized, but the buildings round St.
George's Circus were erected in accordance with
his directions. In about 1790 he made designs for
the 1st Earl Camden for the layout of the
Camden estate in Kentish Town, but after the
building of Camden High Street this degenerated
into haphazard development. A recurrent feature
of Dance's town-planning schemes is the circus
and crescent layouts which he transplanted from
John Wood's Bath, and which subsequently
became a commonplace of London's building development in the late eighteenth and early nineteenth centuries. From 1796 onwards he prepared a series of bold and imaginative designs for
the improvement of the Port of London with new
docks and warehouses and, in place of the old and
narrow London Bridge, two parallel bridges with
a drawbridge in each, to enable traffic to cross on
one while the drawbridge was raised in the other
to give passage to ships. These schemes, illus-

trated in an appendix to the *Report of the Select Committee upon the Improvement of the Port of London* (*Parliamentary Reports* xiv, 1803, 574–6), found realization only as the subject of a fine engraving by William Daniell (1802), but the simple, monumental character of the warehouses envisaged by Dance was not without influence on the design of those subsequently built by Alexander and others. With Sir Robert Taylor, Dance was responsible for drafting the Building Act of 1774, which so largely determined the character of London Street architecture for the next seventy years, and in 1815, when improvements in the City gaols were contemplated, he visited a number of prisons throughout the country, publishing in 1816 a *Report on Inspection, with a Committee of Aldermen, of Several Gaols of this Kingdom.*

In 1768 Dance was one of the original members of the newly founded Royal Academy. In 1798 he was elected Professor of Architecture, but failed to deliver any of the statutory lectures and resigned in 1806. He was also a Fellow of the Royal Society and of the Society of Antiquaries, and a member of the Architects' Club. In 1794 he was Master of the Merchant Taylors' Company, of which his father and grandfather had both been Freemen. Architecture was by no means Dance's only interest. He played well on the violin, flute and 'cello, and in later life spent much of his time making skilful but rather stereotyped pencil portraits of his contemporaries. Seventy-two of these were engraved by Daniell and published in two volumes in 1808–14 as *A Collection of Portraits sketched from the Life since the Year 1793*, but a further eighty-four prints were made and remain in proof in the British Museum, together with the original drawings. Portraits of fifty-three Royal Academicians by Dance are in the possession of the Royal Academy. For both collections see W. Roberts, 'Portraits by George Dance' in *Notes and Queries*, 9th ser. iv, 1899, 1–3.

Sir John Soane was Dance's principal pupil. James Peacock was his assistant for many years, and William Mountague was his clerk. When Peacock died in 1814, Mountague took his place as assistant Clerk of the City Works, and when Dance himself retired in 1815, Mountague succeeded him. Dance died at his house in Gower Street on 14 January 1825, and was buried in St. Paul's Cathedral. A portrait by Sir Thomas Lawrence is in the Guildhall Art Gallery and there is an engraved portrait by S. W. Reynolds (1820) after J. Jackson. A self-portrait is reproduced by Stroud (frontispiece). A bust by Rossi was in the possession of the Poynder family (descendants of one of Dance's nieces) in the nineteenth century. There is a plaster version of it in Sir John Soane's Museum.

It is as a pioneer of neo-classicism that the younger Dance has his place in English architectural history. In All Hallows, London Wall (1765–7), he showed how elegantly and effectively a classical order could be simplified in accordance with the precepts of the Abbé Laugier. Already in the '70s he was experimenting with those pendentive vaults which were later to form so characteristic a feature of Soane's personal style. In some of his later works (notably Coleorton and Ashburnham Place) he attempted a curious stripped Gothic style which is more interesting than beautiful, but which (in the age of Wyatt and Nash) amply demonstrates his original and independent approach to architectural design. In Newgate Prison he designed a monumental building of the first rank. In spirit its forbidding walls, unbroken save for blind niches and chain-festooned doorways, were evocative of the *Invenzioni di Carceri* of Piranesi (whom Dance had in fact met in Rome). But Piranesi's fantastic interiors afforded no guidance to the designer of a real prison in which the architectural expression must necessarily be concentrated in the exterior, and here Dance combined themes from Palladio and Giulio Romano to create a façade that forcibly expressed the drama of retributive justice. The result, in contemporary opinion, was a building whose 'nobleness and grandeur approaches the true sublime in architecture'.

There is a large collection of Dance's drawings in Sir John Soane's Museum. This relates chiefly to his private practice. Drawings made by him and his assistants for the City of London's works are in the City Record Office. A copy of Leoni's edition of Palladio in the R.I.B.A. Collection contains a number of architectural sketches by Dance (see the *Catalogue*). Dance's library was sold in 1837. The catalogue is printed in *Sale Catalogues of Libraries of Eminent Persons* iv, ed. Watkin, 1972, 193–216.

[*Gent's Mag.* 1825 (i), 184–5; S. Angell, 'Sketch of the Professional Life of George Dance', *Builder* v, 1847, 333; *A.P.S.D.*; *D.N.B.*; J. Nichols, *Literary Anecdotes* ix, 1815, 522–3; The Farington Diary, *passim*; Sir R. Blomfield, 'The Architect of Newgate', in *Studies in Architecture*, 1905; Helen Rosenau, 'George Dance the Younger', *R.I.B.A. Jnl.*, 3rd ser., liv, Aug. 1947, 502–7; John Summerson, *Heavenly Mansions*, 1949, 103–5 (on Dance's town-planning); M. Hugo-Brunt, 'George Dance as Town-Planner', *Jnl. of the Society of Architectural Historians* (of America), xiv, 1955, 13–22; *Survey of London* xxv (*St. George's Fields*), chap. 6; Dorothy Stroud, *George Dance, Architect, 1741–1825*, 1971; *George Dance the elder and younger*, catalogue of exhibition at the Geffrye Museum, Shoreditch, 1972; Georges Teyssot, *Città e utopia nell' illuminismo inglese: George Dance il giovane*, Rome 1974.]

PUBLIC BUILDINGS IN LONDON

ALL HALLOWS CHURCH, LONDON WALL, 1765–7 [Stroud, 74–77, citing minutes now in Guildhall Library].

WHITECROSS STREET, Coach Houses and Stables for Lord Mayor and City Officers, 1769–71; dem. [Stroud, 87].

SESSIONS HOUSE, OLD BAILEY, 1769–74; dem. 1902 [Stroud, 100–3].

NEWGATE PRISON, 1770–80; damaged in Gordon Riots 1780 and repaired with alterations 1780–4; altered internally 1835 and 1858; dem. 1902 [Stroud, chap. 5; 'Newgate Gaol: Catalogue of Drawings in Sir John Soane's Museum', *Architectural History* ii, 1959] (Britton & Pugin, *The Public Buildings of London* ii, 1828, 54–66; A. E. Richardson, *Monumental Classic Architecture in Great Britain*, 1914, 29].

BRIDGE HOUSE, SOUTHWARK, alterations including new muniment room, 1771–2; dem. [City Records *ex inf*. Mr. H. D. Kalman].

MANSION HOUSE, added small portico to west door, 1775 (removed 1845); roofing over of cortile, removal of Grand Staircase and lowering roof of Egyptian Hall, 1795–6. The plain coffered ceiling inserted in the Egyptian Hall by Dance was enriched by J. B. Bunning in the 1840s [S. Perks, *History of the Mansion House*, 1922, 195–8].

GUILDHALL, new COMMON COUNCIL CHAMBER, 1777–8 (dem. 1908); CHAMBERLAIN'S COURT and OFFICES, 1787–9 (dem. 1882); rebuilt south façade in quasi-oriental style 1788–9; Justice Rooms on west side of Guildhall Yard 1795–7 (dem. 1969); fitted up banqueting hall for entertainment of the allied sovereigns 1814 (see *Gent's Mag.* 1814 (ii), 179, and the painting by Daniell in the Guildhall Art Gallery) [Stroud, chap. 6 and pp. 219–20].

ST. LUKE'S HOSPITAL, OLD STREET, 1782–9; converted into Bank of England Printing Works 1917–20; dem. *c*. 1955–60 [Stroud, 141–2].

SOUTHWARK, THE BOROUGH COMPTER (Debtors' Prison), TOOLEY STREET, 1785–7; dem. 1855 [Stroud, 108–9].

THE GILTSPUR STREET COMPTER (Debtors' Prison), 1787–91; dem. 1855 [Stroud, 109–10; A. Stratton, 'Two Forgotten Buildings by the Dances', *Arch. Rev.* xl, 1916, 23].

HONEY LANE MARKET, 1788–9; dem. [Stroud, 147–8].

THE SHAKESPEARE GALLERY, NO. 52 PALL MALL, for Alderman John Boydell, 1788–9; from 1805 the British Institution; dem. 1868–9 [A. Stratton, 'Boydell's Shakespeare Gallery', *Arch. Rev.* xli, 1917, 49; *Survey of London* xxix, 335–7; Stroud, 160–2].

ST. BARTHOLOMEW-THE-LESS CHURCH, SMITHFIELD, rebuilt in timber with an octagonal nave, retaining medieval tower, 1789–90, Gothic;

rebuilt in stone by Thomas Hardwick, 1823–5, following Dance's plan [Stroud, 158–9].

ST. BARTHOLOMEW'S HOSPITAL, Surgeons' Theatre and other buildings, 1791–6; dem. [Stroud, 157].

MARTIN'S BANK, NO. 68 LOMBARD STREET, 1793–5; dem. 1930 [Stroud, 159–60].

LEADENHALL MARKET, alterations, *c*. 1795; dem. [Stroud, 149].

SOUTHWARK, COURT HOUSE, TOOLEY STREET, reconstruction of façade, 1796; dem. [Stroud, 109].

BILLINGSGATE MARKET HOUSE, 1798; dem. [Stroud, 149].

BRIDGE HOUSE YARD, WAREHOUSES, 1802–4; dem. [P.R.O., MR 80 (elevation); information from Mr. H. D. Kalman].

ROYAL COLLEGE OF SURGEONS, LINCOLN'S INN FIELDS, in collaboration with James Lewis, 1806–13; rebuilt 1835–7 by Sir Charles Barry, who retained the portico but fluted the columns [Stroud, 193–5].

PUBLIC BUILDINGS ELSEWHERE

BATH, THE THEATRE ROYAL, BEAUFORD SQUARE, elevation and interior of auditorium, 1804–5, for John Palmer, who was responsible for the remainder; interior rebuilt after fire in 1862 [W. Ison, *Georgian Buildings of Bath*, 1948, 102–4; Stroud, 205–6].

MICHELDEVER CHURCH, HANTS., rebuilt nave at expense of Sir Francis Baring, Bart., 1808–10, Gothic; altered 1881 [Winchester Diocesan records, Faculty papers; drawings in Soane Museum].

EAST STRATTON CHURCH, HANTS., wholly or partly rebuilt at expense of Sir Francis Baring, Bart., 1810, Gothic; dem. 1885 [Winchester Diocesan records, Faculty papers: 'according to designs by Sir Francis Baring's architect'; drawings in Soane Museum].

COUNTRY HOUSES

PITZHANGER MANOR, EALING, MIDDLESEX, additions for Thomas Gurnell, 1768; remodelled by Sir John Soane 1800–2; now Ealing Public Library [Stroud, 87–9 and pls. 20–1].

unidentified house for — Webb, 1772 [Stroud, 92 and pl. 27a].

CRANBURY PARK, HANTS., remodelled principal rooms for Thomas Dummer, *c*. 1780 [Stroud, 93–5 and pls. 23–6] (*C. Life*, 25 Oct., 8–15 Nov. 1956).

CAMDEN PLACE, CHISLEHURST, KENT (now Golf Club House), alterations for the 1st Earl Camden, 1788 [J. Newman, *West Kent* (The Buildings of England), 1969, 213]; further alterations for Thomson Bonar, 1807 [Stroud, 211].

LANGDOWN HOUSE, HYTHE, HANTS., designs (perhaps not executed) for George Tate, soon after 1790; dem. 1961 [Stroud, 239].

BOWOOD HOUSE, WILTS., minor alterations for the 1st Marquess of Lansdowne, c. 1795; dem. [Stroud, 164].

PAUL, CORNWALL, house designed for (Sir) Rose Price, 1797, but abandoned after foundations had been laid, when Price purchased an existing house at Trengwainton instead [Stroud, 245 and pl. 76b; D. Gilbert, *Parochial History of Cornwall* iii, 1838, 289].

WILDERNESS (now DORTON HOUSE), nr. SEVENOAKS, KENT, alterations, probably for the 2nd Earl Camden, c. 1800; remodelled 1855 [Stroud, 245].

STRATTON PARK, HANTS., remodelled for Sir Francis Baring, Bart., 1803–6; dem. (except portico) 1960 [Stroud, 200–3 and pls. 64–5].

COLEORTON HALL, LEICS., for Sir George Beaumont, Bart., 1804–8, Gothic; upper storey added by F. P. Cockerell 1862 [inscription on roof of porch; D. Stroud, 'George Dance and Cole Orton House', in *The Country Seat*, ed. Colvin & Harris, 1970].

LAXTON HALL, NORTHANTS., entrance hall for George Freke Evans, c. 1812 [Neale, *Views of Seats*, 2nd ser., i; Stroud, 216].

ASHBURNHAM PLACE, SUSSEX, extensive alterations and additions for the 3rd Earl of Ashburnham, 1813–17, externally Gothic; refaced in red brick 1853; dem. 1959; also bridge in park [Stroud, 216–19] (*C. Life*, 16, 23 and 30 April 1953).

KIDBROOKE PARK, nr. EAST GRINSTEAD, SUSSEX, rebuilt south front, with colonnade, for Charles Abbot (later Lord Colchester), 1815 [Abbot's diaries for 1814–15 in P.R.O., Gifts and Deposits, 30/9/35].

DOMESTIC ARCHITECTURE IN LONDON

LANSDOWNE HOUSE, BERKELEY SQUARE, alterations for the 1st Marquess of Lansdowne, 1788–91, including library (remodelled by Smirke as a gallery 1816–19); dem. [Stroud, 163–5].

ST. GEORGE-IN-THE-EAST RECTORY, alterations for the Rev. Robert Farington, 1802–4 [Stroud, 206].

HILL STREET, MAYFAIR, NO. 33, alterations to Sir Francis Baring's house, 1803; dem. [Stroud, 204].

PICCADILLY, NO. 143, for Sir Nathaniel Dance-Holland, 1807–9 [Stroud, 210–11].

MONUMENTS

PUTNEY COMMON, obelisk to commemorate the invention of David Hartley's fire-plates, 1788 [Stroud, 241].

WESTMINSTER ABBEY CLOISTER, tablet to Scipio

and Alexander Duroure, 1766 [signed] (Stroud, pl. 15).

KEW CHURCH, SURREY, monument to Jeremiah Meyer, R.A., 1790 [signed drawing in B.M. Print Room, reproduced in Geffrye Museum Catalogue, 381.

UNEXECUTED WORKS

For doubtful and unexecuted works see Stroud, 238–45. Dance's designs for LOWTHER CASTLE, WESTMORLAND (1803), are in the Cumberland and Westmorland Record Office at Carlisle. They do not resemble the sketches illustrated by Stroud (pl. 71c), and it is doubtful whether the latter are connected with Lowther.

Dance's design for the Bedford Charity School (Stroud, p. 238) was not carried out.

DANCE, THOMAS (–1733), is described in his obituary in the *London Magazine* of 1733 as 'an eminent Surveyor and Master-Builder, who built Guy's Hospital in Southwark'. The Minute Books of the Hospital show that on 14 April 1725 it was 'Resolved that Mr. Dance be continued in the employment of Surveyor of the Buildings necessary to this Hospital on the same conditions and with the same salary of Fifteen Guineas per Quarter as was agreed on with him in the Lifetime of Thomas Guy Esq.' The central building (1722–5) which he designed still exists, but was refronted in stone in 1777–8. The east wing was added in 1738–9 by James Steer, the west wing in 1774–7 by R. Jupp (see *Survey of London* xx, 1950, 37–8, where, however, Dance's name is wrongly given as 'Lane' – an error due to a misprint in *Gent's Mag.* 1733, 439). In his will, dated 8 December 1732, Dance is described as living in the parish of St. Paul, Covent Garden, and as being a plasterer by trade. He left considerable property, and made many charitable bequests. He mentions his brothers Richard, William and Joseph, and his nephew Richard Dance, but there is no indication that he was related to Giles Dance (d. 1751) or to his son George [S. Perks, *The History of the Mansion House*, 1922, 218; R. A. Cawson & T. H. E. Orde, 'The Design and Building of Mr. Guy's Hospital', *Guy's Hospital Reports*, vol. 118, 1969, 223–6]. On 21 December 1725 the *Daily Post* reported that 'a fine large Square, to be call'd Leman Square, is to be built in Goodman's Fields [Whitechapel], after a plan drawn by Mr. Dance of Covent Garden', but nothing came of this project. For Thomas Dance's connections with the Pulteney estate in Westminster see *Survey of London* xxxi, 9.

DANGERFIELD, EDWIN J—, was presumably the 'J. Dangerfield' who exhibited student's drawings at the Royal Academy in 1808 and 1809. He was then a pupil of either George or Lewis

Wyatt, giving their Albany office as his address. In the 1830s he was practising in London as an architect and surveyor. His only known work is the clumsy Greek Revival CLOCK TOWER on the promenade at HERNE BAY, KENT, 1837, which bears the signature 'Edwin J. Dangerfield' (J. M. Crook, *The Greek Revival*, 1972, pl. 213).

DARLEY, JAMES (–1822), was employed as clerk of the works at CHARLTON HOUSE, WILTS., during the alterations by Matthew Brettingham in 1772–6. An inscription on the roof mentions 'the careful superintendence of James Darley Clerk of the Works'. In 1788 he made an estimate for the repair of MALMESBURY ABBEY CHURCH, WILTS., [*Trans. Royal Historical Soc.* x, 1882, 49]. He died at Hullavington, Wilts., in 1822, leaving all his books and architectural drawings to his son John Darley [information from Mr. R. C. Hatchwell]. John Darley practised as an architect, surveyor and land agent in Chippenham. Documents in the author's possession show that he was concerned in alterations to BOX CHURCH, WILTS., in 1824. 'John Darley and Sons (R. & J. Darley)' of High Street, Chippenham, are listed as architects in the *Architects, Engineers and Building Trades Directory* of 1868.

DARLY, MATHIAS, 'Professor and Teacher of Ornament', exhibited at the Society of Arts between 1765 and 1770, and at the Free Society of Artists in 1771, showing chiefly designs for vases, etc. He published *The Ornamental Architect, or Young Artist's Instructor, consisting of the Five Orders drawn with their Embellishments by Various Masters*, 1770, and *A Compleat Body of Architecture: wherein the Five Orders are exactly described in many Elegant Examples, Compiled, Drawn, and Engraved by Mathias Darly*, 1773.

DAUNEY, WILLIAM, was a native of Aberdeen, but spent some time in Jamaica, where he practised as an architect. He returned to Aberdeen in later life and lived in Marischal Street. Archibald Simpson (*q.v.*) was his nephew. [G. M. Fraser, 'Archibald Simpson, Architect, and his Times', *Aberdeen Weekly Jnl.*, 19 April 1918].

DAVIES, JOHN (–1865), was a pupil of George Maddox [*A.P.S.D., s.v.* 'Maddox']. He began to exhibit at the Royal Academy in 1819, and travelled in Italy in 1820–1 in company with a friend called Samuel Paterson. He subsequently practised from an office in the City and became a Fellow of the R.I.B.A. In 1858 he made a second visit to Italy. He died at Grove Hill, Woodford, Essex, on 30 April 1865 [Principal Probate Registry]. He was District Surveyor for Tower Hamlets from 1839 until his death.

Davies was a very competent architectural draughtsman. In 1821 the Italian engraver Ros-

sini made a fine etching of the temples at Paestum from a drawing by Davies, and several of the plates in the *A.P.S. Dictionary* were from drawings provided by him. Examples of his draughtsmanship, and evidence of his foreign travels, were provided by the contents of an album sold at Sotheby's on 18 November 1971, and subsequently broken up. Davies was an able designer in the eclectic styles expected of an early nineteenth-century architect. His best works appear to have been Highbury College (Greek Ionic), the Synagogue in Great St. Helen's (with a rich classical interior) and the tower and rectory of St. Martin Orgar Church (in the style of Wren). In 1832 he won the second prize in the competition for Fishmongers' Hall.

HIGHBURY COLLEGE (for Dissenters), ISLINGTON, 1825–6 [exhib. at R.A. 1825] (J. Elmes, *Metropolitan Improvements*, 1829, 145 and plate).

SOUTHGATE, MIDDLESEX, ST. PAUL'S CHAPEL, WINCHMORE HILL, 1827–8, Gothic [exhib. at R.A. 1828].

NORTHAMPTON, THE COMMERCIAL STREET CONGREGATIONAL CHURCH, 1829 [letter-book preserved in the church, *ex. inf.* Mr. V. A. Hatley].

RICHMOND, SURREY, THE CONGREGATIONAL CHAPEL, 1830, 'Norman' [*Congregational Magazine*, Feb. 1833, 65–71; *Memoir of Thomas Wilson*, by his son, 1846, 417].

WEST WYCOMBE CHURCH, BUCKS., repairs, 1832 [I.C.B.S.].

STOCKWELL GRAMMAR SCHOOL, LAMBETH, 1833–4, Tudor Gothic [exhib. at R.A. 1833; *Companion to the Almanac*, 1835, 238–42, with illustrations].

THE GROVE, COOKHAM, BERKS., for W. H. Fleming, 1834 [exhib. at R.A. 1834].

BOSSINGTON HOUSE, HANTS., for J. M. Elwes, 1834, Tudor [exhib. at R.A. 1834].

BURE HOMAGE, MUDEFORD, HANTS., for Baroness de Feuchères, 1836; dem. 1956 [exhib. at R.A. 1836 by S. Gompertz as 'erecting from the designs and under the superintendence of Mr. J. Davies', but cf. Donthorne, W. J.].

LONDON, ST. SWITHIN'S LANE, offices for Solomon Rothschild, 1836 [*Architectural Mag.* iii, 1836, 40; exhib. at R.A. 1836].

LONDON, CORNHILL, MARINE INSURANCE OFFICE, 1837; dem. [*Civil Engineer and Architect's Jnl.* i, 29; exhib. at R.A. 1837].

LONDON, NEW SYNAGOGUE, GREAT ST. HELEN'S, BISHOPSGATE, 1837–8; dem. [*Companion to the Almanac*, 1839, 223; exhib. at R.A. 1837] (*A New Survey of London*, John Weale 1853, ii, 535, view of interior).

LONDON, CROSBY HALL, BISHOPSGATE, restoration of medieval hall and design of new buildings (dem.), *c.* 1837–40 [H. J. Hammon, *The Architectural Antiquities of Crosby Place, London*, 1844, 12–13].

LONDON, CAMDEN TOWN CONGREGATIONAL CHAPEL, 1843 [*Congregational Magazine*, 1843, 69 and frontispiece].

LONDON, ST. MARTIN ORGAR CHURCH, rebuilt tower, 1851–2[1] [P. Norman, *The London City Churches*, 1923, 29; exhib. at R.A. 1853].

LONDON, ST. MARTIN ORGAR RECTORY, ST. MARTIN'S LANE (E.C.), 1852 [exhib. at R.A. 1853].

LONDON, NO. 14 CANNON STREET, façade for Messrs. Fisher, 1854 [drawing sold at Sotheby's 18 Nov. 1971, inscribed 'Fisher's stone front, 14 Cannon Street West erected 1854, J. Davies Archt.'].

DAVIES, DANIEL (–1819), was a surveyor with an office in Bloomsbury Square, London. In 1809 he exhibited at the Royal Academy a design for rebuilding Covent Garden Market 'with the Piazza restored agreeably to the original intention of Inigo Jones'. His death was reported in *Gentleman's Magazine* 1819 (ii), 187. H. J. Elmes was his pupil.

DAVIS, EDWARD (*c.* 1802–1852), was a pupil of Sir John Soane from 1824 to 1826. Soane subsequently described him as 'a modest, unassuming young man' [A. T. Bolton, *The Portrait of Sir John Soane*, 1927, 226]. He was awarded a medal by the Society of Arts in 1825, and exhibited at the Royal Academy from 1828 to 1844. He practised in Bath, dying there on 30 April 1852, aged 50 [*Gent's Mag.* 1852 (i), 637]. C. E. Davis, City Architect of Bath from 1862 to 1902, was related to him and may have been his nephew.

Davis's earliest recorded work was the Gothic houses on ENTRY HILL, BATH, which he exhibited at the R.A. in 1828 as 'now building'. He subsequently occupied one of them himself. He laid out VICTORIA PARK, BATH, opened 1830, with a Gothic farm-house and an entrance-screen in the manner of Soane [W. Ison, *The Georgian Buildings of Bath*, 1948, 45]. In 1833 he restored PRIOR BIRDE'S CHAPEL in BATH ABBEY CHURCH, subsequently (1834) publishing a series of engravings entitled *Gothic Ornaments, etc., of Prior Birde's Oratory*, from drawings by S. Burchell. His exhibits at the R.A. show that he also designed TWERTON HOUSE, nr. BATH, for Charles Wilkins, 1838, and BARCOMBE, PAIGNTON, S. DEVON, for N. H. Nugent, 1838, and that he remodelled MARSTON BIGOT CHURCH, SOMERSET, in the Norman style for the Hon. and Rev. R. C. Boyle, 1844–5. In 1846 he won the competition for rebuilding LLANDILO CHURCH in CARMARTHENSHIRE [*Builder* iv, 1846, 329], but the commission eventually went to Gilbert Scott.

DAVIS, JAMES DORDON, made the Gothic plans for rebuilding KILMARTIN KIRK, ARGYLLSHIRE, which were accepted by the heritors in 1833 and carried out in 1835 [S.R.O., HR 369/1].

DAVIS, VALENTINE (1784–1869), was a pupil of Samuel Robinson and probably also of D. R. Roper. A note in the R.I.B.A. Drawings Collection records that he was the son of Richard Davis of Davis's Wharf, Horselydown. According to the same source he 'built Portleven Harbour' and 'was much employed by Rennie, MacAdam & Lord Lowther, but till about 40 years of age was not required to follow his profession'. His exhibits at the Royal Academy included a view of Davis's Wharf (1807) and several designs for villas. In the R.I.B.A. Drawings Collection there is a set of drawings of Crosby Hall, Bishopsgate, made by Valentine Davis and Frederick Nash in about 1804 [*Catalogue: C–F*, 76].

DAVISON, WILLIAM, exhibited at the Royal Academy in 1797 and 1798 from 3 Swinton Street, Battle Bridge, London. In 1816 he published a folio volume entitled *A Series of Original Designs for Shop-Fronts*. In the Avery Library of Columbia University there is an album of 59 designs for public and private buildings dating from about 1825 and entitled 'Memorandum of Mr. William Davison's Designs for Buildings' [John Harris, *Catalogue of British Drawings for Architecture, etc., in American Collections*, 1971, 94].

DAVY, CHRISTOPHER (*c.* 1803–1849), practised as an architect and civil engineer in Furnival's Inn, Holborn, where he died on 18 February 1849, aged 46 [*Gent's Mag.* 1849 (i), 439]. He was the author of two architectural publications: *The Architect, Engineer and Operative Builders' Constructive Manual*, 1839, 2nd. ed. 1841, and *Architectural Precedents*, 1841. The latter work contains an account of the building acts and specifications and working drawings of various typical buildings, including John Newman's Girls' School in Southwark, H. E. Kendall's Spilsby Gaol and Sessions House, an engine factory at Bromsgrove, and the steam-kitchen at the Reform Club.

Davy's own works, as recorded in his exhibits at the Royal Academy, were the Romanesque ST. THOMAS'S CHURCH in THE LIBERTY OF THE ROLLS, CHANCERY LANE, in association with J. Johnson, 1842, dem. (see *The Surveyor, Engineer and Architect*, 1843, plates at 257); offices at OUNDLE, NORTHANTS., for the Oundle Union Brewery Company, 1841; and the entrance to the EQUITABLE GAS COMPANY'S WORKS in LUPUS STREET, VAUXHALL, 1843. Between 1833 and 1846 he also exhibited several drawings of a topographical

---

[1] The church itself had been demolished in 1830. The tower and the adjoining rectory were rebuilt by Davies as one structure.

character, including (1838) an elevation and section of the steeple of St. Vedast's Church, Foster Lane, 'taken from actual measurement during the recent repairs (1837) under the direction of Mr. S. Angell'.

DAWSON, JOSHUA (*c.* 1812–), was in practice in Preston in about 1840. In the 1841 Census he gave his age as 29. At present his only recorded work is ST. BARTHOLOMEW'S R.C. CHURCH, RAINHILL, LANCS., an ambitious classical building completed in 1840 [*London and Dublin Orthodox Journal*, no. 272, 12 Sept. 1840, 174–5] (N. Pevsner, *South Lancashire*, pls. 48–9).

DAY, CHARLES, was the only pupil of Thomas Allason (*q.v.*) [*A.P.S.D.*, *s.v.* 'Allason, Thomas']. He was perhaps the son of a surveyor of this name who was involved in building DORSET SQUARE and GLOUCESTER PLACE, MARYLEBONE, in the 1820s [deeds in Middlesex Land Registry, *ex inf.* Mr. A. F. Kelsall]. He practised in Worcester, where in the 1830s he held the post of County Surveyor. His principal work was THE SHIRE HALL, WORCESTER, 1834–8, an orthodox Greek Revival design in the manner of Smirke [exhib. at R.A. 1835 and 1838]. He also designed the Roman Catholic churches of ST. FRANCIS XAVIER at HEREFORD, 1837–8 [exhib. at R.A. 1838], and ST. EDMUND, in WESTGATE STREET, BURY ST. EDMUNDS, SUFFOLK, 1838 [exhib. at R.A. 1838]. These too are both Grecian designs, but the Chapel which he designed for the nuns of STANBROOK ABBEY, POWICK, WORCS., is said to have been in the 'Georgian Nonconformist' manner [B. Little, *Catholic Churches since 1623*, 1966, 110]. His practice was continued by Henry Day, who was probably his son. Henry Day was succeeded in turn by his nephew Ernest Augustus Day (1846–1915) [information from Mr. B. Brotherton].

DAY, R—, exhibited at the Royal Academy between 1827 and 1841 from various addresses in South London. His only recorded work appears to be the singular Greek monument to Henry Budd in the churchyard of St. Matthew's Church, Brixton, which he designed and erected in 1825 [*Survey of London* xxvi, 134 and pl. 71A]. His son R. Day, junior, exhibited at the Academy in 1843–7.

DEANE, JAMES (*c.* 1699–1765), was a carpenter of Colchester. He was the 'ingenious ... Mr. James Deane' who drew the plates for Morant's *History of Colchester* (1748), and a volume of architectural drawings in the Essex County Record Office (D/DRc 227) has been identified as his work. It contains designs for farm-houses, barns, cottages and similar buildings, with estimates. Deane is known to have designed the west wing which was added to HOLLYTREES HOUSE,

COLCHESTER, for Charles Gray, M. P., in 1748 [Essex C.R.O., D/DRe], and in his will [P.C.C. 327 RUSHWORTH] he bequeathed his books to Gray for the Castle Book Club. They are still preserved in Colchester Public Library, and include editions of Serlio and Palladio, Perrault's *Vitruvius* (1673) and Batty Langley's *Ancient Masonry*. Deane died in August 1765, aged 66, and was buried at All Saints Church, Colchester [information from Mr. J. Bensusan-Butt].

DEANE, JOHN, 'of Reading, surveyor', was paid £10 by the 6th Duke of Somerset in 1683/4 'for surveying and drawing of a Platforme in order to the building a new house' at MARLBOROUGH CASTLE, WILTS. This appears to establish John Deane as the probable designer of the large house which now forms the nucleus of Marlborough School [*Report of the Marlborough College Natural History Soc.* no. 99, 1958–9, 47, 72].

It is possible that this John Deane was the son of Anthony Deane (d. 1679), a master mason of Uffington, Berks., but a John Deane was Master Mason to the City of London from 1696 until his death in 1705.

DEARN, THOMAS DOWNES WILMOT (1777–1853), was presumably the 'T. Dearn' who exhibited designs for mausolea at the Royal Academy in 1798 and 1799. As 'T. D. W.' Dearn' he exhibited in 1806 'a frame containing six designs: a private bath, a cenotaph to the memory of the late Marquis Cornwallis, Gothic entrance, Grecian entrance, villa in the castle style, private chapel and cemetery', and in 1808 a picture entitled 'Tomb of Geraldus, in the Castle court of St. Davids'. He practised at Cranbrook in Kent, where he died on 17 January 1853 [information from Mr. B. R. D. Price].

Dearn was the author of the following works: *Sketches in Architecture, consisting of Original Designs for Public and Private Buildings*, 1806, on the title-page of which he describes himself as 'Architect to the Duke of Clarence'; *Sketches in Architecture, consisting of Designs for Cottages and Rural Dwellings*, 1807; *The Bricklayer's Guide*, 1809, with a dedication to Sir John Soane; *Designs for Lodges and Entrances to Parks, Paddocks and Pleasure-Grounds*, 1811, 1823, dedicated to Sir Walter James, Bart.; *An Historical, Topographical and Descriptive Account of the Weald of Kent*, Cranbrook 1814; and *Hints on an Improved Method of Building*, 1821. He also published an engraving of the interior of Cranbrook Church, 1810 (B.M., Add. MS. 32359, ff. 167, 169), and an aquatint of the Surrey Chapel, Blackfriars Road, 1812 (B.M., *King's Maps* xxvii, 60 C). He designed a lodge (illustrated in *Designs for Lodges*, pl. ix) at ANGLEY, nr. CRANBROOK, for Sir Walter James, Bart., in 1809, and in 1808 exhibited at the R.A. his designs for a house called ATTWATERS at HAWKHURST, KENT, for J. D. Mercer. This does not appear to have been built.

DE BERLAIN, D—, submitted a 'Memorial' to the Mayor and Corporation of London in November 1735, in which he stated that 'Having had the honour to serve the Nation above 40 years, and being a Mathematician, Engineer, and Architect', he wished to submit a design for the new Mansion House, in which he had introduced 'the Corinthian, the Britannical, or Protestant, and the Dorick Orders'. He attended in person with his plan, but the Committee 'did not think fit to Receive it, and the same was delivered back to him and he was dismist' [S. Perks, *The History of the Mansion House*, 1922, 169].

At Christ Church, Oxford, there is a design for a large house presented to General John Guise by D. De Berlain in October 1734.

DE CAUX, or **CAUS**, ISAAC, was a native of Dieppe and either a son or a nephew of Salomon de Caux (*c*. 1577–1626), a French garden-designer and hydraulic engineer who was in the service of Queen Anne of Denmark and of her son Henry, Prince of Wales, in 1611–12. After Prince Henry's death in November 1612 Salomon de Caux returned to the Continent, and was employed by the Elector Palatine and his English wife Princess Elizabeth to lay out the elaborate gardens at the Castle of Heidelberg (described in De Caux's *Hortus Palatinus a Friderico Rege Boemiae Electore Palatino Heidelbergae exstructus*, Frankfurt, 1620). He eventually died at Paris in 1626 [*D.N.B.*; Thieme-Becker; *History of the King's Works* iii, 124–5]. Isaac de Caux, however, remained in England, where he was naturalized in 1634 [*Huguenot Society's Publications* xviii, 1911, 53]. Like Salomon, he was primarily a designer of gardens and waterworks, but he described himself as 'ingenyeur et architecte', and there is evidence that in the latter capacity he had connections with Inigo Jones. In 1623–4 he constructed a grotto in the basement of Jones's Banqueting House in Whitehall [Per Palme, *Triumph of Peace*, 1957, 66], and in 1633–4 he appears to have been acting as the executant architect of the houses in Covent Garden designed by Jones for the 4th Earl of Bedford. He himself lived from 1630 to 1634 in a newly built house on the Bedford estate in (Little) Russell Street [*Survey of London* xxxvi, 28]. In 1630–3 he designed a grotto in the garden of SOMERSET HOUSE for Queen Henrietta Maria [P.R.O., LR6/191], and the still existing grotto at WOBURN ABBEY, BEDS., can be attributed to him, for it was constructed for the Earl of Bedford in about 1630, and is unlikely to have been designed by anyone else.

From the service of the Earl of Bedford De Caux moved to that of the 4th Earl of Pembroke,

who in 1636 employed him to rebuild the south front of WILTON HOUSE, WILTS., and to lay out an elaborate formal garden in front of it. De Caux's employment at Wilton is documented by a warrant dated 14 March 1635/6 in which the Earl authorizes him 'to take down ... that side of Wilton House which is towards the Garden and such other parts as shall bee necessary & rebuild it anew with additions according to the Plott which is agreed'. Here, as at Covent Garden, there is reason to think that Inigo Jones was in the background, for John Aubrey says that it was on Jones's recommendation that De Caux ('an ingeniouse architect') was employed, and that the latter performed his task 'very well; but not without the advice and approbation of Mr. Jones'. The grand scheme for a classical façade nearly 400 feet in length is represented by a drawing now in the Library of Worcester College, Oxford. Only half of it was carried out, in the form of the existing south front with its pavilion towers, derived probably from an illustration in Scamozzi's *Idea della Architettura Universale* of 1615. This was gutted by fire in 1647 or 1648, after which the interior was rebuilt by John Webb, again 'by the advice of Inigo Jones'. Though the façade of the house was curtailed, the garden layout was fully carried out, and a few years later De Caux published a set of 26 engravings entitled *Wilton Gardens* (n.d.). He presumably designed the grotto illustrated in *Vitruvius Britannicus* ii, pl. 65 [H. M. Colvin, 'The South Front of Wilton House', *Archaeological Jnl.* cxi, 1955; A. A. Tait, 'Isaac de Caus and the South Front of Wilton House', *Burlington Mag.* cvi, 1964, 74].

In 1639 Nicholas Stone (*q.v.*) supplied 11½ feet of white marble cornice for the Earl of Pembroke by De Caux's order, no doubt for use at Wilton, and in 1637 it was also by De Caux's order that he made a black and white marble chimney-piece for the Countess of Home's house in Aldersgate Street, London [*The Note-Book of Nicholas Stone*, ed. W. L. Spiers, *Walpole Soc.*, 1918–19, 117, 127].

The only other building for which De Caux is known to have furnished designs is STALBRIDGE PARK, DORSET. In 1638 the 1st Earl of Cork gave £5 to 'Monsieur decon [*sic*] the french architect who belongs to my L. chamberleyn [*i.e.* Pembroke] ... for drawing me a plott, for contriving my new intended buylding over the great sellar at Stalbridge' [*Lismore Papers*, ed. A. B. Grosart, 1st ser., v, 1886, 64]. Nothing remains of the seventeenth-century house at Stalbridge, and no representation of it has so far come to light.

According to Aubrey the Earl of Pembroke rewarded De Caux with a pension 'of, I think, a hundred pounds per annum for his life, and lodgings in the house'. Aubrey adds that he 'died about 1656' and that 'his picture is at Mr. Gauntlet's house at Netherhampton' [*The Natural His-*

tory of Wiltshire, ed. Britton, 1847, 83–4]. The will of his mother Mary de Caus, dated 18 July 1655, shows that he was still alive in that year [P.C.C. 377 AYLETT].

In 1644 he had published a book entitled *Nouvelle Invention de lever l'eau plus hault que sa source avec quelques machines mouvantes par le moyen de l'eau et un discours de la conduite d'icele, par Isaac de Caus, Ingenyeur et Architecte, natif de Dieppe. Imprimé à Londre l'an 1644*. The original drawing for the title-page is in the Burlington-Devonshire Collection in the R.I.B.A. Drawings Collection, together with an elevation for the south front of Wilton House attributed to De Caux. Other drawings attributed to him are in the Clarke Collection at Worcester College, Oxford.

DECKER, PAUL, was the author of *Chinese Architecture, Civil and Ornamental, adapted to this climate*, 2 parts, 1759, and of *Gothic Architecture Decorated, consisting of a large collection of Temples, Banqueting, Summer and Green Houses etc. . . . Being a taste entirely new, likewise Designs of the Gothic Orders, and Rules for Drawing Them*, 2 parts, 1759.

DEERING, J. P., *see* GANDY, J. P.

DEFFERD, JAMES (*c.*1750–*c.*1813), is said to have come of a Somerset family, but to have settled near Bangor in about 1790, and to have worked on the Penrhyn estate. He is recorded to have designed two country houses in Anglesey: PENRHOS HALL for Lady Stanley, and BODORGAN for O. P. Meyrick [J. Evans, *The Beauties of England and Wales* xvii (i), 1812, 245, 257]. In 1795–6 ABERGLASLYN BRIDGE at BEDDGELERT, CAERNARVONSHIRE, was widened under his direction [R.C.A.M., *Caernarvonshire* iii, 127–8]. Defferd died at Llandegai in 1813 or early in 1814, aged 63 [*Gent's Mag.* 1814 (i), 523].

DE GOMME, Sir BERNARD, *see* GOMME

DE GREY, EARL, *see* GREY

DE KEYSER, WILLEM (1603–   ), was one of the three sons of Hendrik de Keyser, architect and sculptor of Amsterdam. He was a talented sculptor and was for some years Master Mason to the city of Amsterdam. He came to England in 1621, probably to be apprenticed to Nicholas Stone (who had married his elder sister Maria in 1613), and while in this country married Walburga Parker. He returned to Amsterdam in 1640, but was back in England at the time of the Restoration [*Nicholas Stone's Note-Book*, ed. Spiers, *Walpole Soc.* vii, 32–3; Thieme-Becker, xx, 235; Elizabeth Neurdenburg, *De Zeventiende Eeuwsche Beeldhouwkunst in de Noordelijke*

Nederlanden, Amsterdam 1948, 143–52]. Very little is known about his work in England, much of which was probably monumental sculpture, but in 1661 he was paid £2 by the Paymaster of the King's Works 'for drawing the draughts with the uprights for the intended Building at Greenwich' [P.R.O., Works 5/2, under Whitehall, July 1661]. This was an abortive scheme for Charles II's intended palace at Greenwich, afterwards superseded by John Webb's design of 1663. Willem was still living in London in 1674, and in 1678 was admitted to the Masons' Company as a 'foreign member' [D. Knoop & G. P. Jones, *The London Mason in the Seventeenth Century*, 1935, 71], but the place and date of his death are not known.

DE LABRIÈRE, ALEXANDRE LOUIS, *see* LABRIÈRE

DE LA ROCHE, PETER, *see* ROCHE

DELIGHT, EZEKIEL, was appointed one of the District Surveyors for London in 1774. He became Surveyor to the Amicable Assurance Company, and designed their premises in Serjeants' Inn, Fleet Street, in 1793 [*N. and Q.*, 11th ser., vi, 67; records of the Amicable Assurance Co. now in possession of the Norwich Union Life Insurance Society]. This very competently designed building, with a façade in the style of Chambers, is illustrated in *The Parlour Book of British Scenery, Architecture and Antiquities*, 2nd ser., 1828, and in A. E. Richardson & C. L. Gill, *London Houses from 1660 to 1820*, 1911, pl. lxxx. The death of Delight's wife is reported in *Gent's Mag.* 1805 (ii), 1182.

DEMPSTER, GEORGE, of Greenock, was a wright by trade. He designed and built the GAELIC CHURCH, CAMPBELTOWN, ARGYLLSHIRE, 1803–6. The original steeple was destroyed by lightning in 1830 and partially rebuilt in 1884–5 [S.R.O., HR 67/1, pp. 44, 46–8; R.C.A.M., *Argyll* i, 105 and pl. 20B].

DEMPSTER, JAMES, is listed as Greenock's only architect in Pigot's *Directory* of 1825–6. In GREENOCK he designed the BLACKHALL STREET CHAPEL, 1823, and the EPISCOPAL CHAPEL, GOUROCK STREET, 1824, Gothic [Daniel Weir, *History of Greenock*, Greenock 1829, 20]. He was also the architect of KILMACOLM PARISH CHURCH, RENFREWSHIRE, 1830–1 [S.R.O., HR 306/1, p. 72, etc.], and (it is said) of CATHCART PARISH CHURCH in the same county, 1830–1, Gothic, dem. except tower *c.* 1929. In 1828–9 he superintended the building of MAUCHLINE CHURCH, AYRSHIRE, to a Gothic design made by a local gentleman, William Alexander of Southbar, and made some modifications that were approved by the heritors [S.R.O., HR 443/2].

DENHAM, Sir JOHN (1615–1669), Surveyor-General of the King's Works from 1660 to 1669, was 'a celebrated Poet, and an eminent Royalist'. It was as a reward for his loyalty that he obtained the Surveyorship, which he claimed had been promised to him by Charles II in 1649. Evelyn, who disagreed with Denham over the siting of Greenwich Palace, described him as 'a better poet than architect', and John Webb, who as Jones's pupil and deputy had hoped to succeed to the latter's post at the Restoration, protested that 'though Mr. Denham may, as most gentry, have some knowledge of the theory of architecture, he can have none of the practice, but must employ another'. The person so employed was Webb himself, who is referred to as Denham's deputy in May 1664 [P.R.O., Works 5/5], and who, in November 1666, was placed in charge of the works at Greenwich Palace as Denham's assistant, 'to execute, act, and proceed there, according to your best skill and judgment in Architecture'. In March 1669, at the King's request, Denham made Wren his 'sole Deputy', and it was Wren who took his place at the Board of Works when he died two weeks later [*History of the King's Works* v, chap. 1].

Though Denham appears (until his mental illness in 1666) to have been a competent administrative head of the Office of Works, there is no evidence that he ever attempted to design a building. During his surveyorship Webb and Samwell acted as the King's architects for Greenwich and Newmarket, respectively, and the house which Denham began to build in Piccadilly in 1665 (afterwards Burlington House) was probably designed by one of his subordinates in the Office of Works [*Survey of London* xxxii, 391]. It is, therefore, only because he held the same office as Inigo Jones and Sir Christopher Wren for eight and a half years that Denham figures in this *Dictionary*. For a full account of his career as a poet and politician see *D.N.B.* and *The Poetical Works of Sir John Denham*, ed. T. H. Banks (Yale 1928).

DERING, HENEAGE (1665–1750), was a wealthy and well-connected clergyman who, after serving as secretary to Archbishop Sharp of York, obtained a number of ecclesiastical preferments, including a canonry at York and the deanery of Ripon, to which he was appointed in 1711 [*D.N.B.*]. Dering was an able and intelligent man who published two poems in Latin verse, and there is some reason to think that he was an amateur architect. Among the Brewster papers in the North Yorkshire Record Office there are plans for a new house at ALDBY PARK, YORKS. (E.R.), the seat of John Brewster, endorsed

'Doct. Dering's Plan for a House'. They are accompanied by a letter from Dering in which he calls himself 'a well wisher to Architecture' and from which it is clear that he drew them himself. They were not adopted when Aldby was rebuilt in 1726, and the name of the architect employed is not known (*C. Life*, 9 Nov. 1935). Some further evidence of Dering's building activities is afforded by his autobiographical memoranda, printed in *Surtees Society* lxv (1875). Immediately after his institution to the rectory of SCRAYINGHAM, YORKS. (E.R.), in 1704 he 'began to rebuild the parsonage house, the old one being ruinous'. Later the same year he 'staid at BISHOPTHORPE, and took care of the alterations then making in the house' (by Archbishop Sharp). At the DEANERY in RIPON he was responsible for 'the brick building towards the garden', completed in 1715.

DESVIGNES, PETER HUBERT (c. 1804–1883), entered the Royal Academy Schools in 1823 at the age of 19, and was awarded a premium by the Society of Arts for an architectural design the same year. He exhibited at the R.A. from 1824 to 1832, and competed for the Houses of Parliament in 1835. He died at Hither Green, nr. Lewisham, on 27 December 1883, leaving an estate valued at £21,000 [Principal Probate Registry, Calendar of Probates].

DEWHURST, JOHN, practised in Preston, where he designed a POLICE STATION (dem.) in AVENHAM STREET, 1831 [P. Whittle, *History of Preston* ii, 1837, 140], and the castellated GOVERNOR'S HOUSE of THE PRISON in STANLEY STREET in 1834 [C. Hardwick, *History of Preston*, Preston 1857, 440]. He designed the Lancashire churches of BLEASDALE, 1835–6, and OUT RAWCLIFFE, 1837–8 [I.C.B.S.], and was presumably the 'Dewhurst' who was the builder of AINSWORTH CHURCH, 1831–2 [G.R.]. Bleasdale Church is in the lancet Gothic style, but Out Rawcliffe is described by Pevsner as being 'a very individual building, Prussian rather than English', with two tiers of small round-arched windows and four corner-turrets [*North Lancashire*, 185].

DE WILSTAR, JOHN JACOB, was a surveyor frequently employed by the Corporation of Bristol in the second quarter of the eighteenth century. In 1740 he submitted a design for a new Exchange, but it was not accepted [W. Ison, *The Georgian Buildings of Bristol*, 1952, 96]. De Wilstar's drawing of the garden front of REDLAND COURT, nr. BRISTOL, is in the British Museum (*King's Maps* xiii, 77-3-b). In 1723 he made 'A new dessein' for rebuilding HEPPINGTON HOUSE, NACKINGTON, KENT, for Bryan Faussett, but the house was not rebuilt until 1732. De Wilstar's drawings are preserved in a scrap-book in the possession of the Godfrey-Faussett family in the Isle of Wight [*ex. inf.* the late Rupert Gunnis]. The house was demolished *c.* 1970.

DEYKES, JOHN, was a native of Great Malvern, where his father Samuel Deykes was a builder.[1] He became a pupil of George Smith and exhibited student's designs at the Royal Academy between 1810 and 1815. He subsequently practised in London, carrying out alterations to the east end of ST. BRIDE'S CHURCH, FLEET STREET, in 1822-3 [W. H. Godfrey, *The Church of St. Bridge, Fleet Street, Survey of London,* 1944]. A statue of Guy, Earl of Warwick, in Warwick Lane, London, restored by 'J. Deykes, Archt.' in 1817, is illustrated by T. H. Shepherd in *London in the Nineteenth Century* (1829). Deykes designed several buildings in GREAT MALVERN, including THE BATHS, THE ASSEMBLY ROOMS and THE CIRCULATING LIBRARY (now Barclay's Bank) [Mary Southall, *A Description of Malvern,* 1822 and 1825].

DICKINSON, WILLIAM (*c.* 1671–1725), is presumed to have been the son of William Dickinson, Chief Clerk of the King's Works from 1660 until his death in 1702, but there is no proof that the two Dickinsons were related. In November 1696 the younger Dickinson was appointed Clerk of the Works at Greenwich Palace, a post which came to an end in 1701 or 1702 following the establishment of the Royal Hospital. It is also in 1696 that he first appears in the accounts of St. Paul's Cathedral as assisting John Oliver, Wren's deputy, as a measurer. He continued in this employment after Oliver's death in 1701, and was described in 1711 as 'clerk for taking the accounts of several materials for the said building' [Hist. MSS. Comm., *Portland* x, 106]. During the early years of the eighteenth century he acted as Wren's assistant in connection with the rebuilding of the City churches, and his entertainment is mentioned in the records of several parishes. He was also, as Wren's deputy, employed in measuring the repairs to Westminster Abbey from 1700 onwards [Bodleian Library, MS. Gough Westminster 1], and in February 1710/11 he succeeded James Broughton both as Deputy Surveyor of the Fabric and as Surveyor to the Dean and Chapter of Westminster. In this dual capacity he was responsible between 1719 and 1722 for the repair of the north transept of the Abbey Church, including the reconstruction of the rose window and porch, and in 1722 for the erection of iron

railings 'in the Gothick manner' across the latter. His drawing of the transept, as approved by Wren, is reproduced in *Wren Soc.* xi, pl. ii, and he initials a design for a proposed central tower over the crossing (pl. v). He also made a number of designs (the earliest dated 1711) for the new Dormitory of Westminster School, which was eventually built in 1722 to Lord Burlington's design (*Wren Soc.* xi, pls. x–xxi).

In 1711 Dickinson was, with Nicholas Hawksmoor, appointed one of the Surveyors to the Commissioners for Building Fifty New Churches in London. In January 1712/13 he 'laid two Models of Churches before the Commissioners', and the plan for a proposed church on the site of St. Mary le Strand (*Wren Soc.* x, pl. 13) is in his hand, but none of the new churches were built to his designs, and in 1713 he resigned to return to the Office of Works as Clerk of the Works at Whitehall, St. James's and Westminster. Two years later he lost this post in the purge following the introduction of Lord Halifax's Orders, but he retained his position as Surveyor to Westminster Abbey until his death on 24 January 1724/5, at the age of 54. He was buried outside the north porch of the Abbey, under a stone (now destroyed) with the inscription: H.S.E./GULIELMUS DICKINSON ARM. ARCHITECTUS;/QUALIS! SUSPICE./OBIIT 24⁰ DIE JANUARII A.D. 1724/SUAEQUE AETATIS 54. The Chapter Book records the payment of 15 guineas to his widow for some of his drawings, including the surviving design for a central tower and one for a 'West Tower', now lost.

Dickinson was, like Hawksmoor, a pupil of Wren, and in a letter to the Duchess of Marlborough written in 1711, Wren's son described him as 'a person that has served [my father] with great fidelity, diligence and skill' [Blenheim Palace archives, F.1.43]. Most of his working life was spent in the performance of the duties of a surveyor or clerk of works rather than in designing new buildings. Few important commissions appear to have come his way, and as a creative architect he has consequently to be judged almost entirely from his unexecuted designs. These make it clear that he was a competent, though not particularly adventurous, designer of the English baroque school. Most of his surviving drawings are to be found in the Gough Collection in the Bodleian Library. Besides many drawings connected with WESTMINSTER ABBEY (Gough Maps 23 and 41 G, ff. 14–19), attention may be drawn to the following: Baron Shutte's house (? in Westminster), 1705 (Gough Maps 22, f. 72); a design for a country house for Sir Charles Pye at CLIFTON CAMPVILLE, STAFFS., 1710 (Gough Gen. Top. 63, p. 440); an unexecuted design for WITNEY RECTORY, OXON., for Dr. Robert Freind, headmaster of Westminster School, 1711 (MS. Top. Oxon. a. 39, ff. 162–4); a plan of a church

---

[1] The 'Foley Arms Hotel' was built in 1810 'from a plan drawn by Mr. Samuel Deykes' (Mary Southall, *A Description of Malvern,* 1822, 61).

at LEEDS, 1722 (Gough Maps 227); a plan of Captain Tufnell's house at NORWOOD (Gough London 127, p. 322); and a miscellaneous sketchbook (MS. Gough Misc. Ant. 17). Two drawings in the Soane Museum show his own (rejected) and Colen Campbell's (successful) designs for PEMBROKE HOUSE, WHITEHALL, side by side (*Wren Soc.* xvii, pl. xlviii, where the building is wrongly identified as Ashburnham House). The design for a pair of houses reproduced in *Architectural History*, vol. 10, fig. 102, and a plan and elevation of a church reproduced by J. Harris, *Catalogue of British Drawings for Architecture etc. in American Collections*, pl. 66, can probably be attributed to him. Dickinson's interest in Gothic is shown by a number of drawings in that style for Westminster Abbey, and by an unexecuted design by him for a Gothic tower for ST. MICHAEL'S, CORNHILL (*Wren Soc.* x, pl. 9). Similarities between the pinnacles of the tower of ST. MARY, ALDERMARY and those envisaged in Dickinson's design for the central tower of Westminster Abbey suggest that at least the detailing of the former tower was due to him. [*Wren Soc.*, *passim* (see index); *History of the King's Works*, v, *passim;* *Westminster Abbey Registers*, ed. J. L. Chester, Harleian Soc. 1876, 312; J. Dart, *Westmonasterium*, vol. i, book 2, chap. 3, 58; *V.C.H. Essex* vi, 191, n. 91 (for his marriage); will in Westminster City Library, No. 1895; information from Mr. T. M. Benton.]

DICKSON, RICHARD (1792–1857) and ROBERT (*c.* 1794–1865), were the sons of John Dickson (1766–1828), an Edinburgh builder. Their mother was Mary Crichton, daughter of James Crichton, mason, and sister of the architect Richard Crichton (*q.v.*). Richard and Robert Dickson were probably pupils of their uncle, and took over his practice at 10 James Street, Edinburgh, when he died in 1817.

Like their predecessor, the two Dicksons were able designers in a variety of styles. They provided their clients with Gothic churches, Grecian academies or castellated houses with equal facility. Their Gothic work is richly detailed but not at all scholarly, and quite unaffected by Puginesque principles. On the other hand their Town Hall at Leith is a most successful synthesis of Renaissance and Greek Revival motifs in the manner of which C. R. Cockerell was the master. Their destroyed Veterinary College in Edinburgh appears to have been a building of similar quality.

Richard Dickson and his parents are commemorated by a monument in the Old Calton Burial Ground in Edinburgh. For the relationship of the Dickson and Crichton families see also Scottish Record Society, *Roll of Edinburgh Burgesses*, 1933.

CHURCHES AND PUBLIC BUILDINGS

KILCONQUHAR CHURCH, FIFE, 1820–1, Gothic [*N.S.A.* ix, 333]. The Heritors' Records show that they wanted the church to be copied from the new church at Cockpen, Midlothian, which the Dicksons were then building to the designs of Archibald Elliot [S.R.O., HR 194/3].

LEITH, MIDLOTHIAN, THE TOWN HALL, 1827–8 [signed 'R. & R. DICKSON ARCHITECTS'] (A. E. Richardson, *Monumental Classic Architecture in Great Britain*, 1914, pl. xxxiv).

EDINBURGH, TRON CHURCH, rebuilt steeple after fire (1824), 1828 [*A.P.S.D.*, *s.v.* 'Edinburgh'].

THE BATHGATE ACADEMY, BATHGATE, WEST LOTHIAN, 1831–3 [Thomas Davidson, *Bathgate Academy 1833–1933*, Bathgate 1933, 20–1].

EDINBURGH, THE VETERINARY COLLEGE, CLYDE STREET, 1833; destroyed by fire 1953 [O. Charnock Bradley, *History of the Edinburgh Veterinary College*, Edinburgh 1923, 31].

MUTHILL, PERTHSHIRE, ST. JAMES'S EPISCOPAL CHURCH, 1836 [*The Scottish Episcopal Church Year Book*, 1973–4, 284].

COLLESSIE CHURCH, FIFE, 1839, Gothic [S.R.O., HR 36/1, p. 101, etc.].

DUNKELD, PERTHSHIRE, THE DUCHESS OF ATHOLL'S INDUSTRIAL SCHOOL, 1853 [drawings at Blair Castle].

KINCARDINE SCHOOL, PERTHSHIRE, 1855–6 [S.R.O., HR 275/1].

BLAIR ATHOLL, PERTHSHIRE, THE 'ATHOLL ARMS' HOTEL, 1856 [drawings at Blair Castle].

LOGIERAIT, PERTHSHIRE, school for the 6th Duke of Atholl, 1863 ['by the Duke of Atholl's architect', S.R.O., HR 38/2].

DOMESTIC ARCHITECTURE

EDINBURGH, NORTH BRIDGE, row of shops, 1817 [drawings in City Architect's Office].

ABERCAIRNY ABBEY, PERTHSHIRE, completed house, begun by R. Crichton, for James Moray (d. 1840) and William Moray (d. 1850), Gothic; dem. 1960 [Mark Girouard in *C. Life*, 9–16 March 1961].

CORTACHY CASTLE, ANGUS, addition of Gothic porch for the 8th Earl of Airlie, 1820–1. This porch was demolished *c.* 1873. [S.R.O., GD 16/27/446 and RHP 5167/1–3] (Jones's *Views of Scottish Seats*, *c.* 1830; A. H. Millar, *Castles and Mansions of Scotland: Perthshire and Forfarshire*, 1890, 307–27).

attributed: MILLEARNE, PERTHSHIRE, for J. G. Home Drummond, 1826–35, Gothic; dem. 1969 [Alistair Rowan in *C. Life*, 24 Feb.–2 March 1972].

BALBIRNIE HOUSE, FIFE, west lodge for General Robert Balfour, 1824 [payment in accounts formerly at Balbirnie, *ex. inf.* Dr. Alistair Rowan].

EDINBURGH, NOS. 1–25 GARDNER'S CRESCENT and 91–107, 109–115 MORRISON STREET, 1826 [S.R.O., Edinburgh Sasines].

BLAIR DRUMMOND, PERTHSHIRE, additions to East Lodge for Henry Home Drummond, 1836 [drawings at Blair Drummond].

DUNIMARLE CASTLE, CULROSS, FIFE, for Mrs. Magdalene Shairp-Erskine, 1840 [drawings at Dunimarle Castle, *ex inf.* Dr. Alistair Rowan].

ARBUTHNOTT HOUSE, KINCARDINESHIRE, estate buildings for the 8th Viscount Arbuthnott, 1839 [drawings at Arbuthnott House, *ex inf.* Mr. J. G. Dunbar].

BLAIR ATHOLL, PERTHSHIRE, BLAIR COTTAGES, 1840 [drawings at Blair Castle].

GARRYSIDE VILLAGE, PERTHSHIRE, for the 6th Duke of Atholl, 1856 [drawings at Blair Castle].

DINGLEY, ROBERT (1708–1781), was the son of a London jeweller, and was himself a prosperous merchant trading in Russia and Portugal. Jonas Hanway was his partner from 1743. Although Dingley shared some of Hanway's philanthropic interests, he was also a connoisseur of the arts, and had a fine collection of coins, antique gems and drawings. In 1736 he was elected a member of the Society of Dilettanti and in 1748 became a Fellow of the Royal Society. For some years (1764–77) he was Secretary to the Dilettanti, and was a member of the committee which sent Chandler and Pars to Asia Minor in 1764. His first wife was Elizabeth, daughter of Henry Thompson of Kirby Hall, Yorkshire. He lived in St. Helen's Place, Bishopsgate, until about 1760, when he moved to Lamorbey, nr. Bexley in Kent.

In 1758 Dingley took a leading part in the foundation of the Magdalen Hospital. The Hospital building in Goodman's Fields, Lambeth, was erected in 1769–72 to the designs of Joel Johnson, and there seems to be no evidence to support Cust's belief that Dingley was its architect. Dingley's ability as an amateur architect is, however, attested both by some engraved designs for temples by him at West Wycombe Park, by three proof engravings of designs for rustic garden buildings signed 'R. D. inv. et delin. J. Noval sculp.' in the collection of Mr. John Harris, and by an elaborate scheme for rebuilding the King's and Queen's Baths at Bath, signed 'R.D. inv. et delin', and engraved by E. Rooker, of which there is a copy in the R.I.B.A. Collection. The architecture is Palladian in character and very competently designed.

[L. Cust & S. Colvin, *History of the Society of Dilettanti*, 1898; H. F. B. Compston, *The Magdalen Hospital*, 1917; *Gent's Mag.* 1781, 395.]

DINNINGHOF, BARNARD, was a glazier by trade, and doubtless a Fleming or German in origin. In 1586 he became a freeman of York, and he was still working in Yorkshire in 1618. At Gilling Castle, Yorkshire (N.R.), the heraldic glass in the Great Chamber is signed 'Bærnard Dinninckhoff fecit Anno 1585'. Among the Temple Newsham papers at Leeds there is a set of competently drawn plans by Dinninghof for a projected house at Sheriff Hutton for Thomas Lumsden, accompanied by a letter dated 2 October 1618 offering to build it for £440. In another document of this date he describes himself as 'of Follyfoot' in the parish of Spofforth, nr. Harrogate. As Follyfoot was a manor-house of the Earl of Northumberland Dinninghof may have had some connection with the Percy household. [S. D. Kitson, 'Barnard Dinninghof', *Jnl. of the British Society of Master Glass-Painters* iii, 1929, 55–8; *Freemen of the City of York* ii, Surtees Soc. 1900, 28; Leeds City Archives Dept., Temple Newsham MSS. SH A3/1–2; information from Dr. E. A. Gee.]

DIXON, CORNELIUS, was an architectural decorator and theatrical scene-painter. A note by Horace Walpole records the fact that he studied in Rome under Clérisseau [A. Graves, *The Royal Academy of Arts, a Dictionary of Exhibitors* ii, 1905, 80]. In 1793–4 he was employed by Walpole at STRAWBERRY HILL, MIDDLESEX, 'new painting the paper of the staircase' and 'the ceiling under the stairs' [*Strawberry Hill Accounts*, ed. P. Toynbee, 1927, 20]. At NO. 15 ST. JAMES'S SQUARE in 1794 he painted 'pilaster pannels', etc., for Thomas Anson under the direction of Samuel Wyatt [E. Croft Murray, *Decorative Painting in England* ii, 1970, 202]. A few years later James Wyatt employed him to paint the pillars in the dining-room at CANWELL HALL, STAFFS., 'in imitation of Italian marble', and he subsequently 'executed similar ones on a smaller scale in Mr. Boulton's dining-room' in his house at SOHO, nr. BIRMINGHAM [S. Shaw, *History of Staffordshire* ii, 1801, 22*]. His firm was still in existence in the 1820s, when 'Cornelius Dixon & Son' were paid £100 for painting the interior of the new COUNTY COURT HOUSE at CARLISLE [Cumberland and Westmorland Record Office, Q.S. Records] and 'Messrs. Dixon' were employed to paint the east wing of the BRITISH MUSEUM [*History of the King's Works* vi, 411, n. 4].

According to E. W. Brayley's *Historical and Descriptive Accounts of the Theatres of London*, 1833, Dixon was the architect as well as the scene-painter of the fourth EAST LONDON THEATRE in GOODMAN'S FIELDS, built in 1785–7 and destroyed by fire in 1802. The scenes that he painted for Isaac Jackman's 'Hero and Leander', produced at the Royalty Theatre, Wellclose Square, in 1787, were acclaimed in the *libretto* as surpassing 'even the genius of Loutherbourg', but there appears to be no evidence that he designed the theatre itself. Some crudely drawn plans of a theatre in the Enthoven Collection in the Victoria and Albert Museum that are inscribed on the back with the names of Dixon and Capon do not correspond to the Royalty, although said to represent it [cf. R. Southern, *The Georgian Playhouse*, 1948, 26, pls. 10–13]. In 1792 Dixon received the first premium of 20 guineas for his designs for rebuilding the THEATRE ROYAL in BIRMINGHAM, but they were subsequently set aside in favour of plans by George Saunders [MS. Minutes of the Proprietors in the Birmingham Reference Library].

DIXON, HENRY (–1859), was a surveyor working in Oxford in the early nineteenth century. From 1820 onwards he was employed by St. John's College to lay out BEAUMONT and ST. JOHN'S STREETS, OXFORD, and was presumably responsible for designing the elevations [St. John's College Register, 17 May and 9 Oct. 1822]. In 1823 Dixon was involved on behalf of the Dean and Chapter of Westminster in a scheme for draining Otmoor [Westminster Abbey Muniments, Chapter Acts 1818–29, f. 214]. In the Bodleian Library (MS. Top. Oxon. a.22 (R)), there is a series of plans of Oxford Colleges made in 1848 'under the supervision of Mr. Henry Dixon of Oxford'. In 1846 he was described as 'Land Surveyor and Civil Engineer'. He died at Leamington on 21 January 1859 according to J. M. Davenport's 'Obituary Book' in the Oxon. County Record Office.

DIXON, JOHN, of Hull, was employed by the Corporation of Lincoln in 1762 to examine the Fish and Butchers' Shambles, and 'to draw a plan of a new Butchers' Shambles and bring in an estimate thereof'. In June 1765 it was decided to build a conduit over the High Bridge 'in the Form of an Obelisk', and on 6 July Dixon was ordered to erect it 'agreeable to the Plan and Estimate delivered in by him' [Lincoln Corporation Minutes, 1710–1800, pp. 442, 444–6] (for an engraving of the obelisk see Thomas Allom, *The Counties of Chester, Derby, Nottingham, Leicester, Rutland and Lincoln Illustrated*, 1836, 28). Dixon was employed by Sir John Hussey Delaval to measure plasterers' and joiners' work executed at Doddington Hall, Lincs., in 1760–2 [Bodleian Library, MS. Top. Lincs. c. 14, ff. 41–5, 56, 63–5, 70].

DIXON, JOHN, was an assistant of James Wyatt. Farington described him in 1794 as 'the artist who is employed by Wyatt to draw for him', and noted that he had been with Wyatt 'from the time of the building of the Pantheon' (opened in 1772). From 1781 to 1796 Dixon exhibited architectural designs at the Royal Academy, but in 1796 Smirke told Farington that 'Wyatt ... will not allow Dixon to exhibit, as he says the designs

are borrowed from his drawings' [Farington's Diary, 21 Jan. 1794, 4 Aug. 1796]. However, Dixon did exhibit again in 1801 and 1803, the subject in the latter year being 'a design for a Gothic hall'. A drawing of Wyatt's New Park, Wilts., formerly in an extra-illustrated copy of Britton's *Beauties of Wiltshire* in the library at Coleshill House, Berks., was stated to be 'by J. Dixon at Mr. Wyatt's': it was probably the view of this house that Dixon exhibited at the Academy in 1784. The name of 'John Dixon Clerk to Jas. Wyatt' is among those inscribed on the plate commemorating the completion of the Radcliffe Observatory, Oxford, to Wyatt's designs in 1794. At the time of Wyatt's sudden death in 1813 he was reported to owe Dixon £900 [Farington's Diary, 18 Sept. 1813]. What became of Dixon subsequently has not been discovered.

DIXON, JOSEPH (–1787), appears to have been one of the sons of Joseph Dixon, a carpenter of Stamford who died in 1777. He established himself in London, where he was active as a mason and surveyor during the third quarter of the eighteenth century. According to the MS. autobiography of Henry Couchman, who as a young man was one of his employees, he lived at first in Air Street, Piccadilly, but afterwards built himself a house and yard in Pimlico near the Chelsea waterworks. Other sources, however, give his address as St. Alban's Street (south of Pall Mall). In 1760–9 he built Blackfriars Bridge to the designs of Robert Mylne, and in 1770 he began to build a new bridge over the R. Exe at Exeter to his own designs, but his workmanship proved defective, and it was swept away by a flood in 1775 before it was complete [G. Oliver, *History of Exeter*, 1861, 169–172].[1] Couchman records that in 1764–5 Dixon built Almack's Rooms in King Street, St. James's to the designs of Robert Mylne, and a house in Piccadilly for the Earl of March to those of Matthew Brettingham. About this time he was also working at Burghley House, Northants., and erecting 'a new house in Gloucestershire'. In 1766 he enlarged COKER COURT, SOMERSET, for John Bullock [Somerset Record Office, DD/WHh Addenda 16 and DD/WHh 2]. In several of his works he was associated with his brother Richard Dixon, a carpenter who became surveyor to the Westminster Lying-in Hospital (built in 1765–7 and dem. *c.* 1830) [*Survey of London* xxiii, 42]. Together they were involved in building houses in Pall Mall in the 1760s [*Survey of London* xxix, 328–9]. This was a development in which Henry Holland was involved, and his account-book in Sir John

---

[1] A new bridge was then built (1776–8) under the direction of John Goodwin, 'who had been an assistant in the former erection' (*A.P.S.D.*, *s.v.* 'Exeter'). This in turn was rebuilt in 1905.

Soane's Museum shows that he often employed Joseph Dixon as a mason. In 1770-2 Joseph and Richard Dixon built the new south wing at Hitchin Priory, Herts., to the designs of R. & J. Adam [Herts. County Record Office, DE 4422/2]. In 1775-7 they were responsible for rebuilding ST. MARY'S CHURCH, BATTERSEA, Joseph as architect and surveyor, Richard as building contractor [J. G. Taylor, *Our Lady of Batersey*, 1925, 99-113]. By then Joseph Dixon was living in Battersea, but Richard was described as 'of Pimlico'. Joseph went bankrupt in March 1778, Richard in November [*Gent's Mag.* 1778, 142, 551]. Joseph Dixon died at Battersea in 1787 [Taylor, *op. cit.*, 120]. In his will [P.C.C. 171 MAJOR], in which he is described as 'Senior Bridge Master of London Bridge', he refers to 'Joseph Dixon, eldest son of my brother Richard Dixon'. This may have been the Joseph Dixon who entered the Royal Academy Schools in 1796 at the age of 20, winning the Silver Medal for Architecture the following year. John Carter (*q.v.*) was for some years Dixon's pupil and assistant [*Gent's Mag.* 1817 (ii), 363].

In his diary C. R. Cockerell recorded (14 May 1825) that a house near Aberystwyth in Cardiganshire called CWMCYNFELIN was 'built by Mr. Davis grandfather to [the then owner] from designs of a Mr. Dixon in London'. This was presumably either Joseph or Richard.

DIXON, JOSEPH, 'Carpenter and House Joyner', 'who has for several years past serv'd Mr. Thomas Ivory in the capacity of Foreman', announced in the *Norwich Mercury* of 11 October 1756 that he had taken over Mr. Thomas Ivory's yard and stock in St. Martin's at Oak, 'where he intends to carry on the said Business in all its Branches'. He was prepared to make 'Plans and Estimates for Gentlemen if required' [S. J. Wearing, *Georgian Norwich: its Builders*, 1926, 58-9].

DOBSON, JOHN (1787-1865), was born at Chirton, North Shields. He showed an early talent for drawing, and at the age of 15 became a pupil of David Stephenson, then the leading builder and architect in Newcastle. At the same time he studied perspective under an Italian refugee artist called Boniface Musso, John Martin being his fellow-pupil. In 1810 he left Stephenson's office and went to London apparently to seek instruction from John Varley, the celebrated water-colour painter. Varley was so impressed by his ability that he agreed to give him lessons at five o'clock each morning – that being the only time which he could spare. A painting entitled 'Dobson's Dream' was the product of this early morning tuition, for it represented the master's version of a dream recounted to him by his recently awakened pupil. While in London Dobson

formed a friendship with the artist Robert Smirke, R.A., who attempted, without success, to dissuade him from returning to the north. Once established in Newcastle, he found that 'although he was (with the exception of Mr. Bonomi of Durham) the only professional architect between Edinburgh and York ... the demand for his services had to be created', and that the employment of builder-architects such as Dodds and Stephenson was still the rule. By characteristic patience and hard work, however, he soon built up a practice for himself in the new industrial towns. Professionally he was unusually well equipped. From Varley he had acquired an enviable facility in producing enticing water-colour perspectives of his designs. To the skill of an artist he added the resourcefulness of an engineer and the practical competence of a surveyor. According to his daughter he 'never exceeded an estimate, and never had a legal dispute with a contractor'. His technical ability was shown in securing the foundations of Lambton Hall, which had been rendered insecure by mining subsidence, and he was equally successful in underpinning and restoring the tower of St. Nicholas Church, Newcastle, when it was in imminent danger of collapse. As an engineer his outstanding achievement was the Central Railway Station at Newcastle, which embodied several structural innovations, one of which earned him a medal at the Paris Exhibition of 1858. He also designed wharves, warehouses, and a graving dock at St. Peter's Shipyard, Newcastle.

Early in his career (*c.* 1824) Dobson made plans for the redevelopment of Newcastle which were not carried out and were eventually superseded by those of the speculative builder Richard Grainger. How far Dobson contributed to the architecture (as opposed to the planning) of Grainger's magnificent new streets is uncertain. He was certainly responsible for the façades of Eldon Square, for the New Markets, and probably for the east side of the curved portion of Grey Street from Mosley Street to Shakespeare Street, but there is no evidence that he designed Grey Street or Grainger Street as a whole, and even his authorship of the Royal Arcade is not quite certain (see p. 360). Nevertheless, Dobson's numerous public buildings and especially the noble portico of the Central Station give him a prominent place among the architects who made Newcastle one of the most handsome Victorian cities in England.

Though Dobson's name is so closely associated with the urban architecture of Newcastle, his practice as a designer of churches and country houses in the north of England was very extensive. In the course of a long career he designed or altered over fifty churches and about a hundred houses. His earliest churches were mostly classical in style. But from the 1820s onwards he was designing churches in a thin refined Gothic style that commands more respect in the twentieth century than it did in the nineteenth. By the 1850s, however, he could produce a conventional 'Decorated' church such as Otterburn that satisfied all the standards of Victorian ecclesiology. As a country-house architect Dobson worked largely for the beneficiaries of the industrial revolution, designing new houses for wealthy manufacturers like Sir William Armstrong or embellishing old ones for established county families enriched by coal royalties. To both he offered Greek Revival or Tudor Gothic dress with equal facility. Though he was probably as competent a purveyor of domestic Gothic as Burn or Blore, it is his classical houses that are most revealing of Dobson's stature as an architect. Carefully sited, and superbly built of meticulously accurate masonry, their sensible planning soon earned for their architect the reputation of 'having the secret of keeping out the cold'. The detailing is always scholarly and precise, but the scale is apt to be over-large and the effect is sometimes rather bleak. As Pevsner observes, the staircase at Meldon Park is 'the size of one in a London club'. Nevertheless they are handsome and habitable houses, and agreeably free from the stereotyped pedantry of so many English Greek Revival houses of the same date.

Dobson never visited the Mediterranean. But as a young man he travelled in England and France. He was a Fellow of the R.I.B.A. and in 1859 became the first President of the Northern Architectural Association. His youngest son Alexander had an architectural training with Sydney Smirke (who had married Dobson's eldest daughter), but died prematurely in 1854 in the explosion at Gateshead. Dobson himself was incapacitated by a stroke about two years before his death at Newcastle on 8 January 1865. A bust of Dobson is reproduced in his daughter's *Memoir*, and an oil portrait is illustrated by Wilkes and Dodds, *Tyneside Classical*, 36. Some topographical drawings by Dobson are in the Laing Art Gallery at Newcastle.

[Margaret Jane Dobson, *A Memoir of John Dobson*, 1885; obituary in *Builder* xxiii, 1865, 27; R. Welford, *Men of Mark 'twixt Tyne and Tweed* ii, 1895, 81–4; L. Wilkes & G. Dodds, *Tyneside Classical: The Newcastle of Grainger, Dobson and Clayton*, 1964; Mark Girouard, 'Dobson's Northumbrian Houses', *C. Life*, 17 and 24 Feb. 1966.]

Unless otherwise stated, the list that follows is a corrected version of the long but very unreliable list of Dobson's works printed by his daughter in her *Memoir* of her father. Some items in that list have been omitted, either because the work in question does not appear to have been carried

out, or because the identification of the building is in doubt.

PUBLIC AND COMMERCIAL BUILDINGS IN NEWCASTLE

THE ROYAL JUBILEE SCHOOL, 1810–11 [E. Mackenzie, *Newcastle* ii, 1827, 452].
WAREHOUSE at BROAD CHARE, 1814.
THE CUSTOM HOUSE, alterations, 1817.
THE OLD THEATRE, alterations to entrance, 1817; dem.
WAREHOUSES at QUAYSIDE for Mr. Sorsbie, 1818.
TOBACCO WAREHOUSE, QUAYSIDE, 1819.
ST. NICHOLAS CHARITY SCHOOL, 1819–20 [E. Mackenzie, *Newcastle* ii, 1827, 446–7].
THE GUILDHALL or EXCHANGE, SANDHILL, added rounded addition to east end containing Fish Market on ground floor, 1823–6.
THE GAOL and HOUSE OF CORRECTION, CARLIOL STREET, 1823–8; dem.
THE LUNATIC ASYLUM, reconstructed 1824 [E. Mackenzie, *Newcastle* ii, 1827, 525–6].
THE LYING-IN HOSPITAL (now Broadcasting House), BRIDGE STREET, 1825–6, Tudor style.
ELDON SQUARE, façades for Richard Grainger, 1825–31 [L. Wilkes & G. Dodds, *Tyneside Classical*, 1964].
ST. MARY'S PLACE, 1829, Tudor Gothic style.
THE NORTHERN ACADEMY OF ARTS, NO. 41 BLACKETT STREET, 1830.
POLICE OFFICES, MANOR CHARE, 1831, Tudor Gothic style.
THE ROYAL ARCADE, 1831–2; dem. 1963.
NORTHERN COUNTIES' CLUB, 1833.
THE NEW MARKETS, 1835–6.
GREY STREET, façades of east side, between Mosley and Shakespeare Streets, for Richard Grainger, c. 1835–9 [L. Wilkes & G. Dodds, *Tyneside Classical*, 1964].
THE SUNDERLAND AND DURHAM UNION JOINT STOCK BANK, MOSLEY STREET, 1836.
THE GENERAL CEMETERY, JESMOND ROAD, Chapels and Entrance Gates, 1836.
THE PUBLIC BATHS, RIDLEY PLACE, 1838–9.
THE CASTLE, restoration of Keep, 1844.
THE RIDING SCHOOL, 1847.
THE CENTRAL RAILWAY STATION, 1847–50 (T. L. Donaldson, *Handbook of Specifications*, 1860, 842).
THE MANORS STATION and GOODS WAREHOUSE, 1849–50 (T. L. Donaldson, *Handbook of Specifications*, 1860, 831).
THE SURGEONS' HALL, RYEHILL, 1851.
THE COLLEGE OF MEDICINE, NEVILLE STREET, 1851–2.
THE INFIRMARY, new wing, 1852–5.
RAGGED SCHOOLS, 1853–4.
PLUMMER'S FLAX MILL.
TOLL-HOUSES, one near the Infirmary, another near St. Thomas's Church.

PUBLIC AND COMMERCIAL BUILDINGS
ELSEWHERE

TYNEMOUTH, NORTHUMBERLAND, HOUSE OF COR-
RECTION, alterations and additions, 1814.

WALLSEND, NORTHUMBERLAND, planned HOWDEN
DOCKS, 1814.

LIVERPOOL, CUSTOM HOUSE, alterations, 1817;
dem. *c.* 1830.

GLASGOW, CUSTOM HOUSE, alterations, 1817; dem.

SOUTH SHIELDS, DURHAM, Glass-works for Mr.
Cookson, 1817.

PONTELAND, NORTHUMBERLAND, SCHOOL, 1817.

MORPETH, NORTHUMBERLAND, COUNTY GAOL and
SESSIONS HOUSE, 1822–31, castellated [E.
Mackenzie, *Northumberland* ii, 1825, 188–9,
with plan; original drawings at Syon House,
Middlesex].

SEAHAM HARBOUR, DURHAM, planned new town for
the 3rd Marquess of Londonderry, 1828.
There are designs by Dobson in the Durham
County Record Office (D/Lo. 596/3
and 6).

HOLY ISLAND, Cross for Henry Collingwood
Selby, 1829 [*Proc. Soc. Antiquaries of Newcastle*, 3rd ser., iii, 1907–8, 286].

MORPETH BRIDGE, NORTHUMBERLAND (R. Wansbeck), 1830– [J. Hodgson, *History of Northumberland* ii (2), 1832, 426].

HENDON, DURHAM, SCHOOL, 1831.

CHOLLERTON, NORTHUMBERLAND, SCHOOL, 1831.

GATESHEAD, DURHAM, Railway Station and Viaduct, 1841.

CARLISLE, LONDON ROAD RAILWAY STATION, for the
Newcastle & Carlisle Railway, 1841.

NORTH SHIELDS, NORTHUMBERLAND, TOWN HALL,
1845, Gothic [J. Latimer, *Local Records 1832–
57*, Newcastle 1857, 202].

TYNEMOUTH, NORTHUMBERLAND, TOWN HALL,
1845 [*History of Northumberland* viii,
352].

TYNEMOUTH, NORTHUMBERLAND, the COLL-
INGWOOD MONUMENT, 1847.

SUNDERLAND, DURHAM, warehouses in Docks,
1850.

HAY HOLE DOCKS, nr. NORTH SHIELDS, NORTHUM-
BERLAND, Dock Offices, 1850.

LYMM, CHESHIRE, SCHOOL, 1850.

WHITBY, YORKS. (N.R.), planned WEST CLIFF development for George Hudson, and designed
EAST TERRACE, *c.* 1850 onwards.

SOUTH SHIELDS, DURHAM, ST. STEPHEN'S NATIONAL
SCHOOL, 1852–3 [*Builder* xi, 1853, 167].

WHIXLEY, YORKS. (W.R.), SCHOOL, 1853.

BISHOPWEARMOUTH, SUNDERLAND, DURHAM,
SCHOOL, 1853.

ROKER, DURHAM, Baths and terraces, 1855.

WARRINGTON, LANCS., LIBRARY AND MUSEUM,
1855–7.

LIVERPOOL, warehouses, 1856.

LEEDS, YORKS. (W.R.), STATION HOTEL, 1857.

MIDDLESBROUGH, YORKS. (N.R.), FREEMASONS'
LODGE, 1858.

NETHERTON, NORTHUMBERLAND, Reformatory.

CHURCHES
(Gothic unless otherwise stated)

NORTH SHIELDS, NORTHUMBERLAND, SCOTCH
CHURCH, HOWARD STREET, 1811, Doric.

NEWCASTLE, NEW ROAD WESLEYAN METHODIST
CHAPEL, 1813, probably classical.

HEXHAM PRIORY CHURCH, NORTHUMBERLAND,
repairs, 1817–18.

ST. JOHN LEE, nr. HEXHAM, NORTHUMBERLAND,
rebuilt east end, 1818–19.

GOSFORTH, NORTHUMBERLAND, enlarged on north
side, 1819, Tuscan.

WHITBURN, DURHAM, restoration, 1819.

NEWCASTLE, ST. NICHOLAS (CATHEDRAL), rebuilt
north window of north transept, 1824;
repaired foundations of west tower (with J.
Green) 1832–3.

WHICKHAM, DURHAM, restoration, 1819; enlarged
1862 (not by Dobson).

ALNWICK, NORTHUMBERLAND, restoration, 1825.

NEWCASTLE, ST. JAMES'S PRESBYTERIAN CHAPEL,
BLACKETT STREET, 1826, Greek Doric; dem.
1859.

GREENHEAD, NORTHUMBERLAND, 1826–8; chancel
added 1900.

MONKWEARMOUTH, SUNDERLAND, DURHAM,
SCOTCH CHURCH, 1826–7, classical [M. A.
Richardson, *The Local Historian's Table-Book*
iii, 356].

BELFORD, NORTHUMBERLAND, largely rebuilt
1828–9 [I.C.B.S.] (F. R. Wilson, *Churches in
the Archdeaconry of Lindisfarne*, 1870, 85).

NEWCASTLE, ST. THOMAS, BARRAS BRIDGE, 1828–9
(B. Allsopp, *Historic Architecture of Newcastle*,
1967, 66–7, with plan).

NEWCASTLE, ST. JOHN, restorations, 1829, 1848
and 1859.

HARTBURN, NORTHUMBERLAND, restoration, 1829
(F. R. Wilson, *Churches in the Archdeaconry of
Lindisfarne*, 1870, 176).

STAMFORDHAM, NORTHUMBERLAND, restoration,
1830; further restoration by B. Ferrey
1848.

BENWELL, NORTHUMBERLAND, ST. JAMES, 1831–2;
chancel, etc., added 1895 [signed drawings in
R.I.B.A. Coll.].

MINSTERACRES, NORTHUMBERLAND, chapel
(R.C.), 1834.

DINNINGTON, NORTHUMBERLAND, 1834–5
[*Builder* xxiii, 1865, 27].

GATESHEAD, DURHAM, HOLY TRINITY CHAPEL, restoration, 1837; enlarged on north side 1893–
4 [J. Latimer, *Local Records 1832–1857*, 1857,
80].

BELLINGHAM, NORTHUMBERLAND, ST. OSWALD
(R.C.), 1837–9 [J. Latimer, *Local Records 1832–*

265

1857, 1857, 112; M. A. Richardson, *Local Historian's Table-Book*, v, 1846, 122].

COWPEN, NORTHUMBERLAND, ST. CUTHBERT (R.C.), 1840.

NEWCASTLE, ST. PETER, OXFORD STREET, 1840–3; dem.

LONG HORSLEY, NORTHUMBERLAND, ST. THOMAS (R.C.), 1841.

FELLING, nr. GATESHEAD, DURHAM, ST. PATRICK (R.C.), 1841; rebuilt 1893–5.

BIRTLEY, DURHAM, ST. MARY AND ST. JOSEPH (R.C.), 1842–3.

NEWCASTLE, ST. ANDREW, restored north and south transepts and chancel, 1844–6.

NORTH SHIELDS, NORTHUMBERLAND, BAPTIST CHAPEL, 1845–6, neo-Norman.

WARWICK BRIDGE CHURCH, CUMBERLAND, 1846, neo-Norman.

GATESHEAD, DURHAM, ST. CUTHBERT, BENSHAM, 1846–8, neo-Norman [drawings and specification in Society of Antiquaries' Library].

MONKWEARMOUTH, SUNDERLAND, DURHAM, ALL SAINTS, 1846–9; dem.

NEWCASTLE, TRINITY PRESBYTERIAN CHURCH, NEW BRIDGE STREET, 1847; dem.

ALSTON, CUMBERLAND, repairs, 1847; rebuilt 1869–70.

SOUTH SHIELDS, DURHAM, PRESBYTERIAN CHURCH, FREDERICK STREET, LAYGATE, 1847–9; largely dem. *c.* 1935.

WINSTON, DURHAM, restoration, 1848.

STELLA, DURHAM, ST. COLUMBA (R.C.), enlarged 1848–9.

KIRKNEWTON CHURCH, NORTHUMBERLAND, restorations, 1849 and 1857 (F. R. Wilson, *Churches in the Archdeaconry of Lindisfarne*, 1870, 71).

BYWELL ST. PETER, NORTHUMBERLAND, restoration, 1849.

BENFIELDSIDE CHURCH, SHOTLEY BRIDGE, DURHAM, 1849–50.

BISHOPWEARMOUTH, SUNDERLAND, DURHAM, addition of transepts, 1849–50 [W. Fordyce, *History of Durham* ii, 1857, 429].

TYNEMOUTH PRIORY CHURCH, NORTHUMBERLAND, restored PERCY CHAPEL, *c.* 1850.

LYMM, CHESHIRE, rebuilt 1850–1; west tower added 1888–90 [*Builder* x, 1851, 631].

EMBLETON, NORTHUMBERLAND, alterations, including rebuilding of Craster aisle, 1850 (F. R. Wilson, *Churches in the Archdeaconry of Lindisfarne*, 1870, 134).

HENDON, DURHAM, ST. PAUL, 1851–2.

NEWCASTLE, UNITARIAN CHURCH, NEW BRIDGE STREET, 1852–4; dem.

FORD, NORTHUMBERLAND, restoration, 1852–3 (F. R. Wilson, *Churches in the Archdeaconry of Lindisfarne*, 1870, 45).

CHATTON, NORTHUMBERLAND, restoration, 1853 (F. R. Wilson, *Churches in the Archdeaconry of Lindisfarne*, 1870, 67).

HARTLEPOOL, DURHAM, CEMETERY CHAPELS and ENTRANCE, 1854–5.

GATESHEAD, DURHAM, ST. MARY, restoration, 1855, after damage by explosion.

OTTERBURN, NORTHUMBERLAND, 1855–7 (F. R. Wilson, *Churches in the Archdeaconry of Lindisfarne*, 1870, 105).

NORTH SHIELDS, NORTHUMBERLAND, WESLEYAN CHAPEL, HOWARD STREET, 1856–7, classical [J. Latimer, *Local Records 1832–1857*, 1857, 381].

NORTH SHIELDS, NORTHUMBERLAND, ST. COLUMBA'S PRESBYTERIAN CHURCH, NORTHUMBERLAND SQUARE, 1856–7, Italianate [J. Latimer, *Local Records 1832–1857*, 1857, 388].

HEXHAM PRIORY CHURCH, NORTHUMBERLAND, rebuilt east end, 1858.

HOUGHTON-LE-SPRING CHURCH, DURHAM, reconstruction of tower arches, 1858–9.

NEWCASTLE, CLAYTON MEMORIAL (PARISH) CHURCH, JESMOND, 1858–61.

WARKWORTH CHURCH, NORTHUMBERLAND, restoration of nave, 1860 (F. R. Wilson, *Churches in the Archdeaconry of Lindisfarne*, 1870, 119).

SUDBROOKE, LINCS., 1860–2, neo-Norman.

SOUTH SHIELDS, DURHAM, ST. MARY, TYNE DOCK, 1860–3.

NEWCASTLE, ST. PAUL, HIGH ELSWICK, 1861.

DOMESTIC ARCHITECTURE

EARSDON, NORTHUMBERLAND, house for J. Nicholson, 1813 [*Builder* xxiii, 1865, 27].

BRADLEY HALL, nr. RYTON, DURHAM, alterations for the 1st Lord Ravensworth, 1813.

FIELD HOUSE, nr. GATESHEAD, DURHAM, for George Barras, 1813.

SEATON DELAVAL, NORTHUMBERLAND, restoration of west wing (gutted by fire in 1752) for Sir Jacob Astley, Bart., 1814–15; central block gutted by fire 1822, after which Dobson was 'consulted with regard to its restoration'.

WATERVILLE HOUSE, NORTH SHIELDS, NORTHUMBERLAND, for R. Rippon, 1815.

FALLODEN HALL, NORTHUMBERLAND, additions for Sir George Grey, Bart., 1815; rebuilt after a fire 19

CRAMLINGTON HALL, NORTHUMBERLAND, for — Lawson, *c.* 1815; dem. [*Builder* xxiii, 1865, 27].

PRESTWICK LODGE, nr. PONTELAND, NORTHUMBERLAND, for P. Fenwick, 1815.

UNTHANK HALL, NORTHUMBERLAND, additions for Dixon Dixon, 1815 and 1860.

BIRTLEY HALL, DURHAM, for J. Warwick, 1813.

BENWELL GROVE, nr. NEWCASTLE, for Charles Cook, 1816.

MINSTERACRES, nr. HEXHAM, NORTHUMBERLAND, enlarged for George Silvertop, 1816.

ELAND HALL, PONTELAND, NORTHUMBERLAND, for William Barkley, 1816.

WHICKHAM, DURHAM, house for J. Errington, 1816.

WEST JESMOND HOUSE (later JESMOND TOWERS), NEWCASTLE, additions for Sir Thomas Burdon, 1817; further additions for Richard Burdon Sanderson, 1823–7; much enlarged by subsequent owners; now La Sagesse Convent School, Gothic.

AXWELL PARK, DURHAM, alterations and additions for Sir John Clavering, Bart., including garden temple, 1817–18.

JESMOND GROVE, NEWCASTLE, for James Losh, 1817.

VILLA REALE (now SANDYFORD PARK), JESMOND, NEWCASTLE, for Capt. John Dutton, 1817.

JESMOND VILLA, NEWCASTLE, additions for Armorer Donkin, 1818.

DOXFORD HALL, NORTHUMBERLAND, for William Taylor, 1818.

BELFORD HALL, NORTHUMBERLAND, alterations and additions for William Clark, 1818.

CHIPCHASE CASTLE, NORTHUMBERLAND, restoration of fenestration and other alterations for John Reed, 1819 (C. Life, 21 June 1956).

CHEESEBURN GRANGE, NORTHUMBERLAND, additions for Ralph Riddell, 1813 and 1819. Dobson appears also to have designed the private Catholic chapel (replaced c. 1860 by the present one designed by J. A. Hansom).

NORTH SHIELDS, NORTHUMBERLAND, PRESTON VILLA, for John Fenwick, 1819.

HEXHAM ABBEY HOUSE, NORTHUMBERLAND, alterations for T. R. Beaumont, 1819 (presumably repairs after the fire which damaged the house in 1818).

THE HERMITAGE, nr. HEXHAM, NORTHUMBERLAND, alterations for R. L. Allgood, 1819 (or ? after 1821, the date of the death of the previous owner John Hunter, whose daughter Allgood had married).

HEBBURN HALL, DURHAM, alterations for Cuthbert Ellison, 1819.

WEST CHURTON HOUSE, NORTH SHIELDS, NORTHUMBERLAND, for Michael Robson, 1819.

BROOME PARK, NORTHUMBERLAND, alterations for William Burrell, 1820; dem. 1953.

BIDDLESTONE, nr. ROTHBURY, NORTHUMBERLAND, alterations for Walter Selby, 1820.

HAWTHORN DENE HOUSE, nr. SEAHAM, DURHAM, for Major Anderson, 1821, Gothic; remodelled as Hawthorn Tower by Thomas Moore of Sunderland c. 1850.

NEWBROUGH HALL, NORTHUMBERLAND, for Rev. H. Wastell, 1821.

SOUTH HILL HOUSE, PLAWSWORTH, DURHAM, for Thomas Fenwick, 1821.

BLACK DENE (afterwards JESMOND DENE) HOUSE, JESMOND, NEWCASTLE, for T. E. Headlam, M.D., 1822.

ANGERTON HALL, NORTHUMBERLAND, for Ralph Atkinson, 1823, Tudor Gothic.

SWANSFIELD HOUSE, nr. ALNWICK, NORTHUMBERLAND, for Henry Collingwood Selby, 1823.

HALTWHISTLE, NORTHUMBERLAND, house for Rev. N. J. Hollingsworth, 1823.

LONGHIRST HOUSE, nr. MORPETH, NORTHUMBERLAND, for William Lawson, 1824–8 (C. Life, 17 Feb. 1966).

FLOTTERTON HOUSE, NORTHUMBERLAND, for C. Wealands, 1825 [E. Mackenzie, Northumberland ii, 1825, 485].

NUNNYKIRK, NORTHUMBERLAND, rebuilt for William Orde, 1825 (C. Life, 17 Feb. 1966).

GORTANLOISK, nr. DUNOON, ARGYLLSHIRE, for Sir John Fife, Bart., 1827.

MATFEN, NORTHUMBERLAND, alterations (probably to the Dower House) for Sir Edward Blackett, Bart., 1828.

LILBURN TOWER, NORTHUMBERLAND, for H. J. W. Collingwood, 1829–37, Tudor style. The stables were added for E. J. Collingwood soon after 1842 (C. Life, 8 Nov. 1973).

EDINBURGH, house for Charles Bruce, 1828.

MITFORD CASTLE, NORTHUMBERLAND, for B. O. Mitford, c. 1828 (C. Life, 17 Feb. 1966).

WOOLSINGTON HALL, NORTHUMBERLAND, alterations for Matthew Bell, 1828.

HARBOTTLE HOUSE, NORTHUMBERLAND, alterations for T. F. Clennell, 1829.

RIDLEY HALL, NORTHUMBERLAND, alterations for Thomas Davison, 1829.

GLANTON HALL, NORTHUMBERLAND, additions for Henry Collingwood, 1829.

TREWHITT HOUSE, nr. ROTHBURY, NORTHUMBERLAND, for J. Smart, 1830.

BENWELL TOWER (since 1881 Bishop of Newcastle's house), nr. NEWCASTLE, for Thomas Crawhall, 1830–1, Tudor style. Three drawings by Dobson in the R.I.B.A. Coll. may relate to this house.

BRINKBURN PRIORY, NORTHUMBERLAND, additions for Major William Hodgson-Cadogan, 1830–7.

CHESTERS, nr. HEXHAM, NORTHUMBERLAND, additions for John Clayton, 1832 and 1837; remodelled by Norman Shaw 1893.

BLENKINSOPP, NORTHUMBERLAND, additions (probably to the Hall, not the Castle) for Col. J. B. Coulson, 1832 and 1837.

MELDON PARK, NORTHUMBERLAND, for Isaac Cookson, 1832 (C. Life, 24 Feb. 1966).

HOLME EDEN, CUMBERLAND, for Peter Dixon, 1833, Tudor style.

NEASHAM HALL, DURHAM, for J. S. Cookson, 1834–7.

DARLINGTON, DURHAM, house for J. Wilson, 1834.

HIGH WARDEN, nr. HEXHAM, NORTHUMBERLAND, for John Errington, 1834.

CHATTON VICARAGE, NORTHUMBERLAND, 1834, Tudor style.

BEAUFRONT CASTLE, NORTHUMBERLAND, rebuilt for William Cuthbert, 1837–41, Gothic (C. Life, 29 Jan., 5 Feb. 1976).

CRASTER TOWER, NORTHUMBERLAND, minor alterations for Thomas Wood-Craster, 1839 [family records, *ex. inf.* the late Sir Edmund Craster].

SWINBURNE CASTLE, NORTHUMBERLAND, alterations for Thomas Riddell, 1840; dem.

EAST BOLDON HOUSE, DURHAM, alterations for William Gray, 1840.

BAMBURGH CASTLE, NORTHUMBERLAND, restoration for Lord Crewe's trustees, 1843.

HACKWOOD HOUSE, HEXHAM, NORTHUMBERLAND, for Charles Head, 1843.

HAUGHTON CASTLE, NORTHUMBERLAND, restoration for William Smith, 1844.

LINETHWAITE, nr. WHITEHAVEN, CUMBERLAND, for H. Harrison, 1845 [*Builder* xxiii, 1865, 27].

THE KNELLS, nr. CARLISLE, CUMBERLAND, works for John Dixon, 1845.

ROCK HALL, NORTHUMBERLAND, restoration for Charles Bosanquet, 1845.

CLEADON COTTAGE, nr. SUNDERLAND, DURHAM, for Robert Swinburne, 1845.

THE BANK HOUSE, NEWBIGGIN, nr. MIDDLETON-IN-TEESDALE, DURHAM, for J. H. Hinde, 1845.

SETTRINGTON RECTORY, YORKS. (E.R.), for the Rev. C. M. Long, soon after 1846 [*Builder* xxiii, 1865, 27].

SANDHOE HOUSE, nr. HEXHAM, NORTHUMBERLAND, for Sir Rowland Errington, Bart., 1850, Jacobean style.

MIDDLESBROUGH, YORKS. (N.R.), house for A. Topham, 1851.

HIGH CROSS (hamlet), BENWELL, NORTHUMBERLAND, 1851.

RYTON, DURHAM, extensive additions to house for R. Leadbitter, 1851.

NEWTON HALL, nr. BYWELL, NORTHUMBERLAND, alterations for W. Blackett, 1851.

WINDSOR, BERKS., CHURCH HOUSE, for Rev. Stephen Hawtrey, 1851.

SUDBROOKE HOLME, LINCS., additions for Richard Ellison, 1851; dem.

NEWCASTLE, DENE HOUSE, for William Cruddace, 1851.

HENDON, SUNDERLAND, DURHAM, ST. PAUL'S RECTORY, 1852.

DALDAWN HOUSE, KIRKCUDBRIGHTSHIRE, for Rev. Dr. Cowan, 1852.

THE LEAZES, nr. HEXHAM, NORTHUMBERLAND, for William Kirsopp, 1853.

CLEADON MEADOW, nr. SUNDERLAND, DURHAM, for Robert Shortridge, 1853.

BISHOPWEARMOUTH RECTORY, SUNDERLAND, DURHAM, 1853.

WALLINGTON HALL, NORTHUMBERLAND, the Central Hall for Sir Walter Trevelyan, Bart., 1853–4 (*C. Life*, 30 April 1970).

INGLETHORPE HALL, nr. WISBECH, NORFOLK, for Edward Metcalfe, 1854.

SEGHILL PARSONAGE, NORTHUMBERLAND, 1855.

SCAR HOUSE, ARKENDALE, YORKS. (W.R.), for J. Gilpin, 1855.

GIBSIDE, DURHAM, additions for the 12th Earl of

Strathmore, 1856; ruinous. An unexecuted design by Dobson for additions to Gibside in 1814 is in the Durham County Record Office, D. St.x.46.

WHITBURN HALL, DURHAM, alterations (including Entrance Hall and Drawing Room) for Sir Hedworth Williamson, Bart., 1856.

HOLEYN HALL, NORTHUMBERLAND, additions for J. James, 1858.

SHAWDON HALL, NORTHUMBERLAND, additions for W. J. H. Pawson, 1858, probably including east lodge and gates (*C. Life*, 5 March 1959).

JESMOND DENE HOUSE, NEWCASTLE, additions and banqueting house for Sir William George Armstrong, 1860–2.

GREENWOOD, nr. EASTLEIGH, HANTS., for George Palmer, 1861; dem.

LAMBTON CASTLE, DURHAM, designs for rebuilding for the 2nd Earl of Durham, carried out by his son-in-law Sydney Smirke 1862–66 (*C. Life*, 24–31 March 1966).

NEWCASTLE, houses for James Morrison (Gresham Place), David Cram (Ellison Place), J. Harvey (Strawberry Place), William Todd (Picton Place), and himself (New Bridge Street).

DODDS, JOHN, was a builder and architect of Newcastle-on-Tyne. In 1784 he was employed by John Reed to carry out minor alterations to CHIPCHASE CASTLE, NORTHUMBERLAND [Gordon Nares in *C. Life*, 14–21 June, 1956], and in 1788 he made an unexecuted design for rebuilding LAMBTON HALL, DURHAM, for General John Lambton [C. Hussey in *C. Life*, 24 March 1966, 667]. In 1786 he and David Stephenson surveyed the church of ALL SAINTS, NEWCASTLE, and decided that it must be completely rebuilt. He submitted designs for a new church, but they were rejected in favour of Stephenson's [T. Sopwith, *An Historical and Descriptive Account of All Saints Church, Newcastle*, 1826, 19, 47]. In 1790–1 he rebuilt LONG BENTON CHURCH, NORTHUMBERLAND, except the chancel. It was Gothicized in the nineteenth century [*Archaeologia Aeliana*, 4th ser., ix, 1932, 135]. GOSFORTH CHURCH, NORTHUMBERLAND, was rebuilt to his designs in 1798–9 [*History of Northumberland* xiii, 336]. Dodds appears to have been a minor Georgian architect of no great distinction.

DODDS, JOSEPH, was a builder and architect of Berwick on Tweed, of which town he was a Bailiff in 1764 and 1769. In 1747 he and George Douglass had leave to work up the clay they had already dug in the Loanen and burn it into bricks, but not to dig any more [Corporation Guild Books, *sub anno*]. Between 1750 and 1754 he built the TOWNHOUSE, BERWICK ON TWEED, to the design of Samuel and John Worrall of London. The inscription, 'JOSEPH DODS. ARCHITECT. 1754', is carved over the doorway, but the Guild Books make it clear that Dodds was the contractor, and not the architect in the modern sense. There was a dispute over the execution of his contract, which was referred to arbitration. In 1769 he received an 'anonymous and incendiary Paper' threatening his life [Guild Books, 28 July 1769].

DONALDSON, JAMES (*c.* 1756–1843), was a member of an Ayrshire family, and eventually inherited an estate in that county called Williamshaw (in Stewarton parish). In 1774 he was apprenticed to Thomas Leverton, and later married his niece Jane (daughter of Andrew) Leverton [P.R.O., Apprenticeship Registers; *V.C.H. Essex* vi, 268, n. 59]. It was 'from Mr. Leverton's' that in 1777 he exhibited his first drawing at the Royal Academy – 'a design for a temple'. In 1782 Robert Mylne engaged him as a clerk, and he remained in Mylne's office for some years. From 1809 until his death he held one of the District Surveyorships for the City of London. He lived in Bloomsbury, and in 1793 exhibited at the Royal Academy a 'Design for the new schoolroom now building in Bloomsbury Churchyard, with an elevation of the Church'. In the British Museum there is (*King's Maps* xxvii, 29 (3)) 'An Ideographical View of the New Chapel, Tavistock Place, Russell Square', signed 'J. Donaldson del. scul. etc. 1802.' The Tavistock (afterwards St. Andrew's) Chapel was built by James Burton in 1801 and demolished in 1900. A survey plan of Culzean Castle, Ayrshire, by James Donaldson, dated 1818, is preserved in a portfolio there. Donaldson died in Bloomsbury on 8 October 1843, aged 87 [*Gent's Mag.* 1843 (ii), 553; P.R.O. PROB. 11/1988, 759].

Donaldson's elder son James supervised the erection of the SURREY THEATRE, BLACKFRIARS ROAD, to the designs of R. Cabanel in 1805–6, but 'fell a sacrifice to his great exertions and anxiety to get the theatre finished within the time that he had engaged', and died in 1806 at an early age [J. Elmes, *Metropolitan Improvements*, 1831, 135]. The most distinguished member of the family was his younger son Thomas Leverton Donaldson (1795–1885), who as a teacher, scholar and virtual founder of the R.I.B.A. was a prominent figure in the Victorian architectural scene. Regarded as 'the father of the profession', he was President of the R.I.B.A. in 1863–4, and was awarded the Royal Gold Medal in 1851. In 1842 he became the first Professor of Architecture at University College, London, and held the post for over twenty years (see Sandra Blutman in *R.I.B.A. Jnl.*, Dec. 1967, 542–4, for a fuller account of his career). As a practising architect he was less distinguished, but his works included HOLY TRINITY CHURCH, BROMPTON, 1826–9, Gothic (criticized in *Gent's Mag.* 1830 (i), 579–80); the handsome classical library of UNIVERSITY

COLLEGE, LONDON, 1848–9; UNIVERSITY HALL (now Dr. Williams's Library), GORDON SQUARE, LONDON, 1848–9, Tudor Gothic; the centre of DALBY HALL, LEICS., for E. B. Hartopp, 1837–8, dem. [exhib. at R.A. 1837]; LAMBOURNE PLACE, BERKS., for Henry Hippisley, 1846, Jacobethan, dem. [exhib. at R.A. 1846]; and the refronting of SHOBROOKE PARK, DEVON, for J. H. Hippisley, dem. 1947 [*Builder*, 8 Aug. 1885, 179].

DONALDSON, THOMAS LEVERTON (1795–1885), *see* DONALDSON, JAMES

DONN, WILLIAM, exhibited at the Free Society of Artists in 1770 and 1775. He competed for the Royal Exchange, Dublin, in 1769, and exhibited his design at the Royal Academy in 1770. He lived in Maddox Street, Hanover Square. From 1769 to 1773 he was Surveyor to the Westminster Commissioners of Sewers. Letters and drawings preserved at CLAYDON HOUSE, BUCKS., show that in the 1770s Donn was employed by Lord Verney to complete the ballroom and rotunda designed by Sir Thomas Robinson, and that at the same time he was engaged in altering the interior of APPULDURCOMBE HOUSE, in the ISLE OF WIGHT, for Sir Richard Worsley, Bart. Here he may have been supervising the execution of designs made by James Wyatt [L. O. J. Boynton, *Appuldurcombe House*, H.M.S.O. 1967, 15]. In 1774 he was in correspondence with Thomas Estcourt, then about to rebuild ESTCOURT PARK, GLOS., dem. 1963 [Glos. Record Office, D 1571/E 356].

DONOWELL, JOHN, was an architectural draughtsman who appears to have made his living mainly by publishing topographical views in much the same way as the Maltons. In 1754 he issued proposals for engraving and publishing by subscription a series of 'Perspective Views of the Colleges and other Public Building of Oxford' [*Jackson's Oxford Jnl.*, 9 Nov. 1754], and eight prints, signed 'J. Donowell Arch.', were issued the following year. Other drawings of his which were engraved include two of St. Giles-in-the-Fields Church (1753), two of the gardens at Chiswick House (1753), one of Ironmongers' Hall (1753), and one of Marylebone Gardens (1761). He exhibited at the Free Society of Artists (1761), at the Society of Artists at Spring Gardens (1762–70), and at the Royal Academy (1778–86). Many of his exhibits were of a topographical character, but they included a design for Skinners' Hall (1781), several for noblemen's houses, and a 'Sketch of a Design for a Palace'. A drawing by him of the south front of Cliveden House, Bucks., is in the Print Room of the British Museum.

It is uncertain to what extent Donowell practised as an architect, but the plan and elevation of WEST WYCOMBE PARK, BUCKS., in the fifth volume of *Vitruvius Britannicus*, are subscribed 'J. Donowell, Archt.' Payments by the hand of J. Donowell are recorded under the year 1755 in the manuscript account-book of Banister Watts, a High Wycombe mason, who was employed by Sir Francis Dashwood in the house and grounds. Moreover, there is among the Dashwood family papers a letter from Donowell about the purchase of Portland stone, dated 22 September 1763, and there are payments to 'Mr. Donowell's men' in the West Wycombe accounts for 1761–3. He appears to have been employed to remodel the house under Dashwood's supervision, acting as draughtsman and clerk of works rather than as an autonomous architect. Even in this subordinate capacity he failed to give satisfaction and was dismissed in 1764. A friend of Dashwood commented: 'I believe the Man is honest & does to the best of his Abilities, but these I am afraid from the experience I have had of him are not very extensive.' The only other evidence of Donowell's activities as an architect so far noted is a statement in Pennant's *Journey from Chester to London*, 1782, 411, that HATFIELD HOUSE, HERTS., had recently 'undergone a complete repair . . . under the conduct of Mr. Donowell the architect'.

DONTHORN, WILLIAM JOHN (1799–1859), was born at Swaffham in Norfolk in May 1799. He became a pupil of Jeffry Wyatville (1817–20) and subsequently practised from 18 Hanover Street, London. He exhibited regularly at the Royal Academy from 1817 to 1853 and at the Norwich Society of Artists from 1818 to 1830. He was a founder member of the R.I.B.A. E. J. Payne was his pupil. He died at Hastings on 18 May 1859, and is commemorated by a tablet in the north aisle of Swaffham Church. A large collection of his drawings is in the R.I.B.A. Drawings Collection. It was originally bound in four volumes titled 'Classic Mansions', 'Gothic Mansions', 'Parsonage Houses' and 'Plans', and appears to have been intended for publication.

Donthorn had an extensive practice as a designer of country houses and parsonages, especially in his native county of Norfolk. His classical houses (nearly all demolished) were remarkably doctrinaire essays in Greek revivalism, their simple geometry and plain external surfaces recalling the work of French neo-classical designers such as Boullée and Ledoux. As a purveyor of Tudor Gothic he was more prolific but less remarkable, and (despite his election to the Cambridge Camden Society in 1843) failed to satisfy the standards of the ecclesiologists. His design for a new square adjoining Westminster Abbey, exhibited at the R.A. in 1846, was condemned in the *Gentleman's Magazine* (1846 (ii), 292) as an outmoded 'resuscitation of Wyatt's darling fancies', and it was characteristic of his

270

approach to Gothic design that the turrets of his parsonage houses often did duty as chimneys. In 1844 he won the competition for the Leicester Memorial at Holkham by methods that were criticized both in the correspondence columns of the *Builder* (ii, 1844, 12, 23, 36) and in the *Narrative* of the proceedings that was subsequently printed. The design consisted of a fluted column surmounted by a wheatsheaf and standing on a pedestal adorned with sculptures symbolizing Coke of Norfolk's agricultural achievements. [*Gent's Mag.* 1859 (ii), 659; *Builder* xvii, 1859, 366; *Catalogue of the R.I.B.A. Drawings Coll.*: C–F, 83–9; *Ecclesiologist* iii, 1843, 44.]

DOMESTIC ARCHITECTURE

MARHAM HOUSE, NORFOLK, added dining-room and circular drawing-room for Henry Villebois, *c.* 1822; dem. [R.I.B.A.D., which includes a rejected Gothic design] (R. H. Mason, *Norfolk Photographically Illustrated*, 1865).

HILLINGTON HALL, NORFOLK, remodelled for Sir William Browne Ffolkes, Bart., 1824–8, Gothic; dem. *c.* 1946 [R.I.B.A.D.; exhib. at R.A. 1824, 1825, 1828, 1841 and at Norwich Soc. of Artists 1823, 1824, 1825].

FELBRIGG HALL, NORFOLK, castellated Gothic stables for Admiral William Windham, 1825, and north corridor 1831 [R.I.B.A.D.; drawings at Felbrigg; exhib. at R.A. 1826 and at Norwich Soc. of Artists 1830].

TWICKENHAM, MIDDLESEX, ULLESWATER COTTAGE, for C. Dufour, 1827 [exhib. at R.A. 1827].

CROMER HALL, NORFOLK, for George Thomas Wyndham, 1827; destroyed by fire 1829 and rebuilt to Donthorne's designs; altered by D. Brandon 1875; Gothic [R.I.B.A.D.; exhib. at Norwich Soc. of Artists 1830; R. W. Ketton-Cremer, *Felbrigg*, 1962, 232].

PICKENHAM HALL, NORFOLK, remodelled for W. L. Wiggett Chute, 1829; rebuilt 1903–4 [R.I.B.A.D.; exhib. at R.A. 1829 and at Norwich Soc. of Artists 1830] (R. H. Mason, *Norfolk Photographically Illustrated*, 1865).

WESTACRE HIGH HOUSE, NORFOLK, refronted for Anthony Hammond, 1829 [R.I.B.A.D.].

WATLINGTON HALL, NORFOLK, for Charles Berners Plestow, 1830; destroyed by fire *c.* 1943 [R.I.B.A.D.; exhib. at Norwich Soc. of Artists 1830].

ELMHAM HALL, NORFOLK, remodelled for the Hon. G. J. Milles, 1830; dem. *c.* 1925 [R.I.B.A.D.; exhib. at Norwich Soc. of Artists 1830] (R. H. Mason, *Norfolk Photographically Illustrated*, 1865; J. Mordaunt Crook, *The Greek Revival*, 1972, pl. 141).

UPTON HALL, nr. SOUTHWELL, NOTTS., for Thomas Wright, *c.* 1830 [R.I.B.A.D.].

WOOLLAND HOUSE, DORSET, alterations and additions for G. C. Loftus, 1833; dem. [R.I.B.A.D.; exhib. at R.A. 1833].

HIGHCLIFFE CASTLE, HANTS., remodelled for Lord Stuart de Rothesay, incorporating the materials of the Norman 'Hotel des Andelys', 1830–4, Gothic [R.I.B.A.D.; exhib. R.A. 1835, 1838; letters printed by Augustus J. C. Hare in *The Story of Two Noble Lives* i, 1893, 177–9] (*C. Life*, 24 April, 1–8 May 1942, where 'Pennethorne' is a mistake for 'Donthorn').

BURE HOMAGE, MUDEFORD, HANTS., remodelled for Baroness de Feuchères, *c.* 1835; dem. 1956 [R.I.B.A.D.; exhib. at R.A. 1835]. But cf. J. Davies.

STANDGROUND, HUNTS., alterations to house for the Rev. William Strong (d. 1842) or for his son the Rev. William Strong [R.I.B.A.D.].

PETERBOROUGH, THE DEANERY (now PRIOR'S GATE), alterations, 1842 [R.I.B.A.D.; exhib. at R.A. 1842] (*C. Life*, 3 April 1958).

FOLKINGTON PLACE, SUSSEX, for Thomas Sheppard, 1844, Tudor Gothic [R.I.B.A.D.; exhib. at R.A. 1844] (*C. Life*, 3 April 1958).

CUCKFIELD PARK, SUSSEX, alterations for Warden Sergison, *c.* 1850 [R.I.B.A.D.] (*C. Life*, 15–22 March 1919).

SHELFORD HOUSE, GREAT SHELFORD, CAMBS., for Capt. Robert G. Wale, *c.* 1850, Gothic [R.I.B.A.D.].

HERONDEN HALL, TENTERDEN, KENT, for W. Whelan, 1853, Tudor Gothic [R.I.B.A.D.].

WALLINGTON HALL, NORFOLK, lodges for Edmund Peel, 1853 [exhib. at R.A. 1853].

PUBLIC BUILDINGS, ETC.

PETERBOROUGH, GAOL and SESSIONS HOUSE, 1841–2 [exhib. at R.A. 1841].

UPPER DICKER, SUSSEX, HOLY TRINITY CHURCH, 1843, neo-Norman [I.C.B.S.].

HOLKHAM, NORFOLK, THE LEICESTER MONUMENT (a column in memory of Thomas Coke, Earl of Leicester), 1845–50 [*Narrative of the Proceedings regarding the Erection of the Leicester Monument*, Norwich 1850].

STOKE FERRY CHURCH, NORFOLK, restoration, 1847–8 [*Ecclesiologist* viii, 1848, 396].

BAGTHORPE CHURCH, NORFOLK, 1853–4, Gothic [G.R.].

PARSONAGES

Donthorn designed or altered the following rectories and vicarages, for nearly all of which there are drawings in the R.I.B.A. Collection. The dates of erection have usually been ascertained from other sources. The style is normally Tudor Gothic: EAST BILNEY RECTORY, NORFOLK, 1848; CHESTERTON RECTORY, HUNTS., *c.* 1851 (?); CHIGWELL VICARAGE, ESSEX, *c.* 1850; DUMMER RECTORY, HANTS., 1850; FINCHAM RECTORY, NORFOLK;

FONTMELL RECTORY, DORSET; HALLATON RECTORY, LEICS., 1844; HARDINGHAM RECTORY, NORFOLK, 1834; HEMPSTEAD PARSONAGE, ? NORFOLK, 1825; HOLME HALE RECTORY, NORFOLK, 1846; HORNBY VICARAGE, YORKS. (N.R.), 1827–8 [exhib. at R.A. 1828]; MOULTON ST. MICHAEL RECTORY, NORFOLK, 1831–2 (Italianate); OUNDLE VICARAGE, NORTHANTS., *c.* 1845; PEASMARSH RECTORY (now HOUSE), SUSSEX, 1839; RUSHBURY RECTORY, SALOP., *c.* 1852; THRAPSTON RECTORY, NORTHANTS., 1837; TITCHWELL RECTORY, NORFOLK, after 1824 (classical); TRUNCH RECTORY, NORFOLK, 1832; WEYBRIDGE RECTORY, SURREY.

WORKHOUSES

THRAPSTON, NORTHANTS., 1836 [*Architectural Mag.* iii, 1836, 482]; WISBECH, CAMBS., 1836 [*Norfolk Chronicle*, 22 Oct. 1836]; SWAFFHAM, NORFOLK, 1836 [*ibid.*, 28 Nov. 1835]; DOWNHAM MARKET, NORFOLK, 1836, dem. [*ibid.*, 17 Sept. 1836]; GAYTON, NORFOLK, 1836 [*ibid.*, 12 March 1836]; ELY UNION, 1837–8 [*ibid.*, 13 Oct. 1838]; AYLSHAM, NORFOLK, 1848–9 [*ibid.*, 1 April 1846] [references to *Norfolk Chronicle ex inf.* Mr. A. P. Baggs, Mr. R. M. O'Donnell and Mr. D. C. Young].

DORMER, HENRY (–1727), was an architect and land-surveyor who was active in Northamptonshire and Leicestershire during the reign of William III. Several estate surveys bearing his name are in the Northamptonshire Record Office. Towards the end of his life he became Master of the Jesus Hospital at Rothwell, Northants., where he died in 1727. Over the door of the hospital is a rhymed inscription signed 'Henry Dormer, Principal, 1721'.

The earliest evidence of Dormer's architectural work is in 1686, when he was paid for 'measuring a room of wainscot ... wrought ... by Henry Jones joyner' at LAMPORT HALL, NORTHANTS. [Sir Gyles Isham, 'Architectural History of Lamport', *Northants. Architectural and Archaeological Soc.'s Report* for 1951, 19]. In the same year he may have been concerned in the rebuilding of the top of the tower of CARLTON CURLIEU CHURCH, LEICS. [*V.C.H. Leics.* v, 80]. In 1693–4 the chapel of ST. MARY IN ARDEN, MARKET HARBOROUGH, LEICS., was rebuilt to his designs [Lincolnshire Record Office, Fac. 9/73]. It is now roofless and disused. From 1694 until early in 1697, when his place was taken by John Lumley, Dormer was employed by the 2nd Earl of Nottingham to supervise the rebuilding of BURLEY-ON-THE-HILL, RUTLAND, but his share (if any) in the design is uncertain[1] [H. J. Habakkuk,

---

[1] From the papers in the Leicestershire Record Office (especially DG 7/1/128) it appears that Lord Nottingham was to a large extent his own architect. Before start-

'Daniel Finch, 2nd Earl of Nottingham: his House and Estate', in *Studies in Social History*, ed. J. H. Plumb, 1955, 148]. In 1706 Dormer made 'the modell of a new steeple' for BURTON OVERY CHURCH, LEICS. [Lincolnshire Record Office, Fac. 9/59]. Though considered 'very proper', it was not carried out. Dormer's original drawing is among the Wake Letters in the Library of Christ Church, Oxford (vol. iii). It shows a traditional battlemented tower with classical west door and cupola. St. Mary in Arden has round-leaded windows with simplified tracery of a type that probably derives from Henry Bell's All Saints Church, Northampton.

DOTCHEN, JOHN, was a minor London architect whose existence is known almost exclusively from his exhibits at the Society of Artists (1772 and 1774) and the Royal Academy (1775–1810). They included 'a villa designed for a gentleman in Middlesex' (1776), 'a small villa just finished for a gentleman in Buckinghamshire' (1781), and 'a design for a Shire Hall in the North of England' (1784). In 1808 he won the third premium in the competition for the New Bethlehem Hospital.

DOUGLAS, JOHN, practised as an architect in Edinburgh in the middle of the eighteenth century. In 1743 he stated that 'since the year 1730 he has built several Houses . . . for private Gentlemen' and that 'he has made Draughts of several Houses, which he has been afterwards imployed to build' [*Depositions in the cause William Adam v. Lord Braco*, 1743, 26]. In 1746 he was described as 'one John Douglas at Edinburgh, next in character to Mr. Adams, [who] has built several houses' [I. G. Lindsay & Mary Cosh, *Inveraray and the Dukes of Argyll*, 1973, 354, n. 40]. Evidently he was a builder-architect of the same sort as his contemporary William Adam, but relatively little is at present known about his career, and still less about his ability as a designer.

In 1734 the mason John Baxter, who was then building a house at Haddo in Aberdeenshire for the Earl of Aberdeen, reported to Sir John Clerk of Penicuik that John Douglas had been there and annoyed him by criticizing his workmanship.

Douglas, he told Clerk, was 'apt to break his toas on stons that lyes not in his road'. He was 'sorry to see such a cub who could nevor work a peice of good work all his days sett up for a Judge'. Douglas had given him 'a hint' of a design he had made for GALLOWAY HOUSE, WIGTOWNSHIRE, which appears to have formed the basis of the house which Baxter eventually built for Lord Garlies in 1740–2 (see p. 99) [S.R.O., GD 18/5005/10: 5246/1/218 and 5246/6, *passim*]. In 1736 Douglas made designs for Palladianizing BLAIR CASTLE, PERTHSHIRE, for the 2nd Duke of Atholl that were not carried out, but are preserved at Blair. In 1737–8 he carried out repairs to ABERCAIRNY HOUSE, PERTHSHIRE, for James Moray that cost nearly £6000 [S.R.O., GD 24/1/624]. In 1746 he contracted to build a new house of three storeys onto the west end of the north front of FINLAYSTON HOUSE, RENFREWSHIRE, for the 13th Earl of Glencairn [S.R.O., GD 39/6/Box 3]. In 1746–50 he was employed to alter TAYMOUTH CASTLE for the 2nd Earl of Breadalbane. His 'plans of the Dining Room, Entry to the House, & other things' are mentioned in the accounts of Lord Glenorchy, who was supervising the estate on behalf of his octogenarian father [S.R.O., GD 112/21/78]. Douglas's plan for KILLIN CHURCH, PERTHSHIRE, is mentioned in 1743 in a letter from Lord Breadalbane's chamberlain [N.R.A. Scotland, Survey 657, bundle 2], and he probably designed the octagonal church that was built in 1744 by Thomas Clark, mason of Dunkeld. In 1754–7 he carried out repairs at HOLYROODHOUSE [Edinburgh University Library, MS. Laing II, 88], and made an estimate for repairing the roof of the Abbey Church which might have been carried out but for the death of the 6th Duke of Hamilton, hereditary keeper of the Palace [National Library of Scotland, MS. 5371, ff. 196–209]. At ST. ANDREWS in 1754–7 he designed a new arcaded building (dem. *c.* 1830) on the north side of St. Salvator's College which 'proved to be an endless source of trouble during the seventy years of its existence' [R. G. Cant, 'St. Andrews Architects', *St. Andrews Preservation Trust Year Book* for 1966–7, 15].

The John Douglas whose career has been traced from 1734 to 1757 was presumably the same as John Douglas, architect of Leith, who became a burgess of Edinburgh in 1745, but may or may not have been the John Douglas, 'architect of Leith', who is listed in Williamson's *Edinburgh Directory* for 1773–4, and the 'John Douglas of Pinkerton, Architect', whose will, dated at Leith on 26 March 1773, was proved in June 1778 [S.R.O., Edinburgh Testaments CC8/8/124 (2)].

DOUGLAS, JOHN (*c.* 1800–1862), though born in Northampton, was for most of his life a builder and surveyor at Sandiway, Weaverham,

---

ing work he had obtained some advice from Wren and had measurements taken at Berkeley and Montagu Houses in London. Sir Henry Sheeres, the military engineer, also volunteered 'some Directions for my Lord Nottingham's building' dated 5 July 1695 (B.M., Sloane MS. 3828, ff. 176–80]. Not only did Nottingham probably determine the design himself, he also drew up memoranda for the workmen's agreements and concerned himself with the minutiae of construction. When his brother Heneage was building at Albury in Surrey in 1698, Nottingham was able to give him some highly professional advice about his plans (see their correspondence in Leics. R.O., bundle 22).

Cheshire. He was the father of John Douglas (1830–1911), the leading architect of Victorian Chester. The only building known to have been designed by the elder Douglas is HARTFORD LODGE (now WHITEHALL), HARTFORD, CHESHIRE, for Thomas Firth, 1835 [Twycross's *Mansions of England: Cheshire* i, 1850, with illustration; information from Mr. Edward Hubbard].

DOULL, WILLIAM (*c.* 1793–), was a pupil of Sir Robert Smirke. He entered the Royal Academy Schools in 1814 at the age of 20, and won the Silver Medal the following year. In 1819 he submitted designs for St. Peter's Eaton Square, London, but they were not accepted [Westminster City Library, minutes of Building Committee among records of St. George's, Hanover Square]. In 1821 he exhibited at the Royal Academy a design for a church at Gibraltar. From 1836 to 1846 he was surveyor or assistant surveyor to the Westminster Commissioners of Sewers.

DOUTHWAITE, RICHARD W—, was in 1788 a pupil of James Paine, from whose office he exhibited a design for a temple at the Royal Academy in that year. In the following year Robert Mylne engaged him as a clerk at £40 p.a., and he remained in Mylne's office until Christmas 1800 [Robert Mylne's diary], exhibiting further designs at the Academy between 1791 and 1796. In 1820 he was acting as assistant to D. A. Alexander [Fishmongers' Company's records, *ex inf.* Miss Priscilla Metcalf]. He subsequently became surveyor to the London Dock Company. A reference in one of Rickman's workbooks (B.M., Add. MS. 37801, f.79ᵛ) suggests that he was still alive in 1832.

DOVE, THOMAS, of Scholes Green, was appointed County Surveyor of Norfolk in 1801. He was a member of the Norwich Tonnage Committee, and in that capacity supervised the building or repair of several bridges in the city. Designs by him for new buildings in Norwich Bridewell (1794 and 1803) are in Norwich City Archives [information from Mr. A. P. Baggs]. As County Surveyor Dove was succeeded in 1806 by Francis Stone (*q.v.*), who in a MS. work on bridges in the County of Norfolk stated that his predecessor had designed those at BUNGAY and DITCHINGHAM DAM [B. Weinreb, *Catalogue No. 9, Bridges*, 1965, no. 88].

DOWBIGGIN, the name of a family of London joiners and surveyors, of which at least three generations are recorded. LAUNCELOT DOWBIGGIN (*c.* 1689–1759) was described as 'citizen and joiner of London' on his monumental tablet in St. Mary's Church, Islington. He was

doubtless related to John Dowbiggin, a Westminster solicitor (d. 1712) who was the son of Launcelot Dowbiggin, a yeoman of High Winder in Lancashire [*ex inf.* Mr. E. Arnold Dowbiggin]. He took the livery of the Joiners' Company in 1731, and was its Master in 1756. In 1737 he was accused of intriguing to get the Common Council to reverse its decision to accept George Dance's designs for the Mansion House [S. Perks, *The History of the Mansion House*, 1922, 170]. However, he was subsequently employed to carry out some of the joiner's work in the building [*C. Life*, 18 Feb. 1954, correspondence]. In 1746 he contracted to rebuild the tower of ST. MARY'S CHURCH, ROTHERHITHE, which the Vestry had decided to erect 'in such a manner as is particularly mention'd in a letter signed by Mr. Benjamin Glanvill surveyor' [MS. Vestry Minutes, *ex inf.*, Canon B. F. L. Clarke] (engraving in *Ecclesiastical Topography ... Views of Churches in the Environs of London*, 1811). It is therefore not clear whether the tower was designed by Glanvill or by Dowbiggin. But Dowbiggin himself designed ST. MARY'S CHURCH, ISLINGTON, built 1751–4 by Samuel Steemson [Parish records in Islington Public Library]. The church was destroyed by bombing in 1940, but Dowbiggin's attractive though somewhat unsophisticated classical steeple survives. A project by him for a bridge over the Thames at Blackfriars, made in 1753, is illustrated in *London Magazine* xxv, 1756, 160. He died on 24 July 1759, aged 70.

SAMUEL DOWBIGGIN (*c.* 1724–1809), son of the above, took the livery of the Joiners' Company in 1754. In 1765 his were among the rejected designs for rebuilding the Church of All Hallows, London Wall [C. Welch, *Churchwardens' Accounts of All Hallows, London Wall*, 1912]. In 1773 he was one of the surveyors employed to inspect Banbury Church, Oxon. [A. Beesley, *History of Banbury*, 1841, 532–3]. He died on 19 November 1809, aged 85, leaving considerable property in London and a farm in Hertfordshire to his sons Launcelot and Samuel [P.C.C. 815 LOVEDAY]. Samuel Dowbiggin signs an unexecuted and rather old-fashioned design for CHISELHAMPTON HOUSE, OXON., built 1767–8 by a City merchant, Charles Peers [Arthur Oswald in *C. Life*, 28 Jan., 4 Feb. 1954].[1] The executed designs (which are better drawn as well as more up to date) are signed by 'Dowbiggin junior', who was presumably Samuel's son Launcelot Dowbiggin, who is listed as a surveyor of 53 Paternoster Row in *The Univeral British Directory of Trade and Commerce* of 1790. In the Soane Museum there is an undated estimate for a house at WINCHMORE HILL, MIDDLESEX, for John Gray, to be built 'agreeable to the several plans and ele-

---

[1] Peers had also built Chiselhampton Church in 1763. There is no evidence to show who designed it.

vations...drawn by Lancelot Dowbiggin of Paternoster Row'.

Thomas Dowbiggin & Co., a well-known firm of cabinet-makers and upholsterers in business during the second quarter of the nineteenth century, were no doubt members of the same family.

[H. L. Phillips, *Annals of the Worshipful Company of Joiners*, 1915, 111; S. Lewis, *History of Islington*, 1842, 210, 233.]

DOWN, RICHARD, is listed in Pigot's *Directory* of 1830 as an 'Architect and Surveyor' of Eastover, Bridgwater, Somerset. He is reported to have designed a Baptist church in Bridgwater in 1837 [N. Pevsner, *South and West Somerset*, 1958, 96].

DOWNE, EDWARD, is referred to as an 'architect' of Truro in the sale catalogue of the furniture from Carhays Castle (1789) [*ex inf.* Mr. H. L. Douch]. William Downe was a builder-architect in Truro in the early nineteenth century. He designed CAMBORNE RECTORY, CORNWALL, in 1818 [Exeter Diocesan Faculty papers in Devon County Record Office, Exeter].

DRAPER, GEORGE, was a pupil of Charles Beazley from 1811 to 1813. He established himself in Chichester, whence he exhibited at the Royal Academy from 1827 to 1841. Some of his works (*e.g.* Chichester Infirmary and St. Bartholomew's Church) are in a somewhat old-fashioned Georgian style; others in the Gothic of the day. He was perhaps the George Draper who published engraved views of Beeleigh Abbey, Essex, in 1818.

FISHBOURNE CHURCH, SUSSEX, enlarged 1821 [I.C.B.S.].

LITTLEHAMPTON, SUSSEX, ST. MARY'S CHURCH, rebuilt 1826, Gothic [I.C.B.S.]; chancel added 1889; whole church rebuilt 1933–4.

NETLEY FORT, HANTS., tower for W. Chamberlayne, 1827 [exhib. at R.A.].

SOUTHAMPTON, PUBLIC BATHS, 1826 [exhib. at R.A. 1827].

WEST PARK, nr. FORDINGBRIDGE, HANTS., column commemorating Sir Eyre Coote, 1827 [*Civil Engineer and Architect's Jnl.* iii, 1840, 288].

MILLBROOK CHURCH, HANTS., rebuilt 1828, octagonal, incorporating old tower and chancel [I.C.B.S.]; dem. *c.* 1880.

CHICHESTER INFIRMARY (now Royal West Sussex Hospital), 1828; enlarged 1839, reconstructed 1913 [*A.P.S.D.*].

CHICHESTER, ST. BARTHOLOMEW WITHOUT, 1830 [*Gent's Mag.* 1830 (ii), 219].

GOODWOOD, SUSSEX, THE RACE STAND, 1830 [W. H. Mason, *Goodwood, its House, Park and Grounds*, 1839, 183 and plate].

LYMINGTON, HANTS., OBELISK commemorating

Admiral Sir Harry Burrard-Neale (d. 1840), 1841 [exhib. at R.A.].

DREGHORN, ALLAN (1706–1764), was the son of Robert Dreghorn, a prosperous Glasgow wright who died in 1760. Allan followed his father's trade, but also had extensive business interests as a timber- and lead-merchant. He was a partner in the Smithfield Iron Company, and one of the founders of the first Glasgow bank. As a member of the ruling oligarchy of merchants he held the municipal offices of treasurer (1739) and bailie (1741). When he died in October 1764 at his country house at Ruchill he was a wealthy man, remembered as the owner of the first four-wheeled carriage to be kept by a citizen of Glasgow. His heir was his nephew Robert Dreghorn, who has a place in Glasgow folklore as the womanizing 'Bob Dragon'.

The number of buildings whose design can at present be ascribed to Dreghorn is small. The plans which he and John Craig (*q.v.*) submitted for the University Library in 1732 were not accepted [Glasgow University, Senate Minutes]. In 1736–8 he was involved in the building of the TOWN HALL, TRONGATE, extended 1758–60, remodelled as the Tontine Hotel 1781 and demolished *c.* 1914. The municipal records contain no explicit reference to the authorship of this building, whose façade was based on Webb's gallery at Somerset House, London, but Dreghorn was employed to measure the masonry and may have been responsible for the design [A. Gomme & D. Walker, *Architecture of Glasgow*, 1968, 52–3, 271; *Extracts from the Records of the Burgh of Glasgow 1718–38*, 495, see also vol. vi, *1739–59*, 14]. His principal architectural work was ST. ANDREW'S CHURCH, 1740–56, a handsome version of Gibbs's St. Martin's-in-the-Fields with a steeple based on another of Gibbs's published designs [*Extracts, etc.* vi, *1739–59*, 72–3, 420] (plan in G. Hay, *Architecture of Scottish Post-Reformation Churches*, 1957, 102). It may be presumed that he also designed the substantial town house which he built for himself in Clyde Street in 1752. For long used as a warehouse, it was finally demolished in 1976, but a water-colour reproduced in *Extracts from the Records of the Burgh of Glasgow* vii, 1912 (frontispiece), shows a handsome mansion in the style of Gibbs.

[*Extracts from the Records of the Burgh of Glasgow*, ed. Renwick, v–vii, *passim*; Senex, *Glasgow Past and Present*, 1884, i, 44, 470–1, ii, 330–1, 528–9, iii, 89; G. Eyre-Todd, *History of Glasgow* iii, 1934, 180–1; *The Regality Club*, 1st ser., 1889, 54–73.]

DREW, THOMAS, a native of Devon, practised as a surveyor in London (Marylebone and Kensington) from about 1770 to *c.* 1815, when he left the country and died abroad. He is said to have been employed by the Duke of Northumberland at Syon House. He was a member of the Surveyors' Club from 1807 to 1817. His practice was carried on by his son Thomas Robert Drew [information from Mr. A. F. Drewe].

DRINKWATER, —. In 1688, when extensive alterations were made to GREAT PARK HOUSE, AMPTHILL, BEDS., by the 2nd Earl of Ailesbury, £3 was paid to 'Mr. Drinkwater coming down and making draughts for the house before the building began' [MS. accounts in Marquess of Ailesbury's archives]. The house was subsequently sold to Lord Ashburnham, and rebuilt by him. 'Mr. Drinkwater' was probably a London master carpenter called Robert Drinkwater who was concerned in the erection of Lord Ailesbury's house on the north side of Leicester Square [*Survey of London* xxxiv, 460].

DRIVER, SAMUEL (–1779), was a London nurseryman and surveyor who appears incidentally to have acted as an architect, *e.g.* at ADLESTROP HOUSE, GLOS., where he was employed as a landscape-gardener by Sir Edward Turner, Bart., and made designs in 1749 for alterations to the house as well as to the grounds [Shakespeare Birthplace Museum, Stratford, Leigh Maps and Plans BN 1]. His sons Abraham and William Driver were also land surveyors, and during the first half of the nineteenth century the business was carried on by their successors Edward and George Neale Driver [F. M. L. Thompson, *Chartered Surveyors*, 1968, 49, 94]. Though primarily surveyors and land-agents, they also called themselves architects, and G. N. Driver exhibited some architectural designs at the Royal Academy between 1813 and 1820. S. T. Driver, described as 'architect', who died in December 1797, was presumably a member of the family [*Gent's Mag.* 1798, 536].

DUBOIS, NICHOLAS (c. 1665–1735), an architect of French birth, was probably a Huguenot refugee who left his country after the Revocation of the Edict of Nantes in 1685. According to his obituary in the *Gentleman's Magazine* for 1735, he 'was appointed by King William III one of the Tutors to the Prince of Friezeland, father of the present Prince of Orange'. In Queen Anne's reign he was serving in the British army. In 1706 he was a bombardier in the artillery train in Spain, and on 2 April was promoted to the rank of Captain. In May 1707 he was appointed quartermaster in the Queen's Own Regiment of Dragoons. From 1709 to 1711 he served as an Engineer in Marlborough's army in Flanders, 'where he exposed his life in many sieges'. After the Treaty of Utrecht (1713) he was retired on half-pay [C. Dalton, *English Army Lists and Commission Registers* vi, 1904, 35, 306; P.R.O., Works 6/15, p. 36].

Hitherto a military engineer, Dubois now turned his attention to architectural practice in London. His choice as the translator of Leoni's edition of *The Architecture of Andrea Palladio* (1715–16) associated him with one of the key books of the English Palladian Revival, but the Translator's Preface which he wrote scarcely suggests that he approached the task in the spirit of a Palladian missionary. In May 1718 he entered into partnership with the Italian architect Alessandro Galilei, with whom he was to be a 'Copartner & Joint Dealer . . . in all Designs, Buildings, Architecture, Drawings, both Military and Civil', for five years. The contract was witnessed by Galilei's patrons John Molesworth and Thomas Hewett [Ilaria Toesca, 'Alessandro Galilei in Inghilterra', *English Miscellany*, ed. Praz, iii, 1952, 212]. The partnership was, however, short-lived, for Galilei returned to Italy the following year. In November 1719 Dubois was appointed Master Mason in the Office of Works in succession to Benjamin Jackson. This appointment, which made Dubois a member of the Board of Works, was presumably due to Thomas Hewett, who had recently become Surveyor of the King's Works. In March 1720/1 Dubois appointed as his deputy the surveyor James Horne, who occasionally took his place at the Board.

Dubois was actively engaged in speculative building in London. Between 1717 and 1720 he was involved in the development of HANOVER SQUARE and ST. GEORGE STREET, on land leased from the Earl of Scarbrough. He was concerned in five sites in the Square, Nos. 19–21 on the west side (of which 19 and 21 have been demolished and 20 altered) and Nos. 8 and 9 on the east side (both demolished). In St. George Street he designed No. 15 for Samuel Hayes [P.R.O., C 11/1805/9 and deeds in Middlesex Land Registry, *ex inf.* Mr. A. F. Kelsall; S.R.O., GD 220/6, vol. 2, p. 22]. In 1720 he attempted to set up a Builders' Company with a monopoly of building in London granted by Royal Charter or Patent. The scheme had the support of the Duke of Bridgewater, Charles Dubourgay (who had financed Dubois in Hanover Square) and James Horne. The company took land in Petty France near Bishopsgate for building, but ran out of funds and failed to secure its patent [P.R.O., C 11/1998/15 and 1999/14; C 78/1486/5, and records in the Guildhall Record Office, *ex inf.* Mr. A. F. Kelsall]. In the 1720s Dubois was involved in building developments on Lord Burlington's estate, and himself took a house in Old Burlington Street in which he lived from c. 1726 to 1729 [*Survey of London* xxxii, 451]. He had previously built himself a house in Brewer Street, in which he lived from 1718 to 1721 [*Survey of London* xxxi, 121–2]. In 1724 a house was to be built for Sir Thomas Webster, Bart., in JERMYN

STREET 'to the satisfaction of Mr. Nicholas Dubois Architect and Surveyor' [MS. builder's notebook at Royal Institution of Chartered Surveyors, 17 Feb. 1723/4].

In 1720 Dubois was one of the architects who submitted designs for rebuilding the church of St. Martin-in-the-Fields, but on 21 July he voluntarily withdrew them [MS. Minutes of the Commissioners for Rebuilding St. Martin's Church, f. 6]. His unexecuted design for some extensive barracks in Hyde Park for the Foot Guards, made c. 1716, and signed 'Nicholas Dubois Architect and Engineer', is illustrated in R.I.B.A. Trans., 1880–1, pl. 1.

In 1718–19 Dubois carried out alterations to LEICESTER HOUSE, LEICESTER SQUARE (dem. 1792), for the Prince of Wales [Survey of London xxxiv, 447]. In 1719–20 he was being employed by the 1st Earl of Tankerville, probably at DAWLEY HOUSE, MIDDLESEX, which the Earl was then enlarging or rebuilding [payments in 'Mr. Robertson's 1st Book' in P.R.O., C 104/82, ex inf. Mr. T. P. Connor]. In 1721 he was invited by the widowed Lady Stanhope to supervise the completion of the alterations to CHEVENING HOUSE, KENT, begun by Thomas Fort for the 1st Earl Stanhope, but hesitated to accept because Governor Pitt (Lady Stanhope's father) 'has employed another surveyor, Mr. James'. However, a note added to his letter by Grizel Lady Stanhope in 1797 states that 'Captain Dubois' was 'the person directed about the great (geometrical) staircase at Chevening, one of the same kind at his House in Brewer Street being liked' [Chevening archives and H. A. Tipping in English Homes, Period V, i, 23]. Between 1722 and 1727 Dubois designed STANMER PARK, SUSSEX (C. Life, 2 Jan. 1932), for Henry Pelham (d. 1725) and his brother and heir Thomas. Dubois' correspondence with the Pelhams shows that he had trouble with the servants at Stanmer, who called him 'the french son of a Bitch', and on 12 August 1727 he protests that he has never 'acted contrary to the rules of a liberal Education, a man of Honour, an old officer to the King, and a Gentleman born, as I am' [B.M., Add. MS. 33085, ff. 59, 112, 235, 285–6, 295, 351–2]. In the course of the correspondence he refers to visits, evidently professional, to 'my lady Effingham in Surry' and to 'Mr. Howard at Audley End in Essex' (both 1726). The nature of his works for Edward Howard at AUDLEY END and for the recently widowed Countess of Effingham at EASTWICK PARK, GREAT BOOKHAM, SURREY (dem., see engraving in Brayley, History of Surrey iv, 470), is not known. Dubois' only other recorded work appears to be the bridge at LEWES, SUSSEX, built in 1727, and widened in 1932, which has his name and that of Arthur Morris, the mason, on the keystone [V.C.H. Sussex iii, 9].

Dubois died on 14 June 1735, aged 70 [Gent's

276

Mag. 1735, 333]. In his will he appointed his wife Anna and the Earl of Essex as guardians of his sons Henry and Richard [P.C.C. 119 DUCIE]. As an architect he has to be judged chiefly by Stanmer Park, the only considerable work by him that is known to survive. This is a plain early Georgian house, competently designed, but not suggesting that Dubois was an architect of any great originality or distinction, still less that he was a convinced Palladian.

DUDDELL, —, was a late seventeenth-century architect of whom nothing is at present known except that in 1694 he went (apparently from London) to STONYHURST, LANCS., where Sir Nicholas Shireburn, Bart., was carrying out improvements. His visit is mentioned in Sir Nicholas's accounts, and among the Shireburn papers in the archives of Sir Joseph Weld of Lulworth Castle there are two coloured elevations for remodelling Stonyhurst which are endorsed 'Mr. Duddell'. Neither was carried out. [J. Gerard, S.J., in Stonyhurst Centenary Record, 1894, 52 n. 3, 69 n. 2, 74–5.]

DUFOUR, ALEXANDER, 'architect', published in 1800 a Letter to the Nobility and Gentry composing the Committee for raising the Naval Pillar, or Monument...in answer to the Letter of John Flaxman, in which he protested against Flaxman's proposals for a colossal statue, 'in preference to an architectural monument'. In 1799 he exhibited at the Royal Academy a 'View of the Queen's new Guard House, St. James's Park', and in 1800 a 'Design for a town gate to record four Naval Victories'. He cannot have been the French architect of the same name (c. 1760–1835) who was employed by Napoleon I at Versailles, but may have been related to a painter of portraits named William Dufour who exhibited at the R.A. between 1765 and 1770.

DUGDALE, J—, is stated in Virtue's Picturesque Beauties of Great Britain: Kent (1832), 11–12, to have been 'the principal architect employed' in designing HADLOW CASTLE, KENT, for W. B. May. The architectural history of this fantastic Gothic house (now mostly demolished) is obscure, but as early as 1821 the young J. B. Bunning had exhibited a design for the south front at the Royal Academy. The 170-foot Gothic tower was added later to the designs of G. L. Taylor (q.v.). No other work by Dugdale is known, but as he is described as 'esq.' he may have been an amateur. Virtue particularly commends his 'taste in the gothic style'.

DUMMER, EDMUND, was Surveyor to the Navy in the reign of William III. He held office from June 1692, when he succeeded Sir John

Tippetts, until August 1699, when he was dismissed. His post was administrative rather than architectural in character, but Dummer seems to have been a competent draughtsman, for several surveys of naval dockyards exist which are beautifully illustrated by drawings which he appears to have made himself. As Surveyor to the Navy his principal achievements were the new Dockyard at Hamoaze, nr. Plymouth (c. 1690–5), which included the first stone-lined dry dock in the British Isles, and the construction of a similar dock at Portsmouth at the same time. The contractor at Portsmouth was John Fitch, and it was accusations of bribery by Fitch that led to Dummer's dismissal in 1699. Dummer's report on the works at Plymouth, presented to the Navy Commissioners in December 1694, contains a detailed account of the Dockyard and its buildings, with a series of engraved 'draughts' showing the officers' dwelling-houses, great storehouse, ropehouse, etc. [B.M., Lansdowne MS. 847]. There is reason, however, to think that Robert Hooke (q.v.) may have been responsible for the architectural part of the design.

The manuscript journal of Dummer's voyage to the Mediterranean in 1682–4, containing 'The Viewes and Descriptions of such remarkable Lands, Cities, Towns and Arsenalls, their severall Planes, and Fortifications, with divers Perspectives of Particular Buildings', is in the British Museum (King's MS. 40). In 1698 he carried out a general survey of the royal dockyards, the results of which are recorded in King's MS. 43. In the same year he made a survey of the ports on the south coast of which there are copies in the National Maritime Museum (P. 34 a and b), the Mellon Collection and the Library of Worcester College, Oxford. Dummer was appointed a Director of Greenwich Hospital in 1695 and served on the Fabric Committee for many years.

[N. Luttrell, *Brief Historical Relation* iv, 1857, 576, 645, 658; J. Ehrman, *The Navy in the War of William III*, 1953, 416–25, 644; B. Pool, *Navy Board Contracts 1660–1832*, 1966, 49, 75–6; *Wren Soc.* vi, 30–63, *passim.*]

DUNCKLEY, SAMUEL (–1714), was a mason of Warwick. He was employed in the rebuilding of ST. MARY'S CHURCH, WARWICK, after the fire of 1694, and is remarkable for having rebuilt the damaged entrance to the BEAUCHAMP CHAPEL in an elaborate and remarkably convincing Gothic style. According to a *Brief Description of the Collegiate Church of Warwick* published in 1757 he 'designed, carved, built and finished' this portal himself, and this is confirmed by accounts cited by P. B. Chatwin in *Trans. Birmingham Archaeological Soc.* lxv, 1943–4, 37. William Stukeley records that Dunckley 'designed and built' the HIGH CROSS erected near WIBTOFT, WAR-WICKS., in 1712 to commemorate the site of the Roman VENONAE [Bodleian Library, Gough Maps 16, f. 43, and cf. engraving in Stukeley's *Itinerarium Curiosum*, 1776, 110]. Dunckley, who was a Baptist, appears to have died in 1714 [*The Restoration of the Beauchamp Chapel*, ed. Sir W. Dugdale, Roxburghe Club, 1956, 8 n.]

DYER, CHARLES (1794–1848), was the son of a surgeon in Bristol, and became a pupil of William Brooks (q.v.). He practised in London, where he was a Fellow of the R.I.B.A., and frequently exhibited at the Royal Academy, but designed many buildings in his native city. His Victoria Rooms, with their handsome octastyle Corinthian portico, were his best-known and most ambitious building. He died on 29 January 1848, aged 54, of 'paralysis induced by too close application'. [*Builder* vi, 1848, 54; *A.P.S.D.*]

BRISTOL, THE FEMALE ORPHAN ASYLUM (now Salvation Army Home), HOOK'S MILLS, ASHLEY HILL (with W. Brooks), 1827–9 [*Gent's Mag.* 1868, 254].

BRISTOL, ST. PAUL'S CHURCH, BEDMINSTER, 1829–31, Gothic; chancel added 1892; gutted 1941 and rebuilt 1958 [exhib. at R.A. 1828–9].

CLIFTON, BRISTOL, LITFIELD HOUSE, 1830 [signed, *ex inf.* Mr. Bryan Little].

CLIFTON, BRISTOL, CAMP HOUSE, 1831 [signed, *ex inf.* Mr. Bryan Little].

ALDBOURNE VICARAGE, WILTS., altered or rebuilt 1833 [Salisbury Diocesan Records].

WALTHAM-ON-THE-WOLDS RECTORY, LEICS., 1833, Tudor Gothic [Lincoln Record Office, Gilbert's Act mortgages, No. 167: *Civil Engineer and Architect's Jnl.* ii, 1839, 449].

BATTLEFIELDS, GLOS. (5 miles north of Bath), Gothic gate-lodge, 1836 [signed, 'Charles Dyer, Architect, 1836', *ex inf.* Mr. J. Lees-Milne].

BRISTOL, THE BISHOP'S COLLEGE and CHAPEL, 1835–9, Tudor Gothic; dem. [exhib. at R.A. 1837] (Arrowsmith's *Dictionary of Bristol*, 1906, 165, plate). This building was designed for the Trustees of the Red Maids' School, but was sold on completion to the Trustees of the Bishop's College (W. A. Sampson, *History of the Red Maids' School*, 1908, 50–2).

CLIFTON, BRISTOL, SAVILE PLACE, extension, 1838 [signed, *ex. inf.* Mr. Bryan Little].

LONDON, DYERS' HALL, NO. 10 DOWGATE HILL, 1839–40; front altered 1856 [*A.P.S.D.*].

BRISTOL, THE VICTORIA ROOMS (now part of Bristol University), 1839–41 [exhib. at R.A. 1838–9; *Companion to the Almanac*, 1839, 243–6, with plan].

LONDON, OLD JEWRY CHAMBERS, OLD JEWRY, 1841–2 [*Civil Engineer and Architect's Jnl.* v, 333].

CLIFTON, BRISTOL, villa for Thomas Wentle, 1842 [exhib. at R.A. 1842].

CLIFTON, BRISTOL, CHRIST CHURCH, CLIFTON DOWN ROAD, cons. 1844, Gothic; steeple 1859; north and south aisles 1885 [*A.P.S.D.*].
BRISTOL, TYNDALL'S PARK, abortive scheme for layout, 1844 [*Builder* ii, 1844, 185].
WICK CHURCH, GLOS., 1845–8; completed by W. Butterfield 1849–50, Gothic [*A.P.S.D.*; Paul Thompson, *William Butterfield*, 1971, 442].
GREAT WALTHAM, ESSEX, NATIONAL SCHOOL, 1847, 'Elizabethan' [exhib. at R.A. 1847].
BRISTOL, ST. MARK, EASTON, 1848; completed by Gabriel, neo-Norman [*A.P.S.D.*].
CLIFTON, Savings Bank [*A.P.S.D.*].

DYER, GEORGE and WILLIAM, were builders and surveyors at Alton in Hampshire. According to W. Curtis, *History of Alton*, 1896, 154, the firm was founded in 1784 by John Dyer, a carpenter, who was probably George Dyer's father. In 1812 John Dyer and George Parfect of Headley, bricklayer, rebuilt the nave of FROYLE CHURCH, HANTS., under the direction of James Harding, surveyor of Farnham [MS. 'Orders of Vestry for rebuilding, etc.']. The simple Gothic tower of NEWTON VALENCE CHURCH, HANTS., has an inscription recording that it was rebuilt in 1813 by 'JOHN DYER & GEORGE PARFECT BUILDERS.' George and William Dyer were responsible for alterations to PELHAM PLACE, HANTS., in 1834 [Pelham Place documents in County Record Office], enlarged HAWKLEY CHURCH, HANTS. (rebuilt 1865) in 1828 [I.C.B.S.], altered or rebuilt PATNEY RECTORY, WILTS., in 1833 [Salisbury Diocesan records], added a south aisle to BENTLEY CHURCH, HANTS., in 1835 [I.C.B.S.], and in 1838 rebuilt the nave of CHAWTON CHURCH, HANTS., destroyed by fire 1872 [W. A. Leigh & M. G. Knight, *Chawton Manor and its Owners*, 1911, 62].

DYER, NATHANIEL (*c.* 1752–1833), of Nailsworth, Glos., designed NAILSWORTH EPISCOPAL CHAPEL, 1793–4, rebuilt 1898–1900 [MS. building accounts at vicarage, 1946]. In 1800 the roof of the nave of WOTTON-UNDER-EDGE CHURCH, GLOS., was rebuilt under his direction, with a Gothic plaster vault [V. R. Perkins, *Guide to the Church of St. Mary, Wotton-under-Edge*, 1912, 15]. According to A. Smith, *Ecclesiastical Edifices in the Borough of Stroud*, 1838, Dyer also 'built several seats in this neighbourhood'. He was buried in a field behind 'The Lawns' at Nailsworth, where his name is inscribed on a stone slab. A tablet in the present church records his benefactions to the parish. In contemporary directories he is described as 'gentleman'.

DYMOND, GEORGE (*c.* 1797–1835), architect of Bristol, died at his house in Castle Green on 29 August 1835 at the age of 38 [*Architectural*

Mag. iii, 1836, 48]. He was a member of the Society of Friends.

In 1827–8 Dymond and R. S. Pope were jointly responsible for the Greek Doric Court of Justice and offices added to the left of Smirke's COUNCIL HOUSE in CORN STREET, BRISTOL [City Archives]. His major work was the extensive HIGHER MARKET at EXETER, with monumental Greek Doric façades very ably composed. Begun in 1835, the Market was completed after Dymond's death by Charles Fowler. It is fully described and illustrated in *Architectural Mag.* iii, 1836, 12–30.

E

EADS, JOHN, of Headley, Hants, was probably a bricklayer by trade. In 1803–4 he designed and built DOGMERSFIELD CHURCH, HANTS., for Sir Henry St. John Mildmay, Bart. [Hants. Record Office, 15 M 50/1294–8]. It is a small brick building with pointed windows. In 1803 Eads submitted plans for rebuilding CHAWTON RECTORY, HANTS. [Winchester Diocesan Records, Faculty papers].

EARLE, JOHN (*c.* 1779–1863), was a mason, sculptor and architect of Hull, where his name first appears in the directories in 1810/11. In 1812 he was working at GRIMSTON GARTH, YORKS. (E.R.), for Thomas Grimston in connection with the castellated gatehouse, then in course of erection, but in what capacity is not clear [M. E. Ingram, *Leaves from a Family Tree*, 1951, 124]. In Hull Earle designed THE PILOT OFFICE, QUEEN STREET, 1819 [*Hull Advertiser*, 25 Dec. 1819]; FERRIES' HOSPITAL, PRINCE'S DOCK STREET, 1822 [*V.C.H. Yorks. E. Riding* i, 407]; THE ASSEMBLY ROOM, NORTH STREET, 1823; dem. [*Hull Advertiser*, 4 July 1823]; ST. CHARLES R.C. CHURCH, JARRATT STREET, 1828–9, remodelled by J. J. Scoles 1834–5 [*V.C.H. Yorks. E. Riding* i, 331]; and THE NEW GAOL, KINGSTON STREET, 1830, dem. [*Hull Advertiser*, 28 May 1830]. Earle appears to have been a competent provincial practitioner in a late Georgian classical style. [references to *Hull Advertiser ex inf.* Mr. A. G. Chamberlain]. As a sculptor he is represented by numerous monumental tablets in local churches. He died on 11 December 1863, aged 84 [J. J. Sheahan, *History of Kingston-upon-Hull*, 1864, 655]. His son Thomas Earle (1810–76) was a successful Victorian sculptor.

EATON, GEORGE, was the 'surveyor' employed to supervise the building of THE COUNTY HALL, DERBY, in 1657–9 [Derbyshire Record Office, archives of Chandos-Pole of Hopton Hall, 60/3]. This is a classical building of some quality, with two mannerist doorways facing the courtyard. No other work by George Eaton is at present recorded, but the west doorway of the Chapel at LOCKO PARK, DERBYSHIRE, dated 1669 (*C. Life*, 5 June 1969, fig. 4), has affinities with the architecture of the Shire Hall.

EAYRE, THOMAS (1691–1757), of Kettering in Northamptonshire, was a versatile man whose activities included clockmaking, bell-founding and surveying. Over 200 bells cast by Thomas Eayre or his son of the same name (d. 1762/70) are recorded, together with a number of turret and long-case clocks. As a surveyor he was responsible for a MS. plan of the town of Peterborough, and for the first large-scale map of Northamptonshire, published in 1779. As a topographical draughtsman he was employed by John Bridges to make several drawings (now in the British Museum, Add. MS. 32467) intended as illustrations for the latter's *History of Northamptonshire*. As an architect he designed a simple classical church at STOKE DOYLE, NORTHANTS, built 1722–5. His drawings, together with his account for making them, are among the Hunt of Boreatton papers in Shrewsbury Public Library. In 1744 he advised the antiquary William Stukeley about the construction of the Gothic bridge which the 2nd Duke of Montagu contemplated building in the park at BOUGHTON, NORTHANTS., to Stukeley's design [*Family Memoirs of the Rev. Wm. Stukeley*, Surtees Soc., i, 1882, 368–9].

After the death of Thomas Eayre and the bankruptcy of his son in 1762, the bell-founding business was continued by his brother Joseph Eayre (1707–72) at St. Neot's in Huntingdonshire. Joseph Eayre was also an ingenious man, whose 'invention for weighing a loaded waggon' was exhibited at the Royal Society in Feb. 1748/9. In 1741 he gave Stukeley a 'model' of a method of securing the steeple of ST. MARY'S CHURCH, STAMFORD, then in danger of collapse [*Family Memoirs, op. cit.* ii, 216–20, 329], and in 1762 the steeple of ST. MICHAEL'S CHURCH, STAMFORD (dem. 1832), was rebuilt 'with a neat tower and six bells agreeable to Mr. Eayre's plan' [MS. Vestry Minutes]. In the Storer Collection in Eton College Library (vol. ii) there is a rather crude design for a bridge at Blackfriars, signed 'Joseph Eayre, St. Neot's Oct. 3, 1759' [P. I. King, 'Thomas Eayre of Kettering and other Members of his Family', *Northamptonshire Past and Present* i, no. 5, 1952, 11–23, and no. 6, 10].

EBBELS, ROBERT (–1860), was active as a church architect in the 1830s. He lived at Trysull, nr. Wolverhampton, until 1841, when he moved to Spring Well Cottage, Tettenhall Wood, near the same town. In the 1850s he retired to Dawlish, where he died in August 1860 [Principal

Probate Registry, Calendar of Probates]. He is described as 'a dapper, energetic little gentleman' by Mark Norman (*Random Recollections*). Most of his churches were undistinguished buildings with wide naves lighted by lancet windows, but his tower at Ewhurst Church is an effective essay in Norman revivalism. Nothing is known about his training as an architect, but in 1829 he exhibited two drawings at the Birmingham Society of Artists which appear to have been student's work: 'the archway and bridge across the approach to the Deepdene' (in Surrey), and the 'Entrance lodge at Garnons' in Herefordshire.

SHIRLEY CHURCH, WARWICKS., 1832, Gothic; enlarged 1883 [I.C.B.S.].

WOLVERHAMPTON, ST. PAUL'S CHURCH, 1834, Gothic [Steen & Blackett's *Wolverhampton Guide*, 1871, 46].

ETTINGSHALL CHURCH, SCHOOLS and PARSONAGE, STAFFS., 1835–7, built in half-timber; the church was rebuilt 1874 [*Civil Engineer and Architect's Jnl.* i, 1837–8, 57].

GUILDFORD, SURREY, ST. NICHOLAS CHURCH, rebuilt 1836–7, Gothic; rebuilt 1870–6 [inscription in church].

READING, BERKS., ST. JOHN'S CHURCH, 1836–7, Gothic; rebuilt 1872 [*Reading Mercury*, 29 April 1837].

VENTNOR, ISLE OF WIGHT, ST. CATHERINE'S CHURCH, for John Hambrough, 1836–7, Gothic; chancel added 1849, south aisle 1897–8 [*Civil Engineer and Architect's Jnl.* i, 1837–8, 57].

HAWLEY CHURCH, HANTS., 1837, Gothic; altered by J. B. Clacy 1857, chancel added 1863, steeple 1882 [*Civil Engineer and Architect's Jnl.* i, 1837–8, 57].

EWHURST CHURCH, SURREY, partial rebuilding, with new central tower in 'Norman' style, 1837–8; also Gothic Rectory for Rev. C. A. Stewart [Brayley, *Surrey* v, 179–80, with views].

WINDLESHAM CHURCH, SURREY, enlarged church and remodelled tower, 1837–8. Ebbels also designed the Gothic Rectory [Brayley, *Surrey* i, 467, 469].

TIPTON, STAFFS., ST. PAUL'S CHURCH, 1838–9, Gothic; altered 1899 [*Civil Engineer and Architect's Jnl.* i, 1837–8, 57].

WOLVERHAMPTON PARISH CHURCH, repairs, 1838–9 [G. P. Mander, *The Wolverhampton Antiquary*, 1933, 256].

HANDSWORTH, STAFFS., ST. JAMES'S CHURCH, 1838–40; enlarged 1895 [*Civil Engineer and Architect's Jnl* i, 1837–8, 57].

SUNNINGDALE, BERKS., HOLY TRINITY CHURCH, 1839–40; chancel added by G. E. Street 1861, nave rebuilt by J. O. Scott 1887–8 [F. C. Hodder, *A Short History of Sunningdale*, 1937, 119].

WOMBOURNE CHURCH, STAFFS., enlarged east end, 1840 [Lichfield Faculty papers]; rebuilt 1867.

WEST BROMWICH, STAFFS., ST. JAMES'S CHURCH, 1839–41, Gothic; tower added c. 1890 [I.C.B.S.].

COVENTRY, ST. PETER'S CHURCH, 1840–1, Gothic [B. Poole, History of Coventry, 1870, 223].

UPPER GORNAL CHURCH, STAFFS., 1840–1, Gothic [Port, 160–1].

CWMAMAN, CARMARTHENSHIRE, CHRIST CHURCH, 1841, Gothic [Port, 170–1].

OLD SWINFORD CHURCH, WORCS., rebuilt nave, 1843, Gothic [J. Noake, The Rambler in Worcestershire, 1848, 210].

WONERSH HOUSE, SURREY, terrace and conservatory for the 3rd Lord Grantley, c. 1840; dem. 1935 [Brayley, Surrey, v, 151].

EBDON, CHRISTOPHER (c. 1744–1824), is described as 'a Durham gentleman', and may have been related to the Rev. Thomas Ebdon, a minor canon of Durham. In 1761 he was apprenticed to James Paine [P.R.O., Apprenticeship Register I.R.1/22], and it was from Paine's address in Salisbury Street, Strand, that he exhibited views of the inside of Durham Cathedral at the Society of Artists in 1767 and 1768. One of these views was subsequently engraved by Tobias Miller. In the summer of 1776 Ebdon was in Rome, whence he moved to Florence in August of that year [Walpole Soc. xxxii, 1946–8, 51 and letter to Henry Holland dated from Florence, 8 Aug. 1776, in Victoria and Albert Museum, 92 D. 28, f. 2ᵛ]. In 1778, 1780 and 1783 he exhibited views of Roman temples at the Society of Artists, giving his address as 'at Earl Cowper's, Great George Street, Hanover Square'. Between 1789 and 1792 he was more than once employed by Sir John Soane as a draughtsman [A. T. Bolton, The Works of Sir John Soane, 1924, Appendix C, xli]. Eventually he appears to have established a practice in the south-west of England, for in 1783 he exhibited designs for lodges to TEHIDY PARK, CORNWALL, for Sir Francis Basset, Bart., and the Carew family papers at Antony House, Cornwall, show that in 1787 he was paid £26 5s. 'for designs for a chapel at Tor Point' (apparently not carried out). Moreover, in the County Museum at Truro there are designs by him for the ASSEMBLY ROOMS at TRURO, opened in 1787. His only other recorded work appears to be the FREEMASONS' LODGE, OLD ELVET, DURHAM, 1810, dem. 1868 [M. A. Richardson, The Local Historian's Table Book iii, 1843, 105]. It was at Durham that he died in 1824, aged 80. [Gent's Mag. 1824 (ii), 572; J. Nichols, Literary Anecdotes viii, 693; monumental inscription in St. Oswald's churchyard, Durham, ex inf. Mr. K. S. Mills.]

EBORAL, WILLIAM (–1795), was 'an eminent builder' of Warwick. In 1786–8 he designed

and built the Gothic Greenhouse at WARWICK CASTLE containing the 'Warwick Vase' [V.C.H. Warwicks. viii, 463]. According to W. Field's History of Warwick, 1815, 81–2, he was the 'architect' of the GREAT BRIDGE at WARWICK, built in 1789–93 to a design closely resembling Robert Mylne's Leafield Bridge nearby. He died suddenly on 16 January 1795 [Gent's Mag. 1795 (i), 348].

EDGAR, WILLIAM (–1746) is described as 'Architect' on the plan of Edinburgh which he published in 1742. He appears to have been the William Edgar who was apprenticed to an Edinburgh wright in 1717 and admitted a burgess in 1736, but his few recorded activities are those of a land surveyor rather than an architect. He is said to have been with the Duke of Cumberland in the '45, and to have 'died of fatigue' in the Highlands in 1746. [W. Cowan, The Maps of Edinburgh 1544–1929, Edinburgh 1932, 30–5; M. K. Meade, 'Plans of the New Town of Edinburgh', Architectural History xiv, 1971, 43–4; E. G. R. Taylor, The Mathematical Practitioners of Hanoverian England, 1966, 205.]

EDGCUMBE, EDWARD, of Tewkesbury, made designs for the refitting of TEWKESBURY ABBEY CHURCH with new pews, galleries in the transepts, and a pulpit of 'peculiarly light and elegant construction', which were executed in 1795 by J. Keyte of Kidderminster [W. Dyde, History of Tewkesbury, 1798, 55]. He also presumably designed the MARKET HOUSE, TEWKESBURY, illustrated by Dyde as the work of 'Rd. Edgecumbe, Archt.' In 1798 he was living at Ellesmere in Shropshire. In 1818 'Edgecombe of Ellesmere' made designs that were not carried out for the insertion of galleries in MALPAS CHURCH, CHESHIRE [Jnl. of the Chester and N. Wales Arch. Soc., N.S. xxxvii (ii), 1949]. George Edgecumbe, who designed STOAK CHURCH, CHESHIRE, 1827, Gothic, may have been a relation [The Cheshire Sheaf xxxvi, 1941, 23–30].

EDGE, CHARLES (–1867), was one of the leading architects in Birmingham from about 1827 until his death in 1867. He began as a designer in the late Georgian Grecian style, but 'ended as a Victorian architect working in Italianate and Gothic'. After the bankruptcy of Messrs. Hansom & Welch in 1834 he was employed to complete the Town Hall. Besides the public buildings listed below he designed a number of commercial premises in Birmingham and several private houses in Edgbaston. Outside his own town his only important work was the CRESCENT at FILEY in YORKSHIRE, designed for the Birmingham solicitor J. W. Unett in 1835–8. In the 1840s he was for a time in partnership with an architect called Avery. Yeoville Thomason and his son C.

A. Edge were his pupils. Four large volumes of drawings by Charles Edge and his son are in the Birmingham Reference Library.[1] He died in Edgbaston on 21 July 1867. [Cornish's *Guide to Birmingham*, 1864, *passim*; Bryan Little, *Birmingham Buildings*, 1971, 124–5.]

BIRMINGHAM: PUBLIC BUILDINGS, ETC.

THE PUBLIC OFFICE, MOOR STREET, enlarged with new Greek Doric elevation, 1829–30; dem. 1957 [drawings 7–24].

THE BANK OF BIRMINGHAM (afterwards Branch Bank of England), BENNETT'S HILL, *c.* 1832 [drawings 29–30; Cornish, 118].

THE MARKET HALL, HIGH STREET, 1832–5; dem. 1940 [drawings 75–87].

THE GENERAL CEMETERY, KEY HILL, Chapel, 1834–6; dem. [drawings 118–29].

THE NORWICH UNION OFFICE, BENNETT'S HILL, 1834 [drawings 88–100].

ST. PETER'S CHURCH, DALE END, reconstruction, 1834–7, after fire; dem. 1899 [drawings 101–4].

THE BIRMINGHAM AND MIDLAND BANK, UNION STREET, 1836 [drawings 167–78].

THE TOWN HALL, completion of building designed by J. A. Hansom and Edward Welch, 1836 onwards [drawings 131–66].

THE NATIONAL PROVINCIAL BANK, BENNETT'S HILL, *c.* 1840 [Cornish, 119].

THE POST OFFICE, 93 NEW STREET, reconstruction of existing premises for use by Post Office, 1841–2; dem. [drawings 228–40].

ASTON, WATERWORKS ENGINE HOUSE, 1851 [drawing 329].

ST. GEORGE'S CHURCH, CALTHORPE ROAD, EDGBASTON, addition of chancel, 1856, Gothic [drawings 349–52].

EDGE, WILLIAM (*c.* 1584–1643), was a freemason living at Raynham in Norfolk, where he died in his 60th year in 1643. From 1619 onwards he was engaged in designing and building RAYNHAM HALL, NORFOLK, for Sir Roger Townshend, Bart. Sir Roger's accounts show that Edge not only executed the masonry, but also made numerous drawings for the house. Moreover he twice accompanied Sir Roger to London, and in 1620 was paid for twenty-eight weeks attending him 'in England and out of England'. The markedly Jonesian character of Raynham's architecture may well have been due to the study by Sir Roger and his mason of buildings by Jones such as the Prince's Lodgings at Newmarket, or even to consultations with Jones himself. Masons named Robert and John Edge were employed at Raynham in 1621, and in his will William Edge

refers to his son William and his nephews Robert and William, sons of his brother Robert [H. L. Bradfer-Lawrence, 'The Building of Raynham Hall', *Norfolk Archaeology* xxiii, 1926–8; John Harris, 'Raynham Hall, Norfolk', *Archaeological Jnl.* cxviii, 1963].

William Edge was also employed by Sir Hamon L'Estrange at HUNSTANTON HALL, NORFOLK, where considerable alterations were in process from 1625 to the early 1640s. In 1625 William Edge and his brother were paid 5s. 'for their travell from Raynham', and in the following year 5s. were again paid to William Edge 'when Sr. Roger Townshend sent him to see the Buylding'. William, Richard, Thomas and John Edge were all employed as masons at Hunstanton during the next fifteen years. Precisely what they did is not clear from the accounts, but, apart from alterations to the house itself, it probably included the octagonal park building illustrated in *Country Life*, 10 April 1926, fig. 6, which is said (no doubt correctly) to have been built in 1640. This elegant classical building is, like Raynham Hall, a notable reflection of the Court style of Inigo Jones in a remote country setting. They were not responsible for the classical gateway, with strapwork cresting, at the entrance to the courtyard, which was built in the years 1623–4, and was the work of Thomas Thorpe of Kingscliffe, Northants. (d. 1625/6), a master mason who was then engaged in building Blickling Hall for Chief Justice Hobart (cf. Summerson, *The Book of Architecture of John Thorpe*, Walpole Soc., 1966, 4). [Norfolk Record Office, L'Estrange papers, General Account 1613–1645, *passim*.]

EDGLEY, —, of Hurley, Berks., an otherwise unknown builder-architect, is stated in the *Picturesque Views of Seats*, published by Harrison & Co. in 1787–8, to have built BEAR PLACE, HARE HATCH, BERKS., for M. Ximenes 'about four years since'.

EDMESTON, JAMES (1791–1867), was the architect to whom Gilbert Scott was articled in 1827. He was chosen more on account of his piety than of his distinction as an architect, which was slight. Although an Independent by descent, he joined the Anglican Church at a comparatively early age, and was the author of numerous hymns, including 'Lead us, Heavenly Father, lead us'. He lived at Homerton and had his office at Salvador House in Bishopsgate Street. His works included HACKNEY GRAMMAR SCHOOL [J. C. Loudon, *Architectural Mag.* v, 1838, 70, where his unexecuted design for another school at Islington is illustrated]; ST. BARNABAS' SCHOOL, HOMERTON, 1855–6 [*Builder* xiii, 1855, 504; xiv, 1856, 320]; ST. PAUL'S CHURCH, ONSLOW SQUARE, 1859–60 [Dorothy Stroud, *The South Kensington*

[1] These are referred to in the list of works above. The drawings for the Crescent at Filey are nos. 107–115.

Estate of Henry Smith's Charity, 1975, 39]; and a Gothic dissenting chapel at LEYTONSTONE, ESSEX. His design (1835) for a lodge for W. G. D. Tyson at FOLEY HOUSE, nr. MAIDSTONE, KENT, is in the R.I.B.A. Drawings Collection. His design for a 'Protestant Church', shown at the Free Architectural Exhibition in 1850, was ridiculed in the *Ecclesiologist* xi, 1850, 173. His pupils included his son James Edmeston, junior (d. 1888), E. H. Springbett and W. B. Moffatt (afterwards Scott's partner). [G. Scott, *Personal and Professional Recollections*, 1879, 53–67; J. Julian, *A Dictionary of Hymnology*, 1907, 321–2.]

EDMONDS, CHRISTOPHER (*c.* 1774–1853), exhibited at the Royal Academy from Southwark addresses between 1795 and 1801. He was surveyor to the Clink Paving Commissioners, and Master of the Tylers' and Bricklayers' Company in 1837–8. In 1801 he exhibited 'An addition to Tidmarsh House (Berks.), new building for R. Hopkins, Esq.' In 1815 he carried out internal alterations to MILTON CHURCH, nr. GRAVESEND, KENT [typed notes in church]. He designed ST. PAUL'S CHURCH, CLAPHAM, a plain brick building consecrated in 1815; chancel added 1879 [C. T. Cracklow, *Views of the Churches in the County of Surrey*, 1827]. He died on 23 August 1853, aged 79 [*Gent's Mag.* 1853 (ii), 428].

Christopher William Crawford Edmonds, junior, exhibited at the Royal Academy between 1834 and 1849. His 1839 exhibit was ST. PETER'S CHURCH, SUMNER STREET, BANKSIDE, SOUTHWARK (dem. 1940), an undistinguished Gothic building illustrated as the work of 'Mr. Chr. Edmonds' in *Companion to the Almanac*, 1840, 128–9, where the interior is described as 'not only exceedingly bald and plain, but mean and ugly; sufficiently dismal without being at all solemn'.

EDMUNDS, WILLIAM, of Margate, Kent, was probably a son of Thomas Edmunds, a builder of the same place. At MARGATE he designed HOLY TRINITY CHURCH, 1825–9, Gothic (dem.); the LIGHTHOUSE (in the form of a Doric column) on the pier, 1828 (dem.); and the OFFICES of the Pier Company (dem.). At DOVER he designed HOLY TRINITY CHURCH, 1833–5, Gothic (dem.), and in 1839 the temporary pavilion erected for the banquet given to the Duke of Wellington by the Cinque Ports. It measured 130 × 120 feet and accommodated some 2000 persons. [S. Lewis, *Topographical Dictionary* iii, 1831, 254–5; M. H. Port, *Six Hundred New Churches*, 1961, 146–7; *Gent's Mag.* 1839 (ii), 416.]

EDWARD, ALEXANDER (1651–1708), was a dispossessed Scottish minister who turned to architecture and landscape-gardening and is emerging as a figure of some importance in the Scottish architectural scene at the end of the

seventeenth century. His father, Robert Edward, minister of Murroes in Angus, was an ingenious man, interested in astronomy, dialling and cartography, who enjoyed the patronage of the Maule family (Earls of Panmure). Alexander, who shared his father's interests, graduated M.A. at St. Andrews in 1670 and entered the Church. He held the living of Kemback in Fife from 1681 until 1689, when he was dispossessed as a nonjuror [Hew Scott, *Fasti Ecclesiae Scoticanae* v, 1925, 206].

The earliest evidence of Edward's architectural activities connects him with Sir William Bruce, the key figure in Scottish architecture after the Restoration. It consists of three plans of Bruce's seat at Kinross in Fife, one of the house itself, one of the gardens, and one of the policies in general.[1] These drawings are attributable to Edward because of their similarity to a garden layout for Hamilton Palace[2] which bears Edward's signature. As the drawing of the house shows it substantially as built, but with minor differences of detail, it must date from *c.* 1685, shortly before work began. Although the design for Kinross must have been Bruce's own work, Edward thus appears to have been acting as his architectural assistant or draughtsman [J. G. Dunbar, 'Kinross House', in *The Country Seat*, ed. Colvin & Harris, 1970, 65–9]. Ten years later he is found in the same role in connection with Bruce's designs for Melville House, Fife. In a letter dated 21 April 1697 Sir William Bruce informed the Earl of Melville that Edward was hard at work 'extending' (*i.e.* drawing out) his designs for Melville House and would be sent to explain them to the Earl before he proceeded to 'extend the draught of the garden and courts' [S.R.O., GD 26/13/272 and 440]. Drawings[3] made in 1698 for remodelling Kinnaird Castle, Angus, for the Earl of Southesk to Bruce's designs are likewise in Edward's hand.

Between 1696 and 1708 Edward was personally responsible for the remodelling of BRECHIN CASTLE, ANGUS, for the 4th Earl of Panmure [David Walker & John Dunbar in *C. Life*, 12 Aug. 1971], and in 1699 he witnessed a contract between Henry Maule of Kellie (the Earl of Panmure's younger brother) and a wright named Hendrie to panel the interior of the principal rooms at KELLIE CASTLE, ANGUS, 'conforme to the lyning of the waiting-room at Panmure' and (in the case of the Drawing Room) 'according to a draught to be given to the said Hendrie with a compleat capitall' [S.R.O., GD 45/18/1233]. He was still giving architectural advice about work

[1] The first two plans belong to the Edinburgh College of Art; the third is among Sir John Clerk's papers at Penicuik House.
[2] At Lennoxlove.
[3] At Kinnaird Castle. They were not carried out.

at Kellie Castle in 1705 [S.R.O., GD 14/332a]. In 1699 he made a 'Draught of the Low Palace at Falkland' (Fife) for its hereditary keeper, the 2nd Marquess of Atholl [Blair Castle Muniments, Box 41, iv, 3]. A surviving letter [S.R.O., GD 45/26/140, loose in pocket] shows that in February 1700 he was concerned in the building of a house (now dem.) at ROSSIE in ANGUS for Patrick Scott. Later Edward assisted Bruce with the layout of the formal gardens at HOPETOUN HOUSE, WEST LOTHIAN [R. Sibbald, *History of the Sheriffdoms of Linlithgow and Stirling*, 1707, 20–1], and in 1708 he made the plan for laying out the grounds of HAMILTON PALACE, LANARKSHIRE, that has already been mentioned. In 1704 he designed the grand architectural monument in DUNKELD CATHEDRAL to the 1st Marquess of Atholl (d. 1703) [*Chronicles of the Atholl and Tullibardine Families*, by the 7th Duke of Atholl, ii, 1908, 43–5].

In 1701–2 Edward undertook a journey to London, Paris and the Low Countries on behalf of a group of Scottish noblemen (mostly of Jacobite sympathies), which included the Earls of Mar, Loudoun, Strathmore, Panmure, Hopetoun, Northesk and Southesk, the Marquess of Annandale, the Master of Balmerino, Sir John Shaw of Greenock and Hercules Scott of Brotherton. He undertook to 'view, observe and take draughts of the most curious and remarkable Houses, Edifices, Gardings, orchards, parks, plantations, land improvements, coall works, mines, water works and other curiosities of nature or art' [S.R.O., GD 124/16/24]. The list of houses he was to inspect included Chatsworth, Lowther, Belvoir and 'Earl Carlil's new designs near Yorke' (*i.e.* Castle Howard). The Earl of Mar particularly wanted drawings of Ranelagh House, Chelsea, and the Earl of Rochester's house at Petersham. As soon as he reached London Edward was to write to various of his patrons, including the Earls of Panmure, Mar and Northesk, and 'to Alex Izit' (a joiner employed by Bruce at Hopetoun and elsewhere) 'about lyning of rooms'. He carried with him a letter of introduction from Sir Robert Sibbald to Sir Hans Sloane in which he was described as having 'acquired much fame by his skill in Architecture and drawing plans of houses and gardens' [B.M., Sloane MS. 4038, f. 167]. His visiting list also included Kneller, Knyff, Robert Kidwell the mason, and several mapsellers. In Paris he purchased prints and noted that the south-east front of the Louvre, the façade of St. Gervais and the Val-de-Grace were 'the best architecture in Paris'. His itinerary included Versailles, Marly and St. Cloud, and he carried letters in cypher to the Pretender's Court at St. Germain. Most of the drawings which he made are lost, but a plan which he made of Marly is among Gibbs's drawings in the Ashmolean Museum (III, 49), and the

notebook which he took with him on the journey is among the Panmure (Dalhousie) papers in the Register House at Edinburgh [S.R.O., GD 45/26/140]. A letter to the Earl of Mar dated from Le Havre on 7 July 1702 also survives [S.R.O., GD 124/15/219].

Edward died in Edinburgh on 16 November 1708, aged 57, and was buried in the Greyfriars Churchyard. Sir Robert Sibbald (*op. cit.*) characterized him as a 'Great Master in Architecture, and contrivance of Avenues, Gardens and Orchards'. His importance as Bruce's architectural adjutant is clear. Brechin Castle, his only independent work so far identified, shows that stylistically he was Bruce's follower, but as an adaptation it does not necessarily reveal his full ability as an architectural designer. His garden layouts are in the formal grand manner of the period.

EDWARDS of Liverpool. Several architects of this name were practising in Liverpool in the first half of the nineteenth century. JAMES EDWARDS appears in the directories as an architect from 1816 to 1829. In 1816 his address was Copperas Hill, but subsequently he lived in Hawke Street. EDWARD EDWARDS of 26 Lawton Street is listed as an architect in 1818–1823. HENRY EDWARDS was at 12 Exchange Street in 1828–9. In the 1830s and early 1840s he was in partnership with his son, HENRY TURBERVILLE EDWARDS, but by 1849 he was living in retirement at Everton. His only architectural work so far identified is the handsome Greek Revival church of ST. JOHN, LISCARD ROAD, EGREMONT, WALLASEY, CHESHIRE, 1832–33 [information from Mr. Edward Hubbard].

In the 1830s STEPHEN LANE EDWARDS was in partnership with Arthur Y. Williams (*q.v.*). In 1836 they designed ST. JOHN'S CHURCH, KNOTTY ASH, LANCS., Gothic [*Architectural Mag.* iv, 351], and in 1837 they exhibited at the Liverpool Academy of Arts their design for the LIVERPOOL MECHANICS' INSTITUTE in Mount Street. The foundation-stone of this building had been laid in 1835 and it was completed in 1837 after being destroyed by fire when almost finished. According to Picton, *Memorials of Liverpool* ii, 1875, 258, 'the front of the building and the portico were designed by Mr. A. H. Holme'. ACCRINGTON CHURCH, LANCS., 1837–8, Gothic, was another building designed by Williams and Edwards [*Architectural Mag.* iv, 1837, 401].

John Foster (*q.v.*) had an assistant called Edwards who was no doubt one of the architects mentioned above. According to Picton (*op. cit.* ii, 243) rumour gave him the credit for being the real designer of Foster's only Gothic church, ST. LUKE'S LIVERPOOL (cons. 1831).

EDWARDS, EDWARD, was a surveyor involved in the rebuilding of the town of Northampton after the great fire of 1675. Together with Henry Bell (*q.v.*) he appears to have been responsible for the two most important public buildings – ALL SAINTS CHURCH (1677–80) and the SESSIONS HOUSE (1676–88). A document in the County Record Office dated 18 January 1676/7 directs 'that Mr. Henry Bell and Mr. Edward Edwards, two experienced Surveyors now residing in the said Towne of Northampton be imployed as Managers' of the works at the church, and 'Mr. Edward Edwards, Surveyor', received £100 in connection with the rebuilding of the Sessions House [C. Markham, *County Buildings of Northampton*, 1805, 40]. It is possible that Edwards, like Bell, came from Norfolk, for a notebook of Sir Edward Turner offered for sale by Jantzen of East Grinstead in 1972 (Catalogue no. 112, item 42) refers to the measurement of a house at Winterton in that county in 1676 'by Mr. Edwards'. The churchwardens' accounts of BLETCHLEY CHURCH, BUCKS., record that in *c.* 1709 one Edwards 'made divers Draughts of the Church in order to alter it, viz. drawings for an Altar piece and screen etc.' [W. Bradbrooke, 'The Reparation of Bletchley Church in 1710', *Records of Bucks.* xii, 1927–33, 248].

EDWARDS, FRANCIS, F.I.B.A. (1784–1857), was born in Southwark and was apprenticed to a cabinet-maker in Moorfields. He showed a strong talent for architectural drawing, and in 1806 entered Soane's office as an 'improver'. He was admitted to the Royal Academy Schools in 1808, was awarded the Silver Medal the same year for measured drawings of the gallery of the British Institution in Pall Mall, and in 1811 won the Gold Medal for his design for a theatre. He exhibited at the Academy between 1809 and 1830. He left Soane's office in 1810, and assisted his former fellow-pupil H. H. Seward (then in partnership with George Byfield) for four days a week until 1823, when he devoted all his time to his own practice. Seward, on retiring soon afterwards, transferred many clients to him. Edwards was much employed in connection with arbitrations, valuations and similar work. He was responsible for the whole of the building and engineering work of the Imperial Gas Company from its incorporation in 1823, and received many commissions from Messrs. Goding, the brewers, for whom he designed the Lion Brewery which for more than a century was one of the landmarks of the South Bank. He died on 15 August 1857 [*A.P.S.D.*].

HOXTON, IMPERIAL GAS COMPANY'S WORKS, 1823 onwards [*A.P.S.D.*].

HOXTON, ST. JOHN BAPTIST'S CHURCH, 1824–6 [drawings in R.I.B.A. Coll.].

HOLMBUSH, nr. CUCKFIELD, SUSSEX, for Thos. Broadwood, 1829, Gothic [T. W. Horsfield,

History of Sussex ii, 1835, 222, and see *Builder* xvii, 1859, 708, for a tower in the park designed by Edwards].

WOTTON HOUSE, SURREY, additions for W. J. Evelyn, 1830–53 [*A.P.S.D.*].

DEPTFORD, houses on the Evelyn estate, 1832–57 [*A.P.S.D.*].

CANNON BREWERY, KNIGHTSBRIDGE, additions for T. Goding, *c.* 1835; dem. [*A.P.S.D.*].

LION BREWERY, GOLDEN SQUARE, additions for Messrs. Goding & Broadwood [*A.P.S.D.*].

LION BREWERY, BELVEDERE ROAD, LAMBETH, for Messrs. Goding & Co., 1836; dem. 1950 [drawings in R.I.B.A. Coll.].

PUBLIC HOUSES, for Messrs. Goding & Co. [*A.P.S.D.*].

NO. 12 ST. GEORGE'S PLACE, HYDE PARK CORNER, for Thos. Goding, 1837 [*A.P.S.D.*].

ROMFORD, ESSEX, UNION WORKHOUSE, 1839, and subsequent additions [*A.P.S.D.*].

ROEHAMPTON, SURREY, additions to MOUNT CLARE for Sir Chas. Ogle, 1840 [*A.P.S.D.*] (*C. Life*, 26 Jan., 2 Feb. 1935).

CHELSEA, WELLINGTON SQUARE, KING'S ROAD, completion of square for Thomas Goding, 1840–7 [G.L.C. Record Office, Westminster Commissioners of Sewers, plans, vol. 38/1207].

VAUXHALL, additions and alterations to Messrs. Burnett's distillery, 1841–57 [*A.P.S.D.*].

BROADWOOD'S MANUFACTORY, HORSEFERRY ROAD, WESTMINSTER, 1856 [*A.P.S.D.*].

EDWARDS, THOMAS (–1775), lived at Greenwich, but enjoyed an extensive practice as an architect in Cornwall, where he also had mining interests. Nothing is certainly known of his early life, but according to the *Parochial History of Cornwall* (who wrongly gives his Christian name as William) he was 'a self-educated architect, the son of a small farmer'. He was living at Greenwich by 1753, when he appears among the subscribers to Francis Price's book on Salisbury Cathedral as 'Mr. Thomas Edwards, Architect of Greenwich', and he is similarly described in the subscription-list to Borlase's *Natural History of Cornwall*, published in 1758. The latter book contains engravings of several of the country houses which he is said to have designed.

Edwards's best-documented work is TREWITHEN, a country house about seven miles north-east of Truro which was under construction in the 1730s. An account 'for the buildings at Trewithen' in 1738–40 contains regular payments to 'Mr. Edwards Surveyor'. The money was generally paid 'per Potter', *i.e.* John Potter, who appears to have been either Edwards's agent or the building contractor. Edwards and Potter also appear in association at NANSWHYDEN, nr. St. Columb Major, the former seat of the Hoblyn family, for one early nineteenth-century writer says it was 'from the designs of Potter', while another attributes it to Edwards. This Potter may conceivably be the carpenter of the same name (*q.v.*) who owned and built the Little Theatre in the Haymarket in 1720.

Two other important houses which Edwards is stated to have designed by the author of the *Parochial History* and by other topographical writers are TEHIDY PARK, nr. Illogan, for J. P. Basset (1736), and CARCLEW, nr. Penryn. The latter house was begun by Samuel Kempe in the 1720s, but was still incomplete in 1749 when it was sold to the mine-owner William Lemon. Lemon is said to have employed Edwards to add the portico and offices to the central block built by Kempe.

The 'London builder renovating the mansion at Carclew' who 'undertook the reconstruction' of ST. GLUVIAS CHURCH, nr. PENRYN, 'after his own plans' can hardly be other than Edwards, and the accounts for rebuilding HELSTON CHURCH in 1756–61 show that the work was done by John Bland of Truro under the direction of Thomas Edwards, 'who is reckoned a very skilful architect'.

Edwards's last work was the addition of the Gothic tower and spire to ST. MARY'S CHURCH, TRURO. In 1765 the Corporation agreed to contribute £500 towards the cost of a steeple 'to be erected and built according to the plans of Mr. Thomas Edwards'. The builder was John Bland and the steeple was finished in 1769. It was not, however, until July 1775 that the Corporation resolved to pay Edwards £70 'for planning and directing the building of the tower at St. Mary's Church'. About thirty years later a local antiquary named Taunton recorded that 'the steeple was built by Mr. Edwards, architect of London', and that 'Mr. Bland was his agent to manage in his absence'. He added that Edwards was 'also the builder of Tehidy, Nanswydden, Mr. Daniell's and Mr. Lemmon's at Truro'. The last-named house was the residence of William Lemon, the builder of Carclew, who died in 1760. It was then the largest and most handsome house in Truro, but soon after Lemon's death his former agent Thomas Daniell, who had married Ralph Allen's niece, bought up Lemon's mining and mercantile interests, and built an equally imposing house in the same street, employing Edwards as his architect.

That Edwards and Daniell were well acquainted appears from the former's will, in which he directs that his mines are to be sold by his executors 'as Mr. Thomas Daniel of Truro in the County of Cornwall shall advise'. Where these mines were is not stated, but it seems likely that Edwards, like Daniell, acquired his mining interests through his association with William

Lemon of Carclew. The will is dated 22 April 1773, and has a codicil witnessed by Mary Potter. It mentions a leasehold estate in Conduit Street and other property, including a share in Covent Garden Playhouse and an eighth share in the East Indiaman *Devonshire*. These were to be sold for the benefit of his wife and his sons John, Francis, James and Thomas. Edwards died at Greenwich on 30 October 1775, and was buried at St. Alphege's Church there on 5 November.

Edwards was a competent Georgian architect, though not a designer of much originality. His country houses derive from the style of Gibbs, to whose *Book of Architecture* he subscribed. Helston Church exhibits several features borrowed directly from Hawksmoor's St. Alphege's, Greenwich. Of his two town houses the earlier is in the Gibbs style, with rich plaster decoration in the interior, while the later adopts the plainer sort of elevation fashionable in London and Bath in the third quarter of the eighteen century.

[*The Parochial History of Cornwall*, 1867–72; Taunton MSS. at Royal Cornwall Institution; P.C.C. 415 ALEXANDER; *Gent's Mag.* 1775, 551; St. Alphege's, Greenwich, burial register; H. Dalton Clifford & Howard Colvin, 'A Georgian Architect in Cornwall', *C. Life*, 4 and 18 Oct. 1962.]

TEHIDY, CORNWALL, for J. P. Basset, 1736; altered and enlarged by Wm. Burn 1861; dem. after a fire 1919 [*Parochial History* ii, 228].

TREWITHEN, CORNWALL, completion of house for the heirs of Philip Hawkins, *c.* 1738–40; altered by Sir Robert Taylor *c.* 1763–4 [Hawkins documents in County Record Office] (*C. Life*, 2–9 April 1953).

CARCLEW, CORNWALL, completed house for William Lemon after 1749; colonnades added 18—; gutted 1934 [*Parochial History* iii, 395] (Richardson & Gill, *Regional Architecture of the West of England*, 1924, 92–3).

NANSWHYDEN, CORNWALL, for Robert Hoblyn (d. 1756); burned 1803 [Taunton MS.] (W. Borlase, *Natural History of Cornwall*, 1758, pl. 9).

ST. GLUVIAS CHURCH, CORNWALL, rebuilt *c.* 1750; rebuilt 1883 [*Parochial History* ii, 85].

TRURO, PRINCE'S HOUSE, PRINCE'S STREET, for William Lemon (d. 1760), now occupied by Farm Industries Ltd. [Taunton MS.].

TRURO, house in PRINCE'S STREET for Thomas Daniell, 1755–62, now known as the Mansion House [Taunton MS.] (Richardson & Gill, p. 96).

HELSTON CHURCH, CORNWALL, 1756–61 [H. S. Toy, *History of Helston*, 1936, 334–40; accounts in Cornwall Record Office, DD. 90. 244–6].

TRURO, ST. MARY'S CHURCH, added Gothic tower and spire, 1766–9; dem. 1880 [F. W. Bullock, *History of the Church of St. Mary Truro*, Truro 1948, 80–1].

EDWARDS, WILLIAM (1719–1789), is celebrated as a bridge-builder in South Wales. He was the youngest son of a farmer at Eglwysilan, nr. Caerphilly in Glamorganshire, and began life as an agricultural labourer. His enterprise and intelligence led him first to learn the technique of dry stone walling, at which he became adept, and then the art of a mason. Though entirely self-taught, he became so skilled at his trade that in 1746 he contracted to build a bridge of three arches over the R. Taff at PONT-Y-PRYDD, GLAMORGANSHIRE, and to maintain it for seven years. When it was destroyed by a flood two years later Edwards boldly decided to replace it by a single span of 140 feet that would offer no obstruction to the flood-waters of the Taff. This bridge was nearly complete when the weight of the masonry in the haunches forced out the keystones and thus caused the arch to collapse. Undaunted, Edwards determined to try again. In order to reduce the mass of masonry he pierced large cylindrical holes through the haunches. Whether this expedient was empirically devised by Edwards or not, it proved entirely successful and the bridge, completed in 1756, still stands today (plans and elevation in *Builder* iii, 1845, 427). Its elegant profile was as much admired as the ingenuity of its constructor, and he subsequently built many other bridges in South Wales. Among the more important were USK BRIDGE, MONMOUTHSHIRE (rebuilt 1836); a bridge of three arches over the R. Tawy in Glamorganshire; PONT-AR-TAWY, about 10 miles above Swansea, of one arch of 80 feet span; BETTWS BRIDGE, GLAM. (one arch, 45 feet span); LLANDOVERY BRIDGE, CARMARTHENSHIRE (one arch, 84 feet span, with one perforation in the haunches); WYCHBREE BRIDGE, over the R. Tawy near Morriston (one arch, 95 feet span, with two perforations); ABERAVON BRIDGE, GLAMORGANSHIRE (one arch, 70 feet span, without perforations); and GLASBURY BRIDGE, over the R. Wye near Hay, of five arches on high piers, afterwards destroyed by a flood. Some of these later bridges represented a considerable technical improvement on the first one at Pont-y-Prydd, whose roadway was so inconveniently steep that the nearby ford remained in use until the middle of the nineteenth century. For Edwards found that, where sufficient abutment was assured, it was possible to construct arches of much larger radius and lower rise than was commonly thought necessary.

Besides building bridges, Edwards continued to erect smelting houses, forges and other industrial buildings, and to carry on the business of a farmer. From 1745 onwards he also officiated

as an Independent minister. He died in 1789, leaving six children. Three of his four sons followed their father's trade, and David, the second, continued the bridge-building business. Among the bridges which he erected were those at LLANDILO, CARMARTHENSHIRE (R. Tawy); EDWINSFORD, CARMARTHENSHIRE (R. Cothy); PONTLOYRIG, nr. Whitland, CARMARTHENSHIRE (R. Taw); BEDWAS, MONMOUTHSHIRE (R. Rhymney); and the five-arch bridge over the Usk at NEWPORT, MONMOUTHSHIRE, completed in 1801. He lived at Beaupre, St. Mary Church, nr. Cowbridge.

[*Gent's Mag.* 1764, 564–5; B. H. Malkin, *The Scenery, Antiquities and Biography of S. Wales*, 1804, 84–94; Samuel Smiles, *The Lives of the Engineers* i, 1861, 266–75; *A.P.S.D.*; *D.N.B.*; *The Dictionary of Welsh Biography*, 1959, 198–9; W. B. Coventry, *A History of Pont-y-ty-Prydd*, 1902; E. I. Williams, 'Pont-y-ty-pridd: A Critical Examination of its History', and S. B. Hamilton, 'Pont-y-ty-pridd: Notes on the Technical Significance of a Remarkable Bridge', *Transactions of the Newcomen Soc.* xxiv, 1943–5.]

EDWIN, RICHARD (–1778), was a pupil of Matthew Brettingham in 1764, when he was awarded a premium of 7 guineas by the Society of Arts [*Register of Premiums*, 1778]. He competed for the Royal Exchange at Dublin in 1769 [*Builder* xxvii, 1869, 781]. He exhibited at the Society of Artists in 1770, and at the Royal Academy in 1774, 1776 and 1777. For the Hon. Edward Stratford, later 1st Earl of Aldborough, he designed in 1773–5 the Adamsian STRATFORD PLACE, OXFORD STREET, a 'longitudinal elevation' of which he exhibited at the Academy in 1774 [A. T. Bolton, 'Stratford Place', *London Topographical Record* xii, 1920; Dorothy Stroud, *George Dance, Architect*, 1971, 90–1]. He also appears to have designed the HANOVER SQUARE CONCERT ROOMS on the east side of HANOVER SQUARE, opened in 1775 by the dancing-master Sir John Gallini, and demolished *c.* 1875, for in 1776 he exhibited 'a longitudinal section of the Concert Room in Hanover Square'. Edwin, who lived in Marylebone, died in October 1778 [P.C.C. 399 HAY].

EGLINGTON was the name of a widespread family of masons working in the Midlands in the latter part of the eighteenth century. They are found in eighteenth-century building records in Derby, Birmingham, Coventry and elsewhere.

JOSEPH EGLINGTON (1746–1810) of Coventry was one of the sons of Benjamin Eglington of Badby, Northants. He appears to have been a prosperous builder-architect, whose will refers to workshops, tenements and other property on the outskirts of Coventry [will in Lichfield Joint Record Office, *ex inf.* Mr. Edward

Saunders]. Between 1775 and 1787 he rebuilt several windows at HOLY TRINITY CHURCH, COVENTRY, and recased the east end [T. Sharp, *Illustrative Papers on the History and Antiquities of Coventry*, 1871, 107]. He designed the classical COUNTY HALL, COVENTRY, 1783–4 [T. Sharp, *The Coventry Guide*, 1824, 53] and in 1792 LEEK WOOTTON CHURCH, WARWICKS., was rebuilt to his designs in a Gothic style, incorporating the medieval tower [Shakespeare's Birthplace, Stratford, Leigh papers, Leek Wotton, 25].

SAMUEL EGLINGTON appears to have been a 'kinsman' of that name living at Kineton in Warwickshire who is referred to in Joseph Eglington's will. In 1773–4 he and a carpenter named John Mantun contracted to rebuild LIGHT-HORNE CHURCH, WARWICKS., in a plain Gothic style [MS. Churchwardens' accounts in Warwick County Record Office]. Their work at Lighthorne was largely paid for by Lord Willoughby de Broke, who also employed both Eglington and Mantun at COMPTON VERNEY HOUSE, *e.g.* in building the Chapel in 1776–8 [Shakespeare's Birthplace, Stratford, Willoughby de Broke papers]. In 1789–90 Eglington was employed on repairs to ASTON CHURCH, WARWICKS. [*Trans. Birmingham and Midland Institute*, 1872, 24].

ELDER. Payments to 'Mr. Elder, Surveyor, for his Journey from London', occur at the beginning of the building accounts of ST. CATHERINE'S HALL, CAMBRIDGE, in 1674, but it is uncertain whether he was the designer of the new buildings which were erected during the next thirteen years [Willis & Clark, ii, 101].

ELGER, JOHN (*c.* 1801–1888), was probably a native of Bedford, where his elder brother Thomas Gwyn Elger was a builder. T. G. Elger was one of the trustees of the Harpur Charity in Bedford, and John Elger acted as surveyor of the trust's estate in Holborn from 1826 to 1846. In 1828 he made classical designs for the new Harpur School in Bedford which were rejected in favour of Blore's Tudor Gothic design [J. Godber, *The Harpur Trust 1555–1973*, 1973, 39, 160, pl. 10]. In London Elger was a highly successful developer on the Grosvenor estate in the 1830s, and in Knightsbridge in the 1840s and 1850s, his best-known speculation being the imposing terrace of houses at PRINCE'S GATE, built *c.* 1845 onwards with architectural help from the young H. L. Elmes [*A.P.S.D.*, *s.v.* 'Elmes']. Elger appears to have retired before 1860. He died at Brighton on 12 August 1888, aged 87, leaving an estate valued at over £115,000 [Principal Probate Registry, Calendar of Probates].

ELISON, THOMAS, 'Architecte du Prince de Wallis', is the name which appears on the title-page of a book entitled *Décorations pour Parcs et Jardins* which was published at Leipzig early in the nineteenth century. This book appears to have been a reprint of *Decorations for Parks and Gardens*, published in London by J. Taylor in *c.* 1810, and usually attributed to Charles Middleton (*q.v.*).

ELLINS, JAMES, succeeded Thomas Dixon as foreman of Lady Oxford's works at WELBECK ABBEY, NOTTS., in 1743. Several architectural designs by him figure in a list of drawings made in 1764, and some of these drawings survive. Most of them are marked as 'not executed'. [Nottingham University Library, Pwf 10052; information from the late Francis Needham; R. W. Goulding, 'Henrietta Countess of Oxford', *Trans. Thoroton Soc.* xxvii, 1924.]

ELLIOT, ARCHIBALD (1760–1823) and JAMES (1770–1810), were the sons of a carrier at Ancrum in Roxburghshire. Archibald was born in August 1760, James in April 1770. Archibald is said to have been brought up as a joiner, and to have worked for a time for a cabinet-maker in London. As a joiner he is said to have worked at Douglas Castle, Lanarkshire, where, upon 'a difference arising between the architect and the proprietor, Elliot took up and completed the work'. He is also said either to have built Castle Mona in the Isle of Man to the designs of James Steuart, or to have completed it after Steuart's death in 1806. From 1794 to 1799 he exhibited architectural designs at the Royal Academy, and soon after 1800 he and his brother James were in joint practice as architects. Archibald had an office in London, while James remained in Scotland to supervise the firm's work there. James's death in October 1810 at the age of 40 brought the partnership to an end, and thereafter Archibald appears to have divided his time between London (Osnaburgh Street) and Edinburgh (Calton Hill). He died in Edinburgh on 16 June 1823, and was buried in the New Calton Graveyard, where he is commemorated by a fluted column topped by a draped urn. His practice was continued by his son Archibald (*q.v.*).

Archibald Elliot was one of the leading Edinburgh architects during the first quarter of the nineteenth century. His Regent Bridge and County Hall were among the best Greek Revival buildings in the 'Modern Athens', and until his death he was strongly favoured by those who wanted a native Scotsman to be chosen as the architect of the National Monument on Calton Hill. As a country-house architect, however, he specialized in castellated houses with Gothic detailing. Externally, these houses are symmetrically designed in a manner which usually derives either from Inveraray (Taymouth and Stobo) or from the Adam castle style (Loudoun and Dreghorn). Often the interiors are classical, but at Taymouth, Lindertis and Newbyth the Elliots provided elaborate Gothic rooms in the style of Wyatt and Atkinson. [Ancrum parish register in New Register House, Edinburgh; *A.P.S.D.*; *Scots Mag.* 1810, 879; testament of Archibald Elliot in Commissariot of Edinburgh, 28 June 1825.]

PUBLIC BUILDINGS

†KIRKCALDY OLD CHURCH, FIFE, rebuilt (incorporating old tower), 1806–7 [S.R.O., HR 239/1, pp. 46, 47, 49, etc.].

DUNFERMLINE, FIFE, THE COUNTY BUILDINGS, 79 HIGH STREET, 1809; spire 1811 [signed plans formerly in possession of the late James Shearer, R.S.A., *ex inf.* Mr. David Walker].

GLENORCHY CHURCH, ARGYLLSHIRE, 1810–11, octagonal Gothic, by James Elliot [*N.S.A.* vii, 100–1; R.C.A.M., *Argyll* ii, 132].

DUNKELD CATHEDRAL, PERTHSHIRE, fitted up choir as parish church, 1814 [drawing at Blair Atholl].

EDINBURGH, THE NEW PRISONS, CALTON HILL, 1815–17, castellated; dem. *c.* 1938 except Governor's house [*A.P.S.D.*] (T. H. Shepherd, *Modern Athens*, 1829, 44–5 and plates).

EDINBURGH, THE REGENT BRIDGE, 1815–19 [signed 'ARCHIBALD ELLIOT, ARCHITECT'; A. J. Youngson, *The Making of Classical Edinburgh*, 1966, 142–7].

EDINBURGH, ST. PAUL'S EPISCOPAL CHURCH, YORK PLACE, 1816–18, Gothic; chancel 1892 [*A.P.S.D.*; W. M. Gilbert, *Edinburgh in the Nineteenth Century*, 1901, 60].

EDINBURGH, THE COUNTY HALL, 1816–19, dem. *c.* 1900 [*Scots Mag.*, Nov. 1816; T. H. Shepherd, *Modern Athens*, 1829, 74 and plate].

EDINBURGH, PARLIAMENT HOUSE, ROOM for LORDS ORDINARY at south end of Parliament Hall, 1818–19 [S.R.O., E 343/3, pp. 7–94, Minutes of the Trustees for Public Buildings].

EDINBURGH, THE CALTON CONVENING ROOMS, WATERLOO PLACE, 1818–19 [part of Waterloo Place, for which see below, under 'Domestic Architecture'].

PAISLEY, RENFREWSHIRE, THE COUNTY BUILDINGS, 1818–20, castellated; enlarged 1850; dem. 1970 [C. Mackie, *Abbey and Town of Paisley*, Glasgow 1835, 148].

COCKPEN CHURCH, MIDLOTHIAN, 1818–20, Gothic [S.R.O., HR 333/6].

EDINBURGH, BROUGHTON PLACE CHURCH (Dr. Brown's Chapel), 1820–1, interior altered 1870 [Anon., *History of Broughton Place U.P. Church*, 1872, 151; Minutes of the Managers in S.R.O., CH 3/564/12, pp. 149, 160].

JEDBURGH, ROXBURGHSHIRE, THE COUNTY PRISON, 1820–3, castellated [*A.P.S.D.*].

BLAIR ATHOLL CHURCH, PERTHSHIRE, 1823–5 [S.R.O., CH 2/430/8].

DOMESTIC ARCHITECTURE, ETC.

LOUDOUN CASTLE, AYRSHIRE, for the Countess of Loudoun and her husband the 2nd Earl of Moira (afterwards 1st Marquess of Hastings), 1804–11, castellated; gutted in 1941 and now in ruins [exhib. at R.A. 1806; G. Richardson, *New Vitruvius Britannicus* ii, 1808, pls. 51–6].

†DREGHORN CASTLE, COLINTON, MIDLOTHIAN, enlarged and remodelled for Alexander Trotter, *c.* 1805, castellated; dem. 1958 [*Scots Mag.*, 1808, 243] (*The Beauties of Scotland* i, 1805, 443; J. Small, *Castles and Mansions of the Lothians* i, 1883).

†STOBO CASTLE, PEEBLESSHIRE, for Sir James Montgomery, Bart., 1805–11, castellated [W. Chambers, *History of Peeblesshire*, 1864, 438–9; R.C.A.M., *Peeblesshire* ii, 308–9].

†AUCHMORE HOUSE, KILLIN, PERTHSHIRE, altered and enlarged for the 4th Earl (1st Marquess) of Breadalbane, 1806–7; rebuilt *c.* 1870 [S.R.O., GDH 112/20/2].

†TAYMOUTH CASTLE, PERTHSHIRE, for the 4th Earl (1st Marquess) of Breadalbane, 1806–10, castellated; subsequently enlarged by W. Atkinson and J. Gillespie-Graham [Alistair Rowan in *C. Life*, 8–15 Oct. 1964].

MINTO HOUSE, ROXBURGHSHIRE, rebuilt for the 1st Earl of Minto, 1809–14; dem. 1973 [National Library of Scotland, Minto Maps and Plans, no. 15; working drawings in N.M.R.S.; cf. *N.S.A.* iii, 367]. The new house followed the unusual V plan of the former one, and incorporated part of its fabric, cf. plan of the former house in Bodleian, Gough Maps 39, f. 28.

LINDERTIS HOUSE, ANGUS, for Gilbert Laing Meason, 1815–16, castellated; dem. [J. P. Neale, *Views of Seats*, 1st ser., ii] (*Forfarshire Illustrated*, 1843, 114).

CALLENDAR HOUSE, STIRLINGSHIRE, Grecian Mausoleum in grounds for trustees of the late William Forbes, 1816 [S.R.O., GD 171/Box 78/5] (R.C.A.M., *Stirlingshire*, pl. 50).

DUNKELD HOUSE, PERTHSHIRE, works for the 4th Duke of Atholl, including castellated gateway and stables (dem.), 1809, restoration of the Low Wing after fire in 1814, and lodges, *c.* 1815 [John, 7th Duke of Atholl, *Chronicles of the Atholl and Tullibardine Families* iv, 1908, 234, 261, 264; drawings at Blair Atholl].

NEWBYTH, EAST LOTHIAN, for David Baird, 1817–18, castellated; interior rebuilt as flats after fire in 1972 [*A.P.S.D.*; contract in S.R.O., GD 236 (unlisted); exhib. at R.A. 1819 by Archibald Elliot, junior].

LOCHNELL HOUSE, ARGYLLSHIRE. Elliot was probably the architect employed by Lt. Gen. Dun-

---

† In conjunction with James Elliot.

can Campbell to enlarge the house in castellated style, 1818–20 [R.C.A.M., *Argyll* ii, 266].

EDINBURGH, WATERLOO PLACE, 1819 (designed 1815) [A. J. Youngson, *The Making of Classical Edinburgh*, 1966, 145].

THE HAINING, SELKIRKSHIRE, enlarged for John Pringle, *c.* 1820 [J. P. Neale, *Views of Seats*, 1st ser., iv] (R.C.A.M., *Selkirkshire*, 49–50).

EDINBURGH, RUTLAND PLACE, STREET and SQUARE were built in 1830–4 to designs by John Tait based on plans made by Elliot in 1819 [S.R.O., Edinburgh Sasines].

ELLIOT, ARCHIBALD, junior (–1843), was the son and successor of Archibald Elliot (*q.v.*). He exhibited at the Royal Academy in 1817–20, showing drawings of recent works by his father. Subsequently he practised in London from Osnaburgh Street, where he was in partnership with his brother Alexander. He altered THE ROYAL BANK OF SCOTLAND, ST. ANDREWS SQUARE, EDINBURGH, 1825–8, designed the handsome Greek Revival ROYAL BANK OF SCOTLAND, GLASGOW, 1827, and THE MILITARY ACADEMY, LOTHIAN ROAD, EDINBURGH, 1829–30 [*A.P.S.D.*; N. Munro, *History of the Royal Bank of Scotland*, Edinburgh 1928, 193–4]. He died in 1843 [P.R.O., P.C.C. Register, 1843, 475].

ELLIOT, WILLIAM, was a builder and architect of Kelso in Roxburghshire. It is possible that he was a brother of Archibald and James Elliot (*q.v.*), for the Ancrum parish register shows that their father, Archibald Elliot, had a son William who was born in December 1766. William Elliot's country houses are attractive examples of late Georgian architecture. Chesters is a conventional Georgian house with flanking wings, Ladykirk a simplified version of Chambers's Dundas House in Edinburgh, and Crailing a compact and elegantly detailed villa. He is presumably the 'Mr. Elliot' who in 1795 built the TEVIOT BRIDGE near KELSO, notable for its use of the motif of engaged Doric columns previously used by Harrison at Lancaster (1783–8) and subsequently by Rennie in his Kelso (1800–3) and Waterloo (1811–17) Bridges [E. Cresy, *Encyclopaedia of Civil Engineering*, 1847, 469]. Walter Elliot, who was practising in Kelso in the middle of the nineteenth century, may have been his successor.

CHESTERS HOUSE, ROXBURGHSHIRE, for Thomas Elliot Ogilvie, 1787–90 [G. Tancred, *Annals of a Border Club*, Jedburgh 1899, 336].

LADYKIRK HOUSE, BERWICKSHIRE, for William Robertson, 1797–9; altered by W. Burn 1845; dem. 1966 [drawings formerly at Ladykirk].

WILTON CHURCH, ROXBURGHSHIRE, enlarged on north side, 1800 [S.R.O., HR 390/2].

CRAILING HOUSE, ROXBURGHSHIRE, for James

Paton, 1803 [G. Tancred, *Annals of a Border Club*, Jedburgh 1899, 348] (*C. Life*, 14 June 1962).

DRUMLANRIG CASTLE, DUMFRIESSHIRE, restoration for the 4th Duke of Buccleuch, 1813 [Mark Girouard in *C. Life*, 8 Sept. 1960, citing accounts at Drumlanrig].

KELSO CHURCH, ROXBURGHSHIRE, internal alterations (chiefly substitution of flat ceiling for domed one), 1823 [S.R.O., HR 651/4].

ELLIOTT, JOHN, was a builder-architect of Chichester. His bankruptcy in 1843 was the subject of a leading article in the *Builder*. He had contracted to build a church at Worthing for £3500, but the design was severely criticized in the *Ecclesiologist*, and alterations were made at the behest of the Cambridge Camden Society which added so much to the cost that Elliot became insolvent [*Builder* i, 1843, 489–90]. He had another encounter with the ecclesiologists in 1849, when he failed to obtain the commission for the monument in Chichester Cathedral to Bishop Otter (d. 1840). According to the *Ecclesiologist* ix, 1849, 272, he claimed that 'those who did not avail themselves of his services, are Papists'; and that long chancels ought properly to be called *transubstantiators*'. He must be distinguished from the London architect of the same name who, with Victor Delassaux, published in 1855 a book entitled *Street Architecture, A Series of Shop Fronts and Façades*.

CHICHESTER, THE CORN EXCHANGE (now a cinema), 1832 [*A.P.S.D.*, *s.v.* 'Chichester'].

PAGHAM CHURCH, SUSSEX, repairs, 1837 [I.C.B.S.].

GOODWOOD HOUSE, SUSSEX, completed east wing for the 5th Duke of Richmond, 1838–9 [W. H. Mason, *Goodwood, its House, Park and Grounds*, 1839, 122].

OVING, SUSSEX, almshouses, school and cottages for Miss Woods of Shopwyke, 1839, Tudor Gothic [Loudon, *Encyclopaedia of Cottage, Farm and Villa Architecture*, 1846, 1242–3].

EMSWORTH CHURCH, HANTS., 1839–40, 'Norman' style [*Ecclesiologist* ii, 1842, 92–3, 170].

WORTHING, SUSSEX, CHRIST CHURCH, 1840–1, Gothic [*Ecclesiologist* i, 1841–2, 78, 148, 210; I.C.B.S.].

MIDDLETON CHURCH, SUSSEX, 1847–9, Gothic [I.C.B.S.].

ELLIS, ANTHONY (1620–1671), built and presumably designed ALTHORP HOUSE, NORTHANTS., as remodelled by the 2nd Earl of Sunderland in 1666–8, and illustrated in *Vitruvius Britannicus* ii, pls. 95–7. The first stone was laid in February 1665/6, and between then and October 1668 Anthony Ellis, 'freemason and surveyor', received at least £2800 'towards the new building' [Blenheim Palace muniments, F.I. 56 and Box XVI/56].

Anthony Ellis was a pupil of Nicholas Stone, to whom he was apprenticed in about 1635 and whose will he witnessed in 1641 [*The Note-Book of Nicholas Stone*, ed. Spiers, Walpole Soc., vii, 1918–19, 30, 147, etc.]. Like Stone, he was a sculptor as well as a builder, and his signature appears on the monument to Sir John Wentworth (d. 1651) at SOMERLEYTON, SUFFOLK. His will [P.C.C. 121 DUKE] shows that he lived in the parish of St. Martin-in-the-Fields, Westminster, and died in 1671.

ELLIS, ROBERT, a carpenter and builder of Fleet in Lincolnshire, designed and built ST. JOHN'S CHURCH in the parish of HOLBEACH, LINCS., 1839, Gothic [G. W. Macdonald, *A Brief Account of the Parish of Holbeach*, n.d., 56].

ELLIS, THOMAS, a carpenter of Sherborne, Dorset, rebuilt SPARKFORD CHURCH, SOMERSET, in a simple Gothic style in 1824, apparently to his own designs [I.C.B.S.].

ELMES, HARVEY LONSDALE (1814–1847), born at Oving, nr. Chichester, was the only son of James Elmes (*q.v.*), and godson of James Lonsdale, the artist, who was his father's intimate friend. He studied architecture under his father, and his uncle Henry John Elmes;[1] also with John Elger (*q.v.*), a speculative builder, for whom he later made a number of designs. In 1831 he was admitted as a student at the Royal Academy Schools, and in 1834 he became an assistant to H. E. Goodridge, in whose office at Bath he remained for three years. After this he returned to London and assisted his father in designing some houses in Queen Anne's Gate, and in the decoration of one of them for the Turkish ambassador.

In July 1839 he obtained the first premium of 250 guineas for the design of St. George's Hall, Liverpool, out of a total of seventy-five competitors. Soon afterwards the Corporation decided to build new Assize Courts, and a premium of £300 was offered for the best design: eighty-nine competitors entered, and Elmes was again successful (April 1840). It was then proposed to unite the two buildings, and Franklin, the city architect, was directed to adapt Elmes's plans. Fortunately he had the generosity not to stand in the way of the young architect, and it was a new design by Elmes himself which was approved on 27 October 1840. It comprised a great central hall, with the crown court at one end, the civil court at the other, and an elliptical concert room

beyond it at a higher level. Work began in 1841, but the architect, whose already poor health had begun to deteriorate under the strain of preparing detailed drawings for this great edifice without adequate assistance, was advised to go abroad, leaving the engineer Robert Rawlinson in charge of the works. In 1842 he visited Belgium and Germany with his friend William Earle, whose account of the tour is printed in R.I.B.A. *Sessional Papers*, 1863–4, p. xi. In the course of it he was able to see some of the new monumental buildings by von Klenze and Schinkel which, through illustrations, may already have influenced his own approach to neo-classical design. On his return, he resumed work on St. George's Hall, but the worry and responsibility involved in its completion – and in particular the problem of vaulting the 73 feet span of the Great Hall – further impaired his health. He was obliged to leave his office, first for Ventnor and then for Jamaica, where he died on 26 November 1847, at the age of 34. The main structure of the building was finished by Rawlinson in the course of the next four years, and between 1851 and 1854 C. R. Cockerell completed the interior, largely to his own designs. The total cost was £400,000.

St. George's Hall is one of the major monuments of neo-classical architecture, 'holding its own in comparison with any classical building of these years in Europe' (Pevsner). The complexity of the brief and the insularity of the site (exposing all the elevations to view) set the architect a problem, both in planning and in composition, which he brilliantly solved. His approach, though controlled by scholarship, was very different from the archaeological pedantry which had inspired much Greek Revival architecture. For Elmes, like Cockerell, the classical orders represented an architectural vocabulary to be manipulated with intelligent understanding rather than a set of rigid precepts to be followed with absolute respect. The result is a building of monumental strength and grandeur in which the architectural vocabulary of Imperial Rome is most successfully used to symbolize the civic pride of a great Victorian industrial city. For a young man still in his twenties it was an astonishing achievement, only to be equalled by the equally precocious performance of Giles Gilbert Scott in the competition for the Anglican Cathedral in 1903.

Before his early death Elmes had time to design only a handful of other buildings: a large Tudor Gothic school of no special distinction, and several private houses in the Liverpool area. A number of his drawings (including those for St. George's Hall) are in the R.I.B.A. Collection, together with some letters and a MS. memoir by his father.

[Obituaries by his father in *Builder* xiii, 1855, 53–4, and *Building Chronicle* i, 1855, 213; others in *Builder* vi, 1848, 24, 71; J. T. Kilpin, 'The

---

[1] H. J. Elmes had an architectural training under Daniel Davis (*q.v.*), but he made a living as a builder in London rather than as an architect.

Late Mr. Elmes and St. George's Hall', *Trans. of the Historic Soc. of Lancs. and Cheshire*, N.S. ix, 1868–9 (giving the text of Elmes's correspondence with Robert Rawlinson); *A.P.S.D.*; R. P. Jones, 'The Life and Work of Harvey Lonsdale Elmes', *Arch. Rev.* xv, 1904, 231; *R.I.B.A. Drawings Coll. Catalogue: C–F*, 103–9.]

LIVERPOOL, ST. GEORGE'S HALL AND ASSIZE COURTS, designed 1840, begun 1841, structure completed 1847–51 by R. Rawlinson, interior by C. R. Cockerell 1851–4 [*Companion to the Almanac*, 1842, 221–6; *Builder* xiii, 1855, 1–5, 23, 26–8, 126–7].

LIVERPOOL, THE COLLEGIATE INSTITUTION, SHAW STREET, 1840–3, Gothic [*Companion to the Almanac*, 1842, 226–7; David Wainwright in *Arch. Rev.*, May 1959].

LONDON, KENSINGTON, façades of houses in ENNISMORE GARDENS and PRINCE'S GATE, for John Elger, speculative builder, c. 1843–6 [drawings in R.I.B.A. Coll.].

RABY HALL, ROCK FERRY, BIRKENHEAD, CHESHIRE, for William Irlam, 1845 [mentioned in his father's memoir as 'a villa at Rock Ferry for William Irlam', and identified by Mr. Edward Hubbard].

WALLASEY, CHESHIRE, REDCLIFFE, WELLINGTON ROAD, NEW BRIGHTON, for Daniel Neilson, 1845, Tudor style [drawings in R.I.B.A. Coll.; N. Pevsner & E. Hubbard, *Cheshire*, 1971, 374].

WALLASEY, CHESHIRE, a villa at NEW BRIGHTON for G. H. Lawrence of Liverpool, c. 1845 [MS. memoir by James Elmes, second version, p. 76].

WOOLTON, LANCS., 'DRUID'S CROSS', villa for Joseph Hornby, 1846–7 [drawings in R.I.B.A. Coll.] (P. Fleetwood-Hesketh, *Murray's Lancashire Architectural Guide*, 1955, 100).

THINGWALL HALL, KNOTTY ASH, nr. LIVERPOOL (now St. Edward's Orphanage), for Samuel Henry Thompson, c. 1846–7 [letter from Elmes to Thompson in the author's possession].

ALLERTON TOWER, ALLERTON, LANCS., for Sir Hardman Earle, c. 1847; dem. 1933 [*A.P.S.D.*].

LANCASHIRE COUNTY LUNATIC ASYLUM, RAINHILL, LANCS., executed by William Moseley, 1847–51; enlarged 1886 [*A.P.S.D.*; exhib. posthumously at R.A. 1853].

LONDON, HANOVER SQUARE, 'houses and chambers built in the garden and stable-yard of a mansion' [*A.P.S.D.*].

ELMES, JAMES (1782–1862), was born in London. His father Samuel and his grandfather John Elmes were both builders by trade and members of the Tylers' and Bricklayers' Company. James was educated at Merchant Taylors'

School and subsequently became a pupil of George Gibson. In 1804 he entered the Royal Academy Schools, winning the Silver Medal in 1805. He exhibited at the Royal Academy from 1801 to 1842. He became Surveyor to the Port of London, and enjoyed a moderate practice in London and in Sussex, where he had a house at Oving, nr. Chichester. He was best known, however, as a prolific writer on artistic and architectural topics, and, in particular, as the editor of Shepherd's *Metropolitan Improvements*. He was Vice-President of the London Architectural Society (founded 1806), lectured on architectural subjects at the Surrey and Russell Institution, and edited a pioneer art journal entitled *Annals of the Fine Arts* (1816–20). He was a friend of Haydon, and through him of Keats, some of whose sonnets first appeared under Elmes's editorship in *Annals of the Fine Arts*. Although essentially an architectural and literary antiquary, whose own writings show no great power of criticism, Elmes has a place in the history of architectural scholarship as the author of the first documented life of Wren, and it was from him that Sir John Soane purchased the important Wren manuscript known as the 'Court Orders' (*Wren Soc.* xviii). Failing sight obliged Elmes to give up practice in 1848. He died at Greenwich on 2 April 1862. His portrait by his friend James Lonsdale (1777–1839), now at the R.I.B.A., is reproduced in *Wren Soc.* xviii, frontispiece. Apart from his more famous son, Elmes's known pupils were John Haviland, Samuel Paterson and George Allen.

The following were Elmes's principal publications: 'A letter to T. Hope ... on the insufficiency of the existing establishments for promoting the fine arts towards that of Architecture', in *The Pamphleteer* iii, 1813; *Hints for the Improvement of Prisons ... partly founded on the principles of John Howard*, 1817; *Lectures on Architecture*, 1821, 2nd ed. 1823; *Memoirs of the Life and Works of Sir Chr. Wren, with a View of the Progress of Architecture in England, from the Reign of Charles I to the End of the Seventeenth Century*, 1823; *The Arts and Artists: or, anecdotes and relics of the Schools of Painting, Sculpture and Architecture*, 3 vols., 1825; *A General and Bibliographical Dictionary of the Fine Arts*, 1826; *A Practical Treatise on Architectural Jurisprudence*, 1827; the 'Historical, Topographical and Critical' introductions to *Metropolitan Improvements or London in the Nineteenth Century*, by T. H. Shepherd, 1827–9; *A Practical Treatise on Ecclesiastical and Civil Dilapidations*, 1829 (3rd ed.); *London Bridge ... with a particular account of the new London Bridge*, 1831; *A Topographical Dictionary of London*, 1831; *A Scientific, Historical and Commercial Survey of the Harbour and Port of London*, 1838; and 'A History of Architecture in Great Britain' in *The Civil Engineer and Architect's Jnl.*

x, 1847. [*Builder* xx, 1862, 275; *Gent's Mag.* 1862 (i), 784–5; *Autobiography of B. R. Haydon*, ed. T. Taylor, i, 1926, 248–9.]

SHERIFF'S COURT, ISLE OF THANET, KENT, 'new principal front, in the Egyptian style of architecture', exhib. as 'to be built' in 1805; probably not built.

STOCKWELL, SURREY, two villas, built 1805–6 [exhib. at R.A. 1807].

OAKWOOD HOUSE, nr. CHICHESTER, SUSSEX, 1809–12 [exhib. at R.A. 1811].

CHICHESTER, KING'S HOLME, 'design for', exhib. at R.A. 1811.

CHICHESTER, ST. JOHN'S CHAPEL, 1812–13, erected under the supervision of John Haviland during Elmes's illness [*A.P.S.D.*, *s.v.* 'Haviland'; *V.C.H. Sussex* iii, 163].

CHICHESTER CATHEDRAL, rebuilt upper part of spire, 1813–14 [*Civil Engineer and Architect's Jnl.* x, 1847, 237].

BEDFORD, THE NEW GAOL, 1819–20; dem. [*Annals of the Fine Arts* iv, 1819, 353; *Notes and Extracts from the Beds. County Records* i [*c.* 1905], 194, 196].

WATERFORD, IRELAND, THE HOUSE OF CORRECTION, 1820 [*Annals of the Fine Arts* v, 1820, 438–9].

LONDON, ST. MICHAEL COLLEGE HILL, interior repairs, 1820 [Guildhall Library, MS. 603].

LONDON, SOCIETY OF BRITISH ARTISTS, SUFFOLK STREET, interior (with J. Nash), *c.* 1823 [J. Summerson, *John Nash*, 1935, 216].

LONDON, BAKERS' HALL, NO. 16 HARP LANE, repairs, 1825 [J. Timbs, *The Curiosities of London*, 1867, 410].

RAVENSCOURT, nr. HAMMERSMITH, MIDDLESEX, a cottage, 1824 [exhib. at R.A. 1824].

LONDON, FARRINGDON STREET, obelisk to Robert Waithman, 1833; moved to Bartholomew Close 1951 [*Architectural Mag.* ii, 1835, 94].

WESTMINSTER, NOS. 6–12 (even) QUEEN ANNE'S GATE (BIRDCAGE WALK), of which No. 6 was for the PARLIAMENTARY AGENCY OFFICES, 1837 [*Architectural Mag.* iv, 75].

WESTWOOD HALL, nr. LEEK, STAFFS., alterations and additions for J. Devonport, M.P., 1837 [exhib. at R.A. 1837].

ELSAM, RICHARD, was a pupil of Robert Browne, Clerk of the Works at Kew Palace. He was living at Richmond at the time of his marriage, in 1793, to Miss Crawley, of Ipswich [*Gent's. Mag.* 1793 (ii), 1050]. He exhibited at the Royal Academy between 1797 and 1807 from an address in Newington Butts. For some years (until *c.* 1803) he was employed in the Barrack Department of the War Office. A design by James Johnson (*q.v.*) for barracks for 2500 officers and men (B.M., *King's Maps* xxvi, 7 tt and uu), dated 1795, is signed by Elsam as draughtsman.

Elsam appears to have been a quarrelsome

character, whose career was marked by frequent disagreements with his clients and others. In 1803 he published *An Essay on Rural Architecture, being an attempt, also to refute the Principles of Mr. James Malton's Essay on British Cottage Architecture*, in which he illustrated several of his executed works, and incidentally accused C. A. Craig, the District Surveyor for Lambeth, of having unreasonably condemned some villas which Elsam had designed for a speculative builder in Vauxhall, on the ground that they were not in conformity with the Building Act of 1774. In 1804 he began to rebuild Chertsey Church, 'but after the general incorrectness of his estimates had been proved by the great outlay, he was superseded by the trustees', and the church was completed by Thomas Chawner. Soon after this episode Elsam emigrated to Northern Ireland, where he set up in practice in Londonderry. It was from Londonderry that in 1808 he published *The Gentleman and Builders Assistant*, 'containing a list of prices of the several artificers works, usually employed in building, together with some Observations on the Customs of Measuring in Ireland which, in many instances, tend not only to injure the employer but the employed'. The frontispiece shows his Tudor Gothic design for 'the Free School now erecting at Londonderry', but he appears to have quarrelled with the authorities soon after, for the building was completed in a 'Regency classical style' by John Bowden [Ulster Architectural Heritage Soc., *List of Buildings in the City of Derry*, 1970, 60]. Elsam subsequently practised in Dublin, but by 1818 he was back in England as surveyor to the Corporation of Dover, for whom he designed a new gaol in 1820–1. But 'owing to litigation with the architect ... the cost to the corporation was very considerable, and is still a charge on the poor-rates'. After this Elsam disappears from record. He had, however, published three further books: *Hints for improving the Condition of the Peasantry, with Plans, Elevations and Descriptive Views of Characteristic Designs for Cottages*, with a dedication to Thomas Coke of Holkham (1816), *A Brief Treatise on Prisons, illustrated with an enlarged design of the New Gaol about to be erected at Dover* (1818), and *The Practical Builder's Perpetual Price-Book* (1825) which contains some designs for houses by the author. Various of his designs are also illustrated in Nicholson's *Practical Builder*. Unexecuted designs by him for a church at Roscrea, Co. Tipperary, 1813, and for a gaol at Monaghan, 1814, are in the National Library of Ireland (MS. 8821(S) 115) and the Dublin Castle records (S.P.O. 558/423/31 and CSORP 1821/547), respectively (*ex inf.* Mr. E. McParland). His exhibits at the R.A. show that he made unexecuted designs for Finborough Hall, Suffolk (1804), and Wilton Castle, Yorks. (1805). Elsam's published designs reveal him as a self-conscious seeker after ingeniously geometrical plans clothed either in neo-classical or picturesque Gothic dress.

IPSWICH, SUFFOLK, a pair of semi-detached Gothic houses for Mr. J. Doughty, 'about to be erected' in 1803 [*Essay on Rural Architecture*, 1803, pl. 14].

HALSTEAD, ESSEX, SLOE FARM, for Mr. Hanbury [*Essay on Rural Architecture*, 1803, pls. 17, 18].

GOSFIELD PLACE, ESSEX, enlarged for J. G. Sparrow, *c.* 1800; dem. *c.* 1940 [*Essay on Rural Architecture*, 1803, pl. 27] (*Excursions in the County of Essex* ii, 1819, 152).

WALMER, KENT, 'Marine pavilion now erecting for A. Gram, Esq.' [*sic* in R.A. Catalogue 1805]; perhaps Walmer Cottage, later the property of J. Gaunt.

LONDON, KENNINGTON, houses in CARDIGAN PLACE built by Thomas Evans, 1806 [*The Practical Builder's Price-Book*, 1825, pl. 5].

CHERTSEY CHURCH, SURREY, 1806–7, Gothic; completed by T. Chawner [Brayley, *Topographical History of Surrey* ii, 193–4].

TUNBRIDGE WELLS, KENT, 'Mr. Baker's chateau', exhib. at R.A. 1807, perhaps Mount Calverley Lodge, later the property of A. St. John Baker.

CAVAN, IRELAND, THE COUNTY PRISON, 1810 [P. Nicholson, *Treatise on the Five Orders of Architecture*, 1834, pls. lxiv, lxv. See also *A Description of Cavan Gaol*, 1810, by R. Elsam or James Neild].

IRELAND, a cottage nr. DEVIL'S BIT, CO. TIPPERARAY, for Daniel Ryan, 1813 [*Hints on improving the Condition of the Peasantry*, 1816, no. x].

DOVER, THE GAOL, 1820–1 [*The Watering-Places of Great Britain and Fashionable Directory*, 1833, 175].

DOVER, THE ROUND HOUSE, for John Shipdem, the Town Clerk; dem. 1945 [J. M. Richards, *The Bombed Buildings of Britain*, 2nd ed. 1947, 186].

ELVINS, THOMAS (–1802), described as 'an eminent architect of Birmingham', died on 27 August 1802 [*Gent's Mag.* 1802 (ii), 879]. He was presumably the Thomas Elvins who had been apprenticed to Thomas Fewster of Birmingham, carpenter, in 1753 [P.R.O., Apprenticeship Register I.R. 1/51/275].

EMBREE, JOHN, a plumber by trade, held the post of Surveyor of Works under the Protectorate government. He had become Sergeant Plumber in Feb. 1639/40, and was put in charge of the Office of Works in March 1653, holding the post until the Restoration of Charles II in 1660. Although there was considerable expenditure on the Protector's residences, little is known of Embree's activity as Cromwell's Surveyor. In 1655 he bought some of the buildings of Exeter Cathedral, including the cloisters, for whose demolition he appears to have been directly or indirectly responsible. Of his career after 1660 nothing is known [*History of the King's Works* iii, 165–8].

EMETT, THOMAS, 'senior', of Preston, is listed as an architect in Baines's Lancashire directory of 1825. He was no doubt related to John Emett, an architect or surveyor who is said to have designed the obelisk erected in the Market Place at Preston in 1782, and to Charles Emett, listed as a 'Joiner and Builder' of Preston in Pigot's *Directory* of 1828–9. Thomas Emett was doubtless the 'Mr. Emmett' who is stated in Twycross's *Mansions of England and Wales: Cheshire* ii, 1850, 114, to have designed SHRIGLEY HALL, nr. PRESTBURY, CHESHIRE, for William Turner, M.P. for Blackburn, in 1825. This is a fine classical house of some size, and indicates that Emett was an architect of ability.

EMLYN, HENRY (*c.* 1729–1815), architect and builder of Windsor, was probably related to the family of Emblin or Emlyn, several of whom were builders at Maidenhead, Berks., in the eighteenth century. He himself was apprenticed in 1744 to William May of Windsor, carpenter [P.R.O., Apprenticeship Register I.R. 1/17/103]. The records of the Office of Works show that he was employed as a carpenter at Windsor Castle from 1761 onwards. From 1784 to 1791 he was also the official carpenter to the Dean and Chapter of ST. GEORGE'S CHAPEL. Between 1787 and 1790 the Chapel was restored under his direction. He designed the elaborate Gothic organ gallery executed in Coade stone, the organ case, the Sovereign's and Prince of Wales's stalls and the pulpit, showing considerable skill in imitating the spirit of the fifteenth-century craftsmen's work, especially in his series of incidents from the life of George III (for illustrations see M. R. James, *St. George's Chapel, Windsor: the Woodwork of the Choir*, 1933) [W. H. St. J. Hope, *History of Windsor Castle*, 389–95]. Engravings of Edward IV's vault in St. George's Chapel by him published in 1796 by the Society of Antiquaries, of which he had become a Fellow in the previous year (*Vetusta Monumenta* iii, pls. 7–9). It is probable that he was the designer of the Gothic screen (in Coade stone) of the Kederminster Chapel in LANGLEY MARISH CHURCH, nr. WINDSOR, for Sir R. Bateson Harvey, 1792. In 1789–90 the spire of ST. GILES CHURCH, READING, was rebuilt in Riga fir, covered with copper, under Henry Emlyn's direction, and a new vestry was built on the north side of the tower [MS. Churchwardens' Accounts]. His work was destroyed when the church was largely rebuilt in 1871–2. He repaired the tower of HUNGERFORD PARISH CHURCH in

1795–6 [MS. Churchwardens' Accounts]. It was subsequently rebuilt in 1812. In 1809–11 WINDSOR PARISH CHURCH was repewed under his direction [MS. Churchwardens' Accounts].

In 1781 Emlyn published *A Proposition for a New Order of Architecture, with rules for drawing the several parts* (2nd ed. 1784, 3rd ed. 1797). This 'British' Order consisted of a shaft that at one-third of its height divided itself into two, the capitals having oak-leaves for foliage, with the Star of the Order of the Garter between the volutes. According to Elmes, George III allowed him 'to execute a specimen of his biforked "British Order" at Windsor: but I believe it has been removed' [*Civil Engineer and Architect's Jnl.* x, 1847, 270]. A version of it, in which Garter plumes are substituted for foliage, was used by Emlyn in the portico of BEAUMONT LODGE, nr. WINDSOR, which he designed for Henry Griffiths, c. 1790 [Neale, *Seats* i, 1818; Sandra Blutman, 'Beaumont Lodge and the British Order', in *The Country Seat*, ed. Colvin & Harris, 1970, 181–4], and in the porch of his own house at Windsor, since demolished. Emlyn died on 10 December 1815, at the age of 86. There is a tablet to his memory in the Bray Chantry in St. George's Chapel. His portrait by A. Livesey survives in private ownership. It shows him standing by a bust of Inigo Jones, with Beaumont College in the background.

[*A.P.S.D.*; *D.N.B.*; *Gent's Mag.* 1815 (ii), 573; Shelagh M. Bond, 'Henry Emlyn of Windsor', *C. Life*, 13 Sept. 1962, reprinted with additions in *Report of the Society of Friends of St. George's Chapel, Windsor* iv, no. 3, 1962.]

EMMETT, MAURICE (*c.* 1646–1694), master bricklayer, was the son of Maurice Emmett, who briefly held the post of Master Bricklayer in the Office of Works at the Restoration in 1660, but was almost immediately superseded by Isaac Corner. However, on Corner's death in 1677, Maurice Emmett, junior (the subject of this entry), took his place, and retained it until his own death in November 1694 at the age of 48.

As a master bricklayer Emmett was employed at Chelsea Hospital from 1682, at Winchester Palace in 1683–4, at Windsor in 1685–6, at Whitehall in 1685–7 and at Kensington Palace in 1689–90 (see *Wren Soc.* xx, 65, index). At Hampton Court in 1689 he was involved in the collapse of some brickwork, which led Wren to declare himself 'very ill used' by Emmett [*Wren Soc.* xviii, 202–3]. His rates for building Sir Philip Warwick's house in St. James's (for which see *Survey of London* xxix, 427–8) are given in *The Architecture of Sir Roger Pratt*, ed. Gunther, 1926, 231. There is considerable evidence of his ability as an architectural draughtsman. In 1665–6 either he or his father made a plan of AUDLEY END [P.R.O., E 351/3379], and in 1667–8 he was paid for making unspecified 'draughts and designs' for the King [E. 351/3281]. He appears both to have designed and built THE COLLEGE OF ARMS in the City of London, begun in 1671 [W. H. Godfrey & A. Wagner, *The College of Arms*, 1963, 11–12], and he was concerned in the reconstruction of WINDSOR CASTLE by Hugh May between 1674 and 1684. There are several payments to him 'for making sundry draughts concerning the Repairs of the said Castle', for his 'Extraordinary Service in drawing the draughts of the Duke's apartment ... and of severall other Roomes and Lodgings, takeing several Admeasurements and setting out the Ground ffor the New Lodgings and other like services' [W. H. St. John Hope, *History of Windsor Castle*, 312–22, 541]. A 'model of a house designed by my father Emmett' was among his son William's possessions in 1714 [inventory in Kent Record Office].

Emmett left two sons, William (*q.v.*) and Maurice. The latter was educated at Merton College, Oxford, and the Inner Temple, and was admitted a Fellow of the Royal Society in March 1697/8 [*The Record of the Royal Society*, 1940, 387]. William Emmett, who executed much carving for royal and other buildings in the 1680s, and who made the altar-piece for the TEMPLE CHURCH, was his elder brother.

THE EMMETT FAMILY

MAURICE EMMETT, 'senior',
Master Bricklayer in 1660

| WILLIAM, carver, b. 1641 | MAURICE, 'junior', Master Bricklayer, c. 1646–1694 | GEORGE, bricklayer, b. 1655 | HENRY, painter-stainer, b. 1657 |

| WILLIAM, of Bromley, 1671–1736 | MAURICE, b. c. 1676, F.R.S., 1698 |

ERSKINE, JOHN

[N. Davenport, 'A Note on the Emmetts', in *Wren Soc.* xiv, p. xxiii; *Walpole Soc.* xxxi, 48, n. 2.]

EMMETT, WILLIAM (1671–1736), eldest son of the above, was baptized at St. Margaret's Church, Westminster, on 14 December 1671. Nothing is known of his upbringing, but in 1694 he was appointed to be Registry Clerk to the Court of Exchequer at a salary of £200 a year with an annuity. In 1698 he sold this place for £500 and went to live at Bromley in Kent. In 1702, when applying for a faculty for a private pew in the parish church, he was stated to be 'a person of very good note and repute', to enjoy 'a plentiful Estate', and to live 'in a very large mansion house which he hath lately rebuilt in the said parish of Bromley'. This may have been Redwood House in the High Street (demolished in 1905), where he was living towards the end of his life. He took an active part in parish affairs, and in 1731 made the plans for a new workhouse, demolished in 1845. He married Eleanor, daughter of John Thornhill of Rossby, Lincs., and died at Bromley on 11 May 1736.

In 1702 Emmett published a series of engravings of St. Paul's Cathedral (*Wren Soc.* xiv, pls. xiii–xvii), and others of the Middle Temple Hall (Bodleian Library, Gough Maps 19, ff. 7 and 9). He also engraved mezzotint portraits of Queen Anne, Prince George of Denmark and Princess Sophia. These engravings were published from a house in New Street, London, which belonged to his younger brother Maurice. He had in his possession some designs for Whitehall Palace attributed to Inigo Jones which Colen Campbell published in *Vitruvius Britannicus* ii, 1717, pls. 2–19. These were given to the British Museum by one of Emmett's descendants in 1848 and are now in the Print Room. With them is the elevation of an unpublished design for the same palace made by Emmett himself between 1710 and 1714. It is in an elaborate but somewhat unsophisticated Italian baroque style. Some of Emmett's papers, including a manuscript treatise on the Orders and a glossary of architectural terms, are among the Norman family papers in the Kent County Record Office at Maidstone.

[N. Davenport, 'Note on the Emmetts', *Wren Soc.* xiv, p. xxiii; *Walpole Soc.* xxxi, 48, n. 2; E. L. S. Horsburgh, *Bromley, Kent*, 1929, 419–20; 'Monumental Inscriptions of Bromley, Kent', in *The British Archivist: Miscellanea*, ed. R. Holworthy; Rochester Diocesan Registry: Muniment Book, 1683–1717, f. 69; *Middle Temple Records*, ed. C. H. Hopwood, iii, 1490; Thieme-Becker, *Künstler-Lexikon* x, 505; British Museum, *Catalogue of British Drawings* i, 1960, 304–6 and pl. 119a.]

ERLAM, SAMUEL B—, exhibited architectural drawings at the Royal Academy in 1815 and 1817 from 20 Green Street, Grosvenor Square, and 40 Brook Street. 'J.' Erlam, who in 1825 exhibited a 'design for a cenotaph' from 16 Green Street, Grosvenor Square, may have been the same person, but a John Erlam of London was a candidate for a surveyorship at Brighton in 1847 [*Builder* v, 1847, 161]. Samuel Erlam is mentioned as an architect and surveyor in Johnstone's *Commercial Street Directory* of 1817, and as a surveyor and builder in Pigot's London *Directory* of 1827–8.

ERSKINE, JOHN, 11TH EARL OF MAR (1675–1732), was the eldest son of the 10th Earl. Of his youth little is known except that he was educated at Edinburgh and Leiden and made the Grand Tour. On his father's death in 1689 he inherited the family seat at Alloa in Clackmannanshire, and an estate much depleted by the heavy debts contracted by his royalist grandfather as well as by his Jacobite father. In these circumstances he prudently adopted a policy of political conformity which enabled him to take his seat in the Scottish parliament in 1698 and secured his appointment as a member of the Privy Council of Scotland. He subsequently supported the Union, and was rewarded first with the office of one of the two Secretaries of State for Scotland (1705) and then with the Keepership of the Scottish Signet. In 1707 he was made a Privy Councillor in England. Despite his second marriage to the daughter of the Whig Duke of Kingston, he accepted office from the Tory government in 1713, and in 1715, finding himself treated with suspicion by the Hanoverians, he put himself at the head of the Pretender's forces in Scotland. His defeat at Sheriffmuir meant exile, attainder and loss of his peerage, penalties only slightly mitigated by the dukedom conferred upon him in 1715 by the grateful James Stuart. In 1717 Mar went to Italy. In 1719 he returned to France by way of Lombardy, where for some time he was held under arrest. He resided in Paris until 1729, when bad health sent him to Aix-la-Chapelle, where he died in May 1732 at the age of 57.

Two passions appear to have dominated Mar's life in exile: political intrigue and architectural design. With the former this *Dictionary* is not concerned, except to record the fact that in 1724 he lost the Pretender's confidence, and in the following year severed his connection with the Jacobite Court, without, however, reconciling himself with the Hanoverian one. How Mar developed his interest in architecture and landscape-gardening is not recorded: it is not known, for instance, whether he was in any way a friend or disciple of Sir William Bruce (*q.v.*). But in 1701 Mar figured prominently among the Scottish magnates who sent Alexander Edward (*q.v.*) on his visit to London and Paris in search of botanical and architectural information, and

295

Edward had for many years been Bruce's right-hand man. In 1712 the Earl of Ranelagh (*q.v.*), himself an amateur architect, left Mar the 'scriptore' in his closet at Chelsea, together with 'all the Mathematicall Instruments Rulers and perspective glasses .... which are in the scriptore'. Mar's patronage of James Gibbs in the days of his political influence is well attested. Already in 1709 Gibbs regarded him as 'very much my friend', and when Gibbs died in affluence in 1754 his sense of obligation to Mar was such as to induce him to leave £1000, three houses and all his plate to Mar's impoverished son Lord Erskine.

Though (as he wrote to his son) Mar was 'never rich enough to undertake the building of a new house all at once', he altered and improved his seat at Alloa so as to make it 'a tolerable good and agreeable one within, tho' not very beautiful and regular without'. The great formal plantations with which he surrounded the castle are described by Macky, and illustrated by a map of Alloa engraved by L. Sturt in 1710 from a survey by Bernard Lens (copy in S.R.O., RHP 13258, no. 2). In his *Journey through England* Macky also mentions the small house at Twickenham, formerly Sir Thomas Skipwith's, which 'was improv'd and inhabited by that great Architect the late Earl of Marr' and had 'hanging gardens to the River'. It was called Copt Hall and was demolished in the nineteenth century (R. S. Cobbett, *Memorials of Twickenham*, 1872, 356–8).[1] According to John Ramsay of Ochtertyre (*Scotland and Scotsmen*, ed. A. Allardyce, ii, 1888, 97, n. 2), Mar was reputed to have designed Tullibody and Tillicoultry Houses in Clackmannanshire and Blair Drummond in Perthshire. The last was in fact designed by Alexander McGill (*q.v.*), but he may have had the benefit of Mar's advice. Tullibody (dem.) appears to have dated from the reign of George I. Tillicoultry was rebuilt in 1806 and nothing is known of the previous house.

Of Mar's architectural activity in exile there is abundant evidence. In April 1716 he wrote to Gibbs from Avignon asking him to take care of his drawings, and in January 1718 he got Gibbs to send him a case of drawing instruments. On one occasion two sheets of his 'large drawing paper' were requisitioned by the Pretender, and when he was received in audience by the Pope it was a bound volume of plans of St. Peter's that he took away as a present. Although it is not quite true that (as Sir Robert Douglas wrote) 'his only

amusement during his exile was to draw plans and designs for the good of his much beloved native country', it was undoubtedly his principal solace. 'I am', he told a correspondent in 1717, 'infected with the disease of building and planting.' Through English or Scottish correspondents he kept in touch with architectural events in Britain, supplying sketches for Gibbs to develop, making suggestions for the improvement of designs that were sent to him for criticism, even contributing (under the guise of 'a person of quality') a grandiose design for a palace to William Adam's projected *Vitruvius Scoticus*. Whigs as well as Tories benefited from these thoughts from abroad, for the large collection of Mar's surviving drawings (S.R.O., Mar and Kellie deposit, RHP 13256–8) includes proposals for Horatio Walpole's house at Wolterton, Norfolk (1725), for Sir Thomas Robinson's at Rokeby (1730), and for Sir William Wentworth's at Bretton Park, Yorks. (1730). Among the papers of his relations the Erskines of Dun (Angus) there is a set of designs for a new house made by him in Paris in 1723, with a note that 'the copier has done no honour by these Draughts to the Designe, but Mr. M[c][Gil]l will understand them' [S.R.O., RHP 13288].[1] As early as 1726 he composed a paper in which he suggested building bridges on the north and south sides of the Old Town of Edinburgh. He had in fact envisaged the principal features of the improvements of the late eighteenth century – the North Bridge, the South Bridge and the siting of George Street, the backbone of the New Town. He also proposed the formation of a navigable canal between the Forth and the Clyde. To the improvement of his own forfeited house and estate at Alloa he devoted an immense amount of thought, drawing plan after plan for intersecting avenues of ever-increasing complexity, and devising a remarkable addition to the parish church incorporating an elaborate family pew and a memorial to himself and his family in the form of a black marble obelisk freestanding beneath a top-lighted dome. Among his more grandiose schemes were plans (anticipating the similar idea of Robert Adam for Syon) for filling the internal quadrangles of Wilton, Longleat and Drumlanrig with domed polygonal halls. Abroad, too, he was ready with designs for acquaintances like a Captain de Wilde, for whose house in Antwerp he devised an ingenious new entrance, the Marquis de Tessé, for whom he designed a Palladian country seat at Chatou, near St. Germain, or the Jacobite Lord Falkland,

---

[1] Among Mar's drawings there are two maps showing a projected house at Twickenham on a different site corresponding approximately to that where Lady Suffolk's Marble Hill was to be built in the 1720s. One of them is dated 1711, before his exile, the other 1719 (RHP 13258, nos. 67–8). Mar also made a design for improving Secretary Johnston's Orleans House nearby (no. 84).

[1] One of these drawings was reproduced by John Fleming, *Robert Adam and His Circle* (1962), pl. 8, but without recognizing its authorship. There are further designs for this house dated April 1731 in the Mar and Kellie Collection. The house was actually built to the designs of William Adam and bears the date 1730.

whose house at Mézières, nr. Orléans he offered to improve in 1720.[1]

Some of Mar's designs are of considerable sophistication, and would repay detailed art-historical analysis. They reflect his no doubt extensive knowledge of French and Italian, as well as of English and Scottish architecture. Dated at Paris, Urbino, Spa or Geneva, they show an acquaintance with the work of architects as diverse as Bramante, Palladio, Le Pautre and Guarini. There are many studies based on Mansart's Marly, and it was a domed version of Marly that he sent to William Adam for publication in *Vitruvius Scoticus*. Although the character of most of these designs is markedly baroque, there are indications that their author may have been more interested in neo-classical design than the surviving drawings suggest. For as early as 1718 he told John Stewart of Invernity that he was designing a house whose elevations were based on the Maison Carrée at Nîmes, and complained that Italian architects 'will be originals and leave the example [of antiquity] and all its noble simplicity for trifling gimcrack insignificant ornaments worthy of nobody but Vanbruge'.

As an architect in exile the Earl of Mar is a unique figure in British architectural history. Though a nostalgic fantasy runs through so many of his designs, no one can examine them without recognizing an able and fertile imagination, or fail to conclude that if Scotland lost a lord of dubious political integrity in 1715, she also lost an amateur architect of some distinction.

[*D.N.B.*; Sir Robert Douglas, *Peerage of Scotland*, 2nd ed. Edinburgh 1813, ii, 217–19; *Macfarlane's Geographical Collections*, ed. Mitchell, Scottish History Soc., i, 309, and J. Macky, *A Journey through Scotland*, 1723, 181–3 (for descriptions of Mar's gardens at Alloa); J. Macky, *A Journey through England* i, 1724, 61–2 (for his house at Twickenham); *The Earl of Mar's Legacies to Scotland and to his Son, Lord Erskine*, ed. S. Erskine, Scottish History Soc., xxvi, 1896, including (192–3) directions for his monument in Alloa Church and (201–2) his scheme for the improvement of Edinburgh; J. Crawford, *Memorials of the Town and Parish of Alloa*, 1874, 89–91; Hist. MSS. Comm., *Egmont* ii, 235–6; *Portland* vi, 120–1, x, 301–2; *Dartmouth* i, 319; *Stuart Papers* ii, 92–3, iv–vi, *passim*; T. C. Smout, 'The Erskines of Mar and the Development of Alloa', *Scottish Studies* vii, 1963; A. J. Youngson, *The Making of Classical Edinburgh*,

1966, 13–14; S.R.O., Mar and Kellie papers, especially GD 124/14, *passim*.]

ESPIN, THOMAS (1767–1822), the son of a farmer, was born at Holton in Lincolnshire, and educated at Wragby. He took up schoolmastering, and in 1790 was appointed Master of the 'Mathematical and Commercial' School at Louth founded by Dr. Mapletoft. His interests were architectural and antiquarian, and he became a competent topographical artist and draughtsman. A number of his drawings were engraved to illustrate such books as Howlett's *Views in the County of Lincoln* (1805). In 1805 he supervised the rebuilding of the belfry windows in the tower of Louth Church, and in 1815 he was invited by the Corporation to make designs for a new Town Hall. In the event this was not built, but Espin had his plans printed as *Plans and Elevations of the New Town Hall which was intended to have been erected in the Market-Place at Louth, Lincolnshire* (Louth 1815). A copy with the original drawings inserted is in the possession of the Louth Natural History and Antiquarian Society. His design for a gallery in Louth Church dated 1817 is in the Lincolnshire Record Office (Fac. 9/44).

For his own occupation Espin designed in 1818 a picturesque Gothic house called Priory Cottage. He died at Louth in 1822, and was buried in a Gothic mausoleum which he had built in the grounds of his house.

A portrait of Espin belongs to the Corporation of Louth. Another, then in private possession, was reproduced by R. W. Goulding in *Notes on Books and Pamphlets printed at Louth 1801–50* (Louth 1920), which contains a short biography. See also R. W. Goulding, *Louth Parish Church*, 1916, 19; E. J. Willson's Lincolnshire Collections in the Library of the Society of Antiquaries; and *Gent's Mag.* 1822 (ii), 570–1.

ESSEX, JAMES (1722–1784), was the son of James Essex (d. 1749), a carpenter and joiner of Cambridge, who executed much of the woodwork in the University during the first half of the eighteenth century and of whom an account will be found in Willis & Clark's *Architectural History of the University of Cambridge* iii, 540–1. He was educated at the grammar school attached to King's College, and afterwards studied architecture under Sir James Burrough, with whom he collaborated in designing several Cambridge buildings. At the same time he continued to practise his father's trade, and in 1749–50, after the latter's death, he built the wooden bridge at Queens' College to the designs of W. Etheridge. He was, however, anxious to establish himself as an architect, and when, in 1748, the Rev. Robert Masters, Fellow and Bursar of Corpus Christi College, who had employed Essex to make a de-

---

[1] Capt. de Wilde's house, for which the designs are dated 1729–30, was in the Vieille Rue de la Monie in Antwerp, near the church of St. Georges. Mar also designed a house for the Bishop of Namur at La Plante, nr. Namur (1731), and one for M. Rotier at Choisy (1721). The design for the Marquis de Tessé is dated 1728.

sign for a proposed new building at that college, had the plan printed and circulated as his own, Essex promptly issued proposals for engraving and printing it himself. Masters replied by asserting that 'Essex was no otherwise employ'd therein than copying out his [Masters'] Design', but in a *Letter to his Subscribers*, published in 1749, Essex was able to demonstrate that this was not the case, and that he was the real author of the design.[1]

Essex was subsequently to carry out many works in Cambridge in the classical style which he had learned from Burrough, but it is as a Gothic architect that he is chiefly remarkable: for, unlike his contemporaries, who regarded Gothic merely as a decorative style, a kind of indigenous rococo with romantic associations, Essex fully appreciated its structural character and had an archaeologist's knowledge of its detail. He was, in fact, the first practising architect to take an antiquarian interest in medieval architecture, and his knowledge of Gothic construction remained unique until the ecclesiological movement of the early nineteenth century. As early as 1756 he issued *Proposals for publishing Plans Elevations and Sections of King's College Chapel, in Fifteen Plates with Observations on the Original Contracts* (printed in Gough's *British Topography* i, 237). This work was never published, but the measured drawings made by Essex are preserved among his papers in the British Museum. He subsequently contributed several pioneer papers on medieval architecture to *Archaeologia*, the journal of the Society of Antiquaries of London, of which he was elected a Fellow in 1772, and he was the author of an unpublished 'History of Gothic Architecture in England', of which the manuscript and drawings are now in the British Museum. He was the friend of Gough, Tyson, Bentham, Cole, Kerrich and other antiquaries, and Horace Walpole employed him at Strawberry Hill. At Ely and Lincoln he carried out technically skilful and aesthetically judicious restorations in a manner that was unique in the eighteenth century, and his own Gothic designs have a scholarly character which sets them apart from other contemporary essays in that style. The cresting with which he crowned the central tower of Lincoln Cathedral, the arch which he built across the west end of the nave, and the apse which he added to the north choir transept are, indeed, frequently mistaken for medieval work.

Essex lived in a house (now dem.) opposite St. Catharine's Hall. He married the daughter of a Cambridge bookseller named Thurlbourn, by whom he had a son, who died in infancy, and a daughter, who married a former fellow of Queens' College. A miniature portrait of Essex from Bowtell's MSS. at Downing College is reproduced in the Cambridge Antiquarian Society's Octavo Publications, vol. 24, together with a silhouette group of Essex, his wife and daughter by Francis Torond that is now in the Worthing Museum. He died at Cambridge on 14 September 1784, of a paralytic stroke, and was buried in St. Botolph's Churchyard, where a tomb commemorates him and his family. There is also a tablet to his memory in the north aisle of the church. His MSS. were presented to the British Museum by the Rev. T. Kerrich, to whom they had been bequeathed on his death, and now form Add. MSS. 6761–73, 6776 and 42569. His original letters to Richard Gough are preserved among the latter's correspondence in the Bodleian Library (MS. Gough Gen. Top. 46, ff. 139–261). Some of them were published by J. Nichols in his *Illustrations of Literary History* vi, 284–310, and there are many references to Essex in Horace Walpole's correspondence (see especially the Yale edition of Walpole's correspondence with Cole). His 'Journal of a Tour through part of Flanders and France in August, 1773' is printed in the Octavo Publications of the Cambridge Antiquarian Society, vol. 24, 1888, with a biographical introduction by W. M. Fawcett.

His own publications were: *Mr. James Essex's Letter to his subscribers to the plan and elevation of an intended addition to Corpus Christi College in Cambridge* (Feb. 1748/9); a 'Letter to Dr. Ducarel, containing observations on Canterbury Cathedral', February 1768, in Nichols, *Bibl. Top. Brit.* i, 470; the 'Plan of the Original Cathedral Church of Ely' and the 'Account of the Old Conventual Church at Ely', in Bentham's *Ely*, 1812, Addenda, pp. 1–10; 'Remarks on the Antiquity and the Different Modes of Brick and Stone Buildings in England', in *Archaeologia* iv, 1776; 'Some Observations on Lincoln Cathedral', *ibid.*; 'Observations on the Origin and Antiquity of Round Churches; and of the Round Church at Cambridge in particular', in *Archaeologia* vi, 1782; 'Observations on Croyland Abbey and Bridge', in Nichols, *Bibl. Top. Brit.* xxii, 1784; 'A Description and Plan of the Ancient Timber Bridge at Rochester', in *Archaeologia* vii, 1785; A description and plan of Denny Abbey, Cambs., 'extracted from Mr. Essex's MSS.', and printed in Lysons, *Magna Britannia* (Cambridgeshire), 1808, 272–4. For his views on the origins of Gothic architecture see T. Kerrich in *Archaeologia* xvi, 1812, 306–10. A list of his engraved designs is given by W. M. Fawcett in the introduction to Essex's 'Tour'.

[*A.P.S.D.*; *D.N.B.*; *Gent's Mag.* 1784 (ii), 718; Willis & Clark, iii, 540–6; J. Nichols, *Literary Anecdotes* v, 117, vi, 624–5, vii, 128, 562, viii, 578, 607, ix, 341–2; J. Nichols, *Illustrations of Literary History* iv, 482, vi, 284–310, 400; D.

---

[1] The design circulated by Masters in 1748 and a revised version of it published by Essex in 1773 are both illustrated in *C. Life*, 17 Oct. 1931, 425.

R. Stewart, 'James Essex', *Arch. Rev.*, Nov. 1950; T. H. Cocke, 'James Essex, Cathedral Restorer', *Architectural History* xviii, 1975.]

CAMBRIDGE UNIVERSITY

Willis & Clark's *Architectural History of the University of Cambridge* is the authority for all the following works.

QUEENS' COLLEGE, built wooden bridge to design of W. Etheridge, 1749–50.

UNIVERSITY LIBRARY, fitted up the 'dome room' for manuscripts, 1750.

GREAT ST. MARY'S CHURCH, executed Doctors' Gallery in the chancel, to designs of Sir J. Burrough, 1754; removed 1863 (*V.C.H. Cambs.* iii, 131).

TRINITY COLLEGE, supervised reconstruction of north and south sides of Nevile's Court, 1755–8.

QUEENS' COLLEGE, chambers at south-west angle of college, 1756–60.

ST. CATHERINE'S HALL, RAMSDEN BUILDING, 1757.

CHRIST'S COLLEGE, ashlared interior of quadrangle, 1758–69.

EMMANUEL COLLEGE, repaired and refitted Hall, 1760–64.

JESUS COLLEGE, refitted Combination Room, 1762.

TRINITY COLLEGE, stone bridge, 1763–5.

CLARE COLLEGE, completed chapel designed by Sir J. Burrough (d. 1764), 1764–9.

SENATE HOUSE, completed west end, 1766–8 (cf. drawings in B.M., Add. MS. 6776, ff. 94–5).

GARRET HOSTEL BRIDGE, 1769; rebuilt 1814 and again 1837.

EMMANUEL COLLEGE, rebuilt street front, 1769–75.

TRINITY COLLEGE, combination rooms, etc., 1770–4.

KING'S COLLEGE, repaired chapel, designed Gothic altar-piece (dem. 1897), and paved ante-chapel, 1770–6.

ST. JOHN'S COLLEGE, altered south side of first court, 1772.

QUEENS' COLLEGE, remodelled interior of chapel, 1772–5; altered 1845.

SIDNEY SUSSEX COLLEGE, rebuilt chapel and library, 1776–82.

OTHER WORKS

CAMBRIDGE, rebuilt the GREAT BRIDGE, 1754; dem. 1823 [*V.C.H. Cambs.* iii, 114].

ELY CATHEDRAL, restored east front to the perpendicular, reroofed the choir, repaired the lantern, and designed a new Gothic screen and organ loft, since removed, 1757–62. Under his direction the choir stalls were removed to the presbytery in 1770. Extracts from his report are given by D. J. Stewart, *Architectural History of Ely Cathedral*, 1868, and in R.I.B.A. *Trans.*, 1875–6, pp. 73–4.[1]

MADINGLEY HALL, CAMBS., minor alterations for Sir John Hynde Cotton, *c.* 1760 [Nichols, *Literary Anecdotes* vi, 625].

LINCOLN CATHEDRAL, carried out extensive repairs, designed Gothic screen wall at west end of nave, apse to northernmost chapel of north choir transept, and arches at west end of choir aisles (carved by Jas. Pink), repaved the church, repaired the choir screen, designed altar-piece, bishop's throne, and battlements and spires of central tower, 1762–5. [Two volumes of designs, estimates and letters in archives of the Dean and Chapter of Lincoln; Venables, 'Architectural History of Lincoln Cathedral', *Archaeological Jnl.* xl, 1883, 187, 396 n., 410, 412, 418; B.M., Add. MS. 6772, ff. 271–82].

THAXTED CHURCH, ESSEX, altered east end, and designed a Gothic altar-piece, 1765–7 [MS. Churchwardens' Accounts. There are drawings for this work in Add. MS. 6776, ff. 60, 61].

CAMBRIDGE, RANDALL HOUSE (now KENMARE), TRUMPINGTON STREET, for John Randall, 1768 [elevation in B.M., Add. MS. 6776, f. 89].

MILTON LODGE, CAMBS., minor alterations to house for Rev. William Cole, 1768–9 [Nichols, *Literary Illustrations* vi, 297].

WIMPOLE, CAMBS., Gothic castle in park for the 2nd Earl of Hardwicke, *c.* 1768–70, in conjunction with L. Brown [B.M., Add. MS. 6771, ff. 99ᵛ, 178ᵛ].

WINCHESTER COLLEGE CHAPEL, advised on repair of tower, 1772; rebuilt 1862–3 by W. Butterfield [Nichols, *Literary Anecdotes* vi, 625].

AMPTHILL, BEDS., Cross in memory of Catherine of Aragon, with an inscription by Horace Walpole, for the 2nd Earl of Ossory, designed 1771, erected 1773 [Yale edition of Walpole's Correspondence, *Letters to Cole* i, 226, 296, 299, 322] (Camden's *Britannia*, ed. Gough, i, plate facing p. 329).

CANTERBURY CATHEDRAL. On 19 Sept 1776, the Rev. William Cole wrote to Walpole that Essex had 'engaged himself to the Chapter there to make out a draft for a new roof for part of their cathedral' [Yale edition of Walpole's Correspondence, *Letters to Cole* ii, 26–7; cf. Add. MS. 6771, f. 271 *et seq.*].

STRAWBERRY HILL, MIDDLESEX, Gothic gateway and the Beauclerk Tower for Horace Walpole, 1776; also designed Offices 1777, executed 1790 by James Wyatt to Essex's drawings [W. S. Lewis, 'The Genesis of Strawberry Hill', *Metropolitan Museum Studies* v (i), 1934].

---

[1] A volume of designs by Essex for a Gothic choir in Ely Cathedral, dated 1768, is in the Fitzwilliam Museum at Cambridge.

ENFIELD, MIDDLESEX, GOUGH PARK, designed Gothic fireplace and window for Richard Gough's new library, 1778–80 [MS. correspondence with Gough in Bodleian Library, MS. Gough Gen. Top. 46, f. 178, etc.].

WINCHESTER CATHEDRAL, report on roof, 1782 [*Hampshire Field Club Trans* iii, 1895–8, 292–3].

CAMBRIDGE, rebuilt the GUILDHALL, 1782–4; dem. 1933 [R.C.H.M., *Cambridge*, 310].

DEBDEN CHURCH, ESSEX, wooden spire, 1786 [an inscription, now in the vestry, records that it was erected 'from a Design of the ingenious Mr. Essex, Architect']; replaced by a spire of different design 1930.

ETHERIDGE, WILLIAM (–1776), is first recorded as a master carpenter employed under Labelye at Westminster Bridge (1744–9). He invented a machine for cutting piles under water of which he published an engraving (copy in Sir John Soane's Museum). He designed the wooden bridge which was built across the Thames at Walton between 1748 and 1750 at the expense of Samuel Dicker, who obtained an Act of Parliament for the purpose in 1747. It consisted of three arches supported on stone piers, with brick abutments and approaches. The arches were formed of straight pieces of timber tangent to a circle, and it was claimed that if any of the members became decayed, they could be removed and replaced without disturbing the adjacent timbers. There is a description and an engraving of the bridge in *Gent's Mag* 1750, 587. See also *ibid.* 1754, 116–17. In 1780, having become decayed, it was rebuilt in stone and brick to the designs of James Paine. According to some accounts, the original bridge was designed by 'White of Weybridge', but he appears only to have been the contractor. In 1749 Etheridge designed a wooden bridge of similar construction over the river Cam at Queens' College, Cambridge. It was erected by James Essex and completed in 1750 [Willis & Clark, ii, 56]. It was rebuilt to the original design in 1902. Etheridge, who afterwards became Surveyor to Ramsgate Harbour, died on 3 October 1776 [*Gent's Mag.* 1776, 483; Brayley, *History of Surrey* ii, 340].

ETTY, JOHN (c. 1634–1708), was a master carpenter at York. He was the son of James Etty, a carpenter of York who died in 1664. The inscription on his monument in All Saints Church, North Street, states that 'by the strength of his own genius and application he had acquired great knowledge of mathematics, especially geometry and architecture in all its parts, far beyond any of his contemporaries in this City'. Thoresby refers to him in 1702 as 'Mr. Etty, sen. the architect', with whom he says that 'the most celebrated Gibbons wrought at York' [*Diary*, ed. Hunter,

i, 1830, 366].[1] He must have been the Etty working for the 2nd Duke of Buckingham at HELMSLEY in 1665–6 [G. Beard, *Georgian Craftsmen*, 1966, 22, citing letter now in Hull University Library, DD/FA/39/2]. In 1674 the roof of the central or west wing of TEMPLE NEWSHAM HOUSE, nr. LEEDS, was rebuilt under his direction after he had 'viewed the decays of the house' for the 2nd Viscount Irwin [*Temple Newsham House*, Leeds Corporation 1951, 41]. In 1677 he designed a classical balustrade (removed 1844) to crown the tower of the church of ST. MARTIN-CUM-GREGORY, YORK [R.C.H.M., *York* iii, 21]. Between 1683 and 1686 there are numerous payments to him in the York Chamberlain's Accounts for building a house in PETERGATE, YORK [York Reference Library, Chamberlain's Accounts, vol. 27, *ex inf.* Mr. J. A. Booth]. In April 1688, when James II contemplated some works at Berwick-on-Tweed, Sir Christopher Wren wrote to 'Mr. John Etty at his house in York', thanking him for his 'description of the palace at Berwick, which was very full and satisfactory' [*Wren Soc.* xviii, 68]. In 1693 he was employed at NEWBY HALL, YORKS. (W.R.), then being completed for Sir Edward Blackett, Bart., to the designs of an unknown architect. Two payments show that Etty was responsible for a windvane, presumably the one crowning the cupola, and may well have been the principal carpenter employed [Northumberland Record Office, Blackett of Matfen papers, ZBL/273/4/25, *ex inf.* Mr. J. A. Booth]. In 1695 Etty contracted with Sir William Robinson, Bart., to build THE MANOR HOUSE at STRENSALL (N.R.), in accordance with a drawing still attached to the document [Leeds City Library Archives Dept., NH 2382]. In a letter-book of Sir Godfrey Copley in Sheffield City Library there are several references to Etty which indicate that he was concerned in the building of SPROTBOROUGH HALL, c. 1696–1700; dem. 1926 (*C. Life*, 11 Feb. 1922). On one occasion he came and stayed four days and on another he wrote when 'ill of a broken leg desirous I would lend him Marrott's book'.

Etty died on 28 January 1707/8,[2] leaving one surviving son William (*q.v*). His eldest son James, a carpenter, had died the previous October, his second son Marmaduke, a painter-stainer, probably died in 1692, and his fourth son John, a limner, also predeceased him [G. Beard, *Geor-*

---

[1] That there was some connection between Gibbons and Etty is indeed proved by a letter dated 10 July 1684 in which the former addresses the latter as 'Deare friend': see Paul Grinke's *Catalogue of Autograph Letters of English Artists and Architects*, 1976, cover illustration.

[2] According to the monument in All Saints Church he died in 1709, but Mr. John Harvey informs me that the date of burial given in the Parish Register is 30 January 1707/8.

gian Craftsmen, 1966, 176; information from Mr. J. H. Harvey]. The somewhat scanty evidence of Etty's ability as an architect given above is supplemented by a drawing among Lord Shaftesbury's archives at Wimborne St. Giles in Dorset. This is a design for the elevation of a late seventeenth-century house of five bays with hipped roof and two giant pilasters supporting a central pediment, signed 'Etty Ebor. delin'. There is a similar (but unsigned) elevation among the Winn archives at Nostell Priory which may possibly be in Etty's hand.

ETTY, WILLIAM (*c.* 1675–1734), master carpenter of York, was the third son of John Etty (*q.v.*). Like his father he combined the functions of carpenter, carver and architect. In 1712 he carved the altar-piece in the church of ST. MICHAEL-LE-BELFRY, YORK [G. Benson, 'The Church of St. Michael le Belfry', *Associated Arch. Socs.' Reports and Papers* xxxvii, 111] and in 1725–6 he designed and executed decorative carving at THE MANSION HOUSE [T. P. Cooper, 'The Mansion House, York', *Associated Arch. Socs.' Reports and Papers* xl, 1930–1, 290]. He laid out the avenue, bridge and park at TEMPLE NEWSHAM HOUSE for the 4th Viscount Irwin in 1712 [*Temple Newsham House*, Leeds Corporation 1951, 46]. In 1718–20 BARROWBY HALL, YORKS. (W.R.), was refronted under his direction for Arthur Ingram in a simple early Georgian style [Christopher Gilbert in *Leeds Arts Calendar*, no. 56, 1965, 9]. Soon afterward he came almost simultaneously into contact with Colen Campbell and Sir John Vanbrugh. For the former he supervised the building of NEWBY (now BALDERSBY) PARK in 1720–1, while for the latter he acted as surveyor or clerk of the works first at SEATON DELAVAL (from 1719 onwards) and then at CASTLE HOWARD (from 1721 onwards, and subsequently for Hawksmoor's Mausoleum from 1729 to 1734) [Lindsay Boynton on Newby in *The Country Seat*, ed. Colvin & Harris, 1970, 97–100; *Vanbrugh's Letters*, ed. Webb, pp. xxxi, 130, etc.; *Walpole Soc.* xix, *passim*]. In 1719 'Mr. Etty Lord Carlisle's Architect' was paid 2 guineas by the Churchwardens of PENRITH, CUMBERLAND, 'for coming over to survey the Church' preparatory to its rebuilding in 1721–2, but he does not appear to have designed the new church [Cumberland and Westmorland Record Office, PR/31/23]. In 1722–7, however, it was to his designs that the important church of HOLY TRINITY, LEEDS, was built in a handsome English baroque style [D. Linstrum in *West Yorkshire Architects and Architecture*, forthcoming]. The existing steeple was the work of R. D. Chantrell in 1839. In 1725 Etty designed a buffet for Lord Langdale's dining-room at HOLME HALL, YORKS. (E.R.), and being in London at the time was 'in hopes to see something that might be newer fashioned & better'

than his first 'draught' [E. Riding Record Office, DDHA 14/25–26]. In 1727 he sent George Bowes designs (now lost) for a country house complete with stables, avenues and 'bastions'. This was presumably an unexecuted scheme for rebuilding GIBSIDE, Bowes's seat in Co. Durham [Glamis Castle, Bowes MSS. 8, f. 28]. In the same year he is reported to have designed the existing bridge at STAMFORD BRIDGE, YORKS. (E.R.) [N. Pevsner, *Yorkshire: York and the East Riding*, 1972, 350]. In 1728–9 he was rebuilding SCRIVEN HALL, YORKS. (W.R.) (dem. 1954), for Sir Henry Slingsby, Bart., but it is not known to whose designs [Yorkshire Archaeological Soc., Leeds, DD 56/10, p. 21]. The attribution to him of some drawings in the R.I.B.A. Collection for alterations to Burton Agnes Hall and Church, though probable, cannot be regarded as certain.

When William Etty died in 1734, Hawksmoor wrote to Lord Carlisle to recommend his son John Etty (1705–38), 'bread up in the way of Building under his father', as likely to be 'sober, carefull, ingenious and industrious' [*Walpole Soc.* xix, 148]. His father's standing as an architect has been much enhanced by the discovery of his responsibility for Holy Trinity Church at Leeds, and further research may establish him as a leading provincial designer of the early eighteenth century.

EVANS, CHARLES, of London, was a carpenter by trade. He is stated by R. Bigland, in his *History of Gloucestershire* i, 1791, 119, to have designed BADMINTON CHURCH, GLOS., for the 5th Duke of Beaufort in 1785, and this is confirmed by building accounts in the Muniment Room at Badminton [403.2:1–5; 304.101:11, the latter giving his Christian name]. In 1777 he supervised internal alterations to NO. 30 UPPER GROSVENOR STREET, LONDON, for Sir Thomas Cave of Stanford Hall, Leics. [Cave MSS. at Stanford]. He was presumably the Evans who built PEMBROKE HOUSE, WHITEHALL, for the 10th Earl of Pembroke, 1757; dem. 1913 [J. Harris, *Sir William Chambers*, 1970, 235] (*Survey of London* xiii, 167–75, pls. 67–88). Badminton Church has a plain classical exterior and a well-designed interior derived from Gibbs's St. Martin's-in-the-Fields (*C. Life*, 25 Nov. 1939, fig. 9).

EVANS, DANIEL (*c.* 1769–1846), was a builder of Oxford who was much employed in the alteration of colleges and other buildings in the University between 1820 and 1840, *e.g.* at MAGDALEN, where he executed J. T. Parkinson's new north front 1822–6, and at PEMBROKE, where he refaced the master's lodgings, the front and the gateway in Gothic style in 1830, apparently to his own designs, and later, with his partner J. R. Symm, erected the New Buildings designed by C. Hayward (1845) [*V.C.H. Oxon.* iii, 292]. He carried out alterations to MERTON COLLEGE CHAPEL in 1823 and restored ST. ALDATE'S CHURCH in 1832. He also built, to the designs of W. Jenkins, the WESLEYAN METHODIST CHAPEL (1817) in New Inn Hall Street and designed a new RECTORY at NUNEHAM COURTENAY, OXON., in 1824 [Bodleian Library, MS. Oxf. Dioc. Papers c. 435, p. 449]. Towards the end of his life he was in partnership with J. R. Symm, whose successors still (1975) carry on the business which he founded. He was a Wesleyan Methodist. He died on 13 November 1846, aged 77 [*Jackson's Oxford Journal*, 21 Nov. 1846].

EVANS, THOMAS (*c.* 1784–1874), was evidently related to William Evans of Wimborne (*q.v.*), for at the time of his marriage in 1819 he was described as 'of Wimborne Minster', and unexecuted designs for rebuilding ETTINGTON HALL, WARWICKS., for E. J. Shirley, dated 1820–1, now in the Warwickshire Record Office and at Shakespeare's Birthplace, Stratford (DR 69/3), are signed in some cases by Thomas, in others by William, Evans. A design for Ettington was exhibited at the Royal Academy by Thomas Evans in 1821, and may be the one now in the R.I.B.A. Collection (*Catalogue: C–F*, fig. 82). In 1824 he showed a design for alterations to CRICHEL HOUSE, DORSET, for H. C. Sturt. Evans married the sister of William Harris (*q.v.*), and after the latter's untimely death in Sicily, he was jointly responsible with Samuel Angell for the publication of the archaeological discoveries that Harris and Angell had made there (*Sculptured Metopes . . . of Selinus*, 1826). Evans died on 22 December 1874, aged 90, and is buried at Lyminster in Sussex, where he had lived for many years [J. Challenor Smith in *Genealogist*, N.S. xxviii, 1911–12, 233].

EVANS, WILLIAM (*c.* 1764–1842), was an architect and surveyor at Wimborne in Dorset, and held the post of County Surveyor from 1824 until his death on 20 January 1842 at the age of 78 [information from Dorset County Record Office]. He designed BOVERIDGE HOUSE, nr. CRANBORNE, DORSET, for Henry Brouncker (d. 1825), altered and enlarged 1887 and 1920, but retaining a fine Greek Doric portico [Hutchins, *History of Dorset* iii, 1868, 385; plan in R.C.H.M., *Dorset*, v, 14]; GAUNT'S HOUSE, nr. WIMBORNE, for Sir Richard Carr Glyn, Bart., 1809, much enlarged 1886–7 [plate in Hutchins, *Dorset* iii, 1868, 244, signed 'Wm. Evans Architect']; and partly rebuilt STURMINSTER NEWTON CHURCH, DORSET, in competent Gothic for its date, 1825–8 [Sir Owen Morshead, *The Parish Church of Sturminster Newton*, 1971]. In 1810 he designed the picturesque cottage at BOURNEMOUTH later known as PORTMAN LODGE for L. D. G. Tregonwell and his wife Henrietta Portman [C. H. Mate & C. Riddle, *Bournemouth 1810–1910*, Bourne-

mouth 1910, 56]. Shortly before 1830 he altered the west end of WIMBORNE MINSTER CHURCH, inserting a gallery and rebuilding the window [P. Hall, *Guide to the Town of Wimborne*, 1830, 28]. His son George Evans (*c.* 1800–1873) succeeded him as County Surveyor and designed a number of churches in Dorset, including those of Holdenhurst (1834), Melbury Abbas (1851–2), Fontmell Magna (1862–3), Compton Abbas (1866–7) and Stanbridge or Hinton Parva (1860).

EVELEIGH, JOHN, was the son of John Eveleigh, 'sergeant-at-mace' of Exeter. He was probably the 'John Eveley' who was apprenticed to James Paine in 1756. In the late 1780s he established himself as an architect and builder in Bath, where he worked both independently and in conjunction with Baldwin, the City Architect. In 1790 he announced that he was prepared to execute 'Designs for Mansions, Villas, Dwellings, etc. in the Gothick or modern taste', to superintend buildings, survey estates, or collect rents. He also acted as a builder's merchant, supplying chimney-pieces and water-closets as well as architectural designs. Many speculative builders availed themselves of his services and in this way he designed CAMDEN CRESCENT, *c.* 1788, for John Morgan, a carpenter and builder; a row of houses called SION ROW in Camden Road for the attorney John Jelly; BEAUFORT BUILDINGS, LONDON ROAD, for Messrs. Gunning & Tanner, 1790; and LAMBRIDGE PLACE for Richard Hewlett, 1792. His other works in Bath included SUMMER HILL PLACE, SION HILL (dem.), for Caleb Hillier Parry, 1789; ST. CATHERINE'S HERMITAGE, LANSDOWN (dem.), for Philip Thicknesse, 1791; and the pedimented central feature to SOMERSET PLACE. Elsewhere Eveleigh designed BAILBROOK LODGE, BATHEASTON, for Dr. Denham Skeet, 1789; a house at ENGLISHCOMBE, SOMERSET, for Matthew Brickdale, 1789; a row of ten houses at TROWBRIDGE, WILTS., for a Mr. Wilkins, *c.* 1788; and 'a new town in America for Lewis Esq.' for which he supplied a plan on vellum in 1788 for £1 11s. 6d. In 1788–9 he made three designs for building developments at CLIFTON (BRISTOL), at least one of which was carried out. This was probably the two terraces flanking THE MALL, and WINDSOR TERRACE may have been another, as it closely resembles his Camden Crescent in Bath. In Bath he began, in 1791, in conjunction with other speculative builders, to develop the Grosvenor Gardens as a housing estate. Only GROSVENOR PLACE (including the Hotel) was completed, when the failure of the Bath City Bank led to Eveleigh's bankruptcy and to the sale of his interest in the Grosvenor project. After this disaster he left Bath and is last heard of at PLYMOUTH, where in 1800 he designed the GUILDHALL (dem. 1941) [R. N. Worth, *History of Plymouth*, 1890, 392].

Eveleigh's work at Bath shows him as an original and, for his period, somewhat unconventional designer, whose façades in Grosvenor and Somerset Places use Adamsian motifs in an almost baroque manner which is engagingly vigorous or vulgarly inelegant according to taste. The destruction of his feeble Gothic Guildhall at Plymouth need, however, cause no regrets.

[Eveleigh's ledgers in Bath Reference Library; W. Ison, *The Georgian Buildings of Bath*, 1948, 40–2; W. Ison, *The Georgian Buildings of Bristol*, 1952, 223, 226, 228; P.R.O., Apprenticeship Register I.R. 1/21, 9 Dec. 1756; *Exeter Freemen* (Devon and Cornwall Rec. Soc. 1973), 325.]

EVELYN, JOHN (1620–1706), qualifies for inclusion in this *Dictionary* as a virtuoso whose theoretical knowledge of architecture was probably as considerable as that of Roger North or Roger Pratt, but who (unlike them) appears rarely to have put it to practical use. His life as a diarist, courtier and country gentleman is too well known to need repetition here, and a well-documented picture of him as an observer and critic of architecture has been given by Kerry Downes in *Concerning Architecture*, ed. Summerson, 1968, 28–39. His English edition of Fréart's *Parallel of the Antient Architecture with the Modern* (1664, 2nd ed. 1707), with its supplementary *Account of Architects and Architecture* dedicated to Wren, shows Evelyn's acquaintance with the principles and vocabulary of classical architecture as then understood in France and England. His scheme for the rebuilding of London after the Great Fire (apparently known only from an eighteenth-century engraving) proves that he knew something of contemporary ideas about town-planning. Drawings in the R.I.B.A. Collection show that he could make intelligible if not elegant sketches of structural and decorative details. His sketch-plan (Bodleian Library, MS. Rawlinson A.195, f. 254) for a naval hospital, made in 1666, soon after his appointment as a commissioner for the sick and wounded from the Dutch War, is absurdly naive, but among his papers at Christ Church, Oxford, there is an elaborate set of designs for a large town-house in the style of a French *hôtel* which shows a more sophisticated approach to architectural design. Although his cousin George Evelyn (1617–99) had (apparently after 1652) designed and built a Doric temple in his garden at WOTTON in SURREY (as well as a 'great room' at ALBURY PARK, SURREY, for Henry Howard, afterwards 6th Duke of Norfolk, *c*. 1655),[1] there appears to be no evidence that John Evelyn built anything significant either at his house at Sayes

Court, Deptford, or at Wotton itself, which he inherited in 1699, though he did much in the gardens at both houses. His diary (and a sheet of sketches in a volume of 'Promiscuous Notes' at Christ Church, Oxford) shows that in 1664 he helped Hugh May to design the chapel at CORNBURY HOUSE, OXON. In 1676 he undertook 'to contrive, & survey, & employ workmen' to build an apartment in WHITEHALL for his friend Sidney Godolphin (*Diary*, 10 Sept. 1676), but it appears from the diary of Robert Hooke (pp. 243–4, 253) that he did not fulfil his task without the latter's help. As the translator of Fréart, a Fellow of the Royal Society, Treasurer of Greenwich Hospital, and a friend of the principal English architects of his day, Evelyn's influence on English architecture may, however, have been greater than the evidence given above may suggest.

EVERARD, WILLIAM (1723–1792), was a Liverpool schoolmaster who commenced business as a surveyor and architect in 1759, building himself premises on the west side of John Street. He was the founder of the Liverpool Library, which was said to have been the first circulating library in the kingdom. It originated in a literary club which met at Everard's former home in St. Paul's Square. When he moved to John Street, he built a room to contain the books and became the first secretary and librarian. He was also one of the original members of the Liverpool Academy of Art, established in 1768, and subsequently delivered lectures on architecture. He was the chief promoter and architect of the LIVERPOOL OBSERVATORY, the first stone of which was laid on 9 September 1766. The building was never completed and Everard lost a considerable sum of money. Everard also designed GREAT CROSBY CHURCH, LANCS., 1769–70; dem. 1864 [*Trans. Hist. Soc. of Lancs. and Cheshire* civ, 1952, 129], and was probably the architect employed by the Rev. Mr. Bragg to design ST. MARY'S CHURCH, HARRINGTON STREET, LIVERPOOL, 1776; dem. 1809. A portrait of Everard was exhibited at a meeting of the Historic Society of Lancashire in 1869. It represented him holding the elevation of the Tuscan garden temple at INCE BLUNDELL HALL, the seat of Henry Blundell, who became president of the Liverpool Academy of Art in 1783 (see illustration of this elegant neoclassical building in *C. Life*, 17 April 1958, fig. 9). [J. A. Picton, *Memorials of Liverpool* i, 205, 208–9, ii, 20, 108; T. J. Kilpin, 'Biographical Sketch of William Everard, Architect and Surveyor', *Trans. Hist. Soc. of Lancs and Cheshire*, N.S. x, 1869–70; information from Mr. S. A. Harris.]

---

[1] For these two buildings see Evelyn's *Diary*, ed. De Beer, i. 55, and ii, 551; *C. Life*, 26 Oct. 1901, 523; and *Architectural Review*, March 1948, 124.

EYES, CHARLES (*c.* 1754–1803), was a member of a family which carried on the profession of surveyor in Liverpool for over 150 years.

The first was James Eyes, a joiner who died in 1723. John Eyes, who succeeded him, was surveyor to the Corporation in the early eighteenth century, and made a number of maps of the town. He was concerned, though in what capacity is not clear, in the building of ST. THOMAS'S CHURCH in 1750. He died in 1773. A design (1761) by him for the west end of a church, with a tower copied from All Saints, Derby, is in the R.I.B.A. Collection [*Catalogue: C–F.*, fig. 86]. John and Charles Eyes carried on the family business in the next generation. They both became members of the Liverpool Academy of Art on its foundation in 1768. Charles, who succeeded his uncle John as Town Surveyor in 1786, designed the OLD MUSIC HALL in BOLD STREET, opened in 1786, and destroyed by fire in about 1840: he also published a large-scale map of Liverpool in 1785. The business was continued by Edward, son of Charles Eyes, and finally came to an end with the death of his son, Edward Eyes, junior, in about 1860. In 1815 Thomas Rickman inspected a house being built by Edward Eyes at WALLASEY, CHESHIRE, for one Warburton, but dismissed it as 'a copy from some of the Villa Books, alter'd & showy outside but not over convenient within' [Diary, 26 Nov. 1815]. [R. Stewart-Brown, 'Maps and Plans of Liverpool and District by the Eyes Family of Surveyors', *Trans. Hist. Soc. of Lancs. and Cheshire* lxii, 1910.]

EYKYN, ROGER (*c.* 1725–1795), was an architect and builder of Wolverhampton. He was born at Worfield, Staffs., in 1724 or 1725, and established himself at Wolverhampton, where he first appears in 1760 as a master joiner, and subsequently as a nurseryman, surveyor and architect. He appears also to have been a mason, as he signs a monument at Broseley, Salop., to Elizabeth Crompton, died 1747, and another (undated) to the Weld family at Willey, Salop., and was paid £4 10s. for carving at STONE CHURCH, STAFFS., *c.* 1758 [W. H. Bowers & J. W. Clough, *Researches into the History of the Parish and Church of Stone,* 1929, 58–61]. He is mentioned frequently in the diary and account-book of William Baker (*q.v.*), who paid him £1 16s. 'for 2 vases' in 1756, and £24 in 1759 for a monument in Leighton Church, Salop. Baker also notes his marriage in 1754. In 1756 Eykyn supplied plans for the rebuilding of RUSHOCK CHURCH, WORCS. [G. K. Stanton, *Rambles and Researches among Worcestershire Churches,* 1884, 193], and he was also the architect of ST. PAUL'S CHURCH, BIRMINGHAM, 1777–9, for which he supplied designs and a model in 1776. His original design, derived from Gibbs's *Book of Architecture,* was modified in accordance with criticisms made by Samuel Wyatt, and the steeple was never completed owing to lack of funds, the present one being added by F. Goodwin in 1823 [L. D. Ettlinger & R. G. Holloway,

'St. Paul's Birmingham', *Arch. Rev.*, June 1947]. He was also consulted when the galleries of ST. MARY'S, BIRMINGHAM, collapsed in 1776. In his own town Eykyn was a Commissioner and a Trustee of the Grammar School, and when he died in 1795, the *Birmingham Gazette* described him as an 'eminent architect and surveyor'.

F

FALLOWS, JOHN (*c.* 1798–1861), of New Street, Birmingham, advertised his services as an architect in *Aris's Birmingham Gazette* for 27 June 1831. The extensive alterations which he had carried out to his own house at No. 100 New Street, 'in a singular yet not inelegant style of combined Grecian and Egyptian architecture', are referred to in West's *Directory of Warwickshire,* 1830, 210. His unexecuted design for a Mechanics' Institute in Bennett's Hill, Birmingham, is mentioned in the same work (p. 789).

In 1831 Fallows submitted a design in the competition for the new Town Hall at Birmingham and was awarded the second premium, the winning design being that of Messrs. Hansom & Welch of Liverpool [Rickman's diary, 7 June 1831]. Fallows's design is preserved in the Birmingham Public Library, but is in bad condition: a sketch based on it is reproduced by A. R. Dent in *Architecture,* 5th ser., iii, 1924–5, 228, where, however, it is wrongly attributed to Barry.

On 18 April 1831, a notice appeared in Aris's *Birmingham Gazette* requesting 'Persons desirous of contracting for building twenty houses and other Buildings near the gaol at Shrewsbury' to apply to 'Mr. Fallows. Architect. New Street. Birmingham'. In 1835 THE HOWARD STREET BUTTER AND CHEESE MARKET at SHREWSBURY was built to the designs of 'Fallows and Hart' of Birmingham [H. Pidgeon, *Memorials of Shrewsbury,* 1851, 179, with illustration].

Designs exhibited by Fallows at the Birmingham Society of Artists included 'A villa erected at Stourbridge', 'A hunting-box erected in Shropshire' and 'An architect's Residence and Offices', all in 1829; and the entrance hall of FOXLYDIATE HOUSE, nr. REDDITCH, WORCS., 1840.

Fallows died at Griffins Hill, Northfield, Birmingham, on 20 December 1861, aged 63 [*Aris's Birmingham Gazette,* 28 Dec. 1861]. F. W. Fiddian of Birmingham was his pupil.

FARQUHAR, COLIN, exhibited at the Royal Academy from London addresses between 1791 and 1799. His drawings included a 'Design of a house intended to be built for a gentleman near Edinburgh' (1791), 'Plans and Sections of a house now building' (1792), and a design for finishing the saloon at Thorndon Hall, Essex, the seat of Lord Petre (1799). He subscribed to Richardson's *New Vitruvius Britannicus* in 1802.

FAULKNER, THOMAS, was the author of several architectural publications, including *Designs for Shop Fronts etc. also the Grecian Orders of Architecture*, 1831, and *Designs for Mural Monuments, Monumental Tombs, and Chimney-Pieces, with Useful Details*, 1835. Two other works, entitled *The Organ-Builder's Assistant* and *Select Designs for Churches*, are mentioned in Loudon's *Architectural Magazine* ii, 1835, 185, and a second edition of *The Organ-Builder's Assistant* was published in 1838. It contains 20 plates of designs for organ-cases, mostly in an elaborate Gothic style.

Faulkner exhibited at the Royal Academy between 1825 and 1833. Thomas Faulkner (1777–1855), the historian of Chelsea and Kensington, may have been a relation, as he is said in *D.N.B.* to have belonged to a family of builders.

FEILDHOUSE, JOHN, designed the SCHOOL HOUSE at CRANBROOK, KENT, a brick building of 1727–9 [John Newman, *West Kent and the Weald*, The Buildings of England, 1969, 236, citing building accounts].

FELLOWS, W—, exhibited at the Royal Academy from 1793 to 1810, his designs including 'An Elevation of a villa now building at Sydenham in Kent' (1793), the new Rectory at Warnford, Hants. (1803), and Farley Hill Castle, nr. Reading, Berks., erected for E. Stephenson in 1809 (1810). FARLEY HILL CASTLE is a Gothic house (now the Hephaistos School) with rainwater heads dated 1808. Fellows was an unsuccessful candidate for election as A.R.A. in 1793 (Farington's Diary, 8 Oct. 1793).

FENTON, JAMES (*c.* 1805–1875), was born at Reading, but established himself in practice in Chelmsford, where in 1830 he married the daughter of John Copland, a wealthy Nonconformist solicitor. He specialized in the designing of chapels for Nonconformist congregations. In addition to the documented examples listed below he may also have been responsible for chapels at Beccles, Suffolk (1836), Longham, Dorset (1841), and Hedingham, Essex (1842), all of which have well-designed fronts resembling those at Wingham and Marlow. In 1839–43 he and two of his Copland relations were partners in a company formed to develop a large area on the south side of Chelmsford. Besides building a cast-iron bridge to carry the principal road across the R. Can, Fenton designed several of the 'highly ornamental mansions' in the new suburb. These included his own house, 'Laurel Grove' (now the Chelmsford Club), and those of his brothers-in-law John and Edward Copland (now

part of the Hospital complex). All these were built of white brick in a free classical style.

In 1850 Fenton was appointed surveyor to the newly formed Chelmsford Local Board of Health, and planned and executed a major water supply and sewerage system for the town. In 1858 he went to Croydon as Engineer and Surveyor to the Local Board of Health, but resigned in 1863 after a dispute. He died in Brixton in 1875, but was buried in the Nonconformist cemetery at Chelmsford which he had designed. [Information from Miss Hilda Grieve.]

WINGHAM, KENT, CONGREGATIONAL CHAPEL, 1835 [*Evangelical Mag.* xiv, 113].

HALESWORTH, SUFFOLK, INDEPENDENT CHAPEL, 1836 [*Evangelical Mag.* xiv, 304, 566].

BILLERICAY, ESSEX, INDEPENDENT CHAPEL, 1837, Gothic [H. Richman, *Billericay and its High Street*, 1963, 154–5].

MARLOW, BUCKS., CONGREGATIONAL CHAPEL, 1839–40 [H. M. Colvin in *Records of Bucks.* xv, 1947, 15].

LINCOLN, THE INDEPENDENT CHAPEL, NEWLAND, 1840, Gothic; converted into school 1874 [F. Hill, *Victorian Lincoln*, 1974, 186].

INGATESTONE, ESSEX, CONGREGATIONAL CHAPEL, 1840, Gothic [Essex Record Office, D/NC 10/49].

CHELMSFORD, ESSEX, INDEPENDENT CHAPEL, NEW LONDON ROAD, 1840; dem. 1971 [*Evangelical Mag.* xviii, 554; *Essex Standard*, 31 July 1840].

CHELMSFORD, ESSEX, development of NEW LONDON ROAD, including iron bridge over R. Can and many detached houses, *c.* 1840–8 [W. White, *History and Directory of Essex*, 1848, 303–4].

DERBY, ST. MARY'S GATE, conversion of house into BAPTIST CHAPEL, 1841 [S. Glover, *History and Directory of Derby*, 1843, 31]. See p. 986

CHELMSFORD, ESSEX, EBENEZER BAPTIST CHAPEL, NEW LONDON ROAD, 1847–8, Gothic [Minutes of the Chapel, *ex inf.* Miss Hilda Grieve].

CHELMSFORD, THE NONCONFORMIST CEMETERY, NEW LONDON ROAD, 1846 [Essex Record Office, D/Z 61].

FERGUS, JOHN, was the son of John Fergus, an Edinburgh merchant. He appears to have been as much a land surveyor as an architect, and was more than once employed by the city authorities in the former capacity. In 1759 he and Robert Robinson published a plan of lands north of the castle belonging to the City and Heriot's Hospital. In 1754 as 'John Fergus, architect', he was a member of the consortium of five (the others were Patrick Jamieson, a mason, and three wrights) who contracted to build the ROYAL EXCHANGE (now CITY CHAMBERS), EDINBURGH, to the designs of John Adam. The foundation-stone had already been laid in 1753, and the building was finally completed in 1761 [R. Miller, *The*

Municipal Buildings of Edinburgh, 1895, 114–7; W. Forbes Gray, 'The Royal Exchange and the City Improvements', *Book of the Old Edinburgh Club* xxii, 1938, 12–13]. In 1755 Fergus was admitted as a burgess of Edinburgh gratis in recognition of his 'good services'. The building of the Exchange did not prove to be a profitable undertaking, and in June 1758 William Mylne, in a letter to his brother Robert about architects in Edinburgh, reported that 'Fergus that was much in vogue is reduced to shelter himself in the Abbey from his creditors. They say he might have done extremely well but ruined himself by bad company' [Mylne family letters].

FERRERS, EARL, *see* SHIRLEY, WASHINGTON

FERRY, GEORGE, was in partnership with John Wallen until about 1826, when his name disappears from the London directories. Their office was in Spital Square, Spitalfields. In 1811 they exhibited 'additions and improvements to a villa at Leyton, Essex' at the Royal Academy, and in 1818 they designed MYDDELTON HOUSE, ENFIELD, MIDDLESEX, for H. C. Bowles [W. Robinson, *History of Enfield* i, 1823, 269–70]. Ferry became a member of the Surveyors' Club in 1806, and was its President in 1818.

FIDEL, JOHN (*c.* 1733–1806), was a native of Lincolnshire, where he served his apprenticeship as a carpenter. In about 1765 he came to Berkshire in order to work on Beckett Park, nr. Shrivenham, then being enlarged by Lord Barrington to the designs of Sanderson Miller. On Lord Barrington's advice he afterwards set up in business as a builder in Faringdon. In 1800 he designed and presumably built KINGSTON BAGPUIZE CHURCH, BERKS. His designs and specification are preserved in the Diocesan Records at Salisbury. Soon after 1800 he handed over the business to his son, J. Fidel, junior. He was a Nonconformist, and 'in the pursuit of his business, would frequently converse with his workmen on the great concerns of their souls'. He allowed services to be held in his workshop at Faringdon until in 1799 he built a chapel there. He died on 30 January 1806, aged 73. [W. H. Summers, *The Congregational Churches of Berkshire*, 1905, 230–1; obituary in *Evangelical Magazine*, xiv, 1806, 557.]

FIDLER, J—, was a pupil of John Yenn. He exhibited student's designs at the Royal Academy from 1784 to 1787. Two unexecuted designs by him for the KYMIN TEMPLE, nr. MONMOUTH, dated Dec. 1798, are in the National Library of Wales.

FIELD, JAMES, was a pupil of Samuel Robinson (d. 1833). He exhibited at the Royal Academy from 1819 to 1836, including a 'Design for a new front to the Sessions House, Newington, Surrey' (1824), a design for 'a literary and scientific institution, intended for the western part of Brighton' (1834), and a design, made in 1832, for the Grammar School at Stockwell, Lambeth (1835). He designed the ST. OLAVE'S GRAMMAR SCHOOL, BERMONDSEY STREET, SOUTHWARK, 1834–5, Tudor style, dem. *c.* 1850 [Brayley, *Topographical History of Surrey* v, 387, with illustrations], THE BRITISH AND FOREIGN SCHOOL SOCIETY'S SCHOOL in BOROUGH ROAD, 1841–2 [*Companion to the Almanac*, 1842, 227], and a METHODIST CHAPEL in GREAT DOVER STREET, SOUTHWARK, *c.* 1835. In partnership with Robinson, he designed additional wings to ST. THOMAS'S HOSPITAL, SOUTHWARK. These were completed by Field after Robinson's death – the north wing in 1836, the south wing in 1842 [*A.P.S.D.*, *s.v.* 'Robinson, Samuel', and Brayley, *op. cit.* v, 395].

FIELD, JOHN, of Bennet Street, St. James's, is described in the London directories as 'carpenter and builder' from 1817 onwards, but as 'architect and surveyor' or 'architect and builder' from 1830 to 1853. The only building he is known to have designed was NO. 6 ST. JAMES'S SQUARE (dem. 1958) which he rebuilt for the 5th Earl of Bristol in 1819–20, with Greek Revival detailing. In 1827 he was working at the Earl's country seat at ICKWORTH, SUFFOLK, where he was presumably concerned in the completion of the unfinished mansion begun by the 4th Earl [*Survey of London* xxix, 105].

FIELD, MARRIOTT (*c.* 1803–), entered the Royal Academy Schools in 1824 at the age of 21. Some porches 'in the Italian manner', illustrated in J. C. Loudon's *Encyclopaedia of Cottage, Farm and Villa Architecture*, 1833 (1846 ed., figs. 1696–8), are stated to be 'from the portfolio of Marriott Field, Esq., a young Architect, lately returned from a professional tour through Italy'. In 1832 he exhibited a design for Fishmongers' Hall at the Royal Academy. Both Loudon and the R.A. Catalogue give his address as Christ's Hospital.

FINDEN, JOHN, practised in London from 41 Upper John Street, Fitzroy Square, from *c.* 1810 to *c.* 1840. He first exhibited at the Royal Academy in 1800, and subsequently showed 'A Cottage near the Church at Finchley, the residence of S. Staples, Esq.' (1810), 'Intended alterations to the Lower Assembly Rooms and West of England Club-House, Bath' (1811), the 'Elevation of a House now building for J. H. Hunt, Esqr. at Compton Pauncefoot' (1821), and a 'Design for the Commercial Benevolent College, intended to be erected at Barrow Hill Road, N. side of

Regents Park' (1830). COMPTON CASTLE, COMPTON PAUNCEFOOT, SOMERSET, which Finden designed for J. Hussey Hunt in 1821, is a castellated house somewhat in the style of Smirke's works in that manner.

FINDEN, THOMAS (*c.* 1785–1861), was the son of John Finden (*q.v.*) and the elder brother of William and Edward Francis Finden, well known as engravers. For some years he practised as an architect and builder from 38 Upper John Street. Subsequently he moved to John Street, Adelphi, where from 1845 to 1857 he was in partnership with T. Hayter Lewis (*c.* 1818–98), and later to Mitcham in Surrey. He was surveyor to Hoare's Brewery and to the Craven and other estates in London. He was elected to the Mastership of the Carpenters' Company, but died (2 Feb. 1861) before he could take office. G. W. Mayhew, A. F. Ashton and W. Snooke were his pupils [*Builder* xix, 1861, 115].

In 1825 or 1826 Finden bought Baron House in Mitcham, Surrey, and in its grounds built three semi-detached houses, of which two survive as NOS. 470/472 and 482/484 LONDON ROAD, MITCHAM [Surrey Land Tax Records, *ex inf.* Mr. Thomas Thorne]. He appears to have designed STAPLEHURST PLACE, KENT, for Henry Hoare, for in 1833 designs for this house (dem.) were exhibited at the R.A. from his address at 38 Upper John Street by H. Finden (*sic*). He certainly designed the SHIP TORBAY TAVERN at GREENWICH, which was exhibited in 1839 by his pupil Mayhew as 'erected from the design of Mr. Thomas Finden'. The following works were exhibited by Finden and his partner Hayter Lewis in 1845: FARRINGDON HALL, DEVON (?), 'lately built for W. Watkin'; a house in KENSINGTON PALACE GARDENS for J. M. Blashfield (not built, see *Survey of London* xxxvii, 158); and 'intended alterations' to two houses in UPPER GEORGE STREET, PORTMAN SQUARE, 'to form an entrance to a new Presbyterian church'. They also designed ST. MARK'S CHURCH, SOUTH NORWOOD, 1852, Gothic [Port, 162], and THE ROYAL PANOPTICON OF SCIENCE AND ART (afterwards the 'Alhambra Palace') in LEICESTER SQUARE, 1852–4, destroyed by fire 1882, which appears to have been exclusively the work of Lewis, whose account of it was printed by the *Builder* xi, 1853, 290–1, 308–9, without any mention of his partner (see also *Builder* xii, 1854, 137, 143, and *Survey of London* xxxiv, 492–9, for this essay in the 'Saracenic' style). In 1841 the principal front of NEW PARK (ROUNDWAY), nr. DEVIZES, WILTS. (dem. 1955), showing 'alterations and new carriage entrance, recently completed', was exhibited at the R.A. by 'Finden and Green' of 25 Regent Street.

FINDLATER, JAMES RATTRAY (*c.* 1803–1873), was the son of a factor. From 1832 he prac-

tised in Dundee and Broughty Ferry, chiefly as a civil engineer. In 1833 he laid out the CONSTITUTION ROAD CEMETERY in DUNDEE, in 1834 he formed the CONSTITUTION BRAE for the Town Council, and in 1845 planned the WESTERN CEMETERY. He died at New Scone on 6 February 1873, aged 69 [information from Mr. David Walker].

FINNEY, JOSEPH, was a watch- and clockmaker at Liverpool. In Gore's *Liverpool Directory* of 1767 he is described as 'Clock and Watchmaker and architect'. The only building he is known to have designed was THE OCTAGON CHAPEL, TEMPLE COURT, 1763; dem. 1820 [J. A. Picton, *Memorials of Liverpool* ii, 1875, 109] (illustrated in E. Meteyard, *Life of Josiah Wedgwood* i, 1865, 314).

FIRMADGE, WILLIAM (1755–1836), of Leicester, was the son of William Firmadge (1726–90), slater and plasterer of Scraptoft, Leicestershire. He became a freeman of Leicester in 1778, and is variously described in directories and other sources as builder, slater, stone-mason, plasterer, architect and surveyor. He did a good deal of work as a monumental mason, and slate headstones carved by him can be seen in several Leicestershire churchyards. As a builder he appears to have been extensively employed, *e.g.* in constructing gaols at Leicester, Worcester and Oakham, but in 1812 he wrote to his sister that he was 'drawing affairs to a narrower compass' by disposing of his stock-in-trade as a builder and that in future he would practise only as an architect. In that capacity his only recorded works of any consequence appear to have been the enlargement of LEICESTER LUNATIC ASYLUM, 1794 [*V.C.H. Leics.* iv, 372], and THE NEW MARKET, LEICESTER, 1824 [*Records of the Borough of Leicester*, ed. Chinnery, v, 464].

Firmadge was a prominent member of the Corporation of Leicester, holding office as Mayor in 1809–10. His pupils included the Leicester architect William Parsons. He died at Leicester on 27 March 1836, aged 80, and was buried at Scraptoft. [J. D. Bennett, *Leicestershire Architects 1700–1850*, Leicester Museum 1968; *Gent's Mag.* 1836 (i), 566; information from family letters *ex inf.* Mrs. J. W. Cole; Rupert Gunnis, *Dictionary of British Sculptors*, 1968, 144.]

FISHER, —, of Bristol, is said to have designed THE SHIRE HALL, MONMOUTH, 1724. The original drawings for the building were seen in the early nineteenth century by a person who noted that 'Fisher of Bristol was the name of the Architect' [Monmouthshire County Records, C. Bu. 0004, letter from T. Phillips].

FISHER, — (*c.* 1762–1817), 'an ingenious architect', died at Stafford in 1817, aged 55 [*Gent's*

Mag. 1817 (ii), 477]. He may have been the architect called Fisher who designed NORTHAW CHURCH, HERTS., for William Strode, 1809–10, Gothic; destroyed by fire 1881 [B.M., Add. MS. 36366, no. 68; cf. J. Nichols, *Literary Anecdotes* viii, 510].

FISHER, JOHN, practised in Glasgow. In 1835 or 1836 he designed a block of buildings in OXFORD STREET, GLASGOW, near the corner of Bridge Street, for Bailie Gourlay [J. Cruikshank, *Sketch of the Incorporation of Masons*, Glasgow, 1879, 93]. John Baird (1816–93) was his pupil.

FISHER, MONEY, a builder at Salisbury who held the post of clerk of works to the Cathedral in the 1830s. He altered or rebuilt parsonages at TROWBRIDGE (1812) and CHILMARK (1814) in WILTSHIRE [Salisbury Diocesan Records] and at AYLESTONE in LEICESTERSHIRE (1813) [Leicestershire Record Office, MGA]. The family business was continued by his son Frederick Richard Fisher.

FISHER, WILLIAM (–1847), was a builder of Oxford. In 1814–16 he rebuilt ST. EBBE'S CHURCH, OXFORD, to his own designs in a simple Gothic style [J. Ingram, *Memorials of Oxford* iii, 1837, 14]. In 1837 he rebuilt MARCHAM CHURCH, BERKS., in a Tudor Gothic style, almost certainly to his own designs [see Berkshire County Record Office, D/P84/6]. The original drawings for the latter church, unsigned, are in the Victoria and Albert Museum (D.1784–D.1787, 98). Fisher also designed and built the ADULLAM CHAPEL, COMMERCIAL ROAD, OXFORD, for Mr. Bulteel, 1832; dem. [*The Oxford University and City Guide*, 1833, 12]. His plan for alterations to FRENCH HOUSE, THAME, OXON., dated 1826, is in the Berkshire Record Office [D/EHP. 3]. He died on 3 April 1847. John Fisher, County Surveyor of Oxfordshire, who died in 1872, was probably his son.

FITCH, Sir THOMAS (1637–1688), was a leading master bricklayer and a prominent figure in the building world of seventeenth-century London. He was the son of William Fitch of Barkway, Herts., and elder brother of John Fitch (below). The earliest reference to his building activities so far noticed is his contract in April 1663 to perform the brickwork of Sir Ralph Bankes's new house at KINGSTON LACY, DORSET, designed by Sir Roger Pratt, in which he is described as 'Thomas Fitts of Farnham, bricklayer' [*The Architecture of Sir Roger Pratt*, ed. Gunther, 1928, 232]. His more important contracts included the work of cutting and wharfing the Fleet Ditch (1672–4), for which he received over £50,000 [T. F. Reddaway, *The Rebuilding of London after the Great Fire*, 1940, 211–16]; fortifications at PORTS-

MOUTH, carried out jointly with John Fitch from 1679 onwards to the designs of Sir Bernard de Gomme [B.M., Add. Charter 32751]; the GARRISON HOSPITAL at PORTSMOUTH, 1680 [C. G. T. Dean, 'Charles II's Garrison Hospital, Portsmouth', *Hampshire Field Club Papers* xiv, 1947, 280–3]; and THE GREAT STOREHOUSE at THE TOWER OF LONDON, 1688–91, a large and imposing building of considerable architectural pretensions which was destroyed by fire in 1841. The design has been attributed to Wren, but the attribution (though stylistically possible) has not been substantiated by documentary evidence [N. Blakiston, 'The Great Storehouse in the Tower', *Arch. Rev.*, June 1957, 453]. It is possible that Fitch designed it himself, for there is evidence that he acted as an architect and surveyor on other occasions, and he was complimented on his 'great knowledge in the Art of Architecture' on two of the plates of the Orders in R. Blome's *Gentleman's Recreation* (1686). In the 1670s he was employed 'as a surveyor to order and direct' the reconstruction of the Bishop of Winchester's Palace at WOLVESEY, WINCHESTER, for Bishop Morley [P.R.O., C 10/230/32; account in B.M., Stowe MS. 541, f. 139ᵛ and duplicate in Portsmouth Guildhall Record Office]. In 1686 a kitchen was to be added to Lord Preston's house in SOHO SQUARE, LONDON, 'according to a draught' signed by the contractor, 'and the direction and satisfaction of Sir Thomas Fitch' [archives of Sir Richard Graham, Bart., at Norton Conyers, Yorks.]. According to Tighe & Davis, *Annals of Windsor* ii, 1858, 423, Fitch designed THE COURT HOUSE, WINDSOR, BERKS., *c.* 1687, and supervised its erection until his death, when the Corporation ordered that it should be completed under the direction of Sir Christopher Wren.

Fitch's efficient performance of the difficult task of constructing the Fleet Ditch earned him a gift of plate from the Corporation, and in December 1679 he was knighted. On 7 September 1688 he was created a baronet by James II, but died nine days later on 16 September. His portrait is in the possession of Mr. Marc Fitch. He had acquired an estate at North Cray in Kent, where he owned, and perhaps built, the mansion called MOUNT MASCALL (dem. *c.* 1960). He married Anne, daughter and heir of Richard Comport of Eltham, and the baronetcy was inherited by his son Sir Comport Fitch (d. 1720) [Hasted, *History of Kent* i, 1778, 156–7; Hist. MSS. Comm., *7th Report*, 474 b; information from Mr. Marc Fitch].

Sir Thomas Fitch's younger brother JOHN FITCH was born at Barkway in 1642 and died early in 1706 [P.C.C. 61 EEDES]. He was a member of the London Grocers' Company. In 1679 he was associated with his brother in the important contract for fortifications at Portsmouth [B.M., Add. Charter 32751], and in 1682 he succeeded Philip

Lanyon as Workmaster to the Office of Ordnance under a reversionary grant of 1678 [Pat. Roll 30 Charles II, Part 3]. He was frequently employed by Robert Hooke, *e.g.* at THE BETHLEHEM HOSPITAL in 1675–6, at THE COLLEGE OF PHYSICIANS in 1674–8, and at MONTAGU HOUSE in 1675–8. He also had the bricklayer's contract for ST. ANNE AND ST. AGNES CHURCH, GRESHAM STREET, 1677–80 [*Walpole Soc.* xxv, 90–6; *Wren Soc.* x, 46, 54]. In 1674 he applied for employment as chief bricklayer at St. Paul's Cathedral, but in spite of Hooke's recommendation, and a present of china to Lady Wren, he was disappointed [*Diary of Robert Hooke*, ed. Robinson & Adams, 118, 132, etc.]. In 1675 he undertook 'several works and buildings' at George, Lord Berkeley's house at CRANFORD, MIDDLESEX [P.R.O., C 6/230/26], and in 1679 he contracted to finish the brick tower of HAMPTON CHURCH, MIDDLESEX (dem. 1829) [B. Garside, *The Parish Church of Hampton-on-Thames during the 16th. and 17th. Centuries*, 1937, 11]. In 1698 he was concerned in the remodelling of ALBURY PARK, SURREY, for Heneage Finch, 1st. Earl of Aylesford. His 'draught' or 'moddell' is mentioned in a letter from Finch to his brother the 2nd Earl of Nottingham [Finch papers, Leicestershire Record Office, bundle 22, no. 116]. In *c.* 1702 he contracted to perform all the mason's, bricklayer's, carpenter's, smith's, glazier's and sawyer's work in building BUCKINGHAM HOUSE, LONDON, for £7000 [London University MS. 533, ff. 9–11]. In 1668 John Fitch married Melior, daughter of William Russell of Kingston Lacy in Dorset, and he subsequently acquired property in that county, including (in 1691) the house at High Hall, nr. Wimborne, which still belongs to his descendants, and where his portrait is preserved [Hutchins, *History of Dorset* iii, 1868, 235–6, 242; N. Luttrell, *Brief Historical Relation* iv, 1857, 481, 576, 645; information from Mr. Charles Gibson].

John Fitch (d. 1706) should not be confused with a master-mason of the same name who died in or about 1700. He was the son of Fabian Fitch, a blacksmith of Higham Ferrers in Northamptonshire, and was made free of the Masons' Company in January 1671. He was concerned in the building of KIVETON HOUSE, YORKS. (W.R.), and contracted in 1700 to build the west front of CHATSWORTH HOUSE, DERBYSHIRE, but evidently died before the work was far advanced [D. Knoop & G. P. Jones, *The London Mason in the Seventeenth Century*, 1935, 46; *Wren Soc.* xvii, 40; F. Thompson, *History of Chatsworth*, 1949, 66, 69].

FLINT, WILLIAM (1801–1862), of Leicester, was the son of John Flint of that town. In 1812 he was apprenticed to a carpenter named Edwyn, and in 1818 to William Parsons, then the leading architect in Leicester. He began independent practice in 1826 and became architect and surveyor to the Corporation. From about 1849 to about 1855 he was in partnership with Charles Wickes, and from 1855 until his death with Henry Shenton, who carried on his practice after his death. Two years later Shenton was joined by Charles Baker, one of Flint's former pupils. Other pupils were William Millican and Isaac Barradale. Flint died on 11 January 1862, aged 60. A portrait in oils is reproduced by J. D. Bennett (see below). Flint's recorded buildings are nearly all classical and show him to have been a competent designer in the Greek Revival style [J. D. Bennett, *Leicestershire Architects 1700–1850*, Leicester Museums 1968].

LEICESTER, NEW HALL, WELLINGTON STREET (now City Lending Library), 1831 [*V.C.H. Leics.* iv, 352–3].
KIBWORTH CHURCH, LEICS., rebuilt tower, 1832–6, Gothic [*V.C.H. Leics.* v, 174].
LEICESTER, NEWS ROOM AND LIBRARY, BELVOIR STREET, 1837; dem. 1901 [*Architectural Mag.* iv, 1837, 78; *Companion to the Almanac*, 1828, 228–9] (Bennett, *op. cit.*, pl. 9).
LEICESTER UNION WORKHOUSE, SPARKENHOE STREET, 1838; rebuilt 1850–1 [*V.C.H. Leics.* iv, 356].
LEICESTER, MIDLAND RAILWAY STATION, CAMPBELL STREET, 1840; dem. 1892 [Bennett, *op. cit.*, with illustration].
LEICESTER, NEW WEST BRIDGE, 1841–2; rebuilt 1890 [Bennett, *op. cit.*] (*Trans. Leics. Archaeological and Hist. Soc.* xxxvi, pl. 18).
LEICESTER, PHOENIX INSURANCE BUILDING, WELFORD PLACE, 1842 [*V.C.H. Leics.* iv, 353] (Bennett, *op. cit.*, pl. 11).
MARKET HARBOROUGH, INDEPENDENT CHAPEL, HIGH STREET, 1844 [Bennett, *op. cit.*].
LEICESTER, CORAH'S WAREHOUSE, 13 GRANBY STREET, 1845; converted into G.P.O. 1865; dem. [*V.C.H. Leics.* iv, 353, n. 66].
LEICESTER, ST. MARY'S CHURCH, repairs, 1846, severely criticized in *Ecclesiologist* vi, 1846, 195–6, vii, 1847, 35–6.

For subsequent works (mostly warehouses) by Flint and Wickes see Bennett, *op. cit.*

FLITCROFT, HENRY (1697–1769), born 30 August 1697, was grandson of Jeffery Flitcroft of Twiss Green, Winwick, Lancs., and son of Jeffery Flitcroft, a labourer employed in the gardens at Hampton Court. He was apprenticed to Thomas Morris, citizen and joiner of London, for seven years from 6 November 1711, and was admitted to the freedom of the Joiners' Company on 3 November 1719. By 1720 he had become draughtsman and architectural assistant to Lord Burlington, a position which it is said he owed to the accident of falling from a scaffold and breaking his leg while working at Burlington House as a 'journeyman carpenter'. The Earl, hearing of his injury, 'interested himself with much humanity concerning the sufferer, and put him under proper care'. In the course of his recovery, Flitcroft was accidentally seen drawing by the Earl, who, 'noticing his more than ordinary talent', took him into his service. As Burlington's assistant, he was employed in surveying the site of the new Dormitory of Westminster School in 1720 [*Memoirs of William Stukeley*, Surtees Soc., i, 1882, 67], and in drawing out designs for, and supervising the works at, Tottenham Park, Wilts., *c.* 1721 [cf. a letter from Flitcroft to Stukeley, dated from Tottenham, in Bodleian, Gough Maps 229, p. 139, and drawings from Chatsworth reproduced in *Archaeological Jnl.* cii, 1945, pl. i]. He subsequently drew out for publication the drawings published by William Kent under Lord Burlington's patronage as *The Designs of Inigo Jones*, 1727; many of the original drawings for these plates are now in the R.I.B.A. Collection. Flitcroft was an accurate and elegant draughtsman, but as works of art his meticulous drawings are dull affairs compared with the lively sketches of his colleague Kent.

In May 1726, Burlington's influence procured Flitcroft the post of Clerk of the Works at Whitehall, Westminster, and St. James's,[1] and for the remainder of his life 'Burlington Harry' was an important figure in the Office of Works. In 1746 he became Master Carpenter, and in 1748 succeeded Kent as Master Mason and Deputy Surveyor. Finally, in 1758 he succeeded Ripley as Comptroller of the Works, a position which he retained until his death in 1769. Although in 1730 he had drawn out Kent's design for rebuilding the Painted Chamber at Westminster [Fiske Kimball, 'William Kent's Designs for the Houses of Parliament', *R.I.B.A. Jnl.*, 6 Aug. 1932, 737], Flitcroft designed no important building in his official capacity, and his principal architectural commissions were due to private patronage. He remained faithful to the Palladian canon throughout his life, and as a careful student of Inigo Jones he showed a special aptitude for designing decorative features such as chimney-pieces in the style of the seventeenth-century master. His architecture, if not distinguished by the creative genius which marks the works of Burlington and Kent, has all the merits of a mature style in practised hands.

Like so many eighteenth-century architects, Flitcroft undertook the erection of buildings as well as their design. In 1730 he supplied marble for the base of the Column of Victory at Blenheim [D. Green, 'Blenheim Column of Victory', *Arch. Rev.*, April 1950, 274], and he contracted to build both the church at Wimpole and that of St. Giles-in-the-Fields. He also took three building sites on the Harley estate in Marylebone as a speculation in 1725, and it is as a 'builder' that he figures in Churchill's poem *The Duellist* (1764).

In 1745 Flitcroft was chosen Sheriff of London and Middlesex, but paid the fine to be excused from serving, as he also did two years later when elected Warden of the Joiners' Company. He lived at Hampstead, where he had bought an estate in 1741, and where he built himself the house known as Frognal Grove. In 1744, when it was proposed to rebuild Hampstead Church, Flitcroft offered to design the new church and to supervise its erection free of charge provided that there was no competition. This offer was, however, refused by the vestry, and the present church was designed by John Sanderson, and not, as is often stated (*e.g.* by Ephraim Hardcastle [W. H. Pyne] in the imaginary dialogue between Flitcroft and Gainsborough which he gives in his *Wine and Walnuts* ii, 1824, 241–9), by Flitcroft [see the Vestry Minutes printed in *C. Life*, 11 Dec. 1937, 610–11]. He died at Hampstead on 25 February 1769, and was buried at Teddington, where a tablet and tombstone record his appointments as 'clerk, Master Mason and Controller' (see Lysons, *Environs of London* iii, 1795, 507, and Park, *Hampstead*, 1818, 222, 337, for the inscriptions). Kenton Couse was his assistant, and, so far as is known, his only pupil. His only son Henry (1742–1826), a barrister by profession, was educated at Corpus Christi College, Cambridge, to which he bequeathed his library. Portraits of Flitcroft, his wife and son are in the R.I.B.A. Library. A bound volume of his drawings of the Five Orders, with designs for a palace, a Doric pavilion, and other buildings, dedicated to the Duke of Cumberland, is in the British Museum (King's MS. 283). From 1733 to 1737 Flitcroft had acted as the Duke's architectural tutor at a salary of £50 a year [Duke of Cumberland's accounts at Althorp House].

[*A.P.S.D.*; *D.N.B.*; *History of the King's Works*, v.]

CHURCHES

LONDON, ST. GILES-IN-THE-FIELDS, 1731–4 [J. Parton, *The Hospital and Parish of St. Giles-in-the-Fields*, 1822, 211–15; *Survey of London* v, 130–2 and pls. 43–51]. The original wooden model is preserved in the church, and drawings by Flitcroft, including an alternative design with a cupola instead of a spire, are in the R.I.B.A. Collection and B.M., *King's Maps* xxiii, 18.

SOUTHWARK, ST. OLAVE'S CHURCH, TOOLEY STREET, 1738–9; restored by G. Allen after a fire in 1843; dem. 1926 [Vestry Minutes, etc., printed in *Builder* ii, 1844, 252–3, 263–5, 420]. The original designs, signed by the architect and

---

[1] From about 1728 until 1746 he was also Clerk of Works at Kew and Richmond.

churchwardens, are in B.M., *King's Maps* xxiii, 32.

WIMPOLE, CAMBS., rebuilt for the 1st Earl of Hardwicke, 1748–9; partly Gothicized 1887 [inscription in church; estimate, specification, etc., in B.M., Add. MS. 35679, ff. 13–17, 20, 28, 53–4] (R.C.H.M., *West Cambridgeshire*, 212 and pl. 126).

STOKE EDITH, HEREFS. A letter from Flitcroft to Thomas Foley dated 27 May 1740, now in the Herefordshire Record Office [Foley Papers, Portfolio 14, f. 564], shows that Flitcroft made a design 'for dressing up the recess on the North side of the Church in the Gothick manner', but no such recess appears to have been built, and there is no other evidence to connect Flitcroft with the rebuilding of the nave and chancel at Foley's expense in 1740–1. The style is classical, not Gothic.

COUNTRY HOUSES, ETC.

CHICHELEY HALL, BUCKS. In Dec. 1722 Sir John Chester paid Flitcroft 5 gns. 'for drawing the designe of the Hall &c.', that is for the entrance hall completed in 1722–3. Whether Flitcroft was himself responsible for the design or whether he was acting as Kent's draughtsman is not clear, but the treatment of the arched screen may be compared with that of a similar screen in the Old Hall at Wentworth Wood-house [Joan D. Tanner, 'The Building of Chicheley Hall', *Records of Bucks.* xvii (1), 1961, 46].

THORESBY HOUSE, NOTTS. The executors' accounts of Evelyn Pierrepont, 1st Duke of Kingston (d. 1726) [Monson MS. xciii, p. 33], contain a payment of 14 gns. to 'Mr. Flitcroft for Drawing Two Drafts for his late Grace of some intended works at Thoresby wch. was delivered the day his Grace died and for supervising setling and adjusting Mr. Jones's bill for the marble Room at Thoresby and for some Instructions in Measuring Drawing and Architecture to Reynolds by his late Grace's special Request and Direction'. The London accounts of the 2nd Duke for 1752 [Nottingham University Library, MS. 4416] contain a payment of £811 19s. 6d. 'To Henry Flitcroft Architect (now and before)', but it is not stated what work he had done.

BOREHAM HOUSE, ESSEX. The ledgers of Hoare's Bank show that in 1729 Flitcroft was paid 8 gns. by Benjamin Hoare 'for the plan of New Hall' (*i.e.* Boreham). The house was built in 1727–8 under the supervision of Edward Shepherd (*q.v.*), but the payment may indicate that he was following a design made by Flitcroft (*C. Life*, 11 July 1914).

THE BOWER HOUSE, HAVERING, ESSEX, for John

Baynes, 1729 [inscription in house, recorded in *C. Life*, 17–24 March 1944].

AMESBURY HOUSE, WILTS., alterations for the 3rd Duke of Queensberry, *c.* 1730, probably including the addition of the wings; rebuilt 1834 by T. Hopper [Drummond's Bank, Duke of Queensberry's account; in 1726 Flitcroft had made a large survey of the Amesbury estate for the duke now in the Wilts. County Record Office (944/1)] (Harrison's *Views of Seats*, 1787).

WENTWORTH WOODHOUSE, YORKS. (W.R.), enlarged and rebuilt east front and added wings for the 1st Earl of Malton, *c.* 1735–*c.*1770; the wings were raised and given engaged Doric porticoes by John Carr later in the century. Flitcroft also designed two temples and the eyecatcher known as HOOBER STAND (erected 1748). Contemporary engravings giving his name as architect of these buildings are in the Hailstone Collection in York Minster Library [A. Booth, 'The Architects of Wentworth Castle and Wentworth Wood-house', *R.I.B.A. Jnl.*, 25 Nov. 1933; Hist. MSS. Comm., *Carlisle*, 174; elevation and two plans in Estate Office inscribed 'Mr. Flitcroft 1737'] (*C. Life*, 20, 27 Sept., 4, 11 Oct. 1924).

DITCHLEY HOUSE, OXON., designed interiors of drawing- and dining-rooms, several chimney-pieces, some table frames, and much internal woodwork, for the 2nd Earl of Lichfield, 1736–40 [bills among Ditchley papers in Oxfordshire County Record Office] (*C. Life*, 9, 16 June 1934; C. Hussey, *English Country Houses: Early Georgian*, 1955, 66–71).

TRENTHAM HALL, STAFFS., alterations for the 2nd Lord Gower, 1737; remodelled 1838, dem. 1910 [Bodleian Library, MS. Eng. Misc. f. 556, p. 20].

MIDGHAM HOUSE, BERKS., additions for the Hon. Stephen Poyntz, 1738–9; dem. *c.* 1965 [bills among Poyntz papers at Althorp House].

WIMBORNE HOUSE, WIMBORNE ST. GILES, DORSET, interiors, including Great Dining Room, Tapestry Room and probably the White Hall, for the 4th Earl of Shaftesbury, 1740–4 [accounts at Wimborne House; R.C.H.M., *Dorset* v, 95–6].

attributed: STOWE HOUSE, BUCKS., interior of THE STATE GALLERY for the 1st Viscount Cobham, *c.* 1742 [Michael Gibbon in *The Stoic*, March 1969, 162, followed by Desmond Fitz-Gerald in *Apollo*, June 1973, 574].

WIMPOLE HALL, CAMBS., refronted and altered house for the 1st Earl of Hardwicke, 1742–5 [R.C.H.M., *West Cambridgeshire*, 216 and plates].

LILFORD HALL, NORTHANTS., staircase, entrance hall and stables for Thomas Powys, *c.* 1744–50 [letters and drawings in Northants. County Record Office, Lilford nos. 3800, 3803, 3805,

3806, 3832; Sir John Soane's Museum, MS. diary of William Freeman (d. 1749), p. 97, referring to stables as Flitcroft's work].

HAMPSTEAD, MIDDLESEX, house (later known as Montagu Grove and now as Frognal Grove) for himself, *c.* 1745; altered by G. E. Street *c.* 1860 and remodelled 1926 [Gordon Nares in *C. Life*, 24 June 1949].

HAMPSTEAD, BRANCH HILL LODGE, alterations for Sir Thomas Clark, Master of the Rolls, *c.* 1745 [T. J. Barratt, *Annals of Hampstead* ii, 1912, 75].

SHOBDON COURT, HEREFS., internal alterations for the 2nd Viscount Bateman, 1746 [Herefordshire County Record Office, Bateman papers, letter of 3 April 1746].

WOBURN ABBEY, BEDS., rebuilt for the 4th Duke of Bedford, 1747–61 [G. Scott-Thompson, *Family Background*, 1949, chap. 1; *Vitruvius Britannicus* iv, 1767, pls. 21–5].

WINDSOR GREAT PARK, works for William Augustus, Duke of Cumberland, including wooden bridge over Virginia Water, and the Belvedere Tower (now the nucleus of Fort Belvedere), *c.* 1750. In 1747 Flitcroft was paid £1900 on account 'for Windsor Great Park' [Duke of Cumberland's accounts at Althorp House; W. Sandby, *Thomas and Paul Sandby*, 1892, 214; E. A. Oppé, *Sandby Drawings at Windsor Castle*, 1947, 42; drawings in Royal Library, Windsor Castle, nos. 17931A, 17927A, etc.].

MILTON HOUSE, NORTHANTS., rebuilt south front and remodelled much of interior for the 3rd Earl Fitzwilliam, 1750–1 [Northants. County Record Office, estimates among Milton House drawings, nos. 88 and 90; payment of Flitcroft's 'salary for surveying the works at Milton' in 'Book of Expences relating to the New Building in 1750 and 1751' (Misc. vol. 156)] (*C. Life*, 18–25 May, 1 June 1961).

CLAPHAM, SURREY, designed house on north side of Common for Henry Hoare, 1753–4; dem. 1851 [Wilts. County Record Office, Henry Hoare's account-book, 383/6] (E. E. F. Smith, *Clapham*, 1976, 44).

REDLYNCH, nr. BRUTON, SOMERSET, alterations for the 1st Earl of Ilchester, executed by Nathaniel Ireson, *c.* 1755; dem. 1913–14 [B.M., Add. MS. 51373A, ff. 37–40].

STIVICHALL HALL, WARWICKS., for Arthur Gregory, 1755; dem. *c.* 1930 [R. Bearman, 'A Lost Warwickshire Country House: Stivichall Hall', *Warwickshire History* i (3), 1970].

PUTNEY, SURREY, designed or altered house for Lady Bruce, 1761 [Wilts. County Record Office, Henry Hoare's account-book, 383/6].

WITLEY COURT, WORCS., portico'd lodge for the 2nd Lord Foley, before 1762 [M. Williams, *The Letters of William Shenstone*, 1939, letter cccii].

STOURHEAD, WILTS., THE TEMPLE OF CERES (now Flora), 1744–5; THE TEMPLE OF HERCULES (based on the Pantheon), 1754–6; THE TEMPLE OF APOLLO (based on the Round Temple at Baalbec), *c.* 1765; ALFRED'S TOWER, designed 1765 but not completed until 1772, for Henry Hoare [K. Woodbridge, *Landscape and Antiquity*, 1970, 26–33, 56].

LONDON HOUSES

MARYLEBONE. The sites of three houses on the Harley estate in Castle Street and Bolsover Street were taken on building leases by Flitcroft in Sept. 1725 [B.M., Add. MS. 18240, f. 14].

CRAVEN STREET, STRAND, layout for William Craven, 1728–30 [copies of plans by Flitcroft in Muniment Room at Syon House, B. xv.5 a–b].

MONTAGU HOUSE, PRIVY GARDENS, WHITEHALL, for the 2nd Duke of Montagu, 1731–3; dem. 1859 [referred to as Flitcroft's design by Batty Langley in his *Ancient Masonry*, 1736, 332] (*Survey of London* xiii, 217).

SACKVILLE STREET, NO. 36, for Edmund Turnor, 1732–3 [*Survey of London* xxxii, 365–6].

ST. JAMES'S SQUARE, NO. 10 (now Chatham House), for Sir William Heathcote, Bart., 1735–6 [*Survey of London* xxix, 122].

DOVER STREET, fitted up house for Isabella, Duchess of Manchester, 1740, at expense of Sarah, Duchess of Marlborough, 1740 [correspondence at Althorp House quoted by Lord Spencer in *C. Life*, 13 March 1942, 517].

GROSVENOR SQUARE, NO. 4, alterations for the 1st Earl of Malton, 1743 [Sheffield Public Library, Fitzwilliam papers: Lord Rockingham's letter-book 1734–50, Flitcroft to Malton, 2 June 1743].

BLOOMSBURY SQUARE, designs for two houses identifiable as Nos. 5–6, 1744 [G. Scott-Thompson, *The Russells in Bloomsbury*, 1940, 356; information from Mr. A. F. Kelsall].

ST. JAMES'S PLACE, NO. 25, for Lady Hervey, 1747–50; dem. *c.* 1940 [*Letters of Mary Lepel, Lady Hervey*, 1821, 111, 125, 170, 261].

BEDFORD HOUSE, BLOOMSBURY, repairs for the 4th Duke of Bedford, 1758; dem. 1800 [documents at Woburn Abbey, *ex inf.* Mrs. M. P. G. Draper].

UNEXECUTED DESIGNS

At Boughton House, Northants., there is a bound set of undated drawings by Flitcroft for a house in DOVER STREET for the 4th Earl of Cardigan. It is not certain whether this house was built.

In one of William Stukeley's notebooks in the Bodleian Library (MS. Top. Gen. d. 14, f. 59ᵛ) there is a drawing of an elevation of a house inscribed 'Flitcroft f. 7 Feb. 1726'. This was the year in which Stukeley moved to Grantham, and it is possible that the drawing represents his architect friend's sketch for a new house there that was never built.

FLOCKTON, WILLIAM (1804–1864), of Sheffield, was the son of Thomas Flockton (1772–1818), a local builder. He designed 'THE MOUNT', GLOSSOP ROAD, SHEFFIELD, a Greek Revival terrace, for James Montgomery, the poet (then editor of the *Sheffield Iris*), *c.* 1835; the WESLEY PROPRIETARY GRAMMAR SCHOOL, SHEFFIELD, now THE KING EDWARD VII GRAMMAR SCHOOL, 1837–40; restored BAKEWELL CHURCH, DERBYSHIRE, 1841–52; and designed HOLY TRINITY CHURCH, WICKER, nr. SHEFFIELD, 1847–8, Gothic [W. Odom, *Memorials of Sheffield: its Cathedral and Parish Churches*, 1922, 134]. He also designed the consecrated part of SHEFFIELD GENERAL CEMETERY (the unconsecrated part being the responsibility of Samuel Worth), *c.* 1836 [H. Schroeder, *The Annals of Yorkshire*, Leeds 1851, ii, 42–3], and laid out the FERHAM ESTATE at ROTHERHAM for James Wheat in 1840. The original plans for the latter are in the Sheffield Public Library (Wheat Collection, 1858), where also are some of his designs (AP43) for the ECCLESALL UNION WORKHOUSE, 1842–3, Tudor Gothic, now part of the Nether Edge Hospital. The Sheffield Grammar School is an ambitious and imposing neo-classical building which shows that Flockton was an architect of some ability. His son, Thomas James Flockton (1823–99), designed a number of churches in and around Sheffield. [R. E. Leader, *Surveyors and Architects of the Past in Sheffield*, 1903; W. Odom, *Hallamshire Worthies*, Sheffield 1926, 148–9.]

FLOOKS, JOHN HARRIS, of Wilton, is listed in Pigot's *Directory* of 1830 as a 'building and land surveyor'. In the *Gardener's Magazine* for 1836 (pp. 506–7) J. C. Loudon describes the villa called THE MOUNT which Flooks had recently built for himself near Wilton, and says that he was 'very extensively employed as a land agent, surveyor, architect, landscape gardener, builder, and, in short, as an adviser in most descriptions of rural business'. In 1824 he altered or rebuilt AMESBURY PARSONAGE, WILTS. [Salisbury Diocesan Records].

FOOKES, CHARLES B—, is said to have designed the MASONIC HALL, WEYMOUTH, 1834, with a Greek Revival façade based on the 'Theseion' [R.C.H.M., *Dorset* ii (2), 340]. Fookes is listed as a 'Builder' of Weymouth in Pigot's *Directory* of 1830.

FOOTE, ROBERT, of Glasgow, is known chiefly as the architect to whom the young 'Greek' Thomson was apprenticed early in the 1830s. He was the son of a Glasgow plasterer called David Foote. According to the *A.P.S. Dictionary* he had been abroad and 'realised the beauties of Greek architecture'. Illness obliged him to retire temporarily from practice in 1838, but by 1842 he was again working from his house at The Peel, Busby. His one known work is a severe Grecian building at the corner of Exchange Place and Buchanan Street [information from Mr. David Walker].

FORBES, JOHN B—, was presumably the John Forbes who was admitted to the Royal Academy Schools in 1815 at the age of 20. In 1826 he told Rickman that he had been in David Laing's office at the time the Custom House was being built, *i.e.* 1813–16 [Rickman's diary, 9 Jan. 1826]. He subsequently established himself in Cheltenham, where he designed THE PITTVILLE PUMP ROOM for Joseph Pitt, 1825–30 [H. Davies, *Cheltenham in its Past and Present State*, 1843, 77], and ST. PAUL'S CHURCH, 1829–31 [Port, 144]. These two handsome and prominent neo-classical buildings should have inaugurated a successful architectural practice, but Forbes's career was cut short in April 1835, when he was convicted of forgery and sentenced to transportation for life. It appears that he had 'connected himself with a person of the name of Prosser in building speculations', had got into financial difficulties, and endeavoured to extricate himself by fraudulent means. 'The Jury found the unhappy man guilty, and sentence of transportation for life was pronounced in a most feeling and impressive manner by the Judge' [contemporary journal in private possession, *ex inf.* Mr. David Verey].

FORD, WILLIAM, was a pupil of D. R. Roper, from whose office he exhibited student's designs at the Royal Academy in 1810 and 1813. He subsequently practised in London, but no executed architectural work by him has so far been identified. For a time (*c.* 1825 onwards) he was in partnership with Samuel Paterson (*q.v.*). From 1823 to 1828 he was a member of the Surveyors' Club.

FORDER, GEORGE (–1864), was an architect and surveyor of Winchester until his retirement in 1861. In 1834 he became surveyor to the Dean and Chapter of Winchester in succession to William Garbett (*q.v.*). He was also surveyor to Winchester College, and in 1832 made designs for refronting the Warden's Lodgings which were rejected in favour of others by G. S. Repton [Winchester College Records, *ex inf.* Mr. J. H. Harvey]. He acted as surveyor for the rebuilding of SLAUGHTERFORD CHURCH, WILTS., in 1823 [I.C.B.S.]. He died at Winchester on 19 March 1864 [Principal Probate Registry, Calendar of Probates].

FORT, ALEXANDER (*c.* 1645–1706), was well known as a master joiner in the latter part of the seventeenth century. He was probably born *c.* 1645, for he was apprenticed to Henry Phillips, a leading London joiner, in May 1659. In 1678 he obtained the reversion of the post of Master Joiner in the Office of Works, which he duly claimed on the death of Thomas Kinward in *c.* 1685. Owing to royal displeasure, which he attributed to his employment on the Duke of Monmouth's house in Soho at the time of the latter's rebellion ('although he was no otherwise concerned than in doeing his work at the said house').[1] he did not obtain full enjoyment of the position until 1689, in which year he also took the livery of the Joiners' Company. He subsequently executed joinery work at several of the royal palaces, including Windsor, Hampton Court and Kensington.

In 1671–2 Fort was engaged in 'new modelling' the furniture in the choir of SALISBURY CATHEDRAL under the direction of Sir Christopher Wren [G. J. Eltringham, 'Alexander Fort and Salisbury Cathedral', *Wiltshire Arch. Mag.* lvii, 1958]. In 1682 he was employed by Sir Stephen Fox as 'Surveyor of building the Hospitall and house' at FARLEY, WILTS., receiving £50 'for several Modells and Journeys about the Worke' [*Wren Soc.* xix, 88]. It seems clear from this evidence that Fort should be regarded as the architect of the Farley Almshouses, and he may also have been responsible for the church built there by Fox a few years later, though documentary evidence is lacking. In 1691–2 he received £50 for measuring and valuing the carvers' and joiners' work at Chatsworth House [accounts at Chatsworth], and he made a wooden model of the design for Sir John Lowther's new house at Lowther, Westmorland, built in 1692–5 [Pearl Finch, *Burley on the Hill*, 1901, 63–4]. In 1696 he built the Ashburnham Pew (destroyed 1877) in AMPTHILL CHURCH, BEDS., for the 1st Lord Ashburnham [Rupert Gunnis, 'A Storm about a Pew', *Bedfordshire Magazine* ii, no. 15, 1950–1, 284].

Fort died impoverished in 1706, leaving a son Thomas (*q.v.*). [*Cal. Treasury Books* viii (3), 1652; *Wren Soc.* xviii, 66, and see General Index; H. L. Phillips, *Annals of the Joiners' Company*, privately printed 1915, 112.]

FORT, THOMAS (–1745), son of the above, applied unsuccessfully for his father's post as Master Joiner on his death in 1706. He said that he had been 'bredd up to Building in generall, and particularly to the Joyner's business, wherein hee was employed by his late Majesty at his

palace at Loe [Het Loo in Holland] as Master Joyner'. The Board of Works report stated that, though well qualified as a master joiner, he lacked capital 'to carry on the works of the Crown, where often the business required is sudden, and seldom ready money' [P.R.O., Works 6/14, ff. 114–15]. However, he was later given the post of Clerk of the Works at Hampton Court, which he held from 1714 until his death early in 1745. He held a similar post at Newmarket from 1719 onwards. A volume of early eighteenth-century survey drawings of Hampton Court and Newmarket Palaces in the library of the Department of the Environment can probably be attributed to Fort.

In his *Vitruvius Britannicus* ii, pl. 46, Colen Campbell gives the plan and elevation of a substantial but rather plain astylar house at SUNBURY, MIDDLESEX (dem.), 'designed and conducted by Mr. Fort, Anno 1712'. In 1717 or 1718 Fort was employed by the 1st Earl Stanhope to add the pedimented wings to the seventeenth-century central block of CHEVENING HOUSE, KENT, and is also said in a letter of 1721 to have 'designed the Figure of a Gladiator standing upon a Pedestal in the middle of the Grass Platt and Military Trophies in the Blank Windows of the Offices' [Stanhope archives at Chevening, Old Library, Shelf C]. Two chimney-pieces in the Drawing Room and Tapestry Room, copied from ones recently designed for Hampton Court by Vanbrugh, may also be attributed to Fort (*C. Life*, 17, 24 April, 1 May 1920). Between 1720 and 1723 he was employed by the 1st Duke of Chandos at CANNONS HOUSE, MIDDLESEX, both as a joiner and as a surveyor; and in 1723 he made plans for houses on the Duke's property in CASTLE STREET, BRIDGWATER, SOMERSET [C. H. & M. I. Collins Baker, *Life and Circumstances of James Brydges, Duke of Chandos*, 1949, 146–8, 222–4]. Fort's will [P.C.C. 42 SEYMER] was proved 7 Feb. 1744/5.

FOSS, JOHN (1745–1827), was the son of James and Elizabeth Foss of Richmond in the North Riding of Yorkshire. His father died when he was still a boy, and his mother then married a mason called Hawkins. Hawkins took his stepson into his business, and gave him a practical training as a mason. Although otherwise quite uneducated, Foss was an intelligent and enterprising man. To the trade of a mason and carver he soon added the skill of a self-taught architect, becoming in due course one of the leading men in the town and holding the office of Mayor in 1811 and 1822. For a time he was also Surveyor to the North Riding, but was eventually dismissed for negligence in the performance of his duties. Foss died on 18 July 1827, aged 82, leaving a son, William Foss, to continue his practice. There is a tombstone to his memory in the parish churchyard.

Foss was an able provincial architect whose

---

[1] He had also been employed at the Duke's country house at Moor Park, Herts., where in 1682/3 he was paid £786 for joinery (S.R.O., GD 224/1059/14).

principal works appear to have been country houses in the neighbourhood of Richmond. Clifton Castle, in particular, is a well-designed house, essentially of the Palladian villa type, but with up-to-date neo-classical detailing.

[Peter Wenham, article in *Ripon and Richmond Chronicle*, 19 Nov. 1955, based on a MS. memoir of Foss by James Arrowsmith.]

BROUGH HALL, YORKS. (N.R.), stables and bridge in park for Sir John Lawson, Bart., before 1790 [W. Angus, *Views of Seats*, pl. xxii, 1790].

SWINTON PARK, YORKS. (N.R.), works for William Danby, including north range 1791–6, south wing 1813–14 and upper part of Quarry Gill Bridge, completed 1822, all castellated [J. P. Neale, *Seats*, 2nd ser., iv, 1828; R. Lugar, *Villa Architecture*, 1828, pls. 24–5; John Cornforth in *C. Life*, 7, 14 and 21 April 1966].

THORPE PERROW, nr. BEDALE, YORKS. (N.R.), 'new modelled and in part rebuilt' for Mark Milbanke, *c.* 1802 [MS. memoir].

CLIFTON CASTLE, nr. MASHAM, YORKS. (N.R.), for Timothy Hutton, 1802–10 [MS. Notebook entitled 'Records and Memoranda, Clifton' in possession of Mrs. Curzon-Howe-Herrick, 1968: 'The Architect of the house was Mr. John Foss'].

SEDBURY PARK, YORKS. (N.R.), rustic tower for Sir Robert Darcy Hildyard [MS. memoir].

FOSTER, JAMES (*c.* 1748–1823), of Bristol, was the pupil and apprentice of Thomas Paty (*q.v.*). Like Paty, he combined architectural practice with the business of a statuary mason, executing (to quote his own advertisement) 'monuments and chimney-pieces in marble with peculiar grace and elegance'. Early in the nineteenth century he was joined by his son and namesake James Foster, junior (d. 1836). From this time onwards the firm's practice appears to have become exclusively architectural in character. In 1820 James Foster & Son were at No. 10 Culver Street, while No. 24 Orchard Street was the address of Thomas Foster, architect, who had become a freeman of Bristol in 1818 on his marriage to a freeman's daughter. He was evidently another son of the elder Foster, for it was 'at the residence of his son, Orchard Street, Bristol', that James Foster died on 1 November 1823, aged 75. James Foster, junior, then joined in practice with his brother at 13 Orchard Street. By 1828 the firm was called 'Foster and Okely', James and Thomas having taken as a third partner the latter's pupil William Ignatius Okely. James Foster, junior, held office as one of the district surveyors for the City of Bristol from 1819 until his death on 5 January 1836. Soon after 1840 Okely left the firm, his place as Thomas Foster's partner being taken by the latter's son John. Thomas died on

6 July 1849, aged 56, leaving the practice to be continued by John Foster (d. 1902) and his partner John Wood.

Clifton Church, the principal independent work of the elder Foster, was designed in a thin Georgian Gothic style comparable to Paty's St. Nicholas, Bristol. Foster & Sons subsequently produced a number of routine early nineteenth-century Gothic (and a few neo-Norman) churches. Foster and Okely were responsible for the competent Greek Revival architecture of the Upper and Lower Arcades, and for the excellent terrace-houses of Clifton Vale, Caledonia Place and the New Mall. In 1835 they competed for the Houses of Parliament, submitting a design in the 'late Gothic style', with a 'castellated effect in the river front'. The works of Foster and Wood fall outside the limits of this *Dictionary*, but according to the *Architects, Engineers and Building Trades Directory* of 1868 they included the Orphan Houses at Ashleydown, the Bristol Athenaeum, the Colston Hall, Foster's and Trinity Almshouses, and the Bristol City Hotel.

[*Gent's Mag.* 1824 (i), 93, 1849 (ii), 219; A. B. Beaven, *Bristol Lists*, 1899, 249; C. F. Dening, *The Eighteenth Century Architecture of Bristol*, 1923, 139; W. Ison, *The Georgian Buildings of Bristol*, 1952, 34.]

ABERGWILI PALACE, nr. CARMARTHEN, remodelled for the Bishop of St. David's, *c.* 1803 onwards [*A.P.S.D., s.v.* 'David's, St.'].

MANGOTSFIELD CHURCH, GLOS., altered and repaired, 1812 [*Bath Chronicle*, 15 Oct. 1812].

BRISTOL, ST. ANDREW'S CHURCH, CLIFTON, 1819–22, Gothic; bombed 1941 and dem. 1954 [W. Ison, *op. cit.*, 29].

KINGSWOOD, nr. BRISTOL, GLOS., HOLY TRINITY CHURCH, 1819–21, Gothic: by 'J. Foster & Sons' [G.R.].

STAPLETON CHURCH, GLOS., 1820–1, Gothic: by 'James Foster & Sons'; rebuilt 1856 [I.C.B.S.].

BRISTOL, THE UPPER and LOWER ARCADES, 1824–5: by 'Foster & Okely' [*A.P.S.D., s.v.* 'Bristol'].

SHIREHAMPTON CHURCH, GLOS., 1827, Gothic: by 'Foster & Okely'; rebuilt 1929 [I.C.B.S.].

OLDLAND CHURCH, GLOS., 1829–30, Gothic: by 'Foster & Okely' [I.C.B.S.].

BEACHLEY CHURCH, GLOS., 1833, Gothic: by 'Foster & Okely' [I.C.B.S.].

MUCH BIRCH CHURCH, HEREFS., 1837, Gothic: by 'Foster & Okely' [I.C.B.S.].

STROUD, GLOS., HOLY TRINITY CHURCH, STROUDS-HILL, 1838–9, Gothic: by Thomas Foster [brass plaque in church].

STROUD, GLOS., ST. PAUL'S CHURCH, WHITESHILL, 1839–41, neo-Norman: by Thomas Foster [Port, 144].

BRISTOL, CLIFTON VALE, CALEDONIA PLACE and

NEW MALL, CLIFTON, c. 1840–3: by Foster & Okely [W. Ison, *op. cit.*, 237–8].

CARDIFF, ST. MARY'S CHURCH, BUTE STREET, 1841–3, neo-Norman: by Thomas Foster [Port, 172].

HANHAM CHURCH, GLOS., 1842, Gothic: by 'Foster & Son' [*Gent's Mag.* 1843 (i), 75].

See p. 986 MINCHINHAMPTON CHURCH, GLOS., rebuilt nave and chancel, 1842, Gothic: by Thomas Foster [*Gent's Mag.* 1842 (ii), 81; H. E. Relton, *Sketches of Churches*, 1883; drawing in R.I.B.A. Coll.].

BRISTOL, THE RED MAIDS' SCHOOL, 1844: by 'Foster & Son'; dem. 1951 [*A.P.S.D., s.v.* 'Bristol'].

BRISTOL, QUEEN ELIZABETH'S HOSPITAL SCHOOL, BERKELEY PLACE, 1845–7, Tudor: by 'Foster & Son' [*Companion to the Almanac*, 1845, 241–2].

FOSTER, JOHN (c. 1759–1827), was for many years a dominant figure in the architectural affairs of Liverpool. His father, John Foster (c. 1730–1801), was a joiner and builder, and he himself continued the joinery business while also practising as an architect. In or about 1790 he took the place of Charles Eyes (*q.v.*) as surveyor to the Corporation, a post which he retained for over thirty years, receiving a salary of £500 a year, with liberty to remain in business as a builder. A contemporary described him as 'a very strong and influential character' who 'set about getting control of the Corporation affairs for himself and his family'. Another remembered him as 'the most influential as well as ... the cleverest man of his day ... who, although not a member of the Council himself, possessed a strange power over its decisions and judgements, and brought to his friends the aid of as much commonsense and as strong an intellect as ever was possessed by any individual'. He was surveyor to the docks as well as to the Corporation, and as his eldest son Thomas (d. 1836) became town clerk in 1832, while his second son John (*q.v.*) succeeded him as municipal architect, it can readily be appreciated that, in Picton's words, the Foster family 'managed the architectural and building affairs of the corporation' before the Municipal Reform Act of 1835 deprived them at once of their offices and of their influence.

The elder Foster designed several public buildings in an elegant late Georgian style comparable to that of James Wyatt, with whom he came into contact over the Exchange (now the Town Hall). In 1787 he was instructed to prepare designs for the building which were to be submitted to some eminent architect in London for his opinion. The architect chosen was James Wyatt, who eventually supplied new designs which were carried out by Foster. In 1795 the interior was destroyed by fire and rebuilt by

Foster under Wyatt's direction. Wyatt may also have had some hand in the New Exchange, a large and important neo-classical building erected by Foster in 1803–9, but demolished in the 1860s. Few of Foster's private commissions have been recorded, but according to a writer in the *Monthly Mirror* for July 1803, it was to his 'taste and ability' that Liverpool was indebted 'for most of our well-built houses all over the town'.

Foster retired in 1824 and died at Newington (Liverpool) on 27 April 1827, in his 69th year. [*A.P.S.D.*; J. A. Picton, *Memorials of Liverpool* i, 1875, 230; *Liverpool a Few Years since*, by an Old Stager, 1852, 33, 104–5; *Trans. Lancs. and Cheshire Hist. Soc.* lxii, 1910, 155; J. Touzeau, *The Rise and Progress of Liverpool* ii, 1910, 714; *Parliamentary Papers*, 1835, xxvi, 2708; obituary notices in Gore's *Liverpool Advertiser* and *Liverpool Mercury*; Liverpool City Library, Underhill MSS. Biography, vol. iii, 94–5 and Treasurer's accounts.]

LIVERPOOL

THE DISPENSARY, CHURCH STREET, 1781; dem. 1830 [Picton, *Memorials* ii, 163].

THE BOROUGH GAOL, GREAT HOWARD STREET, 1786 [*Gent's Mag.* 1813 (ii), 332].

THE EXCHANGE (now TOWN HALL), enlarged by Foster to designs of James Wyatt, 1789–92; rebuilt interior after fire of 1795, completed 1797; dome and cupola added 1802, portico 1811 [J. A. Picton, *Liverpool Municipal Records 1700–1835*, 1886, 265–72] (*C. Life*, 23 July 1927).

THE ATHENAEUM, completed 1799; dem. [G. Richardson, *New Vitruvius Britannicus* ii, 1808, pls. 43–4].

THE UNION NEWSROOM (corner of Duke and Slater Streets), 1800 [Picton, *Memorials* ii, 269–70].

THE THEATRE ROYAL, WILLIAMSON SQUARE, enlarged 1802–3; dem. c. 1965 [*Monthly Mirror*, July 1803, commending the skill of 'Mr. Foster, the architect'].

THE NEW EXCHANGE, 1803–9; dem. c. 1863 [Picton, *Architectural History of Liverpool*, 1858, 11, where Wyatt's share in the design is left in doubt].[1]

THE CORN EXCHANGE, 1807; rebuilt 1851 [*Lancashire Illustrated*, 1831, 15].

ST. LUKE'S CHURCH, begun for the Corporation in 1811 from designs made by Foster in 1802, but left unfinished until 1826–31, when it was completed by his son, who in 1827 proposed some alterations 'in the plans of the interior and exterior', Gothic; gutted 1940–1 [Picton,

---

[1] In 1819 a correspondent told Soane that the Exchange was 'partly by Mr. Harrison' [F. Copland to Soane, 3 Sept. 1819, incorrectly printed by Bolton, *Portrait of Soane*, 288].

Memorials ii, 242–3; *Liverpool Municipal Records 1700–1835*, 396–7].[1]

LEASOWE CASTLE, CHESHIRE, enlarged for Mrs. Boode, 1818 [W. W. Mortimer, *Hundred of Wirral*, 1847, 295].

FOSTER, JOHN (*c.* 1787–1846), second son of the above, was a pupil of Jeffry, and also, according to some accounts, of James Wyatt. He exhibited at the Royal Academy from the former's office in Lower Brook Street in the years 1804–6. In 1809 he went abroad, and spent some time in Greece in company with Haller, Linckh and C. R. Cockerell, taking part in the excavations at Ægina and Phigaleia. Cockerell described him in his journal as 'a most amusing youth, but too idle to be anything more than a dinner companion'. He returned to England in 1816 and entered into partnership with his brother in the family building business. From this he withdrew in 1824, when he succeeded his father as architect and surveyor to the Corporation, at a salary of £1000 per annum. This post he held until 1835, when, on the reform of the Corporation, he lost his office and retired on a pension of £500 a year. He designed many important public buildings in Liverpool, mainly in a scholarly Greek Revival style comparable to Smirke's in London. His greatest work was the Custom House, an imposing Ionic building whose dome and portico were one of the architectural landmarks of Liverpool until their destruction in World War II. His St. John's Market was the first large-scale covered market in England. Few of his buildings survive, but contemporary engravings of many of them will be found in *Lancashire Illustrated* (1831) or *The Stranger in Liverpool* (11th. ed. 1837).

Foster became a member of the Liverpool Academy of Arts in 1810, and was its President from 1822 to 1841. He was a Fellow of the Society of Antiquaries. In 1831 he had a house at Norris Green, West Derby, but at the time of his death he was living in Hamilton Square, Birkenhead. He died on 21 August 1846, aged 59, and was buried in the St. James's Cemetery in Liverpool which he had designed. A collection of his drawings of antique architecture in Greece and Asia Minor is in the Walker Art Gallery, Liverpool.

[*A.P.S.D.*; J. A. Picton, *Memorials of Liverpool* i, 1875, 470; Peter Fleetwood-Hesketh,

Murray's *Lancashire Architectural Guide*, 1955, 88–9; Liverpool City Library, Underhill MSS. Biography, vol. iii, 94–5, and Liverpool Epitaphs, vol. vi, p. 13.]

LIVERPOOL

ST. MICHAEL'S CHURCH, PITT STREET, 1816–26; dem. 1941 [*A.P.S.D.*].
ST. MARY'S CHURCH FOR THE INDIGENT BLIND, HOTHAM STREET, 1818–19; taken down in 1850 and re-erected in Hardman Street by A. H. Holme; dem. *c.* 1935 [*A.P.S.D.*].
ST. GEORGE'S CHURCH, rebuilt 1819–25; dem. 1897 [*A.P.S.D.*].
ST. JOHN'S MARKET, 1820–22; dem. *c.* 1965 [*A.P.S.D.*; *Architectural Mag.* ii, 129; *Gent's Mag.* 1822 (ii), 113–14].
THE ROYAL INFIRMARY, BROWNLOW STREET, 1822–4; dem. [*A.P.S.D.*].
ST. ANDREW'S SCOTTISH CHURCH, RODNEY STREET, 1823–4 [J. A. Picton, *Memorials of Liverpool* ii, 1875, 245].
THE NECROPOLIS CEMETERY, CHAPEL, ENTRANCE, etc., 1823–4 [*The Stranger in Liverpool*, 11th ed. 1837, 163; J. A. Picton, *Memorials of Liverpool* ii, 1875, 369].
LORD STREET and ST. GEORGE'S CRESCENT, street architecture, 1825–7; dem. 1940–1 [*A.P.S.D.*].
ST. MARTIN'S CHURCH, OXFORD STREET NORTH, 1825–8, Gothic; dem. [Port, 132].
ST. DAVID'S WELSH CHURCH, BROWNLOW HILL, 1826–7; dem. [J. A. Picton, *Memorials of Liverpool* ii, 1875, 214].
PUBLIC BATHS, ST. GEORGE'S DOCK, 1826–9; dem. [*A.P.S.D.*].
THE ROCK LIGHTHOUSE, 1827–30 [*Lancashire Illustrated*, 1831, 83].
THE LUNATIC ASYLUM, BROWNLOW HILL, 1828–30; dem. [*The Stranger in Liverpool*, 11th ed. 1837, 74].
THE CUSTOM HOUSE, 1828–35; bombed 1940–1 and dem. [J. H. Rideout, *The Custom House, Liverpool*, 1928; original drawings in P.R.O., Works 30/155–7].
AINTREE RACECOURSE, THE GRANDSTAND, 1829 [*A.P.S.D.*, *s.v.* 'Grandstand'].
ST. JAMES'S CEMETERY, CHAPEL and layout, 1827–9 [*The Stranger in Liverpool*, 11th ed. 1837, 35].
ST. CATHERINE'S CHURCH, ABERCROMBIE SQUARE, 1829–31; bombed 1940–1 and dem. *c.* 1965. [*The Stranger in Liverpool*, 11th ed. 1837, 61–2].
LIVERPOOL & MANCHESTER RAILWAY, Moorish arch connecting engine-houses, 1831; dem. [*A.P.S.D.*].
LIME STREET RAILWAY STATION (Liverpool & Manchester Railway), screen-wall to street, 1835–6; dem. [*A.P.S.D.*].

---

[1] In his *Architectural History of Liverpool* Picton reported that although the design was 'nominally that of Mr. John Foster', the latter knew little about Gothic architecture and 'common report ... ascribes the design to his assistant Mr. Edwards'. A drawing of the church was exhibited at the Liverpool Academy by Foster in 1813, but Thomas Rickman was told that it was 'Gandy's sent in in Foster's name' (Diary, 4 July 1813).

ST. JAMES'S CEMETERY, circular temple (with statue by John Gibson) in memory of William Huskisson, 1834 [*Architectural Mag.* iv, 77–8] (T. S. R. Boase, *English Art 1800–1870*, 1959, pl. 51).

ELSEWHERE

KNOWSLEY HALL, LANCS., alterations and castellated additions for the 12th Earl of Derby, *c.* 1820 [J. P. Neale, *Seats*, 2nd. ser., i, 1824].

BANGOR CATHEDRAL, alterations to interior, 1825–8; removed 1868 [M. L. Clarke, 'Bangor Cathedral, 1700–1828', *Caernarvonshire Historical Soc.'s Trans.* xiii, 1952, 33].

GARSWOOD NEW HALL, ASHTON-IN-MAKERFIELD, LANCS., for Sir John Gerard, Bart., 1826; dem. *c.* 1920 [Twycross, *Mansions of England: Lancs.* iii, 1847, 24].

BOLLINGTON, CHESHIRE, ST. GREGORY'S CHURCH (R.C.), 1834; dem. [*Catholic Magazine* v, 1834, p. lxiv].

FOTHERGILL, RICHARD (1789–1851), amateur architect, was the son of Richard Fothergill of Lowbridge House, Selside, Westmorland, and of Caerleon, Monmouthshire [see Burke's *Landed Gentry*, 8th ed. 1894]. In 1837 he moved from Caerleon to Lowbridge, where he built a new house for himself, and in 1838 a new Gothic church was built to his designs at SELSIDE. His drawings and correspondence are in the I.C.B.S. records.

FOULON, JOHN (*c.* 1794–*c.* 1882), obtained his training as a clerk in the office of John Nash. After travelling abroad, he became architect to Meux's Brewery. He designed the MINERVA INSURANCE OFFICE, CANNON STREET, LONDON, 1852, dem. 1944, and worked for the banking firm of Mills. Towards the end of his life he was dependent on charity. The records of the Distressed Architects Fund established by Sir John Soane show that he was still alive in 1881 at the age of 87 [information from Sir John Summerson].

FOULSTON, JOHN (1772–1842), was a pupil of Thomas Hardwick. He commenced practice in 1796 from St. Alban's Place, Pall Mall, but what (if anything) was built to his designs at this stage of his career is unknown. In 1803 he won the second award of 150 guineas in the competition for the conversion of the Houses of Parliament at Dublin into the Bank of Ireland, and in the following year exhibited his design at the Royal Academy. In 1811 he won the competition for a group of buildings in Plymouth, comprising the Royal Hotel, Assembly Rooms, and Theatre. His design was remarkable both for the extensive use of cast iron in the 'fire-proof' theatre, and for the way in which he combined three distinct buildings into a single architectural composition. His success in obtaining this important commission established his local fame: and taking up residence in Plymouth, he remained for twenty-five years the leading architect of the neighbourhood, which he did much to transform, both by new public buildings and by well-designed street architecture. Most of his work was in the classical style of the Regency 'improvements' in London, with Greek orders accentuating stucco terraces, but at Devonport he indulged in a flight of eclectic fancy by combining in one picturesque group an 'Egyptian' library, a 'Hindoo' nonconformist chapel, a 'primitive Doric' town hall, and a street of houses dressed with an orthodox Roman Corinthian order. The influence of Soane is strongly apparent in several of his buildings, notably in the façade of St. Andrew's Chapel and the interior of the Proprietary Library, with its segmental arches supporting a circular clerestory of windows.

Towards the end of his career Foulston was for a short time in partnership with George Wightwick, who succeeded to his practice, and who wrote an amusing account of his colleague in retirement. He 'lived a pleasing amateur life for some years, decorating his pretty cottage and grounds in the suburb, and seeking to rival, in little, the famed falls of Niagara, by an artistic spreading of the Plymouth watercourse, or leet, over some yards of spa and rockwork, greatly enhancing the beauty of his shrubbery ... The vehicle which served him as a gig ... was built in the form of an antique *biga*, or war-chariot; with a seat furtively smuggled into the service of comfort, though he ascended it from behind with true classical orthodoxy and looked (as far as his true English face and costume allowed) like Ictinus of the Parthenon, "out for a lark" ...' It was during his retirement that Foulston published *The Public Buildings erected in the West of England, as designed by J. Foulston, F.R.I.B.A.*, 1838, with 117 lithographic plates and a portrait. He also made a set of 19 water-colour drawings of his buildings which is now in the City Art Gallery at Plymouth. He died on 13 January 1842, aged 69, and was buried in St. Andrew's New Cemetery. M. A. Nicholson, E. W. Gribble and T. J. Ricauti were his pupils.

[*A.P.S.D.* (memoir by Wightwick); *Civil Engineer and Architect's Jnl.* v, 1842, 68; A. E. Richardson & C. L. Gill, *Regional Architecture of the West of England*, 1924, 67–73; Frank Jenkins, 'John Foulston and his Public Buildings in Plymouth, Stonehouse, and Devonport', *Journal of the Society of Architectural Historians* (of America), xxvii, 1968; J. W. Dawe, 'John Foulston', *Proceedings of the Plymouth Athenaeum* ii, 1971; J. Mordaunt Crook, 'Regency Architecture in the West Country', *Journal of the Royal Society of Arts* cxix, 1971, 438–51; F. G. Hall &

others, *The Bank of Ireland*, 1949, 460; George Wightwick, *Nettleton's Guide to Plymouth, Stonehouse, Devonport and to the Neighbouring Country*, 1836.]

PUBLIC BUILDINGS, ETC., IN PLYMOUTH AND DEVONPORT

ROYAL HOTEL, ASSEMBLY ROOMS, and THEATRE, 1811–13, east wing completed 1822; dem. 1939–41 [*Public Buildings*, pls. 3–47] (Richardson & Gill, *op. cit.*, 66, 69).

THE PUBLIC or PROPRIETARY LIBRARY, 1812; enlarged and refronted by G. Wightwick as the Plymouth and Cottonian Libraries 1850; destroyed by bombing 1941 [*Public Buildings*, pls. 54–8] (Richardson & Gill, *op. cit.*, 68–9).

THE EXCHANGE, 1813 (based on plans made by Foulston, but not carried out under his direction); dem. [*Public Buildings*, pls. 76–9].

THE ATHENAEUM, 1818–19; destroyed by bombing 1941 [*Public Buildings*, pls. 48–53].

PRINCESS SQUARE, completed 1821; destroyed by bombing 1941 [G. Wightwick, *Nettleton's Guide*, 1836, 14].

THE TOWN HALL, DEVONPORT, 1821–3 [*Public Buildings*, pls. 81–4].

ST. ANDREW'S CHAPEL (afterwards St. Catherine's Church), 1823; dem. 1958 [*Public Buildings*, pls. 59–66].

THE CIVIL AND MILITARY (or PUBLIC) LIBRARY (now Oddfellows' Hall), DEVONPORT, 1823, Egyptian style [*Public Buildings*, pls. 90–4].

MOUNT ZION BAPTIST CHAPEL, DEVONPORT, 1823–4, Indian style; dem. *c.* 1925 [*Public Buildings*, pls. 95–8].

THE COLUMN, DEVONPORT, 1824 [*Public Buildings*, pls. 85–9].

ST. ANDREW'S CHURCH, altered and refitted 1826, Gothic; 'restored' by Gilbert Scott 1874–5; gutted 1941 [*Public Buildings*, pls. 67–74].

ST. PAUL'S CHAPEL, DURNFORD STREET, STONEHOUSE, 1830–1, Gothic; chancel added 1891 [*Public Buildings*, pl. 99].

OTHER WORKS

ATHENIAN COTTAGE, TOWNSEND HILL, PLYMOUTH, for himself, *c.* 1813; dem. [J. C. Loudon, *Gardener's Mag*, xviii, 1842, 543] (*Proceedings of the Plymouth Athenaeum* i, 1967, 20).

BODMIN, CORNWALL COUNTY LUNATIC ASYLUM, 1818; enlarged 1842, 1847–8 and 1867 [*Public Buildings*, pls. 104–11].

SALTRAM HOUSE, DEVON, alterations, including addition of Doric porch and formation of library, for the 1st Earl of Morley, 1818 [Britton & Brayley, *Devonshire Illustrated*, 1832, 52; National Trust, *Saltram*, 1967, 6] (*C. Life*, 27 April, 4–11 May, 14 Sept. 1967).

ST. ERME CHURCH, CORNWALL, rebuilt except west tower, 1819–20, Gothic [inscription in church].

ST. MICHAEL'S TERRACE, STOKE DAMAREL, *c.* 1825 [*A.P.S.D.*; Britton & Brayley, *Devonshire Illustrated*, 1832, 84].

ALBEMARLE VILLAS, STOKE DAMAREL, *c.* 1825 [Britton & Brayley, *Devonshire Illustrated*, 1832, 84].

BELMONT HOUSE, STOKE DAMAREL, for John Norman, *c.* 1825 [G. Wightwick, *Nettleton's Guide*, 1836, 89] (R. Ackermann, *Views of Country Seats* ii, 1830, 123).

TAVISTOCK, DEVON, THE BEDFORD ARMS INN, *c.* 1825; Gothic [Britton & Brayley, *Devonshire Illustrated*, 1832, 48; cf. *Public Buildings*, pl. 103].

WARLEIGH HOUSE, TAMERTON FOLIOT, DEVON, alterations for the Rev. Walter Radcliffe, 1825–32, Gothic [signed receipt for drawings dated 1825, at Warleigh House, *ex. inf.* Mr. Peter Reid].

TAVISTOCK, DEVON, restoration of ABBEY GATEWAY, 1829, Gothic [*Public Buildings*, pls. 101–3, showing unexecuted design for interior].

TORQUAY, THE PUBLIC BALLROOM (adjoining the Royal Hotel), 1830; dem. [*Public Buildings*, pl. 100].

TRAVERS HOUSE, STOKE DAMAREL, for R. Bromley [G. Wightwick, *Nettleton's Guide*, 1836, 89].

PARK WOOD HOUSE, nr. TAVISTOCK, DEVON [G. Wightwick, *Nettleton's Guide*, 1836, 157–8].

FOUNTAINE, Sir ANDREW (1676–1753), of Narford in Norfolk, was a well-known virtuoso and to some extent an amateur architect. He was educated at Christ Church, Oxford, under Dean Aldrich, was knighted by William III in 1699, and succeeded to the estate at Narford on his father's death in 1706. He was later Vicechamberlain to Caroline, Princess of Wales, tutor to her son William, Duke of Cumberland, and Master of the Mint. His collection of pictures, books, china and coins was celebrated [*D.N.B.*].

In his *Essay in Defence of Ancient Architecture* (1728), Robert Morris calls Fountaine a 'practitioner of architecture' and couples his name with those of Lords Burlington and Pembroke. William Halfpenny also compliments him on his knowledge of architecture in the dedication of his *Art of Sound Building*. Narford Hall had been built by Fountaine's father in about 1700, but George Vertue, who visited the house in 1739, noted that the gardens were laid out in 'the best manner, wholly I believe by his own direction' [Walpole Soc., *Vertue* v, 120]. Colen Campbell, giving a plan of the garden in *Vitruvius Britannicus* iii, 1725, pl. 95, illustrates an Ionic temple and an ornamental deer-house and states that Fountaine 'has given Marks of his good Taste and Affection for Architecture, in several Pieces lately erected there'. Horace Walpole records

319

that he designed 'a large ugly room ... 36 feet long, 24 high, & 24 wide' for Sir Matthew Decker at his house on Richmond Green, Surrey ['Visits to Country Seats', *Walpole Soc.* xvi, 40].

FOWLER, CHARLES (1792–1867), was born at Cullompton in Devonshire, where his family had lived for several generations. At the age of 15 he was articled to John Powning, an architect and builder of Exeter. On the completion of his apprenticeship in 1814 he left Exeter for London to work as an assistant in the office of David Laing. He began independent practice in 1818. His success in 1822 in obtaining the first premium in the competition for rebuilding London Bridge ended in disappointment, for his designs were eventually set aside in favour of Rennie's. However, by 1830 he had become well known as a result of two recent works: Covent Garden Market and the great glazed conservatory at Syon House. The former established his reputation as the leading designer of covered markets, while the latter demonstrated his mastery of construction in cast iron. The structural refinement of his Hungerford Market, London, and Lower Market, Exeter, was matched by an appropriately simplified classical style derived from French neo-classical architects such as Durand. It is these buildings which give Fowler the distinction of being one of the few nineteenth-century architects who, like the engineers Telford and Rennie, were able to handle structure and form with equal assurance. Fowler maintained his connection with his native county of Devon, where he designed several churches, and had an influential patron in the 10th Earl of Devon, for whom he remodelled the exterior of Powderham Castle. It was the Earl who was instrumental in obtaining for him the commission for the London Fever Hospital in 1848.

Fowler was closely involved in the establishment of the Institute of British Architects in 1835. For over seven years he was one of its two Honorary Secretaries and in 1850–1 was elected a Vice-President. He contributed several papers to its *Transactions*, as well as to Loudon's *Architectural Magazine*. In addition he published a *Description of the plan for the revival of Hungerford Market, with some particulars of the buildings proposed to be erected* (1829). Many of his designs were exhibited at the Royal Academy.

In 1852 Fowler gave up practice because of ill-health and retired first to Wrotham and then to Western House, Great Marlow, Bucks., where he died on 7 September 1867. His son Charles Fowler practised in London, where he became District Surveyor for the parishes of St. Giles-in-the-Fields and St. George, Bloomsbury. Henry Roberts and J. M. Allen (1809–83) of Crewkerne were his pupils. His drawings for the Hungerford Market are in the R.I.B.A. Collec-

tion. What appears to be his winning design for London Bridge is in the Guildhall Record Office. A design in the P.R.O. (C 108/322) for a coach-house in Duke Street, Westminster, for William Courtenay, M.P., dated 1818, shows that his connection with the Earl of Devon's family went back to the early years of his practice.

[Obituaries in *Builder* xxv, 1867, 761, and *R.I.B.A. Trans.* xviii, 1867–8; Jeremy Taylor, 'Charles Fowler, Master of Markets', *Arch. Rev.*, March 1964, and 'Charles Fowler: a centenary memoir', *Architectural History* xi, 1968.]

LONDON, COURTS OF BANKRUPTCY, BASINGHALL STREET, 1818–21; dem. [*Builder* xxv, 1867, 761].

GRAVESEND, KENT, THE NEW MARKET, 1818–22; dem. [R. P. Cruden, *History of Gravesend*, 1843, 490].

TEFONT EWYAS CHURCH, WILTS., rebuilt 1824–6, Gothic [I.C.B.S.].

TOTNES BRIDGE (R. Dart), DEVON, 1826–8 [signed].

LONDON, ST. PAUL'S CHURCH, KILBURN, 1826; remodelled *c.* 1890, dem. 1934 [G.R.; *R.I.B.A. Trans.* xviii, 1867].

SYON HOUSE, ISLEWORTH, MIDDLESEX, conservatory for the 3rd Duke of Northumberland, 1827–30 [J. C. Loudon, *Encyclopaedia of Cottage, Farm and Villa Architecture*, 2nd ed. 1846, 979].

LONDON, COVENT GARDEN MARKET, for the 6th Duke of Bedford, 1828–30 [J. C. Loudon in *Gardener's Mag.* vii, 1831, 265–77, and *Architectural Mag.* v, 1838, 665–77].

EXETER, NO. 14 THE CLOSE (formerly Archdeaconry of Cornwall), for the Dean and Chapter of Exeter, 1829–30, Tudor Gothic [Exeter Diocesan Records, 1190].

LONDON, ST. JOHN'S CHURCH, OXFORD SQUARE, PADDINGTON, 1829–31, Gothic [W. Robins, *Paddington Past and Present*, 1853, 144–5].

LONDON, HUNGERFORD MARKET, 1831–33; dem. 1862 to make way for Charing Cross Railway Station [drawings in R.I.B.A. Coll.; described in Loudon's *Architectural Mag.* i, 1834, 53–62, L. Förster's *Allgemein Bauzeitung*, 1838–9, and (by Fowler himself) in *R.I.B.A. Trans.* xiii, 1862, 54–7].

'VILLA in the Old English Manner', executed before 1833, but unidentified [J. C. Loudon, *Encyclopaedia of Cottage, Farm and Villa Architecture* ii, 1833, 846–50, 2nd ed. 1846, 846–50].

TAVISTOCK, DEVON, THE CORN MARKET, for the 6th Duke of Bedford, 1835 [*Builder* xxv, 1867, 761].

EXETER, THE LOWER MARKET, 1835–7; dem. 1942 [*Builder* xxv, 1867, 761] (A. E. Richardson & C. L. Gill, *Regional Architecture of the West of England*, 1924, 39–40).

EXETER, THE HIGHER MARKET, supervised construction to the designs of George Dymond, after the latter's death, 1835–8 [J. C. Loudon, *Architectural Mag.* i, 1834, 352, and iii, 1836, 12].

CHARMOUTH CHURCH, DORSET, rebuilt 1835–6, Gothic [J. C. Loudon, *Architectural Mag.* v, 1838, 509–10].

POWDERHAM CASTLE, DEVON, castellated alterations and additions for the 10th Earl of Devon, probably begun 1837 (date on rainwater-heads), but not completed until 1848, when Fowler exhibited his design for the entrance at the R.A. Loudon reported in 1842 that the castle was 'being altered by Mr. Fowler' [*Gardener's Mag.* xviii, 1842, 532] (*C. Life*, 4, 11 and 18 July 1963).

HONITON CHURCH, DEVON, 1837–8, Norman style [*Builder* xxv, 1867, 761; *Gent's Mag.* 1842 (ii), 410].

HAINES HILL, BERKS., stables and coach-house for Capt. Garth, R.N., 1838 [signed drawings at Haines Hill].

BICKLEIGH CHURCH, DEVON, rebuilt (except tower) for Sir Ralph Lopes, Bart., 1838, Gothic; altered by J. D. Sedding, 1882 [*Builder* xxv, 1867, 761].

MARISTOW HOUSE, DEVON, lodges for Sir Ralph Lopes, Bart., c. 1839 [exhib. at R.A. 1839].

COFTON CHAPEL, nr. DAWLISH, DEVON, rebuilt 1838–9 for the 10th Earl of Devon, Gothic [W. G. Hoskins, *Devon*, 1954, 387].

EXETER, DEVON COUNTY LUNATIC ASYLUM, 1842–5 [*Builder* iv, 1846, 349; *Companion to the Almanac*, 1849, 239–40; plan in M. Parchappe, *Asiles d'Aliénés*, Paris, 1853, 234].

LONDON, sale-room at 16 ST. PAUL'S CHURCHYARD for Mr. Toplis, 1846; dem. [*Builder* iv, 1846, 91].

THE LONDON FEVER HOSPITAL, ISLINGTON, 1848–52 [*Builder* xxv, 1867, 761].

LONDON, WAX CHANDLERS' HALL, 13 GRESHAM STREET WEST, 1852–5; dem. 1940 [*Builder* xxv, 1867, 761] (*Builder* cxii, 1917, 413).

FOWLER, WILLIAM (1761–1832), was born at Winterton, nr. Brigg in Lincolnshire, and lived there all his life. He was 'brought up to the business of a master builder and architect', and had a considerable local practice as a builder of farm-houses, parsonages and the like. He is best known, however, as one of the greatest antiquarian artists of his time. His first drawing, a Roman pavement, was made in 1796, and three great albums of coloured engravings were published by subscription in 1804, 1809 and 1824. His principal subjects were Roman pavements and medieval glass, in whose representation he showed great skill. All the time which he could spare from his business was devoted to his antiquarian pursuits, and his children assisted him by colouring the engravings which he had

learned to execute himself. He was a member of the Wesleyan connection, but remained a regular churchgoer, and had many clergymen among his patrons and clients. He spent the last years of his life in the 'Gothic Cottage' which he built for himself in West Street, Winterton, in 1827–8. Joseph Fowler (1791–1882), his eldest son, was sent to Oxford in 1812 to become a pupil of John Plowman, but did not remain owing to an illness. He took charge of the business during his father's latter years, but gradually gave it up after his marriage in 1828.

The Correspondence of William Fowler was edited and privately printed by his grandson in 1907. The works mentioned in it include repairs or alterations to the churches of MANTON, 1809, APPLEBY, 1820–3, WINTERINGHAM, 1827, and ADLINGFLEET, 1828; works at CLEATHAM HALL (coach-house, etc., 1802), NORMANBY PARK, 1815–17, LEADENHAM RECTORY, 1821–3, APPLEBY HALL, 1821–3 and 1827, GATE BURTON HALL, 1824–7, CAYTHORPE VICARAGE, 1827, and CAENBY HALL (billiard-room 1829); alterations for Archdeacon H. V. Bayley at the SUBDEANERY, LINCOLN, and at his VICARAGE at MESSINGHAM, 1813–18; a NATIONAL SCHOOL at NEWARK, NOTTS., 1826, and a LIBRARY and READING-ROOM in the Market Place at the same town, 1826–7.

FOXHALL, EDWARD MARTIN (1793–1862), was the son of Edward Foxhall, a carver and furniture-maker who was among Sir John Soane's oldest friends. He entered Soane's office in 1812, and remained there until January 1821. He drew many of the diagrams used to illustrate Soane's lectures, and Soane left him £100 in his will, besides making him his residuary legatee. He became District Surveyor to the parish of St. George Hanover Square in 1825, and was also surveyor to the London estates of Sir John Sutton, Bart., and the Duke of Norfolk. 'His practice was principally confined to the appointments he held', and the only buildings which he is known to have designed are a Roman Catholic chapel at Southampton, another in Romney Terrace, Horseferry Road, Westminster (1853, dem. c. 1903), and the premises at the corner of Bond and Conduit Streets (dem.). He was a member of the Institute of British Architects. [Obituary in *Builder*, 3 Jan. 1863, 8; A. T. Bolton, *The Portrait of Sir John Soane*, 55, 431–2; *The Tablet*, 25 Dec. 1853, 819.]

FRANKLIN, JOSEPH (c. 1785–1855), was a native of Stroud in Gloucestershire, and probably a son of Joseph Franklin, who had a business as a monumental mason there at the end of the eighteenth century. Nothing is known of his career before 1835, when he became Surveyor to the Corporation of Liverpool. He retired in 1848, and died on 12 September 1855, aged 70. He is commemorated by a tablet in the Congregational Church at Stroud.

In LIVERPOOL Franklin designed the CRESCENT CONGREGATIONAL CHAPEL, EVERTON ROW, 1835–6, THE PEMBROKE BAPTIST CHAPEL, 1839 (dem.), and the handsome GREAT GEORGE STREET CON-GREGATIONAL CHAPEL, 1840–1, all in the classical style [J. A. Picton, *Memorials of Liverpool* ii, 288, 346, 442]. His honourable behaviour towards H. L. Elmes in connection with the competition for St. George's Hall deserves to be remembered [see R. P. Jones, 'The Life and Work of H. L. Elmes', *Arch. Rev.*, June 1904, 236].

FRASER, ALEXANDER (*c.* 1790–1841), of Aberdeen, combined the professions of architect, landscape-painter and drawing master. He was one of the original members of the Aberdeen Artists' Society, and exhibited paintings of an architectural character at its exhibition. He appears to have died in 1841, when his office equipment was sold. [G. M. Fraser, 'Archibald Simpson and His Times', *Aberdeen Jnl.*, 14 June 1918; information from Mr. David Walker.]

WILLIAMSTON HOUSE, nr. INSCH, ABERDEENSHIRE, 1825–6 [*Aberdeen Jnl.*, 28 May 1825, 8 March 1826].

POWIS HOUSE, OLD ABERDEEN, entrance gateway for John Leslie, 1830–4, castellated [*Powis Papers*, ed. J. G. Burnett, Third Spalding Club 1951, 366].

BRAEMAR PARISH KIRK, ABERDEENSHIRE, 1832; altered 1878 [*Aberdeen Jnl.*, 19 Dec. 1832].

PORT ELPHINSTONE, ABERDEENSHIRE, warehouse and granary for the Aberdeen Lime Co., 1835 [*Aberdeen Jnl.*, 6 May 1835].

ABERDEEN, HOLBURN U.P. CHURCH, 1836; since reconstructed [*Aberdeen Jnl.*, 7 Sept. 1836].

ABERDEEN, layout of JOHN KNOX'S CHURCHYARD, 1837 [*Aberdeen Jnl.*, 31 May 1837].

FRAZER, ANDREW (–1792), an officer in the Engineers, was the son of George Frazer, a deputy surveyor of excise in Scotland. Either he or his father must be the 'Mr. Fraser of the Excise Office' mentioned by William Mylne in 1758 as 'another [architect] got up lately' in Edinburgh. He joined the Engineers in 1759 as an ensign, and rose to the rank of lieutenant-colonel in 1788. He retired in about 1790, and died on his way to Geneva in the summer of 1792.

In 1781, at a time when he held the position of chief engineer for Scotland, Frazer won the competition for the design of the new church of St. Andrew in George Street, Edinburgh. He generously insisted on relinquishing the premium in favour of a drawing master named Robert Kay, whose design had been commended. Frazer's design, for an oval church with a Corinthian portico and a small tower and cupola, was

illustrated in the *Scots Magazine* for March 1781, and carried out in 1782–5. A steeple was subsequently (1786–7) substituted for the tower and cupola. This feature is said to hve been designed by William Sibbald (*q.v.*), but as it figures in a portrait of Frazer by Zoffany now at Houghton House, Norfolk, he may have designed it himself. In June 1781 Frazer was made a burgess of Edinburgh in recognition of 'his services to his King and Country in general and to this city in particular in the line of his profession'.

[*D.N.B.*; *Notes on the History of St. Andrew's Church, Edinburgh*, 1884; *Scots Mag.*, 1781, 119; *Roll of Edinburgh Burgesses*, Scottish Record Soc. 1933, 60.]

FREDERICK, Sir CHARLES (1709–1785), was the second son of Sir Thomas Frederick. He was educated at Westminster School and New College, Oxford, and made the Grand Tour in 1737–9. From 1741 to 1784 he was M.P., first for Shoreham and then for Queenborough. In 1746 he was appointed to a place in the Office of Ordnance and from 1750 to 1782 held the post of Surveyor-General of the Ordnance. He was created K.B. in 1761 and died on 18 December 1785.

Frederick was a keen antiquary and a man of taste. A collection of drawings of monuments and ancient buildings by him and Smart Lethieullier, formerly in the possession of Horace Walpole and now in the British Museum (Add. MS. 27348), shows that he was a competent draughtsman. He designed the monument in HAGLEY CHURCH, WORCS., to Lucy, Lady Lyttelton (d. 1747), which was executed by Roubiliac [Dr. Pococke, *Travels in England*, Camden Soc., i, 229; *Connoisseur*, May 1954, 256], and that in HIGHCLERE CHURCH, HANTS., to Thomas Milles, Bishop of Waterford (d. 1740), which is signed *Charles Frederick Invt. L. F. Roubiliac Sculpt.*

[Manning & Bray, *Surrey* ii, pedigree facing p. 767; Walpole Society, *Vertue Note Books* iii, 107, 134, 152–3, v, 12; R. Sedgwick, *The House of Commons 1715–54* ii, 1970, 52.]

FREEBAIRN, CHARLES, was the son of James Freebairn, a teacher of French in Edinburgh. As 'Charles Freebairn, Architect in Edinburgh', he was employed at ABERCAIRNY HOUSE, PERTHSHIRE, by James Moray to design and build a new Dining Room in 1755–9 [S.R.O., GD 24/1/624]. This was destroyed when the house was rebuilt early in the nineteenth century. In 1758–62 he designed the charming LIBRARY at INNERPEFFRAY, MUTHILL, PERTHSHIRE, founded under the will of David Lord Madderty [records at Innerpeffray, *ex inf.* Mr. David Walker]. In 1761, when he was admitted a burgess of Edinburgh, by right of his father, he was described as a wright by trade [*Roll of Edinburgh Burgesses 1761–1841*, Scottish Record Soc. 1933, 60]. In

1756 he was elected a member of the Royal Company of Archers [J. Balfour Paul, *History of the Royal Company of Archers*, 1875, 368].

FREEMAN, JOHN (*c.* 1689–1752), was the owner of Fawley Court, Bucks., which he inherited on the death of his uncle in 1707. There is evidence in the family papers that he was an amateur architect of some ability. His principal works were the octagonal saloon at HONINGTON HALL, WARWICKS., and the FREEMAN FAMILY MAUSOLEUM in the churchyard at FAWLEY. The saloon at Honington is an octagonal domed room with coffered ceiling and elaborate plaster decoration of high quality (*C. Life*, 27 Nov. 1920; C. Hussey, *English Country Houses: Early Georgian*, 1955, 175–80). Letters and drawings show that Freeman designed in 1751 for his friend Joseph Townsend, and that it was executed under the direction of William Jones (*q.v.*). In 1748 Freeman refitted the interior of Fawley Church at his own expense, reusing furniture from the recently demolished chapel at Cannons House, Middlesex, and in 1750 he built the mausoleum, a domed building based on Roman prototypes, for which his drawings survive. Freeman was buried in the mausoleum when he died on 9 August 1752. [Gloucestershire Record Office: Strickland of Apperley papers, D1245, FF38; D. & S. Lysons, *Magna Britannia* i, 1806, 562.]

FRENCH, GEORGE RUSSELL (1803–1881), was born in London in 1803. Between 1821 and 1832 he exhibited at the Royal Academy from Wanstead in Essex, and in 1836 he was living at Leytonstone, but in the 1840s he was practising from London, where he was surveyor to the Ironmongers' Company. He had antiquarian interests, and published several genealogical works, including *The Ancestry of Queen Victoria and Prince Albert* (1841), *The Royal Descent of Nelson and Wellington* (1853) and *Shakespereana Genealogica* (1869). He was a member of the Society of Freemasons of the Church (cf. Alfred Bartholomew), a vice-president of the London and Middlesex Archaeological Society and a keen temperance reformer. He died in London on 14 October 1881, aged 78. [*Builder* xli, 1881, 586; F. Boase, *Modern English Biography* i, 1892, 1106; *D.N.B.*]

According to his obituary in the *Builder* French was 'better known by his literary labours than his professional practice', and his executed works were certainly not remarkable. They included ST. MARY'S NATIONAL SCHOOL, PLAISTOW, ESSEX, 1831, Tudor Gothic [exhib. at R.A. 1831; *V.C.H. Essex* vi, 147]; alterations to the hall at BEDDINGTON PARK, SURREY, for Admiral Sir B. H. Carew, 1832 [exhib. at R.A. 1832]; LEAVENHEATH CHURCH, SUFFOLK, 1836, Gothic, enlarged 1883

[I.C.B.S.]; WESTMARSH CHURCH, KENT, 1841, Gothic [I.C.B.S.]; and ALL SAINTS CHURCH, BOTTLE END, nr. STANWAY, ESSEX, 1844–5, Gothic [*Builder* ii, 1844, 482]. In 1835 he entered a Tudor Gothic design for the new Houses of Parliament.

FRESON, LANCELOT (*c.* 1615–), described as gentleman of Leeds, aged 50, gave evidence in 1665 in a case in the Court of Arches concerning dilapidation in the Archbishop of York's houses in Yorkshire. He stated that 'for the space of these twenty yeares last past' he had been 'employed about and undertaken the Building and reparacons of manye houses and structures for divers gentlemen and persons of quality within the County of York' [Lambeth Palace Library, Court of Arches Records Bbb 69].

FRITH, RICHARD (–1695), a bricklayer by trade, was a speculative builder active in London in the reign of Charles II. In the 1670s he was much involved in transactions relating to property in the new St. James's Square, where he was himself responsible for building the Earl of St. Albans' House in the north-west corner, afterwards known as Ormonde, and finally as Chandos House; dem. 1735 [*Survey of London* xxix, 119, etc.]. He developed land in Soho, and Hatton, in his *New View of London*, 1708, described Frith Street as 'so called from Mr. Fryth, a great (and once rich) builder'. He was one of the builders of Monmouth House, Soho Square, begun in 1681, but still unfinished at the time of the Duke of Monmouth's execution in 1685. In 1687–8 he was concerned in a project for the rebuilding of the Royal Mews in St. James's Park, with a 'new intended street leading from Berkeley House to the new intended Mews at St. James's' [*Cal. Treasury Books* viii (iii), 1704, 1716, 1801; *History of the King's Works* v, fig. 13]. His agreement with the respective tradesmen (B.M., Add. MS. 16370, ff. 115–18) shows that 'for every £200 worth of worke wrought, or goods sold and delivered to such like Vallue', each was to receive a proportionate share in the proposed new street, 'being part of his Majesties' park neere St. James, as is set out in a draft of the same. For the terme of 99 yeares, at 18 yeares purchase' – an interesting indication of the speculative builder's methods at this date. Frith eventually got into financial difficulties, and died in debt in 1695. For a full account of his career, see B. H. Johnson, *Berkeley Square to Bond Street*, 1952; also C. L. Kingsford, *Early History of Piccadilly, Leicester Square and Soho*, 1925, 68–9.

FROME, W—, exhibited two architectural drawings at the Royal Academy in 1831. His address is not stated in the catalogue. In 1828 he designed a Gothic tower (since destroyed) for WITHAM PRIORY CHURCH, SOMERSET [I.C.B.S.].

FULCHER, THOMAS (*c.* 1737–1803), was a carpenter, builder, surveyor and timber-merchant at Ipswich. Advertisements in the *Ipswich Journal* show that he built a workhouse at BULCHAMP, nr. BLYTHBURGH, SUFFOLK, in 1765 and a Theatre and Assembly Rooms at BECCLES in 1785. He also built the Theatre at YARMOUTH in 1778 [J. Preston, *History of Yarmouth*, 1819]. Just before his death he obtained a patent for a 'Water Proof Composition in imitation of Portland Stone, for stuccoing and colouring New and Old Brick and Stone Buildings'. According to an advertisement published in the *Ipswich Journal* (19 April 1806), 'specimens of its admired colour and lasting qualities may be seen at Major Heron's and Robert Collins, Esq. Ipswich; Richard Frank's D. D., Alderton; Rev. Samuel Kilderbee's, Campsey Ash; Sir Hyde Parker's Bart., Benhall, Suffolk; Col. Drake Garrard's, Wheathampstead, Hertfordshire; Jn. Rook's Esq. Catton, near Norwich; Thomas Needham's Esq. Dublin; and at the proprietor's Ipswich'. Some of these houses were evidently designed by Fulcher, for in the 'Red Book' which Humphry Repton prepared for Col. Drake Garrard of LAMER, nr. WHEATHAMPSTED, HERTS., in 1792, he states that he has departed somewhat from 'Mr. Fulcher's design'. The house (dem. 1950) was altered in accordance with the design in the 'Red Book' [*ex inf.* Mr. Simon Houfe].

Fulcher died in June 1803, aged 66, leaving his drawing books, drawings and instruments to his sons Robert and Thomas. His will [Ipswich Record Office, IC/AAI/223/72] includes coloured plans of his house and timber yards in Ipswich. His business was carried on by his son Robert Fulcher (d. 1813). Robert Fulcher's only recorded architectural work appears to have been the Bridewell at WOODBRIDGE, SUFFOLK, 1804 [*Report from the Committee of Aldermen appointed to visit several Gaols in England*, 1816, 152]. He continued to advertise the patent composition, whose merits were further urged in a book by— Fulcher (perhaps his son) published at St. Albans in 1813, and entitled *Hints to Noblemen and Gentlemen of Landed Property, how they may build farm-houses, cottages, and offices, in a cheap and durable manner, without going to the timber merchant's yard for assistance.* In the preface the author states that the stucco was 'the same as that used by the Signor Carrabellas,[1] two Italian Artists, at the Right Honourable the Earl of Bristol's Palace at Ickworth ... which has stood fifteen years, in ornamental Pannels, at a Height of eighty feet from the Ground.' He also declared his willingness to make estimates and superintend buildings.

[Information from Mr. J. Bensusan-Butt.]

FULKES, THOMAS, of Reading, was employed as surveyor by the churchwardens of UFTON NERVET, BERKS., in connection with some repairs to their church in 1809 [MS. Parish Records]. He was similarly employed at ST. MARY'S READING, in 1818 [MS. Parish Records], and in 1833 he submitted designs for enlarging and altering CHURCH OAKLEY PARSONAGE, HANTS. [Winchester Diocesan Records]. He entered a Doric design for the Royal Berkshire Infirmary competition in 1837 [*Reading Mercury*, 11 Feb. 1837].

FURNESS, RICHARD (1791–1857), born at Eyam in Derbyshire, and subsequently schoolmaster and parish clerk at Dore in the same county, was a self-educated man who is best known as a poet, though he also showed ability in several other capacities, including those of surveyor and architect. His only considerable work in an architectural capacity appears to have been the rebuilding of DORE CHURCH, DERBYSHIRE, in a simple Gothic style in 1828–9. He not only made the design, but also 'carved the ornamental figures' himself [G. C. Holland, *The Poetical Works of Richard Furness*, 1858, 45; *D.N.B.*; I.C.B.S.]

G

GADSDON, ISAAC, was the author of a work entitled *Geometrical Rules Made Easy for the Use of Mechanicks Concern'd in Buildings: Containing New and Infallible Methods for Striking out from proper Centres, the Groyns of Arches ... also an Essay, on the Nature ... of Arches in general ... with some Remarks on the intended Bridge at Westminster. With a Proposal for Building the Piers, by a method ... to keep out the Water while erecting,* 1739. He was no doubt the Isaac Gadsden of (High) Wycombe who was one of the executors of Robert Morris (*q.v.*), and to whom Morris left money for a ring in his will (1754).

GALILEI, ALESSANDRO (1691–1737), was a Florentine architect who came to England in 1714 at the invitation of John Molesworth, the British envoy to the Tuscan court from 1710 to 1714. Molesworth and his father (created Lord Molesworth in 1716) were men of taste who, together with Sir Thomas Hewett (*q.v.*) and Sir George Markham, formed what they called 'the new Junta for Architecture'. Their aim appears

---

[1] Perhaps Francesco and Donato Carabelli, who decorated the façade of the Palazzo Serbelloni in Milan with a neo-classical relief *c.* 1790 (C. Meeks, *Italian Architecture 1750–1914*, 80).

to have been to introduce a more classical and less baroque style into British architecture, and Galilei was to be their chosen architect. As members of the Whig aristocracy, they were in a position to introduce him to such influential persons as Baron Kielmansegg, Lord Stanhope and the 1st Duke of Newcastle. Although Galilei made designs for several potential patrons, including the Duke of Newcastle, few commissions resulted, and nothing came of an ambitious scheme for a royal palace to replace Whitehall. Designs offered by Galilei for some of the Fifty New Churches in London had equally little success. In May 1718 he entered into an agreement with Nicholas Dubois (*q.v.*) 'to become Copartners & Joint Dealers together in all Designs, Buildings, Architecture, Drawings, both Military and Civil' for five years. During the summer of the same year he visited Ireland, where the Molesworths had their seat (Breckdenstown, nr. Dublin). This led to a commission to design a country house for Speaker William Conolly at CASTLETOWN, CO. KILDARE. Although not begun until about 1722, and then carried out under the direction of Sir Edward Lovett Pearce, Castletown was essentially Galilei's design, and its palazzo-like façade clearly betrays its Italian origin [Maurice Craig & the Knight of Glin, 'Castletown, Co. Kildare', *C. Life*, 27 March, 3–10 April 1969]. In 1718–19 Galilei also designed the Doric portico on the east front of KIMBOLTON CASTLE, HUNTS., for the 1st Duke of Manchester. His original drawing is in the Record Office at Huntingdon [Arthur Oswald in *C. Life*, 26 Dec. 1968, and see also *C. Life*, 1 Feb. 1973, 270].

Despite these encouragements, and his marriage in September 1718 to an English girl, Letitia Martin, Galilei decided in the following year to return to Florence, where the Grand Duke promised him employment. He and his wife accordingly left England in August 1719. In Florence he found little more opportunity than he had in England, but eventually he became well known as the architect of the façade of St. John Lateran in Rome (1734), and of the Corsini Chapel in the same church (1731). He died in Rome on 21 December 1737.

A number of Galilei's unexecuted designs for English buildings are preserved in the state archives at Florence. Some of them are unexpectedly baroque in character, but they include a very neo-classical design for a church in the form of a Doric temple. In 1726 Sir Edward Gascoigne of Parlington in Yorkshire commissioned Galilei to design a monument to his parents. This was executed in Florence in coloured marbles and set up in BARWICK-IN-ELMET CHURCH in 1729, but was destroyed when the church was altered in 1858.

[Ilaria Toesca, 'Alessandro Galilei in Inghilterra', *English Miscellany*, ed. M. Praz, iii,

1952; Elizabeth Kieven, 'Galilei in England', *C. Life*, 25 Jan. 1973; Elizabeth Kieven, 'The Gascoigne Monument by Alessandro Galilei', *Leeds Arts Calendar* No. 77, 1975; Hist. MSS. Comm., *Various Collections* viii, 287, 307, etc.]

GALL, JOHN, of Aberdeen, was the architect employed in 1827–8 to convert BLAIRS HOUSE, KINCARDINESHIRE, into a Catholic seminary [P. F. Anson, 'Catholic Church Building in Scotland', *Innes Review* v, 1954, 128, n. 6].

GALLIER, JAMES (1798–1866), was the son of an Irish builder. He went to Liverpool in 1816 and walked to Manchester, where he worked in the building of a cotton mill. He returned to Ireland, but came to London in 1822, and was employed in 1826–8 as clerk of works at Huntingdon Gaol, then being built to the designs of William Wilkins. While in Huntingdon he offered 'to teach young men the art of drawing the Orders of Roman and Grecian Architecture', and designed a 'small wooden bridge, of an original design, across a branch of the Ouse at Godmanchester'. This was the 'Chinese Bridge', built in 1827 and rebuilt in accordance with the original design in 1869 and again in 1960. He was once more in London in 1828–9, where he was engaged to supervise the building of houses in South Street, Park Lane, to the designs of J. P. Gandy (*q.v.*). In 1832 he left for America, and settled in New Orleans, where he 'made a signal contribution to the style of the Louisiana plantation houses'. He published *The American Builder's General Price Book and Estimator* in 1833. His autobiography was published in Paris in 1864. At Tulane University, New Orleans, there are drawings by him for alterations to Mr. Robson's house in South Audley Street, London, dated 1829, and a competently drawn axonometric view of Huntingdon Gaol [John Harris, *Catalogue of British Drawings for Architecture, Decoration, Sculpture and Landscape Gardening in American Collections*, 1971, 99–100].

GANDON, JAMES (1743–1823), was born in London in February 1742/3, at the house of his grandfather, a Huguenot refugee. His father, Peter Gandon,, was originally a man of substance, but nearly ruined himself by a passion for alchemy. Owing to his father's financial difficulties James's schooling was curtailed, but he afterwards studied at Shipley's Drawing Academy in St. Martin's Lane, and in 1758 means were found to apprentice him to Sir William Chambers. He began to practise on his own in about 1765. In 1767, in conjunction with John Woolfe of the Office of Works, he began to publish a continuation of Campbell's *Vitruvius Britannicus*. Although the second volume (1771) contained his own designs for the county hall at

Nottingham, the venture seems to have been less an advertisement than a genuine attempt to provide a record of recent English architecture. A third volume was contemplated. Though stated in the list of subscribers to the second to be 'in great forwardness', it was never published. In 1767 Gandon also published a set of *Six Designs of Frizes*, followed in 1778 by *A Collection of Antique and Modern Ornaments* and *A Collection of Frizes Capitals and Grotesque Ornaments*.

Gandon exhibited at the Free Society of Artists in 1762 and 1763, at the Society of Artists from 1765 to 1773, and at the Royal Academy from 1774 to 1780. On the establishment of the Royal Academy Schools in 1769 he became a student, and won the first gold medal awarded for architecture. His first recorded commissions dated from 1768, and in 1769 he obtained the second premium of 30 guineas in the competition (won by T. Cooley) for a design for the Royal Exchange in Dublin. Nottingham County Hall, his first public building, was begun in 1770, and in 1776 he won the first prize of 100 guineas for a design for a large lunatic asylum in London (not built, but exhibited at the R.A. by Gandon in 1778).

The origins of Gandon's connection with Ireland can be traced to the years 1768–9, when he was placed second in the competition for the Royal Exchange at Dublin and was employed to alter the Bishop's Palace at Ferns in Co. Carlow. In 1774 his first exhibited drawing at the Royal Academy was 'a design for a villa for a gentleman in Ireland'. As a pupil of Chambers, he had met the latter's client Lord Charlemont, the chief patron of the arts in Ireland, and his friend Paul Sandby introduced him to Lord Carlow, afterwards Earl of Portarlington, who gave him an introduction to John Beresford, later Chief Commissioner of the Irish Revenue. After refusing a tempting but uncertain offer of employment at the Russian Court, he was persuaded to go to Dublin in 1781 in order to superintend the construction of the new docks, stores and Custom House, designs for which he had made in 1780 at the instance of Lord Carlow. The building of the Custom House was attended by great difficulties, both physical and human. The site was liable to flooding, the whole project was opposed by the Corporation, and there was a serious lack of skilled workmen. But with the support of Beresford, and by his own determined conduct, Gandon successfully overcame all obstacles, and this great building, 'the Dublin counterpart to Somerset House', was completed in 1791. At the same time he was engaged on several important buildings in the Irish capital, including the Four Courts and the portico of the Parliament House, now the Bank of Ireland. The year before the rebellion of 1798 he thought it prudent to remove his family to London, but in 1799 he returned

to Dublin in order to complete the Inns of Court. In 1808 he handed over control to his pupil H. A. Baker, and retired to the estate called Canonbrook which he had bought at Lucan, nr. Dublin, where he died of gout on 24 December 1823. He was buried in the churchyard of Drumcondra in the same grave as his friend Francis Grose the antiquary.

Although constantly subjected to hostile criticism from those who considered his buildings too pretentious and too costly, Gandon could always rely on the support of his powerful friends in the government, under whose patronage he was able to make an outstanding contribution to the architectural embellishment of the Irish capital. Like his master Sir William Chambers, he rejected what he regarded as the meretricious elegance of the current Adam style, and looked to French neo-classicism to reinvigorate the expiring tradition of English Palladianism. French influence is evident in the simplified Doric façade of his County Hall at Nottingham, and it is also apparent in many features of his public buildings in Dublin. But the dome of the Custom House and the façade of the Four Courts show that Gandon was also indebted to Wren, and this readiness to learn from a pre-Palladian architect helps to explain why Gandon's public buildings are so much more effectively monumental than Chambers's Somerset House.

Gandon became a Fellow of the Society of Artists in 1771, but failed to secure election as A.R.A. in 1776. In 1791 he was made an honorary member of the London Architects' Club on its foundation, and he was an original member of the Royal Irish Academy. A biographical memoir, based on materials arranged by his son James, was published in Dublin in 1846. It incorporates the texts of two writings by Gandon entitled 'The Progress of Architecture in Ireland' and 'Hints for erecting Testimonials'. A new edition by Maurice Craig (1969) includes a list of portraits of the architect (of which the most important is the one by Tilly Kettle and William Cuming in the National Gallery of Ireland) and a hand-list of his surviving drawings (several of which are illustrated in the catalogue of *Irish Architectural Drawings*, 1965). H. A. Baker (1753–1836) and Sir Richard Morrison (1767–1849) were Gandon's pupils.

[Obituaries in *Gent's Mag.* 1824 (i), 464–5, and *Literary Gazette*, no. 372, 6 March 1824, 156; *The Life of James Gandon*, from materials collected by his son, edited by T. Mulvany, Dublin 1846, new edition by Maurice Craig, London 1969; 'Memoirs of Thomas Jones', *Walpole Soc.* xxxii, 1946–8, 15–17, 20, 21, 23; *A.P.S.D.*; *D.N.B.*; Constantia Maxwell, 'James Gandon, Architect of Georgian Dublin', *C. Life*, 22 Oct. 1948; Maurice Craig, *Dublin 1660–1860*, 1952, chap. xxi; Maurice Craig, 'Burlington, Adam and Gandon', *Jnl. of the Warburg and Courtauld Institutes*, xvii, 1954, 381–2; E. McParland, 'James Gandon and the Royal Exchange Competition, 1768–69', *Jnl. of the Royal Society of Antiquaries of Ireland* 102 (i), 1972].

THE WOOD (or WODE) HOUSE, WOMBOURNE, STAFFS., mausoleum to memory of Handel, 'erected in a wood belonging to Sir Samuel Hellier in Staffordshire', exhibited at Society of Artists, 1768. This no longer exists, but may be the same as 'Music Room' built in 1767 which is mentioned in the N.R.A. list of Hellier papers, or with a 'domed temple flanked by busts' of which a water-colour exists (see *Life of Gandon*, ed. Craig, Appendix 1).

FERNS PALACE, CO. CARLOW, IRELAND, alterations for the Hon. Joseph Dean Bourke, Bishop of Ferns, 1768; rebuilt 1790, gutted 1798 [*Life*, 26].

? KILLALOE DEANERY, CO. CLARE, IRELAND, for the Hon. Joseph Dean Bourke, Dean of Killaloe and Bishop of Ferns, 1768–9; probably not executed [*Life*, 29].

NOTTINGHAM, THE COUNTY HALL, HIGH PAVEMENT, 1770–2; extended 1876–80 [*Vitruvius Britannicus* v, pl. 72, showing the executed design, and pls. 73–7 an alternative scheme not adopted].

? HEYWOOD, CO. LAOIS, IRELAND, for Michael Frederick Trench, *c.* 1770; dem. [in 1771 S. White exhibited at the Society of Artists the 'Front of Mr. Trench's house in Ireland' and a 'Section of the County Hall at Nottingham', both 'from a design of Mr. Gandon's']. Trench was an amateur architect and is supposed to have designed Heywood himself: see T. U. Sadleir & P. L. Dickinson, *Georgian Mansions in Ireland*, Dublin 1915, 96.

MILL HOUSE, EASTBOURNE, SUSSEX, for John Hamilton Mortimer, *c.* 1770; dem. [exhib. at Society of Artists, 1773; *Walpole Soc.* xxxii, 23].

WYNNSTAY, DENBIGHSHIRE, THE THEATRE, for Sir Watkin Williams-Wynn, Bart., 1772; dem. 1858 [National Library of Wales, Wynnstay Coll. 115/4, p. 1].

WARLEY PLACE, nr. BRENTWOOD, ESSEX. The 'elevation of the principal front' which Gandon exhibited at the R.A. in 1777 may not have been carried out, as Warley (dem.) was still described as an 'ancient seat' in 1818.

DUBLIN, THE CUSTOM HOUSE, 1781–91; interior destroyed 1921 [*Life*, 220] (A. E. Richardson, *Monumental Classic Architecture in Great Britain*, 1914, pls. xi–xii).

DUBLIN, CHARLEMONT HOUSE, RUTLAND SQUARE, THE ROCKINGHAM LIBRARY, for the 1st Earl of Charlemont, *c.* 1783; dismantled 1865 [M. J. Craig, *The Volunteer Earl*, 1948, 132–3 and pl. xiii].

WATERFORD, IRELAND, COURT HOUSE AND GAOL, 1784; dem. 1837–49 [*Life*, 68–70].

NEW GENEVA, CO. WATERFORD, IRELAND, model town for refugee Genevan craftsmen, begun *c.* 1783 but abandoned soon afterwards [*Life*, 220; Hubert Butler, 'New Geneva in Waterford', *Jnl. of the Royal Society of Antiquaries of Ireland* lxxvii, 1947, 150–5].

DUBLIN, THE ROTUNDA ASSEMBLY ROOMS, heightening of exterior and embellishment with neo-classical frieze, 1784 [C. P. Curran, *The Rotunda Hospital*, Dublin 1945, 27]. The entrance-block on the south side can also be attributed to Gandon on stylistic grounds.

COOLBANAGHER CHURCH and MAUSOLEUM, CO. LAOIS, IRELAND, for the 1st Earl of Portarlington, 1785; chancel added in nineteenth century [drawing in church] (Maurice Craig & the Knight of Glin, *Ireland Observed*, 1970, 34, illustration of mausoleum).

DUBLIN, THE PARLIAMENT HOUSE (now Bank of Ireland), added east (Corinthian) portico to House of Lords and curved screen-wall, 1785–9 (the three-quarter Ionic columns were added by Francis Johnston in 1804–5). Gandon made designs for the west (Ionic) portico to the House of Commons, built *c.* 1790–2, but was not responsible for the execution, and the final result cannot be attributed to him [C. P. Curran, 'The Architecture of the Bank of Ireland', in F. G. Hall, *The Bank of Ireland*, 1949, 440–6].

DUBLIN, THE FOUR COURTS, 1786–1802, incorporating south and west sides of quadrangle designed by T. Cooley 1776–84; interior destroyed 1922 [*Life*, 220].

DUBLIN, THE MILITARY INFIRMARY, PHOENIX PARK, 1786 (executed by W. Gibson) [*Life*, 154–5] (*C. Life*, 22 Oct. 1948, fig. 7).

ABBEVILLE, nr. MALAHIDE, CO. DUBLIN, IRELAND, alterations and additions for John Beresford, *c.* 1790 [J. N. Brewer, *The Beauties of Ireland* i, 1825, 249; drawing for kitchen dated 1790, listed in *Life of Gandon*, ed. Craig, Appendix 3].

SANDYMOUNT, DUBLIN, villa (now Roslyn Park) for William Ashford, *c.* 1790 [*Life*, 142; information from Mr. E. McParland].

CARRIGLAS, CO. LONGFORD, IRELAND, office court and gateway for Sir William Gleadowe Newcomen, Bart., *c.* 1790–5 [The Knight of Glin, 'James Gandon's Work at Carriglas', in *The Country Seat*, ed. Colvin & Harris, 1970].

EMO PARK (DAWSON COURT), CO. LAOIS, for the 1st Earl of Portarlington, *c.* 1790–1800; altered by L. Vulliamy 1834–6. The portico is dated 1796 [drawing for portico dated 1796, listed in *Life of Gandon*, ed Craig, Appendix 3; E. McParland in *C. Life*, 23, 30 May 1974].

DUBLIN, CARLISLE BRIDGE (R. Liffey), 1791–4; replaced 1880 by O'Connell Bridge [*Life*, 155–6].

EMSWORTH, CO. DUBLIN, IRELAND, for J. Woodmason, 1794 [drawing listed in *Life of Gandon*, ed. Craig, Appendix 3].

For further uncertain and attributed works see Appendix 1 in Maurice Craig's edition of Mulvany's *Life of Gandon*.

GANDY, JOSEPH MICHAEL (1771–1843), was the son of a man employed at White's Club, St. James's. When James Wyatt rebuilt the clubhouse in 1787–8, he was shown some of Gandy's sketches, and offered to take their author, then aged 15, into his office. In 1789 Gandy entered the Royal Academy School, winning the Silver Medal the same year, and the Gold Medal in 1790. In 1794 John Martindale, the proprietor of White's, sent him to Italy at his own expense. He travelled in company with C. H. Tatham, and achieved the distinction of being awarded a special medal by the Academy of St. Luke.[1] But Martindale's bankruptcy in 1797, combined with the advance of Napoleon's armies into Italy, put him in a serious plight, from which he was luckily rescued by a King's Messenger known to his family, who brought him home late in 1797.

Arriving in England in wartime, Gandy saw little prospect of establishing himself in practice immediately. Instead, he found employment as a draughtsman in the office of Sir John Soane, to whom he was, in one way or other, to be indebted for financial assistance for the rest of his life. He practised on his own from 1801, and in 1803 was elected A.R.A., perhaps through Soane's influence, as he had so far done little independent work. In 1808 he undertook to act as tutor to Soane's eldest son, and in 1809 he and his pupil went to Liverpool, where Gandy had entered into a short-lived partnership with the sculptor and modeller George Bullock (d. 1818).[2] In 1811 he returned to London, and, in the intervals of a never very extensive practice, was employed by Soane to make elaborate watercolour perspectives of his architectural designs. But with a wife and nine children to support, Gandy was constantly in financial difficulties, and in 1816, rather than declare himself a bankrupt, he allowed himself to be imprisoned in the Fleet. He is said to have been 'odd and impracticable in disposition', and it seems likely that he was temperamentally unsuited to the exacting routine of a working architect's office. In default of commissions, he devoted most of his energies to painting the architectural fantasies which he exhibited at the Royal Academy almost without a break from 1789 to 1838. It is these extraordinary compositions, highly eclectic in their stylistic sources, but all inspired by a romantic vision akin to that of Coleridge or Turner, that give Gandy a unique place in English architectural history. His independent approach to architectural aesthetics is also seen in his designs for cottages, whose studied simplicity is in pointed contrast to the picturesque artificiality of the *cottage orné*. These he published in 1805 in two separate works entitled *The Rural Architect* and *Designs for Cottages, Cottage Farms and Other Rural Buildings*, the latter being dedicated to Thomas Hope. Gandy also made drawings to illustrate topographical works such as Britton's *Architectural Antiquities*. His only other recorded publication was a paper entitled 'The Philosophy of Architecture', printed in *The Magazine of the Fine Arts* i, 1821, 289, 370.

Gandy died in December 1843. He left a son, Thomas, who became a portrait-painter. At Liverpool he had a pupil called R. Elland, of whom nothing further is known, and he also gave instruction to his younger brother Michael (*q.v.*).

Many of Gandy's drawings are preserved in the collections of the Soane Museum, the R.I.B.A. and the Victoria and Albert Museum. See also J. Harris, *Catalogue of British Drawings for Architecture, etc. in American Collections*, 1971, 103. His unexecuted designs for the Government House at Quebec, exhibited at the R.A. in 1812, and now in the Public Archives at Ottawa, are described by J. F. C. Smith, 'Drawings from the Archives, Ottawa', *Jnl. of the Royal Architectural Institute of Canada* xv, 1938.

[*A.P.S.D.*; *D.N.B.*; S. Redgrave, *Dictionary of Artists of the English School*, 1878, 166; A. T. Bolton, *The Portrait of Sir John Soane*, 1927, *passim*; John Summerson, 'The Vision of J. M. Gandy', in *Heavenly Mansions*, 1949].

LANCASTER CASTLE, completed COUNTY COURTS and GAOL begun by Thomas Harrison, 1802–23, and designed FEMALE PENITENTIARY, 1818–21 [drawings in Soane Museum, xxxv, 7; *The Farington Diary*, ed. J. Greig, ii, 167, vi, 227; drawings exhibited by Gandy at R.A. in 1817, 1822 and 1823; for the extent of Gandy's responsibility for the design of the interiors see J. M. Crook in *C. Life*, 15 April 1971, 878–9].

STORRS HALL, WINDERMERE, WESTMORLAND, boathouse for Sir John Legard, Bart., exhib. at R.A. 1804. In 1804 Sir J. Legard built an octagonal temple on the shore of the lake which may have been designed by Gandy (*C. Life*, 29 Nov. 1962, 1338).

---

[1] His *prova* (a design for a triumphal arch) is in the Cooper Union Museum, New York.

[2] For the identity of Gandy's partner I am indebted to Mr. S. A. Harris of Liverpool. Mr. Harris points out that J. M. Gandy may well have been related to a Liverpool painter named Samuel Gandy (d. *c.* 1790), which would explain why several of his architectural commissions were in the north-west of England.

LONDON, THE PHOENIX FIRE AND PELICAN LIFE IN-SURANCE OFFICES, CHARING CROSS, 1804–5; dem. [exhib. at R.A. 1805] (*Survey of London* xvi, pls. 89–90).

LANCASTER, PUBLIC BATH, NO. 43 BATH STREET, exhib. at R.A. 1806.

BOLTON HALL, BOLTON-BY-BOWLAND, YORKS. (W.R.), rebuilt south front and other alterations in the Gothic style for John Bolton, 1806–8 [*Gent's Mag.* 1841 (i), 581].

STORRS HALL, WINDERMERE, WESTMORLAND, remodelled for John Bolton, 1808–11 [exhib. at R.A. 1808, 1811].

LIVERPOOL, ASSEMBLY ROOM, exhib. at R.A. 1810 and probably to be identified with the Assembly Room built at the rear of the LIVER-POOL ARMS HOTEL, CASTLE STREET, *c.* 1808; dem. (cf. *The Stranger in Liverpool*, 1810).

BATH, 'DORIC HOUSE', SION HILL, for Thomas Barker, 1818 [exhib. at R.A. 1818 as 'now building', but apparently begun some years earlier; W. Ison, *The Georgian Buildings of Bath*, 1948, 182 and pl. 107].

LEYTONSTONE, ESSEX, house near, exhibited at R.A. 1819 as 'building': possibly Wallwood House, rebuilt for William Cotton *c.* 1820; dem. *c.* 1905.

BIRMINGHAM, villa 'to be built near' exhib. at R.A. 1819.

CLUMBER HOUSE, NOTTS., 'proposed addition' for the 4th Duke of Newcastle, exhib. at R.A. 1820, perhaps not carried out. The house was partly rebuilt 1879 and dem. 1938.

SWERFORD HOUSE, nr. CHIPPING NORTON, OXON., alterations and additions for Sir Robert Bolton, 1824 [exhib. at R.A. 1824 as 'now erecting'].

LONDON, LAMBETH: in 1825 Gandy exhibited at the R.A. 'Dwelling houses etc. now building in Vauxhall Road, and other places'. These probably included NO. 363 KENNINGTON LANE, built in 1824 (*Survey of London* xxvi, 38) and NOS. 238–46 WANDSWORTH ROAD (dem. 1953) [John Summerson, *Georgian London*, 1945, 288–9].

LIVERPOOL, 'subscribers' billiard-room', exhibited at R.A. 1826 as built under Gandy's superintendence and presumably to be identified with the Rotunda in Bold Street, a circular building erected 1809 for the exhibition of panoramic views, but subsequently converted into a subscribers' billiard-room; dem. *c.* 1864 (cf. J. A. Picton, *Memorials of Liverpool* ii, 1875, 237).

INCE BLUNDELL, LANCS., design for an entrance hall for Henry Blundell (d. 1810), exhibited at the R.A. 1832 and probably not executed.

GANDY, MICHAEL (1778–1862), was a pupil of his elder brother Joseph. He entered the Royal Academy Schools in 1796, and became an assist-

ant of James Wyatt. Soon afterwards he accepted an appointment in the Indian naval service and served in India and China. In 1812 he exhibited at the Royal Academy a view of the burning of Onrust and Kupers Islands, Batavia, in 1800, 'taken on the spot'. On his return, he was employed as a draughtsman by Edward Holl, civil architect to the Navy, also by Francis Goodwin, and afterwards by Sir Jeffry Wyatville, with whom he had been for thirty-three years at the time of the latter's death in 1840. In conjunction with Benjamin Baud, he published *Architectural Illustrations of Windsor Castle*, with an introduction by J. Britton, fol., 1842 [*A.P.S.D.*].

GANDY, afterwards **DEERING,** JOHN PETER (1787–1850), was the younger brother of Joseph and Michael Gandy (*q.v.*). He showed artistic leanings at an early age, and became a pupil of James Wyatt. He was admitted to the Royal Academy Schools in 1805, and was awarded the Silver Medal the following year. After leaving Wyatt's office he secured a post in the Barrack Office which he was allowed to retain when, in 1811–13, he undertook a journey to Greece and Asia Minor on behalf of the Society of Dilettanti, in company with Sir William Gell and F. Bedford. The results of their researches were published in 1817 as the *Unedited Antiquities of Attica*, and in the third volume of the *Ionian Antiquities*, issued in 1840 (see above, p. 103). With Gell, he was co-author of *Pompeiana*, 1817–19, which was for many years the standard work on the excavations then in progress at Pompeii. In 1830 he was elected a member of the Society of Dilettanti.

In 1810 Gandy was awarded the first prize in the competition for the new Bethlehem Hospital. His design, submitted under the motto *Dum spiro, spero*, was not, however, carried out. The original drawings are in St. Bartholomew's Hospital archives. The plan is illustrated in *Survey of London*, xxv, pl. 38. His design for a new House of Commons is among those illustrated in *Parliamentary Papers*, 1833 (487), xii, and his plan for a Public Record Office is given in *Proceedings of the Record Commissioners*, ed. C. P. Cooper, 1833, 227–9. An unexecuted design for Broomhall, Fife, made for Lord Elgin and exhibited at the Royal Academy in 1827 and 1829, is preserved at that house. With the exception of the Tudor Gothic hospital at Stamford, all Gandy's executed works were in an elegant and sophisticated neo-classical style of which the Greek Revival St. Mark's Church in North Audley Street is a characteristic example.

In 1828 Gandy assumed the name of Deering, on inheriting the estate known as The Lee, nr. Great Missenden, Bucks., which had been left to him by his friend Henry Deering. After this he gradually gave up the practice of his profession,

329

and devoted himself to public life and the management of his property. He was appointed High Sheriff of Bucks. in 1840, and was elected M.P. for Aylesbury in 1847. He was elected A.R.A. in 1826, and R.A. in 1838 – an honour scarcely justified by the professional inactivity of his later life. He had, however acquired a considerable reputation both as an authority on Greek architecture and as a practising architect, before his conversion into a country gentleman cut short his professional career. [*A.P.S.D.*; *D.N.B.*; *The Times*, 6 June 1952 ('A Greek Bas-Relief').]

LONDON, THE UNITED UNIVERSITY CLUB-HOUSE, PALL MALL EAST, in collaboration with W. Wilkins, 1822–6. An attic storey was added in 1850–1. The building was dem. 1906 [*A.P.S.D.*] (plan and elevation in *A New Survey of London*, J. Weale, 1853, i, 294).

LONDON, ST. MARK'S CHURCH, NORTH AUDLEY STREET, 1825–8; interior reconstructed by A. W. Blomfield, 1878 [*Gent's Mag.* 1829 (ii), 393].

LONDON, NO. 28 UPPER GROSVENOR STREET, 1826–7; dem. [T. L. Donaldson, *Handbook of Specifications.* 1860, 670].

STAMFORD, LINCS., THE INFIRMARY, 1826–8, Tudor Gothic [exhib. at R.A. 1827; G. Burton, *Chronology of Stamford*, 1846, 201].

DUMFRIES HOUSE, AYRSHIRE, lodge for the 2nd Marquess of Bute, 1827 [exhib. at R.A. 1827].

LONDON, UNIVERSITY COLLEGE, GOWER STREET, in collaboration with W. Wilkins, to whom the design was mainly due, 1827–8 [*A.P.S.D.*].

LONDON, houses on south side of SOUTH STREET, PARK LANE, 1828; dem. except Nos. 14 and 24 [J. Harris, *Catalogue of British Drawings for Architecture etc. in American Collections*, 1971, 99; cf. 'the elevation of the west end of a house for a nobleman in Park Lane' exhibited by Gandy at the R.A. in 1828].

LONDON, THE PIMLICO LITERARY INSTITUTION, EBURY STREET, 1830 [*A.P.S.D.*]

LONDON, EXETER HALL, STRAND, 1830–1; dem. 1907 [exhib. at R.A. 1830] (*Survey of London* xviii, pl. 111).

SHRUBLAND PARK, SUFFOLK, alterations and additions for Sir W. F. Middleton, Bart., 1831–3; subsequently altered by Sir Charles Barry 1848–52 [exhib. at R.A. 1831] (*C. Life*, 19–26 Nov. 1953).

GANE, JESSE (*c.* 1798–1855), was a builder at Evercreech in Somerset. Between 1825 and 1835 he was responsible for reseating EVERCREECH CHURCH and inserting a gallery in the north aisle, as recorded by an inscription. He probably designed and built the south aisle as enlarged in 1843 to match the medieval north one, for an inscription shows that he was churchwarden at the

time. He also rebuilt the bodies of STOKE LANE (1838) and CHILCOMPTON (1839) churches and the north aisle of HIGH LITTLETON CHURCH (1842), all in Somerset [I.C.B.S.]. A tablet in Evercreech Church shows that he died on 18 April 1855, aged 57.

GARBETT, EDWARD WILLIAM, was the son of William Garbett of Winchester (*q.v.*). By 1819 he was established in practice in Reading, where in that year he surveyed the tower of St. Lawrence's Church [*Berkshire Arch. Jnl.* liv, 1954–5, 80]. In 1821 he was thanked by the vestry of ST. GILES' CHURCH, READING, 'for the liberal and able manner in which he has afforded the committee [for enlarging the church] his gratuitous assistance' [MS. Vestry Minutes, *ex inf.* Canon B. F. L. Clarke]. In 1820–2 he designed THEALE CHURCH, BERKS., in a remarkably precocious and accurate 'Early English' style derived from Salisbury Cathedral [*Quarterly Review* xxvii, 1822, 323]. The tower was added in 1827–8 by John Buckler, among whose drawings in the British Museum is 'Mr. Garbett's original design' [Add. MS. 36357, 5–66]. The apse was added in 1892. Garbett also designed the church of HOLY TRINITY, READING, begun by him in 1825, but 'completed under the superintendence of Mr. Finlayson' [J. Doran, *History of Reading*, 1835, 167–8]. Garbett's west front was rebuilt by J. Billing in 1846 [*Ecclesiologist* vi, 1846, 196].

Garbett must subsequently have returned to Winchester, probably to assist his father, for in 1833–4 'Mr. Edward Garbett of Winchester' was consulted by the Corporation of Bath over the repair of the tower of BATH ABBEY CHURCH [Council Minutes, *ex inf.* Mr. J. Orbach]. In 1843–5 he was living in London at 17 Fludyer Street, but no further record of him has been found thereafter.

GARBETT, WILLIAM (*c.* 1770–1834), was for twenty-five years surveyor to the Dean and Chapter of Winchester, for whom he carried out extensive repairs to the Cathedral during the years 1812–28, including the reconstruction of two defective piers. The Dean and Chapter thought it necessary to take advice from John Nash as to the manner in which this should be done. Garbett resented the intervention of one who showed 'a pre-disposition to dictate rather than to consult', and in 1824 he published a pamphlet entitled *Observations and Correspondence occasioned by the Failure and Renovation of a Principal Pier in Winchester Cathedral*. There is a copy in Sir John Soane's Museum. Garbett's work at Winchester included the design of the episcopal throne and of a stone choir-screen, replaced by Scott in 1875 [*Gent's Mag.* 1827 (ii), 194, 411, 1828 (ii), 310–14; Winkles, *Illustrations* of the Cathedral Churches of England and Wales i, 1836, 133–4].

Other works by Garbett were: Tudor Gothic additions to HERON COURT, HANTS., for the 1st Earl of Malmesbury, 1807–15 [G. F. Prosser, *Select Illustrations of Hampshire*, 1833; *Views of the Principal Seats and Landscape Scenery in the Neighbourhood of Lymington*, drawn by L. Haghe, 1832]; the restoration in 1817 of the hall of WINCHESTER COLLEGE [T. F. Kirby, *Annals of Winchester College*, 1892, 42]; the stucco Gothic vault inserted in the nave of CHRISTCHURCH PRIORY CHURCH, HANTS., in 1819 [*Gent's Mag.* 1820 (i), 232]; the existing north and south blocks of the street front of MAGDALEN HALL (now HERTFORD COLLEGE), OXFORD, 1820–22 [*Gent's Mag.* 1820 (i), 463: by 'Mr. Garbett of Winchester', and not, as is wrongly stated in most modern works, by his son]; UPHAM RECTORY, HANTS., 1820 [Winchester Diocesan Records]; BINFIELD RECTORY, BERKS., 1821 [Salisbury Diocesan Records]; a Greek Revival boat-house and temple combined on AWBRIDGE DANES WATER, HANTS., 1822, upper part rebuilt 1925 but see reproduction of Garbett's original design in R.I.B.A. Collection in Alistair Rowan, *Garden Buildings*, R.I.B.A. Drawings Series 1968; and the new (Gothic) buildings of ST. JOHN'S HOSPITAL in THE HIGH STREET, WINCHESTER, whose erection was in progress at the time of his death [*Hampshire Chronicle*, 8 Sept. 1834].

Garbett was the author of the account of Winchester in Britton's *Picturesque Antiquities of the English Cities*, 1830, and a letter from him about the history of the Cathedral was printed by Britton in his *Cathedral Antiquities*. He died on 31 August 1834, in his 65th year, and is commemorated by a tablet in the north transept of the Cathedral. He was the father of Edward William Garbett (*q.v.*), and the grandfather of Edward Lacy Garbett (d. 1900), the author of a *Treatise on the Principles of Design in Architecture* (1850) and of numerous religious tracts [will in Hants. Record Office].

GARDINER, JOHN BULL (1786–1867), was a pupil and afterwards a partner of Robert Chapman (*q.v.*). He was admitted to the Royal Academy Schools in 1808, and exhibited from 1803 to 1813. He became surveyor to the parish of St. Olave, Hart Street, London, and in 1823 repaired ST. OLAVE'S CHURCH, inserting Gothic tracery in the east window [G. Godwin, *The Churches of London* i, 1838; *Gent's Mag.* 1823 (i), 206–7, 315–17]. His work was destroyed by bombing in 1940–1. He was also surveyor to the Wise estate in Westminster. Gardiner, who was a Fellow of the Institute of British Architects, died at Brighton on 7 January 1867, aged 81. Three drawings by him for the decoration of the SPANISH AND PORTU-

GUESE SYNAGOGUE, BEVIS MARKS, LONDON, are in the R.I.B.A. Collection.

GARDNER, THOMAS (c. 1737–1804), was an architect and builder at Uttoxeter in Staffordshire. By trade he was a carpenter, and his forbears had been carpenters and farmers in Leicestershire for at least a century. In 1764 he was still a journeyman, working on the Derby Assembly Rooms under Joseph Pickford at 2s. a day. Shortly afterwards he became Pickford's clerk and worked for him both at Etruria and at Sandon Hall. In 1772 after the death of his father he had sufficient capital to set up in partnership with Thomas Freeman, a builder of Derby. The partnership was dissolved in March 1776, and for the remainder of his life Gardner carried on an independent business as an architect and builder at Uttoxeter, where he died on 8 October 1804 and is commemorated by a tablet in the parish church. He designed several country houses in the vicinity in a plain Georgian style. [Edward Saunders in *Derbyshire Life*, Aug. 1972, 41; will, P.C.C. 345 NELSON.]

UTTOXETER, STAFFS., house overlooking churchyard for Thomas Hart, 1777 [advertisement in *Derby Mercury*, 3 Jan. 1777, announcing the recent dissolution of the partnership between Gardner and Freeman, but stating that 'the buildings now carrying on for Sir Henry Cavendish Bart. at Doveridge and Mr. Thomas Hart of Uttoxeter ... are to be jointly carried on by the said T.G. and T.F.'].

DOVERIDGE HALL, DERBYSHIRE, works for Sir Henry Cavendish, Bart., 1777; dem. 1934 [advertisement cited above; Edward Saunders, 'Doveridge Hall', *Derbyshire Life*, Aug. 1972].

attributed: WIGGINTON CHURCH, STAFFS., 1777; chancel added 1862 [design among Faculty Papers in Lichfield Joint Record Office attributed to Gardner by Mr. Edward Saunders].

LONGTON HALL, STAFFS., extensive alterations for J. E. Heathcote, 1777; dem. 1939 [E. Meteyard, *Life of Josiah Wedgwood* ii, 1866, 373].

attributed: THORPE CONSTANTINE CHURCH, STAFFS., rebuilt (except tower), 1778; rebuilt 1883 [design among Faculty Papers in Lichfield Record Office attributed to Gardner by Mr. Edward Saunders].

UTTOXETER, STAFFS., conduit in Market Place, 1780; dem. c. 1850 [F. Redfern, *History of Uttoxeter*, 1886, 418].

FARLEY HALL, STAFFS., altered and refronted for C. Bill, 1782 [drawings and agreement in Staffs. Record Office, D554, bundle 105].

ROLLESTON HALL, STAFFS., alterations for Sir Oswald Mosley, Bart., c. 1785; dem. 1928 [Sir O. Mosley, *Family Memoirs*, 1849, 64].

CHURCH GRESLEY CHURCH, DERBYSHIRE, repairs, 1786; restored 1872 [bill among Gresley papers in Derbyshire Record Office].

SUDBURY HALL, DERBYSHIRE, built and presumably designed a lodge for the 1st Lord Vernon, 1787 [Derbyshire County Record Office, Vernon papers, general account-book, 1787, *ex inf.* Mr. Edward Saunders].

STRELLEY HALL, NOTTS., for T. W. Edge, 1789–92 [drawings and building accounts in Notts. County Record Office, DDE 46/60].

WILLERSLEY CASTLE, DERBYSHIRE, works for Richard Arkwright, *c.* 1792–5, including reconstruction after fire of 8 Aug. 1791 and design of stables and entrance gates [account-book belonging to Col. P. Arkwright].

STRATTON AUDLEY HOUSE, OXON., alterations and additions for Admiral Sir J. Borlase Warren of Stapleford Hall, Notts., 1797–8 [Derbyshire County Record Office, Vernon papers, volume of 'Papers relating to Stapleford, Stratton Audley, etc.', ff. 264–81].

THORPE CONSTANTINE HALL, STAFFS., remodelled for William Inge, 1799 [signed drawings at Thorpe Hall, *ex inf.* Dr. Andor Gomme].

GARLAND, ROBERT (*c.* 1808–1863), entered the Royal Academy Schools in December 1827 at the age of 19. He exhibited student's work at the Academy from 1826 to 1831. His name appears on the title-page of Winkles's *Cathedral Churches of England and Wales,* 1836–42, as the author of the drawings engraved in that work. In the 1840s he was in partnership with another architect called Henry Christopher at 11 John Street, Adelphi. A design for a terrace of houses on the north side of Eccleston Square, Westminster, signed 'Garland & Christopher Architects', is in the Cooper Union Museum, New York [J. Harris, *Catalogue of British Drawings for Architecture, etc. in American Collections,* 1971, 103]. Garland died in Hammersmith on 2 April 1863 [Principal Probate Registry, Calendar of Probates].

GARLING, HENRY (1789–1870), was articled to Samuel Page (*q.v.*). Immediately after the expiration of his articles, he assisted Page to carry out alterations to GRIMSTHORPE CASTLE, LINCS., for the 2nd Lord Gwydyr (afterwards 19th Lord Willoughby de Eresby). Framed drawings at Grimsthorpe are dated 1811 and endorsed 'Samuel Page Architect, Henry Garling fecit'. According to the writer of Garling's obituary, 'Mr. Page never answering any letters ... Mr. Garling acted for him in superintending (in fact, designing and doing everything), in the remodelling of Grimsthorpe Castle'. In 1815 Garling was admitted to the Royal Academy Schools, winning the Silver Medal in 1818. He commenced practice on his own at about this time, and was extensively employed in making valuations for leases, mortgages, dilapidations, etc. In about 1821 he became surveyor to the estates of Rugby School.

332

His principal architectural work was the CORN MARKET at GUILDFORD, erected by subscription in 1818, of which he published a print the following year. The market was closed in 1901, but the Tuscan portico survives. He also designed an entrance lodge and gates for Lord St. John at MELCHBOURNE PARK, BEDS., which he exhibited at the Royal Academy in 1833, and the HOLBORN UNION WORKHOUSE. He carried out work for Baron Vaughan and Earl Spencer and for the Carron Iron Company of Thames Street, London. He retired in 1847 after a successful career. He was a member of the Institute of British Architects, a governor of Christ's Hospital, St. Thomas's Hospital, The Bethlehem Hospital and other institutions, and possessed a fine library. He died on 9 April 1870. His son, Henry Bayly Garling (1822–1909), succeeded to his practice. [Obituary in *Builder* xxviii, 1870, 384.]

GARLIVE, JOHN, was the person in accordance with whose plans the parish church of KNUTSFORD, CHESHIRE, was rebuilt in 1741–4. On 3 September 1741, it was unanimously agreed by the Commissioners that there should be a meeting on 11 September 'in order to receive the proposalls of workmen for building a Church according to the modell or plan drawn by John Garlive ...' The mason employed was John Gatley, who undertook to supply ashlar stone 'out of his dell in Millington' [transcript of the Commissioners' minutes in Cheshire Record Office, P 7/8/2]. Garlive is presumably to be identified with the 'John Gatlive' who was paid 20s. in 1741 by the churchwardens of Rostherne, Cheshire, 'for drawing plans and [making an] estimate' for rebuilding their church tower. They were not adopted, but Gatlive, who appears to have been a master mason from Macclesfield, was employed as builder. [F. H. Crossley, 'Post Reformation Church Building in Cheshire', *Jnl. of Chester and N. Wales Architectural Society,* N.S. xxv (i), 1942, 45–8; R. Richards, *Old Cheshire Churches,* 1947, 286–7.]

GARRETT, DANIEL (–1753), was one of Lord Burlington's protégés, assisting him as clerk of works in many of his early building projects. In 1736, when proposing to bring Garrett to Castle Howard, in order to give advice on the completion of the Mausoleum, Sir Thomas Robinson wrote to Lord Carlisle that 'My Ld Burlington has a much better opinion of Mr. Garret's knowledge and judgment than of Mr. Flitcroft's or any person whatever, except Mr. Kent, he lives in Burlington House and has had care and conduct of the Duke of Richmond's house [in Whitehall], my Ld Harrington's [at Petersham] and all my L^{ds} designs he ever gave'. In 1727 Garrett was given a subordinate post in the Office of Works as Labourer in Trust at Richmond New Park Lodge, where his immediate superior was Roger Morris, and subsequently in 1729 at Windsor also. In due course he might have risen to a clerkship of the works, but in 1737 he was dismissed for 'not attending his duty'. By now he had in fact begun to build up an architectural practice of his own which, being largely in the north of England, was no doubt incompatible with the performance of his duties at Windsor and Richmond. From about 1735 onwards he was engaged in remodelling Wallington Hall in Northumberland for Sir Walter Blackett; in 1736 his services were in demand at Castle Howard; and in 1737 Sir Thomas Robinson reported that he had introduced Garrett to Lord Derby, 'for whom he has drawn some plans, and who is greatly pleased with his works'. In 1741 Garrett was one of the architects consulted by Sir James Dashwood before rebuilding his house at Kirtlington in Oxfordshire, and in the course of the next few years he is known to have designed two country houses in Northumberland and various buildings at Gibside in Durham. In 1747 he published a book of engravings entitled *Designs and Estimates of farm-houses, etc. for the County of York, Northumberland, Cumberland, Westmoreland and Bishoprick of Durham*. This was the first publication ever to be devoted entirely to farm-houses, and originated 'from the great complaint of gentlemen, who have built farmhouses, that they were irregular, expensive, and frequently too large for the farms they were intended for'. At a time when many new farm-houses were required as a consequence of enclosure, the book appears to have had some success, for there were two further editions, in 1759 and 1772. Garrett died intestate early in 1753, leaving an only daughter. James Paine was his successor in so many instances (*e.g.* at Wallington, Gibside and Northumberland House) as to suggest that there may have been some connection between these two men, both of whom were remarkable (among London-trained architects) in having an extensive North Country clientèle.

Garrett was, as might be expected, a conscientious disciple of Lord Burlington. He does not appear to have been a very original designer, but provided his clients with handsome houses in a straightforward Palladian style. Thus the entrance to Nunwick has obvious Burlingtonian prototypes, the stairs at the Castle Howard Mausoleum are taken from Chiswick, and the pilastered front at Forcett derives presumably from Lindsey House in Lincoln's Inn Fields. In internal decoration, however, he was something of a pioneer in the use of rococo plasterwork, and he designed several Gothick buildings in the manner of William Kent. The best authenticated of these are the Banqueting House at Gibside and the additions to Kippax Park. Other Gothick

buildings which may be by Garrett, including the Temple at Aske and the Culloden Tower at Richmond in Yorkshire, are discussed by Peter Leach in the article cited below.

[Peter Leach, 'The Architecture of Daniel Garrett', *C. Life*, 12, 19, 26 Sept. 1974; *History of the King's Works* v, 89; P.R.O., Works 4/7, 11 Aug. 1737; P.R.O., PROB 6/129, f. 162; *London Evening Post*, 3–6 March 1753.]

WALLINGTON HALL, NORTHUMBERLAND, reconstructed south front, north front and interior, and probably designed service court, for Sir Walter Blackett, *c.* 1735–53 [drawings by Garrett at Wallington; mid-eighteenth-century list of country houses in library at Alnwick Castle gives 'Mr. Garret' as architect of Wallington; John Cornforth in *C. Life*, 16–23 April 1970]. Garrett was also responsible for the adjoining folly known as Rothley Castle [*C. Life*, 26 Sept. 1974, 834 and fig. 3].

attributed: NEWCASTLE, ST. NICHOLAS CHURCH (now Cathedral), addition of classical library on south side at expense of Sir Walter Blackett of Wallington, 1736 [stylistic attribution].

FORCETT HALL, YORKS. (N.R.), for Richard Shuttleworth (d. 1748), *c.* 1730–40; altered 1795 [list at Alnwick Castle (see above) gives 'Mr. Garret' as architect of 'Forcet, for Richard Shuttleworth'].

CASTLE HOWARD, YORKS. (N.R.), THE MAUSOLEUM, added balustraded steps and outer court for the 3rd and 4th Earls of Carlisle, 1737–42 [G. F. Webb, 'Letters ... relating to the building of the Mausoleum at Castle Howard', *Walpole Soc.* xix, 160–2].

GIBSIDE, CO. DURHAM, works including New Laundry, 1744, Stables, 1748, and Gothic Banqueting House, 1751, for George Bowes [drawings by 'Mr. Garret' in Charter Room at Glamis Castle]. Garrett may also have been responsible for a Gothic tower built in 1743 (*C. Life*, 8 Feb. 1952, illustrates stables and banqueting house).

FENHAM HALL, NORTHUMBERLAND, for William Ord, *c.* 1744–8; refronted and wings added by W. Newton *c.* 1770 [list at Alnwick (see above) gives 'Mr. Garret' as architect of Fenham 'for Wm. Ord'].

TEMPLE NEWSHAM HOUSE, YORKS. (W.R.), designed decoration of 'the Long Passage' executed by Thomas Perritt, plasterer, 1745 [Leeds City Libraries, Archives Dept., Temple Newsham papers, EA 12/10, *ex inf.* Mr. P. Leach]. Garrett may well have been responsible for the decoration of the Long Gallery executed by Perritt in 1738–45, and perhaps also for the contemporary stables.

NUNWICK, NORTHUMBERLAND, for Lancelot Allgood, 1746–50; altered by I. Bonomi 1829 [payments to Daniel Garrett in Allgood's accounts: Northumberland County Record Office, ZAL 46/1, 4 June and 1 July 1946] (*C. Life*, 12–19 July 1956).

RABY CASTLE, CO. DURHAM, internal alterations for the 2nd Duke of Cleveland, including the state rooms in Clifford's Tower, *c*. 1745–50 [Alistair Rowan in *Architectural History* xv, 1972, figs. 3a, 4a, and in *C. Life*, 1 Jan. 1970].

LONDON, NO. 19 ST. JAMES'S SQUARE, internal alterations, including staircase, for the 2nd Duke of Cleveland, 1747–8; dem. 1894 [accounts at Raby Castle, *ex inf.* Mr. Peter Leach] (*Survey of London* xxix, 161–3).

LONDON, NORTHUMBERLAND HOUSE, STRAND, extensive works for the 7th Duke of Somerset, 1748–50, continued by the 1st Duke of Northumberland, 1750–3, including the rebuilding of the north front to the street (of which Garrett published an engraving in 1752) and the addition of the wings extending south and containing the Ball Room and Gallery. The latter was completed by James Paine *c*. 1754–7. The house was dem. 1874 [Alnwick Castle muniments, U IV 2a: Duke of Somerset's accounts with Messrs. Child and Messrs. Hoare 1748–50, *ex inf.* Mr. Peter Leach] (*London and its Environs described*, R. & J. Dodsley, 1761, v, 53 and 59, engravings after Samuel Wale showing Garrett's work before later alterations).

HORTON HOUSE, NORTHANTS. According to Horace Walpole ('Visits to Country Seats', *Walpole Soc.* xvi, 52) Garrett was employed by George Montagu, 1st Earl of Halifax (d. 1739), to alter and refront this house, which was subsequently further altered by Thomas Wright (*q.v.*) and dem. 1936. However, a letter from Sanderson Miller in B.M., Stowe MS. 753, f. 145, shows that Garrett was at Horton in 1750, designing 'Gothic Bridges etc.' for the 2nd Earl. Either he worked there for both Earls over a period of some years, or else Walpole's account was confused. The house is illustrated in Neale's *Views of Seats*, 1st ser., i, 1818, *V.C.H. Northants.* iv, 259–60, and *C. Life*, 26 Aug. 1971, 495.

KIPPAX PARK, YORKS. (W.R.), alterations for Sir John Bland, *c*. 1750, partly Gothic [unsigned drawings among Bland papers in Leeds City Libraries, Archives Dept., identified as in Garrett's hand by Mr. Peter Leach. The house was in course of reconstruction in 1750; see Dr. Pococke's *Travels through England*, Camden Soc. 1888, i, 62] (Neale's *Views of Seats* v, 1822).

GARRETT, JAMES, of Exeter, a joiner by trade, received an annual salary as surveyor at POWDERHAM CASTLE, DEVON, and was paid in 1754 and 1755 for 'drawings for buildings' and for 'designs and directing works' there for Sir William Courtenay. He presumably designed the great staircase, which he supplied [Mark Girouard in *C. Life*, 11 July 1963]. He was described as 'architect' in 1760, when his son John was admitted to St. John's College, Cambridge, in that year [*Admissions to St. John's College, Cambridge*, ed. R. F. Scott, iii, 1903]. In 1753 he supplied a classical altar-piece for KENN CHURCH, DEVON, removed 1862 [F. W. Vining, *Kenn*, *c*. 1910, 80].

GATLIVE, JOHN, *see* GARLIVE

GAYFERE, THOMAS (1755–1827), was the son of Thomas Gayfere (*c*. 1721–1812), who was appointed Master Mason to Westminster Abbey in 1766 and was Master of the London Masons' Company in 1773. The younger Gayfere exhibited a view of Norton Church, Leics., at the Society of Artists in 1774, and a drawing of the ruins of Furness Abbey in 1777. He subsequently exhibited topographical views at the Royal Academy in 1778, 1779 and 1780. In December 1802 he was appointed Master Mason to Westminster Abbey jointly with his father, and retained the post until his retirement in 1823. In 1807–8, when funds were voted by Parliament for the restoration of Henry VII's Chapel, he was commissioned to visit stone-quarries in various parts of the country to select the best stone for the purpose, and pronounced in favour of Combe Down Bath stone. The repairs were begun in 1809 and completed in 1822, at a total cost of £42,000. Although James Wyatt, as Surveyor to the Abbey, was nominally in charge, it was Gayfere who really directed as well as executed the restoration. Before starting work, he examined every part of the decaying structure and took plaster casts of such fragments of mouldings and other details as survived. From these, full-size working drawings were made at his house in Abingdon Street, and he took great pains to discover suitable masons and to instruct them in what was then an unfamiliar style of architecture. The result was an authentic restoration carried out in a manner unique in the eighteenth and early nineteenth centuries. In 1819–22 Thomas Gayfere restored the north front of Westminster Hall with Bath stone under the direction of J. W. Hiort of the Office of Works. He died at Burton-on-Trent on 20 October 1827, and was buried at Newton Solney in Derbyshire, where a tombstone commemorates his 'qualities as a Man' and 'his Abilities as an Architect'. [*A.P.S.D.*; obituary in *Gent's Mag.* 1828 (i), 275; P.R.O., Works 10 B/11; *Gent's Mag.* 1811 (i), 341; J. L. Chester, *Westminster Abbey Registers*, Harleian Soc. 1875, 483; J. P. Neale & E. W. Brayley, 'Henry VII's Chapel', *Abbey Church of Westminster* i, 1818, 21–7; L. N. Cottingham, *Plans, etc. of King Henry VII's Chapel at Westminster* i, 1822, 7–24; sale catalogue of Gayfere's Library (B.M., S.C.S. 138/7).]

GEARY, STEPHEN (1797–1854), entered the Royal Academy Schools in 1817 at the age (according to the Register) of 20. He exhibited a student's design in 1814, and another in 1816. In 1830 he designed KING'S CROSS, BATTLE BRIDGE, LONDON, exhibited at the R.A. that year, but not completed until 1836 [J. C. Loudon, *Architectural Mag.* iii, 41]. This consisted of a statue of George IV set on a high pedestal which was at first used as a police-station and afterwards as a public-house. The statue, caricatured by John Leech in *The Comic Latin Grammar*, 1840, 131, was removed in 1842, and the whole structure was demolished in 1845. It figures in Pugin's *Contrasts*, 1836.

In 1830 Geary was involved, with Signor Gesualdo Lanza, in a scheme for a 'Grand Panharmonium Theatre' (or music and drama centre) on an island site facing the Euston Road. Geary designed the buildings, which were to be connected by an overhead railway. Work started in 1830, but the scheme was abandoned in 1832 [*Survey of London* xxiv, 103].

Geary also designed the ST. PANCRAS COLLEGIATE SCHOOL, ARGYLL SQUARE, KING'S CROSS, of which he exhibited a view at the R.A. in 1837. He is best known, however, as the architect of HIGHGATE CEMETERY, opened in 1839 by a company of which Geary was the founder. Its architectural features, which included an 'Egyptian Avenue' and a 'Gothic Catacomb', are described by Hugh Ross Williamson in *Arch. Rev.* xcii, 1942, 87, and by J. Stevens Curl in *The Victorian Celebration of Death*, 1972, 86–102. In 1840 Geary published *Designs for Tombs and Cenotaphs*, a folding sheet with twenty-one of his characteristically crude designs for funeral monuments, of which there is a copy in the Bodleian Library. A shop-front in ISLINGTON designed by him is illustrated by N. Whittock, *On the Construction and Decoration of the Shop Fronts of London*, 1840, pl. vii.

Geary was clearly more of an entrepreneur than an artist. He is said to have designed the first gin palace in London in about 1830, and took out patents for artificial fuel, paving streets, water supply, motive power and other inventions. He died in Euston Place on 28 August 1854 and was buried in Highgate Cemetery, where a tombstone records his death in his 57th year.

[F. Boase, *Modern English Biography* i, 1892, 1133; F. T. Cansick, *The Monumental Inscriptions of Middlesex* ii, 1872, 78 (where his age at death is wrongly given as 75 instead of 57); *Gent's Mag.* 1854 (ii), 413.]

GEE, THOMAS, designed the spire which was added to the tower of ST. NICHOLAS CHURCH, LIVERPOOL, in 1746, the contractors being Messrs. Henry Sephton and William Smith. It fell in 1810, when a new steeple was designed by Thomas Harrison of Chester [J. A. Picton, *Memorials of Liverpool* ii, 58–9; *Gent's Mag.* 1814 (i), 115]. W. H. Gee, an architect practising in Liverpool in the mid nineteenth century, may have been a descendant.

GERBIER, SIR BALTHAZAR (1592–1663), courtier, diplomatist, miniature painter and architect, figures in this *Dictionary* only in the last capacity. Born on 23 February 1591/2 at Middelburg in Zeeland, he was the son of Anthony Gerbier, a Huguenot *émigré*, but claimed a certain 'Anthony Gerbier, Baron Douvilly' as his great-grandfather, and on occasion used the title himself. Nothing is known of his upbringing, but he may have been a pupil of the artist Hendrik Goltzius. According to Sanderson he was 'a common Pen-man', and the art of calligraphy was certainly among his attainments. He himself claimed to speak 'several languages' and to have 'a good hand in writing, skill in sciences as mathematics, architecture, drawing, painting, contriving of scenes, masques, shows and entertainments for great Princes ... as likewise for making of engines useful in war.' It was his knowledge of the 'framing of warlike machines' that brought him to the notice of Prince Maurice of Orange, who recommended him to the Dutch Ambassador in London, with whom he came to England in 1616. For the next twelve years he was in the service of George Villiers, Duke of Buckingham, who employed him to paint miniatures, embellish his houses, and collect works of art on a large scale. He was also sent on various diplomatic missions abroad, and in 1623 accompanied Buckingham and Prince Charles to Spain, where he painted a portrait of the Infanta for the royal inspection. In Paris in 1625 he met Rubens, with whom he afterwards became intimate. It was with Gerbier that Rubens lodged when he came to London in 1629, and during this visit the artist painted a portrait group of Gerbier's family, now in the Royal Collection at Windsor. After Buckingham's assassination in 1628 Gerbier was naturalized (Jan. 1629) and taken into the king's service as an 'esquire of his Majesty's body extraordinary'. He continued to be employed on a combination of diplomatic and artistic business, and despite more than dubious loyalty to Charles I, was knighted in 1638. In May 1641 he was appointed Master of Ceremonies in succession to Sir John Finet and was (according to his own account) promised the reversion of Inigo Jones's place as Surveyor-General of the Works which he had long coveted (see below). But soon afterwards a political feud with Lord Cottington led to his disgrace. In July 1641 Charles Cotterell was appointed nominally to 'assist', but in practice to supersede Gerbier as Master of Ceremonies.

Gerbier's career as a courtier was now at an end, and in the course of the next few years he tried to make a living by various means, which included banking in Paris, keeping an academy at Bethnal Green, and seeking for gold in America. During the Interregnum, far from regarding himself as a royalist, he dedicated a lecture on military architecture to Lord Fairfax (1650), and associated himself (c. 1651) with a proposal to decorate the palace of Whitehall with portraits and battlepieces illustrating the 'memorable achievements' of the Parliament. When in 1660 he returned to London to claim the mastership of the ceremonies, he was promptly suspended from office, a decision afterwards confirmed by the Privy Council (*Cal. S.P. Dom. 1660–1*, 415, 522, 589; P.R.O., PC 2/56, f. 153). Excluded from the court, Gerbier decided to advertise his talents as an architect by publishing in 1662 a short tract entitled *A Brief Discourse concerning the Three Chief Principles of Magnificent Building*, and in 1663 a more substantial treatise called *Counsel and Advise to All Builders*. About this time Lord Craven (in whose regiment Gerbier's son had served as a Captain) engaged him to design or remodel a large house at Hampstead Marshall in Berkshire. It was at Hampstead Marshall that Gerbier died, apparently in 1663, leaving the unfinished house to be completed by William Winde. A tombstone in Hampstead Marshall Church commemorates 'Sr. Balthazer Gerbier, Kt. Archt. who built a stately pile of Building in the years 1662 to 1665 for the Rt. Hon. William Earl of Craven at Hampsted Marshall, the greatest part of which was destroyed by Fire in the year 1718. He died in the year 1667.' This long posthumous inscription is the only authority for stating that Gerbier died in 1667, and he must have been dead by August 1663, when his daughters were petitioning the king for relief from the starving condition in which they said they had been left by their father's death (see F. H. Cheetham in *Notes and Queries*, 11th ser., vii, 1913, 407–8).

Gerbier's architectural activity falls into two periods, the first in the 1620s when he was Buckingham's artistic adviser, the second in the 1660s. Letters to Buckingham in the Bodleian Library (Tanner MS. 73, ff. 491ᵛ, 510ᵛ) show that in 1624–5 he was busy with alterations both at York House in the Strand and at New Hall in Essex. For the latter house he had commissioned a wooden model for Buckingham's approval. Subsequently he reported that the 'cabinet de marbre' was being paved and that he was about to whiten the vaults. His work here appears to have been chiefly decorative in character (see *Vetusta Monumenta* ii, 1789, pls. xli–xlii and text). At York House, where the 'grande chambre' was being paved, he reported a visit from Inigo Jones in terms which make their

336

rivalry clear. The Surveyor of the Works, he wrote, 'a esté a Jorckhouse pour veoir la Mayson et estoit comme confus et honteux, il ne me faudroit plus que la reversion de la plasse pour luy faire aveoir la gravelle car il en est fort jaloux'. Gerbier's works at York house are also mentioned in his *Brief Discourse*, where he boasts that King Charles I was 'graciously pleased to avouch he had seen in Anno 1628 (close to the Gate of York-House, in a Roome not above 35 Foot square) as much as could be represented (as to Sceans) in the great Banquetting Room of Whitehall'. York House was pulled down in the 1670s, but the Water-Gate survives (*Survey of London* xviii, pls. 31–3). It is mentioned twice in Gerbier's tract, a circumstance which supports its attribution to Gerbier by Sir John Summerson. The main grounds for this attribution are 'the fact that Gerbier is known to have been in charge of York House, the resemblance of the water-gate to the Fontaine de Médicis, which Jones never saw and Gerbier certainly will have seen in 1625, and the resemblance of the design to an indubitable drawing by Gerbier in the Bodleian' (*Architecture in Britain 1530–1830*, 1963, 351). The drawing in question is for a gateway at Hampstead Marshall in the manner of Francini (MS. Gough Drawings a.2, ff. 24–5). It dates from the 1660s and is signed by Gerbier. The mannerist cartouches on the piers should be compared with those framing Gerbier's portraits of the Prince of Orange and Frederick V of Bohemia in the British Museum (*Catalogue of British Drawings*, 1960, pls. 133–4). As Hampstead Marshall was destroyed by fire in 1718 it is now difficult to distinguish the respective shares of Gerbier and Winde in this house, but Kip's view and plans in the Bodleian Library (MS. Gough Drawings a.2) both suggest that they were engaged in remodelling an old Jacobean house rather than building a new one. As work on the first floor did not begin until July 1664, and as several designs for ceilings are dated in the 1670s and 1680s, it is clear that much remained to be done after Gerbier's death.

One other architectural work can be attributed to Gerbier with some confidence. This was the design of the triumphal arches erected in the City of London to celebrate the coronation of Charles II in 1661. According to J. Ogilby's *Relation of His Majestie's entertainment passing through the City of London to his coronation with a description of the triumphal arches*, 1661, 2nd ed. 1662, these arches were designed jointly by Peter Mills (*q.v.*) 'and another Person, who desired to have his name conceal'd'. In Gerbier's *Brief Discourse* they are referred to in terms which suggest that he was their designer, and his banishment from court would explain his desire for anonymity at the time. There are, moreover, resemblances between the London arches and those designed by Rubens for the entry of the Cardinal Infante Ferdinand into Antwerp in 1635 and published in 1642 (*Pompa introitus*), with which Gerbier would certainly have been familiar. The original drawings for the London arches are in the R.I.B.A. Collection (see *Catalogue: G–K*, 18–19).

Gerbier's place in English architecture is difficult to assess because of the destruction, almost without record, of nearly all his known works. Despite his association with Peter Mills in 1661, and the influence of Rubens's *Palazzi di Genova* on English architectural taste in the mid seventeenth century, it is doubtful whether Gerbier had much to do with the formation of the 'artisan mannerist' style. He would, however, appear to have imported into England a florid Netherlandish baroque that might well have affected English architecture much more profoundly but for the chastening influence of his rival Inigo Jones.

[The best accounts of Gerbier's artistic activities will be found in E. Croft-Murray & Paul Hulton, *Catalogue of British Drawings in the British Museum*, 1960, 328–30, and Lita-Rose Betcherman, 'The York House Collection and its Keeper', *Apollo* xcii, 1970, both with further references; for his political career see *D.N.B.* and H. Ross Williamson, *Four Stuart Portraits*, 1949. See also A. E. Richardson, 'Seventeenth-Century Buildings in Search of an Architect', *R.I.B.A. Jnl.*, 17 June 1933, E. Croft-Murray, *Decorative Painting in England* i, 1962, 202, and M. J. Power, 'Sir Balthazar Gerbier's Academy at Bethnal Green', *East London Papers* x (i), 1967, 19–33. Several of his letters to the Duke of Buckingham were printed in Godfrey Goodman's *Court of King James I*, 1839. MS. sources include P.R.O., E 178/5973, which throws light on Gerbier's position in Buckingham's household, and B.M., Add. MS. 32093, ff. 302–7, a protestation of his loyalty to the Commonwealth government made in 1652/3.]

GETHIN, JOHN (1757–1831), a mason of Kingsland, Herefordshire, held the office of Surveyor of Bridges for the county from before 1800 until his death at the Brick House, Kingsland, on 24 May 1831. A list of the bridges which he built or rebuilt (none of much architectural importance) is given by G. H. Jack, 'John Gethin', *Woolhope Naturalists' Field Club Trans.*, 1930–2, 86.

GIBBS, JAMES (1682–1754), was the younger son of Peter or Patrick Gibb(s), a merchant of Footdeesmire, or Fittsmyre, on the outskirts of Aberdeen. He was brought up a Catholic, and in 1703, after a sojourn in Holland with relatives, made his way to Rome to be entered at the Scots College there as a candidate for the priesthood. Within a year, he was driven out by the tyrannical

régime of an over-zealous rector, and turned instead to architecture. As a boy he had 'had a great genius to drawing', and in the course of the journey to Rome (which took him through France, Switzerland and Germany) he had not been insensitive to the artistic attractions of the towns through which he had passed, especially those of northern Italy. Abandoning a clerical career, he became a pupil of Carlo Fontana, then the leading Roman architect. While in Rome he made drawings for some of the visiting English nobility and gentry, establishing contacts that were to be of service in his later career. When in 1709 he returned to Britain, he had had a professional training at the fountain-head of Italian baroque that was unique among contemporary English architects. Only his religion stood in the way of a successful career, and that was an obstacle that may have seemed less serious under Queen Anne than it was to do after the Jacobite Rising of 1715. His first important patron was, indeed, a fellow-Catholic. John, Earl of Mar (*q.v.*), himself an amateur architect, was 'very much his friend', and employed him, *inter alia*, to alter the official house in Whitehall which he shared with the Earl of Loudoun. It was through Mar's influence with Harley,[1] reinforced by a recommendation from Wren, that in 1713 Gibbs succeeded William Dickinson as one of the two surveyors to the Commissioners for building Fifty New Churches in London. The church of St. Mary-le-Strand, which he designed in this capacity, was his first public building, and 'got him great reputation in his business'. But the intended column to Queen Anne, which was to have stood in the Strand in front of the church, and for which Gibbs made designs, was abandoned after the Queen's death in 1714, and when the Commission was reconstructed in the following year, Gibbs, suspect both as a Tory and a Scot, was dismissed (Jan. 1715/16).

Although the loss of his post must have been a serious blow (made more bitter because he believed it was due to the machinations of a 'countryman' almost certainly identifiable as Colen Campbell), Gibbs was by now sufficiently well established to make his own way without the security of a salaried post. His professional training in Italy was an asset that none of his rivals

---

[1] Mar and Harley were related by marriage. Harley's daughter Abigail married the 7th Earl of Kinnoull, whose sister Margaret was Mar's first wife. At Worcester College, Oxford, there is a pair of unique engravings signed 'J.G.', one for the 'Earl of Mar's lodge' (probably at Comley Bank, on Mar's Alloa estate), the other for a house for Lord Kinnoull (presumably at Dupplin Castle, Perthshire) on a plan derived from Boffrand's Malgrange and similar to the palace which Juvarra was later to build at Stupinigi (reproduced in H. M. Colvin, *Catalogue of Architectural Drawings . . . at Worcester College, Oxford*, 1964, pls. 115–16).

had enjoyed, and if Tory patronage could not provide him with official employment, it brought him an abundance of commissions for country houses. In early Georgian England Gibbs was indeed the Tory architect *par excellence*, and most, but not all, of his clients were of that political persuasion. It was the younger Harley's patronage that gave him a stake in the profitable development of the family estate in Marylebone, where in about 1730 he built himself a substantial house on the corner of Wimpole Street and Henrietta Place. But it was the Whig Duke of Argyll who employed him to design his English seat at Sudbrooke in Surrey and who, as Master-General of the Ordnance, gave him in 1727 the post of Architect of the Ordnance. Worth £120 a year, it was 'almost if not merely a sinecure', and Gibbs was to hold it until his death twenty-seven years later.

In 1728 Gibbs advertised his success as an architect by the publication of *A Book of Architecture*, a folio containing 150 plates of his designs, both executed and otherwise. There was a second edition in 1739. This was followed in 1732 by his *Rules for Drawing the Several Parts of Architecture*, of which there were further editions in 1738 and 1753. He also published his designs for the Radcliffe Camera at Oxford in a volume entitled *Bibliotheca Radcliviana*, 1747. The *Book of Architecture* served more than one purpose. By devoting a whole volume to his own works Gibbs more than made up for the deliberate omission of his name from Campbell's *Vitruvius Britannicus*. At the same time, by the inclusion of a number of well-conceived designs for monuments, chimney-pieces, garden buildings, urns and cartouches, he converted a personal advertisement into a general architectural pattern-book of high quality. Its success was immediate and long-lasting. In fact it was 'probably the most widely used architectural book of the century', well known to master builders both in the British Isles and in the American Colonies. It was the source of several stock features of Georgian vernacular architecture, and a host of church steeples on both sides of the Atlantic owe their form to Gibbs's engravings. Gibbs himself told George Vertue that he had made £1500 by his books, and that he afterwards sold the plates for £400 more.

In 1749, 'having been long much afflicted with the stone and gout', Gibbs visited Spa for the sake of his health. He died on 5 August 1754, aged 71, according to the tablet in St. Marylebone Church (for the inscription see Lysons, *Environs of London* ii, 1811, 554). He was unmarried, and he left £1000, three houses in Marylebone, and all his plate, to Lord Erskine, 'in gratitude for favours received from his father the late Earl of Mar'. He left his own house in London to the Scottish portrait-painter Cosmo Alexander, and

another in Cavendish Square to Robert Pringle, one of his executors. To John Borlach, 'for many years my draughtsman', he left £400. He bequeathed all his books, prints and drawings to the Radcliffe Library in Oxford of which he had been the architect.[1]

Gibbs was a highly accomplished architectural designer whose work, if rarely equal in imaginative quality to that of his contemporaries Vanbrugh and Hawksmoor, always shows the practised hand of one who had been a fellow-pupil of Juvarra. His style was a successful synthesis of ideas and motifs derived partly from Italian sources (both baroque and Palladian), and partly from English ones. His steeples, in particular, show an intelligent appreciation of the work of Wren. In 1720, when he submitted his designs for the church of St. Martin's-in-the-Fields, he took the committee on a tour of Wren's churches, and the steeple of St. Martin's is clearly inspired by the example of Wren's City spires. The combination of portico and steeple is not beyond criticism, but this baroque equivalent of a Gothic spire rising from the roof of a classical temple was to be the stereotype of the urban Anglican church for the next hundred years. If St. Martin's was a brilliant development of the type of church started by Wren, the Radcliffe Library at Oxford owed a good deal to Wren's pupil Hawksmoor. Both architects made several designs before the Trustees came to a decision, and although Gibbs was ultimately appointed as architect after Hawksmoor's death in 1736, there is reason to think that it was to Hawksmoor that he owed the idea of a centrally planned domed building (his own designs were for a more utilitarian building on a rectangular plan). Having adopted the idea he transformed Hawksmoor's essentially classical conception of a stately colonnaded drum into a sophisticated piece of Italianate architecture of which Maderno or Fontana would not have disapproved. Gibbs's most conspicuously Italianate building is, however, St. Mary-le-Strand, whose elaborate external dress has echoes of Cortona and Borromini as well as of Palladio and Inigo Jones. In his later works the direct influence of Italian baroque prototypes is much less evident: in many of them, indeed, it persisted only in the elaborate plasterwork (usually executed by the Italians Artari and Bagutti) with which he decorated the halls and saloons of his country houses. For, in spite of his Italian experience, Gibbs was by no means insensitive to the change which came over English architectural taste in the 1720s, and although he never became a disciple of Lord Burlington, he

---

[1] Many of the books were sold as duplicates in 1894, but a MS. catalogue exists (Bodleian, MS. Eng. Misc. c. 28). For the drawings, now in the Print Room of the Ashmolean Museum, see below.

tended in his later years to conform to the fashion for plain pedimented blocks which represented the common form of English Palladianism in domestic architecture.

In 1729 Gibbs was elected a Fellow of the Royal Society, and in 1749, on the opening of the Radcliffe Library, he received the honorary degree of M.A. at Oxford. A number of portraits are recorded. Gibbs presented a half-length by J. M. Williams to the Bodleian Library, and a Kit-Kat to St. Mary Hall, Oxford (now Oriel College). A duplicate of the Bodleian portrait is at the National Portrait Gallery. There is a portrait possibly by Andrea Soldi in the vestry of St. Martin's-in-the-Fields and another by Bartholomew Dandridge is in the Ionides Collection at Orleans House, Twickenham. A portrait by Kneller, formerly at Alloa House, is now in the collection of Mr. Derek Sherborne. Busts by Rysbrack can be seen at St. Martin's-in-the-Feilds and the Radcliffe Library (both dated 1726). An engraved portrait by Hans Huysing is reproduced by Little in his biography, together with a bookplate incorporating a profile portrait dated 1736.

Eight volumes of Gibbs's drawings and one of prints collected by him are now in the Print Room of the Ashmolean Museum at Oxford. They include the original drawings for the *Book of Architecture*, the *Rules* and *Bibliotheca Radcliviana*, and provide many examples of his precise and elegant draughtsmanship. Seventy-two sheets of drawings, nearly all duplicates of those for the *Book of Architecture*, are in the Victoria and Albert Museum. There are also a few drawings (including that for the Strand column) in the Print Room of the British Museum, and several in the R.I.B.A. Drawings Collection (see the *Catalogue*), the Bodleian Library (Gough Collection) and the Soane Museum. At the Soane Museum there is also an important MS. memoir of the architect. This was included in the catalogue of books left to the Radcliffe Library, but marked as not received. Before its acquisition by Soane it belonged to the architect Henry Holland. It contains a fairly complete list of Gibbs's works, and a brief account of his early life and travels. There is reason to think that, despite some minor inaccuracies, it was written by Gibbs himself, or from information supplied by him, and it constitutes the principal source of information about his career. In the same volume there are some 'Cursory Remarks on some of the finest Antient and modern Buildings in Rome, and other parts of Italy', made 'by Mr. Gibbs while he was studying Architecture there' (cf. *Wren Soc.* xii, pl. xli).

Other important sources for Gibbs's life are the records of the Commissioners for Building Fifty Churches in Lambeth Palace Library; letters and references in Hist. MSS. Comm.,

Egmont ii, *Bath* iii, *Stuart Papers* ii, iv and v, and *Portland, passim*; *Vertue's Note Books* (Walpole Society) iii, 17, 133; a brief memoir in *Scots Magazine*, 1760, 475–6; records of his Ordnance post in P.R.O., WO 48/68, p. 186, and WO 54/210; and Gibbs's will (P.C.C. 228 PINFOLD). The modern literature includes Marcus Whiffen, 'The Progeny of St. Martin in the Fields', *Arch. Rev.*, July 1946; A. S. MacWilliam, 'James Gibbs, Architect, 1682–1754', *The Innes Review* v, 1954; S. Lang, 'Gibbs: a bicentenary review of his architectural sources', *Arch. Rev.*, July 1954; John Holloway, 'A James Gibbs Autobiography', *Burlington Mag.*, May 1955; Bryan Little, *The Life and Works of James Gibbs*, 1955; H. E. Stutchbury, 'Palladian Gibbs', *Trans. of the Ancient Monuments Soc.*, N.S. viii, 1960; John Field, 'Early Unknown Gibbs', *Arch. Rev.*, May 1962; Arthur Oswald, 'James Gibbs and his Portraits', *Country Life Annual*, 1963; John Summerson, *Architecture in Britain 1530–1830*, 1970, chap. 21; and T. Friedman, 'James Gibbs 1682–1754: the formation of his architectural style' (unpublished thesis, Courtauld Institute of Art, London, 1971).

PUBLIC BUILDINGS

CAMBRIDGE, THE SENATE HOUSE, 1722–30. This building was intended to form the north wing of a three-sided group of university buildings, as shown in *Book of Architecture*, pl. 36. The west end, originally designed to be engaged with the central block, was not faced until 1767–8 [Willis & Clark, iii, chap. 3; T. P. Hudson, 'James Gibbs's Designs for University Buildings at Cambridge', *Burlington Mag.*, Dec. 1972].

LONDON, THE OXFORD MARKET, MARYLEBONE, for Edward Harley, 2nd Earl of Oxford, 1724–*c.* 1730 [though not specifically mentioned in the Soane MS., it can hardly be doubted that this was among the 'several buildings' there stated to have been designed for Harley by Gibbs].

CAMBRIDGE, KING'S COLLEGE NEW BUILDING, 1724–49 [Willis & Clark, i, 560–3; *Book of Architecture*, pls. 32–5].

LONDON, ST. BARTHOLOMEW'S HOSPITAL, SMITHFIELD, 1730 onwards; repaired by Thomas Hardwick 1814–20 and refaced by P. Hardwick 1851. Gibbs was a governor of the Hospital and made no charge for his designs [Soane MS.; Little, *op. cit.*, 113–16, citing the Hospital records].

OXFORD, THE RADCLIFFE LIBRARY, 1737–48 [J. Gibbs, *Bibliotheca Radcliviana*, 1747; *The Building Accounts of the Radcliffe Camera*, ed. S. G. Gillam, Oxford Historical Soc., N.S. xiii, 1958, with introduction and illustrations of many of the drawings; S. Lang, 'By Hawksmoor out of Gibbs', *Arch. Rev.*, April 1949].

OXFORD, ST. JOHN'S COLLEGE, stone screen in hall, 1743 [College archives, *Computus Annuus*, 1743, f. 45].

CHURCHES

LONDON, ST. MARY-LE-STRAND, 1714–17 (consecrated Jan. 1723/4), for the Commissioners for Building Fifty New Churches. The steeple was an afterthought, designed by Gibbs when the column to Queen Anne, which was to have taken its place, was abandoned. There are two contemporary models of the church in the R.I.B.A. Drawings Collection (formerly at Westminster Abbey and at Burleigh House, Stamford). The interior was refitted by R. J. Withers in 1871 [*Book of Architecture*, pls. 16–23, 31].

LONDON, ST. CLEMENT DANES. The upper stages of the steeple were added to Gibbs's design in 1719–20, replacing Wren's wooden cupola [*Book of Architecture*, pl. 28]. Gibbs also repaired the roof, 1720.

LONDON, ST. PETER, VERE STREET, formerly known as the Oxford or Marylebone Chapel, 1721–4, for Edward Harley, later 2nd Earl of Oxford. There is a copy of the contract, dated 8 Aug. 1721, in the British Museum (Add. MS. 18238, f. 37 ᵛ), and a section signed by Gibbs, Harley and the contractors, in the Ashmolean collection of Gibbs's drawings, vol. i, no. 12b. The interior was altered by J. K. Collings in 1881 [*Book of Architecture*, pls. 24–5].

LONDON, ST. MARTIN-IN-THE-FIELDS, rebuilt 1722–6. Gibbs's designs were chosen in 1720 after the Committee had considered those submitted by John James, Sir James Thornhill, Nicholas Dubois and George Sampson [MS. Minutes of the Commissioners for Rebuilding St. Martin's Church, Westminster City Library]. Gibbs's model, showing a variant treatment of the spire, is preserved in the R.I.B.A. Drawings Collection, and there are other alternative designs in the Ashmolean Museum (see vol. vii). The interior was altered by Sir A. W. Blomfield in 1887. [*Book of Architecture*, pls. 1–15, 29, 30; *Survey of London* xx, 24–8, pls. 10–27; J. McMaster, *A Short History of St. Martin in the Fields*, 1916; K. A. Esdaile, *St. Martin in the Fields*, 1944.]

SHIPBOURNE CHURCH, KENT, rebuilt 1722 for Christopher Vane, Lord Barnard; rebuilt 1879 [Soane MS.] (M. Whiffen, *Stuart and Georgian Churches*, pl. 52).

DERBY, ALL SAINTS (now the Cathedral), rebuilt 1723–5, except the west tower. The interior was altered in 1876 by J. Young, and there was a restoration by Temple Moore in 1904–5. [*Book of Architecture*, pls. 26–7; J. C. Cox & W. H. St. J. Hope, *Chronicles of All Saints, Derby*, 1881, chap. iv.]

LINCOLN CATHEDRAL, strengthened west towers by building up arches at west end, c. 1726 [Hist. MSS. Comm., *Portland* vi, 84; J. W. F. Hill, 'The Western Spires of Lincoln Cathedral and their Threatened Removal in 1726', *Lincolnshire Architectural Soc.'s Reports*, N.S. v (ii), 1954].

DULWICH COLLEGE CHAPEL, the marble font for Rev. Jas. Hume, who records in his diary that in Sept. 1729 he 'agreed with Mr. Van Spanger to make a Font of the Dimensions and form of the Draught made by Mr. Gibbs Architect' [*N. and Q.*, vol. 184, 1943, 173].

CAMBRIDGE, GREAT ST. MARY'S CHURCH, supervised erection of galleries in north and south aisles, 1735–6 [W. D. Bushell, *The Church of St. Mary the Great, Cambridge*, 1948, 134].

KIRKLEATHAM CHURCH, YORKS. (N.R.), mausoleum for Turner family on north side of chancel, 1740; restored 1839 [drawings in Ashmolean Museum, vol. ii, 94; A. C. Taylor, 'Kirkleatham', *Arch. Rev.*, Oct. 1958].

attributed: KIRKLEATHAM, YORKS. (N.R.), THE HOSPITAL CHAPEL, for Cholmondely Turner, c. 1740–8. As Gibbs designed the mausoleum and also made a design for a house for Turner (Ashmolean, vol. iv, 23), it is very probable that he also designed the Hospital Chapel, which has all the characteristics of his style (H. Field & M. Bunney, *English Domestic Architecture of the XVII and XVIII Centuries*, 1905, pls. xlv, xlvi).

PATSHULL CHURCH, STAFFS., for Sir John Astley, Bart., cons. 1743; reconstructed 1874–8 by W. C. Banks, who added a north aisle and rebuilt the upper stage of the tower to a different design [Soane MS.] (S. Shaw, *History of Staffordshire* ii, 1801, pl. xxvi*).

ABERDEEN, ST. NICHOLAS CHURCH WEST, rebuilt 1751–5. Gibbs supplied his designs gratis in 1741, but it was not until 1751 that funds permitted building [Ashmolean Museum, vol. iii, 130–2, vol. iv, 1–5; *Aberdeen Fifty Years Ago*, Aberdeen 1868, 46–7].

HOUSES

ABBOTSTONE, HANTS., see HACKWOOD.

ACTON PLACE, nr. SUDBURY, SUFFOLK. This appears to be the 'large Dwelling house with offices built by Mr. Jenings near Stowmarket (*sic*)' referred to in the Soane MS. It was begun by Robert Jennens (d. Feb. 1725/6), whose widow and son both subscribed to Gibbs's *Book of Architecture* (1728), but it was never completed, and the central block was demolished in 1825, leaving only the wings, one of which was formed into a house. A painting of the house is reproduced by N. Pevsner, *Suffolk*, pl. 58a. [W. Copinger, *Manors of*

Suffolk i, 10–12; Harrison & Willis, *The Great Jennens Case*, 1879, 85–6, 98–100, 113–14.]

ANTONY HOUSE, CORNWALL. This house, built 1720–4 for Sir William Carew, Bart., is stated to have been designed by Gibbs by D. & S. Lysons, *Magna Britannia* i, 1814, 16. Gibbs cannot have designed the main block, which is not in his style. However, the forecourt corresponds closely to the one shown in pl. 57 of Gibbs's *Book of Architecture* (to which Carew subscribed), and the width of the front of the house shown in that plate is the same (101 feet) as that of the existing house [*ex inf.* Mr. M. Trinick & Mr. H. Dalton Clifford]. The existing house may therefore have been based on a design by Gibbs which was modified by John Moyle, the master mason employed, or alternatively Gibbs may have designed the forecourt as an addition to a house already under construction. (*C. Life*, 19, 25 Aug. 1933; W. Borlase, *Natural History of Cornwall*, 1758, plate at p. 92.)

BALVENY HOUSE, nr. MORTLACH, BANFFSHIRE, for William Duff of Braco, 1724–5; dem. 1929 [W. Adam, *Vitruvius Scoticus*, pls. 90–1].

BANK HALL, WARRINGTON, LANCS. (now Warrington Town Hall), for Thomas Patten, 1750 [Soane MS.] (measured drawings in *Arch. Rev.* lxiv, 1928, 30–1).

BEAUMONT LODGE, OLD WINDSOR, BERKS., 'additions' to Lord Weymouth's house, 'besides other things for his Lordship' [Soane MS.]. Among the Gibbs drawings at the Ashmolean (vol. ii, 25a) there is a section of 'An Icehouse for Lord Weymouth at Old Windsor', and accounts at Longleat show that in 1743 Gibbs received £21 'for surveying of works at Longleat and Old Windsor'. The house was rebuilt by H. Emlyn (*q.v.*) in 1785.

BYFLEET, SURREY, 'a very convenient small Hunting Box' for General Henry Cornwall (d. 1756); dem. *c.* 1795 [Soane MS.; O. Manning & W. Bray, *History of Surrey* iii, 1814, 181].

CALKE ABBEY, DERBYSHIRE, designed balustraded flight of steps up to main entrance for Sir John Harpur, Bart., 1727–8; removed *c.* 1790 [accounts at Calke Abbey] (K. Downes, *English Baroque Architecture*, 1966, pl. 383).

CANHAM HEATH, HANTS., see HACKWOOD.

CANNONS HOUSE, MIDDLESEX. According to the Soane MS. 'James Duke of Chandos ordered Mr. Gibbs to rebuild his House and Chapel at Cannons, which was done at a vast Expence'. Work on the new house had, in fact, begun in 1713, three years before Gibbs was consulted, but there is reason to think that he largely determined the design of the south and east elevations, and the chapel was wholly his work. He was dismissed in 1719, and the house was completed by John Price (who published the

elevations with his own name as architect) and Edward Shepherd. The house was pulled down after a demolition sale in 1747. According to the memoir, 'Lord Foley bought all the pictures [in the chapel], and everything else which could be moved, and ordered Mr. Gibbs to fitt them to his Chapel' (completed 1735) at Great Witley, Worcs. These included ten windows with glass dated 1719–21, by Joshua Price after Sebastiano Ricci, and paintings by Bellucci which were reset in the ceiling of the chapel (*C. Life*, 8 June 1945). The pews, pulpit, etc., from the Cannons chapel are now in Fawley Church, Bucks. [C. H. and M. I. Collins Baker, *The Life and Circumstances of James Brydges, First Duke of Chandos*, 1949, 124–5, 142–4; drawings for the chapel in G.L.C. Record Office, CC 262/50/60–61].

CHISWICK, MIDDLESEX, 'repaired and made additions to' the dowager Duchess of Norfolk's house, afterwards known as Corney House, *c.* 1748 [Soane MS.; Lysons, *Environs of London* ii, 1811, 126] (*Historical Collections relating to Chiswick*, ed. W. P. W. Phillimore & W. H. Whitear, 1897, plate facing p. 29).

COMPTON VERNEY, WARWICKS., the stables, for Lord Willoughby de Broke [drawing in Ashmolean, vol. ii, 76] (*C. Life*, 18 Oct. 1913, 535).

DAWLEY HOUSE, nr. HARLINGTON, MIDDLESEX, 'new modelled' with 'large additions' for the 1st Viscount Bolingbroke, *c.* 1725; dem. *c.* 1770 [Soane MS.] (*Gent's Mag.* 1802 (ii), 725). In the Ashmolean, vol. iii, 90a, there is a design for a bridge for Lord Bolingbroke.

DITCHLEY HOUSE, OXON., for the 2nd Earl of Lichfield, 1720–31 [*Book of Architecture*, pl. 39] (*C. Life*, 9–16 June 1934; C. Hussey, *English Country Houses: Early Georgian*, 1955, 66–71). The Dillon papers in the Oxfordshire County Record Office show that Francis Smith of Warwick acted as mason-contractor and surveyor, and that the dining-room and drawing-room were decorated 1736–41 to the designs of Henry Flitcroft.

EAST BARNET, HERTS., house known as NEW PLACE or LITTLE GROVE, for John Cotton, 1719; dem. *c.* 1927 [Soane MS.; *V.C.H. Herts.* ii, 339] (F. C. Cass, *East Barnet*, 1885–92, plate).

FAIRLAWN, SHIPBOURNE, KENT, additions for Christopher Vane, Lord Barnard, *c.* 1722, including 'a very handsome Room 20 ft. by 30 ft. with a fine fretwork ceiling', for which there is a drawing in the Ashmolean (vol. iv, 41) [Soane MS.; payments in Lord Barnard's account at Hoare's Bank] (*C. Life*, 30 Oct., 6 Nov. and 27 Nov. 1958, 1247).

GATESHEAD, DURHAM, PARK HOUSE, alterations for Henry Ellison, 1730 [E. Hughes, *North Country Life in the Eighteenth Century*, 1952, 29]. The house is now within the works of Messrs. Clarke, Chapman & Co.

GUBBINS or GOBIONS, HERTS., added a large room for Jeremy Sambrook 'and did other building for that gentleman' [Soane MS.]. There are designs for a dovecote and ceiling 'for Mr. Sambrooke at Gubbins' in the Ashmolean (vol. iii, 87, iv, 40). The house was dem. soon after 1836. (Neale, *Views of Seats*, 1st ser., i, 1818; drawings by Buckler in B.M., Add. MS. 32350, ff. 143–6, and Herts. County Record Office.)

HACKWOOD PARK, HANTS., 'built a great many temples and ornamental buildings for [Charles, 1st] Duke of Bolton at Hackwood, and a House for him at Cannam Heath [nr. Kingsclere] about 12 miles from Hackwood, and made a great many drawings for a new House to be built there, as likewise a large design for a building to be erected at Abbotstone [nr. Alresford, Hants.], another seat belonging to his Grace', which were not executed owing to the 'finances failing' [Soane MS.]. See *Book of Architecture*, pls. 72–4, 84, for the temples, etc., at Hackwood, and Ashmolean Museum, vol. iv, 25, for design of a house 'for ye Duke of Bolton'.[1] In 1740 George Vertue mentions 'a new stone portico ... design'd by Mr. Gibbs' on the south front of Hackwood (*Note Books* v, 127). This was removed *c.* 1805, and of Gibbs's garden buildings only the Menagerie Temple (*Book of Architecture*, pl. 84) survives. The house at Cannam or Canham Heath was dem. in 1805, Abbotstone *c.* 1760.

HAMPSTEAD MARSHALL, BERKS., In 1739 'he laid the foundation and carried up the walls a considerable height of a large house' for the 3rd Lord Craven, to replace that burned in 1718, but work was abandoned on Lord Craven's death the same year [Soane MS.]. There is a complete set of drawings for the house in vol. v of the Gibbs Collection in the Ashmolean Museum.

HARTWELL HOUSE, BUCKS., designed 'several ornamental buildings' for Sir Thomas Lee, Bart., including the temple illustrated on the right-hand side of pl. 77 of the *Book of Architecture* [Soane MS.]. Gibbs was probably also responsible for the decoration of the hall and some of the drawings for the interior of Hartwell in Bodleian, MS. Top. Gen. b.55, appear to be in his hand (*C. Life*, 14 and 21 March 1914).

HOUGHTON HALL, NORFOLK, the four stone cupolas, for Robert Walpole, 1st Earl of Orford, 1725–8. In 1732 the 2nd Earl of Oxford noted that the roofs of the four towers 'were altered by Mr. Gibbs from the first design' (*i.e.* that published in *Vitruvius Britannicus*) [Hist. MSS. Comm., *Portland* vi, 160]. This is confirmed by a contemporary statement that these cupolas were 'obstinately raised by the master

... in defiance of all the virtuosi' [*Lord Hervey and his Friends*, ed. Lord Ilchester, 1950, 70] (*C. Life*, 1 Jan. 1921).

ISLEWORTH, MIDDLESEX, SHREWSBURY HOUSE, for George Talbot, afterwards 14th Earl of Shrewsbury, *c.* 1720; dem. *c.* 1810 [Soane MS.].

ISLEWORTH, MIDDLESEX, SOMERSET HOUSE, additions for 'Sir John Chester' (really Cheshire); dem. 1803 [Soane MS.].

ISLEWORTH, GUMLEY HOUSE, additions for John Gumley, cabinet-maker [Soane MS.] (M. Jourdain & R. Edwards, *Georgian Cabinet-Makers*, 1944, pl. 89; G. J. Aungier, *History of Syon Monastery and the Parish of Isleworth*, 1840, 228).

KELMARSH HALL, NORTHANTS., for William Hanbury, *c.* 1728–32 [Soane MS.; *Book of Architecture*, pl. 38 (not as executed); volume of drawings in R.I.B.A. Coll. (more or less as executed)] (*C. Life*, 25 Feb. 1933).

LEIGHTON HOUSE, LEIGHTON BUZZARD, BEDS., work for the Hon. Charles Leigh; dem. *c.* 1810 [Soane MS.] (Gibbs may have designed the Doric garden temple illustrated by R. Richmond, *Leighton Buzzard*, 1928, pl. 7).

LONDON, ARLINGTON STREET, NO. 16 for the Duchess of Norfolk, 1734–5 [Soane MS.; bill among Weld papers in Lancs. County Record Office].

LONDON, BURLINGTON HOUSE, PICCADILLY, works for the 3rd Earl of Burlington, *c.* 1715. According to the Soane MS. 'the Earl of Burlington had him to build and adorn his house and offices in Piccadilly. They are all built with solid Portland stone, as is likewise the fine circular colonnade fronting the house, of the Dorick Order'. This identifies Gibbs with the unnamed architect mentioned by Colen Campbell as having rebuilt the east block in the forecourt before he (Campbell) was employed to remodel the house and build the great gateway in 1718. Gibbs's responsibility for the colonnade (dem. 1868) has, however, been questioned. For illustrations and a careful discussion of the problem see *Survey of London* xxxii, 398.

LONDON, NO. 49 GREAT ORMOND STREET, library for Dr. Richard Mead, *c.* 1734; dem. *c.* 1870 [Soane MS.] (*C. Life*, 24 Sept. 1970, 765, for illustration of interior).

LONDON, LEICESTER SQUARE, rebuilt No. 25 for Sir Philip Parker Long, Bart., 1733–4; dem. [Soane MS.; *Survey of London* xxxiv, 491].

LONDON, LEICESTER SQUARE, SAVILE HOUSE, added attic storey and refitted interior for Sir George Savile, Bart., 1733; dem. 1865 [*Survey of London* xxxiv, 460].

LONDON, MARYLEBONE, supervised design of houses on the Cavendish-Harley estate for Edward Harley, 2nd Earl of Oxford, and built

---

[1] See p. 807.

four houses (dem.) in HENRIETTA STREET (now Henrietta Place), including one (No. 5) which he occupied himself, *c.* 1727–30 [B.M., Harley estate papers, Add. MSS. 18238, ff. 40–1, 18240, ff. 16–18; John Summerson, 'Henrietta Place, Marylebone and its Associations with James Gibbs', *London Topographical Record* xxi, 1958].

LONDON, PRIVY GARDENS, WHITEHALL, divided house into two dwellings for the 11th Earl of Mar and the 3rd Earl of Loudoun, 1715; dem. [P.R.O., Works 6/6, p. 78].

MARBURY HALL, nr. COMBERBACH, CHESHIRE, appears to be the house for 'the Hon. John Barry Smith' (really Smith-Barry) referred to in the Soane MS., but there incorrectly identified as 'Aston Park in Cheshire'. Marbury Hall was remodelled by A. Salvin *c.* 1850 and dem. *c.* 1970; cf. Ormerod, *History of Cheshire* i, 1882, 635 (Neale, *Views of Seats*, 2nd ser., v, 1829).

MOOR PARK, HERTS., designed a room with a coved ceiling to be executed for Benjamin Styles by G. Bagutti, *c.* 1730 [Ashmolean, vol. iv, 24].

PATSHULL HALL, STAFFS., rebuilt for Sir John Astley, Bart., *c.* 1750–4, completed by William Baker (*q.v.*); altered by W. Burn 1855 [Soane MS.].

QUARRELL, STIRLINGSHIRE, enlarged for John Drummond, 1735–6; dem. [S.R.O., GD 24/1/495, ff. 506, 520–1, 527].

RAGLEY HALL, WARWICKS., works for the 1st Earl of Hertford, *c.* 1750–55, including completion of interior and decoration of hall [Soane MS.; plan attributed to Gibbs in B.M., Add. MS. 31323, W[3]] (*C. Life*, 1–8 May 1958).

ROEHAMPTON, SURREY, repaired house (called Elm Grove) for Bartholomew Clarke and his brother-in-law Hitch Young and added 'a fine new room 20 ft. by 30 ft. and 20 ft. high, coved', with paintings by Amiconi and a chimney-piece by Rysbrack, *c.* 1725–30; destroyed by fire *c.* 1788 [Soane MS.; *Book of Architecture*, pl. 92].

attributed: ROTHERWAS, HEREFS., for Charles Bodenham, 1732; dem. 1926 [stylistic attribution supported by the fact that Charles Bodenham was among the subscribers to Gibbs's *Book of Architecture* in 1728] (Neale, *Views of Seats*, 2nd ser., ii).

STANWELL PLACE, MIDDLESEX, 'repaired and made additions' for Richard Phillips, Governor of Nova Scotia; rebuilt in nineteenth century [Soane MS.].

STOWE HOUSE, BUCKS., additions to the house (subsequently remodelled) and the following ornamental buildings, for Viscount Cobham: GIBBS'S BUILDING, *c.* 1726, dem.; THE BOYCOTT PAVILIONS, *c.* 1726, altered by Borra, who substituted domes for the original pyramidal termi-

nations; THE TEMPLE OF FRIENDSHIP, 1739; THE GOTHIC TEMPLE, 1741–44; THE LADIES' TEMPLE, *c.* 1744–8, altered *c.* 1775 and renamed THE QUEEN'S TEMPLE; THE IMPERIAL CLOSET; and THE COBHAM MONUMENT, 1747–8 [L. Whistler, 'The Authorship of the Stowe Temples', *C. Life*, 29 Sept. 1950].

SUDBROOK HOUSE, PETERSHAM, SURREY, rebuilt for the 2nd Duke of Argyll and Greenwich, *c.* 1717–20; north front altered *c.* 1767 [*Book of Architecture*, pl. 40; Ashmolean drawings, vol. i, 65a, vol. iii, 97b; Mary Cosh in *C. Life*, 13 July 1972[1]] (measured drawings in *Arch. Rev.* xxxii, 1912, 309; *C. Life*, 19 Oct. 1918).

TRING PARK, HERTS., ornamental buildings for William Gore (d. 1739) [Soane MS.]. A pyramid and several other garden buildings are visible in Badeslade & Rocque, *Vitruvius Brittanicus* iv, 1734, pls. 104–5.

TWICKENHAM, MIDDLESEX, 'new modelled' CROSS DEEP, the house of Barnaby Backwell, banker [Soane MS; R. S. Cobbett, *Memorials of Twickenham*, 1872, 261].

TWICKENHAM, MIDDLESEX., octagon room for James Johnston, Secretary for Scotland, 1720 [*Book of Architecture*, pl. 71]. This stood in the grounds of what later became known as Orleans House. The latter was dem. 1927, but Gibbs's building survives as an art gallery (*C. Life*, 15 Sept. 1944).

TWICKENHAM, MIDDLESEX, added 'a fine Room' to house of Sir Chaloner Ogle [Soane MS.].

TWICKENHAM, MIDDLESEX, additions to Alexander Pope's villa; dem. *c.* 1810 [Soane MS.; *The Correspondence of Alexander Pope*, ed. Sherborne, ii, 1956, 4].

WENTWORTH CASTLE, YORKS. (W.R.), interior of the gallery for the 1st Earl of Strafford, 1724 [B.M., Add. MS. 22239, f. 128] (*C. Life*, 18 April 1903).

WHITTON PLACE, MIDDLESEX, offices and greenhouse for the Earl of Ilay (afterwards 3rd Duke of Argyll), 1725–6; dem. *c.* 1935 [Soane MS.; Mary Cosh in *C. Life*, 20 July 1972].

WIMPOLE HALL, CAMBS., alterations and additions for Edward Harley, later 2nd Earl of Oxford, 1719–21, including library and chapel [Soane MS.; *Wren Soc.* xvii, 10–11; R.C.H.M., *West Cambs.* 215]. Drawings in the Soane Museum connected with this commission are reproduced in *Wren Soc.* xii, pl. xxxv, and xvii, pl. xvi. A design by Gibbs for a vase for Wimpole is in Bodleian, Gough Maps 46, nos. 266–8. (*C. Life*, 21–28 May 1927).

---

[1] The revised date for this house (*c.* 1717–20) proposed by Miss Cosh is confirmed by a pair of sketch-plans and an elevation by W. Dickinson in Bodleian, Gough London 125, p. 400, inscribed 'Feb. 26, 1717/18 Duke of Argiles at Petersum near Richmond per Mr. Gibbs'. They show the house as built.

343

UNEXECUTED

Among many unexecuted designs by Gibbs, attention may be drawn to the following:

ADDERBURY HOUSE, OXON., designs for a recessed portico and for garden buildings, for the 2nd Duke of Argyll and Greenwich, *c.* 1725 [drawings among Buccleuch papers in S.R.O.].

ARUNDEL CASTLE, SUSSEX, designs for rebuilding, for the 9th Duke of Norfolk [Soane MS.].

BADMINTON HOUSE, GLOS., designs for flanking pavilions and alterations to north front for the 3rd Duke of Beaufort [H. M. Colvin in *C. Life*, 4 April 1968].

CATTON HALL, DERBYSHIRE, design for new house for Christopher Horton, *c.* 1740 [Andor Gomme, 'Catton Hall', in *The Country Seat*, ed. Colvin & Harris, 1970, 157–63].

DOWN HALL, ESSEX, designs for a house for Matthew Prior, 1720 [*Book of Architecture*, pl. 55; drawings in Bodleian, Gough Misc. Ant. fol. 4, no. 12, Gough Maps 46, ff. 260–4, and B.M., Portland papers, Loan 29/357, set 2].

KEDLESTON HALL, DERBYSHIRE, designs for two pavilions for Sir John Curzon, Bart. (d. 1727) [*Book of Architecture*, pl. 70]; probably made in 1726, when Curzon paid Gibbs 10 guineas [Kedleston archives, Day-Book 1718–50]. An elevation for a new house attributable to Gibbs is among the drawings at Kedleston.

KIRKLEATHAM HALL, YORKS. (N.R.), design for a new house for Cholmondely Turner [elevation in Ashmolean, vol. iv, 23].

KIRTLINGTON PARK, OXON., designs for a new house for Sir James Dashwood, Bart., for which Gibbs was paid £30 in 1741. The drawings are now in the possession of Mrs. H. M. Budgett.

KIVETON PARK, YORKS. (W.R.), designs for additions and garden buildings, including a Gothic ruin, for the 4th Duke of Leeds, 1741 [Ashmolean Museum, drawings acquired in 1953].

LONDON, THE MANSION HOUSE, designs submitted in competition in 1737 [S. Perks, *The History of the Mansion House*, 1922, 170, pls. 41–4; Ashmolean, vol. ii, 119–24].

LONDON, ST. JOHN'S CHURCH, MARYLEBONE, *c.* 1740 [drawings in Ashmolean, vol. iv, 17].

LOWTHER CASTLE, WESTMORLAND, projects for remodelling or rebuilding for the 3rd Viscount Lonsdale, *c.* 1717–18 [R.I.B.A. Drawings Coll. – see *Catalogue: G–K*, 22–3, figs. 22–3; *Vitruvius Britannicus* iii, pl. 76; Hist. MSS. Comm., *Stuart* iv, 568].

MILTON HOUSE, NORTHANTS., designs for a new house for the 2nd Earl Fitzwilliam (d. 1728) [*Book of Architecture*, pls. 48–51; Northants. Record Office, portfolio of drawings dated 1726 (nos. 59–77)].

RABY CASTLE, DURHAM, design for the high hall for Christopher Vane, Lord Barnard (d. 1723) [the

drawings reproduced by Alistair Rowan in *Architectural History* xv, 1972, figs. 5–6, are duplicated in Ashmolean, vol. ii, 48 and 50].

SACOMBE PARK, HERTS., house for Edward Rolt (d. 1722) [*Book of Architecture*, pls. 52–3].

TREWITHEN, CORNWALL, a set of designs for a new house for Philip Hawkins, probably *c.* 1730, unsigned but in Gibbs's hand; preserved at Trewithen. The ground-plan is reproduced *C. Life*, 2 April 1953, fig. 9.

WENTWORTH WOODHOUSE, YORKS. (W.R.). A plan in the R.I.B.A. Collection for remodelling this house, probably for Thomas Watson-Wentworth, afterwards 1st Earl of Malton, who inherited the house in 1723, has been attributed to Gibbs by W. Ison in *The County Seat*, ed. Colvin & Harris, 1970, 106–9, and by T. Friedman in *R.I.B.A. Drawings Catalogue: G–K*, 23. In the writer's opinion this attribution should be viewed with caution.

WESTON UNDERWOOD, BUCKS., designs for Sir Robert Throckmorton, Bart. (d. 1720), 'which his son proposes to build' [Soane MS.].

WHITTON PLACE, MIDDLESEX, designs for a new house for the Earl of Ilay (afterwards 3rd Duke of Argyll), *c.* 1725 [*Book of Architecture*, pls. 59–62].

WISTON PARK, SUSSEX, designs for rebuilding for Sir Robert Fagg, Bart. [Ashmolean, vol. vi].

WITHAM PARK, SOMERSET, designs for remodelling garden front for Sir William Wyndham, Bart., *c.* 1716 [Ashmolean, vol. iv, 22; *Vitruvius Britannicus* ii, 1717, pls. 91–2 (where Gibbs's authorship is not acknowledged); R.I.B.A. Drawings Coll., reproduced in John Harris, *Georgian Country Houses*, 1968, pl. 9, and discussed by T. Friedman in *R.I.B.A. Drawings Catalogue: G–K*, 24]. This house was at Witham Friary, south-west of Frome, which belonged to the Wyndhams (see Collinson, *History of Somerset* ii, 1791, 234).

MONUMENTS

Gibbs was the first English architect who made a practice of designing monuments. In WESTMINSTER ABBEY he designed the monuments to John Holles, 1st Duke of Newcastle (d. 1711) [*Book of Architecture*, pl. 111; cf. alternative designs in *Wren Soc.* xii, pl. xxxiii; xvii, pl. xiii, and in vol. vi of the 'London and Westminster Prints' in the Library of the Society of the Antiquaries (f. 18)]; Sophia, Marchioness of Annandale (d. 1716), John Smith (d. 1718), Matthew Prior (d. 1721), James Craggs (d. 1721) [drawings in Ashmolean, vol. ii, 13, and V. & A. 3641–1913], Mrs. Katherine Bovey (d. 1727), Dr. John Freind (d. 1728), John Dryden (erected 1720), and Ben Jonson, all of which (with the exception of the Craggs monument) are either listed in the Soane MS. or illustrated in *Book of Architecture*, pls. 112–24.

Elsewhere he designed the monuments to Robert Stuart (d. 1714) in ST. MARGARET'S CHURCH, WEST-MINSTER [*ibid*., pl. 127], to Sir John Bridgeman (d. 1710) in ASTON CHURCH, WARWICKS. [*ibid*., pl. 123], to Edward Colston (d. 1721) in ALL SAINTS CHURCH, BRISTOL [*ibid*., pl. 113], to Montague Drake and his wife in AMERSHAM CHURCH, BUCKS. [*ibid*., pl. 121], to Lord and Lady Barnard (d. 1723/5) in SHIPBOURNE CHURCH, KENT [Ashmolean drawings, vol. iii, 86], to Sir Edward Seymour (d. 1708) in MAIDEN BRADLEY CHURCH, WILTS., erected 1730, under contract dated 11 June 1728 [P.R.O., C 107/126], to Robert Lovell (d. 1740) in SOULBURY CHURCH, BUCKS. [signed], to the 4th Lord Widdrington (d. 1743) in NUNN-INGTON CHURCH, YORKS. (N.R.) [signed], and to Henry, 2nd Duke of Newcastle and his family in BOLSOVER CHURCH, DERBYSHIRE [*Book of Architecture*, pl. 114].

ENGRAVING

Gibbs signs the (very baroque) engraving framing the dedication of J. Flamsteed's *Historia Coelestis* (1712).

GIBSON, GEORGE, was, according to James Elmes,[1] the eldest son of another architect surnamed Gibson who had been employed by Queen Caroline. The elder Gibson 'had travelled in Italy, studied architecture in Rome, collected many curiosities in Art, and deposited them in a singular Villa that he built on Loam-pit Hill, Lewisham, long known ... by the name of the Comical House. It is now inhabited by Mr. Alderman Wire, and is called Stone House, Lewisham.' STONE HOUSE, LOAMPIT HILL, LEWISHAM, is illustrated by S. C. Ramsey & J. D. M. Harvey, *Small Houses of the Late Georgian Period* ii, 1923, pls. 80–2. It appears to have been built in or about 1766, and is a small, ingeniously planned and elegantly finished villa whose stylistic affinities are more French than Italian. The records of St. Paul's Church, Deptford (in whose parish the house stands), show that in 1772 Michael, son of George and Ann Gibson of Loampit Hill, was baptized, and that in 1776 George Gibson paid for two seats. Neither the burial of the elder Gibson nor the birth of the younger one is, however, recorded there.

Elmes, who was a pupil of the younger Gibson, says that, like his father, he had travelled in Italy before commencing practice. He was, however, too much a man of taste to be an effective supervisory architect. 'He would rather sip his claret, drink his Madeira, chat about Art and Music, and take snuff with a gusto, than ascend ladders, tramp scaffolds to see how Bricklayers filled in

their work, or try the scantlings of wall plates and bond timbers ... [like] the practical men of Sir Robert Taylor's working school'. Nevertheless 'he had good connections among the wealthy merchants of the City, for some of whom he designed and superintended some London residences and country mansions'. For Sir Richard Neave, Bart., he designed offices in BROAD STREET, a town-house, NO. 6 ALBEMARLE STREET, and a country seat, DAGNAM PARK, PIRGO, ESSEX.[1] For Neave's son Thomas he altered BRANCH HILL LODGE, HAMPSTEAD, soon after 1799 [Elmes]. In 1774 the banker John Julius Angerstein employed him to design WOODLANDS HOUSE, GREENWICH, an elegant neo-classical villa now in Mycenae Road [*Copperplate Magazine* ii, 1794, pl. lxxx]. In LEWISHAM he designed ST. MARY'S CHURCH, with its handsome portico, in 1775–7 (damaged by fire 1830, chancel added 1881–2) [L. L. Duncan, *The Parish Church of St. Mary, Lewisham*, 1892, 12–16], and built himself a 'little box' adjoining his father's villa. Elmes adds that he spelled his name 'Gibsone' in order to distinguish himself from Jesse Gibson of Hackney (*q.v.*).

GIBSON, JESSE (*c.* 1748–1828), of Hackney in Middlesex, was the District Surveyor of the eastern division of the City of London from 1774 until his death in 1828. He was appointed Surveyor to the Saddlers' Company in 1774, to the Drapers' Company in 1797, and was employed by the Vintners' Company between 1800 and 1820.

Gibson made an estimate for alterations to MONOX'S ALMSHOUSES, WALTHAMSTOW, ESSEX, in 1788 [S. J. Barns, *Walthamstow Vestry Minutes*, Walthamstow Antiquarian Soc. 1925–7, 79–81]; rebuilt the church of ST. PETER-LE-POER, OLD BROAD STREET, LONDON, 1788–92, dem. 1908 [minutes of Rebuilding Committee in Guildhall Library, MS. 2863; Britton & Pugin, *Public Buildings of London* ii, 1828, 72]; designed a house at WEST HILL, nr. WANDSWORTH, for J. A. Rucker in about 1790 [S. Lysons, *Environs of London* i, 1810, 390], and CLAYBURY HALL, ESSEX, for James Hatch, about the same time [*Essex Review* xxxvii, 99–108]; repaired LEYTON CHURCH, ESSEX, 1794 [J. Kennedy, *History of Leyton*, 1894, 53]; and rebuilt the SADDLERS' HALL, CHEAPSIDE, LONDON, 1822–3, refronted 1865, dem. [*Record of the Saddlers' Company*, 1937, 115].

Gibson died on 24 June 1828, aged 80, and was buried at Wimbledon [*A.P.S.D.*]. There is a portrait at Drapers' Hall. He appears to have been a designer of only moderate ability. Despite its circular nave, St. Peter-le-Poer was not a particularly interesting example of a centrally planned

---

[1] In an autobiographical passage prefaced to his MS. memoir of his son H. L. Elmes (R.I.B.A. Library).

[1] Probably soon after 1772, when Neave purchased the estate.

church, and in Britton's opinion its tower was 'far from graceful, either in its general form, or in its embellishments'.

GIBSON, THOMAS, designed MARCHMONT HOUSE, BERWICKSHIRE, for the 3rd Earl of Marchmont, 1750–4. A rare engraving of the house as completed bears the signature 'Thos. Gibson Arch.'', and a note among the archives at Mellerstain records: 'Marchmont House begun to be built 14 June 1750, began to be liv'd in 4th. October 1754'. The master mason was Robert Burns of Dalkeith [National Library of Scotland, Tweeddale papers, Box 98 F.2]. Nothing else is at present known about Thomas Gibson, but his employment at Marchmont is confirmed by a single payment recorded in the Earl's private accounts on 5 December 1750: 'To cash Tho.ˢ Gibson as per Journal' [S.R.O., Marchmont papers, under arrangement].

In the past the house has sometimes been attributed to William Adam, because in 1724–5 he made some designs for the 2nd Earl which were not proceeded with [S.R.O., GD 157/1/25, and cf. W. Warrender, *Marchmont and the Humes of Polwarth*, 1894, 99–100]. By 1750 William Adam had been dead two years, and from a letter which John Adam wrote to Lord Tweeddale in June 1750 [Nat. Lib. Scot., as above] it is quite clear that the Adam family had nothing to do with the building of Marchmont. The house was enlarged and much altered by Lorimer in 1913–16, but the originally severe character of its exterior, and some distinctive features of the internal decoration, show that Gibson was an accomplished designer with a style easily distinguishable from that of William or John Adam (*C. Life*, 28 Feb., 7 March 1925).

GIBSON, THOMAS, was the author of an unexecuted design for a new Town and County Hall at Forfar in about 1785 [photo at N.M.R.S. of drawing at Forfar]. No other reference to him has so far been found.

GILBERT, THOMAS (*c.* 1706–1776), designed and built ST. GEORGE'S CHURCH, REFORNE, PORTLAND, DORSET, 1754–66, a sturdy classical building of some pretensions in a style derived from the school of Wren rather than from contemporary architectural fashions. A tablet commemorates Thomas Gilbert 'of this island, Gent. Architect and Master Builder of this church', who died on 25 July 1776, aged 70 [R.C.H.M., *Dorset* ii (2), 247–9].

Gilbert was descended from a family of masons who carried on the stone-quarrying business in the Isle of Portland. Thomas Gilbert (d. *c.* 1695) was 'probably the largest purveyor of Portland stone during the last quarter of the seventeenth century', and supplied stone for St. Paul's Cath-

edral, Winchester Palace and Hampton Court. His business was carried on by his sons, Thomas (d. 1704, aged 28) and John, both, like their father, Liverymen of the London Masons' Company. Thomas (d. 1776) was presumably the son of John. [D. Knoop & G. P. Jones, *The London Mason in the Seventeenth Century*, 1935, 28–9; *Wren Soc., passim*; J. H. Bettey, *The Island and Royal Manor of Portland*, Portland, 1970; Bodleian Library, Tucker papers, will of Thomas Gilbert (d. 1704).]

GILES, ROBERT, designed a Gothic R.C. Church at NORTH SHIELDS, NORTHUMBERLAND, in 1821 [B. Little, *Catholic Churches since 1623*, 1966, 61]. Nicholas Giles is listed as an architect and surveyor of Newcastle in Pigot's *Directory* of 1828–9.

GILKIE, ALEXANDER (*c.* 1756–1834), was a master builder at Coldstream, Berwickshire. Between 1791 and 1795 he was employed at FORD CASTLE, NORTHUMBERLAND, by Lord Delaval. According to a confused document printed in the *Proceedings of the Society of Antiquaries of Newcastle-on-Tyne* v, 1891–2, 63, 'The great gateway, lodges and towers, amongst other buildings, were remodelled by him', but some of these features were the work of James Nesbit (*q.v.*), who died in 1781. An estimate by Gilkie for a further addition to the east side of the castle in 1801 is in the Northumberland Record Office [2 DE 18/1/30], but is marked 'laid aside'. According to the same writer Gilkie 'was recommended by Lord Delaval to Lord Strathmore for the rebuilding of Gibside'. At GIBSIDE, CO. DURHAM, he was presumably responsible for the remodelling of the south front for the 10th Earl of Strathmore in about 1805. This front, Jacobean in style, with Gothick details, is illustrated in *C. Life*, 8 Feb. 1952. In the R.I.B.A. Drawings Collection there is a design by Gilkie for a bridge at BLACKADDER HOUSE, BERWICKSHIRE, and at Kimmerghame House, Berwickshire, there are two designs by him for courts of offices for Archibald Swinton, one at Kimmerghame (1790), the other at Broadmeadows House, Hutton, Berwickshire (1807). From these recorded works it is evident that Gilkie was a provincial designer of no great ability whose works nevertheless have considerable naive charm. An inscription in Lennel Churchyard, Coldstream, shows that he died on 3 May 1834, aged 78, and that his son Alexander Gilkie, 'surveyor of buildings in Edinburgh', died on 21 November 1852, aged 56.

GILKS, WILLIAM (–1727), was a builder and surveyor at Burton-on-Trent. He was probably a mason by trade, for in 1696 a William Gilks was among the masons employed in building Burley-on-the-Hill, Rutland [accounts in Leicestershire Record Office]. Between 1712 and 1723 he was frequently employed by Sir John Harpur, Bart., at CALKE ABBEY, DERBYSHIRE, where in 1712 he contracted to build the handsome brick stables. In February 1719/20 he was paid £10 8s. 6d. 'for several draughts and his Directions upon several occasions', and in 1721–2 he built a school at the adjoining village of TICKNALL [accounts at Calke Abbey]. In 1720–1 he was supervising alterations at MELBOURNE HALL, DERBYSHIRE, for Thomas Coke and made an estimate for a new vicarage house there [account of 'my time in surveying and directing the workmen at Melbourne Hall' in the muniment room there]. When Burton-on-Trent Church was rebuilt in 1719–26 by Francis Smith of Warwick, Gilks was one of the parishioners who were deputed to negotiate with him over the performance of his contract [C. H. Underhill, *History of Burton upon Trent*, 1941, 133–4]. Gilks died at Burton in April 1727, and was buried at the parish church on the 23rd of that month [Parish Register, *ex inf.* Mr. Edward Saunders].

GILL, ABRAHAM (–1834), son of William Gill of Houghton-on-the-Hill, grazier, was apprenticed to William Parsons of Leicester (*q.v.*) in 1821, and subsequently went into partnership with him. He died young on 8 December 1834, 'greatly respected by a large circle of friends' [H. Hartopp, *Leicester Freemen*, 1927, 576; obituary in *Leicester Journal*, 12 Dec. 1834, quoted by J. D. Bennett, *Leicestershire Architects 1700–1850*, Leicester 1968].

GILL, WESTBY (1679–1746), was the eldest son of Col. John Gill of Carr-house in the parish of Rotherham, nr. Sheffield. He was christened Westby because Carr-house had come to his family through his grandmother Elizabeth Westby. He was educated at Jesus College, Cambridge, where he took his M.A. in 1702. In September 1719 he was appointed Deputy Surveyor of the Works by his neighbour Sir Thomas Hewett (*q.v.*). In 1735 he succeeded William Kent as Master Carpenter, retaining the post until his death in October 1746. After his father's death he sold the family estate and lived in London.

Little is known about Gill's architectural ability, but he is recorded to have designed one medium-sized country house and a funeral monument. The country house is BURROW HALL, LANCS., and documents in private possession show that Gill made the unsigned elevation illustrated in *C. Life*, 14 April 1960, fig. 5. The house was built by George Platt of Rotherham in accordance with a contract dated 20 January 1740 [*ex inf.* Mr. W. J. Smith]. The monument is in ABBOTS LANGLEY CHURCH, HERTS. It commemorates Chief Justice Raymond (d. 1732), was

executed by Cheere, and is signed 'Westby Gill Ar. invenit'. In addition a reference in Andrews Jelfe's letter-book (B.M., Add. MS. 27587, f. 45ᵛ) points to Gill as the architect of the circular Ionic temple built by the 2nd Earl of Macclesfield in 1741 in the grounds of SHIRBURN CASTLE, OXON., for which Jelfe supplied the Portland stone. It may be noted that in 1739 Gill was elected a Fellow of the Royal Society, of which Macclesfield was a leading member.

[J. Hunter, *Hallamshire*, 1819, 234; Venn, *Alumni Cantabrigienses* i, 217; *History of the King's Works*, v.]

GILLESPIE, JAMES, *see* GRAHAM

GILLOW, RICHARD (1734–1811), was a member of a firm of Lancashire carpenters and joiners who became well known as cabinetmakers during the latter part of the eighteenth century. They were strict Catholics and the name of Gillow is well known in the annals of North-Country Catholicism. The firm was founded by Robert Gillow, from Great Singleton in the Fylde, who became a freeman of Lancaster in 1728 and died there in 1773. His books, which survive from 1731 onwards, show that he and his son Richard, whom he took into partnership in 1757 at the age of 23, acted as surveyors and architects as well as joiners, and that they designed a number of local buildings, including several private houses in Lancaster and ST. THOMAS'S CHAPEL at GARSTANG, 1770. In 1764 Richard designed the handsome CUSTOM HOUSE at LANCASTER, which is mentioned as his work in Pennant's *Tour in Scotland*, 1771, 220. He died in 1811 and was succeeded by his eldest son Richard (1772–1849), who acquired the estate of Leighton Hall which still belongs to the family. By the third quarter of the eighteenth century the Gillows were among the leading English cabinetmakers, with a branch in London and a large export business to the West Indies. The architectural side of the business was abandoned and the subsequent history of the firm lies outside the scope of this *Dictionary*. [J. Gillow, *Bibliographical Dictionary of the English Catholics* ii, 1885, 484–5, *Gillow's, its History and Associations*, 1901; Arthur Oswald, 'Leighton Hall, Lancashire', *C. Life*, 11–18 May 1951; Mary E. Burkett, Mrs. Edith Tyson & Mrs. Davidson Low, *The Furniture of Gillow of Lancaster* (typescript, Lancaster Museum, 1971); Gillow records in Westminster City Library; information from Dr. L. O. Boynton.]

GLANVILLE, BENJAMIN (–1774), held the post of Surveyor of Works to the Victualling Office and Inspector of Repairs to the Admiralty from 1731 until his death in 1774 [J. C. Sainty, *Admiralty Officials 1660–1870*, 1975, 76]. He surveyed ST. BOTOLPH'S CHURCH, ALDGATE, prior to its rebuilding in 1741–4 [*Commons' Jnls.* xxiii, 633], and was concerned in the completion of the steeple of ST. MARY'S CHURCH, ROTHERHITHE, by Launcelot Dowbiggin (*q.v.*) in 1746.

GLASCODINE, SAMUEL (–*c.* 1760), of Bristol, was a carpenter by trade. He was admitted to the freedom of the city in January 1737 on payment of a fine of £8. In 1741 he obtained the contract for the carpenter's work at the new Exchange, and in 1746 he was similarly employed at Clifton Hill House. For the Corporation he designed and built in 1744–5 the MARKETS behind the Exchange, with a narrow elevation to the High Street, and in 1746 the old POST OFFICE (now offices) in Corn Street adjoining the Exchange. He also designed the new church and vicarage of ST. GEORGE, KINGSWOOD, nr. BRISTOL, erected in 1752–6, and rebuilt after a fire in 1878. The original plans and elevations are preserved in the minute-book of the Commissioners for building the church (Bristol City Archives). The handsome house in Stokes Croft that Glascodine built for his own occupation now forms part of the former Baptist College there. Glascodine was a fairly competent imitator of John Wood's Palladian style. He must have died shortly before 1761, when the business passed to his son Joseph, who was described as a millwright and carpenter when he was admitted a free burgess in 1772. Joseph Glascodine lived at Stokes Croft until 1805, when he sold the property to the Baptists shortly after becoming one of the District Surveyors for the City of Bristol under the Act of 1788. The only building he is known to have designed is a house in Church Street, Warminster, Wilts., for William Wansey [*V.C.H. Wilts.* viii, 94]. He died in December 1817, when Richard Glascodine (presumably his son) succeeded to his surveyorship, dying on 8 May 1819 [W. Ison, *The Georgian Buildings of Bristol*, 1952, 34–5, 106–8; A Beaven, *Bristol Lists*, 1899, 248–9].

GLOVER, THOMAS (*c.* 1639–1707), was formerly commemorated by the following inscription (now destroyed) in the cemetery on the north side of Salisbury Cathedral: 'In memory of Thomas Glover Architect who having erected many Stately curious and Artful edifices for others, himself is here lodged under this single Stone in full expectation however of a building with God eternal in the Heavens. ob. Dec. 2, A.D. 1707, Aetat 68' [James Harris, *Copies of the Epitaphs in Salisbury Cathedral, Cloisters and Cemetery*, 1825, 133]. The will of Thomas Glover, of the Close of New Sarum, dated 9 Nov. 1707, was proved on 2 Jan. 1707/8 [P.C.C. 8 BARRETT].

In 1682 Thomas Glover of Harnham, nr. Salisbury, contracted to build the MATRONS' COL-

LEGE or almshouses in SALISBURY CATHEDRAL CLOSE for Bishop Seth Ward for £1193. The work was to be under the inspection of Thomas Naish, clerk of works to the Cathedral, but there is nothing in the contract to indicate the authorship of the design [Salisbury Diocesan Record Office]. The building is illustrated in H. Field & M. Bunney, *English Domestic Architecture of the XVII and XVIII Centuries*, 1905, pls. lxxxi–lxxxii.

In a memorandum book of the 1st Earl of Shaftesbury (d. 1683) at WIMBORNE HOUSE, WIMBORNE ST. GILES, DORSET, there are notes on a contract whereby Thomas Glover undertook to make substantial additions to that house for the Earl.

GODEFROY, MAXIMILIAN (1765–?1840), was a French architect of the revolutionary period who emigrated to America after he had fallen foul of the Napoleonic régime. His buildings in Baltimore (notably the Unitarian Church) are important monuments of neo-classical architecture. In 1819, hoping to achieve a European reputation, he came to England and settled in Somers Town. Although he exhibited regularly at the Royal Academy he failed to build up an English practice, and in 1827 returned to France, where he became architect to the *département* of Mayenne. In 1821 Godefroy was awarded the third premium in the competition for SALTERS' HALL, LONDON. The building, erected in 1823–7 to the designs of Henry Carr, the Company's surveyor, incorporated features from the prize-winning designs, and some elements of the façade may be attributed to Godefroy's influence. The only English building known to have been designed in its entirety by Godefroy was the CATHOLIC CHARITIES SCHOOL, CLARENDON SQUARE, LONDON, a simple astylar building in the manner of Durand, built 1825–6 and demolished *c.* 1950 after war-damage. [R. L. Alexander, *The Architecture of Maximilian Godefroy*, Baltimore 1974.]

GODWIN, GEORGE (1789–1863), of Brompton, was an architect of whom little is known beyond the fact that he was the father of George Godwin, junior (1815–88), architect, antiquary, and editor of the *Builder* from 1844 to 1883. The elder Godwin exhibited a drawing of the Théâtre Français in Paris at the Royal Academy in 1811. His designs (1834) for a gardener's lodge at Tottenham Park, Wilts., are in private possession. His younger son Henry (1831–1917) also became an architect. He died on 23 June 1863, aged 73 [*Gent's Mag.* 1863 (ii), 246; monumental inscription in Holy Trinity Church, Brompton Road, London; obituary of George Godwin, junior, in *Builder*, liv, 1888, 75].

GOFF, ELIJAH, junior, was the son of Elijah Goff, 'surveyor and coal-merchant' of Wellclose

Square, London. He exhibited a 'Design for a pavilion intended to be built in North Wales' at the Royal Academy in 1792, and 'Elevations of the east fronts of two houses lately erected' in 1797. He was elected a member of the Surveyors' Club in 1799.

GOLD, JAMES, see GOULD

GOLDEN, ROBERT (c. 1738–1809), was in 1774 appointed District Surveyor for the parishes of St. George the Martyr, St. Andrew Holborn and the Liberty of the Rolls. He was then aged 36, and was described as 'Robert Golden junior' of Lamb's Conduit Street [Middlesex County Records, General Orders, no. 10]. He became a member of the Surveyors' Club in 1795, and died on 28 September 1809, aged 72 [*Gent's Mag.* 1809, 1174]. In 1768 he made designs for 'a set of baths' at Brighton which were built the following year by Dr. Awsiter, and he also designed the Card Room of the Old Ship Tavern in the same resort [*A Description of Brighthelmstone*, 1788, 16, 17].

An architect named R. Golden, who was probably his son, exhibited at the Royal Academy from Rome in 1794, and from London in 1796. He married in 1796, but died on 6 January 1797, aged 28 [*Gent's Mag.* 1796, 81; 1797, 82].

GOLDICUTT, JOHN (1793–1842), a pupil of Henry Hakewill, was admitted to the Royal Academy Schools in 1812, gained the Silver Medal in 1814, and in 1815 that of the Society for the Encouragement of Arts. In 1815 he entered the school of A. Leclère at Paris, and competed for the monthly prizes offered by the Académie des Beaux Arts. He then visited Italy, where he spent four years collecting materials for the books which he afterwards published. In 1817–18 he made an elaborate drawing of the transverse section of St. Peter's at Rome, showing the paintings and decorations, for which he was presented with a gold medal by the Pope. The drawing was exhibited at the Royal Academy on his return in 1819. He remained in Hakewill's office until the latter's death in 1830, but appears also to have practised independently, and being by nature ambitious, rarely missed an opportunity of entering for any public competition that was advertised. In 1820 he obtained the third premium in the competition for the Post Office, London, and in 1829, in association with Henry Hakewill, a premium for the Middlesex Lunatic Asylum. He also competed for the University Observatory at Cambridge in 1821, for the new buildings for King's College, Cambridge, in 1823, for the Fishmongers' Hall in 1830, for the Royal Exchange in 1839, and for the Nelson Monument in 1841. He was an accomplished draughtsman who specialized in the production of highly finished coloured drawings. His designs were characterized by an elegant and fastidious neo-classical taste based on a close study of antique sources. Gundimore, for instance, was described by Augustus Hare as 'from a Pompeian model'. His style was probably too archaeological to be popular, and his practice appears to have been very limited.

He was one of the first two honorary secretaries of the Institute of British Architects, and took a prominent part in the presentation of a testimonial to Sir John Soane in 1835, himself designing the decoration of Freemasons' Hall for the occasion. He was elected a member of the Academy of St. Luke at Rome, and of the Academy of Fine Arts at Naples. His publications were *Antiquities of Sicily*, fol., 1819, *Specimens of Ancient Decorations from Pompeii*, 1825, *Heriot's Hospital, Edinburgh*, 1826 (with plates etched by himself), and a pamphlet showing his designs for the Nelson Monument, 1841.[1] In 1828 he was appointed Surveyor for the combined districts of St. Clement Danes and St. Mary-le-Strand. J. H. Hakewill was his pupil. He died on 3 October 1842, aged 49, and was buried in the Kensal Green Cemetery. A collection of his drawings is in the R.I.B.A. Library. A sketch-book in the Mellon Collection, containing drawings made in northern Italy in 1832–3, has been attributed to him because of the similarity of the draughtsmanship to the drawings at the R.I.B.A. [*A.P.S.D.*; obituary in *Civil Engineer and Architect's Jnl.* v, 372; anon., 'John Goldicutt and his Times', *Arch. Rev.* xxxi, 1912, 321.]

GUNDIMORE, nr. CHRISTCHURCH, HANTS., for W. S. Rose, 1818–19 [R.I.B.A. drawings, no. 365; exhib. at R.A. 1819].

WEST COWES, ISLE OF WIGHT, Marine Villa for Simon Halliday, 1827–8 [R.I.B.A. drawings, nos. 370–5; exhib. at R.A. 1828 as 'now building'].

THE DELL, nr. WINDSOR, BERKS., alterations for the Rt. Hon. H. R. Westenra, M.P., c. 1830 [exhib. at R.A. 1830].

WORTHING, SUSSEX, CASINO on the Esplanade, 1830 [exhib. at R.A. 1830 as 'lately erected'].

DINGLEY HALL, NORTHANTS., new terrace and proposed alterations to the west front for H. H. Hungerford, 1836 [exhib. at R.A. 1836].

PADDINGTON, ST. JAMES'S CHURCH, SUSSEX GARDENS, with G. Gutch, 1841–3, Gothic, remodelled by G. E. Street 1882 [R.I.B.A. drawings, nos. 393–401; exhib. at R.A. 1842].

LONDON, two houses 'proposed to be erected in Park Lane for Mr. Thomas Martin and Mrs. Susanna Curtis' [R.I.B.A. drawings, no. 376].

---

[1] In 1833 he had published a lithograph showing an earlier design for a naval monument in Trafalgar Square, but with a statue of King William IV as the principal feature.

LONDON, WHITE'S CLUB-HOUSE, ST. JAMES'S STREET, alterations [*A.P.S.D.*].

Design for stables for George Watson Taylor, Esq., M.P., probably intended for STOKE PARK, WILTS. [R.I.B.A. drawings, no. 368].

GOLDRING, GEORGE, was a pupil of William Pilkington. He exhibited student's designs at the Royal Academy between 1792 and 1802. He was President of the Surveyors' Club in 1820. In 1821 he was appointed joint surveyor of the London Orphan Asylum with William Inman (*q.v.*).

GOLDSMITH, ROBERT, practised in Manchester during the second quarter of the nineteenth century. He was presumably the 'Goldsmith' who, with one John Day, designed a villa called GREEN HILL at STOCKPORT, CHESHIRE, for George Andrew, *c.* 1810 [Twycross, *Mansions of England: Cheshire* ii, 130].

GOLLOP, GEORGE, a carpenter and joiner of Poole in Dorset, designed Congregational chapels at WAREHAM, 1790, and SWANAGE, 1837 [R.C.H.M., *Dorset* ii (2), 292, 315].

GOMME, Sir BERNARD DE (1620–1685), was born at Lille. As a young man he served in the campaigns of Frederick Henry, Prince of Orange, and afterwards accompanied Prince Rupert to England. From 1642 to 1646 he served in the royal army as engineer and quartermaster-general 'with conspicuous ability', and was knighted by Charles I. His plan of the fortifications of Liverpool, dated 1644, is in the British Museum (Sloane MS. 5027 A, f. 69), and plans of the battles of Naseby, Marston Moor, etc., by him are in Add. MSS. 16370 and 16371.

After the Restoration Gomme was (March 1661) made engineer-general of all the King's fortifications and castles in England and Wales by Charles II, and in 1667 he was naturalized by Act of Parliament. According to the 'Rules and Orders for the Office of the Ordnance' drawn up in 1683, the Principal Engineer was 'to be perfect in Architecture, civil and military', and 'to make Plots and Models of all manner of Fortifications ... commanded by us to be erected for our service' (B.M., King's MS. 70, ff. 31ᵛ–32). In this capacity Gomme supervised the repair of Dover pier, and the construction of fortifications at Dunkirk. In August 1665 instructions were given for fortifying PORTSMOUTH according to Gomme's plans (*Cal. State Papers Domestic 1664–5*, 510), and his estimates and plans for the work are in B.M., Add. MSS. 2448, 16370 and 28088, f. 26. In 1679 Thomas and John Fitch contracted to carry out further fortifications at Portsmouth designed by Gomme (Add. Charter 32751). In November 1665 he was commissioned

to build a new citadel on the Hoe at PLYMOUTH, which was built under his direction in 1670–7, the former date appearing on the handsome baroque gateway, for whose design he was presumably responsible (*Cal. S.P.D. 1665–6*, 57, 61; *1668–9*, 371; *Addenda 1660–85*, 144; volume of accounts in library at Badminton House, Glos.). A coloured plan of the Citadel by Gomme, dated 1666/7, and a 'Plan of the King's House at Plymouth', also attributed to him, but unsigned, were sold at Sotheby's on 9 March 1948, from the Dartmouth Collection (lot 464), and there is a plan of Plymouth by him dated 1668 in B.M., Add. MS. 16371. He also designed the new fort built at TILBURY, ESSEX, in 1670–83, with a gatehouse similar to the one at Plymouth [A. D. Saunders, *Tilbury Fort*, H.M.S.O. 1960]. In 1673 he was in Ireland, where he made designs for a citadel at Ringsend, nr. Dublin. In his report he specifies that the gateway shall be of Portland stone, 'in the same forme as at Plymouth' [Sir J. Gilbert, *Calendar of Ancient Records*, Dublin, 1889–98, v, 568]. See also the 'Observations explanatory of a plan and estimate for a citadel at Dublin, designed by Sir Bernard de Gomme, Engineer-General, in the year 1673', privately printed by Charles Haliday of Dublin in 1861.

On the death of Sir Jonas Moore the younger in 1682, Gomme succeeded him as Surveyor-General of Ordnance. He died on 23 November 1685, and was buried in the chapel of St. Peter within the Tower of London. There is a miniature portrait of him in a collection of plans in B.M., King's Library, cii, 21. [*D.N.B.*]

GOMME, STEPHEN (–1858), of Hammersmith, exhibited at the Society of British Artists in 1835, 1837 and 1838 and at the Royal Academy in 1839 and 1845. In 1838 he showed a BRITISH SCHOOL at HAMMERSMITH erected to his designs, and in 1839 'improvements' carried out for O. May at COCKBURN HOUSE, SHEPHERD'S BUSH, HAMMERSMITH. He died at Hammersmith on 8 July 1858 [Principal Probate Registry, Calendar of Probates].

GOOD, JOSEPH HENRY (1775–1857), was the eldest son of the Rev. Joseph Good, a clergyman with a living in Somerset. From 1795 to 1800 he was a pupil of Sir John Soane. In 1803 he entered the competition for the conversion of the Houses of Parliament at Dublin into the Bank of Ireland. According to his son he won the first two premiums offered, but this claim is not substantiated by the Bank's records. There is also some doubt about the younger Good's claim that his father was associated with W. C. Lochner in winning the Bethlehem Hospital competition of 1810, for there is no mention of Good in the Hospital's records, and in 1811 the design was exhibited at the Royal Academy under Lochner's name without any reference to Good. In about 1814 Good was appointed surveyor to the Thavie estate in Holborn and subsequently became surveyor to the parish of St. Andrew, Holborn. He succeeded W. Cresswell as surveyor to the Armourers' and Braziers' Company in about 1819, and was surveyor to the Hope Assurance Company for many years before its dissolution in 1843. In 1826 he succeeded Edward Mawley as Surveyor to the Commissioners for Building New Churches, a post which he retained until the abolition of the Commission in January 1857. From 1830 to 1832 he also held a post in the Office of Works, first as Clerk of the Works at the Tower of London, Mint, Somerset House, King's Bench, Fleet and Marshalsea Prisons, etc., and then at Kensington Palace and the Horse Guards. He lost this post in the reorganization of the Office in 1832, but was allowed by William IV (who employed him at Brighton) to retain the official residence at Kensington until his death. He was one of the original Fellows of the Institute of British Architects, and exhibited occasionally at the Royal Academy. He died on 20 November 1857. Among his pupils were Henry Ashton, Alfred Bartholomew, R. Chapman, P. F. Page and Robert Wallace. His eldest son, Joseph Henry Good, F.R.I.B.A., followed his father's profession and wrote the memoir in *A.P.S.D.* which forms the basis of this entry.

Good appears to have been a competent architectural practitioner who designed nothing of any great significance. His only surviving building of any consequence, the Armourers' and Braziers' Hall, is (to quote Pevsner) 'a modest late neoclassical building'.

LONDON, ST. ANDREW'S CHURCH, HOLBORN, internal alterations, 1818; redecorated by S. S. Teulon 1872, destroyed by bombing 1941 [*A.P.S.D.*].

APPS COURT, WALTON-ON-THAMES, SURREY, for John Hambrough, 1821–2; dem. *c.* 1970 [*A.P.S.D.*; working drawings by A. Bartholomew in R.I.B.A. Drawings Coll.].

BLENDWORTH LODGE, nr. HORNDEAN, HANTS., for Sir William Knighton, Bart., 1821–8 [*A.P.S.D.*].

LONDON, ST. ANDREW'S VESTRY HALL, HOLBORN, 1823 [*A.P.S.D.*].

AVINGTON RECTORY, HANTS., 1828–9 [John Harris, *Catalogue of British Drawings for Architecture, etc., in American Collections*, 1971, 108].

LONDON, NATIONAL SCHOOL, HOLBORN, 1830; dem. [*A.P.S.D.*].

LONDON, ST. ANDREW'S HOLBORN WORKHOUSE, SHOE LANE, 1831; dem. [*A.P.S.D.*].

BRIGHTON, ROYAL PAVILION: works for King William IV, including SOUTH LODGE, 1831,

dem. 1851; DORMITORIES, 1831, dem.; STABLES, 1832, converted into Museum and Art Gallery 1872; NORTH LODGE (oriental style), 1832 [*A.P.S.D.*; *History of the King's Works* vi, 260].

BROADWINSOR VICARAGE, DORSET, altered or rebuilt 1839 [Salisbury Diocesan Records].

LONDON, ARMOURERS' AND BRAZIERS' HALL, COLEMAN STREET, 1839–41; interior altered 1872 [*A.P.S.D.*; exhib. at R.A. 1834, by his son].

GOODING, GEORGE, practised in Ipswich, where he designed the CORN EXCHANGE, 1812, dem. [J. Wodderspoon, *Memorials of Ipswich*, 1850, 11].

GOODRIDGE, HENRY EDMUND (1797–1864), was the son of James Goodridge, a successful builder of Bath who carried out much of the later work in Bathwick. He was articled to John Lowder (*q.v.*), proved to be an able and intelligent pupil, and by the 1820s was established in independent practice in Bath. Brisk, conscientious and thoroughly professional in every way, Goodridge soon obtained numerous commissions in Somerset and Wiltshire, and his choice by the exacting Beckford as the architect of Lansdown Tower led to his later employment by Beckford's son-in-law the Duke of Hamilton at Hamilton Palace in Scotland. His earlier work was mostly in the Greek Revival style, but he also designed several Gothic churches (including Archdeacon Daubeny's bizarre chapel at Rode Hill), a neo-Norman castle at Devizes and an Italian Romanesque nonconformist chapel. Both his own house and Beckford's Lansdown Tower are eclectic compositions in which Greek, Romanesque and Italian forms are wilfully combined to create eccentric but highly picturesque architecture. His design for the Houses of Parliament (1835) envisaged an octagonal House of Commons and a House of Lords in the form of a 'baronial hall with minstrel gallery'.

Goodridge visited France in or shortly before 1818 and Italy in 1829. He exhibited occasionally at the Royal Academy. He married in 1822 and had a son, Alfred Samuel Goodridge, by whom his practice was continued after his death, which occurred on 26 October 1864. He was buried in the cemetery at Lansdown. H. L. Elmes and W. H. Campbell were his pupils.

[Memoir by A. S. Goodridge in *R.I.B.A. Sessional Papers* 1864–5, extra pagination, 3–5; *Gent's Mag.* 1822 (ii), 88; W. Ison, *The Georgian Buildings of Bath*, 1948, 45.]

BATH

ARGYLE CHAPEL, BATHWICK, enlarged east and west ends and rebuilt façade, 1821; façade altered 1862 [*A.P.S.D.*, *s.v.* 'Bath'].

351

LANSDOWN TOWER, for William Beckford, 1824–7 [memoir] (E. F. English & W. Maddox, *Views of Lansdown Tower, Bath*, 1844; J. Millington, *Beckford's Tower, Lansdown, Bath*, 1973).

HIGH STREET, 'THE CORRIDOR', 1825 [memoir].

CLEVELAND BRIDGE and TOLL-HOUSES, 1827; the bridge was reconstructed in 1928–9 [inscription on bridge].

BATH, villas on BATHWICK ESTATE, including MON-TEBELLO (now BATHWICK GRANGE) for himself, 1828, CASA BIANCA, and FIESOLE, 1846 [R. E. M. Peach, *Street-Lore of Bath*, 1893, 96; *Bath Chronicle*, 24 April 1915; D. Watkin, *Thomas Hope*, 1968, 142–3 and pls. 48–9].

PRIOR PARK, stone staircase leading to portico, and other works connected with the conversion of the mansion into Prior Park R.C. College, 1829–34. Goodridge was probably the architect employed to reconstruct the interior after the fire of 1836 [Ison, 137]. A large perspective by Goodridge showing an ambitious scheme for further additions is in the Mellon Collection.

attributed: LANSDOWN CRESCENT, NO. 19, remodelled interior for William Beckford, *c.* 1835 [J. Lees-Milne, 'Beckford in Bath', *C. Life*, 29 April 1976].

JEWISH SYNAGOGUE, CORN STREET, 1841; dem. [S. D. Major, *Notabilia of Bath*, 1879, 80].

THE EASTERN DISPENSARY, CLEVELAND PLACE, 1845 [memoir] (plan in *Builder* vii, 1849, 160].

ARGYLE CHURCH SCHOOLS, GROVE STREET, 1845; dem. [S. D. Major, *Notabilia of Bath*, 1879, 97].

LANSDOWN CEMETERY, entrance archway, 1848, Romanesque style [memoir].

INDEPENDENT (now CONGREGATIONAL) CHAPEL, CHARLOTTE STREET, 1854, with A. S. Goodridge, Italian Romanesque style [*A.P.S.D.*, *s.v.* 'Bath'].

OTHER WORKS

WIDCOMBE CHURCH, SOMERSET, enlarged 1820 [I.C.B.S.].

DOWNSIDE ABBEY, SOMERSET, chapel and other buildings, 1822–3, Gothic; subsequently partly remodelled and incorporated in other buildings [B. Little, *Catholic Churches since 1623*, 1966, 62, 111, 164 and pl. 34a].

RODE HILL, SOMERSET (formerly WILTS.), CHRIST-CHURCH, 1822–4, Gothic [C. Daubeny, *A Guide to the Church*, 3rd. ed. 1830, Appendix, p. lxxxvi; *Bath Chronicle*, 9 Sept. 1824; *V.C.H. Wilts.* viii, 230].

SOUTH WRAXHALL CHURCH, WILTS., north aisle, 1823, Gothic [I.C.B.S.].

MALMESBURY ABBEY CHURCH, WILTS., designed west window and other alterations, 1823 [*Gent's Mag.* 1823 (ii), 170; a lithograph by Goodridge shows the alterations].

THE HOOD MONUMENT, BUTLEIGH, SOMERSET, 1831 [memoir].

ROWDE CHURCH, WILTS., rebuilt except west tower, 1831–3, Gothic [accounts, correspondence and drawings in parish chest, 1959; drawings in R.I.B.A. Coll.].

ATWORTH CHURCH, WILTS., rebuilt 1832, Gothic [I.C.B.S.].

COMBE DOWN CHURCH, SOMERSET, 1832–5, Gothic; chancel added 1884 [*Gent's Mag.* 1835 (ii), 196].

POTTERNE CHURCH, WILTS., repewed 1833 [I.C.B.S.].

BRISTOL, THE R.C. PRO-CATHEDRAL OF THE TWELVE APOSTLES, PARK PLACE, CLIFTON, begun 1834 but abandoned *c.* 1840 in an incomplete state; eventually completed by C. Hansom to a different design 1847–8 [B. Little, *Catholic Churches since 1623*, 1966, 102–3]. Goodridge's design is illustrated by B. Little, *The City and County of Bristol*, 1954, pl. 29, and by Pevsner, *North Somerset and Bristol (Buildings of England)*, pl. 34a.

LYME REGIS, DORSET, ST. MICHAEL'S R.C. CHURCH, 1835–7, Gothic; tower and spire rebuilt 1937 [inscription in church].

FROME, SOMERSET, HOLY TRINITY CHURCH, 1837–9, Gothic [I.C.B.S.].

DEVIZES CASTLE, WILTS., castellated mansion on site of medieval castle for V. Leach, *c.* 1840; much enlarged *c.* 1860 onwards [exhib. at R.A. 1842].

HAMILTON PALACE, LANARKSHIRE, library for the 10th Duke of Hamilton, *c.* 1845; dem. *c.* 1920 [*Builder* v, 1847, 271]; cf. the projected alterations at Hamilton Palace exhibited by Goodridge at the R.A. in 1842. Goodridge's unexecuted designs for the Hamilton Mausoleum, dated 1846, are among the Hamilton archives at Lennoxlove (photos. at N.M.R.S.).

ECCLESGREIG HOUSE, ST. CYRUS, KINCARDINESHIRE, alterations and additions for Forsyth Grant, 1846 [exhib. at R.A.; memoir].

GOODWIN, FRANCIS (1784–1835), was born on 23 May 1784 at King's Lynn, and became a pupil of J. Coxedge of Kensington. Later he was a pupil or assistant of John Walters, for whose Gothic church of St. Philip, Stepney (1818–20), he claimed the credit. By 1819 he was in independent practice, seeking commissions by every means in his power. Although the unsolicited designs for rebuilding Magdalen College which he submitted in 1822 merely earned him a rebuke as a 'bold speculator' (see J. C. Buckler's *Observations on the Original Architecture of Magdalen College*, 1823, 148–9), the 'inundation of pictures and promises' with which he flooded the church building committees of the Midlands had more success, and he soon had more churches in hand than the Commissioners for Building Churches thought proper. Some of these churches he contrived to pass on to others in return for a suitable consideration, but between 1820 and 1830 he designed and built nine churches paid for by the Commissioners, besides five others otherwise financed. Two of these churches (St. Leonard, Bilston, and St. Paul, Walsall) were designed in a spare neo-classical manner derived from Soane, but all the others were in the showy late Gothic style of which Goodwin was a skilful purveyor. By the mid 1820s Goodwin had a considerable practice in the Midlands, where he was responsible for several competently designed municipal buildings, of which the Grecian Town Hall at Manchester was the most important. At the same time he was assiduously seeking national fame by entering designs for competitions. Among those for which he entered were: King's College, Cambridge (1823), the Middlesex Lunatic Asylum (1828), and King Edward's School, Birmingham (1830), for which he gained the third premium. In 1830 he made designs for a 'National Cemetery' on Primrose Hill, consisting of an outer area 'disposed somewhat after the manner of Père Chaise' at Paris, and an inner enclosure containing temples and mausolea which were to be 'facsimiles of some of the most celebrated remains of Greek and Roman architecture' (Gent's Mag. 1830 (i), 351; lithograph in Soane Museum, lix, set 2, no. 29). These designs he exhibited in Parliament Street, but his proposals were not taken up by the recently formed General Cemetery Company, which eventually laid out Kensal Green Cemetery under the direction of another architect. In 1833 Goodwin was one of the architects invited to submit proposals for a new House of Commons to a Select Committee, and his designs, which are reproduced in the Report (Parliamentary Papers 1833 (487) xii), were 'said to have been the best of those sent in by the witnesses examined'. In 1834 Goodwin was associated with Capt. S. Browne, R.N., in a scheme for a suspension bridge over the Thames on the site of the present Lambeth Bridge, but although it was 'approved by the provisional committee' and exhibited at the Royal Academy, nothing came of the project. In the same year he was in Ireland making designs for additions to the College at Belfast, and for public baths at Dublin, neither of which were executed.

In 1835, when the competition for the new Houses of Parliament was announced, Goodwin naturally determined to compete. The task, however, proved fatal. For his concentration on the designs led first to insomnia and then to the apoplexy from which he died on 30 August 1835. Throughout his career he had been in chronic financial difficulties, and his estate was valued for probate at less than £1000. Benjamin Baud (q.v.)

and Thomas Allom (1804–72), the architectural illustrator, were his pupils.

In 1833–4 Goodwin published Domestic Architecture ... A Series of Designs in the Grecian, Italian and Old English Styles, in two volumes, with descriptive text by W. H. Leeds. In 1835 this was reissued with the alternative title of Rural Architecture, with additional designs for cottages, lodges, etc. There was a second edition in 1843, and a third in 1850. Goodwin also published Plans of the New House of Commons proposed by Francis Goodwin, fol. 1833.

[Obituaries in Loudon's Architectural Mag. ii, 1835, 476, and Gent's Mag. 1835 (ii), 659–60; A.P.S.D.; D.N.B.; Michael Port, 'Francis Goodwin: an Architect of the 1820s', Architectural History i, 1958.]

Unless otherwise stated, the following list of Goodwin's works is based on the information given in his Rural Architecture ii, 1843, p. xiii and passim.

PUBLIC BUILDINGS

MANCHESTER, TOWN HALL AND ASSEMBLY ROOMS, 1822–5; dem. 1912, when façade was re-erected as a screen in Heaton Park (Lancashire Illustrated, 1831, plate).

MACCLESFIELD, CHESHIRE, TOWN HALL AND ASSEMBLY ROOMS, 1823–4.

DERBY, THE COUNTY GAOL, 1823–7; remodelled 1880 (plan and elevation in S. Glover, History of the County of Derby ii, 1833, 450–3).

LEEDS, THE CENTRAL MARKET, 1824–7; dem. (engraving in T. Allen, History of the County of York ii, 1831, 536).

SALFORD, THE MARKET (at the rear of Lane's Town Hall), 1825.

BRADFORD, YORKS. (W.R.), THE PUBLIC ROOMS, 1828; afterwards known as EXCHANGE BUILDINGS, and from 1867 to 1887 used as the Post Office; now offices, known as 'Post Office Chambers, Piccadilly'.

CHURCHES

KING'S LYNN, NORFOLK, rebuilt TRINITY CHAPEL on north side of ST. MARGARET'S CHURCH, 1809 [H. J. Hillen, History of Lynn ii, 1907, 657].

SOUTHSEA (PORTSEA), HANTS., ST. PAUL, 1820–2; Gothic; dem.

WALSALL PARISH CHURCH, STAFFS., rebuilt nave, 1820–1, Gothic.

BIRMINGHAM, HOLY TRINITY, BORDESLEY, 1820–3; Gothic (Gent's Mag. 1827 (ii), 201).

ASHTON-UNDER-LYNE, LANCS., ST. PETER, 1821–4, Gothic.

KIDDERMINSTER, WORCS., ST. GEORGE, 1821–4, Gothic.

WEST BROMWICH, STAFFS., CHRIST CHURCH, 1821–8, Gothic; altered 1878–84.

BIRMINGHAM, ST. PAUL, added steeple, 1823, classical.

BURTON ON TRENT, STAFFS., HOLY TRINITY, 1823–4, Gothic; rebuilt 1882 by J. O. Scott. There is a set of the architect's drawings for this church in the William Salt Library (Staffordshire Views ii, 183–9).

MANCHESTER, ST. PETER, added tower and spire, 1824, classical; dem. 1907.

BILSTON, STAFFS., ST. LEONARD, 1826, classical; tower rebuilt 1882–3, interior remodelled 1893. There are drawings for this church in the R.I.B.A. Collection.

WALSALL, STAFFS., ST. PAUL, 1826, classical; rebuilt by J. L. Pearson 1891–2 (plans, elevations, etc., in R. Tress, *Working Drawings of Churches*, 1841).

DERBY, ST. JOHN, 1826–8, Gothic; chancel added 1871.

MANCHESTER, ST. GEORGE, HULME, 1826–8, Gothic; altered 1884.

OLDHAM, LANCS., ST. JAMES, 1827–8, Gothic; chancel added 1883.

SOUTHAMPTON, ST. MICHAEL, rebuilt nave arcades to accommodate galleries, 1828. The galleries were removed in 1872.

BILSTON, STAFFS., ST. MARY, 1829–30, Gothic.

PENDLETON, LANCS., ST. THOMAS, with R. Lane, 1829–31, Gothic [Port, 148].

DOMESTIC ARCHITECTURE

MEYNELL LANGLEY, DERBYSHIRE, refronted for Godfrey Meynell, 1829 [building accounts and MS. commonplace book at Meynell Langley] (R. Innes-Smith & C. H. Wood, *Notable Derbyshire Houses*, Derby 1972, 96–7).

BILSTON PARSONAGE, STAFFS., for Rev. William Leigh, *c*. 1830 (cf. *Rural Architecture* i, pl. 23).

LISSADELL COURT, CO. SLIGO, IRELAND, for Sir Robert Gore Booth, Bart., 1830–5 (*Rural Architecture* ii, pls. 31–4).

MARKREE, CO. SLIGO, IRELAND, castellated gatelodge to Dublin entrance, for E. J. Cooper, 1832 (*Rural Architecture* i, pl. 40).

CULLAMORE, nr. LISSADELL, CO. SLIGO, IRELAND, House for Henry Gore Booth, before 1833 (*Rural Architecture* i, pls. 30–3).

CURRAGHMORE, CO. WATERFORD, IRELAND, row of seven cottages designed for the 3rd Marquess of Waterford, *c*. 1834 (*Rural Architecture* ii, supplement).

DUNSTALL LODGE, nr. WOLVERHAMPTON, STAFFS., lodge to Stafford Road entrance, for Henry Hordern, before 1833 (*Rural Architecture* ii, pls. 7–8).

TEDDESLEY HALL, STAFFS., a lodge for the 1st Lord Hatherton, 1835 [*A.P.S.D.*].

GORHAM, JOHN (–1801), was described as 'an eminent surveyor and builder' when he died in 1801. He was a bricklayer by trade, and was Master of the Tylers' and Bricklayers' Company in 1755–6. He was surveyor to Gray's Inn, the Inner Temple, the Drapers' and Fishmongers' Companies, and the Duke of Bedford's London estate. His father, Thomas Gorham, had been bricklayer to Gray's Inn since 1726, and in 1738 Thomas and his son were jointly appointed 'surveyor of the new buildings in Holborn Court', *i.e.* Nos. 2–3 South Square. In 1776 John Gorham was associated with Charles Cole (*q.v.*) in the laying out of ELY PLACE, HOLBORN, and soon after 1781 he built several houses in CHANCERY LANE on the site of the present Law Society's offices. He rebuilt the front of DRAPERS' HALL, THROGMORTON STREET, in 1778; again rebuilt 1868–9 [A. H. Johnson, *History of the Drapers' Company* iii, 1922, 286]. He retired in 1797, a wealthy man, but 'lived in habits of the strictest economy, though reputed to be worth upwards of £200,000'. [*Gent's Mag.* 1801, 768; *The Pension Book of Gray's Inn*, ed. R. J. Fletcher, ii, 1910, 200, 230, 378; *Trans. London and Middlesex Archl. Soc.*, N.S. vi, 1929–32, 446; D. J. Oleson, *Town Planning in London in the 18th and 19th Centuries*, Yale 1964, 183.]

GOSLING, CHARLES FLICK (–1865), exhibited at the Royal Academy from London addresses in 1836, 1838 and 1845. In 1836 he showed a 'Design for a mansion now erecting near Ipswich'. He died on 7 October 1865 [Principal Probate Registry, Calendar of Probates].

GOTT, JOHN (1720–1793), of Woodhouse in the parish of Calverley, nr. Leeds, was active as a bridge- and canal-builder in Yorkshire. He was resident engineer of the Aire and Calder Navigation from 1760 to 1792, and Surveyor of Bridges for the West Riding of Yorkshire from 1777 until his death in 1793, when he was succeeded by his son William (1745–1810). His younger son Benjamin (1762–1840) was the well-known woollen manufacturer in Leeds.

Among the Yorkshire bridges designed by John Gott were those at FERRYBRIDGE, 1764–5, replaced in 1797–1804 by the present bridge designed by John Carr; CASTLEFORD, 1770, replaced in 1805 by the existing bridge designed by Bernard Hartley; METHLEY, 1776–9, and HEBDEN, 1789 [West Riding County Records, *ex inf.* Prof. A. W. Skempton]. He also built (1760–1) the ornamental bridge at NOSTELL according to a design made by Sir George Savile [M. W. Brockwell, *The Nostell Collection*, 1915, 44–5, 385], and in 1767–70 designed HEXHAM BRIDGE, NORTHUMBERLAND, destroyed by a flood in 1771 [M. A. Richardson, *The Local Historian's Table-Book* ii, 1842, 168].

GOUD, ANTHONY, was a mason of Springfield, nr. Chelmsford in Essex. In 1726–31 he was working at Boreham House, Essex, and in 1729–41 under Leoni at Moulsham Hall in the same county [R. Gunnis, *Dictionary of British Sculptors 1660–1851*, 1968, 178]. An inscription commemorates the fact that in 1732 he rebuilt the west tower of TERLING CHURCH, ESSEX, in a vernacular classical style. In 1741 he covenanted to erect eight substantial brick houses on land he had leased in DUKE STREET, CHELMSFORD. He subsequently moved to Chatham in Kent, where he died some time before 1774 [Essex Record Office, D/DU/132/1 and 5].

GOULD, or **GOLD,** JAMES (–1734), was a surveyor in London, where in February 1722/3 he was engaged to value building materials on the Harley estate [B.M., Add. MS. 18240, f. 28]. He was very likely the 'John Gould' who in 1720 was associated with Colen Campbell as surveyor of Sir Theodore Jansen's new house at Wimbledon [*The Particulars and Inventories of the Estates of the Late ... Directors of the South Sea Company*, 1721, 43]. In 1723 he was appointed by the South Sea Company to 'Survey and measure the works' of their new premises in Threadneedle Street, at a salary of £100 p.a. As no other architect is mentioned in the minutes, it would appear that it was to Gould's designs that SOUTH SEA HOUSE was erected in 1724–5 (dem. 1902). His salary as 'Surveyor of the new Buildings' was paid up to Christmas 1726 [B.M., Minute Books of the South Sea Company, Add. MSS. 25501, f. 76, 25502, ff. 89, 108^v, 152^v, 177^v, 257^v].

In 1719 Gould's daughter Elizabeth married George Dance (senior), and in 1725–9 Dance and Gould were jointly responsible for rebuilding the church of ST. BOTOLPH, BISHOPSGATE, in a style derived from Wren's City churches. Dance may also have been involved in the building of GOULD or GOLD SQUARE, off Cooper's Row, undertaken by his father-in-law as a speculation in about 1730 [Dorothy Stroud, *George Dance, Architect*, 1971, 29–30]. The death of 'Mr. Gould, Surveyor to the South Sea Company', occurred on 31 January 1734 [*Gent's Mag.* 1734, 107].

GOVER, WILLIAM, an architect and surveyor of Winchester, rebuilt LONGPARISH VICARAGE, WILTS., in 1823 [Bodleian Library, records of Queen Anne's Bounty], enlarged HINDON CHURCH, WILTS., in 1836 [I.C.B.S.], and largely rebuilt ST. MAURICE'S CHURCH, WINCHESTER, in 1842; dem. (except medieval tower) [I.C.B.S.].

GOWAN, GEORGE (–1843), was the son of Alexander Gowan (d. 1776), a builder of Edinburgh. He is described as 'architect' on the family tombstone in the Canongate Churchyard, which shows that he was over 80 at the time of his death

on 23 October 1843. In 1791 he designed a house in GEORGE STREET, EDINBURGH, for the Countess of Balcarres [S.R.O., Edinburgh Sasines].

GOWAN, WILLIAM, was the surveyor responsible for rebuilding TOTTERIDGE CHURCH, HERTS., in 1790–6 [Herts. County Record Office, 69897, 69900]. This small classical church was much altered in the nineteenth century.

GRAHAM, HENRY (*c.* 1795–1819), was the third son of the Rev. John Graham, rector of St. Saviour's, York. Nothing is known of his architectural training, but at the age of 19 he undertook the restoration of the remarkable thirteenth-century church of SKELTON, YORKS. (N.R.), carried out in 1814–18 [E. Christian, *Architectural Illustrations of Skelton Church*, 1846, 4–5]. In 1818 or 1819 Graham set out for Italy, where in May 1819 he met a premature death in Naples. He is commemorated by a monument in the Protestant Cemetery at Rome, set up by 'two of his fellow students' to 'testify their freindship', and by another at Skelton which refers to 'the ardent pursuit of improvement in his profession as an Architect' which exposed him to 'the dissipating and corrupting air of foreign lands'.

GRAHAM, JAMES GILLESPIE (1776–1855), was born at Dunblane in Perthshire on 11 June 1776. His father, Malcolm Gillespie, is described as 'writer' (*i.e.* solicitor) in the Register of Births. James is said to have started life as a working joiner or mason, but nothing is known of his early career before the first decade of the nineteenth century, when for some years he was employed as superintendent of the 2nd Lord Macdonald's works on the Isle of Skye. These were mostly of a utilitarian character, consisting of piers, schools, inns, manses and the like, and offered relatively little scope for architectural design. Indeed at first Gillespie's status appears to have been rather that of a clerk of works than an architect. However, by 1810 he had secured several architectural commissions on the mainland, including a country house at Achnacarry in Inverness-shire and the County Buildings at Cupar in Fife. In 1815 he had the good fortune to marry an heiress. She was Margaret, daughter of William Graham, laird of Orchill in Perthshire. Gillespie now 'elongated his surname' to 'Gillespie Graham', and when his father-in-law died in 1825 he and his wife inherited the estate. She died in 1826, leaving two daughters, the elder of whom, Mrs. Graeme-Oliphant, ultimately succeeded to the property. In 1830 Gillespie Graham took a second wife, Elizabeth, the daughter of Major John Campbell of the 76th Regiment of Foot. There were no children by this marriage. He died in Edinburgh on 21 March 1855 after four years' illness, and was buried in the Greyfriars Cemetery. A portrait at Ardblair Castle, Perthshire, by Watson Gordon, shows him attired in Highland dress, and there is a caricature by Crombie in his series of *Modern Athenians*.

Gillespie Graham had an extensive practice in Scotland, specializing in Gothic churches and castellated country houses. Though basically symmetrical, the latter are generally given a picturesque outline by the addition of a large round tower at one side. The same components tend to recur in his designs, and on one occasion he even went so far as to use almost identical plans and elevations for two houses – Edmonstone and Torrisdale Castles – one in Lanarkshire, the other in Argyllshire. The exteriors of his castles are mostly coarse and unscholarly, but the interiors often show a considerable facility in devising rich Gothic rooms based on more or less authentic medieval sources. Notable examples are Duns Castle and the Banner Hall at Taymouth Castle. Though not in the first rank of Gothic Revivalists, Gillespie Graham provided Scotland with many churches that were greatly superior to the humble and artless kirks of the early nineteenth century. Muthill, for instance, was considered in 1837 to be 'unequalled by any country church in the land'. To modern eyes his best ecclesiastical works were the steeple at Montrose (an effective version of the one at Louth in Lincolnshire) and the spire of Tolbooth St. John's in Edinburgh. His reputation as a Gothic architect was strengthened by an intermittent association with A. W. N. Pugin, whom he is said to have befriended after the latter was shipwrecked on the coast near Leith. It is certain that he gave Pugin a pair of compasses of which the latter thought highly, for they appear in Pugin's portrait by Herbert, clearly inscribed 'James Gillespie Graham, architect, Edinburgh 1830'. In return Pugin helped Graham professionally. Thus in 1829–30 he made designs and supplied a quantity of carvings for the house at Murthly which Graham was building for Sir John Stewart [for the designs see Phoebe Stanton, *Pugin*, 1971, 195, and for the carvings, payments to Pugin in S.R.O., GD 121/Box 68]. In 1835 Pugin appears to have assisted Graham with the chapel of St. Margaret's Convent in Edinburgh [Stanton, 21], and in 1840–1 the latter paid him £200, perhaps for drawings in connection with the refitting of St. Mary's Catholic Church in the same city [*ibid.*, 200], and certainly for help with the designs for Tolbooth St. John's Church, the drawings for which, among the Dean of Guild Records in City Chambers, Edinburgh (Extracted Processes, 4 Feb. 1841), are in Pugin's hand. Pugin's most notable service to his Scottish friend was, however, to make the finished drawings for Gillespie Graham's entry in the competition for the new Houses of Parliament in 1835 [B. Ferrey, *Recol-*

lections of A. N. Welby Pugin, 1861, 241]. Pugin's draughtsmanship was probably the best feature of this badly composed design, of which Graham published a lithograph. Perspective drawings of the interiors of the proposed Houses of Lords and Commons in elaborate Puginesque frames are preserved at Ardblair Castle. As a classical designer, Gillespie Graham is best represented by Gray's Hospital at Elgin and by his work on the Moray estate in the New Town at Edinburgh. Here, instead of continuing the grid-plan of the adjoining streets, Graham exploited the terrain to produce a masterpiece of urban planning, of which the polygonal Moray Place is the centrepiece. The elevations are boldly treated in a monumental manner derived from Robert Adam's Charlotte Square.

Gillespie Graham appears to have been ambitious, pushing and none too scrupulous. In 1818 he styled himself 'Architect in Scotland of the Prince Regent' [see S.R.O., GD 51/6/1963 and 2012], and in 1822 took advantage of the Royal visit to Scotland to convert the title to 'Architect to His Majesty for Scotland', to the justifiable annoyance of Robert Reid, who had enjoyed a similar title since 1808 [National Library of Scotland, MS. 351, ff. 102–3]. Two years later he did his best to acquire the sinecure Mastership of the Works in Scotland, vacant by the death of James Brodie, but was defeated by Reid, who succeeded in getting that office merged with his own [National Library of Scotland, MS. 1056, f. 141]. Graham was elected a Fellow of the Society of Antiquaries of Scotland in 1817 and became a burgess of Edinburgh in 1838 [*Roll of Edinburgh Burgesses*, Scottish Record Society, 68].

[*A.P.S.D.*; *D.N.B.*; Burke's *Landed Gentry*, 1858; James Brown, *Epitaphs and Monumental Inscriptions in Greyfriars Churchyard, Edinburgh*, Edinburgh 1867, 226–7; article on 'Edinburgh Architects' in *Builder*, 10 June 1882; *Scots Mag.* lxxvii, 1815, 556; James Macaulay, 'James Gillespie Graham in Skye', *Bulletin of the Scottish Georgian Soc.* iii, 1974–5.]

PUBLIC BUILDINGS

EDINBURGH, PICARDY PLACE, alterations to premises for Commercial Bank, 1810 [J. L. Anderson, *The Story of the Commercial Bank of Scotland*, Edinburgh 1910, 6].

CUPAR, FIFE, COUNTY BUILDINGS, ST. CATHERINE STREET, 1810; extended by W. Burn 1835–6 and again subsequently [S.R.O., B 13/18/1, f. 60].

EDINBURGH, remodelled premises (now Masonic Chapel) for THE COMMERCIAL BANK in NEW ASSEMBLY CLOSE, 142 HIGH STREET, 1813 [Edinburgh, Dean of Guild plans].

CUPAR, FIFE, COUNTY PRISON, 1813–14 [S.R.O., B 13/18/1, with plan; *Parliamentary Papers*,

1818, vi, Report on Scottish Jails, p.17, with elevation].

ELGIN, MORAYSHIRE, GRAY'S HOSPITAL, 1815–19 [R. Young, *Annals of Elgin*, Elgin 1879, 251, 400].

attributed: DUNS, BERWICKSHIRE, THE MARKET HOUSE, 1816, Gothic; dem. 1966 [the attribution is based on the fact that G.G. designed Duns Castle contemporaneously].

INVERARAY, ARGYLLSHIRE, COURT HOUSE, 1816–20 [I. G. Lindsay & Mary Cosh, *Inveraray and the Dukes of Argyll*, 1973, 317–18].

EDINBURGH, THE DEAF AND DUMB INSTITUTE, HENDERSON ROW, 1823; extended 1893 [J. Stark, *Picture of Edinburgh*, 6th ed. 1835, 260].

LEITH, THE TOLBOOTH or GAOL, 1824–7, dem. [*The Private Letter-Books of Sir Walter Scott*, ed. W. Partington, 1930, 309].

HADDINGTON, EAST LOTHIAN, addition of spire to TOWN HOUSE, 1830–1 [James Miller, *History of Haddington*, 1900, 228].

ABERDEEN, COMMERCIAL BANK OF SCOTLAND, KING STREET, 1836 [G. M. Fraser, 'Archibald Simpson and his Times', *Aberdeen Weekly Jnl.*, 9 Aug. 1918].

EDINBURGH, VICTORIA HALL, *see* TOLBOOTH ST. JOHN'S CHURCH.

CHURCHES

KILMUIR, ISLE OF SKYE, 1810; now in ruins [J. Macaulay, 'James Gillespie Graham in Skye', *Bulletin of the Scottish Georgian Soc.* iii, 1974–5, 8].

FALKIRK, STIRLINGSHIRE, rebuilt (except central tower), 1810–11, Gothic [S.R.O., GD 171/122; R.C.A.M., *Stirlingshire* i, 150 and pl. 35].

MONIMAIL, FIFE, reconstruction of tower, 1811 [S.R.O., HR 432/2, pp. 2, 11].

LINLITHGOW, WEST LOTHIAN, restoration of chancel, 1812–13 [J. Ferguson, *Eccelsia Antiqua, or the story of . . . St. Michael's, Linlithgow*, 1905, 105–9].

EDINBURGH, ST. MARY'S CHURCH, now CATHEDRAL (R.C.), BROUGHTON STREET, 1813–14, Gothic [*A.P.S.D.*]. Internal alterations in 1840–1 may have been designed by Pugin in collaboration with Graham [Phoebe Stanton, *Pugin*, 1971, 200]. There have been many subsequent alterations, including the addition of a new chancel in 1896.

GLASGOW, ST. ANDREW'S CHAPEL, now CATHEDRAL (R.C.), GREAT CLYDE STREET, 1814–17, Gothic; enlarged 1870 and 1890–2 [*A.P.S.D.*].

LIBERTON, MIDLOTHIAN, rebuilt 1815, Gothic [*N.S.A.* i, 11].

CLACKMANNAN, 1815, Gothic [S.R.O., HR 633/1].

DUNOON, ARGYLLSHIRE, 1816, Gothic; enlarged by D. Hamilton 1834 [*N.S.A.* vii, 610].

ALLOA, CLACKMANNANSHIRE, 1817–19, Gothic

[James Lothian, *Alloa and its Environs*, Alloa 1871, 32].

DUNBLANE CATHEDRAL, PERTHSHIRE, alterations to choir, 1817–19; Graham's work was undone in 1890 [A. B. Barty, *History of Dunblane*, Stirling 1944, 203].

STIRLING, HOLY RUDE CHURCH, restoration of West Church (nave), 1818. Graham's plaster vault was removed in 1911–14 [R.C.A.M., *Stirlingshire* i, 130].

GLASGOW, GEORGE STREET INDEPENDENT CHURCH, 14 WEST GEORGE STREET (now British Rail Offices), 1819, Doric [J. Pagan, *Sketch of the History of Glasgow*, 1847, 180].

EDINBURGH, NICHOLSON STREET CHAPEL (DR. JAMIESON'S CHAPEL), 1819–20, Tudor Gothic; altered 1932 [*A.P.S.D.*].

DUNBAR, 1819–21, Gothic [*N.S.A.* ii, 80].

SHOTTS, LANARKSHIRE, 1819, Gothic, executed with modifications by John Brash (*q.v.*) [S.R.O., HR 739/2].

DOUNE, PERTHSHIRE, for the 10th Earl of Moray, 1822, Gothic [S.R.O., HR 245/4, p. 80].

INVERKEITHING, FIFE, rebuilt 1826 incorporating old tower [W. Stephen, *The Story of Inverkeithing and Rosyth*, 1938, 42].

RAFFORD, MORAYSHIRE, 1826, Gothic [*N.S.A.* xiii, 254].

DUNINO, FIFE, 1826, Gothic [S.R.O., HR 64/1] (G. Hay, *Architecture of Scottish Post-Reformation Churches*, 1957, pl. 19b).

MUTHILL, PERTHSHIRE, 1826–8, Gothic [S.R.O., HR 155/2].

PERTH, ST. JOHN'S CHURCH, repairs and alterations, begun in 1828 but not fully completed [*Perthshire Illustrated*, 1843, introduction by W. Hooker, 14; W. Douglas Simpson, *A History of St. John's Kirk, Perth*, 1958, 31–2].

DALGETY, FIFE, 1830, Gothic [S.R.O., HR 185/1, minute of 19 Aug. 1830].

ERROL, PERTHSHIRE, 1831–3, Romanesque [*N.S.A.* x, 386–7; L. Melville, *Errol*, Perth 1935, 117–18].

MONTROSE, ANGUS, Gothic tower and spire, 1832–4 [*N.S.A.* xi, 282].

EDINBURGH, ST. MARGARET'S CONVENT CHAPEL (R.C.), 1835, Romanesque [James Grant, *Old and New Edinburgh* iii, *c.* 1880, 45].

EDINBURGH, GREENSIDE CHURCH, ROYAL TERRACE, 1836–8, Gothic; tower 1851/3 [*A.P.S.D.*].

EDINBURGH, HERIOT'S HOSPITAL CHAPEL, refitted interior, 1837 [*A.P.S.D.*; *Builder*, 10 June 1882, 716] (*C. Life*, 13 March 1975, fig. 8).

EDINBURGH, TOLBOOTH ST. JOHN'S CHURCH or VICTORIA HALL (Hall of Assembly for the Church of Scotland), in association with A. W. N. Pugin, 1841–4, Gothic [*A.P.S.D.*].

MURTHLY, PERTHSHIRE, CHAPEL OF ST. ANTHONY THE EREMITE, rebuilt 1846 [*The Chapel of St. Anthony the Eremite of Murthly*, Edinburgh 1850, folio].

See p. 986

357

GASK, PERTHSHIRE, EPISCOPAL CHAPEL, 1845–6, Romanesque [*Life and Songs of the Baroness Nairne*, ed. C. Rogers, 2nd ed. 1869, 134].

COUNTRY HOUSES, ETC.

ACHNACARRY, INVERNESS-SHIRE, for Donald Cameron, begun 1802, but not completed internally until 1837, castle style; restored 1952 after war-damage [A. Mackenzie, *History of the Camerons*, 1884, 255; *N.S.A.* xiv, 122] (Sheila Forman, *Scottish Country Houses and Castles*, 1967, 161–5).

ALLANTON CASTLE, CAMBUSNETHAN, LANARKSHIRE, enlarged for Sir Henry Steuart, Bart., before 1809 and again *c.* 1820; dem. [*N.S.A.* vi, 620, and information from Dr. A. A. Tait].

KINLOCHMOIDART, INVERNESS-SHIRE, design for offices for Col. Hector Macdonald Buchanan, 1803 [National Library of Scotland, MS. 3983, f. 198].

SLEAT MANSE, ISLE OF SKYE, *c.* 1810, Gothic [J. Macaulay, 'James Gillespie Graham in Skye', *Bulletin of the Scottish Georgian Soc.* iii, 1974–5, 8–9].

CULDEES CASTLE, PERTHSHIRE, for General Andrew John Drummond, *c.* 1810, castle style; restored after fire in 1887; altered by Sir R. Lorimer *c.* 1910 [J. P. Neale, *Views of Seats* v, 1822].

attributed: BOWLAND, STOW, MIDLOTHIAN, new castellated front for General Alexander Walker, *c.* 1811 [stylistic attribution] (J. Small, *Castles and Mansions of the Lothians* i, 1883).

CRAWFORD PRIORY, CULTS, FIFE, for Lady Mary Lindsay Crawford, 1811–13, succeeding David Hamilton, Gothic; enlarged *c.* 1870; dem. 1971 [inscription quoted by A. H. Millar, *Fife, Pictorial and Historical* i, 1895, 191–2] (R. Chambers, *A Description of Crawford Priory*, 1830).

ROSS PRIORY, DUNBARTONSHIRE, remodelled for Hector Macdonald Buchanan, 1812, Gothic, based on T. D. W. Dearn, *Sketches in Architecture* (1807), pl. vi [J. P. Neale, *Views of Seats* vi, 1823].

AUCHTERTOOL MANSE, FIFE, 1812, Gothic, 'in the cottage style' [*N.S.A.* ix, 258].

DRUMTOCHTY CASTLE, FORDOUN, KINCARDINE-SHIRE, for George Harley Drummond, *c.* 1815, castle style [*N.S.A.* xi, 88–9].

EDMONSTONE CASTLE, nr. BIGGAR, LANARKSHIRE, for James Brown, 1815, castle style [*N.S.A.* vi, 364] (G. V. Irving, *Upper Ward of Lanarkshire* i, 1864, 329, plate).

attributed: TORRISDALE CASTLE, KINTYRE, ARGYLL-SHIRE, for General Keith MacAlister, *c.* 1815, castle style; wings added *c.* 1900–10. Closely resembles Edmonstone Castle [R.C.A.M., *Argyll* i, 192 and pls. 84–5].

attributed: GLENBARR ABBEY (NOW BARR HOUSE),

KINTYRE, ARGYLLSHIRE, enlarged and altered for Col. Matthew MacAlister, *c.* 1815, Gothic. The owner was the brother of General K. MacAlister, who probably employed Graham at Torrisdale Castle, and in style the house resembles Ross Priory [R.C.A.M., *Argyll* i, 188 and pl. 78].

KILKERRAN HOUSE, DAILLY, AYRSHIRE, addition of classical wings and staircase for Sir James Fergusson, Bart., *c.* 1815 [Alistair Rowan in *C. Life*, 1–8 May 1975].

ARMADALE CASTLE, ISLE OF SKYE, for the 2nd Lord Macdonald, *c.* 1815–20, castle style [J. P. Neale, *Views of Seats*, 2nd ser., i, 1824, illustrating a more ambitious design than the one actually executed].

CAMBUSNETHAN HOUSE, WISHAW, LANARKSHIRE, for Robert Lockhart, 1816–19, Gothic [J. M. Leighton, *Select Views on the Clyde*, 1830, 35; *N.S.A.* vi, 615].

DUNS CASTLE, BERWICKSHIRE, remodelled for William Hay, 1818–22, castle style [J. P. Neale, *Views of Seats* vi, 1823] (D. MacGibbon & T. Ross, *Castellated and Domestic Architecture of Scotland* v, 1892, 265 for plan).

KILMARON CASTLE, CUPAR, FIFE, for Admiral Sir Frederick Maitland, *c.* 1820, castle style; much altered *c.* 1860; dem. 1970 [J. M. Leighton, *History of Fife*, Glasgow 1840, ii, 35] (A. H. Millar, *Fife, Pictorial and Historical* i, 1895, 130).

MOUNT MELVILLE, FIFE, new front block for John Whyte-Melville, 1820–1, classical; dem. *c.* 1900 [drawings at N.M.R.S. and National Library of Scotland, Advocates MS. 33.8.4] (J. P. Neale, *Views of Seats*, 2nd ser., ii, 1825).

LEE PLACE, LANARKSHIRE, for Sir Charles Lockhart, Bart., 1820–49, castle style [J. M. Leighton, *Select Views on the Clyde*, 1830, 25; *N.S.A.* vi, 18; J. P. Neale, *Views of Seats*, 2nd ser., iv, 1828; drawings in R.I.B.A. Coll.].

BLYTHSWOOD HOUSE, RENFREWSHIRE, for Major Archibald Campbell, completed 1821, Greek Revival; dem. *c.* 1929 [J. P. Neale, *Views of Seats*, 2nd ser., iii, 1826][1] (*The Old Country Houses of the Old Glasgow Gentry*, Glasgow 1870, no. xii).

MILNE GRADEN, nr. COLDSTREAM, BERWICKSHIRE, for Admiral Sir David Milne, 1822, classical [book of drawings at Milne Graden].

SPRINGWOOD PARK, KELSO, ROXBURGHSHIRE, mausoleum and entrance gate by Kelso Bridge

---

[1] A contemporary reference in Sir Walter Scott's Journal (ed. Andrews, 1972, 349) implies that this house was designed by Robert Smirke, but Graham's employment at Blythswood is confirmed by the existence of an engraved 'plan of the town of Blythswood extended agreeably to the design by James Gillespie, Esq. architect', dated 1820, and the classical detai ing also points to Graham rather than to Smirke.

for Sir John James Douglas, Bart., *c.* 1822 [*N.S.A.* iii, 320; drawings at N.M.R.S.] (R.C.A.M., *Roxburghshire* i, fig. 206).

DUNNINALD HOUSE, CRAIG, ANGUS, for Peter Arkly, 1823–4, castle style [Alistair Rowan in *C. Life*, 14–21 Aug. 1969] (plan in J. G. Dunbar, *Historic Architecture of Scotland*, 1966, fig. 93).

attributed: WESTERTOWN HOUSE, nr. ELGIN, MORAYSHIRE, for Lt.-Col. Alexander Hay, 1824, castle style [stylistic attribution].

WISHAW HOUSE, MOTHERWELL, LANARKSHIRE, enlarged and remodelled for the 8th Lord Belhaven and Stenton, 1825, castle style; additions by W. Burn 1858; dem. 1953 [J. P. Neale, *Views of Seats*, 2nd ser., iv, 1828; *N.S.A.* vi, 616] (*Scottish Field*, April 1950).

DOUGLAS MANSE, LANARKSHIRE, 1828 [*N.S.A.* vi, 490].

MURTHLY HOUSE, nr. DUNKELD, PERTHSHIRE, for Sir John A. Drummond-Stewart, Bart. (who was partly responsible for the design), 1829–32, left unfinished, Elizabethan style; dem. *c.* 1950 [building accounts in S.R.O., GD 121, Box 68; *The Journal of Sir Walter Scott*, ed. J. G. Tait, 1950, 685] (*C. Life*, 2 Oct. 1915).

BONNINGTON HOUSE, LANARKSHIRE, addition of porch for Sir Charles Lockhart-Ross, Bart., *c.* 1830; destroyed by fire *c.* 1900 [*N.S.A.* vi, 18].

ARDMADDY CASTLE, ARGYLLSHIRE, court of offices for the 2nd Marquess of Breadalbane, 1837–9. A design by Graham for a Jacobethan addition to the house was partly carried out in 1862 by David Bryce [R.C.A.M., *Argyll* ii, 248–9].

TAYMOUTH CASTLE, PERTHSHIRE, remodelled west wing for the 2nd Marquess of Breadalbane, 1838–9, castle style [Alistair Rowan in *C. Life*, 15 Oct. 1964].

BRODICK CASTLE, ARRAN, castellated addition for the 10th Duke of Hamilton, 1844 [*Building Chronicle* i, 1855, 170; *A.P.S.D.*] (*C. Life*, 1 March 1941; D. MacGibbon & T. Ross, *Castellated and Domestic Architecture of Scotland* iii, 1889, 285–9).

AYTON HOUSE, BERWICKSHIRE, for W. Mitchell Innes, 1851, castle style [*Building Chronicle* i, 1855, 170; *A.P.S.D.*].

WESTER BOGIE HOUSE, ABBOTSHALL, FIFE, for James Thomson, castle style; now in ruins [*N.S.A.* ix, 154].

MINARD CASTLE, GLASSARY, ARGYLLSHIRE, for H. W. Askew [*Builder*, 10 June 1882, 716].

EDINBURGH: DOMESTIC ARCHITECTURE

HOWARD PLACE, 1809–20 [S.R.O., Edinburgh Sasines].

THE EARL OF MORAY'S ESTATE, comprising AINSLIE PLACE, ALBYN PLACE, DARNAWAY STREET, DOUNE TERRACE, FORBES STREET, GLENFILAS STREET, GREAT STUART STREET, MORAY PLACE, RANDOLPH CLIFF, CRESCENT AND PLACE, GREAT COLME STREET and WEMYSS PLACE, all designed by *c.* 1822 and built by *c.* 1830 [A. J. Youngson, *The Making of Classical Edinburgh*, Edinburgh 1966, 216–25].

ALVA STREET, 1823 [S.R.O., Edinburgh Sasines].

BLACKET PLACE, layout, 1825 [*Book of the Old Edinburgh Club* xxiv, 1942, 177].

MELVILLE STREET and WALKER STREET area, general layout only for Sir Francis Walker and the Heriot Trustees, *c.* 1825 [A. J. Youngson, *op. cit.*, 215–16].

QUALITY STREET, 1827 [S.R.O., Edinburgh Sasines].

QUEENSFERRY STREET, NOS. 18–20, 1830 [S.R.O., Edinburgh Sasines].

BIRKENHEAD, CHESHIRE

HAMILTON SQUARE, designed for the Scotsman William Laird in 1825 as part of a larger street plan for which Graham was also responsible. The north and east sides were begun immediately, but the south and west sides were not built until 1839–44 [*A.P.S.D.*; W. W. Mortimer, *Hundred of Wirral*, 1847, 327].

MONUMENT

DUNIRA, nr. COMRIE, PERTHSHIRE, monument to the 1st Lord Melville, 1812 [*Aberdeen Jnl.*, 23 May 1812].

GRAINGER, RICHARD (1797–1861), was a speculative builder of exceptional vision who transformed the centre of Newcastle-on-Tyne during the second quarter of the nineteenth century. He was the son of a quay porter at Newcastle who died young. After going to a charity school he was apprenticed to a carpenter and builder named Brown. Having by a fortunate marriage (to the daughter of Joseph Arundale, a wealthy tanner) acquired considerable capital, he was able not only to set up as a builder on his own account, but to embark on the extensive building projects which made him the Cubitt of the north. In 1825 he began the erection of ELDON SQUARE, and between 1829 and 1834 he built LEAZE'S CRESCENT and TERRACE, consisting of seventy first- and sixty second-class houses. This speculation proved so successful that in 1834 he purchased 12 acres of land in the centre of Newcastle, upon which he proceeded to build a magnificent sequence of handsome and well-planned streets reminiscent of Georgian Edinburgh and Regency London. By 1840 Grainger had built GREY STREET, GRAINGER STREET, MARKET STREET, CLAYTON STREET, NUN STREET, NELSON STREET and various lesser streets in the neighbourhood. Clayton Street was named after John Clayton, the Town Clerk, who assisted Grainger financially and did all in his power to promote his develop-ments. Grainger's activities included the erection or rebuilding of a number of important public buildings, including the MARKETS, the THEATRE ROYAL, the EXCHANGE, the ROYAL ARCADE, the BRANCH BANK OF ENGLAND, LAMBTON'S BANK and the SALEM METHODIST CHAPEL in Hood Street.[1] In 1839 Grainger overreached himself by purchas-ing the Elswick estate immediately to the west of Newcastle for £114,100, but with Clayton's help he managed to extricate himself from an awkward financial predicament without resorting to bank-ruptcy, and although he died in debt (4 July 1861), his estate ultimately proved able to satisfy his creditors.

There can be no doubt that the new Newcastle was largely Grainger's own conception, and that he was an exceptionally able and enlightened de-veloper and town-planner. What is doubtful is to what extent he was responsible for the design of any individual building or street. Among the architects who collaborated with him were John Dobson, Thomas Oliver, John and Benjamin Green, John Wardle and George Walker. Thus Dobson was responsible for the Market, the Greens designed the Theatre Royal, and Oliver planned Leazes Terrace. But individual re-sponsibility for the designs of many of Grainger's other buildings remains undetermined and some of them may have been designed in his office by draughtsmen working under his immediate direction. The Royal Arcade (1831–2) is a case in point. Although Rose's *Westmorland ... and Northumberland Illustrated* (1832) implies that Grainger was its 'architect', it is attributed to Dobson both by his daughter and on the plate illustrating it in Collard & Ross's *Architectural and Picturesque Views in Newcastle upon Tyne* (1841). At a time when the distinction between architect and builder was still far from absolute, and in the exceptional circumstances created by a great town-planning enterprise, the question of artistic authorship may never be satisfactorily resolved. There is, however, an obvious sense in which the Town Council was right, in 1861, to commemorate Grainger as 'one of the greatest architects of his age'.

[Obituaries in *Gent's Mag.* 1861 (ii), 216–17, and *Builder* xix, 1861, 476; Harriet Martineau, 'Self-Made Men – Richard Grainger', *Once a Week* v, 1861, 401–6; R. Welford, *Men of Mark 'twixt Tyne and Tweed* ii, 1895, 321–6; R. Turley, 'Early Victorian City Planning: the work of John Dobson and Richard Grainger at Newcastle upon Tyne', *Arch. Rev.*, May 1946; L. Wilkes & G. Dodds, *Tyneside Classical: the Newcastle of Grainger, Dobson and Clayton*, 1964; B. Allsopp, *Historic Architecture of Newcastle upon Tyne*, 1967.]

GRANTHAM, LORD, *see* ROBINSON, THOMAS

GRAVATT, WILLIAM (1806–1866), had a distinguished career as a mathematician and civil engineer. He was the son of Col. Gravatt, R.E., of the Royal Military Academy at Woolwich, was a pupil of the civil engineer Bryan Donkin, then an assistant of I. K. Brunel, and ultimately engineer to several canal and railway companies. He was a Member of the Institution of Civil Engineers and was elected a Fellow of the Royal Society in 1832. As Engineer to the Calder and Hebble Navigation in Yorkshire he designed several bridges, 'the arches of which were re-markable for their stability and cheapness'. In Somerset, where he was Surveyor and Engineer to the Parrett Navigation, the three-arched bridge at Langport was built by him in 1839–40. While in Yorkshire he had designed the LITERARY AND PHILOSOPHICAL SOCIETY'S HALL at HALIFAX, 1832. [Obituary in *Minutes of Proceedings of the Institution of Civil Engineers* xxvi, 1866–7, 565–75; J. Crabtree, *History of Halifax*, 1836, 352; drawings for Langport Bridge in Somerset River Board's offices at Bridgwater, *ex inf.* Mr. Bryan Little.]

GRAY, (Sir) GEORGE (–1773), younger son of Sir James Gray, Bart., and Colonel of the 37th Foot, was one of the original members of the Society of Dilettanti in 1734, and took a promi-nent part in its affairs. He acted as secretary and treasurer of the Society from 1739 to 1771, and was well known as an amateur of architecture. His portrait by Knapton is still in the possession of the Society. Gray succeeded to the baronetcy on the death of his brother in January 1773, but himself died only a few weeks later.

Gray is said (*e.g.* by Horace Walpole, *Anecdotes of Painting* v, ed. F. W. Hilles & P. B. Daghlian, 1937, 161) to have designed SPENCER HOUSE, GREEN PARK, LONDON, built by John Vardy for the 1st Earl Spencer in 1756–65 (*C. Life*, 30 Oct., 6 Nov. 1926). That he exercised a close control over its design is shown by the existence in the Soane Museum[1] and the R.I.B.A. Collection of several drawings for the house by Vardy with endorsements recording that they had been approved by Gray at various dates between 1755 and 1758. Also in the R.I.B.A. Collection is a drawing for a gateway at 'Lord Cadogan's' (*i.e.* CAVERSHAM PARK, OXON.), 'designed by Coll. George Gray'. A design for the 'Great Door to the Armoury in the Tower [of London], by Mr.

---

[1] Grainger was himself a Wesleyan Methodist. His wife was 'a class-mate at chapel'. She is said to have 'kept his accounts and managed his correspondence'.

[1] Among drawings acquired in 1931.

G. Gray' is in the British Museum, *King's Maps* xxiv, 23 *v*.

[L. Cust & S. Colvin, *History of the Society of Dilettanti*, 1898; *D.N.B.*, supplement, *s.v.* 'Gray, Sir James'; will in P.C.C. 58 STEVENS.]

GRAY, JOHN (*c.* 1773–1824), 'architect in Kelso and tenant at Heriotfield', is commemorated by a monument in the churchyard at Kelso, Roxburghshire. In 1819 the name of John Gray, architect of Kelso, appears among the subscribers to Peter Nicholson's *Architectural Dictionary*.

GRAY, GIDEON, practised in Stirling, where he extended the TOWN HOUSE eastwards in 1785 and in 1788 designed the OLD GRAMMAR SCHOOL in CASTLE WYND [R.C.A.M., *Stirlingshire* ii, 284, 293].

GRAY, JOHN, was an architect and builder of Hampton, nr. Leominster in Herefordshire, and held the post of County Surveyor. In 1843 he designed STAUNTON PARK, HEREFS., for James King, a fact recorded on the trowel used in laying the foundation-stone [family information; original drawings in County Record Office, A.13/1–23]. This mansion, designed in a conservative Georgian style, was dem. *c.* 1925.

GRAY, JOHN HOBDAY, exhibited architectural designs at the Royal Academy in 1834, 1835 and 1837, at the Society of British Artists in 1832, 1835, 1836 and 1837, and at the Liverpool Academy in 1840 and 1842. Up to 1840 he gave London addresses, but by 1841 he was at Holt Hill, Tranmere, Cheshire.

GRAYSON, W——, of Banner Street, Moorfields, exhibited at the Royal Academy from 1791 to 1801, including the 'Elevation of a nobleman's house intended to be built near Sedburgh in Yorkshire' (1791), a 'Design for a gentleman's seat to be built near Lancaster' (1793) and a 'Design of a gentleman's seat to be built at Kingmoor, near Carlisle' (1794). J. Grayson, junior, evidently his son, exhibited from the same address in 1800 and 1803.

GREEN, JAMES (1781–1849), was born in Birmingham, where his father was an engineer. After working under his father he found employment in 1801 with John Rennie. In 1808 he was appointed County Surveyor of Devon, a post which he retained until 1841. In 1843 he moved to London, where he died on 13 February 1849. Green was primarily a civil engineer, whose main responsibilities were roads, bridges and canals. His most important bridges were COWLEY BRIDGE over the R. Creedy near Exeter, 1813–14, and the BEAM BRIDGE AQUEDUCT carrying the Torrington

and Bideford Canal over the R. Torridge, 1824 [obituary in *Minutes of Proceedings of the Institution of Civil Engineers* ix, 1849–50, 98–100; Miles Hadfield, 'James Green as Canal Engineer', *Journal of Transport History* i, 1953–4]. As an architect Green's only recorded works appear to be BUCKLAND FILLEIGH HOUSE, DEVONSHIRE, for J. I. Fortescue, 1810 [R. Ackermann, *Repository of Arts*, 3rd ser., x, 1828] and ST. DAVID'S CHURCH, EXETER, 1816–17, dem. 1897 [brass foundation inscription in new church] (*Devonshire Illustrated*, 1829, 70). The church was an ambitious Greek Doric building of the type later erected in London under the 'Million Act' of 1818. The house was an essay in the same style, the interior as well as the exterior being consistently designed in the Greek Doric manner (David Watkin, 'Buckland Filleigh', in *The Country Seat*, ed. Colvin & Harris, 1970). These two buildings give Green a place after Harrison of Chester as an early prophet of the Greek Revival in the provinces.

GREEN, JOHN, was a surveyor and builder at Yarmouth. He was perhaps the Green who was one of the builders of the PASTON GRAMMAR SCHOOL, YARMOUTH, in 1764–5 [C. R. Forder, *History of the Paston Grammar School*, 1934, 84], and probably the 'John Green, of Southtown, architect' who contracted to build the drawbridge at Yarmouth in 1785 [John Preston, *Picture of Yarmouth*, 1819]. In 1805, when he advertised his services as an architect in the *Ipswich Journal*, he referred to his 'many years experience in the above line', and in 1816, in a similar advertisement, he stated that he had had 'many years experience in the Building Line in the counties of Norfolk, Suffolk and Cambridge' and that he had 'been employed in making Designs for Building a New Street, and superintending all the Public Works lately executed at Yarmouth' [*ex inf.* Mr. J. Bensusan-Butt].

GREEN, JOHN, 'Architect in Salisbury', edited the 8th edition of William Salmon's *Country Builder's Estimator* (1770) and the 5th edition of his *London and Country Builder's Vade Mecum* (1773).

GREEN, JOHN (1787–1852), and his son BENJAMIN (*c.* 1811–1858) had an extensive practice as architects and civil engineers in Northumberland and Durham. John Green was born on 20 June 1787 at Newton Fell House, Nafferton, where his father carried on a business as a carpenter and agricultural implement-maker. Soon after coming of age John joined his father. 'With the talent and energy which he threw into the affairs of the firm, business increased until Nafferton became too small to hold it, and the workshops were removed to Corbridge.' Here the Greens extended their activities to general building work. John Green turned his attention to the architectural side of the business, and in about 1820 left Corbridge for Newcastle, where he practised as an architect and civil engineer. He had two sons, John (c. 1807–68) and Benjamin (c. 1811–58), both of whom became architects. Benjamin, who was a pupil of the elder Pugin, joined his father early in the 1830s, and thereafter they practised together until the former's death in 1852. The elder Green is said to have been 'a plain practical, shrewd man of business', Benjamin 'an artistic and dashing sort of a fellow' whose style was 'ornamental, florid and costly, while the father's was plain, severe and economical'. Between them they designed a number of Gothic churches of no especial distinction and ruthlessly altered some old ones in a manner which showed that they were no antiquaries. Their abilities were better shown in the Greek Doric temple erected on Penshaw Hill as a monument to the 1st Earl of Durham and in the handsome theatre which they designed in Newcastle. They were active as railway architects, and in 1846 George Hudson, the 'Railway King', commissioned them to design all the railway stations between Newcastle and Berwick. The elder Green specialized in the erection of bridges, and in 1841 he was awarded the Telford Medal of the Institution of Civil Engineers for a system of laminated timber arches with which he had experimented as early as 1827, and which he employed successfully in the Willington and Ouseburn railway bridges ten years later. All his wooden laminated bridges have now been replaced, but his wrought-iron suspension bridge at Whorlton in County Durham still stands as the oldest bridge of its type in the country still supported unaided by its original chains. The Greens also had a reputation as designers of farm-houses, and were much employed for this purpose on the Duke of Northumberland's estates. The elder Green died at Newcastle on 30 September 1852, his son in a mental home at Dinsdale Park, Durham, on 14 November 1858, aged 47.

[Memoir in *Minutes of Proceedings of the Institution of Civil Engineers* xiii, 1853–4, 138–40; R. Welford, *Men of Mark 'twixt Tyne and Tweed* ii, 1895, 326–30; T. Fordyce, *Local Records of Northumberland and Durham* ii, 1876, 17; M. A. Richardson, *The Local Historian's Table-Book of remarkable occurrences connected with the Counties of Newcastle-upon-Tyne, Northumberland and Durham*, 8 vols., 1841–6; *Newcastle Weekly News*, 1 Jan. 1887; W. W. Tomlinson, *The North Eastern Railway*, Newcastle 1914, 323, 335, 350, 446, 483; Henry Hagger, 'The Bridges of John Green', *Northern Architect*, no. 8, April 1976.]

PUBLIC AND DOMESTIC ARCHITECTURE

STYFORD, nr. BYWELL, NORTHUMBERLAND, for Charles Bacon, c. 1820 [*Proceedings of the Inst. of Civil Engineers* xiii, 1853–4, 138].

NEWCASTLE, LITERARY AND PHILOSOPHICAL SOCIETY'S LIBRARY, WESTGATE STREET, 1822–5; added MUSEUM for the Natural History Society 1833–5 [W. Collard & M. Ross, *Architectural and Picturesque Views of Newcastle upon Tyne*, 1843, 46].

BEAUFRONT ESTATE, nr. HEXHAM, NORTHUMBERLAND, made 'twenty plans and estimates' for rebuilding or renovating the farms on this estate for J. Errington, 1824. Several of them are given by J. C. Loudon, *Encyclopaedia of Rural Architecture*, 1846, 476–7, 486–96.

SCOTSWOOD, nr. NEWCASTLE, suspension bridge over R. Tyne, 1829–31; dem. 1967 [J. Sykes, *Local Records* ii, 1866, 295–7; exhibited at R.A. 1837].

WHORLTON, nr. BARNARD CASTLE, DURHAM, suspension bridge over R. Tees, 1829–31 [E. Mackenzie & M. Ross, *History of Durham* i, 1834, 193; *Table-Book* iv, 89].

WYNYARD PARK, DURHAM, small suspension bridge in grounds, 1831 [E. Mackenzie & M. Ross, *History of Durham* i, 1834, 450].

BLACKWELL BRIDGE, nr. DARLINGTON, DURHAM (R. Tees), 1832; a stone bridge widened 1961 [J. Sykes, *Local Records* ii, 1866, 362].

BELLINGHAM, NORTHUMBERLAND, stone bridge over R. Tyne, 1834–5 [inscription; see also *Table-Book* iv, 206, 252].

LINTZFORD, DURHAM, stone bridge (R. Derwent), 1834–5 [H. Hagger in *Northern Architect*, no. 8, April 1976, 28].

NEWCASTLE, WESTGATE HILL CEMETERY, monument to John Bruce (d. 1834), 1835 [R. Welford, *Men of Mark 'twixt Tyne and Tweed*, 1895, i, 414; ii, 328].

NEWCASTLE, THE THEATRE, 1836–7; interior destroyed by fire 1899 [*Table-Book* iv, 342–4; original drawings now in Metropolitan Museum of Art, New York, reproduced by R. Southern in *The Georgian Playhouse*, 1948, pls. 51–4].

SOUTH SHIELDS, DURHAM, UNION WORKHOUSE, 1837 [*Table-Book* iv, 390].

TYNEMOUTH, NORTHUMBERLAND, THE MASTER-MARINERS' ASYLUM, 1837, Tudor style [*Table-Book* iv, 395].

OUSEBURN and WILLINGTON DENE RAILWAY BRIDGES, NORTHUMBERLAND, 1837, both of laminated timber construction. The former was rebuilt in iron in 1867, the latter in 1869 [*Table-Book* iv, 337–8; *Civil Engineer and Architect's Jnl.* iv, 284, xi, 33].

NEWCASTLE, THE GREY COLUMN, 1837–8, with statue by E. H. Baily [exhib. at R.A. 1837].

NEWCASTLE, THE CORN EXCHANGE, CLOTH MARKET,

1838–9; largely dem. 1854 and completely 1972 [*Table-Book* v, 42].

NETHER POPPLETON, nr. YORK, stone bridge carrying York and Newcastle Railway over R. Ouse, 1838–40 [*Proceedings of the Inst. of Civil Engineers* xiii, 1853–4, 139].

DALKEITH, MIDLOTHIAN, colliery railway viaduct over R. Esk for the 5th Duke of Buccleuch, 1840–1; dem. [*Newcastle Weekly News*, 1 Jan. 1887].

STREATLAM CASTLE, DURHAM, added portico and three stone cupolas on roof for John Bowes, 1841–2; dem. c. 1925 [Durham County Record Office, St. x81, original drawings].

PENSHAW HILL, DURHAM, Doric monument to the 1st Earl of Durham (d. 1840), 1844 [J. Latimer, *op. cit.*, 189–90].

PONTELAND, NORTHUMBERLAND, THE CASTLEWARD UNION WORKHOUSE, 1848–9 [Whellan's *History and Directory of Northumberland*, 1855, 549].

SUNDERLAND, DURHAM, ST. BEDE'S TOWER, RYHOPE ROAD, for A. J. Moore (Mayor of Sunderland 1854–5), Italianate [*Newcastle Weekly News*, 1 Jan. 1887].

SUNDERLAND, DURHAM, NICHOLSON HOUSE, for W. Nicholson (Mayor of Sunderland 1869–71), Gothic [*Newcastle Weekly News*, 1 Jan. 1887].

CHURCHES

NEWCASTLE, SCOTCH CHURCH, BLACKETT STREET, 1821–2, Gothic; dem. [E. Mackenzie, *History of Newcastle* i, 1827, 390].

FALSTONE, NORTHUMBERLAND, rebuilt 1824–5, Gothic; destroyed by fire 1890 [County Record Office, ZSW 629–30].

USWORTH, DURHAM, HOLY TRINITY, 1831–2, Gothic; chancel added 1903 [*Table-Book* iv, 86].

STELLA, DURHAM, ST. COLUMBA (R.C.), 1831–2, Gothic; enlarged by J. Dobson 1848–9 [E. Mackenzie & M. Ross, *History of Durham* i, 1834, 193].

NEWBURN, NORTHUMBERLAND, enlarged north aisle, 1832, Gothic [I.C.B.S.].

NEWCASTLE, ST. NICHOLAS, repaired west tower (with J. Dobson), 1832–3, added north-west and south-west transepts, refaced north aisle, etc., 1834–44 [H. L. Honeyman & T. Wake, 'St. Nicholas, Newcastle', *Archaeologia Æliana*, 4th ser., ix, 1932, 142–4].

STOCKTON-ON-TEES, DURHAM, HOLY TRINITY, 1834–5, Gothic; altered 1882–90, chancel added 1906–9 [W. Fordyce, *County Palatine of Durham* ii, 1857, 163–4].

NORTH SHIELDS, NORTHUMBERLAND, HOLY TRINITY, 1834–6, Gothic [*Table-Book* iv, 212–14].

ALNWICK, NORTHUMBERLAND, ST. MARY'S R.C. CHAPEL, 1836, Gothic [*Table-Book* iv, 316].

DALTON (DISSINGTON), NORTHUMBERLAND, HOLY TRINITY, 1836–7, Gothic [*Table-Book* iv, 309].

SUGLEY, NORTHUMBERLAND, HOLY SAVIOUR, 1836–7, Gothic [*Table-Book* iv, 309].

EARSDON, NORTHUMBERLAND, 1836–7, Gothic; chancel 1889 [I.C.B.S.].

EGLINGHAM, NORTHUMBERLAND, altered and enlarged, 1837 [*History of Northumberland* xiv, 370].

MIDDLESBROUGH, YORKS. (N.R.), rebuilt 1838–40, Gothic; chancel 1889 [I.C.B.S.; J. Harris, *Catalogue of British Drawings for Architecture, etc. in American Collections*, 1971, 108].

TYNEMOUTH, NORTHUMBERLAND, HOLY SAVIOUR, 1839–41, Gothic; altered 1882, spire removed c. 1955 [J. Latimer, *Historical Register of Remarkable Events in Northumberland and Durham 1832–57*, 1857, 116].

WHITTINGHAM, NORTHUMBERLAND, extensive alterations, 1840–2, Gothic; chancel 1870 [*History of Northumberland* xiv, 490].

CAMBO, NORTHUMBERLAND, 1841–2, Gothic [I.C.B.S. and drawings at Wallington Hall signed 'B. Green' 1837].

WOODHORN, NORTHUMBERLAND, restored, refaced and refenestrated, 1843 [F. R. Wilson, *Churches in the Archdeaconry of Lindisfarne*, 1870, 181].

HORSLEY, nr. OTTERBURN, NORTHUMBERLAND, 1843–4, neo-Norman [I.C.B.S.].

SEGHILL, NORTHUMBERLAND, 1848–9, Gothic [J. Latimer, *op. cit.*, 245–6].

GREENSHIELDS, THOMAS (c. 1800–c. 1845), was a minor Oxford architect of the 1830s. His most important work was probably the new front of St. Peter's Hall, an ambitious Greek Revival design of which only one wing was built.

OXFORD, THE BATHS, BATH STREET, opened 1827; dem. 1877 [N. Whittock, *A Description of the Oxford Baths*, c. 1835].

OXFORD, THE INDEPENDENT CHAPEL, GEORGE STREET, 1832, Gothic; dem. 1936 [*Congregational Magazine*, 1833, 260; *The Oxford University and City Guide*, 1833, 12].

OXFORD, ST. PETER'S HALL, south wing, 1832, as part of a new front which was never completed, but is illustrated by Ingram, *Memorials of Oxford* ii, 1837 ('New Inn Hall', 16). Greenshield's wing was remodelled in 1897 by W. K. Shirley and called 'Hannington Hall'.

OXFORD, ST. GILES' SCHOOL, c. 1835; dem. c. 1955 [Bodleian, MS. Top. Oxon. d. 501, f. 86].

BAMPTON ASTON CHURCH, OXON., 1838–9, Gothic; altered 1885–9 [*Jackson's Oxford Jnl.*, 24 June 1837].

IPING, SUSSEX, THE RECTORY (now HAMMERWOOD HOUSE) for the Rev. H. D. Clarke, 1838–9 [drawings and specification in possession of the Hon. R. W. Morgan-Grenville].

363

IPING CHURCH, SUSSEX, rebuilt 1840, Gothic; altered 1885 [I.C.B.S.].
MARKET LAVINGTON VICARAGE, WILTS., altered or rebuilt, 1841 [Salisbury Diocesan Records].
BLACK BOURTON VICARAGE, OXON., 1842 [Bodleian, MS. Oxf. Dioc. Papers b. 102].

GREENWAY, FRANCIS HOWARD (1777–1837), was the youngest son of Francis Greenway, or Grinway, a mason of Mangotsfield in Gloucestershire. He went to London in order to become the pupil of John Nash, from whose office he exhibited two drawings at the Royal Academy in 1800. It was probably as a result of his connection with Nash that he came to be employed at Carmarthen, where he later claimed to have designed the 'market house'–presumably the quadrangular cheese and meat market built by the Corporation in 1801. In 1802 he exhibited at the Royal Academy a 'Chapel, Library etc., designed for the side of a quadrangle at Bristol', and a drawing of 'Thornbury Castle restored, with a canal brought from the river Severn up to Thornbury'. In about 1805 he and his elder brothers Olive and John Tripp Greenway opened a yard in Bristol, and announced their intention of doing business as 'stonemasons, architects, builders etc.' At the same time Francis took the opportunity of 'offering his services to the public in the capacity of Architect, Statuary, and Landscape-Gardener'. As the architect member of the partnership he designed in 1806 the HOTEL AND ASSEMBLY ROOMS in THE MALL at CLIFTON, which the firm contracted to build. At the same time he and his brothers were speculating by buying unfinished houses in Clifton which they completed and then sold. In May 1809 they were overtaken by bankruptcy, and the Assembly Rooms were completed by Joseph Kay. Some time after the failure Francis Greenway was accused of forgery in connection with a previous contract to complete a house in Cornwallis Crescent, pleaded guilty, and was sentenced to death at Bristol Assizes on 23 March 1812. His motive appears to have been to benefit his creditors rather than himself, and the sentence was commuted to one of transportation for life. He was sent to Australia, where he found a patron and protector in Governor Macquarie, who employed him to carry out his ambitious plans for public works in the colony. In 1816 he was appointed government architect, and in this capacity designed many of the public buildings in Sydney, including St. James's Church, the stables of Government House, the Hyde Park Barracks (now Law Courts) and the Macquarie Tower. The stables are castellated, but most of Greenway's work was designed in a bold, simple, classical manner of considerable merit. [M. H. Ellis, *Francis Greenway*, Sydney 1949; W. Ison, *The Georgian Buildings of Bristol*, 1952, 35–6; M.

Herman, *The Early Australian Architects and their Work*, 2nd ed. 1970.]
Olive and John Tripp Greenway recovered from their bankruptcy and continued their business in Bristol. Olive built, and probably designed, DOWNEND CHURCH, GLOS., in a feeble Gothic style in 1831 [I.C.B.S.].

GREENWAY, THOMAS, mason and carver, had his yard at Widcombe, nr. Bath. He built the COLD BATH HOUSE, CLAVERTON STREET, WIDCOMBE, c. 1704, 'one of the earliest buildings in Bath to show a competent use of Renaissance detail', and houses in ST. JOHN'S COURT, BATH, 1720. Other houses in Bath attributed to him on stylistic grounds are those in Trim Street, begun in 1707, and one in the Abbey Church Yard with superimposed pilasters. He and his sons acquired a considerable reputation as carvers of vases and other architectural ornaments, and were often employed by John Wood, e.g. on the Bristol Exchange. In 1730 he visited Dublin, taking with him 'a large number of Flower Potts, urns and vases' for sale. [W. Ison, *The Georgian Buildings of Bath*, 1948, 30, 116–24; J. Wood, *A Description of the Exchange of Bristol*, 1745; Faulkner's *Dublin Journal*, 15–19 Dec. 1730, *ex inf.* the Knight of Glin.]

GREIG, SAMUEL ALEXANDER (–1846), was Surveyor to the County of Devon from 1841, when he succeeded James Green (*q.v.*), until his death in 1846 [County Records]. In 1839 he exhibited two works at the Royal Academy: a 'Villa in the old English style, lately erected near Exeter on the property of Mr. James Veitch', and an 'Elizabethan villa' for W. B. King, identifiable as THE HENNONS, TEIGNMOUTH, DEVON. He competed for the Assize Courts at Liverpool in 1840, winning the second premium of £200.

GRELLIER, WILLIAM (1807–1852), born at Peckham, Surrey, was articled to George Smith in 1823. He was admitted to the Royal Academy Schools in 1824, winning the Silver Medal in 1826 and the Gold Medal in 1829. He became a member of the Architectural Society on its formation in 1831, contributed largely to its portfolio of measured drawings, acted as its honorary secretary for four years, and was presented with a testimonial by its members on its union with the R.I.B.A. in 1842. In 1838 he obtained the second premium of £30 for a town hall and market-place for St. John's, Newfoundland [*Civil Engineer and Architect's Jnl.* i, 174], and in 1839 the first premium of £300 for a design for the Royal Exchange, London, from amongst thirty-eight competitors. The assessors did not, however, consider that it was 'practicable, advisable, or capable of being advantageously adopted', and the designs eventually executed were those of Sir

William Tite. Grellier's drawings are now in the R.I.B.A. Collection. In 1834–5 he gratuitously designed and supervised the building of the Tylers' and Bricklayers' Almshouses: the Company subsequently presented him with its freedom, elected him to the court, and in 1849 to the Mastership. He was appointed District Surveyor of Whitechapel in November 1838. He exhibited at the Royal Academy from 1828 to 1848. He died on 7 January 1852, and was buried in Norwood Cemetery. There is a privately printed memoir by Dr. H. C. Barlow [*A.P.S.D.*; *Builder* xxvii, 1869, 65].

MACCLESFIELD, CHESHIRE, ST. GEORGE'S SUNDAY SCHOOLS, 1835 [exhib. at R.A.].

TYLERS' AND BRICKLAYERS' ALMHOUSES, BALLS POND, ISLINGTON, 1834–5, north block 1838–9, Gothic [W. G. Bell, *The Tylers' and Bricklayers' Company*, 1938, 56 and plate].

LONDON, ST. ETHELBURGA'S CHURCH, BISHOPSGATE, rebuilt roof, *c.* 1835 [G. Godwin, *Churches of London* ii, 1839].

LONDON, ST. ETHELBURGA SOCIETY'S CHARITY SCHOOLS, WORMWOOD STREET, BISHOPSGATE, *c.* 1839 [exhib. at R.A.].

ISLINGTON, THE DRY METER GAS COMPANY'S WORKS, NEW NORTH ROAD, *c.* 1839 [exhib. at R.A.].

WATFORD, HERTS., NATIONAL SCHOOLS, 1841, Elizabethan style [engraving published Nov. 1841].

LIVERPOOL, ROYAL EXCHANGE INSURANCE BUILDINGS, DALE STREET, 1846–8; dem. [*Builder* vi, 1848, 619].

GREY, THOMAS PHILIP DE, EARL DE GREY (1781–1859), was the elder son of Thomas Robinson, 2nd Baron Grantham (d. 1786), by Mary, 2nd daughter of Philip Yorke, 2nd Earl of Hardwicke, and Jemima, Marchioness Grey, of Wrest Park in Bedfordshire. At the age of five he succeeded his father as 3rd Baron Grantham, inheriting with the title the family seat of Newby (now Baldersby) Park in the North Riding of Yorkshire, built by Sir William Robinson to the designs of Colen Campbell.[1] Under the will of William Weddell (a distant relative), he later inherited the latter's extensive estates in Yorkshire, including Newby Hall in the West Riding, thus becoming the owner of two seats of the same name. Finally in 1833, on the death of his maternal aunt Amabel, Countess de Grey, he inherited Wrest Park together with the titles of Earl de Grey and Baron Lucas. In 1803 he had changed his surname from Robinson to Weddell, and he now changed it again to De Grey. In 1805 he married Henrietta, 5th daughter of the Earl of Enniskillen, by whom he left two daughters.

He died at his London home, 4 St. James's Square, on 14 November 1859.

Lord Grantham was educated at St. John's College, Cambridge, where he took his M.A. in 1801. The Napoleonic Wars would have prevented him from immediately undertaking the usual foreign tour, but he was in Rome in 1816, when Ingres drew a portrait of him (now at Newby Hall).[1] He had a brief political career as First Lord of the Admiralty in Peel's first administration (1834–5) and was sworn of the Privy Council. From 1841 to 1844 he served as Lord Lieutenant of Ireland, a position he filled with credit. On his return he was created a Knight of the Garter. But unlike his younger brother Lord Goderich, De Grey was not dedicated to a political career, preferring 'to move among men of letters and artists at the various learned societies of which he was a member'. Above all he was seriously interested in architecture. This may have been an inherited taste, for it was shared by his father, the 2nd Lord Grantham (*q.v.*). Soon after he had come into possession of Newby Hall he added a dining-room on the north side, apparently to his own designs. It is a simple rectangular room with a coffered recess and restrained neo-classical detailing. His major achievement as an amateur architect was, however, Wrest Park, which he completely rebuilt in a very competent French Louis XV style between 1834 and 1839. In a MS. account of the house (Bedfordshire Record Office, CRT 190/45/2, 1–19) he states explicitly that 'I was strictly and in every sense of the word my own architect ... I had my French books always under my hand [and] referred to them for authority whenever I could find anything to suit me.'[2] To make the working drawings he employed 'a Mr. Brown, who had been Nash's clerk', and as executant architect he engaged a north-countryman called James Clephan (*q.v.*). Earl de Grey's claim to have been his own architect is confirmed by the survival of very competent architectural drawings signed G with a symbol for a coronet. The result was a *tour de force* of French eighteenth-century architectural design on English soil, carried out with consistent skill both inside and out (*C. Life*, 25 June, 2 July 1970).

The only other buildings for which de Grey is known to have been personally responsible are the Silsoe lodges to Wrest Park, which he designed for his aunt in 1826 (*C. Life*, 13 Aug. 1970, 405), and Silsoe Church, which was rebuilt

---

[1] Lord de Grey sold Newby Park in 1845.

[1] Illustrated in *Burlington Magazine* lxxv, 1939, pl. iii A.

[2] The names of 'Blondel', 'Mansard' and 'Le Pautre' are inscribed on the spines of symbolical volumes over the south door of the entrance hall, and the source of the south front is to be found in Blondel's *Maisons de Plaisir* (1737).

in 1830–1 in a remarkably authentic Perpendicular Gothic style. De Grey records that he 'furnished all the designs' but that 'the detail and execution was left' to Thomas Smith of Hertford. De Grey's drawings for the church are in the Bedfordshire Record Office. In addition de Grey played an important part in the design of two prominent buildings in London, the United Service Club in Pall Mall (by John Nash, 1827), and the enlargement of Buckingham Palace (by Edward Blore, 1846–50). As chairman of the building committee of the Club he refused to allow Nash to re-use Henry Holland's beautiful but too constricted staircase from Carlton House, and instead provided a sketch of a more capacious staircase of the kind that was eventually built. At Buckingham Palace he was an active member of the commission set up by Peel to superintend the erection of Blore's new entrance front, and probably exercised some influence over its design. In 1848 he was the Lords' representative on the royal commission appointed to supervise the completion of the new Houses of Parliament. In 1835 de Grey was asked to become President of the recently established Institute of British Architects, a position which he continued to hold until his death some twenty-five years later. It was an appropriate and successful choice, for de Grey brought to the new institution a combination of social distinction and political influence that was invaluable in its early years. [G.E.C., *Complete Peerage*; *D.N.B.*; obituaries in *R.I.B.A. Trans.*, 1860, and *Builder* xviii, 1859, 756; Simon Houfe, 'Wrest Park, Bedfordshire', *C. Life*, 25 June, 2 July 1970; *History of the King's Works* vi, 1973, 233, 289–90.]

GRIFFIN, JOHN, of Hemel Hempstead, designed BOXMOOR CHURCH, HERTS., 1830, Gothic; dem. *c.* 1870 [I.C.B.S.], and added a north aisle to MARKYATE STREET CHURCH, HERTS., in 1842 [I.C.B.S.].

GRIFFITH, JAMES (1761–1821), a prebendary of Gloucester from 1816 and Master of University College, Oxford, from 1808 until his death, had some skill as an amateur artist and architect. Several of the topographical illustrations to Whitaker's *History of Craven* (1805) were supplied by him. 'Poker painting' was his speciality. His *chef d'œuvre* in this medium was a *Salvator Mundi* after Carlo Dolci which formerly hung over the altar in University College Chapel. As an architect he was responsible for redesigning the south side of the main quadrangle of the College when it was refaced in 1802. He replaced the former classical frontispiece by a gabled central feature with Gothic detailing. He also made a Gothic design for a new Master's Lodging which was not executed [*V.C.H. Oxon.* iii, 78, 80]. At Gloucester Cathedral he designed the

Gothic choir-screen erected in 1820, as recorded by an inscription on the north-west pier of the crossing. [J. Britton, *History and Antiquities of Gloucester Cathedral*, 1829, 60 and Appendix, p. 9, n. 18; G. W. Counsel, *History of Gloucester*, 1829, 98; W. Carr, *University College*, 1902, 193–4, 212.]

GRIFFITH, JOHN WILLIAM (*c.* 1790–1855), of St. John's Square, Clerkenwell, London was surveyor to the parish of St. Botolph, Aldersgate, whose church he is said to have enlarged and decorated. He may therefore have been responsible for the design of the east front, as executed in Roman cement by Messrs. John Ward & Son, builders, in 1830 (G. Godwin, *Churches of London* ii, 1839, plate), though his name does not appear in the Vestry Minutes (now Guildhall Library, MS. 3863/2). He was also surveyor to the London estates of St. John's College, Cambridge, and to the Islington estate of James Rhodes. He designed the Islington Parochial Schools, and many villas built between 1816 and 1855 in Islington, Hornsey, Highgate and Kentish Town. He died on 27 November 1855, aged 65, and must not be confused with John Griffith of Finsbury (1796–1888), F.R.I.B.A. and Chairman of the Kensal Green Cemetery Company. His son, William Pettit Griffith (1815–84), was well known as an architect and antiquary [obituary in *Builder* xiii, 1855, 620; W. J. Pinks, *History of Clerkenwell*, 1881, 638, 691–3].

GRIFFITHS, J—, exhibited at the Royal Academy from 27 Francis Street, Bedford Square, from 1807 to 1811. His exhibit in the latter year was a 'Mansion to be erected for E. Ruppel, Esq. opposite the Government House at Memel, in Prussia'. George Griffiths, of the same address, was a member of the Surveyors' Club from 1792 to 1810.

GRINWAY, FRANCIS HOWARD, *see* GREENWAY

GROVES, JOHN THOMAS (–1811), was an architect whose origins are obscure. He exhibited views of Westminster at the Royal Academy in 1778 and 1780,[1] and in 1791, on his return from Italy, a view of the Temple of the Sybil at Tivoli. In 1794 he was appointed Clerk of the Works at Whitehall, Westminster and St. James's on the resignation of Sir John Soane, who is said to have 'been the means of obtaining' the post for Groves. He also held the posts of architect to the General Post Office and surveyor to the Commissioners for the Improvement of Westminster. At the Office of Works he proved to be an indolent

---

[1] The view of Westminster Abbey which he exhibited in 1780 is now in the Museum of London.

administrator who took advantage of James Wyatt's lax régime to neglect his duties. He was Master of the Tylers' and Bricklayers' Company in 1810–11. Charles Bacon (*q.v.*) was his pupil. He died at his home in Scotland Yard on 24 August 1821 after a stroke. As an architect he designed some elegant late Georgian houses, but his most original work is the unusual pierced obelisk at Garbally in Ireland. His portrait by P. Reinagle was exhibited at the Royal Academy in 1790. [*A.P.S.D.*; *Gent's Mag.* 1811 (ii), 287, 494; *The Farington Diary*, ed. J. Greig, i, 74, iv, 149; *History of the King's Works* vi, 67–71; will (P.C.C. 411 CRICKETT).]

BROOMFIELD LODGE, CLAPHAM COMMON (west side), for the Hon. E. J. Eliot, *c.* 1797; dem. [G. Richardson, *New Vitruvius Britannicus* i, 1810, pls. xvii, xviii].

TEWIN WATER, HERTS., for Henry Cowper, Clerk of the House of Lords, *c.* 1798; dem. [Couse is referred to as the architect of this house in Repton's 'Red Book', now in the Herts. Record Office, C.2404] (Neale, *Views of Seats*, 1st ser., i, 1818).

MORDEN, SURREY, house for Abraham Goldsmid, *c.* 1800; dem. [*A.P.S.D.*] (D. Hughson, *Circuit of London* v, 1808, 293, plate).

ELY CATHEDRAL, repaired west front in association with James Wyatt and designed a marble pulpit 'in imitation of the Norman architecture', 1800–2 [*A.P.S.D.*; G. L. Taylor, *Memoirs of an Octogenarian Architect*, 1870–2, 39; *Gent's Mag.* 1805 (i), 122].

TUNBRIDGE WELLS, KENT, THE BATHS, for Mrs. Shorey, *c.* 1804 [P. Amsinck, *Tunbridge Wells and its Neighbourhood*, 1810, plate facing p. 34].

PORTSDOWN HILL, HANTS., monument to Lord Nelson, 1807 [exhib. at R.A. 1807].

GARBALLY PARK, CO. GALWAY, IRELAND, obelisk for the 2nd Earl of Clancarty, 1811 [inscription recording that it was 'erected from a design presented gratuitously by J. T. Groves Esq.'].

EAST GRINSTEAD CHURCH, SUSSEX, completed west tower of Gothic church designed by James Wyatt, 1811–13. His design was accepted 2 August 1811, and was carried out after his death by H. W. & W. Inwood [minutes of committee in East Sussex Record Office].

GRUMBOLD, ROBERT (1639–1720), was the best known of a family of freemasons who practised their trade in Northamptonshire and Cambridgeshire in the sixteenth, seventeenth and eighteenth centuries. They originated in the quarrying villages of Weldon and Raunds, and their names occur frequently in building records from the end of the sixteenth century. WILLIAM GRUMBOLD was a freemason much employed by Sir Thomas Tresham of Rushton, contracting with him in 1578 to build the MARKET HOUSE at ROTHWELL [Hist. MSS. Comm., *Var. Coll.* iii, pp. xxxiii–xxxiv, 2]. Later, from 1594 onwards, 'the Grumbolds' were working on Tresham's NEW BUILDING at LYVEDEN [*ibid.*, xxxv, xlix, liv, 134]. William Grumbold was employed in the construction of FOTHERINGHAY BRIDGE in 1573–4 [P.R.O., Exchequer K.R. 463/33], and may well have been the same as the 'William Grombole master workman and freemason' who, together with 'Robert Grombole our master workman freemason', was engaged in rebuilding the spire of ST. MARY THE GREAT, CAMBRIDGE, in 1593–4 [J. E. Foster, *Churchwardens' Accounts of St. Mary the Great, Cambridge*, Cambridge Antiquarian Soc. 1905, 248].[1] 'John Grombole freemason and brother of Robert Grombole' also worked at St. Mary's in 1594 [*ibid.*, 248–61]. Robert Grombole was given a reward of 2s. 6d. in October 1593 'when he went home at the end of the year', but his place of origin is not stated.

The accounts for building HARROLD HOUSE, BEDS. (dem. 1961), in 1608–10 show that Weldon freestone for the porch, corbel-table and windows was supplied by 'old Grumbold' and Thomas Grumbold ['The Building Accounts of Harrold Hall', ed. John Weaver, *Beds. Historical Record Soc.* xlix, 1970, 79], and there are numerous references to Grumbolds in the parish registers of Weldon from their commencement in 1594. The most prominent member of the family there in the seventeenth century was ARTHUR GRUMBOLD (1603–1670), who had a lease of the Weldon quarries from Lord Hatton [Northants. Record Office, Finch-Hatton papers, 3643]. His initials and the date 1654 can still be seen on the front of a stone-built house in the main street of Weldon. In his will [Peterborough Registry, Liber Q, f. 73] he left 'all my workinge tooles both for hardstone and freestone and my steele two foot rule' to his younger son Thomas. All the rest of his 'Quarrye tooles plotts bookes compasses moldes' and all his 'stone at home and abroad' was to go to his elder son John (1643–1718), who was to take Thomas as apprentice 'to teach him his trade the which I taught him'.

Meanwhile other members of the family had established themselves at Cambridge. The first to settle there appears to have been THOMAS GRUMBOLD, who was paid for work at ST. JOHN'S COLLEGE LIBRARY in 1625, at CLARE HALL in 1639–40, and at KING'S COLLEGE in 1651. He died at Cambridge in 1657. Robert Grumbold, the principal subject of this entry, was the son of Edward Grumbold of Raunds, where he was born in 1639. Whether he learned his trade in the

---

[1] An estimate for the spire, with rough drawings, in B.M., Cotton MS. Faust. C.III, ff. 487–8, 490–1, is very likely in the hand of one of the Grumbolds.

quarries at Raunds or with Thomas Grumbold at Cambridge is not known. He must already have been a master mason of repute when, in 1667–8, he was paid £10 15s. 6d. by the Dean and Canons of Worcester 'for his journey from Cambridge to survey the [cathedral] church' of Worcester [Treasurer's account, 1667–8, *ex inf.* Mr. D. A. Whitehead]. In 1669 he and a partner named Bradwell executed the masonry of the west range of CLARE HALL. From 1674 onwards he was concerned in the building of ST. CATHERINE'S COLLEGE, where payments to him 'for surveying' may indicate that he was responsible for the architectural design. In 1676 he was master mason for the building of the new LIBRARY of TRINITY COLLEGE to the designs of Sir Christopher Wren. In 1678 he superintended a general repair at the REGENT HOUSE; in 1679 he made the north window of EMMANUEL COLLEGE LIBRARY; in 1680–1 he was working in NEVILE'S COURT at TRINITY COLLEGE; in 1681–2 he built Dr. Babington's chambers and the 'TRIBUNAL' in NEVILE'S COURT at the same college; in 1682–6 he designed and built the north range of CLARE HALL, containing the HALL and BUTTERY; in 1687 he gave a design for a new chapel for ST. JOHN'S COLLEGE, which was not, however, carried out; in 1695 he was concerned in laying out the PHYSIC GARDEN; in 1696 he designed the new printing-house in Queen's Lane, and began work on the stone bridge and gate-piers at ST. JOHN'S COLLEGE, which he completed in 1712. This bridge he appears to have designed himself, though the siting of it had been discussed in correspondence with both Wren and Hawksmoor before the work began, and there is a payment to John Longland, a London master carpenter, 'in advising about a modell for the Bridge' [*Wren Soc.* xix, 103–7]. In 1701 he put sash-windows into the MASTER'S LODGE at TRINITY COLLEGE; in 1703 he built the piers at the entrance-gate of JESUS COLLEGE; in 1705–6 he finished the west front of CLARE HALL; in 1709 the north and south cloisters flanking PETERHOUSE CHAPEL were rebuilt 'according to a paper delivered by Mr. Grumbold'; in 1714 he ashlared the gatehouse and part of the west front of CHRIST'S COLLEGE; in 1715 he altered the CIVIL LAW SCHOOL, later the west room of the University Library, for the reception of Bishop Moore's books; in 1716 he rebuilt the fountain at TRINITY COLLEGE; and in 1719–20 he began the building of the WESTMORELAND BUILDING at EMMANUEL COLLEGE under the supervision of John Lumley (*q.v.*), but died before the work was completed [J.B.P., 'The College Buildings in the Eighteenth Century', in *Emmanuel College Magazine* ix (2), 1898, 87].

Outside Cambridge, Grumbold contracted in 1681 to rebuild two turrets at AUDLEY END, ESSEX, for the Board of Works [P.R.O., Works 5/145, p. 118], and he was employed by the 1st Earl of Ailesbury at GREAT PARK HOUSE, AMPTHILL, BEDS., in 1687–9 [accounts at Tottenham Park, Wilts.], and by the 11th Earl of Kent, for whose seat at WREST PARK, BEDS., he made in 1693–5 two stone basins in the garden and a pair of gate-piers with heraldic wyverns [Beds. Record Office, L 31/288]. After the collapse of the north-west angle of the north transept of ELY CATHEDRAL in 1699, Grumbold was employed to rebuild it. He submitted a plan, but Wren was consulted, and may have been responsible for the design of the new doorway to the transept, which resembles that of St. Mary-le-Bow [W. D. Caröe, *Tom Tower*, 1923, 19; *Wren Soc.* xix, pl. 14].

Robert Grumbold died at Cambridge on 7 December 1720, aged 82, and was buried in St. Botolph's Churchyard, where his monument can be seen on the south side of the chancel (*Cambridge Antiquarian Soc.'s Procs.* xxxiv, 1934, pl. ii). His will, proved in the court of the Archdeaconry of Ely on 23 December 1720, shows that he owned a considerable amount of leasehold property in Cambridge. His house and yard stood in Trumpington Street on a site now occupied by the forecourt of St. Catherine's College.

Grumbold was the principal figure in Cambridge architecture at the end of the seventeenth century. Though he never learned the full discipline of classical architecture he achieved an attractive vernacular style compounded of artisan mannerism and baroque elements that he had picked up from Wren and others.

[Willis & Clark, iii, 533 and *passim*; D. Knoop & G. P. Jones, 'The Rise of the Mason Contractor', *R.I.B.A. Jnl.*, 17 Oct. 1936, 1069–70; G. F. Webb, 'Robert Grumbold and the Architecture of the Renaissance at Cambridge', *Burl. Mag.*, Dec. 1925–Jan. 1926; R.C.H.M., *Cambridge*, *passim.*]

GUMMOW, BENJAMIN, practised at Ruabon in Denbighshire. He appears to have been a pupil of S. P. Cockerell, who employed him as clerk of works for the alterations to St. Margaret's Church, Westminster, in 1799–1802 [Westminster Public Library, Minutes of the committee for the repair of the church, MS. 2625]. He probably settled in North Wales as the result of his employment as supervising architect at Eaton Hall, Cheshire, then (1803–12) being rebuilt for Lord Grosvenor to the designs of William Porden. He was also employed by Sir Watkin Williams-Wynn at Wynnstay, and in 1827 he told C. R. Cockerell that he 'has always had £300 per ann. from Lord Grosvenor and Sir W.W. and is not allowed any other charge or profits – but has his lodgings and living – out of this he has saved an easy independence' [C. R. Cockerell's diary, 5 Sept. 1827]. His house at Ruabon was no doubt on the Wynnstay estate. Michael and James Reynolds Gummow, who practised in Wrexham in the mid nineteenth century, were probably Benjamin's son and grandson, respectively. The latter was the author of *Hints on House Building*, published at Wrexham in 1874.

In 1807 Porden told Lord Grosvenor that Gummow 'speaks without thinking and is the most inconsistent man I ever met with' [Eaton Hall muniments]. Though not an architect of the first rank, his additions to Eaton Hall successfully maintained the elegant rococo Gothic of the main block designed by Porden, and at Brogyntyn his Ionic portico is a handsome addition to an existing classical house.

HALKIN MOUNTAIN, FLINTSHIRE, building (probably ornamental) for the 2nd Earl Grosvenor, 1804; dem. [letter dated 20 Aug. 1804, Eaton Hall muniments].

LITTLETON, nr CHRISTLETON, CHESHIRE, for Thomas Dixon, 1806; since much altered [E. Twycross, *Mansions of England: Cheshire* i, 1850, 43].

NERQUIS HALL, FLINTSHIRE, addition of castellated Gothic wings, stable archway, Gothic porch and Gothic orangery for Miss Gifford, 1813–20; wings dem. 1964 [drawings in Clwyd Record Office].

BROGYNTYN (PORKINGTON), SHROPSHIRE, addition of portico and other alterations for Mary Jane Ormsby and her husband William Gore, 1814–15 [P.R.O., Coade Stone Co.'s letter-book, C 111/106, ff. 176, 123, 130, 136, 191, 199, 211].

EATON HALL, CHESHIRE, added wings for the 2nd Earl Grosvenor, 1823–5, Gothic; altered by W. Burn 1846–51; rebuilt by A. Waterhouse 1870; dem. 1963 [*A.P.S.D.*, *s.v.* 'Porden, William'] (*C. Life*, 11, 18 Feb. 1971). Gummow also designed a Gothic temple to contain a Roman altar found in 1821 [R. Ackermann, *Views of Country Seats* i, 1830, 31].

HALKIN CASTLE, FLINTSHIRE, supervised construction of house designed by J. Buckler (*q.v.*) for the 2nd Earl Grosvenor, 1824–7, Tudor Gothic [Eaton Hall, Grosvenor archives nos. 1147–8, building accounts initialled 'B.G.'].

WYNNSTAY, DENBIGHSHIRE, probably responsible for recasing and altering the house for Sir Watkin Williams-Wynn, Bart., *c.* 1825; destroyed by fire 1858 [Peter Howell in *C. Life*, 30 March 1972].

POOL PARK, DENBIGHSHIRE, probably supervised building of house for the 2nd Lord Bagot, *c.* 1827–8, to the designs of John Buckler, whose designs for this 'Tudor' timber-framed building were exhibited by him at the R.A. in 1830 as executed [*Correspondence of Lady Williams Wynn*, ed. R. Leighton, 1920, 330; C. R. Cockerell's diary, 5 Sept. 1827, where Gummow tells him of a 'house built by him for Lord Bagot'].

CHIRK CASTLE, DENBIGHSHIRE, work for Robert Myddelton-Biddulph, 1831, connected with a 'porch' [National Library of Wales, Chirk E 3081, *ex inf.* Mr. Peter Howell].

GUNNERY, JAMES, designed a Gothic church at DELAMERE, CHESHIRE, 1816–17, altered 1878 [inscription on brass plate].

GUTCH, GEORGE (*c.* 1790–1874), was the fifth and youngest son of the Rev. J. Gutch, registrar and historian of Oxford University, and for sixty-two years chaplain of All Souls College. He showed an early aptitude for drawing and at the age of 15 won a medal from the Society of Arts for a view of Wrexham Church. In 1806 his father was 'enquiring for some Architect to place him with', and soon afterwards he became a pupil of George Saunders. It was Saunders's recommendation that in 1825 secured him the post of District Surveyor for Paddington that he was to hold for nearly fifty years. In 1827 he succeeded S. P. Cockerell as surveyor to the Bishop of London's estate in Paddington, and it was under his direction that this important estate, lying between Hyde Park and Paddington Station, was laid out for building. His plan, published in 1838, 'fixed the architectural pattern of the whole district until the late 1930s' and created the stucco terraces characteristic of Sussex Gardens and its neighbourhood. In conjunction with J. Goldicutt, Gutch designed the Gothic church of ST. JAMES, PADDINGTON, which forms the terminal feature at the west end of Sussex Gardens. It was built in 1841–3 and rebuilt (except the steeple) by G. E. Street in 1882.

Gutch appears to have done little work outside Paddington. In 1830 he succeeded Henry Hakewill as Surveyor to the Radcliffe Trustees, but the Trustees did not commission any building of importance during his tenure of the post. In 1839 he and E. W. Trendall jointly submitted a competent but unremarkable Greek Revival design in the competition for the Ashmolean Museum at Oxford (Bodleian, MS. Top. Oxon. a. 9). He became a Fellow of the R.I.B.A. in 1835. He died in November 1874, in his 84th year, and was buried in Paddington Cemetery.

[*Builder* xxxii, 1874, 998, 1002, xxxv, 1877, 384; *Gent's Mag.* 1861 (ii), 684 n.; G. Toplis, 'The History of Tyburnia', *C. Life*, 15, 22 Nov. 1973.]

GWILT, GEORGE (1746–1807), son of Richard Gwilt, peruke-maker, was born in Southwark on 9 June 1746. At the age of 14 he was apprenticed to Moses Waite, a London mason whose yard was in Southwark. Later he was in the office of George Silverside, a surveyor with a considerable practice in London, and also worked occasionally for one of the Jupps. In about 1770 he became Surveyor to the County of Surrey, in 1771 Surveyor to the Commissioners of Sewers for Surrey, and in 1774 District Surveyor for St. George's Parish, Southwark, under the Metropolitan Building Act. He was also Surveyor to the Clink Paving Commissioners and architect to the West India Dock Company. As a young man he was employed by Henry Thrale, whose brewery was in Southwark, and through him met Samuel Johnson, though 'from a dislike to Johnson's unpleasant temper, cordiality never existed between them'. He himself is said to have been 'a person of irascible temper but easily pacified, kind hearted and an excellent father and husband'. He was the father of George and Joseph Gwilt (*q.v.*), and his pupils included John Young (apprenticed to him 1772), Henry Ashley Keeble (1783) and John Shaw (1790). He was Master of the Masons' Company in 1790. He died in Southwark on 9 December 1807, and is commemorated by an inscription on the family monument on the south (exterior) side of Southwark Cathedral.

Gwilt was a hard-working surveyor rather than an architectural artist. When he retired in 1805 the magistrates of Surrey paid tribute to the 'integrity and ability with which as Surveyor of public works, he has served this County during the course of five and thirty years'. Nearly all his buildings were of a utilitarian character. His biggest and finest work was the great range of warehouses for the West India Dock Company which was designed by himself and his eldest son in 1800. The Company received proposals from a number of other architects, including Nash, Soane, George Dance and the two Wyatts, but the Gwilts were given the commission in preference to their more famous rivals. Within two years they had built at least six of the nine 'stacks' (*i.e.* blocks), each five floors high, which together made a range of warehouses nearly two-thirds of a mile long and (until their partial destruction in 1940) were the finest examples of London's dock architecture.

[Joseph Gwilt, 'Parentalia of Gwilt', MS. in Surrey County Record Office, Acc. 390; *Gent's Mag.* 1807, 1181; 1821 (ii), 380; *A.P.S.D.*; *D.N.B.*; Guildhall Library, records of the Masons' Company.]

SOUTHWARK, THE SURREY COUNTY BRIDEWELL, ST. GEORGE'S FIELDS, 1772; dem. [*A.P.S.D.*].

SOUTHWARK, ST. SAVIOUR'S WAREHOUSE (now London Fire Brigade Training Centre), 1777, since altered [Southwark Borough archives, accounts of Workhouse treasurer].

STREATHAM PLACE, STREATHAM, SURREY, alterations for Henry Thrale, 1780; dem. 1863 [*The Queeney Letters*, ed. Lord Lansdowne, 1934, 130, 135].

WEST MALLING CHURCH, KENT, rebuilt nave, 1780;

again rebuilt by J. T. Micklethwaite 1900–1 [MS. Vestry Minutes].

COBHAM BRIDGE, SURREY, rebuilt 1782; destroyed by flood 1968 [*A.P.S.D.*].

LEATHERHEAD BRIDGE, SURREY, rebuilt 1782 [*A.P.S.D.*].

GODALMING BRIDGE, SURREY, rebuilt 1782–3 [*A.P.S.D.*].

LONDON, ST. MARY AT HILL CHURCH, rebuilt tower and west end, 1787–8 [MS. Vestry Minutes in Guildhall Library, 1240/42].

SOUTHWARK, houses on north side of UNION STREET, including No. 18 (dem. *c.* 1890) as his own residence, *c.* 1789 [*Survey of London* xxii, 84 and pl. 62].

SOUTHWARK, SURREY COUNTY GAOL, HORSE-MONGER LANE, 1791–8; dem. 1880–92 [*A.P.S.D.*].

CAMBERWELL, THE CAMDEN CHAPEL, 1797; enlarged 1829, chancel added 1854 [Parish Records].

SOUTHWARK, SURREY COUNTY SESSIONS HOUSE, NEWINGTON CAUSEWAY, 1798–9; dem. 1912 [*A.P.S.D.*].

ISLE OF DOGS, WAREHOUSES for the West India Dock Co., with George Gwilt, junior, 1800–2; all but one destroyed by bombing 1940 [exhib. at R.A. 1801; *A.P.S.D.*; S. H. Kessels, 'A Great Georgian Warehouse', *Arch. Rev.*, Sept. 1955, 191–2].

GWILT, GEORGE (1775–1856), elder son of the above, was born in Southwark on 8 February 1775. He was apprenticed to his father in 1789, and eventually succeeded him in his practice. His inclinations 'led him rather towards the study than the active practice of architecture', and he contributed many papers to *Archaeologia* and *Vetusta Monumenta*, the publications of the Society of Antiquaries, of which he was elected a Fellow in 1815. In 1818–20 he superintended the repair of the steeple of the church of ST. MARY-LE-BOW, CHEAPSIDE, the upper part of which had to be taken down and rebuilt in consequence of the rusting and swelling of the iron cramps which held it together. The crowning obelisk was reduced in height on the grounds that its tenuity rendered it too liable to decay, and the columns beneath were renewed in Aberdeen granite. The foundations of the church were also strengthened, a work which resulted in the identification by Gwilt of the remains of the original eleventh-century structure. His account of the discovery, read to the Society of Antiquaries in June 1828, was published in *Vetusta Monumenta* v, 343–6. Between 1822 and 1825 he carried out the restoration of the choir and tower of the present SOUTHWARK CATHEDRAL at a cost of £35,000 (for details see W. Taylor, *Annals of St. Mary Overy*, 1833). In 1824 he visited Italy. On his return he rebuilt the first ten almshouses of

CURE'S COLLEGE, PARK STREET, SOUTHWARK, and in 1832–3 gratuitously supervised the restoration of the LADY CHAPEL of SOUTHWARK CATHEDRAL, as described in *Gent's Mag.* 1833 (i), 254. He had made the antiquities of Southwark his particular study, and contributed two articles on the remains of Winchester Palace to the *Gent's Mag.* for 1815. He also formed a collection of local antiquities at his house in Union Street. He was Master of the Masons' Company on three occasions, in 1835, 1846 and 1854. He died on 27 June 1856, and was buried in the family vault on the south side of the choir of Southwark Cathedral. There is a lithographic portrait dated 1847 in J. S. Gwilt's *Slight Memoir of Joseph Gwilt* in the R.I.B.A. Drawings Collection. Of the four sons mentioned on his monument, only Alfred survived him, becoming Master of the Masons' Company in 1850, 1869 and 1879. George, the eldest, and Charles Edwin were both promising architects, but died young. S. T. Bull was a pupil. [*A.P.S.D.*; *D.N.B.*; obituary in *Builder* xiv, 1856, 386.]

GWILT, JOSEPH (1784–1863), younger son of George Gwilt the elder, was born in Southwark on 11 January 1784. He was educated at St. Paul's School, and in 1799 entered his father's office. He was admitted to the Royal Academy Schools in 1801, obtaining the Silver Medal in 1801. He exhibited at the Academy from 1800 onwards, and was practising as an architect before he had reached the age of 25. Between 1814 and 1818 he made a series of continental tours, visiting Paris in 1814, Flanders in 1815, Rome in 1816 (with the artist J. S. Hayward) and Paris again in 1818. In or about the latter year he took up residence at No. 20 Abingdon Street, Westminster. He succeeded his father as Surveyor to the Commissioners of Sewers for Surrey, but resigned the office in 1846. He was also Surveyor to the Grocers' and Waxchandlers' Companies, and to the Imperial Fire Assurance Company. Much of his practice consisted in consultations with the Office of Woods and Forests and other official bodies, and with F. C. Penrose he assisted in drawing up a proposition for the new Metropolitan Building Act of 1855. For Sir T. Maryon Wilson he drew up a scheme for laying out his Hampstead estate for building, but it proved abortive. In 1839 he was one of the three assessors in the competition for the new Royal Exchange, and a volume containing his correspondence, etc., in this connection is now in the Guildhall Library. Though an elegant draughtsman, and the author of some accomplished neo-classical designs, he himself erected comparatively few buildings, and it is as a writer on architectural and antiquarian topics that he is best known. He was elected F.S.A. in 1815 and a Fellow of the Royal Astronomical Society in 1833. He died on

14 September 1863, at South Hill, Henley-on-Thames. Among his pupils were J. L. Wolfe, G. Herron, and his younger son John Sebastian Gwilt (1811–90), who became an architect and made all the drawings for his father's *Encyclopaedia of Architecture*. In the R.I.B.A. Drawings Collection there is a volume by J. S. Gwilt entitled *Slight Memoir of Joseph Gwilt* (1882). It contains photographic portraits of Joseph Gwilt dated 1858 and a number of his drawings, with brief notes by his son. [*A.P.S.D.*; *D.N.B.*; obituaries in *Builder* xxi, 1863, 701; R.I.B.A. *Trans.*, 1863–4; *Gent's Mag.* 1863 (ii), 647–52; *Jnl. of the British Archaeological Assoc.* xx, 1864, 178–81; MS. 'Parentalia of Gwilt' by Joseph Gwilt, in Surrey County Record Office, Acc. 390.]

Gwilt's publications were: *A Treatise on the Equilibrium of Arches*, 1811, 1826 and 1838. The 2nd edition contained his design for London Bridge, placed first by the referees, but not awarded a premium. *Notitia Architectonica Italiana, or Concise Notices of the Buildings and Architects of Italy*, originally prepared for his own use when visiting Italy, and published in 1818. *A Cursory View of the Origin of Caryatides*, privately printed 1822 and reprinted in his edition of Chambers's *Treatise. Sciography, or Examples of Shadows, with Rules for their Projection*, 1822, 1824, 1833.[1] *The Conduct of the Corporation of London considered, in respect of the designs submitted to it for rebuilding London Bridge, in a Letter to G. H. Sumner, Esq., M.P., by an Architect*, 1823. *An Historical, Descriptive, and Critical Account of the Cathedral Church of St. Paul, London*, read to the Architects' and Antiquaries' Club, 1823, and printed in Britton & Pugin, *Public Buildings of London* i, 1825. An engraving, entitled a *Comparative View of the Four Principal Modern Churches in Europe by means of Transverse Sections to the Same Scale*, 1824. A new edition of Chambers's *Treatise on the Decorative Part of Civil Architecture*, with an introductory essay on Grecian architecture, 1825. A translation of the *Architecture of Vitruvius*, 1826. *Rudiments of Architecture, Practical and Theoretical*, 1826, 1835, 1839. The *Ordinary* to N. H. Nicolas, *A Roll of Arms*, 1829. *Observations on the Communication of Mr. Wilkins relative to the National Gallery*, 1833. The article on *Music* for the *Encyclopaedia Metropolitana*, 1835. *Rudiments of the Anglo-Saxon Tongue*, 1835. *Elements of Architectural Criticism*, 1837, 1839, in reply to articles on German architecture in the *Foreign Quarterly Review. A Project of a National Gallery on the Site of Trafalgar Square* (with his son), 1838. *An Encyclopaedia of Architecture*,

---

[1] For his MS. translation of a French treatise on shadows by C. Stanislas l'Eveillé, made in 1820, see J. Harris, *Catalogue of British Drawings for Architecture, etc. in American Collections*, 1971, 108.

Historical, Theoretical and Practical, 1842, 1845, 1854, 1859, 1867, 1876, 1889, the last three editions by Wyatt Papworth. All the articles relating to architecture, music, and the fine arts in Brande, *Dictionary of Science, Literature and Art,* 1842, 1853. A pamphlet with I'Anson and Newman on *Sewers, Surrey and Kent,* 1843. A new edition of P. Nicholson's *Principles of Architecture,* 1848.

ST. IVES VICARAGE, HUNTS., 1804 [Lincolnshire Record Office, MGA 44].

HOUGHTON COTTAGE, nr. ST. IVES, HUNTS., for John Ansley, 1807, and proposed alterations 1810 [exhibited at R.A. 1807, 1810].

HOARWITHY, HEREFS., proposed timber bridge of five spans, probably not built [exhibited at R.A. 1813; drawing in J. S. Gwilt's *Memoir*].

LEE, KENT, Tudor cottage for Thomas Brandram, 1813 [F. H. Hart, *History of Lee,* 1882, 21–2].

LEE, KENT, ST. MARGARET'S CHURCH, 1813–14, Gothic; dem. 1841 [*A.P.S.D.*; view of interior in J. S. Gwilt's *Memoir*].

SOUTHWARK, design for FLOOR CLOTH MANUFACTORY, NEWINGTON CAUSEWAY, for W. Hayward, 1814, perhaps not executed [alternative elevations in J. S. Gwilt's *Memoir*].

SOUTHWARK, planned approaches to Southwark Bridge, 1819 [*A.P.S.D.*].

LEE, KENT, conservatory at LEE GROVE (afterwards THE CEDARS) for Thomas Brandram, 1820 [F. H. Hart, *History of Lee,* 1882, 23; exhibited at R.A. 1820; drawings in J. S. Gwilt, *Memoir*].

BANBURY CHURCH, OXON., monument to Anne Brocas (d. 1824), executed by H. R. Hartley [signed].

LONDON, GROCERS' HALL, POULTRY, alterations, including interior of hall and front to Princes Street, 1838; rebuilt 1889–93 [*A.P.S.D.* (giving date 1828); engraving in J. S. Gwilt's *Memoir,* showing interior of hall as altered by Joseph Gwilt, 1838].

LONDON, ST. THOMAS (formerly STAMFORD HILL CHAPEL), CLAPTON COMMON, SURREY, enlarged with addition of east tower, 1828–9 [I.C.B.S.].

MARKREE CASTLE, CO. SLIGO, IRELAND, additions for E. J. Cooper, 1842–3, in conjunction with J. S. Gwilt [exhibited at R.A. 1843 as 'completing by Joseph and J. S. Gwilt'; drawings in J. S. Gwilt, *Memoir,* dated 1842].

CHARLTON, KENT, ST. THOMAS'S CHURCH, MARYON ROAD, 1847–50, 'Byzantine' [*A.P.S.D.*].

GWYNN, JOHN (1713–1786), was the son of John Gwyn of Shrewsbury, where he was born in November 1713. Nothing is known of his father's occupation, or of his own early life. In 1760 he was described as 'till of late of another profession'. According to Joseph Farington he 'was originally a carpenter, and by industrious study acquired knowledge sufficient to become

an Architect, in which capacity he was little employed till towards the latter part of his life'. This last statement is borne out by the list of his recorded works printed below. He had, however, published in 1749 *An Essay on Design, including proposals for erecting a Public Academy to be supported by Voluntary Subscription (until a Royal Foundation can be obtained)*[1] and two engravings, *A Plan for Rebuilding the City of London after the Great Fire in 1666, designed by that Great Architect Sir Christopher Wren* (1749), and a *Transverse Section of St. Paul's Cathedral, decorated according to the original intention of Sir Christopher Wren,* engraved by E. Rooker and dedicated to the Prince of Wales (1755). In preparing this he was assisted by Samuel Wale, who supplied the figures. While taking measurements of the dome for this plate, Gwynn missed his footing and slipped down some distance until stopped by a projecting piece of lead, where he remained in peril until rescued. The plate was reissued in 1801.

Gwynn and Wale were neighbours in Little Court, Castle Street, Leicester Fields, and are said to have given each other much mutual assistance, Gwynn providing architectural backgrounds for his friend's compositions, and receiving help from Wale in his literary work. In 1758 they published a plan of St. Paul's Cathedral, engraved by James Green, showing the dimensions. Gwynn was also aided by Dr. Johnson, who, according to Boswell, 'lent his friendly assistance to correct and improve' his next publication, entitled *Thoughts on the Coronation of George III,* 1761. Johnson also composed the dedication to the King accompanying Gwynn's last and most important work, *London and Westminster Improved, to which is prefixed a discourse on Public Magnificence,* 1766. In this remarkable book, Gwynn 'urged that the map of London should be considered as a whole and future activity controlled by a general plan'. By means of coloured plans he put forward a carefully thought-out scheme of 'improvement', many features of which have since been carried out, and nearly all of which were both handsome and realistic. Nash's Regent Street, Rennie's Waterloo Bridge, the Thames Embankment and Trafalgar Square are all foreshadowed in this enlightened and prophetic work.

In 1755 Gwynn took part in the unsuccessful attempt to establish a 'Royal Academy of London for the improvement of Painting, Sculpture, and Architecture'. In 1760 he began to exhibit at the recently formed Society of Artists of Great Britain, of which he became a member, and continued to do so until the foundation of the Royal Academy in 1768, when he became one of the

---

[1] Other pamphlets attributed to him in *A.P.S.D.* and *D.N.B.* are now known to be by Robert Morris (*q.v.*).

first Academicians. He subsequently exhibited at the Academy annually from 1769 to 1772.

In 1759 he competed for the proposed Black-friars Bridge, and his design was one of the eight short-listed by the Committee. Mylne's design was eventually adopted, after much dispute over the relative merits of semicircular and elliptical arches, the latter being advocated by Mylne and the former by Gwynn and Smeaton.[1] Out of 'regard for his friend Mr. Gwyn', Dr. Johnson took part in the controversy, writing letters in favour of semicircular arches in the *Daily Gazetteer* of 1, 8 and 15 December 1759 (reprinted in *The Architect*, 7 Jan. 1887, 13–14; cf. Hawkins, *Life of Johnson*, 373–5). Subsequently Gwynn designed several important bridges, including that at Worcester, with its fine approaches. In December 1783 he was presented with the freedom of the city of Worcester as a token of appreciation for his services. In May 1771, he was appointed Surveyor to the Commissioners of the Oxford Paving Act at a salary of £150 per annum 'for three years certain and for one year more if necessary'. In this capacity he demolished the east and north gates of the city, and rebuilt Magdalen Bridge. He also designed the new Markets and the Workhouse, and undertook to supervise the reconstruction of the west wing of Queen's College in accordance with the designs of Kenton Couse after the fire of December 1778 [*Letters of Radcliffe and James*, ed. Evans, Oxford Historical Society, 1888, 270–2].

Gwynn died at Worcester on 27 February 1786, and was buried in the graveyard of St. Oswald's Hospital, where tablets, now no longer legible, record his name and that of his natural son Charles, who died in 1796. He left money in trust for the latter's apprenticeship to a painter, sculptor, architect or engraver, and directed him to publish the 'most useful' of Gwynn's own drawings. In the event of Charles's own death without issue, the money was to be divided between the Royal Society and the Royal Academy for the establishment of prizes to be awarded by the former to the best essay on 'Which promotes the happiness of mankind most, ... the establishment of societies of learning, literature, and the dead languages, or ... societies of ingenious, honest, industry', and by the latter 'to the best die engraver, or for a bust, statue, or composition'. Both Societies appear to have refused the bequests, the Royal Society in particular considering them 'totally foreign to the purposes for which the Society was instituted'. None of Gwynn's drawings were ever published, but several of them are preserved in the King's

Collection of Maps in the British Museum, and there are others in the Prattinton Collection in the Society of Antiquaries' Library.

Boswell describes Gwynn as 'a fine, lively, rattling fellow', and relates an anecdote which shows that he was Dr. Johnson's match in conversation. Owen, the historian of Shrewsbury, remembered him as 'lively, quick and sarcastic, of quaint appearance and odd manners'. But the latter were not so pronounced that Shenstone could not write of him in 1757 as 'a very well-bred and ingenious man, one Mr. Gwyn from London'. There is a portrait of him by Zoffany in the Shrewsbury Museum. William Hayward, the architect of Henley Bridge and a native of Shrewsbury, was his pupil and assistant.

[Wyatt Papworth, 'John Gwyn, R.A.', *Builder* xxi, 1863, 454; 1864, 27; J. L. Hobbs, 'The Parentage and Ancestry of John Gwyn', *Notes and Queries*, Jan. 1962, 21–2; *A.P.S.D.*; *D.N.B.*; obituary in *Berrow's Worcester Jnl.*, 2 March 1786; *The Farington Diary*, ed. J. Greig, i, 180; *The Letters of William Shenstone*, ed. M. Williams, 1939, 466; Mulvany's *Life of Gandon*, 1846, 162–3; J. Chambers, *Biographical Illustrations of Worcestershire*, 1820, 504–6; J. Summerson, *Georgian London*, 1945, 103–6; Gwynn's will (P.C.C. 220 NORFOLK).]

SHREWSBURY, THE ENGLISH BRIDGE, 1769–74. The original intention was to widen the old bridge according to a plan made by Robert Mylne, but it was eventually decided to build a new bridge designed by Gwynn. This bridge was rebuilt 1925–7, the original elevations being adapted to a flattened roadway [A. W. Ward, *The Bridges of Shrewsbury*, 1935].

ATCHAM BRIDGE, SALOP., 1769–71 (for the inscription on the foundation-stone, see Camden, *Britannia* ii, 1789, 417).

WORCESTER BRIDGE and approaches, 1771–80. The original plans are in the Prattinton Collection in the Society of Antiquaries' Library, vol. v (folio), 70, and in the B.M., *King's Maps* xliii, 67 *a.a.*

OXFORD, MAGDALEN BRIDGE, 1772–90; widened 1882–3. The original plans are in the B.M., *King's Maps* xxxiv, 33 (3 *a–c*). Gwynn's original design is illustrated in the *New Oxford Guide*, 1772 [T. W. M. Jaine, 'The Building of Magdalen Bridge', *Oxoniensia* xxxvi, 1971].

OXFORD, THE HOUSE OF INDUSTRY or WORKHOUSE, 1772–5; dem. 1864. The original design is in the B.M., *King's Maps* xxxiv, 33 (1).

OXFORD, THE MARKETS, 1773–4. The four houses facing the High Street (Nos. 13–16) were built by the Duke of Marlborough 'in conformity with the architect's suggestion'. The Market was reconstructed by Thomas Wyatt in 1839 and the south end of No. 3 Avenue was rebuilt by W. H. Castle in 1894. Gwynn's colonnade

---

[1] In 1766 it was on Smeaton's recommendation that Gwynn was employed to report on the proposed bridge over the R. Tay at Perth (see *Reports of the late John Smeaton* i, 1812, 184–7).

has been destroyed. The original design is in the B.M., *King's Maps* xxxiv, 32 (e).

PITCHFORD, SALOP., PARK FARM-HOUSE, *c.* 1774 [*V.C.H. Salop.* viii, 117].

LONDON, PICCADILLY, house for Mr. Deards, probably John Deards, of 46 Dover Street, Piccadilly [*The Farington Diary*, ed. J. Greig, i, 180].

BLEDLOW CHURCH, BUCKS., altar-piece (with painting by Samuel Wale); removed to south aisle, 1877 [C. O. Skilbeck, 'Notes on Bledlow Parish Church', *Records of Bucks.* xii, 1927–33, 145].

GYFFORD, EDWARD (1773–1856), was a pupil of J. Lewis. He was admitted to the Royal Academy Schools in 1789 at the age of 17, was awarded the Silver Medal in 1791, and the Gold Medal in 1792 for a 'Design for a House of Lords and Commons'. He exhibited at the Academy from 1791 to 1801, and published two small volumes entitled *Designs for Elegant Cottages and Small Villas* (1806) and *Designs for Small Picturesque Cottages and Hunting Boxes* (1806–7), which together formed 'a series of Select Architecture'. The original drawings for the latter book are in the collection of Mr. Paul Mellon. In 1819 he attempted without success to obtain the commission for the new church of St. Luke, Chelsea, submitting designs now in the R.I.B.A. Collection. In 1821 he obtained a church-building commission in Leeds, but was eventually dismissed as unsatisfactory [Port, 54 n.]. His only executed work so far known is BELLEVUE HOUSE, WALTHAMSTOW, ESSEX, for Charles Cooke, bookseller, dem. 1936, which is illustrated in his 1806 publication (plates 23–4) and in Hughson's *London* vi, 1809, 302. In default of commissions, Gyfford appears to have made a living as a draughtsman, making drawings for, *e.g.* Hughson's *London* (1805–9). Redgrave says that he was 'a rapid, clever, draughtsman, but managed only to gain a poor subsistence by his profession'. He died on 23 June 1856, aged 83, and was buried in Fulham Churchyard. His son Edward A. Gifford or Gyfford, junior, won the R.A. Gold Medal for Architecture in 1837, but gave up architecture for painting.

H

HABERSHON, MATTHEW (1789–1852), came of a family connected with Rotherham in Yorkshire, and, showing much talent for drawing, was articled to William Atkinson in 1806. He began to exhibit in 1807, and entered the Royal Academy Schools in the following year. He subsequently remained in Atkinson's office for some years as an assistant. While designing classical public buildings and Gothic churches like most of his contemporaries, Habershon became an early enthusiast for the picturesque timber-framed houses of the sixteenth and seventeenth centuries, about which he published a pioneer book, *The Ancient Half-Timbered Houses of England*, in 1836. In the text he revealed himself as an opponent of Pugin's crusade for 'Catholic architecture', subjecting the *Contrasts* to a detailed and hostile analysis. He was in fact a zealous Anglican, and was the author of *A Dissertation on the prophetic scriptures* (1834, 2nd ed. 1840) and other similar works. In 1842 he went to Jerusalem on behalf of the London Society for Promoting Christianity among the Jews, in order to give directions for the completion of the Anglican Cathedral there begun by J. W. Johns (*q.v.*), whose unsatisfactory conduct of the works had led to his dismissal. Habershon took with him a clerk of works called Critchlow whom he left in charge. On his return journey in 1843 he had an interview with the King of Prussia, who was one of the promoters of the cathedral. The King subsequently conferred on him a gold medal for his book on timber-framed houses. Habershon died in London on 5 July 1852 and was buried in Abney Park Cemetery. His sons Edward and William Gilbee Habershon both practised as architects. At first they were in partnership, but in 1863 they separated and W. G. Habershon joined A. R. Pite in a successful London practice which had an offshoot at Newport in Monmouthshire. Among Matthew Habershon's other pupils were Ewan Christian and C. Yoget, who practised at Cape Town. [*A.P.S.D.*; *Builder* ii, 1844, 561; Bodleian Library, minute books of the London Society for Promoting Christianity among the Jews.]

LONDON, COVENTRY STREET, ROYAL WORCESTER PORCELAIN WAREHOUSE, for Messrs. Flight & Barr, 1810 [exhibited at R.A.].

BELPER, DERBYSHIRE, ST. PETER'S CHURCH, 1824, Gothic [exhibited at R.A.].

MERE HALL, nr. DROITWICH, WORCS., alterations and additions for E. H. Bearcroft, *c.* 1826 [*Ancient Half-Timbered Edifices*, 17].

HADZOR HOUSE, nr. DROITWICH, WORCS., for J. H. Galton, 1827 [exhibited at R.A.].

STANMORE, MIDDLESEX, AYLMORE GROVE COTTAGE, for J. Marks, 1827 [exhibited at R.A.].

DERBY, COUNTY COURTS at rear of County Hall, 1828–9 [S. Glover, *History of the County of Derby* ii, 1833, 446–9, with plan].

DERBY, THE TOWN HALL and MARKET, 1828–30; in 1841 the interior of the Town Hall was destroyed by fire, after which the portico was removed and the front rebuilt with a clock-tower to the designs of Messrs. Duesbury & Lee [S. Glover, *History of the County of Derby* ii, 1833, 441–3, with plan].

HADZOR, WORCS., farm-house for J. H. Galton, *c.* 1830 [*Ancient Half-Timbered Edifices*, 10].

KINGSTON-ON-SOAR CHURCH, NOTTS., rebuilt 1832, except chancel, Gothic; reconstructed 1900 [I.C.B.S.].

THE GRANGE, SEACROFT, nr. LEEDS, YORKS. (W.R.), for John Wilson, 1834 [*Ancient Half-Timbered Edifices*, 21].

HADZOR CHURCH, WORCS., alterations 1835 [I.C.B.S.].

ASTON SANDFORD RECTORY, BUCKS., for the Rev. H. Alford, 1836–7 [*Ancient Half-Timbered Edifices*, 18; Lincolnshire Record Office, MGA 208].

BRAMPTON, HUNTS., half-timbered cottages for Lady Olivia Sparrow, *c.* 1837 [*Ancient Half-Timbered Edifices*, 13].

DERBY, CHRIST CHURCH, NORMANTON ROAD (BISHOP RYDER'S CHURCH), 1838–40, Gothic; chancel added 1865 [F. White, *History, Gazeteer and Directory of the County of Derby*, 1857, 58].

KIMBERWORTH CHURCH, YORKS. (W.R.), 1840–2, Gothic; chancel 1882 [I.C.B.S.].

WINSTER CHURCH, DERBYSHIRE, rebuilt 1842, incorporating old tower, Gothic; altered 1884–5 [*A.P.S.D.*].

BURBAGE CHURCH, LEICS., rebuilt 1842, Gothic [I.C.B.S].

HARDWICK HOUSE, SUFFOLK, architectural features of parterre gardens for Sir Thomas Cullum, Bart., *c.* 1845 [Suffolk County Record Office, E 2/23/4].

HACKER, FREDERICK, was a member of a family of builders and architects at Canterbury. He may well have been a son of James Hacker, a carpenter who in 1789 agreed to build a market-place at the Bullstake in Canterbury, 'agreeable to his plan' [Corporation Minutes]. Frederick became a pupil of John Nash and by 1825 was in independent practice in the Edgware Road. But he evidently failed to make a success of it, for Pigot's *Directory* shows that in 1827–8 he was back in Kent, giving addresses both in Canterbury and Dover. In 1832 he left England for Canada. By June of that year he was established at 14 Palace Street, Quebec. In 1834 he designed No. 43 D'AUTEUIL STREET, a stone-fronted house with a Greek Doric doorcase. In 1838 he petitioned the Governor to be 'continued in the situation of Expert in which he has heretofore acted . . . and . . . be honoured with the appointment of architect to the Civil Government' [*Quebec Mercury*, 14 June 1832; Public Archives of Canada, MSS. R. G. 4, AL, S–401; information from Sir John Summerson].

HACKER, SAMUEL, was another member of the Canterbury family referred to above. He established himself at Herne Bay as an 'Architect,

Builder and Estate Agent' and in 1830–1 began to lay out a new seaside resort there of which only the promenade was completed more or less in accordance with his plans [*The Watering Places of Great Britain and Fashionable Directory*, 1833, 48; John Newman, *North East and East Kent*, 'the Buildings of England', 1969, 336].

HADFIELD, GEORGE (1763–1826), was born at Leghorn in Italy, where his father kept a hotel. In 1779, after her husband's death, his mother returned to England, and in September 1781, a few days after his eighteenth birthday, George Hadfield was admitted to the R.A. Schools as an architectural student. He was an immediate success, winning the Silver Medal in his first year and the Gold Medal in 1784. In the latter year he became a pupil of James Wyatt. On leaving Wyatt's office in 1790 he became the first recipient of the Travelling Scholarship in Architecture awarded by the Academy, and spent some time in Italy. In 1791, in conjunction with an Italian architect called Colonna, he made drawings, now in the R.I.B.A. Collection, for a restoration of the temple at Palestrina or Praeneste. In 1795 he exhibited drawings of the temples of Mars and Jupiter Tonans at the Royal Academy.

Hadfield had by now acquired a considerable reputation as a young architect of promise, but when, in January 1795, he was proposed for election to the Architects' Club by Henry Holland and James Wyatt, he was excluded by a single black ball which Wyatt attributed either to Soane or to Brettingham. It may have been this setback which induced Hadfield to accept an invitation to go to America to superintend the building of the Capitol at Washington. For this difficult task, requiring far more experience both of men and of building than he then possessed, Hadfield was by no means well equipped, and in 1798 he was dismissed after struggling in vain against 'the ignorance and the dishonesty of the commissioners and of the workmen'. Meanwhile his real abilities as an architect were largely wasted. In 1806 Benjamin Latrobe doubted whether his 'irritable pride and neglected study [will] ever permit him to take the station in the art which his elegant talent ought to have obtained'. During the last ten years of his life, however, his fortunes recovered, and he designed a number of neo-classical buildings of distinction in Washington, including the City Hall, now the District of Columbia Courthouse (1820), the Greek Doric portico of Arlington House (1818), the Assembly Rooms (1822), the United States Bank (1824), and Van Ness's mausoleum (1826), now in Oak Hill cemetery at Georgetown.

[*A.P.S.D.*; *D.N.B.*; Fiske Kimball in *Dictionary of American Biography*; H. F. & E. Withey, *Biographical Dictionary of American Architects*, 1956; G. L. M. Goodfellow, 'George

375

Hadfield', *Arch. Rev.* July 1965, 35–6; R. A.
Admission Register; *The Farington Diary*, ed. J.
Greig, i, 85; *The Journal of Latrobe*, ed. J. H. B.
Latrobe, New York, 1905, 133–4.]

HAGUE, DANIEL (*c.* 1736–*c.* 1816), son of
Daniel Hague, late of Corsham, yeoman, was
apprenticed to Thomas Manley, mason of
Bristol, in April 1750, and was admitted to the
freedom of the City of Bristol in August 1762
[Bristol City archives]. He developed a successful
business as a builder and surveyor which was
taken over by his son when he retired in about
1805. In 1784 he designed the ROYAL INFIRMARY
in association with Thomas Paty. He also
planned PORTLAND SQUARE in 1790, and was the
architect of ST. PAUL'S CHURCH, PORTLAND
SQUARE, built 1789–94 in an engagingly unscholarly Gothic style, with a tower whose receding
upper stages recalled that of the Royal Exchange
in London. A classical design by James Allen had
previously been approved, and it was believed at
the time that the adoption of Hague's Gothic design was due to the influence of Dr. Small, the
first incumbent of St. Paul's [W. Ison, *The Georgian Building of Bristol*, 1952, 36–7, 76–81, 220–
23].

HAKEWILL, GEORGE, was a son of John
Hakewill (1742–91), painter and decorator, and a
younger brother of Henry and James Hakewill,
the architects. He exhibited at the Royal Academy from 1806 to 1810, including a 'Design for
the Garden front of a Marine Villa building in
Norfolk' (1808). This appears to be his only
recorded work.

HAKEWILL, HENRY (1771–1830), was the
eldest son of John Hakewill (1742–91), painter
and decorator. He became a pupil of John Yenn,
was admitted to the Royal Academy Schools in
1790, and won the Silver Medal the same year.
He exhibited at the Academy from 1792 to 1809.
In the latter year he became architect to the trustees of Rugby School, an appointment which he
retained until his death. He was also architect to
the Radcliffe Trustees, and to the Benchers of the
Middle Temple. He wrote *An Account of the
Roman Villa discovered at Northleigh, Oxfordshire, in the years 1813–14–15–16*, printed in
Skelton's *Antiquities of Oxfordshire* 1823, and
reissued separately in 1826. He died on 13 March
1830, aged 59, and was buried at North Cray,
Kent. He was a liveryman of the Fishmongers'
Company. His two sons, John Henry (1811–80)
and Edward Charles (1812–72), both practised as
architects. Among his other pupils were John
Turner, T. M. Cook, John Winckworth and John
Goldicutt, who, after his Italian tour, returned
to Hakewill's office until the latter's death, and
was associated with him in the competition for

the Hanwell Lunatic Asylum, in which they
obtained the third premium.

Hakewill was a competent but rather un-
inspired architect who specialized in Tudor
Gothic. His best works are, however, in the
Greek Revival style (St. Peter, Eaton Square,
Stisted Hall and Wormington Grange). His
church at Wolverton is an early example of neo-
Norman. [*A.P.S.D.*; *D.N.B.*]

FOOTS CRAY PLACE, KENT, alterations for Benjamin
Harenc, 1792; further 'improvements' for
Nicholas Vansittart, Lord Bexley, *c.* 1825;
dem. after a fire in 1950 [*A.P.S.D.*; exhibited
at R.A. 1792, and cf. J. Dunkin, *History of
Dartford*, 1844, 468].

NORTH WALES, an unidentified villa, exhibited at
the R.A. 1795.

RENDLESHAM HALL, SUFFOLK, extensive alterations
for P. I. Thellusson, *c.* 1801, Gothic; destroyed by fire 1830 [exhibited at R.A. 1801]
(J. P. Neale, *Views of Seats*, 1st ser., iii, 1820).

CAVE CASTLE, YORKS. (E.R.), for H. B. Barnard,
1804, Gothic; altered 1873–5; reduced in size
1938 [exhibited at R.A. 1804] (R. A. Alec-
Smith, 'Cave Castle', *E. Yorkshire Georgian
Soc.* iv (2), 1956–8).

LONDON, enlarged the OLD ARGYLL ROOMS, 1806;
dem. [plans and correspondence in Sir John
Soane's Museum].

WALTON HALL, WARWICKS., alterations for Sir
Charles Mordaunt, Bart., *c.* 1810; rebuilt 1860
[J. Britton, *Beauties of England and Wales* xv,
1814, 188].

RUGBY SCHOOL, WARWICKS, BUILDINGS 1809–15
and CHAPEL 1818–21, Gothic; chapel rebuilt
1867–98 [*A.P.S.D.*; exhibited at R.A. 1809].

WOLVERTON CHURCH, BUCKS., for the Radcliffe
Trustees, 1810–15, 'Norman' style [Bodleian
Library, minutes of the Radcliffe Trustees
1792–1815].

PACKINGTON HALL, WARWICKS., south and west
terraces for the 5th Earl of Aylesford, 1812. In
1828 Hakewill also designed the interiors of the
billiard room and upper library [G. C. Tyack
in *Archaeological Jnl.* cxxviii, 1971, 242].

FARNBOROUGH HALL, WARWICKS., designed
stables and minor internal alterations for
William Holbech, 1813–16 [drawings and
accounts at Farnborough Hall].

WARWICK, THE JUDGES' HOUSE, 1814–16; extended
1955 [Warwick County Records, Class 24 (36–
7)].

HOLME PARK, nr. READING, BERKS., works for
Robert Palmer, *c.* 1815; dem. 1881 [*A.P.S.D.*]
(J. P. Neale, *Views of Seats*, 2nd ser., iv, 1828).

BLENHEIM PALACE, OXON., the Aviary, for the 4th
Duke of Marlborough, *c.* 1815; dem. [J. P.
Neale, *Views of Seats*, 1st ser., v.
1822].

OXFORD, ORIEL COLLEGE, remodelled PROVOST'S

LODGINGS, 1815–17, Gothic [*V.C.H. Oxon*, iii, 128.]

BADBY VICARAGE, NORTHANTS., remodelled 1817 [Peterborough Diocesan records in Northants. Record Office].

LAMPORT HALL, NORTHANTS., various works for Sir Justinian Isham, Bart., including rebuilding of north-west front in Tudor Gothic style (1819), entrance gates on Northampton Road (1824) and pediment on south-west front (1829). The north-west front was subsequently rebuilt by Burn [Sir Gyles Isham, 'The Architectural History of Lamport', *Reports and Papers of the Northants. Architectural and Archaeological Soc.* No. 106, 1951, 25–6].

BILLING HALL, NORTHANTS., alterations for R. C. Elwes, 1820; dem. *c.* 1955 [bills in Northants. Record Office].

CORNBURY PARK, OXON., alterations for Lord Churchill *c.* 1820, probably unimportant and now unrecognizable [*A.P.S.D.*].

ALBURY PARK, SURREY, alterations and additions for Henry Drummond, *c.* 1820, Tudor style [J. P. Neale, *Views of Seats*, 2nd ser., iii, 1826] (*C. Life*, 1 Sept. 1950).

LONDON, THE MIDDLE TEMPLE: designed PARLIAMENT CHAMBERS, including former library, 1822–4; restored screen, porch and louver of Hall; designed Nos. 1–2 PLOWDEN BUILDINGS, Elizabethan style, executed after his death by J. Savage, 1831–3, enlarged 1896 and renovated 1933 [*A.P.S.D.*].

STISTED HALL, ESSEX, for C. S. Onley, 1823–5 [J. A. Rush, *Seats in Essex*, 1897, 166].

LONDON, ST. PETER'S CHURCH, EATON SQUARE, 1824–7. His first design for a Gothic church was rejected. The church was gutted by fire in Jan. 1837, and reconstructed by J. H. Hakewill from the original drawings. The chancel was added by Sir A. W. Blomfield in 1873 and he remodelled the interior of the nave in 1875 [*A.P.S.D.*].

DINGLEY HALL, NORTHANTS., works for H. H. Hungerford, probably *c.* 1825 [*A.P.S.D.*].

SOUTH WEALD VICARAGE, ESSEX, for the Rev. C. A. Belli, 1824. Belli was related to C. R. Cockerell, whom he consulted, and who revised the designs [C. R. Cockerell's diary, 12 March 1824].

SHRUBLAND HALL, LEAMINGTON PRIORS, WARWICKS., for Matthew Wise, *c.* 1825 [*A.P.S.D.*].

STONE CASTLE, nr. GRAVESEND, KENT, alterations for Robert Talbot, probably *c.* 1825, Tudor style [*A.P.S.D.*].

WORMINGTON GRANGE, GLOS., enlarged for Josiah Gist, 1826–7 [Arthur Oswald in *C. Life*, 21 Sept. 1940].

HAKEWILL, JAMES (1778–1843), was the second son of John Hakewill, painter and decorator. On his father's death in 1791, his elder brother Henry, then a pupil in the office of John Yenn, settled the family business on James, who exhibited decorative and architectural designs at the Royal Academy from 1800 onwards. His talents, however, were literary and antiquarian rather than practical, and it is for his architectural publications that he is best known. In 1813 he published *The History of Windsor and its Neighbourhood*, illustrated from his own drawings. After the Peace of Vienna he visited Italy in 1816–17 in company with his wife, who was herself a talented artist. On his return he exhibited his drawings in Bond Street, and in 1818–20 published *A Picturesque Tour of Italy*, some of the plates of which were engraved after J. M. W. Turner's finished drawings from Hakewill's own sketches. In 1820–21 he visited Jamaica, and in 1825 published *A Picturesque Tour in the Island of Jamaica*, fol. In 1828 he published *Plans, Sections, and Elevations of the Abattoirs of Paris, with considerations for their adoption in London*, and in 1835 *An Attempt to determine the exact character of Elizabethan Architecture*, with plans of Dorton House, Bucks., and other Elizabethan buildings. In 1830 he was engaged on drawings for a work on the Rhine, intended to be a companion volume to his *Italy*, but it was never published. He is also said to have written a novel, *Coelebs Suited, or the Stanley Letters*, 1812.

His only recorded architectural works were a house at YARMOUTH for Thomas Penrice, *c.* 1805; dem. 1844 [C. J. Palmer, *Perlustration of Great Yarmouth*, ii, 1876, 161]; the elegant domed Pump Room, at DORTON SPA, BUCKS., for C. S. Ricketts, 1834, now dem., described and illustrated by J. Knight, *History of the Dorton Chalybeate*, 1835 and in *The Mirror of Literature, Amusement and Instruction*, No. 965, 31 Aug. 1839; a lodge at the Rostherne entrance to TATTON PARK, CHESHIRE, for W. Egerton, 1833; a lodge and eating-room at HIGH LEGH, CHESHIRE, for G. C. Legh, 1833–4; and THE CHRISTIAN UNION ALMSHOUSES, JOHN STREET, EDGWARE ROAD, 1834, for all of which he exhibited drawings at the Royal Academy. In 1835 he submitted a design for rebuilding the Houses of Parliament in a sixteenth-century classical style derived from Longleat and Hatfield. A design by him for a house for G. W. Aylmer (1829) is in the R.I.B.A. Drawings Collection. He died on 28 May 1843, and was buried in Paddington churchyard. He had four sons, Arthur William (1808–56), an architect and pupil of Decimus Burton, Frederick, a portrait painter, Henry James (d. 1834, aged 20), a sculptor, and Richard Wentworth.

[*A.P.S.D.*; *D.N.B.*; obituaries in *Civil Engineer and Architect's Jnl.* vi, 1843, 324 and *Gent's Mag.* 1843 (ii), 209–10, reprinted in *Builder*, 2 Sept. 1843; Farington's Diary, 27 June 1818.]

HALDANE, —. According to the anonymous author of *Forfarshire Illustrated* (Dundee, 1843), 23, THE TABERNACLE, later ST. DAVID'S CHURCH, DUNDEE, 'a large plain looking edifice', was built in about 1800 'by the Messrs. Haldane'.

HALDANE, JAMES, practised in Edinburgh and appears to have died soon after 1830. He first appears in the Edinburgh directories in 1800 as a 'teacher of mathematics'. By 1804–5 he was described as 'architect'. He was responsible for the design of houses on the Morrison Estate in MAITLAND STREET WEST (Nos. 1–14), MORRISON STREET (Nos. 252–70) and TORPHICHEN STREET (Nos. 2–24), all begun in about 1825 [S.R.O., Edinburgh Sasines]. In 1806 he designed the fountain or well-head in front of the Town Hall at LINLITHGOW in an elaborate sixteenth-century style based on its decayed predecessor. It was executed by an Edinburgh mason called Robert Gray [Town Council Minutes in S.R.O., B 48/9/14, pp. 455, 460, 461, 494].

HALFPENNY, WILLIAM, *alias* MICHAEL HOARE (–1755), described as 'architect and carpenter' on the title-page of several of his works, is mentioned by Batty Langley in his *Ancient Masonry*, 1736, p. 147, as 'Mr. William Halfpeny, *alias* Hoare, lately of Richmond in Surry, carpenter'. His recorded architectural works are not numerous, and he is best known as the author of many architectural pattern-books, written for the benefit of 'those who are engaged in the noble art of building'. They are mainly devoted to domestic architecture, and it was, in the words of the poet Lloyd, 'from Halfpenny's exact designs' that many a 'cit's country box' was erected. His more ambitious designs for country seats are in the Palladian vernacular of the period, though often enlivened externally by features of baroque extraction and internally by rococo decoration. There was, indeed, a fanciful element in his taste which found congenial expression in the Chinese and Gothic designs of which he was one of the earliest popularizers. His son John Halfpenny was associated with him in some of his later publications.

Halfpenny's career is still somewhat obscure. As a practical architect he first appears as the author of an unexecuted design for HOLY TRINITY CHURCH, LEEDS. On 8 May 1723 William Halfpenny was paid £1 11s. 6d. 'for his draughts of the new Church', and the design is illustrated in his *Art of Sound Building* of 1725. It shows a building of six bays ornamented with Corinthian pilasters. The (externally Doric) design adopted and carried out in 1722–7 was, however, the work of William Etty (*q.v.*) [D. Linstrum, citing newly-discovered documents in his forthcoming *West Yorkshire Architects and Architecture*, and superseding R. S. Shapely, 'Holy Trinity

Church, Leeds', *Jnl. of the W. Yorkshire Society of Architects* xiv, no. 1, March 1955]. This employment at Leeds may suggest that Halfpenny was a native of Yorkshire, where his surname is not uncommon. By 1726 he was evidently established in Surrey, for in that year he was among those who submitted designs for a timber bridge across the river Thames at Fulham [minutes of the Fulham Bridge Commissioners, P.R.O., GD 26/12, ff. 12–13]. He is next found in Ireland, designing a HORSE BARRACKS at HILLSBOROUGH, COUNTY DOWN, for the 1st Viscount Hillsborough in 1732 [C. E. B. Brett, *Court Houses and Market Houses of the Province of Ulster*, Belfast 1973, 73]. In 1739 he was at Waterford, surveying the cathedral there and making unexecuted designs, now in the R.I.B.A. Drawings Collection, for its replacement by a modern classical church.

When Halfpenny made these Irish designs he may already have been based in Bristol, for his *Perspective Made Easy*, published in 1731, includes views of the Drawbridge, the Hotwell, the north side of Queen Square, and his own design for an Exchange. He was certainly established in Bristol by 1739–40, when he submitted several designs to the committee for building an Exchange, and also tendered unsuccessfully for the carpenter's work when the commission was given to John Wood.[1] In 1742 he was equally unsuccessful in a scheme for adding wings to the Infirmary, but the COOPERS' HALL in KING STREET was built to his designs in 1743–4. It presents a handsome though far from academically correct Palladian facade to the street (Dening, *Eighteenth-Century Architecture of Bristol*, pl. xxx).

According to Shiercliff's *Bristol and Hotwell Guide* for 1789, Halfpenny was the designer of the REDLAND CHAPEL, BRISTOL, an elegant and highly-finished building which was erected at the expense of John Cossins of Redland Court between *c.* 1740 and 1743. Halfpenny's name is also connected with the Chapel by a view of it in the British Museum signed 'William Halfpenny Architect delin. 1742' (King's Maps, Supplementary volume 24, f. 37). But the original building accounts[2] show that it was not until 22 May 1742, that Halfpenny agreed with Cossins 'to Give proper Directions as is Usuall By Archi-

[1] Several sets of alternative designs by Halfpenny are preserved in the Bristol City Archives (1024), and on 28 April 1740, Mr. Halfpenny was ordered to be paid 5 guineas in part for the trouble he had been at in drawing plans for the Exchange and Markets (Minutes of the Committee for Building the Exchange in Bristol City Archives). There are two surveys by Halfpenny, dated 1742, in Plan Book B.

[2] In the custody of Messrs. Osborne, Ward, Vassall, Abbott & Co., solicitors, of Broad Street, Bristol, who kindly allowed them to be examined by the writer. Extracts from them are printed by J. Charlton and D. M. Milton in *Redland 791 to 1880*, 1951, Appendix II.

tects and Directors of Buildings, to all his Workmen Employ'd at his Chapple at Redland and to see Said Workmen do their work in a Workmanlike Manner... and to See the Whole Compleated for the Sum of ten pounds ten shillings sterling'. It is not certain exactly when the building was begun, but it was already well advanced by 1742, when Halfpenny came on the scene, and the original estimate, which has been preserved, is not in his hand. It would appear therefore that the chapel had already been begun to the designs of another architect, and that architect was probably John Strahan, recently deceased, who had been employed by Cossins to design Redland Court a few years earlier. Halfpenny's functions would therefore have been confined to the completion of the chapel and the only specific feature which he is known to have designed is the altarpiece, which was made in 1742 by William Brooks, a London joiner, 'according to a draught drawd by William Halfpenny'. The elaborate wood-carving is stated in a contemporary account of the chapel to have been designed as well as executed by Thomas Paty of Bristol.

Other buildings that have been attributed to Halfpenny on stylistic grounds are No. 40 PRINCE STREET, BRISTOL, 1740–1, dem. (C. F. Dening, *The Eighteenth-Century Architecture of Bristol*, 1923, pl. xxxi); CLIFTON COURT, CLIFTON GREEN, for Martha Dandervall, *c.* 1742–3; UPTON HOUSE, TETBURY, GLOS., for Thomas Cripps, 1752 [Marcus Binney in *C. Life*, 15 Feb. 1973]; and THE ASSEMBLY ROOMS, BRISTOL, 1754–5, dem. [C. F. Dening, *The Eighteenth-Century Architecture of Bristol*, 1923, 102]. Halfpenny's only other recorded works appear to be the monument to Islesworth Parish Church, Middlesex, to Mrs. Ann Dash (*alias* Tonson), died 1750, which bears his signature, and a Chinese bridge at CROOME COURT, WORCESTERSHIRE, illustrated as his work in *Improvements in Architecture and Carpentry* (1754). He died in debt in 1755 [P.C.C. Admon. Register].

Halfpenny's publications were: *Magnum in Parvo, or the Marrow of Architecture*, 1722, 1728; *Practical Architecture*, 1st ed., n.d., 1724, 1730, 1736 (5th ed.), 1748, 1751; *The Art of Sound Building demonstrated in Geometrical Problems*, 1725, with a dedication to Sir Andrew Fountaine; *Builder's Pocket Companion*, 1728, 1731, 1747 (by 'Michael Hoare'); *Perspective Made Easy*, 1731; *The Modern Builder's Assistant* (with John Halfpenny, Robert Morris, and T. Lightoler), ?1742[1], 1757; *Arithmetic and Measurement Improved by Examples*, 1748, *A Perspective View*

of the sunk Pier and the two Adjoining Arches at Westminster (one folio plate), 1748; *A New and Compleat System of Architecture, delineated in a Variety of Plans and Elevations of Designs for Convenient and Decorated Houses*, 1749, 1759; *A Plan and Elevation of the Royal Fireworks Perform'd in St. James's Park* (one folio sheet), 1749; *New Designs for Chinese Temples etc.*, 1750; *Twelve Beautiful Designs for Farm Houses*, 1750, 1759, 1774; *Andrea Palladio's First Book of Architecture*, n.d. (*c.* 1750); *Six New Designs for Farm Houses, ... adapted more particularly to the Western Counties... and the Principality of Wales*, 1751; *Useful Architecture in Twenty-One New Designs for erecting Parsonage-houses, Farmhouses and Inns*, 1752, 1755, 1760 (with additional matter, including designs for bridges); *Thirteen New Designs for Parsonages and Farm-houses*, 1752; *Rural Architecture in the Gothic Taste* (with John Halfpenny), 1752; *Chinese and Gothic Architecture properly ornamented* (with John Halfpenny), 1752; *Geometry, Theoretical and Practical*, 1752; *Rural Architecture in the Chinese Taste*, 1752, 1755, in four parts, of which nos. ii, iii and iv were the joint work of William and John Halfpenny; *The Country Gentleman's Pocket Companion and Builder's Assistant* (with John Halfpenny), 1753–6; *Twenty-six New Designs of Geometrical Paling* (one folio sheet), 1750; *Improvements in Architecture and Carpentry*, 1754.

[*A.P.S.D.*; *D.N.B.*; E. Shiercliff, *Bristol and Hotwell Guide*, 1789, 42, 91; C. F. Dening, *The Eighteenth-Century Architecture of Bristol*, 1923, 95–7; K. A. Esdaile, 'The Small House and its Amenities in the Architectural Handbooks, 1749–1847', *Trans. Bibliog. Soc.* xv, 1917–19; W. Ison, *The Georgian Buildings of Bristol*, 1952, 37–8.]

HALL, JAMES (1769–1809), was the third son of Henry Hall, Principal Clerk to the Commissioners of Sewers for the City of London and Surveyor to the Sun Fire Office, who died in 1796. James Hall succeeded his father as Surveyor to the Sun Fire Office, and was also Surveyor to St. Bartholomew's Hospital and the Inner Temple. He died in Bloomsbury Place on 14 July 1809, in his 40th year [*Gent's Mag.* 1796, 173; 1809 (ii), 686]. In 1806 he had been consulted by the Rev. Charles Mayo about THE GREAT HOUSE, CHESHUNT, HERTS., and may have been responsible for remodelling it in a thin Gothic style [C. H. Mayo, *A Genealogical Account of the Mayo and Elton Families*, 2nd ed. 1908, 579–80].

HALL, JOHN, practised as an architect in Bangor, North Wales, during the third decade of the nineteenth century. Between 1824 and 1828

---

[1] This date rests on an emendation of the date given on the title page (MDCCVLII) to MDCCXLII, but 1742 is perhaps unduly early for the participation of Timothy Lightoler and John Halfpenny.

he acted as superintending surveyor for the repairs and alterations then in progress at BANGOR CATHEDRAL to the designs of Joseph Turner of Whitchurch and John Foster of Liverpool. He also designed the NATIONAL SCHOOL in DEAN STREET, 1821–2, a terrace of six houses on the Green at BEAUMARIS, 1824–5, and in 1825 carried out some alterations and repairs to BEAUMARIS CHURCH. After 1828 there is no further evidence of his architectural activities, and he appears to have attempted unsuccessfully to make a living as an inn-keeper. [M. L. Clarke, 'A Bangor Architect of the Early Nineteenth Century', *Trans. of the Caernarvonshire Historical Society*, 1954, 49–50].

HALL, SYLVANUS (–1792), was 'an eminent builder and carpenter' who died in Paternoster Row, London, on 23 November 1792 [*Gent's Mag.* 1792, 1062]. He had been Carpenter to the City of London since 1784. He designed CORDWAINERS' HALL, No. 7 CANNON STREET, in 1788, with interiors in the Adam style. It was demolished in 1909 [C. H. W. Mander, *History of the Guild of Cordwainders*, 1931, 113, with illustrations].

HALLAM, JOHN, became Clerk of the Works at Whitehall, Westminster, and St. James's, and Secretary to the Board of Works in 1719, in succession to Benjamin Benson, whose dismissal had followed that of his brother William, Surveyor-General from April 1718 to August 1719. Hallam was a protégé of the new Surveyor-General, Sir Thomas Hewett, and, like him, was a native of Nottinghamshire. Sir John Vanbrugh, who was hostile to Hewett, described Hallam as 'a poor mean Country Joyner who never has executed the office since he had it, not being capable', and alleged that Hewett merely 'put him in for form', taking the revenues of his office himself, and giving him 'only a small allowance out of the Income of the Place' [*The Works of Sir John Vanbrugh* iv, *The Letters*, ed. G. F. Webb, 169–70]. When Hewett died in 1726, Hallam was immediately deprived of his posts, which were given to Flitcroft and Hawksmoor respectively.

It is probable that Vanbrugh was correct in describing Hallam as a joiner, for in 1691 a joiner of that name was employed at Chatsworth [Chatsworth archives, 70.4], but the allegation that he was incapable of carrying out the duties of his office is refuted by references to his making estimates for works at St. James's Palace in 1722 [*Wren Soc.* vii, 221–2]. Moreover in 1721–3 he was employed to measure the artificers' work in connection with the new library designed by Hewett for Lord Sunderland in Piccadilly [Blenheim Palace Muniments, F.I.57], and in 1729 he designed a garden building at RUFFORD ABBEY,

380

NOTTS., for Sir George Savile called the BATH SUMMER-HOUSE, for which some of his drawings have survived in the Nottinghamshire Record Office [202/2, 3, 10, 15, 16, 22 and 211/58/16].

HALLETT, JOHN (–1841), of Mortimer Street, Cavendish Square, London, was President of the Surveyors' Club in 1836 and died in 1841. He exhibited at the Royal Academy from 1827 to 1835, including 'a church proposed to be built in Northamptonshire' (1827) and 'designs for cottages to be erected in Essex' (1829).

HAMILTON, DAVID (1768–1843), was for thirty years Glasgow's leading architect. Apart from the fact that he was born in Glasgow on 11 May 1768, the son of William Hamilton, mason, and admitted to the Incorporation of Masons there in 1800, very little is known about his early life. He appears, however, to have worked as a mason before becoming an architect, and his earliest recorded buildings were not designed until he was in his thirties. He must have had some contact with the Adam family, for he made many copies of Adam drawings to which he would not otherwise have had access. Hutcheson's Hospital, his first building of any consequence, is a remarkably assured neo-classical design which suggests a familiarity with the work of Wyatt and Soane as well as of Robert and James Adam. Within a few years he had assimilated the Greek Revival, using a Greek Doric order in his Town Steeple at Falkirk (1813–14) and a rich Corinthian one in the portico of the Glasgow Royal Exchange (1829–30). Never a pedantic purist, he moved on to Jacobean (Dunlop House, 1831–4) and even Norman Revival (Lennox Castle, 1837–41). The Western Club (1840) has an Italianate facade, the Union Bank (1841) shows a return to complete classical purity. Whatever the style Hamilton was never its slave, but used it to produce an effective and often original design. As a Gothic Revivalist he was responsible for one symmetrical house in the Adam castle tradition (Kincaid House, *c.* 1812), and one romantically asymmetrical one (Castle Toward, 1820–1) in the manner of Wyatville. His planning was resourceful and ingenious.

In 1836 Hamilton was one of the four prize-winners in the competition for the new Houses of Parliament. His designs (P.R.O., Works 29/48–57) were in the Scottish Jacobean style he had employed at Dunlop House. Though well planned and richly detailed, his scheme lacked any tower or other dominant feature to mark it as a public building, and it reminded one critic of 'a splendid patrician mansion rather than of an edifice intended for any grand national purpose' (*Gent's Mag.* 1836 (i), 637). In 1813 he competed for the Wellington Monument in Dublin, submitting an effective design for an obelisk rising from a cluster of Doric columns (National Library of Ireland, MS. 7778), and in 1838 for Donaldson's Hospital at Edinburgh, winning the third premium. Apart from these three bids for national fame, Hamilton's practice was largely confined to Glasgow and the south-west of Scotland, where he deservedly enjoyed a high reputation, both as an architect and as an individual. In 1840 he was entertained at a public dinner at which he was presented with £500 in a gold box. He died on 5 December 1843 after an attack of paralysis.

Hamilton had three sons. William, the eldest, died young. Another, John had a stone and marble-cutter's business, known as 'David Hamilton and Sons', from which he retired in 1840. James (d. 1862) was in partnership with his father during the latter's last years. He was a talented designer, and his share in Hamilton's later works may have been important. After his father's death James carried on for a year or two in partnership with his brother-in-law James Smith (1808–63), but withdrew after financial troubles. Hamilton had several pupils and assistants, including John Baird (1816–93), Thomas Gildard (1822–95), J. T. Rochead (1814–78) and Charles Wilson (1810–63).

According to Gildard, Hamilton was 'a man of most impressive presence, frank and kindly in manner...and in social intercourse distinguished by much grace and courtesy'. He 'knew how to deport himself in the society of dukes and earls'. A marble bust by Patric Park is in the City Art Gallery at Kelvingrove. Another by William Mossman, 'considered a better likeness', belonged in the nineteenth century to Hamilton's family. An oil portrait by Sir Daniel Macnee was shown at the Old Glasgow Exhibition in 1894. Another by James Saxon is mentioned by Gildard.

Most of Hamilton's drawings were destroyed by the carelessness of an architect who got them by a misunderstanding and consigned them to a damp cellar, but three volumes of drawings, formerly the property of the Glasgow Philosophical Society, are now in Glasgow University Library. Drawings from his office were often elaborately washed in colour, and the inscriptions are always written in a distinctive back-sloping script done with a quill pen.

[Glasgow birth register in New Register House, Edinburgh; *A.P.S.D.*; *D.N.B.*; *Builder* i, 1843, 537–8; Thomas Gildard, 'An Old Glasgow Architect on some Older Ones', *Trans. of the Philosophical Soc. of Glasgow* xxvi, 1894–5, 97–106; Glasgow City Archives, Register of the Incorporation of Masons; Andor Gomme & David Walker, *The Architecture of Glasgow*, 1968, 271–2.]

PUBLIC BUILDINGS

GLASGOW, HUTCHESON'S HOSPITAL, INGRAM STREET, 1802–5 [L. Hill, *Hutcheson's Hospital*, 1855, 137].

GLASGOW, THE THEATRE ROYAL, QUEEN STREET, 1803–5, destroyed by fire 1829 [R. Chapman, *Picture of Glasgow*, 1812, 130] (elevation in J. Denholm, *History of Glasgow*, 3rd ed. 1804, 214).

GLASGOW, THE NELSON MONUMENT (an obelisk), GLASGOW GREEN, 1806 [R. Chapman, *Picture of Glasgow*, 1812, 132–4].

GLASGOW, THE TRADES HOUSE, GLASSFORD STREET, extensions at rear, 1838; rebuilt 1887 [*Glasgow Ancient and Modern or Glasghu Facies*, ed. J. F. S. Gordon, Glasgow 1872, ii, 992].

GLASGOW, rebuilt THE TOLBOOOTH, TRONGATE for James Cleland, 1813, Gothic; dem. *c.* 1921 [J. Cleland, *Annals of Glasgow* i, 1816, 75].

FALKIRK, STIRLINGSHIRE, THE TOWN STEEPLE, 1813–14 [R.C.A.M. *Stirlingshire*, 311 and pl. 145].

IRVINE, AYRSHIRE, THE ACADEMY, 1814–16 [A. F. McJannet, *The Royal Burgh of Irvine*, Glasgow 1938, 231].

PORT GLASGOW, RENFREWSHIRE, TOWN BUILDINGS, 1815–16 [W. F. Macarthur, *History of Port Glasgow*, Glasgow 1932, 179].

GLASGOW, THE ROYAL EXCHANGE, QUEEN STREET, 1827–9, incorporating the former Stirling Mansion [*A.P.S.D.*].

GLASGOW, entrance to THE NECROPOLIS, the 'BRIDGE OF SIGHS' over Molendinar Burn, 1833–9 [J. M. Leighton, *Strath-Clutha, or the Beauties of Clyde, c.* 1840, 91].

GLASGOW, THE NORMAL SCHOOL (now DUNDAS VALE SCHOOL), 6 NEW CITY ROAD, 1835–7 [*A.P.S.D.*; Gildard, 103].

GLASGOW, HUTCHESON'S BOYS' SCHOOL, 211 CROWN STREET, 1839–41, since altered [L. Hill, *Hutcheson's Hospital*, 1855, 215; Gildard].

GLASGOW, THE WESTERN CLUB, BUCHANAN STREET, 1840; St. Vincent Street frontage subsequently enlarged by Honeyman [Gildard, 99–102] (*Art Journal*, Oct. 1889).

GLASGOW, COMMERCIAL AND DOMESTIC ARCHITECTURE

CALTON GREEN, layout and elevations of new houses, 1812 [*Records of the Burgh of Glasgow*, ed. Renwick, x, 144].

THE CLELAND TESTIMONIAL BUILDING at corner of Buchanan and Sauchiehall Streets, 1835–6 [Gildard, 104].

THE CLYDESDALE BANK, QUEEN STREET, 1840, dem. [J. Pagan, *Sketch of the History of Glasgow*, 1847, 180–1; Gildard, 99].

THE WESTERN BANK, MILLER STREET, 1840;

enlarged 1845 by W. Burn and D. Bryce; dem. [J. Pagan, *op. cit.*, 178; Gildard, 99].

THE BRITISH LINEN COMPANY'S BANK, 110 QUEEN STREET, 1840–1; upper floors added *c.* 1905; dem. [J. Pagan, *op. cit.*, 184; Gildard, 103].

THE GLASGOW AND SHIP (later the UNION) BANK, INGRAM STREET, 1841; facade rebuilt 1876–9, when the columns were reused at the Royal Princess's Theatre [Gildard, 102–3].

CHURCHES

AYR, THE NEW CHURCH, 1807–12 [S.R.O., B 6/39/77, 9 and 11].

GLASGOW, GORBALS (now JOHN KNOX) CHURCH, CARLTON PLACE, 1810 [R. Chapman, *Picture of Glasgow*, 1812, 92–3]. Only the auditorium, west front and steeple were completed to Hamilton's design, and the spire was subsequently destroyed by lightning.

GLASGOW CATHEDRAL, alterations including restoration of west window and niche for organ in choir, 1812 [R. Chapman, *Picture of Glasgow*, 1812, 83; J. Pagan, *History of the Cathedral and See of Glasgow*, 2nd ed., Glasgow, 1856, 62].

ERSKINE, BISHOPTON, RENFREWSHIRE, 1813–14, [S.R.O., HR 135/2].

GLASGOW, ST. JOHN, BELL STREET, 1817–19, Gothic; dem. [R. Chapman, *Picture of Glasgow*, 1822, 129].

LARBERT, STIRLINGSHIRE, 1818–20, Gothic [*N.S.A.* viii, 357] (R.C.A.M. *Stirlingshire*, pl. 31*c*).

BOTHWELL, LANARKSHIRE, new church to west of ruined chancel of collegiate church, *c.* 1825–33, Gothic [S.R.O., RHP 5567–8, original drawings dated 1824].

GLASGOW, ST. ENOCH, rebuilt 1827–8 incorporating steeple of 1780; dem. [J. M. Leighton, *Select Views of Glasgow*, 1829, 198].

CAMPSIE HIGH CHURCH, LENNOXTOWN, STIRLINGSHIRE, 1827–8, Gothic [J. Cameron, *The Parish of Campsie*, Kirkintilloch 1892, 15, 33–4, 36] (R.C.A.M. *Stirlingshire* 160–1 and pl. 39*c*).

DUNOON, ARGYLLSHIRE, enlarged church of 1816 by J. Gillespie Graham, 1834 [*N.S.A.* vii, 610].

GLASGOW, ST. PAUL, JOHN STREET, 1835; dem. [*A.P.S.D.*; Gildard, 104].

ASCOG, ISLE OF BUTE, FREE CHURCH, *c.* 1843 [Gildard, 99–100].

COUNTRY HOUSES

MOORE PARK, GOVAN, LANARKSHIRE, for — Hagart, *c.* 1805 [J. Guthrie Smith, *Old Country Houses of the Glasgow Gentry*, 1870, lxxiv].

?AITKENHEAD HOUSE, KING'S PARK, GLASGOW for John Gordon, 1806 [*see below*].

KENMURE HOUSE, LANARKSHIRE, for Charles Stirling, *c.* 1806 [J. Guthrie Smith, *op. cit.*, lxiii].

AIRTH CASTLE, STIRLINGSHIRE, north-west front, castellated, for T. G. Stirling, 1807-9 [J. P. Neale, *Views of Seats*, 2nd ser., iii, 1826; R.C.A.M. *Stirlingshire*, 230–6].

AUCHINRAITH, BLANTYRE, LANARKSHIRE, for — Coulter, 1809 [J. Guthrie Smith, *Old Country Houses of the Glasgow Gentry*, 1870, iii].

CRAWFORD PRIORY, CULTS, FIFE, begun for Lady Mary Lindsay Crawford, 1809; completed by J. Gillespie Graham 1811–13, Gothic; dem. 1971 [inscription quoted by A. H. Millar, *Fife, Pictorial and Historical* i, 1895, 191–2].

RALSTON HOUSE, nr. PAISLEY, RENFREWSHIRE, for William Orr, 1810; enlarged 1864; dem. 1934 [Glasgow University, Hamilton Drawings vol. iii, Nos. 374–84] (A. H. Millar, *Castles and Mansions of Renfrewshire*, 1890).

GERMISTON HOUSE, nr. GLASGOW, enlarged for Lawrence Dinwiddie, 1810 [J. Guthrie Smith, *op. cit.*, xlix].

BARNTON CASTLE, MIDLOTHIAN, porch for William Ramsay Ramsay, *c.* 1810; dem. *c.* 1920 [Glasgow University, Hamilton Drawings, vol. i, no. 39] (J. Small, *Castles and Mansions of the Lothians* i, 1883).

?BROADMEADOWS HOUSE, HUTTON, BERWICKSHIRE, for John Swinton, *c.* 1810; dem. *c.* 1915. This was probably the house for which Hamilton's designs, dated 1811, remain among the Swinton family papers at Kimmerghame House, Berwicks.

KINCAID HOUSE, STIRLINGSHIRE, enlarged for — Kincaid, *c.* 1812, Gothic [Glasgow University, Hamilton Drawings, vol. i, no. 110] (R.C.A.M. *Stirlingshire*, pl. 202).

BARSKIMMING, MAUCHLINE, AYRSHIRE, alterations and additions for Sir William Miller, Bart., *c.* 1816 [*N.S.A.* v, 643].

CADDER HOUSE, LANARKSHIRE, drawing-room for Charles Stirling, *c.* 1817 [*N.S.A.* vi, 407; Sir William Fraser, *The Stirlings of Keir*, 1858, 78].

LADYLAND, KILBIRNIE, AYRSHIRE, for William Cochrane, 1817–21 [drawings preserved at Ladyland].

KEIR, DUNBLANE, PERTHSHIRE, lodge and gates for Archibald Stirling, 1820, resited 1969 [photos of signed drawings at N.M.R.S.]; enlarged house by addition of drawing-room and gallery, 1829–34 [Alistair Rowan in *C. Life*, 7 and 14 August 1975].

GARNKIRK HOUSE, CADDER, nr. GLASGOW, rebuilt *c.* 1820, retaining facade of *c.* 1790, for Mark Sprott [J. Guthrie Smith, *op. cit.*, xliv].

CASTLE TOWARD, nr. ROTHESAY, ARGYLLSHIRE, for Kirkman Finlay, 1820–1, castellated [*N.S.A.* vii, 610; J. P. Neale, *Views of Seats* vi, 1823].

LARBERT HOUSE, STIRLINGSHIRE, for Sir Gilbert Stirling, 1822–5 [J. C. Gibson, *Larbert and Dunipace Parishes*, Glasgow 1908, 10].

AITKENHEAD HOUSE, KING'S PARK, GLASGOW, added wings for John Gordon, 1823 [J. Guthrie Smith, *op. cit.*, i]. Gordon had built the house in 1806, very likely to Hamilton's designs.

HAMILTON PALACE, LANARKSHIRE, rebuilt north front for 10th Duke of Hamilton, 1822–5; dem. *c.* 1920 [*N.S.A.* vi, 271–2] (*C. Life*, 7, 14 and 21 June 1919).

CASTLE HOUSE (now Public Library), DUNOON, ARGYLLSHIRE, for James Ewing, 1823–4 [J. M. Leighton, *Strath-Clutha or the Beauties of Clyde*, *c.* 1830, 208].

SCOTSTOUN, nr. RENFREW, refronted for Miss Elizabeth Oswald, 1825 [J. Guthrie Smith, *op. cit.*, lxxxvii].

CALLENDAR HOUSE, FALKIRK, STIRLINGSHIRE, Library for William Forbes, 1827 [drawings at Callendar, photographs at N.M.R.S].

DUNLOP HOUSE, AYRSHIRE, for Sir James Dunlop, Bart., 1831–4; Scots Jacobean style [*A.P.S.D.*; Gildard, 104].

LENNOX CASTLE, LENNOXTOWN, STIRLINGSHIRE, for J. L. Kincaid Lennox, 1837–41, 'Norman' style [*N.S.A.* viii, 244; J. Cameron, *The Parish of Campsie*, Kirkintilloch 1892, 162–4].

MOSESFIELD HOUSE, SPRINGBURN PARK, GLASGOW, for — Duncan, 1838; Elizabethan style [inscription].

CAMISEKAN HOUSE, DUNBARTONSHIRE, additions for Colin Campbell, *c.* 1840 [Gildard, 99] (J. Irving, *The Book of Dumbartonshire* iii, 1879, pl. ix).

ST. FILLAN'S VILLA, LARGS, AYRSHIRE, for — Stewart (?), *c.* 1840 [Gildard, 99–100].

STONEBYRES HOUSE, LESMAHAGOW, LANARKSHIRE, additions for James Monteath (?), *c.* 1840, Jacobethan; dem. 1934 [Gildard, 99–100].

LONDON

HAMILTON HOUSE, 12 (later 15) PORTMAN SQUARE, alterations for the 10th Duke of Hamilton, *c.* 1820 [*A.P.S.D.*].

HAMILTON, GEORGE ERNEST, practised as an architect and surveyor in Staffordshire. In 1831 he was living at Stone, in 1844 at Wolverhampton. In 1836 he published a volume of *Designs for Rural Churches*, castigated in the *Gentleman's Magazine* as exhibiting 'all the peculiar marks of the genuine "carpenters' Gothic"'. His work as a church architect was indeed not such as to commend him to the ecclesiologists. It included EARL STERNDALE CHURCH, DERBYSHIRE, 1828–9, Gothic, gutted 1940 [I.C.B.S.]; WOORE CHURCH, SALOP., 1830–1, classical, chancel added

1887 [I.C.B.S.]; CHRIST CHURCH, STAFFORD, 1838–9, Romanesque, enlarged 1863 [I.C.B.S.]; PELSALL CHURCH, STAFFS., 1843–4, Gothic [I.C.B.S.]; the addition of aisles to ST. JOHN'S, BARLASTON, STAFFS., *c.* 1831, since rebuilt [I.C.B.S.], and alterations to CHRIST CHURCH, COSELEY, STAFFS., 1747–8 [*Gent's Mag.* 1848 (i), 76]. Hamilton also designed an obelisk at LILLESHALL, SALOP., to the memory of the 1st Duke of Sutherland, 1833 [*Gent's Mag.* 1833 (ii), 459], and SHARESHILL PARSONAGE, STAFFS., 1844–5 [records of Queen Anne's Bounty in Bodleian Library].

HAMILTON, JAMES, was in practice in Weymouth in the reign of George III. He designed the monument erected in that town in 1809 to commemorate the fiftieth year of the king's reign, which bears the signature 'J. Hamilton, Arch.' He also designed Nos. 1–4 GLOUCESTER ROW [*C. Life*, 18 Oct. 1946, correspondence], ST. MARY'S CHURCH, 1815–17 [J. Dugdale, *British Traveller* ii, 1819, 259; R.C.H.M. *Dorset* ii (2), 332 and pls. 177–8], and a monument in the Greek Revival style on the exterior of WYKE REGIS CHURCH, commemorating the wreck of the ship 'Alexander' in 1815 [*ibid.*, pl. 176]. A plan of Weymouth showing developments proposed by him is in the Bodleian Library, together with a design for an obelisk at MORETON, DORSET, to the memory of James Frampton, Esq. [Gough Maps 6, ff. 79, 105ᵛ]. This was erected in 1785–6 [*Gent's Mag.* 1787 (i), 49]. Unexecuted designs in the R.I.B.A. Drawings Collection for Langton House, Dorset, for J. J. Farquharson, dated 1810 and signed JH, are attributable to Hamilton.

HAMILTON, THOMAS (1784–1858), was one of the principal Edinburgh architects of the early nineteenth century, and a Greek Revivalist of distinction. His father, Thomas Hamilton, was a wright and builder in Edinburgh, but appears to have removed for some years to Glasgow, where Thomas was born on 11 January 1784. However the family was back in Edinburgh by 1794, when the father took up his freedom as a burgess, and in the following year Thomas entered the High School, where he received the usual classical education. After leaving school in 1801 he was apprenticed to his father and spent the next 16 years working for him and his uncle (also a builder). In 1813 he married, and in 1819 became a burgess of Edinburgh. The first evidence that he was proposing himself for architectural practice was the exhibition, in 1815, of an 'architectural design' at the short-lived Edinburgh Exhibition Society. Then in the following year he entered the public competition for the completion of Adam's unfinished University building. W. H. Playfair was the successful competitor, but Hamilton published a pamphlet describing his own designs (*Observations explanatory of the two designs for completing the College of Edinburgh*, 1816). He followed this with an anonymous article in the *Scots Magazine* for March 1817 proposing large-scale road-developments to open up the Old Town to the south and west. At the time this bore no fruit, but it appears to have been the first suggestion of the ideas which were eventually implemented by the Edinburgh Improvements Commissioners from 1827 onwards. The winning in 1818 of the competition for the Burns Monument at Alloway was an important success which must have done much to establish Hamilton's reputation as an architect. A free interpretation of the Choragic Monument of Lysicrates, the Monument is an elegant and effective essay in Grecian design by an architect whose only knowledge of ancient Greek architecture was derived from books. It was his 'acquaintance with all the most eminent authors on Greek, Roman and Gothic architecture' that Hamilton emphasized when in 1819 he applied unsuccessfully for the vacant post of Superintendent of the Edinburgh City Works. In 1825, however, the new High School gave him an opportunity to demonstrate his ability to design a major monumental building. Admirably composed, impeccably detailed, and magnificently situated, this Scottish version of the Theseion immediately took its place as one of the major monuments of the 'Modern Athens'. It was followed by the Hopetoun Rooms in Queen Street, now destroyed and inadequately recorded, but regarded by C. R. Cockerell as 'admirably disposed', and later (1844–6) by the elegant and refreshingly unconventional College of Physicians.

Although Hamilton's best-known works are Grecian, he also designed several Gothic churches and one Romanesque one (at Alyth). These are in no way outstanding, and his attempts at the domestic Jacobethan style so successfully exploited by his contemporary Burn are disappointing. At Ayr, however, he handled a traditional Scottish theme – the municipal steeple – with great success, and in the Dean Orphanage he experimented effectively with the drama of Vanbrughian towers. As a town-planner he was largely responsible for the ideas which (already adumbrated in his 1817 article, and described in detail in the *Report relative to the proposed approaches from the South and West to the Old Town of Edinburgh* which he wrote jointly with William Burn in 1824) were eventually set on foot by the Edinburgh Improvements Commission set up by Act of Parliament in 1827. Hamilton was immediately appointed architect to the Commissioners, and carried out the two major improvements for which they were responsible – the George IV and King's Bridges, together with their associated thoroughfares. Controversy and the financial difficulties which bedevilled the Commission led to his resignation in 1834.

Hamilton was a Fellow of the Institute of British Architects from 1836 to 1846. He was one of the original founders of the Royal Scottish Academy in 1826, and acted as its treasurer until 1829 and again from 1845 onwards. He took a prominent part in the projects for building galleries for the Academy on the Mound, writing in 1830 *A Report relative to Proposed Improvements on the Earthen Mound at Edinburgh* which was printed by the Improvements Commissioners. In 1850 he published *A Letter to Lord John Russell ... on the Present Crisis relative to the Fine Arts in Scotland*, setting out his 'views of what ought to be done for the promotion of art in this city, and for the architectural adornment of the Mound', and illustrated with lithographs. There is a drawing of his design at the R.S.A. and there are water-colour sketches of his proposals in the Print Room of the National Gallery of Scotland. In 1855 he won a gold medal at the Paris International Exhibition, exhibiting drawings of the proposed galleries on the Mound and of the illfated 'John Knox's Church' (Flemish Gothic) which the City had commissioned him to build on Castle Hill in 1829. The foundation stone was laid in 1829, but the financial difficulties of the Town Council led it to abandon the scheme in 1831, and the site remained vacant until 1841, when Tolbooth St. John's Church was built on it to the designs of J. Gillespie Graham.

Hamilton died at 9 Howe Street, Edinburgh on 24 February 1858, after a few days' illness. He suffered from deafness in his last years and his will indicates some confusion in his financial affairs. He was buried in the Calton Cemetery near the Martyrs' Memoral, in the lair of his uncle John Hamilton (d. 1812). A bronze plaque was set up in 1829. Apart from his son Peter (d. 1861), his only recorded pupil was John Henderson (1804–62). There is a portrait by William Nicholson at the Royal Scottish Academy, and a caricature in Crombie's *Modern Athenians*. A few of Hamilton's drawings are in the Print Room of the Scottish National Gallery. A list of other surviving drawings will be found in the thesis by Ian Fisher cited below.

[*A.P.S.D.*; *D.N.B.*; *Builder* xvi, 1858, 146, xvii, 1859, 243; *Gent's Mag.* 1858 (i), 451; F. C. Mears, 'Measured Drawings of Lawnmarket and Castlehill made by Thomas Hamilton, Architect', *Book of the Old Edinburgh Club* xii, 1923; T. H. Hughes in *Royal Incorporation of the Architects of Scotland Quarterly*, no. 20, 1926; A. J. Youngson, *The Making of Classical Edinburgh*, 1966; Ian Fisher, thesis entitled 'Thomas Hamilton of Edinburgh', copy at N.M.R.S.]

PUBLIC BUILDINGS

EDINBURGH, NORWICH INSURANCE COMPANY'S OFFICE, 32 PRINCE'S STREET, 1820; dem. c. 1890 [drawings in Edinburgh Dean of Guild records].

KINGHORN, FIFE, THE TOWN HOUSE, 1822, Gothic [A. Reid, *Kinghorn*, Kirkcaldy 1906, 19].

EDINBURGH, THE ROYAL HIGH SCHOOL, REGENT ROAD, 1825–9 [Edinburgh Town Council Minutes; working drawings in City Architect's Office; T. L. Donaldson, *Handbook of Specifications*, 1860, 260].

EDINBURGH, THE HOPETOUN (ASSEMBLY) ROOMS, 72 QUEEN STREET, c. 1827; dem. 1967 [C. R. Cockerell's diary, 17 March 1828, with sketch-plan; Edinburgh Dean of Guild records 22 July 1831].

EDINBURGH, KING'S BRIDGE, carrying Johnston Terrace over King's Stables Road, 1827–31 [Edinburgh City Archives, minutes of the Improvements Commissioners; A. J. Youngson, *The Making of Classical Edinburgh*, 1966, 180–2 and pl. 51].

EDINBURGH, GEORGE IV BRIDGE and associated town planning, 1827–34 [Edinburgh City Archives, minutes of the Improvements Commissioners; A. J. Youngson, *The Making of Classical Edinburgh*, 1966, 180–7].

AYR, THE MUNICIPAL BUILDINGS AND STEEPLE, 1828–30; enlarged 1880–1 [Ayr Town Council Minutes in S.R.O., B6/18/26–7; *N.S.A.* v, 23; preliminary design illustrated in *R.I.A.S. Quarterly*, no. 20, 1926].

KINGHORN, FIFE, THE SCHOOL, 1829 [*Edinburgh Evening Courant*, 6 Aug. 1829].

AYR, THE WALLACE TOWER, 1831–4, Gothic [Ayr Town Council Minutes in S.R.O., B 6/18/27; contract B 6/39/101/15; drawings in Ayr Burgh Architect's Office and S.R.O., RHP 2561].

EDINBURGH, THE DEAN ORPHANAGE (now Education Centre), BELFORD ROAD, 1833–6 [*A.P.S.D.*; J. Grant, *Old and New Edinburgh*, n.d. iii, 67].

EDINBURGH, EARL GREY PAVILION, a temporary pavilion in High School Playground for dinner in honour of Earl Grey, 1834 [MS. description by Hamilton in R.I.B.A. Library, MS. SP 10/17, printed in *R.I.B.A. Trans.* 1835–6, vol. i with engraving; J. C. Loudon, *Architectural Magazine* iii, 1836, 388; *Edinburgh Evening Courant* 1–21 Sept. 1834, *passim*].

EDINBURGH, ROYAL COLLEGE OF PHYSICIANS, QUEEN STREET, 1844–6; hall enlarged by D. Bryce, 1864 [A. J. Youngson, *The Making of Classical Edinburgh*, 1966, 279–80].

CHURCHES

ALYTH, PERTHSHIRE, 1837–9, Romanesque [*N.S.A.* x, 1119; J. Meikle, *History of Alyth Parish Church*, 1933, 268–78; account in S.R.O., GD 16/46/91].

EDINBURGH, ST. JOHN'S ('DR. GUTHRIE'S') FREE CHURCH (now ST. COLUMBA'S FREE CHURCH), JOHNSTON TERRACE, 1843–5, Gothic [*A.P.S.D.*; D. K. & C. J. Guthrie, *Memoir of Thomas Guthrie*, 1874, 512].

EDINBURGH, NEW NORTH (FREE) CHURCH, FORREST ROAD (north end of George IV Bridge), 1846, Gothic [Josiah Livingston, *History of the New North Road Church, Edinburgh*, 1893, 37].

SOUTH LEITH, ST. MARY'S CHURCH, rebuilt 1848, Gothic [*A.P.S.D.*; J. Grant, *Old and New Edinburgh*, n.d. iii, 219–20, with illustrations; J. Campbell Irons, *Leith and its Antiquities* i, 1897, 82].

DUNBAR, FREE CHURCH, 1850 [James Miller, *History of Dunbar*, 1859, 210].

KENNOWAY, FIFE, 1850, Romanesque [A. H. Millar, *Fife, Pictorial and Historical*, 1891, ii, 62; S.R.O., HR 293/3].

DOMESTIC ARCHITECTURE

EDINBURGH, NOS. 1–12 CASTLE TERRACE, in collaboration with Robert Wright, 1826 [S.R.O., Edinburgh Sasines].

LATHALLAN (LAURENCE PARK) HOUSE, STIRLINGSHIRE, 1826, Elizabethan style [exhib. at Royal Scottish Academy, 1828].

COMPSTONE HOUSE, TWYNHOLM, KIRKCUDBRIGHTSHIRE, for Adam Maitland of Dundrennan, c. 1827–9; enlarged by W. H. Playfair 1845, and again 1896; Tudor Gothic [exhib. at Royal Scottish Academy, 1828].

KIRKHILL HOUSE, nr. GOREBRIDGE, MIDLOTHIAN, for John Tod, c. 1828 [exhib. at Royal Scottish Academy, 1828].

attributed: ARTHUR LODGE (originally SALISBURY COTTAGE), 60 DALKEITH ROAD, EDINBURGH, for W. Cunningham, jeweller, c. 1827–30 [stylistic attribution].

EDINBURGH, NOS. 5, 6, 7, 10–11, CLAREMONT PARK, LEITH, 1827–c. 1830 [advt. in *Edinburgh Evening Courant*, 2 June 1827].

COLDSTREAM, BERWICKSHIRE, THE MANSE, 1830–2 [*N.S.A.* ii, 211].

EDINBURGH, NO. 93 GEORGE STREET, 1833; altered 1900 [Edinburgh Dean of Guild records, 6 Aug. 1833, *ex inf.* Mr. David Walker].

EDINBURGH, NO. 7 NORTH ST. ANDREW STREET, conversion of house into shop, 1839; dem. [S.R.O., RHP 1388].

DUNBEATH CASTLE, CAITHNESS, addition for Mrs. Sinclair of Freswick, 1858; addition dem. [photographs of drawings signed T. H. at N.M.R.S.].

MONUMENTS

ALLOWAY, AYRSHIRE, THE BURNS MONUMENT, 1820–3 [J. C. Ewing, 'History of the Monument' (based on the Trustees' minutes) in the *Burns Monument Catalogue*, Ayr 1966; drawings in collection of the Royal Incorporation of Architects of Scotland].

GLASGOW NECROPOLIS, JOHN KNOX MONUMENT, 1825 [G. Blair, *Sketches of Glasgow Necropolis*, Glasgow 1857, 171].

GOGAR CHURCHYARD, MIDLOTHIAN, monument to Sir Robert & Lady Liston, 1829 [National Library of Scotland, MS. 5683, f. 140].

PENICUIK, MIDLOTHIAN, VALLEYFIELD MILLS, monument to FRENCH PRISONERS, 1830 [*N.S.A.* i, 34].

EDINBURGH, BURNS MONUMENT, REGENT ROAD, 1830–2 [*A.P.S.D.*, *s.v.* 'Edinburgh'].

EDINBURGH, CALTON OLD BURIAL GROUND, monument (obelisk) to POLITICAL MARTYRS of 1794, 1844 [*A.P.S.D.*].

HAMILTON, WILLIAM, practised in Glasgow in the reign of George III. In 1781, when he was employed to alter and enlarge the former Assembly Rooms at the Town Hall as the TONTINE HOTEL, he was described as 'an architect from London' [J. Cleland, *Annals of Glasgow* i, 1816, 74; *The Regality Club* ii, 1893, 75–6]. For the Burgh of Glasgow he designed in 1785 a weigh-house and in 1786 the layout and elevations of ST. ANDREW'S SQUARE [*Extracts from the Records of the Burgh of Glasgow*, ed. Renwick, viii, 1913, 175, 212, 214, 215–17]. It is possible that he was the Hamilton (father of William Hamilton, R.A.) who was employed by the Adam brothers as a clerk of works at Kenwood and elsewhere [A. T. Bolton, *The Architecture of R. & J. Adam* i, 1922, 316].

HAMPDEN, ROBERT, *see* TREVOR

HANNAFORD, JOSEPH, was an architect and builder at Christchurch, Hampshire. Together with John Kent of Southampton he designed and built ST. JAMES'S CHURCH, POOLE, DORSET, in 1819–21 [R.C.H.M. *Dorset* ii (2), 192 and pl. 118]. He also designed BRANSGORE CHURCH, HANTS., in 1822 [Port, 132–3]. Both are characteristic Gothic churches of their period.

HANSOM, JOSEPH ALOYSIUS (1803–82), *see* WELCH, EDWARD

HARCOURT, CHARLES, *see* MASTERS

HARDING, JAMES, practised in Farnham, Surrey, where several members of his family

were in the building trade [Nigel Temple, *Farnham Buildings and People*, Farnham 1963, 183–4]. It was his father, James Harding senior, a mason by trade, who in 1812 made the plans for rebuilding the nave of FROYLE CHURCH, HANTS. [MS. 'Orders of Vestry for rebuilding etc. 1812']. James Harding, junior, rebuilt the nave of BRAMSHOTT CHURCH, HANTS., in 1836 (again rebuilt 1872) [I.C.B.S.]; and designed WRECCLESHAM CHURCH, SURREY, 1840 (rebuilt 1877) [I.C.B.S.] and CROOKHAM CHURCH, HANTS., 1840–1 (chancel added 1876–7) [tender advertised in *Reading Mercury*, 28 Jan. 1840].

HARDWICK, PHILIP (1792–1870), younger son of Thomas Hardwick (d. 1829), was educated at Dr. Barrow's School in Soho Square. In 1808 he entered the Royal Academy Schools, and at the same time became a pupil in his father's office. He exhibited at the Academy from 1807 to 1844. In 1815 he went to Paris to see the Louvre, then filled with the pictures collected by Napoleon from all parts of Europe, and in 1818–19 he spent about twelve months in Italy. On his return he entered into partnership with his father, to whose practice he eventually succeeded. He became architect to the Bridewell and Bethlehem Hospitals in 1816, to the St. Katherine's Dock Company in 1825, to St. Bartholomew's Hospital in succession to his father in 1826, to the Goldsmiths' Company in 1828, to the Westminster Bridge Estates in 1829, and to the London and Birmingham Railway Company in 1839. He was also architect to the Duke of Wellington and surveyor to the Portman estate in London. He held the surveyorship of the Bridewell and Bethlehem Hospitals for twenty years, and resigned that of St. Bartholomew's to his son in 1856.

Hardwick was elected F.S.A. in 1824, F.R.S. in 1831, F.G.S. in 1837, A.R.A. in 1840, and R.A. in 1841. From 1850 to 1861 he was treasurer of the Royal Academy. He was elected a member of the Institution of Civil Engineers in 1824, and was an original member of the Institute of British Architects in 1834. He was vice-president in 1839 and 1841, and received the Royal Gold Medal in 1854. He was awarded a Gold Medal at the Paris Exhibition of 1855, at which he exhibited drawings of Goldsmiths' Hall and Lincoln's Inn. He was an efficient man of business, and was much employed as a referee, notably in connection with the Royal Exchange Competition of 1840. He was one of the examiners of candidates for district surveyorships under the Metropolitan Building Act of 1843. As an architect he is best known for his monumental Doric gateway to Euston Station – a magnificent tribute of transport to early nineteenth-century taste that was wantonly destroyed in 1962 – but at Goldsmiths'

Hall he produced a noble facade in the English baroque tradition, and at Lincoln's Inn and elsewhere he used Tudor Gothic in an exceptionally scholarly and convincing manner.

Hardwick's health broke down in 1843, when he was little more than 50 years old, and he was obliged to confine himself to such practice as could be conducted from his own room, though he continued, in spite of serious physical disabilities, to serve on the Royal Academy committee of which he was a member. From this time onwards his practice was virtually in the hands of his son, Philip Charles Hardwick (1822–92), and in 1861 he gave up all work and retired from public life. He died at his son's home, Westcombe Lodge, Wimbledon Common, on 28 December 1870, and was buried at Kensal Green. He married in 1819 a daughter of John Shaw, the architect, by whom he had two sons, Thomas and Philip Charles. T. H. Wyatt was his pupil. Several of his drawings and sketch-books are in the R.I.B.A. Collection. [*D.N.B.*; obituaries in *Builder* xxix, 1871, 24 and *Minutes of Proceedings of the Institution of Civil Engineers* xxxiii, 1871–2 (i), 215.]

STRETTON CHURCH, CHESHIRE, 1826–7, Gothic; rebuilt 1870 [Port, 140; drawings in R.I.B.A. Collection].

LONDON, ST. KATHERINE'S DOCKS, WAREHOUSES and OFFICES, 1827–9 [*Companion to the Almanac*, 1829, 219–21; exhib. at R.A. 1825 and 1830].

LAMBETH, THE HOUSE OF OCCUPATIONS (a school), 1829–30; dem. *c.* 1923 [Bethlehem Hospital archives, *ex inf.* Miss P. Allderidge].

BABRAHAM HOUSE, CAMBS., for H. J. Adeane, 1829–32, Jacobethan; enlarged 1864 [exhib. at R.A. 1840].

LONDON, GOLDSMITHS' HALL, FOSTER LANE, 1829–35 [exhib. at R.A. 1831, 1839, 1842].

KNELLER HALL, WHITTON, MIDDLESEX, addition of wings for Charles Calvert, *c.* 1830; remodelled by George Mair as the Kneller Hall Training School, 1849–50 [*Builder* viii, 1850, 67–8].

ENFORD CHURCH, WILTSHIRE, restoration 1830–1, after damage by lightning in 1817 [I.C.B.S.].

STOCKPORT, CHESHIRE, THE FREE GRAMMAR SCHOOL, for the Goldsmiths' Company, 1830–32, Tudor Gothic; dem. 1923 [*Companion to the Almanac*, 1833, 219].

WAINFLEET ST. MARY SCHOOL, LINCS., for the Governors of Bethlehem Hospital, 1830–2 [Bethlehem Hospital archives, *ex inf.* Miss P. Allderidge].

HEREFORD, THE BISHOP'S PALACE, alterations 1833 [*D.N.B.*; exhib. at R.A. 1840; drawing in Bodleian Library, MS. Top. gen. c. 28, f. 21].

LONDON, THE CITY CLUB–HOUSE, NO. 19 OLD BROAD STREET, 1833–4 [original drawing in Sir Albert Richardson's Collection; engraved plan and elevation by Baynes & Harris].

CHADACRE HALL, SHIMPLING, SUFFOLK, for Thomas Hallifax, *c.* 1834 [letter from Benjamin De Carle, mason of Bury St. Edmunds, to Hardwick, soliciting employment at Chadacre 6 Aug. 1834, in De Carle's letter-book, W. Suffolk Record Office, Acc. 468].

DOVER, WATERLOO CRESCENT, 1834–8 [J. C. Loudon, *Architectural Mag.* i, 1834, 209–10].

LONDON, EUSTON STATION: THE EUSTON and VICTORIA HOTELS, DORIC GATEWAY and LODGES, 1836–40; dem. 1962. A building linking the two hotels was erected 1880–1. The Great Hall of the station was by P. C. Hardwick, 1846–9 [*Survey of London* xxi, 107–14; *Companion to the Almanac*, 1839, 233–5].

LONDON, GLOBE INSURANCE COMPANY'S OFFICE, CORNHILL, 1837–8 [*Companion to the Almanac*, 1838, 233].

LONDON, FREEMASONS' HALL, GREAT QUEEN STREET, alterations 1838; remodelled by F. P. Cockerell 1867 [*Civil Engineer & Architect's Jnl.* i, 1837–8, 204].

EVERTON CHURCH, BEDS., repairs 1838 [I.C.B.S.].

BIRMINGHAM, CURZON STREET STATION, 1838–42 [*Companion to the Almanac*, 1838, 236–7].

WESTWOOD PARK, WORCS., addition of kitchens and other alterations in Elizabethan style for J. S. Russell Pakington, *c.* 1840 [*V.C.H. Worcs.* iii, 234] (*C. Life*, 14, 21 July 1928).

RHYMNEY, MONMOUTHSHIRE, ST. DAVID'S CHURCH, 1840–3 [I.C.B.S.] (J. B. Hilling, *Cardiff and the Valleys*, 1973, 115).

LONDON, LINCOLN'S INN, completion of south wing of Sir Robert Taylor's STONE BUILDINGS, 1842–5; designed new HALL, LIBRARY, etc. in conjunction with his son P. C. Hardwick, 1843–5, Tudor Gothic [published *Drawings of the Hall and Library, Lincoln's Inn*, 1842; *Companion to the Almanac*, 1844, 235–8, 1845, 241, 1846, 238–40; *Builder* iii, 1845, 521–2, 526].

LONDON, BELGRAVE SQUARE, house in south-east angle for the 3rd Earl of Sefton, 1842–5; portico since removed [*Companion to the Almanac*, 1842, 205].

SUSSEX, a 'mansion to be built near Maresfield', exhib. at R.A. 1842. For possible identifications see M. A. Lower, *Compendious History of Sussex* ii, 1870, 42.

HALL, nr. BARNSTAPLE, DEVON, for Robert Chichester, 1844–7, completed by P. C. Hardwick and R. D. Gould of Barnstaple, 1847–9, Tudor Gothic [exhib. at R.A. 1844; inscription in Great Hall].

LONDON, KENSINGTON PALACE GARDENS, house (No. 10) for S. H. Sutherland, 1846–7 [*Survey of London* xxxvii, 165].

LIVERPOOL, THE DOCK TRAFFIC OFFICE, ALBERT DOCK, 1846–7 [Quentin Hughes, *Seaport*, 1964, 30].

PENGE, KENT, KING WILLIAM NAVAL ASYLUM,

1847–9, Tudor Gothic [*Illustrated London News*, 8 December 1849].

PEPER HAROW, SURREY, entrance to kitchen garden for the 5th Viscount Midleton, 1847 [W. Keane, *The Beauties of Surrey*, 1849, 128].

LONDON, ST. ANNE'S CHURCH, LIMEHOUSE, restoration after fire, in collaboration with John Morris, 1850–1 [*Builder* x, 1852, 39].

LONDON, ST. BARTHOLOMEW'S HOSPITAL, additions and repairs to Gibbs's building, 1851 [*Minutes of . . . the Institution of Civil Engineers*, loc. cit.; *D.N.B.*; cf. *Archaeological Jnl.* viii, 1851, 103].

WANDSWORTH, SURREY, THE ROYAL FREEMASONS' SCHOOL FOR GIRLS, 1851, Tudor Gothic [*Builder* ix, 1851, 722–3; exhib. at R.A. 1852 by P. C. Hardwick, who was no doubt the effective architect].

BIRMINGHAM, ST. MARTIN'S CHURCH, restoration of tower and spire, 1854–5, by 'Messrs. Hardwick' [*A.P.S.D.*, *s.v.* 'Birmingham']. J. T. Bunce, *History of Old St. Martin's Birmingham*, 1875, 22, makes it clear that P. C. Hardwick was the effective architect.

LONDON, BRANCH BANK OF ENGLAND, No. 7 BURLINGTON GARDENS, alterations including addition of Doric porch, 1855 [*Survey of London* xxxii, 465].

HARDWICK, THOMAS (1725–1798), lived at New Brentford, Middlesex, where he carried on the business of a mason, and subsequently that of an architect. In 1764 the nave of ST. LAURENCE'S CHURCH, BRENTFORD, was rebuilt to his designs, and in 1781–2 he rebuilt HANWELL CHURCH, MIDDLESEX, rebuilt by Scott and Moffatt in 1841. His will was proved on 24 Sept. 1798 [P.C.C. 600 WALPOLE]. He was the father of Thomas Hardwick (1752–1829) [*A.P.S.D.*].

HARDWICK, THOMAS (1752–1829), son of the above, became in 1767 a pupil of Sir William Chambers. He was admitted to the Royal Academy Schools in 1769, winning the first Silver Medal for architecture the same year. He began to exhibit at the Academy in 1772, and continued to do so almost every year until 1805. In 1776 he set out for Italy, via Paris, where he joined forces with the artist Thomas Jones. Together they reached Rome in December. In the course of the next three years Hardwick made measured drawings of many antique and some more recent buildings in Rome and its vicinity, and also visited Naples, Paestum, Pompeii and Venice. In Rome he worked for a time in collaboration with the young John Soane, but their friendship did not last. Hardwick returned to England in May 1779, bringing with him a number of sketchbooks filled with neo-classical examples. Most of these are now in the R.I.B.A. Drawings Collec-

tion, but three belong to Mr. J. G. Dunbar and one is in the Fowler Collection at Baltimore, U.S.A.[1]

Soon after his return Hardwick won the competition for the best design for a female prison offered by the Commissioners for Penitentiary Houses established under the Penitentiary Act of 1779. This building was never erected, but Hardwick was subsequently employed as the architect of the important Millbank Penitentiary begun in 1812 on marshy ground on the site of the present Tate Gallery. After building the boundary wall and gateway he resigned the post in 1813 on the ground that the remuneration of $2\frac{1}{2}$ per cent offered by the commissioners was inadequate, and because 'the management of this extensive concern took up a larger portion of his time and attention than he could conveniently spare from his other business'. His place was taken by John Harvey, and ultimately by Robert Smirke, who found that, despite elaborate precautions, the foundations laid under Hardwick's direction had not been adequate.

In 1809 Hardwick became surveyor to St. Bartholomew's Hospital, and in 1810 he obtained a post in the Office of Works as Clerk of the Works at Hampton Court, a position which he retained until his death. From 1815 onwards his responsibilities also included Kew Palace and its gardens. He was elected F.S.A. in 1781 and was an original member of the Architects' Club founded in 1791, but failed to secure election as A.R.A. although he was a candidate on several occasions. He died on 16 January 1829, at his house in Berners Street, and was buried in the family vault in the churchyard at Brentford, where there is a tablet to his memory. A pencil portrait by George Dance is reproduced in the latter's *Collection of Portraits sketched from the Life* (1808–14). The original drawing is in the Victoria and Albert Museum. His pupils included Samuel Angell, John Foulston, John MacDonnell, John Williams, and his younger son Philip Hardwick

[1] See *R.I.B.A. Drawings Catalogue: G–H*, 89–95; J. G. Dunbar, 'An English Architect at Naples', *Burlington Mag.* cx, 1968, 265–6 and J. Harris, *Catalogue of British Drawings for Architecture etc. in American Collections*, 110. Hardwick wrote a paper on the Colosseum for the Society of Antiquaries (MS. in Soane Museum, AL, Pc47 and printed version in *Archaeologia* vii, 1786, 369–73). A large cork model of the building that he had made in Rome was presented to the British Museum by Philip Hardwick in 1851 but can no longer be found and is presumed to have been destroyed. A volume of drawings by Hardwick entitled 'Sketches of Sundry Buildings already executed and Original Designs on various subjects, commencing about the year 1773' belongs to Mr. A. P. Lyons, who kindly allowed the writer to examine it. Mr. Lyons also has the diaries kept by Hardwick on visits to Flanders in 1816 and Paris in 1822.

(*q.v.*), who eventually succeeded to his practice. His elder son John (1791–1875) was a barrister and stipendiary magistrate. J. M. W. Turner was in his office for a time, but abandoned architecture for painting on his advice. He wrote the memoir of Sir William Chambers which was first published in Gwilt's edition of Chambers's *Civil Architecture* (1825).

Hardwick was, as James Wyatt expressed it, 'a regular bred, classical architect' [Farington's *Diary*, 20 Jan. 1799]. He was an accomplished draughtsman and a competent designer in a conservative neo-classical manner which he inherited from Chambers. But, unlike Chambers, he never became a fashionable designer of houses for the wealthy, and he made a living chiefly as a surveyor and as a designer of churches and minor public buildings. His failure to secure election to the Royal Academy is no doubt indicative of his relatively modest standing as an architectural artist. His best surviving works are St. Marylebone Church in London, Wanstead Church in Essex and St. John's Church at Workington in Cumberland, all of which have handsome porticos.

[*A.P.S.D.*; *D.N.B.*; *Gent's Mag.* 1829 (i), 92; 'Memoirs of Thomas Jones', *Walpole Soc.* xxxii, 1946–8, 40–45, 58–65, 68, 79, 89; P. de la Ruffinière du Prey, 'Soane and Hardwick in Rome: a neo-classical partnership', *Architectural History* xv, 1972].

?STOVER LODGE, DEVONSHIRE, for James Templer, 1776. The volume of drawings by Hardwick belonging to Mr. A. P. Lyons contains plans and elevations for Stover Lodge which correspond closely to the house as built. The rain-water heads are dated 1776. It would be surprising if Hardwick had designed a substantial country house so early in his career, and before the visit to Italy which completed his architectural education. There must therefore be some hesitation in taking the evidence of the drawings at their face-value.

RUPERRA CASTLE, GLAMORGAN, rebuilt interior for Charles Morgan 1784–9, after a fire; gutted *c.* 1945 [National Library of Wales, Tredegar MS. 150].

WANSTEAD CHURCH, ESSEX, 1787–90 [*V.C.H. Essex* vi, 333; exhib. at R.A. 1791] (plans and elevations in Stieglitz, *Plans et Desseins*, Paris, 1801, pls. 53–4).

LONDON, ST. PAUL'S CHURCH, COVENT GARDEN, extensive repairs, including recasing of exterior in Portland stone, 1788–9. The church was gutted by fire in 1795 and restored by Hardwick 1796–8, adhering closely to Inigo Jones's original design. Hardwick's interior was altered by Butterfield in 1871–2 and his ceiling was replaced in 1887–8. [*Survey of London*

xxxvi, chap. 5: pl. 17 shows the interior as designed by Hardwick].

LONDON, ST. BARTHOLOMEW THE GREAT, SMITHFIELD, examined and reported on the state of the church in 1790–1, and by judicious repairs saved it from demolition. Hardwick carried out further repairs in 1808 [Vestry Minutes in Guildhall Library, MS. 3990/4, pp. 8–21, 225]. He presented measured drawings of the church to the Society of Antiquaries (*Red Portfolio London*, A–B, pp. 12–16).

LONDON, ST. JAMES'S CHAPEL, HAMPSTEAD ROAD, 1791–2; dem. *c.* 1965 [minutes of the building committee, with plans, elevations and sections, in Westminster Public Library among the records of St. James's parish, Piccadilly, for whom the chapel was built] (measured drawings in *Arch. Rev.* xli, 1917, 62–4).

DORCHESTER, DORSET, THE SHIRE HALL, 1796–7 [Hutchins, *History of Dorset* ii, 1863, 372].

GALWAY, IRELAND, THE COUNTY GAOL, 1802–3, executed under the superintendence of R. Morrison [James Hardiman, *History of Galway*, 1820, 302; cf. the 'design for a gaol to be built in Ireland' exhibited by Hardwick at the R.A. in 1803].

LONDON, ST. JAMES'S CHURCH, PICCADILLY, repairs and alterations, 1803–4 [*Survey of London* xxix, 37, 41].

HEREFORD, THE NELSON COLUMN, CASTLE GREEN, 1806–9, executed by Thomas Wood of Hereford, who modified Hardwick's design [*The Hereford Guide* 2nd ed. 1808, 43].

LONDON, ST. PANCRAS WORKHOUSE, KING'S ROAD, CAMDEN TOWN, 1809 [*A.P.S.D.*].

SYON HOUSE, MIDDLESEX, THE EVIDENCE ROOM (a detached building) for the 2nd Duke of Northumberland, 1809 [Alnwick Castle, MS. 94, f. 49].

OXFORD, ST. JOHN'S COLLEGE, stables afterwards forming east side of North Quadrangle, 1811; dem. 1959. The stables were built 'according to a plan alter'd from Mr. Hardwick's and deliver'd by Mr. Hudson', who erected them under Hardwick's supervision [College Register viii, pp. 188–90].

LONDON, THE MILLBANK PENITENTIARY. The parts erected under Hardwick's direction in 1812–13 were the boundary wall, the lodge and gateway, the main drain, and the foundations of the first Pentagon and of the chapel. The foundations subsequently proved inadequate, and were rebuilt by R. Smirke. The prison was demolished in 1902 [G. Holford, *An Account of the Penitentiary at Millbank*, 1828, xxv–xxix].

LONDON, ST. MARYLEBONE NEW CHURCH, 1813–17. This church was begun as a chapel of ease, but completed as a parish church. To give it more consequence, the original Ionic order was altered to Corinthian when the church was half built, and the portico was enlarged from four to six columns. The apse was added in 1883–4 [Britton & Pugin, *The Public Buildings of London* i, 1825, 167–79].

LONDON, ST. JAMES'S VESTRY HALL, PICCADILLY, 1814; dem. 1861 [*Survey of London* xxix, 55 and xxx, pl. 18a].

LONDON, ST. JOHN'S CHAPEL, ST. JOHN'S WOOD, 1814 [J. Elmes, *Metropolitan Improvements*, 1829, 165 and plate].

LONDON, ST. BARTHOLOMEW'S HOSPITAL, a 'general repair', 1814–20 [*Builder* iii, 1845, 78].

BANGOR CATHEDRAL, CAERNARVONSHIRE, survey of fabric, c. 1820 [M. L. Clarke, 'Bangor Cathedral 1700–1828', *Caernarvonshire Hist. Soc's Trans.* xiii, 1952, 33].

LONDON, ST. JAMES'S WORKHOUSE, POLAND STREET, 1821; dem. [*Survey of London* xxxi, 212].

KEW, SURREY, ST. ANNE'S CHURCH, extended east end, 1822 [Surrey Archdeaconry Records].

WORKINGTON, CUMBERLAND, ST. JOHN'S CHURCH, 1822–3; tower added 1847 [Port, 132].

LONDON, CHRIST CHURCH, COSWAY STREET, LISSON GROVE, MARYLEBONE, 1822–4 [Port, 136]. Philip Hardwick evidently completed this church, as he exhibited a view of the interior at the R.A. in 1826.

LONDON, ST. BARNABAS CHURCH, KING SQUARE, FINSBURY, 1822–6; damaged 1941, restored 1954 [Port, 134].

LONDON, ST. BARTHOLOMEW THE LESS, SMITHFIELD, rebuilt Dance's octagonal nave in stone with iron roof, 1823–5 [G. Godwin, *The Churches of London* ii, 1839].

BOLTON, LANCS., HOLY TRINITY CHURCH, 1823–5, Gothic [Port, 132].

LONDON, ARCHBISHOP TENISON'S CHAPEL (ST. THOMAS), REGENT STREET, redecorated interior 1824 [*Survey of London* xxxi, 183–4].

FARNWORTH (KEARSLEY), LANCS., ST. JOHN'S CHURCH, 1824–5, Gothic [Port, 132].

KEW PALACE, SURREY, lodges for King George IV, 1824–7; dem. [*History of the King's Works* vi, 359].

HARGRAVE, JOSEPH (c. 1754–1802), was an architect and surveyor of Hull, where he died on 15 October 1802, aged 48 [*Gent's Mag.* 1802, 977]. He was the son of Jeremiah Hargrave, a carver who was responsible for the finely-executed rococo relief in the pediment of Trinity House, Hull, in 1753 [G. Hadley, *History of Hull*, 1788, 821]. Joseph Hargrave made the drawings of buildings which illustrate Hadley's *History of Hull* (1788). The engraving of THE CHARTERHOUSE HOSPITAL, built in 1780, is the only one which he signs as 'Architect', and it may therefore be presumed that he designed it. He also designed THE SUBSCRIPTION LIBRARY in PARLIAMENT STREET,

1801 (dem.) [J. N. Crosse, *Account of ... Subscription Library*, 1810, 5, 14; *V.C.H. Yorks. East Riding* i, 425].

HARLOW, JOHN, designed a new altar-piece for the church of ST. MARY ABBOTS, KENSINGTON, in 1685, and in the following year supervised the enlargement of the north aisle. The church was rebuilt in 1696 and again in 1869 [J. D. G. Scott, *St. Mary Abbots, Kensington*, 1942].

HARPER, JAMES BENJAMIN (–1873), was a builder and surveyor at Henley-in-Arden in Warwickshire. He rebuilt the nave of CLAVERDON CHURCH, WARWICKS., in 1828–30 [I.C.B.S., letter in Nuthurst file], designed a small Gothic church at NUTHURST, WARWICKS., 1835, rebuilt 1879 [I.C.B.S.], and another at SALTER STREET, near TANWORTH-IN-ARDEN, WARWICKS., 1840 [I.C.B.S.], to which a tower was added in 1860. He later moved to Great Malvern, where he combined the functions of a surveyor, agent and auctioneer. He died at Great Malvern on 16 April 1873 [Principal Probate Registry, Calendar of Probates].

HARPER, JOHN (1809–1842), was born at Dunkenhalgh Hall, near Blackburn, Lancashire, on 11 November 1809. He was apparently the son of John Harper, the estate agent there. He became a pupil of Benjamin and Philip Wyatt, whom he assisted in preparing the designs for Apsley House, York House and the Duke of York's Column. He began to practise on his own in York, and was employed by the Duke of Devonshire at Bolton Abbey, by Lord Londesborough, and others. He competed for the Houses of Parliament in 1835, paying particular attention to the acoustics and ventilation of the two chambers. Most of his recorded works are in the Gothic style, and one or two of his churches (e.g. All Saints, Elton, and St. Marie's, Bury) show an ability to get away from the standard formulae of early-nineteenth-century church design.

Harper died of malaria while on a visit to Italy in 1842. He was a friend of David Roberts, Clarkson Stanfield and William Etty, and his own 'sketches of scenery, antiquity and architecture' were highly commended by the last-named artist. Many of them were, in 1890, in the possession of his brother, Edward Harper of Brighton, who also had a portrait of him by Etty. [S. Redgrave, *Dictionary of Artists of the English School*, 1878, 198; *D.N.B.*; Chetham Soc. vol. 85, 1926, 73.]

YORK, Gothic piazza to Theatre Royal, 1834–5; dismantled 1879 and re-erected at No. 73 Fulford Road [R.C.H.M. *York* iv, 53].

SHIBDEN HALL, nr. HALIFAX, YORKS. (W.R.), addition of tower and offices for Miss Anne Lister, *c.* 1835 [*Castles and Country Houses in Yorkshire*, Bradford 1885].

EVERINGHAM PARK, YORKS. (E.R.), CATHOLIC CHAPEL for William Constable-Maxwell, 1836–9, based on designs supplied by Agostino Giorgioli of Rome [Arthur Oswald in *C. Life*, 22 Feb. 1968].

YORK, ST. PETER'S SCHOOL, CLIFTON, 1838, Gothic [*D.N.B.*] (R.C.H.M. *York* iv, 53).

CLAYTON-LE-MOORS CHURCH, LANCS., 1838–40, Gothic; chancel rebuilt 1882 [R. Trappes-Lomax, *A History of Clayton-le-Moors*, Chetham Soc. vol. 85, 1926, 146].

CRAKEHALL CHURCH, YORKS. (N.R.), 1840, Gothic [I.C.B.S.].

BLACKTOFT CHURCH, YORKS. (E.R.), 1841, Gothic [I.C.B.S.].

BURY, LANCS., ST. MARIE'S CHURCH (R.C.), 1841, Gothic [*Companion to the Almanac*, 1841, 234–6].

ELTON, nr. BURY, LANCS., ALL SAINTS CHURCH, 1841–3, Romanesque [B. T. Barton, *History of Bury*, 1874, 201].

HARRIS, DANIEL (–*c.* 1835), was an architect and builder of Oxford who also acted as Keeper of the County Gaol. This was built to the design of William Blackburn between 1785 and 1805. It was begun by Edward Edge, a mason from Gloucestershire, but was completed by Harris, who contrived that the greater part of the work should be done by the convicts themselves. He subsequently (1805–11) built the COUNTY BRIDEWELL at ABINGDON to the designs of Jeffry Wyatt(ville) [*Report from the Committee of Aldermen appointed to visit several Gaols in England*, 1816, 25; D. Linstrum, *Sir Jeffry Wyatville*, 1972, 258]. He was also employed by the Thames Commissioners to supervise the construction of locks at Oseney (1789–90), Godstow (1790) and Pinkhill (1791), and was in charge of the reconstruction of Sandford Weir in 1795. Oseney lock was built by the Castle felons, and a contemporary pamphlet on the Thames Navigation observes ironically that 'the Thames must flourish while Mr. Harris, the *Oxford Gaoler*, is employed as an extra official Engineer' [J. Nichols, *Literary Anecdotes of the Eighteenth Century* iii, 698; F. S. Thacker, *The Thames Highway: General History*, 1914, 151; *The Thames Highway, A History of the Locks and Weirs*, 1920, 91, 114, 135]. A mill at Eynsham that Harris had built is mentioned by J. C. Loudon in his booklet on *Paper Roofs used at Tew Lodge*, Oxon. (1811).

For some years Harris was in partnership with John Plowman (*q.v.*). The association probably dated from 1812, when Harris advertised in the *Oxford Herald* that 'his arrangements with his late foreman J. Plowman now allow him to attend to [his clients'] favours in the architectural way'. His ability as a draughtsman is shown by the fact that he made the drawings for the University Almanacs annually from 1780 to 1792, and in 1799 exhibited at the Royal Academy an elegant view of BRAZIERS, nr. IPSDEN, OXON., a Gothic house which he had built for I. G. Manley. His drawings (1797) for a small house at HEADBOURNE WORTHY, HANTS., are in the Public Record Office (C 133/33). In about 1796 he was employed to examine the spire of MERTON CHURCH, OXON., and advised that it should be taken down, which was accordingly done [Bodleian, Oxford Archdeaconry Papers, Oxon. b. 25, f. 238]. He made estimates for repairing or rebuilding parsonages at BAMPTON (1799), SWYNCOMBE (1803) and STOKE TALMAGE (1820) in Oxon. [Bodleian, Oxford Diocesan Faculty Registers 1737–1804, 190, 227; 1804–27, 225] and at FLORE in Northants. (1816) [Peterborough Diocesan Records]. In Oxford he designed a Gothic palisade in front of WADHAM COLLEGE in 1806, replaced 1822 [T. G. Jackson, *Wadham College, Oxford*, 1893, 218] and in 1812 repaired the Warden's Lodgings at MERTON COLLEGE [*Illustrations of Oxford*, J. Ryman, 1839].

HARRIS, THOMAS (*c.* 1688–1763), of Cublington in Bucks., was descended from a family of joiners. Both his father Thomas Harris (1654–1724), his grandfather William Harris (1616–84), and his elder brothers George (b. 1684) and John Harris (1686–1730) followed the same trade. In 1663 the churchwardens of Soulbury, Bucks., paid £2 to 'Goodman Harris of Cublington for y^c Communion table', and his timber-framed house, with his initials and the date 1661 over the mantelpiece, still stands at the west end of Cublington village. George Harris is described as 'architect' in a Quarter Sessions record of 1713, and Thomas also had some architectural ability. In 1720 he was one of the two 'surveyors' who submitted 'plans, ground plots and models' for rebuilding the PRISON and COUNTY HALL at AYLESBURY, BUCKS. The other was a 'Mr. Brandon'. Both designs were submitted to Sir John Vanbrugh, who chose the one made by Harris and charged a fee of 20 guineas for his advice. Work began in 1722–4, but was then suspended owing to lack of funds, and was not completed until 1737–40. Harris received £21 for his 'draughts and model', and £100 'for upwards of two years surveyorship'. He also performed some of the carpentry work of the building, and was presumably responsible for the handsome joinery of the Court Room. The main elevation to Market Square is Palladian in character, but is handled in a slightly clumsy manner which shows that Harris was not a complete master of the style. The Prison was demolished in 1847, but the Court Room survives [G. R. Crouch, 'The Building of the County Hall, Aylesbury', *Records of Bucks*. xii].

According to local tradition Harris designed or built the LOVETT SCHOOL at SOULBURY, BUCKS. (*c.* 1724), but the building is so conservative in style that the attribution would be more credible if applied to his father. When Dr. Pococke visited EYTHROPE HOUSE, BUCKS., in 1751, he saw 'a handsome new front before the court, of good architecture, designed by Harris' for Sir William Stanhope [*Dr. Pococke's Travels in England*, ed. Cartwright, i, 161]. This appears to have been the screen-wall on either side of the west front of the chapel, which stood in the middle of a courtyard between the house and the stables. It was demolished in 1810–11 [H. M. Colvin, 'Eythrope House', *Records of Bucks*. xvii, 1964].

In 1738 the mansion of the Fortescue family at Salden, Bucks., was sold for demolition. Browne Willis records that one half of the house was bought by Thomas Harris for £400 or £500 and pulled down by him [Bodleian Library, MS. Willis 101, f. 179].

Harris died at Cublington in June 1763, and is described in the register of burials as 'Mr. Thomas Harris, Joiner and house carpenter'. His annotated copies of Vitruvius, Palladio and Gibbs remained in the possession of his descendants until the present century [information from Miss Dorothy M. Harris of Wing].

HARRIS, WILLIAM (*c.* 1796–1823), was the son of William Harris, a London merchant. He became a pupil of Sir Jeffry Wyatville, was admitted to the Royal Academy Schools in 1819, and won the Silver Medal the same year. He exhibited designs at the Academy from 1815 to 1818. In 1821 he joined Samuel Angell in Paris, and with him travelled through the south of France to Rome, Naples and Sicily, where he assisted in the discovery of the sculptures at Selinus. He died of malaria in Palermo on 16 July 1823. A monument in the English cemetery at Rome commemorates his 'ardor in the study of his profession' and laments the loss of 'an artist of talent and taste'. His sister married Thomas Evans (*q.v.*), who with Angell was responsible for the publication of the sculptures in 1826 [*A.P.S.D.*].

HARRIS, WILLIAM, was one of the District Surveyors for the City of Bristol from 1840 until his resignation in 1847 [A. B. Beaven, *Bristol Lists*, 1899, 249]. He designed two Greek Revival Market Houses in Cornwall, one at HELSTON, 1837–8 [*The Parochial History of Cornwall* ii, 1868, 177], the other at BODMIN, 1839 [J. Maclean, *Deanery of Trigg Minor* i, 1873, 111]. The latter is based on a building on the island of Delos illustrated by Woods in the *Antiquities of Athens* (cf. J. M. Crook, *The Greek Revival*, 1972, pl. 191), and shows that Harris was a

serious student of Greek architecture. In 1838 he rebuilt the INDEPENDENT CHAPEL at CLIFTON, nr. BRISTOL [*Civil Engineer and Architect's Jnl.* i, 1837–8, 235]. In 1838–41 he rebuilt the chancel and transepts of CHEPSTOW CHURCH, MONMOUTHSHIRE, in Norman style [*Civil Engineer and Architect's Jnl.* i, 1837–8, 235]. His work was partly rebuilt by Seddon in 1890.

HARRIS, WILLIAM (–1863), practised at 55 Park Street, Grosvenor Square, from about 1830 until his death on 1 April 1863. In 1840 he exhibited a design for 'A tomb in memory of the late H. Salisbury, Esq.' at the Royal Academy. His designs for a watermill at Feltham, Middlesex, dated 18 March 1839, are in the Public Record Office (LRRO 1/867).

HARRISON, HENRY (*c.* 1785–*c.* 1865), was the son of John Harrison, a London surveyor and builder. He stated in 1828 that he had been 'brought up as a builder and architect', but that 'within about the last five years' he had practised solely as an architect. His brother George was, however, a builder, and had built Richmond Terrace, Whitehall, as a speculation from his designs.[1] Henry appears subsequently to have resumed business as a builder, for he was described as such when he went bankrupt in 1840. In 1856, when he was among the applicants for the post of Architect to the Metropolitan Board of Works, he furnished a long list of buildings that he had built or altered. It shows that he had a considerable practice as a designer of minor country houses and parsonages, especially in Sussex and Cornwall, and that he built or altered many town houses in the West End of London. Richmond Terrace, Bignor Park and the Lying-in-Hospital at Lambeth are typical of the somewhat tame Greek Revival style which he favoured in the 1820s, but he also designed some poorly-detailed Tudor or Jacobean houses (e.g. Swyncombe House and Hadleigh Deanery), and his Guards' Club in Pall Mall of 1848–9 had a façade of fashionably Italian character.

In the 1830s Harrison was living at 31 Park Street, Grosvenor Square, in a house of his own building, but at the time of his bankruptcy he was in Bruton Street, and later he moved to Bedford Square. He was still alive in 1861 at the age of 75, but his name disappears from the London Directories in 1864. His specification for concrete for use in foundations has been preserved (Museum of the History of Science, Oxford, MS. Gunther 9, f. 95^v).

[*Report from the Select Committee on the Office*

---

[1] George Harrison did, however, submit a design for the Houses of Parliament in his own name. He was Clerk of Works to the East India Company from *c.* 1837 onwards.

of Works and Public Buildings, 1828, 86–91; G.L.C. Record Office, M.B.W. 213 (Harrison's letter of 1 Feb. 1856);[1] will of John Harrison in Middlesex Land Registry 1828/1/794; P.R.O. Census Returns of 1851 and 1861; *Survey of London* xxxvii, 103–4].

COUNTRY HOUSES, PARSONAGES, ETC.

ADDINGTON PARK, SURREY, added Chapel, Library and other rooms for William Howley, Archbishop of Canterbury, 1829–30 [M.B.W.; E. W. Brayley, *Topographical History of Surrey* 1841, iv, 28].

AUBERIES, BULMER, ESSEX, alterations for Col. Augustus Meyrick, *c.* 1835 [M.B.W.].

AUDLEY END, ESSEX, restored house and designed 'Ice-house Lodge' for the 3rd Lord Braybrooke, *c.* 1825–7 [M.B.W.; Lord Braybrooke, *History of Audley End and Saffron Walden*, 1836, 132, 137].

BARMING RECTORY, KENT, alterations for the Rev. C. H. Barham [M.B.W.].

BARON HILL, ANGLESEY, extensive works for Sir Richard Williams-Bulkeley, Bart., *c.* 1836 [M.B.W.]. This house was 'totally destroyed by fire' on 5 May 1836, when 'nearly completed' [*Gent's Mag.* 1836 (i), 654]. It was subsequently rebuilt in the form illustrated by T. Nicholas, *Annals of the County Families of Wales* i, 1875, 6, and is now a ruin.

BEXHILL RECTORY, SUSSEX, for the Rev. Mr. Baker [M.B.W.].

BIGNOR PARK, SUSSEX, for John Hawkins, 1826–8 [M.B.W.; Dallaway, *Rape of Arundel*, ed. Cartwright, ii (1), 1832, 249; Gordon Nares in *C. Life*, 26 April, 3 May 1956].

BLETCHLEY RECTORY, BUCKS., 1834, Gothic [Lincs. Record Office, MGA 186].

BRAXTED PARK, ESSEX, work for Peter Du Cane (d. 1841) [M.B.W.].

CARCLEW, CORNWALL, alterations for Sir Charles Lemon, Bart., *c.* 1830; gutted 1934 [M.B.W.; memoirs of Mrs. Loveday Sarah Gregor in Cornwall County Record Office].

EAST WOODHAY RECTORY, HANTS., for the Rev. T. D. Hodgson, 1828–9 [M.B.W.; Winchester Diocesan Records].

ENYS, CORNWALL, for J. S. Enys, 1833 [M.B.W.; signed drawings at Enys].

FAIRLIGHT RECTORY, SUSSEX, for the Rev. Mr. Pearce, 1839, Tudor [M.B.W.].

FELTWELL RECTORY, NORFOLK, for the Rev. E. P. Sparke [M.B.W.].

GOODRICH COURT, HEREFS., alterations or repairs for Col. Augustus Meyrick, *c.* 1850; dem. 1950 [M.B.W.].

GREAT HAMPDEN RECTORY, BUCKS., addition of new drawing and dining rooms, 1820 [Lincs. Record Office, MGA 107].

[1] Cited below as M.B.W.

HADLEIGH DEANERY (RECTORY), SUFFOLK, for the Rev. H. J. Rose, 1831, Tudor [M.B.W.].

HAM MANOR, ANGMERING, SUSSEX, for W. Gratwicke, *c.* 1835 [M.B.W.].

HELIGAN, CORNWALL, alterations for J. H. Tremayne, *c.* 1830 [M.B.W.; memoirs of Mrs. Loveday Sarah Gregor in Cornwall County Record Office].

?HESSENFORD CHURCH, CORNWALL, 1832–3. In June 1830 the incumbent wrote to the I.C.B.S. to say that Lord St. Germans had employed Harrison 'to inspect the plan [for rebuilding the church submitted by some local architect] and perhaps to furnish a new one'. The outcome is not known. The church was again rebuilt in 1871.

KINGSEY VICARAGE, BUCKS., remodelled 1834, Gothic [Lincs. Record Office, MGA 191].

LULLINGSTONE CASTLE, KENT, alterations or repairs for Sir Percival Hart-Dyke, probably *c.* 1850 [M.B.W.] (*C. Life*, 1 Nov. 1913).

MARLBOROUGH, WILTS., ST. PETER'S RECTORY, 1832–3 [records of Queen Anne's Bounty in Bodleian Library].

NORMAN COURT, HANTS., enlarged for C. B. Wall, 1818–20; further alterations, including addition of Ionic pilasters, *c.* 1910 [M.B.W.; G. F. Prosser, *Select Illustrations of Hampshire*, 1833].

OAKHAM VICARAGE, RUTLAND, for the Rev. Heneage Finch [M.B.W.].

PENDARVES, CORNWALL, alterations for E. W. W. Pendarves, 1832 [M.B.W.; memoirs of Mrs. Loveday Sarah Gregor in Cornwall County Record Office; drawing by Harrison for a lantern for Pendarves dated 1832 among drawings at Enys].

PORT ELIOT, CORNWALL, Gothic entrance hall and porch for the 2nd Earl of St. Germans, 1829 [M.B.W.; C. Hussey in *C. Life*, 22–29 Oct. 1948].

PRIDEAUX, nr. LUXULYAN, CORNWALL, alterations for Sir Colman Rashleigh (d. 1847) [M.B.W.].

PUTNEY, SURREY, house in Putney Park Lane for Seymour Larpent [M.B.W.].

SAFFRON WALDEN, ESSEX, ALMSHOUSES, 1829–33, Gothic [Lord Braybrooke, *History of Audley End and Saffron Walden*, 1836, 236; drawings, specification etc., in papers of Nash, Son & Rowley in Cambridge Record Office].

STEEPLE ASHTON VICARAGE, WILTS., altered or rebuilt 1829 [Salisbury Diocesan Records].

SWYNCOMBE HOUSE, OXON., for the Rev. C. E. R. Keene, *c.* 1830–40, Jacobean [M.B.W.].

TREWARTHENICK, CORNWALL, alterations and additions for C. W. F. Gregor, 1831; wings added by Harrison dem. 1925 [M.B.W.; J. Britton & E. W. Brayley, *Cornwall Illustrated*, 1831, 44; Gregor papers in Cornwall County Record Office].

WARBOYS RECTORY, HUNTS., enlarged or rebuilt

for the Rev. William Finch, 1829 [M.B.W.; Lincs. Record Office, MGA 152].[1]

WARNHAM COURT, SUSSEX, for Henry Tredcroft,[2] 1829, Elizabethan [M.B.W.] (L. Jewitt & S. C. Hall, *The Stately Homes of England*, 2nd ser., n.d., 280–9).

WINWICK RECTORY, LANCS., alterations for the Rev. J. J. Hornby [M.B.W.].

WISBECH RECTORY, CAMBS., for the Rev. Mr. Fardell [M.B.W.].

LONDON HOUSES AND OTHER BUILDINGS

CAMBRIDGE SQUARE, No. 7 for Charles Harrison [M.B.W.].

THE GENERAL LYING-IN HOSPITAL, YORK ROAD, LAMBETH, 1828 [M.B.W.; *Survey of London* xxxiii (1), 42].

GROSVENOR SQUARE, No. 42 (formerly 37) for the 2nd Lord Wenlock, 1853; dem. [M.B.W.].

THE GUARDS' CLUB-HOUSE, ST. JAMES'S STREET, 1828; dem. [M.B.W.; *Select Committee*, 86, 90].

THE GUARDS' CLUB-HOUSE, NO. 70 PALL MALL, 1848–9; dem. 1922 [M.B.W.; *Survey of London* xxix, 380] (plan and elevation in *A New View of London*, J. Weale, 1853, i, 300–1).

LOWER GROSVENOR STREET, No. 20 [M.B.W.].

OXFORD SQUARE, No. 22, for Frederick Harrison [M.B.W.].

PARK STREET, GROSVENOR SQUARE, Nos. 31 and 32 (No. 31 was occupied by Harrison himself from 1828 to 1839) [M.B.W.].

PICCADILLY, No. 82, BATH HOUSE, rebuilt for Alexander Baring, cr. Lord Ashburton, 1821; interior remodelled *c.* 1900; dem. 1963 [M.B.W.; *Select Committee*, 86].

RICHMOND TERRACE, WHITEHALL, 1822–5 [M.B.W.; *Select Committee*, 86].

UPPER BROOK STREET, No. 11, for Lt. Col. Sir Thomas Brotherton [M.B.W.].

UPPER GROSVENOR STREET, Nos. 10 and 11 and No. 62 PARK STREET [M.B.W.].

In addition, Harrison stated in 1856 that he had 'repaired or altered' the following houses: No. 61 GREEN STREET, GROSVENOR SQUARE, for the 3rd Viscount Hampden (d. 1824); Sir Jacob Astley's house in GROSVENOR STREET; No. 3 GROSVENOR SQUARE, for James Balfour, dem.; No. 27 BERKELEY SQUARE for Col. Meyrick; No. 51 GROSVENOR STREET for the 10th Earl of Kinnoull; No. 58 GREEN STREET for the 10th Earl of Kinnoull;

No. 48 BERKELEY SQUARE, 'late in the occupation of Henry Baring'; No. 14 CARLTON HOUSE TERRACE for General Robert Balfour. *c.* 1831; Lady Glynn's house in Berkeley Square; No. 46 UPPER GROSVENOR STREET for the Earl of Carysfort, dem.; THE ALFRED CLUB, No. 23 ALBEMARLE STREET; Col. Holder's house in CHARLES STREET, BERKELEY SQUARE; the Ladies Cornwallis's house in CHARLES STREET, BERKELEY SQUARE; No. 10 CHARLES STREET, BERKELEY SQUARE, for the 2nd Earl of Chatham (d. 1835), and subsequently for Lady De Dunstanville; NO. 21 ST. JAMES'S SQUARE for the Bishop of Winchester, probably *c.* 1830, dem. 1934; and NO. 23 ST. JAMES'S SQUARE for James Angerstein.

HARRISON, J—, practised from addresses in Clerkenwell and Pentonville in the 1830s and 1840s. His exhibits at the Royal Academy show that he designed the following buildings: HALSON WOOD VILLA, SOUTH DEVON, for Richard Peck, 1831; THE HOLT, SOUTH DEVON, for William Jackson, 1833; DODBROOKE RECTORY, nr. KINGSBRIDGE, SOUTH DEVON, for the Rev. C. G. Owen, 1834 (exhibited 1837); a villa at TENBY, PEMBROKESHIRE, for Capt. Wells, 1839; and KENSAL HOUSE, HARROW ROAD, N.W. LONDON, for Alfred Haines, 1846.

HARRISON, JAMES, formerly a builder, practised as an architect in Sheffield in the second quarter of the nineteenth century. In 1828 he entered into a short-lived partnership with Samuel Worth (*q.v.*), in conjunction with whom he designed in 1829 the MEDICAL SOCIETY's building or SURGEONS' HALL in SURREY STREET. In 1836 he designed the CIRCUS AND THEATRE. This was a building 'adapted both for dramatic performances and equestrian exercises'. It had 'a stately portico of the Ionic order'. [R. E. Leader, *Surveyors and Architects of the Past in Sheffield*, 1903; W. White, *Directory of the West Riding of Yorkshire* i, 1837, 85; S. Lewis, *Topographical Dictionary of England* iv, 1848, 62].

HARRISON, JOHN, was the nephew of the better-known Thomas Harrison (*q.v.*), whom he assisted in his practice in Chester. The relationship is made clear by correspondence between the two Chester architects and a Scottish baronet, Sir William Forbes, who in 1801 invited them to submit a design (not executed) for a house to be built at Colinton near Edinburgh [Fettercairn papers, National Library of Scotland, box 27, and N.M.R.S.].

How far John Harrison practised independently is not clear, but in 1806 he was paid £20 'for planning and superintending the building of' SHERDLEY HALL, nr. ST. HELENS, LANCS. (dem.) for Michael Hughes [J. R. Harris, 'The Hughes Papers', *Trans. Hist. Soc. of Lancs. and*

---

[1] Harrison was probably responsible for rebuilding the chancel of WARBOYS CHURCH in yellow brick in 1832, for in the same year he was employed to design new pews and galleries in the nave [I.C.B.S.].

[2] In his letter to the M.B.W. Harrison names his client at Warnham Court as Edward Tredcroft, who succeeded his father Henry in 1844. But it was Henry who built the house in 1829.

Cheshire, ciii, 1951, 115], and he evidently designed THE JEWISH SYNAGOGUE, SEEL STREET, LIVERPOOL, 1807, dem. 1874, for a view of it in Thomas Troughton's *History of Liverpool*, 1810, is dedicated to 'Mr. John Harrison Architect'. Sherdley Hall and the synagogue were both competently designed classical buildings.

HARRISON, JOSHUA (*c.* 1772–1837), of Leicester, was a carpenter and builder who also acted as an architect and surveyor. He may have been a son of William Harrison (*q.v.*). In Leicester he built a new House of Correction for St. Mary's Parish in 1815 and was responsible for alterations to the ASSEMBLY ROOMS in 1817–18 [J. D. Bennett, *Leicestershire Architects 1700–1850*, 1966]. He designed a small Gothic church at ISLEY WALTON, LEICS., in 1819 [I.C.B.S.] and rebuilt HATHERN RECTORY, LEICS., in 1819–20 [drawings, etc. in Leicestershire Record Office]. He died on 24 April 1837, aged 65.

HARRISON, ROBERT, a mason, was concerned in the rebuilding of PENRITH CHURCH, CUMBERLAND, in 1721–3. He was paid £3 10s. 'for Drawing Plans for the Church', and, together with Joseph Simpson of Hawkside in the parish of Dalston, received £330 for carrying out the masonry work. It is not, however, certain that he designed the building, as William Monkhouse (the clerk who kept the building accounts) was also paid 'for drawing the plans for the church' [Cumbria Record Office, PR/31/23].

HARRISON, THOMAS (1744–1829), the son of a joiner, was born at Richmond in Yorkshire, where he was baptised on 7 August 1744. He showed an early talent for arithmetic, mechanics and drawing, and attracted the attention of Sir Lawrence Dundas of Aske, by whose liberality he was sent to Italy in 1769 in company with his friend George Cuitt, the landscape-painter. While in Rome, he submitted to Pope Clement XIV a design for converting the Cortile del Belvedere in the Vatican into a museum which was favourably received, though not in the end adopted. In 1773 he competed for the annual architectural prize offered by the Academy of St. Luke, which carried with it eligibility for membership of the Academy. The subject (chosen by James Byres) was a town gateway decorated with columns and pilasters. The judges did not favour Harrison's design, but he appealed to the Pope against their verdict, claiming that he had been unfairly passed over, and was eventually admitted to the Academy by an exceptional exercise of the Pope's personal prerogative as patron of the institution. Harrison was subsequently commissioned to make a design for an alteration to the sacristy of St. Peter's, but the work was not carried out, probably owing to Pope Clement's death in 1774.[1]

Harrison returned to England in 1776, and in 1777 exhibited at the Royal Academy two drawings for remodelling the Piazza del Popolo in Rome. These showed that he was a master of the elegant neo-classical style fashionable on the Continent in the 1770s, though not yet aspiring to the simplified compositions which were to be characteristic of his later work as a Greek Revivalist. In 1779–80 he was back in Richmond, but in the 1780s he was living in Lancaster, and in 1793 he moved to Chester. At Lancaster he had in 1783 obtained an important commission for a bridge over the river Lune. The first stone was laid by George III, and the work was completed in 1788. This bridge was remarkable as the first large bridge to be built in England with a level road surface from bank to bank. Its architectural treatment was highly effective, and Harrison's elliptical arches separated by pairs of Doric columns provided a formula which was afterwards employed by Rennie at Kelso Bridge, Waterloo Bridge and London Bridge. Further bridges followed at Derby and Kendal, and at Warrington and Cranage Harrison experimented successfully with a form of laminated timber construction. In 1776–8 he made designs for a triumphal bridge over the Thames on the site of the future Waterloo Bridge, but when the idea of a bridge in that position finally came to fruition in 1809 he was not employed, though his criticisms of the design made by the engineer Dodd are said to have played their part in persuading the commissioners to engage John Rennie instead. Harrison was also unsuccessful in putting forward a plan for a quay along the Thames from Westminster to the City which would have anticipated the Victorian Embankment. His biggest work as a bridge-builder was the Grosvenor Bridge at Chester, begun in 1827, and not completed until after his death. At the time of its construction its 200 foot span constituted the largest stone arch in the world. In view of Harrison's age and ill-health, its execution was entrusted to his pupil William Cole and the civil engineer Jesse Hartley, who (apart from raising the abutments one foot in height) adhered faithfully to Harrison's design.

Although Harrison designed several country houses, of which the most notable was Lord Elgin's Broomhall, it was as a civic architect that he made his reputation. The public buildings with which he adorned Manchester, Liverpool and Chester demonstrate his ability as a designer of monumental neo-classical architecture. His Chester Castle complex forms the finest group of Greek Revival buildings in Britain – the neo-

---

[1] The Pope also gave Harrison two medals which are now in the Chester City Record Office.

classical counterpart to Greenwich Hospital—and the Hill and Anglesey Columns, the Memorial Arch at Holyhead and the Jubilee Tower on Moel Fammau were among the most notable public monuments of their age. Though Harrison was best known as a classical architect, handling the Greek Doric and Ionic Orders with unfailing assurance and sensitivity, he also used Gothic on occasion, notably at Lancaster Castle and in the highly effective steeple which he added to St. Nicholas Church in Liverpool. In either style his bold sense of mass and his capacity to design in three dimensions set his work apart from the stereotyped Gothic boxes and Grecian porticos characteristic of so much early nineteenth-century British architecture. Although his practice was limited geographically to the north-western counties, Harrison enjoyed a high reputation among contemporary architects. 'Harrison', wrote C. R. Cockerell in 1823, 'has a spark divine'. 'Almost, if not quite, the first architectural genius in the kingdom' was the verdict of his first biographer, Canon Blomfield, in 1863. Only his isolation in Chester and a natural diffidence prevented him from becoming a national figure like Soane or Smirke. The diffidence is well attested: 'a plain man in person and manners, with an embarrassed delivery in conversation; but very clear and ready in explaining with his pencil' was how Joseph Farington remembered him in 1795. 'A man of great modesty and diffidence—shy, reserved and abrupt in his manner', wrote Canon Blomfield, 'He ... followed the profession from a mere love of the art, and not with a view to pecuniary emoluments ... His personal qualities in some measure hindered his popularity with the world, and prevented him from becoming the public man which his genius and talents certainly entitled him to be.'

Harrison held only one public office, the county surveyorship of Cheshire, to which he was appointed in 1815 at £100 per annum. He died at his house (St. Martin's Lodge) facing the Castle on 29 March 1829 aged 84, and was buried in St. Bridget's churchyard. He left a widow and two daughters. A portrait in oil by H. Wyatt is in the Town Hall at Chester, and another by the same artist is in the Crown Courts in Chester Castle. A portrait in chalk by John Downman, dated 1815, is in the Grosvenor Museum. An engraving of a portrait by A. R. Burt was published in 1824. There is also a lithograph by M. Gauci of one of Wyatt's portraits. The R.I.B.A. has a silhouette profile (reproduced in C. Life, 15 April 1971, fig. 1). A marble bust by George Caldwell, exhibited at the Liverpool Academy in 1824, is now in the Lyceum there. Harrison's principal pupils were William Cole, junior, Thomas Penson, John Hargrave of Cork and his nephew John Harrison (q.v.). James Harrison

396

(1814–1866), who was in practice in Chester in the mid nineteenth century, was apparently not a relation. The most important collections of Harrison's drawings are in the Chester City Archives and the Cheshire Museum Head-quarters at Northwich. The former collection was presented to the Chester Archaeological Society by Miss Harrison in 1849. Other drawings are in the Grosvenor Museum at Chester, the County Record Office, the R.I.B.A. Drawings Collection and the Mellon Collection.

[*A.P.S.D.*; *D.N.B.*; obituary in *Gent's Mag.* 1829 (i), 468–70; Michaud, *Biographie Universelle* xviii, 1857, 496–7; memoir by Canon Blomfield in *Builder* xxi, 1863, 203–5; J. Hemingway, *History of Chester* 1831, i, 364–5, ii, 362–4; *The Cheshire Sheaf*, 3rd ser., i, 1896, 74 (for Harrison's will); *The Farington Diary* ed. J. Greig, i, 126, ii, 167, v, 101, vi, 227; Luigi Pirotta, 'Thomas Harrison architetto inglese accademico di San Luca per sovrano motu proprio', *Strenna dei Romanisti* xxi, 1960, 257–63; J. Mordaunt Crook, 'The Architecture of Thomas Harrison', *C. Life*, 15 & 22 April, 6 May 1971; information from Mr. F. R. Altmann, Dr. J. Mordaunt Crook and Mr. Peter Howell].

PUBLIC BUILDINGS, ETC.

LANCASTER, cupola of TOWN HALL, 1782 [K. H. Docton in *Lancashire and Cheshire Historian*, August 1965, 146–7].

LANCASTER, SKERTON BRIDGE (R. Lune), 1783–8 [*A.P.S.D.*].

LANCASTER, ST. JOHN'S CHAPEL, tower and spire, 1784 [*A.P.S.D.*].

LANCASTER CASTLE, reconstruction, including new SHIRE HALL, GRAND JURY ROOM, GAOL, etc., 1788–99, Gothic; completed by J. M. Gandy 1802–23 [*A.P.S.D.*; J. M. Crook in *C. Life*, 15 April 1971, with illustrations].

CHESTER CASTLE, THE COUNTY COURTS, PRISON, ARMOURY, BARRACKS, EXCHEQUER and GATEWAY, 1788–1822. The Shire Hall was built 1791–1801, the flanking wings in 1804–10 and the gateway or propylaeum in 1811–13 [*A.P.S.D.*; J. M. Crook in *C. Life*, 15 April 1971, with illustrations].

DERBY, ST. MARY'S BRIDGE (R. Derwent), 1788–93 [*A.P.S.D.*].

KENDAL, WESTMORLAND, STRAMONGATE BRIDGE (R. Kent), 1793–4 [A. C. Taylor, 'Thomas Harrison and the Stramongate Bridge, Kendal', *Trans. Cumberland and Westmorland Arch. Soc.* N.S. lxix, 1969, 275–9].

LIVERPOOL, THE LYCEUM (Library and Newsroom), BOLD STREET, 1800–3 [*The Stranger in Liverpool*, 1837, 39].

MANCHESTER, THE PORTICO LIBRARY, MOSLEY STREET (now Lloyd's Bank), 1802–6 [*A.P.S.D.*; T. Pratt, *The Portico Library, Manchester*, 1922].

CHESTER, ST. PETER'S CHURCH, refaced south side 1804 and tower 1811 [F. Simpson, *History of St. Peter's Church, Chester*, 1909, 12; *Cheshire Sheaf* xl, 1945, 120].

WHITTINGTON CHURCH, SHROPSHIRE, rebuilt nave 1805–6; tracery inserted in windows and other alterations 1894 [W. Cathrall, *History of Oswestry*, 1855, 281; D. H. S. Cranage, *Churches of Shropshire*, 1894–1901, ii, 836].

MANCHESTER, THE THEATRE ROYAL, 1806; burned 1844 [*A.P.S.D.*].

MANCHESTER, THE EXCHANGE AND COMMERCIAL BUILDINGS, 1806–9; enlarged by A. W. Mills 1847–8; dem. 1871–2 [E. Simpson, *A Sketch of the History of the Manchester Royal Exchange*, 1875; J. G. C. Parsons, *The Centenary of the Manchester Royal Exchange*, Manchester 1904].

CHESTER, THE NEWS-ROOM (now restaurant and City Club), NORTHGATE STREET, 1808 [*A.P.S.D.*; John Broster, *A Walk round the Walls and City of Chester*, 6th ed., 1821, 70].

CHESTER, THE NORTH GATE, for the 2nd Earl Grosvenor, 1808–10 [inscription].

MOEL FAMMAU, DENBIGHSHIRE, OBELISK to commemorate King George III's Jubilee, 1810; damaged by a storm 1862 and now totally ruined [R. J. Edwards, *A History of the Jubilee Tower on Moel Vammau*, 1885].

LIVERPOOL, ST. NICHOLAS CHURCH, Gothic steeple 1811–15 [J. A. Picton, *Memorials of Liverpool* ii, 1875, 59].

CHESTER, HOLY TRINITY CHURCH, report on spire advising its demolition, 1811, printed by Hemingway, *History of Chester* ii, 1831, 93–4.

CHESTER, WESLEYAN METHODIST CHAPEL, ST. JOHN STREET, 1811; refronted 1906 [John Broster, *A Walk round the Walls and City of Chester*, 6th ed., 1821, 60].

WARRINGTON, LANCS., timber bridge (R. Mersey), 1812 [*A.P.S.D.*; contract in Cheshire County Record Office, QAR 18].

SHREWSBURY, LORD HILL'S COLUMN, 1814–16, minor modifications to design by Edward Haycock (*q.v.*) [T. J. Howell, *The Stranger in Shrewsbury*, 1816, 79–80; *Gent's Mag.* 1817 (ii), 393].

HIGH LEGH, CHESHIRE, WEST HALL CHAPEL, 1814–16 (Ionic); burned 1891 and rebuilt as parish church [J. H. Hanshall, *History of Cheshire*, 1817, 398].

LLANFAIRPWLL, ANGLESEY, THE ANGLESEY COLUMN, 1816 [*A.P.S.D.*].

LIVERPOOL, ST. PAUL'S CHURCH, inserted ceiling in dome, 1818; dem. 1932 [*Gent's Mag.* 1829 (ii), 511].

CHESTER CATHEDRAL, repairs to exterior, 1818–19 [C. Hiatt, *Chester Cathedral*, 1905, 17; R. V. H. Burne, 'Chester Cathedral 1787–1837', *Jnl. of the Chester and N. Wales Arch. Soc.* xliii, 1956, 16–17].

HOLYHEAD, ANGLESEY, MEMORIAL ARCH to commemorate the landing in 1821 of King George IV, 1824 [*A.P.S.D.*] (R.C.H.M. *Anglesey*, pl. 128).

OXFORD, MAGDALEN COLLEGE, completed the unfinished ends of the NEW BUILDING, 1824 [*V.C.H. Oxon.* iii, 206]. Harrison also made unexecuted designs for rebuilding the College: see T. S. R. Boase, 'An Oxford College and the Gothic Revival', *Jnl. of the Warburg and Courtauld Institutes* xviii, 1955, 157–8.

CHESTER, widened the OLD DEE BRIDGE, 1825–6 [City Archives].

CHESTER, THE GROSVENOR BRIDGE, 1827–33, executed by James Trubshaw under the supervision of William Cole, junior, with Jesse Hartley, C.E., as clerk of works [J. W. Clarke, 'The Building of the Grosvenor Bridge', *Trans. Chester and N. Wales Arch. Soc.* xlv, 1958]. Some of Harrison's drawings are in the Mellon Collection.

CRANAGE, CHESHIRE, timber bridge (R. Dane) [S. Lewis, *Topographical Dictionary of England* i, 1831, 536].

CHESTER, THE EXCHANGE, NORTHGATE STREET, alterations to interior; destroyed by fire 1862 [John Broster, *A Walk round the Walls and City of Chester*, 6th ed. 1821, 72].

DOMESTIC ARCHITECTURE

KENNET HOUSE, CLACKMANNANSHIRE, for Robert Bruce, 1793–4; dem. 1967 [Sir J. Sinclair, *Statistical Account of Scotland* xiv, 1795, 616].

BROOMHALL, FIFE, for the 7th Earl of Elgin, 1796–9. The north front was left incomplete until 1865–6 when the existing porch was built to the designs of C. H. Wilson and David Thomson of Glasgow [J. M. Crook in *C. Life*, 29 Jan. 1970].

attributed: GLAN-YR-AFON, nr. MOLD, FLINTSHIRE, for Henry Potts, *c.* 1810; enlarged 1890 [Henry Potts was Clerk of the Peace for Cheshire and as such closely involved in the building of the County Court at Chester Castle by Harrison, who later designed Watergate House, Chester, for him].

TABLEY HOUSE, CHESHIRE, formation of Picture Gallery for Sir John F. Leicester, Bart., *c.* 1810 [R. Ackermann, *Repository of Arts*, 3rd ser., ii, 1823; cf. D. & S. Lysons, *Magna Britannia* ii, (2), 1810, 532].

GREDINGTON, nr. HANMER, FLINTSHIRE, for the 2nd Lord Kenyon, 1810–15 [S. Lewis, *Topographical Dictionary of Wales* i, 1849, 399; unsigned drawings at Gredington].

OUGHTRINGTON HALL, LYMM, CHESHIRE, entrance-lodge and gates for Trafford Trafford, *c.* 1810/20 [Mogg's edition of *Paterson's Roads*, 1826, 467].

WOODBANK, nr. STOCKPORT, CHESHIRE, for Peter

Marsland, 1812 [E. Twycross, *The Mansions of England: Cheshire* ii, 1850, 127].

DEE HILLS, nr. CHESTER, for Robert Baxter, 1814 [J. Hemingway, *History of Chester* i, 1831, 429].

ALLERTON, LANCS., GROVE HOUSE for Jacob Fletcher, *c.* 1815 [R. Stewart-Brown, *History of Allerton*, 1911, 184–5].

CHIRK CASTLE, DENBIGHSHIRE, Gothic vaulting, probably in the south-east tower, for Robert Myddelton-Biddulph, *c.* 1820 [J. Parker, *The Passengers*, 1831, 6].

CHESTER, ST. MARTIN'S LODGE, for himself, *c.* 1820 (*C. Life*, 22 April 1971, 944, fig. 2).

CHESTER, WATERGATE HOUSE, for Henry Potts, 1820 [*A.P.S.D.*].

HARDWICK GRANGE, nr. HADNALL, SHROPSHIRE, for General Lord Hill, *c.* 1820, Gothic; dem. [J. P. Neale, *Views of Seats*, 2nd ser., iii, 1826].

HAWKSTONE, SHROPSHIRE, THE CITADEL, for Sir Rowland Hill, Bart., 1824–5, castellated [Arthur Oswald in *C. Life*, 21 Aug. 1958].

HOOLE HOUSE, CHESHIRE, added veranda, conservatory, etc. for Lady Broughton [J. C. Loudon, *Gardener's Mag.* xiv, 1838, 353–62].

RUSSIA

Harrison designed a tower or lighthouse on the Black Sea coast for Count Michael Woronzow, the Russian ambassador to Britain. He also made designs, *c.* 1822, for a Greek Revival palace for Count Woronzow to be built in the Ukraine on the banks of the Dnieper, but these were never carried out [*Gent's Mag.* 1829 (i), 470]. The drawings are among those in the City Archives and Grosvenor Museum at Chester.

Note: The following ascriptions must be regarded as erroneous or unsubstantiated: Ashburton House, Piccadilly, London (by Henry Harrison, *q.v.*); the Sessions House at Knutsford, Cheshire (by George Moneypenny, *q.v.*); The Liverpool Athenaeum (by John Foster, *q.v.*); Quernmore Park Hall, Lancs. (unsubstantiated); Seggieden, Perthshire (apparently by John Paterson, *q.v.*); Swarkestone Bridge, Derbyshire (by Samuel Lister, *q.v.*), Talacre Hall, Flintshire (by Thomas Jones, *q.v.*). The 'house for General Abercrombie' mentioned in *A.P.S.D.* was almost certainly not built.

HARRISON, WILLIAM (*c.* 1742–1794), was an architect and surveyor of Leicester, where he died on 21 November 1794, 'after a long illness'. He designed the LUNATIC ASYLUM that was added to Leicester Infirmary in 1781 and supervised the building of the COUNTY GAOL to the designs of George Moneypenny in 1790–2. His own (rejected) designs for the Gaol, dated 1789, are among the County Records (QS 32/3/8). [J. D.

398

Bennett, *Leicestershire Architects 1700–1850*, 1966; *Gent's Mag.* 1794, 1154, 1797, 79; *V.C.H. Leics.* iv, 372].

HARTLEY, BERNARD, was the name of three generations of masons and architects of Pontefract in Yorkshire. Bernard Hartley I (*c.* 1745–1834) may have been the son of Hugh Hartley, a mason active in Yorkshire in the reign of George II. In 1797 Bernard Hartley I was appointed Surveyor of Bridges to the West Riding of Yorkshire, a post which he retained until his death in 1834 at the age of 89. An inscription on FERRYBRIDGE BRIDGE shows that Hartley built it to the designs of John Carr in 1797–1804, and in 1803 the West Riding magistrates gave him a gratuity of £200 for the trouble he had taken in this work, and for inventing a pile-driving machine worked by one horse and two men 'and capable of doing the work of 40 men'. In 1805 he built CASTLEFORD BRIDGE, evidently to his own designs, for it is inscribed 'BERNARD HARTLEY ARCHITECT 1805'. In 1819 Bernard Hartley II (1779–1855) was appointed Surveyor of Bridges jointly with his father, and when he died in 1855 he was succeeded by his son Bernard Hartley III, who retired in 1882. Thus for nearly a hundred years the maintenance of the county bridges was in the hands of this family.

Bernard Hartley I designed the TOWN HALL at PONTEFRACT, built in 1785 in a style similar to that of John Carr [*The Book of Entries of the Pontefract Corporation 1653–1726*, ed. R. Holmes, Pontefract 1882, 26]. In 1806 Bernard Hartley II submitted designs for the Court House at Wakefield, but those of Charles Watson were preferred. His designs for a vicarage at LEDSHAM, YORKS. (W.R.), dated 1821, are at the Borthwick Institute (MGA 1821/2; see also 1814/2 for his designs for enlarging KELLINGTON VICARAGE). Jesse Hartley (1780–1860), well known as the Surveyor to the Liverpool Dock Trustees from 1824 to 1860 and as the designer of the Albert Dock there, was the younger son of Bernard Hartley I, and was born at Pontefract in Dec. 1780. He was succeeded by his son John Bernard Hartley (1814–69).

[West Riding Quarter Sessions Order Books; Bishop's Transcripts of Pontefract Parish Registers at Borthwick Institute, York; *Gent's Mag.* 1834 (i), 342; obituary of Jesse Hartley in *Minutes of Proceedings of the Institution of Civil Engineers* xxiii, 1871–2 (i), 219.]

HARVEY, FREDERICK E—, of Ipswich, is described as a 'builder' in Pigot's *Directory* of 1830. He built, and perhaps designed, LEVINGTON HOUSE, nr. IPSWICH, SUFFOLK, for Major Charles Walker shortly before 1830 [G. R. Clarke, *History and Description of Ipswich*, 1830, 377]. In 1833 he exhibited at the Royal Academy a design for a cast-iron aqueduct in the Gothic style. He designed HOLY TRINITY CHURCH, IPSWICH, in 1836 [J. Wodderspoon, *New Guide to Ipswich*, 1842; B.M., Add. MS. 19179, f. 5].

HARVEY, JACOB (1783–1867), was a speculative builder who, with his sons John Tapley Harvey and William Harvey, was responsible for the developments which made Torquay a Victorian seaside resort. The initiative came from the principal landowner, Sir Lawrence Palk, but Harvey and his sons supplied the designs and did the building. Harvey came to Torquay a poor man, but when he died in January 1867 at the age of 84 he was a leading figure in the town he had so largely built. One of the earliest of Harvey's developments was HIGHER TERRACE (*c.* 1811), followed by PARK PLACE, PARK CRESCENT, VAUGHAN PARADE (*c.* 1830) and BEACON TERRACE. HESKETH CRESCENT, designed in a quite sophisticated style reminiscent of Brighton or Cheltenham, was the firm's most ambitious development. It was built in 1845–8 to the designs of J. T. and W. Harvey, who (unlike their builder father) described themselves as 'architects'. Their later works included THE MARKET (1852), a house called ROCKWOOD for the Hon. J. Boyle (1857) and the TORBAY HOTEL (1866). [A. C. Ellis, *An Historical Survey of Torquay*, 1930, *passim*].

HARVEY, JOHN, was the name borne by three generations of masons working in Bath during the early part of the eighteenth century. The second of the name designed and built the first PUMP ROOM in 1706, and it was probably his son, the third John Harvey, who rebuilt the church of ST. MICHAEL EXTRA MUROS in 1734. John Wood had offered to rebuild the church partly at his own expense on conditions which were rejected by the vestry, and his displacement by Harvey explains the severe criticism to which St. Michael's is subjected in Wood's *Essay towards a Description of Bath*. It was in fact a handsome Georgian classical church ingeniously planned to fit an awkward site, but the architecture belonged to the age of Archer and Hawksmoor rather than to that of Colen Campbell and John Wood. It was demolished *c.* 1835 to make way for the existing church by G. P. Manners. [W. Ison, *The Georgian Buildings of Bath*, 1948, 30, 60–1, 70–1, fig. 9; plan of St. Michael's Church in I.C.B.S. records].

HARVEY, JOHN, was probably the pupil and certainly the assistant of Samuel Wyatt, whose office he entered in or before 1785. In 1792, when he was elected to membership of the Surveyors' Club, he was described as being 'at Mr. Wyatt's, Berwick Street, Soho', and in 1794, when Wyatt's designs for Trinity House were exhibited at the Royal Academy, they were attributed to Wyatt in the text, but to Harvey in the index,

of the Catalogue. Harvey continued to occupy Wyatt's house at 36 Berwick Street after the latter moved to Albion Place in 1803, and he was still living there in 1819, twelve years after Wyatt's death. He was probably related to Wyatt, for the latter's uncle William Wyatt (d. 1772) married a Mary Harvey.

Harvey's first important commission was the SHIRE HALL at STAFFORD, built in 1794 and illustrated as his work in Richardson's *New Vitruvius Britannicus* ii, 1808, pls. 7–10. Stafford was in the Wyatts' territory, and Harvey no doubt owed the commission to Samuel's good offices: indeed the building appears to have been a joint design, for the Quarter Sessions Order Book shows that on 14 November 1793 it was resolved 'that Mr. Wyatt's plan of the proposed New County Hall ... with Mr. Harvey's elevation marked A be adopted subject to such alterations as have been suggested by the Magistrates respecting the Grand Jury Room'.

In 1805 Harvey succeeded James Wyatt as Deputy Surveyor to the Office of Woods and Forests, but was dismissed for incompetence after little more than a year in office [P.R.O., Crest 8/2–3]. In 1813 he took the place of Thomas Hardwick as architect in charge of the erection of the MILLBANK PENITENTIARY, but proved unable to cope with the legacy of insecure foundations left by his predecessor, and was superseded by Sir Robert Smirke [G. Holford, *An Account of the Penitentiary at Millbank*, 1828, xxix–xxxii]. His only other recorded work appears to be the interior of the library at LITTLE GLEMHAM HALL, SUFFOLK, designed for Dudley North in 1811 [drawings in Kent Record Office, U 471, P 6].

Harvey was President of the Surveyors' Club in 1803. He exhibited regularly at the Royal Academy from 1785 to 1810, showing *inter alia* a design for a stone bridge of 400 foot span over the Menai Straits (1787), the river front of a design for new Houses of Parliament (1790) and a design for a new London Bridge constructed of cast iron (1801) – all of which may well have been ideas suggested by Samuel Wyatt. J. L. Harvey, who entered the R.A. Schools in 1809, and exhibited an architectural drawing at the Academy the same year, was probably Harvey's son, for his address is given as '62 Berwick Street'.

HASSALL, RICHARD, *see* BAKER, RICHARD

HASTIE, WILLIAM (*c.* 1755–1832), was a Scot who had a distinguished career as an architect in Russia. Nothing is known of his early life in Scotland, but he was one of a number of Scottish artisans who went out to Russia in 1784 in response to an advertisement published in the *Edinburgh Evening News* (21 Jan.). He was then described as a stone-mason, but by 1794 he was (perhaps as a result of Charles Cameron's tuition) making technically accomplished architectural designs, and between 1795 and 1799 he was employed as an architect in the Crimea by Prince Platon Zubov, the Governor of the Ekaterinoslav and Taurida regions. He subsequently worked in St. Petersburg, where he was the pioneer in the design and construction of cast-iron bridges and was much employed as a town-planner. The lay-out of Tsarskoe Selo was designed by him in 1808, and he was also concerned in town-planning projects at Kiev, Vilna, Smolensk, Eka-terinoslav, Tomsk and elsewhere. In 1813 he made a plan for rebuilding Moscow after its de-struction by fire, and, although it was not accepted, many of his ideas were adopted in the plan finally approved in 1818. Hastie died at Tsarskoe Selo on 4 June 1832. [Miliza Kor-shunova, 'William Hastie in Russia', *Architec-tural History* xvii, 1974.]

HASWELL, GEORGE (–1784), was for many years the Duke of Argyll's chief wright at INVERARAY CASTLE, ARGYLLSHIRE, where he was responsible for the carpentry work from 1750 onwards. In 1778, as 'Mr. Haswell, architect, of Inveraray', he designed CASTLEHILL CHURCH, CAMPBELTOWN, which was built to his designs by an Inveraray mason named John Brown in 1778–80 [S.R.O., HR 67/1; R.C.A.M., *Argyll* i, 103], and in the Scottish Record Office there is a plan for seating SOUTHEND CHURCH, KINTYRE, ARGYLLSHIRE, signed by him and dated 1779 [RHP 7175]. He died at Inveraray on 24 March 1784 [I. G. Lindsay & Mary Cosh, *Inveraray and the Dukes of Argyll*, 1973, 417].

HATCHARD, CHARLES, was an architect and surveyor practising from Lower Belgrave Place, Pimlico. He was elected to membership of the Surveyors' Club in 1826 and was President of the Club in 1830. In 1824–5 he rebuilt EPSOM CHURCH, SURREY, in the Gothic style, retaining the medieval tower [E. W. Brayley, *Topographi-cal History of Surrey* iv, 1850, 357]. He also designed the front of ALDRIDGE'S CATTLE AUCTION ROOMS on the west side of St. Martin's Lane, London, 1843; dem. 1955 [Hermione Hobhouse, *Lost London*, 1971, 189].

HATTON, THOMAS, was a pupil of Samuel Robinson and exhibited student's designs at the Royal Academy from his office from 1799 to 1801. In 1802 he began independent practice from 16 Dean Street, Southwark. His subsequent exhibits at the R.A. indicate that he was respon-sible for the following buildings: a cottage at MOUNT PLEASANT, nr. CROUCH END in north Lon-don for H. St. John, 1802; a house on DARTMOUTH HILL, BLACKHEATH, for J. Green, 1806; and the

'PUBLIC PORTER' BREWHOUSE, WESTON STREET, SOUTHWARK, 1809. He was still at Dean Street in 1825–6, but disappears from the directories soon afterwards.

HAUDUROY, S—, was a French Huguenot architect employed by William Blathwayt at DYRHAM PARK, GLOS., where he designed the west front in 1692. He is referred to in the building records as 'Mr. Hauduroy', but in his one surviv-ing letter signs himself 'S. Hauduroy'. He may have been the Samuel Hauduroy who appears as a godfather in the records of the Huguenot church in Threadneedle Street in 1691. A draw-ing at Dyrham of the 'Porte de la Chambre du Conseil', offered as a pattern for a doorway, is presumably in his hand. Two other members of the family, Louis and Mark Antony Hauduroy, were painters. Louis was responsible for decora-tive painting (now destroyed) on the staircase at CULVERTHORPE HALL, LINCS., in 1704–5, and signs the illusionist architectural paintings in Archer's pavilion at WREST PARK, BEDS., which are dated 1712 [Mark Girouard, 'Dyrham Park, Glos.', *C. Life*, 15 Feb. 1962; E. Croft-Murray, *Decorative Painting in England* i, 1962, 248, ii, 1970, 218].

HAVILAND, JOHN (1792–1852), born at Gun-denham Manor, nr. Taunton, Somerset, on 15 December 1792, was the son of James Haviland, a country gentleman. On his mother's side he was connected with the artist Benjamin Haydon. He became a pupil of James Elmes, who, while ill, entrusted the erection of the chapel of St. John at Chichester to him (1812). His mother's sister had married Admiral Count Mordwinoff, then minister of works to the Emperor Alexander, and at his uncle's invitation he went to Russia to enter the Imperial Corps of Engineers; but meeting there representatives of the American govern-ment, he was induced to visit America, where he landed in September 1816. He settled in Phila-delphia, where he designed a number of public buildings. He became well known as a prison architect, and his Eastern State Penitentiary at Philadelphia was the first prison built in the United States in accordance with the ideas of Howard and other prison reformers. He also designed many churches and private houses, principally in the Greek revival style. A manu-script 'Description of the Halls of Justice or House of Detention, New York', with drawings, is in the R.I.B.A. Drawings Collection, and twelve volumes of his sketches, specifications, and business correspondence are in the Somerset County Record Office at Taunton.

[Fiske Kimball in *Dictionary of American Bio-graphy* viii, 1932; *A.P.S.D.*; obituaries in *Builder* x, 1852, 341; *Gent's Mag.* 1852 (i), 629–30; and *Civil Engineer and Architect's Jnl.* xv, 227.]

HAWKSMOOR, NICHOLAS (*c*. 1661–1736), was a native of Nottinghamshire, and was probably born either at Ragnall or at East Drayton, both villages near Tuxford where members of the Hawksmoor or Hawksmore family were yeomen farmers in the seventeenth century. Nothing is known of his education, but according to George Vertue he was employed as a clerk by Samuel Mellish of Doncaster, a J.P. whose family had property in Hawksmoor's part of Nottinghamshire. From Mellish's service he passed to that of Sir Christopher Wren, who hearing of his 'early skill and genius' for architecture, took him as his clerk at about the age of 18. A topographical sketch-book now in the R.I.B.A. Drawings Collection contains some of Hawksmoor's early drawings, including a view of Bath Abbey dated 1683.[1] Their somewhat amateurish draughtmanship shows that at the age of 22 Hawksmoor was still learning the techniques of his new profession. As Wren's 'domestic clerk' he was to be associated with the Surveyor-General in nearly all his architectural works from *c*. 1684 onwards, either as draughtsman, measurer, or clerk of the works. Thus he is said to have been employed as 'supervisor' under Wren at Winchester Palace (begun in 1683), for which he witnessed the brickmaker's contract in 1684, and to have acted in a similar capacity at Chelsea Hospital, where, at some date between 1687 and 1692, he was paid £10 'for drawing designs for the Hospitall'. His name as Wren's 'gentleman' occurs also in connection with the City churches, and there are many payments to him for assisting Wren in making working drawings for St. Paul's Cathedral between 1691 and 1712. In 1689 Wren obtained for Hawksmoor the post of Clerk of Works at William III's newly-purchased palace of Kensington, and in 1698 that of Clerk of Works at Greenwich Hospital in succession to Henry Symonds. The latter post Hawksmoor retained until 1735, the former until 1715, when he succeeded William Dickinson as Clerk of the Works at Whitehall, Westminster and St. James's. At the same time he obtained the newly-established post of Secretary to the Board of Works which, in accordance with the new regulations of 1715, went with his Clerkship of the Works and carried with it an additional salary of £100 per annum. Hawksmoor was now a senior official of the Royal Works and a likely candidate for further promotion. But in 1718, when Wren was superseded by William Benson, Hawksmoor was deprived of his dual office in order to provide a place for Benjamin Benson, the new Surveyor's brother. Only in 1726, when Benson's successor Hewett died, was Hawksmoor restored to his Secretaryship, though not to the Clerkship of the Works, which was given to Flitcroft. In 1696 Hawksmoor was appointed surveyor to the Commissioners of Sewers for Westminster, but was dismissed in 1700, 'having neglected to attend the Court several days last past' [G.L.C. Record Office, minutes of the Commissioners of Sewers].

In 1711, on the passing of the Act imposing a duty on coals for the purpose of building fifty new churches in London, Hawksmoor was one of the two surveyors appointed by the commissioners at a salary of £200 to carry the Act into effect, and it was in this capacity that he designed the six churches which are his best-known works. This appointment came to an end in 1733 on the termination of the commission, but Hawksmoor and his colleague John James were still being paid 'for carrying on and finishing the works under their care' up to the time of the former's death. After the death of Wren in 1723, Hawksmoor succeeded him as Surveyor to Westminster Abbey, a post which carried a salary of £100 out of the money voted by Parliament for the repair and completion of the Abbey in 1698. The west towers of the Abbey were designed by Hawksmoor in the course of his duties as Wren's successor, although they were not completed until after his death.

Meanwhile Hawksmoor had come into contact with Vanbrugh, who since 1702 had held the office of Comptroller of the Works, and who in 1716 succeeded Wren as Surveyor of Greenwich Hospital. Vanbrugh, like Wren, found Hawksmoor an able assistant, and employed him both at Castle Howard and at Blenheim Palace, where he acted as assistant surveyor from 1705 onwards, and ultimately took Vanbrugh's place as architect in charge after the latter's final breach with Sarah, Duchess of Marlborough. It was to Vanbrugh that Hawksmoor owed his advancement in 1715, and it was Vanbrugh who subsequently did his best to protect Hawksmoor from the predatory Benson and his successor Hewett. In July 1721 Vanbrugh made Hawksmoor his deputy as Comptroller of the Works, a position which he retained until Vanbrugh's death in 1726.

Hawksmoor suffered all his life from 'the vile distemper of the gout', and it was from gout in the stomach that he died at his house in Millbank, Westminster, on 25 March 1736, leaving a widow, Hester, to whom he bequeathed all his property in Westminster, Highgate, Shenley (Herts.) and East Drayton (Notts.). He was buried at Shenley, where he is commemorated by a ledger-stone with a Latin inscription cut by the mason Andrews Jelfe. The inscription is given by Downes (*Hawksmoor*, 1959, 7). Hawksmoor's only child was a daughter, Elizabeth, whose second husband, Nathaniel Blackerby, was treasurer to the Commissioners for building the Fifty

---

[1] Some pages have been cut out of this book. One of them (a drawing of the cross at Coventry) is in the Bodleian Library (Gough Maps 233, f. 33).

New Churches. It was Blackerby who wrote the obituary of his father-in-law which appeared in *Read's Weekly Journal*, No. 603, for 27 March 1736. The only known portrait of Hawksmoor is the bust by Cheere in the buttery of All Souls College, Oxford.

As the assistant and then the colleague first of Wren and then of Vanbrugh, Hawksmoor was brought into intimate contact with two of the greatest figures in the history of English architecture. There can be no doubt that he gave to the latter the expertise that he had gained from the former, and that it was Hawksmoor's collaboration that enabled Vanbrugh's heroic designs to be translated into actuality in spite of their author's lack of previous architectural experience. What influence Hawksmoor, having worked with Vanbrugh, had on Wren's later work, is a more difficult problem that cannot be discussed here; but it is at least arguable that Wren's own architectural development owed a good deal to the persuasion and example of his former pupil. For by 1700 Hawksmoor had emerged as a major architectural personality in his own right. In the course of the next twenty years he was to prove himself to be one of the great masters of the English baroque, more assured in his command of the classical vocabulary than the untrained Vanbrugh, more imaginative in his vision than the intellectual Wren. No one understood better than Hawksmoor the dynamic deployment of architectural form or the dramatic possibilities of light and shade. The complex forms of the London churches, whether in internal planning or in external embellishment, are as eloquent as anything by Borromini, the Italian architect with whom Hawksmoor most obviously invites comparison. Although it is the fantastic side of baroque that is apparent in so many of his unexecuted designs, he could also be gravely classical, as in the Clarendon Building, St. George's, Bloomsbury, or the Mausoleum at Castle Howard. He could also be romantically Gothic, not only in situations (as at All Souls) where collegiate or ecclesiastical associations justified the adoption of that style, but also in the ostensibly classical towers of some of his churches, which recall the silhouette of a medieval steeple crowned with a lantern. Hawksmoor was indeed a master of architectural form, for whom Antiquity, the Renaissance, the English Middle Ages and contemporary Italian baroque (studied in engravings, for he never went abroad) were all exploited and transfused into a powerful personal style that constitutes one of the highest achievements of English classical architecture.

Hawksmoor had no pupil – unless Henry Joynes, his friend and assistant, can be regarded as such – and even before his death, the romantic approach to the classical past for which he stood

had begun to give way to the more rigid canons of Palladian correctitude. Both at Castle Howard, where the mausoleum which he had designed was given a staircase copied from that of Lord Burlington's villa at Chiswick, and at Blenheim, where the Column of Victory, for which he had made so many sketches, was finally 'conducted by my Lord Herbert', his work was subjected to Palladian discipline. At Oxford, his designs for the Radcliffe Camera, first made in 1712, and represented by a wooden model which is still preserved, remained in abeyance for lack of funds. At Cambridge he had seen his place as architect of the new buildings at King's College taken by Gibbs. These disappointments, coupled with the loss of his offices in 1718, and the appointment of Thomas Ripley to the surveyorship of Greenwich Hospital over his head in 1729, may perhaps account for the somewhat querulous tone of some of his letters to the Duchess of Marlborough, and for the disillusionment which is so clear in his portrait-bust. 'Poor Hawksmoor', wrote Vanbrugh in 1721, 'what a Barbarous Age have his fine, ingenious, parts fallen into. What wou'd Monsr. Colbert in France have given for such a man?' But something may have been due to Hawksmoor's own diffidence, for Vanbrugh thought it necessary to apply to the Duke of Marlborough on his behalf 'for some opportunity to do him good, because he does not seem very solicitous to do it for himself', and in 1734 Sir Thomas Robinson told Lord Carlisle that he 'never talk'd with a more reasonable man, nor one so little prejudiced in favour of his own performances'.

The materials for Hawksmoor's life are comparatively extensive. Over 500 of his drawings survive and have been listed by Downes (*Hawksmoor*, 1959) who also prints many of his letters. More drawings now missing are listed in the sale catalogue of Hawksmoor's collection, printed in part by Downes in *Burlington Mag.* xcv, 1953, 332–5 and in full in *Sale Catalogues of Libraries of Eminent Persons*, vol. 4, ed. D. J. Watkin, 1972, 45–106. A small notebook in Hawksmoor's hand dealing with materials and prices is in the National Maritime Museum (MS. 63/030). All previous accounts of Hawksmoor have been superseded by Kerry Downes's monograph *Hawksmoor*, 1959. *Hawksmoor*, 1969, by the same author, is a shorter introductory work which supplements but does not supersede the monograph. Attention should also be drawn to J. H. V. Davies's stylistic appraisal, 'Nicholas Hawksmoor' in *R.I.B.A. Jnl.* Oct. 1962, 368–75.

PUBLIC AND DOMESTIC ARCHITECTURE

BROADFIELD HALL, HERTS., repairs and alterations for James Forester, 1690–93; dem. *c.* 1875 [R. L. Hine, *Relics of an Un-Common Attorney*, 1951, 6–7 and endpapers].

LONDON, CHRIST'S HOSPITAL, designed SIR JOHN MOORE'S WRITING SCHOOL under Wren's direction, 1692–5; dem. 1902 [E. H. Pearce, *Annals of Christ's Hospital*, 1908, 151; cf. *Wren Soc.* xi, pls. xlviii–li].

GREENWICH HOSPITAL. As Clerk of the Works from 1698 to 1735 Hawksmoor was more closely associated with the building of the Hospital than any other person. At first, however, he was working to Wren's designs, and although he may well have been personally responsible for designing the east range of Queen Anne's Court, begun in 1701, and the dormitories in King William's Court, begun in 1699, it cannot be proved that he was their effective as well as their executant architect. He subsequently made many designs for enlarging the Hospital that were not carried out, including a grandoise scheme for a monumental chapel dominating the whole complex. See *Wren Soc.* vi, *passim* and his own *Remarks on the Founding and Carrying on the Buildings of the Royal Hospital at Greenwich*, 1728 (reprinted in *Wren. Soc.* vi, 17–27, in which he pleaded for the completion of the hospital on the scale originally intended).

EASTON NESTON, NORTHANTS., for Sir William Fermor, cr. Baron Leominster in 1692. This house was built *c.* 1685–95 to a design probably made in Wren's office and executed under Hawksmoor's direction, but the exterior was remodelled by Hawksmoor *c.* 1700–02. The model in the R.I.B.A. Drawings Collection may be connected with the building of the house in *c.* 1685–95, but may represent an alternative scheme for remodelling it *c.* 1695–1700. The engravings in *Vitruvius Britannicus* i, 1715, pls. 98–100 show the house as remodelled by Hawksmoor, but with wings, a forecourt and other additions that were never built. According to Campbell the works were concluded in 1713. [H. M. Colvin, 'Easton Neston Reconsidered', *C. Life*, 15 Oct. 1970] (*C. Life*, 7–14 Nov. 1908; *C. Life*, 20–27 Aug. 1927; H. A. Tipping, *English Homes*, Period iv, vol. ii, 1928, 119–40; J. Kenworthy-Browne in *Connoisseur*, Oct. 1964).

?ADDISCOMBE HOUSE, SURREY, for William Draper, 1702–3; dem. *c.* 1861 (illustrations in Downes, *English Baroque Architecture*, 1966, pl. 163 and *National Views and History of London*, 1832, 118). The incomplete building accounts in B.M. Add. MS. 38480, ff. 406–12, show that the carpenter's and joiner's work was measured by Hawksmoor in 1703, but the house may have been designed by Edward Strong, the master-mason employed. Draper was Treasurer to the Commissioners for Greenwich Hospital, where Hawksmoor was Clerk of Works at the time.

KENSINGTON PALACE, THE ORANGERY was built in 1704–5 under Hawksmoor's direction as Clerk of the Works, but Wren as Surveyor General was officially responsible for the design, and a Treasury minute shows that it was revised by Vanbrugh [*History of the King's Works* v, 193–4].

KENSINGTON CHARITY SCHOOL, 1711–12; dem. 1875 [J. D. G. Scott, *St. Mary Abbots Kensington*, 1942, 115–17].

LONDON, NO. 3 ST. JAMES'S SQUARE, advised the 3rd Lord (later 1st Earl of) Ashburnham on construction, 1712; dem. 1930 [*Survey of London* xxix, 84].

OXFORD, THE CLARENDON BUILDING, 1712–15 [*V.C.H. Oxon*. iii, 54–55] (plan in R.C.H.M. *Oxford*, 12).

OXFORD, ALL SOULS COLLEGE, North Quadrangle, Hall, Buttery and Codrington Library, 1716–35, externally Gothic [*V.C.H. Oxon*. iii, 190–3; H. M. Colvin, *Catalogue of Architectural Drawings in Worcester College Library*, 1964, pls. 59–81].

WESTMINSTER HALL, temporary Court of Judicature for trial of rebel Lords, 1716 [P.R.O., Works 4/1, 78].

ST. JAMES'S PALACE, THE BRICK ARCADE, STABLE COURT, 1716–17 [*History of the King's Works* v, 240].

WESTMINSTER, THE JEWEL TOWER, alterations 1718–19 [*History of the King's Works* v, 410].

PANTON HALL, nr. WRAGBY, LINCS., for Joseph Gace, *c.* 1720; enlarged and remodelled by John Carr *c.* 1775; dem. 1960 [W. Angus, *Select Views of Seats*, 1792, pl. xxx; H. M. Colvin in *Lincolnshire Historian* No. 7, 1951, but note that demolition revealed structural evidence that the centre was earlier in date than the wings].

OXFORD, WORCESTER COLLEGE. Hawksmoor assisted Dr. George Clarke to plan the new buildings that were begun in 1720, and was closely involved in the designing of the library [*V.C.H. Oxon*. iii, 307–8; H. M. Colvin, *Catalogue of Architectural Drawings in Worcester College Library*, 1964, xxiii–xxiv and pls. 8–23].

KENSINGTON, COLBY HOUSE, for Sir Thomas Colby, *c.* 1722 [J. H. V. Davies, 'Colby House' in *The Country Seat*, ed. Colvin & Harris, 1970, 94–5].

BLENHEIM PALACE, OXON. First as Vanbrugh's assistant from 1705 to 1716, and later as sole architect in charge of the completion of the palace for Sarah, Duchess of Marlborough, from 1722 to 1725, Hawksmoor was closely associated with every stage in the designing and building of Blenheim. The decoration of the Long Library, with its elaborate plasterwork by Isaac Mansfield, was carried out entirely to his designs, and it has been said that while 'Blenheim as a whole is Vanbrugh's . . .

yet there is not one detail of which one could say with certainty that Hawksmoor had not designed it' (L. Whistler, *Sir John Vanbrugh*, 1938, 128). He also designed the Triumphal Gateway at the Woodstock entrance to the Park, built in 1722–3, and made a number of designs for the Column of Victory, though the Doric pillar completed in 1730 was 'conducted by' Lord Herbert, afterwards Earl of Pembroke. [David Green, *Blenheim Palace*, 1951.]

CASTLE HOWARD, YORKS. (N.R.), works for the 3rd Earl of Carlisle, including the PYRAMID, 1728, THE MAUSOLEUM, 1729–36, and the TEMPLE OF VENUS, 1731–5 (dem.) [G. F. Webb, 'The Letters and Drawings of Nicholas Hawksmoor relating to the Building of the Mausoleum at Castle Howard', *Walpole Soc*, xix, 1930–1; H. A. Tipping, 'The Outworks of Castle Howard', *C. Life*, 6–13 August 1927].

OCKHAM PARK, SURREY, alterations for Lord Chancellor King, 1729; altered in nineteenth century and dem. 1949 after a fire [L. Whistler, 'Ockham Park, Surrey', *C. Life*, 29 Dec. 1950; R. N. Bloxam, 'The "Big House" in Ockham Park', *Surrey Arch. Colls*. lxii, 1965; J. Harris, *Catalogue of British Drawings for Architecture etc. in American Collections*, 1971, 112–15].

OXFORD, THE QUEEN'S COLLEGE, screen-wall to High Street, 1733–6, executed by William Townesend with some modifications to the cupola [K. Downes, *Hawksmoor*, 1959, 107, note 14].

LONDON, No. 5 NEW BURLINGTON STREET, interior for Anne Viscountess Irwin, 1735; dem. [*Survey of London* xxxii, 490–1].

CHURCHES

London[1]

ST. ALPHEGE, GREENWICH, 1712–14. Of the steeple designed by Hawksmoor (known from an engraving published by J. Kip in 1714) only the lower stage was built. The upper part was designed by John James in 1730. The church was gutted in 1941 and reopened in 1963 after restoration.

ST. ANNE, LIMEHOUSE, 1714–30; damaged by fire 1850 and restored by P. Hardwick and J. Morris 1851–4.

ST. GEORGE-IN-THE-EAST, WAPPING STEPNEY, 1714–29; gutted 1941, exterior restored as a shell containing a modern hall, church and rectory, 1960–4.

CHRIST CHURCH, SPITALFIELDS, 1714–29; the spire was stripped of its original ornaments in 1822–

3 and the interior was altered in 1851 and 1866 (when the galleries were removed) (*Survey of London* xxvii, chap. xii). Hawksmoor also designed the rectory in 1726.

ST. MARY WOOLNOTH, CITY, 1716–24. The interior was altered by Butterfield in 1875–6, when the galleries were removed and their fronts set back against the walls.

ST. GEORGE, BLOOMSBURY, 1716–31, refitted by G. E. Street 1871, when the lions and unicorns were removed from the steeple; orientation changed to north–south in 1781, but recently restored to east–west. Hawksmoor also designed the rectory in 1726.

ST. GEORGE, QUEEN SQUARE, alterations 1717–20, including ceiling; altered 1867.

ST. MICHAEL, CORNHILL, CITY, steeple 1718–24, Gothic. The rebuilding of the steeple was begun by Wren in 1715–17, suspended, and completed by Hawksmoor to his own designs.

ST. JOHN, HORSELYDOWN, SOUTHWARK, with John James, 1727–33; gutted 1940–1, and subsequently dem.

ST. LUKE, OLD STREET, FINSBURY, with John James, 1727–33; dismantled 1960.

Elsewhere

attributed: CANTERBURY CATHEDRAL, archbishop's throne (now in south transept) for Archbishop Tenison, *c.* 1704 [Downes, *Hawksmoor*, 1959, 277].

BEVERLEY MINSTER, YORKS. Hawksmoor repaired the north transept, employing machinery devised by W. Thornton, a carpenter of York, to restore it to the perpendicular, placed an ogival cupola over the crossing, and refitted the interior, introducing a stone screen (Gothic), a Corinthian baldachino over the altar, and galleries in the nave aisles, *c.* 1716–20. See appeal (1716) and engravings by Hawksmoor in Bodleian, Gough Maps, 35, ff. 3–4; 44, f. 67, and descriptions in *The Diary of a Tour in 1732* (Roxburghe Club, 1890), 199–201, and by Dr. Pococke in B.M., Add. MS. 14259, f. 133. Hawksmoor's work has been largely destroyed (R. H. Whiteing, 'Georgian Restorations at Beverley Minister 1715–40', *Trans. Georgian Soc. for E. Yorks* III (i), 1951; Downes, *Hawksmoor*, 1959, 6, note 11).

ST. ALBAN'S ABBEY, HERTS.[1] Hawksmoor carried out repairs soon after 1721, when he published a plate of the Abbey in order to raise funds [B.M., *King's Maps* xv, 49, and Bodleian, MS. Rawlinson B. 376, f. 261]. There was a Brief for £5775 in 1723–4.

---

[1] The authority for all Hawksmoor's London churches will be found in H. M. Colvin, 'Fifty New Churches', *Arch. Rev.*, March 1950 and Kerry Downes, *Hawksmoor*, 1959.

[1] There is a bird's-eye view of the town of St. Albans, 'done by N. Hawksmoor Architect, anno 1721 May y[e] 12', in the Sutherland Collection in the Ashmolean Museum, Oxford (c. iii, 555).

WESTMINSTER ABBEY. The Gothic west towers were designed by Hawksmoor in 1734, and completed by his successor, John James, c. 1745 [*Wren. Soc.* xi, 11, 31, 33]. The gable is dated 1735.

UNEXECUTED DESIGNS

Hawksmoor's many unexecuted designs include schemes for INGESTRE PARK, STAFFS., 1688;[1] HERRIARD PARK, HANTS., 1696;[2] WINDSOR CASTLE, BERKS., 1698;[3] a MAUSOLEUM for KING WILLIAM III, c. 1702;[4] GREENWICH HOSPITAL, c. 1702 onwards;[5] THIRKLEBY PARK, YORKS (N.R.), 1704;[6] THE QUEEN'S COLLEGE, OXFORD, 1708–9;[7] ALL SOULS COLLEGE, OXFORD. 1708–9;[8] ST. PAUL'S CATHEDRAL BAPTISTERY, c. 1710;[9] KING'S COLLEGE, CAMBRIDGE, 1712–13;[10] THE RADCLIFFE LIBRARY, OXFORD, 1712–15 and 1733;[11] OXFORD, steeple for ALL SAINTS CHURCH, c. 1713–15;[12] WOTTON HOUSE, SURREY, 1713;[13] BRASENOSE COLLEGE, OXFORD, 1720–34;[14] MAGDALEN COLLEGE, OXFORD, 1724;[15] an elaborate altar in YORK MINSTER, 1726;[16] OCKHAM PARK, SURREY, 1727–9;[17] ST. GILES-IN-THE-FIELDS CHURCH, LONDON, 1730;[18]

[1] See Downes, *Hawksmoor*, 1969, 24–5.
[2] Unpublished drawings in Hampshire Record Office (Jervoise papers).
[3] *Wren Soc.* viii, pls. xi–xv.
[4] See *History of the King's Works* v, 455, and Downes, *Hawksmoor*, 1959, 66 and pl. 10b.
[5] *Wren Soc.* vi.
[6] Unpublished design for stables in Yorkshire Archaeological Society's Library, Leeds; cf. the 18 drawings 'for Sir Thomas Frankland's' in Hawksmoor's Sale Catalogue.
[7] See Downes, *Hawksmoor*, 1959, 102–7.
[8] H. M. Colvin, *Catalogue of Architectural Drawings in Worcester College Library*, 1964.
[9] *Wren Soc.* iii, pls. xxiii, xxiv.
[10] Drawings at King's College and Bodleian Library: see Downes, *Hawksmoor*, 1959, 278.
[11] See S. Lang, 'By Hawksmoor out of Gibbs', *Arch. Rev.* April 1949, and the plates in *The Building Accounts of the Radcliffe Library*, ed. S. G. Gillam, Oxford Historical Soc. 1958.
[12] H. M. Colvin, 'The Architects of All Saints Church, Oxford', *Oxoniensia* xix, 1954, 112–16.
[13] See *R.I.B.A. Drawings Catalogue G–K*, 99.
[14] See E. W. Allfrey, 'The Architectural History of the College', *Brasenose Quatercentenary Monograph* No. iii, 1909, and H. M. Colvin, *Catalogue of Architectural Drawings in Worcester College Library*, 1964, pls. 87–90.
[15] See Colvin, *op. cit.*, p. xxii and Nos. 84–5.
[16] Drawings in York Minster archives (M/P 644 and 1021) and British Museum (King's Maps xlv, 7 ff. 2).
[17] J. Harris, *Catalogue of British Drawings for Architecture, etc., in American Collections*, 1971, 112–15 and plates. Further drawings in Minet Library, Camberwell.
[18] B.M., Add. MS. 15506.

and WESTMINSTER BRIDGE, 1736.[1] For Hawksmoor's town planning schemes for Oxford and Cambridge see S. Lang, 'Cambridge and Oxford Replanned; Hawksmoor as a Town-planner', *Arch. Rev.* April 1948, and *The Town of Cambridge as it ought to be Reformed, the plans of Nicholas Hawksmoor interpreted in an Essay by David Roberts and a set of eight drawings by Gordon Cullen*, privately printed, Cambridge 1955.

HAYCOCK, EDWARD (1790–1870), was the second son of J. H. Haycock (*q.v.*). He became a pupil of Sir Jeffry Wyatville, studied at the R.A. Schools, and exhibited student's work at the Royal Academy in 1808, 1809 and 1810. He also exhibited at the Liverpool Academy in 1812, 1813 and 1814. Returning to Shrewsbury, he joined his father in the family building firm, and continued, in conjunction with his younger brother Robert, to combine the business of a builder with the practice of an architect until about 1845, after which he worked only as an architect. From 1834 to 1866 he was County Surveyor of Shropshire, and for many years he played an important part in the social and political life of Shrewsbury. He sat on the Council as a Conservative for 34 years, became an Alderman, and served as Mayor in 1842. He died in December 1870, and was buried in the family vault in St. Chad's churchyard. His practice was continued by his son Edward Haycock, junior (d. 1882).

Haycock had an extensive practice in Shropshire, the Border Counties and South Wales. Clytha Court and Millichope Park show that he was a Greek Revivalist of some ability, and Glynlliffon in Caernarvonshire is another considerable house in the same style which may have been designed by him (see below). His numerous Gothic churches, mostly in the lancet style, are, however, routine productions of their time which do nothing to enhance his reputation.

[Obituary in *Eddowes's Shrewsbury Journal*, 28 Dec. 1870; J. L. Hobbs, 'The Haycocks', *Shropshire Magazine*, Feb. 1960.]

PUBLIC BUILDINGS

SHREWSBURY, LORD HILL'S COLUMN, 1814–16, assisted by Thomas Harrison of Chester. There was a competition, in which the first premium was won by the sculptor, (Sir) Richard Westmacott, the second by Edward Haycock, and the third by John Carline (*q.v.*). However, it was 'unanimously agreed' to adopt Haycock's design, but to 'put [it] into the

[1] See Hawksmoor's publication, *A Short Historical Account of London Bridge, with a Proposition for a new Stone Bridge at Westminster*, 1736, and a drawing at the R.I.B.A.

hands of Mr. Harrison, of Chester, Architect, who made some alterations [chiefly to the pedestal] that were finally adopted'. Haycock exhibited his design at the Liverpool Academy in 1814. [*A Description of the Column in honour of Lord Hill erected at Shrewsbury*, J. Watten, Shrewsbury, 1818; *Gent's Mag.* 1817 (ii), 393–4, with engraving; T. J. Howell, *The Stranger in Shrewsbury*, 1816, 79–80].

SHREWSBURY, THE BUTTER MARKET, PRIDE HILL, 1819–20; dem. 1830 [Shrewsbury Public Library, Henry Pidgeon's 'Salopian Annals' 1823–30, vol. v, p. 87, *ex inf.* the late J. L. Hobbs].

COED-CWNWR, LLANTRISANT FAWR, MONMOUTH-SHIRE, ALMSHOUSES for Roger Edwards's Charity, 1825 [J. H. Clark, *The Usk Gleaner*, 1878].

MONMOUTH, SHIRE HALL, enlarged and remodelled interior, 1829–30 [Monmouthshire County Records, C. Bu. 5–11; C7 Bu. P.S5].

SHREWSBURY, SAVINGS BANK, COLLEGE HILL, 1839 [H. Pidgeon, *Memorials of Shrewsbury*, 1851, 168].

SHREWSBURY, THE MUSIC HALL, THE SQUARE, 1839–40 [H. Pidgeon, *Memorials of Shrewsbury*, 1851, 166].

SHREWSBURY, THE NEW BUTTER MARKET, PRIDE HILL, 1844; dem. 1877 [H. Pidgeon, *Memorials of Shrewsbury*, 1851, 177].

DOWLAIS, GLAMORGANSHIRE, THE MARKET HALL, 1844; dem. 1971 [J. B. Hilling, *Cardiff and the Valleys*, 1973, 109].

PRESTON HOSPITAL, PRESTON-ON-THE-WEALD-MOORS, SALOP., stone bell-turret on hall, replacing wooden cupola, 1844 [contract advertised in *Builder* ii, 1844, 84] (*C. Life*, 16 April 1964, fig. 3).

SHREWSBURY, LANCASTERIAN SCHOOL, nr. Railway Station, 1851 [H. Pidgeon, *Memorials of Shrewsbury*, 1851, 194].

SHREWSBURY, ST. CHAD'S SCHOOL, BRIDGE STREET, 1859; dem. except master's house [obituary in *Eddowes's Shrewsbury Journal*, 28 Dec. 1870].

BICTON HEATH, nr. SHREWSBURY, SHROPSHIRE COUNTY LUNATIC ASYLUM, alterations [obituary in *Eddowes's Shrewsbury Journal*, 28 Dec. 1870].

CHURCHES

CAERPHILLY, GLAMORGANSHIRE, 1826; dem. [I.C.B.S.].

MACHYNLLETH, MONTGOMERYSHIRE, 1827, Gothic [I.C.B.S.].

TAI-BACH (MARGAM), GLAMORGANSHIRE, 1827, Gothic [I.C.B.S.].

SHREWSBURY, ST. GEORGE, FRANKWELL, 1829–32, Gothic [D.H.S. Cranage, *The Churches of Shropshire* ii, 1903, 914].

BARMOUTH, MERIONETHSHIRE, 1830, Gothic [I.C.B.S.].

ABERYSTWYTH, ST. MICHAEL, 1830–3, Gothic; rebuilt 1894 [National Library of Wales, parish records of St. Michael's Aberystwyth, 12–114].

ABERSYCHAN, MONMOUTHSHIRE, 1831–2, Gothic [*Monmouthshire Merlin*, 30 April 1831].

TREVETHIN, MONMOUTHSHIRE, ST. THOMAS, 1831–2, Gothic [Port, 172].

HAY, BRECKNOCKSHIRE, 1833–4, Gothic; chancel added 1867 [I.C.B.S.].

TILSTOCK, SALOP., rebuilt 1835, Gothic [Salop. Record Office, Bridgewater papers 212 (plan)].

ABERAYRON, CARDIGANSHIRE, 1835 [I.C.B.S.].

CARMARTHEN, ST. DAVID, 1835–6, Gothic [Port, 170].

WHITCHURCH, SALOP., ST. CATHERINE, DODINGTON, 1836–7, classical [Shrewsbury Public Library, Watton's cuttings].

CRUCKTON, SALOP., 1840, Gothic [I.C.B.S.; elevations in Bodleian, MS. Top. Salop. c. 2, ff. 619–20].

LLANON, CARMARTHENSHIRE, 1841, Gothic [I.C.B.S.].

CRESSAGE, SALOP., 1841, Gothic [*Gent's Mag.* 1852 (ii), 60; elevations in Bodleian, MS. Top. Salop. c. 2, ff.621–2].

HOPE, SALOP., 1843, Gothic [I.C.B.S.; drawings in Stackhouse Library, St. Leonard's, Bridgnorth].

CHAPEL LAWN, nr. CLUN, SALOP., 1843, Gothic [I.C.B.S.].

BAYSTONHILL, SALOP., 1843, Gothic; chancel added 1886 [I.C.B.S.].

MIDDLETON IN CHIRBURY, SALOP., 1843, Gothic [I.C.B.S.].

LLANDEVAUD, MONMOUTHSHIRE, 1843, Gothic [I.C.B.S.].

DORRINGTON, SALOP., 1843–5, Gothic [*V.C.H. Salop.* viii, 55; Bodleian, MS. Top. Salop. c. 2, f. 179].

LLANWDDYN, MONTGOMERYSHIRE, c. 1844 [I.C.B.S., referred to as Haycock's design in Chapel Lawn, Salop., bundle].

NEWCASTLE, SALOP., 1848, Gothic [Shrewsbury Public Library, Watton's cuttings, vol. 7, p. 4; plans in Stackhouse Library, St. Leonard's, Bridgnorth].

COUNTRY HOUSES, ETC.

HODNET RECTORY, SALOP., for Bishop Heber, 1812, Tudor Gothic [*The Cambrian Traveller's Guide*, 1840, 528].

ONSLOW HALL, SALOP., remodelled for John Wingfield, c. 1815–20; dem. 1957 [drawings in R.I.B.A. Drawings Collection; exhib. at R.A. 1820].

LOTON PARK, SALOP., alterations for Sir Baldwin Leighton, Bart., 1819 [Drawings at Loton Park, *ex inf.* Mr. John Harris and Mr. J. B. Lawson].

CLYTHA COURT, MONMOUTHSHIRE, for William Herbert, *c.* 1830 [*The Cambrian Traveller's Guide*, 1840, 528].

ORLETON HALL, SALOP., refronted for Edward Cludde, *c.* 1830 [*The Cambrian Traveller's Guide*, 1840, 528; cf. Salop. Record Office 665/ 6040] (F. Leach, *The County Seats of Shropshire*, 1891, 305).

SHOBDON COURT, HEREFS., alterations for William Hanbury, afterwards 1st Lord Bateman, with advice from Sir Jeffry Wyatville, *c.* 1830–5; dem. [D. Linstrum, *Sir Jeffry Wyatville*, 1972, 248] (*C. Life*, 10 Nov. 1906).

LEATON KNOLLS, SALOP., for J. A. Lloyd, *c.* 1835; dem. 1955 [obituary in *Eddowes's Shrewsbury Journal*, 28 Dec. 1870; but in his *Reminiscences of a Literary Life* i, 1836, 396, T. F. Dibdin refers to 'the mansion of Mr. Lloyd, recently erected on his own plan (for he is his own *Vitruvius*)'].[1]

WALFORD MANOR, SALOP., for R. A. Slaney, 1831–5 [Salop. Record Office, specification, 665/ 1223–4].

MILLICHOPE PARK, SALOP., for the Rev. R. N. Pemberton, 1835–40 [obituary in *Eddowes's Shrewsbury Journal*, 28 Dec. 1870; views of the old and new houses and an elevation probably by Haycock in Bodleian, MS. Top. Salop. c. 2, ff. 377–8].

? GLYNLIFFON, CAERNARVONSHIRE, for the 3rd Lord Newborough, *c.* 1836–40 [National Library of Wales, Glynliffon No. 2492 is an award by Edward Haycock in a dispute between Lord Newborough and a plasterer about the value of ornamental plasterwork recently executed at Glynliffon, made in April 1842. Haycock's arbitration does not necessarily prove that he designed the house] (T. Nicholas, *Annals of the County Families of Wales* ii, 1875, 799).

LONGNOR HALL, SALOP., alterations for Panton Corbett, 1838–42 [Salop. Record Office, 567] (*C. Life*, 13–20 Feb. 1964).

NANTEOS, CARDIGANSHIRE, work for W. E. Powel, *c.* 1839–49, presumably including portico and stables [accounts at National Library of Wales, *ex inf.* Mr. D. B. Hague].[2]

KELMARSH HALL, NORTHANTS., enlargement of morning room for William Hanbury, 1st Lord Bateman, 1842 [Northants. Record Office H(K) 275, specification, estimate and account].

STANAGE PARK, RADNORSHIRE, alterations including dining-room, for the Rev. John Rogers, 1845 [newspaper cutting at Stanage].

---

[1] There are unsigned drawings for this house at Wheaton College, Norton, Mass., U.S.A.

[2] There are also some payments during this period to an Aberystwyth architect called Coulthart, perhaps William Coulthart (*q.v.*).

CHURCHSTOKE VICARAGE, MONTGOMERYSHIRE, enlarged 1846–7 [Bodleian Library, records of Queen Anne's Bounty].

NETLEY HALL, SALOP., for T. H. Hope-Edwardes, 1854–8 [F. Leach, *County Seats of Shropshire* i, 1891, 179: 'by the late Mr. Edward Haycock', which could mean either Edward Haycock senior (d. 1870) or his son (d. 1882)].

HAYCOCK, JOHN HIRAM (1759–1830), was the second son of William Haycock (1725–1802), a carpenter, joiner and builder of Shrewsbury. William Haycock had two other sons who were builders or architects, but William, the eldest, died in 1779 at the age of 27 and Edward, the youngest, in 1791 at the age of 23, leaving John as the only survivor. He had been apprenticed to his father in 1774, was admitted a freeman of the Shrewsbury Carpenters' and Bricklayers' Company in 1780, and became a burgess of Shrewsbury in 1796. In 1824 he was appointed County Surveyor of Shropshire. He died at Shrewsbury on 6 January 1830, aged 70, and was buried at St. Chad's Church. He was a competent provincial architect whose most important work was probably the Shirehall, a classical building with an engaged Ionic portico. He was the father of Edward Haycock (*q.v.*) [*Gent's Mag.* 1830 (i), 380; J. L. Hobbs, 'The Haycocks', *Shropshire Magazine*, Feb. 1960, 17; Shrewsbury Public Library, 13487, register of the Shrewsbury Carpenters' and Bricklayers' Company; pedigree in *Trans. Salop. Arch. Soc.*, 4th ser., ix, 1923, 29].

SHREWSBURY, THE GUILDHALL and SHIREHALL, 1783–5; dem. 1835 [T. Minshull, *The Shrewsbury Guide*, 1786, 47; H. Owen, *Some Account of the Ancient and Present State of Shrewsbury*, 1808, 411].

OAKLY PARK, SALOP., alterations for the 2nd Lord Clive (afterwards 1st Earl of Powis), *c.* 1784–90; subsequently remodelled by C. R. Cockerell [C. Hussey, *English Country Houses, Late Georgian*, 1958, 153].

SHREWSBURY, MILLINGTON'S HOSPITAL, FRANKWELL, remodelled central feature with portico and cupola, 1785–6 [J. B. Lawson, 'The Architect of Millington's Hospital, Shrewsbury', *Shropshire News Letter* no. 42, May 1972, 10].

SHREWSBURY, THE COUNTY GAOL, 1787–93; executed by Thomas Telford with modifications suggested by John Howard [H. Owen, *Some Account of the Ancient and Present State of Shrewsbury*, 1808, 430; A. Gibb, *The Story of Telford*, 1935, 323].

ATCHAM UNION WORK-HOUSE (now Berrington Hospital), CROSS HOUSES, SALOP., 1792–3 [Salop. Record Office, 13/5, minute-book 1792–1801].

MORETON CORBET CASTLE, SALOP., unexecuted designs for rebuilding for Andrew Corbet, 1796

[Shrewsbury School Library, S.IX 100, *ex inf.* Mr. J. B. Lawson].

SHREWSBURY, ALLATT'S CHARITY SCHOOL (now Health Centre), MURIVANCE, 1799–1800 [*Gent's Mag.* 1830 (i), 380].

ACTON REYNALD HALL, SALOP., enlarged for Sir Andrew Corbet, Bart., 1800 [order for chimney-pieces from Haycock in Carline's order-book in Salop. Record Office, 30 Sept. 1800].

SHREWSBURY, house for Anthony Kynnersley, 1800 [in 1800 Carline supplied stone sills for 8 windows 'for Mr. Haycock to Major Kynnersley's House', *ibid.*].

SWEENEY HALL, SALOP., for Thomas Netherton Parker, 1805 [Salop. Record Office, 1060/26].

THE ROVERIES, nr. LYDHAM, SALOP., house for John Oakeley, 1810 [specification and estimate in Salop. Record Office, 1079, Box 13].

GUNLEY HALL, MONMOUTHSHIRE, for Richard Pryce, *c.* 1810 [National Library of Wales, Gunley papers, parcel 14, proposed plan and elevation by J. H. Haycock, similar to house as built] (T. Nicholas, *Annals of the County Families of Wales* ii, 1875, 799).

OAKELEY HOUSE, nr. BISHOP'S CASTLE, SALOP., alterations and additions for the Rev. Herbert Oakley, 1814–16, dem. [Salop. Record Office, 1079/13].

SHREWSBURY SCHOOL (now Public Library), remodelled Elizabethan library by removing attic storey and inserting Gothic windows and roof, 1815 [specification and estimate in Salop. Record Office, 3356, box lx, bdl. 2613, *ex inf.* Mr. J. B. Lawson].

PRADOE, SALOP., alterations for the Hon. Thomas Kenyon, 1816 [plan and specification in scrapbook at Pradoe, *ex inf.* Miss M. C. Hill].

SHREWSBURY, Headmaster's House in School Lane, refronted for Dr. Samuel Butler by J. H. & E. Haycock, 1818, Tudor style [Shrewsbury School Trustees' minutes 1798–1881, p. 60, *ex inf.* Mr. J. B. Lawson].

PRESTON HOSPITAL, PRESTON-ON-THE-WEALD-MOORS, SALOP., addition of curved arcades and outer blocks, 1827 [Weston Hall, Staffs., Preston Hospital papers 13/8; agreement between the trustees and J. H. & E. Haycock] (plan in *C. Life*, 16 April 1964, fig. 6).

HAYDEN, —, described as 'Surveyor at the Building of the Right Hon. the Lord Grosvenor', designed THE EASTGATE, CHESTER, 1768–9 [Chester Assembly Book 1725–85].

HAYLEY, WILLIAM (–1860), practised in Manchester from the late 1820s onwards. Until 1840 he was in partnership with Thomas Brown, in conjunction with whom he designed several Commissioners' churches. Brown died in 1840 [Port, 178], and Hayley thereafter practised on

his own until he was joined by his son William Henry Hayley. He died at Broughton near Manchester on 30 June 1860. W. H. Hayley subsequently entered into partnership with William Dawes. Richard Tattersall (*q.v.*) was a pupil of the elder Hayley.

Buildings designed by the firm of Hayley and Brown are listed below. Hayley's independent works included the Italianate tower of ST. THOMAS'S CHURCH, ARDWICK GREEN NORTH, MANCHESTER, which he built in *c.* 1836 to the designs of a Mr. Frayer [Church Notes of the Rev. Richard Loxham in Manchester Central Library, ii, f. 98]; the neo-Norman ALL SOULS CHURCH, ANCOATS, MANCHESTER, 1839–40 [Port, 148–9]; the Gothic ST. MATTHEW'S CHURCH, STRETFORD, LANCS., 1841–2 [Port, 148–9] and ST. PAUL'S CHURCH, MACCLESFIELD, CHESHIRE, 1843–4 [Port, 140–1]. A design by him dated 1839 for a Post Office in Manchester is in the Public Record Office (MPD 137).

BOLLINGTON, CHESHIRE, ST. JOHN'S CHURCH, 1832–4, Gothic [Port, 140–1].

NORBURY, CHESHIRE, ST. THOMAS'S CHURCH, 1833–4, Gothic [Port, 140–1].

CHORLTON-ON-MEDLOCK, LANCS., ST. SAVIOUR'S CHURCH, cons. 1836, Gothic [C. Stewart, *The Architecture of Manchester: An Index of the Principal Buildings and their Architects,* Manchester 1956, 32, citing *Manchester Guardian,* 12 Nov. 1836].

TONG, LANCS., ST. MICHAEL'S CHURCH, 1838–9, Gothic [Port, 150–1].

NEWTON MOOR, nr. HYDE, CHESHIRE, ST. MARY'S CHURCH, 1838–9; chancel 1876–7; neo-Norman [I.C.B.S.].

WITHINGTON, nr. MANCHESTER, ST. PAUL'S CHURCH, 1840–1, neo-Norman [C. Stewart, *op. cit.,* citing *Manchester Courier,* 23 Oct. 1841].

HAYWARD, ABRAHAM (1692–1747), was a native of Whitchurch in Shropshire, but established himself as a mason and master builder in Lincoln. According to family tradition he went to Lincoln to build St. Peter at Arches Church, but as this church was in fact designed and built (1720–4) by William Smith of Warwick it is likely that Hayward was working for Smith, perhaps as his foreman. In 1735 he was one of the builders who gave evidence before the House of Commons as to the condition of Gainsborough Church [*Commons' Journals* xxii, 556–7, 619–21; xxiii, 582, 618]. He built the town house of the Disney family in Disney Place, Lincoln, in 1736, and lived in a house which he had built for himself on the east side of St. Peter at Arches churchyard, on the site of the former Taylors' Hall. He died at Lincoln in 1747 and was buried at St. Peter at Arches. His younger brother John Hayward (1708–78), also a mason by trade, accompanied him to Lincoln, purchased the freedom

THE HAYWARDS AND THE CARLINES

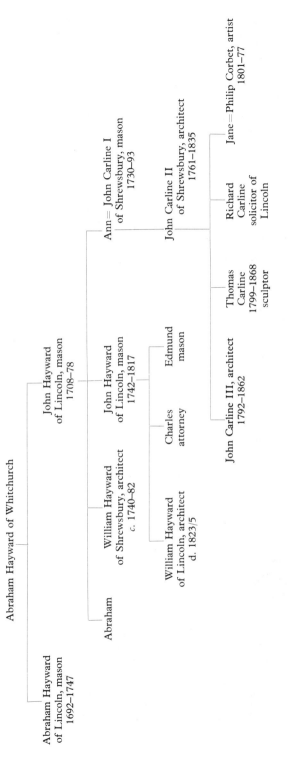

Abraham Hayward of Whitchurch

Abraham Hayward
of Lincoln, mason
1692–1747

John Hayward
of Lincoln, mason
1708–78

Ann = John Carline I
of Shrewsbury, mason
1730–93

Abraham

William Hayward
of Shrewsbury, architect
c. 1740–82

John Hayward
of Lincoln, mason
1742–1817

John Carline II
of Shrewsbury, architect
1761–1835

William Hayward
of Lincoln, architect
d. 1823/5

Charles
attorney

Edmund
mason

Thomas
Carline
1799–1868
sculptor

Richard
Carline
solicitor of
Lincoln

Jane = Philip Corbet, artist
1801–77

John Carline III, architect
1792–1862

409

of the city in 1753, and died there in 1778. In 1753 St. Mary's Bridge, Lincoln, was rebuilt 'pursuant to a plan and estimate made by John Hayward, mason' [Lincoln Corporation Minutes 1710–1800, pp. 341, 342]. John Hayward was the grandfather of William Hayward, surveyor to Lincoln Cathedral (q.v.), and probably the father of the architect William Hayward of Shrewsbury (q.v.). His daughter Ann married John Carline (q.v.), a Lincoln man who afterwards established himself in Shrewsbury.

[E. Venables, *Walks through the Streets of London*, 1888, 30; Society of Antiquaries, E. J. Willson's Collections, v, 74, and Thomas Sympson's MS. *Adversaria* in the same collection, p. 126; *Lincolnshire Notes and Queries* ix, 1906–7, 66; J. L. Hobbs, 'The Hayward Family of Whitchurch', *Shropshire Magazine*, Jan. 1960; information from Mr. Richard Carline].

HAYWARD, WILLIAM (c. 1740–1782), was probably one of the sons of John Hayward of Lincoln (d. 1778) and grandson of Abraham Hayward (q.v.). In 1766 he was appointed to be deputy to John Gwynn as surveyor in charge of the rebuilding of the English Bridge at Shrewsbury [A. W. Ward, *The Bridges of Shrewsbury*, 1935, 84–5]. Thereafter (if not before) he was resident in Shrewsbury. In the 1770s he was again associated with Gwynn at Oxford, for the latter's plans for paving the city and rebuilding Magdalen Bridge are accompanied by a note that they 'were executed by William Hayward of Shrewsbury, under Mr. Gwynne Architect' [B.M., *King's Maps* xxxiv, 33, 3a–c].

Hayward himself designed at least three bridges. The first was the bridge over the river Tern at ATCHAM, SHROPSHIRE, which (in the words of the inscription on the parapet) 'was erected at the Expense of the County A.D. MDCCLXXX, and decorated at the Expense of Noel Hill, Esq. William Hayward, Architect'. It was widened in 1932. The second was the important bridge over the river Thames at HENLEY, OXON., for which Hayward made designs in 1781. He died before work had started, as a result of a 'cold and fever' contracted by 'giving up his place inside a coach to a woman on a stormy night'. He is said to have expressed a wish to be buried under the centre arch of the bridge, but was in fact interred in Henley Parish Church, where there is a tablet to his memory (now in the tower). The bridge was built by John Townesend of Oxford and completed in 1786 in accordance with Hayward's designs. The heads of 'Thames' and 'Isis' on the keystones were carved by Mrs. Damer, the daughter of General Conway, of Park Place nearby. Hayward's third bridge was the TERN BRIDGE over the river Tern about half a mile from his Atcham Bridge, which was built by subscription in 1782, and bears an inscription on the

central arch recording that it was 'the last Edifice erected by that ingenious Architect William Hayward'.

[*A.P.S.D.*; J. S. Burn, *History of Henley*, 1861, 298; J. L. Hobbs, 'The Hayward Family of Whitchurch', *Shropshire Magazine*, Jan. 1960].

HAYWARD, WILLIAM (–1823/5), was the son of John Hayward (d. 1817) and grandson of John Hayward (d. 1778). His father, like his grandfather, was a mason by trade, and was twice Mayor of Lincoln, dying in office in 1817 at an advanced age [*Gent's Mag.* 1817 (i), 381]. William Hayward held the post of Surveyor to Lincoln Cathedral from 1799 to 1823 and is generally described as 'architect'. He had a considerable local practice, and the Judges' Lodgings at Lincoln show that he was a competent designer in the 'Regency' style. His reconstruction of Kirton-in-Holland Church in 1804 shows that he also had an understanding of Gothic architecture quite remarkable at this date, and suggests that he may have been a pupil of William Lumby, his predecessor as surveyor to the cathedral. He succeeded his father as Mayor in 1817 and appears to have died in 1823 or 1825. [J. L. Hobbs, 'The Hayward Family of Whitchurch', *Shropshire Magazine*, Jan. 1960; information from Mr. Richard Carline; Lincoln Cathedral archives, Bij.2.12, p. 403].

LINCOLN, ST. SWITHIN'S CHURCH, rebuilt 1802–3; rebuilt 1868–9 [E. Venables, 'History of St. Swithin's Church, Lincoln', *Associated Architectural Societies' Reports and Papers* xix, 1887–8, 27].

LINCOLN, SHIRE HALL, rearranged interior; dem. 1823 [Lincolnshire Record Office, Minutes of County Meetings, 1792–1823].

LINCOLN CATHEDRAL, rebuilt gable on south side of west transept, 1804 [C. Wild, *The Cathedral Church of Lincoln*, 1819, 23 note †].

KIRTON-IN-HOLLAND CHURCH, LINCOLNSHIRE, demolished central tower and transepts, shortened chancel and built new west tower closely resembling and incorporating some features of the demolished central tower, 1804–5 [*Churches in the Division of Holland*, 1843, Kirton, 5; Lincolnshire Record Office, plans in Fac. 9/34] (F. J. Allen, *The Great Church Towers of England*, 1932, 129 plate).

LINCOLN, THE CITY GAOL AND SESSIONS HOUSE (now Police Station), MONKS ROAD, 1805–9 [*The Date Book for Lincoln and Neighbourhood*, Lincoln 1866, 255, 268].

METHERINGHAM VICARAGE, LINCS., altered or rebuilt 1808 [Lincolnshire Record Office, MGA 58].

LINCOLN, ST. MARTIN'S CHURCH, rebuilt north aisle 1809; dem. c. 1875 [MS. Vestry Minutes].

LINCOLN, THE JUDGES' LODGINGS, CASTLE HILL,

1810–11 [Lincolnshire Record Office, Grand Jury Minute Book, p. 282].

LINCOLN, THE GOWTS BRIDGE, 1813; since rebuilt [*A.P.S.D.*, *s.v.* 'Lincoln'].

SILK WILLOUGHBY RECTORY, LINCS., west wing, 1813 [Lincolnshire Record Office, MGA 71].

HAMBLETON VICARAGE, RUTLAND, repairs 1817 [Northants. Record Office, Peterborough Diocesan Records].

TORKSEY CHURCH, LINCS., alterations 1821–2 [accounts in parish records].

HAYWOOD, JOHN (1751–), entered the Royal Academy Schools in 1772, and gained the Silver Medal in 1774. He exhibited at the Academy from 1773 to 1794, including an 'Elevation for a market house at Bridgewater' (1780), a 'Design for a lodge to be built at Clehonger, Herefordshire' (1785),[1] and a 'Plan and Elevation for a Mausoleum to the memory of the late Mr. John Smeaton, F.R.S.' (1793), none of which are known to have been built. J. J. Haywood, junior, exhibited student's designs at the Royal Academy from 1790 to 1793 from the same address (75 Long Acre).

HEAN, Messrs., were builders at Dundee and wrights by trade. The firm appears to have been founded by David Hean, senior, during the first quarter of the nineteenth century. Later members of the family were James (who lectured on domestic architecture at the Watt Institute on 27 January 1830), Alexander (d. 1865), Peter (d. 1877) and David, junior (d. 1878). The last was a Town Councillor, Baillie and Dean of Guild. The principal architectural works for which the firm was responsible before 1840 were ST. PETER'S FREE CHURCH, DUNDEE, 1836 [*ex inf.* Mr. David Walker] and the enlargement in 1837 of the south side of ST. AIDAN'S CHURCH, BROUGHTY FERRY, DUNDEE [*Dundee Advertiser*, 1 March 1837]. [Information from Mr. David Walker.]

HEATHER, CHARLES of Hereford, was appointed Surveyor of Bridges to the county of Hereford in 1831, in place of the late John Gethin [*Woolhope Club's Transactions*, 1931–2, 89]. In 1836 he added a Gothic porch to ST. PETER'S CHURCH, HEREFORD [I.C.B.S.].

HEDGELAND, CHARLES, practised in Exeter during the second quarter of the nineteenth century. His marriage in 1823 is noted in *Gent's Mag.* 1823, 82. He was probably the son of Caleb Hedgeland (*c.* 1760–1839), a builder of

Exeter who made a model of the city afterwards in the possession of the Devon and Cornwall Institution. Charles Hedgeland designed MANATON RECTORY, DEVON, in 1825 [Exeter Diocesan Records]; enlarged the nave of SOUTH MOLTON CHURCH, DEVON in 1825–9 [I.C.B.S.]; designed a small Greek Revival church at STARCROSS, nr. DAWLISH, DEVON, in 1826–7 [Port, 142–3]; and reconstructed ST. PETROCK'S CHURCH, EXETER, in 1828 [G. Oliver, *Ecclesiastical Antiquities in Devon*, 1840, ii, 196; R. Dymond, *Calendar of Deeds and Documents belonging to the Feoffees of the Parish Property*, Exeter 1889, 38].

HEDGELAND, JOHN PIKE, was awarded the silver medal of the Society of Arts for an architectural drawing in 1819. In the same year he was an unsuccessful competitor for the church of St. Peter, Eaton Square, Westminster. He exhibited architectural drawings at the Royal Academy in 1822 and 1823, and was the author of a work entitled *First Part of a Series of Designs for Private Dwellings*, 1821, containing 20 lithographic plates. He appears subsequently to have given up architecture for work as an artist in stained glass. In 1826–9 he supervised the careful restoration of the early sixteenth-century glass in the windows of ST. NEOT'S CHURCH, CORNWALL, subsequently publishing in 1830 *A Description, accompanied by Sixteen Coloured Plates, of the Windows of St. Neot's Church, Cornwall*. In 1841–5 he was similarly employed to repair the windows of King's College Chapel, Cambridge, and filled a vacant half-window at the south-east end of the chapel with glass representing the Brazen Serpent in the Wilderness after Rubens [Willis & Clark, i, 515]. As a glass-painter he was succeeded by his son George Hedgeland, whose major work was the west window of Norwich Cathedral [*Jnl. of the British Society of Master Glass Painters* xiii, 1959–63, 392–3].

HEDGER, WILLIAM, of South Street, West Square, Southwark, was a member of a family of speculative builders active in Southwark at the end of the eighteenth century [*Survey of London* xxv, 52–6]. In 1807–8 he supervised extensive internal alterations to ST. GEORGE'S CHURCH, SOUTHWARK, after a survey by S. P. Cockerell. They included new north and south galleries and a new ceiling with painted decoration [Surrey Archdeaconry Records]. William Hedger, junior, of the same address, exhibited a view of St. Pancras Church at the Royal Academy in 1827.

HEITON, ANDREW (*c.* 1793–1858), practised in Perth. He designed GARTH HOUSE, PERTHSHIRE, for General Sir Archibald Campbell, Bart., *c.* 1840, Gothic [A. H. Millar, *Castles and Mansions of Perthshire and Forfarshire*, 1890, 64]; enlarged REDGORTON CHURCH, PERTHSHIRE, 1840–1

---

[1] The seat of the Aubrey family at Clehonger was destroyed by fire in 1785. The estate was bought by Col. John Matthews, who in 1788–90 built a new house called Belmont to the designs of James Wyatt (C. J. Robinson, *The Mansions of Herefordshire*, 1872, 66).

[S.R.O., HR 311/2, p. 92 *et seq.*]; and rebuilt ST. MARTIN'S CHURCH, PERTHSHIRE, 1842–3 [S.R.O., HR 514/1]. His son Andrew Heiton, junior (1823–94), was a pupil of David Bryce. In 1848 he joined his father in partnership, and ultimately became City Architect. He specialized in Scottish Baronial country houses. The family practice was continued by Andrew Heiton III (born Andrew Heiton Grainger), who died in the 1920s [information from Mr. George Hay and Mr. David Walker].

HEMSLEY, HENRY (*c.* 1764–   ), a pupil of Henry Holland, was admitted to the Royal Academy Schools in 1787 at the age of 23, and was awarded the Silver Medal in 1788. He exhibited student's designs at the Academy from 1785 to 1790. In 1805 he was appointed architect to the Barrack Department of the War Office in succession to James Johnson.

The Henry Hemsley who died in Vincent Square on 30 May 1825, at the age of 33, leaving a widow and six infant children, was presumably his son [*Gent's Mag.* 1825 (i), 572]. This younger Hemsley had exhibited at the Academy from Vincent Square in 1819, 1821 and 1822, and had made designs for ST. GEORGE'S CHURCH, RAMSGATE, KENT, 'but in consequence of his death, shortly after the commencement of the building, the completion of it devolved on Mr. H. E. Kendall, who made some few alterations' [*The Watering Places of Great Britain and Fashionable Directory*, 1833, 217].

HENDERSON, DAVID (–*c.* 1787), was a mason from Sauchie near Alloa who established himself in Edinburgh. In February 1765, while still resident at Sauchie, he was awarded the prize of 30 guineas offered for the best design for the North Bridge, but in May the committee declared that as he 'had failed in finding security to execute the Bridge agreeable to his estimates', the design and estimate of William Mylne (*q.v.*) would be accepted instead. However in 1769 Henderson was among those who reported on the state of Mylne's bridge after its partial collapse, and in 1784 he was employed to carry out some work on its structure. In 1785–6 he was responsible for designing and building the important bridge of four arches which carries the main road from Edinburgh to Berwick over the Pease Dean near Cockburnspath. He was also employed to make designs and estimates for the Borrowstounness Canal Company. In Edinburgh, when the idea of rebuilding the University was first contemplated in 1767, he was paid 10 guineas for making a plan, and in 1773, as 'David Henderson, Architect', he contracted to build INVERLEITH HOUSE (now within the Edinburgh Botanic Gardens) for James Rocheid, evidently to his own designs [Edinburgh Public Library, MS.

412

decreet referring to tne contract]. Inverleith House is a small villa with quadrant wings in the Palladian tradition. It was extensively repaired after a fire in 1876.

Henderson had two sons, David and John. David was in business in Alloa as a mill-wright, but John was destined to be an architect, for in or about 1774 his father sent him to Rome. There he became friendly with Thomas Hardwick, and competed with the young Soane for the fickle patronage of the Bishop of Derry, who wanted a design for a summer dining-room at his Irish seat of Downhill [P. de la R. du Prey in *Architectural History* xv, 1972, 52]. In 1785 he exhibited a 'plan, elevation and section of a temple' at the Royal Academy in London. The only buildings known to have been erected to his designs are the wings which he added to AMISFIELD HOUSE, EAST LOTHIAN in 1785 for the Hon. Francis Charteris-Wemyss (afterwards 6th Earl of Wemyss), dem. *c.* 1928 [J. Miller, *History of Haddington*, 1894, 527],[1] and THE ASSEMBLY ROOMS, GEORGE STREET, EDINBURGH, 1784–7, to which the portico was added in 1818 [S.R.O., GD 15/798, minutes of the committee for building the Assembly Rooms].

John Henderson died at Edinburgh on 16 February 1786 [*Scots Mag.* xlviii, 1786, 103], and his father appears to have died within the next two years. The 'heirs and creditors' of 'the two Mr. Hendersons' are referred to in the minutes of the committee for building the Assembly Rooms in August 1788, and in June 1789 the surviving son David was claiming money due to himself as heir to both. But for John Henderson's premature death he might well have emerged as one of Edinburgh's leading Georgian architects.

In 1765 David Henderson was stated in the *Edinburgh Advertiser* to have published proposals for printing 'a book of architecture', but this evidently came to nothing. A design by him for a vine-house is among the Fairlie papers in the Scottish Record Office (GD 237/113/4).

[*A.P.S.D.*; J. Grant, *Old and New Edinburgh* i, n.d., 337; A. J. Youngson, *The Making of Classical Edinburgh*, 1966, 62–5, 124; *Scots Mag.* xxxvi, 1774, 108; H. M. Register House, Edinburgh Testaments, 18 June 1789.]

HENDERSON, JOHN (–1786), *see* HENDERSON, DAVID.

HENDERSON, JOHN (*c.* 1813–1844) was the eldest son of John Henderson, a builder of Edinburgh who died in 1860 aged 76. On the family monument in St. Cuthbert's Churchyard, Edinburgh, John Henderson is described as 'Archi-

---

[1] Cf. an engraving of the house from a drawing by 'that ingenious architect, Mr. John Henderson' in *Archaeologia Scotica* i, 1792, p. 46.

tect', but he died in May 1844 at the early age of 31, and no building designed by him has so far been identified. His sister Margaret married Robert Brown (q.v.). He must be distinguished from John Henderson (1804–62), originally of Brechin, who had an extensive architectural practice in Edinburgh in the 1840s and 1850s, and is buried in the Grange Cemetery.

HENDERSON, *alias* **ANDERSON, WILLIAM** (c. 1737–1824) and his son **JOHN** (c. 1761–1800) were architects and builders at Loughborough in Leicestershire, where their surname usually appears in local records as 'Henderson' but sometimes as 'Anderson'. In 1768–70 William Henderson 'of Staunton' built the LEICESTER INFIRMARY under the direction of Benjamin Wyatt. He had previously submitted designs which may have been modified by Wyatt [minutes of the committee in Leicester Museum Archives Dept.]. At this time (1762–75) he was engaged in rebuilding STAUNTON HAROLD HALL, LEICS., for Washington, 5th Earl Ferrers (q.v.), who, according to Throsby's *Select Views of Leicestershire* i, 1759, 126, designed the house himself [building accounts in Leicestershire Record Office]. 'Mr. Anderson' was the 'architect and undertaker' of STANFORD HALL, NOTTS., for Charles Vere Dashwood in 1771–4 [Thoroton's *History of Nottinghamshire*, ed. Throsby, 1797, i, 9] (Neale, *Views of Seats*, 1st ser., ii, 1819), and in 1781 Samuel Stretton of Nottingham built WILFORD HALL, NOTTS., for Samuel Smith, 'under the direction of Anderson of Loughborough, Architect' [*The Stretton Manuscripts*, ed. G. C. Robertson, 1910, 227]. Stanford and Wilford are substantial Georgian houses with restrained neo-classical detailing in the style of Adam. Unexecuted designs for a lunatic asylum at Leicester made by William Henderson in 1781 are in the Department of Archives at Leicester Museum. William Henderson died at Loughborough in March 1824, aged 87 [Burial Register]. His son John predeceased him, dying on 8 June 1800, aged 39. John and his mother are commemorated by a slate tombstone in All Saints churchyard, Loughborough [information from Mr. Edward Saunders].

HENWOOD, LUKE (–1830), 'architect', was admitted to the freedom of the City of Bristol on 19 September 1789, on payment of 15 guineas [City Archives]. He was one of the District Surveyors for Bristol from 1804 until his death, which took place on 19 March 1830 [A. Beaven, *Bristol Lists*, 1899, 248; *Gent's Mag.* 1830 (i), 379]. In 1807–8 he repaired the tower of ALL SAINTS CHURCH, BRISTOL, and reconstructed the stone cupola, altering the outline of the dome. The cupola was again rebuilt in 1930 [MS. Vestry Minutes]. At Trewithen, Cornwall, there are un-

dated drawings signed by Henwood for alterations to NO. 30, ARGYLL STREET, LONDON, for Christopher Hawkins, M.P. The works included a new front door with elegantly designed detail.

HEPPER, DENT, practised in Chelmsford. In 1812, when he was one of the unsuccessful candidates for the County Surveyorship of Essex, he stated that he had been in practice in the county for 25 years [Essex Record Office, Q/SO 22, pp. 40–1; advt. in *Chelmsford Chronicle*, 18 Sept. 1812]. In 1818 he designed a south gallery for CHELMSFORD CHURCH similar to an earlier design by him for a north gallery [Essex Record Office, Chelmsford Vestry Minutes, D/P 94/8/3]. His designs for a new mansion at Eye in Suffolk for Thomas Wythe, Esq., dated 1815, are in the Suffolk Record Office at Ipswich [S1/2/300, *ex inf.* Miss Nancy Briggs].

HERBERT, HENRY, 9TH EARL OF PEMBROKE (c. 1689–1750), was the eldest son of Thomas, 8th Earl of Pembroke, whom he succeeded in 1733. He was educated at Christ Church, Oxford, where he matriculated in 1705 at the age of 16. His presence in Venice in 1712 is evidence that he subsequently went on the Grand Tour. On the accession of George I he was appointed a lord of the bedchamber to the Prince of Wales, a post which he retained on the latter's accession to the throne as George II in 1727. In 1735 he was made First Lord of the Bedchamber and Groom of the Stole. He also held various military commands, attaining the rank of Lieutenant-General in 1742. His friendship with the antiquary William Stukeley and his election to the Royal Society in 1743 are indications of his intellectual interests. He died suddenly at his house in Privy Gardens, Whitehall, on 9 January 1749/50.

Pembroke inherited his father's fondness for the arts, but architecture was his special interest. As befitted the owner of Wilton, he favoured the Palladian style which Inigo Jones had been the first to introduce into England, and which in his own time 'was being revived through the influence of Lord Burlington. In the absence of personal papers or correspondence, the development of his architectural taste is undocumented, but the fact that he was at Christ Church in the time of Dean Aldrich should not be overlooked.[1]

That Pembroke was more than merely an intelligent patron of architecture is clearly implied by Vertue, Walpole and other eighteenth-century writers. Walpole indeed thought him a better architect – *i.e.* a purer Palladian – than either Burlington or Kent, and it is true that most of the buildings with which he was associated adhere closely to Palladian prototypes – notably

[1] As an undergraduate he subscribed £20 to the building of Peckwater Quadrangle to Aldrich's designs.

the bridge at Wilton and three villa-like houses reminiscent of Palladio's Villa Emo at Fanzolo, *i.e.* his own house in Whitehall (designed 1723), Marble Hill, Twickenham (begun 1724), and the White Lodge at Richmond (begun 1727).[1] The English prototype is Colen Campbell's Newby Park in Yorkshire, begun in 1720, and Campbell also made an unexecuted design for a house of this type to be built at Ardkinglas in Argyllshire (above p. 185). Lord Herbert and Campbell had a link in their common association with the Prince of Wales (Herbert as a lord of the bedchamber from 1715, Campbell as the Prince's architect from 1719), and in 1723 it was Campbell who designed Herbert's house in Whitehall. He may also have had a hand in Marble Hill, but from about 1725 his place as Herbert's architectural collaborator was taken by Roger Morris, who was to be concerned in nearly all of his patron's subsequent building activities.

A list of buildings for whose design Pembroke appears to have been in some way responsible is given below. The problem is to determine whether, like Aldrich and Burlington, the 'Architect Earl' could envisage a building in detail and express his ideas on paper in a form intelligible to others, or whether he worked entirely through architectural amanuenses. No authenticated drawings by Pembroke have yet been discovered, though a plan and two elevations for the Water Tower at Houghton may possibly be in his hand.

Apart from the buildings which he and Morris erected, Lord Pembroke's interest in architecture was demonstrated by the prominent part which he took in the construction of Westminster Bridge, of which he laid the first stone in 1739, and the last in 1747. He used his influence to defend the Swiss architect Labelye against the attacks of Batty Langley, Hawksmoor and others, whose designs had been rejected. Drawings and minutes connected with the bridge are preserved among the Earl's papers at Wilton.

[G.E.C., *Complete Peerage*; *A.P.S.D.*; *D.N.B.*; Walpole, *Anecdotes of Painting*, ed. Dallaway & Wornum, iii, 1862, 771–2; J. Lees-Milne, *Earls of Creation*, 1962, 59–100.]

BUILDINGS ASSOCIATED WITH LORD PEMBROKE

LONDON, WHITEHALL, house (afterwards PEMBROKE HOUSE) for himself, 1724; rebuilt 1757, dem. 1913. The plate in *Vitruvius Britannicus* iii, 1725, pl. 48, is signed 'Co: Campbell Architectus'. An original elevation, dated August 1723, is in the Lister Collection in the Treasury Library, Whitehall, no. 52 b. The hand

does not appear to be Campbell's. At Wilton there is another elevation signed 'Rog^r. Morris Delt.' (reproduced by Draper & Eden, *Marble Hill House*, pl. 5). For an alternative design by William Dickinson dated 1723 see *Wren Soc.* xvii, pl. xlviii. The house is described in *Survey of London* xiii, 167–75.

MARBLE HILL, TWICKENHAM, MIDDLESEX, for Henrietta Howard, Countess of Suffolk, mistress of George II, 1724–9. Illustrated by Campbell in *Vitruvius Britannicus* iii, pl. 93, but without naming any architect. Ascribed by Walpole to Pembroke. The bills, among the Hobart papers in the Norfolk and Norwich Record Office, show that Roger Morris was in charge, but that most of the money was 'Received of the Honble Mrs. Howard by the Hands of the R^t Honble Lord Herbert'. An unsigned design for the house preserved at Wilton may be in Campbell's hand. The history of the house is fully discussed by Marie P. G. Draper and W. A. Eden, *Marble Hill House*, 1970.

THE WHITE LODGE, RICHMOND NEW PARK, begun 1727 for George I, completed 1728 for George II. Ascribed by Walpole to Pembroke, but Roger Morris was in charge of the building operations and is described as architect in *Vitruvius Britannicus* iv, 1767, pls. 1–4. The wings were added in the 1760s. See *History of the King's Works* v, 230–3 for documentation and further details.

CASTLE HILL, DEVONSHIRE, remodelled for Lord Clinton (afterwards 1st Lord Fortescue) by Roger Morris under the direction of Lord Burlington and Lord Herbert, 1729 onwards [see above, p. 131 and below, p. 561].

WESTCOMBE HOUSE, BLACKHEATH, KENT, was bought by Lord Herbert after the death of Capt. Galfridus Walpole (brother of Sir Robert), who was Treasurer of Greenwich Hospital from 1715 to 1721 and died in 1726. Sarah, Duchess of Marlborough, described the house in 1732 in terms which make it clear that it was designed by Herbert, and it closely resembled Whitton Place, Middlesex, designed for the Earl of Islay by Herbert's collaborator Roger Morris *c.* 1732. It may therefore be concluded that the house was rebuilt by Herbert and Morris *c.* 1730. It was demolished in 1854 [Larking, *Hundred of Blackheath*, ed. Drake, 1886, 53; *Letters of a Grandmother*, ed. G. Scott Thompson, 1944, 21–3, 53] (Watts, *Views of Seats*, pl. 1, 1779; Sandby, *Select Views in England etc.* i, 1781, pl. 24).

BLENHEIM PALACE, OXON., THE COLUMN OF VICTORY, for Sarah, Duchess of Marlborough, 1730–1. Hawksmoor, who had previously made designs for the column which were not adopted, described it in 1731 as 'conducted by my Ld. Herbert' and there is evidence that

---

[1] For South Dalton Hall, Yorkshire, another house of this group, see W. A. Eden in *The Country Seat*, ed Colvin & Harris, 1970.

Roger Morris was concerned in its construction [David Green, 'Blenheim Column of Victory', *Arch. Rev.*, April 1950; Angela Green, 'Letters of Sarah, Duchess of Marlborough, on the Column of Victory at Blenheim', *Oxoniensia* xxxi, 1966].

WIMBLEDON HOUSE, SURREY, for Sarah, Duchess of Marlborough, 1732–3; destroyed by fire 1785. Walpole, writing in the 1750s, says the house was designed 'by Henry Earl of Pembroke', but Roger Morris is given as architect in *Vitruvius Britannicus* v, 1771, pls. 20–22. A letter from the Duchess to Pembroke (then Lord Herbert), dated 25 March 1732, mentions Morris in connection with the works then in progress, but implies that he was following Herbert's directions (Blenheim Palace muniments, GI, 20). Others published in *Letters of a Grandmother*, ed. G. Scott Thompson, 1943, 35, 70, 104, 123, indicate that Francis Smith of Warwick was employed as surveyor. There is a plan of the house at Wilton. Plans for the layout of the grounds are in Bodleian, MS. Gough Drawings a.3, f. 31 and a.4, f. 44. [M. P. G. Draper in *C. Life*, 2 August 1962].

WILTON HOUSE, WILTS., THE PALLADIAN BRIDGE, 1736–7. Vertue, writing in 1740, says 'this is the design of the present Earl of Pembroke and built by his direction' [Walpole Society, *Vertue Note Books* v, 130]. Roger Morris is, however, described as 'Architect' on the plate in *Vitruvius Britannicus* v, 1771, pl. 89, and in the Royal Library at Windsor there is a drawing of the bridge signed 'R. Morris'. Copies of the Wilton Bridge were later erected at Stowe (before 1742), Prior Park, Bath (1756), Hagley (before 1764) and Amesbury (1777).

HOUGHTON HALL, NORFOLK, THE WATER HOUSE, for Robert Walpole, 1st Earl of Orford, probably *c.* 1730. Drawings in the Metropolitan Museum of Art from the grangerised manuscript of Horace Walpole's *Aedes Walpolianae* are inscribed by Walpole 'The Water-House in the Park, designed by Henry Lord Herbert, afterwards Earl of Pembroke' [John Harris, 'The Water Tower at Houghton', *Burl. Mag.* cxi, 1969, 300: John Harris, *Catalogue of British Drawings for Architecture etc. in American Collections*, 1971, 122 and pls. 88–9].

HIGHCLERE, HANTS. Pembroke's brother the Hon. Robert Herbert (1693–1769), who inherited Highclere under the will of his maternal grandfather Sir Robert Sawyer (d. 1692), may well have obtained his help in embellishing his grounds with certain garden buildings which, although undocumented and undated, appear to have been erected by him. Indeed, in his *Historic Lands of England* ii, 1849, 152, Sir Bernard Burke states, no coubt correctly, that Pembroke was responsible for the Palladian MILFORD LAKE HOUSE, the most important of

these buildings. The Ionic Temple (remodelled by Barry) may date from the second half of the 18th century, but the Corinthian Temple known as JACKDAW'S CASTLE is clearly of earlier date, and was probably built in the 1730s, as it is said to incorporate columns salvaged from the ruins of Devonshire House, Piccadilly, when it was burned in 1733 [letter from Charles Lyttelton to Sanderson Miller in Warwicks. Record Office, 1757].

HERBERT, WILLIAM (*c.* 1792–1863), was a successful London builder and surveyor who lived in Farm Street, Berkeley Square. He was one of the builders associated with Thomas Cubitt in the development of Belgravia, and established his own saw-mills on a site in Pimlico. When Cubitt moved to a new house in Clapham Park in 1832 it was Herbert who took over and enlarged his former residence, Cavendish House on Clapham Common, and in 1841 Herbert's daughter married Cubitt's lawyer, James Hopgood [Hermione Hobhouse, *Thomas Cubitt*, 1971, 90, 185, 253–4; E. E. F. Smith, *Clapham*, 1975, 78].

Herbert was the builder responsible for the West Strand Improvements of 1830–2. These included the surviving stuccoed block opposite Charing Cross Station now occupied by Coutts's Bank and the Lowther Arcade demolished in 1902. In an illustrated article on 'The Improvements near Charing Cross' in the *Gentleman's Magazine* for 1831 (i), 201–6, it is stated that 'the architect and builder of the whole comprised in this triangle is Mr. William Herbert, of Farm Street, Berkeley Square', but although some details may have been left to Herbert it is clear that the whole scheme, including the elevations and the Arcade, was designed by Nash [M. V. Stokes, 'The Lowther Arcade in the Strand', *London Topographical Record* xxiii, 1972, 119–28].

For over 40 years Herbert was Surveyor of Buildings to the Excise Office. It was in this capacity that in 1829 he made plans [P.R.O., MPD 68] for internal alterations to the EXCISE OFFICE, OLD BROAD STREET, LONDON (dem. 1854) and designed the EXCISE OFFICE at BRISTOL, 1833–40 (dem.) [*A.P.S.D.*, *s.v.* 'Bristol']. He also designed a lead works at BIRMINGHAM in 1837 [B. Little, *Birmingham Buildings*, 1971, fig. 46]. He retired in 1861 and died on 18 September 1863 [*Parliamentary Papers*, 1862 (Superannuation Allowances, 260), 1864 (Increase and Diminution of Public Offices, Sessional Paper No. 169)].

HERBERTSON, JOHN, practised in Glasgow, where in 1809, as 'John Herbertson, junior, architect', he was admitted to the Incorporation of Wrights [*The Incorporation of Wrights in Glasgow*, Glasgow 1880, 55]. In early life he was in David Hamilton's office. For many years he was architect to the Lanarkshire Prison Board. John Baird (1798–1859), John Carrick (1819–90) and Alexander Munro are all stated by Gildard to have been his assistants. He reseated the OUTER HIGH CHURCH, GLASGOW, in 1812–13, designed the new COUNTY BRIDEWELL c. 1823, submitted a design for ST. DAVID'S CHURCH in 1824 that was not accepted, and designed BALFRON CHURCH, STIRLINGSHIRE, 1832 [advt. in *Stirling Journal and Advertiser*, 5 April 1832, *ex inf.* Mr. David Walker], HAGGS CHURCH, DENNY, STIRLINGSHIRE, designed 1832, completed 1840 [*Stirling Journal and Advertiser*, 24 May 1832, *ex inf.* Mr. David Walker] and ST. COLUMBA'S CHURCH, HOPE STREET, GLASGOW, 1838–9; dem. c. 1900. He supervised the building of the Royal Exchange to David Hamilton's designs in 1827–9 [C. C. Brewsher, *The Glasgow Royal Exchange . . . Centenary*, 1927].

[Thomas Gildard, 'An Old Glasgow Architect on some older Ones', *Trans. Royal Philosophical Soc. of Glasgow* xxvi, 1895, 108; *A.P.S.D.*, *s.v.* 'Glasgow'; *Extracts from the Records of the Burgh of Glasgow*, ed. Renwick, x, 133, 220–1, xi, 196.]

HERING, FREDERICK (c. 1799–1869), appears to have been an elder brother of the artist G. E. Hering (1805–79). Their father was a German bookbinder established in London. Frederick Hering began to exhibit architectural designs at the Royal Academy in 1825. They included a 'Sketch for a boat-house and fishing-lodge to be built in Hampshire' (1825), and a library and cottages erected at the 'new watering-place at Hayling Island', Hampshire (1834). In 1839 he gratuitously made designs for an almshouse for the Bookbinders' Provident Asylum Society, but the building eventually erected in the Balls Pond Road in 1843 was designed by Charles Dunning [*First Report of the Bookbinders' Provident Asylum Society*, 1839]. Other recorded works were a shop-front in the Regent Street Quadrant for Messrs. Swan & Edgar [*Builder* xxvii, 1869, 373] and ALL SAINTS' CHURCH, CLAPHAM, 1859, Gothic, in association with T. Talbot Bury [B. F. L. Clarke, *Parish Churches of London*, 1966, 216]. His most interesting building was, however, the house, NO. 2 PALACE GREEN, KENSINGTON, which he designed for the novelist W. M. Thackeray in 1860 in an early Georgian style prescribed by his client [Priscilla Metcalf, 'Postscript on Thackeray's House', *Journal of the Society of Architectural Historians* [of America] xxviii, 1969, 118]. An unexecuted design by him for a church in the Romanesque style is in the R.I.B.A. Drawings Collection. According to the *Builder* xxvii, 1869, 373, he was 'an accomplished and amiable man, but seems to have obtained few opportunities to distinguish himself in his profession'. He died at

416

2 Argyll Street, Regent Street, on 2 May 1869, in his 70th year.

HEWETT, SIR THOMAS (1656–1726), was a Whig country gentleman and *virtuoso* who from 1719 to 1726 held the post of Surveyor-General of the King's Works. He was the great-grandson of a London merchant who had acquired the estate of Shireoaks near Worksop in Nottinghamshire, where Thomas was born on 9 September 1656. He was educated at Shrewsbury and Christ Church, Oxford, and then 'travelled about 5 years in France, Holland and Switzerland, Italy and Germany'. He is known to have visited Padua in February 1688 [*Architectural Review*, Nov. 1957, 344], and he married his wife (Frances, daughter of Sir Edward Bettinson of Scadbury in Kent) at Geneva in September 1689. He subsequently obtained some minor government posts, including the Surveyorship of Woods North of Trent in 1696 and of Woods both North and South of Trent in 1715. In 1716 Walpole dismissed him from the latter in favour of another claimant, but in 1719 Walpole's rival Sunderland made him Surveyor of the Royal Works in place of the disgraced Benson. He was knighted the same year and retained the post until his death.

The Surveyor-Generalship was an appropriate post for Hewett to hold, for he was seriously interested in architecture. He had been a leading member of the 'new Junta for Architecture' which was already trying to steer British architecture in a neo-classical direction before Lord Burlington's Palladian revival.[1] As Surveyor-General to George I his opportunities were limited, but he was proud of the new state rooms at Kensington Palace 'exactly done according to the Grecian tast', and George Vertue reported that in his own gardens at Shireoaks he built a 'greek Tempietto' decorated with 'pillasters of 3 greek Orders, the floors marble, ceilings painted by . . . Trench . . . [and a] Bust of Sr. Th. in Marble by [Rysbrack]'. How far he was his own architect it is difficult to say, but in his will he states that he has 'begun the building of a House in the Wood called Scratoe', and enjoins his executors to complete 'severall cutts and ornaments in and about the said wood according to a draught and design which I have made and drawn thereof'. It was under his directions – and presumably to designs prescribed if not actually drawn by him – that Lord Sunderland's celebrated library in Piccadilly was built in 1719–20 [*Survey of London* xxxii, 368]: described by Macky as 'the finest in Europe, both for the disposition of the Apartments, as of the Books', it was demolished in 1758. In 1724 Lord Chancellor Macclesfield proposed to consult him

[1] See 'GALILEI, ALESSANDRO' for further details.

about fitting up a library at SHIRBURN CASTLE, OXON. [Hist. MSS. Comm., *Various Collections* viii, 371]. And Hawksmoor (who was prejudiced against Hewett for not restoring him to his places in the Office of Works) tells us that he was responsible for the stables at THORESBY HOUSE, NOTTS., which he dismisses as 'the only piece of Building that Sr. Tho. Hewett was Guilty of, dureing his being Architect Royall . . . [and] the most infamous that ever was made' [*Walpole Soc.* xix, 1931, 126]. They were built *c.* 1725 and demolished in the nineteenth century.

Hewett died on 9 April 1726, and was buried at Wales Church, Yorks., where there is an inscription to his memory. An inventory of his possessions at Shireoaks includes several works of art, including his own portrait by Bombelli [Arundel Castle MSS. In. 4]. A fragment of the Elizabethan house of Shireoaks survives in ruins, and the vaulted basement of his unfinished house still exists in Scratta Wood.

[*History of the King's Works* v, 71–3; Walpole Soc., *Vertue Note Books* ii, 36 and vi, 23, 70; Ilaria Toesca, 'Alessandro Galilei in Inghilterra' in *English Miscellany*, ed. M. Praz, iii, 1952; Hist. MSS. Comm. *Various Collections* viii, 368; J. Holland, *History of Worksop*, 1826, 175–7; P.C.C., 99 PLYMOUTH; inscription in Wales Church.]

HIDE, EDWARD, was an architect and builder at Worthing in Sussex. 'Messrs. Hides' designed the THEATRE ROYAL in ANNE STREET, 1806, closed 1855 and subsequently used as a warehouse [M. T. Odell, *The Old Theatre, Worthing*, Aylesbury 1938, 14]. In 1812 Edward Hide completed the interior of ST. PAUL'S CHURCH, WORTHING, designed by J. B. Rebecca [*The Watering-Places of Great Britain and Fashionable Directory*, 1833, 69]. In 1828 he supervised the repewing of SOMPTING CHURCH, SUSSEX [I.C.B.S.]. Charles Hide (*c.* 1810–76), for many years Town Surveyor of Worthing, was probably his son [cf. *Builder* xxxiv, 1876, 645].

HIGGINS, JAMES WHITE (*c.* 1783–1854) was articled to Thomas Bush, but bought off a portion of his term of apprenticeship in order to become fully employed as a surveyor in measuring the extensive Government works then being carried out by Messrs. Holland, Copland, Rowles and others. Before he was 22 he had begun speculative building in Chelsea, on the Sloane Street estate developed by Henry Holland. In later life he was chiefly employed in valuation for dock and railway companies, the Office of Woods and Forests, the Boards of Ordnance and Admiralty, and other bodies. He was extensively employed as an arbitrator, and was one of the first referees appointed under the Metropolitan Buildings Act of 1844, but retired after holding the office for

only one year, 'not liking the confinement of official life'. He usually handed over architectural commissions to others. He was a member of the Surveyors' Club, and was elected President in 1814, but did not take the Chair. He lived latterly at Hormead, Herts., and died on 13 May 1854, aged 71. His daughter Catherine married T. E. Owen of Portsmouth (*q.v.*). [*A.P.S.D.*; obituary in *Builder* xii, 1854, 293.]

HIGGINS, WILLIAM MULLINGER, was an architect and surveyor practising in London during the second quarter of the nineteenth century. He designed the LITERARY and SCIENTIFIC INSTITUTION in CLARENCE STREET, STAINES, MIDDLESEX, 1835, now the Public Library, his signature and the date being inscribed on the door-jamb. He was also the architect of the CONGREGATIONAL CHURCH, THAMES STREET, STAINES, 1836, dem. 1956, which had an inscription recording his authorship. He was presumably the architect called Higgins who designed a METHODIST CHAPEL in the NEW ROAD, LONDON [noted by C. R. Cockerell in his Diary, June 1823], and the GRANDSTAND at ASCOT RACE-COURSE in 1838–9 [G. Tattersall, *Sporting Architecture*, 1841, 92]. Higgins was the author of a work entitled *The House Painter: or, Decorator's Companion: being a complete treatise on the origin of colour . . . the manufacture of pigments, oils and varnishes; and the art of house painting, graining and marbling*, 1841, in which he is described as 'formerly professor of mechanical and experimental philosophy at Guy's Hospital'.

HIGHWAY, ISAAC, was a builder-architect of Walsall, Staffs. He designed ST. PETER'S CHURCH, WALSALL, in a lancet Gothic style in 1839–41, and was probably the 'Mr. Highway' who designed ST. JOHN'S CHURCH, WALSALL WOOD, in a plain Gothic style in 1836–7 [*V.C.H. Staffs.* xvii, 237, 282].

HILL, CHARLES HAMOR (–1863), of Islington, was one of the London District Surveyors in the 1830s and 1840s. His only recorded architectural work appears to be the Tudor Gothic LEATHERSELLERS' ALMSHOUSES at BARNET, HERTS., 1843, of which there is an engraving naming him as the architect. He died at Canonbury Tower, Islington, on 4 February 1863 [Principal Probate Registry, Calendar of Probates].

HILL, DAVID, of Arbroath, was the son of James Hill, 'an ingenious man, who spent a great deal of time in trying to invent perpetual motion'. He designed THE TRADES HALL (later THE SHERIFF COURT HOUSE), ARBROATH, ANGUS, 1814–15 [G. Hay, *History of Arbroath*, 1876, 289].

HILL, JAMES (–1734), of Cheltenham, was one of the two master masons employed to rebuild NEWENT CHURCH, GLOS., of which he and Francis Jones of Hasfield laid the first stone on 31 July 1675. The church was completed in 1679, the medieval steeple being retained. Externally, it is Gothic in style, but there are Ionic pilasters in the interior, and the nave was covered by a roof of exceptionally wide span designed by Edward Taylor (*q.v.*) on the model of that of the Sheldonian Theatre, Oxford [MS. account of the building of Newent Church by Walter Nourse, of Kilcot, *c.* 1725.] A memorandum in the vestry minutes of CHELTENHAM PARISH CHURCH records that in 1693 'was the steeple of Cheltenham repayred from the upper hole to the top by James Hill, of Cheltenham, stone-mason' ['Cheltenham Vestry Minutes', *Glos. Notes and Queries* viii (i), 1901, 38]. In 1700 Hill was employed to rebuild the central tower of BISHOP'S CLEEVE CHURCH, GLOS. The former tower had collapsed in 1696, and the churchwardens' accounts for 1699 include a payment of 16s. 'to James Hill for a draught of ye tower'. It is traditional in character, with battlements and pinnacles [MS. Churchwardens' Accounts in Gloucester County Record Office]. Hill's will, dated 19 January 1733/4, was proved at Gloucester on 11 February 1733/4.

HILLIER, WILLIAM CURRY, junior (*c.* 1815–1840), of Rochester, went to Jerusalem to build a church and hospital there for the Society for promoting Christianity among the Jews, but died soon afterwards at the age of 25 [*Gent's Mag.* 1840 (ii), 676; J. W. Johns, *The Anglican Cathedral Church at Jerusalem*, 1844].

HILLYER, WILLIAM (–1782), of Moorfields, designed the church of ST. ALPHEGE, LONDON WALL, LONDON, 1775–7, incorporating the old tower. The church was dem. in 1923–4, with the exception of the tower, which was gutted in 1940–41 [Vestry Minutes in Guildhall Library, MS. 1431/4]. In 1777 Hillyer supervised repairs to the church of ST. MARY, ALDERMANBURY, gutted in 1940 [P. C. Carter, *The History of St. Mary Aldermanbury*, 1913, 23].

At the time of his death in 1782 Hillyer held the post of Surveyor to the County of Essex, in which capacity he had designed the COUNTY GAOL at CHELMSFORD, ESSEX, 1773–7, as stated in the *Report from the Committee of Aldermen appointed to visit several Gaols in England*, 1816, 52. It was subsequently much altered by his successor, John Johnson. He also designed the bridge over the river Stour at NAYLAND, on the county boundary with Suffolk, in 1775 [*Essex Review* lxi, 1952, 225–32] and began the HOUSE OF CORRECTION at HALSTEAD, ESSEX, which was completed by Johnson after his death [J. Simmons, 'John Johnson', *Leicester Arch. Soc. Trans.* xxv, 1949, 145–6]. His

unexecuted designs for a County Hall at Chelmsford, dated 1771, are preserved in the County Record Office (Q/AS 1/3 and Q/SO 12, p. 53). In 1779 Hillyer carried out alterations to the COUNTY GAOL at HERTFORD [Herts. County Records].

In 1847 a folio album of drawings by Hillyer was advertised for sale by the bookseller Bohn in his catalogue (item 224). It included designs for the Gaol and County Hall at Chelmsford; drawings of, or designs for rebuilding Saffron Walden Church, Essex; designs for Bamber Gascoyne's house at Bifrons, nr. Barking, Essex (dem. 1815–16); and for 'Gibbs esq. at Horkesley Park', Essex (dem.). Whether any of these designs (other than those for the County Gaol) were carried out it is now impossible to say.

From about 1780 until his death Hillyer was also Surveyor to the Bridewell and Bethlehem Hospitals [*ex inf.* Miss P. Allderidge, Archivist to the Hospitals].

HINSBEY, WILLIAM, was an architect and surveyor at Norwich in the 1830s and 1840s. His designs for a range of cottages next to St. Martin's Church are in the City Archives [*ex inf.* Mr. A. P. Baggs].

HINSBY, ROBERT (–1820), an 'eminent architect and builder' of Halesworth, Suffolk, died there on 27 November 1820 [*Gent's Mag.* 1820, 571].

HIORNE, FRANCIS (1744–1789), was the elder son of William Hiorne of Warwick, and succeeded to his business as an architect and builder. His father had already executed works in the Gothic manner at Arbury and Stratford-on-Avon, and Francis became well known as an architect who specialized in that style. In 1785 the poet Mason wrote that 'Tetbury church gave me the very highest opinion of his Gothic taste', and commended Lord Harcourt for thinking of employing him as the architect of a projected 'Courtenay Castle' in the grounds of Nuneham Park, Oxon. Two years later a correspondent of Richard Gough, the antiquary, reported that 'At Greystoke Castle I found Mr. Hiorne, the gothic architect, whom the Duke of Norfolk had invited there to consult with relative to his intended repairs at Arundel Castle; and we made a party to see Alnwick Castle, etc. in Northumberland, for Mr. Hiorne's information'. 'Hiorne's Tower' still stands in the Home Park at Arundel, but proposals for restoring and remodelling the Castle, described in Dallaway's *Western Division of the County of Sussex*, ed. Cartwright, ii (i), 1832, 188–9, were not carried out owing to his death.

Hiorne was one of the most accomplished designers of the elegant, decorative Gothic of the late eighteenth century, of which Tetbury church is an excellent example. As a classical designer he is represented by St. Anne's, Belfast, whose domed tower appears to have derived from Archer's church at Birmingham, and by Tardebigge church, whose steeple is elegantly refined in a manner which suggests that Hiorne was sensitive to neo-classical taste.

Hiorne was elected an alderman of Warwick in October 1773, and held office as Mayor for the years 1773–4, 1782–3 and 1787–8. He also acted as Treasurer to the Corporation from 1781 to 1789, and as Bridge-master to the county of Warwick during the same period. He was elected F.S.A. in 1784, and bequeathed to the Society of Antiquaries 'the ancient volume called Milles Honour[1] corrected by the hand of Sir William Dugdale', and such of his coins and medals as the Society chose to select. His other legacies included the bust of Francis Smith by Rysbrack, which he left to the Radcliffe Library at Oxford, 50 guineas to the Corporation of Warwick to buy a piece of plate, and his silver drawing instruments, which he gave to William Callow of Tardebigge 'as a token of esteem'. To his wife Elizabeth he left, *inter alia*, his newly erected house called Kyte's Nest at Beausale, near Warwick, in the occupation of himself and Richard Kyte, with instructions to his executors 'to perfect the plan by me already begun for the improvement of the said Messuage, Garden and Shrubbery'. He died on 9 December 1789, aged 45, and is commemorated by a tablet in St. Mary's, Warwick.

[*A.P.S.D.*; Field, *History of Warwick*, 1815, 113; *Gent's Mag.* 1789 (ii), 1211; 1800 (ii), 1144–5; J. Nichols, *Literary Anecdotes* iii, 642; ix, 553; *Literary Illustrations* vi, 423; F. W. Harcourt, *The Harcourt Papers* vii, 1883, 110; *Aris's Birmingham Gazette*, 21 Oct. 1776. His will is P.C.C. 24 BISHOP, and the sale catalogue of his library (1791) is in the B.M. (129.1.19).]

WARWICK. ST. MARY'S CHURCH. In 1769 Francis Hiorne made designs for reconstructing the galleries, which are preserved among the Faculty Records now in the County Record Office, Warwick. A faculty was obtained, but nothing was done until 1777, when Edward Croft took the galleries down and rebuilt them according to Hiorne's plan. Hiorne also carried out extensive repairs to the Beauchamp Chapel in 1779, and converted the vaulted chamber under the Vestry into a burial vault for the Earl of Warwick in 1769. [T. Kemp, *History of Warwick*, 1905, 111, 125; *Notices of the Churches of Warwickshire*, 1847, i, 64; P. B. Chatwin, 'The Rebuilding of St. Mary's Church, Warwick', *Trans. Birmingham Arch. Soc.* lxvi, 1949, 33–4.]

[1] i.e. Thos. Milles, *The Catalogue of Honour*, 1610.

BELFAST, ST. ANNE'S CHURCH, completed 1776; dem. 1900 [C. E. B. Brett, *Buildings of Belfast 1700–1914*, 1967, 4; cf. A. Gordon, *Historic Memorials of the First Presbyterian Church at Belfast*, 1887].

TARDEBIGGE CHURCH, WORCS., 1777; chancel rebuilt 1879–80 [M. Dickens, *A Thousand Years of Tardebigge*, 1931, 85–90].

STONY STRATFORD CHURCH, BUCKS., rebuilt, incorporating old tower, 1776–7, Gothic. The tracery in the nave windows was inserted by Street in 1876, and the present chancel is by C. G. Hare, 1928 [J. Dugdale, *British Traveller* i, 1819, 183].

attributed: BUCKINGHAM PARISH CHURCH, rebuilt 1777–81, Gothic; altered 1862 by G. G. Scott, who added the chancel. The parish records contain no information as to the architect employed, but the style is characteristic of Hiorne, and 'Mr. Hearn' is mentioned twice in a letter dated 22 April 1777 from Charles Webb to Lord Verney about the erection of the church [Verney archives at Claydon House].

TETBURY CHURCH, GLOS., rebuilt, except steeple, 1777–81, Gothic [A. T. Lee, *History of Tetbury*, 1857].

ARUNDEL CASTLE, SUSSEX, triangular tower in Home Park for the 11th Duke of Norfolk, *c.* 1787, Gothic [T. W. Horsfield, *History of Sussex*, 1835, ii, 128].

ALTHORP HOUSE, NORTHANTS., repairs to STABLES for the 2nd Earl Spencer, 1788 [drawings at Althorp].

WARWICK, rebuilt ST. PETER'S CHAPEL over the east gate, 1788, Gothic [J. Chambers, MS. *Biography of English Architects* in R.I.B.A. Library].

KYTE'S NEST, nr. BEAUSALE, WARWICKS., for himself and Richard Kyte, 1788 [Referred to in Hiorne's will P.C.C. 24 BISHOP].

HIORNE, or **HIORNS**, WILLIAM (*c.* 1712–1776) and DAVID (–1758) were brothers who established themselves as the leading masons and architects in Warwick in the middle of the eighteenth century. They came from Great Tew in Oxon., where members of their family had been masons since at least the early seventeenth century. They appear to have been the sons of John Hiorne of Great Tew, whose father John, described in his will as a mason, left small legacies to his grandsons William and David when he died in 1718. A specimen of their grandfather's work still survives in the village, for in the attic of a stone cottage on the east side of the Square there is an inscription recording that it was built in 1680 by John Stow and his wife, and round the tablet is cut the distich,

JOHN HIORN THAT IS MY NAME
AND WITH MY HANDS I MAD THIS SAME.

During the first half of the eighteenth century the building trade in Warwick was dominated by the family of Smith, and there is reason to think that it was as masons in the Smiths' employment that the Hiornes became established in Warwick. It is certain that members of the family were employed by the Smiths, and the building accounts of Ditchley House, Oxon., which was built by Francis Smith for Lord Lichfield between 1720 and 1726, show that 'John Hyron' was his chief mason on the site. In his will, dated 19 January 1735/6, Francis Smith left one guinea to John Hiorn, 'my workman', David Hiorn witnessed William Smith's report on Tetbury Church in July 1742 [Gloucester Public Library, MS. RR. 300.1, p. 16] and Edward Knight's notebook (Kidderminster Public Library, MS. 294) refers to Kirtlington Park, Oxon., as having been built 'by Smith & Hiorns'. Moreover, when Francis Hiorne died in 1789, he had in his possession a bust of Francis Smith by Rysbrack, which he left to the Radcliffe Library at Oxford. It therefore seems probable that when William Smith died unmarried in 1747, William and David Hiorn succeeded to his business. During the next twenty years, they designed and built churches and country houses in many parts of the Midlands, in a style which is basically Palladian, though some of their designs for interior decoration are rococo in character, and the influence of Gibbs is also apparent.

David Hiorne predeceased his brother William, dying on 8 April 1758. He left three sons, John, Edward and David. Edward became a druggist in Coventry, and neither John nor David appears to have followed their father's trade. William died on 22 April 1776, leaving two sons by his first wife Mary Duncalfe. Francis, the elder, succeeded to the family business and became a well-known architect. William, the younger, became a merchant and perished at sea off the coast of Georgia. Their father was an alderman of Warwick at the time of his death, and held the office of Mayor in 1765–6. There is a tablet to his memory in the church of St. Mary, Warwick. He lived in a house on the north side of Warwick High Street [notes on the family by F. R. Hiorns, published in *C. Life*, 18 Aug. 1923, 218; the wills of William and Francis (P.C.C., 271 BELLAS; 24 BISHOP), and of John Hiorn of Great Tew (Oxford Archdeaconry Court, Reg. II, vol. 15, f. 133ᵛ; see also vol. 7, f. 167*b*)].

COVENTRY, HOLY TRINITY CHURCH: in 1742 the spire was examined by 'Mr. Hiorn of Warwick' [T. Sharp, *Illustrations of the History of Holy Trinity Church, Coventry*, 1818, 32].

COVENTRY, ST. MICHAEL'S CHURCH (now the CATHEDRAL). In 1747 'Mr. Hiorne of Warwick, engaged to take down the old Altar-piece, and make two wings, in stucco-work, according to

420

his design given in, for £43:18s.' [T. Sharp, *Illustrations of the History and Antiquities of St. Michael's Church, Coventry*, 1818, 40–41].

ARBURY HALL, WARWICKS. William Hiorne acted as executant architect for Sir Roger Newdigate's alterations in the Gothic style from *c.* 1748 onwards. Hiorne was paid 2 guineas for a 'plan of Arbury' on 23 Dec. 1748, and Sir Roger Newdigate's MS. account-book, now in the County Record Office at Warwick, contains several payments to him and his brother between 1750 and 1755. (C. Hussey, *English Country Houses: Mid Georgian*, 1956, 41–8).

EDGBASTON HALL, WARWICKS., internal alterations by W. & D. Hiorne for Sir Henry Gough, 1751–2 [account and letter in Edgbaston Estate Office, *ex inf.* Mr. D. N. Cannadine].

BIRMINGHAM, KING EDWARD'S SCHOOL, fitted up library 1752 [*Records of King Edward's School*, ed. Chatwin, Dugdale Soc. iv, pp. xxi, 101].

DAVENTRY PARISH CHURCH, NORTHANTS., 1752–8, by William and David Hiorne [*Gent's Mag* 1826 (ii), 402; a note in William Baker's MS. diary indicates that David was concerned, but it was William who gave evidence in connection with the Faculty which was granted in Jan. 1752 [Peterborough Diocesan Records].

BIRMINGHAM, ST. BARTHOLOMEW'S CHURCH. In 1753 'Messrs. W. and D. Hiorn' gave an estimate and a design for an altar-piece in this church, which had been built in 1749–50, and may be attributed to the same architects. [*Aris's Birmingham Gazette*, 6 Aug. 1753]. It was closed in 1935 and subsequently dem.

BIRMINGHAM, ST. MARTIN'S CHURCH; the spire was repaired by William Hiorne in 1753, and the vestry and lobby at the east end of the north aisle were built by William and David Hiorne in 1760. [J. T. Bunce, 'St. Martin's Church', *Trans. Birmingham and Midland Institute*, 1870, 15–16; J. T. Bunce, *Old St. Martin's Church, Birmingham*, 1875, 19.] The spire was recased by P. C. Hardwick in 1852–5, and the whole church was reconstructed by J. A. Chatwin in 1872–5.

KYRE PARK, WORCS., was remodelled by W. & D. Hiorne for Edmund Pytts in 1753–6 [H. Avray Tipping in *C. Life*, 17 & 24 March 1917, citing accounts now in Worcestershire Record Office].

WARWICK, THE SHIRE HALL was built 1754–8 to the designs of Sanderson Miller by William and David Hiorn and Job Collins as contractors. An inscription on a plate fixed to the roof timbers records the names of 'MR. WILLIAM AND DAVID HIORN OF WARWICK SURVEYORS AND BUILDERS OF THIS HALL RICHARD NEWMAN MASON DAVID SANDERS CARPENTER1754.' Estimates, bills, etc., are preserved among Sanderson Miller's papers now in the County Record

Office, Warwick. Francis Hiorne afterwards published a plan and elevation of the building, engraved by Edward Rooker, but had no connection with its design or erection.

GREAT HOUGHTON CHURCH, NORTHANTS., was rebuilt in 1754 in a style which suggests that the Hiornes were the architects employed and this is confirmed by an advertisement in the *Northampton Mercury* of 31 March 1755 offering for sale 'All the OLD LEAD belonging to Great-Houghton Church', and instructing prospective purchasers to apply to 'Mr. David Hiorn, or Mr. Smith, his Foreman, at Great Houghton aforesaid'. The architectural character of the church has been impaired by alterations in 1875 and 1910–11, but its original appearance is illustrated in M. Whiffen, *Stuart and Georgian Churches*, 1948, pl. 79.

CHARLECOTE, WARWICKS., bridge over river Avon, built by David Hiorn, 1755 [F. R. Hiorns in *C. Life*, 18 Aug. 1923, 218].

DERBY COUNTY GAOL., 1755–6; rebuilt by F. Goodwin in 1823–7. By 'Mr. Irons, of Warwick' [J. C. Cox, *Three Centuries of Derbyshire Annals* ii, 10].

FOREMARK HALL, DERBYS., for Sir Robert Burdett, 1759–61. The architect was David Hiorne, who based his design on Isaac Ware's Wrotham Park (1754) [*Vitruvius Britannicus* v, 1771, pls. 31–5; Burdett papers in Berkshire County Record Office, accounts A1/1] (*C. Life*, 18 Aug. 1923).

NOTTINGHAM, ST. MARY'S CHURCH. The west end was rebuilt in classical style, with a pediment and Doric doorcase, in 1762, the architect being 'one Hirons of Warwick' [*The Stretton Manuscripts*, ed. G. C. Robertson, 1910, 137].

PACKINGTON HALL, WARWICKS., work for the 3rd Earl of Aylesford, 1762–5, probably comprising the Stables [accounts 1725–66 at Packington Hall] (*C. Life*, 9 July 1970).

STRATFORD-ON-AVON CHURCH, WARWICKS., tower and spire were rebuilt in Gothic style in 1763–4 by William Hiorn, perhaps to designs made by Timothy Lightoler [*V.C.H. Warwicks.* iii, 271; Hist. MSS. Comm. *Correspondence of Joseph Greene*, ed. Fox, 99–100].

GOPSALL HALL, LEICS., works for Charles Jennens (d. 1773), *c.* 1750–60. According to J. Throsby, *Select Views of Leicestershire* i, 1789, 280, the house was designed by Alderman Westley of Leicester but 'the offices, through a misunderstanding, were built by Mr. Hiorn of Warwick'. A volume of designs for Gopsal in the R.I.B.A. Collection includes several designs by the Hiornes for the interiors and also for various garden buildings. Owing to the demolition of the house in 1951 it is not clear which drawings were executed, but some of the garden buildings were certainly built. [*R.I.B.A. Drawings Catalogue: G–K*, 130–2;

A. Rowan, *Garden Buildings*, R.I.B.A. 1968, pls. 12,15,17] (L. G. G. Ramsay, 'Gopsal Hall', *Connoisseur* vol. 128, 1951).

OVER WHITACRE CHURCH, WARWICKS., rebuilt 1766, may be attributed to William or David Hiorne on stylistic grounds, but there are no parish records of the period by which this attribution can be tested. The tower originally terminated in a dome, the present spire being substituted in 1850.

HIORT, JOHN WILLIAM (1772–1861), the son of a Swedish father and an English mother, was born in London on 16 April 1772. After spending a year with Peter Simon, a miniaturist and engraver, he entered the office of C. A. Craig in January 1787. Craig was the Chief Resident Clerk in the Office of Works, and in 1793 Hiort was engaged to take the place of George Horsley, an Assistant Clerk who had become insane. Hiort was recommended to the Treasury by Sir William Chambers, the Surveyor General, as 'a very intelligent young man, very industrious and attentive to business, very sober and tractable'. He was subsequently promoted to be Resident Clerk (1805) and Chief Examining Clerk (1815). He retired in 1832, when the Office of Works was merged with that of Woods and Forests. He proved to be a thoroughly capable and reliable member of the staff, and it was upon him that the main burden of administration was to fall during the negligent surveyorship of James Wyatt.

In his official capacity Hiort had few opportunities to design new buildings, but he was much employed in arranging public ceremonies, such as the funerals of William Pitt and Lord Nelson, and the coronation of George IV in 1820. For the coronation banquet in Westminster Hall he designed the Gothic triumphal arch and galleries (illustrated in *Gent's Mag.* 1821 (ii), 109). In a semi-official capacity, assisted by J. B. Papworth, he designed various ancillary buildings at CLAREMONT HOUSE, SURREY, for Princess Charlotte, including the Gothic 'Retreat' which was converted into a chapel or cenotaph after her death [Ackermann, *Repository of Arts*, 1819, 154]. His private works included DDERW, nr. RHAYADER in RADNORSHIRE, for N. S. Prickard, 1799, rebuilt *c.* 1860; considerable works for Nicholas Vansittart, Lord Bexley, at FOOTS CRAY PLACE, KENT, and at his house in GREAT GEORGE STREET, WESTMINSTER; alterations for Col. William Elliott (or Eliot) at NO. 34 OLD BURLINGTON STREET, *c.* 1808; and to the London residences of Charles Arbuthnot, Secretary to the Treasury, and John Johnson, afterwards Lord Mayor of London.

Hiort invented and patented (8 Nov. 1825) bricks for building circular flues in a manner adopted at Buckingham Palace and elsewhere, and founded the London, Surrey, and Kent Safety Brick Company to carry out these and similar inventions. In 1826 he published a *Practical Treatise on the Construction of Chimneys, etc.*, and in 1847, after many years of retirement at Bath, returned to London in order to readvocate some of his ideas in a *Report of the Aeronomic Association*, 1852. He died at Bedford Place, Kensington, on 8 February 1861, and was buried in Kensal Green Cemetery. C. Hiort, who may have been a nephew, was an assistant in Soane's office, 1822–3. [Obituary in *Building News* vii, 1861, 460–61; privately printed memoir in B.M. (10826 h.20); *A.P.S.D.; History of the King's Works* vi, *passim*.]

HIRD, JOHN, was an eighteenth-century Lancashire architect. He was probably the 'John Herd, house carpenter of Kendal', who became a freeman of Lancaster in 1763–4 [*Lancs. and Cheshire Record Soc.* vol. 87, 1938, 148]. He designed LEIGHTON HALL, LANCS., for George Townley, 1765, 'a neat but rather dull little essay in the Palladian style' that was subsequently remodelled in picturesque Gothic [Arthur Oswald in *C. Life*, 11 May 1951, where Hird's drawings are illustrated]; rebuilt the nave of PRESTON PARISH CHURCH in 1770–1 (again rebuilt 1853–8) [C. Hardwick, *History of Preston*, 1857, 466]; and in 1777 was invited to submit plans for rebuilding FLOOKBURGH CHAPEL, nr. CARTMEL, LANCS. [J. Stockdale, *Annales Caermoelenses*, 1872, 284].

HIRST, THOMAS (*c.* 1779–1842), was the son of a schoolmaster at Sheffield. From *c.* 1817 to *c.* 1822 he was in partnership with William Unwin (*q.v.*) [P. Eden, *Dictionary of Land Surveyors 1550–1850*, 1975–6, 133].

HISCOCK, WILLIAM, was a mason at Christchurch, Hants., where he carried on a business as a builder and monumental sculptor. Several well-carved tablets signed by him can be seen in Christchurch Priory Church, which he repaired in 1809 [R. Gunnis, *Dictionary of British Sculptors*, 1968, 203]. In 1825–6 he designed HAMWORTHY CHURCH, DORSET, rebuilt 1958–9 [I.C.B.S.] (Sydenham, *History of Poole*, 1839, 458), and in 1831 MILTON CHURCH, HANTS., in a weak Gothic style [I.C.B.S.].

HITCHCOCK, JOHN THOMAS (1812–44), was born in Amsterdam. He went to London as a youth, exhibited at the R.A. in 1827–9, became a pupil of Philip Hardwick, and entered the R.A. Schools in 1834. In the following year he made designs for the Fitzwilliam Museum at Cambridge which, although not accepted, are preserved in the museum's library. After eight years in England, he returned to Amsterdam, when he built a club-house and other houses. He migrated to the Dutch East Indies in 1841, and died at Batavia in 1844 [*A.P.S.D.*].

HOARE, —, appears to have been the architect and builder of Alderman William Beckford's magnificent Palladian house at FONTHILL, WILTSHIRE begun *c.* 1757 but not completed until *c.* 1770 and demolished by his son in 1807 (*Vitruvius Britannicus* iv, 1767, pls. 82–7; John Harris, 'Fonthill, Wiltshire', *C. Life*, 24 Nov. 1966). 'Mr. Hoore' is given as the architect of Fonthill in an eighteenth-century list of country houses in the library at Alnwick Castle, and in April 1763 a correspondent of Sir Charles Farnaby wrote to him that 'there is one Hoar a Builder in the City of whom I have heard a Good character. He built Beckford the present Lord Mayor's house in Wiltshire and he is employed now in Building the new Court House at Maidstone...' [Hertfordshire County Record Office, DE 43213]. The employment of 'Mr. Hoare' to design the COURT HOUSE or TOWN HALL at MAIDSTONE in 1763–4 confirmed by the Corporation Minutes, which record the decision that it should be 'new built and enlarged agreeable to the plan produced ... by Mr. Hoare'.

HOARE, MICHAEL, *see* HALFPENNY

HOBCROFT, or **HOBCRAFT,** JOHN, was a carpenter and builder of Titchfield Street, London, who also acted as an architect. He was probably born shortly before 1730, for in 1743 John, son of Nicholas Hopcroft, was apprenticed to Joseph Harris, citizen and joiner of London [Guildhall Library, index to Apprenticeship Registers in P.R.O.]. He is first found working at STOWE HOUSE, BUCKS., where in 1755 he submitted an account which was mainly for architectural joinery supplied, but also included 10s. for 'Drawing a Plan for State Bedchamber' [Desmond Fitz-Gerald in *Apollo*, June 1973, 577, 584–5 (n. 36)]. He next appears as a builder carrying out work of high quality at various country houses designed or altered by Lancelot Brown in the 1760s, including Broadlands, Corsham, Redgrave and Newnham Paddox [Dorothy Stroud, *Capability Brown*, 1975, *passim*]. He drew out the Gothic elevations for Donnington Grove designed by John Chute which now hang framed at the Vyne,[1] and in 1768 he appears to have designed the elaborate Gothic chapel at AUDLEY

[1] This was presumably the 'Design for the house of a gentleman in the county of Berkshire' which Hobcroft exhibited at the Society of Artists in 1771, for Horace Walpole noted in his copy of the catalogue that it was 'designed by John Chute Esq. and executed'.

END, ESSEX, for Sir John Griffin, later Lord Howard de Walden [J. D. Williams, *Audley End, The Restoration of 1762–97*, Chelmsford 1966, 31]. An album at Audley End contains two drawings signed by him, including (f. 64) a design for the chapel screen. Later, in 1778–9, he remodelled Sir John Griffin's town house at No. 10 New Burlington Street to the designs of the Adam brothers [*Survey of London* xxxii, 493]. In Berkshire Hobcroft himself designed two country seats, PADWORTH HOUSE for Christopher Griffith, 1769, for which his plans and elevations, signed and dated 1769, survive [H. Avray Tipping in *C. Life*, 16 & 23 Sept. 1922] and WASING HOUSE, nr. NEWBURY, for John Mount, 1772, destroyed by fire 1945 [Berkshire County Record Office, D/EMcA. 21]. Externally these were both plain brick buildings of no special distinction, but the interiors at Padworth are elegantly decorated in a style derived from the Adam brothers. Hobcroft probably worked for the Adams at other houses besides Sir John Griffin's. He took a building site in Mansfield Street on the Portland estate which they laid out [A. T. Bolton, *The Works of R. & J. Adam* ii, 102], and he subscribed to Robert Adam's *Spalatro* (1764).

Hobcroft's son John, born in 1747, entered the R.A. Schools as an architectural student in 1771, but appears to have died young, as 'Dead' is written against his name in the R.A. Register.

HOBDEN, HENRY WILLIAM, was a builder and surveyor at Warrington in Lancashire. He rebuilt the churches of LYTHAM and NEWTON-LE-WILLOWS, LANCS., in 1834–5, and added a north aisle to that of NEWCHURCH-IN-ROSSENDALE in 1833 [all I.C.B.S.].

HOBSON, WILLIAM, was brother-in-law of William Blackburn, the prison architect (*q.v.*). Writing from Southwark after Blackburn's death in 1791, Hobson told the Bedfordshire Justices that he had been 'bred up in the architectural line' and claimed to have enjoyed Blackburn's 'unbounded friendship and confidence, which has been extended to his taking my opinion for almost every plan for a gaol that he has made' [Bedfordshire County Records, QSR 17/173–4]. He was employed to complete at least one prison designed by Blackburn, the HOUSE OF CORRECTION at LEWES, SUSSEX [East Sussex Record Office, QAP/2/11 and 12/E12]. A W. Hobson exhibited a design for a museum at the Royal Academy in 1801, but not further trace of him has been found after that date.

HODKIN, DANIEL, of Chesterfield, is described as 'architect and surveyor of County bridges' in Pigot's *Directory* of 1828–9. One of the Registers records that in 1795 Daniel Hodkin made a new altar-piece in CHESTERFIELD PARISH CHURCH, and according to a MS. note in a copy of Ford's *History of Chesterfield* he designed the METHODIST CHAPEL, SALTERGATE, CHESTERFIELD, in 1822–3. He is presumably the 'David Hodkin' who according to J. C. Cox designed and built BLACKWELL CHURCH, DERBYSHIRE, in 1827–8, again rebuilt 1879 [*Churches of Derbyshire* i, 1875, 95].

HOLDEN, THOMAS, was a surveyor and architect practising in London in the reign of George II. The only building which he is known to have designed is IRONMONGERS' HALL, FENCHURCH STREET, built in 1748–50 and demolished in 1917. His name was inscribed on the façade [J. Nicholl, *Some Account of the Worshipful Company of Ironmongers*, 1866, 451; *A.P.S.D.*]. In 1753 Holden made designs for rebuilding CLAPHAM CHURCH, SURREY, but they were not carried out [B. F. L. Clarke, *The Building of the Eighteenth-Century Church*, 1963, 25]. He must not be confused with Strickland Holden (d. 1765), a London carpenter who also acted as a building surveyor.

HOLL, EDWARD (–1824), may have been the son of Edward Holl (*c.* 1751–1815), a mason at Beccles in Suffolk. Under various titles he was the official architect in charge of naval works from 1804 onwards, and in that capacity was responsible for several buildings in the Royal Dockyards, notably at Sheerness, where he began extensive works that were completed by his successor, G. L. Taylor (*q.v.*). The large Dockyard Chapels at CHATHAM, 1808–11 and DEVONPORT, 1816–17 (dem. *c.* 1941) were designed by him [drawings in P.R.O., Adm. 140/68 and 233]. At Portsmouth he designed THE SCHOOL OF NAVAL ARCHITECTURE, 1815–17 [H. & J. Slight, *Chronicles of Portsmouth*, 1828, 164], and according to J. Dugdale's *British Traveller* iii, 1819, 610, he also designed the large and monumental ROYAL NAVAL HOSPITAL (afterwards barracks and now St. Nicholas Hospital) at YARMOUTH, 1809–11, though other sources say the architect was William Pilkington (*q.v.*).

HOLLAND, HENRY (1745–1806), born on 20 July 1745, was the eldest son of Henry Holland (1712–85), a successful Georgian master builder who was Master of the Tylers' and Bricklayers' Company in 1772–3. Henry's architectural training appears to have been obtained in his father's yard in Fulham, for there is no evidence that he was the pupil of any professional architect. In 1771, however, he became the partner of Lancelot Brown, the landscape-gardener, who was then living only a few miles away at Hampton Court, and with whom his father was acquainted. The partnership appears to have been of an informal character, and did not necessarily involve one partner in every commission that the other secured. It did, however, mean that Holland largely took over the architectural side of Brown's practice, and in this way obtained an introduction to the latter's large and influential clientèle. The alliance was strengthened in 1773 by Holland's marriage to Brown's daughter Bridget. The couple took up residence at No. 17 Hertford Street, a London house which had recently been built by Holland and his father.

Despite his lack of professional pupilage or foreign travel, Holland soon emerged as one of the leading English architects of the reign of George III. His first important work was Brooks's Club in St. James's Street, a commission which brought him into contact with those members of the Whig aristocracy who were to be his principal patrons, and which led, through them, to his employment by the Prince of Wales. The Gallic sympathies of the Whig circle into which Holland was thus introduced were reflected in the French influence which is apparent in his architecture. This was derived chiefly from the publications of French architects. For it was not until shortly before the Revolution that he actually visited France, and the French elements in his style appear to have been based less on personal observation than on a close study of French sources such as Peyre, Patte and Gondoin and on the employment of a French assistant, J. P. Trécourt, and of French craftsmen and decorative painters. In this way Holland developed a neoclassical style of his own that was as elegant and refined as that of the Adam brothers, and as valid as an alternative to the outmoded Palladianism of the mid-eighteenth century. Holland's ability in planning was demonstrated at Carlton House, where he created an elaborate sequence of rooms inside the shell of an existing building and devised a forecourt which gave consequence to the entrance in a manner very suggestive of Rousseau's Hôtel de Salm in Paris, begun in the same year. Both at Carlton House and at Berrington Hall he designed staircases of great beauty and sophistication. In his sober exteriors, his adventurous staircases and his interest in contemporary French architecture, Holland was carrying on the tradition established by Chambers. But, unlike Chambers, he did not despise the Greek Revival, using at Woburn both Doric and Ionic orders of strictly Grecian origin with more or less archaeological accuracy.

Like most eighteenth-century architects, Holland turned to speculative building to supplement the proceeds of his architectural practice, and in 1771, with the aid of capital supplied by his father, he took a lease of 89 acres of land in Chelsea from Lord Cadogan. Upon this site Holland later erected the estate known as Hans Town, comprising Sloane Street, Cadogan Place and the polygonal Hans Place, at one end of

424

which he built himself a large detached villa known as Sloane Place.

Holland was a man of retiring disposition who did not seek public notice, and never exhibited his work at the Royal Academy. 'Pray no more public compliments to me', he admonished David Hartley in 1789. 'I began the world a very independent man and wish to hold it at arms length ... I find myself already more the object of public notice than suits my disposition or plan of life.' Nevertheless he became a J.P. for Middlesex in 1778 and held two public offices, the one a District Surveyorship under the Act of 1774, the other the Clerkship of the Works at the Royal Mews at Charing Cross, an Office of Works appointment which he obtained in 1775 through the influence of Lord North. He lost the latter post as a result of the reforms of 1782, but it is doubtful whether a career in the Office of Works had an important place in his ambitions. In 1799 he succeeded Richard Jupp as Surveyor to the East India Company. From 1782 to 1793 he was also Surveyor to the Bridewell and Bethlehem Hospitals. He devoted much time to methods of preventing fire, notably by the use of David Hartley's 'fire-plate', which he used at Althorp and elsewhere, and was responsible for the publication of the *Resolution of the Associated Architects, with the Report of a Committee appointed to consider the causes of the frequent fires*, etc., 1793. He also contributed two papers to the *Communications of the Board of Agriculture* in 1797, one a practical essay on the construction of cottages, the other on the use of *pisé* as described by A. M. Cointereaux in his *Traité sur la construction des Manufactures et des Maisons de Campagne*, Paris 1791. According to Papworth's *Rural Residences* (1818), the use of *pisé* was 'introduced into England by the late Mr. H.'

Holland died in Sloane Place on 17 June 1806, aged 60, and was buried in the family tomb in Fulham churchyard. He left two sons, named Henry and Lancelot, and five daughters. Soane began his architectural career in 1772 as an assistant in Holland's office and C. H. Tatham became his draughtsman in about 1789. H. Hemsley, J. Jagger and W. Plumridge were also his pupils. Marble busts by Garrard are preserved at Woburn Abbey and Southill Park, and there is an oil portrait by Opie (illustrated in Miss Stroud's biography). Holland's drawings and papers appear to have been largely destroyed by his nephew and executor Henry Rowles after his death, but two sketchbooks relating to Carlton House and a volume of drawings, chiefly of interior decoration, are in the R.I.B.A. Collection (see the *Catalogue: G-K*, 134–9).

[H. B. Hodson, 'Holland, the Architect', *Builder* xiii, 1855, 437; *A.P.S.D.*; Dorothy Stroud, *Henry Holland*, 1950; Dorothy Stroud, *Henry Holland, His Life and Architecture*, 1966;

David Hartley's papers in the Berkshire Record Office, DEHy].

HALE HOUSE, HANTS., alterations for Lady Elizabeth Archer, 1770 [Stroud, 24].

HILL PARK (now VALENCE), nr. WESTERHAM, KENT, work for the 1st Earl of Hillsborough, c. 1770; since much altered [Stroud, 25].

BATTERSEA BRIDGE, MIDDLESEX (timber), built for 15 proprietors, 1771–2; dem. 1881 [D. Lysons, *Environs of London* i, 1810, 33].

*CLAREMONT HOUSE, nr. ESHER, SURREY, for the 1st Lord Clive, 1771–4 [G. Richardson, *New Vitruvius Britannicus* i, 1802, pls. 61–3].

*BENHAM PLACE, BERKS., for the 6th Lord Craven, 1774–5; attic storey added and pediment removed c. 1870 [Stroud, 36–7].

*CADLAND, nr. SOUTHAMPTON, HANTS., for the Hon. Robert Drummond, 1775–8; wing added by Holland 1782; enlarged by Wyatville 1837–8; dem. 1953 [Stroud, 39–40; Linstrum, *Wyatville*, 138–9, 233].

*TRENTHAM HALL, STAFFS., alterations for the 2nd Earl Gower, 1775–8; reconstructed by Barry 1834–40 and 1840–9; dem. 1910 [Stroud, 40–1] (*C. Life*, 25 Jan. 1968, fig. 8).

LONDON, BROOKS'S CLUB-HOUSE, NO. 60 ST. JAMES'S STREET, 1776–8 [Stroud, 50–2].

*CARDIFF CASTLE, GLAMORGANSHIRE, reconstruction in Gothic style for Lord Mount Stuart, 1777–8; rebuilt 1875 [Stroud, 56–7] (*C. Life*, 6 April 1961).

LONDON, HANS TOWN, CHELSEA, comprising SLOANE STREET, SLOANE PLACE, CADOGAN PLACE and HANS PLACE, 1777 onwards [Stroud, 43–9].

BERRINGTON HALL, nr. LEOMINSTER, HEREFS., for the Hon. Thomas Harley, 1778–81 [Stroud, 52–6; Christopher Hussey in *C. Life*, 2, 9 & 16 Dec. 1954].

STONE, STAFFS., THE CROWN INN, new front to street, 1779–80 [Stroud, 58].

CHART SUTTON CHURCH, KENT, rebuilt, except tower, 1779–82; remodelled 1896–8 [E. Hasted, *History of Kent* ii, 1782, 407 note; Stroud, 58].

*NUNEHAM PARK, OXON., alterations including heightening of wings for the 2nd Earl Harcourt, 1781–2 [Stroud, 58; M. L. Batey, *Nuneham Courtenay, Oxfordshire*, 1970, 11–12].

LONDON, NO. 7 ST. JAMES'S SQUARE, probably refronted the house, which Holland bought in 1782 and sold to Richard Barwell in 1783 [*Survey of London* xxix, 112].

GRANGEMOUTH, STIRLINGSHIRE, layout plan for Sir Thomas Dundas, Bart., 1783 [Stroud, 59–60].

LONDON, CARLTON HOUSE, PALL MALL, works for George, Prince of Wales, 1783–96; dem. 1827–8. Holland added the Corinthian portico and the Ionic screen to Pall Mall and remodelled

the interior [Stroud, 61–85; *History of the King's Works* vi, 307–12].

LONDON, SPENCER HOUSE, GREEN PARK, internal alterations for the 2nd Earl Spencer, 1785–92 [*Survey of London* xxx, 521; Stroud, 103].

BRIGHTON, THE MARINE PAVILION, for George, Prince of Wales, 1786–7; subsequently remodelled by John Nash [G. Richardson, *New Vitruvius Britannicus* i, 1810, pls. 6–7; Stroud, 86–90].

LONDON, YORK, formerly FETHERSTONHAUGH, afterwards MELBOURNE, and now DOVER HOUSE, WHITEHALL, added portico and domed entrance hall for Frederick, Duke of York, 1787 [*Survey of London* xiv, 60–4; 92–3].

LONDON, BEDFORD, HOUSE, BLOOMSBURY, remodelled eating-room for the 5th Duke of Bedford, 1787; dem. 1800 [Stroud, 106].

KNIGHT'S HILL, NORWOOD, SURREY, house for the 1st Lord Thurlow, 1787; dem. 1810 [Stroud, 137–8; *Picturesque Views of the Principal Seats of the Nobility and Gentry*, Harrison & Co., plate dated 1788, mentioning Holland as the architect; *The World*, 18 April, 7 May, 3 July, 12 July 1787].

STANMORE HOUSE or PARK, MIDDLESEX, alterations for George Drummond, 1787; dem. [*The World*, 4, 22 Aug. 1787, *ex inf.* Mr. P. A. Bezodis; W. Keane, *Beauties of Middlesex*, 1850, 138].

WOBURN ABBEY, BEDS., remodelled south façade, added entrance portico, enlarged stables, and added the conservatory (now sculpture gallery), Chinese dairy, riding-school, tennis court and park-entrance to London Road, for the 5th Duke of Bedford, 1787–1802. The portico, riding-school and tennis court were dem. 1954 [Stroud, 106–15] (*C. Life*, 1–8 Sept. 1955).

ALTHORP, NORTHANTS., recased house in white mathematical tiles and remodelled much of interior, for the 2nd Earl Spencer, 1787–9 [Stroud, 97–102] (*C. Life*, 11, 18 & 25 June, 2 July 1921, 19–26 May 1960).

LONDON, NO. 105 PALL MALL, remodelled interior for Mrs. Fitzherbert, 1787; dem. 1838 [*The World*, 17 Oct., 30 Nov. 1787, *ex inf.* Mr. P. A. Bezodis] (*Survey of London* xxix, 349).

ALLERTON MAULEVERER, YORKS. (W.R.), remodelled house for Frederick, Duke of York, 1788; rebuilt 1848–51 [*The World*, 28 March 1788, *ex inf.* Mr. P. A. Bezodis].

BROADLANDS, HANTS., east Ionic portico, vestibule and interior decoration for the 2nd Viscount Palmerston, 1788–92 [Stroud, 133] (*C. Life*, 31 March, 7 April 1923).

OAKLEY HOUSE, BEDS., alterations for the 5th Duke of Bedford, 1789–92 [Stroud, 113–14] (Neale, *Views of Seats* vi, 1823).

WOBURN, BEDS., THE GEORGE INN, repairs for the 5th Duke of Bedford, c. 1790 [Stroud, *Holland*, 1950, 37].

---

* In collaboration with L. Brown.

BEDFORD, THE SWAN HOTEL, for the 5th Duke of Bedford, 1792 [Stroud, 114–15].

HOUGHTON CONQUEST, BEDS., unidentified inn designed for the 5th Duke of Bedford, c. 1792 [Stroud, 114].

BIRCHMORE FARM, WOBURN, BEDS., alterations for the 5th Duke of Bedford, c. 1792 [Stroud, 115].

LONDON, DRURY LANE THEATRE, rebuilt for R. B. Sheridan, 1791–4; burned 1809 [Stroud, 116–25; see also *The Georgian Playhouse*, Arts Council Exhibition 1975, nos. 227–8].

LONDON, COVENT GARDEN THEATRE, alterations for Thomas Harris, 1792; burned 1808 [Stroud, 123–5].

OATLANDS HOUSE, WEYBRIDGE, SURREY, for Frederick, Duke of York, 1794–1800, with Gothic detailing by John Carter (*q.v.*); dem. [Stroud, 95] (*Gent's Mag.* 1808 (i), 9; *The Ambulator*, 1807, 225).

ABERDEEN, THE THEATRE, MARISCHAL STREET, 1795; dem. [W. Kennedy, *Annals of Aberdeen*, 1818, ii, 280].

DEBDEN HALL, ESSEX, for R. M. T. Chiswell, 1795; dem. 1936 [Stroud, 131–3] (Neale, *Views of Seats*, 1st ser., ii, 1819).

SOUTHILL HOUSE, BEDS., remodelled for Samuel Whitbread, 1796–1800 [Stroud, 127–30] (A. E. Richardson and others, *Southill: A Regency House*, 1951).

PARK PLACE, nr. HENLEY-ON-THAMES, BERKS., alterations for the 1st Earl of Malmesbury, c. 1796; remodelled 1871 [J. Britton & E. W. Brayley, *Beauties of England and Wales* i, 1801, 183; Stroud, 133].

DUNIRA, PERTHSHIRE, design for enlargement for the 1st Viscount Melville, 1798, carried out 1802 onwards by William Stirling (*q.v.*); rebuilt by W. Brown 1851–2 [Dundas papers at Comrie House, *ex inf.* Dr. A. A. Tait].

LONDON, EAST INDIA HOUSE, LEADENHALL STREET, completed building after death of Richard Jupp (*q.v.*), 1799–1800; dem. 1861–2. For the extent of Holland's responsibility for this building, see below, p. 479. (Britton & Pugin, *The Public Buildings of London* ii, 1828, 77–89.)

LONDON, WAREHOUSES adjacent to Middlesex Street and Harrow Place for the East India Company, 1799–1800, following designs by Richard Jupp, but with a modified layout [India Office Records B/130, ff. 1092–3 and A/1/1, ff. 490, 507].

WIMBLEDON PARK HOUSE, SURREY, for the 2nd Earl Spencer, 1800; dem. 1949 [Stroud, 104–5].

LONDON, ALBANY, PICCADILLY, conversion of Melbourne House into residential chambers and erection of additional buildings, 1803–4 [Stroud, 142–4; *Survey of London* xxxii, 373–85].

HERTFORD CASTLE, alterations to GATEHOUSE for

temporary accommodation of the East India College, 1805 [Stroud, 142].

GLASGOW, THE ASSEMBLY ROOMS, INGRAM STREET, added terminal pavilions to building designed by R. & J. Adam, completed 1807; dem. c. 1889 [*A.P.S.D.*].

WESTPORT, COUNTY MAYO, IRELAND, gateway at north-east end of town, for the 1st Marquess of Sligo, being built 1808 'from designs of Holland'; dem. c. 1958 [Diary of the Rev. D. A. Beaufort, Trinity College, Dublin, MS. K.6.63, f. 75].

DOUBTFUL WORKS

COLEHILL HOUSE, FULHAM, MIDDLESEX, is stated by Britton & Brayley, *Beauties of England and Wales* x (part 5), 1816, 96–7, to have been 'built in 1770 from the design of its late proprietor [James Madden] and under the direction of Mr. Holland, architect'. This was probably Henry Holland, senior. A letter from Henry Holland in the Somerset County Record Office dated Oct. 1783 refers to proposed works at KINGWESTON HOUSE, SOMERSET, for William Dickinson, but what, if anything, was done is uncertain. According to J. Stoddart, *Remarks on Local Scenery and Manners in Scotland* ii, 1801, 274, IRVINE HOUSE, LANGHOLM, DUMFRIESSHIRE, was 'a neat villa, designed by Holland'. What are probably Holland's designs for this house, signed and dated 1783, are preserved in a portfolio at Bowhill, Selkirkshire. But they were rejected as too expensive, and the modest house actually built c. 1792 appears to have been designed by a builder in London [Buccleuch archives, S.R.O., *ex inf.* Dr. A. A. Tait]. The house still exists, enlarged in 1836–7 by William Burn (*q.v.*). The 'works at Little Willenham, Staffordshire', attributed to Holland in *A.P.S.D.*, have not been identified.

HOLLAND, JOHN J—, 'Architect and Draftsman', of 25 Warren Street, London, signs two architectural drawings in the Metropolitan Museum of Art at New York, one of them dated 1802 [J. Harris, *Catalogue of British Drawings for Architecture, etc. in American Collections*, 1971, 125]. He was probably the J. Holland, of 24 Upper Edmund Street, St. Pancras, who exhibited a design for a Military Depot at the R.A. in 1815.

HOLLAND, RICHARD (1752–1827), a cousin of Henry Holland (*q.v.*), exhibited at the Royal Academy in 1771, 1772 and 1773, having been admitted to its Schools in October 1770, at the age of 18. He was awarded the Silver Medal the same year. His subsequent career was, however, to be that of a successful builder rather than an architect. In 1786 he was employed by R. M. T. Chiswell to design a Coade stone font for Debden

Church, Essex, which attracted much interest and was exhibited to the King at Buckingham Palace. It is described and illustrated in the *European Magazine* for 1786. Richard Holland is said also to have designed Debden Hall, Essex, for the same patron, but it appears in fact to have been designed by his cousin Henry. He retired in about 1804 to Madley, nr. Hereford, but moved in 1810 to Combe Royal, Kingsbridge, Devon, and ultimately to Moreton Hampstead in the same county, where he died on 28 September 1827. He was a friend of Sir John Soane, with whom he corresponded. [*A.P.S.D.*; A. T. Bolton, *Portrait of Sir John Soane*, 1927, 165–76; information from Miss Dorothy Stroud.]

HOLLINS, WILLIAM (1763–1843), architect and sculptor, was born at Shifnal on 18 March 1763, but went to Birmingham as a boy and lived there for the rest of his life. Originally a journeyman stonemason, he taught himself drawing and perspective and became a successful architect, sculptor and wax-modeller. In 1793 he assisted George Saunders of London to make the working drawings for the new Theatre Royal in New Street, and subsequently himself designed several public buildings in Birmingham in a competent Greek Revival style. He was one of the architects employed by the Earl of Shrewsbury to design the picturesque garden buildings at Alton Towers, though precisely what he did there does not appear to be recorded. He is said to have 'declined an offer to enter the service of the Empress of Russia at St. Petersburg, but made plans for the Royal Mint in that city'. As it stands this story is doubtful, but Hollins may have been concerned in some way with Matthew Boulton's commission to supply minting machinery from his Soho Works at Birmingham for the new Royal Mint at St. Petersburg designed by A. Porta (1805). In 1806 he produced a design for the Birmingham memorial to Nelson consisting of a column 100 feet high, rising from 'an appropriate building with two fronts suitable for a dispensary and post-office', but a simpler design by Westmacott was adopted. A list of his executed buildings is given below. For his activity as a sculptor see Rupert Gunnis's *Dictionary of British Sculptors*. He was also interested in lettering, and published *The British Standard of the Capital Letters contained in the Roman Alphabet*, Birmingham 1813.

Hollins had 16 children, 'through the whole of whom was to be traced the varied genius of the original'. His eldest son Peter (1800–86) was a well-known Victorian sculptor. Hollins died on 12 January 1843, and is buried under a granite obelisk in St. Paul's churchyard at Birmingham. He and his family are also commemorated by a glass window in the church with a sculptured surround incorporating his bust by Peter Hollins.

[H. H. Horton, *Birmingham A Poem*, 2nd ed. 1853, 285–9 (biographical notes); J. A. Langford, *Modern Birmingham* i, 1873, 31–2; *D.N.B.*; R. Gunnis, *Dictionary of British Sculptors*, 1968, 206–7; Bryan Little, *Birmingham Buildings*, 1971; I. G. Spassky, *The Russian Monetary System*, Amsterdam 1967, 222; Cornish's *Guide to Birmingham*, 1864.]

BIRMINGHAM, THE OLD LIBRARY, UNION STREET, 1798; enlarged 1845 by D. R. Hill [Langford, *Modern Birmingham* i, 31–2].

BIRMINGHAM, THE PUBLIC OFFICE and PRISON, MOOR STREET, 1805–7; enlarged 1829–30; dem. 1911 [Langford, *Modern Birmingham* i, 31–2].

BIRMINGHAM, THE GENERAL DISPENSARY, UNION STREET, 1806–8; dem. 1957 [Langford, *Modern Birmingham* i, 31–2].

BIRMINGHAM, THE BULL RING PUMP, 1807; dem. 1836 [J. A. Langford, *A Century of Birmingham Life* ii, 1871, 199].

ALTON ABBEY (later TOWERS), STAFFS., works for the 15th Earl of Shrewsbury, *c.* 1813–17, Gothic [papers in the Staffs. Record Office show that in Dec. 1817 it was ordered that the Hall should be 'finished agreeably to Mr. Hollins's plan', *ex inf.* Mr. J. M. Frew].

HANDSWORTH CHURCH, STAFFS., enlargement of north side 1820–1, Gothic [A. E. Everitt, 'Handsworth Church', *Trans. Birmingham Arch. Soc.* 1876, 62].

BIRMINGHAM, THE ATHENAEUM, TEMPLE ROW, for the Birmingham Institute for Promoting the Fine Arts, 1828; dem. [J. Hill & W. Midgley, *The Royal Birmingham Society of Artists*, 1928, 15, 26 and pl. 20].

HOLLIS, CHARLES, exhibited architectural designs at the Royal Academy in 1801–3. After this no further references to him have been found until 1820, when his designs for rebuilding WINDSOR PARISH CHURCH in the Gothic style were accepted, though Jeffry Wyatt was also concerned, apparently as a consultant. The church was completed in 1822 [*A.P.S.D.*; Parish Records]. Hollis also designed WINDSOR BRIDGE, consisting of three arches of iron, 1822–4 [*A.P.S.D.*], and the classical church of ALL SAINTS, POPLAR, with its parsonage house, 1821–3, illustrated in Britton & Pugin, *Public Buildings of London* ii, 1828, 202–4.[1] In 1820–5 Hollis was practising from Fenchurch Street, London, but his name then disappears from the London directories, and his death in or about 1826 may be presumed. He appears to have been a competent but unremarkable early nineteenth-century architect.

---

[1] J. J. Scoles also made designs for this church which were not accepted. He exhibited them at the R.A. in 1821.

HOLLOWAY, BENJAMIN, a local carpenter and builder, was employed by James Brydges, Duke of Chandos, in his building developments at Bridgwater in Somerset during the years 1723–8. Holloway designed at least four of the houses which he built for the Duke in New, or Castle, Street, but others may have been designed by the Duke's London surveyors, Fort and Shepherd. Holloway also built houses in Chandos Street, and one on the quay known as 'The Lions', which he occupied himself. This handsome house is illustrated in William Halfpenny's *Perspective Made Easy* (1731), with the inscription 'Benjamin Holloway invenit'. Chandos thought Holloway 'a very great knave. But being a good workman and the only one thereabouts 'tis necessary to employ him'. Stylistically he was a provincial master builder who had picked up some baroque details and made effective use of them to enliven his street-fronts. [C. H. & M. I. Collins Baker, *James Brydges, Duke of Chandos*, 1949, chap. x.]

HOLMES, WILLIAM (*c*. 1761–1847), 'of Lewisham, architect', is commemorated by a tablet on the north wall of Lewisham parish church. He died on 13 August 1847, aged 86. He designed the church of ST. JOHN, CAMPHILL ROAD, SOUTH END, LEWISHAM, *c*. 1823 [I.C.B.S.]. In the Public Record Office there is a 'sketch' by him for farm buildings at ELTHAM COURT FARM, KENT, dated 1828 [MPE 723].

HOLT, THOMAS (–1624), see AKROYD, JOHN

HOOKE, ROBERT (1635–1703), was born at Freshwater in the Isle of Wight, where his father, John Hooke, was then curate of the parish. He showed an early aptitude for drawing which led to his being apprenticed to Lely, but he soon gave up painting and entered Westminster School, where he lived in the house of Dr. Busby and astonished his teachers by his progress in learning. In 1653 he went up to Oxford as a chorister or servitor at Christ Church, matriculating in 1658, and proceeding M.A. in 1663. Here he became intimate with Wren, and attended the meetings of the 'Experimental Philosophical Club' which was the precursor of the Royal Society. His flair for scientific enquiry led to his appointment as curator of experiments to the Royal Society in 1662, and his election as a fellow in the following year. In 1665 his curatorship was made perpetual, with a salary of £30 and apartments in Gresham College, Bishopsgate Street, where he lived for the rest of his life. Later in the same year he was appointed Professor of Geometry at Gresham College, where Wren had been Professor of Astronomy, and from 1677 to 1682 he acted as Secretary to the Royal Society.

As a scientist, his fertility of invention and his genius for discerning the principles underlying chemical and physical processes were outstanding, and he was a pioneer in almost every branch of scientific enquiry.

Hooke's career as an architect began in September 1666, when he laid before the Common Council his plan (now lost) for rebuilding the City, and was told by the Lord Mayor that the court of aldermen 'had approved of it, and greatly preferring it to that of the city surveyor [Peter Mills] desired it might be shown to his Majesty'.[1] In October Hooke was nominated as one of the three surveyors whom the City was required to appoint under the Act for rebuilding London, the others being Peter Mills and Edward Jerman. In this capacity he was closely associated with Wren (one of the three surveyors nominated by the King) in the reconstruction of the City, surveying the sites of houses to be taken in in order to widen the streets, discussing the problems of the Fleet Ditch, agreeing with contractors, and negotiating with landowners. Both Wren and Hooke were concerned in the design and erection of the Monument on Fish Street Hill and it is not easy to decide which of them was its principal architect.[2] Hook also collaborated with Wren in connection with the City Churches, and there are several references to him as one of the three 'Surveyors for the building of the churches in London', the third being Edward Woodroffe, Surveyor to the Dean and Chapter of Westminster. It was 'on the City Churches account' that Hooke received substantial payments from Wren, and much of his time was spent in visiting them with or without the Surveyor-General, in passing accounts, and in attending vestry meetings. Hooke's share in the designing, as distinct from the building, of the City churches, is difficult to define. The existence of a drawing for the west front of St. Edmund, Lombard Street, in his hand (*Wren Soc.* ix, pl. 15) shows that on occasion he might design a major architectural feature, but the approbatory initials 'CW' also show that Wren retained ultimate control. Though Wren as Surveyor-General was the senior officer, Hooke must not be thought of merely as his junior assistant. In the eyes of the City he was Wren's colleague, not his deputy, and his diary shows that 'he met Wren as a friend and dined with him as an equal'; indeed they were related, one of Wren's sisters having married a member

---

[1] John Ward, *Lives of the Professors of Gresham College* (1740), 175. The formal entry in the Journal of the Court of Common Council (vol. 46, f. 121) is as follows: 'Mr. Hooke haveing upon the Mocion and Encouragement of this Court prepared & presented an Exquisite Modell or draught for rebuilding of this City doth declare their good Acceptance & Approbacion of the Same'.

[2] See below p. 924.

of Hooke's family,[1] and in correspondence Wren addressed Hooke as 'Cousin'. Despite their kinship and their close association in both architectural and scientific matters, Hook never took one of the Office of Works posts that were in Wren's gift. In January 1690/1, however, he was appointed Surveyor to the Dean and Chapter of Westminster at an annual salary of £20.[2] In this capacity he was consulted about repairs to the exterior of the Abbey Church in 1693. He presumably resigned in January 1696/7, when his place was taken by James Broughton. Hooke was an active, restless little man who slept little and often worked all night, taking a short nap during the day. Estimates of his character differ, but it is clear that although as a young man he had been 'very communicative of his philosophical discoveries and inventions', as he grew older he became increasingly mistrustful and secretive. In person he was 'but despicable', being 'crooked and low in stature', 'pale faced', and as he grew older, more and more deformed. He died at Gresham College on 3 March 1702/3, at the age of 67, and was buried in the church at St. Helen Bishopsgate.

For Hooke architecture was always a secondary activity, and he never gave himself up to it in the same way as Wren did. Nor do any of his architectural works or drawings suggest that he was a designer of outstanding ability. Nevertheless he was a competent architect whose contribution to English architecture has been obscured by the destruction of his most important works: the domed octagonal theatre of the Royal College of Physicians, the carefully articulated blocks of the Bethlehem Hospital, and the *cour d'honneur* of Montagu House, designed (as Evelyn noted) 'after the French pavilion-way'. French planning and Dutch detailing are the most obvious characteristics of Hooke's architectural style, and his diary shows that he purchased architectural books and prints from both France and Holland. A projected visit to France is mentioned in 1676, but it did not eventuate, and if Hooke ever visited Holland the occasion is not recorded, though an elevation of the Nieuwe Kerk at the Hague is among his drawings at the British Museum.

A volume of seventeenth-century architectural drawings in the British Museum (Add. MS. 5238) contains a number by Hooke or his assistant Henry Hunt. A few drawings by Hooke (including a section of the dome of the Physicians'

College) are among the Feilding family papers at Newnham Paddox, Warwicks. A design for a barracks at the R.I.B.A. and one for rebuilding the Royal Mews in the Library of the Department of the Environment (Dartmouth Collection) may be in his hand.

The primary source for Hooke's life in general and for his architectural work in particular, is his diary, the surviving portions of which extend from August 1672 to May 1683 (Guildhall Library), from November 1688 to March 1690, and from December 1692 to August 1693 (B.M. Sloane MS. 4024). The Guildhall MS. was published in 1935 in *The Diary of Robert Hooke*, ed. H. W. Robinson & W. Adams, omitting the entries for 1681, 1682 and 1683, the B.M. MS. in *Early Science in Oxford*, ed. R. T. Gunther, x, 1935, 69–265. [Aubrey's *Brief Lives*, ed. A. Clark, 1898, and O. L. Dick, 1949; *D.N.B.*; Margaret 'Espinasse, *Robert Hooke*, 1956; Geoffrey Keynes, *A Bibliography of Dr. Robert Hooke*, 1960; M. I. Batten, 'The Architecture of Dr. Robert Hooke', *Walpole Soc.* xxv, 1936–7; *Early Science in Oxford*, ed. R. T. Gunther, vols. vi, vii, viii, x, 1930–5; *Wren Society, passim*; T. F. Reddaway, *The Rebuilding of London after the Great Fire*, 1940; E. G. R. Taylor, 'Robert Hooke and the Cartographical Projects of the late 17th-Century', *Geographical Jnl.* 90, 1937; S. R. Pierce, 'A Drawing for a Thames Embankment by Robert Hooke', *Antiquaries' Jnl.* 44, 1964; Westminster Abbey Muniments; Sale catalogue in B.M.]

?BUNTINGFORD, HERTS., BISHOP SETH WARD'S ALMSHOUSES, founded under a charter of December 1684, but probably not built until 1689, when Hooke's assistant Hunt 'brought designs of Sarums almes houses at Buntingford' [*Diary*, 2 April 1689].

CAMBRIDGE, MAGDALENE COLLEGE, designs 1677, probably in connection with the Pepys Building, which was under construction in 1679 [Batten, 105–6; R.C.H.M. *Cambridge* ii, 139].

CANTERBURY CATHEDRAL, panelling in choir 1676; removed *c.* 1826 [*Archaeologia* lxii (2), 1911, 357; cf. *Diary*, 14 & 22 July 1676; C. E. Woodruff & W. Danks, *Memorials of Canterbury Cathedral*, 1912, plate facing p. 342].

ESCOT HOUSE, DEVONSHIRE, designs for Sir Walter Yonge, Bart., 1677–8, perhaps executed *c.* 1680–8. The house illustrated in *Vitruvius Britannicus* i, pls. 78–9 as 'Sir Walter Yonge's house in Devonshire' was Escot, not Colyton: see the engraving of Escot in Polwhele's *Devon* (1793–1806). Hooke made designs for a country house for Yonge in 1677–8 [Batten, 109], but Yonge did not complete the purchase of the estate at Escot until 1680, and the new house was not finished until *c.* 1688. It was

---

[1] Either Rachel or Katherine Wren married John Hooke (d. 1674), rector of Blechingdon, Oxon., and formerly Fellow of Magdalen College, Oxford. See Wood, *Life & Times*, ed. A. Clark, ii, 1892, 282. The exact relationship between Robert and John Hooke is not clear, but they appear both to have belonged to the Hampshire family of Hooke.

[2] He had previously given advice about repairing the choir (Diary, 18 July, 21 Aug., 8–10 Oct. 1676).

subsequently altered by James Wyatt and destroyed by fire in 1808.

LONDESBOROUGH HOUSE, YORKS. (E.R.), designs for the 1st Earl of Burlington, including garden layout, 1676–8. How much was done is uncertain. The house was demolished in 1811 [Batten, 104–5].

LONDON, ASKE'S HOSPITAL, HOXTON, for the Haberdashers' Company, c. 1690–3; rebuilt by D. R. Roper, 1825–6 [Batten, 103–4 and pl. xl].

LONDON, BETHLEHEM HOSPITAL, MOORFIELDS, 1675–6; wings added 1733; dem. 1815–16 [Batten, 91–3; drawings in B.M., Add. MS. 5238 and Bodleian, Gough Maps 44, no. 119].

LONDON, CHRIST'S HOSPITAL, NEWGATE STREET, THE WRITING SCHOOL, with John Oliver, 1675–6; dem. 1902 [Batten, 110 and Diary, 28 Aug. 1676] (Wren Soc. xi, pls. xliv, xlv).

LONDON, MERCHANT TAYLORS' HALL, THREAD-NEEDLE STREET, hall screen 1673, destroyed by bombing 1940–1 [Batten, 90–1 and pl. xxxvi].

LONDON, MERCHANT TAYLORS' SCHOOL, SUFFOLK LANE, 1674–5, with Lem, the bricklayer employed, 1674–5; dem. 1875 [Diary, 28 & 29 Jan., 3 & 11 Feb. 1674] (F. R. Nixon, History of Merchant Taylors' School, 1823, with lithographs).

LONDON, MONTAGU HOUSE, BLOOMSBURY, for Ralph Montagu, cr. Duke of Montagu, 1675–9; gutted Jan. 1685/6 and rebuilt 1687, apparently by the French architect Pouget (q.v.); sold to the British Museum Trustees 1754 and opened as Museum 1759; dem. c. 1850 [Batten, 93–6]. The only known representation of the house before the fire of 1687 is the small-scale view in Ogilvy & Morgan's map of 1682, reproduced by K. Downes, English Baroque Architecture, 1966, fig. 24. A comparison between this and engravings of the house after its reconstruction suggests that, even if the walls were partially retained, the elevations were considerably altered by Pouget. Hooke's forecourt and gateway, however, survived until the nineteenth century and are illustrated, e.g. by drawings by J. C. Buckler reproduced in C. Life, 14 Sept. 1951.

LONDON, THE MONUMENT, FISH STREET HILL, 1671–6, in association with Wren (see p. 924).

LONDON, THE ROYAL COLLEGE OF PHYSICIANS, WARWICK LANE, 1672–8. The domed octagonal theatre was dem. 1866 and the remainder of the buildings were destroyed by fire in 1879 [Batten, 89–90 and pls. 36–7; cf. Wren Soc. v, pl. xxxiii, which may be an alternative design for the elevation] (Britton & Pugin, The Public Buildings of London ii, 1828, 44–53).

LONDON, ST. JAMES'S SQUARE, probably supervised completion of nos. 6–7 for John Hervey and the 1st Earl of Ranelagh, 1676–7; dem.

[Batten, 107–8; Survey of London xxix, 103, 109].

LONDON, SOMERSET HOUSE, STRAND, THE STABLES for Queen Catherine of Braganza, probably c. 1669–70; dem. c. 1780 [History of the King's Works v, 258; Wren Soc. v, pl. xxxii].

LONDON, SPRING GARDENS, probably designed house for Sir Robert Southwell, 1684–5; dem. [a payment of 5 guineas to Hooke by Southwell on 17 June 1684, recorded in Thomas Thorpe's Catalogue of Southwell MSS. 1837, 296–7 probably relates to this house, which was built by Richard Frith, B.M. Egerton MS. 1627, ff. 62ᵛ, 68].

LONDON, STRAND, designed five houses for John Hervey, 1678 [Batten, 108].

LONDON, WHITEHALL, house in Privy Gardens for the 20th Earl of Oxford, 1676; dem. 1691 or 1698 [Batten, 106–7].

?LOWTHER CHURCH, WESTMORLAND, for Sir John Lowther, Bart., c. 1686. In Jan. 1679 Hooke 'gave Sir J. Lowther a Designe of church and estimate', and Lowther subsequently reconstructed the medieval church, crowning the centre tower with a dome and lantern which Hooke could well have designed. This feature was removed in 1824, but is shown in drawings by Machell (Carlisle Cathedral Library) and Buckler (B.M., Add. MS. 36390, f. 146). The date of the reconstruction is given as 1686 in Nicholson and Burn's History of Westmorland (1777), but the termination of Hooke's diary in 1683 makes it impossible to ascertain whether he made any further designs in that year. Among the Lonsdale papers in the Cumberland and Westmorland Record Office there is a large design on vellum for the façade of Lowther Castle which can be attributed to Hooke. It presumably dates from c. 1690, when Sir John Lowther was about to rebuild the Castle, though not, in the event, to Hooke's design.

?PLYMOUTH, ROYAL DOCKYARD, HAMOAZE, THE OFFICERS' DWELLING-HOUSES, GREAT STORE-HOUSE, ROPEHOUSE, etc. c. 1690–1700. A set of the designs for these buildings, as engraved for the benefit of the Navy Commissioners, is preserved among the Hooke drawings in B.M. Add. MS. 5238, and they closely resemble the Bethlehem Hospital in style. Moreover the Deputy-Governor of the Citadel at this time was Henry Hook, who may have been a relation of Robert's. Edmund Dummer (q.v.) was in charge of the work, but it seems possible that Hooke was responsible for the designs, especially as he had been involved in the design of the Navy Office in London in 1674 (Batten, 85–6). There is another set of these engravings in Add. MS. 9329, ff. 156–81. The buildings were not yet finished in 1698: see the view in King's MS. 43, f. 130.

430

RAGLEY HALL, WARWICKS., for the 1st Earl of Conway, 1679–83. Hooke extensively revised a design already made by William Hurlbatt or Hulbert (*q.v.*). The interior was altered by Gibbs *c.* 1750–5 and the portico was added by James Wyatt *c.* 1780 [Batten, 97–103; P. Leach, 'Ragley Hall', *Archaeological Jnl.* cxxviii, 1971, 230–3] (*C. Life*, 22, 29 March 1924, 1, 8 May 1958).

RAMSBURY MANOR, WILTS., for Sir William Jones, Attorney General, *c.* 1680–3. Hooke 'drew designes' for Jones in 1673 and in 1680 designed or altered a house for him in London. It is therefore likely that Jones would have employed Hooke to design the new house which he shortly afterwards began to build at Ramsbury (*C. Life*, 2, 9 Oct. 1920, 30 Nov., 7 Dec. 1961), and the fact that in August 1682 Hooke visited Ramsbury in company with Lem (bricklayer), Avis (carpenter) and Davis (joiner), three London craftsmen regularly employed by him, makes it virtually certain that he was the architect of Ramsbury [H. Colvin, 'Robert Hooke and Ramsbury Manor', *C. Life*, 23 Jan. 1975].

SHENFIELD PLACE, ESSEX for Richard Vaughan, 1689 [Batten, 111: 'House in Essex' identifiable as Shenfield Place] (R.C.H.M. *Essex* ii, 214).

WILLEN CHURCH, BUCKS., for Dr. Richard Busby, 1680 [Batten, 96–7]. The lead cupola on the tower was removed in 1814 and the apse is an addition of 1862. An alternative design is illustrated in *Wren Soc.* ix, pl. 37. An engraving in *Gent's Mag*, 1792, 1168 shows the cupola.

HOPE, JOHN (1734–1808), and SAMUEL (1737–*c.*1770), were the sons of John Hope, an architect and builder of Millington, near Altrincham in Cheshire. The father is said to have designed 'several residences' in Cheshire, and in particular to have been employed by the Earl of Stamford at Dunham Massey and Enville Hall (Staffs.) His sons succeeded to his practice, but moved to Liverpool in about 1763. In 1769 they competed jointly for the Royal Exchange in Dublin, but Samuel's death soon afterwards left John to carry on the practice alone for over 30 years. He died in 1808 in his 73rd. year, leaving his practice to be continued by his son-in-law William Byrom (*q.v.*). From 1770 onwards he kept a detailed diary of both private and professional matters whose present whereabouts is unknown, though it was still in existence in 1869 [*Builder* xxvii, 1869, 781, 803–4, 909].[1]

In 1766 John Hope designed a vaulted room in the LIVERPOOL EXCHANGE in order to contain the Corporation Records, and in 1777, when it was proposed to build a new gaol, he was authorised to send for plans of Newgate Prison, London, 'as lately rebuilt' [J. A. Picton, *Liverpool Muncipal Records 1700–1835*, 1886, 256, 264]. In 1773 he made an unexecuted design, now in the R.I.B.A. Drawings Collection, for the front of ENVILLE HALL, STAFFS., for the 5th. Earl of Stamford, and at about the same time one for GWYDYR CASTLE, NORTH WALES, for the 3rd. Duke of Ancaster, now in the Lincolnshire Record Office [3 Anc/5]. He designed the PIECE HALL at HALIFAX, YORKS. (W.R.), in 1774–9 [D. Linstrum, *West Yorkshire Architects and Architecture*, forthcoming], the BLUECOAT SCHOOL at WARRINGTON, LANCS., in 1779–82 [J. Bowes, 'The Warrington Blue Coat School', *Trans. of the Historic Soc. of Lancs. and Cheshire* N.S. x, 1869–70, 101–2], rebuilt HIGH LEGH HALL, CHESHIRE (dem.), for Henry Cornwall Legh in 1781–4 [accounts among Legh papers in John Rylands Library, Manchester], and altered RODE HALL, CHESHIRE for Randle Wilbraham *c.* 1800 [Wilbraham papers, *ex inf.* Mr. J. M. Robinson]. In 1802 he was employed at INCE BLUNDELL, LANCS., by Henry Blundell, probably as executant architect of the latter's new Pantheon Gallery [Lancashire Record Office, DD/N. 53/114 and cf. C. Hussey in *C. Life*, 17 April 1958]. In 1789 the tower of ST. NICHOLAS'S CHURCH, LIVERPOOL, was repaired by Thomas Wainwright under his direction [*Gent's Mag*. 1814 (i), 116] and in 1803 he was paid £2 14s. 6d. for planning alterations to the same church [*Liverpool Vestry Books*, ed. Peet ii, 37].

In 1790 his designs for St. John's Church, Wakefield, were rejected in favour of those of Charles Watson [J. W. Walker, *Wakefield*, 1939, 300], but in 1794 he designed HOLY TRINITY CHURCH, WAVERTREE, nr. LIVERPOOL, with a prominent classical steeple in the Wren tradition [*Builder* xxvii, 1869, 909].

HOPE, THOMAS (1769–1831), was the eldest son of John Hope, a wealthy merchant of Scottish descent whose family had been established in Amsterdam for several generations. Thomas Hope was brought up in luxurious and cultivated surroundings at his father's country house near Haarlem, and was given every opportunity to develop a natural taste for the arts. As a young man he travelled extensively in Europe and the Near East and acquired a considerable knowledge of architecture and sculpture. When the French occupation of Holland obliged him and his family

---

[1] The Hopes of Liverpool must be distinguished from Samuel and J. Hope, statuary masons of Manchester, for whom see R. Gunnis, *Dictionary of British Sculptors 1660–1851*, 1968, 208. Samuel Hope of Manchester was described as 'architect' in the *Gentleman's Magazine*

when he died at Altrincham in 1817, aged 76. [*Gent's Mag*. 1817, 568]. As the Liverpool Hopes were natives of Millington in the same parish, the two families were no doubt related.

to leave the country of their adoption he came to England (1795) and established himself as a connoisseur and patron of the arts. He built up a large collection of antique sculpture and vases which was augmented by the works of contemporary artists such as Flaxman, Canova, Thorwaldsen, Haydon, Westall and West. He also did his best to influence the taste of others by showing his own collections and by publishing works on architecture and furniture. In 1800 he was elected a member of the Society of Dilettanti, and in 1804 he was asked by Francis Annesley, the first Master of Downing College, Cambridge, to pronounce on James Wyatt's designs for the college buildings. Hope's report, which he published as *Observations on the Plans and Elevations designed by James Wyatt, Architect, for Downing College, Camb.; in a letter to Francis Annesley, Esq., M.P.*, 1804, was intended to discredit Wyatt's Roman Doric design and to advocate one of the most uncompromisingly Grecian character. Although pretentious and pedantic, Hope's report was not without its effect, for other architects were invited to submit plans, among them William Wilkins, whose Greek design was eventually adopted. Wyatt's defeat by Wilkins in this opening battle of the Greek Revival was an important artistic event. Although it embroiled Hope with the Royal Academy (of which Wyatt was the President), it established him – at least in the eyes of his supporters – as 'Judge Supreme of Architecture'.

Hope himself was a competent draughtsman, but as an amateur architect he confined himself to his own two houses, both of them very remarkable buildings. In 1799, in order to accommodate his collections, he bought a house in Duchess Street, Portland Place, which had been built by Robert Adam for General Robert Clerk. This house Hope gradually enlarged and remodelled, adding in 1819 a Picture Gallery designed by himself in order to display the collection of Flemish and Dutch pictures belonging to his brother Henry Philip Hope. This gallery was decorated in a sophisticated neo-classical style and contained furniture to match designed by its owner. There were also a Sculpture Gallery, a second Picture Gallery suggestive of a Greek temple, Indian and Egyptian rooms, a 'Flaxman Room' (enshrining the sculptor's 'Aurora and Cephalus'), and three rooms for the display of Greek vases. All these rooms were regularly open to the public, and made Hope's house (like Soane's) half-museum, half-residence. With its hard, bright colours, its uncomfortable but archaeologically correct furniture, and its esoteric symbolism, the Hope style was too uncompromising to be universally admired, but it played an important part in disseminating neo-classical ideas among contemporary architects and interior decorators. The house was

432

demolished by Hope's son in 1850 but was recorded in Hope's *Household Furniture and Interior Decoration* (1807), in C. M. Westmacott's *British Galleries of Painting and Sculpture* (1824), and in Britton & Pugin's *Public Buildings of London* i, 1825, 308–12.

Hope's country house, the Deepdene, near Dorking in Surrey (purchased in 1807 from Sir Charles Merrick Burrell) was similarly enlarged and embellished by its owner, who employed William Atkinson (*q.v.*) to carry out his plans (apparently in two main stages, dated by Dr. Watkin 1818–19 and 1823). Here, although the architectural components were mostly classical, the planning was asymmetrical and the effect picturesque. The interior was furnished in the same style as Hope's London house, and here again there was much classical statuary and 'Egyptian' ornament, including a bed copied from a plate in Denon's *Egypte* (1802). The house was subsequently enlarged in an Italianate style by Hope's son Henry Beresford Hope. The contents were dispersed in 1917, and the fabric was demolished in 1967. Two volumes of an elaborately-illustrated *History of the Deepdene* by John Britton are in the R.I.B.A. Drawings Collection and the Minet Library at Camberwell.

A complete list of Hope's publications will be found in Dr. Watkin's book. The most important were *Household Furniture and Interior Decoration executed from Designs by Thomas Hope*, fol., 1807; *Costume of the Ancients*, 2 vols. 1809; *Designs of Modern Costume*, 1812; *An Essay on the Origin and Prospects of Man*, 1831, and *An Historical Essay on Architecture by the late Thomas Hope, illustrated from Drawings made by him in Italy and Germany*, posthumously published in 2 vols. in 1835. In 1819 he published anonymously a picaresque novel entitled *Anastasius, or Memoirs of a Modern Greek, written at the Close of the Eighteenth Century*, which was at first ascribed to Byron, and achieved considerable popularity.

Hope married in 1806 Louisa Beresford, daughter of William Beresford, Archbishop of Tuam. He died on 3 February 1831, leaving three sons, Henry Thomas Hope (1808–62), founder of the Art Union, Adrian John Hope (1811–63), and Alexander James Beresford Hope (1820–87), ecclesiologist and leader of the Gothic Revival, who became President of the R.I.B.A. in 1865.

[D.N.B.; H. W. & I. Law, *The Book of the Beresford Hopes*, 1925; S. Baumgarten, *La Crépuscule Néo-Classique: Thomas Hope*, Paris 1958; David Watkin, *Thomas Hope and the Neo-Classical Idea*, 1968.]

HOPKINS, JOHN DOUGLAS (–1869), was a pupil of J. B. Papworth. He won a premium from the Society of Arts in 1830–1, exhibited at the Royal Academy in 1831, and was admitted to the R.A. Schools in 1832. In 1835 he competed for the Houses of Parliament in conjunction with H. E. Kendall. Their design was in a Gothic style of 'a character sufficiently decorated to stand the extraordinary test of comparative richness with Henry VII's Chapel'. The only buildings erected to Hopkins' designs that have been noted are: HOLY TRINITY CHURCH, WOOLWICH, KENT, a small stuccoed building erected in 1833–4 [Drake, *Blackheath Hundred*, 1886, 161 n.] and the SWEDENBORG CHAPEL, ARGYLE STREET, KING'S CROSS, in the Norman style, 1844 [J. Timbs, *Curiosities of London*, 1855, 176]. He was Hon. Secretary of the Committee formed in 1834 to establish the Institute of British Architects. According to Wyatt Papworth he was 'also eminent in the engineering profession' [*J. B. Papworth*, 1879, 96]. He had two architect sons.

HOPKINS, ROGER, of Plymouth, civil engineer and architect, designed the BRIDGE at TEIGNMOUTH, DEVONSHIRE, which was executed under his supervision between 1825 and 1827: it was 1671 feet long, and was considered at the time to be the longest bridge in the kingdom. He also designed the ROYAL UNION BATHS at PLYMOUTH, 1829 [*Devonshire Illustrated, with Historical and Descriptive Accounts by J. Britton and E. W. Brayley*, 1828, 96, 99]. He was the father of Rice Hopkins (1807–1857), civil engineer [*Minutes of Proceedings of the Institution of Civil Engineers* xviii, 1859, 192].

HOPPER, THOMAS (1776–1856), was born at Rochester, where his father was a measuring surveyor, 'clever and prominent in his business, but of intemperate habits'. Apart from the practical training which Thomas received in his father's office, his architectural knowledge was apparently self-acquired. Early in his career he carried out extensive alterations to Craven Cottage, Fulham, for Walsh Porter, converting it into the elaborate *cottage orné* described by Croker in his *Walk from London to Fulham* (1860). There were three reception-rooms. 'The centre, or principal saloon, [was] supported by large palm-trees of considerable size, exceedingly well executed, with their drooping foliage at the top, supporting the cornice and architraves of the room.' This room led to a large Gothic dining-room, and there was also a semi-circular library with an 'Egyptian' doorway. Walsh Porter's 'cottage' was much admired by his friend the Prince Regent, who commissioned Hopper to make alterations to Carlton House, including the addition of a large Gothic conservatory, *en suite* with the dining-room. This was a brilliant conceit, designed in the style of Henry VII's Chapel, but constructed of cast-iron so that the tracery of the vaulting could be pierced to admit light through coloured glass. This royal patronage brought

Hopper a fashionable practice as a country-house architect, which he combined with the more mundane duties of County Surveyor of Essex, a post (worth £250 p.a.) which he obtained in 1816 and held for 40 years. He was also surveyor to the Atlas Fire Assurance Company, whose London offices he designed. From time to time Hopper competed for major public buildings such as the General Post Office (1820), the Houses of Parliament (1835), the Conservative Club (1842) and the Carlton Club (1844), but he derived more vexation than advantage from these efforts,[1] and the list of his public works contains nothing more important than the Essex County Gaol, Arthur's Club in St. James's, St. Mary's Hospital, Paddington (for which he gave his services gratis) and a handful of country churches. Nevertheless, Hopper was among the best-known of early nineteenth-century architects, and is said to have declined a knighthood from George IV, as well as offers from the Tsar of Russia and the Duchess of Oldenburg to settle in St. Petersburg. Like all successful nineteenth-century architects he lived an active and energetic life. 'In his best days his flow of spirits was exuberant; his powers of conversation remarkable; his memory most tenacious. He never drank anything stronger than water, and could bear a marvellous amount of fatigue.' His office was first at 42 Berkeley Street, then at 40 Connaught Terrace, Edgware Road, but he had a private residence at 1 Bayswater Hill, where he died on 11 August 1856. A bust of Hopper by J. Ternouth was exhibited at the Royal Academy in 1838, and it is said that 'his form and features' can be seen in the bas relief on the east side of the base of Nelson's Column, where they were given by the same sculptor to a sailor who is supporting a wounded boy. Hopper's pupils included F. J. Francis, S. Hutchins, T. Lloyd, J. Miller, R. Papworth, G. J. Robinson and G. A. Burn, who latterly had charge of his practice. He never became a member of the R.I.B.A., but exhibited at the Royal Academy from time to time.

Hopper was an eclectic designer who held the belief that 'it is an architect's business to understand all styles, and to be prejudiced in favour of none'. He carried out his own precept, using Greek Doric at Springfield Gaol, Greek Ionic at

---

[1] He claimed that his design for the Post Office had been made use of by Smirke, the architect eventually employed (see his pamphlet entitled *A Letter to Lord Melbourne on the rebuilding of the Royal Exchange*, 1839), and after the Houses of Parliament competition he not only published two pamphlets, *A Letter to Lord Viscount Duncannon*, 1837, and *Hopper v. Cust, on the New Houses of Parliament*, 1837, but went to the expense of having his own entry published in a large folio volume entitled *Designs for the New Houses of Parliament*, 1840. His designs for the Carlton Club are in the R.I.B.A. Drawings Collection.

Leigh Court, North Stoneham and Kinmel Park, Palladian classical at Arthur's Club, Boreham House and Amesbury, Tudor Gothic at Margam Abbey, Danbury Place, Rood Ashton, and Easton Lodge, Jacobethan at Llanover House and Wivenhoe Park, and Norman Revival at Gosford and Penrhyn Castles. He handled all these styles with competence, but his Grecian façades were somewhat banal and his most interesting and original works were the two Norman castles, in which he effectively combined picturesque massing with a remarkable repertoire of Romanesque detailing which owed something to his familiarity with the twelfth-century keeps of Rochester and Hedingham. A certain coarseness of touch runs through all his work, and nothing he did in later life would seem quite to have equalled the brilliant *jeu d'esprit* at Carlton House with which he began his career.

[Obituary in *Builder* xiv, 1856, 481; *A.P.S.D.*; Charlotte Fell Smith, 'Thomas Hopper', *Essex Review* xxiii, 1914, 145–8; Robin Fedden, 'Neo-Norman', *Architectural Review* Dec. 1954; Arthur Searle, 'Thomas Hopper', *Essex Journal* v, Oct. 1970, 132–40.]

PUBLIC BUILDINGS

LONDON, THE ROYAL SOCIETY OF MUSICIANS, 11–13 LISLE STREET, 1808–9; dem. 1931 [*Survey of London* xxxiv, 474–5].

SOUTHMINSTER CHURCH, ESSEX, new roof, apse and plaster vaulting, 1819 [I.C.B.S.].

CHELMSFORD, ESSEX, THE COUNTY GAOL, SPRINGFIELD, 1822–6, and alterations, 1845–8 [Essex County Records].

RAWRETH CHURCH, ESSEX, rebuilt except tower, 1823; rebuilt 1882 [I.C.B.S.].

CANTERBURY CATHEDRAL, report on north-west tower, 1824 [C. E. Woodruff & W. Danks, *Memorials of Canterbury Cathedral*, 1912, 360–1].

HATFIELD PEVEREL CHURCH, ESSEX, enlarged 1826 [I.C.B.S.].

LONDON, ARTHUR'S (now THE CARLTON) CLUB, NOS. 69–70 ST. JAMES'S STREET, 1826–7 [*Survey of London* xxx, 475–7 and pls. 66–7] (*C. Life*, 1 June 1940).

ILFORD, ESSEX, THE HOUSE OF CORRECTION, 1828–31 [Essex County Records].

SALISBURY, WILTS., GUILDHALL, enlarged 1829, forming existing portico [contract in Salisbury Corporation MSS.; R.C.H.M. *Salisbury*, forthcoming].

LONDON, THE ATLAS FIRE ASSURANCE OFFICE, NO. 92 CHEAPSIDE, 1834–6 [*A.P.S.D.*].

LONDON, THE LEGAL AND GENERAL LIFE INSURANCE OFFICE, NO. 10 FLEET STREET, 1838; dem. 1885 [*A.P.S.D.*].

LONDON, COUTTS'S BANK, NO. 59 STRAND, alterations 1838–9; dem. 1923 [*A.P.S.D.*].

BROMLEY COMMON, KENT, HOLY TRINITY CHURCH, 1839–42; Gothic; altered 1884 [I.C.B.S.].

SOUTHEND, ESSEX, ST. JOHN'S CHURCH, 1841–2, Gothic; aisles added 1869, chancel 1873 [I.C.B.S.].

BUTTERTON CHURCH, STAFFS., 1844–5, Norman style, at the expense of Sir William Pilkington, Bart. [*Staffordshire Advertiser*, 8 Feb. 1845].

EPPING, ESSEX, ST. JOHN'S CHURCH, addition of porch c. 1848; dem. 1889 [*V.C.H. Essex* v, 136].

LONDON, ST. MARY'S HOSPITAL, PADDINGTON, 1845–51 [*Builder* iii, 1845, 299, 304, 321, iv, 1846, 182, 238, 245].

DOMESTIC ARCHITECTURE

CRAVEN COTTAGE, FULHAM, MIDDLESEX, alterations for Walsh Porter, c. 1806; destroyed by fire 1888 [*Builder* xiv, 481] (C. J. Fèret, *Fulham Old and New* iii, 1900, 91–2; T. C. Croker, *A Walk from London to Fulham*, 1860, 190–1).

LONDON, CARLTON HOUSE, PALL MALL, Gothic Conservatory and other works for George, Prince of Wales, 1807; dem. 1827–8 [*History of the King's Works* vi, 313, fig. 6 and pls. 12–13].

DROMOLAND CASTLE, CO. CLARE, IRELAND, Greek Doric entrance lodge for Sir Edward O'Brien, Bart., 1812 [drawings in National Library of Ireland, *ex inf.* Mr. Nicholas Sheaff].

MELFORD HALL, LONG MELFORD, SUFFOLK, library and staircase for Sir William Parker, Bart., 1813 [*Melford Hall, Suffolk*, National Trust guidebook, 1975] (*C. Life*, 7 Aug. 1937).

LEIGH COURT, nr. BRISTOL, SOMERSET, for P. J. Miles, 1814 [*Builder* xiv, 1856, 481] (Robert Cooke, *West Country Houses*, 1957, 155–8).

PURLEY HALL, BERKSHIRE, remodelled for John Wilder, 1818–20 [C. Hussey in *C. Life*, 5–12 Feb. 1970].

NORTH STONEHAM PARK, HANTS., house and 'Belvedere Lodge' for John Willis Fleming, 1818 and reconstruction after fire in 1831; dem. [Ackermann, *Views of Country Seats* ii, 1830; G. F. Prosser, *Select Illustrations of Hampshire*, 1833].

ALSCOT PARK, WARWICKS. (formerly Glos.), added porch for James Roberts West, shortly before 1820 [Neale's *Views of Seats* iii, 1820; original drawing in Bodleian, Gough Misc. Ant. fol. 4, 19] (*C. Life*, 29 May 1958, fig. 1).

ALTON TOWERS, STAFFS., works for the 15th Earl of Shrewsbury, c. 1820 [*A.P.S.D.*].

SLANE CASTLE, CO. MEATH, IRELAND, designs for alterations for the 1st Marquess Conyngham, probably c. 1820 [*Builder* xiv, 481; Alistair Rowan in *Bulletin of the Irish Georgian Soc.* Jan–March 1964, 29, n. 32].[1]

---

[1] Hopper was also employed at SHANE'S CASTLE, CO. ANTRIM, to arbitrate between John Nash and Lord

GOSFORD CASTLE, CO. ARMAGH, IRELAND, for the 2nd Earl of Gosford, *c.* 1820, Norman style [*Builder* xiv, 481]. In 1859 G. A. Burn, who had been Hopper's principal assistant, designed a new entrance front, which he exhibited at the R.A.

TERLING PLACE, ESSEX, alterations, including addition of wings, for Col. J. H. Strutt, 1818–21 [Essex Record Office, D/DR a, E 25,89, *ex inf.* Miss Nancy Briggs].

WOOLVERSTONE HALL, SUFFOLK, additions for Charles Berners, 1823 [W. A. Copinger, *Manors of Suffolk* vi, 1910, 125].

PENRHYN CASTLE, CAERNARVONSHIRE, for G. H. Dawkins Pennant, *c.* 1825–*c.* 1844, Norman style [exhib. at R.A. 1836 and 1838] (*C. Life*, 21, 28 July 1955; C. Hussey, *English Country Houses: Late Georgian*, 1958, 181–92).

KENTWELL HALL, SUFFOLK, reconstructed interior for R. H. Logan after fire, *c.* 1825 [S. Tymms in *Proc. Suffolk Inst. of Archaeology* ii, 1854, 72; Rickman's diary, 3 July 1828].

ERDIGG PARK, DENBIGHSHIRE, remodelled dining-room for Simon Yorke, 1827–8 [letter and accounts at Erdigg, *ex inf.* Mr. Gervase Jackson-Stops].

BOREHAM HOUSE, ESSEX, added wings and flanking gateways for Sir John Tyrell, Bart., 1827–8 [Charlotte Fell-Smith in *C. Life*, 11 July 1914].

DUNKELD HOUSE, PERTHSHIRE, design for a new house for the 4th Duke of Atholl, 1828. Only the foundations were laid and work was abandoned after the Duke's death in 1830. Hopper's drawings remain in the Charter Room at Blair Atholl [*Chronicles of the Atholl and Tullibardine Families*, by the 7th Duke of Atholl, 1908, iv, 388, 392; exhib. at R.A. 1843].

LLANOVER HOUSE, MONMOUTHSHIRE, for Sir Benjamin Hall, Bart., 1828–39, Elizabethan style; dem. 1935 [J. A. Bradney, *History of Monmouthshire* ii, 1906, 385].

BERWICK PLACE, HATFIELD PEVEREL, ESSEX, for A. Johnson, *c.* 1830 [B. Burke, *Visitations of Seats and Arms*, 2nd. ser., i, 1854, 68].

MARGAM ABBEY, GLAMORGANSHIRE, for C. R. Mansel Talbot, 1830–5, Tudor Gothic [exhib. at R.A. 1833, 1835] (*C. Life*, 5 April 1902).

CRICHEL, DORSET, alterations to entrance for H. C. Sturt, 1831 [Wiltshire Record Office, Penistone papers, letter-book, 7 and 21 Feb., 1 March 1831].

DANBURY PLACE, ESSEX, for John Round, 1832, Tudor Gothic [T. Wright, *History of Essex*, 1831–5, i, 685].

WELFORD PARK, BERKSHIRE, added bow-win-

dowed dining-room for J. A. Houblon, 1831–3 [drawings and accounts at Welford Park].

AMESBURY HOUSE, WILTS., rebuilt for Sir Edward Antrobus, Bart., 1834–40 [exhib. at R.A. 1841] (*C. Life*, 1 March 1902).

ROOD ASHTON HOUSE, nr. TROWBRIDGE, WILTS., alterations for Walter Long, 1836, Gothic, now ruinous [*Builder* xiv, 481].

KIRTLINGTON PARK, OXON., repairs and/or minor alterations for Sir George Dashwood, Bart., 1838 [note among drawings formerly at Kirtlington Park].

BUTTERTON HALL, STAFFS., for Sir William Pilkington, Bart., *c.* 1840–50, Tudor Gothic; dem. 1921 [exhib. at R.A. 1840 as 'proposed to be built'] (a drawing by J. Buckler in the William Salt Library at Stafford, II, 211, shows the house 'now building' in 1847).

STANSTEAD HOUSE, SUSSEX, alterations for Charles Dixon, *c.* 1840; destroyed by fire 1900 [*Builder* xiv, 481].

KINMEL PARK, DENBIGHSHIRE, rebuilt for the 1st Lord Dinorben, 1842–3; rebuilt by W. E. Nesfield 1875 [*Builder* xiv, 481] (B. Burke, *Visitations of Seats and Arms*, 2nd ser., i, 1854, frontispiece; *C. Life*, 4 Sept. 1969, fig. 2).

BIRCH HALL, ESSEX, for C. G. Round, 1843–7; dem. 1954 [J. A. Rush, *Seats in Essex*, 1897, 40].

WIVENHOE PARK, ESSEX, remodelled for J. Gurdon Rebow, 1846–9, Jacobean [*A.P.S.D.*; Rosemary Feesey, *A History of Wivenhoe Park*, Colchester, 1963].

EASTON LODGE, nr. DUNMOW, ESSEX, rebuilt for the 3rd Viscount Maynard, after a fire in 1847, Tudor Gothic; reconstructed by Philip Tilden after a fire in *c.* 1918 [J. A. Rush, *Seats in Essex*, 1897, 73].

HOPPERTON, WILLIAM (–1853), practised from Pimlico, London, from about 1810 to 1850. He competed unsuccessfully for the New Bethlehem Hospital in 1810 and exhibited his design at the Royal Academy the following year. He appears to have designed the INDEPENDENT CHAPEL, DORKING, SURREY, built in 1834–5 by William Shearburn (*q.v.*) [Brayley, *Surrey* v, 103]. The probate of his will in January 1854 (P.C.C.) indicates that he probably died in 1853.

HOPPUS, EDWARD (–1739), was appointed surveyor to the London Assurance Corporation in 1729 in succession to John Shepherd, and retained the post until his death in April or May 1739. He is best known as the author of *Practical Measuring* (1st ed. 1736), a manual for building surveyors that was many times reissued in the course of the eighteenth, nineteenth and early twentieth centuries. The last edition was in 1942 and the book went out of print only in 1973 when it was made obsolete

---

O'Neil, who began to rebuild the house after a fire had destroyed the old castle in 1816, but stopped the work before it was finished [information from Mr. Robin Fedden].

by metrication. Hoppus made the drawings for the engravings which illustrate the English translation of *The Third and Fourth Books of Palladio's Architecture*, published by the engraver B. Cole in 1733–5. This was an unscholarly work that was superseded a few years later by Ware's translation of all four books. Hoppus also published a collection of largely second-hand architectural designs entitled *The Gentleman's and Builder's Repository, or Architecture Displayed*, 1737, 1738, 1748, 4th ed. 1760, edited W. Salmon's *Palladio Londinensis, or London Art of Building*, 1738, and revised the same author's *Country Builder's Estimator*, 1737 [*A.P.S.D.*].

HORN, R—, is known only from two exhibits at the Royal Academy: in 1812 'a Design for a museum', and in 1815 a 'Model of a design of a capital for the columns of the Caledonian Asylum', i.e. the ROYAL CALEDONIAN ASYLUM, CHALK ROAD, COPENHAGEN FIELDS, ISLINGTON, established in 1813–15.

HORN, WILLIAM, was a successful Glasgow builder. He was a wright by trade, and was Deacon of the Glasgow Wrights in 1769 [*The Incorporation of Wrights of Glasgow*, Glasgow 1880, 44]. He built Horn's Court off St. Enoch's Square, Glassford Street (*c.* 1792), and many of the houses in Argyll Street [Senex, *Glasgow Past and Present*, 1884, i, 100, 462, ii, 102, 239, 450, iii, 285]. In 1796 he designed the wings which were added to GLASGOW BRIDEWELL [*Records of the Burgh of Glasgow*, ed. Renwick, ix, 7, 142].

HORNE, JAMES (–1756), was probably the James Horne, joiner, who is mentioned in 1711 as the son of Thomas Horne, a citizen and joiner of London. James first appears in association with Nicholas Dubois (*q.v.*), for whom he deputised at the Office of Works on several occasions in the years 1721–4. He also acted as measurer at Stanmer Park, Sussex, a house designed by Dubois and built in 1722–7. Early in George II's reign he acted as clerk of works for the formation of the Serpentine Lake in Hyde Park. In 1740 he was one of the three arbitrators in the case between John Cordwell, the City Carpenter, and the Corporation of London, over the former's payment for making the model of the Mansion House. In 1742 he undertook to act gratuitously as surveyor to the Foundling Hospital, and supervised the erection of its buildings to the designs of the amateur architect Theodore Jacobsen. His 'ability and integrity' are praised in a letter from William Pulteney, Earl of Bath, to Zachary Pearce, Dean of Winchester, dated 1 Sept. 1742. In 1746 he succeeded John James as surveyor to the fabric of Westminster Abbey. His resignation in 1752 may have been occasioned by his appointment as surveyor of the Naval Hos-

436

pital at Gosport, another building designed by Theodore Jacobsen. The death of 'Mr. Horn, surveyor of Gosport Hospital', took place on 19 Aug. 1756. Some 'Remarks and Observations in several parts of Civil Architecture, alphabetically digested, and collected by Mr. Horne', form part of an anonymous MS. in the library at Ardkinglas, Argyllshire, entitled *The Architects Remembrancer, or Surveyors Pocket Companion, being a Parallel of Antient and Modern Architecture, set forth in Tables*.

As an architect Horne appears to have been employed chiefly to design churches in a handsome but rather pedestrian style which may be described as 'vernacular Palladian'. Of these Holy Trinity at Guildford is now the only surviving example.

[*A.P.S.D.*; G.L.C. Record Office, Middlesex Land Register 1711/4/20; *History of the King's Works* v, 87, 203; *Wren Soc.* vii, 68, 192–5, 205, 221–2; S. Perks, *The Mansion House*, 1922, 184; R. H. Nichols and F. A. Wray, *History of the Foundling Hospital*, 1935, 43; W.A.M. 64662; *Gent's Mag.*, 1756, 412].

EALING, MIDDLESEX, ST. MARY'S CHURCH, 1735–40, rebuilt by S. S. Teulon, 1866–74 [MS. Vestry Minutes: there is a set of plans and elevations in B.M., *King's Maps* xxix, 9b. 1–8].

attributed: SOUTHWARK, CHRISTCHURCH, BLACK-FRIARS ROAD, 1738–41; altered by C.R.B. King, 1891, and gutted 1941. There is a set of plans and elevations in B.M., *King's Maps* xxvii, 50 a–g, by the same hand as those of St. Mary, Ealing, and St. Katherine Coleman, whose design Christchurch closely resembled (*Survey of London* xxii, 101).

LONDON, ST. KATHERINE COLEMAN, FENCHURCH STREET, 1739–40; dem. 1925. There is a set of plans and elevations in B.M., *King's Maps* xxiii, 22b 1–7 [MS. Minutes of Trustees for Rebuilding the church in Guildhall Library, MSS. 1133–4] (G. Godwin, *The Churches of London* ii, 1839).

WESTMINSTER, ST. JOHN'S CHURCH, reconstructed roof and interior in 1744–5 after fire of 1742, removing the twelve columns which supported the original roof designed by Archer. The interior was rearranged by W. Inwood 1824–5, gutted 1940–41 and restored 1965–8 [MS. Minutes of Committee for Repair of Church in Westminster Public Library, MS. 2626].

GUILDFORD, SURREY, HOLY TRINITY CHURCH, 1749–63 [MS. Vestry Minutes].

HORTON, JOHN (–1825), builder of Deritend, Birmingham, designed the GUNBARREL PROOF HOUSE, BIRMINGHAM, 1813, as recorded by the following inscription on a drawing preserved in the board-room: 'This building was designed and executed by John Horton Architect and

Builder Bradford Street Derritend' [Mrs. Margaret Jones in *C. Life*, 24 May 1956, 1125]. Horton died on 13 March 1825 [*Aris's Birmingham Gazette*, 14 March 1825].

HOSKING, WILLIAM (1800–1861), was born at Buckfastleigh in Devon, but in 1809 his parents emigrated to New South Wales, where he was apprenticed to a builder and surveyor. Returning to England in 1819, he was in 1820 articled to William Jenkins, of Red Lion Square, for three years, and afterwards travelled in France and Italy (including Sicily) studying architecture and engineering works in company with Jenkins's son John (*q.v.*). In 1827 they jointly published *A Selection of Architectural Ornaments, Greek, Roman and Italian*. In 1834 Hosking became engineer to the Birmingham, Bristol and Thames Junction Railway Company, for which he designed the complicated arrangement of bridges near Kensal Green by which the Paddington Canal was carried over the railway and a public road over the canal. In 1840 King's College, London, made him Professor of 'the Art of Construction', and afterwards of 'the Principles and Practice of Architecture'. In 1844 he was appointed one of the referees under the Metropolitan Buildings Act. He became a Fellow of the Institute of British Architects in 1835, and served on its council in 1842–3. He was elected F.S.A. in 1830. He died on 2 August 1861.

From an early age Hosking wrote and lectured about architecture, emphasizing the importance of practical and technical considerations in a manner which earned him the reputation of being an 'anti-Vitruvianist'. Some lectures which he gave to the Western Literary and Scientific Institution led to his being invited to write the articles on 'Architecture' and 'Building' for the seventh edition of the *Encyclopaedia Britannica*. These were afterwards republished as a separate volume in 1832, 1846, 1860 and (revised by Ashpitel) in 1867. He also published an inaugural lecture entitled *The Principles and Practice of Architecture* (1842), and (with J. Hann) a standard work on *The Theory, Practice and Architecture of Bridges*, 1843. His work in connection with the Metropolitan Buildings Act led him to write *A Guide to the proper Regulation of Buildings in Towns, as a means of promoting and securing the Health, Comfort and Safety of the Inhabitants*, 1848, reissued in 1849 as *Healthy Homes*.

Hosking appears to have designed relatively few buildings. He begun to exhibit designs at the Society of British Artists in Suffolk Street in 1825, and in 1827 showed a 'mansion for W. Redfern, to be erected on his estate of Campbellfield, New South Wales'. In 1839–43 he designed ABNEY PARK CEMETERY, NORTH LONDON, with a pretentious but poorly designed Gothic chapel, and in 1840–1 TRINITY INDEPENDENT CHAPEL,

POPLAR, in an interesting blend of Grecian and Italian Renaissance styles [*Companion to the Almanac* 1842, 210–12, with illustrations]. Later, in the 1850s, he was responsible for some business premises for Messrs. Berens on the south side of Cannon Street. In 1849 he submitted to the Trustees of the British Museum a scheme for filling the vacant quadrangle with a circular building which he envisaged as 'a modified copy of the Pantheon in Rome'. It was illustrated in the *Builder* for 1850 (pp. 295–6), and when Panizzi's plan for the circular reading-room was adopted in 1854 Hosking regarded it as 'an obvious plagiarism', although it had nothing in common with his proposal except the circular form. In 1858, to substantiate his claim, he published a pamphlet entitled *Some Observations upon the recent Addition of the Reading-room to the British Museum*.

[*Builder* xix, 1861, 560; *D.N.B.*; application (with *curriculum vitae*) for post of architect to Metropolitan Board of Works, 1856, in G.L.C. Record Office, MBW 213.]

HOWELL, JAMES (*c.* 1787–1866), of 1 Vincent Square, Westminster, was the nephew and pupil of William Pilkington. He was President of the Surveyors' Club in 1832 and 1849, and died on 31 July 1866, aged 79 [*A.P.S.D., s.v.* 'Pilkington'; J. W. Penfold, *A Century of Surveyors*, privately printed 1892, and MS. supplement among records of the Surveyors' Club]. He designed SOUTHWICK HOUSE, HANTS., for Thomas Thistlethwayte, 1841, after the former house had been destroyed by fire. Sydney Howell, of the same address, exhibited a view of the house at the R.A. in 1841, as then erecting 'from the designs and under the superintendence of Mr. James Howell'.

HUBERT, SAMUEL MORTON, of Mount Gardens, Lambeth, was the architect of two churches in Essex: ST. JOHN, EPPING, 1832, dem. 1889 [I.C.B.S.; Essex Record Office D/Q.19/30] and ST. PAUL, HIGH BEECH, 1835–6, dem. 1885 [I.C.B.S.]. The latter church is included in the list of L. Vulliamy's works in *Builder* xxix, 142, but this is not supported by the I.C.B.S. records.

HUDSON, HENRY BATEMAN (*c.* 1792–1865), practised in London as an architect and surveyor. In 1837 he restored THE PREBENDAL HOUSE at THAME, OXON., and converted it into a private residence for Charles Stone [lithograph in Bodleian, MS. Top. Oxon. a. 39, f. 138ᵛ]. He also 'restored' THAME CHURCH in 1843–5 [F. G. Lee, *History of Thame Church*, 1883, 179]. Hudson, who was President of the Surveyors' Club in 1837 and 1846, died on 7 May 1865, aged 73.

HUDSON, JOHN, was an Oxford mason who held the post of surveyor of bridges to the county in the 1820s. Although chiefly employed as a builder, he sometimes acted as an architect. Thus in 1810–11 he designed and built a Porter's Lodge at the entrance to the RADCLIFFE OBSERVATORY [Bodleian Library, Minutes of the Radcliffe Trustees 1792–1815]. The classical front of the BAPTIST CHAPEL at the corner of New Inn Hall Street and the New Road was added in 1819 to the designs of 'the architect Hudson of Oxford' [R. Lascelles, *The University and City of Oxford displayed*, 1821, 238], and in 1821–5 the Gothic tower of CHIPPING NORTON CHURCH, OXON., was rebuilt to his designs [Bodleian Library, MS. Oxford Archdeaconry Papers Oxon. *c.* 61, f. 101]. He also designed or altered parsonages at EAST HENDRED, BERKS., 1807 [Salisbury Diocesan Records]; CULHAM, OXON., 1816 [Bodleian, Diocesan Faculty Register 1804–27, p. 87]; and FOREST HILL, OXON., 1830–1 [Bodleian, MS. Oxford Diocesan Papers b. 103, no. 2d.]. He was presumably the father of John Hudson, a successful Oxford builder who died on 16 January 1869, aged 67, leaving an estate valued at 'under £40,000' [*Jackson's Oxford Journal* 23 Jan. 1869; Principal Probate Registry, Calendar of Probates, 1869].

HUÉ, WILLIAM BURNELL, was from 1801 to 1809 a pupil or assistant of William Jupp, junior. Then in 1816–19 he was living in Bloomsbury, but after that there is no trace of him in the London directories. He exhibited at the Royal Academy from 1801 to 1819, showing in 1809 a design for a 'monumental pillar' in memory of Sir John Moore, in 1816 'The grand quadrangle building before Carlton House', and in 1819 'Annett's Crescent, now building in Lower Road Islington'. J. Mullins was his pupil.

HULLS, RICHARD (1773–1841), was the son of Jonathan Hulls (1732–93), a builder of Broad Campden, Glos., and grandson of Jonathan Hulls (1699–1758), the inventor of steam propulsion as applied to water transport. He practised as an architect and builder at Chipping Campden for forty-seven years, as recorded on his gravestone in the parish churchyard, and left £200 to the poor of the town [P. C. Rushen, *History of Chipping Campden*, 1911, 146, 174].

Hulls was no doubt responsible for much unrecorded work in Campden. Rushen says that he built two houses on the north side of Broad Campden churchyard in 1829 and considered that the early nineteenth-century rebuilding of CHIPPING CAMPDEN TOWN HALL 'looks like' his work [Rushen, *op. cit.*, 80, 162]. Outside Campden Hulls probably designed the Gothic lodges at the entrance to ALSCOT PARK, WARWICKS., for which he tendered in 1813 [West of

Alscot papers], and in 1832–4 he built the Picture Gallery at NORTHWICK PARK, GLOS., for the 2nd Lord Northwick. No evidence has been found in the Northwick Papers in the Worcestershire County Record Office to support the attribution of this building to C. H. Tatham, and the documents [5 (i) and 67] suggest that Hulls acted as architect as well as builder. In 1838 Hulls rebuilt the east wall of the chancel of the adjoining church of BLOCKLEY [Rushen, 79].

HUMFREY, CHARLES (1772–1848), was the eldest son of Charles Humfrey, a Cambridge carpenter and joiner. In 1789 he became a pupil of James Wyatt, was admitted to the Royal Academy Schools, and exhibited four drawings at the Academy's exhibitions in the next two years. He married in 1796 and was practising as an architect in Cambridge from *c.* 1800 onwards. He designed several churches, parsonage houses, etc., and in 1820–2 a Gaol and Shire Hall at Ely, but failed to secure any major commission from the university. In 1820 his scheme for alterations at Sidney Sussex College was rejected in favour of one by Wyatville, and in 1824 his proposals for a new wing at Emmanuel College also came to nothing. His best (and also his most remunerative) works were the admirable speculative building developments which he carried out between 1815 and 1828 in the area south-east of Christ's Piece and probably elsewhere in Cambridge. By the 1840s his annual income from property was over £1000. For some years he had also been the co-proprietor of a bank in Trinity Street, and in 1829 he published an open letter to Lord Melbourne on the reform of the currency. He took an active part in local politics, was elected a Councillor after the Municipal Reform Act and served as Mayor in 1837–8. From 1819 to 1830 he was Surveyor to the Cam Conservancy Board. Early in the 1840s he got into financial difficulties which culminated in 1845 in the closure of his bank and the sale of all his Cambridge property in order to satisfy his creditors. He died in Islington in March 1848 aged 75. He left several children, one of whom (Mary Anne) became the wife of Professor Willis, the architectural historian. [Information from Mr. D. E. Chaffin].

SWAFFHAM PRIOR CHURCH (ST. CYRIAC), CAMBS., rebuilt 1806–8 incorporating old tower, Gothic; now ruinous [Ely Diocesan Records, Faculty Book 1791–1829, f. 15; MS. Churchwardens' accounts].

GRANSDEN MAGNA VICARAGE, HUNTS., altered or rebuilt 1812 [Lincolnshire Record Office, MGA 67].

CAMBRIDGE, DOLL'S CLOSE development, comprising houses in MAID'S CAUSEWAY, WILLOW WALK, SHORT STREET and FAIR STREET, 1815–26 [R.C.H.M. *Cambridge* ii, 363–4].

WILLIAN VICARAGE, HERTS., altered or rebuilt 1816 [Lincolnshire Record Office, MGA 87].

SWAFFHAM BULBECK VICARAGE, CAMBS., 1818 [Ely Diocesan Records, Faculty Book 1791–1829, ff. 79–84].

CAMBRIDGE, NOS. 9–10, ST. ANDREW'S HILL, porches and railings 1818 [R.C.H.M. *Cambridge* ii, 334].

CAMBRIDGE, ST. CLEMENT'S CHURCH, new west tower, 1821–2, Gothic. The spire (known as 'Humfrey's Extinguisher') was removed in 1928 [R.C.H.M. *Cambridge* ii, 269].

ELY, CAMBS., SHIRE HALL and GAOL, 1821–2; gaol enlarged by Basevi 1845 [*A.P.S.D.*, s.v. 'Ely'].

CAMBRIDGE, NOS. 4–12 TENNIS COURT ROAD and (probably) NO. 15 FITZWILLIAM STREET, c. 1822–5 [R.C.H.M. *Cambridge* ii, 357].

CAMBRIDGE, ADDENBROOKE'S HOSPITAL, addition of wings and colonnade, 1823–5 [R.C.H.M. *Cambridge* ii, 312].

CAMBRIDGE, CLARENDON HOUSE (dem.) for himself and range of mews in MILLER LANE facing Christ's Piece, 1825–8 [R.C.H.M. *Cambridge* ii, 361–2].

CAMBRIDGE, ANATOMICAL LECTURE ROOM AND MUSEUM etc., DOWNING STREET, 1832–3; dem. [Willis & Clark, iii, 156].

CAMBRIDGE, PHILOSOPHICAL SOCIETY'S PREMISES, DOLPHIN LANE, 1832–3; dem. [ex inf. Mr. D. E. Chaffin].

CAMBRIDGE, TRINITY COLLEGE, LECTURE ROOM COURT, 1833–4, Tudor Gothic [R.C.H.M. *Cambridge* ii, 243].

HUNT, THOMAS (1737–1809/18), of Wadenhoe near Oundle in Northamptonshire, appears to have been an amateur architect. He inherited Wadenhoe Manor from his father, Edward Hunt, a merchant of Oundle, and died without issue some time between 1809 and 1818. The only evidence of his architectural interests consists of an album of drawings now in the R.I.B.A. Drawings Collection. This contains a number of plans and designs, some of existing buildings, and others apparently representing projects by Hunt for small houses and other buildings, none of which is known to have been executed. The contents of the album are fully described in the *R.I.B.A. Drawings Catalogue: G–K*, 148–151.

HUNT, THOMAS FREDERICK (c. 1791–1831), joined the Office of Works in 1813 as Labourer in Trust at St. James's Palace, and was promoted in 1829 to the Clerkship of the Works at Kensington Palace, where he died on 4 January 1831, aged 40. He was well thought of both at the Office of Works and in Court circles. But he lived beyond his means, was always in debt and was constantly harassed by bailiffs. At one time he was obliged to take refuge in the gatehouse of

St. James's Palace in order to escape their attentions, and could only venture out on Sundays for fear of arrest.

Hunt was an able architect who made a special study of the picturesque Tudor style, upon which he published several books listed below. He designed the elegant neo-classical BURNS MAUSOLEUM in ST. MICHAEL'S CHURCHYARD at DUMFRIES, 1815 [exhib. at R.A. 1816]. This is a domed Ionic version of James Wyatt's pyramidal Doric mausoleum at Cobham in Kent, and was originally intended to have sarcophagi standing over the columns as at Cobham [W. McDowall, *Memorials of St. Michael's Churchyard, Dumfries*, 1876, 103]. This commission, won in competition, led to his employment as architect of the OLD EPISCOPAL (now Wesleyan) CHURCH in BUCCLEUCH STREET, DUMFRIES, with a prominent Ionic portico [P. Gray, *Dumfriesshire Illustrated*, 1894, 70]. Other works, all exhibited by him at the Royal Academy, were a cottage in Hertfordshire (1825); a house 'in the old English domestic style' to be erected at SYDNEY, NEW SOUTH WALES, 'for one of the principal government officers' (1828); DANEHURST, nr. DANEHILL, SUSSEX, for — Davies (1828), illustrated in the third edition of his *Hints*; and a design for REDRICE, nr. ANDOVER, HANTS., for the Hon. William Noel Hill, afterwards 3rd Lord Berwick (1828). According to the journalist William Jerdan, who knew him well, one of Hunt's most characteristic works in the Tudor style was BIFRONS, PATRIXBOURNE, KENT, for the Marquess Conyngham, c. 1825, dem. 1948.

The titles of Hunt's publications were: *Half-a-dozen Hints on Picturesque Domestic Architecture in a series of designs for Gate Lodges, Gamekeepers' Cottages, and other rural residences*, 1825, 2nd ed. 1826, 3rd ed. 1833, reprinted 1841; *Designs for Parsonage-houses, Alms houses, etc., with examples of gables, and other curious remains of old English Architecture*, 1827; *Architettura Campestre, displayed in Lodges, Gardeners' Houses, etc. in the Modern or Italian Style*, 1827; *Exemplars of Tudor Architecture adapted to modern habitations, with illustrative details, selected from Ancient Edifices; and observations on the Furniture of the Tudor Period*, 1830, 1841. [*A.P.S.D.*; obituary in *Gent's Mag.* 1831 (i) 376; *The Autobiography of William Jerdan* iv, 1853, 52–5].

HUNTER, JAMES (1755–   ), was a pupil of James Arrow (q.v.). He was admitted to the Royal Academy Schools in 1773 at the age of 17, and won the Silver Medal in 1775. He exhibited drawings at the Academy in 1776 and 1777. He was probably not the same person as James Hunter of 25 Fetter Lane, who exhibited 'A plan and elevation for a gentleman's house in Somersetshire' at the Free Society of Artists in 1774.

HURLBATT, FRANCIS (c. 1754–1834), was a surveyor at Newington in Surrey, where he rebuilt the parish church of St. Mary in 1791–3 (dem. 1876) [C. T. Cracklow, *The Churches of Surrey*, 1827]. In Lambeth Palace Library there is an elevation of the church which is perhaps by him [V.P. III. 6b./112]. In 1793 an Act of Parliament enabled the Dean and Chapter of Canterbury to grant building leases on their Newington property to Hurlbatt [cf. *Commons' Jnls.* xlviii, 30 May 1793]. In the British Museum there is (Add. MS. 12553g) a plan of premises in New Road, Newington, made by Francis Hurlbatt and John Leachman (q.v.). In 1798 Hurlbatt exhibited a design for 'Almshouses erected near Brighton' at the Royal Academy. In 1812 he added a portico to HOLY TRINITY CHURCH, CLAPHAM [Cracklow, *op. cit.*]. He died in 1834 aged 78, and is buried in St. Mary Newington churchyard [*ex inf.* Miss P. G. Mann].

HURLBUTT, ROGER and WILLIAM, were master carpenters in Warwickshire during the latter part of the seventeenth century. William was living at Stareton near Coventry in the 1670s, but both worked in Warwick, and Roger was a freeman of the town by 1684. In 1670 William contracted to build a MARKET HOUSE at WARWICK (now the Museum) [T. Kemp, *History of Warwick*, 1905, 190–1], and in 1676–81 he was both surveyor and contractor for the new SHIRE HALL [*Warwickshire County Records: Proceedings in Quarter Sessions* vii, 1946, pp. cxiii, cxlix, 77, 183, etc.]. The market house is a stone building of traditional character, but the Shire Hall (again rebuilt 1753–8), had quite an ambitious classical façade with Ionic pilasters and Corinthian centre-piece. In 1669–78 the two Hurlbutts were jointly responsible for remodelling the state rooms in WARWICK CASTLE for the 4th Lord Brooke in a very handsome manner. The accounts show that William was sent down to Dorset to see the interiors at Kingston Lacy recently designed for Sir Ralph Bankes by Sir Roger Pratt, which were evidently the model for the new rooms at Warwick [Michael Farr in *V.C.H. Warwicks* viii, 460–1].

Either Roger or William may be identified as the 'Mr. Holbert', by trade a carpenter, who in 1679 began to build RAGLEY HALL, WARWICKS., for the 1st Earl of Conway. The original 'model' for this large country house appears to have been provided by Hurlbutt himself, but the design was considerably modified by Robert Hooke (q.v.), and the latter may have been responsible for the projecting corner pavilions which distinguish Ragley from most other contemporary houses [see letters from Hooke printed in *Walpole Soc.* xxv, 99–103; Arthur Oswald in *C. Life*, 1–8 May 1958; and P. Leach in *Archaeological Jnl.* cxxviii, 1971, 230–2]. In 1671 Lord Conway had already

employed Hurlbutt to build a large stable for him at his house at PORTMORE, CO. ANTRIM in IRELAND (dem. 1761) [*Cal. S.P. Dom. 1671*, 116, 349, 364, 375, 427], and he appears subsequently to have recommended him to his cousin Sir Edward Seymour, Bart. Seymour was the builder of MAIDEN BRADLEY HOUSE, WILTS., a house partly demolished in 1821, but illustrated in *Vitruvius Britannicus* ii, pl. 56, and in 1683 Conway, in a letter to Sir Edward Harley, says that Seymour has taken 'Mr. Halbert' with him to Maiden Bradley [Hist. MSS. Comm., *Portland* iii, 374].

In 1683–4 William Hurlbutt was employed by the Trustees of the TEMPLE BALSALL HOSPITAL, WARWICKS., to build the original courtyard of the Hospital (in its present form largely an early 18th-century rebuilding, cf. SMITH, FRANCIS) [MS. Minutes, *ex inf.* Mr Anthony Wood].

In 1692 Roger Hurlbut, joiner of Warwick (perhaps the same as the Roger mentioned above, but more likely his son or nephew), contracted to build LANDOR HOUSE, WARWICK, for Dr. William Johnson. The contract [County Record Office, records of Ann Johnson's charity] is accompanied by a competent but unsigned drawing showing alternative treatments of the elevation, one of which (not adopted) incorporates heavily keystoned architraves derived from the south front of Chatsworth. In September 1694, after the great fire which devastated Warwick, Roger Hurlbut helped to put a temporary covering on the chancel of St. Mary's Church, and he appears elsewhere in the accounts for rebuilding the town.

In 1671 a carpenter called John Hurlbut became a freeman of the City of London, where he was engaged in rebuilding after the Great Fire [City Repertory 76, f. 148 b]. It is possible that further investigation would show that he was the link between the Warwickshire Hurlbutts of the seventeenth century and Francis Hurlbatt of Newington (q.v.) in the eighteenth.

HURST, AARON HENRY (1762–1799), was admitted to the Royal Academy Schools in 1788 at the age of 26, and exhibited at the Academy from 1778 to 1796. That he was an elegant draughtsman and a sophisticated neo-classical architect can be seen from the two designs for Wimbledon Lodge illustrated in John Harris, *Georgian Country Houses* (R.I.B.A. 1968), 46–7. Peterborough House, Fulham, closely resembled the alternative design on p. 47. Hurst practised in London, but died at Brighton on 23 June 1799, and was buried in the chapel at Pentonville which he had designed [*Gent's Mag.* 1799 (ii), 622].

LONDON, ST. JAMES'S CHAPEL, PENTONVILLE, 1787–8, cons. 1791; altered 1933. Hurst also designed 'four houses adjoining' [exhib. at R.A. 1787] (B. F. L. Clarke, *Parish Churches of London*, 1966, fig. 35).

LONDON, WINCHESTER PLACE (on the north side of what is now Pentonville Road), ISLINGTON, 1788 [exhib. at R.A. 1788].

HAMMERSMITH, a house, 1792 [exhib. at R.A. 1792].

WIMBLEDON LODGE, WIMBLEDON COMMON (south side), SURREY, for Gerard de Visme, 1792; dem. [exhib. at R.A. 1792; elevations in R.I.B.A. Drawings Coll.] (D. Hughson, *London*, 1805–9, v, 393).

PETERBOROUGH HOUSE, PARSONS GREEN, FULHAM, MIDDLESEX, for John Meyrick, 1796; dem. *c.* 1900 [exhib. at R.A. 1796] (C. J. Fèret, *Fulham Old and New* ii, 1900, 150).

HURST, WILLIAM (1787–1844), was a native of Doncaster, and was articled to William Lindley of that town (*q.v.*). In 1811 he exhibited two drawings at the Royal Academy. He afterwards joined the firm of Lindley and Woodhead, subsequently Woodhead and Hurst, and was extensively employed in Yorkshire and the neighbouring counties. In partnership with John Woodhead, he designed a number of Gothic churches (including three for the Parliamentary Commissioners), of which the most ambitious were St. George's, Sheffield and Christ Church, Doncaster. After Woodhead's death in *c.* 1838, Hurst, who had recently (1836) become a Fellow of the R.I.B.A., entered into partnership with W. L. Moffatt (1808–82), a Scottish pupil of William Burn, in conjunction with whom he was responsible for more churches, including some (*e.g.* Goole) of an ecclesiologically more advanced character, and many public buildings in Leeds and Wakefield principally designed by Moffatt.[1] Hurst died on 8 December 1844, aged 57, and was buried in Doncaster churchyard. Moffatt subsequently returned to Edinburgh, where he specialized in workhouses and lunatic asylums. J. G. Weightman (1801–72) and M. E. Hadfield (1812–85) were both pupils of Woodhead and Hurst [*A.P.S.D.*].

BUILDINGS DESIGNED BY WOODHEAD AND HURST

FIRBECK PARK, YORKS. (W.R.), alterations for Henry Gally Knight, *c.* 1820 [drawing in R.I.B.A. Collection].

FIRBECK CHAPEL, YORKS. (W.R.), rebuilt for Henry Gally Knight, 1820, Gothic [I.C.B.S.].

SNEATON CASTLE, YORKS. (N.R.), for Col. James Wilson, *c.* 1820, castellated [*Whitby Magazine*

---

[1] In 1836, before entering into partnership with Hurst, Moffatt had won the competition for the Wakefield Corn Exchange, built 1836–8, enlarged 1864, demolished 1964 [C. E. Camidge, *History of Wakefield*, 1866, 22; J. W. Walker, *Wakefield*, 1939, 521].

iii, 1829, frontispiece; signed drawing in R.I.B.A. Collection].

SNEATON CHURCH, YORKS. (N.R.), rebuilt for Col. James Wilson, 1823–5, Gothic [*Whitby Magazine* iii, 1829, frontispiece; unsigned drawings in P.R.O. MPD 113].

SHEFFIELD, ST. GEORGE'S CHURCH, 1821–5, Gothic [Port, 138–9].

SHEFFIELD, THE MUSIC HALL, SURREY STREET, 1823; dem. [R. E. Leader, *Surveyors and Architects of the Past in Sheffield*, 1903, 31] (T. Allen, *History of the County of York* iii, 1831, 70].

DONCASTER, YORKS. (W.R.), THE RACECOURSE GRANDSTAND, alterations 1824; dem. 1969 [*A Skilful Master-Builder*, ed. H. E. C. Stapleton, York 1975, 46].

GOOLE, YORKS. (W.R.), designed new town for the Aire and Calder Navigation Company, 1824–40; largely dem. 1965–6 [J. D. Porteous, 'Goole: a pre-Victorian Company Town', *Industrial Archaeology* vi, 1969, 105–13].

SHEFFIELD, THE GRAMMAR SCHOOL, CHARLOTTE STREET, 1824–5, Gothic; dem. [Leader, *op. cit.*].

SHEFFIELD, THE BOYS' CHARITY SCHOOL, 1825–6 [report of the Charity for 1826–9 in City Library].

SHEFFIELD, THE SHREWSBURY ALMSHOUSES, NORFOLK ROAD, 1825–7, Gothic [T. Allen, *History of the County of York* iii, 1831, 59 and plate].

PATELEY BRIDGE CHURCH, YORKS. (W.R.), 1825–7, Gothic [Port, 168–9].

ARMTHORPE CHURCH, YORKS. (W.R.), north aisle 1826; rebuilt 1885 [I.C.B.S.].

THE OAKES, NORTON (nr. SHEFFIELD), DERBYSHIRE, alterations for W. J. Bagshawe, 1827, lodges 1834 [drawings at the Oakes and inscription on lead flat].

LEEDS, warehouse in Call Lane for Aire and Calder Navigation, 1827–8; destroyed by fire *c.* 1965 [drawings in Inland Waterways office, *ex inf.* Dr. D. Linstrum].

DONCASTER, YORKS. (W.R.), CHRIST CHURCH, 1827–9, Gothic [*Gent's Mag.* 1830 (ii), 489, with engraving].

STANNINGTON CHURCH, YORKS. (W.R.), 1828–9, Gothic [Port, 170–1; drawings in R.I.B.A. Collection].

SHEFFIELD, THE CORN MARKET, 1830; dem. [*Sheffield Mercury*, 6 Nov. 1830].

NEW BRAMPTON, nr. CHESTERFIELD, DERBYSHIRE, ST. THOMAS'S CHURCH, 1830–1, Gothic [Port, 142–3].

DONCASTER, YORKS. (W.R.), THE MANSION HOUSE, alterations 1831 [J. Tomlinson, *Doncaster*, 1887, 226; *A Skilful Master-Builder*, ed. H. E. C. Stapleton, York 1975, 47].

DONCASTER, YORKS. (W.R.), PRIORY PLACE METHODIST CHAPEL, 1832 [C. W. Dolbey, *The Architectural Expression of Methodism*, 1964, 149].

SHEFFIELD, TOWN HALL, enlargement 1832–3; dem. [drawings in City Library].

RIDGEWAY CHURCH, DERBYSHIRE, 1838–40, Gothic; tower added 1883–4 [I.C.B.S.].

BUILDINGS DESIGNED BY HURST IN PARTNERSHiP WITH MOFFATT

CHATSWORTH, DERBYSHIRE, unspecified work (probably on the estate) for the 6th Duke of Devonshire, 1839 [G. F. Chadwick, *The Works of Sir Joseph Paxton*, 1961, 162].

LEEDS, THE NEW INDEPENDENT CHAPEL, EAST PARADE, 1839–41; dem. [J. Mayhall, *The Annals of Yorkshire*, 1861, 462] (D. Linstrum, *Historic Architecture of Leeds*, 1969, 48).

ROTHERHAM, YORKS. (W.R.), THE SHIP HOTEL and WESTGATE improvements, 1840 [*A.P.S.D.*].

GROSMONT CHURCH, YORKS. (N.R.), 1840, Gothic; rebuilt 1875–84 [engraving inscribed 'Hurst & Moffatt, Architects, Doncaster'].

WOODSETTS CHURCH, YORKS. (W.R.), 1841, Gothic [I.C.B.S.].

ARDSLEY, YORKS. (W.R.), CHRIST CHURCH, 1841, Gothic [I.C.B.S.].

BIRKENHEAD, CHESHIRE, ST. PETER'S CHURCH, ROCK FERRY, 1841–2, Romanesque [*A.P.S.D.*].

RAWCLIFFE CHURCH, YORKS. (W.R.), rebuilt 1842, Gothic [I.C.B.S.].

WELBECK ABBEY, NOTTS., CLIPSTONE ARCHWAY for the 4th Duke of Portland, 1842–4 [*A.P.S.D.*].

DONCASTER, THE CORN MARKET, 1843 [*Surveyor, Engineer and Architect* iv, 1843, 197].

GOOLE CHURCH, YORKS. (W.R.), 1843–8, Gothic [*A.P.S.D.*].

HOOK CHURCH, YORKS. (W.R.), restoration 1844 [*Builder* ii, 1844, 275].

LEEDS, THE BOROUGH GAOL, 1844–7 [*Builder* ii, 1844, 643].

HUTCHENS, CHARLES (*c.* 1781–1834), was born at Buryan in Cornwall, but practised from Torpoint in the parish of Antony near Plymouth. A tombstone in Antony churchyard records his death on 17 November 1834 at the age of 53. He designed THE CRESCENT at PLYMOUTH [G. Wightwick, *Nettleton's Guide to Plymouth, etc.*, 1836, 15] and three Commissioners' churches in Cornwall at CHASEWATER, 1826–8 (rebuilt 1892 except tower), ST. DAY, 1826–8, and ST. MARY, REDRUTH, 1827–8 [Port, 183]. He also designed MILLBROOK CHURCH, CORNWALL, 1827 (rebuilt 1893–5) [I.C.B.S.] and ST. MARY'S CHURCH, PENZANCE, CORNWALL, 1832–6 [G. B. Millet, *Penzance Past and Present*, 1880, 14].

HUTCHESON, JOHN, a land-surveyor and architect of Montrose, designed the handsome Palladian TOWN HALL, MONTROSE, ANGUS, 1763–4 [J. G. Low, *Highways and Byways of an Old Scottish Burgh*, Montrose 1938, 99].

HUTCHINSON, EDMUND, is said to have been a pupil of William Sands, architect and mason of Spalding, and to have cut the latter's epitaph in Spalding church when he died in 1751 [J. Nichols, *Literary Anecdotes* vi, 72]. He may have been the 'Mr. Hutchinson' who is reputed to have designed the Georgian church at LANGTON-BY-SPILSBY, LINCS. [E. H. R. Tatham in *Associated Architectural Societies' Reports and Papers* xxx, 1910, 368] (Jack Yates & Henry Thorold, *Lincolnshire*, Shell Guides, 1965, 88–9).

HUTCHINSON, HENRY (1800–1831), born at Ingleby in Derbyshire, was the younger brother of Thomas Hutchinson, an architect who practised briefly in Birmingham before dying in his 24th year. Henry began his architectural training in his brother's office, but at the age of 18 went to Liverpool to become Thomas Rickman's first pupil. In 1820 he was transferred to the new office which Rickman had opened in Birmingham, and in the following year, on attaining his majority, was taken into partnership by him. During the next ten years the firm enjoyed an extensive practice, especially as church architects. Hutchinson's contribution to its success was probably considerable, for there is evidence that he was an able designer in his own right: the Gothic bridge at St. John's College, Cambridge, for instance, was his idea (see Rickman's diary, 10 Feb. 1827: 'Henry has made a beautiful design for the Cambridge Bridge'). A list of the buildings erected by the partnership will be found below under Rickman's name. Hutchinson fell ill in 1830, of a 'similar disease' (probably consumption) to the one that had killed his brother, and went abroad for the sake of his health. But he never fully recovered, and died at Leamington on 22 November 1831. He was buried in the church at Hampton Lucy which he and Rickman had designed. [T. M. Rickman, *Notes on the Life of Thomas Rickman*, 1901, 22, 26–7, 42, 44–5; *Gent's Mag.* 1831 (ii), 568; B.M., Add. MS. 37800, f. 96.]

HUTCHINSON, WILLIAM (*c.* 1779–1869), was a builder at Hull. He was responsible for the following churches: CHRIST CHURCH, SCULCOATES, HULL, *c.* 1815–22; dem. 1962 [*V.C.H. Yorks. E.R.* i, 305]; SPROATLEY CHURCH, YORKS. (E.R.), 1820 [*Hull Advertiser*, 18 Aug. 1820, but see p. 73 for evidence that P. Atkinson was also involved]; DRYPOOL CHURCH, nr. HULL, 1823–4, dem. 1941 [I.C.B.S.]; and ST. JOHN, NEWLAND, HULL, 1833 [I.C.B.S.]. The last was Romanesque in style, the others Gothic. He retired in 1860 and died on 15 December 1869 in his 91st year. His business was continued by his son Charles Hutchinson (d. 1875). [*Hull Advertiser*, 7 Jan. 1860; *Hull News*, 18 Dec. 1869; information from Mr. A. G. Chamberlain.]

HUTCHISON, JAMES (*c.* 1751–1801), 'late architect in Dumfries', is commemorated by a tombstone in St. Michael's Churchyard, Dumfries. He died on 16 May 1801, aged 50.

HUTCHISON, ROBERT, practised in Fife. In 1824 he was living at Coalton of Balgonie near Markinch. He designed THE TOWN HALL, ST. CATHERINE STREET, CUPAR, FIFE, 1815–17 [Cupar Town Council Minutes, S.R.O., B13/14/8, p. 261]. In 1824 he inspected ABDIE CHURCH, FIFE, and pronounced it past repair [S.R.O., HR 649/1, pp. 58–9], in 1833 he made the working plans and specifications for KENNOWAY MANSE on the basis of a plan produced by Captain Lundin of Auchtermainey [S.R.O., HR 293/1], and in 1838 he was consulted over the repair of CUPAR PARISH CHURCH [S.R.O., HR 3/15].

I

I'ANSON, EDWARD (1775–1853), was born in London, and was articled at an early age to an architect and surveyor named Healey, who practised in the West End. He was admitted to the Royal Academy Schools in 1791, and exhibited at the Academy from 1792 to 1798. For some time he was chiefly employed as a measuring surveyor, but gave up his own business to become first the assistant, and shortly after the partner, of D. A. Alexander. On Alexander's retirement he continued their practice on his own account, acting as surveyor to large ecclesiastical and other estates in Southwark and the City of London. He was also much engaged in the compensation cases arising out of the formation of the approaches to the new London Bridge, and in superintending the erection of new houses in the streets leading to the bridge, though their external architecture was designed by Sir Robert Smirke for the Corporation of London.

I'Anson was surveyor to the Commissioners of Sewers for Surrey and Kent from 1804 until the Commission was superseded in 1846. In conjunction with Joseph Gwilt and John Newman he drained and laid out for building extensive tracts on the south side of the Thames, and with them published a *Report relating to the Sewage, etc.*, 1843. It was under his immediate supervision that large areas of Bermondsey, Walworth, Kennington and St. George's Fields were drained by sewers and outlets, whose design and construction became the model for such works elsewhere in England and abroad.

I'Anson was also much engaged in designing warehouses, chiefly in Southwark, and offices and houses in the City of London. During the latter part of his career, however, he acted chiefly as a referee, a function which he fulfilled with characteristic tact and good judgment. He became a member of the Surveyors' Club in 1815, and was elected President in 1823. In about 1842 he gave up practice and fulfilled a life-long ambition by visiting Rome. He died on 13 November 1853 at the age of 78, and was buried in Norwood Cemetery. There is a drawing of his cottage at Wandsworth in B.M., Add. MS. 36389, ff. 61–2. His eldest son, Edward I'Anson, junior (1812–88), was President of the R.I.B.A. in 1886–8. Charles Purser was his pupil [*A.P.S.D.*].

INGLEMAN, RICHARD (1777–1838), was the son of Francis Ingleman, a surveyor or builder of Southwell in Nottinghamshire, and the grandson of Richard Ingleman, a mason employed to repair Southwell Minster after damage by lightning in 1711 [P.R.O., Eccles 2/118/4463, 8/9]. From 1801 to 1808 he was paid £10 a year as Surveyor of the Fabric to the Minster, and during this period carried out a general repair of the church, which had hitherto been in a neglected state. He appears to have been responsible for the removal of the two western spires, which were then thought to be too heavy for the towers, but were replaced in 1880 without any ill effects.

Although primarily a local architect, Ingleman obtained commissions as far afield as Oxford and Devizes. The lunatic asylum which he planned at Nottingham led to his employment to design similar buildings at Lincoln and Oxford, and in 1810 he was one of the unsuccessful competitors for the New Bethlehem Hospital in London. The minutes of the Oxford Asylum testify to the trouble he took in designing what was then a relatively novel type of building. Architecturally Ingleman's asylums were classical buildings of no special distinction, but his unexecuted design for rebuilding Shelton Church, Notts. in 1819 (Borthwick Institute, York) is an essay in 'Early English' of quite creditable character for its date. Ingleman died at Southwell on 11 January 1838. [Notts. County Record Office, DD 113/14/1–2 and will in PRSW 207/12; information from Dr. N. Summers.]

SOUTHWELL MINSTER, NOTTS., repairs to fabric, 1801–8 [N. Summers, *Southwell Minster*, 1972, 23].

SOUTHWELL, NOTTS., ASSEMBLY ROOMS adjoining Saracen's Head Inn, 1805 [Notts. County Record Office, minutes in DDM 71/40].

SOUTHWELL, NOTTS., THE RESIDENCE HOUSE, extensive improvements *c.* 1805 [Southwell Minster records, *ex inf.* Dr. N. Summers].

SOUTHWELL, NOTTS., THE HOUSE OF CORRECTION, 1807–8; enlarged 1817 [R. P. Shilton, *A History of Southwell*, 1818].

DEVIZES, WILTS., THE COUNTY GAOL, 1810 [J. Waylen, *Chronicles of the Devizes*, 1839, 318] (plan in *V.C.H. Wilts.* v, 187).

NOTTINGHAM, THE LUNATIC ASYLUM, 1810–12 [Brenda Parry-Jones, *The Warneford Hospital, Oxford*, 1976, 8–9].

CONOCK HOUSE, nr. DEVIZES, WILTS., added Ionic porch and wings for E. Warriner, 1817 [Wiltshire Record Office, 451/74 (ix)] (*C. Life*, 29 June 1951].

ORDSALL RECTORY, NOTTS., designs for rebuilding 1819 [Borthwick Institute, MGA 1819/1].

LINCOLN, THE LUNATIC ASYLUM, 1819–20 [*A.P.S.D.*, *s.v.* 'Lincoln'].

SOUTHWELL, NOTTS., THE GRAMMAR SCHOOL, CHURCH STREET, 1820 [Southwell Chapter Decree Book, 7 Dec. 1819, *ex inf.* Dr. N. Summers].

OXFORD, THE WARNEFORD LUNATIC ASYLUM, HEADINGTON, 1821–6; enlarged 1877 [Brenda Parry-Jones, *The Warneford Hospital, Oxford*, 1976, 8–12].

INMAN, WILLIAM SOUTHCOTE (1798–1879), was the son of Captain Henry Inman, R.N. He was admitted to the Royal Academy Schools in 1818 and exhibited at the Academy up to 1838. In 1821 he won the competition for the LONDON ORPHAN ASYLUM at CLAPTON, but because of his youth and inexperience George Goldring was appointed joint surveyor to assist in the execution of the building [Minutes of the Board of the London Orphan Asylum, *ex inf.* Mr. F. Kelsall]. This ambitious Greek Doric building, now the Salvation Army Congress Hall, was completed in 1823 and is illustrated in Shepherd's *Metropolitan Improvements* (1831). Inman subsequently competed for the new buildings at King's College, Cambridge, in 1823, obtaining the second premium for a design illustrated in *Architect and Building News*, 23 June 1933, for the Fitzwilliam Museum and the Houses of Parliament in 1835, for the Royal Berkshire Infirmary in 1837, and for a public building at St. John's, Newfoundland, in 1838. For the last design (exhibited at the Royal Academy) he obtained the first premium of £50 [*Civil Engineer and Architect's Jnl.* i, 174].

Despite the ability he had shown in these competitions Inman appears to have obtained very few commissions, and in 1844 he secured the senior architectural post of Surveyor of Works and Buildings in the Office of Woods and Works. He retained this after the separation of Woods from Works in 1851, finally retiring in 1856. His duties were chiefly administrative, and he does not appear to have designed any building of importance in his official capacity.

Inman became a Fellow of the R.I.B.A. in 1835, and was later a Vice-President. In the R.I.B.A. Library there is a photograph of his portrait by Pickersgill. In 1836 he published, with notes, an abbreviated version of the *Report of the Committee of the House of Commons on Ventila-*

tion, *Warming, and Transmission of Sound*. He also published in Weale's *Quarterly Papers on Architecture* iii, 1845, a translation of a paper on 'Symbolic Colours' by Frédéric, Baron Portal.

INWOOD, CHARLES FREDERICK (*c.* 1799–1840), second son of William Inwood, entered the Royal Academy Schools in 1822. He assisted his father in some of his buildings, in particular the Westminster Hospital. He designed MARLOW PARISH CHURCH, BUCKS., 1832–5, Gothic, chancel added by J. O. Scott, 1875–6, and arcades inserted *c.* 1898, of which he exhibited designs at the R.A. in 1832 and 1834; the ST. PANCRAS NATIONAL SCHOOLS, SOUTHAMPTON STREET, EUSTON SQUARE, and NO. 22 OLD BOND STREET for Mr. Tinkler. He died on 1 June 1840, aged nearly 42 years; but other accounts say 40 years, and according to the Royal Academy Register he was only 21 on his admission in 1822 [*A.P.S.D.*; *Gent's Mag.* 1840 (ii), 107].

INWOOD, EDWARD (*c.* 1803–   ), third son of William Inwood, entered the Royal Academy Schools in 1822 at the age of 19. He exhibited at the Academy from 1821 to 1827. His only known work is a memorial tablet at Pangbourne, Berks., to the Rev. J. S. Breedon, D.D. (d. 1826), and his wife Elizabeth (d. 1827), which bears his signature.

INWOOD, WILLIAM (*c.* 1771–1843) and HENRY WILLIAM (1794–1843). William Inwood, the father, was the son of Daniel Inwood, bailiff to Lord Mansfield at Kenwood, Highgate. He became steward to Lord Colchester and was surveyor to several other landowners. He published *Tables for the Purchasing of Estates . . . and for the Renewal of Leases held under . . . Corporation Bodies*, 1811. A second edition of this well-known work, which was based on the tables of Baily and Smart, appeared in 1820, and it reached its twenty-first edition in 1880. Inwood is said to have designed 'numerous mansions, villas, barracks, warehouses, etc.', but nearly all his known works were carried out in conjunction with his eldest son, Henry William Inwood, who contributed the Grecian scholarship so characteristic of their buildings. In his later years Inwood was in poor circumstances and received assistance from Sir John Soane's Fund for Distressed Architects. He died in Upper Seymour Street on 16 March 1843, aged 72, and was buried in the family vault in St. Pancras New Church. Besides H. W. Inwood, he had two architect sons, Charles Frederick and Edward Inwood, who are noticed separately above. H. Lane, R. Parker, W. Railton and Thomas Tayler were among his pupils, and William Butterfield was in his office for a short time.

Henry William Inwood was born on 22 May 1794. He was trained in his father's office, and began to exhibit at the Royal Academy when he was only fifteen years old. In 1818–19 he travelled in Italy and Greece, visiting Athens in order to make a careful study of its architectural monuments.[1] His subsequent publication, *The Erectheion at Athens: Fragments of Athenian Architecture and a few remains in Attica, Megara and Epirus*, 1827, became the standard work on the Erectheion. The fruits of his Grecian scholarship soon became apparent in St. Pancras New Church, designed in conjunction with his father in 1819. This was a landmark in the history of the Greek Revival and the most expensive church of its day. It is a Grecian version of the type of steepled Anglican church established by Gibbs at St. Martin-in-the-Fields, all the architectural features being ingeniously adapted from authentic Greek prototypes. The result is a *tour-de-force* whose elegance compels admiration despite the architectural pedantry which it embodies. W. H. Inwood was also associated with his father in the design of All Saints, Camden Town, and St. Peter's, Regent Square, both in the Grecian style, and shares with him responsibility for the Somers Town Chapel, a meagre Gothic building held up to deserved ridicule by Pugin in his *Contrasts* (1836). In conjunction with his pupil E. N. Clifton (1817–89) he designed another Grecian church, St. James's, Holloway, 1837–8, and a dull Gothic one, St. Stephen's, Islington, 1837–9. Most of these buildings are named by W. H. Inwood in a letter of 1840 to John Place of Nottingham (Notts. Record Office DD 67/3/1–8). Other recent works mentioned in the same letter are a temple at Clandon Park, Surrey, for Lord Onslow, a new church near Rochester (unidentified), a hotel at Windsor, and (among 'less important works'), 'Schools, Country and Town Residences'.

Inwood's career was prematurely terminated in March 1843, when a ship in which he had sailed for Spain was lost with all on board. Besides the book already mentioned he had also published in 1834 *The Resources of Design in the Architecture of Greece, Egypt, and other Countries obtained by the Studies of the Architects of those Countries from Nature*, in which he drew parallels between the fluting of Doric columns and the formation of certain shells. He was a Fellow of the Society of Antiquaries. E. N. Clifton, G. G. Place (of Nottingham), F. B. Russell and J. D. Wyatt were his pupils. There are drawings by him in the Victoria and Albert Museum and the R.I.B.A. Drawings Collection [*A.P.S.D.*;

[1] In the letter cited further on Inwood states that he was in Greece and Rome in 1818–19. He must, however, have returned very early in the latter year, for work on St. Pancras Church started on 1 May 1819.

D.N.B.; *Builder* ix, 1851, 682, 689, xvi, 1858, 251; *Gent's Mag.* 1843 (i), 547].

EAST GRINSTEAD CHURCH, SUSSEX, completion of tower 1811–13 after death of J. T. Groves [minutes of committee for building church in East Sussex Record Office; exhib. at R.A. 1812 by H. W. Inwood, 1817 by W. Inwood].

RADWINTER RECTORY, ESSEX, 1812 [exhib. at R.A. 1812 by H. W. Inwood].

LONDON, ST. PANCRAS NEW CHURCH, 1819–22; redecorated by Crace 1880 [exhib. at R.A. 1819 and 1821 by W. & H. W. Inwood; Britton & Pugin, *The Public Buildings of London* i, 1825, 145–66; drawings in R.I.B.A. Collection].

LONDON, CAMDEN CHAPEL, PRATT STREET, CAMDEN TOWN, 1822–4 (known at one time as St. Stephen's, but dedicated to All Saints in 1920 and in 1948 leased to the Greek Orthodox Church) [exhib. at R.A. 1823 by W. & H. W. Inwood; *Gent's Mag.* 1824 (ii), 489].

LONDON, ST. PETER'S CHAPEL, REGENT SQUARE, 1822–5; damaged by bombing and dem. 1967 [exhib. at R.A. 1823 by W. & H. W. Inwood; *Gent's Mag.* 1828 (i), 393].

LONDON, WOBURN LODGE, UPPER WOBURN PLACE, ST. PANCRAS, 1824; dem. 1930 [*Survey of London* xxi, 105] (*Architect and Building News*, Jan.–March 1930).

LONDON, ST. MARY'S CHAPEL, SOMERS TOWN, ST. PANCRAS, 1824–7, Gothic; chancel added 1878 [*Gent's Mag.* 1827 (ii), 393].

LONDON, ST. JOHN'S CHURCH, WESTMINSTER, rearranged interior (destroyed by fire 1940–1) and cut two new doorways in west towers, 1824–5 [MS. parish records in Westminster City Library].

LONDON, THE NEW WESTMINSTER HOSPITAL, BROAD SANCTUARY, 1832–4; remodelled 1923–4; dem. 1951 [exhib. R.A. 1832–3 by W. & C. Inwood].

CLANDON PARK, SURREY, Ionic temple for the 3rd Earl of Onslow, 1838 [exhib. at R.A. 1838 by W. & H. W. Inwood] (*C. Life*, 24 Sept. 1927, p. 439, fig. 12).

LONDON, ST. JAMES'S CHURCH, CHILLINGWORTH ROAD, HOLLOWAY, 1837–8; subsequently much enlarged; by H. W. Inwood & E. N. Clifton [S. Lewis, *History of Islington*, 1842, 373].

LONDON, ST. STEPHEN'S CHURCH, CANONBURY ROAD, ISLINGTON, 1837–9, Gothic; reconstructed 1957 after war-damage; by H. W. Inwood & E. N. Clifton [H. W. Inwood's letter cited in text; exhib. at R.A. 1839 by E. N. Clifton; S. Lewis, *op cit.*, 410].

WINDSOR, BERKS., a hotel, 1840 [H. W. Inwood's letter cited in text].

IONS, JOHN (*c.* 1785–1826), of Gateshead, was a mason by trade. In 1824–5 he built the Gothic church of GATESHEAD FELL, CO. DURHAM, and when he died on 26 November 1826, at the age of 41, he was commemorated as 'architect and builder of this church'. Ions's design is, however, known to have been improved by the professional hand of Ignatius Bonomi [E. Mackenzie & M. Ross, *County Palatine of Durham* i, 1834, 107–8; Port, 132, 183].

IRELAND, JOSEPH (*c.* 1780–1841), belonged to an old Roman Catholic family from Crofton near Wakefield in Yorkshire. It is possible that he was a pupil of Joseph Bonomi, for he began to exhibit at the Royal Academy from No. 12 Great Titchfield Street, London, in 1808, the year in which Bonomi died at No. 76. For the next thirty years he worked for an almost exclusively Catholic clientèle, providing them with well-designed chapels and churches in either Gothic or Grecian style. He died at Moorcroft House, Hillingdon, Middlesex, on 16 November 1841, aged 60. J. J. Scoles became his pupil in 1812. [*Catholic Directory*, 1842, 134; *Gent's Mag.* 1842 (i), 112; information from Mr. Denis Evinson.]

LONDON, R. C. CHAPEL, ROMNEY TERRACE, HORSE-FERRY ROAD, WESTMINSTER, 1813; dem. [*Downside Review* viii, 1889, 115].

TRANBY PARK, HESSLE, YORKS. (E.R.), for John Todd, 1816 [exhib. at R.A. 1816].

HASSOP HALL, DERBYSHIRE, R. C. CHAPEL for Francis Eyre, titular Earl of Newburgh, 1816–18, Grecian [exhib. at R.A. 1819].

LEICESTER, R. C. CHAPEL, WELLINGTON STREET, 1817–19, Gothic [B. Little, *Catholic Churches since 1623*, 1966, 55].

IRNHAM HALL, LINCS., R. C. CHAPEL for the 6th Lord Clifford, 1822–3, Grecian; dem. 1855 [exhib. at R.A. 1822].

TIXALL HALL, STAFFS., 'restoration' for Sir Thomas Clifford Constable, Bart., 1823; dem. 1930 [exhib. at R.A. 1823].

HINCKLEY, LEICS., R. C. CHAPEL (ST. PETER), 1825, Gothic; enlarged 1885; dem. 1976 [C. L. Eastlake, *History of the Gothic Revival*, 1872, 130].

WALSALL, STAFFS., ST. MARY'S R. C. CHURCH, 1825–7, Grecian [S. Lewis, *Topographical Dictionary of England* iv, 1831, 373; B. Little, *Catholic Churches since 1623*, 1966, 64].

WOLVERHAMPTON, STAFFS., GIFFORD HOUSE R. C. CHAPEL (SS. PETER & PAUL), 1827–8, Grecian; enlarged 1901 [*Catholic Magazine* v, 1834, 306–7; B. Little, *Catholic Churches since 1623*, 1966, 64–5].

HOUGHTON HALL, YORKS. (E.R.), R. C. CHAPEL for the Hon. Charles Langdale, 1827–9, Grecian; dem. 1959 [*Catholic Miscellany*, 1829, 238–9] (*Trans. Georgian Soc. for E. Yorkshire* v (ii), 1961–3, fig. 8).

TIXALL HALL, STAFFS., conversion of existing

building into a domestic R.C. chapel for Sir Clifford Constable, Bart., 1828; dem. [exhib. at R.A. 1830]. In 1836 Ireland exhibited at the Liverpool Academy the 'Interior of the Chapel at Tixall, Staffordshire, the seat of Sir George Clifford Constable, Bart.' This was presumably the elaborate Tudor Gothic R.C. chapel at Great Haywood, Staffs., which formerly stood at Tixall and was rebuilt at Haywood in 1845.

WEST BROMWICH, STAFFS., ST. MICHAEL'S R. C. CHURCH, 1830–2, Gothic; rebuilt 1877 [F. W. Hackwood, *History of West Bromwich*, 1895, 45].

BURGHFIELD, BERKSHIRE, cottage for the 16th Earl of Shrewsbury, *c.* 1836 [exhib. at Liverpool Academy, 1836].

TUNBRIDGE WELLS, KENT, R. C. CHURCH (ST. AUGUSTINE), GROSVENOR ROAD, 1837–8, classical; dem. *c.* 1970 [Colbrand's *Guide to Tunbridge Wells*, 1840, 109] (H. R. Hiscock, *Early Victorian Architecture in Britain* ii, 1954, pl. III, 4).

IRESON, NATHANIEL (1686–1769), master builder, was a native of Warwicks., but may have been related to the Iresons of Yarwell, Northants., who were master masons there in the seventeenth and eighteenth centuries, and whose descendants are still in business as builders in Stamford. He is said to have been born in the neighbourhood of Nuneaton, probably at Ansley, but subsequently lived at Ladbrooke, where a daughter was born in 1711. He served his apprenticeship with Francis Smith of Warwick (*q.v.*), who subsequently recommended him as 'a young man ... that understands his business very well' [National Library of Wales, Penrice & Margam MSS. L 945, 958]. By 1720 he was established at Stourton in Wilts., where he built Stourhead House for Henry Hoare to the designs of Colen Campbell. In Stourton Church there is an inscription recording that 'This church was newly paved and seated and beautified 1722/3. Nathl. Ireson, John Butcher, Churchwardens', but it is not known whether Ireson executed the work himself. His daughter Mary died here in 1723, and was buried in the church, where Nathaniel erected a tablet to her memory the following year. In about 1726 he purchased Windmill Farm at Wincanton in Somerset, and built Ireson House, where he lived until his death on 18 April 1769, at the age of 83. In 1733 he opened a quarry on his land at Wincanton, which not only produced an excellent freestone, but also yielded an over-burden of clay suitable for brickmaking and the manufacture of pottery. He made the most of these natural resources, becoming a skilled potter as well as a quarry-owner, brickmaker and master builder. As a sculptor he is represented by the signed tablet to the memory of the Rev. Robert

Kingston (d. 1748) in St. Cuthbert's Church, Wells, and he is reputed to have carved the statue to himself which stands in Wincanton Churchyard, 'keeping it ready to be erected after his death'. As an architect he did not attempt to follow Campbell's new Palladianism, but designed and built in a vigorous provincial baroque style which invites comparison with the work of the Smiths of Warwick in the Midlands, and with that of the Bastards of Blandford in Dorset. With the Bastards Ireson shared a fondness for the Borrominesque capitals with inturned volutes which are used at Crowcombe Court and also in an unexecuted design for the north front of Corsham Court which bears Ireson's signature (reproduced in C. Hussey, *English Country Houses: Early Georgian*, 1955, 229).

In his will, dated 24 September 1765 (P.C.C. 212 BOGG), Ireson, who describes himself as a mason, leaves Crosses or Crases House, Wincanton to his daughter Mary Ireson Kittermaster, and all his books, tools and marble to John Ireson, a relation who was evidently not his son. His descendants continued to live in Wincanton until the early nineteenth century, and the quarry on Windmill Farm was not exhausted until 1900. Portraits of Ireson and his wife, painted in 1725 and 1745 respectively, were in 1896 in the possession of Mrs. William Bewsey of Wincanton, but their present ownership is unknown.

[W. Phelps, *History of Somerset*, 1836–9, i, 162, 167; G. Sweetman, *History of Wincanton*, 1903, 209–11; H. St. George Gray, 'N. Ireson, Master-Builder and Potter', *C. Life*, 12 April 1939; H. St. George Gray, 'Nathaniel Ireson of Wincanton, Master-Builder', *Procs. of the Somerset Arch. Soc.* lxxxvii, 1941.]

KINGSTON DEVERILL CHURCH, WILTS., work by Ireson is recorded in the parish records in 1724 [*Procs. of Somerset Arch. Soc.* lxxxvii, 1941, 82].

VEN HOUSE, MILBORNE PORT, SOMERSET, enlarged and rebuilt house for James Medlycott (d. 1731), probably *c.* 1725, incorporating as west elevation the front of a smaller house built in 1698–1700 [information from accounts formerly at Ven *per* Mr. J. Lees-Milne] (*C. Life*, 24 June 1911; H. A. Tipping, *English Homes* iv (i), 385–96).

MELLS PARK, SOMERSET, for Thomas Horner, 1725; canted bows added later in the 18th century; alterations by Soane 1810–24; dem. after fire in 1917 [contract in volume of drawings by Soane at Mells Manor House] (*C. Life*, 24 May 1962, p. 1254).

BERKLEY HOUSE, nr. FROME, SOMERSET, for Abigail Prowse, 1730–2 [contract in Warwickshire Record Office, Mordaunt papers CR 711, box 3].

CROWCOMBE COURT, SOMERSET, for Thomas Carew, 1734; damaged by fire 1963. On 6 July 1734 Ireson contracted to build a house 'on foundations some time since laid and carried up by Thomas Parker Architect ... according to Modells fformes, plans and Representations of the four fronts and of the Severall Rooms ... drawn up prepared and signed by the said N. Ireson' [C. Hussey in *C. Life*, 22–9 April 1933].

BRUTON CHURCH, SOMERSET, the chancel, for Charles Berkeley of Stratton, 1743 [Sweetman, 211].

WINCANTON CHURCH, SOMERSET, rebuilt chancel, added clerestory, re-roofed and rewindowed nave at his own expense, 1748. The altar bore an inscription that it was 'given by Nathaniel Ireson Architect 1748'. His work was destroyed by J. D. Sedding in 1887–9 [Sweetman, 45].

REDLYNCH, SOMERSET. According to Sweetman (p. 211) he built the CHAPEL in the grounds of Redlynch House in 1750, and documents in B.M., Add. MS. 51373 A., ff. 37–40 show that in *c.* 1755 he was carrying out alterations to the house for the 1st Earl of Ilchester in conjunction with Henry Flitcroft; dem. 1913–14.

WINCANTON, SOMERSET. According to Sweetman Ireson was responsible for the following works in Wincanton: IRESON HOUSE for himself, *c.* 1726, altered *c.* 1851; HILLSIDE HOUSE; the rebuilding of THE WHITE HORSE INN in 1733; and alterations to BALSAM HOUSE, RODBER HOUSE (*c.* 1730), and 'THE DOGS', TOUT HILL, *c.* 1745.

IVORY, THOMAS (1709–1779), was a leading architect and builder in Norwich in the eighteenth century. The place of his birth is unknown, but the fact that, in September 1745, he purchased his freedom of the city as a carpenter indicates that he was neither born nor apprenticed in Norwich. In 1751 he was nominated to do all the carpenter's work for the Great Hospital 'in the room of Agabus Molden', an appointment which he held to the time of his death. He is described in his will as a builder and timber merchant, and by his son William as 'a publick spirited Man, with great activity of Mind and resolution, and great knowledge in his business as a Master builder, and employing ... a considerable number of Workmen, and having always on his own premises, a large Assortment of Deals and Timber, being considerably employed in the profession of a Merchant in Exporting the Norwich Manufactory and other English Manufactures into the Northern Countries and Importing from thence large Quantities of Deals, Timber, Iron, etc., into this Country'. His timber yard was in Bishopsgate Street. From 1752 onwards he built as speculations a number of houses on sites leased from the Corporation and the Great Hospital, and in 1757 he not only undertook the erection of a theatre out of his own capital, but continued to be its sole proprietor until 1766, when he 'offered his whole Theatrical Estate to Publick Sale, to be divided into Thirty shares – reserving two shares to himself'. He was responsible for some excellent Georgian architecture in Norwich, his most notable building being the octagonal Nonconformist chapel in Colegate, which has quite an ambitious interior with giant Corinthian columns supporting the dome.

Thomas Ivory of Norwich is not to be confused with Thomas Ivory of Dublin (d. 1786), an architect with whom, so far as is known, he was unconnected. He died in Norwich on 28 August 1779, aged 70, as a result of an injury due to 'a large firr baulk going over his legg and thigh'. He is commemorated by a memorial tablet in the cathedral (now in the triforium), executed by his nephew John Ivory, who was a carver and monumental mason, and also by an inscription on the floor of the north transept. He left two sons, Thomas, who was employed in the Revenue Office at Fort William in Bengal, and William, who succeeded his father as an architect and builder in Norwich [S. J. Wearing, *Georgian Norwich: its Builders*, 1926, 11–36 (in which evidence will be found for the list of buildings that follows); *D.N.B.*; Norfolk and Norwich Record Office, 19180, letters from William Ivory to the Earl of Buckinghamshire, 1779].

NORWICH

THE METHODIST MEETING-HOUSE, BISHOPSGATE, 1751–3.

HOUSE IN ENTRANCE COURT tO THE GREAT HOSPITAL, 1752–3.

attributed: HOUSE IN BISHOPSGATE adjoining MEETING-HOUSE, for 'Mr. Wheatley the Methodist Preacher', 1753.

THE OCTAGON CHAPEL, COLEGATE, 1754–6.

THE ASSEMBLY ROOMS, 1754. The interior was designed by Sir James Burrough (*q.v.*).

THE THEATRE, 1757, enlarged and altered by W. Wilkins 1800, and again altered 1819; dem. 1825.

SURREY STREET, NOS. 29–35, 1761–2; NOS. 25 and 27, *c.* 1770.

THE ARTILLERY BARRACKS, 1771–2.

KING STREET, NO. 31, for Sir Edward Astley, *c.* 1774; dem.

ELSEWHERE

COLCHESTER, THE THEATRE, 1764; dem. *c.* 1820.

BLICKLING HALL, NORFOLK, alterations for the 2nd Earl of Buckinghamshire 1767 onwards, in conjunction with his son Thomas, who appears to have made most of the designs. The Elizabethan staircase was moved and altered, and new ceilings were inserted in the hall, Peter the

Great Room and State Dressing Chamber. (*C. Life*, 28 June 1930).

IVORY, WILLIAM (1746–1801), was the son and successor of Thomas Ivory of Norwich (d. 1779). At the age of 24 he gratuitously designed, and superintended the erection of, the NORFOLK AND NORWICH HOSPITAL, 1770–5. He was associated with his father in the alterations at BLICKLING HALL from about 1770 onwards, making many of the designs, and completing the works there after his father's death. In 1780 and 1781 he acted as honorary auditor to the Infirmary, and in 1768 he became one of the proprietors of the Norwich Theatre. He is believed to have lived in St. Helen's Place, a substantial house possibly designed and built by himself, and in 1780 he erected in the south transept of St. Helen's Church a Gothic pew for his family and his servants. In 1784 he left Norwich for Ipswich, where he died on 24 June 1801. He held the rank of Captain in the East Norfolk Militia, and there is a portrait of him, wearing uniform, in the Christchurch Museum at Ipswich.

[S. J. Wearing, *Georgian Norwich: its Builders*, 1926, 37–41; *Ipswich Journal*, 24 June 1801; letters to the Earl of Buckinghamshire in Norfolk and Norwich Record Office, 19180; information from Mr. J. Bensusan-Butt].

IVORY, WILLIAM (*c.* 1747–1837), carpenter and builder of Saffron Walden, carried out works at AUDLEY END, ESSEX for the 4th Lord Howard de Walden. These included repairs to the house, and a new VICARAGE in SAFFRON WALDEN, erected in 1793 [Essex County Record Office, Audley End papers, Annual Account for 1793]. His designs for the vicarage are preserved in an album of architectural drawings in the library at Audley End (f. 101). This also contains a set of plans of Audley End made by Ivory in 1787 (ff. 48–51). He died in the Edward VI Almshouses at Saffron Walden in his 91st year, and was buried in the churchyard there [J. C. Loudon, *Architectural Magazine* iv, 1837, 96; S. J. Wearing, *Georgian Norwich: its Builders*, 1926, 40–1].

J

JACKSON, —, was an otherwise unidentified surveyor employed in connection with the building of the new river front of CLARE COLLEGE, CAMBRIDGE, in 1669–71. On 24 April 1669 £1 was paid 'to Jackson for his journey hither to surveigh the building'. It is possible, but unlikely, that he was the Cambridge bricklayer called George Jackson who contracted to build Pembroke College Chapel in 1663 [Willis & Clark, i, 102, 155].

JACKSON, GEORGE (*c.* 1805–1842) was almost certainly the son of Thomas Jackson, a builder of Durham, who in 1838–40 designed SHADFORTH CHURCH, CO. DURHAM, Gothic, largely rebuilt 1889–91 and 1917 [I.C.B.S.]. Thomas Jackson died in 1840, and the certificate sent to the Incorporated Church Building Society was signed by George. George Jackson subsequently designed the following churches in County Durham, all in the 'Early English style': WINGATE, 1840–1 [J. Latimer, *Local Records*, 1857, 149]; COLLIERLY (ANNFIELD PLAIN), 1840–1 [I.C.B.S.]; PELTON, 1841–2 [J. Fordyce, *History of Durham* ii, 1855, 620]; SEATON CAREW, chancel only, 1842 [I.C.B.S.]; and SOUTHWICK-ON-WEAR, 1842–5 [I.C.B.S.]. In 1841 he made designs for a new vicarage at BLACKTOFT, YORKS. (E.R.), in the Gothic style [Borthwick Institute, MGA 1841/1]. George Jackson died on 26 August 1842, aged 37, and is commemorated by a tombstone in Durham Cathedral graveyard.

JACKSON, GEORGE, of Hull, appears to have been the son of George Jackson, a joiner of that town. He designed the HULL SAVINGS BANK, POSTERNGATE, 1828–9, dem. [*Hull Advertiser*, 6 June 1828, *ex inf.* Mr. A. G. Chamberlain].

JACKSON, JOHN (*c.* 1602–1663), was a master mason much employed in Oxford in the middle of the seventeenth century. He came to Oxford from London in 1634 in order to superintend the building of the CANTERBURY QUADRANGLE at ST. JOHN'S COLLEGE after the failure of the original mason-contractors. He was paid a pound a week for overseeing the work, and is always referred to in the accounts as 'Mr. Jackson'. The design had already been settled before his employment, and there is no evidence that he was called upon to make any further drawings [St. John's College Muniments, lxii, 13; Arthur Oswald in *C. Life*, 9 Nov. 1929; *V.C.H. Oxon.* iii, 262]. After the completion of the new quadrangle at St. John's in 1636 Jackson settled in Oxford, where he was employed on various jobs, such as carving the niche for Charles I's bust in the Bodleian Library, for which he received £6 in 1641, building a buttress at the north-west corner of the Schools in 1650, and 'cleansing and polishing' the antique marbles given to the University by John Selden in 1660 [Wood, *Life and Times*, Oxford Hist. Soc., i, 320, iv, 57, 62]. In 1635–6 he was paid 10s. for his advice about the new tower and gateway being built at UNIVERSITY COLLEGE, and in 1637–8 provided the 'draughts' for the wooden gates [*V.C.H. Oxon.* iii, 75, see also 76]. A more important commission was the porch of ST. MARY'S CHURCH, which he built in 1637, apparently to the designs of Nicholas Stone (*q.v.*) [T. G. Jackson, *Church of St. Mary the Virgin*,

Oxford, 1897, 128]. In 1656 he undertook to act as 'overseer' of the new Chapel and Library at BRASENOSE COLLEGE at one pound a week, and in 1659 was paid £20 'for his modell of the Roof of the new Chapple, and his paynes taken about it' [E. W. Allfrey, 'The Architectural History of the College', *Brasenose Quatercentenary Monographs* iii, 1909, 18–28.] From this it may be concluded that Jackson was probably the designer of the whole building, in which Gothic and classical motifs are combined in a quite sophisticated manner reminiscent of St. Mary's porch. In 1663 he made a 'modell' for completing the 'great gate' (i.e. Tom Tower) at Christ Church [W. G. Hiscock, *A Christ Church Miscellany*, 1946, 202], but nothing was done for nearly twenty years, and by then Jackson was dead. He died on 22 December 1663, and was buried in St. Mary Magdalen Church, where an inscription commemorated him as 'John Jackson, stone-carver, an ingenious artist, a loyall subject, an honest man and a good neighbour' [Wood, *City of Oxford*, ed. Clark, iii, 143]. His will, dated 7 December 1663, is witnessed by John Stone (*q.v.*) and Simon White, another Oxford mason and carver [Bodleian Library, Oxford Archdeaconry Wills 136/4/9].

JACKSON, JOHN GEORGE (*c.* 1798–*c.* 1852], was a pupil of P. F. Robinson, and was admitted to the Royal Academy Schools in 1817 at the age of 19. He exhibited at the Academy from 1817 onwards and at the Society of British Artists in 1824 and 1831. In 1828–9 he published a volume of *Designs for Villas . . . adapted to the vicinity of the Metropolis, or large Towns*, all classical or Italianate in style. Soon after 1830 he established himself at Leamington in Warwicks., where he designed JEPHSON GARDENS, 1834, the classical EPISCOPAL CHAPEL, MILVERTON, 1836, dem., the Gothic ST. MARY'S CHURCH, 1838–9, and the TENNIS COURTS in BEDFORD STREET, 1844 [T. B. Dudley, *History of Leamington*, 1896–1900, 204, 209, 223, 237] (R. P. Ross Williamson, 'Leamington Spa', *Arch. Rev.*, May 1942). He was the architect first employed by the Rev. John Craig to realize the latter's ambitious designs for rebuilding the PARISH CHURCH of ALL SAINTS, LEAMINGTON, in a continental Gothic style, but was dismissed in 1843 in favour of another local architect named Edmund Mitchell, who continued the building on lines already laid down by Jackson. Jackson defended himself vigorously in the *Builder* (see vol. i, 1843, 305, 335, 337, 367, 381, 388; also *Ecclesiologist* ii, 1842, 93–4) and exhibited his design at the Birmingham Society of Artists in 1844. He also designed a new chancel for LEEK WOOTTON CHURCH, WARWICKS., 1843 (rebuilt 1899) which he likewise exhibited at Birmingham in 1844, and in 1847 added a north aisle to LILLINGTON CHURCH, WARWICKS. [*Ecclesiologist* viii, 1848, 260].

JACOBSEN, THEODORE (–1772), was descended from a family of German origin which managed the London Steelyard on behalf of the Hanseatic merchants. After the death of his brother Sir Jacob Jacobsen in 1735, Theodore became the senior member of the family, and carried on a successful business in the Steelyard. He latterly resided in Basinghall Street, and, though actively engaged in commerce, found time to practise as an amateur architect. His first recorded work was for the East India Company, who in 1726 decided to adopt 'the ground plat and front presented by Theodore Jacobsen, Esqr.' for their new buildings in Leadenhall Street (rebuilt 1799–1800 and demolished 1861–2). On its completion in 1729 the Directors were sufficiently pleased with the result to offer Jacobsen their formal thanks, together with a piece of plate worth 200 guineas, afterwards exchanged, at his own request, for a ring of equal value. The erection of the building was, however, supervised by John James, a surveyor possessed of the technical knowledge necessarily lacking in a busy City merchant, who at the time the EAST INDIA HOUSE was being built, was prosecuting a lawsuit of long standing with the Hanse Towns.

Jacobsen's best-known work was the FOUNDLING HOSPITAL, LONDON, erected between 1742 and 1752, and demolished in 1928 (*Arch. Rev.* lviii, 1925, 127–32). Four other architects submitted plans, but the fact that Jacobsen offered his gratuitously may have influenced the Governors in his favour. The execution of his designs was entrusted to James Horne (*q.v.*) who also gave his services free of charge. Designs for the interior of the chapel are in the collection of Mr. & Mrs. Paul Mellon. In 1745 Jacobsen made the designs for another charitable institution, the ROYAL NAVAL HOSPITAL FOR SICK SAILORS at HASLAR, GOSPORT, nr. PORTSMOUTH, HANTS., of which there is an engraving in *Gent's Mag.* 1751, 408. The building was not completed until 1761. James Horne appears again to have acted as executant architect. A third public building for which Jacobsen furnished designs was the main quadrangle of TRINITY COLLEGE, DUBLIN, as built in 1752–9. In 1755 Hugh Darley, the surveyor in charge, wrote to John (*sic*) Keene in London to say that the north range and the north-west pavilion were ready for the cornice, but that suggestions had been made for alterations to 'Mr. Jacobsen's elevation' which the College was unwilling to adopt 'without the consent and approbation of Mr. Jacobsen'.[1] The proposed modifications involved the elimination of a dome

over the central pediment and of cupolas on the pavilions and an adjustment of the position of the pilasters in the main elevation. It was no doubt as a result of these suggestions that the dome and cupolas were omitted, but in other respects the elevations presumably follow Jacobsen's design, and the rôle of Henry Keene and John Sanderson in providing plans and elevations (for which they were paid £74 11s. 8d.) must have been to make detailed working drawings from Jacobsen's no doubt relatively simple ones. It may be noted that there was evidently some connection between Keene and James Horne, who had been executant architect for Jacobsen's two previous buildings, and that one of Jacobsen's few surviving architectural designs (the elevation of a house) is among Keene's drawings in the Victoria and Albert Museum (see below).

In about 1732 Jacobsen offered a design for the Bank of England's new building in Threadneedle Street, but that of George Sampson (*q.v.*) was preferred. The only record of Jacobsen's design appears to be an engraving of the main elevation among the Bank's records (see *An Historical Catalogue of Engravings, Drawings and Paintings in the Bank of England*, 1928, p. 3, no. 10).

Jacobsen's three executed public buildings have in common a quadrangular layout with corner pavilions. The architectural treatment is in each case fairly simple, an order being used only at Trinity College, where it is handled in a slightly clumsy manner consistent with an amateur designer. His proposed elevation for the Bank of England was that of a conventional English Palladian villa, with Ionic pedimented centre-piece.

On the strength of a portrait of Jacobsen by Hogarth, signed and dated 1742, in which he is shown holding the plan of a triangular house, it has been assumed that he was the architect employed by Sir Jacob Bouverie to remodel the interior of Longford Castle, Wilts., from 1737 onwards. The plan depicted, however, is not that of Longford Castle, but corresponds with the 'section, plan, and elevation of a design for a triangular house, by Theodore Jacobsen, Esqr.', engraved by Fourdrinier, of which there is an impression in Bodleian, Gough Maps 30, f. 75. It is possible that the idea of designing such a house was suggested by Longford Castle, and it is certain that Bouverie, who was himself a prominent London merchant, and Vice-President of the Foundling Hospital in 1740–1, must have known Jacobsen. Moreover, the portrait itself is said to have belonged to his descendants, the Earls of Radnor. There is, however, apparently no mention of Jacobsen in the building accounts preserved at Longford, and it can only be conjectured that Bouverie may have asked Jacobsen to advise him about the alterations to his house.

The only other building known to have been

---

[1] For a copy of this letter I am indebted to Mr. Edward McParland of Trinity College.

designed by Jacobsen was his own house near Dorking in Surrey, known as LONESOME LODGE or TILLINGBOURNE, which he built in 1740 and made his summer residence until 1763, when he sold the estate to Jeremiah Joyce. The house, later known as Fillbrook Lodge, was demolished early in the nineteenth century, but there is an engraving of 'Lonesome Lodge at Wootton in Surry belonging to Theodore Jacobsen Esqr., designed by himself' in Bodleian, Gough Maps 30, f. 76. Vertue, who dined with Jacobsen here in 1747, confirms that the house was of 'his own design and building' (Walpole Society, *Vertue Note Books* v, 155).

In his will (P.C.C., 137 TAVERNER), Jacobsen refers to his books of architecture, to a portfolio containing architectural drawings by himself, and to copper-plates of his designs. Two of the latter (of the triangular house and of the Foundling Hospital) are now in the Soane Museum. There is an elevation of a house 'Design'd by T. Jacobsen' in the Victoria and Albert Museum (E. 850–1921, A. 189). He died at an advanced age on 25 April 1772, and was buried in the family vault in the churchyard of All Hallows the Great, Upper Thames Street. He was a Fellow of the Royal and Antiquarian Societies, a member of the Society of Arts, and a Governor of the Foundling Hospital, where there is a full-length portrait of him painted by Hudson in 1746 (reproduced by Nichols and Wray, *History of the Foundling Hospital*, 1935, 42). The half-length portrait by Hogarth referred to above is now in the Museum at Oberlin, Ohio, U.S.A. It is reproduced in *C. Life*, 27 March 1942. It shows a jewelled ring on Jacobsen's left hand which is doubtless the one presented to him by the East India Company in 1729. Another portrait, showing Jacobsen holding a plan titled 'Portsmouth 1761' was for sale in London in 1972.

[*A.P.S.D.*; *D.N.B.*; W. Foster, *The East India House*, 1924; R. H. Nichols and F. A. Wray, *History of the Foundling Hospital*, 1935; P. Norman, 'Notes on the later History of the Steelyard in London', *Archaeologia* lxi (ii), 1909; *C. Life*, 27 March 1942, 621; Brayley, *History of Surrey* v, 69; *V.C.H. Surrey* iii, 155.]

JAFFRAY, ALEXANDER (1677–   ), laird of Kingswells near Aberdeen, came of a Quaker family well-known in Aberdeen. His wife Christian was a daughter of Robert Barclay, the Quaker apologist. Alexander was active as an agricultural improver, and was also an amateur architect. In 1730 he visited London in order to see 'all the fine buildings and gardens'. In the following year he became the first surveyor of roads and bridges in Aberdeenshire. At KINGSWELLS he carried out alterations commemorated by his initials over the doorway, and in 1719–20 he was consulted by Sir Archibald Grant of MONYMUSK

HOUSE, ABERDEENSHIRE. Jaffray offered to design a new house, but Grant preferred to alter the old house with Jaffray's advice. ['Alexander Jaffray's Recollections of Kingswells 1755–1800', ed. G. M. Fraser, *Third Spalding Club Miscellany* i, 1935; *Monymusk Papers*, ed. H. Hamilton, Scottish Historical Soc. 1945, xi, xlv, 77–9; Alistair Rowan, 'House of Monymusk', *C. Life*, 19–26 Oct. 1972.]

JAFFRAY, GEORGE, was a builder and architect of Aberdeen, where he designed THE TOWN HOUSE, OLD ABERDEEN, 1787–8, in a simple Palladian style. A payment to him in the accounts for building POWIS HOUSE, OLD ABERDEEN, for Hugh Leslie in 1802–4 probably indicates that he designed that house, now part of the University [*Powis Papers*, ed. J. G. Burnett, Third Spalding Club 1951, 101, 335].

JAFFREY, *or* **JEFFRAY,** JAMES, is described in the 1787 Glasgow directory as 'architect, cabinet-maker and house wright'. In 1780 he designed ST. ENOCH'S CHURCH, GLASGOW, rebuilt (except the steeple) by David Hamilton in 1827–8; dem. [R. Chapman, *Picture of Glasgow*, 1822, 125]. In the Glasgow University Archives [832] there is an unexecuted design by him for the termination of College Street. His unexecuted designs for the Trades House, dated 1791, are in the City Archives [T-KF 1/1, 23]. The inscription on his tomb in the Cathedral graveyard (lair 37) describes him as 'architect and builder', but does not give the date of his death [*ex inf.* Mr. J. Stevens Curl].

JAMES, JOHN (*c.* 1672–1746), is stated on his monument in Eversley Church, Hants., to have been the eldest son of the Rev. John James, master of the Holy Ghost School at Basingstoke (1673), and afterwards vicar of Basingstoke (1697–1717), and rector of Stratfield Turgis (1717–33). In a letter to the Duke of Buckingham, dated 20 October 1711, James describes himself as 'a Parson's son',[1] and there is no evidence to support the statement in *D.N.B.* that his parents were Thomas and Eleanor James, the printers. Nothing is known of his early upbringing, but in his own estimation there was 'no person pretending to Architecture among us, Sir Chr. Wren excepted, [who] has had the advantage of a better Education in the Latin, Italian, and French Tongues', besides 'a competent share of Mathematicks and ten years Instruction in all the practical parts of Building by Mr. Banks, who was well known in their Majesty's Works'.[2]

---

[1] Bodleian Library, MS. Rawlinson B.376, f. 8.

[2] It may be noted that at this date he does not mention foreign travel among his qualifications, and it is scarcely possible that he can have been the J. James who signed the Visitors' Book of Padua University on 4 December

Matthew Bancks was Master Carpenter to the Crown from 1683 to 1706, and it was as a carpenter that James began his architectural career. In 1698 he was an unsuccessful applicant for the post of Clerk of the Works at Greenwich Hospital, but was told that the Committee, 'being well satisfied with his qualifications, will, as any opportunity shall offer, be ready to prefer him accordingly'. He was, in fact, employed as Store-Keeper and assistant Clerk of the Works at Greenwich from 1705 until 1718, when he became joint Clerk of the Works with Hawksmoor, the successful candidate of 1698, and remained in charge of the buildings of the Hospital until his death. In 1711, when Richard Jennings was dismissed from the works at St. Paul's Cathedral for fraud and embezzlement, James secured his position as master carpenter to the cathedral, and in 1715 he took Thomas Bateman's place as Assistant Surveyor under Sir Christopher Wren. On Wren's death in 1723, James succeeded him as Surveyor to the Fabric. Meanwhile, he had failed to secure one of the surveyorships to the Commissioners for Building Fifty New Churches under the Act of 1711, but had obtained the carpenter's contract for four of the new churches in partnership with Robert Jelfe of Westminster. In 1716, however, when James Gibbs, one of the two surveyors appointed by the Commissioners, was dismissed, John James was given his vacant post as Hawksmoor's colleague. By this time the designs of most of the new churches had been settled, but it was left to James to design St. George's, Hanover Square, and, in conjunction with Hawksmoor, two other churches that were to be 'as cheap as possible', namely St. Luke, Old Street, and St. John Horselydown. This appointment ceased in 1733, but Hawksmoor and James were paid 'for carrying on and finishing the Works under their Care' for some time afterwards, and the Commissioners were so pleased with the latter's services that they presented him with a gratuity of £52 10s. 'for his More than Ordinary attendance upon the works and the Commissioners'. In January 1724/5, James succeeded William Dickinson as Surveyor to the Dean and Chapter of Westminster, and in 1736, on Hawksmoor's death, he became also Surveyor to the Fabric of Westminster Abbey, under the Act of 1698 providing funds for its repair. It was in this capacity that between 1736 and 1745 he completed the west towers of the Abbey, in accordance with Hawksmoor's designs. He drew a 'North-West Prospect of Westminster Abbey with the Spire as design'd by Sr Christopher Wren' which was engraved by Four-

drinier and published in 1737 (*Wren Soc.* xi, pl. vi). James was a member of the Carpenters' Company, and was elected Master in 1734.

James was a competent architect, but he lacked inventive fancy, and his buildings are for the most part plain, unadorned and somewhat stolid. The exception is Appuldurcombe, whose elaborate decorative treatment differs so much from that of all his other works as to raise some doubt whether it can have been wholly his design. His earlier buildings are all articulated by giant orders, and fall in with the English baroque tradition. In 1711 James made a statement which at first sight suggests some sympathy with the Palladian revival then imminent. In the letter to the Duke of Buckingham already quoted he declared that his ambition was to show 'that the Beautys of Architecture may consist with the greatest plainness of the structure', something he claimed that 'has scarce ever been hit on by the Tramontani unless by our famous Mr. Inigo Jones'. Though James's buildings are plain in the sense that they lack baroque enrichments, Wricklemarsh is the only one that attempts to be conventionally Palladian, and James must be regarded as a rather sober disciple of Wren and Vanbrugh rather than as an effective pioneer of Palladianism.

As a surveyor James was eminently competent and trustworthy, and was much employed in this capacity, particularly by ecclesiastical patrons. In 1725, when he was a candidate for the under-surveyorship of Westminster Abbey, the subcommittee reported that 'tho' many persons well recommended both for their skill and honesty, did lately apply . . to succeed Mr. Dickenson as Surveyor of the College, yet the Dean and Chapter did unanimously chuse Mr. James into that office, who neither was recommended by any Person, nor did appear himself a Candidate for the same' (Westminster Abbey Muniment 34885), and in the same year Baron Comyns characterized him as 'a person of unquestioned skill and fidelity', in connection with a survey of Serjeants' Inn which he had carried out for the Dean and Chapter of York (Bodleian, MS. Rawl. C.441, f. 26). In 1711 he had been able to send Harley a long list of 'Persons of Quality' who would vouch for his character, and many of whom he had 'served in the business of their Buildings'. The list is as follows: 'Duke of Buckingham, Duke of Leeds, E. of Pembroke &c., Ld. Vic^t. Weymouth, Ld. Lempster, Mr. Benson Chancel^r. of the Excheq^r, Mr. Aislabie [and] Mr. Geo: Clark Lds. of ye Admty., Mr. John Hill, Sr. Charles Hedges, Sr. James Bateman, Sr. Willm. Gifford, Mr. James Johnston, Mr. Geo: Pitt of Hampshire &c.' (B.M., Harley Papers, xlvi).

After the death of Archbishop Tenison (Dec. 1715), James carried out a survey of the archiepiscopal palaces at Lambeth and Croydon, which

1717 (*Arch. Rev.*, Nov. 1957, 344), for the Minutes of the Commissioners for St. Paul's Cathedral make it clear that he was in England in June 1717 and February 1718 (*Wren Soc.* xvi, 129, 131).

was made the basis of a demand for dilapidations by his successor Archbishop Wake. This was contested by Tenison's executors, and James took part in the pamphlet warfare which ensued, publishing in 1717 *The Survey and Demand for Dilapidations in the Archiepiscopal See of Canterbury Justified against the Cavils and Misrepresentations contained in Some Letters lately printed by Mr. Archdeacon Tenison*. Copies of Tenison's printed letter, which attacks James personally, and quotes from his report, are preserved in Cambridge University Library, MS. 2508, and in Bodleian, Gough Kent 16. James also engaged in the controversy over the design of Westminster Bridge, publishing *A Short Review of the several Pamphlets and Schemes that have been offered to the Publick in relation to the Building of a Bridge at Westminster*, 1736, in which he criticized those of John Price, Nicholas Hawksmoor, and Batty Langley (the last of whom published a reply in 1737). James's own design, though not accepted by the Commissioners, was stated by Ripley, the assessor, to be 'clearly and well described' (Commissioners' Minutes, vol. i, f. 83 [P.R.O., Works 6/28]). A drawing by him for the central part of a large bridge is among Lord Burlington's drawings from Chatsworth now in the R.I.B.A. Drawings Collection (F. 14). James also made unexecuted designs for All Souls College and the Clarendon Building, Oxford, both *c.* 1710 (Colvin, *Catalogue of Architectural Drawings at Worcester College*, pls. 50, 104), for St. Martin's-in-the-Fields Church, 1720, for the Senate House at Cambridge, 1722, and for the Mansion House, London, 1734 (S. Perks, *The Mansion House*, 1922, pls. 37–40).

In 1729 James was induced to join with his brother Thomas, a typefounder, William Fenner, a stationer, and James Gedd, in their unsuccessful attempt to carry out William Gedd's system of block-printing or stereotyping. He is said to have been 'taken into partnership as having money, and as being universally acquainted with the nobility and dignified clergy'. His loss was proportionately severe when the venture became a total failure in 1738. He died at Greenwich, after a lingering illness, on 15 May 1746. His will (P.C.C., 155 EDMUNDS) directs that his estate at Eversley in Hants. shall be sold for the benefit of his widowed daughter-in-law, Mrs. Frances James, and that his property on Croom's Hill, Greenwich, shall be similarly disposed of for the benefit of his wife Mary. He was buried in the churchyard at Eversley, and there is an inscription to his memory in the north aisle of the church.[1] Besides the pamphlets already mentioned, he published *Rules and Examples of Perspective, proper for Painters and Architects*,

from the Italian of Andrea Pozzo (Rome, 1693), 1707, *A Treatise of the Five Orders of Columns in Architecture*, from the French of Claude Perrault (Paris, 1683), published in 1708 with the 'approbation' of Wren, Vanbrugh and Hawksmoor,[1] and *The Theory and Practice of Gardening* from the French of Dezallier D'Argenville (Paris, 1709), 1712, 2nd ed. 1728, 3rd ed. 1743. James's interest in gardening is also attested by his membership of the society of gardeners which published a *Catalogus Plantarum* or *Catalogue of Trees, Shrubs, etc. for sale in the Gardens near London* in 1730.

[*A.P.S.D.; D.N.B.; Wren Soc., passim*; Walpole, *Anecdotes of Painting*, ed. Wornum, 1862, 696; H. M. Colvin, 'Fifty New Churches', *Arch. Rev.*, March 1950; Willis & Clark, i, 195; iii, 44, 54; Hist. MSS. Comm., *Portland* x, 120–1; *Biographical Memoirs of William Ged* (S. Hodgson, Newcastle Reprints, 1819); K. A. Esdaile in *Times Literary Supplement*, 5 July 1941, 328.]

ECCLESIASTICAL WORK

DEAL, KENT, ST. GEORGE'S CHURCH, surveying and advice 1712–16. The church was designed and built by a Deal man, Samuel Simmons, in 1706, but completion was delayed by local squabbles, and a fresh contract for the carpentry of the roof was made in 1712 with James's advice. 'Plain modillion eaves' were substituted for parapets at his suggestion [John Laker, *History of Deal*, 1917, 258–63; Kent Record Office, Chapelwardens' Accounts, De QC1, p. 32].

TWICKENHAM, MIDDLESEX, ST. MARY'S CHURCH, rebuilt, except west tower, 1713–15 [D. Lysons, *Environs of London* ii (2), 1811, 788]. The galleries were altered in 1859.

WHITCHURCH, MIDDLESEX, ST. LAWRENCE'S CHURCH, rebuilt for the 1st Duke of Chandos, 1714–16 [C. H. & M. I. Collins Baker, *The Life of James Brydges, Duke of Chandos*, 1949, 116–24].

TIVERTON, DEVONSHIRE, ST. GEORGE'S CHAPEL, 1714–33; re-roofed 1841–2. There are no building records, but in 1716 a benefactor left £1000 towards the cost of construction on condition that the church was completed according to a model given by 'Mr. James, surveyor' [W. Harding, *History of Tiverton* ii, 1849, 236].

WORCESTER CATHEDRAL, 'viewed the dilapidations' for the Dean and Chapter, 1718 [Treasurer's Book, 1718, *ex inf.* Mr. D. Whitehead].

CAMBRIDGE, GONVILLE AND CAIUS COLLEGE CHAPEL, rebuilt east end and designed altarpiece 1718–26; dem. 1870 [Willis & Clark, i, 195].

LONDON, ST. GEORGE'S CHURCH, HANOVER SQUARE,

[1] Printed in *Collectanea Topographica et Genealogica* viii, 1834, 64.

[1] A proof copy presented to Sir William Gifford is in Worcester College Library (B.2.2.)

1720–5; redecorated by B. Ferrey 1871 [Lambeth Palace Library; records of the Commissioners for building Fifty New Churches; a drawing by James for the north elevation is in the R.I.B.A. Collection].

LINCOLN CATHEDRAL, advised on strengthening of west towers, 1726 [J. W. F. Hill, 'The western spires of Lincoln Minster and their threatened removal in 1726', *Lincolnshire Architectural Soc's Reports* N.S. v(ii) 1954].

LONDON, ST. JOHN'S CHURCH, HORSELYDOWN, SOUTHWARK, 1727–33; bombed 1940 and subsequently dem.; designed jointly with Hawksmoor [Lambeth Palace Library, Minutes of the Commissioners for Building Fifty New Churches, vol. ii, 415, 418].

LONDON, ST. LUKE'S CHURCH, OLD STREET, 1727–33; dismantled 1960; designed jointly with N. Hawksmoor [Lambeth Palace Library, Minutes as above].

GREENWICH, KENT, ST. ALPHEGE'S CHURCH, added the steeple to Hawksmoor's church, 1730; rebuilt 1813 after damage by lightning [Lambeth Palace Library, Minutes as above, vol. iii, 34].

ROCHESTER CATHEDRAL, KENT, repaired south transept, c. 1730 [G. H. Palmer, *The Cathedral Church of Rochester*, 1897, 29].

LONDON, ST. MARGARET'S CHURCH, WESTMINSTER, repaired and refaced tower with Portland stone and raised it 20 ft., adding a Gothic belfry storey, 1735 [Westminster City Library, MS. Parish records].

SALISBURY CATHEDRAL, advice about repairs, 1736–7 [Salisbury Diocesan Record Office, bills and accounts, 1736–7].

WESTMINSTER ABBEY, completed west towers to designs of N. Hawksmoor, 1736–45, Gothic [*Wren Soc.* xi, 11–12].

PUBLIC AND DOMESTIC ARCHITECTURE

TWICKENHAM, MIDDLESEX, house (afterwards ORLEANS HOUSE), for the Hon. James Johnston, Secretary for Scotland, 1710, to which James Gibbs added the octagon room in 1720. The house was restored by J. B. Papworth 1837–9, but dem. 1927 except the octagon room [*Vitruvius Britannicus* i, 1715, pl. 77].

HERRIARD PARK, HANTS., for Thomas Jervoise, c. 1700–4; dem. 1965. James is stated to have been the architect of this house by G. F. Prosser, *Select Illustrations of Hampshire*, 1833, and this is confirmed by a reference to James in 1701 in a MS. notebook formerly at Herriard. Drawings for the house attributable to James are among the Jervoise papers in the Hants. County Record Office, together with a set of unexecuted designs attributable to Hawksmoor dated 1696. It appears that William Talman had also made a rejected design: see F.

H. J. Jervoise in *The Ancestor* ii, 1902, 7. (*C. Life*, 1 July 1965).

APPULDURCOMBE HOUSE, ISLE OF WIGHT, for Sir Robert Worsley, Bart., c. 1701–13; dismantled but preserved as an Ancient Monument. The evidence for John James's responsibility for this house is set out by L. O. J. Boynton, *Appuldurcombe House*, H.M.S.O. 1967, 10–11. It is not sufficient to prove beyond doubt that the design of this unusual house was wholly due to James, but if any other architect was involved, his identity remains unknown. (*Vitruvius Britannicus* iii, 1725, pl. 61.)

CANNONS HOUSE, MIDDLESEX. James was called in by the 1st Duke of Chandos after Talman had been dismissed in 1714. James made designs for remodelling the old house which were in part executed before James Gibbs took his place as the Duke's architect in 1715. A design for the west front in the G.L.C. Record Office (Acc. 262/50/59) is in James's hand [C. H. & M. I. Collins Baker, *The Life of James Brydges, Duke of Chandos*, 1949, 116–24].

PARK HALL, CROOMS HILL, GREENWICH, intended as his own residence but never in fact occupied by him, 1717–19, since much altered [P.R.O. Cres. 6/32, f. 247, *ex inf.* Mr. Frank Kelsall].

HURSLEY LODGE (now PARK), HANTS., for Sir William Heathcote, Bart., c. 1720; enlarged c. 1905 [G. F. Prosser, *Select Illustrations of Hampshire*, 1833, s.v. 'Herriard'] (*C. Life*, 13 Dec. 1902, showing the house before enlargement; 23–30 Oct. 1909, showing it after enlargement).

SWALLOWFIELD PARK, BERKS., alterations and additions (including bridge in park), for Thomas Pitt, c. 1720–2; remodelled by W. Atkinson 1820 [accounts in P.R.O., C104/424].

WARBROOKS HOUSE, EVERSLEY, HANTS., for himself, 1724 [inscription on his monument: 'The said John James Built the House called Warbrooks in this Parish Anno 1724'] (*C. Life*, 11–18 March, 1939).

WRICKLEMARSH, BLACKHEATH, KENT, for Sir Gregory Page, Bart., c. 1725; dem. 1787 [*Vitruvius Britannicus* iv, 1767, pls. 58–64] (Watts's *Views of Seats*, pl. xlvii, 1782; elevation by T. Milton in B.M. Print Room). The portico and other materials were re-used by John Cator at Beckenham Place, Kent, and four chimney-pieces were removed to the First Lord's House, Whitehall (illustrated in *C. Life*, 24 Nov. 1923, 723). When Beckenham Place was demolished some chimney-pieces from Wricklemarsh were removed to Woodbastwick Hall, Norfolk.

LONDON, THE EAST INDIA HOUSE, LEADENHALL STREET, supervised erection to designs of Theodore Jacobsen, 1726–9; rebuilt 1796–9 [W. Foster, *The East India House*, 1924, 131–2].

LONDON, BISHOPSGATE GATE, 1733; dem. 1760 [B. Langley, *Builders' Prices*, 1748, 246; 'Built by Mr. James, late of Greenwich'] (W. G. Bell *et al.*, *London Wall*, 1937, 80).

BAYLIES HOUSE, SLOUGH, BUCKS., altered and enlarged for Francis Godolphin, 1733–5 [accounts in Duke of Leeds's papers in Bucks. County Record Office].

WELBECK ABBEY, NOTTS., reconstructed south wing and remodelled west front for Henrietta, Countess of Oxford, 1742–6. The west front was remodelled by Repton in 1790 and the south front was rebuilt in 1860 and again in 1901 [A. S. Turberville, *Welbeck Abbey and its Owners* i, 1938, 394–6].

JAMES, WILLIAM, of Stone, near Berkeley in Gloucestershire, may have been the son of Richard James, who built Coleford Church to the designs of the Rev. Henry Poole (*q.v.*) in 1820–1 [I.C.B.S.]. He designed the RECTORY at SLIMBRIDGE, GLOS., in 1818–20 [Gloucester Public Library, R.F. 274.15], the POORHOUSE at ALDERLEY, GLOS., in 1825 [*ibid.*, RF. 7.9], rebuilt EASTON GREY CHURCH, WILTS. in 1836 [I.C.B.S.], enlarged STANDISH VICARAGE, GLOS., in 1839 [D. Verey, *Gloucestershire* ii, 345], and rebuilt LITTLE SODBURY CHURCH, GLOS., in 1859 [I.C.B.S.].

JANSSEN, BERNARD, was one of the sons of Gerard or Garet Janssen or Johnson, a native of Amsterdam who came to England in about 1567, settled in Southwark, married an English wife, and had several sons, of whom Bernard, John, Nicholas and a younger Gerard all followed his profession. In about 1620 Bernard Janssen made a finely-carved altar-tomb in REDGRAVE CHURCH, SUFFOLK, to support the effigies of Sir Nicholas and Lady Bacon made by Nicholas Stone [*Walpole Soc.* vii, 52]. In 1619–20 he also made in London a monument to Marcel Bax, governor of Bergen-op-Zoom, which was set up in the church there but destroyed during a bombardment in 1622 [*Messager des Sciences Historiques des Arts de Belgique*, 1858, 93–4]. Stone's great nephew Charles Stoakes told George Vertue that Janssen was the surveyor of NORTHUMBERLAND HOUSE, STRAND (*c.* 1605–9, dem. 1874), AUDLEY END, ESSEX (*c.* 1603–16, partly dem. 1708), 'and many other buildings' [Walpole Soc., *Vertue* ii, 49]. As the 1st Earl of Northampton, who built Northumberland House, was also responsible for the construction of Audley End for his nephew the 1st Earl of Suffolk, it is very probable that the same surveyor was employed for both buildings, and the same repertoire of Anglo-Flemish ornament was a prominent feature of both houses.

JARMAN, EDWARD, *see* JERMAN

JARRAT, THOMAS, appears to have been an amateur architect. In 1781 he designed the TOWN HALL at LANCASTER, with a handsome Roman Doric façade, and was given the freedom of the corporation in a silver box 'for his trouble in drawing the plan'. In the following year, however, it was concluded that the cupola shown on Jarrat's drawings would be 'inexpedient and dangerous to build', and one designed by Thomas Harrison of Chester was substituted [K. H. Docton, 'The Lancaster Town Hall', *The Lancashire and Cheshire Historian*, August 1965, 146–7]. According to *V.C.H. Lancs.* viii, 45 n., Jarratt had the title of 'Major'.

JAY, WILLIAM (*c.* 1793–1837), was the son of a nonconformist minister at Bath. He was articled to D. R. Roper, and began to exhibit student's work at the Royal Academy in 1809. He designed the ALBION CHAPEL, MOORFIELDS, LONDON, 1815–16, dem. 1879, a building which, according to Elmes, possessed 'a character of original thinking in its design that is highly pleasing' [*Metropolitan Improvements*, 1831, 170]. In 1817 Jay emigrated to Savannah, U.S.A., where he designed several public buildings and some houses, of which the best-known example is now the Owens-Thomas House Museum. His Telfair and Scarbrough Houses are notable as being among the earliest monuments of the Greek Revival in America. In 1824 he returned to England and appears to have worked for a time in Cheltenham, for in June 1825 he offered to make designs for a new church there for the Church Building Commissioners [Church Commissioners records, C.B.C. M B. 18, 21 June 1825], and in the Gloucestershire Record Office there is a set of designs by him for a terrace [D. 1388] which closely resembles COLUMBIA PLACE, WINCHCOMBE STREET, CHELTENHAM. Another plan in the same collection marked 'Mr. Mullings' house' establishes Jay as the designer of WATERMOOR HOUSE, CIRENCESTER, GLOS., for J. R. Mullings, a business associate of Joseph Pitt, of Pittville, Cheltenham. A drawing in the Cheltenham Museum dated 1826 and inscribed 'design by Mr. Jay for Pitville Parade' shows that he also designed PITTVILLE PARADE, now NOS. 2–34 EVESHAM ROAD, CHELTENHAM. In 1829 Jay enlarged the CONGREGATIONAL CHURCH at HENLEY–ON–THAMES, OXON., of which his brother-in-law, the Rev. Robert Bolton, was minister [*Berkshire Chronicle*, 6 June 1829], and in the same year he married a Henley girl named Louisa Coulson. In 1836, failing to establish a successful practice in England, he obtained a post as Assistant Chief Architect and Inspector of Works in the Colony of Mauritius, where he died on 17 April 1837. [*The Autobiography of the Rev. William Jay*, 1855, ed. G. Redford & J. A. James, 94; B. St. J. Ravenel, *Architects of Charleston*, Charleston, U.S.A., 1945, chapter 17; G. L. M.

Goodfellow, 'William Jay and the Albion Chapel', *Jnl. of the Society of Architectural Historians* [of America], xxii, No. 4, Dec. 1963, 225; information from Mr. David Verey and Canon B. F. L. Clarke.]

JEANS, JOHN (–1808), was an architect and builder of Aberdeen, where he died in 1808 aged 80 [Aberdeen City Library, G. M. Fraser's MS. Notes and Jottings, vol. 17, p. 73]. In Aberdeen he designed THE MEAL MARKET, 1770 [G. M. Fraser's Notes and Jottings, vol. 17, p. 75, citing Council Register vol. 63, pp. 151, 161]. His estimate, dated 17 January 1759, for adding wings to BELVIL or BELLEVILLE HOUSE, INVERNESS-SHIRE, is in the Scottish Record Office, together with a competently-drawn survey plan of the house as then existing [S.R.O., GD 1/32/4].

JEANS, THOMAS, was the son of Dr. T. Jeans, of Christchurch, Hants. He was a pupil of Sir John Soane from 1792 to 1797, and exhibited a drawing of the Countess of Salisbury's chapel at Christchurch at the Royal Academy in the latter year. He subsequently obtained a post in the Barrack Department. He was in Italy in 1819, and on his return became one of the original members of the Architects' and Antiquaries' Club. He was an F.S.A. [A. T. Bolton, *The Works of Sir John Soane*, 1924, Appendix C, p. xli].

JEARRAD, ROBERT WILLIAM (–1861), practised from 260 Oxford Street, London, from about 1810 onwards. For some years he was in partnership with Charles Jearrad, who was probably his brother. He died on 14 January 1861, leaving a son, R. W. Jearrad, junior, who had assisted his father since the 1840s.

The Jearrads were both architects and builders, and in 1830 they took over an extensive speculative building development on the Lansdowne estate in CHELTENHAM from the banker Henry Thompson, dismissing his architect J. B. Papworth and managing the whole concern themselves. They completed LANSDOWNE CRESCENT on the lines indicated by Papworth, built the Italianate villas in LANSDOWNE COURT, perhaps to Papworth's designs, but more probably to their own, and built LANSDOWNE PARADE to their own designs in 1838–41. They also designed the LITERARY AND PHILOSOPHICAL INSTITUTION, with Greek Doric portico, in the Promenade in 1835–6 (dem.), the imposing QUEEN'S HOTEL, 1837–8, and the Gothic CHRIST CHURCH, MALVERN ROAD, 1838–40, of which they exhibited a model at the Royal Academy in 1838. The Jearrads must accordingly be classed with Burton and Cubitt as leading developer-architects of the early nineteenth century, and Cheltenham is as much their monument as it is Papworth's [H. Davis, *Cheltenham in its Present and Past State*,

1843, 113, 187, 190; Rowe's *Illustrated Cheltenham Guide*, 1845, 18; David Verey, *Gloucestershire* (Buildings of England) ii, 1970, 124, 141–2].

Elsewhere R. W. Jearrad is known to have designed the following buildings:

HAMPTONS, WEST PECKHAM, KENT, for the Dalison family, exhibited at R.A. as 'now building' in 1813, but said by Greenwood, *Epitome of County History: Kent*, 1838, 140, to have been built in 1820; interior reconstructed after fire in 1883.

BADSWORTH RECTORY, YORKS. (W.R.), designs for alterations and additions, 1822 [Borthwick Institute, MGA 1822/2].

WELBECK ABBEY, NOTTS., alterations in the castellated style for the 4th Duke of Portland, *c.* 1826 [A. S. Turberville, *Welbeck Abbey and its Owners* ii, 1938, 392].

HEREFORD, ST. MARTIN'S CHURCH, 1845, Gothic [I.C.B.S.; *A.P.S.D.*, *s.v.* 'Hereford'].

BIRKENHEAD, CHRIST CHURCH, CLAUGHTON, 1844–9, Gothic [*A.P.S.D.*, *s.v.* 'Birkenhead'].

In 1835 R. W. Jearrad competed for the Houses of Parliament, but nothing is known about the character of his design. In 1815 C. Jearrad exhibited at the R.A. designs for alterations to a mansion in Poland for General Count Pack.

JEFFERY, THOMAS, is known only as the designer of a fantastic Gothic villa called BELMONT CASTLE at GRAYS THURROCK in ESSEX, which he designed for Zacharias Button in 1795; dem. *c.* 1945. Jeffery published two engravings of the house of which there are copies in B.M., *King's Maps* xiii, 20, a, b. One of these is reproduced in *Essex Homes* (Essex County Council, 1965), fig. 47.

JELFE, ANDREWS (–1759), master mason, was the son of William Jelfe of South Weald, Essex. His mother's maiden name was Andrews. He was made free of the London Masons' Company in 1711 by service with Edward Strong, to whom he had been apprenticed in 1704, and was subsequently in partnership with Edward Strong, junior, and Christopher Cass, until December 1728, when Strong withdrew [B.M., Stowe MS. 412, f. 98, no. 77]. His partnership with Cass continued until the latter's death in 1734. Jelfe was later in partnership with George Mercer, who succeeded Cass as Master Mason to the Board of Ordnance. He himself held a post in the Office of Works as Clerk of the Works at Newmarket from 1715 to 1718, and Clerk Itinerant from 1715 to 1728. In January 1719 he was appointed 'Architect and Clerk of the Works of all buildings erected or to be erected in the several garrisons, forts, castles, fortifications etc., belonging to the Office of Ordnance in Great Britain', and went up to Scotland to begin the erection of the barracks at Ruthven and Bernera as well as to continue those at Kiliwhimen and Inversnaid already begun by his predecessor James Smith. In the following year he was transferred to Plymouth, to supervise the construction of a new Gun Wharf or Ordnance Yard there [P.R.O., WO 47/32, ff. 21, 83, 105, 270, 47–33, ff. 16, 17, 36, 58, 158, 51/101, ff. 4, 41; 55/490]. Some of his drawings (for the Scottish fortifications) are in the National Library of Scotland (Z2/2, 2a, 10, 26a, etc.). While in Scotland he was made a burgess of Edinburgh [Edinburgh Town Council Minutes, vol. 48, p. 11].

In England Jelfe was chiefly employed as a mason-contractor. He had the masonry contracts for several of the 'Fifty New Churches' built in London under the Act of 1711, and his account and letter-book, now B.M., Add. MS. 27587, shows that he also executed monumental sculpture, chimneypieces, and other statuary work. His biggest contract was the building of WESTMINSTER BRIDGE to the designs of Charles Labelye. For this he was in partnership with Samuel Tufnell, the Master Mason to Westminster Abbey. The contracts were signed on 22 June 1738, and the bridge was completed in 1747. Jelfe successfully overcame the structural problems caused by the sinking of the central pier by springing relieving arches across the spandrels of the adjacent arches, an expedient apparently suggested to him by his friend William Stukeley, the antiquary. [Manning & Bray, *Surrey* ii, 308; Bodleian, Gough Maps 23, f. 57b, and MS. Top. Gen. b. 53, f. 90; B.M., Crace Coll., Portfolio v, No. 93.] Designs by Jelfe for a house (unexecuted) for Mr. Butler on Barn Hill, Stamford (1731), and for an ornamental alcove (1753), are preserved among Stukeley's collections in the Library of the Wiltshire Archaeological Society at Devizes, and in the Bodleian Library (MS. Top. Gen. d. 14, p. 59). While in Scotland in 1719, Jelfe made measured drawings of the Roman monument known as 'Arthur's O'on', which Stukeley afterwards had engraved (see Bodleian, Gough Maps 40, ff. 6ᵛ, 7ᵛ, and Stukeley's *Account of a Roman Temple and other Antiquities near Grahams-Dike in Scotland*, 1720). There is a portrait of Jelfe by Stukeley, dated January 1722/3, in Bodleian, MS. Eng. Misc. e. 136, f. 30. In 1744 he was fined for the office of sheriff of London and Middlesex [*Gent's Mag.* xiv, 333].

Jelfe's most important work as an architect was probably the COURT HOUSE or TOWN HALL at RYE in SUSSEX, which was built to his designs in 1743 [L. A. Vidler in *N. & Q.*, 177, 1939, 11, and Add. MS. 27587, f. 106ᵛ]. A contemporary model is preserved in the building, and there are measured drawings in *Arch. Rev.* lx, 1926, 76–7. It is a competently-designed building in what by 1743 was

the somewhat outmoded style of the early eighteenth century. Jelfe's letter-book shows that he rebuilt WARESLEY CHURCH, HUNTS., in 1728 (dem. 1856), and that in 1734 he carried out works at EXNING HOUSE, SUFFOLK, where he added a stone door-case for Francis Shepherd, and at ABINGTON, CAMBS., for Col. Vachell. In 1741 he built thirteen houses 'in Two Rows adjoyning together on the North side of New Palace Yard and on the South side of Bridge Street, Westminster', of which he afterwards purchased the freehold from the Westminster Bridge Commissioners. His yard and wharf were in New Palace Yard: their position is shown on a plan in the Crowle Pennant in the British Museum, ii, f. 100. In 1747 Jelfe bought for his own residence Pendrell House at Bletchingley, Surrey, where he formed the entrance courtyard and built the wall at the west end of the garden [U. Lambert, *Bletchingley* i, 1921, 316–17]. This property he left to his elder son, Captain Andrew Jelfe, R.N. He left his stone-built dwelling-house in New Palace Yard to his daughter Elizabeth, wife of Griffen Ransom, a timber merchant, together with his wharf and yard, then in occupation of his nephew William Jelfe (perhaps a son of Robert Jelfe, master carpenter), whom he had taken into partnership, and who died in 1771 (*London Magazine*, 1771, 472). He also left £10,000 to his daughter, and a similar sum to his younger son William, 'who has proved very idle and extravagant' [P.C.C., 173 ARRAN]. He desired to be buried at South Weald, where the 'surcophragus' which he had erected to the memory of his parents can still be seen on the south side of the tower. He died on 26 April 1759.

JELLY, THOMAS (–1781) was an architect and builder of Bath who made very competent designs in the Palladian manner and was probably responsible for many buildings in that town that have been ascribed to his better-known contemporary, John Wood. His best surviving buildings are KING EDWARD'S GRAMMAR SCHOOL, BROAD STREET, 1752–4, and the houses in ABBEY STREET, which he built in partnership with a mason called Henry Fisher on land leased from the Duke of Kingston in 1762 [B. M., Egerton MS. 3647, f. 113]. He also designed the adjoining KINGSTON BATHS, 1763–6, dem. *c.* 1885. He was for a time in partnership with John Palmer (*q.v.*), and to either Jelly or Palmer must be attributed the design of houses such as NORTH PARADE BUILDINGS and those in MILSON STREET, in whose erection Jelly is known to have been concerned. [W. Ison, *The Georgian Buildings of Bath*, 1948, 42, 54–5, 73–5, 100–1, 149, 151–3.] Jelly died on 19 May 1781 [*Bath Chronicle*, 23 May 1781].

JENKINS, EDWARD, practised for a time in Cheltenham, where he designed ST. JAMES'S

CHURCH, SUFFOLK SQUARE, 1825, Gothic. He got into difficulties with the enormous span of the roof, and J. B. Papworth had to be called in to help [Wyatt Papworth, *J. B. Papworth*, 1879, 74; David Verey, *Gloucestershire* ii, 1970, 128–9]. Jenkins's original designs are among Papworth's drawings in the R.I.B.A. Collection. Several of the plates in Griffith's *Description of Cheltenham* (1826) were from drawings by Jenkins, but it is not stated that he had designed any of the buildings illustrated. Pigot's *Directory* shows that by 1828 he had moved to Leamington in Warwickshire.

JENKINS, J—, exhibited architectural designs at the Royal Academy from 1788 to 1795, his address being 13 Hanover Street, Hanover Square. Joseph Salway (*q.v.*) was his pupil. An architect of this name from London entered a design in the competition for the Royal Exchange at Dublin in 1769 [*Builder* xxvii, 1869, 781].

JENKINS, JOHN, appears to have been the younger son of the Rev. William Jenkins (*q.v.*). He was admitted to the Royal Academy Schools in 1821 at the age of 23, and was awarded the Silver Medal in 1823. In company with his father's pupil William Hosking he travelled in the Mediterranean in 1823–5, and subsequently exhibited several drawings of temples at Rome, Pompeii, Paestum and Athens at the Academy. In 1827 he and Hosking were the joint authors of *A Selection of Architectural Ornaments, Greek, Roman and Italian*. At this period he was living with his father at 6, Red Lion Square.

In 1835–6 John Jenkins ('of 6 Red Lion Square, London') designed ST. GEORGE'S CHURCH, TREDEGAR, MONMOUTHSHIRE [*Monmouthshire Merlin*, 4 July 1835]. In 1841 he refronted the METHODIST CHAPEL in GREAT QUEEN STREET, LONDON, designed by his father in 1816–17 (dem. 1910), adding an Ionic portico [*Companion to the Almanac*, 1842, 213] (*Survey of London* v, pl. 32).

JENKINS, the Rev. WILLIAM (*c*. 1763–1844), is said to have received an architectural training before becoming a Wesleyan Methodist minister. After some twenty years as an itinerant preacher, he retired from the ministry in 1810 for reasons of health, and set up practice as an architect in Red Lion Square, London. He specialized in designing Methodist Chapels and has been described as 'the outstanding figure in Methodist building' during the early nineteenth century. His Carver Street Chapel in Sheffield (designed while he was still a minister) was regarded at the time as 'one of the best planned, most elegant and commodious places of worship in this country' and provided an effective formula for the architectural treatment of the broad many-windowed fronts characteristic of nonconformist chapels.

458

Jenkins died on 19 July 1844, aged 81, and was buried in Wesley's Chapel, Finsbury. William Jenkins, junior, and John Jenkins (*qq.v.*) appear to have been his sons, and William Hosking (*q.v.*), became his pupil in 1819 or 1820 [*Wesleyan Magazine*, 1844, 775; John Telford, *Wesley's Chapel and Wesley's House*, ?1906, 107–8; G. W. Dolbey, *The Architectural Expression of Methodism*, 1964].

SHEFFIELD, THE CARVER STREET METHODIST CHAPEL, 1804 [R. E. Leader, *Surveyors and Architects of the Past in Sheffield*, 1903].

LONDON, METHODIST CHAPEL, HINDE STREET, 1809–10; rebuilt 1886 [N. Curnock, *The Hinde Street Chapel*, 1910, 24].

ROCHESTER, KENT, METHODIST CHAPEL, 1810 [G. W. Dolbey, *op. cit.*, 161].

CANTERBURY, METHODIST CHAPEL, ST. PETER'S STREET, 1811 [J. Telford, *op. cit.*].

DARLINGTON, CO. DURHAM, METHODIST CHAPEL, BONDGATE, 1812 [W.H.D. Longstaffe, *History of Darlington*, 1854, 253].

EXETER, THE MINT METHODIST CHAPEL, FORE STREET, 1813; front rebuilt 1868 [guide to chapel].

HULL, YORKS. (E.R.), WALTHAM STREET METHODIST CHAPEL, 1814; dem. [*V.C.H. Yorks. E.R.* i, 326].

LEICESTER, METHODIST CHAPEL, BISHOP STREET, 1815 [*Proceedings of the Wesley Historical Soc.* xxv, 1945–6, 106–7].

BATH, SOMERSET, THE WALCOT METHODIST CHAPEL, 1815–16 [W. Ison, *The Georgian Buildings of Bath*, 1948, 80].

NORTHAMPTON, GOLD STREET METHODIST CHAPEL, 1816 [Chapel Account Book, 1816–1890, *ex inf.* Mr. V. A. Hatley].

LONDON, METHODIST CHAPEL, GREAT QUEEN STREET, LINCOLN'S INN FIELDS, 1816–17; refronted 1841; dem. 1910 [J. Telford, *op. cit.*] (*Survey of London* v, 86–8).

OXFORD, METHODIST CHAPEL, NEW INN HALL STREET, 1817–18; dem. *c.* 1970 [R. Lascelles, *The University and City of Oxford displayed*, 1821, 237].

LONDON, METHODIST CHAPELS in LAMBETH, KING'S CROSS, SLOANE TERRACE (1812) and SOUTHWARK [J. Telford, *op. cit.*; W. W. Pocock, *Memoir of W. F. Pocock*, 1883, 21].

JENKINS, WILLIAM WESLEY (–1864), appears to have been the elder son of the Rev. William Jenkins (*q.v.*). His exhibits at the Royal Academy (1822 and 1823) show that he was in Athens in 1820, and that his address (6, Red Lion Square) was the same as his father's. In 1823 he was one of the unsuccessful competitors for the new buildings at King's College, Cambridge [*Exhibitions of Designs for completing King's College, Cambridge*, 1823, in Soane Museum, P.C. 55]. He later practised from 20 Bartlett's Buildings, winning in 1853 the second prize in the competition for the Wesleyan College in Horseferry Road, Westminster, and in 1854 exhibiting at the R.A. his executed designs for altering and enlarging GELLY DÊG, CARMARTHENSHIRE, for Richard Jennings. He may have been the architect named Jenkins who designed a proprietary chapel and some houses at GRAVESEND, KENT, in the 1830s [*Gent's Mag.* 1836 (i), 654; W. E. Trotter, *Select Illustrated Topography of Thirty Miles Round London*, n.d., 158]. He died in Southend on 24 July 1864 [Principal Probate Registry: Calendar of Probates].

JENNER, JOHN (–1728), a bricklayer by trade, was active as a builder and surveyor in London in the 1720s. In 1723–5 the Earl of Tankerville had a new stable built at UPPARK, SUSSEX, according to 'a Plan or Model drawn by Mr. Jenner',[1] and in 1727 Jenner was concerned in some alterations to the Earl's London house in St. James's Square. As a speculative builder he was in 1726 engaged in building six new houses on the Grosvenor Estate in Mount Row, Mount Street [P.R.O., C105/21, Montigny *v.* Jenner].

JENNINGS, J—, of Hawkhurst, designed a poor Gothic church at SISSINGHURST, KENT, in 1837–8 [C. C. R. Pile, *Cranbrook*, 1955, 95–6].

JERMAN, or **JARMAN, EDWARD** (– 1668), belonged to a family who had been carpenters in the City of London since the reign of Queen Elizabeth. He was the elder son of Anthony Jerman (d. 1650), Master of the Carpenters' Company in 1633.[2] He held the office of City Carpenter until he resigned it in October 1657. He was also Surveyor to the Fishmongers' Company from April 1654 until his death in November 1668.

Sir Robert Pratt described Jerman as 'an experienced man in buildings', and after the Great Fire of 1666 he was one of the three surveyors appointed on behalf of the Corporation to control the rebuilding of the City in conjunction with Wren, May and Pratt, the other two being Robert Hooke and Peter Mills. He declined, however, to undertake the detailed survey of the devastated area required by the Rebuilding Act, which was

carried out mainly by Mills and Hooke. Together with the two latter he was also directed by the Committee for Gresham Affairs to report on the rebuilding of the Royal Exchange, and on 25 April 1667, 'the committee being very sensible of the greate burthen of businesse lying upon him [Mills] for the city att this time; and considering that Mr. Jerman is the most able known artist (besides him) that the city now hath; therefore the committee unanimously made choice of Mr. Jerman to assist the committee in the agreeing for, ordering, and directing of that worke; and haveing declared the same unto him, hee, after much reluctancy and unwillingness (objecting, it might bee thought an intrenchment upon Mr. Mills his right), at length accepted, being assured first, by the lord mayor and the committee, that itt was no intrenchment, and that this wholle committee, at all times, would acquit him from any scandall in that behalfe'. On 9 December, the committee, 'considering that Mr. Jerman hath not yet received any gratification for his paines about drawing drafts and directing the building', ordered £50 to be paid to him on account. The last mention of Jerman occurs on 22 October 1668, and it is clear that he died soon afterwards. The appointment of a surveyor to take his place was considered, but Thomas Cartwright, the contracting mason, 'declared himself master of the wholle designe intended for that buildinge' and no appointment was made. The committee afterwards found it necessary to consult Hooke and Wren in view of 'the greatnesse of the charge given in by the workmen since Mr. *Jerman's* death, for exceeding the estimate by him', but it was substantially in accordance with Jerman's designs that the Royal Exchange was completed in 1671. The bricklayer's work was performed by John Tanner, the City Bricklayer, and the master carpenter was Edward's younger brother Roger Jerman, who held the office of City Carpenter from 1662 until his death on 24 October 1678. What were reputed to be Jerman's original drawings on vellum were in 1846 in the possession of R. W. Jupp, Clerk to the Carpenters' Company [W. Tite, 'The Old 'Changes of London', *Builder* iv, 1846, 2].

After the Great Fire Jerman was employed to make designs for rebuilding several of the City Companies' Halls, though he did not live to see most of them completed. In 1667 he provided the 'draughts' for the new Weavers' Hall, and in January 1668 the Court instructed Mr. Lewis, the master carpenter, so 'see Mr. Jerman's directions performed by all the workmen concerned'. There is similar evidence that Jerman designed new halls for the Drapers', Fishmongers', Mercers' and Wax Chandlers' Companies, and supervised the repair of the Barber-Surgeons' and Goldsmiths' Halls, which had not been totally destroyed. His plans for the Mercers' Hall were carried out after

[1] This was presumably one of the two outbuildings shown in the view of Uppark by Pieter Tillemans (d. 1734), which do not correspond with the ones seen in Kip's view published in 1714. The existing stables date from *c.* 1750.

[2] In 1634 Anthony Jerman was one of those who offered designs for the Goldsmiths' Hall [J. Newman in *Architectural History* xiv, 1971, 31], and in 1638 he and a Mr. Holmes were paid £1 by the churchwardens of St. Michael le Querne for making a 'modell' of their church, then about to be rebuilt with advice from Inigo Jones [Guildhall Library, MS. 2895/2].

his death under the superintendence of John Oliver. In the case of the Apothecaries' Hall, the accounts show that Jerman was consulted in 1667–8, but that the surveyor responsible was a Mr. Lock (*q.v.*). Jerman may also have designed the new Vintners' Hall, for which his brother Roger was master carpenter, but documentary evidence is lacking.

Jerman was essentially a City artisan who appears to have done little work outside London, though in 1666–8 there are payments to him in the Works accounts for surveying Windsor Castle (P.R.O., E 351/3280–1). The Royal Exchange was no doubt his most important work. It was elaborately detailed in the manner characteristic of the City artizans, and its tower formed a picturesque feature rising somewhat awkwardly from a triumphal arch. It was a handsome enough building, but one whose architectural treatment looked back to the reign of Charles I and hardly reflected the new influences soon to be seen in the works of Pratt, Hooke and Wren. What remains of Jerman's City Halls is regrettably small, but enough is recorded to show that their interiors were lavishly decorated with the finest carpentry and joinery of their day.

[*A.P.S.D.*; T. F. Reddaway, *The Rebuilding of London after the Great Fire*, 1940, 55, 59, 108 n., 268–9; S. Perks, *The History of the Mansion House*, 1922, 148; *The Architecture of Sir R. Pratt*, ed. R. T. Gunther, 1928, 12; *Wren Soc.* xx, 112; E. B. Chancellor, *Lives of the British Architects*, 1909, 109–13; E. B. Jupp, *A History of the Carpenters' Company*, 1848; Malcolm Pinhorn, 'The Jerman Family', *Blackmansbury* i, nos. 5–6, 1965, 3–9.]

LONDON

THE ROYAL EXCHANGE, 1667–71; destroyed by fire Jan. 1838 [*A.P.S.D.*, *s.v.* 'Jerman'] (engraving published by the mason Cartwright in 1671, of which there is a copy in B.M. *King's Maps* xxiv, 11a 1; *Vitruvius Britannicus* ii, 1717, pls. 23–5; Britton & Pugin, *The Public Buildings of London* i, 1825, 287–97).

BARBER–SURGEONS' HALL, MONKWELL STREET, repairs after Great Fire; rebuilt 1863–4 [*ex inf.* Mr. Beck].

DRAPERS' HALL, THROGMORTON STREET, rebuilt to Jerman's designs by T. Cartwright 1668–71; street front rebuilt 1778; rebuilt 1868–9 [A. H. Johnson, *History of the Drapers' Company* iii, 1922, 286].

FISHMONGERS' HALL, LONDON BRIDGE, rebuilt 1667–72; rebuilt 1831–3 [Priscilla Metcalf, *The Halls of the Fishmongers' Company*, forthcoming].

GOLDSMITHS' HALL, FOSTER LANE, repairs after Great Fire; rebuilt 1829–35 [J. Newman,

'Nicholas Stone's Goldsmiths' Hall', *Architectural History* xiv, 1971, 34].

MERCERS' HALL and CHAPEL, CHEAPSIDE, rebuilt to Jerman's designs by John Oliver, *c.* 1668–72; front to Cheapside rebuilt 1873; destroyed by bombing 1941 [Philip Norman in *Builder*, 31 March 1916, 252; A. F. Rayden, *Mercers' Hall*, 1947, 10] (plan in R.C.H.M. *London: The City*, 69).

WAX CHANDLERS' HALL, MAIDEN LANE, rebuilt 1668–70; rebuilt 1792–3 and again 1852–5; destroyed by bombing 1940 [J. Dummelow, *The Wax Chandlers of London*, 1973, 85].

WEAVERS' HALL, BASINGHALL STREET, rebuilt 1667–9; dem. 1856 [A. Plummer, *The London Weavers' Company 1600–1970*, 1972, 202].

JERNEGAN, or **JERNINGHAM**, GEORGE (*c.* 1760–1815), of London, was elected a member of the Surveyors' Club in 1805. He died on 13 December 1815, aged 55 [*Gent's Mag.* 1815 (ii), 643]. In 1793 he exhibited a drawing of 'Buildings erecting in Grosvenor Place' at the Royal Academy.

JERNEGAN, WILLIAM (*c.* 1751–1836), was for many years the principal architect practising in Swansea. He was a native of the Channel Islands, but had settled in Swansea by the 1780s, and died there in 1836. He is said to have designed 'many public buildings, churches and houses in Swansea and district', including a house called MARINO, built (1783) on an octagonal plan, which was later incorporated in the Vivians' mansion at SINGLETON (now the University College of Wales), and WOODLAND HOUSE, later, as CLYNE CASTLE, the seat of W. G. Vivian. Other buildings known to have been designed by Jerneghan were THE COUNTESS OF HUNTINGDON'S CHAPEL at SWANSEA, 1789 [Countess of Huntingdon's papers, *ex inf.* Mr. Alan Harding]; STEETLY HALL, GLAMORGANSHIRE, for Ralph Sheldon [letter from Sheldon to Matthew Boulton, 26 Oct. 1800, in Birmingham Assay Office, *ex inf.* Mr. John Cornforth]; the MUMBLES LIGHTHOUSE, 1793 [W. H. Jones, *History of the Port of Swansea*, Carmarthen 1922]; CARDIFF GAOL, 1795–6 [Glamorgan County Record Office, Q.G.P.1]; SKETTY PARK, GLAMORGANSHIRE, for Sir John Morris, Bart., *c.* 1820, dem. 1975 [*The New Swansea Guide*, 1823]; and the enlargement of ST. JOHN'S CHURCH, SWANSEA, in 1824 [I.C.B.S.]. He died at his house in Adelaide Place on 12 January 1836, in his 86th year [*Cambrian*, 16 Jan. 1836]. According to Ralph Sheldon he was 'an architect of much merit and taste'. His unexecuted design for a Town Hall at Swansea, made in 1825, is illustrated in *Plans and Prospects: Architecture in Wales 1780–1914* (Welsh Arts Council Exhibition 1975), no. 35.

JERNINGHAM, EDWARD (1774–1822), was the youngest son of Sir William Jerningham of Cossey (or Costessey) Hall, Norfolk. He was a barrister by profession and acted as Secretary to the General Board of British Catholics. For his brother Sir George Jerningham he designed an elaborate Perpendicular Gothic Catholic chapel (dem.) at COSSEY HALL in about 1810. He also Gothicised the CATHOLIC CHAPEL at STAF-FORD, and in 1810–15 began to rebuild STAFFORD CASTLE, which was on his brother's property. This project was never completed, but Jern-ingham created a picturesque castellated land-mark, recently demolished but illustrated in Cal-vert & West's *Picturesque Views in Staffordshire and Shropshire* (1830) and Mark Hughes, *The Story of Staffordshire* (1924). His interest in architecture may have been hereditary, for at Swynnerton Hall there is a portrait of his father holding an architectural plan, with a Gothic land-scape tower in the background.

[*Gent's Mag.* 1822 (i), 564–5; J. P. Neale's *Views of Seats*, 2nd ser., i, 1824; J. Gillow's *Dic-tionary of English Catholics*, iii, 1887, 627–8; J. Gillow, *St. Thomas's Priory, Stafford*, n.d., 105–7; B.M., Add. MS. 36387, ff. 200–1.]

JERSEY, THOMAS (–1751), is an obscure figure of whom all that is at present known is that he subscribed to West and Toms' *Views of the Ancient Churches in the Cities of London and West-minster*, published in 1739, acted as Clerk of Works for the building of the Radcliffe Library in Oxford from 1737 to 1745, and was the 'man of genius' under whom James Paine 'began the study of architecture'. The date of his death is given in *D.N.B., s.v.* 'Paine'.

JOHNS, JAMES WOOD (*c.* 1810–), was admitted to the Royal Academy Schools in 1833 and exhibited a 'Design for a botanical institu-tion' at the Academy in 1835. In 1836–7 he designed a proprietary school at HULL called HULL COLLEGE (dem.). It was near Spring Bank and had an octastyle Corinthian portico [*Hull Advertiser*, 9 Sept. 1836, *ex inf.* Mr. A. G. Chamberlain].

In 1841 Johns was engaged by the London Society for promoting Christianity among the Jews to go out to Jerusalem to design and build an Anglican Cathedral there. After work had been in progress for some months he got at cross-purposes with the committee and was dismissed in the winter of 1842–3. His place was taken by Matthew Habershon (*q.v.*), who carried the building forward to designs that, although modi-fied in detail, appear to have been substantially those originally made by Johns. In 1844 Johns published a folio volume entitled *The Anglican Cathedral Church of St. James, Jerusalem*, in which he described the erection of the building,

but made no reference to his dismissal. [Bodleian Library, minutes of the London Society for pro-moting Christianity among the Jews.]

JOHNSON, JAMES (–1807), held the post of architect to the Barrack Department of the War Office until 1805, when he retired owing to ill-health, dying two years later, in June 1807 [*Gent's Mag.* 1807 (ii), 684]. A design for a bar-racks to accommodate 2500 men and their officers, signed 'J. Johnson Archt. Rd. Elsam delt. June 1795', is in the British Museum (*King's Maps* xxvi, 7 tt, uu). The CAVALRY BARRACKS in FULFORD ROAD, YORK, built to the designs of Johnson and his fellow surveyor James Sanders (*q.v.*) are de-scribed and illustrated in R.C.H.M. *York* iv, 46. In 1794 he became surveyor to the Mint, and shortly before his death he designed the new ROYAL MINT on TOWER HILL, LONDON. His origi-nal designs are in the R.I.B.A. Collection. The Mint was built under the direction of his suc-cessor Robert Smirke between 1807 and 1812 and was enlarged in 1881–2 [*History of the King's Works* vi, 452–60].

JOHNSON, JOEL (*c.* 1721–1799), was probably a son of the builder of the same name who took several building leases on the Harley estate in Marylebone in 1719–21 [B.M., Add. MS. 18240, ff. 7–8]. He is said in his obituary notice in *Gent's Mag.* lxix (i), 1799, 358, to have designed the church of ST. JOHN, WAPPING, 1756, destroyed, except for the tower, in 1940–1: the MAGDALEN HOSPITAL, ST. GEORGE'S FIELDS, 1769, dem. 1869; the LONDON HOSPITAL, WHITECHAPEL ROAD, 1752–9; the 'Asylum',[1] and many chapels and other edifices. Johnson was named as 'architect' in the inscription on the foundation-stone of the Mag-dalen Gospital, given by D. Hughson, *London* iv, 1807, 509. He was, however, only the carpenter employed at the London Hospital under B. Mainwaring, and it may be noted that the latter was among the surveyors who gave evidence before the House of Commons on 9 March 1756, in connection with the rebuilding of St. John's Wapping. In 1774 Johnson made plans for a gallery to be built in the south aisle of WAL-THAMSTOW PARISH CHURCH, ESSEX. He was a public-spirited man who was 'always usefully or innocently employed', and took 'indefatigable pains' in establishing and regulating the Wal-thamstow House of Industry. He was a Warden of the Carpenters' Company in 1780, 1787 and 1788, and Master in 1789. He died at Dedham Place, Essex, on 17 April 1799, at the age of 78 [*A.P.S.D.*; S. J. Barnes, *Walthamstow Vestry Minutes, etc.*, Walthamstow Antiquarian Society, 1925–7, 58].

[1] Presumably the Asylum founded in 1787 as an adjunct to the Lock Hospital in Grosvenor Place, Lon-don (dem. 1842).

JOHNSON, JOHN, may have been an architect of importance in the north of England in the early seventeenth century. In 1620 or 1621 John Johnson, 'surveyor', was at the head of a body of workmen who reported on the state of the CASTLE at NEWCASTLE-UPON-TYNE [P.R.O., E 178/4366]. In 1622 John Johnson of Little Langton, Yorkshire (N.R.), contracted to enlarge DILSTON HALL, NORTHUMBERLAND, for Sir Francis Radcliffe. The house was rebuilt in 1710–14 and demolished in 1765, but Johnson's very competently drawn plan survives and is illustrated in *History of Northumberland* x, 289–91. In the Yorkshire Archaeological Society's library at Leeds there is an elevation of a Jacobean doorway (MD 59/21) with an annotation 'this must be altered according to this line per me Johnson'.

JOHNSON, JOHN (1732–1814), was born in Southgate Street, Leicester, on 22 April 1732. Little is known of his early life. His father, John Johnson, was apparently a joiner by trade, and he himself was probably brought up as a carpenter. At the time of his death it was stated that he 'left Leicester in early life, possessing little more than strong natural abilities, which soon found their way in the metropolis'. He was established in London by 1759. In the late 1760s he was engaged in speculative building on the Berners estate in Marylebone, and by 1767 had himself taken up residence in one of the houses he had built in Berners Street. He exhibited once (1773) at the Royal Academy, and fairly regularly at the Society of Artists between 1775 and 1783. In 1782 he succeeded William Hillyer as Surveyor to the County of Essex, and it was in this capacity that he designed his most important work, the Shire Hall at Chelmsford, on whose completion he was presented with a piece of plate worth 100 guineas, 'as a public testimony of his integrity and professional abilities'. When in 1812 he retired from the county surveyorship at the age of 80, he received the formal thanks of the Justices 'for his long, active, faithful and meritorious services to this county during the space of more than thirty years'.

Johnson's private practice was considerable. He designed more than twenty country houses, chiefly in Essex and the Midlands, but including some as far afield as Devon and Glamorgan. He also built several town houses for aristocratic clients, and prepared an abortive scheme for a new square in Leicester. In 1777 he attempted to patent a stucco composition similar to the one purveyed by the brothers Adam. The Adams went to law in defence of their composition and obtained a favourable judgement in the Court of King's Bench from Lord Chief Justice Mansfield. Mansfield, as a fellow-countryman and friend of the plaintiffs, was open to the charge of partiality (see *Observations on Two Trials at*

Law respecting Messieurs Adams's new-invented Patent-Stucco and a *Reply* thereto, both published in 1778). In 1779 Johnson obtained another patent for 'a particular manner of securing buildings from damage by fire'. Johnson was also involved in banking. He was a partner with Sir Herbert Mackworth in a bank established in Bond Street by 1785. For a time Johnson prospered on the profits of his architectural and financial activities. In 1790 he assigned a considerable amount of leasehold property in various parts of London to his eldest son John, and in 1792–5 he was able to build and endow a small charitable foundation in Leicester for the benefit of his poor relations. This family almshouse, which he called the 'Consanguinitarium', contained five small dwellings, and was endowed with £70 a year from an estate in Lubbenham together with the rents of four adjacent houses built by Johnson. But the bank ended in bankruptcy in 1803 and towards the end of his life Johnson was in such financial straits that in 1813 the magistrates and gentlemen of the county of Essex got up a subscription to pay him an annuity for the rest of his life.

After the bankruptcy Johnson moved from Berners Street to Camden Town, but in 1812 he retired to his native town. He died in Leicester on 17 August 1814, and was buried in St. Martin's Church, where there is an inscription to his memory on the base of the monument (executed by Bacon) which he had erected to his parents (Nichols, *Leicestershire* i, pl. xliv). A miniature was formerly preserved in the County Rooms and a portrait was in 1974 in the possession of Mrs. Brooke-Johnson of Richmond, Surrey. His eldest son John Johnson, junior, was also a surveyor, but appears to have designed nothing of importance, and died the year before his father, on 26 February 1813, in his fifty-second year: there is a tablet to his memory in Finchley Church. His second son Charles (d. 1841) entered the Church and became a Canon of Wells. His third son, Dr. Joseph Johnson, died in 1802 in his thirty-second year.

Johnson was an able designer in a late Georgian manner somewhat akin to that of the Wyatts. Although not marked by much individuality, his work is always elegant and he was an accomplished designer of staircases. The basic authority for his architectural works is a list given in Nichols's *History of Leicestershire*. There is evidence that Nichols and Johnson were acquainted, so the list was probably based on information supplied to the historian by the architect himself.

[J. Nichols, *History of Leicestershire* i, 1815, 528; *Gent's Mag.* 1793 (ii), 1046; 1813 (i), 387; 1814 (ii), 296; *A.P.S.D.*; J. Simmons, 'Notes on a Leicester Architect; John Johnson', *Trans. Leicestershire Archl. Soc.* xxv, 1949, reprinted with alterations in *Parish and Empire*, 1952, 128–45; J. D. Bennett, *Leicestershire Architects 1700–1850*, Leicester Museums 1968; F. G. Hilton Price, *Handbook of London Bankers*, 2nd ed. 1890–1, 54; *London Gazette*, 1803, 535, 1697; 1811, 1122, 1538 (for bankruptcy); will, P.C.C., 204 WYNNE; information from Miss Nancy Briggs and Mr. Peter Robb.]

PUBLIC BUILDINGS, ETC.

NEWMARKET, SUFFOLK, THE NEW ROOMS (now Jockey Club), HIGH STREET, 1771–2; refronted 1933 [Nichols] (*C. Life*, 1 Oct. 1932).

HALSTEAD, ESSEX, completed HOUSE OF CORRECTION designed by W. Hillyer, *c.* 1782; dem. [Simmons, 146].

CHELMSFORD, ESSEX, COUNTY GAOL, alterations and additions, 1782–94; dem. [Simmons, 146].

WIMBLEDON CHURCH, SURREY, rebuilt 1787–8; rebuilt 1843 [Nichols; W. A. Bartlett, *History of Wimbledon*, 1865, 72] (*Ecclesiastical Topography: A Collection of One Hundred Views of Churches in the Environs of London*, 1811).

CHELMSFORD, ESSEX, conduit in Tindal Square with Coade stone naiad, 1787–91; dem. 1814 (naiad now in Chelmsford Museum) [Essex Record Office, Mildmay Charity Trustees' Accounts D/P 94/25/24] (*Essex Countryside* xii, Oct. 1964, 604–6).

CHELMSFORD, ESSEX, THE SHIRE HALL, 1789–91 [J. Johnson, *Plans, Sections and Perspective Elevations of the Essex County Hall at Chelmsford*, 1808; see *Builder* xiv, 1856, 133, 151 for the fall of the stairs in 1856].

BARKING, ESSEX, HOUSE OF CORRECTION, 1791–2; dem. *c.* 1835 [*V.C.H. Essex* v, 243–4].

LEICESTER, THE CONSANGUINITARIUM, SOUTHGATE STREET, with four adjacent houses (dem. *c.* 1965), forming part of the endowment, 1792–3; dem. 1878, when a new building was erected at 11–19 Earl Howe Street [Nichols; *Gent's Mag.* 1793 (ii), 1046] (Nichols i (2), pl. xxxv and *Gent's Mag.* 1820 (i), 17).

LEICESTER, THE COUNTY ROOMS, HOTEL STREET, 1792–1800; designed as a Hotel and later used as Judges' Lodgings [Nichols] (Simmons, pls. 5–6).

LEICESTER, THE BOROUGH GAOL, HIGHCROSS STREET, 1792–3; dem. 1837 [Nichols] (J. D. Bennett, *Leicestershire Architects 1700–1850*, 1968, pl. 18).

CHELMSFORD, ESSEX, GRAMMAR SCHOOL HOUSE, alterations 1797–9; dem. [Essex Record Office, D/DBe 04; DQ 12/3].

FELSTED, ESSEX, NEW SCHOOL HOUSE (now IN-GRAMS), 1799–1802 [M. Craze, *A History of Felsted School*, Ipswich 1955, 124–6].

LEICESTER, THE THEATRE, opened 1800; dem. 1836 [Simmons, 157].

CHELMSFORD, ST. MARY'S CHURCH (now CATH-EDRAL), rebuilt nave 1801–3, Gothic; since considerably enlarged [J. F. Williams, 'The Rebuilding of Chelmsford Church 1800–3', *Essex Review*, July 1931].

CHELMSFORD, ESSEX, HOUSE OF CORRECTION, 1802–7; dem. [Simmons, 146].

THAXTED CHURCH, ESSEX, repairs to spire, 1807 [Essex County Record Office, MS. Vestry Minutes D/P 16/5].

GREAT HALLINGBURY CHURCH, ESSEX, repairs for J. A. Houblon, 1807 [accounts at Welford Park, Berks.].

LEWES, SUSSEX, THE COUNTY HALL, 1808–12 [R. F. Dell, 'The Building of the County Hall, Lewes', *Sussex Arch. Colls.* c, 1962].

COUNTRY HOUSES

NEWMARKET, SUFFOLK, stables for Lord March, *c.* 1770 [Essex Record Office, T/B 181/1/2].

TERLING PLACE, ESSEX, for John Strutt, *c.* 1772–8; wings etc. added 1818–21 [Nichols; exhib. 1778] (*Excursions in the County of Essex*, i, 1818, 42).

SADBOROW HOUSE, THORNCOMBE, DORSET, for John Bragge, 1773–5; west wing added 1843 [Nichols; accounts in Dorset County Museum] (*R.C.H.M. Dorset, West*, 246–7, pls. 75, 120).

KINGSTHORPE HALL, NORTHANTS., for James Fremeaux, 1774–5 [Nichols; accounts in County Record Office] (J. A. Gotch, *Squires' Homes of Northamptonshire*, 1939, pls. 84–6).

PITSFORD HALL, NORTHANTS., for Col. James Money, *c.* 1775; altered 1910 [Nichols].

CLASMONT, nr. MORRISTON, GLAMORGANSHIRE, for (Sir) John Morris, *c.* 1775; dem. *c.* 1820 [Nichols].

HOLCOMBE HOUSE (now St. Mary's Abbey), MILL HILL, MIDDLESEX, for Sir John Anderson, Bart., *c.* 1775–8 [Nichols; exhib. 1778].

WOOLVERSTONE HALL, SUFFOLK (now School), for William Berners, 1776 [Nichols; exhib. 1777].

GNOLL CASTLE, nr. NEATH, GLAMORGANSHIRE, for Sir Herbert Mackworth, Bart., *c.* 1776–8, castellated; dem. 1956 [Nichols; exhib. 1778] (Neale's *Views of Seats* i, 1818).

HALSWELL PARK, SOMERSET, THE TEMPLE OF PAN, for Sir Charles Kemeys Tynte, Bart., *c.* 1777; dem. [exhib. 1778].

CARLTON HALL, EAST CARLTON, NORTHANTS., for Sir John Palmer, Bart., 1777–81; enlarged 1823, rebuilt 1870 [Nichols; exhib. 1778] (Neale's *Views of Seats* vi, 1823).

KILLERTON PARK, DEVON, for Sir Thomas Acland, Bart., 1778–9; since rebuilt [Nichols] (J. Britton & E. W. Brayley, *Devonshire Illustrated*, 1829, 34–5).

BRADWELL LODGE, BRADWELL-ON-SEA, ESSEX, for the Rev. (Sir) Henry Bate-Dudley, 1781–6 [Nichols] (*C. Life*, 7 July 1966).

463

LANGFORD GROVE, LANGFORD, ESSEX, for N. West-combe, 1782; dem. 1952 [Nichols].

BENHALL LODGE, SUFFOLK, for Sir William Beau-maris Rush, c. 1785; rebuilt c. 1810 [Nichols].

HATFIELD PLACE, HATFIELD PEVEREL, ESSEX, for Col. John Tyrell, 1792–4 [Nichols; accounts in Essex Record Office, D/DKe F4].

ST. LEONARD'S LODGE, LOWER BEEDING, SUSSEX, for Charles G. Beauclerk, c. 1801; dem. c. 1860 [Nichols].

WHATTON HALL or HOUSE, LONG WHATTON, LEICS., for Edward Dawson, c. 1802; restored after fire in 1876 [Nichols; Neale's *Views of Seats*, 2nd ser., iii, 1826].

BOREHAM HOUSE, ESSEX, alterations for Sir John Tyrell, Bart., 1802–3 [Essex Record Office, D/DKe. A3] (*C. Life*, 11 July 1914).

BRAXTED PARK, GREAT BRAXTED, ESSEX, north front and staircase for Peter Du Cane, 1804–6 [Nancy Briggs in *Essex Journal* v, June 1970, 100].

HALLINGBURY PLACE, ESSEX, repairs for J. A. Hou-blon, 1807; dem. 1924 [accounts at Welford Park, Berks] (*C. Life*, 19 Sept. 1914).

BROOMFIELD LODGE, BROOMFIELD, ESSEX, for John Judd, c. 1808 [Nichols; *The Chelmsford Guide*, n.d., 17].

THE LAWN, STROUD GREEN, ROCHFORD, ESSEX, enlarged for Major G. D. Carr, after 1798 [Nichols].

FOREST HALL, WILLINGALE DOE, ESSEX, for the Rev. John Bramston-Stane, c. 1805; dem. 1957 [Nichols] (J. A. Rush, *Seats in Essex*, 1897, 85–6).

TORRILE'S HALL, WILLINGDALE DOE, ESSEX, new front block for John Crabb [Nichols].

LONDON HOUSES

NEW CAVENDISH STREET, NO 63 (formerly No. 7) for Sir Charles Bampfylde, Bart. (afterwards occupied by the 3rd Earl of Hardwicke), 1776–7 [Nichols; exhib. 1775 and 1778; D. Stroud in *Report of the Institute of Psycho-Analysis*, 1953, 69–72] (*C. Life*, 13–20 Oct. 1917).

NEW CAVENDISH STREET, NO. 61 for William Udny, 1776–7 [Nichols; exhib. 1775] (*C. Life*, 20 Oct. 1917; M. Jourdain, *English Interiors in Smaller Houses* 1923, figs. 65–73).

CHARLES STREET, ST. JAMES'S SQUARE, house (No. 19) for the 7th Earl of Galloway, 1775–6; dem. 1912 [Nichols; exhib. 1778].

PORTMAN SQUARE, house (No. 9) for the Hon. Charles Greville, c. 1778; dem. [Nichols].

PORTMAN SQUARE, house (No. 10) for the Hon. Henry Willoughby (afterwards 5th Lord Middleton), probably c. 1775; dem. [Nichols].

PALL MALL, reconstructed house for Sir Hugh Palliser, Bart., c. 1779; dem. 1866 [Nichols].

HARLEY STREET, house (originally No. 27, ulti-mately No. 68) for the Rev. Sir John Hotham, Bart., Bishop of Ossory; dem. [Nichols].

HARLEY STREET, house (originally No. 43, now No. 63) for John Pybus, before 1780; dem. [Nichols].

BRIDGES

In his capacity as County Surveyor of Essex Johnson built a number of bridges in that county. Most of them were small structures of no great architectural pretension, but the Moulsham Bridge at Chelmsford is elegantly designed. The following list of the principal bridges built or rebuilt by Johnson is based on the Quarter Sessions Records in the Essex Record Office: AKINGFORD (timber), 1806, dem. 1913; BATTLE BRIDGE (R. Crouch), 1795–6; BAYTHORN (BIRD-BROOK), 1795–6; CHELMSFORD, MOULSHAM BRIDGE (R. Can), 1787; DEDHAM, c. 1787, destroyed by a flood 1795 and rebuilt by Johnson 1796, dem. 1876; HIGH ONGAR, 1787, rebuilt 1913; LOUGH-TON, 1781; MORETON, 1783; PASSINGFORD, 1785, dem. c. 1966–9; SUTTON FORD, nr. ROCHFORD, 1784, dem.; WEALD BRIDGE, NORTH WEALD BAS-SETT, 1785; WIDFORD, 1803.

ATTRIBUTED AND UNEXECUTED WORKS

1. The 'Dining-Parlour for a nobleman in Rut-land', for which Johnson exhibited a capital at the Society of Artists in 1778, may have been the one at BURLEY-ON-THE-HILL, RUT-LAND, designed for the 8th Earl of Winchilsea about this time (*C. Life*, 17 Feb. 1923, fig. 7).

2. EAST HADDON HALL, NORTHANTS., for Henry Sawbridge, 1780–3, may with great probability be attributed to Johnson on stylistic grounds: see Sir Gyles Isham in *Reports and Papers of the Northants. Antiquarian Soc.* lxiv (1962–3), 37.

3. WIMBLEDON HOUSE, SURREY, was inherited in 1783 by Sir William Beaumaris Rush (1750–1833), who 'much enlarged and improved' the house. The façade was very similar to that of the Shire Hall at Chelmsford, and as Rush employed Johnson to design Benhall Lodge, Suffolk, for him at about the same time, the enlargement of Wimbledon House (dem.) can confidently be attributed to him. (G. F. Prosser, *Select Illustrations of Surrey*, 1828).

4. The following unexecuted designs may be noted: drawings for enlarging MAMHEAD, DEVONSHIRE [Victoria and Albert Museum 2187–2194: 1896]; a 'Design of Embellish-ment' to the front of THORPE HALL, THORPE-LE-SOKEN, ESSEX, 1782 [Essex Record Office, D/DHf T92/76]; a project for a 'BRUNSWICK SQUARE' in LEICESTER, 1792 [Simmons, 157].

JOHNSON, THOMAS (–1800), was an architect and builder of Warwick. In 1779–80 the church of ST. NICHOLAS, WARWICK, was rebuilt in accordance with his designs. In May 1778, it was 'agreed and finally determin'd to adopt Mr. Thomas Johnson's Plan Estimate and Model for the Rebuilding of the said Church'. His wooden model, which still exists, had previously been sent up to London in a box 'to be inspected by Mr. [John?] Johnson the Architect there'. A copy of the plan and elevation, signed 'J. L. Johnson Delin., T. Johnson Archt.' and dated 'Warwick 1779', is among the Faculty Petitions in the County Record Office (DRO 92). Johnson was the contractor as well as the architect, and the statement in Field's *History of Warwick*, 1815, p. 131, that the church was 'built under the direction of Job Collins' appears to be incorrect. The church is in the Gothic style, the present chancel being an addition of 1869. The parish records, upon which the above is based, are also in the Record Office.

At the same time, Johnson was being employed by the Justices of Warwick to design and build the COUNTY GAOL on a site immediately to the north of the Shire Hall. He made two models, now preserved in the County Museum, one showing how the octagonal chapel could be arranged in such a way 'that the Prisoners shall not see each other yet see and hear distinctly the Minister', the other of the proposed Doric façade to Sheep (now Northgate) Street. The contracts were signed in 1779, and the buildings were completed in 1782. It was found, however, that in several respects Johnson had failed to comply with the terms of his contract. In particular, the columns of the façade had not been fluted 'as was intended',[1] and the brick partitions in the interior had not been carried up to the height of the roof 'by way of security'. As regards the fluting, Johnson claimed that it had been omitted at the desire of the Justices themselves. But the other shortcomings were less easy to justify, and he was eventually obliged to make good such of the deficiencies as could be remedied, and to allow for the remainder in his account [Warwick County Records, Class 24 (671)]. The Gaol was extended on its north side in 1789 by Henry Couchman, the County Surveyor, and reconstructed as the County Council Officers in 1929–30. Johnson's façade, however, remains substantially as he left it. It is remarkable as one of the earliest attempts to adapt Greek Doric to the purposes of an English public building.

After this somewhat discreditable episode in his career, Johnson removed to Worcester, where he continued to practise as an architect until his death. In 1786 he refitted the interior of KIDDERMINSTER CHURCH in accordance with designs made by James Rose (*q.v.*), and on 6 April of that year *Berrow's Worcester Jnl.* Published an advertisement inviting tenders for supplying timber for the purpose, in accordance with a bill of scant-

lings to be seen on application to 'Mr. Johnson, Architect, at his house in Worcester'. A postscript notifies the reader that 'All kinds of business in the building line' are 'planned, surveyed, or undertaken by the public's much obliged and very humble servant Thomas Johnson'. In 1789–92 Johnson re-roofed the nave and rebuilt the east and west windows of WORCESTER CATHEDRAL, himself making designs for the painted glass borders of the west window; both windows have been altered in the course of subsequent restorations. Johnson's drawings for a new gallery for the church of ST. NICHOLAS, WORCESTER, dated 1790, are preserved among the parish records, and those for SHELSLEY BEAUCHAMP RECTORY, signed and dated 1791, are among the Faculty papers in the Worcester Diocesan Records.

In 1792–5 HANBURY CHURCH, WORCS., was largely rebuilt to Johnson's designs. The Gothic tower is virtually a reproduction of the one which he had built at St. Nicholas, Warwick, in 1779–80 [*V.C.H. Worcs.* iii, 378; Society of Antiquaries, Prattinton Collections, xvii, f. 122]. In 1795 he made plans and elevations for a church at ETTINGTON in WARWICKS. for Evelyn Shirley, apparently that built *c.* 1800, but demolished, except for the tower, in 1902. These drawings are in the Record Office at Warwick. Johnson also designed the PRESBYTERIAN CHAPEL at STOURBRIDGE, WORCS., which was built in 1788 [W. Scott, *History of Stourbridge*, 1832, 471] and the church at ASTON SUBEDGE, GLOS., a minute Gothic chapel built in 1797 largely at the expense of the 1st Lord Harrowby [Harrowby archives, 70].

Johnson died in Worcester in December 1800,[1] and was buried in the cathedral behind the choir. He bequeathed to Miss Mary Pitt, his late wife's niece, two pieces of needlework representing the 'Entrance Front of Warwick Castle and Mr. Dewes's House at Wellesbourne in Warwickshire'. His real estate he left to his son-in-law, Henry Lamb, who was his sole executor. According to the obituary notice in *Berrow's Worcester Jnl.* for 11 December 1800, Johnson lived in the part of Worcester known as Sidbury, and it was in the roof of a small building behind a house in Sidbury that the wooden models already referred to were discovered in about 1915. In all there were six models as shown overleaf. No. 4 is now in the Museum of the Bartlett School of Architecture at University College, London. The remainder are at Warwick. With the exception of No. 6, all of them probably represent designs by Johnson, and there is no reason to associate them

---

[1] They are fluted in the model.

[1] In his *Biographical Illustrations of Worcestershire*, 1820, p. 469, J. Chambers wrongly ascribes Johnson's death to the year 1806, and refers also to the death of an architect of the same name in Worcester in 1786. Both statements appear to be inaccurate versions of the obituary notice in the *Worcester Jnl.* for 1800.

	Architect
1. St. Nicholas, Warwick, with alternative spires	T. Johnson, 1778
2. Warwick County Gaol, façade, with fluted columns	T. Johnson, 1778
3. Warwick County Prison, to show chapel	T. Johnson, 1778
4. A classical church, unidentified, probably never built (*c.* 1780).	
5. A circular building, ? a prison.	
6. Warwick Shire Hall, façade	S. Miller, *c.* 1753

with Thomas White of Worcester (*d.* 1748), as suggested in *Trans. Worcs. Arch. Soc.* for 1943, p. 25, and in *Burlington Magazine*, May 1944.

[*A.P.S.D.*; J. N. Brewer, *Introduction to the Beauties of England and Wales*, 1818, 662; copy of Johnson's will (dated 6 Nov. 1800) in Birmingham Probate Registry; J. Noake, *The Monastery and Cathedral of Worcester*, 1866, 338–40; *Aris's Birmingham Gazette*, 24 Jan. 1791; *The Register of Worcester Cathedral 1693–1811* (Worcester Parish Register Society, 1913), 86.]

JOHNSON, THOMAS (–1814), of Leeds, was probably the son of William Johnson (*q.v.*). He was a competent classical architect, and may conceivably have been the person of this name who was admitted to the Royal Academy Schools in 1782 at the age of 20, and was awarded the Silver Medal the same year. He was recently dead in August 1814, when L. Ingham advertised that he would complete buildings Johnson had designed. Joseph Cusworth was his pupil. [F. Beckwith, *Thomas Taylor*, Thoresby Society, 1946, 16, 89.]

LEEDS, R. C. CHAPEL, 1793–4, dem. [B. Little, *Catholic Churches since 1623*, 1966, 44].

HALIFAX, YORKS. (W.R.), HOLY TRINITY CHURCH, 1795–8 [F. Beckwith, *op. cit.*, citing *Leeds Intelligencer*, 17 Aug. 1795] (wrongly attributed to J. Oates in T. Allen, *History of the County of York* iii, 1831, 239–40).

TEMPLE NEWSHAM HOUSE, YORKS. (W.R.), rebuilt south wing for Frances, Lady Irwin, in a style externally approximating to that of the Jacobean mansion of which it forms part, 1796 [Guidebook to Temple Newsham House, 1967, 10].

CAWTHORNE CHURCH, YORKS. (W.E.), added north aisle 1805 [Sheffield City Library, Sp. s. Maps, which also shows a south aisle that was not built].

LEEDS, THE LEEDS LIBRARY, COMMERCIAL STREET, 1808 [F. Beckwith, *op. cit.*, 16, n. 23].

SEWERBY HALL, YORKS. (E.R.), added bow-fronted wings and portico for John Greame, 1807–8 [*V.C.H. Yorks.*, *E. Riding* ii, 96].

JOHNSON, WILLIAM (–1795), of Leeds, was probably the father of Thomas Johnson (*q.v.*). When William died in 1795 the *Leeds In-*

telligencer described him as 'many years architect at Temple Newsham'. He appears in fact to have been agent and surveyor to Lord Irwin, the owner of Temple Newsam, and it was probably in that capacity that in 1786, when the old White Cloth Hall in Leeds was sold, he was paid 'for valuing the old White Cloth Hall, taking down the cupola and clock and removing them to the new White Cloth Hall' [*ex inf.* Dr. D. Linstrum]. It is possible that Johnson designed the NEW WHITE CLOTH HALL (dem. 1868), and T. Allen's *History of the County of York*, 1831, records (ii, 510) that he designed ST. PAUL'S CHURCH, LEEDS, 1791–3; dem. 1905 (illustrated by T. D. Whitaker, *Loidis and Elmete*, 1816, 69).

JOHNSON, WILLIAM, appears to have been a surveyor at Nottingham. In 1690 'Mr. Johnson of Nottingham' was employed to survey works then in progress at THE RESIDENCE, SOUTHWELL [P.R.O., Eccles. 2/118]. In 1701 Sir John Harpur of CALKE ABBEY, DERBYSHIRE, paid £2 3s. 0d. to 'Mr. Johnson the Surveyor' for unspecified services in connection with the new mansion he was then building [accounts at Calke Abbey], and in 1708 the borough of Nottingham decided that Mr. William Johnson was 'to survey part of the free School in order to rebuild it' [*Records of the Borough of Nottingham* vi, 40–1].

JOHNSTON, CORNELIUS, 'painter and architect', published in January 1754 a 'design for a British Musaeum' to contain in a quadrangular building the Cottonian Library, the Royal and Antiquarian Societies, and a Royal Academy of Painting, Sculpture and Architecture. There are impressions in the Print Room of the British Museum and in *King's Maps* xxiv, 17a, and an illustration will be found in J. Mordaunt Crook, *The British Museum*, 1972, fig. 14. The design has a strongly rococo character unusual in English eighteenth-century architecture. No other reference to Cornelius Johnston has so far come to light.

JOHNSTON, JOHN, was an English architect who went out to Brazil in 1815 in order to superintend the erection of a replica of the gateway at Syon House, Isleworth (by Robert Adam) which the 2nd Duke of Northumberland had commissioned from the Coade Stone factory as a present to the Prince Regent of Portugal, who was then living in exile at Rio de Janeiro. Johnston established himself in Rio, where in the course of the next few years he reconstructed the Prince's house, the QUINTA DA BOA VISTA at SAO CHRISTOVAO, and was responsible for various other buildings in a recognizably English style, notably the ENGLISH CHURCH in RIO DE JANEIRO, 1820; dem. [Michael Teague, 'An English Architect in Brazil', *C. Life*, 18 Aug. 1960].

JOHNSTON, ROBERT, of Kilmarnock, designed THE MANSE at IRVINE, AYRSHIRE, 1820 [S.R.O., HR 719/10]; TARBOLTON CHURCH, AYRSHIRE, 1820–1 [S.R.O., HR 718/1 and 2]; and THE KING STREET U.P. CHURCH at KILMARNOCK, 1832 [A. McKay, *History of Kilmarnock*, Kilmarnock 1880, 248]. The last was one of the earliest Nonconformist churches in Scotland to have a spire.

JOHNSTONE, ALLAN, was a builder-architect of Stirling, where he is known to have built NOS. 13–14 MELVILLE PLACE (now TERRACE), *c.* 1810 and a number of houses in QUEEN STREET. He also designed THE ERSKINE CHURCH, STIRLING, a simple but effective pedimented building of 1824–6; dem. [David Walker in *C. Life*, 28 Aug. 1969]. In 1815–16 he built THE ATHENAEUM in KING STREET to the designs of William Stirling (*q.v.*) [David Walker in *Bulletin of the Scottish Georgian Soc.* i, 1972, 46–7].

JOHNSTONE, JOHN, a wright by trade, lived on the estate of Sir John Clerk of Penicuik (*q.v.*), and worked with the elder John Baxter (*q.v.*) at Mavisbank, Midlothian, Haddo House, Aberdeenshire, and Galloway House, Wigtownshire. In October 1738 he wrote to Clerk to say that he was occupied in supervising the building of LOCHNELL CASTLE, ARGYLLSHIRE, for Sir Duncan Campbell. It is possible either that he designed the house himself or that he was executing designs made by his colleague Baxter [R.C.A.M., *Argyll* ii, 265–6].

JOINET, M—, exhibited a 'Design for a house to be built in Scotland' at the Royal Academy in 1804. His address was 6 Noel Street, Berwick Street, London. He may have been the artist named Joinet who was employed by Messrs. Eckhardt to finish by hand their printed wallpapers [E. Croft-Murray, *Decorative Painting in England* ii, 1970, 225]. A watercolour by him of Guy's Cliff House, Warwickshire, dated 1807, is in the Victoria and Albert Museum.

JONES, EDWARD, was a pupil of John Wallen. He evidently travelled in Greece, for in 1835 he published a thin folio volume entitled *Athenian or Grecian Villas, being a series of original designs for Villas or Country Residences* dedicated to Sir Robert Smirke. He exhibited at the Royal Academy in 1819, 1826, 1831 and 1835. In 1826 he

showed a drawing of the Temple of Jupiter at Athens, in 1831 a design for an ornamental temple based on the Temple on the Ilissus, 'proposed to be built' by Mrs. Powys of Berwick House, Salop., and in 1835 a 'Design for an Athenian Cottage'. In 1834 he exhibited a 'Design for a Villa in the Athenian style of Architecture' both at the Society of British Artists in Suffolk Street and at the Liverpool Academy of Arts. He was probably the 'Mr. Jones' who in 1823 made an unexecuted design for Broomhall, Fife, the seat of the 7th Earl of Elgin [J. Mordaunt Crook in *C. Life*, 29 Jan. 1970, 245–6].

JONES, EVAN, was a Flintshire master-carpenter of the early seventeenth century. In 1637 it was according to 'a plott ... drawen by Evan Jones Carpenter' that Ralph Booth, a freemason of Chester, undertook to build NERCWYS (NERQUIS) HALL, FLINTS., for John Wynne. All the architectural details were to be similar to those at RHUAL, FLINTS., recently built for Evan Edwards, and any defects noted in the work at Rhual were to be avoided at Nercwys 'accordinge to the direccion of the said Evan Jones' [Clwyd Record Office, D/NH 1007 A]. Jones must therefore be regarded as the designer of Nercwys Hall (which bears the date 1638), but his model at Rhual (1634) was inspired by English houses and may have had an English architect (see *C. Life*, 25 June 1943).

JONES, FRANCIS, of Hasfield, Glos., was one of the master masons employed to rebuild NEWENT CHURCH, GLOS., of which he and James Hill of Cheltenham laid the first stone on 31 July 1675. The roof of the Gothic nave was to have been supported by three stone columns, but the parish was persuaded by a carpenter named Edward Taylor (*q.v.*), who had worked in London after the Great Fire, to do away with the columns and erect the roof in a single span. The church was completed in 1679, the medieval steeple being retained. Soon after he had finished the church, Jones rebuilt the bridge over the Severn at OVER, nr. Gloucester; this was demolished in 1834, after the erection of the present bridge to the designs of Telford [MS. account of the building of Newent Church by Walter Nourse, of Kilcot, *c.* 1725]. Francis Jones may have been the master mason employed by Uvedall and Mary Tomkins to rebuild the nave and chancel of MONNINGTON-ON-WYE CHURCH, HEREFS., in 1679–80, as the windows and finials are similar in design to those at Newent.

JONES, INIGO (1573–1652), was the son of Inigo Jones, a London clothworker of Welsh origin. He was baptised in the church of St. Bartholomew-the-Less, Smithfield, in July 1573. Very little is known about his early life, but according to George Vertue, Sir Christopher Wren had information that he was apprenticed to a joiner in St. Paul's Churchyard. It is, however, as a painter or artist that he first appears in record, for in 1603 a payment of £10 to 'Henygo Jones, a picture maker', occurs in a list of gifts and rewards in the household accounts of the Earl of Rutland. In that year Jones may have accompanied the Earl on a diplomatic visit to the Danish court, but what is more important is evidence that at this period of his life Jones spent some time ('many years' according to his pupil Webb) in Italy. In 1605 he was described as 'a great traveller', and in 1606 a friend who gave him a copy of *De Rebus Gestis a Sixto V Pon: Max.* (Rome, 1588), wrote an inscription in Latin on the fly-leaf which expressed the hope that through Jones's agency, 'sculpture, modelling, architecture, painting, acting and all that is praiseworthy in the elegant arts of the ancients, may one day find their way across the Alps into our England'. By the early years of James I's reign, therefore, Inigo Jones had already acquired sufficient expertise abroad to see himself as an artistic missionary capable of introducing the sophisticated arts of Italy into an England which as yet had little conception of what the Renaissance meant in terms of the visual arts.

It was in the service of Queen Anne of Denmark that Jones first enjoyed the patronage of the royal court, and it was the court masque in which he revealed his skill as an Italian-trained designer. Between 1605 and 1640 he was responsible for staging over fifty masques, plays and other court entertainments, often in collaboration with Ben Jonson. Both poet and designer were assertive men jealous of their respective skills and reputations, and their relationship was not an easy one. More than once what Jonson saw as Jones's arrogance and pedantry were exposed to ridicule in his verses, but Jones prevailed in 1631, when Jonson retired discomfited from the court after the poor reception of his masque *Chloridia*.[1] Although nothing can now recapture the magic of these ephemeral performances to which Jones devoted so much of his time, over 450 drawings for scenery and costumes survive to demonstrate his virtuosity as a draughtsman and his familiarity with Italian stage designs, especially those of Alfonso and Giulio Parigi at Florence. All these drawings have been described and illustrated by Stephen Orgel and Roy Strong, who point out that they reveal a marked development in Jones's style between 1605 and 1609. The earliest drawings of 1605 'belong directly to an existing artistic tradition and betray

no knowledge of Italian Renaissance draughtsmanship', whereas by 1609 Jones was drawing freely in an accomplished Italianate manner. This development might seem to add strength to Gotch's hypothesis of a visit to Italy in 1606, but of this there is no definite evidence, and it was not until the summer of 1609 that Jones is known to have made a short foreign journey, not however to Italy but to France.

Jones had made a name for himself as a theatrical designer some years before he became actively involved in architecture. Architectural settings are of course to be found in the early masque drawings, but they are of a romantic and insubstantial character, and do not suggest any deeper interest in architectural composition. The earliest design by Jones for a real structure that has so far been identified is for a monument to Lady Cotton (d. 1606) at Norton-in-Hales in Shropshire. A strapwork cartouche framing the inscription shows that at this date Jones had not yet wholly emancipated himself from the decorative conventions of Jacobean mannerism, but the sarcophagus supporting the effigy is classical in intention. Drawings of *circa* 1608 for the New Exchange in the Strand and for the completion of the central tower of St. Paul's Cathedral are evidence at once of a nascent architectural ambition, of an imperfect assimilation of classical themes from such sources as Serlio, Palladio and Sangallo, and of a total lack of practical architectural experience. They are, in the words of Sir John Summerson, 'obviously the work of somebody who had had little to do with architecture and nothing with building'. At Hatfield House in 1609 Jones appears in the role of an architectural consultant, apparently modifying certain features of a building already in progress, but not as an architect in general control of the whole operation.

In 1610 Jones's appointment as Surveyor to Henry, Prince of Wales, brought him a little closer to practical architecture, for besides devising a masque and a dramatic tourney for the Prince, he may have been involved in some internal alterations to St. James's Palace, where the Prince was establishing a library and picture gallery. However the Prince's death in 1612 brought this appointment to an end, and it was not until the following year that Jones was granted the reversion of the place of Surveyor of the King's Works (27 April 1613).

The second Italian journey which Jones made in 1613–14 was of crucial importance in his education as an architect. He went in the train of the young Earl of Arundel, destined to be one of the greatest of English patrons and collectors of art. The Earl himself was escorting Princess Elizabeth and her husband the Elector Palatine to Heidelberg after their wedding in England, but, that duty completed, he spent over a year

---

[1] Jonson's final gibe at Jones was the character of 'Colonel Iniquo Vitruvius' in *Love's Welcome at Bolsover*, an entertainment written by Jonson for the Earl of Newcastle in 1634.

in Italy accompanied by Jones. In 1613 they visited Milan, Padua, Parma, Siena, Florence, Bologna and Vicenza. After spending the winter of 1613–14 in Rome they visited Naples, Venice, Vicenza, Genoa and Turin before returning home via Paris. A surviving sketchbook shows that Jones was still preoccupied with the work of Italian painters such as Parmigianino, Schiavone and Guercino, on whom his own style of draughtsmanship was largely based, but his annotated copy of Palladio's *Quattro Libri* shows that he was also systematically visiting the buildings illustrated in it and acquiring a detailed knowledge of the theory and grammar of classical architecture. He also bought other architectural text-books and in Venice he met Scamozzi, on whom the mantle of the great Palladio had fallen. The acquisition of a large number of Palladio's drawings was a coup which provided a valuable supplement to the crude woodblocks of the *Quattro Libri*.

Jones's second visit to Italy gave him the necessary equipment to exploit the Surveyor-General's place, to which he succeeded on Simon Basil's death in September 1615. Though much routine administration fell to the Surveyor-General, the holder of the office had the opportunity to design whatever buildings were called for by the King, and in James I Jones had a patron whose expenditure on his palaces was lavish compared with Queen Elizabeth's careful economy. The Whitehall Banqueting House, the Queen's House at Greenwich and the chapel at St. James's are the surviving products of his period of office under James I. They show him not only as a careful student of Palladio and Scamozzi but also as a mature architectural designer whose skill in composition was controlled by an intellectual grasp of the principles of Renaissance architecture. Nothing like these buildings had previously been seen in England, and in a baroque Europe they were an unexpected reaffirmation of High Renaissance principle which found no contemporary parallel in France or Italy. In England they remained isolated monuments of an art which few even of Jones's own staff at the Office of Works could emulate. On contemporary English taste their influence was limited, because Jones himself designed very little outside the immediate circle of the court, and his style was too esoteric to be easily absorbed by provincial master builders.

Between 1625 and 1640 Jones's principal architectural works were the repair and remodelling of St. Paul's Cathedral and the designing of Covent Garden for the Earl of Bedford. His work at St. Paul's provided precedents for a classical church architecture which were to be taken up by Wren in the reign of Charles II, but the outstanding feature of the building as Jones left it was the great Corinthian portico, the largest

north of the Alps, in which he demonstrated the grandeur of classical architecture in a manner for which none of his other works gave an opportunity. In Covent Garden he not only designed the first wholly classical church in England, but also carried out a piece of uniform planning that was to be of immense importance in the history of English urban architecture. What might have been his greatest work was, however, never begun. This was the replacement of the old incoherent palace of Whitehall by a new architectural complex symmetrically grouped round a series of monumental courtyards, into one of which the Banqueting House was to be incorporated. This scheme, frustrated by Charles I's financial and political difficulties, is represented today by a large and confusing series of drawings, mostly in the hand of Jones's pupil and assistant John Webb, which have been ably analysed by Dr. Margaret Whinney. Of the many variant schemes distinguished by Dr. Whinney, only one can confidently be attributed to Jones himself, and even this is known only from drawings by Webb. It was, however, the starting point of all the projects for a new Whitehall which stretch from the reign of Charles I to that of William III, and for this reason it has an importance which transcends its ephemeral character as the abortive dream of a powerless monarch.

After his appointment as Surveyor-General Jones had little time to spare for private commissions. In the 1630s, when Charles I himself was anxious to offer Jones's services to his Lord Chamberlain, the Earl of Pembroke, at Wilton House, Jones had to delegate the commission to Isaac de Caux because of pressure of work at Greenwich. Only the greatest courtiers such as the Duke of Buckingham, the Earl of Salisbury or the Earl of Bedford could normally command his services, and the attribution of undocumented private works to Jones has to be tested not only by stylistic criteria but also by the standing of the patron at court. Apart from Wilton, the only country houses that pass both these tests are Houghton and Stoke Bruern. Chevening (c. 1630)[1] and the screen at Castle Ashby (c. 1630)[2] both fail the stylistic test, and although Raynham (c. 1620) was a remarkable epitome of motifs that appear in Jones's earlier drawings, it appears to be rather an intelligent reflection of his style than a personal work.[3] Apart from John Webb there

---

[1] Illustrated in *Vitruvius Britannicus* ii, pl. 85 and *C. Life*, 17 & 24 April and 1 May 1920.

[2] The building accounts are in the Warwickshire Record Office (CR 556/274), but unfortunately fail to identify the architect. References to 'the surveyor', however, make it clear that he was not Inigo Jones, who is always referred to in contemporary records as 'Mr. Surveyor'.

[3] See John Harris, 'Raynham Hall', *Archaeological Jnl.* cxviii, 1963, and above, p. 281.

were other architects such as Edward Carter, Isaac de Caux, Sir Balthazar Gerbier and Nicholas Stone whose style, though not measuring up to the exacting standards which Jones set himself, would probably have satisfied many patrons who wanted something fashionable, but could not command the services of the King's Surveyor.

For Jones, as for his royal master, the 1640s were years of distress. 'As the conductor of ruinously expensive court entertainments, as the executor of arbitrary proclamations about London building, and, most especially, as the accomplice of Archbishop Laud (in the rebuilding of St. Paul's Cathedral) he was marked out for trouble.' In December 1641 he was brought before the House of Lords to answer a charge of high-handed conduct towards the parishioners of St. Gregory's, a church whose fabric stood in inconvenient proximity to the south-west corner of St. Paul's. He was not impeached, but the Lords directed that part of the materials collected for the repair of the cathedral were to be given to the parishioners for the restoration of their church. In January 1642 the King left Whitehall, and later in the year Jones was with him in Yorkshire, no doubt to assist in the intended siege of Hull, for which his knowledge of fortification would (though hitherto untested) be useful. In July, when the court was at Burleigh, the King signed a receipt for £500 lent to him by his Surveyor. In 1643 Jones was ousted from his place as Surveyor of the Royal Works by Edward Carter (q.v.). In 1644–5 he was among the royalists caught in Basing House, Hampshire, and was captured when Cromwell took the place by siege in October 1645. The sequestration of his estate followed, but it was restored on the payment of a fine. According to Vertue, he and Nicholas Stone had successfully hidden 'their joint store of ready money' in Lambeth Marsh, and when he made his will on 22 July 1650 Jones was able to leave a modest fortune to be divided between John Webb, who had married his 'kinswoman' Anne Jones, Richard Gammon (q.v.), who married Elizabeth Jones, another kinswoman, and other legatees. He appears to have had lodgings in Somerset House, where he died unmarried on 21 June 1652. He was buried with his parents at St. Benet's, Paul's Wharf. A monument decorated with reliefs of the Banqueting House and St. Paul's Cathedral was destroyed in the Great Fire. Aubrey's sketch of it is reproduced in The King's Arcadia (1973), 405.

There is no evidence that Jones was ever a Roman Catholic. On the contrary the fact that he was an M.P. (1621) and a Justice of the Peace means that he must have been a conforming Anglican. Furthermore in 1636 a papal agent in England characterized him as puritanissimo fiero, by which he appears to have meant that he was

an irreligious person and certainly not a Catholic.

The portraits of Inigo Jones are described in the articles by C. F. Bell and Oliver Millar listed below and also in The King's Arcadia, nos. 406–12. The most important are (1) a print by Francesco Villamena, made in Italy before 1624, presumably in 1613–14; (2) three self-portraits of various dates at Chatsworth; (3) the drawing by Van Dyck at Chatsworth from which Robert van Voerst made his engraving for Van Dyck's Iconographiae (1640); (4) an oil portrait by Van Dyck at the Hermitage, Leningrad; (5) an oil portrait by Dobson at Chiswick House dateable c. 1644.

Jones's drawings passed into the possession of his pupil John Webb, who bequeathed them to his son William Webb, with strict injuctions that they should not be dispersed. It appears, however, that they were sold by William's widow. In the 1680s John Aubrey noted that 'John Oliver, the City Surveyor, hath all [Jones's] papers and designs, not only of St. Paul's Cathedral, etc. and the Banquetting House, but his designe of all Whitehall'. After Oliver's death in 1701 his collection appears to have been acquired by William Talman, from whose son John (q.v.), it passed in the 1720s to Lord Burlington. When Burlington died in 1753 his collections passed to his daughter Charlotte, who had married the 4th Duke of Devonshire. In 1894 the 8th Duke gave the architectural drawings to the Royal Institute of British Architects (see R.I.B.A. Drawings Catalogue: Inigo Jones & John Webb, by John Harris, 1972), but retained the masque designs, which are the subject of a separate catalogue by Orgel and Strong. Meanwhile another collection of drawings by Jones and Webb had been acquired by Dr. George Clarke (q.v.) from an unknown source. These drawings were bequeathed by Clarke to Worcester College, Oxford, in 1736, and are described in a forthcoming catalogue by John Harris and A. A. Tait which will supersede the one published by Gotch in the R.I.B.A. Journal for 29 March 1913. They include a number of drawings of a theoretical character which might suggest that Jones contemplated a systematic treatise on classical architecture that was never written. Many of the drawings in Lord Burlington's possession were published in William Kent's Designs of Inigo Jones (1727), Isaac Ware's Designs of Inigo Jones and Others (n.d.) and John Vardy's Designs of Mr. Inigo Jones and Mr. William Kent (1744), but without distinguishing between Jones's hand and Webb's. Scholarly analysis of the drawings in the two collections began with Gotch and Grant Keith and has been continued by Whinney, Harris and Tait (see bibliography).

Over 40 books from Jones's library are in the library of Worcester College, Oxford. Many of them contain annotations in his hand. There is

470

a list in *The King's Arcadia*, Appendix III. Jones's annotated copy of Serlio (1560–2) is in the Library of The Queen's College, Oxford.

SELECT BIBLIOGRAPHY

1. *General and Biographical*

P. Cunningham, *Inigo Jones : a life of the Architect*, Shakespeare Soc. 1848–9, reissued 1853.

A.P.S.D., vol. iv, 1865, *s.v.* 'Jones, Inigo', article by Wyatt Papworth.

D.N.B., vol. x, 1891–2, *s.v.* 'Jones, Inigo', article based on notes by A. P. Horne.

W. G. Keith, 'Inigo Jones as a Collector', *R.I.B.A. Journal* xxxiii, 1925–6, 94–108.

J. A. Gotch, *Inigo Jones*, 1928.

C. F. Bell, 'Portraits of Inigo Jones', *R.I.B.A. Journal*, 11 Sept. 1937, 1007.

J. A. Gotch, 'Inigo Jones's Principal Visit to Italy in 1614: the Itinerary of his Journeys', *R.I.B.A. Journal*, 21 Nov. 1938, 85–6.

E. S. De Beer, 'Notes on Inigo Jones', *Notes and Queries*, 30 Dec. 1939, 27 April and 4 May 1940.

R. Wittkower, 'Inigo Jones, Puritanissimo Fiero', *Burlington Mag.* xc, 1948, reprinted in *Palladio and English Palladianism*, 1974.

D. J. Gordon, 'Poet and Architect: the Intellectual Background to the Quarrel between Ben Jonson and Inigo Jones', *Journal of the Warburg and Courtauld Institutes* xii, 1949.

Oliver Millar, 'Dobson's portrait of Inigo Jones', *Burlington Mag.* xciv, 1952, 207.

Margaret Whinney, 'Inigo Jones, a revaluation', *R.I.B.A. Journal*, 3rd ser., lix, 1952.

Geoffrey Webb, 'Inigo Jones Tercentenary', *C. Life*, 20 June 1952.

R. Wittkower, 'Inigo Jones, Architect and Man of Letters', *R.I.B.A. Journal*, 3rd ser., lx, 1953.

J. Lees-Milne, *The Age of Inigo Jones*, 1953.

John Summerson, *Architecture in Britain 1530–1830*, 1953 (4th ed. 1963), chapters 7–9.

Lawrence Stone, 'Inigo Jones and the New Exchange', *Archaeological Jnl.* cxiv, 1959.

John Summerson, 'Inigo Jones', *Proceedings of the British Academy*, 1, 1965.

John Summerson, *Inigo Jones*, 1966.

Inigo Jones on Palladio (facsimile of Jones's annotated Palladio), ed. B. Allsopp, 2 vols. 1970.

A. A. Tait, 'Inigo Jones – Architectural Historian', *Burlington Mag.* cxii, 1970, 235.

The King's Arcadia : Inigo Jones and the Stuart Court, Catalogue of Exhibition by John Harris, Stephen Orgel and Roy Strong, 1973.

J. A. Skovgaard, *A King's Architecture*, 1973, Appendix IV : 'Inigo Jones and Christian IV [of Denmark]'.

John Harris, 'Inigo Jones and the Courtier Style', *Architectural Review*, July 1973.

John Summerson, 'The Surveyorship of Inigo Jones' in *The History of the King's Works*, ed. Colvin, iii, 1975.

2. *Drawings*

J. A. Gotch, 'The Original Drawings for the Palace at Whitehall attributed to Inigo Jones', *Architectural Review*, June 1912.

W. G. Keith, 'Some hitherto unknown drawings by Inigo Jones', *Burlington Mag.* xxii, 1913, 218–26.

Margaret Whinney, 'John Webb's Drawings for Whitehall Palace', *Walpole Soc.* xxxi, 1942–3.

C. Rowe, *The Theoretical Drawings of Inigo Jones, their Sources and Scope*, unpublished thesis, University of London, 1947.

Roy Strong, *Festival Designs by Inigo Jones*, 1967.

John Harris, 'A Prospect of Whitehall by Inigo Jones', *Burlington Mag.* Feb. 1967.

Margaret Whinney, 'An Unknown Design for a Villa by Inigo Jones', in *The Country Seat*, ed. Colvin & Harris, 1970.

John Harris, *Catalogue of the R.I.B.A. Drawings Collection : Inigo Jones & John Webb*, 1972.

Stephen Orgel & Roy Strong, *Inigo Jones, The Theatre of the Stuart Court*, 2 vols. 1973.

John Harris & A. A. Tait, *Catalogue of Drawings by Inigo Jones and John Webb in the Library of Worcester College, Oxford*, forthcoming.

3. *Jones as a Theatrical Designer*

W. G. Keith, 'A Theatre Project by Inigo Jones', *Burlington Mag.* xxxi, 1917.

P. Simpson & C. F. Bell, 'Designs by Inigo Jones for masques and plays at Court', *Walpole Soc.* xii, 1924.

Oskar Fischel, 'Inigo Jones und der Theaterstil der Renaissance', in *England und die Antike*, 1932.

A. Nicoll, *Stuart Masques and the Renaissance Stage*, 1937.

M. T. Jones-Davies, *Inigo Jones, Ben Jonson et le Masque*, Paris 1967.

Roy Strong, *Festival Designs by Inigo Jones* (exhibition catalogue), 1967.

Frances Yates, *The Theatre of the World*, 1969.

Glynne Wickham, 'The Cockpit reconstructed', *New Theatre Magazine* vii, 1967.

Stephen Orgel & Roy Strong, *Inigo Jones, The Theatre of the Stuart Court*, 2 vols. 1973.

4. *Sources and Style*

Joan Sumner Smith, 'The Italian Sources of Inigo Jones's style', *Burlington Mag.* xciv, 1952, 200–6.

John Harris, 'Inigo Jones and his French Sources', *Metropolitan Museum Bulletin*, May 1961.

John Harris, 'The Link between a Roman second-century sculptor, Van Dyck, Inigo Jones and Queen Henrietta Maria', *Burlington Mag.* cxv, 1973, 526.

5. *Attributions*

A comprehensive list of the many buildings that have been attributed to Jones without

471

adequate evidence will be found in *A.P.S.D.*
J. Lees-Milne, *The Age of Inigo Jones*, 1953,
contains a useful survey of buildings influenced by Jones's style.

FULLY AUTHENTICATED WORKS

NORTON-IN-HALES CHURCH, SALOP., monument to
Lady Cotton (d. 1606), later modified to
accommodate the effigy of her husband Sir
Rowland Cotton (d. 1634) [John Newman, 'An
early drawing by Inigo Jones and a monument
in Shropshire', *Burlington Mag.* cxv, 1973,
360].

NEWMARKET PALACE, SUFFOLK, brew-house,
stable, dog-house, riding-house and stables for
Sir Thomas Compton and Mr. Dupper, 1615–
17; the Prince's Lodging and clerk of works'
house, 1619–21; dem. *c.* 1650 [John Harris,
'Inigo Jones and the Prince's Lodging at Newmarket', *Architectural History* ii, 1959; *History
of the King's Works* iv].

GREENWICH PALACE, KENT, THE QUEEN'S HOUSE,
begun for Queen Anne of Denmark, 1616–19,
completed for Queen Henrietta Maria, 1630–
5; altered 1661 by John Webb, who added the
bridges over the east and west entrances [G.
H. Chettle, *The Queen's House, Greenwich*,
London Survey monograph, 1937: *History of
the King's Works* iv].

ST. JAMES'S PALACE, WESTMINSTER, the Prince's
Buttery, 1617–18; dem.; the Queen's Chapel,
1623–5; Sculpture Gallery and pergola to
Queen's Withdrawing Chamber, 1629; dem.;
gateway in park wall, 1631; dem. [*History of
the King's Works* iv].

SOMERSET HOUSE, STRAND, lantern over the hall,
1617–18; Queen's Cabinet Room, 1626; river
stairs, 1628–31; the Queen's Chapel, 1630–5;
refitted Cross Gallery, 1635; new cabinet
room, 1637; all dem. 1776–90 [*History of the
King's Works* iv].

OATLANDS PALACE, SURREY, great gate to park,
silk-worm house and gateway to vineyard, for
Queen Anne of Denmark, 1617–18; arbour in
garden for Queen Henrietta Maria, 1631; bal-
cony to Queen's lodgings, 1635; all dem. 1650
[*History of the King's Works* iv; *R.I.B.A.
Drawings Catalogue: Inigo Jones & John
Webb*, 16–17; W. G. Keith, 'The Palace of
Oatlands', *Arch. Rev.* xxxix, 1916].

LONDON, ARUNDEL HOUSE, STRAND, alterations for
the 14th Earl of Arundel, including a gateway
dated 1618, and probably the addition of the
sculpture gallery; dem. *c.* 1678 [*R.I.B.A.
Drawings Catalogue: Inigo Jones & John Webb*,
13].

LONDON, STRAND, entrance with 'pergola' to
house of Sir Edward Cecil, *c.* 1618; destroyed

by fire 1628 [*R.I.B.A. Drawings Catalogue:
Inigo Jones & John Webb*, 13].

WHITEHALL PALACE, lodgings for George Villiers,
Marquis of Buckingham, 1619–20; lodgings
for the Countess of Buckingham, 1620–1; park
stairs 1624 (remodelled 1628); clock-house
1626; Cockpit reconstructed as a theatre 1629;
masquing room, 1637; all dem. [*History of the
King's Works* iv].

WHITEHALL PALACE, THE BANQUETING HOUSE,
1619–22; used as a Chapel Royal from 1698 to
1808, as a military chapel from 1808 to 1891
and as the Royal United Service Institution
from 1891 to 1963. The exterior was progressively refaced in Portland stone in 1774, 1785
and 1828 [*History of the King's Works* iv; *Survey of London* xiii, chap. 4; Per Palme, *Triumph
of Peace, a study of the Whitehall Banqueting
House*, 1957].

CHELSEA, BEAUFORT HOUSE, classical gateway for
Lionel Cranfield, 1621; reerected at Chiswick
House, Middlesex, by the 3rd Earl of Burl-
ington, 1738 [*R.I.B.A. Drawings Catalogue:
Inigo Jones & John Webb*, 13].

THEOBALDS PALACE, HERTS., new stable, 1623;
banqueting house, 1625; dem. *c.* 1650 [*History
of the King's Works* iv].

WESTMINSTER PALACE, HOUSE OF LORDS, new
ceiling 1623–4; dem. 1823 [*History of the
King's Works* iv].

GREENWICH PALACE, KENT, remodelling of
Chapel; great gate to park, 1623–4; dem. *c.*
1700 [*History of the King's Works* iv].

BAGSHOT PARK, SURREY, lodge, 1631–2; dem.
[*History of the King's Works* iv].

LONDON, ST. PAUL'S CHURCH, COVENT GARDEN, for
the 4th Earl of Bedford, 1631–3; repaired and
cased in Portland stone by Thomas Hardwick
1788–9; gutted by fire 1795 and rebuilt by
Hardwick closely following Jones's design,
1796–8; altered internally by W. Butterfield
1871–2; refaced in brick 1887–8 [*Survey of
London* xxxvi, chap. v; John Summerson,
'Inigo Jones', *Proceedings of the British
Academy* 1, 1965, 170–82].

LONDON, COVENT GARDEN, THE PIAZZA, for the 4th
Earl of Bedford, 1631–7; for subsequent
alterations and demolitions see *Survey of London*. None of the original houses now survive,
but Bedford Chambers (by Henry Clutton,
1877–9) follows the character of the original
design [*Survey of London* xxxvi, chap. iv].

LONDON, ST. PAUL'S CATHEDRAL, general repair,
remodelled exterior of nave and transepts and
added west portico, 1633–42; ruined by Great
Fire of London 1666 and subsequently dem.
[John Summerson, 'Inigo Jones', *Proceedings
of the British Academy* 1, 1965, 182–91; *History
of the King's Works* iii, 147–52].

LONDON, ST. GILES-IN-THE-FIELDS CHURCH, monument to the poet George Chapman (d. 1634),

in the form of a Roman altar: inscribed 'Georgius Chapman poeta 1634 Ignatius Jones Architectus Regius ob honorem bonarum literarum familiari suo hoc mon DSPFC' (*Survey of London* v, 136).

LONDON, HYDE PARK, lodge 1634–5; dem. [*History of the King's Works* iv; *The King's Arcadia*, 1973, 265].

LONDON, THE BARBER SURGEONS' HALL, MONKWELL STREET, ANATOMY THEATRE, 1636–7; dem. 1783 [J. Harris & A. A. Tait, *Catalogue of Drawings by Inigo Jones and John Webb in the Library of Worcester College, Oxford*, forthcoming] (Isaac Ware, *Designs of Inigo Jones and Others*, 1736, pls. 8–9).

WINCHESTER CATHEDRAL, HANTS., choir-screen, 1637–8; dismantled 1820: the central portion is now in the Museum of Archaeology at Cambridge [*History of the King's Works* iii, 153; *R.I.B.A. Drawings Catalogue: Inigo Jones & John Webb*, 17] (*The King's Arcadia*, 1973, 256).

WIMBLEDON HOUSE, SURREY, alterations and additions for Queen Henrietta Maria, 1640–1; dem. *c.* 1717 [C. S. S. Higham, *Wimbledon Manor House under the Cecils*, 1962, 31–2; *R.I.B.A. Drawings Catalogue: Inigo Jones & John Webb*, 17].

INADEQUATELY DOCUMENTED WORKS

ASCOTT HOUSE, WING, BUCKS., apartment for the 1st Earl of Carnarvon (d. 1643). According to Browne Willis (1682–1760), who lived in Buckinghamshire, 'This was a large house, and the Earl of Carnarvon, temp. Charles I, added a Noble Apartment to the old house, by the Plan of Inigo Jones: but it was never entirely finished' [B.M., Add. MS. 5840, f. 159ᵛ]. Willis says that the house was 'suffered to go to ruin' in the 1720s, but Luttrell says it was 'lately burnt down' in 1691 [*Diary of Narcissus Luttrell* ii, 233].

BYFLEET HOUSE, SURREY, as rebuilt or remodelled by Queen Anne of Denmark *c.* 1617, had a classical portico in a style strongly suggestive of Inigo Jones, but known only from a sketch by John Aubrey reproduced in *Surrey Archaeological Colls.* 1, 1946–7, pl. xvi. The house was dem. *c.* 1686.

HALE CHURCH, HANTS., 1631–2; chancel rebuilt and transepts added by Thomas Archer, 1717; roof and cornice rebuilt in nineteenth century. Stylistic attribution [Peter Burman, 'Inigo Jones at Hale?', *C. Life*, 7 Feb. 1974].

HATFIELD HOUSE, HERTS. In 1609 Jones visited Hatfield, then being built for Robert Cecil, 1st Earl of Salisbury, and was subsequently paid £10 'for drawinge of some Architecture'. It is

possible that he modified the design of the arcaded south front, and probable that he designed the classical clock-tower [Lawrence Stone, 'The Building of Hatfield House', *Archaeological Jnl.* cxii, 1955].

HOUGHTON HOUSE, HOUGHTON CONQUEST, nr. AMPTHILL, BEDS., classical frontispieces for Mary, Dowager Countess of Pembroke (d. 1621), probably soon after 1615. Stylistic attribution [*The King's Arcadia*, 1973, 109–11; see also H. Clifford Smith, *The Haynes Grange Room*, Victoria and Albert Museum, 1935].

LONDON, MARSHALSEA PRISON, SOUTHWARK, THE PALACE COURT, *c.* 1630; dem. 1803. Stylistic attribution (*Gent's Mag.* 1803 (ii), 1205, engraving).

LONDON, ST. MICHAEL-LE-QUERNE CHURCH, CHEAPSIDE, 1638; destroyed by fire 1666. Jones's involvement in the building of this church was an act of interference on the part of the Council, who wanted the new building to be an ornament to the street. A 'modell' for a new church had already been made by Anthony Jerman and a Mr. Holmes before the Privy Council attempted to impose a new one made by Jones, and the outcome is not clear either from the legal records referred to by Gotch, *Inigo Jones*, 185–8, or from the churchwardens' accounts in the Guildhall Library (MS. 2895/2), which refer to numerous meetings between the parishioners and 'Mr. Surveyor'. No representation of the church is known.

LONDON, house in Strand for Sir Fulk Greville, before 1619: destroyed by fire 1666: although no design for this house survives, it had several features characteristic of surviving designs for London houses by Jones [*The King's Arcadia*, 104–5].

NEW HALL, BOREHAM, ESSEX, alterations for George Villiers, Duke of Buckingham, 1622–3. Jones's involvement in New Hall is referred to in a letter from John Chamberlain to Sir Dudley Carleton dated 5 Sept. 1622, and is attested by a fragmentary memorandum dated 1622 and by a design for a gateway dated 1623 [Gotch, 127; *R.I.B.A. Drawings Catalogue: Inigo Jones & John Webb*, 14 (no. 14), 16 (no. 56)]. Jones appears to have been superseded by Sir Balthazar Gerbier (*q.v.*) who was employed here in 1624–5.

STOKE PARK, STOKE BRUERN, NORTHANTS., for Sir Francis Crane, *c.* 1630; central block destroyed by fire 1886, leaving the pavilion and quadrants. The ultimate authority for the attribution of this house to Jones is Colen Campbell, who says that 'This Building was begun by Inigo Jones; the Wings, and Collonades, and all the Foundations, were made by him; but the Front of the House was designed by another Architect, the Civil Wars having also interrupted this Work' [*Vitruvius Britannicus* iii, 1717, pl. 9]. Bridges (d. 1724), in his *History of Northamptonshire*, ed. Whalley, i, 1791, 328, says that Crane, 'brought the design from Italy, and in the execution of it received the assistance of Inigo Jones'. The pavilions are illustrated in *C. Life*, 23 July 1953.

WHITEHALL, THE BANQUETING HOUSE, 1606–9, destroyed by fire 1619. The possibility of Jones's participation in the design of this building is discussed by Summerson in *History of the King's Works* iv.

WILTON HOUSE, WILTS. The evidence for Jones's involvement in the rebuilding of the south front for the 4th Earl of Pembroke in 1636 is John Aubrey's statement that 'King Charles the first did love Wilton above all places, and came thither every summer. It was he that did put Philip ... Earle of Pembroke upon making this magnificent garden and grotto, and to new build that side of the house that fronts the garden, with two stately pavilions at each end, all *al Italiano*. His Majesty intended to have it all designed by his own architect, Mr. Inigo Jones, who being at that time ... engaged in his Majesties buildings at Greenwich, could not attend to it: but he recommended it to an ingeniouse architect, Monsieur [Isaac] de Caus [*q.v.*], who performed it very well; but not without the advice and approbation of Mr. Jones.' When the interior was gutted in 1647 or 1648 it was rebuilt by John Webb, again 'by the advice of Inigo Jones', now too old to 'be there in person'. The existence of several designs for ceilings at Wilton in Jones's hand is evidence of his participation, probably in the design of the interior in the 1630s, for the existing drawings for the exterior are by De Caux, and those for the interiors of 1649 are by Webb [H. M. Colvin, 'The South Front of Wilton House', *Archaeological Jnl.* cxi, 1955].

JONES, RICHARD, 3RD VISCOUNT and 1ST EARL OF RANELAGH (?1638–1712), was an Irish peer who as a young man enjoyed the favour of the Duke of Ormonde. Under Charles II he was Chancellor of the Irish Exchequer and manager of the Irish revenues. William III made him Paymaster of his Army (1691). A clever and plausible man, he was allowed with impunity to make large sums of money from public office. Building and gardening were his great enthusiasms, and according to Macky he 'spent more money, built more fine houses, and laid out more on household-furniture and gardening, than any other Nobleman in England'. As Treasurer of Chelsea Hospital (1685–1702) he built himself (*c.* 1688–9) a handsome house (dem. 1805) immediately adjoining the hospital which, according to Bowack's *Antiquities of Middlesex* (1705), was 'Designed and built by himself'. This is sup-

ported by the fact that in 1683 Ranelagh House was taken as a model for the Earl of Rochester's new house at Petersham, in the contract for which the Earl of Ranelagh himself is named as arbitrator in the event of any dispute between owner and builder [Surrey County Record Office, SC13/26/102–3]. Ranelagh had, moreover, given architectural advice to Lord Conway in connection with his buildings at Newmarket and at Ragley in Warwickshire [*Cal. S.P. Dom. 1679–80*, 623; *1683* (i), 105, 128, 166, 172], and in 1704–5 it was he who supervised the enlargement of the Duke of Ormonde's house at Richmond in Surrey [Hist. MSS. Comm. *Seventh Report*, Appendix, 774–6]. The house called Cranbourn Lodge in Windsor Park which Ranelagh bought from Lord Lexington in 1700 was of fairly recent erection, but here too his activities either as architect or as gardener are attested by a letter from Sidney Godolphin dated 18 July 1700 in which he says that 'at Cranborn ... my Lord Ranelagh to all his usuall improvements has added more expedition than any other man could have been capable of' [Sotheby's, 6 Feb. 1973, lot 258]. An eighteenth-century view of Cranbourn Lodge by Sandby is reproduced by Oppé, *Sandby Drawings at Windsor Castle*, and there is a plan of the grounds by London and Wise in P.R.O., Works 32/1155.

It was doubtless Ranelagh's reputation both for taste and for getting things done that in June 1700 led William III to make him 'Sur-intendent generall of oure Buildings & of our works in our parks' at a salary of £400 a year. This made Ranelagh in effect a minister of Works, with authority both over Wren as Surveyor-General of Works and over Talman as the officer in charge of the royal gardens. His tenure of the post lasted for less than two years before it was brought to an end by the King's death in March 1702. Ranelagh himself died on 5 January 1711/12. Among the legacies provided for in his will were two drawers of mathematical instruments, rulers and perspective glasses, which he left to his 'dear friend, John Earl of Mar' (*q.v.*), £20 each to John Churchill, Master Carpenter and Henry Wise, Master Gardener, 'to buy silver in remembrance of me who was heartily their friend', £50 to Richard, son of the joiner Sir Charles Hopson, £25 to 'honest Hugh Warren joyner', and smaller sums to his gardeners at Chelsea and Cranbourn.

[*D.N.B.*; *History of the King's Works* v, 35, 218; C. G. T. Dean, *The Royal Hospital, Chelsea*, 1950, chap. xviii; David Ascoli on Ranelagh and Chelsea Hospital in *C. Life*, 5 June 1975; *Survey of London* xxix, 67, 109–12, 299, 517; John Macky, *Memoirs of the Secret Services of John Macky*, 1733, 82; P.C.C., 99 BARNES.]

JONES, RICHARD (1703–   ), was the son of a cordwainer at Bath. He served an apprenticeship to a local mason and worked for some years at his trade before becoming in about 1730 clerk of the works to Ralph Allen, in whose service he remained until Allen's death in 1764. In 1765 he was appointed City Surveyor of Bath, but gave up the post when he was appointed Sergeant at Mace in 1772. In the City Library at Bath there is a nineteenth-century transcript of some somewhat rambling reminiscences written or dictated by Jones. From these it is apparent that he had taught himself to draw and that he designed a number of buildings in and around Bath, besides building others to the designs of architects such as John Wood.

For Ralph Allen Jones began the building of PRIOR PARK to the designs of John Wood in 1735. After a disagreement between Allen and Wood in 1748 the house was completed by Jones, who altered the design of the east wing and was responsible for various outbuildings. In 1755–6 he built the Palladian Bridge in the park, but does not claim to have designed it. He does, however, state twice that the SHAM CASTLE on Claverton Down was built 'to my plan' or 'design'. Seven years earlier Sanderson Miller had been approached for a design for the eye-catcher, but there is no evidence that he was again consulted in 1762, and Jones's claim to have designed the Castle may well be correct. For Allen Jones also claimed to have built NEWTON BRIDGE at WESTON, c. 1752–4, altered CLAVERTON HOUSE (dem. c. 1820), altered or repaired CLAVERTON CHURCH ('restored' 1858), and rebuilt the nave and south aisle of BATHAMPTON CHURCH in 1754 ('restored' 1858). When William Warburton, who had married Allen's favourite niece, became Dean of Bristol (1757), Jones was employed to reconstruct the DEANERY at a cost of £900, and in 1760, when Warburton was promoted to the bishopric of Gloucester, Jones dealt with the dilapidations at the BISHOP'S PALACE there. His final service to Ralph Allen was to design his elaborate pyramidal monument in CLAVERTON CHURCHYARD (1764).[1]

Among many other buildings which Jones says he was concerned with as builder or clerk of works, the only ones of which he specifically claims to have been the architect were the remodelling of the LOWER ASSEMBLY ROOMS at BATH in 1750 and the 'altering' of the OLD BRIDGE, by which he presumably meant its rebuilding in 1754. In 1766 he was one of several architects

---

[1] Jones specifically mentions his designs for Allen's monument, and relates that the latter 'sent for me to bring him the drawings of the burial place' some five days before his death, and gave him orders to have them carried out. The mason Robert Parsons, who was also consulted by Allen (cf. Gunnis, Dictionary of British Sculptors, 292), was probably employed to carry out Jones's design.

who made designs for the new Market and Guildhall, but nothing was done for several years and it was eventually built to the designs of Thomas Baldwin [W. Ison, The Georgian Buildings of Bath, 1948, 35]. A cryptic reference to his 'drawings of the other piece at Widcombe, done for one Squire Bennet, and his summer house in his garden', may indicate that Jones designed the delightful classical garden house at WIDCOMBE MANOR, illustrated by Ison, op. cit., p. 30.

JONES, RICHARD (c. 1756–1826), 'an eminent architect and surveyor', died at Worcester on 17 January 1826, aged 70. He published The Builder's Vade-Mecum, or practice of Surveying etc., with Specifications, 1809, and Every Builder his own Surveyor, 1809. He had earlier practised in Birmingham, where his son Richard (1779–1851) was born. The latter was trained as an architect, but, at the age of 18, 'an unfortunate speculation' of his father's 'caused so much embarrassment in his affairs', that, having some abilities as an actor, he decided to adopt the stage as his profession [A.P.S.D.; D.N.B.; 'Memoirs of Mr. Jones, Comedian' in Monthly Magazine, Aug. 1808, 68; obituary in Gent's Mag. 1826 (i), 94].

JONES, ROBERT, was a London tradesman who practised as a building surveyor in the reign of Queen Anne. He appears to have been a carpenter or joiner by trade, and in 1707 he told Lord Cholmondeley's agent that 'sence I left my trade of' he was 'daily out upon vews and serveays and sumetymes in the Contry'. He said that his chief employment was fixing prices for the employment of workmen and settling their bills. The first Earl of Cholmondeley employed him at his house in Arlington Street, and in 1702 Jones was consulted about the rebuilding of CHOLMONDELEY CASTLE in CHESHIRE. Work appears to have started under his direction, but in view of the difficulty of supervising it at a distance he subsequently recommended Lord Cholmondeley to employ the Smiths of Warwick instead [Chester County Record Office, Cholmondeley archives; Mark Girouard in C. Life, 19 July 1973, 156].

Jones was the surveyor employed by the South Sea Company to fit up the premises in Threadneedle Street occupied by the Company before the erection of its new buildings in 1723–7. On 31 January 1711/12, the Deputy Governor reported that 'Mr. Jones the Surveyor had laid before them a Plan of the General Court in the nature of an Ampitheatre' and it was 'Resolved that a Gallary Ampitheatrewise correspondent with the lower part [of the design] be added'. In July 1712 it was ordered that Mr. Jones should be paid £50 'as Rated by Mr. Robt. Jones the Surveyor of the work done for the Company's House'. No further reference to Jones occurs after this date [B.M., Minutes of the South Sea Company, vol. i, Add. MS. 25494, ff. 52ᵛ, 199].

JONES, THOMAS (c. 1794–1859), practised in Chester. He was County Surveyor of Flintshire from 1827 to 1855, when he resigned from ill-health. He died at Barmouth on 2 October 1859, aged 65. His most celebrated work was the Grosvenor Lodge to Eaton Hall, which was based on the gateway of St. Augustine's Abbey, Canterbury. His principal recorded works are:

TALACRE HALL, FLINTSHIRE, for Sir Piers Mostyn, 1824–7, 'old English' style [J. Hicklin, *Excursions in N. Wales*, 1851, 141].

ST. ASAPH CATHEDRAL, Gothic altar tomb to Bishop John Luxmoore (d. 1830) [J. Hemingway, *Panorama of N. Wales*, 4th ed. 1848, 284].

LOTON PARK, SALOP., additions for Sir Baldwin Leighton, Bart., 1830 and 1838 [drawings at Loton Park, *ex inf.* Mr. John Harris].

PENSAX CHURCH, WORCESTERSHIRE, 1832–3, Gothic [I.C.B.S.].

EATON HALL, CHESHIRE, THE GROSVENOR LODGE for the 1st Marquess of Westminster, 1835, Gothic; dem. [J. Hemingway, *Panorama of N. Wales*, 4th ed. 1848, 133].

RHYL, FLINTSHIRE, HOLY TRINITY CHURCH, 1835–6 [D. R. Thomas, *A History of the Diocese of St. Asaph*, 1870, 304; I.C.B.S.].

WREXHAM CHURCH, DENBIGHSHIRE, Gothic monument to Sir Foster and Lady Cunliffe, c. 1835 [J. Hemingway, *Panorama of N. Wales*, 4th ed. 1848, 318]; altar-piece [J. Hicklin, *Excursions in North Wales*, 1851, 211].

KINMEL, DENBIGHSHIRE, ST. GEORGE'S CHURCH, mausoleum to Lady Dinorben (d. 1835) [J. Hemingway, *Panorama of N. Wales*, 4th ed. 1848, 41].

TREVALYN HALL, DENBIGHSHIRE, alterations for Thomas Griffith, 1836–8 [National Register of Archives, List of Sources for Architectural History, iii, no. 13673] (*C. Life*, 12 July 1962).

CHESTER, CHRIST CHURCH, NEWTOWN, 1838, Gothic; dem. 1876 [*A.P.S.D.*, *s.v.* 'Chester'].

BALA UNION WORKHOUSE, 1838 [*N. Wales Chronicle*, 26 June 1838].

FFESTINIOG, MERIONETHSHIRE, ST. DAVID'S CHURCH, 1840, Gothic [*N. Wales Chronicle*, 4 Aug. 1840].

LLANGELYNEN CHURCH, CARNARVONSHIRE, 1840 [*N. Wales Chronicle*, 24 Sept. 1840].

HARLECH, MERIONETHSHIRE, CHURCH, 1841, Gothic [*N. Wales Chronicle*, 12 Oct. 1841].

BARMOUTH, NATIONAL SCHOOL, 1841 [J. Hemingway, *Panorama of N. Wales*, 4th ed. 1848, 83].

MOLD, FLINTSHIRE, COUNTY HALL, c. 1843, 'Old English' style [J. Hicklin, *Excursions in N. Wales*, 1851, 172].

LLANARMON (DYFFRYN CEIRIOG) CHURCH, DEN-

BIGHSHIRE, rebuilt 1846 [*N. Wales Chronicle*, 6 Oct. 1846; I.C.B.S.].

JONES, WILLIAM (–1757), was a minor Georgian architect best known as the designer of THE ROTUNDA in RANELAGH GARDENS, CHELSEA, a large circular building with an elegant galleried interior in which people of fashion drank tea and coffee and listened to music. It was opened in 1742 and demolished in 1805. There is an engraving in Bodleian, Gough Maps 17, f. 36, signed 'William Jones, Architect', and various bills and contracts connected with the erection of the building are among the Chancery Masters' Exhibits in the Public Record Office (C 105/37/32).

Of Jones's earlier career all that is known is that he was the author of the 26 'Designs for Frontispieces' etc., which were appended to James Smith's *Specimen of Antient Carpentry* (1736), and which he republished in 1739 as a separate book entitled *The Gentleman's or Builder's Companion containing Variety of usefull Designs for Doors, Gateways, Peers, Pavilions, Temples, Chimney-Pieces, etc.*, 'Printed for the Author, and sold at his house near the Chapple in King Street Golden Square'. In 1752 he became Surveyor to the East India Company, and designed the Warehouses, Pay Office and Deputy Secretary's Office at EAST INDIA HOUSE, LEADENHALL STREET, in 1754; dem. 1861–2 [W. Foster, *The East India House*, 1924, 136]. In 1757 he submitted a design for NEWGATE GAOL which in layout closely followed one by the elder Dance but was treated externally in a bleak and rather amateurish castellated style [Harold Kalman in *Architectural History* xii, 1969, 52–3 and fig. 28b].

As a country-house architect Jones is found at EDGCOTE HOUSE, NORTHANTS., where he followed William Smith as architect after the latter's death in 1747, and was largely if not wholly responsible for designing the house built by Richard Chauncey in 1747–52 [H. A. Tipping in *C. Life*, 10 Jan. 1920 and *English Homes*, Period V, vol. i, 1921, 289–300]; at WALLINGTON HALL, NORTHUMBERLAND, where in 1750 he made an unexecuted design, preserved in a portfolio, for a garden building; and at HONINGTON HALL, WARWICKS., where he supervised the building of the octagonal saloon for Joseph Townsend to the designs of the amateur architect John Freeman (q.v.) [Gloucester County Record Office, Strickland-Freeman papers, D 1245, FF 38] (*C. Life*, 27 Nov. 1920).

Though Jones was mainly a 'second-generation Palladian' of no special distinction, the Ranelagh Rotunda was an unusual building of some originality for which he deserves considerable credit, and it is likely that further works remain to be identified. William Newton became his pupil in 1750, Jacob Leroux in 1753.

JOPLING, JOSEPH, was the son of Joseph Jopling of Cotherstone, near Barnard Castle. It is not known whether he was related to the J. Jopling who in 1786 submitted a design for rebuilding All Saints Church, Newcastle [T. Sopwith, *All Saints Church, Newcastle*, 1826, 47], or with John Jopling, a Newcastle marble-mason of the early nineteenth century who is said to have been 'a good sculptor' and to have had 'a fine taste for miniature painting' [E. Mackenzie, *Newcastle* ii, 1827, 589]. Nothing is known of his training, but he was probably the J. Jopling who exhibited a 'Design for a Gothic church' at the Royal Academy in 1816. He subsequently practised in London as an architect and civil engineer. His only recorded works in the former capacity appear to have been the Greek Revival PANTECHNICON (a furniture repository) in MOTCOMB STREET, BELGRAVIA, which he designed for Seth Smith in 1830–1 [C. Hussey in *C. Life*, 31 March 1966], and the COLUMN at AMMERDOWN PARK, SOMERSET, in memory of T. S. Jolliffe, 1853, of which he published an elaborate account in the *Builder* xi, 1853, 633–4. He was best known as an authority on theories of proportion and the finer points of architectural draughtsmanship, on both of which subjects he wrote some abstruse treatises. The Society of Arts gave him a Gold Medal for an improvement in the construction of the ribs of groined arches. He was also the inventor of a method of drawing curves which he published as *The Septenary System of generating Curves by continued motion including sundry observations ... on its application and utility in civil and naval architecture [and] sculpture ...* 1823. His subsequent publications included *The Septenary System of generating lines: No. 1. Description of Jopling's Double Cranks*, 1825; *The Practice of Isometrical Perspective*, 1833; *Blackfriars Bridge and Thames Navigation*, 1833; *The Septenary System of Generating Lines, No. 2*, 1844; *Letter to T. L. Donaldson ... on the necessity of numerous correct examples of Mathematical Lines*, 1847; *Examples of Entasis*, 1848; *An Impulse to Art: or Ancient Greek Practical Principles for Volutes and Lines of Beauty* 1849; *A Key to the Proportions of the Parthenon*, 1855, and *A Key to the Proportions of the Parthenon, No. 2*, 1856. As literary executor of his uncle, Charles Waistell (d. 1825), he published in 1827 *Designs for Agricultural Buildings, Labourers' Cottages etc., by the late Charles Waistell, Esq., Chairman of the Committee of Agriculture of the Society of Arts.* He also contributed articles to the *Builder* (vol. ii, 1844, 532, 557, 585) and the *Mechanics' Magazine*.

JOYCE, JAMES, designed MACKRELL'S CHARITY SCHOOL, ALMER, DORSET, 1832, which bears the inscription 'James Joyce, Architect' [R.C.H.M. *Dorset* ii, part 2, 286]. He was probably a local builder.

JOYNES, HENRY (*c.* 1684–1754), was, as stated on his monument in Hendon churchyard, 'Comptroller and Conductor of the Building of Blenheim House in Oxfordshire from 1705 to 1715'. His duties were, in fact, those of a resident clerk of the works, and there are frequent references to him in Vanbrugh's letters, and in the papers relating to Blenheim in the British Museum (Add. MSS. 19602–10). He also assisted Hawksmoor in connection with the erection of the Clarendon Building in Broad Street, Oxford, to the latter's designs in 1712–13 [Add. MS. 19607, ff. 14, 83, 90–100]. In 1715, when Hawksmoor became Clerk of the Works at Whitehall, Joynes succeeded him as Clerk of the Works at Kensington Palace, an appointment which he owed to the influence of Sir John Vanbrugh as Comptroller of the Works. He remained in charge of the works at Kensington until his death.

It is clear from the Blenheim papers that Joynes was a competent draughtsman, and there is evidence that he had a private practice as an architect. Letters and drawings preserved at LINLEY HALL, SALOP., show that he designed that house in 1743–6 for Robert More, M.P., F.R.S. It is an unusual house for its date, combining the strength and movement of a Vanbrughian design with the decorative conventions of the current Palladianism, and shows that Joynes was an architect of ability and originality [Arthur Oswald in *C. Life*, 7–14 Sept. 1961]. References in the letters make it clear that Joynes was also responsible for designing NORMANTON PARK, RUTLAND, for Sir John Heathcote, Bart., *c.* 1735–40. This house was altered and enlarged by K. Couse in 1763–7 and demolished *c.* 1920 (*C. Life*, 8 Feb. 1913). The letters also afford evidence that Joynes was, as stated by Batty Langley (*Ancient Masonry*, 1736, 227), the architect of the house in LINCOLN'S INN FIELDS (now Nos. 57–8) built by Lord Chancellor Charles Talbot in 1730. This has a Palladian elevation designed to harmonize with the adjoining Lindsey House (*Survey of London* iii, 90–1, pls. 73–5). In view of this commission it is possible that Joynes was also employed by Lord Talbot to design his country house at BARRINGTON PARK, nr. BURFORD, GLOS., built in 1734 with a handsome Palladian façade (P. Sandby, *Select Views* i, 1781, no. 15).

A payment to 'H. Joynes Surveyor' in the accounts of Sir John Fellowes, Bart., as printed in *The Particulars and Inventories of the Estates of the late ... Directors of the South Sea Company* i, 1721, shows that Joynes was employed at CARSHALTON HOUSE, SURREY, in about 1720. Here it is possible that he designed the Water Pavilion, a markedly Vanbrughian building illustrated by Field & Bunney, *English Domestic Architecture of the Seventeenth and Eighteenth Centuries*, 1905, pls. lxviii and described in *C. Life*, 4 March 1949.

477

From 1723 to 1748 Joynes was Surveyor to the Commissioners of Sewers in Westminster. He married Mary, daughter of Bartholomew Peisley of Oxford, a master-mason whose son was employed at Blenheim. He died at Kensington on 2 July 1754, at the age of 70, leaving his house in Kensington Gore to his elder son Samuel. He desired to be buried in Hendon churchyard near the east end of the chancel, beneath a monument of Portland stone to be erected 'according to a Draught prepar'd by me'. The monument, which still exists, consists of a square pedestal with a moulded cornice.

[*A.P.S.D.*; *History of the King's Works* v, 475; *The Complete Works of Sir John Vanbrugh* iv: *The Letters, passim*, esp. 244; *Wren Soc.* xx, 116; David Green, *Blenheim Palace*, 1951, *passim*; B.M., Add. MS. 24327; P.C.C., 200 PINFOLD].

JULIAN, GEORGE HANSON, was in partnership with Robert Cornish of Exeter (*q.v.*) in the 1830s. He subsequently became City Surveyor of Exeter, but was practising in London in 1860. He was presumably the George Julian of whom William Moseley (*q.v.*) was a pupil.

JUPP, RICHARD (1728–1799), was the youngest son of Richard Jupp of Clerkenwell, Master of the Carpenters' Company in 1768, who built Sunbury Church to the designs of Stephen Wright in 1751–2. Nothing is known of Jupp's early training, but the fact that he was one of the original members of the Architects' Club would imply that, in accordance with its rules, he had studied architecture in Italy or France.

Jupp succeeded James Steere (d. 1759) as architect to GUY'S HOSPITAL, where he supervised the building of the west wing in *c.* 1774–7 and remodelled the principal façade in 1777–8 [R. A. Cawson and T. H. E. Orde, 'The Design and Building of Mr. Guy's Hospital', *Guy's Hospital Reports* 118(2), 1969]. He also designed DYERS' HALL, DOWGATE HILL, 1768–70, rebuilt 1839–40 [Dyers' Company minutes, Guildhall Library MS. 8164/5, pp. 216–17, 219, 221, 237]. According to Harrison's *Views of Seats* (1787) he designed PAIN'S HILL HOUSE, nr. COBHAM, SURREY, for the Hon. Charles Hamilton in 1774. However Hamilton was obliged by financial difficulties to sell Pain's Hill in 1775, and by 1778, when Jupp exhibited the 'Principal front of the villa in the gardens at Pain's Hill' at the Royal Academy, the owner of the house was Benjamin Bond Hopkins. The house was enlarged by Decimus Burton in 1831–2, and Jupp's portico, awkwardly placed between flanking bows, was removed in the nineteenth century (*C. Life*, 2 Jan. 1958). In about 1790 Jupp altered or remodelled WILTON PARK, nr. BEACONSFIELD, BUCKS. (dem. 1967) for Josias Dupré, Governor of Madras [J. Dugdale, *The British Traveller* i, 1819, 138]. LEE MANOR-HOUSE,

KENT, built in 1772 by Thomas Lucas, has been attributed to him for reasons given in E. & J. Birchenough, *The Manor House, Lee*, Lewisham 1971, 61–3.

For over thirty years (1768–99) Jupp was surveyor to the East India Company, which explains his employment in 1784 to design SEVERNDROOG CASTLE, SHOOTER'S HILL, KENT, a triangular Gothic tower erected by the widow of Sir William James 'To Commemorate that Gallant Officer's Achievements in the East Indies during his Command of the Company's Forces in those Seas', and in particular his capture in 1755 of the fortress of Severndroog on the coast of Malabar [J. Dugdale, *The British Traveller* iii, 1819, 245]. For the East India Company Jupp designed several warehouses in London, including the BENGAL WAREHOUSE in NEW STREET, 1769–70, those between Houndsditch and Middlesex Street, 1792–9, and others on the south side of Crutched Friars, 1796–9 [Minutes of the Court in India Office Records, B 116, ff. 62, 772, B 125, ff. 151–2 and A/1/1, ff. 402, 490, 507]. In 1796 it was decided to rebuild the EAST INDIA HOUSE in LEADENHALL STREET, and the Company, anxious to secure a worthy design for their new building, and evidently uncertain whether their surveyor was equal to the task, decided that he should be asked to take the advice of some of the leading architects of the day. Dance, Wyatt, Holland and Soane were mentioned, but Soane's name was eventually withdrawn at Jupp's instance because he feared that this young and ambitious man, already Architect to the Bank of England, would seek to deprive him of the commission altogether. Unfortunately for Jupp, Soane was at this time the victim of some scurrilous writings which James Wyatt was unwise enough to read aloud at a meeting of the Architects' Club (of which Jupp was a member), and when the unhappy Jupp, in an endeavour to placate Soane by exposing his enemies, sent him a copy of one of these pamphlets, he merely succeeded in identifying his conduct over the East India House with the personal attack on Soane. An interview, at which, according to Soane, Jupp made himself seem 'a knave talking like an honest man', did nothing to mend matters, and in spite of Dance's counsels of moderation, Soane, while privately preparing plans for the new East India House, endeavoured unsuccessfully to bring Jupp's conduct before the General Court of Proprietors.

Meanwhile Jupp had addressed a pathetic letter to the Directors, reminding them of his twenty-nine years of faithful service, and imploring them not to deprive him of this opportunity of distinguishing himself. This had its effect. On 9 August 1796 Jupp was directed to prepare plans without any reference to other architects, and on 23 September these plans were accepted. The building was begun under Jupp's direction the following year, and was substantially complete by the time of his death on 17 April 1799. Jupp's place as Surveyor to the Company was then filled by Henry Holland, who had the task of finishing off the interior and settling the accounts. It has often been claimed that although Jupp was the nominal architect of the East India House, the design was really made for him by Holland. The basis of this allegation appears to be a note by H. B. Hodson in *The Builder* for 15 September 1855 (p. 437) recording that in 1807 he found a quantity of working drawings for the building in Holland's office. These drawings are now in the Victoria and Albert Museum (boxes A.175–6), but they relate almost exclusively to the interior, and the fact that they came from Holland's office does not prove that they were his work. Several of them are drawn on paper watermarked 1796, and one of them is a 'Section of the Lime Street Front as settled by Mr. Jupp, April 31st. 1797'. Jupp himself claimed credit for the design both by exhibiting it at the Royal Academy in 1798 and by issuing a printed description of the façade, with a key to the sculpture in the pediment. The building (demolished 1861–2) was illustrated as his work in Britton & Pugin's *Public Buildings of London* ii, 1828, 77–89, and Holland's alleged participation in its design must be regarded as unsubstantiated.

At the time of his death Jupp held office as Master of the Carpenters' Company. William Tyler told Joseph Farington that he died worth £35,000.

[*A.P.S.D.*; *D.N.B.*; A. T. Bolton, *The Portrait of Sir John Soane*, 1927, 59–79; India Office Library, records of the East India Company, especially B1/123, pp. 498, 642 (minutes of 9 Aug. and 23 Sept. 1796); Farington's Diary, 17 Aug. 1799; information from Mr. N. Kitz.]

JUPP, WILLIAM (–1788), was the elder brother of Richard Jupp (d. 1799). He exhibited two designs for gentlemen's seats at the Society of Artists in 1763 and 1764, and an unexecuted design for a country house signed by him is at the Platt Hall Art Gallery, Rusholme, Manchester. He rebuilt the LONDON TAVERN, BISHOPSGATE STREET WITHIN (dem. 1876), after its destruction by fire in 1765; drawings connected with this work are in Sir John Soane's Museum (Drawer 57, 7). The entrance hall and principal staircase of CARPENTERS' HALL, LONDON WALL, were erected to his designs, c. 1780. The entrance hall was decorated in stucco work with figures and implements emblematic of carpentry, and with the heads of Vitruvius, Palladio, Inigo Jones and Wren, executed by Bacon. The archway forming the entrance to the street was also designed by Jupp, with a bust of Inigo Jones by Bacon on the keystone. The staircase was

damaged by fire in 1849 and the Hall itself was demolished in 1876. Both at Carpenters' Hall and at the London Tavern, Jupp appears to have been assisted by William Newton, who certainly designed the Eating-Room and Ballroom of the latter building. Jupp was a warden of the Carpenters' Company in 1781. He was the father of William Jupp (d. 1839) and of Richard Webb Jupp, solicitor (1767–1852), who was Clerk to the Carpenters' Company from 1796 to 1852. The latter's son, Edward Basil Jupp, F.S.A. (1812–77), Clerk to the same Company from 1852 to 1877, was the author of an *Historical Account of the Worshipful Company of Carpenters*, 1848, 2nd ed., 1887, from which the above particulars are largely derived [*A.P.S.D.*; *D.N.B.*; C. H. L. Woodd, *Pedigrees and Memorials of the Family of Woodd and the Family of Jupp*, privately printed 1875].

JUPP, WILLIAM (–1839), was the elder son of William Jupp (d. 1788). He exhibited at the Royal Academy from 1794 to 1804, including a design for a room at the 'Star and Garter' Hotel at Richmond, Surrey (1803). He was architect and surveyor to the Skinners', Merchant Taylors', Ironmongers' and Apothecaries' Companies, and was also District Surveyor for Limehouse, Blackwall, Wapping, Mile End Old Town, Poplar and Ratcliff. In 1801–3 he carried out alterations to SKINNERS' HALL, DOWGATE HILL [J. F. Wadmore, *Account of the Skinners' Company*, 1902, 133], and as surveyor to the Merchant Taylors' Company was presumably the architect of that Company's Almshouses at Lee, Kent, erected in 1826. He was Master of the Carpenters' Company in 1831 [*A.P.S.D.*; E. B. Jupp, *Historical Account of the Company of Carpenters*, 1887].

K

KAY, JOSEPH (1775–1847), was a pupil of S. P. Cockerell. He travelled on the Continent from 1802 to 1805, for part of the time in company with Robert Smirke. The journal which he kept in Rome in 1803–4 is in the British Museum (Add. MS. 45545, ff. 1–34). In 1807 he married the eldest daughter of William Porden, whom he assisted in the erection of EATON HALL, CHESHIRE [Neale, *Views of Seats* i, 1818]. In the same year he was appointed surveyor to the Foundling Hospital in succession to Cockerell, and in this capacity laid out the garden in MECKLENBURGH SQUARE and designed the block of houses on the east side, begun in 1810, but not completed until 1821. He exhibited the design at the Royal Academy in 1812. In 1811 he succeeded J. T. Groves as architect to the Post Office, and in 1818–19 designed the POST OFFICE in WATERLOO PLACE, EDINBURGH [P.R.O., Works 1/13]. In 1814 he made preliminary designs for a new General Post Office in London, but, after much bureaucratic wavering and an indecisive competition, they were set aside in favour of plans by Robert Smirke which were executed in 1823–9. Kay's design is preserved in P.R.O., Works 30/414–5, and in Sir John Soane's Museum (Drawer 38, 6). He keenly felt the disappointment, and from that time onward never entered into competition for any public works, confining himself to private practice and to the duties of his appointments. In 1823 he succeeded H. H. Seward as Clerk of Works to Greenwich Hospital. In this capacity he carried out extensive improvements in the town, forming NELSON STREET and the new MARKET in 1829.

Kay's private clients included the Thornhill family, for whom he supervised the development of their ISLINGTON estate from 1813 onwards [see many letters from Kay among the Thornhill papers in the Hunts. Record Office]; the Earl of Chichester, for whom in 1824–8 he carried out a handsome piece of town-planning at HASTINGS, consisting of PELHAM CRESCENT with the church of ST. MARY-IN-THE-CASTLE as its central feature; the Marquis Camden, who employed him on his CAMDEN TOWN estate in London; and the Earl of Radnor, for whom in 1843 he made an unexecuted scheme for housing at FOLKESTONE which is preserved in the Radnor Estate Office there. In 1828 he made designs for alterations to Lord Radnor's seat, LONGFORD CASTLE, WILTS., but these were apparently not carried out. It is also uncertain whether the 'small library and picture gallery designed for D. W. Acraman, Esqr.', which he exhibited at the Royal Academy in 1808, was built. In 1809–11 he completed the MALL ASSEMBLY ROOMS at CLIFTON, BRISTOL, after the bankruptcy of F. H. Greenway, the original architect and builder. His designs for the decoration of the ceilings, signed and dated 1811, are in the Victoria and Albert Museum [93 H.23, nos. 3 and 20]. One drawing by Kay connected with Greenwich Hospital is in the R.I.B.A. Drawings Collection, and at Rougham Hall, Norfolk there are plans by him dated 1828 for enlarging a house at Hastings for Frederick North.

Kay was secretary of the London Architects' Club. He also took an active part in the formation of the Institute of British Architects, and became one of its first vice-presidents. He died on 7 December 1847, aged 72, at his house, No. 6 Gower Street, and was buried in the Foundling Hospital Chapel. His eldest son, William Porden Kay, born in 1809, assisted his father for many years before going out to Australia in 1842 as Director of Public Works. His daughter Eliza married Edward Basil Jupp, grandson of William Jupp (*q.v.*). Charles Matson was a pupil.

[*A.P.S.D.*; John Summerson, *Georgian London*, 1969, 168–9; *History of the King's Works* vi, 431–2; P.R.O., Greenwich Hospital Records; F. T. Cansick, *Epitaphs of Middlesex* ii, 1872, 247.]

KAY, ROBERT (1740–1818), was an Edinburgh architect and drawing master. He was a distant relative of John Kay, the Scottish caricaturist, who was the son of a mason of Dalkeith. He himself was born at Cairnton, nr. Penicuik, and began life as a wright or carpenter. 'But, gradually advancing himself by steady application and industry, he became a builder and architect, and attained to no small degree of respectability and professional reputation'. In 1781 he entered the competition for St. Andrew's Church in the New Town, which was won by Captain Frazer (*q.v.*) with a design for an oval church. Frazer, however, 'declined accepting the premium, desiring it might be given to Mr. Robert Kay, drawing master in Edinburgh, whose drawings and section of a square church were thought highly meritorious' [*Scots Mag.*, 1781, 119]. In the Scottish Record Office there is an unexecuted design by Kay for a proposed church at Wick in Caithness, dated 1796 [RHP 12365]. In 1787–8 he made drawings of lighthouses for Thomas Smith, the first engineer to the Commissioners of Northern Lighthouses [D. B. Hague & R. Christie, *Lighthouses*, 1975, 220].

Kay made a modest fortune by successful speculations in building in South Bridge Street and from property in Hunter Square. On his retirement in about 1806 he built a house at Wester Duddingston on the south-east outskirts of Edinburgh. When he died in 1818 he was buried in a lair in the Calton Old Burial Ground which has the name 'Robert Kay Architect' carved on the lintel. His fortune was mostly bequeathed to charity. A portrait caricature is given in John Kay's *Original Portraits* ii, 1838, 378, together with a short biography. See also *Book of the Old Edinburgh Club* xxiv, 167 n.

KECK, ANTHONY (1726–1797), had an extensive practice in the West Midland counties during the second half of the eighteenth century. His works are mostly of the type described in contemporary literature as 'a neat brick edifice', the interiors being in the Adam style. His finest work was the great Orangery, 327 feet in length, at Margam Abbey in Glamorganshire. Keck lived for many years at Beech House, King's Stanley, Gloucestershire, where he died in August 1797. He became a Freeman of Worcester in 1768. Unexecuted drawings by him for alterations to Allensmore House, Herefs., are in the R.I.B.A. Drawings Collection. [*A.P.S.D.*; *Berrow's Worcester Journal*, 12 Oct. 1797.]

BEVERE HOUSE, NORTH CLAINES, WORCS., for Dr. T. R. Nash, probably *c.* 1760 [*A.P.S.D.*] (illustrated on the title-page of T. R. Nash's *History of Worcestershire* i, 1781).

WORCESTER, THE COUNTY INFIRMARY, 1767–70; altered by W. J. Hopkins *c.* 1855 [V. Green, *History of Worcester* ii, 1796, 12; engraved plan and elevation signed by Keck in Bodleian, Gough Maps 33, f. 54].

WORCESTER, ST. MARTIN'S CHURCH, 1768–72; altered by W. J. Hopkins, who inserted Gothic tracery in the east window, 1855–62 [V. Green, *History of Worcester* ii, 1796, 62].

UPTON-ON-SEVERN CHURCH, WORCS., added cupola to tower, 1769–70 [MS. 'Parish Book' under date 18 July 1769] (H. Field & M. Bunney, *English Domestic Architecture of the 17th and 18th Centuries*, 1905, pl. cvii].

HAM COURT, UPTON-ON-SEVERN, WORCS., for John Martin, 1772; dem. [accounts partly reproduced in copy of 1914 sale catalogue of house in Birmingham Reference Library].

PENRICE CASTLE, GLAMORGANSHIRE, for Thomas Mansel Talbot, 1773–80 [C. A. Maunsell, *The Family of Maunsell* i, 1917, 231; John Cornforth in *C. Life*, 18, 25 Sept. 1975].

DURSLEY, GLOS., designs for WORKHOUSE, 1774 [Gloucester Public Library, MS. RF 115, 72].

MOCCAS COURT, HEREFS., for Sir George Cornewall, Bart., 1776–83; semicircular porch added 1792 [W. Angus, *Views of Seats*, 1787, pl. xix][1].

FLAXLEY ABBEY, GLOS., reconstruction after fire in 1777, for Thomas Crawley-Boevey, 1780 [volume of drawings by Keck preserved in the house; J. & H. S. Storer, *Delineations of the County of Gloucester*, 1824, 127] (*C. Life*, 29 March, 5–12 April 1973).

BARNSLEY PARK, GLOS., redecoration of dining-room for James Musgrave, *c.* 1780 [C. Hussey in *C. Life*, 9 Sept. 1954].

HILL HOUSE (later RODBOROUGH MANOR), RODBOROUGH, GLOS., extensions for Sir G. O. Paul, 1784; burned 1906 [*Gloucester Jnl.*, 23 Aug. 1784, *ex inf.* Mr. N. M. Herbert].

WORCESTER COUNTY GAOL, enlarged 1784–88 [V. Green, *History of Worcester* ii, 1796, 28–9].

GLOUCESTER, inspected and altered the plans made by William Price for the EASTGATE and SOUTHGATE STREET MARKETS, which were erected by Price in 1785–6 under Keck's supervision [extracts by C. H. Dancey from Gloucester City Council Books in Gloucester Public Library, 17270].

attributed: CANON FROME COURT, HEREFS., for

---

[1] Alternative designs made by Robert & James Adam in 1775 were not carried out, but in 1781 they supplied some further designs for chimney-pieces and a ceiling to decorate the house designed by Keck [Soane Museum, vol. xxiii, 136–9, and information from Mr. Nicholas Thompson].

Richard Cope Hopton, 1786 [stylistic attribution, based on resemblance to Moccas Court].

MARGAM ABBEY, GLAMORGANSHIRE, THE ORANGERY, for Thomas Mansel Talbot, 1787–90 [drawing at Penrice Castle signed 'A. Keck Oct. 4 1787' and entitled 'greenhouse now building', *ex inf.* Mr. O. E. Craster, 1961; Patricia Moore, 'The Orangeries at Margam', *The Glamorgan Historian* iv, 1967, 25].

LONGWORTH HALL, HEREFS., for Robert Phillipps, *c.* 1788 [Neale, *Views of Seats*, 2nd ser., iv].

KEEBLE, HENRY ASHLEY, was apprenticed in 1783 to George Gwilt the elder. He exhibited at the Royal Academy from 1797 to 1806, and competed unsuccessfully for the New Bethlehem Hospital in 1810. Under a lease dated December 1830 he designed and built NOS. 45–57 FALMOUTH ROAD, SOUTHWARK, a row of stucco-fronted houses illustrated in *Survey of London* xxv, 116.

KEENE, HENRY (1726–1776), born on 15 November 1726, was the son of Henry Keene, probably the carpenter of that name who was one of the builders of Ealing Church, Middlesex, to the designs of James Horne in 1739–40. He was 'bred to the profession of architecture', and in 1746 succeeded Thomas Hinton as Surveyor to the Dean and Chapter of Westminster. In 1752 James Horne resigned his post as Surveyor to the Fabric of Westminster Abbey in favour of Keene, who thus combined both the Abbey surveyorships until his death. There are many references in the Chapter Acts to his duties in connection with the estates of the Dean and Chapter, and details of his architectural work in the Abbey are given below. A letter in which he described the opening of Edward I's tomb in 1774 is printed in Hist. MSS. Comm., *Third Report*, Appendix, 276*b*.

In 1761 Keene was taken to Ireland by Lord Halifax, the newly appointed Lord-Lieutenant, and according to a letter written by the Dean of Westminster to Lord le Despenser in the following year[1] he was 'appointed by him Architect of the Kingdom of Ireland for his Majesty's Works there'. No such office appears to have been in existence at this date, but from 1763 to 1766 Keene is referred to in Irish records as 'Architect to the Barrack Board' in Dublin, and it was from the Barrack Board that the Irish Board of Works later developed. Nothing is at present known of any works which Keene may have carried out in this capacity, but in the 1750s he had already been employed, in conjunction with John Sanderson, to make the working drawings for the west front of Trinity College, Dublin, designed by the amateur architect Theodore Jacobsen (*q.v.*). Accord-

---

[1] Bodleian Library, Oxford, MS. D. D. Dashwood (Bucks.) c. 7.

ing to the Dean of Westminster, he also held the post of 'Gentleman of the Privy Chamber' to his patron the Lord-Lieutenant, at whose Sussex seat he and his son were afterwards to be employed.[1]

As a private architect, Keene is chiefly remarkable as one of the first to exploit the fashion for Gothic which became so characteristic a feature of English taste in the latter part of the eighteenth century. He was not a serious student of Gothic architecture in the same way as James Essex; but as Surveyor to Westminster Abbey he was in daily contact with a famous medieval building, and details from Westminster recur frequently in his Gothic work. At Arbury, for instance, the Drawing Room fireplace is copied from the tomb of Aymer de Valence, and in 1766 a joiner was taken to the Abbey to make exact copies of foliage and other Gothic details for Sir Roger Newdigate's house. The Gothicization of Arbury had begun under Sanderson Miller's direction, and it may well have been through Miller that Keene first became interested in Gothic, for as early as 1749 Keene was helping Miller to make drawings for Hagley,[2] and about the same time Miller records in his diary that he repaired Nelmes in Essex 'by means of Mr. Henry Keene (then a young beginner in architecture)'. The octagonal Hartwell Church (now in ruins) was Keene's *chef d'œuvre* in this style, but characteristic examples of his elegant rococo Gothick can still be seen at Hartlebury Castle and Harefield Church.

As a classical architect, Keene is best known for his work in Oxford, and for the handsome Town Hall which he built for Lord Shelburne at High Wycombe. What appears to be the interior of this building is shown in a conversation-piece painted by Robert Pyle in 1760.[3] The principal figure is Keene himself, who is pointing to a plan of an unidentified building, which is laid on the table. The other persons present are Ben Carter (a statuary mason), 'Euclid Abfray' (? Euclid Langley), Devereux Fox, Thomas Dryhurst (a carver), Thomas Hefford (a plasterer), George Mercer (Master of the Masons' Company in 1763), Edmund Rawlinson (landscape-painter), Thomas Gayfere (Master Mason to Westminster Abbey), J. Pratt (Master Bricklayer

to the Crown), William Cobbett (a glazier), 'John Devet' (? John Devall, Serjeant Plumber), Jeremiah Hutchins (a painter) and Thomas Collins (a builder).

Keene invested in house property in Golden Square, London, where he had a town residence (No. 13, dem. 1906). He also took a building site on the Portland estate in Harley Street at the time of its development by the Adam brothers, and possessed property in Oxford.[1] He had a country house at Drayton Green, Ealing, where he died on 8 January 1776, at the age of 50.

Keene died in mid-career. But there are indications that in Oxford at least, where a few years earlier he had been thought of as 'a very ingenious man', his reputation was declining. In 1773 it was James Wyatt who was chosen to design the Canterbury Quadrangle at Christ Church, although Keene had earlier been employed there to alter the Library, and in the same year Keene's design for the Radcliffe Observatory had been set aside in favour of 'another Elevation', almost certainly that of Wyatt, by whom the building was completed after his death. Keene was, in fact, an architect of minor stature in comparison with Wyatt, 'in whose hands the design for the Observatory acquired a distinction and an originality of treatment altogether beyond the powers' of his predecessor, and it is only in the history of the Gothic revival that he has a place of some importance.

He married Anne, daughter of M. Deval, a French Huguenot refugee, and had numerous children, of whom only two sons and a daughter survived him. Theodosius, who appears to have been the eldest, followed his father's profession. Thomas became the father of Henry George Keene, the Persian scholar. Elizabeth married William Parry, Welsh harper to George III. There is a small collection of drawings by Henry Keene in the Victoria and Albert Museum (A.189). It includes the design for the fireplace at University College, Oxford, an elevation of an unidentified house, and drawings for an octagonal Gothic Pavilion resembling Hartwell Church.

[*A.P.S.D.*; *D.N.B.*; H. Clifford Smith, 'A Georgian Architect', *C. Life*, 30 March 1945, and subsequent correspondence; *An Eighteenth-Century Correspondence*, ed. Dickins & Stanton, 1910, 179–80; Westminster Abbey muniments; A. T. Bolton, *The Architecture of R. & J. Adam* ii, 1922, 102; Keene's will is P.C.C. 22 BELLAS.]

WESTMINSTER, THE FLESH MARKET, *c.* 1749–50; dem. 1805. Keene's designs are preserved in Westminster Abbey Muniments (P) 733, 733

[1] For information about Keene's career in Ireland I am indebted to Mr. M. J. Craig and Mr. E. McParland.

[2] Warwick County Record Office, Sanderson Miller's correspondence, 125B/350.

[3] This picture was formerly in the possession of the Hon. Mrs. Ionides, but was unfortunately burned in the fire which destroyed Buxted Park, Sussex, in 1940. It is reproduced in *C. Life*, 30 March 1945, 556. Seven of the thirteen craftsmen depicted were employed by Keene in the building and decoration of Nos. 17–18 Cavendish Square in 1756–7, and four of them in altering Sir Roger Newdigate's house in Spring Gardens in 1763.

[1] Among Keene's Oxford property was No. 65 St. Giles', whose lease he bought in 1768. The house was refronted before 1793, possibly during the period of Keene's tenancy.

A-B, see also W.A.M. (P) 734 and 24887. For a view of the Market, see *Views of Westminster by William Capon*, London Topographical Society 1923–4.

GRAY'S INN, NO. 4 SOUTH SQUARE, 1750 (in conformity with Nos. 2–3, already built under the direction of Mr. Gorham, bricklayer to the Society). [*Records of Gray's Inn*, ed. R. J. Fletcher, ii, 263, 268].

HARTLEBURY CASTLE, WORCS., refitted and reroofed the Castle Chapel for Bishop Maddox in Gothic style, c. 1750 [E. H. Pearce, *Hartlebury Castle*, 1926, 243] (*C. Life*, 23 Sept. 1971).

WORCESTER CATHEDRAL. In May 1750 it was ordered 'that Mr. Kean, or some other skilful architect, be applied to for a draught of a proper ornamental Portico in the Gothick style to be erected over the great Gate of the Cathedral instead of a mean, deformed covering now over the Gate, falling into Ruins'. It is doubtful whether this was executed. [J. Noake, *The Monastery and Cathedral of Worcester*, 1866, 336.]

NELMES, HORNCHURCH, ESSEX, repairs for Godfrey Webster under the direction of Sanderson Miller, c. 1750; dem. 1967 [Sanderson Miller's diary].

TRINITY COLLEGE, DUBLIN. Although it appears from the *Journal of the House of Commons of the Kingdom of Ireland* vi, 1757–60, Appendix, p. cclxiii, no. xxxv, that £74 11s. 8d. were paid to 'Messrs. Keene and Saunderson for the Plans and Elevations' of the building erected in 1752–9, it is clear from the evidence cited above (p. 450) that they were in fact implementing designs made by the amateur architect Theodore Jacobsen.

HARTWELL CHURCH, BUCKS., for Sir William Lee, Bart., 1753–5, Gothic; fell into ruin 1951 [W. H. Smythe, *Addenda to the Aedes Hartwellianae*, 1864, 20–1; there are some alternative designs for the church in Bodleian, MS. Top. Gen. b. 55, ff. 29–34].

HIGH WYCOMBE CHURCH, BUCKS., added Gothic parapet and pinnacles to tower, and designed Gothic pew, font-cover and west door for the 1st Earl of Shelburne, 1754. Keene's drawing for the Shelburne pew is reproduced by F. Skull in *Records of Bucks*. ix, 1908. The pew itself was removed to the west end of the church in 1858 and to Wycombe Abbey School in 1891. It original position over the chancel screen is shown in Addleshaw & Etchells, *The Architectural Setting of Anglican Worship*, 1948, pl. 5 [A. T. Bolton, *Architecture of R. and J. Adam* i, 1922, 204].

EALING GROVE, MIDDLESEX, for Joseph Gulston, c. 1755; altered by J. Yenn c. 1780; dem. [elevation signed by Keene in Northumberland Record Office, ZBU B 5/6 (28)].

BOWOOD HOUSE, WILTS., for the 1st Earl of Shel-

burne, 1755–60. The portico was added or altered, the office block remodelled, and the interior of the house decorated by R. Adam for the 2nd Earl of Shelburne, 1761–4. The chapel by C. R. Cockerell was added in 1824, and C. Barry carried out general alterations in 1834–5, including the addition of the gallery between the Diocletian wing and the house. The main block designed by Keene was dem. 1956 [A. T. Bolton, *Architecture of R. and J. Adam* i, 1922, 204, 215].

LONDON, NOS. 17–18 CAVENDISH SQUARE, for Thomas Bridges and William Lloyd, 1756–7 [drawings and building accounts in Middlesex County Record Office, 85/223–64].

HIGH WYCOMBE, BUCKS., THE GUILDHALL, for the 1st Earl of Shelburne, 1757 [A. T. Bolton, *Architecture of R. and J. Adam* i, 1922, 204; *Records of Bucks*. x, 1916, 301] (measured drawings in *Arch. Rev.* xlvii, 1920, 26–7).

CORSHAM COURT, WILTS., rebuilt north front, etc., for Peter Methuen, 1759–60; reconstructed by T. Bellamy 1850 [C. Hussey in *C. Life*, 20–27 Nov. 1937; C. Hussey, *English Country Houses: Early Georgian*, 1955, 228–33].

HARTWELL HOUSE, BUCKS., rebuilt east front, etc., for Sir William Lee, Bart., 1759–63. Keene also designed a bridge in the park, which was completed by James Wyatt in 1780, but has since been destroyed. It is illustrated in W. H. Smythe, *Addenda to the Aedes Hartwellianae*, 1864, 21. Keene's bills and estimates for his work at Hartwell were sold at Sotheby's on 8 March 1939, lot 665. Some papers connected with the house are in the Bucks. Record Office and the library of the Victoria and Albert Museum (Reserve L 4), and there are drawings in Bodleian, MS. Top. Gen. b. 55. (*C. Life*, 14–21 March 1914).

ARBURY HALL, WARWICKS., assisted Sir Roger Newdigate, Bart., in connection with the remodelling of the house in Gothic style which had been in progress since c. 1750 and was not completed until c. 1790. Keene does not appear to have been employed at Arbury until 1761 (he was paid 15 guineas 'for drawings &c' in 1762) and after his death his place as Newdigate's architectural collaborator was taken by Henry Couchman (*q.v.*) [Warwickshire Record Office, Newdigate family papers; A. C. Wood, 'The Diaries of Sir Roger Newdigate', *Trans. Birmingham Archaeological Soc.* lxxviii, 1962, 48–53] (*C. Life*, 8, 15, 29 Oct. 1953).

LONDON, SPRING GARDENS, repairs and alterations to house for Sir Roger Newdigate, Bart., 1763; dem. c. 1882 [Warwickshire Record Office, Newdigate family papers].

OXFORD, UNIVERSITY COLLEGE, remodelled interior of Hall in Gothic style, 1766, the chimney-piece being the gift of Sir Roger Newdigate. Keene's Gothic ceiling and woodwork were destroyed 1904 [A. Wood, *Colleges and Halls*, ed. Gutch, 1786, Appendix, 236; design for fireplace in V. and A., E 903, 1921] (Acker-mann, *History of the University of Oxford*, 1814, plate).

OXFORD, CHRIST CHURCH, designed the ANATOMY SCHOOL (later Chemical Laboratory), 1766–7, and enclosed and fitted up ground floor of LIBRARY, 1769–72 [W. G. Hiscock, *A Christ Church Miscellany*, 1946, 70–1, 210].

OXFORD, SHELDONIAN THEATRE, inserted sash-windows, 1767–8; replaced 1959 [University Archives, Theatre Account, 1767–9].

HAREFIELD CHURCH, MIDDLESEX, new chancel arch and Gothic plasterwork in chancel, for Sir Roger Newdigate, Bart., 1768 [Warwickshire Record Office, Newdigate family papers].

attributed: ASTLEY CHURCH, WARWICKS., Gothic stalls and plasterwork in chancel, for Sir Roger Newdigate, Bart.

OXFORD, MAGDALEN COLLEGE. Keene is said to have been 'engaged at Magdalen College for about 20 years'. A plan for paving the ante-chapel, as 'executed by Mr. H. Keene in Octr. 1768', is preserved in a volume of drawings in the College Library (f. 26), and the President's Lodgings are said to have been altered by him in 1769.

OXFORD, BALLIOL COLLEGE, THE FISHER BUILDING, 1768–9; north side refaced 1877 and 1963, south side refaced and altered by Waterhouse 1870 [J. Nichols, *Literary Anecdotes* 1812–15, viii, 248].

WESTMINSTER ABBEY. Keene remodelled the interior of the JERUSALEM CHAMBER in Gothic style, 1769 [W.A.M. 24836], designed Gothic gates for the entrance to the cloister from Dean's Yard, 1769 [W.A.M. 24836], and Gothic choir-stalls, pulpit, etc., 'contrived so as to be removable on public occasions', 1775 [W.A.M., Register 46, ff. 170ᵛ–172ᵛ]. The choir-furniture was removed by Blore in 1848. The pulpit is now in Trottiscliffe Church, Kent.

WESTBOURNE CHURCH, SUSSEX, Gothic spire (timber) for the Earl of Halifax, 1770. The inscription 'HENRY KEENE ARCHITECT 1770' is painted on a beam inside the spire. The crockets, quatrefoils, etc., which originally decorated the spire were removed by H. Woodyer in 1865.

SPELSBURY CHURCH, OXON., monument to 3rd Earl of Lichfield (d. 1772), signed 'H. KEENE Archs. invt. W. Tyler sculpt.' (K. A. Esdaile, *English Church Monuments 1510–1840*, 1946, pl. 127).

OXFORD, THE RADCLIFFE OBSERVATORY, begun 1772 to Keene's designs, but in March 1773, after public criticisms of the design, notably by Edward Tatham in *Oxonia Explicata et Ornata* (1773), the Trustees decided to adopt 'another elevation' (by James Wyatt), which Keene

carried out until his death in 1776, whereupon the Trustees ordered 'that Theodosius Keene his son be employed to finish the same under the Direction of Mr. Wyatt'. The building was completed in 1794 [Bodleian Library, MS. Minute Books of the Radcliffe Trustees] (*C. Life*, 10 May 1930).

OXFORD, WORCESTER COLLEGE, THE PROVOST'S LODGINGS, 1773–6. Keene also completed the north range of the College, of which he built the central portion and the two staircases to the west, repeating the design of the two staircases to the east erected by Dr. Clarke's trustees between 1753 and 1759 [*V.C.H. Oxfordshire* iii, 308–9; Arthur Oswald in *C. Life*, 5 Nov. 1948].

UPPARK, SUSSEX, THE VANDALIAN TOWER, for Sir Matthew Fetherstonhaugh, Bart., 1774, Gothic [C. Hussey in *C. Life*, 21 June 1941 and 28 June, 569; Margaret Meade-Fetherston-haugh & Oliver Warner, *Uppark and its People*, 1964, 46 and fig. 12].

KEENE, THEODOSIUS (*c.* 1754–), was the elder son of Henry Keene, who left him all his freehold, copyhold and leasehold estates in Middlesex, Oxford and elsewhere. He exhibited an 'Elevation of a house and offices' at the Society of Artists in 1770, and in 1772 'A View of Stan-stead Castle, near Emsworth'. This is the tri-angular Gothic folly now known as RACTON TOWER, which was built by Lord Halifax, of Stan-stead Park, Sussex, who in 1770 had employed Henry Keene to design the spire of Westbourne Church. An elevation of the tower is among the Keene drawings in the Victoria and Albert Museum (E.876, 1921, reproduced in *C. Life*, 18 Sept. 1969, 682). The only other known work by Theodosius Keene is MAIDENHEAD TOWN HALL, erected to his designs in 1777, but remodelled 1879–80 and dem. *c.* 1960. [J. W. Walker, *History of Maidenhead*, 1931, 75–6]. He exhibited 'A De-sign for a nobleman's mansion' at the Royal Aca-demy the same year, and in 1786 Sir Roger Newdigate paid him £500 for work at his house in Spring Gardens [*Trans. Birmingham Arch. Soc.* lxxviii, 1962, 48]. In 1787 he was responsible for some 'small alterations' to Sir Charles Asgill's villa at RICHMOND, SURREY [*The World*, 16 June 1787, *ex inf.* Mr. P. A. Bezodis], but after this no further references to him have been found. His Italian sketch-book, bearing the inscription 'KEENE, Archt. 1775' on the fly-leaf, is in the Vic-toria and Albert Museum (D.443.88). It contains a design for a bridge.

KELSALL, CHARLES (1782–1857), eccentric, author, traveller and amateur architect, was the son of the prosperous Thomas Kelsall who was on the Council of the East India Company and whose cousin had married at Madras Clive of

India. He was educated at Eton and Trinity College, Cambridge, and published many books of which the most remarkable was *Phantasm of an University*, 1814, in which he outlined an enlightened programme of educational and intellectual reform. His other publications included *A Letter from Athens addressed to a Friend in England*, 1812, *A Letter to the Society of Dilettanti on the Works in Progress at Windsor*, 1827, *Esquisse de mes travaux, de mes voyages et de mes opinions*, Frankfurt, 1830, and *Horae Viaticae*, 1836. By 1841 he had purchased Knightons, a house at Hythe, nr. Southampton, which he called the Villa Amalthaea. He adorned the garden with a row of busts and a small tower which still survive. On his death he left his library to Morden College, Blackheath, where a building to house it was added to designs by P. C. Hardwick. Some of his MSS. are preserved in the library, including three drawings for a monument to Milton in the grounds of Christ's College, Cambridge, and four drawings for a new library at Morden College in the Elizabethan style. [D. J. Watkin, 'Charles Kelsall: the Quintessence of Neo-Classicism', *Arch. Rev.* cxl, 1966, 109–12, and *Thomas Hope and the Neo-Classical Idea*, 1968.]

KELSEY, RICHARD (1791–1856), was admitted to the Royal Academy Schools in 1818 at the age of 27. He was awarded Silver Medals for architectural designs by the Society of Arts in 1819 and 1820, and in 1821 gained the Gold Medal of the Royal Academy. He subsequently became David Laing's principal assistant and later practised from Finsbury [S. Redgrave, *Dictionary of Artists*, 1878, 247]. In 1829 he designed the south tower-porch of EAST BARNET CHURCH, HERTS., in a Romanesque style [I.C.B.S.], and in 1842 the circular pedestal for Samuel Nixon's statue of King William IV, now in Greenwich Park but originally in King William Street, London [*Companion to the Almanac*, 1842, 204]. He died on 7 August 1856, aged 65 [*Gent's Mag.* 1856 (ii), 394].

KEMP, GEORGE MEIKLE (1795–1844), was born at Hillrigs in the parish of Biggar.[1] His father was a shepherd, and George's childhood was spent in pastoral surroundings. A boyish interest in carving and model-making led to his apprenticeship to a carpenter in Peeblesshire (1809–13). Subsequently he worked as a mill-wright at Galashiels. While travelling on foot to his new job he was given a lift by Walter Scott, though he did not discover the identity of his

benefactor until he had been set down at the end of the journey.

While working as a journeyman at Galashiels, Kemp developed a latent interest in architecture by studying and drawing the monastic churches at Melrose, Dryburgh and Jedburgh. Subsequent employment in Edinburgh, Lancashire and Glasgow enabled him to extend his knowledge of Gothic architecture. In 1824 he reached London and saw some of the southern cathedrals, including Canterbury. In the following year he set out on a tour of Europe, intending (though ignorant of any foreign language) to maintain himself as a mill-wright and see the principal churches abroad. After two years travelling in northern France the news of his mother's death recalled him to Scotland. Failing to establish his own business as a carpenter in Edinburgh, he was employed as a draughtsman by William Burn (*q.v.*), and in 1831–2 made a large wooden model of Burn's design for a proposed new palace for the Duke of Buccleuch at Dalkeith. He also made drawings for a volume of Scottish ecclesiastical antiquities projected by an Edinburgh printer, but abandoned after the latter's death.

Though entirely self-taught, Kemp had by now acquired a first-hand knowledge of Gothic architecture unrivalled in Scotland, and in England equalled only by that of J. C. Buckler, Edward Blore and Thomas Rickman. In 1834 he made unsolicited drawings for the restoration of Glasgow Cathedral which were taken up by a local committee and formed the basis of a scheme for which J. Gillespie Graham (*q.v.*) unscrupulously took the sole credit, allowing the committee to publish them without acknowledgement to Kemp (*Plans and Elevations of the Proposed Restorations and Additions to the Cathedral of Glasgow, with an Explanatory Address by the Local Committee*, folio, 1836). In 1840 Kemp vindicated himself in an open letter to the committee, but the whole project fell through, and it was not until 1843 that the Cathedral was restored under the direction of Edward Blore.

In 1836 Kemp entered the competition for the Scott Monument in Edinburgh. He gained the third prize,[1] the first being awarded to Thomas Rickman and the second to Charles Fowler in collaboration with the sculptor Sievier. However, the committee decided on a second competition, and this time Kemp was the winner. His elaborate openwork Gothic monument, based on his studies of late Gothic churches in Scotland, was built in 1840–6. This brilliant and much-admired work would doubtless have assured Kemp's future as an architect, but on 6 March 1844 he was accidentally drowned by falling into a canal while returning home on a foggy

---

[1] Not at Moorfoot in Midlothian, where his father was living at a later date (see *Border Magazine* xv, 1910, 137, 156, for his birthplace).

[1] One of his original drawings for this design is in the Peebles Museum.

night. He was buried in St. Cuthbert's Cemetery, where a monument with a medallion portrait by Alexander Handyside Ritchie was erected by public subscription. A bust by Ritchie and a portrait by his brother-in-law, William Bonnar, are in the Scottish National Portrait Gallery. An attractive picture of his simple and engaging personality is given by Thomas Bonnar in his *Biographical Sketch of George Meikle Kemp*, 1892. See also James Colston, *History of the Scott Monument*, Edinburgh 1881, and Ann Martha Wrinch, 'George Kemp and the Scott Monument', *C. Life*, 5 Aug. 1971. The only other buildings which Kemp appears to have designed are MAYBOLE WEST CHURCH, AYRSHIRE, 1836–40 (see Bonnar, *op. cit.*, 81), and the south wing (dem. 1965) of WOODHOUSELEE, MIDLOTHIAN, for James Tytler, 1843 [J. Small, *Castles and Mansions of the Lothians* ii, 1883]. There are two drawings by him in the Print Room of the Scottish National Gallery. Some beautifully drawn details for the Scott Monument are in the collection of the Royal Incorporation of the Architects of Scotland.

KEMPSHED, JOHN, was an obscure early nineteenth-century architect. His name appears among the subscribers to Richard Elsam's *Essay on Rural Architecture* (1803), and in 1816 he was an unsuccessful candidate for the County Surveyorship of Essex. He was then living in Whitechapel [Essex County Records, Q/SO 24, p. 194]. A design by him for a castellated park entrance, dated 1808, formerly among papers at Hinton St. George, Somerset, is now in the collection of Mr. Paul Mellon.

KEMPSHOT, WILLIAM, of Pentonville, contributed a plan of 'an Inn in the Italian Style' to Loudon's *Encyclopaedia of Rural Architecture*, 1833, in which he is said to have built 'numerous public houses, and also some country churches, and one or two mausoleums' (1846 ed., p. 685).

KEMPSTER, CHRISTOPHER (1627–1715), master mason, was the son of William Kempster of Burford, Oxfordshire. He owned a quarry there from which stone was being sent to London as early as 1668. He was made free of the Masons' Company and of the City by redemption on 4 August 1670, and was Master of the Company in 1691 and 1700. In London, his first contract was for St. Stephen's, Walbrook, 1672–9 (jointly with Thomas Strong). He was also mason-contractor at St. James, Garlickhythe, 1674–87, St. Mary Abchurch, 1681–7, and St. Mary, Somerset, 1686–94. Elsewhere he was the mason-contractor for Abingdon Town Hall, 1678–80, and for Tom Tower at Christ Church, Oxford, 1681–

2 (in partnership with Thomas Robinson). He also had contracts at Winchester Palace in about 1683. His connection with St. Paul's began in 1691 or 1692, from which time until 1707 he worked there more or less continuously in partnership with Ephraim Beauchamp, first on the legs of the Dome and then on the Dome itself. From 1707 to 1709 he was employed on his own account, chiefly in repairing the vaults. Wren had a high opinion of him and told Dean Fell in 1681 that he was 'a very able man, modest, honest and treatable ... I have used him on good works, he is very careful to work true to his design and does strong well-banded work and I can rely on him'.

In 1687 Kempster built the Perrot Chapel on the north side of NORTH LEIGH CHURCH, OXON., for James Perrot in a classical style reflecting that of Wren's City churches [Bodleian Library, MS. Oxf. Dioc. papers c. 455, f. 103]. In 1698 he refronted a house at UPTON, nr. BURFORD, for himself, leaving the inscription 'Christopher Kempster built this in 1698' on a window architrave. He died here on 12 August 1715, aged 88, and was buried in the parish church, where there is a monument to his memory erected by his son William (*Wren Soc.* xix, pl. lix). He left his quarry to his second son, John. His brother, William Kempster the elder, continued to work at St. Paul's after his death and was Master of the Masons' Company in 1705. Kempster's 'Day Book', found in his house in 1884 and now in St. Paul's Cathedral Library, gives some details of his business from about 1667 onwards, but adds little to what is known from other sources. [D. Knoop & G. P. Jones, *The London Mason in the Seventeenth Century*, 1935, 45–6; W. D. Caröe, *Wren and Tom Tower*, 1923, chap. 10–11; *Wren Soc., passim.*]

KEMPTHORNE, SAMPSON (1809–1873), a native of Gloucester, became a pupil of Annesley Voysey. He was admitted to the R.A. Schools in 1833. In December of that year he was in Rome, and he exhibited drawings made in Italy at the Royal Academy in 1835 and 1836. He began practice in London, and with S. S. Teulon competed for the new town hall and market-place at Penzance in 1835. Soon afterwards he became architect to the Poor Law Commissioners, whose *First Report*, 1835, contains designs by him for workhouses that served as models for many built in the 1830s and 1840s. The one which he designed at Abingdon was the first completed under the provisions of the Poor Law Amendment Act: it cost £8500. The *Rules to be observed in planning and fitting up Schools*, published by the Committee of the Council on Education in 1839–40, contains twenty-three sheets of schoolhouses drawn from his designs.

His designs for a school at Cranleigh in Surrey are in the Surrey Record Office (264/15/1–2).

Kempthorne's father-in-law, the Rev. Josiah Pratt, was secretary of the Church Missionary Society. In 1836 he made designs for a mission church at North Waimate in New Zealand,[1] and in 1841–2 he emigrated to that country, where he continued to practise until his death in 1873. In New Zealand his connection with the Church Missionary Society provided him with several commissions, but he does not appear to have designed any building of great importance there. [*A.P.S.D.*; John Stacpoole, *William Mason, the First New Zealand Architect*, Auckland 1971, 12–13, 125, 128.]

KEMPSHOTT HOUSE, HANTS., remodelled exterior for E. W. Blunt, 1832 [G. F. Prosser, *Select Illustrations of Hampshire*, 1833].

WANTAGE, BERKS., THE TOWN HALL, 1835; dem. 1877 [A. Gibbons & E. C. Davey, *Wantage Past and Present*, 1901, 53].

WORKHOUSES at ABINGDON, BERKS., 1836; BRAD-FIELD, BERKS., c. 1835; BANBURY, OXON., c. 1835; CHERTSEY, SURREY, 1836; TICEHURST, SUSSEX, 1836; EPPING, ESSEX, 1836; BISHOP'S STORT-FORD, HERTS., 1836; BATH, 1837–8 [*Architectural Mag.* iii, 1836, 330, 532; *Companion to the Almanac*, 1836, 234–6; *Bath Guide*, 1853].

HADZOR, WORCS., LODGE (Italianate), designed for J. H. Galton [exhib. at R.A. 1837].

LONDON, alterations to MESSRS. BARNETT, HOARES & CO.'S BANK, 62 LOMBARD STREET, 1838 [exhib. at R.A.].

BUCKHOLD CHURCH, BERKS., 1836, Gothic [G.R.].

ROTHERHITHE, HOLY TRINITY CHURCH, 1837–8, Gothic; dem. [*Gent's Mag.* 1837 (ii), 526].

GLOUCESTER, ST. JAMES'S CHURCH, BARTON, 1837–41; chancel rebuilt 1879 [*A.P.S.D.*].

HASELBURY PLUCKNETT CHURCH, SOMERSET, rebuilt nave, 1839 [I.C.B.S.].

ROTHERHITHE, ALL SAINTS CHURCH, 1838–40; Gothic; dem. [*A.P.S.D.*].

ASH CHURCH, SOMERSET, 1840; chancel 1889, tower 1920 [I.C.B.S.].

MISTERTON CHURCH, SOMERSET, rebuilt 1840 [I.C.B.S.].

HOLYWELL CHURCH, nr. GUILSBOROUGH, NORTH-ANTS., 1840, Gothic [exhib. at R.A.].

KENDALL, HENRY EDWARD (1776–1875), the son of a banker, was born at York on 23 March 1776. He became a pupil of Thomas Leverton and, it is said, of John Nash. He joined the Barrack Department of the War Office, in whose employment he remained until 1823, when he became District Surveyor for the parishes of St. Martin's-in-the-Fields and St. Anne's, Soho, an appointment which he held for over fifty years. He was one of the founders of

[1] Described in *Gent's Mag.* 1836 (ii), 192.

the Institute of British Architects, and the early meetings of the committee formed in 1834 to bring it into existence were held in his house in Suffolk Street. He exhibited at the Royal Academy from 1799 to 1843. He is described as a man of 'gentlemanly manners, noble and generous in disposition, tall and handsome in person'. He married twice, and had a son and two daughters. One of the latter married his pupil Lewis Cubitt. The son, Henry Edward Kendall, junior (1805–85), was trained in his father's office and became a successful Victorian architect.[1] Kendall died on 4 January 1875, in his 99th year.

Kendall was a prolific architect whose work included churches, town and country houses, gaols and workhouses, and he was equally at home with Greek Revival or Tudor Gothic. His ability in the latter style was shown in the designs he submitted for Kensal Green Cemetery in 1832 and subsequently published as *Sketches of the Approved Designs of a Chapel and Gateway Entrances, intended to be erected at Kensal Green, for the General Cemetery Company*. They were awarded the first prize in the competition, but were set aside by Sir John D. Paul, the chairman of the company, who wanted Grecian buildings. Kendall's proposed layout was an able essay in picturesque landscaping, and 'a scenic and picturesque effect' was what he aimed for in the design for the Houses of Parliament which he and J. D. Hopkins submitted jointly in 1835. The same qualities were shown in the town-planning schemes at Brighton and Rosherville (on the banks of the Thames near Gravesend) for which Kendall and his son were responsible. Their designs for the development of the latter place were, however, too grandiose for realization, and it eventually degenerated into an amusement park. [Obituary by T. L. Donaldson in *Builder* xxxiii, 1875, 33; *ibid*, 60; J. S. Curl, *The Victorian Celebration of Death*, 1972, 60–4; *Survey of London* xxxvii, 336–7.]

PUBLIC BUILDINGS

SPALDING, LINCS., THE HOUSE OF CORRECTION, 1824 [*Builder* xxxiii, 1875, 33].

SPILSBY, LINCS., SESSIONS HOUSE and HOUSE OF CORRECTION, 1824–6 [plans in C. Davy, *Architectural Precedents*, 1841].

RAMSGATE, KENT, ST. GEORGE'S CHURCH, 1825–7,

[1] For H. E. Kendall, junior, see F. W. Leakey, 'Baudelaire et Kendall', *Revue de littérature comparée*, Trentième Année, no. 1, 1956, his entry in *The Architects, Engineers and Building Trades Directory* (1868), and the obituary in *Builder* xlviii, 1885, 883–4. His works included the remodelling of Knebworth House, Herts. (1844), and Shuckburgh Hall, Warwicks. (1844), and the Tudor Gothic house at Twickenham known as 'Pope's Villa'.

Gothic: designed by H. Hemsley of the Barrack Department (*q.v.*), who died in 1825, and carried out by Kendall with 'some few alterations' [*The Watering-Places of Great Britain and Fashionable Directory*, 1833, 217].

KEMP TOWN, BRIGHTON, SUSSEX, Esplanade and Tunnel, 1828–30, with H. E. Kendall, junior [A. Dale, *Fashionable Brighton*, 1947, 81–92 and pls. 46–7].

LOUTH, LINCS., HOUSE OF CORRECTION, *c.* 1828 [exhib. at R.A. 1829].

SLEAFORD, LINCS., THE SESSIONS HOUSE, 1830, Gothic [exhib. at R.A. 1831].

SLEAFORD, LINCS., CARR'S HOSPITAL, east range 1830, Gothic [exhib. at R.A. 1832]. Kendall may also have designed the south range built in 1841–6.

ROSHERVILLE, NORTHFLEET, KENT, Hotel, Pier and Gardens, 1837, with H. E. Kendall, junior [*Builder* xxxiii, 1875, 33; F. W. Leakey, 'Baudelaire et Kendall', *Revue de littérature comparée*, Trentième Année, no. 1, 1956, 58–9].

LONDON CONSERVATIVE ASSOCIATION'S BANQUET, PAVILION for, 1837 [H. E. Kendall, *Plan, etc. of the Pavilion erected for the Banquet of the London Conservative Association*, 1837].

COCKFOSTERS, MIDDLESEX, CHRIST CHURCH, 1839, Gothic [G.R.].

ST. JOHN'S WOOD, SCHOOL FOR THE BLIND, AVENUE ROAD, 1838 [E. Walford, *Old and New London* v, 250].

CLAYGATE CHURCH, SURREY, 1840, Romanesque [exhib. at R.A. 1841]. Steeples, transept and apse were added in 1860 in conformity to what may have been Kendall's original design.

SUDBURY, SUFFOLK, THE CORN EXCHANGE, 1841–2 [Suffolk Record Office, minutes of the Sudbury Market House Company, 1841].

LONDON, BEDFORD CHAPEL, NEW OXFORD STREET, remodelled 1846 [*Builder* iv, 1846, 79–80].

BANTRY, CO. CORK, IRELAND, a church [*Builder* xxxiii, 1875, 33].

WORKHOUSES at UCKFIELD, SUSSEX, and MELKSHAM, WILTS.' [*Builder* xxxiii, 1875, 33].

PRIVATE WORKS

MISTERTON HOUSE, LEICS., 'intended improvements' for J. H. Franks, exhib. at R. A. 1804; rebuilt *c.* 1845.

MAUSOLEUM 'to be erected' in the park of S. Forster, Esq., in Yorkshire, exhib. at R.A. 1813.

TILLINGTON RECTORY, SUSSEX, for the Rev. J. S. Clarke, 1818 [exhib. at R.A. 1818].

MAUSOLEUM 'to be erected' in SHROPSHIRE for H. Smith, Esq., exhib. at R.A. 1820.

FISHTOFT RECTORY, LEICS., 1826 [Lincoln Record Office, MGA 139].

LONDON, NO. 24 BELGRAVE SQUARE (later DOWNSHIRE HOUSE), for T. R. Kemp, 1827–33 [Brit-

ton & Pugin, *The Public Buildings of London* ii, 1828, 290–4].

attributed: BRIGHTON, NO. 12 CHICHESTER TERRACE, *c.* 1828 [A. Dale, *Fashionable Brighton*, 1947, 109].

attributed: BRIGHTON, NO. 14 CHICHESTER TERRACE, interior for the 6th Duke of Devonshire, 1828 [A. Dale, *Fashionable Brighton*, 1947, 98, 109].

BRIGHTON, NOS. 19–20 SUSSEX SQUARE, for the 1st Marquess of Bristol, 1829–31 [A. Dale, *Fashionable Brighton*, 1947, 83].

HAVERHOLME PRIORY, LINCS., remodelled for Sir Jenison Gordon, Bart., 1830, Tudor Gothic; dem. 1927 [exhib. at R.A. 1830] (*C. Life*, 24 Jan. 1903).

ASHURST LODGE (later WENTWORTH HALL.), MICKLEHAM, SURREY, for William Strachan, *c.* 1835 [exhib. at R.A. 1835] (Brayley, *History of Surrey* iv, 457, plate).

ASWARBY PARK, LINCS., additions for Sir Thomas Whichcote, Bart., 1836–8; dem. 1951 [exhib. at R.A. 1836–8].

CHIDDINGSTONE CASTLE, KENT, additions for Henry Streatfield, *c.* 1837–8 [exhib. at R.A. 1838; Kent Record Office, drawings by Kendall, U 908/P 94].

WIMPOLE HALL, CAMBS., alterations to north-east wing, addition of balustrades to house, etc., 1842, stables, Arrington entrance gates and Queen's Lodge (dem.), 1849–51, for the 4th Earl of Hardwicke [*Builder* xxxiii, 1875, 33, 60; C. Hussey in *C. Life*, 21–28 May 1927; R.C.H.M., *Cambs. West*, 218].

KENDALL, JOHN (1766–1829), was the son of Edward Kendall (d. 1796), a mason and monumental sculptor of Exeter. He appears to be identical with the John Kendall who became a pupil of James Paine and exhibited architectural designs at the Royal Academy in 1781–4. In 1796 he succeeded his father as stonemason to Exeter Cathedral, and retained the post until his death in September 1829, at the age of 63. Apart from his work as a monumental sculptor, his chief employment was the repair and embellishment of Exeter Cathedral, upon which he was more or less continuously engaged from *c.* 1805 onwards. His works included the refacing of the chapterhouse and chapel of the Holy Ghost, 1814, a new reredos (subsequently removed by Scott), 1818, the restoration of the west front, 1817–19, additions to the organ-screen, 1819, a new gallery-screen (since removed) at the west end of the chapter-house and the chimney-piece there, 1821, the refitting of the Lady Chapel, 1822, and various external repairs, 1821–7. Like a medieval master mason he himself designed all the works that he executed, and he was probably the last man of his trade in whom these two capacities were thus combined. [*A.P.S.D.*; *Gent's Mag.*

1796 (ii), 1059, 1829 (ii), 572; archives of the Dean and Chapter of Exeter.]

Kendall published *An Elucidation of the Principles of English Architecture, usually denominated Gothic*, 1818 (reissued 1842), with 23 plates of examples taken from Exeter Cathedral, and a folio print of the 'Elevation of the east end, showing the window, and the new altar-piece, stalls, etc.' (Bodleian, Douce Prints, N 8 (134)). According to Lysons, *Magna Britannia* vi (2), 1822, 250, a new Gothic altar-piece, stone screen and stone pulpit were made in 1822 for HACCOMBE CHURCH, DEVON, at the expense of Sir Henry Carew, Bart., by 'Mr. Nicholas Kendall' – almost certainly a mistake for John Kendall.

KENT, I— J—, of Paddington, exhibited student's work at the Royal Academy in 1809 and 1811. He subsequently specialized in building schools and designed, among others, the PADDINGTON CHARITY SCHOOLS, the design of which is given in J. C. Loudon's *Encyclopaedia of Rural Architecture*, 1846, 740–50 (see also pp. 751–7). He was also the author of 'Instructions for choosing a dwelling-house' in Loudon's *Architectural Mag.* i, 1834, 34, 166.

KENT, JOHN, practised in Southampton from about 1800 to 1830. He rebuilt LEIGH PARK, HANTS., for William Garrett, 1802 [G. F. Prosser, *Select Illustrations of Hampshire*, 1833], and remodelled PAULTONS, nr. ROMSEY, HANTS., for Hans Sloane-Stanley in 1805–7; dem. 1955 [Hants. Record Office, contracts in Sloane-Stanley papers, bundle 117] (*C. Life*, 17 Sept. 1938). According to A. E. Richardson and H. D. Eberlein he also designed CHESSEL HOUSE, BITTERNE, HANTS., 1802 (dem.), and a house in SOUTHAMPTON dated 1806 [*The Smaller English House of the Later Renaissance*, 1925, 34, 180]. Among J. B. Papworth's drawings in the R.I.B.A. Drawings Collection there is a plan of a house with hollow walls built by Kent 'in or near Southampton', with a note that 'it did not answer'.

KENT, WILLIAM (?1685–1748), was born at Bridlington in Yorkshire, and can probably be identified with the William, son of William and Esther Cant, or Kent, whose baptism on 1 January 1685/6 is recorded in the parish register. He is said to have been apprenticed to a coach-painter in Hull, but left his master before he had served his full term. He had evidently shown promise of unusual talent, for although 'his parents' ... circumstances [were] not in a condition to forward his practice & the expence of a profession', he 'had the good fortune to find some Gentlemen ... to promote his studyes', who 'raised a contribution and recommended him to proper persons at London to direct him to Italy', whither he travelled in 1709 in company with John Talman and a young man named William Locke. Kent's patrons were Sir William Wentworth of Bretton Park in Yorkshire, Burrell Massingberd of Ormsby in Lincolnshire, and the latter's friend Sir John Chester of Chicheley in Buckinghamshire. In return for their remittances, Kent bought paintings and objects of virtu for their country houses, while he learned to paint in the studio of Benedetto Luti in Rome. There 'he became acquainted with many English Noblemen', including Thomas Coke, the future Earl of Leicester, in whose company he toured northern Italy in the summer and autumn of 1714, making notes on the pictures which they saw in a notebook which is now in the Bodleian Library (MS. Rawlinson D.1162). By this time Kent's reputation as an artist was established in the eyes of his countrymen. In 1713 he had won one of the prizes awarded for painting by the Accademia di S. Luca, and according to Thoresby he was admitted a member of the Tuscan Academy in Florence. In 1717 he 'gave the first proof of my painting in fresco' in the church of S. Giuliano dei Fiamminghi in Rome, whose ceiling he decorated with the apotheosis of its patron saint, St. Julian.[1]

It was as a painter that the Earl of Burlington, who had first met Kent in Rome in the winter of 1714/15, brought him back to England with him in 1719. At Burlington House Kent painted several ceilings for his new patron, the Duke of Chandos employed him at Cannons, and Earl Tylney at Wanstead. At Kensington, with the support of Burlington, Sir Thomas Hewett (whom he had met in Italy) and Vice-Chamberlain Coke, he displaced Sir James Thornhill, the Sergeant Painter, as the decorator of the new state rooms, thereby incurring the life-long enmity of Thornhill's son-in-law William Hogarth. Burlington 'promoted him on all occasions to everything in his power, to the King, to the Court works, & Courtiers declared him the best History painter – & the first that was a native of this Kingdom'. As a 'history-painter' Kent was in fact second-rate, and certainly inferior to his rival Thornhill, but he showed some skill in the 'grotesque' style of antique decoration which he used in the Presence Chamber at Kensington, and in the Cube Room he provided a simulated coffered ceiling which was more in accord with the neo-classical aspirations of the room than anything in Thornhill's baroque repertoire. However, despite his victory over Thornhill, it was as an architect rather than as a painter that Kent was to show his real ability.[2]

---

[1] Kent's drawing for this painting is illustrated in *Connoisseur*, Aug. 1954, 7. For the painting itself see E. Croft-Murray, 'William Kent in Rome', *English Miscellany*, ed. M. Praz, i, 1950.

[2] Kent appears to have painted few easel-pictures, but

In about 1724 Burlington had given Kent the task of editing the *Designs of Inigo Jones, with some Additional Designs* (by Lord Burlington and himself) which were published in two volumes in 1727 (republished 1770, and reprinted 1835 and 1967). The drawings, however, were made by Flitcroft from the originals in the Earl's collection, and 'apart from painting, it was on the designing of stuccos, frames, chimney-pieces, door-surrounds and similar decorations that Kent specialised in those years, not the planning of houses'. Professor Wittkower has shown that his work as an architect did not begin until the early 1730s, by which time the character of English Palladianism had already been established by Lord Burlington. But so far the new style had been confined to the country houses of Burlington's friends, and to one or two public buildings, such as the Dormitory of Westminster School and the Assembly Rooms at York; it still remained to bring Palladio into the Office of Works and thus to influence the design of the Royal Palaces and other buildings in its charge. This was to be the function of Kent when, in May 1726, Burlington's influence procured him a seat on the Board of Works as Master Carpenter. In 1735 he succeeded Nicholas Dubois as Master Mason and Deputy Surveyor, positions which he retained until his death in 1748. He never obtained the post of Sergeant Painter held by his rival, Thornhill, but in 1728 'Mr. Kent received as an additional favour by the interest of Lord Burlington his patron ... a new constituted place purposely for him'. This was the post of Surveyor or Inspector of Paintings in the Royal Palaces, to which he was appointed on 24 January 1727/8, at a salary of £100 a year. It was in this capacity that he restored Rubens's painting in the Banqueting House at Whitehall – an operation which was the occasion of a flattering visit from the King and Queen, of which Kent made the following memorandum at the end of a MS. version of Ovid's *Metamorphoses*, 'istoricamente spiegate e descritte da Guglielmo Kent', which is now in the Bodleian Library (MS. Rawlinson D.540):

> The 12th day of January 1733/4 the King & Queen came to the Banquiting House at WhiteHall, and came upon the scaffold forty foot High to see the paintings of Ruben's, that I had restor'd – his Majesty was pleas'd to tell me I had done them exceeding well the Queen told me I not only deserv'd thanks from the

King but to all lovers of Painting – from thence I waited on them to the Muse [*sic*] to look upon that Building of my Designe.

Finally, on the death of Charles Jervas in 1739, Kent became Portrait Painter to the King, although, according to Vertue, George II 'declared he would never sit to him for his picture'. Nevertheless, 'his true friend' the Duke of Grafton, then Lord Chamberlain, employed him to paint official portraits of the King to send abroad, and one of these, signed and dated 1741, is preserved at Rokeby, Yorkshire (*C. Life*, 19 May 1955, fig. 9).

It was as a member of the Board of Works that Kent designed his best-known works – the Horse Guards, the Royal Mews, and the Treasury Buildings, all of which were, like his project for a Royal Palace (represented by a wooden model now exhibited at Kew), and his designs for rebuilding the Houses of Parliament, directly inspired by Burlington's ideals. They show that, so far as external architecture was concerned, Kent had become as complete a Palladian as his patron could have wished – so much so that Burlington is said to have declared that 'if Kent was not the first or best painter in England – he was certainly the best architect'. Externally all his classical works were closely based on Palladian or Jonesian formulas, handled, however, with an unfailing sense of scale and composition which saves them from ever degenerating into mere reproductions. Internally the Palladian precedents were less precise, and here Kent, while still making use of approved motifs from Jones and antiquity, produced some theatrical effects (notably the hall at Holkham and the staircase at 44 Berkeley Square) which suggest that in a different climate of taste he might have been equally successful as a baroque architect. His decoration, always bold and architectural in character, may have lacked the elegance of the rococo or the neo-classical, but has its own virtues of richness and three-dimensional solidity. The same may be said of the excellent furniture which he designed for many of his buildings, thus anticipating the later role of Robert Adam as a creator of complete interior ensembles.

Though Holkham and the Horse Guards are serious, even solemn buildings, Kent's delightful sketches, often animated by human and animal figures, prove that he was far from being a humourless architectural pedant. His pioneer Gothic designs, moreover, show him exercising a fancy uncontrolled by Palladian constraints and establish him as the creator of an English rococo Gothick happily free from antiquarian preoccupations. His versatility extended to the illustration of books (notably Gay's *Poems*, 1720, Thomson's *Seasons*, 1730, and Spenser's *Faerie Queen*, 1751), the designing of sculpture (see

---

attention should be drawn to his 'Battle of Crécy' and 'Meeting and Marriage of Henry V and Catherine of France' in the Royal Collection at Kensington Palace, as they show Kent as probably the first English painter to attempt historical subjects drawn from the Middle Ages. The 'Marriage' is signed and dated 1729.

below), and even, it is said, of a lady's dress decorated with columns of the Five Orders, so that she seemed 'a walking Palladio in petticoats'.[1]

Finally, Kent has a very important place in the history of English landscape-gardening. As Horace Walpole saw it, Kent 'leaped the fence, and saw that all Nature was a Garden': in other words it was Kent who led the revolt against the formal gardening of the seventeenth century, and who first realized Addison's vision of 'a whole estate thrown into a kind of garden by frequent plantations'. Modern research has shown that the change from formality to informality was less abrupt than Walpole implied, and that others besides Kent had a hand in it. Nevertheless Kent's contribution to English landscape-gardening was crucial. It was he who combined the formality of Palladian architecture with the studied informality of the surrounding park, and it was he who (as can still be seen at Rousham) set out to create on English soil a series of three-dimensional pictures comparable to (if not directly inspired by) the ideal compositions of Albani or Poussin. These were to be the essential characteristics of English landscape-gardening for the rest of the eighteenth century, and it was to Kent that its practitioners were to look back as the founder of their art.

Kent did not fail to arouse hostility in those who envied the ease with which he attracted the patronage of the great. But it is clear that the 'Signior' was an amiable and easy-going companion as well as a gifted designer, and the combination was enough to secure for him the friendship and support of one of the most influential patrons in the history of English art. For much of his life Burlington House was his home, and when he died on 12 April 1748, of 'an inflammation in his bowels and foot, which turned to a general mortification', he was buried in his patron's vault at Chiswick. He was unmarried, but kept a mistress, Elizabeth Butler of Covent Garden, by whom he had two children.

Several portraits of Kent are known or recorded (see M. Jourdain, *The Work of William Kent*, 43–4).[2] The best known is that by Bartholomew Dandridge in the National Portrait Gallery. A number of his architectural designs were published by John Vardy in *Some Designs of Mr.*

Inigo Jones and Mr. William Kent, 1744, and others by Isaac Ware in *Designs of Inigo Jones and Others* (n.d.). Drawings by him are preserved in several places, notably at Chatsworth, the R.I.B.A. Drawings Collection,[1] the Public Record Office, Sir John Soane's Museum, the Victoria and Albert Museum, the British Museum (Print Room) and the Ashmolean Museum at Oxford. His letters to Burrell Massingberd of Ormsby are in the Library of the Society of Genealogists. They are the subject of an article by Margaret Jourdain in *C. Life*, 25 Aug. 1944. Four letters to Lord Burlington at Althorp were published in *Architectural Review* lxiii, 1928, 180 and 210. Copies of the Sale Catalogue of his library and works of art are in the Bodleian Library (Mus. Bibl. III 4to 17, 8° 20).

[*A.P.S.D.*; *D.N.B.*; Walpole Society, *Vertue Note Books* i, 100, iii, 139–140, vi (index), 131–2; Basil S. Long, 'Some Drawings by William Kent', *Connoisseur* lxxviii, 1927, 93–5; Trenchard Cox, 'William Kent as Painter', *Artwork* vii, 1931; Fiske Kimball, 'William Kent's Designs for the Houses of Parliament', *R.I.B.A. Jnl.*, 6 Aug. and 10 Sept. 1932, see also 9 Jan. 1939; Margaret Jourdain, 'Early Life and Letters of William Kent', *C. Life*, 25 Aug. 1944; R. Wittkower, 'Lord Burlington and William Kent', *Archaeological Jnl.* cii, 1945, reprinted in *Palladio and English Palladianism*, 1974; R. Wittkower, *The Earl of Burlington and William Kent* (York Georgian Society 1948); Margaret Jourdain, *The Work of William Kent*, 1948; Hugh Honour, 'John Talman and William Kent in Italy', *Connoisseur*, Aug. 1954; U. Middeldorf, 'William Kent's Roman Prize in 1713', *Burlington Mag.*, April 1957, 125; J. P. Eichholz, 'William Kent's Career as Literary Illustrator', *Bulletin of the New York Public Library* lxx, 1966, 620–46; E. Croft-Murray, *Decorative Painting in England* ii, 1970, 229–35; K. Woodbridge, 'William Kent as Landscape-Gardener: a Re-Appraisal', *Apollo*, Aug. 1974; K. Woodbridge, 'William Kent's Gardening: the Rousham Letters', *Apollo*, Oct. 1974; Geoffrey Beard, 'William Kent and the Cabinet-makers', *Burlington Mag.*, Dec. 1975; *The History of the King's Works* v, 1976, *passim*.]

PRIVATE COMMISSIONS

LONDON, BURLINGTON HOUSE, PICCADILLY, some internal decoration for the 3rd Earl of Burlington, before 1727 [Kent, *Designs of Inigo Jones* i, 1727, pls. 63, 67; *Survey of London* xxxii, 401].

CHISWICK HOUSE, MIDDLESEX, internal decoration of the principal rooms for the 3rd Earl of Burl-

---

[1] In December 1731 Frederick, Prince of Wales, gave a masquerade in which he appeared as a shepherd attended by eighteen huntsmen 'dressed after a drawing of Kent's, in green waistcoats, leopard-skins and quivers at their backs, ... tragedy buskins upon their legs, ... antique gloves with pikes up to their elbows, and caps and feathers upon their heads like a Harry the 8th by Holbein' (*Lord Hervey and His Friends*, ed. Lord Ilchester, 1950, 115–16).

[2] To those mentioned by Miss Jourdain should be added a portrait by Benedetto Luti at Chatsworth, painted at Rome in 1718.

---

[1] Including a set of unexecuted designs for remodelling Honingham Hall, Norfolk, in the Gothic style, dated 1737.

ington, *c.* 1726–9 [Jourdain, *Kent*, 67; John Charlton, *Chiswick House*, H.M.S.O. 1962, 6–8].

HOUGHTON HALL, NORFOLK, internal decoration, *c.* 1726–31, of house designed by Colen Campbell for Sir Robert Walpole. The stables built *c.* 1733–5 may also have been designed by Kent. Thirteen plates of ceilings and chimney-pieces by Kent are given in Isaac Ware's *Plans, Elevations and Sections of Houghton*, 1735. A design for the interior of the Cabinet Room by Kent is in the Print Room of the Ashmolean Museum, Oxford. It is inscribed 'For Houghton W.K.' A design for a chimney-piece for Houghton signed 'W. Kent 1726' is in the Witt Collection of the Courtauld Institute of Art, London. (Tipping, *English Homes, Period V* (i), 1921, 78–110; Jourdain, *Kent*, 63–4 and figs. 57–63; Hussey, *English Country Houses: Early Georgian*, 1955, 76–86.)

SHERBORNE HOUSE, GLOS., designs (probably for internal decoration and furniture) for Sir John Dutton, Bart., 1728 [Christopher Gilbert, 'James Moore the Younger and William Kent at Sherborne House', *Burlington Mag.* cxi, 1969, 148–9].

STOWE HOUSE, BUCKS., garden buildings for the 1st Viscount Cobham, *c.* 1730 onwards: THE TEMPLE OF VENUS, before 1732; THE TEMPLE OF ANCIENT VIRTUE, *c.* 1734; THE TEMPLE OF BRITISH WORTHIES, *c.* 1735; CONGREVE'S MONUMENT, 1736; THE OXFORD GATE; THE HERMITAGE; THE SHEPHERD'S COVE [B. Seeley, *Stowe: a Description of the House and Gardens*, 1773, *passim*; L. Whistler *et al.*, *Stowe, a Guide to the Gardens*, 1968].

TWICKENHAM, MIDDLESEX, POPE'S VILLA, designs for garden buildings and ornaments for Alexander Pope, *c.* 1730; dem. [James Boardman, 'Pope's Essay in the Picturesque', *C. Life*, 7 March 1968; designs for two vases for Pope in Vardy's *Designs of Jones and Kent*, pl. 25; *The Correspondence of Alexander Pope*, ed. G. Sherborne, iii, 1956, 314, 322, 329, 341].

RICHMOND GARDENS, SURREY, works for Queen Caroline, including THE HERMITAGE, 1730, dem. *c.* 1775, and MERLIN'S CAVE, 1735, dem. 1766 [J. Vardy, *Some Designs of Mr. Inigo Jones and Mr. William Kent*, 1744, pls. 32, 33; *History of the King's Works* v, 224].

RAYNHAM HALL, NORFOLK, internal alterations for the 2nd Viscount Townshend, *c.* 1731 [Jourdain, *Kent*, 65].

KEW HOUSE, SURREY, for Frederick, Prince of Wales, 1731–5; dem. 1802 [*History of the King's Works* v, 227].

ESHER PLACE, SURREY, addition of wings and other alterations to 'Wolsey's Tower' for the Hon. Henry Pelham, *c.* 1733, Gothic. The wings have been demolished. Some of the original designs are in an extra-illustrated copy of

Brayley's *Surrey* in Wimbledon Public Library. One is dated 1733 [J. W. Lindus Forge in *Arch. Rev.*, Sept. 1949, with plans; John Harris in *C. Life*, 14 May 1959].

HOLKHAM HALL, NORFOLK, for the Earl of Leicester and his trustees, 1734–65. The general design for the house was made 'by the Earls of Burlington and Leicester, assisted by Mr. William Kent', but was carried out, with modifications, by Matthew Brettingham. In 1761 Brettingham published *The Plans and Elevations of the late Earl of Leicester's House at Holkham*, without acknowledgement to Kent, but in a second edition in 1773 his son admitted Kent's responsibility for the design, and Kent's drawings remain at Holkham to prove it (see *Archaeological Jnl.* cii, 1945, pls. 4, 5, 7, 10). It is further stated in the 1773 edition of the book that 'The stone Bridge at the commencement of the lake, the obelisk, the Temple-building contiguous, the Seat upon the Mount, the two Arches which enclose the pleasure garden, as well as the distant building called the Triumphal Arch at the entrance of the approach, were all deduced from sketches by Mr. Kent, with considerable alterations made in the designs, long before these works were erected'.

LONDON, DEVONSHIRE HOUSE, PICCADILLY, for the 3rd Duke of Devonshire, 1734–5; altered by James Wyatt and D. Burton; dem. 1924–5 [*Vitruvius Britannicus* iv, 1767, pls. 19–20].

EASTON NESTON, NORTHANTS., chimney-pieces in hall and 'next room' for the 1st Earl of Pomfret, before 1735 [G. Baker, *History of Northants.* ii, 1822–30, 145; description of the house *c.* 1735, Alnwick Castle Library, Percy family letters, vol. 25, f. 225; see also *C. Life*, 7 Feb. 1974, 250] (Tipping, *English Homes, Period IV* (ii), 1928, figs. 183, 192).

attributed: ASKE HALL, YORKS. (N.R.), the Gothic Temple for Sir Conyers D'Arcy, *c.* 1735 [unsigned design in R.I.B.A. Collection attributed to Kent on grounds of draughtsmanship: Peter Leach in *C. Life*, 26 Sept. 1974, 837].

CLAREMONT, SURREY, garden buildings for the 1st Duke of Newcastle. Two buildings at Claremont by Kent are illustrated in Ware's *Designs of Inigo Jones and Others* (n.d.), pls. 40–1. One of these is identified as the BOWLING GREEN HOUSE on Rocque's engraving of the grounds at Claremont, dated 1738. In addition Rocque shows a domed temple on the island in the lake which must be attributed to Kent, who was responsible for the formation of the lake. This temple survives in ruins, but the other two have been demolished. Two drawings by Kent for the gardens at Claremont are illustrated in *C. Life*, 8 Feb. 1952 (correspondence).

SHOTOVER PARK, OXON., octagonal garden building and obelisk for Col. James Tyrrell, before

1733 [I. Ware, *Designs of Inigo Jones and Others* (n.d.), pls. 38–9, 42; original drawings in Mellon Collection] (Tipping, *English Homes, Period IV* (ii), figs. 366, 372).

ROUSHAM HOUSE, OXON., addition of wings to north front and garden buildings for General James Dormer, 1738–41 [C. Hussey in *C. Life*, 17–24 May, 14–21 June 1946; Jourdain, *Kent*, 54–5; K. Woodbridge in *Apollo*, Oct. 1974].

BADMINTON HOUSE, GLOS., works for the 3rd Duke of Beaufort, *c.* 1740, including the WORCESTER LODGE, several garden buildings no longer in existence, and almost certainly the remodelling of the north front with pediment, twin cupolas and flanking pavilions [H. M. Colvin in *C. Life*, 4 April 1968] (*C. Life*, 25 Nov., 1–8 Dec. 1939).

STANWICK HALL, YORKS. (N.R.), was remodelled, *c.* 1730–40, by Sir Hugh Smithson, Bart. (afterwards 1st Duke of Northumberland), in a style suggestive of Lord Burlington's circle. An engraving of the Dining Room dated 1818 shows a ceiling supported by large console brackets similar to those in the Blue Velvet Room at Chiswick. This room at least may probably be attributed to Kent. The house was demolished in 1923 (*C. Life*, 17 Feb. 1900).

LONDON, NO. 22 ARLINGTON STREET, for the Hon. Henry Pelham, 1741–50. The building accounts are in the R.I.B.A. Library. They show that Stephen Wright completed the house after Kent's death in 1748.

LONDON, NO. 44 BERKELEY SQUARE, for Lady Isabella Finch, 1742–4 [building accounts in Sir John Soane's Museum, 39B] (*C. Life*, 27 Dec. 1962).

LONDON, NO. 16 ST. JAMES'S PLACE, for Sir John Evelyn, Bart.; dem. 1899–1900. Evelyn built this house early in the 1740s, and on 8 July 1743 paid 'Mr. Kent architect for his directions about the house in St. James Place' [account-book among Evelyn archives at Christ Church, Oxford]. Among the Evelyn archives there is a design by Kent for the interior of a room which may have been connected with this commission.

OATLANDS HOUSE, WEYBRIDGE, SURREY, garden building for the 9th Earl of Lincoln, probably *c.* 1745; dem. 'Mr. Kent's pretty building on the old Terrace' at Oatlands is referred to in a letter from Joseph Spence dated 24 March 1766 [Nottingham University Library, Newcastle Collection, Ne C], and Kent refers to a proposed visit to Oatlands in a letter to Lady Lincoln dated 6 July 1745 [*ibid.*, Ne C 3, 111].

EUSTON HALL, SUFFOLK, THE TEMPLE or BANQUETING HOUSE, for the 2nd Duke of Grafton, 1746 [J. Dugdale, *British Traveller* iv, 1819, 277; Arthur Oswald in *C. Life*, 24 Jan. 1957, reproducing drawings by Kent].

WAKEFIELD LODGE, NORTHANTS., for the 2nd Duke

of Grafton, *c.* 1748–50 [Jourdain, *Kent*, 59–60, Marcus Binney in *C. Life*, 2 Aug. 1973].

PUBLIC BUILDINGS

YORK MINSTER, figured pavement, 1731–5. According to John Carter in *Gent's Mag.* 1807 (ii), 630, this was designed by Lord Burlington, but in 1744 Philip Yorke was told that it was 'from a design of Mr. Kent's' [Travel Journal in *Beds. Hist. Rec. Soc.* xlvii, 1968, 129]. No doubt Burlington was the moving spirit and Kent the executant. The Dean and Chapter's archives show that the work was carried out between 1731 and 1735.

LONDON, THE ROYAL MEWS, CHARING CROSS, THE GREAT MEWS, 1731–33; dem. 1830 [*History of the King's Works* v, 212–13; A. Stratton, 'The King's Mews at Charing Cross', *Arch. Rev.* xxxix, 1916].

HAMPTON COURT PALACE, Gothic gateway in Clock Court and reconstruction of adjoining apartment for occupation by Duke of Cumberland, 1732 [*History of the King's Works* v, 181].

KENSINGTON PALACE, revolving garden seat on mount, 1733; dem.; *attributed:* the QUEEN'S TEMPLE (now part of Temple Lodge), 1734–5 [J. Vardy, *Some Designs of Mr. Inigo Jones and Mr. William Kent*, 1744, pl. 38; *History of the King's Works* v, 203–4].

LONDON, THE TREASURY BUILDINGS, WHITEHALL, 1733–7 [*History of the King's Works* v, 431–3; *Survey of London* xiv, chap. 3].

LONDON, ST. JAMES'S PALACE, THE QUEEN'S LIBRARY, for Queen Caroline, 1736–7; dem. 1825 [*History of the King's Works* v, 242–3].

LONDON, WESTMINSTER HALL, Gothic screen enclosing Courts of Chancery and King's Bench, 1739; heightened 1755; dem. *c.* 1825 [*History of the King's Works* v, 389–90; J. Vardy, *Some Designs of Mr. Inigo Jones and Mr. William Kent*, 1744, pl. 48].

YORK MINSTER, Gothic pulpit and choir furniture, 1741; removed. The pulpit is now in Bridlington Church [J. Vardy, *Some Designs of Mr. Inigo Jones and Mr. William Kent*, 1744, pl. 51; drawings and contract in Dean and Chapter's archives, YM/F 90, 239, and M/P 1140/1–4].

GLOUCESTER CATHEDRAL, Gothic choir-screen, 1741; removed 1820 [J. Vardy, *Some Designs of Mr. Inigo Jones and Mr. William Kent*, 1744, pl. 49].

LONDON, THE HORSE GUARDS, WHITEHALL, designed by Kent shortly before his death and built, 1750–9, under the direction of the Board of Works [*History of the King's Works* v, 436–40; *Survey of London* xvi, chap. 2].

MONUMENTS

CHESTER CATHEDRAL, John and Thomas Wainwright (d. 1720), signed *G. Berkley S.T.P. & Gul. Kent inven.*

WESTMINSTER ABBEY, HENRY VII'S CHAPEL, George Monck, Duke of Albemarle (d. 1670), ex. Scheemakers, 1730(?) [E. W. Brayley & J. P. Neale, *History of the Abbey Church of Westminster* i, 1818, Henry VII's Chapel, 71].

YORK MINSTER, Thomas Watson Wentworth (d. 1723), ex. Guelfi, probably in 1731 [engraving in Bodleian, Gough Maps 41K, f. 37, signed *W. Kent arch.*].

WESTMINSTER ABBEY, Isaac Newton (d. 1727), ex. Rysbrack, completed 1731 [signed].

KIRKTHORPE CHURCH, YORKS. (W.R.), Thomas and Catherine Stringer, ex. Guelfi, 1731–2 [M. I. Webb in *Burlington Mag.*, May 1955, 143–4].

BLENHEIM PALACE CHAPEL, OXON., John Churchill, 1st Duke of Marlborough (d. 1722), ex. Rysbrack, designed 1730, completed 1733 [David Green, *Blenheim Palace*, 1951, 160, 274].

WESTMINSTER ABBEY, James, 1st Earl Stanhope (d. 1721), ex. Rysbrack, completed 1733 [signed].

WESTMINSTER ABBEY, William Shakespeare (d. 1616), ex. Scheemakers, 1740 [signed].

ASHBY-DE-LA-ZOUCHE CHURCH, LEICS., Theophilus Hastings, 9th Earl of Huntingdon (d. 1746), ex. Rysbrack [signed].

MISCELLANEOUS WORKS

(excluding paintings, furniture and book illustrations)

WESTMINSTER HALL, triumphal arch for coronation of King George II, 1727, of which there is a print signed *Wm. Kent invt. & delin.* (Bodleian, Gough Maps 23, f. 49^v). Drawings by Kent exist in P.R.O., Works 36/68/46, and Westminster City Library, Pennant, vol. iii, f. 48.

THE ROYAL STATE BARGE, made in 1732 for Frederick, Prince of Wales, used until 1849, now in the National Maritime Museum, Greenwich [A. E. Richardson, 'The Royal Barge, Notes on the Original Drawings by William Kent', *R.I.B.A. Jnl.* xxxviii, 1931; G. W. Beard, 'William Kent and the Royal Barge', *Burlington Mag.*, Aug. 1970].

KING'S THEATRE, HAYMARKET, designed the scenery for Nicolo Porpora's cantata *La Festa d'Imeneo*, produced in 1736 in honour of the marriage of Frederick, Prince of Wales [E. Croft Murray in *C. Life*, 4 Sept. 1939, 269].

PLATE, CANDELABRA, etc., for various persons, illustrated by J. Vardy, *Some Designs of Mr. Inigo Jones and Mr. William Kent*, 1744, pls. 19–31, including a pair of silver chandeliers (pl. 23) made for King George II's palace at Herrenhausen in 1736, and now at Anglesey Abbey, Cambs. (see *C. Life*, 22 April 1954, 1229).

KEYS, HENRY LENT (*c.* 1801–), was admitted to the Royal Academy Schools in 1823 at the age of 22. He lived at No. 6 Regent Square, London, from 1834 to 1852 and was described as an architect, but nothing is known about his practice [*Survey of London* xxiv, 76].

KEYTE, JOHN, of Kidderminster, was the 'able architect' who in 1795 repewed and refitted TEWKESBURY ABBEY CHURCH to the designs of Edward Edgcumbe [W. Dyde, *History of Tewkesbury*, 1798, 55]. He appears to have designed ST. MARTIN'S CHURCH, TIPTON, STAFFS., in 1797 [B. F. L. Clarke, *The Building of the Eighteenth-Century Church*, 1963, 102].

KILLIGREW, WILLIAM, of Bath, was a joiner who 'laid his Apron aside about the year 1719' and thereafter practised as an architect. His few recorded buildings have all been demolished. They were vigorous examples of pre-Palladian architecture which met with the disapproval of John Wood but appear to have had considerable merit. Wood states that he added a new ballroom to the LOWER ASSEMBLY ROOMS in 1720 (remodelled 1750, gutted 1820, demolished 1933); designed THE BLUECOAT SCHOOL, UPPER BOROUGH WALLS, 1721–2 (demolished 1859–60), and the south front of the old GUILDHALL, *c.* 1725 (dem. *c.* 1775). WEYMOUTH HOUSE, 1720 (partially demolished 1826 and wholly in 1896), and NO. 3 ST. JAMES'S STREET SOUTH (demolished 1959) have also been attributed to him. [John Wood, *Essay towards a Description of Bath*, 1749, 318, 319, 321; W. Ison, *The Georgian Buildings of Bath*, 1948, 30, 49, 99–101, 122–3, 126.]

The Bath architect was probably not the same person as William Killigrew, described as a builder of Chippenham, who in 1740 contracted to enlarge the market house at Tetbury, Glos., and in 1742 surveyed Tetbury Church [Glos. Record Office, D 566/B12, *ex inf.* Mr. N. M. Herbert; Gloucester Public Library, MS. R.R. 300.1, p. 6].

KIMPTON, W—, of 199 Strand, London, exhibited at the Royal Academy in 1784 a plan and elevation of the seventeenth-century Lyveden New Building, nr. Thrapston in Northamptonshire. In 1785 he made a set of five measured drawings of another seventeenth-century building, Houghton House, nr. Ampthill, Beds., one of which is illustrated by H. Clifford Smith in *The Haynes Grange Room* (Victoria and Albert Museum 1935, pl. xii). He was perhaps the clerk named Kimpton who was in Robert Mylne's office until December 1781.

KING, JAMES, of St. Martin's Lane, Westminster, a carpenter by trade, submitted in 1737 a design for building a wooden bridge at Westminster, which so favourably impressed the Commissioners that they asked him to make detailed specifications for a timber bridge to be carried on stone piers designed by Charles Labelye. It was eventually decided to build a bridge entirely of stone, but King's original design is known from an engraving in the British Museum, *King's Maps* xxii, 36b [Minutes of the Westminster Bridge Commissioners, P.R.O., Works 6/28]. In 1737, King, by mechanical means, saved the ceiling of the portico of St. Martin's-in-the-Fields Church from collapse owing to shrinkage of the timbers [parish records in Westminster City Library]. He is said to have built the timber obelisk containing the cistern of the York Buildings Waterworks Company, which stood on the north bank of the Thames at the bottom of Villiers Street, and which forms a prominent feature in Canaletto's paintings of the river.

KING, JOHN, was a clerk or assistant of Francis Goodwin [*Architectural History* i, 1958, 63]. He exhibited at the Royal Academy from 1817 to 1829. His drawings included a 'Design for a hunting seat proposed to be erected for a gentleman in Derbyshire' (1821), the new Commissioners' Church at Kidderminster designed by Goodwin (1822), and a 'monumental building proposed to be erected in the County of Wicklow' (1823). In 1820 he carried out repairs and alterations to TONBRIDGE CHURCH, KENT [B. Wadmore, *Some Details of the History of the Parish of Tonbridge*, 1906, 5].

KINNARD, WILLIAM (*c.* 1788–1839), the son of a magistrate, was admitted to the Royal Academy Schools in 1805 at the age of 17, and was awarded the Gold Medal the same year. In 1807 he became District Surveyor for the parishes of St. Giles-in-the-Fields and St. George, Bloomsbury, and in 1812 laid an information under the Building Act against John Soane for building a projection on to the front of his house in Lincoln's Inn Fields. The case was heard in October 1812, and was dismissed in Soane's favour. In 1817–19 Kinnard travelled in Italy and visited Greece and Turkey in company with Charles Barry and Charles Eastlake. He subsequently exhibited at the Royal Academy a number of drawings of buildings he had visited, and edited the fifth or supplementary volume of the *Antiquities of Athens* published in 1830, to which he contributed an account of buildings in Athens and Delos.

Kinnard's architectural practice appears to have been small. In 1811 he exhibited at the Academy a view of a villa 'now being erected for a gentleman at Ham Frith in Essex', and in 1813 he published an engraved 'View of a Triumphal

Arch, proposed to be erected at Hyde Park Corner, commemorative of the victories achieved by the British Arms during the Reign of His Majesty King George the Third', of which there are copies in the British Museum (*King's Maps* xxvii *i*), and the Bodleian Library (Douce Prints N.8). He designed the monument in East Retford Church, Notts., to Sir Wharton Amcotts (d. 1807), which bears his signature. He died on 12 October 1839. His library was auctioned on 9 January 1840 (Sale Catalogue in B.M., S.C. Sg.53 (14)).

[*A.P.S.D.*; *The Farington Diary*, ed. J. Greig, vii, 283; A. T. Bolton, *The Portrait of Sir John Soane*, 181, 257.]

KINSMAN, EDMUND, was a leading London master mason of the early seventeenth century. The dates of his birth and death have not been ascertained, but he was Master of the Masons' Company in 1635. In 1613–14 he was working at THE CHARTERHOUSE under Francis Carter, and presumably built the new north aisle of the Chapel [Arthur Oswald in *C. Life*, 15 Oct. 1959]. In 1615–16 he was associated with Nicholas Stone in the contract for the monument to Thomas Sutton, the founder of the Charterhouse [*Walpole Soc.* vii, 41]. Inigo Jones subsequently employed him at NEWMARKET, OATLANDS and ST. PAUL'S CATHEDRAL [*Architectural History* ii, 1959, 33; *Arch. Rev.*, xxxix, 1916, 76; *History of the King's Works* iii & iv]. In *c.* 1630 he was concerned in some ambitious proposals, not carried out, for alterations to COPT HALL, ESSEX, for Lionel Cranfield, 1st Earl of Middlesex, and may have built the classical loggia (dem. 1748) [John Newman in *The Country Seat*, ed. Colvin & Harris, 1970, 25]. The Churchwardens' Accounts of ST. ALBAN'S CHURCH, WOOD STREET, show that Kinsman was (with Matthew Banckes, senior) involved in the rebuilding of the church in 1633–4, for in 1634 he was paid 50s. 'for his paynes draught & valuacon of the worke about the church' [Guildhall Library, MS. 7673/1]. In 1636 he rebuilt the 'lanthorn' on the tower of ST. MARY-LE-BOW CHURCH, which was crowned by a stone lantern supported by four flying buttresses [*Cal. State Papers Domestic 1635–6*, 149], and in 1638 he was one of the three London masons responsible for rebuilding the west tower of GOUDHURST CHURCH, KENT [*Archaeologia Cantiana* xxviii, 10–13].

The evidence at present available does not make it clear whether Kinsman was an architectural designer of any consequence or not. Although he executed strictly classical works for Inigo Jones, his church commissions suggest that he was more at home in the mixture of classical and Gothic of which the undocumented St. Katherine Cree (1628–31) is the outstanding example.

KIRBY, JOHN JOSHUA (1716–1774), born at Wickham Market in Suffolk, was the eldest son of John Kirby, author of *The Suffolk Traveller*, 1735, and of a *Map of the County of Suffolk*, 1736. He was apprenticed to a coach and house painter in Ipswich, but formed a friendship with Gainsborough, by whose persuasion he is said to have attempted landscape-painting. He made a number of topographical drawings intended to illustrate a projected history of Suffolk, twelve of which he published in 1748 together with an *Historical Account*. He made himself an authority on perspective, upon which he lectured at the St. Martin's Lane Academy in London. In 1754 he published at Ipswich *Dr. Brook Taylor's Method of Perspective made Easy, both in Theory and Practice*, with a frontispiece by Hogarth. Soon afterwards, through the influence of the Earl of Bute, he became drawing master to the Prince of Wales (afterwards George III), and in 1761 he and his son William were appointed joint Clerks of the Works at Richmond and Kew Palaces. Several of the drawings which he exhibited at the Society of Artists during the next few years were said to be the work of his royal pupil, and it was at the King's expense that in 1761 he published *The Perspective of Architecture deduced from the principles of Dr. Brook Taylor*, fol.[1] He also published *Dr. Brook Taylor's Method of Perspective compared with the examples published as Sirigatti's by Isaac Ware ... In which the superior excellence of Taylor's is shown, c.* 1767. He was secretary of the Incorporated Society of Artists, and in 1768 was elected president by a 'discontented clique', but resigned soon after on grounds of ill-health. He was elected F.R.S. in March 1767, and F.S.A. in June of the same year. He died on 21 June 1774, aged 58, and was buried in Kew Churchyard. His son William, who had been sent to Italy to study architecture at the King's expense, died suddenly at Kew in 1771 at the age of 28.[2] A portrait of Kirby and his wife by Gainsborough is in the Tate Gallery.

In 1744 Kirby designed an altar-piece for HADLEIGH CHURCH, SUFFOLK, which has since been removed. His drawing is attached to the contract between the Rev. David Wilkins and Josias Harris, an Ipswich joiner [Kent Record Office, U 23, Q 3/1–3]. In 1768 KEW CHAPEL or CHURCH was enlarged by Kirby at the King's expense. In 1766 he communicated to the inhabitants 'a Most Gracious offer from His Majesty to enlarge the Chapel according to a plan now laid before them for that purpose' [Surrey Archdeaconry Records]. In the King's Collection in the British Museum (*King's Maps* xl, 46 *h*) there is a 'Plan and Elevation of Kew Chapel with the proposed Alterations', signed J.K., and dated February 1768. The chapel was enlarged by adding north and south aisles (not, as shown in the plan, by an extension to the west end). It was subsequently extended to the west in 1805 (by R. Browne) and again in 1837–8 (by Sir J. Wyatville). Kirby also designed ST. GEORGE'S CHAPEL, OLD BRENTFORD, MIDDLESEX, 1762, enlarged 1828, dem. 1887.

[*A.P.S.D.*; *D.N.B.*; T. Faulkner, *History of Brentford*, 1845, 128, 131, 156; W. H. Pyne, *Wine and Walnuts* i, 1824, 175–6 n.; *Walpole Soc.* xxvii, 70; W. T. Whitley, *Artists and their Friends in England* i, 1928, 225.]

KIRK, WILLIAM (1749–1823), of Leicester, was born into a family long connected with the building trade, and was himself a surveyor and monumental mason. For some years he was County Surveyor of Leicestershire. In that capacity he was, with Henry Couchman (*q.v.*), jointly responsible in 1810 for the rebuilding of BENSFORD BRIDGE, on the boundary between Leicestershire and Warwickshire [Warwickshire County Records, Class 24, 28 (x)]. In 1814–15 he designed a new HOUSE OF CORRECTION at LEICESTER [Leicestershire County Records, Q.S. 32/3/12/1–6], in 1818 he added a Fever Ward to LEICESTER INFIRMARY [drawings in Leicester Museum, Dept. of Archives], and in 1822 he designed the bridge at MELTON MOWBRAY, LEICS. He died on 21 January 1823, aged 73 [J. D. Bennett, *Leicestershire Architects 1700–1850*, Leicester Museums 1968].

KIRSHAW, LUKE (*c.* 1770–1821), practised as an architect and surveyor in Northampton. In 1792–3 he was clerk of the works in charge of the building of Northampton Infirmary to the designs of Samuel Saxon [F. F. Waddy, *History of Northampton General Hospital*, Northampton 1974]. From 1802 onwards he also acted as an auctioneer, and he was successively the proprietor of the Goat Inn in Gold Street and (from 1813) of the Peacock Inn in Market Square. He was elected Mayor in 1807 and died on 26 April 1821, in his 51st year [*Northampton Mercury*, 20 Feb. 1802, 28 April 1821, etc., *ex inf.* Mr. B. A. Bailey]. George Papworth (1781–1855) joined his office in 1804, but left in 1806 in order to start practice in Dublin [*Builder* xiii, 1855, 150].

The following evidence of Kirshaw's architectural activity has been noted: plans of the GEORGE HOTEL, NORTHAMPTON, 1800 [Northants. Record Office, George Inn Tontine papers]; a payment to him by the Radcliffe Trustees for making unexecuted designs for rebuilding WOLVERTON

---

[1] The design for a house engraved on pl. lxiv of this work was drawn by George III. The original drawing is at Windsor (E. A. Oppé, *English Drawings of the Stuart and Georgian Periods at Windsor Castle*, 1950, 10–20).

[2] Some of the drawings made by him in Rome in 1767–8 are preserved in the Royal Collection at Windsor Castle.

CHURCH, BUCKS., in 1803 [Bodleian Library, Minutes of the Radcliffe Trustees, 1792–1815]; survey plans of BOUGHTON HALL, nr. NORTHAMPTON, with unexecuted proposals for alterations, 1809 [Northants. Record Office, Howard-Vyse papers, Box 1, parcel 20]; a new gallery designed by him for ALL SAINTS CHURCH, NORTHAMPTON, 1815 [Peterborough Diocesan Records]; a plan and elevation of the lodges at ALTHORP HOUSE, NORTHANTS., 1818 [Althorp House, Lord Spencer's archives].

KITCHEN, HENRY (*c.* 1793–1822), may have been the son of a Surrey bricklayer of the same name. He became a pupil of James Wyatt, and exhibited student's work at the Royal Academy from Wyatt's office in 1810 and 1811. By 1813 he was practising on his own at 36 St. James's Place, and in that year exhibited at the Academy his designs for EWELL HOUSE or CASTLE, SURREY, a castellated house built in 1814 by Thomas Calverley. About the same time he designed a gallery in EWELL CHURCH [Surrey Archdeaconry Records].

In 1816 Kitchen emigrated to Australia, where he died six years later at the age of 29, having failed to make a successful career for himself in the colony in competition with F. H. Greenway, the Government architect [M. Herman, *The Early Australian Architects and their Work*, 1970, 97–100].

KNIGHT, DANIEL (*c.* 1784–1843), was an architect, surveyor and timber merchant at Leicester, where he died on 16 February 1843, aged 59. He also owned a public house, the 'Keck's Arms', in Archdeacon Lane. He was practising as an architect at least as early as 1816. His works included additions to GREAT GLEN VICARAGE, LEICS., 1819 [Lincolnshire Record Office, MGA 102]; repairing BARKBY CHURCH, LEICS., 1826 [specifications in Leicester Museum]; and adding a south aisle to MARKFIELD CHURCH, LEICS., in 1827, altered 1865 [I.C.B.S.]. His designs for a NATIONAL SCHOOL at ANSTEY, LEICS., dated 1831, are in the Leicester Museum. [J. D. Bennett, *Leicestershire Architects 1700–1850*, Leicester Museums, 1968.]

KNIGHT, WILLIAM (–1832), was employed in the offices both of J. B. Papworth and of Sir John Rennie. For the latter he acted as resident architect or clerk of the works for the construction of Plymouth Breakwater (begun 1812) and of London Bridge (begun 1824). He exhibited at the Royal Academy from 1807 onwards, his drawings including 'the west front of Hillingdon House [Middlesex], the seat of J. D. Porcher, Esq., M.P.' (1808), the 'interior of the cathedral of Barcelona' (1819), a plan and elevation of Rennie's Southwark Bridge (1822),

a 'design for a nobleman's residence in the Castle style' (1823), and 'the works of the new London Bridge in progress as they appeared in August 1827' (1832). Knight was an enthusiastic antiquary, and made several communications to the Society of Antiquaries, of which he was a Fellow, on the subject of old London Bridge. The sale of his library and collections at Sotheby's in December 1832 included a number of architectural drawings and 'the Lower Jaw, and three other Bones, of Peter of Colechurch, the original Architect of London Bridge, found on removing the foundation of the Ancient chapel'. [*Gent's Mag.* 1832 (i), 201–6, 1833 (i), 67–8; W. Papworth, *Memoir of J. B. Papworth*, 1879, 96; sale catalogue in Bodleian Library, Mus. Bibl. III.]

KNIGHT, WILLIAM, was an architect practising in Kidderminster. In 1822 he was acting as clerk of works for Francis Goodwin at St. George's Church, Kidderminster [Rickman's diary, 21 June 1822]. In 1829–30 he was paid £23 19s. 2d. for surveying in connection with the building of the new SEBRIGHT SCHOOL at WOLVERLEY, WORCS., whose striking Gothic façade (illustrated in Pevsner's *Worcestershire*) he may therefore have designed. However, at the same time a Mr. Pinches was paid 5s. a day for 10 days 'making drawings for Wolverley School' [A. L. Murray, *Sebright School, Wolverley*, Cambridge 1954, 126].

In 1830 Knight designed a new Gothic tower for EASTHAM CHURCH, WORCS. In the course of his correspondence with the Incorporated Church Building Society the incumbent described Knight as 'an Architect, whose simplicity of design and good taste the Society has been pleased to approve in more, I believe, than one instance' [I.C.B.S.]. Knight was also concerned in the rebuilding of the nave of HARTLEBURY CHURCH, WORCS., to the designs of Thomas Rickman in 1836–7. From Rickman's 'work-book' [B.M., Add. MS. 37802, f. 75ᵛ] it appears that in 1834, after he had made the necessary designs, the churchwardens proposed to employ another architect, and Knight signs the drawings submitted to the Incorporated Church Building Society about this time. However, they evidently represented Rickman's design, and it was Rickman who was named as architect on the foundation-stone laid in 1836 [*Gent's Mag.* 1836 (i), 654].

KNOWLES, GEORGE (*c.* 1776–1856), was 'an able and successful civil engineer'. In that capacity he designed WHITWORTH BRIDGE over the R. Liffey in DUBLIN in 1816–17 [M. Craig, *Dublin 1660–1860*, 1952, 289]. He lived at Lucan House, Sharow, Yorkshire (W.R.), and in 1821–5 'designed and superintended the building' of SHAROW CHURCH in a competent Perpendicular

Gothic style. He died at Scarborough on 23 June 1856, aged 80, and was buried at Sharow, where an inscription records his responsibility for the design of the church, which is confirmed by the I.C.B.S. records.

L

LABELYE, CHARLES (1705–?1781), was the son of François Dangeau Labelye, a French Protestant refugee living at Vevey in Switzerland. He probably came to England in about 1725, in which year he joined a French Masonic Lodge in London of which his friend J. T. Desaguliers was also a member.[1] This is consistent with his own statement that he 'never heard a word of English spoken till I was near twenty years of age'. His first employment in England appears to have been as a teacher of mathematics to naval personnel, for the 'Mapp of the Downes ... together with the Soundings at low water, Places of Anchorage and all the necessary leading marks' which he produced in 1736 was 'By Charles Labelye, Engineer, late Teacher of the Mathematics in the Royal Navy' (P.R.O., MPH 218). In 1727–8 he was in Madrid, but by November 1728 he was back in England, practising as an expert in harbours and waterways. In 1734 he supplied maps and plans of the Thames to the promoters of the project for a new bridge over the river at Westminster. In June 1737 he was one of the five persons who were 'desired to attend the Commissioners with surveys of the river', and in July his were among the many plans for a wooden bridge which were submitted to them.[2] On 10 May 1738 he was appointed 'engineer' at a salary of £100 a year, with 10s. a day subsistence money. His commission extended only to the stone piers, as it was intended to build a bridge which could support either a timber or a stone superstructure, and the decision in favour of the latter was not taken until later. The employment of a foreigner[3] caused some jealousy among English architects, and led to the publication of a series of pamphlets in which the authors of the rejected designs gave vent to their disappointment by criticizing each other and denouncing 'the Swiss impostor' (see John James, *A Short Review of the Several Pamphlets and Schemes ... in relation to Building a Bridge at Westminster,* 1736.) Labelye had, however, a strong supporter in the Earl of Pembroke, by whom the first stone was laid on 29 January 1738/9. Richard Graham acted as 'surveyor and comptroller of the works' at £300 a year, and the contractors for the masonry were Andrews Jelfe and Samuel Tufnell.

The method of construction employed, involving the use of caissons in which to build the piers, was one not hitherto used in England. The caissons were huge timber boxes, 80 feet long and 16 feet deep, which were floated into position over the sites of the piers and sunk into excavations dug in the bed of the river to receive them. The water was then pumped out, and each pier was built inside the caisson up to water level. The sides of the caisson were then removed, leaving the flat bottom beneath the pier. In this way piling was avoided, and the piers were built of accurately laid masonry from their foundations upwards. In spite of these improved methods of construction, a subsidence occurred in one of the piers when the bridge was nearly complete, and it was not till November 1750 that it was eventually opened to the public. The accident occasioned a fresh outbreak of pamphlets, including a ballad entitled *The Downfall of Westminster Bridge, or my Lord in the Suds* (n.d.), in which Lord Pembroke, the Commissioners and Labelye were all severely handled. Batty Langley took the opportunity to publish *A Survey of Westminster Bridge, as 'tis now Sinking into Ruin,* 1748, containing a virulent attack on the Commissioners for employing 'an INSOLVENT IGNORANT, ARROGATING SWISS', and an engraved frontispiece showing his own rejected design for the bridge with a figure of Labelye hanging from a gallows in one corner. The Commissioners were, however, unimpressed by these taunts, and in February 1751 resolved to present Labelye with an honorarium of £2000 'for his great fidelity and extraordinary labour and attendances, skill and diligence'. Unfortunately for Labelye his patron the Earl of Pembroke died later that year, and he told a friend that in fact he was 'cutt off with only half the recompence promised' to him. He was now in poor health and 'voluntarily banished himself' from a country where he felt that he had been shabbily treated. In 1753 the architect Stephen Riou (*q.v.*) found him in Naples, but he appears eventually to have returned to France. The *Gentleman's Magazine* reported his death in Paris in 1762, but other sources indicate that it did not occur until 17 December 1781.

As the first major bridge to be built over an English river for more than a century, Westminster Bridge attracted much attention. Labe-

---

[1] Labelye contributed a paper on the laws of motion to Desaguliers' *Course of Experimental Philosophy,* 2nd ed. 1745, ii, 77–95. See also his account of the railway which conveyed stone from Ralph Allen's quarry near Bath to the R. Avon, *ibid.* i, 283–4 and pls. 21–3.

[2] Their authors were Thomas Lediard & Thomas Cotton, John James, Robert Browne, John Henslow & John Lock, Charles Labelye, John Simmonds, Samuel Perry, Thomas Innys, James King, Batty Langley, William & John Westley, and Messrs. Wyatt & Bartlett.

[3] In 1746 Labelye was naturalized by Act of Parliament (19 Geo. II, cap. 26).

lye himself published in 1739 *A Short Account of the Methods made use of in Laying the Foundation of the Piers of Westminster Bridge*, and *The Present State of Westminster Bridge ... in a letter to a Friend*, published anonymously in 1743, is also believed to have been written by him. He intended to publish a full description of the bridge, and in 1744 he issued a prospectus of the proposed work, which was to have been in two volumes. *The Description of Westminster Bridge* which he published in 1751 is, however, little more than an enlarged edition of the *Short Account*, and neither work contains the promised engravings. The original drawings, together with others relating to the bridge, are preserved in the Library of the Institute of Civil Engineers, bound up with a copy of Labelye's *Short Account*. They are signed by Thomas Gayfere, Andrews Jelfe's clerk, who apparently acted as Labelye's draughtsman. There is also in the same library a MS. *History and Construction of Westminster Bridge* by F. Wishaw, 1837, which is based on the Minutes of the Commissioners, now in the Public Record Office (Works 6). The original contracts are P.R.O., Works 16/D/1–17 and 16/E/1–6. Andrews Jelfe's letter-book in the British Museum (Add. MS. 27587) contains many letters relating to the construction of the bridge. One volume of the Commissioners' Minutes for 1741 is among the Parish Records of St. Margaret's, Westminster, in the Westminster City Library, and the Accounts of the Commissioners' Clerk for 1736–9 are in the Bodleian Library (MS. Gough London, 1). Some drawings and other documents relating to the bridge are among the 9th Earl of Pembroke's papers at Wilton House. There is a collection of engravings of the bridge in Bodleian, Gough Maps 23, and also a volume of pamphlets relating to its construction (Gough Westminster 22). Labelye's bridge was replaced by the present structure in 1854–62. It was illustrated in the *Gentleman's Magazine* for 1746, pp. 683–4, in a work entitled *Gephyralogia; an Historical Account of Bridges, ancient and modern, including a more particular History and Description of the new Bridge at Westminster*, 1751, and in Britton & Pugin's *Public Buildings of London* ii, 1828, 295. See also Patricia Carson, 'The Building of the First Bridge at Westminster', *Jnl. of Transport History* iii, 1957–8.

The only other English bridge for which Labelye is known to have been responsible was BRENTFORD BRIDGE, MIDDLESEX, which he rebuilt in brick and stone in 1740–2 [Middlesex Sessions Records, Orders of Court, iv, ff. 171–2, 211–12].

In 1746, for the Bridgehouse committee, Labelye made drawings of London Bridge designed to show how the waterway could be doubled by reducing the size of the starlings. These were published in Maitland's *History of London* ii, 1756, 826–32. Several of his reports on

harbours and waterways were published: namely *The Result of a View of the Great Level of the Fens*, 1745; *The Result of a Particular View of the North Level of the Fens taken in August 1745*, 1748; *Abstract of Mr. C. L.'s Report, relating to the Improvement of the River Wear and Port of Sunderland in 1748*, Newcastle c. 1748; and *The Result of a View and Survey of Yarmouth Haven, taken in the year 1747*, Norwich 1775. His plan of a projected harbour at Sandwich was engraved by Harris, c. 1740.

[D.N.B.; A.P.S.D., *Ars Quatuor Coronatorum* xl, 1927, 37, 244; MS. Tour in Greece by S. Riou in Mellon Collection; sources mentioned in text.]

LABRIÈRE, ALEXANDRE-LOUIS DE, was a French architect who came to England as a refugee during the Revolution. Before 1785 his career is difficult to distinguish from that of his relative and contemporary, Jean-Jacques de Labrière, who died in that year, but one or other of them was 'Contrôleur des bâtiments du roi' at Fontainebleau in 1772 and at Meudon in 1778, and architect both to the Comte d'Artois and to Mme. Elizabeth (sister of Louis XVI), for whom he designed the Château de Montreuil.

In England de Labrière was employed by Henry Holland at CARLTON HOUSE, LONDON, and at SOUTHILL HOUSE, BEDS., where he was responsible for the decoration of the boudoir (c. 1796–1800) in an elegant French neo-classical style. In the muniment-room at BEECHWOOD, HERTS., there are drawings by de Labrière which show that he designed a chimney-piece in the library there c. 1804, and also the interior of the library in Lord Marchmont's house in CURZON STREET, LONDON, which is stated to have been 'executed with good effect'.

[M. Gallet, *Demeures Parisiennes, l'époque de Louis XVI*, Paris 1964, 187; Dorothy Stroud, *Henry Holland*, 1966, 74, 128.]

LAING, ALEXANDER (–1823), practised in Edinburgh, first as a mason, then as an architect. He first appears in the Edinburgh directories as a mason in 1774. He was still described as a mason in 1777, when he became a member of the Royal Company of Archers, whose new Hall he had just built, and in 1782, when he was admitted as a burgess of Edinburgh [J. Balfour Paul, *History of the Royal Company of Archers*, 1875, 370; *Roll of Edinburgh Burgesses, 1761–1841*, Scottish Record Soc., vol. xc]. Thereafter, however, he described himself as an architect. His buildings are designed in a plain, masculine Georgian style without much elegance or refinement. The Edinburgh Marriage Register shows that he was married three times, first in 1772, and again in 1786 and 1789. He died at Portobello on 17 September 1823 [*Scots. Mag.*, 1823, 512].

EDINBURGH, THE ARCHERS' HALL, BUCCLEUCH STREET, 1776; altered and enlarged 1900 [Minutes of the Royal Company of Archers, 27 July 1776] (J. Grant, *Old and New Edinburgh* ii, 1882, 352–3).

EDINBURGH, THE HIGH SCHOOL, INFIRMARY STREET (now Edinburgh University Geographical Dept.), 1777; reconstructed 1905 [Edinburgh Dean of Guild Records] (unsigned engraving of design in *Scots Mag.*, 1777, 332–4).

EDINBURGH, designed and built THE SOUTH BRIDGE, 1786–8 [A. J. Youngson, *The Making of Classical Edinburgh*, 1966, 112].

INVERNESS TOLBOOTH, Steeple, 1789 [*Old Inverness*, ed. Eveline Barron, 1967].

BRECHIN CASTLE, ANGUS, alterations for William Ramsay, 1st Lord Panmure, 1796–7 [John Dunbar & David Walker in *C. Life*, 19 Aug. 1971].

DYSART CHURCH, FIFE, 1802–3 [building records in S.R.O., GD 164/7/284].

INVERMAY, nr. FORTEVIOT, PERTHSHIRE, designed or supervised alterations for Col. J. Hepburn Belshes, 1802, including stables, west lodges, game larder, dairy and gazebo [N.M.R.S., extracts from factor's letter-book at Invermay].

DARNAWAY CASTLE, MORAYSHIRE, for the 8th Earl of Moray, 1802–12, castellated [N.M.R.S., extracts from Moray muniments at Darnaway Castle, vol. vi, Box 18] (Sheila Forman, *Scottish Country Houses and Castles*, 1967, 141–3).

PETERHEAD OLD CHURCH, ABERDEENSHIRE, 1804–6 [J. T. Findlay, *History of Peterhead*, Aberdeen 1933, 143–4].

? SNIZORT CHURCH, ISLE OF SKYE, 1805; enlarged 1839 [probably the church for which Laing provided a design in 1801: J. Macaulay, 'James Gillespie Graham in Skye', *Bulletin of the Scottish Georgian Soc.* iii, 1974–5, 5].

HUNTLY CHURCH, ABERDEENSHIRE, 1805 [S.R.O., Gordon Castle papers, GD 44/37/47].

DRUMSHEUGH HOUSE, EDINBURGH, gateway and lodge for the 8th Earl of Moray, 1808–9; dem. [N.M.R.S., extracts from Moray muniments at Darnaway Castle, vol. vi, box 18, 701].

ABERDOUR MANSE, ABERDEENSHIRE, 1822 [*Aberdeen Jnl.*, 18 May 1822]. This was the outcome of a protracted dispute in which Laing acted initially as arbitrator, but was eventually employed to modify a plan submitted by William Robertson of Elgin: see the printed *Abstract of the Law Proceedings in the Case of the Manse of Aberdour, Aberdeenshire*, 1823 (S.R.O., GD 16/46/89).

LAING, DAVID (1774–1856), son of D. Laing, of Tower Street, London, 'cork cutter', was articled to Sir John Soane in 1790. He was still in Soane's office in 1795, when he exhibited a 'design for a saloon' at the Royal Academy, but left

in 1796 to begin independent practice. In 1800 he published *Hints for Dwellings, consisting of original designs for Cottages, Farm-Houses, Villas, etc.*, which was reprinted in 1804, 1823, 1841 and 1972. This was a typical work of its kind, offering designs for villas, ornamental cottages, etc., in a style which shows the influence of his master Soane. Several of them were intended for specific patrons in England, Ireland[1] and (in one case) Germany, where Laing was later to build at least one house (at Brunswick). In 1810 Laing succeeded Pilkington as Surveyor to the Customs, and immediately designed a new Custom House at Plymouth whose elegantly accented simplicity reveals him as a student of contemporary French architecture. In 1812 he was commissioned to rebuild the London Custom House, which was completed to his designs in 1817. Here again he produced an elegant neo-classical design of considerable merit. Unfortunately he failed to supervise a delinquent contractor with sufficient care, and in 1825 part of the façade collapsed owing to the inadequacy of the beech piling employed in the foundations. Subsequent investigations revealed faulty work on a scale which indicated either gross incompetence or collusion on the part of the architect, and Sir Robert Smirke had to be called in to reconstruct the building at great expense. Laing was dismissed from his office and was obliged to retire from practice. Professionally ruined, he lived on until 1856, dependent upon the charity dispensed by the Artists General Benevolent Institution, the Fund for Distressed Architects established by Soane, and the Surveyors' Club, a society over which he had once (1821) presided.[2] He died at Brompton on 27 March 1856, aged 82.

In addition to the work already mentioned, Laing published in 1818 *Plans etc. of Buildings, Public and Private, executed in various parts of England, including the Custom House*. He drew many of the illustrations of public buildings for Nicholson's *Practical Builder*, 1837. In the Royal Collection at Windsor there is a design by him dated 1818 for converting Hyde Park and Kensington Gardens into the site of a royal palace. There are unexecuted designs by him for Banks Hall, nr. Lanercost, Cumberland, 1828 (Cumbria Record Office) and for a Corn Exchange at Winchester, 1835 (Richardson Collection at Ampthill). His pupils included T. Bellamy,

---

[1] The 'Mansion designed for a Nobleman, and intended to be built at — in the County of Kildare, on the Banks of the Liffey', was almost certainly for Lord Cloncurry at Lyons. It was not built, but the design is interesting as a neo-classical version of the 'Villa Rotonda'. Lord Cloncurry was among the subscribers to Laing's *Plans* in 1818.

[2] In 1815–16 he had also been Master of the Tylers' and Bricklayers' Company.

Charles Fowler, R. Kelsey, T. Lee and William Tite (in conjunction with whom he designed St. Dunstan's Church). His son C. D. Laing was a wood-engraver whose work often appeared in the *Builder*.

[*A.P.S.D.*; *Gent's Mag.* 1856 (i), 650; *Builder* xiv, 1856, 189; A. T. Bolton, *The Works of Sir John Soane*, 1924, Appendix C, p. xli; J. M. Crook, 'The Custom House Scandal', *Architectural History* vi, 1963.]

PUBLIC BUILDINGS

PLYMOUTH, DEVON, THE CUSTOM HOUSE, 1810 [G. Wightwick, *Nettleton's Guide to Plymouth*, 1836, 25] (A. E. Richardson & C. L. Gill, *Regional Architecture of the West of England*, 1924, 76).

LONDON, THE CUSTOM HOUSE, THAMES STREET, 1813–17; central portion reconstructed by Sir Robert Smirke 1825–7 after collapse [*Plans* pls. 1–41; Britton & Pugin, *Public Buildings of London* i, 1825, 46–54; *History of the King's Works* vi, 1973, 422–30].

LONDON, ST. DUNSTAN-IN-THE-EAST-CHURCH, rebuilt body of church, excluding steeple, 1817–21, Gothic; destroyed by bombing 1941 [exhib. at R.A. 1818, 1819 and 1822; *Plans*, pls. 54–7] (G. Godwin, *The Churches of London* i, 1838).

COLCHESTER, THE CORN EXCHANGE, HIGH STREET (now ESSEX & SUFFOLK INSURANCE SOCIETY'S FIRE OFFICE), *c.* 1820; upper storey since added [T. Wright, *History of Essex* i, 1836, 307].

LONDON, THE ROYAL UNIVERSAL INFIRMARY FOR CHILDREN, WATERLOO ROAD, 1833–4; rebuilt 1903–5 [*A.P.S.D.*; lithograph signed by Laing as architect in Berkshire Record Office, D/EBy F.24].

PRIVATE HOUSES

ABBOTS LANGLEY, HERTS., house for Griffith Jones, *c.* 1800 [*Hints*, pls. 15–18].

BALLYMAHON, CO. LONGFORD, IRELAND, 'design for a villa to be erected for a gentleman', *c.* 1800 [*Hints*, pl. 11].

BRUNSWICK, GERMANY, 'mansion constructed for J. Retburgh, Esq.', before 1818 [*Plans*, pls. 45–6].

CASTLE TAYLOR, ARDRAHAN, CO. GALWAY, IRELAND, house 'erected' for General Sir J. Taylor, before 1818 [*Plans*, pl. 47].

COLEY PARK, nr. READING, BERKS., villa for John McConnell, before 1818; remodelled *c.* 1840 [*Plans*, pl. 48].

DEDHAM, ESSEX, house for Stephen Teissier (d. 1816) [*Plans*, p. 33].

EASTHAMPSTEAD, BERKS., cottages, etc., for the 3rd Marquess of Downshire, 1803 [Berkshire Record Office, D/ED. E80].

GUERNSEY, Gothic villa 'intended to be erected for Mr. Macculloch' [*Plans*, pls. 43–4].

JERSEY, villa 'erected' for J. Emery, before 1818 [*Plans*, pl. 49].

LAVENDER HILL, WANDSWORTH, SURREY, villa 'erected' before 1818, probably for Ephraim Gompertz [*Plans*, pl. 42].

LEXDEN PARK HOUSE (now Endsleigh School), ESSEX, for J. F. Mills, 1825; remodelled *c.* 1850 [T. Cromwell, *History of Colchester*, 1825, 238].

THEBERTON, SUFFOLK, 'design for a lodge to be built at', *c.* 1800 [*Hints*, pl. 4].

LAMB, WILLIAM, was a builder-architect of Leith, where he designed 1–8 VANBRUGH PLACE, 1826 [S.R.O., Edinburgh Sasines]. He also built and probably designed NOS. 1–13 BERNARD STREET and 30–34 CONSTITUTION STREET, LEITH, 1815–16 [Scottish Development Department, typescript *List of Buildings of Special Architectural or Historic Interest in Edinburgh*, nos. 596, 2137].

LANDI, GAETANO, was a native of Bologna, and perhaps a relative of the Bolognese architect and painter, Giuseppe Antonio Landi. He described himself as 'Professor in the University of Bologna and Member of the Clementine Academy', but no record of him can be found in the archives of either institution. He was in England by 1810, when he published the first and only part of a series of aquatint plates entitled *Architectural Decorations: A Periodical Work of Original Designs invented from the Egyptian, the Greek, the Roman, the Etruscan, the Attic, the Gothic etc. for Exterior and Interior Decoration of Galleries, Halls, Apartments etc. either in Painting or Relief*, dedicated to the Marquess of Douglas, of which there is a copy in the Soane Museum. Letters in the same museum indicate that in 1810 he was in financial difficulties and about to depart for Russia. [E. Croft-Murray, *Decorative Painting in England* ii, 1970, 236–7.]

LANDMANN, ISAAC, was a Professor at the Royal Military Academy at Woolwich from 1777 to 1815 [O. F. G. Hogg, *The Royal Arsenal* i, 1963, 191, n. 50]. He was the author of *A Course of the Five Orders of Civil Architecture with a Plan and Some Geometrical Elevations of Town Gates of Fortified Places*, 1785, and of *The Principles of Fortification reduced into Questions and Answers for the Use of the Royal Military Academy at Woolwich*, 1796. The former work was partly based on Chambers's *Civil Architecture*.

501

LANE, H— (*c.* 1787–   ), a pupil of William Inwood, entered the Royal Academy Schools in 1808 at the age of 21. He exhibited at the R.A. from Inwood's office in 1808 and 1809, but by 1810 he appears to have begun independent practice, exhibiting a 'Design for a villa intended to be erected in Sussex' from 60 Berwick Street.

LANE, JOHN (–1753), held the combined posts of Surveyor of the Horse Guards and Clerk of the Works at Chelsea Hospital from January 1728/9 until his death in 1753. In 1732–3 he was responsible for building the new PAYMASTER-GENERAL'S OFFICE in WHITEHALL immediately to the north of the Horse Guards [*Survey of London* xvi, chap. 3 and Treasury records there cited]. He was presumably the Mr Lane who in 1741–2 designed and built the old parish church of ST. JOHN, MARYLEBONE, LONDON (dem. 1949), after a design by James Gibbs had been rejected [F. H. W. Sheppard, *Local Government in St Marylebone 1688–1835*, 1958, 31].

LANE, RICHARD, practised in Manchester from 1821, when he was appointed Land Surveyor to the Manchester Police Commissioners, until 1858. Nothing is known of his training, but he was presumably the R. Lane who exhibited a drawing of Southill House, Beds. at the Royal Academy in 1815 from a London address. He soon became the leading Manchester architect of his day, and was the first President of the Manchester Architectural Society founded in 1837. For some years he was in partnership with P. B. Alley. Alfred Darbyshire and Alfred Waterhouse were his pupils. The date of Lane's death has not been ascertained with certainty, but he may have been the Richard Lane of Fir Bank, Ascot, Berks., who died there on 25 May 1880, aged 85, for one of the latter's executors lived in Manchester [*The Times*, 27 May 1880; will in Principal Probate Registry].

Though he designed some Gothic churches (marked, according to J. C. Loudon, by 'many little disagreeable negligences of style'), Lane favoured a correct, dignified and rather unenterprising Greek Revival style reminiscent of Smirke's work in London. 'His practice', wrote Alfred Darbyshire, 'was almost exclusively devoted to an attempt to force upon a commercial nineteenth-century town, with a sunless and humid climate, the refinement and beauty of the art of the Greeks in the golden age of Pericles' [Cecil Stewart, *The Stones of Manchester*, 1956, 28–30; Alfred Darbyshire, *An Architect's Experiences*, 1897, 21].

STOCKPORT, CHESHIRE, TIVIOT DALE WESLEYAN METHODIST CHAPEL, 1825–6 [H. Heginbotham, *Stockport, Ancient and Modern* ii, 1892, 70–1].

SALFORD, LANCS., THE TOWN HALL AND ASSEMBLY ROOMS, 1825–7 [B. Love, *Handbook to Manchester*, 1842, 250].

OLDHAM, LANCS., ST. MARY'S CHURCH, 1827–30, Gothic [*V.C.H. Lancs.* v, 104].

MANCHESTER, THE FRIENDS' MEETING-HOUSE, MOUNT STREET, 1828–30 [plate in *Lancashire Illustrated* inscribed 'R. Lane Architect'].

OLDHAM, LANCS., THE BLUE-COAT SCHOOL, 1829–30, Gothic [G. N. Wright, *Lancashire, its History, Legends and Manufactures, c.* 1850, 135].

PENDLETON (SALFORD), LANCS., ST. THOMAS'S CHURCH, with F. Goodwin, 1829–31, Gothic [Port, 148].

CHORLTON-ON-MEDLOCK, MANCHESTER, THE TOWN HALL, 1830 [S. Lewis, *Topographical Dictionary of England* iii, 1831, 242].

MANCHESTER, THE CONCERT HALL, PETER STREET, 1831; dem. [T. Swindells, *Manchester Streets and Manchester Men* i, 1906, 165].

STOCKPORT, CHESHIRE, THE INFIRMARY, WELLINGTON ROAD SOUTH, 1832–3 [H. Heginbotham, *Stockport, Ancient and Modern* ii, 1892, 382].

WAKEFIELD, YORKS. (W.R.), THE WEST RIDING PROPRIETARY (later Grammar) SCHOOL, NORTHGATE, 1833–4, Tudor Gothic [*Architectural Mag.* i, 1834, 142].

MANCHESTER, THE ROYAL INFIRMARY, PICCADILLY, refaced 1835, enlarged 1848–53; dem. 1909 [B. Love, *Handbook to Manchester*, 1842, 120; *A.P.S.D.*].

MANCHESTER, THE CORN EXCHANGE, HANGING DITCH, 1835–7; dem. [B. Love, *Handbook to Manchester*, 1842, 234].

MANCHESTER, THE UNION CLUB-HOUSE, MOSLEY STREET, 1836 [B. Love, *Handbook to Manchester*, 1842, 238].

MANCHESTER, HENSHAW'S BLIND ASYLUM AND DEAF AND DUMB SCHOOL, OLD TRAFFORD, 1836–7, Gothic [*A.P.S.D.*, s.v. 'Manchester'].

SALFORD, ST. JOHN'S CHURCH, HIGHER BROUGHTON, 1836–8, Gothic; chancel by J. E. Gregan 1846 [*A.P.S.D.*, s.v. 'Manchester'; drawings in Manchester Reference Library].

MANCHESTER, VICTORIA PARK, layout and lodges (dem.), 1837 [*Architectural Mag.* iv, 487; v. 701].

BOWDEN HALL, CHAPEL-EN-LE-FRITH, DERBYSHIRE, for John Slack, 1844, Tudor [S. Bagshaw, *History and Directory of Derbyshire*, 1846, 464].

HENBURY CHURCH, CHESHIRE, 1844–5, Gothic [I.C.B.S.].

SALFORD, LANCS., ST. SIMON'S CHURCH, 1845–9, Gothic; dem. [*Builder* iii, 1845, 187, 547].

SALFORD, LANCS., THE RICHMOND INDEPENDENT CHAPEL, BLACKFRIARS ROAD, 1845, Gothic [*Builder* iii, 1845, 547].

PENDLETON (SALFORD), LANCS., THE INDEPENDENT CHAPEL, 1846, Gothic [*Builder* iv, 1946, 452].

STOCKPORT ETCHELLS, CHESHIRE, THE MANCHESTER

ROYAL LUNATIC ASYLUM, 1848–9, Elizabethan [*A.P.S.D.*, *s.v.* 'Manchester'].

ST. JOHN'S CHURCH, ISLE OF MAN, 1849, Gothic [L. D. Butler, *An Architectural History of the Churches of the Isle of Man*, typescript 1970, 13].

STRANGEWAYS, LANCS., BAPTIST CHAPEL, CLARE-MONT TERRACE, BRIDGE STREET, 1851, Gothic [*Builder* ix, 1851, 296].

MANCHESTER, ARDWICK CEMETERY, THE DALTON MEMORIAL, 1854 [*Builder* xii, 1854, 36].

LANE, WILLIAM, was a carpenter and builder at Eton. He rebuilt TAPLOW CHURCH, BUCKS., in 1826–8 (again rebuilt 1912) [parish records, *ex inf.* Canon B. F. L. Clarke]. In 1829 he rebuilt the south aisle of BISHAM CHURCH, BERKS., to his own plans [Bodleian Library, MS. Oxford Arch-deaconry Papers, Berks, c. 160, f. 63 *et seq.*; drawings in Salisbury Diocesan Registry].

LANG, CHARLES EVANS, exhibited a view of the Column and Town Hall at Devonport at the Royal Academy in 1831, giving his address as 'Dockyard, Deptford'. In 1833 he exhibited part of a design for a royal palace at the Society of British Artists, and in 1842 he showed at the Royal Academy a design for the Assize Courts at Liverpool submitted in 1840. He became an Associate of the R.I.B.A. in 1842 and a Fellow in 1848.

LANGDON, JOHN HARRIS, a London builder, appears to have designed the Greek Re-vival GUILDHALL at ANDOVER, HANTS. In January 1825 he submitted a plan and estimate which were accepted [Andover town records, *ex inf.* Mr. Richard Warmington]. Pigot's *Directory* shows that in 1825 Langdon was living at 14 Hadlow Street, Burton Crescent, London.

LANGLEY, BATTY (1696–1751), was the son of Daniel and Elizabeth Langley of Twickenham, where he was baptized on 14 September 1696. His father was a gardener, and Batty appears at first to have practised as a landscape-gardener (see his *Practical Geometry*, p. 35, and several books on the subject which he published in the 1720s). For some years he lived in Twickenham, but removed to Parliament Stairs, Westminster, in or before 1735, and to Meard's Court, Dean Street, Soho, in about 1740. There he established a school or academy offering lessons in archi-tecture and drawing, in which he was assisted by his brother Thomas, an engraver. An advertise-ment published in *The City and Country Builder's Treasury* (1740) indicates that Langley was pre-pared to make 'Designs for Buildings, Gardens, Parks, etc. in the most grand Taste', to design and build 'Grottos, Cascades, Caves, Temples, Pavillions, and other Rural Buildings of

Pleasure', to survey estates, and to construct 'Engines for raising Water in any Quantity, to any height required, for the service of Noblemen's Seats, Cities, Towns, etc.' He also manufactured an artificial stone, of which he made statues, busts and architectural ornaments. He was best known, however, as the author of numerous publications designed to enable the master builder to keep abreast with current fashions, and in particular of an attempt to sys-tematize Gothic architecture.

As a practising architect Langley appears to have had little success. The extremely jejune de-sign which he submitted in the competition for the Mansion House in 1735 (illustrated by S. Perks, *The History of the Mansion House*, 1922, pl. 49, from an engraving by Langley) suggests that his abilities as an architectural designer were small, and the only buildings actually known to have been built under his direction were an orna-mental temple for Nathaniel Blackerby, whose house adjoined his own at Parliament Stairs, and a new dining-room, greenhouse and brewhouse for the Duke of Kent at Wrest Park in Bedford-shire (1735). Langley's membership of a 'Society of Artizans' which included some 'newswriters' led, much to the Duke's annoyance, to the announcement of the latter commission in the press, and it was no doubt due to the same channel of communication that in 1735 the *St. James's Evening Post* as able to publish a descrip-tion of the 'curious grotesque temple in a taste entirely new, finely decorated within with busts of King William III, George I and five gentlemen of the Club of Liberty', which Langley had designed for Blackerby at Parliament Stairs [J. P. Malcolm, *Londinium Redivivum* iv, 1807, 172]. In 1736–7 Langley's were among the many pro-jects for a bridge across the Thames which were submitted to the Westminster Bridge Commis-sioners, and he not only had his design engraved (1736, with descriptive text) but took a promi-nent part in the subsequent pamphlet con-troversy, publishing *A Reply to Mr. John James's Review of the Several Pamphlets and Schemes... for the Building of a Bridge at Westminster*. 1737, and *A Survey of Westminster Bridge, as 'tis now sinking into Ruin*, 1748, reviewed in *Gent's Mag.* 1748, 96. Under the pseudonym of 'Hiram' he published in the *Grub Street Journal* (11 July 1734 *et seq.*), a 'continuation' of the well-known *Critical Review of the Publick Buildings in London and Westminster* by James Ralph (see his admission of authorship in a letter to the Lord Mayor, printed by Perks, *op. cit.*, 165).

It was, no doubt, Langley's failure to succeed as a practising architect that induced him to make a living chiefly by his architectural publications. Most of these were manuals designed for artisans and craftsmen, but the 494 plates of *Ancient Masonry* (2 vols. folio, 1734–6), derived from a wide range of sources from Vredeman de Vries to Gibbs, made it one of the largest and most comprehensive treatises in the literature of English architecture. Langley's most celebrated book, *Ancient Architecture Restored and Improved by a Great Variety of Grand and Usefull Designs, entirely new in the Gothick Mode for the ornamenting of Buildings and Gardens* (1741–2), reissued in 1747 as *Gothic Architecture, improved by Rules and Proportions in many Grand Designs of Columns, Doors, Windows, Chimney-Pieces . . . Temples and Pavillions* etc. was remarkable as a pioneer attempt to make Gothic architecture intelligible to an age brought up on the classical orders. By attempting to reduce Gothic to a formula Langley incurred the ridicule of later Revivalists, but the book enjoyed considerable success in its day, and Langley's engaging but unscholarly designs for Gothic doorways and chimney-pieces found willing imitators all over the country (see examples illustrated by Rowan, of which the most striking are the Gothic Octagon at Bramham Park, Yorks. (1750), and a fireplace at Tissington Hall, Derbyshire).

Langley died at his house in Soho on 3 March 1751, aged 55. A mezzotint portrait by J. Carwitham, who engraved the plates for several of his works, was published in 1741. It is reproduced by E. Beresford Chancellor, *Lives of the British Architects*, 1909, 231. He married twice, and had a large family. Several of the sons were given Christian names (Euclid, Vitruvius, Archimedes and Hiram) indicative both of Langley's architectural pretensions and of his interest in Freemasonry.

In addition to the works already mentioned, Langley published: *An Accurate Account of Newgate . . . together with a Faithful Account of the Impositions of the Bailiffs . . . by B. L.* of Twickenham, 1724; *Practical Geometry, applied to the Useful Arts of Building, Surveying, Gardening and Mensuration*, dedicated to Lord Paisley, 1726, 1729; *The Builder's Chest Book, or a Compleat Key to the Five Orders of Columns in Architecture*, 1727, 1739, also published in Dublin as the *Builder's Vade Mecum*, 1729, 1735; *New Principles of Gardening; or the laying out and planting Parterres, Groves, Wildernesses, Labyrinths, Avenues, Parks*, etc., 1728; *A Sure Method of Improving Estates by Plantations of Oak, Elm, Ash, Beech*, etc., 1728, republished as *The Landed Gentleman's Useful Companion*, 1741; *Pomona, or the Fruit Garden Illustrated*, 1729; *A Sure Guide to Builders, or the Principles and Practice of Architecture Geometrically Demonstrated*, dedicated to Thomas Scawen of Carshalton, 1729; *The Young Builder's Rudiments, or the Principles of Geometry, Mechanics*, etc., *Geometrically Demonstrated*, 1730, 1734; *The Builder's Compleat Chest Book*, 1738; *The City and Country Builder's and Workman's Treasury of Designs*, 1740, 1745, 1750, 1756, 1770, reprint of 1745 ed. 1969; *The Builder's Compleat Assistant*, c. 1741, 4th. ed. 1766; *The Builder's Jewel, or the Youth's Instructor, and Workman's Remembrancer*, 1741 and many subsequent editions, including one at Dublin 1768 and another at Edinburgh 1808; *The Measurer's Jewell*, 1742; *A Plan of Windsor Castle*, 1743; *The Builder's Director or Bench-Mate*, 1747, 1751, 1761, 1763, 1767; *London Prices of Bricklayers' Materials and Works*, 1748, 1749, 1750; *The Workman's Golden Rule for Drawing and Working the Five Orders in Architecture*, 1750, 1756. He was probably also the author of the anonymous *Observations on a Pamphlet lately published entitled Remarks on the Different Construction of Bridges . . . by Charles Marquand, in which the Puerility of the Performance is considered*, 1749.

[*A.P.S.D.*; *D.N.B.*; Walpole Soc., *Vertue Note Books* iii, 3, 5, 51; *Ars Quatuor Coronatorum* xlv, 1932, 101–2 (on Langley as a Freemason); R. Gunnis, *Dictionary of British Sculptors*, 1968, 233; Alistair Rowan, 'Batty Langley's Gothic', in *Studies in Memory of David Talbot Rice*, Edinburgh 1975; Bedfordshire Record Office, Wrest Papers, L30/8/43/1–2, L31/246–252 and L28/22.]

LANGSTAFFE, or **LONGSTAFFE**, JOHN (1622–1694), was a master mason of Bishop Auckland, Co. Durham. He was the son of Thomas Langstaff, a mason of the same place. Between 1662 and 1666 he was employed by Bishop Cosin to carry out extensive alterations to BISHOP AUCKLAND CASTLE, and he was probably the mason who reconstructed the twelfth-century Great Hall as the Bishop's Chapel. Like other seventeenth-century master masons, he probably designed the buildings he executed, and a drawing by him of a scheme for the 'outward court walls of Auckland Castle', dated 1655, is preserved in Mickleton and Spearman MS. 91 in the Library of the University of Durham. In the same MS. there is a plan and elevation by Langstaffe for the School and Almshouses which Cosin built on Palace Green, Durham, in 1666. The almshouses as built do not, however, correspond to Langstaffe's 'draught', which shows a building of more classical character with pedimented doorway and rusticated coins.

Langstaffe was an active member of the Society of Friends, whose meetings were regularly held in his house at Bishop Auckland. He appears to have become a Quaker in 1654, and was repeatedly fined for refusing to take the oath of allegiance during the remainder of his life. His cattle were also distrained on for unpaid tithes by Cosin's officials, but the bishop seems to have adopted a tolerant attitude towards his mason's nonconformity, and in 1664 gave him the job of rebuilding the COUNTY HALL on Palace Green,

Durham, partly (it was said) in order to reimburse him. As Langstaffe was not a freeman of Durham, it was only with the bishop's support that he was able to undertake this important contract. The 'County House' built by Langstaffe was demolished early in the nineteenth century.

Langstaffe was also employed by Cosin in connection with the LIBRARY which he founded on Palace Green in 1669. There is reason to think that the building was designed by Langstaffe, for in 1670 Cosin asked him to provide a drawing of it as a pattern for a projected library at Caius College, Cambridge, and later in the same year he got Langstaffe to make 'a handsome draught' of an addition to the Durham library which was soon afterwards built and is now known as 'Cosin's Small Room'.

Another work in Durham which Langstaffe may have carried out was the refronting of the house whose lease was bought for Cosin's son-in-law Samuel Davison in 1670. The bishop desired that 'no patcher (be employed), but that John Langstaffe should set on neat workmen to doe it'. In the following year Langstaffe was employed by Cosin to make alterations to the manor-house at BRAFFERTON, Co. Durham, which belonged to the Bishopric. They included the addition of a library and alterations to 'the kitchen-side Court'.

Langstaffe died at Middlestone, nr. Auckland, on 26 May 1694. Besides his mason's tools his possessions included 'some books' and surveying instruments. Four of his sons followed their father's trade: Thomas, of Bishop Auckland (1655–1703),[1] John, of Whitby (1649–1719), Bethwell, who appears to have migrated to Philadelphia, and Amos, of Middlestone (d. 1693). [G. B. Longstaffe, *The Longstaffs of Teesdale and Weardale*, 1923, chap. 7; *The Correspondence of John Cosin, Bishop of Durham* ii (Surtees Soc. 1870), 229, 233–4, 249, 251–2, 253, 254, 255; University of Durham Library, Mickleton and Spearman MS. 91.]

LANGWITH, JOHN (*c.* 1715–1795), was a carpenter and builder of Grantham in Lincolnshire. Accounts in the Lincolnshire Record Office suggest that he designed SYSTON NEW HALL, LINCS., for Sir John Thorold, Bart. He worked on the 'new building' there between 1766 and 1775, and in the latter year a contract was made with a bricklayer for work on the north wing 'according to Mr. Langwith's plan'. The house, demolished *c.* 1930, was a plain building with fenestration of 'Palladian' character. In 1785

Langwith was one of three architects who submitted designs for the Castle Gaol at Lincoln, but those of William Lumby were accepted [Lincolnshire Record Office, Quarter Sessions Records, 1785–8]. Langwith retired to Harston, nr. Grantham, where he died in January 1795 at the age of 80, and was succeeded by his son, John Langwith, junior. He left a considerable amount of property, and according to the *Gentleman's Magazine* 'by his death the poor have lost a good benefactor' [*Gent's Mag.* 1795 (i), 355; Grantham Parish Registers, *ex inf.* the Rev. Henry Thorold].

LANGWITH, JOHN (*c.* 1753–1825), son of the above, continued his father's business as a builder and surveyor at Grantham, where he was buried on 3 June 1825, aged 72. His recorded works include GRANTHAM VICARAGE, which he rebuilt in 1789 in a pleasant vernacular Georgian style; BARKSTON RECTORY, LINCS., 1801; and designs (perhaps not executed) for a prison at GRANTHAM, 1811. He was succeeded by his son Joseph Silvester Langwith (*q.v.*). [Lincolnshire Record Office, MGA 6 and 33; Grantham Borough Records; Grantham Parish Registers, *ex inf.* the Rev. Henry Thorold; Arthur Oswald, 'Grantham, Lincolnshire', *C. Life*, 17 Sept. 1964.]

LANGWITH, JOSEPH SILVESTER (1787–1854), son of the above, was baptized at Grantham on 31 December 1787. He continued the family practice as an 'Architect and Surveyor', but apparently gave up the building business. In the Lincolnshire Record Office there are designs by him for enlarging or rebuilding the parsonages at NORTH and SOUTH STOKE, LINCS., 1825, GREAT PONTON, LINCS., 1826, HACEBY, LINCS., 1828, BARKSTON, LINCS., 1829, and KNIPTON, LEICS., 1830 [MGA 122, 136, 144, 150, 157]. HARSTON CHURCH, LEICS., was rebuilt to his designs in 1821–2, but was again rebuilt later in the nineteenth century [I.C.B.S.]. He died on 12 May 1854, and is commemorated by a tombstone in Grantham Churchyard.

LANSDOWN, JAMES (*c.* 1796–1838), was a pupil of P. F. Robinson. He was admitted to the Royal Academy Schools in 1817 at the age of 21, and exhibited student's work at the Academy in 1817 and 1818. He appears to have been involved in the building developments round Regent's Park, for in 1828 he exhibited drawings of CHESTER TERRACE, and of STRATHERNE VILLA (*i.e.* 12 and 14 GLOUCESTER GATE), 'now erecting on the east side of Regent's Park'. His own address was given as Chester Terrace, and it was in Chester Place that he died on 18 October 1838 [*Gent's Mag.* 1838 (ii), 667]. Shortly before his death he had designed offices (dem.) for the Phoenix Fire

---

[1] This was no doubt the mason who made the column erected at Burgh-on-Sands, Cumberland, in 1685 in memory of King Edward I. It was signed 'Tho. Langstaff Fecit 1685' (St. Edmund Hall, Oxford, MS. 7/3, f. 191).

Insurance Company in Lombard Street. These were completed by John Shaw [Anon., *Phoenix Assurance Company Ltd.*, privately printed 1915]. He had been elected a member of the Surveyors' Club in 1836.

LAPIDGE, EDWARD (1779–1860), was the eldest son of Samuel Lapidge of Hampton Wick (d. 1806), a former assistant of Lancelot Brown, who held the post of Chief Gardener at Hampton Court Palace.[1] Edward was appointed Surveyor to the County of Surrey in 1824, and it was in this capacity that he designed his most important work, the bridge of five elliptical arches over the Thames at Kingston. His interest in civil engineering was also shown by the design for a suspension bridge 'upon a new principle of construction, whereby oscillation and undulation will be counteracted', which he exhibited at the Royal Academy in 1850. As an architect Lapidge appears to have been a competent but fairly conventional practitioner of his day. His chief surviving works are dull Gothic churches in yellow stock brick, but he entered some more ambitious designs for public competitions. The elaborate town-planning scheme for Westminster which he submitted to the Commissioners for improving the access to the Houses of Parliament is now in the R.I.B.A. Drawings Collection. It was dismissed by the Commissioners as too 'visionary' for serious consideration. In 1823 he entered a classical design for the new buildings at King's College, Cambridge, which is illustrated in *Architect and Building News*, 23 June 1933, and in 1835 his designs for the Fitzwilliam Museum were among the four finally considered by the Senate. He also competed for the Houses of Parliament in 1835, submitting a design described as 'collegiate, Henry VIII and Elizabethan' in style.

Lapidge was elected a Fellow of the R.I.B.A. in 1838. He had a son named Samuel who trained as an architect, but got into financial difficulties and emigrated to New Zealand. His younger brother, William Lapidge (1793–1860), had a distinguished naval career and rose to the rank of Rear Admiral. George Wightwick and H. H. Russell were his pupils. He died in February 1860, and was buried at Hampton Wick. As a young man Lapidge was concerned in the discovery of a fine Roman pavement on the site of the East India House in Leadenhall Street, and in 1803 published a short description of it with an engraving. A volume of drawings by him belongs to Mr. Michael Darby. [*A.P.S.D.*; *D.N.B.*]

ESHER PLACE, SURREY, for John Spicer, *c.* 1806–8; enlarged and remodelled 1895–8 [exhib. at R.A. 1808; E. W. Brayley, *History of Surrey* ii, 1841–8, 437].

HILDERSHAM HALL., CAMBS., for Thomas Fawcett, *c.* 1814 [exhib. at R.A. 1814].

WALTHAM ABBEY CHURCH, ESSEX, proposed alterations, 1818 [Essex Record Office, DP 75/8].

NORBITON PLACE, SURREY, works (including a dairy) for C. N. Palmer, who enlarged the house and added an Ionic portico [exhib. at R.A. 1821].

KINGSTON BRIDGE, SURREY (R. Thames), 1825–8; widened 1914 [exhib. at R.A. 1828; plans in Surrey County Record Office (Q.S. Parl. Deposits, 106); *Proceedings of the Institution of Civil Engineers* ii, 1842, 184–6].

HAMMERSMITH, MIDDLESEX, ST. PETER'S CHURCH, 1827–9, Doric [Port, 152–3].

HAMPTON WICK, MIDDLESEX, ST. JOHN'S CHURCH, 1829–31, Gothic [Port, 156–7].

HAMPTON CHURCH, MIDDLESEX, rebuilt 1830–1; Gothic; chancel 1888, tracery inserted in nave windows 1907–25 [H. Ripley, *History and Topography of Hampton*, 1885].

HAM COMMON, SURREY, ST. ANDREW'S CHAPEL, 1830–2, Gothic; chancel 1900–1 [E. W. Brayley, *History of Surrey* iii, 1841–8, 111].

KINGSWOOD CHURCH, SURREY, 1835–6; Romanesque: dem. [I.C.B.S.].

PUTNEY CHURCH, SURREY, rebuilt 1836–7, incorporating medieval west tower, nave arcades and Bishop West's Chapel [E. W. Brayley, *History of Surrey* iii, 1841–8, 477].

DODDINGTON CHURCH, CHESHIRE, 1836–7, Gothic [R.I.B.A. Drawings Coll., J7/33].

STEPNEY, ST. JAMES'S CHURCH, RATCLIFF, 1837–8, Gothic; dem. *c.* 1950 [*A.P.S.D.*].

FULHAM CHURCH, MIDDLESEX, alterations and enlargement, 1840; rebuilt 1881 [C. J. Fèret, *Fulham Old and New* i, 1900, 200].

BETCHWORTH BRIDGE, SURREY (R. Mole), 1842 [Surrey County Record Office, P22/8/166–171, with drawings].

REIGATE, SURREY, POLICE STATION, 1852 [*A.P.S.D.*; *Builder* x, 1852, 414].

SOUTHWARK, SURREY COUNTY SESSIONS HOUSE, NEWINGTON CAUSEWAY, additions, 1853; dem. 1912 [*A.P.S.D.*].

LATHAM, GEORGE (–1871), of Nantwich, had a local practice in Cheshire during the second quarter of the nineteenth century. His works included WISTASTON CHURCH, in an old-fashioned Georgian style, 1827–8 [I.C.B.S.]; a gallery in DAVENHAM CHURCH, 1832 [I.C.B.S.]; alterations to MALPAS CHURCH in 1840 [*Jnl. of the Chester and N. Wales Arch. Soc.* xxxvii (2), 1949, 38–9], and a new rectangular dome to the COURT HOUSE, PRESTON, LANCS., in 1849 [C. Hardwick, *History of Preston*, 1857, 441]. In 1833–42 he

---

[1] For some information about Samuel Lapidge as a landscape-gardener see J. C. Loudon's *Gardener's Magazine* iv, 1828, 116.

designed ARLEY HALL, NORTHWICH, for Rowland Egerton Warburton, 'in imitation of a Cheshire house of the period of James I' [E. Twycross, *Mansions of Cheshire* ii, 1850, 61]. In the 1840s Lord Tollemache thought of employing him to design Peckforton Castle before he gave the commission to Salvin, but generously paid him £2000, 'chiefly compensation for his great disappointment at another architect being appointed' [Mark Girouard in *C. Life*, 29 July 1965, 287]. In 1853 he published a *History of Stydd Chapel and Preceptory near Ribchester, Lancashire*. He died at Nantwich on 8 August 1871, leaving a son, Edwin Davenport Latham, in practice as a civil engineer and surveyor at Middlesbrough [Principal Probate Registry, Calendar of Probates].

LATHAM, JOHN (*c.* 1805–), of Preston, designed several churches in that town and its vicinity in the 1830s and 1840s. He specialized in a 'Norman revival' style of some singularity (cf. descriptions in Pevsner's *North Lancashire*).

PRESTON, LANCS., CHRIST CHURCH, 1836, Romanesque [C. Hardwick, *History of Preston*, 1857, 476–7 and engraving at p. 468].

PRESTON, LANCS., ST MARY'S CHURCH, 1836–8, Romanesque [C. Hardwick, *History of Preston*, 1857, 477 and engraving].

PRESTON, LANCS., ST. THOMAS'S CHURCH, LANCASTER ROAD, 1837, Romanesque [C. Hardwick, *History of Preston*, 1857, 477].

CROSSENS CHURCH, LANCS., 1837; rebuilt 1883–5 [I.C.B.S.].

FRECKLETON CHURCH, LANCS., 1837–8, Romanesque [I.C.B.S.].

PRESTON, LANCS., ALL SAINTS CHURCH, LANCASTER ROAD, 1846–7, Ionic [C. Hardwick, *History of Preston*, 1857, 478 and engraving].

LATROBE, BENJAMIN HENRY (1764–1820), born at Fulneck, nr. Leeds, was the second son of the Rev. Benjamin Latrobe, the head of the Moravian congregation in England. In 1776 he was sent to the Moravian college at Niesky in Saxony, where he received a good education. On his return to England in 1784 he was placed in the Stamp Office, but soon afterwards decided to take up architecture and became a pupil of S. P. Cockerell. According to family tradition he also studied engineering under Smeaton, the builder of the Eddystone Lighthouse. He left Cockerell's office in 1790, and was encouraged to begin practice on his own by a Mr. Sperling, who commissioned him to design HAMMERWOOD LODGE, in EAST GRINSTEAD, SUSSEX, in an advanced neoclassical style inspired by French architects of the Boullée-Ledoux school. Other works of the same period included ASHDOWN HOUSE, nr. FOREST ROW, SUSSEX, for Trayton Fuller, and alterations

to BARHAM COURT, TESTON, KENT, for the 1st Lord Barham, to FRIMLEY PARK, SURREY, for James Laurell, and to SHEFFIELD PLACE, SUSSEX, for J. B. Holroyd. He also obtained a minor public post as surveyor of the London Police Offices established under the Middlesex Justices Act of 1792. Latrobe now seemed established in a successful career, but the death of his wife in 1793 led to a period of personal distress and professional confusion which resulted in his emigration to North America in 1896.

In America Latrobe was soon engaged on important works, including the Bank of Pennsylvania in Philadelphia, which has been described as 'the first monument of the Greek Revival in America'. In 1803 he became surveyor of public buildings to the Federal Government, built the south wing of the Capitol at Washington, containing the Hall of Representatives, and remodelled the whole interior after its destruction by the British in 1814. He also designed the elegant neo-classical Cathedral at Baltimore, and the important Exchange in the same town. He was concerned in various engineering projects, including the supply of water to Pennsylvania and New Orleans. He died of yellow fever on 3 September 1820, having resigned his surveyorship two years previously.

[Fiske Kimball in *Dictionary of American Biography*; Talbot Hamlin, *B. H. Latrobe*, 1955.]

LATTIMER, JOHN, was a carpenter and surveyor at Stratford-on-Avon. He designed BIDFORD CHURCH, WARWICKS., 1835 [I.C.B.S.], and may have designed BISHOPTON CHURCH, WARWICKS., 1844, attributed by Pevsner to Joseph Lattimer, who was in practice in Stratford in the 1860s and 1870s and was presumably his son.

LAXTON, WILLIAM ROBERT (*c.* 1776–), entered the Royal Academy Schools in 1797 at the age of 21 and subsequently practised from various addresses in London. He exhibited at the Royal Academy from 1796 to 1813. His exhibits included 'A Saxon gateway, designed for a place of arms, King's Mews' (1799), a 'Design for a cottage, building for Mr. E. Thomas, at Sydenham' (1799), a 'Design for a villa for R. Storey, Esq. to be built near Newcastle' (1799), 'Meux & Co's Brewery, Liquorpond Street' (1800), a 'Proposed improvement at the north end of Leather Lane' (1804), 'The front next the river Medway, of the Crown Inn, Rochester, now rebuilding' (1806), 'A recent improvement entering Rochester' (1809), a 'Court House now building for the parish of St. Pancras' (1810), 'The Mary Brewery, Mary Street, built for Mr. J. Raymond' (1810), 'The Union Brewery, Wapping, as rebuilt for Mr. R. Bowman' (1810), 'Stabling, now building at Mrs. Clarke's Cottage, Putney' (1810), a 'Design for rebuilding the river front of St. John's College, Cambridge' (1813). He was evidently the Mr. Laxton, described as having 'had great experience in fitting up public houses', who contributed a design for 'A Suburban Public House in the Old English Style' to Loudon's *Encyclopaedia of Cottage, Farm and Villa Architecture* (1833).

G. Colebatch, H. L. Holland and Thomas Nicholls were Laxton's pupils. He was the father of William (1802–54) and Henry Laxton, who were both in practice as architects and surveyors. William established the *Civil Engineer and Architect's Journal*, of which he and his brother were successively editors. They were also the authors of a well-known manual known as *Laxton's Builders' Price Book*. Henry Laxton was the architect responsible for designing the Castelnau estate at Barnes (1842–3). [*Builder* xii, 1854, 361; *The Architects, Engineers and Building Trades Directory*, 1868, 123; *Gent's Mag.* 1854 (ii), 199–200; *D.N.B.*, s.v. 'Laxton, William'.]

LEACH, JOHN (1760–1834), was the son of a copper-smith at Bedford. He was articled to Sir Robert Taylor, and while in his office is said to have made the working drawings for Stone Buildings, Lincoln's Inn. He subsequently assisted his fellow-pupil S. P. Cockerell, but decided to abandon architecture for the law, and entered himself at the Middle Temple in 1785. After a distinguished legal career he was knighted in 1818, and died Master of the Rolls in 1834. According to Foss he designed HOWLETTS, nr. BEKESBOURNE, KENT, for Isaac Baugh, but this is open to doubt, as Baugh did not acquire Howletts until 1789, two years after Leach had abandoned his architectural career. [*Gent's Mag.* 1834 (ii), 647; E. Foss, *The Judges of England* ix, 1864, 92–5; Wheatley & Cunningham, *London Past and Present* iii, 1891, 319; *A.P.S.D.*; *D.N.B.*].

LEACH, WILLIAM, spent his life in the service of the Office of Works. He was first Labourer in Trust at the Queen's House, Greenwich, then Clerk of the Works at Greenwich from 1774 to 1782, and at Greenwich, Newmarket, Winchester and the Tower of London from 1782 to 1790. In March 1790 he was appointed Clerk of Works at Windsor, a post from which he retired in 1805 [*History of the King's Works* v and vi]. It is possible that he was the architect named Leach who largely rebuilt HUNSDON HOUSE, HERTS., for Nicolson Calvert in a Tudor Gothic style in 1805 [Mrs. W. Blake, *An Irish Beauty of the Regency*, 1911, 49–50].

LEACHMAN, JOHN (*c.* 1795–   ), was a pupil of James Medland. He was admitted to the Royal Academy Schools in 1816 at the age of 21, and exhibited at the Academy from 1812 to 1834. Among his exhibits were 'Design for an entrance

to the grounds of Sulby Hall, Northants., the seat of George Payne, Esq.' (1826) and the 'Entrance Gates to Warnford Park, Hants., the seat of W. Abbot, Esq.' (1829). He was responsible for two dreary Gothic churches in Wiltshire at WARMINSTER (CHRIST CHURCH), 1830–1 [Port, 164–5], and CORSLEY, 1831–3 [inscription in church].

LEADBETTER, STIFF (–1766), may have been related to Thomas Stiff, a London carpenter of the late seventeenth century. He was apprenticed in 1719 to Henry Leadbetter, a carpenter at Thurfield in Hampshire [Guildhall Library, index to Apprenticeship Registers]. He subsequently established himself as a carpenter, builder and surveyor at Eton in Buckinghamshire, where he had his yard and wharf. He became Surveyor to St. Paul's Cathedral on the death of Henry Flitcroft in 1756. He died at Eton on 18 August 1766, leaving a son named Henry [P.C.C. 311 TYNDALL]. He had a brother named John who may have been the author of *The Gentleman and Tradesman's Complete Assistant in the Art of Measuring and Estimating made easy*, 'by J. Leadbetter and assistants' (3rd ed. 1770).

Leadbetter was a competent but rather dull architect working in the Palladian tradition. Langley Hall, Bucks., Newton Park, Somerset, and Nuneham Park, Oxon., were his most important works. His unexecuted design for rebuilding one of the wings of Woburn Abbey, Beds., made in 1765, the year before his death, is in the Victoria and Albert Museum (7076.11). His bills for carpenter's work for Francis Godolphin at Baylies House, Bucks., and elsewhere (1733–5) are among the Duke of Leeds's papers in the Bucks. Record Office.

MAIDENHEAD BRIDGE, BERKS., repairs in 1750 to the timber bridge which was replaced by the existing stone bridge in 1772 [J. W. Walker, *History of Maidenhead*, 1931, 13–14].

LONDON, FOLEY HOUSE, PORTLAND PLACE, LONDON, for the 2nd Lord Foley, 1753–8; dem. *c.* 1815 [C. H. Smith, 'The Site of Foley House', *Builder* xxi, 1863]. In the Fauntleroy Pennant in the Soane Museum there is an elevation of the house which may possibly be by Leadbetter.

LANGLEY PARK, LANGLEY MARISH, BUCKS., for the 3rd Duke of Marlborough, 1755–8; alterations *c.* 1850–60 [drawings by Leadbetter dated 1755 and 1758 in the Bucks. County Record Office; others in album at Hovingham Hall, Yorks.; payments to Leadbetter in the accounts of the Duke's Trustees at Althorp, Northants.] (Neale, *Views of Seats* iv, 1821).

NUNEHAM PARK, OXON., for the 1st Earl Harcourt, 1756–64; alterations by L. Brown 1781–2; south wing added by R. Smirke *c.* 1834; entrance front remodelled 1904 [*Vitruvius Bri-*

tannicus v. 1771, pls. 99–100] (*C. Life*, 7–14 Nov. 1941).

GLOUCESTER, THE GENERAL INFIRMARY, built by Leadbetter to the designs of Luke Singleton, *c.* 1758–61 [George Whitcombe, *The General Infirmary at Gloucester*, 1903, 18].

SHARDELOES HOUSE, BUCKS., reconstruction for William Drake, 1758–66: begun by Leadbetter to his own designs, but completed with modifications by R. Adam, who designed the portico and the interior decoration (1759–63) [G. Eland, *Shardeloes Papers* 1947, chap. ix; A. T. Bolton, *Architecture of R. and J. Adam*, 1922, chap. viii].

HARTLEBURY CASTLE, WORCS., unspecified work for James Johnson, Bishop of Worcester, 1759 [J. Lees-Milne in *C. Life*, 23 Sept. 1971, 742].

WORCESTER, BISHOP'S PALACE, repairs and addition of 'a room with a bow window to the river' for James Johnson, Bishop of Worcester, probably *c.* 1760 [MS. 'Account of what was done at Hartlebury Castle and the Palace by Bishop Johnson' at Hartlebury Castle].

ETON COLLEGE, BUCKS., added upper storey to north and east sides of Cloister Court, 1759–62 [Willis & Clark, i, 459].

OXFORD, THE RADCLIFFE INFIRMARY, 1759–70; designed and built by Leadbetter and completed after his death by John Sanderson [Bodleian Library, Minutes of the Radcliffe Trustees, 1752–91].

DITCHLEY HOUSE, OXON., Leadbetter probably designed the Temple in the Park, built 1760–3, as he examined the bills in 1763 [Ditchley papers in Oxfordshire Record Office].

NEWTON PARK, nr. BATH, SOMERSET, for Joseph Langton, *c.* 1761 [letter from George Lucy dated 29 March 1761, referring to 'Ledbiter' as the architect, cited by Dorothy Stroud in *Humphry Repton*, 1962, 97 n.].

FULHAM PALACE, MIDDLESEX, rebuilt south and east sides for Richard Terrick, Bishop of London, 1764–5, castellated Gothic; again rebuilt 1814–15 by S. P. Cockerell [Lambeth Palace Library, F. P. 453].

LONDON, ST. PAUL'S (also called Portland or Foley) CHAPEL, GREAT PORTLAND STREET, 1766; dem. 1908 [C. H. Smith, 'The Site of Foley House', *Builder* xxi, 1863, 703].

ELVILLS, ENGLEFIELD GREEN, SURREY, for Sir John Elvill, completed 1766, Tudor Gothic [R. Ackermann, *Views of Country Seats* ii, 1830, 104] (W. Watts, *Seats of the Nobility and Gentry*, pl. lxvi, 1784; P. Sandby, *A Collection of One Hundred and Fifty Select Views* i, 1781, pl. 61).

STOKE PARK, STOKE POGES, BUCKS., repaired the 'Great Apartments' for Thomas Penn; dem. 1789 [*Historical and Descriptive Account of Stoke Park*, 1813, 45].

LEATHER, JOHN, practised as a surveyor and architect in Sheffield. A plan of Sheffield made by him in 1823 is mentioned by R. E. Leader, *Surveyors and Architects of the Past in Sheffield*, 1903. In 1827 he prepared a specification for building DORE CHURCH, DERBYSHIRE, apparently to the designs of Richard Furness (*q.v.*) [I.C.B.S.].

LEE, ADAM (*c.* 1772–1843), was trained as a carpenter and worked as a foreman carpenter on barracks at Bridport and at the Military Hospital at Portsmouth before joining the Office of Works in 1801 as a subordinate clerk of works at Richmond. In 1806 he was promoted to be Labourer in Trust at Whitehall and Westminster and from 1832 until his retirement in 1841 he was Clerk of Works for Whitehall and the Horse Guards.

Lee was an able and energetic man who did not always distinguish sufficiently between initiative and insubordination. He had a private business as a builder, and was a competent architectural draughtsman. In his official capacity he made plans for alterations to the Privy Council Office in Whitehall (*c.* 1810), and designed a new front for the Office of the Auditors of Land Revenue in Scotland Yard. In 1833 he was among those who submitted a design for a new House of Commons (see *Parliamentary Papers*, 1833, xii, 568 and plate), and in 1835 he competed for the new Houses of Parliament. His design included a restoration of St. Stephen's Chapel, for which he made elaborate drawings (sold at Sotheby's 4 June 1962, lot 154). Various drawings by him connected with the Palace of Westminster are in the R.I.B.A. Drawings Collection. He exhibited a 'Design for a public building' at the Royal Academy in 1838. [*Builder* iii, 1845, 104; *History of the King's Works* vi, 119–20.]

LEE, THOMAS (1794–1834), was the son of Thomas Lee (1756–1836) of Barnstaple in Devonshire. The father was a pupil of William Rhodes and won the Royal Academy's Silver Medal in 1776, but soon after coming of age he inherited an independent fortune and went to live at Barnstaple, where he died on 17 June 1836. The son was educated at the grammar school at Barnstaple. He spent a short time in Sir John Soane's office in 1810, but soon transferred to that of David Laing. He was admitted to the Royal Academy Schools in 1812, and in 1816 won the Silver Medal for a drawing of Lord Burlington's villa at Chiswick. In the same year the Society of Arts awarded him a Gold Medal for a design for a British Senate House, which is now in the R.I.B.A. Drawings Collection together with two preparatory drawings of Chiswick House. Lee exhibited at the Royal Academy from 1814 to 1824, showing in 1815 a view of the cathedral at Antwerp (subsequently engraved by

509

Woolnoth), made while staying in that town in July 1814 in order to attend his brother, Frederick Lee, R.A., who had been taken ill there; in 1817 a section of the chapel forming part of his design for a British Senate House; and in 1820 a reconstruction of Pliny's villa at Laurentinum, prepared for submission in competition for the R.A. Gold Medal. Lee was drowned on 5 September 1834, while bathing at Morthoe in Devonshire, and is commemorated by an inscription on the exterior of St. Anne's Chapel, Barnstaple.

Lee was an eclectic designer whose works included a plain classical house with Soaneic interior (Arlington Court), a large Tudor Gothic mansion (Eggesford), several Gothic churches of the Commissioners' type, and one neo-Norman one (at the early date of 1822).

[*A.P.S.D.*; A. T. Bolton, *The Works of Sir John Soane*, Appendix C, p. xlv.]

THE WELLINGTON MONUMENT, BLACKDOWN HILL, SOMERSET, 1817–18 [exhib. at R.A. 1818]. This triangular obelisk was intended to be surmounted by a cast-iron statue of the Duke of Wellington, but was left incomplete owing to lack of funds: see *R.I.B.A. Jnl.*, 24 April 1920, and *The Times*, 18 May 1960, 16.

NYNEHEAD COURT, SOMERSET, bridge in grounds for W. A. Sandford, *c.* 1818 [exhib. at R.A. 1818].

ARLINGTON COURT, DEVONSHIRE, for Col. J. P. Chichester, 1820–3 [exhib. at R.A. 1822; drawings in Exeter City Library].

THE ELLOWS, nr. WOLVERHAMPTON, STAFFS., alterations for J. Fereday, 1821 [*A.P.S.D.*].

EGGESFORD HOUSE, DEVONSHIRE, for the Hon. Newton Fellowes, 1822, Tudor Gothic; dismantled 1917 and now a ruin [exhib. at R.A. 1822] (F. O. Morris, *Views of Seats* vi, 17).

WORCESTER, ST. CLEMENT'S CHURCH, 1822–3, neo-Norman [I.C.B.S.; exhib. at R.A. 1824].

PRIORY HALL, DUDLEY, WORCS., for Francis Downing, *c.* 1825, Tudor Gothic [Rickman's diary, 17 May 1832].

BARNSTAPLE, DEVONSHIRE, THE GUILDHALL, 1826–8 [*A.P.S.D.*].

SEDGLEY CHURCH, STAFFS., for the 1st Earl of Dudley, 1826–9, Gothic [*A.P.S.D.*].

COSELEY, STAFFS., CHRIST CHURCH, 1827–9, Gothic [Port, 160].

NETHERTON CHURCH, nr. DUDLEY, WORCS., 1827–30, Gothic [Port, 138].

DISLEY CHURCH, CHESHIRE, added north and south aisles, 1828, Gothic [I.C.B.S.].

LEEDS, WILLIAM HENRY (1786–1866),

was an architectural critic and journalist. He was born in Norfolk, but nothing is known of his early life and it is uncertain whether he had any formal architectural training. In 1815 he showed a design for a monument at the Norwich Society of Artists, and between 1829 and 1849 he exhibited several architectural drawings at the Royal Academy and at the Society of British Arists. None of them, however, represented an actual commission, and there appears to be no evidence that he was ever in regular practice as an architect. A small private income made it unnecessary for him to work for a living, and he devoted the proceeds of his literary activity to the formation of a large architectural library. He was an excellent linguist, bought many foreign books, and made it his business to communicate their contents to English architects by means of articles and reviews. As a young man he is said to have been something of a dandy, but in later life he became careless of appearances and had 'an air of oddity which repelled rather than attracted new acquaintances'. He died in Charlotte Street on 1 May 1866, aged 79. The sale of his library by Puttick and Simpson lasted four days (29 April to 2 May 1867).

One of Leeds's earliest literary works was the text of the description of Sir John Soane's house in Lincoln's Inn Fields published by John Britton in 1827 as *The Union of Architecture, Sculpture and Painting*. He subsequently quarrelled with Britton, but in 1838 produced for the publisher John Weale an enlarged edition of Britton & Pugin's *Public Buildings of London*, containing descriptions of several buildings erected since the original publication in 1825–8. His other principal publications were a translation of Georg Moller's work on German Gothic architecture (1815–21) entitled *Moller's Memorials of German Gothic Architecture*, 1836; *Studies and Examples of the Modern School of English Architecture: The Travellers' Club House by Charles Barry, Architect*, 1839; *Rudimentary Architecture for the Use of Beginners: The Orders and their Aesthetic Principles*, 1848, 2nd. ed. 1852; and an edition of Chambers's *Civil Architecture*, 1862. To his friend E. B. Lamb's *Studies of Ancient Domestic Architecture*, 1846, he contributed an essay entitled 'Observations on the Application of Ancient Architecture to the Pictorial Composition of Modern Edifices'. From 1838 to 1850 he wrote the accounts of 'Public Improvements' for the *Companion to the Almanac*. Leeds is believed, with good reason, to have been the author of the articles, generally controversial in tone and hostile to the Greek Revival, which were contributed to Loudon's *Architectural Magazine* and to the *Civil Engineer and Architect's Journal* under the name of 'Candidus'. His design for a 'Villa Residence in the Tudor or Old English Style' will be found in Loudon's *Encyclopaedia of Cottage, Farm and Villa Architecture* (1846 ed.), 897–913. At the Architectural Association's first exhibition in 1849 he showed a design for a 'Victorian' capital, with a 'V' on each face, and 'a series of A's on the cresting' (*Ecclesiologist* ix, 1849, 305). Two letters from him to Soane are printed in A. T. Bolton, *The Portrait of Sir John Soane*, 1927, 416–18. [Hyde Clarke, 'W. H. Leeds, Architectural Critic', *Building News* xiv, 1867, 681–2, 697–8, 717–18; Boase, *Modern English Biography* ii, 1897, 362.]

LEES, WILLIAM, was an architect and wright living at Pittenweem in Fife. In the former capacity he was responsible for refitting the choir of CRAIL CHURCH, FIFE, in 1828 [S.R.O., HR 242/2, pp. 56–7], for alterations to CRAIL MANSE in 1829 [*ibid.*, pp. 63–4], and for designing KINGSBARNS MANSE, FIFE, in 1835 [S.R.O., HR 184/2].

LEGG, WILLIAM DANIEL (–1806), may have been the William Legg, of Coleman Street, carpenter, who in 1774 applied unsuccessfully for one of the London District Surveyorships. He was then stated to be 31 years of age [Middlesex County Records, General Orders, No. 10]. William Legg of Coleman Street exhibited designs for 'a nobleman's seat', 'a town house', etc., at the Royal Academy in 1773, 1774 and 1775, and was doubtless the William Legg (no address given) who in 1776 exhibited at the Free Society of Artists the 'Elevation of a stable, now building at a gentleman's seat, near Wragby, in Lincolnshire'. This was probably the stable at PANTON HALL, nr. WRAGBY, LINCS., which bore the date 1777.

As William Legg was working in Lincolnshire in 1776, it is likely that he was the architect of the same name whose career in that county can be traced from the 1780s onwards. He was evidently resident in Stamford by about 1785, when he designed The Vale House. In 1787 he examined the tower and spire of St. Mary's Church there [bill among parish records]. In 1796, as 'William Legg, Architect and Surveyor', he became a freeman on payment of £8, evidently to qualify himself for his election as a member of the Common Council the same day. He died in Stamford on 27 March 1806. His works included the attractive Gothick front of Casewick House, the entrance gate and lodge to Burghley House, competently designed in a neo-Jacobean style as early as 1799, and the handsome Tuscan portico to the Stamford markets, now incorporated in the Public Library. [Stamford Corporation Hall-Books, *sub annis* 1796 and 1804; J. Simpson, *The Obituary and Records for Lincolnshire, Rutland and Northants., 1800–1850*, 1861, 57; *Gent's Mag.* 1806 (i), 385.]

STAMFORD, THE VALE HOUSE, KING'S MILL LANE, for Joseph Robinson, *c.* 1785 [R.C.H.M., *Stamford*, forthcoming].
CASEWICK HOUSE, LINCS., rebuilt west front for Sir Thomas Trollope, Bart., 1786–9, Gothic [Arthur Oswald in *C. Life*, 24–31 Dec. 1964].
BURGHLEY HOUSE, NORTHANTS., lodge and gateway at west entrance, for the 1st Marquess of Exeter, 1799–1801, neo-Jacobean [signed 'w. D. LEGG ARCHITECT'; exhib. at R.A. 1801].
STAMFORD, LINCS., THE BUTCHERS', FISH AND BUTTER MARKETS, 1804–7; dem. 1906 except Tuscan portico incorporated in Public Library [J. Drakard, *History of Stamford*, 1822].
BULWICK HALL, NORTHANTS., enlarged and altered house for Thomas Tryon, 1805–6 [Northants. Record Office, TB. 636].
AYSTON HALL, RUTLAND, rebuilt for George Fludyer, *c.* 1806–7 [drawings at Ayston Hall, *ex inf.* Sir Nikolaus Pevsner].

LEMYINGE, or **LIMINGE**, ROBERT (– 1628), was a carpenter by trade. His origins are unknown, and his earliest recorded employment was some carpentry for the almshouses at Theobalds in Hertfordshire in 1607. In 1607–12 he was the surveyor employed by the 1st Earl of Salisbury to design and supervise the construction of HATFIELD HOUSE, HERTS. This is proved by several references to his plots and drawings, for which he was handsomely rewarded by the Earl. Advice was, however, given by Simon Basil, the Surveyor of the King's Works, and in 1609 Inigo Jones was also consulted and probably modified the design of the south front (see p. 473) [Lawrence Stone, *Family and Fortune*, 1973, 64–78] (H. A. Tipping, *English Homes, Period III* (ii), 1927, 305–52).

In 1616–17 Lemyinge designed another great Jacobean house, BLICKLING HALL, NORFOLK, for Sir Henry Hobart, Bart., Lord Chief Justice. His cypher RL appears in various places on the building, and the Blickling Parish Register records in 1628 that 'Robert Liminge the architect and builder of Blickling Hall was buried the 8th January' [H. A. Tipping in *C. Life*, 7 June 1930].

LEONI, GIACOMO (*c.* 1686–1746), described himself as a 'Venetian', and was presumably born in Venetian territory. Nothing, however, is known of his early life before 1708, when a manuscript now in McGill University Library shows that he was in Düsseldorf. Leoni's subsequent description of himself as 'Architect to the Elector Palatine', whose court was at Düsseldorf, may have been an exaggeration, but he certainly assisted the Venetian architect Count Matteo de' Alberti to build a hunting-seat for the Elector at Schloss Bensberg, nr. Cologne, where work was in progress between 1705 and 1716. The McGill manuscript is a treatise on the Five Orders based on Palladio, and show that the idea of a revised version of Palladio had already engaged Leoni's attention in his early twenties.

At what date, and in what circumstances, Leoni arrived in England is at present unknown. The earliest evidence of his presence in England consists of the edition of Palladio which he published in 1715–20 and of a manuscript treatise entitled *Compendious Directions for Builders* which is dedicated to Henry, Duke of Kent, and contains the Duke's bookplate dated 1713.[1] The bookplate may have been affixed to the manuscript at any time after 1713, but the preparations for publishing the Palladio must have taken some months, and it is reasonable to suppose that Leoni was already in England by 1714 at the latest. The translator was Nicholas Dubois, who states in his preface that Leoni had 'spent several years in preparing the Designs from which the following cuts have been engrav'd', and that having 'seen most of the Originals of those Designs that are in the second, third and fourth Books of this Work; that is, the Houses, Palaces, Churches, and other Buildings, both publick and private, raised by Palladio himself', he had been able to add many details to the crude 'wooden cuts' by which Palladio's work had originally been illustrated. In his own preface to the second part of the second volume, Leoni states that 'after five Years' continual Labour, I have at last happily finish'd the Edition which I undertook of Palladio's Architecture', and offers his services, 'either in person or otherwise, to such of my subscribers and others, as may have occasion for me in the way of my Profession'. The full title was *The Architecture of A. Palladio, Revis'd, Design'd, and Publish'd by Giacomo Leoni, a Venetian: Architect to his most Serene Highness, the Elector Palatine.* The text was in English, French and Italian. It was published in five instalments, of which the last did not appear until 1720. Leoni's edition was not only the first adequate reprint of Palladio since 1642, but also the first to substitute large engraved plates for Palladio's woodcuts. Although he took undue liberties in redrawing some of the illustrations, the book was an immediate success, and a second edition (in English only) was published almost immediately (in 1721). A third, with the addition of 'Notes and Remarks of Inigo Jones now first taken from his original Manuscript in Worcester College, Oxford', appeared in 1742.

Leoni's *Palladio* was one of the text-books of the English Palladian revival. Together with Campbell's *Vitruvius Britannicus* it appears to have been instrumental in arousing Lord Burlington's interest in architecture, and it remained the standard edition of Palladio until Isaac Ware produced a more scholarly one in 1738. Unlike Campbell, Leoni does not, however, appear to

have enjoyed Burlington's patronage. When, in 1726, he published his three-volume translation of *The Architecture of L. B. Alberti* (2nd. ed. 1739), he complimented Burlington on his initiative in re-establishing Palladian architecture in England, but there is no evidence that Leoni was ever employed by Burlington, either at Burlington House or elsewhere, and his first English patron appears to have been the Duke of Kent, to whom the manuscript already mentioned is dedicated, and for whom 'Signor Leoni' was making designs as early as August 1715.

Leoni's subsequent life in England is not well documented. Apart from his publications and his architectural commissions, all that is known about him is that he lived at various addresses in London.[1] As a Catholic he would have been ineligible for public employment, and he appears to have been dependent for his income entirely upon what he could make as an architect. At a time when most architectural designers were either builders or salaried officials of the Office of Works, this was inevitably a precarious means of livelihood, and it is clear that Leoni died in poor circumstances. Lord Fitzwalter of Moulsham Hall was paying him £50 a year during the last years of his life, more, as he said, out of charity than in return for services rendered, and the final entry in his account-book (in the Essex Record Office) is as follows: 'June 8, 1746. Mr. Leoni, my Italian Architect, dy'd this day, sent him during his illness, which lasted about one month pour charite £8 8s. 0d.' Leoni was buried in St. Pancras Old Churchyard, where an inscription gave his age as 60 years. He died intestate, leaving a widow, Mary, and two sons, John Philip and Joseph.[2]

Leoni was chiefly a country-house architect. Of the eighteen architectural commissions listed below, ten were for country houses, but of these two were never completed, two were destroyed early in the nineteenth century, and only four survive today. The demolished houses are not adequately recorded, but the designs which

[1] In 1726 he was in Charles Street, St. James's (*Survey of London* xxix, 90), between 1731 and 1742 in Vine Street, north of Piccadilly (ratebooks in Westminster City Library), and in 1744–6 at 52 Poland Street, off Oxford Street (*Survey of London* xxxi, 245). In the Westminster rate-books, as in *Vitruvius Britannicus* iv, 1767, pl. 31, he is sometimes called 'Battista Leoni'.

[2] In December 1739 Joseph Leoni signed a receipt on behalf of the decorative painter Francis Sleter for a payment for work done by the latter at Mereworth Castle, Kent (Bodleian, MS. DD. Dashwood, Bucks, c. 8/10). 'Mr. Leoni my clerk' is mentioned in Matthew Brettingham's account-book (P.R.O., C 108/362) in 1748–50 in connection with Norfolk House, London.

[1] In the possession of Lady Lucas and Dingwall (cf. Hist. MSS. Comm., *Second Rept.*, Appendix, p. 7, no. 48).

Leoni appended to his edition of Alberti[1] afford some further specimens of his style.

Leoni had a first-hand knowledge of Palladio's buildings, and borrowings from both Palladio and Inigo Jones are apparent in his own works. The plan of Carshalton House, for instance, was based on Palladio's unexecuted design for the Villa Mocenigo, and his design for a house dedicated to Lord Peterborough (*Alberti*, pls. 16–17) was conceived 'in Imitation of the Stile of Inigo Jones'. But he was hardly an orthodox Palladian of the Burlington school. His interpretation of the Palladian canon was less purist than Burlington's, and he was prepared to introduce features of baroque origin, especially in the interiors of his buildings. The alternating pediments, Venetian windows and pavilion towers which became the clichés of English Palladianism are scarcely to be found in his work, which in many ways has more in common with that of Gibbs, with whom Leoni shared a somewhat doubtful conformity to Palladian precept. Indeed, one of his last works, Lathom Hall, might easily be mistaken for a work of Gibbs himself.

[*A.P.S.D.*; *D.N.B.*; Walpole Society, *Vertue Note Books* iii, 131; R. Wittkower, 'Giacomo Leoni's Edition of Palladio's *Quattro Libri dell'Architettura*', *Arte Veneta*, 1954, 310; P. Collins, 'The McGill Leoni', *Jnl. of the Royal Architectural Institute of Canada* xxxiv, 1957; P. Collins, 'New Light on Leoni', *Arch. Rev.* cxxvii, April 1960, 225–6; Timothy Hudson, 'A Venetian Architect in England', *C. Life*, 3 April 1975; information from Mr. Timothy Hudson.]

LONDON, QUEENSBERRY HOUSE, NO. 7 BURLINGTON GARDENS, begun 1721 for John Bligh, cr. Lord Clifton, completed 1722–3 for Charles Douglas, 3rd Duke of Queensberry; enlarged *c.* 1785–9 by J. Vardy and J. Bonomi as Uxbridge House and now the Royal Bank of Scotland [Leoni's *Alberti*, pls. 14–15; *Survey of London* xxxii, 455–66 and pls. 75–9].

LONDON, ARGYLL HOUSE, KING'S ROAD, CHELSEA, for John Pierene or Perrin, 1723 [Leoni's *Alberti*, p. 4[v] and pls. 20–2; *Survey of London* iv, 82–3 and pls. 84–99].

CARSHALTON PARK, SURREY, house for Thomas Scawen, to be built under the will of his uncle Sir Thomas Scawen (d. 1722), who left him £10,000 to build the house 'as neare to and agreeable to the Modell I now have as may be' [P.C.C. 233 MARLBOROUGH]. A letter from Leoni among the Lyme Park papers shows that work was in progress in 1725, but the house was never completed owing to financial diffi-

culties. Leoni's designs are illustrated in his *Alberti*, pls. 3–13, which are dated 1723 and 1727.

LYME PARK, CHESHIRE, remodelled for Peter Legh, *c.* 1725–35. Leoni was making designs in 1725, but major work does not seem to have begun until 1729. The roof over Leoni's portico was altered in 1817–18 [Lady Newton, *The House of Lyme*, 1917, 341–2, 370; John Cornforth in *C. Life*, 5, 12, 19, 26 Dec. 1974].

MOULSHAM HALL, ESSEX, for the 1st Earl Fitzwalter, 1728–45; dem. 1816 [accounts in the Essex County Record Office; *Vitruvius Britannicus* iv, 1767, pls. 30–1] (P. Muilman, *History of Essex* i, 1770, plate).

BOLD HALL, nr. ST. HELENS, LANCS., for Peter Bold, *c.* 1730–2; dem. 1901 except stable-block [E. Twycross, *Mansions of England* iii, 1847, 27–8].

CLANDON PARK, SURREY, for the 2nd Lord Onslow, *c.* 1730–3 [Walpole, *Visits to Country Seats*, Walpole Soc. xvi, 61; *Beauties of England and Wales* xiv, 1813, 274; Neale, *Views of Seats*, iii, 1826] (*C. Life*, 10, 17, 24 Sept. 1949, 4, 11 Dec. 1969). The architectural history of this house presents some difficulty, as there is evidence that it was already being 're-edified' in the 1720s (see addenda to vol. i of Defoe's *Tour*, published in 1724), and it is possible that Leoni took over the carcase of a house begun by another architect. The rainwater leads are dated 1733, but work on the interior appears to have continued into the 1740s (see Vertue in *Walpole Soc.* xxvi, 153).

THORNDON HALL, ESSEX, partially remodelled for the 8th Lord Petre, 1733–42, but left unfinished on Lord Petre's death in 1742 and demolished by his successor in 1763. The stones cut for Leoni's portico were used by James Paine to form the portico of his new house built 1764–70 on an adjoining site [drawings by Leoni dated 1733 in Essex Record Office, D/DP.P.145 A; cf. description in Defoe's *Tour*, 1738 ed., i, 124–5, and J. C. Ward, *Old Thorndon Hall*, Essex Record Office, 1972].

CLIVEDEN HOUSE, BUCKS., octagonal temple (now chapel) and 'Blenheim pavilion' for the 1st Earl of Orkney, *c.* 1735; also unexecuted designs for a new house dated 1727 [G. Jackson-Stops, 'The Cliveden Album: drawings by Archer, Leoni and Gibbs', *Architectural History* xix, 1976] (*C. Life*, 11 July 1931).

LONDON, NO. 82 PICCADILLY, BATH HOUSE, for William Pulteney, cr. Earl of Bath, 1735; dem. 1821 [album of drawings at Cliveden House, letter from Leoni to Lord Orkney dated London, 20 June 1735, in which he says he is 'obliged to attende Mr. Pulteny and Governor Worsley in order to begin their buildings'] (A. I. Dasent, *Piccadilly*, 1920, 72).

---

[1] They have a separate title-page with explanatory text: *Some Designs for Buildings both Publick and Private* by James Leoni Architect, and the date 1726. However, as some of the plates are dated 1727, 1728 and 1729, the book cannot in fact have appeared before 1729.

LONDON, NO. 4 NEW BURLINGTON STREET, for
Henry Worsley, formerly Governor of Barbados, 1735; dem. [*ibid.*; *Survey of London*
xxxii, 552–3].

ALKRINGTON HALL, LANCS., for Sir Darcy Lever,
1735–6 [P. Fleetwood-Hesketh, 'Alkrington
Hall', in *The Country Seat*, ed. Colvin &
Harris, 1970, 139–44].

LONDON, NO. 21 ARLINGTON STREET, for the 2nd
Viscount Shannon, 1738; subsequently altered
by Chambers (1769) and others [drawings by
Leoni in the possession of R. Fleetwood-
Hesketh, Esq., of Meols Hall, Lancs.].

BURTON or BODECTON PARK, SUSSEX, for Richard
Biddulph, 1738; destroyed by fire 1826 [Neale,
Views of Seats, 2nd ser., i, 1824]. A view in
B.M., Add. MS. 5674, f. 50, shows the date
1738 in the pediment.

LATHOM HOUSE, LANCS., for Sir Thomas Bootle,
c. 1740; altered by T. H. Wyatt 1862; dem.
1929 [*Vitruvius Britannicus* iv, 1767, pls. 94–
8; R. Kerr, *The Gentleman's House*, 1864, pl.
24; for the date of building see Defoe's *Tour*
iii, 1742, 225].

? LONDON, NO. 4 WHITEHALL YARD, alterations for
the 4th Earl of Holderness, *c.* 1740; dem. 1793.
This may have been 'the Building' for which
Leoni was paid £260 'on account' by the Earl
of Holderness in 1740 [B.M., Egerton MS.
3497]. It was altered for his occupation soon
after 1738 [*Survey of London* xiii, 153].

WORTLEY HALL, YORKS. (W.R.), the south front, for
Edward Wortley Montagu, 1743; arms in
pediment added after 1826 [Sheffield City
Library, Wortley papers, Wh. M 58 (49),
elevation inscribed 'Rough Draught of the
Upright of Wortley by Sig^r. Leoni, Apr.
1743';[1] cf. J. Hunter, *South Yorkshire* ii, 1831,
323].

STOWE HOUSE, BUCKS., two gateways flanking
north front of house, for the 1st Viscount Cobham, date uncertain, perhaps *c.* 1740 [B. Seeley, *Stowe: A Description of the House and
Gardens*, 1744].

WESTMINSTER ABBEY, monument in cloisters to
Daniel Pulteney (d. 1731), executed by Rysbrack [signed 'Ia. Leoni Archs.'].

QUAINTON CHURCH, BUCKS., monument to Piggott
family, after 1735 [signed].

UNEXECUTED DESIGNS

WREST PARK, BEDS., designs for rebuilding house
for the 1st Duke of Kent, 1715 [drawings in
Bedfordshire Record Office; T. Hudson in *C.
Life*, 17 Jan. 1974].

LONDON, HYDE PARK, TRIUMPHAL ARCH commissioned by the 1st Earl Stanhope, 1719
[Leoni's *Alberti*, pls 1–2].

---

[1] I am indebted to Mr. Richard Hewlings for telling
me of this drawing.

514

CLIVEDEN HOUSE, BUCKS., designs for a house for
the 1st Earl of Orkney, dated 1727 [drawings
belonging to the National Trust].

SHARDELOES HOUSE, BUCKS., designs for remodelling the house for Montagu Garrard Drake,
1728, abandoned after his death that year [G.
Eland, *Shardeloes Papers*, 1947, 129].

LONDON, THE MANSION HOUSE, designs submitted
in competition, 1735 [S. Perks, *History of the
Mansion House*, 1922, 166–7].

LEROUX, JACOB, architect and speculative
builder, was articled in 1753 to William Jones
(*q.v.*). He exhibited at the Society of Artists in
1761, and at the Royal Academy in 1771–2 and
1782–4. In 1769 he competed for the Royal
Exchange at Dublin. At Southampton he
designed the Polygon, a description of which is
given in the *Southampton Guide*, 4th ed. 1787.
'This intended assemblage of elegant buildings
was devised about the year 1768 by Mr. Leroux,
an architect of Great Russel Street; it was to consist of twelve sides, having a house in the center
of each, with the proper offices low and detached.
The principal fronts were contrived to appear
outwards, and the gardens to converge towards
a bason of water in the center, which was to
supply the several houses.... At the extremity a
capital building was erected with two detached
wings and colonades; of which the center was an
elegant tavern, with assembly, and card rooms,
&c. and each wing were the hotels, to accommodate the Nobility and gentry.' The 'tavern' was
taken down within a few years of its erection, the
wings being converted into private houses. In
1771 Leroux exhibited at the Royal Academy 'A
view of part of the Polygon, now building at
Southampton', and in 1772 'A design for a
publick chapel and shops, forming a forum, intended to be built in the Polygon, Southampton'.
The latter buildings, however, do not appear to
have been erected.

In 1793 Leroux erected a second Polygon on
the Somers estate in North London. He himself
was the principal speculator, and the same layout
was adopted as at Southampton, the houses facing outwards, with gardens converging on a
central point. At first the scheme prospered, but
before the Polygon was complete, 'some unforseen cause occurred which checked the
fervour of building and many carcases of houses
were sold for less than the value of the materials'.
Leroux, however, continued to live in a house on
the south side of Clarendon Square (which
enclosed the Polygon) until his death, when it
became the residence of the Abbé Carron. The
Polygon itself was demolished early in the nineteenth century, but other houses built by Leroux
in Canonbury Square and Compton Terrace in
about 1800 still remain.

Leroux also remodelled CAMS HALL, nr. FARE-

HAM, HANTS., for John Delmé, exhibiting an elevation of the front at the R.A. in 1771, and refronted BUCKDEN VICARAGE, HUNTS., in 1783 [Lincolnshire Record Office, MGA4]. In 1784, as a Justice of the Peace for Middlesex, he was a member of a committee for building a new MIDDLESEX HOUSE OF CORRECTION in COLDBATH FIELDS, CLERKENWELL, other members of which were Sir Robert Taylor and Henry Holland. Leroux was appointed architect and made plans for the prison which after much revision by the committee appear to have formed the basis of the design which the Justices had engraved by Charles Middleton (*q.v.*) in order to attract competitive tenders. These designs were carried out in 1788–94 under the direction of a clerk of works (first S. P. Cockerell and then Thomas Rogers). The building was demolished in 1889 [minutes of the Committee in G.L.C. Record Office, MA/G, CBF1].

Leroux's activities as a speculative builder are denounced by Charles Dibdin in his *Musical Tour*, published in 1788 (pp. 10–11). Dibdin claimed to have lost £290 'by building a castle in the air near Pancras, by virtue of an agreement with the famous – I had almost added another syllable – JACOB LEROUX, Esq. architect, brick-maker, and trading-justice in the district of Clerkenwell. This gentleman, with a dastardly speciousness for which a Hyena might envy him, promised me a license in the name of several magistrates *who opposed the motion*, and . . . erected the skeleton of a building which was blown down by the first high wind after the licence was refused'.

The date of Leroux's death has not been ascertained, but there is a tomb in the churchyard of St. Laurence's Church, Reading, to Mary, relict of Jacob Leroux, who died on 7 February 1831, aged 86.

[Guildhall Library, typescript index to Apprenticeship Registers in P.R.O.; *Gent's Mag.* 1813 (ii), 428–9; *Builder* xxvii, 1869, 781; John Summerson, *Georgian London*, 1969 ed., 314–15; *Survey of London* xxiv, 120–1.]

LESLIE, ALEXANDER (1754–1835), was the son of Robert Leslie (1723–1804), a wright and cabinet-maker of Largo in Fife, and the elder brother of Sir John Leslie (1766–1832) the mathematician. His mother, Anne Carstairs, was almost certainly a sister of another local architect-builder, David Carstairs (*q.v.*). In 1807 KILRENNY CHURCH, FIFE, was rebuilt to Alexander Leslie's designs [S.R.O., HR 21/1, 5 June 1807], and his reconstruction of LARGO CHURCH in 1817 in a quite creditable Gothic style is commemorated by an inscription in the nave.

Alexander Leslie and his father are commemorated by a tombstone in Largo Churchyard, and a portrait silhouette remains in the posses-

sion of his descendants. He was the father of James Leslie, C.E. (*q.v.*).

LESLIE, JAMES (1801–1889), was the son of Alexander Leslie (*q.v.*) of Largo in Fife, where he was born on 25 September 1801. He was educated in the local parish schools, then at Mackay's Academy in Edinburgh, and finally at Edinburgh University. In 1818 he was apprenticed to W. H. Playfair, with whom he remained for six years. Having decided to become a civil engineer rather than an architect, he went to London in 1824 to work in the office of Messrs. G. & J. Rennie. In 1828 he obtained his first post as Clerk of Works to the Leith Dock and Harbour Commissioners, and in 1832 he was appointed Resident Engineer for the Dundee Harbour Works. He subsequently had a distinguished career as a civil engineer specializing in harbour and water works, and in 1846 moved to Edinburgh as Engineer to the Edinburgh Water Company. He died in Edinburgh on 29 December 1889, in his 89th year, and is commemorated by a monument in the Dean Cemetery. His practice was continued by his only son Alexander Leslie, C.E. (1844–93), and his son-in-law R. C. Reid. His grandson Alexander Leslie (1881–1921) and his great-grandson of the same name (b. 1910) were also civil engineers, and the family's long connection with the profession was only recently broken by the latter's retirement. [Obituary in *Minutes of Proceedings of the Institution of Civil Engineers*, vol. c, 1889–90, part ii; information from Mr. Alexander Leslie of Kilconquhar, Fife.]

Though James Leslie did not follow the profession of an architect, his early training enabled him to furnish designs for buildings from time to time. Of these the most important were WOOD'S HOSPITAL at his native village of LARGO, which he designed in a competent Jacobean style in 1830 [J. M. Leighton, *History of Fife* iii, 1840, 140], and the handsome classical CUSTOM HOUSE at DUNDEE, which he designed in 1839–40 in conjunction with John Taylor (*q.v.*), Surveyor to H.M. Customs [London Custom House Records, MS. 160]. A number of plans and drawings in the Scottish Record Office illustrate his activities as a harbour and railway engineer from 1831 onwards.

LETHBRIDGE, JOHN (–*c.* 1830), practised in Exeter, where he designed the Greek Revival BATHS at Southernhay, opened in 1821; dem. [J. Britton & E. W. Brayley, *Devonshire Illustrated*, 1832, 67, where he is described as 'the late Mr. Lethbridge']. He was also the architect of the Grecian ST. JOHN'S CHURCH, TORQUAY, 1822–3, rebuilt *c.* 1870 [R. J. E. Boggis, *History of St. John's Church, Torquay*, 1930, 7], and of the

Gothic HOLY TRINITY CHURCH, EXMOUTH, 1824, reconstructed 1909–10 [G.R.].

LEVERTON, THOMAS (1743–1824), was the son of Lancelot Leverton, a builder of Woodford in Essex, where he was born. After learning his father's business, he 'was subsequently enabled, by influential patrons, among whom were Mr. Kendall, a banker, to perfect himself in architecture'. Nothing, however, is known of his architectural training or career before 1771, when he began to exhibit his works at the Royal Academy. He designed a number of town and country houses, and may have been responsible for the planning of Bedford Square (1775–80), though all that is certain is that (as he wrote in 1797) he 'had a principal concern in promoting the finishing of Bedford Square, and built among other houses in it that of the Lord Chancellor [Loughborough, Nos. 6 and 6a], besides several on my own account, in one of which I now reside [No. 13]'. As several of the houses in the square are decorated in a style similar to Leverton's, it is possible that, as the editors of the *Survey of London* were inclined to believe, 'he was the author of the general scheme and the designer of the houses'.

Leverton was Surveyor to the Grocers' Company and to the Phoenix Fire Insurance Company, for whom he designed both their offices in Lombard Street and a striking fire-engine house at Charing Cross. For some years he appears to have assisted John Marquand at the Land Revenue Office, and when Marquand retired in 1809 Leverton and Thomas Chawner succeeded him as joint architects to that department. In 1811 they submitted a scheme for the development of Marylebone (afterwards Regent's) Park. Their plan, which would have involved extensive building in the form of new streets and squares, was rejected in favour of Nash's more imaginative idea of a park surrounded by terraces and occupied only by a small number of villas designed like miniature country houses. It is illustrated in the *First Report* of the Commissioners of Woods, Forests and Land Revenue, 1812.

Leverton's architectural style was at first closely modelled on that of the Adam brothers. Watton Wood Hall and Plaistow Lodge, for instance, both have exquisite interiors in a neo-classical style akin to that of the Adam brothers. It may be significant that Joseph Bonomi, who had been in the Adams' employment, was in Leverton's office for some time in the 1770s. The subsequent development of Leverton's style is obscured by the destruction of most of his buildings, but at Scampston Hall (1803) the domed exterior probably reflects a favourite motif of the Wyatts, while the interior is designed in a style of refined simplicity without decorative elaboration.

516

Leverton was a J.P. for Westminster, Middlesex, Surrey and Kent. He died on 23 September 1824, in his 81st year, and was buried in Waltham Abbey Church, where there is a tablet to his memory. He left a considerable fortune, of which about £50,000 went to his relations and friends, and £12,000 to various charitable purposes. He left no children, his only son having died in boyhood, but his nephew William Leverton (*q.v.*) practised as a surveyor, while his niece Jane married his pupil James Donaldson (*q.v.*) and was the mother of Thomas Leverton Donaldson, Professor of Architecture at London University. Other pupils were H. E. Kendall, J. Lotan and R. Walker.

A portrait of Leverton is in the vestry of the church of St. Giles–in–the–Fields, whose charities benefited largely under his will. Another, by John Russell, R.A., belongs to the Phoenix Insurance Company, which also possesses a silver salver presented to Leverton on his retirement from the Company's service in 1811. Many surveys and other drawings by him are among the Land Revenue Records in the Public Record Office. His designs for a new Exchequer Office are to be found in P.R.O., Works 30/317, and Sir John Soane's Museum (Drawer 38, 5). The R.I.B.A. Drawings Collection has some designs for lodges at Culford Hall, Suffolk, dated 1803.

[*A.P.S.D.*; *D.N.B.*; *V.C.H. Essex* vi, 268 n.; *Gent's Mag.* 1784 (i), 237, 1789 (i), 182, 1793 (i), 424, 1802 (ii), 879, 1824 (ii), 469; P.C.C. 558 ERSKINE; D. J. Oleson, *Town Planning in London*, Yale 1964, 48, n. 21.]

WOODFORD HALL, ESSEX, for William Hunt, 1771; dem. *c.* 1900 [exhib. at R.A. 1771].

LONDON, NO. 65 LINCOLN'S INN FIELDS, for Henry Kendall, 1772 [*A.P.S.D.*; *Survey of London* iii, 108, pls. 86, 97].

KENT, an unidentified villa exhibited at the R.A. as 'now building' in 1773.

LONDON, BEDFORD SQUARE, interior of No. 13, begun 1775, and perhaps of other houses in the square [*Survey of London* v, 150–1, 163].

ESSEX, unidentified stables and offices exhibited at R.A. as 'erected' in 1775.

BOYLES COURT, GREAT WARLEY, ESSEX, exhibited at R.A. 1776.

An unidentified chapel exhibited as 'now building' in 1777.

WATTON WOOD HALL (now WOODHALL PARK), HERTS., for Sir Thomas Rumbold, Bart., 1777–82; wings enlarged after 1791 [G. Richardson, *New Vitruvius Britannicus* i, 1810, pls. 27–8] (*C. Life*, 31 Jan., 7 Feb. 1925).

LONDON, unidentified 'house of a person of distinction' exhibited at R.A. as 'now building' in 1778.

PLAISTOW LODGE (now Quernmore School), BROMLEY, KENT, for Peter Thellusson, 1780:

almost certainly the 'gentleman's seat building in Kent' which Leverton exhibited at the R.A. in 1780, as it closely resembles Watton Wood Hall [J. Newman, *West Kent and the Weald*, Buildings of England, 1969, 182].

PARLINGTON HOUSE, YORKS. (W.R.), triumphal arch in park to commemorate the War of American Independence, for Sir Thomas Gascoigne, Bart., exhibited at R.A. as 'now building' in 1781. The arch bears the inscription 'LIBERTY IN N. AMERICA TRIUMPHANT MDCCLXXXIII'. Leverton's original drawing is among the Gascoigne papers in Leeds City Library Archives Dept., together with an unexecuted design by him for a single-storey quadrangular house dated 1782 (T. F. Friedman in *Leeds Arts Calendar*, no. 66, 1970, figs. 1 and 5).

LONDON, THE PHOENIX FIRE OFFICE, LOMBARD STREET, *c.* 1787; dem. [*exhib.* at R.A. 1787].

ENFIELD CHURCH, MIDDLESEX, extensive repairs, 1789 [Bodleian Library, MS. Gough Middlesex 8, ff. 44–6].

RIDDLESWORTH HALL, NORFOLK, for Silvanus Bevan, 1792; rebuilt 1900 after fire in 1892 [exhib. at R.A. 1792] (J. P. Neale, *Views of Seats* vi, 1823).

TOWN HILL PARK, SOUTH STONEHAM, HANTS., for Nathaniel Middleton, 1792; since reconstructed [exhib. at R.A. 1792].

LONDON, THE PHOENIX FIRE-ENGINE HOUSE, CHARING CROSS, 1794; dem. *c.* 1830 [exhib. at R.A. 1794; drawings in P.R.O., MPE 380] (*Arch. Rev.* xxix, 1916, 118).

LONDON, LOMBARD STREET, BANK for Messrs. Robarts & Curtis, 1796; dem. [exhib. at R.A. 1796].

LONDON, HAYMARKET OPERA HOUSE, design for façade, partially executed 1796, never completed [*Survey of London* xxix, 237–8].

LONDON, GROCERS' HALL, POULTRY, 1798–1802; altered by Joseph Gwilt 1838; rebuilt 1889–93 [G. Richardson, *New Vitruvius Britannicus* ii, 1808, pls. 5–6].

LONDON, NO. 23 ST. JAMES'S PLACE, for Sir John Lubbock, Bart., 1801–2; dem. [A.P.S.D.].

attributed: LONDON, THE SCOTTISH PRESBYTERIAN CHAPEL, SWALLOW STREET, with J. Marquand, 1801–4; dem. 1915 [*Survey of London* xxxi, 63–4].

NEW YORK, U.S.A., a sugar-house, exhibited as 'now building' in 1803.

SCAMPSTON HOUSE, YORKS. (E.R.), remodelled for W. T. St. Quintin, 1803 [exhib. at R.A. 1803] (*C. Life*, 1–8 April 1954).

LISLEE, CO. CORK, IRELAND, 'marine villa' for the Rev. Dr. Synge, 1803. Although exhibited at the R.A. in 1803 as 'now building' and illustrated in G. Richardson's *New Vitruvius Britannicus* ii, 1808, pls. 45–50, it is doubtful

whether this house was ever completed and no trace of it now remains.

HERRINGSTON, WINTERBORNE HERRINGSTON, DORSET, remodelled for Edward Williams, soon after 1803, Gothic [Arthur Oswald, *Country Houses of Dorset*, 1959, 88; R.C.H.M., *Dorset*, ii (2), 388–9].

LONDON, HAMILTON PLACE, PICCADILLY, layout for the Crown, 1806 [*Third Report of the Surveyor-General of Woods, Forests and Land Revenues*, 113; P.R.O., CREST 2/1729]. The Earl of Lucan's papers at Althorp House, Northants., show that he and the 4th Earl of Buckinghamshire both built houses in Hamilton Place to Leverton's designs in 1807.

LONDON, CHELSEA HOSPITAL, house for General J. W. Gordon, 1810; altered 1825 and 1931–2 [C. G. T. Dean, *The Royal Hospital, Chelsea*, 1950, 258].

LONDON, WHITEHALL PLACE, SCOTLAND YARD, *c.* 1810–20, in conjunction with T. Chawner; dem. [*Survey of London* xvi, 220; *History of the King's Works* vi, 541].

LEVERTON, WILLIAM, was the son of Thomas Leverton's younger brother Andrew. He evidently became a pupil of his uncle, from whose address he exhibited at the Royal Academy in 1780–2. He continued to exhibit up to 1807, showing designs for unspecified lodges, theatres, baths., etc., from his office in Gate Street, Lincoln's Inn Fields, but no executed works, and it appears that he was chiefly employed as a builder and surveyor. The firm of 'Leverton and Moore', builders and surveyors, was still in business in Gate Street in the 1820s. Leverton was elected a member of the Surveyors' Club in 1797 and was its President in 1809.

LEWIS, JAMES (*c.* 1751–1820), was probably born at Brecon in South Wales. He went to Italy in 1770, at the age of 19, returning in December 1772. A volume of drawings of friezes, urns, classical ornaments, etc., which he made in Rome is in the Mellon Collection. He told Farington that he got to know Piranesi well, and that he kept a journal which he subsequently destroyed because he was ashamed of the bad Italian in which it was written. From 1774 to 1778 he exhibited at the Society of Artists, and in 1779–80 he published a volume of *Original Designs in Architecture, Consisting of Plans, etc. for Villas, Mansions, Town Houses, etc.*, which was evidently intended to advertise his talents, since it contained very few executed buildings. In preparing this work Lewis was apparently assisted by an Italian draughtsman called Vincenzo Berrarese, who told Milizia in a letter that he had been responsible for the drawings although his name did not appear in the book. A second volume was published in 1797.

517

In 1792 Lewis succeeded R. Norris as surveyor to Christ's Hospital, and in November 1793 he received a gratuity of 100 guineas 'for his great attention during the building of the new grammar schools', as he had charged only 2½ per cent, instead of the usual 5 per cent. In 1793 he made a design for many additions to the Hospital to cost about £15,400, and in 1794 a model was made of a design he had prepared 'for the uniform and gradual rebuilding of the hospital'. This model, which is probably identical with one now preserved at Christ's Hospital, Horsham, comprised a three-storied edifice, 360 feet by 285 feet, round a colonnaded court 264 feet by 190 feet. He also made a smaller design in 1795, but neither was carried out, though drawings were exhibited at the Royal Academy in 1799 and 1800. One of these schemes is represented by a drawing in the R.I.B.A. Collection.

In 1793 Lewis was appointed surveyor to the Bridewell and Bethlehem Hospitals. In 1810 a competition was held for designs for a new Bethlehem Hospital for lunatics in St. George's Fields, Southwark. The first premium was awarded to W. C. Lochner,[1] the second to J. A. & G. S. Repton, and the third to John Dotchen. None of these designs was, however, adopted, but instead Lewis was instructed to incorporate their best features in a new design of his own, which was approved in 1811 and carried out between 1812 and 1815 at a cost of about £100,000. The result was a well-planned but somewhat barrack-like building whose chief architectural ornaments were a large portico and a low saucer-dome rising behind it. The present more lofty dome was substituted by Sydney Smirke in 1844–6.

Long-continued ill-health led Lewis to resign his office at Christ's Hospital in January 1816, and the surveyorship of the Bethlehem Hospital the following year. He died in Powis Place on 16 July 1820, aged 69, leaving a considerable fortune to his two sons and two daughters. He had a house at Totteridge in Hertfordshire, to which his elder son John retired. His portrait by George Dance was in 1899 in the possession of E. E. Wellesley (N. and Q., 9th ser., iv, 1899, 2). E. Gyfford, W. C. Lochner and A. P. Moore were his pupils, and George Hawkins was in his office as a clerk.

Lewis was an elegant neo-classical architect whose best works were country houses such as Bletchingdon, Eydon, Hackthorn and Lavington. These are neo-classical versions of the Palladian villa with interiors treated in a restrained style of Adamsian character. His unexecuted designs included a villa at Hadleigh in Suffolk (Original Designs i, pl. 2), a country house

---

[1] Not to J. M. Gandy, as stated in Survey of London xxv, 76–80.

for R. P. Thelwall (i, pls. 12, 13), an opera-house in Pall Mall (ii, pls. 19–22), a villa and temple at Lodore, nr. Keswick, Cumberland, for Edward and Rowland Stephenson (ii, pls. 9 and 25–6), a park entrance and stable courtyard (1799) at Longleat House, Wilts. (ii, pl. 35 shows the former), a market house and a theatre at Limerick in Ireland, 1788 (ii, pls. 1, 2 and 21–4), a casino at Lough Cutra, Co. Galway, for J. P. Smyth (ii, pls. 13, 14), a design for Coole House, Co. Galway, for Robert Gregory (ii, pls. 29–30), and a villa near Cork for Silver Oliver, 1789 (ii, pls. 31–4).

[A.P.S.D.; The Farington Diary, ed. J. Greig, iv, 192; P.C.C. 481 KENT.]

LONDON, GREAT ORMOND STREET, three houses with a uniform façade, before 1780 [Original Designs i, pl. 7].

BLETCHINGDON HOUSE, OXON., remodelled for Arthur Annesley, 1782 [Original Designs ii, pls. 3–8].

HAWNES or HAYNES, BEDS., a greenhouse for the 1st Lord Carteret, 1782 [Original Designs ii, pl. 15]. The rebuilding of the south front of the house for Lord Carteret in 1790 may also be attributed to Lewis. A view of it was exhibited at the R.A. in 1797 by his pupil A. P. Moore, who regularly exhibited drawings of his master's recent works. The original designs are (or were) preserved in the house, but are not signed (C. Life, 29 Dec. 1934).

SUTTON PARK, BEDS., alterations for Sir Montagu Burgoyne, Bart., c. 1786, and a proposed temple for Lady Burgoyne, c. 1795 [Original Designs ii, pls. 19–20].

EYDON LODGE, NORTHANTS., for the Rev. Francis Annesley, 1788–9 [Original Designs ii, pls. 16–18] (C. Life, 21 Jan. 1971).

LAVINGTON HOUSE, SUSSEX, for John Sargent, 1790–4; enlarged 1903 and 1912–13 [Original Designs ii, pl. 12*] (C. Life, 25 July 1925).

LONDON, CHRIST'S HOSPITAL, the Grammar Schools, 1793; dem. 1903 [A.P.S.D.].

LONDON, CLEVELAND HOUSE, ST. JAMES'S, remodelled south front and interior for the 3rd Duke of Bridgewater, 1795–7; dem. 1840 [Survey of London xxx, 494 and pl. 233].

NAZEING PARK, ESSEX, alterations for William Palmer, c. 1797 [Original Designs ii, pls. 27–8].

HACKTHORN HOUSE, LINCS., for J. Cracroft, c. 1798 [exhibited at R.A. 1798 by A. P. Moore as 'designed and built under the direction of Mr. J. Lewis, architect'].

WELWYN RECTORY, HERTS., 1798 [Huntingdon Archdeaconry papers in Herts. County Record Office].

HERTFORD, CHRIST'S HOSPITAL SCHOOL FOR GIRLS, Dining Hall and Infirmary, 1800 [A.P.S.D.].

WOOLMERS, HERTINGFORDBURY, HERTS., alterations for the 3rd Duke of Bridgewater, 1802

[Bridgewater papers in Herts. County Record Office].

BRIDEWELL HOSPITAL, BLACKFRIARS, pedimented entrance to New Bridge Street, c. 1802; dem. 1864 [E. G. O'Donoghue, *Bridewell Hospital*, 1929, 244].

DELAFORD PARK, IVER, BUCKS., remodelled for Charles Clowes, c. 1802; burned 1845, dem. 1959 [*The Ambulator*, 1811, 270; J. N. Brewer, *The Beauties of England and Wales* x (iv), 1816, 539–40 and plate].

LONDON, THE ROYAL COLLEGE OF SURGEONS, LINCOLN'S INN FIELDS, in collaboration with George Dance, 1806–13; rebuilt 1835–7 by Sir Charles Barry [Dorothy Stroud, *George Dance Architect*, 1971, 193–5].

LONDON, THE BETHLEHEM HOSPITAL, SOUTHWARK (now the Imperial War Museum), 1812–15; new dome, addition of chapel, etc., by Sydney Smirke 1838–46; wings truncated 1930 [Britton & Pugin, *The Public Buildings of London* i, 1825, 298–304; original designs in P.R.O., MR 76; *Survey of London* xxv, 76–80].

CLAVERING VICARAGE, ESSEX, rebuilt under a faculty granted in 1822, of which a copy is preserved among the Leicester Archdeaconry Records (Faculties 230 j). The designs are stated to have been made by James Lewis, presumably shortly before his death in 1820.

LEWIS, THOMAS, was surveyor to the Harpur Trust Estate in Holborn. In 1765–7 he made plans for redeveloping property in Lambs Conduit Street, Theobalds Road and the surrounding area, but in 1767 he was dismissed because his charges were too high [Harpur Trust Minutes at Bedford]. He designed the WELSH CHARITY SCHOOL in GRAYS INN LANE, LONDON, built in 1771–2; dem. He was a trustee of the school, and gave his services gratis. His portrait, showing him with a plan of the school, now hangs in the Welsh Girls' School at Ashford, Middlesex [Rachel Leighton, *Rise and Progress, the Story of the Welsh Girls' School*, 1950, with illustration of the portrait].

LEWIS, THOMAS, of Bath, is described as 'Builder and Surveyor' in Pigot's *Directory* of 1830. In his *Rambles Round Bath*, 1848, 287, J. Tunstall records that Lewis designed a new tower for BATHFORD CHURCH, SOMERSET. The existing tower dates from 1879.

LIDDELL, THOMAS (1800–1856), was the second son of Sir Thomas Henry Liddell, 1st Baron Ravensworth. In 1808 his father began to rebuild RAVENSWORTH CASTLE, CO. DURHAM, to the designs of John Nash, but the work went on for over twenty years, and in its later stages was superintended by Thomas. According to Britton [*Illustrations of Toddington*, 1840, 26], 'The

Honourable Thomas Liddell . . . has devoted some years to the pleasing and arduous task of superintending these works, and, I am well informed, has manifested both architectural skill and taste in the different parts of the mansion, which have been raised from his designs'. This elaborate castellated mansion, demolished in 1952–3, is illustrated in Morris's *Views of Seats* v. For Nash's original drawings see *R.I.B.A. Drawings Catalogue: L–N*, 107–9, and note the inscription 'Plan suggested by Thomas' on No. 10, a sketch elevation of the south front dating probably from the 1820s. A Gothic gate-lodge at Ravensworth designed by Liddell is described and illustrated in Loudon's *Encyclopaedia of Cottage, Farm and Villa Architecture*, 1846, 1152–3.

In 1823 Liddell's sister married the 6th Viscount Barrington and in 1843 Liddell himself married Lord Barrington's sister. According to E. Churton, *The Railroad Book of England*, 1851, BECKETT PARK, BERKS., Lord Barrington's seat, was built in 1831 'from designs of the Hon. Thomas Liddell, and under his superintendence'. This is confirmed by Earl de Grey (*q.v.*), who in a MS. in the Bedfordshire Record Office [CRT 190/45/2, pp. 1–19] records that in 1834 he took over his clerk of works James Clephan (*q.v.*) from Lord Barrington, 'whose house was built by an amateur architect, his brother [-in-law], Tom Liddell'. William Atkinson (*q.v.*) had made designs for rebuilding Beckett Park for the 5th Lord Barrington as early as 1805 [Lysons, *Magna Britannia* i, 1806, 366], but nothing appears to have been done until Shute Barrington, Bishop of Durham, who died in 1826, left £10,000 for a mansion to be built for Lord Barrington at Beckett 'according to the plan delivered by Mr. Atkinson, architect' [J. B. Nichols, *Literary Illustrations* v, 1828, 628]. As the 5th Viscount died in 1829, it was left to his successor to erect the new Gothic house with the help of his brother-in-law. How far the design was Atkinson's or Liddell's requires further investigation.

Liddell's reputation as a Gothic expert was such that in 1835 he was one of the members of the committee appointed to select the design for the new Houses of Parliament [*History of the King's Works* vi, 576]. Shortly before his death he designed a classical 'memorial room' at WYNYARD PARK, CO. DURHAM, to commemorate the 3rd Marquess of Londonderry (d. 1854). This was decorated with marble Corinthian pilasters, between which were niches containing military trophies of the Peninsular War, etc. [W. Fordyce, *County Palatine of Durham* ii, 1855, 321].

LIDSTONE, JOSEPH, of Dartmouth, was probably a son of Thomas Lidstone, a carpenter and builder of that place who designed ALL SAINTS CHURCH, LOWER BRIXHAM, DEVON, c. 1819–24,

519

Gothic; rebuilt 1885–1900 [Port, 132–3]. Joseph Lidstone designed SOUTH POOL RECTORY, DEVON, 1828 [Exeter Diocesan Registry], ST. PETROC'S CHAPEL, HIGHER STREET, DARTMOUTH, 1831–3 [I.C.B.S.], and STRETE CHURCH, DEVON, 1836, Gothic [I.C.B.S.].

LIGHTFOOT, JOHN JACKSON (1795–), was a Liverpool accountant who made the acquaintance of Thomas Rickman (*q.v.*) at the time when the latter was similarly employed in the same town. Encouraged by Rickman he became a keen amateur architect, entering for several competitions and exhibiting from time to time at the Liverpool Academy. Among the drawings which he showed were a design for the General Post Office in London (1822), 'a Grecian Temple . . . being one of the unsuccessful designs for the Assize Courts, Liverpool' (1840), 'a Gothic interior' (1842), and an elevation of the north front of 'The Wray, Windermere, ... designed by J. Lightfoot' (1842), presumably WRAY CASTLE, nr. HAWKSHEAD, LANCS., which was built by Dr. James Dawson in 1840–7, it is said to the designs of H. P. Horner of Liverpool. [Rickman's diaries, *passim*, especially 29 May 1816.]

LIGHTOLER, TIMOTHY, was a Georgian architect whose career remains in some respects obscure. The use of the initial T. on the title-page of his book and elsewhere has permitted the supposition that his Christian name was Thomas, but in several contemporary records it is given as Timothy, and no authenticated reference to him as 'Thomas Lightoler' has been found. By trade he was a carver. Sanderson Miller's correspondence shows that in 1758 Lightoler gave an estimate for carving the tympanum in the pediment of the newly built Shire Hall at Warwick, and that in 1759 he was making moulds for decorative work at Belhus in Essex. In about 1760 he designed a Gothic altar-piece for the Beauchamp Chapel at Warwick that was executed by the sculptor William Collins, and about the same time he and Collins were again associated in the redecoration of some of the principal rooms at Burton Constable in Yorkshire. Some of his work here is remarkable for the introduction of neo-Jacobean motifs. In 1761 a prospectus was issued announcing that 'Mr. Lightoler is at this Time making a Tour of England, to take Perspective Views and Plans of the Chief Seats of all the Peers'. Some of his drawings were subsequently engraved, with elegant rococo frames, as illustrations to William Guthrie's *Complete History of the English Peerage* (1763).

As an architect Lightoler's most important works were the Church of St. Paul at Liverpool and the Octagon Chapel at Bath, both domed buildings of considerable merit. His other Liverpool church (St. John) was in the Gothic style,

and some Gothic designs appear in the book, entitled *The Gentleman and Farmer's Architect*, which he published in 1762 (later editions 1764 and 1774). This consists of designs for ornamental farm-houses, offices, etc., and one plate entitled 'Facades to place before disagreable Objects' includes artificial ruins in the manner of Sanderson Miller. As 'T. Lightoler, Carver', he also contributed a number of plates to Half-penny's *Modern Builder's Assistant*, ?1742[1] and 1757, some of a markedly rococo character. In 1766 he made designs for a new Town Hall at Bath that were not accepted, and in 1769 (as 'Timothy Lightoler') he was among the unsuccessful competitors for the Exchange at Dublin [*Builder* xxvii, 1869, 781]. His normal place of residence is not clear. His numerous commissions in Warwickshire suggest a connection with that county, but the name Lightoler is associated with Lancashire, and in particular with Ollerton in Withnell, nr. Blackburn, where a Timothy Lightoler was in fact born in 1701 [*ex inf.* Mr. R. Sharpe France]. It may be noted that in 1769 Lightoler's designs for the Dublin Exchange were sent from Chester. The date of his death has not been ascertained, but he is referred to as 'the late Mr. Lightholder' in Watts's *Seats* of 1779.

WARWICK, ST. MARY'S CHURCH, designed Gothic altar-piece in Beauchamp Chapel executed by William Collins, *c.* 1760 [*Notices of the Churches of Warwickshire* i, 1847, 71, where the date is wrongly given as 1735].

BURTON CONSTABLE, YORKS. (E.R.), designed quadrangular stable-block and interiors of Great Hall, staircase hall and dining-room for William Constable, *c.* 1760 [W. Watts, *Seats of the Nobility etc.*, pl. 12, 1779; C. Hussey in *C. Life*, 27 Aug., 3 Sept. 1932].

THE SOHO MANUFACTORY, HANDSWORTH, nr. BIRMINGHAM, began construction for Matthew Boulton 1761, but was superseded by Benjamin Wyatt & Co., probably in 1763. In 1766 William Wyatt described Lightoler as 'the greatest lyar I have yet met' [Birmingham Assay Office, Tew MSS., William Wyatt to Boulton, 26 Jan. 1766].

MANCHESTER, ST. MARY'S CHURCH, addition of spire to classical church, 1762; dem. 1854 [*Lancs. and Cheshire Antiquarian Soc.'s Trans.* x, 1892, 135].

STONELEIGH ABBEY, WARWICKS., internal alterations for the 5th Lord Leigh, 1763–5 [Shakespeare's Birthplace Museum, Stoneleigh muniment no. 51; drawings in volume at Stoneleigh Abbey, one signed 'Tim° Lightoler'].

LIVERPOOL, ST. PAUL'S CHURCH, 1763–9; dem.

---

[1] See note on p. 379.

1932 [J. A. Picton, *Memorials of Liverpool*, ii, 1875, 39–40, where the architect's Christian name is given as 'Thomas'].

BIDSTON HILL, CHESHIRE, signal house for shipping, 1763; dem. [Minutes of the Liverpool Common Council, 11 May 1763, *ex inf.* Mr. S. A. Harris].

? PLATT HALL, RUSHOLME, LANCS., for John Worsley, *c.* 1763. [A set of designs for the interiors of the principal rooms signed 'T. Lightoler' is preserved at Platt Hall (now the City of Manchester Gallery of English Costume). Some of these were probably carried out, but only one room in Lightoler's style survives. Unexecuted designs for the house itself by R. Jupp and John Carr are also preserved, and it is possible that the whole building was designed by Lightoler.]

WARWICK CASTLE, new dining-room and other alterations for the 1st Earl of Warwick, 1763–9 [*V.C.H. Warwicks.* viii, 462, by 'Timothy Lightoler'].

STRATFORD-ON-AVON CHURCH, WARWICKS., designs for spire, 1763–4 [*Correspondence of the Rev. Joseph Greene*, ed. L. Fox, Hist. MSS. Comm., 1965, 100, where it is stated that two designs for the spire by 'Timothy Lightoller' are in the Halliwell-Phillipps Collection in the Folger Shakespeare Library, U.S.A.]. See above, p. 421.

TEDDESLEY HALL, STAFFS., designs for chimney-pieces for Sir Edward Littleton, Bart., 1766; dem. 1954 [Staffordshire County Record Office, Hatherton papers D260/M/E/116, payment to 'Timothy Lightoler'].

BATH, THE OCTAGON CHAPEL, MILSOM STREET, 1766–7 [engraving signed 'T. Lightoler' reproduced by W. Ison, *The Georgian Buildings of Bath*, 1948, pl. 23]. For his unsuccessful design for a new Town Hall, see Ison, p. 35. The Chamberlain's vouchers among the Bath City archives show that in 1766 he signed his name as 'Tim° Lightoler'.

STRATFORD-ON-AVON, WARWICKS, a payment of £10 in connection with the rebuilding of the Town Hall, 1770 [*The Correspondence of the Rev. Joseph Greene*, ed. L. Fox, Hist. MSS. Comm., 1965, 100 n.].

LIVERPOOL, ST. JOHN'S CHURCH, 1775–83, Gothic; dem. 1898 [J. A. Picton, *Memorials of Liverpool* ii, 1875, 188, where the architect's Christian name is given as 'Thomas'].

LIMINGE, ROBERT, *see* LEMYINGE

LINDLEY, WILLIAM (*c.* 1739–1818), of Doncaster, may have been related to Joseph Lindley (1710–91), of Heath, nr. Wakefield, whose son Joseph (1756–1808) was a surveyor and cartographer. William Lindley began life as John Carr's draughtsman and assistant. In September 1774, when advertising his services as an architect in the *York Courant*, he stated that he had been 'an Assistant to Mr. Carr of York upwards of 20 years'. In October 1774 the Corporation of Doncaster applied to 'Mr. Lyndley of York to draw a plan for a playhouse', and the theatre was built to his designs in the following year. In 1783 he became a freeman of Doncaster, where he lived for the rest of his life. The house which he built for himself in South Parade was evidently of some size and elegance, for the Prince of Wales lodged in it in 1806. In the 1790s Lindley was in partnership with Charles Watson (*q.v.*), and from about 1810 with John Woodhead (*q.v.*). William Hurst (*q.v.*), afterwards Woodhead's partner, was his pupil. Lindley died in February 1818 at the age of 79, and was buried in Doncaster Church. He was a competent but unadventurous architect who never deviated from the basically Adamsian style that he had learned from Carr. Drawings by him are to be found in the Hailstone Collection in York Minster Library, in the Fitzwilliam and Elmhirst archives at Sheffield, the Drake papers in the Buckinghamshire Record Office, and elsewhere. A drawing by him of a Roman altar found at Doncaster is in the Bodleian Library (Gough Maps 36, f. 49), and was engraved in *Gentleman's Magazine*, 1781, 361. [J. Hunter, *South Yorkshire* i, 1828, 46; Doncaster Corporportation archives; MS. History of Lindley family in Yorkshire Archaeological Society's Library, MS. MD 280 (22); R. B. Wragg, 'Two Architects of York', *York Georgian Society's Report*, 1957–8, 38–40.]

DONCASTER, THE THEATRE, 1775–6; altered (by Lindley) 1814; dem. [John Tomlinson, *Doncaster*, 1887, 238].

KIRKLEES PARK, YORKS. (W.R.), designs for interior of 'new room' (probably drawing-room) for Sir George Armytage, Bart., 1777 [*C. Life*, 22 Aug. 1808, 265].

ACKWORTH SCHOOL, YORKS. (W.R.), THE OLD MEETING HOUSE, 1779 [H. Thompson, *History of Ackworth School*, 1879, 32]. Lindley's design for a Cold Bath House here is in the Hailstone Collection in York Minster Library.

DONCASTER TOWN HALL, rebuilt Common Council Room, 1784–6 [R. B. Wragg, *op. cit.*, citing Order Books of the Corporation].

DONCASTER VICARAGE, design for enlargement, 1785 [plan and elevation in Yorkshire Archaeological Society's library, MS. 387].

BECCA HALL, YORKS. (W.R.), for William Markham, probably *c.* 1785 [drawing in Hailstone Collection, York Minster Library].

OSSINGTON HALL, NOTTS., alterations and additions for John Denison, *c.* 1790; dem. 1963 [drawings formerly at Ossington].

ECCLESALL, nr. SHEFFIELD, COURT HOUSE AND GAOL for the 4th Earl Fitzwilliam, 1791; dem. [Sheffield City Library, Fitzwilliam papers, MP 36].

WAKEFIELD, YORKS. (W.R.), ST. JOHN'S CHURCH, with Charles Watson, 1791–5 [engraving by Malton in Soane Museum, drawer lix, inscribed 'Lindley & Watson Archts.'].

SHEFFIELD, ST. PETER'S CHURCH (now Cathedral), alterations, 1791–1802 [Sheffield City Library, R. E. Leader's Notes, 141, p. 39].

DONCASTER, YORKS. (W.R.), THE INFIRMARY, FRENCH STREET, 1793–4; dem. 1969 [G. Swann, *The Doncaster Royal Infirmary, 1792–1972*, 1973, 13–15].

WATH-UPON-DEARNE VICARAGE, YORKS. (W.R.), with Charles Watson, 1793 [Borthwick Institute, York, MGA 1793/1].

OWSTON HALL, YORKS. (W.R.), for Bryan Cooke, 1794–5[1] [G. A. Usher, *Gwysaney and Owston*, 1964, 191].

OGSTON HALL, DERBYSHIRE, internal alterations for William Turbutt, 1795 [drawings formerly at Ogston].

WAKEFIELD, YORKS. (W.R.), ALL SAINTS CHURCH (now Cathedral), with Charles Watson surveyed spire, 1796 [J. W. Walker, *Wakefield*, 1939, 260].

DONCASTER, YORKS. (W.R.), NOS. 19, 20, 21 SOUTH PARADE, c. 1797 [MS. account of Lindley at The Oaks, Norton, Derbyshire, *ex inf.* Mr. Angus Taylor].

DONCASTER, YORKS. (W.R.), houses at junction of PRINCES STREET and HALLGATE, c. 1799 [ibid.].

STANTON HALL, STANTON-IN-THE-PEAK, DERBYSHIRE, enlarged on south side for Bache Thornhill, 1799 [family papers, *ex inf.* Mrs. Thornhill].

DONCASTER, YORKS. (W.R.), NO. 15 SOUTH PARADE, c. 1800 [MS. at The Oaks cited above].

CAMPSMOUNT, CAMPSALL, YORKSHIRE (W.R.), minor alterations for George Cooke Yarborough, 1802; dem. 1940 [T. Connor, 'The Building of Campsmount', *Yorks. Arch. Jnl.* xlvii, 1975, 129].

DONCASTER, THE MANSION HOUSE, added attic storey, 1800–1; new dining-room 1806 [J. Tomlinson, *Doncaster*, 1887, 225; *A Skilful Master-Builder*, ed. H. E. C. Stapleton, York 1975, 37, 44].

CANTLEY HALL, YORKS. (W.R.), design for alterations for J. W. Childers, 1802 [drawing in Hailstone Collection, York Minster Library].

GAUTBY HALL, LINCS., designs for alterations for Robert Vyner, 1803; dem. 1874 [drawings at Newby Hall, Yorkshire].

ROSSINGTON RECTORY, YORKS. (W.R.), 1804 [MS. at The Oaks cited above].

DONCASTER, YORKS. (W.R.), RACECOURSE GRANDSTAND, alterations, 1804; dem. 1969 [*A Skilful*

---

[1] The 'Design for Owston' exhibited by William Porden at the Royal Academy in 1797 was evidently a rejected design.

Master-Builder, ed. H. E. C. Stapleton, York, 1975, 40–1].

THE OAKS, NORTON, DERBYSHIRE, designs for alterations for Sir William Chambers Bagshawe, 1811 [drawings at The Oaks, *ex inf.* Mr. P. Leach].

CANTLEY VICARAGE, YORKS. (W.R.), with J. Woodhead, rebuilt 1812 [Borthwick Institute, York, MGA 1812/1].

SERLBY HALL, NOTTS., with J. Woodhead remodelled house for the 5th Viscount Galway, 1812 [Arthur Oswald in *C. Life*, 26 March, 2 April 1959].

LISTER, SAMUEL, was a master mason of Bramley, nr. Leeds. In 1795 the County of Derby advertised for designs and estimates for rebuilding SWARKESTONE BRIDGE near Burton-on-Trent. Lister's plan and estimate were accepted, and the existing five-arch bridge was built by him in 1795–7 [Derbyshire Record Office, Quarter Sessions Order Book and draft contract]. In a letter dated 25 December 1795 Lister says that he has four brothers who are all masons, and the John Lister of Rotherham to whose designs the nave of WICKERSLEY CHURCH, YORKS. (W.R.), was rebuilt in 1835 [I.C.B.S.] was no doubt a relation.

LLOYD, JOHN (–1867), practised in Caernarvon, where in 1831–2 he designed the MARKET HALL (which bears his signature). He died at Twthill, Caernarvon, on 24 October 1867 [Principal Probate Registry, Calendar of Probates].

LLOYD, JOHN, practised in Mold, Flintshire. He designed CHRIST CHURCH, PONTBLYDDYN, FLINTSHIRE, 1836, reconstructed 1865 [D. R. Thomas, *History of the Diocese of St. Asaph*, 1870, 597]; HOLY TRINITY, GWERNAFIELD, FLINTSHIRE, 1838, rebuilt 1870 [drawings in R.I.B.A. Coll.]; ST. MARY, BRYMBO, DENBIGHSHIRE, 1838, dem. c. 1870 [Port, 172–3]; EMMANUEL CHURCH. BISTRE (BUCKLEY), FLINTSHIRE, 1841–2, remodelled 1881 [Port, 172–3]; and CHRIST CHURCH, LLANFYNYDD, FLINTSHIRE, 1842–3, altered 1868 [Thomas, *op. cit.*, 597]. These were mostly cheap churches of poor design and (as proved to be the case at Brymbo, Gwernafield and Pontblyddyn) bad construction as well. Thomas states that the one at Bistre was copied from Casterton Church in Westmorland, a model illustrated by its builder, the Rev. W. Carus Wilson, in *Helps to the Building of Churches, Parsonage Houses and Schools* (c. 1840).

LLOYD, LEONARD WILD (–1868), was a pupil of William Brooks. He exhibited at the Royal Academy from 1821 to 1830, at the Norwich Society of Artists in 1823 and at the Society of British Artists in 1825. He practised in London, dying at 29 Gilbert Street, Grosvenor

Square, on 10 January 1868 [Principal Probate Registry, Calendar of Probates]. G. T. Bower, J. M. Clark and H. B. Parry were his pupils.

Lloyd designed a MASONIC LODGE at PETERSFIELD, HANTS., 1826 [exhibited at R.A.]; the Greek Revival ASYLUM FOR FEMALE ORPHANS, LAMBETH, 1827, dem. 1866 [exhibited at R.A. 1827] (J. Elmes, *Metropolitan Improvements*, 1831, 170 and plate); three villas near Richmond Bridge for George Topham, 1828 [exhibited at R.A.]; and TWICKENHAM PARK, MIDDLESEX, for Joseph Todd, 1828, dem. [exhibited at R.A.]. His designs for Butterton Hall, Staffs., for Thomas Swinnerton, exhibited as 'about to be built' in 1830, were not in fact carried out.

LOAT, SAMUEL (*c.* 1802–1876), was admitted to the Royal Academy Schools in 1823 at the age of 21. In 1825 he was awarded a premium by the Society of Arts and a Silver Medal by the Royal Academy, and in 1827 he gained the Royal Academy's Gold Medal. In the following year he was given a Travelling Scholarship, and in 1832 he exhibited a 'Section of the Corsini Chapel in the church of S. Giovanni in Laterano, Rome'. He subsequently emigrated to Canada, dying at Kingston, Ontario, on 12 October 1876 [Principal Probate Registry, Calendar of Probates]. His only recorded work in England is a tablet in East Retford Church, Notts., to the memory of Beaumont Marshall (d. 1826), which bears the signature 'S. Loat Archt. London'.

LOCHNER, WILLIAM CONRAD (*c.* 1780–1861), was a pupil of James Lewis. He was admitted to the Royal Academy Schools in 1800 at the age of 20. He won the Silver Medal in 1800 and the Gold Medal in 1805. He exhibited at the Academy from 1798 onwards. In 1810 he obtained the first premium in the competition for the new Bethlehem Hospital, but his design was not carried out (see p. 518). He rebuilt the south aisle of ENFIELD PARISH CHURCH in 1824 [*V.C.H. Middlesex* v, 247], and designed the churches of ST. JAMES, ENFIELD HIGHWAY, MIDDLESEX, 1829–31 [Port, 156–7], and ST. PETER, DE BEAUVOIR TOWN, HACKNEY, 1840–1 [W. Robinson, *History of Hackney* i, 1842, 180], both in the thin, starved Gothic of the period. He may also have designed the houses in DE BEAUVOIR SQUARE, HACKNEY, for the De Beauvoir Estate records in the G.L.C. Record Office show that he was the lessee of Nos. 1 and 2. Lochner, who was a Fellow of the R.I.B.A., died at Haxted, nr. Edenbridge in Kent, in September 1861 [Principal Probate Registry, Calendar of Probates]. He had been Surveyor to the Royal Exchange Assurance Company.

LOCK, DANIEL (*c.*1682–1754), son of Daniel Lock of London, was educated at St. Paul's School and entered Trinity College, Cambridge, as a sizar on 8 April 1699, aged 17. He became a scholar in 1702, took his B.A. in 1702–3 and his M.A. in 1706. He is said to have been 'an architect of some eminence' who 'retired from business with an ample fortune' and lived in Surrey Street off the Strand. He was buried in Trinity College Chapel, where there is a monument to him (with a bust by Roubiliac) which records his death on 15 January 1754, at the age of 69 (*sic*). He is described in the inscription as ARCHITECTURAE, SCULPTURAE, PICTURAE, MUSICAE, OMNIUMQUE BONARUM ARTIUM AMANTISSIMUS. There is a mezzotint portrait of him by J. McArdell after Hogarth, in which he is shown holding the plan and elevation of a house. He presented busts of Newton and Bacon by Roubiliac to Trinity College Library. [Venn, *Alumni Cantabrigienses* i, part 3, 97; *The Works of William Hogarth* (Simkin Marshall, n.d.), 80; Willis & Clark, ii, 549, 550; K. A. Esdaile, *Roubiliac's Work at Trinity College, Cambridge*, 1924, pl. xviii.]

LOCK, THOMAS, was a carpenter by trade and a member of the Fishmongers' Company. As a master carpenter he was employed by Wren in rebuilding the London City churches of St. Magnus Martyr, St. Mary at Hill and St. Mildred, Poultry, and by Sir Roger Pratt at Horseheath Hall, Cambs., in 1665. He was also the master carpenter for the rebuilding of FISHMONGERS' HALL in 1667–72 under Edward Jerman, and when Jerman died in 1668 Lock took his place as the surveyor in charge, for there is a payment to him in 1672 for surveying and drawing draughts for the Hall. He was evidently the 'Mr. Locke' who in April 1668 similarly succeeded Jerman as surveyor of the new APOTHECARIES' HALL, completed in 1670. [*Wren Soc.* xx, 127; *The Architecture of Sir Roger Pratt*, ed. R. T. Gunther, 1928, 118, 129; Fishmongers' Company's archives, *ex inf.* Miss Priscilla Metcalf; Arthur Oswald, 'The Hall of the Worshipful Company of Apothecaries', *C. Life*, 10 Oct. 1947, and additional information from Mr. Oswald.]

LOGAN, DAVID, practised in Montrose, where in 1791 he designed THE PARISH CHURCH [J. G. Low, *Memorials of the Parish Church of Montrose*, Montrose 1891, 138, 142]. His design for a steeple, dated 1811, is preserved among the burgh records: it was not carried out, the existing Gothic steeple being erected to the designs of J. Gillespie Graham in 1834. Logan's most distinguished work is the MONTROSE ACADEMY, 1815, with a Greek Ionic façade of some originality and much charm [drawings at the Academy]. At FORFAR ACADEMY in 1815 he used the same formula of an engaged order (here Greek Doric) recessed between slightly projecting wings [contracts advertised in *Dundee Advertiser*, 28 April 1815]. He also designed the TOWN HALL, ARBROATH, ANGUS, 1803, altered 1844 [G. Hay, *History of Arbroath*, 1876, 365]. A set of drawings for farm buildings signed 'David Logan' is in the Mellon Collection.

Other members of the Logan family were civil engineers. David Logan (d. *c.* 1839) and his father Peter Logan were both concerned in the building of Robert Stevenson's Bell Rock Lighthouse in 1807–10, the former as clerk of works at the yard in Arbroath where the stone was prepared, the latter as foreman builder at the lighthouse itself [Robert Stevenson, *Account of the Bell Rock Lighthouse*, 1824]. David became resident engineer at Dundee Harbour under Telford (1816–20), and was subsequently responsible for the construction of harbours at Donaghadee and Ardglass in Northern Ireland under Sir John Rennie [E. R. R. Green, *Industrial Archaeology of County Down*, 1963, 76, 79]. In 1834 he was appointed engineer to the River Clyde Trustees. His death was reported in *Minutes of Proceedings of the Institution of Civil Engineers* for 1840 (i, 12). At Dundee he had been succeeded by his cousin Peter Logan, who subsequently worked at St. Catherine's Dock in London under Telford. It seems likely that David Logan of Montrose and Peter Logan the foreman were brothers, and that David Logan, junior, was therefore the architect's nephew. [Information from Prof. A. W. Skempton.]

LONG, F—, of Liverpool, exhibited two designs at the Royal Academy in 1834 in conjunction with R. J. Barrow: 'an elevation for a cathedral' and a design for Fishmongers' Hall, London. He subsequently designed the Greek Revival ROYAL INSTITUTION OF SOUTH WALES at SWANSEA, 1838–40 [*Companion to the Almanac*, 1840, 241–2].

LONGWORTH, JAMES and his son THOMAS, practised in Liverpool in the early nineteenth century. In 1817 the nave of LEYLAND CHURCH, LANCS., is said to have been rebuilt to the designs of 'a man named Longworth, more celebrated as a combatant at Waterloo than as a skilled or competent architect' [*Trans. Lancashire and Cheshire Antiquarian Soc.* v, 1887, 337].

LOUDON, JOHN CLAUDIUS (1783–1843), was the eldest son of a Scottish farmer at Gogar, nr. Edinburgh. As a child he showed a fondness for gardening, and after a schooling in Edinburgh he was apprenticed to a nurseryman and landscape-gardener at Easter Dalry. In 1803 he left Scotland for London, where he began a successful practice as a landscape-gardener. The Duchess of Brunswick employed him at Brunswick House, Blackheath, and Lord Mansfield engaged him to improve the grounds at Scone

Palace in Perthshire. In 1804 he exhibited three drawings at the Royal Academy and published his first book, entitled *Observations on the Formation and Management of Useful and Ornamental Plantations, on the Theory and Practice of Landscape Gardening and on Gaining and Embanking Land from Rivers or the Sea*. For the rest of his life he was to combine his practice as a landscape-gardener with incessant literary activity. In 1806 he published a two-volume *Treatise on forming, improving and managing Country Residences*, in 1812 *Observations on laying out Farms in the Scotch Style, adapted to England*, and *Hints on the Formation of Gardens and Pleasure Grounds*, in 1822 an *Encyclopaedia of Gardening*, in 1825 an *Encyclopaedia of Agriculture*, in 1829 an *Encyclopaedia of Plants*, in 1833 an *Encyclopaedia of Cottage, Farm and Villa Architecture and Furniture*, in 1838 *The Suburban Gardener and Villa Companion* and an encyclopaedia of British trees and shrubs entitled *Arboretum et Fruticetum Britannicum*, and in 1843 a work *On the Laying Out, Planting and Management of Cemeteries*. These were merely his principal publications. In addition he conducted three periodicals: *The Gardener's Magazine* (1826–42), *The Magazine of Natural History* (1829–36) and *The Architectural Magazine* (5 vols., 1834–8), all replete with information assembled by their indefatigable editor, who frequently worked all night in order to get his copy to the printer in time.

In 1809 Loudon rented a farm at Great Tew in Oxfordshire, where he took pupils in agriculture, and by 1812 he had made a profit of £15,000. He then gave up the farm and went on a tour of Northern Europe, studying foreign methods of farming and gardening. On his return he found that his investments had failed, and further financial difficulties followed the publication of the financially disastrous *Arboretum* in 1838. His health had been poor since an attack of rheumatic fever in 1806, and he was disabled both by a stiff leg and, more seriously, by the amputation of his right arm in 1825. Nevertheless, with the help of his wife Jane, whom he married in 1830, he remained active as a writer, botanist and landscape-gardener up to the time of his death in December 1843.

As a landscape-gardener Loudon was a follower of Payne Knight and Uvedale Price, whose belief in irregularity and picturesque grouping he shared. Though at first critical of Repton, he eventually recognized that Repton's ideas combined 'all that was excellent in the former schools [of landscape gardening]', and in 1840 he gave fresh currency to Repton's theories by reprinting all his works on the subject in one volume. In the introduction he recognized the emergence of a new approach to landscape-gardening which he called 'the Gardenesque'. The object of the Gardenesque was to combine the picturesque grouping of the past with the display of individual trees and shrubs for their botanical interest. In applying these principles to the smaller scale of the suburban villa and the public park, Loudon helped to establish the characteristics of the Victorian garden. The arboretum perfectly embodied his ideas, and his Derby Arboretum (1839–41) was a pioneer example of its kind. Ornamental buildings figured prominently in such layouts, and it was no doubt as a picturesque adjunct to gardening that Loudon first approached architecture. It would, however, have been uncharacteristic of him not to make himself the master of any subject that he chose to take up, and in 1831 he wrote that 'though we are not a practising architect, yet we pretend to as thorough a knowledge of the principles of architecture, as of those of landscape-gardening' (*Gardener's Magazine* vii, 404–5). The result was *The Encyclopaedia of Cottage, Farm and Villa Architecture* (1833, 2nd ed. by Mrs. Loudon 1846) and *The Architectural Magazine*. Both had the same object – 'to diffuse among general readers a taste for architectural beauties and comforts, and to improve the dwellings of the great mass of society in all countries'. Unlike most previous architectural publications (including the numerous slim volumes offering elegant designs for picturesque cottages) the *Encyclopaedia* and the *Magazine* were addressed to the middle classes rather than to the aristocracy. Comfort and convenience were studied in detail and it is the farm-house and the suburban villa rather than the country seat whose siting, planning, construction and embellishment form the main theme of the *Encyclopaedia*. In fulfilling his task Loudon had the help of a number of contributors, who provided him with plans, elevations and descriptions of appropriate buildings. One of his most faithful assistants was Edward Buckton Lamb, a young architect then in his twenties upon whom he relied particularly for Gothic designs. At the end of the *Encyclopaedia* Loudon summarized his architectural theory in terms largely derived from the tradition of Scottish rationalist philosophy as set out in Alison's *Essays on the Nature and Principles of Taste* (1790). Guided by Alison, Loudon rejects the niceties of the orders for fitness of purpose and the appropriate expression of function. The latter did not necessarily mean functionalism in the modern sense. But it did mean that architectural forms – whether Gothic or classical – had to be chosen because they were actually or symbolically expressive of the building's function. Having discovered 'the beauty of truth' (*Encyclopaedia*, 1846 ed., 1113), Loudon was on the same road as Pugin and the ecclesiologists, though stylistically he accepted a degree of eclecticism which to them was anathema. With its numerous illustrations Loudon's *Encyclopaedia* therefore has an important place in the formation of Victorian architectural taste, especially at the suburban level with which loftier theorists such as Ruskin or Pugin scarcely condescended to concern themselves.

Although he did not regard himself as a practising architect, there is evidence that in his early days as a landscape-gardener Loudon did occasionally act in that capacity. In 1804 he exhibited at the Royal Academy an 'Elevation of a house proposed to be built at Balliad in Perthshire for P. Campbell, Esq.', and in 1806 he appears to have remodelled the exterior of BARNBARROW, WIGTOWNSHIRE (burned 1942), whose grounds he landscaped for R. V. Agnew (see original drawings by Loudon in Mr. Paul Mellon's Collection and his *Treatise on forming ... Country Residences*, pls. xiii–xiv and one opposite p. 613). His principal architectural work appears to have been GARTH, nr. WELSHPOOL, MONTGOMERYSHIRE (dem. 1947), which he designed for R. Mytton in 1809–10. This crudely detailed Gothic house is described and illustrated in his *Observations on laying out Farms in the Scotch Style, adapted to England*, 1812. In the same work he states that 'extensive improvements to house and grounds are now executing from my designs' at HOPE END, nr. LEDBURY, HEREFS., for E. M. Barrett. Hope End (mostly demolished 1873) was a most eccentric building coarsely designed in a pseudo-Moorish style, presumably at the owner's behest, but certain resemblances to Garth confirm Loudon's responsibility for the architecture (cf. Sandra Blutman in *C. Life*, 19 Sept. 1968). Later in life Loudon designed NOS. 3 and 5 PORCHESTER TERRACE, LONDON, a 'double detached villa' which he built in 1823–4, occupying No. 3 himself, and was responsible for the singular monument, consisting of a sarcophagus projecting from an obelisk, which he erected in PINNER CHURCHYARD, MIDDLESEX, to the memory of his parents.

[Jane Loudon, 'A Short Account of the life and Writings of John Claudius Loudon', in *Self-Instruction for Young Gardeners*, 1844; *D.N.B.*; Geoffrey Taylor, *Some Nineteenth Century Gardeners*, 1951, chap. 2; John Gloag, *Mr. Loudon's England*, 1970; G. L. Hersey, 'J. C. Loudon and Architectural Associationism', *Arch. Rev.*, Aug. 1968; L. Fricker, 'John Claudius Loudon: the Plane Truth', in *Furor Hortensis: Essays on the History of the English Landscape Garden in Memory of H. F. Clark*, ed. P. Willis, Edinburgh 1974. All Loudon's papers were destroyed by bombing during the Second World War.]

LOVELL, WILLIAM, practised as a surveyor in Pentonville. In 1828 he designed the CLERKENWELL PAROCHIAL SUNDAY SCHOOL, altered by W. P. Griffith in 1858 [W. J. Pinks, *History of Clerkenwell*, 1881, 178]. He appears to have been the father of a District Surveyor named William Lovell who died in 1874.

LOVEN, or **LOVIN,** JOHN (–1679), was a master mason of Peterborough. In February 1660/1 he contracted to build THORNEY ABBEY HOUSE, CAMBS., for the 5th Earl of Bedford 'according to the draught and order of works designed for the same and now delivered in to the said Earl under the hand of the said John Lovin' [G. Scott Thompson, *Family Background*, 1949, 180–4]. The house, which has features recalling Thorpe Hall, is illustrated in *C. Life*, 27 Sept. 1919. Loven repaired the BISHOP'S PALACE at PETERBOROUGH after damage done during the Commonwealth, and in 1671 built the arcaded MARKET HOUSE there [W. T. Mellows, *History of Peterborough's Public Buildings*, 1934; B.M., Lansdowne MS. 1027, f. 200]. Loven's will, dated 11 May 1679, was proved at Peterborough on 7 June the same year [Northants. Record Office]. He left sons named Thomas and John.

LOVI, Father WALTER, a Roman Catholic priest, is reputed to have designed several Catholic chapels in Scotland, including those of KEITH, BANFFSHIRE, 1831; WICK, CAITHNESS, 1837; and BRAEMAR, ABERDEENSHIRE, 1839. The chapel at Keith is a classical building with a west front of Italian baroque character [G. Hay, *The Architecture of Scottish Post-Reformation Churches*, 1957, 158].

LOWDER, JOHN, was a member of a wealthy family of bankers at Bath. He exhibited a design for the interior of a mausoleum at the Royal Academy in 1803. In January 1817 he was appointed Surveyor to the City of Bath at a salary of £100 p.a., but resigned in July 1823. He designed the BATH AND DISTRICT NATIONAL SCHOOL, 1816, dem. 1896, which was built on a circular plan, with wedge-shaped classrooms. He also designed the Gothic HOLY TRINITY CHURCH, JAMES STREET, BATH, 1819–22, dem. 1957, and the simple but elegant BISHOPSTONE RECTORY (now HOUSE), HANTS., for the Rev. Thomas Bromley, c. 1816–20 [Salisbury Diocesan Records; C. Hussey in *C. Life*, 12 Nov. 1959]. His original designs for Holy Trinity, Bath, were in the Grecian style, but in deference to the wishes of the building committee he substituted the Gothic design which was carried out at a greatly increased cost. The ensuing difficulties are said to have hastened his death. H. E. Goodridge was his pupil. [W. Ison, *The Georgian Buildings of Bath*, 1948, 82; Bath City Archives.]

LUCY, EDWARD and JAMES, were carpenters and surveyors of Worcester. James Lucy was admitted a freeman of the city in 1809. In the *Worcester Journal* for 11 June 1816 he offered himself to the public as a builder who was prepared to act as a surveyor or architect. It appears that he also owned a verandah factory in Sidbury. In 1821 he was responsible for laying out a new street which became known as Carden Street [*Berrow's Worcester Jnl.*, 24 May 1821]. For the Parliamentary Commissioners he designed the small Gothic chapel of ST. GEORGE at CLAINES, nr. WORCESTER, 1829–30, dem. 1894, which was completed by Lewis Belling after Lucy's bankruptcy (3 December 1829) and death [Port, 164–5; *Berrow's Worcester Jnl.*].HALLOW CHURCH,WORCS., 1829–30, dem. 1867, was apparently designed by James Lucy but completed by Edward Lucy [*Berrow's Worcester Jnl.*, 2 April 1829; I.C.B.S.]. [Information from Mr. D. A. Whitehead.]

LUGAR, ROBERT (c. 1773–1855), was the son of Edward Lugar, a carpenter of Colchester. He practised in London from about 1799 onwards, and exhibited regularly at the Royal Academy for the next twenty years. In 1812 he succeeded John Johnson as County Surveyor of Essex, but resigned four years later. He retired from practice some years before his death in Pembroke Square, Kensington, on 23 June 1855, at the age of 82 [*A.P.S.D.*]. Archibald Simpson of Aberdeen was his pupil.

Lugar was a skilful practitioner of the picturesque, exploiting the fashion for *cottages ornés* and castellated Gothic mansions in the manner of John Nash. His two Dunbartonshire castles were among the first to introduce the picturesque formula into Scotland (where the symmetrical Adam castle style was still in vogue), and at Shoreham in Kent he designed an early example of an Italianate villa in 1806. He published *Architectural Sketches for Cottages, Rural Dwellings, and Villas*, 1805, dedicated to George Ward, reprinted 1815 and 1823; *The Country Gentleman's Architect; Designs for Farm Houses and Yards*, 1807; *Plans and Views of Buildings executed in England and Scotland in the Castellated and Other Styles*, 1811, 2nd. ed. 1823; and *Villa Architecture, a Collection of Views, with Plans, of Buildings executed in England, Scotland, etc.*, 1828, with a dedication to William Crawshay. In 1835 he entered a design for the new Houses of Parliament jointly with J. Burrell (q.v.). It was in the Gothic style, based on 'the best examples of its date' in England and on the Continent, 'and so disposed as to unite (in connection with Westminster Hall, the Abbey towers, &c.) in forming a dignified and characteristic composition' [*Catalogue of the Designs for the New Houses of Parliament*, 1836, 12–13].

BALLOCH (now ARDOCH) CASTLE, DUNBARTONSHIRE, additions for John Buchanan, 1809, castellated [*Plans and Views*, 1823, pls. 10–13;

Neale, *Seats* vi, 1823; exhib. at R.A. 1809] (J. Irving, *Book of Dumbartonshire* iii, 1879, pl. vii).

BETTESHANGER HOUSE, KENT, for F. E. Morrice, before 1828, Tudor style; rebuilt by George Devey 1856 onwards [*Villa Architecture*, 1828, pls. 17–19].

BOTURICH CASTLE, DUNBARTONSHIRE, repaired for John Buchanan, *c.* 1830; burnt [J. B. Burke, *Visitations of Seats* ii, 1853, 249].

BRANDON COTTAGE or LODGE (now Brandon Hall Hotel), nr. WOLSTON, WARWICKS., for the 19th Lord Grey de Ruthyn (d. 1810) [*Plans and Views*, 1823, pls. 14–16].

CHEPSTOW, MONMOUTHSHIRE, WYELANDS ESTATE, advertised in 1846 as 'lately erected from the designs of Lugar' [*Monmouthshire Merlin*, 18 July 1846].

attributed: COLCHESTER, ESSEX, THE TURRETS, LEXDEN ROAD, for Francis Smythies, 1818, Gothic [stylistic attribution supported by the fact that Lugar became a freeman of Colchester during Smythies' mayoralty in 1812].

CROSBY HALL, LANCS., bailiff's cottage for William Blundell, before 1828 [*Villa Architecture*, 1828, pl. 4].

CULZEAN CASTLE, AYRSHIRE, cottage and pheasantry for the 12th Earl of Cassilis, before 1823 [*Plans and Views*, 1823, pl. 31; cf. design for a lodge attributable to Lugar in portfolio at Culzean Castle, no. 39].

CYFARTHFA CASTLE, GLAMORGANSHIRE, for William Crawshay, 1825; since enlarged, castellated [*Villa Architecture*, 1828, pls. 41–2] (T. Nicholas, *Annals of the County Families of Wales* i, 1875, 474].

DEDHAM, ESSEX, a cottage 'to be built', exhibited at the R.A. 1803.

DENHAM MOUNT, DENHAM, BUCKS., for Nathaniel Snell, before 1823 [*Plans and Views*, pls. 24–5].

DUDDESTONE HOUSE, WARWICKS., designs, perhaps unexecuted, for a fishing lodge, etc., for Samuel Galton, 1818–19 [Warwickshire Record Office, CR 1198/85, 92].

EASTWOOD, CO. TIPPERARY, IRELAND, a cottage 'to be built', exhibited at the R.A. 1802.

FINGRINGHOE BRIDGE, ESSEX, 1814; a wooden bridge dem. 1923 [G. M. Burton, 'Fingringhoe Bridge', *Essex Arch. Soc. Trans.*, N.S. xx, 1933].

GLANUSK PARK, BRECONSHIRE, for Joseph Bailey, Elizabethan style [MS. copy of Burke's *Visitation of Seats, ex inf.* Mr. Peter Reid] (J. B. Burke, *Visitations of Seats* i, 1852, 209–11, plates).

GLENLEE, nr. NEW GALLOWAY, KIRKCUDBRIGHTSHIRE, enlarged for Lady Ashburton, 1823 [*Villa Architecture*, 1828, pls. 30–1].

GOLD HILL (now DUNSTALL PRIORY), SHOREHAM, KENT, 1806, Italianate [exhib. at R.A. 1806].

GWLITH-FAES, BRECON, house 'to be built' for William West, exhibited at R.A. 1841.

HENSOL, nr. CASTLE DOUGLAS, KIRKCUDBRIGHTSHIRE, for John Cunningham, *c.* 1825 [*Villa Architecture*, 1828, pls. 26–9].

HOLDERS HILL COTTAGE, nr. HENDON, MIDDLESEX, alterations and additions for William McInerheny, before 1823; dem. [*Plans and Views*, 1823, pls. 26–7].

HORSLEY PLACE (TOWERS), SURREY, lodge for William Currie, before 1828 [*Villa Architecture*, 1828, pl. 2].

KIRBY HALL, OUSEBURN, YORKS. (W.R.), lodge for R. J. Thompson, before 1828 [*Villa Architecture*, 1828, pl. 6].

LEE HALL, GATEACRE, LANCS., lodge for John Okill, before 1828 [*Villa Architecture*, 1828, pl. 1].

MAESLWCH CASTLE, RADNORSHIRE, for Walter Wilkins, 1828–39, castellated; partly dem. *c.* 1965 [exhib. at R.A. 1841] (T. Nicholas, *Annals of the County Families of Wales* ii, 1875, 913).

MARKYATE CELL, HERTS., alterations for D. G. Adey, 1825–6, Elizabethan style [*Villa Architecture*, 1828, pls. 39–40].

NEWLAITHES HALL, HORSFORTH, YORKS. (W.R.), for Charles Greenwood, before 1828, Tudor Gothic [*Villa Architecture*, 1828, pls. 22–3].

OXNEY PARK, KENT, enlarged for John May, 1816, Gothic; now in ruins [*Villa Architecture*, 1828, pls. 20–1] (Neale, *Seats*, 2nd ser., ii, 1825).

PUCKASTER COTTAGE, nr. NITON, ISLE OF WIGHT, for James Vine, before 1828 [*Villa Architecture*, 1828, pls. 11–12].

THE ROOKERY, WOODFORD, ESSEX, picturesque cottages for John Hanson, before 1823 [*Plans and Views*, 1823, pl. 32].

ROSE HILL COTTAGE, WARGRAVE, BERKS., for J. F. Nicholas [signed drawing in Bodleian Library, MS. Top. Oxon. b. 91, f. 193, no. 298].

THE RYES LODGE, LITTLE HENNY, ESSEX, for N. Barnardiston, 1809 [*Plans and Views*, 1823, pls. 7–9; exhib. at R.A. 1809].

ST. MARGARET'S, ISLEWORTH, MIDDLESEX, lodge for the 12th Earl of Cassilis, before 1828 [*Villa Architecture*, 1828, pl. 3; see above under Culzean Castle].

STANFORD (? STAMFORD) HILL, house 'to be built' for Mr. Bayley, exhibited at the R.A. 1806.

SWINTON PARK, YORKS. (N.R.), remodelled in castellated style for William Danby, 1821–4; tower heightened 1889 [*Villa Architecture*, 1828, pls. 24–5; John Cornforth in *C. Life*, 7, 14, 21 April 1966].

TULLICHEWAN CASTLE, DUNBARTONSHIRE, for John Stirling, 1808, castellated; dem. 1954 [*Plans and Views*, 1823, pls. 1–6; exhib. at R.A. 1808; drawing in R.I.B.A. Coll.] (J. Irving, *Book of Dumbartonshire* iii, 1879, pl. xx).

WARLEY HALL, WORCS., for Hubert Galton, *c.* 1820, Gothic; dem. *c.* 1940 [*Villa Architecture*, 1828, pls. 32–5].

WEDDINGTON HALL, WARWICKS., for Lionel Place, before 1823, castellated; dem. *c.* 1928 [*Plans and Views*, 1823, pls. 28–30].

YAXHAM RECTORY, NORFOLK, for the Rev. J. Johnson, 1820–2, classical [*Villa Architecture*, 1828, pls. 13–14].

LUMBY, THOMAS and his son WILLIAM (–1804), were master carpenters at Lincoln. Thomas Lumby 'did a great deal of business in that line of building', but went bankrupt in 1775. He rebuilt the roof of the Chapter House of Lincoln Cathedral under the direction of James Essex, who told the Bishop in 1775 that 'I am well satisfied no one in Lincoln knows better the business of a Carpenter in general, and I much doubt if there is a man in the County of Lincoln who is so good a judge of the work that is wanting in the Cathedral'. William Lumby was brought up to his father's business, but succeeded William Jepson clerk of the works to the cathedral in about 1775, and thereafter practised as an architect. He was closely associated with James Essex in the refitting of the cathedral in 1777–9, and several of his designs for Gothic screens intended to conceal the beams over the lateral gateways to the choir are in a volume of designs and estimates made by himself and Essex and now among the Dean and Chapter's records (A4, 15). According to an account of his work in the cathedral, preserved by E. J. Willson, he designed 'the ornaments upon the beams over the choir-side-gates', and 'the tabernacles opposite to the bishop's throne in the choir. The antient stained glass was removed into the transepts, and to the two eastern windows in the aisles of the presbytery under him. The iron rails before the altar were removed from the steps on which the table stands, and put across in a straight line by him.' When the cathedral was repaved, he made a plan of the old pavement, showing all the grave-stones, which was engraved by Gough in his *British Topography*. The original drawing is in the Bodleian Library, Gough Maps 16, f. 10. He also drew the plan and elevation of the cathedral published in *Vetusta Monumenta* iii, 1791, pls. 10, 11.

E. J. Willson described William Lumby as being 'of a very ingenious turn of mind, mild and gentle'. He died at Greatford, nr. Stamford, on 18 August 1804, 'before the age of 50, after falling into a low and nervous state of health, which almost rendered him incapable of attending to business'.

As a secular architect William Lumby was competent but unremarkable. But his drawings for the interior of Lincoln Cathedral show that he was a pioneer Gothic Revivalist of the same sort as James Essex. The church at Doddington which Thomas Lumby reconstructed in 1770–5 is also notable for its Gothic detailing. It is

natural to suppose that it was designed by the son, but if E. J. Willson was correct about his age at the time of his death this would hardly be feasible. The possibility that Essex himself helped cannot be excluded.

A design by William Lumby for a Palladian lodge on the Dashwood estate at Dunston, Lincolnshire, is preserved at West Wycombe Park.

[*Gent's Mag.* 1775, 47, 1804 (ii), 795, 983; E. J. Willson's MS. Lincolnshire Collections in the Library of the Society of Antiquaries of London, v, f. 71, vii, f. 99, xiii, f. 54, and Folder Q; Records of the Dean and Chapter of Lincoln, A4, 13 and 15; B.M., Add. MS. 6772, f. 281 (letter from T. Lumby to Essex).]

DODDINGTON HALL, LINCS., internal alterations for Sir John Hussey Delaval, Bart., carried out by Thomas Lumby in 1761–2. They included a new staircase and the refitting of the principal rooms [Bodleian, MS. Top. Lincs. c. 14, and R. E. G. Cole, *History of Doddington*, 1897, 149, where, however, the elder Lumby is confused with his son].

DODDINGTON CHURCH, LINCS., reconstructed by Thomas Lumby for Sir John Hussey Delaval, Bart., 1770–5, Gothic [building accounts in Bodleian, MSS. Top. Lincs. c. 23, 24, 25, 26, 29; letters from the steward at Doddington in Northumberland County Record Office, 2 DE 20/6/1–27].

REDBOURNE CHURCH, LINCS., partially rebuilt by 'Mr. Lumby' for the Rev. Robert Carter, 1772–4, Gothic; subsequently altered [Lincolnshire Record Office, Red. 3/1/4/6, 1772].

STAMFORD, LINCS., surveyor's work by Thomas Lumby for the 9th Earl of Exeter in connection with building activity in the town, 1781–94 [Burghley archives, *ex inf.* Dr. E. R. Till].

LINCOLN, THE BLUE COAT SCHOOL, designed by William Lumby, 1784–5 [Society of Antiquaries, E. J. Willson's Collections, v, f. 71].

LINCOLN, THE CASTLE GAOL, designed by William Lumby, 1786–8. According to E. J. Willson this was designed by John Carr of York, but the Grand Jury Minute Book shows that although Carr did make a design in 1774 nothing was done for over ten years. No reference was made to Carr's plan in 1785, when Messrs. Legg, Langwith and Lumby submitted designs and Lumby's were adopted [Lincolnshire Record Office, Q.S. Records 1785–88].

SOUTHWELL, NOTTS., THE RESIDENCE HOUSE, designed by William Lumby, 1786 [Chapter Decrees, 21 Jan. 1785 and signed drawing in Minster Library, *ex inf.* Dr. N. Summers].

LINCOLN, house opposite St. Mary's Church designed by William Lumby for Alderman Gibbeson [Society of Antiquaries, E. J. Willson's Collections, xiii, f. 54].

LUMLEY, JOHN (1654–1721), was the only son of John Lumley of Harlestone, Northants., where his family had been masons since the Middle Ages. In 1648 he was made free of the London Masons' Company as a 'Foreign Member', and in 1703 he became a freeman of Northampton gratis in repayment of a debt owed to him by the Corporation. He established a yard in Northampton and carried on business as a surveyor and master mason there until his death in November 1721. In his will he left half his marble and alabaster and all his working tools to his apprentice William Swan and the other half to the stone-carver Samuel Cox, whom he describes as 'my loving kinsman' [L. G. Horton-Smith, 'The Later Lumleys of Harlestone', *Trans. of the Northants. Natural History and Field Club* xxx, 1943, 103; Shelagh M. Lewis, 'The Coxes of Northamptonshire', *Northamptonshire Past and Present* i, 1953, 21–2].

In 1697 Lumley took the place of Henry Dormer (*q.v.*) as the surveyor employed by the 2nd Earl of Nottingham to supervise the building of his mansion at BURLEY-ON-THE-HILL, RUTLAND. The foundations had been laid in 1694, and the main features of the design had already been determined by the time Lumley took charge.[1] There are, however, several references to moulds, draughts, etc., made by Lumley, and some of the architectural details may have been determined by him. The house was structurally complete by 1700, but Lumley was still in correspondence with Lord Nottingham in connection with the stables as late as 1705 [H. J. Habakkuk, 'Daniel Finch, 2nd Earl of Nottingham: his House and Estate', in *Studies in Social History* ed. J. H. Plumb, 1955; Pearl Finch, *Burley on the Hill*, 1901, 30, 64–5, 73, 110].

It was by Lord Nottingham's advice that his friend the 1st Lord Ashburnham employed Lumley as surveyor at GREAT PARK HOUSE, AMPTHILL, BEDS., in 1704–7. Hawksmoor had previously been consulted, but letter-books formerly at Ashburnham Park, Sussex, show that Lumley was making plans, elevations and estimates for rebuilding the house in the winter of 1704–5, and that he remained in control of the works for the next two years. In 1706–7 Lord Ashburnham was consulting William Winde about the decoration of the interior and the employment of 'Tissue the french iron worker', but Winde's name does not occur until the house was structurally complete, and it seems clear that Lumley was the principal architect of this typical house of the 1700s.

In 1719 Lumley was employed to 'draw the plan' for rebuilding the south range of the Front Court of EMMANUEL COLLEGE, CAMBRIDGE, and superintended the work until his death two years later [J.B.P., 'The College Buildings in the

Eighteenth Century', *Emmanuel College Magazine* ix (2), 1898]. The principal benefactor to the work was the 6th Earl of Westmorland (after whom the new range was named 'The Westmorland Building') and as Lumley is described in the accounts as the Earl's 'overseer' at Apethorpe, it is evident that his employment at Cambridge was due to Westmorland's patronage. At APETHORPE, NORTHANTS., he may have been responsible for the orangery forming the south side of the second court, which was built in 1718 (cf. *V.C.H. Northants.* ii, 545). The Westmorland Building is a three-storied range somewhat clumsily dignified by a pair of giant Ionic pilasters and a swept-up balustrade.

Other references to Lumley show him surveying the house at AYNHO PARK, NORTHANTS., in 1698 (a date when no structural work was carried out) [account-book among Cartwright family papers in Northants. Record Office] and examining the defective spire of GREENS NORTON CHURCH, NORTHANTS., in 1718 [Peterborough Diocesan Records].

M

MABERLEY, WILLIAM (*c.* 1798–   ), was admitted to the Royal Academy Schools in 1817 as an architectural student at the age of 19. Pigot's *Directory* shows that ten years later he was practising as an architect in Davies Street near Berkeley Square.

McBRIDE, JAMES (*c.* 1785–1845), 'architect in Elgin', is commemorated by a tombstone in the churchyard of Elgin Cathedral. He died on 7 October 1845, aged 60. He is described as 'carpenter and architect' in Pigot's *Directory* for 1825–6.

McCANDLISH, WILLIAM, of Dalry, Kirkcudbrightshire, designed GLENCAIRN CHURCH, DUMFRIESSHIRE, 1836, in an elementary Gothic style enlivened by a dramatically arched north transept [S.R.O., HR 116/1].

MACDONNELL, JOHN (1770–   ), son of J. MacDonnell, of Mount Street, Berkeley Square, carpenter, was a pupil of Sir John Soane from 1786 to 1791, and afterwards of Thomas Hardwick from 1792 to 1794. He entered the Royal Academy Schools in 1793, and exhibited at the Academy from 1788 to 1804. His exhibited designs included 'a theatre intended to be built at Lewes, Sussex' (1789) and a 'Design for a government house for the island of Antigua' (1804) [A. T. Bolton, *The Works of Sir John Soane*, Appendix C, p. xl, where his name is wrongly given as 'McDowell'].

---

[1] Above, p. 271, n. 1.

MACFARLANE, JAMES, was a mason-architect at Doune in Perthshire, where he lived at Woodside Cottage. He was a prominent elder of the parish church, and was several times Master of the local Freemasons' Lodge [M. S. Mackay, *The Parish of Kilmadock and Borough of Doune,* typescript 1952, 111]. In 1834–5 he designed BEATH CHURCH, FIFE [S.R.O., HR 56/1, pp. 3–6]. He signs a design dated 1838 for enlarging a lodge to REDNOCK HOUSE, PERTHSHIRE [drawing at Rednock]. He was still active in 1855–6, when he supervised the building of KINCARDINE SCHOOL to the designs of R. & R. Dickson [S.R.O., HR 275/1].

McGILL, ALEXANDER (–1734), was the son of George McGill, minister of Arbirlot in Angus. Owing to a gap in the Arbirlot parish registers the date of his birth cannot be ascertained, but in June 1697 he was apprenticed to Alexander Nisbet, mason of Edinburgh. In 1710 he was admitted to the Edinburgh masons' lodge gratis as 'architector'. He became one of the leading Scottish architects of the early eighteenth century, and in November 1720 was appointed to the newly constituted post of City Architect of Edinburgh, with a salary of £50 a year. In December 1725 this salary was discontinued as a measure of economy at a time when 'no publick work of importance' was in progress, but McGill continued to be employed from time to time on an *ad hoc* basis. From the business correspondence of the 2nd Earl of Bute (for whom McGill designed Mount Stuart), we learn that he had the reputation of 'knowing his business very well', and that he was in London in December 1717.

Early in his career McGill was associated with James Smith, for Yester House is stated in *Vitruvius Scoticus* to have been their joint work, and among the Seafield papers in the Scottish Record Office [RHP 2541] there is an unexecuted design for Cullen House, Banffshire, endorsed as 'Mrs. Smith & McGill's 3rd design of Cullen House 1709'. The connection between the two architects appears to have continued up to the time of Smith's death in 1731, for in 1727 McGill appears as Smith's assignee in a lawsuit brought by the latter against the Earl of Leven for non-payment of money due for the building of Melville House, and in the same year he witnessed an agreement concerning a pumping-engine which Smith had installed in a coalmine on his estate at Whitehill. In 1729 McGill and Smith were employed jointly by the City of Edinburgh to inspect a defect in the quay at Leith [Edinburgh City Records, Sederunt Book of the Sub-Committee for managing the Ale Duty, 2 Sept. 1729]. Yester is, however, the only executed building for which Smith and McGill are at present known to have been jointly responsible.

To judge by his independent work McGill favoured a simple, dignified style of country-house architecture probably derived largely from Sir William Bruce. Indeed at Nairne he appears to have been involved in the completion of a house begun to Bruce's design, and at Kellie Castle he had dealings with Bruce's associate Alexander Edward. Although he provided his houses with extensive subsidiary buildings, the main block was usually rectangular, with hipped roof and regular fenestration without any of the baroque ornamentation favoured by William Adam. In one of his last works, Donibristle Chapel, he used blocked architraves and other features characteristic of James Gibbs.

McGill died in Edinburgh in May 1734.

[Hew Scott, *Fasti Ecclesiae Scoticanae* v, 1925, 421; *Edinburgh Register of Apprentices 1666–1700,* Scottish Record Soc. 1929–59; Edinburgh Town Council Minutes, vol. 48, pp. 282, 288, and Sederunt Book of the Sub-Committee for managing the Ale Duty, 6 Dec. 1725; Ale Duty accounts 1718–68, *passim*; J. G. Dunbar, 'The Building of Yester House', *Trans. of the E. Lothian Antiquarian and Field Naturalists' Soc.* xiii, 1972, 23–4; extracts from letters to 2nd Earl of Bute at N.M.R.S.; S.R.O., Edinburgh Testaments, 28 Feb. 1737, 28 May 1756.]

DOMESTIC ARCHITECTURE

KELLIE CASTLE, ANGUS, alterations for Henry Maule, in association with Alexander Edward, 1699–1705 [S.R.O., GD 45/18/1233, 1236; GD 14/332].

YESTER HOUSE, EAST LOTHIAN, for the 2nd Marquess of Tweeddale, in partnership with James Smith, *c.* 1700–15; altered by W. Adam 1730 and by Robert Adam 1788 [*Vitruvius Scoticus*, pls. 28–9; J. G. Dunbar, 'The Building of Yester House', *Trans. of the E. Lothian Antiquarian and Field Naturalists' Soc.* xiii, 1972] (*C. Life*, 23–30 July 1932, 9, 16 and 23 Aug. 1973).

CRAIGIEHALL HOUSE, WEST LOTHIAN, ornamental gates for the 1st Marquess of Annandale, 1708 [letters from McGill to the Earl of Mar, S.R.O., GD 124/15/752/1–2].

HOUSE OF NAIRNE, PERTHSHIRE, advice or designs for completion of house in March 1710 after death of Sir William Bruce, who appears to have designed it for the 2nd Lord Nairn [J. G. Dunbar, *Sir William Bruce* (exhibition catalogue), 1970, 20].

BLAIR DRUMMOND, PERTHSHIRE, for George Drummond, 1715–17; dem. 1870 [*Vitruvius Scoticus*, pls. 83–5].

GLASGOW, recons. house in Dry Gate for the 1st Duke of Montrose, 1718–19; dem. *c.* 1855 [designs by McGill in S.R.O., RHP 6285]. The Duke's accounts in S.R.O., GD 220/6, vol. 11, show that the house cost £28,481 (presumably

Scots). Macky, *Journey through Scotland*, 1723, 296, implies that it was unfinished.

MOUNT STUART, ISLE OF BUTE, for the 2nd Earl of Bute, 1718–22; main block apparently rebuilt by W. Adam *c*. 1740 and destroyed by fire 1877, leaving McGill's pavilions [drawings at Mount Stuart, *ex inf*. Dr. A. A. Tait and Mr. J. G. Dunbar].

DONIBRISTLE HOUSE, nr. ABERDOUR, FIFE, for the 6th Earl of Moray, 1719–23; main block destroyed by fire 1858 [*Vitruvius Scoticus*, pls. 92–4; N.M.R.S., extracts from Moray muniments, vol. vi, box 16].

INVERARAY CASTLE, ARGYLLSHIRE, temporary 'pavilion' or lodging for the 2nd Duke of Argyll, 1720–2; dem. 1745 [I. G. Lindsay & Mary Cosh, *Inveraray and the Dukes of Argyll*, 1973, 25–6, 350–1, n. 62].

BRUNSTANE HOUSE, MIDLOTHIAN, plan for alterations, perhaps not executed, for Andrew Fletcher, Lord Milton, 1730 [letters in National Library of Scotland, Saltoun Papers, Box 15].

PICARDY VILLAGE, BROUGHTON, EDINBURGH, layout of village for Picardy weavers, 1730; dem. *c*. 1800 [John Mason, 'The Weavers of Picardy', *Book of the Old Edinburgh Club* xxv, 1945, 9].

CHURCHES

EDINBURGH, GREYFRIARS WEST CHURCH, 1719–22 [G. Hay, *The Kirk of the Greyfriars, Edinburgh*, 1959, 9].

DUMFRIES NEW CHURCH, 1724–7; dem. 1866 [W. McDowall, *History of Dumfries*, Edinburgh 1867, 616].

NEWBATTLE CHURCH, MIDLOTHIAN, 1727–8 [Dalkeith Presbytery Records, S.R.O., CH2/424/11, pp. 411–14, 420].

DONIBRISTLE CHAPEL, FIFE, for the 6th Earl of Moray, 1729–32 [inscription in gallery and N.M.R.S., extracts from Moray muniments, vol. vi, box 16].

PUBLIC BUILDING

STIRLING, alterations to the 'court place' in the TOLBOOTH, 1710 [*Extracts from the Records of the Royal Burgh of Stirling 1667–1752*, ed. Renwick, 1889, 122, and cf. 188 and 194 for his advice about a ford in 1726].

UNEXECUTED DESIGNS

The following unexecuted designs have been noted: for rebuilding ALLOA CHURCH, CLACKMANNANSHIRE, 1709 [S.R.O., RHP 13258, no. 29, unsigned but in McGill's hand]; for CULLEN HOUSE, BANFFSHIRE, 1709 [S.R.O., RHP 2541, in McGill's hand and endorsed as 'Mrs. Smith &

McGill's 3rd. design of Cullen House']; for alterations to ALLOA HOUSE, CLACKMANNANSHIRE, for the 11th Earl of Mar, 1710 [S.R.O., RHP 13258, no. 5, unsigned but in McGill's hand]; for refronting MAKERSTOUN HOUSE, ROXBURGHSHIRE, 1714 [in private hands, photos at N.M.R.S.]; and for adding wings to the old castle at INVERARAY, ARGYLLSHIRE, in 1720 [I. G. Lindsay & Mary Cosh, *Inveraray and the Dukes of Argyll*, 1973, 26]. At Dunrobin Castle, Sutherland, there is a survey plan of the Castle *c*. 1720 which is attributed to McGill.

McGOWAN, WILLIAM, was a mason who became a burgess of Dumfries in 1825. He designed the small and unpretentious CHURCH at WAMPHRAY, DUMFRIESSHIRE, in 1834 [S.R.O., HR 562/1, pp. 58–63].

MACHELL, the Rev. THOMAS (1647–1698), was the second son of Lancelot Machell of Crackenthorpe Hall, Westmorland, where he was born in 1647. He was probably educated at Appleby Grammar School before going up to The Queen's College, Oxford, where he graduated B.A. in 1668, proceeded to M.A. in 1672, and became a Fellow of the College the same year. Five years later he was presented by the 3rd Earl of Thanet to the well-endowed rectory of Kirkby Thore in Westmorland, and for the rest of his life he remained the parson of this remote parish, where he died in November 1698.

In Oxford Machell had become acquainted with some of the leading intellectuals of the time, notably with Sir Joseph Williamson, a fellow-Cumbrian at whose expense the Williamson Building at Queen's was built to Wren's designs in 1671–4, and with the antiquaries Dugdale and Wood. He shared their interests and in 1684 was elected a member of the Oxford Philosophical Society. Far away in Westmorland he saw himself as a lone representative of the new historical and aesthetic attitudes that he had learned in Oxford. Emulating Dugdale, he set about making collections for a history of the two Cumbrian counties, copying deeds, drawing Roman inscriptions and making sketches of notable buildings. At the same time, being interested in 'the most Beautifull Art of Architecture', he determined to introduce classical architecture into an area where every manor-house was still a fortified tower and the classical orders were almost unknown. In one of his manuscripts he claims that he and the master mason Edward Addison (*q.v.*) were 'the first introducers of Regular building into these Parts; Hutton Hall in the County of Cumberland was Altered by Addison; Rose Castle in Cumberland, Caesar's Tower, Howgill Castle & Crackenthorp Hall in the County of Westmorland by Mr. Machell'. In Appleby parish church he demonstrated his architectural skill by designing a Doric organ case 'which has the extraordinary fancy in it [of] the Guttae & Triglyphy being rendered Musicall, & the fluting turn'd into Organ pipes'.

The houses which Machell and Addison designed were in fact the earliest attempts to introduce classical architecture into Cumbria. At CRACKENTHORPE HALL he designed in 1685 a pedimented front for his brother Hugh, 'exactly uniforme & of such a surprising symetry, that it semeth greater by far than it is'. On the roof he built two cupolas, 'one being designed for pleasure only, the other for a stack of chimneys'. For William Sandford he regularized HOWGILL CASTLE '(with much art and small cost) from an old & irregular piece of Building to a very elligent & uniform structure', but the 'Ionic Bellcony' and 'double transom windows curiously carved' with which he embellished the front have been removed, as have the 'railes & Ballisters' which he substituted for the medieval battlements. At ROSE CASTLE his alterations are no longer distinguishable, but at APPLEBY CASTLE ('Caesar's Tower') he was presumably responsible for the east range built by the 6th Earl of Thanet in 1686–8 in a handsome classical style (*C. Life*, 13, 20 April 1940). It was no doubt from Machell that Addison learned his architectural vocabulary, and a whole group of early classical buildings in Cumbria can be attributed to Machell's influence, although he claimed personal credit only for the four mentioned above.

Six volumes of Machell's Cumbrian collections are preserved in Carlisle Cathedral Library. Among Francis Douce's MSS. in the Bodleian Library there are notes by him on a note-book of Machell's then in the possession of James Bindley (d. 1818), which contained drawings of various buildings, including Crackenthorpe Hall, the library of Queen's College, Oxford, and the Sheldonian Theatre, 'taken immediately after the front was finished'. A letter from Machell to Dugdale, describing an ancient well at Kirkby Thore, was printed in *Philosophical Transactions of the Royal Society* xiii, 1683–4, 559–63.

[Machell MSS. in Carlisle Cathedral Library; T. Rogan & Eric Birley, 'Thomas Machell the Antiquary', *Trans. Cumberland and Westmorland Antiquarian Soc.*, N.S. lv, 1955; Jane M. Ewbank, *Antiquary on Horseback*, 1963; Bodleian Library, MSS. Tanner 22, ff. 97, 112, 134, Douce e.64, ff. 101–110.]

McINNES, A—, exhibited two drawings at the Royal Academy in 1807 from 7 Salisbury Street, Strand. One was a 'view of the altars in the chapel at Roslin, near Edinburgh', the other a design for alterations at TAPLOW LODGE, BUCKS., for P. C. Bruce, M.P.

In the British Museum (*King's Maps* xlix, 47.2) there is an engraved design, signed 'Edin-

burgh. A. McInnes delt. 1801', for a 'Washington Monument' to be built 'on a natural mound opposite the New Town of Thurso, Co. Caithness'. It is in the form of a circular castellated tower.

MACKENZIE, DAVID, was the second son of Alexander Mackenzie (d. 1827), and younger brother of W. M. Mackenzie (*q.v.*). By 1830 he was established at Dundee, where in 1831 he entered unsuccessfully for the Seminaries competition and in 1833 for the Courthouse and Bridewell competitions. However, in June 1833 his scheme for the layout of the Chapelshade grounds for building was accepted in preference to that of his principal rival George Angus (*q.v.*). In or shortly after 1842 Mackenzie died or left Dundee. His place was subsequently taken by his nephew David Mackenzie (1832–75), the son of W. M. Mackenzie of Perth [information from Mr. David Walker].

MONIFIETH MANSE, ANGUS, 1830 [*Dundee Advertiser*, 6 May 1830].

BALDOVAN HOUSE, ANGUS, stables for Sir John Ogilvy, Bart., 1832 [*Dundee Advertiser*, 19 Jan. 1832].

FORFAR, ANGUS, 20–26 HIGH STREET, 1832 [*Dundee Advertiser*, 19 April 1832].

DUNDEE, feued FLEUCHAR CRAIG, LOGIE, for villas, 1833 [*Dundee Advertiser*, 12 Dec. 1833].

DUNDEE, TAY SQUARE U.P. CHURCH (now Halls), 1833 [G. Jamieson, *Tay Square Church, Dundee: A Centenary Retrospect*, 1932, 22–3].

INVERGOWRIE, ANGUS, West Toll House, 1834 [*Dundee Advertiser*, 4 July 1834].

INCHTURE CHURCH, PERTHSHIRE, 1835, Gothic [*N.S.A.* x, 833].

MONIFIETH, ANGUS, SCHOOLHOUSE, 1836 [*Dundee Advertiser*, 13 May 1836].

KINGOLDRUM CHURCH, ANGUS, 1840 [drawings in S.R.O., RHP 7874–5].

MACKENZIE, WILLIAM MACDONALD (–1856), was the eldest son of Alexander Mackenzie, architect of Scone (d. 1827), the founder of a dynasty of Scottish architects. W. M. Mackenzie practised in Perth, where he held the post of City Architect for thirty years, dying there on 15 February 1856. His younger brother Thomas Mackenzie (1814–54) was apprenticed to him before becoming assistant to Archibald Simpson of Aberdeen. Thomas practised in Elgin from 1841 onwards in partnership with James Matthews (1820–98), and was the father of A. Marshall Mackenzie of Aberdeen (1848–1933). W. M. Mackenzie was the father of David Mackenzie II of Dundee (1832–75). [*Builder* xii, 1854, 593, xiv, 1856, 174; information from Mr. David Walker.]

PUBLIC BUILDINGS

KINFAUNS, PERTHSHIRE, Schoolhouse, 1832 [S.R.O., HR 323/1, pp. 29–35].

KINNAIRD, PERTHSHIRE, Schoolhouse, 1834 [S.R.O., HR 418/1, pp. 32–3].

PERTH, THE CITY AND COUNTY INFIRMARY, YORK PLACE (now County Council Offices), 1836: wing added later [N.S.A. x, 129].

PERTH, THE EXCHANGE COFFEE ROOMS, 26–32 GEORGE STREET, 1836 [D. Peacock, Perth, 1849, 501].

PERTH, Triumphal Arch for Queen Victoria's visit, 1842 [D. Peacock, Perth, 1849, 406].

PERTH, THE CITY HALL, 1845; dem. 1877 [D. Peacock, Perth, 1849, 506].

CHURCHES

METHVEN, PERTHSHIRE, enlarged 1825–6 [S.R.O., HR 315/1].

CARGILL, PERTHSHIRE, 1831 [S.R.O., HR 453/1].

PERTH, ST. LEONARD, 1834 [N.S.A. x, 86].

LIFF AND BENVIE CHURCH, ANGUS, 1838–9 [N.S.A. xi, 586; A. B. Dalgety, The Church and Parish of Liff, Dundee 1940, 42].

KINFAUNS OLD PARISH CHURCH, PERTHSHIRE, enlargement, 1838; dem. [S.R.O., HR 323/1, pp. 47, 59].

CLUNIE, PERTHSHIRE, 1839–40, Gothic [S.R.O., HR 334/1].

DOMESTIC ARCHITECTURE

MEGGINCH CASTLE, PERTHSHIRE, additions for Admiral Sir Adam Drummond, 1817–20 [drawings at Megginch, ex inf. Mr. David Walker].

Manses at ARNGASK, PERTHSHIRE, 1828–9 [S.R.O., HR 457/2]; KINNAIRD, PERTHSHIRE (now 'MANSFIELD'), 1831 [S.R.O., HR 418/1]; DRON, PERTHSHIRE, 1838 [S.R.O., HR 320/1, pp. 33–5]; KINFAUNS, PERTHSHIRE (enlargement), 1840 [S.R.O., HR 323/1, pp. 65–76].

ELCHO CASTLE, PERTHSHIRE, farmhouse [J. C. Loudon, Encyclopaedia, 1846, 537–44].

MACKIE, WILLIAM, was a pupil of Samuel Robinson. He exhibited student's work at the Royal Academy in 1810–13, and Pigot's Directory shows that he was practising from Charles Street, Blackfriars Road, London, in 1827–8.

MACKINTOSH, THOMAS, was a pupil of Robert Abraham. He exhibited student's work at the Royal Academy in 1818 and 1820. In 1840 he was practising from 106 Fenchurch Street, London.

McLERAN, JAMES, of Edinburgh, is mentioned in the contract (1790) for building

NETHERURD HOUSE, PEEBLES-SHIRE, for William Lawson. He was to superintend the work failing 'Mr. Burns' [S.R.O., GD 120/415]. He was presumably the author of some rather crude working drawings for TARBAT HOUSE, ROSS-SHIRE, c. 1790, now at Castle Leod, which are signed 'J. McL.' In 1789, when James McLeran made a report on the state of Kettins Church, Angus, he wrote to the heritors from Tarbat House [S.R.O., HR 10/1]. He is doubtless to be identified with the 'J. McLaren, architect', whose name appears in the Edinburgh directories from 1791/2 to 1793/4.

MAC PACKE, JOSE, see PEACOCK, JAMES

McWILLIAM, ROBERT, exhibited at the Royal Academy from 5 Furnival's Inn, London, in 1818, 1821 and 1823. He showed in 1818 a 'View of a Gothic mansion, with the late alterations and improvements', in 1821 a 'View of Weeting Hall, Norfolk, the residence of Sir R. Sutton, Bt.' and in 1823 a 'View of a Gothic mansion in the county of Southampton'. In 1818 he published An Essay on the Origin and Operation of the Dry Rot, with a View to its Prevention and Cure, to which are annexed, Suggestions on the Cultivation of Forest Trees, and an Abstract of the Several Forest Laws, with a dedication to the Duke of Gordon. In 1837 he wrote two controversial pamphlets about the Grand Junction Railway.

MADDOX, GEORGE (1760–1843), was the son of a builder of Monmouth, to whom he was apprenticed. Having served his term, he went to London, became for a time an assistant in the office of Sir John Soane, but soon found the latter's régime intolerable and left in disgust. In 1789 he was employed to make designs for a new opera house on the north side of Leicester Square to replace the burnt-out King's Theatre in the Haymarket. This came to nothing, but Maddox's design is said to have been adopted for the Grand Theatre at Moscow, which was completed in 1796, but destroyed by fire in 1812. Instead of building in Leicester Square the promoters of the opera house proceeded to convert the Pantheon in Oxford Street for the purpose, with James Wyatt as architect. Maddox appears to have been one of the shareholders who suffered serious loss when the building was destroyed by fire in 1792. This may have contributed to his subsequent failure to establish himself in regular architectural practice, though for this he appears in any case to have been temperamentally unfitted. In 1796 he was assisting S. P. Cockerell in his office in Savile Row, and for the rest of his life he made a living chiefly by tuition and by designing and drawing for other architects. He died on 7 October 1843, in his 83rd year.

In 1824 Maddox was employed by Messrs.

Woolcott & Browning of London to design STRENSHAM COURT, WORCS. (dem. 1974), which they had undertaken to build for a banker named John Taylor. He was not, however, responsible for the Ionic portico and internal furnishings, which were carried out later. In 1825 he was engaged by the same firm to superintend the works at LANCASTER HOUSE, ST. JAMES'S, then being built by them for the Duke of York to the designs of Benjamin Wyatt. In London he designed a number of shop-fronts: one for a chemist in the Strand opposite St. Mary's Church, one for Messrs. Godfrey & Cooke in Southampton Street, another in Tavistock Place, Woburn Square (exhibited at Society of British Artists, 1827), and a long front in High Holborn for a glazier named Tucker. The fronts which he designed for Hammersley's Bank at 69 Pall Mall and for Jones & Loyd's Bank in Lothbury are praised in the *Monthly Magazine* for June 1817, p. 399. In 1819 he exhibited a 'design for a church to be built at Greenock' at the Royal Academy, but it is doubtful whether it was erected.

Maddox was chiefly celebrated as an architectural drawing-master and among his pupils were W. J. Booth, W. M. Brooks, Decimus Burton, John Davies, W. Hosking, Edwin Nash, Charles Parker and Gilbert Scott. In his *Recollections* Scott pays a tribute to Maddox's 'wonderful power of drawing', but describes him as an 'infidel', whose 'conversation on such subjects was truly appalling'. He exhibited occasionally at the Royal Academy, but more often at the Society of British Artists, showing architectural compositions, in oils as well as water-colours, which are said to have been 'as interesting as those of Gandy'. An album of his sketches of classical compositions, etc., is in the R.I.B.A. Drawings Collection, to which it was presented by Decimus Burton in 1869. At the time of his death Maddox is said to have been engaged on a series of about forty etchings of 'architectural groups and fragments'.

[*A.P.S.D.*; *Civil Engineer and Architect's Jnl.* vii, 1844, 6, 118; *Building News* xii, 1865, 659.]

MADDOX, GEORGE VAUGHAN (1802–1864), was the only son of James Maddox of Monmouth, and was no doubt related to George Maddox (*q.v.*). He had a local practice as an architect and builder. In Monmouth his principal work was THE NEW MARKET, PRIORY STREET, opened in 1839, damaged by fire 1964. This formed part of a new street built on arches, and Maddox was presumably responsible for the whole scheme, which formed a handsome new entrance to the town from the north [*Monmouthshire Merlin*, 29 Nov. 1834, 28 Dec. 1839]. Maddox also designed CLEARWELL CHURCH, GLOS., 1829, rebuilt 1866 [I.C.B.S.]; a small house near Monmouth called THE HENDRE, which he

designed as a shooting-lodge for John Rolls in 1829–30, and altered and enlarged in 1833–4 for J. E. W. Rolls, who subsequently employed T. H. Wyatt to enlarge it still further in 1837–40 and 1858 [Monmouthshire Record Office, FIF. 32, 35, 36]; alterations to PENTWYN HOUSE, ROCKFIELD, MONMOUTHSHIRE, which he owned, *c.* 1834 [*Monmouthshire Merlin*, 25 March 1837]; and two houses and shops in PONTYPOOL, MONMOUTHSHIRE, 1840 [*Monmouthshire Merlin*, 30 May 1840]. He died at Hempsted Rectory, Glos., the home of his brother-in-law, the Rev. Thomas Jones, on 27 February 1864, aged 62, and is commemorated by a tablet in Hempsted Church [references to *Monmouthshire Merlin ex inf.* Mr. A. G. Chamberlain].

MAINWARING, BOULTON, described as son of Mary Mainwaring of Audley, Staffordshire, was apprenticed in or about 1715 to John Beech of Barthomley in Cheshire, a joiner [Guildhall Library, index to Apprenticeship Registers in P.R.O.]. By the 1750s he was practising as a surveyor in Bedford Row, London. He was a J.P. for Middlesex, and between 1750 and 1764 carried out some surveying for the county for which, in 1774, he claimed remuneration at the rate of 5 per cent. This was refused, on the grounds that his services had been voluntary [Middlesex County Records, General Order Book No. 10, ff. 4, 7, 11]. He passed carpenters' bills for work done at OSTERLEY PARK, MIDDLESEX, in 1756–9 [accounts at Victoria and Albert Museum], and in 1770 examined the plasterers' bills at BENHAM PLACE, BERKS., then being built to the designs of Lancelot Brown [Berkshire County Record Office, Craven Papers D/EC.A.9]. His unexecuted designs for a gallery in WALTHAMSTOW CHURCH, ESSEX, are referred to in *Walthamstow Vestry Minutes* (Walthamstow Antiquarian Soc., 1925–7, 29–40, 46).

Mainwaring was surveyor to the LONDON HOSPITAL, WHITECHAPEL ROAD, built in stages between 1752 and 1771. The hospital is stated to have been 'Designed by Boulton Mainwaring' on an engraving published in 1753 and reproduced by N. Brett-James, *The Growth of Stuart London*, 1935, 286, and this is confirmed by the minutes of the Building Committee quoted in E. W. Morris, *A History of the London Hospital*, 1910, 83–7. However, the elevation resembled a 'Design for a proposed Infirmary' in the Avery Library, Columbia University, which has been attributed to Isaac Ware: see John Harris, *Catalogue of British Drawings for Architecture, etc., in American Collections*, 1971, 267 and pls. 209–10. The plan is given in *Gentleman's Magazine*, 1752, 103. Mainwaring resigned from the surveyorship of the Hospital on 4 December 1771, on account of advanced age and bad health. Andrew Thornthwaite was a pupil. [*A.P.S.D.*]

MALIPHANT, GEORGE (*c.* 1788–), was probably related to a monumental sculptor called Maliphant who lived at Kidwelly in South Wales,[1] and perhaps to Richard Maliphant, a London builder or surveyor who carried out some alterations and repairs to GATTON PARK, SURREY, for Sir Henry Harpur-Crewe, Bart., when the latter rented that house in 1809 [letter at Calke Abbey, Derbyshire]. George Maliphant became a pupil of Charles Beazley. He was admitted to the Royal Academy Schools in 1809 at the age of 21, and exhibited at the Academy between 1806 and 1829. He also exhibited at the Society of British Artists from 1824 to 1833. He practised in London until the 1840s. He was the author of a volume of *Designs for Sepulchral Monuments.* Unexecuted designs by him for Gothic alterations to HORNBY CASTLE, YORKS. (N.R.), dated 1815, are preserved there. Other works by Maliphant were a conservatory 'proposed to be erected for Sir R. Levinge, Bart., in Ireland', presumably at KNOCKDRIN CASTLE, CO. WESTMEATH [exhib. at R.A. 1812]; the EPISCOPAL JEWS' CHAPEL, BETHNAL GREEN, in collaboration with G. A. Busby, 1813–14, dem. 1895 [exhib. at R.A. 1814 and see p. 175 above]; a villa 'designed to be erected in the Highlands for R. Douglas, Esq.' [exhib. at R.A. 1815]; HAVERSTOCK LODGE, HAMPSTEAD, for J. Lund [exhib. at R.A. 1821 as 'erected']; some cottages at EMBERTON, BUCKS., for John Osmond [exhib. at R.A. 1829 as 'erected']; a design for a proposed 'Gallery of Arts' at Bolton, Lancs. [exhib. at Soc. of British Artists 1831]; and a villa at WEST HILL, WANDSWORTH, SURREY, for W. Newton [exhib. at Soc. of British Artists as 'erected', 1833].

MALPAS, T—, exhibited architectural designs at the Royal Academy from various London addresses between 1796 and 1806, but nothing further is known about him. In 1834–5 Henry Malpas was practising as an architect and surveyor in Nottingham [P. Eden, *Dictionary of Land Surveyors 1550–1850,* 1975–6, 173]. In 1837 he designed a Gothic church at GILLINGHAM, DORSET [*Somerset and Dorset Notes and Queries* xv, 1917, 33; I.C.B.S.]

MALTON, JAMES (–1803), was the younger son of Thomas Malton (1726–1801), architectural draughtsman and writer on perspective. He was born in England, but accompanied his father to Dublin when financial difficulties obliged the latter to live in Ireland. For some time he was employed as a draughtsman in James Gandon's office, but 'he so frequently betrayed all official confidence, and was guilty of so many irregulari-

ties, that it became quite necessary to dismiss him from the employment'. He returned to London in the 1790s, and made a living chiefly as a topographical artist, publishing in 1797 *A Descriptive View of Dublin.* However, his numerous exhibits at the Royal Academy included architectural designs, and he published two early works on picturesque cottages, *An Essay on British Cottage Architecture: being an attempt to perpetuate on Principle, that peculiar mode of building, which was originally the effect of Chance* (1798, 2nd ed. 1804), and a *Collection of Designs for Rural Retreats ... principally in the Gothic and Castle styles of architecture* (1802). These two books establish Malton as a pioneer of the *cottage orné.* Attention should also be drawn to the 'Elevation of a country mansion in the Norman style of architecture' which he exhibited at the Royal Academy in 1801, as it probably represents the earliest recorded attempt to design a modern building in the Norman style. Malton died in Marylebone of brain fever on 28 July 1803. Two designs by him for *cottages ornés,* dated 1798, are in the Victoria and Albert Museum, and a design for a hunting lodge in the castle style dated 1803 now in the Mellon Collection is reproduced in B. Weinreb's *Catalogue* No. 2, 1963, item 84. [*D.N.B.*; J. Gandon, *The Life of James Gandon,* ed. Mulvany, 1846, 67; *Gent's Mag.* 1803 (ii), 791.]

MALTON, THOMAS (1726–1801), born in London in 1726, is said originally to have kept an upholsterer's shop in the Strand. In 1766 he exhibited at the Society of Artists a view of St. Stephen's Church, Walbrook, the first of a number of architectural and perspective drawings which he showed at London exhibitions. He never practised as an architect, but appears to have taught perspective at his house in Poland Street, Soho. In 1776 he published *The Royal Road to Geometry* and in 1775 *A Compleat Treatise on Perspective.* Financial difficulties are said to have led to his removal to Dublin, where he lived for many years and died on 18 February 1801. He was the father of Thomas Malton, junior, and James Malton (*qq.v.*). [S. Redgrave, *Dictionary of Artists,* 1878, 284; *Gent's Mag.* 1801 (i), 277; *D.N.B.*]

MALTON, THOMAS (1748–1804), was the elder son of Thomas Malton (1726–1801), architectural draughtsman and writer on perspective. Having been admitted to the Royal Academy Schools in 1773 as an architectural student, he gained in 1774 the Silver, and in 1782 the Gold, Medal. From 1773 onwards he was a regular exhibitor at the Academy, showing an occasional architectural design for a bath, a temple or a theatre, but chiefly appearing as a topographical artist of considerable skill. He was one of the first to make use of the newly invented process

---

[1] A cottage at Kidwelly was the subject of a drawing exhibited by George Maliphant at the Society of British Artists in 1826.

of aquatinta, and in 1792–1801 published the work by which he is now best known, *A Picturesque Tour through the Cities of London and Westminster*, containing 100 aquatint plates which form a valuable topographical record of Georgian London. At the time of his death he was engaged upon a similar series of views of Oxford, some of which appeared in parts in 1802, and were reissued in 1810. He was also responsible for the series of aquatint views of buildings by Sir Robert Taylor which were published after the latter's death. Several of the original drawings for this series are in the Ashmolean Museum, Oxford. Other drawings attributed to him are in the R.I.B.A. Collection.

Although he never practised as an architect, Malton attempted in 1795 to secure election as an Associate of the Royal Academy, but was rejected on the ground that he was 'only a draughtsman of buildings, but no architect'. From 1783 to 1787 he lived in Conduit Street, where he held evening classes in perspective which were attended by Thomas Girtin and J. M. W. Turner as young men. He died on 7 March 1804, leaving a widow and six children. One of his sons, Charles Malton, became a pupil of Sir John Soane, and won the Royal Academy's Silver Medal in 1807, but does not appear ever to have practised as an architect. [*D.N.B.*; *The Farington Diary*, ed. J. Greig, i, 74, 107, 124, ii, 208; A. T. Bolton, *The Works of Sir John Soane*, 1924, Appendix C, p. xliii.]

MANDEY, VENTERUS (1645–1701), held the post of bricklayer to Lincoln's Inn from 1667 to the time of his death. He was buried at Iver, Bucks., where in the north aisle of the church there is a tablet with the following inscription:

Beneath this place lyes interred the Body of VENTERUS MANDEY of the Parish of St. Giles in the Fields, in the County of Middlesex, Bricklayer; son of MICHAEL MANDEY, Bricklayer, & Grandson to VENTERUS MANDEY, of this parish, Bricklayer, Who had ye honour of being Bricklayer to the Honble Society of Lincoln's Inn from the year of our Lord 1667 to the day of his Death, He was studious in the Mathematicks & wrote & published three Books for Publick Good: one Entituled Mellificium Mensionis or ye Marrow of Measuring; Another of Mechanic powers or the Mystery of Nature & Art Unvayled: the third An Universal Mathematical Synopsis. He also translated into English Directorum Generale Vranometricum and Trigonometria Plana & Sphærica Linearis & Logarithmica: Auctore Fr. Bonaventura Cavalerio Mediolanesi: & some other tracts which he designed to have Printed if Death had not prevented him. He Dyed the 26th day of July *Anno Domini* 1701 aged 56 years & upwards.

536

The work entitled *Mellificium Mensionis* (1682) went through several editions, the fourth of which was published in 1727. It contains a portrait of the author at the age of 37. *Mechanick Powers; or the Mistery of Nature and Art Unvail'd* was written by Mandey in collaboration with James (not Joseph) Moxon and published as their joint work in 1696. There were later editions in 1699, 1702 and 1709. *The Synopsis Mathematica Universalis* was a translation from the Latin of John James Heinlin. It was dedicated to the Benchers of Lincoln's Inn, who, in 1701, acknowledged the gift of a copy by making the author a present of £8 [*The Black Book of Lincoln's Inn* iii, 1899, 100, 147, 209]. Several payments to 'Mr. Mandey the measurer' are recorded in the accounts for building a house at BARN ELMS, SURREY, for Thomas Cartwright of Aynho in 1694–5 [Northants. Record Office, Cartwright papers]. Mandey's library was sold by auction on 15 March, 1713/14. There is a copy of the sale catalogue in the B.M. (S.C. 301(2)). His will is P.C.C. 99 DYER.

MANNERS, GEORGE PHILLIPS (c. 1789–1866), practised in Bath, where he held the post of City Architect from 1823 to 1862. Early in his career he was working with C. Harcourt Masters, and from about 1845 onwards he was in partnership with J. E. Gill. He was a prolific architect who appears to have designed nothing of great distinction. He died at Send Lodge, Ripley, Surrey, on 28 November 1866, aged 77 [Principal Probate Registry, Calendar of Probates; *Gent's Mag.* 1867 (i), 120].

BATH, ST. CATHERINE'S HOSPITAL, 1829, Tudor style [*A.P.S.D.*, *s.v.* 'Bath'].

BATH, reconstructed HOT BATH and added TEPID SWIMMING BATH (dem. 1923) to designs of Decimus Burton, 1830 [W. Ison, *Georgian Buildings of Bath*, 1948, 64].

BATH, ST. MARK'S CHURCH, LYNCOMBE, 1830–2, Gothic; chancel 1883 [*A.P.S.D.*, *s.v.* 'Bath'].

BATH ABBEY CHURCH, restored exterior and repaired interior, 1835 [*Companion to the Almanac*, 1837, 229–31].

BATH, ST. MICHAEL'S CHURCH, 1835–6, Gothic [*Architectural Mag.* iii, 483; iv, 78–9].

BATH, ROYAL VICTORIA PARK, obelisk, 1837 [*A.P.S.D.*, *s.v.* 'Bath'].

WESTON, nr. BATH, SOMERSET, ST. JOHN'S CHURCH, 1838, Gothic; enlarged 1869 by C. E. Davis [I.C.B.S.].

TWERTON CHURCH, SOMERSET, rebuilt 1839; rebuilt 1885–6 [I.C.B.S.].

GODNEY CHURCH, SOMERSET, 1839–40, 'Norman'; chancel 1902 [I.C.B.S.].

EAST HUNTSPILL CHURCH, SOMERSET, 1839, 'Norman' [I.C.B.S.].

CLEEVE CHURCH, nr. YATTON, SOMERSET, 1840, 'Norman' [I.C.B.S.].

BATH, THE CATHOLIC APOSTOLIC CHURCH, VINEYARDS, 1841, 'Norman' [A.P.S.D., s.v. 'Bath'].

BRADFORD-ON-AVON, WILTS., CHRIST CHURCH, BEARFIELD, 1841, Gothic; chancel 1878 [I.C.B.S.].

SHEPTON MALLET, SOMERSET, rebuilt upper part of Market Cross, 1841 [note by F. J. Allen accompanying photograph in National Monuments Record].

BATH, THE COUNTESS OF HUNTINGDON'S SCHOOLS, VINEYARDS, 1842 [S. D. Major, Notabilia of Bath, 1879, 98].

SOUTH BRENT CHURCH, SOMERSET, organ gallery, 1843 [Builder i, 1843, 360].

BATH, THE NEW PRISON, TWERTON, 1843 [A.P.S.D., s.v. 'Bath'].

BROMHAM CHURCH, WILTS., restoration of interior, 1843–4 [Salisbury Diocesan Records].

BATH, THE ABBEY CEMETERY CHAPEL, 1843–4, 'Norman' [A.P.S.D., s.v. 'Bath'].

BERROW CHURCH, SOMERSET, repewed 1844 [I.C.B.S.].

SOUTH STOKE CHURCH, SOMERSET, repaired and enlarged, 1845, Gothic [J. Tunstall, Rambles round Bath, 1848, 135].

TWERTON VICARAGE, SOMERSET, 1845 [Bath Reference Library, R. Naish's MS. collections for a history of Twerton, ex inf. Mr. J. Orbach].

*BATH, ST. MATTHEW'S CHURCH, WIDCOMBE, 1846–7, Gothic [G. N. Wright, Historic Guide to Bath, 1864, 244].

*WESTON-SUPER-MARE, SOMERSET, EMMANUEL CHURCH, 1846–8, Gothic [Builder iv, 1846, 140; Gent's Mag. 1848 (i), 76].

*KINGSTON DEVERILL CHURCH, WILTS., rebuilt 1847, Gothic [Gent's Mag. 1847 (ii), 417].

*HINTON HOUSE, HINTON CHARTERHOUSE, SOMERSET, extensive alterations, 1847 [drawings at Hinton House].

*CLANDOWN CHURCH, SOMERSET, 1847, Gothic [Gent's Mag. 1848 (i), 75].

*TROWBRIDGE CHURCH, WILTS., alterations, 1847–8 [Salisbury Diocesan Records; Ecclesiologist ix, 1849, 106–7].

*BATH, ST. JAMES'S CHURCH, rebuilt tower and remodelled nave, 1848, Italianate; gutted 1942, dem. 1957 [G. N. Wright, Historic Guide to Bath, 1864, 216; W. Ison, Georgian Buildings of Bath, 1948, 74].

BATH, THE ROYAL UNITED HOSPITAL (now Technical College), BEAU STREET, the Chapel, 1849 [A.P.S.D., s.v. 'Bath'].

*FROME, SOMERSET, CHRIST CHURCH, alterations 1851 onwards [G.R.].

*BATH, THE ROYAL MINERAL WATER HOSPITAL, additions (including the Chapel), c. 1850–9 [W. Ison, Georgian Buildings of Bath, 1948, 91].

*BATH, THE CORN MARKET, WALCOT STREET, 1855

[Bath Express, 10 Nov. 1855, ex inf. Mr. J. Orbach].

WESTON-SUPER-MARE, SOMERSET, CHRIST CHURCH, 1855, Gothic [G.R.].

*CLAVERTON CHURCH, SOMERSET, enlarged and altered, 1858 [The Church Rambler i, 1876, 254].

KINGSTON DEVERILL RECTORY, WILTS., altered or rebuilt, 1858 [Salisbury Diocesan Records].

*BATH, THE BLUECOAT SCHOOL, 1859–60, Jacobean style [R. E. M. Peach, Bath Old and New, 1888, 139].

*BATH, CHAPELS in ST. MICHAEL'S CEMETERY, LOWER WESTON, 1862 [advt. in Bath Express, April 1860, ex inf. Mr. J. Orbach].

*BATH, THE GAS WORKS OFFICES, UPPER BRISTOL ROAD, 1858–9 [S. D. Major, Notabilia of Bath, 1879, 10].

MANOCCHI, GIUSEPPE, was an Italian architectural draughtsman employed by the Adam brothers in the 1760s. He may have been engaged by James Adam during his Italian tour in 1760–3, for dated drawings and payments in the Adam bank accounts show that he was in their employment in London by 1765. Manocchi was an accomplished draughtsman of the neo-classical and arabesque ornament that was an important feature of the decorative style created by the Adam brothers. How much he contributed to the Adam repertoire is difficult to say. Some of his drawings are inscribed 'di Mia invenzione', but according to Dr. Stillman 'none of Manocchi's renderings appear to have served as sources for specific Adam decorations'. Manocchi himself considered that he had been 'treated very ungenerously by the Adamses'. In October 1774 Lord Arundell was told by a correspondent in Rome that Manocchi 'has been above a year out of England, and is by no means disposed to return'. A number of his drawings are to be found in the Soane Museum, R.I.B.A. Drawings Collection, Victoria and Albert Museum, Royal Library at Windsor, and Metropolitan Museum of Art, New York. [D. Stillman, The Decorative Work of Robert Adam, 1966, 42–3; John Harris, Catalogue of British Drawings for Architecture, etc. in American Collections, 1971, 136–7; R.I.B.A. Drawings Catalogue: L–N, 63; letter from Fr. Thorpe, S.J., to Lord Arundell, 22 Oct. 1774, at Ugbrooke Park, Devonshire.]

MANSFIELD, GEORGE, belonged to a family of builders established in Gray's Inn Lane, London. He was employed as a surveyor by the Office of Woods and Forests, and also received a small salary from Sir John Soane for surveyor's work between 1797 and 1800. In January 1797 he succeeded John Gorham (q.v.) as bricklayer or sur-

---

* In partnership with J. E. Gill.

veyor to Gray's Inn. He exhibited at the Royal Academy from 1799 to 1803, showing in 1801 a 'Design for a chapel, hall, library and offices, for an Inn of Court', and in 1803 'Chambers now building for the Honourable Society of Gray's Inn'. In 1837 another member of the family named R. J. Mansfield exhibited at the Royal Academy 'An Elevation of Sopwell Hall proposed to be built near St. Albans, Herts.' [A. T. Bolton, *The Works of Sir John Soane*, 1924, p. xliii; *The Pension Book of Gray's Inn*, ed. R. J. Fletcher, ii, 1910, 378].

MAR, EARL OF, *see* ERSKINE

MARDELL, CHARLES, signs three competently drawn elevations for a Georgian mansion among the Bromley-Davenport papers in the John Rylands Library at Manchester. They appear to be connected with Capesthorne Hall, Cheshire, and probably date from about 1730. One of them is reproduced by A. H. and S. M. Gomme in *Trans. Historic. Soc. of Lancs. and Cheshire* cxxi, 1969, 36. No other reference to Mardell has so far been found, and the character of his handwriting suggests that he may have been trained on the Continent.

MARKS, J—, exhibited at the Society of Artists in 1791 and at the Royal Academy from 1790 to 1799. Most of his exhibits were of a topographical character, but they included a 'Design for a town hall and assembly rooms' (1794) and a 'Design for a villa' (1796). He may have been the Joseph Marks who signs two sheets of plans for a house for Lord Suffield in Albemarle Street, London [Soane Museum, lvii, 7].

MARQUAND, JOHN (*c.* 1723–1810), was probably the son of Charles Marquand, a carpenter who in 1741 was one of the contractors for rebuilding Brentford Bridge, Middlesex, to the designs of Charles Labelye [Middlesex Sessions Records, Orders of Court, iv, ff. 200, 211]. In 1736, immediately after the passing of the Act for building a bridge at Westminster, Charles Marquand had gone to Paris in company with Captain (later Admiral) Charles Knowles for the express purpose of gathering information from French engineers about the foundation of piers in deep water. In 1749 he published *Remarks on the Different Construction of Bridges, and Improvements to secure their Foundations on the Different Soils where they are intended to be built.* John Marquand was employed as a surveyor by the Navy Board in the 1780s, and in that capacity probably designed the DOCKYARD CHAPEL of ST. ANNE at PORTSMOUTH in 1784 (cf. Alexander Gibb, *The Story of Telford*, 1935, 9). For many years he was also a surveyor in the Land Revenue Office. He retired in 1809 and died at Brixton on

24 April 1810, aged 87 [*Gent's Mag.* 1810 (i) 498; P.C.C. 260 COLLINGWOOD]. He was a member of the Smeatonian Society of Civil Engineers. The attribution to him of Gwydyr House, Whitehall, by Richardson & Gill, *London Houses from 1660 to 1840* [1911], 70, appears to be without foundation.

MARSH, SAMUEL, is stated by George Vertue to have been the architect employed by the 1st Duke of Newcastle at Nottingham Castle in the 1670s, and at Bolsover Castle, Derbyshire, 'about the same time' [Walpole Soc., *Vertue Note Books* ii, 33]. His employment at BOLSOVER CASTLE in the 1660s is confirmed by documents in the Portland papers at Nottingham University (Pwl 624, a–c), but these do not specify the building in question, and appear to relate to repairs and alterations rather than to new construction. It is probable, however, that Marsh was responsible for the façade and interior of the Hall on the west side of the Great Court. The date of this is uncertain (cf. M. Girouard, The *Smythsons*, 1966, 178, 221, and P. A. Faulkner, *Bolsover Castle*, H.M.S.O. 1972), but the stylistic resemblance to Nottingham Castle is unmistakable, and confirms Vertue's statement.

NOTTINGHAM CASTLE was begun by the Duke of Newcastle in 1674 and completed after his death in 1676. According to Charles Deering's *Historical Account of the Ancient and Present State of Nottingham*, 1751, 186–7, 'the Architect was one March, a Lincolnshire man, who with [others] was made Joint Trustee for finishing the work'. There is, however, no mention of Marsh in the Duke's will, which provides for an expenditure of £2000 a year out of his personal estate on finishing the building 'according to the fforme and modell thereof by me laid and designed' [P.C.C. 22 HALE]. An inscription recorded that the Castle was completed in 1679 in accordance with the Duke's will, 'and by the model he left' [Deering, *op. cit.*]. The building was gutted by fire in 1831 but restored as a Museum and Art Gallery in 1878. A plan and measured drawings made before the fire are in the Victoria and Albert Museum (E.2118–21, 1909), and a wooden model, still known in 1925 as 'Mr. Marsh's model' (*R.I.B.A. Jnl.*, 3rd ser., xxxii, 1925, 520), is preserved in the Museum. The elevations are designed in an elaborate Italian mannerist style with ornament reminiscent of Alessi (some of whose works were illustrated in Rubens's *Palazzi di Genova* of 1622): see photograph and measured drawings in Belcher & Macartney, *Later Renaissance Architecture in England*, 1901.

Marsh was also employed by the Duke of Newcastle at WELBECK ABBEY, NOTTS., for a letter exists in which the Duke directs an agent to 'gett Mr. Marshe to come to Welbeck, – & make a draughte, for the makinge of a good stare to my Ridinge house Chamber' [S. A. Strong, *Catalogue of Letters and other Historical Documents exhibited in the Library at Welbeck*, 1903, 56].

Deering states that Marsh was a Lincolnshire man, and records connect him with the quarries at Haydor and Culverthorpe, nr. Grantham. A rental of Haydor and Culverthorpe in the British Museum shows that Samuel Marsh paid £3 a year for 'Haydor pitts' from 1678 to 1695 [Add. MS. 28647, ff. 3, 157]. Samuel Marsh 'the elder', described as 'gentleman', was living at Culverthorpe in 1666, and Samuel Marsh 'the younger', variously described as 'freemason', 'stonecutter' and 'architect', is found there between 1670 and 1697 [Lincolnshire Record Office, Welby of Denton deeds and BRA 866/5/1]. The elder Marsh was doubtless the 'Mr. Marsh' who supplied stone for building Belton House from a quarry at Haydor in 1684–6 and died in 1686 or the following year [accounts at Belton].

Samuel Marsh was clearly an important architect of the mid seventeenth century with a distinctive style derived from sources different from those which formed the origin of the more restrained manner of Pratt and May which dominated English architecture from 1660 to 1700. In 1654–5 and 1667 he is known to have been carrying out masonry at BELVOIR CASTLE, LEICS. [Belvoir Castle archives, Account 461 and Misc. MS. 67], but here the controlling architect was John Webb (*q.v.*). There was, however, one other important house which may have reflected Marsh's Italian mannerist style. This was THORESBY HOUSE, NOTTS., now known to have been built by William Pierrepont before 1660, though subsequently remodelled in the 1680s (below, p. 804). The ornamentation of the lower windows as illustrated in *Vitruvius Britannicus* i, pl. 91, is similar to that of Marsh's work at Nottingham Castle, and if these windows formed part of the house built *c.* 1650, then it would be logical to attribute them to Marsh.

MARSHALL, EDWARD (*c.* 1598–1675), was a prominent London master mason in the seventeenth century. He was apprenticed to John Clarke (probably the mason of that name who built Lincoln's Inn Chapel), was made free of the Masons' Company in January 1626/7, was admitted to the Livery in 1630/1, was Warden in 1643, and Master in 1650. He carried on business as a stone-mason in Fetter Lane, and was much employed as a monumental mason. In June 1660, despite the claims of John Stone to the post, he was appointed Master Mason to the Crown: in his petition he professed to have 'constantly endeavoured to promote His Majesty's interest in the late Common Council', though according to his rival he was 'a Pretender ... who in no kind served Your Majestie' [*Cal. State Papers Domes-*

tic 1660–1, 13; *Walpole Soc.* vii, 28]. He resigned in 1673 in favour of his son Joshua, and died on 10 December 1675, at the age of 77 years, as recorded on the family monument in the church of St. Dunstan-in-the-West.

Buildings where Marshall worked as a mason-contractor included THE VYNE, HANTS., where in 1654 he built the portico to the designs of John Webb, NORTHUMBERLAND HOUSE, STRAND, where in 1655–7 he carried out work valued at nearly £900, including the 'great stone staires which leads from the dyning room downe to the Terrace', and GUNNERSBURY HOUSE, MIDDLESEX (1658), where he was again working to Webb's designs [W. G. Keith in *R.I.B.A. Jnl.*, 22 July 1933, 733; accounts at Alnwick Castle, V.III.3]. In 1662 he was one of those consulted by the vestry of St. Martin-in-the-Fields about rebuilding the tower of their church [MS. Vestry Minutes in Westminster City Library, vol. iii]. He seems to have been employed by John Cartwright of Aynho, Northants., to supervise the rebuilding of AYNHO PARK after the Restoration, for in several of the surviving contracts (*e.g.* for the staircase and the piers in the garden) it is stated that the work shall be carried out 'according to Mr. Marshall's direction' or 'according to Mr. Edward Marshall's draught' [Northants. Record Office, Aynho papers, book of 'Agreements with the Workmen'] (*C. Life*, 2, 9 and 16 July 1953). He also provided a design for a gallery in Aynho Church, and when John Cartwright advertised his house at BARN ELMS, SURREY, to be let in 1659, prospective tenants were directed to 'enquire further of Mr. Edward Marshall, stone cutter' (*Mercurius Politicus*, 5 May 1659).

Joshua Marshall (1629–78), Edward's eldest son, had, like his father, an extensive business as a monumental sculptor and mason-contractor. He was Master of the Masons' Company in 1670 and again in 1677, and in 1673 succeeded his father as Master Mason to the King. He was one of the mason-contractors for St. Paul's Cathedral, and built the Monument, Temple Bar (in conjunction with Thomas Knight, the City Mason) and six of the City churches. He died in April 1678, and was buried with his father in the church of St. Dunstan-in-the-West.

[*A.P.S.D.*; *D.N.B.*; D. Knoop & G. P. Jones, *The London Mason in the Seventeenth Century*, 1935, 34–5; K. A. Esdaile, *English Monumental Sculpture since the Renaissance*, 1927, 136–7; R. Gunnis, *Dictionary of British Sculptors*, 1968, 254–6; *Wren Soc.* xx, 139; *History of the King's Works*, v.]

MARSHALL, WILLIAM (−*c.* 1793), designed the church of BOURTON-ON-THE-WATER, GLOS., 1784 [D. Royce, *A History of the Church of Bourton-on-the-Water*, 1874, 12]. The nave was rebuilt by T. G. Jackson in 1873–8 and 1891–2, but the domed west tower remains. In 1787 the church of LONGDON, WORCS., was rebuilt to Marshall's designs, incorporating the medieval tower and spire [MS. Vestry Minutes and Churchwardens' Accounts]. The original drawings, signed 'Wm M.', are in the Worcester Diocesan Registry. A new chancel was added in 1868. Marshall appears to have lived at Bourton-on-the-Water. His will, dated 19 July 1789, was proved at Gloucester on 6 May 1793.

MARTYR, THOMAS (*c.* 1777–1852), was the son of a builder. He became a pupil of S. P. Cockerell, and exhibited student's work at the Royal Academy from 1794 to 1799. He subsequently made a continental tour in company with his fellow-pupil, Joseph Kay, and on his return to England commenced practice in about 1805. But on his marriage he entered into partnership with his father, then established 'with a good government connection' at Greenwich. He died on 2 January 1852, aged about 75 years. His son, Richard Smirke Martyr (1811–54), became a pupil of his godfather, Robert Smirke, and after a short continental tour established himself in practice in Greenwich. He was much engaged in surveys and valuations of property in connection with the building of railways in south-east London and Kent. He was surveyor to several local charities and trusts, to the Burney estate, and to the newly created district of Deptford. He was a member of the Architectural Society, and in 1842 became a fellow of the Institute of British Architects on its union with that body. He died at Greenwich on 10 October 1854, aged 43 [*A.P.S.D.*].

MARVIN, JOSEPH, exhibited architectural and topographical drawings at the Royal Academy from 1815 to 1819. He subsequently practised as an architect and surveyor in the Edgware Road. In 1819 he had a pupil named B. May, who exhibited a design for a mausoleum at the Royal Academy from his office.

MASON, GEORGE, was a builder-architect of Ipswich, where he allegedly designed the NEW ASSEMBLY ROOMS [G. Clarke, *History and Description of Ipswich*, 1830, 352]. He was still in business in 1830. He was the father of William Mason (1810–97), who became a pupil of Edward Blore and practised for a few years in Ipswich before emigrating first to New South Wales (1838) and then to New Zealand (1840), where he had a successful career and ranks as the colony's pioneer architect. William Mason's principal works in England were the churches of ST. JAMES, BRIGHTLINGSEA, ESSEX, 1837, Gothic [*Architectural Mag.* iv, 1887, 79–80], ST. BOTOLPH, COLCHESTER, 1837–8, in the 'Norman style' [H. E. von Stürmer, *Historical Guide to Colchester*, 1852, 25], and EAST DONYLAND, ESSEX, 1837–8,

Gothic, on an octagonal plan. The last was intended to be a copy in white brick of the chapter-house at York [G. M. Benton, 'The Destroyed Church of St. Laurence, East Donyland' *Essex Arch. Soc.'s Trans.*, N.S. xix, 1930, 99]. He also designed several Gothic vicarages, and poor-houses at Ipswich, Eye, Epsom and Stroud. [J. Stackpoole, *William Mason, the First New Zealand Architect*, 1971; *Architectural Mag.* iii, 484].

MASON, JOHN, was a London mason who began as an assistant to William Stanton (*q.v.*), and was, through him, employed at Stonyhurst in Lancashire, where he worked as a stone-carver between 1702 and 1713. He later had a yard in the parish of St. Sepulchre's, Holborn [R. Gunnis, *Dictionary of British Sculptors*, 1968, 258]. In 1707 Mason designed the SHIREBURN ALMSHOUSES at STONYHURST. The contract between Sir Nicholas Shireburn, Bart., and Richard Rideing of Waddington, Yorkshire, mason, dated 17 October 1707, specifies that the almshouses are to be built 'according to Mr. John Mason's draught', and Rideing's workmanship was afterwards measured by Mason [contract and account-book among archives of Weld of Lulworth]. These very handsome almshouses, originally built on a remote site, were re-erected at Hurst Green, Stonyhurst, in 1946. They are illustrated in *C. Life*, 22 Oct. 1910, 582–3.

MASON, JOHN, practised in Derby during the second quarter of the nineteenth century. He acted as clerk of works during the building of the County Gaol to the designs of Francis Goodwin in 1823–7, and when it was complete the committee formally recorded their 'approbation of his conduct in the discharge of every part of his duty'. After the riots of 1831 Mason designed eight 'martello towers' to defend the gaol [S. Glover, *History of the County of Derby* ii (1), 1833, 455]. Mason subsequently became surveyor of bridges for the southern part of the county, a post which he still held in 1846. He designed the Gothic LIVERSAGE ALMSHOUSES, LONDON ROAD, DERBY, 1835–6 [S. Glover, *History and Directory of Derby*, 1843, 41], and undistinguished Gothic churches at OCKBROOK, 1835, HULLAND, 1838, and TANSLEY, 1839–40 [all I.C.B.S.].

MASON, WILLIAM, drew three drawings of gateways among the Fitzwilliam papers from Milton House, Northants., in the Northants. Record Office (nos. 37, 38, 39). One is signed 'William Mason June 28 [16]75', another is described as 'A Patterne of ye L. Berkeley's Gate drawn by Wm. Masonne'.

MASON, WILLIAM, was the surveyor responsible for rebuilding DAGENHAM CHURCH, ESSEX, in an unsophisticated Gothic style in 1801–5. His name appears on the west porch [Vestry Minutes in Essex Record Office; *V.C.H. Essex* v, 296 and plate].

MASON, WILLIAM (1810–1897), *see* MASON, GEORGE

MASSEY, EDWARD, *see* SCOLTOCK, SAMUEL

MASSIE, JAMES (–1816), was a builder-architect of Aberdeen, where he had a yard on Castlehill. In 1803–4 he designed the Gothic ST. PETER'S CHURCH, ABERDEEN (R.C.) [minute book at church, *ex inf.* Mr. David Walker]. He is said to have been responsible for the remodelling of FETTERNEAR HOUSE, ABERDEENSHIRE, for John Leslie, but this may not be correct, as the work was apparently not carried out until 1818, two years after his death. The house has been roofless since a fire in 1919. Archibald Simpson (*q.v.*) was in Massie's office for a time. [G. M. Fraser, 'Archibald Simpson and his Times', in *Aberdeen Weekly Jnl.*, 19 April 1918; Charles Leslie, *Historical Records of the Family of Leslie*, 1869; H. Gordon Slade, 'The House of Fetternear', *Proceedings of the Society of Antiquaries of Scotland* ciii, 1970–1.]

MASTERS, CHARLES HARCOURT (1759–), the son of Benedict Masters, a goldsmith of Bath, practised there as an architect and surveyor. In 1786–7 he made a fine set of maps of the roads managed by the Bath Turnpike Trust which are now in the Somerset Record Office at Taunton. In 1789 he constructed a model of Bath to the scale of 30 feet to 1 inch, which he exhibited at his house, and afterwards in London. It was based on a survey of the city which he published in 1794. Masters was much employed as a land surveyor, and was concerned in the development of property in Widcombe and Lyncombe, where he designed several small houses, including those in Cottage (now Bloomfield) Crescent. His most important work was the SYDNEY HOTEL, built in 1796–7 at one end of the hexagonal SYDNEY GARDENS, for whose layout Masters was also responsible. The house, heightened by J. Pinch in 1836, and remodelled by Sir Reginald Blomfield in 1915, is now the Holburne of Menstrie Museum. According to Bryan Little, *The Building of Bath*, 1947, 129, Masters also designed the Gothic BATTLEFIELD HOUSE at LANSDOWN, nr. BATH, in 1802, and a plan for the layout of the grounds of HARPTREE COURT, SOMERSET, made by him *c.* 1802, is in private hands.

Towards the end of his life, Masters 'practised under the name of Harcourt, at first on his own account and later in partnership with George P. Manners'. It was in conjunction with the latter that in 1817–18 he designed the neo-classical

COTHELSTONE HOUSE, SOMERSET (dem. 1968), for E. J. Esdaile [Somerset Record Office, DD/ES, Box 15] (J. P. Neale, *Views of Seats* 2nd ser., iv, 1828).
[W. Ison, *The Georgian Buildings of Bath*, 1948, 43, 95–8; information from Mr. I. P. Collis, Mr. Bryan Little and Mr. J. Orbach.]

MASTERS, GEORGE, was the architect employed by Thomas Stonor to carry out alterations to the interior of STONOR PARK, OXON., in 1834. They included the formation of a drawing-room with a screen of Greek Ionic columns. He was dismissed before the work was completed [C. Hussey in *C. Life*, 20 Oct. 1950; *V.C.H. Oxon.* viii, 143].

MATHEWS, CHARLES JAMES (1803–1878), was the son of Charles Mathews (1776–1835), a well-known actor. In 1819 he became a pupil of Augustus Pugin. On the expiry of his articles in 1823 he went over to Ireland to build a house for Lord Blessington at Mountjoy Forest, Co. Tyrone. No progress was made with the house, but Mathews became intimate with Lord Blessington, who invited him to spend some time in Naples with a party of aristocratic friends, whom he delighted by his humour and vivacity. In 1824 he became architect to an iron and coal company at Coed Talwyn in North Wales, and while in this employment designed an inn, a bridge, some cottages and a house for the director called HARTSHEATH HALL, nr. MOLD in FLINTSHIRE, 1825. Two years later he returned to London, where for a short time he worked in Nash's office. An allowance from his father allowed him to make another visit to Italy in 1827 in company with James D'Egville. In 1832 he became District Surveyor for Bow and Bethnal Green, but in 1835 he finally abandoned architecture for the stage, where he achieved some celebrity. A sketch of a vase made by Mathews in Rome is in the R.I.B.A. Drawings Collection. [*The Life of C. J. Mathews*, ed. C. Dickens, 1879; *Builder* xxxvi, 1878, 695; *D.N.B.*; Dudley Harbron, 'Charles Mathews', *Arch. Rev.* lxxx, 1936, 77–80.]

MATHEWSON, GEORGE, practised in Dundee from 1832 or 1833 until about 1853, the date of his death or retirement. His unexecuted designs for the Watt Institute at Dundee are in Dundee Public Library [information from Mr. David Walker].

? CUNMONT HOUSE, NEWBIGGING, nr. DUNDEE, 1834 [probably the house whose contract was advertised in *Dundee Advertiser*, 27 Jan. 1834].
DUNDEE, ST. ANDREW'S R.C. CHURCH, NETHERGATE, 1836, Gothic [C. Mackie, *Historical Description of Dundee*, 1836, 129].

DUNDEE, ELM LODGE and houses in MAGDALEN PLACE, 1836–40 [*Dundee Advertiser*, 12 Feb. 1836].

DUNDEE, new street on the CROFT OF BLAIRGOWRIE, 1836 [*Dundee Advertiser*, 16 Sept. 1836].

BEACH COTTAGE, 23 DOUGLAS TERRACE, WEST FERRY, DUNDEE, for himself, *c.* 1838.

DUNDEE LUNATIC ASYLUM, additions, 1838 [*Dundee Advertiser*, 23 March 1838].

DUNDEE, north-east corner of UNION STREET, 1839 [*Dundee Advertiser*, 14 Aug. 1840].

DUNDEE, DUDHOPE CHURCH (now Repertory Theatre), LOCHEE ROAD, 1839, Romanesque [*Dundee Advertiser*, 7 Oct. 1839].

DUNDEE, WALLACETOWN CHURCH, 1840, Romanesque; altered 1876 [*Forfarshire Illustrated*, Dundee, 1843, 23].

INVERARITY, ANGUS, SCHOOL, 1840 [*Dundee Advertiser*, 20 March 1840].

DUNDEE, MAINS SCHOOL (now private house called 'St. Malo'), 1841 [*Dundee Advertiser*, 22 Jan. 1841].

MONIFIETH, ANGUS, LINLATHEN SCHOOL, 1841 [*Dundee Advertiser*, 26 Feb. 1841].

DUNDEE, ST. DAVID'S PARISH SCHOOL, LARCH STREET, 1842; dem. [*Dundee Advertiser*, 7 Jan. 1842].

DUNDEE, ST. DAVID'S FREE CHURCH, 1843 [*Dundee Advertiser*, 28 July 1843].

ARBROATH, ANGUS, ST. THOMAS'S R.C. CHURCH, 1846–8 [article in *Dundee Advertiser*, 9 Sept. 1899].

DUNDEE, ST. MARY'S R.C. CHURCH, FOREBANK, 1850; towers added 1900–1 [*Dundee Advertiser*, 18 Oct. 1850].

MATSON, CHARLES (*c.* 1797–   ), was a pupil of Joseph Kay. He entered the Royal Academy Schools in 1815, aged 18, and exhibited at the Academy from 1816 to 1819, his last exhibit being a 'View of Heath Lodge, Hampstead, the seat of C. King Esq.'

MATSON, JOHN (1760–1826), the son of a builder, was in business as a master builder at Bridlington from about 1790 until 1823, when he removed to London. As a young man he was trepanned into the Indian Army, and underwent a series of adventures which earned him some celebrity. He had received instruction in draughtsmanship, and may have designed some of the buildings which he erected in Bridlington, which included the Baths and 'several good houses'. In 1806 he built the lighthouse on Flamborough Head to the designs of Samuel Wyatt. His son John moved to London in 1817, and presumably built Matson Terrace, Kingsland Road, Shoreditch, where his father died on 23 February 1826. [*Indian Warfare; or the Extraordinary Adventures of John Matson, the Kidnapped Youth late of Kingsland Road, London, and formerly of*

Bridlington Quay in the county of York, *Architect and Builder*, 1842; information from Mr. Francis Johnson, F.R.I.B.A.]

MATTHEWS, JAMES TILLY (–*c.* 1814), was a London tea merchant who became insane and was an inmate of the Bethlehem Hospital from 1797 until 1813. While in confinement he amused himself with drawing and engraving, and was the author of a publication entitled *Useful Architecture*, in which he proposed to give designs for buildings 'from the £50 Cot to the £200,000 Mansion, mostly grounded on the Grecian, Roman, Gothic, and Plain Styles of Architecture'. The first and only part was published in 1812.

MATTHEWS, WILLIAM LAUGHER (*c.* 1798–1827), was the son of W. Matthews of Birmingham. He died at Penzance on 10 May 1827, aged 29 [*Aris's Birmingham Gazette*, 21 May 1827]. He exhibited architectural designs at the Royal Academy in 1822–6 and at the Birmingham Society of Artists in 1827.

MATTHEWS, WILLIAM (*c.* 1780–1847), was a builder and surveyor of Ashby-de la-Zouche in Leicestershire, where he died on 18 June 1847, aged 67. In 1825 he was the surveyor who supervised the rebuilding of the nave of SWANNINGTON CHURCH, LEICS. (not necessarily to his own designs) [G.R.], and in 1831 he altered STONEY STANTON RECTORY, LEICS. (rebuilt 1844) [J. D. Bennett, *Leicestershire Architects 1700–1850*, Leicester 1968].

MAUND, ARTHUR (*c.* 1722–1803), 'architect of this town and county', died at Brecon on 24 March 1803, aged 81, and is commemorated by a monument in the north transept of the cathedral. An architect called Andrew Maund was practising in Worcester in 1828–9.

MAWLEY, EDWARD (–1826), was an architect of whose career little is known before 1821, when he was appointed architect to the Commissioners for Building New Churches. He was a member of the Painter-Stainers' Company and an original member of the Surveyors' Club, of which he was President in 1799. In 1807 he exhibited at the Royal Academy a 'Design for a gentleman's house, now building in Oxfordshire'. In 1824 he was staying at STANFORD HALL, NORTHANTS., in order to give Mrs. Otway Cave advice about some proposed alterations there [Church Commissioners, file 21744, part 5]. He died on 30 January 1826, as the result of a carriage accident, and was succeeded as the Commissioners' architect by J. H. Good. J. Starkey was a pupil.

Henry Mawley (d. 1871), Edward's son, followed the same profession and was in turn succeeded by his son Septimus Mawley. His works included HOLY TRINITY CHURCH, HOUNSLOW, MIDDLESEX, Gothic, 1828–9 [G. J. Aungier, *History of Syon Monastery and Isleworth*, 1840, 508–9]; some chambers in DEVEREUX COURT, MIDDLE TEMPLE [exhibited at R.A. 1841]; and TWINING'S COFFEE HOUSE, 215 STRAND [exhibited at R.A. 1841].

MAY, HUGH (1621–1684), was the seventh son of John May, a Sussex gentleman with an estate at Rawmere in the parish of Mid Lavant, three miles north of Chichester.[1] He was baptized at Mid Lavant on 2 October 1621. Nothing is known of his early life, but in 1669 he told Pepys that he had served the Duke of Buckingham 'for twenty years together, in all his wants and dangers'. This statement is confirmed by the account-book of Sir Charles Cottrell, the Duke's steward, which in 1650–1 records 'My charges to Rotterdam and the Hagh, going to meet Mr. May when he came out of Scotland', and indicates that the latter was engaged in effecting the transfer of works of art from York House to Holland, where they were to be sold for the Duke's benefit.[2] Letters from May to Cottrell, written in London during this period, show that he was living with 'my friend Mr. Lely' in Covent Garden, and in 1656, when Lely had a pass to go to Holland, May was allowed to accompany him as his 'servant'. This was presumably an expedient designed to get May out of the country without attracting unwelcome attention. For the object of his journey was to join the exiled Court, and the favour shown to May after the Restoration shows that he must have rendered not inconsiderable services to the Royalist cause. On 29 June 1660, he was appointed Paymaster of the Works and in that capacity dealt with the financial side of the great overhaul of the royal palaces which occupied the years immediately after 1660. In April 1666 he received a warrant to act as Surveyor of the Works during the illness of Sir John Denham, and when the latter died in 1669 he hoped to be his successor. But he was (as he told Pepys) 'put by' in favour of Wren, and had to be content with the Comptrollership, to which he had been promoted in June 1668. This gave him an income of less than £200 a year, whereas

Wren as Surveyor was receiving nearly £400, besides the many incidental perquisites of his office. In conversation with Pepys, May attributed this disappointment to the ingratitude of the Duke of Buckingham. 'But he tells me', Pepys noted, 'the King is kind to him, and hath promised him a pension of £300 a year out of the Works' – an increment which was, in fact, granted to him on 24 March 1669, 'as a mark of the King's gracious acceptance of his loyal and faithfull service'. Moreover in the following year he succeeded his brother Adrian both as Clerk of the Recognizances in the Courts of Common Pleas and King's Bench and as inspector of French and English gardeners at Whitehall, St. James's, Greenwich and Hampton Court. The latter post was worth £200 a year, while the former entitled him to a fee of 3s. 4d. for each recognizance. Finally, in November 1673, within a few days of Wren's appointment as architect to St. Paul's, May succeeded Hartgill Baron as Comptroller of the Works at Windsor, and took charge of the reconstruction of the Castle for Charles II.

May's ability as a practising architect had already been shown at Eltham Lodge and Cornbury House, and as Pepys's Diary shows, he had the reputation of being 'a very ingenious man'. He does not seem to have shared Wren's scientific interests, but both John Evelyn and Roger North were his friends, and it was with his help that in 1664 the former published his translation of Freart's *Parallel of Architecture*, 'perhaps the most influential work of its kind in English'. In 1665–6 he was involved, with Pratt, Webb and Wren, in the problem of how best to repair the decrepit fabric of old St. Paul's Cathedral. After the Great Fire, he was one of the three surveyors nominated by the King to supervise the rebuilding of the City in conjunction with three representatives chosen by the Lord Mayor and Corporation. As a public official with experience of the finance of building, he was well qualified to act in this capacity, and although he did not himself design any of the new churches and public buildings, his duties as a commissioner took up so much of his time that in March 1667 he was allowed to have a deputy at the Office of Works on account of his 'extraordinary business'.

As Comptroller of the Works, and architect to Windsor Castle, May was a well-known figure in the Court of Charles II, and it was for Court acquaintances that most of his recorded works were erected. The houses which he designed for them are remarkable for the introduction of what has been described as 'a mature baroque style of interior treatment', which he achieved with the aid of Verrio, the painter, and Grinling Gibbons, who owed his first important commissions to May. Unfortunately, few of his works survive, and his career has been overshadowed by that of

[1] Pedigrees of the family are printed in Dallaway's *Western Division of Sussex*, 1815, 114, Nichols's *Leicestershire* iv (2), 548, and *Harleian Soc.* viii, 229–30.

[2] I am indebted to Mr. T. Cottrell-Dormer for allowing me to examine his ancestor's account-book, preserved at Rousham Park, Oxon. There is a story that May fought at the Battle of Worcester under the Duke of Buckingham, and was entrusted with the latter's George, which he preserved through all dangers and eventually restored to his master in Holland (Collins's *Peerage* iii, 1812, 783).

his rival, Wren. But of his importance as one of the two or three men who determined the character of English domestic architecture after the Restoration there can be no doubt, and his work at Windsor is of the greatest interest in the history of English baroque architecture. Of his ability as a draughtsman, nothing is known, for no drawings by his hand have so far been identified.[1] But that he understood the technicalities of architecture is shown by an observation of John Aubrey that ''twas Mr. Hugh May that brought in the Staff-moulding on solid right Angles, after the Restauration of the King. The fashion has taken much' (*Chronologia Architectonica*, 1671 – Bodleian, MS. Top. Gen. c. 25, f. 179).

May's association with Lely – first recorded during the Commonwealth – was to be one of long standing, for in later years May asked Lely's advice when designing Cassiobury Park, and they were both consulted by Sir Ralph Verney about the value of a monument executed by Grinling Gibbons. At Audley End there is a portrait of May by Lely which shows him in company with the painter, and when Lely died in 1680, May was one of his executors. May himself died on 21 February 1683/4, aged 62, and was buried in the family vault in Mid Lavant Church. When the vault collapsed in 1829, May's coffin-plate was removed to the chancel. The inscription on it is as follows:

Hugh May Esqr Comptroller of the Works to King Charles the Second. Comptroller to the Castle of Windsor and by his Maj.^tie appointed to be Sole Architect in Contriving and Governing the Works in the Great Alterations made by his Maj.^tie in that Castle Dyed the 21th day of February 168¾ in the Sixty Second yeare of his Age.

By his will [P.C.C. 32 HARE], dated 19 January 1683/4, and witnessed by, among others, Nicholas Hawksmoor, May left to his nephew Thomas, son of his elder brother John, £1000, all the silver plate given to him by the Earl of Essex, and the leases of certain properties which he had purchased 'for the greater conveniency they are to Rawmeare estate'. He also left £100 towards the repair of Mid Lavant Church, 'in case I doe not see and procure it to bee repaired in my Lifetime', and a similar sum to the fabric of Chichester Cathedral. His executors were Sir Henry Capell, Thomas May and Nathaniel Cole, the King's Chaplain. A miniature portrait of May painted by Samuel Cooper in 1653 was acquired for the Royal Library at Windsor in 1958. It is

reproduced in *The History of the King's Works* v, pl. 2.

[*A.P.S.D.*; *Wren Soc.* xx, 141–2; *Cal. State Papers Domestic: Charles II, passim; Cal. Treas. Books 1667–8* ii, pp. xxx–xxxiii; *Builder* xi, 645; C. H. Collins Baker, *Lely and the Stuart Portrait Painers*, 1912, i, 142, 149, ii, 132–3; the *Diaries* of Evelyn and Pepys; *Sussex Arch. Colls.* cvii, 1969, 1–3; T. F. Reddaway, *The Rebuilding of London after the Great Fire*, 1940, 57; G. F. Webb, *Wren* (Great Lives series); G. F. Webb, 'The Architectural Antecedents of Sir Christopher Wren', *R.I.B.A. Jnl.*, 27 May 1933, 582; G. F. Webb, 'Baroque Art', *Proceedings of the British Academy* xxxiii, 1947; Kerry Downes, *English Baroque Architecture*, 1966, *passim*; *History of the King's Works* v, 1976, *passim*.]

CORNBURY HOUSE, OXON., rebuilt east front and designed stables and chapel for the 1st Earl of Clarendon, 1663–8 [Evelyn's *Diary*, 18 Oct. 1664; memoir of the Strong family in R. Clutterbuck, *History of Hertfordshire* i, 1815, 167; accounts in Bodleian, MS. Clarendon 78, f. 167, and P.R.O., C 104/109] (*C. Life*, 22 Sept. 1950). The interior has been completely altered at various times.

ELTHAM LODGE, KENT, for Sir John Shaw, Bart., 1664 [*The Architecture of Sir Roger Pratt*, ed. R. T. Gunther, 1928, 232] (*C. Life*, 9–16 Aug. 1919; H. A. Tipping, *English Homes, Period IV* (i), 1929, 93–110).

LONDON, BERKELEY HOUSE, PICCADILLY, for the 1st Lord Berkeley of Stratton, 1665; dem. 1733 [Evelyn's *Diary*, 25 Sept. 1672; *The Architecture of Sir Roger Pratt*, ed. R. T. Gunther, 1928, 139, 261].

*LONDON, BURLINGTON HOUSE, PICCADILLY, supervised completion of house, 1667–8, for the 1st Earl of Burlington after the latter had bought it in an unfinished state from Sir John Denham; completely remodelled in the eighteenth and nineteenth centuries. It is possible that May had also been Denham's architect, but evidence is lacking [*Survey of London* xxxii, 391–2 and illustrations].

*HOLME LACY HOUSE, HEREFS., was built by Anthony Deane of Uffington for the 1st Viscount Scudamore, by a contract dated 16 Feb. 1673/4, in which it is stated that many of the details were to be copied from those of Sir John Duncombe's house at Battlesden, Beds. It was agreed that in the event of any dispute both parties should submit to the 'finall Arbitrament and determination of Hugh May Esqr.', who may possibly have made the designs [P.R.O., Chancery Masters' Exhibits, 'Duchess of Norfolk Deeds', Box M, bundle 24, no. 7789] (*C. Life*, 12–19 June 1909).

---

[1] He may have relied to some extent on draughtsmen, for the Cornbury accounts (Bodleian, MS. Clarendon 78) contain two payments 'For Drawing the first Draft of Cornbury for Mr. May' and 'For Drawing the 2nd. Draft of Cornbury for Mr. May'.

---

* Doubtful or inadequately documented works.

WINDSOR CASTLE, remodelling of the Upper Ward, including St. George's Hall and the King's Chapel, 1675–84 [W. H. St. J. Hope, *Windsor Castle*, 1913, 312 *et seq.*; *History of the King's Works* v, 315–28]. Nearly all May's work has since been destroyed or altered.

CASSIOBURY PARK, HERTS., for the 1st Earl of Essex, *c.* 1677–80; remodelled by James Wyatt *c.* 1800; dem. 1922 [Evelyn's *Diary*, 18 April 1680; a letter from May to the Earl of Essex about 'severall meetings and consultations concerning the frontis's peece on the courteside at Caishobury' which he had had with Lely is printed in part by C. H. Collins Baker, *Lely and the Stuart Portrait Painters* ii, 1912, 133; what appear to be some of the original working drawings for the plasterwork are in Bodleian, MS. Gough Drawings a.3] (J. Britton, *Cassiobury Park*, 1837, gives plans and views; *C. Life*, 17 Sept. 1910).

*MOOR PARK, HERTS., was built *c.* 1680–4 for James, Duke of Monmouth, by a team of Office of Works craftsmen, whose names are given in a summarized account in S.R.O., GD 224/1059/14. A surviving contract for mason's work between the Duke and Thomas Wise, the King's Master Mason, dated March 1680/1, provides that both parties shall abide by the judgement of Hugh May in case of disagreement [B.M., Add. MS. 51326, ff. 4–5]. It is therefore possible that the house was designed by May. It was rebuilt *c.* 1725.

*KILKENNY CASTLE, CO. KILKENNY, IRELAND, was altered and embellished, *c.* 1682, for the 1st Duke of Ormonde. Sir William Robinson, the Surveyor-General of Ireland, was probably the architect [cf. Bodleian, Carte MS. 54, f. 74], but in December 1681 the Earl of Longford wrote to the Duke of Ormonde from England to say that he had gone 'immediately to Mr. May to consult with him about the Proportion of the Peeres [presumably of a gateway] in which as yett he is not of opinion to make any alteration from the draught he sent & your Grace returned' [National Library of Ireland, Ormonde papers, MS. 2417, f. 237, misquoted in Hist. MSS. Comm., *Ormonde*, N.S. vi, 282–3, *ex inf.* Dr. R. Loeber].

CHISWICK, MIDDLESEX, house for Sir Stephen Fox, 1682–3; dem. 1812 [Evelyn's *Diary*, 30 Oct. 1682; T. Faulkner, *History of Brentford, Ealing and Chiswick*, 1845, 372–3].

*DINGLEY HALL, NORTHANTS., was rebuilt in the 1680s by Sir Edward Griffin. He was Groom of the Chamber to Charles II and his sister Anne married Hugh May's cousin James May of Coldrey, Hants. As Sir Gyles Isham has suggested, he may well have obtained the de-

sign from Hugh May (*C. Life*, 16–23 April 1921).

MAYHEW, JAMES GRAY (1771–1845), was born on 8 February 1771. He exhibited architectural designs at the Royal Academy from 1792 to 1796. In 1798 he became Surveyor to the Westminster Fire Office and in 1823 District Surveyor of the Parish of St. James, Westminster. Mayhew's practice consisted chiefly in surveying and repairing buildings for the Fire Office. In 1808–10 he was responsible for converting premises in King Street, Covent Garden, as offices for its use [Westminster Fire Office Records, *ex inf.* Mr. G. F. Osborn]. Mayhew died on 24 March 1845, aged 75, leaving a son, Charles Mayhew, who succeeded him in both his surveyorships. Several notebooks and sketch-books belonging to J. G. Mayhew and his son were sold at Sotheby's on 27 October 1970. [*A.P.S.D.*]

MEAD, JOHN CLEMENT (1798–1839), born 3 April 1798, was the son by his second wife of C. Mead, a London surveyor who in 1794 designed BRYNBELLA, DENBIGHSHIRE, for Gabriel Piozzi [exhib. at R.A. 1794; letters from Mead to Piozzi in John Rylands Library, Manchester, English MS. 607]. Mead received his training in his father's office, and was admitted to the Royal Academy Schools in 1815. In 1820 he obtained the second premium in the competition for the new General Post Office in London, drawings of which he exhibited at the Academy in 1824 and 1826. In 1821 he won the competition for the new hall of the Salters' Company, but the designs executed were by the Company's surveyor H. Carr. In 1823 he competed for the completion of King's College, Cambridge, and in the following year made designs (reproduced in *Arch. Rev.*, July 1946, p. lxii), which were not adopted, for a new court at St. John's College, Cambridge. In 1822–4 he designed and erected the CAMBRIDGE OBSERVATORY, which is described and illustrated in Weale's *New Survey of London* ii, 1853, 670–2: see also Willis and Clark, iii, 195. His other works included the premises of Messrs. Rundell, Bridge & Rundell on Ludgate Hill, built 1825, the designs for which he exhibited in 1827. He visited France, where he was professionally employed, and became much interested in the system of abattoirs as well as the casting of works of art in bronze. He died, after a long illness, on 15 January 1839, at the age of 41, and was buried at Piddletrenthide, Dorset, to which place he had retired. He left a widow and three sons. [*A.P.S.D.*; *The Farington Diary*, ed. J. Greig, viii, 42, 114, 115.]

MEADOWS, JOHN (*c.* 1732–1791), practised as an architect and surveyor in New Peter Street, Westminster. Most of his recorded works were,

---

* Doubtful or inadequately documented works.

however, in Devonshire. In 1779 he rebuilt HART-LAND ABBEY for Paul Orchard in a Gothic style [R. P. Chope, *The Book of Hartland*, 1940, 65]; in 1782 he repaired EGGESFORD RECTORY [Exeter Diocesan Records]; and in *c.* 1790 he rebuilt ARL-INGTON COURT for J. P. Chichester in a plain Georgian style [R. Polwhele, *History of Devonshire* iii, 1797, 401]. The last house was again rebuilt in 1820–3, owing it is said to the defective construction of Meadows's building. In about 1780–5 Meadows supervised the rebuilding of HURSTBOURNE PARK, HAMPSHIRE, for the 2nd Earl of Portsmouth to the designs of James Wyatt [Harrison's *Views of Seats*, 1787]. This house was destroyed by fire in 1870. It was at Hurstbourne that Meadows made his will on 15 November 1786 [P.C.C. 583 BEVOR]. He died at Arlington on 26 September 1791, aged 59, and is commemorated by a tablet on the south wall of the church there. His daughter Jane married as her second husband the Devonshire surveyor James Rendle, or Rendel, and was the mother of the civil engineer James Meadows Rendel (1799–1856).

MEAR, STEPHEN (*c.* 1752–1827), and his son WILLIAM, were architects and builders in Norwich. Stephen Mear died on 15 August 1827, in his 76th year, and is commemorated by a tablet in the church of St. John de Sepulchre. William Mear designed the CORN EXCHANGE and the adjoining EXHIBITION ROOM for the Norwich artists, 1826–8, dem. [Chambers, *Norfolk Tour* iii, 1829, 1109–10]. He is also said to have remodelled MOUSEHOLD HOUSE, NORWICH, in 1821 [letter in *C. Life*, 5 May 1966]. He and Stephen Mear (junior) were declared bankrupt in 1837 [*Norfolk Chronicle*, 5 June 1841, *ex inf.* Mr. D. C. Young].

MEDLAND, JAMES, was a pupil in 1789 of Charles Beazley, and in 1790 of Samuel Robinson. He exhibited at the Royal Academy from 1789 to 1828, and at the Society of British Artists in 1826 and 1827. He practised first in Newington Butts and later (in the 1820s) in the New Kent Road. J. Leachman and J. P. Pritchett were his pupils. In 1805 he erected a terrace of five houses, now NOS. 17–25 CLAPHAM ROAD, BRIXTON [*Survey of London* xxvi, 107]. In 1813–14 he altered BEDD-INGTON HOUSE, SURREY, for Henry Bridges [exhib. at R.A.]. His last exhibit at the Royal Academy (1828) was a 'Design for a villa intended to be erected in Kerry'. He was presumably the father of James Medland of Gloucester (*c.* 1808–94).

MEDWORTH, JOSEPH (*c.* 1754–1827), was a native of Wisbech, Cambs. He began life as a bricklayer, and became a builder in Bermondsey. By 1793 he had acquired sufficient capital to be able to buy the seventeenth-century house known as Wisbech Castle, which was then being offered for sale by the Bishop of Ely. He developed its grounds by building the Crescent 'according to a design which he had previously drawn'. Subsequently he built further houses to form a circus, and began to lay out approach roads to the bridge, the market and the churchyard. In 1811 he offered the Castle itself to the Corporation for £2000 for use as a grammar school. The offer was refused, whereupon Medland pulled the house down and on its site erected the present low, two-storied building as his own residence. When the Corn Exchange (now the Exchange Hall) was built in 1811, Medworth was asked to oversee the work, though it is not certain that he made the designs. He was Bailiff of Wisbech in 1819. He died on 17 October 1827, aged 73. There is a monument to his memory in Wisbech Churchyard.

[N. Walker and T. Craddock, *History of Wisbech and the Fens*, 1849, 278–9; F. J. Gardiner, *History of Wisbech and Neighbourhood 1848–98*, 1898, 15, 473 ff.; anonymous article on 'The Five Castles of Wisbech' in *The Isle of Ely and Wisbech Advertiser*, 28 Dec. 1932; F. J. Rudsdale, 'Wisbech Castle', Wisbech Society's *Annual Report* for 1946; Arthur Oswald, 'Wisbech, Cambridgeshire', *C. Life*, 23–30 May 1947.]

MEE, ARTHUR PATRICK (1802–1868), son of Joseph Mee, of Upper Berkeley Street, London, was a pupil of Sir John Soane from 1818 to 1823. He was admitted to the Royal Academy Schools in 1822, and subsequently travelled in Italy. He began to exhibit at the Academy in 1824. In 1838–9 he was associated with Alexis de Châteauneuf of Hamburg in competing for the new Royal Exchange in London; they obtained the second premium of £200 for a design whose principal features appear to have been due to Châteauneuf [*Civil Engineer and Architect's Jnl.* ii, 1839, 437; *Architectural Review* cxl, 1966, 366–7, figs. 4–5]. Mee was a Fellow of the R.I.B.A. and in 1849–56 a member of its Council. He died on 19 September 1868 [*A.P.S.D.*; A. T. Bolton, *The Works of Sir John Soane*, Appendix C, p. xlvi].

HARE PARK, nr. NEWMARKET, CAMBS., additions for General Thomas Grosvenor, 1834 [exhib. at R.A. 1834].

GRAVESEND, KENT, a proprietary school, 1835, 'Elizabethan' style [*Gent's Mag.* 1836 (i), 654].

HAMBURG, GERMANY, villa, In de Bost 39/40, Hamburg-Nienstedten, for R. Godeffroy, 1836 [exhibited at R.A. 1837; cf. G. Dehio, *Handbuch der Deutschen Kunstdenkmäler*, Hamburg, Schleswig-Holstein, ed. Johannes Habich, 1971, 68].

WOOD GREEN, MIDDLESEX, FISHMONGERS' AND POULTERERS' ALMSHOUSES, in association with W. Webb, 1847–8, 'Elizabethan' style [*A.P.S.D.*].

LONDON, ST. GEORGE'S HOSPITAL, GROSVENOR PLACE, extensive alterations, 1850, addition of upper storey, 1859, addition of new wing, 1868 [*A.P.S.D.*].

MEIKLEHAM, ROBERT STUART (*c.* 1782–   ), was admitted to the Royal Academy Schools in 1813 at the age of 21. All that is known of his subsequent career is that he published several books on steam engines under his own name and wrote, under that of 'Robert Stuart, Architect and Civil Engineer', *A Dictionary of Architecture* in three volumes that was published in or about 1830 by Jones & Co. at the Temple of the Muses in Finsbury Square.

MENELAWS, ADAM (–1831), was an architect of Scottish origin who, like William Hastie (*q.v.*), found employment in St. Petersburg. Little appears at present to be known of his activities in Russia, but he is credited with the design of several ornamental buildings in the Alexander Park at Tsarskoe Selo, including a ruined chapel (1827), a Turkish elephant house (1828), and the Egyptian Gate, consisting of two cast-iron pylons covered with Egyptian decoration [G. H. Hamilton, *The Art and Architecture of Russia*, 1954, 222].

MEREDITH, GEORGE (1762–   ), born on 1 December 1762, was articled to John Yenn in 1780 and was admitted to the Royal Academy Schools the same year. He remained in Yenn's office until 1795, and exhibited at the Academy from 1782 to 1799. His exhibits consisted chiefly of measured drawings of medieval architecture, and he was elected a Fellow of the Society of Antiquaries. He was probably the architect called Meredith who wrote a life of Sir William Chambers for C. G. Dyer's *Biographical Sketches of Illustrious and Eminent Men*, 1819.

MEREDITH, JAMES, was paid £78 10s. for 'drawing and attendance' in connection with the building of HOLY TRINITY CHURCH, WARRINGTON, LANCS., in 1758–60. No other architect is mentioned in the detailed building accounts [W. Beamont, *Warrington Church Notes*, 1878, 140–1].

MEREDITH, MICHAEL (–1865), was admitted to the Royal Academy Schools in 1809. He subsequently practised in London, dying at 99 Guilford Street on 16 June 1865 [Principal Probate Registry, Calendar of Probates]. In 1827 he altered or rebuilt the VICARAGE at OLD WINDSOR, BERKS. [Salisbury Diocesan Records], and in 1828–30 he designed ALL SAINTS CHURCH, SKINNER STREET, BISHOPSGATE, Gothic, dem. 1869 [*Architectural Mag.* iii, 1836, 498].

MEW, HENRY, was an architect and builder at Brighton, where he designed the classical church of ALL SOULS, EASTERN ROAD, 1833–4, remodelled by G. Scott in 1879 [*V.C.H. Sussex* vii, 260]. In 1830, in conjunction with — Stroud, he built a Gothic school in CHURCH STREET [A. Dale, *Fashionable Brighton*, 1947, 62]. He was still in practice in 1853.

MEYMOTT, WILLIAM, junior (*c.* 1761–   ), was admitted to the Royal Academy Schools in 1787 at the age of 26. He exhibited at the Academy from Church Street, Southwark, in 1784 and 1788. A 'large handsome house' on the south side of St. George's Road, Southwark, adjoining Pitt Street, is described by James Edwards, *A Companion from London to Brighthelmston* (published 1801, but compiled *c.* 1789), i, 7, § x, as 'belonging to Mr. Maymott, architect'. J. and W. G. Maymott were both District Surveyors in the early nineteenth century.

MICHELL, JOHN, contracted in 1691 to recase the walls of the nave of ST. THOMAS'S CHURCH, PORTSMOUTH, but abandoned the undertaking [H. J. Lilley & A. J. Everitt, *Portsmouth Parish Church*, Portsmouth 1921, 91]. He is probably to be identified with the 'Mr. Michell' who in 1670 was paid £389 5s. 4d. for building the tower of LYMINGTON CHURCH, HANTS. [C. Bostock, *History of Lymington Parish Church*, 1912].

MIDDLETON, CHARLES (1756–   ), was a pupil of James Paine, from whose office he exhibited at the Society of Artists in 1778 a 'section of the Great Staircase at Wardour Castle, built by James Paine, Esq.' He was admitted to the Royal Academy Schools in 1779 at the age of 22, and was awarded the Silver Medal the same year. He exhibited architectural designs at the Royal Academy from 1779 to 1793, but none of them represented executed buildings, and for some years he appears to have been employed in Henry Holland's office. In one of his publications he refers to 'my having had the superintendence of the building of Carlton House', and in the G.L.C. Collection there is a perspective by him of Holland's design for that house. Moreover among drawings from Holland's office in the Victoria and Albert Museum there are several drawings of classical ornament signed by Middleton (Box 176, D. 1752–1773–98). In 1786 a committee of Middlesex Justices of the Peace, of whom Holland was one, commissioned Middleton to produce a set of engravings of their designs for a new prison in Coldbath Fields, Clerkenwell, in order to attract tenders. This appeared in 1788 as *Plans, Elevations and Sections of the House of Correction for the County of Middlesex to be erected in Cold-Bath Fields, London*, engraved ... from the original drawings, with the authority of the

Magistrates, by Charles Middleton, Architect, 1788. Middleton had no other connection with this building, which appears to have been chiefly designed by Jacob Leroux (*q.v.*), and was erected in 1788–94 under the direction of S. P. Cockerell and Thomas Rogers [G.L.C. Record Office, Minutes of the Committee, MA/G. CBF/1]. Middleton subsequently practised in Lambeth in partnership with James Bailey (*q.v.*). He was District Surveyor for the parish, and in 1797 designed the turnpike at Lower Marsh. Sir Charles Barry was a pupil in Middleton and Bailey's office from 1810 to 1816. Middleton probably died before 1818 [*A.P.S.D.*].

Middleton was the author of *Picturesque and Architectural Views for Cottages, Farm Houses, and Country Villas*, engraved by himself, 1793, 1795; *The Architect and Builders Miscellany, or Pocket Library*, containing a series of small-scale designs 'through all the gradation of Buildings, from the Primitive Hutt, to the superb Mansion', 1799; *Designs for Gates and Rails suitable to Parks, Pleasure Grounds, Balconys, etc.*, n.d.; and *An Abstract of the Building Act* (of 1774), 1810. The anonymous book entitled *Decorations for Parks and Gardens* that was formerly attributed to Middleton is now known to have been the work of Thomas Elison (*q.v.*). Middleton's name appears on two large plates of carefully measured elevations of the north and west fronts of Westminster Abbey, published in 1803.

MIDDLETON, SIR CHARLES (1799–1867), *see* MONCK

MIDDLETON, WILLIAM (1730–1815), was the leading builder in Beverley during the reign of George III. He was a joiner by trade, but did considerable business as a builder's merchant besides acting as an architect. His excellent reputation as a builder is referred to in a letter of 1769 from Charles Hotham of South Dalton [East Riding Records, DD Ho/13/5]. He became an Alderman in 1778 and served as Mayor in 1779, 1789, 1794 and 1802. His portrait hangs in the Guildhall. Middleton's most important works in Beverley were the remodelling of the GUILDHALL in 1762–5 and the reconstruction of the BEVERLEY ARMS HOTEL in NORTH BAR in 1794. He was also responsible for NO. 39 NORTH BAR WITHOUT, 1769, NO. 40 NORTH BAR WITHIN, 1793–4, NOS. 72–74 LAIRGATE, and for a number of other attractive examples of Georgian vernacular architecture in the town. [K. A. MacMahon, 'William Middleton', *Trans. of the Georgian Soc. for East Yorkshire* iv (1), 1953–55, 68–82; Ivan & Elizabeth Hall, *Historic Beverley*, 1973, *passim*.]

MILLAR, JAMES, 'a local architect', carried out internal alterations to the East Church of

HOLY RUDE CHURCH, STIRLING, in 1803 [R.C.A.M., *Stirlingshire*, 130].

MILLER, JOHN, is said to have studied in Italy and then to have practised in London. He published *Andrea Palladio's Elements of Architecture, restored to its Original Perfection, with a Geometrical Explanation of its True Principles of Perspective*, c. 1748, 1759, and *The Country Gentleman's Architect, in a Great Variety of New Designs for Cottages, Farm Houses, Country Houses, Villas, Lodges for Park or Garden Entrances, etc.*, 1787, 1791, 1805. He is confused by Redgrave and the *D.N.B.* with James Miller, a topographical artist who exhibited at the Society of Artists and the Royal Academy during the last quarter of the eighteenth century. The four plates entitled *The Ruins of Paestum or Posidonia, a Town of Magna Graecia*, 1767, which have been attributed to him, appear in fact to be those by E. Berkenhout.

MILLER, SANDERSON (1716–1780), was the son of Sanderson Miller, a wealthy merchant of Banbury. He was born at Radway Grange, a Tudor house near Edgehill which his father had recently acquired. He matriculated at St. Mary Hall, Oxford, in 1734, and studied there for the next two or three years, but did not take a degree. His father's death in 1727 made him master of an independent fortune at the age of 21, and he settled down to the life of a country gentleman with a taste for literature, landscape-gardening and architecture. His first experiments in building were at Radway itself. In 1744 he built a picturesque thatched cottage on Edgehill and proceeded to give a more pronouncedly Gothic character to his Cotswold manor-house by rebuilding the south-east front with pointed arches and by setting small crocketed pinnacles on the angles. Shortly afterwards he built an octagonal Gothic tower on the summit of Edgehill and decorated it with stained-glass windows and heraldic shields. These were pioneer buildings of their kind, more effectively picturesque than anything by Kent, and making a strong appeal to an enthusiastic if somewhat uncritical antiquarianism. For others besides Horace Walpole, Miller's ruined tower at Hagley had 'the true rust of the Barons' Wars', and an ever-widening circle of aristocratic friends and neighbours was soon demanding the services of the squire of Radway in the embellishment of their houses and parks. As a Gothic architect Miller had two highly successful formulae. One was the two-storied bay window, with cusped panelling, which he used at Radway, Arbury, Adlestrop and Rockingham Hall. The other was the half-ruined tower or castle, of which he furnished much-admired examples for Hagley, Ingestre and Wimpole. Elsewhere – notably at Hagley Hall and the Shire

Hall, Warwick – Miller showed that he knew something of orthodox classical architecture, but it was as a purveyor of Gothic that he was chiefly in demand.

Miller was essentially a gentleman architect whose architectural activities formed part of an active social life. Like other amateur architects he had professional assistants. His plans for Hagley – based, as Horace Walpole was at pains to point out, on those of Houghton – had to be drawn out by John Sanderson before they could be given to the workmen, and his other major work, the Shire Hall at Warwick, was executed by William and David Hiorn of Warwick, master masons who were themselves competent architects, and who described themselves as 'surveyors' as well as 'builders' of the Hall. Miller normally operated in conjunction with a mason called William Hitchcox whom Sir Edward Turner aptly called his 'mason a latere'. Hitchcox no doubt understood the practical details of construction in which Miller may not have been fully versed. Very few drawings by Miller survive. There are some sketches for Arbury among the Newdigate papers in the Warwickshire Record Office (CR 764) and four designs for the tower at Wimpole which may be by him are in an album preserved at Wimpole. The R.I.B.A. Collection has two drawings attributed to him (see *Catalogue: L–N*, 71 and fig. 45).

Miller married in 1746 Susannah, daughter of Edward Trotman of Shelswell in Oxfordshire, by whom he had several children. From 1759 onwards Miller became subject to fits of insanity, which recurred four or five times before his death on 23 April 1780, at the age of 63. He is commemorated by a monument in Radway Church. There is a portrait at Lacock Abbey. Another, now believed to be in Canada, forms the frontispiece to the book by Dickins & Stanton cited below. A large collection of letters from Miller's friends is preserved in the Warwickshire Record Office. It formed the basis of *An Eighteenth-Century Correspondence*, ed. Lilian Dickins & Mary Stanton, 1910. Miller's copy of Leoni's *Architecture of L. B. Alberti* (1726) is in the library of the Faculty of Architecture at Cambridge.

[L. Dickins & M. Stanton, *An Eighteenth-Century Correspondence*, 1910; references in the *Letters of William Shenstone*, ed. M. Williams, 1939, and in Horace Walpole's Correspondence; letters and two diaries (CR 1382/1 and 32) in Warwickshire Record Office; A. C. Wood & W. Hawkes, *Sanderson Miller of Radway*, Banbury Historical Society, 1969; information from Mr. A. C. Wood, Mr. W. Hawkes and Mr. Michael McCarthy.]

Unless otherwise stated, the following list of Miller's principal executed works is based on his correspondence in the Warwickshire Record Office.

For a fuller list including uncertain, unexecuted and attributed works, see Wood & Hawkes, *op. cit.*, 108–10.

EDGEHILL, WARWICKS., thatched cottage, 1743–4 (*C. Life*, 13 Sept. 1946, figs. 6 and 8).

RADWAY GRANGE,* WARWICKS., rebuilt south and east fronts, 1744–6, Gothic (*C. Life*, 6 Sept. 1946).

AMBROSDEN HOUSE, OXON., assisted Sir Edward Turner, Bart., with the completion of his new house, 1745 onwards. The house had been begun c. 1739 to the designs of an unknown architect (possibly Miller himself), was not completed until the 1760s, and was demolished soon after Turner's death in 1766. Miller designed a Gothic front to a barn (1747) and new offices (1761) [Sir Edward Turner's accounts among Leigh papers at Shakespeare's Birthplace, Stratford-on-Avon] (*V.C.H. Oxon.* v, 16).

EDGEHILL, WARWICKS., octagonal castellated Gothic tower, 1745–7 (*C. Life*, 13 Sept. 1946).

WROXTON ABBEY, OXON., designs for the 1st Earl of Guilford, including Gothic window in east wall of chapel, 1747, an octagonal Gothic temple, 1750 (dem.), and Hall ceiling in Jacobean style, 1753 [W. Hawkes, 'Miller's Work at Wroxton', appended to Wood & Hawkes, *op. cit.*, 99–106].

WROXTON CHURCH, OXON., Gothic tower surmounted by an 'octagon of stone' for the 1st Earl of Guilford, 1747–8. The octagon 'fell down the first winter' and was not rebuilt [Bodleian Library, MS. North b. 29, ff. 175–7; cf. Walpole to Chute, 4 Aug. 1754] (Wood & Hawkes, *op. cit.*, fig. 11).

HAGLEY PARK, WORCS., Gothic castle for the 1st Lord Lyttelton, 1747–8 (*C. Life*, 16 Oct. 1915).

HONINGTON HALL, WARWICKS., advised Joseph Townsend on layout of grounds and designed grotto, 1749.

MIDDLETON PARK, OXON., designs for the 3rd Earl of Jersey, 1749, probably for the Gothic gate lodge at the south-east corner of the park, on the road from Middleton to Weston.

WIMPOLE HALL, CAMBS., Gothic castle designed for the 1st Earl of Hardwicke, 1749–51, but not built until 1772 under the direction of James Essex or Lancelot Brown [R.C.H.M., *West Cambridgeshire*, 216, 223 and pl. 137; B.M., Add. MSS. 6771, f. 99ᵛ, 35679, f. 55].

INGESTRE HALL, STAFFS., Gothic tower for the 2nd Viscount Chetwynd, c. 1750; dem. c. 1850.

ENVILLE HALL, STAFFS., Gothic greenhouse for the 4th Earl of Stamford, 1750 [*Letters of William Shenstone*, ed. M. Williams, 1939, 262] (N. Pevsner, *Staffordshire*, 1974, pl. 55).

HANWORTH HOUSE, MIDDLESEX, designs for stables for Lord Vere Beauclerk, 1750, evidently for the existing eighteenth-century Gothic stables [diary, 1749–50] (W. H. Tapp, *The Royal Manor of Hanworth*, n.d., pl. l).

OXFORD, ALL SOULS COLLEGE, fitted up Old Library in Gothic style to serve as rooms for Robert Vansittart, 1750–1; partitions since removed but panelling, etc., remains.

ARBURY HALL, WARWICKS., advice and designs for Sir Roger Newdigate, Bart., *c.* 1750–2, including Gothic dressing-room for Lady Newdigate, 1750, and bay window of library, 1750–2 [Newdigate archives, including original drawing for dressing-room, CR 764; C. Hussey, *English Country Houses, Mid Georgian*, 1956, 43].

ADLESTROP PARK, GLOS., alterations, including rebuilding of south-west front in Gothic style for James Leigh, 1750–4 and 1759–62 [agreements, etc., among Leigh muniments at Shakespeare's Birthplace, Stratford-on-Avon, Series B–Box 7, bundle 4] (Neale, *Views of Seats* vi, 1823; David Verey, *Gloucestershire: The Cotswolds, Buildings of England*, 1970, pl. 77).

HAGLEY, WORCS., reconstructed house known as ROCKINGHAM HALL for Admiral Thomas Smith (half-brother of the 1st Lord Lyttelton), 1751, Gothic.

CHART PARK, SURREY, designs for a Gothic greenhouse for Henry Talbot, 1751 [*Eighteenth-Century Correspondence*, 179–80; Bodleian Library, MS. North d. 19, ff. 68–9].

CROOME COURT, WORCS., built for the 6th Earl of Coventry in 1751–2 by the landscape-gardener Brown, may have owed something to Miller's advice, for it closely resembles Hagley, and when both house and garden were finished Lord Coventry wrote to Miller to say that 'whatever merits it [Croome] may in future time boast it will be ungrateful not to acknowledge you the primary Author'. Miller's surviving diary for 1749–50 shows that in 1750 he 'drew stables' for Lord Deerhurst, who succeeded as 6th Earl of Coventry in the following year.

DURHAM CASTLE, internal alterations, including dining-room (now Senior Common Room), for Joseph Butler, Bishop of Durham, 1751–2.

BELHUS, ESSEX, advised Thomas Barrett Lennard, afterwards 17th Lord Dacre, on alterations to interior, 1752–7, and perhaps also on the rebuilding of the south and west fronts in Tudor Gothic style, 1745–7; dem. 1956 (*C. Life*, 15, 22 May 1920).

WARWICK, THE SHIRE HALL, 1754–8, built by William & David Hiorn & Job Collins.

LACOCK ABBEY, WILTS., Great Hall and Gothic gateway for John Ivory Talbot, 1754–5 (*C. Life*, 17 March 1923; for the statuary by V. A. Sederbach in the Hall see N. Pevsner in *Arch. Rev.*, May 1958).

HAGLEY CHURCH, WORCS., rebuilt chancel for the 1st Lord Lyttelton, 1754–6, Gothic; rebuilt 1858. Miller also designed the monument to Sir Thomas Lyttelton (d. 1751). See R. Pococke, *Travels through England*, Camden Soc. 1889, ii, 235–6, for a description of Miller's work, written in 1756.

HAGLEY HALL, WORCS., for the 1st Lord Lyttelton, 1754–60, assisted by Thomas Prowse and John Sanderson [Michael McCarthy, 'The Building of Hagley Hall', *Burlington Mag.*, April 1976] (*Vitruvius Britannicus* v, 1771, pls. 14–15; *C. Life*, 19–26 Sept. 1957).

GOSFIELD HALL, ESSEX, addition to west front for the 1st Lord Nugent, 1755.

BATH, SOMERSET, design for a sham castle on Claverton Down for Ralph Allen, 1755. The sham castle built here by Allen in 1762 may have been based on Miller's design, but Richard Jones (*q.v.*) claimed to have designed it himself.

KINETON CHURCH, WARWICKS., rebuilding of nave and transepts in Gothic style for the Rev. William Talbot, 1755–6; remodelled 1873–80 [Miller's diary, 1756–7, contains several references to his supervision of this work].

STOWE HOUSE, BUCKS. Miller's diary shows that on 15 July 1756 he was at Stowe 'contriving a finishing to Gibbs building', which suggests that he may have designed the two Gothic lanterns which surmount the two lower towers of Gibbs's Gothic temple. These are not shown on Gibbs's original drawing (cf. illustrations in *C. Life*, 29 Sept. 1950, figs. 6–7).

KILKENNY CATHEDRAL, IRELAND, designs for restoration of choir, etc., for Bishop Richard Pococke, made in 1756–7 but not executed [Michael McCarthy, 'Eighteenth-Century Cathedral Restoration: Correspondence Relating to St. Canice's Cathedral, Kilkenny', in *Studies*, Dublin, Winter 1976, Spring 1977].

PARK PLACE, nr. HENLEY, BERKS., library for General Henry Seymour Conway, 1757; destroyed by fire 1768 [Miller's diary, 1756–7; for the fire see P. Noble, *Anne Seymour Damer*, 1908, 48].

WOTTON HOUSE, WOTTON UNDERWOOD, BUCKS., bridge for George Grenville, 1758.

ADLESTROP CHURCH, GLOS., alterations including building of south transept (containing Leigh family pew), 1758–9, Gothic [Shakespeare's Birthplace, Stratford, Leigh papers, Series B, Box 2, bundle 6].

LONDON, POMFRET HOUSE, ARLINGTON STREET, for the Countess of Pomfret, 1758–60, Gothic; dem. 1920 [Horace Walpole, *Anecdotes of Painting* v, ed. F. W. Hilles & P. B. Daghlian, 1937, 161] (photographs in *Country Life Annual*, 1970, 138–9, and drawing by W. Stukeley in Bodleian, Gough Maps 22, f. 39ᵛ).

BECKETT PARK, BERKS., stables and minor alterations to house for the 2nd Viscount Barrington, 1766; house dem.

ECTON HALL, NORTHANTS., rebuilding of south front in Gothic style for Ambrose Isted, 1755–6 [stylistic attribution combined with the fact that Ambrose Isted was a friend of several of Miller's patrons: see *Memoirs of George Cumberland*, 1806, 121–3] (J. A. Gotch, *Squires' Homes of Northamptonshire*, 1939, pl. 76).

SISTON COURT, GLOS. Miller may have been responsible for the octagonal entrance-lodges for his Trotman relations. In 1759 he designed a classical almshouse at Siston, but it does not seem to have been built (*C. Life*, 7 Oct. 1905).

MILLS, JOHN, of Worcester, rebuilt ST. PETER'S CHURCH, WORCESTER, in a poor Gothic style in 1838–9 [I.C.B.S.]. In 1839–40 the nave and chancel of ELMLEY LOVETT CHURCH, WORCS., were rebuilt in accordance with his designs. The Vestry Minutes show that he was instructed to 'keep in view the utmost economy consistent with durability'.

MILLS, PETER (1598–1670), was the son of John Mills, a tailor of East Dean in Sussex, where he was baptized on 12 February 1597/8. On 30 November 1613 he was apprenticed to John Williams, a tyler and bricklayer of London. Mills took his first apprentice in 1629, and on 17 October 1643 he was appointed Bricklayer to the City of London. He was Master of the Tylers' and Bricklayers' Company in 1649–60. He ceased to be City Bricklayer at about the time of the Restoration, perhaps because by then he had come to be increasingly employed as a surveyor and architect. In 1661 he and 'another person' (almost certainly Sir Balthazar Gerbier, *q.v.*) were commissioned by the City to design the triumphal arches erected to celebrate Charles II's coronation. In 1664 he acted as the City's surveyor in negotiations with the Dean and Chapter of St. Paul's, and after the Great Fire of 1666 he was one of the four surveyors appointed by the City to supervise the rebuilding of London in conjunction with Wren, May and Pratt. He was himself the author of a plan for the City of which nothing is known except that it was thought inferior to the one submitted by Hooke. Together with Hooke and Oliver he was responsible for making a detailed survey of the destroyed areas and for directing the staking out of the new and widened streets. Mills also played an active part in rebuilding the property of St. Bartholomew's Hospital, of which he had been a Governor since December 1644. In 1667–8 he was acting as surveyor to Christ's Hospital, and the Gresham Trustees would have employed him to rebuild the Royal Exchange, but for 'the great burthen

of businesse lying upon him for the city att this time', which induced them instead to appoint Edward Jerman as 'the most able knowne artist (besides him) that the city now hath'. Mills's own losses in the Fire included the destruction of three tenements in Budge Row which he held under the Master and Fellows of Pembroke College, Cambridge, by a lease dated 10 April 1662. This was to have expired in 1702, but in July 1668 the College, 'in consideration of his (Mills's) great 'losse susteyned by the Fire', agreed to extend it for a further period of thirty-four years on condition that he rebuilt the houses 'with all convenient speed', and in accordance with the 'Act of Parliament lately made for the Rebuilding the City of London'. The tenements in question occupied the site of No. 26 Budge Row. Mills himself lived in a house in Bartholomew Close which he rented from St. Bartholomew's Hospital, and when he made his will in July 1670 he left 10s. apiece to the twenty Governors 'that most frequently meet at the Compting House about the affairs of the Hospital whom I desire may be at my Funerall ... to buy each of them a Ring'. He left money for the same purpose to 'every person of the Kindred meeting att the Greene Dragon whereof I am a member'. He died in the following month and was buried in the middle aisle of the church of St. Bartholomew the Less on 25 August.

Mills's activity as a surveyor and architect can be traced at least as far back as 1638, when he and a mason called Llewellyn made a ground plan of the church of St. Michael-le-Querne and were involved on behalf of the churchwardens in subsequent negotiations with Inigo Jones over the design of a new church to replace it [Guildhall Library, MS. 2895/2]. The most important of his known works was Thorpe Hall, nr. Peterborough, which he designed for Oliver St. John in 1653–4. Thorpe Hall is a major monument of what has been called the 'artisan mannerist' style, whose characteristics are also evident in the houses which Mills had built in Great Queen Street, Lincoln's Inn Fields, in *c.* 1640. Other important examples of the style are Cromwell House, Highgate (for Robert Sprignell, *c.* 1637–8), Tyttenhanger, Herts. (for Sir Henry Blount, *c.* 1655), and Wisbech Castle, Cambs. (for John Thurloe, *c.* 1658, dem. 1815). Tyttenhanger (*C. Life*, 4–11 Oct. 1919) is a brick house which Mills may well have built, and the resemblances between Wisbech Castle and Thorpe Hall are so striking as to suggest that he was probably Thurloe's architect. As Cromwell's Secretary of State and Chief Justice, respectively, Thurloe and St. John must have been well known to each other, and in 1642 Thurloe had actually witnessed an agreement whereby Mills had undertaken to build houses on land in Holborn leased to him by St. John [Huntingdonshire Record Office, dd.

M 69/4/1]. It may be added that Mills's own sympathies evidently lay with the Parliamentary party, for in May 1648 he was appointed a member of the Committee for the City of London Militia, an office which he still held in Feb. 1659/60 [*Acts and Ordinances of the Interregnum*, ed. Firth & Rait, i. 1138; *The Diurnall of Thomas Rugg*, ed. Sachse, Camden Soc., 1961, 45].

Whatever Parliamentary connections Mills may have had, they did not prevent his employment at the Restoration both to design the triumphal arches to celebrate Charles II's coronation, and to organize the 'shews and pageants' on the Thames with which the City welcomed Charles and his Queen to Whitehall on 23 August 1662 [John Tatham, *Aqua Triumphalis*, 1662]. Nor did the royalist Duke of Lennox scruple to employ Mills to rebuild the centre of his house at Cobham in Kent in the 1660s. At Cobham Hall, moreover, Mills showed that he had largely assimilated the new domestic style associated with architects such as May and Pratt: only in the main doorway are some traces of 'artisan mannerism' still perceptible. The interior was handsomely fitted up by the same team of London craftsmen whom Mills had employed to construct and decorate the coronation arches.

[*A.P.S.D.*, *s.v.* 'Mills' and 'Jerman'; Malcolm Pinhorn, note on date of Mills's birth in *Blackmansbury* i (3), 1964, 21; Guildhall Library, records of the Tylers' and Bricklayers' Company; Guildhall Record Office, City Repertories; T. F. Reddaway, *The Rebuilding of London after the Great Fire*, 1940, *passim*; S. Perks, *The History of the Mansion House*, 1922, 143–52; *The Survey of Building Sites in the City of London after the Great Fire of 1666*, ed. W. H. Godfrey, London Topographical Soc. 1946, 1956; Gweneth Whitteridge, 'The Fire of London and St. Bartholomew's Hospital', *London Topographical Record* xx, 1952; R. A. Beddard, 'Church and State in Old St. Paul's', *Guildhall Miscellany* iv (3), 1972; Wren Soc. xi, 63–4 (Christ's Hospital); P.C.C. 147 PENN.]

LONDON, houses on the south side of GREAT QUEEN STREET, LINCOLN'S INN FIELDS, *c.* 1640; dem. George Vertue states that it was Mills who 'design'd & built the great houses in Great Queen Street', *Vertue Note Books*, Walpole Soc., i, 130. This is confirmed by the lease of the site of Nos. 66–68 to Mills on 15 Sept. 1639. The whole south side of the street was rebuilt at approximately the same time to a uniform pattern for which Mills was evidently responsible [*Survey of London* v, 42–5, 56 and pls. 16–22, cf. J. Parton, *Some Account of the Hospital and Parish of St. Giles in the Fields*, 1817, 290, and R. W. Paul, *Vanishing London*, 1894, pl. xxvii].

LONDON, houses in CASTLE (now FURNIVAL)

STREET, HOLBORN, on the site of a 'great garden' leased to Mills by Oliver St. John in Feb. 1642. The houses were to be of brick, three storeys high, and were to be 'in the same uniformitie and beauty' as the adjoining houses to be built under a royal licence to St. John dated 5 Aug. 1641. [Huntingdonshire Record Office, dd. M 69/4/1].

THORPE HALL, NORTHANTS., for Oliver St. John, 1654–6 [B.M., Add. MS. 25302, f. 153, contract dated 8 Feb. 1653/4 (printed in *Fenland Notes and Queries* iv, 1898–1900, 272–3), whereby John Ashley and Sampson Frisbey of Ketton, freemasons, undertake to execute the windows of the north and south fronts 'as is expressed & sett forth in a Draught or map of the said intended House made by Peter Mills of London Surveyor']. The date 1656 is carved on the stable-block. The house was restored by F. Ruddle of Peterborough in 1850–1, and in 1852 A. W. Hakewill published a *General Plan and External Details of Thorpe Hall*. The panelling in the library was removed to Leeds Castle, Kent, *c.* 1920. [H. M. Colvin, 'The Architect of Thorpe Hall', *C. Life*, 6 June 1952; Sir Gyles Isham, 'Thorpe Hall', *Northants. Antiquarian Soc.'s Report* for 1958–9, 37–45] (J. Belcher & M. E. Macartney, *Later Renaissance Architecture in England* ii, 1901, 97–99 and plates; Oliver Hill & John Cornforth, *English Country Houses: Caroline*, 1966, 102–10).

attributed: WISBECH CASTLE, CAMBS., for John Thurloe, *c.* 1658; dem. 1815 [Arthur Oswald in *C. Life*, 23 May 1947, 955–6; H. M. Colvin in *C. Life*, 6 June 1952, 1733–4].

LONDON, TRIUMPHAL ARCHES to celebrate coronation of King Charles II, 1661, in association with 'another Person, who desired to have his name conceal'd', who can probably be identified as Sir Balthazar Gerbier (*q.v.*) [J. Ogilby, *Relation of His Majestie's Entertainment passing through the City of London to his Coronation with a Description of the Triumphal Arches*, 2nd ed. 1662]. For the original drawings see *R.I.B.A. Drawings Catalogue: G–K*, 18–19. See also E. Halfpenny, 'The Citie's Loyalty Display'd', *Guildhall Miscellany*, no. 10, 1959.

CAMBRIDGE, PEMBROKE COLLEGE, THE HITCHAM BUILDING, 1659–61, was measured by Mills on its completion in 1661, and he may probably be regarded as its designer [A. Attwater, *Pembroke College, Cambridge*, 1936, 76] (R.C.H.M., *Cambridge* ii, pl. 212).

COBHAM HALL, KENT, remodelled central block (or 'Cross Wing') for Charles Stuart, 3rd Duke of Richmond and 6th Duke of Lennox, 1661–3; attic storey altered *c.* 1767–70 [H. M. Colvin, 'Peter Mills and Cobham Hall', in *The Country Seat*, ed. Colvin & Harris, 1970].

LEWISHAM, KENT, COLFE'S ALMSHOUSES for the

Leathersellers' Company, 1664–5; dem. *c.* 1955 after bomb-damage [L. Duncan, *History of the Borough of Lewisham*, 1908, 126].

LONDON, five warehouses on BREWERS' QUAY, THAMES STREET, 1667–8; dem. [Northants. Record Office, B (D) 282, item 3, a Fire Court case which suggests that Mills had designed the warehouses].

LONDON, CHRIST'S HOSPITAL, designed in 1667–8 a 'Compting House, Court Roome, and Schoole, with a house for the Treasurer, and houses for other Officers of this Hospital', which were built, at least in part, before his death in 1670 [*Wren Soc.* xi, 63–4].

LONDON, BUDGE ROW, houses on site leased from Pembroke College, Cambridge, 1668–9; dem. ['A Copie of the agremt. between ye College & Mr. Mills about Rebuilding the Wrastlers, Budgrow', as confirmed by the Fire Court on 26 June 1668, among the title-deeds of No. 26 Budge Row, formerly in the muniment-room of St. John's College, Oxford].

MILLWARD, JOHN, is described in Pigot's *Directory* (1830) as a 'carpenter, joiner and stone-cutter' at Hay-on-Wye. In 1806–8 he built and presumably designed RIDGEBOURNE, nr. KINGTON, HEREFS., for Edmund Cheese [Parry's *History of Kington*, 1845, 224].

MILNE, JAMES, is listed among the architects practising in Edinburgh from 1809 to 1834. He was doubtless the James Milne, mason, who was admitted as a burgess of Edinburgh in 1809 [*Roll of Edinburgh Burgesses*, Scottish Record Soc., 112], but must be distinguished from the 'James Milne, Builder' (d. 3 Jan. 1826) who is comme-morated on a tombstone in Leith Churchyard, and also from the James Miln or Milne (*c.* 1792–1863) who was County Surveyor of Northamptonshire from 1826 until 1863.

EDINBURGH

LYNEDOCH PLACE, NOS. 3–22, 1820–3 [S.R.O., Edinburgh Sasines].

SAXE COBURG PLACE, NOS. 1–8 and 25–32, 1822–30 [S.R.O., Edinburgh Sasines].

ST. BERNARD'S CHURCH (originally CLAREMONT STREET CHAPEL), SAXE COBURG STREET, 1823; apse, etc., added 1888 [J. Stark, *Picture of Edinburgh*, 6th ed. 1835, 226].

CARLTON STREET, 1824 [S.R.O., Edinburgh Sasines].

DANUBE STREET, 1824 [S.R.O., Edinburgh Sasines].

DEAN TERRACE, 1824 [S.R.O., Edinburgh Sasines].

DEANHAUGH STREET, 1824–5 [S.R.O., Edinburgh Sasines].

ST. BERNARD'S CRESCENT, 1824 [S.R.O., Edinburgh Sasines].

MILNE, JOHN, practised in Edinburgh in the 1830s, appearing in the directories as 'civil engineer and teacher of architecture'. He appears to have been an expert on ventilation, for he con-tributed two articles on the subject to Loudon's *Architectural Magazine* i (1834), 64–70, and ii (1835), 27–31. He designed a house in RANDOLPH CRESCENT, EDINBURGH, for Sir John Robison which incorporated an elaborate ventilation sys-tem [J. C. Loudon, *Cottage, Farm and Villa Architecture*, 1846, 1197–1205].

In 1842 he applied unsuccessfully for the vacant post of Master of the School of Archi-tecture run by the Royal Dublin Society [*Pro-ceedings*, vol. 78, 128, *ex inf.* Mr. E. McParland], but evidently obtained some other employment as his name disappears from the Edinburgh directories in the same year. He must not be con-fused with John Milne (1823–1904), a pupil of John Henderson who practised in St. Andrews from about 1850 onwards.

MILNER, THOMAS, is stated in Campbell's *Vitruvius Britannicus* ii, 1717, pl. 47, to have designed GREGORIES, nr. BEACONSFIELD, BUCKS., for John Waller in 1712. Nothing else is known about Milner except that he is described as 'esquire' and subscribed to volumes ii and iii of *Vitruvius Britannicus*. Gregories was destroyed by fire in 1813. A late eighteenth-century eleva-tion of the house is preserved in the Aylesbury Museum (V. G. Garvin, 'Gregories, Bucks.', *Arch. Rev.* lxvii, 1930, 169–74).

MITCHELL, ROBERT, is said to have been born in Aberdeen, but his exhibits at the Royal Academy show that he was practising in London from 1782 onwards. In 1801 he published *Plans, etc. of Buildings erected in England and Scotland; with An Essay to elucidate the Grecian, Roman, and Gothic Architecture*. He was presumably also the author of a work advertised in an early nine-teenth-century bookseller's catalogue as 'Mit-chell's Designs for Rural Villas on Economical Principles, 8°, 25 plates, 1785', of which no copy has so far been found. Mitchell designed mainly in the manner of James Wyatt, but his larger houses combine the neo-classical detail of the late eighteenth century with a liking for the large Palladian porticoes and attached office blocks characteristic of the earlier Georgian period. His book includes a design for a country house in the form of a Greek Doric temple, anti-cipating Wilkins's Grange Park.

Mitchell probably had a son or younger rela-tive named George Mitchell, for in June 1796 a person of this name wrote from Tobago to Mr. T. Webster (*q.v.*) at Robert Mitchell's office in Newman Street to say that he had given up archi-tecture and become a planter. He was probably the George Mitchell who had been admitted to the Royal Academy Schools as an architectural student in 1795 at the age of 20 [*R.I.B.A. Drawings Catalogue: L–N*, 72].

COTTESBROOKE HALL, NORTHANTS., alterations for Sir James Langham, Bart., *c.* 1770–80, probably including the bridge and lodges in the park [*Plans*, pls. 7–8] (*C. Life*, 17–24 March 1955, 19 Feb. 1970).

MOORE PLACE, MUCH HADHAM, HERTS., for James Gordon, 1777–9 [*Plans*, pls. 7–8] (*C. Life*, 26 Jan, 2 Feb. 1956).

PRESTON HALL, MIDLOTHIAN, for Sir John Callender, Bart., *c.* 1794 [*Plans*, pls. 9–13; exhibat R.A. 1794] (*C. Life*, 24–31 Aug. 1961).

LONDON, THE ROTUNDA, LEICESTER SQUARE, for Mr. Barker, 1793–4; reconstructed 1865–8 as the R.C. Church of Notre Dame [*Plans*, pl. 14].

SILWOOD PARK, BERKS., for Sir James Sibbald, Bart., 1796; rebuilt 1876 [*Plans*, pls. 1–4; exhib. at R.A. 1796–7] (Neale's *Views of Seats*, 1st ser., iv, 1821).

TWICKENHAM, MIDDLESEX, HEATH LANE LODGE, for Isaac Swainson, before 1801 [*Plans*, pls. 5–6].

MONTREAL, CANADA, THE NELSON COLUMN, 1808–9 [Elizabeth Collard in *C. Life*, 24 July 1969, 210–11].

MITCHELL, ROBERT, was a builder-architect of Peterhead, Aberdeenshire. In 1804–6 he and his brother John appear to have built PETER-HEAD OLD CHURCH to the design of Alexander Laing of Edinburgh (*q.v.*). Robert subsequently designed ST. PETER'S EPISCOPAL CHURCH, PETER-HEAD, 1813–14, Gothic [J. T. Findlay, *History of Peterhead*, Aberdeen 1933, 143–4, 171].

MOFFAT, JOHN, an 'architect' then resident in Liverpool, was in 1704 employed to go to Dumfries and 'furnish a modall' for a new Town Hall and steeple there. His design, which was based on the steeple of the College at Glasgow, appears to have been the one carried out in the following year by Tobias Bachop (*q.v.*) [W. McDowall, *History of Dumfries*, Edinburgh 1867, 539–42].

MOFFAT, WILLIAM LAMBIE (1808–1882), see HURST, WILLIAM

MONCK, Sir CHARLES (1779–1867), was the third but only surviving son of Sir William Middleton, Bart., of Belsay Castle, Northumberland, whom he succeeded in 1795. His mother was Jane Monck, only child and heiress of Lawrence Monck of Caenby Hall, Lincolnshire. On Lawrence Monck's death in 1798 he inherited the Caenby estate and took the name of Monck in accordance with his father-in-law's will.

Monck received a good classical education at Rugby School. He was prevented by the Napoleonic War from making the usual Grand Tour, but immediately after his marriage in 1804 he and his wife made an extended visit to Greece, where he studied the temples in company with his friend Sir William Gell. Soon after his return in 1806 he decided to build a new house at BELSAY in the Grecian style. The foundations were laid in 1807 and the house was first inhabited ten years later. Monck was entirely his own architect, making his own drawings and supervising the work himself. Surviving drawings show that he was a neat and accurate draughtsman, and it was only when confronted with such difficult tasks as drawing the volutes of an Ionic capital that he was obliged to seek the professional assistance of John Dobson of Newcastle. He demanded exceptionally high standards from his craftsmen, and according to Dobson he did much raise the standard of masonry in the North of England. Belsay is one of the outstanding monuments of the Greek Revival. It represents a personal and exceptionally uncompromising approach to the problem of adapting ancient Greek architecture to domestic purposes. Planned round a peristyle, it recalls internally the layout of a Graeco-Roman villa. Externally every detail from the stylobate to the cornice has classical authority, but archaeological nicety is subordinated to a noble simplicity which redeems the house from being no more than a monument of architectural pedantry.

Monck designed one other country house in Northumberland. This was LINDEN HOUSE, nr. MORPETH, which he planned for his friend Charles William Bigge in 1812–13. Here the design is more conventional, and the Doric order is confined to a portico. Monck's designs are among the family papers in the County Record Office (5/223–6). The house is illustrated by B. Allsopp & Ursula Clark, *Historic Architecture of Northumberland*, 1970, 70 (where it is wrongly ascribed to Dobson).

At Belsay Monck also designed the stables (with a belfry based on the 'Tower of the Winds'), a row of houses with arcaded lower storey probably inspired by a visit to Italy and Sicily in 1830–1, and the Gothic school (1842). He was an improving landlord who took a keen interest in farming, and created a remarkable romantic garden from the quarry out of which the house was built.

Monck, who was a prominent figure in the public life of Northumberland, and represented the county in Parliament from 1812 to 1820, died on 20 July 1867. His diaries and other papers are deposited in the Northumberland Record Office, together with a MS. memoir by his son Sir Arthur Middleton.

[MS. memoir by Sir Arthur Middleton; R. Welford, *Men of Mark twixt Tyne and Tweed* iii,

1895, 206–12; J. Dobson in *Building News* vi, 1859, 404; *C. Life*, 5, 12 Oct. 1940; C. Hussey, *English Country Houses: Late Georgian*, 1958, 83–90; J. M. Crook, *The Greek Revival*, 1972, 126–7.]

MONEYPENNY, GEORGE (1768–), was the son of George Moneypenny, a sculptor and carver of Derby, who died in 1807. He was baptized at St. Werburgh's Church on 21 July 1768. Prisons were his speciality, and he appears to have succeeded William Blackburn (d. 1790) as the leading designer of such buildings. He could express their purpose effectively. Pevsner describes his Winchester Gaol as 'among the most impressive in the country', and at Leicester he showed a 'knowledge of grand design' which, according to a contemporary critic, 'bordered on the terrific'. His Sessions House at Knutsford (often supposed to be the work of Harrison of Chester) has a polite Ionic portico flanked by two frowning Vanbrughian doorways. At Leicester, where he was the contractor as well as the architect, Moneypenny got into financial difficulties, and was one of the first to be imprisoned for debt in his own building. He eventually moved to London, where he was still in practice in the 1820s. In 1813 the *Gentleman's Magazine* printed a letter from him criticizing the centering designed for the construction of Waterloo Bridge. [*A.P.S.D.*; register of St. Werburgh's and St. Alkmund's churches, Derby, *ex inf.* Mr. Edward Saunders; J. Dugdale, *The British Traveller* iii, 1819, 570; N. Pevsner & D. Lloyd, *Hampshire*, 1967, 54; *Gent's Mag.* 1809 (ii), 1019, 1813 (i), 124–6, 225, 411–12, 1813 (ii), 221–3.]

LEICESTER, THE COUNTY GAOL, 1790–2; dem. *c.* 1880 [J. Dugdale, *The British Traveller* iii, 1819, 570; J. Flower, *Views of Ancient Buildings in the Town and County of Leicester, c.* 1826, 4].

SOUTHAMPTON, HANTS., NORTHAM BRIDGE, 1799 [P. Brannon, *Picture of Southampton*, 1850, 59].

WINCHESTER, THE COUNTY GAOL, JEWRY STREET, 1805; largely dem. [J. Dugdale, *The British Traveller* ii, 1819, 556; *Gent's Mag.* 1808 (i), 204].

EXETER, THE COUNTY HOUSE OF CORRECTION, 1807–9; dem. 1848–50 [J. Dugdale, *The British Traveller* ii, 1819, 136–7; *Gent's Mag.* 1810 (i), 121].

PETWORTH, SUSSEX, THE COUNTY PRISON, alterations, 1816; dem. 1835 [*A.P.S.D.*, *s.v.* 'Wyatt, James'].

KNUTSFORD, CHESHIRE, THE SESSIONS HOUSE AND HOUSE OF CORRECTION, 1817–19 [J. H. Hanshall, *History of Cheshire*, 1817, 389; G. Ormerod, *History of Cheshire* i, 1819, 380].

TABLEY HOUSE, CHESHIRE, reinstatement of east wing for Sir John Leicester, Bart., after damage by fire, 1819–20 [Cheshire Record Office, Leicester-Warren papers, uncatalogued 1976].

MONTAGU, JOHN, 2ND DUKE OF MONTAGU (1690–1749), was the son of Ralph, 1st Duke of Montagu, and succeeded him in 1709 as the owner of Boughton House, Northants., Clitheroe Castle, Lancs., and Montagu House, Bloomsbury. He was a Knight of the Garter and a Fellow of the Royal Society, and his status as a great nobleman brought him various offices, including those of Master-General of the Ordnance (1740–1 and 1743–9). In private he was a Man of Feeling before his time, and shared with his friend William Stukeley many unfashionable enthusiasms, including a precocious taste for Gothic architecture. It was to him that Batty Langley dedicated his *Ancient Architecture Restored* in 1742, and it was for him that Stukeley designed (1744) a Gothic bridge to be erected in the park at Boughton, and a Gothic mausoleum to be added to Weekley Church. Neither was built (though a wooden model of the bridge survives at Boughton), but the Duke himself was something of an amateur architect in his own right. Stukeley records that he had 'a very good knack of drawing and designing'. Among a list of drawings formerly in the Ordnance Office (P.R.O., WO 55/2281) there appears a 'Plan and elevation for building Barracks at Woolwich by His Grace the Duke of Montagu 1741', and at Boughton there are two drawings which show him as an early designer of buildings in the castle style. One (marked 'Box, 3, No. 32') is a scheme for some castellated farm-buildings to be built on an ancient moated site on his Northamptonshire estate. This does not seem to have been carried out, but is remarkable for the deliberately irregular layout which the Duke envisaged, giving the impression of a picturesque fortified manor-house, at a time when such follies were invariably conceived in strictly symmetrical terms. The other drawing (marked 'Box 3, No. 49') is for a house to be built within the walls of CLITHEROE CASTLE, LANCS., and is inscribed 'Plan for a New House at Clithero drawn by the Duke in 1740, and since built'. Though the draughtsmanship is crude, the annotations show that the Duke knew exactly what he wanted – a building in 'comon ordinary plane stone work the same as common farm houses are built of', without plinth, cornice, architraves or other ornaments. There were to be no sash windows, but only 'plane comon iron casements', and none of the rooms were to be wainscoted, but only plastered and whitewashed. These were architectural precepts of which Pugin might have approved. For 1740 they were astonishingly precocious. The existing building corresponds closely to the Duke's drawing, and although the windows have since been sashed, the rubble stonework is so convincing that it is difficult to decide what is medieval and what is Georgian.

[*D.N.B.*; G.E.C., *Complete Peerage*; *The Family Memoirs of the Rev. William Stukeley*, Surtees Soc., i, 1880, 114–15; T. D. Whitaker, *History of the Parish of Whalley and the Honor of Clitheroe*, 1872, i, 253–4, ii, 69 n. 2; Stuart Piggott, *William Stukeley*, 1950, 144–6, 150–1, 153.]

MONTGOMERY, JOHN, was a mason of Old Rayne, Aberdeenshire. In 1685 he was made an honorary burgess of Old Aberdeen for 'the good service' he had done in making Bishop Scougal's monument in ST. MACHAR'S CATHEDRAL CHURCH [*Records of Old Aberdeen*, New Spalding Club, i, 277]. In 1686 he built the MERCAT CROSS at ABERDEEN for £100 sterling in accordance with 'ane moddell and frame therof of timber and pasteboard' which he had 'formed and given in'. It is a polygonal structure with an elaborately decorated parapet supported by an Ionic order and was extensively repaired in 1821. [*Extracts from the Council Register of the Burgh of Aberdeen 1643–1747*, Scottish Burgh Record Society 1872, 306–7; D. MacGibbon & T. Ross, *The Castellated and Domestic Architecture of Scotland* v, 1892, 212–13; G. M. Fraser, 'The Market Cross of Aberdeen', *Scottish Historical Review* v, 1907–8, 178–9.]

MONTIER, JOHN, was a builder and architect of Tunbridge Wells. 'William Montier' is listed as an architect and surveyor at Tunbridge Wells in Pigot's *Directory* of 1827–8, and the names of John Montier 'senior' and 'junior' appear among the architects subscribing to Horsfield's *History of Sussex* in 1835. John Montier rebuilt the chancel of BRENCHLEY CHURCH, KENT, in 1814 [archives of Lord Courthope, *ex inf.* the late Rupert Gunnis], and rebuilt FRANT CHURCH, SUSSEX, in 1819–22 [H. S. Eeles, *Frant, a Parish History*, 1947, 194]. Between 1810 and 1830 he designed and built a number of picturesque lodges and cottages on the ERIDGE estate, nr. Tunbridge Wells [Kenneth Clark, *The Gothic Revival*, 1928, 141, n. 1]. A farm-house 'in the style of a yeoman's house of the Tudor times . . . built by Messrs. Montier and Douch from their own designs' is illustrated in Colbran's *New Guide to Tunbridge Wells*, 1840, 144.

MOOR, THOMAS, was a Leicestershire master builder of the 1720s. Among the Herrick papers in the Leicestershire Record Office (DG/9/2134) there is an estimate submitted by Moor in about 1725 for building a mansion at Beaumanor to a design drawn by himself. It was not adopted, the accepted design being by John Westley (*q.v.*). In 1725–6 Moor rebuilt the nave and tower of

Sibson Church to the designs of Francis Smith (*q.v.*).

MOORE, ALEXANDER, POOLE (*c.* 1777–1806), was a pupil of James Lewis. He was admitted to the Royal Academy Schools in 1792 at the age of 15, and was awarded the Silver Medal in 1794. He was subsequently employed in the Surveyor's office at Christ's Hospital. He died on 11 July 1806 at the age of 28, after a short illness, leaving a father who had long depended upon him for support. He is described as 'a young man of very eccentric habits but a clever Artist'. He exhibited regularly at the Royal Academy, showing views and drawings of various buildings, including St. Paul's Cathedral, St. Stephen's, Walbrook, and St. Mary's, Taunton. [*Gent's Mag.* 1806 (ii), 686; J. Chambers, MS. *Collections for a Biography of British Architects* in R.I.B.A. Library; S. Redgrave, *Dictionary of Artists*, 1878, 296.]

MOORE, FRANCIS, rebuilt the tower and reroofed the nave of EAST BRIDGFORD CHURCH, NOTTS., in 1778, as recorded by a tablet on the south wall of the tower giving the name of 'Moore, archt.' [A. Du Boulay Hill, *East Bridgford*, Notts., 1932, 119, 158]. He was no doubt the same as Francis Moore, carpenter, who received nearly £100 in 1776 for repairs to CHESTERFIELD CHURCH, DERBYSHIRE [Churchwardens' Accounts, *ex inf.* Canon B. F. L. Clarke].

MOORE, GABRIEL, was the surveyor employed by Sir John Strode to design his house, CHANTMARLE, DORSET, in 1612. In a surviving notebook Strode describes Moore as 'a skilfull architect', and says that he was 'born about Chinnock' and 'had of me 20s. monethly, with his dyet, for his paines only, to survey and direct the building to the forme I conceived and plotted it' [Dorset Record Office, MW/M4, f. 24ᵛ]. The house, designed in a rather conservative style for its date, is described in Arthur Oswald, *Country Houses of Dorset* (2nd ed. 1959), 97–9, and R.C.H.M., *Dorset* (*West*), 71–2.

MOORE, GEORGE (*c.* 1777–1859), began his career in partnership with William Leverton, the builder, and afterwards established himself as an architect in Lincoln's Inn Fields. He exhibited at the Royal Academy between 1797 and 1810. He was surveyor to the Skinners' Company, a member of the Society of Arts, a Fellow of the Royal Society, and an original member of the Institute of British Architects. He was President of the Surveyors' Club in 1817. He died in Grenville Street, Brunswick Square, in November 1859, in his 83rd year [*Builder* xvii, 1859, 765].

MOORE, GEORGE, (*c.* 1810–), was a pupil of Edward Blore. He was admitted to the Royal Academy Schools in 1830, at the age of 20, and exhibited at the Academy from 1831 to 1840. He was an able architectural draughtsman and artist, and in that capacity accompanied Henry Gally Knight on his tour of Norman architecture in Sicily. In 1835–6 he travelled extensively in eastern Europe, reaching Moscow. A volume of fine topographical sketches, mostly from this tour, and including buildings in Copenhagen, Stockholm, Novgorod, Gdansk, Lübeck, Potsdam, Nürnberg, Bamberg, Zwickau and Regensburg, is in the R.I.B.A. Drawings Collection. On his return he exhibited a view of Prague at the Royal Academy. Other drawings exhibited by him at the Academy show that he designed the following buildings: THE ARCHERS' LODGE in REGENT'S PARK, LONDON, 1833; a new Tudor Gothic front to LITCHBOROUGH HOUSE, NORTHANTS., for William Grant, 1838; some (half-timbered) houses at MUCH HADHAM, HERTS., for N. G. Times, 1840; and a cottage at WALLINGTON, SURREY, for T. F. Reynolds, 1840. He, rather than his elderly namesake (*q.v.*), was presumably the George Moore who designed YAZOR CHURCH, HEREFS., in 1843 [*Hereford Times*, 1 April 1843, 539]. The R.I.B.A. Collection has designs by Moore for a Gothic cathedral and a neo-Grecian villa, and a view of a room in Exeter Hall, Strand, as arranged for a conversazione of the Architectural Society [*Catalogue*: *L–N*, 91 and figs. 53–4]. Moore's career ended in 1846, when he became an imbecile. A fund for his support was raised by subscription through the *Builder* [*Builder* iv, 1846, 80, 345].

MORGAN, JAMES, was a Welshman who began his career in the office of John Nash. From 1806 to 1815 he was the latter's assistant as architect to the Department of Woods and Forests. As such he was responsible for the routine work of repairs to the buildings in the royal parks and forests. Through Nash's influence he was in 1812 appointed engineer to the Regent's Canal Company, for which he designed the MACCLESFIELD BRIDGE, REGENT'S PARK, built in 1815–16 to carry a road over the canal [J. Elmes, *Metropolitan Improvements*, 1831, 57–8]. In REGENT STREET he built No. 326, and in PARK PLACE he collaborated with Nash and the elder Pugin in the design of the DIORAMA (1823), an ingenious revolving spectacle for which he devised the machinery [Elmes, *op. cit.*, 81]. In 1828–30 he designed ST. GEORGE'S CHURCH, WOLVERHAMPTON, for the Church Building Commissioners in a classical style [Port, 162], and in 1834 he rebuilt the south side of BUSHBURY CHURCH, STAFFS. [I.C.B.S.]. Morgan exhibited occasionally at the Royal Academy, showing in 1802 a 'Design for a Gothic mansion', in 1807 a 'Design for rebuilding Sholbrook

Lodge, Whittlebury Forest', Northants., and in 1819 and 1821 designs for mausolea. [John Summerson, *John Nash*, 1935, *passim*.]

MORGAN, JAMES DAVIES, exhibited at the Royal Academy in 1830 (a view of part of the crypt of Kirkstall Abbey, Yorkshire) and 1831 (a lodge for D. Cheetham, Esq., of Stalybridge Cheshire, 'now erecting under the direction of Mr. J. W. Atkinson'.) In 1835 he competed for the Houses of Parliament with a 'Perpendicular' Gothic design, and in 1839 for the Ashmolean Museum at Oxford [Bodleian Library, MS. Top. Oxon. c. 202]. He was then living at Castle Hedingham in Essex. In 1840, when he designed ST. JOHN'S CHURCH, CORNISH HALL END, ESSEX, in the 'Early English' style, his address was given as Chelmsford [I.C.B.S.].

MORISON, DAVID, was Secretary of the Literary and Antiquarian Society at Perth, and not a professional architect. In 1822 he designed a building in George Street originally known as THE MONUMENT in order to accommodate the Society and the Public Library. It was remodelled in 1854 as the Perth Art Gallery [D. Peacock, *Perth*, 1849, 505].

MORISON, ROBERT (–1825), appears to have been a pupil of Robert and James Adam. Writing to the Earl of Buchan to introduce Morison in 1807, Joseph Bonomi said he was a native of Edinburgh and described him as 'a clever architect' whom he had known for forty years. They had, he said, been 'companions many years in the study of the Messrs. Adams of the Adelphi' [Sotheby's, 22 Feb. 1972, lot 599].

In July 1791 Morison was engaged by Sir John Soane as an assistant at a salary of £100 per annum [A. T. Bolton, *The Works of Sir John Soane*, 1924, Appendix C, xli]. In the same year he exhibited a design for a villa at the Royal Academy, and in 1794 he published the first part of a little-known work, entitled *Designs in Perspective for Villas in the Ancient Castle and Grecian Styles*, with a dedication to the Duchess of Gordon. The Edinburgh directories show that he was practising there from 1807 until his death.

In 1789 Morison submitted a design for the new Edinburgh University of which the original section is preserved in the Scottish National Monuments Record (EDD/220/1), and in 1815 he was one of the selected architects who competed for the completion of Adam's building [D. C. Horn in *University of Edinburgh Jnl.* xxiii, 1967–8, 321, and xxiv, 1969–70, 39]. Alternative designs by him for a toll-house (1798) are in the Scottish Record Office (RHP 10318–9). The only architectural work at present known to have been carried out to his design is NOS. 24, 26, 28 and 30 HOWE STREET, EDINBURGH, 1807, which originally formed a symmetrical group [Edinburgh Dean of Guild plans, 26 June 1807].

Morison died at Raeburn Place, Stockbridge, Edinburgh, on 9 August 1825 [*Scots Mag.* xvii, 1825, 384].

MORLIDGE, JOHN, acted as clerk of the works at Longleat House, Wilts., under Jeffry Wyatville from 1807 to 1813 [D. Linstrum, *Sir Jeffry Wyatville*, 1972, 26]. According to *Gentleman's Magazine*, 1814 (ii), 491, and J. Dugdale's *British Traveller* iv, 1819, 463, he designed EVERLEY CHURCH, WILTS., built in the Gothic style in 1813–14 at the expense of Francis Dugdale Astley. Pigot's *Directory* of 1825–6 lists John Morlidge as a builder in Horseferry Road, Westminster, and Samuel Morlidge as a carpenter at the same address.

MORRIS, JOHN (*c.* 1716–1792), was the successor, and almost certainly the son, of Arthur Morris (d. 1744), the principal stonemason in Lewes in the first half of the eighteenth century. From 1750 onwards he did a great deal of work at GLYNDE PLACE, SUSSEX, for Richard Trevor, Bishop of Durham. Between 1753 and 1756 he built the stable range in accordance with designs submitted by himself, and in 1758–9 he remodelled the interior of the hall. He also rebuilt the southern of the two bow-windows on the east front, and added the bay window on the north front. In 1763–5 he was employed by the Bishop to rebuild GLYNDE CHURCH to the designs of Sir Thomas Robinson [*Sussex Arch. Colls.* xx, 1868, 78–9]. Morris's craftsmanship at Glynde is of a very high standard, and his use of dressed stone, flint and brick shows a subtle appreciation of their contrasting effects of colour and texture [Trevor archives in East Sussex Record Office and *C. Life*, 14–28 April 1955]. Morris was also employed in the rebuilding of ASHBURNHAM PLACE, SUSSEX, between 1757 and 1761 [*C. Life*, 23 April 1953], and it has been suggested by Mr. Arthur Oswald that he may have been concerned in the remodelling of FIRLE PLACE, SUSSEX, in the middle of the eighteenth century [*C. Life*, 17–24 Feb. 1955]. In 1761–3 he designed and built the TOWN HALL or SESSIONS HOUSE at LEWES, dem. 1810 [E. Sussex County Records, QAF/2/1/E1, and a letter among the Glynde archives dated 24 Aug. 1760, in which Morris refers to his plans for the Sessions House], and a ground plan of the west gate at Lewes made by him in 1777 is in the British Museum [Add. MS. 5677, f. 8]. In 1776–8 he carried out alterations at COOMBE PLACE, HAMSEY, SUSSEX, for Sir John Bridger [Shiffner MS. 1379].

Morris was one of the constables of Lewes in 1751 and 1765, and died there in 1792, aged 76 [Register of All Saints, Lewes]. In his will he is described as 'Surveyor and Stone Mason' [E.

558

Sussex Record Office: Wills of the Archdeaconry of Lewes, A 66, f. 423]. His business was continued by the firm of Parsons (afterwards Bridgeman) of Eastgate Street, Lewes.

MORRIS, ROBERT (*c.* 1702–1754), was related to Roger Morris (*q.v.*), for the second part of his *Lectures* is dedicated to the latter, and in the dedication he refers to him as his 'kinsman', and acknowledges the 'erudition' he has received 'in your service'. He practised as an architect and surveyor, but is chiefly notable as the author of several architectural publications. Their titles were: *An Essay in Defence of Ancient Architecture or, A Parallel of the Ancient Buildings with the Modern: showing the Beauty and Harmony of the Former, and the Irregularity of the Latter*, 1728; *Lectures on Architecture, consisting of Rules founded upon Harmonick and Arithmetical Proportions in Building*, 1734, 2nd. ed. 1759; *An Essay upon Harmony, as it relates to Situation and Building*, published anonymously, 1739; *The Art of Architecture, A Poem in imitation of Horace's Act of Poetry*, published anonymously, 1742; *Rural Architecture*, 1750, reissued as *Select Architecture*, 1755, 2nd. ed. 1757 (reprint New York 1973); *The Architectural Remembrancer: being a Collection of New and Useful Designs, of Ornamental Buildings and Decorations for Parks, Gardens, Woods, etc., to which are added, A variety of Chimney-Pieces, after the Manner of Inigo Jones and Mr. Kent*, 1751; reissued as *Architecture Improved*, 1755, 1757; *The Qualifications and Duty of a Surveyor, Explained in a Letter to the Earl of —*, published anonymously, 1752; and *A Second Letter to the Rt. Hon. the Earl of — concerning the Qualifications and Duty of a Surveyor*, published anonymously, 1752. The last work contains a list of 'some tracts wrote by the author of this letter' which includes the *Essay upon Harmony*, the *Art of Architecture*, and two poetical effusions entitled *Rupert to Maria. An Heroic Epistle* (1748) and *An Inquiry after Virtue* (n.d.). These latter works have been attributed (*e.g.* in *A.P.S.D.* and *D.N.B.*) to John Gwynn (*q.v.*), but internal evidence makes it clear that the *Essay upon Harmony, The Art of Architecture* and *Rupert to Maria* are in fact by Morris, who must therefore have been the author of the two essays on the *Qualifications of a Surveyor*. In addition Morris is stated by D. E. Baker, *Biographica Dramatica* ii, 1812, 230, to have been the author of *Fatal Necessity: or, Liberty Regain'd*, a political play published in Dublin in 1742, soon after the general election of that year, and dedicated by the author, under the character of 'An Independent Elector', to Charles Edwin, one of the M.P.s elected for the City of Westminster. The *Lectures* are stated to have been 'Read to a Society Establish'd for the improvement of Arts and Sciences'. No other reference to that society has been found, but it was evidently more than a literary fiction, for Morris gives the date upon which each lecture was read (starting on 22 October 1730).

Morris's publications – especially his *Essay in Defence of Ancient Architecture* and his *Lectures* – are important as the chief exposition in writing of the architectural theory of English Palladianism. Although several volumes of engravings were published under Lord Burlington's auspices they were accompanied by very little text, and it was Morris's function to supplement the fundamental law of Palladio with an aesthetic theory which he set out in prose in his two *Essays* and *Lectures*, and in verse in *The Art of Architecture*. His belief in a strict adherence to the canon of the Orders and in the virtues of a classical simplicity is exemplified in the designs that he published in *The Architectural Remembrancer* and *Select Architecture*.

Morris's published designs are competent but somewhat pedestrian. They hardly suggest that he was an architect of much distinction, and no building of any importance can confidently be attributed to him. There is, however, evidence to connect him with the building of the south front of Culverthorpe in Lincolnshire (*c.* 1730–5) for Sir Michael Newton. It was to Newton that his *Lectures* (1734) were dedicated, and plate 23 of his *Select Architecture* (1755) is a variation on the design of Culverthorpe. The building accounts (now among the Halliwell-Phillipps MSS. in the Library of Congress at Washington and kindly examined for me by Mr. A. A. Tait) show that Robert Morris was in control of the work, charging in 1731 'Board wages 37 weeks at 4s. per week', and passing the craftsmen's bills. But as Sir Michael Newton was simultaneously employing Roger Morris to alter his London house, it is likely that the latter was also involved at Culverthorpe, which has several features found in his documented works elsewhere (see plan and measured drawings in H. Field & M. Bunney, *English Domestic Architecture of the XVII and XVIII Centuries*, 1905, 46–7 and pl. xlix; *C. Life*, 15, 22 Sept. 1923).

In 1740 Morris was called in to value the model of George Dance's design for the Mansion House made by John Cordwell, the City Carpenter [City of London records; S. Perks, *History of the Mansion House*, 1922, 184], in 1743 he was paid £1 6s. for 'surveying or measuring' some brickwork in Twickenham for the banker George Middleton [Coutts Bank, P/L 1735–55, f. 135], and in 1753–4, at the behest of Christopher Lee, a carpenter of Norwich, he supplied plans for building an octagonal chapel in that city, for which he was paid 8 guineas by the Committee, although in the event another design was adopted [S.J. Wearing, *Georgian Norwich: Its Builders*, 1926, 23]. A letter in the possession of Mr. Geoffrey Beard shows

that in 1753 he was altering a house in London for an unnamed bishop on the instructions of Sir Edward Hales. Some designs for chimney-pieces in the R.I.B.A. Drawings Collection are attributed to him on the strength of their resemblance to plates in his *Architecture Improved*.

In 1728 Morris described himself as 'of Twickenham', but by 1740 he was living in Hyde Park Street, near Grosvenor Square, and in his will [P.C.C. 334 PINFOLD] he is described as 'of George's, Hanover Square, Surveyor'. According to a contemporary note in a copy of his *Essay in Defence of Ancient Architecture* in the R.I.B.A. Library he died on 12 November 1754 in his 53rd year. He directed that all his 'real and personal estate, goods, books, copper plates, copyright to Books wrote printed and published by me, my drawings, manuscripts, etc.' were to be sold for the benefit of his children Thomas, Mary, James and Hannah, with the exception of 'the silver tankard, the silver cup and salver given me by John Cope, which I would have preserved in my family'. His executors were his friend Mr. William Perritt of Farm Street and his cousins James Thornton of Kew and James Morris, painter in Berkeley Square.

[*A.P.S.D.*; *D.N.B.*; John Fleming, *Robert Adam and his Circle*, 1962; information from Dr. Eileen Harris.]

MORRIS, ROGER (1695–1749), was born in London on 19 April 1695 and baptized in the church of St. Martin-in-the-Fields. Nothing is known of his father, Owen Morris, or of his own early life. The first record of his activities as a builder occurs in 1724, when he took a lease of a plot on the Harley estate in Oxford Street, and built a house for his own occupation. He was then described as a bricklayer. By 1730, when he moved to a larger house which he had built in Green Street, he was described by the rate collector as 'gentleman'. Later he was to be concerned in extensive speculative building developments in Argyll Street (1736) and on the approaches to Westminster Bridge (1740–2), and it may be presumed that speculative building formed the basis of his prosperity.

As an architect, Morris's career appears to have been closely linked with two persons: Colen Campbell and Henry Herbert, the 'Architect Earl' of Pembroke. On loan to the R.I.B.A. Drawings Collection there is a set of drawings for rebuilding Goodwood House. These drawings correspond to the designs for Goodwood by Colen Campbell which he published in the third volume of *Vitruvius Britannicus* (1725). But the draughtsmanship is certainly not Campbell's and may be Morris's. At Wilton there is an elevation signed by Morris which represents a variant version of Campbell's design for Pembroke House, Whitehall (built in 1724), and in 1729, shortly before Campbell's death, Morris was acting on his behalf in connection with the building of the stables at Studley Royal in Yorkshire. Campbell (as Morris explained in a letter to John Aislabie, the owner of the estate) had been taken ill in Norfolk and was got back to London only with 'grate difficulty'. In a letter written a fortnight later from his sick-bed Campbell dismisses two drawings by Morris as 'very ugly' and says that he has 'ordered him to correct' a third.

It would appear, therefore, that as a young man Morris acted, at least on occasion, as Campbell's assistant, and it may have been through Campbell that he came into contact with the future Earl of Pembroke, whose architectural collaborator he was to be at Marble Hill (1724–9), the White (New Park) Lodge at Richmond (1727–8), the Column of Victory at Blenheim (1730–1), Wimbledon House (1732–3), the Palladian Bridge at Wilton (1736–7), and probably at Westcombe House, Blackheath. Herbert evidently valued Morris's services highly, for in 1734 he presented him with a large silver cup as a token of his regard. Still preserved by Morris's descendants, it bears the inscription: 'Given by my Noble Patron Henry, Earl of Pembroke, By whose favour alone I am Enabled to fill it. R. Morris 1734.' Above there is a portrait of Inigo Jones framed in a cartouche of architectural instruments (see illustration in *C. Life*, 31 Oct. 1952, 1409).

As the former assistant of Colen Campbell and the acknowledged collaborator of the Architect Earl, Morris was now well placed to attract a wider patronage. The accuracy of the estimates provided by 'the noted architect Mr. Morris' had already been commended by Edward Laurence in *The Duty of a Steward to his Lord* (1727), and in 1731–2 Morris gave himself the benefit of foreign travel, for between June 1731 and November 1732 he was reported to be 'absent from the Kingdom and beyond the seas'.[1] In 1727 he had been given the newly created Office of Works post of Clerk of the Works at Richmond New Park Lodge, and in 1734 he succeeded Sir William Ogbourne as Master Carpenter to the Office of Ordnance – a post which he undoubtedly owed to the 2nd Duke of Argyll, who was Master-General of the Ordnance from 1725 to 1740, for whom he had recently enlarged Adderbury House, and with whom he is said to have 'stood high in favour and on terms of great

friendship'. It was a valuable appointment which brought him work at Woolwich and elsewhere that was worth £2000 or £3000 a year.

Despite his association with Campbell and Herbert, Morris was by no means a tamely orthodox Palladian. Marble Hill and the lodge at Richmond were, of course, Palladian villas *par excellence*. But elsewhere, notably at Combe Bank and Whitton Place, Morris developed a villa style of his own which, if it had basically Palladian antecedents, had some markedly individual features, notably the pyramidal roof, the *œil-de-bœuf* windows, and the distinctive porch. The arcaded wings which he added to Adderbury House are his most obvious, but not his only, borrowing from Vanbrugh, while for the stables at Althorp he designed a Tuscan portico which followed the lead of Inigo Jones's St. Paul's, Covent Garden, in a manner which has no obvious parallel in contemporary Georgian architecture. Most remarkable of all are his two castellated houses, Clearwell (*c.* 1728) and Inveraray (1745). In its appreciation of the simple massing of genuine medieval domestic architecture Clearwell is unique, having no affinity with either Vanbrugh's castellated villas or Hawksmoor's transvestite Gothic churches and colleges. Inveraray, on the other hand, was to be the progenitor of a whole sequence of symmetrical Georgian castles, and must itself be related to a sketch in Vanbrugh's Elton album which shows that he had envisaged just such a castle-like house as Morris designed for the Duke of Argyll at Inveraray. Though Morris had little understanding of Gothic detail, he therefore emerges as a figure of some importance in the long and complex history of neo-medieval architecture in Britain.

Morris died on 31 January 1749. He had been twice married. Both his wives appear to have been members of a family of London merchants called Jackson who established themselves as country gentry at Pontrilas in Herefordshire. His first wife, Mary, died in 1729, and in 1731 Roger married Elizabeth, daughter of Sir Philip Jackson of Pontrilas. By his first marriage he had two sons, James and Roger, and by his second, one son and four daughters. All the daughters appear to have married well, and the eldest son, who succeeded to his post as Master Carpenter to the Ordnance, lived the life of a gentleman in Surrey, of which county he was High Sheriff in 1764. The second son, Col. Roger Morris, married Mary Philipse and became the ancestor both of the family of Morris of New York and of an English family of Morris which figures in Burke's *Landed Gentry*.

[Wyatt Papworth in *Builder* xxxiii, 1875, 881–2; correspondence in *C. Life*, 25 Feb., 17–24 March, 7 April 1944; Marie P. G. Draper, *Marble Hill House*, 1970, 17–19; O. F. G. Hogg, *The Royal Arsenal* i, 1963, 285; *Survey of London*

---

[1] An allusion to Morris's visit to Italy will be found in a letter from Martin Folkes, then at Venice, to the Duke of Richmond (1733) printed by the Earl of March in *A Duke and his Friends* i, 1911, 251–2: 'I am confident that Mr. Morris was mistaken who as I understand said at your Graces [that the Rialto Bridge] is a bigger arch than that at Verona [which Morris] said he measured.' See also *Survey of London* xxxv, 73, for another reference to Morris's foreign journey.

xxxi, 284, 290; G. L. M. Goodfellow, 'Colen Campbell's Last Years', *Burlington Mag.* cxi, 1969, 189–90; Burke's *Landed Gentry* under 'Morris of York' or 'Morris of Netherby'; P.C.C. 49 LISLE.]

MARBLE HILL, TWICKENHAM, MIDDLESEX, for Henrietta Howard, Countess of Suffolk, mistress of George II, 1724–9 [see above, p. 414].

COMBE BANK, nr. SUNDRIDGE, KENT, for Col. John Campbell, later 4th Duke of Argyll, *c.* 1725; subsequently much altered by D. A. Alexander, G. Legg (1835–9) and others [*Vitruvius Britannicus* iv, 1767, pls. 75–7; Mary Cosh in *C. Life*, 13 July 1972, 80, and 28 Sept. 1972, 723].

THE WHITE BANK, LODGE, RICHMOND NEW PARK, begun 1727 for George I, completed 1728 for George II [see above, p. 414].

CLEARWELL CASTLE, GLOS., for Thomas Wyndham, *c.* 1728, castellated Gothic [National Library of Wales, Dunraven papers 347, an estimate by Roger Morris dated 29 Dec. 1727 and 1 Jan. 1728, corresponding to the building as erected] (Alistair Rowan, 'Clearwell Castle', in *The Country Seat*, ed. Colvin & Harris, 1970, 145–9).

CASTLE HILL, DEVONSHIRE, remodelled for Lord Clinton (afterwards 1st Lord Fortescue) under the direction of Lord Burlington and Lord Herbert, 1729–*c.* 1740. Morris's contract for the Portland stonework of the exterior, dated 22 Feb. 1728–9, specifies that the proportions of the entablature 'shall be made as the Earl of Burlington or Lord Herbert shall direct and the carving of . . . all other parts of the said cornice [shall be] according to the plan or drawing thereof signed by the said Roger Morris' [Devon County Record Office, Fortescue papers, E1/93]. For further evidence of Lord Burlington's participation in the design, see above, p. 131. The centre was gutted by fire in 1934, and subsequently restored (*C. Life*, 17, 24 March 1934, 29 Oct. 1938).

attributed: BEECHWOOD PARK, HERTS., library for Sir Thomas Sebright, Bart., *c.* 1730; internally remodelled by Thomas Cundy 1804 [drawings preserved at Beechwood include designs by Roger Morris for a new west front. These were not carried out, but are similar to the existing library] (*C. Life*, 12 Nov. 1938, fig. 4).

LONDON, GREEN STREET, house (now No. 61) for himself, *c.* 1730 [M. P. G. Draper, *Marble Hill House*, 1970, 17–18].

*WESTCOMBE HOUSE, BLACKHEATH, KENT, rebuilt for Lord Herbert, *c.* 1730; dem. 1854 [above, p. 414].

*BLENHEIM PALACE, OXON., THE COLUMN OF VICTORY, for Sarah, Duchess of Marlborough, 1730–1 [above, p. 414].

attributed: CULVERTHORPE HALL, LINCS., rebuild-

ing of south front for Sir Michael Newton, Bart., *c.* 1730–5 [above, p. 559].

LONDON, NO. 6 ST. JAMES'S SQUARE, repairs or alterations for the 1st Earl of Bristol, 1731; dem. 1819 [*Survey of London* xxix, 104].

CHICHESTER, SUSSEX, THE COUNCIL HOUSE, 1731 [Walpole Soc., *Vertue Note Books* v, 144; for Lord Burlington's involvement see above, p. 132].

ADDERBURY HOUSE, OXON., added arcaded wings, including gallery, for the 2nd Duke of Argyll, 1731; south wing and gallery dem. 1808 [signed drawings among Duke of Buccleuch's papers in S.R.O.] (plan in *V.C.H. Oxfordshire* ix, 8; *C. Life*, 7 Jan. 1949).

*LONDON, PEMBROKE HOUSE, WHITEHALL, addition of outbuildings for Henry, Lord Herbert, 1731–2; house rebuilt 1757, dem. 1913 [accounts at Wilton House, *ex inf.* Mr. T. P. Connor; cf. Ralph's *Critical Review of the Publick Buildings in London and Westminster*, 1734, 45].

LONDON, NO. 30 OLD BURLINGTON STREET, interior decoration for Sir Michael Newton, Bart., 1731–2; dem. 1935 ['Mr. Matthew Lamb's Accounts with Sir Michael Newton 1728–40' at Welford Park, Berks., record payments to Roger Morris and a number of London craftsmen (including Isaac Mansfield, plasterer, James Richards, carver, and James Morris, painter) in the years 1731–2. The building is not specified, but was evidently 30 Old Burlington Street, whose interior Newton embellished after acquiring the lease in 1725: see *Survey of London* xxxii, 505 and plates].

WHITTON PLACE (or PARK), MIDDLESEX, for the Earl of Ilay (afterwards 3rd Duke of Argyll), *c.* 1732–9; dem. *c.* 1847 [Mary Cosh in *C. Life*, 20 July 1972; cf. related designs, not necessarily for Whitton, reproduced by John Harris, *Catalogue of British Drawings for Architecture, etc. in American Collections*, 1971, pls. 98–104].

*WIMBLEDON HOUSE, SURREY, for Sarah, Duchess of Marlborough, 1732–3; destroyed by fire 1785 [above, p. 415].

ALTHORP HOUSE, NORTHANTS., THE STABLES, for the 5th Earl of Sunderland, *c.* 1732–3 [Woburn Abbey archives, letter from Sarah, Duchess of Marlborough, to the Duchess of Bedford, 11 Sept. 1733, referring to Morris as the architect of the stables and of some other buildings in the park, no doubt including the Palladian Gardener's House: *ex inf.* the late Lord Spencer and Mr. David Green].

EASTBURY PARK, DORSET, completed interior of house for George Bubb Dodington after death of Sir John Vanbrugh, *c.* 1733–8; dem. 1775 [F. J. B. Watson in *C. Life*, 11 Feb. 1949, 317;

---

* Buildings designed in conjunction with Henry, Lord Herbert, afterwards 9th Earl of Pembroke.

L. Whistler, *The Imagination of Vanbrugh*, 1954, 174–5 and fig. 76].

*WILTON HOUSE, WILTS., THE PALLADIAN BRIDGE, for the 9th Earl of Pembroke, 1736–7 [above, p. 415].

LONDON, NO. 59 STRAND, for George Middleton, banker, 1739–40; dem. [Coutts & Co., P/L 1735–55, ff. 95, 102, *ex inf.* Miss Mary Cosh].

LONDON, WESTMINSTER, houses on north side of NEW PALACE YARD, 1740–2; dem. [P.R.O., Works, records of the Westminster Bridge Commissioners] (*Architectural History* ix, 1966, fig. 51).

LONGFORD CASTLE, WILTS., unidentified building for the 1st Viscount Folkestone, perhaps not executed, 1742. Accounts at Longford show that on 31 May 1742 Lord Folkestone paid 'Mr. Morris for drawing a design for the building at Longford'.

attributed: GOODWOOD HOUSE, SUSSEX, CARNÉ'S SEAT, for the 2nd Duke of Richmond, 1743. Vertue states that the Duke of Richmond was the 'greatest promoter' of the Council House at Chichester, which Morris designed, and a letter in B.M., Add. MS. 27587, f. 83, shows that Morris was obtaining Portland stone for building operations at Goodwood in the autumn of 1742: see also C. Hussey in *C. Life*, 17 March 1744, Correspondence (*C. Life*, 16 July 1932).

INVERARAY CASTLE, ARGYLLSHIRE, for the 3rd Duke of Argyll, 1745–60, castellated Gothic, centre damaged by fire 1877, restored 1878–9 [Ian G. Lindsay & Mary Cosh, *Inveraray and the Dukes of Argyll*, 1973].

INVERARAY, ARGYLLSHIRE, THE GARRON BRIDGE, 1747–9 [W. Adam, *Vitruvius Scoticus*, pl. 74; Ian G. Lindsay & Mary Cosh, *Inveraray and the Dukes of Argyll*, 1973, 125].

KIRBY HALL, OUSEBURN, YORKS. (W.R.), elevation for Stephen Thompson, in association with the 3rd Earl of Burlington, 1747–c. 1755; dem. 1920 [above, p. 131].

LONDON, NO. 19 ST. JAMES'S SQUARE, alterations for the 2nd Duke of Cleveland, 1746–7; dem. 1894. In 1747 Morris's place was taken by Daniel Garrett after a disagreement between himself and the Duke [accounts at Raby Castle, *ex inf.* Mr. Peter Leach] (*Survey of London* xxix, 161–3).

BRANDENBURG HOUSE, HAMMERSMITH, MIDDLESEX, rebuilt for George Bubb Dodington, who bought the house in 1748; gallery added by J. N. Servandoni; dem. 1822 [*Vitruvius Britannicus* iv, 1767, pls. 26–7].

Note: Further buildings which may prove to have been designed by Roger Morris are LYDIARD

HOUSE, LYDIARD TREGOSE, WILTS., as remodelled by the 2nd Viscount St. John *c.* 1743 [C. Hussey in *C. Life*, 19–20 March 1948], and a group of buildings commissioned by the 7th Earl of Westmorland: the remodelling of the inner quadrangle of APETHORPE, NORTHANTS., *c.* 1740–2 (cf. plan in *V.C.H. Northants.* ii, 544), the wings which he added to MEREWORTH CASTLE, KENT, about the same time, and the remarkably neoclassical church which he built at MEREWORTH in 1744–6. These suggestions are prompted by stylistic considerations too complex to set out in this *Dictionary* and too tentative to justify a firm attribution. The possibility that Morris designed ARGYLL HOUSE, ARGYLL STREET, LONDON, for the Earl of Ilay (afterwards 3rd Duke of Argyll) is discussed in *Survey of London* xxxi, 296.

Unexecuted designs by Morris include a bound volume of drawings for a new house at MILTON, NORTHANTS. (Northants. Record Office, Milton Drawings 99–111); a design for rebuilding the garden front of BEECHWOOD PARK, HERTS. (at Beechwood); designs for a coach-house, stable, etc., dated 1742 at BLAIR ATHOLL, PERTHSHIRE (at Blair); and drawings in the Mellon Collection for a house supposed to be WHITTON PLACE, MIDDLESEX (John Harris, *Catalogue of British Drawings for Architecture, etc., in American Collections*, 1971, pls. 98–104). It may be noted that there is so close a similarity between some of Roger Morris's drawings and those published by Robert Morris in his *Rural Architecture, etc.*, as to indicate close collaboration between the two.

MORTON, HENRY PENNY SELBY, rebuilt LOWICK CHURCH, NORTHUMBERLAND, in 1794, as recorded by an inscription on the tower giving his name as 'Architect'. The church was much altered in the nineteenth century [F. R. Wilson, *Churches in the Archdeaconry of Lindisfarne*, 1870, 24; *History of Northumberland* xiv, 91]. In 1810 the foundation of a masonic lodge at Tweedmouth was laid by 'brother Selby Morton', acting master' [J. Sykes, *Local Records* ii, 1866, 60].

MORTON, RICHARD (–1814), was apprenticed to a carpenter and cabinet-maker of Worcester in 1768. He subsequently became a carpenter and builder in that city, and held various offices in the Corporation, including that of Mayor in 1797. As an architect his works included the MARKET HALL in HIGH STREET, WORCESTER, 1804, dem. 1954, which is illustrated as a vignette on the title-page of T. Eaton's *Concise History of Worcester* (1816) [Worcester City Chamber Order Book, 16 July 1801], and extensions to NASH'S HOSPITAL in NEW STREET, 1809 [Chamber Order Book, 1809] [information from Alderman B. Brotherton and Mr. D. A. Whitehead].

---

* Buildings designed in conjunction with Henry, Lord Herbert, afterwards 9th Earl of Pembroke.

MOSELEY, WILLIAM (c. 1799–1880), was a pupil of George Julian. He practised in London from the late 1820s until his death on 29 July 1880, in his 82nd year [*Times*, 31 July 1880]. He held the post of County Surveyor of Middlesex from 1829 to 1846, and that of District Surveyor for West Islington from 1853 onwards. Latterly he was in partnership with his brother Andrew Moseley. Charles Henman (d. 1884) was his pupil.

Moseley designed the following churches in Sussex: HOLTYE COMMON, cons. 1836, dem. 1892 [I.C.B.S.]; FOREST ROW, cons. 1836, enlarged 1879 [I.C.B.S.]; HADLOW DOWN, 1836, rebuilt 1913 [I.C.B.S.]; UCKFIELD, incorporating old tower and chancel, 1839 [I.C.B.S.; *Civil Engineer and Architect's Jnl.* ii, 1839, 316]; and ST. MARK'S, HORSHAM, 1840–1, remodelled 1870 [exhib. at R.A. 1841]. None of them satisfied nineteenth-century ecclesiological standards. In 1843–4 his designs for ST. MARY'S CHURCH, KINGSTON, PORTSEA, HANTS., were rejected in favour of less expensive ones by T. E. Owen (*q.v.*).

Moseley's public works included the enlargement of the MIDDLESEX HOUSE OF CORRECTION in COLDBATH FIELDS, CLERKENWELL, 1830, dem. [exhib. at R.A. 1833]; the addition of wings to the COUNTY LUNATIC ASYLUM at HANWELL, MIDDLESEX, 1838 [exhib. at R.A. 1838]; the COUNTY LUNATIC ASYLUM FOR SURREY at WANDSWORTH, 1839–41 [exhib. at R.A. 1839; Brayley, *Surrey* ii, 498]; the MIDDLESEX HOUSE OF DETENTION at CLERKENWELL, 1845–6 [*Builder* iv, 1846, 277, 282–3; W. G. Pinks, *History of Clerkenwell*, 1881, 185]; and the completion of the COUNTY LUNATIC ASYLUM at RAINHILL, LANCS., after the death of H. L. Elmes, 1847–51 [exhib. at R.A. 1853]. He also designed a GIRLS' SCHOOL at NEW BRENTFORD, MIDDLESEX, 1840 [exhib at R.A.], and a house called SUTTON HURST at BARCOMBE in SUSSEX for Capt. Thomas Richardson, 1838 [exhib. at R.A.]. In conjunction with Andrew Moseley he designed THE CITY BANK in THREADNEEDLE STREET, LONDON, 1856 [exhib. at R.A.], a branch bank in BROAD STREET, and THE WESTMINSTER PALACE HOTEL, VICTORIA STREET, 1859–61, said to have been the first hotel in London to be equipped with lifts [*Builder* xx, 1862, 165–7]. [*The Architects, Engineers and Building Trades Directory*, 1868, 127; *Builder* xxxix, 1880, 171.]

MOSS, WILLIAM (1754–), was admitted to the Royal Academy Schools in 1774 at the age of 20. He was awarded the Silver Medal in 1775, and the Gold Medal in 1778. He exhibited at the Academy from 1775 to 1782. According to Redgrave's *Dictionary of Artists* (1878), he 'painted some landscapes and both drew and etched'. An architect of this name was employed to rebuild the tower and part of the nave and chancel of LUD-

DENHAM CHURCH, KENT, after they had collapsed in 1807 [C. E. Woodruff, *An Inventory of Parish Registers and Records in the Diocese of Canterbury*, 1922, 114].

MOUNTAGUE, JAMES (c. 1776–1853), was the younger brother of William Mountague, and, like him, began his architectural career as a clerk in the office of George Dance. In 1821 he became District Surveyor for the North Division of the City of London. He was also Surveyor to the Port of London (1806–28) and of Blackfriars Bridge. He designed, in c. 1820, the SCHOOLS of the Benevolent Society of St. Patrick in STAMFORD STREET, SOUTHWARK, now the London School of Printing [*Survey of London* xxiii, 18; *Gent's Mag.* 1822 (i), 497]. He died on 24 April 1853, aged 77 [*A.P.S.D.*; *Gent's Mag.* 1853 (i), 675].

MOUNTAGUE, WILLIAM (1773–1843), was the son of William Mountague (d. 1791), a minor City official who was for a time a clerk in the office of George Dance, the Surveyor to the City of London. After being employed by Dance in a similar capacity for some years, the younger Mountague succeeded James Peacock as Assistant Clerk of the City Works in 1814, and in 1816 succeeded Dance himself as City Surveyor. He had, in 1812, been appointed surveyor to the City Improvement Committee, and in this capacity was responsible for the formation of Finsbury Circus, planned by Dance in 1802, but not carried out until the demolition of the Bethlehem Hospital in 1815. Among the buildings which he designed were the DEBTORS' PRISON in WHITECROSS STREET, 1813–15, dem. 1873; the COURTS of KING'S BENCH and COMMON PLEAS at GUILDHALL, 1823, dem.; THE CITY LIBRARY, 1828, dem. 1871; FARRINGDON MARKET, 1828–9, dem. 1873 and 1892; the Gothic panelling under the window at the east end of GUILDHALL, 1838, removed 1866; and the lobbies and committee rooms at GUILDHALL, 1842. He was also responsible in 1842 for the removal of the attic storey over the Ballroom of the MANSION HOUSE, and for designing the existing new coffered ceiling to take its place.

Besides these works, he made the valuations for purchasing the property required for various improvements in the City, including the widening of St. Martin's le Grand and the erection of the new Post Office in 1824, the formation of King William Street, and of Wellington Street in the Borough, as north and south approaches to London Bridge; and for the formation of Moorfields Pavement, Sir Robert Smirke being employed as architect of the new houses in each case. He was similarly employed in clearing the site for the new Royal Exchange, begun in 1841, and in valuations preparatory to the construction

563

of Moorgate Street, Prince's Street and Gresham Street. The enlargement of Smithfield Market was also carried out under his direction. He was District Surveyor for the West Division of the City from 1808, and was surveyor to the estates of Sir Charles Morgan, the Sons of the Clergy, Baroness von Zandt, and the Thames Tunnel Company. He died on 12 April 1843, aged 70, and was interred in the Bunhill Fields Burial Ground. His only son and chief assistant, Frederick William Mountague (c. 1801–41), was a successful surveyor with a considerable practice, but predeceased his father, dying on 2 December 1841, aged 40, after being thrown from his gig. [A.P.S.D.; D.N.B.; S. Redgrave, A Dictionary of Artists of the English School, 1878, 301; Dorothy Stroud, George Dance, 1971, 137, 155–6, 221–2, 246; The Farington Diary, ed. J. Greig, vi, 63.]

MOUNTAIN, CHARLES (c. 1743–1805), was prominent as an architect and builder in Hull during the last quarter of the eighteenth century. He was much employed by the wealthy merchant J. R. Pease, for whom he designed a country house at HESSLE called HESSLEWOOD, and probably a town house in CHARLOTTE STREET, HULL (dem.). He also designed a house in MOSLEY STREET, MANCHESTER, for Pease's Robinson connections, the TRINITY HOUSE NAVIGATION SCHOOL, HULL, 1786–7, dem. 1844, and a plain row of houses in MYTON PLACE, HULL. From about 1781 onwards he was involved in the development of the Hull Dock Company's estate on the north side of the Queen's Dock, and probably designed most of the handsome houses in GEORGE STREET, CHARLOTTE STREET, NORTH STREET and CARROLL PLACE (formerly PARADISE ROW), some of which survive. His style was late Palladian in character, with internal detailing influenced by the Adam brothers. Mountain died on 7 August 1805, aged 62, leaving his practice to be continued by his son Charles Mountain, junior (q.v.). [A. G. Chamberlain & I. Hall in V.C.H. Yorks.: E. Riding i, 349, 445, 447–8, 451–2; Gent's Mag. 1805 (ii), 781.]

MOUNTAIN, CHARLES (c. 1773–1839), only son of the above, appears to have practised in Lincoln until his father's death in 1805, when he returned to Hull. Under the terms of his father's will he inherited his architectural books, papers, etc., the materials of his building business, and his copyhold property in the manor of Myton. He was declared bankrupt in 1812, whereupon his assets were offered for sale, one of them being an estate of twenty-one houses and tenements lately erected at Brigg in Lincolnshire. His affairs soon recovered, and in 1820, while continuing to practise as an architect, he started a new business as a slater and slate merchant. In or shortly before

1835 he moved to Malton, and subsequently to Wakefield, where he died on 23 April 1839, aged 66.

Mountain was Hull's first neo-classical architect. His work was nearly all in a competent Greek Revival style which he sometimes handled with considerable elegance (e.g. at Goodmanham Rectory).

[A. G. Chamberlain, 'Mountain of Hull', Arch. Rev., Oct. 1968, 299; J. Greenwood, Picture of Hull, 1835, 126 n.]

HULL, THE MEAT MARKET or SHAMBLES, 1806; dem. [Monthly Magazine, 1806 (i), 575].

HULL, THE THEATRE ROYAL, HUMBER STREET, 1809–10; destroyed by fire 1859 [J. Greenwood, Picture of Hull, 1835, 136].

BRIGG, LINCS., twenty-one houses and tenements, 'lately erected' in 1812 [Hull Advertiser, 4 Sept., 27 Nov. 1812].

WAKEFIELD PARISH CHURCH (now Cathedral), rebuilt upper 15 feet of spire, 1823 [J. L. Sisson, Historic Sketch of the Parish Church of Wakefield, 1824, 10].

GOODMANHAM RECTORY (now HALL GARTH), YORKS. (E.R.), 1823–4 [Borthwick Institute, York, MGA 1822/1; Arthur Oswald in C. Life, 23 Feb., 2 March 1961].

HULL, THE TRINITY ALMSHOUSE, POSTERNGATE (now offices), 1828; portico destroyed 1941 [J. Greenwood, Picture of Hull, 1835, 95].

HULL, WHITEFRIAR GATE, rebuilt south side, including Smith's Bank (now Woolworth's stores), for Trinity House, 1829–31 [V.C.H. Yorks.: E. Riding i, 449].

HULL, THE MECHANICS' INSTITUTE, CHARLOTTE STREET, 1830; dem. [J. Greenwood, Picture of Hull, 1835, 126].

HULL, THE PUBLIC ROOMS, KINGSTON SQUARE, 1830–4. Though given the credit of having designed this building by Greenwood (p. 134), Mountain appears only to have been 'superintending architect' for a design made by R. H. Sharp of York. The building was completed by H. R. Abraham after Mountain had moved to Malton [V.C.H. Yorks.: E. Riding i, 420].

BEVERLEY, YORKS. (E.R.), added portico to GUILDHALL, 1832 [R. H. Whiteing, 'The Guildhall, Beverley', Trans. Georgian Soc. for E. Yorkshire ii, part iv, 1948–9].

HULL, THE MASTER MARINERS' ALMSHOUSES, CARR LANE, for Trinity House, 1834; dem. 1941 [J. Greenwood, Picture of Hull, 1835, 95].

WAKEFIELD, YORKS. (W.R.), THE SAVINGS BANK, 1834 [Architectural Mag. i, 1834, 142].

MOXSON, JOHN, appears to be known only as the designer of the MIXED CLOTH HALL at LEEDS, built in 1756–8 and demolished in 1889. An engraving records that the building was 'Design'd, delineated and superintended by John

Moxson'. There is a reproduction in *Johnson's England*, ed. A. S. Turberville, i, 1933, 250.

MOYLE, JOHN, of Exeter, was a master builder of some importance in the south-western counties in the reign of George I, and was probably capable of making his own architectural designs, although no direct evidence of this has so far been found. In 1713, as 'John Moyle of the Citty of Exeter, Bricklayer', he contracted to build a garden wall at Antony in Cornwall for Sir William Carew, Bart., and in 1718 to build the shell of ANTONY HOUSE 'according to a draught agreed upon' [Carew papers at Antony, CE/E/22] (*C. Life*, 19, 25 Aug. 1933). Between 1710 and 1727 'Mr. Moyle the Builder' carried out considerable works at POWDERHAM CASTLE, DEVON, for Sir William Courtenay, Bart. [Mark Girouard in *C. Life*, 4 July 1963], and in 1721 he was working for Thomas ('Governor') Pitt in Cornwall, presumably at BOCONNOC HOUSE, which Pitt had recently bought, and to which he added an east wing that was demolished in 1834 [P.R.O., C 104/424, Pitt's Letter-Book No. 14, no. 513, 1721].

MOYSER, JAMES (*c.* 1693–1753), was the son of John Moyser (*c.* 1660–1738) of Beverley, M.P. for that town in 1705–8. In 1692 his father had married Catherine, widow of Sir John Hotham, a local landowner, and John was their eldest child. His early life was spent in the Army, first as an officer in Sir Charles Hotham's regiment of foot, and subsequently as a Colonel in the 1st Regiment of Foot Guards. He saw active service in Spain, where in 1710 he was Stanhope's Adjutant. The rest of his life was spent in Beverley, where he died in 1753.

The elder Moyser had taken a leading part in raising money for the repair of Beverley Minster in the reign of Queen Anne, but although he subscribed to the third volume of *Vitruvius Britannicus* (1725), there is no evidence that he had any architectural skill. In the 1730s and 1740s, however, his son was active as an amateur architect. Both the Moysers were on friendly terms with Lord Burlington, and the Colonel appears to have been one of his provincial disciples. The first building with which he can be connected is BRETTON HALL, YORKS. (W.R.), which was built by Sir William Wentworth in about 1730 in a plain style of Palladian character (*C. Life*, 21–28 May 1938; D. Linstrum in *Leeds Arts Calendar*, no. 68, 1971). According to a list of houses found by Dr. Eileen Harris in a copy of the *Builder's Dictionary* (1734) in the Metropolitan Museum at New York, Bretton was designed 'by Sir Wm. and Col. Moyser'. This is confirmed by a note added to a letter of Moyser's to Godfrey Bosvile of Gunthwaite in which he is identified as the person 'who gave Sr. William Wentworth

the plan of Britton House, and was his most intimate friend' [E. Riding Record Office, Bosvile-Macdonald papers, DD BM/32/8].

The list already cited also names 'Col. Moyser' as the architect of NOSTELL PRIORY, YORKS. (W.R.), built by Sir Rowland Winn *c.* 1737 onwards.[1] A plan at Nostell [C3/1/1/2] shows that the basic design, with four wings connected to the main block by quadrants in the manner of Palladio's Villa Mocenigo, had been envisaged as early as 1731. It is related to a similar design for a large country house by Colen Campbell (now in the R.I.B.A. Drawings Collection) which Moyser may have seen. The supervision of the work was entrusted to the young James Paine, who was responsible for a good deal of the detailed designing as the work proceeded. He did not, however, claim to have been the architect of the house, stating quite correctly in the preface to his *Plans* (1767) that 'at the age of nineteen (he) was entrusted to conduct a building of consequence in the West Riding of Yorkshire'. Nostell is illustrated in *Vitruvius Britannicus* iv, 1767, pls. 70–3, and in *C. Life*, 16–30 May 1952.

In 1741 Moyser made a design for a new house at Gunthwaite, nr. Penistone, Yorks. (W.R.), for Godfrey Bosvile, but it was not built, although Moyser assured him that it would be 'the most convenient, the hansomest & the cheapest of any House in Yorkshire' [E. Riding Record Office, Bosvile-Macdonald papers, DD BM/32/8]. In 1746 Moyser was one of the architectural experts consulted by Stephen Thompson before he began to build Kirby Hall, nr. Ouseburn. He provided Thompson with a plan which the latter admired and described as 'a perfect Model of Ld. Orford's at Houghton'. In the event Thompson progressively altered the plan until it no longer met with Moyser's approval. But he took the Colonel's advice in consulting Roger Morris, who was persuaded to call at Kirby on his way to Scotland in the summer of 1747. Lord Burlington also helped, and the final outcome was a house planned by the owner, with elevations by Burlington and Morris (p. 131) [E. Riding Record Office, Grimston papers, DD GR/41/3–7].

The only other executed design by Moyser that has so far come to light is ANNE ROUTH'S HOSPITAL in KELDGATE, BEVERLEY, which was built in 1749 'pursuant to a plan drawn by Mr. Moyser' [*Beverley Corporation Minute Books*, ed. K. A. MacMahon, Yorks. Arch. Soc. Record Series 1958, p. xvii].

No drawings of Moyser's have so far been

---

[1] A contemporary note in a book of plans of Kirtlington Park, Oxon., in the Oxfordshire County Record Office (Dash. III/xlix/1) records that 'The idea of the House is taken from Sr Rowland Winn's which was originally planned by Col. Moyser of Beverley'.

identified, and his ability as an architect is difficult to assess on the strength of the few buildings for which he is known to have been responsible. Bretton is merely a rectangular block dressed up with 'Palladian' windows. Though Nostell is a large and ambitious mansion there is a certain stolidity about the main elevations which shows that Moyser was not an architect of the same calibre as his friend Lord Burlington. In short, although James Moyser was evidently a competent amateur, there is no reason to suppose that he made a contribution of any importance to English Palladian architecture.

[J. W. Clay, 'Dugdale's Visitation of Yorkshire, with Additions', *Genealogist*, N.S. xxv, 1909, 111; G. Poulson, *Beverlac* ii, 1829, 678; G. Oliver, *History of Beverley*, 1829, 241, 326; *Yorkshire Diaries*, Surtees Soc. 1875, 349; Dalton, *English Army Lists and Commission Registers* i, 172, v, 19, vi, 169; *Beverley Corporation Minute Books*, ed. K. A. MacMahon, Yorks. Arch. Soc. Record Series 1958, pp. xiii, 7, 13; Chatsworth House, Lord Burlington's Correspondence, 127/9 and 10 (1735); Borthwick Institute of Historical Research, York Probate Register vol. 86, f. 252 (will of John Moyser).]

MULLINS, JOHN (–1880), was in 1816–17 a pupil of W. B. Hué. In the 1820s he was practising from Fenchurch Street. He exhibited at the Royal Academy between 1814 and 1827. He designed the IMPERIAL PLATE GLASS MANUFACTORY on the north bank of the Thames opposite Greenwich, of which he exhibited a drawing in 1826. A monument in ORPINGTON CHURCH, KENT, to William Dredge (d. 1820) is signed 'J. Holder Sculp. John Mullins Arch.' Mullins was District Surveyor for Streatham and Brixton from 1844 until his death on 22 November 1880 [*Builder* xxxix, 1880, 683; Principal Probate Registry, Calendar of Probates].

MÜNTZ, JOHANN HEINRICH (1727–1798), was an artist of German–Swiss origin born at Mülhausen. As a young man he travelled in Spain as well as in France, Germany and Italy. He arrived in England in 1755 via the Channel Islands, where he was discovered by Richard Bentley (*q.v.*). 'I have a painter in the house', wrote Horace Walpole to Sir Horace Mann in 1758, 'who is an engraver too, a mechanic, an everything. He was a Swiss engineer in the French service, but, his regiment being broken at the peace, Mr. Bentley found him in the Isle of Jersey, and fixed him with me. He has astonishing genius for landscape, and added to that all the patience and industry of a German.' For four years he worked for Walpole before being dismissed 'for some amorous misdemeanour' with one of Walpole's female servants. At STRAWBERRY HILL he painted the ceiling of the China Closet

with 'convolvulus's on poles' in a manner suggested by a ceiling in the Borghese Villa at Frascati, and designed several Gothic features, including probably the doorway of the Gallery and the niches in the Chapel or Cabinet. For Richard Bateman's 'half Gothick, half Attic, half Chinese and completely fribble house' at OLD WINDSOR, BERKS., he designed in 1761–2 an octagonal Gothic room with a pyramidal roof like a chapterhouse, which still survives although the rest of the house has been rebuilt. For the Earl of Charlemont he designed in 1762 an 'Egiptian Room' (really a Gothic room with Egyptian figures) for his house at MARINO, nr. DUBLIN, which does not appear to have been built, but in 1768 he was making further designs for Lord Charlemont which may have been carried out. And at KEW GARDENS he not only designed the 'Gothic Cathedral' in about 1759 (see W. Chambers, *Plans etc. of the Gardens and Buildings at Kew in Surrey*, 1763, pl. 29), but may have provided the original drawing from which the Moorish 'Alhambra' was developed.

Müntz's interest in Gothic architecture is shown not only by the measured drawings which he made of doorways in St. Albans Abbey Church in 1759 and 1762, but also by his proposals for publishing by subscription *A Course of Gothic Architecture*, of which there is a prospectus, dated 12 April 1760, among James Essex's MSS. in the British Museum (Add. MS. 6771, f. 215). This was to have demonstrated 'The Fundamental Principles and Rules for the Disposition, Proportions, Use and Intentions of all the Parts and Members of that Stile of Building ... Exemplified by Designs and Measures taken from the finest Fabrics and Monuments still existing in ENGLAND and abroad'. Had it been published, it would have been one of the pioneer works on Gothic architecture.[1] Müntz was also interested in the process of encaustic painting, upon which he published a treatise in 1760 entitled *Encaustic: or, Count Caylus's Method of Painting in the Manner of the Ancients*. The five drawings which he exhibited at the Society of Artists in 1762 included a landscape painted in encaustic as well as his designs for Richard Bateman's Gothic room and for Lord Charlemont's Egyptian one.

In 1763 Müntz went to Holland. From 1780 to 1783 he was in Poland, where he designed a villa for Prince Poniatowski. He eventually died

---

[1] Richard Gough was, however, sceptical of Müntz's pretensions as an architectural historian. In a MS. note in his own copy of his *British Topography* in the Bodleian Library he wrote that 'Munz was totally incapable of executing this work; nor knew what Gothic Architecture was, but by living 4 years with Mr. Walpole, and drawing some Antiquities for him while Strawberry Hill was building'. I owe this reference to Mr. J. M. Frew.

in Kassel in 1798. Drawings by Müntz exist in several European collections. Mr. W. S. Lewis's collection at Farmington, U.S.A., contains a number of his English drawings, including those made for Richard Bateman, Lord Charlemont and Horace Walpole, and also an album of drawings of vases 'entrepris et commencé à Rome en 1751 a reduit a ce terme à Amsterdam 1772 par J. H. Muntz, Ingénieur et Architecte' (see John Harris, *Catalogue of British Drawings for Architecture, etc. in American Collections*, 1971, 143–8 and pls. 105–8.

[Thieme & Becker, *Allgemeines Lexikon der Bildenen Künstler* xxv, 253; Walpole's *Letters*, especially 9 Sept. 1758, to Sir Horace Mann; Hist. MSS. Comm., *Charlemont* i, 286; A. Graves, *The Society of Artists and The Free Society of Artists*, 1907, 180; John Harris, *Sir William Chambers*, 1970; J. M. Crook, 'Strawberry Hill Revisited', *C. Life*, 14 June 1973, 1728–9.]

MURRAY, GEORGE, practised in Glasgow, when he added the FEVER HOSPITAL to the ROYAL INFIRMARY in 1825–32 and designed the CITY HALL, CANDLERIGGS, 1840, and the OBSERVATORY, VICTORIA CRESCENT, 1840, Tudor, dem. [*A.P.S.D.*, *s.v.* 'Glasgow']. The City Hall was built on arches over the Bazaar, and originally had no façade to the street. The existing front dates from 1885, when the building was altered and enlarged by John Carrick.

MURRAY, JAMES (–1634), was the son of James Murray (d. 1615), a master wright who had been appointed overseer of the King's works in Scotland in 1601. The son was appointed Master Wright in 1601, and in 1605 his father surrendered the office of overseer in his favour. In 1607 he succeeded David Cunningham of Robertland as 'principal master of all his majesties works in Scotland', with a yearly fee of 500 merks. He was knighted at the coronation of Charles I in 1633, and died in December 1634. In 1612 he was granted an estate at Baberton (or Kilbaberton), nr. Currie in Midlothian, where in 1622–3 he proceeded to build a house which still exists. Though traditional in character, it is decorated with classical detail reminiscent of Heriot's Hospital. Further evidence of Murray's ability as an architect is afforded by the Edinburgh Town Council Minutes, which record that in 1633 he was paid £1000 (Scots) for past services in the town's works, 'and for drawing up of the modell of the workes of the Parliament and Counsel hous presentlie intendit'. This was the PARLIAMENT HOUSE begun in 1633 and completed in 1640, whose structure still exists, though embedded in later buildings by Robert Reid and others. Engravings show an L-shaped building

decorated with small turrets and mannerist detail akin to that at Baberton House.

[D. MacGibbon & T. Ross, *The Castellated and Domestic Architecture of Scotland* iv, 1892, 67–8 (for Baberton House), v, 547; R. S. Mylne, 'The Masters of Work to the Crown of Scotland', *Proceedings of the Society of Antiquaries of Scotland*, 3rd ser., vi, 1895–6; R. K. Hanney, 'The Building of the Parliament House', *Book of the Old Edinburgh Club* xiii, 1924; *Accounts of the Masters of Works*, ed. H. M. Paton, i, 1957, xxix.]

MYLNE, JOHN (–1621), is the first of his family to come within the chronological limits of this *Dictionary*. Traditionally he was the second John Mylne to be a leading Scottish master mason, the first having 'come from the North Country' some time in the sixteenth century. However, if the conjectures of the family historian can be accepted, the first John Mylne practised his craft in the reigns of James III and IV (1460–1513), and the second John Mylne was the son of Thomas Mylne, a Dundee master mason who may have been a native of Elgin. Certainly the John Mylne who is the subject of this entry was established in Dundee during the last decade of the sixteenth century. According to a document drawn up by the masons' lodge at Perth in 1658 he and his father successively held the post of King's Master Mason. Although no official or contemporary record appears to confirm this statement, it may be noted that John Mylne is also referred to as royal master mason in the memoirs of James, Lord Somerville (d. 1690). Writing in 1679, Lord Somerville recalled that in 1584–5 the 7th Lord Somerville employed 'John Millne, the king's master meassone', to build the family seat called THE DRUM, MIDLOTHIAN (rebuilt by William Adam *c.* 1725) [*Memorie of the Somervilles*, ed. Walter Scott, Edinburgh 1815, i, 460].

During the 1580s John Mylne was engaged in various works at Dundee, where in September 1587 he was admitted a burgess 'for services done and to be done' in the burgh, 'and especially for repairing the whole harbour' [R. S. Mylne, *Master Masons*, 66]. He erected in 1586 the market cross in the High Street, a polygonal shaft surmounted by an heraldic unicorn [Alexander Maxwell, *The History of Old Dundee*, Dundee 1884, 245] (R. S. Mylne, *op. cit.*, plate at p. 65). In February 1589/90 he and another Dundee mason named George Thomson contracted to build a gallery and other additions for Thomas Bannatyne at BANNATYNE HOUSE, NEWTYLE, ANGUS [R. S. Mylne, *op. cit.*, 66–9]. In 1604 he undertook the major task of building a new bridge of eleven arches over the R. Tay at Perth [R. S. Mylne, *op. cit.*, 93]. This bridge was eventually completed in 1617, but was destroyed by a great flood in October 1621.

JOHN MYLNE = Helen Kinnereis
d. 1621

JOHN MYLNE = Isobel Wilson
d. 1657

JOHN MYLNE
1611–67

ALEXANDER MYLNE = Anna Vegilman
1613–43

ROBERT MYLNE = Elizabeth Meikle
1633–1710

WILLIAM MYLNE =   Janet = JAMES SMITH
1662–1728   d. 1699   c. 1645–1731

THOMAS MYLNE = Elizabeth Duncan
d. 1763

ROBERT MYLNE = May Home   WILLIAM MYLNE
1733–1811   1734–90

WILLIAM C. MYLNE = Mary Coxhead
1781–1863

ROBERT W. MYLNE = Hannah Scott
1817–90

In 1607 Mylne was admitted to the freedom of Perth gratis. As Master of the Lodge of Scone he entered King James VI by his own desire as 'frieman Meason and Fellow Craft' [R. S. Mylne, *op. cit.*, 128]. Mylne died early in 1621 and was buried in the Greyfriars burial ground at Perth, where there is a stone (originally the top of a table-tomb, restored in 1849 and again in 1913) with a quaint epitaph in verse to his memory. The architect Robert Mylne added a mural tablet in 1774. By his wife Helen Kinnereis John Mylne had a son John (d. 1657) (*q.v.*).

[R. S. Mylne, *The Master Masons to the Crown of Scotland*, Edinburgh 1893; *A.P.S.D.*; *D.N.B.*]

MYLNE, JOHN (–1657), was the son of John Mylne (d. 1621), and assisted him for some years

in the erection of the Tay Bridge at Perth. In 1616 he left Perth for Edinburgh, in response to an invitation from the town council to complete a statue of King James I and VI for the Netherbow Port after the sudden death of the original sculptor, a Frenchman named Benjamin Lambert [R. S. Mylne, *Master Masons*, 105–6]. In conjunction with a mason called Tailefer he was subsequently employed to take down and re-erect the Market Cross, and in June 1617 he was made a burgess of Edinburgh [*op. cit.*, 106–7]. In 1618 he appears to have returned to the north (whether to Perth or Dundee is not clear), and in January 1620 he contracted with David Murray, Lord Scone, to rebuild FALKLAND CHURCH, FIFE (again rebuilt 1850) [*op. cit.*, 110–11]. His next engagement was in Aberdeen, where he executed the masonry of the new Tolbooth steeple in 1622–

3 [*Aberdeen Burgh Records*, Spalding Club 1848, ii, 379]. In consequence he was in May 1622 made a burgess of the city *ex gratia* [R. S. Mylne, *Master Masons*, 113]. In 1627 he became a burgess of Dundee in right of his late father [*op. cit.*, 113]. In 1629–30 he carried out some works at DRUMMOND CASTLE, PERTHSHIRE, for the 2nd Earl of Perth [*op. cit.*, 114]. These included the elaborate faceted sundial in the garden, which is dated 1630 (D. Macgibbon & T. Ross, *The Castellated and Domestic Architecture of Scotland* v, 1892, 417–18).

By 1629 John Mylne was back in Edinburgh constructing a pond at Holyroodhouse for King Charles I, and in 1631 he succeeded William Wallace (*q.v.*) as Master Mason to the Crown [R. S. Mylne, *Master Masons*, 114–15]. The principal memorial to his tenure of this office is the sundial in the gardens of Holyroodhouse, which he constructed in 1633 with the aid of his sons John and Alexander [D. Macgibbon & T. Ross, *op. cit.* v, 441–2]. In 1636 he resigned his office in favour of his elder son John, and returned to Dundee, where between 1643 and 1651 he was employed upon various works, including the repair of the church steeple and the fortification of the town [Alexander Maxwell, *The History of Old Dundee*, Dundee 1884, 151, 213–14, 492; R. S. Mylne, *op. cit.*, 127]. His admission in 1643 as a burgess of Kirkcaldy may have been connected with the repair and enlargement of the parish church there in that year [R. S. Mylne, *op. cit.*, 126].

Like his father, John Mylne was master of the masons' lodge at Scone. He married Isobel Wilson of Perth in 1610, and died in 1657. A portrait is reproduced by R. S. Mylne in his *Master Masons*, 104. His elder son John (d. 1667) is noticed below. His younger son Alexander (1613–43), commemorated by a monument in Holyrood Abbey, was a sculptor and carver.

[R. S. Mylne, *The Master Masons to the Crown of Scotland*, Edinburgh 1893; *A.P.S.D.*; *D.N.B.*]

MYLNE, JOHN (1611–1667), son of John Mylne (d. 1657), was born in Perth in 1611. On 9 October 1633 he was admitted a burgess of Edinburgh by right of patrimony, and on the same day was made 'fellow of craft' in the Edinburgh masonic lodge. In February 1636, at the age of 25, he succeeded his father as Master Mason to the Crown, and in 1646 he was appointed Captain of Pioneers and Master Gunner of Scotland. For over thirty years he was a prominent figure in the Scottish capital. He repeatedly served as Deacon of the Edinburgh masons, and was for several years a member of the town council. In 1652 he was sent to London as one of the Scottish Commissioners to negotiate a Treaty of Union with the English Parliament,

and from 1654 to 1659 represented Edinburgh at the convention of royal burghs. In 1662 he was elected M.P. for Edinburgh in the Scottish Parliament, and attended the second and third sessions of Charles II's first parliament in Edinburgh.

John Mylne was married three times, but his only son died in infancy, and it was his nephew Robert (1633–1710) who succeeded him as Master Mason to the Scottish Crown. John died in Edinburgh on 24 December 1667, and was buried in the Greyfriars Cemetery, where he is commemorated by a handsome monument erected by Robert. Another inscription to his memory was erected over the door of St. Mary's Chapel (the masons' meeting-place) by the Incorporated Trades of Scotland, in which he was described as

.... the Fourth John
And by descent from Father unto Son
Sixth Master Mason to a Royal Race
of seven successive Kings...
Rare man he was, who could unite in one
Highest and lowest occupation.
To sit with Statesmen, Councillors to Kings
To work with Tradesmen, in Mechanick
things.

His portrait, now in the Scottish National Portrait Gallery, shows him with a bust and an architectural plan. Another is in the possession of his descendants.

Early in his career Mylne was commissioned to make designs for the two new churches required to house the congregations displaced by Charles I's decision (1633) to erect St. Giles' Church into a cathedral. One church was begun on Castle Hill, but later abandoned; the other was THE TRON CHURCH in the High Street, begun in 1637 but not completed until 1647. Though truncated in 1788 and partly rebuilt after a fire in 1824, the Tron Church is a striking example of Scoto-Flemish mannerism and as such indicative of Mylne's style [see *Extracts from the Records of the City of Edinburgh 1626–41*, ed. M. Wood, 307–11 for the estimate, and *op. cit. 1642–55*, 40; also R.C.A.M., *Edinburgh*, 35, *Book of the Old Edinburgh Club* xxix, 1956, 99–103, and plan in G. Hay, *The Architecture of Scottish Post-Reformation Churches*, 1957, fig. 15]. His next recorded work was COWANE'S HOSPITAL, STIRLING, built to his designs by a Stirling mason in 1637–48. Though the E-shaped plan was unusual for Scotland, the architectural character of the building was traditional, with restrained mannerist detailing [R.C.A.M., *Stirlingshire*, 289–92]. In 1642 Mylne reported on the dangerous state of the fabric of the ABBEY CHURCH at JEDBURGH, ROXBURGHSHIRE [R. S. Mylne, *Master Masons*, 138–9]. In 1643 he succeeded William Aytoun (*q.v.*) as master mason to HERIOT'S HOSPITAL, begun in

1628, but still incomplete owing to the political and financial troubles of the time. In 1648 he was instructed to take down the upper part of the south-west tower and rebuild it uniform with the others [*Extracts, etc. 1642–55*, 142]. He was still employed at the Hospital as late as 1659 [R. S. Mylne, *op. cit.*, 139–40]. In 1648 he also repaired the openwork crown of ST. GILES' CATHEDRAL, then in a dangerous state [R. S. Mylne, *op. cit.*, 144]. In 1649–50 he fortified Leith [*Extracts etc. 1642–55*, 41, 130, 204, 226, 228, 249, 293] and in February 1650/1 made an estimate for adding a frontispiece, etc., to NEWBATTLE ABBEY, MIDLOTHIAN, for the 1st Earl of Lothian, 'in a perfect manner off gudlie Architect[ure]' [S.R.O., GD 40/xviii/1, 82]. In 1655–6 he was employed to divide the GREYFRIARS CHURCH, EDINBURGH, to accommodate two congregations [*Extracts from the Records of the City of Edinburgh 1642–55*, ed. M. Wood, 391–2]. In 1656 he undertook to build a professor's house and six chambers at the COLLEGE in EDINBURGH [*Extracts etc. 1655–65*, 34, 109; *Book of the Old Edinburgh Club* iv, 1911, 148]. These were demolished in 1790 to make way for the new College designed by R. & J. Adam, but the monument to Bartholomew Somervell (d. 1640) which ornamented the building survives at Craighall Rattray in Perthshire.

After the Restoration Mylne was confirmed in his office of Master Mason to the Crown, and in October 1663 made a survey of the second floor of HOLYROODHOUSE showing how 'it is intendet to be finished' [Bodleian Library, Gough Maps 39, f. 1ᵛ, reproduced by R. S. Mylne, *op. cit.*, 148–9]. Nothing, however, was done until after his death, when Sir William Bruce and Robert Mylne reconstructed the palace in its existing form.

In 1661 the repair and partial rebuilding of COLDINGHAM CHURCH, BERWICKSHIRE, was to be carried out 'by the sight of John Milne master mason or any other they shall bring to visite the same after finishing thereof' [S.R.O., Register of Deeds, Dal. 7, 223, Warrant No. 1930 (1662)]. The draft of a contract exists whereby in November 1661 Mylne was to execute the masonry of a 'great addition' to ADDISTON HOUSE, RATHO, MIDLOTHIAN, for Sir John Gibson, but it is not known whether this was carried out [S.R.O., GD 45/17/299]. In 1665–6 he was employed to build, and apparently to design, FORT CHARLOTTE in SHETLAND [R. G. Bell, 'The Shetland Garrison 1665–1666', *Jnl. of the Society for Army Historical Research*, vol. 43, 1965, 5–26; R.C.A.M., *Shetland*, 63].

In 1666 Mylne contracted to build PANMURE HOUSE, ANGUS, for the 2nd Earl of Panmure, 'according to the maner forme and dimensions of the said structure and edifice designed and set down by the said John Mylne in draughts' [R.

S. Mylne, *op. cit.*, 153–4]. On his death in the following year the work was completed by Alexander Nesbit, mason of Edinburgh, 'according to the maner, forme and dimensions alredy begun' [S.R.O., GD 45/18/565]. With its quadrangular plan and picturesque silhouette of cupola'd towers the house (dem. 1955, illustrated in *Vitruvius Scoticus*, pls. 129–31) bore a certain resemblance to Heriot's Hospital. Like Drumlanrig Castle it looked backwards to the early seventeenth century, and showed little evidence that John Mylne was participating in the new architectural ideas already current in England and soon to be introduced into Scotland by Sir William Bruce. The unexecuted design which he made for LINLITHGOW TOLBOOTH just before his death in 1667 [Mylne, *op. cit.*, 240–1] was also somewhat old-fashioned.[1] In the same year he was engaged by the 7th Earl (1st Duke) of Rothes to enlarge and remodel LESLIE HOUSE, FIFE, but here Bruce's advice was sought, and the house as completed by Robert Mylne in 1672 was rather more up to date in style. John Mylne must therefore be seen as the leading master of the last phase of Scottish mannerism.

[R. S. Mylne, *The Master Masons to the Crown of Scotland*, Edinburgh 1893; *A.P.S.D.*; *D.N.B.*; *Extracts from the Records of the City of Edinburgh*, ed. M. Wood, *1642–55* and *1655–65*, *passim*; information from Mr. J. G. Dunbar].

MYLNE, ROBERT (1633–1710), was the eldest son of Alexander Mylne (1613–43), younger son of John Mylne (d. 1657). He was apprenticed to his uncle John Mylne (d. 1667), and in 1668 succeeded him as Master Mason to the Scottish Crown.

His earliest recorded work appears to be WOOD'S HOSPITAL at LARGO, FIFE, which he built in 1665: it was rebuilt in 1830 [*The Chronicles of Fife, being the diary of John Lamont of Newton 1649–1672*, 1810, 223–4]. In 1668 he built a MARKET CROSS at PERTH to replace one destroyed by Cromwell's army in 1652: it was completed in 1669 and stood in the High Street until 1765, when it was demolished [R. S. Mylne, *Master Masons*, 214–16]. At the same time he was completing LESLIE HOUSE, FIFE, which had been begun by his uncle for the 7th Earl (1st Duke) of Rothes shortly before his death [J. G. Dunbar, *Sir William Bruce* (exhibition catalogue, 1970), citing Rothes papers in Kirkcaldy Museum]. In 1669 he contracted with the 2nd Earl of Wemyss to build an addition to WEMYSS CASTLE, FIFE, which was completed in 1672 [Sir William Fraser, *Memorials of the Family of Wemyss of*

---

[1] The minutes of the Linlithgow Town Council show that after Mylne's death they found a new master mason (John Smith), and it was to his design that the existing Tolbooth was built in 1668–73 [S.R.O., B 48/9/3].

Wemyss i, 1888, 284; *Scottish Diaries and Memoirs 1550–1746*, ed. J. G. Fyfe, Stirling 1927, 129–30]. In 1671 he began work on the rebuilding of HOLYROODHOUSE under the direction of Sir William Bruce. His name and the date July 1671 are cut on the north-west pillar of the quadrangle. Although Bruce was responsible for the design, much of the practical planning must have fallen to Mylne as master mason, and a set of drawings formerly in the possession of the Mylne family and now in the British Museum (Egerton MSS. 2870–1) appears to be in his hand. The palace was completed in 1679. Another work which he carried out at that period under Bruce's direction was the remodelling of THIRLESTANE CASTLE, BERWICKSHIRE, for the Duke of Lauderdale, *c.* 1670–80. He also made gate-piers to Bruce's designs for the Duke's English seat of HAM HOUSE, SURREY [J. G. Dunbar, 'The Building-activities of the Duke and Duchess of Lauderdale, 1670–82', *Archaeological Jnl.*, vol. 132, 1975]. In 1662 and again in 1677 and 1685 Mylne was employed in repairing the fortifications of EDINBURGH CASTLE, where a battery on the north side formerly bore his name [R. S. Mylne, *op. cit.*, 203–5, 233; R.C.A.M., *Edinburgh*, 8; J. Grant, *Old and New Edinburgh* i, 75].

Between 1674 and 1681 Robert Mylne, under the direction of Sir William Bruce, constructed cisterns in various parts of Edinburgh in connection with the new water-supply from Comiston [*Extracts from the Records of the City of Edinburgh 1665–80*, ed. M. Wood, 426–31]. In 1674 he built the west tower of SOUTH LEITH PARISH CHURCH (taken down 1836) [D. Robertson, *South Leith Records*, 1911, 128–9] (view in J. Grant, *Old and New Edinburgh* iii, 217). In 1682 he contracted to build a bridge of one arch over the R. Clyde at Ramelwell Crags or Ram's Horn Pool, 29 miles above Lanark. This no longer exists, but the site is shown on a map in R. S. Mylne's *Master Masons*, 226 [for the contract, etc., see 221–5]. In 1693, having undertaken to complete the steeple of HERIOT'S HOSPITAL in accordance with a drawing which he had submitted, he built the existing octagonal stone cupola [R. S. Mylne, *op. cit.*, 232]. In 1703 he made a draught for NEWHALL HOUSE, nr. PENICUIK, but one by Sir John Clerk was preferred [S.R.O., GD 18/5188, no. 17]. In 1709 he began the burial place of the Trotter family of Mortonhall in the GREYFRIARS CHURCHYARD, but it was unfinished at the time of his death and was completed by his son William [MS. notes on the history of the family by Robert Mylne, d. 1811].

Robert Mylne engaged in a considerable amount of speculative building. In 1678 he built a block of ten dwellings on waste land which he had acquired on the Shore of Leith [cf. *Extracts etc. 1665–80*, 339]. The date and his initials appeared in the pediment [survey drawings from

Mylne family archives in N.M.R.S.]. In Edinburgh he built MYLNE'S SQUARE opposite the Tron Church in 1684–6 (dem. 18—) [I. A. Stirling, 'Mylne Square', *Book of the Old Edinburgh Club* xiv, 1925], MILNE'S COURT in the High Street opposite the West Bow (1690), and MILNE'S LAND outside the Potter-Row Gate. Contracts in the S.R.O. show that he also built tenements for others in HART CLOSE, HIGH STREET, 1687 [Register of Deeds, Dal. 74.44], SIMPSON'S CLOSE, 1689 [Dal. 70, 497 (1689)], WRITER'S COURT, HIGH STREET, *c.* 1695–6 [*Book of the Old Edinburgh Club* xii, 1923, 28, xxix, 1956, 125–7], and WEIR'S LAND, ST. JOHN STREET, 1705 [Register of Deeds 1709, Dur. Warrant No. 710].

The profits of his trade and his rents were sufficient to enable Mylne to acquire two estates, one at Balfargie in Fife, the other at Inveresk, nr. Edinburgh, 'where he generally retired to live free from the hurry of business'. In 1672 he had registered a coat of arms [R. S. Mylne, *op. cit.*, 213]. He died at Inveresk on 10 December 1710, aged 77, and was buried in the family vault in the Greyfriars Churchyard. He is commemorated on the monument he had erected to his uncle John. A portrait by Roderick Chalmers is reproduced by R. S. Mylne, *op. cit.*, 217.

Robert Mylne married in 1661 Elizabeth Meikle, by whom he had eight sons and six daughters. His eldest daughter Janet married the architect James Smith (*q.v.*). He was succeeded as head of the family by his eldest son William. William Mylne (1662–1728) did not play as important a part in Scottish architecture as his father, and does not require a separate biography. He was admitted a burgess of Edinburgh in 1687 and was a prominent member of the Edinburgh masonic lodge. In 1711 he sold the Balfargie estate to George Balfour of Balbirnie, and lived at Leith in one of the houses built by his father. He died on 9 March 1728, aged 66, and was buried at South Leith. He is commemorated by an inscription cut on the left-hand column of the family monument in the Greyfriars Cemetery. The only building for which he is known to have been wholly responsible was a land of houses in HALKERSTON'S WYND, EDINBURGH, which bore the inscription 'BUILT BY WILLIAM MYLNE MASON 1715'. It was partially destroyed by fire in 1756. He was succeeded by his son Thomas Mylne (*q.v.*).

[R. S. Mylne, *The Master Masons to the Crown of Scotland*, Edinburgh 1893; *A.P.S.D.*; *D.N.B.*; S.R.O., Mylne papers (GD 1/51); *Extracts from the Records of the City of Edinburgh*, ed. Wood & Armet, *1665–80, 1681–9, 1689–1701, 1701–18, passim.*]

MYLNE, ROBERT (1733–1811), was descended from the long line of Scottish master masons whose genealogy is set out on page 568.

His father Thomas Mylne (*q.v.*) was one of the leading Edinburgh masons in the reign of George II. Robert, his eldest surviving son, was born in Edinburgh on 4 January 1733. In 1747 he was apprenticed to Daniel Wright, a carpenter, for six years, and the Edinburgh Lodge of Freemasons of which he became an honorary member in 1754 was by now a 'speculative' fraternity only tenuously connected with the masons' craft. After working for a time as a woodcarver at Blair Atholl he determined to qualify himself as an architect and persuaded his father to allow him to go abroad, first to Paris, where he joined his brother William (Oct. 1754), and then to Rome (Dec. 1754). Robert Adam was making the same journey at the same time, but the two Mylne brothers lacked his financial resources and travelled as cheaply as they could, even 'footing a good deal of it'. Nevertheless Robert was sure that 'a little studye will make more than one family of Architects in Scotland', and made the most of his opportunities. In 1758 he had the satisfaction of winning the Silver Medal for architecture in the *Concorso Clementino* at St. Luke's Academy, a distinction never before achieved by a Briton. The subject was a palatial public building, which Mylne treated in an elaborate neo-classical manner. In the following year he was elected a member of the Academy, and, through the good offices of Prince Altieri, obtained the necessary dispensation to take his seat. He was also made a member of the academies of Florence and of Bologna. In Rome he became friendly with Piranesi and made useful contacts with several members of the British aristocracy to whom he was later to be indebted for employment, including Lord Garlies, Sir Wyndham Knatchbull and William Fermor of Tusmore. In 1757 a connoisseur named Richard Phelps took him to Sicily, where he made drawings of the Greek temples with the intention of publishing a volume on the 'Antiquities of Sicily'. This was never completed, but Piranesi and Winckelmann were both indebted to Mylne for information about the Sicilian temples. Mylne's notes were still in manuscript at the time of his death. After travelling through northern Italy and the Rhineland to Holland he reached London in July 1759, bringing with him an introduction to Lord Charlemont which had been given to him by the Abbé Grant in Rome.

Mylne's arrival coincided with the scheme to build a bridge over the Thames at Blackfriars. This was one of the major public works of the eighteenth century, and the competition attracted sixty-nine entries. Eight of these were short-listed (Barnard, Chambers, Dance, Gwynn, Mylne, Phillips, Smeaton and Ware). All except Mylne's were adversely criticized in a pamphlet entitled *Observations on Bridge-Building, and the several Plans offered for a New*

Bridge, which there is reason to believe was written by Mylne himself. When, in February 1760, Robert Mylne was adjudged the winner, it was nevertheless an astonishing triumph for a young and totally untried man. 'The English nation' (he wrote to his father) 'holds up their hands – and my countrymen stare. Nay I cannot account for it myself – [that] a young man just arrived in a great city, where he knew nobody, should, against the cabballing interests of city factions, contrary to the interests of the Prince of Wales's court [which no doubt supported Chambers], and in spite of the specious plausibility of the Royal Society, step at once into the head of his profession, and several hundreds a year'. Mylne's design was both handsome and efficient. It spanned the river in only nine arches (Westminster Bridge needed twelve), the masonry was beautifully detailed, and the pair of Ionic columns which adorned each pier was a nicely calculated concession to contemporary architectural taste. A feature which gave rise to much discussion at the time was the use of elliptical arches, an innovation which Dr. Johnson was induced to criticize in print (*Daily Gazeteer*, 1, 8 and 15 Dec. 1759) on behalf of his friend John Gwynn, who had been among the unsuccessful competitors. Further attacks on Mylne were made during the construction of the bridge, and popular feeling against the employment of an unknown Scot was exploited by Charles Churchill in his poem *The Ghost* (1763). The bridge was opened on 19 November 1769, and cost £152,840, which was £163 less than the original estimate. A view of Mylne's design was engraved in 1760, and in 1766 a plan and elevation were published by his assistant R. Baldwin.[1] In the same year Mylne himself published a fine oblique view showing the centering which he had had engraved in Rome by Piranesi. Mylne was also responsible for planning the approaches to the bridge on both sides of the river, and for designing the obelisk erected in 1771 to mark the junction of the roads which radiated from St. George's Circus. The bridge itself was taken down in 1868 and replaced by the present iron structure.

Blackfriars Bridge proved Mylne's ability as civil engineer as well as architect, and bridges and canal-works formed an important part of his practice throughout his life: indeed, in the 1790s most of his time was taken up by business connected with water-ways, including many appearances before parliamentary committees considering canal bills. His most important engineering

---

[1] Baldwin was also responsible for seven plates entitled *Plans, Elevations and Sections of the Machines and Centering used in erecting Black-Friars Bridge, drawn and engraved by R. Baldwin, Clerk of the Work*, which was published by Taylor in 1787.

works were the planning of the Gloucester and Berkeley Ship Canal and the improvement of the fen drainage by means of the Eau Brink Cut above King's Lynn. The latter project, though authorized by Act of Parliament, was delayed by opposition until 1817, when it was carried out by Rennie. In 1772, after the destruction of the old Tyne bridge at Newcastle, Mylne gave advice on the form and situation of the new bridge; in 1775 he surveyed the harbour at Yarmouth, and in 1781 that at Wells-next-the-Sea in Norfolk. In 1783 he reported on the disaster to Smeaton's bridge at Hexham; in 1784 on the Severn navigation; on 1789 on the state of the mills and waterworks of the city of Norwich; in 1790 on the Worcester Canal; in 1791–4 on the Thames navigation;[1] in 1800 on the problems connected with the Port of London and the proposed reconstruction of London Bridge;[2] in 1807 on the East London Waterworks; and in 1808 on Woolwich Dockyard. In 1800 both he and George Dance submitted designs for a new London Bridge, but neither was proceeded with.

As an architect Mylne had to compete with Robert Adam and James Wyatt, and he never rivalled their celebrity as fashionable designers. However, in Shropshire he obtained a number of country-house commissions from a group of interrelated county families, and at Inveraray he had the opportunity of carrying out extensive works for the Duke of Argyll, who also employed him at Rosneath. Outside Shropshire his principal country houses were Cally, Kirkcudbrightshire (1763–5), Tusmore, Oxon. (1766–70), Wormleybury, Herts. (1767–70), Addington, Surrey (1773–9), and Bickley Place, Kent (c. 1780). The exteriors of his houses are characterized by a fastidious restraint that is prophetic of the neo-classical simplicity of the 1790s, while the portico at Woodhouse (Salop.) and the obelisk at Woolverstone (Suffolk) show that occasionally he could design something as strikingly original as anything by Dance or Soane. In his interiors he developed a decorative style very similar to Adam's. How far this was the result of his own studies in Rome, how far it derived from Adam, and how far it was dependent on the help of George Richardson (whom he paid for drawings from time to time) it is not easy to say. He rarely Gothicized, but deserves to be remembered as the designer of Blaise Castle, a well-known castellated folly near Bristol.

In 1764 Mylne applied for the vacant post of Master of the Works in Scotland, but this was a political sinecure which he could hardly hope to secure. In 1767, however, he obtained the congenial post of surveyor to the New River Company (the precursor of the Metropolitan Water Board). At first this was a joint appointment with his aged predecessor Henry Mill, who died in 1770. The salary was £200 per annum, and a house was provided at Islington. Mylne was assiduous in his attention to his duties, and in 1806 the Company expressed its appreciation by the gift of a silver-gilt cup. In 1770 he had rebuilt its offices in Clerkenwell, and in 1800 he commemorated Sir Hugh Myddelton, the founder of the Company, by placing an elegant urn near the source of the New River at Great Amwell in Hertfordshire.

Other appointments which Mylne held were the surveyorships of St. Paul's (Oct. 1766) and Canterbury (Oct. 1767) Cathedrals and the Clerkship of the Works at Greenwich Hospital (Nov. 1775). He was also Surveyor to the Stationers' Company. Though he performed his duties at the two cathedrals with credit, a dispute with James Stuart over the rebuilding of the chapel at Greenwich Hospital led to his dismissal by the governors in September 1782.

Mylne's aspirations were scientific rather than artistic. He never exhibited at the Royal Academy and never sought election to that body. But he became a Fellow of the Royal Society in 1767 and was a member of the group of literary and scientific men which met at Slaughter's Coffee House in St. Martin's Lane. He was a prominent member of the Society of Civil Engineers founded in 1771 and one of the original members of the Architects' Club founded in 1791. He is described by Elmes as 'a man of austere manners, (and) of violent temper, (who) appeared to have a contempt for every art but his own, and for every person but himself'. One of his workmen said that 'Mr. Mylne was a rare jintleman, but as hot as pepper and as proud as Lucifer'. He was, however, punctilious in the performance of his duties, and Farington describes him as a sociable man, 'much addicted to conversation', as well as one who was 'extremely exact in all his affairs'. His principal pupils and assistants were Robert Baldwin, Thomas Cooley, R. W. Dowthwaite and James Donaldson. His son W. C. Mylne succeeded to his practice.

Mylne married in 1770 May, daughter of Robert Home, a surgeon, by whom he had ten children, five of whom survived him. He died on 5 May 1811, in his 79th year, and was, at his own request, buried in the crypt of St. Paul's Cathedral near the remains of Sir Christopher Wren. The rest of his family were buried at Great Amwell in Hertfordshire, where he built himself a small country house in 1794–7, and where he erected a plain brick mausoleum in the churchyard. His portrait, drawn by Brompton in Rome

---

[1] His report on the navigation between Lechlade and Abingdon was printed by the Thames Commissioners in 1791. They also printed his *Report on a Survey of the River Thames from Boulter's Lock to the City Stone near Staines* in 1793.

[2] See *Parliamentary Papers* xiv, 1793–1802, 550–4.

in 1757, was engraved in Paris by Vangeliste in 1783 (see reproductions in Nichols, *Literary Anecdotes* ix, 233, and R. S. Mylne, *Master Masons*). A pencil portrait by Dance in the National Portrait Gallery shows him in later life: it was published in W. Daniell's *Collection of Portraits*, 1808–14.

Mylne's professional diaries and his early letters from Rome and London remain in the possession of his descendants. A grossly inaccurate transcript of the diaries was published by A. E. Richardson in 1955 in his *Robert Mylne*. Brief notes made on a visit to Edinburgh in 1781 are among the Mylne papers in the Scottish Record Office (GD 1/51/37). There is a volume of drawings by Mylne in the Richardson Collection at Ampthill; others are in the R.I.B.A. Drawings Collection. His unexecuted designs for Mersham Hatch, Kent, made for Sir Wyndham Knatchbull in 1761, are among the Arundell of Wardour papers.

[*A.P.S.D.*; *D.N.B.*; *Gent's Mag.* 1811 (1), 499–500; J. Nichols, *Literary Anecdotes* ix, 1815, 231–3; *Builder* xxii, 1864, 8; J. Elmes in *Civil Engineer and Architect's Jnl.* x, 1847, 340; Cussans, *Hertfordshire* ii, 1870, 126–7; R. S. Mylne, *The Master Masons to the Crown of Scotland*, Edinburgh 1893, chap. xiii; Hist. MSS. Comm., *12th Report* x, 252 (Abbé Grant's letter); Bodleian Library, Gough Norfolk 1(4), a printed exchange of letters between Mylne and George Hardinge following the latter's allegations at the Wells Harbour case at Norwich in 1782–3; *The Farington Diary*, ed. Greig, vi, 271–2; *Memoirs of R. L. Edgeworth* i, 1821, 183; *The Whitefoord Papers*, ed. W. A. S. Hewins, 1898, 176, 184; K. A. Esdaile, 'A Forgotten Episode in the History of Robert Mylne', *R.I.B.A. Jnl.*, Feb. 1944; Lesley Lewis, 'The Architects of the Chapel at Greenwich Hospital', *Art Bulletin* xxix, 1947; C. Gotch, 'The Missing Years of Robert Mylne', *Arch. Rev.*, Sept. 1951; C. Gotch, 'Mylne and Adam', *Arch. Rev.*, Feb. 1956; A. E. Richardson, *Robert Mylne, Architect and Engineer*, 1955; J. Harris, 'Robert Mylne and the Academy of St. Luke', *Arch. Rev.*, Nov. 1961; D. Wiebenson, *Sources of Greek Revival Architecture*, 1969, 124–5 (for Mylne's Sicilian expedition); Damie Stillman, 'British Architects and Italian Architectural Competitions, 1758–1780', *Jnl. of the Society of Architectural Historians* (of America), xxxii, 1973, 45–50; *I disegni di architettura dell'Archivio storico dell'Accademia di San Luca*, 1974, nos. 535–6; *Numismatic Chronicle*, 4th ser., iv, 1904 (for Mylne's medals); A. W. Skempton, *The Smeatonian Society of Civil Engineers*, 1971.]

BRIDGES

BLACKFRIARS BRIDGE, LONDON (R. Thames), 1760–9; dem. 1868. A parapet was substituted for the original balustrading in 1839, in the course of repairs by Walker and Burgess (cf. A. T. Bolton, *The Portrait of Sir John Soane*, 524). For Mylne's own account of the building of this bridge, see *Parliamentary Papers* xiv, 1793–1802, 580–5. His design was illustrated in the *London Magazine* for 1760.

WELBECK ABBEY, NOTTS., bridge in park for the 3rd Duke of Portland, 1765–7; dem. [Diary, April and June 1765; Nottingham University Library, Portland papers, PwF. 7087–7130].

WARWICK, LEAFIELD BRIDGE in the Park (R. Avon) for the 1st Earl of Warwick, 1772–6 [*V.C.H. Warwicks.* viii, 472]. In 1773–4 Mylne was asked to survey the GREAT BRIDGE over the R. Avon by the corporation. He condemned it and recommended the building of a new bridge on a different site. This advice was followed in 1789–93, when the existing bridge was built by W. Ebboral to a design closely resembling the Leafield Bridge. There appears, however, to be no evidence that Mylne furnished the drawings or gave further advice (cf. *V.C.H. Warwicks.* viii, 463).

GLASGOW, THE NEW (JAMAICA) BRIDGE (R. Clyde), 1768–72 [*The Picture of Glasgow*, Glasgow 1812, 132]. Designed in conjunction with his brother William Mylne and built by John Adam (*q.v.*). In the R.I.B.A. Drawings Collection there is an elevation of this bridge, inscribed 'The Original Design, by which the New Bridge over the River Clyde at Glasgow was constructed, after the scale was enlarged for a wider part of the River than this Drawing was intended for. Robert Mylne.'

NEWCASTLE, NORTHUMBERLAND (R. Tyne), 1774–81, in association with John Wooler; dem. 1873. The Bishop of Durham and the Corporation of Newcastle were each responsible for half the bridge: Mylne was the Bishop's engineer, Wooler the Corporation's [J. Sykes, *Local Records*, Newcastle 1865, i, 294; C. Gotch, 'Robert Mylne and Tyne Bridges', *Archaeologia Æliana*, 4th ser., xxxiii, 1955, 88–91].

GLASGOW, widened the OLD BRIDGE (R. Clyde), 1774–5 [Diary, 12 Sept., 26 Oct. 1774, 5 Feb., 30 Aug. 1775; R. S. Mylne, *Master Masons*, 270–3].

INVERARAY, ARGYLLSHIRE, ARAY BRIDGE, 1774–6, and DUBH LOCH (DOWLOCH) BRIDGE, 1786–7, for the 5th Duke of Argyll [I. G. Lindsay & Mary Cosh, *Inveraray and the Dukes of Argyll*, 1973, 234–5, 243].

TONBRIDGE, KENT (R. Medway), 1775–6; dem. 1888 [Diary, Nov. 1773, July, Aug. 1775; J. Dugdale, *British Traveller* iii, 1819, 259]. The original design is in the U.D.C. offices.

ROMSEY, HANTS. (R. Test), 1782–3; rebuilt to original design 1933 [Diary, 1 Oct. 1782 etc.; *The Southampton Guide*, 1787, 70].

HEXHAM BRIDGE (R. Tyne), 1785–93 [J. Sykes, *Local Records*, Newcastle 1865, i, 301; E. Mackenzie, *Northumberland* ii, 1825, 295].

RIDLEY HALL BRIDGE, NORTHUMBERLAND (R. Tyne), *c.* 1788–92 [Diary, 8–9 Oct. 1785, 16 Oct. 1786, 30 July 1788].

SHERBORNE CASTLE, DORSET, PINFORD BRIDGE in the park for the 1st Earl Digby, 1790(?) [Hutchins, *History of Dorset* iv, 1873, 279] (R.C.H.M., *Dorset* i, pl. 113).

CLACHAN BRIDGE, SEIL, ARGYLLSHIRE, probably revised design made by John Stevenson of Oban and executed by the latter in 1791 [R.C.A.M., *Argyll* ii, 294–5].

PUBLIC BUILDINGS

EDINBURGH, ST. CECILIA'S HALL, NIDDRIE STREET, for the Musical Society of Edinburgh, 1761–3; restored 1966 [Diary, 10 March 1763; *Book of the Old Edinburgh Club* xix, 1933, 225] (*C. Life*, 15 Aug. 1968).

LONDON, ALMACK'S CLUB (afterwards WILLIS'S ROOMS), KING STREET, ST. JAMES'S, 1764–5; destroyed by bombing 1939/45 [*Survey of London* xxix, 304–6 and plates].

LONDON, rebuilt NEW RIVER COMPANY'S OFFICES, CLERKENWELL, 1770; dem. [R. S. Mylne, *Master Masons*, 268] (W. Maitland, *History of London*, ed. Entick, ii, 1775, pl. 128).

LONDON, THE CITY OF LONDON LYING-IN HOSPITAL, CITY ROAD, 1770–3; dem. *c.* 1903 [Diary, 7 April 1770; Sir Albert Richardson's plans; R. S. Mylne, *Master Masons*, 269; W. Maitland, *History of London*, ed. Entick, ii, 1775, pl. 127: 'Mylne Architect'].

ROCHESTER CATHEDRAL, directed structural repairs, 1780–1 [Diary, 29–30 March, 21 Aug., 10–11 Sept. 1780, 22 March 1781, 13–14 Sept. 1782].

ST. PAUL'S CATHEDRAL, repairs to south transept, 1781; designed new pulpit 1805 ['The Fabric of St. Paul's 1760–1810', *R.I.B.A. Jnl.*, 3rd ser., xxiii, 1916; Lambeth Palace Library MS. 1489, Mylne's report on the fabric dated 1781; see also MS. 2027].

TOBERMORY, ISLE OF MULL, ARGYLLSHIRE, CUSTOM HOUSE and INN for the British Fisheries Society, 1789–90 [S.R.O., GD 9/4, ff. 169, 313, 439–43; Diary, 16 March 1789, 14 May 1790].

INVERARAY, ARGYLLSHIRE, CHURCH for the 5th Duke of Argyll, 1795–1800 [I. G. Lindsay & Mary Cosh, *Inveraray and the Dukes of Argyll*, 1973, chap. viii].

LONDON, STATIONERS' HALL, LUDGATE HILL, rebuilt east front, 1800–1 [R. S. Mylne, *Master Masons*, 280; Diary].

DOMESTIC ARCHITECTURE

LONDON, NO. 1 STRATTON STREET (NO. 79 PICCADILLY), for the 10th Earl of Eglinton, 1763 [Diary, 16 and 22 Dec. 1763, recording the passing of bills totalling £3195 on Lord Eglinton's behalf]. In 1771 an attic storey was added by Sir W. Chambers for Lord Fitzwilliam. In 1795 Mylne surveyed the house for a new owner, Thomas Coutts [Diary, 20 Oct. 1795; A. I. Dasent, *Piccadilly*, 1920, 68–9]; dem. 1929 (A. E. Richardson & C. L. Gill, *London Houses from 1660 to 1820*, 1911, pls. lxxv, lxxvi, where the attribution to R. F. Brettingham should be disregarded.)

CHISWICK, MIDDLESEX, alterations to house for the 16th Earl of Morton, 1763 [Diary, 1763, esp. 7 Dec.].

LONDON, NO. 47 BROOK STREET, alterations or repairs for the 16th Earl of Morton, 1763 [Diary, 1 Sept., 7 Dec. 1763].

CALLY HOUSE, KIRCUDBRIGHTSHIRE, for James Murray, 1763–5 [*N.S.A.* iv, 297; Diary; S.R.O., GD 10/1421/287, 288A (plan and elevation)]. The wings were raised in 1794 by Thomas Boyd (*q.v.*), and the house was extensively altered in 1833–7 by J. B. Papworth.

KINGS WESTON, GLOS., stables and alterations to interior (including saloon) for Edward Southwell, Lord de Clifford, 1763–8 [Diary; accounts of Lord de Clifford's executors at Badminton House, Glos.; Christopher Gotch, 'Mylne and Kings Weston', *C. Life*, 23 Jan. 1953].

LONDON, ARGYLL HOUSE, NO. 7 ARGYLL STREET, alterations for the Marquess of Lorne (afterwards 5th Duke of Argyll), 1764–5; dem. 1864–5 [Diary, 9, 28 Feb. 1764, etc.]. At Inverary Castle there is an engraved survey plan of the house, probably the 'printed plan' referred to in Mylne's Diary on 10 Feb. 1774.

TWICKENHAM, MIDDLESEX, alterations to house, including new hall and portico, for — Briscoe, 1764 [Diary, 5 May, 22 Sept. 1764].

GALLOWAY HOUSE, GARLIESTOWN, WIGTOWNSHIRE, alterations for Lord Garlies, 1764 [Diary, 10 April 1764; *A.P.S.D.*].

NORWICH, house in SURREY STREET (now Norwich Union Fire Office) for T. Patterson, 1764 [Diary, 29 Jan., 21 Aug. 1764, etc.; drawings in Richardson Collection; *A.P.S.D.*].

LONDON, house in HIGHGATE ROAD, KENTISH TOWN, for H. S. Woodfall, 1766 [contract drawings in Richardson Collection].

BLAISE CASTLE, nr. BRISTOL, GLOS., a castellated tower for Thomas Farr, 1766 [Diary, Jan. 1766: 'Sent finished Drawings of . . . a Castle to Mr. Farr'; drawing of a variant design in Richardson Collection].

AMISFIELD HOUSE, EAST LOTHIAN, alterations for Francis Charteris, 1766 [Diary, 12, 14 Aug. 1766]. The house was dem. *c.* 1928, but the 'castle' mentioned in Mylne's diary may be the surviving castellated folly by the main road.

CONDOVER HALL, SALOP., designs for internal

alterations for Miss Anna Maria Leighton, 1766 [Diary, 22 May, 10, 26 June 1766]. T. F. Pritchard (*q.v.*) also made designs for Condover at the same time. As the Georgian interiors have been destroyed it is not certain what was done.

HALSTON HALL, SALOP., alterations for John Mytton, 1766–8, including interior of saloon [Diary, 1766–8, *passim*].

TUSMORE HOUSE, OXON., for William Fermor, 1766–70; altered by W. Burn 1858; dem. 1961 [G. Richardson, *New Vitruvius Britannicus* i, 1802, pls. 3–5; Diary, 1766–70, *passim*] (*C. Life*, 30 July, 6 Aug. 1938; *V.C.H. Oxon.* vi, 334–5 and plate).

CAVERSHAM GROVE, OXON., alteration for — Bindley, 1767 [Diary, 2 April, 14 and 16 May, 6 June 1767].

LONDON, NO. 16 GREAT WINDMILL STREET, for Dr. William Hunter, 1767; remodelled 1887 and later [*Survey of London* xxxi, 48–50 and pl. 135].

WORMLEYBURY, WORMLEY, HERTS., for Sir Abraham Hume, 1767–70. The principal rooms were decorated by Robert Adam, 1777–9 [Diary, 19 May 1767, etc.; drawings by Mylne in R.I.B.A. Drawings Coll.] (*C. Life*, 30 Jan. 1915).

HANWELL, MIDDLESEX, house for Henry Berners, 1768–9 [Diary, 16 April 1768, etc.; drawings in Richardson Collection] (A. E. Richardson, *Robert Mylne*, pl. 31).

ARDINCAPLE CASTLE, DUNBARTONSHIRE, alterations (?) for Lord Frederick Campbell, 1769; dem. 1958 [*A.P.S.D.* The Diary records a visit to Ardincaple on 11 Sept. 1769, but it is doubtful what, if anything, was done here to Mylne's design].

EDINBURGH, WHITEFOORD HOUSE, 53 CANONGATE, for Sir John Whitefoord, 1769–70 [Diary, 18 Sept. 1769: 'Sent Sir John Whitefoord plans elevations and sections of a house to be built at Edinburgh'].

GOODNESTONE PARK, KENT, alterations for Sir Brook Bridges, Bart., probably including the decoration of the two bow-ended rooms on the east front, 1770 [Diary, 4 March 1770, etc.].

LONDON, NEW BRIDGE STREET, CHATHAM PLACE and ALBION PLACE, forming the approaches to Blackfriars Bridge, 1772–c. 1790; dem. [C. Gotch, 'Blackfriars Bridge', *Arch. Rev.*, Oct. 1952].

ADDINGTON LODGE, SURREY, for Barlow Trecothick, 1773–9; enlarged 1829–30 by H. Harrison (*q.v.*) [G. Richardson, *New Vitruvius Britannicus* i, 1802, pls. 32–3].

LOTON PARK, SALOP., alterations for Sir Charlton Leighton, Bart., 1773–4 [Diary, 27 Jan.–9 April 1773, 24–25 June 1774].

TERN HALL, ATTINGHAM, SALOP., proposed alterations and additions for Noel Hill (d. 1782),

1773–4, probably not carried out; dem. c. 1785 [Diary, 16 Feb., 26 March 1773, 18–19, 26 June 1774; design for semicircular stables 'for Mr. Hills Shropshire' in Richardson Collection].

WOODHOUSE, nr. WHITTINGTON, SALOP., for William Mostyn-Owen, 1773–4 [Diary, 14 April 1773, 22–23 June 1774]

BRYNGWYN HALL, MONTGOMERYSHIRE, works for William Mostyn-Owen, 1773–4; damaged by fire c. 1800 and largely rebuilt [Diary, 22 Sept. 1771, 26 Jan., 10 Feb., 23 Dec. 1773, 20 and 30 April, 24 June, 20 and 23 Oct. 1774].

SUNDORN HALL, SALOP., alterations to offices for John Corbet, 1774 [Diary, 19–20 June, 1 Nov. 1774].

ONSLOW HALL, SALOP., additions for Richard Morhall, 1774; rebuilt 1780 by G. Steuart for Rowland Wingfield [Diary, 20 June, 8 Oct. 1774].

PITLOUR HOUSE, STRATHMIGLO, FIFE, for General Philip Skene, 1775–6 [Diary, 24–26 Aug. 1774, 2 Sept. 1776] (A. E. Richardson, *Robert Mylne*, pls. 48–9).

THE WICK, RICHMOND HILL, SURREY, for Lady St. Aubyn, 1775 [Diary, 10 Dec. 1774, 3 June 1775; contract drawings in Richardson Collection] (*C. Life*, 1 Feb. 1941).

CLOWANCE, nr. CROWAN, CORNWALL, advised on rebuilding of defective front for Lady St. Aubyn, 1775–6 [Diary, 28 March, 17 May, 28 June 1775, 10 May 1776]: cf. 'C. Rawlinson'.

INVERARAY CASTLE, ARGYLLSHIRE, alterations to windows on main floor, 1777, and redecoration of principal rooms, 1782–9, for the 5th Duke of Argyll [I. G. Lindsay & Mary Cosh, *Inveraray and the Dukes of Argyll*, 1973, 200, 208–16, etc.].

INVERARAY ESTATE, ARGYLLSHIRE, works for the 5th Duke of Argyll, including FISHERLAND BARN, 1774–5, MALTLAND COURT (barns, etc.), 1774–82, GARRON LODGE, 1783–4, and a semicircular court of farm-buildings at MAAM STEADING, GLENSHIRA, 1787–9. In Inveraray town Mylne was responsible for two rows of tenements called ARKLAND and RELIEF LAND, 1774–6, as well as for the arched screen-wall which forms the façade to Loch Fyne, 1787 [I. G. Lindsay & Mary Cosh, *op. cit., passim*].

LONDON, NO. 17 HILL STREET, alterations for Sir Abraham Hume, c. 1777 [Diary, 31 May 1777, payments in March 1781 and April 1782].

BOLESWORTH CASTLE, CHESHIRE, alterations to dining-room for John Crewe, 1777 [Diary, 15 May, 30 Oct. 1777]. The house was rebuilt in 1829.

BICKLEY PLACE, KENT, for John Wells, c. 1780; dem. c. 1968 [drawings in Richardson Collection] (J. P. Neale, *Views of Seats*, 1st ser., iii, 1820). As this commission is not mentioned in Mylne's diaries it is just possible that the drawings were copied by Mylne from those of another architect, but as the house had all the characteristics of his style this is unlikely.

EDGMOND RECTORY, SALOP., enlarged for the Rev. William Pigott, 1780 [Diary 14 April, 25 July 1780].

BERWICK HOUSE, SALOP., alterations and additions (since removed) for Thomas Jelf Powys, 1780 [Diary, 17 July, 4 Sept. 1780].

SOUTHWARK, house on east side of GREAT SURREY (now Blackfriars) STREET (afterwards the YORK HOTEL) for himself, 1780; dem. 1864 [*Survey of London* xxii, 115].

EDINBURGH, WEST BOW, shop and tenement, his own property, 1782; dem. 1830 [Edinburgh Dean of Guild plans].

POWDERHALL, nr. EDINBURGH (his own property, on lease to a tenant), new lodge and gate, *c.* 1782–4 [sketch in S.R.O., GD 1/51/37 (1781); payments in Diary, Sept.–Oct. 1785].

ROSNEATH, DUNBARTONSHIRE, castellated alterations for the 5th Duke of Argyll, 1784–6; destroyed by fire 1802 [Diary, especially 24 April, 15 May and 2 June 1784; I. G. Lindsay & Mary Cosh, *Inveraray and the Dukes of Argyll*, 1973, 382, n. 51].

LITTLE WOODCOTE, CARSHALTON, SURREY, additions to house and offices for — Durand, 1790 [Diary, 29 May, 19 June, 24 July 1790].

THE GROVE, GREAT AMWELL, HERTS., for himself, 1794–7; since enlarged [Diary, 4 Aug. 1794, etc.; drawings preserved in house].

SYON HOUSE, MIDDLESEX, domed Ionic BOATHOUSE for the 2nd Duke of Northumberland, 1803 [Diary, 19 July, 6 Aug., 8 and 31 Oct. 1803] (measured drawings in S. C. Ramsey & J. D. M. Harvey, *Small Houses of the Late Georgian Period* ii, 1923, pls. 72–3).

BUTE HOUSE, PETERSHAM, SURREY, alterations for the 1st Marquess of Bute, 1805–6; dem. [Diary, 1804–6, *passim*].

MAUSOLEA AND MONUMENTS

ASKHAM RICHARD CHURCHYARD, YORKS. (W.R.), monument (urn on column) to Elizabeth Berry (d. 1767), erected 1770, signed 'MYLNE FECIT 1770'.

ADDINGTON CHURCH, SURREY, monument (urn) to Barlow Trecothick (d. 1770), erected 1776 [Diary, 3 Jan. 1776].

CLOWANCE, CORNWALL, St. Aubyn family mausoleum, 1778 [Diary, 16 Nov. 1777, 26 March 1778].

LUNDIE CHURCHYARD, ANGUS, mausoleum in memory of Sir William Duncan, Bart. (d. 1774), built 1787–9 for Lady Mary Duncan [Diary, 6 Oct. 1786, 31 Jan., 3 Feb. 1787].

DUBLIN, ST. CATHERINE'S CHURCH, tablet to his brother William Mylne (d. 1790) [R. S. Mylne, *Master Masons*, 260].

WOOLVERSTONE HALL, SUFFOLK, obelisk in memory of William Berners, erected by Charles Berners, 1791–3; dem. 1945 [Diary, 14 Feb., 18 Sept. 1791] (H. R. Barker, *East Suffolk Illustrated*, 1908–9, 539).

GREAT AMWELL, HERTS., Mylne family mausoleum in churchyard, 1800; urn in memory of Sir Hugh Myddelton on island in New River, 1800.

FAREHAM, HANTS., HOLY TRINITY CHURCH, monument (originally in parish church) to Admiral Sir Charles Thompson (d. 1799), 1802, Flaxman sculptor [Diary, 25 Oct. 1802].

ST. PAUL'S CATHEDRAL, monument in crypt to Sir Christopher Wren, 1807 [Diary, 21 May, 20 June 1807, 12 March 1808].

MYLNE, THOMAS (–1763), was the son and successor of William Mylne (d. 1728). In 1729 he was admitted a burgess of Edinburgh and a member of the Edinburgh Masonic Lodge, of which he was subsequently (1735–6) master. Although in origin an association of working masons, this lodge was by now assuming the social and 'speculative' character associated with modern freemasonry. In 1736 the Grand Lodge of Edinburgh was established, and Thomas Mylne appears to have been a prominent member of this purely 'speculative' society, of which he was Grand Treasurer from 1737 to 1755.

In 1743 Thomas Mylne was one of the witnesses in William Adam's lawsuit against Lord Braco. His evidence shows that he was active as a mason-contractor in Edinburgh and its neighbourhood, but that (unlike the more enterprising Adam) he 'never built a House of his own undertaking above three miles from Edinburgh'. However, he stated that he sometimes provided plans for houses which he did not himself build, for instance at Fisherrow and Inveresk, both near Musselburgh, Midlothian. The only other buildings whose design can at present be attributed to him are a 'land' near the cross on the north side of High Street, Edinburgh, which bore the Mylne mark[1] and the date 1744 on the lintel, and his own house at Powderhall on the north-east outskirts of the city (illustrated by J. Grant, *Old and New Edinburgh* iii, 93 (6)).

Thomas Mylne died on 5 March 1763, and is commemorated on the family monument in the Greyfriars Churchyard. A portrait by Mossman, painted in 1752, remains in the possession of his descendants, and is illustrated by R. S. Mylne, *Master Masons*, 251. By his wife Elizabeth Duncan he had seven children, of whom Robert (1733–1811) and William (1734–90) are the subjects of separate entries [R. S. Mylne, *The Master Masons to the Crown of Scotland*, Edinburgh 1893; *A.P.S.D.*; *D.N.B.*].

---

[1] ⋈

MYLNE, WILLIAM (1734–1790), was the second son of Thomas Mylne of Edinburgh (*q.v.*). After a period of apprenticeship as a mason he went (1754) to France and then to Italy with his elder brother Robert. He returned in 1758 and took over his father's business as a mason. In 1759 he designed a bridge over the Tweed at FAIRNILIE, SELKIRKSHIRE, which he appears to have built the following year [letter to Robert Mylne, 27 Feb. 1759], and in 1768–72 he was jointly responsible with his brother Robert for the design of the NEW (JAMAICA) BRIDGE over the Clyde at GLASGOW, for which the Glasgow mason John Adam (*q.v.*) was the contractor [R. S. Mylne, *Master Masons*, 258–9; *N.S.A.* vi, 219; *The Picture of Glasgow*, Glasgow 1812, 132; Robert Mylne's Diary, 11 Sept. 1772, 11 Sept. 1773]. In 1770–2 he was employed by the 5th Duke of Argyll at INVERARAY CASTLE, ARGYLL-SHIRE, where he was responsible for rearranging the interior, though not for the subsequent re-decoration to the designs of his brother Robert [I. G. Lindsay & Mary Cosh, *Inveraray and the Dukes of Argyll*, 1973, 196–7]. Meanwhile in 1765 he had submitted a design for the NORTH BRIDGE linking the New and Old Towns of Edinburgh. The design was pedestrian, but Mylne (unlike his principal competitor, David Henderson) was able to find security to execute the bridge according to his proposals, and contracted to build it for £10,140. In 1769, when it was almost finished, part of the southern abutment gave way, burying five people in the ruins. Mylne made good the damage, but he was now in serious financial difficulties, and in 1772 he decided to leave Scotland and settle in America. At first he tried the life of a planter in South Carolina, but in 1774 he moved to New York in the hope of obtaining employment as an architect. Finding, however, that there was little prospect of success unless he 'turned undertaker' again, he migrated to Ireland, where he became engineer to the Dublin Water Works. His success in this capacity is testified by a silver salver which was presented to him by the Lord Mayor and Aldermen of Dublin in 1786 to record 'their entire approba-tion of the laudable exertion of his great abilities in rescuing those important works from the very bad condition they were in, and bringing them to a state of perfection'. Mylne died at Dublin in March 1790, aged 56. His brother erected a tablet in St. Catherine's Church 'to inform Pos-terity of the uncommon Zeal, Integrity and Skill with which he formed, enlarged, and established on a perfect system the water works of Dublin'. [A. J. Youngson, *The Making of Classical Edin-burgh*, 1966, 60–5; R. S. Mylne, *The Master Masons to the Crown of Scotland*, Edinburgh 1893, 235–60; *Reports of the late John Smeaton* iii, 1812, 218 (report on failure of North Bridge); Mylne family papers.]

578

MYLNE, WILLIAM CHADWELL (1781–1863), second son of Robert Mylne, was born in London on 5 or 6 April 1781. As early as 1797 he was assisting his father to stake out the lands purchased for the Eau Brink Cut, and he was also employed on the Gloucester and Berkeley Ship Canal. In 1804 he was appointed assistant engineer to the New River Company, and on his father's death in 1811 succeeded him in control of the works. He held this appointment for fifty years, retiring only two years before his death. He also succeeded his father as surveyor to the Stationers' Company in 1811, and held the post until 1861.

Although mainly engaged in engineering works connected with water-supply and drainage, Mylne also practised as an architect, and is said to have altered or enlarged several country houses. He was also much employed as a surveyor and valuer. As surveyor to the New River Company he laid out their property at Clerkenwell for building purposes. The new streets, including MYDDELTON SQUARE, AMWELL, INGLEBERT and RIVER STREETS, were begun in 1819. Mylne also designed ST. MARK'S CHURCH, MYDDELTON SQUARE, 1826–8, Gothic [*Gent's Mag.* 1829, 579–81], and the CLERKENWELL PAROCHIAL CHARITY SCHOOLS in AMWELL STREET, 1828, Gothic [W. J. Pinks, *History of Clerkenwell*, 1881, 577]. His work in Clerkenwell is described and illustrated in *C. Life*, 28 Jan. 1939.

In 1815 he supervised the repair of CAVERSHAM BRIDGE, nr. READING, for Lord Cadogan [Treacher papers in Reading Public Library], and he designed GARRET HOSTEL BRIDGE over the R. Cam at Cambridge, 1835–7; dem. 1960 [R.C.H.M., *Cambridge*, 309]. It was a single iron arch, with Gothic detailing, and is illustrated in Hann & Hosking, *Bridges*, 1843. In 1827 he was one of the unsuccessful competitors for Clifton Bridge, Bristol. For the Stationers' Company he designed an octagonal card-room at STATIONERS' HALL in 1825 [C. Blagden, *The Stationers' Com-pany*, 1960, 225–6].

Mylne designed HARPOLE RECTORY, NORTH-ANTS., in 1816 [Northants. Record Office, Peter-borough Diocesan Records], and in 1842–4 built THE FLINT HOUSE, AMWELL, HERTS., for himself to take the place of his father's house (The Grove), whose situation near the river he regarded as un-healthy.

Mylne was elected a Fellow of the Royal Society in 1826, and of the Institute of British Architects on its foundation in 1834. He was Treasurer of the Smeatonian Society of Civil Engineers for forty-two years, and in 1842 became a member of the Institution of Civil Engineers. He retired from his profession in 1861, and died at Amwell on 25 December 1863, in his 83rd year. His portrait by H. W. Phillips is given in R. S. Mylne's *Master Masons*. His son,

Robert William Mylne (1817–90), architect, engineer and geologist, was the last of the family to practise architecture.

[*A.P.S.D.*; *D.N.B.*; *Builder* xxii, 1864, 7; *Minutes of Proceedings of the Institution of Civil Engineers* xxx, 1869–70, 448–51; R. S. Mylne, *The Master Masons to the Crown of Scotland*, 1893, chap. xiv.]

N

NASH, JOHN (1752–1835), was probably born in London. His father, an engineer and millwright in Lambeth, died when John was still a boy. He was employed in the office of Sir Robert Taylor, at first 'in a subordinate capacity', but later as a draughtsman. By 1777 he had left Taylor to establish himself as an architect and speculative builder in London. But in 1783 he was declared bankrupt, and removed to Carmarthen, where he seems to have been on familiar terms with the local gentry. He maintained an association with the London architect Samuel Saxon (*q.v.*). Together they reroofed the parish church and carried out other works of minor importance. In 1788 Nash designed his first public building, the County Gaol at Carmarthen. Other commissions followed, and by 1793 he was employing the refugee Augustus Charles Pugin as a draughtsman. In 1796 he was able to return to London as an architect with an established practice and a distinctive style.

Nash's Welsh exile had not been fruitless, for it was there that he emerged as the leading architect of the Picturesque. Nash's initiation into the Picturesque can probably be traced to his contacts with Thomas Johnes, the creator of the romantic landscape of Hafod, and with Uvedale Price, the author of a celebrated *Essay on the Picturesque* (1796), for whom he designed a triangular castellated house on the shore of Cardigan Bay at Aberystwyth. Through Price he may also have met Payne Knight, whose 'Castle' at Downton in Herefordshire was the prototype of the picturequely asymmetrical country house of which Nash was soon to be the acknowledged master. Most of Nash's country houses were, like Downton, to affect a castle air externally, but he offered his clients an alternative formula in which a simple Italianate architecture, almost vernacular in character, was used to form picturesque houses composed like buildings in a landscape by Claude. A few suburban villas (notably Southgate Grove) showed that he could also design in a sophisticated neo-classical style which owed something to recent French architecture (studied of course in engravings, for France was enemy territory from 1793 onwards, and Nash's first

recorded visit to that country took place in 1814[1]).

Back in London Nash formed a partnership with Humphry Repton who, as a fashionable landscape-gardener, had many opportunities to obtain architectural commissions. Between them Nash and Repton transformed many old-fashioned houses into elegant seats with grounds carefully landscaped to enhance their picturesque character. By 1802, when the partnership was dissolved, Nash had executed commisions in many parts of the country. At the Royal Academy that year he showed designs for four houses – one in Surrey, one in Shropshire, one in Wales and one in Scotland. He could also claim royal patronage, for in 1798 he had designed a conservatory for the Prince of Wales, presumably at Carlton House. It is likely that he owed this commission to Repton, but in the same year he married a young woman who appears to have had connections of a different sort with the Prince. That Mary Ann Nash was the Prince's mistress cannot be proved, but in her lifetime it was commonly believed that Nash was a complaisant husband who had married her more to oblige the Prince than to please himself.

In 1806 Nash was appointed architect to the Department of Woods and Forests, with James Morgan, one of his early assistants, as his colleague. In this capacity he prepared a plan for the layout of Marylebone Park, an estate on the northern outskirts of London which in Jan. 1811 reverted to the Crown on the expiration of the lease. This, as laid out by Nash with the approval of his royal patron, became The Regent's Park, a carefully landscaped open space containing a small number of private villas and surrounded by palatial 'terraces', most of which were designed by Nash himself. In this way the amenities of a park were combined with the development of the estate as a fashionable residential area. In order to connect the park with the West End and the seat of government at Westminster, Nash designed a new street running north to south in such a way as to provide 'a boundary and complete separation between the Streets and Squares occupied by the Nobility and Gentry' to the west, and the 'narrow Streets and meaner Houses occupied by mechanics and the trading part of the community' on the east. It was also intended to form a royal route from Carlton House to a villa or pavilion which was to be erected for the Prince Regent in the new park: though, as the villa was not built, and as Carlton House itself

---

[1] In the Coade Stone firm's letter-book there is a letter to Nash's assistant James Morgan dated 25 Oct. 1814, which begins, 'If Mr. Nash is returned from France' (*Architectural History* xi, 1968, 46, n. 20). He visited Paris again in January 1818 (*The Farington Diary*, ed. J. Greig, viii, 159).

was demolished in 1827, this idea was never realized. The Bill authorizing the building of Regent Street was passed in 1813. Nash himself designed many of the buildings along its route, including the colonnaded Quadrant and the church of All Souls, Langham Place, which were its most striking architectural features. In Lower Regent Street he built an ingeniously planned double residence for his own occupation and that of his relative, John Edwards. Like an Italian *palazzo*, it occupied the upper parts of a block whose ground floor was divided into shops.

On the sudden death of James Wyatt in 1813, Nash was the Prince Regent's choice for his place as Surveyor-General of the Works. He was in fact given responsibility for the maintenance of the royal palaces until a successor should be formally appointed. But Wyatt's inefficiency resulted in the suppression of his office and a reorganization of the Works with three 'attached architects' under an administrative head who enjoyed the title of Surveyor-General. With Soane and Smirke, Nash was one of the triumvirate. As a working arrangement the three architects divided the royal palaces between them. Carlton House, Kensington, St. James's and the royal lodges in Windsor Great Park fell to Nash. It was, however, as the Regent's personal architect that he remodelled the Royal Pavilion at Brighton in 1815–21, and when the Prince became King in 1820 it was by his personal direction that Nash received orders to reconstruct Buckingham House on a palatial scale, regardless of the claims of Sir John Soane as the architect officially responsible for that building. At a time when the King himself had forfeited the affections of his subjects, such partiality was not calculated to make his architect a popular figure, and when the extravagant expenditure on Buckingham Palace became a national scandal, Nash had to undergo the ordeal of being interrogated by a Select Committee of the House of Commons (1828). Although its findings were scarcely to his credit, there was 'no actual reflection on his professional ability or his integrity'. But in the following year he was accused by Colonel Davies, the member for Worcester, of malversation and fraud in connection with his building activities in Regent Street. Once more he was exonerated on every charge, but the committee added a rider to the effect that 'it was undesirable for official architects to acquire a financial interest in property for which they might be called upon to give a valuation', and Baring voiced the general feeling when he declared that although 'from what he had heard of Mr. Nash, he should be inclined to think that he was incapable of dishonesty; ... he must say that, as a manager of public money and as an exhibitor of taste, he was sorry the public ever had anything to do with him'. Nash himself issued a printed *Statement* in which he declared

that while 'claiming no greater dislike for fair emolument' than any other architect, he had been induced to assume the role of a speculator solely by the desire to see his own designs carried out. The King, who regarded the attack on Nash as a personal affront, would have vindicated both his own injured dignity and the reputation of his architect by making Nash a baronet, but the Duke of Wellington dissuaded him from conferring the honour until the completion of Buckingham Palace – an event which George IV did not live to see. When the King died in 1830, Nash's career as a public architect was virtually at an end. The direction of Buckingham Palace was taken out of his hands and he was dismissed from the Office of Works. A third Select Committee enquired into the expenditure on the Palace and employed a committee of architects to investigate its alleged structural weaknesses. Once more nothing positively discreditable to Nash was found, but the design of the Palace was universally criticized, and both the building and its architect shared in the odium which the name of George IV inspired. When Nash himself died in 1835, his reputation as an architect was at its lowest ebb, and Victorian taste did nothing to vindicate the name of one who showed so marked a predilection for the 'fatal facility of stucco'. For his picturesque castles were far removed in style and intention from the earnest Gothic of Pugin or Scott, while his use of the orders was too slipshod to commend itself to an age in which scholarship was the first requisite of the classical architect. Though he had little interest in the finer points of architectural design, he had a remarkable gift for composition on a large scale which was the secret of his success both as a country-house architect and as a town-planner. In London he brilliantly applied the principles of the Picturesque to the problems of urban development presented by Regent's Park and Regent Street; and he alone had the enthusiasm and the organizing ability to carry through the great schemes of metropolitan improvement which were his major contribution to English architecture.

Nash died at his country house, East Cowes Castle, on 13 May 1835, and was buried in East Cowes Churchyard, where a tomb marks his grave. He may have had a son by an early marriage, and his second wife brought up five children named Pennethorne whose parentage is a mystery. Officially, they were the offspring of a cousin, but the possibility that some of them were royal bastards cannot be discounted. James Pennethorne (1801–71) was brought up as an architect in Nash's office, assisted him in his later years, and succeeded to his practice. He carried out many public works in London and was knighted in 1870. Nash's other principal assistants were Augustus Pugin, James Morgan and John Foulon. George Stanley and John Adey Repton, F. H. Greenway, Anthony Salvin and the brothers Henry, James and George Pain were among his pupils. The last two established themselves in Ireland, where they designed a number of houses in a picturesque castle style derived directly from that of their master.

The finest portrait of Nash is one by Lawrence painted in 1824–5 and now in the possession of Major Allan J. Cameron of Lochiel (photograph in National Portrait Gallery). Another portrait by Lawrence is at Jesus College, Oxford. A wax miniature by J. A. Couriguer is in the National Portrait Gallery. A marble bust by J. C. F. Rossi was exhibited at the Royal Academy in 1823. The whereabouts of a marble bust by Behnes (exhibited at the R.A. 1831) appears to be unknown, but there is a plaster cast at the R.I.B.A. Drawings Collection.

[John Summerson, *John Nash: Architect to George IV*, 1935, 2nd ed. 1949; Terence Davis, *The Architecture of John Nash*, introduced with a critical essay by John Summerson, 1960; Terence Davis, *John Nash*, 1966; R. Liscombe on Nash's specimen designs for the Church Building Commission of 1818 in *Architectural History* xiii, 1970; *Catalogue of the R.I.B.A. Drawings Coll.: L–N*, 1973; *History of the King's Works* vi, 1973, *passim*; papers in P.R.O., CREST 2/1616.]

PUBLIC BUILDINGS, ETC.

CARMARTHEN CHURCH, new roof and ceiling, 1785; destroyed 1860 [W. Spurrell, *Carmarthen*, 1879, 32, 129].

CARMARTHEN, THE 'SIX BELLS' INN (now one of a row of houses), c. 1785 [W. Spurrell, *Carmarthen*, 1879, 51 n.].

CARMARTHEN, THE COUNTY GAOL, 1789–92; dem. [W. Spurrell, *Carmarthen*, 1879, 51].

ST. DAVID'S CATHEDRAL, PEMBROKESHIRE, rebuilt west front and designed new Chapter-House, 1791–3. The west front was again rebuilt by Scott in 1862, and the Chapter-House was demolished in 1829 [I. Wyn Jones, 'John Nash at St. David's', *Arch. Rev.*, Oct. 1952].

TRE-CEFEL BRIDGE, CARDIGANSHIRE, 1792–3 [National Library of Wales, Cardiganshire Q.S. Order Book, 17 July 1793].

CARDIGAN, THE COUNTY GAOL, 1793; dem. [S. Lewis, *Topographical Dictionary of Wales* i, 1849, 161].

ABERGAVENNY, MONMOUTHSHIRE, THE MARKET HOUSE, 1794–5; altered by J. Westcott 1825; dem. [Summerson].

HEREFORD, THE COUNTY GAOL, 1795–6; dem. 1928 [J. Duncumb, *History of the County of Hereford* i, 1804, 425].

ABERYSTWYTH, CARDIGANSHIRE, bridge over R. Rheidol, c. 1797–1800; destroyed by flood 1886 [National Library of Wales, Cardiganshire Q.S. Order Book, 13 Oct. 1792, 8 Oct. 1794].

STANFORD-ON-TEME, WORCS., iron bridge over R. Teme for Sir Edward Winnington, Bart., 1797; dem. 1905 after collapse [Summerson]. A copy of Nash's design for a previous bridge, which collapsed soon after its erection in 1795, is in the Prattinton Collection in the Library of the Society of Antiquaries (Box IV). Nash patented an iron bridge in 1797 (Patent No. 2165).

CHICHESTER, SUSSEX, THE MARKET HOUSE, NORTH STREET, 1807–8; top storey added 1900 [T. W. Horsfield, *History of Sussex* ii, 1835, 11].

NEWPORT, ISLE OF WIGHT, THE ISLE OF WIGHT INSTITUTION (library and news-room), 1811 [Summerson].

HIGHGATE, LONDON, THE ARCHWAY, 1812; dem. 1901 [Summerson].

LONDON, ST. JAMES'S PARK, bridge, pagoda, polygonal ballroom and other temporary buildings for fête in honour of the allied sovereigns, 1814. The ballroom was re-erected at Woolwich Arsenal as a military museum in 1819 [Summerson, 147–51; *History of the King's Works* vi, 317–19].

NEWPORT, ISLE OF WIGHT, MARKET HOUSE AND GUILDHALL, 1814–16 [Summerson].

WEST COWES CHURCH, ISLE OF WIGHT, tower, incorporating a mausoleum, for George Ward, 1816 [Summerson].

LONDON, THE ROYAL OPERA HOUSE, HAYMARKET, remodelled in collaboration with G. S. Repton, 1816–18; interior destroyed by fire 1867 and rebuilt in 1868–9; dem., except the Arcade, c. 1895 [Britton & Pugin, *The Public Buildings of London* i, 1825, 72–9].

OXFORD, JESUS COLLEGE, advice on altering roofs, battlements, etc., of both quadrangles, 1815–18 [*V.C.H. Oxfordshire* iii, 275; J. Ingram, *Memorials of Oxford* iii, 1837, 15].

OXFORD, EXETER COLLEGE, the hall was repaired in 1818 'from the designs of Mr. Nash, under the superintendence of Mr. Repton' [J. Ingram, *Memorials of Oxford* i, 1837, 12–13].

LONDON, THE OPHTHALMIC INSTITUTION, ALBANY STREET, 1818 [Summerson].

LONDON, THE ARGYLL ROOMS, REGENT STREET, in collaboration with G. S. Repton, 1819–20; destroyed by fire 1830 [Summerson; drawing by Repton in the Mellon Collection].

LONDON, NEWMAN STREET, PICTURE-GALLERY for Benjamin West's sons, 1820–1; dem. [Summerson; *The Farington Diary*, ed. J. Greig, viii, 300].

LONDON, THE HAYMARKET THEATRE, 1820–1 [Britton & Pugin, *The Public Buildings of London* i, 1825, 262–72].

ASCOT RACECOURSE, ROYAL STAND, 1822; dem. [*History of the King's Works* vi, 257].

581

LONDON, ST. JAMES'S SQUARE, Ionic garden seat, 1822 [*Survey of London* xxix, 69–70].

LONDON, THE ROYAL MEWS, PIMLICO, 1822–4 [*History of the King's Works* iv, 303–7].

LONDON, ALL SOULS CHURCH, LANGHAM PLACE, 1822–5 [Britton & Pugin, *The Public Buildings of London* ii, 1825, 99–101].

LONDON, SUFFOLK STREET, GALLERY for the Society of British Artists, in collaboration with James Elmes, 1823 [Summerson].

LONDON, THE ADULT ORPHAN ASYLUM, ST. ANDREW'S PLACE, REGENT'S PARK (later Someries House), 1823–4; dem. *c.* 1960.

CARMARTHEN, THE PICTON MONUMENT, 1825–7; dem. [W. Spurrell, *Carmarthen*, 1879, 53–6].

BUCKINGHAM PALACE, LONDON, 1825–30; completed by Edward Blore, 1832–7; east front to Mall rebuilt to Blore's designs 1847–50 and again rebuilt by Sir Aston Webb 1913. The Marble Arch designed by Nash to stand in front of the Palace was removed in 1851 and re-erected at Cumberland Gate. [Britton & Pugin, *The Public Buildings of London, Supplement* by W. H. Leeds, 1838, 103–23; H. Clifford Smith, *Buckingham Palace*, 1931; John Harris, G. de Bellaigue & O. Millar, *Buckingham Palace*, 1968; *History of the King's Works* vi, 263–302.]

LONDON, CLARENCE HOUSE, ST. JAMES'S, rebuilt for the Duke of Clarence, 1825–8; altered 1874–5 [C. Hussey, *Clarence House*, 1949; *History of the King's Works* vi, 323–6].

LONDON, ST. MARY'S CHURCH, HAGGERSTON, 1826–7, Gothic; remodelled by James Brooks 1861–2; dem. 1940/1 [Summerson].

LONDON, THE UNITED SERVICE CLUB, PALL MALL, 1826–8; altered and enlarged by D. Burton 1858–9 [*Survey of London* xxix, 386–94].

BEMBRIDGE CHURCH, ISLE OF WIGHT, 1827; built under the supervision of Jacob Owen of Portsmouth to a plan and estimate supplied gratuitously by Nash; rebuilt 1845 [I.C.B.S.].

WINCHESTER, HOSPITAL OF ST. CROSS, completed restoration begun by S. P. Cockerell, 1827–9 [Summerson].

LONDON, THE WEST STRAND IMPROVEMENTS, 1830–2, including THE LOWTHER ARCADE (dem. 1902), executed by W. Herbert (*q.v.*) [M. V. Stokes, 'The Lowther Arcade in the Strand', *London Topographical Record* xxiii, 1972, 119–28].

LONDON, ST. MARTIN'S VICARAGE, VESTRY HALL and NATIONAL SCHOOLS, ST. MARTIN'S PLACE, *c.* 1830 [P.R.O., CREST 26/32, ff. 59, 268; Vestry Minutes in Westminster City Library, and file at the National School Society, *ex inf.* Mr. A. F. Kelsall] (*Survey of London* xx, 55, pl. 34).

EAST COWES CHURCH, ISLE OF WIGHT, 1831–3; Gothic; rebuilt, except tower, by T. Hellyer, 1868 [I.C.B.S.].

582

DOMESTIC ARCHITECTURE

LONDON, built NOS. 66–71 GREAT RUSSELL STREET for Sir John Rushout, Bart., 1777–8 [bond in Bedford Estate Office, *ex. inf.* Sir John Summerson].

LONDON, NO. 17 BLOOMSBURY SQUARE (formerly two houses, but now the premises of the Royal Pharmaceutical Society), *c.* 1782 [Summerson].

CARMARTHEN, ORCHARD STREET, house ('Green Gardens', now 'Nolton House') said to have been built for himself, *c.* 1785; partly dem. [W. Spurrell, *Carmarthen*, 1879, 51 n.].

GOLDEN GROVE nr. CARMARTHEN, bathroom for John Vaughan, *c.* 1787; dem. 1829 [*The Farington Diary*, ed. J. Greig, viii, 301].

CLYTHA COURT, MONMOUTHSHIRE, Gothic folly known as Clytha Castle for William Jones, 1790 [Monmouthshire Record Office, payment to Nash in M 413/2114, Jones's accounts].

FFYNONE, PEMBROKESHIRE, for John Colby, 1792–6; remodelled 1904 [Summerson; bills in National Library of Wales, Owen & Colby papers, 1139–1267].

HAFOD HOUSE, CARDIGANSHIRE, work for Thomas Johnes, probably including the octagonal library, built in 1794; destroyed by fire 1807 [Summerson; D. Watkin, *C. R. Cockerell*, 1974, 5].

HAVERFORDWEST, PEMBROKESHIRE, FOLEY HOUSE, GOAT STREET, for Richard Foley, 1794 [sale advt. in *Cambrian*, July 1821].

LLANAYRON, CARDIGANSHIRE, for Major Lewis, *c.* 1794 [James Baker, *Guide through Wales* ii, 1795, 200].

WHITSON COURT, MONMOUTHSHIRE, for William Phillips, *c.* 1794 [James Baker, *Guide through Wales* i, 1795, 47].

LLYSNEWYDD, HENLLAN BRIDGE, CARDIGANSHIRE, for Col. Lewes, *c.* 1795; remodelled in nineteenth century, dem. *c.* 1970 [Summerson].

TEMPLE DRUID, MAENCLOCHOG, PEMBROKESHIRE, for Henry Bulkeley, *c.* 1795 [sale advt. in *Cambrian*, 8 Sept. 1821].

DOLAUCOTHI, CARMARTHENSHIRE, remodelled for John Johnes, 1795; dem. [National Library of Wales, Dolaucothi papers].

TENBY, PEMBROKESHIRE, SION HOUSE (later WOOFFERTON GRANGE), for William Routh, *c.* 1795; subsequently enlarged, destroyed by fire 1937 [Summerson].

CARDIGAN, CARDIGAN PRIORY, for Thomas Johnes, senior, *c.* 1795; since remodelled as a War Memorial Hospital [Summerson].

ABERYSTWYTH, CARDIGANSHIRE, THE CASTLE HOUSE, for Sir Uvedale Price, *c.* 1795; dem. 1895 [*Cambrian Directory*, 1800, 65] (*C. Life*, 4 July 1952, 33).

KENTCHURCH COURT, HEREFS., remodelled for John Scudamore, *c.* 1795, Gothic [J. P. Neale,

Views of Seats, 2nd ser., iv, 1828] (*C. Life*, 15, 22 and 29 Dec. 1966).

HARROW-ON-THE-HILL, MIDDLESEX, THE PARK, HIGH STREET, for Richard Page, *c.* 1795–1803; since altered [letters in wallpaper-maker's letter-book in G.L.C. Record Office, B/TRL/9, pp. 20–1, 24–6, *ex inf.* Survey of London; E. D. Laborde, *Harrow School*, 1948, 184].

CORSHAM COURT, WILTS., alterations including remodelling of north front, for P. C. Methuen, in collaboration with J. A. Repton, 1797–8, Gothic; with the exception of the library nearly all Nash's work was destroyed by T. Bellamy in 1844–9 [exhib. at R.A. 1797; J. P. Neale, *Views of Seats*, 2nd ser., ii, 1825; J. Britton, *Historical Account of Corsham House*, 1806; D. Stroud, *Humphry Repton*, 1962, 95–6] (*C. Life*, 20, 27 Nov. 1937; C. Hussey, *English Country Houses: Early Georgian*, 1955, 228–33).

HIGH LEGH HALL, CHESHIRE, alterations and additions for G. J. Legh, 1797–1818; dem. *c.* 1963 [correspondence among Legh papers in John Rylands Library, Manchester].

SOUTHGATE GROVE, MIDDLESEX, for Walker Gray, 1797 [exhib. at R.A. 1797; G. Richardson, *New Vitruvius Britannicus* i, 1802, pls. 29–31].

CASINA, DENMARK HILL, DULWICH, SURREY, for Richard Shawe, 1797; dem. 1906 [exhib. at R.A. 1797].

BANK FARM or POINT PLEASANT, KINGSTON-ON-THAMES, SURREY, for Major-General St. John, 1797; dem. [Summerson].

EAST COWES CASTLE, ISLE OF WIGHT, for himself, 1798 onwards, castellated; dem. 1950 [exhib. at R.A. 1800; Summerson] (*Builder*, 1 Sept. 1950, 270–3).

LONDON, NO. 29 DOVER STREET, for himself, *c.* 1798; mutilated 1934, dem. 1940/1 [Summerson].

SUNDRIDGE PARK, nr. BROMLEY, KENT, for Sir Claude Scott, Bart., in association with Humphry Repton, 1799. Samuel Wyatt (*q.v.*) was responsible for the interior, and also for the stables [exhib. at R.A. 1799; W. Angus, *Seats of the Nobility and Gentry*, pl. lvi, 1804; J. P. Neale, *Views of Seats*, 2nd ser., v, 1829; John Newman, *West Kent and the Weald*, Buildings of Britain, 1969, 182–3].

HELMINGHAM HALL, SUFFOLK, alterations for the 6th Earl of Dysart, 1800, Tudor Gothic style [exhib. at R.A. 1800; Arthur Oswald in *C. Life*, 23 Aug. 1956].

BARR HALL, GREAT BARR, STAFFS., Gothic gateway from grounds to churchyard, for Joseph Scott, *c.* 1801; dem. [S. Shaw, *History of Staffordshire* ii, 1801, 106 and engraving p. 103].

CHALFONT HOUSE, BUCKS., remodelled exterior for Thomas Hibbert, *c.* 1800; again remodelled by A. Salvin 1836 [*The Gardener's Magazine*, ed.

J. C. Loudon, iv, 1828, 119–20; for Salvin's alterations see *Builder* xli, 1881, 810].

LUSCOMBE CASTLE, DAWLISH, DEVON, for Charles Hoare, 1800–4 [exhib. at R.A. 1800] (*C. Life*, 9, 16 and 23 Feb. 1956; C. Hussey, *English Country Houses: Late Georgian*, 1958, 55–65).

KILLYMOON CASTLE, CO. TYRONE, IRELAND, for Col. William Stewart, *c.* 1801–3, castellated [exhib. at R.A. 1803].

CRONKHILL, nr. CROSS HOUSES, SHREWSBURY, for Francis Walford, *c.* 1802 [exhib. at R.A. as 'house near Shrewsbury', 1802; Summerson].

HOLLYCOMBE, nr. LINCH, SUSSEX, for Sir Charles Taylor, Bart., *c.* 1805; rebuilt *c.* 1895 [T. W. Horsfield, *History of Sussex* ii, 1835, 103].

MOCCAS, HEREFS., 'BRIDGE LODGE' and 'DAW'S LODGE' for Sir George Cornewall, Bart., *c.* 1805 [Summerson].

MERLY HOUSE, DORSET, stables for Ralph Willett, *c.* 1805 [Summerson].

HARPTON COURT, RADNORSHIRE, outbuildings for Frankland Lewis, *c.* 1805 [Summerson].

LYNDHURST, HANTS., house near, probably THE WARRENS, BRAMSHAW, for Mr. Eyre, *c.* 1805 [Summerson].

LONGNER HALL, SALOP., for Robert Burton, *c.* 1805, Gothic [Summerson].

WITLEY COURT, WORCS., alterations including addition of Ionic portico on west side for the 3rd Lord Foley; altered *c.* 1860, now ruinous [Summerson; *R.I.B.A. Drawings Catalogue: L–N*, 109] (sketch-plan by C. R. Cockerell reproduced in *Architectural History* xiv, 1971, fig. 24; *C. Life*, 8, 15 June 1945).

SANDRIDGE PARK, STOKE GABRIEL, DEVON, for Lady Ashburton, *c.* 1805 [exhib. at R.A. 1805].

HALE HALL, LANCS., south front, etc., for John Blackburne, 1806; dem. [Summerson].

GARNSTONE CASTLE, HEREFS., for Samuel Peploe, *c.* 1806, castellated; dem. 1958 [J. P. Neale, *Views of Seats*, 2nd ser., iv, 1828].

BARNSLEY PARK, GLOS., lodge, conservatory and interior of library for Sir James Musgrave, Bart., 1806–10 [Bodleian Library, Wykeham-Musgrave papers; C. Hussey in *C. Life*, 2–9 Sept. 1954].

CHILDWALL HALL, LANCS., for Bamber Gascoyne, 1806–13, castellated; dem. 1949 [J. P. Neale, *Views of Seats*, 2nd ser., ii, 1825].

HAMSTEAD FARM, nr. NEWTOWN, ISLE OF WIGHT, for himself, *c.* 1806; since rebuilt [Summerson].

LISSAN RECTORY, CO. DERRY, IRELAND, for the Rev. John Staples, 1807 [Summerson; E. M. Jope, 'Lissan Rectory – and the Buildings in the North of Ireland designed by John Nash', *Ulster Jnl. of Archaeology* xix, 1956].

KILWAUGHTER CASTLE, CO. ANTRIM, IRELAND, for E. J. Agnew, 1807, castellated; dismantled 1951 [E. M. Jope, *op. cit.*].

ATTINGHAM HALL, SALOP., picture gallery and

staircase for the 2nd Lord Berwick, 1807–10 [Summerson; Michael Rix in *C. Life*, 21 Oct. 1954] (C. Hussey, *English Country Houses: Mid Georgian*, 1956, 195–202). Nash also appears to have planned a model village at Atcham, which was at least partly built, and of which there are some traces opposite the park gates [Nigel Temple, 'A Recent Discovery at Attingham; *Arch. Rev.*, Aug. 1976].

PARNHAM HALL, DORSET, additions for Sir William Oglander, Bart., 1807–11, Gothic [Dorset County Record Office, MW/M8] (*C. Life*, 29 Aug. 1908; Arthur Oswald, *The Country Houses of Dorset*, 2nd ed. 1959, 58–9).

AQUALATE HALL, STAFFS., enlarged for Sir John F. Boughey, Bart., 1808, Gothic; destroyed by fire 1910 [Summerson].

SOUTHBOROUGH PLACE, ASHCOMBE AVENUE, SURBITON, SURREY, for Thomas Langley, 1808 [Summerson].

CAERHAYS CASTLE, ST. MICHAEL CAERHAYS, CORNWALL, for J. B. Trevanion, *c.* 1808, castellated [E. Twycross, *The Mansions of England and Wales: Cornwall*, 1846, 52].

CALEDON, CO. TYRONE, IRELAND, alterations and additions for the 2nd Earl of Caledon, 1808–10; portico added 1833 by Thomas Duff of Newry [Summerson and information from Dr. Alistair Rowan] (*C. Life*, 27 Feb., 6 March 1937).

INGESTRE HALL, STAFFS., alterations including reconstruction of north front for the 2nd Earl Talbot, 1808–13; Nash's work was destroyed by fire in 1882 [Summerson] (*C. Life*, 17, 24 and 31 Oct. 1957).

RAVENSWORTH CASTLE, CO. DURHAM, for the 1st Lord Ravensworth, begun 1808 to Nash's designs, but still in progress 1824, and eventually completed under the direction of the Hon. Thomas Liddell (*q.v.*), the owner's son; dem. 1952–3 [Summerson; drawings in R.I.B.A. Coll., including one (E 4/3(16)) by Nash dated 1824].

KNEPP CASTLE, WEST GRINSTEAD, SUSSEX, for Sir Charles Burrell, Bart., *c.* 1809, castellated; damaged by fire 1904 [signed drawings formerly at Knepp; cf. J. Harris, *Catalogue of British Drawings for Architecture etc. in American Collections*, 1971, 150].

WEST GRINSTEAD PARK, SUSSEX, for Walter Burrell, *c.* 1809, Gothic; enlarged *c.* 1865, now in ruins [Summerson; D. G. C. Elwes & C. J. Robinson, *Castles and Mansions of West Sussex*, 1867, 108].

BETLEY COURT, STAFFS., alterations to drawing-room for Sir Thomas Fletcher, 1809–10 [T. R. Twemlow, *The Twemlows*, 1910, 218].

ROCKINGHAM HOUSE, CO. ROSCOMMON, IRELAND, for the 1st Viscount Lorton, 1810; altered 1822; destroyed by fire 1957 [Summerson;

building accounts in National Library of Ireland, MS. 3775].

PRESHAW HOUSE, HANTS., additions for Walter Long, 1810 [G. F. Prosser, *Select Illustrations of Hampshire*, 1833].

CHARBOROUGH PARK, DORSET, alterations for Richard Erle Drax Grosvenor, *c.* 1810 [J. B. Burke, *A Visitation of Seats and Arms* ii, 1853, 166] (R.C.H.M., *Dorset* ii, 163–8).

BLAISE CASTLE, HENBURY, GLOS., group of picturesque cottages forming BLAISE HAMLET for J. S. Harford, 1810–11. Nash also designed a conservatory in 1806 [Summerson] (*C. Life*, 28 Dec. 1901, with plan, 14 Oct. 1939, 3 Sept. 1943, 429).

LOUGH CUTRA CASTLE, CO. GALWAY, IRELAND, for the Hon. Charles Vereker, 1811, castellated; enlarged 1856, restored 1967 [Summerson; D. Guinness & W. Ryan, *Irish Houses and Castles*, 1971, 177–80].

HOPTON COURT, SALOP., added portico and additional storey for Thomas Botfield, 1811–13 [J. B. Burke. *A Visitation of Seats and Arms* i, 1852, 268; B. Botfield, *Stemmata Botevilliana*, 1858, p. ccxxi].

RHEOLA, nr. NEATH, GLAMORGANSHIRE, enlarged for John Edwards, *c.* 1812 [Summerson]; also designed Steward's House *c.* 1818 [R.I.B.A.D., K1/18/1, 2 (wrongly captioned as 'Blaise'), *ex inf.* Mr. Nigel Temple].

WINDSOR, ROYAL LODGE in THE GREAT PARK, for the Prince Regent, 1813–16; dem. 1830 [O. Morshead, *George IV and Royal Lodge*, 1965; *History of the King's Works* vi, 399–401].

LONDON, CARLTON HOUSE, PALL MALL, remodelled basement storey for the Prince Regent, 1813; dem. 1827–8 [*Survey of London* xx, 74–5].

LONDON, LANGHAM HOUSE, PORTLAND PLACE, for Sir James Langham, Bart., 1813–15; dem. *c.* 1864 [Summerson].

LONDON, LANGHAM PLACE, houses on west side, 1813; dem. [Summerson].

attributed: WOODHALL, SWINE, YORKS. (E.R.), for H. W. Maister, 1814–15 [a house of the Cronkhill type, described in a sale advt. in *Hull Advertiser* of 19 May 1820 as 'erected about four years since by an eminent London architect'].

BRIGHTON, THE ROYAL PAVILION, remodelled for the Prince Regent, 1815–21 [John Nash, *The Royal Pavilion at Brighton*, 1826, 2nd ed. 1838; H. D. Roberts, *History of the Royal Pavilion, Brighton*, 1939; C. Musgrave, *Royal Pavilion*, 1959].

SHANE'S CASTLE, CO. ANTRIM, IRELAND, designs for a new house for the 2nd Viscount O'Neil, to replace one destroyed by fire in 1816, and partially executed before work was stopped by Lord O'Neil. Thomas Hopper (*q.v.*) was then employed to arbitrate between Nash and Lord O'Neil [account-book in Estate Office at Gosford Castle, *ex inf.* Mr. Robin Fedden]. Nash's design is illustrated by Davis, *John Nash*, pl. 29, and the unfinished walls in *C. Life*, 18 Aug. 1955, 344. It is doubtful whether (as has been supposed) Nash made any designs for Shane's Castle before the fire of 1816.

GRACEFIELD LODGE, CO. KILDARE, IRELAND, for Mrs. Kavanagh, 1817, executed by William Robertson of Kilkenny [J. N. Brewer, *The Beauties of Ireland* ii, 1826, 105].

SHANBALLY CASTLE, CO. TIPPERARY, IRELAND, for the 1st Viscount Lismore, completed 1819, castellated; dem. 1960 [Summerson].

WEST COWES, ISLE OF WIGHT, Gothic villa for Sir J. Coxe Hippisley, Bart., *c.* 1825; now incorporated in premises of Royal Corinthian Yacht Club [R. Ackermann, *Views of Country Seats* i, 1830, 112].

NORTHERWOOD, nr. LYNDHURST, HANTS., 'improved ... at the suggestion of ... Mr. Nash', probably by the addition of pavilions and veranda, for Capt. Charles William Mitchell, date uncertain; later enlarged by Thomas Cubitt [G. F. Prosser, *Select Illustrations of Hampshire*, 1833; *R.I.B.A. Drawings Catalogue: L–N*, 110].

NORTHWOOD HOUSE, WEST COWES, ISLE OF WIGHT, two classical lodges for George Ward, date uncertain [Summerson]. The house was remodelled by G. J. Mair in 1838–9 and 1843 (see drawings in B.M., Add. MSS. 18157–8).

WORCESTER PARK, nr. EWELL, SURREY, enlarged for William Taylor, date uncertain; dem. [G. F. Prosser, *Select Illustrations of Surrey*, 1828].

LONDON: REGENT STREET, REGENT'S PARK, ETC.

Besides planning REGENT STREET and REGENT'S PARK as a whole, Nash himself designed THE QUADRANT, 1818–20 (colonnades removed 1848, Quadrant as a whole rebuilt by R. N. Shaw and Sir R. Blomfield 1906–23); NO. 15 REGENT STREET for C. T. Blicke, 1819 (dem. *c.* 1838); NOS. 14–16 REGENT STREET as a double mansion for himself and John Edwards, 1822–4 (dem., illustrated in Britton & Pugin, *Public Buildings of London* ii, 1828, 287–9); and CARLTON HOUSE TERRACE, 1827–33 (described in *Survey of London* xx, 77–87).

In REGENT'S PARK Nash was responsible for the terrace façades generally, for the siting of the villas, and for the planting. The façades of CORNWALL TERRACE and CLARENCE TERRACE were, however, delegated to Decimus Burton, and elsewhere the executant architects employed by the builders sometimes modified Nash's designs, notably in the case of GLOUCESTER GATE (see 'Scoles, J. J.'). For CUMBERLAND GATE and CUMBERLAND TERRACE the executant architect was James Thomson. The other terraces with façades

by Nash are ULSTER TERRACE, YORK TERRACE (E. and W.), YORK GATE, SUSSEX PLACE, HANOVER TERRACE, KENT TERRACE, CHESTER TERRACE, CAMBRIDGE TERRACE, ST. ANDREWS TERRACE and PARK SQUARE (E. and W.), all of which were building during the period 1821–30. PARK CRESCENT, built 1812–22, was rebuilt to the original elevations, but with new interiors, in 1963–5. The PARK VILLAGES, forming a satellite model suburb, were completed by Sir James Pennethorne.

Of the detached houses in the park, only one was designed by Nash himself: HANOVER LODGE (now part of Bedford College) for Sir Robert Arbuthnot, *c.* 1827 [P.R.O., CREST 2/768].

Nash's first plan for Regent's Park (1811), showing the proposed building sites planted as nurseries, is in the Public Record Office (MPEE 58), together with two panoramic drawings of the whole design (MR 1045 and 1047). For these and other plans and drawings connected with Nash's metropolitan improvements see *Maps and Plans in the Public Record Office* i, 1967. See also Ann Saunders, *Regent's Park*, Newton Abbot 1969.

LEAMINGTON, WARWICKSHIRE

A 'Plan of Newbold Comyn at Leamington Priors the Estate of Edw. Willes Esq. as now laid out for building on by Jno. Nash & Jas. Morgan Architects 1827' [Warwickshire Record Office, CR 1247/8 and 9] shows that Nash was involved in the planning of Leamington Spa. But other architects were employed, and how far any of the existing town can be regarded as Nash's design is uncertain: see Robin Chaplin, 'The Rise of Royal Leamington Spa', *Warwickshire History* ii (2), 1972, 22.

NASH, WILLIAM THOMAS, was from 1821 onwards a partner in the firm of Cockett & Nash (subsequently Nash, Son & Rowley), auctioneers and land surveyors of Royston, Herts. Nash appears to have had some architectural training, and during the following quarter of a century the firm undertook a number of minor architectural commissions in Royston and neighbourhood. Among these were ROYSTON MARKET-HOUSE, 1829–30, ICKLETON VICARAGE, CAMBS., *c.* 1832, and HINXTON GRANGE, CAMBS., for Charles Nash, *c.* 1840. The firm's records, including many architectural drawings, are now in the County Record Office at Cambridge.

NASMITH, ROBERT (–1793), was an architect of whom little is known except that he designed STOKE PARK, STOKE POGES, BUCKS., for John Penn in 1789. He died in Upper Norton Street, Marylebone, on 30 August 1793, leaving the house to be completed by James Wyatt. At HACKWOOD PARK, HANTS., there is an undated drawing endorsed 'Nasmith' showing 'the alteration proposed in [the] Withdrawing room'.

Owing to subsequent alterations it is impossible to say whether this was carried out. [J. Penn, *An Historical and Descriptive Account of Stoke Park*, 1813, 60–1; J. P. Neale, *Views of Seats* i, 1818; R. Ackermann, *Repository of Arts*, 3rd ser., iii, 1824, 313; *Gent's Mag.* 1793 (ii), 866; *Scots Mag.* lv, 1793, 467; will, P.C.C. 517 DODWELL.]

NASMYTH, ALEXANDER (1758–1840), was descended from a family of Scottish masons. His father, Michael Nasmyth (d. 1803), was a successful Edinburgh builder with a workshop in the Grassmarket.[1] Alexander was educated at the High School and apprenticed to a coach-builder, but attracted the notice of Allan Ramsay the portrait-painter, who employed him in his London studio. In 1778 he returned to Edinburgh and established himself as a portrait-painter, and in 1782–4 he visited Italy. Although Nasmyth enjoyed considerable success as an artist, his liberal political views alienated his aristocratic clients, and during the latter part of his life his work was increasingly restricted to landscape subjects.

Nasmyth was an ingenious and intelligent man who took a great interest in scientific and mechanical matters and who also practised occasionally as an architect. In this capacity his best-known work is the elegant circular temple which he erected over ST. BERNARD'S WELL in the DEAN VALLEY, EDINBURGH, in 1789 at the expense of Lord Gardenstone (see J. C. Nattes, *Scotia Depicta*, 1804, pl. 33, for an early view).[2] In 1807 he submitted a design for the Nelson Monument on Calton Hill (illustrated in his *Autobiography*, p. 45), and in 1813 he was one of the prize-winners in the competition for the layout of the area to the north of Calton Hill [A. J. Youngson, *The Making of Classical Edinburgh*, 1966, 307]. Among his drawings in the Print Room of the National Gallery of Scotland are unexecuted designs for a new house at DUNGLASS, EAST LOTHIAN, for Sir James Hall (*c.* 1807); rebuilding TAYMOUTH CASTLE for the 4th Earl of Breadalbane (*c.* 1806); a bridge at TONGLAND, KIRKCUDBRIGHTSHIRE (*c.* 1804);[3] and a bridge at THE MOUND in EDINBURGH (1826). There are also drawings for

'bow and string' bridges and roofs, a form of construction of which Nasmyth was apparently the inventor in 1794. Nasmyth was employed by the Dukes of Atholl and Argyll in laying out their grounds at Blair and Inveraray Castles. At Inveraray his works included a 'Bee-hive Cottage' in the wood (1801), and at Rosneath he fixed the site for the new house and himself designed the Gothic offices and a tower [I. G. Lindsay & Mary Cosh, *Inveraray and Dukes of Argyll*, 1973, 252–3, 428].

Nasmyth died in Edinburgh on 10 April 1840. He was the father of Patrick Nasmyth (1787–1831), landscape-painter, and of James Nasmyth (1808–90), engineer.

[*The Autobiography of James Nasmyth*, 1883; *D.N.B.*; National Gallery of Scotland, *Catalogue of Scottish Drawings*, 1960, 145–9.]

NAYLOR, WILLIAM RIGBY (–1773), then of London, in 1769 submitted two designs in the competition for the Royal Exchange at Dublin [*Builder* xxvii, 1869, 781]. He subsequently emigrated to North America, practising as an architect and surveyor in Charleston, South Carolina, until his death in October 1773. [Beatrice St. J. Ravenal, *Architects of Charleston*, Charleston 1945, 33–4.]

NEALE, WILLIAM (–1822), and his son William (*c.* 1794–1838), were architects and builders at Melton Mowbray in Leicestershire. The father was responsible for alterations and additions to EASTWELL RECTORY, LEICS., in 1814. The son was Surveyor to the Oakham Canal Company, and died suddenly at the house of the Company's treasurer on 12 October 1838, aged 44 [J. D. Bennett, *Leicestershire Architects*, Leicester Museums 1968].

NEAVE, DAVID (1773–1841), was the son of Thomas Neave, a mason of Forfar, where he was born on 17 March 1773. He practised in Dundee, where he succeeded Samuel Bell (d. 1813) as the leading architect. No formal appointment has been traced, but in June 1833 he resigned the post of Town's Architect which he appears to have held for some twenty years. He died at Dundee on 23 January 1841.

Neave was a competent architect whose best work is in the Greek Revival style, sometimes with Soaneic mannerisms. A large volume of his architectural drawings is in the possession of Mr. T. H. Thoms of Dundee. Two MS. plans of parts of Dundee made by Neave in 1813 are in the S.R.O. (RHP 37 and 64). [David Walker, *Architects and Architecture in Dundee*, Abertay Historical Society's Publications No. 2, 1955, 6–8; information from Mr. David Walker.]

---

[1] Michael Nasmyth built and probably designed BARNS HOUSE, PEEBLESSHIRE, for James Burnet, *c.* 1773–80 [R.C.A.M., *Peeblesshire* ii, 280].

[2] He did not, however, design the Dean Bridge, as stated in *D.N.B.* It was designed by Thomas Telford.

[3] The *Scots Magazine* for 1807, 883, credits Nasmyth with the design for the existing bridge at Tongland built in 1805–6, but (although the building of this bridge requires further investigation) it seems clear that Telford was the effective designer (cf. A. Gibb *The Story of Telford*, 1935, 156–7), and it should be noted that Nasmyth's drawing is for a three-arched bridge, not a single-arched bridge as built.

PUBLIC BUILDINGS

MONIKIE CHURCH, ANGUS, 1811–12, Gothic [drawings in S.R.O., GD 45/25/28].

EDZELL CHURCH, ANGUS, 1818 [vol. of drawings].

KILSPINDIE CHURCH, PERTHSHIRE, 1821 [S.R.O., HR 417/1].

DUNDEE, reconstructed THE TABERNACLE, N. TAY STREET, as ST. DAVID'S CHURCH, 1822–4 [Dundee Town Council Minutes, 6 April 1822].

HIGH or WEST LIGHTHOUSE at SOUTH FERRY, nr. TAYPORT, FIFE, 1823, apparently in connection with Robert Stevenson; since heightened [vol. of drawings].

FORFAR, THE COUNTY BUILDINGS, 1823–4 [signed drawings and specifications preserved in the building 1972; also in vol. of drawings].

DUNDEE LUNATIC ASYLUM, additions, 1824–5 [*Dundee Advertiser*, 2 Dec. 1824].

DUNDEE INFIRMARY (later Victoria Road School), completion of John Paterson's original designs of 1793–8, 1824–6; dem. [*Dundee Advertiser*, 12 Sept. 1824, 6 Mar. 1826].

DUNDEE, THISTLE HALL, UNION STREET, 1826–9; largely rebuilt, but façade survives as part of Royal Hotel [David Walker, *op. cit.*, 8, with illustration].

LIFF AND BENVIE SCHOOL, ANGUS, 1828 [*Dundee Advertiser*, 29 May 1828].

ABERNYTE SCHOOL, PERTHSHIRE, 1829; dem. [*Dundee Advertiser*, 2 July 1829].

LOCHEE, ANGUS, ST. NINIAN'S CHAPEL, 1829–30; remodelled 1880 [*Dundee Advertiser*, 21 May 1829].

DUNDEE, CHAPELSHADE CHURCH, reconstructed 1830–1 [David Walker, *op. cit.*, 81 from Kirk Session Minutes].

DOMESTIC ARCHITECTURE

Most of Neave's private commissions were for villas and small houses in and around Dundee. BALRUDDERY HOUSE, LIFF, ANGUS, for James Webster, for which there are drawings in the Neave volume, appears to have been his only country house; is was rebuilt in 1889 after a fire, but there is a small engraving in *Forfarshire Illustrated*, Dundee 1843, plate at end. In 1823–4 he designed LONGFORGAN MANSE, PERTHSHIRE [S.R.O., HR 441/1].

In DUNDEE Neave was responsible for the layout of UNION, DOCK and EXCHANGE STREETS, 1828 [Town Council Minutes, 17 Jan. and 20 March 1828, *ex inf.* Mr. David Walker], and designed a terrace of houses comprising NOS. 1–27 SOUTH TAY STREET, *c.* 1818–20, one of which he occupied himself [David Walker, *op. cit.*, 7].

The drawings in the volume mentioned above include the following: a cottage at STRATHMARTINE, ANGUS, for the heirs of Admiral Laird; a cottage at IDVIES, ANGUS, for John Baxter (dem.);

a villa (dem.) at CHAPELSHADE for James Soot; a lodge at LOGIE HOUSE, DUNDEE, for Isaac Watt, 1817 (dem.); a house at BINROCK, DUNDEE, for Mr. Clayhills; a house in PERTH ROAD, DUNDEE, for Thomas Miller, brewer; a house for James Davidson in SEAGATE, DUNDEE; a small house at MILNBANK, DUNDEE, for James Reid; a large house in PERTH ROAD called UNION MOUNT for Mr. Alison; remodelling a house at ROSEANGLE for the Rev. Mr. McVicar, 1819; a house at ROSEANGLE for David Martin; a house (dem.) at BONNYBANK, DUNDEE, for William Straton; a house (166 NETHERGATE) for Mr. Gray, 1817; a house (dem.) in PARK PLACE for James Ogilvie, 1820; a villa in FERRY ROAD for William Small, Town Clerk of Dundee, 1818; houses in MAGDALEN YARD ROAD for Capt. Shaw and Mr. Watt; a villa (dem.) at ANNFIELD for Capt. Black, 1818; a villa at ROSEANGLE for Robert Adie, 1819; a house (dem.) in FERRY ROAD for James Souter; refronting THE NEW BANK, 65 MURRAYGATE, for William Roberts (dem.); and a house at ROSEANGLE (now LAING'S HOTEL) for Mr. Calman.

NEILL, JOHN (1781–1837), 'Architect', is commemorated by a monument in the Calton Old Burial Ground at Edinburgh. He was probably the John Neill, 'builder', who was admitted a burgess in June 1809 in right of his father, Andrew Neill, builder [*Roll of Burgesses of the City of Edinburgh, 1761–1841*, Scottish Record Soc. 1933, 119].

NEILSON, SAMUEL, was an Edinburgh master mason. He was the son of William Neilson, a merchant who was Lord Provost of the City in 1717, and himself became a burgess in 1733 in right of his father [*Roll of Edinburgh Burgesses 1701–60*, Scottish Record Soc. 1929, 152]. In 1743 he gave evidence in William Adam's lawsuit against Lord Braco. He stated that besides carrying on his business as a mason he sometimes made designs for country houses. As an example he mentioned MONKTON HOUSE, AYRSHIRE, for Hugh Baillie, *c.* 1740. He had also advised Mr. Blair of ADAMTON, nr. MONKTON, 'about repairing an old House' [*Depositions in the Cause William Adams v. Lord Braco*, 1743, 14–15]. In 1750–4 he built the ROYAL BANK OF SCOTLAND in the Old Town, following (with some modifications) the designs made by William Adam some years previously [John Fleming, *Robert Adam and his Circle*, 1962, 336].

NELSON, S—, was a pupil of Joseph Bonomi, from whose address he exhibited at the Royal Academy from 1790 to 1795. By 1800 he was in independent practice at 9 Pratt Street, Hampstead Road. A 'design for a gentleman's villa', circular in plan and neo-classical in style, which he exhibited in 1790, is now in the Metropolitan Museum at New York and is illustrated by John Harris, *Catalogue of British Drawings for Architecture, etc. in American Collections*, 1971, pl. 109. In 1800 Nelson exhibited 'a design for a pavilion to be erected at the Mote, the seat of Lord Romney', evidently the circular Greek temple or 'pavilion' at MOTE PARK, nr. MAIDSTONE, KENT, erected in 1801 by the Volunteers of Kent as a tribute to the Lord Lieutenant, Lord Romney (*Gent's Mag.* 1801 (ii), 1046; *C. Life*, 7 Sept. 1951, 737).

NEVIS, ROBERT, practised as an architect and surveyor in Hull in the 1820s. In 1829 he designed a house – apparently PROSPECT PLACE – at BARTON-ON-HUMBER, LINCS., for R. Hall of Hull. His designs are in the Lincolnshire Record Office [B.H. 12].

NEWALL, WALTER, practised in Dumfries. Several of the buildings which he designed are illustrated in Loudon's *Encyclopaedia of Cottage, Farm and Villa Architecture* (1846 ed.): a villa near Dumfries for Mr. Hannay, formerly known as HANNAYFIELD, and now as LADYFIELD WEST HOUSE, *c.* 1830 [850–3]; and farm-houses at HALSTONE, GATESTACK, INGLESTONE, ALTON, GREBTEN (GRIBTON) and RIDDENWOOD [454–71]. In vol. vii of the *Gardener's Magazine* (1831), p. 529, Loudon illustrates two monuments in St. Michael's Churchyard at Dumfries designed by Newall. Newall is also known to have designed NETHER CORSOCK HOUSE (now GLENLAIR), KIRKCUDBRIGHTSHIRE, for John Clerk Maxwell, 1830, remodelled 1884 [drawings in the office of Messrs. Dick, Peddie & McKay, Edinburgh, *ex inf.* Mr. Richard Emerson]; the tower of KIRKBEAN CHURCH, KIRKCUDBRIGHTSHIRE, 1835 [S.R.O., HR 759/1, p. 23]; and GLENCAIRN MANSE, DUMFRIESSHIRE, 1840 [J. Corrie, *Glencairn*, Dumfries 1911, 50]. In 1822–3 he probably designed, and certainly superintended the erection of, a church at KIRKMAHOE, DUMFRIESSHIRE, in a Gothic style relatively advanced for its date [S.R.O., HR 148/1]. In 1836 he was employed to convert a windmill in Dumfries into an OBSERVATORY (now the DUMFRIES MUSEUM), adding a doorway and window surrounds of 'Egyptian' character [*ex inf.* the Curator]. In the S.R.O. there is an ingenious design by him for an episcopal church and manse combined as one building [RHP 3545].

NEWCOURT, RICHARD (–1679), was a gentleman with a small estate at Somerton in Somerset. He is best known as a surveyor and topographical draughtsman. For his friend Sir William Dugdale he made a number of drawings of cathedrals, etc., in the south-west of England

to illustrate the *Monasticon Anglicanum* (1655–73). These were subsequently reused by Daniel King in his *Cathedrall and Conventuall Churches of England and Wales orthographically delineated* (1656, 2nd ed. 1672). In 1658 Newcourt published an important map of London which was engraved by Faithorne, and after the Great Fire he was the author of an ambitious but impracticable plan for rebuilding the city on a rectilinear grid of streets with fifty-five arcaded piazzas each containing a parish church in the centre [Guildhall Library, MS. 3441]. In the accompanying text he refers to a design he had made for rebuilding Whitehall Palace. The only other evidence of Newcourt's activity as an architect so far noted is a design by him for a Gothic chapel, dated 29 July 1670, which survives among the Longleat archives (Box xxx, vol. lxxvii, f. 19).

Newcourt died in 1679 and was buried at Somerton. He was the father of Richard Newcourt (d. 1716), registrar of the diocese of London and author of *Repertorium Ecclesiasticum Parochiale Londinense* (1708–10).

[*D.N.B.*; T. F. Reddaway in *Town Planning Review* xviii, 1939, 155 *et seq.*; will, P.C.C. 89 KING.]

NEWDIGATE, Sir ROGER (1719–1806), was a wealthy landowner whose architectural activities at Arbury Hall, Warwicks., Harefield Church, Middlesex, and elsewhere, give him a place of some importance in the history of the Gothic Revival. The 7th son of Sir Richard Newdigate, 3rd Bart., he was educated at Westminster School and University College, London, and made the Grand Tour in 1738–40. He succeeded his brother as 5th Bart. in 1734, and sat in the House of Commons from 1742 to 1747 as M.P. for Middlesex and from 1751 to 1780 as M.P. for Oxford University. He visited Italy again in 1774–5 after the death of his first wife.

Sir Roger was a man of taste who is more important as a patron than as an architectural designer in his own right. At Arbury, Sanderson Miller, the Hiornes, Henry Keene and Henry Couchman successively helped him to make his family seat the Strawberry Hill of the Midlands, and elsewhere (*e.g.* at University College, Oxford, and Harefield Church) Henry Keene was much employed by him or through his influence. Nevertheless, he was himself a sufficiently competent draughtsman to make a drawing of the Roman arch at Aosta which served as the basis for an engraving by Piranesi (1774), and besides many preliminary drawings for Arbury he made designs in the 1740s for a new Palladian house at Copt Hall in Essex for his brother-in-law John Conyers. These were not carried out, and Arbury remains the principal monument to

Newdigate's architectural enthusiasm.[1] At Oxford he is remembered by the Newdigate Prize for Poetry which he endowed and by the two candelabra constructed by Piranesi from antique fragments which he presented to the University in 1776.

[*D.N.B.*; L. B. Namier & J. Brooke, *The House of Commons 1754–1790*, 1964, 196–9; A. C. Wood, 'The Diaries of Sir Roger Newdigate', *Trans. Birmingham Arch. Soc.* lxxviii, 1962; C. Hussey, *English Country Houses: Mid Georgian*, 1956; Michael McCarthy, 'Sir Roger Newdigate and Piranesi', *Burlington Mag.*, July 1962, 466–72; Michael McCarthy, 'Sir Roger Newdigate: Drawings for Copt Hall, Essex and Arbury Hall, Warwickshire', *Architectural History* xvi, 1973.]

NEWEY, ISAAC (*c.* 1810–1861), practised at Birmingham. For a time he appears to have been in partnership with F. W. Fiddian, for in 1834 Messrs. Fiddian & Newey exhibited at the Birmingham Society of Artists a 'villa erecting at Edgbaston' and in 1835 a 'villa now erecting in Wellington Road for James Kimberley, Esq.' Thereafter, however, they exhibited separately. In 1838 Newey designed ST. MICHAEL'S CHURCH, BARTLEY GREEN, nr. BIRMINGHAM, a simple Gothic building consecrated in 1840 [I.C.B.S.]. He died on 16 February 1861, aged 51 [*Aris's Birmingham Gazette*, 23 Feb. 1861]. Christopher Isaac Newey, who was in practice in Birmingham in 1868, was no doubt his son.

NEWHAM was the name of a family of architects and builders who were active in King's Lynn throughout the first half of the nineteenth century. The founder of the firm appears to have been Samuel Newham (1749–1816), a Methodist, who built the WESLEYAN CHAPEL, TOWER STREET, KING'S LYNN, in 1813 [H. J. Hillen, *History of King's Lynn* ii, 1907, 549]. He may have been the father of William Newham, who became a pupil of James Wyatt, exhibiting two architectural designs at the Royal Academy from Wyatt's office in 1796–7. The name of William Newham, as architect, builder or joiner, thereafter appears in directories of Lynn until the 1870s, and evidently represents two generations of the family. In 1809 it was William Newham who built the TRINITY CHAPEL at ST. MARGARET'S CHURCH to the designs of Francis Goodwin [H. J. Hillen, *op. cit.* ii, 657], and 'Mr. Newham' is described as 'the ingenious architect' of THE THEATRE ROYAL, KING'S LYNN, 1815, demolished *c.* 1910/20 [J.

Burley, *Playhouses and Players of East Anglia*, 1928, 128]. In 1827 William Newham was responsible for improvements to the ASSEMBLY ROOMS at SWAFFHAM, NORFOLK [*Norfolk Chronicle*, 17 Nov. 1827, *ex inf.* Mr. D. C. Young], and in 1832–3 STOKE FERRY CHURCH, NORFOLK, was enlarged at the east and west ends by him [I.C.B.S.]. The name of William Newham, architect of St. Austin's Street, King's Lynn, appears in *The Architects, Engineers and Building Trades Directory* of 1868.

NEWMAN, JOHN (1786–1859), was born in London and baptized in St. Sepulchre's Church on 8 July 1786. His father, John Newman, was a wholesale dealer in leather in Skinner Street, Snow Hill, and a common councillor of the ward of Farringdon Without. His grandfather was Sheriff of London in 1789–90.

Nothing is known of Newman's architectural training, but he evidently visited Italy, for in 1807 he exhibited at the Royal Academy a drawing of the remains of the Temple of Jupiter Tonans in Rome. He was employed under Sir Robert Smirke in the erection of Covent Garden Theatre in 1809, and at the General Post Office in 1823–9. Early in life he obtained an appointment in the office of the Bridge House estates, and eventually succeeded to the clerkship, which he held for more than thirty years. From about 1815 he was one of the three surveyors to the Commission of Sewers for Surrey and Kent, and in conjunction with his colleagues (Joseph Gwilt and Edward I'Anson) published a *Report relating to the Sewage, etc.*, in 1843. He held several surveyorships, including that to the commissioners of pavements and improvements for the west division of Southwark, and to Earl Somers's estate at Somers Town, St. Pancras. He was honorary architect to the Royal Literary Fund from 1846, and to the Society of Patrons of the Charity Children's Anniversary Meeting in St. Paul's Cathedral. He exhibited at the Royal Academy between 1807 and 1838. As an architect he was responsible for one outstanding building, the ambitious and cleverly designed Catholic Church in Moorfields. Here, for the first time in nineteenth-century London, the mass was given a dramatic setting comparable to that in continental churches. At the east end, concealed lighting, contrived in a manner which Newman had observed in France, illuminated a panorama of Calvary painted by Agostino Aglio and viewed through a screen of marble columns.

In the course of his professional work Newman was able to form a valuable collection of antiquities found in London and the neighbourhood. Some bronzes in his possession from the bed of the Thames were described by C. Roach Smith in a paper read to the Society of Antiquaries in June 1837 (*Archaeologia* xxviii), and Smith again

---

[1] Mr. Keith Goodway informs me that among the Sneyd MSS. at Keele University (S. 1458) there is evidence that Sir Roger Newdigate made designs for Gothick alterations to Keele Hall, Staffs., that were carried out by William Baker, either in 1757–9 (see p. 84) or later.

referred to Newman's collections when reading another paper to the Society of Antiquaries in 1842 (*Archaeologia* xxix). His antiquities were sold by auction at Sotheby's in 1848. Among them was the bronze head of Hadrian now in the British Museum. He was a Fellow of the Society of Antiquaries from 1830 to 1849, and an original Fellow of the Institute of British Architects, whose travelling fund he originated. He retired in 1851, and died at the home of his son-in-law, Dr. Alexander Spiers, at Passy, nr. Paris, on 3 January 1859, aged 72. He had married in 1819 a daughter of the Rev. B. Middleton, Sub-Dean of Chichester, and left a son, Arthur Shean Newman (1828–73), who succeeded to some of his father's appointments, and in 1858 entered into partnership with Arthur Billing [*A.P.S.D.*; *D.N.B.*].

LONDON, ST. MARY'S R.C. CHURCH, BLOMFIELD STREET, MOORFIELDS, 1817–20; dem. 1899 [Britton & Pugin, *Public Buildings of London* ii, 1828, 5–10].

SOUTHWARK, terrace of houses in DUKE STREET, with wharves and warehouses at the back, facing the river, erected when the line for the new London Bridge was settled in 1824 [*A.P.S.D.*].

ISLINGTON, THE PROPRIETARY SCHOOL, BARNSBURY STREET, 1830 [*A.P.S.D.*].

SOUTHWARK, SCHOOL FOR THE INDIGENT BLIND, ST. GEORGE'S FIELDS, 1834–8, Tudor Gothic [*Civil Engineer and Architect's Jnl.* i, 1838, 207–12; *Companion to the Almanac*, 1836, 220–1].

SOUTHWARK, ST. OLAVE'S GIRLS' SCHOOL, MAZE ROAD, 1839–40 [plans, elevations, and sections in C. Davy, *Architectural Precedents*, 1841].

NEWMAN, W— S—, exhibited at the Royal Academy in 1792, 1794 and 1798, giving his address in 1792 as 'At Mr. Smith's, Knightsbridge'. In 1794 he showed a 'Design for the floor cloth manufactory building at Knightsbridge'. He does not appear to have been the same person as William Newman, who was admitted to the Royal Academy Schools in 1778 at the age of 22 and won the Silver Medal in 1780.

NEWNHAM, W— H—, was a pupil or assistant of Joseph Walker (*q.v.*), from whose office at 21 Earl Street, Blackfriars, he exhibited at the Royal Academy in 1822 and again in 1830. In the latter year his exhibit was an 'Interior View of a tomb near the Pyramids of Saccara the scite of ancient Memphis, taken on the spot in 1828'.

NEWTON, WILLIAM (1730–1798), christened at St. Andrew's Church, Newcastle, on 20 Dec. 1730, was the son of Robert Newton, a shipwright who turned his attention to architecture and practised as a builder-architect in Newcastle-upon-Tyne. In 1762 Robert and William Newton were both concerned in repairs and alterations

to Simonburn Church, Northumberland, whose aisles were rebuilt under their direction in the following year [*History of Northumberland* xv, 179]. Newton spent the whole of his life in Newcastle and had a considerable local practice. He was a competent but conventional Georgian architect whose work is sometimes elegant, always pleasing, but never remarkable. In 1763 he married Dorothy Bell of Gateshead, by whom he had six sons and six daughters. In 1769 he obtained a lease of land from the Corporation upon which he built Charlotte Square, the first development of its kind in the city. He occupied one of the houses himself for the next twenty years. He died at Newcastle on 29 April 1798, aged 68, and was buried in St. Andrew's Church. His tombstone is now covered by the organ. Some drawings by Newton for unexecuted alterations to Wallington Hall, Northumberland, are preserved in a portfolio at that house. [*Proceedings of the Society of Antiquaries of Newcastle-on-Tyne*, 3rd ser., vi, 1913–14, 28–9; Terence Scott, *William Newton, Architect and Builder*, 1971, unpublished dissertation, Architecture Seminar Library, Newcastle University.]

NEWCASTLE-UPON-TYNE

ST. ANNE'S CHAPEL, CITY ROAD, 1764–8 [J. Dugdale, *The British Traveller* iii, 1819, 721] (B. Allsopp, *Historic Architecture of Newcastle*, 1967, 36–7).

THE LUNATIC ASYLUM, 1765–7; reconstructed by J. Dobson 1824; dem. *c.* 1866 [E. Mackenzie, *Account of Newcastle* ii, 1827, 525].

CHARLOTTE SQUARE, *c.* 1770 [*Proc. Soc. Antiq. Newcastle-on-Tyne*, 3rd ser., vi, 1913–14, 28].

THE ASSEMBLY ROOMS, WESTGATE, 1774–6 [E. Mackenzie, *Account of Newcastle* i, 1827, 231] (B. Allsopp, *Historic Architecture of Newcastle*, 1967, 38–9).

attributed: ST. ANDREW'S CHURCH, refitting of interior, *c.* 1780 [H. L. Honeyman, 'The Church of St. Andrew, Newcastle', *Archaeologia Æliana*, 4th ser., xix, 1941].

THE ROYAL FREE GRAMMAR SCHOOL, added the porch, 1782; dem. [E. Mackenzie, *Account of Newcastle* ii, 1827, 443].

ST. NICHOLAS CHURCH, refitted interior in conjunction with David Stephenson, 1783–5 [M. A. Richardson, *The Local Historian's Table Book* ii, 1842, 284–8].

THE EXCHANGE AND GUILDHALL, rebuilt north front, 1795, in collaboration with David Stephenson [E. Mackenzie, *Account of Newcastle* i, 1827, 216].

COUNTRY HOUSES

CASTLE EDEN, CO. DURHAM, for Rowland Burdon, *c.* 1760 [*Proc. Soc. Antiq. Newcastle-on-Tyne*,

3rd ser., vi, 1913–14, 28; E. Mackenzie & C. Ross, *County Palatine of Durham* i, 1834, 403].

FENHAM HALL, NORTHUMBERLAND, addition of wings and new front for William Ord, *c.* 1770 [E. Mackenzie, *History of Northumberland* ii, 1825, 410].

HEATON HALL, NORTHUMBERLAND, remodelled for Sir Matthew Ridley, Bart., *c.* 1770–80; dem. [E. Mackenzie, *History of Northumberland* ii, 1825, 478].

KEILDER CASTLE, NORTHUMBERLAND, for the 1st Duke of Northumberland and Earl Percy, 1772–5, Gothic [memorandum in Keilder Castle Game Book in Alnwick Castle Library, shelf 49/3] (Watts's *Views of Seats*, pl. 58, 1783).

BACKWORTH HALL, NORTHUMBERLAND, for R. W. Grey, 1778–80 [estimate, etc., in Northumberland Record Office, ZBU B7; *Proc. Soc. Antiq. Newcastle-on-Tyne*, 3rd ser., vi, 1913–14, 28].

HOWICK HALL, NORTHUMBERLAND, for Sir Henry Grey, Bart., 1781–2; north front rebuilt 1808–9 to designs of George Wyatt; remodelled internally 1928 after a fire [M. A. Richardson, *The Local Historian's Table Book* ii, 1842, 269] (F. O. Morris, *Views of Seats* vi, 1880, 63).

WHITFIELD HALL, NORTHUMBERLAND, for William Ord of Fenham, 1785; storey added 1856 [J. Hodgson, *History of Northumberland*, part ii, vol. iii, 1840, 105].

CAPHEATON HALL, NORTHUMBERLAND, rebuilt north front for Sir John Swinburne, Bart., 1789–90 [Northumberland Record Office, Capheaton papers ZSw 452] (*C. Life*, 12 Aug. 1965).

HESLEYSIDE, NORTHUMBERLAND, rebuilt east front for William Charlton, 1796–1800 [*History of Northumberland* xv, 253].

HEXHAM ABBEY HOUSE, NORTHUMBERLAND, work for Col. Beaumont, interrupted by illness, 1797; altered by J. Dobson after fire in 1818 [Northumberland Record Office, ZBL 226/2] (B. Allsopp & U. Clark, *Historic Architecture of Northumberland*, 1969, 78).

LEMINGTON HALL, NORTHUMBERLAND, for Nicholas Fenwick (?), date uncertain; dem. before 1913 [*Proc. Soc. Antiq. Newcastle-on-Tyne*, 3rd ser., vi, 1913–14, 28–9].

ALNWICK, NORTHUMBERLAND, house at foot of Clayport occupied successively by families of Farquhar, Dawson and Drysdale, date uncertain [*Proc. Soc. Antiq. Newcastle-on-Tyne*, 3rd ser., vi, 1913–14, 29].

NEWTON, WILLIAM (1735–1790), born on 27 October 1735, was the eldest son of James Newton, a cabinet-maker of Holborn, who claimed to be related to Sir Isaac Newton. His mother was the daughter of a clergyman who was mathematical master at Christ's Hospital. William was admitted to Christ's Hospital in November 1743, and on leaving the school in

December 1750 was apprenticed to the architect William Jones (*q.v.*). He was afterwards in the London office of Matthew Brettingham. He began to exhibit at the Society of Artists in 1760, and was practising on his own by 1764. He also exhibited at the Free Society of Artists in 1761 and 1783, and at the Royal Academy in 1776. In 1766 he visited Rome, returning to England early in the following year. Newton's drawings in the R.I.B.A. Collection indicate a fairly extensive practice in and around London, but major commissions eluded him. In 1769 he competed unsuccessfully for the Royal Exchange at Dublin, in 1774 for the church of St. Alphege, London Wall, and in 1775 for that of St. Mary, Battersea. From time to time he appears to have acted as 'ghost' to William Jupp the elder, for whom he designed the Ballroom and Eating-Room of the London Tavern (1768), and probably also the entrance to Carpenters' Hall (1779), for which there is a design among his drawings. His drawings suggest that he was trained in the Palladian tradition, but developed a neo-classical style for which his visit to Rome was no doubt a preparation. For Battersea Church he produced a competent neo-classical design in 1775, and his interiors were decorated in an elegant 'antique' style comparable to that of the Adam brothers.

In 1771 Newton published the earliest English translation of the first five books of Vitruvius, under the title *De Architectura libri decem, written by Marcus Vitruvius Pollio*. He was also the author of *Commentaires sur Vitruve*, written in French, but published in London in 1780, and helped to edit and complete the second volume of Stuart's *Antiquities of Athens*, which, though dated 1787, was not published until after its author's death in 1788. After Newton's death a complete edition of Vitruvius, including a translation of the remaining five books, was published by his brother and executor James Newton 'from a correct manuscript prepared by himself'. This was entitled *The Architecture of M. Vitruvius Pollio translated*, 1791, and was illustrated by numerous engravings.

In September 1782 Newton succeeded Robert Mylne as Clerk of the Works at Greenwich Hospital. Mylne had been dismissed by the Governors after a disagreement with their Surveyor, James Stuart, who was then engaged in rebuilding the Chapel after its destruction by fire in 1779. Newton had already been acting as Stuart's assistant since the previous February, and as Clerk of the Works he was largely responsible for the design as well as for the execution of the Chapel, whose rebuilding was not completed until 1790. When Stuart died in February 1788, Newton not unnaturally hoped to succeed him as Surveyor, but was passed over in favour of Sir Robert Taylor. The latter died within a year, but Newton's claims were again set aside by the appointment of John Yenn. Newton now thought of resigning, 'as it will be displeasing to me to be placed under a younger man and perhaps I may say less eminent in the profession than myself'. In the event he did not do so, but endeavoured to obtain from the Governors an admission that, as the real architect of their Chapel, he was entitled to professional remuneration in addition to his salary as Clerk of the Works. There can be little doubt that the former claim was substantially justified, though the Governors did not admit that it involved them in any additional financial obligation towards him.

In February 1790, Newton, whose health was failing through overwork, obtained three months' leave of absence from Greenwich in order to take a course of sea-bathing. He died at Sidford, nr. Sidmouth, on 6 July 1790. A portrait, engraved by James Newton after R. Smirke, R.A., is given in the 1791 edition of his *Vitruvius*, and there is a self-portrait (*aetat.* 26) in the Print Room of the British Museum. A collection of over one hundred drawings by Newton was presented to the R.I.B.A. in 1891.

[Wyatt Papworth, 'W. Newton and the Chapel of Greenwich Hospital', *R.I.B.A. Jnl.*, 1891, 417–20; *D.N.B.*; Lesley Lewis, 'The Architects of the Chapel at Greenwich Hospital', *Art Bulletin* xxix, 1947; *R.I.B.A. Drawings Catalogue: L–N*, 128–44.]

DURDANS, nr. EPSOM, SURREY, rebuilt for Charles Dalbiac, 1764–8; altered by George Devey 1878 and recently by Claude Phillimore. [A tablet over the entrance is inscribed 'Chas. Dalbiac Rest./1764/Wm. Newton Ar^t.' and there are drawings in the R.I.B.A. Collection dated 1764 and 1768].

LONDON, THE LONDON TAVERN, BISHOPSGATE STREET WITHIN, assisted William Jupp, senior, in designing, 1765–8; dem. 1876 [drawings in R.I.B.A. Coll.].

HIGHAMS, WOODFORD GREEN, WALTHAMSTOW, ESSEX (now Woodford County High School for Girls), for Anthony Bacon, 1768 [drawings in R.I.B.A. Coll.].

HUNGERFORD PARK, BERKS., for Charles Dalbiac, 1768; altered 1934, dem. [drawings in R.I.B.A. Coll.].

ISLEWORTH, MIDDLESEX, house at SMALLBERRY GREEN for Lewis Chauvett, 1769; dem. 1795 [drawings in R.I.B.A. Coll.; D. Lysons, *Environs of London* ii (2), 1811, 457].

Unidentified house exhibited at R.A. in 1780 as 'now building in Berkshire'.

GREENWICH HOSPITAL, assisted James Stuart in rebuilding the CHAPEL, 1782–88, and completed the building after Stuart's death in 1788 [Lesley Lewis, 'The Architects of the Chapel at Greenwich Hospital', *Art Bulletin* xxix,

1947, and 'Greece and Rome at Greenwich', *Arch. Rev.*. cix, 1951, 17–24].

GREENWICH HOSPITAL, THE BOYS' SCHOOL, KING STREET, 1782–3; incorporated in Nurses' Home 1929 [*R.I.B.A. Drawings Catalogue: L–N*, 131–2].

The list above comprises all the buildings certainly known to have been built to Newton's designs. In addition the drawings in the R.I.B.A. Collection include designs by Newton for the following buildings, some of which may have been executed, others not: a house for Mr. Fellows, 1763; a house for Mr. Lewis at CHESHUNT, HERTS., 1765; a house at EWELL, SURREY, for Philip Rowden, the builder of BOURNE or GARBRAND HALL, EWELL, c. 1765, dem. 1962; a house at SPITALFIELDS for Mr. Ouvry, 1765; a house 'building in the country' for a Mr. Vilion, 1768; an addition to a house for Mr. Nouaille, 1768; a house at WALTHAMSTOW, ESSEX, for Mr. Fullager (*i.e.* Fulger), 1769; a villa at TWICKENHAM for Daniel Giles, the builder of the house known as SPENCER GROVE or TWICKENHAM MEADOWS, c. 1775; a villa at LITTLE MARLOW, BUCKS., for Sir John Borlase Warren; a house in Yorkshire for the Lascelles family; a building for the Society of Dilettanti, probably c. 1764; an Assembly Room at SNOW HILL, HOLBORN, for Mr. Warford, 1767; THE ORPHAN SCHOOL, CITY ROAD, ISLINGTON, 1772 (probably built to Newton's designs, but dem.); ST. ALPHEGE CHURCH, LONDON WALL, 1774–5 (rejected); and ST. MARY'S CHURCH, BATTERSEA, 1775 (rejected).

Drawings by Newton for a villa on LUNDY ISLAND for Sir John Borlase Warren, made c. 1775, were in 1973 in the custody of the Curator of the Lundy Museum. The designs which he submitted for the Dublin Royal Exchange competition in 1769 are in the Murray Collection at the National Library of Ireland (Portfolio I). Another drawing for the Exchange is in the Print Room of the British Museum, together with a section through the east end of Newton's design for Battersea Church.

NICHOL, JOHN, of Wellesbourne, 'Civil Engineer', held the office of Surveyor of Bridges to the County of Warwick. He designed bridges at WHITLEY, nr. COVENTRY, over the R. Avon, 1831, at NUNEATON, over the Hinch Brook, 1835, and at BARSTON, over the R. Thame, 1838 [Warwickshire County Records, Class 24, No. 28, *passim*]. COMBROKE CHURCH, WARWICKS., was rebuilt to his designs in 1831; it was again rebuilt 1866–7 [I.C.B.S.].

NICHOLLS, THOMAS, was a pupil of W. R. Laxton, from whose office in Tottenham Court Road he exhibited at the Royal Academy in 1810 and 1811. He subsequently practised as an architect and surveyor from various London addresses. The Thomas Nicholls who exhibited architectural designs at the Royal Academy in 1832 and 1836 and at the Society of British Artists in the latter year was probably his son, for in the British Artists' Catalogue he appears as 'Thomas Nicholls, junior'.

NICHOLSON, GEORGE (–1793), a mason by trade, was surveyor to the Dean and Chapter of Durham until his death in 1793, when he was succeeded by William Morpeth. In 1772–7, with some advice from Robert Mylne, he designed and built the PREBENDS' BRIDGE over the R. Wear for the Dean and Chapter. From about 1773 onwards he carried out repairs to DURHAM CATHEDRAL which included an unfortunate attempt to restore the west and north fronts by paring off the decayed surface of the stone. The present parapets of the two western towers, the upper parts of the north transept and the twin turrets of the north face of the Chapel of the Nine Altars were his work, and he also rebuilt the north porch. His unexecuted design for rebuilding the church of St. Mary the Less, Durham, is described and illustrated by C. W. Gibby in *Transactions of the Architectural and Archaeological Society of Durham and Northumberland* x (iii), 1950. [Durham Cathedral Chapter Act Books; W. Hutchison, *History of the County Palatine of Durham* ii, 1787, 226, 317; correspondence in *R.I.B.A. Jnl.*, Oct., Nov. 1955, Jan., March 1956.]

NICHOLSON, MICHAEL ANGELO (*c.* 1796–1842), was the son of Peter Nicholson by his first wife. He studied architectural drawing at the school of Richard Brown (*q.v.*), and then became a pupil of John Foulston. He was admitted to the Royal Academy Schools in 1814 at the age of 18, and exhibited occasionally at the Academy between 1812 and 1828. He engraved plates for his father's works, and collaborated with him in the publication of *The Practical Cabinet Maker*, 1826. He drew the frontispiece for Richard Elsam's *Practical Builder's Perpetual Price Book*, 1825, and lithographed the plates for Inwood's *Erectheion*, 1826. His own publications were: *The Carpenter and Joiner's Companion*, 1826; *The Five Orders, Geometrical and in Perspective* 1834; and *The Carpenter's and Joiner's New Practical Work on Hand-Railing*, 1836. He kept a school for architectural drawing in Melton Place, Euston Square, and rarely, if ever, practised as an architect. He claimed some responsibility for CARSTAIRS HOUSE, LANARKSHIRE, for he exhibited a view of it at the Royal Academy in 1823, and a plan and elevation of the house, 'Designed by M. A. Nicholson, Architect', appear in his father's *Practical Builder*. It is possible that he designed the MARKET HOUSE, EGLIN-

TON, CO. DERRY, IRELAND, for in 1823 he was paid £5 13s. 9d. for three plans connected with it [C. E. B. Brett, *Court Houses and Market Houses of the Province of Ulster*, 1973, 85]. He left two daughters, one of whom married Alexander ('Greek') Thomson of Glasgow, and the other Thomson's partner John Baird. [*A.P.S.D.*; *D.N.B.*]

NICHOLSON, PETER (1765–1844), born on 20 July 1765, at Prestonkirk, East Lothian, was the son of a stone-mason. Disliking his father's trade, he was apprenticed to a cabinet-maker at Linton, Haddingtonshire. On the conclusion of his apprenticeship, he worked as a journeyman in Edinburgh, and at the age of 23 went to London, where he taught in an evening school for mechanics as well as pursuing his craft. In this way he acquired sufficient capital to finance his first publication, *The New Carpenter's Guide*, 1792, for which he engraved his own plates. In it he described an original method of constructing groins and niches of complex forms. This was followed by *The Principles of Architecture*, 1795–8, 2nd ed. 1809, and *The Carpenter's and Joiner's Assistant*, 1797. In 1800 he returned to Scotland and went to Glasgow, where he practised as an architect until 1808. During this period he designed several buildings listed below, and laid out the town of Ardrossan in Ayrshire for the 12th Earl of Eglinton. The harbour at Ardrossan was constructed under the direction of Thomas Telford, whose recommendation is said to have been instrumental in obtaining for Nicholson the post of Surveyor to the county of Cumberland in 1808 on the death of John Chisholme. In this capacity Nicholson supervised the building of the new Courts of Justice at Carlisle to Telford's designs until 1810, when he returned to London, leaving the courts to be completed by Sir Robert Smirke.

In 1812–19 Nicholson produced *The Architectural Dictionary*, 2 vols., which contains plates of many of his executed works. A second edition, largely rewritten, was published by Lomax & Gunyon in 1852–4. In 1827 he began the publication of a work entitled *The School of Architecture and Engineering*, intended to have been completed in twelve numbers, but abandoned after the fifth number owing to the bankruptcy of the publishers. Nicholson lost heavily, and probably for this reason went in 1829 to live at Morpeth on a small property left him by a relative. In 1832 he moved to Newcastle-upon-Tyne, where he opened a school. It does not appear to have been a financial success, for, in July 1834, he was presented with £320 by public subscription. In the following year he was elected president of the Newcastle Society for the Promotion of the Fine Arts, and received many other honours locally. During his last years he was supported by the generosity of Thomas Jamieson of Newton, Northumberland. He died at Carlisle on 18 June 1844, and was buried in the Christ Church graveyard. A monument to his memory, curiously designed by R. W. Billings in the form of two interpenetrating obelisks, was erected in the Carlisle Cemetery in 1856 (see illustration in the Edinburgh *Building Chronicle* i, 1855, 175). His portrait is given in several of his own works, *e.g.* the *Builder and Workman's New Director* and the *Guide to Railway Masonry* (edition of 1846). He was twice married, and had two sons and a daughter. His elder son, Michael Angelo (*q.v.*), shared his father's interests and engraved the plates for some of his books.

Nicholson was one of the leading intellects behind nineteenth-century building technology. He used his great ability as a mathematician to simplify many old formulae used by architectural draughtsmen as well as to devise new ones. His improvements in the construction of handrailing were recognized by the award of the Gold Medal of the Society of Arts in 1814, and although he never derived financial advantage from his inventions, his contribution to the mechanics of building was very considerable. He was the first author to write on the construction of hinges and the hanging of doors, and was also the first to notice that Grecian mouldings were conic sections. His invention of the 'centrolinead', an instrument for drawing lines which are required to converge towards an inaccessible point, brought him a gift of £20 from the Society of Arts in 1814, and a silver medal for its improvement later in the same year.

His principal publications, apart from those already mentioned, were: *The Student's Instructor in drawing and working the Five Orders of Architecture*, 1795; *Mechanical Exercises, or the Elements and Practice of Carpentry, Joinery, etc.*, 1811; *A Treatise on Practical Perspective*, 1815; *An Introduction to the Methods of Increments*, 1817; *Essays on the Combinatorial Analysis*, 1818; *The Rudiments of Algebra*, 1819; *Essay on Involution and Evolution*, 1820; *A Treatise on the Construction of Staircases and Handrails*, 1820; *Analytical and Arithmetical Essays*, 1820; *Popular Course of Pure and Mixed Mathematics*, 1822; *The Rudiments of Practical Perspective*, 1822; *The New Practical Builder and Workman's Companion*, 1823; *The Builder and Workman's New Director*, 1824; *The Carpenter and Builder's Complete Measurer*, 1827; *Popular and Practical Treatise on Masonry and Stone-Cutting*, 1827; *Practical Masonry, Bricklaying, and Plastering*, 1830; *A Treatise on Dialling*, Newcastle 1833; *A Treatise on Projection, with a Complete System of Isometrical Drawing*, Newcastle 1837; *The Guide to Railway Masonry, containing a Complete Treatise on the Oblique Arch*, Newcastle 1839; *The Carpenter, Joiner, and Builder's Companion*, 1846;

Carpentry (ed. Ashpitel), 1849; *Carpentry, Joining and Building*, 1851; with John Rowbotham Nicholson, published *A Practical System of Algebra*, 1824; and with his son, Michael Angelo Nicholson, *The Practical Cabinet Maker, Upholsterer, and Complete Decorator*, 1826. Further editions of nearly all Nicholson's books were published, only the first edition being listed above in each case. For a fuller list giving the later editions see *D.N.B.*

[*A.P.S.D.*; *D.N.B.*; *Architectural Mag.* i, 1834, 140–1; *Civil Engineer and Architect's Jnl.*, iii, 1840, 152–3, vii, 1844, 425–7; memoir in *Builder and Workman's New Director* (reprinted in *Mechanic's Magazine*, 1825); *Builder* iv, 1846, 514, vii, 1849, 615–16.]

GLASGOW, CARLTON PLACE, LAURIESTON, 1802–18 [*Architectural Dictionary* ii, 1819, 912].

GLASGOW, timber bridge over R. Clyde, *c.* 1805; dem. [*A.P.S.D.*].

CRUXTON, nr. GLASGOW, cottage for Mr. Buchanan, *c.* 1805 [*Architectural Dictionary* i, 1819, 102–3].

GLASGOW, house for Mr Grey, jeweller, *c.* 1805 [*Architectural Dictionary* i, 1819, 102–3].

PAISLEY, RENFREWSHIRE, Coffee House (? executed), *c.* 1805 [*Architectural Dictionary* i, 1819, 102–3].

PARTICK, LANARKSHIRE, house called YORKSHIRE HO! for Fulton Alexander, 1806; dem. [*Architectural Dictionary* i, 1819, 102–3; frontispiece to *Practical Builder*, 1825].

HOUGHTON HOUSE, HOUGHTON, CUMBERLAND, library for William Hodgson, Clerk of the Peace (? executed), *c.* 1810 [*Architectural Dictionary* ii, 1819, 908].

CASTLETOWN HOUSE, ROCKLIFFE, CUMBERLAND, for Robert Mounsey, 1811, in conjunction with William Reid, *q.v.*

GLASGOW, OLD COLLEGE, THE HAMILTON BUILDING, executed 1811–13 to a modified design by John Brash, *q.v.*

CORBY CASTLE, CUMBERLAND, enlarged and remodelled for Henry Howard, 1812–17 [*Architectural Dictionary* i, 1819, 102–3] (*C. Life*, 7–14 Jan. 1954).

CLIVEDEN, BUCKS., Tea Room at the Spring, 1813 [*Architectural Dictionary* ii, 1819, 913].[1]

TAPLOW, BUCKS., house for a country baker [*Architectural Dictionary* i, 1819, 102–3].

NICOL, W—, is at present known only as the author of two designs made for J. H. Belshes of Invermay, Perthshire, in 1802, one for a teahouse, the other for a 'Gothic Temple for the point near the Hummel-bummel' [Fettercairn papers, National Library of Scotland].

---

[1] In 1816 Nicholson published an engraved design for rebuilding Cliveden House for the Countess of Orkney in the castellated style.

NISBET, DAVID (1790–1853), is described as 'Architect' on his monument in the Calton Old Burial Ground in Edinburgh. He died on 4 October 1853. He figures in the Edinburgh directories from 1811/12 onwards as 'builder' or 'architect'.

NISBET, JAMES (–1781), of Kelso, was a mason by trade. He may have been the James, son of James Nisbet, who was born at Kelso on 2 December 1746 [Register in New Register House, Edinburgh], and his recent death is mentioned in the Wedderburn papers in November 1781 [S.R.O., GD 267/1/3]. His first recorded work appears to be EDNAM HOUSE, KELSO, built for James Dickson in 1761, and described in the *New Statistical Account of Scotland* iii, 1845, 320, as 'one of the most elegant private mansions that Nisbet ever designed' (for description see R.C.A.M., *Roxburghshire*, 248–9, where Nisbet is wrongly stated to have been of Berners Street, London).

From 1771 onwards Nesbit was at work remodelling FORD CASTLE, NORTHUMBERLAND, for Sir John Hussey Delaval, afterwards 1st Lord Delaval, in the Gothick style [Northumberland Record Office, Hussey Delaval papers, M 17/29 and 2 DE 18/1] (for plans and illustrations see *History of Northumberland* xi, 420–2 and *C. Life*, 11–18 Jan. 1941). From one of Sir John Delaval's letters to Nesbit [2 DE 18/1/7] it appears that in 1771 the latter was being employed by Mr. (later Sir) Francis Blake, presumably at TWIZEL CASTLE, NORTHUMBERLAND, which Blake was then engaged in building. Twizel was a fantastic Gothick building in a romantic situation on the Tweed: it was never finished and is now a ruin. There are survey drawings in the Northumberland Record Office [2BU B 5/6]. It is possible that Nesbit was also employed by Sir Francis Blake when he remodelled FOWBERRY TOWER, NORTH-UMBERLAND, in the Gothick style in 1776–8, but documentary evidence is lacking.

In 1771–5 Nisbet superintended the building of WEDDERBURN CASTLE, DUNS, BERWICKSHIRE, to the designs of Robert Adam [drawings at Paxton House, *ex inf.* Dr. A. Rowan]. In 1771 he designed the octagonal church at KELSO in conjunction with two fellow-builders, John Laidlaw (a mason) and John Purves (a carpenter): it was completed in 1773. In 1823 a flat ceiling was substituted for the original domed one [S.R.O., HR 651/3 and 4: cf. RHP 8462 and 8466] (for illustrations see R.C.A.M., *Roxburghshire*, figs. 105, 304).

In December 1774 Nisbet made a report, now in the Charter Room at Floors Castle, on the state of BROXMOUTH HOUSE, EAST LOTHIAN.

The subject of this entry should not be confused with James Nisbet, an Edinburgh plasterer who was active from about 1780 to 1810 and is occasionally referred to as an architect.

NISBET, ROBERT, was a mason in Newbiggin, Musselburgh, Midlothian. In 1802 his design for a new church at INVERESK, MIDLOTHIAN, was chosen from five submitted, and the building was erected under his supervision in 1803–5. The handsome classical steeple was added in 1805–10. The design was made by Nisbet, who in 1808 submitted an account for his 'plan & other necessary information'. William Sibbald, to whom the design has been incorrectly attributed, was merely asked to settle the contract price in conjunction with John Thin [S.R.O., HR 6/1, pp. 17, 22, 41, 94, 97–8].

NIXON, ROBERT FEAKE, was a builder and surveyor at Woburn in Bedfordshire. He rebuilt LIDLINGTON CHURCH, BEDS., in 1809–10, dem. [*Gent's Mag.* 1849 (ii), 481], and may have rebuilt HEATH AND REACH CHURCH, BEDS., in 1829, as he reported on its condition in 1828 [I.C.B.S.]. Neither was a building of any architectural merit.

NIXON, WILLIAM (–1824), was one of the bridge-masters for the County of Cumberland from 1816 until his death on 2 March 1824. His district was Allerdale Wards 'above and below Derwent'. In 1822, when the County accepted the plans of J. Orridge (*q.v.*) for a new gaol at Carlisle, directions were given that the building should be supervised by Christopher Hodgson five days a week and by William Nixon one day [Cumberland and Westmorland Record Office, Q.S. Order Books 1816–24 and Gaol Committee's Second Report AG/4]. Nixon lived at Chalk Lodge, Dalston. Although described as 'Architect' in the Carlisle Probate Records, he appears to have been principally a builder and surveyor, and was probably related to the Nixon family of masons who in the eighteenth century lived at Cumdivock, nr. Dalston. Paul Nixon or Nixson (1766–1850), a local sculptor, was no doubt a member of the same family.

NIXON, WILLIAM (*c.* 1810–1848), may have been the elder son of William Nixon (d. 1826), Nash's clerk of works at Brighton and elsewhere. Like the elder Nixon, he was employed in the public service as a Clerk of Works, and was in April 1840 transferred from Phoenix Park, Dublin, to head the small establishment of the Office of Works at Edinburgh. In this capacity he was responsible for the maintenance of Holyroodhouse and the law courts in Parliament Square, and for the repair of several cathedrals (Glasgow, Elgin, Kirkwall, etc.) which were Crown property. It was to his designs that the interior of Gillespie Graham's TOLBOOTH ST. JOHN'S CHURCH was furnished in 1842–5 [S.R.O., RHP 6501]. The POLICE OFFICE at 192 HIGH STREET was designed by him in 1845 in conformity with the architecture of the adjoining buildings in Parliament Square [Edinburgh Dean of Guild plans]. In 1845 he undertook the completion of the buildings of the UNITED COLLEGE at ST. ANDREWS begun by Robert Reid in 1829–31. The north wing and the 'cloister' behind the church were built to his designs between 1845 and 1849. At ST. ANDREWS he also designed the MARTYRS' MONUMENT (an obelisk with neo-classical detailing) in 1842 and the (WEST) INFANT SCHOOL (Romanesque) in 1844. He died on 24 March 1848, aged 38, and was succeeded by his assistant Robert Matheson. [*History of the King's Works* vi, 1973, 253–4; R. G. Cant, 'St. Andrews Architects', *St. Andrews Preservation Trust Year Book*, 1966–7, 12; C. Roger, *History of St. Andrews*, 1849, 54; information from Mr. L. Russell Muirhead.]

NOBLE, JAMES (–1875), was the nephew of Charles Noble (died 1827, aged 72), who had for many years been a trusted clerk in S. P. Cockerell's office, and who received a legacy of £500 under the latter's will in recognition of his 'long attachment to me through life . . . and faithful and constant service'. James Noble became pricipal assistant to C. R. Cockerell, but was dissatisfied with his subordinate status, and eventually established himself in independent practice. He was an original member of the Institute of British Architects in 1834, and exhibited designs for churches at the Royal Academy in 1837 and 1838, but no building designed by him has been identified, and he is best known as the author of the first book on architectural practice, entitled *The Professional Practice of Architects, and that of Measuring Surveyors . . . from the time of the celebrated Earl of Burlington*, 1836. He died at Florence Villa, Warwick Gardens, Kensington, on 14 April 1875 [Principal Probate Registry, Calendar of Probates].

NOLLORTH, SAMUEL, of East Dereham, Norfolk, announced in the *Norfolk Chronicle* of 29 June 1771 that he was in practice as an architect, having had '3 years regular instruction under Ward of Bury St. Edmunds and many years of his own experience'. He was presumably the Mr. Nolloth who was paid for making a plan of Kimberley Hall, Norfolk, in 1755 [Kimberley accounts, *ex inf.* Mr. T. P. Connor].

NORRIS, JOHN, was, according to Lysons, *Magna Britannia* ii, 1810, 513, the architect from whose designs DUNHAM MASSEY HALL, CHESHIRE, was rebuilt by the 2nd Earl of Warrington between 1732 and 1740. An account-book preserved in the house records several payments to 'Mr. Norris about the New Building' [J. Swarbrick, 'Dunham Massey Hall', *Trans. Lancs. and Cheshire Antiq. Soc.* xlii, 1927]. A payment of £16 19s. 0d. to 'Mr. Norris Architect' in 1750 has

been noted by Mr. T. P. Connor in the accounts of the Atherton family of Atherton Hall, Lancashire [Lancashire Record Office, DD Li/Cash Account 1749–61]. Atherton and Dunham Massey are only ten miles apart and Norris no doubt came from Manchester or some other town in that vicinity.

NORRIS, RICHARD (*c.* 1750–1792), was the eldest son of Richard Norris (*c.* 1719–79), a builder and surveyor who lived at Hampstead, but had premises in Holborn. In 1767 the elder Norris was among those who submitted designs for the Shire Hall at Hertford, but although they were at first accepted, they were ultimately set aside in favour of drawings by James Adam [Hertfordshire Quarter Sessions records]. In 1773–5 he remodelled BROKE HALL, NACTON, SUFFOLK, for Philip Broke, but the house was rebuilt to the designs of James Wyatt less than twenty years later [E. Suffolk Record Office, HA 93/722/159, *ex inf.* Mr. J. M. Frew]. Norris died on 24 May 1779 at the age of 60, and was buried at Finchley. In 1766 the younger Norris exhibited a drawing at the Free Society of Artists. It represented 'a Triumphal Arch, proposed for the reception of her Majesty on her intended landing at Greenwich, from a design of Mr. Stuart'. This suggests that he may have been Stuart's pupil. He must have travelled on the Continent, for he would not otherwise have been eligible for membership of the Architects' Club, of which he was a founder-member in 1791. He became surveyor to Christ's Hospital, the Clothworkers' Company, the Charterhouse estates, the London Assurance Corporation, the Sun Fire Insurance Office and (from October 1790) the Corporation of Trinity House. He died suddenly on 7 January 1792, aged 42, 'oppressed with overweight of business, the loss of a beloved consort about 15 months ago, and of a useful foreman and clerk lately', and was buried at Finchley, where he is commemorated on the family monument. His only recorded architectural works appear to be a design for a new dining-room at WANLIP HALL, LEICS. (dem.), for Charles Grave Hudson, *c.* 1780 [drawings in Leics. Record Office], and some alterations to FETCHAM PARK, SURREY, for Thomas Hankey in 1789–91 [Surrey County Record Office, S.C. 19/175/2]. As surveyor to the Clothworkers' Company he was succeeded by his younger brother Philip Norris, who retired in 1797 and died in 1806, aged 52. [*A.P.S.D.*; *Gent's Mag.* 1792 (i), 91, 485; information from Miss P. G. Mann.]

NORTH, ROGER (?1653–1734), was the sixth and youngest son of Dudley, 4th Lord North. Like his brother Francis, afterwards Lord Chancellor Guilford, Roger was educated for the law, and partly by his own abilities, partly through his brother's influence, he had a not unsuccessful career. He was called to the Bar in 1675, and became in due course a Bencher of the Middle Temple, steward to Archbishop Sancroft, and Solicitor-General to the Duke of York. But although the law provided North with a profession, it by no means monopolized his mind, and in the course of a long life he found time to study optics and mathematics, to listen to, and to theorize about, music, to collect pictures, to plant, and to build. Although never a member of the Royal Society, North was nevertheless in touch with the intellectual and scientific ideas of his time. He had read Descartes at Cambridge at a time when 'the new philosophy was a sort of heresy'; he had attempted to arrive 'at a system of nature, upon the Cartesian or rather mechanical principles'. He was an expert at dialling, and as a 'dabbler in mathematics ... fell into that disease that all tyros in that art do, a conceit of having found a perpetual motion'. For a person of these tastes, the transition from science to architecture was an easy one, as it had been for Robert Hooke and Sir Christopher Wren before him.

It was the fire which destroyed the Temple in January 1678/9 which first led Roger North to number building among his 'mechanical entertainments'. For he played a prominent part in the negotiations with Nicholas Barbon, the 'undertaker' of the new buildings, and it was in 'drawing the model of my little chamber and making patterns for the wainscot' that he learned the use of a scale and tasted for the first time 'the joys of designing and executing known only to such as practise or have practised it'. This, however, was 'but a beginning'. Soon he was buying the architectural text-books of the day, Palladio, Scamozzi, and Evelyn's *Parallel of the Orders*. He learned the principles of perspective, and spent many happy hours in drawing 'which might have been better and more profitably employed'. Architecture, in fact, became for him a passion second only to that for music, and North's active mind delighted in the technicalities of building just as it did in the niceties of draughtsmanship.

In 1683–4 the building of the Great Gateway leading from the Temple into Fleet Street gave him an opportunity to display his talents as an architect. The gateway has traditionally been ascribed to Wren, but a passage in North's essay on building (B.M., Add. MS. 32540, f. 37ᵛ) makes it clear that it was he and not Wren who made the designs.

> When I built the Temple gate, I designed 4 pilaster columes, and a frontoon.[1] But it being necessary for preserving the dignity of such a fabrick, between very high houses to rais the frontoon eves, above the Cornish of the houses,

... I raised the first story with Rustick stone, & made a flatt arch for the coaches to pass, whereby I gained the Greatest passage height I could: & compass ones for the shopps, lower so as to lay the thrust of the other upon the solid, clear of the void, and set balconys over these compass arches. Then a fillett of stone, and above that a deep plane, which served as Stylobate, or foundation for the Columnes, being more in height than ordinary, & upon that sett the bases, by which means the Columnes were brought into due proportion to the height, and altogether hath no ill aspect. I could not compass the Midle Arch, & flatt the side ones, because the Story above must be preserved, but that bin much more proper.

Wren did indeed offer his advice, suggesting that it might save expense if the pediment and entablature were made of wood and plaster, 'but' (North tells us) 'out of a proud high spirit I declined it, and made the whole intablature & frontoon of stone, & it is as lusty, as most are'. He was, however, on excellent terms with the Surveyor-General, for he records several conversations of great interest which passed between them, and he and his brother made regular visits to St. Paul's to inspect the progress of the works. He was also a friend of Hugh May, the Comptroller of the Works, and his essay 'Of Building', now in the British Museum (Add. MS. 32540), shows that he was familiar with all the most important architectural works of his time, whose design and construction he criticizes freely.

Roger North's own contribution to English architecture was not large, for unlike Sir Roger Pratt, he never became a 'profest architect', and did not 'pretend either to great publick designes, nor new models of great howses'. There are, however, some highly competent designs by him in the British Museum (Add. MS. 23005), and between 1680 and 1685 he assisted his brother, Lord Guilford, to make considerable alterations to the latter's country seat, Wroxton Abbey in Oxfordshire [*V.C.H. Oxon.* ix, 172–3; B.M., Add. MS. 32510, ff. 136–9]. In 1690–1 he bought a large but old-fashioned house at Rougham in Norfolk, which he remodelled gradually, as his purse allowed, adding a gallery at the back, and an Ionic portico in front. He also built a library on the north side of Rougham Church, to which he proposed to leave his large collection of books. But before the end of the eighteenth century 'not one stone was left upon another' of the house which he had reconstructed, the library too had been destroyed, and the books dispersed. Fortunately his papers survived. Most of them were acquired by the British Museum in 1885, and some others (including a variant version of the treatise on building) are still at Rougham. Also at Rougham are some drawings in North's hand,

---

[1] *I.e.* a pediment.

including two plans of Wroxton Abbey, and an elevation of the Temple Gateway. Roger North died at Rougham on 1 March 1733/4, and is commemorated by a monument in the church. His portrait by Lely hangs in the present Rougham Hall, formed in the nineteenth century from the outbuildings of Roger's house.

[*D.N.B.*; *The Autobiography of the Hon. Roger North*, ed. A. Jessopp, 1887; *The Lives of the Norths*, ed. A. Jessopp, 1890; H. M. Colvin, 'Roger North and Sir Christopher Wren', *Arch. Rev.*, Oct. 1951.]

NORTON, CHARLES, was a builder and surveyor of Birmingham. In 1793–4 he was jointly employed with George Saunders to rebuild the THEATRE ROYAL in NEW STREET after the fire of 1792, and acted as 'superintendent in the erecting and finishing the Theatre and Buildings adjoining' [MS. Minutes of the Proprietors in Birmingham Reference Library]. In 1795, having obtained plans from the architect Charles Rawstorne, he issued *Proposals with the Plan and Specification for Building the Crescent at Birmingham*, of which there is a copy in the Birmingham Reference Library. The Crescent was to have consisted of a 'superb range of twenty-three stone houses, elevated upon a terrace 1182 feet long and 17 feet wide', but only the wings were, in fact, built. There is an engraving of the original project in the British Museum (*King's Maps* xlii, 82m).

In 1786–8 Norton rebuilt ALL SAINTS CHURCH, WEST BROMWICH, STAFFS. (again rebuilt 1870–2) [agreement among parish records, *ex inf.* Mr. D. A. Johnson], and it was apparently to designs made by him jointly with a surveyor named William Whitmore that CHRIST CHURCH, BIRMINGHAM, was built in 1806–14 (dem. 1899) [minute book in Birmingham Reference Library, *ex inf.* Mr. G. W. Beard].

NOSWORTHY, MATTHEW (1750–1831), a speculative builder of Exeter, was responsible for much of the excellent late eighteenth-century domestic architecture of that city. He was born at Widecombe-in-the-Moor, but came to Exeter at an early age and proved to be a man of 'great industry and perseverance' in his business as a builder. He died in Exeter on 14 March 1831, aged 81.

The Exeter City accounts show that in 1789 Nosworthy was paid 8 guineas 'for drawing plans of the buildings on Southernhay' – that is for the terraces of brick houses built in SOUTHERNHAY during the next few years. In 1792 he contracted to build BARNFIELD CRESCENT [*Flying Post*, 24 May 1792], and he subsequently designed and built DIX'S FIELD, begun 1806, and probably COLLETON CRESCENT, 1802–5. He also designed THE NEW LONDON INN, HIGH STREET, EXETER, 1793–4

(dem.). [A. E. Richardson & C. L. Gill, *Regional Architecture of the West of England*, 1924, 26–31; *Devon and Cornwall Illustrated*, with text by J. Britton & E. W. Brayley, 1832, 67; information from Prof. W. G. Hoskins.]

NOVOSIELSKI, MICHAEL (1750–1795), was born in Rome of Polish parents and is said to have come to London as a young man in order to assist James Wyatt at the time when he was building the Pantheon (1770–2). In 1772 he was living at the house of the artist Bartoli in Golden Square.

In 1785 Novosielski leased some 14 acres of land on the south side of Brompton Road, Kensington, on which he proceeded to build, as a speculation, MICHAEL'S PLACE (forty-two houses), MICHAEL'S GROVE (ten houses), BROMPTON CRESCENT (twenty-five houses) and a large detached house (dem. 1843) for his own occupation. Some of these houses remained in an unfinished state for many years, and the whole development was demolished in 1886 to make way for Egerton Gardens and Egerton Place [T. C. Croker, *A Walk from London to Fulham*, 1860, 43, 50; Dorothy Stroud, *The South Kensington Estate of Henry Smith's Charity*, 1975, 16–17]. Three houses built by Novosielski 'opposite Lord William Gordon's' in PICCADILLY are mentioned in *The World* for 22 May, 30 June and 3 August 1787, where it is stated that he had also begun to build in GROSVENOR PLACE.

After the fire of 27 June 1789, Novosielski reconstructed the OPERA HOUSE in the HAYMARKET in 1790–1, exhibiting his designs at the Royal Academy in 1794. This was then the largest theatre in Europe, except La Scala at Milan. It was reconstructed by J. Nash and G. Repton in 1816–18, incorporating Novosielski's auditorium, and the interior was redecorated in 1846. The interior was destroyed by fire in 1867, rebuilt in 1868–9, and finally demolished in the 1890s [Britton & Pugin, *Public Buildings of London* i, 1825, 72–9]. Novosielski was also concerned with Francis Pasquali in fitting up the CONCERT ROOM in the TOTTENHAM COURT ROAD for the 'Concerts of Ancient Music' which were held from 1786 onwards. This building, later known as the Queen's Theatre, was demolished in 1882 [*Survey of London* xxi, 36–9]. Novosielski was a scene-painter as well as an architect, and it was probably his theatrical connections which led to his employment by the 7th Earl of Barrymore to design a house for him in Piccadilly (No. 105, at the corner of Brick Street). In 1850–1 it was reconstructed as Hertford House [*Builder* ix, 1851, 227]. An engraving of the original front is reproduced by A. I. Dasent, *Piccadilly*, 1920, 117.

Novosielski died at Ramsgate on 8 April 1795, aged 45. At the time of his death he was engaged in a new speculative building venture at SID-

MOUTH, then beginning to be a fashionable sea-side resort. In a letter from C. H. Tatham to Henry Holland dated 10 July 1795, he writes: 'Mr. Jenkins ... informed me of Mr. Novo-sielski's death, by which he is a sufferer on account of a Crescent of considerable magnitude contracted for by the deceased and now erecting near the sea at Sidmouth in Devonshire, the property of Mr. Jenkins' [Victoria and Albert Museum, 92.D.28, f. 16]. 'Mr. Jenkins' was the 'antiquary' and archaeologist Thomas Jenkins who, though long resident in Rome, was a native of Devon and lord of the manor of Sidmouth. The terrace is identifiable as FORTFIELD TERRACE, begun in about 1790, and still existing in the in-complete state in which it was left by Novosielski [cf. Anna Sutton, *A Story of Sidmouth*, 1959, 23].

A portrait of Novosielski by Angelica Kauff-mann is in the National Gallery of Scotland and is reproduced in *Survey of London* xxx, pl. 30.

[*A.P.S.D.*; *Gent's Mag.* 1795 (ii), 616; J. Boaden, *Life of Kemble* ii, 1825, 141; Horace Walpole, *Anecdotes of Painting* v, ed. F. W. Hilles & P. B. Daghlian, 1937, 189–90; will, P.C.C. 269 NEWCASTLE.]

O

OAKLEY, EDWARD, is thought to have been a native of Carmarthenshire. Some time before 1725 he had been living in the town of Car-marthen, where he was senior grand warden of the freemasons' lodge. But in 1721 he applied un-successfully for the post of clerk of the works at the church of St. Martin in the Fields, London, then about to be rebuilt to the designs of James Gibbs, and in 1725 he was one of the wardens of a lodge meeting at the 'Three Compasses' in Silver Street, Golden Square, where, on 31 December 1728, as master of the lodge, he de-livered a speech mainly concerned with archi-tecture. He stated in 1730 that he had been in government service abroad, where he had 'long contemplated a famous republic' [*Magazine of Architecture*, part 2, Preface]. In that year he was residing 'over against Tom's Coffee House, in St. Martin's Lane', and advertising as follows:

Estates Survey'd, Designs made, and Esti-mates calculated, for Building or repairs; Articles and Contracts for Agreements with Workmen fairly drawn; Artificers' works measured, and Bills adjusted; And all Affairs relating to Building carefully managed, By Edward Oakley.

He designed the greenhouses and hothouses for the PHYSIC GARDEN at CHELSEA, the first stone of which was laid by Sir Hans Sloane on 12 August 1732. They were completed in 1734. Plans and elevations of these buildings, drawn by Oakley and engraved by B. Cole, are in the British Museum (*King's Maps* xxviii, 4 g). In 1735 he made three designs for a bridge across the Thames at Westminster, of which he published an engraving. In 1756 he reissued the same engraving as a design for Blackfriars Bridge, merely altering the date and lettering. In the lat-ter form it appears as an illustration to W. Mait-land's *London*, 1756, 1387.

Oakley published in 1730 a substantial archi-tectural treatise entitled *The Magazine of Archi-tecture, Perspective and Sculpture*, with a dedica-tion to Sir Robert Walpole, a second edition of which was appearing in parts in 1732–3. He was also the author of *Every Man a Compleat Builder; or Easy Rules and Proportions for Drawing and Working the several Parts of Architecture*, 1738(?), 1766, 1774. In 1750 he published an engraved plan of Calais (B.M., *King's Maps* lxix, 40). The exact date of his death is not known, but it occurred between 1756 and 1766 [*A.P.S.D.*; *D.N.B.*; *Ars Quatuor Coronatorum* xxvii, 1914, and xl, 1927, 134; MS. Minutes of the Commis-sioners for Rebuilding St. Martin's Church, f. 78].

OATES, JOHN (–1831), practised in Halifax from before 1820 until his death early in 1831. He probably came from Manchester, for in 1813 he gave a Manchester address when exhibiting a design for a villa at the Liverpool Academy. He designed a number of Commissioners' churches, some of which (*e.g.* Sowerby Bridge and Wilsden) are described by Pevsner as more solid and substantial in character than most of their kind. His Infirmary at Huddersfield has a hand-some Greek Doric portico. Oates died early in 1831 [Church Building Commissioners' Records, Surveyors' Reports, iv, f. 170]. Two of his churches were completed by Matthew Oates and Thomas Pickersgill, who both subsequently practised in York.

PUBLIC BUILDINGS

HALIFAX, YORKS. (W.R.), ASSEMBLY AND CONCERT ROOMS, 1828 [J. Crabtree, *History of Halifax*, 1836, 347].

RISHWORTH GRAMMAR SCHOOL, YORKS. (W.R.), 1827–8 [J. H. Priestley, *History of Rishworth School*, Halifax n.d., 51].

HUDDERSFIELD, YORKS. (W.R.), THE INFIRMARY, 1829–31 [W. White, *History, Gazeteer and Directory of the West Riding of Yorkshire* i, 1837, 365].

CHURCHES

SOWERBY BRIDGE, YORKS. (W.R.), CHRIST CHURCH, 1819, Gothic; chancel 1873–89 [I.C.B.S.].

*BUCKLEY, FLINTSHIRE, 1821–2, Gothic; rebuilt [Port, 138–9].

WINKSLEY, YORKS. (W.R.), 1822–4; dem. 1917 [I.C.B.S.].

*WILSDEN, YORKS. (W.R.), 1823–5, Gothic [Port, 138–9].

BIRDSALL, YORKS. (E.R.), 1824, Gothic, for the 6th Lord Middleton; chancel 1879–81 [design exhibited by Oates at Northern Society for the Encouragement of the Arts, Leeds, 1823].

BISHOP THORNTON, YORKS. (W.R.), rebuilt 1825; dem. 1888 [I.C.B.S.].

*SHIPLEY, YORKS. (W.R.), ST. PAUL, 1823–5, Gothic [Port, 138–9].

*LINDLEY, YORKS. (W.R.), ST. STEPHEN, 1828–9, Gothic [Port, 168–9].

*PADDOCK, YORKS. (W.R.), ALL SAINTS, 1828–9, Gothic [Port, 168–9].

*HUDDERSFIELD, YORKS. (W.R.), ST. PAUL, 1828–30, Gothic [Port, 168–9].

*IDLE, YORKS. (W.R.), HOLY TRINITY, 1828–30, Gothic [Port, 168–9].

HARROGATE, YORKS. (W.R.), CHRIST CHURCH, 1830–1, Gothic; chancel and transepts 1862 [W. Grainge, History of Harrogate, 1882, 159].

*HALIFAX, YORKS. (W.R.), ST. JAMES, 1830–1, Gothic; dem. 1955 [Port, 166–7].

*SHELTON, nr. HANLEY, STAFFS., ST. MARK, 1831–3, Gothic, completed by M. Oates & T. Pickersgill [Port, 160–1].

*HEBDEN BRIDGE (MYTHOLM), YORKS. (W.R.), ST. JAMES, 1832–3, Gothic, erected by M. Oates & T. Pickersgill [Port, 166–7].

OGBOURNE, Sir WILLIAM (c. 1662–1734), was a prominent London master carpenter. After an apprenticeship to John Olley (q.v.) he was admitted a freeman of the Carpenters' Company on 20 October 1693. For many years he was Master Carpenter to the Board of Ordnance. He was Master of the Carpenters' Company in 1724 and 1726, and was knighted in 1727 after serving as Sheriff of London the previous year. He died on 13 October 1734, aged 72, and was buried in St. Olave's Church, Hart Street, where there was formerly a monument to his memory. From time to time Ogbourne is found acting as a surveyor in contemporary records, and his 'draught' for alterations to two houses in St. James's Place is mentioned in 1699. In 1694–7 he built the TRINITY ALMSHOUSES, MILE END, STEPNEY, for the Corporation of Trinity House, who also employed him in 1704 to erect a sea-mark in the Isle of Wight. Documents in Streatham Public Library show that he certified the bills for building STREATHAM HOUSE for Mrs. Howland in 1706. [Guildhall Library, Carpenters' Company records, MSS. 4329/11 and 15; A. Povah, Annals

---

* Designed for the Commissioners for building New Churches.

of St. Olave Hart Street and All Hallows Staining, 1894, 31, 115; Survey of London xxx, 514–15; Corporation of Trinity House Cash Books.]

OGILVY, JAMES (c. 1700–), was a Scottish master mason from a place in Morayshire called Pettinscar. In 1743, in the course of giving evidence in William Adam's lawsuit against Lord Braco, Ogilvy stated that as a young man he had worked at Mereworth Castle, Kent, Sir Gregory Page's house at Blackheath, and the church of St. Martin-in-the-Fields. He said that 'the works he has performed in the North-country consisted of repairing of Kirks and building one Kirk, also building and repairing Ministers' Manses, and putting up Ministers' Monuments'. The church he had built was at SPEYMOUTH, MORAYSHIRE (1732), and here he was 'Architect and Undertaker for the mason-work', though he and the minister had 'contrived' the building between them [Depositions of the witnesses adduced by William Lord Braco, 1743, 14–15].

OGLE, JOHN, of High Ongar, Essex, was an unsuccessful candidate for the office of County Surveyor of Essex in 1812 and again in 1816 [Essex County Records, Q/So 24]. He designed ASHWELL VICARAGE, HERTS., in 1814 [Lincolnshire Record Office, MGA 73].

OLDFIELD, HENRY GEORGE (–1791?), was the son of John Oldfield (d. 1788), a bricklayer of Wingham in Kent. He practised as an architect in Great Scotland Yard, exhibiting architectural designs at the Royal Academy in 1787 and 1788 and at the Society of Artists in 1790. In 1788 he was described as 'architect to the late Princess Amelia'. His only recorded work appears to be the rebuilding of the parish church of CHATHAM, KENT, after a fire. In 1786 plans were made by 'Mr. Oldfield of Scotland Yard' [Vestry Minutes in Kent Record Office, P85/18/1]. The church, completed in 1788, was again rebuilt 1884–1903. Oldfield had antiquarian interests, collaborating with R. R. Dyson in writing a History of the Parish of Tottenham High Cross (1790), and publishing in 1791 Anecdotes of Archery, Ancient and Modern. He is believed also to have been the author of a brief description of St. Giles's Church, Camberwell, printed without title or date. A drawing by him of the west front of St. Giles-in-the-Fields Church is in the R.I.B.A. Collection together with the elevation of a rusticated gateway [D.N.B.; Gent's Mag. 1788 (i), 271].

OLDHAM, WILLIAM (c. 1740–1814), was an architect and builder of Leicester. He was a prominent member of the corporation, serving as Mayor in 1783–4. He was married three times, his third wife, Ann, being the daughter of Alderman John Westley (*q.v.*). Oldham died at his house in Leicester High Street on 25 March 1814, aged 74, and was buried in St. Martin's Church. His son, Thomas Westley Oldham of Atherstone, was High Sheriff of Leicestershire in 1826 [J. D. Bennett, *Leicestershire Architects 1700–1850*, Leicester Museums 1968].

LEICESTER RACECOURSE, GRANDSTAND, 1770 [Bennett, *op. cit.*].

BRAUNSTONE HALL, LEICS., for Clement Winstanley, 1776 [J. Throsby, *Select Views in Leicestershire* i, 1789, 257].

LEICESTER, RECORDER'S HOUSE (BOWLING GREEN HOUSE), addition of attic storey, 1785 [Bennett, *op. cit.*].

LEICESTER, ALDERMAN NEWTON'S SCHOOL, Master's House, 1789 [Bennett, *op. cit.*].

LEICESTER, COUNTY GAOL, HIGHCROSS STREET, alterations 1803; dem. *c.* 1880 [Bennett, *op. cit.*].

LEICESTER, NEW HOUSE OF CORRECTION, FREE SCHOOL LANE, 1803 [Bennett, *op. cit.*].

OLIVER, JOHN (*c.* 1616–1701), was a glazier by trade, a surveyor by profession, and a master mason by virtue of office. He stated in 1687 that he had practised surveying for forty years, and from January 1685/6 until his death he held the office of Master Mason to the Crown, with a seat on the Board of Works. He was not, however, a mason by trade, and his will contains a small legacy to the Glaziers' Company. Payments to him in the St. Paul's Cathedral accounts for glazing confirm that this was his trade, and it follows that he must have been the John Oliver who gave a painted glass window to Oxford Cathedral which bore the inscription 'John Oliver aetatis suae lxxxiv, A° 1700 pinxit deditque'. This establishes his birth as having occurred *c.* 1616 and his age at the time of his death in 1701 as 85.

After the Great Fire of London Oliver was one of the four surveyors appointed by the corporation to supervise the rebuilding of the City in conjunction with Wren, May and Pratt. Like Jerman, he at first declined to assist in carrying out the detailed survey of the devastated area provided for by the Rebuilding Act, but offered to act without pay when Mills was ill during the summer of 1667. He was ultimately prevailed upon to accept the post, and was sworn on 27 January 1667/8. His surveys were more careful and detailed than those of either Hooke or Jerman, and many more of them contain plans of the site concerned. Oliver's name is frequently mentioned in connection with the rebuilding of the City churches, and, like Wren, he was the recipient of gratuities from more than one parish 'for his help in forwarding the building of the Church', or for 'coming to direct the building (of) the Steeple'. He appears to have been a parishioner of St. Michael's Queenhithe, a church

in whose records he is often mentioned, and to which he presented a bell in 1685. He also assisted in supervising the building of the Monument, and in 1675 he succeeded Edward Woodroffe as assistant surveyor of St. Paul's Cathedral, a post which he retained for over twenty-five years.

Little is known of his architectural works, but the records of the Mercers' Company show that it was he who supervised the erection of their new hall and chapel in Cheapside after the death of Edward Jerman in November 1668. He was also appointed surveyor to the Skinners' Company, and designed their Hall on Dowgate Hill which was completed *c.* 1670 [*Builder*, 14 July 1916, 26]. In 1673 he and Hooke prepared designs for the new Boys' and Girls' Wards at Christ's Hospital, which were built at the expense of Erasmus Smith. They also designed the Writing School in 1675–6. In 1683 Oliver was thanked for 'the great paines' he had taken in the erection of the new Mathematical School built in 1682–3 and attributed to Wren (*Wren Soc.* xi, 60 ff.). He also supervised the building of the Christ's Hospital Girls' School at Hertford in 1691–5, and presumably made the designs for this attractive work (*Wren Soc.* xi, 81–3). He was himself a Governor of Christ's Hospital and left money in his will for an annual dinner of roast meat for the boys. In 1676 he and Edward Pierce made designs for the woodwork of the Chapel of Emmanuel College, Cambridge, which were executed by Cornelius Austin [Willis & Clark, ii, 707].

Oliver was a cartographer as well as a building surveyor. He was the author of *A Mapp of the Cityes of London & Westminster & Burrough of Southwark, with their suburbs as it is now rebuilt since the late dreadfull Fire*, published in or about 1680, of engraved maps of the counties of Hertford (1695) and Essex (1696), and of the town plan of St. Albans in Chauncy's *History of Hertfordshire* (1700).

Oliver's will was proved on 18 November 1701 (P.C.C., 157 DYER). He left property in Ironmonger Lane and elsewhere in the City to his wife Susanna. He desired to be buried in the vault under the choir of St. Paul's Cathedral. His portrait in crayons was the last done by W. Faithorne, who died in 1691 (Walpole Society, *Vertue Note Books* i, 140). Aubrey, writing between 1681 and 1691 (*Brief Lives*, ed. Clark, ii, 10), recorded that all Inigo Jones's 'papers and designes, not only of St. Paul's Cathedral etc., and the Banquetting House, but his designe of all Whitehall . . .' were then in Oliver's possession. These appear to have been the drawings subsequently in the possession of William Talman, and later of Lord Burlington. A copy of Palladio's *Quattro Libri* (1570), with a MS. translation and Oliver's name on the title-page, was sold at Sotheby's on 29 November 1972.

OLIVER, THOMAS

[*A.P.S.D.*; *D.N.B.*; Walpole Society, *Vertue Note Books* ii, 60; D. Knoop & G. P. Jones, *The London Mason in the Seventeenth Century*, 1935, 6; T. F. Reddaway, *The Rebuilding of London after the Great Fire*, 1940, 108 n.; *Wren Soc.* xx, 152–3].

OLIVER, THOMAS (1791–1857), the son of a weaver, was born at Crailing, near Jedburgh, on 14 January 1791, and was educated at Jedburgh School. As a youth he went to Newcastle, where he is said to have been for some time in John Dobson's office. In 1814 he married Margaret Lorrimer, the daughter of a Kelso mason, and in 1821 he began independent practice as a 'land surveyor and architect'. Although best known in the former capacity, Oliver shares with Dobson the credit for much of the early nineteenth-century development of the city. In 1824 he designed for Dr. John Baird two houses at the junction of Northumberland Street and Elswick Court, which he claimed were the first stone-fronted dwelling-houses to be built in Newcastle for over a century. At the same time he was consulted by the Common Council in connection with the laying out of the new streets between Newgate and the Fickett Tower, and the new houses in BLACKETT STREET were built in accordance with his plans and elevations. For Richard Grainger (*q.v.*) he designed LEAZES CRESCENT and the adjoining houses and the handsome block known as LEAZES TERRACE, built 1829–34. He also designed the triangular VICTORIA BAZAAR, 1836–7, dem. *c.* 1965 [*The Topographical Conductor*, 1851, 65], warehouses on the banks of the River Tyne at HILLGATE, GATESHEAD, for Messrs. Bertram and Spencer, 1843–4, destroyed by fire 1854 [drawings in Gateshead Public Library], and the INDEPENDENT CHAPEL in WEST CLAYTON STREET, NEWCASTLE, 1850 [J. Latimer, *Local Records*, 1857, 277].

In addition to the excellent engraved plans of Newcastle which he issued in 1830, 1844, 1849, 1851, and (posthumously) in 1858, Oliver was the author of *The New Picture of Newcastle upon Tyne*, 1831, and of *The Topographical Conductor, or descriptive Guide to Newcastle and Gateshead*, 1851. On the title-page of the former work he is described as the author of *The Geographical Synopsis of the World* and of a *Topographical View of Great Britain and Ireland*. Neither of these works is, however, to be found in the British or Bodleian Libraries.

Oliver died at Newcastle in December 1857, leaving four sons, Adam (born 1815), James (born 1820), Thomas (born 1824), and John (born 1826). Thomas practised as an architect in Sunderland until his father's death, when he returned to Newcastle, afterwards becoming the founder of the firm of Oliver, Leeson and Wood. Among his works was the Greek Revival LON-

602

DONDERRY INSTITUTE at SEAHAM HARBOUR, DURHAM, 1853–5 [J. Latimer, *Local Records*, 1857, 327–8]. Adam and James both became civil engineers.

[M. E. Jones and H. L. Honeyman, 'Thomas Oliver and his Plans for Central Newcastle', *Archaeologia Aeliana*, 4th ser., xxix, 1951; L. Wilkes & G. Dodds, *Tyneside Classical*, 1964, *passim*; John Noddings, 'Thomas Oliver 1791–1857', unpublished dissertation, School of Architecture, University of Newcastle, 1971.]

OLLEY, JOHN, was appointed Clerk of the Works to the City of London on 14 December 1693, and resigned on 29 September 1711. He was succeeded by his son, Isaac Olley, a carpenter by trade, who retained the post until his death early in 1724. John Olley designed the EMANUEL ALMSHOUSES in TOTHILL FIELDS, WESTMINSTER, which were built in 1699–1701. His plans are preserved in the Guildhall Record Office [Rep. 106, f. 119]. These handsome almshouses were demolished in 1893. They are illustrated by R. W. Paul, *Vanishing London*, 1894, pls. i–ii. In *c.* 1700 John Olley and a bricklayer named Richard Smith built WATERSTOCK HOUSE, OXON., for Sir Henry Ashurst, Bart., dem. 1787 [Bodleian Library, MS. Top. Oxon. d. 385, f. 28 and MS. d. d. Ashurst d. 8]. In 1710 Olley was one of the three surveyors who reported on the condition of the City church of St. Mary Woolnoth [*Wren Soc.* xix, 35].

ORAM, WILLIAM (–1777), held the post of Master Carpenter in the Office of Works from May 1748 until his death in 1777. Horace Walpole says that he 'was bred an architect, but taking to landscape painting arrived at great merit in that branch. He was made Master Carpenter to H.M. Board of Works, by the interest of Sir Edward Walpole, who has several of his pictures and drawings' (*Anecdotes of Painting*, ed. Wornum, 1862, 711). According to J. Mulvany (*Life of James Gandon*, 1846, 214), he 'painted in the manner of Wooton, to whom probably he had been a pupil'. He designed the Triumphal Arch erected in Westminster Hall for the Coronation of George III in 1761, of which he published a print (B.M., Crowle Collection, iii, 172, and Bodleian, Gough Maps 23, f. 49ᵛ). He was known as 'Old' Oram, in order to distinguish him from his son Edward, who assisted de Loutherbourg as scene-painter to the Drury Lane Theatre [J. T. Smith, *A Book for a Rainy Day*, ed. W. Whitten, 1905, 98]. His will (P.C.C., 124 COLLIER) was proved on 17 March 1777. For his work as a decorative painter see E. Croft-Murray, *Decorative Painting in England* ii, 1970, 251–2.

ORRIDGE, JOHN, was the governor of the County Gaol at Bury St. Edmunds in Suffolk.

As a young man he studied the law, but found it uncongenial and at the age of 21 became a prison governor. In 1819–20 Bury Gaol was enlarged by William Wilkins (*q.v.*) on lines indicated by Orridge, who published the plan in his *Description of the Gaol at Bury St. Edmunds*, 1819. This work also contains plans of a prison made by him for the Emperor of Russia at the request of T. F. Buxton, M.P. In 1822 he and John Dobson competed for the design of the new County Gaol at Carlisle. Orridge's plans were preferred as those of 'a man of long experience' in the management of gaols, and were carried out between 1822 and 1825 under the direction of two local surveyors, Christopher Hodgson and William Nixon (*q.v.*). His brother Robert was governor of Cambridge Gaol, and in 1824 his son John Orridge junior was appointed keeper of the new Carlisle Gaol at the same early age of 21 as his father [Cumbria Record Office, Gaol Committee's Second Report, QAG/4].

OSBORNE, ROBERT (*c.* 1798–), was admitted to the Royal Academy Schools in 1816 at the age of 18, and was awarded the Silver Medal in 1821. He was a pupil of H. H. Seward, and exhibited architectural drawings at the Royal Academy between 1817 and 1822.

OVER, CHARLES, published in 1758 a work entitled *Ornamental Architecture in the Gothic, Chinese and Modern Taste, being above fifty entire new designs ... (Many of which may be executed with roots of trees) for gardens, parks, forests, woods, canals, etc., containing paling of several sorts, gates, garden-seats both close and open, umbrellos, alcoves, grottoes and grotesque seats, hermitages, triumphal arches, temples, banqueting houses and rooms, rotundos, observatories, ice-houses, bridges, boats and cascades ... from the designs of Charles Over.* Nothing is known about Over, but his book has been described as 'the most elegant, the most inventive (in a true rococo way) and in many details the most influential of the "Chinese" pattern books before Chambers' (B. Weinreb's Catalogue 17, 1966, no. 111).

OVERTON, THOMAS COLLINS, exhibited architectural designs at the Free Society of Artists in 1764, 1765 and 1766. They included a design for a Gothic pavilion, an elevation of the façade of St. Peter's, Rome, and designs for a large country house. In 1766 he published fifty plates of designs for garden temples, etc. Some copies of this work are entitled *The Temple Builder's Most Useful Companion, being fifty entire new original designs for pleasure and recreation ... in the Greek, Roman and Gothic taste.* others are entitled *Original Designs of Temples, and other ornamental Buildings for Parks and Gardens, in the Greek, Roman and Gothic taste.*

With the exception of the title-page the contents are identical. Plate 30 shows a Gothic temple 'built for Mr. Richards at Spittle Croft near Devizes', plate 34 a rustic cottage 'designed for Edward Goddard to be built near Cliffhill Copse, Wiltshire', and plate 41 a triangular building 'built for Mr. Maynard near Devizes'.

Overton was no doubt a member of a family of land surveyors of that name practising in Devizes in the eighteenth century (for whom see P. Eden, *Dictionary of Land Surveyors and Cartographers 1550–1850*, 1975–6, 196).

OWEN, JACOB (1778–1870), was born in North Wales on 28 July 1778, and received his training under William Underhill, a civil engineer much engaged in canal works, principally in South Staffordshire. Having in 1804 joined the Royal Engineers Department of the Ordnance, he became Clerk of the Works at Portsmouth. In 1832 he was tranferred to Dublin as architect and engineer to the Irish Board of Works, and remained there until 1856, when he retired. He died at Tipton in Staffordshire on 26 October 1870.

In England Owen designed two Gothic Commissioners' churches, ALL SAINTS, LANDPORT, PORTSMOUTH, 1825–7, and ST. JOHN, FORTON, nr. GOSPORT, HANTS., 1829–30, the latter in conjunction with his son T. E. Owen [Port, 132–3, 144–5]. In 1827 he acted as executant architect for a church at BEMBRIDGE, ISLE OF WIGHT, designed by John Nash [I.C.B.S.]. It became unsafe and was replaced in 1845. In Ireland he was responsible for MOUNTJOY PRISON, 1850, the CRIMINAL LUNATIC ASYLUM at DUNDRUM, 1848, additions to the FOUR COURTS and to the KING'S INNS in DUBLIN, and for several model schools and other government buildings in various parts of the country.

Owen married the daughter of his master Underhill, and by her had seventeen children. Five of the sons followed their father's profession: Thomas Ellis Owen (d. 1862) is the subject of the next entry. David Price Owen was in the Royal Engineers' Department. William Henshaw Owen practised as an architect and civil engineer at Limerick, Henry Owen at Waterford, while James Higgins Owen (d. 1891) succeeded his father as architect to the Irish Board of Works. One of the daughters married Sir Charles Lanyon, architect and civil engineer of Belfast, who was her father's pupil [*A.P.S.D.*, memoir by J. H. Owen; *D.N.B.*].

OWEN, THOMAS ELLIS (1804–1862), was one of the sons of Jacob Owen, clerk of the works at Portsmouth (*q.v.*). He became the pupil of an 'eminent' (but unidentified) 'architect and civil engineer' in London, and then went to Italy to complete his professional education. The 'architect' in question may have been the surveyor J. W. Higgins (q.v.), whose daughter Owen married soon after his return from Italy. Surveying and land valuation were certainly skills in which Owen was proficient, and they formed the basis of his later success as a developer in Southsea. His earliest architectural works were Gothic churches, some of which he designed in collaboration with his father. These were characteristic works of their period, but in his later churches (notably St. Jude's, Southsea) Owen endeavoured to develop a more 'ecclesiological' style, and his Greek Orthodox church in London was an essay in the Byzantine style.

Owen also designed one or two public buildings in Portsmouth, and was involved in railway and civil engineering works (e.g. in the Camber Docks), but he was chiefly notable as an enterprising and successful speculative builder who was responsible for some extensive and attractive residential development in Southsea, first (c. 1835–51) in the form of stuccoed brick terraces and Italianate villas in the area to the west of Grove and Palmerston roads, and later (c. 1851–60) of informal layouts of detached villas in various styles to the east of those roads.

By the 1830s Owen was a prominent figure in Portsmouth. In 1831 he became a member of the unreformed corporation, and after the Municipal Reform Act he was first a councillor, then an alderman and Mayor (1847–8 and again in 1862). He died suddenly on 11 December 1862 aged 58, and was buried at Milton in the same grave as his father-in-law J. W. Higgins. His practice was continued by George Rake, who had been his partner since the 1850s. In the 1870s Rake joined forces with A. E. Cogswell, whose practice is now in its third generation [Tony Preedy & Ian Stewart, 'Thomas Ellis Owen 1804–1862', unpublished dissertation, Portsmouth Polytechnic School of Architecture, 1972].

CHURCHES AND OTHER PUBLIC BUILDINGS

EAST STOKE CHURCH, DORSET, 1828–9, Gothic; chancel 1885 [I.C.B.S.].
FORTON, HANTS., ST. JOHN'S CHURCH, in collaboration with Jacob Owen, 1829–30, Gothic; rebuilt 1905 [Port, 144–5].
GOSPORT, HANTS., HOLY TRINITY CHURCH, galleries, etc., in collaboration with Jacob Owen, 1829–30; removed 1887–8 [I.C.B.S.].
WATERLOOVILLE CHURCH, HANTS., 1830–1, Gothic; remodelled 1969 [I.C.B.S.].
PORTSEA ISLAND CEMETERY, Greek Doric entrance screen, 1831; dem. [Preedy & Stewart, 16–18].
PORTSMOUTH, THEATRE ROYAL, HIGH STREET, alterations 1831 [Preedy & Stewart, 34–5].
HORDLE CHURCH, HANTS., rebuilt 1831, Gothic; rebuilt 1872 [I.C.B.S.].

HAVANT CHURCH, HANTS., rebuilt west end of nave, 1831–2; rebuilt 1874 [I.C.B.S.].
ALVERSTOKE CHURCH, HANTS., repairs and alterations, 1832 [I.C.B.S.].
FAREHAM, HANTS., HOLY TRINITY CHURCH, 1834–6, Gothic; chancel 1911 [Southern Daily Mail, 31 Oct. 1896].
REDHILL, nr. HAVANT, HANTS., ST. JOHN'S CHURCH, 1838, Gothic; chancel rebuilt 1853 [I.C.B.S.].
PORTSMOUTH, ST. MARY'S CHURCH, HIGHBURY STREET, 1839, Gothic; dem. 1921 [I.C.B.S.].
LONDON, FRENCH PROTESTANT CHURCH, ST. MARTIN-LE-GRAND, 1842–3, Gothic; dem. 1888 [exhib. at R.A. 1843; H. B. Wheatley & P. Cunningham, London Past and Present ii, 1891, 78].
PORTSMOUTH, ST. THOMAS'S CHURCH (now Cathedral), restoration of chancel in collaboration with Jacob Herbert, surveyor to Winchester College, 1843 [Builder i, 1843, 187].
PORTSEA, HANTS., ST. MARY'S CHURCH, KINGSTON, 1843–4, Gothic; rebuilt 1887–9 [R. Hubbuck, Portsea Island Churches, Portsmouth 1969, 9–10].
PORTSMOUTH, THE PORTSEA ISLAND UNION WORKHOUSE (now St. Mary's Hospital), with A. F. Livesay, 1843–5 [Preedy & Stewart, 133].
PORTSEA, BAPTIST CHAPEL, off KENT STREET, 1846; dem. [Preedy & Stewart, 134].
LONDON, THE GREEK CHURCH, LONDON WALL, 1850, Byzantine style; dem. [J. Timbs, The Curiosities of London, 1867, 227].
SOUTHSEA, HANTS., ST. JUDE'S CHURCH, KENT ROAD, 1850–1, Gothic; galleries, Bishop Ingham's Chapel and south transept added later by Owen [R. Hubbuck, Portsea Island Churches, Portsmouth 1969, 23].
HADLEY CHURCH, SALOP., 1856, Gothic [I.C.B.S.].

RESIDENTIAL DEVELOPMENT

The first phase of Owen's activity as a speculative builder began in 1834–5 with the development of the area north of Kent Road. Here he was responsible for QUEEN'S TERRACE, 1834–7, a terrace (dem.) in SUSSEX PLACE, 1835–7, SUSSEX TERRACE, 1837–8, etc. Later terraces to the south of Kent Road included NETLEY TERRACE, RICHMOND TERRACE and CLIFTON TERRACE, all completed in the 1840s. The largest was PORTLAND TERRACE, built 1845–6. The detached villas built by Owen in the neighbourhood of Elm Grove, Grove Road South, Albany Road, Merton Road, Nelson Road, Clarendon Road and The Circle are too numerous to particularize, but special mention must be made of his own house, DOVER COURT, PORTLAND ROAD, a Gothic mansion built in 1848–50 and now a school. For a detailed study of these developments see the dissertation by Preedy and Stewart cited above.

P

PACE, RICHARD (*c.* 1760–1838), was a builder and architect of Lechlade in Gloucestershire. Little would be known about him but for the large tradecard issued by him and his son in 1830. This gives small engraved views of twenty-seven buildings, described as 'a part of their designs which they have executed'. It shows that they designed and built a number of parsonages and small country houses in the neighbourhood of Fairford, and a few further afield. These are mostly in a simple late Georgian style, sometimes with fashionable Grecian or Gothic detailing. The information given on the tradecard is not wholly to be trusted, for one of the buildings illustrated, Dancers Hill, South Mimms, Middlesex (not 'Herts.') appears never to have been enlarged in the manner indicated, while at Broadwell Grove, Oxfordshire, the Paces appear merely to have been carrying out designs by William Atkinson. Richard Pace died on 28 April 1838, aged 78, and is commemorated by a monument in the churchyard at Lechlade. The business was continued by his son Richard Pace, junior. A lithographic copy of the trade-card is preserved in the Bodleian Library, together with some of Pace's business correspondence [MS. Eng. Hist. c. 298].

LONDON, premises in LEICESTER SQUARE* for Messrs. Gedges, 1788.

LONDON, house in Soho Square* for Robert Hervey Gage, 1791.

LUSHILL HOUSE*, nr. HIGHWORTH, WILTS., for William Peek, 1795.

BIBURY RACE STAND,* GLOS., 'for H.R. Highness the Prince of Wales, Noblemen etc. of Bibury Club', 1800; dem.

BOWDENDALE,* WILTS., for R. Broome, 1803.

WOODHILL PARK,* CLYFFE PYPARD, WILTS., added south-east range for B. Pinneger, 1804.

BROADWELL,* OXON., house for William Hervey, occupied by Mr. Large, 1804.

BROADWELL GROVE,* nr. BURFORD, OXON., for William Hervey, 1804, Gothic. A view of this house was, however, exhibited at the Royal Academy in 1810 by William Atkinson as executed to his own design, and there can be little doubt that Pace was merely employed as the builder.

SHRIVENHAM RECTORY,* BERKS., for Rev. Mr. Berens, 1805.

LECHLADE RECTORY,* GLOS., for Rev. Mr. Bennet, 1805; façade since altered.

BROADLEASE,* nr. CRICKLADE, WILTS., for E. Lovden Lovden, 1808.

BROUGHTON POGGS RECTORY,* OXON., for Rev. Mr. Goodenough, 1808.

FILKINS HALL,* OXON., stables for E. Colston, 1809.

COLN ST. DENNIS RECTORY,* GLOS., for Rev. Mr. Price, 1810.

LITTLE HINTON RECTORY,* WILTS., for Rev. Mr. Moysey, 1810.

KINGSTON LISLE,* BERKS., addition of wings, etc., for A. E. M. Atkins, 1812 (*C. Life*, 17 June 1971).

CHINNOR RECTORY,* OXON., for Sir James Musgrave, Bart., 1813.

COXWELL RECTORY,* BERKS., for Rev. Mr. Cleaver, 1816.

SALPERTON PARK,* nr. NORTHLEACH, GLOS., for J. Brown, 1817.

SHIPTON-UNDER-WYCHWOOD VICARAGE,* OXON., for Rev. Mr. Phillimore, 1818 (cf. Bodleian Library, Oxford Diocesan Papers, Faculty Register 1804–27, pp. 113–14).

SHERBORNE,* GLOS., STONE FARM HOUSE for the 1st Lord Sherborne, 1819.

ODDINGTON,* GLOS., house (?rectory) for Hon. and Rev. Dr. Rice, 1820.

WILLIAMSTRIP PARK,* nr. FAIRFORD, GLOS., Gothic lodge for M. Hicks Beach, 1822.

LITTLECOTE PARK, WILTS.,* stables and Gothic lodge for General E. W. Popham, 1822.

LECHLADE CHURCH, GLOS., repairing and refitting, including Gothic altarpiece and insertion of north and south galleries, 1823, all removed 1882 [A. Williams, *Lechlade*, 1888, 85].

COBERLEY RECTORY,* GLOS., for Rev. W. Hicks, 1826.

FAIRFORD,* GLOS., house (probably CROFT HOUSE) for J. Wane, 1826.

BURFORD CHURCH, OXON., refitted interior 1826–7; altered by G. E. Street 1870–2 [I.C.B.S.; cf. W. J. Monk, *History of Burford*, 1891, 38–9].

BROADWELL CHURCH, OXON., gallery and other fittings, 1829 [I.C.B.S.].

LANGFORD CHURCH, OXON., repewing 1829 [I.C.B.S.].

HATHEROP RECTORY (now SEVERALLS), GLOS., 1833 [Glos. Diocesan Records F4/1].

PACEY, JEPTHA, was an architect and builder at Boston in Lincolnshire. His plans for altering or rebuilding WIGTOFT VICARAGE, LINCS., dated 1817, are in the Lincolnshire Record Office [MGA 90]. In 1821 he designed WHAPLODE DROVE CHURCH, LINCS., in a classical style in conjunction with W. Swansborough of Wisbech [I.C.B.S.], and in 1826–7 the chapel at CHAPEL HILL, nr. TATTERSHALL, LINCS., remodelled 1884 [I.C.B.S.]. Several other churches said to be in his style are mentioned in Pevsner's *Lincolnshire*.

PAGE, JOSEPH (–1775), has been described as 'probably the first recognisable architect to work in Hull'. He was trained as a bricklayer and

---

* Buildings shown on the trade-card.

plasterer and completed his apprenticeship in 1740. For Henry Maister he designed MAISTERS HOUSE, NO. 160 HIGH STREET, HULL, in 1743. This showed the influence of contemporary Palladianism in a manner which was also apparent in two other Hull mansions, ETHERINGTON HOUSE (c. 1750, dem. 1947) and BLAYDES HOUSE, for both of which Page may have been responsible. His last recorded work was the redecoration of the court room suite at TRINITY HOUSE, HULL, in 1773–4 [*V.C.H. Yorkshire: E. Riding* i, 445–7].

PAGE, SAMUEL (1771–1852), was a builder, surveyor and architect with an office at 14 King's Road, Gray's Inn. In 1803 he exhibited a 'design for a gentleman in Kent' at the Royal Academy. In the same year he altered HAREWOOD HOUSE, HANOVER SQUARE, LONDON, for the 1st Earl of Harewood [Harewood archives]. In 1806–9 he rebuilt SAVILE HOUSE, NOS. 5–6 LEICESTER SQUARE, LONDON, as premises for Mary Linwood, an artist in needlework, in association with a surveyor called George Boyd. A Chancery suit which ensued over the payments due to Page became a *cause célèbre* which is said to have gone on for forty years, and involved an appeal to the House of Lords in 1841. Savile House was destroyed by fire in 1865 [J. Timbs, *The Curiosities of London*, 1868, 512; *Survey of London* xxxiv, 462–3]. In 1811 Page was responsible for alterations to GRIMSTHORPE CASTLE, LINCS., for the 2nd Lord Gwydyr (afterwards 19th Lord Willoughby de Eresby), assisted by his pupil Henry Garling (*q.v.*). He died at Dulwich on 2 April 1852, aged 80 [A. P. Burke, *Family Records*, 1897, 462–3; *Gent's Mag.* 1852 (i), 535; Foster, *Alumni Cantabrigienses, 1752–1900* v, 5].

Page was married three times, and had nine children. His two eldest sons by his first wife, Mary Flood, were Samuel Flood Page (1796–1854) and Philip Flood Page (b. 1798). Samuel began his career as an architect, but was subsequently ordained. Philip became a pupil of J. H. Good, from whose office he exhibited student's work at the Royal Academy in 1814, 1816 and 1817. In 1825–7 Samuel Flood Page and his brother jointly designed the Greek Revival PARTIS' COLLEGE at WESTON, nr. BATH [*A.P.S.D.*, *s.v.* 'Bath'; lithograph in Baker Collection, Bath Reference Library, vol. xviii, 29]. Samuel Flood Page also designed ST. PAUL'S CHURCH, MILL HILL, MIDDLESEX, 1829–36, in a cheap Gothic style with cement-rendered walls [*V.C.H. Middlesex* v, 35].

PAGETT, a family of Shropshire master masons who probably made their own designs. In 1714 Henry Pagett the elder, freemason of Bridgnorth, together with William Higgins of Pitchford, freemason, rebuilt the nave and west tower of QUATFORD CHURCH, SALOP., in traditional Gothic style

[contract in parish records]. The churchwardens' accounts of RYTON, nr. SHIFNAL, SALOP., contain what is doubtless a reference to Henry Pagett and his son, when they record the payment in 1710 of 12s. to 'the two Patchetts for Measuring the Steeple' after it had been built by Roland Richards, mason. The 'Mr. Paget, head workman', who laid the first stone of the new MARKET HOUSE at NEWPORT in SALOP. in June 1662 was probably a member of the same family [E. C. Peele and R. S. Clease, *Shropshire Parish Documents*, 1903, 247]. Several building-leases in Bridgnorth obtained by Henry Pagett at the end of the seventeenth century are in Shrewsbury Public Library (8663–5). A monument in St. Alkmund's Church, Shrewsbury, by James Paget (1702) is recorded by Pevsner, *Shropshire*, 1958, 257.

PAIN, WILLIAM, called in his publications 'architecture and joiner', or 'architect and carpenter', was the author of numerous architectural pattern-books published during the second half of the eighteenth century. They were as successful in popularizing the 'Adam style' as the earlier books of William Halfpenny had been in disseminating Palladian and rococo motifs, and nearly all of them went into several editions. Their titles, with the date of the first edition in each case, were: *The Builder's Companion and Workman's General Assistant*, 1758; *The Builder's Pocket Treasure; or, Palladio delineated and explained*, 1763; *The Practical Builder*, 1774; *The Carpenter's and Joiner's Repository; or, a new System of lines, etc. for Doors, etc., Staircases, Soffits, etc.*, 1778; *The Builder's Golden Rule; or, Youth's sure Guide in Architecture and Carpentering*, 1781; *A Supplement to the Builder's Golden Rule*, 1782; *The Carpenter's Pocket Directory*, 1781; *The Practical House Carpenter*, date of 1st ed. uncertain, 2nd ed. 1788; *The British Palladio; or, Builder's General Assistant*, 1786; *The Builder's Sketch Book*, 1793; and *List of Prices of Materials*, 1793. A selection of plates from his works was published in 1946 as *Decorative Details of the Eighteenth Century by William and James Pain*, with an introduction by A. E. Richardson.

Apart from his publications, nothing is known of Pain's career, unless he is to be identified with the William Paine of Bellyard, Temple Bar, carpenter and builder, who was one of the unsuccessful candidates for a District Surveyorship in 1774, when he was 56 years of age [Middlesex County Records, General Orders, No. 10]. In *The British Palladio* Pain was assisted by his son James, 'builder and surveyor'. This James Pain was the father of James, George Richard, Henry and Thomas Pain. All except the last became pupils of John Nash, who was instrumental in establishing James (c. 1779–1877) and George Richard (c. 1793–1838) as architects and builders in Ireland, where they had an extensive practice as designers of churches and castellated houses. Henry Pain practised as an architect and surveyor in London until the 1840s. William Pain, who exhibited architectural designs at the Royal Academy in 1802–9 from the same address (1 Diana Place, Fitzroy Square) as G. R. Pain, was presumably another of James Pain's sons. [*A.P.S.D.*; *D.N.B.*, *s.v.* 'Pain, James'; James Wicks, 'Narrative Pedigree of the Pain Family', *Blackmansbury* ix, 1972, 79–80.]

PAINE, JAMES (1717–1789), was born in Hampshire and was probably the son of John Pain, a carpenter at Andover. The baptism of 'James, son of John Pain' took place there on 9 October 1717. Very little is known about Paine's early life, but in the preface to the first volume of his *Plans*, published in 1767, he stated that he 'began the study of architecture in the early part of his life, under the tuition of a man of genius', identified in a footnote as 'the late Mr. Thomas Jersey'. Jersey (*q.v.*) is in fact an obscure figure, and a more significant influence on Paine's early life may have been the St. Martin's Lane Academy, where he is believed to have been a student, and where he would have come into contact with some of the leading artistic personalities of the time, including the architect Isaac Ware. Paine's first commission suggests that he had found favour in Lord Burlington's circle, for it was to act as clerk of the works or superintending architect at Nostell Priory, a large Palladian house in Yorkshire about to be built to the designs of Col. James Moyser (*q.v.*), a friend and disciple of Burlington's. The building of Nostell occupied Paine for some seven years. It established him in architectural practice in Yorkshire, and led, in 1741, to his marriage to Sarah, the daughter of a gentleman of Pontefract named Jennings. In the course of the 1750s Paine appears to have taken over the north-country practice of Daniel Garrett (*q.v.*), and between 1745 and 1770 he designed or altered nearly thirty country houses in the northern counties, including Alnwick, Chatsworth, Kedleston, Sandbeck and Worksop. His practice was never, however, confined exclusively to the north. From 1746 onwards he was again resident in London, and it was commissions such as Melbourne House, Whitehall (1754–8), Brocket Hall, Herts. (*c.* 1760–75), Thorndon Hall, Essex (1764–70), and Wardour Castle, Wilts. (1770–6), as well as his numerous northern houses, that prompted Hardwick's well-known remark that Paine and Sir Robert Taylor 'nearly divided the practice of the profession between them, for they had few competitors till Mr. Robert Adam entered the lists'.[1]

---

[1] In his introduction to Gwilt's 1825 edition of Chambers's *Treatise on Civil Architecture*.

Like many other Georgian architects, Paine aspired to a place in the Office of Works. In January 1745 he was appointed Clerk of the Works at the Queen's House at Greenwich, a post which he is said to have owed to the patronage of a former Surveyor-General, the Hon. Richard Arundell. In December 1746 he was promoted to be Clerk of the Works at the Mews at Charing Cross, but in 1750 exchanged this post with Kenton Couse for the almost sinecure clerkship of the works at Newmarket, which he retained until 1780. From 1758 onwards he was also Clerk of the Works at Richmond New Park Lodge. Paine's acceptance of these offices must have been due more to the hope of promotion to a senior post than to the small salaries which they commanded. With Arundell's help he did in fact aspire to succeed Ripley as Comptroller in 1758, but it was Flitcroft who got the job, and it was not until 1780 that Paine obtained a seat on the Board of Works as one of the two Architects of the Works, only to lose it two years later as a result of Burke's reform of the Civil Service.

In July 1755 Paine obtained a year's leave from the Board of Works in order 'to make the Tour of Italy'. Very little is known about this journey, and it does not appear to have played an important part in Paine's artistic development. Indeed, in the preface to his *Plans* (1767), he writes deprecatingly about the value of foreign travel to an architect, emphasizing the importance of practical experience rather than the pursuit of 'inconsistent antiquated modes' abroad. For him the publications of Palmyra and Baalbec were 'curious' rather than 'useful' works which 'furnish no new lights on the great parts of architecture, and are only valuable for the ornaments'. As for the ancient Greek architecture studied by Stuart and Revett, he dismissed it as 'despicable ruins'. As these passages make clear, Paine was no neo-classicist. His architecture is basically Palladian in character, but he was by no means a slavish imitator of Kent and Burlington, and his work is distinguished by several characteristic features that give it a strong individuality. Prominent among these were tripartite grouping (derived from the wings at Holkham, but frequently used by Paine for the principal blocks of his houses), very wide pediments (e.g. at Serlby Hall and originally at South Ormsby Hall), 'open' pediments with a vestigial strip of cornice at the base, and the hollowing of solid surfaces by niches. Like his rivals Taylor and Chambers he was one of the pioneers of the country house designed as a compact, centrally-planned villa, and he was an accomplished designer of staircases, of which the finest surviving example is at Wardour Castle. In interior decoration he was from the first attracted towards lighter rococo forms, and eventually devised a type of compartmented ceiling elegantly patterned into coiling

607

festoons which was offered as an alternative to Adam's neo-classical repertoire. Though charming enough (as can be seen in the Ballroom at Sandbeck or the Temple of Diana at Weston Park), it failed to hold its own against Adam's brilliant decorative schemes, and at Kedleston, Nostell and Alnwick Paine had the mortification of seeing Adam supersede him as the interior decorator.

Paine was for some years a prominent member of the Society of Artists of Great Britain, and many of his designs were shown at the Society's exhibitions between 1761 and 1772. In 1770, at time when the Society was shaken by the recent defection of a group led by Chambers, Paine was elected President, and shortly afterwards he designed for the Society the academy or exhibition-room in the Strand, of which he laid the first stone on 16 July 1771. The first exhibition was held in the new premises in May 1772, but the Society was heavily in debt and losing ground rapidly to the newly-established Royal Academy headed by Reynolds and Chambers. Paine resigned the Presidency in October 1772, leaving the Society to its fate. The traditional story that it was rivalry between himself and Chambers that led to the break-up of the Society appears to be unfounded, but Paine's loyalty to the older Society in 1768 may help to explain why he never became a Royal Academician. The only occasion when he exhibited at the Academy was in 1783, when he showed the designs for the three bridges that he built across the Thames. In 1767 he published a folio volume of *Plans, Elevations and Sections of Noblemen and Gentlemen's Houses . . . executed in the Counties of Derby, Durham, Middlesex, Northumberland, Nottingham and York* as the first instalment of his collected works. The second volume, illustrating a number of further buildings, was published in 1783. A second edition of the former volume was issued at the same time. A reprint of both was published by the Gregg Press in 1967.

In 1754 Paine built a new house for himself in St. Martin's Lane. At the end of the garden, facing onto Little Court, Castle Street, were three smaller houses, in one of which he established his friends John Gwynn and Samuel Wale. He removed in 1766 to Salisbury Street, Strand, which he was building as a private speculation on land leased from the Earl of Salisbury, and in 1773 acquired a country retreat at Sayes Court near Chertsey in Surrey. Here he assumed the status of a country gentleman, serving as J.P. for Middlesex and Surrey and in 1785 as High Sheriff for the latter county. His death took place in France in the autumn of 1789, in circumstances which have never been satisfactorily explained. According to the obituary in the *Gentleman's Magazine*, 'some months preceding his decease, finding the infirmities of age steal fast

upon him, and a family occurrence of a singular nature preying upon his spirits', he 'retired' to the Continent, where he died at the age of 72.

Paine's first wife died after only a few years of marriage, and in 1748 he made a second, and socially superior, marriage to Charlotte, youngest sister of Richard Beaumont of Whitley Beaumont near Huddersfield. By his first wife he had a son James (*q.v.*) and by the second two daughters, the younger of whom married Tilly Kettle the painter. Paine's principal pupils were R. W. Dowthwaite, Christopher Ebdon, John Eveleigh, John Kendall and John Sanderson.

A portrait of Paine by P. Falconet, intended as one of a 'set of artists', was engraved by D. Pariset in 1769; Grignion's engraving of another, by Paine's friend Francis Hayman, is prefixed to his volume of designs for the Mansion House at Doncaster, published in 1751. The finest portrait, however, is that of Paine and his son by Sir Joshua Reynolds, which was painted in 1764. It was bequeathed to Oxford University by the younger Paine in 1829 and now hangs in the Ashmolean Museum. There is a companion portrait of the second Mrs. Paine and her two daughters in the Lady Lever Art Gallery at Port Sunlight. Several drawings by Paine are in the Victoria and Albert Museum, and there are others in the R.I.B.A. Drawings Collection, the Soane Museum (xlvi, 9 no. 14, a design for a country house), and among the Fitzwilliam papers in Sheffield Public Library (unexecuted design for a grandstand on Knavesmire race-course, 1754).

[*A.P.S.D.*; *D.N.B.*; will (P.C.C. 260 BISHOP); sale catalogue of library (B.M., S.C.S. 24(6)); obituary in *Gent's Mag.* 1789 (ii), 1153; J. Nichols, *Literary Illustrations* vi, 373; *History of the King's Works* v, 1976, 90–1; Marcus Binney, 'The Villas of James Paine', *C. Life*, 20, 27 Feb., 6 March, 1969; Peter Leach, 'The Life and Work of James Paine', unpublished D.Phil. thesis, Oxford University, 1975.]

PUBLIC BUILDINGS

DONCASTER, YORKS (W.R.), THE MANSION HOUSE, 1745–8; attic storey added by W. Lindley 1801 [J. Paine, *Plans, Elevations, Sections, and other ornaments of the Mansion House of Doncaster*, 1751].

LONDON, THE MIDDLESEX HOSPITAL, MARYLEBONE, 1755–78; remodelled in nineteenth century; dem. 1928 [B.M., Crace views, Portfolio xxix, 16, engraved view signed 'James Pain, Arch^t.'; elevation by Paine in V. & A., 93H.19, 807].

NORWICH, ROMAN CATHOLIC CHAPEL, MUSEUM COURT, for the 9th Duke of Norfolk, 1764 [Arundel Castle MS. MD18, part 1, i, *ex inf.* Mr. Peter Leach].

LONDON, ST. ANNE'S, SOHO, WORKHOUSE, NO. 14

MANETTE STREET, 1770–1; heightened 1804 [*Survey of London* xxxiii, 190–1].

LONDON, ACADEMY or EXHIBITION ROOMS in STRAND for Incorporated Society of Artists, 1771–2; converted into Lyceum Theatre 1790, reconstructed as the English Opera House 1809; dem. 1815 [W. T. Whitley, *Artists and their Friends in England 1700–1799* i, 1928, 242].

BALLYMOTE, CO. SLIGO, IRELAND, scheme for projected market-house and other buildings for the Hon. Thomas Fitzmaurice, *c.* 1775 [Arthur Young, *Tour in Ireland*, 2nd ed. 1780, i, 270].

BRIDGES (PUBLIC)

WALLINGTON BRIDGE, NORTHUMBERLAND, for Sir Walter Blackett, 1755 [signed drawing at Wallington].

CAVENDISH BRIDGE, SHARDLOW, DERBYSHIRE (R. Trent), 1758–61; collapsed 1947 [Paine, *Plans* i, pls. 10–11, where it is called 'Welden Bridge'].

RICHMOND BRIDGE, SURREY (R. Thames), in collaboration with Kenton Couse, 1774–7; widened 1937 [Paine, *Plans* ii, pls. 82, 83; drawing in R.I.B.A. Collection].

CHERTSEY BRIDGE, SURREY (R. Thames), 1780–5; partly rebuilt 1894 [exhibited at R.A. 1783].

WALTON BRIDGE, SURREY (R. Thames), 1783; rebuilt 1863–4 [exhibited at R.A. 1783].

KEW BRIDGE, SURREY (R. Thames), for Robert Tunstall, 1783–9; rebuilt 1903 [contract and drawings in B.M., Add. Charter 16155; exhibited at R.A. 1783].[1]

LONDON: DOMESTIC ARCHITECTURE

ST. MARTIN'S LANE, NO. 76, and three small houses in LITTLE COURT, CASTLE STREET, the former for himself, the others as speculations, 1754; dem. 1843 [J. T. Smith, *Nollekens and his Times* ii, 1828, 222–3].

NORTHUMBERLAND HOUSE, STRAND, completion of Gallery begun by Daniel Garrett, for the 1st Duke of Northumberland, *c.* 1754–7; dem. 1874 [Alnwick Castle muniments U IV 2a, *ex inf.* Mr. Peter Leach].

WHITEHALL, house for Sir Matthew Fetherstonhaugh, Bart, afterwards MELBOURNE and now DOVER HOUSE, 1754–8. The portico and entrance were added by Henry Holland, who also

rebuilt the west front [*Plans* i, pls. 26–32] (*Survey of London* xiv, 60–4 and pls. 38–56).

ST. JAMES'S SQUARE, NO. 19, completed remodelling of house for the 2nd Duke of Cleveland, 1754–60, succeeding Daniel Garrett; dem. 1894 [accounts at Raby Castle, *ex inf.* Mr. Peter Leach] (*Survey of London* xxix, 161–3).

LEICESTER SQUARE, NO. 47, chimney-piece for Sir Joshua Reynolds, *c.* 1760; dem. [*Plans* ii, pl. 97]. Paine may have designed the gallery and painting-room built by Reynolds in 1760–1 [*Survey of London* xxxiv, 508–9].

SALISBURY STREET, STRAND, 1765–73. This was a personal speculation by Paine on land leased to him by the 6th Earl of Salisbury in 1765 [Guildhall Library MS. 1955]. The two end houses facing the Strand, illustrated in Tallis's *London Street Views*, 1838–40, pl. 19, were demolished in 1888, the remainder in *c.* 1923.

SOUTH AUDLEY STREET, LUMLEY HOUSE, alterations and repairs for the 4th Earl of Scarbrough, 1766 [accounts at Sandbeck Park, *ex inf.* Mr. Peter Leach].

ST. JAMES'S SQUARE, NO. 17, chimney piece for Sir Henry Bridgeman, Bart., 1766; dem. 1865 [Weston Park, Staffs., Bradford MSS 3/11A, *ex inf.* Mr. Peter Leach].

PARK LANE, house for the 9th Lord Petre, 1766–70; dem. [*Plans* ii, pls. 72–5, 89, 98].

PALL MALL, NO. 79, for Dr. William Heberden, 1769–71; dem. 1866 [*Plans* ii, pls. 76–8; *Survey of London* xxix, 378].

SACKVILLE STREET, NO. 28, chimney-piece for the 1st Lord Melbourne, *c.* 1770; dem. [*Plans* ii, pl. 100].

STRAND, NO. 59, COUTTS'S BANK, alterations for James Coutts, 1770–1, and for Thomas Coutts, 1780–3; dem. 1923 [Messrs, Coutts & Co., Private Ledgers 1769–71, ff. 114, 195–6; 1775–80, f. 273; 1780–5, ff. 17, 60, 125, 188, *ex inf.* Mr. Peter Leach].

MELBOURNE HOUSE (now ALBANY), PICCADILLY, chimney-pieces for the 1st Lord Melbourne, 1773; one removed 1803 and now at Renishaw Hall, Derbyshire [*Plans* ii, pls. 99, 100].

attributed: KING STREET, COVENT GARDEN, NO. 37, for John Lane, 1773–4 [*Survey of London*, xxxvi, 160–5 and pls. 69b, 82].

PALL MALL, NO. 105, alterations for the Hon. Thomas Fitzmaurice, 1779–80; dem. 1838 [*Plans* ii, pls. 79–81] (*Survey of London* xxix, 349).

COUNTRY HOUSES

NOSTELL PRIORY, YORKS. (W.R.), acted as executant architect for house designed by the amateur architect James Moyser (*q.v.*), for Sir Rowland Winn, Bart., *c.* 1737–*c.* 1750. Paine was left to make his own designs for the interior

---

[1] An engraving of a more ambitious design dated 1 January 1792 states 'The Building as executed is the joint Product of Messrs. James Paine Architects, who conducted the design, but much alter'd from their intended mode of finishing, as well as the proposed breadth of the road, to reduce the expense'. A copy of this engraving is exhibited at Kew Palace.

decoration, but this was never completed under his direction, and the principal rooms were designed by Robert Adam between 1765 and 1775 [Winn archives at Nostell; *Vitruvius Britannicus* iv, 1767, pls. 70–3] (*C. Life*, 16–30 May 1952).

HEATH HOUSE, nr. WAKEFIELD, YORKS. (W.R.), enlarged for Robert Hopkinson, 1744–5 [*Plans* i, pls. 61–2].

HICKLETON HALL, YORKS. (W.R.), for Godfrey Wentworth, 1745–8; enlarged *c.* 1775 and altered 1857–60 [Paine is stated to have been the architect in an eighteenth-century list of country houses in a copy of *The Builder's Dictionary* (1734) in the Metropolitan Museum, New York].

WILSFORD HALL, LINCS., east end enlarged for Matthew Lamb, 1749–51; dem. 1918 [contract and drawings in muniment-room at Melbourne Hall, Derbyshire].

CUSWORTH HALL, YORKS. (W.R.), alterations, including addition of wings containing Chapel and Library for William Wrightson, 1749–53 [*Vitruvius Britannicus* iv, 1767, pls. 88–9; W. Angus, *Select Views of Seats*, pl. xvi (1788); Leeds City Libraries, Archives Dept., Battie-Wrightson MSS.].

WADWORTH HALL, YORKS. (W.R.), for Josias Wordsworth, *c.* 1750 [Leeds City Library, Archives Dept., Battie-Wrightson MSS. A22, letter from Paine to Wm. Wrightson, 7 March 1750] (*C. Life*, 1 Sept. 1966).

SPROTBOROUGH HALL, YORKS. (W.R.), unidentified work for Godfrey Copley, *c.* 1750; dem. 1926 [Paine's responsibility for work here is referred to in a letter from James Norris to Samuel Popplewell in Leeds City Library, Archives Dept., Harewood papers, 1 July 1755, *ex inf.* Mr. Peter Leach].

YORK, work for the Rev. John Fountayne, Dean of York, *c.* 1750 (presumably at the Old Deanery, dem. 1831) [Paine's responsibility for work here is referred to in a letter from James Norris to Samuel Popplewell in Leeds City Library, Archives Dept., Harewood papers, 1 July 1755, *ex inf.* Mr. Peter Leach].

attributed: MILNSBRIDGE HOUSE, nr. HUDDERSFIELD, YORKS. (W.R.), for William Radcliffe, *c.* 1750; altered 1795–6 [stylistic attribution] (J. P. Neale, *Views of Seats*, 1st ser., iv, 1821).

BRAMHAM, YORKS. (W.R.), THE BIGGIN, remodelled for Mr. Allison, *c.* 1750–6 [referred to as a work of Paine's in a letter from James Norris to Saml. Popplewell in Leeds City Library, Archives Dept., Harewood papers, 1 July 1755].

FELBRIGG HALL, NORFOLK, built quadrangular service-wing, fitted up Gothic library, designed staircase, added bow window at north end of west block, and decorated several rooms, including the dining-room, for William Windham, 1751–6 [drawings and correspondence at Felbrigg; drawings in Sheffield City Library, A.P. 508, 5 and 7 (i)] (*C. Life*, 22 Dec. 1934).

SOUTH ORMSBY HALL, LINCS., for William Burrell Massingberd, 1751–6 [signed drawings and accounts in Lincolnshire Record Office] (*C. Life*, 26 March, 2 April 1959).

attributed: DINNINGTON HALL, YORKS. (W.R.), alterations and additions for Henry Athorpe, 1752 [stylistic attribution].

attributed: THE GRANGE (now Beckett Park College), HEADINGLEY, nr. LEEDS, YORKS. (W.R.), for Walter Wade, 1752 [stylistic attribution].

BLAGDON HALL, NORTHUMBERLAND, new south range for Sir Mathew White, Bart., 1752–6 [Northumberland Record Office, Ridley MSS., cash-book 1753–61, and drawings at Blagdon, *ex inf.* Mr. Peter Leach].

COWICK HALL, YORKS. (W.R.), alterations for the 3rd Viscount Downe, 1752–60, including remodelling of north front and internal alterations (the latter since largely destroyed) [*Plans* i, pls. 12–14; J. Killeen, *A Short History of Cowick Hall*, 1967].

RABY CASTLE, CO. DURHAM, alterations and repairs for the 1st Earl of Darlington, including suite of rooms in west range, Raby Hill House (Gothic) and the Home Farm, *c.* 1752–8 [drawings at Raby Castle, *ex inf.* Mr. Peter Leach; Alistair Rowan in *C. Life*, 1 Jan. 1970 and *Architectural History* xv, 1972].

WHITLEY BEAUMONT, YORKS. (W.R.), redecoration of Great Hall for his brother-in-law Richard Beaumont, *c.* 1752–4; dem. 1953–5 [Huddersfield Central Library, Whitley Beaumont Papers DO/WRC/127, *ex inf.* Mr. Peter Leach].

GLENTWORTH HOUSE, LINCS., east front for the 4th Earl of Scarbrough, 1753; façade mutilated *c.* 1950. This was a fragment of a grandiose scheme for rebuilding the house for which Paine's drawings, dated 1753, remain at Sandbeck Park, Yorks. Two of them are illustrated in *C. Life*, 7 Oct. 1965, p. 883, figs. 8–9; cf. *Plans* i, p. 12.

attributed: COXHOE HALL, CO. DURHAM, alterations for John Burdon, *c.* 1754; dem. [Burdon was employing Paine at Hardwick at the same time].

HARDWICK, nr. SEDGEFIELD, CO. DURHAM, the Temple, Banqueting House, Bath House, Gothic Ruin and other ornamental buildings for John Burdon, 1754–7 [E. Mackenzie & M. Ross, *County Palatine of Durham* i, 1834, 440]. Designs by Paine for a Banqueting House and a large mansion (never built) are in the County Record Office (D/Br.). The latter is illustrated in *C. Life*, 20 Feb. 1969, p. 406, fig. 1.

ALNWICK CASTLE, NORTHUMBERLAND, reconstruction of keep as residence for the 1st Duke of Northumberland, *c.* 1754–68, Gothic; destroyed *c.* 1854. Paine's work included the great staircase and the state bedrooms. Robert Adam, who succeeded him, was responsible for the saloon, drawing room and library [Alnwick Castle archives, *ex inf.* Mr. Peter Leach] (plans in *Castles of Alnwick and Warkworth &c.* from sketches by C. F. Duchess of Northumberland, privately printed 1823 and *R.I.B.A. Sessional Papers* 1856–7, 14).

SERLBY HALL, NOTTS., for the 2nd Viscount Galway, 1754–73; remodelled by Lindley & Woodhead 1812 [*Plans* i, pls. 37–40] (*C. Life,* 26 March, 2 April 1959).

GOSFORTH HOUSE, NORTHUMBERLAND, for Charles Brandling, *c.* 1755–64 [*Plans* i, pls. 15–25]. In 1880 the house was converted into a club and grandstand for the Newcastle Races, with a hotel in one wing and stables in the other. It was gutted by fire in 1914 and reconstructed internally in 1921.

BELFORD HALL, NORTHUMBERLAND, for Abraham Dixon, 1754–6; altered and enlarged by J. Dobson 1818 [*Plans* i, pls. 33–6].

CHATSWORTH, DERBYSHIRE, works for the 4th Duke of Devonshire, including the office wing, 1756–60 (dem. *c.* 1820), the stables 1758–63, and the bridge in the park over the river Derwent, 1760–4 [*Plans* i, pls. 1–9; Francis Thompson, *A History of Chatsworth,* 1949, 90–1; John Cornforth in *C. Life,* 18 July 1968].

attributed: HIGH MELTON HALL, YORKS (W.R.), rebuilt for John Fountayne, Dean of York, 1757 [stylistic attribution confirmed by Paine's documented employment by Fountayne at York].

AXWELL PARK, CO. DURHAM, for Sir Thomas Clavering, Bart., 1758; altered and enlarged by J. Dobson 1817–18 [*Plans* i, pls. 56–60].

STOCKELD PARK, nr. WETHERBY, YORKS. (W.R.), for William Middleton, 1758–63; enlarged 1895 [*Plans* i, pls. 41–6].

RAVENSWORTH CASTLE, CO. DURHAM, alterations for the 1st Lord Ravensworth, before 1759; rebuilt 1808 onwards [Alnwick Castle, Northumberland, MS. 121, Notebook of the Duchess of Northumberland: 'alter'd & improved . . . by the Advice of the late Ld. Leicester & Mr. Payne'].

ST. IVES, nr. BINGLEY, YORKS. (W.R.), for Benjamin Ferrand, 1759; dem. 1859 [*Plans* i, pls. 63–6].

SYON HOUSE, ISLEWORTH, MIDDLESEX, Gothic bridge for the 1st Duke of Northumberland, 1760; dem. [Horace Walpole, 'Visits to Country Seats', *Walpole Soc.* xvi, 36].

BYWELL HALL, NORTHUMBERLAND, enlarged for William Fenwick, *c.* 1760; west wing added 1817 [*Plans* i, pls. 53–5].

BRAMHAM PARK, YORKS. (W.R.), temple, now chapel, for George Fox, Lord Bingley, *c.* 1760 [*Plans* i, pl. 73]; *attributed:* the pavilions at

either end of the stables (*C. Life,* 1 Oct. 1921, figs. 5 and 7).

GIBSIDE, CO. DURHAM, chapel and mausoleum for George Bowes, 1760–6 [*Plans* i, pls. 67–9] (*C. Life,* 15 Feb. 1952); also interior decoration in house, *c.* 1756–60 [Bowes papers at Glamis Castle and in Durham County Record Office, *ex inf.* Mr. Peter Leach].

BROCKET HALL, HERTS., rebuilt for Sir Matthew Lamb, Bart., and his son Sir Peniston Lamb, *c.* 1760–75; also bridge in park 1772–4, and entrance screen and lodges, *c.* 1770–5 [*Plans* ii, pls. 53–9, 84–5, 90–2; designs for ceilings in R.I.B.A. Collection; design for entrance screen etc. at Raby Castle] (*C. Life,* 4, 11, 18 July 1925).

KEDLESTON HALL, DERBYSHIRE, for Sir Nathaniel Curzon, Bart. (cr. Lord Scarsdale), 1759–60. Paine superseded Matthew Brettingham, who had already built the north-east wing, and was himself superseded by R. & J. Adam after he had built the north-west wing and started work on the central block and quadrants. Paine's design, evidently conditioned by Brettingham's, was exhibited at the Society of Artists in 1759 and is illustrated in his *Plans* ii, pls. 42–52.

FORCETT HALL, YORKS. (N.R.), banqueting house for James Shuttleworth, 1762; dem. [*Plans* i, pls. 70–2].

WORKSOP MANOR, NOTTS., for the 9th Duke of Norfolk, 1763–7, never completed and dem. 1843 apart from triumphal arch, screen-wall and basement of north front. Paine had also been responsible for internal decorations in the old house, burnt down in 1761 [*Plans* ii, pls. 1–16, 96, 101; Marcus Binney in *C. Life,* 15–22 March 1973].

SANDBECK PARK, YORKS. (W.R.), remodelled for the 4th Earl of Scarbrough, *c.* 1763–8 [*Plans* i, pls. 47–52; Mark Girouard in *C. Life,* 7, 14, 21 Oct. 1965].

GOPSALL HALL, LEICS., garden temple for Charles Jennens, *c.* 1764; dem. 1835 [*Plans* i, pl. 74]. Drawings in R.I.B.A. Collection for internal decoration in the house (dem. 1951) were probably not carried out.

THORNDON HALL, ESSEX, for the 9th Lord Petre, 1764–70; gutted 1878 [*Plans* ii, pls. 17–29, 88; building accounts in Essex Record Office, D/ DPA 58; two elevations by Paine in B.M., Add. MS. 31323, U, V]. Though on a different site, Paine's house incorporated the portico designed by Leoni for the house begun by the 8th Lord Petre in 1733, but never completed owing to the latter's death in 1742.

WESTON PARK, WESTON-UNDER-LIZARD, STAFFS., TEMPLE OF DIANA, 'ROMAN BRIDGE', and chimney-pieces, for Sir Henry Bridgeman, Bart., *c.* 1765–70 [*Plans* ii, pls. 68–71, 86, 95, 97] (*C. Life,* 23 Nov. 1945, 26 April 1946, p. 760).

BAGSHOT PARK, SURREY, remodelled for the 3rd Earl of Albemarle, 1766–72; dem. [E. Suffolk Record Office, Albemarle MSS. R II/6–7, *ex inf*. Mr. Peter Leach; there are two designs for ceilings in the R.I.B.A. Collection] (Paul Sandby, *Select Views in England, Wales etc.*, pl. 66 (1777); G. F. Prosser, *Select Illustrations of the County of Surrey*, 1828).

BURTON HALL, LINCS., addition of new south range for the 2nd Lord Monson, 1767–71 [Lincolnshire Record Office, Monson family papers 7/45]. Paine's range was retained when the remainder of the house was demolished in 1959.

WARDOUR CASTLE, WILTS., for the 8th Lord Arundell, 1770–6 [*Plans* ii, pls. 30–41, 93–4, drawings by Paine in the Arundell archives belonging to Mr. R. J. R. Arundell] (*C. Life*, 22–9 Nov. 1930).

attributed: ST. PAUL'S WALDEN BURY, HERTS., north range for Mrs. Bowes, widow of George Bowes of Gibside, 1767 [stylistic attribution supported by Paine's documented employment at Gibside] (*C. Life*, 15–22 March 1956).

HARE HALL, ROMFORD, ESSEX, for J. A. Wallinger, 1769–70 [*Plans* ii, pls. 60–3].

MOOR PARK, SURREY, remodelled for Basil Bacon, *c*. 1770 [design for ceiling by Paine in R.I.B.A. Drawings Collection, K 3/18] (*C. Life*, 25 Nov. 1949).

SHRUBLAND PARK, SUFFOLK, for the Rev. John Bacon, 1770–2; remodelled by J. P. Gandy Deering 1831–3 and Sir Charles Barry 1848–52 [*Plans* ii, pls. 64–7; designs for ceilings in R.I.B.A. Collection] (*C. Life*, 19–26 Nov. 1953).

GAYNES PARK, UPMINSTER, ESSEX, for Sir James Esdaile, 1771–6; dem. 1820 [T. L. Wilson, *Sketches of Upminster*, 1856, 75].

CHILLINGTON HALL, STAFFS., bridge in park for Thomas Giffard, *c*. 1770 [*Plans* ii, pl. 87] (*C. Life*, 13 Feb. 1948, p. 328, fig. 7).

SAYES COURT, ADDLESTONE, SURREY, alterations for himself *c*. 1773; dem. 1925 [*A.P.S.D.*] (*Blackmansbury* viii, 1971, 83).

HAMPTON, MIDDLESEX, alterations to a house for James Coutts, 1774–5 [Messrs. Coutts & Co., Private Ledger 1772–5, ff. 166–8, Ledger 63, 1774–5, f. 497, *ex inf*. Mr. Peter Leach].

PONSONBY HALL, CUMBERLAND, built by Edward Stanley *c*. 1780, is stated by Col. J. Thornton in his *Sporting Tour through the Northern Parts of England etc.*, 1896 ed., 308 (written *c*. 1786), to have been 'built under the direction of that eminent architect, Mr. Paine'. The house is virtually a duplicate of Paine's St. Ives, built in 1759, and was probably copied from Paine's published designs without his knowledge.

PAINE, JAMES (1745–1829), the only son of James Paine (*q.v.*), was born at Pontefract in

August 1745. His father brought him up as an architect, employing him as clerk of works at Thorndon Hall. But he appears to have vacillated between architecture, painting and sculpture, exhibiting a mixture of paintings, water-colour drawings and sculptures at the Society of Artists between 1761 and 1773. In 1769–70 he visited Rome and following his marriage in 1773 he lived there for some years. His failure to settle down to a regular career did not please his father, from whom he was for some time estranged. The latter's death in 1789 presumably brought him some property, and it is doubtful whether he made any attempt to practise after that date. He was elected a Fellow of the Society of Antiquaries in 1771, and of the Architects' Club in 1791. He died at Sunninghill, Berks., in May 1829, aged 83. His pictures, casts and architectural books were sold at Christie's on 12 March 1830. They included Nicholas Stone's account-book, now in the Soane Museum, where there is also a copy of the sale catalogue. Nineteen volumes of 'Architectural Drawings and Memoranda by Mr. Paine of Ascot Heath' (close to Sunninghill) were sold by Puttick and Simpson on 12 November 1863, lot 1413. Among these may have been various drawings by Paine now in the Victoria and Albert Museum, including some made in Rome in 1774 (93 H.19), and others now in the British Museum (Add. MS. 31,323). The joint portrait of the two Paines painted by Reynolds in 1764 is mentioned above (p. 608). A half-length portrait of himself by Romney, described as 'a shew performance' of the latter's ability, is also mentioned in the younger Paine's will. He left three daughters. His son, James Thomas Paine, born in Rome in 1774, died in boyhood.[1]

The only building known to have been erected to the younger Paine's designs is a villa called BELMONT at MILL HILL, MIDDLESEX, for which the elevation, inscribed 'villa erected at Mill Hill for Peter Hammond, Esq.' is in the British Museum (Add. MS. 31,323, A³). According to a marginal note in the Bodleian copy of his father's *Works* ii, 17, the chimney-piece in the Saloon at BROCKET HALL, HERTS., was 'the Design and Performance of Ja. Paine Junʳ. A.D. 1771'. The drawings in the Victoria and Albert Museum include several designs for monuments, and the following monuments signed by Paine have been noted: to William Powell the actor (d. 1769) in Bristol Cathedral; to Lady Sondes (d. 1777) in Rockingham Church, Northants. (for which there is a drawing in the V. & A.); and to Mrs. Sarah Proby (d. 1783) in Chatham Parish Church, Kent. Paine's architectural designs, one of which is reproduced in *Country Life*, 5 Oct. 1967, p.

[1] A portrait of 'Master James Thomas Paine' was painted by Romney in 1776 and engraved by John Dean in 1780 (H. Ward & W. Roberts, *Romney* ii, 1904, 115).

792, fig. 6, are in a Greek Revival style quite different from that of his father. Among the Marquess of Salisbury's papers at Hatfield House there is a perspective by him of a scheme for laying out some land on Millbank, Westminster, for building (1787). His design for a bridge across Lough Foyle at Derry, exhibited at the Royal Academy in 1788, was published as an engraving in 1791.

[*A.P.S.D.*; *D.N.B.*; Rupert Gunnis, *Dictionary of British Sculptors*, 2nd ed. 1968, 286–7; *The Farington Diary*, ed. J. Greig, ii, 123, 208; iii, 210; v, 155, 190; viii, 26; will, P.C.C. 438 LIVERPOOL.]

PAINE, JOHN DAVIS (*c.* 1807–   ), was admitted to the Royal Academy Schools in 1824 at the age of 17. He was awarded the Gold Medal in 1833, and exhibited at the Academy from 1828 to 1843. From 1828 to 1832 he worked for Jeffry Wyatville at Windsor Castle, and then he was in the office of Benjamin Dean Wyatt [*C. Life*, 14 Nov. 1968, 1257]. He appears to have started independent practice from 57 Lincoln's Inn Fields in 1836. He designed a London terminus for the Westminster and Greenwich Railway Company (not executed), and the new bridge across the Water of Leith for the Edinburgh, Leith, and Newhaven Railway Company. He also designed the terminus of the St. Petersburg and Tsarsköe Selo Railway in Russia. His other works included CHRIST CHURCH, NEWARK-ON-TRENT, NOTTS., 1836, an unidentified church in Hampshire, 1839, the GRAMMAR SCHOOL at DAGENHAM in ESSEX, 1840, a residence for Henry Fownes at BATTERSEA, 1840, the LIGHTHOUSE on GOODWIN SANDS, 1842, and some VILLAS at OSTERLEY PARK in MIDDLESEX for the 5th Earl of Jersey, 1841–3, for all of which he exhibited designs at the Royal Academy. A volume of his engraved *Plans and Sections of the Proposed Westminster Bridge, Deptford and Greenwich Railway* is in the Bodleian Library (Gough Adds., fol. D. 28). The design which he submitted for the Royal Exchange competition in 1839 was engraved, and is illustrated in *London as it might have been* (Guildhall Library exhibition catalogue, 1975). He was still in practice in London in 1860, but the date of his death has not been ascertained.

PAINTER, J—, junior, of Emsworth, Hants., exhibited at the Royal Academy in 1807–8. His exhibits were: 1807 – the 'elevation of a villa now building near Portsmouth'; 1808 – a 'villa now building at Widley, near Portsmouth', and a 'Design for the intended improvement of an old building near Chichester'.

PALMER, HENRY (*c.* 1805–1830), was the son of Robert Palmer of Reading. He was admitted to the Royal Academy Schools in 1825 at the age of 20, and won the Silver Medal in 1827. He exhibited views of buildings in Reading at the Academy in 1828 and 1829. He died at Paris in 1830 'on his return from Italy, where he had been completing his education as an architect' [*Gent's Mag.* 1830 (ii), 574].

PALMER, JOHN (*c.* 1738–1817), was the son of Thomas Palmer, a successful glazier of Bath, who had been associated with Thomas Jelly, the architect and builder. John Palmer was taken into partnership by Jelly in about 1765, and was associated with him in offering to build a new Guildhall in return for a ninety-nine years' lease of the shops and houses which were to be included in the layout. The rejection of their proposal by the Corporation in 1775 occasioned a violent controversy between Palmer and Atwood, the city's architect, which was terminated only by the latter's death. Jelly and Palmer subsequently rebuilt the nave of St. James's Church, and there can, as Mr. Ison has pointed out, be little doubt that Palmer also designed St. Swithin's, Walcot, whose interior closely resembles that of St. James's.

In September 1792, Palmer was elected Supervisor of Bounds, and soon afterwards he succeeded Thomas Baldwin as city architect. In this capacity he completed the Pump Room and built the Theatre Royal in Beauford Square, largely from designs by George Dance the younger, though it appears that Palmer did his best to take the whole credit for the building.

Palmer died on 19 July 1817, at the age of 79, and was buried in St. Swithin's Church, where there is a memorial tablet. Although not an architect of the first stature, his works maintain the high standards of design and craftsmanship characteristic of eighteenth-century Bath [W. Ison, *The Georgian Buildings of Bath*, 1948, 36–7, 42–3].

BATH

ST. JAMES'S CHURCH, rebuilt nave 1768–9, with Thomas Jelly, Gothic; interior altered by Manners & Gill, 1848, gutted 1942, dem. 1957 [Ison 73–6; plan in B.M., Egerton MS. 3647, f. 158].

attributed: ST. SWITHIN'S CHURCH, WALCOT, 1777–88; spire completed 1790 [Ison, 76–7].

ORCHARD STREET THEATRE, remodelled auditorium 1775; closed 1805; since dem. [Ison, 101–2].

LANSDOWN CRESCENT, for Charles Spackman, 1789–93 [Ison, 169–70].

ST. JAMES'S SQUARE, for Richard Hewlett & James Broom, 1791–4 [Ison, 170–2].

attributed: SEYMOUR STREET and part of GREEN PARK BUILDINGS, 1792–6; partly dem. at various dates [Ison, 174–5].

THE ROYAL MINERAL WATER HOSPITAL, addition of attic storey, c. 1793 [Ison, 91].

ALL SAINTS CHAPEL, LANSDOWN, 1794, Gothic; altered 1878, dem. 1942 [Ison, 77–8].

KENSINGTON CHAPEL, LONDON ROAD, and adjacent houses, for John Jelly, 1795 [Ison, 78–9].

CHRIST CHURCH, MONTPELIER ROW, 1798, Gothic; chancel added 1866 [Ison, 79–80].

THE THEATRE ROYAL, BEAUFORD SQUARE, 1804–5, built by Palmer largely to the designs of G. Dance, junior; rebuilt internally after fire of 1862 [Ison, 102–4].

NEW BOND STREET, 1805–7 [Bath Council Minutes, 2 Jan. 1801, 4 Jan. 1803, 27 Feb. 1805, *ex inf.* Mr. J. Orbach].

PALMER, JOHN (1785–1846), was the fourth son of a humble family at Bishop Middleham, Co. Durham, where he was born on 28 January 1785. At the age of sixteen he was apprenticed to his uncle, a mason at Durham, and it was as a mason that in 1804 he obtained employment at Scone Palace in Perthshire, then being built to the designs of William Atkinson (*q.v.*). By now he had taught himself to read and write, and, with Atkinson's help, he 'learned the rudiments of architecture'. After two years in London (1806–8) he went to Yarmouth in order to assist in the building of the Naval Hospital, and while there married. In 1811 he returned to London, but in August 1813 he removed to Manchester, where he established a successful practice as an ecclesiastical architect. Himself a Catholic, he designed at least two churches for his co-religionists as well as several for the Church of England. His most notable work was the Catholic Church at Pleasington, a remarkably ambitious Gothic design of 1816–19 with a large traceried rose window and other elaborate decorative features.

Palmer had antiquarian interests which found expression in a book entitled *The History of The Siege of Manchester by the King's Forces* (1822) and in his *Guide to the Collegiate Church of Manchester* (Manchester, 1829). With Dr. S. Hibbert-Ware and W. R. Whatton he collaborated in writing a *History of the Foundations in Manchester* (1834), to which he contributed the detailed description of the Collegiate Church in volume ii. Some of his papers and antiquarian collections are in the Chetham Library and Manchester Central Library. Towards the end of his life he lived in Chorlton-on-Medlock, where he died on 23 August 1846, aged 61. [R. W. Procter, *Memorials of Manchester Streets*, 1874, 191–2; J. Gillow, *Bibliographical Dictionary of English Catholics*, 1885, v, 238–9.]

MANCHESTER, COLLEGIATE CHURCH (NOW CATHEDRAL), alterations and restorations, 1814–15 [Joseph Aston, *A Picture of Manchester*, 1816, 45 n., 56].

PLEASINGTON, LANCS., SS. MARY AND JOHN (R.C.),

1816–18, Gothic, for J. F. Butler [*Catholic Gentleman's Magazine* 1818, 146, 241–2].

BLACKBURN, LANCS., ST. PETER'S CHAPEL, 1819–21, Gothic [W. A. Abram, *History of Blackburn*, 1877, 352].

MANCHESTER, ST. AUGUSTINE'S CHAPEL, GRANBY ROW (R.C.), 1820, Gothic [S. Lewis, *Topographical Dictionary of England* iii, 1831, 244].

BLACKBURN, LANCS., ST. MARY (formerly Parish Church, now CATHEDRAL), 1820–6, Gothic; damaged by fire 1831 and restored by Thomas Stones, clerk of works, with advice from T. Rickman [W. A. Abram, *History of Blackburn*, 1877, 306; I.C.B.S.].

ABRAM, LANCS., ST. JOHN'S CHURCH, 1837–8, Gothic; rebuilt 1936–7 [I.C.B.S.].

ASHTON-IN-MAKERFIELD, LANCS., HOLY TRINITY CHURCH, NORTH ASHTON, 1837–8, Gothic; chancel 1914, top of tower 1938 [G.R.].

PALMER, ROBERT, was a surveyor practising in Westminster in the latter part of the eighteenth century. In 1771 he was employed by the Hertfordshire justices to survey the new Shire Hall at Hertford designed by R. & J. Adam, and in 1774–6 he supervised the building of a new County Gaol there [L. Turner, *History of Hertford*, 1830, 293; Hertfordshire Quarter Sessions Records, *ex. inf.* Mr. P. Walne].

PALMER, T—, junior, exhibited at the Royal Academy from 17 Abchurch Lane, London, between 1798 and 1804. In the latter year he exhibited 'Tolworth Farm, nr. Kingston, Surrey, the property of T. Stanton, Esqr.', presumably TOLWORTH COURT HOUSE, on the road from Kingston to Ewell, which was occupied as a farm-house in the nineteenth century.

PANCHARD, R—, of Bath, exhibited a design for a cathedral at the Royal Academy in 1804. In 1811 he was one of the architects who submitted plans for rebuilding the tower of Hungerford Church, Berks. They were not accepted [MS. minutes of trustees for rebuilding Hungerford Church].

PAPENDIEK, CHARLES EDWARD (– 1835), was the youngest son of Christopher Papendiek, a member of the royal household staff at Kew. He was a pupil of Sir John Soane from 1818 to 1824, and exhibited at the Royal Academy between 1823 and 1831. At the time of his death in 1835 he had a post in the Office of Works as a writing clerk. He was the author of a series of 24 coloured lithographs of Kew Gardens, published by Ackermann in about 1820, and of *A Synopsis of Architecture, for the information of the Student and Amateur*, 1826. [A. T. Bolton, *The Works of Sir John Soane*, 1924, Appendix C, p. xlvi; *History of the King's Works* vi, 185.]

PAPILLON, DAVID (1581–1659), was a
Huguenot refugee who was brought to England
as a child in 1588. He became an architect and
military engineer and is said to have 'built houses
in the city and suburbs of London'. During the
Civil War he fortified Leicester and Gloucester
for the Parliamentary forces. He established himself near Lubenham in Leicestershire, where he
built an octagonal house called PAPILLON HALL,
rebuilt by Lutyens in 1903 and demolished *c.*
1950 (see eighteenth-century drawing reproduced in *C. Life,* 15 Aug. 1957, fig. 13). In the
1650s Sir Justinian Isham sought his advice
about rebuilding Lamport Hall in Northamptonshire, which Papillon condemned as a 'structure
si fort repugnant aux regles de l'art'. His plans
for replacing it were not, however, adopted. He
was the author of *A Practicall Abstract of the Arts
of Fortification and Assailing,* dedicated to Fairfax
(1645). [A. F. W. Papillon, *Memoirs of Thomas
Papillon,* 1887; J. Nichols, *History of Leicestershire* ii, 1798, 708; Sir Gyles Isham, 'The Architectural History of Lamport', *Reports and Papers
of the Northants. Architectural and Archaeological
Soc.* lvii, 1953, 17.]

PAPWORTH, JOHN BUONAROTTI (1775–
1847), born in Marylebone, London, on 24
January 1775, was the second son of John Papworth (1750–99), the leading stuccoist of his day,
who was much employed by the Office of Works
in the time of Sir William Chambers. John was
intended by his father for a medical career, but
he showed an early talent for drawing which
attracted the attention of Sir William Chambers,
by whose advice it was decided to give him an
architectural training. He received instruction in
drawing from John Deare, the sculptor, and
acquired the rudiments of a knowledge of perspective from Thomas Malton. On Sir William
Chambers's advice he spent two years in the
office of John Plaw, and in November 1789 he
was apprenticed for three years to Thomas Wapshott, a builder, in order to learn the practical side
of his profession. Subsequently he worked for a
year at Sheringham's, a well-known firm of
decorators in Great Marlborough Street, and he
also assisted Michael Novosielski for a time. He
exhibited at the Royal Academy from 1794
onwards, and was admitted to the Schools in
December 1798. Owing to the outbreak of war
with France, he was unable to complete his training in the usual way by a foreign tour, and it was
not until much later in life that he went abroad,
and then only to Paris (1824) and other places in
Northern Europe.

In 1796–7 he supervised the building of a
house at Woodford in Essex for Sir James
Wright. The nominal architect was Philip
Norris, then upon the point of retirement, who
introduced Papworth to his client as clerk of the

works and allowed him to take complete charge
of the building. This employment continued until 1799, and brought him other commissions in
the neighbourhood. By the time he was 25, Papworth was well established in practice, and in
1803 he took up the freedom of the Clothworkers'
Company and accepted his first pupil, Samuel
Benwell, a nephew of John Plaw.

Papworth was a prolific architect, who was
much employed in the alteration and decoration
of country houses, in which he showed considerable skill. But his interests were not confined to
his professional work, and he acted as honorary
secretary to the Associated Artists in Water-
colours from 1808 to 1810, himself exhibiting a
work entitled 'The Hall of Hela', which had been
shown at the Royal Academy the previous year,
and was bought by Lord Tankerville. His 'Sketch
for an Altar-piece in the private chapel at the Seat
of a Nobleman', intended to combine in its
structure architecture, painting, and sculpture',
exhibited at the Academy in 1815, is now in the
R.I.B.A. Drawings Collection. He was a member
of the Society of Arts, and joined the Graphic
Society on its foundation in 1833. His facility in
drawing figure subjects as well as those of an
architectural character is shown by the nine volumes of his drawings now in the R.I.B.A.
Collection. His friends included John Varley,
Henry Pickersgill, W. H. Pyne, James Ward, who
painted his portrait, T. C. Hofland, for whom he
designed the architectural part of the latter's
picture of Jerusalem, and M. C. Wyatt, after
whom he named his younger son. He contributed
four illustrations (the breakfast-room, the dressing-room, the dining-room, and the architectural
part of 'the carriage at the portico') to Peter
Coxe's poem *The Social Day,* 1823, and he was
a regular contributor to Ackermann's *Repository
of Arts,* 1809–28. In it appeared *Select Views
in London,* consisting of seventy-six coloured
plates, reprinted under his name in 1816: in 1813
and 1814 a series of papers entitled *Architectural
Hints,* and in 1816 and 1817 a second series of
Architectural Hints, which were republished as
*Rural Residences, consisting of a Series of Designs
for Cottages, small villas, and other ornamental
Buildings,* 1818, 2nd ed. 1832. This was followed
by a series of designs for garden buildings, which
appeared between 1819 and 1820, and was
reprinted under the title of *Hints on Ornamental
Gardening* in 1823. Of the *Poetical Sketches of
Scarborough,* 1813, illustrated by the drawings of
James Green, he wrote fourteen of the twenty-
one chapters, and he was also the author of an
unpublished farce entitled *The Artist, or Man of
Two Masters,* and of some verses. In 1818–19 he
assisted W. H. Pyne in the descriptions of Marlborough House, St. James's, and Kensington
Palace for his *Royal Residences,* 1820, and in 1823
he wrote for Pyne's *Somerset House Gazette* the

article on 'Antony Pasquin and Somerset House', which was reprinted by Gwilt in the preface to his edition of Chambers's *Civil Architecture* in 1825. He also wrote several descriptions of buildings for Britton and Pugin's *Public Buildings of London*, 1825–8, and edited in 1826 the fourth edition of Chambers's *Treatise on the Decorative Part of Civil Architecture*, adding copious notes, and *An Essay on the Principles of Design in Architecture, with nine plates, illustrative of Grecian Architecture*. In 1803 he had published a pioneer *Essay on the Causes of Dry Rot in Timber*. His 'Explanation of the method adopted in 1820, to confine the lateral walls, then inclining outwards, of Trinity Church, on Clapham Common', was printed in *The Architect, Engineer and Surveyor* iv, 1843, 187, and his paper on 'The Benefits resulting to the Manufactures of a Country from a well-directed cultivation of architecture, and of the art of ornamental Design', read at the R.I.B.A. in 1835, was published in the first volume of its *Transactions*.

Papworth's skill as a designer procured him many commissions to make 'artistic designs' for furniture, manufactured articles, silverwork, ornamental glassware, etc., as well as for testimonials, such as the salver given to Serjeant Onslow, M.P., in 1816 for his parliamentary services. He designed the glass throne made by John Blades for the Shah of Persia, and an elaborate sherbet service for the Pasha of Egypt; the figurehead and other decorations of the 'London Engineer' paddle-steamer, the first of its kind to ply on the Thames below London Bridge; the covers of the *Forget-me-not Annual* from 1825 to 1830; three blinds with Greek ornamentation for the Phoenix Bank at New York, 1827; and a Gothic lantern for Eaton Hall, Cheshire. The monument which he erected to Colonel Gordon on the field of Waterloo was the first to be made in the form of a 'broken column', and other features regarded as characteristic of nineteenth-century taste could probably be traced to his designs. At a time when the improvement in the manufacture of glass permitted larger windows, Papworth was much in demand as a designer of shop-fronts, and he also built a number of warehouses, in which he made an early use of iron-framed construction. He was extensively employed as a landscape-gardener and town-planner. In the latter capacity he was responsible for Lansdowne Place and Crescent at Cheltenham, for the layout of the Brockwell estate at Dulwich and for the formation of St. Bride's Avenue in Fleet Street. Between 1825 and 1830 he planned and surveyed a proposed 'London Central Street' in continuation northwards of the Fleet Market, and a 'Greshambury New Street' from Cheapside to Queen Street – schemes which, although not carried out at that time, have since been largely effected. For William Bullock,

the former owner of the Egyptian Hall, Piccadilly, he made a design for laying out an estate on the river Ohio opposite Cincinnati, upon which it was proposed to build a town called 'Hygeia', but this was not carried out (for a description of the estate, see W. Bullock, *Sketch of a Journey through the Western States of North America*, 1827).

Between 1817 and 1820 he was commissioned to make three sets of designs for a palace to be erected at Cannstatt for Wilhelm I, King of Württemberg, who had expressed the 'intention to anglicize some of the Royal Domains'. Drawings of the entrance and south fronts of one of these designs were exhibited at the Royal Academy in 1823, and those of the east and west fronts in 1827. None, however, were carried out, but Papworth's design for laying out the park at Cannstatt in the English fashion was partly executed, and in 1820 he received a diploma conferring upon him the title of 'architect to the King of Württemberg'. One of his designs for the palace, now at Broomhall, Fife, is illustrated in *Country Life*, 29 Jan. 1970, p. 245, fig. 11.

Papworth's versatility was recognized by his contemporaries, and when in 1815 he produced a design for a 'Tropheum' to commemorate the victory of Waterloo, his friends hailed him as a second Michelangelo. He was thereupon induced to add 'Buonarotti' to his name. The drawing was, however, rejected by the Royal Academy.

In 1835 he gave evidence before Mr. Ewart's select committee on arts and manufactures, and in the following year he was appointed director of the Government School of Design, which occupied the rooms vacated by the Royal Academy on its removal to the west wing of the National Gallery. The detailed organization of the school was left in his hands, and he was assisted by his son John as secretary. The school was opened in May 1837, but a reduction in the government grant after it had been in existence only fifteen months necessitated his retirement in the interests of economy.

Papworth was one of the twelve architects who, on 2 July 1834, signed the resolution which led to the foundation of the Institute of British Architects. He was several times vice-president, and was made an honorary member on his retirement in December 1846. In January 1847 he was presented with a salver inscribed by a number of his pupils and other architects 'as a tribute of their respect and esteem for his talents as a distinguished architect, and for his worth as a man'.

Failing health led to Papworth's retirement from professional life at the end of 1846, and in February 1847 he left London to take up residence at Little Paxton, near St. Neots in Hunts., in a house designed by him many years before for his aunt Mary Papworth. Here he died on 16 June 1847. He was buried in the churchyard, near other members of his family who had been connected with the place. His portrait was painted by James Ward, R.A., in 1813; another was painted in the following year by James Green, and engraved in mezzotint by William Say. A third was painted in 1833 by F. R. Say.

Papworth was twice married: first, in 1801, to Jane, daughter of Thomas Wapshott, his former master; she died in 1809; and secondly, in 1817, to Mary Anne, the eldest daughter of William Say, mezzotint engraver, by whom he had two sons and one daughter. The elder son, John Woody Papworth (1820–70), architect and antiquary, is best known as the author of Papworth's *Ordinary of British Armorials*, a standard work of heraldic reference. His brother, Wyatt Angelicus Van Sandau Papworth (1822–94),[1] was the founder of the Architectural Publication Society and the editor of its *Dictionary of Architecture*.

Papworth's pupils included his brother George (1781–1855), who had a successful career as an architect in Ireland, Samuel Benwell, James Thomson, W. A. Nicholson, J. D. Hopkins, Samuel West, who became a portrait-painter, and Charles Edwards, who also gave up architecture. William Knight, George Guillaume, G. H. Stokes, and Thomas Latter were in his office.

[Wyatt Papworth, *John B. Papworth, A Brief Record of his Life and Works*, privately printed, 1879; abstract of his diaries by Wyatt Papworth, typescript in R.I.B.A. library; *A.P.S.D.*; *D.N.B.*; R. P. Ross Williamson, 'John Buonarotti Papworth', *Arch. Rev.* lxxix, 1936.]

The following list of works is based on Wyatt Papworth's privately printed memoir of his father, supplemented by reference to his abstract of the latter's diaries.

RAY LODGE, WOODFORD, ESSEX, for Sir James Wright, Bart. (as a residence for his son George), 1796–7; dem.

CHIGWELL, ESSEX, minor works for Mr. Wilkins, Mr. Noble, Mr. Hodgson, Mr. Richmond, Mr. St. Albans, and Miss Harrison, *c.* 1798–1802.

DENNE HILL, BARHAM DOWNS, nr. CANTERBURY, KENT, additions for Mr. Harrison, 1802; replaced *c.* 1870 by a new house by George Devey.

COBHAM LODGE, COBHAM, SURREY, for Col. Joseph Hardy, 1803–4.

LALEHAM PARK, MIDDLESEX, for Richard, 2nd Earl of Lucan, 1803–6, with additions 1827–30, and further alterations in 1839 for the 3rd Earl, including the model farm, stables, etc.

WANDSWORTH, SURREY, additions to residence of George Tritton, 1805–8.

CHIGWELL ROW, ESSEX, villa for Sir David Wedderburn, Bart., 1807–10.

WOOLWICH RECTORY, KENT, for the Rev. H. Fraser, 1807–11; dem.

FISHERWICK PARK, STAFFS., alterations for Lord Spencer Chichester, *c.* 1810; dem. 1816.

YEADING BRIDGE, MIDDLESEX, 1812.

WHITE KNIGHTS, BERKS., rustic seats, etc., for the Marquess of Blandford, 1815–1816 (Mrs. Hofland, *A Descriptive Account of the Mansion and Gardens of White-Knights*, 1819).

FYFIELD HOUSE, ESSEX, additions for George Dorrien, 1815–17.

WATERLOO, BELGIUM, monument to Col. Gordon, 1815.

KNEBWORTH, HERTS., mausoleum for Mrs. Bulwer Lytton, 1817 (executed by Whitelaw).

GWYNNE HOUSE, WOODFORD BRIDGE, ESSEX (now Dr. Barnardo's Home), large additions for H. Burmester, 1816.

CLAREMONT, SURREY, assisted J. W. Hiort in designing (1816) many of the works for Prince Leopold and Princess Charlotte, including the conservatories, entrance gates, cottages, coach-houses, stabling, etc., and the Gothic summer-house which was eventually remodelled as a memorial to the Princess after her death in Nov. 1817.

FYFIELD CHURCH, ESSEX, repairs and wooden steeple, 1817.

HARESFOOT, nr. BERKHAMSTEAD, HERTS., for Thos. Dorrien, 1817–19; dem. *c.* 1965.

ST. JULIAN'S, nr. SEVENOAKS, KENT, for Robert Herries, 1818–20, Gothic; enlarged by Sir James Pennethorne, 1835–7.

ALTON TOWERS, STAFFS., bridge of seven arches, Grecian and Gothic temples, park entrance, garden seats, etc., for the Earl of Shrewsbury, 1818–22.

TAMWORTH, additions to Dr. Woody's Lunatic Asylum, 1819.

NORTH END, HAMMERSMITH, MIDDLESEX, remodelled for Wm. Jones, 1819–30.

LEIGHAM COURT, STREATHAM, for J. G. Fuller, 1820–2, and added to it a second and larger house in 1823–44; dem.

GRANADA, SPAIN, monument to Mrs. Duncan, wife of Thomas Duncan, *c.* 1829.

BALHAM HILL, SURREY, redecorated residence of James Morrison, 1821–3.

KEW PRIORY, SURREY, additions and landscape-gardening for Miss Dougherty, 1823.

HOW HATCH, nr. BRENTWOOD, ESSEX, landscape-gardening for W. Willan, 1824.

MONNEY HILL HOUSE, RICKMANSWORTH, HERTS., landscape-gardening for Thos. Fellows, 1824.

CLAPTON, MIDDLESEX, landscape-gardening for Wm. Amory, 1825.

BRAMPTON PARK, HUNTS., extensive alterations for Lady Olivia Sparrow, 1825; destroyed by fire 1907 (*V.C.H. Hunts.* iii, 12–13).

---

[1] Andrew Van Sandau, of 34 Dowgate Hill, was one of J. B. Papworth's clients in the 1820s. Was he Wyatt Papworth's godfather?

BRAMPTON SCHOOLS, HUNTS., for Lady Olivia Sparrow, c. 1825.

GRAFHAM SCHOOL, HUNTS., for Lady Olivia Sparrow, c. 1825.

HOLLY LODGE, HIGHGATE, MIDDLESEX, landscape-gardening, including a conservatory and new room, for Mrs. Coutts, afterwards Duchess of St. Albans, 1825.

HAREFIELD GROVE, MIDDLESEX, landscape-gardening for W. Flower, 1826.

TURRET HOUSE, SOUTH LAMBETH, SURREY, landscape-gardening for William Heseltine, 1826.

DULWICH, laid out Brockwell estate for John Blades, 1825–30; built two houses in Brockwell Terrace for John Blades, 1828–30; dem. 1908; altered or repaired Brockwell Hall for John Blades, 1824–9; designed Brockwell (later Clarence) Lodge for Mrs. Emma Murray, 1825–6; dem. [Survey of London xxvi, 161–4].

CHELTENHAM, GLOS., designed MONTPELLIER PUMP ROOM (ROTUNDA) and laid out MONTPELLIER GARDENS, for Pearson Thompson, 1825–6.

CHELTENHAM, GLOS., designed LANSDOWNE PLACE and CRESCENT for R. W. & C. Jearrad, 1825–9.

CHELTENHAM, GLOS., a 'large detached house' for Dr. John Shoolbred, c. 1824; a terrace for Robert Morris, probably on the north side of Suffolk Square, 1825; Charlton House for Capt. F. Cregoe, 1825; a house near St. John's Chapel for Capt. Daniel Capel, 1828.

CHELTENHAM, GLOS., completed ST. JAMES'S CHURCH, SUFFOLK SQUARE (begun by E. Jenkins), 1826–32, Gothic.

CHELTENHAM, GLOS., ST. JOHN'S CHURCH or BERKELEY STREET CHAPEL, for the Rev. W. Spencer Phillips, 1827–9; dem. 1967.

HUNTLY, ABERDEENSHIRE, design for a Court House for the Marquess of Huntly, 1826 (not carried out).

DOVER, KENT, planned Maison Dieu estate for William Taswell, 1827 (not carried out).

DENFORD HOUSE, BERKS., drawing-room, offices, lodge, entrance gates, dairy, etc., for G. H. Cherry, 1827–8.

BLACKHEATH, landscape-gardening for R. Paterson, 1828.

PRICKLER'S HILL, nr. FINCHLEY, MIDDLESEX, new wing for Thos. Wyatt, 1828–32.

LITTLE GROVE, EAST BARNET, HERTS., extensive alterations and farm buildings for Frederick Cass, 1828–46; dem. c. 1927.

CLAPHAM, SURREY, SOUTH SIDE, added picture gallery, saloon, and stables for John Allnutt, 1829–33; dem. c. 1863 (E. E. F. Smith, Clapham, 1975, 71–2).

NEVILL HOLT, LEICS., alterations for Charles Nevill, 1829–32, Tudor Gothic.

TWICKENHAM PARK, MIDDLESEX, landscape-gardening, with conservatory, aviary, etc., for Thos. Todd, 1829.

FONTHILL, WILTS., lodges, entrance gateway, and other alterations for James Morrison, 1829–42.

PARK HILL, STREATHAM, SURREY, billiard-room, conservatories, lodge and garden buildings, etc., for William Leaf, 1830–41.

HOLY TRINITY CHURCH, CLAPHAM COMMON, repairs, 1829, including new foundations and screwing up lateral walls to upright, as described in Architect, Engineer and Surveyor, 1843, p. 187.

CRANBURY PARK, HANTS., interior of library, fountain and other works for Thomas Chamberlayne, c. 1830 (C. Life, 15 Nov. 1956).

DENFORD CHURCH, BERKS., for G. H. Cherry, 1830–4, Gothic; dem. c. 1957.

ST. JOHN'S WOOD, house and cottage for Edward May, c. 1830.

FROGNAL, HAMPSTEAD, large additions to two houses for C. P. Sullivan, c. 1830.

CHICKLADE CHURCH, WILTS., 1832, Gothic.

DULWICH, SURREY, stables and landscape-gardening for James Hannen, 1832.

CROUCH END, nr. HORNSEY, pavilion for J. G. Booth, 1832.

KIRBY HALL, YORKS. (W.R.), landscape-gardening and conservatory for R. J. Thompson, 1833.

CALLY, KIRKCUDBRIGHTSHIRE, remodelled house for Alexander Murray, 1833–7.

HILFIELD, YATELEY, HANTS., alterations and additions for Capt. H. B. Mason, R.N., 1834.

KILLIBEGS, CO. DONEGAL, IRELAND, chapel, stables, and alterations to house for Alexander Murray, 1834–9.

ORNHAMS HALL, nr. BOROUGHBRIDGE, YORKS., house and farm buildings for Geo. Crow, 1835–6.

CLAPHAM COMMON, SURREY, landscape-gardening and conservatory for J. T. Betts, 1835–9.

HERNE HILL, works for Mrs. Simpson, 1835.

ALEXANDRIA, EGYPT, RAILWAY STATION for Messrs. Galloway, engineers, 1835.

ALEXANDRIA, EGYPT, monument to Thomas Galloway Bey, 1837.

GLASSERTON CHURCH, WIGTOWNSHIRE, tower 1836 [B. Burke, Visitation of Seats, ser, i, vol. ii, 1853, 91; S.R.O., RHP 7697, no. 2, drawing probably by J.B.P.].

ORLEANS HOUSE, TWICKENHAM, MIDDLESEX, restored for Alexander Murray, 1837–9; dem. 1927.

CHURCH LANE, KENSINGTON, additions to house for Princess Sophia of Gloucester, 1838.

BASILDON PARK, BERKS., completion of interior, including the principal ceilings, etc., and the cottages, octagonal lodges, entrance gates, park farm, etc., for James Morrison, 1839–44.

PENSHURST, KENT, added attic storey to Mrs. Yates's house, c. 1840.

CASTLEBAR, CO. MAYO, IRELAND, farmyard,

bailiff's cottage etc. for the 3rd Earl of Lucan, c. 1840–4.

MORDEN, SURREY, stabling, etc., for the Rev. R. Garth, 1841.

BEDDINGTON RECTORY, SURREY, landscape-gardening for the Rev. James Hamilton, 1842.

HYLANDS, ESSEX, alterations for John Attwood, 1842.

CHOBHAM LODGE, SURREY, repairs for Sir Denis le Marchant, 1842.

CLAPHAM PARK, house in King's Road for J. E. B. Stevenson, 1844–6.

FIR GROVE, WEYBRIDGE, SURREY, lodges and other buildings for Sir John Easthope, 1844.

HENDON, MIDDLESEX, alterations to house for George Morant.

BEAULIEU LODGE, WINCHMORE HILL, MIDDLESEX, landscape-gardening for Frederick Cass.

CHORLEY WOOD, RICKMANSWORTH, HERTS., landscape-gardening for John Barnes.

KENSAL GREEN CEMETERY, Galloway family monument, 1838, and monument to Sir Charles Grey, Bart., 1839.

LONDON

STRAND, No. 101, showroom for R. Ackermann, 1812, and new premises at corner of Beaufort Buildings, 1826 (*Repository of Arts*, 3rd ser., ix, 363).

NEW BOND STREET, No. 88, shop-front for George Morant, 1817–19.

PICCADILLY, EGYPTIAN HALL, gallery for William Bullock, 1819; dem. 1905 (Ackermann, *Repository of Arts*, 2nd ser., viii, 153).

MARYLEBONE, porch and verandah of house at corner of Brook Street for John Braithwaite, c. 1820–9; dem.

BOODLE'S CLUB, ST. JAMES'S, Reading Room and other alterations, 1821; Dining Room (now kitchen), 1833–4 [*Survey of London* xxx, 443].

WEST STREET, W. SMITHFIELD, factory for Alexander Galloway, 1821–2, enlarged 1835 and 1840; dem.

BERKELEY SQUARE, No. 24, repairs for Wm. Snell, 1822–3.

YORK STAIRS, WATERGATE, repairs, 1822–3.

LUDGATE HILL, No. 8, façade to Messrs. F. & R. Sparrow's Tea Warehouse, 1822–3, Chinese style; dem.

COVENTRY STREET, No. 17, shop-front for Messrs. Clarkson & Turner, 1822–7.

RICHMOND GARDENS, WHITEHALL, house for J. Irvine, 1824; dem.

LUDGATE HILL, No. 5, shop-front for John Blades, 1824–30.

MILTON STREET, warehouses for Messrs. Morrison & Co., 1824–35; dem. 194–.

LEICESTER SQUARE, No. 47, interior arrangement and addition of lecture theatre for the Western

Literary and Scientific Institution, 1826; dem. 1937 (cf. *Survey of London* xxxiv, 510–11).

ST. BRIDE'S AVENUE, FLEET STREET, 1825–30 (J. Elmes, *Metropolitan Improvements*, 1831, 149 and plate).

FORE STREET, alterations, etc., to premises of Messrs. Morrison & Co., 1829–30.

BELGRAVE ROAD, workshop for Messrs. Wm. & Edward Snell, 1829–35.

GREAT CORAM STREET, No. 57, shop-front for — Dutton, 1829.

HOLBORN HILL, No. 94, 'gin-palace' for Messrs. Thompson & Fearon & Co., 1829–32.

CHARLES STREET, No. 10, reconstructed façade for John Howell, 1833–8.

GRAY'S INN ROAD, workshops for Messrs. G. & T. Seddon, cabinet-makers, 1830–2; afterwards used as a hospital.

HARLEY STREET, No. 57, redecorated interior, including library, for James Morrison, 1831–3.

ACADEMY COURT, CHANCERY LANE, two houses for Alexander Galloway, 1832; dem.

FRITH STREET, SOHO, shop-front for Messrs. Sewell & Cross, linen drapers, 1832.

CHEAPSIDE, shop-front for Messrs. Collard & Co., 1834.

NO. 2 SEAMORE PLACE, PARK LANE, alterations, including iron verandahs, for the 1st Earl of Ducie, 1835.

GLOUCESTER LODGE (12, GLOUCESTER GATE), REGENT'S PARK, additions for J. Cryder, 1836.

OXFORD STREET, No. 314, shop-front for Messrs. Duppa & Collins, c. 1840.

WHITE'S CLUB HOUSE, ST. JAMES'S, repairs and decorations for Henry Raggett, 1842–3.

PORTLAND PLACE, No. 56, repairs and alterations for Sir Roger Palmer, Bart., 1843.

WEYMOUTH STREET, No. 41, work for George Dorrien.

PORTMAN SQUARE, No. 1, work for Thomas Dorrien.

FINCH LANE, premises for Messrs. Dorrien, Magens & Co.

WESTMINSTER BRIDGE ROAD, shop-front for Messrs. Collinge.

HOLBORN, No. 69, factory for Alexander Galloway.

PICCADILLY, shop-fronts to Nos. 29 and 117.

MANSFIELD STREET, PORTLAND PLACE, improvements to mansion for the 2nd Marquess of Sligo.

FLEET STREET, No. 43, alterations for Joseph Butterworth.

GLOUCESTER TERRACE, REGENT'S PARK, No. 4, conservatory for Mrs. T. Wyatt.

PARKE, HENRY (?1792–1835), was the son of John Parke, an eminent oboist. He was intended for the Bar, and studied for a time under a special pleader. But owing to an impediment in his speech he decided to give up the law, and after taking up several subjects without pursuing them, he developed a strong interest in architecture and was apprenticed to Sir John Soane in 1814. He became proficient in mathematics, geometry, mechanics and drawing, and some of the finest of the diagrams which were used by Soane to illustrate his lectures were made by Parke. These are still preserved in Sir John Soane's Museum, together with other drawings made by him at this time. He was awarded five Silver Medals by the Society of Arts, and in 1812 received their Gold Medal for a sea-piece.

Between 1820 and 1824 he travelled in Italy, Sicily and Egypt, ascending the Nile in 1824 with his fellow-student J. J. Scoles. In 1829 he published a 'Map of Nubia, comprising the country between the first and second cataracts of the Nile', showing the positions of all the temples, rock-cut tombs, and other ancient monuments on the banks of the river. At Rome and elsewhere in Italy, he worked with Catherwood, T. L. Donaldson, and others, laboriously measuring the buildings of antiquity as well as those of the Renaissance. On returning to England, he worked up his sketches, and made a large number of fine architectural drawings, many of which were presented to the R.I.B.A. Library by his widow. Some drawings of Pompeii by Parke are in the Victoria and Albert Museum. He frequently exhibited at the Royal Academy from 1815 onwards, but most of his exhibits were of a topographical character, and he appears never to have practised as an architect. 'Diffident and retiring', he was 'ill fitted for the jarring warfare of life, and consequently was little known beyond the immediate circle of his friends'. He was a member of the committee of architects who, in 1835, presented a Gold Medal to Sir John Soane, and was largely responsible for the design of the medal, from the die of which the Soane medallion awarded annually by the R.I.B.A. is reproduced. He built a house in Queen Square, Westminster, facing St. James's Park, where he died on 5 May 1835, aged about 43. Many of Parke's works in oil and water-colour were sold at Sotheby's in May 1836. In 1838 a bust of Parke was presented to the R.I.B.A. by J. J. Scoles.

[*A.P.S.D.*; *D.N.B.*; *Gent's Mag.* 1835 (ii), 325, 670, 1838 (i), 528; A. T. Bolton, *Portrait of Sir John Soane*, 1927, 289–93; S. Rowland Pierce, 'Some Early R.I.B.A. Travellers', *R.I.B.A. Jnl.* Nov. 1962, 412].

PARKER, CHARLES (1799–1881), was a pupil of Sir Jeffry Wyatville, and attended the drawing school run by George Maddox. He subsequently spent several years in Italy. He began practice in London in about 1830, and became a Fellow of the Institute of British Architects on its foundation in 1834. He contributed a number of papers to its sessional meetings until his retirement in

1869. In 1834 he was elected a Fellow of the Society of Antiquaries, but resigned in 1844. He was steward and surveyor to the Bedford Estate in London from 1859 to 1869. Towards the end of his life his sight failed and he became totally blind. He died on 9 February 1881, aged 81, and was buried at St. Thomas's Church, Fulham, where a tombstone gives the date of his birth as 1799 (not 1800 as stated in *D.N.B.*).

Parker published in monthly parts an influential work entitled *Villa Rustica*, containing 93 lithographic plates 'selected from Buildings and Scenes in the Vicinity of Rome and Florence, and arranged for Lodges and Domestic Dwellings, with Plans and Details', 1832–41, 2nd ed. 1848. It showed how Italian domestic architecture could be adapted to English needs, and was one of the principal sources for the Italianate architecture of the early Victorian period.

Parker designed MESSRS. HOARE'S BANK in FLEET STREET, 1829–32 [C. Hussey in *C. Life*, 6 March 1958] and in about 1840 was employed by Sir Hugh Hoare to add the portico to STOURHEAD HOUSE, WILTS., in accordance with the original design, and to make other alterations [R. Colt Hoare, *Modern Wiltshire* v, 1837, Addenda, 15]. He also designed the west tower of KIMPTON CHURCH, HANTS., 1837–8, in flint and brick in a distinctive 'lancet' style [I.C.B.S.]; the R.C. CHURCH OF ST. RAPHAEL, SURBITON, in a neo-Lombardic style for Alexander Raphael, M.P. for St. Albans, 1846–7 [*Builder* v, 1847, 602–3]; and presumably CHRIST CHURCH, ST. ALBANS, which was built by the same patron in a similar style in 1850–1, but sold to the Church of England in about 1860. He altered the R.C. SPANISH CHAPEL in MANCHESTER SQUARE, in 1846, heightening the campanile [H. B. Wheatley & P. Cunningham, *London Past and Present* iii, 1891, 290]. His designs for an Italianate R.C. Church in Hastings, illustrated in the *Catholic Magazine* v, 1834, 673 and vi, 1835, cxiv, cxv, were not executed.

PARKER, THOMAS, was paid £73 10s. in 1729 'for making the screens, flooring and wainscotting the Altar' of CROWCOMBE CHURCH, SOMERSET [*Proceedings of the Somerset Archaeological Society* liv, 1908, 61]. Parker's screen survived alterations to the church in 1856. The agreement, dated 6 July 1734, between Nathaniel Ireson of Wincanton and Thomas Carew to build CROWCOMBE COURT stipulates that it is to be erected 'on foundations sometime since laid and carried up by Thomas Parker Architect'. The identification of the 'Architect' with one Thomas Parker of East Quantoxhead appears to be due to a misreading of the *Calendar of Taunton Wills* published by the British Record Society [*C. Life*, 15 Oct. 1938, and 22 April 1939, 424; *Proceedings of the Somerset Archaeological and Natural History Soc.* lxxxvii, 1941, 84].

PARKER, WILLIAM, of Hereford, designed
the GENERAL INFIRMARY at HEREFORD, 1781–3,
after the rejection of designs made by Thomas
Symonds [*Hereford Journal*, 10 Oct. 1776, 16 Jan.
1777, 13 July and 16 Aug. 1780; engraving dated
1783, with Parker's name as architect, in B.M.,
King's Maps, xv, 9]. He also designed the
THEATRE, *c.* 1790, and the SWAN INN, 1791 [*Hereford Journal*, 1790–1, especially 2 March 1791].

PARKINSON, JOSEPH T — (1783–1855), was
the son of James Parkinson, a land agent, and was
articled to William Pilkington. As a young man
he was a member of James Burton's volunteer
force, 'The Loyal British Artificers', and acted
as secretary to the Emigrant Office for refugees
from Revolutionary France. One of his earliest
works was to design a picturesque castellated
house for Burton's own residence in a style
reminiscent of Nash. Another was the conversion
of the Leverian Museum in Blackfriars Road into
the Surrey Institution. The building, erected by
his father in order to house the collections of Sir
Ashton Lever, which he had acquired in a lottery
in 1784, had been sold to the newly-established
Institution in 1806. In about 1811 Parkinson
became surveyor to the Union Fire Assurance
Office, a post which he retained until about two
years before his death. He was also District Surveyor of Westminster. The Duke of Buckingham
employed him on his property in the Isle of
Wight. In London he designed the stuccoed
façades of Montagu and Bryanston Squares.
Elsewhere, e.g. at Magdalen College, Oxford, he
specialized in a somewhat coarse variety of
Gothic. He exhibited at the Royal Academy from
1806 onwards.

Parkinson became a Liveryman of the Fishmongers' Company in 1821. His pupils included
John Haies, afterwards on the Stock Exchange,
Joseph Jennings, Raphael Brandon, Professor T.
Hayter Lewis, and his nephew F. C. J. Parkinson.
G. L. Taylor and Edward Cresy were also in his
office as young men. He died in May 1855, and
was buried in Kensal Green Cemetery
[*A.P.S.D.*; *D.N.B.*].

MABLEDON PARK, QUARRY HILL, TONBRIDGE, KENT,
for James Burton, *c.* 1805, castellated;
enlarged by Decimus Burton 1829 [exhib. at
R.A. 1810] (E. W. Brayley, *Beauties of England
and Wales* viii, 1808, 1295).

LONDON, THE SURREY INSTITUTION, BLACKFRIARS
ROAD, conversion of premises for use by the Institution, including addition of library and
Reading Room, *c.* 1807–8 [exhib. at R.A.
1809].

HAMPSTEAD, MIDDLESEX, villa in BELSIZE LANE,
HAVERSTOCK HILL., for G. Todd, 1810 [exhib.
at R.A. 1810].

TOOTING, SURREY, BEDFORD COTTAGE, TOOTING
COMMON, 1810 [exhib. at R.A. 1810].

LONDON, BRYANSTON SQUARE, MONTAGU SQUARE,
and adjacent streets on the Portman estate, *c.*
1811 [exhib. at R.A. 1811; G. L. Taylor, *Auto-Biography of an Octogenarian Architect* i, 1870,
1].

ROTHERFIELD PARK, HANTS., for James Scott,
1818–21, Tudor Gothic; refaced in stone *c.*
1885 [exhib. at R.A. 1818, 1831; G. F. Prosser,
Select Illustrations of Hampshire, 1833] (*C.
Life*, 23 & 30 April, 7 May 1948).

BAGSHOT, SURREY, ST. ANNE'S CHAPEL, 1819–21;
dem. 1882 [I.C.B.S.].

OXFORD, MAGDALEN COLLEGE, rebuilt north and
east sides of Quadrangle, reconstructed the
cloisters, and refitted the Library with plaster
ceiling (destroyed 1940), 1822–8, Gothic
[exhib. at R.A. 1824; T. S. R. Boase, 'An
Oxford College and the Gothic Revival', *Jnl.
of the Warburg and Courtauld Institutes* xviii,
1955, 158–68].

FRIMLEY CHURCH, SURREY, 1825, Gothic; chancel
etc. 1882–4 [I.C.B.S.].

STREATHAM CHURCH, SURREY, rebuilt nave and
Gothicised tower and spire, 1830–1; spire
rebuilt 1841, apse rebuilt 1863–4, church
altered by B. Ferrey in 1870s [*D.N.B.*].

WEALD PARK, GREAT STANMORE, MIDDLESEX, for
William Windle, before 1825 [*A.P.S.D.*].

PARKYNS, SIR THOMAS (1662–1741), was
the son and heir of Sir Thomas Parkyns, first
baronet, of Bunny in Nottinghamshire. He was
educated at Westminster School and Trinity
College, Cambridge, and in 1684 succeeded his
father as the squire of Bunny. For the rest of
his life he was active as a landowner and magistrate, but his less conventional activities included wrestling and architecture. Not only did
he practice the former sport himself, but he also
wrote an entertaining work on the subject
entitled *The Inn-Play: or, The Cornish Hugg-Wrestler* (1713), and designed a monument for
himself in Bunny Church which shows him 'in
the primary posture of wrestling'. The inscription records, *inter alia*, that he 'Built the Schoolhouse and Hospital. . . . the Mannor Houses in
Bunney and East Leake . . . the Vicaridge House
& most of the Farm Houses in Bunney and Bradmore. He . . . . had a Competent knowledge of
most part of the Mathematicks, especially Architecture & Hydraulics, & Contriving & Drawing
all his Planns without an Architect'.

BUNNY HALL (dated 1723) is a highly eccentric
building dominated by a castellated tower which
interpenetrates with a huge segmental pediment.
On the face of the tower beneath the pediment
there is a colossal achievement of the Parkyns
arms. All this is at one end of a rectangular house
clasped by four giant Ionic pilasters. EAST LEAKE
MANOR HOUSE (1704, dem. *c.* 1785) has not survived, but at Bunny Parkyns's SCHOOL AND ALMS-

HOUSES (1700) still stand, as do several of the farm-buildings which he built for his tenants, notably HIGHFIELDS FARM, COSTOCK (1729), and RANCLIFFE FARM, BRADMORE (1736). These are relatively conventional buildings of traditional character, but Bunny Hall belongs to the lunatic fringe of the Baroque.

[Ellis Flack, 'Sir Thomas Parkyns of Bunny Hall', *Trans. Thoroton Soc.* xlix, 1945; B. Twelvetrees, *Sir Thomas Parkyns of Bunny*, Nottingham, 1973.]

PARSONS, WILLIAM (1796–1857), was one of the leading Leicester architects of the early nineteenth century. He was born at Scraptoft, educated at Billesdon School, and apprenticed to William Firmadge in 1809. In 1819 he succeeded his father as Surveyor to the Harborough-Loughborough Turnpike Trust, and in 1823 he was appointed County Surveyor of Leicestershire. He was active both as a road-builder and as a railway architect, and had a considerable private practice. His most important works were Caythorpe Hall, the County Lunatic Asylum and the County Gaol. His pupils included William Flint (1818), Henry Webb (1823), Frederick Plant (1826), James Ray (1833), and Abraham Gill (1821), with whom he went into partnership for a time. In about 1845 he took M. J. Dain into partnership, and Dain took over his practice after his death. Parsons died at his house, No. 21 St. Martin's, on 4 January 1857, aged 60, and was buried in Scraptoft churchyard. He was an amateur artist, and three of his drawings appeared in a volume of lithographic views entitled *Sketches in Leicestershire* which was published at Leicester in 1846. [*A.P.S.D.*; J. D. Bennett, *Leicestershire Architects 1700–1850*, Leicester Museums 1968; W. Hartopp, *Leicester Freemen*, 1927.]

HINCKLEY, LEICS., THE NATIONAL SCHOOL, 1820 [*Leicester Journal*, 26 May 1820, cited by Bennett, *op. cit.*].

LEICESTER, ST. GEORGE'S CHURCH, 1823–6, Gothic; burnt 1911 and rebuilt 1913 [J. Curtis, *Topographical History of Leicestershire*, 1831, 106].

BIRSTALL CHURCH, LEICS., rebuilt nave 1826; remodelled 1860 [I.C.B.S.].

CAYTHORPE HALL, LINCS., for Col. G. H. Packe, 1824–7 [*The Correspondence of William Fowler of Winterton*, ed. J. T. Fowler, 1907, 475 ff.; building accounts in Packe papers, Leicestershire County Record Office, 700 (xxiv)].

LEICESTER, THE NEW COUNTY GAOL, WELFORD ROAD, 1825–8 and additions 1844–6, castellated [J. Curtis, *Topographical History of Leicestershire*, 1831, 111].

STONEY STANTON, LEICS., STONEY BRIDGE, 1826 [plan and specification in County Record Office, cited by Bennett, *op. cit.*].

GALBY RECTORY, LEICS., altered or rebuilt 1829. [Lincolnshire Record Office, MGA 153].

LOUNT LODGE, LEICS., work for Mr. Burton, 1831 [papers in Dept. of Archives, Leicester Museum, cited by Bennett, *op. cit.*].

KEYHAM BRIDGE, LEICS., 1832 [*Leicester Journal*, 6 April 1832, cited by Bennett, *op. cit.*].

DISEWORTH VICARAGE, LEICS., enlarged 1833 [Lincolnshire Record Office, MGA 182].

BELGRAVE BRIDGE, LEICS., 1834; since enlarged [*V.C.H. Leics.* iv, 424].

BURY HOUSE, COTTINGHAM, NORTHANTS., alterations, including new staircase, for the Hon. Mrs. Cockayne Medlicote, 1835 [plans etc. in Northants. Record Office, Map 639 a, b, c].

LEICESTER, THE LEICESTERSHIRE AND RUTLAND LUNATIC ASYLUM (now part of Leicester University), 1837 and additions 1844 [*V.C.H. Leics.* iv, 374].

THURMASTON VICARAGE, LEICS., rebuilt 1838 [Lincolnshire Record Office, MGA 220].

LEICESTER, ST. MARGARET'S VICARAGE, additions and repairs, 1838; dem. 1964 [Lincolnshire Record Office, MGA 227].

LEICESTER, CHRIST CHURCH, 1839, Gothic; dem. 1957 [*V.C.H. Leics.* iv, 359].

EVINGTON VICARAGE, LEICS., rebuilt 1839 [Lincolnshire Record Office, MGA 237].

AYLESTONE RECTORY, LEICS., rebuilt 1839 [Lincolnshire Record Office, MGA 225].

BOTTESFORD, LEICS., Bridge over Winter Beck, 1841 [plan in County Record Office cited by Bennett, *op. cit.*].

QUORNDON CHURCH, LEICS., added north aisle 1842, Gothic [I.C.B.S.].

HATTON PARSONAGE, WARWICKS., alterations *c.* 1845 [Bodleian Library, MS. Top. Warwicks, a.2, f. 7].

RAILWAY STATIONS at REARSBY, BROOKSBY, FRISBY, ASFORDBY, MELTON MOWBRAY and SAXBY, for the Midland Railway Co., 1846–8 [Bennett, *op. cit.*, citing Minute Book of the Syston-Peterborough Committee of the Midland Railway].

BITTESWELL, LEICS., ALMSHOUSES, 1847 [*A Reply to the Question: 'Where and What is Bitteswell?'*, Lutterworth 1848, 23].

LEICESTER, STAMFORD STREET, warehouse for Mr. Jacques, 1851 [plan in Dept. of Archives, Leicester Museum, cited by Bennett].

LEICESTER, THE CASTLE HALL, altered interior, 1856 [*V.C.H. Leics.* iv, 345].

LEICESTER, a pair of semi-detached Greek villas designed by Messrs. Parsons and Gill 'for a particular situation in the suburbs of Leicester' are described and illustrated in Loudon's *Encyclopaedia of Rural Architecture*, 1846, pp. 870–7, but have not been identified.

PASCOE, JOSEPH, of Bodmin, new seated ST. NEOT'S CHURCH, CORNWALL, in 1832 [I.C.B.S.], and designed THE JUDGES' LODGINGS at BODMIN *c.* 1840 [J. Maclean, *Deanery of Trigg Minor* i, 1870, 109].

PATCH, JOHN, of Crewkerne, Somerset, is described in Pigot's *Directory* of 1830 as 'carpenter, builder and surveyor'. In 1834 he largely rebuilt LOPEN CHURCH, SOMERSET [I.C.B.S.].

PATERSON, DAVID, was a local Scottish architect living at Newton of Airlie in Angus. In 1828–9 he designed CORTACHY CHURCH, ANGUS, Gothic, for the 8th Earl of Airlie [S.R.O., GD 16/46/97 and drawings in RHP 5160 and 5165]. In the Scottish Record Office there are designs by him for BOTTOM STEADING, LINTRATHEN, ANGUS, 1833 [RHP 5023], and for additions to CRAIG HOUSE, ANGUS, 1833, dem. [RHP 5127].

PATERSON, GEORGE (–1789), practised as an architect in Edinburgh, but was at the same time the owner of a small estate at Monimail in Fife called Cunnochie. In 1793, in the course of legal proceedings, he was described as 'the deceased George Paterson Architect in Edinburgh, father of George Paterson of Cunochy', and the death of 'George Paterson of Cunoquhy, Esq.' on 26 February 1789 is recorded in the *Scots Magazine* for that year. He appears to have had a connection with Robert Mylne (*q.v.*), for whom in 1761–3 he superintended the building of St. Cecilia's Hall, Edinburgh [*Book of the Old Edinburgh Club* xix, 1933, 227], and in 1766 some alterations to Amisfield House, E. Lothian, for Francis Charteris [Robert Mylne's diary, 12 & 14 Aug. 1766]. In 1758 he was elected a member of the Royal Company of Archers, and in 1776 was a member of the Committee for building Archers' Hall, Edinburgh [J. Balfour Paul, *History of the Royal Company of Archers*, 1875, 368; minutes of the Royal Company of Archers, 27 July 1776].

ROSSIE HOUSE, FIFE, addition of wings for Henry Cheape, 1753 [St. Andrews University Library, Rossie Papers 7/305].

MARLEFIELD HOUSE, nr. ECKFORD, ROXBURGHSHIRE, repairs and alterations for William Nisbet, 1754 onwards; reconstructed 1891 [S.R.O., GD 6/1649, lawsuit 1793].

BOTHWELL CASTLE, LANARKS., alterations for the Duke of Douglas, 1759–60; remodelled by J. Playfair, 1788 [papers in Douglas Estate Office, *ex inf.* Dr. A. A. Tait].

ST. ANDREWS, FIFE, COLLEGE CHURCH (ST. LEONARD'S), alterations 1759–61 [R. G. Cant, 'St. Andrews Architects', *St. Andrews Preservation Trust Year Book*, 1966–7, 15].

KINGSBARNS MANSE, FIFE, 1765; dem. [S.R.O., HR 184/1, p. 5].

CUPAR, FIFE, some houses 'built ten years before to plans by George Paterson', i.e. *c.* 1769 [advertisement in *Ruddiman's Weekly Mercury*, 13 Jan. 1779].

DALHOUSIE CASTLE, MIDLOTHIAN, repairs for the 8th Earl of Dalhousie, 1778–9 [S.R.O., GD 45/19/123].

PATERSON, JAMES (–1838), came to Dundee with George Angus (*q.v.*) to superintend the building of the seminaries. In July 1832 he opened a class for architectural drawing at 22 Union Street. In 1837 he advertised for contractors for additions to the DUNDEE ASYLUM. He began building the WATT INSTITUTION to Angus's designs, but died on 18 February 1838 before the building was finished and was buried in the Constitution Road cemetery. His place was taken by his brother William [information from Mr. David Walker].

PATERSON, JOHN (–1832), was probably the son of George Paterson (*q.v.*), whom he succeeds in the Edinburgh directories as the occupant of a house in St. John's Street. He was living at this address from 1777 to 1784, but appears subsequently to have removed to Elgin, for he dates a drawing [S.R.O., RHP 9064–5] at Elgin in July 1789, and when he was appointed clerk of works for the new Edinburgh University buildings later that year he was described as 'Mr. John Paterson, late Architect and Builder at Elgin'. The Edinburgh appointment he owed to Robert Adam, with whom he appears to have been closely associated, and whose Scottish practice he helped to manage. In December 1791 his place as clerk of works at the University was taken by Hugh Cairncross, and thereafter he practised as an architect in Edinburgh for over 40 years, first from 2 North Bridge Street, and later from 24 Buccleuch Place. He died on 19 November 1832 at what must have been a fairly advanced age. [Edinburgh City Records, College Trust Minute Book, 18 Nov. 1789 and 15 Dec. 1791; S.R.O., Edinburgh Commissariot Records, testament dated 1833.][1]

Paterson had a considerable practice in Scotland and the north of England. After the death of the Adam brothers he became the leading practitioner of the 'Castle style' that they had developed. He was also an accomplished designer of elegant classical interiors, with a special predilection for oval and circular rooms. Statements by Paterson of his terms of employment as an architect (1% for designs and 4% for superinten-

[1] John Paterson the architect must be distinguished from John Paterson, civil engineer in charge of Leith Docks from *c.* 1803 until his death on 4 January 1823 (*Scots Magazine*, 1823, 256). It was John Paterson of Leith who briefly held the post of Superintendent of Public Works in Edinburgh from May to December 1809 (Edinburgh Town Council Minutes, 24 May 1809). In June 1809 he was also appointed Surveyor or Superintendent of Works to the Heriot Trustees, but resigned in July of the following year (Minutes of the Heriot Trust, vol. 18, pp. 199, 438).

623

dence) will be found in the Abercairny and Breadalbane papers in the S.R.O. (GD 112/16/7 and
GD 24/1/624).

The following unexecuted designs by Paterson
have been noted: the addition of wings to GRANT
LODGE, ELGIN, MORAYSHIRE, for Sir James Grant,
1789 [S.R.O., RHP 9064–6]; an oval drawing-
room at ABERCAIRNY, PERTHSHIRE, 1797 [letter in
S.R.O., GD 24/1/624]; a tontine inn and
assembly rooms at AYR, 1802 [drawings at Culzean Castle]; additions to CASTLE FORBES, ABER-
DEENSHIRE, 1807 and 1811 [drawings at Castle
Forbes]; a house at DALGUISE, PERTHSHIRE, for
Charles Stewart, 1794 [specification in Paterson's
hand in S.R.O., GD 38/1/1143]; alterations to
PITFIRRANE HOUSE, FIFE, 1811 [National Library
of Scotland MSS. 6509 and 6511]; and a scheme
for the enlargement of KINRARA HOUSE, INVER-
NESS-SHIRE, c. 1814, initialled 'J.P.' and probably
by Paterson [S.R.O., GD 44/48/70]. Houses
which might be attributed to him on stylistic
grounds include: ST. BRYCEDALE HOUSE, in KIRK-
CALDY, FIFE, for George Heggie, 1786 (oval
rooms); HARVIESTOUN CASTLE, CLACKMANNAN-
SHIRE, remodelled for Crawfurd Tait, 1804, dem.
1965; and FASQUE CASTLE, KINCARDINESHIRE, for
Sir Alexander Ramsay, Bart., c. 1809, to which
may be added the stables at PINKIE HOUSE, MUS-
SELBURGH, MIDLOTHIAN. SEGGIEDEN, PERTHSHIRE,
is said in *The Scots Magazine* for June 1808, 403,
to have been 'built fourteen or fifteen years ago,
upon a plan by Paterson'. Although the oval
saloon and drawing-room suggest Paterson,
building accounts preserved in the house appear
to indicate that it was built in 1772–5, several
years before any other recorded work of Paterson's.

PUBLIC BUILDINGS

DUNDEE, THE INFIRMARY (later Victoria Road
School), 1794–8; completed by D. Neave,
1824–6; dem. [C. Mackie, *Historical Description of Dundee*, 1836, 156].

GLASGOW, THE BRIDEWELL, 1795, castellated;
dem. [*Extracts from the Records of the Burgh
of Glasgow*, ed. Renwick, viii, 1913, 595].

PERTH, ST. PAUL'S CHURCH, c. 1800–7, Gothic
(octagonal plan) [Perth Town Council
Minutes, 5 March 1799].

attributed: LEITH, THE LEITH (now National Commercial) BANK, 1805–6 [façade almost identical
with that of Coilsfield House, Ayrshire, listed
below].

FETTERESSO CHURCH, STONEHAVEN, KINCARDINE-
SHIRE, 1810–12, Gothic (octagonal plan)
[S.R.O., GD 105/781].

LEITH, THE SEAFIELD BATHS, SEAFIELD PLACE,
1812–13 [signed engraving in *Edinburgh
Almanack*, 1812].

COUNTRY HOUSES

CASTLE FRASER, ABERDEENSHIRE, offices for Alex-
ander Mackenzie, 1794 [Report of Scottish
National Register of Archives on Castle Fraser
MSS: plans by Paterson dated 1794].

COILSFIELD (or MONTGOMERIE) HOUSE, nr. TAR-
BOLTON, AYRSHIRE, for the 12th Earl of Eglin-
ton, 1798; dem. 1971 [B. Burke, *Visitation of
Seats*, 2nd ser., i, 1854, 187] (A. H. Millar,
Castles and Mansions of Ayrshire, 1885).

MONZIE, PERTHSHIRE, for General Alexander
Campbell, c. 1795–1800, castellated; recon-
structed by Sir R. Lorimer after a fire in 1908
[J. C. Nattes, *Scotia Depicta*, 1804, pl. 15]
(Neale's *Seats* vi, 1823).

EGLINTON CASTLE, AYRSHIRE, rebuilt for the 12th
Earl of Eglinton, 1798–1803; castellated;
alterations by W. Railton of Kilmarnock 1857–
60; dem. 1925 [J. C. Nattes, *Scotia Depicta*,
1804, pl. 22: for the alterations of 1857–60 see
S.R.O., RHP 2058] (A. H. Millar, *Castles and
Mansions of Ayrshire*, 1885).

BARMOOR CASTLE, NORTHUMBERLAND, for Francis
Sitwell, 1801, castellated [signed drawings at
Barmoor].

TAYMOUTH CASTLE, PERTHSHIRE, began to rebuild
for the 4th Earl (1st Marquess) of Breadalbane,
1801, but was dismissed 1805 before the building was complete: it was then demolished by
A. & J. Elliot, who designed a new house on
a different site [Alistair Rowan in *C. Life*, 8
Oct. 1964].

CHILLINGHAM CASTLE, NORTHUMBERLAND, rebuilt
east side for the 4th Earl of Tankerville after
a fire, 1803; castellated [*History of Northumberland* xiv, 336].

WINTON HOUSE, EAST LOTHIAN, castellated addition for Col. John Hamilton, 1805 [payment
in S.R.O., RH 15/119/98].

MILBOURNE HALL, NORTHUMBERLAND, for Ralph
Bates, 1807–10 [B. Burke, *Visitation of Seats*,
2nd ser., i, 1854, 187; *History of Northumberland* xii, 542].

FETTERESSO CASTLE, KINCARDINESHIRE, alterations
and additions for Col. Robert William Duff,
1808; gutted 1954 [tracing of plan at
N.M.R.S.].

BRANCEPETH CASTLE, DURHAM, alterations including addition of Russell Tower, for Matthew
Russell, 1818–19, castellated [M. A. Richardson, *The Local Historian's Table-Book* iii, 1843,
194; A. T. Bolton, *The Portrait of Sir John
Soane*, 1927, 306].

attributed: LENNEL HOUSE, COLDSTREAM, BER-
WICKSHIRE, for the 8th Earl of Haddington, c.
1820 [the unusual plan closely resembles an
unexecuted design by Paterson for Castle
Forbes dated 1811].

PATERSON, ROBERT (c. 1790–1846), 'architect and surveyor' of Edinburgh, who died on 6

July 1846, aged 56, is commemorated in the Warriston Cemetery there.

PATERSON, SAMUEL (c. 1788–), a pupil of James Elmes, was admitted to the Royal Academy Schools in 1809 at the age of 21. He was awarded the Silver Medal in 1817. In 1820 he went to Rome with John Davies (q.v.), and subsequently exhibited drawings of St. Peter's and the church at Loreto at the Royal Academy. Nothing is known of his subsequent career.

PATEY, ANDREW (–1834), is said to have begun life as a mason in Yorkshire before establishing himself as an architect in Exeter [*A.P.S.D.*, *s.v.* 'Paty']. His best work was the Fire Assurance Office in the High Street, whose façade derived from Soane's Bank of England. Of the several churches which he designed, that at West Teignmouth, which is octagonal in plan, with a central lantern supported on thin cast-iron Gothic pillars, is the most ambitious. Patey died at Teignmouth on 2 September 1834, having gone there for the sake of his health [*Gent's Mag.* 1834 (ii), 443].

WEST TEIGNMOUTH, DEVON, ST. JAMES'S CHURCH, cons. 1821, Gothic [Vestry Minutes].
EAST TEIGNMOUTH, DEVON, ST. MICHAEL'S CHURCH, 1822–3, 'Norman' style; chancel added 1875, steeple 1887–9 [I.C.B.S.].
DAWLISH CHURCH, DEVON, rebuilt (except tower), 1824; chancel and transepts added 1874 [J. Britton & E. W. Brayley, *Devonshire and Cornwall Illustrated*, 1832, 90].
EAST TEIGNMOUTH, THE PUBLIC ROOMS (later Riviera Cinema), forming the central feature of Den Crescent, 1826 [J. Britton & E. W. Brayley, *Devonshire and Cornwall Illustrated*, 1832, 76].
EXETER, ST. THOMAS'S CHURCH, rebuilt chancel 1829–30, Gothic [Vestry Minutes in Exeter City Library].
EXETER, ST. LEONARD'S CHURCH, 1831–3; dem. 1876, 'in the Grecian style' [Davidson's Church Notes in Exeter City Library].
EXETER, THE WEST OF ENGLAND FIRE ASSURANCE OFFICE (afterwards the Commercial Union), HIGH STREET, 1833, destroyed by bombing 1942 [*The Exeter Guide*, 1836, 53, with illustration].

PATIENCE, JOHN THOMAS (c. 1774–1843), began his career as a mason in Colchester and Bury St. Edmunds. In 1812 he went bankrupt, leaving an unfinished mansion in Westgate, Bury St. Edmunds, to be sold by his assignees [*Ipswich Journal*, 7 Nov. 1812]. By 1820 he was practising as an architect in Norwich, where in 1836 he became City Surveyor. He exhibited at the Norwich Society of Artists from 1820 to 1830, and

made several designs for public buildings which are preserved in the City Archives. He died on 10 April 1843, aged 69 [*Gent's Mag.* 1843 (ii), 107; information from Mr. J. Bensusan-Butt and Mr. A. P. Baggs].

NORWICH, ST. PETER'S METHODIST CHAPEL, LADY'S LANE, 1824 [John Chambers, *Norfolk Tour* iii, 1829, 1151, 1260].
NORWICH, THE FRIENDS' MEETING-HOUSE, UPPER GOAT LANE, 1825 [John Chambers, *Norfolk Tour* iii, 1829, 1151, 1169–70].
NORWICH, THE CATHOLIC CHURCH, WILLOW LANE, 1827, converted into a Catholic school 1894 [John Chambers, *Norfolk Tour* iii, 1829, 1151–2].
RAVENINGHAM, NORFOLK, cast-iron milestone for Sir Edmund Bacon, 1831, signed 'Patience Archt. 1831'.
NORWICH, THE NORFOLK AND NORWICH SUBSCRIPTION LIBRARY, GUILDHALL HILL, 1835; rebuilt 1898–9 after fire, retaining Doric portico [*Norfolk Chronicle*, 24 Oct. 1835, ex inf. Mr. D. C. Young].
NORWICH, DISTRICT SCHOOLS, ST. AUGUSTINE'S GATES, 1838; dem. [contemporary booklet in City Library, ex inf. Mr. D. C. Young].

PATIENCE, JOSEPH (c. 1739–1797), of Wormwood Street, Bishopsgate, London, was an unsuccessful candidate for a District Surveyorship in 1774 [Middlesex County Records, General Orders, No. 10]. He was elected a member of the Surveyors' Club in 1793 and died on 27 September 1797, aged 58. He is commemorated by a monument in All Hallows Church, London Wall. He was the father of Joseph Patience, junior (q.v.). A design for an organgallery in St. Michael Bassishaw Church by 'the late Jos. Patience', 1780, is in the collection of the late Sir Albert Richardson.

PATIENCE, JOSEPH (c. 1767–1825), son of the above, practised from the same address in Wormwood Street, Bishopsgate, until his death on 14 May 1825, aged 58. He was elected a member of the Surveyors' Club in 1797 and was its President in 1817. He exhibited at the Royal Academy from 1786 onwards. He designed new offices at BEAVER HALL, SOUTHGATE, MIDDLESEX (dem. 1870), exhibited 1793 and 1806; completed GREAT SAXHAM HALL, nr. BURY ST. EDMUNDS, SUFFOLK, for T. Mills, exhibited in 1797 and 1808 (cf. N. Scarfe, 'Great Saxham Hall', *Proceedings of the Suffolk Institute of Archaeology* xxvi, 1954, 230–1); and designed a villa at DULWICH for J. Willes, exhibited in 1804. In 1807 he was consulted by the vestry of HANWORTH, MIDDLESEX, about repairing their church [MS. Vestry Minutes]. He made plans for rebuilding FRINGFORD RECTORY, OXON., in 1818, and for that

625

of ODDINGTON in the same county in 1821 [Bodleian Library, Oxford Diocesan Records, Faculty Register 1804–27, pp. 97, 241]. A drawing by him for alterations to premises in COVENT GARDEN, LONDON, 1801, is in the R.I.B.A. Drawings Collection. He is commemorated on the monument to his father in the church of All Hallows, London Wall. This is signed by 'T. Patience', who appears to have been a sculptor member of the family (see Rupert Gunnis, *Dictionary of British Sculptors*, 293, where he is confused with Joseph Patience).

PATON, DAVID (–1882) was a member of a family of builders in Edinburgh. They were wrights by trade, and there is a monument in St. Cuthbert's Churchyard to John Paton, 'wright and builder', who died in 1834 aged 71. The names of John Paton, senior and junior, variously described as 'builder' or 'architect', occur in the Edinburgh directories round about 1820. David Paton was already practising as an architect in 1824, when he designed Nos. 1–3, YORK PLACE and 15–19 NORTH ST. ANDREW STREET [Edinburgh Dean of Guild plans]. In the following year he appears to have been in Paris, for several plans of buildings in the French capital, signed by Paton and dated 1825, were among the drawings from the Signet Library sold in 1960. In November 1829 Paton entered the office of Sir John Soane in London as an assistant, but left in the following May [A. T. Bolton, *The Works of Sir John Soane*, 1924, xlvii]. In 1832 he emigrated to Carolina, where he was one of the architects of the State Capitol at Raleigh [T. Hamlin, *Greek Revival Architecture in America*, 1944, 197]. He died in America in 1882.

PATTERSON, WILLIAM, was a builder at Nottingham, where he designed a Gothic INDEPENDENT CHAPEL in FRIAR LANE in 1828 [J. Orange, *History of Nottingham* ii, 1840, 812]. He was later in partnership with T. C. Hine (1813–99), in conjunction with whom he designed a school and parsonage at STAPLEFORD, NOTTS., in 1836 [Northants. Record Office, Map 734], and a rectory at AVERHAM, NOTTS., in 1838 [Borthwick Institute, York, MGA 1838/1].

PATY, JAMES (–1779), was a member of a large and complex family of masons, carvers and architects who were active in Bristol throughout the greater part of the eighteenth century. It is possible that the family originated in Chipping Norton, Oxfordshire, where several freemasons of this surname followed their trade in the late seventeenth and early eighteenth centuries. The first member of the family to work in Bristol was evidently not a native of the city, for he was required to pay a fine of £15 for his freedom in 1721. He was the first James Paty, and he died

before 1760, when James, 'son of James Paty of Bristol, carver, deceased', was apprenticed to Thomas Kilby, mason. James Paty, junior, was made free on 9 March 1768. The James Paty who designed the THEATRE ROYAL, KING STREET, BRISTOL in 1764–6 cannot have been the same person, and is probably to be identified with a third James Paty who died on 1 February 1779. He was succeeded by his son John Paty, 'Carver, Marble Mason, etc.', who announced in *Felix Farley's Journal* that he would 'continue the Business in all its branches of his late Father, James Paty, at his Yard under the Bank', and that in addition to supplying 'Monuments, Chimney-Pieces, etc.', he was prepared to undertake land surveying and measuring. [W. Ison, *The Georgian Buildings of Bristol*, 1952, 40; R. Gunnis, *Dictionary of British Sculptors*, 1968, 294; J. R. Edwards, 'The Theatre Royal, Bristol', *Archaeological Jnl.* xcix, 1942; John Summerson, 'The Theatre Royal, Bristol', *Arch. Rev.* Nov. 1943.]

PATY, THOMAS (*c.* 1713–1789), of Bristol, was probably the most talented member of his family, working with equal facility as an architect and surveyor, and as a carver and statuary mason. Between 1741 and 1743 he executed the wood- and stone-carving in the chapel built by John Cossins at Redland, near Bristol. He also supplied the font in 1755. All his work here is of the finest quality, and a contemporary note on the chapel, preserved with the original bills,[1] observes that Paty 'is generally esteemed one of the best Carvers in England, either in Wood or Stone', and that 'all the Ornaments in the Chapel were designed and carved' by him. In 1741–2 he was employed by John Wood to carve the architectural ornamentation of the Bristol Exchange [J. Wood, *A Description of the Exchange of Bristol*, 1745]. He was responsible for the dressed masonry and carving at Clifton Hill House, designed by Isaac Ware in 1746, and the carving at the Royal Fort and at Arno's Court may also be his work. In 1762–5 he was employed in 'grinding, gageing and laying' the tiles in the grotto at Goldney House, Clifton [*C. Life*, 13 Aug. 1948]. He and his sons John and William Paty had an extensive business as monumental masons, and tablets signed by them are to be found in many churches in Bristol and the neighbouring counties.

As an architect Paty enjoyed a considerable reputation, and the street-elevations designed by him and his sons set the standard for many of the terrace-houses built in Bristol during the second half of the eighteenth century. Clare, High, Bridge, Union, and Bath Streets were laid out by him, and there is evidence that he and his sons

---

[1] In the custody of Messrs. Osborne, Ward, Vassall, Abbott & Co., of Bristol, solicitors.

provided the elevations not only for the buildings lining these streets, but also for many of those in College, Park, Great George, Charlotte, and Lodge Streets, and in Berkeley Square and Crescent and Upper Berkeley Place. Between 1763 and 1769 he carried out James Bridges' plans for rebuilding Bristol Bridge and the adjoining church of St. Nicholas. Bridges had proposed to retain the steeple of the old church, but it proved to be insecure, and Paty replaced it with a Gothic tower and spire of his own designing. It is an indication of Paty's professional standing that in 1775 he should have been invited to arbitrate in the dispute over the building of the Guildhall at Bath, and his fame was celebrated in verse by a local poet in the lines:

Palladio's stile in Patty's plans appear.
Himself a master with the first to stand,
For Clifton owes her beauties to his hand.
      (*Clifton, a Poem*, by the late Henry Jones,
            2nd ed. 1773, Canto 1, p. 8)

Paty died on 4 May 1789, in his 77th year, leaving, besides his two sons, a daughter Elizabeth, who had married Thomas King, a statuary of Bath. His business was continued by his sons, but their partnership was cut short by John Paty's premature death on 10 June 1789, leaving William Paty as the sole survivor. [W. Ison, *The Georgian Buildings of Bristol*, 1952, 40–3; R. Gunnis, *Dictionary of British Sculptors*, 1968, 294–5.]

BRISTOL

BRISTOL BRIDGE, to designs of James Bridges, 1763–8; widened 1873–4 [Ison].

ST. NICHOLAS CHURCH, completed to designs of James Bridges, 1763–9, himself designing the Gothic tower and spire; gutted 1940 [Ison].

ST. MICHAEL'S CHURCH, 1775–7, Gothic, retaining medieval tower [Ison].

ST. JAMES'S MARKET, UNION STREET, *c.* 1775 [Ison].

ALL SAINTS' CHURCH, repaired cupola, 1781 [MS. Vestry Minutes].

THE MERCHANTS' HALL, remodelled 1783; destroyed by bombing 1940 [Ison].

THE ROYAL INFIRMARY, central portion, with Daniel Hague, 1784–8 [Ison].

ST. AUGUSTINE'S CHURCH, alterations [Ison].

WELLS, SOMERSET, THE TOWN HALL, 1776–80, since rebuilt: according to *Felix Farley's Journal* of 17 Aug. 1776, 'The Corporation of Wells have agreed to rebuild the assize hall and market house, after a plan of the Rev. Dr. Camplin's, ... to be completed under the direction of Mr. Paty of this city'.

PATY, WILLIAM (1758–1800), of Bristol, was the younger son of Thomas Paty of that city. He

was admitted to the Royal Academy Schools as an architectural student in December 1775, and it is stated in the Academy's Register that he would attain the age of 18 in the following February. After the deaths of his father and elder brother in 1789 he carried on the family business of a statuary mason, and executed many monumental tablets. He was one of the three city surveyors appointed under the Act of 1788[1] and he was admitted a freeman in December 1790, paying a fine of 15 guineas.

As his father's partner and assistant, Paty played an important part in the Georgian development of Bristol, and he was probably responsible for the design of many of the buildings erected in Clifton during the last decade of the eighteenth century. He appears to have been the architect of CHRIST CHURCH, BRISTOL, which was built under the direction of his firm in 1786–90 (altered internally in 1883), and he also designed NO. 7 GREAT GEORGE STREET (now THE GEORGIAN HOUSE MUSEUM) for John Pretor Pinney, a successful West Indian merchant, 1789–91. According to J. & H. S. Storer, he was the architect employed to design BLAISE CASTLE HOUSE, nr. BRISTOL, for J. S. Harford, *c.* 1795, but 'he received, in his professional exertions, the assistance of Mr. Nash' [*Delineations of the County of Gloucester*, 1824, 105]. Paty died on 11 December 1800, aged 43, and is commemorated by a tablet in the south aisle of St. Augustine's Church. His will, dated 22 September 1795, contains legacies to his wife Sarah, to his son, George William Paty (then under age), and to his nephew, John Paty, 'son of my late brother John Paty' [P.C.C., 54 ABERCROMBIE]. James Foster was his pupil and assistant, but his business and yard in College Place were bought by Henry Wood, a London mason and architect. A volume of his designs for monumental tablets is referred to as extant by Dening in 1923. Drawings in the R.I.B.A. Collection for rebuilding Butleigh Court, Somerset, signed 'WP', are attributed to him.

[*A.P.S.D.*; C. F. Dening, *The Eighteenth-Century Architecture of Bristol*, 1923, 132–4, 138–9; J. Evans, *History of Bristol* ii, 1816, 169; W. Ison, *The Georgian Buildings of Bristol*, 1952, 43; R. Gunnis, *Dictionary of British Sculptors*, 1968, 295.]

PAUL, ROWLAND (–1850), practised in Cheltenham from before 1820 until his death on 20 November 1850. He was latterly in partnership with his two sons Andrew and Charles Paul. Charles, who had been secretary to the Cheltenham and Oxford Railway Company, died at

---

[1] Cf. A. B. Beaven, *Bristol Lists*, 1899. There are several plans drawn by him in this capacity in the 'Plan Books' in the City Record Office. They include a design for an Oyster Market, dated 1794.

Charlton Kings on 10 April 1854, aged 44 [Gloucester Probate Act Book 1842–52, p. 183; *Gent's Mag.* 1854 (i), 666]. The firm's works included the Greek Doric st. mary's cemetery chapel in lower high street, cheltenham, 1831 [J. Goding, *History of Cheltenham*, 1863, 550], and dowdeswell court, glos., for Mrs. Hester Rogers, 1833–5 [Glos. Record Office, D. 269 A/F 9]. This house, designed in the style of the early 18th century, is illustrated in Burke's *Visitation of Seats*, ser. I (i), 247. The interior of the hall was remodelled by Samuel Onley, junior, in 1848, and the attic storey was removed in the present century.

PEACOCK, ALEXANDER (*c.* 1733–1818), who died at Burdiehouse Mains, nr. Edinburgh, on 11 May 1818, aged 85, is described as 'architect' in his obituary notice in the *Edinburgh Magazine* ii, 1818, 598. He was doubtless the 'Mr. Peacock' who designed leuchie house, north berwick, east lothian for Sir Hew Dalrymple in 1779–85, with elaborate decoration in the Adam style [Mark Girouard in *C. Life*, 12 Oct. 1961; information from Mr. John Giffard].

PEACOCK, JAMES (? 1738–1814), was for over forty years assistant Clerk of the Works to the City of London. In 1771 George Dance the younger, who had succeeded his father as Clerk of the Works in 1768, asked for the appointment of an assistant, as he found that his duties often required his presence in two places at the same time. The City Lands Committee agreed, provided that the arrangement involved no charge to the City, and in December 1771 Peacock was appointed on Dance's recommendation, and presumably at his expense [Lands Committee Jnl., vol. 105, f. 156']. Nothing is known of Peacocks's origins or early life, though according to Sir John Soane he had become acquainted with Dance soon after the latter's return from Italy in 1765 (*Memoirs of Professional Life*, 1835, 11). He became Dance's lifelong assistant, and remained in his office until his death in 1814. Peacock's only independent work of importance was the stock exchange in capel court, which was built to his designs in 1801–2, but reconstructed by Allason in 1853–4. He also carried out repairs to st. anne and st. agnes church, gresham street, in 1781–2 [W. McMurray, *A City Church Chronicle*, 1914, 63], and to st. stephen's, walbrook, in 1803–4. A drawing of the elevation of the Mines Royal, Dowgate Hill, by him and a plan of proposed quays between London Bridge and the Tower (1795), are in the British Museum (*King's Maps* xxi, 28 and xxv, 16). He took up the livery of the Joiners' Company in 1774, and appears at one time to have held a post in the Ordnance Office, whose loss in 1780 he attributed to the machinations of James Wyatt, then Surveyor of the Ordnance.

Peacock published several works on architectural subjects. The most important of these was entitled Οἰκίδια or *Nutshells*, and was published under the anagrammatic pseudonym of 'Jose Mac Packe, bricklayer's labourer', in 1785. It contains 'ichnographic distributions' (*i.e.* plans) for small villas, together with some satirical directions for prospective builders.

Peacock's 'Account of Three Simple Instruments for Drawing Architecture and Machinery in Perspective' was printed in the *Philosophical Transactions of the Royal Society* for 1785, and he also published *A New Method of Filtration by Ascent*, 1793, and *Subordinates in Architecture*, 1814. A MS. volume compiled by him, on 'Terms of Contracts for Bricklayers', Slaters' and Joiners' Works', on the Peace Establishment, for the Service of the Board of Ordnance', is in Sir John Soane's Museum.

Peacock was also interested in social and economic questions, and published several small treatises on these subjects which are of considerable interest in the history of social welfare. His *Outlines of a Scheme for the General Relief, Instruction, Employment, and Maintenance of the Poor*, was published in 1777, and is described by its author as 'an imperfect and crude performance' in the *Proposals for a Magnificent and Interesting Establishment for the Employment of the Poor*, which he issued in 1790. He also published *Superior Politics*, 1789, and *The Outlines of a Plan for establishing a United Company of British Manufacturers*. His object in all these projects was to give 'protection and suitable incitement, encouragement, and employ to every class of the destitute, ignorant, and idle poor, who shall be healthy, able to work, and willing to conform ... to such ... regulations as the company shall exact, and which are intended to be of mutual benefit and advantage to the company and the workpeople, and eventually so to society at large'.

Peacock died on 22 February 1814, 'in the 76th year of his age', as stated on the headstone formerly in the cemetery of St. Luke's Church, Old Street. Little is known of his personality, but he was friendly with Sir John Soane as well as with George Dance, and in his edition of Chambers's *Civil Architecture*, Gwilt paid a tribute to his 'virtues and moral excellence', which 'will be honoured as long as the memory of his surviving friends remains sound'.

[*A.P.S.D.*; *D.N.B.*; A. T. Bolton, *The Portrait of Sir John Soane*, 1927, 59, 96–8; Dorothy Stroud, *George Dance, Architect*, 1971, *passim*.]

PEARCE, EDWARD, *see* PIERCE

PEARCE, SIR EDWARD LOVETT (– 1733), was the son of General Edward Pearce and his wife Frances, daughter of Christopher Lovett, a prominent Dublin merchant. His connections were chiefly with Ireland, but his family had a property at Witlingham near Norwich, and he may have been brought up in England. In 1716 he entered the Army as a cornet in Col. Richard Morris's Dragoons, but he does not appear to have persisted in a military career, and in 1723–4 he was in Italy studying architecture. By 1726 he was established in Dublin. In the following year he was elected a Member of the Irish Parliament, and in 1730 he succeeded Thomas Burgh as Surveyor of Works and Fortifications in Ireland. He was knighted in 1732, and died on 7 December 1733 while still in his thirties.

Nothing is known of Pearce's architectural education, but it is evident from his drawings that at some stage he came under the tutelage of Sir John Vanbrugh, who was his father's first cousin. Subsequently he was in contact with Lord Burlington's circle, and in Ireland he became the leading Palladian architect of his day. As the designer of Bellamont Forest, Cashel Palace, the Parliament House, and probably of the State Apartments at Dublin Castle, Pearce was in fact a major figure in the history of Irish architecture. It is unlikely that in the course of his brief but brilliant career he had time or opportunity to do much architectural work in England. However, his drawings, now at Elton Hall in Huntingdonshire, show that he made a survey of the seat of the Earle family at HEYDON HALL in NORFOLK, and that he designed additions to ASHLEY PARK, nr. WALTON in SURREY (dem.) for Richard Boyle, 2nd Viscount Shannon, which probably included the long gallery illustrated in Oliver Brackett's *Encyclopaedia of English Furniture* (1927), 195. At Elton Hall there is also a set of unexecuted designs by Pearce for a large Palladian 'lodge' at Richmond, probably made for George II soon after his accession. In about 1725 he helped John Buxton (*q.v.*) to design his new house at SHADWELL PARK, NORFOLK, providing him with 'the first design for the front', but how far this was followed is uncertain [Mark Girouard in *C. Life*, 2 July 1964].

[T. U. Sadleir, *Sir Edward Lovett Pearce*, Dublin, 1927; H. Colvin & M. Craig, *Architectural Drawings in the Library of Elton Hall by Sir John Vanbrugh and Sir Edward Lovett Pearce*, Roxburghe Club, 1964; *History of the King's Works* v, 220; Maurice Craig and the Knight of Glin, 'Castletown, Co. Kildare', *C. Life*, 27 March, 3–10 April 1969; John Cornforth, 'Dublin Castle', *C. Life*, 6 Aug. 1970; Maurice Craig, 'Sir Edward Lovett Pearce', *Bulletin of the Irish Georgian Soc.* Jan.–June 1974.]

PEARCE, MATTHEW (–1775), was described as 'Architect' of WHITEFIELD'S TABERNACLE, TOTTENHAM COURT ROAD, LONDON, of which he was also the builder. It was erected in 1756, enlarged in 1759–60, damaged by fire in 1857, and entirely rebuilt in 1890–2. Pearce is commemorated by a tablet in the chapel [*Survey of London* xxi, 1949, 67, 71].

PEARS, JAMES (*c.* 1740–1804), of Oxford, was a builder much employed by James Wyatt, for whom he carried out alterations at NEW COLLEGE in 1789–93 [Bodleian Library, MS. Top. Oxon, a.29, ff. 65–7], at MERTON COLLEGE in 1790–1 [College Register 1731–1822], and at MAGDALEN COLLEGE in 1792–5 [College Archives]. He was also the builder of the RADCLIFFE OBSERVATORY, which was completed by him to Wyatt's designs in 1794, and his name is inscribed on the copper ball which surmounts its roof. In 1783 he repaired and improved the President's Lodgings at CORPUS CHRISTI COLLEGE [College Archives]. In 1790 he was employed to carry out alterations to the interior of ST. JOHN'S COLLEGE CHAPEL, and in 1795 he erected the HOLMES BUILDING at the same College, apparently to his own designs. He also designed and built a secondary staircase in the President's Lodgings at St. John's in 1797 [St. John's College Archives: Bills and Receipts and Registers VII, 636, VIII, 32, 44]. A design by Pears for a proposed screen wall at WORCESTER COLLEGE is among drawings preserved there (No. 491 B). He became a freeman of Oxford in 1776, was for many years a member of the Council, and served as Mayor in 1793 [*Oxford Council Acts 1752–1801*, ed. Hobson, Oxford Historical Soc. 1962, 120, 219 etc.]. He died at Woodperry House on 1 Jan. 1804, aged 64, and is commemorated by a brass inscription on the floor of Iffley Church.

PEISLEY, BARTHOLOMEW, was the name of three generations of Oxford master masons. Bartholomew Peisley and partners supplied Headington stone for the building of St. Paul's Cathedral in 1686–7 and in 1697 [*Wren Soc.* xiv, 19–21; xv, 28, 30, 35], and it is safe to assume that, like the Strongs of Taynton, they were quarry-owners as well as master-builders.

In 1673–6 the elder Peisley (*c.* 1620–94) built the SENIOR COMMON ROOM of ST. JOHN'S COLLEGE [College Archives, *Computus Annuus*, 1673–8, f. 150ᵛ], and in 1685–6 he completed the LIBRARY and CHAPEL of ST. EDMUND HALL, which had been begun by William Byrd in 1680–2 [A. B. Emden, *An Account of the Chapel and Library Building, St. Edmund Hall, Oxford*, 1932, 22]. In November 1681, when giving evidence in a lawsuit, he stated that he was 61 years of age, and that he had built a stone house in ST. GILES' (No. 62, now demolished), 'wherein Esqr. Bateman lately lived' [Oxford University Archives, Vice-Chancellor's Court, 1681 M]. Either he or his son Bartholomew, who had been apprenticed to him in July 1669, was the master-mason employed to build TRINITY COLLEGE CHAPEL in 1691–4 [Wood, *Life and Times* iii, 364], and the New Building at the south-west corner of WADHAM COLLEGE facing the Parks Road in 1693–4 [Wadham College Archives]. He died in 1693/4, dividing his property in St. Giles' and St. Ebbe's between his two sons, Bartholomew and Charles, and his daughter Miriam. He desired to be buried in St. Giles' Church [Bodleian Library, Oxford Consistory Court Register, f. 209].

Bartholomew Peisley II (c. 1654–1715) stated in 1689 that he had 'severall times been chief contriver of buildings of about £200 and 300 value' [Oxford University Archives, Vice-Chancellor's Court, 1689 Easter, bundle 54]. In 1695 Sir William Trumbull intended to employ him to build a proposed gallery at EASTHAMPSTEAD PARK, BERKSHIRE [Hist. MSS. Comm., Downshire I (ii), 501, 507, 655]. In 1697 he contracted to build STONE'S ALMSHOUSES, ST. CLEMENT'S, OXFORD [Strickland Gibson, 'Stone's Hospital', Bodleian Quarterly Record viii, 1935]. It may have been Bartholomew II who built ST. GILES' HOUSE, OXFORD, for Thomas Rowney in 1702 – the date which appears on the leadwork of the roof – for a note among the St. John's College Muniments records that 'Bath. Piesly's 2 tenements were pull'd down when the New House was built', and in 1709 Peisley is referred to in a letter of Sir John Vanbrugh as bringing him 'Mr. Rowney's Draught' in London [The Complete Works of Sir J. Vanbrugh iv, The Letters, ed. G. F. Webb, 227]. There are measured drawings of the house in Arch. Rev., vol. 57, 1925, 122–5. Peisley was one of the principal contractors at BLENHEIM PALACE, where he built the Great Bridge. When he died in 1715 his will referred to a 'debt of £1200 due to me for worke done at Blenheim House' [copy in B.M., Add. MS. 24327, f. 12]. His daughter married Henry Joynes, the Comptroller at Blenheim, to whom he left £300. His business was continued by his eldest son, Bartholomew Peisley III (c. 1683–1727), who had been apprenticed to him in July 1698.

The third Bartholomew appears to have entered into partnership with William Townesend, for they are found in association in several important contracts, and Hearne wrote of Peisley that 'he and one Townsend carried (as it were) all the business in masonry before them, both in Oxford and all the Parts about it'. It was Townesend and Peisley who built the RADCLIFFE QUADRANGLE at UNIVERSITY COLLEGE between 1717 and 1719 [Bodleian Library, Minutes of the Radcliffe Trustees, 1717–20], and the CODRINGTON LIBRARY at ALL SOULS from 1715 onwards [College Archives], and it was with the same two master masons that Sir John Stonehouse contracted for the erection of RADLEY HALL, BERKSHIRE, in June 1721 [V. Hope, 'The Architect of Radley Hall', C. Life, 27 Jan. 1950]. At All Souls they were carrying out the designs of Hawksmoor, but at University College their work is traditional in

630

character, and the vaulting of the Radcliffe Gateway shows that they were skilled in the technicalities of Gothic masonry as well as in the classical detail which they executed at Radley. Like his father, Peisley worked at Blenheim, where he and Townesend built the WOODSTOCK GATE to Hawksmoor's designs in 1722–3 [W. J. Churchill, 'Some Unpublished Letters of Sarah, Duchess of Marlborough, relating to the Building of Blenheim Palace', Trans. Birmingham and Midland Institute, 1884–5].

Peisley died at his house in New Inn Hall Lane on 29 August 1727, aged 44 or 45, and was buried in St. Giles' churchyard. He is described on the monument erected to his memory in the south aisle of the church, as 'in Re Architectonica Peritus Artifex', and the ungracious Hearne, who had no love for his partner Townesend, admitted that Peisley 'was looked upon as a very courteous well behaved man'. He left a widow, described by Hearne as 'a very pretty woman', who afterwards married President Hudsford of Trinity [Hearne's Collections ix, Oxford Historical Society, 1914, 343].

PENISTON, JOHN (c. 1779–1848) established himself as an architect and surveyor in Salisbury, where he lived in the Close. Farmhouses, cottages and other utilitarian buildings formed the bulk of his practice, but, being a Catholic, he was also employed to design several chapels for members of the same faith. After his death on 22 June 1848 at the age of 69 his office was continued by his son John Michael Peniston (1807–58) and by his grandson Henry Peniston (born 1832) who held the post of County Surveyor from 1858 to 1864. A large collection of the firm's drawings, letter books and other records is preserved in the Wiltshire County Record Office and is the principal source of the list of works given below.

POULSHOT RECTORY, WILTS., altered or rebuilt, 1823 [Salisbury Diocesan Records].

WYLYE RECTORY, WILTS., altered or rebuilt, 1827 [Salisbury Diocesan Records].

CLARENDON PARK, WILTS., additions and alterations (including stuccoing of exterior) for Sir Frederick Henry Bathurst, 1828 [Letter-book, 6 Oct. 1828 etc.].

EAST KNOYLE CHURCH, HANTS., gallery, c. 1828 [I.C.B.S.].

BRAMSHAW CHURCH, HANTS., repaired and enlarged, 1829 [I.C.B.S.].

SPETTISBURY, DORSET, Catholic Chapel, 1829–32 Gothic [Wilts. R.O. 451/200].

CANNINGTON PRIORY (now Somerset Farm Institute), SOMERSET, octagonal Catholic Chapel 1830 [Wilts. R.O. 451/74 (ix); B. Little, Catholic Churches since 1623, 1966, 110].

UPTON HOUSE, DORSET, enlarged (Kitchen, Conservatory and Chapel), 1830 [Wilts. R.O. 451/72 (iii)].

LANDFORD HOUSE, WILTS., drawing-room for — Bolton, 1831 [Wilts. R.O. 451/74 (xxiiiA)].

IBSLEY CHURCH, HANTS., 1832, Gothic [inscription in church].

CHUTE CHURCH, WILTS., paving and window, 1832; rebuilt 1869–72 [Wilts. R.O. 451/72 (xix)].

DEVIZES, ST. JAMES'S CHURCH, SOUTHBROOM, rebuilt (except tower) 1833–4, Gothic, following designs made by Benoni White of Devizes (d. 1833) [Wilts. R.O. 451/72 (xii)].

WINCANTON, SOMERSET, house for E. Yalden Cooper, 1835 [Wilts. R.O. 451/72 (xxii)].

WESTMEAD HOUSE, WESTBURY-ON-TRIM, GLOS., Catholic Chapel, 1835 [Wilts. R.O. 451/74 (vii) & 231].

THORNHILL HOUSE, DORSET, altered interior of entrance hall for W. Boucher [Wilts. R.O. 451/73 (xxii)].

FRYERN COURT, HANTS., alterations 1845 [Wilts. R.O. 451/73 (xxiv)].

SOMERLEY PARK, HANTS., proposed alterations for the 2nd Earl of Normanton, c. 1830–40 [Wilts. R.O. 451/73 (xxxiv)].

PENNEL, MARMADUKE, was a successful bricklayer and alderman of Nottingham in the early eighteenth century, holding the office of Mayor in 1718–19 and 1724–5. He built ST. MARY'S WORKHOUSE in 1714, and during his second mayoralty he paved St. Peter's Square, established a Monday Market there for butter, fruit, and vegetables, and erected a MARKET CROSS, consisting of a tiled roof supported by four Tuscan columns. 'Pennel's Cross', as it was called, was converted into a fire-engine house in 1733, and demolished in 1787. In 1724–5 Pennel built (and presumably designed) the front rooms of the NEW EXCHANGE (illustrated in C. Deering, *Nottinghamia Vetus et Nova*, 1751, 8) and on 19 March 1724/5, he was appointed surveyor to design and build a new County Hall in the city. He visited Worcester in order to make drawings of the new Guildhall there, but nothing came of the scheme, as it was eventually decided to repair the old County Hall. [*The Stretton Manuscripts*, ed. G. C. Robertson, 1910, 156, 159, 165; *Records of the Borough of Nottingham* vi, 99, 140; *Nottinghamshire County Records of the Eighteenth Century*, ed. K. T. Meaby, 1947, 47–9.]

PENRICE, JOHN, practised in Colchester. In 1823–5 he supervised the building of STISTED HALL, ESSEX, for C. S. Onley to the designs of Henry Hakewill [*Ipswich Journal*, 7 May 1825]. On 26 December 1834 the *Essex Standard* reported that the BAPTIST MEETING HOUSE in ELD LANE, COLCHESTER, had recently been erected 'under the superintendence of Mr. Penrice,

architect', and on 19 September 1845 the same journal advertised building plots in new roads in Colchester (Osborn, Forster, Cross and Arthur Streets) for which Penrice was the superintending architect. He was still in practice in 1847, when he designed public baths in the town [*Builder* v, 1847, 277], but was dead by 1860.

Penrice was the principal architect involved in the development of WALTON-ON-THE-NAZE, ESSEX, as a seaside resort in the 1830s. In his *Descriptive Account of Walton on the Naze*, Colchester 1860, Thomas Wilmshurst states that Penrice built the wooden pier in 1830, and that he also designed Kent's Hotel (1832), while Pigot's *Directory* of c. 1835 says 'Many of the dwellings present peculiar neatness and taste, particularly those erected by Mr. Penrice, architect, of Colchester'. Another hotel at Walton designed by him is illustrated in *An Historical Account of Walton-on-the-Naze*, published at Colchester in 1829. [Information from Mr. J. Bensusan-Butt.]

PENSON, THOMAS (–1824), was the founder of a dynasty of architects practising in Chester and North Wales. He himself lived at Wrexham, where he combined the function of architect, auctioneer and County Surveyor of Flintshire (from 1810 to 1814, when he was dismissed for reasons unknown). In 1799 he bought a large house in Charles Street, Wrexham, which he subsequently rebuilt before moving in about 1818 to a house which he built for himself in Theatre Lane behind the THEATRE which he erected in Beast Market. In 1784 he designed THE COUNTY GAOL at CAERNARVON [W. H. Jones, *Old Karnarvon*, 1889, 115]. He died on 30 March 1824 and was buried in the Old Cemetery at Wrexham [A. N. Palmer, *History of Wrexham*, 1893, 123, 128, 215].

Thomas Penson had two sons. The younger, John William Todd Penson, was an artist and died at the age of 36 in 1826. The elder, Thomas Penson (c. 1790–1859), became a pupil of Thomas Harrison of Chester and established himself in practice at Oswestry in Shropshire. He was County Surveyor of Denbighshire and Montgomeryshire for over thirty years, a Fellow of the R.I.B.A. and a member of the Institution of Civil Engineers. He revolutionized the road system of Montgomeryshire, and designed many bridges, including NEW BRIDGE over the river Dee near Wynnstay and one at LLANYMYNECH over the river Virniew. Other works by him included HOLY TRINITY CHURCH, OSWESTRY, 1836–7, with the unusual feature for its date of a vaulted apse [I.C.B.S.], ST. DAVID'S CHURCH, DENBIGH, 1838–40, the new PARISH CHURCH at NEWTOWN, MONTGOMERYSHIRE, 1843–5, LLANYMYNECH CHURCH, SALOP., 1845, in the Norman style, HOLY TRINITY CHURCH, GWERSYLLT, DENBIGHSHIRE, 1850–1, a cruciform church in Norman style at RHOS LLANERCHRUGOG, DENBIGHSHIRE, 1852–3, and the alteration or rebuilding of two 'Elizabethan' houses, VAYNOR PARK, MONTGOMERYSHIRE, and LLANRHAIADR HALL, DENBIGHSHIRE [*A.P.S.D.*; *Minutes of Proceedings of the Institution of Civil Engineers* xx, 1860–1, 156; D. R. Thomas, *History of the Diocese of St. Asaph*, 1870, 340, 365, 634, 660, 812, 841].

The younger Thomas Penson had two sons, Thomas Mainwaring Penson (d. 1864) and Richard Kyrke Penson (d. 1886), both architects in Chester, where the latter had a considerable practice.

PEPPER, WILLIAM, may have been the son of George Pepper, a surveyor practising in Westminster who was President of the Surveyors' Club in 1801. In 1808 William Pepper exhibited at the Royal Academy a design for a monumental building in memory of Admirals Howe, Duncan, Vincent and Nelson, giving his address as Park Prospect, Westminster. He subsequently established himself in Kingston-on-Thames, where in 1823 he was responsible for altering the galleries in the parish church [Surrey Archdeaconry Records]. His designs for a new north aisle for Cobham Church, Surrey, dated 1821–2, are among the parish records [*ex inf.* Mr. J. H. Harvey].

PERCY, EDWARD THOMAS, was practising as an architect and surveyor in Sherborne in the early nineteenth century. In 1828 he repaired the central tower of SHERBORNE ABBEY CHURCH (see his report, of which there is a copy in Sir John Soane's Museum, Soane Case, 'Misc. MSS. relating to Architecture', I).

PERCY, J—, was a pupil of James Wyatt, from whose office at 3 Newman Street he exhibited drawings of two of Wyatt's buildings (the Pantheon and Bryanston House) at the Royal Academy in 1793 and 1795. He subsequently moved to Norwich, and in 1806 exhibited a design for a monument to Lord Nelson at the Norwich Society of Artists.

PERRY, EBENEZER, practised in London from the 1820s until the 1850s. In 1825–7 FOLLY BRIDGE, OXFORD, was built to his designs [J. M. Davenport, *Oxfordshire Bridges*, Oxfordshire County Council 1869, 11]. In 1832 he was employed by Messrs. Dunston, Robinson and Flanders to lay out their Battle Bridge estate in St. Pancras [*Survey of London* xxiv, 106].

PERRY, GEORGE, practised at Bewdley in Worcestershire. In 1773 he rebuilt one arch of BRIDGNORTH BRIDGE at a cost of £1300 [*Trans. Salop. Archaeological Soc.* xlix, 1937, 208]. He

was the author of some designs for Gothic almshouses, 'proposed to be built in Park Lane' Bewdley in 1802, which are in the Prattinton Collection in the Library of the Society of Antiquaries (Portfolio v, 72/2 and 3(i)). Another drawing in the same collection shows that he designed the Gothic monument in the churchyard at Hartlebury to Bishop Hurd (d. 1808).

PERRY, JOHN, was an architect and surveyor of Godalming, Surrey, where in 1814 he designed the attractive TOWN HALL [Brayley, *Topographical History of Surrey* v, 201]. Several of his executed works are illustrated in Loudon's *Encyclopaedia of Rural Architecture*, 1846, including a 'Bailiff's Cottage, in the Old English Style', built at BURY HILL, nr. DORKING, for Charles Barclay in 1831, a farm at the same place, and a stable nr. GODALMING. In 1839 he reported on the condition of GODALMING CHURCH, and in the following year carried out a number of alterations, all of which were swept away by Gilbert Scott in 1879 [S. Welman, *The Parish and Church of Godalming*, 1900, 45–6]. His design for a new rectory in the Tudor style at PUTTENHAM, SURREY, is preserved among the Surrey Archdeaconry Records. He also 'enlarged and rearranged' LEA (now WHITLEY) PARK, SURREY, for John Leech [Brayley, *op. cit.* v, 255]. R. Varden was his pupil.

PETIT, C—A—, exhibited 'A Ceiling for Stuco ornaments and painted pannels' at the Free Society of Artists in 1771, and a 'Design for a Prison' at the Royal Academy in 1814.

PHILLIPS, AMBROSE (*c.* 1707–1737), was the owner of GARENDON PARK, LEICS., which he inherited from his father William Phillips in 1729. He travelled extensively in Italy, making drawings of Roman antiquities that are now in the R.I.B.A. Collection, and on his return was probably one of the original members of the Society of Dilettanti. He was quite a competent architectural draughtsman, and the drawings at the R.I.B.A. include several designs by him of a Palladian character. At Garendon he designed and built a Triumphal Arch, a Temple of Venus, and an Obelisk, and had begun to rebuild the house before his early death in 1737 at the age of 30. The Triumphal Arch is based on the Arch of Titus in Rome, of which only the central portion then remained, embedded in medieval fortifications. The Garendon Arch is therefore an essay in archaeological reconstruction which shows that Phillips was a serious student of Roman architecture. The Temple of Venus is inspired by the Temple of Vesta in Rome and the coffered ceiling of the portico of the new house derived from the barrel-vault of the Temple of the Sun and Moon at Rome. The façade was moreover flanked by two gateways based on the well-known archways by Inigo Jones which Lord Burlington re-erected at Chiswick. The house, completed by Ambrose Phillips's successor, was remodelled in the French chateau style in 1866 and demolished in 1964, but the Arch, Temple and Obelisk remain as monuments to their builder's taste. On his monument in Shepshed church his architectural enthusiasm is commemorated by an inscription which claims that *Ex Italia reversus/Inspectis antiquorum aedificiorum Reliquijs Artes Romanas in Patriam transtulit,/Et inter Principes viros qui jam Architecturam/in Anglia restituere et perpolire coeperant/Enituit pene Primus.*

[Mark Girouard, 'Ambrose Phillips of Garendon', *Architectural History* viii, 1965; *Catalogue of the R.I.B.A. Drawings Collection O–R*, 52.]

PHILLIPS, HENRY (–*c.* 1851), of Bermondsey, London, exhibited a design for a public library to be erected in Dublin at the Royal Academy in 1820. He was elected to membership of the Surveyors' Club in 1829, and was President in 1834. He was still practising from Bermondsey in 1850, but he must have died soon afterwards, for in 1852 the Surveyors' Club voted a sum from its Charitable Fund to his widow [records of the Surveyors' Club]. The R.I.B.A. Drawings Collection has an unexecuted design by him for the Public News Room at Leicester, dated 1837.

PHILLIPS, JOHN (*c.* 1709–1775), was a London master carpenter of considerable repute in the reigns of George II and George III. He was the son of Matthew Phillips, of East Hagbourne in Berkshire, and grandson of another Matthew Phillips, a mason or bricklayer of the same place. His uncle Thomas Phillips (*c.* 1689–1736) was another well-known London master carpenter of the early eighteenth century, whose 'skill and diligence in his profession' are commemorated on his monument in East Hagbourne churchyard. The latter (who had been apprenticed to Jeremiah Franklin of Oxford, carpenter, on 5 July 1705) was active as a speculative builder in London, *e.g.* on the Harley estate between 1723 and 1730 [B.M., Add. MS. 18240] and in Sackville Street in 1730 [*Survey of London* xxxii, 345]. He had the carpenter's contract for two churches designed by Gibbs, St. Martin's-in-the-Fields and St. Peter's, Vere Street, and for several buildings erected by the Office of Works, including Kent's Treasury Buildings [*Gent's Mag.* 1736, 488]. In 1729 he built the wooden bridge across the Thames between Fulham and Putney 'according to a scheme and principles laid down by' Dr. William Cheselden of St. Thomas's Hospital [G.L.C. Record Office, Commissioners' Minutes, 2 July 1730, etc.].

John Phillips appears to have succeeded to his uncle's business in London, and to have been in partnership with George Shakespear (d. 1797). In

London he was responsible for the development of CHARLES STREET, MAYFAIR (1750), and of a block of land with frontages to KING STREET, WESTMINSTER, and PALL MALL (1759) [B. H. Johnson, *Berkeley Square to Bond Street*, 1952, 179; *Survey of London* xxix, 328–9]. In Oxford he built the wooden dome of the RADCLIFFE LIBRARY to the designs of James Gibbs and made the fine joinery for the interior of the building (1742–50) [*Building Accounts of the Radcliffe Camera*, ed. Gillam, Oxford Historical Soc. 1958, *passim*]. Together with Shakespear he was responsible for the even finer joinery in CHRIST CHURCH LIBRARY (1752–62) [W. G. Hiscock, *A Christ Church Miscellany*, 1946, 69]. It was also in partnership with Shakespear that he demolished the east wing of AUDLEY END, ESSEX, for Lady Portsmouth in 1749 [Lord Braybrooke, *History of Audley End*, 1836, 93–4] and between 1750 and 1764 rebuilt ALSCOT HOUSE, WARWICKS., for James West in a Gothick style akin to that of Batty Langley [accounts at Alscot; Mark Girouard in *C. Life*, 15, 22, 29 May 1958]. In 1767–9 he carried out alterations to AUBREY HOUSE, NOTTING HILL, for Lady Mary Coke [*Letters and Journals of Lady Mary Coke* ii, 1889, 45, 221, 388–9, iii, 1892, 15, 24, 38, 54, 114], and in 1771 he built the wooden bridge (dem. 1881) at BATTERSEA under the direction of Henry Holland [Dorothy Stroud, *Henry Holland*, 18, 25, 97]. In 1772–4 he acted as surveyor on behalf of the Society of Arts during the building of their premises in the Adelphi by the brothers Adam [A. T. Bolton, *The Architecture of R. & J. Adam* ii, 42–3]. Though more notable as a master builder than as an architect, Phillips was undoubtedly capable of making his own designs, and he was presumably the 'Phillips' who in 1760 was short-listed by the Committee for the selection of a design for Blackfriars Bridge. According to the anonymous *Observations on Bridge Building and the several Plans offered for a New Bridge* (1760), he 'submitted 11 different designs'.

Phillips lived in Brook Street[1] and died, a wealthy man, on 28 December 1775, aged 66. He was the lord of the manor of Blewbury in Berkshire, and since 1763 had been the lessee of the rectorial manor of Culham, near Abingdon, where he occupied and rebuilt CULHAM HOUSE (OXON.). When he died childless in 1775 he left his property first to his father (who died two years later) and then to his brother William (d. 1782), whose descendants continued to live at Culham until 1935.

[Oxford City Records (apprenticeship of Thomas Phillips); Bodleian Library, MS. Wills

---

[1] His house, now 39 Lower Brook Street, was built by Thomas Phillips, who lived there from 1724 until his death in 1736 (*ex inf.* Survey of London). A later occupant was Sir Jeffry Wyatville, who remodelled it.

Berks. 21, f. 127ᵛ (will of Matthew Phillips the elder), MS. Oxf. Dioc. Papers *c.* 2115, nos. 4–15 (lease of Culham); P.R.O. PROB 6/112, f. 34 (administration of Thomas Phillips); P.C.C. 87 BELLAS (will of John Phillips); *Passages from the Diary of Mrs. Lybbe Powys*, ed. Climenson, 1899, 153; *V.C.H. Berkshire* iii, 281; *V.C.H. Oxon.* vii, 29, 36; monumental inscriptions at East Hagbourne.]

PHILLIPS, JOHN (*c.* 1771–), a pupil of George Byfield, was admitted to the Royal Academy Schools in 1791 at the age of 20, and gained the Silver Medal in 1793. He exhibited at the Academy from Byfield's office in 1790–3 and thereafter from various London addresses. He was still in practice in Kensington in 1817.

Phillips's first exhibit at the Academy, a 'Perspective view of the two new fronts intended for the seat of Thomas Bund, Esqr.', i.e. WICK HOUSE, ST. JOHN IN BEDWARDINE, WORCESTER, probably represented a building designed by Byfield. But subsequent exhibits indicate that he designed THE ROYAL NAVAL HOSPITAL at DEAL in KENT (1799); an unidentified house for a gentleman in East Kent (1804); UPTON HOUSE, WORTH, KENT, for Robert Small (1809); and 'improvements' to GREAT DOODS, nr. REIGATE, SURREY (1810).

PHILLIPS, MATTHEW (*c.* 1781–1825), of York, was in partnership with Peter Atkinson II until 1819, when he set up office in New Bridge Street [York Public Library, Knowles MSS.]. He died in February 1825 in his 45th year, and is commemorated by a tomb in the churchyard at Acomb, nr. York. J. A. Hansom (1803–82) was his pupil.

PHIPPS, JOHN (*c.* 1796–1868), spent his life in the service of the Office of Works. He entered the Office in 1819 as a temporary clerk, became an Examining and Measuring Clerk in 1822, and in 1832 was promoted to the new post of Assistant Surveyor of Works and Buildings. He was regarded as 'an excellent draughtsman' and an 'active, zealous and intelligent' member of the staff. His architectural opportunities were confined to minor works at Windsor, Frogmore and elsewhere. [*History of the King's Works* vi, 185 and *passim; Builder* xxvi, 1868, 117.]

PICKERNELL, JONATHAN (*c.* 1738–1812), was sent from London[1] to assist John Wooler in investigating the site for Hexham Bridge, Northumberland, in 1775, and subsequently supervised the building of the bridge (destroyed by a flood in 1782) to the designs of John Smeaton [Samuel Smiles, *Lives of the Engineers* ii, 1861, 62]. In 1776 he was appointed Surveyor of Bridges in the County of Northumberland, and held the post until his resignation in January 1781 [Northumberland Record Office, QS Order Books 11, p. 306 and 12, p. 99]. In that year he became Harbour Engineer at Whitby, where he remained until his death in August 1812 at the age of 74. At WHITBY he built the west pier of the harbour and designed in 1788 the TOWN HALL in an attractive but somewhat old-fashioned classical style. His name is recorded on an oval plaque. His son, of the same name, was harbour engineer at Sunderland from 1795 to 1804 and built the lighthouse on the north pier there. A design by the younger Pickernell for centering to support the single arch of the great iron bridge over the river Wear at Sunderland during its construction in 1793–6 is preserved in Sir John Soane's Museum (Portfolio 3, no. 56). Francis Pickernell, Harbour Engineer at Whitby from 1822, was probably the grandson of Jonathan Pickernell senior. [G. Young, *History of Whitby* ii, 1817, 526; *Parliamentary Reports* xiv, 1803, 334; information from Prof. A. W. Skempton].

PICKERSGILL, THOMAS (*c.* 1807–1869), started practice in York in 1829. He held the post of Surveyor to the Corporation from 1854 until his death on 5 May 1869, aged 62 [information from Dr. E. A. Gee]. His earliest recorded work was the WESLEYAN METHODIST CHAPEL in LADY PECKITT'S YARD, built in 1829, and demolished in 1874–5 [*New Guide to York*, 1838, 162]. In 1831 he was employed to restore the portion of the City wall between Micklegate Bar and North Postern [*R.C.H.M. York* ii, 32]. He designed SEATON CAREW CHURCH, CO. DURHAM, in 1831 [I.C.B.S.], rebuilt the tower and arcades of ST. DENYS CHURCH, YORK, in 1846 [I.C.B.S.], and largely rebuilt ST. MARGARET'S CHURCH, YORK, in 1851–2 [I.C.B.S.].

PICKFORD, JOSEPH (*c.* 1736–1782), was the leading architect in Derby in the reign of George III. He was the son of William Pickford, a mason of Warwick, and nephew of Joseph Pickford, a sculptor and monumental mason with a yard at Hyde Park Corner in London.[1] His father died when he was a boy, and in 1748 he went to London to be trained in his uncle's yard. By 1759 he was working in the Midlands, and in about 1760 he settled in Derby, marrying (1762) the daughter of the agent at Longford Hall. Here he combined the business of a mason with the practice of an architect, and designed a number of

---

[1] He probably came from Hampshire, for in 1769 Jonathan Pickernell of 'East Wasdy', Southampton, carpenter, took William Pickernell as an apprentice (P.R.O., Apprenticeship Registers).

[1] For Joseph Pickford the sculptor see R. Gunnis, *Dictionary of British Sculptors*. He appears, however, to have died *c.* 1759 and not in 1762 as stated by Gunnis.

small country houses and other buildings in a competent late Palladian style which owes something to James Paine. In Derby he built a handsome house for himself in Friargate, became a member of the corporation, and was a close friend both of the artist Joseph Wright, who painted a portrait of his two sons as children, and of John Whitehurst, the clockmaker, mathematician, and author of an *Inquiry into the Original State and Formation of the Earth* (1778). He died in July 1782, aged 45, leaving a widow and two sons, the elder of whom became a Fellow of Oriel College, Oxford. His business was not carried on by his family, but he had two pupils, Thomas Gardner and James Pollard (*qq.v.*). [Edward Saunders, 'Joseph Pickford of Derby', *C. Life*, 9 Nov. 1972; T. Mozley, *Reminiscences*, 1882, i, chap. 9.]

PUBLIC BUILDINGS

DERBY, THE ASSEMBLY ROOMS, built under Pickford's supervision 1762–5, probably to designs by Washington, Lord Ferrers (*q.v.*); interior completed by Robert Adam 1774; gutted by fire 1963; dem. 1971; façade re-erected at Crich [Derbyshire Record Office, account-book signed by Pickford among Strutt papers] (*C. Life*, 16 Aug. 1930, 215).

NOTTINGHAM, THE COUNTY HALL, built by Pickford to the designs of James Gandon, 1770–2 [*Nottingham County Records of the Eighteenth Century*, ed. K. T. Meaby, 1947, 54].

NOTTINGHAM, ST. MARY'S CHURCH, design for restoration of Gothic windows, 1770 [Nottingham University Library, MAB 115].

WIRKSWORTH, DERBYSHIRE, THE MOOT HALL, for the Duchy of Lancaster, 1772–3; rebuilt 1814 [P.R.O., DL 42/175, f. 346, 176, f. 86[v], *ex inf.* Sir Robert Somerville].

BIRMINGHAM, ST. MARY'S CHURCH, 1773–4, on an octagonal plan with circular tower; dem. 1925 [sources cited by Saunders, *C. Life*, 9 Nov. 1972, 1208].

SOLIHULL CHURCH, WARWICKS., rebuilt spire 1774–5 [E. C. Sheppard, *The Tower and Bells of Solihull Church*, 1950, 20].

COVENTRY, HOLY TRINITY CHURCH, rebuilt three windows at east end, 1774 and all windows on south side, 1775 [T. Sharp, *Illustrative Papers on the History and Antiquities of Coventry*, 1871, 107 n.].

LEICESTER, TRINITY HOSPITAL, reconstructed 1776 [*V.C.H. Leics.* iv, 408].

OTHER WORKS

LONGFORD HALL, DERBYSHIRE, work for Wenman Coke, 1762 [Keele University, Sneyd papers, letter from Pickford to Ralph Sneyd, 13 May 1762].

attributed: ASHBOURNE, THE MANSION, refronted

for the Rev. John Taylor, *c.* 1765 [stylistic attribution] (*C. Life*, 28 March 1968).

OGSTON HALL, DERBYSHIRE, design for remodelling house for William Turbutt, 1767, executed with modification by E. Stanley of Chesterfield (*q.v.*) 1768–9; altered *c.* 1840–50 and remodelled 1864 [drawings formerly at Ogston].

ETRURIA HALL, nr. BURSLEM, STAFFS., for Josiah Wedgwood, 1767–9 [E. Meteyard, *Josiah Wedgwood* ii, 1866, 37, 82–3, 126–9].

BANK HOUSE, ETRURIA, nr. BURSLEM, STAFFS., for Thomas Bentley (Wedgwood's partner), 1767–9; dem. 1819 [E. Meteyard, *op. cit.*, 83].

THE ETRURIA WORKS, nr. BURSLEM, STAFFS., for Josiah Wedgwood, 1767–73; dem. [E. Meteyard, *op. cit.*, 37, 82–3, 126–9].

HAMS HALL, nr. COLESHILL, WARWICKS., work for C. B. Adderley, 1768. A letter from Josiah Wedgwood to Bentley, 15 Sept. 1768 [Wedgwood archive at Barlaston], mentions Pickford's employment at Hams. He may have designed this house, which according to Neale's *Seats* iii, 1820, was built in 1760, and according to Burke, *Visitation of Seats* ii, 1853, 67, in 1764. It was reconstructed internally after a fire in 1890 and dem. *c.* 1920, when the upper part of the façade was rebuilt at Coates, Glos., as part of what is now Bledisloe Lodge.

SANDON HALL, STAFFS., for Lord Archibald Hamilton, 1769–71; destroyed by fire 1848 [*Vitruvius Britannicus* v, 1771, pls. 90–3].

DERBY, NO. 41 FRIARGATE, for himself, *c.* 1770 [T. Mozley, *Reminiscences* i, 1882, chap. 9; E. Saunders in *C. Life*, 9 Nov. 1972].

TRENTHAM HALL, STAFFS., lodges for the 2nd Earl Gower (later 1st Marquess of Stafford), 1774–6 [John Cornforth in *C. Life*, 25 Jan. 1968, 179–80, and *Correspondence*, 1 Feb. 1968, 240].

DARLEY ABBEY, DERBYSHIRE, alterations for Robert Holden, 1775–8; dem. 1962 [drawings in Derbyshire Record Office].

PIERCE, or PEARCE, EDWARD (*c.* 1630–1695), was the son of Edward Pierce (d. 1658), a member of the London Painter-Stainers' Company. The elder Pierce was, in Vertue's words, 'a good History and Landskip Painter, in the Reigns of King Charles the First and II. He also drew Architecture, Perspective, etc; and was much esteem'd in his time'. The exact date of his son's birth is not known, and the first recorded event in his career is his admission to the freedom of the Painter-Stainers' Company by patrimony in 1656. He was 'chosen of the Livery' in 1668, and was Master of the Company in 1693. Of his early life and training nothing is known, but he married in 1661, and he was working as a mason under Sir Roger Pratt at Horseheath, Cambs., in 1665 [R. T. Gunther, *The Architecture of Sir Roger Pratt*, 1928, 130]. He became well known as a sculptor, and, as Vertue observes, 'was much employed by Sr Chr. Wren in his Carvings and Designs'. After the Great Fire he had masonry contracts in connection with ST. LAWRENCE JEWRY, 1671–81 (£7586), ST. CLEMENT DANES, 1680–2, in partnership with John Shorthose (£3200), ST. MATTHEW, FRIDAY STREET, 1682–7 (£710), and ST. ANDREW, HOLBORN, 1684–7, in partnership with William Stanton (£4050). He also worked on the GUILDHALL between 1671 and 1673, and held masons' contracts for the building of ST. PAUL'S CATHEDRAL. As a sculptor, Pierce is best known for his fine portrait-busts of Oliver Cromwell and Sir Christopher Wren, now in the Ashmolean Museum at Oxford. He worked with equal facility in either stone or wood, and much of his best carving in the latter material has been erroneously attributed to Grinling Gibbons. In 1680 he carved the wooden model for the copper dragon which forms the weathervane on the steeple of St. Mary-le-Bow, and he executed carving in several other churches, including the fonts at St. Andrew, Holborn, and St. Matthew, Friday Street.

In 1676 Pierce was associated with John Oliver in designing the fittings of EMMANUEL COLLEGE CHAPEL, CAMBRIDGE, in whose erection Archbishop Sancroft was closely concerned [Willis & Clark, ii, 707]. It was to Sancroft that Pierce owed what was probably his most important architectural commission, the BISHOP'S PALACE at LICHFIELD, which was built under his supervision and to his designs in 1686–7 [H. Colvin & A. Oswald in C. Life, 30 Dec. 1954]. The palace was rebuilt under the archbishop's direction during a sequestration of the see, and its erection is described in a series of letters from Dean Addison to Sancroft which are preserved in the Bodleian Library [Tanner MS. 131, ff. 170–88]. In addition to his remuneration as architect, Pierce received £14 for carving, probably in the pediment [Church Commissioners, Muniment 123828]. In Staffordshire, Pierce was also employed at WOLSELEY HALL (dem. 1966), where he executed the woodwork in the dining-room for Sir Charles Wolseley, Bart. [R. Plot, Natural History of Staffordshire, 1686, 383] (C. Life, 12 Feb. 1910), and he carved the staircase at SUDBURY HALL, DERBYSHIRE, in 1676–7 [C. Hussey in C. Life, 15–22–29 June, 1935]. In 1680–1 he probably designed the screen and panelling in WINCHESTER COLLEGE CHAPEL, subsequently removed to Hursley Park, but now reinstalled in the New Hall at Winchester [J. H. Harvey, 'Winchester College', Jnl. of the British Archaeological Assn. 3rd ser., xxviii, 1965, 126; John Cornforth in C. Life, 11 May 1961 and 26 March 1964].

In 1682–3 Pierce was employed by William Winde to design and carve the pediment of COMBE ABBEY, WARWICKS., for the 1st Earl of Craven [Bodleian Library, MS. Gough War-

wicks. 1, ff. 14, 31, 45, 47], and he also worked at the house at HAMPSTEAD MARSHALL, BERKSHIRE, which Winde built for the same nobleman in the years following the Restoration. A design for a gate-pier at Hampstead Marshall, inscribed 'E. Peirce F^{ct}', is in the Bodleian Library [MS. Gough Drawings a.2, f. 36]. In 1694 Pierce was employed to design the pillar at Seven Dials in the parish of St. Giles-in-the-Fields, London. His original drawing is in the Print Room of the British Museum. The pillar was removed in 1773, and is now at Weybridge, Surrey (Survey of London v, pl. 40).

Pierce died at his house in Surrey Street in March 1695, and was buried at St. Clement Danes. He left a curious memorandum of his 'Dues Debts and Disposalls' which on 20 April 1695 was proved as his will in the Archdeaconry Court of Middlesex. In it he states that he 'may justly be supposed to be worth 2516 pounds'. This sum was to be shared between his son John Pierce, his son-in-law John Killingworth, and his widow. In addition there was his 'Clositt of Books, prints and drawings', of which his 'very good freind' William Talman was 'to have the choise and picking of what therein shall seeme to make up the worthy colection he intends'. The 'sirpluce' was to be divided between his son and son-in-law, and evidently supplied the material for the 'curious collection of Books, Drawings, Prints, Models, and Plaster Figures' that was sold by auction in February 1696, together with that of the landscape-painter Thomas Manby, who had died in November 1695. Anne Pierce, his widow, died in 1703. A portrait of Pierce by Isaac Fuller at Sudeley Castle is reproduced in Walpole Society xi, pl. 24. The sculptor William Kidwell (d. 1736) was his pupil [H. Potterton in Burlington Mag. Dec. 1972, 864].

Talman evidently availed himself of the opportunity to select drawings from Pierce's 'closet', for several drawings by Pierce formerly in Talman's collection are in the Print Room of the British Museum,[1] and others bearing indications of Talman's ownership are in the Victoria and Albert,[2] Soane and Ashmolean[3] Museums, the R.I.B.A. Drawings Collection and the Art Institute at Chicago.[4] Some of these drawings are reproduced in Wren Soc. xvii, pls. 22, 23, 24 and

[1] See E. Croft-Murray & P. Hilton, Catalogue of British Drawings i, 1960, 451–5 and plates.
[2] Numbered 3436. 318–20, 421, 432, 433, 441. No. 421 is reproduced by John Physick, Designs for English Sculpture, 1969, 46–7.
[3] Gibbs Collection iii, 99 and 110, and Talman album, f. 87 (sketch for a bust identified by Dr. Margaret Whinney as that of Baldwin Hamey at the Royal College of Physicians, which is known to have been executed by Pierce in 1675).
[4] John Harris, Catalogue of British Drawings for Architecture, etc. in American Collections, 1971, 160–1.

26, where they are wrongly ascribed to Talman. In addition there is a design by Pierce for a monument to Archbishop Matthew Parker at the end of Bodleian, Tanner MS. 89. This was made for Archbishop Sancroft but was not executed.

Pierce was the author of a set of 12 engraved designs for friezes, of which there is a copy in the British Museum (Department of Prints and Drawings). The set is undated, but no. 1 is titled: 'Edward Pearce Inventer. Sould by John Overton att ye White horse without Newgate neere the Fountaine Tavern'.

[Rachel Poole, 'Edward Pierce, the Sculptor', *Walpole Soc.* xi, 1922–3; D. Knoop & G. P. Jones, *The London Mason in the Seventeenth Century*, 1935, 25–6; K. A. Esdaile in *The Architect*, 2 Sept. 1921; June Seymour, 'Edward Pearce: Baroque Sculptor of London', *Guildhall Miscellany*, No. 1, 1952; R. Gunnis, *Dictionary of British Sculptors*, 1968, 296–7; Walpole Soc. *Vertue Note Books, passim; Wren Soc.* xx, 160; abstract of will published by J. H. Harvey in *Jnl. of the British Archaeological Assn.*, 3rd ser., xxviii, 1965, 127].

PIERCE, THOMAS, was an architect and surveyor of Stamford, Lincs. A new GAOL behind the Town Hall at STAMFORD was built to his designs in 1821 [advt. in *Lincoln, Rutland and Stamford Mercury*, 23 Feb. 1821], and he also designed the Tudor Gothic SNOWDEN'S HOSPITAL in the same town, as rebuilt in 1822–3 by Robert Goodwin, mason [Stamford Corporation Records, Mayor's Accounts for 1823–4].

PILKINGTON, REDMOND WILLIAM (1789–1844), the younger son of William Pilkington (*q.v.*), followed his father's profession, succeeding him in 1824 as surveyor to the Charterhouse, in 1826 as architect to the Earl of Radnor, and in 1838 as Surveyor to the Sun Fire Assurance Office. At the CHARTERHOUSE he rebuilt PREACHER'S and PENSIONERS' COURTS in 1825–30, apparently to designs provided by Edward Blore (*q.v.*), though in 1827 he exhibited at the Royal Academy under his own name a 'view of one of the quadrangles now erecting' at the Charterhouse. He died suddenly on 22 May 1844, aged 54. He had purchased an estate called Ash Hill near his father's property in Yorkshire. In London, where he was a magistrate, he lived in Hyde Park Gate, Kensington Gore. His son Lionel Scott Pilkington, *alias* Jack Hawley, was well known as a sportsman and eccentric. [*A.P.S.D.; D.N.B.*]

PILKINGTON, WILLIAM (1758–1848), born on 7 September 1758, at Hatfield, near Doncaster, was the elder son of William Pilkington of that place. He became a pupil of Sir Robert Taylor, whom he assisted until the latter's death

in 1788. In 1781 he was appointed Surveyor to the Board of Customs, resigning in 1810. He also became District Surveyor to the parishes of St. Margaret and St. John, Westminster (1784), and was surveyor to the Sun Fire Assurance Office (1792) and to the Charterhouse (1792). He was employed as surveyor and architect by the Earl of Radnor, for whom he built the Council House at Salisbury to the designs of Sir Robert Taylor in 1788–95. He exhibited occasionally at the Royal Academy between 1780 and 1790. He retired in about 1842 to his estate at Hatfield, where he died in 1848. He married in 1785 Sarah, daughter and co-heiress of John Andrews of Knaresborough, Yorks., by whom he had two sons. The elder, Henry, was called to the Bar; the younger, Redmond William (*q.v.*), followed his father's profession, and succeeded to several of his posts. His pupils included Joseph Parkinson, G. Goldring, and his nephew, James Howell. [*A.P.S.D.; D.N.B.;* H. Walpole, *Anecdotes of Painting* v, ed. F. W. Hilles & P. B. Daghlian, 1937, 199.]

PORTSMOUTH, THE CUSTOM HOUSE, 1785; dem. [*A.P.S.D.*].

LIVERPOOL, THE CUSTOM HOUSE, enlargement of accommodation 1786; dem. 1828 [E. H. Rideout, *The Custom House, Liverpool*, Liverpool 1928, 46].

EALING, MIDDLESEX, LONDON STYLE HOUSE, for Luke Wetten, 1790–1; dem. [*A.P.S.D.*].

LONDON, DOVER STREET, NO. 38, for the Hon. W. H. Bouverie, 1791 [*A.P.S.D.*].

LONDON, HALF MOON STREET, house for the 3rd Duke of Grafton (who himself lived in Clarges Street), 1798 [*A.P.S.D.*].

CHILTON LODGE, nr. HUNGERFORD, BERKSHIRE, rebuilt for John Pearse, 1800; altered by Sir A. W. Blomfield; dem. *c.* 1969 [J. Britton, *Beauties of Wiltshire* iii, 1825, 266–7]. Pilkington also designed the PEARSE MAUSOLEUM in CHILTON FOLIAT CHURCHYARD [*ibid.*].

FOLKESTONE, KENT, gaol for the 2nd Earl of Radnor, 1801; dem. [*A.P.S.D.*].

OTTERDEN PLACE, KENT, rebuilt for Granville Hastings Wheler, 1802, Tudor style [J. Lees-Milne in *C. Life*, 27 Aug. 1970].

LONDON, THE CHARTERHOUSE, the 'BIG SCHOOL', 1803; dem. *c.* 1872 [*Chronicles of Charter-House*, by a Carthusian, 1847, 175].

YARMOUTH, NORFOLK, THE ROYAL NAVAL HOSPITAL (later barracks and now St. Nicholas Hospital), 1809–11, is said to have been designed by Pilkington by J. Preston, *Picture of Yarmouth*, 1819, 7 and J. H. Druery, *Great Yarmouth*, 1826, 89, but according to J. Dugdale's *British Traveller* iii, 1819, 610, it was designed by Edward Holl, the official Architect to the Navy (*q.v.*).

CLERMONT HALL, LITTLE CRESSINGHAM, NORFOLK,

for T. H. Fortescue, 1st Earl of Clermont, 1812 [*A.P.S.D.*].

WYCKHILL HOUSE, nr. STOW-ON-THE-WOLD, GLOS., for Charles Pole, 1812, with large alterations 1815; enlarged and remodelled *c.* 1880–90 [*A.P.S.D.*].

WESTMINSTER, THE TRANSPORT OFFICE (afterwards the India Board of Control), CANNON ROW, WHITEHALL, 1816; dem. [*A.P.S.D.*].

POLSTEAD HALL, SUFFOLK, improvements for Thomas Cooke, 1816–19 [*A.P.S.D.*].

NORK HOUSE, BANSTEAD, SURREY, alterations, including addition of wings, for the 2nd Lord Arden, 1812 onwards; dem. *c.* 1930 [*A.P.S.D.*].

CALVERTON HOUSE, nr. STONY STRATFORD, BUCKS., alterations for the 2nd Lord Arden, 1819 onwards [*A.P.S.D.*].

CALVERTON CHURCH, BUCKS., for the 2nd Lord Arden, 1818–24, Gothic, with neo-Norman tower [contract in Bucks. Record Office].

LONDON, THE TEMPLE PRINTING OFFICE, NO. 13 BOUVERIE STREET, for James Moyes, 1824 [drawings by 'Mr. Pilkington' in St. Bride Printing Library, Bride Lane, Fleet Street, cf. Iain Bain, 'James Moyes and his Temple Printing Office', *Jnl. of the Printing Historical Soc.* iv, 1968].

An unexecuted design by Pilkington for PARLINGTON HALL, YORKS. (W.R.) 1810, is illustrated by Angus Taylor in *Leeds Arts Calendar*, No. 77, 1975, 27.

PINCH, JOHN (*c.* 1770–1827), of Bath, began his career as a builder but went bankrupt soon after 1800, and thereafter practised as an architect and surveyor with considerable success. Most of his recorded work was on the Earl of Darlington's estate in Bathwick, to which he acted as surveyor. His terraces are marked by great elegance and refinement, and represent the final phase of Georgian building in Bath. His churches are also attractive examples of late Georgian ecclesiastical Gothic. Pinch died at his house in Duke Street on 11 March 1827, aged 57. His practice was continued by his son John Pinch, junior (*q.v.*). [W. Ison, *The Georgian Buildings of Bath*, 1948, 44 and *passim*; J. M. Hunt, 'A Little-known Architect of Bath', *C. Life*, 14 June 1962].

BATH, terraces on Darlington estate in BATHWICK, including NEW SYDNEY PLACE, 1807–8, DANIEL STREET, 1810, and RABY PLACE, 1825 [Ison].

BATH, terraces on Lansdowne slopes, including CAVENDISH PLACE, 1808–15, CAVENDISH CRESCENT, 1817–30, and SION HILL PLACE, 1817–20 [Ison].

BATH, ST. MARY'S CHURCH, BATHWICK, 1814–20, Gothic; chancel 1873 [G. N. Wright, *Historic Guide to Bath*, 1864, 248].

HUNGERFORD CHURCH, BERKSHIRE, 1814–16, Gothic [*V.C.H. Berks*, iv, 197].

BISHOPSTROW HOUSE, WILTS., for William Temple, 1817–21 [*V.C.H. Wilts.* viii, 7].

CAMERTON CHURCH, SOMERSET, Gothic mausoleum in churchyard for Sir Richard Hoare, Bart., 1819; dem. [*Journal of a Somerset Rector 1803–34*, ed. Coombs, 1971, 121].

TWERTON CHURCH, SOMERSET, enlarged 1824; rebuilt by G. P. Manners 1839 [I.C.B.S.].

BATH, THE ROYAL UNITED HOSPITAL (now Technical College), BEAU STREET, 1824–6; Albert Wing added by J. E. Gill, 1864 [S. D. Major, *Notabilia of Bath*, 1879, 40].

PINCH, JOHN, junior (–1849), was the son of John Pinch of Bath, to whose practice he succeeded. In 1823, when he was employed by General Goldie-Taubman to design his new house in the Isle of Man, the general's wife described him in her diary as 'a very intelligent young man ... a very clever Architect in the Gothic style especially – the Father and Son built two beautiful new Churches, the Houses in New Sidney Place and some Gentlemen's Seats'. His churches are, in fact, all in the Gothic style, but his domestic work in Bath shows the influence of the Greek revival. It is possible that the designs for St. Saviour's Bath, which Pinch carried out in 1829–31, were made in collaboration with his father before the latter's death in 1827. He himself died at Bath on 23 December 1849 [W. Ison, *The Georgian Buildings of Bath*, 1948, 44, 83, 95, 132; *Gent's Mag.* 1850 (i), 229].

THE NUNNERY, ISLE OF MAN, for General Goldie, 1823, Gothic [family papers, *ex inf.* Capt. J. W. L. Fry-Goldie-Taubman].

BATH, ST. SAVIOUR'S CHURCH, WALCOT, 1829–31, Gothic; chancel 1882 [Port, 158–9].

BATH, QUEEN SQUARE, central block on west side, 1830 [Ison, 132].

MIDSOMER NORTON CHURCH, SOMERSET, rebuilt (except tower), 1830–1, Gothic [I.C.B.S.].

WESTON CHURCH, SOMERSET, rebuilt (except tower), 1832, Gothic [I.C.B.S.].

BATH, SYDNEY HOTEL, addition of attic storey, 1836 [Ison, 95].

GRITTLETON CHURCH, WILTS., added south aisle and porch, 1836, Gothic [J. E. Jackson, *History of Grittleton*, Wilts. Topographical Soc. 1843].

DOWNSIDE, SOMERSET, CHRIST CHURCH, 1837–8, Gothic [I.C.B.S.].

PAULTON CHURCH, SOMERSET, rebuilt (except tower), 1839, Gothic [I.C.B.S.].

BATH, ST. MARY'S SCHOOLS, HENRIETTA ROAD, 1840, Gothic [S. D. Major, *Notabilia of Bath*, 1879, 103].

FARRINGTON GURNEY CHURCH, SOMERSET, 1843–4, Norman style [I.C.B.S.].

PITT, JOHN (*c.* 1706–1787), of Encombe in Dorset, was the second son of George Pitt of Stratfieldsaye and a distant cousin of Thomas Pitt, Lord Camelford (*q.v.*). His public career as M.P., Lord of Trade and Surveyor General of Woods and Forests will be found in the *History of Parliament.* His activities as an amateur architect are less well documented. He appears, however, to have designed two garden buildings, an Ionic rotunda and an octagon seat, at HAGLEY, WORCS., for the 1st Lord Lyttelton in 1748–9, and his architectural skill is praised in an ode addressed to him by a clerical relation, the Rev. Christopher Pitt. It may be concluded that Pitt was his own architect at ENCOMBE, DORSET, a small country house that he gradually enlarged and rebuilt from 1734 onwards in an individual style that owes something to Vanbrugh (*C. Life*, 24, 31 Jan. 1963 and R.C.H.M., *Dorset* ii(1), 78–80).[1] Family connections and stylistic affinities suggest that Pitt may also have designed WEST LODGE, nr. IWERNE MINSTER, DORSET (R.C.H.M., *Dorset* iv, 38); remodelled BINFIELD LODGE, BERKSHIRE, for his elder brother William soon after 1754; altered STRATFIELDSAYE HOUSE, HANTS., for his nephew George Pitt, 1st Lord Rivers, in 1755 (*C. Life*, 10–17 April 1975); and designed STRATFIELDSAYE CHURCH (*C. Life*, 15 June 1967) and RECTORY for the same nephew soon afterwards.[2] In these buildings conventional Palladian elements have been invigorated by ideas of Vanbrughian origin to produce a distinctive personal style of considerable interest and merit. Pitt, who was a member of the Society of Dilettanti, died in February 1787. [Edward Marsden, 'John Pitt of Encombe: an 18th Century Dilettante Architect', *C. Life*, 9 Sept. 1976.]

PITT, THOMAS, 1st BARON CAMELFORD (1737–1793), was the only son of Thomas Pitt of Boconnoc in Cornwall, elder brother of William Pitt, first Earl of Chatham. His mother was Christian, daughter of Sir Thomas Lyttelton, Bart., of Hagley. He was admitted to Clare College, Cambridge, as a fellow-commoner in January 1754, and took the degree of M.A. in 1759.

Pitt suffered from ill health from an early age, and it was for the sake of his health that he accompanied Lord Kinnoull on his embassy to Lisbon in 1760.[3] From Lisbon he passed through Spain

to Barcelona, sailed thence to Genoa, and spent some time in Italy. He was staying at Florence with his uncle, Sir Richard Lyttelton, when news reached him of his father's death. Besides the family estate of Boconnoc, Pitt now inherited the rotten borough of Old Sarum, and a considerable interest in that of Okehampton in Devonshire. As member for the former, he entered Parliament in December 1761, and continued to sit for one or the other until he was raised to the peerage in 1784 as Baron Camelford, through the influence of his cousin, the younger Pitt.

In March 1762, Pitt took a small house at Twickenham which he referred to facetiously as the 'Palazzo Pitti'. Horace Walpole welcomed him as a neighbour, and described him in a letter to Montagu as 'very amiable and very sensible, and one of the very few that I reckon quite worthy of being at home at Strawberry'. He was, in fact, privileged to advise on the internal decoration of Walpole's Gothic villa, and himself designed the 'ornaments' of the Gallery and Chapel. From this time onwards there is considerable evidence of Pitt's activities as an amateur architect. In 1763 he appears to have designed the Gothic cottage, the bridge of rocks and a conservatory, at PARK PLACE, nr. HENLEY-ON-THAMES, for Walpole's friend General Conway. In 1764 Dr. Richard Pococke noted that the PALLADIAN BRIDGE at HAGLEY, WORCS., was built 'after young Mr. Pitt's design' [B.M., Add. MS. 14260, f. 178]. At STOWE HOUSE, BUCKS., he not only designed the CORINTHIAN ARCH (erected in 1765–6) for his near relative Richard Grenville, Lord Temple, but was also responsible for the final form of the south front, as rebuilt between 1772 and 1777 [M. J. McCarthy, 'The Rebuilding of Stowe House, 1770–7', *Huntingdon Library Quarterly* xxxvi, 1973]. For his uncle, Bishop Charles Lyttelton, he made a design, executed in 1765, for refurnishing the choir of CARLISLE CATHEDRAL in the Gothic style.[1] [J. Nichols, *Literary Illustrations* iii, 1818, 310; J. Dugdale, *The British Traveller* i, 1819, 573.] He also had a hand in some similar alterations at NORWICH CATHEDRAL a few years later [B.M., Stowe MS. 754, f. 235 *et seq.*]. At BOCONNOC he added in 1772 a new south wing containing a library and picture-gallery,[2] and in the previous year he erected an obelisk in the park to the memory of his uncle, Sir Richard Lyttelton (d. 1770). After his marriage in 1771 he built CAMELFORD HOUSE at the Oxford Street end of Park Lane, presumably to his own designs.

In 1763 Pitt was elected a member of the

---

[1] The interior of Encombe was largely remodelled by J. & J. Belcher in the 1860s, and by A. Salvin in 1871–4.

[2] The church was dedicated by the Bishop of Salisbury on 1 Sept. 1758.

[3] Lord Strathmore was his travelling companion, and B.M., Add MS. 5845, ff. 111–46 is a transcript by William Cole of 'Observations in a Tour to Portugal and Spain 1760 by John Earl of Strathmore and Thos. Pitt Esq.' It contains some interesting passages on Gothic and Moorish architecture.

---

[1] Pitt's woodwork was ejected by Ewan Christian in 1856, but the reredos went to Featherstone Castle, Northumberland, and some fragments are preserved in St. Mary's Church, Carlisle.

[2] This was built by Charles Rawlinson (*q.v.*).

Society of Dilettanti, and he proposed in 1785 that the shell of two adjoining houses built by him in Hertford Street should be converted into a museum by the Society: but the project was not carried out on grounds of expense. In 1778 he met the young John Soane in Italy, and became one of the architect's earliest patrons, introducing him to his cousin William Pitt the younger, and himself employing him in 1781–2 to repair Petersham Lodge, Surrey, of which he had taken a lease, in 1783 to alter and enlarge Westgate House, Burnham Market, Norfolk, which he had inherited through his wife, and in 1786 to carry out some repairs at Boconnoc [Dorothy Stroud, *The Architecture of Sir John Soane*, 1961, 14, 24, 33, 157, 158].

Soane, who owed much to Pitt, not only paid tribute in his *Memoirs* to the latter's 'classical taste and profound architectural knowledge', but in one of his lectures coupled his name with those of Burlington and Pembroke as leaders of English architectural taste. If Pitt was not quite a neo-classical Burlington, he was certainly an able and influential amateur, and at Stowe he had an important share in creating one of the major monuments of Georgian architecture.

Pitt married in 1771 Anne, daughter and co-heiress of Pinckney Wilkinson, a wealthy London merchant, by whom he had one son, Thomas, whose misspent life ended in his death in a duel in 1804. He himself died at Florence in 1793, and was buried at Boconnoc, where his portrait is preserved (reproduced in Tresham Lever, *The House of Pitt*, 268).

[*D.N.B.*; Horace Walpole's *Letters*, *passim*; J. Nichols, *Literary Illustrations* vi, 1831, 67–119; *An Eighteenth-Century Correspondence*, ed. Dickins & Stanton, 1910, 369, 444; J. Soane, *Lectures on Architecture*, ed. Bolton, 1929, 56; A. T. Bolton, *The Portrait of Sir John Soane*, 1927, 16, 21–5; Tresham Lever, *The House of Pitt*, 1947; L. Namier & J. Brooke, *The House of Commons 1754–1790* iii, 1964, 286–90.]

PLATT, a family of mason-architects who originated at Lyme Park in the parish of Disley in Cheshire in the seventeenth century, and were the leading architects and builders at Rotherham in Yorkshire in the eighteenth century. As early as 1680 a mason called John Platt was employed to build the New Parlour at LYME PARK for Richard Legh, and between 1727 and 1730 several members of the family were engaged in rebuilding the house for Peter Legh to the designs of Giacomo Leoni [John Cornforth in *C. Life*, 19 Dec. 1974]. Those principally concerned were Edmund, John and George Platt, the sons of Edmund Platt (d. 1715).

JOHN PLATT, whose death in 1730 is noted in the Lyme Steward's book now in Stockport Public Library, appears to have designed ST.

PAUL'S CHURCH, SHEFFIELD, a handsome baroque building in the style of Thomas Archer, built in 1720–1, but not wholly finished until 1772. In his *History of Hallamshire* (1819, p. 158), Joseph Hunter states that the church was built by 'Platts of Rotherham', whom he describes elsewhere as 'an architect of no slender merit', and in 1769 John Platt II recorded in his journal that he made drawings for 'finishing the steeple of St. Paul's Church in Sheffield, which was built [by] Mr. Tunnicliffe [*q.v.*] and my uncle John Platt ... but never finished'. For measured drawings etc., of the church, which was demolished in 1937, see *Building News*, vol. c, 23 June 1911, p. 876.

GEORGE PLATT (1700–1743), the third son of Edmund Platt, left Lyme in about 1730 and established himself in the neighbourhood of Rotherham. He lived at the Red House, Woodlaithes, and owned a quarry at Thrybergh. In 1731–3 he partly rebuilt the church of CHAPEL-EN-LE-FRITH, DERBYSHIRE, whose steeple had been taken down by his brother John in 1729 [W. M. Bunting, *The Parish Church of Chapel-en-le-Frith*, 1925, 157], and in 1738 he took down and rebuilt the top of the spire of HATHERSAGE CHURCH, DERBYSHIRE, as recorded by a memorandum in the parish records. In 1740 he contracted to build BURROW HALL, LANCS., for Robert Fenwick to the designs of Westby Gill (*q.v.*). His most important recorded work was CUSWORTH HALL, YORKS. (W.R.), a house of Palladian character which he designed and built for William Wrightson, M.P., in 1740–1. An engraving dated 1743 is inscribed '*Geo: Platt Architecto*', and there are payments to Platt in the building accounts in the Leeds Archives Department (BW/Ma 5, A 22, 32 etc.). The wings containing the chapel and library were added to the designs of James Paine in 1750–3 (see *Vitruvius Britannicus* iv, pls. 88–9, which also shows modifications to the main elevation by Paine). George Platt contracted consumption, and died at Bristol Hot Wells on 9 November 1743, aged 43. He was buried in Rotherham churchyard, where a monument (destroyed in 1950) described him as 'Architect and Builder' and as 'a Man of great abilities in his profession and of the strictest integrity in his dealings'. His widow carried on the business until her eldest son John was able to take charge of it.

JOHN PLATT (1728–1810) was only 15 when his father died, but took charge of the business at Rotherham as soon as he was old enough, and had a very successful career as an architect, builder and statuary mason. Later he took over the quarries of black marble at Ashford nr. Matlock, together with the works for sawing and polishing the marble established by Henry Watson of Bakewell earlier in the century. He also worked the quarries of grey marble at Richlow Dale, nr. Monyash. In 1765 he established pottery works, which (after a period of partnership) he eventually sold to the ironmaster Samuel Walker.

Platt's journal, which extends from 1763 to 1796, throws considerable light on his activities as an architect and builder. As a contracting mason he was employed at Wentworth Castle (where in 1762 he carved the pediment of the portico), Wentworth Woodhouse, and elsewhere. He made numerous monuments and chimney-pieces, and was responsible for the marble staircases at Aston Hall (1776–7) and Clifton Hall (1783–4). Surviving drawings[1] show that he was quite a competent draughtsman, and it is clear from his journal that he designed a number of minor country houses and public buildings in the neighbourhood of Sheffield and Rotherham, a list of which is given below.

In 1757 John Platt married Anne Fitzgerald, the illegitimate daughter of one of the locally influential family of Buck. They had ten children, none of whom chose to follow their father's trade. John (1763–1832) was sent to York to become a pupil of Thomas Atkinson, but after running away he was allowed by his father to enter the Navy and eventually rose to the rank of Captain. Charles (1770–1817) was apprenticed to Westmacott, the sculptor, but in 1794 joined the Army and fought in the Napoleonic Wars. George Edmund (1779–1850) was articled to the architect John Rawstorne, but like his brothers he preferred a military career and took part in the Peninsular Campaign. William (1775–1811) became an engraver, but lost his sight and died at the age of 36. John Platt himself died at Halifax on 14 December 1810, aged 85, and was buried in Rotherham churchyard.

[J. H. Cockburn, 'A Rotherham Architect and his Family', *Rotherham Advertiser*, 8 Feb. 1936; J. D. Potts, *Platt of Rotherham, Mason-Architects 1700–1810*, Sheffield, 1959; A. J. B. Kiddell, 'John Platt of Rotherham, Potter and Mason-Architect', *Trans. of the English Ceramic Circle* v (iii), 1961, 172–5; Rupert Gunnis, *Dictionary of British Sculptors*, 1968, 308; J. Dugdale, *The British Traveller* ii, 1819, 21; J. Guest, *Historic Notices of Rotherham*, 1879, 410–11; B.M., Strafford Papers, Add. MS. 22241, ff. 130–3, 140 *et seq.*].

DOMESTIC ARCHITECTURE

WORTLEY HALL, YORKS. (W.R.), is stated by Hunter, *South Yorkshire* ii, 1831, 323, to have been rebuilt by Edward Wortley Montagu in stages, beginning in 1743, 'with the assistance of Platts of Rotherham'. The Platts probably built the south front designed by G. Leoni (*q.v.*) in 1743, and surviving accounts show that John Platt was employed more or less continuously from 1749 to 1789. In 1757–9 he built the east wing, probably to the designs of Matthew Brettingham (*q.v.*), but the house was still unfinished when Montagu died in 1761, and in the 1780s Platt built a new west wing and offices for Montagu's daughter Lady Bute. Further work was done (not apparently by Platt) when Lady Bute's grandson James Archibald Stuart Wortley (later 1st Lord Wharncliffe) came to live at Wortley *c.* 1800 [Wortley papers in Sheffield City Library; information from Mr. Richard Hewlings].

GATE BURTON HALL, LINCS., temple or summer-house for Thomas Hutton, 1747–8 [drawing in Sheffield City Library, AP 508 (1) inscribed 'Built for T. Hutton at Burton nr. Gainsbro' per J. Platt 1747 & 1748'] (B. Howlett, *Views in the County of Lincoln*, 1797).

MOORGATE HALL, nr. ROTHERHAM, YORKS. (W.R.), office buildings for Samuel Tooker, 1764 [Potts, 11].

CANKLOW HOUSE, nr. ROTHERHAM, YORKS. (W.R.), for J. Taylor, 1767 [Potts, 12].

MASBROUGH HALL, nr. ROTHERHAM, YORKS. (W.R.), for Samuel Walker, 1768; dem. except stables [Potts, 12].

TONG HALL, YORKS. (W.R.), gateway (1773) and alterations to house for Major John Tempest [Potts, 13]. These alterations must have included the addition of the top floor and of the bow windows to the north front.

WORSBROUGH HALL, YORKS. (W.R.), drawing room for Francis Edmunds, 1775 [Potts, 14].

PAGE HALL, nr. ECCLESHALL, YORKS. (W.R.), for Thomas Broadbent, *c.* 1775 [Potts, 13].

MOUNT PLEASANT, nr. SHEFFIELD, YORKS. (W.R.), for Francis Hurt Sitwell, 1777 [Potts, 15].

THUNDERCLIFFE GRANGE, ECCLESFIELD, YORKS. (W.R.), for the 3rd Earl of Effingham, 1777–8 [Potts, 15].

ROTHERHAM, FERHAM HOUSE, KIMBERWORTH ROAD, for Jonathan Walker, 1787 [MS. Journal, 4 Sept. 1787].

ROTHERHAM, house in WESTGATE for himself, 1794; dem. [Potts, 19].

OTHER BUILDINGS

WORTLEY CHURCH, YORKS. (W.R.), rebuilt steeple and chancel for Edward Wortley Montagu, 1753–4; rebuilt 1815 [Sheffield City Library, Wortley papers M.58 (1–9)].

DONCASTER, YORKS. (W.R.), THE MARKET CROSS AND SHAMBLES, 1756; dem. [engraving in Hailstone

---

[1] Of which there is a small collection in Sheffield City Library (AP 508). Others in private ownership are illustrated in Mr. J. D. Potts's booklet cited below. Platt may have helped Lord Strafford to design the south front of Wentworth Castle (see the drawing illustrated by Potts, and another at Temple Newsam House signed 'Per John Platt' which shows the front as completed in 1764).

Collection, York Minster Library, signed
'Platt Archt.'; Potts, 8].

ECKINGTON CHURCH, DERBYSHIRE, rebuilt south
aisle, 1763 [Potts, 10].

DONCASTER CHURCH, YORKS. (W.R.), galleries,
1764; dem. [Potts, 11].

PENISTONE, YORKS. (W.R.), THE CLOTH HALL AND
SHAMBLES, designed 1763, erected 1768?
[Potts, 10].

BARNSLEY, YORKS. (W.R.), THE SHAMBLES, 1768;
dem. [Potts, 12].

ROTHERHAM, CHARITY SCHOOL and HOUSE in THE
CROFTS, 1776 [Potts, 14].

DONCASTER, THE GREEN INN, 1778 [MS. Journal,
Jan. 1778].

ROTHERHAM, THE MARKET HOUSE, 1780–1; dem.
[Potts, 16].

ROTHERHAM, THE BREWERY (now Mappin's
Brewery), 1791 [MS. Journal, April 1791].

PLAW, JOHN (*c.* 1745–1820), was presumably
the John Plaw who in 1759 was apprenticed to
Thomas Kaygill, a member of the Tyler's and
Bricklayers' Company [Guildhall Library. MS.
3053/3, under 1768]. He was described as an
'architect and master builder in Westminster',
when in 1763 he was awarded a premium by the
Society of Arts for a drawing of the Banqueting
House in Whitehall (*Register of Premiums*, p. 39).
He was a member of the Incorporated Society of
Artists, and was the last president elected before
its dissolution in 1791. He exhibited with the
Society in 1773, 1790 and 1791, and at the Royal
Academy from 1775 onwards. A Miss P. Plaw,
who appears to have been his daughter, exhibited
drawings of architectural subjects at the Society
of Artists in 1791. In about 1795 he moved to
Southampton, where he prepared ambitious
plans for residential development at Albion Place
and Brunswick Place of which little or none was
carried out, and is said to have designed the Barracks on the site of the present Ordnance Survey
Office. In about 1810 he emigrated to Canada,
settling in Charlottetown, Prince Edward Island.
Here he designed several buildings before his
death at the age of 75, on 24 May 1820. There
is an illustration of his tombstone in *Arch. Rev.*
xlv, 1919, 130. J. Taylor and J. B. Papworth were
his pupils, and Samuel Benwell was his nephew.

Plaw published *Rural Architecture; or Designs
from the Simple Cottage to the Decorative Villa*,
1785, 1794, 1796, 1800, 1802 and 1804, in which
many of his executed designs were illustrated;
Ferme Ornée or Rural Improvements, 1795, 1813;
and *Sketches for Country Houses, Villas and Rural
Dwellings*, 1800, 1803. These were among the
earliest of the cottage and villa books which
became so popular during the first quarter of the
nineteenth century. Plaw's best-known works are
the romantically-sited and unusually planned
circular house on an island in Lake Windermere,

642

and the neatly geometrical church at Paddington.
[*A.P.S.D.*; *D.N.B.*; *Gent's Mag.* 1820 (ii), 376.]

BELLE ISLE, LAKE WINDERMERE, WESTMORLAND, for
Thomas English, 1774–5 [exhib. at R.A. 1775;
Rural Architecture, pls. 25–30] (*C. Life*, 3–10
Aug. 1940).

LONDON, an unidentified villa at VAUXHALL, 1781
[*Rural Architecture*, pls. 14–15].

WOOTTON COURT, nr. CANTERBURY, KENT,
refronted for the Rev. E. T. Bridges, 1781;
dem. [*Rural Architecture*, pl. 33; *Topographical Miscellanies* i, 1792, p. xviii].

LONDON, CHRIST CHURCH, NEWGATE STREET,
monument to Peter Dore (d. 1781), executed
by Robert Chambers [K. A. Esdaile, *English
Monumental Sculpture since the Renaissance*,
1927, 99].

SELSDON FARMHOUSE, nr. CROYDON, SURREY, additions for Thomas Lane, before 1785 [*Rural
Architecture*, pls. 8–9].

LONDON, GREEN PARK LODGE, a 'hermitage' in the
garden, before 1785 [*Rural Architecture*, pl.
1;* original design in B.M., *King's Maps* xxvi,
7-*n*-2].

BELMONT, nr. THROWLEY, KENT, pair of cottages
'in the American style' (now house named 'New
York') for Col. John Montresor, before 1787
[*Ferme Ornée*, pl. 17, identified by Dr. Jesse
P. Poesch].

HARESFOOT, nr. BERKHAMSTEAD, HERTS., 1787;
rebuilt by J. B. Papworth 1817–19; dem. *c.*
1965 [exhib. at R.A. 1787].

LONDON, ST. MARY'S CHURCH, PADDINGTON, 1788–
91 [exhib. at Society of Artists 1791; Stieglitz,
Plans, etc., Paris 1801, pls. 45–6; working
drawings in R.I.B.A. Collection] (*C. Life*, 1
Nov. 1973).

THORNVILLE ROYAL (i.e. ALLERTON MAULEVERER),
YORKS. (W.R.), farm-buildings, etc., for Col.
Thomas Thornton, *c.* 1790 [*Ferme Ornée*, pls.
1, 24, 25].

BROCKENHURST HOUSE, HANTS., domed bath-
house and fishing-lodge for John Morant,
before 1795 [*Ferme Ornée*, pls. 1, 14–15].

SEACLIFF, EAST LOTHIAN, for Robert Colt, M.P.,
c. 1795; rebuilt by William Burn 1841 [*Rural
Architecture*, pls. 42–3].

LYMINGTON, HANTS., cottage orné near, before
1800 [*Sketches*, pls. 16, 17].

UNEXECUTED

Among the designs in Plaw's *Rural Architecture*,
and apparently not executed, are a 'Design made
for—Scott Esqr. of Ireland' (pls. 44–5), 'Designs
made for Glenfiddoch in Scotland for the Duke
of Gordon' (pls. 52–3), and a 'Design for a House
for Humberston Mackenzie Esq. intended to be
built in Scotland' (pl. 56). *Sketches for Country
Houses* includes a shooting box for the Marquis

of Huntly (pl. 25) and a design for Wodehouse, Wombourne, Staffs., for the Rev. Shaw Hellier (pls. 29–31), neither of which appears to have been carried out.

Plaw's exhibited designs included a 'Design for a bridge over the River Suir from the city of Waterford to the County of Kilkenny in Ireland' (1779), a 'Design for a bridge across the Thames at Fulham' (1780), a 'Design for an assembly room, intended to be built at Harrogate' (1790), and a 'Design for a house in Third Street, Philadelphia' (1790).

At Penicuik House, Midlothian, there is a set of drawings for an unexecuted park entrance, signed 'J. Plaw Arch^t', and his plans and elevations for an 'Admiral's House, Halifax, Nova Scotia', signed and dated 1813, are preserved in the Public Record Office (MPI/166).

PLAYFAIR, JAMES (1755–1794), born on 5 August 1755, was the fourth son of the Rev. James Playfair, minister of Liff and Benvie in Angus. His elder brother John (1748–1819) became a distinguished mathematician and geologist, while his younger brother William (1759–1823) gained a precarious living and some notoriety as an inventor and pamphleteer. Nothing is known about James's early life or training as an architect, but the last ten years of his life are well documented owing to the survival of his professional journal for the years 1783–93 (National Library of Scotland, Advocates MS. 33.5.25) and many of his drawings are preserved in Sir John Soane's Museum and the R.I.B.A. Drawings Collection. By 1783 he was established in London, with an office in Bloomsbury, and began to exhibit regularly at the Royal Academy. His practice was largely in Scotland (where he had the good fortune to secure Henry Dundas as a patron), but no doubt he hoped to acquire an English clientèle in the course of time, and the commission (1790) to design a picture-gallery in Grosvenor Square for Sir George Beaumont must have been encouraging. In 1783 he had published *A Method of Constructing Vapour Baths*.

Playfair made at least two visits to the continent. A drawing in the R.I.B.A. Collection shows that he was in Paris in August 1787, probably on a visit to his brother William, who was the Paris agent of the Scioto Land Company of Ohio. The drawing is of the Baths of the Emperor Julian in the Rue de la Harpe, but Playfair no doubt inspected the latest French architecture besides this Roman antiquity. In 1792–3 he made an Italian tour. In October 1791 he obtained an introduction to Canova from the painter Henry Tresham [Canova archive, Bassano, 5188], and a set of drawings for Townley Hall in the National Library of Ireland was dated by him at 'Rome, April 13, 1792'. A design for a 'Casina' in the R.I.B.A. Collection is dated at Rome on 24 April

1793. On his return Playfair exhibited at the Royal Academy views of the Appian Way nr. Capua and of one of the Greek temples at Paestum.

Playfair's career was terminated prematurely by his death at Edinburgh on 23 February 1794 at the age of 39. According to Joseph Farington he 'died of a broken heart in consequence of the death of his eldest boy' [Diary, 18 April 1794]. Soane and Farington helped his widow to dispose of his books and drawings, which were sold at Christie's on 10 January 1795 (catalogue in Soane Museum). It was then that Soane acquired the portfolio of drawings now in his Museum. Playfair was the father of James George Playfair, M.D. (1786–1857), who practised medicine in Florence, and of the architect W. H. Playfair (*q.v.*), who was only three at the time of his death.

Playfair was an elegant architectural designer with a strong predilection for a refined neoclassical simplicity. The simplicity is already apparent in Forfar Town Hall and Kirriemuir Church (both begun in 1786), but in later buildings a more sophisticated taste appears which shows an evident interest in the works of both Soane and Ledoux. This is most manifest in the remarkable mausoleum at Methven in Perthshire (1793), which takes the form of a Greek temple embedded in rusticated masonry, in his unexecuted designs for a house at Ardkinglas in Argyllshire (1790), and in the clear-cut geometrical forms of Cairness, with its hemicycle of offices, bold semi-circular arches, primitivist Doric columns and Egyptian billiard room. Most of these features have parallels or prototypes in the works of Boullée or Ledoux, and were no doubt the first-fruits of the French visit of 1787. Playfair's interest in neo-classical architecture in general and French architecture in particular is confirmed by the sale catalogue of his library, which includes such items as Winckelmann's *Histoire des Arts Anciens*, 'Ruines de Pestum', '4 French books on building' and 'A portfolio with architectural designs and the Halles aux Grains'. But for his premature death he would probably have emerged as an important figure in the neoclassical movement. As it is, the remote and in some respects immature Cairness remains as a remarkable testimony to his advanced architectural ideas. None of his other classical houses was of comparable significance. The exteriors of Kinnaird and Melville Castles were perfunctory and ineffective essays in castellation which compared poorly with the contemporary works of Robert Adam, but at Farnell in Angus Playfair designed a small Gothic church of unusual and precocious character. The designs for 'an American City' which he made in 1790, apparently at the behest of his brother William, are not known to have survived, but might well show further evidence of French neo-classical influence.

[*A.P.S.D.*; A. G. Playfair, *Notes on the Scottish Family of Playfair*, 1932; W. W. Robertson, 'The Journal of James Playfair', *Trans. of the Edinburgh Architectural Assn.* iii, 1894; David Walker & Colin McWilliam in *C. Life*, 28 Jan. 1971.]

PUBLIC BUILDINGS, ETC.

FORFAR, TOWN AND COUNTY HALL, 1786–8 [W. S. McCulloch, *Forfar Town and County Hall*, 1968].

KIRRIEMUIR CHURCH, ANGUS, 1786–90. The heritors employed Playfair in preference to a local builder because they wanted the church to be 'an ornament to the village', but some serious deficiencies in the internal accommodation made them regret their choice [drawings in Soane portfolio and set of engraved plans etc. in S.R.O., RHP. 176 and 8086–93; legal proceedings against Playfair in S.R.O., HR 479/4/1].

FARNELL or FARNWALL CHURCH, ANGUS, Gothic, exhibited by Playfair at R.A. as 'now building' in 1789, but said in *N.S.A.* xi, 112 to have been built in 1806. His diary shows that he made the working drawings in 1788 and the specification in 1789.

METHVEN, PERTHSHIRE, mausoleum in churchyard for Thomas Graham cr. Lord Lynedoch (whose wife had died in 1792), 1793 [Diary].

EDINBURGH, ST. PETER'S EPISCOPAL CHAPEL, ROXBURGH PLACE, 1790–1 [*Scots Mag.* 1790, 359, recording inscription on foundation stone as 'ARCHITECTO JOANNE PLAYFAIR' (*sic*)].

DOMESTIC ARCHITECTURE

HAWKHEAD PARK, RENFREWSHIRE, repairs and alterations for the Countess of Glasgow, 1784–6 [exhib. at R.A. 1785 and cf. his letters to Lord Findlater in S.R.O., GD 248/589/2].

KINNAIRD CASTLE, ANGUS, remodelled for Sir David Carnegie, Bart., 1785–93, castellated; enlarged and remodelled by D. Bryce 1855–62 [drawings in Soane portfolio; exhib. at R.A. 1791] (*Forfarshire Illustrated*, Dundee, 1843, 86).

ANNISTON HOUSE, ANGUS, for John Rait, 1785–6; dem. [drawings in Soane portfolio].

RAITH PARK, FIFE, gateway and lodge for William Ferguson, 1786 [drawings in Soane portfolio, and cf. letter to Lord Findlater, S.R.O., GD 248/591/2].

CLAPHAM, SURREY, house for David Webster, 1786 [Diary; drawings in Soane portfolio].

LANGHOLM LODGE, DUMFRIESSHIRE, additions for the 3rd Duke of Buccleuch, 1786–7; rebuilt after fire in *c.* 1790; dem. 1953 [drawings in Soane portfolio].

DALKEITH HOUSE, MIDLOTHIAN, added bow window to library for the 3rd Duke of Buccleuch, 1786 [drawings in Soane portfolio]. Playfair

also made unexecuted designs for an entrance gate and lodges.

PETERSHAM, SURREY, DOUGLAS HOUSE, greenhouse for Archibald Douglas, 1786 [drawings in Soane portfolio].

MELVILLE CASTLE, MIDLOTHIAN, for Henry Dundas, 1st Viscount Melville, 1786–91, castellated [Diary; letters to Lord Findlater; working drawings in S.R.O., RHP 6699].

MOLESEY HURST, SURREY, alterations to house for the 8th Earl of Winchilsea (who had it on a lease), 1787–8 [drawings in Soane portfolio].

BOTHWELL CASTLE, LANARKS., remodelled house for Archibald Douglas, 1787–8; dem. 1926 [Diary: exhib. at R.A. 1787].

CULLEN HOUSE, BANFFSHIRE, probably designed THE TEMPLE OF POMONA, for the 7th Earl of Findlater, *c.* 1788 [*cf.* drawings in Soane portfolio and S.R.O., RHP 2545–6]. Playfair made numerous unexecuted designs for Lord Findlater about this time, including a complete scheme for a new house.

BURLEY-ON-THE-HILL, RUTLAND, 'farm offices', etc. for the 8th Earl of Winchilsea, 1788–9 [Diary; letters to Lord Findlater; drawings in Soane portfolio].

BROOKSBY HALL, LEICS., minor alterations for Thomas Graham (cr. Lord Lynedoch), 1788–9 [Diary].

DUPPLIN CASTLE, PERTHSHIRE, works for the 9th Earl of Kinnoull, including a 'Temple of Virtue and Honour', 1789 (dem.); the house was destroyed by fire 1827 and rebuilt by W. Burn [Diary].

BUCHANAN HOUSE, STIRLINGSHIRE, enlarged for Lord Graham, afterwards 3rd Duke of Montrose, 1789 [Neale, *Seats*, 1st ser., i, 1818; letter to Earl of Findlater, S.R.O., GD 248/588].

WESTER OGLE (GLENOGIL), ANGUS, design for house for William Lyon, 1788, probably not built [Diary, f. 50].

LYNEDOCH LODGE, PERTHSHIRE, offices, etc. for Thomas Graham, cr. Lord Lynedoch, 1789 [Diary].

INCHMURRIN, LOCH LOMOND, design for tower for Lord Graham, afterwards 3rd Duke of Montrose, 1789 [letter to Earl of Findlater, S.R.O., GD 248/588]. It contained a dining-room and drawing-room, and appears to have been intended as a hunting-lodge, disguised as an old 'Gothic tower of strength'.

LONDON, 29 (later 34) GROSVENOR SQUARE, picture gallery for Sir George Beaumont, Bart., 1790–2 [Diary, ff. 68ᵛ, 69, 69ᵛ, 70, 76. The entries in the diary are not conclusive, but this must be the building Playfair exhibited at R.A. in 1790 as 'Design in perspective of a gallery now building'].

SKENE HOUSE, ABERDEENSHIRE, additions for George Skene, 1790; remodelled 1847–50 [Diary].

LONDON, house and premises in LONG ACRE for Mr. O'Keefe, coach-maker, 1791 [drawings in Soane portfolio].

CAIRNESS HOUSE, ABERDEENSHIRE, for Charles Gordon, 1791-7 [drawings in Soane portfolio and Aberdeen University Library: David Walker & Colin McWilliam in *C. Life*, 28 Jan.–4 Feb. 1971].

UNEXECUTED DESIGNS

The following unexecuted designs have been noted: alterations to BLACKADDER HOUSE, BERWICKS., 1782 [R.I.B.A. Drawings Collection]; a small house at BALDOVIE, KINGOLDRUM, ANGUS, for Alexander Anderson, 1785 [Soane portfolio]; house, village and market for David Scott at DUNNINALD, ANGUS, 1787 [Soane portfolio and separate folio of drawings]; remodelling URIE, KINCARDINESHIRE, for Robert Barclay, 1789 [Soane portfolio]; additions to MURIE, PERTHSHIRE, for James Yeoman, 1789 [Soane portfolio]; alterations and additions to KIPPENROSS, PERTHSHIRE, for John Stirling, 1789 [Soane portfolio]; a house at EASTER ELCHIES, MORAYSHIRE, for the 7th Earl of Findlater, 1789 [S.R.O., RHP 2547]; a house at ARDKINGLAS, ARGYLLSHIRE, for Sir Alexander Campbell, Bart., 1790 [drawings at Ardkinglas and in Soane portfolio: see Colin McWilliam, 'James Playfair's designs for Ardkinglas' in *The Country Seat*, ed. Colvin & Harris, 1970]; additions to DOUGLAS CASTLE, LANARKS., 1791 [drawings in possession of Sir Alexander Douglas-Home]; and a design for TOWNLEY HALL, CO. LOUTH, IRELAND, for B. T. Balfour, 1792 [National Library of Ireland, Portfolio 23, Nos. 62–71 and R.I.B.A. Drawings Collection G 6/5].

PLAYFAIR, WILLIAM HENRY (1790–1857), was a younger son of James Playfair (*q.v.*). Although he is stated in *D.N.B.* and elsewhere to have been born in London in July 1789, the inscription on his monument in the Dean Cemetery at Edinburgh gives the date of birth as 28 August 1790. As he himself celebrated his 27th birthday on 7 July 1817, it may be concluded that he was born in the summer of 1790. In 1804, at the age of 14, he went to live with his uncle, Professor John Playfair, in Edinburgh. In due course he became a pupil of William Stark (*q.v.*). After Stark's death in 1813, he is said to have gone to London to work in the offices of 'Wyatt and Smirke'. In the summer of 1816 he made a short visit to France in the company of his uncle before returning to Edinburgh. Later that year he won the first prize in the competition for the completion of Adam's University building. In 1818 he was entrusted with the planning of the important Calton Hill estate on the northern outskirts of the city. These early successes suggest that

Playfair may have been regarded as the architectural heir of the brilliant Stark, and in the Calton Hill scheme he certainly adhered closely to the principles of town-planning previously advocated by Stark.

For the next thirty years Playfair was, with his rivals Burn and Gillespie Graham, at the top of the Scottish architectural profession. Quantitatively, his practice never equalled theirs. Fastidious and scholarly, he had no desire to emulate their mass-production of country houses and churches. Of the former, he could show a mere score to put beside Burn's hundreds, of the latter only two to compete with Graham's large ecclesiastical output. But as a designer of public buildings in the Scottish capital he was pre-eminent. The Royal Institution, the Surgeons' Hall, the National Gallery, Donaldson's Hospital and the Free Church College were among the most prominent and important buildings in nineteenth-century Edinburgh. The first three, like the monumental Dollar Academy, were academic exercises in the classical tradition of the 'Modern Athens'. But the Gothic towers of the Free Church College, and the Jacobethan cupolas of Donaldson's Hospital showed that Playfair could master other styles besides the Grecian, while St. Stephen's Church has all the dramatic power – as well as the stylistic ambivalence – of a church by Hawksmoor. His early houses were conceived as picturesque Italianate villas, but by 1830 he was following Burn and Blore in the revival of the Scottish and English vernacular styles of the sixteenth and seventeenth centuries. The remodelling of Floors Castle was his biggest work in this manner. Though undeniably picturesque at a distance, at close quarters its coarse and overcrowded detailing repels. Lurgan, Bonaly and Islay were serious and relatively successful attempts to recapture the Elizabethan or Stuart past.

In his practice Playfair was very much a professional. All his designs were worked out with immense care. 'Nothing good in Architecture', he wrote, 'can be effected without a monstrous expenditure of patience and Indian Rubber.' A perfectionist himself, he expected the highest standards from his builders, relentlessly insisting on precise conformity to his specifications. To his pupils and staff he was equally exacting, and David Cousin (who was one of them) 'used to tell with great glee many stories of the strictness and rigour of Mr. Playfair's rule, and the devices to which his assistants had to resort to escape detection if at fault'.

Playfair never visited Rome or Greece. His early visit to France has already been mentioned. In 1842, after a long period of increasing ill-health, he went to Florence in order to obtain the advice of his elder brother James, who practised medicine there. Architecturally this journey was of little or no significance, for in Florence he found 'little to admire and a great deal to shudder at'. Back in Edinburgh, despite increasing deafness, crippling rheumatism and chronic bronchitis, he managed to struggle on for another decade, but illness compelled him to refuse a number of commissions during the last years of his life. He died at Edinburgh on 19 March 1857, and was buried in the Dean Cemetery next to his great friends Andrew and Sophia Rutherford. He was unmarried. There is a water-colour portrait of Playfair as a young man in the R.I.B.A. Drawings Collection. An engraving of a portrait by John Watson Gordon, P.R.S.A., is reproduced by A. J. Youngson. *The Making of Classical Edinburgh*, 1966, fig. 60.[1]

A large collection of Playfair's drawings is preserved in Edinburgh University Library, and there are others in the collection of the Royal Incorporation of the Architects of Scotland. In the same library are a diary for the year 1817 with accounts for 1817–22, and two surviving volumes of an elaborate series of letter-books (vol. 4, covering the years 1830–3, and vol. 7 for 1840–5). A brief journal of a visit to the island of Arran in 1811 is in Cambridge University Library (Add. MS. 6305). Many letters to Andrew Rutherford and his family from 1834 onwards are in the National Library of Scotland (MS. 9704). The sale catalogue of his library (National Library of Scotland KR.16, f. 5(1)) shows that he owned a large number of views of Athens by his friend H. W. ('Grecian') Williams.

[*A.P.S.D.; D.N.B.*; obituaries in *Builder* xv, 1857, 208; xviii, 1860, 140; *Building News*, 10 April 1857, 359–60; and Edinburgh *Building Chronicle* ii, 1857, 181–2; J. M. Graham, 'Notice of the Life and Works of W. H. Playfair', *Trans. of the Architectural Institute of Scotland* v, part iv, 1859–61, 13–28; T. H. Hughes, 'W. H. Playfair', *Quarterly of the Incorporation of Architects in Scotland*, Nos. 17–18, 1926; see also *Builder*, 10 June 1882, 717 (for David Cousin's recollections of Playfair's office), and the MS sources cited above.]

In the following list, drawings by Playfair in Edinburgh University Library are referred to by the letter U.

PUBLIC BUILDINGS

EDINBURGH, THE UNIVERSITY, completion (to modified designs) of the buildings commenced by R. & J. Adam in 1789–93, 1817–26; dome added by Sir Rowand Anderson 1887 [D. C. Horn, 'The Building of the Old Quad, 1767–

_____

[1] The present whereabouts of the original oil portrait is not known, but there is an old photograph of it at N.M.R.S.

1841', *University of Edinburgh Jnl.* xxiv, 1969–70, 43; U 10 and 15].

EDINBURGH, THE CITY OBSERVATORY, CALTON HILL, 1818; boundary wall and Playfair Monument, 1825–7 [U 45].

DOLLAR, CLACKMANNANSHIRE, THE ACADEMY, 1818–20; enlarged 1867 [U 16].

EDINBURGH, THE ROYAL INSTITUTION (now the ROYAL SCOTTISH ACADEMY), 1822–6; enlarged and altered by Playfair, 1832–5 [U 29].

EDINBURGH, premises in ALBYN PLACE for the Highland Society, 1823–41 [U 28].

EDINBURGH, THE NATIONAL MONUMENT, CALTON HILL, in collaboration with C. R. Cockerell, 1824–9 (unfinished) [U 43; correspondence with Cockerell in National Library of Scotland, MS 639].

EDINBURGH, ST. STEPHEN'S CHURCH, 1827–8; refurnished 1880, interior reconstructed 1956 [U 50].

EDINBURGH, HERIOT'S HOSPITAL, gateway and terraces, Jacobean style, 1828–30 [U 26].

EDINBURGH, THE ADVOCATES' (now SIGNET) LIBRARY, staircase for the Faculty of Advocates, 1819–20; remodelled by William Burn for the Writers to the Signet, 1833. The Corinthian columns at the top are by Playfair, the Ionic columns below and the stairs themselves by Burn. [U 1 and Portfolio 6; *History of the Society of Writers to the Signet*, 1890, 439: cf. Letter-Book 4, pp. 57–60.]

EDINBURGH, THE ADVOCATES' LIBRARY, 1829–30 [U 1 and Portfolio 6; P.R.O., MPD 102 shows Playfair's unexecuted scheme for a monumental library on the site of the present National Library].

EDINBURGH, THE SURGEONS' HALL, NICOLSON STREET, 1830–2 [U 13].

MINTO CHURCH, ROXBURGHSHIRE, 1830–1, Gothic [U 39].

DALCRUE BRIDGE, REDGORTON, PERTHSHIRE (R. Almond), 1832–6, at the expense of Thomas Graham, Lord Lynedoch [U 19].

EDINBURGH, DONALDSON'S HOSPITAL, 1842–54, Jacobethan style [U 20]. Won in a limited competition with Gillespie Graham and David Hamilton.

EDINBURGH, THE FREE CHURCH COLLEGE, 1846–50; Gothic. The Assembly Hall was added by D. Bryce 1858–9 [U, Supplementary].

EDINBURGH, THE NATIONAL GALLERY OF SCOTLAND, 1850–7 [U 44].

EDINBURGH: DOMESTIC ARCHITECTURE

In 1818 Playfair was appointed architect for the development of the area to the north of Calton Hill, and in 1819 produced a printed *Report to the Lord Provost, Magistrates and Council of the City of Edinburgh on a Plan for laying out the new Town between Edinburgh and Leith*. In this he followed the ideas of his master William Stark (*q.v.*) in paying 'the strictest attention to the nature of the ground, and none whatever to the neatness of the plan, as it appears on paper'. As a result the following streets were laid out under Playfair's direction, and in most cases built to his designs, from 1821 onwards: BLENHEIM PLACE, BRUNSWICK STREET, BRUNTON PLACE, CARLTON TERRACE, ELM ROW, HILLSIDE CRESCENT, LEOPOLD PLACE, MONTGOMERY STREET, REGENT TERRACE, ROYAL TERRACE, WINDSOR STREET [A. J. Youngson, *The Making of Classical Edinburgh*, 1966, 152–6; drawings in U 2, 3, 4, 6, 12, 21, 27, 31, 37, 48, 51].

In 1820 Playfair designed ROYAL CIRCUS for the Trustees of Heriot's Hospital. With CIRCUS PLACE and CIRCUS GARDENS it was built in 1821–3 [Youngson, *op. cit.*, 206–8; drawings in U 49]. In 1824 he designed NO. 8, INVERLEITH ROW for Daniel Ellis [drawings in U 22], and in 1825 NO. 20 INVERLEITH PLACE [minutes of the Caledonian Horticultural Soc., Oct. 1825].

COUNTRY HOUSES, ETC.

GLEN HOUSE, PEEBLESSHIRE, additions for William Allan, 1821; dem. *c.* 1853 and rebuilt by D. Bryce [U 24; W. Chambers, *History of Peeblesshire*, 1864, 389–90].

MINTO MANSE, ROXBURGHSHIRE, 1827; 'a Tuscan villa' [U 38].

DUMPHAIL HOUSE, MORAYSHIRE, for C. L. Cumming Bruce, 1828–9; enlarged 1842; remodelled 1965; Italianate [U 17].

BELMONT, CORSTORPHINE, MIDLOTHIAN, for Thomas Mackenzie, Lord Mackenzie, 1828–30, Italianate [U 7].

DRUMBANAGHER HOUSE, CO. ARMAGH, IRELAND, for Maxwell Close, 1829; Italianate; dem. [U 18].

PRESTON GRANGE, PRESTONPANS, EAST LOTHIAN, enlarged for E. Grant Suttie, 1830; stables for Sir George Grant Suttie, 1845; additions for same 1850; Scottish vernacular style [U 46] (J. Small, *Castles and Mansions of the Lothians*, 1883).

GRANGE HOUSE, GRANGE LOAN, nr. EDINBURGH, alterations for Sir Thomas Dick Lauder, 1830–1, Scottish vernacular style; dem. *c.* 1936 [U 25] (J. Small, *Castles and Mansions of the Lothians*, 1883; T. Hannan, *Famous Scottish Houses: The Lowlands*, 1928, 165–8].

LYNEDOCH LODGE, PERTHSHIRE, drawing-room for Thomas Graham, Lord Lynedoch, 1832; dem. [U 32].

DALCRUE, PERTHSHIRE, Italianate farm-house for Thomas Graham, Lord Lynedoch, 1832 [U 19].

LURGAN, or BROWNLOW HOUSE, CO. ARMACH, IRELAND, for the Right Hon. William Brownlow, 1833–5, 'Elizabethan' style [U 33].

MEADOWBANK HOUSE, KIRKNEWTON, MIDLOTHIAN,

additions for Alexander Maconochie, Lord Meadowbank, 1835 [U 40] (J. Small, *Castles and Mansions of the Lothians*, 1883).

CRAIGCROOK CASTLE, CRAMOND, MIDLOTHIAN, enlarged for Francis Jeffrey, Lord Jeffrey, 1835; further additions 1891; Scottish vernacular style [U 14] (J. Small, *Castles and Mansions of the Lothians*, 1883; T. Hannan, *Famous Scottish Houses: the Lowlands*, 1928, 69–72; J. Taylor, *Lord Jeffrey and Craigcrook*, Edinburgh 1892].

BONALY TOWER, MIDLOTHIAN, for Henry Thomas Cockburn, Lord Cockburn, 1836–8; wings added 1874 and 1886–9; Scottish vernacular style [U 9] (J. Small, *Castles and Mansions of the Lothians*, 1883; T. Hannan, *Famous Scottish Houses: the Lowlands*, 1928, 33–6).

BARMORE (now STONEFIELD HOUSE), LOCH FINE, ARGYLLSHIRE, for John Campbell, 1836–8, Scottish vernacular style [U 8].

MINTO HOUSE, ROXBURGHSHIRE, alterations for the 2nd Earl of Minto, 1837; dem. 1973 [National Library of Scotland, Minto Maps 15; Letter Book 7, p. 85].

FLOORS CASTLE, ROXBURGHSHIRE, remodelled for the 6th Duke of Roxburghe, 1837–45, Jacobethan style [U 23].

ISLAY HOUSE, ISLAY, INNER HEBRIDES, offices, etc. for W. F. Campbell, 1841–5, Scottish vernacular style [U 30].

COLINTON HOUSE (now Merchiston Castle School), MIDLOTHIAN, kitchen offices for James Abercromby, Lord Dunfermline, 1840–2 [Letter Book 7, *passim*].

COMPSTONE HOUSE, TWYNHOLM, KIRKCUDBRIGHTSHIRE, additions for Thomas Maitland, 1845 [Letter Book 7, pp. 475, 478, 483].

LAURISTON CASTLE, MIDLOTHIAN, alterations and additions, including staircase and two porches, for Andrew Rutherford, 1845 [Letter Book 7, *passim*].

MONUMENTS

EDINBURGH, CALTON HILL, monument to Professor John Playfair (d. 1819), 1825 [U 45].

ST. QUIVOX, AYRSHIRE, Doric mausoleum in churchyard for James Campbell, 1822 [U 35, portfolio 10].

EDINBURGH, HERIOT'S HOSPITAL, monument to James Denholm, 1824 [U, portfolio 11].

EDINBURGH, CALTON HILL, monument to Dugald Stewart, 1831 [U 42].

DUTHIL, INVERNESS-SHIRE, mausoleum for Seafield family, 1837 [*N.S.A.* xiii, 132].

KENSAL GREEN CEMETERY, MIDDLESEX, monument to Robert Ferguson of Raith, 1842 [Letter Book 7, pp. 217–19, 383].

KELSO, ROXBURGHSHIRE, monument to — Robertson of Ednam, 1844; dem. [Letter Book 7, p. 387].

EDINBURGH, DEAN CEMETERY, monument to Francis Jeffrey, Lord Jeffrey, 1851 [National Library of Scotland, MS. 9704, f. 179ᵛ].

EDINBURGH, DEAN CEMETERY, pyramidal monument to Sophia Rutherford (d. 1852) [National Library of Scotland, MS. 9704, ff. 193, 197].

EDINBURGH, DEAN CEMETERY, monument to himself (d. 1857) [U, portfolio 39].

PLEVINS, JOSEPH, was a builder in Birmingham. According to Francis White's *History, Gazeteer and Directory of Warwickshire*, 1850, 612, he designed the Greek Revival BATHS in BATH STREET, LEAMINGTON, WARWICKS., 1836, dem. 1867. He was the father of the Birmingham architect Thomson Plevins (1825–97).

PLOWMAN, JOHN (*c.* 1773–1843), was an architect and builder of Oxford. After working for some time as foreman to Daniel Harris (*q.v.*), he was from 1812 to 1837 the latter's partner in business. His most ambitious works were the demolished St. Martin's Church at Carfax, Oxford, and the church at Churchill, with a tower copied, on a smaller scale, from that of Magdalen College. Plowman died in Oxford on 12 August 1843, aged 70. He was the father of Thomas and John Plowman. Thomas, who predeceased his father, is noticed below. John, who was born on 2 April 1807, and died on 1 October 1871, began to practise in Oxford in the 1830s, and assisted his father during the last years of the latter's life. In 1839 he won the second prize in the competition for the Ashmolean Museum. Sir Robert Smirke, the assessor, considered his designs 'more like a distinguished residence than a collegiate establishment'. His principal work was the Shire Hall on the site of Oxford Castle, for which he provided a 'Norman' façade guarded by fasces of cast-iron battle-axes.

[*Oxford Herald*, 2 May 1812; *Jackson's Oxford Jnl.* 19 Aug. 1843; Bodleian Library, MSS. Wills Oxon. 103, f. 283, 109, f. 160; transcript of St. Michael's, Oxford, baptism register for 1807.]

The following list contains works by both John Plowmans. All buildings before *c.* 1835 must be the father's, and those known to be by the son are indicated.

OXFORD, ST. MARTIN'S CHURCH, rebuilt (except tower), 1820–2, Gothic, in collaboration with D. Harris; dem. 1896 [J. Ingram, *Memorials of Oxford* iii, 1837, 2].

CHURCHILL CHURCH, OXON., 1826–8, Gothic [Bodleian Library, MS. Oxford diocesan papers c. 2166].

BAVERSTOCK RECTORY, WILTS., altered or rebuilt 1826 [Salisbury Diocesan Records].

LONG WITTENHAM VICARAGE, BERKSHIRE, altered or rebuilt 1827 [Salisbury Diocesan Records].

ADDERBURY CHURCH, OXON., west gallery (removed 1866) and font, 1831–2 [*V.C.H. Oxon.* ix, 35–6].

OXFORD, ST. MICHAEL'S CHURCH, rebuilt North Chapel, 1833 [J. Ingram, *Memorials of Oxford* iii, 1837, 5].

RAVENSTHORPE VICARAGE, NORTHANTS., enlarged and refronted 1835 [Northants. Record Office, Peterborough Diocesan Records].

OXFORD, ST. PETER'S-IN-THE-EAST CHURCH, repaired and reseated, 1836 [Bodleian Library, Vestry Minutes 1769–1842, f. 129; *Gent's Mag.* 1836 (ii), 637].

BICESTER, OXON., THE UNION WORKHOUSE, 1835–6, *by J.P. junior* [*V.C.H. Oxon.* vi, 40].

CUBLINGTON RECTORY, BUCKS., remodelled 1837 [Lincolnshire Record Office, MGA 210].

ROSS-ON-WYE, HEREFS, THE ROYAL HOTEL, 1837, *by J.P. junior* [*Jackson's Oxford Jnl.* 30 Sept. 1837].

LAUNTON RECTORY, OXON., enlarged 1838 [*V.C.H. Oxon.* vi, 233].

OXFORD, THE FLOATING CHAPEL for BOATMEN, 1839; foundered *c.* 1868 [Bodleian Library, MS. Top. Oxon. d. 505, f. 272].

BISHOPSWOOD CHURCH, HEREFS., 1839–41, *by J.P. junior* [G.R.].

OXFORD, THE SHIRE HALL, 1839–41 *by J.P. junior* [*A.P.S.D., s.v.* 'Oxford'].

BENSON CHURCH, OXON., repaired and re-roofed south aisle 1841 [Parish records, *ex inf.* Canon B. F. L. Clarke].

WARBOROUGH CHURCH, OXON., alterations 1842 [*Oxford Herald*, 2 April 1842].

STEEPLE ASTON CHURCH, OXON., restoration 1842 [W. Wing, *History of Steeple Aston*, 1845, 61–2].

STANTON ST. JOHN RECTORY, OXON., *c.* 1842, *by J.P. junior* [plans in parish chest].

AYLESBURY CHURCH, BUCKS., repaired and refitted 1843, *by Messrs. Plowman* [*Ecclesiologist* ii, 168; R. Gibbs, *History of Aylesbury*, 1885, 41].

BODICOTE CHURCH, OXON., rebuilt 1843–4, Gothic [*V.C.H. Oxon.* ix, 38].

PLOWMAN, THOMAS (*c.* 1805–1828), elder son of John Plowman of Oxford, was awarded medals for architectural designs by the Society of Arts in 1822 and 1824. After spending some time in the office of Sir Jeffry Wyatville he returned to Oxford in order to assist his father. He had already, in 1823, submitted a Gothic design in the competition for the completion of King's College, Cambridge, and in 1826 his designs for refitting ST. MARY'S CHURCH, OXFORD, with Gothic pews and galleries, were approved by Convocation. The drawings were exhibited at the Royal Academy in 1826. Plowman died on 19 February 1828, aged 22 or 23, a few days before the completion of the work (some of which was removed in 1900).

[*A.P.S.D*; *Jackson's Oxford Jnl.*, 23 Feb. 1828; *Oxford Herald*, 23 Feb. 1828; *Gent's Mag.* 1828 (i), 380; T. G. Jackson, *The Church of St. Mary the Virgin, Oxford*, 1897, 139–43.]

POCOCK, WILLIAM FULLER (1779–1849), was the eldest son of William Pocock, a carpenter, joiner and maker of patent extensible furniture, then resident in the City of London, but subsequently at Leyton in Essex.[1] He was at first apprenticed to his father, who wished him to follow the same trade as himself. Pocock, however, had made up his mind to be an architect, and eventually persuaded his father to cancel his articles and allow him to enter the office of Charles Beazley as a pupil. In 1799 he began to exhibit at the Royal Academy, and in 1801 he was admitted to the Academy Schools. After leaving Beazley's office he acted for some years as an assistant to Thomas Hardwick. By 1802 or 3 he was beginning independent practice, and in 1804 secured a commission from a London business firm (Messrs. Warner of Rood Lane) to which he was to be indebted for much subsequent employment. In 1811 he leased some land in Knightsbridge from Lord Dungannon, and began to build houses in Trevor Place as a speculation. One of these, No. 5, was reserved for his own occupation.[2] Pocock was now well established as an architect and surveyor, with a number of City clients, and several estates to administer, including those of Lord Dungannon and the Brewers' Company. He was an early member of the Institute of British Architects, and was Master of the Carpenters' Company in 1840. He died on 29 October 1849, aged 69, leaving a son, William Willmer Pocock (1813–99), who succeeded to his practice. F. Wehnert (1801–71) was a pupil.

Pocock, who was a member of the Wesleyan Church, was a meticulous, hard-working man, reserved in manner and 'scrupulously clean and neat' in appearance. His probity and business efficiency do much to explain his extensive practice as a surveyor. As an architect he was competent but unremarkable, his best work being in the Greek Doric style. In 1835 he made a somewhat pedestrian design for the Houses of Parliament competition, of which there is a lithograph made by his son, under whose name it is described in the *Catalogue* of designs exhibited in 1836. He published the following works: *Archi-*

---

[1] George Pocock, the builder of Cornwall Place, George's Place, and other streets on the Marquis of Northampton's estate in Islington (*c.* 1800), and of Nos. 120–2 Maida Vale (1819), was probably a member of the same family: see S. Lewis, *History of Islington*, 1842, 370 and *C. Life*, 25 Jan. 1936, 103.

[2] In 1827 he moved to No. 10, where he continued to live until his death.

tectural Designs for Rustic Cottages, Picturesque Dwellings, Villas, etc. with appropriate scenery, dedicated to Sir J. Courtenay Honywood, Bart., 1807, 1819, 1823 (reprinted 1971); *Modern Finishings for Rooms: a series of designs for vestibules, staircases, boudoirs, libraries, etc., to which are added some designs for villas and porticos*, 1811, 1823, 1837; *Designs for Churches and Chapels*, 1819, 3rd ed. 1835; and *Observations on Bond in Brickwork*, 1839. An album of prints and drawings collected by him is in the R.I.B.A. Drawings Collection.

[*A.P.S.D.*; MS. Memoir by W. W. Pocock in R.I.B.A. Library; W. W. Pocock, *William Fuller Pocock, F.R.I.B.A.*, privately printed 1883, reprinted in *Blackmansbury* ix, 1972; E. T. Joy, 'Pocock's – the ingenious inventors', *Connoisseur* clxxiii, Feb. 1970, 88–92; information from Miss M. A. Powel.]

Unless otherwise stated, the following list is based on the privately printed memoir by W. W. Pocock.

LEYTON, ESSEX, house for Mr. Banks, 1802.

LEYTON CHURCH, ESSEX, monument to Wildman family [exhib. at R.A. 1802].

HAFOD, WALES, obelisk to memory of the 5th Duke of Bedford, for Thomas Johnes, 1803 [exhib. at R.A.].

ESSEX, villa, probably at WHIPS CROSS, WALTHAMSTOW, for E. Warner, 1804 [exhib. at R.A.].

EVINGTON PLACE, KENT, work (unspecified), for Sir John Honywood, 1806; dem. 1938.

QUEX PARK, KENT, work (unspecified), for — Powell, 1806–9.

BLACKHEATH, cottage orné for Sir John Eamer [exhib. at R.A. 1811].

KNIGHTSBRIDGE, TREVOR TERRACE, Nos. 5–8, 1811, Nos. 9–10, 1826.

MONTREAL, CANADA, MANSION HOUSE HOTEL, ballroom for Mr. Moulson, 1817 [exhib. at R.A. 1819].

RANELAGH CHAPEL, GEORGE STREET, SLOANE SQUARE, 1818; dem. 1887 (illustrated in *Belgrave Presbyterian Church, Jubilee Memorial*, 1896, 13, 17, 30).

FAN GROVE (now COURT), nr. CHERTSEY, SURREY, for Genl. Sir Herbert Taylor, 1818–20: since enlarged and remodelled.

LONDON, LEATHERSELLERS' COMPANY'S HALL, GREAT ST. HELEN'S PLACE, BISHOPSGATE, 1820–2 (used as offices from 1878); dem. *c.* 1930.

KNIGHTSBRIDGE, Messrs. Smith & Baber's Floorcloth Manufactory, 1822.

HORNSEY PRIORY, MUSWELL HILL, for Henry Warner, 1823–5, Tudor Gothic, dem. 1902 [exhib. at R.A. 1825–7].

THE 'CLOCK CASE' TOWER, VIRGINIA WATER, SURREY, alterations for Henry Willmer, 1824 (this building, named in W. W. Pocock's Memoir, had been built by the Duke of Cumberland in the 18th century, and must be the 'Cumberland Tower' exhibited by Pocock at the R.A. in 1824. It was later sold to George IV, as it overlooked Virginia Water).

GLENRIDGE, CALLOW HILL, VIRGINIA WATER, SURREY, for himself, 1825, *cottage orné* style.

ALDENHAM GRAMMAR SCHOOL, HERTS., for the Brewers' Company, 1825 [exhib. at R.A. 1828; drawings in R.I.B.A. Collection].

HIGHGATE, MIDDLESEX, THE LITTLE PRIORY, for Henry Willmer, 1826.

LONDON, restored BREWERS' HALL, ADDLE STREET, 1828 [*A.P.S.D.*].

LONDON, HEADQUARTERS OF THE LONDON MILITIA, BUNHILL ROW, 1828 [*A.P.S.D.*].

COWES, ISLE OF WIGHT, buildings for Mr. Broster, junior, 1829.

LONDON, NO. 66 PATERNOSTER ROW, 1833, 'ostensibly for Rev. J. Mason'.

CLIMPING VICARAGE, SUSSEX, for the Rev. Owen Marden, *c.* 1833.

CHELSEA DISPENSARY, 1835.

THE WESTERN GRAMMAR SCHOOL (now ALEXANDER HOUSE), NORTH TERRACE, SOUTH KENSINGTON, 1835–6.

DOWN COTTAGE, HARTING, SUSSEX, *c.* 1835; for Henry Willmer: subsequently enlarged by W. W. Pocock and known thereafter as DOWN PLACE.

KENSINGTON, WESLEYAN CHAPEL, 1836.

GUNNERSBURY HO., MIDDLESEX, entrance gates and lodges for Mr. Farmer, 1837; improvements to stables, 1844.

ANTIGUA, W. INDIES, a chapel, 1837.

VIRGINIA WATER, SURREY, CHRIST CHURCH, 1837, Gothic.

LONDON, WESLEYAN CENTENARY HALL, BISHOPSGATE, 1840; dem. [exhib. at R.A.] (*Companion to the Almanac*, 1841, 246–7).

TWICKENHAM, CARPENTERS' COMPANY'S ALMSHOUSES, 1841; dem. *c.* 1951 [*A.P.S.D.*].

VIRGINIA WATER, SURREY, SCHOOLS, 1843.

POGMIRE, ALEXANDER, was the 'excellent skillful mayson and carver' employed by Sir John Lowther, 1st Bart., to 'beautify the hall porch' at LOWTHER HALL, WESTMORLAND, 'with pilasters and other cuttwork' in 1642, and to build the gallery on the east side of the forecourt in 1655–6 ['Memorable observations' by Lowther in Cumbria Record Office, D./Lons./L/A1/1, ff. 273, 276]. This gallery, demolished *c.* 1805, is illustrated in Kip's *Britannia Illustrata* i, 1714, pl. 41. It so closely resembled the gallery still remaining on the north side of the forecourt of HUTTON-IN-THE-FOREST, CUMBERLAND, and built by Sir Henry Fletcher, Bart., some time between 1641 and 1645 (*C. Life*, 4 Feb. 1965), as to make it virtually certain that the latter was also Pogmire's work.

POLLARD, JAMES, was a pupil of Joseph Pickford of Derby. He was awarded premiums for architectural designs by the Society of Arts in 1764 and 1765. He is described as being under 18 years of age on both occasions [*Register of Premiums*, 1778]. He was still in Pickford's office in 1771 [University of Keele, Sneyd papers 10095–11.]

PONTON, ALEXANDER, was a wright and surveyor of Edinburgh active during the last quarter of the eighteenth century. He was a sworn measurer and as such measured John Baxter's masonry at GORDON CASTLE in 1778–9 [S.R.O., GD 44/49/16]. In 1792 he was one of the arbitrators in a dispute over work performed at YESTER HOUSE, EAST LOTHIAN [J. G. Dunbar, 'The Building of Yester House', *Trans. of the E. Lothian Antiquarian and Field Naturalists' Soc.* xiii, 1972, 36]. The death in Jamaica of his son Lieut. Thomas Ponton is noticed in *Gent's Mag.* 1802, 181.

POOL, JOHN LIDBURY, practised in London during the first quarter of the nineteenth century. He exhibited at the Royal Academy from 1802 onwards, showing in 1804 a 'Design for a mausoleum to the memory of the late unfortunate Lord Camelford', who had been killed in a duel, in 1810 a 'Design for a Theatre', and in 1817 a 'design for a villa, now building for a gentleman, in the Coburg road, near Peckham'. In 1811 his designs for rebuilding Hungerford Church, Berkshire, were selected in a competition, but he was dismissed the following year, apparently because his estimates were considered excessive. His place was taken by John Pinch of Bath. [MS. Minutes of the Trustees.] An elevation of his design for the tower, signed and dated 1812, is among the Treacher papers in Reading Public Library.

POOLE, the Rev. HENRY (*c.* 1785–1857), appears to have had some architectural training before being ordained in 1811 at the age of 26. After a curacy at Ossett, nr. Wakefield, he moved to Corsham in Wiltshire, and then in 1818 to the living of Coleford and Bream in the Forest of Dean. Here he was able to gratify a long-felt desire to design and build a church, first at COLEFORD (1820–1; dem. except the tower in 1880), then at PARK END (cons. 1822), and finally at BREAM (1823). He also designed a new tower for BERRY HILL CHURCH in 1822. His drawings for Coleford and Bream churches (the latter signed 'Henry Poole, Minister and Surveyor') are among the I.C.B.S. records now in Lambeth Palace Library. His Gothic detailing was typical of its date, but his churches at Coleford and Park End were unconventional in having octagonal plans. Poole died on 22 December 1857, aged 72, and was buried in the churchyard at Park End, which he had 'long endeavoured to render as attractive as possible, by regulating the character of the tomb-stones erected in it'. [H. G. Nicholls, *The Forest of Dean*, 1858, 166, 169; H. G. Nicholls, *The Personalities of the Forest of Dean*, 1863, 152–60; *Something about Coleford and the old Chapel*, 1877].

POPE, RICHARD SHACKLETON (*c.* 1792–1884), was the son of a clerk of works employed by Sir Robert Smirke, and as a young man was himself employed in the same capacity by both Smirke and C. R. Cockerell. In 1821–3 Cockerell sent him to Bristol to supervise the building of the Philosophical Institution, and he decided to settle in that city, where he remained for the rest of his life. He had a large practice, designing many commercial buildings, and holding the office of District Surveyor with monopolistic tenacity for forty years from 1831 to 1872. His principal works in Bristol were the Gothic Guildhall and the church of St. Mary-on-the-Quay, dignified by a handsome Corinthian portico. His unexecuted designs for a new Mansion House are in the Bristol Archives Office. From 1849 onwards he was in partnership with John Bindon and J. A. Clark, and from the 1860s with his son Thomas Shackleton Pope. He died at Shirehampton on 10 February 1884, in his ninety-second year [*Builder* xlvi, 1884, 426; Principal Probate Registry, Calendar of Probates].

WORKS PRIOR TO 1849

BRISTOL, COURT OF JUSTICE adjoining the Council House in Corn Street, in collaboration with George Dymond, 1827–8 [City Archives].

BRISTOL, THE CATTLE MARKET, TEMPLE MEADS, 1830; rebuilt 1874 [*A.P.S.D.*, *s.v.* 'Bristol'].

BRISTOL, THE GAOL, repairs 1831–2; dem. 1895 [*A.P.S.D.*].

BRISTOL, THE BRIDEWELL, BRIDEWELL LANE, 1832; dem. 1865 [*A.P.S.D.*].

BRISTOL CATHEDRAL, restoration of CHAPTER-HOUSE, 1833 [*A.P.S.D.*].

BRISTOL, THE ROYAL WESTERN HOTEL (now Brunel House), COLLEGE PLACE (St. George's Road), 1837–8 [*Builder* xlvi, 1884, 426].

OKEFORD CHURCH, DEVON, 1838, Gothic [I.C.B.S.].

BRISTOL, ST. MARY-ON-THE-QUAY CHURCH, 1839–40, built originally for the Irvingites, but purchased by the Roman Catholics in 1843 [*A.P.S.D.*].

BRADFORD-ON-AVON VICARAGE, WILTS., altered or rebuilt 1840 [Salisbury Diocesan Records].

WINSLEY CHURCH, WILTS., 1841, Gothic [I.C.B.S.].

BRISTOL, THE GUILDHALL, 1843–6, Gothic [*Companion to the Almanac*, 1845, 248–50].

BRISTOL, THE CENTRAL POLICE STATION, 1844; dem. [*A.P.S.D.*].

BRISTOL, THE BUCKINGHAM BAPTIST CHURCH, CLIFTON, 1844–7, Gothic [*A.P.S.D.*].

BRISTOL, with S. C. Fripp planned VICTORIA STREET, 1845 (carried out 1870) [Builder iii, 1845, 399].

BRISTOL, THE MEAT MARKET, 1848–9 [J. Latimer, *Annals of Bristol*, 1887, 307].

POPE, THOMAS (–1805), was an architect and builder of Bristol, where he held the office of District Surveyor from 1801 to 1805 [A. Beavan, *Bristol Lists*, 1899, 248]. In the City Archives (Plan Book B, nos. 111b, 119a) there are designs by him for two houses for John Wadham at the corner of Bell Lane and Broad Street (1802), and for additions to a house in Lower Park Row (1804).

POPE, WILLIAM (–1678), was a Warden of the Carpenters' Company in 1670, 1673 and 1674, and its Master in 1675. In 1664 he was among those who made signs for the Company's new Court Room, but the Committee (of which he was a member) preferred those of John Wildegos. In May 1671, however, when it was resolved 'that the ceiling of the Hall be handsomely done', it was decided to leave this 'to the discretion of Warden Pope'. Carpenters' Hall was demolished in 1876 [E. B. Jupp and W. W. Pocock, *Historical Account of the Carpenters' Company*, 1887, 229, 232]. After the Great Fire, Pope was one of the carpenters employed in the rebuilding of the Guildhall [Guildhall Library, MS. 184/41]. In 1674 he and Thomas Clarke contracted to enlarge the Synagogue in Cree Church Lane, London, for some £760 [L. D. Barnett, *Bevis Marks Records* i, 1940, 10]. The translation by Godfrey Richards of Palladio's *First Book of Architecture*, 1663, contains an appendix on the framing of Roofs 'By that ingenious Architect Mr. William Pope of London'. At his death in 1678, Pope left a rent charge of £3 10s., to be paid out of some property in Colman Street to seven poor members of the Carpenters' Company or their widows. He was then living in Whitehorse Lane, Stepney. His will is P.C.C., 9 KING.

PORDEN, CHARLES FERDINAND (1790–1863), was the son of Isaac Porden, an obscure architect who is said to have practised in Birmingham. He was articled to his uncle, William Porden, and was also in the office of George Wyatt. In 1806 he gained a gold medal for architectural design offered by the Society of Arts, and in 1809, having been admitted to the Royal Academy School, he was awarded the Silver Medal of the Academy. He exhibited at the Academy between 1810 and 1825 and provided drawings

651

for some of the plates in Rutter's *Delineations of Fonthill* (1823). He supervised the building of ST. PANCRAS CHURCH for Messrs. Inwood between 1819 and 1822, and designed the fine Greek Doric church of ST. MATTHEW, BRIXTON, 1822–4, skilfully solving the problem of combining a steeple with a portico'd temple by placing the tower at the east end [*Survey of London* xxvi, 132–4 and plates]. He was for ten years in the office of Sir William Tite, whom he assisted in the erection of the Royal Exchange, London. He died on 6 March 1863, aged 73 years, and was buried in Highgate Cemetery, where a tombstone states that he was 'nephew of William Porden, architect to King George the 4th, and grandson of Roger [*sic*] Pourden of York, architect'. [*A.P.S.D.*]

PORDEN, WILLIAM (*c.* 1755–1822), was baptised at St. Mary's Church, Hull, on 29 January 1755. His father, Thomas Purden or Porden, was described as 'Labourer'. In 1774 he became a pupil of James Wyatt, to whom he had been introduced by the poet Mason. He was in Wyatt's office in 1778, when he exhibited at the Royal Academy for the first time, and in 1779, when he was responsible, with the elder Smirke and a young painter called Watson, for an amusing skit on the Royal Academy entitled *The Exhibition, or a second Anticipation:*[1] *being Remarks on the principal works to be exhibited next month at the Royal Academy: by Roger Shanhagan, Gent.* Porden was presumably responsible for the architectural portion of the text, in which Chambers, Sandby, Paine and other members of the architectural establishment were criticized or ridiculed, while Wyatt was praised. According to Redgrave he was 'afterwards the pupil of S. P. Cockerell' (though he and Cockerell were almost the same age), 'then became secretary to Lord Sheffield, who appointed him paymaster to the 22nd Dragoons, a regiment raised by his Lordship', and eventually 'turned again to architecture after the reduction of this regiment'. As Sheffield's regiment was raised in 1779 (not 1770 as stated by Redgrave) and disbanded by 1783, Porden would have returned to architecture about the latter year. It may be noted that although he exhibited at the Royal Academy in 1778 he did not do so again until 1784. There is some evidence that for a time Porden returned to Wyatt's office as a senior assistant,[2] but his

appointment as Lord Grosvenor's surveyor appears to date from *c.* 1785, and he must by then have been in independent practice.

Porden obtained several commissions for country houses, and enjoyed a considerable reputation as a Gothic architect in the manner of his master Wyatt. The Prince of Wales employed him at Brighton, and at Eaton Hall he designed 'the most extravagant Gothic house of the Regency period'. But he failed to secure election as A.R.A. in 1797, and in 1805 he was unsuccessful in the competition for Downing College, Cambridge (his designs for which are in the R.I.B.A. Collection). His connection with Lord Grosvenor was also to end unhappily, for in 1821 his retirement from the surveyorship of the Grosvenor Estate in London was hastened by the failure of a scheme, for which he had been responsible, to rebuild the north side of Berkeley Square on a speculative basis. According to Redgrave, 'this preyed upon his spirits' and he died 'two years after', on 14 September 1822, aged 67. He was then living at 59 Berners Street, and was buried in St. John's Wood Chapel. He had a large family, all of whom died young, except two daughters. The elder married Joseph Kay, the younger (Eleanor) married Sir John Franklin, and became a well-known figure in literary circles. Henry Rhodes, P. F. Robinson, J. Temple and John Young were Porden's pupils. His portrait by W. Stavely was exhibited at the Royal Academy in 1795. His younger brother Charles (born 1762) had an architectural training under James Wyatt, but does not seem to have practised independently. In 1785 he was engaged as a draughtsman by the engineer James Watt on the recommendation of Samuel Wyatt.

[*A.P.S.D.*; F. T. Cansick, *Epitaphs of Middlesex* ii, 1872, 85; will P.C.C., 35 RICHARDS; S. Redgrave, *Dictionary of Artists of the English School,* 1878, 338–9; *D.N.B.*; *The Farington Diary,* ed. J. Greig, i. 165, ii, 270, iii, 230, vii, 137; A. T. Bolton, *The Portrait of Sir John Soane,* 1927, 155, 217, 288; W. T. Whitley, *Artists and their Friends in England 1700–1799,* 1928, i, 343–4, ii, 216; Hermione Hobhouse, *Thomas Cubitt,* 1971, 53, 88–9; Birmingham City Library, Boulton & Watt Collection, S. Wyatt to J. Watt, 31 Jan. 1785.]

LONDON, PHILLIMORE PLACE, KENSINGTON, 1787–9; dem. *c.* 1935 [exhib. at R.A. 1788; J. Summerson, *Georgian London,* 1945, 263].

LONDON, THE EBURY CHAPEL, FIVE FIELDS, CHELSEA, 1790 [cutting recording laying of foundation stone in Westminster Public Library, 'Cuttings relating to the Dukes of Westminster'].

ALDWARK HALL, nr. ROTHERHAM, YORKS. (W.R.), stables, dairy and farmyard, for Francis F. Foljambe, *c.* 1790 [exhib. at R.A. 1790 and 1792].

---

[1] The first *Anticipation* was a well-known political satire published by Richard Tickell in 1778.

[2] See the letter from Samuel Wyatt cited at the end of this biography. It was presumably as Wyatt's assistant that, as Redgrave records, Porden made the arrangements for the Handel Commemoration in Westminster Abbey in 1785, for Wyatt was the Surveyor to the Abbey, and had been responsible for the arrangements for the first Commemoration in 1784.

PUTNEY PARK, nr. ROEHAMPTON, SURREY, enlarged and remodelled for Beilby Thompson, 1794; enlarged by D. Burton 1837–8 [exhib. at R.A. 1794; G. Richardson, *New Vitruvius Britannicus* i, 1810, pls. 19–21].

SOUTH KELSEY CHURCH, LINCS., rebuilt (except tower) 1795–6, Gothic; remodelled by Butterfield 1853 [exhib. at R.A. 1797].

'A house in the Gothic style of the fourteenth century', exhibited at R.A. 1796, and said by Graves (*The Royal Academy of Arts, Dictionary of Contributors* vi, 1906, 183), to have been 'for R. T. Gordon Esq.'

An unidentified 'house in Sussex for W. Breton, Esq.', exhibited at R.A. 1796 and perhaps not built.

OWSTON HALL, nr. DONCASTER, YORKS. (W.R.), 'design' for Bryan Cooke, exhibited at R.A. 1797, but apparently not executed (cf. 'W. Lindley').

WINDSOR FOREST, BERKSHIRE, 'design for a chapel', exhibited at R.A. 1797, but probably not executed.

OSBORNE HOUSE, ISLE OF WIGHT, 'design for the West front' for B. P. Blachford (?), exhibited at R.A. 1797; rebuilt for Queen Victoria 1845–8.

SWAINSTON HOUSE, CALBOURNE, ISLE OF WIGHT, rebuilt principal front for Sir John Barrington, Bart. 1798; damaged by bombing 1941 but subsequently restored [exhib. at R.A. 1798] (W. Cooke, *New Picture of the Isle of Wight*, 1808, 75).

HAMPTON LODGE, nr. FARNHAM, SURREY, design for south and east fronts for N. Snell, exhibited at R.A. 1798, but not executed.

LONDON, design for a market 'proposed to be erected on the estate of the Earl of Darnley, nr. Finsbury Square', exhibited at R.A. 1802, but apparently not executed.

EATON HALL, CHESHIRE, rebuilt for the 2nd Earl Grosvenor, 1804–12, Gothic; wings added by B. Gummow, 1823–5; altered by W. Burn, 1846–51; rebuilt by A. Waterhouse, 1870; dem. 1963 [exhib. at R.A. 1804, 1805, 1807, 1810, 1812; drawings etc. in Cheshire County Record Office; J. & J. C. Buckler, *Views of Eaton Hall*, 1826; G. Aclocque & J. Cornforth in *C. Life*, 11–18 Feb. 1971].

BRIGHTON, THE PAVILION, stables, riding-house, tennis-court and other alterations for George, Prince of Wales, 1804–8. The stables (now known as The Dome) were converted into an Assembly Room in 1867 and remodelled internally as a Concert Hall in 1934–5; the riding-house was later used as a Corn Exchange [H. D. Roberts, *History of the Royal Pavilion, Brighton*, 1939].

BRIGHTON, house on the Steyne (now Y.M.C.A.) for Mrs. Fitzherbert, 1804 [exhib. at R.A. 1805].

HARE PARK, DULLINGHAM, CAMBS., alterations for

the 2nd Earl Grosvenor, 1805–6 [Grosvenor archives, *ex inf.* Survey of London].

ECCLESTON CHURCH, CHESHIRE, for the 2nd Earl Grosvenor, *c.* 1806–9, Gothic; dem. 1899 [exhib. at R.A. 1809, 1813].

SHOTTESBROOKE PARK, BERKSHIRE, enlarged and remodelled for Arthur Vansittart, 1807, Gothic [drawings at Shottesbrooke] (*C. Life*, 1 Feb. 1913).

LONDON, GROSVENOR HOUSE, UPPER GROSVENOR STREET, alterations and extensive redecoration for the 2nd Earl Grosvenor, 1807–8; dem. 1927 [correspondence and accounts in Cheshire Record Office; John Cornforth in *C. Life*, 15 Nov. 1973].

BROOMHALL, FIFE, proposed north front for the 7th Earl of Elgin, exhibited at R.A. in 1808 as 'now building', but not in fact executed (design illustrated by J. M. Crook in *C. Life*, 29 Jan. 1970, fig. 7).

PORTER, GEORGE (*c.* 1796–1856), was a pupil of Thomas Chawner. He was admitted to the Royal Academy Schools in 1816 at the age of 20, and exhibited at the Academy from 1815 onwards. He subsequently practised from Fort Place, Bermondsey, and is said to have laid out part of the West estate in that neighbourhood. From 1824 onwards he was District Surveyor for Newington and North Lambeth. He was a Fellow of the Institute of British Architects and a member of the Surveyors' Club, of which he was President in 1839. He died in October 1856. S. S. Teulon was his pupil.

GUILDFORD BRIDGE, SURREY, widened 1825 by 'Mr. Porter, engineer and architect', presumably George Porter [Brayley, *Topographical History of Surrey* i, 1841, 384].

BERMONDSEY, ST. MARY'S CHURCH, remodelled west front 1830, Gothic [C. Mackeson, *Guide to the Churches of London*, 1894].

SURREY, a villa 'now erecting for a gentleman', exhibited at R.A. 1834.[1]

BERMONDSEY, premises for London Leather Company, *c.* 1837 [exhibited at R.A.].

FINSBURY, LONDON, DUTCH ALMSHOUSES, CROWN STREET, *c.* 1837 [exhibited at R.A.].

BERMONDSEY, ST. JAMES'S SCHOOLS, *c.* 1840 [Brayley, *Topographical History of Surrey* iii, 195].

PENGE, KENT, WATERMEN'S COMPANY'S ALMSHOUSES, 1840–1 [H. Humpherus, *History of the Watermen's Company*, n.d. iii, 349].

PORTWOOD, GEORGE (–1742), of Stamford, was probably the most prominent of the master masons who had their yards in that

[1] The original drawing, executed by S. S. Teulon, is now in the possession of Sir John Summerson.

653

town in the first half of the eighteenth century. He was Chamberlain of Stamford in 1736, and held office as Mayor at the time of his death on 3 May 1742. The Chamberlains' accounts record many payments to him for minor repairs to the Corporation's buildings between 1711 and 1741, and bills among the Marquis of Exeter's archives show that he did a good deal of repair work at BURGHLEY HOUSE in the 1720s for the 8th Earl of Exeter, who also employed him to take down the steeple of the ruinous church of PICKWORTH, RUTLAND, in 1723, and to refront the GEORGE HOTEL, STAMFORD, in 1724 [Exeter Archives 51/21/23, *ex inf.* Mr. P. I. King]. In 1722 he rebuilt the bridge over the river Nene at FOTHERINGHAY, NORTHANTS. [H. K. Bonney, *Historic Notices relating to Fotheringhay*, 1821, 2.] In 1729 he was employed at ST. MARY'S CHURCH, STAMFORD, where he repaved the space within the altar-rails, repaired the gable of the chancel, and altered a window on the south side [bills preserved among the parish records]. In 1737 he was paid 5 guineas by the churchwardens of WITHAM-ON-THE-HILL, LINCS., 'for Drawing Several designs for the rebuilding of there Church Steeple', which were carried out in the following year in Ketton stone by Messrs. Jackson and Chaplin for £318 [bill and accounts in parish chest]. In 1741 he made a design for rebuilding the front of Dr. William Stukeley's house on BARN HILL, STAMFORD, which has been preserved among Stukeley's papers in the Bodleian Library [Gough Maps 16, f. 52]. It was not executed, but similar elevations, with blocked architraves and prominent keystones, are to be seen on other eighteenth-century houses in Stamford, some of which were probably designed and built by Portwood.

In his will, dated 16 April 1742 [P.C.C., 51 ANSTIS], Portwood left his elder son George a note of £5 which he had lent him, and gave his younger son Samuel 'one shilling only', observing that 'neither of them had been so dutiful as they ought to a loving Father'. George Portwood, junior, was admitted to scot and lot in 1737 and appears to have died in 1761. He was also a mason by trade, but nothing is known of his building activities.

POTTER, JOHN, a carpenter by trade, was the builder and proprietor, and no doubt also the architect, of the LITTLE THEATRE, HAYMARKET, LONDON, which was erected in 1720 and replaced by Nash's Haymarket Theatre in 1820 [*Survey of London* xx, 98–9]. He is presumably to be identified with 'J. Potter Archt.', who signed the monument to James Cart (d. 1706) formerly in St. Mary-le-Bow Church, which was executed by Samuel Tufnell [K. A. Esdaile, *English Monumental Sculpture since the Renaissance*, 1927, 98], and may have been the Potter who was associated

with Thomas Edwards of Greenwich (*q.v.*), in some of his building activities in Cornwall.

POTTER, JOSEPH (*c.* 1756–1842), was an architect and builder of Lichfield with a considerable practice in Staffordshire and the neighbouring counties in the early nineteenth century. Early in his career he was employed by James Wyatt to supervise the latter's alterations to the cathedrals at Lichfield (1788–93) and Hereford (1790–3). He was also associated with Wyatt in the repair of St. Michael's Church, Coventry (1794), and the rebuilding of Plas Newydd for the first Marquess of Anglesey. At Lichfield he became the established Cathedral architect, carrying out further repairs after Wyatt's employment had ceased, including the repair of the south-west spire (1794), the restoration of the vaults of the north transept (1795–7) and of the west front (1820–2). By the standards of the early nineteenth century he was a competent Gothic architect, but he designed nothing of great distinction. He was County Surveyor of Staffordshire for 45 years, and also Engineer to the Grand Trunk Canal Company. He died at Lichfield on 18 August 1842, in his 87th year. His three sons all followed their father's profession in one of its branches. Robert (*c.* 1795–1854), the eldest, is noticed separately below. Joseph (*c.* 1797–1875) took over his father's office, and had an extensive local practice in the mid-nineteenth century. James (1801–1857), the youngest, became a civil engineer working chiefly for canal and railway companies. Thomas Johnson of Lichfield (1794–1865) was a pupil of the elder Potter, and James Fowler of Louth (1828–1892) was in the office of his son. A number of Potter's drawings (including those for Oscott College) are among the portfolios of his son's drawings in Sheffield City Library.

[*Gent's Mag.* 1842, 556; J. Hewitt, *Handbook to Lichfield Cathedral*, 1875, 49; *Proceedings of the Institution of Civil Engineers* xvii, 1858, 94.]

As it is not always possible to distinguish between the later works of Joseph Potter senior and the earlier works of his son, the following list contains all the recorded products of the Potter office up to the former's death in 1842.

HANBURY VICARAGE, STAFFS., 1793 [P.R.O., MPC 203, designs dated 1791].
COVENTRY, ST. MICHAEL'S CHURCH, repaired tower 1794, after a joint survey with James Wyatt; further repairs 1818 [T. Sharp, *Illustrations of the History of St. Michael's Church, Coventry*, 1818, 48–9].
LICHFIELD, NEWTON'S COLLEGE, THE CLOSE, 1800–2 [building contract, *ex inf.* Lichfield Joint Record Office].
HANDSWORTH CHURCH, STAFFS., rebuilt west end

c. 1800 [A. E. Everitt, 'Handsworth Church', *Trans. Birmingham Arch. Soc.* 1876, 52].

OKEOVER HALL, STAFFS., demolition of west wing for H. F. Okeover, *c.* 1810 [Arthur Oswald in *C. Life*, 12 March 1964].

TEDDESLEY HALL, STAFFS., unexecuted design for addition of wings for E. J. Littleton, 1814 [Staffs. Record Office D 260/M/E 359–71].

POLESWORTH SCHOOLS, WARWICKS., 1817–18, Tudor Gothic [Warwicks. Record Office, DRB 16/262–9].

POLESWORTH VICARAGE, WARWICKS., alterations 1817–18 [Warwicks. Record Office, DRB 16/271–8].

PENKRIDGE, STAFFS., NATIONAL SCHOOL, 1818 [Staffs. Record Office, D 260/M/E, 399–400].

BURNTWOOD CHURCH, STAFFS., 1819–20, Gothic [I.C.B.S.].

CAERNARVON, BATHS and ASSEMBLY ROOMS, for the 1st Marquess of Anglesey, 1822; subsequently converted into a Training College [University College of N. Wales, Bangor, Plas Newydd MSS. ii, 1392–1549, *ex inf.* Prof. M. L. Clarke].

PLAS NEWYDD, ANGLESEY, works for the 1st Marquess of Anglesey, completed 1823. Potter had already been employed here from 1795 onwards as executant architect under Wyatt, and appears to have been solely responsible for the Gothic chapel (dem.) built in 1805–9 [drawings in R.I.B.A. Collection; G. Jackson-Stops in *C. Life*, 1 July 1976].

CHETWYND BRIDGE, ALREWAS, STAFFS., 1823–4 (cast-iron) [*N. Staffs Jnl. of Field Studies* ii, 1962, 97].

BAKEWELL CHURCH, DERBYSHIRE, report on spire with Lewis Wyatt, 1824 [parish records].

GRENDON HALL, WARWICKS, rebuilt for Sir George Chetwynd, Bart., *c.* 1825, Elizabethan style; dem. 1932 [W. White, *Directory of Warwickshire*, 1874, 1359; designs for chimney-pieces by Potter dated 1825 in Victoria and Albert Museum and Metropolitan Museum, New York].

GRENDON CHURCH, WARWICKS., alterations and repairs 1824–5 [account loose in Vestry Minutes 1845–1906].

FREEFORD HALL, STAFFS., enlarged for General William Dyott, 1826–7 [Staffs. Record Office, D 661/8/1/2/6].

SHEFFIELD, ST. MARY'S CHURCH, 1826–9, Gothic [Port, 138–9; W. Odom, *Memorials of Sheffield*, 1922, 111]. An inscription on the roof records the names of 'Jos. Potter architect' and 'R. Potter resident architect'.

BEAUDESERT, STAFFS., alterations to the Gothic hall for the 1st Marquess of Anglesey, 1826–31; dem. *c.* 1925. Potter added a lantern and plaster rib vaulting to the Gothic hall designed by James Wyatt in 1771–2 [Staffs. Record

Office, uncatalogued drawings and accounts, *ex inf.* Mr. J. M. Frew].

ARMITAGE, STAFFS., HIGH BRIDGE, 1829–30 (cast-iron) [*N. Staffs. Jnl. of Field Studies* ii, 1962, 97].

TAMWORTH, STAFFS., ST. JOHN BAPTIST CHURCH (R.C.), 1829–30, classical; enlarged 1954–6 [*Catholic Mag*, i, 1831, 512 and v, 1834, 324, with illustration at p. 301].

PENKRIDGE CHURCH, STAFFS., report and estimate for internal alterations, 1830 [I.C.B.S.].

NEWPORT, SALOP., STS. PETER AND PAUL CHURCH (R.C.), 1832 [*Catholic Record Soc.* xiii, 1913, 338].

WADSLEY CHURCH, YORKS. (W.R.), 1833–4, Gothic [plans in Sheffield City Library].

LICHFIELD, HOLY CROSS CHURCH (R.C.), addition of sanctuary 1835 [*Catholic Mag.* v, 1834, 322 and frontispiece].

ST. MARY'S R.C. COLLEGE, NEW OSCOTT, SUTTON COLDFIELD, WARWICKS., 1835–8, with some alterations by A. W. N. Pugin, especially to the Chapel [*Companion to the Almanac*, 1839, 222; drawings by Potter in Sheffield City Library; Bryan Little, *Catholic Churches since 1623*, 1966, 77–8].

POTTER, ROBERT (*c.* 1795–1854), was the eldest son of Joseph Potter of Lichfield (*q.v.*). In 1826–9 he acted as 'resident architect' in charge of the building of St. Mary's Church, Sheffield, to the designs of his father, as recorded by an inscription on the roof. He subsequently established himself in Sheffield, where he designed CHRIST CHURCH, FULWOOD, 1837–9, Gothic, enlarged by G. G. Pace 1953–5 [printed record of the laying of the foundation stone in Sheffield City Library]. In Sheffield City Library there is a collection of his drawings, which includes designs for several schools, the SAVINGS BANK in SURREY STREET, SHEFFIELD (1831), alterations to ST. PETER'S CHURCH (now the Cathedral), including screen, singers' gallery and altar-piece (1841), and Tudor Gothic stables for STUMPERLOWE HALL, FULWOOD (1844). Potter died on 26 July 1854, aged 59, and was buried in the Churchyard of St. Chad's Church at Lichfield.

POUGET, —, was a French architect said to have been employed by Ralph, 1st Duke of Montagu, at MONTAGU HOUSE, BLOOMSBURY. Montagu was Charles II's ambassador at the Court of Louis XIV in 1676–7 and became a great admirer of French art and artists. In 1675–9 he built Montagu House 'after the French pavilion way', employing Robert Hooke as his architect. The house designed by Hooke was destroyed by fire in Jan. 1685/6 and rebuilt by Montagu the following year. It was sold to the British Museum Trustees in 1754 and demolished *c.* 1850 to make way for the existing Museum. Illustrating the rebuilt house in *Vitruvius Britannicus* i, 1715, pls. 34–6, Colen Campbell stated that 'the Architecture was conducted by Monsieur Pouget, 1678'. George Vertue, who says that the house was designed 'by an architect brought over on purpose', adds that the decorative painter Jacques Rousseau (1630–93) acted as 'assistant surveyor and designer for the building of (the) house' [*Note Books*, Walpole Soc., ii, 85, iii, 24]. As the 1678 house was in fact designed by Hooke, it has generally been supposed that what Pouget and Rousseau were employed to do was to rebuild it after the fire. No other reference to Pouget's presence in England has, however, been found, and his identity remains uncertain. For several reasons it is unlikely that he was Pierre Pouget (1622–94), a well-known French sculptor and architect who worked chiefly in Toulon and Marseilles. That a French architect was employed is, however, substantiated by the existence in France (ownership at present unknown) of a contemporary painting showing 'le Duc et la Duchesse de Montaigu arrètant le Plan de Montaigu-house qui leur est presenté par un Architecte francais' (photograph in Department of the History of Art, Oxford University).

POUGET, FRANCIS (1794–1867), was admitted to the Royal Academy Schools in 1818 at the age of 24. He subsequently practised as an architect and surveyor from Trinity Square, Southwark. In 1821 he won the second premium in the competition for Salters' Hall, exhibiting his design at the Royal Academy in 1823. Later works included a house called MOUNT HILL at SPRINGFIELD, nr. CHELMSFORD, ESSEX, for A. R. Chalk [exhib. at R.A. 1844]; a house at OATLANDS, SURREY, for R. Mathews [exhib. at R.A. 1849]; the CONGREGATIONAL CHURCH, SNELL'S PARK, EDMONTON, MIDDLESEX, 1849, dem. 1955 [F. Fisk, *History of Edmonton*, 1914, 86]; and an Italianate hotel near the Crystal Palace in Upper Norwood, 1853 [*Civil Engineer and Architect's Jnl.* xvi, 1853, 361]. Pouget died at Grove Lodge, Tottenham on 14 January 1867. [Principal Probate Registry, Calendar of Probates; information from Mr. P. J. Seaman.]

POULTON, CHARLES (–*c.* 1820), was a cabinet-maker at Reading, of which town he was mayor in 1798 and again in 1809. The town hall was built to his designs in 1786 [J. Man, *History of Reading*, 1816, 77]. It is a plain brick structure which still exists behind the present municipal buildings by Alfred Waterhouse. William Ford Poulton (*c.* 1820–1900), who practised in Reading in the 1840s and 1850s, may have been a relation.

POWER, JOSEPH, was a builder and architect of Colyton in Devon. He designed WISCOMBE

PARK, nr. SOUTH LEIGH, DEVON, for C. Gordon in an unsophisticated Gothic style in 1826 [J. R. W. Coxhead, *Honiton and the Vale of the Otter*, 1949, 74]. The I.C.B.S. records show that in 1820 he made an unexecuted design for enlarging SOUTH LEIGH CHURCH.

POWNING, JOHN (1763–1832), was an architect and builder of Exeter. His designs for STOWFORD RECTORY, DEVON, are among the Exeter Diocesan Records. A tablet in St. Mary the Great Church recorded his birth on 6 June 1763 and his death on 16 July 1832. Charles Fowler (1792–1867) was his pupil.

POWSEY, JOHN (*c.* 1734–), was a builder and surveyor of Poplar. In 1770 he supervised alterations to the premises of John Steinmetz, gingerbread and biscuit-maker of Limehouse [contract in R.I.B.A. Library, MS. 728.3 (42.13)]. In 1774, at the age of 40, he was appointed District Surveyor for Wapping and Limehouse [Middlesex County Records, General Orders No. 10]. In 1789–90 he acted as engineer for the construction of BRUNSWICK DOCK at Blackwall for the famous shipwright John Perry [*ex inf.* Prof. A. W. Skempton]. In 1794 he made a plan for docks at Wapping [*East London Papers* x, 1967, 77].

POYNTER, AMBROSE (1796–1886), born in London on 16 May 1796, was the second son of Ambrose Lyon Poynter, a surgeon of Huguenot descent. From 1814 to 1818 he was a pupil in the office of John Nash (who does not appear to have liked him). Afterwards he travelled in Italy, Sicily and the Ionian Islands, before starting practice in Westminster in 1821. In 1831–2 he spent some time in Paris, where he took lessons in water-colour painting from Thomas Shotter Boys, becoming a competent water-colourist in a style reminiscent of his teacher. It was in Paris that in 1832 he married his first wife, Emma Forster, a grand-daughter of the sculptor Thomas Banks.

Poynter was one of the founder-members of the Institute of British Architects in 1834, served as Secretary in 1840, 1841 and 1844, and as Vice-president in 1847–8. He was also a Fellow of the Society of Antiquaries, and a member of the Arundel Society, the Graphic Society and the Archaeological Institute. At meetings of the Institute of British Architects he read several papers, chiefly on antiquarian topics (including one on the arabesques in the Loggie of the Vatican[1] which was regarded as particularly valuable), and was the author of an anonymous essay 'On the Introduction of Iron in the Construction

---

[1] Printed in *Civil Engineer and Architect's Journal* vi, 1843, 1–6.

of Buildings',[1] to which the silver medal of the Institute was awarded in 1842. He wrote the essay on the history of Windsor Castle which forms part of *Illustrations of Windsor Castle by the late Sir Jeffry Wyatville*, ed. H. Ashton (1841), and he helped Charles Knight by providing illustrations for his popular *History of England* (1837–43) and *Pictorial Shakespere* (1838–41), to the former of which he also contributed the articles on literature, science and art. He took much interest in artistic education, and in 1850 gladly accepted the post of Inspector of the Government Schools of Design. In professional practice he was often employed in arbitration cases and was one of the official referees under the Metropolitan Building Act of 1844.

As an architect Poynter is best known for his earliest work, St. Katharine's Hospital and Chapel in Regent's Park (1826–8). This is an attractive essay in Tudor Gothic, carried out in yellow stock brick with stone dressings. It belongs to the 'pre-ecclesiological' phase of the Revival, but by 1833 Poynter was experimenting with Romanesque at Osberton Church and by 1842 he was designing an archaeologically correct church in Westminster in late thirteenth-century style, complete with a steeple from the Nene Valley. Despite his early travels in the Mediterranean he appears to have done little classical work, unless the premises which he is stated to have designed for the National Provincial Bank 'in several towns' were in that style.

In about 1860 Poynter began to go blind, and was obliged to retire prematurely at the height of his career. He died at Dover on 20 November 1866. His son Sir Edward John Poynter (1836–1919) was a successful artist and first Director of the National Gallery. Many of Ambrose Poynter's travel drawings are in the R.I.B.A. Collection. Some of them were reproduced in a small volume entitled *Drawings by Ambrose Poynter*, which was privately printed in *c.* 1932. His letters to the Rev. Robert Finch (1821–30) are in the Bodleian Library (MS. Finch d. 13, ff. 429–92).

[*R.I.B.A. Proceedings* N.S. iii, 1887, 113–15, 137; *D.N.B.*; *Catalogue of the R.I.B.A. Drawings Collection O-R*, 96–7.]

LONDON, ST. KATHERINE'S ROYAL HOSPITAL, REGENT'S PARK, 1826–8, Gothic [*History of the King's Works* vi, 479–80].

HODSOCK PRIORY, nr. WORKSOP, NOTTS., for Mrs. Chambers, 1829–33, Gothic [building accounts in Nottingham University Library, Mellish papers].

WARWICK CASTLE, re-roofed and repaired Great Hall for the 3rd Earl of Warwick, 1830–1, Gothic, destroyed by fire 1871 [exhib. at R.A. 1831; *V.C.H. Warwicks.* viii, 464].

SCOFTON-WITH-OSBERTON CHURCH, NOTTS., for G. S. Foljambe, 1833, Romanesque [Foljambe papers at Osberton; Charles Anderson, *Ancient Models; or, Hints on Church Building*, 2nd ed., 1841, 181–6, with plan and elevation].

CAMBRIDGE, CHRIST CHURCH, 1837–9, Tudor [Port, 140–1] (R.C.H.M. *Cambridge*, 255).

CAMBRIDGE, ST. PAUL'S CHURCH, 1840–1, Tudor Gothic; enlarged 1864 and 1893 [Port, 140–1] (R.C.H.M. *Cambridge*, 287). This church was singled out for attack in the first issue of the *Ecclesiologist*.

CAMBRIDGE, CHURCH OF ST. ANDREW THE GREAT, rebuilt 1842–3, Gothic [I.C.B.S.] (R.C.H.M. *Cambridge*, 260–1).

LONDON, CHRIST CHURCH, BROADWAY, WESTMINSTER, 1842–3, Gothic; dem. [*Companion to the Almanac*, 1843, 239–40].

CAMBRIDGE, ST. CLEMENT'S CHURCH, restoration 1843 [*Ecclesiologist* ii, 1843, 138].

WHITFORD CHURCH, FLINTSHIRE, rebuilt tower 1843 and church 1846, Gothic [D. R. Thomas, *History of the Diocese of St. Asaph*, 1870, 488].

MOSTYN QUAY, WHITFORD, FLINTSHIRE, CHRIST CHURCH, 1844–5, Gothic [S. Lewis, *Topographical Dictionary of Wales* ii, 1849, 429].

CILCAIN CHURCH, FLINTSHIRE, repairs 1845 [D. R. Thomas, *History of the Diocese of St. Asaph*, 1870, 459].

LONDON, THE FRENCH PROTESTANT CHURCH, BLOOMSBURY STREET, 1845, Gothic; dem. [*R.I.B.A. Proceedings* N. S. iii, 1887, 113–14].

LONDON, PARK STREET (now QUEEN ANNE'S GATE), house and offices for himself (later occupied by J. P. Seddon), *c.* 1846 [*R.I.B.A. Proceedings* N.S. iii, 1887, 113].

RHESYCAE CHURCH, FLINTSHIRE, 1846, Gothic [I.C.B.S.].

FLINT, ST. MARY'S CHURCH, rebuilt 1847–8, Gothic [D. R. Thomas, *History of the Diocese of St. Asaph*, 1870, 485].

LONDON, ST. JOHN'S LODGE, REGENT'S PARK, decoration of ballroom etc. designed by C. Barry for Baron de Goldsmid, 1847–8 [*R.I.B.A. Proceedings* N.S. iii, 1887, 114; A. T. Bolton in University of London: *Institute of Archaeology's First Annual Report*, 1937, 15].

DEAL, KENT, ST. ANDREW'S CHURCH, 1848–50, Gothic [I.C.B.S.].

MOSTYN HALL, FLINTSHIRE, alterations and additions, including new library, for the Hon. Edward M. Lloyd Mostyn, 1848–9, Elizabethan style [exhib. at R.A. 1849; S. Lewis, *Topographical Dictionary of Wales* ii, 1849, 427; Parry, *Railway Companion from Chester to Holyhead*, 1848, 57].

PYNES, nr. EXETER, DEVON, alterations, including new entrance hall, for Sir Stafford Henry Northcote, Bart., 1852 [exhib. at R.A.].

---

[1] Printed *ibid*, 291–6.

CASTLE MAELGWYN, PEMBROKESHIRE, for A. A. Gower, before 1840; dem. [*R.I.B.A. Proceedings* N.S. iii, 1887, 114].

PRATT, Sir ROGER (1620–1685), was descended from a family of country gentlemen who had their seat at Ryston, nr. Downham in Norfolk. His father, Gregory, was the younger brother of Francis Pratt, the owner of Ryston, and a lawyer by profession. Roger Pratt matriculated at Magdalen College, Oxford, on 12 May 1637, at the age of 19, and entered the Inner Temple in 1639. His father died in 1640, leaving him an income which enabled him in 1643 to set out on a six years' tour of France, Italy, Flanders and Holland, in order to avoid the Civil War and 'to give myself some convenient education'. In January 1645 he matriculated in the faculty of law at Padua, and about the same time he was 'cohabitant' with John Evelyn in Rome. It is evident from his notebooks that architecture was already a major interest, and although he resided in the Inner Temple for some time after his return to England in 1649, he seems to have had no desire to resume his legal studies. Within a year or two he had entered on the architectural career which, if it did not bring him wealth, was to give him congenial employment and eventually a knighthood. He had a fine collection of architectural books, and his notebooks display more than a merely amateur interest in architecture, with their eminently practical 'Rules for the Guidance of Architects' and 'Notes on the Building of Country Houses'. In these, the new rôle of the gentleman architect is made clear: the prospective builder is advised to 'get some ingenious gentleman who has seen much of that kind abroad and been somewhat versed in the best authors of Architecture: viz. Palladio, Scamozzi, Serlio etc. to do it for you, and to give you a design of it in paper'. In this capacity Pratt himself was to become one of the pioneers of classical architecture in England. Although his output was limited (so far as is known) to four large houses, they were all of considerable importance in establishing a new type of astylar 'double-pile' house that was to be the norm until the reign of Queen Anne. The one which he built in Piccadilly for Lord Clarendon was, indeed, to be one of the most influential buildings in the history of English domestic architecture. Evelyn considered it 'the best contrived, the most usefull, gracefull and magnificent house in England', and, although demolished in 1683, only sixteen years after its completion, it was the model upon which gentlemen's seats all over the country were being erected in the reigns of Charles II and James II.

After the Restoration Pratt was, with Webb, May, Hooke, Evelyn and Wren, one of the few educated Englishmen with any serious interest in

architecture. Together with May and Wren he was called in to advise the commissioners for the repair of St. Paul's Cathedral shortly before the Great Fire of 1666, and after the Fire he was one of the three commissioners appointed by the King to supervise the rebuilding of the City. His notebooks show how seriously he took his duties in this capacity, and in 1668 his services were rewarded by knighthood. In the same year he married Anne, daughter and coheiress of Sir Edmond Monins, Bart. of Waldershare in Kent, and set about rebuilding the house at Ryston which he had recently inherited under the will of his cousin, Edward Pratt (d. 1664). This appears to have been his last architectural work, and his later years were spent in leading the life of a country gentleman. But some notes, made probably in 1672, concerning a projected palace on the Thames for 'the Prince' – probably the Duke of York, who had married Lord Clarendon's eldest daughter, and had since 1664 been in possession of the site of the old royal palace of Richmond-on-Thames – show that he still maintained his architectural interests. Pratt died at Ryston on 20 February 1684/5, and was buried in the parish church which stands in the park. His portrait by Lely is preserved at Ryston, together with his library and the elaborate manuscript notebooks in which he set down his architectural experience. His intention was probably to publish a systematic architectural treatise. This was never completed, but in 1928 the notes were edited by R. T. Gunther as *The Architecture of Sir Roger Pratt*, which constitutes the principal source of information about Pratt's architectural career.

[R. T. Gunther, *The Architecture of Sir Roger Pratt*, 1928; *D.N.B.*; Francis Blomefield, *History of Norfolk* vii, 1807, 393; *Students admitted to the Inner Temple*, ed. Cooke, 1877, 302; *The Diary of John Evelyn*, ed. de Beer, 1959, 360, 493, 494, 541; *Wren Soc.* xiii, 4, 14–15, 18; J. W. Stoye, *English Travellers Abroad*, 1952, 206–9; Jane Lang, *Rebuilding St. Paul's*, 1956; John Summerson, *Architecture in Britain 1530–1830*, 1963, 85–88].

COLESHILL HOUSE, BERKSHIRE, for Sir George Pratt, Bart., *c.* 1650–62; repaired 1744–5 'by the Direction of the Earls of Burlington and Leicester' (as recorded by a brass plate), again repaired 1814–16 by D. A. Alexander; demolished after a fire in 1952.

The circumstances of the building of this house are confused. The will of Sir Henry Pratt, Sir George Pratt's father, dated 1645, nearly 4 years before his death in 1649, shows that he was then building a house at Coleshill, for he directed his executors to finish it. This may explain a story recorded by Sir Mark Pleydell (1692–1768), a later owner of Coleshill, to the effect that Sir George Pratt was persuaded by his distant 'cousin', Sir Roger Pratt, to abandon a house that had been begun on a different site ('in the cucumber garden'). According to this story, Pratt was supported by Inigo Jones, who came down to advise at the age of 78, i.e. in 1651, the year before his death, and 'was also consulted about the ceiling' (evidently the one in the hall, which resembled that at the Queen's House at Greenwich). This tradition of Inigo Jones's participation in the design of Coleshill is both supported and complicated by the existence in the Chatsworth 'Book of Capitals' of three designs by Webb described as for 'Sir George Pratt at Coleshill neere Faringdon in Barkshyre' and by the presence in the R.I.B.A. Collection of a design for a chimney-piece for Coleshill by Webb. These designs do not correspond with the house as built, and the share (if any) of Webb in the design remains problematical. [H. A. Tipping in *C. Life*, 26 July, 2 Aug. 1919; R. T. Gunther, *The Architecture of Sir Roger Pratt*, 1928, 4, 5, 92–7; W. Grant Keith in *R.I.B.A. Jnl.* 22 July 1933, 732–3; M. Pinhorn, 'A Note on the date of construction of Coleshill, Berks.', *Blackmansbury* i (1), 1964, 5–7; John Harris, *Catalogue of the R.I.B.A. Drawings Collection: Inigo Jones and John Webb*, 1972, 23] (*Vitruvius Britannicus* v, 1771, pls. 86–7).

KINGSTON LACY, DORSET, for Sir Ralph Bankes, 1663–5; cased in stone and altered by Sir C. Barry 1835–9 [R. T. Gunther, *op. cit.*, 98–116; A. S. Oswald, *Country Houses of Dorset*, 1935, 76–9].

HORSEHEATH, CAMBS., for William Lord Alington, 1663–5; enlarged *c.* 1700 by John Bromley and dem. in 1777 by his son Lord Mountford [R. T. Gunther, *op. cit.*, 117–31; Miss C. Parsons in *Proceedings of the Cambridge Antiquarian Society* xli, 1941–7] (*Vitruvius Britannicus* iii, 1725, pls. 91–2).

CLARENDON HOUSE, PICCADILLY, for Edward Hyde, 1st Earl of Clarendon, 1664–7; dem. 1683 [R. T. Gunther, *op. cit.*, 9–11, 135–66].

RYSTON HALL, NORFOLK, for himself, 1669–72; altered by Sir John Soane 1786–8 [R. T. Gunther, *op. cit.*, 167–93].

PRICE, FRANCIS (*c.* 1704–1753), held the post of Surveyor or Clerk of the Works to Salisbury Cathedral from 1737 until his death. He made a general survey of the cathedral soon after his appointment, and carried out considerable repairs in the following years. In 1736–8 he also altered and repaired the BISHOP'S PALACE for Bishop Sherlock [drawings and estimates in Diocesan Record Office]. He appears to have designed the west end of ELLINGHAM CHURCH, HANTS., as rebuilt in brick in 1747, for in October

he was paid one guinea by the churchwardens for his 'Estimate and advice' [MS. Churchwardens' Accounts]. If so, it is possible that he was also the architect of HEMINGSBY HOUSE, NO. 56 THE CLOSE, SALISBURY, as its design resembles the contemporary work at Ellingham. In 1753 he was consulted by Ivory Talbot concerning the alterations which the latter was about to make to LACOCK ABBEY, WILTS., but his suggestions for a Gothic front with bow windows were not adopted [*An Eighteenth-Century Correspondence*, ed. Dickins and Stanton, 1910, 304]. He appears to have been well thought of, for in William Hanbury's directions for the management of his projected collegiate foundation at Church Langton, Leics. (*c.* 1760), he stated that the 'diligence of Mr. Price, of Salisbury, affords a laudable pattern for him (the Resident Surveyor) to copy after' [J. H. Hill, *History of Langton*, 1867, 137–9].

In 1733 Price published *The British Carpenter, or a Treatise on Carpentry*, dedicated to Algernon Seymour, Earl of Hertford, afterwards 7th Duke of Somerset, a work recommended by Nicholas Hawksmoor, John James and James Gibbs, as 'a very Usefull and Instructive Piece'. Later editions appeared in 1735, 1753, 1759, 1765 and 1768, and the book was long regarded as one of the best of its kind. It contains a description of a trammel for describing an ellipse, which, as 'Price's Trammel', was still in current use in builders' workshops in the nineteenth century. He was also the author of *A Series of particular and useful Observations ... upon ... the Cathedral Church of Salisbury*, published in 1753. This is notable as the first serious attempt to describe and analyse the structure of a major Gothic building. It was based on a survey undertaken at the request of Bishop Sherlock, and formed the basis of many subsequent accounts of the cathedral. The anonymous *Description of ... the Cathedral Church of Salisbury* published in 1787 was in effect a second edition, with additional material derived from Price's manuscripts.

Price died on 20 March 1753, in his 50th year, and was buried in the cloisters at Salisbury, where a monument was erected to his memory. His portrait by George Bear, dated 1747, is in the National Portrait Gallery. [*A.P.S.D.*; *D.N.B.*; *Gent's Mag.* 1789 (ii), 875; James Harris, *Copies of the Epitaphs in Salisbury Cathedral*, 1825, 127; *Builder* xxxi, 1873, 765; Peter Ferriday, 'Francis Price, Carpenter', *Arch. Rev.*, Nov. 1953.]

PRICE, JOHN (–1736), 'of London', was the architect and builder of the church of ST. MARY–AT–THE–WALLS, COLCHESTER, 1713–14. With the exception of the tower, the church was rebuilt by A. W. Blomfield in 1871–2 [G. O. Rickword, 'The Rebuilding of the Church of St. Mary-at-the-Walls, Colchester, 1713–14', *Essex*

Arch. Soc.'s Trans., n.s., xxiii (2), 1945]. There can be no doubt that he was the same as the John Price 'of Richmond', who designed ISLEWORTH CHURCH, MIDDLESEX, 1705–7, gutted 1943 [Bodleian, MS. Rawlinson B. 389c, ff. 111–26; M. Robbins in *The London and Middlesex Historian* i, 1965, 4], and who, in conjunction with his son John Price, junior (also of Richmond), designed and built ST. GEORGE' CHAPEL, YARMOUTH, in 1714–16. In 1715 Messrs. Price and Son also contracted to build a new TOWN HALL and ASSEMBLY ROOM at YARMOUTH, 'according to a draft and plans delivered . . . by the said Messrs. Price' [J. Preston, *Picture of Yarmouth*, 1819, 23–4, 191–2]. The latter building was enlarged in 1772 and 1842 and demolished in 1882. It is illustrated in A. W. Yallop, *Ancient Yarmouth*, 1905, pl. 80. John Price subsequently designed the church of ST. GEORGE, SOUTHWARK, whose foundation stone was laid on 23 April 1734, by the deputy of King George II, *adjuvante Johanne Price armiger, architecto*. It was completed in 1736, and refitted internally by William Hedger in 1808. The present ceiling, designed by Basil Champneys in 1897, replaces one of 1808. [Manning & Bray, *History of Surrey* iii, 1814, 637; *Survey of London* xxv, chap. 4].

The evidence set out above establishes Price as a designer of early Georgian churches in a pleasant but rather unsophisticated vernaclar style derived from Wren. In 1720 he was responsible for a remarkable project for residential development at HEADLEY in SURREY, not far from Epsom, then a fashionable watering place. This is known from an engraving (found separately, and as plates 96–7 of Badeslade and Rocque's *Vitruvius Brittanicus* iv of 1739) inscribed 'the Elevation or West Prospect of Part of a Design of Building already began to be Erected on the Lawne at Headly in Surrey/Design'd by John Price, Architect, 1720'. It shows a grand central building with portico and mansard roofs (presumably some sort of Assembly Rooms) flanked by two identical ranges each of nine houses treated as a uniform composition. Though poorly composed, this design is remarkable as 'the earliest English essay in urban terrace composition' since Inigo Jones's Covent Garden, anticipating Colen Campbell's designs for Grosvenor Square by five years (C. Hussey in *C. Life*, 6 June 1968, 1539). It was never completed, but Manning and Bray record that some traces of Price's unfinished buildings were still be to seen at Headley in the early nineteenth century (*History of Surrey* ii, 1814, 637, and cf. the printed 'Proposals for Building in the Parishes of Headly and Walton on the Hill in the County of Surrey' in Bodleian, MS. North b. 1, f. 15). Price had already had some experience of speculative building in London, having in 1718 taken several leases on the Harley estate in Holles, Oxford,

Margaret and Prince's Streets [B.M., Add. MS. 18240, f. 7].

The elder Price was the fourth architect employed by the Duke of Chandos at CANNONS HOUSE, MIDDLESEX, in 1720–1. By this time the structure was largely complete, and Price's contribution, so far as original designs were concerned, was probably small. However, the elevations of Cannons published by Hulsbergh at this time are inscribed 'John Price Architect, Built Anno 1720', although what they show was largely the work of his predecessors in the Duke's service. The engraved elevation of the Duke's projected mansion in Cavendish Square is similarly described as 'Design'd by John Price, architect 1720'. Its design obviously owed much to Cannons. It was never built, and by 1723 Price's place as the Duke's surveyor had been taken by Edward Shepherd [C. H. & M. I. Collins Baker, *James Brydges, Duke of Chandos*, 1949, *passim*].

Price was among those who made designs for a bridge to be built across the Thames between Fulham and Putney. He published *Some considerations for building a [stone] Bridge over the Thames from Fulham to Putney, humbly offer'd to the Commissioners appointed*, and *Mr. Price's Second Letter to one of the Commissioners for Building a Bridge over the Thames from Fulham to Putney, together with some Proposals for building a Wooden Bridge*. Neither design was, however, accepted by the Commissioners, and fresh plans were invited in 1728. Price again submitted a design for a stone bridge, together with 'draughts of the most famous Bridges in Europe both Ancient and Modern' for comparison. The Commissioners' minutes show that the timber **bridge which was built by Thomas Phillips** in 1729 was constructed 'according to a scheme and principles laid down by' Dr. William Cheselden of St. Thomas's Hospital [G.L.C. Record Office, Commissioners' Minutes, 2 July 1730; H. Humpherus, *History of the Watermen's Company*, n.d., ii, 127]. In 1735 Price took part in the Westminster Bridge controversy by publishing *Some Considerations humbly offered to the House of Commons, for building a Stone-Bridge over the River Thames from Westminster to Lambeth*, with an engraved design. This was criticised by John James in his *Short Review of the Several Pamphlets and Schemes . . . in relation to Building a Bridge at Westminster*, 1736.

John Price the elder died in November 1736 [*Historical Register*, 1736, 60], where he is described as 'Architect of St. George's Church in Southwark'.[1] It is doubtful whether he is to be identified with the 'Mr. Price of Wandsworth' whose design for a stable at King's Weston, nr. Bristol, dated 1720, is among drawings connected

---

[1] Reference to the parish registers of Richmond and Wandsworth shows that he was buried in neither place.

with that house reproduced in *Architectural History* x, 1967 (fig. 24), or with the 'Mr. Price of York Buildings, Surveyor and Architect', to whose designs the tower of LALEHAM CHURCH, MIDDLESEX, was rebuilt in 1730–1 [MS. Vestry Minutes]. In both cases there is a Vanbrughian character about the designs which does not altogether accord with John Price's recorded works. In the John Johnson Collection in the Bodleian Library there is a MS. prospectus by John Price of Wandsworth announcing his intention to publish a book entitled *Vignola Revived, being a Translation of Daviller's Architecture*, a proposal endorsed by Wren, Vanbrugh and Talman as 'highly useful and deserving of encouragement'.

Not much is known of the career of John Price, junior. In 1737 he was one of the several surveyors who reported on the state of the City church of St. Katherine Coleman before its rebuilding [MS. Churchwardens' Accounts in Guildhall Library], and it is possible that he was the same as 'John Price of Hounsditch' who submitted estimates for enlarging the church of St. John Hackney in 1756 [R. Simpson, *Memorials of St. John at Hackney*, 1881, 156–7]. He was a Warden of the Carpenters' Company in 1751–2, and was elected Master in 1753. He acted as Surveyor to the Fishmongers' Company, and his death on 17 October 1765 is recorded in the Company's records [MS. 5573/3, p. 344, *ex inf.* Miss Priscilla Metcalf].

PRICE, WILLIAM, was an architect and builder of Gloucester. In 1785–6 he built the new MARKETS (dem.) in EASTGATE and SOUTHGATE STREETS, in accordance with plans and estimates made by himself and altered by Anthony Keck, who was employed by the Corporation to inspect them, and to act as surveyor during their execution; and in 1788–9 he built the Gothic almshouses known as ST. BARTHOLOMEW'S HOSPITAL, in accordance with his own designs, and without the supervision of a surveyor. [Extract from Gloucester Corporation Records by C. H. Dancey in Gloucester Public Library, Ref. 17270.]

PRICE, WILLIAM LAKE, described as 'Architect and Painter', exhibited at the Royal Academy between 1828 and 1841, and at the Society of British Artists in 1830. His exhibits included designs for a mausoleum (1828), a palace and gardens (1829), 'the square of a city with a triumphal bridge and arch' (1830), views of buildings in Rouen (1831–2), and a 'design for a marine residence for a nobleman, suggested by the Palace of the King of Naples' (1841). From 1828 to 1832 his address was 46 Warren Street, London, but in 1841 it was Corbetstye, nr. Upminster in Essex.

PRIDDEN, Rev. JOHN, F.S.A. (1758–1825), was a clergyman of antiquarian tastes who also

had 'a considerable knowledge and natural taste for architecture and civil engineering'. He was one of the founders of the Sea-Bathing Infirmary at Margate, whose buildings were erected to his designs in 1796 (see engravings in *Gent's Mag.* lxvii (ii), 841 and lxxxvi (i), 17). He shortly afterwards became vicar of Caddington in Beds., where in 1812 he rebuilt the vicarage (dem. 1970), acting as his own architect and surveyor. He made an elaborate design for uniting the summits of Snow Hill and Holborn Hill by means of a bridge, 'under which the road from Black Friars to the great North road might conveniently have been carried', for which he received the thanks of the Corporation of London. The project was considered too expensive at the time, but eventually found realization in the modern Holborn Viaduct. For a full account of Pridden's many-sided career, see *Gent's Mag* 1825 (1), 467–8; Nichols, *Literary Illustrations* viii, 676–7; and *D.N.B.* His MS. journal of a tour in Wales in 1780, with sketches, is in the National Library of Wales (MS. 15172 D), and two volumes of 'Topographical Collections' by him (1783–97) are in the Essex Record Office.

PRINCE, JOHN, acted as agent and surveyor to Edward Harley in connection with the laying out of the Harley estate in Marylebone. He was responsible for the planning of the new streets, and a plan signed by him was engraved in 1719,[1] although alterations were subsequently made in execution. There are several references to him in an inventory of Harley estate documents now in the British Museum, *e.g.*:

Draughts for rebuilding Marybone Church and an Estimate of the Charge thereof by John Prince.

An Estimate of the Charge of making a French Chapell out of the Barn by the Mansion House,[2] by the same.

A Plan of the Building Ground set out in Marybone Fields on Vellom by Mr. John Prince, 1720.

A Plan of Coll°. Guise's House by Mr. J. Prince, 1723. (Add. MS. 18240, ff. 30–6.)

Prince appears to have been a bricklayer by trade, and was himself one of the principal speculators who built on the estate. He appears to have given his name to Prince's Street, and was in the habit of calling himself the 'Prince of Surveyors' – a boast which brought on him a violent

---

[1] It is entitled 'A Design of Buildings already begun to be built in the Parish of St. Mary la Bonne Belonging to the Rt. Honble Edward Ld. Harley and ye Rt. Honble Lady Henrietta Cavendish Holles Harley, AD. 1719', 'Design'd and Delineated by John Prince' and is reproduced by Baker, *James Brydges, Duke of Chandos*, 1949, 272.

[2] The old Manor House of Marylebone.

attack in the *Weekly Medley* for September 1719 [T. Smith, *St. Marylebone*, 1833, 157].

It was presumably the same John Prince who designed COUND HALL, SALOP., for Edward Cressett in 1703–4. An elevation for this house, signed 'John Prince Inv^t. et Delineavit', was seen by Tipping in 1918 and is reproduced in his *English Homes*, Period IV, vol. i, 1929, 420.[1] The house is remarkable for the ambitious but inept use of a giant Corinthian order applied to the main elevations in a manner perhaps suggested by the King William block at Greenwich Hospital. The name of 'Mr. John Prince' appears in the list of subscribers to James Gibbs's *Book of Architecture*, published in 1728.

Certain resemblances between Cound Hall and Rosewell House, Virginia (*c.* 1725), 'the largest and most magnificent house known to have been built in the American colonies', have led to the suggestion that Prince may have been its architect. There is, however, no evidence that Prince visited America, and until more is known about his career, the possibility that he was 'the founder of the Shropshire school of Virginia building' cannot be regarded as more than a speculation [T. T. Waterman, 'English Antecedents of Virginia Architecture', *Proceedings of the American Philosophical Society* lxxx, 1939, 57–63].

PRITCHARD, EDWARD (*c.* 1783–1863), of Tarrington in Herefordshire, designed the north aisle that was added to TARRINGTON CHURCH in 1835 in a late Gothic style [I.C.B.S.]. As 'Edward Pritchard, surveyor', he was concerned in repairs to WESTON BEGGARD CHURCH, HEREFS., in 1826 [I.C.B.S.]. A monument in Tarrington churchyard praises his 'integrity and uprightness' and records that he died on 23 March 1863, aged 83, having been for 'upwards of sixty years Head Builder for the Foley family Stoke Edith'.

PRITCHARD, THOMAS FARNOLLS (1723–1777), was baptised at St. Julian's Church, Shrewsbury, on 11 May 1723. Like his father he was a joiner by trade, but developed a considerable practice as an architect in Shropshire and the neighbouring counties. The discovery in the library of the American Institute of Architects at Washington of an album of drawings for chimney-pieces, interior decoration and monuments, and its identification by Mr. John Harris as the work of Pritchard, shows that he was a competent designer of decorative features in the rococo style, and that he also made gothic designs in the manner of Batty Langley. His houses and churches are no more than pleasant examples of mid-Georgian provincial architecture, but in the history of bridge-building Pritchard has a place of national importance. In 1767 he made a design for rebuilding the English Bridge at Shrewsbury that was not accepted, but ten years later he was the key figure in the building of the cast-iron bridge over the R. Severn in Coalbrookdale – the first of its kind in the world. In 1773 he had made designs for a timber bridge with stone abutments to span the same river at Stourport, and the contract to build such a bridge under his direction was advertised in *Berrow's Worcester Journal* on 15 December 1773. But being dissatisfied with this method of construction he designed a single-arch brick bridge on an iron centre, with circular perforations in the haunches of the arch to allow for the passage of flood–water. The bridge actually built in 1775 (and destroyed by a flood in 1794) was of three stone arches, but Pritchard continued to explore the possibility of employing iron in the construction of bridges, and in 1775 he made the designs for a bridge of completely iron construction which (with some modifications) were executed by Abraham Darby in Coalbrookdale in 1777–9. Pritchard's designs both for this bridge and for the one at Stourport are described and illustrated in a note by his grandson John White published in *The Philosophical Magazine and Annals of Philosophy* N.S. xi, 1832, 81–2, and also printed separately in White's booklet *On Cementitious Architecture as applicable to the Construction of Bridges, with a prefatory notice of the first introduction of iron as the constituent material for arches of large span, by Thomas Farnolls Pritchard in 1773*, 1832.

Pritchard did not live to see his iron bridge constructed, dying on 23 December 1777. Since about 1770 he had been living at Eyton-on-Severn, in a Jacobean garden-building converted into a house known as 'Eyton Turret'. He was buried at St. Julian's Church, Shrewsbury, where there is a tablet to his memory. His wife Eleanor had died in 1768. Three of their children died young, but their surviving daughter became the wife of John White (*q.v.*), whose son published the account of Pritchard's bridge-building activities already referred to. A copy of a portrait of Pritchard, made in 1824 from an original by Thomas Worlidge, is in the R.I.B.A. Collection. Drawings by Pritchard for a house for a Mr. Good (unidentified) are in the same collection.

[*A.P.S.D.*; J. L. Hobbs, 'Thomas Farnolls Pritchard', *Shropshire Magazine*, Aug.–Sept. 1959; John Harris, 'Pritchard Redivivus', *Architectural History* xi, 1968; Robin Chaplin, 'New Light on T. F. Pritchard', *Shropshire News Letter*, No. 34, 1968; John Harris, *Catalogue of British Drawings*

---

[1] On p. 418 Tipping quotes the words 'Prince, architect, Salop' as if they were inscribed on the drawing, which is not the case. The inscription is clearly legible on a print kindly provided by *Country Life*, Ltd., and reads 'John Prince Inv^t. et Delineavit', without any reference to 'Salop.'

for Architecture etc. in American Collections, 1971, 162–8; Rupert Gunnis, *Dictionary of British Sculptors*, 1968, 311; A. W. Ward, *The Bridges of Shrewsbury*, Shrewsbury, 1935, 40–1; information from Mr. J. B. Lawson.]

HILL COURT, ROSS–ON–WYE, HEREFS., unexecuted design for addition of wings, etc., which indicates that Pritchard was probably responsible for the enlargement carried out for the Clarke family, *c.* 1745–50 [J. Harris in *Architectural History* xi, 1968, 19] (*C. Life*, 27 Jan., 3 Feb. 1966).

SHREWSBURY, three shops in CARRIERS INN (now SHOPLATCH) for the Shrewsbury Drapers' Company, 1749; dem. [Salop. Record Office, estimate and contract in records of Shrewsbury Drapers' Co., *ex inf.* Mr. J. B. Lawson].

SHREWSBURY, ST. JULIAN'S CHURCH, rebuilt, incorporating medieval tower, 1749–50 [D. H. S. Cranage, *The Churches of Shropshire*, 1894–1912, ii, 921].

attributed: BROCKHAMPTON HALL, nr. BROMYARD, HEREFS., for Bartholomew Barneby, *c.* 1750 [John Cornforth, letter in *C. Life*, 4 April 1968, 815].

LUDLOW, SALOP., HOSYER'S ALMS-HOUSES, 1758–9 [*V.C.H. Salop.* ii, 109].

SHREWSBURY, CANN OFFICE (now Kingsland Bank) for the Shrewsbury Drapers' Company, 1759 [Salop. Record Office, accounts of Drapers' Company, *ex inf.* Mr. J. B. Lawson].

TERN HALL, ATTINGHAM, SHROPSHIRE, for Thomas Hill, 1759–61; replaced by Attingham Hall 1783–5 [R. Chaplin in *Shropshire News Letter*, No. 34, 1968, 3–4] (*C. Life*, 5 Feb. 1921, p. 162, fig. 6).

SHREWSBURY, THE FOUNDLING HOSPITAL (now Shrewsbury School), 1759–63; remodelled by Sir Arthur Blomfield 1878–82 [*ex inf.* Mr. J. B. Lawson, Librarian of Shrewsbury School].

LUDFORD HOUSE, nr. LUDLOW, SALOP., remodelled east front for Sir Francis Charlton, Bart., 1761 [estimate and specification in Salop. Record Office, 783/box 8, *ex inf.* Mr. J. B. Lawson].

SHREWSBURY, SWAN HILL COURT HOUSE for the trustee (the Earl of Bath) of John Newport, 1761–2 [P.R.O., C 110/6 and C 110/4].

ACTON ROUND CHURCH, SALOP., mortuary chapel and monument to Sir Whitmore Acton, Bart. (d. 1732) for Sir Richard Acton, Bart., 1761–3 [accounts in Salop. Record Office, 1093, *ex inf.* Mr. J. B. Lawson; monument signed by Pritchard].

WOLVERHAMPTON, STAFFS., enlarged and largely rebuilt THE RED LION INN for the trustee of John Newport, 1764–5; dem. [P.R.O., C110/6; designs for picture-frame and chimney-piece in Pritchard album].

LUDLOW, SALOP., GAOLFORD TOWER, 1764–5; dem. [Salop. Record Office, accounts of Ludlow bai-

liffs and chamberlains, 356, box 32, *ex inf.* Mr. J. B. Lawson].

WOLVERHAMPTON, STAFFS., THE DEANERY, additions and repairs for the trustee of John Newport, 1764–5; dem. [P.R.O., C 110/6].

HATTON GRANGE, SHROPSHIRE, for Plowden Slaney, 1764–8 [John Cornforth in *C. Life*, 29 Feb. 1968].

CROFT CASTLE, HEREFS., internal decorations, including Gothic staircase, for Thomas Johnes, 1765 [J. Harris in *Architectural History* xi, 1968, 21; National Trust Guidebook to Croft Castle] (*C. Life*, 5 May 1960).

GAINES, WHITBOURNE, HEREFS., internal alterations, including a Gothic saloon, for John Freeman, probably *c.* 1765 [J. Harris in *Architectural History* xi, 1968, 21].

SHREWSBURY, NOS. 10–11 HIGH STREET, for John Ashby, 1766 [designs for chimney-pieces in Pritchard album; Salop. Record Office, 3460/5/1, *ex inf.* Mr. J. B. Lawson].

EYTON TURRET, EYTON–ON–SEVERN, SALOP., conversion of one of two Jacobean turrets in the garden of the demolished seat of the Newport Earls of Bradford into a dwelling-house for his own occupation, 1767–9 [P.R.O., C 110/6] (Mrs. S. Acton, *The Castles and Old Mansions of Shropshire*, 1868, 45).

WYNNSTAY, DENBIGHSHIRE, work for Sir Watkin Williams-Wynn, Bart., 1768–73, probably including 'Great Room'; dem. [National Library of Wales, Wynnstay Estate Rentals 1768–73, *ex inf.* Mr. J. B. Lawson; lost drawing by Pritchard listed *ibid.*, 115/28; P. Howell & T. W. Pritchard in *C. Life*, 23 March 1972, 689].

RUABON CHURCH, DENBIGHSHIRE, repairs and alterations to chancel for Sir Watkin Williams-Wynn, Bart., 1769–70 [P. Howell & T. W. Pritchard in *C. Life*, 23 March 1972, 688].

BITTERLEY COURT, SHROPSHIRE, alterations, probably including south front, for Charles Walcot, 1769 [J. Harris in *Architectural History* xi, 1968, 20].

SHREWSBURY, THE ABBEY, internal alterations, probably including the drawing room, for Henry Powys, *c.* 1769; dem. [J. Harris in *Architectural History* xi, 1968, 23].

DOWNTON CASTLE, HEREFS., made designs and assisted Payne Knight in initial stages of building, 1772 [Alistair Rowan, 'Downton Castle' in *The Country Seat*, ed. Colvin & Harris, 1970].

KINNERLEY CHURCH, SHROPSHIRE, rebuilt 1773–4 [D. H. S. Cranage, *The Churches of Shropshire*, 1894–1912, ii, 794–5].

LUDLOW, SALOP., THE GUILDHALL, MILL STREET, rebuilt exterior 1774–6, with Gothic doorway [Salop. Record Office, 356/box 461, No. 9676 and vouchers in box 436, *ex inf.* Mr. J. B. Lawson].

SUDBOROUGH MANOR, NORTHANTS., proposed

repairs and additions for the trustee of John Newport, 1775–6; dem. [plan, estimate etc. in P.R.O., C 110/6].

POWIS CASTLE, MONTGOMERYSHIRE, works including conversion of Long Gallery into Ballroom, for the 2nd Earl of Powis, 1775–7 [J. Lawson & M. Waterson, 'Pritchard as Architect and Antiquary at Powis', *National Trust Year Book 1975–6*].

KYRE PARK, WORCS., proposed alterations for Jonathan Pytts, rejected as too ambitious, 1776 [H. A. Tipping in *C. Life*, 24 March 1917, citing report now in Worcestershire Record Office, BA 4707/4].

SHIPTON HALL, SHROPSHIRE, redecoration of hall etc., for Henry or Thomas Mytton [design for chimney-piece in Pritchard album: see Harris, 23] (*C. Life*, 19 March 1910).

attributed: COTON HALL, SHROPSHIRE, the Gothic chapel for Lancelot Lee [a design for a frame for Lancelot Lee in the Pritchard album connects Pritchard with this house].

THE IRON BRIDGE, COALBROOKDALE, SHROPSHIRE, 1777–9 [J. White, *On Cementitious Architecture*, etc., 1832; R. Maguire & P. Matthews, 'The Iron-bridge at Coalbrookdale', *Architectural Assoc. Jnl.*, July–Aug. 1958, 31–45].

MONUMENTS AND CHIMNEY-PIECES

The following monuments designed by Pritchard are recorded: ACTON ROUND, SALOP., Gothic monument to Sir Whitmore Acton (d. 1732), erected 1763 [signed]; ALBERBURY SALOP., Richard Lyster [d. 1766) [Harris, 20]; LUDFORD, SALOP., Dr. Samuel Sprott, 1759 [signed]; MAMBLE, WORCS., Sir Edward Blount, Bart. (d. 1765) [Harris, 22]; MORETON CORBET, SALOP., Richard Corbet (d. 1770) [Gunnis]; PONTESBURY, SALOP., R. W. Offley, 1769 [Harris, 22]; SHREWSBURY, ST. MARY'S CHURCH, Rev. John Lloyd (d. 1758) and Mary Morhall (d. 1765) [Gunnis]; SHREWSBURY, OLD ST. CHAD'S, Richard Hollings [signed]; WREXHAM, DENBIGHSHIRE, Ann Wilkinson (d. 1756) [Gunnis].

Designs by Pritchard exist for chimney-pieces, etc., in the following houses: BROSELEY, SALOP., THE LAWNS; CONDOVER HALL, SALOP.; HIGH HATTON, SALOP.; KINSHAM COURT, HEREFS.; LONGNER HALL, SALOP.; LOTON PARK, SALOP.; LUDLOW, NO. 27 BROAD STREET; PENDEFORD HALL, STAFFS.; SHAWBURY PARK, SALOP.; several houses in SHREWSBURY; TATTON PARK, CHESHIRE [Harris, 20–4].

PRITCHETT, JAMES PIGOTT (1789–1868), born at St. Petrox, Pembrokeshire, on 14 October 1789, was the fourth son of Charles Pigott Pritchett, rector of St. Petrox and Stackpole Elidor and prebendary of St. David's. He was articled to James Medland of Southwark and afterwards spent two years in the office of D. A. Alexander.

He became a student at the Royal Academy in 1808, and exhibited there in 1808 and 1809. After a short period in the Barrack Office, he began practice in London in 1812, but soon afterwards removed to York, where from January 1813 he was in partnership with Charles Watson (*q.v.*). The partnership was dissolved on 1 January 1831, when Pritchett opened his own office at 13 Lendal. He had an extensive practice in Yorkshire, especially as an ecclesiastical architect, and was for over fifty years architect and surveyor to Earl Fitzwilliam at Wentworth Woodhouse, where he was responsible for various buildings on the estate.[1] Pritchett was a prominent congregationalist, and took part in many philanthropic and religious activities at York. He died there on 23 May 1868. By his first wife, Peggy Terry, he had three sons and one daughter: the latter married John Middleton of York, and was the mother of John Henry Middleton (1846–96), architect and archaeologist. By his second wife, Caroline Benson, he had three sons and two daughters. The eldest son, James Pigott Pritchett (1830–1911), worked in his father's office before setting up practice in Darlington in 1854. Two other sons, Charles and George E. Pritchett, also joined the family firm before establishing their own offices. Pritchett's pupils were Walter Blackett, S. W. Daukes, James Medland of Gloucester, John Middleton and J. C. Gilbert of Nottingham.

Pritchett was a competent but never a brilliant designer. His favourite style was Perpendicular or Tudor Gothic. His earlier churches were preaching houses scarcely distinguishable from his nonconformist chapels (at Norton in 1816 he and Watson even used the Scottish T-shaped plan for an Anglican church), and it was only in his later works that he made some attempt to conform to Camdenian ideas. His classical buildings included the dignified portico of the York Assembly Rooms, the elegant Greek Revival cemetery chapel, the handsome railway station at Huddersfield, and the Soaneic façade of the Savings Bank in St. Helen's Square, York. In such matters as heating and ventilation his buildings were among the best equipped of their day.

[*A.P.S.D.: D.N.B.; Builder* xvi, 1868, 406; G. H. Broadbent, 'The Life and Work of Pritchett of York', in *Studies in Architectural History*, ed. Singleton ii, 1956.]

CHURCHES, CHAPELS AND PUBLIC BUILDINGS

* YORK, LENDAL INDEPENDENT CHAPEL, 1816; now a department store [*A.P.S.D.*].

[1] His unexecuted designs for a library at the Fitzwilliams' Northamptonshire seat at Milton, nr. Peterborough, are in the Northamptonshire Record Office. The most ambitious scheme is dated 1837 and 1854.
* Designed in partnership with Charles Watson.

*NORTON CHURCH, YORKS. (E.R.), rebuilt 1816; dem. 1899; classical (T-shaped plan) [Borthwick Institute, York, Fac. 1814/2].

* WAKEFIELD, THE WEST RIDING LUNATIC ASYLUM, 1816–18 [*Plans etc. of the Pauper Lunatic Asylum lately erected at Wakefield*, York, 1819].

* YORK, THE FRIENDS' MEETING HOUSE, 1816–19 [plans, etc., in W. Alexander, *Observations on the Construction of Meeting Houses*, York, 1820].

*WAKEFIELD, YORKS. (W.R.), library and newsroom (later Mechanics' Institution, now Museum), 1820–1 [Yorkshire Archaeological Society's Library, MS. 1142, *ex inf*. Dr. D. Linstrum].

* HUDDERSFIELD, YORKS. (W.R.), THE RAMSDEN STREET NONCONFORMIST CHAPEL, 1824; dem. 1936 [Broadbent, 110, citing Sykes, *History of the Ramsden St. Chapel*].

*GREASBROUGH CHURCH, YORKS. (W.R.), rebuilt 1826–8, Gothic [Port, 166–7].

* SHEFFIELD, NETHER CHAPEL (INDEPENDENT), 1827; altered 1878 [R. E. Leader, *Surveyors and Architects of the Past in Sheffield*, 1903].

* YORK, ASSEMBLY ROOMS, new façade and portico, 1828 [*A.P.S.D.*].

* YORK, ST. PETER'S SCHOOL (now Choir School), MINSTER YARD, 1829, Tudor Gothic [*A.P.S.D.*].

* YORK, THE SAVINGS BANK, ST. HELEN'S SQUARE, 1829–30 [W. Camidge, *History of the York Savings Bank*, 1886, 49–51].

* NETHER HOYLAND CHURCH, YORKS. (W.R.), 1830, Gothic [Port, 168–9].

BRAFFERTON CHURCH, YORKS. (N.R.), rebuilt nave 1831, Gothic [I.C.B.S.].

OAKAMOOR CHURCH, STAFFS., 1832, Gothic [I.C.B.S.].

HUDDERSFIELD, YORKS. (W.R.), ST. PETER'S CHURCH, rebuilt 1834–6, Gothic [I.C.B.S.; Borthwick Institute, York, Fac. 1834/1].

YORK, CEMETERY CHAPEL, 1836–7, Greek Revival [Broadbent, 114].

MELTHAM CHURCH, YORKS. (W.R.), west tower and north aisle, 1835, classical to match existing church of 1787 [I.C.B.S.].

BREARTON CHURCH, YORKS. (W.R.), 1836, Gothic [I.C.B.S.].

BRADFORD, YORKS. (W.R.), AIREDALE COLLEGE CHAPEL, HIGH STREET, 1837–9; dem. [*Bradford Observer*, *ex inf*. Mr. David Griffiths].

CHEADLE CHURCH, STAFFS., 1837–9, Gothic [I.C.B.S.].

WORSBOROUGH CHURCH, YORKS. (W.R.), remodelled aisles, 1838, Gothic [I.C.B.S.].

MELTHAM MILLS CHURCH, YORKS. (W.R.), 1838, Gothic; rebuilt by Pritchett on a larger scale 1845–6 [*Civil Engineer and Architect's Jnl*. ii, 1839, 28; *Gent's Mag*. 1846 (i), 84].

TINSLEY CHURCH, YORKS. (W.R.), enlarged 1838 [I.C.B.S.].

YORK, SALEM CHAPEL, ST. SAVIOUR'S PLACE, 1838–9; dem. 1964 [*A.P.S.D.*] (R. Willis, *Nonconformist Chapels of York*, York Georgian Soc. 1964).

RAWMARSH CHURCH, YORKS. (W.R.), 1839, Gothic; tower added 1855, chancel 1898 [I.C.B.S.].

HUDDERSFIELD, YORKS. (W.R.), HUDDERSFIELD COLLEGE, NEW NORTH ROAD, 1839–40, Gothic [*Bradford Observer*, 4 April 1839, *ex inf*. Mr. David Griffiths].

BURLEY-IN-WHARFDALE, YORKS. (W.R.), INDEPENDENT CHAPEL, 1839–40, Gothic [*Bradford Observer*, 17 Oct. 1839, *ex inf*. Mr. David Griffiths].

BRADFORD, YORKS. (W.R.), WESTGATE CHAPEL, remodelled 1840 [*Bradford Observer*, 6 Feb. 1840, *ex inf*. Mr. David Griffiths].

YORK, LADY HEWLEY'S HOSPITAL, ST. SAVIOURGATE, 1840, Gothic [*A.P.S.D.*].

GATE HELMSLEY, YORKS. (N.R.), THE RETREAT (a private Mental Asylum), enlarged and altered for James Martin, *c.* 1840 [advt. at end of Pigot's *National and Commercial Directory of York, Leicester, Rutland etc.*, 1841].

BROTHERTON CHURCH, YORKS. (W.R.), rebuilt 1842–3, Gothic [I.C.B.S.].

ACKWORTH, YORKS. (W.R.), THE FRIENDS' MEETING HOUSE, 1846 [Leeds Public Library, Archives Dept., Nettleton papers, *ex inf*. Dr. D. Linstrum].

ACKWORTH, YORKS. (W.R.), THE FLOUNDERS INSTITUTE, 1847–8 [*ibid.*].

HUDDERSFIELD, YORKS. (W.R.), THE RAILWAY STATION, 1846–7 [C. Barman, *An Introduction to Railway Architecture*, 1950, 100].

YORK, THE EBENEZER CHAPEL, LITTLE STONEGATE (now printing works), 1851 [*V.C.H. York*, 414].

HUDDERSFIELD, THE LION ARCADE, 1852–4 [*Huddersfield Chronicle*, 14 Jan. 1854, cited by Broadbent, 123–4].

BRAMPTON BIERLOW CHURCH, YORKS. (W.R.), 1854–5, Gothic [Port, 166–7].

DOMESTIC ARCHITECTURE

*WOOLLEY PARK, YORKS. (W.R.), lodge and gateway for Godfrey Wentworth, 1814 [D. Linstrum in *Leeds Arts Calendar* lxviii, 1971, 11].

* BURGHWALLIS RECTORY, YORKS. (W.R.), rebuilt 1815 [Borthwick Institute, York, MGA 1815/2].

* *attributed*: RISE PARK, YORKS. (E.R.), for Richard Bethell, 1815–20 [design for Doric lodge at Rise in album at Stoneleigh Park, Warwicks., signed 'Watson & Pritchett 1818'].

* BRAFFERTON VICARAGE, YORKS. (N.R.), enlarged 1818 [Borthwick Institute, Yorks, MGA 1818/3].

---

* Designed in partnership with Charles Watson.

665

* SLEDMERE HOUSE, YORKS. (E.R.), gates to main road for Sir Mark Sykes, Bart., 1818 [drawings at Sledmere].
*SALTMARSHE HALL, YORKS. (E.R.), for Philip Saltmarshe, 1825; stables 1842 [drawings in the possession of Mr. J. E. Scott of Huyton, 1971].
YORK, THE DEANERY, 1827–31, Gothic [Hargrove, *Guide to York*, 1838; drawings in Minster Library].
* LOTHERTON HALL, YORKS. (W.R.), probably designed interior of drawing room for R. O. Gascoigne, *c.* 1828 [Angus Taylor in *Leeds Arts Calendar*, No. 77, 1975, 28].[1]
* NOSTELL PRIORY, YORKS. (W.R.), north and east sides of stable block for C. W. Winn, 1828–9, adopting Robert Adam's design (1776) for the cupola [drawings at Nostell].
BOSSALL VICARAGE, YORKS. (N.R.), 1838 [Borthwick Institute, York, MGA 1838/2].
NEW MALTON VICARAGE, YORKS. (N.R.), 1840 [Borthwick Institute, York, MGA 1840/2].
THORNTON DALE RECTORY, YORKS. (N.R.), altered or rebuilt 1841–2 [Borthwick Institute, York, MGA 1841/4].
NUNBURNHOLME RECTORY, YORKS. (E.R.), 1853 [Borthwick Institute, York, MGA 1853/2].

PROSSER, HENRY (*c.* 1802–), became a pupil at the Royal Academy in 1822 at the age of 20. He was subsequently taken into partnership by John Staff of Croydon. In 1825 SUTTON CHURCH, SURREY, was enlarged to their designs [I.C.B.S.]. In 1828 Prosser exhibited at the Royal Academy his designs for 'a college proposed to be erected by the Honourable Artillery Company for widows and orphans of deceased members'. This does not appear to have been built. In the same year he exhibited a drawing of All Saints, Beaulah Hill, Upper Norwood, 'executing under the direction of His Majesty's Commissioners for building new churches', although this church is known to have been designed by James Savage. A number of topographical drawings by Prosser are in an extra-illustrated copy of Brayley's *Surrey* in Wimbledon Public Library. He may have been related to George Frederick Prosser, the author of *Select Illustrations of the County of Surrey* (1828) and of *Select Illustrations of Hampshire* (1833).

PROSSER, THOMAS, exhibited a design for a villa at the Royal Academy in 1819, giving a London address. He was presumably the architect of the same name who was practising in Worcester in 1828–9 and in Hereford in 1830 (Pigot's *Directory*), and who contributed a design for a

cider-press to Loudon's *Encyclopaedia of Rural Architecture* (pp. 609–15 in 1846 edition). Either this or another Thomas Prosser was practising in the north of England by 1835–7, when SEAHAM HARBOUR CHURCH, CO. DURHAM, was built to his designs [I.C.B.S.]. He was architect to the North-Eastern Railway Company at Newcastle from 1854 to 1874 and in that capacity designed the RAILWAY STATION at LEEDS in 1869 [W. W. Tomlinson, *The North Eastern Railway*, 1914, 634, 773].

PROWSE, THOMAS (*c.* 1708–1767), was a country gentleman and an amateur architect. He was the son of John Prowse of Compton Bishop and Berkley in Somerset. In 1731 he married Elizabeth Sharp, through whom he inherited the estate of Wicken in Northamptonshire, and on his mother's death in 1763 he inherited Berkley House nr. Frome in Somerset. He represented Somerset in Parliament continuously from 1740 to 1767, and declined the Speakership in 1761 because of ill-health.

Prowse was on friendly terms with Sanderson Miller (*q.v.*), and helped him in his designs for Hagley Hall and the Shire Hall at Warwick. He was also involved in the projects for rebuilding Copt Hall in Essex for John Conyers in the 1740s. The principal buildings for which he was himself responsible (usually with John Sanderson as executant architect) are listed below. Both at Hatch Court and at Kimberley Hall he used Palladian pavilion towers like those at Hagley, but Hatch Court has the attractive and unusual feature of an arcade across the main front between the flanking towers. His work at Wicken Church is in a Gothic style similar to that of his friend Sanderson Miller.

Prowse died on 1 January 1767, aged 59, and was buried at Axbridge. A portrait of him attributed to Gainsborough belongs to Mr. Derek Sherborne. Another portrait reproduced in *R.I.B.A. Journal* xlvi, 1939, 536, and supposed to be of John Wood of Bath, may represent Prowse, as it was among the pictures at Berkley House.

[R. Sedgwick, *The House of Commons 1715–1754*, 1970, 371; E. F. Wade, 'Notes on the Family of Prowse', *Miscellanea Genealogica et Heraldica* N.S. iii, 1880, 162, 165; *An Eighteenth-Century Correspondence*, ed. Dickins & Stanton, 1910, 286, 289, 290, 314; *Architectural History* xvi, 1973, 28; *Gent's Mag.* 1763, 565, 1767, 47; *London Magazine*, March 1760 (letter from Prowse about the use of elliptical arches in bridges); will (P.C.C., 24 LEGARD)].

WICKEN CHURCH, NORTHANTS., rebuilt except tower 1753–67, Gothic; windows altered and transepts added 1897 [An inscription records that 'This Church was designed and built by

---

* Designed in partnership with Charles Watson.
[1] Unexecuted designs for Gascoigne's family seat at Parlington Hall, Yorks. (W.R.) are illustrated in the same article.

Thomas Prowse Esqr. in the year 1758 and finished after his Death'. However it appears from the Peterborough Faculty Register that the chancel was already being rebuilt under Prowe's direction in 1753, and Mr. Sanderson's plan for the chancel is mentioned in a letter from Thomas Prowse written in that year (Prowse papers in Northants. Record Office). In a letter from John Sanderson to John Conyers dated 10 June 1758 (Essex Record Office D/D W.E. 36/7), he states that he intends to go to Wicken 'to give directions for finishing the groyned ceiling of Esqr. Prowse's Church there, the carcase of which has been built and used for service these 4 years past'. The diary of Prowse's daughter-in-law Elizabeth Prowse records that the church was 'new paved' in 1770, when 'Mr. Sanderson came down to give directions'.

HATCH COURT, SOMERSET, for John Collins, 1755 [described by Edward Knight of Wolverley in 1761 as 'built by Prowse': Kidderminster Public Library MS. 294] (C. Life, 22–9 Oct. 1964).

KIMBERLEY HALL, NORFOLK, remodelled for Sir Armine Wodehouse, Bart., c. 1755–7 [Kymber: a Monody, by the Rev. Robert Potter, 1759, contains the following lines about Kimberley: '... fix'd by Prowse's just palladian hand/its towred honours stand', and Sir Armine's 'cautions about Gentlemen-Architects' in general and Prowse in particular are referred to in a letter in the Mordaunt of Walton MSS. in the Warwicks. Record Office, letter-book v, opp. f. 57, ex inf. Mr. Anthony Wood. John Sanderson's employment here in 1757 is documented by family accounts seen by Mr. T. P. Connor, and there are drawings by him for this house in the R.I.B.A. Collection.

SWINDON HOUSE ('THE LAWN'), WILTS., advice about refronting house for Richard Goddard, 1757; dem. 1952 [Warwicks. Record Office, Mordaunt of Walton MSS., letter-book v, letter opp. f. 57, ex inf. Mr. Anthony Wood].

WICKEN HOUSE, NORTHANTS., enlarged and altered for himself, 1765–6 [diary of Elizabeth Sharpe penes Col. Lloyd-Baker of Hardwicke Court, Glos.] (J. P. Neale, Views of Seats 1st ser., i, 1818).

PUGIN, AUGUSTUS CHARLES (1769–1832), came to this country as a refugee from France at the time of the French Revolution. He claimed to be of aristocratic birth, but little is known about his ancestry. It is said that he fell fighting for the King, was thrown, supposedly dead, into a pit near the Place de la Bastille, came to his senses, and escaped by swimming the Seine. Eventually he landed in Wales, 'a penniless foreigner' ignorant of the English language

and without any qualifications except some slight ability in drawing.

An advertisement in a newspaper proved his salvation. Mr. John Nash, by now an architect with a considerable practice in Wales, required a draughtsman – if possible a foreigner. The significance of this curious preference is uncertain, but Pugin was given the post. When Nash moved permanently to London in 1796, Pugin accompanied him and soon became known as one of the best architectural draughtsmen of the day. In 1799 he began to exhibit at the Royal Academy on his own account, and within the next four years he formed connections with topographical writers and publishers such as Ackermann, Britton and Brayley, for whose works he drew and etched many plates. In this antiquarian company he developed an interest in medieval architecture which made him something of an authority on the subject. His publications were among the first to provide accurate drawings of medieval architectural detail at a time when many architects were beginning to work in the Gothic style. In London he established a flourishing school of architectural drawing and colouring, and among his many pupils were J. Amos, Francis Arundale, Benjamin Green, Talbot Bury, T. Cramer, J. D'Egville, F. T. Dollman, Benjamin Ferrey, R. Grantham, C. E., C. J. Mathews, G. B. Moore, Joseph Nash, J. Pennethorne, W. Lake Price, W. Shoubridge, T. L. Walker and F. Whitaker. In 1808 he was elected an associate of the Old Water Colour Society, and was a frequent exhibitor at its annual exhibitions.

Pugin was a draughtsman and drawing-master rather than a practising architect. His exhibits at the Royal Academy were mostly of a topographical character, but in 1826–7 he showed three designs for cemeteries, and early in 1830 he was concerned in the layout of the cemetery at Kensal Green. In 1823 he designed the interior of the Diorama in Regent's Park in conjunction with James Morgan [J. Elmes, Metropolitan Improvements, 1831, 81], and the Vicarage at Portbury in Somerset appears to have been his work, for in 1832 Thomas Rickman went to see 'Pugin's Parsonage at Portbury [which] looks well outside but is miserable within' [diary, 1 Feb. 1832]. Pugin may also have designed the Picture Gallery which his friend Charles Mathews, the actor, added to Ivy Cottage, his house in Kentish Town [J. T. Smith, A Book for a Rainy Day, ed. Whitten, 1905, 85, n. 2], and according to the obituary in Arnold's Magazine of the Fine Arts N.S. i, 1833, 326, he was employed as an architect by the Earl of Essex and the Marquess of Downshire.

As well as being an accomplished artist, Pugin was an agreeable companion whose social talents no doubt contributed to his success. They may also account for his marriage, while still a far from affluent refugee, to Catherine, the daughter of

667

William Welby of Islington, a barrister-at-law and member of an old Lincolnshire family. Their only child, born in 1812 at their house in Stone Street, Bedford Square, was Augustus Welby Northmore Pugin. Pugin died on 19 December 1832, at No. 106 Great Russell Street, Bloomsbury. The sale catalogue of his library is in the Bodleian Library (Mus. Bibl. III, 80, 413). His portrait is given in Ferrey's *Recollections of A. W. N. Pugin*, 1861, facing page 26.

The following is a list of the principal publications with which he was associated: R. Ackermann, *The Microcosm of London* (with plates by Pugin & Rowlandson), 1808–10; with F. Mackenzie, *Specimens of Gothic Architecture ... Selected from ancient buildings at Oxford* [1816]; with E. W. Brayley, *A Series of Views in Islington and Pentonville*, 1819; *Specimens of Gothic Architecture*, 2 vols. 1821–3, with descriptions by E. J. Willson; with J. Britton, *Illustrations of the Public Buildings of London*, 2 vols. 1825–8, 2nd ed. by W. H. Leeds, 1838; *Gothic Furniture*, 1827, consisting of plates previously published in Ackermann's *Repository of Arts* in 1825–7;[1] with J. Britton and J. & H. Le Keux, *Specimens of the Architectural Antiquities of Normandy*, 1827–8; *Examples of Gothic Architecture*, vol. i, 1828–9, vol. ii, 1836 with text by E. J. Willson, vol. iii with text by Pugin's executor T. L. Walker, 1836; translated Normand, *New Parallel of the Orders of Architecture*, with 2 extra plates, 1829; with C. Heath, *Paris and its Environs*, 1829–31; *Gothic Ornaments from Ancient Buildings in England and France*, 1828–31; *A Series of Ornamental Timber Gables, from existing examples in England and Wales*, 1831, drawn by B. Ferrey under Pugin's direction, with text by E. J. Willson.

[*A.P.S.D.*; *D.N.B.*; *Gent's Mag.* 1833 (i), 278–9; B. Ferrey, *Recollections of A. W. N. Pugin*, 1861; M. Trappes Lomax, *Pugin*, 1933; John Summerson, *John Nash*, 1935.]

PURSER, CHARLES (*c.* 1802–   ), may have been a younger brother of William Purser (*q.v.*). He was a pupil of Edward I'Anson, became a student at the Royal Academy in 1820 at the age of 18, and was awarded the Silver Medal in 1822. He exhibited at the academy in 1821 and 1824. In 1833 he published a pamphlet entitled *The Prospects of the Nation in regard to the National Gallery*, in which he severely criticized the designs of William Wilkins.

PURSER, WILLIAM, junior (*c.* 1790–   ), was the son of William Purser, of whom little is

known except that he was one of the original members of the Surveyors' Club in 1792. The younger Purser was admitted to the Royal Academy Schools in 1807 at the age of 17, and began to exhibit architectural designs in 1805. From 1817 to 1820 he travelled in Italy and Greece with John Sanders, acting as his draughtsman, and taking part in the discovery of the Lion of Chaeronea. On his return to England he exhibited at the Royal Academy from 1820 to 1834 as 'architect and painter'. Among his exhibits was a 'Design for a villa, proposed to be erected on the banks of the Ouse near Bedford' (1820), but it is not known whether this was built. He appears to have made a living chiefly as an illustrator of books such as Finden's *Landscape Illustrations to the Bible* [information from Mr. R. G. Searight].

PYCOCK, GEORGE (*c.* 1749–1799), was the principal architect and builder in Hull in the latter part of the eighteenth century. Among his works in that town were the GENERAL INFIRMARY, 1784 (façade altered by H. F. Lockwood 1840–2); the NEW GAOL at MYTON GATE, 1786 (dem.); and THE NEPTUNE INN, WHITEFRIARSGATE (later known as Custom House Buildings), 1794–6 [G. Hadley, *History of Hull*, 1788, 837–9 and plates facing pp. 349, 356; *V.C.H. Yorks. E. Riding* i, 383, 449]. Some houses he had built in HANOVER SQUARE were advertised for sale in the *Hull Advertiser*, 3 May 1800. In 1793 he designed MARFLEET PARISH CHURCH, YORKS. (E.R.), rebuilt 1884 [Borthwick Institute, York, Fac. 1793/2]. His design for a small house at Tealby, Lincs., for George Tennyson (1797) is among the Tennyson d'Eyncourt papers in the Lincolnshire Record Office (T.D.E.H. 169).

Pycock died at Hull on 27 March 1799, aged 50 [*Gent's Mag.* 1799, 349]. His business was carried on by his son Marmaduke Ward Pycock, who died on 8 August 1815, aged 35 [*Hull Advertiser*, 12 Aug. 1815, *ex inf.* Mr. A. G. Chamberlain]. A plan and elevation for an 'intended New House' for D. Sykes at EPPLEWORTH, nr. HULL, signed by M. W. Pycock and dated 1803, are in the Gott Collection at Wakefield Museum (vol. 6, p. 98).

R

RAEBURN, JAMES (1787–1851), was born at Boyndie, nr. Banff, on 20 February 1787. From 1827 to 1839 he held the post of First Clerk in the Scottish Office of Works at Edinburgh. On the abolition of the Office in 1839 he retired with a pension. He died in Edinburgh on 30 September 1851, and is commemorated by a monument in St. Cuthbert's Churchyard. His practice

---

[1] This was not, as is sometimes said, the first edition of the younger Pugin's *Gothic Furniture in the style of the 15 Century* (1835), which is an entirely different book.

was continued by his son Robert R. Raeburn (1819–88). In the Register House there is a copy of a sheet of lithographs, 'drawn and presented by Robert R. Raeburn' 1845, representing designs for Free Churches, manses and schools by James Raeburn [RHP 970/20]. The buildings illustrated include THE TRINITY AND ALVAH CHURCH at BANFF, designed by James Raeburn in 1834, and a 'Design of a Church proposed to be built in Montreal'. The Trinity and Alvah Church presents a competently designed Ionic portico to the street.

RAFFIELD, JOHN, was the son of George Raffield, a Northumbrian joiner who was largely responsible for alterations to FORD CASTLE, NORTHUMBERLAND, which were carried out by Sir John Hussey Delaval in the 1760s 'without the aid of any architect'. The son appears first as a joiner working at Ford Castle under James Nisbet in the early 1770s, and subsequently as an assistant of the Adam brothers in their office in the Adelphi. In this capacity he wrote in 1781 to Lord Delaval about alterations that were being made to his house in Hanover Square, and in 1788 about the house in Claremont Lane, Esher, recently designed for him by Robert Adam. By 1797 Raffield was in independent practice in Great Portland Street, exhibiting a design for a castle in Scotland at the Royal Academy. In 1792 he showed a design for a cast-iron bridge over the Thames 'from the Strand, in the vicinity of the Adelphi, to Lambeth', and in 1805 a design for a suspension bridge over the Danube at Vienna. In 1818 or 1819 he was declared bankrupt, and in 1825 he exhibited at the Royal Academy for the last time. Adam influence is apparent in his work, notably in the 'Chain Gate' at Easton Neston, which is based on the screen at Sion House. [*Proceedings of the Society of Antiquaries of Newcastle-on-Tyne* v, 1891–2, 62–3; Northumberland Record Office, Delaval papers, M 17/29, 2 DE, *passim.*]

NEW CROSS, OLD KENT ROAD, KENT, villa for John Rolls, 1804–5; dem. [exhib. at R.A. 1805; Monmouthshire Record Office, Rolls papers, E4. A2–3; cf. D. Hughson, *London* v, 1808, 59, for a view of the house based on a drawing by Raffield].

LONDON, ST. JOHN'S LODGE, REGENT'S PARK, for C. A. Tulk, 1818–19 [exhib. at R.A. 1818–19]; wings, entrance screen and upper storey added by C. Barry 1847; small library and circular chapel added 1892 (J. Elmes, *Metropolitan Improvements*, 1831, 79–80; A. T. Bolton in *1st Annual Report of the Institute of Archaeology*, 1938, 14–17).

EASTON NESTON, NORTHANTS., THE 'CHAIN' GATE and LODGES for the 3rd Earl of Pomfret, 1822–

3 [exhib. at R.A. 1825]. The decorative features are of Coade stone, dated 1822 (*C. Life*, 7 Nov. 1908, 635).

RAILTON, WILLIAM (*c.* 1801–1877), was a pupil of William Inwood. He became a student at the Royal Academy in 1823 at the age of 22, and travelled abroad in the years 1825–7, visiting Greece and Corfu. His 'Account of the newly-discovered Temple at Caldachio, in Corfu' was published in 1830 in the supplementary volume of Stuart's *Antiquities of Athens*. He exhibited regularly at the Royal Academy from 1829 onwards. From 1838 to 1848 he was architect to the Ecclesiastical Commissioners, for whom he designed a number of parsonage houses in an economical style of vaguely Italianate character which was strongly disapproved of by the *Ecclesiologist*. His Gothic churches, mostly in the Early English style, do not reward the architecturally minded visitor. Railton did, however, secure the approval of his contemporaries on two occasions. The first was in 1835, when his design for rebuilding the Houses of Parliament was awarded the fourth premium on the ground that it was well planned, and in other respects 'inferior to none in attention to the instructions and specifications delivered to the competitors'. The other was in 1839, when he won the competition for the Nelson Memorial in Trafalgar Square with the conventional but unexceptionable idea of a column surmounted by a statue. Railton died on a visit to Brighton on 13 October 1877. He should not be confused with William A. Railton (1820–1902), an architect practising at Kilmarnock to whom he appears to have been unrelated. [*A.P.S.D.*; *D.N.B.*; *Ecclesiologist* ii, 1843, 145–7; A. Savidge, *The Parsonage in England*, 1964, 135, 145, 151; *R.I.B.A. Drawings Catalogue*: O–R, 111.]

RANDALLS, nr. LEATHERHEAD, SURREY, for N. Bland, *c.* 1830, Gothic; dem. *c.* 1935 [exhib. at R.A. 1830] (Brayley, *History of Surrey* iv, 433, engraving).

GRACE-DIEU MANOR, LEICS., house and R.C. chapel for Ambrose Lisle March-Phillipps, 1833–4, Gothic [exhib. at R.A. 1834].

GARENDON PARK, LEICS., lodges at Dishley and Hathern entrances for Charles March-Phillipps, 1838, Gothic [exhib. at R.A. 1838].

DUDDON CHURCH, CHESHIRE, 1835, Gothic [I.C.B.S., under 'Tarvin'].

COPT OAK (CHARLEY) CHURCH, LEICS., 1836–7, Gothic; chancel 1889 [*Gent's Mag.* 1836 (ii), 648].

WOODHOUSE EAVES CHURCH, LEICS., 1836–7, Gothic; altered 1880 [*Gent's Mag.* 1836 (ii), 648].

WILDEN CHURCH, BEDS., repaired and repewed, 1837 [I.C.B.S.].

RIPON, YORKS. (N.R.), residence (now Spring Hill Schools) for the Bishop of Ripon, 1838–9, and the chapel, 1848, Gothic [exhib. at R.A. 1839, 1849].

LAUNDE ABBEY, LEICS., 'chapel erecting at Launde Abbey for E. Dawson, Esq.' exhibited at Society of British Artists 1839. According to W. White's *History, Gazetteer and Directory of Leicestershire*, 1877, the chapel 'was repaired and newly fitted up with carved oak seats in 1839'.

ANSTEY PASTURES HALL, LEICS., alterations for the Rev. R. Martin, *c.* 1839–40 [Leicestershire Record Office, DG6/C/25–28].

LONDON, NELSON'S COLUMN, TRAFALGAR SQUARE, 1840–3 [exhib. at R.A. 1846]. The statue is by E. H. Baily; the lions were added in 1867.

RISEHOLME HALL, LINCS., enlarged and altered as residence for the Bishop of Lincoln, 1840–5 [exhib. at R.A. 1846].

WOLVERHAMPTON, STAFFS., ST. MARY'S CHURCH, 1842–3, Gothic [*Gent's Mag.* 1843 (i), 75].

RIPON MINSTER, YORKS. (W.R.), repair of south-west tower and gable of west front and insertion of sham Romanesque vaulting in north and south transepts, 1843–4 [*A.P.S.D.*; *Gent's Mag.* 1844 (i), 182–3]. Railton's plaster and papier-mâché vaulting was removed by Scott in *c.* 1865.

LONDON, ST. MARY'S CHURCH, BROMLEY ST. LEONARD'S, rebuilt 1843, Romanesque; destroyed by bombing 1941/3 [exhib. at R.A. 1844, 1851].

LONDON, ST. BARTHOLOMEW'S CHURCH and SCHOOLS, BETHNAL GREEN, 1843–4, Gothic [exhib. at R.A. 1844].

THORPE ACRE CHURCH, LEICS., 1845, Gothic [I.C.B.S.].

BEAUMANOR PARK, LEICS., for W. P. Herrick, 1845–6, Jacobean style [exhib. at R.A. 1845; Herrick papers in Leicestershire Record Office].

LONDON, HOLY TRINITY CHURCH, HOXTON, 1846–8, Gothic [exhib. at R.A. 1849].

MEANWOOD, nr. LEEDS, YORKS. (W.R.), HOLY TRINITY CHURCH, 1849, Gothic [exhib. at R.A. 1849–50; *Ecclesiologist* x, 1850, 237–40].

PARSONAGE HOUSES

The many parsonage houses designed by Railton for the Ecclesiastical Commissioners in the 1840s included those of ST. BARNABAS, BRISTOL; ST. JOHN, CARISBROOKE, ISLE OF WIGHT; CHURCHSTOW, DEVON; CORRINGHAM, LINCS.; ST. JAMES, MUSWELL HILL, MIDDLX.; HOLY TRINITY, ROTHERHITHE, SURREY; and UPLEADON, GLOS. His designs for all but the last are in the R.I.B.A. Collection.

RAINEY, EDWARD, was a builder of Spilsby in Lincolnshire in the second quarter of the nine-

670

teenth century. In 1838 he designed and built CANDLESBY CHURCH, LINCS., in a poor Gothic style [I.C.B.S.].

RALPHS, JOHN, was architect of Warminster. He designed the new Gothic tower which was built on the north side of the nave of WALTON CHURCH, SOMERSET, in 1836, in place of a former central tower [I.C.B.S.]. In the correspondence with the I.C.B.S. he is mentioned as being seriously ill.

RAMPLING, CLARK (–1875), was in C. H. Tatham's office in Queen Street, Mayfair, in 1818–19. He was also a pupil of Richard Brown [*Builder* vii, 1849, 615]. He went first to Manchester (where he was living in 1825–9), and then to Birkenhead and Liverpool. He was still practising in Birkenhead in 1866, but by 1868 had retired to Quarry Bank, Tranmere, Cheshire, where he died on 7 March 1875. He exhibited at the Royal Academy in 1815–19 and at the Liverpool Academy in 1831, 1832 and 1834. His principal work was the Greek Revival Medical Institution at Liverpool, ingeniously planned to make the most of a triangular site. R. B. Rampling, who practised from Preston in the 1850s, was presumably his son.

BRANDON, SUFFOLK, design for parsonage house, exhibited at R.A. 1818.

BIRCH, nr. MIDDLETON, LANCS, ST. MARY'S CHURCH, 1827–8, Gothic [Port, 146–7].

MILL BANK, nr. WEST DERBY, LANCS., villas 'now erecting', exhib. at Liverpool Academy 1832.

WEST DERBY, LANCS., house for Spencer Jones, *c.* 1834 [exhib. at Liverpool Academy 1834].

LIVERPOOL, THE MEDICAL INSTITUTION at angle of HOPE and MOUNT STREETS, 1836–7 [*Architectural Mag.* iv, 1837, 383; *Companion to the Almanac*, 1838, 229–31].

LIVERPOOL, THE FISH HALL, MURRAY STREET, for the Liverpool Fish Company, 1837 [*Architectural Mag.* iv, 402–3].

BIRKENHEAD, THE MAGISTRATES' OFFICES, 1840 [*A.P.S.D.*, *s.v.* 'Birkenhead'].

BUGLAWTON CHURCH, CHESHIRE, 1840, Norman [I.C.B.S.].

BIRKENHEAD, THE TOWN HALL, MARKET, etc., 1845; dem. [W. W. Mortimer, *Hundred of Wirral*, 1847, 362].

RAMSAY, ALEXANDER (*c.* 1777–1847), was a builder in Edinburgh. He became a burgess in 1829 [*Roll of Edinburgh Burgesses*, Scottish Record Soc., 129]. A stone in the Warriston Cemetery records his death on 18 May 1847 in his 71st year. He rebuilt CRAIGEND CASTLE, STIRLINGSHIRE, for James Smith of Craigend. At first it was intended only to enlarge the existing house to the designs of Smith's cousin James Smith of Jordanhill (*q.v.*), but 'after the erection had gone some length, it was found more suitable to pull down the old house entirely, and the present building was completed according to plans furnished by Mr. Alexander Ramsay, architect and builder, Edinburgh, preserving as much as possible the internal arrangement as designed by Mr. Smith' [Jones's *Views of Scottish Seats*, n.d.]. This castellated house, completed in 1812, is illustrated in *The Old Country Houses of the Glasgow Gentry*, Glasgow 1870, xxvi.

RAMSAY, JAMES (–1800), was a Scottish architect and landscape-gardener. According to J. C. Loudon [*Encyclopaedia of Gardening*, 1828, 82], he began life as a mason in Ayrshire, where he was employed by John Robertson (*q.v.*), 'but soon displayed a taste for disposing of verdant scenery, and afterwards became a landscape-gardener of considerable repute. He gave ground-plans and drawings in perspective, both of the buildings and ... scenery. Leith Head, a small place near Edinburgh, is entirely his creation. His style was that of Brown. ... He died at Edinburgh in 1794.' Ramsay's activities as a landscape-gardener are documented at Cally House, Kirkcudbrightshire, Gosford House, East Lothian, and elsewhere [*ex inf.* Mr. A. A. Tait]. Loudon was, however, mistaken in the date of his death, for the *Scots Magazine* records that he died on 22 May 1800 [*Scots Mag.*, 1800, 432]. As an architect he is represented by a plan dated 1782 for an 'Intended New Street' at STEWARTON, AYRSHIRE [S.R.O., RHP 1202], by designs at REDNOCK HOUSE, PERTHSHIRE, for a stable-block there dated January 1797, and by CATHKIN, CARMUNNOCK, LANARKSHIRE, an agreeably unpretentious and rather old-fashioned house illustrated in *The Old Houses of the Glasgow Gentry*, Glasgow 1870, xxi, where is is stated to have been built by Walter Ewing Macrae in 1799, 'from designs of James Ramsay of Edinburgh'. Ramsay must be distinguished from a man of the same name who figures in the Edinburgh directories from 1774/5 to 1796/7 as a 'slater and builder', and was one of the 'ordained measurers' for the City (cf. S.R.O., RHP 591).

RAMSHAW, WILLIAM, was a joiner and builder at Bishop Auckland, Co. Durham. He designed churches at SADBERGE (1831) and ETHERLEY (1832), CO. DURHAM, both altered later in the nineteenth century [I.C.B.S.].

RANDALL, JAMES (*c.* 1778–1820), is stated in *A.P.S.D.* to have been born in 1782, but in announcing his death in 1820, the *Gentleman's Magazine* gave his age as 42. He published *Designs for Mansions, Casinos, Villas, Lodges and Cottages in the Grecian, Gothic and Castle Styles*, 1806, and *A Philosophical Enquiry on the Cause, with Directions to Cure, the Dry Rot in Buildings*,

1807. His exhibits at the Royal Academy between 1798 and 1814 provide almost the only record of his activity as an architect. They included a 'design for an entrance to Merton Grove' (or Place), Surrey, then the property of a Mr. Graves (1798); a 'design for a casino intended to be erected in Oxfordshire' (1801); a 'lodge and gateway for Lord Hobart at Roehampton' (1803); a 'design for a villa for J. S. Collenguin, Esq. in Dorsetshire' (1807); a 'design for a conservatory for Col. E. Agar, M.P.' (1809); a 'bath, now erecting for J. Colingridge, Esq.' at Sunbury Villa, Middlesex (1810); and 'A gallery, as it was intended to have been erected in the garden of Leicester Square by B. West, P.R.A.' (1814). His front to the ESSEX STREET UNITARIAN CHAPEL, STRAND, is praised in the *Monthly Magazine*, June 1817, 399. He practised from various addresses in London, and died on 27 October 1820.

RANGER, WILLIAM (*c.* 1800–1863), was the son of a builder and surveyor of the same name at Brighton (see the list of subscribers to Horsfield's *History of Sussex* ii, 1835). He practised in London, chiefly as a civil engineer, and in that capacity was much employed by the Board of Health in enforcing the Public Health Act. He was also known as the patentee of an 'artificial stone' or cement composition (1832), and of a concrete block designed to be used as a substitute for masonry (1834). The latter was used by Barry in the College of Surgeons in Lincoln's Inn Fields, and the former by Ranger himself at WESTLEY CHURCH, SUFFOLK, which he built in 1835–6 to his own designs in a poor Gothic style [I.C.B.S.]. Ranger's 'Patent Stone Manufactory' was in Lambeth, and he died in St. George's Square, Southwark, on 12 September 1863, aged 63 [*Builder* xxi, 1863, 672].

RATHBONE, THOMAS, sometimes called 'Captain Rathbone', is referred to as a building surveyor in London records of the early eighteenth century. In 1694 he built a watch-house for the parish of St. Giles in the Fields and in 1703 made a survey of houses in Portugal Row [J. Parton, *Some Account of the Hospital and Parish of St. Giles-in-the-Fields*, 1822, 229, 292]. He was also employed by Gray's Inn and by Lord Scudamore on his estate at Battle Bridge [P.R.O., Chancery Masters' Exhibits, Duchess of Norfolk Deeds, Box C, bundle 10, nos. 1178, 1180, 1182]. He is best known, however, as the speculative builder of Rathbone Place, 1718.

RAWLINS, THOMAS (–1646?), described as 'gentleman', was employed to supervise the erection of a new royal lodging in TUTBURY CASTLE, STAFFS., in 1634–6. This was demolished in 1751 with the exception of its south wall. It was of some interest as a provincial essay in classical architecture. Whether Rawlins designed it himself is not clear. He may have been a Thomas Rawlins of Alton who died in 1646. [*History of the King's Works* iii, 297.]

RAWLINS, THOMAS, was the son of Thomas Rawlins, a worsted weaver of Norwich. He appears to have been apprenticed to a statuary mason in London, for in an advertisement he claimed to have 'worked at the most eminent Carvers in London'. Returning to Norwich, he ran a successful business as a monumental mason from about 1743 to 1780, specializing in tablets incorporating coloured marbles. He also practised as an architect, exhibiting designs at the Society of Artists in London in 1767, 1769 and 1770, and at the Royal Academy in 1773, 1774 and 1776. Some of these were of quite an ambitious character, *e.g.* a 'design for a palace' (1769), a 'section of a rotunda' (1773) and 'three designs for a Forum, for the Four Courts of Judicature, designed to be built in Lincoln's Inn Fields' (1774). In 1769 he competed for the Royal Exchange at Dublin. In 1765 the *Ipswich Journal* contained an advertisement for a proposed work on architecture by Rawlins, and in 1768 he published *Familiar Architecture; or Original Designs of Houses for Gentlemen and Tradesmen; Parsonages; Summer Retreats; Banqueting-Rooms; and Churches*, with an excursus on the masonry of semicircular and elliptical arches. There was a second edition in 1789 and a third in 1795. The character of the designs is Palladian, with some affinity to the works of James Paine. Plate xlvi shows the unexecuted design which he submitted in 1753 for the Octagon Chapel at Norwich. His only documented architectural works are the entrance to ST. ANDREWS HALL, NORWICH, 1774, since rebuilt [Chambers, *Norfolk Tour* iii, 1829, 1193], and WESTON HOUSE, WESTON LONGVILLE, NORFOLK, for John Custance, 1781, dem. 1926 [*Woodforde's Diary*, ed. Beresford, i, 1924, 317, 323], but several buildings in Norwich can be attributed to him on stylistic grounds, notably NO. 94 ST. GILES and NOS. 10–12 THE CLOSE. [S. J. Wearing, *Georgian Norwich: its Builders*, Norwich 1926, 53–5; C. L. S. Linnell & S. J. Wearing, *Norfolk Church Monuments*, Norwich 1952, 25–6, 30–1; R. Gunnis, *Dictionary of British Sculptors*, 1968, 315; information from Mr. A. P. Baggs.]

RAWLINSON, CHARLES (1729–1786), was a carpenter and joiner at Lostwithiel in Cornwall, where he is buried in the parish church. He signs the design for rebuilding REDRUTH CHURCH, CORNWALL, completed *c.* 1768, among the Faculty papers in the Exeter Record Office, and the minutes of the committee for building ST. AUBYN'S CHAPEL, DEVONPORT, 1770–1, show that he was probably the designer and certainly

the surveyor in charge [Plymouth City archives]. In 1772 Thomas Pitt (*q.v.*) employed him to build the new south wing of BOCONNOC, CORNWALL, containing a library and picture-gallery. This was probably designed by Pitt himself [B.M., Add. MS. 59489]. In 1775–6 Rawlinson rebuilt or rectified the leaning front of CLOWANCE HOUSE, CORNWALL, for Lady St. Aubyn after consultation with Robert Mylne [Mylne's *Diary*, ed. Richardson, 102–3, 109], and in about 1780 he partly rebuilt CATCHFRENCH, nr. LISKEARD, CORNWALL, for Mrs Glanville [memoirs of Sarah Loveday Gregor in Cornwall County Record Office]. From the same source it appears that he had designed a long gallery at PORT ELIOT for Edward (afterwards 1st Lord) Eliot. This was demolished in 1829, but is illustrated in *C. Life*, 22 Oct. 1948, fig. 4. Mrs Gregor thought Rawlinson 'a very dull architect', a verdict which his surviving works do nothing to upset.

RAWLINSON, GEORGE (*c.* 1734–1823), was described as 'architect' on his monument in All Saints Church, Derby. He died at Belle View, Matlock Bath, on 26 October 1823, aged 89 [J. C. Cox, *Chronicles of All Saints Derby*, 1881, 148; *Derby Mercury*, 5 Nov. 1823].

RAWSTORNE, JOHN (*c.* 1761–1832), was the son of the Rev. William Rawstorne, rector of Badsworth, nr. Doncaster, and his wife Elizabeth, daughter of Samuel Walker of Stapleton Park. He became a pupil of James Wyatt, and subsequently practised in Birmingham, Doncaster and York. In 1787 he exhibited two architectural designs at the Royal Academy from Wyatt's office, but soon afterwards he moved to Birmingham, where he designed the BLUE COAT SCHOOL in ST. PHILIP'S CHURCHYARD, 1792–4, dem. 1935 (measured drawings in *Architect and Building News*, 1 May 1936), and the CAVALRY BARRACKS in GREAT BROOK STREET. For a speculative builder called Charles Norton (*q.v.*) he designed in 1790 THE CRESCENT, a large terrace of twenty-three stone houses, of which only the extremities were ever built. An engraving, of which there is a copy in B.M., *King's Maps* xlii, 82 *m*, shows the complete design [B. Walker, 'Some Eighteenth-Century Birmingham Houses', *Trans. Birmingham Arch. Soc.* lvi, 1932, 27; *V.C.H. Warwickshire* vii, 48]. His unexecuted designs for rebuilding MOSELEY HALL, destroyed in the Birmingham riots of 1791, are in the Birmingham City Library. His elegant trade card, inscribed 'RAWSTORNE Architect BIRMINGHAM. Estates Surveyed, Pleasure Grounds Laid out &c.', is illustrated in *C. Life*, 13 Sept. 1956, 539.

In 1793 Rawstorne designed THE ROYAL INFIRMARY at SHEFFIELD, opened in 1797 [*Aris's Birmingham Gazette*, 9 Sept. 1793; J. Hunter,

History of Hallamshire, 1869, 323–4]. Soon afterwards he moved to Doncaster. His designs, in an Adamsian style, for redecorating the drawing-room at CUSWORTH HALL, nr. DONCASTER, are among the Battie-Wrightson papers in Leeds City Libraries Archives Department (BW/Ma3). From Doncaster he exhibited at the Royal Academy in 1798 his design for the Sheffield Infirmary, in 1800 an elevation of 'Bilham Belvedere, Yorkshire', a building (dem.) in the grounds of BILHAM HALL, nr. HICKLETON, YORKSHIRE (W.R.), and in the same year a design for proposed additions to CHEVET HALL, nr. WAKEFIELD (dem. 1955), for his nephew Sir Thomas Pilkington.[1] Soon afterwards he appears to have moved again, for in 1802 the *Monthly Magazine* reported (p. 434) that 'Mr. Rawsthorne, the architect, who resides near York, has lately invented a new kind of bricks, dove-tailed into each other, for constructing arches for the cieling of rooms, &c. in lieu of timber', and in 1805 the *York Chronicle* reported the opening of the NEW STREET METHODIST CHAPEL 'after a design of Mr. Rawstorne, architect in this city' [R. Willis, *Nonconformist Chapels of York*, York Georgian Soc. 1964, 22]. In 1809 he was awarded the second prize in the competition for the Ouse Bridge [*York Courant*, 25 Sept. 1809]. Later he moved to Sheffield (see a design by him for houses to be built on Little Sheffield Moor, dated 1819, in Sheffield City Library, F. Maps 37), but after this his practice appears to have collapsed, and during his latter years he was in serious financial straits. In 1821 he was reduced to begging for money to enable him to move from Sheffield 'to another part of Yorkshire' [Farington's Diary, 3 April 1821]. It was from Manchester that in 1822 he issued the prospectus of a proposed book of *Designs in Architecture* that was never published [prospectus in Sheffield City Library, F66/108]. Eventually he died in Liverpool on 24 August 1832, aged 71 [*Gent's Mag.* 1832 (ii), 286]. He appears to have had at least three architect sons, George, who was apprenticed to John Platt of Rotherham in 1793 [J. D. Potts, *Platt of Rotherham*, 1959, 19], Walker (*q.v.*) who practised in Bradford, and William, born in about 1798, who was looking for work in London in 1821 [Farington's Diary, 3 and 20 April, 30 Nov. 1821] and who subsequently practised in Liverpool [Pigot's *National Commercial Directory* ii, 1828–9, 292].

RAWSTORNE, WALKER (–1867), was evidently the son of John Rawstorne (*q.v.*), whose mother's maiden name was Walker. He practised

in Bradford from about 1835 to 1854. He designed a number of churches in the lancet or Norman styles. He died at Headingley, nr. Leeds, on 21 June 1867 [Principal Probate Registry, Calendar of Probates; information from Mr. D. Griffiths].

BINGLEY CHURCH, YORKS. (W.R.), north chapel for Walker Ferrand, 1834, Gothic [Borthwick Institute, York, Fac. 1834/4].

BRADFORD, YORKS. (W.R.), ST. JAMES'S CHURCH, 1836–8, Gothic; dem. 1966 [J. James, *History of Bradford*, 1841, 222].

BUTTERSHAW CHURCH, YORKS. (W.R.), 1838, Gothic [*Bradford Observer*, 22 March 1838].

STOCKTON-ON-TEES, CO. DURHAM, EXCHANGE BUILDINGS, later Mechanics' Institute and now Literary and Philosophical Society's Institute, 1839–40 [*Bradford Observer*, 7 June 1838].

BRADFORD, YORKS. (W.R.), THE INFIRMARY, WESTGATE, 1840–3, Tudor Gothic; heightened 1864, dem. 1936 [John James, *Continuation and Additions to the History of Bradford*, 1866, 212].

MANNINGHAM, YORKS. (W.R.), ST. JUDE'S CHURCH, 1840–3, Norman [*Bradford Observer*, 19 March 1840].

BURLEY-IN-WHARFEDALE CHURCH, YORKS. (W.R.), 1841–3, Gothic [R. V. Taylor, *Churches of Leeds*, 1875, 233].

YEADON CHURCH, YORKS. (W.R.), 1841–4, Gothic [Port, 170–1; *Leeds Intelligencer*, 19 Oct. 1841].

INGROW CHURCH, YORKS. (W.R.),[1] 1841–2, Romanesque [Port, 168–9].

ECCLESHILL CHURCH, YORKS. (W.R.), 1846–8, Gothic [Port, 166–7].

BURNLEY, LANCS., ST. PAUL'S CHURCH, 1852–3, Norman [Port, 146–7].

READ, THOMAS, of Deal, enlarged ST. LEONARD'S CHURCH, DEAL, in 1819 [I.C.B.S.], and reseated ST. GEORGE'S CHURCH, DEAL, in 1822 [I.C.B.S.]. He designed the BAPTIST (now the UNITARIAN) CHAPEL, ADRIAN STREET, DOVER, in 1819–20 [*The Watering-Places of Great Britain and Fashionable Directory*, J. Robins, 1833, 178], and was probably the 'Mr. Read' who won the first prize in the competition for the esplanade at Brighton in 1828, though in the event his design was not carried out [Hermione Hobhouse, *Thomas Cubitt*, 1971, 367].

REBECCA, JOHN BIAGIO (–1847), was the son of Biagio Rebecca (1735–1808), a decorative painter who worked in England from 1761 onwards and was elected A.R.A. in 1771. J. B. Rebecca appears to have practised partly from London and partly from Worthing in Sussex. His works included an aggressively Greek Doric

---

[1] Rawstorne's sister Isabella married Sir Michael Pilkington (d. 1788) and was mother of Sir Thomas Pilkington (d. 1811). A design for a lodge at Chevet Hall by Rawstorne (1797) is among the Pilkington papers in the Central Library at Wakefield.

[1] Otherwise known as St. John, Paper Mill Bridge, nr. Keighley.

church, Tudor Gothic alterations to two country houses, and the extraordinary fantasy of Castle Goring, suavely neo-classical on one side and romantically castellated on the other. Rebecca died in London on 3 June 1847 [*Gent's Mag.* 1847 (ii), 105; will, P.R.O., PROB 11/2058, f. 144].

CASTLE GORING, nr. ARUNDEL, SUSSEX, for Sir Bysshe Shelley, Bart., *c.* 1795–1815 [J. Evans, *Picture of Worthing*, 1805, 96; Sandra Blutman, 'Castle Goring', in *The Country Seat*, ed. Colvin & Harris, 1970].

WORTHING, SUSSEX, ST. PAUL'S CHURCH, 1812 [*The Watering Places of Great Britain and Fashionable Directory*, J. Robins, 1833, 69].

KNEBWORTH HOUSE, HERTS., partly rebuilt for Mrs. Bulwer Lytton, 1813, Tudor Gothic; reconstructed by H. E. Kendall 1844 [contract at Knebworth dated 18 Sept. 1813] (J. P. Neale, *Views of Seats*, 2nd ser., i, 1824).

PENSHURST PLACE, KENT, alterations and additions for Sir John Shelley Sidney, *c.* 1818 onwards, Tudor Gothic [exhib. at R.A. 1818 and 1820; *The Farington Diary*, ed. J. Greig, viii, 206] (*C. Life*, 9, 16 March, 4 May 1972).

attributed: PENSHURST CHURCH, KENT, rebuilding of SIDNEY CHAPEL for Sir John Shelley Sidney, 1820, Gothic.

BUCKINGHAM PLACE, SHOREHAM, SUSSEX, for H. Bridger, 1820; now preserved as a shell at Woodville, The Drive, Shoreham [exhib. at R.A. 1820].

WORTHING, SUSSEX, BEACH HOUSE, for — Helmes, 1820 [David Watkin, *Thomas Hope*, 1968, 192] (*C. Life*, 29 Jan. 1921).

CROWELL RECTORY, OXON., 1822 [Bodleian Library, Oxford Diocesan Faculty Register, 1804–27, p. 351].

WORTHING, SUSSEX, THE SEA HOTEL, THE ESPLANADE, *c.* 1826 [exhib. at R.A. 1827].

REDGRAVE, JOHN, of Harleston (presumably Suffolk), is shown by the building accounts (now at Welford Park, Berks.) to have been the architect or surveyor responsible for rebuilding HALLINGBURY PLACE, ESSEX, for Jacob Houblon in 1771–3; dem. 1924 (*C. Life*, 19 Sept. 1914). In 1763–4 he had carried out alterations to COOPERSALE, ESSEX, for John Archer, Houblon's father-in-law [Dorothy Stroud, *Capability Brown*, 1950, 165]. He may have been the 'Mr. J. Redgrave' (presumably a carpenter by trade) who refloored all the rooms in the Jockey Club's premises at Newmarket in 1783 [Jockey Club accounts, *ex inf.* Mr. P. A. Robb].

REED, BENJAMIN (*c.* 1780–1853), practised in Old Broad Street, London, from about 1826 until his death on 11 December 1853, aged 73 [*Gent's Mag.* 1853 (i), 110]. He was succeeded by his son William Candler Reed.

REEVES, EDWARD, is said to have been the surveyor employed by the 1st Lord Strafford to supervise the building of the east front of WENTWORTH CASTLE, YORKS., to the designs of Johann von Bodt from about 1710 onwards [A. Booth, 'The Architects of Wentworth Castle and Wentworth Woodhouse', *R.I.B.A. Jnl.*, 25 Nov. 1933, 65; cf. B.M., Add. MS. 22241, f. 5]. In a volume of Strafford papers in Sheffield City Library there is (f. 178) a crude design by him for enlarging the house.

REID, ROBERT (1774–1856), was the principal government architect in Scotland during the first half of the nineteenth century. He was born in Edinburgh on 8 November 1774 (not 1776 as stated in *A.P.S.D.* and *D.N.B.*), and was the son of Alexander Reid, a mason in the Tron Kirk parish [inscription on monument in Dean Cemetery; New Register House, Edinburgh, Baptism Register No. 35]. Nothing is at present known of his early life or architectural training. His long career as a public architect began in 1803 when he was commissioned by the Trustees for Public Buildings to design the new Law Courts in Parliament Square, Edinburgh. In 1808, on the strength of this important public work, he obtained a warrant authorizing him to use the title of 'King's Architect and Surveyor in Scotland'. This was purely honorary and conferred no emoluments on its holder, but when the titular Master of Works to the Scottish Crown, James Brodie of Brodie, died in 1824, Reid succeeded in getting that office merged with his own. As 'Master of Works and Architect' to the King in Scotland he was to receive a salary of £200 a year. His next move was to persuade the government to establish a properly constituted Scottish Office of Works, with himself at its head, an office in Parliament Square and a salary of £500 a year (1827). In 1839, as a measure of economy, Reid's office and title were abolished, and the Scottish Works were henceforth administered from London. Reid was retired on full pay, and went to live at a house called Lowood which he had acquired near Melrose.[1] He died in Edinburgh on 20 March 1856, and was buried in the Dean Cemetery, where he is commemorated by a monument with a bronze portrait medallion.

In his exteriors Reid adhered closely to the style of the brothers Adam. Their Edinburgh University was the source of his Parliament Square façade, and most of his public buildings are designed in a slightly coarsened version of the Adams' monumental manner. This did not command universal approval, and both the Faculty of Advocates and the Writers to the Signet in-

---

[1] This house was rebuilt in 1914, but an old photograph shows a small early nineteenth-century villa which Reid had enlarged for himself.

sisted on employing a different architect (William Stark) for the interiors of their respective libraries, which formed part of the Parliament Square complex. St. George's Church and the Custom House at Leith (a pedestrian essay in Greek Doric) were also the subjects of adverse criticism, and an Aberdeen professor regarded it as a deliverance when Archibald Simpson was employed to design the new Marischal College there instead of 'the King's Architect ... a dull, staid personage who had acquired much discredit by the plans for the new Custom House at Leith and his repairs at St. Andrews'. To modern eyes Reid's slightly ponderous public buildings make a by no means contemptible contribution to the fabric of Edinburgh, and his sector of the New Town forms a distinctive and well-planned portion of the whole. His finest work, however, is the little-known picture gallery at Paxton House, Berwickshire, whose interior was (before its modern subdivision) an ambitious neo-classical composition of considerable merit. So far as is known this was Reid's only country-house commission, for (as he informed the Barons of the Exchequer in 1837) his official duties obliged him first 'to restrict my private practice, and ultimately to relinquish it altogether' [S.R.O., T 1/4381].

[*A.P.S.D.*; *D.N.B.*; *History of the King's Works* vi, 1973, 251–3; G. M. Fraser, 'Archibald Simpson, Architect', *Aberdeen Weekly Jnl.*, 26 July 1918; *Gent's Mag.* xlv, 1856, 547.]

PUBLIC BUILDINGS

PERTH, THE ACADEMY (now County Library), ROSE TERRACE, 1803–7[1] [photographs of original drawings in N.M.R.S.] (*C. Life*, 10 Oct. 1968, 916, fig. 1).

EDINBURGH, THE BANK OF SCOTLAND on THE MOUND, jointly with Richard Crichton, 1802–6 [Bank of Scotland Minutes, 29 Oct. 1800: 'Resolved to employ Robert Reid and Richard Chrichton, Architects in Edinburgh, jointly']; remodelled by D. Bryce 1865–70 (T. H. Shepherd, *Modern Athens*, 1829, 74).

EDINBURGH, NEW LAW COURTS, PARLIAMENT SQUARE, including façade to square, 1804–10, and eastern extensions, 1825–40 [S.R.O., E 343/1–5, minutes of the Trustees for Public Buildings; drawings in RHP 6525/13–15 and P.R.O., MPD 103].

EDINBURGH, THE LUNATIC ASYLUM (EAST HOUSE), MORNINGSIDE, 1809–10; largely rebuilt by W. Burn 1839–40 and enlarged by D. Bryce 1856 and W. L. Moffat 1874–86 [*A.P.S.D.*] (plan and elevation in *Scots Mag.*, March 1808). In

1809 Reid published *Observations on the Structure of Hospitals for the Treatment of Lunatics ... to which is annexed an account of the intended establishment of a Lunatic Asylum at Edinburgh.*

EDINBURGH, external shell of THE SIGNET AND ADVOCATES' LIBRARIES (now the UPPER AND LOWER SIGNET LIBRARY), PARLIAMENT SQUARE, 1810–12. Reid originally designed interiors for these libraries, which form two storeys of the same building, but both the Writers to the Signet and the Faculty of Advocates commissioned William Stark (*q.v.*) to design the interiors. Reid as the government architect supervised the execution of Stark's designs in 1812–16. The staircase to the Advocates' Library on the upper floor was designed by W. H. Playfair in 1819–20, but altered by W. Burn for the Writers to the Signet after they had acquired the upper library from the Advocates in 1826. [S.R.O., E 343/1–5, minutes of the Trustees for Public Buildings; *History of the Society of Writers to the Signet*, 1890, lxxiii–lxxvi, 430–1.]

PERTH, THE PRISON, EDINBURGH ROAD, 1810–12, originally designed as a military prison but remodelled in 1841–2 as the General Prison for Scotland [J. Morison, *A Guide to the City of Perth*, 1812, 6].

EDINBURGH, ST. GEORGE'S CHURCH, CHARLOTTE SQUARE, 1811–14; converted into Register House annexe 1965–70 [T. H. Shepherd, *Modern Athens*, 1829, 43 and plate].

LEITH, THE CUSTOM HOUSE, 1811–12 [*A.P.S.D.*].

EDINBURGH, completed THE REGISTER HOUSE, designing the north wing, 1822–30 [*Book of the Old Edinburgh Club* xvii, 167–8].

DOWNPATRICK GAOL. CO. DOWN, IRELAND, 1824–30 [Dublin Castle, S.P.O., Chief Secretary's Office, RP 1823/6726 and 1827/1956, *ex inf.* Mr. E. McParland].

ST. ANDREWS, FIFE, THE UNITED COLLEGE, begun 1829–31, when the east wing only was built. The buildings were eventually completed 1845–9 by William Nixon in a simplified version of Reid's Jacobethan design [R. G. Cant, 'St. Andrews Architects', *St. Andrews Preservation Trust Year Book* for 1966–7, part ii, 12].

ST. ANDREWS, FIFE, remodelled ST. MARY'S COLLEGE, 1829–30 [R. G. Cant, *op. cit.*].

ST. ANDREWS, FIFE, extended THE UNIVERSITY LIBRARY, 1829 [R. G. Cant, *op. cit.*].

EDINBURGH, HOLYROODHOUSE, general repair, 1824–35. Reid rebuilt the south-east quarter which had been damaged by subsidence and refaced the south front, originally built of rubble, in ashlar. He also took down and rebuilt the sixteenth-century Abbey Court House [S.R.O., General Report on Works executed at Holyroodhouse by Reid, 1836].

---

[1] The attribution of this building to William Burn in *N.S.A.* x, 85, is incorrect.

DOMESTIC ARCHITECTURE

PERTH, NOS. 1–28 MARSHALL PLACE, 1801 [S.R.O., Perth Sasines].

PAXTON HOUSE, BERWICKSHIRE, east wing containing Library and Picture Gallery (now Chapel) for George Home, 1812–13 [Alistair Rowan in *C. Life*, 31 Aug. 1967].

EDINBURGH, NEW TOWN. In conjunction with William Sibbald (*q.v.*), Reid was responsible for the layout of the northern extension of the New Town comprising ABERCROMBY PLACE, CUMBERLAND STREET, DUBLIN STREET, DUNDAS STREET, DUNDONALD STREET, DRUMMOND PLACE, FETTES ROW, GLOUCESTER PLACE, GREAT KING STREET, HERIOT ROW, INDIA STREET, MANSFIELD PLACE, NELSON STREET, NORTHUMBERLAND STREET, ROYAL CRESCENT and SCOTLAND STREET. The plan was drawn up in 1802, and building was in progress from 1803 onwards. Reid designed the principal elevations, including those of Heriot Row (1803–8) [A. J. Youngson, *The Making of Classical Edinburgh*, 1966, 206–11].

EDINBURGH, NOS. 33–46 CHARLOTTE SQUARE, 1807–15 [*Book of the Old Edinburgh Club* xxiii, 25–28].

UNEXECUTED DESIGNS

These include a project for a new town at DUNKELD, PERTHSHIRE, 1806 [drawings at Blair Castle, D.l. 27–8]; a COURT HOUSE at INVERARAY, ARGYLLSHIRE, 1807–8 [I. G. Lindsay & Mary Cosh, *Inveraray and the Dukes of Argyll*, 1973, 316–17]; a design for rebuilding GOSFORD HOUSE, EAST LOTHIAN, for the 8th Earl of Wemyss, *c.* 1810 [*C. Life*, 21 Oct. 1971, 1050]; a design for the MERCHANT MAIDEN HOSPITAL, EDINBURGH, 1810–12 [*Book of the Old Edinburgh Club* xxix, 21–2]; the COUNTY BUILDINGS at PERTH, 1812–4 [drawings in Perth Art Gallery]; a design for a new building for Edinburgh University on the south side of Leith Walk, exhibited at the R.A. in 1818; and a design for 'a National Monumental Church for Scotland, in the style of the Parthenon at Athens, to perpetuate the memory of the great Naval and Military Achievements of the late war', designed to be built on the Mound in Edinburgh, and exhibited at the R.A. in 1819.

REID, WILLIAM (1772–1849), was a quarry-owner, builder and architect at Lochee on the outskirts of Dundee. In all three capacities he was largely employed in assisting the expansion of Dundee in the early nineteenth century. In Lochee itself he was a prominent figure, known popularly as 'the Baron'. Most of the buildings erected in Lochee during the early nineteenth century are said to have been designed and built by him, including THE WEAVERS' HALL, 1824, and

ST. LUKE'S U.P. CHURCH (afterwards Church of Scotland), 1826–7, remodelled 1856. An elaborate monument in Mains Churchyard records his death on 19 September 1849 at the age of 77 [Alexander Elliot, *Lochee*, Dundee 1911, 61, 185–6].

REID, WILLIAM, practised in Glasgow in the early nineteenth century. He was probably the 'Mr. Reid' referred to by Joseph Bonomi in 1807 as a 'young architect of Glasgow' who was friendly with his sons [letter to Duke of Argyll's factor among papers at Inveraray]. In 1813 he was one of the prize-winners in the competition for laying out the Calton Hill area of Edinburgh [A. J. Youngson, *The Making of Classical Edinburgh*, 1966, 307]. He designed some bonded warehouses in Howard Street, Glasgow, 1818 [Chapman's *Picture of Glasgow*, 1820, 193], and a 'villa in the old Scotch style' at SPRINGFIELD, BISHOPBRIGGS, LANARKSHIRE, for D. S. Cleland, 1831, described and illustrated in Loudon's *Encyclopaedia*, 1846, 879–84. At PAISLEY he designed ST. GEORGE'S CHURCH, an able classical work of 1819–20 [Town Council Minutes, 9 Sept. 1816, *ex inf.* Mr. David Walker]. He may also have designed the castellated COUNTY (now MUNICIPAL) BUILDINGS at PAISLEY, 1818–20, but in his *Abbey and Town of Paisley*, 1835, 148, C. Mackie states confusingly that 'The plan of the building was drawn by William Reid, Esq. The architect was Archibald Elliot, Esqr., Edinburgh.' Some drawings by Reid are in the R.I.B.A. Collection. They comprise two designs (1795) for steeples in a manner derived from Gibbs, a plan and elevation of a villa at LARGS, AYRSHIRE, for Dr. Brown, 1811, probably to be identified as BROOMFIELD HOUSE, dem. 1963, and a perspective of CASTLETOWN HOUSE, ROCKLIFFE, CUMBERLAND, a Greek Revival mansion designed 'by Reid & Nicholson architects' for Robert Mounsey, 1811. This house is illustrated in Peter Nicholson's *Architectural Dictionary* i, 1819, 102–3, where, however, it is stated that 'This design was made from a sketch by Thomas Telford, Esqr., but the working drawings were made, and the work was superintended, by the Author'. In 1833 Reid read a paper on the acoustics of public buildings to the Edinburgh Society of Arts [Loudon's *Architectural Mag.* i, 1834, 212]. His unexecuted design for a gaol at Carlisle (1822) is in the Cumbria Record Office (Q.AG/5).

RENDLE, JOHN, was a builder and surveyor at Teignmouth in Devon. His only known work was KINGSTEIGNTON VICARAGE (now 'The Coach House', No. 6 Elmfield), which he designed in 1815 for Thomas Whipham, D.D., in the form of a thatched *cottage orné*, with oval rooms arranged in a plan of some sophistication [Exeter Diocesan Records]. Rendle was probably a

676

relation, and perhaps the uncle, of James Meadows Rendel (1799–1856), a celebrated civil engineer who was the son of James Rendle, a land surveyor at Okehampton who married Jane, daughter of the architect John Meadows (*q.v.*). J. M. Rendel's third son Stuart, also a civil engineer, entered politics and was raised to the peerage in 1895 as Lord Rendel. The latter's grandson was Harry Stuart Goodhart-Rendel (1887–1959), architect and architectural critic. [Genealogical information from Mr. Vincent Rendel; *D.N.B.*, *s.v.* 'Rendel, James Meadows'.]

RENNIE, JOHN (1761–1821), the younger son of a Scottish farmer, was born at Phantassie in East Lothian on 7 June 1761. As a child he showed a remarkable aptitude for mechanical pursuits, and he afterwards found congenial employment with a millwright. His earnings enabled him to study at Edinburgh University for three years before establishing himself as a millwright and general engineer. In 1784 he went to Birmingham in order to assist Boulton and Watt in designing and executing the machinery for the Albion Flour Mills at Southwark. Although destroyed by fire in 1791, these power-driven mills had attracted great interest, and Rennie's connection with them established his reputation as a mechanical engineer. It was, however, as a planner of docks and harbours, as a drainer of fens, and as a builder of bridges that Rennie eventually became famous, and it is chiefly in the last capacity that he figures in this *Dictionary*.

Rennie began his career as a bridge-builder at the age of 22 and in the course of his life he designed many minor bridges over canals, etc., as well as major ones over rivers such as the Thames and the Tweed. All of them are admirable as architecture as well as engineering, and Rennie ranks as one of the great British bridge-builders of the nineteenth century. His first major bridge was the one over the Tweed at Kelso, which, with its semi-elliptical arches separated by pairs of Doric columns, its boldly defined masonry and its level roadway, anticipates the chief characteristics of his later bridges across the Thames at London.

In 1809 he and William Jessop were asked to report on the plans for a new bridge across the Thames at Somerset House which had been prepared by the engineer George Dodd with the assistance of J. L. Bond. As a result of their unfavourable criticism, Rennie himself was asked to prepare the designs which were adopted, and in June 1810 he undertook to supervise the construction of the bridge as a salary of £1000 a year. Foreseeing that the eventual removal of Old London Bridge would result in an increased scour higher up the river, Rennie laid the foundations

of the piers in coffer dams instead of in the caissons advocated by Dodd, thus securing an absolutely firm basis for his bridge. The Strand Bridge, as it was at first called, was opened by the Prince Regent in 1817. Rennie was then offered a knighthood, which he refused.

In 1813 a company was formed to provide a bridge across the Thames between Blackfriars and London Bridge, of which Rennie was appointed Engineer. This (Southwark) bridge consisted of three cast-iron arches designed to allow the largest possible waterway. It was completed in 1819 and replaced in 1920–1.

Rennie's last great work was to design a new bridge to take the place of the medieval London Bridge, with its narrow roadway, decrepit arches and battered starlings. The Corporation had already taken the advice of its surveyor, George Dance, in consultation with Messrs. Chapman, Alexander and Mountague. They recommended that eight of the arches should be removed and replaced by four larger ones: but Rennie, in a report which he submitted on 12 March 1821, showed convincingly that it would be better in the end to build a new bridge rather than to spend large sums of money in altering the old one. An Act of Parliament was accordingly obtained, but Rennie died in October 1821, and in 1823 a competition was held in which about one hundred designs were submitted. The assessors were Messrs. Soane, Smirke and Nash, of the Office of Works, with whom was associated Mountague, the City Architect. Prizes of £250, £150 and £100 were awarded to the authors of the three best designs (Charles Fowler, John Boorer and Charles Busby), but as none of these was considered to be entirely satisfactory, the competition was set aside, and it was Rennie's original design which was eventually executed under the direction of his son, Sir John Rennie, and completed in 1831. The original specification is in the Library of London University (MS. 158).

Rennie died on 4 October 1821, and was buried in the crypt of St. Paul's Cathedral. His practice as a civil engineer was continued by his younger son John (1794–1874), who was knighted in 1831 on the completion of London Bridge. As engineer to the Admiralty, a post in which he succeeded his father, Sir John Rennie completed various works in the royal dockyards, including the great breakwater across Plymouth Sound which had been begun by his father in 1811, of which he published an *Account* in 1848. He also planned and designed the ROYAL WILLIAM VICTUALLING YARD at STONEHOUSE, nr. PLYMOUTH, completed in 1832, a group of buildings, monumental in scale and massive in construction, which is amongst the finest works of the engineer-architect in England (A. E. Richardson & C. L. Gill, *Regency Architecture of the West of England*, 1924, 59–63). This, however, was his only important architectural work,[1] and his achievements as an engineer fall outside the scope, as well as the chronological limits, of this book. Sir John Rennie retired in about 1862 and died on 3 September 1874. [S. Smiles, *Lives of the Engineers* ii, 1861, part vii; Edward Cresy, *Encyclopaedia of Civil Engineering*, 1847; *The Autobiography of Sir John Rennie*, 1875; *A.P.S.D.*; *D.N.B.*; C. G. T. Boucher, *John Rennie*, Manchester 1963; Rennie papers in the Library of the Institution of Civil Engineers; letters in the National Library of Scotland, MS. 2909.]

PRINCIPAL BRIDGES DESIGNED BY JOHN RENNIE (1761–1821)

Bridge over Water of Leith, nr. Stevenhouse Mill, Midlothian, 1784; dem. (Smiles, ii, 131).

DUNDAS AQUEDUCT, LIMPLEY STOKE, WILTS., carrying the Kennet and Avon Canal over R. Avon, c. 1795–7.

LUNE AQUEDUCT, nr. LANCASTER, carrying the Lancaster Canal over the R. Lune, 1794–7.

WOLSELEY BRIDGE, nr. COLWICH, STAFFS., 1798–1800.

KELSO BRIDGE, ROXBURGHSHIRE (R. Tweed), 1800–3 (Cresy, 434).

WHITEADDER BRIDGE, BERWICKSHIRE, 1800.

MUSSELBURGH BRIDGE, MIDLOTHIAN (R. Esk), 1803 (Cresy, 435).

BOSTON BRIDGE, LINCS.* (R. Witham), 1804–7; dem. 1913 (Smiles, ii, 176).

VIRGINIA WATER, SURREY, bridge on Great West Road, 1805.

DARLASTON BRIDGE, STAFFS. (R. Trent), 1805.

LONDON, bridge* over R. Lea at East India Dock Road, 1809; dem.

FOSDYKE BRIDGE,* LINCS. (R. Welland), 1810; dem.

LONDON, WATERLOO BRIDGE (R. Thames), 1811–17; dem. 1938 (Cresy, 436–41).

NEWTON STEWART BRIDGE, WIGTOWNSHIRE (R. Cree), 1812–13 (Cresy, 435).

LUCKNOW, INDIA,* bridge over R. Goomtee, 1814.

STONELEIGH ABBEY, WARWICKS., NEW BRIDGE, GRECIAN DRIVE, for J. H. Leigh, 1814–15 [Shakespeare's Birthplace, Stratford, Leigh MSS. Ser. D. Warwicks., bundles 17 and 37–8] (Cresy, 436).

LONDON, SOUTHWARK BRIDGE* (R. Thames), 1815–19; dem. 1920 (Smiles, ii, 190).

LEEDS, YORKS. (W.R.), WELLINGTON BRIDGE (R. Aire), 1817–19.

NAPLES, ITALY,* bridge, 1818.

BRIDGE OF EARN, PERTHSHIRE, 1819–21.

CRAMOND BRIDGE, MIDLOTHIAN (R. Almond), 1819–23.

KEN BRIDGE, NEW GALLOWAY, KIRKCUDBRIGHTSHIRE, 1820–1.

CHEPSTOW BRIDGE,* MONMOUTHSHIRE (R. Wye), 1815–16.

LONDON BRIDGE (R. Thames), designed by John Rennie, but carried out by his sons, 1824–31; dem. 1967 and rebuilt at Lake Havasu City, Arizona, U.S.A., 1970–1 (Cresy, 442–58).

RENNY, WILLIAM, was paid £2 3s. in 1699 for drawing the 'draught' for the TOWN HALL at SHEFFIELD, and £200 for building it in the following year. It was demolished in 1810 [J. D. Leader, *Extracts from the Earliest Book of Accounts of the Town Trustees of Sheffield*, Sheffield 1879, 139–41; R. E. Leader, *Surveyors and Architects of the Past in Sheffield*, 1903, 32].

REPTON, GEORGE STANLEY (1786–1858), the fourth and youngest son of Humphry Repton, was born on 30 January 1786. He exhibited his first drawing at the Royal Academy at the age of 15,[1] and soon afterwards became a pupil of John Nash, in whose office he remained long enough to become his chief assistant.[2] In 1817 he married Lady Elizabeth Scott, the daughter of Lord Chancellor Eldon, secretly, and in defiance of her father's wishes. Lord Eldon was at first furious, but relented after the birth of his daughter's first child in 1820, and in his will her children were placed on the same footing as those of his other daughter. As a young man, Repton assisted his father and elder brother in their designs for the Pavilion at Brighton, and in conjunction with John Nash he remodelled the Royal Opera House in the Haymarket. After about 1820 he practised on his own, and achieved a considerable reputation as a designer of country houses, especially in the west of England. A number of his architectural designs are in the R.I.B.A. Collection. They show that he was an excellent draughtsman and a versatile architect, whose classical work forms part of the brief Palladian revival which preceded the introduction of the Italianate style by Barry. His picturesquely composed Tudor Gothic country houses owed much to his early training in Nash's office.

Repton appears to have retired from practice

* Iron bridges.
[1] He subsequently exhibited sometimes as 'G. Stanley Repton' and sometimes as 'G.S.R.'. In Graves's *Royal Academy Exhibitors* the latter exhibits will be found in the 'Anonymous' section.
[2] Two sketch-books used by G. S. Repton while in Nash's office survive, one in the R.I.B.A. Drawings Collection, the other in the Royal Pavilion Art Gallery, Brighton.

[1] According to J. Britton, *The Original Picture of London*, 26th ed., c. 1828, 122, the STAMFORD STREET UNITARIAN CHAPEL in BLACKFRIARS was 'built in 1823 by Mr. Rennie'. When it was demolished in 1966 the Greek Doric portico was preserved as the entrance to the London Nautical College.

in about 1845. He died on 29 June 1858, and was buried at Kensal Green. His only son, George William Repton, was for many years M.P. for St. Albans and afterwards for Warwick.

[*A.P.S.D.*; *D.N.B.*; *The Farington Diary*, ed. J. Greig, viii, 159; John Summerson, 'A Repton Portfolio', *R.I.B.A. Jnl.*, 25 Feb. 1933; John Summerson, *John Nash*, 1935, 281–2; Dorothy Stroud, *Humphry Repton*, 1962, 25; *Catalogue of the R.I.B.A. Drawings Coll.*]

LONDON, ROYAL OPERA HOUSE, HAYMARKET, remodelled in collaboration with John Nash, 1816–18; interior destroyed by fire 1867 and rebuilt 1868–9; dem. except the Arcade *c.* 1895 [Britton & Pugin, *The Public Buildings of London* i, 1825, 72–9].

COBHAM HALL, KENT, the library for the 4th Earl of Darnley, 1817–20 [J. P. Neale, *Views of Seats* vi, 1823, where the library is stated to have been 'lately fitted up' by G. S. Repton; R.I.B.A.D.].

OXFORD, EXETER COLLEGE, the hall was repaired in 1818 'from the designs of Mr. Nash, under the superintendence of Mr. Repton' [J. Ingram, *Memorials of Oxford* i, 1837, 12–13].

LONDON, ST. PHILIP'S CHAPEL, REGENT STREET, for his brother, the Rev. Edward Repton, 1819–20; dem. [Britton & Pugin, *The Public Buildings of London* i, 1825, 102–6].

ABERYSTWYTH, CARDIGANSHIRE, THE ASSEMBLY ROOMS, 1820 [Nicholson's *Cambrian Traveller's Guide*, 1840, 25; J. Hemingway, *Panorama of North Wales*, 1835, 41; R.I.B.A.D.].

THE RIDGE, WOTTON-UNDER-EDGE, GLOS., for Edward Sheppard, *c.* 1820; dem. *c.* 1930 [T. & H. S. Storer, *Delineations of the County of Gloucester*, 1824, 142; R.I.B.A.D.].

KITLEY HOUSE, DEVONSHIRE, remodelled for E. P. Bastard, *c.* 1820–5, Elizabethan [R. Ackermann, *Views of Seats* ii, 1830; R.I.B.A.D.; building accounts in Plymouth Public Library, bundle 625] (*C. Life*, 7 Oct. 1939; C. Hussey, *English Country Houses: Late Georgian*, 1958, 168–74).

SANDGATE CHAPEL, KENT, for the 4th Earl of Darnley, 1822; dem. 1849 or later [R.I.B.A.D.].

SARSDEN HOUSE, OXON., added portico, colonnade and conservatory for J. H. Langston, *c.* 1823–5 [R.I.B.A.D.]. The domed hall appears to have been built earlier by Humphry or perhaps J. A. Repton. Humphry submitted a 'Red Book' for landscaping the park in 1795, and he says in his book (ed. Loudon, 270) that he 'advised covering the inner court entirely, and converting it into a hall of communication'.

SARSDEN CHURCH, OXON., reconstructed *c.* 1823–5 [Bodleian Library, Oxford Diocesan Faculty Register 1804–27, 408].

FOLLATON HOUSE (now Council Offices), nr. TOTNES, DEVONSHIRE, rebuilt for S. Cary, *c.*

1826–7 [R. Ackermann, *Views of Seats* ii, 1830; R.I.B.A.D.].

WOLTERTON HOUSE, NORFOLK, added east wing and perron to south front for the 3rd Earl of Orford, 1828–9 [drawings at Wolterton dated 1828; R.I.B.A.D.; Gordon Nares in *C. Life*, 18, 25 July 1957].

WIDWORTHY COURT, nr. HONITON, DEVONSHIRE, for Sir Edward Marwood Elton, 1830 [R.I.B.A.D., showing portico, etc., not built].

DUMBLETON HALL, nr. EVESHAM, GLOS., for Edward Holland, *c.* 1830, Tudor Gothic [R.I.B.A.D.].

SARSGROVE COTTAGE (now HOUSE), OXON., remodelled for J. H. Langston, *c.* 1830 [R.I.B.A.D.; *Connoisseur* cxxxviii, 1956, 222–5].

PEAMORE HOUSE, EXMINSTER, DEVONSHIRE, remodelled for S. T. Kekewich, *c.* 1825–30 Tudor Gothic [*A.P.S.D.*; R.I.B.A.D.].

WINCHESTER COLLEGE, HAMPSHIRE, refronted Outer Court of Warden's Lodgings, 1832–3, and designed New Commoners, 1837–9, and Headmaster's House, 1839–41 [College Archives, *ex inf.* Mr. J. H. Harvey].

KINGSTON CHAPEL (now Church Hall), nr. CORFE, DORSET, for his father-in-law, Lord Eldon, 1833, Gothic [R.I.B.A.D.].

HURSLEY PARK, HANTS., addition of porch for Sir William Heathcote, Bart., 1834; porch dem. *c.* 1905 [J. Harris, *Catalogue of British Drawings for Architecture, etc., in American Collections*, 1971, 171; R.I.B.A.D.] (*C. Life*, 13 Dec. 1902).

HURSLEY CHURCH, HANTS., alterations to tower, 1834 [J. Harris, *Catalogue of British Drawings for Architecture, etc., in American Collections*, 1971, 171].

CAMERTON COURT, SOMERSET, for John Jarrett, 1838–40 [R.I.B.A.D.].

? SHIRLEY RECTORY, HANTS., for the Rev. William Orger, 1839 [R.I.B.A.D., inscribed 'Parsonage-Shirley-Surrey' (*sic*)].

CHIPPING NORTON TOWN HALL, OXON., 1842; damaged by fire 1950 [R.I.B.A.D.].

MEDMENHAM CHURCH, BUCKS., restored chancel, 1844–5, including new stone altar (removed 1846), reredos (removed 1906), aumbry and font [R.I.B.A.D.].

SOUTHAMPTON, HANTS., BECKFORD HOUSE, conservatory for F. L. Beckford [R.I.B.A.D.].

BURGH HALL, nr. AYLSHAM, NORFOLK, design (perhaps not executed) for addition of porch, etc., for J. H. Holley, probably *c.* 1830. Holley built a new house in the 1840s.

REPTON, HUMPHRY (1752–1818), was born at Bury St. Edmunds on 21 April 1752. His father had for many years held 'the honourable and lucrative situation of a Collector of Excise', and designed a mercantile career for his son. It was, in fact, as a general merchant in Norwich that Repton began his career in about 1773, but his business soon failed, and he decided to retire to Sustead, nr. Aylsham, where his sister had married a solicitor named John Adey. Here he followed his natural inclinations by studying botany and gardening, and living the life of a country gentleman. One of his neighbours was William Windham of Felbrigg, whom he accompanied to Ireland as private secretary on the latter's appointment as Chief Secretary in 1783. On his return to England, he removed to a cottage at Hare Street in Essex, where he lived for the rest of his life. Having lost more money in a project for establishing mail-coaches, he was obliged to find some way of supporting his family. All his life he had been keenly interested in gardening, and now at the age of 39 he resolved to 'turn his hobby into a profession' and become a 'landscape gardener'. The death of Lancelot Brown in 1783 had made way not only for new men but for new ideas, and Repton exploited and systematized the current desire for something at once more natural and more picturesque than Brown's Arcadian landscapes. Repton had both the theoretical knowledge and the practical ability to make a success of his art, and his facility as a water-colourist enabled him to illustrate his proposed 'improvements' by means of charming perspective views furnished with flaps designed to allow the prospective client to make a direct comparison between his park in its improved and unimproved condition. In the case of his more important commissions Repton was in the habit of presenting his client with an elaborately illustrated report bound in red morocco and known as a 'Red Book'. Very soon he became famous; he was mentioned by name in Jane Austen's *Mansfield Park*, and as 'Mr. Milestone' he figures in T. L. Peacock's *Headlong Hall*. By the time of his death in March 1818, at the age of 65, Repton had established himself as one of the great figures in the history of English landscape-gardening. Over seventy 'Red Books' are recorded,[1] and a total of nearly two hundred commissions have been listed by Miss Stroud.

Repton was not trained as an architect, but architecture was, as he himself put it, 'an inseparable and indispensable auxiliary' to the art of landscape-gardening. In planning a park, he could never ignore the architectural character of its mansion: he might, and did, recommend alterations which he thought essential to his proposals: and his opinion might be asked by a gentleman who intended to build and plant at the same time. Brown had found the ideal solution for this problem in his partnership with Henry Holland, and Repton established a somewhat similar but short-lived relationship with John Nash, to whom he turned over most of the architectural commissions which came his way in return for $2\frac{1}{2}$ per cent on the cost of the work executed. Nevertheless he 'occasionally acted as architect', until in his later years he was able to rely on his sons for increasing assistance in this direction. His most ambitious plans – those for remodelling Brighton Pavilion in the Hindu, and Magdalen College, Oxford, in the Gothic style – were both prepared in collaboration with his sons, but neither was executed, though the designs for both are still in existence, the former in the volume dedicated to the Prince Regent which Repton published in 1808, the latter in Magdalen College Library. The assistance of his eldest son 'in the architectural department' was specifically acknowledged by Repton in the cases of 'Brenty Hill, Cotham Bank, Organ Hall, Stapleton, Stratton Park, Scarisbrick, Panshanger, Bayham, &c.', and can be documented in several other instances. Only in one or two early commissions does it appear that Humphry Repton was indebted neither to Nash nor to his sons for architectural assistance. At WELBECK ABBEY, NOTTS., it was he who dictated the remodelling of the east and west fronts in 1790 [A. S. Turberville, *Welbeck Abbey and its Owners* ii, 1938, 312–16].[1] In 1792 he advised certain minor alterations to HONING HALL, NORFOLK, for Mrs. Cubitt [R. W. Ketton-Cremer, *A Norfolk Gallery*, 1948, 205], in 1793–4 he added an iron balcony, etc., to HIGHAM HILLS, nr. WALTHAMSTOW, ESSEX, for John Harman [*V.C.H. Essex* vi, 260], in 1795 he advised the conversion of the central courtyard of SARSDEN HOUSE, OXON., into a domed 'hall of communication' [Loudon, 270], and the 'Red Book' for WARLEY HALL, WORCS., dated 1795 (now in Warley Public Library), includes a design for a Doric temple which existed until about 1940. In 1805 he designed a new entrance to UPPARK, SUSSEX, for Sir Harry Fetherstonhaugh, Bart. [C. Hussey in *C. Life*, 14, 21, 28 June 1941; C. Hussey, *English Country Houses: Mid Georgian*, 1956, 30, fig. 34 (plan)]. More significant than these

[1] A useful but incomplete list will be found in Loudon, 27–8. Those now in public collections include Armley, Yorks. (Mellon Collection), Brandesbury, Middlesex (Dumbarton Oaks Garden Library, Washington, U.S.A.), Claybury, Essex (G.L.C. Record Office), Ferney Hall, Salop. (Pierpont Morgan Library, New York, U.S.A.), Hatchlands, Surrey (*ibid.*), Hill Hall, Essex (Essex Record Office), Hooton Hall, Cheshire (Architectural Association Library), Langley Park, Kent (R.I.B.A.), Little Green, Sussex (W. Sussex Record Office), Rose Hill, Sussex (Bodleian Library), Royal Fort, Bristol (Yale University Library, U.S.A.), Stonelands, Sussex (*ibid.*), Tewin Water, Herts. (Hertfordshire Record Office), and Trewarthenick, Cornwall (Cornwall Record Office). Facsimiles of the Antony, Attingham and Sheringham Red Books were published in a limited edition by the Basilisk Press in 1976, with commentary by Edward Malins.

[1] For Repton's Welbeck 'Red Books', which include designs for a completely new house, see John Steegmann in *C. Life*, 30 Sept. 1933.

minor architectural works was the 'lodge of a new and singular description' illustrated as Repton's work by William Cooke in his *New Picture of the Isle of Wight*, 1808, 90. It consisted of two thatched cottages, one on either side of the drive, and was evidently one of the first of its kind.[1] In 1791 the Hon. John Byng had already commented on the thatched roof of a Lincolnshire rectory (at Scrivelsby) 'repair'd upon Mr. Repton's plan' [*The Torrington Diaries*, ed. C. B. Andrews, ii, 1935, 377], and it is evident that Repton was, with his associate Nash, one of the pioneers of the picturesque cottage style so successfully exploited by the latter in the early years of the nineteenth century.[2]

Repton's principal publications on the subject of landscape-gardening – which include his observations on architectural design – were reprinted with a memoir by J. C. Loudon in 1840 as *The Landscape Gardening and Landscape Architecture of the late Humphry Repton.* Between 1789 and 1809 Repton contributed vignettes of country seats, etc., to the almanack called *Peacock's Polite Repository*. In the collection of Mr. Paul Mellon there is a set of some forty of these small engravings, mounted on a decorated sheet and inscribed 'Proof Impressions of Plates engraved from Drawings by H. REPTON of Scenery improving under his directions'. Other sources for Repton's career are the obituary notices in *Gent's Mag.* 1818 (i), 372, 648, and (ii), 102, and a list of views of Norfolk drawn by him printed in *Collectanea Topographica et Genealogica* viii, 1843. The standard modern biography is Dorothy Stroud, *Humphry Repton*, 1962. See also *A.P.S.D.*; *D.N.B.*; C. Hussey, *The Picturesque*, 1927; J. Steegman, 'Bayham Abbey, Designs for a House and View by Humphry Repton', *Arch. Rev.* lxxx, 1936; J. Steegman, 'Humphry Repton at Blaize Castle', *Arch. Rev.* lxxxiii, 1938; N. Pevsner, 'Humphry Repton: A ᵣorilegium', *Arch. Rev.* ciii, 1948; R. W. Ketton-Cremer, 'Humphry Repton in Norfolk', in *A Norfolk Gallery*, 1948; C. Hussey, 'Humphry Repton 1752–1818', *Country Life Annual*, 1952; Margaret Meade-Fetherstonhaugh & Oliver Warner, *Uppark and its People*, 1964, chap. 4; Hugh Prince, *Parks in England*, 1967; J. Harris, *Catalogue of British Drawings for Architecture, etc., in American Collections*, 1971, 172–8; Edward Hyams, *Capability Brown and Humphry Repton*, 1971.

REPTON, JOHN ADEY (1775–1860), eldest son of Humphry Repton, was born at Norwich on 29 March 1775. He became a pupil of William Wilkins of Norwich (the father of William Wilkins, R.A.), for whom he made complete measured drawings of Norwich Cathedral which are now in the Library of the Society of Antiquaries.[1] In 1796 he entered the office of his father's friend, John Nash, as an assistant. Nash found his knowledge of Gothic a useful asset, and Repton afterwards claimed the credit for the alterations to Corsham Court which were carried out by Nash in 1797–8. Repton's partial responsibility for this and other buildings was, however, never publicly acknowledged by Nash, and rather than act as a 'ghost', he joined his father at Hare Street, in order to collaborate with him in his publications and in the architectural side of his practice. From 1802 (the date he left Nash's office) until 1818, J. A. Repton was concerned in the alteration of many country houses whose gardens his father was improving. After his father's death in the latter year, he practised from Springfield in Essex. He was stone-deaf from infancy and for this reason lived a very retired existence, though his handicap did not prevent him from visiting the Continent in 1821–2, in order to improve various estates in Holland and Germany, including those of Prince Pückler-Muskau at Muskau in Silesia (cf Ackermann, *Repository of Arts*, 3rd ser., xi, 1828, 313–14) and of Prince Hardenburg at Neu Hardenburg, nr. Frankfort-on-Oder, and at Glienicke, nr. Potsdam.

Repton specialized in the enlargement and restoration of country houses in an Elizabethan style that owed something to East Anglian manor-houses. He also designed some classical houses, of which Sheringham Hall is the most attractive example, and one neo-Romanesque church. In 1809 he and his brother shared with C. Bacon the first prize for the design of public buildings then intended to be built in Westminster [P.R.O., Works 8/10B, 24], and in 1810 they gained the second prize in the competition for the Bethlehem Hospital. Repton also competed for the Houses of Parliament. He exhibited at the Royal Academy between 1798 and 1804.

Repton's inclinations were antiquarian, and in later years he took a strong interest in the Camdenian movement, even contributing a paper on Gothic mouldings to the *Ecclesiologist*. He was elected F.S.A. in 1803, and was a frequent contributor to *Archaeologia* (see vols. xv, xvi, xix, xxi, xxiv and xxvii). Many articles by him appeared in the *Gentleman's Magazine* from 1795 onwards, and in the *Jnl. of the British Archaeological*

---

[1] Mr. Nigel Temple kindly informs me that he has identified drawings for these lodges in a sketch-book (now at the Royal Pavilion Art Gallery, Brighton) used by G. S. Repton while working in John Nash's office.

[2] Some 'remarkably neat rustic cottages' designed by Repton at Norman Court, Hants., are mentioned by G. F. Prosser in his *Select Illustrations of Hampshire* (1833).

---

[1] These were published by the Gregg Press in 1965 as J. A. Repton, *Norwich Cathedral at the End of the Eighteenth Century*, with an introduction by S. Rowland Pierce.

Association (cf. xvii, 175–80). In 1820 he printed eighty copies of an 'olden-tyme romance', entitled *A Trew Hystorie of the Prince Radapanthus*, and in 1839 a paper on beards and moustaches which he had read to the Society of Antiquaries. The drawings of Norwich Cathedral in Britton's *Cathedral Antiquities* (vol. ii, 1816) were his work. He died unmarried at Springfield on 26 November 1860. Frederick Mackenzie was a pupil.

[*A.P.S.D.*; *D.N.B.*; obituaries in *Gent's Mag.* x, 1861, 107–10, and *Jnl. of the British Archaeological Assn.* xvii, 1861, 175–80; J. Summerson, 'A Repton Portfolio', *R.I.B.A. Jnl.*, 25 Feb. 1833; *Catalogue of the R.I.B.A. Drawings Coll.*]

CORSHAM COURT, WILTS., assisted John Nash in alterations, including remodelling of north front for P. C. Methuen, 1797–8, Gothic; destroyed 1844–9 [above, p. 583; drawing for north front in Mellon Collection attributed to Repton].

*BRENTRY HILL, nr. BRISTOL, GLOS., for William Payne, c. 1802 [exhib. at R.A. 1802; Loudon, 282–3].

*COTE or COTHAM BANK, OLVESTON, GLOS., for William Broderip, before 1803; dem. [Loudon, 130, 284 n.].

*ORGAN HALL, ALDENHAM, HERTS., designs (? executed) for William Towgood, before 1803; dem. [Loudon, 131, 284 n.].

*STAPLETON, nr. BRISTOL, GLOS., designs (? executed) for Dr. Lovell, M.D., before 1803 [Loudon, 131, 284 n.].

*STANAGE PARK, RADNORSHIRE, enlarged for Charles Rogers, 1803–7; further additions by E. Haycock 1845 ['Red Book' at Stanage; J. Williams, *History of the County of Radnor*, 1905 (written c. 1810), 241].

*BARNINGHAM HALL, NORFOLK, alterations to south front for John Thruston Mott, 1805, Elizabethan style [Loudon, 435–9].

*LAXTON HALL, NORTHANTS., for George Freke Evans, 1805–11, with hall by George Dance, junior [J. P. Neale, *Views of Seats*, 2nd ser., i, 1824; Loudon, 506–7 and fig. 207; Stroud, 148; Sir Gyles Isham, 'Laxton Hall', *Northants. Antiquarian Soc.* lxvi, 1969, 18–21].

*HARLESTONE HOUSE, NORTHANTS., remodelled for Robert Andrew, 1809–11; dem. 1939 [drawings at Althorp House and in the Northants. Record Office; Loudon, 428–9] (J. A. Gotch, *Squires' Homes of Northamptonshire*, 1939, figs. 94–6).

*UPPARK, SUSSEX, alterations, including remodelling of dining-room, for Sir Harry Fetherstonhaugh, 1810–13 [C. Hussey in *C. Life*, 14, 21, 28 June 1941].

*SHERINGHAM HALL, NORFOLK, for Abbot Upcher, 1813–19 [C. Hussey in *C. Life*, 31 Jan., 7 Feb. 1957].

*COBHAM HALL, KENT, alterations and additions for the 4th Earl of Darnley, c. 1813–31, including ceiling of Queen Elizabeth's Room (1817), and Brewer's Gate and Shepherd's Gate lodges, Elizabethan style [Loudon, 418–19, 564; Stroud, 52; drawings in library of Cambridge University School of Architecture and R.I.B.A. Coll.].

*BOURN HALL, CAMBS., reconstructed for the 5th Earl De La Warr, 1817–19, Elizabethan [J. P. Neale, *Views of Seats*, 1st ser., vi, 1823].

SPRING (WOODCHESTER) PARK, nr. STROUD, GLOS., alterations, including library and dining-room, for the 1st Earl of Ducie, c. 1820; dem. c. 1845 [J. & H. S. Storer, *Delineations of the County of Gloucester*, 1828, 40; cf. drawings in R.I.B.A. Coll.].

BUCKHURST (formerly STONELANDS) PARK, WITHYHAM, SUSSEX, remodelled for the 5th Earl De La Warr, c. 1830–5, Elizabethan [Colbran's *New Guide for Tunbridge Wells*, 1840, 284; B. Burke, *Visitation of Seats and Arms* ii, 1853, 162; cf. J. Harris, *Catalogue of British Drawings for Architecture, etc., in American Collections*, 1971, 178].

SPRINGFIELD, nr. CHELMSFORD, ESSEX, HOLY TRINITY CHURCH, 1842–3, Romanesque [*Gent's Mag.* 1843 (ii), 421].

ATTINGHAM PARK, SALOP., Tern Lodge for the 2nd Lord Berwick, date uncertain [R.I.B.A.D.].

Note: J. A. Repton's designs for BAILBROOK HOUSE, BATHEASTON, SOMERSET (c. 1805), BAYHAM ABBEY, SUSSEX (c. 1800), GREAT TEW PARK, OXON. (1803), PANSHANGER, HERTS. (1800), and SCARISBRICK HALL, LANCS. (1802), were not carried out.

REVELEY, WILLEY (1760–1799), born on 14 March 1760, was the son of William Reveley (d. 1806), a member of a North Country family which had inherited the estate of Newby Wiske in Yorkshire by the marriage of William Reveley (d. 1725 and probably the architect's grandfather) to Margery, daughter and heiress of Robert Willey. Willey became a pupil of Sir William Chambers in 1777 and was admitted to the Royal Academy Schools the same year. From July 1781 to December 1782 he was employed by Chambers as assistant clerk of works at Somerset House. From 1784 to 1789 he accompanied Sir Richard Worsley as 'architect and draughtsman' on his tour through Italy, Greece and Egypt, in the course of which he spent some time in Athens studying the temples made famous by Stuart and Revett. The MS. journal describing his journey from Rome to Malta, Crete, Athens and Delos in 1785 is in the R.I.B.A. Collection.

On his return to England, Reveley appeared

---

* In association with his father.

to have every prospect of a successful career. He had already begun to exhibit at the Royal Academy, and he had acquired a considerable reputation as an authority on Greek architecture. He was a friend of Thomas Holcroft and William Godwin, and assisted Jeremy Bentham in preparing the plans for a panopticon prison which were published by the latter in 1791. In 1792–5 the church of ALL SAINTS, SOUTHAMPTON, was erected to his designs by a builder named John Hookey: it was an interesting essay in neo-classical design with an Ionic portico and a segmental, coffered ceiling 61 feet wide. It was destroyed by bombing in 1940. He also designed a mansion at WINDMILL HILL, SUSSEX, for W. H. Pigou, completed in 1798, and illustrated in G. Richardson, *New Vitruvius Britannicus* i, 1810, pls. 24–6: and he was the architect of the lodges at PARHAM in SUSSEX, the seat of Sir Cecil Bisshopp, Bart. (1789), and of those at STOURHEAD, WILTS. (1793), designs for which he exhibited at the Royal Academy in those years. References in Sir John Soane's journal suggest that in 1798 Reveley may also have made designs for a house for W. Moffat at WESTON, nr. SOUTHAMPTON (dem.).

In 1794 he was chosen to edit the third volume of Stuart's *Antiquities of Athens*, and in the introduction showed himself an enthusiastic champion of the use of the Greek orders in contemporary architecture. Indeed, he did not hesitate to take Sir William Chambers himself to task for his strictures on the 'gusto Greco'. 'Sir William', he wrote, 'seems to insinuate that the Parthenon would gain considerably with respect to beauty by the addition of a steeple. A judicious observer of the fine arts would scarcely be more surprised were he to propose to effect this improvement by adding to it a Chinese pagoda.' This was not in the best of taste, nor was it prudent in a young architect to make fun of the Surveyor-General of His Majesty's Works. 'But Mr. Reveley had rather an awkward way of letting loose his opinions; and had habituated himself to a sarcastic mode of delivering them.' It had already, in 1789, been responsible for his separation from Worsley, who finished his tour alone, and if it alienated even those who could appreciate his talents, it was fatal with the less enlightened clientele of aldermen and churchwardens. At Canterbury it was exasperating to learn that his plans for the County Infirmary were to be executed under the supervision of a 'common Carpenter', 'in order to save the expense of an architect'; but his annoyance was so unconcealed that it cost him the commission altogether. Some such incident may have led to the rejection of his designs for the new Pump Room at Bath, which were said to be 'of great beauty and elegance, replete with convenience, full of rare contrivance, and disposed in an original style of accommodation', and a similar lack of success attended the

plans for wet docks on the Thames which he submitted to Parliament in 1796 (see *Parliamentary Reports* xiv, 1803, 342b, 422, 424, etc., *Monthly Magazine*, 1799, 147, and Sir Joseph Broodbank, *History of the Port of London* i, 1921, 87). Even at Southampton, his plans for the new church had to be 'modified somewhat drastically to suit the prejudice of the mayor and aldermen of that city'.

Reveley died, 'after a few hours illness, in the prime of life', on 6 July 1799. His widow married John Gisborne and became intimate with the poet Shelley in Italy. A portrait of Reveley is in the possession of Mr. C. E. Kenney. Some of his drawings of buildings in Egypt and Greece are in the Victoria and Albert Museum. A folio volume of his 'Tracings and Drawings of Architectural Ornaments' and the sale catalogue of his drawings, designs and books (Christie's, 11–12 May 1801) are in Sir John Soane's Museum. Measured drawings by him of the Pyramids, formerly in the library of New College, Oxford, cannot now be found.

Reveley's son Henry Willey Reveley (*c.* 1789–1875) practised first in Cape Town, where in 1828 he obtained the post of Civil Engineer and Superintendent of Buildings, and then in Australia. At Cape Town his work included St. Andrew's Presbyterian Church (Doric) and St. George's Church (Ionic). He returned to England and died at Reading in 1875, aged 86. He and his wife Cleobulina are buried in Reading Cemetery.

[*A.P.S.D.*; *D.N.B.*; J. Nichols, *Literary Anecdotes of the Eighteenth Century* ix, 1815, 148–50; *Gent's Mag.* 1799 (ii), 627, 1801 (i), 419–20, 1806 (i), 587; A. T. Bolton, *The Portrait of Sir John Soane*, 1927, 25, 60; *The Works of Jeremy Bentham*, ed. J. Bowring, x, 1843, 251–2; F. L. Jones, *Maria Gisborne and Edward E. Williams: their Journals and Letters*, Oklahoma 1951, 3 *et seq.*; *C. Life*, 19 June 1958, 1382; *Catalogue of the R.I.B.A. Drawings Coll.*]

REVETT, NICHOLAS (1720–1804), was the second son of John Revett of Brandeston Hall, nr. Framlingham in Suffolk, where he was born. He left England for Italy in September 1742, and studied painting in Rome under Cavaliere Benefiale. Here he became friendly with James Stuart, Matthew Brettingham, junior, and Gavin Hamilton, the painter. In April 1748 he accompanied them on an expedition to Naples, in the course of which they decided to visit Athens in order to measure the Greek antiquities there. This proposal was encouraged by many of the English dilettanti in Rome and money was raised to finance the expedition. Hamilton and Brettingham were unable to take part, but Stuart and Revett left Rome for Venice in March 1750. At Venice they made the most of an enforced delay by visiting the antiquities at Pola in Dalmatia. They became acquainted with Sir James Gray, the British resident in Venice, through whose agency they were elected members of the Society of Dilettanti in 1751. Reaching Athens in the spring of 1751, they remained there, with some intervals, until March 1753. In spite of the difficulties caused by the disturbed state of the city's government and an outbreak of plague, they measured and drew all the principal monuments of antiquity in Athens. Revett was responsible for the architectural part of the drawings and it was from him that, according to a writer in the *Gentleman's Magazine* of March 1788, 'Mr. Stuart first caught the ideas of that science, in which (quitting the painter's art) he afterwards made so conspicuous a figure'. On their return to England in 1755, they obtained support from the Society of Dilettanti for the publication of their discoveries, and the first volume of *The Antiquities of Athens, measured and delineated by James Stuart, F.R.S. and F.S.A., and Nicholas Revett, Painters and Architects*, appeared in 1762. The book enjoyed an immediate success, but all the profits, as well as most of the credit, went to Stuart, who had bought out Revett's interest before the publication of the first volume. Revett, however, remained an active member of the Society of Dilettanti, and was chosen by them to go on an expedition to the coast of Asia Minor with Richard Chandler (a Fellow of Magdalen College, Oxford, and author of *Marmora Oxoniensia*, 1763) and William Pars ('a young painter of promising talents'). They left England in June 1764, returning in September 1766. Revett undertook the measuring of the architectural antiquities, and a selection of the drawings was afterwards published by the Society of Dilettanti under his editorship as *The Antiquities of Ionia* (2 fols. 1769–97). His original drawings are now in the R.I.B.A. Drawings Collection and the British Museum (Add. MSS. 21152–3). Thus Revett was the leading figure in the production of two books which were to be of great importance both in disseminating a knowledge of Greek architecture in Europe, and in providing sources for the later Greek Revival in England.

Revett, having private means, did not practise extensively as an architect, and his chief works were undertaken for friends like Henry Dawkins, for whom soon after 1766 he added a portico to STANDLYNCH (now TRAFALGAR HOUSE), WILTS., and designed the ceilings, chimney-pieces, and many internal decorations [*Vitruvius Britannicus* v, 1771, pls. 78–81; C. Hussey in *C. Life*, 13, 20 July 1945]. For Sir Francis Dashwood (afterwards Lord Le Despenser), a member of the Dilettanti Society, he added the Ionic portico to the west front of WEST WYCOMBE PARK, BUCKS. This was based on the Temple of Bacchus at Teos which Revett had measured in 1764–6.

According to a MS. note in the copy of Langley's *Hundred of Desborough* in the Library of the Society of Antiquaries, it was completed in 1771. The Dashwood papers (now in the Bodleian Library, Oxford) show that Revett was still working at West Wycombe in 1778, 1779 and 1780, presumably in connection with the Temple of Flora (dem.) and the 'Music Room' or Island Temple, both of which he is stated to have designed in a letter from James Dawkins, junior, to the publisher of the fourth volume of the *Antiquities of Athens*. Some of his drawings for the Music Temple are in the Bodleian Library (Gough Misc. Ant. fol. 4). There is no documentary evidence that he designed the church at West Wycombe, which was rebuilt by Lord Le Despenser in the years 1761–3, and Dawkins specifically told Joseph Taylor in 1809 that Revett was not its architect. Dawkins's claim that Revett designed the east (Doric) portico of the house is incorrect, as it was built in 1754–5, long before he had any connection with West Wycombe.

The only other building of importance of which Revett is known to have been the architect is the church at AYOT ST. LAWRENCE, HERTS., which he designed for Sir Lionel Lyde in 1778. It was consecrated on 28 July 1779 (*Gent's Mag.* 1779, 374; 1789 (ii), 972). As at Standlynch, he employed the Order of the Temple of Apollo at Delos, whose shafts were fluted at the extremities only.

From a letter in the Bodleian Library (Gough Misc. Ant. fol. 4, no. 174), it appears that in 1757 Revett designed an ornamental 'portico' which was built in the garden of his brother's house at Brandeston in Suffolk. This, if Grecian in character, would have been one of the earliest recorded buildings in that style. He also designed the memorial tablet to Alexander Ballantyne, M.D., in Salisbury Cathedral (erected 1783), and the monument to James Dawkins (d. 1766) in Chipping Norton Church, Oxon.

In 1791 Revett was made an Honorary Member of the Architects' Club on its foundation. Towards the end of his life he is said to have been in financial difficulties. He died on 3 June 1804, aged 84, and was buried in Brandeston Churchyard. There is an inscription to his memory in the north pavilion of Ayot St. Lawrence Church. His library was sold at Christie's on 26–27 June 1804. There is a copy of the catalogue in Sir John Soane's Museum. A portrait of Revett in old age by G. Dance, R.A., is engraved in W. Daniell's *Collection of Portraits* (1808–14). There is an engraving of a portrait by Allan Ramsay at the R.I.B.A., and E. B. Jupp, in his *Catalogue of Original Drawings, illustrating the Catalogues of the Society of Artists*, 1871, 7, notes an engraving by William Wollett of a 'Portrait of Revett sketching Ruins' by James Stuart (1765).

A large volume containing some drawings by Revett and a number of proof engravings (chiefly for the *Ionian Antiquities*) is in the Bodleian Library (Gough Misc. Ant. fol. 4). Other drawings by him are at West Wycombe Park. His copies of Chandler's *Travels in Asia Minor*, 1775, and *Travels in Greece*, 1776, with MS. notes, were bought at his sale by George Saunders, who presented them to the British Museum: they were republished in 1825 with the notes.

[*A.P.S.D.*; *D.N.B.*; Lesley Lawrence, 'Stuart and Revett; their Literary and Architectural Careers', *Jnl. of the Warburg Institute* ii, 1938–9; memoirs in Wood, *Antiquities of Athens*, vol. iv, 1816, pp. xxviii–xxxi; *Gent's Mag.* lxxiv (ii), 1804, 690, 860; lxxix (ii), 1809, 596–7; xci (ii), 1821, 423; letter from James Dawkins, junior, in B.M., Add. MS. 22152, f. 35, describing his architectural works; Dora Wiebenson, *Sources of Greek Revival Architecture*, 1969; J. Mordaunt Crook, *The Greek Revival*, 1972; Gervase Jackson-Stops, *West Wycombe Park* (National Trust guide-book, 1973).]

REYNOLDS, ESAU (1725–1778), was the son of Jonathan Reynolds, a prosperous carpenter and joiner at Trowbridge in Wiltshire. Esau followed his father into the family business, but, with the advantage of a better education, also practised as an architect. He designed the TOWN BRIDGE at TROWBRIDGE in 1777, altered the BRIDEWELL at DEVIZES in 1775, and was responsible for repairs and alterations to several local churches, notably at RODE, where he rebuilt the clerestory in 1773, replacing the original window by 'segmental-headed substitutes' which were in turn removed in 1872. His principal work was the almshouses known as HEYTESBURY HOSPITAL, which were built to his designs in 1766–8. In the R.I.B.A. Drawings Collection there is a design for a Palladian gateway signed 'Esau Reynols Delin. 1748'. On 29 September 1778 Reynolds was returning from a visit to Bath when his horse bolted, he 'struggled to stop him for above two miles' but eventually fell and was killed on the spot. He left a number of books, pictures, busts, statues and medals. [K. H. Rogers, *Esau Reynolds of Trowbridge*, Trowbridge 1967.]

REYNOLDS, SAMUEL WILLIAM (1773–1835), is best known as an artist and engraver (see *D.N.B.*). There is evidence that he also acted as an architect. In 1810–11 Lee Antonie of Colworth, to whom Reynolds had been introduced by their mutual friend Samuel Whitbread, employed him to supervise various alterations to the offices and grounds at COLWORTH HOUSE, BEDS. [Bedfordshire Record Office, UN 370, 457, 509, etc.] In 1813 he fitted up a house in STRATFORD PLACE, LONDON, for Lord Henry Fitzgerald [*ibid.*, 384, 387], and in 1815 he designed FOSTON

RECTORY, LEICS. [Leicestershire Record Office, Faculty papers]. Reynolds exhibited regularly at the Royal Academy, but none of his exhibits were of an architectural character.

REYNOLDS, THOMAS, of London, contracted in 1759 to build WIVENHOE PARK, ESSEX, for Isaac Rebow, apparently to his own designs [Rosemary Feesey, *Wivenhoe Park*, 1963, 10–14]. A person of this name signs an elevation of the Pantheon in Rome among drawings collected by William Stukeley and now in the Bodleian Library (Gough Maps 230, p. 373). In 1774 Thomas Reynolds of Islington, surveyor, then aged 39, was appointed District Surveyor for the parishes of St. Mary, Islington, and St Sepulchre, Holborn [Middlesex County Records, General Orders No. 10].

RHODES, HENRY (–1846), was articled at an early age to William Porden. In about 1808 he entered the Land Revenue Office as a clerk. He subsequently succeeded Thomas Leverton as one of the two surveyors to the Office of Woods, Forests and Land Revenue (amalgamated in 1832 with the Office of Works). Owing to ill-health he reitred on a pension in 1840 and was succeeded by James Pennethorne. He exhibited occasionally at the Royal Academy, and was one of the first members of the Council of the Institute of British Architects. He had antiquarian interests, and was a member of the Royal Archaeological Institute. As an architect he has to be judged chiefly by Egham Church, a somewhat clumsy essay in the style of Sir John Soane. Rhodes died at his house in Margaret Street, Cavendish Square, on 27 January 1846. His library and collection were sold by Christie's on 24 March and the following days. [*Gent's Mag.* 1846 (i), 329; *Builder* iv, 1846, 58; *A.P.S.D.*]

CHEQUERS, BUCKS., alterations for Sir George Russell, Bart., 1802, Gothic [L. Fleming, *Memoir and Select Letters of Samuel Lysons*, 1934, 35–6; exhib. at R.A. 1805].

FIRLE PLACE, SUSSEX, proposed alterations for the 3rd Viscount Gage, 1807 [drawings now or formerly at Firle].

HALTON CHURCH, BUCKS., 1813, Gothic; reconstructed 1886–7 [*Builder* v, 1846, 58].

EGHAM CHURCH, SURREY, 1818–20 [exhib. at R.A. 1817].

LONDON, premises at corner of PALL MALL EAST and COCKSPUR STREET for Messrs. Hancock & Rixon, glass manufacturers, *c.* 1830; dem. [J. Elmes, *Metropolitan Improvements*, 1831, 155] (N. Whittock, *On the Construction and Decoration of the Shop Fronts of London*, 1840, pl. ix).

BARRINGTON HALL, ESSEX, unexecuted designs for extensive alterations for Sir William Barrington, Bart., 1833 [Essex Record Office].

LONDON, ST. JAMES'S PARK, entrance from Duke Street, Whitehall, in conjunction with T. Chawner, 1834; dem. [*Architectural Mag.* i, 1834, 316].

LONDON, COX'S HOTEL, NOS. 53–55 JERMYN STREET, in conjunction with T. Chawner, 1836–7; dem. 1923–4 [*A.P.S.D.*; *Survey of London* xxix, 275].

LONDON, stabling at corner of HAYMARKET and COVENTRY STREET, in conjunction with T. Chawner; dem. [*A.P.S.D.*].

RHODES, WILLIAM, was an obscure London architect of the eighteenth century. In 1772, as 'William Rhodes of St. James's Westminster, architect and surveyor', he took an apprentice named Robert Greening [P.R.O., Apprenticeship Registers], and in 1774 and 1776 Thomas Lee (*q.v.*) exhibited architectural designs at the Royal Academy from 'Mr. Rhodes', Great Marlborough Street'. Rhodes subscribed to George Richardson's *Book of Ceilings* (1776), and was presumably the William Rhodes who in 1771–4 redecorated the drawing-room and dining-room at DRAYTON HOUSE, NORTHANTS., for Viscount Sackville [*Associated Architectural Societies' Reports and Papers* xxxiii, 1915–16, 78–80] (*C. Life*, 3 June 1965).

RIBBANS, WILLIAM PARKES (–1871), practised in Ipswich, where he died on 15 January 1871 [Principal Probate Registry, Calendar of Probates]. In 1835 he won the competition for the EAST SUFFOLK HOSPITAL at IPSWICH, which was erected to his designs in 1835–6. It has a striking but awkwardly composed façade [J. Woodderspoon, *Memorials of Ipswich*, 1850, 10; *Ipswich Jnl.*, 13 June 1835, 6 August 1836]. F. B. Ribbans, a schoolmaster who in 1843 published *An Essay on Perspective ... intended for Architectural Students and Civil Engineers*, was presumably a relation.

RICAUTI, T— J—, was a pupil of John Foulston. He published two books, entitled *Rustic Architecture*, 1840, containing 42 plates of designs for picturesque cottages, etc., and *Sketches for Rustic Work including Bridges, Park and Garden Buildings, Seats and Furniture*, 1842, 2nd ed. 1848. The latter was dedicated to Sir Robert Howland of Orwell Park, Suffolk, whom the author acknowledged as his first patron. Both were intended to demonstrate 'the picturesque and pleasing appearance of rough wood, thatch etc., when applied as the only decorations of rural buildings'. A design for a half-timbered cottage by Ricauti is given by Loudon, *Encyclopaedia of Rural Architecture*, 1846, 1145–6. In the list of contributors Loudon described Ricauti as 'deceased', so he must have died between 1842 and 1846.

RICE, WILLIAM (*c.* 1734–1789), was successively Clerk of Works at Richmond from 1751 to 1758, and at Hampton Court from 1758 until his death in 1789. He was also Surveyor of the Horse Guards, and from 1768 to 1780 Surveyor of Buildings to H.M. Customs. As Surveyor of the Horse Guards he was succeeded by his nephew Thomas Rice, who also held his uncle's former post at Hampton Court from 1808 until his death in 1810. A portrait of William Rice at the age of 10, painted by R. Scadder in 1744, is in the possession of the proprietors of Lord's Cricket Ground.

RICHARDBY, JAMES (*c.* 1776–1846), practised in Bradford for many years until his death on 6 August 1846 at the age of 70. He was a prominent Liberal and in 1838 received a presentation silver cup in recognition of forty years' service to the Liberal cause. His works in Bradford included a MARKET HOUSE built at HALL INGS in 1823, but demolished two years later because it infringed the manorial market rights [John James, *Continuation to the History of Bradford*, 1866, 98]; the COURT HOUSE, HALL INGS, 1834–5, a handsome classical building demolished *c.* 1960 [W. Cudworth, *History of Bradford Corporation*, 1881, 72]; and FIELD HOUSE, SMITH LANE (now part of the Royal Infirmary), for Mrs. Susannah Ward, 1835–6 [W. Cudworth, *History of Manningham, Heaton and Allerton*, 1896, 55] [information from Mr. D. N. Griffiths].

RICHARDS, GEORGE, of Rotherhithe, submitted a design for rebuilding London Bridge in 1823 [*Catalogue of the Exhibition of Designs for rebuilding London Bridge*, 1823, Soane Museum, P.C. 55]. He may have been the author of some designs for stables signed 'George Richards Archt. Truro 10 April 1826' [J. Harris, *Catalogue of British Designs for Architecture, etc., in American Collections*, 1971, 178].

RICHARDS, JOHN (1690–1778), was born at Mariansleigh, N. Devon, and received 'some little instruction at a Grammar School'. As 'his Genius chiefly inclined him to Mathematical studies', he was apprenticed to a joiner in Exeter named Abraham Voysey 'who also made and sold Gunther's scales and Sea-Quadrants'. Voysey died in 1710 and in the following year Richards, then only 20, married his widow and carried on his business. Eventually he gave up joinery and building and was chiefly employed as a valuer, accountant and surveyor of land and buildings. He was the author of two tracts on Life Annuities, etc. (1730, 1739), and of another on Cask Gauging (1740). In 1741–3 he gratuitously designed THE DEVON AND EXETER HOSPITAL in SOUTHERNHAY, EXETER, enlarged in 1772, 1856, 1896, etc. Towards the end of his life he became

686

insane, dying in January 1778 at the age of 87. [W. G. Hoskins, *Two Thousand Years in Exeter*, 1960, 89; obituary in *Exeter Flying Post* of Jan. 1778, *ex inf*. Prof. W. G. Hoskins; *Trans Devonshire Association* civ, 1972, 176.]

RICHARDS, WILLIAM, of Penzance, designed the COINAGE HALL at HELSTON, CORNWALL, in 1807 [Cornwall Reccrd Office, 37A/BAR/33, signed drawings]. He was presumably the architect called Richards who designed SAUNDERS HILL, nr. PADSTOW, CORNWALL, for Thomas Rawlings in about 1810 [J. P. Neale, *Views of Seats*, 2nd ser., ii, 1825; S. Lysons, *Magna Britannia* iii, 253]. As the latter is somewhat Soaneic in character it is possible that its author was the William Richards who was a clerk in Sir John Soane's office from 1789 to 1803 [A. T. Bolton, *The Works of Sir John Soane*, 1924, p. xl].

RICHARDSON, GEORGE (–*c*. 1813), began life as a draughtsman in the office of Robert and James Adam. He may have been apprenticed to their elder brother John Adam, for on 10 March 1759 he was described as 'apprentice' when witnessing the latter's will in Edinburgh. From 1760 to 1763 he accompanied James Adam on his Grand Tour, gaining in this way a first-hand knowledge of the antique sources that formed the basis of the Adam style. He was not, however, treated at all generously by his master, and complained in a letter to a friend that he was obliged to conceal such sketches as he had made for his own use, as Adam would be very angry if he discovered them, although they were made in Richardson's own time. On his return to Britain he had, however, little prospect of establishing an independent practice, 'well knowing my own incapacity, small fortune, want of books, and little hopes of interest'. For some years he continued to be employed as a draughtsman in the Adams' London office. Exactly when he left their service is not known. The fact that in 1765 he obtained a premium from the Society of Arts for an architectural design may indicate his emancipation, and from 1766 onwards he exhibited at the Society of Artists under his own name. According to the Society of Arts register he was under 30 in 1765, and in 1774 he stated that he had been 'draughtsman and designer' to the Adam brothers for 'upwards of eighteen years'.

Although he was an accomplised draughtsman and designer of internal decoration in the Adam style, Richardson appears to have designed few complete buildings, and to have made a living chiefly by his publications and by acting as a drawing-master (see advertisement in his *New Designs in Architecture*). Towards the end of his life he was in seriously reduced circumstances. Joseph Nollekens is known to have helped him

financially, and Joseph Farington records that he received 30 guineas out of the Royal Academy Charity Fund in 1807. The exact date of his death is not known, but news of it reached Joseph Farington on 16 May 1814, and in March of the same year the *Gentleman's Magazine* reported that the drawings and prints of 'the late Mr. George Richardson' had been sold on 29 November 1813.

Richardson competed for the Royal Exchange at Dublin in 1769. In 1783 he exhibited at the Royal Academy the 'Elevation of a church building at Stapleford, in Leicestershire, for the Earl of Harborough'. This elaborately Gothic church was one of three built by the 4th Earl of Harborough, the others being Teigh, Rutland (1782, Gothic), and Saxby, Leics. (1789, classical). It is likely that the same architect was responsible for all three. According to J. Throsby's *Select Views in Leicestershire* i, 1790, 153, the 'architect' of Stapleford Church was Christopher Staveley of Melton Mowbray, but he may have been carrying out plans provided by Richardson.

As a decorative designer Richardson appears to have played an important part at KEDLESTON HALL, DERBYSHIRE, in the late 1760s, for there are a number of drawings for ceilings, etc., signed by him both at Kedleston and in the Soane Museum, and in 1776 he exhibited at the Royal Academy 'The Ceiling executed in the Grecian Hall at Keddlestone'. Ceilings designed by him at Kedleston, Drapers' Hall, London, and Sir Lawrence Dundas's house in Edinburgh are illustrated in his *Book of Ceilings*. He was also employed at BROCKENHURST PARK, HAMPSHIRE, in 1775 [*Antique Collector*, Aug. 1954, 134], and a design by him for a ceiling at BENTON HOUSE, NORTHUMBERLAND, is illustrated by John Harris, *Catalogue of British Drawings for Architecture, etc., in American Collections*, 1971, 180–1.

Richardson's publications were, in order of date: *Ædes Pembrochianae*, 1774 (an account of the classical antiquities at Wilton House); *A Book of Ceilings composed in the Stile of the Antique Grotesque*, dedicated to Lord Scarsdale, 1774, 1776, 1793; *Iconology, or a Collection of Emblematical Figures*, 2 vols. 1779–80 (an English version of Cesare Ripa's *Iconologia* of 1593); *A New Collection of Chimney Pieces*, dedicated to Sir Lawrence Dundas, 1781; *A Treatise on the Five Orders of Architecture* (with observations on antiquities in Rome, Pola and Southern France, made in 1760–3), dedicated to Thomas Sandby, 1787; *New Designs in Architecture* (dedicated to Henry, Earl of Gainsborough), 1792; *New Designs of Vases, Tripods, etc.*, 1793; *Capitals of Columns and Friezes from the Antique*, 1793; *Original Designs for Country Seats or Villas*, 1795; *The New Vitruvius Britannicus*, 2 vols. 1802–8 and 1808–10; and *A Collection of Ornaments in the Antique Style*, by G. Richardson & Son, 1816.

The most ambitious of these works was the *New Vitruvius Britannicus*, which attempted to do for English architecture of the late eighteenth century what Colen Campbell and Woolfe and Gandon had done for earlier decades. Except in the case of *Iconology* Richardson engraved in aquatint all the plates for his books. In his later works he was assisted by his son William, who himself exhibited decorative designs at the Royal Academy in 1783, 1784, 1793 and 1794.

[*A.P.S.D.*; *D.N.B.*; *Gent's Mag.* 1814 (i), 210; Joseph Farington's diary, 12 July 1807, 12 July 1812, 16 May 1814; J. T. Smith, *Nollekens and his Times* i, 1829, 110–12; *Builder* xxvii, 781; John Fleming, *Robert Adam and his Circle*, 1962, 368–9, 377, etc.]

RICHARDSON, JOHN (1774–*c.* 1865), practised in Kendal, Westmorland, where he designed the NEW THEATRE, 1828–9 [C. Nicholson, *Annals of Kendal*, 1861, 297], THE INFANTS' SCHOOL, 1829 [*ibid.*], and the WHITE HART HOTEL, *c.* 1830 [drawings in Cumbria Record Office, Kendal].

RICHMOND, JOHN, appears to have designed RICCARTON CHURCH, AYRSHIRE, 1823, as his name appears on a set of drawings preserved in the church [G. Hay, *The Architecture of Scottish Post-Reformation Churches*, 1957, 135]. The façade of this otherwise unremarkable Georgian church is enlivened by two pediments with an unusual concave profile.

RICKETTS, JOHN, was one of a family of masons and carvers who were active in Gloucester throughout the eighteenth century (see Rupert Gunnis, *Dictionary of British Sculptors*, 1968, 321–2). He was probably a grandson of John Ricketts (d. 1734), the founder of the firm. In addition to designing and carving a number of elegant monuments, he appears to have designed the triumphal arch erected in Gloucester in 1777 in honour of William Bromley Chester, M.P. for that city. An engraving of the arch in Bishop Hooper's Museum is signed 'John Ricketts, Statuary at Gloucester'. In 1784 Ricketts was among those who surveyed the tower of St. Nicholas Church, Gloucester, receiving £1 11s. 6d. for his plan [Gloucester Public Library, extracts from Vestry Minutes]. Documents in private hands are said to show that he built and presumably designed EASTGATE HOUSE, GLOUCESTER, *c.* 1780.

RICKMAN, THOMAS (1776–1841), born on 8 June 1776, was the eldest son of Joseph Rickman, an apothecary at Maidenhead. The Rickmans were a large, close-knit, Quaker family of long standing. Thomas was destined by his father for a medical career, but he found medicine un-

congenial, and after various vicissitudes gave it up in favour of commerce. In 1804 he started business in London as a corn-factor and married his first cousin Lucy Rickman. Both actions proved to be disastrous. The marriage was not sanctioned by the Friends, who proceeded to disown Thomas and his wife,[1] and in 1807 the business failed and left him heavily in debt. He found employment in the office of a Liverpool insurance-broker, but the death a few weeks later of his wife, coupled with his other misfortunes, reduced him to a state of near despair from which he recovered only gradually. It was during this period of acute depression that he began to take the long country walks in the course of which he developed a latent interest in medieval architecture. Being 'very minute in his observation on any subject which he selected', he began to classify the window-tracery and other architectural details which he noted and to arrange them in a typological sequence which he labelled 'Norman', 'Early English', 'Decorated English' and 'Perpendicular English' (terms which he was already using in his diary as early as 1811). Soon afterwards he joined a small Philosophical Society in Liverpool in which scientific subjects were discussed, and it was to this society that in September 1811 he gave the first of a series of lectures on medieval architecture. In 1812, with the encouragement of George Harrison, an ironfounder of Chester with whom he became friendly, he wrote an account of the architectural history of Chester Cathedral (eventually printed in the *Journal of the Architectural, Archaeological and Historic Society of Chester*, 1864, 277–8). He also wrote a long article on Gothic architecture for *Smith's Panorama of Arts and Sciences* (Liverpool 1812–15), which was reprinted separately in 1817 as *An Attempt to discriminate the Styles of English Architecture from the Conquest to the Reformation*. This, the first systematic treatise on Gothic architecture in England, soon became well known, and Rickman's nomenclature was followed by all subsequent writers on the subject. The book was reprinted, with additions, several times during its author's lifetime. A seventh edition, edited by J. H. Parker, appeared in 1881.

In addition to the works already mentioned, Rickman published 'A Tour in Normandy and Picardy in 1832' (*Archaeologia* xxv, 1833), 'Four Letters on the Ecclesiastical Architecture of France and England' (*ibid.*) and an important paper on pre-Conquest architecture (*Archaeologia* xxvi, 1836, 26–46). He contributed the 'architectural observations' to J. S. Cotman's *Specimens of Architectural Remains*, 1838. He was elected a Fellow of the Society of Antiquaries in

[1] The marriage of first cousins was contrary to Quaker rules. Rickman was readmitted in 1813, shortly before his second marriage to Christiana Hornor.

1829, and was an early member of the British Association for the Advancement of Science. His achievement as an architectural scholar lay in the application of elementary scientific method to a subject that hitherto had been the preserve either of antiquaries like Britton who lacked his analytic powers, or of topographical artists whose approach was picturesque rather than historical. Rickman's acute observation of architectural detail, coupled with his grasp of evolutionary principle, enabled him to demonstrate once and for all the essential stylistic sequence to which all English medieval architecture conforms.

As an architect, Rickman was self-taught. As early as 1794–7 he is said to have drawn and coloured several thousand figures wearing army uniforms, which he cut out and arranged against an architectural background of military buildings. But draughtsmanship did not come easily to him, and it was not until 1810–11 that he developed a thoroughly professional technique. In 1812 he began to show his drawings at the annual exhibitions of the Liverpool Academy, and in the same year he met John Cragg, a wealthy ironmaster with an interest in church-building. In 1813–14 he assisted Cragg to build a Gothic church at Everton, nr. Liverpool, in whose construction iron entered largely, and two more churches designed jointly by Rickman and Cragg were built at the latter's expense in 1814–16. At the same time Rickman was helping the Liverpool builder-architect John Slater to remodel Scarisbrick Hall in Lancashire in the Gothic style. These and other such tasks gave Rickman valuable practical experience, and in December 1817 he gave up his job and opened an architect's office in Liverpool. During the next few years Rickman assiduously sought commissions. He entered for every architectural competition that was announced, and having persuaded the Church Building Commissioners of his competence, gained a large share of their patronage in the West Midlands. By 1820 he was beginning to be well known as a church architect, and for the next fifteen years he was one of the busiest architects in England. In 1820 he started a second office in Birmingham, to which his pupil Henry Hutchinson was transferred, becoming in December 1821 Rickman's partner. Hutchinson died in 1831, after much illness. Meanwhile a brother, Edwin Swan Rickman, had become an assistant in the Liverpool office, and was for a short time (1831–3) Rickman's partner in Birmingham (to which town the entire practice had by then been transferred). By 1833 Edwin was already showing signs of the mental illness which was later to incapacitate him. His place was taken by R. C. Hussey (1802–87), who became Rickman's partner in 1835. Failing health now began increasingly to interfere wth Rickman's practice. In the spring of 1838 he handed over the office

entirely to Hussey, and he died on 4 January 1841, in his 64th year. He was buried in the churchyard of St. George's, Birmingham, where a monument was erected in 1845 by several of his friends. Though for the greater part of his life he had been a conscientious member of the Society of Friends, he joined the Irvingites a few years before his death. His first wife, Lucy Rickman, had died in 1807. His second wife, Christiana Hornor, sister of Thomas Hornor, the proprietor of the Colosseum in Regent's Park, died in child-birth in 1813. In 1825 he married his third wife, Elizabeth Miller of Edinburgh, by whom he had several children, one of whom, Thomas Miller Rickman (1827–1912), became a pupil of R.C. Hussey and followed his father's profession.[1] Rickman's pupils included J. A. Bell of Edinburgh, John Broadbent of Liverpool, S. C. Fripp of Bristol, Thomas Fulljames of Gloucester, A. H. Holme of Liverpool, John Smith of Cambridge, G. Vose and Zugheer of Zurich. A. E. Perkins of Worcester was also in his office for some years.

In 1823 Rickman & Hutchinson competed unsuccessfully for the new buildings at King's College, Cambridge, and in 1829 were placed third in the limited competition for the new University Library. In the course of the subsequent controversy they published an *Answer to Observations* [by G. Peacock] *on the Plans for the New Library*, Birmingham 1831. In 1831 they won the third prize in the competition for Birmingham Town Hall. In conjunction with Hussey Rickman also competed in 1835 for the Fitzwilliam Museum at Cambridge and for the Houses of Parliament at Westminster. For the former building they submitted three designs, one Gothic, one Roman and one Grecian in the manner of Schinkel [Ann James, 'Rickman and the Fitzwilliam Competition', *Arch. Rev.*, April 1957; John Cornforth in *C. Life*, 22 Nov. 1962]. For the latter they proposed a building 'in the decorated style, as it prevailed in the time of King Edward III' [*Catalogue of the Designs for the New Houses of Parliament*, 1836, 8]. In 1836 they won the first prize in the competition for the Scott Monument in Edinburgh, but the committee eventually set their design aside in favour of one submitted by G. M. Kemp (*q.v.*) [T. Bonnar, *G. M. Kemp*, 1892, 83].

Rickman's considerable success as an architect rested partly on his enormous capacity for work

[1] Another architect member of the Rickman family was Thomas Rickman, who died at Harting in Sussex in 1849 at the age of 23. He is said to have been a cousin of the subject of this entry, and to have made designs for refitting Harting Church in 1845 [M. C. W. Hunter, *The Restorations of Harting Church, 1796–1876*, Harting 1970]. Some drawings by him are in the R.I.B.A. Collection.

('he could', Hussey wrote, 'without material inconvenience, pass two nights of three in travelling'), and partly on his reputation as an expert on Gothic architecture. He and his friend Edward Blore (whom he first met in 1811 sketching at Doncaster) were probably the first English architects since James Essex who had a thorough knowledge of medieval architectural detail. Not only could Rickman date an ancient building correctly: he could reproduce its characteristic mouldings and enrichments accurately in a new one. But he was no ecclesiologist. If the detailing of his buildings was unusually scholarly, the planning remained Georgian, and the total effect of most of his churches is thin and brittle, if by no means unattractive. Many of them are in the Perpendicular style disliked by later revivalists, and Rickman did not scruple to make use of cast-iron tracery and to admit galleries and other features that were anathema to the next generation of church-builders. Many of his churches were economical jobs for the Church Building Commissioners, but Hampton Lucy, Ombersley, Oulton and Stretton-on-Dunsmore show what he could do if funds permitted. Rickman's most ambitious secular buildings were the classical Exhibition Room for the Birmingham Society of Artists (demolished in 1928) and the Gothic New Court at St. John's College, Cambridge, which exploits to the full the picturesque possibilities of Gothic architecture. The most brilliant feature of the latter building – the Bridge of Sighs – was designed by his partner Hutchinson, who must share the credit for everything built by the firm between 1821 and 1831.

Fifty-seven of Rickman's diaries, covering the years 1807 to 1834, are in the R.I.B.A. Library, together with a number of drawings. His 'work books' or professional journals for the years 1821–37 are in the British Museum (Add. MSS. 37793–37802). Besides constituting a day-by-day record of Rickman's architectural practice they contain many notes on and sketches of medieval churches made by him in the course of his professional journeys. With them is a volume (Add. MS. 37803) of drawings of churches made by Rickman, chiefly in the years 1809–12. The first draft of the *Attempt* forms part of a notebook in the possession of Mr. John Baily, R.I.B.A. Notes and sketches for the 3rd edition (1825) are in the Bodleian Library (MSS. Top. eccles. c. 3–4). A large collection of Rickman's sketches of medieval architecture was purchased by the Oxford Architectural Society in 1842 and is described in the Society's *Report* for 1846, pp. 37–56. It is now in the Bodleian Library (MS. Dep. b. 140). A number of Rickman's architectural designs are in the R.I.B.A. Collection.

[*A.P.S.D.* (with list of works contributed by T. M. Rickman); T. M. Rickman, *Notes on the Life of Thomas Rickman*, 1901 (based on the

diaries); *Gent's Mag.* 1841 (i), 322, 1861 (i), 523; *D.N.B.*; A. T. Brown, *How Gothic came back to Liverpool*, Liverpool 1937; M. H. Port, *Six Hundred New Churches*, 1961, chap. 6; *R.I.B.A. Drawings Catalogue*; information from Mr. John Baily.]

The principal sources for Rickman's architectural work are his diaries and work-books (see above), which together provide an almost complete record of his working life. In addition there is the list of buildings contributed to the *A.P.S. Dictionary* by his son T. M. Rickman, and a list of churches left by Rickman himself in one of his work-books (Add. MS. 37802, f. 290ᵛ). Many of the minor commissions present problems of identification, and the following list attempts only to give Rickman's principal executed works.

Buildings designed in partnership with H. Hutchinson are marked by an asterisk (★), those designed in partnership with R. C. Hussey by a dagger (†).

CHURCHES[1]

LIVERPOOL, ST. GEORGE, EVERTON, in conjunction with John Cragg, 1813–14; altar 1817.

LIVERPOOL, ST. MICHAEL, TOXTETH, in conjunction with John Cragg, 1814–15.

LIVERPOOL, ST. PHILIP, HARDMAN STREET, in conjunction with John Cragg, 1815–16; dem. 1882.

BIRKENHEAD, CHESHIRE, ST. MARY, for Francis Price, 1819–21; transepts added 1832–5; dem. 1976 [see also R.I.B.A.D.].

BIRMINGHAM, ST. GEORGE, 1819–22; enlarged 1883–4; dem. 1960.

WARRINGTON, LANCS., HOLY TRINITY CHURCH, rebuilt classical tower, 1820–1; rebuilt 1862.

BARNSLEY, YORKS (W.R.), ST. MARY'S CHURCH, rebuilt 1820–1 retaining medieval west tower.

★BARNSLEY, YORKS. (W.R.), ST. GEORGE, 1821–2.

★ERDINGTON, WARWICKS., ST. BARNABAS, 1822–3; enlarged 1883; reroofed 1893.

★GLOUCESTER, CHRIST CHURCH, BRUNSWICK SQUARE, 1822–3, classical; remodelled in Romanesque style 1899–1910.

★CHORLEY, LANCS., ST. GEORGE, 1822–5.

★PRESTON, LANCS., ST. PETER, 1822–5; spire added 1851–2.

★HAMPTON LUCY, WARWICKS., for the Rev. John Lucy, 1822–6; apse added by Scott 1856.

★CHILDWALL, LANCS., alterations, 1823–4, probably including north aisle (rebuilt 1906).

★HANBURY, STAFFS., rebuilt north aisle, 1823–4 [see also I.C.B.S.]

★MOSELEY, WORCS., rebuilt 1823–4; rebuilt 1886, 1897, 1909–11 and 1940 [see also I.C.B.S.].

★PRESTON, LANCS., ST. PAUL'S CHURCH, 1823–5; chancel 1882.

---

[1] All Gothic unless otherwise stated.

*GLASGOW, ST. DAVID, INGRAM STREET (RAMSHORN CHURCH), 1824–6; interior remodelled 1887.

*BEVERLEY MINSTER, YORKS. (E.R.), alterations to choir and removal of galleries in nave, 1825 [cf. G. Poulson, *Beverlac*, 1829, 683].

*BIRMINGHAM, ST. PETER, DALE END, 1825–7, classical; reconstructed 1834–7 by C. Edge after fire in 1831; dem. 1899.

*OMBERSLEY, WORCS., for the Marchioness of Downshire, 1825–9.

*HANDSWORTH, STAFFS., ST. MARY, THE WATT CHAPEL, 1826.

*COVENTRY, WARWICKS., HOLY TRINITY, recased tower, etc., 1826 onwards [cf. B. Poole, *History of Coventry*, 1870, 202].

*GREAT TEW, OXON., repaired and repewed, 1826–7 [see also I.C.B.S.].

*BIRMINGHAM, ST. THOMAS, 1826–9, classical; refitted 1893; damaged by bombing 1940/1 and dem. except tower [see also R.I.B.A.D.].

*HAGLEY, WORCS., added north aisle, 1827–8 [see also I.C.B.S.].

*DARWEN, LANCS., ST. JAMES, LOWER DARWEN, 1827–8.

*DARWEN, LANCS., HOLY TRINITY, OVER DARWEN, 1827–9.

*MELLOR, LANCS., 1827–9; altered 1899.

*OULTON, YORKS., (W.R.), for John Blayds, 1827–9.

*HARBORNE, WARWICKS., rebuilt 1827–9 retaining medieval tower; rebuilt 1867 [see also I.C.B.S.].

*CLITHEROE, LANCS., ST. MARY MAGDALENE, rebuilt 1828–9 retaining medieval tower, etc. [see also I.C.B.S.].

*CARLISLE, CUMBERLAND, CHRIST CHURCH, 1828–30; dem. 1952.

*CARLISLE, CUMBERLAND, HOLY TRINITY, 1828–30.

*WHITTLE-LE-WOODS, LANCS., 1828–30; dem. 1880.

CANTERBURY CATHEDRAL, survey of north-west tower, etc., 1828–31.

*BRISTOL, HOLY TRINITY, 1829–31 [see also R.I.B.A.D.].

*RUGBY, WARWICKS., ST. ANDREW, added south aisle, c. 1830; rebuilt 1877–9.

*HAIGH WITH ASPULL, LANCS., ST. DAVID, 1830; chancel 1886–7.

*PEMBERTON, nr. WIGAN, LANCS., ST. JOHN, 1830–2.

*COVENTRY, WARWICKS., CHRIST CHURCH, 1830–2, incorporating medieval steeple; dem. after bombing in 1941, except steeple.

*LIVERPOOL, ST. JUDE, LOW HILL, 1831; altered 1882; dem.

*BLACKBURN, LANCS., ST. MARY (now Cathedral), survey after fire of 1831 and advice about subsequent restoration conducted by Thomas Stones as 'clerk of works' [cf. I.C.B.S.].

*SAFFRON WALDEN, ESSEX, rebuilt belfry and spire, 1831–2.

*TOCKHOLES, LANCS., ST. STEPHEN, 1831–3; dem. 1965.

LOWER HARDRES, KENT, rebuilt 1831–2.

WORCESTER CATHEDRAL, repairs, 1832.

BIRMINGHAM, ALL SAINTS, NINEVEH, 1832–3; chancel 1881; dem.

REDDITCH, WORCS., OUR LADY (R.C.), BEOLEY ROAD, 1833–4.

BAVERSTOCK, WILTS., alterations, 1833; much altered by Butterfield 1880–2.

BRISTOL, ST. MATTHEW, KINGSDOWN, 1833–5 [see also R.I.B.A.D.].

MELLOR BROOK CHAPEL, MELLOR, LANCS., remodelled Independent Chapel for use by Established Church, 1834.

HENBURY, GLOS., repairs and alterations, 1834–5; altered by G. E. Street 1875–7 [see also *Trans. Bristol and Glos. Arch. Soc.* xxviii, 1915, 182–3].

STRETTON-ON-DUNSMORE, WARWICKS., rebuilt 1835–7.

LOUGHBOROUGH, LEICS., EMMANUEL CHURCH, FOREST ROAD, 1835–7.

HARTLEBURY, WORCS., rebuilt nave, 1836–7 [the inscription on the foundation-stone is given in *Gent's Mag.* 1836 (i), 654].

SETTLE, YORKS. (W.R.), 1836–8.

CLEVEDON, SOMERSET, CHRIST CHURCH, 1838–9.

†BIRMINGHAM, BISHOP RYDER'S MEMORIAL CHURCH, 1838; chancel 1894; dem. 1960.

†HALESOWEN, WORCS., internal alterations, 1838–9 [see also I.C.B.S.].

†SNEINTON, NOTTS., 1838–9; dem. 1912.

†HORSLEY, GLOS., rebuilt 1838–9 retaining medieval tower.

†GOODNESTONE, KENT, rebuilt nave and chancel, 1838–41 [S. Lewis, *Topographical Dictionary of England* ii, 1848, 315].

PUBLIC BUILDINGS, ETC.

LIVERPOOL, PARADISE STREET, premises for Messrs. Cropper, Benson & Co., merchants, 1816; later the 'Museum of Anatomy'; dem. 1941.

LIVERPOOL, CHARLOTTE STREET, Riding School for the Liverpool Light Horse Volunteers (later Lucas's Repository for Horses and Carriages), 1817.

CLITHEROE, LANCS., THE TOWN HALL, 1820–1, Gothic.

*PRESTON, LANCS., THE COURT HOUSE, STANLEY STREET, 1825; dome removed 1849.

*GLOUCESTER, THE INFIRMARY, south wing, 1826–7 [cf. G. W. Counsel, *History of Gloucester*, 1829, 176; G. Whitcombe, *The General Infirmary at Gloucester*, 1903, 18].

*CAMBRIDGE, ST. JOHN'S COLLEGE, THE NEW COURT, 1827–31, Gothic [cf. Willis & Clark, ii, 278; Marcus Whiffen in *Arch. Rev.*, Dec. 1945, 160–5].

691

*BIRMINGHAM, PUBLIC NEWS ROOM, additions, 1828; dem.

*BIRMINGHAM, EXHIBITION ROOM in NEW STREET for the Birmingham Society of Artists, 1829; dem. 1928 [see also J. Hill & W. Midgley, *History of the Royal Birmingham Society of Artists*, 1928, 16].

*EDGBASTON, BIRMINGHAM, DEAF AND DUMB ASYLUM, designed Master's House, 1829.

*COVENTRY, WARWICKS., THE DRAPERS' HALL, 1829–32.

*CARLISLE, CUMBERLAND, NEWSROOM AND LIBRARY (later Barclay's Bank), ENGLISH STREET, 1830–1, Gothic (S. Jefferson, *History of Carlisle*, 1838, frontispiece).

*BIRMINGHAM, THE BIRMINGHAM BANKING COMPANY'S OFFICE (now Midland Bank), BENNETT'S HILL, 1830.

*BORDESLEY, nr. BIRMINGHAM, HOLY TRINITY SCHOOL, 1831; dem. 1854.

*COVENTRY, BOND'S HOSPITAL, partial reconstruction, 1832, timber-framed Tudor style [cf. B. Poole, *History of Coventry*, 1870, 295].

*COVENTRY, THE BABLAKE BOYS' SCHOOL, 1832–3, Tudor Gothic; dem. 1890 [cf. *V.C.H. Warwicks.* viii, 141].

WHITEHAVEN, CUMBERLAND, THE TRUSTEE SAVINGS BANK, LOWTHER STREET, 1832–3.

†BRISTOL, ASYLUM FOR THE BLIND, PARK STREET, 1835–7, Gothic; dem. *c.* 1914.

DOMESTIC ARCHITECTURE

SCARISBRICK HALL, LANCS., remodelled for Thomas Scarisbrick in conjunction with John Slater (*q.v.*), 1812–16, Gothic; remodelled by A. W. N. Pugin 1837 onwards.

RHIWLAS, nr. BALA, MERIONETHSHIRE, Gothic gateway for R. Thelwall Price, 1813; house dem. 1951.

LEE HALL, GATEACRE, LANCS., stables for John Okill, 1815, castellated; dem. *c.* 1960.

EVERTON, nr. LIVERPOOL, stables, etc., for Colin Campbell, 1815; dem.

GATEACRE, LANCS., house for John Bibby, 1816.

GWRYCH CASTLE, DENBIGHSHIRE, Gothic designs for L. B. Hesketh, 1816 onwards. Some of Rickman's drawings are in the National Library of Wales. Hesketh designed the house himself with help from C. A. Busby, Rickman and others. The foundation-stone was not laid until 1819 (J. P. Neale, *Views of Seats*, 2nd ser., ii, 1825).

GREAT TEW, OXON., work for M. R. Boulton, 1820–1. Rickman appears to have been responsible for some elements of the picturesque village created by Boulton, for a farm-house (with carefully designed chimneys) and an ornamental well are both mentioned in his diary (*C. Life*, 29 July 1949).

*THE DOWN HOUSE, nr. REDMARLEY, GLOS., for George Dowdeswell, 1822–2.

*SANDWELL PARK, STAFFS., minor works for the 4th Earl of Dartmouth, 1822 onwards, including alterations to stables; dem. 1928.

*ETTINGTON PARK, WARWICKS., alterations for E. J. Shirley, 1824; rebuilt by John Prichard of Llandaff 1862 [cf. E. P. Shirley, *Lower Ettington*, 1880].

*LOUGH FEA HOUSE, CO. MONAGHAN, IRELAND, for E. J. Shirley, began 1825, Elizabethan [cf. E. P. Shirley, *Lough Fea*, 1869].

*THE GROVE, KIRKPATRICK-IRONGRAY, DUMFRIESSHIRE, for Wellwood Maxwell (of Liverpool), 1825 [cf. *N.S.A.* iv, 270].

*BADGEWORTH COURT, GLOS., for J. Ellis Viner, 1827–8, Gothic; rebuilt 1895.

*BRUNSTOCK HOUSE, nr. CARLISLE, CUMBERLAND, for George Saul, 1828–30, Gothic.

*BURFIELD LODGE, nr. BRISTOL, SOMERSET, for E. B. Fripp, 1827–8.

*HARBORNE, nr. BIRMINGHAM, WARWICKS., house for George Simcox, 1828–9.

*BURY, HUNTS., house for John Julian, 1828–9.

*ROSE CASTLE, CUMBERLAND, alterations and additions for Hugh Percy, Bishop of Carlisle, 1828–9.

*LAUNDE ABBEY, LEICS., new offices, etc., for E. Dawson, 1829.

*BIRMINGHAM, NO. 12 ISLINGTON ROW, house for himself, 1830.

*WESTON HALL, WESTON-UNDER-LIZARD, STAFFS., alterations for the 2nd Earl of Bradford, 1830–1 [cf. Bradford archives 3/32] (*C. Life*, 9, 16, 23 Nov. 1945).

STANWICK, YORKS. (N.R.), works on estate for Lord Prudhoe, 1830–1, including farm-houses at ALDBOROUGH, MELSONBY and probably at STANWICK [cf. drawings for further unexecuted works among Percy archives at Alnwick Castle].

TETTENHALL WOOD, nr. WOLVERHAMPTON, STAFFS., for Miss Hinckes, 1831–6; dem. *c.* 1968.

MATFEN HALL, NORTHUMBERLAND, for Sir Edward Blackett, Bart., 1832–5. Blackett was a difficult client who insisted on the 'Elizabethan' style for the exterior. He was to some extent his own architect, made many changes as the work progressed, and eventually dismissed Rickman in 1835, when the house was nearly finished.

SOHAM VICARAGE, CAMBS., for the Rev. H. Tasker, 1833.

RUGBY, WARWICKS., BROOKSIDE, DUNCHURCH ROAD, for H. S. Gibbs, 1833; dem.

BAYNARDS PARK, CRANLEIGH, SURREY, additions for the Rev. Thomas Thurlow, 1833–41, Tudor Gothic; further alterations and additions by B. Ferrey after 1841.

GREAT OAKLEY RECTORY, ESSEX, for the Rev. W. Tatham, 1834–5.

AUDLEY END, ESSEX, THE MAIN GATE LODGE, for the 3rd Lord Braybrooke, 1834 [cf. Lord Braybrooke, *History of Audley End*, 1836, 137].

†OUSDEN HALL, SUFFOLK, alterations, including north and west porticoes, for T. J. Ireland, 1835–6; dem. 1955.

†CASTLE BROMWICH HALL, WARWICKS., alterations and repairs for the 2nd Earl of Bradford, 1837–8 [see also Bradford archives at Weston Hall, 8/5; G. W. Beard in *C. Life*, 9 May 1952].

MONUMENTS

Monuments (nearly all Gothic) designed by Rickman were erected in the following churches: ASHTON-BY-SUTTON, CHESHIRE (Catherine Harrison, 1813); BANGOR CATHEDRAL (Major Hoyland); BUCKDEN, HUNTS. (Robert Whitworth, d. 1831); DURHAM CATHEDRAL; EVERTON, ST. GEORGE, nr. LIVERPOOL (R. P. Buddicum); GLOUCESTER CATHEDRAL (Richard Raikes, d. 1823); HAMPTON LUCY, WARWICKS. (Henry Hutchinson, d. 1831); HINDLEY CHAPEL, WIGAN, LANCS. (John Layland, 1813); KINGS NORTON, WORCS.; LISMORE CATHEDRAL, IRELAND (J. H. Lovett); PRESTON PARISH CHURCH, LANCS. (three monuments); WALTON, LANCS.; WARRINGTON, LANCS.; WHITFORD, FLINTS. (Caroline Pennant).

RIDDELL, THOMAS, of Hull, is recorded to have designed the MERCHANT SEAMEN'S HOSPITAL there in 1781 in conjunction with one Hammond, and also NO. 8 CHARLOTTE STREET, HULL, *c.* 1796–9 [*V.C.H. Yorks. E.R.* i, 407, 447, 451].

RIDE, WILLIAM, was surveyor to the Dukes of Richmond at Goodwood in Sussex. He corresponded with George Vertue on the subject of some ancient paintings in Chichester Cathedral [Walpole Society, *Vertue Note Books* v, 74], and in a volume of prints in the Library of the Society of Antiquaries there is an engraving of the recently repaired Market Cross at Chichester dedicated to the Duke of Richmond and inscribed 'Wm. Ride delin. A° 1749 G. Vertue sculpsit'. In 1750 the rebuilding of ST. PANCRAS CHURCH, CHICHESTER, was carried out by William Ride, master builder, 'according to a plan already made'. The Duke was among the subscribers to the building fund [MS. parish records]. In 1775 'Mr. Ride' was paid £21 for his set of plans for the new SUSSEX COUNTY GAOL at HORSHAM. They were produced at Quarter Sessions by the Duke of Richmond, and executed between 1778 and 1779 [W. Albery, *A Horsham and Sussex Millennium of Facts*, 1947, 392–3].

It is possible that the Duke of Richmond's surveyor was related to a London master carpenter of the same name who was employed by Earl Temple at Stowe House, Bucks., between 1756 and 1778 [Michael McCarthy, 'The Rebuilding of

Stowe House, 1770–1777', *Huntingdon Library Quarterly* xxxvi, 1973, 274]. This Ride lived in Westminster, and in 1763 took an apprentice named John Ride, who was probably his son [P.R.O., Apprenticeship Registers]. John Ride subsequently exhibited architectural designs at the Royal Academy from addresses in Westminster in 1773 and 1781.

RIDER, RICHARD, *see* RYDER

RIDER. On 15 June 1688, it was agreed by the Society of Gray's Inn that Mr. Rider should be 'chiefe surveyor to this Society, and to supervise and direct the buildings of the Gate . . . and all publique structures belonging to this Society'. The gatehouse was rebuilt that year [*The Pension Book of Gray's Inn: Records of the Honourable Society, 1669–1800* ii, 1910, 97]. This may have been Richard Rider, who in 1705 directed the building of a Rectory and Watch House for the parish of St. Anne's, Soho [Vestry Minutes in Westminster City Library]. The latter was probably the elder son of Richard Ryder (d. 1683), *q.v.*

RIOU, STEPHEN (1720–1780), was the son of Stephen Riou, a London merchant of Huguenot origin who had become naturalized in 1702. Stephen was therefore 'born a subject of Britain', and served in Flanders in the war of 1741 as a Captain in the 2nd troop of Horse Grenadier Guards. He eventually retired on his pay and studied architecture 'in a foreign protestant academy'. This was the University of Geneva, where Riou in 1743 wrote in French a MS. treatise on civil architecture based on Vignola, Daviler, etc., that is now in the Mellon Collection. In 1746 he published *The Elements of Fortification, translated and collected from the works of the most celebrated authors*, vol. i only. Another MS. in the Mellon Collection shows that he subsequently travelled in Italy and Greece, acting as *cicerone* to a Mr. Barton. It is entitled 'Itineral Remarks from Italy to the Archipelago and Constantinople by Sea and thence by land thro' Rome to Bulgaria Servia Hungary to Vienna in the years 1753 & 1754 with designs'. In Smyrna he met Stuart and Revett on their way to Athens and spent some time in their company. After returning to England Riou (who had met Charles Labelye, *q.v.*, in Naples) published *Short Principles for the Architecture of Stone Bridges*, 1760, and *The Grecian Orders of Architecture delineated and explained from the Antiquities of Athens*, with a dedication to James Stuart, 1768. This was intended to give wider currency to the discoveries of Stuart and Revett, and included a number of plates drawn by the author to show how Grecian features could be incorporated in buildings of basically Palladian character.

No executed building by Riou is known, but a volume of architectural designs made by him in Rome in 1752 is in the Mellon Collection, and in the Metropolitan Museum at New York there is a sketch by him for an elevation of Palladian character described as 'a Museum or Repository to preserve Works of Sculpture, Painting, etc.' (J. Harris, *Catalogue of British Drawings for Architecture, etc., in American Collections*, 1971, pl. 132). In the Royal Library at Windsor there is a volume of designs by Riou for a royal palace, begun at Rome in 1751–3, and completed in London in 1754. A design by him for a villa, dated 1758, is in a copy of Du Cerceau's *Livre d'Architecture* in the Library of the Queen's University, Ontario. He competed for the Royal Exchange at Dublin in 1769, and in the same year was an exhibitor at the Free Society of Artists, showing his designs both for the palace and for the exchange. In 1760 he was living at Herne Hill in Kent, and in 1769 at Canterbury. He died in Bentinck Street, Cavendish Square, on 12 March 1780, and was buried in Marylebone Churchyard. He left two sons, Col. Philip and Capt. Edward Riou. The latter's gallantry as one of Nelson's commanders earned him a monument in St. Paul's Cathedral. Stephen Riou's granddaughter Charlotte married Moses George Benson of Lutwyche Hall, Salop., where his portrait was formerly preserved.

[*A.P.S.D.*; *Gent's Mag.* 1780, 153; S. Lysons, *Environs of London* ii (2), 1811, 558; *Builder* xxvii, 1869, 781; H. Wagner, 'Pedigree of Riou', *Miscellanea Genealogica et Heraldica*, 3rd ser., iv, 1900–1, 190; P. H. Ditchfield, 'The Family of Riou', *Proceedings of the Huguenot Society of London* x (2), 1913, 236–64.]

RIPLEY, THOMAS (*c.* 1683–1758), rose from humble origins to the status of a senior officer of the Board of Works. He was born in Yorkshire and is said to have walked to London to seek his fortune. He was admitted to the Carpenters' Company on 14 March 1705, and at first he combined the trade of a carpenter with keeping a coffee-shop in Wood Street, off Cheapside. His subsequent career was due to the patronage of Sir Robert Walpole, one of whose servants he married. In April 1715 he was appointed Labourer in Trust at the Savoy and in February 1716 Clerk of the Works at the Mews. In September 1721 he succeeded Grinling Gibbons as Master Carpenter, and on the death of Sir John Vanbrugh in 1726 he became Comptroller of the Works. In 1729 Walpole obtained for him the further appointment of Surveyor of Greenwich Hospital, and he also held the sinecure post of Surveyor of the King's Private Roads from 1737 until his death in 1758. In 1742 he obtained a grant of arms from the College of Heralds, and in 1744 was fined for the office of Sheriff of London and Middlesex. He was a Warden of the Carpenters' Company in 1740 and 1741, and Master in 1742.

As an architect Ripley has not been much esteemed either by his contemporaries or by posterity. Certainly the ill-proportioned portico of the Admiralty was a poor advertisement of his abilities as a designer, and none of his other works quite atones for this notorious failure. Wolterton Hall and the demolished Blatherwycke were, however, handsome enough houses, and the former suggests that Ripley's employment as executant architect at Houghton was not without a salutary effect on his style. Many other second-rate Georgian architects did no better without incurring public censure, but it was Ripley's misfortune that his inferior professional ability, combined with his dependence on Walpole, earned him the contempt both of Vanbrugh and of Burlington. When, in 1721, the former 'met with his name (and Esquire to it) in the Newspaper; such a Laugh came upon me, I had like to Beshit my Self'; while the latter's disapproval found its echo more than once in Pope's scathing couplets:

Heav'n visits with a taste the wealthy fool,
And needs no rod but Ripley with a rule.
Epistle to the Earl of Burlington,
ll. 17–18 (1731)

Who builds a bridge that never drove a pile?
(Should Ripley venture, all the world would smile).
Imitations of Horace, Bk. II,
Ep. 1, ll. 185–6 (1737)

See under Ripley rise a new White-hall,
While Jones' and Boyle's united labours fall.
Dunciad, Bk. III, ll. 327–8 (1743)

That Ripley did, in fact, aspire to build bridges is shown by the Minutes of the Commissioners appointed in 1726 to erect a bridge across the Thames from Fulham to Putney. For Ripley attended the first meeting in person, was subsequently employed to survey the river, and produced a design for a timber bridge which was accepted by the Commissioners on 22 August. But for some unexplained reason it was not executed, and in 1728, when further plans were invited, Ripley again submitted one for a timber bridge, this time with stone piers. The timber bridge that was finally built in 1729 was, however, constructed 'according to a scheme and principles' laid down not by Ripley but by William Cheselden, a surgeon at St. Thomas's Hospital [G.L.C. Record Office, Fulham Bridge Minutes]. In 1737 Ripley was employed as an assessor by the Commissioners for building a bridge at Westminster, and his report on the plans submitted is preserved among the minutes now in the Public Record Office [Works 6/28, f. 83]. He himself submitted a design for a bridge of fifteen arches, but that of Charles Labelye was eventually adopted.

Like most eighteenth-century architects, Ripley engaged in speculative building, though little is at present known of his activities in this direction.[1] In 1732 the Duke of Chandos was endeavouring to persuade him to build in St. James's Square on the site of Chandos House, and wrote that he 'is very rich and though he is in good employments continues still this sort of business' [Baker, *Life and Circumstances of James Brydges, Duke of Chandos*, 1949, 216]. He also engaged, with Richard Holt, in the manufacture of 'a compound liquid metall, by which artificiall stone and marble is made by casting the same into moulds of any form, as statues, columns, capitalls', for which they took out a patent in 1722. A manuscript in the British Museum (Additional 11394, ff. 45–6) shows that the chief ingredients of Holt's 'secret formula' were powdered glass and clay. In 1730 Holt published *A Short Treatise of Artificial Stone* in which he alleged that the composition had been pirated by Batty Langley [K. A. Esdaile, 'Coade Stone', *Architect and Building News*, 19–26 Jan. 1940; S. R. Hamilton, 'Coade Stone', *Arch. Rev.*, Nov. 1954].

Ripley's first wife died in November 1737. On 22 April 1742 he married a Miss Bucknall of Hampton, Middlesex, who is said to have had a fortune of £40,000. She died in September 1752, aged 48, and Ripley himself died at Hampton on 10 February 1758, aged 75. He is commemorated by a ledger-stone, formerly in the chancel, but now in the tower, of Hampton Church. There is a portrait of Ripley by Gardiner at Wolterton Hall, and a Kit-Kat portrait by Joseph Highmore was in the possession of Ripley's descendants in 1851. A bust by Rysbrack was sold at the latter's sale in 1765 (lot 28).

Ripley left three sons, named Richard, Thomas and Horatio. Richard is said to have been called to the Bar, but did not pursue a legal career. Through his father's influence he was appointed Chief Clerk of the King's Works in April 1756, and on the reorganization of the Office of Works in 1782 became Resident Clerk. He died on 22 January 1786. Richard Ripley, junior, who was apprenticed to Sir William Chambers in 1771, admitted to the Royal Academy Schools in 1776 at the age of 21, and exhibited a design for a casino at the Academy in 1779, was presumably his son.

[*A.P.S.D.*; *D.N.B.*; H. Walpole, *Anecdotes of Painting*, ed. Dallaway & Wornum, iii, 1862, 769–70; *Gent's Mag.* 1737, 702; 1742, 274; 1744, 333; 1758, 94; *Builder* ix, 1851, 2–3; xx, 1862, 563; *Walpole Soc.* xix, 145; *The Works of Sir John*

---

[1] His interest in the Grosvenor Estate 'as a small speculator' is noted by Sir John Summerson (*Georgian London*, 1945, 87).

Vanbrugh iv: *The Letters*, ed. G. F. Webb, 1928, 138; Sir J. Hawkins, *Life of Samuel Johnson*, 1787, 375–6; *History of the King's Works* v; will (P.C.C. 53 HUTTON)].

LONDON, THE CUSTOM HOUSE, reconstruction after fire, 1718–25, and additional buildings on north side, 1738–40; destroyed by fire 1814 [T. F. Reddaway, 'The London Custom House 1660–1740', *London Topographical Record* xxi, 1958; *History of the King's Works* v, 347–8].

LIVERPOOL, THE CUSTOM HOUSE, 1719–21; dem. 1828 [E. H. Rideout, *The Custom House, Liverpool*, Liverpool 1928, 5–8; *Customs Letter-Books of the Port of Liverpool 1711–1812*, ed. R. C. Jarvis, Chetham Soc. 1957, 13–14]. See also S. A. Harris, 'The Old Blue Coat Hospital, Liverpool: was it designed by Thomas Ripley?' *Trans. Historic Soc. of Lancs. and Cheshire* cix, 1957.

BLATHERWYCKE HALL, NORTHANTS., for Henry O'Brien, 1720–4; dem. 1948 [Northants. Record Office, OBB/12, contract dated 26 July 1720 to build the house 'according to the plan and designe thereof made by Thomas Ripley of London Gent'] (J. A. Gotch, *Squires' Homes of Northamptonshire*, 1939, pl. 5).

HOUGHTON HALL, NORFOLK, supervised erection of house for Sir Robert Walpole to designs of Colen Campbell and William Kent, 1722–35 [Isaac Ware, *The Plans, Elevations and Sections of Houghton in Norfolk*, 1735; H. A. Tipping in *C. Life*, 1 Jan. 1921, 21–2].

LONDON, THE ADMIRALTY, WHITEHALL, 1723–6; entrance screen by R. Adam, 1760 [*Builder* ix, 1851, 3; *Survey of London* xvi, 57–64] (*C. Life*, 17–24 Nov. 1923).

WOLTERTON HALL, NORFOLK, for the 1st Lord Walpole, 1727–41; east wing, stone stairs and-perron added by G. S. Repton 1828 [H. Walpole, *Anecdotes of Painting* iii, 1862, 769–70; Gordon Nares in *C. Life*, 18–25 July 1957].

GREENWICH HOSPITAL: Ripley was responsible for the completion of the QUEEN MARY BLOCK *c.* 1735. The central pediment, popularly known as 'Ripley's Saddle', was removed and replaced by a balustraded attic in 1777 (see drawing in Westminster City Library). Ripley was also responsible for the roof and interior of the CHAPEL 1735–9, destroyed by fire 1779 [*A.P.S.D.*]

LONDON, PALL MALL, NO. 71 for Sir Edward Walpole, *c.* 1737–8; dem. *c.* 1830 [*Survey of London* xxix, 378–9].

ROBERTS, HENRY (1803–1876), was a pupil of Charles Fowler. In 1824 he was awarded two medals by the Society of Arts, and in the following year he was admitted to the Royal Academy Schools. He subsequently spent some years in the office of Sir Robert Smirke, 'whose tastes, habits, modes of construction, and method of making working drawings, he thoroughly imbibed'. A continental tour followed, in the course of which he visited Naples (1829). On his return, he set up in practice in Suffolk Street. In 1832 he won the competition for Fishmongers' Hall with an elegant Greek Revival design in the manner of Smirke. Escot House is in a similar style, but many of Roberts's subsequent works were Gothic designs of no special distinction. Having independent means, he was able to retire from practice in 1856, and for reasons of health went to live in Italy, where he spent the last twenty years of his life. He died in Florence on 9 March 1876. Gilbert Scott, who entered his office in 1832, describes him as 'a gentlemanly, religious, precise, and quiet man'.

Roberts is best known as a pioneer of working-class housing. From the 1840s onwards he devoted most of his energies to improving the appalling housing conditions of the Victorian working classes, and even after his retirement to Italy he continued to be active in this cause. He was a founder-member and honorary architect to Lord Shaftesbury's Society for Improving the Conditions of the Labouring Classes, formed in 1844, and also acted as honorary architect to the society founded by Prince Albert to improve working-class housing in Windsor. On this subject he published a number of works, of which the principal were *The Dwellings of the Labouring Classes*, 1850 (revised edition 1867), of which a translation was published in France the same year; *House Reform; or, what the Working Classes may do to improve their dwellings* [1852]; *The Improvement of the Dwellings of the Labouring Classes*, 1859; *The Essentials of a Healthy Dwelling, and the extension of its benefits to the Labouring Population*, 1862; *Proposed People's Palace and Gardens for the Northern and Midland Counties*, 1863; *The Physical Condition of the Labouring Classes, resulting from the State of their Dwellings*, 1866; and *Efforts on the Continent for improving the Dwellings of the Labouring Classes*, Florence 1874.

[*A.P.S.D.*; *D.N.B.*; *Builder* viii, 1850, 37; G. G. Scott, *Personal and Professional Recollections*, 1879, 73–5; N. Pevsner, 'Model Houses for the Labouring Classes', *Arch. Rev.*, May 1943; A. M. Foyle, 'Henry Roberts', *Builder*, 2 Jan. 1953, 5–8; J. N. Tarn, *Five Per Cent Philanthropy: an account of housing in urban areas between 1840 and 1914*, Cambridge 1973.]

LONDON, FISHMONGERS' HALL, LONDON BRIDGE, 1832–5 [W. H. Leeds, *Supplement* to Britton & Pugin's *Public Buildings of London*, 1838, 21–32] (*C. Life*, 19 Jan. 1939).

CAMBERWELL, SURREY, THE COLLEGIATE SCHOOL, 1834–5, Tudor Gothic; dem. 1867 [*Companion to the Almanac*, 1836, 219–20; W. H. Blanch, *Ye Parish of Camberwell*, 1875, 307].

696

LONDON, THE SAILORS' HOME, WELL STREET, LONDON DOCKS, 1835 [*A New Survey of London*, John Weale, i, 1853, 268].

SOUTHBOROUGH, KENT, THE GLEBE HOUSE, 1836 [drawings and contract in R.I.B.A. Drawings Coll.].

YOXFORD CHURCH, SUFFOLK, added north aisle, 1837, Gothic [I.C.B.S.].

MANCHESTER, GROSVENOR SQUARE CHAPEL, 1838 [exhib. at R.A. 1838].

ESCOT HOUSE, DEVONSHIRE, rebuilt for Sir John Kennaway, Bart., 1838 [exhib. at R.A. 1838; drawings in Devon County Record Office, 961 M/E29].

ESCOT CHURCH, DEVONSHIRE, for Sir John Kennaway, Bart., 1839–40, Gothic [W. Spreat, *Picturesque Sketches of the Churches of Devon*, 1842, no. 69].

CLAYDON HOUSE, BUCKS., minor alterations for Sir Harry Verney, Bart., 1839–40 [plans at Claydon House].

ELVETHAM CHURCH, HANTS., rebuilt for the 3rd Lord Calthorpe, 1840–1, Norman [exhib. at R.A. 1841, specifically mentioning 'new towers and porch'].

LONDON, LONDON BRIDGE RAILWAY STATION, in conjunction with George Smith & Thomas Turner, c. 1841–44; rebuilt 1851, dem. 1969 [*Companion to the Almanac*, 1843, 248–9; 1844, 239–41].

NORTON MANOR, NORTON FITZWARREN, SOMERSET, for C. Noel Welman, c. 1842, Tudor Gothic [exhib. at R.A. 1842].

LONDON, ST. PAUL'S CHURCH FOR SEAMEN, DOCK STREET, WHITECHAPEL, 1846–7, Gothic [*Builder* iv, 1846, 241; *Illustrated London News* viii, 321; *Ecclesiologist* vi, 1846, 34–5].

NORBITON, SURREY, ST. PETER'S PARSONAGE, 1846–7, Tudor [Surrey Record Office, Acc. 1056/441].

LONDON, NATIONAL SCOTCH CHURCH, CROWN COURT, COVENT GARDEN, enlarged 1848, with two schools adjoining; rebuilt 1905 [*A.P.S.D.*].

NORBITON, SURREY, NATIONAL SCHOOL, 1851 [Surrey Record Office, 264/51/1–5].

EXTON HALL, RUTLAND, rebuilt centre for the 1st Earl of Gainsborough, 1851–2, Elizabethan style [*The Architects, Engineers and Building Trades Directory*, 1868, 133].

TOFT HALL, CHESHIRE, additions for Ralph Leycester [*The Architects, Engineers and Building Trades Directory*, 1868, 133].

KIMBOLTON CASTLE, HUNTS., additions for the 6th Duke of Manchester [*The Architects, Engineers and Building Trades Directory*, 1868, 133].

See p. 980

MODEL DWELLINGS

As architect to the Society for Improving the Conditions of the Labouring Classes, etc.,

Roberts designed houses in LOWER ROAD, PEN-
TONVILLE, 1844, dem. [*Builder* ii, 1844, 630; iii,
1845, 1]; houses in GEORGE STREET, BLOOMSBURY,
1846–7 [*Builder* v, 1847, 286–7]; houses in
STREATHAM STREET, BLOOMSBURY, 1849–50
[*Builder* vii, 1849, 325–6; viii, 1850, 49, 250];
THANKSGIVING BUILDINGS, PORTPOOL LANE,
GRAY'S INN ROAD [*Builder* viii, 1850, 369]; model
houses exhibited at the Great Exhibition of 1851
and subsequently re-erected as lodges in Kennington Park [*Builder* ix, 1851, 311–12]; and
houses at WINDSOR, BERKS., 1852 [*Builder* x, 1852,
468–9].

ROBERTS, JOHN and WILLIAM, were
builders at Nottingham in the second half of the
eighteenth century. They built the GREYHOUND
YARD at NOTTINGHAM in 1754 [*The Stretton
Manuscripts*, ed. G. C. Robertson, 1910, 216]. In
1768 'Mr. Roberts' made designs (which were
not adopted) for the new COUNTY HALL, and in
1770–2 William Roberts acted as clerk of the
works during its erection to the designs of James
Gandon [*Nottinghamshire County Records of the
Eighteenth Century*, ed. K. T. Meaby, 49, 55]. He
also made estimates for enlarging BULWELL
CHURCH in 1767 and (jointly with John White and
Samuel Stretton) for repairing EAST BRIDGFORD
CHURCH in 1769 [*ibid.*, 160–1].

ROBERTS, WILLIAM, a carpenter, designed
and built the TOLSEY or COUNCIL HOUSE at GLOU-
CESTER in 1750–1 [extracts by C. H. Dancey from
Gloucester Council Books in Public Library,
Book B, p. 108]. It was demolished in 1893–4.
There is an illustration in *Trans. Bristol and
Gloucester Arch. Soc.* xix, facing p. 185.
Roberts's will, dated 20 January 1754, was
proved at Gloucester on 27 October 1773.

ROBERTSON, DANIEL, appears to have
been related to the family of Robert and James
Adam, whose mother was a Robertson of Gladney. He was probably their pupil, for among
some Adam drawings in the Victoria and Albert
Museum there is one (3436–52) signed 'Daniel
Robertson fecit'. He certainly had connections
with their younger brother William Adam. At
Blair Adam there are several drawings for lodges
and cottages in the park signed 'Daniel Robertson *delt.*', and among the family papers there are
letters which show that Daniel Robertson was an
improvident character who contributed (in
exactly what way is not clear) to William Adam's
financial difficulties. In January 1821 Adam
formally undertook, 'at the express desire of my
nearest and best friends', to 'give up all connection with Alexander and Daniel Robertson'
[S.R.O., GD 18/4996].

Speculative building may have been the
trouble, for in 1812 Daniel Robertson exhibited

at the Royal Academy an elaborate project for a
new square between Covent Garden and Drury
Lane theatres, and in 1813 he and Alexander
Robertson (who was presumably his brother)
were involved in an abortive scheme for speculative building on the Grosvenor estate [Hermione
Hobhouse, *Thomas Cubitt*, 1971, 89]. In 1817 (at
a time when his father-in-law, Dr. Thomas Clarke
of Greenwich, was trying to persuade him to take
a post in Dublin – see S.R.O., GD 18/4992),
Daniel was preparing a design (now in the Royal
Library at Windsor) for a vast building in Whitehall to accommodate 'all the offices which form
the Executive Departments of the Government
of the United Kingdom'.

Robertson's first recorded architectural
commission was the alteration of premises in Pall
Mall for the Travellers' Club in 1821. Between
1825 and 1828 he obtained several commissions
in Oxford, notably the design of the new
Clarendon Press building in Walton Street, for
whose handsome Graeco-Roman façade he was
responsible. He also restored the Gothic front of
All Souls College and designed two local
churches in a starved Romanesque style which
earned one of them the nickname of 'the Boiled
Rabbit'.

In 1829 Robertson left Oxford for Ireland.
That something discreditable had occurred is
evident from a remark in a contemporary periodical that 'We regret the loss of Mr. Robertson to
Oxford; but the reason for his departure is no
subject for public discussion' (*The Crypt* iii,
1829, 200). In Ireland he had several commissions for country houses, particularly in Co.
Wexford, and on his drawings he described himself as of 'Dublin and Gorey'.[1] He is last heard
of at Powerscourt, where he designed the Upper
Terrace in 1843. Improvident as ever, he was on
one occasion hidden in the dome of the house
when sheriff's officers came to arrest him for
debt. 'He was' (Lord Powerscourt recalled)
'given to drink, and always drew best when he
was excited with sherry. He suffered from gout,
and used to be driven about in a wheel-barrow
with a bottle of sherry; while that lasted he was
always ready to direct the workmen, but when
it was finished he was incapable of working any
more' (Lord Powerscourt, *Description and History of Powerscourt*, 1903, 77).

Unexecuted designs by Robertson are illustrated in Colvin, *Architectural Drawings in the
Library of Worcester College, Oxford*, 1964, pl. 36
(new front for Worcester College), and Harris,
*British Drawings for Architecture, etc., in Ameri-
can Collections*, 1971, pls. 133–6 (Burton Park,
Lincs.).

LONDON, NO. 49 PALL MALL, alterations for the

---

[1] He must not be confused with the Irish architect
William Robertson of Kilkenny (1770–1850).

Travellers' Club, 1821; dem. [*Survey of London* xxix, 400, but see above, p. 224].

OXFORD, THE CLARENDON PRESS, WALTON STREET 1826–7; north wing completed by E. Blore 1829–30 [J. Ingram, *Memorials of Oxford* iii, 1837, 16].

OXFORD, WADHAM COLLEGE, fireplace in Hall, 1826 [T. G. Jackson, *Wadham College, Oxford,* 1893, 178].

OXFORD, ORIEL COLLEGE, rebuilt west side of north (St. Mary Hall) quadrangle, *c.* 1826 [*V.C.H. Oxon.* iii, 131].

OXFORD, ST. JOHN'S COLLEGE, the inner Senior Common Room, 1826–7 [the College Register viii, 325–6, refers to the architect as 'Mr. Robinson', but in the accounts (*Computus Annuus*, 1826) he is 'Mr. Roberson'].

OXFORD, ALL SOULS COLLEGE, restored High Street front and refronted Warden's house, 1827 [exhib. at R.A. 1828; original designs in Sir John Soane's Museum, drawer xv, 4].

OXFORD, ST. CLEMENT'S CHURCH, 1827–8, 'Norman' style; altered internally by E. G. Bruton 1874 [*A.P.S.D.*; Thomas Rickman's diary, 8 June 1826].

DINTON CHURCH, BUCKS., reseated 1827 [I.C.B.S.].

attributed: KENNINGTON CHURCH, BERKS., 1828, 'Norman' style [stylistic attribution].

CRICK RECTORY, NORTHANTS., 1829; dem. *c.* 1960 [Northants. Record Office, drawings in Peterborough Diocesan Records].

JOHNSTOWN CASTLE, CO. WEXFORD, alterations and additions for Hamilton Knox Grogan Morgan, *c.* 1833–6, castellated [*Connoisseur* clxvii, 1961, 282–3].

CARRIGLAS, CO. LONGFORD, IRELAND, for Anthony Lefroy, 1837–8, Tudor style [The Knight of Glin in *The Country Seat*, ed. Colvin & Harris, 1970, 192, n. 10].

DUBLIN, ST. MATTHIAS CHAPEL, WELLINGTON SQUARE, 1840 [drawings in National Library of Ireland, Portfolio 1, *ex inf.* Mr. E. McParland].

WELLS HOUSE, CO. WEXFORD, for Robert Doyne, *c.* 1840, Jacobethan [drawings formerly at Wells, *ex inf.* Mr. J. O'Callaghan].

BALLINKEEL HOUSE, CO. WEXFORD, for John Maher, *c.* 1840–3 [drawings at Ballinkeel, *ex inf.* Messrs. E. McParland & J. O'Callaghan].

KILRUDDERY HOUSE, CO. WICKLOW, garden layout for the 10th Earl of Meath, *c.* 1840 [drawings at Kilruddery, *ex inf.* Mr. E. McParland].

CASTLEBORO HOUSE, CO. WEXFORD, for the 1st Lord Carew, soon after 1840; now a ruin [C. L. Adams, *Castles of Ireland*, 1904, 102] (*C. Life,* 30 May 1974, 1357, fig. 3).

POWERSCOURT, CO. WICKLOW, IRELAND, the Upper Terrace for the 6th Viscount Powerscourt, 1843 [inscription: 'The Upper Terrace was designed by Daniel Robertson Archt. after the Villa Butera in Sicily'].

ROBERTSON, JAMES, of Edinburgh, designed REDHALL HOUSE, COLINTON, MIDLOTHIAN (now a suburb of Edinburgh), for George Inglis in 1758 [James Steuart, *Notes for a History of Colinton Parish*, 1938]. In 1770 he and Alexander Gowan were the 'architects' by whose advice COLINTON CHURCH was condemned as beyond repair [S.R.O., HR 728/1].

ROBERTSON, JOHN, was a nephew of Robert and James Adam. He practised in Glasgow, where in 1798 he built the BARONY CHURCH to the designs of James Adam [*Glasgow Delineated*, 1826, 73]. In the Scottish Record Office there are designs by him for various public buildings in Ayr, including a Market (1799), Assembly Rooms (1802) and Church (1804–6) [RHP 2554–5, 2558, 2563, 2582, 2585]. None of these appear to have been built, but Robertson did design the AYR ACADEMY in 1800. This elegant astylar building was rebuilt in 1895 [*Air Academy and Burgh Scule 1233–1895*, Ayr 1895, 100, with illustration]. Robertson appears to have been a competent late Georgian architect.

ROBERTSON, JOHN, of Bayswater, was employed as a draughtsman in the office of J. C. Loudon from 1829 onwards, and was responsible for many of the figures which illustrate the latter's *Encyclopaedia of Cottage, Farm and Villa Architecture,* 1833 (2nd ed. 1846). In 1833 he published under his own name a *Supplement to Loudon's Manual of Cottage Gardening, Husbandry and Architecture containing Thirty Designs for Dwellings in the Cottage Style.* Robertson subsequently became architectural assistant to Sir Joseph Paxton, and in this capacity helped to design the picturesque village of EDENSOR, nr. Chatsworth in Derbyshire, for the 6th Duke of Devonshire, *c.* 1839–45. Robertson may also have been concerned in some other of Paxton's works, such as the Cemetery at Coventry and the Park at Birkenhead, but in 1846 or 1847 he appears to have left Paxton's office, his place being taken by G. H. Stokes [G. F. Chadwick, *The Works of Sir Joseph Paxton*, 1961, 160–6, 186–8, 198–9].

ROBERTSON, W—, was the author of a book entitled *Designs in Architecture for Garden Chairs, Small Gates for Villas, Park Entrances, Aviarys, Temples, Boat Houses, Mausoleums, and Bridges,* 1800. Nothing else appears to be known about him, and it is unlikely that he was the Irish architect William Robertson of Kilkenny (1770–1850).

ROBERTSON, WILLIAM, of Leven in Fife, was active in Dundee as a designer of industrial buildings in the middle of the eighteenth century and is described as 'architect' in contemporary records. In 1752 he reconstructed and refitted the

TOWN'S MILLS, in 1755 he contracted to build the PACKHOUSES (or Public Warehouse) on a well-designed symmetrical plan, and in 1757 he designed a large WINDMILL of novel construction described by Dr. Pococke in his *Tours in Scotland* (Scottish History Soc. 1887, 224). He took a lease of the Town's Mills in 1766 [Dundee Town Council Minutes, 10 May, 13 Nov. 1752, 29 March 1755, 4 April 1757, and 1766, *ex inf.* Mr. David Walker].

ROBERTSON, WILLIAM (*c.* 1786–1841), practised in Elgin, where he died on 12 June 1841, aged 55, and is commemorated by a tombstone in the cathedral churchyard. In 1826 W. Clarke published *A Series of Views of the Ruins of Elgin Cathedral . . . with ground plan and table of measurements by Mr. Robertson, architect* (Elgin 1826). In the following list all references to the *Aberdeen Journal* are due to Mr. David Walker.

GRANGE MANSE, BANFFSHIRE, 1814 [mentioned as Robertson's design in the printed *Abstract of the Late Proceedings in the Case of the Manse of Aberdour, Aberdeenshire,* 1823; S.R.O., GD 16/46/89].

CULLEN, BANFFSHIRE, TOWN HALL, POST OFFICE, SEAFIELD HOTEL, etc., for Col. F. W. Grant, 1822–3 [S.R.O., GD 248/784/5].

ELGIN, EPISCOPAL CHURCH and PARSONAGE (32 NORTH STREET), 1825 [*Aberdeen Jnl.*, 13 April 1825].

ORTON HOUSE, MORAYSHIRE, additions for Richard Wharton Duff, 1826 [*Aberdeen Jnl.*, 20 Sept. 1826].

ARNDILLY HOUSE, BANFFSHIRE, additions for — McDowall, 1826 [*Aberdeen Jnl.*, 11 Oct. 1826].

WESTER ELCHIES HOUSE, MORAYSHIRE, additions for Charles Grant, 1828; dem. 1970 [*Aberdeen Jnl.*, 9 Jan. 1828].

GLENGUNNERY, or CLUNE COTTAGE (a shooting lodge), KNOCKANDO, MORAYSHIRE, for Charles Grant, 1828 [*Aberdeen Jnl.*, 16 Jan. 1828; cf. *N.S.A.* xiii, 70].

BOHARM CHURCH, BANFFSHIRE, porches, 1828 [*Aberdeen Jnl.*, 2 July 1828].

BOHARM SCHOOL, BANFFSHIRE, 1828 [*Aberdeen Jnl.*, 2 July 1828].

BUCKIE CHAPEL, BANFFSHIRE, 1835; dem. *c.* 1880 [*Aberdeen Jnl.*, 22 July 1835].

DUFFUS HOUSE, MORAYSHIRE, large addition for Sir Archibald Dunbar, Bart., 1835 [*Aberdeen Jnl.*, 26 Aug. 1835].

DINGWALL, ROSS AND CROMARTY, NATIONAL BANK, 1835 [*Aberdeen Jnl.*, 27 July 1835].

ELGIN, COURT HOUSE AND PUBLIC OFFICES, 1837; rebuilt *c.* 1930 [*Aberdeen Jnl.*, 22 Nov. 1837].

BANFF ACADEMY, 1838 [*N.S.A.* xiii, 55].

INVERNESS, a hotel, 1838 [*Aberdeen Jnl.*, 1 Aug. 1838].

ABERLOUR HOUSE, BANFFSHIRE (now Gordonstoun Preparatory School), for Alexander Grant, 1838; also the stables and a Tuscan column [*Aberdeen Jnl.*, 28 Nov. 1838].

ABERLOUR CHURCH, BANFFSHIRE, tower ('Saxon'), 1838 [*Aberdeen Jnl.*, 28 Nov. 1838].

PORTKNOCKIE CHURCH, BANFFSHIRE, 1838 [*Aberdeenshire Jnl.*, 8 Aug. 1838].

FORRES, MORAYSHIRE, TOWN HOUSE, 1838–9 [R. Douglas, *Annals of Forres*, Elgin 1934, 285].

DOCHFOUR HOUSE, INVERNESS-SHIRE, work for Evan Baillie, 1839 [*Aberdeen Jnl.*, 12 June 1839].

ROTHES MANSE, MORAYSHIRE, 1839 [*Aberdeen Jnl.*, 23 Oct. 1838].

KININVIE HOUSE, BANFFSHIRE, addition and square of offices for Archibald Young Leslie, 1840 [*Aberdeen Jnl.*, 16 Dec. 1840].

BLAIRSHANNOCK (a farm-house), ABERLOUR, BANFFSHIRE, 1841 [*Aberdeen Jnl.*, 3 March 1841].

ROBINS, GREENWAY (–1853), of Crosby Row, Walworth, designed EDEN PARK, BECKENHAM, KENT, for John Woolley, exhibiting a drawing of the house at the Royal Academy in 1827 as 'lately erected'. The house (dem.) is illustrated by C. Greenwood, *Epitome of County History: Kent*, 1838, 32. Robins also designed ST. JAMES'S CHURCH, RYDE, ISLE OF WIGHT, 1827–8, Gothic [Stephen Green, *St. James's Church, Ryde*, Ryde 1975, 3]. He was elected a member of the Surveyors' Club in 1827 and was its President in 1831. His will was proved in the Prerogative Court of Canterbury in June 1853.

ROBINSON, —, of Middleton in Lancashire, is stated by J. P. Neale, *Views of Seats*, 2nd ser., v, 1829, to have designed additions to SOMERFORD HALL, CHESHIRE, for C. W. S. Shakerley. The house was remodelled in 1860 and demolished in 1926. Drawings formerly at Rudding Park, Yorkshire, show that in 1795–6 Robinson of Middleton made designs for minor alterations to MILNSBRIDGE HOUSE, YORKS. (W.R.). He may have been the 'L. Robinson' who signs a design for the enlargement of WINSTANLEY HALL, LANCS., dated 1785 [framed drawing at Winstanley Hall, *ex inf.* Mr. John Harris], and if so may probably be identified with the Lawrance Robinson whose name appears in the 1786 Land Tax assessment for Middleton in the Lancashire Record Office.

ROBINSON, L—, *see* ROBINSON, —

ROBINSON, PETER FREDERICK (1776–1858), was a pupil of Henry Holland. He afterwards became an assistant of William Porden, and in 1801–2 supervised the execution of the latter's works at the Royal Pavilion, Brighton. He was a prolific designer of country mansions and picturesque cottages. His published works show that he was prepared to provide his clients with residences in either the 'Old English', 'Edwardian', 'Tudor', 'Elizabethan' or half-timber styles, and he even proposed to build a 'Norman' villa in Hampshire with a tower copied from Christchurch Priory, windows derived from Barfreston Church, and a hall like the nave of a Romanesque cathedral. His most exotic work was the 'Egyptian Hall' in Piccadilly, designed as a museum for William Bullock, naturalist and antiquarian. This was a famous architectural novelty in its day, and represented the first attempt to graft Egyptian features on to an English building.

In 1816 Robinson travelled on the Continent, visiting Rome, and returning by way of Switzerland, thus enabling him to add the 'Swiss chalet' to his architectural repertoire. He became an F.S.A. in 1826 and was one of the first vice-presidents of the Institute of British Architects. He exhibited at the Royal Academy from 1795 to 1833. James Lansdown, H. F. Lockwood, J. G. Jackson of Leamington and Josiah Taylor, afterwards the architectural publisher, were his pupils. Financial difficulties obliged him to live at Boulogne from about 1840 onwards, and he died there on 24 June 1858, aged 82.

Robinson was employed by E. Willes of Leamington to make plans for the development of his property there in 1823–6. Several of his plans are in the Warwickshire Record Office, and the layout which he proposed is illustrated by H. G. Clarke, *Royal Leamington Spa*, 1947, 88–9. The streets round Beauchamp Square were developed under his direction in 1825–6. His designs (1827) for re-erecting the portico of Carlton House as a memorial to the Duke of York are preserved in the Royal Library at Windsor. In 1831 he made designs, now in the Library of the Society of Antiquaries (pressmark 64, I), for a building on the north side of Trafalgar Square to accommodate the Royal and Antiquarian Societies. In 1835 he competed for the Houses of Parliament, submitting a Tudor Gothic design whose detailing was derived from Hengrave Hall, Suffolk. In the Monmouthshire Record Office there are unexecuted designs by him dated 1838 for a castle-style house for Pryse Powell.

Robinson projected a continuation of *Vitruvius Britannicus*, publishing plates of *Woburn Abbey*, 1827; *Hatfield House*, 1833; *Hardwicke Hall*, 1835; *Castle Ashby*, 1841; and *Warwick Castle*, ?1842. He also published *Rural Architecture; or a Series of Designs for Ornamental Cottages*, 1823, 5th ed. 1850, with landscapes redrawn by J. D. Harding; *Designs for Ornamental Villas*, 1825–7, 1836, 4th ed. 1853; *Designs for Village Architecture, being a Series of Designs illustrating the Observations contained in the Essay on the Picturesque by Sir Uvedale Price*, 1830, 4th ed. 1837;

Designs for Farm Buildings, 1830, 3rd ed. 1837; *Designs for Lodges and Park Entrances*, 1833, 3rd ed. 1837; *Domestic Architecture in the Tudor Style*, 1837; *A New Series of Designs for Ornamental Cottages and Villas*, 1838. He was also the author of *An Attempt to ascertain the Age of Mickleham Church in Surrey*, 1824; and read papers to the Institute of British Architects on 'The Newly Discovered Crypt at York Minster' (6 July 1835), 'Observations relating to the proposal for removing the choir screen', and 'Oblique arches' (5 Dec. 1836).

[*A.P.S.D.*; *D.N.B.*; *Builder* xvi, 1858, 458.]

LONDON, THE HANS TOWN ASSEMBLY ROOMS, CADOGAN PLACE, 1807 [exhib. at R.A.].

HUTTON BUSHELL, nr. SCARBOROUGH, YORKS. (N.R.), stabling for G. Osbaldeston, *c.* 1807–8; dem. [exhib. at R.A.]. The house was largely destroyed by fire about this time, and not rebuilt. Robinson exhibited designs for 'alterations and additions' in 1808, and for a 'banqueting-seat' at Yedmandale, on the same estate, in 1809, but it is unlikely that these were built. After the fire Osbaldeston went to live at Ebberston Lodge (see p. 184), and in 1823 Robinson exhibited another abortive design for a new house for Osbaldeston there.

WESTPORT, CO. MAYO, IRELAND, Marine Bath for the 1st Marquess of Sligo, 1807 [exhib. at R.A.].

SANDGATE, KENT, 'Seaman's Cottage' for Capt. Waller, R.N., 1808 [exhib. at R.A.].

CAMPDEN HILL, KENSINGTON, villa for W. Phillimore, 1808 [exhib. at R.A.].

KEW CHURCHYARD, SURREY, monument to Luke Wetten (d. 1807) [exhib. at R.A. 1808].

LONDON, THE EGYPTIAN HALL, PICCADILLY, for W. Bullock, 1811–12; dem. 1905 [exhib. at R.A. 1811; Wyatt Papworth in *Notes and Queries*, 5th ser., iii, 1875, 284–5; *Survey of London* xxix, 266–70].

LAMPETER, CARDIGANSHIRE, TOWN HALL AND MARKET PLACE for R. H. Davis, 1813; dem. 1879 [exhib. at R.A.].

MILLFIELD COTTAGE, BOOKHAM, SURREY, for Major-General Bayley Wallis, 1814; enlarged 1863 [exhib. at R.A.].

FERNACRES, nr. FULMER, BUCKS., for J. Woodcock, 1815 [exhib. at R.A.].

KIPLIN HALL, nr. CATTERICK, YORKS. (N.R.), drawing-room for the 4th Earl of Tyrconnel, 1819 [exhib. at R.A.].

SHINFIELD HOUSE, BERKS., remodelled east front for E. Willes, 1820, and further alterations *c.* 1826 [Warwickshire County Record Office, Willes drawings 58–60, etc.].

NORBURY PARK, nr. DORKING, SURREY, additions for F. Maitland, including castellated lodge, 1821–3; front remodelled *c.* 1860 and again by Mewès and Davis 1920 [exhib. at R.A. 1820–

3] (*Arch. Rev.*, 1, 1921, 40–2; engraving of lodge in Brayley, *Surrey* iv, 453).

MICKLEHAM CHURCH, SURREY, alterations in Norman style, including rebuilding of south arcade to support a new gallery and refitting of interior, 1822–3 [exhib. at R.A. 1821–4]. All Robinson's work was removed in 1891.

KEW CHURCH, SURREY, minor alterations, 1823 [Surrey Archdeaconry Records].

CHESHUNT, HERTS., cottage for E. Clarke, 1824 [exhib. at R.A.].

TRELISSICK HOUSE, nr. TRURO, CORNWALL, for Thomas Daniell, 1824 [R. Ackermann, *Repository of Arts*, 3rd ser., ix, 1827, 64; cf. *Ornamental Villas*, no. 3].

LEAMINGTON, WARWICKS., BINSWOOD COTTAGE for E. Willes, 1824 [*New Series of Designs*, 1838, part 2, pls. 1–4].

LEAMINGTON, WARWICKS., CHRIST CHURCH, for E. Willes, 1825, Norman; dem. [T. B. Dudley, *History of Leamington*, 1896–1900, 180, 272].

THE QUERNS, nr. CIRENCESTER, GLOS., for Charles Laurence, 1825–7 [*Ornamental Villas*, no. 5].

YORK, CASTLE GAOL, rebuilt Prison, Governor's House, Gatehouse, etc., 1826–35, castellated; dem. 1935 [*Companion to the Almanac*, 1834, 219–22; T. P. Cooper, *History of the Castle of York*, 1911, 236–41].

LEAMINGTON, WARWICKS., COPP'S ROYAL HOTEL, 1826–7; dem. 1847 [exhib. at R.A. 1828; T. B. Dudley, *History of Leamington*, 1896–1900, 187].

THE HOLMWOOD, nr. DORKING, SURREY., for Miss Arnold, 1827 [*Ornamental Villas*, no. 7].

WOOLMER LODGE, BRAMSHOTT, HANTS., for Sir James Macdonald, Bart., 1827–8 [exhib. at R.A. 1830; *Ornamental Villas*, 1836 ed., p. 28].

SAMPFORD HOUSE, LITTLE SAMPFORD, ESSEX., for John Hinxman, 1828; destroyed by fire 1836 [exhib. at R.A. 1832; *New Series of Designs*, 1838, part 2, pls. 13–16].

LONDON, THE SWISS COTTAGE, in the grounds of THE COLOSSEUM, REGENT STREET, for Thomas Hornor, c. 1828 [*A.P.S.D.*; Thomas Rickman's diary, 26 June 1828] (*The Mirror* xx, 1832, 257–9).

STORA SUNDBY, SÖDERMANLAND, SWEDEN, remodelled castle in 'Anglo-Norman' style, 1830 [exhib. at R.A. 1830; information from Mr. R. Tatchell, F.R.I.B.A.].

WARTER HALL, YORKS. (E.R.), additions for the 3rd Lord Muncaster, c. 1830; dem. c. 1973 [*Ornamental Villas*, 1836 ed., 16].

HEVER CASTLE, KENT, drawing-room for Mrs. Waldo, c. 1830 [exhib. at R.A. 1831; *Colbran's New Guide for Tunbridge Wells*, 1840, 261].

SINGLETON HOUSE (now UNIVERSITY COLLEGE), SWANSEA, remodelled for J. H. Vivian, 1831 [*Domestic Architecture in the Tudor Style*, 1837].

BLAIR DRUMMOND, PERTHSIRE, toll-house for H.

H. Drummond, 1831 [signed drawing: photograph at N.M.R.S.].

BRIDEHEAD, LITTLE BREDY, DORSET, remodelled for Robert Williams, 1831–3, Tudor [exhib. at R.A. 1831, 1833].

COOLHURST, nr. HORSHAM, SUSSEX, for the Dowager Marchioness of Northampton, 1831–3, Elizabethan [exhib. at R.A. 1831; T. W. Horsfield, *History of Sussex* ii, 1835, 265, with engraving].

YORK, BOOTHAM BAR., rebuilt inner face, replacing Georgian elevation, 1834 [R.C.H.M., *York* ii, 117, pl. 33].

NOTTINGHAM, THE PARK, a villa, c. 1835 [*New Series of Designs*, 1838, part 2, pls. 8–12].

KEMBLE HOUSE, GLOS., THE GARDEN HOUSE for Robert Gordon, 1835 [*Ornamental Villas*, 1836 ed., 37].

? TICKTON GRANGE, nr. BEVERLEY, YORKS. (E.R.), for Smith Wormald, 1836, dem.: apparently the house stated on p. 40 of *Ornamental Villas*, 1836 ed., to be 'now erecting near Beverley for Smyth Wyndham, Esq.'

DUNSLEY MANOR HOUSE, nr. STOURBRIDGE, STAFFS., for H. H. Foley, c. 1838 [*New Series of Designs*, 1838, part 2, pls. 17–20].

PRESTWOOD, nr. STOURBRIDGE, STAFFS., farmhouse for H. H. Foley [*New Series of Designs*, 1838, part 2, pls. 5–8].

BROMLEY HILL HOUSE, KENT, design said to have been 'partially adopted' by Sir Charles Long, cr. Lord Farnborough [*Ornamental Villas*, 1836 ed., 43].

CASSIOBURY PARK, HERTS., conservatory for the 5th Earl of Essex [*Ornamental Villas*, 1836 ed., 10].

OYSTERMOUTH, GLAMORGANSHIRE, seaside villa [*New Series of Designs*, 1838, part 2, pls. 21–4].

ROBINSON, ROBERT (1734–), was a younger brother of William Robinson (*q.v.*) [*A.P.S.D.*]. He appears to have begun life as an assistant to Lancelot Brown, the landscape-gardener, subsequently practising in Edinburgh as an architect and landscape-gardener. In an advertisement in the *Caledonian Mercury* for 8 March 1760, Robert Robinson, 'late Draughtsman and Executor of the Designs of Lancelot Brown, Esq.', announced that he and William Boutcher had entered into partnership 'for designing, drawing and executing all kinds of policy and gardening', but that he would continue to 'give Designs, and carry on buildings, as formerly'. In 1764 he was at Castle Grant, Morayshire, in order to make a plan of the grounds for James Grant [S.R.O., GD 248/178/2 and 248/250]. Designs by him exist for laying out the grounds of Balbirnie House, Fife (1779), and Paxton House, Berwickshire [Alistair Rowan in *C. Life*, 29 June 1972, 1671]. In 1773, as Robert Robinson, 'architect', he was made a burgess of Edinburgh gratis 'for good services' [*Roll of Edinburgh Burgesses 1761–1841*, Scottish Record Soc., 136]. He was presumably the 'Robert Robertson, architect', who occurs in the Edinburgh directories up to 1782, when he was declared bankrupt, but is to be distinguished from George Robertson, 'designer in gardening', who appears in the same directories up to 1784/5.

ROBINSON, SAMUEL (1752–1833), was admitted to the Royal Academy Schools in 1775 at the age of 23, and exhibited at the Academy between 1775 and 1821. He was surveyor to the estates of St. Thomas's Hospital, those of St. Olave's Grammar Schools, the Cordwainers' Company, and the parishes of St. Magnus Martyr and St. Margaret Lothbury. He specialized in the design of warehouses and similar buildings, and was much employed in valuations, particularly those connected with the formation of the new Regent Street, which he carried out in conjunction with D. R. Roper. D. A. Alexander, V. Davis, T. Hatton, W. Mackie, J. Medland, Edwin Nash and W. Strutt were his pupils. He died on 4 September 1833, aged 82, and was buried in front of the almshouses at Hackney which he had built and endowed [*A.P.S.D.*].

A brewhouse for Edmund Dawson [exhib. at R.A. 1783].

WOODFORD CHURCHYARD, ESSEX, monument to Edward Keepe (d. 1781), executed in Coade stone [exhib. at R.A. 1784] (*Architect and Building News*, 26 Jan. 1940, 114).

LONDON, 'Buildings now erecting on the bank of the River, where the late great fire happened opposite the Tower', exhib. at R.A. 1786.

HACKNEY, THE WIDOWS' RETREAT ALMSHOUSES, 1812, Gothic [W. Robinson, *History of Hackney* ii, 1842, 320].

ST. THOMAS'S HOSPITAL, SOUTHWARK, anatomical theatre, 1814–15. In about 1833, in partnership with J. Field, he designed the north wing, entrance gates and lodges as part of a general plan of rebuilding. The south wing was completed by Field in 1842.

SOUTHWARK, premises of BRITISH AND FOREIGN SCHOOL SOCIETY, BOROUGH ROAD, 1817 [*A.P.S.D.*].

THE PROTESTANT DISSENTERS' COLLEGE, HOMERTON, 1823 [W. Robinson, *History of Hackney* ii, 1842, 282].

SOUTHWARK, ST. OLAVE'S GRAMMAR SCHOOL, MAGDALEN STREET, 1824; dem. [*A.P.S.D.*].

ROBINSON, Sir THOMAS (*c.* 1702–1777), was the eldest son and heir of William Robinson of Rokeby, Yorks. As a young man he travelled widely on the Continent and acquired the taste for architecture which was to be his dominant interest in later life. In 1727 he was returned to

Parliament as Member for Morpeth through the influence of George Bowes. In the following year he married Elizabeth, the eldest daughter of Charles Howard, 3rd Earl of Carlisle, and widow of Nicholas, Lord Lechmere. He was created a baronet in 1731, and was a commissioner of excise from 1735 to 1742. Both in London, where he 'gave balls to all the men and women in power and in fashion', and at Rokeby, where he rebuilt the mansion and enclosed the park, his expenditure was extravagant, and it was chiefly in order to relieve his finances that in 1742 he accepted the post of Governor of Barbados. Here his love of building led him into further difficulties, for he ordered extensive alterations to his official residence at Pilgrim without consulting the assembly, and also undertook to build an armoury and arsenal. The assembly refused to vote sufficient money, and in the end he had to pay most of the building expenses himself. After further troubles over the command of the armed forces in the island, he was recalled in 1747. His first wife had died in 1739, and while in Barbados he married the widow of a rich ironmonger who brought him a considerable fortune, but refused to accompany him back to England.

On his return, Robinson acquired shares in Ranelagh Gardens, and undertook the congenial duties of master of ceremonies. Under his management the Gardens reached the height of their celebrity, and the tall figure of 'Long Sir Thomas' figures largely in the social satires of the time. He built a house called Prospect Place on a site adjoining the Gardens, and once more gave the magnificent entertainments for which he had been famous as a young man. But renewed extravagance brought a return of his financial troubles, and in 1769 he was obliged to sell Rokeby, which had been in the possession of his family since 1610. He died at his house in Chelsea on 3 March 1777, at the age of 76, and was buried in the chancel of Merton Church, Surrey, where a monument was erected to his memory. A second monument, with busts of himself and his wife by John Walsh, was erected in Westminster Abbey in accordance with his will. He was succeeded in the baronetcy by his brother William. His portrait by Frans van de Mijn, formerly at Farnham Royal, Bucks., was exhibited at the Royal Academy exhibition of 'English Taste in the Eighteen Century' in 1955–6 (No. 85).

It is as a man of fashion that Sir Thomas Robinson is chiefly celebrated: but in the eighteenth century building was a fashionable occupation, and Sir Thomas counted architecture among his polite accomplishments. He was on friendly terms with Lord Burlington, whose Palladian principles he did his best to follow. It was in the Palladian style that he rebuilt ROKEBY between 1725 and 1730. A design had been made by the Yorkshire architect Wakefield in 1724 and was published in *Vitruvius Britannicus* iii, 1725, pl. 90. But Robinson rejected Wakefield's design in favour of one for which he claimed the credit himself, issuing in 1735–41 a set of engravings signed 'T. Robinson Bar. architectus'.[1] Though Robinson built his design up out of established Palladian elements, he combined them into an original and highly effective composition that had no precedent among English country houses. Out of the Park he created the romantic landscape which, nearly a hundred years later, was to form the setting for Sir Walter Scott's poem *Rokeby* (*C. Life*, 22–29 Sept. 1917, 19 May 1955; H. A. Tipping, *English Homes, Period V*, vol. i, 1921).

Sir Thomas maintained a long correspondence on architectural and other matters with his father-in-law, Lord Carlisle, and criticized Hawksmoor's designs for the mausoleum which the latter was building at CASTLE HOWARD. After Hawksmoor's death in 1736, it was by his advice that Daniel Garrett was employed to complete the dual stairway and the surrounding wall in a manner which, although it may have been more 'Palladian', accorded ill with Hawksmoor's intentions [G. F. Webb, 'The Letters and Drawings ... relating to ... the Mausoleum at Castle Howard', *Walpole Soc.* xix, 1931]. Later on, between 1753 and 1759, Robinson was allowed to carry out alterations to the mansion itself which were designed to give it as far as possible a Palladian character. The western court had been left incomplete on Vanbrugh's death in 1726, and Robinson, instead of completing it in accordance with the published designs, built a new wing extending to the corner of the garden front, and terminating in a pavilion which gives the façade an unfortunately lop-sided appearance. It is likely that he hoped to remodel the eastern court to correspond, but this he was not permitted to do [L. Whistler, *The Imagination of Vanbrugh*, 1954, 48–50] (H. A. Tipping, *English Homes, Period IV*, vol. ii, 1928, 36, figs. 54–6).

For Ralph, 2nd Lord Verney, one of the proprietors of Ranelagh Gardens, Robinson designed a new house at CLAYDON, BUCKS, with a central rotunda and a large ballroom occupying one wing. The work proceeded slowly, and was still incomplete at the time of Robinson's death in 1777. The ballroom and rotunda were pulled down in about 1790, but one wing remains as designed by Robinson. His correspondence with Lord Verney was published by Margaret Lady Verney and Patrick Abercrombie as 'Letters of an Eighteenth Century Architect', *Arch. Rev.*,

June–September 1926. For the house see C. Hussey in *C. Life*, 24–31 Oct., 7 Nov. 1952.

For Richard Trevor, Bishop of Durham, Robinson designed in 1760 the Gothic gateway at BISHOP AUCKLAND CASTLE, CO. DURHAM [W. Fordyce, *History of Durham* i, 1857, 549, confirmed by a contemporary drawing of the gateway preserved at the Palace, on which Robinson is named as the architect, illustrated *C. Life*, 24 Feb. 1972, 462], and in 1763–5 the classical church at GLYNDE, SUSSEX [T. W. Horsfield, *History of Lewes* ii, 1827, 125; W. de St. Croix, 'Parochial History of Glynde', *Sussex Arch. Colls.* xx, 1868, 78–9]. He may also have designed the stable block built at Glynde in 1753–6 by John Morris of Lewes and illustrated in *C. Life*, 28 April 1955. For the Rt. Hon. Arthur Onslow, Robinson designed an addition to EMBER COURT, SURREY, of which there is a signed engraving (B.M., *King's Maps* xl, 20, 2a, and Bodleian, Gough Maps 30, f. 51ᵛ), but it is not known whether this was built.

According to Surtees [*History of Durham* iv, 1840, 35], Robinson designed the bridge over the R. Tees at WINSTON, CO. DURHAM, in 1762–3, but the attribution to him of Greta Bridge near Rokeby is incorrect, as it was designed and built by John Carr of York in 1773, four years after Robinson had parted with the Yorkshire estate. It is also doubtful whether he had anything to do with the design of Rokeby Church, completed in 1778, though a design by him for a proposed parsonage at Rokeby is illustrated by Isaac Ware in his *Complete Body of Architecture* (1756). Several of the Rokeby engravings have Ware's name as draughtsman, and he evidently acted as Robinson's architectural amanuensis.

Robinson's personal papers were destroyed after his death, but a portfolio of his architectural designs remains at Rokeby.

[*A.P.S.D.*; *D.N.B.*; R. Sedgwick, *The House of Commons* ii, 1970, 388–9; R. Blunt, *Mrs. Montagu* ii, 1923, 28; Hist. MSS. Comm., *Carlisle, passim*; J. H. Round, 'Family History from Private Manuscripts', *The Ancestor* ix, 1904, 6–19; Dudley Harbron, 'The Modern Proteus', *Arch. Rev.* lxxx, 1936, 167–70.]

ROBINSON, THOMAS, BARON GRANTHAM (1738–1786), was the son of Sir Thomas Robinson of Newby Hall, Yorks., whom he succeeded as 2nd Baron Grantham in 1770. He was the grandson, through his mother, of Thomas Worsley of Hovingham (*q.v.*), and the father of Earl de Grey (*q.v.*). A portfolio of drawings at Newby Hall shows that he had some ability as an amateur architect. It includes designs for a 'Triumphal arch to be erected across the Great Western Road near St. George's Hospital between Hyde Park & the Green Park, 1761', for offices and stables for Newby (now Baldersby)

---

[1] Sets of these engravings can be seen in B.M. (*King's Maps* xlv, 26), Bodleian Library (Gough Yorks. 52) and York Minster Library, Hailstone Collection. They show stairs in place of the existing Doric porch or portico, which is clearly a later addition, though possibly one made by Robinson himself.

Park, and for an octagonal tower for Saltram House, Devonshire, the seat of his brother-in-law John Parker, cr. Lord Boringdon (cf. the National Trust guide-book to Saltram, 7 and 27). For Robinson's political career see *D.N.B.* and Namier & Brooke, *The House of Commons 1754–1790* iii, 1964, 367.

ROBINSON, WILLIAM, is known only as the author of a small volume consisting of 32 pages of engraved plates and text entitled *Proportional Architecture, or the Five Orders regulated by equal parts*, 1733, 2nd ed. 1736.

ROBINSON, WILLIAM (–1767), Surveyor to the Gresham Trustees, was, on 7 August 1767, appointed to supervise the expenditure of the £10,000 voted by the House of Commons for the repair of the Royal Exchange. According to Britton & Pugin, *Public Buildings of London* i, 1825, 292, 'almost the whole of the western side was rebuilt' under his direction. He also held the post of Surveyor to the East India Company from 1757 onwards. He died on 25 December 1767, leaving large sums to London charities. [*Gent's Mag.* 1767, 611; *A.P.S.D.*]

ROBINSON, WILLIAM (*c.* 1720–1775), born at Keyper, Co. Durham, was the eldest son of William Robinson of Durham. He came to London at an early age, served under Thomas Ripley, the Surveyor of Greenwich Hospital, and in 1746 was appointed Clerk of the Works at the Hospital, retaining the post until his death. From about 1752 to 1767 he was Surveyor of Buildings to the Board of Customs, and in 1754 he was appointed to the Office of Works post of Clerk of the Works at Whitehall, Westminster and St. James's. In 1762 he was promoted to be Secretary to the Board of Works and Clerk Itinerant. From 1762 onwards he was also Clerk of the Works at the Queen's (Buckingham) House.

Robinson was chiefly an official architect. In 1750–9 he and John Vardy supervised the building of the Horse Guards building in Whitehall to the designs of William Kent (d. 1748), and at Greenwich he supervised the erection of the Infirmary to the designs of James Stuart in 1763. His most important work was the EXCISE OFFICE in OLD BROAD STREET, built in a competent but conservative Palladian style in 1769–75 and demolished in 1854. His death in 1775 deprived him of the commission for the new public offices on the site of Somerset House which then fell to Sir William Chambers.

In a private capacity Robinson was employed by Horace Walpole to make the first alterations to STRAWBERRY HILL, TWICKENHAM, in 1748, but this was 'before there was any design of further improvements to the house', and they were not 'truly Gothic' – that is, they were in the kind of

Gothic devised by William Kent which no longer satisfied Walpole's antiquarian tastes. It was in the same sort of Gothic that in 1753 Robinson designed a church for the parish of STONE in STAFFORDSHIRE, which was built in 1754–8 under the direction of William Baker (*q.v.*) [W. H. Bowers & J. W. Clough, *Researches into the History of the Parish of Stone*, 1929, 58–61].

Robinson died suddenly of gout on 10 October 1775, and was buried in the Chapel at Greenwich Hospital. His brother Thomas (1727–1810) was a master gardener at Kensington, while another brother, Robert (*q.v.*), practised as an architect and landscape-gardener in Edinburgh.

[*A.P.S.D.*; P.R.O., Adm. 65/106; *History of the King's Works* v; Horace Walpole, *Works* ii, 1798, 421.]

ROBINSON, WILLIAM (*c.* 1744–), of Hackney, architect and surveyor, was, in 1774, a candidate for a District Surveyorship [Middlesex County Records, General Orders No. 10]. He published *The Gentleman and Builders' Director* [1775], which contains a commentary on the regulations laid down in the Building Act of 1774 and 'Directions to build Chimneys to prevent their Smoking'.

ROBINSON, WILLIAM (1762–1820), was the son of William Robinson, a builder of Saffron Walden in Essex. He followed his father in the business and died in April 1820, aged 58. On his tombstone in Saffron Walden Churchyard he is styled 'Architect and Builder'. Apart from the house called 'The Grove' which he built for himself, no buildings designed by Robinson appear to be recorded, but in 1784 a view of Saffron Walden Church by him was engraved, and in 1818 he published *The Sawyer's Ready Reckoner, an entire new work formed on equitable principles*. In 1816 he was a candidate for the County Surveyorship of Essex [Essex Record Office, Q/SO 24, p. 194]. [R. Heffer, 'William Robinson, Architect and Engraver of Saffron Walden', *Essex Review* xxx, 1921, 20–3.]

ROBSON, JOHN, practised in Great Marlborough Street, London. He exhibited at the Royal Academy between 1797 and 1833. His exhibits included a 'Design for a cottage intended to be built in Hunts.' (1803), a 'Design for a cottage to be built in Northumberland' (1806), a 'Design for a Cottage for Mr. Keats, to be built at Paddington' (1810), a 'Design for a castellated mansion for A. Bonelli, Esq.' (1815), a 'Design for the west end of the church at Norwood' (1819), a 'Design for a ball-room executed in Harley Street' (1820). Some unexecuted designs by him for additions to Littlecote House, Wilts., are described in a letter in *C. Life*, 27 Jan. 1966. He was one of the architects who submitted designs for rebuilding Hungerford Church, Berks., in 1811, and he competed for the University Observatory at Cambridge in 1821.

ROCHE, PETER DE LA, was the author of *An Essay on the Orders of Architecture, in which are contained some considerable alterations in their proportions etc., and the introduction of a new great order, called the Britannic Order*, 1769. In the introduction, he explains that although he had received no architectural training, he had 'always had a strong propensity to the study of this art, and that from my youth, as far back as I can remember, I have often amused myself in drawing elevations and plans of buildings; and being disgusted with the way of life I had hitherto led, I resolved to take another course and to give myself entirely to the study and practice of ARCHITECTURE'. He competed for the Royal Exchange at Dublin in 1769 [*Builder* xxvii, 1869, 781].

ROGERS, THOMAS (*c.* 1744–   ), was Surveyor to the County of Middlesex from *c.* 1773 to 1802, and District Surveyor of the parish of St. Marylebone from 1774 onwards. He exhibited at the Society of Artists (of which he was elected Director in 1774) from 1766 to 1790, and at the Royal Academy in 1786 and 1787. Among his exhibits was (1776) the 'Elevation of a new Front, erected to an old villa at Chigwell, Essex'. He was the successful competitor for the MIDDLESEX COUNTY SESSIONS HOUSE at CLERKENWELL GREEN, built in 1779–82. John Carter, however, claimed quite unjustifiably that Rogers had merely copied a design published by himself in the *Builder's Magazine* (pls. xc, xci). The building is illustrated in G. Richardson, *New Vitruvius Britannicus* i, 1802–8, pls. xxxiv–xxxv, and the original drawings and contracts are in the Middlesex Record Office. Rogers was President of the Surveyors' Club in 1795. He died after 1808 [*A.P.S.D.*].

ROLFE, WILLIAM EDWARD, son of W. Wolfe of East Ham, Essex, a builder, was a pupil in the office of Sir John Soane from 1801 to 1804. He exhibited at the Royal Academy between 1802 and 1820. He designed KEMPTON PARK, nr. HAMPTON, MIDDLESEX, with lodges and Gothic entrance-gates, for J. Fish, 1808–10; dem. [A. T. Bolton, *The Works of Sir John Soane*, 1924, Appendix C, p. xliii].

ROMER, JOHN LAMBERTUS (1680–?1754), was the son of Wolfgang William Romer (1640–1713), a military engineer in the service of William III. In 1708 he was appointed assistant engineer to his father at Portsmouth, and in 1715 he became engineer at Sheerness, with charge of the defences of the Thames and Medway. In July 1719, he took part in the expedition to Vigo under Lord Cobham, and on his return was (Jan. 1720) appointed surveyor in charge of the northern district and Scotland in succession to Andrews Jelfe. In Scotland he was responsible for the completion of barracks at Inversnaid, Ruthven, Bernera and Kiliwhimen, as well as for important defence works at Forts Augustus, William and George. In 1723 he was promoted engineer-in-ordinary, and went to the Board of Ordnance in London as officer in charge of the administration of Scotland and the northern engineer districts. In 1745–6 he served under the Duke of Cumberland, and was wounded at Culloden. He retired in 1751 [*D.N.B.*; P.R.O., Ordnance Office records].

In the British Museum there is a 'Plan and Section of a Cistern built at Sheerness in the year 1716 by John Romer Engineer' (*King's Maps* xvii, 19k), and in the Public Record Office there is a copy made by Isaac Swan in 1781 of the 'Plans and Sections of a Market House and stables built at Sheerness in the year 1718', signed 'Romer' (MPH 15). From their similarity of style, which has a markedly Vanbrughian character, it is possible that he was also responsible for the designs for a Barracks and Storehouse at Upnor Castle, dated 1717/18 (*King's Maps* xviii, 58 c–d), and for a 'Plan and Elevation of the New Store-House at Chatham begun in the year 1717' (*ibid.* xvi, 42 g). Drawings connected with his Scottish works are in the National Library of Scotland (MS. 1648).

ROOKS, JOHN (*c.* 1760–1833), practised in Norwich, where for twenty-seven years he was Surveyor to the Paving Commissioners. He was also Surveyor to the Commissioners of Sewers and to the Trustees of the Great Hospital. He died on 24 June 1833, aged 73, and was commemorated by a tombstone in St. Stephen's Churchyard.

ROPER, DAVID RIDDALL (*c.* 1774–1855), was a well-known surveyor who, in partnership with Samuel Robinson, made the valuations of property in connection with the formation of Regent Street. He exhibited at the Royal Academy between 1797 and 1822, and was President of the Surveyors' Club in 1813. He died on 11 April 1855, in his 82nd year. W. Ford, T. Hatton, W. Jay and T. Ruck were his pupils. Joshua and David Roper, who exhibited architectural designs from his Blackfriars office at the Royal Academy in 1815–17 and 1820, respectively, were his sons. A. B. Clayton (*q.v.*) was an assistant in his office, and is said to have been the effective designer of two of his principal buildings, St. Mark's Church, Kennington, and the Shot Tower at Lambeth. [*A.P.S.D.*; letter from H. C. Barlow in *Builder* xxvii, 1869, 65; *The Times*, 14 April 1855.]

SOUTHWARK, ALBION FIRE OFFICE, NEW BRIDGE STREET, BLACKFRIARS, c. 1805 [A.P.S.D.].

ACTON, MIDDLESEX, a villa in Horn Lane for N. Selby, c. 1807 [exhib. 1807].

BROCKWELL HALL, nr. DULWICH, for John Blades, 1811–13, repaired by J. B. Papworth 1824–9 [Brayley, Topographical History of Surrey iii, 379; Survey of London xxvi, 161].

SOUTHWARK, SURREY CHAPEL ALMSHOUSES, 1812 [exhib. at R.A. 1814].

CAMBERWELL, SURREY, GROVE CHAPEL, 1819 [Brayley, Topographical History of Surrey iii, 275].

LONDON, ST. MARK'S CHURCH, KENNINGTON, 1822–4; reconstructed internally by S. S. Teulon 1873–6; damaged by bombing 1941 [exhib. at R.A. 1822].

LONDON, HABERDASHERS' (ASKE'S) ALMSHOUSES, HOXTON, 1825–6, now the Shoreditch Technical Institute [A.P.S.D.] (J. Elmes, Metropolitan Improvements, 1831, 143 and plate).

LAMBETH, THE SHOT TOWER, for Messrs. Maltby, 1826; dem. [Survey of London xxiii (i), 47].

GRAVESEND, KENT, improvement of Town Quay, 1828–9 [R. P. Cruden, History of Gravesend, 1843, 496].

ROPER, ROBERT, practised in Preston. He rebuilt the east front of LEAGRAM HALL, LANCS., for George Weld in 1822; dem. [J. Weld, History of Leagram, Chetham Soc. 1913, 81]. In 1822–3 he designed HOLY TRINITY CHURCH, HOUGHTON, LANCS., Gothic, for the Church Building Commissioners [Port, 132–3]. He also rebuilt KIRKHAM CHURCH, LANCS., 1822, retaining the medieval tower [Lancashire Record Office, Bourne of Stalmine papers]; LUND CHAPEL, nr. PRESTON, 1824 [I.C.B.S.]; and BROUGHTON CHURCH, nr. PRESTON, retaining the Tudor tower, 1826 [I.C.B.S.].

ROSE, HENRY, practised in Southwark. His principal work was THE LICENSED VICTUALLERS' ASYLUM, OLD KENT ROAD, 1827–8, an ambitious classical building with a pedimented portico. According to A.P.S.D. he was also responsible for the subsequent addition of the north and south wings, 1831–3, the ladies' wing, 1849, and the chapel, board room, court house and four additional houses, 1850, but a medal commemorating the laying of the foundation-stone of the ladies' wing in 1849 gives the name of C. J. Kemp as architect. He also designed THE LICENSED VICTUALLERS' SCHOOL, KENNINGTON LANE, 1835–6, now the headquarters of the N.A.A.F.I. and renamed 'Imperial Court' [Architectural Mag. iii, 1836, 140], and the BOROUGH MARKET, SOUTHWARK, 1851, rebuilt 1863–4. In 1839–40 he rebuilt the nave of ST. SAVIOUR'S CHURCH, SOUTHWARK (now the CATHEDRAL), in a feeble Gothic style caricatured by Pugin in his Contrasts, pl. 18. It was again rebuilt

by Sir A. W. Blomfield in 1890–7. The church of ST. MARK, ROSHERVILLE, KENT, which Rose designed in 1851–3 in conjunction with Edward Rose (presumably his son) was better calculated to satisfy Camdenian critics [Builder xii, 1854, 175]. [A.P.S.D.]

ROSE, JAMES (c. 1731–1796), was a Worcestershire mason and architect. In 1786 he is referred to as 'Mr. James Rose of Bewdley', but according to J. S. Roper he is to be identified with a James Rose whose tomb in Chaddesley Corbett Churchyard records his death on 14 May 1796 at the age of 65. Probably he was a native of Chaddesley Corbett who spent his working life in Bewdley.

In 1768–9 Rose designed and built STANFORD-ON-TEME CHURCH, WORCS., for Sir Edward Winnington, Bart., in the Gothic style. According to J. Noake, The Rambler in Worcestershire ii, 1854, 172, Rose hewed and laid with his own hands 'every outside stone'. In the Prattinton Collection in the Library of the Society of Antiquaries of London there is (Box IV) the plan and elevation of a bridge of three arches proposed to be built at Stanford-on-Teme, with an estimate signed by James Rose and dated 15 Feb. 1768. It is doubtful whether this was ever built. In 1778–82 the tower and spire of CHADDESLEY CORBETT CHURCH, WORCS., were rebuilt in quite a creditable Gothic style to Rose's designs. An entry in the Parish Register records the laying of the first stone on 12 April 1778, and names 'the architect James Rose; James Hayward, builder' [J. Noake, The Rambler in Worcestershire iii, 1854, 227; Associated Architectural Societies' Reports and Papers iv, 1856, 64; J. S. Roper, History of Chaddesley Corbett Church, 1969]. LOWER MITTON CHAPEL, STOURPORT, WORCS., was rebuilt to Rose's designs in 1790–1; enlarged 1834; demolished c. 1920 [W. A. Trippas, The Church of St. Michael, Stourport, 1946, 10–11].

A plan in the Worcester Diocesan Records indicates that Rose was involved, either as a witness or as a principal, in litigation over buildings erected at Shelsley Beauchamp Rectory in 1784–5, and 'Mr. Rose's first plan for New Rooms at Besford Court' was among architectural drawings formerly at Beechwood House, Herts.

ROSS, CHARLES, was a London carpenter and joiner who sometimes acted as an architect or surveyor. As a carpenter and joiner he is recorded to have worked under Matthew Brettingham at the 2nd Earl of Strafford's house in St. James's Square in 1748–9 [Survey of London xxix, 100] and at Marble Hill, Twickenham, in 1750–1 [M. P. G. Draper, Marble Hill House, 1970, 43–4]; to have been employed at St. James's Church, Piccadilly, under James Horn in 1756 [Survey of London xxix, 37]; and to have made furniture for the Royal Society of Arts in 1760 [*Jnl. of the Royal Society of Arts* cxiv, 1966, 431–2]. As an architect Ross (described as 'of Piccadilly, carpenter') undertook on 30 August 1748 to rebuild the west front of KIRTLING HALL, CAMBS. (dem. 1801), for the 1st Earl of Guilford, 'according to a plan given by him' [Bodleian Library, MS. North adds. b. 1, ff. 1–2]. He may have been the 'Mr. Ross' who seems to have finished off the works at BLAIR CASTLE, PERTHSHIRE, after the death of Roger Morris in 1749 [Blair Castle archives D.2.13 (38)], and in 1759 he undertook 'to superintend' the building of the Palladian south-east wing of WENTWORTH CASTLE, YORKS. (W.R.), for the 2nd Earl of Strafford. He was 'to provide a clever man that understands drawing and the several branches of building' and 'to anser all letters and draw what planes is relating to the building' [agreement printed in *R.I.B.A. Jnl.*, 25 Nov. 1933, 70, from B.M., Add. MS. 22241, f. 137]. Receipts show that Ross continued to superintend the new building until its completion in 1764. As contemporary writers are unanimous in stating that Lord Strafford (*q.v.*) designed the new building himself [see Horace Walpole, *Walpole Soc.* xvi, 65 : 'entirely designed by the present Earl himself' (1768); Lord Verulam, Hist. MSS. Comm., *Verulam*, 239 : 'Lord Strafford himself is his own architect and contriver in everything' (1768); W. Bray, *Sketch of a Tour into Derbyshire and Yorkshire*, 2nd ed. 1783, 249 n. : 'This front is from a design drawn by his lordship'], it is clear that Ross's function was to act as his draughtsman and executant architect.

ROSS, CHARLES (1722–1806), of Greenlaw, nr. Paisley, was a land surveyor much employed in Scotland during the second half of the eighteenth century. In 1773 he published an engraved map of Lanarkshire, and numerous estate plans signed by him are in the Scottish Record Office. He was also the author of a *Traveller's Guide to Lochlomond* (Paisley 1792), in which he illustrates an eccentric Gothic gateway at GARSCADDEN HOUSE, DUNBARTONSHIRE (dem.), which he says was 'designed and executed by the author of this work' for James Colquhoun, the owner of the house. This is his only known architectural work.

ROSS, WILLIAM, of Bristol, contributed designs for farm-buildings and for a 'Tudor' public-house and ale-house to Loudon's *Encyclopaedia of Cottage, Farm and Villa Architecture* (1833). He was a native of Ross-shire and one of the farms illustrated had been built in the parish of Tarbat in that county in accordance with his designs. In or about 1834 he emigrated to New York, where he was employed to revise the designs for the interior of the Customs House (now Sub-Treasury), as described in Loudon's *Architectural Mag.* ii, 1835, 525–33.

ROUCHEAD, ALEXANDER (–1776), was a mason by trade. He became free of the London Masons' Company by redemption on 27 May 1728 [Guildhall Library, MS. 5308], but was already active as a builder, *e.g.* on the Harley estate in Oxford Street, where he took a plot in 1726 [B.M., Add. MS. 18240, f. 15; see also *Survey of London* xxix, 90–1, Addendum]. He appears to have been identical with the 'Alexander Rovehead' of London who apparently designed, and certainly superintended the erection of, the NAVAL HOSPITAL at STONEHOUSE, PLYMOUTH, in 1758–64 [*A.P.S.D.*]. This building, designed on what was then a novel plan of insulated but linked blocks, marked an important step forward in the planning of hospitals, and was commended by J. R. Tenon in his *Mémoires sur les hôpitaux de Paris*, 1788, 385–6, and illustrated in plate 29 of Durand's *Recueil et parallèle des édifices anciens et modernes*, 1800. A contemporary plan, perhaps drawn by Rouchead, is in the Public Record Office (ADM 140/321). Alexander Rouchead, of the parish of St. George, Hanover Square, died intestate in 1776 [P.C.C. 472 BELLAS].

ROUMIEU, ABRAHAM, son of John Roumieu of London, refiner, was a member of a Huguenot family. He was apprenticed first to Isaac Ware (1748), and then to Thomas Reynolds (1753) [Guildhall Library, Records of the Carpenters' Company, MSS. 4329/16–17 and 4335/4, *ex inf.* Mr. Roger White]. An architectural book seen in the sale-room in 1972 was inscribed 'Abraham Roumieu Architect 1756'. No building designed by Roumieu appears to be known, but in the 1760s he was in the service of the 4th Duke of Gordon, for whom he made unexecuted designs for Gordon Castle, Morayshire, that are now in the Register House, Edinburgh (Gordon Castle Plans 1072–4, dated 1766–7). According to *A.P.S.D.* he was the grandfather of the Victorian architect Robert Lewis Roumieu, F.R.I.B.A. (1814–77).

ROWE, HENRY (1787–1859), practised in Worcester, where he designed the METHODIST CHAPEL, PUMP STREET, 1813 (dem.) [*Worcester Jnl.*, 16 July 1812]; THE CITY GAOL, 1823–5, dem. [Worcester Corporation Archives, Gaol Ledger 1823–31]; and ST. GEORGE'S (R.C.) CHURCH, SANSOME PLACE, 1829, façade rebuilt 1887 [G.R.]. His plans for a new vicarage for St. Swithin's Church are among the Worcester Diocesan Records. In 1829 he was appointed City Surveyor, an office in which he was succeeded by his son Henry Rowe, junior. He died on 6 June 1859, aged 72 [information from Mr. D. A. Whitehead].

ROWE, ISAAC, was a seventeenth-century architect who appears to have worked chiefly in Northamptonshire. No coherent account of his career can at present be given, but the following evidences of his architectural activity have been noted:

1663–6 payments in the accounts of Sir Thomas Proby of Elton Hall, Hunts., two totalling £50 'to Mr. Roe' or 'Rowe' in 1663, and one of 10s. 'To Roe for drawing a Chymney peice' in 1666. These payments relate to the building of the west wing of ELTON HALL in 1664–6 (see *C. Life*, 21 Feb. 1957, fig. 3, and plan in R.C.H.M., *Huntingdonshire*, 79) [Proby MSS. at Elton Hall].

1667 an elegantly drawn design for a large cupboard or wardrobe among the Isham papers at Lamport Hall, Northants., signed 'Isaac Rowe 1667'.

1672 a plan and elevation of a small house with pedimented central feature, signed 'Isaac Rowe November 25, 1672' [Hampshire Record Office, Cope papers in Mildmay Collection].

?1674 a drawing in the R.I.B.A. Collection (G1/4) signed 'I Rowe' in a monogram with a date which may be 1674. It consists of three alternative plans of a small house, roughly drawn.

1676 a contract dated 1 May between the 2nd Earl of Peterborough and Richard Warner of Weldon, stone-mason, to erect a building 'on either side of the New Gate' at DRAYTON HOUSE, NORTHANTS., 'According to a Draught Designed by Isaac Rowe now servant to the said Earle of Peterborough' [Stopford-Sackville papers at Drayton]. The buildings in question are presumably those on either side of the seventeenth-century outer gateway (*C. Life*, 13 May 1965).

1676 an elevation of a doorway signed 'I. Rowe 1676' in a monogram [Northants. Record Office, Fitzwilliam papers from Milton Hall].

1680 a design for a hexagonal pedestal signed 'I. Rowe April ye 28 1680' in a monogram [among drawings by Robert Hooke in B.M., Add. MS. 5238, f. 85].

1686 drew a 'platform' for a square of thirty houses (later reduced to twenty-eight) in the parish of St. Margaret, Westminster, for Bevis Lloyd, staked out 1687 and largely built by 1688 [P.R.O., C7/210/8, *ex inf.* Mr. Frank Kelsall].

ROWE, JOSEPH, a joiner by trade, was a builder and surveyor of Exeter. He designed KENTISBURY RECTORY, DEVON, in 1779, and enlarged and refronted CORNWORTHY VICARAGE, DEVON, in 1784 [Exeter Diocesan Records]. He was probably the father of Joseph Rowe, who built (and no doubt designed) the elegant Regency houses

in PENNSYLVANIA PARK, EXETER, in 1822–3 [W. G. Hoskins, *A Thousand Years in Exeter*, 1960, 146], and who reroofed and remodelled ST. STEPHEN'S CHURCH, EXETER, in 1826 [MS. Vestry Minutes in Exeter City Library]. A third generation of the family is represented by Joseph's son Joseph Coplestone Rowe, who took up his freedom in 1828 [*Exeter Freemen*, Devon and Cornwall Rec. Soc. 1973, 359].

ROWLAND, SAMUEL (–c. 1845), was the nephew and successor of William Byrom of Liverpool (*q.v.*). He had a considerable practice and is said to have 'accumulated a large fortune'. In Liverpool he designed some excellent Greek Revival buildings, notably the Ionic portico of St. Bride's Church and the former Royal Bank in Dale Street. He left no successor to his practice when he died childless in about 1845. [*Builder* iv, 1846, 530, xxvii, 1869, 803–4.]

LIVERPOOL, THE NORTHERN DISPENSARY, VAUXHALL ROAD, c. 1826; dem. [J. A. Picton, *Architectural History of Liverpool*, 1858, 69].

LIVERPOOL, THE SCOTCH PRESBYTERIAN CHAPEL, MOUNT PLEASANT, 1827; dem. [J. A. Picton, *Memorials of Liverpool* ii, 1875, 212].

WARRINGTON, LANCS., ST. JAMES'S CHURCH, WILDERSPOOL CAUSEWAY, 1829–30, Gothic [I.C.B.S.].

LIVERPOOL, ST. BRIDE'S CHURCH, PERCY STREET, 1830–1 [J. A. Picton, *Memorials of Liverpool* ii, 1875, 261].

LIVERPOOL, THE ROYAL BANK (later Queen Insurance Buildings), DALE STREET, 1837–8 [J. A. Picton, *Memorials of Liverpool* ii, 1875, 106].

ROWLAND, THOMAS, held the post of Clerk of the Works at Windsor Castle from 1715 until 1729, when he was dismissed. He was a carpenter by training, and had previously been foreman to John Churchill, the Master Carpenter at Windsor. A 'plan and upright of the Engine House at Windsor with the Dimensions of Measurement of the Severall Artificers' Works', drawn up by himself and Thomas Fort in 1718, is in the Bodleian Library (Gough Maps 1, f. 23).

As an architect, Rowland's most important recorded work was the LIBRARY at ETON COLLEGE. In 1719–20 the Hall at Eton was repaired 'according to Mr. Rowland's model', and in December 1725 the Provost and Fellows agreed 'to proceed to the building of a new Library According to Mr. Rowland's Plan'. He received £50 for 'surveying' in 1726, and a like sum in 1729 for 'surveying the Inside Works of the Library' [Willis & Clark, i, 452, 455]. Soon after 1725, Dr. Godolphin, the Provost of Eton, employed Rowland to design a new attic storey which he added to his residence, BAYLIES HOUSE, nr. SLOUGH. The house was considerably altered a few years later by John James [R. A. Austen-Legh in *The Times*, 22 July 1938, citing documents among the Godolphin family papers now in the Bucks. County Record Office]. In 1727–8 Rowland was employed by Charles Aldworth to make an estimate for repairs to FROGMORE HOUSE, nr. WINDSOR, of which Aldworth was then the lessee [Berkshire County Record Office, Account Book of Charles Aldworth, D/EN F.30].

Rowland was the author of three books: *A General Treatise of Architecture ... containing all that is necessary to be known in Building*, 1732 (of which there is a copy in the Soane Museum); *Mensuration of Superfices and Solids, by Tables of Feet, Inches and Parts, chiefly applied to the several Artificers' Works in Building*, 1739; and *Compleat Tables for measuring Round and Square Timber*, 1745.

ROWSON, JOHN, of Macclesfield, mason, designed and built the tower of ROSTHERNE CHURCH, CHESHIRE, in 1742–3, after the fall of its predecessor in 1741. He was paid £3 'for drawing plans and estimates' in the latter year. [F. H. Crossley, 'Post-Reformation Church Building in Cheshire', *Jnl. of Chester and N. Wales Architectural Society*, N.S. xxxv (i), 1942, 45–8 and plate.]

ROYLE, THOMAS, appears in Manchester directories of the 1820s as an architect and land agent. In W. Westall & T. Moule's *Great Britain Illustrated* (1830), there is an engraving of the Greek Revival façade of Messrs. Cunliffe's & Brookes's Bank in Market Street, Manchester, as built in 1827 to the designs of 'Messrs. Royle and Unwin architects'. The name of Robert Unwin, architect, is found in contemporary directories.

RUDD, JOHN (1754–), was apprenticed to Sir William Chambers in 1770 or 1771 [P.R.O., Apprenticeship Registers], and was admitted to the Royal Academy Schools in 1772, winning the Silver Medal in the same year. He exhibited a design for a villa at the Academy in 1774. Measured drawings of the Banqueting House, Whitehall, by him are in the R.I.B.A. Collection.

RUDHALL, WILLIAM (*c.* 1660–1733), was a mason living at Henley-in-Arden in Warwickshire. In *c.* 1700 he was one of three architects or master builders who submitted designs for Hanbury Hall, Worcs. It is not clear which of them was eventually employed [J. Lees-Milne in *C. Life*, 4 Jan. 1968, where Rudhall's drawing is reproduced; genealogical information about the Rudhall family from Mr. William Hawkes].

RUMLEY, HENRY, practised in Bristol in the 1830s. He designed Grecian terrace-houses in QUEEN SQUARE, BRISTOL, in 1833 [W. Ison, *The*

Georgian Buildings of Bristol, 1952, 147], and a Gothic church at FRENCHAY, GLOS., in 1832–3 [I.C.B.S.]. He was no doubt the father of Charles Frederick Rumley, who was in practice in Bristol in the 1860s.

RUNDLE, ABRAHAM (–1750), was a joiner by trade and lived at Tavistock, where he died in November 1750 [parish register]. He designed KELLY HOUSE, DEVONSHIRE, for Arthur Kelly, 1743–5, in a competent Georgian style with handsome interiors. Documents at Kelly show that he provided an estimate for the new house in December 1742, and that £340 was paid to 'Mr. Rundle, Architect, Joiner, etc.' [Kelly family archives, E 4/7–9]. A design for a Tudor Gothic fireplace signed 'John Rundle Arct.' is in the collection of the Hon. Christopher Lennox-Boyd.

RUSSELL, HENRY HEATHCOTE, is said to have been a nephew of Admiral Sir Henry Heathcote (1777–1851). He became a pupil of Edward Lapidge, exhibited designs at the Royal Academy in 1829 and 1845, and competed for the Ashmolean Museum at Oxford in 1839.

RUSSELL, JOHN, practised in Leamington, Warwicks., where he was for a time in partnership with Edmund Mitchell. He designed STOCKINGFORD CHURCH, WARWICKS., for the Church Building Commissioners in a simple classical style in 1822–3 [Port, 138–9]; ST. PETER'S (R.C.) CHURCH, LEAMINGTON, 1828, Greek Ionic, dem. 1863 [T. B. Dudley, *History of Leamington*, 1896–1900, 189]; and the CONGREGATIONAL CHURCH, SPENCER STREET, LEAMINGTON, 1836, Greek Ionic [Dudley, *op. cit.*, 203]. His design for the addition of a veranda to NEWBOLD COMYN HOUSE, WARWICKS., for Edward Willes, 1821, is in the Warwickshire Record Office (CR 1247/38). He was presumably the father of William Russell, who was in practice in Leamington in the 1850s and 1860s.

RUSSELL, W—, exhibited at the Royal Academy in 1834 and 1837, and competed unsuccessfully for the Houses of Parliament in 1835.

RYDER, RICHARD (–1683), was a master carpenter by trade, and in 1668 succeeded John Davenport as Master Carpenter in the Office of Works. He frequently acted as an architect and surveyor, and was also active as a speculative builder in London. He is first referred to in 1647–50 in connection with the repairs and alterations to the Manor House at Cranborne in Dorset for William Cecil, 2nd Earl of Salisbury. This house had recently been damaged by the Royalist army, and Ryder was employed to carry out repairs and to rebuild the west wing in a style that was quite advanced for its date (H. Field & M. Bunney, *English Domestic Architecture of the XVII and XVIII Centuries*, 1905, 16, *C. Life*, 7 June 1924, 3–10 May 1973; R.C.H.M., *Dorset* v, 9–10, pl. 44). The plans are described as 'Captain Ryder's plott', and a letter has been preserved in which Thomas Fort, the mason employed, asks his employer:

> To lett Capt. Rider draw a platt for the gate and for the tarrasse to his Lordshipp's liking ... that I may have stone for every use now att the beginning of the summer ... As for the forme of the roofs in that design wch. Captaine Rider drew, it is more agreeable to the forme of the house than any other as yet demonstrated. Consider the high turrets and the low turrets, and looke upon Captain Rider's roofe, and they doe agree. [Hatfield Muniments, General 74/11.]

That Ryder was at this time in touch with John Webb may be inferred from the fact that, in addition to his bill for 'a design for the new building at Cranborne', he charged for coming over on two occasions to Cranborne from Wilton, where Webb was then engaged in restoring the Earl of Pembroke's house after a fire [Hatfield Muniments, Bills 239].

After the Restoration Ryder is found repairing Bedford House in Bloomsbury for the 5th Earl of Bedford, 1660 [accounts at Woburn Abbey], surveying with John Davenport the decayed tower of St. Martin's-in-the-Fields, and eventually reconstructing it, 1662–8 [Vestry Minutes in Westminster City Library] (*Survey of London* xx, pls. 8–9), valuing houses to be pulled down in connection with the repair of St. Paul's Cathedral, 1665 [minute-book of Commissioners for repair of St. Paul's Cathedral in Guildhall Library, p. 7], estimating, with Davenport, for carpenter's and joiner's work at Clarendon House, 1666/7 [*The Architecture of Sir Roger Pratt*, ed. Gunther, 153–5], playing some part in the completion of Burlington House, Piccadilly, 1667 [*Survey of London* xxxii, 392], surveying Syon and Northumberland Houses for the Earl of Northumberland, 1667 [Alnwick Castle, Percy archives U.I. 43], surveying, with Edward Jerman, the site of Apothecaries' Hall, 1667 [Apothecaries' Company records, *ex inf.* Mr. Arthur Oswald], designing a window in the chapel at Gorhambury House in Hertfordshire, 1673 [J. C. Rogers, 'The Manor and Houses of Gorhambury', *Trans. St. Albans and Herts. Arch. Soc.* 1933, 41], and supervising repairs at Great Park House, Ampthill, for the 1st Earl of Ailesbury, 1676 [accounts among Ailesbury archives formerly at Tottenham Park, Wilts.]. In his official capacity as King's Master Carpenter he was responsible in 1675 for constructing the elaborate

scenery designed by Robert Streeter for the production in the Whitehall Theatre of the play *Calisto* [E. Boswell, *The Restoration Court Stage*, 1932, 208]. The possibility that he was involved in the building of the Theatre Royal in Brydges Street in 1662–3 (destroyed by fire 1672) is discussed in *Survey of London* xxxv, 41–2.

One of Ryder's principal building speculations was on land in Newport Street leased from the Earl of Salisbury in 1653. On 2 April of that year he undertook that within the next seven years he would lay out at least £500 in erecting and new building two fair new brick houses in Newport Street 'answerable to any twentie foot howse built in Covent Garden' and in rebuilding four other tenements in the street 'towards Newport House'. A further indenture dated 18 December 1657 states that he has pulled down all but one of the old houses in Newport Street and has built in their stead nine fair messuages, five of which face on to Newport Street on the south, the rest on to St. Martin's Lane on the east [Hatfield Muniments, Leases 1649–57, ff. 46ᵛ, 47ᵛ, 48, 140, 142]. Ryder's will shows that in 1683 he owned houses in Newport Street in the occupation of Sir Christopher Musgrave, Lady Hewitt, Charles Bertie and Lady Exeter, and others in Suffolk Street and Russell Street, leased from the Earls of Suffolk and Bedford. In 1664 he was himself resident in Newport Street, but at the time of his death he was living in Swan Close off Leicester Fields, and he appears to have given his name to Ryder's Court at the north-east corner of Leicester Square, described by Strype in 1720 as 'newly built and neat' [C. L. Kingsford, *Piccadilly, Leicester Square and Soho*, 1925, 55, 63]. Ryder Street, St. James's, laid out in the 1670s, may also owe its name to Captain Ryder, but his connection with the street has not been established [*Survey of London* xxix, 317].

Ryder died in the early months of 1683, leaving a widow Joan and sons named Richard and George [P.C.C. 61 DRAX]. It is possible that one of these sons was the 'Mr. Rider' whose employment as surveyor to Gray's Inn is noted above (p. 693).

S

SALISBURY, JAMES, was brought from London to Edinburgh in or about 1774 in order to superintend the building of the Register House to the designs of R. & J. Adam. When he was made a burgess of Edinburgh in 1778 he was described alternatively as 'carpenter' or 'architect' [*Roll of Edinburgh Burgesses 1761–1841*, 139]. In the same year he was consulted by the Writers to the Signet about a new library which they then thought of building [*History of the Society of*

Writers to the Signet, 1890, 409]. In 1783, when he was employed as a mediator in a dispute between the Duke of Gordon and John Baxter (*q.v.*), he was stated to be employed by the Duke of Roxburghe and to have 'a job of consequence' at Lawers for Mr. Drummond [S.R.O., Gordon Castle papers, GD 44/49/16, letter of 4 July 1783]. In 1798–1800 he was responsible for altering and refitting the interior of HOLY TRINITY CHURCH, ST. ANDREWS, FIFE [*The Parish Church of Holy Trinity, St. Andrews*, 1920, 5].

SALMON, ROBERT (1763–1821), was the youngest son of William Salmon, a carpenter and builder of Stratford-on-Avon, where he was born. He was employed by Henry Holland as a clerk of works at Carlton House and subsequently at Woburn Abbey. Here he attracted the notice of the 5th Duke of Bedford, who in 1794 gave him employment as resident estate surveyor and agricultural manager. It was in the latter capacity that he showed the remarkable ability as an inventor that won him considerable celebrity and several medals from the Society of Arts. The haymaking machine which he patented in 1814 was only the best known of his many inventions. As an architect he was chiefly employed in designing model farms on the Woburn estate in Bedfordshire, but he is also credited with the rebuilding in 1800, at the Duke's expense, of the body of SOULDROP CHURCH, BEDS., again rebuilt in 1860–1. He was the author of *An Analysis of the General Construction of Trusses*, 1807. [*D.N.B.*; Kelly's *Directory of Bedfordshire*, 1914, *s.v.* 'Souldrop'.]

SALMON, WILLIAM (*c.* 1703–1779), was the son of a carpenter and joiner at Colchester, and followed the same trade himself. He died at Colchester in March 1779, in his 77th year [*Ipswich Jnl.*, 3 April 1779, and will in Essex Record Office (D/ABR 27/82), *ex inf.* Mr. J. Bensusan Butt]. Salmon was the author of a number of builders' manuals whose success may be judged from the number of editions through which they passed. Their titles were: *The Country Builder's Estimator: or, the Architect's Companion*, date of 1st edition uncertain, 2nd ed. by E. Hoppus, 1737, 8th ed. by John Green of Salisbury, 1770; *Palladio Londinensis, or the London Art of Building*, 1734, 2nd ed. by E. Hoppus, 1738, 8th ed. 1773; *The Builder's Guide and Gentleman's and Trader's Assistant*, 1736; *The London and Country Builder's Vade Mecum: or, the Complete and Universal Estimator*, 1745, 5th ed. by John Green of Salisbury, 1773. The manuscript of an unpublished work by Salmon entitled *The Vitruvian Principles of Architecture Practically Demonstrated*, with a title-page dated 1737, is in the Mellon Collection.

SALWAY, JOSEPH, was a pupil of J. Jenkins of London and exhibited drawings at the Royal Academy from his office in 1785–9. He was among the subscribers to George Richardson's *New Vitruvius Britannicus*, published in 1802.

SAMBELL, PHILIP (1798–1874), was born at Devonport on 15 August 1798. He was deaf and dumb from birth, but appears nevertheless to have had a successful architectural practice in Devon and Cornwall. In the 1830s he was living in Truro, but he moved later to Falmouth, and died at Stonehouse, nr. Plymouth, on 5 December 1874. In 1840 Caroline Fox attended a lecture at Falmouth 'written by Sambell, the deaf and dumb architect, and read by young Ellis. It was a good lecture, and beautifully illustrated, principally by subjects of Egyptian architecture.' Sambell was the author of an 'Essay on Architecture' published in the *Journal of the Royal Institute of Cornwall* for 1840, and of a letter 'On the construction of chapels' which was printed in *The Baptist Magazine* xxxiii, 1841, 355. Sambell designed ST. JOHN'S CHURCH, TRURO, CORNWALL, 1827–8, Grecian [*Port*, 142–3]; a DORIC COLUMN in LEMON STREET, TRURO, to commemorate the explorer Richard Lander, 1835 [*Architectural Mag.* ii, 1835, 137–8]; THE BAPTIST CHAPEL, CLARENCE STREET, PENZANCE, 1835–6, Norman [J. S. Courtney, *Guide to Penzance*, 1845, 42]; and THE BAPTIST CHAPEL, HELSTON, 1836 (later a cinema) [H. S. Toy, *History of Helston*, 1936, 353]. He competed for the Houses of Parliament in 1835.

[G. C. Boase & W. P. Courtney, *Bibliotheca Cornubiensis* ii, 1878, 619; *The Journals and Letters of Caroline Fox*, ed. H. N. Pym, 1882, 58.]

SAMPSON, GEORGE, was given the posts of Clerk of the Works at the Tower of London and Somerset House by William Benson in 1718, his predecessor, Thomas Kynaston, being deprived to make way for him. After Benson's dismissal in 1719, he was himself deprived and Kynaston was restored through the influence of Sir John Vanbrugh, then Comptroller of the Works (cf. *The Letters of Sir John Vanbrugh*, ed. G. F. Webb, 118).

Sampson subsequently became Surveyor to the Bank of England, and was the architect of the central portion of the old Bank, erected in 1732–4, altered by Sir John Soane, and demolished in 1925 [H. R. Steel & F. R. Yerbury, *The Old Bank of England*, 1930, pp. 3–5, pl. xi]. It was described by Soane as being 'in a grand style of Palladian simplicity' [*Works*, 32]. What appear to be contemporary copies of Sampson's original designs are in Sir John Soane's Museum (Drawings 1, 1). He was also employed as a surveyor by the Fishmongers' Company, St. Thomas's Hospital and Guy's Hospital. He may have died in 1764, the year in which Sir Robert Taylor succeeded him as Surveyor to the Bank.

Sampson's only other known work is the monument in HURSLEY CHURCH, HANTS., to Mrs. Elizabeth Cromwell (*d.* 1731), which is signed 'G. Sampson architect. John Huntington fecit.' In 1720 he had submitted a design for rebuilding the church of St. Martin-in-the-Fields, and 'attended' the committee 'about his Planns and Estimate'; but they do not seem to have been further considered [MS. Minutes of the Commissioners for rebuilding the church, f. 16]. In 1726–7 he appears to have supervised the building of the stables at THORESBY HOUSE, NOTTS., to the designs of Sir Thomas Hewett (*q.v.*) [Manvers papers, Nottingham University Library]. In 1739 Sir Hans Sloane consulted him about the cost of repairing BEAUFORT HOUSE, CHELSEA, which he had recently purchased. Sampson said it would cost £500, but Sloane did nothing, and Sampson eventually persuaded him to pull it down and sell the materials to two acquaintances of his, one a master bricklayer, the other a master carpenter [R. Davies, *The Greatest House at Chelsey*, 1914, 230–4].

SAMWELL, WILLIAM (1628–1676), was the eldest son of Anthony Samwell, of Dean's Yard, Westminster, who was the fourth son of Sir William Samwell of Upton Hall, Northants., Auditor of the Exchequer in the reign of Queen Elizabeth. He was admitted to the Middle Temple in 1648 and lived in chambers there until 1656 (the year of his father's death), but was never called to the Bar.

Aubrey describes Samwell as 'an excellent architect, that has built severall delicate houses (Sir Robert Henley's, Sir Thomas Grosvenor's in Cheshire)', and Evelyn mentions him as the architect of Charles II's 'new building' at Newmarket. He was, in fact, a gentleman architect of the same sort as Hugh May and Roger Pratt, and his houses are excellent examples of the type which became fashionable in England immediately after the Restoration. Nearly all his works have been mutilated or destroyed, but the planning of Grange Park and Eaton Hall shows considerable sophistication, and suggests that Samwell was an able designer whose contribution to English seventeenth-century architecture may have been under-estimated. In 1668 a 'Mr. Samuel' was among the six applicants for the post of surveyor to the new Royal Exchange in succession to Edward Jerman. It is probable, however, that this was not Samwell but a master bricklayer of that name who is mentioned more than once in Hooke's diary. The design of Euston Hall, Suffolk, built *c.* 1670 by Henry Bennet, 1st Earl of Arlington, has been attributed to Samwell (cf. *Wren Soc.* xix, p. xiii), but upon what evidence is not clear. Some connection (not necessarily of

an architectural nature) between Arlington and Samwell is, however, indicated by a document among the Shaftesbury papers in the Public Record Office (P.R.O., 30/24/VI B, no. 394).

Samwell purchased the manor of Watton in Norfolk some time after 1660, and remained its owner until his death in 1676. He married Anne, daughter of Sir Denner Strutt of Little Warley in Essex, by who he had two daughters, Anne and Mary. Anne married William Henry Fleming of Suffield, High Sheriff of Norfolk in 1736. By his will, dated 25 April 1676, and proved on 26 June, Samwell directed that his body should be buried at Upton in Northants. 'in a private manner and without Funerall Pompe'. There are monuments at Watton to his daughter and widow.

[Aubrey's *Brief Lives*, ed. A. Clark, i, 288, 293; Burke's *Extinct Baronetcies*, 1838, 465; Blomfield's *History of Norfolk* iii, 315–17; Baker's *History of Northants.* i, 225; *Middle Temple Records*, ed. C. H. Hopwood, 1904–5, ii, 968, 982, iii, 1071, 1099; P.C.C. 71 BENCE.]

attributed: LOWER LODGE (now BUSHY HOUSE), BUSHY PARK, MIDDLESEX, for Edward Proger, 1664–5; altered and enlarged in eighteenth century [Peter Foster & Edward Pyatt, *Bushy House*, National Physical Laboratory, 1976].

NEWMARKET, SUFFOLK, THE KING'S HOUSE, for King Charles II, 1668–71; partly dem. after 1814 (south-east block survives as 'Palace House Mansion') [*History of the King's Works* v, 214–16].

GRANGE PARK, nr. ALRESFORD, HANTS., for Sir Robert Henley, *c.* 1670; remodelled by W. Wilkins, 1809 [E. Mercer, 'William Samwell and the Grange', in *The Country Seat*, ed. Colvin & Harris, 1970, 48–54; J. Redmill in *C. Life*, 8 May 1975].

HAM HOUSE, PETERSHAM, SURREY, remodelled for the 1st Duke and Duchess of Lauderdale, 1672–4 [J. G. Dunbar, 'The Building-activities of the Duke and Duchess of Lauderdale, 1670–82', *Archaeological Jnl.* cxxxii, 1975].

LONDON, THE ROYAL MEWS, CHARING CROSS, coach-house, etc., 1673–4; dem. [*History of the King's Works* v, 208].

FELBRIGG HALL, NORFOLK, added the west wing for William Windham, completed 1686. Samwell's designs, signed and dated 1674, are preserved at Felbrigg [*C. Life*, 22 Dec. 1934; R. W. Ketton-Cremer, *Felbrigg*, 1962].

EATON HALL, CHESHIRE, for Sir Thomas Grosvenor, Bart., 1675–82; rebuilt by W. Porden, 1804–12 [Aubrey's *Brief Lives*, ed. A. Clark, i, 293; C. T. Gatty, *Mary Davies and the Manor of Ebury* i, 1921, 210–11, citing accounts in Eaton Hall MS. 68] (*Vitruvius Britannicus* ii, 1717, pls. 35–6).

SANDBY, THOMAS (1721–1798), was the elder son of Thomas Sandby, a gentleman with property at Babworth in Nottinghamshire. He was born in Nottingham, where he and his brother Paul appear to have been apprenticed to Thomas Peat, of Messrs. Peat & Badder, land surveyors. The drawings which decorate the margins of the map of Nottingham published by Peat & Badder in 1744 were made by Thomas Sandby during his apprenticeship. In 1741 or 1742 the brothers left Nottingham in order to take up situations in the military drawing office in the Tower of London which had been procured for them by John Plumptre, the Member for Nottingham, who held the office of Treasurer of the Ordnance. From 1743 onwards Thomas was attached to the Commander-in-Chief, William Augustus, Duke of Cumberland. He was present at the Battle of Dettingen in 1743, and was with the Duke on the Culloden campaign in 1745–6. He made a sketch of the latter battle which is now in the Royal Library at Windsor Castle, together with views of Fort Augustus and other military scenes. He afterwards accompanied the Duke on his campaigns in the Netherlands, and probably remained there until the Peace of Aix-la-Chapelle in 1748. In 1750 he was appointed Draughtsman to the Duke at a salary of £100, and in 1764 he became his Steward and Clerk of the Stables at Windsor. In 1746 the Duke had become Ranger of Windsor Great Park, and either he or his nephew Frederick, who succeeded him in 1765, appointed Sandby his deputy. The Duke's previous steward is said also to have acted in this capacity, and whether Sandby's appointment dated from 1746 or 1765, he held the position of Deputy Ranger for the rest of his life.[1]

As Deputy Ranger Sandby enjoyed financial independence and was provided with a residence in Lower Lodge (afterwards rebuilt by John Nash). Here he was joined by his brother Paul, who assisted him in the landscape-gardening activities which became his principal occupation at Windsor. Chief among these was the formation of Virginia Water, then the largest artificial lake in the kingdom. The original dam, constructed only of sand and clay, gave way as a result of a storm in 1768, earning for its engineer the nickname of 'Tommy Sandbank'. It was reconstructed in more enduring materials with the assistance of Charles Cole (q.v.), and Sandby constructed a series of grottoes and artificial ruins at the head of the Water which were completed

in 1785. He also designed the stone bridge over the northern arm of the Water, replacing a wooden one erected by Flitcroft in the reign of George II. A number of plans and drawings connected with these works are preserved in the Royal Library at Windsor Castle, Sir John Soane's Museum, the Bodleian Library (Gough Maps 41 A, ff. 4–23), the Victoria and Albert Museum (3436, 172–9), and the Achenbach Foundation at San Francisco.

Another project with which Sandby was associated at this time was for the re-erection in Windsor Great Park of the 'Holbein' Gateway at Whitehall, which had been taken down in 1759. His design for its reconstruction, with Gothic additions on either side, is given in J. T. Smith's *Antiquities of Westminster*, 1807, facing p. 21. This was never carried out, but two of the terracotta busts with which the gateway was decorated were incorporated by Sandby in a keeper's lodge at Virginia Water, whence they were removed in the nineteenth century to Hampton Court. In 1754 he published a set of eight folio plates, engraved on copper by his brother Paul, illustrating the works at Virginia Water. They were reissued by Boydell in 1772.

Sandby enjoyed the favour not only of William Augustus, Duke of Cumberland, and of his successor Henry Frederick, Duke of Cumberland, but also of George III, who retained him as Deputy Ranger when he took the management of the Park into his own hands on Frederick's death in 1790. In April 1777 he was appointed Architect of the King's Works in succession to Sir Robert Taylor, and in November 1780 he became Master Carpenter in the Office of Works. The latter office was, however, abolished two years later as a result of Burke's Act. He was one of the committee of artists which was formed in 1753 with the object of establishing an Academy of Art, and in 1759 he became a member of the committee of the newly formed Society of Artists. But he exhibited only once with the Society (in 1767), and after his nomination as one of the original Royal Academicians in 1768 he exhibited at the Academy. He was chosen to be the first Professor of Architecture, and in 1770 delivered the first of six lectures which he repeated annually until the last two years of his life, when they were read for him. The sixth was illustrated by about forty drawings and designs, including one for a 'Bridge of Magnificence' across the Thames at Somerset House, based on a similar idea of Piranesi's. It was shown at the Academy's exhibition in 1781 and attracted much attention. Several versions of this design are in existence (at Windsor, the R.I.B.A. and the National Gallery of Scotland). The manuscript of Sandby's lectures is in the R.I.B.A. Library, but the illustrations were sold with his other drawings after his death. There is another copy of the lectures

---

[1] This was not an official post and the appointment is consequently not noticed in the Court Kalendars. It is very unlikely that (as has usually been assumed) it dated from the Duke's appointment as Ranger in 1746, and it is significant that 'Windsor Great Park' became Sandby's permanent address only from 1765, in which year he gave up his house in London (see F. H. Ramsden, 'The Sandby Brothers in London', *Burlington Magazine* lxxxix, Jan. 1947).

in Sir John Soane's Museum. Sandby was elected an honorary member of the Architects' Club on its foundation in 1791.

In February 1769 Sandby competed for the Royal Exchange at Dublin, obtaining the third premium [*Builder* xxvii, 1869, 781]. His drawings for this building are in the R.I.B.A. Library and the Library of Vassar College, U.S.A. His most important executed work was the FREEMASONS' HALL in QUEEN STREET, LINCOLN'S INN FIELDS, which was built in 1775–6, reconstructed by F. P. Cockerell in 1864–6 (preserving Sandby's Great Hall), damaged by fire in 1883, and finally demolished in 1932. The fine interior is illustrated by Britton & Pugin, *Public Buildings of London* i, 1825, 321–33. Some of the original drawings are in Sir John Soane's Museum, and there are two sections in the British Museum (Crowle Pennant, vii, 36–7).

Sandby also designed the Gothic wainscoting round the altar in ST. GEORGE'S CHAPEL, WINDSOR, carved with emblems of the Order of the Garter, which was executed by Henry Emlyn in 1782 [W. H. St. J. Hope, *Windsor Castle*, 398–95]; the BLEACH-WORKS at LLEWENNI in the VALE OF CLWYD, nr. DENBIGH, c. 1785 [plate 9 of Colt Hoare's *Views of Seats, etc., in North and South Wales*, shows this building as originally designed by Sandby for the Hon. Thomas Fitzmaurice]; and a stone bridge over the R. Thames at STAINES which was built in 1792–7 but failed in 1799 and was replaced by an iron bridge in 1801–3. For the Duke of Cumberland Sandby enlarged and refronted the GREAT LODGE in WINDSOR PARK in c. 1757. The house was largely rebuilt in 1869 (after a fire) and in 1912, and is now known as Cumberland Lodge [Oppé, no. 103 and pl. 144]. He also designed a few private houses, including ST. LEONARD'S HILL, nr. WINDSOR, for the Dowager Countess Waldegrave, afterwards Duchess of Gloucester, remodelled in French Renaissance style in the nineteenth century [J. P. Neale, *Views of Seats*, 1st ser., iii, 1820, with distant view: see a closer view by Neale in Bodleian, MS. Top. Berks. d. 13, f. 21]; and HOLLY GROVE, OLD WINDSOR, for Col. Deacon [*D.N.B.*].

Sandby was an accomplished topographical artist, whose water-colour drawings cannot easily be distinguished from those of his brother Paul. As an architect he is less easy to evaluate, because his restricted practice and the destruction of virtually all his executed works leave only his drawings for the architectural historian to study. It is clear, however, that he was an able designer in a neo-classical style closely akin to that of Chambers, and the influence that he exerted through his lectures at the Royal Academy should not be under-estimated.

Sandby died at the Deputy Ranger's Lodge on 25 June 1798, and was buried in the churchyard

714

at Old Windsor. There is no monument, but a memorial brass was put up in 1883. There are several portraits of Sandby, of which the most accessible is the one by Beechey in the National Portrait Gallery. Many of Sandby's drawings were sold with his library in 1799 (catalogue in B.M., S.C.5.34(14)). Another sale of drawings (from the collection of William Sandby, author of *Thomas and Paul Sandby*, 1902) took place at Christie's in 1959. Two volumes of architectural drawings are in Sir John Soane's Museum, and there are others at Windsor Castle, the British and Victoria and Albert Museums, the R.I.B.A. Collection, and in various American collections (see John Harris, *Catalogue of British Drawings for Architecture, etc., in American Collections*, 1971).

[*A.P.S.D.*; *D.N.B.*; W. H. Stevenson's articles on Badder & Peat's map of Nottingham in *Nottinghamshire Weekly Express*, 25 Sept.–23 Oct. 1896; T. Mulvany, *Life of James Gandon*, 1846, 189, 296; J. T. Smith, *A Book for a Rainy Day*, ed. W. Whitten, 1905, 92, 102–3, 303; *The Farington Diary*, ed. J. Greig, i, 233, iv, 106; W. Sandby, *Thomas and Paul Sandby*, 1902; F. H. Ramsden, 'The Sandby Brothers in London', *Burl. Mag.* lxxxix, 1947; E. A. Oppé, *Sandby Drawings at Windsor Castle*, 1947.]

SANDERS, JOHN (1768–1826), born on 27 April 1768, was the son of Thomas Sanders, a tallow-chandler of the parish of St. Dunstan-in-the-East, London. In 1784 he became Sir John Soane's first pupil, and at the end of the following year he was admitted to the Royal Academy School. In 1786 he began to exhibit his designs, and in 1788 he was awarded the Gold Medal of the Academy. After leaving Soane's office in 1790, he began to practise on his own, and from 1794 onwards was architect to the Barrack Department of the War Office with James Johnson. His principal works were the ROYAL MILITARY ASYLUM (now the Duke of York's Barracks) at CHELSEA, 1801–3 [G. Richardson, *New Vitruvius Britannicus* ii, 1808, pls. 39–42], and the ROYAL MILITARY COLLEGE at SANDHURST, BERKS., 1807–12, the designs for which he exhibited at the Royal Academy in 1811 and 1813. This is a long plain building dignified by an impressive Greek Doric portico (*C. Life*, 26 June 1969). Sanders also made additions to BEOLEY HALL, WORCS., for Thomas Holmes, 1791 [exhib. at R.A.]; restored HOLLAND HOUSE, KENSINGTON, for the 3rd Lord Holland in 1796–7 [*A.P.S.D.*]; designed a drawing-room for the 1st Marquess of Headfort, probably for his London house at 13 STANHOPE STREET, MAYFAIR [exhib. at R.A. 1804]; enlarged KINRARA HOUSE, INVERNESS-SHIRE, for the Duchess of Gordon in 1805 [S.R.O., RHP 2498 and GD 44/51/279]; and altered the unfinished ROYAL PALACE at WINCHESTER for use as a barracks in 1810 [exhib. at R.A. 1812]. In 1808 he issued a printed *Letter to the Lords Commissioners of His Majesty's Treasury* replying to criticisms of the Barrack Department made in the *Fourth Report of the Commissioners of Military Inquiry*. There is a copy in Sir John Soane's Museum.

In later life Sanders was very well off. He was able to retire early from practice, and travelled on the Continent from 1817 to about 1820. He employed William Purser as a draughtsman, and was joined in Rome by G. L. Taylor and Edward Cresy, two young architects who were similarly engaged in investigating the architectural antiquities of Italy. Together they explored the Mediterranean, drawing and sketching wherever they went. 'They measure every thing; even the Gothic buildings in Sicily have not escaped them', wrote John Soane, junior, to his father. At Chaeroneia in Boeotia they discovered the lion commemorating the Thebans who fell in the battle of 338 B.C. [*Builder* xx, 1862, 908; and W. S. W. Vaux, 'On the Discovery of the Lion at Chaerona, by a Party of English Travellers in 1818', *Trans. Royal Society of Literature*, 2nd ser., viii, 1866]. On his return, Sanders became the first president of the Architects' and Antiquaries' Club, founded by ten gentlemen who had seen the value of architectural academies abroad, and were resolved to establish one in their own country. He himself had a fine library and collection of antiquities at his house at Reigate, where he died early in 1826. His collection of architectural casts was bought by Sir Thomas Lawrence, who offered them in his will to the Royal Academy for £250.

[*A.P.S.D.*; A. T. Bolton, *The Portrait of Sir John Soane*, 1927, 129–30, 252–70, 276, 281–2; A. T. Bolton, *The Works of Sir John Soane*, 1924, Appendix C, p. xl; G. L. Taylor, *Memoirs of an Octogenarian Architect*, 1870–2; *The Farington Diary*, ed. J. Greig, vii, 26, 96, 135, 200, 230, viii, 67; will P.C.C. 181 SWABEY.]

SANDERSON, JAMES (*c.* 1791–1835), born at East Grinstead, Sussex, was the son of a local builder of the same name. He was a pupil of Jeffry Wyatville from 1813 to 1816. He afterwards practised from Cork Street, London, where he died on 1 March 1835, in his 45th year [*Gent's Mag.* 1835 (i), 443; P.C.C. 452 GLOSTER]. His exhibits at the Royal Academy included 'Stanmore Cottage [at Great Stanmore, Middlesex], now building for Dr. Hooper' (1817), a 'House [Baldornie Tower] erected at St. Clare, near Ryde, for E. V. Utterson, Esqr.' (1824), the 'garden front of St. Leonard's near Stanmore, now erecting for Henry Stone, Esqr.' (1825), a 'Gothic House proposed to be built near Ryde' (1826), and alterations to Ryde Church, Isle of Wight, carried out at the expense of George Player in 1827 (1828). The 'Gothic House' near Ryde was probably

STEEPHILL CASTLE, which was designed by Sanderson for John Hambrough and is described as newly built in 1833 [G. Brannon, *The Pleasure Visitor's Companion to the Isle of Wight*, 1833, 71–2]. It was demolished in 1964, but is illustrated by Brannon, and by J. B. Marsh, *Steephill Castle*, privately printed 1907. According to a later edition of Brannon's *Companion*, Sanderson 'gave the designs for nearly all the principal buildings of Ryde', including BRIGSTOCK TERRACE, and the Ionic TOWN HALL is mentioned as his work in W. B. Cooke's *Bonchurch, Shanklin and the Undercliff*, 1849, 109. He was probably the author of some unexecuted designs for a library at KIDBROOKE PARK, SUSSEX, for the 1st Lord Colchester, signed 'Sanderson' and dated 1813 [P.R.O., Colchester papers 9/10, pt. 2, no. 19].

SANDERSON, JAMES WRIGHT (–1813), was a pupil of James Wyatt, from whose office he exhibited at the Royal Academy in 1790 and 1791. He was admitted to the Royal Academy Schools in 1789 and won the Silver Medal in 1790. He was an unsuccessful candidate for election as A.R.A. in 1797 [W. T. Whitley, *Artists and their Friends in England 1700–1799* ii, 1928, 216]. He afterwards practised in Reading, where he died in 1813 [*Gent's Mag.* 1813 (i), 393; P.C.C. 218 HEATHFIELD].[1] His trade card is illustrated in Sotheby's Belgravia Catalogue, 13 April 1976, lot 80.

Sanderson's exhibits at the Royal Academy show that he designed COOMBE LODGE, nr. WHITCHURCH, OXON., for Samuel Gardiner, 1794–5, dem. *c.* 1950; additions to PROSPECT HILL, nr. READING, for J. E. Liebenrood, 1800; 'peasants' cottages' at WOODLEY, BERKS., for the Rt. Hon. Henry Addington, 1801; and a Gothic lodge at BILLINGBEAR, BERKS., for the 2nd Lord Braybrooke, 1801. He also appears to have designed a house at BEARWOOD, nr. WOKINGHAM, BERKS., for John Walter II, though it was not built until after his death and was demolished in 1865 [Mark Girouard in *C. Life*, 17 Oct. 1968, 964 and fig. 9].

SANDERSON, JOHN (–1774), was a Georgian architect about whom little is known other than the list of works given below. His will [P.C.C. 349 BARGRAVE] suggests that he may have had connections with Norfolk, but he practised in London, and lived, at least during the latter part of his life, at Parkgate, Hampstead. He died in 1774, leaving, *inter alia*, 'two terra cotta figures

---

[1] J. W. Sanderson should not be confused with James Sanderson of Reading (d. *c.* 1787), a land surveyor who laid out the grounds of Claydon House, Bucks., between 1768 and 1776 [bills at Claydon House], and partly rebuilt Chalfont St. Peter parsonage in 1780, dem. 1966 [Muniments of St. John's College, Oxford, xli, 16].

of the Crouching Venus and Roman Charity done by Delvaux' to John Wodehouse of East Lexham in Norfolk. To 'John Sanderson, late Chamberlain of Lynn Co. Norfolk, Gent., but now residing with Mr. Johnson in Berners St., Builder' he left £10. Neither wife nor children are mentioned in the will, the principal legatees being Anne Lejolivet, of Laval in France, and Beaumont, son of George Stubbs. According to J. J. Park's *History of Hampstead* (1818), 'the articles disposed of at his sale' included 'the model of a very large seat, his own design; with a capital, said to have been brought from the ruins of Herculaneum; [and] some of the better authors on architecture'.

Sanderson was a competent 'second-generation Palladian' who designed several handsome country houses of what by then was a conventional Georgian type. At Stratton Park the interior decoration, as illustrated in *Vitruvius Britannicus*, was also of a standard Palladian character, but at Kirtlington and Kimberley, and perhaps also at Hagley, he showed himself to be an accomplished designer of rococo decoration. At Hagley he had helped the amateur architect, Sanderson Miller, to draw out the plans for the main structure 'properly figured for the direction of the workmen', and he assisted Theodore Jacobsen and Thomas Prowse in a similar fashion at Trinity College, Dublin,[1] and Wicken Church, respectively. His unexecuted designs for a large Palladian mansion at Woburn for the 4th Duke of Bedford, dated 1733, are preserved in Woburn Abbey MS. 151. Other drawings by, or attributed to, him are described in the *Catalogue of the R.I.B.A. Drawings Collection* and in John Harris's *Catalogue of British Drawings for Architecture, etc., in American Collections*, 1971.

KELHAM HALL, NOTTS., for the executors of the 2nd Lord Lexington, *c.* 1730; destroyed by fire 1857 [Belvoir Castle Muniments, Account No. 377] (J. P. Neale, *Views of Seats*, 1st ser., iv, 1821).

STRATTON PARK, HANTS., for the 3rd Duke of Bedford, 1731; said to have been partly demolished by the 4th Duke (1732–71) for fear his successors should prefer it to Woburn; remodelled by George Dance, junior, for Sir Francis Baring, 1803–6; dem. 1960 [*Vitruvius Britannicus* iv, 1767, pls. 52–5].

CHEAM CHURCH, SURREY, design and estimate for rebuilding, 1741, possibly the one carried out in 1746; rebuilt 1862–4 [Surrey County Record Office, Q.S. Roll 1741, *ex inf.* Miss Mary Jackson].

ELY CATHEDRAL, monument to Humphry Smith

<hr>

[1] Also, it appears, at the Foundling Hospital, London: see R. H. Nichols & F. A. Wray, *History of the Foundling Hospital*, 1935, 261.

(d. 1743), erected 'by John Sanderson of London Architect' [inscription].

HAMPSTEAD, MIDDLESEX, ST. JOHN'S CHURCH, 1745–7 [Vestry Minutes printed by C. H. Collins Baker in *C. Life*, 11 Dec. 1937, 610–11; cf. J. J. Park, *History of Hampstead*, 1818, 222–3]. The small copper spire was added in 1784. In 1843–4 the church was lengthened and transepts were added, and in 1878 an apsidal chancel designed by F. P. Cockerell was added at the west end.

KIRTLINGTON PARK, OXON., completed house for Sir James Dashwood, Bart., 1747–8, succeeding William Smith (d. 1747). Sanderson designed the interiors and probably the wings [drawings and accounts formerly at Kirtlington; *Vitruvius Britannicus* iv, 1767, pls. 32–6] (*C. Life*, 13 April 1912). The dining-room was dismantled and sold in 1931 and has since been re-erected in the Metropolitan Museum of Art at New York: see P. Remington in *Metropolitan Museum Bulletin* xiv, no. 7 (March 1956), and *C. Life*, 1 Oct. 1970, 823, fig. 3.

PUSEY HOUSE, BERKS., for John Allen Pusey, *c.* 1750 [in 1754 Sanderson proposed to show his next client, John Conyers, two large framed drawings of 'Mr. Pusey's house in Berkshire', which he had evidently designed: Essex Record Office, D/DW. E 36/6].

TRINITY COLLEGE, DUBLIN. Although it appears from the *Journal of the House of Commons of the Kingdom of Ireland* vi (1757–60), Appendix, p. cclxiii, that £74 11s. 8d. were paid to 'Messrs. Keene and Sanderson for the Plans and Elevations' of the building erected in 1752–9, it is clear from the evidence cited above (p. 450) that they were in fact implementing designs made by the amateur architect Theodore Jacobsen.

COPPED HALL, ESSEX, rebuilt for John Conyers, 1753–8, under the amateur direction of Sir Roger Newdigate and Thomas Prowse; altered internally by James Wyatt 1775–7; enlarged *c.* 1895; damaged by fire 1917 [letters from Sanderson in Essex Record Office, D/DW E. 29–36; drawings in R.I.B.A. Coll.] (T. Muilman, *History of Essex* 1770–2, iv, 152; *C. Life*, 29 Oct., 5 Nov. 1910).

WICKEN CHURCH, NORTHANTS., assisted Thomas Prowse (*q.v.*) to rebuild church, 1753 onwards, and completed it after his death in 1767 [above, p. 667].

KIMBERLEY HALL, NORFOLK, assisted Thomas Prowse (*q.v.*) to remodel the house for Sir Armine Wodehouse, Bart., *c.* 1755–7, as shown by accounts seen by Mr. T. P. Connor. Drawings in the R.I.B.A. Collection show that Sanderson was designing interiors here as late as 1770.

HAGLEY HALL, WORCS., assisted Sanderson Miller

(*q.v.*) by drawing out his plans 'properly figured for the direction of the workmen' in 1754 [*An Eighteenth-Century Correspondence*, ed. Dickins & Stanton, 1910, 290], and may, as Mr. Michael McCarthy has suggested, have been responsible for the interior decoration as completed in 1760 (*C. Life*, 16 Oct. 1915, 19, 26 Sept. 1957; C. Hussey, *English Country Houses: Early Georgian*, 1955, 195–9).

OXFORD, THE RADCLIFFE INFIRMARY, completed building, 1766–70, after death of Stiff Leadbetter (*q.v.*) [Bodleian Library, Minutes of the Radcliffe Trustees, 1752–91].

SANDERSON, JOSEPH (–1747), was a carpenter and joiner by trade, and a cousin of John Sanderson (*q.v.*). He lived in Little Queen Street, Bloomsbury, but a legacy to the poor of Hatfield Broad Oak in Essex may indicate that he was a native of that parish. The Leak of Okeover papers show that in 1745–7 he enlarged OKEOVER HALL, STAFFS., for Leak Okeover to his own designs in a style akin to that of Gibbs [Arthur Oswald in *C. Life*, 23–30 Jan. 1964]. From his letters to Leak Okeover it appears that in 1745 he was also working at GARENDON PARK, LEICS., and in 1746 was building BASSINGBOURNE HALL, TAKELEY, ESSEX, for Francis Bernard. On 22 November he wrote to say that he hoped 'to keep at home pretty much from Essex having near compleated the Parsonage and quite covered in Mr. Bernard's house' [Arthur Oswald in *C. Life*, 2 April 1964, correspondence]. In 1745 he refers to a quarrel with 'Mr. Jno. Sanderson (my cozen)', but in his will he left John Sanderson 'my gold ring of Inigo Jones's head and a small book of my own drawings of the five Orders . . . as a token of our former freindship'. Leak Okeover was to receive 'two pictures of fish and fowls painted by Ross and six of my principal Books of Architecture'. Other legatees were his 'much honoured master John Barrington Esquire' of Barrington Hall, nr. Hatfield Broad Oak (which Sanderson may possibly have designed), and John Silvester, to whom he left his silver drawing instruments and his remaining books of architecture. He died on 17 August 1747 [P.C.C. 214 POTTER].

SANDFORD, GEORGE, was apprenticed to the architect Henry Keene in 1759 [P.R.O., Apprenticeship Register 1R1/22]. He evidently became Keene's clerk or draughtsman, for in 1775 Keene left him £100 in his will. Among Keene's drawings in the Victoria and Albert Museum there is a design for a 'Dog Kennell for Lord Boyle in Ireland' signed 'G. G. Sandford delin'. [E. 866, 921).

SANDS, JAMES, was a pupil of Lewis Wyatt. He exhibited at the Royal Academy from Wyatt's office in 1813 and 1816, and from Warwick Street, Golden Square, in 1819 and 1820. In 1813–16 he showed designs for intended alterations to TORRIE HOUSE, TORRYBURN, FIFE, for Sir William Erskine, Bart. (d. 1813), and his successor Sir John Erskine. In 1824 he was among the unsuccessful competitors for St. David's Church, Glasgow [R. Renwick, *Extracts from Glasgow Records* xi, 196], but he had more success in Ireland, where in 1824, as 'James Sands of London, architect', he agreed, in conjunction with Thomas Alfred Cobden of Carlow, to build RUSSELLSTOWN HOUSE, CO. CARLOW, for William Duckett [National Library of Ireland, Sir John Ainsworth's Report – private MSS. No. 259]. He is subsequently found in County Down, making a plan of HILLSBOROUGH HOUSE for the 3rd Marquess of Downshire in 1844, and designing a terrace at ROSEMOUNT, GREYABBEY, in 1846 [P.R.O. N. Ireland, D 671/C173/C, P 8/15A and P 13/5, *ex inf.* Mr. E. McParland].

SANDS, WILLIAM (–1751), was an architect and mason of Spalding, Lincs., where he was Master of the local Freemasons' Lodge and a member of the Gentlemen's Society. His estimate for 'Ceiling the Town Hall in Spalding in a Circular Arch to the upper Beames' was laid before the Society on 26 February 1740/41, and among the Society's records is a design for a Triumphal Archway to be erected in Spalding Market Place to celebrate the peace of 1749 which bears the signatures 'M. J[ohnson][1] designavit, W. S[ands]Architectus',and 'J. Newstead del'. According to J. Nichols, Sands 'drew three plans and designs of stages and uprights for a new mansion-house at Burton Pedwardine, near Sleaford, in Lincs., for Thomas Orby Hunter, esq., Lord of that manor: who was himself a curious draughtsman, and designed the house himself, but altered his mind and added to his house at Croyland'. In 1722 Sands designed the octagonal MOULTON CHAPEL, nr. SPALDING, for Maurice Johnson [J. R. Jackson, 'Moulton Chapel', *Fenland Notes and Queries* iii, 1897, 172–4]: and Robert Harmstone records in his *Notices of Remarkable Events and Curious Facts connected with the History of Spalding*, 1846, 8, that 'Towns End Manor House was pulled down in 1746 and materials sold to Mr. William Sands, Architect, and Mr. John Heals, Builder, who built two houses, one occupied by Mr. Byford, Boot Maker, Bridge-Street, and the other [now No. 12 High Street] by Mr. Capps, Builder'. In 1729 John Proudlove of Kirton-in-Holland, carpenter, undertook to rebuild MONKS HALL, GOSBERTON, LINCS., 'according to a Plan or Form drawn by Mr. William Sands' [contract printed by M. W. Barley, *The English Farmhouse and Cottage*, 1961, Appendix C].

---

[1] The founder of the Society.

Sands executed monumental sculpture, examples of which, bearing his signature, can be seen in the churches of Weston (nr. Spalding) and Crowland. He died on 2 October 1751, and was buried in Spalding Church, where a tablet (which no longer exists) cut by his pupil Edmund Hutchinson was erected to his memory. He left a son, William Sands, junior, who built HOLLAND HOUSE, HIGH STREET, for John Richards in 1768, and the two houses on either side of the brewery in Cowbit Road known as WESTBOURNE HOUSE (now the brewery offices) and LANGTON HOUSE. [J. Nichols, *Literary Anecdotes of the Eighteenth Century* vi, 111; E. H. Gooch, *A History of Spalding*, 1940, 357; records of the Spalding Gentlemen's Society.]

SANDYS, FRANCIS, was a native of Ireland, and is described as 'of Kilrea' (Co. Londonderry) in the entries in the parish register of Ickworth, Suffolk, which record the baptism of his children. He may have been a son of the Irish architect of the same name who designed Sallymount, Co. Kildare, and a Gothic 'dining-room' in the grounds of Bellevue, Co. Wicklow, in 1788 [J. N. Brewer, *The Beauties of Ireland* ii, 1826, 53; J. Ferrar, *Ancient and Modern Dublin*, 1796, 111]. His brother Joseph was domestic chaplain to Frederick Hervey, 4th Earl of Bristol and Bishop of Derry, and it was probably at Hervey's expense, and certainly with his encouragement, that Francis went to Italy in 1791, taking with him a letter of introduction to Canova [Canova archive, Bassano, 2433]. He was in Rome in 1793 [B.M., Add. MS. 39790], and did not return until 1796, when Flaxman called on Joseph Farington in company with 'Mr. Sandys an Architect; a young man who left Rome at the beginning of April, and is now employed, as he says, in beginning to build a Palace at Ickworth for Lord Bristol' [*The Farington Diary*, ed. J. Greig, i, 152].

The 'palace' which Sandys began to build at Ickworth in 1796 (and of which he exhibited a design at the Royal Academy in the following year) was an eccentric building consisting of an oval domed rotunda connected to wings by quadrants. Lord Hervey had already (1787) begun a similar house at Ballyscullion, Co. Londonderry, which is said to have been inspired by John Plaw's circular house on an island in Lake Windermere. Ickworth House was a neo-classical version of Ballyscullion, apparently worked out in Rome by the Italian architect Mario Asprucci (whose responsibility for the design, first mentioned in print in the *Civil Engineer and Architect's Jnl.* for 1846, has been confirmed by two drawings discovered by Mr. John Harris and published in *C. Life*, 17 May 1973) and executed, with modifications, in Suffolk by Sandys.

Besides supervising the building of Ickworth House, Sandys enjoyed for the next few years a

modestly successful practice, chiefly in Suffolk. He continued to exhibit at the Royal Academy, and became a Fellow of the Society of Antiquaries. But in 1809 he contracted to design and build a new court house and gaol at Durham. The work was carried out by local builders in a fraudulent manner and much of it had to be taken down and rebuilt. Sandys was superseded, first by George Moneypenny and ultimately by Ignatius Bonomi, to whose design the building was completed in 1811. Public controversy ensued, in the course of which Moneypenny attacked Sandys in print. Sandys brought an action for libel against Moneypenny which was heard in the Court of King's Bench and resulted in a verdict of £100 in Sandys's favour. But he lost the much more serious action which was brought against him by the Durham magistrates, who were awarded £20,000 damages against their architect. According to Sir Robert Smirke, Sandys was the victim of 'a juggling trick' by the Durham workmen, but whether his own conduct was fraudulent or merely negligent, he was legally responsible, and must have been financially as well as professionally ruined. No further record of him has been found, and for practical purposes his career terminates in 1814 [*Annual Register*, 1814, 298–9; W. Fordyce, *History of Durham* i, 1857, 292–3].

ICKWORTH HOUSE, nr. BURY ST. EDMUNDS, SUFFOLK, begun 1796 for the 4th Earl of Bristol and Bishop of Derry, on the basis of a design by Mario Asprucci, left unfinished on the Earl's death in 1803, completed by the 1st Marquess of Bristol c. 1825–30 [*Civil Engineer and Architect's Jnl.* ix, 1846, 60–1; Pamela Tudor-Craig, 'The Evolution of Ickworth', *C. Life*, 17 May 1973] (*C. Life*, 31 Oct., 7 Nov. 1925; C. Hussey, *English Country Houses: Mid Georgian*, 1956, 239–46).

FINBOROUGH HALL, GREAT FINBOROUGH, SUFFOLK, for Roger Pettiward, 1795 [Britton & Brayley, *Beauties of England and Wales* xiv, 1813, 207; exhib. at R.A. 1800].

WORLINGHAM HALL, SUFFOLK, remodelled for Robert Sparrow, c. 1800 [exhib. at R.A. 1800] (*C. Life*, 12 March 1970).

CHIPPENHAM PARK, CAMBS., entrance lodges for John Tharp, c. 1800 [J. Dugdale, *The British Traveller* i, 1819, 245; exhib. at R.A. 1802].

BURY ST. EDMUNDS, SUFFOLK, THE ASSEMBLY ROOMS (now the Athenaeum), 1804 [exhib. at R.A. 1806].

AYSTON HALL, RUTLAND, unexecuted design for alterations and additions for George Fludyer, 1808 [drawings at Ayston Hall, *ex inf.* Sir Nikolaus Pevsner].

WEST DEAN PARK, SUSSEX, design for the 2nd Lord Selsey for completion of house begun by James

Wyatt for his father (d. 1808); rebuilt 1893 [exhib. at R.A. 1809].

WORCESTER, THE COUNTY PRISON, 1809–13; dem. Plans had been made by George Byfield, but he disagreed with the Justices over his professional charges, and was superseded by Sandys, who is named as architect of the prison both in the *Report from the Committee of Aldermen appointed to visit Several Gaols in England*, 1816, 155, and by J. Chambers, *History of Worcester*, 1819, 350. Sandys's specification is among the County Records.

DURHAM, THE COUNTY COURTS AND GAOL, begun 1809 to the designs of Sandys but completed by George Moneypenny and Ignatius Bonomi after the failure of part of the building and Sandys's dismissal [W. Fordyce, *History of Durham* i, 1857, 292–3].

DORCHESTER BRIDGE, OXON. (R. Thames), 1813–15 [*Gent's Mag.* 1816 (ii), 297; J. M. Davenport, *Oxfordshire Bridges*, 1869, 3].

SAUL, WILLIAM, was a builder at Norwich. He exhibited a design for a Catholic Chapel at the Norfolk and Norwich Society of Artists in 1818, and his design for a new Gaol at St. Giles, Norwich, 1823, is in the City Archives [information from Mr. A. P. Baggs].

SAUNDERS, GEORGE (*c.* 1762–1839), practised in Oxford Street, London. He was a magistrate for the County of Middlesex and for twenty-eight years chairman of the Commission of Sewers for that county. In 1826 he was a member of the committee of three magistrates appointed to report on the county bridges, and was joint author of the printed *Report* (1826). Although not apparently an architectural designer of special distinction, he had a reputation for administrative efficiency which led to his employment by the Treasury to investigate the accounts of the Office of Works at a time (1809–12) when it was suffering from the incompetent management of James Wyatt. He was particularly interested in improved methods of construction such as fireproof floors made of hollow earthenware pots, and had apparently been to Paris to study their use in such buildings as the Théâtre du Palais Royal (1789–90). On the subject of theatres he wrote a systematic work (*A Treatise on Theatres*, 1790), describing the principal European theatres and discussing scientifically the optical, acoustic and other problems connected with theatre design. He was a Fellow of the Royal Society (1812) and of the Society of Antiquaries, and published papers on 'The Origin of Gothic Architecture' and 'The Situation and Extent of London at Various Periods' in *Archaeologia* xvii, 1814, and xxvi, 1836. The former was an important contribution to the study of vaulting and the first clear exposition of the connection between vaulting and the pointed arch. His 'Observations on Brick Bond as practised at various periods' were printed in the *Civil Engineer and Architect's Jnl.* i, 1838. Saunders died at his house in Oxford Street in the summer of 1839, aged 77. A bust in ivory by B. Cheverton after Sir Francis Chantrey is in the collection of the R.I.B.A. His brother Thomas Saunders, who died on 11 May 1798, is said to have been an architect in the notice of his death in *Gent's Mag.* 1798 (i), 448.

[*A.P.S.D.*; *Gent's Mag.* 1839 (ii), 321; R. S. Fitton & A. P. Wadsworth, *The Strutts and the Arkwrights*, Manchester 1958, 201–3; Paul Frankl, *The Gothic*, Princeton, 1960, 499–502; *History of the King's Works* vi.]

BIRMINGHAM, rebuilt THE THEATRE ROYAL, NEW STREET, and adjoining ASSEMBLY ROOMS, etc., 1793–4, retaining the façade by Samuel Wyatt (1780); executed under the direction of Samuel Norton (*q.v.*); destroyed by fire 1820 [MS. Minutes of the Proprietors in Birmingham City Library].

KEN (CAEN) WOOD HOUSE, HIGHGATE, MIDDLESEX, alterations for the 2nd Earl of Mansfield, 1793–6 [*A.P.S.D.*; *The Farington Diary*, ed. J. Greig, i, 17; A. T. Bolton, *The Architecture of R. and J. Adam* i, 1922, 304].

LONDON, THE STAG BREWERY, PIMLICO, for John Elliott, 1797–1802; internally reconstructed 1860; dem. *c.* 1960 [B. Spiller, 'The Georgian Brewery', *Arch. Rev.*, Nov. 1957, 322].

OXFORD, THE SHELDONIAN THEATRE, reconstruction of roof, 1801–2 [*V.C.H. Oxon.* iii, 53].

OXFORD, BODLEIAN LIBRARY, designed the 'Antiquaries' Closet' for the reception of the MSS. of Dodsworth, Tanner, Browne Willis, etc., *c.* 1805 [J. Nichols, *Literary Illustrations* v, 553–5]. There is a sketch of the 'Closet' in Bodleian, MS. Top. Oxon. a. 36, f. 79.

LONDON, BRITISH MUSEUM, THE TOWNLEY GALLERY, 1804–8; dem. *c.* 1850 [J. Mordaunt Crook, *The British Museum*, 1972, 68–70 and figs. 21–4].

DARTINGTON HALL, DEVON, survey of medieval house for Arthur Champernowne, 1805 [A. Emery, *Dartington Hall*, 1970, 85 and plates, pp. 162–3].

SAVAGE, JAMES (1779–1852), born at Hackney on 10 April 1779, was articled to D. A. Alexander, under whom he served for several years as clerk of the works. In 1798 he became a student at the Royal Academy, and subsequently exhibited at the Academy between 1799 and 1832. In 1800 his design for improving the city of Aberdeen obtained the second premium of £150. In 1805 he was the successful competitor for a design for rebuilding Ormonde Bridge over the R.

Liffey at Dublin. This was not carried out, but in 1808 his designs for Richmond Bridge in the same city were accepted, and subsequently executed. In 1806 he read a paper on 'Bridge-building' to the London Architectural Society (of which he was a member), which was printed in the second volume of the Society's *Essays*, 1810, 119–67. In 1823 he made a design for rebuilding London Bridge which was highly thought of; but the chairman of the committee of the House of Commons gave his casting vote in favour of that submitted by Sir John Rennie. Savage thereupon published a pamphlet entitled *Observations on the proposed new London Bridge*, in which he criticized Rennie's design, and claimed that his proposed centering was deficient in construction, 'implicating stability and security'. In 1825 he published a plan for improving the south bank of the R. Thames by forming a 'Surrey Quay' to extend from London Bridge to Bishop's Walk, Lambeth. He competed for the Houses of Parliament in 1835, submitting a design in 'the castle style of Gothic'.

The interest in construction which made Savage a successful bridge-builder is also apparent in the church of St. Luke at Chelsea, which was built to his plans in 1820–4. Over forty designs were submitted, and Savage's, although pronounced by the Attached Architects to the Board of Works to be of 'extremely difficult construction', were accepted, though he was not allowed to carry into execution his plans for a stone spire constructed like that of St. Dunstan-in-the-East. With its flying buttresses supporting a genuine stone vault, St. Luke's is remarkable as one of the first serious attempts to revive medieval forms of construction, and it was recognized at the time as a landmark in the history of the Gothic revival. None of Savage's other Gothic churches has the same interest or importance as St. Luke's, but his one classical church, St. James, Bermondsey, has the merit of demonstrating an original and effective solution to the problem of combining a Grecian portico with a steeple.

Savage was much employed as an adviser in legal cases concerning architecture or engineering, and in 1827–30 he gave evidence on behalf of Henry Peto, the builder, in the action consequent upon the failure of the foundations of the Custom House.

In about 1830 he succeeded Henry Hakewill as architect to the Society of the Middle Temple, for whom he designed Plowden Buildings and other works noted below. In 1840 he began the restoration of the Temple Church for the Societies of the Inner and Middle Temples, but was superseded by Sydney Smirke and Decimus Burton after grossly exceeding his estimates. This affair no doubt had an adverse effect on his practice, and he appears to have had relatively

few commissions between 1842 and his death ten years later.

Savage was President of the Surveyors' Club in 1825, and was a vice-president of the London Architectural Society. He was also chairman of the Committee of Fine Arts of the Society for the Promotion of Arts, Manufactures, and Commerce, a member of the Institution of Civil Engineers, a member of the Graphic Society from its foundation in 1831 and, for a short time, a Fellow of the Institute of British Architects, from which he resigned after a 'difference of views upon some matters of regulation'. He was a freeman of the City of London, and a member of the Skinners' Company.

He died at North Place, Hampstead Road, London, on 7 May 1852 in his 74th year, and was buried at St. Luke's Church, Chelsea. His books and drawings were sold on 9 December 1853. Several of the latter were presented to the R.I.B.A. Library in 1854. His designs (1841) for a new Armoury at the Tower of London are in the British Museum (Add. MS. 16368, A–B).

In addition to the work already mentioned, he published, with L. N. Cottingham, *St. Saviour's Church, reasons against pulling down the Lady Chapel*, 1832; and *Observations on Style in Architecture, with suggestions on the best mode of procuring Designs for Public Buildings, and promoting the improvement of Architecture, especially in reference to a Recommendation in the Report of the Commissioners on the Designs for the New Houses of Parliament*, 1836, in which he took exception to the proposal that the architect's drawings should 'be submitted from time to time to competent judges of their effect, lest from over-confidence, negligence, or inattention ... we fail to obtain that result to which our just expectations have been raised'. He is also believed to have been the author of *Observations on the Varieties of Architecture used in the Structure of Parish Churches*, 1812.

[*A.P.S.D.*; *D.N.B.*; obituaries in *Builder* x, 1852, 377, *Civil Engineer and Architect's Jnl.* xv, 1852, 226, *Gent's Mag.* 1852 (ii), 206–7.]

CHURCHES

LONDON, ST. LUKE, CHELSEA, 1820–4, Gothic [*Gent's Mag.* 1826 (ii), 201–5; Britton & Pugin, *Public Buildings of London* ii, 1828, 205–18].

LONDON, ST. MARY-AT-HILL, repairs, 1827–8, and refitting of interior, 1848–9, after a fire [*Gent's Mag.* 1852 (ii), 207].

UPPER NORWOOD, SURREY, ALL SAINTS, BEULAH HILL, 1827–9, Gothic; chapel added 1861 [Port, 162–3].

LONDON, ST. JAMES, BERMONDSEY, assisted by George Allen, 1827–9 [Port, 134–5; *A.P.S.D.*].

LONDON, HOLY TRINITY, SLOANE STREET, CHELSEA, 1828–30, Gothic; dem. 1890 [*Gent's Mag.* 1831 (i), 298–300, with engraving].

TOTTENHAM GREEN, MIDDLESEX, HOLY TRINITY, 1828–9, Gothic; damaged by bombing 1940/1 [Port, 158–9].

ILFORD, ESSEX, ST. MARY, 1829–31, Gothic; tower 1866, chancel 1920 [Port, 144–5].

SPEENHAMLAND, BERKS., 1829–31, Gothic; chancel by G. E. Street 1879; nave rebuilt by A. E. Street 1911 [*Gent's Mag.* 1852 (ii), 207; exhib. at R.A. 1830].

NEWPORT PAGNELL, BUCKS., rebuilt south aisle and added pinnacles and battlements to tower, 1830 [I.C.B.S.].

GREAT MARLOW, BUCKS., reported on old church and made unexecuted designs for a new one [*Records of Bucks.* xv, 1947, 14].

LONDON, ST. MICHAEL, BURLEIGH STREET, STRAND, 1832–3, Gothic; dem. *c.* 1906 [*Gent's Mag.* 1852 (ii), 207]. The fittings are in St. Michael's Church, Sutton Court, Chiswick.

BRENTWOOD, ESSEX, ST. THOMAS, 1835, Gothic; chancel rebuilt by J. Clarke 1866, the remainder by E. C. Lee 1882–90 [*Gent's Mag.* 1852 (ii), 207].

ADDLESTONE, SURREY, ST. PAUL, 1836–8, Gothic; subsequently altered at various dates [*Gent's Mag.* 1852 (ii), 207].

LINCOLN CATHEDRAL, new floor and bell-frame in central tower for 'Great Tom', 1836 [*Gent's Mag.* 1852 (ii), 207].

LONDON, ST. MARY-LE-BOW, CHEAPSIDE, repaired belfry floor and bell-frame [*Gent's Mag.* 1852 (ii), 207].

LONDON, TEMPLE CHURCH, commenced restoration 1840–1, was superseded by Sydney Smirke and Decimus Burton [J. Mordaunt Crook, 'The Restoration of the Temple Church: Ecclesiology and Recrimination', *Architectural History* viii, 1965].

OTHER WORKS

DUBLIN, RICHMOND BRIDGE (R. Liffey), 1813–16 [*Gent's Mag.* 1852 (ii), 207].

TEMPSFORD BRIDGE, BEDS. (R. Ouse), 1815–20 [R.I.B.A.D.; *Gent's Mag.* 1852 (ii), 207].

LONDON, PAROCHIAL SCHOOLS, CHELSEA, 1824–6, Gothic [T. Faulkner, *Chelsea*, 1829, i, 98–101; ii, 92, engraving].

READING, BERKS., two bridges on road made through Crown lands, *c.* 1825 [R.I.B.A.D.; *Gent's Mag.* 1852 (ii), 207].

LONDON, BAPTIST COLLEGE, STEPNEY GREEN, 1830; mostly dem. [*Gent's Mag.* 1852 (ii), 207].

LONDON, 'BULL AND MOUTH' INN (later Queen's Hotel), ST. MARTIN'S-LE-GRAND, 1830–1; dem. 1887 [*A.P.S.D.*].

LONDON, THE MIDDLE TEMPLE, built domed louvre (destroyed 1944) and north entrance to Hall to

designs of Henry Hakewill, 1830; designed Clock Tower 1830–1, and completed Plowden Buildings (begun by Hakewill) 1831–3 [*A.P.S.D.*].

ILFORD, ESSEX, CHURCH SCHOOLS, 1831 [*A.P.S.D.*].

LONDON, ST. MARY-AT-HILL RECTORY, 1834 [*A.P.S.D.*].

BRENTWOOD, ESSEX, CHURCH SCHOOLS, *c.* 1835, Gothic [*A.P.S.D.*].

DARTFORD UNION WORKHOUSE (now West Hill Hospital), DARTFORD, KENT, 1836 [*A.P.S.D.*].

TENTERDEN UNION WORKHOUSE, KENT, 1843–7 [*Gent's Mag.* 1852 (ii), 207].

BROMLEY UNION WORKHOUSE, LOCK'S BOTTOM, FARNBOROUGH, KENT [*Gent's Mag.* 1852 (ii), 207].

BROXBOURNE VICARAGE, HERTS. [*A.P.S.D.*].

HAMPSTEAD, LONDON, house for — Husband [*A.P.S.D.*].

LUTON, BEDS., house for R. Vyse [*A.P.S.D.*].

'House for Sir J. Shaw' [*A.P.S.D.*], probably STAPLEFIELD PLACE, SUSSEX, since completely rebuilt.

House (unidentified) for Samuel Cartwright [*A.P.S.D.*].

SAXON, SAMUEL (1757–), born on 30 June 1757, became a pupil of Sir William Chambers. He was admitted a student at the Royal Academy in November 1776, and exhibited at the Academy between 1778 and 1782. He was appointed a Labourer in Trust at Whitehall in 1780, and would no doubt have been promoted to a clerkship of the works but for the reforms which abolished many Office of Works posts in 1782.

Saxon designed the GENERAL INFIRMARY at NORTHAMPTON, 1791–3, enlarged 1840 and 1887 [F. F. Waddy, *History of the Northampton General Hospital*, Northampton 1974]; and two elegant country houses: COURTEENHALL, NORTHANTS., for Sir William Wake, Bart., 1791–4 (*C. Life*, 12–19 Aug. 1939), and BUCKMINSTER PARK, LEICS., for Sir William Manners, Bart., *c.* 1795–8, dem. 1950, both illustrated in G. Richardson's *New Vitruvius Britannicus* i, 1810, pls. 67–72. No other buildings by Saxon are known, and as no trace of him has been found after 1800, it is possible that he died about that time.

SCAMP, WILLIAM (1801–1872), was born on 5 June 1801, at Georgeham, nr. Barnstaple, where his father was a prosperous maltster and shipowner. He showed an early aptitude for geometry and surveying, and but for his father's early death he would doubtless have received a regular professional training. As it was, he was largely self-taught, and it was his success in winning the competition for the ASSEMBLY ROOMS at ILFRACOMBE which brought him to the notice of Sir Jeffry Wyatville. For thirteen years he served

Wyatville as a clerk of the works during the rebuilding of Windsor Castle, proving himself a man of untiring energy with 'an iron frame and a good constitution'. During this period, he designed the parish church at UPTON-CUM-CHALVEY, nr. SLOUGH, BUCKS., a building in the Lombardic style, which was completed in 1837 and rebuilt by J. O. Scott between 1876 and 1918 [P. W. Phipps, *Records of Upton-cum-Chalvey*, 1886, 24]. On the completion of the work at Windsor, he was appointed assistant engineer to the Works Department at Woolwich Dockyard, and in 1841 he accompanied Capt. Brandreth, Director of Engineering Works to the Admiralty, on a visit to Malta in order to report on the naval accommodation there. It was he who supervised the construction of the first dry dock in 1841–8, and he subsequently remodelled the Dockyard by designing a new bakery, coal stores, officers' quarters, and other buildings. He was also put in charge of the dockyard at Gibraltar, where the new Mole and other works were completed under his direction, largely by convict labour.

Shortly after his arrival in Malta, he was asked to report on the half-finished Anglican Cathedral of St. Paul which had been founded by Queen Adelaide in 1839. Its architect was Richard Lankersheer, the English Director of Public Works, who, although a gentleman of taste, was not altogether competent in structural matters. In particular, he failed to appreciate the peculiar properties of the local stone, and certain 'cracks, splits and crushings began to appear' which caused the Building Committee to seek the professional advice of the Admiralty architects. Their report showed that the Ionic portico was in danger of collapse and that the whole building must be condemned as insecure. The incompetence of the Director of Public Works gave unwelcome force to a campaign against the English monopoly of Government posts which then occupied the Maltese press: and when the unfortunate Lankersheer died in 1841 at the age of 38, the completion of Queen Adelaide's church became a matter involving the prestige of the British Government in Malta. It was in these circumstances that the Committee turned to Scamp as the only competent representative of his profession available. He proved equal to the occasion and not only saved the church from collapse, but designed and built the handsome tower and spire which form one of the principal landmarks of Valetta. On his return to England in 1845, Queen Adelaide presented him with a silver candelabrum 'in grateful remembrance of his services in completing the Collegiate Church of St. Paul, at Malta'. He was now promoted to be Chief Assistant to the Admiralty Director of Engineering and Architectural Works, and in 1852 he became Deputy Director under G. T. Greene, with whom he shares the credit for designing some of the impor-

722

tant iron-framed structures built by the Admiralty in the 1850s. Between 1845 and 1867 he was engaged in re-equipping British naval bases in all parts of the world for the new fleet of ironclads, and in 1860 the Director of Admiralty Works wrote that 'The present Admiralty establishments at Malta, Gibraltar, and Bermuda, are almost entirely projected by him. Deptford, Woolwich, Sheerness, Portsmouth and Pembroke, owe many of their best buildings to his professional talent. Keyham is almost entirely his own, from first to last.' Scamp died on 13 January 1872, five years after his retirement in 1867. He was a member of the Institution of Civil Engineers. [Obituary in *Proceedings of the Institution of Civil Engineers* xxxvi, 1872–3, 273–8; H. M. Colvin, 'Victorian Malta', *Arch. Rev.*, June 1946, 179–80; A. W. Skempton, 'The Boat Store, Sheerness (1858–60) and its Place in Structural History', *Trans. Newcomen Soc.* xxxii, 1959–60, 63–4; *Gent's Mag.* 1844 (ii), 632–3.]

SCAMPION, JOHN, was employed in the construction of a new building in MONTGOMERY CASTLE for the 1st Lord Herbert of Chirbury in the 1620s. Between 1622 and 1625 the parish register of Montgomery records the baptisms of two of his children and the burial of his wife, and refers to him as *Johannes Scampion, artificiossimus jam architectus novi operis in Castello de Mountgomeri*. He appears to have been a master carpenter by trade, to have lived previously in Whitechapel, London, and to have been a native of Great Hormead in Essex [J. D. K. Lloyd, 'The New Building at Montgomery Castle', *Archaeologia Cambrensis* cxiv, 1965, 60–8].

SCARBOROUGH, JOHN (–1696), was Clerk of the Works at Greenwich Palace from 1681 until his death in November 1696. In May 1696, on the commencement of the new Hospital at Greenwich, he was appointed Clerk of the Works there, still retaining his former post. He was also appointed Clerk of the Works at Winchester soon after the commencement of the new Palace there in 1682, and was Surveyor to the Westminster Commissioners for Sewers from 1691 to 1696. He was frequently employed by Sir Christopher Wren as a measuring clerk – *e.g.* at St. Paul's from 1687, at Hampton Court from 1689, and in connection with several of the new City churches. He also assisted Robert Hooke in a similar capacity [*Wren Soc.* xx, 204; *Walpole Soc.* xxv, 93]. In 1680 he was the measurer employed at ABINGDON TOWN HALL [Arthur Oswald in *C. Life*, 21 Sept. 1929, 394, referring to B.M., Add. MS. 28666, ff. 338–9], and in 1690 he spent a week at PETWORTH HOUSE, SUSSEX, measuring work carried out on the Duke of Somerset's great new mansion, a task for which he received £10 15s. [*Sussex Arch. Colls.* xcvi, 1958, 98].

SCHOFIELD, JOHN, of Jewin Street, London, exhibited a 'Design for a mausoleum for the interment of warlike heroes' at the Royal Academy in 1802. Pigot's *Directory* shows that he was practising as architect from the same address in 1827–8.

SCOLES, JOSEPH JOHN (1798–1863), born in London on 27 June 1798, was the son of Matthew Scoles, a joiner. His parents were Roman Catholics, and Scoles was apprenticed in 1812 to Joseph Ireland, the leading Roman Catholic architect of the time, to whom he was related through his mother. While in his office, Scoles came into contact with John Carter, who corrected his drawings of medieval detail and encouraged his interest in ecclesiastical architecture. In 1820 he was admitted to the Royal Academy Schools, and began to exhibit his designs.

In 1822 Scoles left England in company with Joseph Bonomi, junior, and travelled extensively on the Continent and in Sicily, Greece, Egypt and Syria, devoting himself to architectural and archaeological research. In Sicily he assisted Angell and Harris in their explorations, and in Syria and Egypt he was the companion of Henry Parke and Frederick Catherwood. In 1829 he and Parke published an engraved Map of Nubia, based on a survey made by them in 1824, and the illustrations to the article 'Catacomb' in the Architectural Publication Society's Dictionary include plans of a catacomb in Alexandria drawn by Scoles, Parke and Catherwood in 1823. His plan of the Church of the Holy Sepulchre at Jerusalem was utilized by Professor Willis in his monograph on that building (1849), and he also made the drawings from which the plate of the temple of Cadacchio (Corfu) in the supplementary volume of the *Antiquities of Athens* was prepared.

On returning to England in 1826, Scoles was employed to plan Gloucester Terrace, Regent's Park, for which John Nash supplied a characteristic elevation. The internal arrangement of the houses forming the terrace was entirely Scoles's work, and he attempted to improve Nash's façade by enlarging the scale of the mouldings. Nash is said to have 'passed the work with the observation that the parts looked larger than he expected'. It was, however, as a designer of churches (nearly all Roman Catholic) that Scoles made his reputation. These were chiefly in a Gothic style which satisfied everyone except Pugin (who criticized St. Mary's Islington in his *Present State of Ecclesiastical Architecture in England*, 1843), but some were 'Norman' and a few, notably at Prior Park College and Ince Blundell Hall, were handsome classical buildings.

Scoles was one of the original fellows of the Institute of British Architects in 1835, acted as its honorary secretary from 1846 to 1856, and was vice-president in 1857–8. At its meetings he read a number of papers, principally on the monuments of Egypt and the Holy Land. He died on 29 December 1863, at his residence Crofton Lodge, Hammersmith, leaving four sons and eight daughters by his wife Harriott, daughter of Robert Cory of Great Yarmouth. Two of his sons, Ignatius and Alexander Joseph, received an architectural training, but subsequently entered the church, and practised only in a clerical capacity. S. J. Nicholl and T. J. Willson were his pupils. [*A.P.S.D.*; *D.N.B.*; *Builder* xxii, 1864, 41; S. J. Nicholl's reminiscences in *Downside Review* viii, 1889, 114–17; J. Gillow, *Bibliographical Dictionary of the English Catholics*, 1885; list of works in *Catholic Annual Register*, 1850, 106–7, cited below as *C.A.R.*; B. Little, *Catholic Churches since 1623*, 1966.]

ESHER, SURREY, WEST END LODGE, for Thomas Roberts, *c.* 1820 [*A.P.S.D.*].

KNOWSLEY, LANCS., conservatory 'proposed to be erected' for the 12th Earl of Derby, exhib. at R.A. 1820.

LONDON, interior of GLOUCESTER TERRACE, REGENT'S PARK, and houses in GLOUCESTER GATE, 1827–8 [*D.N.B.*].

YARMOUTH, NORFOLK, suspension bridge over R. Bure, 1830, failed 1845 [*Builder* iii, 1845, 253–4].

YARMOUTH, NORFOLK, ST. PETER'S CHURCH, 1831–3, Gothic [Port, 158–9].

YARMOUTH, NORFOLK, ST. MARY'S CHAPEL, SOUTH TOWN, 1831–2, Gothic; enlarged 1893 [*A.P.S.D.*].

HOLYWELL, FLINTSHIRE, ST. WINIFRIDE'S CHURCH (R.C.), 1832–3, classical; enlarged 1895–8 [*C.A.R.*].

STONYHURST COLLEGE, LANCS., ST. PETER'S CHURCH (R.C.), 1832–5, Gothic [*C.A.R.*].

LONDON, OUR LADY'S CHAPEL (R.C.), GROVE ROAD, ST. JOHN'S WOOD, 1833–6, Gothic [*C.A.R.*].

PRESTON, LANCS., ST. IGNATIUS' CHURCH (R.C.), 1833–6, Gothic; chancel by J. A. Hansom 1858 [*C.A.R.*].

YARMOUTH, NORFOLK, ST. NICHOLAS' CHURCH, repaired tower, 1834 [*Norfolk Chronicle*, 8 March 1834, *ex inf.* Mr. D. C. Young].

BANGOR, CAERNARVONSHIRE, ST. MARY'S CHURCH (R.C.), 1834–44, Gothic [*C.A.R.*].

HULL, YORKS. (E.R.), ST. CHARLES' CHURCH, JARRATT STREET (R.C.), alterations, 1835, classical [*C.A.R.*].

PRINCETHORPE, WARWICKS., ST. MARY'S PRIORY, altar, 1835 [*C.A.R.*].

WOOLTON, nr. LIVERPOOL, LANCS., THE MAGDALEN ASYLUM (R.C.), 1835 [*C.A.R.*].

BIRMINGHAM, ST. GEORGE'S CHURCH, EDGBASTON,

1836–8, Gothic; chancel by C. Edge, 1856; rebuilt 1884–5 by J. A. Chatwin [*A.P.S.D.*].

COLCHESTER, ST. JAMES'S CHURCH (R.C.), 1837, Norman; enlarged 1904–10 [*C.A.R.*].

STONYHURST COLLEGE, LANCS., OBSERVATORY, 1838 [*C.A.R.*].

NEWPORT, MONMOUTHSHIRE, ST. MARY'S CHURCH (R.C.), 1838–40, Gothic [*C.A.R.*].

CARDIFF, GLAMORGANSHIRE, ST. DAVID'S CHURCH (R.C.), 1841–2, Norman; rebuilt 1884–7 [*C.A.R.*].

LONDON, ST. JOHN'S CHURCH, DUNCAN TERRACE, ISLINGTON (R.C.), 1841–3, Norman [*C.A.R.*; *Builder* i, 1843, 98–9].

HAMMERSMITH, MIDDLESEX, CONVENT OF THE GOOD SHEPHERD, 1843 [*C.A.R.*].

BERRYMEDE PRIORY, ACTON, MIDDLESEX (CONVENT OF SACRED HEART), new lodge, etc., 1843 [*C.A.R.*].

INCE BLUNDELL, LANCS., school, 1843 [*Builder* i, 1843, 487].

PRESTON, LANCS., ST. WILFRID'S CHURCH (R.C.), added Lady Chapel, 1844; rebuilt 1879–80 [*C.A.R.*].

DOWLAIS, GLAMORGANSHIRE, ST. ILLTYD'S CHURCH (R.C.), 1844–6, Gothic; enlarged 1894 [*C.A.R.*].

PONTYPOOL, MONMOUTHSHIRE, ST. ALBAN'S CHURCH (R.C.), 1844–6, Norman [*C.A.R.*].

PRIOR PARK COLLEGE, BATH, SOMERSET, CHURCH (R.C.), begun 1844, not completed until after 1863, classical [exhib. at R.A. 1844].

LIVERPOOL, ST. FRANCIS XAVIER'S CHURCH, EVERTON (R.C.), 1845–9, Gothic; Lady Chapel 1888 [*C.A.R.*].

LONDON, CHURCH OF THE IMMACULATE CONCEPTION, FARM STREET (R.C.), 1846–9, Gothic [*C.A.R.*] (*Builder* vii, 1849, 258).

CHELMSFORD, ESSEX, CHURCH OF THE IMMACULATE CONCEPTION (R.C.), 1847, Gothic [*C.A.R.*; *Builder* v, 1847, 545].

BURGH CASTLE CHURCH, SUFFOLK, restoration and refitting, 1846 [*D.N.B.*]. In 1847 Scoles read a paper on the 'Construction of the Roof of St. Peter's Church, Burgh, Suffolk' to the R.I.B.A.

YARMOUTH, NORFOLK, ST. MARY'S CHURCH (R.C.), 1848–50, Gothic [*C.A.R.*].

BLUNDESTON CHURCH, SUFFOLK, restoration of roof, 1849 [*D.N.B.*].

LONDON, THE ORATORY, BROMPTON, KENSINGTON, for the Oratorians, 1849–53 [*C.A.R.*]. Scoles's residential building remains, but his temporary church was replaced in 1878.

HEREFORD, ST. FRANCIS XAVIER'S CHURCH (R.C.), altar and ciborium, *c.* 1850 [*C.A.R.*].

LYDIATE, LANCS., OUR LADY'S CHURCH (R.C.), 1854–5, Gothic [*A.P.S.D.*].

INCE BLUNDELL HALL, LANCS., CHAPEL (R.C.) for Thomas Weld Blundell, 1858–9, classical [*D.N.B.*]. Scoles may also have been respon-

sible for the redecoration of the Drawing Room, Gallery, etc., as he exhibited 'intended alterations to Ince Blundell Hall' at the R.A. in 1854 (cf. *C. Life*, 10, 17, 24 April 1958).

ST. HELEN'S, LANCS., HOLY CROSS CHURCH (R.C.), 1860–2, Gothic [*A.P.S.D.*; *D.N.B.*].

NEW HALL CONVENT, BOREHAM, ESSEX, alterations [*C.A.R.*].

LONDON, schools in CHARLES STREET, DRURY LANE [*A.P.S.D.*].

SCOLTOCK, SAMUEL (*c.* 1739–1819), is described as 'architect' on a tablet to his memory in Shrewsbury Abbey Church. He died on 18 March 1819, aged 80. He was a bricklayer by trade and was no doubt the successor of Richard Scoltock, a bricklayer who, with Edward Massey, a carpenter, jointly designed and built MILLINGTON'S HOSPITAL, FRANKWELL, SHREWSBURY, in 1747–8 (central feature altered by J. H. Haycock in 1785–6). In an affidavit to the estimate Massey stated that he and Scoltock had 'for several years ... been very much employed in making plans of Publick and other great Buildings and making calculations of the expences of the building thereof' [J. B. Lawson, 'The Architect of Millington's Hospital, Shrewsbury', *Shropshire News Letter*, no. 42, May 1972, 10]. Jonathan Scoltock of Sutton, nr. Shrewsbury, also described as 'architect', is mentioned in 1791 in the Salop Fire Office Policy Books.

SCOTT, ARCHIBALD (*c.* 1798–1871), practised in Edinburgh for many years. Shepherd's *Modern Athens* (p. 77) records that he designed the STOCKBRIDGE MARKET, ST. STEPHEN PLACE, 1825, of which only the entrance archway now remains. He was probably the 'Mr. Scott of Edinburgh' who is said to have designed the spire of NEWCASTLETON CHURCH, ROXBURGHSHIRE, in 1835 [G. Hay, *The Architecture of Scottish Post-Reformation Churches*, 1957, 274]. He died on 3 July 1871, aged 73.

SCOTT, G—, of Furnival's Inn, exhibited a 'Design for a house at Demerary, for R. Fernier Esq.' at the Royal Academy in 1802. He also exhibited a drawing of Louth Church, Lincs., in 1832. A person of this name was appointed District Surveyor of the Western District of the City of London in 1774.

SCOTT, JOSEPH, junior, advertised in the *Leicester Journal* (23 Nov. 1810) and the *Northampton Mercury* (15 Dec. 1810) that having been 'many years in the employ of James Wyatt, Esq.' he was established in Market Harborough, where he 'engages to design and execute in a masterly and workmanlike manner, MODERN, GOTHIC, and GROTESQUE Architecture, on the most reasonable terms'. Joseph Scott figures as a 'builder and surveyor' under Market Harborough in Pigot's *Directory* of 1828–9.

SCOTT, ROBERT (–*c*. 1840). J. Pagan, *Sketch of the History of Glasgow*, 1847, 182, states that ST. MARY'S EPISCOPAL CHAPEL, RENFIELD STREET, GLASGOW, 1825, Gothic, was designed 'by the late Robert Scott, architect'. This was presumably the Robert Scott of the 'Architectural Academy, Glasgow', who appears among the subscribers to Peter Nicholson's *Architectural Dictionary* (1819). In 1830 he was in partnership with — Wilson, and in 1834 he was a member of the firm of 'Scott, Stephen and Gale'. He died about 1840 [information from Mr. David Walker]. In 1834 he was working at BOTURICH CASTLE, DUNBARTONSHIRE, for John Buchanan [*Glasgow Herald*, 29 Aug. 1834]. He appears to have designed the POLICE OFFICES in ALBION STREET, GLASGOW, completed in 1825, for in February 1824 Thomas Rickman saw the plans in his office [Rickman's diary, 16 Feb. 1824].

SCOUGAL, DAVID, a mason of Crail in Fife, was the carver of the Glencairn Monument in the Glencairn Aisle of KILMAURS CHURCH, AYRSHIRE. It was erected in 1600 and bears the inscription WROCHT BE DAVID SCWGAL MASSON BURGES IN CAREL, together with Scougal's mark.[1] The same mark is found on the monument in DUNFERMLINE ABBEY CHURCH to William Schaw, Master of the King's Works in Scotland, who died in 1602.

SEABROOKE, WILLIAM, was apparently a bricklayer by trade, but also acted as a surveyor. In 1723 and 1729/30 he was remunerated for making drawings, plans and estimates, etc., for buildings in CLEMENTS INN, STRAND (dem. 1868) [*The Pension Book of Clements Inn*, ed. C. Carr, Selden Soc. vol. lxxviii, 1960, 107, 152–3].

SEARLES, MICHAEL (1750–1813), was the son of Michael Searles of Greenwich, a surveyor, and was brought up to his father's profession.[2] He married in 1771 and appears shortly afterwards to have begun to practise on his own in Bermondsey, where he became surveyor to the Rolls estate. The Rolls family owned a considerable amount of freehold land in St. George's Fields and Walworth, and Searles was probably concerned in its development. By 1792, when he entered into partnership with one Robert Roberts, he was already describing himself as an architect as well as a surveyor. A large collection of his drawings in the R.I.B.A. Collection shows

---

[1] ⋈

[2] A survey of Mr. Swindon's estate at Greenwich, taken in May 1773 by M. Searles & Son, is in the B.M. (*King's Maps* xvii, 13y). The elder Searles was the author of *The Young Surveyor's Assistant*, 1779.

that he was an able designer of domestic architecture in an elegant late Georgian style, but in general his 'opportunities do not seem to have equalled his talents', and most of his time was spent building small houses and shops in southeast London and in repairs and alterations to existing buildings. His ability can, however, still be appreciated at the Paragon at Blackheath, a crescent of semi-detached houses attractively linked by colonnades, and at Clare House, East Malling, Kent, a skilfully composed sequence of geometrically planned rooms, circular, oval and octagonal. Other small town-planning schemes for which he was responsible were Gloucester Circus, Greenwich, and Surrey Square, Southwark. He may well have designed Colonnade House, Blackheath, whose name draws attention to a feature which constantly recurs in Searle's designs, and of which he made highly effective use.

Searles died at Lee on 20 October 1813, after a road-accident in which his chaise was overturned. As surveyor to the Rolls estate he was succeeded by his son Richard and by his second son Robert Thomas Searles, who died in 1863 [A. R. Martin in *C. Life*, 14 Oct. 1949, 1149–50; *Gent's Mag.* 1813 (ii), 507; *Survey of London* xxv, 122; P.C.C. 582 BRIDPORT; *R.I.B.A. Drawings Catalogue.*]

SOUTHWARK, SURREY PLACE (now NOS. 228–250), OLD KENT ROAD, 1784 [R.I.B.A.D.].

DEPTFORD, KENT, UNION PLACE, 1786 [R.I.B.A.D.].

STREATHAM, SURREY, house for William Wilkinson, probably THE ROOKERY, STREATHAM COMMON SOUTH, rebuilt 1786; dem. [R.I.B.A.D.].

LAMBETH, MARLBOROUGH HOUSE, NO. 317 KENNINGTON ROAD, for William Edridge, *c*. 1787 [R.I.B.A.D.; *Survey of London* xxvi, 50–1]

SOUTHWARK, THE PARAGON, NEW KENT ROAD, 1789–90; dem. 1898 [James Edwards, *A Companion from London to Brightelmston* i, 1801, 7, §9; *Survey of London* xxv, 118–23 and pl. 86].

LAMBETH, PRINCES PLACE (now NOS. 114–135), KENNINGTON PARK ROAD, flanking the entrance to Princes (now Cleaver) Square, 1790 [R.I.B.A.D.; *Survey of London*, xxvi, 52, pl. 50].

GREENWICH, GLOUCESTER CIRCUS, designed as a double crescent, of which only one side was built, 1790–1 [R.I.B.A.D.].

DARTFORD CHURCH, KENT, repairs, 1792 [J. Dunkin, *History of Dartford*, 1844, 46–9].

BLACKHEATH, THE PARAGON, *c*. 1793; restored 1946–58 after bomb-damage [R.I.B.A.D.] (S. C. Ramsey, *Small Houses of the Late Georgian Period*, 1919, pls. 71–2, ii, 1923, pls. 65–6).

CLARE HOUSE, EAST MALLING, KENT, for John Larking, 1793 [R.I.B.A.D.] (*C. Life*, 16–23 Sept. 1949).

725

SOUTHWARK, NO. 155 OLD KENT ROAD (later the Rolls estate office) for himself, 1795 [*Survey of London* xxv, 122; cf. R.I.B.A.D.].

SOUTHWARK, SURREY SQUARE, 1795–8 [R.I.B.A.D.; *Survey of London* xxv, 89–90 and pl. 56].

attributed: BLACKHEATH, COLONNADE HOUSE, *c.* 1800 [stylistic attribution] (S. C. Ramsey, *Small Houses of the Late Georgian Period*, 1919, pl. 73).

REIGATE PRIORY, SURREY, alterations to west front for George Mowbray, 1802 [R.I.B.A.D.] (*C. Life*, 6–13 April 1918).

SEPHTON, HENRY (*c.* 1686–1756), was the leading mason and architect in Liverpool during the second quarter of the eighteenth century. His most important work was Ince Blundell Hall, for which an original drawing bearing his signature survives. This is a handsome Georgian house with a façade derived, with variations, from that of Buckingham House, London. He also designed the classical tower of Prescot Church and the demolished church of St. Thomas, Liverpool. In *c.* 1726 he made plans for St. George's Church which were not adopted, those of Thomas Steers being preferred [J. A. Picton, *Liverpool Municipal Records* ii, 1886, 70–1]. In 1738 he was paid 20s. 'for viewing the steeple' of Rostherne Church, Cheshire [*Trans. Chester and N. Wales Arch. Soc.* xxxv (i), 45–8], and in 1746 'Messrs. Sephton and Smith' contracted to build the spire of St. Nicholas Church, Liverpool, in accordance with designs made by Thomas Gee (*q.v.*). As a master mason Sephton was also employed at Knowsley Hall and at the Exchange in Liverpool.

Sephton died on 2 June 1756, aged 70, and was buried at Walton, nr. Liverpool, where a tablet (destroyed by bombing during the Second World War) also commemorated his wife Esther (d. 1759) and his son Daniel, 'late of Manchester, Eminent in Carving', who died on 11 January 1759, aged 45. A fine example of the latter's work is the monument to William Wright (d. 1753) at Stockport, Cheshire.

INCE BLUNDELL HALL, LANCS., for Robert Blundell, probably *c.* 1720; enlarged 1800 and 1847–50 [elevation among Everingham papers in Hull University Library, with damaged signature 'Hen[ry] S[ep]hton Invenit & Delin', ref. DDEv/13(j)] (*C. Life*, 10 April 1958).

PRESCOT CHURCH, LANCS., rebuilt tower and spire, 1729 [MS. parish books].

LIVERPOOL, ST. THOMAS'S CHURCH, 1748–50; spire removed after damage by storm in 1822; dem. *c.* 1907 [obituary of Sephton's widow in *Williamson's Liverpool Advertiser*, 12 Jan. 1759, which stated that he was 'an eminent architect and mason, who built St. Thomas's Church'].

LANCASTER, ST. MARY'S CHURCH, designed new Gothic west tower, built by William Kirkby of Lancaster, mason, 1753–4 [*V.C.H. Lancs.* viii, 24, n. 229].

SERJEANTSON, THOMAS, was a master mason at Coventry in the early seventeenth century. In 1611 Sir Edward Pytts of Kyre Park in Worcestershire invited 'Sergianson of Coventry' to make a 'platt' for extending his house, but the latter 'did nothing' [Mrs. Baldwyn-Childe, 'The Building of Kyre Park', *The Antiquary* xxii, 1890, 26]. Subsequently Thomas Serjeantson is found repairing the spire of HOLY TRINITY CHURCH, COVENTRY, in 1623 [T. Sharp, *Illustrations of the History of Holy Trinity, Coventry*, 1818, 30]; measuring mason's work at JOYCE POOL HOUSE, WARWICK, for William Fetherston in 1634 [Warwickshire Record Office, calendar of Fetherston-Dilke papers, pp. 97–100, no. 42] (for a view of the house see B.M., Add. MS. 29264, ff. 77–8); building fortifications for Richard Greville in 1645 at either Coventry or Warwick [P.R.O., E 101/634/32]; and working under John Webb at LAMPORT HALL, NORTHANTS., in 1655 [see letter from him in Isham archives dated 19 Aug. 1655].

SERVANDONI, GIOVANNI NICCOLÒ (1695–1766), was born in Florence, became a pupil of the painter Pannini in Rome, and later studied architecture under G. I. Rossi. He was primarily a theatrical scene-painter, and as such worked in Portugal, France and England. He first came to London in about 1722 and was employed as scene-painter to the Italian Opera at the King's Theatre in the Haymarket. In 1724 he removed to Paris, where in 1732 he designed the façade of S. Sulpice in a style obviously influenced by the west front of St. Paul's Cathedral, but returned to London early in 1747 and provided the scenery for a number of productions at Covent Garden Theatre. In 1749 he designed the structure of the elaborate firework display staged in the Green Park to celebrate the Peace of Aix-la-Chapelle. This took the form of a Doric temple with flanking pavilions, ornamented with 'Frets, Gilding, Lustres, Artificial Flowers, Inscriptions, Statues, Allegorical Pictures &c', and was constructed by the Office of Ordnance. During the performance the left-hand pavilion caught fire and the agitated architect (who was notoriously irascible) so far forgot himself as to draw his sword and affront Charles Frederick (*q.v.*), then Comptroller and later Surveyor of the Ordnance, for which he was 'disarmed and taken into custody, but discharg'd the next day on asking pardon before the Duke of Cumberland'.

According to J. F. Blondel's *Architecture Française* ii, 1752, 37, n. *a*, Servandoni was employed by Frederick, Prince of Wales, and this is confirmed by a document in the Hartwell Sale at Sotheby's on 8 March 1939 (lot 667) which included a payment of £100 by way of 'Cash Advanced to Mr. Salvadoni (*sic*) in consideration of his pains & expences in making & drawing Designs at Kew & for his attendances thereon' (1751). His principal architectural work in England was the interior of the gallery at George Bubb Dodington's house at Hammersmith (then known as 'La Trappe' but later as Brandenburg House, demolished in 1822), which is illustrated as his design in *Vitruvius Britannicus* iv, 1767, pls. 28–9. He returned to Paris in May 1751 and, after visits to Lisbon, Dresden, Vienna and Poland, died there on 19 January 1766.

[E. Croft-Murray, *Decorative Painting in England* ii, 1970, 274–6; Walpole Soc., *Vertue Note Books* iii, 134; letters from Servandoni to Dodington in Paul Grinke's *Catalogue of Autograph Letters of Artists and Architects*, spring 1976, no. 145; *Description of the Machine for the Fireworks*, published by the order of the Board of Ordnance, 1749; account of fireworks in *Gent's Mag.* 1749, 187, and engraving in Bodleian, Gough Maps 22, f.34ᵛ, B.M., Crace Collection, etc., reproduced in E. Walford, *Old and New London* iv, 181; L. Hautecœur, *Histoire de l'architecture classique en France* iii, 1950, 266–9.]

SEWARD, HENRY HAKE (*c.* 1778–1848), was articled to Sir John Soane in May 1794. He remained in Soane's office for some time after the expiration of his articles, leaving in 1808 to become District Surveyor of the parishes of St. Martin in the Fields and St. Anne Soho. In 1810 he entered into partnership with George Byfield, in consequence of whose ill-health he was appointed joint surveyor with him of the estates of the Dean and Chapter of Westminster. In the same year he was appointed Clerk of the Works at Greenwich Hospital, and in 1821 succeeded John Yenn as Surveyor to the Hospital. It was in this capacity that he designed four new churches in the parish of Simonburn in Northumberland on its division in 1811, the Governors of Greenwich Hospital being the patrons and lords of the manor. On the death of George Byfield in 1813, he took Francis Edwards as his assistant. In 1823, on the retirement of Robert Browne, he was appointed Assistant Surveyor-General and Cashier of the Office of Works, following which he resigned the surveyorship of Greenwich Hospital and relinquished general practice. On the amalgamation of the Works with the Department of Woods and Forests in 1832, Seward became first Surveyor of Works and Buildings. He resigned on account of ill-health in 1844, and died on 19 January 1848, aged 70. He exhibited at the Royal Academy between 1797 and 1823. George Aitchison, R. Osborne, and H. J. Underwood were pupils. Seward's career was largely devoted to his official duties,

and he had neither the opportunity nor perhaps the ability to design a building of distinction. His four Northumbrian churches are small Gothic buildings of the simplest kind.

[*A.P.S.D.*; A. T. Bolton, *The Works of Sir John Soane*, 1924, Appendix C, p. xlii; *History of the King's Works* vi; MS. Memoir by Francis Edwards in R.I.B.A. Library.]

NEW COURT, LUGWARDINE, HEREFS., reconstructed for the Rev. J. Lilly, 1808–10, Gothic [exhib. at R.A. 1810; drawings in R.I.B.A. Coll.].

EAST WITTON CHURCH, YORKS. (N.R.), 1809–12, Gothic; altered 1872 [exhib. at R.A. 1812].

GREENWICH HOSPITAL, KENT, rebuilt west façade of King Charles Block, in association with John Yenn, 1811–14 [Hasted's *History of Kent: Hundred of Blackheath*, ed. Drake, 1886, 69].

STEVENTON VICARAGE, BERKS., design for the Dean and Chapter of Westminster, 1815 [W.A.M., P. 743].

WARK-ON-TYNE CHURCH and parsonage, NORTHUMBERLAND, 1815–17, Gothic [exhib. at R.A. 1816] (E. Mackenzie, *Northumberland* i, 1825, 244).

GREYSTEAD CHURCH and parsonage, NORTHUMBERLAND, 1815–17, Gothic [exhib. at R.A. 1816].

HUMSHAUGH CHURCH and parsonage, NORTHUMBERLAND, 1815–17, Gothic [exhib. at R.A. 1816].

THORNEYBURN CHURCH and parsonage, NORTHUMBERLAND, 1815–17, Gothic [one of the four new churches built for the Governors of Greenwich Hospital].

LONDON, ST. MARTIN'S ALMSHOUSES, BAYHAM STREET, CAMDEN TOWN, 1818 [J. McMaster, *St. Martin-in-the-Fields*, 1916, 282].

BRISTOL, THE COUNTY GAOL, 1819–20; dem. [exhib. at R.A. 1817, 1819].

BRISTOL, THE PUBLIC BATHS AND READING ROOM, CLIFTON HOT WELLS, 1820; dem. 1867 [exhib. at R.A. 1820].

LEDBURY PARK, HEREFS., improvements for J. Biddulph, *c.* 1820 [exhib. at R.A. 1820].

SHAKESPEAR, GEORGE, *see* PHILLIPS, JOHN.

SHARMAN, JOHN, was an architect and builder working in the Peterborough area in the mid eighteenth century. In 1757 the Corporation of Wisbech, Camb., resolved to build a stone bridge to a design submitted by George Swaine and John Sharman provided that James Burrough, Master of Caius College, Cambridge, was satisfied that it was 'likely to stand and answer the purposes of a bridge' [N. Walker & T. Craddock, *History of Wisbech and the Fens*, 1849, 419]. The bridge was erected in 1758–9, but demolished in 1855. An engraving of it was published in 1761, with the inscription 'J. Sharman, Archt. and G. Swain, Builders' (B.M., *King's Maps* viii, 79*d*). Among the papers from Milton House, nr. Peterborough, now in the Northamptonshire County Record Office, are estimates by J. Sharman submitted in 1747 for building a new house to the alternative designs of Henry Flitcroft and Matthew Brettingham. Edward Sharman of Peterborough, 'statuary and mason', who died on 9 July 1805, aged 32, was probably his son [*Gent's Mag.* 1805 (ii), 686].

SHARP, RICHARD HEY (*c*. 1793–1853), was the eldest son of Richard Sharp, a member of a Yorkshire family with property at Gildersome, nr. Bradford. He became a pupil of Peter Atkinson, junior, at York. In 1816–19 he travelled through France to Rome, Naples and Greece. In Paris he met Joseph Woods (*q.v.*), who was to be his travelling companion for much of the journey. On his return he exhibited two drawings of Roman antiquities at the Royal Academy. His former master Atkinson now took him into partnership, and together they designed and built several Gothic churches for the Church Building Commissioners (listed at p. 73). In addition Sharp collaborated with William Wilkins in the erection of the Greek Revival York Museum in 1827–30. According to the *Library of the Fine Arts* 'the exterior design was made by Mr. Wilkins, but most of the internal arrangements were adopted from plans prepared in 1825 by Mr. Sharp, though subsequently much enlarged and improved'. In 1827 Sharp left Atkinson's office to start practice on his own at 18 St. Saviour Gate, assisted by his young brother Samuel Sharp, whom he took into partnership in 1831. In about 1830 they were commissioned to prepare a scheme for the development of the Valley at Scarborough, of which a print was published in 1832 (*C. Life*, 18 April 1974, 942, fig. 5). Some features of this, including the Crescent, were carried out during the 1830s and 1840s. Sharp had already designed the circular Museum in 1828. He died at Heyworth Moor on 25 February 1853, aged 59.

[*A.P.S.D.*; John James, *History of Bradford*, 1841, 421; *York Chronicle*, 29 July 1831; J. Woods, *Letters of an Architect*, 1828, i, 137, ii, 211, 287, 294; *Gent's Mag.* 1853 (i), 452.]

YORK, THE MUSEUM, in collaboration with William Wilkins, 1827–30 [*Gent's Mag.* 1827 (ii), 457; *Library of the Fine Arts* i, 1831, 172–3].

SCARBOROUGH, YORKS. (N.R.), THE MUSEUM, 1828–30 [*Theakston's Guide to Scarborough*, 1845, 71; F. D. Klingender, 'Scarborough Museum', *Arch. Rev.*, Dec. 1951].

HULL, YORKS. (E.R.), THE ASSEMBLY ROOMS (now part of the New Theatre), KINGSTON SQUARE, 1830–4, executed by C. Mountain and com-

pleted by H. R. Abraham [*V.C.H. Yorks. E.R.* i, 420; drawings by Sharp in Gott Collection, Wakefield Museum, vol. 7, pp. 1–7].

SCARBOROUGH, YORKS. (N.R.), TRINITY HOUSE, ST. SEPULCHRE STREET, 1832–3 [*Theakston's Guide to Scarborough*, 1845, 74].

CRAMBE VICARAGE, YORKS. (N.R.), rebuilt 1836 [Borthwick Institute, York, MGA 1836/3].

BRADFORD, YORKS. (W.R.), ST. JOHN'S CHURCH, MANCHESTER ROAD, 1838–9, Gothic; dem. *c.* 1873 [*Bradford Observer*, 13 Sept. 1838, *ex inf.* Mr. D. Griffiths].

HOWDEN CHURCH, YORKS. (E.R.), repairs after damage by storm, 1839 [*Bradford Observer*, 28 Feb. 1839, *ex inf.* Mr. D. Griffiths].

BOWLING CHURCH, YORKS. (W.R.), 1840–2, Gothic [W. Cudworth, *Bolton and Bowling*, 1891, 274].

KIRBY UNDERDALE RECTORY, YORKS. (E.R.), alterations, 1843 [Borthwick Institute, York, MGA 1843/4].

ROECLIFFE CHURCH, YORKS. (W.R.), 1843–4, Norman [*Builder* ii, 1844, 598].

YORK, ST. SAVIOUR'S CHURCH, largely rebuilt 1844–5, Gothic [*Yorkshire Gazette*, 3 and 31 May 1845; drawings in Diocesan Faculty Register 1816–58, pp. 485–90, *ex inf.* Dr. E. A. Gee].

HORBURY NATIONAL SCHOOL, YORKS. (W.R.), 1845, Gothic [*Civil Engineer and Architect's Jnl.* viii, 1845, 307].

YORK, ST. SAVIOUR'S CHURCH, monument to the Rev. John Graham, 1846 [*Builder* iv, 1846, 212].

SHARP, SAMUEL (1808–1874), was a younger brother of Richard Hey Sharp and, like him, began his architectural career in the office of Peter Atkinson, junior, at York. In 1831 he was taken into partnership by his brother, but later practised in Leeds, where he died in 1874, aged 66. In 1838 he was awarded the Soane Medal of the R.I.B.A. for a restoration drawing of St. Mary's Abbey at York, and in 1839 another with a gold rim for drawings of Sheriff Hutton Castle (now in the R.I.B.A. Drawings Collection). His only independent architectural work appears to have been the classical church of ST. JAMES at THORNES, nr. WAKEFIELD, 1829–31. [*A.P.S.D.*; John James, *History of Bradford*, 1841, 421; W. Cudworth, *Rambles round Horton*, Bradford 1886, 132; Port, 170–1; *York Chronicle*, 29 July 1831; *Gent's Mag.* 1838 (i), 299, 528–9, 1839 (i), 193, 296.]

SHAW, JOHN, was the surveyor responsible for repairs to CHESTER CASTLE soon after the Restoration of Charles II [*History of the King's Works* iii, 241].

SHAW, JOHN (1776–1832), was born at Bexley, Kent, on 10 March 1776. He was apprenticed to

George Gwilt the elder in 1790, and commenced practice in 1798. He exhibited his designs at the Royal Academy from 1799 onwards. They included a project for a 'British Circus, proposed to be built by subscription between the Paddington-road and Hampstead, on the freehold estate of H. S. Eyre, Esq., the inner circle consists of 36 detached houses, with appropriate offices; the outer circle of 66 houses. There will be about one acre and a quarter of land to each house, besides the enjoyment of the central pleasure-ground which contains 42 acres. The road between the two circles is about one mile in circumference.' The date of this entry is 1803, but a plan of the Eyre estate showing the whole layout had already been engraved in 1794 under the names of Spurrier & Phipps, auctioneers of Copthall Court, London. As Shaw was still in his pupilage at this time, he cannot have been the originator of the scheme, which is remarkable for its use of semi-detached houses. It was not, however, carried out.

In 1816 Shaw succeeded James Lewis as architect and surveyor of Christ's Hospital, London, to which he made extensive additions costing about £30,000. They were in the Gothic style which Shaw also used with picturesque effect in the church of St. Dunstan, Fleet Street, at Ilam Hall and in his alterations to Newstead Abbey for Col. Wildman.[1]

Shaw was also architect to the trustees of Ramsgate harbour, where he designed the clock-house and the obelisk to commemorate the visit of King George IV in 1821. He was extensively employed in the valuation of property in London for street improvements, and was architect to the Phoenix Assurance Company. He was a member of the Architects' Club, a Fellow of the Royal and Linnean Societies, of the Society of Antiquaries, and of the Institute of British Architects. He died suddenly at Ramsgate on 30 July 1832, and was buried at Bexley. He left six sons and two daughters. His practice was continued by his eldest son, John Shaw (q.v.). His youngest son, Thomas Budge Shaw, became professor of English literature at St. Petersburg. T. Johnson of Lichfield (1794–1865) was in his office after leaving that of Joseph Potter. [A.P.S.D.; D.N.B.; John Summerson, Georgian London, 1945, 158–9.]

Villa 'intended to be built in Surrey for G. Whitfield', exhibited at R.A. 1799.

---

[1] It is natural to suppose that Shaw was the 'modern Goth ... call'd an architect' whose 'restoration' of a country house called the Abbey was so savagely satirized by Byron (the former owner of Newstead) in Don Juan, canto xvi, 58, but Mrs Rosalys Coope tells me that this is unlikely, as the reports that reached Byron of Col. Wildman's alterations were favourable.

PUTNEY HILL, SURREY, 'a suite of rooms lately erected', exhibited at R.A. 1801.

PUTNEY HILL, SURREY, villa for William Leader, 1804 [exhib. at R.A. 1804].

FLAMBARDS, HARROW, MIDDLESEX, 'proposed alterations' for the 1st Lord Northwick, exhibited at R.A. 1806.

LONDON, THE RUSSELL INSTITUTION, GREAT CORAM STREET, reroofed c. 1812 [Builder xiv, 1856, 72].

LAMORBEY PARK, SIDCUP, KENT, alterations for — Malcolm, after 1812 [A.P.S.D.].

BEAUDESERT, STAFFS., lodge at Lichfield entrance to park for the 2nd Earl of Uxbridge, 1814 [exhib. at R.A. 1814].

BLENDON HALL, nr. BEXLEY, KENT, remodelled for John Smith, c. 1815, Gothic; dem. 1934 [exhib. at R.A. 1815].

RAMSGATE, KENT, CLOCK-HOUSE, and steps called 'Jacob's ladder', c. 1815; obelisk to commemorate visit of King George IV, 1821–2 [A.P.S.D.].

HEATH HOUSE, TEAN, STAFFS., lodge for John Philips, c. 1816 [exhib. at R.A. 1816].

SPURN HEAD LIGHTHOUSE, 1816; dem. [D. B. Hague & R. Christie, Lighthouses, 1975, 224].

CHILHAM CASTLE, KENT, alterations for James B. Wildman, after 1816 [A.P.S.D.].

NEWSTEAD ABBEY, NOTTS., remodelled for Col. Thomas Wildman, 1818–c. 1830, Gothic [exhib. at R.A. 1820; R.I.B.A.; Gervase Jackson-Stops in C. Life, 9, 16 May 1974].

ROOKSNEST (now Croome House), nr. GODSTONE, SURREY, for C. H. Turner, c. 1818 [A.P.S.D.].

LONDON, UXBRIDGE HOUSE, stables in Boyle Street for the 1st Marquess of Anglesey, 1819 [Hermione Hobhouse, Thomas Cubitt, 1971, 25].

CRESSWELL HALL, NORTHUMBERLAND, for A. J. Baker Cresswell, 1820–4; dem. 1931 [A.P.S.D.; drawing by Shaw in author's possession]. Mackenzie, Northumberland ii, 1825, 127, says the house was erected 'under the superintendence of Mr. Green of Newcastle', but Shaw's name was cut in the masonry (N. Lloyd, The English House, 1931, 270, fig. 294).

LONDON, CHRIST'S HOSPITAL, NEWGATE STREET, the Infirmary and west side of quadrangle, 1820–2; the Great Hall (Gothic), 1825–9; the Mathematical and Grammar Schools, 1832; all dem. 1902 [A.P.S.D.] (Britton & Pugin, The Public Buildings of London ii, 1828, 187–92, for plan and elevation of Hall; for the interior see London Interiors, 1841–4).

ILAM HALL, STAFFS., for J. Watts Russell, 1821–6, Gothic; partly dem. c. 1935 [R.I.B.A.; A.P.S.D.] (F. O. Morris, Picturesque Views of Seats i, 1880, 41).

DUNHAM MASSEY HALL, CHESHIRE, alterations for the 6th Earl of Stamford, 1822 [A.P.S.D.].

LEYTON CHURCH, ESSEX, addition of south aisle and vestry, 1822 [J. Kennedy, History of the Parish of Leyton, 1894, 62].

AUDLEY END, ESSEX, interior of library for the 3rd Lord Braybrooke, c. 1825–7 [Lord Braybrooke, *History of Audley End*, 1836, 132].

DUNSTON VICARAGE, LINCS., 1827–8 [Bodleian Library, records of Queen Anne's Bounty].

PARKHURST, BEXLEY, KENT, alterations for himself, 1831, Elizabethan style; dem. 1955 [C. Greenwood, *Epitome of County History: Kent*, 1838, 47].

LONDON, ST. DUNSTAN'S CHURCH, FLEET STREET, 1831–3, Gothic; completed by his son [Britton & Pugin, *The Public Buildings of London*, ed. Leeds, i, 1838, 187–93].

SHAW, JOHN (1803–1870), born in London on 17 May 1803, was the son and pupil of John Shaw (*q.v.*), whom he succeeded in 1832 as architect of Christ's Hospital. He also became surveyor to Eton College, for whom he designed the Tudor Gothic buildings in Weston's Yard at Eton and developed their Chalk Farm estate in Hampstead. His employment by the Church Building Commissioners to design a new church in London led him to write *A Letter on Ecclesiastical Architecture as applicable to Modern Churches: addressed to the Lord Bishop of London*, 1839, in which he advocated the use of the Romanesque style as most practical and economical for the purpose. It was, however, as a designer of buildings in a revived 'Renaissance' style that Shaw was most successful and original. His reputation as a designer in the manner of Wren was remarked on by the *Builder* as early as 1843, and his Wellington College was a *tour de force* of revived Anglo-French baroque. Like his father, the younger Shaw was much engaged in valuations, and was one of the official referees under the Metropolitan Buildings Act of 1844. He died on 9 July 1870, and was buried at Kensal Green. [*A.P.S.D.*; *D.N.B.*].

BOGNOR REGIS, SUSSEX, SUDLEY LODGE, 1827, exhibited at the R.A. as the 'first of a series of detached houses to be built on the property of the Earl of Arran'.

LONDON, CHRIST'S HOSPITAL, NEWGATE STREET, completed the Grammar Schools to his father's design, 1832, and designed the east range of dormitories, 1836, the entrance from Newgate Street, 1836, and the baths, 1868–9; all dem. 1902 [*A.P.S.D.*].

LONDON, LAW LIFE ASSURANCE OFFICE, NO. 187 FLEET STREET, 1834, Jacobean [exhib. at R.A. 1833].

LONDON, HOLY TRINITY CHURCH, GOUGH SQUARE, 1837–8, Romanesque; altered 1873; dem. 1913 [G. Godwin, *The Churches of London* ii, 1839, with plate].

LONDON, CHRIST CHURCH, WATNEY STREET, STEPNEY, 1840–1, Romanesque; apse 1870; dem. after war damage 1940–1 [Port, 156].

HILMARTON CHURCH, WILTS., rebuilt west tower, 1840, Gothic [*Wiltshire Arch. Mag.* xxxvii, 1911–12, 431].

WALTHAMSTOW, ESSEX, ST. PETER'S CHURCH, 1840, Romanesque; much altered [*Christian Guardian*, 1840, 477; *V.C.H. Essex* vi, 292].

LONDON, CHALCOTS ESTATE, CHALK FARM, HAMPSTEAD, laid out Adelaide Road, Provost Road, and Eton College Road, etc., for Eton College, 1840–50 [D. J. Olsen in *The Victorian City*, ed. H. J. Dyos & M. Wolff, 1973, i, 348–52 and pls. 285–6].

ETON COLLEGE, BUCKS., altar, altar-rails and pulpit in Chapel, 1842; new buildings in Weston's Yard, 1844–6, Tudor Gothic [Willis & Clark, i, 450, 463; Eton College archives; R.I.B.A.D.].

DEPTFORD, KENT, ROYAL NAVAL COLLEGE (now Goldsmiths' College), 1843–4, Renaissance style; CHAPEL, 1853 [*Builder* i, 1843, 218–19; *A.P.S.D.*].

STOKE POGES CHURCH, BUCKS., alterations (including rebuilding of chancel arch), 1844–5 [parish records].

BOURNE PARK, KENT, repairs and internal alterations for Matthew Bell, 1848–9 [H. A. Tipping in *C. Life*, 6, 13 May 1922] (*C. Life*, 10, 17 Nov. 1944).

LONDON, ST. DUNSTAN'S PAROCHIAL SCHOOL, FETTER LANE, 1849, Jacobean [*A.P.S.D.*].

LONDON, ST. BRIDE'S CHURCH, FLEET STREET, 'repaired, painted, marbled and gilded' the interior, 1852; gutted 1940 [*Builder* x, 1852, 397].

LONDON, LONDON AND PROVINCIAL LAW LIFE ASSURANCE OFFICE, NO. 21 FLEET STREET, 1853–5, 'Renaissance' style; dem. [*Builder* xiii, 1855, 474].

WELLINGTON COLLEGE, SANDHURST, BERKS., 1855–9, 'Renaissance' style [*Builder* xiv, 1856, 86–7; T. L. Donaldson, *Handbook of Specifications*, 1860, 549–636] (*C. Life*, 18 June 1959).

SHEARBURN, WILLIAM (1798–1860), was the son of Joseph Shearburn, joiner and resident clerk of works on the Earl of Ripon's estate at Nocton Park, Lincs. He established himself as an architect and builder at Dorking in Surrey, where in 1834–5 he built the INDEPENDENT CHAPEL (now Congregational Church) in WEST STREET 'under the superintendence of' William Hopperton of London, and in 1839 designed the WORKHOUSE on ROSE HILL, now part of the County Hospital. He also designed HERSHAM NATIONAL SCHOOL, SURREY, 1841, and the north aisle that was added to MICKLEHAM CHURCH, SURREY, in 1842 [Brayley, *History of Surrey* iv, 464, v, 103–4; Surrey County Record Office, S.C. 19/30/4 and 264/84/1]. Several houses in Falkland, Arundel and Howard Roads, Dorking, are detailed in a similar way to the workhouse, and may have been built by Shearburn. His biggest work was the rebuilding of NOCTON PARK, LINCS., for his father's employer, the 1st Earl of Ripon, between 1841 and 1846. The house (dem.) was in the Elizabethan style (*C. Life*, 28 Sept. 1901) and is stated to have been designed by Shearburn both in *Builder* iii, 1845, 549, *Gent's Mag.* 1846 (i), 83, and in an annotated copy of *Some Notes for a History of Nocton*, 1900, in Lincoln Public Library. Shearburn died at Dorking on 22 June 1860, leaving a son of the same name to continue his practice [Principal Probate Registry, Calendar of Probates].

SHELTON, THEOPHILUS (–1717), is said to have been 'the son of a clergyman in one of the eastern counties', but established himself at Wakefield in Yorkshire and lived, or owned property, in the neighbouring villages of Heath and Darrington.[1] He appears to have been a lawyer by profession, for he was Clerk of the Peace for the West Riding and in 1704 became the first Registrar of Deeds for the same County. He married Margaret, daughter of the Rev. Joshua Witton, rector of Thornhill, and died at Nottingham in November 1717 [J. W. Walker, *Wakefield, its History and People* ii, 1939, 497–8; *Surtees Soc.* lxxvii, 1883, 127–8; will at Borthwick Institute, York].

Shelton's skill as an architect is attested by several contemporary records. When Sir George Tempest rebuilt TONG HALL, YORKS. (W.R.), in 1700–2 he recorded in an inscription that it was erected 'Domini Theophili Sheltoni de Heath Ingenio Prudentiaque vere Architectonica' [Thoresby's *Ducatus Leodiensis*, ed. Whitaker, 1816, 204]. An original elevation of the house, perhaps in Shelton's hand, is in the muniment-room at Nostell Priory. In about 1710 the Corporation of Pontefract proposed to build a cupola on the newly built tower of ST. GILES' CHURCH 'pursuant to such a modell thereof as Theophilus Shelton, Esq. shall draw for that purpose'. It is not, however, certain that it was carried out, and the tower itself was rebuilt in its present form in *c.* 1789 [*The Book of Entries of the Pontefract Corporation 1653–1726*, ed. R. Holmes, Pontefract 1882, 283].

Shelton also designed the existing MARKET CROSS at BEVERLEY, a polygonal building supported by four pairs of Doric columns and surmounted by a dome and lantern, and probably designed the similar MARKET CROSS at WAKEFIELD, built in 1707 but demolished in 1866 (illustrated Walker, *op. cit.*, 475, and *C. Life*, 9 Nov. 1945,

[1] He bought Heath Hall in 1694, and he probably built and designed the house that forms the nucleus of the existing Hall (cf. Ivan & Elizabeth Hall, *Heath*, 1975, 14). He may also have designed Lupset Hall, nr. Wakefield, for his brother-in-law Richard Witton.

828). In 1710 Shelton had already designed a CHARITY SCHOOL in HIGHGATE, BEVERLEY, and in July 1711 the Chamber of Beverley sent a carpenter over to Wakefield 'to consult and advice with Mr. Shelton' about building the proposed Cross. 'The draught of a new cross drawn by Mr. Shelton' was approved in September, and it was completed in 1714 [K. A. MacMahon, 'The Building of the Beverley Market Cross', *Trans. Georgian Soc. for East Yorkshire* iii (3), 1952–3].

SHEPHERD, EDWARD (–1747), was an architect and builder who is best known as the proprietor of Shepherd's Market and other buildings in Mayfair. According to Vertue, he began his career as a plasterer, and his brother John certainly followed that trade. He is first found in the service of James Brydges, 1st Duke of Chandos, who employed him to supervise the completion of his mansion at Cannons in 1723–5, and for whom he soon afterwards built two houses on the north side of Cavendish Square in place of the mansion which the Duke originally intended to erect on that site. He was also in charge of the Duke's building operations at Bridgwater and Bath, though, except in one or two cases, he does not seem to have been responsible for the designs executed by the local master builders; and he carried out repairs to the Duke's property in Scotland Yard and at Shaw House in Berkshire. In 1730, when he was, with Gibbs and Flitcroft, one of the candidates for rebuilding the church of St. Giles-in-the-Fields, the *Daily Post* described him as 'that ingenious architect Edward Shepherd Esq., who built the Duke of Kent's fine house in St. James's Square, the Earls of Thanet's and Albemarle's in Grosvenor Square, and many other magnificent Buildings for his Grace the Duke of Chandos and other Persons of Quality and Distinction'.

In 1735 Shepherd engaged in a successful speculation of his own by building Shepherd's Market and the adjoining streets on the site of the ancient fairground in Mayfair. The Market House consisted of two stories, the lower containing butchers' shops, while the upper was used as a theatre in fairtime. In March 1738 Shepherd obtained permission to hold a market for live cattle here, and at the time of his death he was stated to be the owner both of the market itself and of 'many other buildings about Mayfair'. He lived in a small house in Curzon Street on the site of the present Crewe House. Shepherd died in October 1747. In his will, dated 13 December 1746, he left the Shepherd's Market estate to his wife Elizabeth, who, as his executrix, was instructed to spend £300 in building an almshouse for ten poor decayed housekeepers of the parish of St. George, Hanover Square. It was to be built 'upon the ground that the Lease belongs to Shepherd's Market', in accordance with a 'Plan and

Elevation drawn and signed by me'. He also left his silver watch and an annuity of £50 to his brother, John Shepherd.

[*A.P.S.D.*; Walpole Society, *Vertue Note Books* iii, 51; C. H. & M. I. Collins Baker, *James Brydges, Duke of Chandos*, 1949, *passim*; *Gent's Mag.* viii, 164, xvii, 497, xx, 40, lxxxvi, 228; *Daily Post*, 31 Dec. 1730, 4 Feb. 1731; E. B. Chancellor, *The Private Palaces of London*, 1908, 222; P.R.O., C 105/32, bundle 1; P.C.C. 266 POTTER.]

LONDON

CAVENDISH SQUARE, designed and built the two end houses on the north side for the Duke of Chandos, 1724–8; dem. [Baker, *Duke of Chandos*, 1949, 276–7; J. Summerson, *Georgian London*, 1945, 92, pl. xvi].

ST. JAMES'S SQUARE, NO. 4, for the Duke of Kent, 1726–8 [*Daily Post*, 31 Dec. 1730; copy of the joiner's contract in Notts. County Record Office, DDR 215/60, in which he is 'to be directed by Edward Shepherd surveyor'; *Survey of London* xxix, 90–1, addendum] (*Survey of London* xxx, pls. 134–9).

GROSVENOR SQUARE, NOS. 18–21 on north side, *c.* 1728–30; dem. [P.R.O., C 105/32; John Summerson, *Georgian London*, 1945, 87] (Richardson & Gill, *London Houses from 1660 to 1820*, 1911, pl. xlvi).

GOODMAN'S FIELDS THEATRE, GREAT ALIE STREET, GOODMAN'S FIELDS, *c.* 1730; dem. *c.* 1746 [H. B. Wheatley & P. Cunningham, *London Past and Present* ii, 1891, 127].

COVENT GARDEN THEATRE, for John Rich, 1731–2; destroyed by fire 1808 [*Survey of London* xxxv, 71–2, 86–7].

SHEPHERD'S MARKET and adjoining streets, Mayfair, *c.* 1735; dem. [*Gent's Mag.* 1747, 497].

SOUTH AUDLEY STREET, NOS. 71–75, 1736–7, built by Shepherd on land leased from Sir Robert Grosvenor, probably to his own designs [Arthur Oswald in *C. Life*, 15 April 1933; information from the Survey of London].

ELSEWHERE

CANNONS HOUSE, MIDDLESEX, supervised completion for the 1st Duke of Chandos, 1723–5; dem. 1747 [Baker, *Duke of Chandos*, 1949, 146, 148–9].

GREAT STANMORE RECTORY, MIDDLESEX, for the 1st Duke of Chandos, 1725 [Baker, *Duke of Chandos*, 1949, 280].

BOREHAM HOUSE, ESSEX, supervised building for Benjamin Hoare, 1727–8, probably executing designs by Henry Flitcroft (*q.v.*) (*C. Life*, 11 July 1914).

SHAW HOUSE, NEWBURY, BERKS., repairs and internal decorations for the 1st Duke of Chandos, 1730 [Baker, *Duke of Chandos*, 1949, 369–70].

GREAT LODGE, ENFIELD CHASE, MIDDLESEX, remodelled for the 1st Duke of Chandos, 1730–2; dem. [Baker, *Duke of Chandos*, 1949, 387–9].

FLITTON CHURCH, BEDS., monuments to Lady Amabell de Grey (d. 1727), wife of John Campbell, afterwards 3rd Earl of Breadalbane, and to Henry de Grey, Duke of Kent (d. 1740). The Breadalbane papers [S.R.O., GD 112/21/77] show that the former monument was designed by Shepherd and set up in 1739. The latter is signed 'Edwd. Shepherd Arch[t].'.

HAMPDEN HOUSE, GREAT HAMPDEN, BUCKS., surveyed works for John Hampden, 1743–6, in particular the curved screen-walls at each end of the garden front [Bucks. Record Office, Hampden papers, day-books 1743–6].

PETERSHAM LODGE, SURREY, added wings with octagonal terminations for the 1st Earl of Harrington, *c.* 1740; dem. *c.* 1835 [Walpole, *Anecdotes of Painting*, ed. Wornum, iii, 1862, 776].

SHEPHERD, RICHARD, was a master mason whose name is connected with two notable seventeenth-century buildings, the banqueting house at SWARKESTONE in DERBYSHIRE, and the church at STAUNTON HAROLD in LEICESTERSHIRE. The former is almost certainly the 'Bowl-alley house' for whose construction Sir John Harpur's executors paid £111 12s. 4d. to 'Richard Shepperd the mason' in 1630–2 [accounts at Calke Abbey]. Shepherd was probably the master mason who built the remarkable Gothic church which Sir Robert Shirley began at Staunton Harold in 1653, for a volume of Shirley accounts in the Warwickshire Record Office shows that he paid £60 'for finishing the battlements' in 1662, and his name RICHARD SHEPHEARD ARTIFEX is prominently carved on the inside of the parapet at the east end [J. Simmons & H. M. Colvin in *Archaeological Jnl.* cxii, 1955, 173–6]. Although it cannot be proved that Shepherd designed either of these buildings, it would be normal practice at this date for the master mason employed to be responsible for the design.

SHEPHERD, VINCENT (*c.* 1750–1812), was apprenticed to George Thompson of Alnwick, carpenter, in 1764 [P.R.O., Apprenticeship Registers]. He spent the greater part of his life working for the Duke of Northumberland at ALNWICK CASTLE, where he appears to have acted as resident architect. He is said to have 'united the powers of execution with those of design', and in Gothic design to have been 'without a rival in the county of Northumberland'. Although the principal Gothic rooms in the Castle were designed by Robert & James Adam, Shepherd was no doubt responsible for their execution. In 1781 he reconstructed the chancel of ALNWICK CHURCH in the Gothic style, giving it a 'fanvaulted' plaster ceiling and a screen of Gothic 'trellis-work' (all destroyed by Salvin in 1863, but illustrated in *Proceedings of the Society of Antiquaries of Newcastle* iii, 1867, 74), and in 1796 he designed a castellated building called 'Mount Athelstan' in the park at RODDAM HALL, NORTHUMBERLAND [drawing at Roddam]. This has been demolished, but the castellated stables may well be Shepherd's design. Shepherd died at Alnwick in May 1812, aged 62 [*Gent's Mag.* 1812 (i), 601].

SHERLOCK, JOHN, junior, was a carpenter of Boston in Lincolnshire. In 1715 he and his father were among the 'able and experienced workmen' who estimated the value of the damage caused by a fire in Spalding [E. H. Gooch, *History of Spalding*, 1940, 264]. The 'Geometrical Plan & South prospect of St. Botolph's att Boston Taken and Drawn by John Sherlock Junr. Carpenter of Boston 1711' is in the Bodleian Library, Gough Maps 16, f. 26, and drawings by him after Scamozzi and Palladio are in Gough Maps 230, ff. 105, 340.

SHIRLEY, WASHINGTON, 5TH EARL FERRERS (1722–1778), was a nephew of the 3rd Earl Ferrers and in 1760 succeeded his brother as 5th Earl. He was in the Navy and rose to the rank of Vice-Admiral. His interests included astronomy and shipbuilding. In 1761 he was elected a Fellow of the Royal Society, and in 1775 he was an honorary exhibitor at the Royal Academy, showing three sectional drawings of different vessels designed by himself.

Both Throsby [*Select Views in Leicestershire*, 1789, 126] and Nichols [*History of Leicestershire* iii (2), 1804, 717] state that it was to his own designs that Ferrers rebuilt STAUNTON HAROLD HALL, LEICS., in 1762–75 in what by then was a somewhat old-fashioned Palladian style (*C. Life*, 5, 12 April 1913, 24 Feb. 1950). It is probable that he also designed the ASSEMBLY ROOMS at DERBY, for he laid the first stone in March 1775, and Joseph Pickford (*q.v.*), who superintended the building (1763–5), was paid £100 for his 'time and trouble' by Ferrers' order [E. Saunders in *C. Life*, 9 Nov. 1972, 1207]. The interior was completed by Robert Adam in 1774. The building was demolished in 1971 after damage by fire, but the Palladian façade (again distinctly old-fashioned for its date) was re-erected as part of the Tramway Museum at Crich, nr. Matlock.

SHORT, WILLIAM (–1753), 'An Architect or Builder at Cirencester', was among those who, in 1751, submitted designs for building the new church of St. George at Kingswood nr. Bristol. They were not adopted, but Short was paid 25 guineas for his trouble [Commissioners' Minutes in Bristol City Archives]. His will, proved at Gloucester on 18 June 1753, shows that he was a carpenter by trade.

SHORTESS, J—, 'Gentleman', was the author of a work entitled *Harmonic Architecture, exemplified in a Plan etc. of a Building, with four different fronts, upon an Harmonic Form or Cube, now made Octangular, Being designed for a Museum, in a retired situation of a Park or Garden*, which was published in 1741 by the 'Society of Booksellers for promoting learning'. It contains plans and elevations of a garden building externally square but internally octagonal, designed on 'harmonic' principles. There is in the Bodleian Library an engraved 'Draught of a Building erected for an Apiary in the Garden of Thomas Hayley Esq., near Erith (now Lord Baltimore's)', which bears the signature 'J. Shortis inv^t & fecit' (Gough Maps 14, f. 10b).

SHOUBRIDGE, WILLIAM, was admitted to the Royal Academy Schools in 1832, was elected an Associate of the R.I.B.A. in 1842 and retired in 1844. He exhibited at the Society of British Artists in 1832 and at the R.A. in 1831, 1837 and 1843. A design by him for a classical water gate, dated 1833, is in the R.I.B.A. Drawings Collection [*R.I.B.A. Drawings Coll. Catalogue*].

SHOUT was the name of a family of masons and civil engineers who were active in the north of England throughout the eighteenth century. Two branches of the family have been identified, one originating in the parish of Weston in the West Riding of Yorkshire, the other at Helmsley in the North Riding.

WILLIAM SHOUT, or SHUTT, born at Weston in 1678, was employed as a mason and carver at Castle Howard in 1720–1. In 1749 he built a temple in the grounds of Hovingham Hall, Yorkshire (N.R.), for which a drawing is preserved at Hovingham [R. Gunnis, *Dictionary of British Sculptors*, 1968, 351].

WILLIAM SHOUT of York (*c.* 1750–1826), was for many years master mason to York Minster. He died on 20 July 1826, aged 75, and was buried at Huntington, nr. York, where his epitaph states that 'for forty years with credit to himself and satisfaction to his employers he conducted the repairs and restoration of York Minster' [Gunnis, *op. cit.*; *Gent's Mag.* 1826 (ii), 190; P.C.C. 659 SWABEY].

BENJAMIN and ROBERT SHOUT, who were probably the Benjamin and Robert named as his brothers in the will of William Shout (d. 1826), kept a mason's yard in Holborn, where they made monuments and plaster casts. As manufacturers of the latter they were evidently well known, for in *A Letter to Maria Gisborne* (1820) Shelley described Leigh Hunt's study as 'adorned with many a cast from Shout'. Robert Shout, who was Master of the London Masons' Company in 1822, handed over to his son Charles Lutwyche Shout in about 1825. The latter, who died in 1855, aged 61, was the father of the architect Robert Howard Shout (1823–82), who practised chiefly in the south-western counties [*A.P.S.D.*; *Gent's Mag.* 1855 (i), 663; *Builder* xlii, 1882, 385; Gunnis, *op. cit.*].

ROBERT SHOUT (*c.* 1702–74), of Helmsley, was Surveyor of Bridges in the North Riding of Yorkshire east of the Hambleton Hills from 1757 to 1765 and himself designed and built several fine bridges, *e.g.* at Newsham, nr. Malton, 1752–3, Scawton, nr. Rievaulx, 1755–7, and Egton, in Eskdale, 1760–1. His son ROBERT SHOUT (1734–97), of Helmsley, also designed and built bridges, *e.g.* at Whitby, 1765–8, Welburn, 1768–9, and Sinnington, 1768–9. From 1781 to 1795 he was harbour engineer of Sunderland, Co. Durham, where he died in March 1797, aged 64. In 1788 he made a design for a stone bridge of large span over the R. Wear at Sunderland. It was not built, but Shout's drawing is in Sir John Soane's Museum (Portfolio 3, nos. 60–2) [*A.P.S.D.*; *Antiquities of Sunderland* xiii, 1913, 113].

JOHN SHOUT (1738–81), a younger son of Robert Shout of Helmsley, worked at Stockton-on-Tees, where he died on 13 June 1781, aged 42. From 1780 to 1781 he was harbour engineer of Sunderland. In 1768 he built the Tuscan column in the Market Place at Stockton [T. Richmond, *Local Records of Stockton*, 1868, 74].

MATTHEW SHOUT (1774–1817), son of the younger Robert Shout, was harbour engineer at Scarborough from 1801 to 1804, and at Sunderland from 1804 to 1817.

[Information from Professor A. W. Skempton and Mr. J. H. Harvey.]

SHURMER, THOMAS MOLAND (– 1872), of Andover, designed APPLESHAW CHURCH, HANTS., 1830–1, Gothic [I.C.B.S. and inscription in church], and altered or rebuilt BOSCOMBE RECTORY, WILTS., in 1836 [Salisbury Diocesan Records]. He subsequently lived at Hackney, and died at Prospect House, Lower Clapton, on 11 April 1872 [Principal Probate Registry, Calendar of Probates].

SIBBALD, WILLIAM (–1809), was an architect and builder of Edinburgh who held the post of Superintendent of Public Works in that city from January 1790 until his death on 29 March 1809 [Edinburgh Town Council Minutes; *Scots Mag.* lxxi, 1809, 319]. He appears to have come from Inverness, for in 1793 the Heritors of St. Cuthbert's Church, Edinburgh, chose the plan for a new manse submitted by 'William Sibbald Surveyor & Builder late of Inverness' [S.R.O., HR 152/2]. He was presumably the 'William Sibbald, mason', who became a burgess of Edinburgh in August 1794 [*Roll of Edinburgh Burgesses, 1761–1841*, Scottish Record

734

Soc., 144]. In 1802 Sibbald was associated with Robert Reid (*q.v.*) in settling the layout of the first extension of the New Town [A. J. Youngson, *The Making of Classical Edinburgh*, 1966, 206–7]. He acted as surveyor or overseer of works for the Heriot Trust who owned the land, and was active in making surveys, laying out the new streets, etc. Though Reid was responsible for the principal elevations, Sibbald must share the credit for the successful planning of the second New Town.

Sibbald's principal architectural works in Edinburgh were the tall classical steeple which was added to ST. ANDREW'S CHURCH in 1786–7 [*Notes on the History of St. Andrew's Church, Edinburgh*, 1884, 5], and LADY YESTER'S CHURCH, which he designed in a neo-Jacobean style at the remarkably early date of 1803 [Edinburgh Town Council Minutes, vol. 138, pp. 419–20, 24 Aug. 1803] (see contemporary illustrations in *Scots Mag.*, 1805, 571, and T. H. Shepherd, *Modern Athens*, 1829, pl. 87). The attribution to him of the steeple of INVERESK CHURCH appears to be unfounded despite its resemblance of that of St. Andrew's (see p. 595). In PORTOBELLO he designed the BATHS, 1805–6 [signed drawings in S.R.O., RHP 4997], and the OLD CHURCH, 1809 [*Report on the Burgh of Portobello*, 1832]. BEECHWOOD, nr. CORSTORPHINE, MIDLOTHIAN, was enlarged by him for Robert Dundas (afterwards 1st Baronet), *c.* 1799 [Dundas papers at Comrie House, Perthshire, *ex inf.* Dr. A. A. Tait]. From his testament in the Scottish Record Office it appears that he had been in partnership with a builder named William Lumley who died in 1808 [CC 8/8/138, f. 487].

William Sibbald is often referred to as 'senior' to distinguish him from William Sibbald, junior, who was also an architect and builder, and died on 12 November 1823 [*Edingburgh Mag.* xiii, 1823, 768]. The younger Sibbald built the Bank of Scotland on the Mound to the designs of Reid & Crichton in 1802–6 [Minutes of the Bank of Scotland]. In 1805 either he or his father was associated with John Thin (*q.v.*) in an abortive design for rebuilding Falkirk Church [S.R.O., HR 139/1].

SIBLEY, ROBERT (1789–1849), was the son of a builder and surveyor (probably James Sibley of Wapping). He became a pupil of S. P. Cockerell and subsequently practised from Great Ormond Street. In 1818 he was appointed County Surveyor of Middlesex, resigning in 1828 to become District Surveyor of Clerkenwell. From 1839 onwards he was also surveyor to the Ironmongers' Company. He was a friend and admirer of Telford, and a member of the Institution of Civil Engineers, on whose Council he served. As County Surveyor he built a number of roads and bridges in Middlesex and supervised the erection of Hanwell Lunatic Asylum to the designs of William Alderson (*q.v.*). The list of his own buildings which he drew up in 1828 does not suggest that he designed anything of much architectural importance, and during the latter part of his life he was chiefly engaged in valuation and arbitration. He died on 31 March 1849, aged 59, leaving a son, Robert Lacon Sibley, to continue his practice. [*Minutes of Proceedings of the Institution of Civil Engineers* ix, 1849–50, 101; *Builder* vii, 1849, 160; G.L.C. Record Office, MRD MA/AJ/1, list of buildings supplied by Sibley to the Committee of Visiting Justices of the Hanwell Lunatic Asylum in 1828.]

SIDNELL, MICHAEL, was a statuary mason working at Bristol during the second quarter of the eighteenth century. A list of monuments signed by him will be found in R. Gunnis's *Dictionary of British Sculptors*, 1968, 351. Among them is the monument to Edward Colston (d. 1721) in All Saints Church, which was designed by James Gibbs, and is illustrated in his *Book of Architecture* (1728), to which Sidnell subscribed. The figure of Colston is by Rysbrack.

Bankruptcy in 1742 [*London Magazine*, 1742, 518] may have put Sidnell out of business as a mason, but in 1742–5 he acted as surveyor of a new house at WESTBURY COURT, WESTBURY-ON-SEVERN, GLOS., for Maynard Colchester, at 3s. a day. That he made the designs is shown by his receipt for £13 9s. 'in full for surveying Drawing and attending the Building', and by his description of himself as 'Master Workeman and Architect' [account-book formerly in possession of the late Sir Francis Colchester-Wemyss]. The house was demolished soon after 1800.

SIM, CHARLES, a Perthshire builder, designed and built the very simple church at STRUAN, PERTHSHIRE, in 1828–9 [S.R.O., CH 2/430/8]. He was also responsible for WEEM MANSE, PERTHSHIRE, 1829–30 [S.R.O., HR 405/1]. In the Weem records he is said to be 'presently residing at Pitnacree' (in Logierait parish). He was probably the same person as a mason from Stanley called Charles Syme who in 1819 repaired DULL CHURCH, PERTHSHIRE, after submitting a design for a new church which was not carried out [S.R.O., HR 658/1].

SIMMONS, JOHN, was the 'undertaker' of the block of houses forming the east side of GROSVENOR SQUARE, LONDON, erected between 1725 and 1735. It is not known whether the design was furnished by an architect [John Summerson, *Georgian London*, 1945, 86]. In 1737 he submitted a design for building a wooden bridge across the Thames at Westminster [P.R.O., Minutes of the Westminster Bridge Commissioners, i, f. 69]. He died in 1737 or 1738 [*ex inf.* Survey of London].

SIMMONS, SAMUEL, of Deal, was the builder and apparently the designer of the church of ST. GEORGE at DEAL, KENT, of which he laid the foundation-stone on 21 July 1707. In 1712 John James of Greenwich was consulted as to the desirability of a parapet. He recommended 'plain mondillion eaves' instead, and the design was altered accordingly. Owing to difficulties over the carpenter's contract, due to local politics, the church was not completed until 1716 [J. Laker, *History of Deal*, 1917, 258–63].

SIMPSON, ARCHIBALD (1790–1847), was the leading architect in Aberdeen during the early nineteenth century, and the designer of many of its principal public buildings. He was the third son of William Simpson, a prosperous clothier of Aberdeen, where he was born in May 1790. After an education at the Grammar School he was at first placed with James Massie (*q.v.*), a local architect-builder, but in 1810 transferred to the more professional London office of Robert Lugar (*q.v.*). By April 1811 he was working for David Laing, but this appears to have been only a temporary situation, and soon afterwards he made a visit to Italy of which no details are known. On his return in 1813 Simpson set up in practice in Aberdeen, a town then entering upon a period of prosperity and expansion which offered many opportunities to an able architect. John Smith (*q.v.*) was already established as the City Architect, and for the next thirty years almost every architectural commission of importance in Aberdeen went to one or the other of these two men, who often found themselves in competition. Though Smith had the advantage of his official post, Simpson was the abler designer, and contributed more to the city's architecture. He made excellent use of the local granite, and it is to the intelligent exploitation of its monumental qualities (hitherto largely neglected) that many of his buildings owe their special distinction. This is most obvious in his Greek Revival designs such as the Music Hall, the church at Elgin, and the country house of Crimonmogate, whose faultless masonry gives them a dignity unattainable in brick or stucco. Simpson's Gothic and castellated buildings are in general less notable, but the group of Free Churches which he built in Aberdeen in 1843–4 is remarkable for the octagonal brick spire of north German derivation – an alien but architecturally effective importation into the 'granite city'. Towards the end of his life Simpson experimented with a simplified classical style of which the most interesting examples are Thainston House and Woodside Church.

Though Simpson was one of the ablest architects of his day, he appears never to have competed for public buildings in Edinburgh and elsewhere. Content with his extensive local practice he spent the whole of a busy and prosperous professional career in Aberdeen, where he died on 23 March 1847, in his 57th year. He was unmarried and died intestate. He is said to have been a man of 'strong and indeed eccentric character', whose main recreation was music. He was a member, and in 1844 the president, of a local dining club known as the Maryculter Club. At least three portraits exist, all by his friend James Giles, R.S.A. One is in the Aberdeen Art Gallery and two are the property of Aberdeen University. There is no major collection of his drawings, many of which were in any case burned in a fire which destroyed his office in February 1826, but some are in Aberdeen Public Library. His principal pupils were Thomas Mackenzie (1814–54) and James Matthews (1820–98), who subsequently practised jointly in Elgin and Aberdeen.

The principal sources for Simpson's life and works are the obituary in *Builder* v, 1847, 217, and a series of unusually scholarly and well-informed articles by G. M. Fraser, entitled 'Archibald Simpson, Architect, and his Times', which appeared in the *Aberdeen Weekly Journal* from 5 April to 11 Oct. 1918. See also *A.P.S.D.*, the catalogue of an exhibition of Simpson's works held in Aberdeen in 1908 (*Aberdeen Journal Notes and Queries* i, 1908, 168–9), and *The Archibald Simpson Centenary Celebrations*, with a memoir by W. Douglas Simpson, reprinted (with amplifications) from the *Quarterly Journal of the Royal Incorporation of Architects in Scotland*, 1947.

PUBLIC BUILDINGS

ABERDEEN, THE MEDICO-CHIRURGICAL SOCIETY'S HALL, KING STREET, 1818–20 [Fraser, v].

ABERDEEN, THE LUNATIC ASYLUM, 1819–22 (dem.), and additions, 1845–6 [Fraser, viii, xxvi].

ABERDEEN, THE COUNTY ASSEMBLY ROOMS (MUSIC HALL), 1820–2 [Fraser, vii].

ABERDEEN, THE ATHENAEUM READING ROOM, UNION STREET, 1822–3 [Fraser, vi].

ABERDEEN, THE TOWN AND COUNTY BANK, 91–93 UNION STREET, 1826; dem. [plans at Clydesdale Bank, Aberdeen].

FORRES, MORAYSHIRE, MASONIC LODGE AND ASSEMBLY ROOMS, 1829 [Fraser, xi; *N.S.A.* xiii, 165].

ELGIN, MORAYSHIRE, THE ELGIN or ANDERSON INSTITUTION, 1830–3 [*N.S.A.* xiii, 9].

ABERDEEN, INFANT SCHOOL, PRINCES STREET, 1831; dem. [*Aberdeen Jnl.*, 2 Feb. 1831].

FOCHABERS BRIDGE, MORAYSHIRE, timber arch to replace central spans of stone bridge over R. Spey destroyed by floods, for the 5th Duke of Gordon, 1831–2; replaced by an iron bridge 1852 [Fraser, xiv; accounts in S.R.O., GD 44/53/Box 1].

ABERDEEN, THE ROYAL INFIRMARY, 1832–40, and additions, 1844 [Fraser, xv, xxiii].

ABERDEEN, DR. BELL'S SCHOOL, FREDERICK STREET, 1834–5; dem. [Fraser, xvii].

PETERHEAD, ABERDEENSHIRE, NORTH OF SCOTLAND BANK, BROAD STREET, 1835 [*Aberdeen Jnl.*, 19 Dec. 1835].

BANFF, NORTH OF SCOTLAND BANK, LOW STREET, 1837 [*Aberdeen Jnl.*, 23 Jan. 1837].

ABERDEEN, MARISCHAL COLLEGE, 1837–44, Tudor Gothic; new front, etc., by Marshall Mackenzie 1903–6 [Fraser, xvii–xviii].

ABERDEEN, MRS. ELMSLIE'S INSTITUTION (later GIRLS' HIGH SCHOOL), ALBYN PLACE, 1838–40 [Fraser, xix; drawings in Aberdeen Public Library].

HUNTLY, ABERDEENSHIRE, THE GORDON SCHOOLS, for the Duchess of Gordon, 1839, Elizabethan style; wings added to north 1888 [Fraser, xxi].

ABERDEEN, NORTHERN ASSURANCE CO.'s premises, KING STREET, 1840 [Fraser, xx].

ABERDEEN, NORTH OF SCOTLAND BANK, CASTLE STREET, 1840–2 [Fraser, xx] (*C. Life*, 19 Aug. 1965, fig. 3).

HUNTLY, ABERDEENSHIRE, NORTH OF SCOTLAND BANK, *c.* 1840 [Fraser, xxi].

ABERDEEN, THE NEW MARKET (dem.) and layout of MARKET STREET, 1840–2 [Fraser, xxi] (*C. Life*, 19 Aug. 1965, fig. 7).

ABERDEEN, THE POST OFFICE, MARKET STREET, 1841–2 [Fraser, xxii].

ABERDEEN, THE MECHANIC'S INSTITUTE, MARKET STREET, 1845–6 [Fraser, xxv].

ABERDEEN, WEST PARISH CHURCH SCHOOL (subsequently part of Training College), GEORGE STREET, 1846; dem. [Fraser, xxvi].

LERWICK, SHETLANDS, UNION BANK OF SCOTLAND, 1846 [Fraser, xxvi].

attributed: EDINBURGH, DUCHESS OF GORDON'S FREE CHURCH SCHOOL (now chauffeurs' quarters), PALACE YARD, HOLYROODHOUSE, 1846, Jacobethan [attribution based on stylistic grounds and Simpson's employment elsewhere by the Duchess].

CHURCHES

ABERDEEN, ST. ANDREW'S EPISCOPAL CHURCH (now CATHEDRAL), KING STREET, 1816–17, Gothic; chancel by G. E. Street 1880, choir fittings, etc., by N. Comper 1941 [Fraser, iv].

KINTORE PARISH CHURCH AND MANSE, ABERDEENSHIRE, 1819, Gothic [Fraser, vi].

ELGIN, MORAYSHIRE, ST. GILES, 1827–8, Greek Revival [Fraser, x; *N.S.A.* xiii, 9].

INVERBROTHOCK CHAPEL, ARBROATH, ANGUS, 1828 [*Aberdeen Jnl. N. and Q.* i, 1908, 168–9].

WOODSIDE CHAPEL (afterwards Free Church), nr. ABERDEEN, 1829–30, Gothic [P. Morgan, *Annals of Woodside and Newhills*, Aberdeen 1886, 82–3].

BANFF, ST. ANDREW'S EPISCOPAL CHURCH, 1833–4, Gothic [Fraser, xvii].

FOCHABERS, MORAYSHIRE, EPISCOPAL CHAPEL AND SCHOOL for the Duchess of Gordon, 1833–4, Gothic [Fraser, xvii].

DRUMOAK PARISH CHURCH, ABERDEENSHIRE, 1835–6, Gothic [Fraser, xvii; *N.S.A.* xii, 895].

ABERDEEN, ST. NICHOLAS EAST, 1835–7, Gothic [Fraser, xvi].

ABERDEEN, UNITED FREE CHURCHES, BELMONT STREET, 1843–4, Gothic [Fraser, xxiv].

ROTHESAY FREE CHURCH, BUTESHIRE, 1844 [*Builder* v, 217].

ABERDEEN, OLD ABERDEEN FREE CHURCH, 1845–6, Gothic, 'simplified greatly from what he intended' [Fraser, xxiv].

WOODSIDE CHURCH OF SCOTLAND, nr. ABERDEEN, 1846 [Fraser, xxiv].

ABERDEEN: DOMESTIC ARCHITECTURE

The following list includes only Simpson's principal domestic commissions in Aberdeen:

UNION BUILDINGS, UNION AND CASTLE STREETS, 1819 [Fraser, v].

House at corner of Union Street and Shiprow for Alexander Galen, 1819 [Fraser, v].

BON-ACCORD SQUARE AND CRESCENT, 1823–6 [Fraser, viii] (*C. Life*, 19 Aug. 1965, fig. 6).

MARINE TERRACE, FERRYHILL, designed 1831, Nos. 9–10 built 1837–8, others later [Fraser, xiii].

WESTBURN HOUSE (now public park) for David Chalmers, 1839 [Fraser, xix].

COUNTRY HOUSES

CASTLE FORBES (formerly PUTACHIE), ABERDEEN-SHIRE, for the 17th Lord Forbes, 1814–15, castellated [*Builder* v, 1847, 217; S.R.O., GD 52/349] (J. P. Neale, *Seats*, 1st ser., i, 1818; F. O. Morris, *Picturesque Views of Seats* v, 61].

PARK HOUSE, ABERDEENSHIRE, for William Moir, 1822 [*Builder* v, 1847, 217].

HEATHCOT, BANCHORY DEVENICK, KINCARDINE-SHIRE, 1822; dem. [*Builder* v, 1847, 217].

HADDO HOUSE, ABERDEENSHIRE, alterations for the 4th Earl of Aberdeen, 1822 [*Builder* v, 1847, 217] (*C. Life*, 18–25 Aug. 1966].

MURTLE HOUSE (now Rudolph Steiner School), ABERDEENSHIRE, for John Thurburn, 1823 [*Builder* v, 1847, 217; Fraser, x].

DURRIS HOUSE, KINCARDINESHIRE, additions for John Innes, 1824 [*Builder* v, 1847, 217].

CRIMONMOGATE, LONMAY, ABERDEENSHIRE, for Sir Alexander Bannerman (?), *c.* 1825; mansard roof added 1875 [*Builder* v, 1847, 217; Fraser, xi].

LETHAM GRANGE, nr. ARBROATH, ANGUS, for John Hay, *c.* 1825–30 [*Builder* v, 1847, 217; Fraser, x] (*Forfarshire Illustrated*, Dundee 1843, 71].

PITLURG (formerly LEASK) HOUSE, SLAINS, ABER-DEENSHIRE, for General William Cumming Skene Gordon, 1826–7; burned 1927 [Fraser, x].

GORDON CASTLE, MORAYSHIRE, alterations and repairs to east wing after fire, for trustees of the 4th Duke of Gordon, 1827 [S.R.O., GD 44/49/16].

TILLERY HOUSE, FOVERAN, ABERDEENSHIRE, for — Hunter, *c.* 1827; gutted [Fraser, x].

STRACATHRO HOUSE, ANGUS, for Alexander Cruickshanks, 1828 [*Builder* v, 1847, 217; Fraser, x] (*Forfarshire Illustrated*, Dundee 1843, 137].

CASTLE NEWE, ABERDEENSHIRE, rebuilt for Sir Charles Forbes, Bart., 1831; dem. [*N.S.A.* xii, 546; Fraser, xii] (*Castles of Aberdeenshire*, Aberdeen 1887, 130).

BOATH HOUSE, NAIRNSHIRE, for Sir James Dunbar, *c.* 1830 [*Builder* v, 1847, 217; photostats at N.M.R.S. of signed drawings].

CRAIG HOUSE, AUCHINDOIR, ABERDEENSHIRE, altered or enlarged for — Gordon, 1832; burned 1942 [*Builder* v, 1847, 217].

LINTON HOUSE, CLUNY, ABERDEENSHIRE, for — Craigie (?), *c.* 1835 [elevation exhibited in 1908, *Aberdeen Jnl. Notes and Queries* i, 1908, 169, no. 65].

MELDRUM HOUSE, ABERDEENSHIRE, rebuilt for B. C. Urquhart, *c.* 1835/40, castellated; altered 1934–7 [*Builder* v, 1847, 217; Fraser, xix] (*Castles of Aberdeenshire*, Aberdeen 1887, 120).

CARNOUSIE NEW HOUSE, BANFFSHIRE, for Capt. Alexander Grant, *c.* 1835/40; dem. *c.* 1930 [*Builder* v, 1847, 217; Fraser, xxi; W. Douglas Simpson in *Banffshire Field Club's Trans.*, 1966].

LESSENDRUM HOUSE, DRUMBLADE, ABERDEENSHIRE, altered and enlarged for William Bisset, 1840, Scottish vernacular style; destroyed by fire *c.* 1925 [*Builder* v, 1847, 217].

PITTODRIE HOUSE, ABERDEENSHIRE, additions for Allan C. Dunlop, 1840; canted bay added 1926 [*Builder* v, 1847, 217].

GLASSAUGH HOUSE, PORTSOY, BANFFSHIRE, for Arthur Abercromby, 1840 [Fraser, xi].

DRUMINNOR HOUSE, AUCHINDOIR, ABERDEENSHIRE, enlarged for Alexander Grant, 1841–3; Simpson's additions dem. *c.* 1965 [*Builder* v, 1847, 217].

GLENFERNESS, NAIRNSHIRE, for John Dougal, 1844–5 [*Builder* v, 1847, 217; Fraser, xxiii].

MORKEU, BANCHORY DEVENICK, KINCARDINESHIRE, *c.* 1845; porch added 1910 [Fraser, xxv].

SCOTSTON HOUSE, nr. OLD ABERDEEN, for Sir Michael Bruce, Bart.; dem. [*Builder* v, 1847, 217].

THAINSTON, nr. KINTORE, ABERDEENSHIRE, remodelled for Duncan Forbes-Mitchell [*Builder* v, 1847, 217] (Colin McWilliam in *Scotland's Magazine*, July 1955, 47].

SKENE HOUSE, ABERDEENSHIRE, designed additions

737

for the 4th Earl of Fife, *c.* 1847, carried out after his death by — Ramage, who published a lithograph of the house [*Builder* v, 1847, 217].

SIMPSON, JAMES (–1864), of Leeds, specialized in designing Nonconformist chapels. His work in Leeds included THE BRUNSWICK METHODIST CHAPEL, 1824–5, with a handsome classical façade [D. Linstrum, *Historic Architecture of Leeds*, 1969, 47, illustrating an engraving on which Simpson is named as architect of the chapel]; ST. PETER'S STREET CHAPEL, 1834; OXFORD PLACE CHAPEL, 1835; WESLEY CHAPEL, MEADOW LANE, 1837; THE LADY LANE CHAPEL, 1840; HANOVER PLACE CHAPEL, 1847, and RICHMOND HILL CHAPEL, 1849 [R. Willis, *Nonconformist Chapels of York*, York Georgian Soc. n.d., 31]. Elsewhere he designed THE CENTENARY METHODIST CHAPEL at YORK, 1839–40 [Willis, *op. cit.*, 31]; THE WESLEYAN CHAPEL, SCARBOROUGH, 1839–40 [*Theakston's Guide to Scarborough*, n.d., 63]; THE METHODIST CHAPEL, KING STREET, DERBY, 1841 (dem. 1967) [S. Glover, *History of Derby*, 1843]; THE PITT STREET METHODIST CHAPEL, BARNSLEY, 1845–6 [Willis, *op. cit.*, 31]; the Gothic ROWLANDS METHODIST CHAPEL, SUMMERSEAT, BURY, LANCS., for John Robinson Kay, 1845–7 [signed drawings formerly preserved in the chapel]; and the WESLEY CHAPEL, YORK, 1855 [Willis, *op. cit.*, 31]. Simpson died at Leeds on 13 March 1864 [Principal Probate Registry, Calendar of Probates].

SIMPSON, JAMES CHARNOCK (–1876), practised at Brighton, where in 1830 he designed the LONDON ROAD CHAPEL [*The Watering Places of Great Britain and Fashionable Directory*, J. Robins, London 1833, 33]. He died in Jersey on 2 July 1876 [Principal Probate Registry, Calendar of Probates].

SIMPSON, JOHN, 'of Budby', made a design for the new County Hall at Nottingham in 1768 which was not accepted, but in the following year John Simpson 'of Thoresby' was paid £43 7s. 6d. for drawing plans and attending Parliament in connection with the Act to build the new County Hall designed by James Gandon. The change of address is explained by the fact that Simpson was then engaged in supervising the building of Thoresby House to the designs of John Carr of York. He was presumably the John Simpson who in 1781–2 designed the GENERAL HOSPITAL at NOTTINGHAM, of which he published a print (Bodleian Library, Gough Maps 26, ff. 21ᵛ–22), and who was concerned in rebuilding the LEEN BRIDGE at NOTTINGHAM in 1764 and GAINSBOROUGH BRIDGE in 1787. But he must not be confused with John Simpson of Shrewsbury (*q.v.*), a builder regularly employed in bridge and canal works during the latter part of the eighteenth century.

738

[*A.P.S.D.*; *Nottinghamshire County Records of the Eighteenth Century*, ed. K. T. Meaby, 1947, 49, 55, 106; J. Blackner, *History of Nottingham*, 1815, 160; T. Whitehead, *Original Anecdotes of the late Duke of Kingston*, 1792, 106; J. F. Sutton, *The Date Book for Nottingham*, 1852, 144; Nottingham University Library, Ne C4, 339, 359, Minutes of the Committee for Gainsborough Bridge.]

SIMPSON, JOHN (1755–1815), was born at Stenhouse in Midlothian, and was probably a mason by trade. He was regularly employed by Telford, who described him as 'a treasure of talents and integrity'. Under Telford's direction he built bridges at Bewdley, Dunkeld, Craigellachie and Bonar, the Chirk and Pont-y-Cysyllte aqueducts, and the locks and basins of the Caledonian Canal. He eventually settled in Shrewsbury, where he superintended the erection of New St. Chad's Church to the designs of George Steuart in 1790–2. Although primarily a builder and clerk of works, he was sometimes described as an architect, and he may have been the 'Sympson' who, according to the antiquary Thomas Prattinton, designed the TOWN HALL at BEWDLEY, WORCS., in 1808 [original drawings in Library of the Society of Antiquaries of London, Prattinton Collection, vol. v, 25/5, inscribed 'Sympson, Architect']. He died at Shrewsbury on 16 June 1815, and is commemorated by a monument in New St. Chad's Church, with a bust by Chantrey. His business was taken over by his nephew, John Straphen (d. 1826), the builder of Lord Hill's Column. [A. Gibb, *The Story of Telford*, 1935, 39; *Gent's Mag.* 1815 (i), 572, 1820 (ii), 303; C. Hulbert, *Memoirs*, Shrewsbury 1852, 191.]

SINCLAIR, JOHN (*c.* 1789–1863), of Hartshill, Warwicks., was for 'upwards of 42 years resident engineer to the Coventry Canal Company', according to the inscription on his tombstone at Mancetter. He died on 17 March 1863, aged 74. An iron bridge at HAWKSBURY, WARWICKS., dated 1837, bears his signature, and in 1847 the west tower of GRENDON CHURCH, WARWICKS., was rebuilt to his (Perpendicular Gothic) design [Vestry Minutes in County Record Office]. The 'John Sinclair, junior' of Coventry who competed for the Ashmolean Museum at Oxford in 1839 was no doubt a relation, and Robert Cooper Sinclair, who practised from Hartshill in the 1870s as 'engineer and architect', was presumably his son.

SINGLETON, LUKE (–1768), of Gloucester, is known only as the designer of the GENERAL INFIRMARY in that city. The minutes of the committee for building the Infirmary show that Singleton's plan was approved in 1755 after consultation with John Wood of Bath. The building was erected by Stiff Leadbetter (*q.v.*) and completed in 1761. A south wing was added in 1827 and a north wing in 1869. When Singleton died in 1768 he was described as 'gentleman' in the probate records and as 'esquire' in the *London Magazine*. [G. W. Counsel, *History of Gloucester*, 1829, 176; George Whitcombe, *The General Infirmary at Gloucester*, 1903, 18; *London Magazine*, 1768, 501; notes from committee book *ex inf.* Mr. Bryan Little.]

SKAE, DAVID (–*c*.1819), was a builder in Edinburgh. The only building he is known to have designed is THE ALBANY STREET INDEPENDENT CHAPEL, EDINBURGH (now the Congregational Church of the Nazarene), 1816 [J. & H. Storer, *Views in Edinburgh* i, 1820]. The façades were designed to conform to the domestic architecture of Broughton and Albany Streets. Skae, who died young, was the father of David Skae (1814–73), a distinguished physician (see *D.N.B.*).

SKAIFE, THOMAS, advertised himself in *Aris's Birmingham Gazette* of 17 August 1789 as a 'Surveyor and Builder from London (No. 9 Fleet Street,)' who 'proposes drawing Plans, Elevations and Sections, and to measure and value the different Artificers' Works in Buildings upon the most reasonable Terms'. He was also prepared to 'Estimate and undertake all Sorts of Building By Contract'. He was a carpenter and joiner by trade and was the author of *A Key to Civil Architecture, or the Universal British Builder*, 1774, 2nd ed. 1776, 3rd ed. 1778.

SKINNER, WILLIAM (1700–1780), was a military engineer who was appointed Chief Engineer of Great Britain in 1757, and rose to the rank of lieutenant-general. His activities as a military engineer fall largely outside the scope of this *Dictionary*, but he may be mentioned here as the designer of FORT GEORGE at ARDESEIR, nr. INVERNESS (1748–69), a major monument of Georgian military architecture. See Iain MacIvor, *Fort George*, H.M.S.O. 1970, and *D.N.B.* for a full account of Skinner's career.

SLATER, JOHN, was a joiner in Seel Street, Liverpool, who also practised as an architect. At the Liverpool Academy's exhibition in 1812 he showed a 'Design for an altarpiece for a Catholic Chapel'. Between 1812 and 1816 he was employed by the Catholic Thomas Scarisbrick to carry out extensive alterations to SCARISBRICK HALL, LANCS. These were in the Gothic style and in making the designs Slater was assisted by Thomas Rickman (*q.v.*), then at the outset of his career as an architect. From 1837 onwards the house was again remodelled in a more advanced Gothic style to the designs of A. W. N. Pugin, but some traces of Rickman and Slater's work can still be seen [Rickman's diaries, 1812–16, *passim*; information from Mr. John Baily]. Slater later designed the classical R.C. church of ST. PATRICK, PARK PLACE, LIVERPOOL, 1821–3 [*Liverpool Mercury*, 23 March 1821], and according to *Gent's Mag.* 1839 (ii), 532, the Gothic parish church of HURDSFIELD, CHESHIRE, but drawings for the latter preserved in the church are reported to be signed by William Hayley of Manchester.

SLOANE, CHARLES (1690–1764), was a native of Dartford, but established himself as a carpenter and builder in Gravesend. In 1731–3 he designed and rebuilt the parish church of ST. GEORGE, GRAVESEND, after its destruction by fire in 1727. He also designed the TOWN HALL, which, before its refronting in 1836 by A. H. Wilds, bore on a stone fascia an inscription recording that it was 'ERECTED IN THE YEAR 1764, JOHN DELAP, ESQ., MAYOR; C. SLOANE ARCHITECT' [R. P. Cruden, *History of Gravesend*, 1843, 408, 425]. In 1746 he designed the COUNTY GAOL, MAIDSTONE, which likewise bore the inscription 'C. SLOANE, ARCHITECT' [*Gent's Mag.* 1809 (ii), 813]; it was enlarged by William Tyler in 1784 and entirely rebuilt in 1810. In 1742–3 he repaired and refitted the choir of ROCHESTER CATHEDRAL, and in 1749 rebuilt the central spire [G. H. Palmer, *The Cathedral Church of Rochester*, 1897, 29–30]. In 1751 two large brick buttresses were erected against the south-east transept in accordance with his advice [*Archaeologia Cantiana* xxiii, 1898, 283]. In 1754 he supplied plans for rebuilding DARTFORD BRIDGE which were carried out in the following year [Kent Record Office, QS. County Bridges]. The bridge was rebuilt in 1790–1 and again in 1922–3.

In 1754 a letter from Sloane concerning Dartford Bridge was written from Calehill, Little Chart, the seat of the Darell family. As CALEHILL HOUSE (dem. 1951) was rebuilt in 1753–4 [Kent Record Office, U386, E1–3], Sloane was probably the architect employed. It was a well-proportioned plain brick house with flanking wings.

Sloane died at Gravesend in 1764 and is commemorated by an inscription in St. George's Churchyard. He appears to have been a competent but undistinguished Georgian architect.

SMALLWOOD, WILLIAM FROME (1806–1834), born at Peasemarsh in Surrey, was the son of the proprietor of the Grand Hotel, Covent Garden. He became a pupil of L. N. Cottingham, but never practised as an architect, preferring the profession of an artist. He specialized in architectural subjects, and exhibited a number of drawings of cathedrals, etc., in Northern France and Belgium at the Royal Academy in 1830–4. Drawings made by him at Amiens and Rouen in 1831–

739

SMALMAN, JOHN

3 are in the Avery Library of Columbia University, New York, and one of Notre Dame at St. Omer, dated 1833, is in the Victoria and Albert Museum. A number of his drawings were engraved for the *Penny Magazine*. According to *Gent's Mag.* 1834 (i), 661, his early death at the age of 27 was due to brain fever, brought on 'by the great exertions made to support a young and increasing family'. Loudon, in reporting his death in the *Architectural Magazine* i, 1834, 184, gave his age as 34.

SMALMAN, JOHN (*c.* 1783–1852), was a builder and architect of Quatford, nr. Bridgnorth in Shropshire. He had pretensions to gentility, and claimed descent from the Smalmans of Wilderhope, but it is likely that he was more closely related to the 'J. Smallman' who signs a monumental tablet in Much Wenlock Church to Thomas and Mary Smyth (d. 1780). He made a fortune as a builder in the Bridgnorth area, but his known architectural works are neither numerous nor distinguished. In about 1816 he enlarged STANLEY HALL, SALOP., for Sir John Tyrwhit Jones, Bart., after designs by Thomas Cundy had been rejected [J. P. Neale, *Views of Seats*, 1st ser., iii, 1820]. In 1823 he widened the two middle arches of BRIDGNORTH BRIDGE by the insertion of the present iron girders [*Trans. Salop. Arch. Soc.* xlix, 1937, 209]; in 1823–4 he designed and built the BRIDGNORTH THEATRE (dem. *c.* 1855), for which some of his designs survive among the Corporation archives; in 1828 he designed DITTON PRIORS VICARAGE, SALOP. [Bodleian Library, records of Queen Anne's Bounty]; and in 1829 he rebuilt the west tower of CHETTON CHURCH, SALOP., in a somewhat perfunctory Gothic style [I.C.B.S.]. A plan of the dining-room at DUDMASTON HALL, SALOP., by Smalman, dated 1826, shows that he was concerned in the early nineteenth-century alterations to that house for W. W. Whitmore, and was very likely responsible for the new attic storey that was added at that time. At Quatford he built himself in 1829–30 a castellated mansion called QUATFORD CASTLE which is somewhat in the style of Wyatville's work at Windsor, and largely rebuilt the village (see George Griffith's poem *The English Village*, 1847, which is dedicated to Smalman).

Smalman, who appears to have been a Whig in politics, was elected an alderman of Bridgnorth immediately after the Municipal Reform Act of 1835, and served as Mayor in 1837–8. He died unmarried on 11 March 1852, aged 69, and is buried at Quatford, where a eulogistic epitaph refers to the 'vigorous will ... simplicity of life, sound judgment and indomitable perseverance' which enabled him to rise to 'Honour and Fortune'. The epitaph also refers to his literary interests, of which evidence survives in the form of

several long manuscript poems of a somewhat eccentric character. Among them are 'Lines addressed to Mrs. Farmer [of] Ludstone Hall on her judicious attention to the preservation of the character and state of that ancient mansion'. A portrait of Smalman hangs in the Mayor's Parlour at Bridgnorth. The architect S. Pountney Smith of Shrewsbury (1812–83) was his nephew and pupil.

[Bridgnorth Corporation Archives; National Library of Wales, Bridgnorth Peculiar records (will); information from Dr. J. F. A. Mason.]

SMART, ALFRED RAWDON (*c.* 1804–1842), was in practice as an architect and surveyor in Leicester by 1827. His career, however, was a short one, for he died of epilepsy in the County Lunatic Asylum on 2 September 1842, aged 38 [J. D. Bennett, *Leicestershire Architects 1700–1850*, Leicester Museums 1968].

SMART, ANDREW (*c.* 1676–1736), is described as 'mason and architect' on his monument (No. 978) in the Houff Cemetery at Dundee. He owned a quarry at Dundee, and according to the inscription 'built the Town House of Dundee [to the designs of William Adam], and many other public and private buildings'. He died on 3 October 1736, aged 60 [James Thomson, *History of Dundee*, Dundee 1847, 149]. The monument was erected by his son Thomas, who may have been the father of Thomas Smart, 'mason and architect' of Dundee, whose death in 1801 in his 76th year is recorded in *Gent's Mag.* 1801, 377. ABERNYTE CHURCH, PERTHSHIRE, was built in 1736 by David Smart, mason in Dundee [S.R.O., HR 499/1, f. 4ᵛ].

SMIRKE, Sir ROBERT (1780–1867), second son of the artist Robert Smirke, R.A., was born in London on 1 October 1780. He was educated at a well-known private school at Aspley Guise in Bedfordshire, where he showed 'an inclination towards drawing'. In May 1796 he entered the office of Sir John Soane, but left a few months later owing to a mutual antipathy between master and pupil. For his subsequent training he was indebted to George Dance, junior, and to the surveyor Thomas Bush (*q.v.*). He had begun to study at the Royal Academy Schools in July 1796, gaining the Silver Medal in that year, and the Gold Medal in 1799. In 1801 he went abroad with his elder brother Richard. Abandoning the risky idea of visiting Paris disguised as Americans, they eventually went there after the Peace of Amiens, and subsequently travelled extensively in Italy and Sicily. Robert also visited Greece, then a wild and bandit-ridden country, and with considerable intrepidity succeeded in drawing most of the ancient buildings in the Morea. He returned to England in 1805, and in the following year

740

published the first and only part of a projected work entitled *Specimens of Continental Architecture*.[1]

As a practising architect in London Smirke enjoyed an immediate success. His father's connections helped to bring him clients, and he soon became the favoured architect of the Tory establishment. It was to Tory patronage that he was indebted for all his official posts and for most of his commissions. George Dance and Sir George Beaumont recommended him to Lord Lonsdale, a Tory magnate who gave him his first major commission as a country-house architect. Earl Bathurst, another Tory, employed him at Cirencester Park and made him architect to the Royal Mint (1807). The painter Sir Thomas Lawrence introduced him to the future Prime Minister Sir Robert Peel, who employed him to design a town house in Whitehall and a country seat in Staffordshire. In fact Smirke became such a favourite of Peel that the Radical press made fun of the 'two Sir Roberts' and wrote derisively of 'the Prime Minister and his pet'.

In 1813, at the age of 33, Smirke rose to the top of his profession by being nominated as one of the three architects attached to the Office of Works, the others being Soane and Nash, both many years his seniors. This appointment brought him several major commissions, notably the British Museum, the General Post Office, the Custom House and King's College in the Strand. In 1819 he became surveyor to the Inner Temple, where he carried out extensive works. From 1820 he was also Surveyor-General for the South Parts of the Duchy of Lancaster, and as such was responsible for the development of the Savoy estate in London. His private commissions were numerous. Outside London he built or enlarged some thirty country houses and designed eight county halls: at Carlisle, Gloucester, Hereford, Bristol, Shrewsbury, Lincoln, Maidstone and Perth. Inside London he was responsible for Covent Garden Theatre, the Royal College of Physicians, four clubs and several churches. His was in fact one of the biggest and most successful architectural practices of the nineteenth century. At the height of his career he was rumoured to have declined commissions for work costing less than £10,000, and he died worth £90,000.

Smirke was elected A.R.A. in 1808, R.A. in 1811, and held the office of Treasurer of the Royal Academy from 1820 to 1850. In 1832, when the Office of Works was reorganized without the three 'attached architects', he received a knighthood in recognition of his services. He was a Fellow of the Royal Society and of the Society of Antiquaries, and an Honorary Fellow of the R.I.B.A., whose Gold Medal was awarded to him

in 1853. He retired from practice in 1845, when Peel made him a member of the Commission for London Improvements. At the same time he was presented by his former pupils and assistants with a bust of himself by Thomas Campbell which is now at the R.I.B.A. In 1859 he resigned from the Royal Academy and retired to Cheltenham, where he died on 18 April 1867, at the age of 87.

Smirke's professional success owed more to a reputation for reliability than it did to brilliance in design. His meticulous and business-like methods commended themselves to a generation that had suffered from the mismanagement first of Wyatt and then of Nash. He rarely exceeded his estimates, and sound construction was his speciality. The frequency with which he was called in to remedy the defective work of others led Croker to call him 'the Dr. Baillie of architects', alluding to the author of a well-known work on morbid anatomy. The Carlisle County Courts, the Millbank Penitentiary and the London Custom House were the most celebrated architectural casualties to benefit from his skill. Technically he was thoroughly up to date. Indeed he was something of a structural innovator, being the first British architect to use load-bearing foundations of lime concrete in measured quantities, and one of the first to make regular use of load-bearing cast-iron beams in public and domestic (as opposed to industrial) architecture.

Aesthetically, Smirke was a dedicated Greek Revivalist. His Covent Garden Theatre was London's first building in the pure Doric style, the British Museum its greatest neo-classical monument. It was not, however, the archaeological niceties of Greek architecture that Smirke admired, so much as its rational simplicity. Once having found one or two Grecian formulae (notably the Order of the Temple on the Ilissus) which satisfied him, he adhered to them with tedious fidelity, repeating them again and again in his churches and public buildings. His public works, though invariably dignified, are in consequence frequently dull. Only in the front of the British Museum did grandeur of scale and the novel combination of a portico with a colonnade enable him to transcend his usual urbane banality and produce a masterpiece of classical dignity. As a country-house architect he was less inhibited by Grecian precept. Indeed, with the exception of Armley, none of his country houses is dominated by the conventional Doric or Ionic portico. Several, like Lowther and Eastnor, are castellated Gothic, a few, like Drayton and Cultoquhey, are Tudor or Jacobean. But others represent a serious attempt to evolve a simplified classical style whose lack of elegance should not be allowed to detract from its originality. Such are Eden Hall, the Homend, Kinmount, Normanby, Whittinghame and Worthy House: cubical com-

---

[1] He also published a paper on 'Gothic Architecture' in Italy and Sicily in *Archaeologia* xv.

positions which represent Smirke's most interesting contribution to British architecture. But what Pugin called 'the New Square Style of Mr. Smirke' did not save him from the reputation of being in general a conventional and unenterprising designer. Already in 1831 a writer in *The Library of the Fine Arts* described him as an architect who (in the words of Pope) was 'content to dwell in decencies for ever', and in 1842 he was the object of a scathing attack in the *Surveyor, Engineer and Architect*. Long before his death in 1867 he had been repudiated by contemporary taste, and modern scholarship has emphasized his constructive virtues without doing much to vindicate his reputation as an artist.

Smirke married in 1819 Laura, the fifth daughter of the Rev. Anthony Freston, a nephew of Matthew Brettingham (see p. 134) by whom he had one daughter. His extensive practice demanded a large and well-organized office, and his many pupils included William Burn, C. R. Cockerell, William Doull, C. C. Nelson, John Newman, Henry Roberts, Lewis Vulliamy, and his younger brother Sydney Smirke (1797–1877).

There is a large collection of Smirke's drawings in the R.I.B.A. Drawings Collection. Many of his continental drawings (1802–4) are in the Mellon Collection. His correspondence with Sir Robert Peel is in the British Museum (Add. MS. 40605). Busts by E. H. Baily (1828) and Thomas Campbell (1845) are in the British Museum and the R.I.B.A. respectively. There is a portrait by George Dance at the Royal Academy.

[*A.P.S.D.*; *D.N.B.*; obituary by Sir E. Smirke in *R.I.B.A. Jnl.*, 1866–7, reprinted in *Builder* xxv, 1867, 604; *Building News* xiv, 567–8; *The Farington Diary*, ed. J. Greig, *passim*; J. Mordaunt Crook, 'The Career of Sir Robert Smirke', Oxford D.Phil. thesis, 1961, and the following articles: 'Sir Robert Smirke: A Pioneer of Concrete Construction', *Trans. Newcomen Soc.* xxxviii, 1965–6; 'Architect of the Rectangular: a Reassessment of Sir Robert Smirke', *C. Life*, 13 April 1967; 'Sir Robert Smirke: a Centenary Florilegium', *Arch. Rev.*, Sept. 1967; 'Sir Robert Smirke: A Regency Architect in London', *Jnl. of the London Society*, March 1968; *History of the King's Works* vi, 1973, *passim*.]

PUBLIC BUILDINGS IN LONDON

SOMERSET HOUSE, STRAND, alterations to the Library of the Society of Antiquaries, 1807–8 [Joan Evans, *History of the Society of Antiquaries*, 1956, 216].

COVENT GARDEN THEATRE, 1808–9; altered 1846–7 and rebuilt by E. M. Barry 1856–8 after a fire [Britton & Pugin, *Public Buildings of London* i, 1825, 193–226; *Survey of London* xxxv, 93–7].

THE ROYAL MINT, TOWER HILL, completion of building begun by James Johnson, 1809–11, and repairs after fire in 1815 [*History of the King's Works* vi, 453–8].

THE BRITISH MUSEUM, MONTAGU HOUSE, BLOOMSBURY, repairs and additions, 1815–16, and temporary rooms for the Elgin Marbles, 1816; dem. *c.* 1840 [*History of the King's Works* vi, 405; J. Mordaunt Crook, *The British Museum*, 1972].

THE MILLBANK PENITENTIARY, completion of building designed by Thomas Hardwick (*q.v.*) after failure of foundations, 1816–19, and further alterations 1824 and 1828; dem. 1903 [G. Holford, *An Account of the Penitentiary at Millbank*, 1828, pp. xxxi–xxxii; *Builder* lxiii, 1892, 474].

THE INNER TEMPLE, alterations to HALL, 1816–17, 1827 and 1837, rebuilt by Sydney Smirke 1867–70, destroyed by bombing 1940–1; LIBRARY and PARLIAMENT CHAMBERS, 1819 and 1827–8, destroyed by bombing 1940–1; refaced CROWN OFFICE ROW, 1827; alterations to NOS. 4 and 5 HARE COURT, 1827 and 1832; repairs and alterations to MASTER'S HOUSE, 1827 and 1831; NOS. 12 and 13 KING'S BENCH WALK, 1829–30; NO. 9 KING'S BENCH WALK, 1836–7; TANFIELD COURT, 1832–3, rebuilt 1896; HARCOURT BUILDINGS, 1832–4, destroyed by bombing 1940–1; PAPER BUILDINGS, rebuilt north front after fire in 1838, south front rebuilt by Sydney Smirke 1847–8, destroyed by bombing 1940–1 [J. M. Crook, 'Career of Sir Robert Smirke', 174–181].

SOMERSET HOUSE, STRAND, THE LEGACY DUTY OFFICE in north-west corner, 1817–19 and 1821–33 [*History of the King's Works* vi, 481].

THE UNITED SERVICE CLUB, CHARLES STREET, ST. JAMES'S, 1817–19; altered by Decimus Burton for the Junior United Service Club 1830; rebuilt 1855–7 [*Survey of London* xxix, 289–91, and xxx, pl. 64].

LANCASTER PLACE, STRAND, and DUCHY OF LANCASTER OFFICES, *c.* 1817–23; dem. [R. Somerville, *The Savoy*, 1960, 111–13; *A.P.S.D.*].

WHITMORE'S BANK, NO. 24 LOMBARD STREET, *c.* 1820; burnt before 1867 [Crook, 'Career of Sir Robert Smirke', 375, n. 7].

THE LONDON OPHTHALMIC INFIRMARY, MOORFIELDS, 1821–2; rebuilt 1898 [*A.P.S.D.*] (J. Elmes, *Metropolitan Improvements*, 1831, plate).

THE MILITARY DEPOT, TOOLEY STREET, SOUTHWARK, 1821–3; dem. [*History of the King's Works* vi, 451–2].

THE ROYAL COLLEGE OF PHYSICIANS (now CANADA HOUSE), TRAFALGAR SQUARE, 1822–5; remodelled 1925, when new south portico was added [Britton & Pugin, *Public Buildings of London* ii, 1828, 219–23].

THE UNION CLUB (now CANADA HOUSE), TRAFALGAR

SQUARE, 1822–7; attic storey added by D. Burton 1841–50; remodelled 1925 [Britton & Pugin, *Public Buildings of London* ii, 1828, 219–23].

attributed: THE WESTERN NATIONAL SCHOOL, BRYANSTON SQUARE, 1824; dem. [erected 'in a corresponding style with the church': T. Smith, *Parish of St. Mary-le-bone*, 1833, 107].

THE BRITISH MUSEUM, 1823–46, completed under direction of Sydney Smirke, 1846–52. The domed reading-room was built to Sydney Smirke's design in 1854-7 [Britton & Pugin, *Public Buildings of London*, ed. Leeds, ii, 1838; *History of the King's Works* vi, 403–21; J. Mordaunt Crook, *The British Museum*, 1972].

THE GENERAL POST OFFICE, ST. MARTIN'S LE GRAND, 1824–9; attic storey added 1892; dem. 1912 [Britton & Pugin, *Public Buildings of London*, ed. Leeds, ii, 1838; *History of the King's Works* vi, 430–7].

THE CUSTOM HOUSE, rebuilding after failure of foundations, 1825–7 [J. Mordaunt Crook, 'The Custom House Scandal', *Architectural History* vi, 1963; *History of the King's Works* vi, 422–30].

THE EQUITABLE ASSURANCE COMPANY'S OFFICE, BRIDGE STREET, BLACKFRIARS, 1829 [*A.P.S.D.*].

LONDON BRIDGE APPROACHES, street façades to KING WILLIAM STREET, BOROUGH HIGH STREET, etc., 1829–35, including BRIDGE HOUSE HOTEL (NO. 4 BOROUGH HIGH STREET), ST. MAGNUS MARTYR RECTORY, 1833–5, and ST. MARY WOOLNOTH RECTORY, 1834–9 (dem.) [*A.P.S.D.*].

KING'S COLLEGE, STRAND, forming the east wing of Somerset House, 1830–5; chapel remodelled by Scott 1861–62; attic storey added 1886–8 [*History of the King's Works* vi, 483].

THE CARLTON CLUB, PALL MALL, 1833–6; rebuilt by Sydney Smirke 1854–6; dem. 1940 [*Survey of London* xxix, 354–5].

WESTMINSTER PALACE, refaced interior of WESTMINSTER HALL, 1834–7; temporary HOUSE OF LORDS in former Painted Chamber and temporary HOUSE OF COMMONS in former House of Lords, 1834–5 [*History of the King's Works* vi, 503, 573–5].

MOORGATE STREET, façades, 1835–9 [*A.P.S.D.*].

THE MANSION HOUSE, alteration of steps to portico, 1836 [*A.P.S.D.*].

THE OXFORD AND CAMBRIDGE CLUB, PALL MALL, 1836–8; staircase altered 1907 [*Survey of London* xxix, 419–22].

SERJEANTS' INN, CHANCERY LANE, largely rebuilt, 1836–9; dem. 1910 [*A.P.S.D.*; R.I.B.A.D.].

ST. JAMES'S PALACE, new lodge at entrance to park from stable yard, 1838 [*History of the King's Works* vi, 370].

PUBLIC BUILDINGS ELSEWHERE

CARLISLE, CUMBERLAND, COUNTY COURTS, completion, after failure of foundations, of buildings begun by Telford, Chisholme and Nicholson, 1810–12, castellated [*A.P.S.D.*; R.I.B.A.D.].

APPLEBY, WESTMORLAND, THE MARKET HOUSE, 1811, Gothic [S. Lewis, *Topographical Dictionary of England* i, 1831, 42].

CARLISLE, CUMBERLAND, THE EDEN BRIDGE, 1812–15; widened 1932 [*A.P.S.D.*].

WHITEHAVEN, CUMBERLAND, THE FISH MARKET, 1813, dem. *c.* 1852; THE BUTTER MARKET, 1813, dem. 1880 [S. Lewis, *Topographical Dictionary of England* iv, 1831, 458].

GLOUCESTER, THE SHIRE HALL, 1814–16; enlarged 1909–11 [*A.P.S.D.*; R.I.B.A.D.].

GLOUCESTER, WESTGATE BRIDGE (R. Severn), 1814–17 [*A.P.S.D.*].

BOLTON, WESTMORLAND, iron chain bridge over R. Eden, 1815–16; collapsed 1822 [J. F. Curwen, *The Later Records relating to N. Westmorland*, Kendal 1932, 345].

HEREFORD, THE SHIRE HALL, 1815–17 [*A.P.S.D.*].

PERTH, THE COUNTY BUILDINGS, 1815–19; enlarged 1866–7 [*N.S.A.* x, 86].

DUBLIN, THE WELLINGTON TESTIMONIAL, PHOENIX PARK, 1817–22, unfinished [*A.P.S.D., s.v.* 'Dublin'; R.I.B.A.D.].

MAIDSTONE, KENT, THE COUNTY GAOL, completion of building designed by D. A. Alexander, 1817–19 [*A.P.S.D.*].

LEDBURY, HEREFS., ST. KATHERINE'S HOSPITAL, 1822–5, Gothic [*A.P.S.D.*].

LINCOLN, THE COUNTY COURTS in THE CASTLE, with repairs and additions to gaol, watch-tower, battlements, etc., 1823–30, Gothic [J. Mordaunt Crook, 'The Building of Lincoln County Hall', *Lincolnshire Arch Soc. Reports* ix, 1962].

BRISTOL, THE COUNCIL HOUSE and adjoining shops in BROAD STREET, 1824–7 [*A.P.S.D.*].

MAIDSTONE, KENT, THE SESSIONS HOUSE, 1826–7; enlarged 1850, 1862 and 1914 [*A.P.S.D.*].

SHREWSBURY, THE INFIRMARY, 1827–30 [archives of the Royal Salop. Infirmary].

OXFORD, THE SCHOOLS QUADRANGLE, repairs to roof, including new ceiling of present Upper Reading Room, 1830 [*Bodleian Library Record* iii, 1951, 89–91].

OXFORD, CLARENDON BUILDING, fitted up interior as university offices, etc., 1831 [*V.C.H. Oxon.* iii, 55].

ST. JOHN'S, NEWFOUNDLAND, GAOL, *c.* 1831 [*A.P.S.D.*].

SHREWSBURY, SHIRE HALL, 1834–7; interior reconstructed after fire in 1880; dem. 1971 [*A.P.S.D.*].

CHURCHES

GLOUCESTER CATHEDRAL, Gothic screen behind altar, 1807; removed 1873 [J. Britton, *History and Antiquities of Gloucester Cathedral*, 1829, 62–3, pl. xvii; R.I.B.A.D.].

CARLISLE CATHEDRAL, repairs and alterations to Fratry, 1809–11; restored 1880 [J. M. Crook, 'The Career of Sir Robert Smirke', 324].

STROOD CHURCH, KENT, incorporating medieval tower, 1812 [*A.P.S.D.*; H. Smetham, *History of Strood*, 1899, 55–75].

LONDON, THE BELGRAVE CHAPEL, HALKIN STREET, 1812; dem. *c.* 1910 [J. Elmes, *Metropolitan Improvements*, 1831, 153–4 and plate].

LONDON, THE SAVOY CHAPEL, rebuilt south wall and added west tower, 1820–1, Gothic [R. Somerville, *The Savoy*, 1960, 128–9].

LUTON HOO PARK CHAPEL, BEDS., 1816, Gothic [H. Shaw, *The History and Antiquities of the Chapel at Luton Park*, 1829].

WANDSWORTH, SURREY, ST. ANNE, 1820–2; chancel 1896 [Port, 136–7].

CHATHAM, KENT, ST. JOHN, 1821–2; altered 1869 [Port, 132–3; R.I.B.A.D.].

BRISTOL, ST. GEORGE, BRANDON HILL, 1821–3; altered 1871–6 [Port, 132–3].

LONDON, ST. JAMES, WEST HACKNEY, 1821–3; altered 1859 by W. White and 1879 by G. F. Bodley; dem. 1958 [Port, 134–5] (J. Elmes, *Metropolitan Improvements*, 1831, plate).

LONDON, ST. MARY, WYNDHAM PLACE, BRYANSTON SQUARE, 1821–3; altered internally 1874 [Port, 136–7].

TYLDESLEY, LANCS., ST. GEORGE, 1821–4, Gothic [Port, 134–5; R.I.B.A.D.].

SALFORD, LANCS., ST. PHILIP, 1822–4; altered 1895 [Port, 134–5].

LONDON, GROSVENOR CHAPEL, GROSVENOR PLACE, *c.* 1825 [*A.P.S.D.*].

LONDON, THE TEMPLE CHURCH, repairs and alterations, 1825–30 [J. Mordaunt Crook, 'The Restoration of the Temple Church', *Architectural History* viii, 1965, 40].

YORK MINSTER, restoration of choir roof after fire, 1830–2. Smirke also made a report after the fire which destroyed the roof of the nave in 1840, but the subsequent repairs were entrusted to Sydney Smirke [E. Wylson, 'York Minster; its Fires and Restorations', *Builder* iii, 1845, 158, 175].

MARKHAM CLINTON, NOTTS., church and mausoleum for the 4th Duke of Newcastle, 1831–2 [W. White, *History and Directory of Nottinghamshire*, 1832, 383].

ASKHAM CHURCH, WESTMORLAND, 1832, Tudor Gothic [I.C.B.S.].

LONDON, CHAPEL ROYAL (*i.e.* BANQUETING HOUSE), WHITEHALL, repairs and internal alterations, 1835–8 [*History of the King's Works* vi, 548–9].

LONDON, CHAPEL ROYAL, ST. JAMES'S PALACE, refitted interior, 1836–7 [*History of the King's Works* vi, 370].

LONDON, ST. JAMES'S CHURCH, PICCADILLY, repair of roof, 1836 [*Survey of London* xxix, 39].

EYWOOD, HEREFS., additions for the 5th Earl of Oxford, 1806–7; dem. *c.* 1955 [R.I.B.A.D.].

OFFLEY PLACE, HERTS., for the Rev. Lynch Burroughs, 1806–10, Gothic [J. P. Neale, *Views of Seats*, 2nd ser., v, 1829].

LOWTHER CASTLE, WESTMORLAND, for the 1st Earl of Lonsdale, 1806–11, castellated; interior gutted 1957 [J. P. Neale, *Views of Seats* ii, 1819].

OFFLEY RECTORY, HERTS., for the Rev. Thelwall Salusbury, 1810 [Farington's Diary, 13 July 1810].

WILTON CASTLE, YORKS. (N.R.), for Sir John Lowther, Bart., *c.* 1807, castellated; enlarged 1887 [J. P. Neale, *Views of Seats*, 2nd ser., iv, 1828].

SHERWOOD LODGE, BATTERSEA, statue gallery for Jens Wolff, Danish consul, 1807–8; dem. [*The Farington Diary*, ed. J. Greig, iii, 97 n.; v, 34].

UPLEATHAM HALL, YORKS. (N.R.), enlarged for Lawrence Dundas, cr. 1st Earl of Zetland, *c.* 1810; dem. 1897 [*V.C.H. Yorks. N.R.* ii, 411] (*Apollo*, Sept. 1967, 175, fig. 14).

BICKLEY PLACE, KENT, added library wing for John Wells, 1810; dem. *c.* 1968 [Farington's Diary, 6 March 1810, 31 Jan. 1811].

LONDON, MORTIMER HOUSE, HALKIN STREET, for the 5th Earl of Oxford, *c.* 1810; remodelled *c.* 1860 [*A.P.S.D.*].

CIRENCESTER PARK, GLOS., added north wing and rebuilt east front for the 3rd Earl Bathurst, 1810–11 and 1830 [*A.P.S.D.*; C. Hussey in *C. Life*, 16 June 1950].

ROSE HILL (now BRIGHTLING) PARK, nr. ROBERTSBRIDGE, SUSSEX, works for John Fuller, including additional wing to house (dem. 1955), temple and observatory, *c.* 1810–12 [T. W. Horsfield, *History of Sussex* i, 1835, 564–5; *A.P.S.D.*; R.I.B.A.D.].

BENTLEY PRIORY, STANMORE, MIDDLESEX, enlarged for the 1st Marquess of Abercorn, 1810–18 [*A.P.S.D.*].

KINMOUNT, DUMFRIESSHIRE, for the 5th Marquess of Queensberry, 1812 [J. P. Neale, *Views of Seats* ii, 1819; R.I.B.A.D.].

BOULTIBROOKE, RADNORSHIRE, for Sir Harford Jones-Brydges, 1812–15 [signed drawing at Kentchurch Court, Herefs., *ex inf.* Mr. Derek Sherborne].

EASTNOR CASTLE, HEREFS., for the 2nd Lord Somers, 1812–20, castellated [J. P. Neale, *Views of Seats* ii, 1819; Alistair Rowan in *C. Life*, 7, 14 and 21 March 1968].

THE HOMEND, STRETTON GRANDISON, HEREFS., enlarged for Edward Poole, 1814–21; altered 1973 [letters in Herefordshire County Record Office, C95].

LONDON, LANSDOWNE HOUSE, BERKELEY SQUARE, remodelled library as a picture gallery for the

3rd Marquess of Lansdowne, 1816–19 [*A.P.S.D.*; J. M. Crook, 'The Career of Sir Robert Smirke', 361] (*C. Life*, 11 May 1935).

NEWTON DON, nr. KELSO, ROXBURGHSHIRE, for Sir Alexander Don, Bart., *c.* 1815 [*A.P.S.D.*; design for lodge in R.I.B.A.D.].

BOWOOD HOUSE, WILTS., designed upper terrace for the 3rd Marquess of Lansdowne, 1817–18 [John Cornforth in *C. Life*, 8 and 22 June 1972].

POWIS CASTLE, MONTGOMERYSHIRE, repairs for the 1st Earl of Powis, 1815–18 [J. M. Crook, 'The Career of Sir Robert Smirke', citing Powis accounts].

LONDON, NO. 45 BERKELEY SQUARE, additions for the 1st Earl of Powis, *c.* 1816 (?) [*A.P.S.D.*].

GLOUCESTER, SOMERSET HOUSE (now JUDGE'S LODGINGS), for John Phillpotts, *c.* 1816 [G. W. Counsel, *History of Gloucester*, 1829, 188].

WORTHY HOUSE, HANTS., for Sir Charles Ogle, Bart., 1816, and addition of *porte cochère* for Charles Wall, 1825 [G. F. Prosser, *Select Illustrations of Hampshire*, 1833].

LUTON HOO, BEDS., additions for the 2nd Marquess of Bute, *c.* 1816 onwards; reconstructed by Sydney Smirke after fire in 1843; remodelled by Mewès & Davis 1903 [*A.P.S.D.*].

STRATHALLAN CASTLE, PERTHSHIRE, additions for James Drummond, cr. Lord Strathallan, 1817–18 [*A.P.S.D.*].

CARDIFF CASTLE, GLAMORGANSHIRE, additions for the 2nd Marquess of Bute, *c.* 1818 [*A.P.S.D.*].

WALBERTON HOUSE, SUSSEX, for Richard Prime, 1817–18; colonnade removed *c.* 1960 [*A.P.S.D.*].

HAFFIELD HOUSE, nr. LEDBURY, HEREFS., for William Gordon, 1817–18 [*A.P.S.D.*].

HARDWICKE COURT, GLOS., for T. J. Lloyd Baker, 1817–19 [*V.C.H. Gloucestershire* x, 182; J. Lees-Milne in *C. Life*, 5 July 1973].

WHITTINGHAME HOUSE, EAST LOTHIAN, for James Balfour, 1817–18; altered 1827 by W. Burn [*A.P.S.D.*; R.I.B.A.D.].

LUDLOW CASTLE, SHROPSHIRE, repairs for the 1st Earl of Powis, 1818 [J. M. Crook, 'The Career of Sir Robert Smirke', citing Powis accounts].

GRANGE PARK, HANTS., additions (dem.) for Alexander Baring, *c.* 1818 [J. Mordaunt Crook in *The Country Seat*, ed. Colvin & Harris, 1970, 223].

ARMLEY HOUSE, nr. LEEDS, YORKS. (W.R.), remodelled for Benjamin Gott, *c.* 1818 [J. P. Neale, *Views of Seats*, iv, 1821].

CULTOQUHEY HOUSE, PERTHSHIRE, for Anthony Maxtone, *c.* 1820, Tudor [*N.S.A.* x, 257].

KINFAUNS CASTLE, PERTHSHIRE, for the 15th Lord Gray, 1820–2, castellated [J. P. Neale, *Views of Seats*, 2nd ser., iv, 1828; R.I.B.A.D.].

HEREFORD, POOL COTTAGE (now THE FOSSE), CASTLE GREEN, for Capt. Pendegrass, 1825 [J. M. Crook, 'Career of Sir Robert Smirke', 275].

EDEN HALL, CUMBERLAND, for Sir Philip Musgrave, Bart., 1821; dem. 1934 [*A.P.S.D.*] (F. O. Morris, *Picturesque Views of Seats* ii, 1880, 63).

OULTON HALL, nr. LEEDS, YORKS. (W.R.), for John Blayds, *c.* 1822; reconstructed by Sydney Smirke after fire in 1850 [*A.P.S.D.*].

LONDON, NO. 4 WHITEHALL GARDENS, for Sir Robert Peel, Bart., 1822–4; dem. 1938 [*A.P.S.D.*; *Survey of London* xiii, 198–200, pls. 89–90].

LONDON, NOS. 5 and 6 WHITEHALL GARDENS, for Sir Alexander Grant and Sir Charles Long, 1822–4; dem. 1938 [J. M. Crook, 'The Career of Sir Robert Smirke', 355–6] (*Survey of London* xiii, 193–7).

WARREN HOUSE, STANMORE, MIDDLESEX, additions for himself, 1824, Jacobean; dem. *c.* 1957 [J. M. Crook, 'The Career of Sir Robert Smirke', 274].

EDMOND CASTLE, CUMBERLAND, enlarged and remodelled for Thomas Graham, 1824, Tudor; wing added 1844–5 [*A.P.S.D.*].

LONDON, BARRYMORE HOUSE, NO. 105 PICCADILLY, addition of Doric porch, etc., for the 3rd Marquess of Hertford, *c.* 1824; rebuilt 1850–1 [*A.P.S.D.*].

LONDON, NO. 13 PORTMAN SQUARE, alterations for the 2nd Earl Manvers, *c.* 1825 [*A.P.S.D.*; B.M., Egerton MS. 3527, f. 144].

NORMANBY PARK, LINCS., for Sir Robert Sheffield, Bart., 1825–30; enlarged 1906 [*A.P.S.D.*; John Cornforth in *C. Life*, 17 Aug. 1961].

SEDBURY PARK, nr. CHEPSTOW, GLOS., alterations for George Ormerod, 1826 [*A.P.S.D.*] (G. Ormerod, *Strigulensia*, 1861, frontispiece).

LONDON, NOS. 5 and 6 CARLTON GARDENS, for J. W. Croker and Henry Baring, 1827–30 [*A.P.S.D.*].

ERSKINE HOUSE, RENFREWSHIRE, for the 11th Lord Blantyre, 1828, Gothic [*N.S.A.* vii, 515] (A. H. Millar, *Castles and Mansions of Renfrewshire*, 1898).

PUTNEY HILL HOUSE, SURREY, for the dowager Countess of Guilford, 1828; dem. 1933 [*A.P.S.D.*] (plans in Bodleian Library, MS. North a.17 (R)).

CHOLMONDELEY CASTLE, CHESHIRE, addition of towers for the 2nd Marquess of Cholmondeley 'under the advice of Sir Robert Smirke', *c.* 1829 [G. Ormerod, *History of Cheshire*, ed. Helsby, ii, 1875, 636; Gervase Jackson-Stops in *C. Life*, 26 July 1973].

DRAYTON MANOR, nr. TAMWORTH, STAFFS., for Sir Robert Peel, 1831–5, Elizabethan; gallery added by Sydney Smirke 1846; dem. 1919 [*A.P.S.D.*] (*C. Life*, 28 March 1908).

NUNEHAM PARK, NUNEHAM COURTENAY, OXON., alterations for Edward Vernon Harcourt, Archbishop of York, including addition of south wing, 1832 [*A.P.S.D.*; Mrs. M. L.

Batey, *Nuneham Courtenay, Oxfordshire*, 1970, 14–15] (*C. Life* 7, 14 Nov. 1941).

CLUMBER PARK, NOTTS., unidentified works for the 4th Duke of Newcastle, *c.* 1830 (?); dem. 1938 [*A.P.S.D.*].

MARKHAM CLINTON VICARAGE, NOTTS., for the 4th Duke of Newcastle, 1832–3 [J. Curtis, *Topographical History of Nottinghamshire*, 1843, 179].

WARFIELD HALL, BERKS., enlarged for General Sir John Malcolm, 1832–3 [*Seats and Mansions of Berkshire*, Beard & Co., Twyford, *c.* 1880].

LONDON, NO. 12 BELGRAVE SQUARE, for the 1st Earl Brownlow, *c.* 1833 [*A.P.S.D.*].

SHILLINGTHORPE HALL, LINCS., additions for Dr. John Willis, 1833; dem. *c.* 1950 [*A.P.S.D.*].

STOURTON CASTLE, KINVER, STAFFS., alterations for James Foster, *c.* 1835 [*A.P.S.D.*; G. & R. M. Grazebrook, *History of Stourton Castle*, 1919, 46–7].

LONDON, STAFFORD (now LANCASTER) HOUSE, ST. JAMES'S, acted as supervisory architect for completion of house by Benjamin Wyatt for the 2nd Duke of Sutherland, 1833–8 [Howard Colvin, 'The Architects of Stafford House', *Architectural History* i, 1958; John Cornforth in *C. Life*, 7, 14 Nov. 1968].

SMITH, CHARLES HARRIOTT (1792–1864), was the son of Joseph Smith, a monumental sculptor of Portland Road, Marylebone. He was intended by his father to follow the same trade, but, with the encouragement of Joseph Bonomi, he decided to study architecture, and was admitted to the Royal Academy Schools in 1814. Here he showed unusual skill in drawing the human figure, and was awarded the Gold Medal for Architecture in 1817. It was, however, as a sculptor that he made his career, and the Corinthian capitals and other architectural enrichments of University College, London, the National Gallery and the Royal Exchange were executed by him. He also carved the cornice and frieze of Dorchester House, London, in 1851–3, and the ornamental stonework of Bridgewater House.

He was an occasional competitor for architectural works, including the Nelson Column and the South Kensington Museum, and his exhibits at the Royal Academy included designs for a villa, a church, etc., as well as works of sculpture. His drawing of the 'interior of a pagan temple', exhibited in 1821, was in the possession of the late Sir Leonard Woolley, and a design for a classical church attributed to him is illustrated in *London Topographical Record* xxiii, 1972, 104–5. He also lectured and wrote many articles (notably in the *Builder*) on architectural and aesthetic topics, and was, in his own words, 'a strange mongrel of art, science, literature, and business'. He had a considerable knowledge of geology and mineralogy,

and in 1838 he was one of the four Commissioners appointed to examine and select the most suitable stone for the new Houses of Parliament (see their *Report*, published in 1839 and reprinted 1845). He was a member of the Society of Arts, and in 1855 was elected an honorary member of the Institute of British Architects, a distinction of which he was very proud. He died on 27 October 1864, leaving one son, Percy Gordon Smith, who was for many years architect to the Local Government Board. [*Builder* xxii, 1864, 802; *A.P.S.D.*; *D.N.B.*; R. Gunnis, *Dictionary of British Sculptors*, 1968, 354–5.]

SMITH, CHARLES S— (*c.* 1790–), a pupil of Sir Jeffry Wyatville, was admitted to the Royal Academy Schools in 1808 at the age of 18. He exhibited at the Academy between 1808[1] and 1816, and again in 1828. He established himself in Warwickshire (either in Warwick or in Leamington), and nearly all his recorded works were in that county. None of them is of special distinction. Unexecuted designs by him are among the Ettington papers in the Warwickshire Record Office and the Wollaton papers in Nottingham University Library.

LEAMINGTON SPA, WARWICKS., THE ROYAL BATHS AND PUMP ROOM, 1813–14; largely rebuilt 1926 [Moncrieff's *Guide to Leamington Spa*, 1833, 17].

STONELEIGH ABBEY, WARWICKS., works for J. H. Leigh, including castellated stables, 1813 [drawings at Stoneleigh].

LEAMINGTON SPA, WARWICKS., THE REGENT HOTEL, 1819 [Moncrieff's *Guide to Leamington Spa*, 1833, 41].

ADDERBURY, OXON., repairs and additions to an unidentified house for Mrs. Holford Cotton, 1823–4 [*V.C.H. Oxon.* ix, 12].

GROVE PARK, WARWICKS., for the 11th Lord Dormer, 1833–8, Gothic [documents at Grove Park].

TEMPLE BALSALL HOSPITAL, WARWICKS., rebuilt MASTER'S HOUSE, 1835–6 [Temple Balsall Hospital Order Books, *ex inf.* Mr. Anthony Wood].

STONELEIGH ABBEY, WARWICKS., alterations for the 1st Lord Leigh, including Gothic entrance hall, etc., 1837–9 [G. H. Parks, 'Stoneleigh Abbey', *Trans. Birmingham Archaeological Soc.* lxxix, 1964, 83–4].

SMITH, DAVID (–*c.* 1845), of Dundee, was an assistant of James Black (*q.v.*) from 1836, and continued his practice after his death in 1841. He designed the PRINCES STREET CONGREGATIONAL CHAPEL, DUNDEE, 1839, dem. [chapel records, *ex inf.* Mr. David Walker]; MENMUIR PARISH

---

[1] He was probably the 'S. Smith' who exhibited at the Academy from Wyatville's office in 1807.

CHURCH, ANGUS, 1842 [S.R.O., HR 565/4–5, bundle 14]; ARBROATH INFIRMARY, 1843–4, illustrated in *Builder* ii, 1844, 494–5; and added a wing to ARBROATH TOWN HALL in 1844 [*Dundee Advertiser*, 19 April 1844].

SMITH, FRANCIS (1672–1738) and WILLIAM (1661–1724), were sons of Francis Smith, a bricklayer of The Wergs, nr. Tettenhall in Staffordshire. William, his second son, was baptized on 1 April 1661, Francis, his youngest son, on 4 January 1671/2. Like their elder brother Richard (1658–1726), they were both brought up in the building trade, William apparently as a bricklayer, Francis as a mason. They often worked in partnership, and by the time of William's death they had become the leading master builders in the Midland counties of England. William died on 21 August 1724, in his 64th year, and was buried at Tettenhall, where Francis erected a monument to his memory on which he was described as an 'Architect Eminent in his profession'. Though he sometimes built to the designs of others (*e.g.* at Whitchurch Church) there can be no doubt that he normally acted as his own architect, *e.g.* at Stanford Hall and the churches at Lincoln, Burton-on-Trent and Newcastle-under-Lyme. Stanford was a somewhat old-fashioned house for its date, and with their large round-headed windows and rather coarse Tuscan arcades, his churches are handsome but provincial works that make no attempt to be original. Their immediate prototype appears to have been the church which Smith built at Whitchurch in Shropshire to the designs of John Barker, who was following the precedents afforded by Wren's City churches in London.

William Smith was based at The Wergs, but it was at Warwick that Francis lived and worked for over thirty years, and as 'Francis Smith of Warwick' he is celebrated as one of the most successful master builders in English history. His connection with Warwick appears to date from 1697 when, in conjunction with his brother, he contracted to rebuild the nave and tower of St. Mary's Church after the fire of 1694, in accordance with the designs of Sir William Wilson (*q.v.*). In 1702, while still engaged in this task, he married a Warwick girl named Anne Lea, and subsequently settled in the town. Although it was the rebuilding of Warwick that gave him an opportunity of which he no doubt took full advantage, his subsequent career was based on the patronage of the Midland gentry, many of whom employed him to build their country houses. A list of the country houses with which he was concerned either as architect or as builder (and usually in both capacities) will be found below. It is divided into those for whose authorship there is documentary evidence, and those whose attribution to Smith rests at present only on stylistic evidence. If this list is analysed topographically it will be seen that there are houses by Francis Smith or his brother William in all the Midland counties except (apparently) Nottinghamshire and Herefordshire, and that nearly all of them fall within a fifty-mile radius of Warwick. Chronologically there are too many imprecise or incomplete dates for a satisfactory analysis, but it is at least evident that there must have been years when Francis Smith had three, four or even five major country houses on hand at once.

Of the business methods which enabled Smith to maintain this remarkable output there is, unfortunately, little evidence. None of his personal accounts or papers are known to have survived, and the documentation of many of his houses is incomplete. By trade a mason, he maintained a yard at the 'Marble House' in Warwick from which he supplied chimney-pieces and statuary marble-work such as the monument to Sir Justinian Isham in Lamport Church, for which he was paid £87 in 1732. But, like other enterprising Georgian master builders, he and his brother were prepared to build a whole house 'by the great', performing the masonry themselves and sub-contracting the carpentry and other trades. In 1700 William Smith was ready to build Stanford Hall for Sir Roger Cave on this basis, and in 1710 he offered 'to performe all Carpenters Bricklayers & Masons worke' at Cholmondeley Hall for a certain sum and to be responsible for the joinery and plasterwork too. There are indications that the Smiths dealt in timber as well as in stone and marble. In 1712 William Smith was buying timber from Lord Cholmondeley's woods in Cheshire to roof the church he was building at Whitchurch, and a reference in Francis Smith's will (1736) to 'all my stock of Marble and Timber' implies some involvement in the raw material of carpentry, if not in its actual workmanship. More research into this aspect of Smith's business is needed. Meanwhile it may be noted that, like other eighteenth-century master builders, he was prepared both to build houses to his own designs and to make designs to be carried out by others. When acting purely in a supervisory capacity he charged the 5 per cent fee which was standard remuneration of an architect throughout the eighteenth and nineteenth centuries. 'One shilling in the Pound' was, he told Sir Justinian Isham, 'my usuall Pay from other Gentlemen', and at Ditchley he asked 'five pounds for every Hundred I have paid, & for my own trouble, Journeys, proffits out of my workmen, & measuring the work'. Whether as builder or as surveyor he enjoyed a reputation for honesty which no doubt helps to explain his popularity among the Midland gentry. In 1707 a London surveyor called Robert Jones considered that it would be greatly to Lord Cholmondeley's advantage to employ 'one Smith that

747

does great deal of busness in the Contry and they have done a great deal of worke thearabout & in Warwick you may easy hear of them for [they] are brothers both masters and very good Workmen'. When the redoubtable Sarah, Duchess of Marlborough, was building a house at Wimbledon in Surrey she insisted 'that Mr. Smith of Warwickshire the Builder may be employed to make Contracts and to Measure the Work and to doe every thing in his Way that is necessary to Compleat the Work as far as the Distance he is at will give him Leave to do'. Francis Smith was almost certainly the unnamed builder whom Sir Roger Cave recommended to Sir John Langham of Cottesbrooke as 'as honest a dealor as the Kingdom has and as retionable', and when he died in 1738 Sir Edmund Isham was not alone in lamenting the loss of 'our honest Builder Mr. Smith of Warwick'.

Honesty and reliability were the qualities which stood Francis Smith in good stead rather than any great distinction as an architectural designer. One eighteenth-century critic who had seen several of his houses noted that although 'all of them (are) convenient and handsome ... there is a great sameness in the plans, which proves he had but little invention'.[1] The typical Smith house is, indeed, easily recognizable. It is three stories in height, and the centre is emphasized by slight projection or recession. The fenestration is uniform throughout, and there is little external ornamentation other than that provided by keystones, architraves, aprons, quoins and a balustraded parapet. On the ground floor the centre contains only two rooms – a hall and a saloon – and the staircase is set to one side in one of the flanks. Superb plasterwork and joinery – there is marquetry too at Davenport and Mawley – may create some splendid interiors, but the spatial effects are simple and unenterprising. Essentially it is the standard late seventeenth-century country house, typified by Belton (Lincs.), brought up to date by the substitution of a balustraded parapet for a hipped roof (at William Smith's Stanford even this concession to modernity is dispensed with). Such are Umberslade, Alfreton, Kinlet, Meriden, Newbold Revel, Wingerworth and Wynnstay. Of the same family, but with variations such as the substitution of pilasters for quoins, are Davenport, Mawley, Shenstone, Swynnerton, Buntingsdale and Berwick. In the first quarter of the century the trimmings are generally of a vernacular baroque character, but thereafter they become progressively more 'correct' under the influence of Gibbs and the Palladians.

The list given below does, however, include four exceptional houses which do not conform to the standard Smith pattern: Kedleston, Chicheley, Stoneleigh and Sutton Scarsdale. Smith's Kedleston (pulled down to make way for the existing house by Paine and Adam) was based on a rectangular plan with projecting corner pavilions and seems to have derived from Ragley in Warwickshire (1679–83), a house with which Robert Hooke was concerned, though the basic design was apparently due to the Warwick master carpenter, Roger Hurlbut. Hanbury in Worcestershire (1701) is another example, though not by Smith, and Calke Abbey in Derbyshire (1701–3) a third. It is tempting to attribute Calke to Smith, but his name does not occur in the building accounts and its authorship remains a mystery. The special characteristics of Chicheley, with its illusionistic baroque front and Borrominesque doorways, are best seen as evidence of the personal taste of its owner, Sir John Chester, and his connoisseur friends, rather than of Francis Smith's unaided invention. Stoneleigh represents a somewhat inept attempt to use a giant order in the grand baroque manner, but at Sutton Scarsdale Smith produced a notable façade in which a giant Corinthian order is used with an assurance that is quite unexpected. Gibbs's engraved design for the University buildings at Cambridge of 1721 could have suggested several of the essential elements of this front, including the three-quarter Corinthian columns and the channelled masonry. Indeed, the contrast between the confident grandeur of Sutton Scarsdale and Stoneleigh's gauche assemblage of overcrowded windows and leggy pilasters is so striking that one cannot help suspecting a helping hand from Gibbs himself. However, it is Francis Smith who alone appears as 'gentleman architect' on the lead plate (now lost) which also recorded the names of Edward Poynton of Nottingham, carver, Thomas Eboral of Warwick, joiner, Francis Butcher of Duckmanton, carpenter, John (?) Reading of Derby, painter, Joshua Needham of Derby, plasterer, and other craftsmen employed in the building and adorning of this magnificent house, now an empty shell since its interiors were dismantled in 1920. As Reading and Needham were employed at Ditchley, and as Poynton and Eboral worked at both Ditchley and Chicheley, it looks as if we have here a list of Smith's regular associates.

In his later years Smith put on the weight that is all too apparent in an unflattering portrait painted by Winstanley. But his energies appear to have been undiminished. 'It is unlucky', wrote Dr. George Clarke of All Souls College in February 1730, 'that Mr. Smith is grown so unweildy and engaged in so much business.' When he died in April 1738 at the age of 66, he left a flourishing business and an estate at Knowle in

---

[1] In a letter from the Hon. Daines Barrington, F.S.A., to the Rev. Mr. Norris, dated 22 December 1784, and read before the Society of Antiquaries on 20 January 1785.

Warwickshire that he had bought from Sir Fulk Greville for £10,000. He had twice been Mayor of Warwick (in 1713–14 and 1728–9). He was buried in St. Mary's Church, but there is no record of any monument to his memory. Several portraits are, however, preserved. One in the Court House at Warwick is reproduced in *Birmingham Arch. Soc.'s Trans.* lix, 1935, pl. iv, and by Christopher Hussey, *English Country Houses: Early Georgian*, 1955, 36. Another, from Stoneleigh Abbey, is now on loan to the Warwick Museum; it is reproduced in *Connoisseur* cxviii, Dec. 1946, 73. A third, by W. Winstanley, belongs to the Thursby family, formerly of Abington Hall, Northants., and now of Culverlands, Burghfield Common, Berks. There is an engraving of it by A. Vanhacken, with a dedication to J. H. Thursby, the builder of Abington Hall. There is also a bust of Smith by Rysbrack, which was bequeathed to the Radcliffe Trustees by Francis Hiorne in 1789, and is now in the Radcliffe Library at Oxford. It is dated 1741 (three years after Smith's death), and appears to be based on the Abington Hall portrait. It was intended by Hiorne to occupy a vacant niche in the Library, of which Smith had been one of the mason-contractors in 1737, although he did not live to see its completion (see E. G. Tibbits, 'A Bust by Rysbrack', *Bodleian Library Record* i, 1941, 230–4).

Francis Smith had four sons and one daughter, but only two of the sons survived their father. William, the elder, to whom he left 'all my stock of Marble and Timber ... in my Marble Yard in Warwick', continued his father's business and is separately noticed below. Richard died in 1753, aged 39. Neither had any children. Elizabeth, the daughter, married John Stokes of Dippens, and it was her son, Francis Stokes, who eventually inherited Smith's property.

Among some Stokes family papers formerly (1947) in the possession of Mrs. Calcott Stokes there is a memoir of Mrs. Nancy Stokes (d. 1838), whose husband was Francis Stokes's second son and eventual heir.[1] In this document Francis Smith is described as 'the architect ... from whose plans the church of St. Philip in Birmingham, the great mansions of Ombersley Court, Kinlet, Patshull, Davenport House etc. arose'. This evidently represents the account of Francis Smith's works handed down in the Stokes family, and although it is demonstrably incorrect in connecting him with St. Philip's, Birmingham, and Patshull House, his responsibility for Ombersley, Davenport and Kinlet is confirmed by other sources. A letter at Ombersley written in 1861 by G. W. L. Childe, then the owner of Kinlet, records an independent tradition that Kinlet,

Ombersley, Mawley and Buntingsdale were designed by Francis Smith, and a MS. history of the Fitzherbert family, compiled in 1828 and preserved at Swynnerton, ascribes Swynnerton, Wingerworth and Mawley to the same architect, but wrongly names him as Carr of York. Apart from these somewhat doubtful family traditions, the list of Smith's works has to be pieced together from the various sources cited below, and it will doubtless be increased as the result of further research.

[*Tettenhall Parish Register*, ed. P. W. L. Adams, Staffordshire Parish Register Soc. 1930; *Warwick County Records*, vii: *Quarter Sessions Records 1674–1682*, 1946, cxii; Francis Smith's will, P.C.C. 162 BRODREPP; B.M., Add. MS. 29265, ff. 227–9 (for Smith's Knowle estate); H. M. Colvin, 'Francis Smith of Warwick 1672–1738', *Warwickshire History* ii (2), 1972/3.]

SECULAR BUILDINGS DESIGNED OR BUILT BY WILLIAM AND FRANCIS SMITH

1. Authenticated Works

UMBERSLADE HALL, WARWICKS., for Andrew Archer, *c.* 1695–1700; altered in nineteenth century [W. Field, *History of Warwick*, 1815, 374, where the house is said to have been built 'by John Smith', referred to elsewhere in the book as the builder of St. Mary's, Warwick] (*Vitruvius Britannicus* iii, 1731, pl. 101; *Wren Soc.* xvii, pl. xlii).

STANFORD HALL, LEICS., designed and built by William Smith for Sir Francis Cave, Bart., 1697–1700. The stables (completed 1737) were added by Sir Verney Cave to the designs of Francis Smith, to whom the remodelling of the east front may also be attributed. The interior of the great hall was altered by William Smith, junior, in 1745 [estimates and contracts at Stanford; drawings and letter among Verney archives at Claydon House, Bucks.] (*C. Life*, 4, 11 and 18 Dec. 1958).

MELBOURNE HALL, DERBYSHIRE, unspecified work by Francis Smith for Thomas Coke, 1698 and 1725–6 [accounts and correspondence at Melbourne].

KEDLESTON HALL, DERBYSHIRE, for Sir Nathaniel Curzon, *c.* 1700; rebuilt 1758 onwards [plan at Kedleston inscribed 'Kedleston built by Smith', reproduced in *Warwickshire History* ii (2), 1972–3, 9].

SUTTON COLDFIELD RECTORY, WARWICKS., built by William Smith for the Rev. John Riland, 1701; dem. 1936 [W. K. R. Bedford, *History of the Rilands of Sutton Coldfield*, 1889, 19–20].

STRATFORD-ON-AVON, WARWICKS., THE VICARAGE (now the Headmaster's House) built by 'Mr. Smith', 1702–3 [Stratford Chamberlains' Accounts, 1702–3, *ex inf.* Miss Molly Barratt].

[1] A version of this document was printed by John Randall, *A Guide to Worfield*, Madeley 1887, 102.

CHOLMONDELEY HALL, CHESHIRE, remodelled by William Smith for the 1st Earl of Cholmondeley, 1704–13; dem. c. 1805 [Gervase Jackson-Stops in C. Life, 19 July 1973] (Vitruvius Britannicus ii, 1715, pls. 31–4, iii, 1725, pls. 79–80).

SANDWELL PARK, STAFFS., rebuilt by William Smith for the 1st Earl of Dartmouth, 1705–11; dem. 1928 [V.C.H. Staffs. xvii, 19, with plan] (S. Shaw, History of Staffordshire ii, 1801, 128, plate).

HEYTHROP HOUSE, OXON., built 'by Smith' to the designs of Thomas Archer (q.v.) for the Duke of Shrewsbury, c. 1705–8 [notebook (1759–61) of Edward Knight in Kidderminster Public Library].

TRENTHAM HALL, STAFFS., built by William Smith for the 1st Lord Gower, c. 1707–10 [Staffordshire Record Office, D 868/9/52, 53, 55]; additions by Francis Smith 1736–7 [ibid., D 593/P/16/2/4/20 and accounts for 1736–7]; altered 1764–78, remodelled 1838; dem. 1910 (C. Life, 25 Jan. 1968).

DUNCHURCH SCHOOL, WARWICKS., built by Francis Smith, 1708–9 [accounts in Warwickshire Record Office].

CLIFTON CAMPVILLE HALL, STAFFS., for Sir Charles Pye, Bart., 'who built the wings before the centre, and was unable to finish it according to his plans'. The wings are said to have been built in 1708. A plan in Francis Smith's hand showing both the existing wings and the projected main building is among Pye papers in Sheffield City Library (Elmhirst 1337). For an alternative design for the main building by William Dickinson dated 1710, see above, p. 259.

BAGINTON HALL, WARWICKS., built by Francis Smith for William Bromley, c. 1710; destroyed by fire 1889 [F. L. Colvile, Worthies of Warwickshire, 1869, 61, note, citing building accounts now lost].

WOLVERHAMPTON, STAFFS., THE GRAMMAR SCHOOL, JOHN STREET, built by William Smith, 1712–14; converted into shops 1877 [G. P. Mander, History of Wolverhampton Grammar School, 1913, 179].

STONELEIGH ABBEY, WARWICKS, largely rebuilt by Francis Smith for the 3rd Lord Leigh, 1714–26 [G. H. Parks, 'Stoneleigh Abbey', Trans. Birmingham Arch. Soc. lxxix, 1964, 78; Andor Gomme in Archaeological Jnl. cxxviii, 1976, 246–51] (C. Hussey, English Country Houses: Early Georgian, 1955, 37–9).

STONELEIGH, WARWICKS., STONE FARM HOUSE, built by Francis Smith for the 3rd Lord Leigh, 1716 [Shakespeare's Birthplace Trust Record Office, Stratford, Leigh papers, Stoneleigh no. 38].

CROOME COURT, WORCS., stables built by 'Mr. Smith' for the 4th Earl of Coventry, 1716–19

[account-book of Gilbert, Earl of Coventry, at Antony House, Cornwall, CVA/H3/22].

CHICHELEY HALL, BUCKS., built by Francis Smith for Sir John Chester, Bart., 1719–21; stables 1723–5 [Joan D. Tanner, 'The Building of Chicheley Hall', Records of Bucks. xvii, 1961; see also Arthur Oswald in C. Life, 9, 16, 23 May 1936, and Marcus Binney in C. Life, 13, 20 Feb. 1975] (J. Lees-Milne, English Country Houses: Baroque, 1970, 227–35).

CAPESTHORNE HALL, CHESHIRE, wings built by William Smith for John Ward, 1720; house rebuilt by Francis Smith for John Ward, 1732–3; enlarged by E. Blore 1839–42; rebuilt by A. Salvin after a fire in 1861 [contract of Jan. 1719/20 and estimate of Feb. 1731/2 among Bromley-Davenport papers in John Rylands Library, Manchester; A. H. & S. M. Gomme, 'Who Designed Capesthorne Hall?' Trans. Historic Soc. of Lancs. and Cheshire cxxi, 1969].

MERIDEN HALL, WARWICKS., remodelled by Francis Smith for Martin Baldwin, c. 1720 [Birmingham Public Library, Digby deposit, 7313L/19–21, 98].

DITCHLEY HOUSE, OXON., built by Francis Smith to the designs of James Gibbs (q.v.) for the 2nd Earl of Lichfield, 1720–31 [Dillon papers in Oxfordshire County Record Office show that Francis Smith acted as mason-contractor and surveyor] (J. Gibbs, Book of Architecture, 1728, pl. 39; C. Life, 9–16 June 1934; C. Hussey, English Country Houses: Early Georgian, 1955, 66–71).

HAMPTON LUCY RECTORY, WARWICKS., built by Francis and William Smith, 1721 [Alice Fairfax-Lucy, Charlecote and the Lucys, 1958, 189].

BUNTINGSDALE HALL., SALOP., built by 'Smith of Warwick' for Bulkeley Mackworth, completed 1721; enlarged 1857 [S. Leighton, Shropshire Houses, 1901, 30; H. A. Tipping in C. Life, 3 Nov. 1917, citing accounts now lost, including an agreement to supply Smith with 'a pad nag to ride hither from Warwick' in order to inspect the works; H. A. Tipping, English Homes, Period V (i), 1921, 193–8].

WILTON, HEREFS., unexecuted project by Francis Smith for mansion for the Duke of Chandos, 1723 [C. H. C. & M. I. Baker, James Brydges, Duke of Chandos, 1949, 213, 276].

OMBERSLEY COURT, WORCS., built by William & Francis Smith for Samuel Sandys, 1723–6; exterior remodelled by John Webb 1812–14 [bills at Ombersley: the first receipt for £400, dated 4 Dec. 1723, is signed by both William and Francis Smith. William died in 1724 and all the other payments, amounting to some £1500, are to Francis] (C. Life, 2, 9, 16 Jan, 1953).

SUTTON SCARSDALE, DERBYSHIRE, built by Francis Smith for the 4th Earl of Scarsdale, begun 1724; unroofed 1920, now a ruin; three rooms are in Philadelphia Museum of Art. An inscription on a lead plate, now lost, recorded that:

> This house was begun to be rebuilt in the year 1724 by the order of the Right Honourable Nicholas, Earl of Scarsdale. Francis Smith of Warwick, gentleman architect, Edward Poynton of Nottingham, gentleman carver, Thomas Eboral of Warwick, gentleman joiner, Francis Butcher of Duckmanton, carpenter, Albert Artari, gentleman, and Francis Vessali, gentleman, Italians, who did the stuke work, Joshua [? John] Reading of Derby, gentleman painter, Joshua Needham of Derby, gentleman plasterer, William Jeffrey of Chesterfield, plumer, Thomas How of Westminster, gentleman upholsterer, John Wilks of Birmingham, gentleman locksmith, John Lillyman, gentleman steward, John Christian, gentleman gardener, John Nott, gentleman keeper.

[H. A. Tipping in *C. Life*, 15 Feb. 1919, and *English Homes, Period V* (i), 1921, 199–206] (*C. Life*, 16 April 1970).

ALFRETON HALL, DERBYSHIRE, for Rowland Morewood, 1724–5; dem. *c*. 1960 [Derby Public Library, Morewood Account Book no. 3. The only reference to Smith is a payment 'for going to Mansfield Post-House to put in a Letter for Mr. Smith', but this, coupled with the architectural character of the house, makes Smith's responsibility for the design almost, if not quite, certain].

TEMPLE BALSALL HOSPITAL, WARWICKS., rebuilt by Francis Smith except Master's Lodge, *c*. 1724–6 [MS. Minutes of the Trustees, *ex inf*. Mr. Anthony Wood].

WARWICK, THE COURT HOUSE, designed and built by Francis Smith, 1725–30 [*Trans. Birmingham Arch. Soc.* lix, 1935, 72–3].

DAVENPORT HALL, SALOP., designed and built by Francis Smith for Henry Davenport, 1726 [F. Calvert & W. West, *Picturesque Views and Descriptions of ... Staffordshire and Shropshire*, 1831, 124] (*C. Life*, 27 June, 4, 11 July 1952).

SHARDELOES HOUSE, BUCKS., 'new building' erected under supervision of Francis Smith for Montague Garrard Drake, 1726–7; house reconstructed 1758–66 by S. Leadbetter and R. & J. Adam [Bucks. Record Office, Shardeloes papers, bundle 9, 21–32; receipt books, bundle 9, 25; accounts, bundle 2/174, *ex inf*. Mr. T. P. Hudson].

KINLET HALL, SALOP., designed and built by Francis Smith for William Lacon Childe, 1727–9; library added 1827 [S. Leighton, *Shropshire Houses*, 1901, 42; Stokes memoir cited above].

CALKE ABBEY, DERBYSHIRE. Francis Smith built a

new flight of steps up to the front door to the designs of James Gibbs in 1727–8; removed *c*. 1790 [accounts at Calke Abbey][1] (K. Downes, *English Baroque Architecture*, 1966, pl. 383).

LAMPORT RECTORY, NORTHANTS., designed and built by Francis Smith for Sir Justinian Isham, Bart., 1727–30 [Isham papers at Lamport Hall, correspondence 2826 and I.L. 3959, estimate].

LAMPORT HALL, NORTHANTS., alterations and additions by Francis Smith for Sir Justinian Isham, Bart., including the addition of the wings, 1732–8, completed by William Smith, junior [Sir Gyles Isham, 'The Architectural History of Lamport', *Reports and Papers of the Northants. Architectural and Archaeological Soc.* lvii, 1951] (*C. Life*, 26 Sept., 3–10 Oct. 1952).

CAPESTHORNE HALL, CHESHIRE, Francis Smith rebuilt house for John Ward, 1732–3 [see above].

WIMBLEDON HOUSE, SURREY, Francis Smith employed as surveyor of house designed by Lord Pembroke and Roger Morris for Sarah, Duchess of Marlborough, 1732–3; destroyed by fire 1785 [M. P. G. Draper in *C. Life*, 2 Aug. 1962].

STANFORD HALL, NORTHANTS., alterations and additions by Francis Smith for Sir Verney Cave, Bart. (d. 1734), including the quadrangular stable-block completed by Sir Thomas Cave in 1737 (the date on the vane) [correspondence at Claydon House, Bucks., including an estimate by Smith of which there is a contemporary copy at Stanford] (*C. Life*, 4, 11, 18 Dec. 1958).

BROGYNTYN, SALOP., built by Francis Smith for William Owen, 1735–6; portico added 1814–15 [National Library of Wales, Owen papers 1582, 1852, 2008].

WYNNSTAY, DENBIGHSHIRE, built by Francis and his son William Smith for Sir Watkin Williams-Wynn, Bart., 1736–9; remodelled by James Wyatt 1785; destroyed by fire 1858 [Peter Howell in *C. Life*, 23, 30 March 1972].

TEMPLE BALSALL HOUSE, WARWICKS., rebuilt 1738–9 after Francis Smith had been asked to provide an estimate [Minutes of the Trustees of Temple Balsall Hospital, *ex inf*. Mr. Anthony Wood].

2. *Attributed Works*

DUDMASTON HALL, nr. BRIDGNORTH, SALOP., for Sir Thomas Wolryche, Bart., *c*. 1695; attic storey and other alterations *c*. 1820 [stylistic

---

[1] There are no references to the Smiths in the accounts for building Calke Abbey in 1701–3, and the authorship of the design is uncertain. The architectural historian will do well to remember the old Derbyshire saying: 'like Calke House, the thing is done but nobody did it'.

attribution, based on close resemblance to
Stanford Hall, supported by a letter dated 10
April 1695 from George Weld of Willey asking
Andrew Archer of Umberslade to lend a plan
or model of his house to his son-in-law Sir
Thomas Wolryche (Salop. R.O., uncatalogued
Forester MSS.)].

COTTESBROOKE HALL, NORTHANTS., for Sir John
Langham, Bart., 1703–13 [Sir Gyles Isham &
Bruce Bailey in C. Life, 19 Feb. 1970] (C. Life,
15, 22 Feb. 1936, 17, 24 March 1955).

ELFORD HALL, STAFFS., for the 4th Earl of Berkshire, begun 1710; dem. 1964 [stylistic attribu-
tion].

KISLINGBURY RECTORY, NORTHANTS., for the Rev.
John Perkins, c. 1710 [stylistic attribution].

SHENSTONE PARK, STAFFS., for John Strickson, c.
1710/20 [stylistic attribution] (S. Shaw, Staffordshire ii, 1801, 46, engraving).

HEWELL GRANGE, WORCS., for the 2nd Earl of Plymouth, 1712; portico added 1815; a ruin since
c. 1890 [stylistic attribution] (T. Nash, History
of Worcs. ii, 1782, 403; J. P. Neale, Views of
Seats vi, 1823).

WARWICK, house in Market Place known as
'Abbotsford', for Francis Smith's father-in-
law, — Lea, 1714; restored 1963.

NEWBOLD REVEL HALL, WARWICKS., for Sir Fulwar
Skipwith, Bart., 1716 [stylistic attribution]
(Vitruvius Britannicus ii, 1717, pl. 94; C. Life,
7 March 1903; S. M. Stanislaus, Newbold
Revel, 1949).

DALLINGTON HALL, NORTHANTS., for Sir Joseph
Jekyll, c. 1720 [stylistic attribution] (J. P.
Neale, Views of Seats, 1st ser., i, 1818; J. A.
Gotch, Squires' Homes of Northants, 1939, 34).

SANDYWELL PARK, GLOS., addition of wings for the
1st Lord Conway, c. 1720/30 [stylistic attribu-
tion] (J. Rudder, History of Gloucestershire,
1779, 414–15).

CHILLINGTON HALL, STAFFS., south front for Peter
Giffard, 1724 [Arthur Oswald in C. Life, 13,
20 Feb. 1948].

SWYNNERTON HALL, STAFFS., for Thomas Fitzherbert, 1725–9; hall altered 1811–12 and 1974;
new entrance 1949–50 [stylistic attribution,
supported by a confused tradition current in
the early nineteenth century that the house was
designed by the architect of Ince Blundell (sic),
Wingerworth and Mawley: see MS. history of
the Fitzherbert family at Swynnerton by
Michael Jones, 1828, p. 160] (J. P. Neale,
Views of Seats, 1st ser., iii, 1820).

WINGERWORTH HALL, DERBYSHIRE, for Sir
Thomas Winsor Hunloke, Bart. 1726–9; dem.
c. 1930 [H. A. Tipping in C. Life, 29 Jan. 1910,
and English Homes, Period V (i), 1921, 207–
16].

MAWLEY HALL, SALOP., for Sir Edward Blount,
Bart., 1730 [H. A. Tipping in C. Life, 2 July
1910; H. A. Tipping, English Homes, Period V

(i), 1921, 217–28; Mary Parry, 'Mawley Hall',
Archaeological Jnl. cxiii, 1956, 194–5].

BERWICK HOUSE, SALOP., for Thomas Powys,
1731; altered by R. Mylne 1780; south-west
front rebuilt 1878 [stylistic attribution] (F.
Leach, The County Seats of Shropshire,
Shrewsbury 1891, 1).

ABINGTON HALL, NORTHANTS., refronted for J. H.
Thursby, c. 1738–43 [stylistic attribution supported by the fact that the Thursby portrait
of Francis Smith came from Abington] (J. A.
Gotch, Squires' Homes of Northamptonshire,
1939, 34–5).

CHURCHES DESIGNED OR BUILT BY
WILLIAM AND FRANCIS SMITH

WARWICK, ST. MARY'S CHURCH, rebuilt by William
& Francis Smith to the designs of Sir William
Wilson, 1698–1704, Gothic [Warwickshire
Record Office, records of the Commissioners
for rebuilding Warwick after the fire of 1694;
P. B. Chatwin, 'The Rebuilding of St. Mary's
Church, Warwick', Trans. Birmingham and
Midland Institute lxv, 1943–4].

attributed: ABBOTS BROMLEY CHURCH, STAFFS.,
west tower, 1702–7 [stylistic attribution: only
the date of the tower is recorded in the parish
records].

WHITCHURCH CHURCH, SALOP., rebuilt by William
Smith to the designs of John Barker (q.v.),
1712–13; interior refaced 1902 [MS. churchwardens' accounts].

attributed: LICHFIELD, STAFFS., ST. MARY'S
CHURCH., 1717–21; rebuilt 1868–70 [stylistic
attribution: see drawings by Buckler in B.M.,
Add. MS. 36386, ff. 219, 251. The churchwardens' accounts show that 'Mr' (probably
William) Smith had been consulted when the
spire threatened in 1715].

BURTON-ON-TRENT CHURCH, STAFFS., rebuilt by
William and Richard Smith, 1719–26, completed by Francis Smith after William's death
in 1724; restored 1886–1904 [W. Molyneux,
Burton-on-Trent, 1869; MS. Vestry Minutes].

NEWCASTLE-UNDER-LYME CHURCH, STAFFS.,
rebuilt by William Smith except west tower,
1720–1; rebuilt 1873–6 [R. Fenton, St. Giles
Parish Church, Newcastle-under-Lyme,
reprinted from the Staffordshire Times, June
1876].

LINCOLN, ST. PETER-AT-ARCHES CHURCH, c. 1720–
4; taken down 1932, and rebuilt in the suburbs
of Lincoln as St. Giles, 1936. The original
church was of Roche Abbey stone: it was
rebuilt in brick with the old stone dressings.
The urns and balustrades had been renewed
in the 1820s, and there were alterations by S.
S. Teulon in 1853–4. A plan of the church by
Teulon is in the Diocesan Records (Fac. 11/
44). The Corporation Minute Book shows (29

Oct. 1723) that the contractor was a 'Mr. Smith' and a visitor noted in 1725 that 'the mason and architect was Smith of Warwick' [Hist. MSS. Comm., *Portland* vi, 84].

DERBY, ALL SAINTS CHURCH, nave and chancel rebuilt by William and Francis Smith to the designs of James Gibbs, 1723–5. In 1719 'Mr. Smith of Warwick' made a design and estimate, but objections were raised, and in 1723 a new plan 'contrived by Mr. Gibbs and Mr. Smiths' was adopted. William and Francis Smith were the joint contractors, but owing to William's death in 1724, only his brother's name appears in the accounts after that date. [J. C. Cox and W. H. St. J. Hope, *Chronicles of All Saints Derby*, 1881, 63–80].

SIBSON CHURCH, LEICS., nave and west tower rebuilt by Thomas Moor 'according to a draught given in by Francis Smith', 1725–6 [contract in Leicestershire Record Office, DE 373/3].

MONMOUTH, ST. MARY'S CHURCH, rebuilt except steeple, 1736–7; remodelled by G. E. Street 1881–2 ['by one Smith of Warwick' according to Thomas Wakeman, 'On the Priory of Monmouth', *Collectanea Archaeologica* i, 1862, 285; no parish records of this period survive].

GAINSBOROUGH CHURCH, LINCS., nave and chancel rebuilt, 1736–44. The 'Report of the Committee for Rebuilding Gainsborough Church' in the Lincoln Diocesan Records (Fac. 9/68) shows that Francis Smith made a plan and estimate in 1734, and this is confirmed by the evidence given in 1735 before the House of Commons (*Commons' Jnls.* xxii, 556–7, 619–21; xxiii, 582, 618). There is no mention of Gibbs, who is said to have been the architect of the new church by the Lincolnshire antiquary, E. J. Willson (1787–1854), and by T. Mozley (b. in Gainsborough 1806) in his *Reminiscences* (1855). The parish records of this period have been lost or destroyed.

SMITH, GEORGE (1783–1869), was born at Aldenham, Herts., on 28 September 1783. He was articled to R. F. Brettingham in October 1797, leaving his office in 1802 to become clerk to James Wyatt, D. A. Alexander and C. Beazley in turn. He exhibited at the Royal Academy from 1801 to 1849. In 1810 he was appointed District Surveyor of the Southern Division of the City of London, and in 1814 surveyor to the Mercers' Company, retaining both posts until his death. He was for a time surveyor to the Coopers' Company, of which he was a member and twice Master; and he was also surveyor to the trustees of Morden College, Blackheath. From 1836 to 1842 he was in partnership with his pupil W. Barnes (1807–68) and subsequently with G. B. Williams, also a pupil. He was a Fellow of the Society of Antiquaries, a member of the Sur-

veyors' Club from 1807, and a Fellow of the Institute of British Architects, of which he was Vice-President in 1844–5. His principal works were Whittington's Almshouses at Highgate (Gothic), St. Paul's School (Greek Corinthian), the Corn Exchange in Mark Lane (Greek Doric) and St. Albans Town Hall (Greek Ionic). These were all handsome civic buildings, and were favourably received by contemporary critics.

Smith was a careful and meticulous man whose office was a model of orderliness. His pupils included H. C. Barlow, W. Barnes, James Barr, David Brandon, W. Grellier, George Low, Arthur Scrivenor and G. B. Williams, T. Nichols and A. B. Clayton were assistants. Smith died on 5 January 1869, aged 87. He should not be confused with the cabinet-maker George Smith, who was the author of *A Collection of Designs for Household Furniture*, 1808, etc.

[*A.P.S.D.*; *Builder* xxvii, 1869, 42, 65, 92.]

ALDENHAM LODGE, HERTS., design (perhaps not executed) for the entrance to the grounds of the late G. Mason, exhibited at R.A. 1807.

COLNEY LODGE, HERTS., south front exhibited at R.A. 1810.

CLAY HALL, HERTS., proposed alterations and additions for J. Gosling, exhibited at R.A. 1810.

HORTON KIRBY CHURCH, KENT, rebuilt tower and chancel and other alterations, 1816–17, Gothic [Edward Cresy's notebook in Dartford Public Library, f. 9].

LONDON, ST. MARY MAGDALENE CHURCH, OLD FISH STREET, repairs, 1816; dem. 1886–7 [Guildhall Library MS. 1349, minutes of committee for repairs].

MITCHAM CHURCH, SURREY, rebuilt 1819–22, Gothic [Brayley, *History of Surrey* iv, 92].

LONDON, THE ROYAL EXCHANGE, rebuilt entrance-front and tower, 1820–6; destroyed by fire 1838 [Britton & Pugin, *Public Buildings of London* i, 1825, 292–7].

LONDON, WHITTINGTON'S ALMSHOUSES, HIGHGATE, for the Mercers' Company, 1822, Gothic; dem. 1966 [J. Elmes, *Metropolitan Improvements*, 1831, 141–2 and plate].

LONDON, ST. MICHAEL'S CHURCH, QUEENHITHE, altar-piece, 1823; dem. 1876 [G. Godwin, *The Churches of London* ii, 1839].

LONDON, ST. PAUL'S SCHOOL, ST. PAUL'S CHURCHYARD, for the Mercers' Company, 1823–4; dem. 1884 [J. Elmes, *Metropolitan Improvements*, 1831, 126 and plate].

LONDON COLNEY CHURCH, HERTS., 1825–6, Romanesque [I.C.B.S.].

BLACKHEATH, BROOKLANDS, BLACKHEATH PARK, for himself, 1825 [*A.P.S.D.*].

LONDON, MERCERS' HALL, entrance to Architect's Office, *c.* 1826 [exhib. at R.A.].

LONDON, THE CORN EXCHANGE, MARK LANE,

assisted by A. B. Clayton, 1827–8; dem. 1941 [*A.P.S.D.*; J. Elmes, *Metropolitan Improvements*, 1831, 146–7 and plate; W. H. Leeds, *Supplement* to Britton & Pugin's *Public Buildings of London*, 1838, 9–20].

FINCHLEY, MIDDLESEX, villa 'lately erected' for R. Hughes, exhibited at R.A. 1827.

MEDBURN BRIDGE, HERTS., repairs, 1829 [*Sessions Records of the Liberty of St. Albans 1770–1840* iv, 1923, 182, 184, 215, 218].

LONDON, MERCERS' SCHOOL, COLLEGE HILL, DOW-GATE, 1829–32; dem. *c.* 1894 [J. Watney, 'Mercers' School', *Trans. London and Middlesex Arch. Soc.*, N.S. i, 1898, 135].

ST. ALBANS, HERTS., COURT-HOUSE AND TOWN HALL, 1829–33 [*Sessions Records of the Liberty of St. Albans 1770–1840* iv, 1923, pp. xxix–xxxiv; *V.C.H. Herts.* ii, 472; drawings in Victoria and Albert Museum].

BLACKHEATH, ST. MICHAEL AND ALL ANGELS CHAPEL, 1828–30, Gothic [*A.P.S.D.*].

BROMLEY CHURCH, KENT, rebuilt 1820 except tower; enlarged 1883–4; destroyed by bombing 1940–1 [I.C.B.S.].

HORNSEY CHURCH, MIDDLESEX, rebuilt 1830–3 except tower, Gothic; dem. 1927 [*A.P.S.D.*].

GREENWICH, CROWN AND SCEPTRE TAVERN, the hall, in collaboration with W. Barnes, 1836 [exhib. at R.A. 1837].

LONDON, ST. THOMAS'S CHURCH, ARBOUR STREET, STEPNEY, in collaboration with W. Barnes, 1838, Gothic [exhib. at R.A. 1838].

HORSHAM, SUSSEX, THE GRAMMAR SCHOOL, 1840–1 [*A.P.S.D.*].

LONDON, ST. GEORGE'S WESLEYAN CHAPEL, BACK ROAD, STEPNEY, 1840 [*A.P.S.D.*].

NOAK HILL, ESSEX, ST. THOMAS'S CHURCH, 1841, Tudor [Port, 144–5].

KILREA CHURCH, CO. LONDONDERRY, IRELAND, rebuilt for the Mercers' Company, 1841–2 [*A.P.S.D.*].

LONDON, LONDON BRIDGE RAILWAY STATION, in collaboration with Henry Roberts, 1841–4; rebuilt 1851; dem. 1969 [*Companion to the Almanac*, 1843, 248–9].

LONDON, GRESHAM COLLEGE, BASINGHALL STREET, 1842–3; rebuilt 1912 [*A.P.S.D.*].

LONDON, CHRIST CHURCH SCHOOLS, JOHNSON STREET, MILE END, STEPNEY, 1848–9 [exhib. at R.A. 1849].

NEWLANDS, COPTHORNE, SUSSEX, for himself, 1848–9 [*A.P.S.D.*].

LONDON, PRINTING OFFICES, PILGRIM STREET, LUD-GATE, in collaboration with G. B. Williams, 1860 [*A.P.S.D.*, *s.v.*. 'Williams, G. B.'].

WOODBASTWICK HALL, NORFOLK, altered or rebuilt for John Cator, date uncertain; destroyed by fire 1882 [*A.P.S.D.*].

SMITH, GEORGE (1793–1877) was born at Aberdeen, where in 1818 he endeavoured to

establish himself as an architect. But making no headway against John Smith and Archibald Simpson, he moved to Edinburgh, where according to Redgrave's *Dictionary of Artists* (1878), he became an assistant of William Burn. He practised independently from about 1827, and in 1834 obtained a salaried post as architect to the Edinburgh Improvement Commissioners. In the same year he won the competition sponsored by the Highland Society for the design of 'Cottages for the Labouring Classes' [J. C. Loudon, *Architectural Magazine* i, 1834, 93]. He published his designs in a small book entitled *Essay on the Construction of Cottages suited for the Dwellings of the Labouring Classes, illustrated by Working Plans* (1834). He was also the author of a manual on the *Elements of Architecture*, intended for the use of students attending the architectural lectures at the Edinburgh School of Arts (1827). In Glasgow on Woodlands Hill he designed several handsome terraces of houses for the well-to-do. Latterly he was in partnership with Henry Hardy (1831–1908). He died in Edinburgh in October 1877, aged 84, and was buried in the Warriston Cemetery [information from Mr. David Walker].

DUNDEE, EXCHANGE COFFEE ROOM, now 8–11 EXCHANGE STREET, 1828–30 [C. Mackie, *Historical Description of Dundee*, 1836, 140].

TAYFIELD HOUSE, FORGAN, FIFE, enlarged and remodelled for William Berry, 1829, Jacobethan [drawings at Tayfield] (A. H. Millar, *Fife, Pictorial and Historical* ii, 1895).

GLASGOW, WOODLANDS HILL, the following terraces, etc.: WOODSIDE CRESCENT, 1831; WOODSIDE TERRACE, 1835–42; WOODSIDE PLACE, 1838; LYNEDOCH CRESCENT and LYNEDOCH STREET, 1845 [J. Pagan, *Sketch of the History of Glasgow*, 1847, 181; A. Gomme & D. Walker, *Architecture of Glasgow*, 1968, 279].

KIMMERGHAME, BERWICKSHIRE, lodge for James Bonar, 1835 [drawings at Kimmerghame].

EDINBURGH, 1–12 MELBOURNE PLACE, 1837 [Edinburgh City Archives, Minutes of City Improvement Trust].

GLASGOW, NEWTON PLACE, SAUCHIEHALL STREET, 1837 [A. Gomme & D. Walker, *Architecture of Glasgow*, 1968, 279].

EDINBURGH, ST. JOHN'S CHURCH OF SCOTLAND, VICTORIA STREET (now furniture store), 1838–40, 'in a mixed style of architecture, with a Saxon doorway' [*A.P.S.D.*, *s.v.* 'Edinburgh'].

EDINBURGH, VICTORIA STREET, shops, Mechanics' Library, etc., *c.* 1840–6 [Edinburgh City Archives, Minutes of City Improvement Trust].

EDINBURGH, NORMAL SCHOOL (now Public Health Chambers), JOHNSTON TERRACE, 1844–5, Jacobethan [A. Morgan, *Two Famous Old Edinburgh Colleges*, 1935, 13].

EDINBURGH, NOS. 37–65 LOTHIAN ROAD, designed

1848, not completed until the 1860s [S.R.O., Edinburgh Sasines].

EDINBURGH, NO. 87 WEST BOW, 1850 [Edinburgh City Archives, Minutes of City Improvement Trust].

EDINBURGH, NO. 22 QUEEN STREET, reconstructed in Jacobethan style, 1852; altered 1892 [Edinburgh Dean of Guild records, 7 May 1852, *ex inf.* Mr. David Walker].

SMITH, GEORGE H— (*c.* 1805–), was a pupil of T. F. Hunt and was admitted to the Royal Academy Schools in 1824 at the age of 19. He exhibited at the R.A. from London addresses between 1825 and 1837, but no trace of him has been found thereafter. His exhibited drawings included STOBARS HALL, nr. KIRKBY STEPHEN, WESTMORLAND, shown as 'now erecting' in 1825; ' 'a roadside inn designed for Chenies, Bucks.' (1830); 'a park lodge designed for Sir William Somerville, Bart.' (1833), probably at SOMERVILLE, NAVAN, CO. MEATH, IRELAND; a cottage designed for the antiquary Nicholas Carlisle, 'to be built in Sussex' (1835); CULVERHOUSE, HOLCOMBE BURNELL, nr. EXETER, 'now erecting' in Tudor Gothic style for the Rev. Richard Stephens (1835); alterations and additions carried out to BIFRONS HOUSE, PATRIXBOURNE, KENT (dem. 1948), for the Dowager Marchioness Conyngham (1835); and the west front of ORTON HOUSE, HUNTS., as remodelled in Tudor Gothic style for Lord Strathavon (1836) (*V.C.H. Hunts.* iii, 190).

SMITH, JAMES (*c.* 1645–1731), was a figure of considerable importance in the history of Scottish, and perhaps also of English, architecture. In Scotland his reputation is well attested. 'Our first architect' was how a Scottish laird described him in 1719 [Hist. MSS. Comm., *Xth Report,* Appendix 1, p. 197], and in 1693 it was 'Mr. Smith' whom the Earl of Lothian wanted to consult about his house at Newbattle because 'he hath really the best skill of them all' [S.R.O., GD 40/ viii/28]. To Colen Campbell he was 'the most experienc'd Architect of that kingdom' (*Vitruvius Britannicus* ii, 1717, 3), and in the reign of George III the Scottish-born Robert Mylne (d. 1811) was aware that Smith had been 'a remarkable man' [notes on Mylne family history in possession of Miss J. M. H. Mylne].

Smith was the son of a master mason of the same name who died in 1684 or early in 1685. The elder Smith was living at Tarbat in Ross-shire in 1656, but became a burgess of Forres (Morayshire) in 1659 [S.R.O., Deeds Mackiness 58.609 and Forres Burgh Records, *ex inf.* Mr. J. G. Dunbar]. According to Robert Mylne's notes, Smith 'was bred to the Church, but afterwards took to building', to which he adds the crucial information that 'He went abroad to Italy and

studied his Art'. The date and circumstances of Smith's visit to Italy are obscure, as is his alleged training for the Church. It is, however, just possible that he went to Italy as a candidate for the Catholic priesthood, for in May 1671 a certain 'James Smith of Morayshire' was admitted to the Scots College in Rome, where he studied rhetoric, philosophy and theology for four years. In October 1675, however, he 'left with permission and promising to return, but became an apostate' [*Records of the Scots Colleges in Douai, Rome, etc.,* New Spalding Club, 1906, i, 118]. Even in the north of Scotland, Smith is too prevalent a name, and Catholicism too common a creed, to justify the conclusion that the apostate of 1675 was the future architect. But whether or not he was at the Scots College in 1671–5, Smith was undoubtedly an educated man. In 1715, when he offered himself as a candidate for election to Parliament as representative for Edinburgh, he claimed to have had a 'liberall education at schools and Colledges at home and abroad and occasion to know the world by traveling abroad'. One journey is documented by a receipt dated December 1677 acknowledging a contribution of 20s. towards 'my . . . necessare expenses on my voyage upon the account of Sr. William Bruce . . .' [S.R.O., GD 29/263], but the destination is not stated, and the document is chiefly of interest because it shows that by 1677 Smith was already in touch with the leading figure in the Scottish architectural scene.

In 1715 Smith stated that he had 'lived with a fair character' in Edinburgh 'for many years'. He had in fact become a burgess of Edinburgh in December 1679 by right of his recent marriage to the eldest daughter of Robert Mylne (d. 1710), Master Mason to the Scottish Crown, and a prominent figure in the Scottish capital. At the time Mylne was engaged in rebuilding Holyroodhouse under the direction of Sir William Bruce, and the accounts show that James Smith had undertaken some of the masonry [R. S. Mylne, *The Master Masons to the Crown of Scotland,* 1893, 200]. He was soon to have a closer connection with the King's Works in Scotland, for the dismissal of Sir William Bruce in 1678 had left them without a superior officer, and in February 1683, on the recommendation of the Duke of Queensberry (for whom he was then working at Drumlanrig), James Smith was appointed Surveyor or Overseer of the Royal Works, with a salary of £100 p.a.[1] His chief responsibility in this capacity was the maintenance of Holyroodhouse, and in 1688 he was engaged in fitting up the former abbey church as a Chapel Royal for King James II. His tenure of the post was not affected by the Revolution, and it was

---

[1] Though less than Bruce's exceptional salary of £300 p.a., Smith's £100 corresponded to the salary of earlier Masters of the King's Works in Scotland.

renewed by Queen Anne's government in 1707. But payment of his salary ceased after the Union, and although he subsequently acted as surveyor of the Highland forts erected by the Board of Ordnance early in the reign of George I, this employment was terminated in 1719 by the appointment of Andrews Jelfe as 'Architect and Clerk of the Works' for all fortifications under the Board's jurisdiction. A visit to London failed to recover either his lapsed salary or his lost employment, and in a long petition to the Barons of the Scottish Exchequer, as well as in a private letter to Sir John Clerk of Penicuik, Smith complained bitterly of the way in which he had been 'disgracefully turn'd out of His Majesty's service in the 73^d year of his age' [S.R.O., E 307/2 and GD 18/5004].

In his letter to Sir John Clerk, Smith wrote that he was forced to 'hunt for my living elsewhere'. From about 1700 he appears to have had some sort of professional association with Alexander McGill (*q.v.*), but after about 1710 he is not known to have received any private architectural commission of consequence, and it was evidently during these years that (as Robert Mylne records), 'he ruined himself by a Drowned Colliery near Musselburgh', eventually obliging himself to part with the estate at Whitehill in the parish of Inveresk that he had purchased in 1686, and from whose possession he was generally known as 'Mr. Smith of Whitehill'.[1]

So far as firm evidence goes, the last ten years of Smith's life are almost a blank, but there is some reason to think that he may have formed a connection with Colen Campbell, then emerging as the publicist of the new Palladianism that was soon to transform English architecture. The evidence consists of a number of drawings, now in the R.I.B.A. Collection, which belonged to Campbell, but are not in his hand. One of them is a plan of Dalkeith House, as remodelled by Smith in 1702–10, another is a design for a mansion with a façade stylistically similar to Dalkeith, and a third is virtually a duplicate (both in content and in draughtsmanship) of Smith's surviving plans (S.R.O., RHP 2541) for Melville House, the mansion which Campbell illustrates as Smith's work in *Vitruvius Britannicus*. Moreover there are certain mannerisms which these drawings share with an unexecuted design made by Smith and McGill for Cullen House, Banffshire, in 1709 (S.R.O., RHP 2541). The bulk of the drawings, however, consists of studies on Palladian themes. There are numerous designs for villas with centralized plans related to Palladio's Villa Rotunda, one with a façade based on the Palazzo Iseppo Porto in Vicenza, and one which

formed the starting-point of Campbell's design for a house 'in the theatrical style' (*Vitruvius Britannicus* ii, 1717, pl. 90). The existence of the last drawing, and of another related to the engraving of Somerset House in vol. i (pl. 16), makes it clear that the drawings in question must have been known to Campbell at least sixteen years before Smith's death in 1731. Whether Campbell was Smith's pupil, or whether he acquired the drawings from Smith at a time when the latter was in financial difficulties, must be a matter for conjecture. It does, however, seem probable that, just as Campbell's Palladianism preceded Burlington's, so Smith's Palladianism preceded Campbell's and it is tempting to go further and suggest that Smith's interest in Palladian architecture went back to his sojourn in Italy in the 1660s or 1670s. If so, it is to James Smith's Italian travels that the origins of British Palladianism must ultimately be traced.

Smith's executed buildings, on the other hand, show little evidence of any Palladian intentions. Though (as Mr. Dunbar had observed) the basilican plan of the Canongate Church 'is more reminiscent of Continental Catholicism than of Scottish Presbyterianism', its façade appears to be of baroque rather than of Palladian extraction. Apart from Drumlanrig Castle, whose romantic design (derived from Heriot's Hospital) may to some extent have been determined by previous plans, Smith's country houses follow the direction indicated by Sir William Bruce. With their hipped roofs and pedimented fronts they are plain, handsome and for the most part undemonstrative houses which hardly betray the classical aspirations revealed by the drawings. Smith was, it seems, a Palladian only on paper.

The death at Edinburgh on 6 November 1731, of 'Mr. James Smith of Whitehill, a famous Architect in that Country', was announced in *The Political State of Great Britain* xlii, 552, and in *The Caledonian Mercury* of 8 November 1731. He was 86 years old, and left a family of patriarchal size. In 1720, in his petition to the Barons of the Exchequer, he mentioned the needs of 'his numerous family of 32 children'. This is corroborated by Robert Mylne, who in his notes on the history of his family records that Smith's first wife, Janet Mylne, 'had 18 children, and died of twins at the age of 37 years in 1699. Her husband [then] married a second wife, named Smith, by whom he had 14 children'. Janet was 'a good Drawer and very Clever'. Smith was evidently proud of her, for after her death he had her portrait by Faithorne engraved, with an inscription in Latin recording her death and the number of her children. The names of all thirty-two children are not known, but Robert Mylne noted that one of Smith's sons by his second wife was christened 'Climacterick Smith, because born in his father's 70th. year'. One of his daughters married

---

[1] According to R. S. Mylne, *Master Masons*, 245–6, he sold part of it in 1706, and in 1726 assigned the remainder to his son-in-law Gilbert Smith as security for a debt of £365 sterling.

Gilbert Smith (d. 1726), an Edinburgh mason who was appointed Master Mason to the Crown in 1715. Gilbert appears to have been James Smith's first cousin, and had been apprenticed to him in 1694, as was Gilbert's elder brother James (d. 1705) in 1680. In contemporary documents the subject of this entry is often distinguished from his cousin and namesake by the title 'Mr. James Smith'.

James Smith's activities were by no means confined to architecture. He was a justice of the peace and in 1704 one of the Commissioners of Supply for the County of Edinburgh [*Acts of Parliament of Scotland* xi, 139]. When offering himself for election as Member of Parliament for the City of Edinburgh in 1715 he claimed to have 'had the honour to be a representative in Scots parliaments and [to] acquit himself to the satisfaction of his constitutents'. Although unsuccessful in 1715, there is no reason to doubt the truth of his statement, and it is likely that he was the James Smith who represented Forres in the Scottish Parliament of 1685–6. According to Robert Mylne he was 'no contemptible sculptor'. Although he supplied the lead statue of King Charles II which stands in Parliament Square, Edinburgh, for £2580 Scots in 1685 (see *Book of the Old Edinburgh Club* xvii, 1930, 83), it is not clear that he made it himself, since £38 was paid for 'shipping it' either from London or from Holland. But in 1683 'Mr. James Smith statuary' was among those paid for recent works at Holyroodhouse [S.R.O., E 26/11/4, p. 317], and the list of his works includes at least one monument.[1]

That Smith was also an engineer is demonstrated by the employment of 'Mr. Smith, Architectour', as arbitrator in a dispute over the construction of a harbour at Cockenzie, East Lothian, because 'he had the repute to be very well skilled in works of this nature' [*Register of the Privy Council of Scotland* vi, 385], by his involvement in 1696 in a scheme to supply Scottish towns with water, and by his obtaining in 1701 the Scottish rights to operate an engine to raise water invented by Captain Thomas Savory [*Acts of Parliament of Scotland* x, 80, 267]. In the 1720s, with William Adam, Alexander McGill and George Sorocold, he carried out a survey to investigate the possibility of a Forth–Clyde Canal [J. Crawford, *Memorials of Alloa*, 1874, 91].

[*Extracts from the Records of the Burgh of Edinburgh, 1681–9*, ed. M. Wood & H. Armet, *passim*; *1689–1701, passim*; *1701–18*, 282–3; *Roll of Edin-*

burgh *Burgesses 1406–1700*, Scottish Rec. Soc., 456; *Cal. Treasury Books* xxii, 469, xxiv, 257, xxv, 52; *Cal. Treasury Papers 1708–14*, 194; R. S. Mylne, *The Master Masons to the Crown of Scotland*, 1893, 245–6; letters from Smith to the Earl of Mar in S.R.O., GD 124/15; H. M. Colvin, 'A Scottish Origin for English Palladianism?' *Architectural History* xvii, 1974.]

INVERNESS BRIDGE, 1680–2 [*Register of the Privy Council of Scotland* xi, 528–30].

DRUMLANRIG CASTLE, DUMFRIESSHIRE, rebuilt for the 1st Duke of Queensberry, *c.* 1680–90, perhaps on the basis of designs by Robert Mylne, Smith's father-in-law [Mark Girouard in *C. Life*, 25 Aug. 1960].

ST. ANDREWS, ST. SALVATOR'S COLLEGE, advised on repair, 1683 [*Proc. Soc. Antiquaries of Scotland* liv, 1919–20, 237].

EDINBURGH, THE CANONGATE CHURCH, 1688–90 [*Register of the Privy Council of Scotland* xiii, p. xlviii; xiv, 22; *Extracts from the Records of the Burgh of Edinburgh 1681–9*, ed. H. Armet, xxxi; *1689–1701*, xxxvi] (plan in G. Hay, *Architecture of Scottish Post-Reformation Churches* 1957, fig. 22).

EDINBURGH, HOLYROODHOUSE, fitted up Abbey Church as Chapel Royal for King James II, 1688; destroyed by mob later same year. The accounts [S.R.O., E 26/12/3, pp. 187, 190, 288] show that Smith was in charge as Surveyor of the Royal Works, and was presumably responsible for the designs, though this cannot be proved. In December 1687, after a visit to James II in Whitehall, he was paid an extra £120 as an expression of the King's satisfaction with 'the performance of his duty' [S.R.O., E 28/369/54]. The interior of the Chapel is illustrated in *Vitruvius Scoticus*, pl. 5. William Morgan, recently employed at Chelsea Hospital, was the Master Carver [S.R.O., E 28/477/2] and 'three image-peeces for the high Altar' were carved by Grinling Gibbons [S.R.O., SP 57/13, p. 181].

WHITEHILL (now NEWHAILES) HOUSE, MUSSELBURGH, MIDLOTHIAN, for himself, *c.* 1690; enlarged in eighteenth century (T. Hannan, *Famous Scottish Houses: the Lowlands*, 1928, 133–6; *C. Life*, 15 Sept. 1917).

EDINBURGH, repaired house in TWEEDDALE'S CLOSE, HIGH STREET, for the 1st Marquess of Tweeddale, 1692–3 [National Library of Scotland, Yester papers, Box 98, F. 3] (J. Grant, *Old and New Edinburgh* i, 277).

NEWBATTLE ABBEY, MIDLOTHIAN, alterations were carried out by the 4th Earl of Lothian in 1693 onwards. Smith's advice was sought, but it is not clear whether he was the effective architect or not [S.R.O., GD 40/viii/53, 58, 76, 108, xviii/1, 77] (*C. Life*, 13 Sept. 1902, 22 Feb. 1941).

---

[1] The James Smith who contracted to erect the monument in Holyrood Abbey Church to the 15th Earl of Sutherland (d. 1703) was probably the younger Smith (d. 1705). He was associated with 'Mr. James Smith' in the contract for the Hamilton monument now in Bothwell Church. The contract for the Sutherland movement is printed in *Book of the Old Edinburgh Club* xxv, 1945, 210.

HAMILTON PALACE, LANARKSHIRE, for the 3rd Duke and Duchess of Hamilton, 1693–1701; wings added by W. Adam 1717; new north front by D. Hamilton 1822–5; dem. *c.* 1920 [*Vitruvius Scoticus*, pl. 8; Rosalind K. Marshall, *The Days of Duchess Anne*, 1973, chap. 9] (*C. Life*, 7, 14 and 21 June 1919).

TRAQUAIR HOUSE, PEEBLESHIRE, alterations for the 4th Earl of Traquair, including the forecourt and gate-piers, *c.* 1695–9 [R.C.A.M., *Peeblesshire* ii, 313 and pls. 89, 90, 116].

DURISDEER, DUMFRIESSHIRE, mausoleum for the 1st Duke of Queensberry, 1695 [contract at Drumlanrig cited by M. Girouard in *C. Life*, 1 Sept. 1960]. The mausoleum forms the north transept of the parish church (rebuilt in 1716–17): see plan in G. Hay, *Architecture of Scottish Post-Reformation Churches*, 1957, fig. 19.

BOTHWELL CHURCH, LANARKSHIRE, monument to 3rd Duke of Hamilton (d. 1694), originally in Hamilton Collegiate Church [contract and drawing dated Feb. 1696 in Hamilton MSS., Box 463/10/2].

EDINBURGH, SURGEONS' HALL AND ANATOMICAL THEATRE, SURGEONS' SQUARE, 1696–7 [G. H. Creswell, *The Royal College of Surgeons of Edinburgh*, 1926, 51].

MELVILLE HOUSE, FIFE, for the 1st Earl of Melville, 1697–1700 [C. Campbell, *Vitruvius Britannicus* ii, 1717, pl. 50; original drawings in S.R.O., RHP 4093; plumber's contract witnessed by Smith in S.R.O., GD 26/6/158; lawsuit over contract in S.R.O., GD 26/6/164].

YESTER HOUSE, EAST LOTHIAN, for the 2nd Marquess of Tweeddale, in partnership with Alexander McGill, *c.* 1700–15; altered by W. Adam 1730 and by Robert Adam 1788 [*Vitruvius Scoticus*, pls. 28–9; J. G. Dunbar, 'The Building of Yester House', *Trans. of the E. Lothian Antiquarian and Field Naturalists' Soc.* xiii, 1972] (*C. Life*, 23–30 July 1932, 9, 16 and 23 Aug. 1973).

DALKEITH HOUSE, MIDLOTHIAN, remodelled for Anne, Duchess of Buccleuch, 1702–10 (*Vitruvius Scoticus*, pls. 23–4; building accounts in S.R.O., GD 224/625/1] (*C. Life*, 7 Oct. 1911).

GIFFORD CHURCH, EAST LOTHIAN, was built in 1710 at the expense of the 2nd Marquess of Tweeddale, and many of the craftsmen engaged at Yester House were employed. It may therefore have been designed by Smith and McGill, the architects of Yester [J. G. Dunbar, 'The Building of Yester House', *Trans. E. Lothian Antiquarian and Field Naturalists' Soc.* xiii, 1972, 40, n. 24].

DUPPLIN CASTLE, PERTHSHIRE, office-wings for the 7th Earl of Kinnoull, *c.* 1720–5; destroyed by fire 1827 [J. Macky, *Journey through Scotland*, 1723, 153–4, where he states that 'Mr. Smith, the Architect, lives there till he finishes it']. Smith may have been responsible for earlier

works here, for in Oct. 1707 he says in a letter to the Earl of Mar that he has been detained at Dupplin by Lord Dupplin, afterwards 6th Earl of Kinnoull (d. 1719) [S.R.O., GD 124/15/663/2].

EDINBURGH, SMITH'S LAND or CLOSE, later known as Paisley's Close, on the north side of the High Street, built by Smith as an investment [*Book of the Old Edinburgh Club* xii, 1923, 45].

SMITH, JAMES, a carpenter by trade, is known only as the author of two books, one entitled *The Carpenters Companion: Being an Accurate and Compleat Treatise of Carpenters Works*, together with the Five Orders of Architecture 'in a more easy and concise Method than any yet Published', dedicated to George Fox, 1733, the other *A Specimen of Antient Carpentry, consisting of Variety of Designs for Roofs, exemplefy'd in common circular mixt spiral & such which have been fram'd in Publick & Private Antique Buildings*, Collected by James Smith, Carpenter. *To which are added, Designs of Frontispieces to Doors, Gateways, Piers, Pavillions, Temples, Chimney Pieces etc.* by William Jones, 66 copper plates, 1736. A second edition of the latter work, consisting of 36 plates only, and omitting Jones's designs, was published in 1787 as *Specimens of Ancient Carpentry, consisting of Framed Roofs, selected from various Ancient Buildings, Public & Private, Also some Specimens of Mouldings for Cornices, Doors & Windows, by the late Mr. James Smith*. There was a reprint by Taylor of Holborn in 1834. *The Specimens of Antient Carpentry* is devoid of text, but the plates constitute the earliest antiquarian study of English medieval carpentry, and are still valuable as a record of some roofs that were destroyed in the eighteenth century.[1] The plates of Gothic mouldings, taken from 'several churches &c. in Town & Country', are likewise the earliest of their kind.

SMITH, JAMES (1734–1807), was the elder son of James Smith of the Coppice Green, nr. Shifnal in Shropshire. He practised as an architect and surveyor from Coppice Green, where he died on 15 January 1807, aged 72 [Shifnal parish register in Salop. Record Office]. In 1776 he acted as arbitrator in a dispute over the contract for building the English Bridge at Shrewsbury [A. W. Ward, *The Bridges of Shrewsbury*, Shrewsbury 1935, 68]. In 1781–2 he was employed by Bishop Hurd to design the library at HARTLEBURY CASTLE,

---

[1] The roofs illustrated include those of Netley Abbey, Westminster School, Burleigh House, Northants., the Savoy Hospital, Staple Inn, Holborn, Gray's Inn, the London Guildhall, Pinners' Hall, London, the Middle Temple, Westminster Hall, Lambeth Palace, Eltham Palace, Hampton Court, Jesus and St. John's Colleges, Cambridge, and eight of the Oxford Colleges.

WORCS., in a style of Adamsian character. His original drawing is illustrated in *C. Life*, 7 Feb. 1931 and 23 Sept. 1971. In 1783 Smith submitted three alternative designs for the Shirehall at Shrewsbury [Salop. Record Office, 348/10]. He also made drawings for improvements at Pitchford Hall, Salop., which are undated and were not executed [J. B. Lawson in *Shropshire Newsletter*, no. 44, June 1973, 19]. His younger brother John (born March 1736/7) appears also to have acted as a surveyor, for in 1793 his advice was taken before it was decided to rebuild St. Alkmund's Church, Shrewsbury [D. H. S. Cranage, *Churches of Shropshire* ii, 1903, 894].

SMITH, JAMES (1782–1867), F.R.S., of Jordanhill, nr. Glasgow, is best known as a geologist and man of letters, but also had some reputation as an amateur architect. He was the son of a prosperous Glasgow merchant and enjoyed a private income which allowed him to devote his life to science, literature and the arts. According to the author of *The Old Country Houses of the Glasgow Gentry* (Glasgow 1870), 'he had a great taste for architecture, and furnished plans for many of his friends' houses'. Among these was CRAIGEND CASTLE, STIRLINGSHIRE, the seat of his cousin James Smith, which was rebuilt by Alexander Ramsay of Edinburgh in 1812, partly in accordance with Smith's plans (see under 'Ramsay'). In 1824 he remodelled his own house at JORDANHILL (dem. *c.* 1960) in a plain style (see *Old Country Houses of the Glasgow Gentry*, pl. lix), and in 1826 designed a Gothic church, since rebuilt, at GOVAN, LANARKS., with a steeple said to have been based on Stratford-on-Avon Parish Church [*N.S.A.* vi, 711] (W. Fraser, *The Kirk and the Manse*, 1857, plate). For the ANDERSONIAN INSTITUTION, GLASGOW, of which he was president from 1830 to 1839, he designed a circular museum and lecture theatre which were added at the back of the Institution's premises (dem.) in George Street [A. H. Sexton, *The First Technical College, the History of the Andersonian Institution*, 1894, 33–4, with illustration]. For further biographical details see *D.N.B.*

SMITH, JAMES, practised in Inverness. He designed two public buildings in TAIN, ROSS-SHIRE – THE ACADEMY, 1810–13, and the PARISH CHURCH (now the Town Hall), 1814 [R. W. & Jean Munro, *Tain through the Centuries*, Tain 1966, 104, 106]. Under Thomas Telford's direction he furnished the plans and specifications for the series of 'Parliamentary kirks' built in the Highlands between 1824 and 1834 [R.C.A.M., *Argyll* ii, 25, n. 4].

SMITH, JOHN, was a master mason working in Linlithgow in the reign of Charles II. In 1667 John Mylne, the King's Master Mason, designed a new Tolbooth for the Town Council of Linlithgow which would doubtless have been built but for his death in December of that year. In January 1668 the Council approved 'the concording with John Smith maister meson for edifeing our Tolbuth in all respects conforme to the draught thereof drawn up be him', and it was completed in 1669 or 1670. It was repaired after a fire in 1847, when Smith's classical façade was carefully reproduced, and the existing external stone stairs were added in 1906. In 1670 Smith built a Grammar School for the town [S.R.O., Linlithgow Town Council Minutes, B48/9/3, 1667–70, *passim*].

SMITH, JOHN, was a Clerk of the Works first at Richmond and Kew Palaces (1758–61) and then at Kensington (1761–82), retiring on a pension in 1782 [*History of the King's Works* v, 475, vi, 24]. Like other members of the Office of Works he evidently had a small private practice, for his designs for a new dining-room for the 1st Earl of Hardwicke, dated 1763, are in the Bedfordshire Record Office (L 31/260–272).

SMITH, JOHN (*c.* 1748–1815), was a mason and builder of Darnick, nr. Melrose in Roxburghshire. Monuments in Melrose Churchyard, and family papers in the Register House at Edinburgh, show that he died on 17 October 1815, aged 67, leaving three sons: JAMES SMITH (1779–1862), an architect and builder in Edinburgh who enjoyed the title of 'H.M. Master Mason for Scotland' (conferred on him in 1819, perhaps through the good offices of his neighbour Robert Reid, 'King's Architect in Scotland'), and JOHN (1782–1864) and THOMAS (1785–1857) SMITH, who continued the family business at Darnick.

John and Thomas Smith, the sons, were intelligent and enterprising men. The first volume of the *R.I.B.A. Transactions* (part i, 1837, 52–60) contains a paper by them on the subject of building bridges in whinstone rubble without the use of ashlar, an economical method of construction which they employed with success on several occasions. They were also responsible for building a chain suspension bridge at Dryburgh, said to have been the first of its kind. Private persons who employed them included Sir Walter Scott, for whom they enlarged ABBOTSFORD, ROXBURGHSHIRE, to the designs of Atkinson in 1822–3, and built CHIEFSWOOD, ROXBURGHSHIRE, to their own designs in 1820–21; the 5th Duke of Buccleuch, for whom they worked at BOWHILL, SELKIRKSHIRE; and the 16th Lord Somerville, to whose house called PAVILION, nr. MELROSE, they added a wing with cavity walls described in their paper to the R.I.B.A.

Bridges built by the two Smiths (evidently to their own designs) included: THE CHAIN BRIDGE,

DRYBURGH, BERWICKSHIRE, 1817, blown down 1818, successfully re-erected 1818, but since demolished (original drawing in R.I.B.A. Collection); the two bridges over the Rivers Tweed and Ettrick between Selkirk and Galashiels, 1831;[1] one over the Hermitage Water in Liddesdale for the 5th Duke of Buccleuch, 1832; YARROW BRIDGE, SELKIRKSHIRE, 1833; the bridge carrying the drive to Bowhill over the Ettrick at FAULDSHOPE, SELKIRKSHIRE, 1834; and LOW PEEL BRIDGE, over the Tweed at ASHIESTEEL, SELKIRKSHIRE, completed 1848 after an initial failure [T. Craig-Brown, *History of Selkirkshire* i, 1886, 388]. In 1834 they widened the TWEED BRIDGE at PEEBLES [R.C.A.M., *Peebleshire* ii, 341].

See p. 986 In the S.R.O. there are designs by them for enlarging ST. BOSWELL'S CHURCH, ROXBURGHSHIRE, 1835 [RHP 7190–1], for a shop and school at the same place, 1836 [RHP 7192–3, 7196], for enlarging KELSO SCHOOL, 1846 [RHP 8429–32], for a manse at DUNS, BERWICKSHIRE, 1847 [RHP 8343–4], for altering ECKFORD CHURCH, ROXBURGHSHIRE, 1848 [RHP 8220–1], for an unidentified school, 1853 [RHP 5525], and for repairs and alterations to DARNICK TOWER for John Heiton, 1861 [GD 1/146].

John Smith was also an occasional sculptor. His best-known work in this capacity was the colossal statue of William Wallace at Dryburgh, carved in 1814.

[*The Journal of Sir Walter Scott*, ed. Tait, 1950, 732; Messrs. Smith of Darnick, 'On Whinstone Construction', *R.I.B.A. Trans.* i (1), 1837, 52–60; R. S. Mylne, *The Master Masons to the Crown of Scotland*, Edinburgh 1893, 247; National Library of Scotland, MS. 3899, f. 199, letter to Scott, 1824; family papers in S.R.O., GD 241/250.]

SMITH, JOHN (1781–1852), was the son of William Smith (d. 1812), a builder and architect of Aberdeen. After learning his father's trade he went to London, where he is said to have become a pupil of James Playfair (who died, however, in 1794, when Smith was only 13). In 1804 or the following year he returned to Aberdeen, where he established himself in practice. At that date he was virtually the only professional architect in Aberdeen, and soon developed an extensive local practice. He was appointed City Architect, and for some forty years directed the public works of a rapidly expanding town in an able and conscientious manner. From about 1820 his virtual monopoly of architectural practice in Aberdeen was challenged by Archibald Simpson (*q.v.*), whose superior ability as a designer was probably a salutary stimulus. Smith's best works were

Greek Revival designs such as the North Church and the Schools in Little Belmont Street, but his numerous works in the vernacular styles of the sixteenth and seventeenth centuries earned him the nickname of 'Tudor Johnny'. Like Simpson he knew how to make the most of granite, and, with Simpson, he must be regarded as the principal creator of the 'granite city' of the nineteenth century. In 1810 he published an engraved plan of Aberdeen City and harbour.

Smith is said to have been personally 'a shy, retiring man, as well as an able and diligent official'. From 1845 he was in partnership with his son William Smith (1817–91), the architect of Queen Victoria's Balmoral Castle. He died at Rosebank, Hardgate, on 22 July 1872, aged 71. Robert Kerr of London, Alexander Ellis of Aberdeen and Thomas Mackenzie of Elgin were his pupils. A number of his professional accountbooks for the years 1807–32 are in the National Monuments Record of Scotland. At the end of vol. viii there is a list of drawings which provides evidence for a number of Smith's commissions. Some of his drawings are in Aberdeen Art Gallery. [Obituary in *Builder* x, 1852, 506; *A.P.S.D.*; G. M. Fraser's articles on Archibald Simpson in *Aberdeen Weekly Jnl.*, 1918; information from Mr. David Walker.]

PUBLIC BUILDINGS IN ABERDEEN

THE COURT HOUSE, 1818–20; dem. 1865 [*Builder* x, 506; *N.S.A.* xii, 104].

THE TOWN HOUSE or TOLBOOTH, new front, Gothic, 1820; dem. 1865 [*Builder* x, 506].

KING'S COLLEGE, rebuilt street front and other alterations, 1825–6 [*Builder* x, 506].

THE BRIDGE OF DON, in association with Thomas Telford, 1827–30 [G. M. Fraser in *Aberdeen Weekly Jnl.*, 14 June 1918].

THE EAST PRISON, 1829–31; dem. [*Builder* x, 506; *A.P.S.D., s.v.* 'Aberdeen'].

ST. NICHOLAS CHURCHYARD, Ionic screen to Union Street, apparently based on a design by Decimus Burton, 1830 [G. M. Fraser in *Aberdeen Weekly Jnl.*, 21 June 1918].

GORDON'S HOSPITAL, addition of wings, 1830–4 [*Builder* x, 506].

THE RECORD OFFICE, KING STREET, 1832 [*Builder* x, 506].

THE ADVOCATES' HALL, NOS. 116–120 UNION STREET, 1838 [*Builder* x, 506].

THE TOWN'S SCHOOLS, LITTLE BELMONT STREET, 1841 [*Builder* x, 506].

THE BRIDGE OF DEE, widened on west side in association with James Walker, C.E., 1841–2 [G. M. Fraser in *Aberdeen Weekly Jnl.*, 30 Aug. 1918].

ASYLUM FOR BLIND, HUNTLY STREET, 1841–3 [G. M. Fraser in *Aberdeen Weekly Jnl.*, 30 Aug. 1918].

---

[1] The foundation-stone of the Tweed bridge was laid by Sir Walter Scott, who records in his diary that 'Mr. Smith gave a proper repast to the workmen'.

TRINITY HALL, UNION STREET, for the Incorporated Trades, 1845–6, Tudor Gothic [G.
M. Fraser in *Aberdeen Weekly Jnl.*, 20 Sept.
1918].

PUBLIC BUILDINGS ELSEWHERE

STRICHEN, ABERDEENSHIRE, THE TOWN HOUSE for
Mrs. Fraser of Strichen, 1816 [List of Drawings, no. 130].

STONEHAVEN, KINCARDINESHIRE, COUNTY HOUSE
AND GAOL, alterations and additions, 1822
[*Aberdeen Jnl.*, 1 Jan. 1822].

MONYMUSK, ABERDEENSHIRE, PAROCHIAL SCHOOL,
1826 [*Aberdeen Jnl.*, 28 June 1826].

CULTS, ABERDEENSHIRE, SUSPENSION FOOT-BRIDGE
over R. Dee to Banchory Devenick, for the
Rev. George Morison, 1837 [*N.S.A.* xi, 185].

DYCE, ABERDEENSHIRE, SCHOOL, 1841 [*Aberdeen
Jnl.*, 26 May 1841].

PETERHEAD, ABERDEENSHIRE, THE PRISON, 1843;
partly dem. and converted into house [*Aberdeen Jnl.*, 8 Feb. 1843].

NEW DEER, ABERDEENSHIRE, SCHOOL, 1845 [*Aberdeen Jnl.*, 26 Feb. 1845].

CLUNY, ABERDEENSHIRE, SCHOOL, 1847 [*Aberdeen
Jnl.*, 10 March 1847].

CRUDEN, ABERDEENSHIRE, SCHOOL, 1847 [*Aberdeen
Jnl.*, 14 July 1847].

CHURCHES

UDNY, ABERDEENSHIRE, 1821, Gothic [List of
Drawings, no. 266; Account-Book, i].

FINTRAY, ABERDEENSHIRE, 1821 [List of Drawings, no. 180].

ABERDEEN, UNION UNITED FREE CHURCH, SHIPROW,
c. 1822; dem. [plans in Aberdeen Public
Library].

FORDOUN, KINCARDINESHIRE, 1828–9, Gothic
[*N.S.A.* xi, 104].

ABERDEEN, ST. CLEMENT, FOOTDEE, 1828–9, Gothic
[G. M. Fraser in *Aberdeen Weekly Jnl.*, 14 June
1918].

NIGG, KINCARDINESHIRE, 1828–9, Gothic [con-
tract in S.R.O., HR 487/6].

NEWHILLS, ABERDEENSHIRE, 1829–30, Gothic
[*Aberdeen Jnl.*, 29 April 1829].

ABERDEEN, NORTH CHURCH (now Arts Centre),
1830–1 [G. M. Fraser in *Aberdeen Weekly Jnl.*,
14 June 1918].

ABERDEEN, SOUTH CHURCH, 1830–1, Gothic [G.
M. Fraser, *op. cit.*].

CRUDEN, ABERDEENSHIRE, additions and alterations, 1833–4 [*Aberdeen Jnl.*, 9 Oct. 1833].

KEIG, ABERDEENSHIRE, 1834, Gothic [*Aberdeen
Jnl.*, 27 Dec. 1834].

LONGSIDE, ABERDEENSHIRE, 1836 [*Aberdeen Jnl.*, 8
April 1835].

TOUGH, ABERDEENSHIRE, 1838 [*Aberdeen Jnl.*, 1
Aug. 1838].

NEW DEER, ABERDEENSHIRE, 1839; tower completed 1865 [S.R.O., HR 403/1, minute of 21
June 1864 referring to the completion of the
tower 'either on the original plan by the late
John Smith, or on a modified plan submitted
to the meeting'].

ABOYNE, ABERDEENSHIRE, 1842 [*Aberdeen Jnl.*, 21
April 1841].

INVERURIE, ABERDEENSHIRE, 1842, Gothic [*Aberdeen Jnl.*, 14 April 1841].

ELLON, ABERDEENSHIRE, a church – probably the
new church at Savoch of Deer completed
1834; altered 1897 [List of Drawings, nos.
157–60].

BETHELNIE CHURCH, ABERDEENSHIRE, repairs,
1844 [*Builder* ii, 1844, 198].

DOMESTIC ARCHITECTURE

ABERDEEN, CRIMONMOGATE HOUSE, UNION STREET
(later Northern Club), for Patrick Milne of
Crimonmogate, *c.* 1810; dem. 1964 [*Builder* x,
506; design for 'finishing hall for Patrick
Milne' in Aberdeen Art Gallery].

PHESDO, FORDOUN, KINCARDINESHIRE, for Alexander Crombie, *c.* 1810–15 [*Builder* x, 506].

BRUCKLAY CASTLE, NEW DEER, ABERDEENSHIRE,
addition of entrance-hall, etc., for John
Dingwall, 1814; remodelled by James Matthews 1849; dem. 1953 [drawings in Aberdeen
Art Gallery; J. B. Pratt, *Buchan*, 1901, 179–
80].

RAEMOIR, BANCHORY, KINCARDINESHIRE, for
William Innes, 1817 [*Builder* x, 506].

DUNECHT HOUSE, ECHT, ABERDEENSHIRE, for
William Forbes, 1820; enlarged by G. E.
Street 1877–81 [*Builder* x, 506].

STRICHEN HOUSE, ABERDEENSHIRE, for Thomas
Fraser, cr. Lord Lovat, 1818–21; gutted
[*Builder* x, 506].

INCHMARLO, KINCARDINESHIRE, reconstructed for
— Douglas, 1823 [Account-Book].

KIRKVILLE (now KIRKTON) HOUSE, SKENE, ABER-
DEENSHIRE, for James Knowles, 1826 [*Builder*
x, 506].

TONLEY HOUSE, ABERDEENSHIRE, alterations and
additions for General Patrick Byres, 1829;
dem. [*Aberdeen Jnl.*, 3 March 1829].

FINTRAY HOUSE, ABERDEENSHIRE, for Sir John
Forbes, Bart., 1829–31, Tudor Gothic; rebuilt
1880; dem. 1952 [*Builder* x, 506; S.R.O., GD
250, Box 41].

AUCHMACOY HOUSE, LOGIE BUCHAN, ABERDEEN-
SHIRE, completed house begun by W. Burn
(*q.v.*) for James Buchan, 1833, Jacobethan
[*Builder* x, 506].

EASTER SKENE, ABERDEENSHIRE, for William
McCombie, 1832, Elizabethan [*Builder* x,
506].

KEMNAY HOUSE, KINTORE, ABERDEENSHIRE, alterations and additions for John Burnett, 1833
[*Builder* x, 506].

BALMORAL, ABERDEENSHIRE, additions for Sir Robert Gordon, 1834–9, Jacobethan style; subsequently remodelled for Queen Victoria by William Smith 1853–6 [*Builder* x, 506]. At Haddo House there is a set of unexecuted designs by John & William Smith for remodelling the house for Queen Victoria, dated 1848.

MONTBLAIRY, ALVAH, BANFFSHIRE, stables for Alexander Morison, 1835 [*Aberdeen Jnl.*, 10 June 1835].

CANDACRAIG, STRATHDON, ABERDEENSHIRE, for Robert Anderson, 1835; burned *c.* 1900 [*Builder* x, 506; *N.S.A.* xii, 546–7].

MANAR HOUSE, INVERURIE, ABERDEENSHIRE, for James Gordon, probably *c.* 1835 [*Builder* x, 506].

HAZELHEAD HOUSE, ABERDEENSHIRE, offices for — Robertson, 1836 [*Aberdeen Jnl.*, 30 March 1836].

MENIE, nr. ABERDEEN, for Col. George Turner, *c.* 1836, Jacobethan [*Builder* x, 506].

SLAINS CASTLE, ABERDEENSHIRE, rebuilt for the 17th Earl of Errol, 1836–7 [*Builder* x, 506].

CLUNY CASTLE, ABERDEENSHIRE, for Lt.-Col. John Gordon, 1836–40, castellated [*Builder* x, 506].

CRAIGSTON CASTLE, ABERDEENSHIRE, porch for William Pollard-Urquhart, 1838 [drawings at Craigston] (*C. Life*, 17–24 Oct. 1963).

LEARNEY HOUSE, ABERDEENSHIRE, rebuilt for — Brebner, after fire, 1838 [*Builder* x, 506; *Aberdeen Jnl.*, 3 Jan. 1838].

WHITEHAUGH, KEITHHALL, ABERDEENSHIRE, added wings for Col. J. J. F. Leith, *c.* 1838–40 [*Builder* x, 506; cf. *N.S.A.* xii, 447–8].

BANCHORY HOUSE, KINCARDINESHIRE, for Alexander Thomson, 1839 [*Builder* x, 506: drawings in house].

CRAIGELLIE HOUSE, MINTLAW, ABERDEENSHIRE, for William Shand, 1840 [*Builder* x, 506].

CORSINDAE HOUSE, nr. MONYMUSK, ABERDEENSHIRE, reconstructed 1840 [accounts in house].

FORGLEN HOUSE, TURRIFF, BANFFSHIRE, for Sir Ralph Abercromby, Bart., *c.* 1840, Tudor [*Builder* x, 506].

WILLOWBANK, nr. ABERDEEN, enlarged for his son-in-law Alexander Gibb, *c.* 1843 [L. M. Rae, *The Story of the Gibbs*, privately printed Edinburgh 1961, 86].

BADENTOY HOUSE, BANCHORY, KINCARDINESHIRE, for — Nicol, 1849 [*Aberdeen Jnl.*, 6 June 1849].

ADEN HOUSE, OLD DEER, ABERDEENSHIRE, for James Russell [*Builder* x, 506].

BUCHANNESS LODGE, PETERHEAD, ABERDEENSHIRE, enlarged for the 4th Earl of Aberdeen [*Builder* x, 506].

DUNLUGAS, ALVAH, BANFFSHIRE, work for — Leslie [*Builder* x, 506].

KEITHHALL HOUSE, ABERDEENSHIRE, stables for the Earl of Kintore [List of Drawings, nos. 226–8, 252].

PITFOUR HOUSE, OLD DEER, ABERDEENSHIRE, for Capt. George Ferguson, dem. 1927 [*Builder* x, 506].

SMITH, ROBERT, junior, figures in Jones's *Glasgow Directory* of 1787 as 'architect, cabinet-maker and house-wright'. J. Cleland, *Annals of Glasgow* i, 1816, 99, records that he was responsible for fitting up the interior of ANDERSON'S INSTITUTION in JOHN STREET, GLASGOW, *c.* 1796.

SMITH, SAMUEL, was a builder-architect at Madeley in Shropshire. His plans for alterations to SHADWELL HALL, SALOP. (perhaps not executed), and for farm-houses at Shadwell and Llanhedrick, made in 1809 for William Botfield, are in the Garnett-Botfield Collection in the Shropshire Record Office. In 1829 he completed the rebuilding of PONTESBURY CHURCH, SALOP. after the death of John Turner (*q.v.*) [I.C.B.S.; *V.C.H. Salop.* viii, 288], and in 1833 he and his son Thomas were jointly responsible for designing the classical HOLY TRINITY CHURCH, WROCKWARDINE WOOD, SALOP. Thomas Smith, who is described in the 1851 Shropshire directory as 'architect, builder and surveyor', designed several minor Shropshire churches, including those of ST. LUKE, IRONBRIDGE, 1836, CHRIST CHURCH, WELLINGTON, 1838, and EATON CONSTANTINE, 1847–9, all Gothic [D. H. S. Cranage, *Churches of Shropshire*, 1903, i, 200, ii, 634, 650; G.R.].

SMITH, THOMAS (1799–1875), practised in Hertford from the 1820s until his death. He was County Surveyor of Hertfordshire from 1837 onwards and held a similar appointment in Bedfordshire for several years. He was Mayor of Hertfordshire in 1868, and died on 1 October 1875, aged 76.

In Hertfordshire Smith designed the County Gaol, the Hospital, the Lunatic Asylum and many smaller buildings and bridges. In Bedfordshire he was employed by Earl de Grey as executant architect for Silsoe Church and the Silsoe lodges to Wrest Park. In London he was surveyor to two Hertfordshire landowners, the Marquess of Salisbury and Baron Dimsdale, and is said to have erected a number of buildings on the latter's property. In Ireland he acted for Lord Ranfurly and Sir Patrick (afterwards Lord) Bellew, and designed or remodelled several country houses in County Louth. In conjunction with his son Thomas Tayler Smith he designed Radlett Church, Herts. (1864), the English Hotel at Nice, the Protestant chapels at Nice, Cannes, Stuttgart and Naples, and the Château Ste-Ursule at Cannes for Lord Londesborough.

[*A.P.S.D.*; *Builder* xxxiii, 1875, 904, 995.]

HERTFORD, ALL SAINTS CHURCH, south aisle and porch, 1824, Gothic; destroyed by fire 1824 [I.C.B.S.].

WREST PARK, BEDS., supervised erection of lodges to designs of Earl de Grey (*q.v.*), 1826.

SILSOE CHURCH, BEDS., supervised erection to designs of Earl de Grey (*q.v.*), 1830–1.

BARMEATH, CO. LOUTH, IRELAND, remodelled for Sir Patrick Bellew, Bart., *c.* 1830 [J. Leslie, *History of Kilsaran*, Dundalk 1908, 125].

CASTLE BELLINGHAM, CO. LOUTH, IRELAND, for Sir Alan Edward Bellingham, Bart., *c.* 1830 [J. Leslie, *History of Kilsaran*, Dundalk 1908, 125].

BRAGANSTOWN HOUSE, CO. LOUTH, IRELAND, remodelled for the Rev. Anthony Garstin, *c.* 1830, Elizabethan [J. Leslie, *History of Kilsaran*, Dundalk 1908, 125].

HERTFORD, THE GENERAL INFIRMARY OF COUNTY HOSPITAL, NORTH ROAD., 1832–3 [reports in local newspaper, *ex inf.* Mr. P. Walne, County Archivist].

HODDESDEN, HERTS., THE CLOCK TOWER, 1835 [J. A. Tregelles, *History of Hoddesden*, 1908, 283].

STEVENAGE RECTORY, HERTS., altered or rebuilt, 1835 [Lincs. Record Office, MGA 184].

LOUTH COUNTY INFIRMARY, DUNDALK, IRELAND, 1835 [*Builder* xxxiii, 1875, 994].

LECKHAMSTEAD RECTORY, BUCKS., altered or rebuilt, 1836 [Lincs. Record Office, MGA 205].

NEWNHAM VICARAGE, HERTS., 1837–8 [Bodleian Library, records of Queen Anne's Bounty].

WESTON VICARAGE, HERTS., altered or rebuilt, 1838 [Lincs. Record Office, MGA 221].

LETCHWORTH RECTORY, HERTS., altered or rebuilt, 1839 [Lincs. Record Office, MGA 238].

ST. ALBANS, HERTS., GAOL AND HOUSE OF CORRECTION (ABBEY GATEWAY), alterations, 1840 [Hertfordshire County Records, *Sessions Records of the Liberty of St. Albans* iv, 1923, 319–22].

WESTON CHURCH, HERTS., rebuilt chancel, 1840, Norman [A. H. Bradbeer, 'Weston Church', *Trans. E. Herts. Arch. Soc.* iv (1), 1908–9, 68].

STEVENAGE CHURCH, HERTS., south transept, 1841, Gothic [I.C.B.S.].

WARESIDE, HERTS., HOLY TRINITY CHURCH, 1841, Norman [G.R.].

HERTFORD, THE COUNTY GAOL, alterations and additions, 1842 [*Builder* i, 1843, 267–8, xxxiii, 1875, 994; *Hertfordshire County Records: Sessions Books* x, 1957, 387–8].

ORSETT RECTORY, ESSEX, 1843–4 [Bodleian Library, records of Queen Anne's Bounty].

WEST HYDE CHURCH, HERTS., 1844–5, Norman [I.C.B.S.].

KILNWICK PERCY VICARAGE, YORKS., rebuilt 1848 [Borthwick Institute, York, MGA 1848/1].

CLOPHILL CHURCH, BEDS., 1848–9, Gothic [I.C.B.S.].

HUNTINGDON COUNTY GAOL, altered 1850 [Cassey's *History, Topography and Directory of Beds., Hunts and Herts.*, 1863, 240].

HUNTINGDON INFIRMARY AND DISPENSARY, 1853 [Cassey's *History, Topography and Directory of Beds., Hunts. and Herts.*, 1863, 242].

SMITH, WILLIAM (1661–1724), *see* SMITH, FRANCIS

SMITH, WILLIAM (1705–1747), was the eldest surviving son of Francis Smith of Warwick (d. 1738), and succeeded him in his business as an architect and master builder. After his father's death he took over the contract for the masonry of the Radcliffe Library at Oxford which (in conjunction with the Oxford mason, John Townesend) he completed shortly before his own death in 1747. He designed a number of country houses in the Midlands in a handsome but unadventurous style that was basically Palladian, with some indebtedness to Gibbs. He died a bachelor in April 1747. His business appears to have been taken over by William and David Hiorne.

RADBOURNE HALL, DERBYSHIRE, for German Pole, *c.* 1740 [a MS. account of the family written by Sacheverell Pole, who inherited Radbourne in 1780, says the house was built by 'Smith of Warwick'].

CATTON HALL, DERBYSHIRE, for Christopher Horton, *c.* 1742–5 [Andor Gomme, 'Catton Hall', in *The Country Seat*, ed. Colvin & Harris, 1970, 157–63] (*C. Life*, 17, 24 March 1960).

KIRTLINGTON PARK, OXON., for Sir James Dashwood, Bart., 1742–7, completed by John Sanderson (*q.v.*) [drawings and accounts formerly at Kirtlington; *Vitruvius Britannicus* iv, 1767, pls. 32–6] (*C. Life*, 13 April 1912).

LAMPORT CHURCH, NORTHANTS., rebuilt chancel, outer walls of nave and south porch, 1743 [Sir Gyles Isham, *All Saints Church, Lamport*, 1950].

BRIXWORTH HOUSE, NORTHANTS., work for John Nicolls Rainsford, 1743; dem. 1954. Smith's employment here is mentioned in a letter from the Rev. Euseby Isham dated 14 Dec. 1743 among the Isham Correspondence at Lamport (no. 2508). He probably rebuilt or at least refronted the house. (J. P. Neale, *Views of Seats*, 1st ser., iii, 1820).

STANFORD HALL, NORTHANTS., work for Sir Thomas Cave, Bart., *c.* 1743–5. Smith was here in 1743 (Isham Correspondence, no. 2508), and documents at Stanford show that the 'improvements' referred to in 1746 (Hist. MSS. Comm., *13th Report*, Appendix IV, 478) were carried out by him during the previous year. They included 'removing entirely the upper row of windows [in the hall] and sinking the ceiling by a cove'. The plasterwork is by John

Wright of Worcester (*C. Life*, 4, 11, 18 Dec. 1958).

MELBOURNE HALL, DERBYSHIRE, rebuilt east front for G. L. Coke, 1744 [accounts at Melbourne] (*C. Life*, 7, 14 April 1928).

THAME PARK, OXON., is said by F. G. Lee, *History of Thame*, 1883, 393, to have been designed for the 6th Viscount Wenman by 'Mr. Smith, an architect of Coventry', *c.* 1745. This is presumably a mistake for 'Smith of Warwick' [Arthur Oswald in *C. Life*, 28 Nov. 1957].

EDGCOTE HOUSE, NORTHANTS. The stables were built by Richard Chauncey in 1745–7, and there is a payment of £40 6s. to William Smith for 'surveying the building'. The house itself was rebuilt between 1747 and 1752 under the direction of William Jones, who was perhaps carrying out a design by Smith [MS. abstract of building accounts at Edgecote; H. A. Tipping in *C. Life*, 10 Jan. 1920, and *English Homes*, Period V (i), 1921, 289–300].

SMITH, WILLIAM (–1786), otherwise unknown, is commemorated as *architector* on a monument in the Calton Cemetery at Edinburgh, with the date 1786.

SMITH, WILLIAM, an architect and builder of Montrose, designed the upper storey which was added to MONTROSE TOWN HALL in 1818 [J. G. Low, *Highways and Byways of an Old Scottish Burgh*, Montrose 1938, 99]. He is also said to have designed ST. JOHN'S FREE CHURCH, MONTROSE, 1829, a Greek Revival building with an Ionic portico and a well-designed cupola [G. Hay, *The Architecture of Scottish Post-Reformation Churches*, 1957, 138].

SMYTHSON, JOHN (–1634), was the son of Robert Smythson (*c.* 1535–1614), a celebrated Elizabethan architect whose works included WOLLATON HALL, NOTTS. (1580–8), WORKSOP MANOR, NOTTS. (*c.* 1585), and HARDWICK HALL, DERBYSHIRE (1591–7). Like his father, John Smythson was by trade a mason, and is first found working as a freemason at Wollaton in 1588. But by the 1590s he was probably helping his father in an architectural capacity, and in 1600, when he married, he was described in the register of St. Peter's Church, Nottingham, as 'gentleman'. In his will he called himself 'Architecter'.

John Smythson's principal patrons were members of the Cavendish family, for whom he worked at Bolsover Castle in Derbyshire, Welbeck Abbey in Nottinghamshire, and Slingsby Castle in Yorkshire. In 1615 Sir Charles Cavendish gave him the lease for life, at a nominal rent, of a farm at Kirkby-in-Ashfield (Notts.), 'in consideration of the just and faithful service to him

heretofore done and hereafter to be done'. The service which Smythson gave in return appears to have included estate management as well as architectural supervision. In 1618–19 he visited London and made a number of drawings of recent buildings by Inigo Jones and others. His own architecture, as seen at Bolsover, was baroque rather than Jonesian in intention, and he delighted in rustication, fractured pediments, exaggerated mouldings and the like. The result is a highly personal style, mannered almost to the point of eccentricity, but unexpectedly attractive as well as whimsical. The drawings made by himself and his father are now in the R.I.B.A. Collection, and constitute a unique record of architectural practice in Elizabethan and Jacobean England.

John Smythson died in November or December 1634, leaving a house in Bolsover and considerable property in Nottinghamshire to his widow and his sons Huntingdon and John Smythson. Huntingdon Smythson (d. 1648), who called himself 'Practioner of the Mathematiqs', appears, like his father, to have been partly a land surveyor and partly an architect. Of the 'skill in architecture' with which he is credited by his epitaph in Bolsover Church there is little evidence, though he probably assisted his father at Bolsover Castle, and may have designed some of the buildings erected by Sir William Cavendish, whose exact dating is in doubt. He died on 27 September 1648, leaving property valued at £960, including unspecified books and mathematical instruments in his study.

['The Smythson Collection of the R.I.B.A.', ed. Mark Girouard, *Architectural History* v, 1962; Mark Girouard, *Robert Smythson and the Architecture of the Elizabethan Era*, 1966].

BOLSOVER CASTLE, DERBYSHIRE, works for Sir Charles Cavendish (d. 1617) and his son Sir William Cavendish (later 1st Duke of Newcastle), *c.* 1612–34, including the interior of the 'Little Castle' or keep (completed *c.* 1621), and the gallery, either 1617–20 (Faulkner) or *c.* 1631–4 (Girouard) [D. Knoop & G. P. Jones, 'The Bolsover Castle Building Account, 1613', *Ars Quatuor Coronatorum* xlix (1), 1936; Girouard, *Robert Smythson*, chaps. 6–7 and Appendix II; P. A. Faulkner, *Bolsover Castle*, H.M.S.O. 1972].

WELBECK ABBEY, NOTTS., RIDING SCHOOL for Sir William Cavendish, 1622–3; remodelled 1889; STABLES 1625, dem. [Girouard, *Robert Smythson*, 187–90].

AULT HUCKNALL CHURCH, DERBYSHIRE, monument to Anne Cavendish, Countess of Devonshire, 1627 [Girouard, *Robert Smythson*, 197].

attributed: SLINGSBY CASTLE, YORKS. (N.R.), for Sir Charles Cavendish (d. 1654), *c.* 1630; now in ruins [Girouard, *Robert Smythson*, 190–2].

CLIFTON HALL, NOTTS., stables and probably other works for Sir Gervase Clifton, 1632; dem. [Girouard, *Robert Smythson*, 197–8].

SOANE, SIR JOHN (1753–1837), born on 10 September, 1753, was the son of John Soan, or Soane, a bricklayer at Goring-on-Thames, nr. Reading. Nothing is known of his early upbringing, but in 1768 he entered the office of George Dance, junior, the City Surveyor, through the good offices of the latter's assistant James Peacock, to whom he had been introduced by 'a near relative'. In October 1771 he was admitted to the Royal Academy Schools, and in the following year he exhibited a design for the 'Front of a Nobleman's Town House', and was awarded the Silver Medal for a measured drawing of the façade of the Banqueting House in Whitehall. He competed unsuccessfully for the Gold Medal in 1774, but won it in 1776 with a design for a triumphal bridge.[1] Meanwhile, in 1772 he had been taken on as an assistant at a salary of £60 a year by Henry Holland, then newly established in practice in Mayfair. Holland was at that time engaged in completing Claremont House for Lord Clive, and Soane afterwards claimed to have been responsible for the design of the entrance hall. His engagement with Holland came to an end in 1778, when, having attracted the attention of Sir William Chambers, he was awarded the King's Travelling Studentship and set out for Italy in company with R. F. Brettingham. In Rome, besides studying the architectural monuments, he made the acquaintance of Thomas Pitt, Lord Camelford, and of Frederick Hervey, Bishop of Derry (afterwards Earl of Bristol). The latter, whose passion for building was well known, offered Soane employment in designing country houses for him at Ickworth in Suffolk and at Downhill in Ireland. Soane, dazzled by 'the magnificent promises and splendid delusions of the Lord Bishop of Derry', cut short his tour in order to follow his patron to Ireland, but after remaining at Downhill for six weeks 'without any prospect of professional employment' he returned to England in June 1780, depressed in spirits and uncertain of the future. A further disappointment awaited him when the prospect of various works at Allanbank, nr. Berwick, for John Stuart also came to nothing. But a series of more modest commissions, chiefly in East Anglia, established him in practice, and in 1784 he was able to marry. His bride was Elizabeth Smith, a niece of George Wyatt, a wealthy builder to whose property he succeeded in 1790. In 1788 he applied unsuccessfully for the vacant surveyorship of Greenwich Hospital, but gained a greater prize in that of the Bank of England, to which he was appointed in October 1788, through the influence of William Pitt. His competitors included James Wyatt, Henry Holland, S. P. Cockerell and Charles Beazley, who had 'transacted the whole of the Bank business' for Sir Robert Taylor during the last years of his life, and who was believed to 'stand well with the governors'. The surveyorship of the Bank gave Soane financial security, professional status and the most important commission of his life, besides introducing him to some of his wealthiest clients. From 1788 onwards he had an established place among the leading English architects, and enjoyed a professional practice second only to that of Wyatt. In 1791 he secured his first government appointment – that of Clerk of the Works at Whitehall, Westminster, and St. James's (£300 a year); in 1795 he became Deputy-Surveyor of H.M. Woods and Forests (£200 a year);[1] and in 1807 Clerk of the Works to Chelsea Hospital. In 1814, on the reorganization of the Board of Works, he was appointed one of the three 'Attached Architects', with personal responsibility for the public buildings in Whitehall, Westminster, Richmond Park, Kew Gardens and Hampton Court Palace. This appointment lasted until 1832, when Soane retired from the Office of Works with a knighthood. He was elected A.R.A. in 1795, and R.A. in 1802. In 1806 he succeeded George Dance as Professor of Architecture at the Royal Academy, and in 1809 began to deliver the elaborately illustrated lectures which he continued to repeat until the year before his death.[2] In 1810–11 they were temporarily suspended in consequence of a vote of censure passed upon him by the Academy for criticizing the work of a 'living artist' in the person of Robert Smirke, whose Covent Garden Theatre had figured in the fourth lecture as an example of the misuse of the Greek Doric Order. The care which he took in the preparation and presentation of his R.A. lectures was characteristic of Soane's interest in architectural education, and both in this way and by his personal influence over his many pupils he did much to raise the standards of architectural practice. He was outspoken in condemnation of what he regarded as unprofessional conduct, and although he was debarred by the rules of the R.A. from accepting the Presidency of the Institute of British Architects which was offered to him on its foundation in 1834, his position as the father of his profession was recognized

---

[1] Cf. Dorothy Stroud, 'Soane's Design for a Triumphal Bridge', *Arch. Rev.*, April 1957.

[1] This proved too small a salary to secure Soane's attention to the duties of his office, and he resigned in 1799 after complaints about his negligence. He had already, in 1793, resigned his Clerkship of the Works at Whitehall after a disagreement about his duties.

[2] They were published in 1929 under the editorship of A. T. Bolton as *Lectures in Architecture by Sir John Soane* (Soane Museum Publications, No. 14).

in the following year by the presentation to him of a Gold Medal on behalf of 350 subscribers. To acknowledge the honour then showed to him Soane gave £5000 as a fund for distressed architects and their dependants. Later in the same year he presented the sum of £750 to the Institute and £250 to the Architectural Society, expressing the hope that they would before long be united. The former gift was commemorated by the foundation of the Soane Medal, which became the principal award offered by the Institute to architectural students.

In 1833, Soane, then in his 80th year, was compelled by failing eyesight to resign the surveyorship of the Bank of England which had been 'the pride and boast' of his life. His connection with the Office of Works had already been terminated in 1832 upon its amalgamation with the Department of Woods, Forests, and Land Revenues. He spent his last years in writing a *Description* of the house in Lincoln's Inn Fields which had been his home since 1812, and which he left to the nation as a museum for 'the study of Architecture and the Allied Arts', obtaining an Act of Parliament to that effect in 1833. Throughout his life, Soane had collected architectural drawings, models and casts, besides paintings, sculpture and miscellaneous antiquities of all kinds. The house had gradually been extended and adapted for their reception until every available space was occupied by a bust or an antique vase, a painting by Hogarth or a drawing by Piranesi, all disposed in accordance with their collector's declared purpose of demonstrating 'the unity of the arts'. The result was a kind of personal Academy of the Arts, contained within the walls of a private residence, but intended for public display; and what had been a museum in its builder's lifetime retains after his death the atmosphere of a private house.

Soane was a man of difficult temperament, austere, exacting, touchy and neurotic. His private life was strained by difficulties with his sons, whose failure to follow their father's profession caused him life-long regret: and the sudden death of Mrs. Soane in 1815 was a tragedy which he never allowed himself to forget. He was punctilious in his relations with his clients, and spared neither himself nor his staff in accomplishing what he admitted to be 'the ruling passion of my life', namely 'to be distinguished as an architect'.

Soane's ambition found its expression in a highly individual architectural style based on an elegantly mannered – it might almost be said 'mannerist' – interpretation of the neo-classical vocabulary. Structurally, the Soaneic style is marked by a fondness for shallow domes associated with clerestory lighting, by the extensive use of segmental arches, and by great ingenuity in planning, particularly in cases where the site was circumscribed by existing buildings: in the

field of decoration, its distinguishing feature was the elimination of the classical column and entablature, together with their appropriate mouldings, and their replacement by a system of linear ornamentation, incised more often than raised, and eked out by the use of antique motifs such as *paterae* and *acroteria*. These characteristic features first appear fully developed in Soane's work at the Bank (from 1792 onwards),[1] where the effect was that of a primitive classicism stripped of its later embellishments: afterwards they were 'recombined and expanded' to obtain the picturesque effects which are so striking a feature of the Museum itself. In its earlier form this personal style owed much to the work of Soane's 'revered master', George Dance, junior, whose Guildhall Council Chamber (1777) anticipated its essential features; later, it absorbed both Gothic and Pompeian elements in the endeavour to achieve what Soane called 'the poetry of Architecture'. To deviate from the accepted canons of classical architecture was inevitably to invite attack, and Soane had his share of abuse in the shape of a facetious article on 'The Sixth or Boeotian Order of Architecture', which appeared in *Knight's Quarterly Magazine* in 1824, and led him to institute an unsuccessful libel action. Although not without influence on his contemporaries, Soane's style found no serious imitator, and his death meant the end of the attempt, begun by George Dance seventy years before, to develop a modern architecture based on classical forms, but freed from the inhibitions of the Vitruvian and Palladian past.

Apart from controversial pamphlets, Soane's published works were *Designs in Architecture, consisting of Plans, Elevations and Sections for Temples, Baths, Casines, Pavilions, Garden-Seats, Obelisks, and Other Buildings,* 1778 (a youthful work which Soane afterwards did his best to suppress); *Plans, Elevations and Sections of Buildings erected in the Counties of Norfolk, Suffolk,* etc., 1788;[2] *Sketches in Architecture, containing Plans and Elevations of Cottages, Villas and Other Useful Buildings,* 1793; and *Designs for Public Improvements* (1827, 25 copies only[3]), reprinted with additions as *Designs for Public and Private Buildings,* 1828. His *Description of the House and Museum on the North Side of Lincoln's Inn Fields,* 1832, of which an enlarged version was printed

---

[1] A comparison between his published designs for the saloon at Chillington, which shows a domed hall in the manner of Wyatt or Holland, and those actually executed in 1785–9 shows that the characteristic Soaneic Hall had already been conceived and executed before the Bank gave its author an opportunity of employing it on a large scale.

[2] The original drawings for pls. 28–32 are in the Hailstone Collection in York Minster Library.

[3] The copy presented by Soane to the Royal Library at Windsor contains a number of original drawings.

in 1835–6, and his *Memoirs of the Professional Life of an Architect*, 1835, were both privately printed.

The Soane Museum contains many portraits of its founder (notably that by Sir Thomas Lawrence), and all his private and professional papers, besides a large collection of his architectural drawings and lecture-diagrams. Several portraits of Soane and some of his drawings are preserved at the Bank of England (see *An Historical Catalogue of Engravings, Drawings and Paintings in the Bank of England*, 1928, 57–8, 69–73). There are also a few drawings by Soane in the R.I.B.A. Collection and the Victoria and Albert Museum.

In the course of his long career Soane had many pupils and assistants. The former included J. Adams, George Bailey (who remained with Soane until his death, and was appointed first Curator of the Museum under his will), George Basevi, S. Burchell, H. Burges, J. Buxton, R. D. Chantrell, Thomas Chawner, F. Copland, E. Davis, E. Foxall, J. H. Good, Thomas Jeans, David Laing, C. Malton, John McDonnell, A. P. Mee, Frederick Meyer (who gave up), David Mocatta, Henry Parke, C. E. Papendiek, C. J. Richardson, W. E. Rolfe, J. Sanders, H. H. Seward, Thomas Sword, B. J. Storace, Charles Tyrrell and Thomas Williams (who ran away to sea). Chief among Soane's assistants was J. M. Gandy, A.R.A., who spent most of his life as Soane's chief draughtsman and illustrator. Others were Christopher Ebdon, J. W. Hiort, G. E. Ives, William Lodder, R. Morrison, D. Paton and G. A. Underwood. George Wightwick was his secretary for about eight months in 1826–7, and wrote a brilliant and amusing account of his eccentric employer.

[*A.P.S.D.*; *D.N.B.*; T. L. Donaldson, *A Review of the Professional Life of Sir John Soane*, 1837; list of works by G. Bailey in *Builder* iv, 1846, 577, 590; A. T. Bolton, *The Works of Sir John Soane, R.A.*, 1924; A. T. Bolton, *The Portrait of Sir John Soane, R.A.*, 1927; H. J. Birnstingl, *Sir John Soane*, 1925; John Summerson, *Sir John Soane*, 1952; Dorothy Stroud, 'The Early Work of Soane', *Arch. Rev.*, Feb. 1957; Dorothy Stroud, *The Architecture of Sir John Soane*, 1961; *History of the King's Works* vi, 1973, *passim*.]

The following list of Soane's principal executed works is based on his publications (referred to as *Plans*, *Sketches* and *Designs*, respectively), on the list of his buildings printed in *A.P.S.D.* and reprinted by A. T. Bolton in *The Works of Sir John Soane*, and on the comprehensive list of commissions compiled by Miss Dorothy Stroud from the journals, account-books and drawings in Sir John Soane's Museum and printed at the end of her book entitled *The Architecture of Sir John Soane*, 1961.

PUBLIC BUILDINGS, ETC.

NORWICH, BLACKFRIARS BRIDGE (R. Wensum), 1783–4; since widened (*Plans*; Stroud, *Architecture*, pl. 7).

WALTHAMSTOW CHURCH, ESSEX, alterations, 1784 (cf. *V.C.H. Essex* vi, 289).

NAYLAND CHURCH, SUFFOLK, pewing, etc., 1785.

HINGHAM CHURCH, NORFOLK, alterations to chancel, including Gothic reredos since removed, 1785.

LONDON, THE BANK OF ENGLAND, rebuilt 1788–1833; rebuilt 1930–40 (*Designs*; Bolton, *Works*; H. R. Steele & F. R. Yerbury, *The Old Bank of England*, 1930; Stroud, *Architecture*, pls. 65–92).

NORWICH CASTLE, rebuilt COUNTY GAOL, 1789–94, castellated; dem. 1825 (*Designs*; Stroud, *Architecture*, pl. 46).

CAMBRIDGE, CAIUS COLLEGE, remodelled interior of Hall, 1792; converted into rooms 1853 [Willis & Clark, i, 197].

LONDON, HYDE PARK, CUMBERLAND GATE and lodge, 1797; dem. (Stroud, *Architecture*, pl. 109).

LONDON, CONSTITUTION HILL, lodge and gateway, 1797.

BRAMLEY CHURCH, HANTS., added BROCAS CHAPEL for Mrs. Brocas, 1802, Gothic.

WAKEFIELD, ALL SAINTS CHURCH (now Cathedral), report on repair of spire, 1892 [J. W. Walker, *Wakefield*, 1939].

READING, BERKS., obelisk in Market Place for Edward Simeon, 1804 (*Arch. Rev.* xlvii, 1920, 110–11, measured drawings).

OXFORD, BRASENOSE COLLEGE, converted cloister into rooms, 1807.

BELFAST, IRELAND, THE ACADEMICAL INSTITUTION, COLLEGE SQUARE, 1809–14, representing a much simplified version of his original designs (C. F. B. Brett, *Buildings of Belfast*, 1967, pls. 14, 15).

CHELSEA HOSPITAL, LONDON, the INFIRMARY, STABLES and additions to Clerk of the Works' House, 1809–17. The house was dem. 1858 and the Infirmary was destroyed by bombing in 1941 (Stroud, *Architecture*, pls. 145–53).

DULWICH COLLEGE, THE PICTURE GALLERY and MAUSOLEUM, 1811–14; restored after bomb damage in 1944 (*Designs*; Bolton, *Works*, 76–82; Stroud, *Architecture*, pls. 156–63).

LONDON, THE NATIONAL DEBT REDEMPTION AND LIFE ANNUITIES OFFICE, OLD JEWRY, 1818–19; dem. *c.* 1900 (*Designs*; Bolton, *Works*, 83–6; Stroud, *Architecture*, pls. 176–7).

WESTMINSTER, THE LAW COURTS, 1822–5; dem. 1883. The exterior was Gothicized against Soane's wishes, in accordance with a design which he disowned. [*History of the King's Works* vi, 1973, 504–12] (*Designs*; Bolton, *Works*, chap. 9; Stroud, *Architecture*, pls. 205–13).

WESTMINSTER, THE HOUSE OF LORDS: royal entrance, royal gallery, library and committee rooms, 1822–7; partly destroyed by fire 1834, remainder dem. 1851 [*History of the King's Works* vi, 1973, 520–5] (*Designs*; Bolton, *Works*, 103–14).

LONDON, ST. PETER'S CHURCH, WALWORTH, 1823–4 (Stroud, *Architecture*, pl. 189).

LONDON, THE INSOLVENT DEBTORS' COURT, PORTUGAL STREET, LINCOLN'S INN FIELDS, 1823–4; dem. 1911 [*History of the King's Works* vi, 438–40] (Stroud, *Architecture*, pls. 196–7).

LONDON, BOARD OF TRADE AND PRIVY COUNCIL OFFICES, WHITEHALL, 1824–6; remodelled by Barry 1845–6 [*History of the King's Works* vi, 1973, 551–62] (*Designs*).

WESTMINSTER, THE HOUSE OF COMMONS: LIBRARY and COMMITTEE ROOMS, 1826–7, Gothic; destroyed by fire 1834 [*History of the King's Works* vi, 527–9].

LONDON, HOLY TRINITY CHURCH, MARYLEBONE, 1826–7; chancel 1878; converted into S.P.C.K. offices 1955–6 (Stroud, *Architecture*, pls. 186–7).

LONDON, ST. JOHN'S CHURCH, BETHNAL GREEN, 1826–8; interior remodelled after fire in 1870 and chancel extended 1888 (Stroud, *Architecture*, pl. 188).

LONDON, FREEMASONS' HALL, GREAT QUEEN STREET, the new COUNCIL CHAMBER, 1828; dem. 1864 (*Designs*; Bolton, *Works*, 116, 119; Stroud, *Architecture*, pl. 221).

LONDON, THE BANQUETING HOUSE, WHITEHALL, restoration of exterior, 1829–33 [*History of the King's Works* vi, 547–8].

WESTMINSTER, THE STATE PAPER OFFICE, DUKE STREET, 1830–4; dem. 1862 [*History of the King's Works* vi, 1973, 567–70] (*Designs*; Bolton, *Works*, 128–31; Stroud, *Architecture*, pls. 222–4).

COUNTRY HOUSES, ETC.

PETERSHAM LODGE, SURREY, repairs and decorations for Thomas Pitt, later 1st Lord Camelford, 1781–2; dem. *c.* 1835.

WALTHAMSTOW, ESSEX, new room for James Neave, 1781, perhaps at CLEVELANDS, dem. 1960.

HAMELS (now Crofton Grange), nr. BUNTINGFORD, HERTS., alterations, entrance lodges and dairy for the Hon. Philip Yorke, 1781–3; house remodelled *c.* 1830/40 (Stroud, *Architecture*, pl. 8).

COOMBE HOUSE, nr. KINGSTON, SURREY, repairs and alterations for the Hon. Wilbraham Tollemache, 1782–5; dem. 1933.

BURN HALL, CO. DURHAM, neo-classical cow-house for George Smith, 1783 [P. de la R. du Prey in *C. Life*, 8 Jan. 1976, 84] (*Plans*).

WALTHAMSTOW RECTORY MANOR, ESSEX, enlarged for William Cooke, 1783–4; dem. *c.* 1897.

BURNHAM WESTGATE HALL, NORFOLK, alterations and additions for Thomas Pitt, later 1st Lord Camelford, 1783–5.

TYTTENHANGER, HERTS., repairs for the Hon. Mrs. Yorke, 1783 and 1789.

MALVERN HALL, SOLIHULL, WARWICKS., added wings, etc., for Henry Greswold Lewis, 1783–6; wings dem. 1899 (*Plans*; cf. *Constable's Correspondence*, ed. R. B. Beckett, iv, 62; Stroud, *Architecture*, pl. 107 for Doric barn).

LETTON HALL, NORFOLK, for B. G. Dillingham, 1783–9 (*Plans*; Stroud, *Architecture*, pls. 1–6).

SAXLINGHAM RECTORY, NORFOLK, for the Rev. J. Gooch, 1784–7 (*Plans*; Stroud, *Architecture*, pls. 9–10).

COSTESSY HALL, NORFOLK, stable and dovecote for Sir William Jerningham, Bart., 1784; probably built but dem.

TAVERHAM HALL, NORFOLK, alterations for M. S. Branthwayt, 1784–8; rebuilt by D. Brandon, 1858–9.

EARSHAM HALL, nr. BUNGAY, NORFOLK, Music Room for William Wyndham, 1784–5 (*Plans*; Stroud, *Architecture*, pls. 17–19).

TENDRING HALL, SUFFOLK, for Sir Joshua Rowley, Bart., 1784–6; dem. 1955 (Stroud, *Architecture*, plus. 11–16).

LANGLEY PARK, NORFOLK, two sets of lodges for Sir Thomas Beauchamp-Proctor, Bart., 1784 onwards (*Plans*; Stroud, *Architecture*, pls. 20–2).

SHOTESHAM PARK, NORFOLK, for R. Fellowes, 1785–8 (*C. Life*, 10 Aug. 1967; Stroud, *Architecture*, pls. 23–7).

BLUNDESTON HOUSE, SUFFOLK, for Nathaniel Rix, 1785–6 (*Plans*, where it appears under the name of 'Oulton'; Stroud, *Architecture*, pl. 36).

CHILLINGTON HALL, STAFFS., remodelled for Thomas Giffard, 1785–9 (*Plans*; *C. Life*, 27 Feb. 1948). There are drawings by Soane in the William Salt Library at Stafford: 'Staffordshire Views' iii, ff. 95–107.

PIERCEFIELD, nr. CHEPSTOW, MONMOUTHSHIRE, rebuilt for George Smith, 1785–93; now in ruins (Stroud, *Architecture*, pls. 44, 45).

LEES COURT, KENT, alterations to house and new stables for L. T. Watson, 1786 (Stroud, *Architecture*, pls. 30–2).

CRICKET LODGE, CRICKET ST. THOMAS, SOMERSET, alterations and additions for Admiral Hood, 1st Viscount Bridport, 1786 and 1801–4; since much altered (Stroud, *Architecture*, pl. 134).

RYSTON HALL, NORFOLK, remodelled for Edward Pratt, 1786–8 (*Plans*; Stroud, *Architecture*, pls. 33–4).

BOCONNOC, CORNWALL, repairs for the 1st Lord Camelford, 1786–88.

MULGRAVE HALL, YORKS. (N.R.), alterations and additions for the 2nd Lord Mulgrave, 1786

(*Plans*); remodelled by William Atkinson as Mulgrave Castle, *c.* 1804–11.

HOCKERILL, nr. BISHOPS STORTFORD, HERTS., house for R. Winter, 1786 (*Plans*).

BEAUPORT, nr. BATTLE, SUSSEX, designs for greenhouse and obelisk for General the Hon. James Murray, 1786 and 1790; house dem. 1923.

NACKINGTON HOUSE, KENT, alterations for R. Milles, 1786; dem.

HOLWOOD HOUSE, KENT, alterations and additions for William Pitt, 1786 and 1797–8; dem. 1823 (*Designs*; Stroud, *Architecture*, pl. 35).

SKELTON CASTLE, YORKS. (N.R.), alterations and additions, including stables, for John Hall (later Wharton), 1787 (*Plans*).

FONTHILL HOUSE, WILTS., picture gallery for Alderman William Beckford, 1787; dem. 1807 (Stroud, *Architecture*, pls. 37–8).

HETHERSETT, NORFOLK, design for house for J. F. Iselin, 1788.

KELSHALL RECTORY, HERTS., designs for alterations for the Rev. Thomas Waddington, 1788.

BENTLEY PRIORY, STANMORE, MIDDLESEX, alterations and additions for the 1st Marquess of Abercorn, 1788–98; enlarged by R. Smirke 1810–18; subsequently much altered (Stroud, *Architecture*, pls. 40–3).

WARDOUR CASTLE, WILTS., enlarged CHAPEL (R.C.) for the 8th Lord Arundell of Wardour, 1788 (*C. Life*, 10 Oct. 1968).

BEMERTON RECTORY, WILTS., designs for alterations for Dr. William Coxe, 1788.

RICHMOND PARK, SURREY, HILL or PEMBROKE LODGE, alterations for the Countess of Pembroke, 1788 and 1796.

GAWDY HALL, nr. HARLESTON, NORFOLK, alterations for the Rev. Gervase Holmes, 1788; dem. 1939.

WOKEFIELD PARK, BERKS., alterations and new gateway for Mrs. Brocas, 1788–9; altered *c.* 1845.

SYDNEY LODGE, HAMBLE, HANTS., for the Hon. Mrs. Yorke, 1789 (G. Richardson, *New Vitruvius Britannicus* i, 1810, pl. 10; Stroud, *Architecture*, pls. 47–9).

TAWSTOCK COURT, DEVON, alterations to exterior (castellated) and new staircase for Sir Bourchier Wrey, Bart., 1789 (*Gent's Mag.* 1817 (i), 489; Stroud, *Architecture*, plus. 50–1).

WRETHAM HALL, NORFOLK, for William Colhoun, 1789; rebuilt in nineteenth century; dem. *c.* 1905.

FAIRFORD PARK, GLOS., alterations for J. R. Barker, 1789; dem. *c.* 1960.

GUNTHORPE HALL, NORFOLK, for Charles Collyer, 1789; altered 1880 and 1900.

HALSNEAD HALL, WHISTON, LANCS., south front for Richard Willis, 1789; dem. 1932 (S. A. Harris in *Trans. Historic Soc. of Lancs. and Cheshire* cvi, 1954, 153–8).

CHILTON LODGE, nr. HUNGERFORD, BERKS., for William Morland, 1789–90; rebuilt by W. Pilkington 1800 (*Sketches*; Stroud, *Architecture*, pl. 53).

WOODEATON MANOR, OXON., new porch and kitchen wing for John Weyland, 1790.

COLNE PARK, ESSEX, Ionic column in park for Philip Hills, 1790.

WILLIAMSTRIP PARK, GLOS., refitted library for Michael Hicks Beach, 1791; altered *c.* 1940.

WISTON HALL, WISSINGTON, SUFFOLK, for Samuel Beachcroft, 1791.

WHICHCOTES, HENDON, MIDDLESEX, repairs for John Cornwall, 1791.

NETHERAVON HOUSE, WILTS., enlarged for Michael Hicks Beach, 1791; since much altered.

BARON'S COURT, CO. TYRONE, IRELAND, additions for the 1st Marquess of Abercorn, 1791–2; rebuilt in nineteenth century (Stroud, *Architecture*, pls. 63–4).

WIMPOLE HALL, CAMBS., alterations and additions, including Yellow Drawing Room and Book Room, for the 3rd Earl of Hardwicke, 1791–3 (*C. Life*, 21, 28 May 1927; R.C.H.M., *West Cambridgeshire*, 217 and plate; Stroud, *Architecture*, pls. 58–62).

TAPLOW, BUCKS., additions to house for Lady Wynn, 1792.

SULBY HALL, NORTHANTS., for René Payne, 1792–5; apparently remodelled *c.* 1830; dem. *c.* 1953 [stated to be by Soane in J. P. Neale, *Views of Seats*, 1st ser., vi, 1823, and confirmed by Soane's ledgers] (J. A. Gotch, *Squires' Homes of Northants.*, 1939, 23–4, illustrating the house after 1830).

TYRINGHAM HALL, BUCKS., including lodge and bridge, for William Praed, 1793–*c.* 1800; interior altered, dome a modern addition (*Designs*; Bolton, *Works*, 12–20; Stroud, *Architecture*, pls. 93–9).

SOUTHGATE, MIDDLESEX, alterations to house for Thomas Lewis, 1793.

CAIRNESS HOUSE, ABERDEENSHIRE, completion, 1794–7, of house designed by James Playfair (*q.v.*) for Charles Gordon.

CUFFNELLS, nr. LYNDHURST, HANTS., south front, etc., for George Rose, 1794–5; dem. *c.* 1950 (G. F. Prosser, *Select Illustrations of Hampshire*, 1833).

PITSHILL, nr. TILLINGTON, SUSSEX, designs for north front for William Mitford, executed in modified form, 1794.

SUNBURY PLACE, MIDDLESEX, designs for alterations for Roger Boehm, 1794.

SOUTHGATE, MIDDLESEX, alterations to house at Palmer's Green for Samuel Boddington, 1795.

BAGDEN or SAVERNAKE LODGE, SAVERNAKE FOREST, WILTS., enlarged for the 1st Earl of Ailesbury as a residence for his son Lord Bruce, 1795; destroyed by fire 1861.

WESTON, nr. SOUTHAMPTON, HANTS., alterations

769

for W. Moffat, 1797; dem. Although Soane was responsible for alterations to this house in 1797, subsequent references in Soane's journal suggest that he may have been superseded by Willey Reveley (*q.v.*).

NORTH MIMMS PARK, HERTS., repairs and new dairy and greenhouse, etc., for the 5th Duke of Leeds, 1797.

CLAPHAM, WANDSWORTH, SURREY, alterations to house for T. A. Green, 1798.

BAGSHOT PARK, SURREY, alterations for the Duke of Clarence, 1798; dem. (G. F. Prosser, *Select Illustrations of Surrey*, 1828; Stroud, *Architecture*, pl. 108).

BETCHWORTH CASTLE, SURREY, alterations to house and new stables, etc., for Henry Peters, 1798–9 (Stroud, *Architecture*, pls. 110–14).

HEATHFIELD LODGE, ACTON, MIDDLESEX, alterations for John Winter, 1798.

RICHMOND PARK, SURREY, THATCHED HOUSE LODGE, alterations to dining-room, etc., for General Sir Charles Stuart, 1798.

DOWN AMPNEY HOUSE, GLOS., alterations for the Hon. John Eliot, 1799.

AYNHO PARK, NORTHANTS., remodelled interior and altered exterior for W. R. Cartwright, 1799–1804 (*C. Life*, 2, 9, 16 July 1953).

ALBURY PARK, SURREY, north front and internal alterations for Samuel Thornton, 1800–2; exterior remodelled by A. W. & E. W. Pugin 1842 onwards (*C. Life*, 25 Aug., 1 Sept. 1950).

PITZHANGER PLACE or MANOR, EALING, MIDDLESEX (now Public Library), largely rebuilt for himself, 1800–3 (G. Richardson, *New Vitruvius Britannicus* ii, 1808, pls. 57–9; Stroud, *Architecture*, pls. 122–30).

RICKMANSWORTH, HERTS., THE MOAT HOUSE, designs for alterations and additions for T. H. Earle, 1800.

SOUTH HILL PARK, BRACKNELL, BERKS., alterations for George Canning, 1801.

NORWOOD GREEN, MIDDLESEX, house for John Robins, 1801; dem. (Stroud, *Architecture*, pl. 133).

COOMBE HOUSE, nr. KINGSTON, SURREY, alterations, including library, for Lord Hawkesbury, later 2nd Earl of Liverpool, 1801; dem. 1933.

GREENWICH, KENT, MACARTNEY HOUSE, alterations for the Hon. G. F. Lyttlelton, 1802.

LITTLE HILL COURT, HERTS., designs for alterations for Mrs. Saunders, 1803.

HAMPSTEAD, LONDON, new entrance and other alterations to house for Daniel Bayley, 1803.

PORT ELIOT, ST. GERMAN'S, CORNWALL, remodelled house and designed new stables for the 2nd Lord Eliot, 1804–6, castellated; entrance hall and porch by H. Harrison 1829 (*C. Life*, 15, 22, 29 Oct. 1948; Stroud, *Architecture*, pls. 136–8).

RAMSEY ABBEY, HUNTS., remodelled for H. Fel-lowes, 1804–7; remodelled by E. Blore 1838–9 (Stroud, *Architecture*, pl. 139).

ROEHAMPTON, SURREY, CEDAR COURT, enlarged for John Thomson, 1804–7; dem. 1910–13.

STOWE HOUSE, BUCKS., Gothic library for the 1st Marquis of Buckingham, 1805–6 (Stroud, *Architecture*, pls. 141–2).

ASTROP PARK, NORTHANTS., additions for the Rev. W. S. Willes, 1805; reduced in size 1961.

ENGLEFIELD HOUSE, BERKS., repairs for Richard Benyon, 1806 [drawings in Berks. County Record Office, D/EBY 23 and C14].

WHITLEY ABBEY, WARWICKS., alterations for the 1st Viscount Hood, 1810; dem. 1953 (J. P. Neale, *Views of Seats*, 1st ser., iii, 1820).

MOGGERHANGER HOUSE, BEDS., rebuilt for Stephen Thornton, 1809–11 (Stroud, *Architecture*, pls. 143–4).

MELLS PARK, SOMERSET, alterations, including entrance and library, for Col. Thomas Horner, 1810–24; dem. after fire in 1917 (*C. Life*, 24 May 1962, 1254; Stroud, *Architecture*, pls. 154–5).

EVERTON HOUSE, BEDS., alterations for William Astell, 1811–12; dem.

WALMER COTTAGE, KENT, additions for Capt. Lee, 1812.

RINGWOULD HOUSE, KENT, for the Rev. John Monins, 1813 (C. Greenwood, *Epitome of County History: Kent*, 1838, 433; Stroud, *Architecture*, pl. 172).

BUTTERTON, STAFFS., BUTTERTON GRANGE FARM-HOUSE, for Thomas Swinnerton, 1815 (Stroud, *Architecture*, pl. 174).

MARDEN HILL, TEWIN, HERTS., new porch and other alterations for C. G. Thornton, 1818–19 (*C. Life*, 22 Aug. 1941; Stroud, *Architecture*, pls. 178–9).

WOTTON HOUSE, BUCKS., reconstructed interior after fire for the 2nd Marquis of Buckingham, 1821–2 (*C. Life*, 15 July 1949; Stroud, *Architecture*, pls. 180–2).

PELLWALL HOUSE, nr. MARKET DRAYTON, STAFFS., for Purney Sillitoe, 1822–8 (*Designs*; Stroud, *Architecture*, pl. 198–204).

HARDENHUISH HOUSE, WILTS., alterations and additions for Thomas Clutterbuck, 1829.

LONDON HOUSES, ETC.

PICCADILLY, NO. 148, completion and decoration for the Hon. Wilbraham Tollemache, 1781–8.

ADAMS PLACE, SOUTHWARK, shops and tenements for Francis Adams, 1781–4; dem.

BERKELEY SQUARE, alterations for the Hon. Mrs. Perry, 1782–3.

NEW CAVENDISH STREET, NO. 63 (formerly NO. 1), alterations for the Hon. P. Yorke, 1782–4.

WIMPOLE STREET, repairs to house for Sir John Stuart of Allanbank, 1783.

SAVILE ROW, NO. 18, alterations to drawing-room for Lady Banks, 1784.

PALL MALL, NO. 103, shop-front for Mr. Crooke, 1790; dem. 1836–7 [*Survey of London* xxix, 350].

HILL STREET, NO. 23, alterations for the 1st Earl Fortescue, 1791.

PALL MALL, NO. 56, alterations for Messrs. Ransom, Morland & Hammersley, 1791.

PHILPOT LANE, NO. 15, repairs and decorations for Peter Thellusson, 1792.

FENCHURCH STREET, NO. 27, repairs and decorations for Charles Thellusson, 1792.

MARK LANE, NO. 17, repairs and alterations for Samuel Boddington, 1792.

UPPER GROSVENOR STREET, NO. 1, repairs for Mrs. Brocas, 1792 and 1819.

BUCKINGHAM HOUSE, NO. 91 PALL MALL, rebuilt for the 1st Marquis of Buckingham, 1792–5; further alterations and repairs 1813–14; dem. 1908 (*Designs*; *Survey of London* xxix, 360–3 and pls. 224–7).

LINCOLN'S INN FIELDS, NO. 12, for himself, 1792–4 (Stroud, *Architecture*, pls. 100–4).

PALL MALL, NO. 104, alterations for Lady Louisa Manners, 1793–4; dem. *c.* 1837 [*Survey of London* xxix, 350].

LINCOLN'S INN FIELDS, NO. 51, alterations for John Pearse, 1794; dem. 1904 (*Survey of London* iii, pls. 61–5).

STRATTON STREET, NO. 12, for Col. Thomas Graham, 1795–7.

SOUTH AUDLEY STREET, NO. 56, repairs and decorations for Miss Anguish, 1795.

LINCOLN'S INN FIELDS, NOS. 57–8, divided into two houses, with new porch, 1795 (*Survey of London* iii, pls. 73–5).

PORTLAND PLACE, NO. 25 (now 70), repairs and alterations for Sir Alan, later 1st Lord Gardner, 1795 and 1810.

ST. JAMES'S SQUARE, NO. 21, completion of house designed by R. F. Brettingham for the 5th Duke of Leeds, 1795; dem. 1934 [*Survey of London* xxix, 175–80, pls. 191–3].

PARK LANE, alterations and repairs to house for the 2nd Earl of Mornington, 1796.

LOWER GOWER STREET, NO. 34, alterations for Mrs. Peters, 1798.

ST. JAMES'S SQUARE, NO. 22, internal alterations for Samuel Thornton, 1799, and repairs, 1805 and 1811; dem. 1847 (*Survey of London* xxix, 180–1).

MANSFIELD STREET, NO. 12, alterations for Charles Mills, 1799.

GEORGE STREET, HANOVER SQUARE, NO. 24, alterations for Dr. Pemberton, 1799.

GROSVENOR SQUARE, NO. 22 (later 25), alterations for the 1st Marquess of Abercorn, 1799.

OLD BOND STREET, CITY, alterations for Stephen Thornton, 1800.

PARK STREET, MAYFAIR, NO. 50 or 51, repairs for Henry Peters, 1800.

NEW NORFOLK (now DUNRAVEN) STREET, NO. 22,

alterations for J. Hammet, 1801, completed by James Spiller.

FLEET STREET, NO. 189, Bank for William Praed, 1801; dem. 1923 (Stroud, *Architecture*, pls. 131–2).

FOUNTAIN COURT, ALDERMANBURY, new premises for W. A. Jackson, Peters & Co., 1802; dem.

GROSVENOR SQUARE, NO. 44, alterations for Robert Knight, 1802; dem. (Stroud, *Architecture*, pl. 135).

PARK LANE, alterations to windows of house for the 4th Earl of Breadalbane, 1803.

UPPER GROSVENOR STREET, NO. 14, alterations for Thomas Raikes, 1803.

CURZON STREET, NO. 19, alterations for Sir John Sebright, Bart., 1803.

ST. JAMES'S SQUARE, NO. 33, alterations for the 2nd Lord Eliot, 1805–7 [*Survey of London* xxix, 207–10].

SOUTH AUDLEY STREET, NO. 6, decorations for Richard Benyon, 1805.

FREDERICK'S PLACE, NO. 4, alterations for Thomas Lewis, 1806.

DEAN STREET, MAYFAIR, alterations to house for Mr. Knight, 1807.

NEW BANK BUILDINGS, PRINCES STREET, LOTHBURY, 1807–10; dem. 1891 (*Designs*; Stroud, *Architecture*, pl. 140).

GROSVENOR SQUARE, NO. 34, alterations for Mrs. Benyon, 1807.

CHARLOTTE (now HALLAM) STREET, NO. 38, mausoleum for Sir Francis Bourgeois, 1807; dem.

WHITEHALL, FIFE HOUSE, repairs and alterations for the 2nd Earl of Liverpool, 1809; dem.

PARK LANE, NO. 22 (later 18), for John Robins, 1812.

LINCOLN'S INN FIELDS, NO. 13, for himself, 1812–13 (John Britton, *The Union of Architecture, Sculpture and Painting*, 1827; John Summerson, *A New Description of Sir John Soane's Museum*, 1955).

WHITEHALL, CARRINGTON HOUSE, stables and minor alterations to house for the 1st Lord Carrington, 1816–18; dem. 1886 (*Survey of London* xvi, pls. 94–5).

GROSVENOR SQUARE, NO. 13, alterations for the 2nd Lord Berwick, 1816.

ST. ALBAN'S STREET, ST. JAMES'S, stabling for the 1st Earl of St. Germans, 1816–18; dem. [*Survey of London* xxix, 208].

THREADNEEDLE STREET, NO. 62, alterations to Bank for Grote, Prescott & Grote, 1818.

ST. JAMES'S SQUARE, NO. 3, alterations and additions for the 4th Earl of Hardwicke, 1818–19; dem. 1930 [*Survey of London* xxix, 85–6].

MONTAGUE PLACE, BLOOMSBURY, NO. 16, alterations for Henry Hase, 1820.

REGENT STREET, NOS. 156–172 on east side, houses and shops for J. Robins and others, 1820–1; dem. (Stroud, *Architecture*, pls. 183–4).

LINCOLN'S INN FIELDS, NO. 14, for himself, 1823–4.

DOWNING STREET, NOS. 10–11, internal alterations, 1825–6 [*History of the King's Works* vi,
565–6] (Stroud, *Architecture*, pls. 217–20).

BELGRAVE PLACE, NO. 30, ante-room to sculpture
gallery for Sir Francis Chantrey, 1830–1; dem.
[*Designs*; Bolton, *Works*, 120, 122].

MISCELLANEOUS WORKS

BURY ST. EDMUNDS, SUFFOLK, NO. 81 GUILDHALL
STREET, enlarged for James Oakes, 1789–90.

READING, BERKS., SIMONDS' BREWERY, new house
and brewery buildings on east side of Bridge
Street, 1789–91; dem. 1900 (Stroud, *Architecture*, pl. 52).

NORWICH, SURREY STREET, additions to house
(now Norwich Union Fire Office) for John
Patterson, 1790 (Stroud, *Architecture*, pls. 56–
7).

WINCHESTER, HANTS., school (now drill-hall) for
the Rev. Mr. Richards, 1795 (Stroud, *Architecture*, pls. 105–6).

MONUMENTS

KENSINGTON, ST. MARY ABBOTS CHURCHYARD,
monument to Miss Elizabeth Johnstone for the
Earl of Bellamont, 1784 (*C. Life*, 8 Oct. 1953,
1135).

FELBRIDGE PLACE, SURREY, column in memory of
James Evelyn, 1785–6, moved to Lemington,
Northumberland, 1928 [B.M., Add. MS.
38480, ff. 372–4].

LONDON, ST. STEPHEN'S CHURCH, COLEMAN STREET,
monument to Claude Bosanquet, 1786; destroyed by bombing 1940.

LEYTONSTONE CHURCHYARD, ESSEX, monument to
Samuel Bosanquet, 1806; dem. 1957–8.

SOUTHWARK CATHEDRAL, tablet in south choir
aisle to Abraham Newland, 1808.

CHISWICK CHURCHYARD, MIDDLESEX, monument
to P. J. de Loutherbourg, R.A., 1812.

CRICKET ST. THOMAS CHURCH, SOMERSET, monument to the 1st Viscount Bridport, 1814
(Stroud, *Architecture*, pl. 173).

ST. GILES' BURIAL GROUND (now St. Pancras
Gardens), monument to Mrs. Soane, 1816
(Stroud, *Architecture*, pl. 175; John Summer-
son in *Revue de l'Art*, No. 30, 1975, 51–4).

LAMBETH PARISH CHURCH, monument to Anna
Storace, 1817; destroyed.

SPEED, JOHN, a mason of Newburgh in Fife,
designed the TOWN HOUSE there with its octagonal
steeple in 1808 [Newburgh Town Council
Minutes, *ex inf.* Mr. David Walker].

SPERRING, JOHN, of Frome, designed COLE-
FORD CHURCH, SOMERSET, in a poor Gothic style
in 1831 [G.R.].

772

SPILLER, JAMES (–1829), was the son of
John Spiller, a speculative builder of Christ
Church, Southwark, who built Highbury Place,
Islington, in 1774–7. James became a pupil of
James Wyatt, and was in his office in 1780, the
year in which he exhibited his first drawing at the
Royal Academy. He began practice soon after-
wards and became surveyor to the Royal
Exchange Assurance Company in about 1790. He
is said also to have been surveyor to the Eagle
Insurance Corporation in Cornhill. He was a
temperamental architect, who was rarely satisfied
with his work and frequently disagreed with his
clients. He corresponded for many years with Sir
John Soane, who occasionally employed him to
survey or supervise works in his care, and took
over at least one commission – that of Mells
Park – which Spiller had abandoned. In 1807 he
and Thomas Spencer were employed to survey
the houses then in course of erection on the
Foundling Hospital estate in London, and in
their report strongly criticized both the architect,
S. P. Cockerell, and the principal builder, James
Burton. Despite this, Cockerell succeeded in re-
gaining the confidence of the Governors, and the
services of Messrs. Spiller and Spencer were dispensed with. They thereupon printed an *Address
to the Governors and Guardians of the Foundling
Hospital ... intended as a Justification of their
Reports and Proceedings* (1807), of which there is
a copy in Sir John Soane's Museum. The Governors replied by printing at length *Reports upon
the Buildings erected on the Estate of the Foundling
Hospital by James Spiller and Thomas Spencer,
Surveyors, with observations on the said Reports by
S. P. Cockerell, Esq., Architect to the said Hospital, together with the Answer of the Surveyors to
the Observations of Mr. Cockerell and the Letter
to the General Court* (1808). This was not
published, but there is a copy in the Soane
Museum. Spiller was also the author of a pamphlet entitled *A Letter to John Soane, Esq. on the
subject of the New Churches*, 1822, in which he
complained of the inferior design of the churches
erected under the Act of 1818. Spiller's own
church of St. John, Hackney, is a striking neo-
classical building which suggests that he was an
architect of considerable originality, though of
very limited performance. He died at his house
in Guildford Street (No. 35) in April or May
1829, after a long illness. The MS. 'Observations'
on the reorganization of the Office of Works in
1814–15 which he prepared on Soane's behalf are
in the Soane Museum, together with some of his
designs for churches (xlvii, 10, nos. 22–31), and
nearly a hundred of his letters. His brothers John
(d. 1794) and Robert were both in business as
masons and sculptors.

[*A.P.S.D.*; A. T. Bolton, *The Portrait of Sir
John Soane*, 1927, *passim*; R. Gunnis, *Dictionary
of British Sculptors*, 1968 (for John and Robert

Spiller); information about John Spiller, senior, from Mr. Frank Kelsall.]

LONDON, THE LONDON HOSPITAL, WHITECHAPEL ROAD, additional buildings, 1781–3 [*A.P.S.D.*].

LONDON, THE GREAT SYNAGOGUE, DUKE'S PLACE, ALDGATE, 1788–90; destroyed 1940/1 [T. Pennant, *London*, 1793, 278].

LONDON, ST. JOHN'S CHURCH, HACKNEY, 1792–7; steeple and porches 1812–13; damaged by fire 1955 [exhib. at R.A. 1792; J. N. Brewer, *Beauties of England and Wales* x (iv), 265; W. Robinson, *History of Hackney* ii, 1843, 113] (Elizabeth & Wayland Young, *Old London Churches*, 1956, pls. 48A, 49).

ROEHAMPTON, SURREY, ELM GROVE for Benjamin Goldsmid, *c.* 1797; bombed 1940, dem. 1957 [exhib. at R.A. 1801; sketch for decoration of one of the rooms in Soane Museum (F.14)].

LONDON, THE ROYAL INSTITUTION, NOS. 20–21 ALBEMARLE STREET, revised designs of Thomas Webster for the Lecture Theatre, Library and Repository, 1800–1; altered 1928–30 [exhib. at R.A. 1801; cf. drawings reproduced in *Architects' Jnl.*, 23 Oct. 1941, 269–70].

WOODFORD, ESSEX, a 'design for a gentleman', exhibited at R.A. 1801.

TOLMERS, or TOLLIMORE, NEWGATE STREET, nr. HATFIELD, HERTS., for Robert Taylor, 1805–6 [exhib. at R.A. 1805; *A.P.S.D.*].

MELLS PARK, SOMERSET, began additions for Thomas Horner, but gave up the commission after a disagreement with his client, who employed Sir John Soane to complete the work to his own designs between 1810 and 1824 [A. T. Bolton, *Works of Sir John Soane*, 101].

SQUIRE, RICHARD (1700–1786), was a mason and monumental sculptor of Worcester, of which city he became a freeman in 1733. On his ledger-stone in All Saints Church he is described as 'one of the Master-Builders of this Church; which, with many Memorial-works here, and throughout this County will be lasting Monuments of his Skill and Abilities'. ALL SAINTS CHURCH was built between 1738 and 1742. Squire's name and that of his brother-in-law William Davis, the master carpenter, were inscribed on the tower, but are now no longer legible. In 1737 Squire gave evidence before the House of Commons about the condition of the old church [*Commons' Jnls.* xxiii, 48], and it is possible that he designed as well as built the new one. According to Nash it was designed by Thomas White (*q.v.*), but there is reason to doubt the accuracy of Nash's information about White's architectural activities. No parish records remain to determine the matter. At UPTON-ON-SEVERN CHURCH in 1755–7 Squire acted as a building surveyor, inspecting the workman-

ship of John Willoughby in rebuilding it, besides himself supplying the marble altar-table and font [MS. 'Parish Book']. Many monuments bearing his signature are to be seen in Worcestershire churches.

SQUIRHILL, CHARLES, practised as an architect and surveyor in Northampton in the 1820s and 1830s. He had previously been in the office of Francis Goodwin [Thomas Rickman's Diary, 15 May 1821]. His works included rebuilding ABINGTON CHURCH, NORTHANTS., in 1824–6 [churchwardens' accounts]; rebuilding the spire of RAUNDS CHURCH, NORTHANTS., in 1826 after it had been struck by lightning [minute-book among parish records]; reconstructing the interior of DENTON CHURCH, NORTHANTS., in 1828 [I.C.B.S.]; reseating BUGBROOK and HARPOLE CHURCHES, NORTHANTS., both in 1828, and designing a new gallery in ALL SAINTS CHURCH, NORTHAMPTON, in the same year [parish records, no. 166]. His work at Abington and Denton reveals him as a purveyor of the feeblest sort of early nineteenth-century Gothic. Daniel Goodman Squirhill (1809–63), who practised at Leamington in the 1840s, may have been his son.

STAFF, JOHN (*c.* 1751–1833), practised in Croydon, where he died in December 1833, aged 82, and was buried in the parish churchyard. He is stated in James Edwards' *Companion from London to Brightelmston*, 1801, part 2, 48, to have designed JUNIPER HILL, MICKLEHAM, SURREY, for Mr. Jenkinson in about 1780. In 1789–90 BETCHWORTH CHURCH, SURREY, was repaired and repewed under his direction [MS. Vestry Minutes]. The minutes of the Croydon Waste Lands Trustees show that the COURT HOUSE at CROYDON, built in 1807-9 and dem. 1894, was designed by Staff after plans by S. P. Cockerell had been rejected.[1] Towards the end of his life Staff evidently took Henry Prosser (*q.v.*) into partnership, for they appear as 'Staff & Prosser, Surveyors and Architects', in Pigot's *Directory* of 1827–8, and in 1825 they were jointly responsible for the enlargement of SUTTON CHURCH, SURREY (rebuilt 1862–4) [I.C.B.S.].

STANDBRIDGE, JOHN, of Warwick, is described as 'an architect of skill' in the Warwick Castle records (1777). He appears to have been a mason by trade. His design and estimate for a stone bridge at ALSCOT PARK, WARWICKS., 1766, is among the West papers there, and he may have been the 'Coventry (*sic*) builder called Stand-

---

[1] This accounts for the erroneous attribution to S. P. Cockerell in Brayley's *History of Surrey* iv, 22, and other topographical works. For extracts from the MS. minute-book of the Trustees I am indebted to Mr. K. Ryde of the Central Library, Croydon.

bridge' who designed and built a wooden bridge at CHARLECOTE HOUSE, WARWICKS., in 1768 [Alice Fairfax-Lucy, *Charlecote and the Lucys*, 1948, 230]. He is recorded to have made unexecuted designs for a stone spire for STRATFORD-ON-AVON CHURCH, 1763 [Hist. MSS. Comm., *Correspondence of the Rev. Joseph Greene*, ed. L. Fox, 99 n.]; for rebuilding the chancel of ST. NICHOLAS CHURCH, WARWICK, 1776-7 [MS. churchwardens' accounts]; for rebuilding MOSELEY HALL, nr. BIRMINGHAM, for John Taylor, 1790 [drawings in Birmingham City Library]; and for CHRIST CHURCH, BIRMINGHAM, in 1804 [minute-book in Birmingham City Library, *ex inf.* Mr. G. W. Beard].

STANDEN, THOMAS, of Lancaster, designed the COUNTY LUNATIC ASYLUM (now known as the Moor Hospital) at LANCASTER, built 1812-16. Though he is described as 'architect' no other work by him has been noted [T. Baines, *History and Gazeteer of Lancashire* ii, 1825, 17; Lancashire County Records, Q.A.M.1/1].

STANLEY, EDMUND, was employed by William Turbutt to design a new front to OGSTON HALL, DERBYSHIRE, in 1768-9, modifying a proposal by Joseph Pickford of Derby [drawings, letters, etc., formerly at Ogston Hall]. In 1768 he submitted designs for the County Hall at Nottingham that were not carried out [*Nottinghamshire County Records of the Eighteenth Century*, ed. K. T. Meaby, 1947, 49].

STANLEY, IGNATIUS, was employed by the 2nd Duke of Portland at WELBECK ABBEY, NOTTS., from 1757 to 1761. Payments to him 'for joiner's work and for drawing plans and overseeing all the building work' are recorded in the accounts, now in Nottingham University Library. A list of plans at Welbeck drawn up in 1764 includes designs by Stanley for a bridge and a pavilion in the garden [PwF 10.052].

STANLEY, JOHN, of Holbeck Woodhouse, nr. Worksop, Notts., was described as 'Mr. Stanley the Surveyor & Carpenter' in 1710, when he was paid £2 3s. 0d. 'for drawing 2 or 3 designs at severall times' for a 'new intended house' for the Duke of Norfolk at Sheffield. At the same time he was employed to view defects in the chancel of Sheffield Parish Church [R. E. Leader's notes in Sheffield City Library, 141, p. 37]. In the same year he was employed by the Nottinghamshire magistrates to consider a draught for a new Shire Hall made by a Mr. Twell and to make 'two new Draughts in Plans and Perspective for the new County Hall' (which was not proceeded with) [*Nottinghamshire County Records of the Eighteenth Century*, ed. K. T. Meaby, 1947, 46].

STANNARD, JOSEPH, senior (1771–1855), and his son JOSEPH STANNARD, junior (1795–1850), practised as architects and builders in Norwich during the first half of the nineteenth century. Their business was evidently on a considerable scale, for in 1824 they contracted to build the new court at King's College, Cambridge, to the designs of William Wilkins for £73,000 [Willis & Clark, i, 565]. The son held the post of City Architect in the early 1840s. His principal recorded work appears to have been the ROYAL HOTEL in the market place at Norwich, built in 1840 and since demolished [G. K. Blyth, *Directory and Guide to Norwich*, 1843, 192]. Father and son were both commemorated by a monument in the churchyard of St. George, Colegate, Norwich.

STANTON was the name of a family prominent as masons and sculptors throughout the greater part of the seventeenth century. Though chiefly famous for their monumental sculpture, they also took important masonry contracts. Their yard was in Holborn, close to St. Andrew's Church, in whose graveyard the family tomb once stood.[1] The earliest recorded member of the family was THOMAS STANTON (1610–74), who was made free of the Masons' Company in February 1630/1. He served as Warden in 1658 and as Master in 1660. He is known to have been established in Holborn by 1635. His son Thomas having predeceased him, he was succeeded in his business by his nephew, WILLIAM STANTON (1639-1705), who, as his apprentice, had been made free of the Masons' Company in 1663. William was Warden in 1681 and 1684 and Master in 1688 and 1689. He erected numerous monuments, many of which are recorded by Le Neve in his *Monumenta Anglicana* (1717–19), from information supplied by his son Edward. In 1684 he was associated with Edward Pierce in the mason's contract for rebuilding ST. ANDREW'S, HOLBORN, to the designs of Wren [*Wren Soc.* x, 95–8]. In 1685 he was the mason-contractor for BELTON HOUSE, nr. GRANTHAM, LINCS., receiving over £5000 for his work. The house was completed in 1688. It is not known who supplied the design, which is based on Pratt's Clarendon House, but it may well have been William Winde (*q.v.*) [MS. building accounts at Belton] (*C. Life*, 26 Aug. 1911; Oliver Hill & John Cornforth, *English Country Houses: Caroline*, 1966, 193–202). In 1688 Stanton began to build another large country house for Sir Roger Hill at DENHAM PLACE, BUCKS. It was completed in 1701 and bears

---

[1] In 1735 William Stanton was stated to have his 'house and shop' in Shoe Lane, which joins Holborn close to St. Andrew's Church. Stonecutter Street on the east side of Shoe Lane may perhaps mark the exact site of the Stantons' yard.

an obvious resemblance to Belton. The identity of the designer is again unknown, but in this case it is possible that it was Stanton himself [John Harris, 'The Building of Denham Place', *Records of Bucks*. xvi, 1957-8] (Hill & Cornforth, *op. cit.*, 203–10). In 1704–5 Stanton and his son Edward were working at CULVERTHORPE HALL, LINCS., then being remodelled for Sir John Newton, Bart., and were presumably responsible for the existing garden front [Newton's banking accounts at Welford Park, Berks.] (*C. Life*, 15, 22 Sept. 1923).

William Stanton died on 30 May 1705, leaving two sons, Thomas and Edward. The elder brother went abroad, leaving EDWARD STANTON (*c.* 1681–1734) to carry on the family business. He had been apprenticed to his father in

furnished house at Highgate, and the library of 'that ingenious Architect Capt. Edward Stanton' was sold with two others as 'Bibliotheca Splendidissima' on 17 November 1735. His elder son William was appointed Master Mason to the Mint and the Navy shortly before 1727, when he entered into a limited partnership with John Churchill, Master Mason to the Board of Ordnance [B.M., Stowe MS. 412, no. 75]. He continued 'to get his living by buying selling and working of severall sorts of Marble Stone Free Stones and divers other work of Stones ... as is usual for Persons of that Employ to do' until 1735, when, falling into debt, he absconded and was declared bankrupt [Stowe MS. 412, no. 80]. His property was sold by auction at Hodgson's Coffee-House in Chancery Lane on 18 May 1736

THE STANTON FAMILY

STANTON

THOMAS,
1610–74

Thomas,
d. before 1665

Thomas,
d. before 1674

Edward,
d. 1686

WILLIAM,
1639–1705

THOMAS
'at Leghorn'

Capt. EDWARD,
c. 1681–1734

WILLIAM,
bankrupt 1735

Edward

1694, and was made free of the Masons' Company in June 1702. He was a Warden in 1713 and 1716 and Master in 1719. It was probably in the latter year that he became Master Mason to Westminster Abbey, a post which brought him work in connection with the repairs to the Abbey and the building of the new Dormitory of Westminster School in 1722–6. He was for many years in partnership with Christopher Horsenaile, whose signature is found with Edward's on many monuments after 1718, and to whom, as 'my honest and industrious copartner', he left £40 in his will. He was a Captain in the Train Bands, and it is as 'Captain Edward Stanton' that he usually figures in contemporary documents. The list of works which he supplied to Le Neve shows that during the ten years after his father's death over 140 monuments were made in his yard in Holborn, and he ranks as one of the greatest of the eighteenth-century sculptor-masons. He died in 1734, leaving two sons, William and Edward. His will shows that he had a well-

(*ibid.*, no. 37). [K. A. Esdaile, 'The Stantons of Holborn', *Archaeological Jnl.* lxxxv, 1929; K. A. Esdaile, 'Some Annotations on John Le Neve's *Monumenta Anglicana*', *Antiquaries' Jnl.* xxii, 1942; D. Knoop & G. P. Jones, *The London Mason in the Seventeenth Century*, 1935, 21; R. Gunnis, *Dictionary of British Sculptors*, 1968.]

STANTON, CHARLEY, of St. Olave's, Southwark, was a carpenter by trade, and was Master of the London Carpenters' Company in 1693. In about 1670 he made designs for houses to be built by the Tallow Chandlers' Company on Dowgate Hill [*Builder*, 10 Aug. 1917], and in 1674 he was paid 10s. by the Corporation of Trinity House 'for a draft of three houses to be built at Southwark'. In 1680 the same Corporation paid him £704 for building eighteen almshouses forming part of TRINITY HOSPITAL, DEPTFORD (dem. 1877), and a further £42 for timber and workmanship in connection with their lighthouse at Scilly [archives of Trinity House Corporation]. He also

STAPLES, SAMUEL

built, and perhaps designed, two churches: ST. MARY MAGDALENE, BERMONDSEY, 1676–9, and ST. NICHOLAS, DEPTFORD, 1697–8, gutted 1940/1 [MS. Vestry Minutes of both parishes, *ex inf.* Canon B. F. L. Clarke]. Both are artisan's versions of a Wren City church.

STAPLES, SAMUEL (–1860), exhibited at the Royal Academy from 1 Staple's Inn, Holborn, between 1824 and 1837. In the latter year he submitted what the *Reading Mercury* described as 'a commonplace design' in the competition for the Royal Berks. Infirmary. He designed a Gothic chapel at SHENLEY, HERTS., illustrated in *The Surveyor, Engineer and Architect*, 1842, 172, and the NATIONAL SCHOOLS, ST. THOMAS'S DISTRICT, STEPNEY, 1841–2 [*ibid.*, 305]. He was President of the Surveyors' Club in 1842, and died in October 1860.

STARK, WILLIAM (1770–1813), was the son of Mark Stark, a manufacturer of Dunfermline, where he was born on 25 May 1770. Nothing is known of his early life or training, apart from the fact that he was in St. Petersburg in 1798. He practised at first in Glasgow, but shortly before his death moved to Edinburgh for the sake of his health. He was only 43 when, on 9 October 1813, he died at Drumsheugh on the western outskirts of Edinburgh. He left a widow named Catherine (*née* Thompson) and a daughter of the same name.

Contemporaries were agreed that Stark was an architect of unusual ability. In 1811 Sir Walter Scott wrote of him as 'a young man of exquisite taste who must rise very high in his profession if the bad health under which he suffers does not keep him down or cut him short', and when he heard of Stark's death he lamented that with him 'more genius has died than is left behind among the collected universality of Scottish architects'. The *Scots Magazine* said that 'his reputation, deservedly high in Scotland, was spreading rapidly in England at the time of his death'. Lord Cockburn thought him 'the best modern architect that Scotland has produced'. Stark was undoubtedly a very able and versatile architect, whose short list of works contains several buildings of distinction. His Glasgow Court House of 1810 disputes with Smirke's Covent Garden Theatre the distinction of being the first public building in Britain to be ornamented with a Greek Doric portico.[1] For St. George's Church he took a Wren steeple and transformed it into an original and effective neo-baroque composi-

tion perfectly adapted to its situation at a focal point in the city. In Edinburgh his Advocates' (now Upper Signet) Library triumphantly overcame the difficulty of making architectural sense of a long narrow room. At Glasgow his Lunatic Asylum was a pioneer attempt to achieve that segregation by sex, social background and mental condition which was considered desirable by contemporary medical opinion (see his *Remarks on the Construction of Public Hospitals for the Cure of Mental Derangement*, Glasgow 1810). Even his two rural churches represent a serious if slightly crude attempt to recapture the sturdy quality of medieval masonry so lacking in the stereotyped Gothic boxes of the early nineteenth century.

Stark also made his mark as a town-planner. His posthumously printed *Report to the Lord Provost, Magistrates and Council of Edinburgh on the Plans for Laying out the Grounds for Buildings between Edinburgh and Leith* (1814: also published in *Scots Mag.* lxxvii, 1815, 576–82) is a remarkably enlightened appreciation of the potentialities of the Edinburgh townscape, and his principles (variety in layout rather than a rigid grid of streets, careful attention to contours, the picturesque value of trees, etc.) were largely embodied in the plan ultimately carried out by his pupil W. H. Playfair (*q.v.*).

[S.R.O., Dunfermline Register; S.R.O., CC 8/8/142, f. 135, testament of William Stark; E. Henderson, *Annals of Dunfermline*, 1879, 569; *A.P.S.D.*; *Scots. Mag.*, 1813, 879; *The Letters of Sir Walter Scott*, ed. Grierson, 1811–14, 34, 65; Henry Cockburn, *Memorials of his Time*, 1910, 278–9; A. J. Youngson, *The Making of Classical Edinburgh*, 1966, 149–52; Andor Gomme & David Walker, *Architecture of Glasgow*, 1968, 69–71, 279–80; memoir by R. Gordon Stark in National Library of Scotland, MS. 1758.]

GLASGOW, THE HUNTERIAN MUSEUM, 1804–5; dem. 1870 [*The Picture of Glasgow*, 1813, 101–3; signed drawings in S.R.O., RHP 1997].

GLASGOW, ST. GEORGE'S CHURCH, BUCHANAN STREET, 1807–8 [*The Picture of Glasgow*, 1813, 90–1].

SALINE CHURCH, FIFE, 1809–10 [S.R.O., HR 411/2, p. 63].

GLASGOW, COURT HOUSE, GAOL and PUBLIC OFFICES, GLASGOW GREEN, 1810–11; remodelled 1845 and 1859 and rebuilt 1910, retaining portico [*Extracts from the Records of the Burgh of Glasgow*, ed. Marwick, x, 43; *The Picture of Glasgow*, 1813, 139–47] (A. Gomme & D. Walker, *Architecture of Glasgow*, 1968, fig. 46).

GLASGOW, THE LUNATIC ASYLUM (later used as workhouse), 1810–11; dem. [*The Picture of Glasgow*, 1813, 135–6].

GLASGOW, THE CATHEDRAL, refitted THE INNER HIGH CHURCH, c. 1810; Stark's fittings were

---

[1] See A. Gomme & D. Walker, *Architecture of Glasgow*, 1968, 70. But it appears from the Glasgow Burgh Records that the Court House was not designed until 1809, whereas Smirke's theatre was designed in 1808 and completed in 1810.

removed *c.* 1890 [*The Picture of Glasgow*, 1813, 84–5].

DUNFERMLINE ABBEY CHURCH, FIFE, rebuilt south-west tower after collapse (1807), 1810–11 [E. Henderson, *Annals of Dunfermline*, 1879, 569].

DUNDEE, THE LUNATIC ASYLUM, 1812–20; altered and enlarged by W. Burn 1830 and 1839 [James Thomson, *History of Dundee*, 1847, 190; *Dundee Delineated*, 1822, 117, with plan].

MUIRKIRK, AYRSHIRE, THE OLD CHURCH, 1812–13, Gothic [S.R.O., HR 287/3, pp. 12, 20, 22, 26; RHP 7651 (plan dated 1810)].

EDINBURGH, interior of THE SIGNET LIBRARY (now Lower Signet Library), PARLIAMENT SQUARE, for the Society of Writers to the Signet, 1812–15 [*History of the Society of Writers to the Signet*, 1890, lxxiv, 430–1].

EDINBURGH, interior of the ADVOCATES' LIBRARY (now Upper Signet Library), for the Faculty of Advocates, 1812–16 [S.R.O., Minutes of the Trustees for Public Buildings, E 343/2, pp. 62, 68–70, 75–81, 86–7, 119–128, 215].

GLOUCESTER, THE LUNATIC ASYLUM, built 1813–23 by J. Collingwood, the County Surveyor, was based on a plan provided by Stark [Ann Bailey, 'The Founding of the Gloucestershire County Asylum', *Trans. Bristol and Glos. Arch. Soc.*, etc., 1971, 184].

GREENOCK, RENFREWSHIRE, MIDDLE CHURCH, monument to Lt.-Col. Henry Crawfurd (d. 1813) [G. Williamson, *Old Greenock*, 1886, 311].

For an unexecuted design for a school at Greenock (1805), with a Greek Doric façade, see G. Williamson, *Old Greenock*, 2nd ser., 1888, 250. Stark's unexecuted design for a mansion at BROOMHALL, FIFE, for Lord Elgin (1808) is illustrated in *C. Life*, 29 Jan. 1970, fig. 9. It is an early essay in Greek Revivalism, but an alternative scheme is reported to envisage 'two storey quadrant colonnades in a mixed Renaissance style'.

STAVELEY, CHRISTOPHER (*c.* 1727–1801), was a member of a Leicestershire family which produced four generations of monumental masons and surveyors. He was probably a son of Stephen Staveley (1705–75) of Melton Mowbray, and was the father of Christopher Staveley (1759–1827) and perhaps also of Edward Staveley (*q.v.*). Good examples of his work as a mason and carver can be seen in Grantham Church and Churchyard. A tomb in Melton churchyard records his death on 31 January 1801, in his 75th year. In the *Monthly Magazine* for that year he was described as an 'eminent architect', and according to Throsby's *Select Views in Leicestershire* i, 1790, 153, he was the 'architect' of STAPLEFORD CHURCH, LEICS., built in 1783 by the Earl of Harborough. But as the design was exhibited

at the R.A. by George Richardson (*q.v.*), Staveley was probably only the builder. He had, however, supervised repairs and alterations to STAPLEFORD HALL for Lord Harborough in 1768–9 [Bray archives, Leicester City Museum, Archives Dept.]. [J. D. Bennett, *Leicestershire Architects 1700–1850*, Leicester Museums 1968].

STAVELEY, CHRISTOPHER (1759–1827), the eldest son of the above, practised as an architect, surveyor and engineer, first at Melton Mowbray, then at Loughborough, and ultimately (from 1819) at Leicester. He was surveyor to several canal companies and also acted as a land agent. As an architect he is recorded to have repaired the tower and spire of ST. MARY'S CHURCH, STAMFORD, in 1787 [Vestry Minutes, churchwardens' accounts, and framed drawings in Vestry]; designed LEADENHAM HOUSE, LINCS., for William Reeve, in 1790–6 [Arthur Oswald in *C. Life*, 17, 24 June 1965]; repaired LOUGHBOROUGH RECTORY, LEICS., in 1799–1800 (dem. 1962) [Lincs. Record Office, MGA 23]; altered THURCASTON RECTORY, LEICS., in 1803 [*ibid.*, MGA 40]; rebuilt SUTTON BONINGTON RECTORY, NOTTS., in 1811 [Borthwick Institute, York, MGA 1811/1]; and altered the interior of LOUGHBOROUGH CHURCH, LEICS., in 1815 [Faculty, etc., in Leics. Record Office]. After his death in 1827 his practice was at first carried on by his elder son Edward (1795–1872). But in 1833 the latter absconded with nearly £1700 of the funds of the Leicester Navigation Company. His brother Christopher, who was involved in the scandal, appears to have committed suicide, but Edward made good his escape to North America, where he worked as a canal and railway engineer, first in Baltimore, and later in Canada. He died in Quebec in 1872. [F. Burgess, *English Churchyard Memorials*, 1963, 269–70; J. D. Bennett, *Leicestershire Architects 1700–1850*, Leicester Museums 1968.]

STAVELEY, EDWARD (–1837), was a member of the Staveley family of Melton Mowbray. In 1796 he was appointed Surveyor to the Corporation of Nottingham at a salary of £20 [*Records of the Borough of Nottingham* vii, 1947, 336]. He remodelled the NEW EXCHANGE in that city in 1814–15 [J. Blackner, *History of Nottingham*, 1815, 410] and designed the GEORGE STREET BAPTIST CHAPEL, 1815 [W. H. Wylie, *Old and New Nottingham*, 1853, 122], and the PLUMPTRE HOSPITAL (almshouses), 1823 [J. F. Sutton, *The Date-Book of Events connected with Nottingham*, 1852, 378]. He died in 1837 [Sutton, *op. cit.*, 454].

STEAD, JOHN, practised in Wakefield in the 1820s. In 1823 he advertised for tenders for the PRIMITIVE METHODIST CHAPEL, and in 1827 he designed the WESLEYAN METHODIST CHAPEL at

WESTGATE END. In 1823 he also advertised for tenders for a large house to be built seven miles from Wakefield. In 1827 he was surveyor to the abortive Wakefield and Ferrybridge Canal. In December of that year he went bankrupt, and by 1830 he had left Wakefield for good [information from Mr. J. Goodchild of Wakefield Library]. In 1830 he exhibited at the Liverpool Academy an elevation of a Gothic church 'intended for Askrigg, Yorkshire'. He may have been the John Stead who was appointed surveyor to the Brighton Commissioners in 1837 [*Builder* v, 1847, 161].

STEAD, THOMAS, (*c.* 1775–1850), was probably starting practice when he exhibited architectural designs at the Royal Academy in 1797 and 1801. He subsequently had an office in Bloomsbury, where he acted as surveyor to the Bedford estate. He died at Hampstead on 8 August 1850, aged 75 [*Gent's Mag.* 1850 (ii), 340]. His only recorded architectural work appears to be the BEDFORD ESTATE OFFICE in MONTAGUE STREET, built in 1841–3 [Bedford Estate records, *ex inf.* Mrs. M. P. G. Draper].

STEDMAN, JAMES, made designs for, and superintended the execution of, extensive alterations to POLESDEN LACEY HOUSE, GREAT BOOKHAM SURREY, for Thomas Moore between 1735 and 1748, as shown by the accounts in the Bodleian Library, MS. North c. 62, f. 28. The house is illustrated in J. P. Neale, *Views of Seats*, 2nd ser., i, 1824, and *C. Life*, 5, 12 March 1948. Stedman was one of the bridge-surveyors for the County of Surrey in the 1740s [Surrey County Records, QS 5/7, 7–9, 59, 61, 67, etc.].

STEEL, THOMAS, of Chichester, a carpenter, appears to have been the architect of SHILLINGLEE PARK, SUSSEX, for Edward Turnour. On 18 October 1734, he agreed 'to survey or carry on a Building or Dwelling house at Shillingly Park According to a Draught signed by the above mencioned partys', for a fee of £100. The house, gutted by fire *c.* 1943, bears the date 1735 [Arthur Oswald in *C. Life*, 8 Aug. 1936]. The names of several boys apprenticed to Steel between 1711 and 1742 are given in *Sussex Apprentices and Masters*, Sussex Rec. Soc., xxviii.

STEER, JAMES (–1759), was by trade a carpenter and joiner. He was made free of the London Carpenters' Company in 1729 after a five years' apprenticeship, and subsequently rose to be a Warden of the Company in 1758. But for his death in the following year he would probably have been elected Master. In 1736 he was appointed Town Surveyor by the Hand in Hand Fire Office, and in the same year he became Surveyor to St. Thomas's Hospital. He died on 28 January 1759. Though chiefly employed in sur-

veying property for his two principal employers, Steer occasionally acted as an architect, designing in 1738 the WELSH CHARITY SCHOOL (now much altered as the Marx Memorial Library), 37–8 CLERKENWELL GREEN, and in 1738–9 the east wing of GUY'S HOSPITAL (destroyed by bombing in the 1940s). The latter was a building of conventional 'Palladian' character (*Survey of London* xxii, pls. 32, 34). Steer was an officer of the City's Trained Bands, and evidently a staunch Protestant, for in 1746 he published an engraved design for an obelisk to be erected in Smithfield, in order to 'Perpetuate the Memory of the Cruel Triumph of Popery, and to instruct Protestants what may again be expected, If the British Crown should ever be plac'd on a Popish Head' (Bodleian Library, Gough Maps 19, f. 41ᵛ).

[Andrew Rothstein, 'Mr. Steere the Surveyor', *Builder*, 27 March 1964; *London Magazine*, 1759, 107.]

STEERS, THOMAS (–1750), engineer and architect, was a pioneer of dock construction whose works at Liverpool laid the foundation of the town's greatness as a seaport. The place and date of his birth are unknown, but as a young man he held a Commission in the 4th Regiment of Foot, which was partially disbanded in 1697 after three years' service in the Netherlands. Thereafter Steers is found living at Rotherhithe at the time when the Howland Great Dock – the first of its kind in England – was under construction. There can be little doubt that Steers was in some way concerned in this work, but in what capacity is at present unknown. In 1710 he went to Liverpool in order to supervise the construction of a wet dock similar to that at Rotherhithe, and for the remainder of his life he played a leading part in the affairs and development of the town. The dock was constructed on land reclaimed from the sea, and was surrounded by new streets laid out by Steers. In 1717 he was appointed Dock Master, and from 1724 combined the offices of Dock Master and Water Bailiff of Liverpool. In 1717–18 he constructed a Dry Dock (now the Canning Dock) adjoining the Old Dock, and he also planned the South (now Salthouse) Dock, which was completed in 1753 after his death. Apart from these and other engineering works, which took him to Ireland in 1736–41 to advise the Newry Navigation Commission, Steers established a lucrative anchor-smithy in Liverpool, and engaged in a good deal of speculative building in that town. In 1740 he built the OLD ROPERY THEATRE as a personal speculation, and the house in PARADISE STREET in which he lived was one of a pair which he had erected on the reclaimed land in the Pool. He designed a large house in HANOVER STREET (damaged by fire 1867 and destroyed by bombing 1941) for Thomas Seel in 1740, but his principal architectural work was ST. GEORGE'S CHURCH, LIVERPOOL, which was erected to his designs between 1726 and 1734. Externally, it was liberally decorated with engaged Doric columns, and had a classical tower and spire. Unfortunately, the tower was built on the edge of the filled-in Castle Ditch, and subsidences led to the removal of the spire in 1809, and to the subsequent reconstruction of the whole church by John Foster between 1819 and 1825. It was finally demolished in 1897. Its architect was elected Mayor of Liverpool in 1739, and died there on 2 November 1750.

[H. Peet, 'Thomas Steers, A Memoir', *Trans. Historic Soc. of Lancs. and Cheshire* lxxxii, 1930; J. A. Picton, *Municipal Records of Liverpool* ii, 1886, 70–1, 398; S. A. Harris, 'Paradise Street, Liverpool: the Derivation of the Name,' *Trans. Historic Soc. of Lancs. and Cheshire* civ, 1952, 143–4.]

STEPHEN, JOHN (*c.* 1807–1850), practised in Glasgow. His works in Glasgow included the gateway and chapel of the SIGHTHILL CEMETERY, 1839 [*A.P.S.D., s.v.* 'Glasgow']; ST. JUDE'S EPISCOPAL CHURCH, 1840, Greek Revival [J. Pagan, *Sketch of the History of Glasgow*, 1847, 181]; THE FREE TRON CHURCH, NORTH DUNDAS STREET [David Thomson, 'The Works of the late Charles Wilson', *Trans. Glasgow Philosophical Soc.*, 1882, 2]; and the monument in THE NECROPOLIS to the Rev. Robert Muter (d. 1842), 1844 [G. Blair, *Sketches of Glasgow Necropolis*, 1857, 233]. He died in November 1850, aged 43, and is buried in the Necropolis [Necropolis records, *ex inf.* Mr. J. Stevens Curl].

STEPHENSON, DAVID (1757–1819), was born on 31 October 1757. His father, John Stephenson (d. 1796), was a master carpenter in Newcastle-on-Tyne who was well known in his day for the construction of a temporary timber bridge across the Tyne after the old one had been destroyed by a flood in 1771. At the age of 24 David went to London to study in the Royal Academy Schools, to which he was admitted in January 1782. If at the same time he became the pupil of a London architect, the fact is not recorded, and early in 1783 he returned to Newcastle to start practice as an architect. He immediately obtained several civic commissions, for some of which he was indebted to the favour of Sir Matthew White Ridley of Blagdon, and in 1786 he won the competition for the new church of All Saints with a bold design for an elliptical building with transverse seating. This was his most important work, and ranks as one of the most striking and original churches built in England in the eighteenth century.

Stephenson appears to have received no country-house commissions, but in 1805 he was appointed Surveyor and Architect to the Duke of Northumberland, and in that capacity designed several farmhouses on the Duke's estate and some minor buildings at Alnwick Castle. He died at Alnwick on 29 August 1819, aged 63, and is commemorated by a tablet in the vestibule of All Saints Church at Newcastle. Although his practice had doubtless been curtailed by the Napoleonic War, he had been sufficiently prosperous to be able to purchase an estate called Walridge, nr. Chester-le-Street in County Durham. His widow was still living there in the 1830s.

[*A.P.S.D.*; R. Welford, *Men of Mark 'twixt Tyne and Tweed* iii, 1895, 434–7; F. Mackenzie & M. Ross, *County Palatine of Durham* i, 1834, 146; D. W. Johnson, 'A Study of the Life and Works of David Stephenson 1757–1819', unpublished dissertation, School of Architecture, The University of Newcastle-upon-Tyne, 1972.]

NEWCASTLE

THE SCALE or KALE CROSS, erected 1783 at the expense of Sir Matthew Ridley, Bart., but taken down in 1807 and presented by the Corporation to its original donor, who re-erected it in his grounds at Blagdon, Northumberland [M. A. Richardson, *The Local Historian's Table Book* ii, 1842, 280; iii, 1843, 66].

THE NEW WHITE CROSS, NEWGATE STREET, erected 1784, removed to the Butcher Market in 1808, Gothic [E. Mackenzie, *Newcastle* i, 1827, 173].

ST. NICHOLAS CHURCH (now the CATHEDRAL) was repaired and repewed under the joint direction of John Dodds and David Stephenson in 1783–5 [Richardson, *op. cit.* ii, 284–8]. Stephenson repaired the church in 1792, and the steeple in 1795 [E. Mackenzie, *Newcastle* i, 1827, 255].

ALL SAINTS CHURCH, 1786–9, spire completed 1796 [T. Sopwith, *An Historical and Descriptive Account of All Saints Church, Newcastle*, 1826].

THE THEATRE ROYAL, MOSLEY STREET, 1787–8; dem. 1836 [E. Mackenzie, *Newcastle* i, 1827, 229].

THE CIRCUS or AMPHITHEATRE (a riding-house), 1789; dem. [E. Mackenzie, *Newcastle* ii, 1827, 594; *Civil Engineer and Architect's Jnl.* vi, 1843, 147].

THE EXCHANGE, rebuilt the north front, with W. Newton, 1796 [E. Mackenzie, *Newcastle* i, 1827, 216].

TYNE BRIDGE, widening, 1801; dem. 1873 [E. Mackenzie, *Newcastle* i, 1827, 214].

NORTHUMBERLAND

NORTH SHIELDS, NORTHUMBERLAND, the NEW QUAY AND MARKET PLACE, 1806–17 [Richardson, *op. cit.* iii, 58].

ALNWICK, NORTHUMBERLAND, farm-houses at

LONGDYKE, DENWICK WATERSIDE and BRISLEY WEST, 1807 [D. W. Johnson, *op. cit.*], and iron bridge in Hulne Park, *c.* 1813 [Alnwick Castle Library, Sir David Smith's Atlas of Northumberland, vol. iii].

ALNWICK, NORTHUMBERLAND, column erected by the Duke of Northumberland's tenantry to commemorate his munificence, 1816 [Richardson, *op. cit.* iii, 166–7; Alnwick Castle Library, MS. 187A/27].

STEUART, GEORGE (*c.* 1730–1806), was a Highland Scot from Atholl in Perthshire. He and his brother Charles are said both to have been Gaelic speakers. Charles was a topographical painter who exhibited at the Royal Academy between 1764 and 1790. Some of his pictures can still be seen at Blair Atholl. George is said to have been a house-painter by trade, but at least from 1770 onwards he was practising as an architect in London, first in Berners and afterwards in Harley Street. His first recorded work was a town house for the 3rd Duke of Atholl, and the patronage of the 3rd and 4th Dukes evidently played an important part in his career. Some of his most important works were, however, in Shropshire, where he had a number of commissions from the local gentry. Towards the end of his life he lived at Douglas in the Isle of Man, where the Dukes of Atholl were the Governors and principal landowners. Steuart died at the Lough House, Douglas, on 20 December 1806, leaving a substantial estate to his son Major Robert Steuart (who subsequently built the Villa Marina overlooking Douglas Bay). His will mentions his intention to be buried 'in the vault of the mausoleum intended to be built upon the summit of his land near Douglas', but in fact he was interred in Kirk Braddan Churchyard, where a simple tombstone records his death at the age of 76.

Nothing is known about Steuart's architectural training, but his buildings show a markedly neo-classical taste. Mr. Lees-Milne has noted his fondness for 'a uniform severity of wall surface broken occasionally by slightly recessed arches containing a window (after the fashion set by J. Wyatt) and a tenuousness of pilaster and column'. These characteristics are found in all his country houses, whose elegant restraint verges on bleakness. At St. Chad's, Shrewsbury, he achieved a bolder and more original composition by the juxtaposition of a circular nave and a massive steeple of three clearly defined stages, one square, one octagonal and one circular. This was probably his most important work and is certainly one of the most striking and original of English Georgian churches. Unexecuted designs by Steuart for rebuilding Onslow Hall, Shropshire, are in the R.I.B.A. Drawings Collection.

[*A.P.S.D.*; *Chronicles of the Atholl and Tulli-*

bardine Families, compiled by the 7th Duke of Atholl, iv, 1908, *passim*; M. M. Rix & W. R. Serjeant, 'George Steuart, Architect, in the Isle of Man', *Jnl. of the Manx Museum* vi, 1962-3, 177-9; information from Mr. B. R. S. Megaw and Mr. M. M. Rix.]

LONDON, GROSVENOR PLACE, house for 3rd Duke of Atholl, 1770; dem. [C. T. Gatty, *Mary Davies and the Manor of Ebury* i, 1921, 181].

MILLICHOPE PARK, SALOP., Ionic temple or cenotaph for More family on rock facing the house, 1770 [J. B. Blakeway, *The Sheriffs of Shropshire*, Shrewsbury 1831, 208].

BLAIR CASTLE and DUNKELD HOUSE, PERTHSHIRE, various subsidiary buildings (lodges, greenhouses, etc.) for the 4th Duke of Atholl, 1777, etc. [drawings at Blair Castle].

PAISLEY, RENFREWSHIRE, inn in Gauze Street, for the 8th Earl of Abercorn, 1780–2 [G. Crawford and W. Semple, *History of the Shire of Renfrew*, Paisley 1782, part 2, 290].

ATTINGHAM HALL, SALOP., for Noel Hill, cr. 1st Lord Berwick, 1783–5 [G. Richardson, *New Vitruvius Britannicus* ii, 1808, pls. 25–30; drawings preserved in house and in John White volume in R.I.B.A. Drawings Coll.] (*C. Life*, 5–12 Feb. 1921, 21 Oct. 1954; C. Hussey, *English Country Houses: Mid Georgian*, 1956, 195–202; J. Lees-Milne, *Guide to Attingham*, National Trust 1949).

LYTHWOOD HALL, SALOP., for Joshua Blakeway, *c.* 1785; converted into flats 1950, destroying portico and other architectural features [H. Owen & J. B. Blakeway, *History of Shrewsbury* ii, 1825, 248].

STOKE PARK, EARL STOKE, WILTS., for Joshua Smith, 1786-91; gutted 1950 [G. Richardson, *New Vitruvius Britannicus* i, 1810, pls. 36–8; original drawings in R.I.B.A. Coll.].

WELLINGTON CHURCH, SALOP., 1788–90 [plan and elevation signed 'G. Stuart Archt.' in B.M., *King's Maps* xxv, 19–1].

SHREWSBURY, NEW ST. CHAD'S CHURCH, 1790–2 [H. Owen & J. B. Blakeway, *History of Shrewsbury* ii, 1825, 248–50].

DOUGLAS, ISLE OF MAN, THE COURTHOUSE, RED PIER AND LIGHTHOUSE, 1793–9; courthouse dem. *c.* 1860, lighthouse 1936, when the pier was remodelled [drawings and accounts in Manx Museum Library, see *Jnl. of the Manx Museum* vi, 1962–3, pls. 264–5].

RAMSEY, ISLE OF MAN, THE COURT HOUSE, 1798 [drawings in Manx Museum Library] (*Jnl. of the Manx Museum* vi, 1962–3, pl. 266).

CASTLE MONA, DOUGLAS, ISLE OF MAN, for the 4th Duke of Atholl, 1801–6 [drawings in Manx Museum Library] (*Jnl. of the Manx Museum* vi, 1962–3, pl. 266).

attributed: KIRK BRADDAN CHURCHYARD, ISLE OF MAN, obelisk in memory of Lord Henry

Murray, 5th son of the 3rd Duke of Atholl (d. 1805).

BARONS COURT, CO. TYRONE, IRELAND, for the 8th Earl of Abercorn (d. 1789); remodelled by Sir J. Soane 1791–2 and again in the nineteenth century [J. Soane, *Sketches in Architecture*, 1793, iv, where he refers to the architect as *Charles* Steuart] (survey drawings of 1791 in Sir John Soane's Museum show the house as designed by Steuart).

STEVENS, ALEXANDER (*c.* 1730–1796), was a Scottish architect and civil engineer. According to his obituary in the *Gentleman's Magazine* he had, 'in the course of the last forty years, erected more stone bridges, and other buildings in water, than any man in these kingdoms ... The North of England and Scotland exhibit numberless works of his execution.' Among them were DRY-GRANGE or LEADERFOOT BRIDGE over the R. Tweed near Melrose, Roxburghshire, 1779–80 [signed 'Alexander Stevens, architect'; contract in S.R.O., GD 244, Box 19]; SARAH BRIDGE, DUB-LIN (R. Liffey), 1783–91 [*A.P.S.D.,s.v.* 'Dublin']; AYR BRIDGE (R. Ayr), 1786–9 [S. Shaw, *A Tour in 1787 from London to the Western Highlands*, 1788, 115]; THE BRIDGE OF DUN, nr. MONTROSE, ANGUS (R. South Esk), 1785–7 [contract in S.R.O., GD 244, Box 19], and HYNDFORD BRIDGE, nr. LANARK (R. Clyde), stated to have been built by Stevens 'a few years ago' in the *Statistical Account of Scotland* xv, 1795, 26. The castellated bridge at OXENFOORD CASTLE, MIDLOTHIAN, can be attributed to him on the strength of an alternative design by him dated 1783 that is preserved at Oxenfoord [Alistair Rowan in *C. Life*, 15 Aug. 1974]. In the R.I.B.A. Drawings Collection there is a design by him for a bridge at Blackadder, Ber-wickshire. He was also responsible for the locks on the 'grand canal of Ireland', and for the execu-tion of John Rennie's aqueduct over the R. Lune at Lancaster. In 1783–4 he built a handsome double-fronted Gothic house close to the Bridge in Ayr. This house he subsequently gave to his daughter Jean on her marriage (1794) to James Fyfe, agent to Lord Mountjoy [Ayr Town Council Minutes and titles, *ex inf.* Mr. David Walker].

Stevens died at Lancaster on 29 January 1796, while supervising the construction of the Lune aqueduct. He was aged 66. He is commemorated by a tablet on the external south wall of Lancaster Parish Church. In 1778 he was described as 'mason in New Preston' and in 1785 as 'Architect at Prestonhall', both in the parish of Cranston in Midlothian. In 1786 his business was said to be at Prestonhall, though he was temporarily resi-dent in Ayr. [*Gent's Mag.* lxvi (i), 1796, 169; *A.P.S.D.*]

STEVENS, ALEXANDER, practised in Edin-burgh, and should not be confused with Alex-ander Stevens, the bridge-builder (*q.v.*). He designed RAEHILLS, nr. MOFFAT, DUMFRIESSHIRE, for the 3rd Earl of Hopetoun, 1786, in imitation of the Adam castle style. The house was subse-quently enlarged by W. Burn [building accounts at Hopetoun, *ex inf.* Mr. Basil Skinner; cf. photo-copy of unsigned drawing at Raehills in S.R.O., RHP 10196]. In a portfolio at Raehills there is a design by Stevens for a small castellated house on paper watermarked 1807. At Culzean Castle there is a plan by him for a projected square on the site of the Citadel at Ayr, together with an elevation of the proposed houses dated 1799.

Stevens was the builder, and perhaps the designer, of the steeple of ST. CUTHBERT'S CHURCH, EDINBURGH. In April 1789 the Heritors decided to build the steeple by subscription according to a plan 'marked by the Praeses as relative hereto' [S.R.O., HR 152/2], and on 8 July 1790 the *Caledonian Mercury* reported that 'The steeple of St. Cuthbert's Church is now finished ... Mr. Stephen, the builder of this elegant structure, was also the builder of St. Andrew's Church steeple; and the drawbridge at Leith,[1] the masterly execution of all which does him great honour as an architect'. In 1792 'Alex-ander Steven Architect' was one of three archi-tects who were asked to survey St. Cuthbert's Manse [S.R.O., HR 152/2, 28 Dec. 1792]. He continues to appear in the Edinburgh directories up to 1811/12.

STEVENS, EDWARD (*c.* 1744–1775), was a pupil of Sir William Chambers from 1760 [P.R.O., IR 1/22] until 1766. He gained premiums offered by the Society for the Encouragement of Arts, Manufactures, and Commerce in 1762 and 1763, and exhibited at the Free Society of Artists in 1762–3, at the Society of Artists in 1765–8, and at the Royal Academy in 1770–3. In 1769 he competed for the Royal Exchange at Dublin, exhibiting his design at the Royal Academy the following year. He was elected A.R.A. in 1770. He went abroad in 1774, and was made a member of the Florentine Aca-demy.[2] He was taken ill soon after his arrival in Rome, and died there on 27 June 1775 at the age of 31, leaving a widow and daughter. He is com-memorated by a monument in the Protestant cemetery.

Stevens's principal executed works were a new front to SPYE PARK, WILTS., for Sir Edward Bayn-ton, Bart., which he exhibited at the Society of Artists in 1767 (demolished 1868); and DOVERIDGE HALL, DERBYSHIRE, for Sir Henry Cavendish, Bart., begun in 1769, which he exhi-bited at the R.A. in 1771 (demolished 1934, des-

---

[1] This was the Upper Drawbridge, built as part of the harbour improvements of 1788.

[2] His diploma is in the R.I.B.A. Collection (E4/20A).

cribed by E. Saunders in *Derbyshire Life*, Aug. 1972). The latter house was in a conservative Palladian style with rusticated basement, pedimented façade and narrow, pavilion-like wings. Stevens was also employed at WREST PARK, BEDS., by the 2nd Earl of Hardwicke, for whom in 1770 he designed a Bridge and a classical Cold Bath [Bedfordshire Record Office, abstract of bills in L 31/318]. Among the Wrest drawings in the same Record Office there is an unexecuted design for a 'Theatre or Colonnade designed for the Gardens at Wrest', signed 'Edw. Stevens Arct. 1769'.

The R.I.B.A. Drawings Collection possesses an album of drawings (mostly of a 'theoretical' character) made by Stevens in Chambers's office, a design for a large town house (probably 'the London House, fit for a person of distinction', which he exhibited at the Free Society of Artists in 1763), and a design for a ceiling for Thomas Collins, who was Chambers's partner in a building speculation in Berners Street in 1770 [*R.I.B.A. Drawings Catalogue*].

The Apprenticeship Registers in the Public Record Office show that Stevens had two pupils, William Wickham (1767) and William Grantham (1769 or 1770).

STEVENS, JOHN, of Wantage, was the surveyor employed in connection with the erection of the COUNCIL CHAMBER at ABINGDON in 1731–3. According to the agreement made between the Corporation and Samuel Westbrook, mason, and Charles Etty, carpenter, on 13 August 1731, the 'ornaments' were 'to be made with the best Heddington Freestone well wrought according to the draught of Mr. John Stevens of Wantage'. Subsequently there are payments to Stevens for unspecified services which probably included surveying. [Contract in Abingdon Corporation records, *ex inf.* Miss A. C. Baker.]

STEVENS, JOHN (–1857), practised as an architect and surveyor from 54 Green Street, Grosvenor Square, during the period 1810–30, and later from 6 Clements Inn. From 1843 until his death in 1857 he was Surveyor of the Western District of the City. In 1813 he supervised repairs and alterations to BEACHBOROUGH HOUSE, HYTHE, KENT (destroyed by fire *c.* 1965), for James Drake-Brockman [accounts in B.M., Add. MS. 42673, ff. 254–5, 269–70, 280] (C. Greenwood, *Epitome of County History: Kent*, 1838, 305). He appears to have been the father of John Hargrave Stevens (d. 1875), District Surveyor of Bethnal Green.

STEWART, DANIEL, was practising in Liverpool from about 1810 onwards. J. A. Picton (1805–89) entered into partnership with him in 1830, and took over his practice when he retired

in 1835 [Boase, *Modern English Biography* ii, 1897, 1525]. He designed the churches of ST. JOHN, BURSCOUGH BRIDGE, LANCS., 1829–31, Gothic [Port, 146–7]; ST. ANNE, STANLEY (OLD SWAN), nr. LIVERPOOL, 1831, rebuilt 1890–1 [G.R.]; and (in partnership with Picton) ST. MATTHIAS, LIVERPOOL, 1832–3, Ionic, dem. 1848 to make way for a railway.

STEWART, JOHN, was an architect and carpenter of Dunkeld in Perthshire. In about 1804 he appears to have moved to Perth, but by 1811 he was back in Dunkeld. He designed the following Perthshire churches: LITTLE DUNKELD, 1798 [S.R.O., HR 470/1, p. 63]; LOGIERAIT, 1804–6 [S.R.O., HR 38/1, p. 23]; COMRIE, 1805 [S.R.O., copies of Heritors' minutes in GD 16/20]; and AUCHTERGAVEN, 1811–13 [S.R.O., HR 663/1, p. 5].

STEWART, JOHN (*c.* 1792–1871), practised in Liverpool, chiefly as a surveyor. He was 'long and intimately connected with the public affairs of the town', and served as Mayor in 1855–6. In 1843 he and Sir William Tite were jointly responsible for framing the Liverpool Health Act. For many years he was in partnership with the Foster family as building contractors under the name of 'Foster & Stewart'. The designs (among the I.C.B.S. records) for NORLEY CHURCH, CHESHIRE, built 1832, replaced 1878–9, are signed 'Foster & Stewart Architects, Liverpool'. [J. A. Picton, *Memorials of Liverpool*, 1875, i, 464, ii, 210; *A.P.S.D.*, *s.v.* 'Liverpool'.]

STIBBS, THOMAS (–1759), was a carpenter in London. He was probably the brother of Joseph Stibbs, who was one of the surveyors considered for rebuilding the church of St. Katherine Coleman, in 1739. James Horne was the successful applicant, but Thomas Stibbs, of the parish of St. Giles, Cripplegate, was the contracting carpenter [Guildhall Library, MSS. 1133, 1134]. The 'Mr. Stibbs' whose designs for the ARMOURY HOUSE, ARTILLERY GROUND, FINSBURY, were in 1729 preferred to those of George Dance [G. A. Raikes, *History of the Honourable Artillery Company* i, 1878, 286, 290] may have been either Joseph or Thomas, but it was the latter who in 1743 built the JEWISH SCHOOL (now the Talmud Torah Classes) in Bride Lane, Stepney [*Survey of London* xxvii, 221]. He was Surveyor to the London Assurance Company, and in 1749–50 built its office in Birchin Lane, Cornhill, to the designs of Joseph Manning (*q.v.*). When he died in 1759 he was succeeded by his son William Stibbs. [Guildhall Library, Minutes of the London Assurance Company, MSS. 8728/6, p. 152, 8728/7, p. 196.]

STICKELLS, ROBERT (–1620), appears to have been a mason by trade, but the surviving records of his career show him acting as an architect, clerk of works and naval engineer. In the 1580s he was one of the 'masters of the work' then in progress at Dover harbour, his main task being raising rocks by barrels and chains and floating them to a jetty in process of construction. Stow's *Chronicle* records that in 1595 'master Stickles, the excellent Artichect of our time', constructed in Leadenhall a small pinnace that could be taken to pieces and reassembled. This was launched in Tower Dock, 'but there came no good of it'. And in the Lansdowne MSS. there is a paper by Stickells proposing to build a ship that would be 'shot free and fire free' and a boat that could be propelled 'without sails or oars'. As an architect Stickells is known to have been employed by Sir Thomas Tresham of Rushton in Northants, and a surviving drawing by him has been identified as a design for an elaborate classical lantern surmounting the cruciform LYVEDEN NEW BUILDING which Tresham started to build in about 1605 but never completed. In 1613 he was paid by Sir Edward Pytts of Kyre in Worcestershire for 'drawing the platt of my house [probably in London] anewe', and two papers survive in which Stickells discusses, in esoteric terms, the proposition whether the 'Antique' or the 'Modern' was the more valid way of building.

In 1595 the Earl of Derby recommended Stickells as a candidate for the Surveyorship of the Queen's Works. In fact he had to be content with a subordinate clerkship of the works, which he held from 1597/8 until his death. From 1598/9 he was stationed at Richmond, where in 1605–6 he designed a new lodge in the park of which there are drawings in the Thorpe MS. in Sir John Soane's Museum. Stickells died in May 1620. In his will he describes himself as a 'citizen and freemason of London' living in the parish of St. Olave Southwark.

[John Summerson, 'Three Elizabethan Architects', *Bulletin of the John Rylands Library* xl, 1957, 216–21, 225–8; *History of the King's Works* iii, 134–5.]

STIRLING, WILLIAM (1772–1838), was the principal member of a family of builder-architects established at Dunblane in Perthshire. He was the eldest son of James Stirling, a wright and cabinet-maker, and continued his business besides acting as an architect. His marriage in 1803 to Jean, daughter of David Erskine, W.S., allied him to the closely related families of Erskine, Graham, Stirling and Masterton who were among the principal Perthshire landowners, and brought him many commissions on their estates. The bulk of his work consisted of stables, offices, manses, farm-houses and country churches, and he never designed any building of the first rank.

His designs reflect the styles current in early nineteenth-century Scotland – neo-Adamsian or Grecian for domestic purposes, simplified Gothic for churches, 'Tudor' for manses, etc. The profits of a highly successful business enabled him to build up a small estate in Dunblane upon which in 1826 he built himself a house (Holmehill) of some pretensions. He died on 5 February 1838, and was succeeded in his practice by William Stirling II (*c.* 1789–1876), who may have been a cousin and had been his 'chief assistant and superintendent' for some years. William Stirling II retired long before his death in 1876 at the age of 87, and handed the business on to his son William Stirling III (born *c.* 1819), who predeceased his father, dying in 1867.

[A. B. Barty, *History of Dunblane*, 1944, 21 231–2; David Walker, 'The Stirlings of Dunblane and Falkirk', *Bulletin of the Scottish Georgian Soc.* i, 1972.]

The following list of works is based on Mr. Walker's article, where full references will be found.

CHURCHES AND OTHER PUBLIC BUILDINGS

LOGIE CHURCH, STIRLINGSHIRE, 1805; reconstructed 1901.

PORT OF MENTEITH CHURCHYARD, PERTHSHIRE, mausoleum for Graham of Gartmore family, *c.* 1810.

STIRLING, THE ATHENAEUM, 1814–16 (R.C.A.M., *Stirlingshire* ii, pl. 134 B).

AIRTH, STIRLINGSHIRE, NORTH CHURCH, 1818–20, Gothic [R.C.A.M., *Stirlingshire* i, 142 and plates].

RATTRAY CHURCH, PERTHSHIRE, 1820, Italianate.

KIPPEN CHURCH, STIRLINGSHIRE, 1823; altered 1928; Gothic.

LECROPT CHURCH, PERTHSHIRE, 1824–6, Gothic.

LECROPT SCHOOL, PERTHSHIRE, 1826.

DRON CHURCH, PERTHSHIRE, *c.* 1825, Gothic [signed drawings among Fettercairn papers in National Library of Scotland].

CRIEFF CHURCH, PERTHSHIRE, completion of church built 1786–7 but left unfinished, 1826.

TILLICOULTRY CHURCH, CLACKMANNANSHIRE, 1827–9, Gothic.

MONZIE CHURCH, PERTHSHIRE, 1830–1, Gothic [*N.S.A.* x, 278].

CREICH CHURCH, FIFE, 1830–3 [S.R.O., HR 273/1].

DUNIPACE CHURCH, STIRLINGSHIRE, 1832–4, Gothic.

TOM A CHAISTEL, STROWAN, PERTHSHIRE, obelisk in memory of Sir David Baird, 1832.

PLEAN HOSPITAL (almshouses), STIRLINGSHIRE, *c.* 1835–7.

DOMESTIC ARCHITECTURE

DUNIRA, PERTHSHIRE, works for the 1st and 2nd Viscounts Melville, 1802–16, based on designs by Henry Holland; rebuilt by W. Burn 1851–2 [Dundas papers, Comrie House, *ex inf.* Dr. A. A. Tait].

COMRIE LODGE, PERTHSHIRE, works for the 4th Earl of Aberdeen, 1803 and *c.* 1820.

TULLIBODY HOUSE, CLACKMANNANSHIRE, repairs for the 2nd Lord Abercromby, *c.* 1803; dem.

CARDROSS HOUSE, PERTHSHIRE, alterations for David Erskine, 1803.

STROWAN, CRIEFF, PERTHSHIRE, for Sir Thomas Stirling, 1804–8; since rebuilt.

ALVA HOUSE, CLACKMANNANSHIRE, stables for James Johnstone, 1805–9.

DOUNE LODGE, KILMADOCK, PERTHSHIRE, stables for the 8th Earl of Moray, 1807–9.

KINNAIRD HOUSE, nr. LARBERT, STIRLINGSHIRE, repairs for James Bruce, 1808–11; rebuilt 1895.

KIPPENROSS, PERTHSHIRE, alterations for John Stirling, 1809; since modified.

AIRTHREY CASTLE, STIRLINGSHIRE, lodges for Sir Robert Abercromby, 1809; one demolished.

METHVEN CASTLE, PERTHSHIRE, work on offices for Robert Smythe, 1810–12.

KEAVIL HOUSE, DUNFERMLINE, FIFE, work for J. R. Barclay, 1810–12.

ALVA MANSE, CLACKMANNANSHIRE, 1810–12.

MONZIE, PERTHSHIRE, lodge to east gate for General Alexander Campbell, 1812.

LECROPT MANSE, PERTHSHIRE, 1812.

DUPPLIN CASTLE, PERTHSHIRE, south-west wing for the 10th Earl of Kinnoull, 1814–15; remodelled by W. Burn 1828–32; dem.

COMRIE MANSE (now TULLICHETTLE HOUSE), PERTHSHIRE, new front block, 1818–20.

KINCARDINE-IN-MENTEITH MANSE, PERTHSHIRE, 1821–3.

LINLATHEN HOUSE, nr. DUNDEE, ANGUS, remodelled for Thomas Erskine, *c.* 1820–6; dem. 1958.

MONCREIFFE HOUSE, PERTHSHIRE, enlarged stable-block for Sir David Moncreiffe, Bart., 1821.

MONCREIFFE, PERTHSHIRE, enlarged the Inn, 1821.

TIBBERMORE MANSE, PERTHSHIRE, 1824.

FORTEVIOT MANSE, PERTHSHIRE, 1825–6.

ARDOCH HOUSE, PERTHSHIRE, addition to offices, etc., for William Moray Stirling, 1826.

HOLMEHILL HOUSE, DUNBLANE, PERTHSHIRE, for himself, 1826, Tudor style.

COLQUHALZIE, CRIEFF, PERTHSHIRE, wing for John Hepburn, 1826.

DUNBLANE MANSE, PERTHSHIRE, 1829; dem.

BRIDGE OF ALLAN, STIRLINGSHIRE, an inn, probably the 'Westerton Arms', 1831.

FALKIRK, STIRLINGSHIRE, RED LION INN (now shop), 148–154 HIGH STREET, 1828.

GARDEN HOUSE, STIRLINGSHIRE, east block for

784

John Stirling, 1830 [R.C.A.M., *Stirlingshire*, 370–1 and pl. 200].

MUCKHART MANSE, PERTHSHIRE, 1832.

STOAKES, CHARLES, was the great-nephew of Nicholas Stone (1586–1647), and ultimately inherited his business as a mason and architect from his sons. He had in his possession the Stone account-books, which are now in Sir John Soane's Museum, and gave George Vertue information about sculptors of his generation. In 1712 he repaired and partly rebuilt the south side of MERE CHURCH, WILTS., as recorded by two circular tablets in the spandrels of the arcade stating that the work was 'performed by Mr. Charles Stoakes of London Surveyor of Buildings' [*Wilts. Arch. Mag.* xxix, 1896–7, 51–2]. A 'Plan of Stafford House and Grounds taken in the year 1725 by Chas. Stokes senior' is in the Library of the Society of Antiquaries (Topographical Drawings of London, vol. vi, f. 5). It appears from Vertue's *Note Books* ii, 25, that there were two Charles Stoakes's (father and son), with both of whom Vertue was acquainted.

STOKES, GEORGE (–1870), is known only as an exhibitor at the Royal Academy between 1827 and 1851. His address was 21 Southampton Street, Bloomsbury, in 1827–31 and Porchester Gardens from 1843 until his death. His exhibits included a 'Design for a Town Hall and Assembly Rooms proposed to be built at Halifax' (1831), 'a Portion of Westbourne Terrace, now completing on the Bishop of London's estate at Paddington' (1843), and a 'Sketch of a proposed new church on the Bishop of London's estate at Paddington' (1844). Thereafter he showed only topographical drawings. As Westbourne Terrace was designed by the Bishop of London's surveyor, G. L. Taylor (*q.v.*), it is possible that Stokes was working in his office as an assistant. He appears to have made, or inherited, sufficient money to give up practice relatively early in life. He died at Ryde on 27 August 1870, leaving a son George Edward Stokes [Principal Probate Registry, Calendar of Probates].

STOKES, ROBERT, exhibited student's work at the Royal Academy in 1828 and 1829. He was admitted to the Royal Academy Schools in 1830, and won the Silver Medal the same year. By 1831 he had moved to Cheltenham, where he designed the Tudor Gothic FEMALE ORPHAN ASYLUM, 1833–4 [H. Davies, *Cheltenham in its Past and Present State*, 1843, 148]. His only other recorded work appears to be OAKRIDGE CHURCH, GLOS., 1836–7, Gothic [I.C.B.S.] (A. Smith, *Ecclesiastical Edifices in the Borough of Stroud*, 1838). See p. 986

STOKOE, JOHN (*c.* 1756–1836), was the son and successor of William Stokoe, a builder and architect of Newcastle-on-Tyne who probably died in about 1810. The son signs the drawings for the Moot Hall, a remarkably competent and precocious Greek Revival design which suggests that he may have had a training in London or Edinburgh. He was presumably the 'Stokoe' by whom two designs for villas were exhibited at the Royal Academy in 1808. He died in Newcastle on 23 August 1836, aged 80. [*Newcastle Courant*, 27 Aug. 1836; All Saints Church Burial Register, *ex inf.* Mr. Terry Scott.]

ELSWICK HALL, NORTHUMBERLAND, for John Hodgson, 'by Mr. Stokoe and his son', 1803 [J. Dobson in *Building News* v, 1859, 403; Margaret J. Dobson, *Memoir of John Dobson*, 1885, 11].

NEWCASTLE, THE MOOT HALL or COUNTY COURTS, designed by John Stokoe, 1810–12 [E. Mackenzie, *Newcastle* i, 1827, 225–6; set of drawings in Evidence Room at Syon House, Middlesex, signed 'Stokoe Junr Architect 1810', B.XVII, 2.c].

NEWCASTLE, ALL SAINTS CHURCH, alterations to improve acoustics, 1812 [T. Sopwith, *Historical and Descriptive Account of All Saints Church, Newcastle*, 1826, 131].

NEWCASTLE, PANDON DEAN BRIDGE, designed by John Stokoe, 1812 [T. Oliver, *New Picture of Newcastle*, 1831, 105].

SUNDERLAND, CO. DURHAM, THE EXCHANGE, designed by 'Mr. Stokoe', 1812–14 [E. Mackenzie & M. Ross, *County Palatine of Durham* i, 1834, 311].

HARTFORD HALL, NORTHUMBERLAND, for William Burdon (d. 1818), by 'Mr. Stokoe' [E. Mackenzie, *Northumberland* i, 1825, 348].

HEWORTH CHURCH, CO. DURHAM, by John Stokoe, 1821–2, Gothic [I.C.B.S.].

STONE, FRANCIS (1775–1834), practised in Norwich, where he held the post of County Surveyor from 1806 until his death. He was a founder member of the Norwich Society of Artists in 1805, and served as President in 1822. He exhibited drawings at the Society's exhibitions from 1805 to 1816, and was the author of a set of lithographs entitled *Picturesque Views of All the Bridges belonging to the County of Norfolk*, 1830–1. A manuscript account of the county bridges, with water-colour drawings by Stone, is described in B. Weinreb's *Catalogue* no. 9, *Bridges*, of 1965. Stone died on 22 August 1835, and is commemorated by a monument in the church of St. George Tombland at Norwich. His son, F. H. Stone, exhibited architectural designs at the Norwich Society of Artists from 1816 to 1825, and at the Royal Academy in 1821, but no further evidence of his architectural activity has been found. [*A.P.S.D.*; *Architectural Mag.* iii, 1836, 48; information from Mr. A. P. Baggs.]

NORWICH, ST. MARY'S BAPTIST MEETING HOUSE, SOUTERGATE, 1811–12; enlarged 1838; dem. 1942 [accounts, *ex inf.* Mr. C. B. Jewson].

NORWICH, THE NORFOLK LUNATIC ASYLUM (now St. Andrew's Hospital), THORPE, 1811–14 [exhib. at Norwich Society of Artists].

NORWICH CATHEDRAL, repaired west front, 1815 [*A.P.S.D.*].

GREAT YARMOUTH, NORFOLK, THE GAOL, 1818 [J. H. Druery, *Great Yarmouth*, 1826, 76].

NORWICH CASTLE, repaired and largely reconstructed the east front, *c.* 1829; further works in progress at the time of his death which were completed by A. Salvin [*A.P.S.D.*].

BRIDGES in NORFOLK at BABURGH, 1815; BARNEY, 1814; BRANDON CREEK; CROSTWICK, 1809; FAKENHAM, 1833; GREAT CRESSINGHAM, 1810–11; HILGAY, 1809 (timber); HONINGHAM, 1810; MODNEY CREEK; NORWICH, FYE BRIDGE, 1829 (iron); ROXHAM DRAIN; SEDGE FEN DRAIN; THETFORD, 1829 (iron) [*A.P.S.D.*; B. Weinreb, *Catalogue* no. 9, *Bridges*, no. 88; *Norfolk Chronicle*, 3 Jan. 1829; *Norwich Mercury*, 30 Nov. 1833].

STONE, JOHN (1620–1667), was the third and youngest son of Nicholas Stone (*q.v.*). According to his near relation Charles Stoakes, he 'was bred a scoller by Docttor Busby'. George Vertue says that he was 'brought up at Oxford, design'd for a clergyman', and if so he was probably the John Stone who was Bible Clerk and Librarian at University College from 1644 until 1648, when he was expelled by the Parliamentary Visitors. According to Vertue he was the author of a book entitled *Enchiridion of Fortification, or a handfull of knowledge in Martiall affairs*, published anonymously in London in 1645. On leaving Oxford he 'went out to serve the King', and subsequently became a fugitive from the Parliamentary forces, living for a whole year concealed in London before escaping to France. He returned to England some time after his father's death, and helped to carry on the family business, which devolved on him after his brother Henry's death in 1653. Stoakes says that he was 'an excelent architect', and like his father he evidently combined the practice of architecture with that of sculpture, though it may be doubted whether he actually carved with his own hands. Caius Gabriel Cibber (*q.v.*) acted as his foreman, and was probably the actual sculptor of most of the monuments which are recorded to have been made in Stone's workshop between 1650 and 1657 (listed in Spiers, 138–42). Stone's principal recorded work as an architect was CHESTERTON HOUSE, WARWICKS., which he probably designed for the royalist Sir Edward Peyto before the latter's death in 1658, and for which he was supplying capitals and other architectural details in 1660. The house was demolished in 1802, but two

785

monuments from the Stone workshop remain in the parish church [H. M. Colvin, 'Chesterton, Warwickshire', *Arch. Rev.*, Aug. 1955].

At the Restoration John Stone went over to Breda to petition the King for the Office of Master Mason held by his father. He was given the Windsor office, but not the Master Masonship of the Works, which went to Edward Marshall. While at Breda he was stricken with paralysis. Cibber brought him home, but he never recovered sufficiently to resume the management of his affairs, and eventually died an inmate of the Hospital of St. Cross at Winchester in 1667.

[*The Note-Book and Account-Book of Nicholas Stone*, ed. W. L. Spiers, *Walpole Soc.* vii, 1918–19, 26–30, 138–42, etc.; *Vertue Note Books*, Walpole Soc., i, 89–93; D. Knoop & G. P. Jones, *The London Mason in the Seventeenth Century*, 1935, 24; *History of the King's Works* v, 3–4.]

STONE, NICHOLAS (1587–1647), sculptor and master mason, was born in Devonshire, where his father was a quarryman. At the age of 16 or 17 he was apprenticed to Isaac James, a sculptor of Dutch origin working in Southwark. When Hendrik de Keyser, master mason to the City of Amsterdam, visited London in 1606, Stone was introduced to him and engaged to work for him in Holland. He eventually married de Keyser's daughter and in 1613 returned to London, where he established himself in Long Acre. He immediately obtained important commissions for monuments, and soon became the leading English monumental sculptor. His large output is documented by a note-book in which he recorded his commissions, and by an account-book covering the years 1631–42. He was a sculptor of considerable ability, whose monuments are often novel and inventive in design, and responsive to new influences such as the antique sculptures acquired by Charles I from Mantua.

Stone's activities were by no means limited to tomb-making. He also acted as a master mason, and was employed in this capacity by Inigo Jones at the building of the Banqueting House in Whitehall in 1619–22, William Cure, the King's Master Mason, having declined the task. In April 1626 Stone was formally brought into the royal works by his appointment as 'master mason and architect' to Windsor Castle, and in October 1632 he succeeded Cure as Master Mason to the Crown, while retaining the parallel office at Windsor. At Windsor he designed a banqueting house which was not built, but carried out other works for whose design his responsibility is less certain. Other recorded architectural commissions are listed below. They show Stone as a designer who had partly absorbed the new classicism of Inigo Jones, but without accepting its full

discipline, and without rejecting some of the mannerist or baroque features that he had learned in London and Amsterdam. The result was a vernacular classical architecture of considerable charm and accomplishment of which regrettably little remains extant today.

Nicholas Stone was a member of the London Masons' Company. He was Warden in 1627 and 1630, and served as Master in 1633 and 1634. His career, like that of Inigo Jones, was no doubt disrupted by the Civil War, and according to Vertue he and Jones joined together to bury their joint stock of ready money, first in Scotland Yard, and later in Lambeth Marsh. Stone died on 24 August 1647, and was buried in the church of St. Martin-in-the-Fields, where a monument (now destroyed, but illustrated in Bodleian, Gough Maps 22, f. 70^v) commemorated his 'knowledge in Sculpture and Architecture'. His business was continued by his sons Henry and John (*q.v.*), his eldest son Nicholas having died in the same year as his father.

The two manuscripts already mentioned, an office note-book kept by Stone from 1614 to 1641, and an account-book for the years 1631 to 1642, are in Sir John Soane's Museum, together with sketch-books belonging to his sons Nicholas and Henry. A diary kept by the younger Nicholas on a visit to Italy in 1638–42 is in the British Museum (Harleian MS. 4049, printed by Spiers, *op. cit. subt.*).

[*The Note-Book and Account-Book of Nicholas Stone*, ed. W. L. Spiers, *Walpole Soc.* vii, 1918–19; D. Knoop & G. P. Jones, *The London Mason in the Seventeenth Century*, 1935, 22–4; Margaret Whinney, *Sculpture in Britain 1530–1830*, 1964, 24–31; *History of the King's Works* iii, 1975, 132–3, 330–1.]

CHILHAM CHURCH, KENT, chapel on south side of chancel, for Sir Dudley Digges, to contain monument by Stone to Lady Digges, 1631–2; dem. 1863 [*Note-Book*, 86].

CORNBURY HOUSE, OXON., partly rebuilt for the 1st Earl of Danby, 1632–3; west front rebuilt by Hugh May 1663–8; interior altered at various dates [*Note-Book*, 70] (*C. Life*, 22 Sept. 1950).

OXFORD, THE BOTANICAL GARDEN, built three gateways at expense of the 1st Earl of Danby, 1632–3 [*Note-Book*, 70]. Though Stone built these gateways it is not certain that he designed them.

LONDON, GOLDSMITHS' HALL, FOSTER LANE, 1635–8; damaged in the Great Fire of 1666 and restored; dem. 1829 [John Newman, 'Nicholas Stone's Goldsmith's Hall', *Architectural History* xiv, 1971].

WINDSOR CASTLE, built gateway to park at east end of terrace, 1636; dem. [*History of the King's Works* iii, 330–1]. It is not certain that Stone designed this gateway himself.

COPT HALL, ESSEX, work for the 1st Earl of Middlesex, including new windows in the gallery, 1638–9; dem. 1748 [*Note-Book*, 120; John Newman, 'Copthall', in *The Country Seat*, ed. Colvin & Harris, 1970, 25–6].

MILCOTE HOUSE, WESTON-ON-AVON, WARWICKS., a 'plot' made for the 1st Earl of Middlesex, 1638, whether executed or not unknown; house destroyed by fire 1644 [letter from Stone among Cranfield papers, Sackville MSS., Kent Record Office, *ex inf.* Mr. John Newman].

LONDON, TART HALL, WESTMINSTER, for the Countess of Arundel, 1638; dem. 1720 [*Note-Book*, 125–6]. For an engraving that may possibly represent this house see *The King's Arcadia* (exhibition catalogue 1973), 202–3.

KIRBY HALL, NORTHANTS., remodelled north front for Sir Christopher, later 1st Lord Hatton, 1638–40 [*Note-Book*, 119, 125, 128–9] (G. H. Chettle, *Kirby Hall*, H.M.S.O. 1937).

ATTRIBUTIONS

John Stoakes, who was related to Nicholas Stone, left a list of 'the most Eminentt Workes' that the latter 'did in England … Holland and Scotland' [*Note-Book*, 136–7]. This list of architectural works includes some, like the Banqueting House, where Stone was merely the executant, others, like Cornbury House and the Goldsmiths' Hall, that are confirmed by documentary evidence, and a residue whose authenticity can neither be proved nor disproved. These last include the WATER-GATE at YORK HOUSE, LONDON (1626), which Stoakes says Stone both 'desined & built'; 'many curious pavements and other workes' within HOLYROODHOUSE, EDINBURGH, which according to Stoakes he 'desined & built' for King James I (cf. *Note-Book*, 43–4); and the 'Virgin Porch' at ST. MARY'S CHURCH, OXFORD (1637), which Stoakes claims Stone 'desind & built', although in fact it is known to have been built by John Jackson (*q.v.*).

Stoakes does not mention LINDSEY HOUSE, LINCOLN'S INN FIELDS, which Stone may well have designed, since it was built *c.* 1640 by Sir David Cunningham, whom Stone described as his 'noble friend', and who in 1639 had commissioned him to make the monument to Sir Thomas Puckering in St. Mary's Church, Warwick (*Note-Book*, 76). Nor does he mention BALLS PARK, HERTS., built by Sir John Harrison in 1638–40 (*C. Life*, 20 April 1912), which shares several distinctive features with Stone's Goldsmiths' Hall, notably the irregularly spaced brackets supporting the cornice and the unusual rusticated basement windows on either side of the front doorway. Harrison, like most of Stone's clients, was a royalist.

STOWEY, PHILIP, of Exeter, exhibited designs for two buildings at the Society of Artists

in 1775. They were the GENERAL HOSPITAL at TAUNTON, SOMERSET, 1772–5, and the SESSIONS HOUSE in the CASTLE at EXETER, 1773–5. The former building is illustrated in J. Toulmin's *History of Taunton*, 1791, 42, where it is said to have been erected by 'Stowey and Jones, architects'. It afterwards became a nunnery, and was known as The Convent. The County Records show that Stowey's designs for the Sessions House were submitted to James Wyatt, who made various recommendations for the improvement of the main elevation, which is illustrated by A. E. Richardson & C. L. Gill, *Regional Architecture of the West of England*, 1924, 100. In 1776 Messrs. Stowey & Jones[1] built a house for the Master of St. John's Hospital at Exeter [Parliamentary Papers, *Report of the Commissioners for Charities* vi, 1821, 86].

STRAFFORD, EARL OF, *see* WENTWORTH, WILLIAM

STRAHAN, JOHN (–*c.* 1740), was an architect of Bristol. According to John Wood, it was in December 1725 that Strahan 'came to Bristol, and by printed Bills, [offered] his services to the Publick, as a land surveyor and Architect' (*Essay towards a Description of Bath*, 1749, 242). In 1727 he was employed by John Hobbs, a Bristol timber merchant who had interests in Bath, to lay out 'Some Meadow and Garden Ground on the West Side of the Body of the City of Bath into Streets for Building'. This new quarter consisted of Kingsmead and Beauford Squares, with Kingsmead, Monmouth and Avon Streets, and the New Quay. John Wood, who resented the intrusion of a Bristol architect, referred scathingly in his *Essay towards a Description of Bath* (p. 341) to what he called 'the Piratical Architecture of … Mr. Strahan', and contrasted the lack of uniformity in the two new squares with the rigid control which he had himself imposed on the builders of Queen Square. Nevertheless, he admitted that 'Beaufort Buildings have a sort of Regularity to recommend them', and the surviving portions of the Kingsmead layout show that Strahan was by no means so negligent a surveyor as Wood would make out.

According to Shiercliff's *Bristol and Hotwell Guide* of 1789, Strahan was 'the architect who built Redland-Court House, and many other capital mansions in and near Bristol'. REDLAND COURT was erected by John Cossins in about 1735, and Shiercliff's statement is confirmed by a contemporary elevation of the garden front in the British Museum (*King's Maps* xiii, 77. 3*b*) which bears the inscription 'Delin. H. de Wilstar. Invented and Executed by I. Strahan Archit.'

---

[1] Jones's Christian name appears to have been Thomas.

None of the 'other capital mansions' designed by Strahan has so far been identified by documentary evidence, but it is possible that it was he who built FRAMPTON HOUSE, GLOS., for Richard Clutterbuck in 1731–3. For Clutterbuck was an official of the Bristol Customs House, and the architecture of his house is, in many respects, very similar to that of Redland Court (C. Life, 8–15 Oct. 1927). In both, Palladian elements are employed in a manner which, although by no means ineffective, shows that their architect had little understanding of Palladian theory. Another building in Strahan's style is the garden house (c. 1730), originally at WOODCHESTER, GLOS., but rebuilt at BODNANT, DENBIGHSHIRE, in 1938 (C. Life, 14 Sept. 1961, 554), and a case has been made for the attribution to him of EARNSHILL, nr. HAMBRIDGE, SOMERSET, built for a Bristol merchant named Henry Combe and completed in 1731 [C. Hussey in C. Life, 13, 20 Oct. 1960].

In Bristol, Strahan's only other recorded work appears to be the former organ case in ST. MARY REDCLIFFE CHURCH, which is mentioned as his by Shiercliff. It is possible, however, that he was the architect of the REDLAND CHAPEL, which was built by John Cossins between 1740 and 1743 (measured drawings in Details, ed. R. R. Phillips, i, 1909, 193–6). William Halfpenny, under whose direction the chapel was completed, did not undertake the supervision of the building until May 1742, when the structure was already finished, and as Wood refers to Strahan as 'deceas'd' in the 1742 edition of his Essay, it is natural to suppose that it was his death in or about that year which led to Halfpenny's employment. The building accounts do not refer to Halfpenny's predecessor by name, but accompanying them is the original 'Roff Computation what Expences the Materials and Workmanship (of) the Chappel will amount to', which may be in Strahan's hand.[1] In the British Museum there is an original design for the gallery and Cossins monuments, and a contemporary view of the interior dedicated to Cossins (King's Maps xiii, 95. a–d).

A bust of 'Mr. John Straughan Surveyor of Bristol' is included in a list of Rysbrack's works compiled by George Vertue in 1732.

[C. F. Dening, The Eighteenth-Century Architecture of Bristol, 1923; W. Ison, The Georgian Buildings of Bath, 1948, 33, 133–4; W. Ison, The Georgian Buildings of Bristol, 1952, 45–6; C. H. & M. I. Collins Baker, Life of James Brydges, Duke of Chandos, 1949, 301; J. Charlton & D. M.

Milton, Redland 791 to 1800, 1951; Walpole Soc., Vertue Note Books iii, 57.]

STRATFORD, FERDINANDO (1719–1766), was a civil engineer and surveyor who appears to have lived at Gloucester before moving to Bristol in about 1760. Before coming to Bristol he had been responsible for a highly commended scheme to make the R. Avon navigable from Bath to Chippenham. He died at Tidenham in Gloucestershire in April 1766, from ague contracted while investigating the possibility of making the R. Chelmer navigable from Chelmsford to Maldon in Essex. At Bristol he was one of the engineers who made designs for rebuilding the bridge, and was involved in the ensuing controversy, publishing in 1760 A Short Account of the Manner proposed for Rebuilding Bristol Bridge (see also Reports of the Late John Smeaton i, 1812, 99–102). As an architect he is known to have enlarged or remodelled BROMSBERROW HOUSE, GLOS. (dem.), for Robert Dobyns Yate in 1758–62 [estimate and account among Yate-Allen papers, on loan to Glos. Record Office in 1955], and to have designed the handsome classical MARKET HOUSE (now TOWN HALL) at NEWTOWNARDS in CO. DOWN, IRELAND, in 1765 [C. E. B. Brett, Court Houses and Market Houses of the Province of Ulster, Belfast 1973, 72–5]. There are estate maps and surveys by Stratford in the Public Record Office, Gloucestershire Record Office and National Library of Wales. [I. E. Gray, 'Ferdinando Stratford of Gloucestershire', Trans. Bristol and Glos. Archaeological Soc. lxvii, 1946–8, 412–15; W. Ison, The Georgian Buildings of Bristol, 1952, 46–7, 114–123; P. Eden, Dictionary of Land Surveyors 1550–1850, 1975–6; will, P.C.C. 246 TYNDALL.]

STRETTON, SAMUEL (c. 1732–1811) and WILLIAM (1755–1828), were the principal builders and architects in Nottingham in the second half of the eighteenth century. They were descended from a family of minor gentry with property at Longdon in Staffordshire, but Samuel's father had 'dissipated' the estate, and in 1750 he was obliged to leave Longdon and establish himself as a builder at Lenton, on the outskirts of Nottingham. Among the many industrial buildings which he erected was Richard Arkwright's cotton mill, the first of its kind in England. He married in 1754, and had two sons, William and Samuel. The elder son was for many years in partnership with his father, and succeeded to his business on the latter's death in 1811. He had his yard in Cow Lane, near Clumber Street, and did a good deal of surveying for the Corporation. In 1790 he introduced the first Welsh slates into Nottinghamshire by bringing a cargo from Lord Penrhyn's quarries at Llandegai in Carnarvonshire. He had anti-

---

[1] See p. 379. Dening (Eighteenth-Century Architecture of Bristol, 1923, 85) claimed to have found documentary evidence that Strahan designed the chapel, but failed to state his source.

quarian interests, and made extensive notes on local antiquities which were privately printed by G. C. Robertson in 1910 as *The Stretton Manuscripts*, with a prefatory memoir of the family. He carried out excavations on the site of the Cluniac priory of Lenton, whose site he had acquired, and built the house known as 'Lenton Priory', where he died in 1828. He married in 1778, and had six children, whom he named Stella, Sempronius, Severus,[1] Salacia, Sabina and Severus.

The following list of the Strettons' principal works is based on *The Stretton Manuscripts*, pp. 180–1, etc., and *Records of the Corporation of Nottingham* vii, 1947.

NOTTINGHAM

COTTON MILL at HUCKLEY, for Richard Arkwright, 1769.

NAVIGATION INN, WILFORD STREET, 1787.

THE NEW TOWN HALL and PRISON, 1789–91, built by William Stones 'according to Messrs. Strettons' Plans and Specifications' [*Records* vii, 236, 239, 254, 262] (J. Throsby, *Antiquities of Nottinghamshire* ii, 1790, 140).

TIMBER HILL, rebuilt Mrs. Freeth's house, 'except the back part', 1790.

RICK'S GARDEN, 'laid out and the first houses built thereon by S. and W.S. for Mr. J. Howard', 1791 (cf. *Records* vii, 259: 'ordered that Mr. William Stretton do draw an elevation of houses proper to be built on Rick's garden', 1791).

BUTT DYKES, 'Mrs. Melville's Warehouse' (S. and W.S.), 1791.

'Dawson's Lace Manufactory, since Beardmore's, now Fellows's, Silk Mill', 1791.

POPLAR PLACE, Messrs. Evans, Storer & Green's Brewery (S. and W.S.), 1792.

BROAD MARSH, Alderman Green's Cotton Mill, 1792–3.

THE BARRACKS, CASTLE PARK (S. and W.S.), 1792–3.

THE 'TEN-ARCH BRIDGE' on the Flood Road, 1796–7.

LENTON, Green and Killingley's Bleach Yard (W.S.), 1797.

RIDING SCHOOL nr. CASTLE GATE for the Nottingham Troop of Yeomanry Cavalry (W.S.), 1798.

THE NEW INN, LONG ROW, bought by W.S. in 1797 and rebuilt soon after.

ST. JAMES'S CHURCH, STANDARD HILL, (W.S.), 1808–9, Gothic; dem. 1935.

STANDARD HILL, three houses 'which cost about £4000 besides land' (W.S.), 1810–14.

ST. MARY'S CHURCH, inserted groined ceiling

(which survives only in the tower) (W.S.), 1811–12.

ST. PETER'S CHURCH, alterations (W.S.), 1812–13.

LENTON PRIORY, LENTON, built by W.S. for himself before 1814.

THE NEW EXCHANGE, alterations to the designs of Edward Staveley, 1814–15.

GREGORY'S PADDOCK, house for Thomas Elliott, (W.S.), 1817.

NOTTINGHAMSHIRE

WILFORD HALL, NOTTS., built by S.S. for Samuel Smith 'under the direction of Anderson of Loughborough, Architect', completed 1781.

WOLLATON HALL, 'Park Gateway erected by W.S. and the urns made by him', 1790.

REMPSTONE, NOTTS., 'Mr. Greg. Williams' House surveyed and in part built by W.S.', 1792.

COLWICK RECTORY, NOTTS., enlarged 1819 [Borthwick Institute, York, MGA 1819/2].

STRIBLING, ROBERT, was a builder at Exeter. He was apprenticed to a carpenter and joiner in 1727. He had a son Robert who was apprenticed to him in 1761. From 1765 onwards he held the post of carpenter and joiner to Exeter Cathedral. In 1773–5 he built the north side of BEDFORD CIRCUS, EXETER, as a speculation. The south side was not completed until 1826, and the whole was destroyed by bombing in 1942. [*Exeter Freemen*, ed. Rowe & Jackson, Devon and Cornwall Record Soc. 1973, 241, 290; A. Jenkins, *History of Exeter*, 1806, 323–4; information from Prof. W. G. Hoskins; A. E. Richardson & C. L. Gill, *The Regional Architecture of the West of England*, 1924, 26–7.]

STRONG was the name of a family of master masons active throughout the seventeenth and early eighteenth centuries, and well known for the important buildings which they executed to the designs of Wren, Vanbrugh, Hawksmoor and other architects. The foundation of the family fortunes was laid in the freestone quarries at Little Barrington in Gloucestershire and Taynton in Oxfordshire, which were acquired by TIMOTHY STRONG early in the seventeenth century. He came from Wiltshire, but settled at Little Barrington, where, according to his grandson's account of the family, printed by Clutterbuck in his *History of Hertfordshire*, 'he had several apprentices, and kept several masons and labourers employed in those quarries, to serve the Country with what they wanted in the way of trade'. In 1632–3 he largely rebuilt CORNBURY HOUSE, OXON., for Henry Danvers, Earl of Danby, to the designs of Nicholas Stone. In 1634 he and his sons were working on the CANTERBURY QUADRANGLE at ST. JOHN'S COLLEGE, OXFORD, having been 'fecht out of my Lord Danvers's work' by

---

[1] The first child of this name died in infancy.

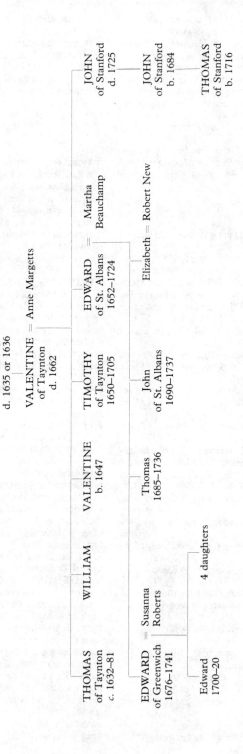

THE STRONG FAMILY

TIMOTHY STRONG
of Little Barrington
d. 1635 or 1636

VALENTINE = Anne Margetts
of Taynton
d. 1662

THOMAS
of Taynton
c. 1632–81

WILLIAM

VALENTINE
b. 1647

TIMOTHY
of Taynton
1650–1705

EDWARD = Martha
of St. Albans   Beauchamp
1652–1724

JOHN
of Stanford
d. 1725

EDWARD = Susanna
of Greenwich   Roberts
1676–1741

Thomas
1685–1736

John
of St. Albans
1690–1737

Elizabeth = Robert New

JOHN
of Stanford
b. 1684

Edward
1700–20

4 daughters

THOMAS
of Stanford
b. 1716

the promise of 'extraordinary rates' which the College 'yeilded to give them but concealed from the other workemen' [St. John's College Muniments lxii, 13]. Timothy Strong died in 1635 or 1636, leaving the quarries to his only son, Valentine Strong, who soon afterwards moved to Taynton.

According to Clutterbuck's manuscript, VALENTINE STRONG (d. 1662) enlarged SHERBORNE HOUSE, GLOS., for John Dutton in 1651–3, and was perhaps responsible for adding wings to the façade of superimposed orders which was reproduced by L. W. Wyatt when he rebuilt the house in 1829–34 (cf. letter from Mark Girouard in *C. Life*, 25 Oct. 1956, 954); and in 1656 he contracted to build LOWER SLAUGHTER MANOR-HOUSE, GLOS., for Richard Whitmore, 'according to one moddell or plattforme by him lately received from the said Mr. Whitmore and according to such moulds as hee hath given to the said Mr. Whitmore concerning the same' [Whitmore papers in Gloucestershire County Record Office, 8 (4/1)]. His last work was at FAIRFORD, where he began to build a new manor-house for Andrew Barker in 1661, but died in 1662 before it was finished.[1] He was buried at Fairford, and is commemorated by the following rhyming epitaph:

Here's one that was an able workman long
Who divers houses built, both fair and Strong;
Though Strong he was, a Stronger came than he
And robb'd him of his life and fame, we see:
Moving an old house a new one for to rear,
Death met him by the way, and laid him here.

Valentine Strong married Anne Margetts of Charlbury in 1631 or 1632. By her he had six sons and five daughters – Ann, Thomas, William, Elizabeth, Lucy, who died young, Sarah, Valentine, Timothy, Edward, John, and Lucy, 'the second of that name'. All his six sons were bred to the mason's trade, and THOMAS STRONG (*c.* 1632–81), the eldest, carried on the family business as a mason and quarry-owner. At the time of his father's death he had been working at LONGLEAT HOUSE, WILTS., where a number of alterations and improvements were being carried out by Sir James Thynne,[2] and he completed the unfinished house at Fairford for Andrew Barker. In

---

[1] His will, dated 3 Oct. 1661, and proved 5 Nov. 1662, is P.C.C. 148 LAUD. But according to the inscription on his tomb in Fairford Churchyard he died on 26 Dec. 1662.

[2] According to a MS. account of Longleat written by the 1st Lord Weymouth (Longleat archives, Box 179B), Sir James Thynne 'made the Stone Terras from the outward Gate to the Hall Door, and made the Door by the direction of Sr. Chr. Wren, now taken away and placed at the School House in Warminster. He also new made the Great Stairs, paved the Hall and passages with stone ... finished the Blew Parlor and Drawing roome ioyning to it ... walled and planted the old Kitchin Garden and made the door out of the Hall into the Greate Parlor'.

about 1663 he built the stables at CORNBURY HOUSE, OXON., which had been designed by Hugh May for the Earl of Clarendon, and in 1665–6 he built the east front to the designs of the same architect, together with the terrace-walls. At the same time he was engaged in building the first part of the new quadrangle at TRINITY COLLEGE, OXFORD, designed by Wren and completed in 1668.

Meanwhile, the Great Fire of London had attracted him to the capital, where he not only obtained several important contracts, but also sold large quantities of stone to other masons. In 1670, taking advantage of the Act for rebuilding the City, which permitted 'foreign' artificers to take up their freedom, Strong was made free of the Masons' Company and of the City by redemption. He was admitted to the Livery on 30 October 1671, and to the Court of Assistants on 10 July 1675. According to his nephew's memoir, he was engaged in building three City churches – ST. STEPHEN, WALBROOK, ST. AUGUSTINE, WATLING STREET, and ST. BENET, PAUL'S WHARF – and although the two latter were completed by his younger brother Edward, there can be no doubt that Thomas was the original contractor. He became one of the principal contractors for St. Paul's Cathedral when work began in 1675, laying the foundation-stone 'with his own hands' on 21 June. In 1678 he was employing thirty-five men on the site. At the same time, he was building 'a front of stone betwixt the wings of Lord Craven's house at Hampstead Marshall, in Berkshire'. He died unmarried in the summer of 1681, leaving everything to his younger brother Edward, whom he made his sole executor [P.C.C. 99 NORTH].

EDWARD STRONG (1652–1724), who now took over his brother's contracts, had probably learned the mason's trade in the family quarries at Taynton and Little Barrington. He had been apprenticed to his brother on 2 January 1671/2, and no doubt came to London in order to assist him. He was made free of the Masons' Company in April 1680, became a Warden in 1694, and Master in 1696. He completed the churches which his brother had begun, and was himself responsible for the masonry of ST. CLEMENT, EASTCHEAP (1683–7), ST. MARY, ALDERMARY (1681–2), ST. MARY MAGDALEN, OLD FISH STREET (1683–7), ST. MICHAEL, COLLEGE HILL (1686–94), ST. MILDRED, BREAD STREET (1681–7), and the tower of ST. VEDAST, FOSTER LANE (1695), representing contracts amounting to over £11,000. At the same time he was working at WINCHESTER PALACE, where, according to his own account, he 'had all the designs of all the masons' work committed to his care, by Sir Christopher Wren, the surveyor'. But the main work of his London career was the building of ST. PAUL'S CATHEDRAL, in which he took a prominent part, supplying large quantities of 'Burford' stone, and contracting for the east end, the north portico, the north side of the nave, and the north-west quarter of the dome. In 1695 he was employing sixty-five masons at St. Paul's, more than twice the number employed by his fellow-contractors, Kempster and Beauchamp. In 1694 he 'performed all the stone work of Sir John Morden's Hospital on Blackheath', *i.e.* MORDEN COLLEGE, and in 1696 he took the first mason's contract for the building of GREENWICH HOSPITAL. For this he was in partnership with Thomas Hill, but in the performance of succeeding contracts he was associated first with Ephraim Beauchamp, and afterwards with his son, Edward Strong, junior. Their MS. Day Book for this work, covering the years 1699 to 1708, is in the Guildhall Library (MS. 233). In 1705 Edward Strong and his son took the chief mason's contract at BLENHEIM PALACE, OXON., where they erected the whole of the main pile. After the dispute between Vanbrugh and the Duchess of Marlborough had brought the works to a standstill in 1712, the Strongs had recourse to litigation in order to recover the considerable sums of money owing to them (see David Green, *Blenheim Palace*, 1951, and *Cal. Treas. Papers 1714–19*, 15, 63, 323).

Edward Strong made the most of his opportunities as a master mason and quarry-owner at a time when unprecedented building activity offered great rewards to the master builder with capital and experience. With the fortune which he had made in London, he established himself as a landowner, not in his native Cotswolds, but in the neighbourhood of St. Albans. In 1714 he bought the manor of Hyde at Abbot's Langley, and in 1716 that of Herons at Wheathampstead. He lived at St. Albans in the house known as New Barnes, where he died on 8 February 1723/4, aged 71. He was buried in St. Peter's Church, where there is a monument with a portrait-bust. The epitaph is given in Cussans's *Hertfordshire*, 1881, 299–301, and in *Builder* xxii, 1864, 700. His will is P.C.C. 45 BOLTON. A portrait of Strong, formerly at Shaloch, Aberdeenshire (*N. and Q.*, 7th ser., i, 1886, 228], was exhibited at the Wren Tercentenary Exhibition at St. Paul's Cathedral in 1932. It subsequently belonged to Miss R. M. Davenport. Ivy House, No. 107 St. Peter's Street and a house in the Market Place on the site of the former north gateway to the abbey precinct are said to have been built by Strong, the former as his own residence [*V.C.H. Herts.* ii, 473; J. C. & C. A. Buckler, *History of the Abbey Church of St. Albans*, 1847, 165]. He married Martha, sister of Ephraim Beauchamp, and left three sons, Edward Strong, junior, who carried on the business, Thomas, who died in 1736, and John, who sold the Wheathampstead estate in 1726, and died at St. Albans in 1737.

EDWARD STRONG, junior (1676–1741),

was apprenticed to his father on 30 July 1691, was made free of the Masons' Company on 18 October 1698, and was called to the Livery the same day. He was admitted to the Court of Assistants in 1702, was Warden in 1712 and 1715, and Master in 1718. He lived at Greenwich, where he was engaged in building the Hospital for many years. In 1702 he contracted to build the NORTH GATE of ST. BARTHOLOMEW'S HOSPITAL, SMITHFIELD, 'according to the model drawn by the said Edward Strong and approved of by the Governors ... of this Hospital for the sum of £550'. This, the existing gateway to Smithfield, was completed in 1703 [Gweneth Whitteridge, 'The Henry VIII Gateway into Smithfield', *St. Bartholomew's Hospital Jnl.*, 1949]. At ST. PAUL'S, Strong assisted his father in building the lantern in 1706–8, and subsequently laid the marble pavement beneath the dome and transepts. He also built the 'lanterns' or spires of CHRISTCHURCH, NEWGATE STREET, ST. VEDAST, FOSTER LANE, ST. STEPHEN, WALBROOK, ST. MICHAEL, COLLEGE HILL, and ST. JAMES, GARLICKHYTHE, and the steeple of ST. MICHAEL, CORNHILL (completed 1722). With Edward Tufnell as partner, he built the churches of ST. JOHN, WESTMINSTER (1713–28), ST. PAUL, DEPTFORD (1713–30), ST. GEORGE IN THE EAST (1714–23), ST. ANNE, LIMEHOUSE (1714–24), and ST. GEORGE, BLOOMSBURY (1716–30). The 'Book of Entry for Masons work' kept by Strong and Tufnell while engaged on these five churches is preserved in the R.I.B.A. Library. Strong was also for a time in partnership with Christopher Cass and Andrews Jelfe, an arrangement which was terminated on 31 December 1728, at Strong's desire (B.M., Stowe MS. 412, no. 77).

Private houses with which Strong is known to have been concerned were William Draper's house at ADDISCOMBE in SURREY, which he built to the designs of an unknown architect in 1702–3; MARLBOROUGH HOUSE, LONDON; and CANNONS HOUSE, MIDDLESEX, of which he built the north front in 1715. In the summer of 1711 he accompanied Sir James Thornhill and his brother Thomas on a visit to Holland. The diary kept by Thornhill is now in the British Museum (Add. MS. 34788).[1]

In 1699 he married Susanna, daughter of Joseph Roberts, Serjeant Plumber, by whom he had a son Edward, who died of smallpox at the age of 20, and four daughters, the eldest of whom married Sir John Strange, Master of the Rolls. Strong died on 10 October 1741, leaving his property in Hertfordshire and elsewhere[2] to be

---

[1] Some extracts from it were printed in the *Proceedings of the Suffolk Institute of Archaeology* xiii, 1907–9, 33–43.

[2] His London property included six houses in Bartlett's Buildings (parish of St. Andrew's, Holborn), and others in Wellclose Square. Some papers relating to his estate are in the Bodleian Library, MS. Top. Herts. c. 2.

divided among his daughters [P.C.C. 284 SPUR-WAY].

Nothing is known of Valentine Strong's second son William, or of his third son Valentine, except that they were both still alive in 1681. But his fourth and sixth sons Timothy and John are mentioned as masons of Stanford-in-the-Vale in Berkshire in some late seventeenth-century documents formerly belonging to the Aston family, who were lords of a moiety of the manor at that time.[1] John, like his father, had many children, and the family continued to live and work in Stanford throughout the eighteenth century. As late as 1866, it was remembered that some of the best of the tombstones in the church-yard were 'the workmanship of a family of the name of Strong, who for many years were masons at Stanford, and who were famous in the country round' [L. G. Maine, *A Berkshire Village, its History and Antiquities*, 1866, 54]. The church-wardens' accounts contain several payments to John Strong for minor repairs to the church between 1694 and 1703, and in 1709 he applied for a faculty to erect a pew for himself at the west end of the nave [Bodleian Library, MS. Oxford Archdeaconry papers, Berkshire, c. 161, ff. 64–74]. He lived in the neighbouring village of Shell-ingford, but was buried at Stanford when he died in August 1725. His will was proved on 4 September [Archdeaconry Court of Berkshire, Register 21, f. 285].

John Strong's eldest son John was baptized at Stanford on 26 October 1684. In January 1733 he was consulted in connection with the building of the new COUNCIL CHAMBER at ABINGDON, for there is a payment of 6 guineas 'to Mr. John Stevens and Mr. John Strong per Bill', and the former is known to have made designs for the 'ornaments' which are referred to in the builders' contract. Either John or his father rebuilt the tower of LONGCOT CHURCH, BERKS., in 1722, as appears by a note on the flyleaf of the Shrivenham Parish Register[2] to the effect that after the old tower had fallen in 1721 'the Estimate for rebuilding it being 226£ was raised by a Tax of 30 shillings on the Yard Lands of Longcote and Furnham. The Contractor for this was – Strong of Standford, who not only finished the Tower for this sum, but added the flower pots. He was a reputable Mason, and built Wadley House for Mr. Charles Pye.' The churchwardens' accounts of UFFINGTON, BERKS., show that 'Mr. Strong' also rebuilt the octagonal central tower of that church after its destruction by lightning in December 1740. The present battlements and pinnacles were substituted in the nineteenth cen-

tury for Strong's parapet with classical orna-ments at the angles. The house at WADLEY, nr. SHRIVENHAM, mentioned above, was rebuilt by Charles Pye in 1768, and must have been the work of a later member of the family, perhaps of Thomas, son of John Strong, junior, who was born on 19 March 1715/16, and repaired Stan-ford Church more than once between 1750 and 1775. In 1766 'Mr. Strong' was working at BECK-ETT PARK, BERKS., for Lord Barrington under Sanderson Miller's direction [Sanderson Miller's correspondence in Warwick Record Office, Let-ters 777, 842–3]. The baptisms and burials of members of the family continue to occur in the parish registers until the end of the century, and as late as 1814–16 a Thomas Strong was employed to carry out repairs to COLESHILL HOUSE, BERKS., under D. A. Alexander.

Other branches of the family were established at Box in Wiltshire, where a Thomas Strong owned one of the quarries in the early nineteenth century, and at Warminster in the same county, where three generations of the family were in business as masons from 1830 until the death of Egerton Strong at the age of 83 in August 1964.
[R. Clutterbuck, *History of Hertfordshire* i, 1815, 167; D. Knoop & G. P. Jones, *The London Mason in the Seventeenth Century*, 1935, 43–5; transcript of Taynton Parish Registers in Bodleian Library, MS. Top. Oxon. c. 526; *V.C.H. Herts.* ii, 302, 324, 412, 420, 473; W. H. Blacker, *Gloucestershire Notes and Queries* ii, 1884, 262–4, iii, 1885–7, 365; *Wren Soc.* xx, 218–20; *A.P.S.D.*; *Warminster Jnl.*, 21 Aug. 1964 (obituary of Egerton Strong).]

STUART, CHARLES, an architect of Darna-way, nr. Forres, designed the castellated NELSON MONUMENT at FORRES, MORAYSHIRE, 1806. A rival design by Richard Crichton was rejected [R. Douglas, *Annals of Forres*, Elgin 1934, 313, 318).

STUART, JAMES (1713–1788), the son of a Scottish mariner, was born in Creed Lane, Lud-gate Street, in 1713. As a boy, he displayed a con-siderable talent for drawing, and when his father died, leaving his mother and the other children without means of support, Stuart obtained employment with Lewis Goupy, the well-known fan-painter. It may have been Goupy who first aroused Stuart's interest in classical antiquity, for George Vertue says that Lord Burlington engaged Goupy to accompany him on his Grand Tour, and many of his fans were decorated with views of classical buildings. While working for Goupy, Stuart studied mathematics, geometry and anatomy to good effect, becoming a skilful draughtsman as well as a competent painter in gouache and water-colours. He also taught him-self Latin and Greek, being led to study the former language 'by the desire of understanding

---

[1] I owe this information to Mr. J. H. Harvey.
[2] Based on 'the books containing the accounts of the Churchwardens of Longcote since the year 1721'. These no longer exist.

what was written under prints published after pictures of the ancient masters'. After his mother's death, his brother and sister being by now in employment, Stuart was able to realize a long-cherished plan to visit Rome, in order to pursue his studies in art. He set out in 1742, travelling most of the way on foot, and earning money as opportunity offered.[1] Having arrived in Rome, he appears to have acquired a considerable reputation as a judge of pictures, and it is very probable that, as Miss Lawrence has suggested, he supported himself in Rome by acting as *cicerone* to English visitors. In 1748 he accompanied Gavin Hamilton, Matthew Brettingham and Nicholas Revett on an expedition to Naples, in the course of which the project of visiting Athens was first discussed. He also occupied himself by making drawings of the obelisk found in the Campus Martius, which were published by Bandini in his treatise *De Obelisco Caesaris Augusti* (Rome 1750). Appended to the book was an account of the obelisk in the form of a letter addressed by Stuart to Charles Wentworth, Earl of Malton (afterwards Marquis of Rockingham).

It was in 1748 that Stuart and Revett issued their 'Proposals for publishing an Accurate Description of the Antiquities of Athems'. Their scheme was well received by the English dilettanti then in Rome, some of whom, including the Earl of Malton, the Earl of Charlemont, James Dawkins and Robert Wood, agreed to finance their projected expedition. They left Rome in 1750, but were delayed for some months in Venice. The British Resident there was Sir James Gray, a prominent member of the Society of Dilettanti, who procured their election to that body in 1751. His brother, Colonel George Gray, secretary and treasurer to the Society, published the *Proposals* in London, while Consul Smith issued a further edition in Venice in 1753. On 19 January 1751, Stuart and Revett embarked for Greece, arriving at Athens on 18 March. Here they enjoyed the protection of Sir James Porter, Ambassador at Constantinople, who was a member of the Dilettanti Society, and experienced comparatively little difficulty in making their survey of the antiquities, one person even pulling down a house to enable them to get a better view of the Tower of the Winds. There was, however, an awkward occasion when Stuart was 'provoked' to knock down a Greek consul with whom he had quarrelled, and he narrowly avoided murder at the hands of some Turks when in the autumn of 1753 he set out for Constantinople to obtain a renewal of the firman granted by the Sultan. Escaping with difficulty, he made his way to the coast and rejoined Revett

at Salonika. After visiting the Greek archipelago, they returned to England early in 1755, in order to prepare their drawings for publication. It was decided to alter the table of contents published in the *Proposal*, and to illustrate the smaller buildings of the town of Athens in the first volume, reserving the major architecture of the Acropolis for a second. The first volume appeared in 1762 as *The Antiquities of Athens measured and delineated by James Stuart, F.R.S. and F.S.A., and Nicholas Revett, Painters and Architects*, with a dedication to the King. It constituted the first accurate survey of Greek classical remains and was to be the principal source book of the Greek Revival in Britain. Though immediately recognized as a major work of architectural scholarship, its effect on contemporary architecture was limited; for the Greek Revival was a phenomenon of the nineteenth rather than of the eighteenth century, and the 'Gusto Greco' of the 1760s was decorative rather than structural in character. It was, in fact, 'the different Greek modes of decorating buildings' which the first volume of the *Antiquities* professed to illustrate, and over twenty-five years were to elapse before the publication of the splendours of the Acropolis. Meanwhile, Stuart had bought out Revett, who 'although his name appears on the title page of all four volumes' had 'resigned his interest in the work before the publication even of the first'. It was Revett, however, who had been responsible for all the measured drawings which gave the *Antiquities* its unique importance as the first accurate survey of the Athenian buildings, and made its publication a major event in the history of classical archaeology. Stuart's contribution was limited to the general topographical views which were engraved from his original gouache drawings, many of which are now in the R.I.B.A. Collection.

But it was Stuart whom the publication of the *Antiquities of Athens* made famous, and for the rest of his life he had as much employment as a painter and architect as he chose to accept. He was elected a Fellow of the Royal Society and of the Society of Antiquaries, and remained a prominent member of the Society of Dilettanti. In 1763 he was appointed painter to the Society in succession to George Knapton, but failing to fulfil his statutory duties by painting portraits of its members, he was superseded by Reynolds in 1768. In 1758 he became surveyor of Greenwich Hospital, a post worth £200 a year which he owed to the influence of his patron Lord Anson, and in 1764 he succeeded Hogarth as Sergeant Painter in the Office of Works. The latter post was abolished in 1782, but he retained the former until his death in 1788.

Stuart exhibited for some years with the Free Society of Artists, showing mainly the watercolour drawings of Athens in which he seems to

---

[1] He apparently acted as an 'itinerant Fan-painter' (see 'Memoirs of Thomas Jones', *Walpole Soc.* xxxii, 1946–8, 74).

have done something of a trade. He also executed a certain amount of decorative painting in the houses of his patrons (*e.g.* the 'Zephyrs and Zephyrettes' in Mrs. Montagu's bedroom at Sandleford Priory), and 'was frequently applied to when anything particularly elegant was required', such as a commemorative medal or a monument.[1] He was constantly consulted by Josiah Wedgwood, and was regarded as an arbiter of taste by all except those who shared Sir William Chambers's contempt for the 'Gusto Greco'.

As an architect, Stuart failed to make the most of his opportunities. The commissions which he received seem (as Miss Lawrence has said) 'to have been executed with reluctance, and, in some cases, to have been completed by other hands'. Mrs. Montagu, who employed him to build 22 Portman Square, 'on account of his disinterestedness and contempt of money', complained bitterly of his failure to deliver designs to the workmen, of his unreliability, and of his carelessness over accounts. Sir Sampson Gideon, she said, had been 'obliged to take many precautions to prevent being imposed on by the workmen whose bills he assented to', and at Greenwich it is clear from surviving correspondence that his conduct was equally unsatisfactory. His architectural practice was, in consequence, very limited, and he owed his principal commissions almost entirely to members of the Dilettanti Society and their friends. Comfortably circumstanced (at least in his latter days),[2] he preferred an easy and convivial life to the exacting routine of a busy architect's office. The success of the brothers Adam in popularizing their architectural innovations is the measure of Stuart and Revett's failure to do the same, and suggests that what they lacked was 'the capacity rather than the opportunity to be leaders of fashion'. Nevertheless, Stuart's place as the pioneer of the Greek Revival is secure. The temples which he designed at Hagley in 1758 and at Shugborough in the 1760s were the first buildings in Europe in which the Greek orders were used[3] and his designs for

neo-classical furniture at Kedleston and Spencer House occupy a comparable position in the history of English taste.

It was largely Stuart's own indolence which delayed for twenty-six years the appearance of the second volume of the *Antiquities*. It was almost ready for the press, when its appearance was further postponed by its author's sudden death at his house in Leicester Square on 2 February 1788. He was buried in the crypt of the church of St. Martin in the Fields. Stuart was twice married, his first wife being his housekeeper, by whom he had a son who died in infancy. By his second wife, whom he married late in life, he had five children, three of whom survived him.

The second volume of the *Antiquities of Athens* was published by Stuart's widow with the help of William Newton, his assistant and former Clerk of Works at Greenwich Hospital. It bore the date 1787 but was not actually published until 1789. The third volume, for which he left the completed drawings, appeared in 1795 under the editorship of Willey Reveley. In 1816 a further volume of miscellaneous papers and drawings by Stuart and Revett was issued by Josiah Taylor, the architectural publisher, with a memoir of its authors by Joseph Woods. A supplementary volume was published by C. R. Cockerell and others in 1830. An edition of the first three volumes on a reduced scale was published in 1825–7, and there were others in 1837, 1841, 1849 and 1858. Stuart is believed also to have been the author of a pamphlet entitled *Critical Observations on the Buildings and Improvements of London*, published anonymously in 1771 (see *Notes and Queries*, 3rd ser., vi, 1864, 71–2, and *Survey of London* xxix, 143 n.).

Miniature portraits of Stuart and his second wife were presented to the National Portrait Gallery in 1858 by his son. An engraved portrait serves as the title-page of an anonymous work entitled *Rudiments of Ancient Architecture*, published by I. & J. Taylor (2nd ed. 1794). A self-portrait of Stuart as a youth is among his drawings in the R.I.B.A. Collection and is reproduced in *R.I.B.A. Jnl.* xlii, 1935, 798. Portraits by J. Basire, Sir J. Reynolds (etched by S. W. Reynolds) and Probon (engraved by W. C. Edwards) are mentioned by E. B. Jupp in his *Catalogue of Drawings illustrating the Catalogues of the Society of Artists*, 1871, 7. A Wedgwood portrait medallion is reproduced by Eliza Meteyard in her *Life of Josiah Wedgwood* ii, 1866, 220.

Twenty of Stuart's gouache drawings for the *Antiquities of Athens* are in the R.I.B.A. Collec-

---

[1] The latter were chiefly executed by Peter Scheemakers and his son Thomas, who exhibited several 'models from the designs of Mr. Stuart' at the Free Society of Artists between 1765 and 1783. Among the medals designed by Stuart was one to celebrate the birth of the Prince of Wales in 1762 [Walpole, *Anecdotes of Painting* v, ed. Hilles & Daghlian, 1937, 109], and the medal awarded by the Royal Society of Arts from 1757 until 1805 [H. T. Wood, *A History of the Royal Society of Arts*, 1913, 316]. He also designed the frontispieces to James Harris's *Hermes* (2nd. ed. 1765) and *Philosophical Arrangements* (1775).

[2] 'Athens Stuart, unexpectedly to most people, has died possessed of much property, chiefly on mortgage on new buildings in Marybone' reported *The World* newspaper (22 Feb. 1788).

[3] The Greek Doric porches or porticoes that were

added to two Yorkshire houses, Rokeby and Kirby, have sometimes been thought to be of earlier date, but the date of the Rokeby portico is at present uncertain, and the one at Kirby was added after 1771.

tion, together with a sketch-book containing notes on Italian painters and sketches of buildings in Venice, Verona, etc. (see the *Catalogue*). Some fine decorative designs in the Pierpont Morgan Library are illustrated by John Harris in his *Catalogue of British Drawings for Architecture, etc., in American Collections*, 1971, 227–31. Stuart's original drawings of monuments in Lydia was Phillipps MS. 16099. [Obituaries in *Gent's Mag.* 1788 (i), 95–6, 181, 216–8, 1809 (ii), 596–7; and in *European Mag.* xiii, 1788, 68, 143, 284; A. Caldwell, *An Account of the Extraordinary Escape of James Stuart*, 1804 (a broadsheet, also printed in *European Mag.* xlvi, 1804, 369); memoir prefixed to vol. iv of the *Antiquities of Athens*, 1816; J. Mulvany, *Life of James Gandon*, 1846, 195–9; Eliza Meteyard, *Life of Josiah Wedgwood* ii, 1866, 219–26; J. T. Smith, *Nollekens and his Times* (World's Classics ed.), 15–16, 27; *Original Letters of Eminent Literary Men*, ed. Ellis, Camden Soc. 1843, 379–89 (for the ('Prospectus' of 1751); B.M., Add. MSS. 22152 (papers used in the preparation of vol. iv of the *Antiquities*), 27576 (memoir written by his son, James Stuart, R.N.); *A.P.S.D.*; *D.N.B.*; *Notes and Queries*, 2nd ser., ii, 80, 100, xi, 163, 3rd ser., ii, 275; Lesley Lawrence, 'Stuart and Revett: their Literary and Architectural Careers', *Jnl. of the Warburg Institute* ii, 1938–9; John Harris, 'Early Neo-Classical Furniture', *Jnl. of the Furniture History Soc.* ii, 1966; Dora Wiebenson, *Sources of Greek Revival Architecture*, 1969; E. Croft-Murray, *Decorative Painting in England* ii, 1970, 283–5; Nicholas Goodison, 'Mr. Stuart's Tripod', *Burlington Mag.* cxiv, 1972, 695–704; J. M. Crook, *The Greek Revival*, 1972.]

WENTWORTH WOODHOUSE, YORKS. (W.R.), internal decoration for the 2nd Marquis of Rockingham, *c.* 1755 onwards. A letter from Stuart to the Marquis [Sheffield City Library, Wentworth Woodhouse Muniments Rl.70, 28 Sept. 1755] shows that he was employed here as early as 1755. Arthur Young [*Six Months Tour through the North of England* i, 1770, 281] mentions the panels over the niches in the hall as Stuart's work, and Horace Walpole ['Visits to Country Seats', *Walpole Soc.* xvi, 71] saw a chimney-piece by Stuart in 1772 (*C. Life*, 4 Oct. 1924).

WESTMINSTER SCHOOL, designed the scenery for the Latin play 1758, last used 1808 [*A Naval Career: the Life of Admiral John Markham*, 1883, 14].

HAGLEY PARK, WORCS., Greek Doric temple for the 1st Lord Lyttelton, 1758–9 [Stuart's design is mentioned by Lord Lyttelton in a letter to Mrs. Montagu dated Oct. 1758, quoted by A. T. Bolton in *C. Life*, 16 Oct. 1915, 528] (J. M. Crook, *The Greek Revival*, 1972, pl. 48).

LONDON, SPENCER HOUSE, GREEN PARK, designed interiors of rooms on first floor for the 1st Earl Spencer, 1759–65 [Earl Spencer in *C. Life*, 30 Oct., 6 Nov. 1926; M. Jourdain, 'Furniture designed by James Stuart at Althorp', *C. Life*, 24 Aug. 1935; E. Croft-Murray, 'A Drawing by Athenian Stuart for the Painted Room at Spencer House', *British Museum Quarterly* xxi, 1957, 14–15].

LONDON, HOLDERNESS (later LONDONDERRY) HOUSE, HERTFORD STREET, was 'largely decorated and perhaps completely designed' by Stuart for the 4th Earl of Holderness, *c.* 1760–5; reconstructed by Benjamin Wyatt 1825–8; dem. *c.* 1964 [Arthur Oswald in *C. Life*, 10 July 1937; Lesley Lawrence, *Jnl. of Warburg Institute* ii, 1938–9, 134, 139].

GREENWICH HOSPITAL, THE INFIRMARY (now Dreadnought Hospital), 1763–4; damaged by fire 1811 [drawings in National Maritime Museum Library].

LONDON, LICHFIELD HOUSE, NO. 15 ST. JAMES'S SQUARE, for Thomas Anson, 1764–6; alterations by Samuel Wyatt 1791–4 [*Survey of London* xxix, 142–53 and plates].

SHUGBOROUGH, STAFFS., buildings in the park for Thomas Anson, including the TRIUMPHAL ARCH (a copy of the 'Arch of Hadrian' at Athens), 1764–7; the TOWER OF THE WINDS, 1764; the GREENHOUSE, 1764, dem. *c.* 1800; the LANTHORN OF DEMOSTHENES (*i.e.* a copy of the 'Monument of Lysicrates'), 1770. The last was surmounted by a tripod and bowl, the former made at Soho and the latter at Etruria. Stuart appears also to have been responsible for some internal alterations to the house, now no longer recognizable [J. P. Neale, *Views of Seats*, 1st ser., iii, 1820; E. Meteyard, *Life of Wedgwood* ii, 1866, 222–3; Philip Yorke's Journal (1763) in *Beds. Hist. Rec. Soc.* xlvii, 1968, 161; C. Hussey in *C. Life*, 25 Feb., 4–11 March, 15–22 April 1954; guide-book published by the National Trust, 1971].

NUNEHAM PARK, OXON., designed chimney-piece in dining-room and ceiling of drawing-room for the 1st Earl Harcourt, *c.* 1760–4. The church, which forms an important feature in the landscape, was built in 1764, 'at the expence of Simon, Earl Harcourt, after a design of his own, slightly corrected by Stuart' [J. N. Brewer, *Beauties of England and Wales* xii (ii), 1813, 273, 275, 278–9] (*C. Life*, 7, 14 Nov. 1941; M. L. Batey, guide-book published 1970).

WINDSOR CASTLE, BERKS., ST. GEORGE'S CHAPEL, altar-piece 'of Grecian architecture', 1771; removed 1786. An alternative Gothic design by Stuart is preserved in the archives of the Dean and Chapter [W. H. St. J. Hope, *Windsor Castle* ii, 1913, 426].

BELVEDERE, nr. ERITH, KENT, rebuilt for Sir Sampson Gideon, cr. Lord Eardley, *c.* 1775; dem.

c. 1960 [Lesley Lawrence, *Jnl. of Warburg Institute* ii, 1938–9, 142].

WIMPOLE HALL, CAMBS., the 'Prospect House', *c.* 1775; dem. [engraving in B.M., *King's Maps* viii, 83*g*, published 1778, inscribed 'Stuart Architect'].

LONDON, MONTAGU (later PORTMAN) HOUSE, NO. 22 PORTMAN SQUARE, for Mrs. Elizabeth Montagu, *c.* 1775–82; saloon by J. Bonomi 1790, portico a later addition; destroyed by bombing 1940 [R. Blunt, *Mrs. Montagu* ii, 1923, 13, 18, 82–3, 101].

MOUNT STEWART, CO. DOWN, IRELAND, the 'TEMPLE OF THE WINDS', for Robert Stewart, cr. Marquis of Londonderry, *c.* 1780 [S. Lewis, *Topographical Dictionary of Ireland* i, 1837, 674; the Knight of Glin, *The Temple of the Winds, Mount Stewart*, National Trust 1966].

GREENWICH HOSPITAL, rebuilt the CHAPEL after a fire, 1780–8, assisted by William Newton, who completed the building after Stuart's death [Lesley Lewis, 'The Architects of the Chapel at Greenwich Hospital', *Art Bulletin* xxix, 1947, and 'Greece and Rome at Greenwich', *Arch. Rev.* cix, 1951, 17–24].

WIMBLEDON HOUSE, SURREY, decorative work for the 1st Earl Spencer, date uncertain; destroyed by fire 1785 [Horace Walpole, *Jnl. of Visits to Country Seats* in *Walpole Soc.* xvi, 1927–8, 15, and Lesley Lawrence, *op. cit.*, 132.

BLITHFIELD HOUSE, STAFFS., conservatory for the 1st Lord Bagot, built by Samuel Wyatt 'from designs and under the immediate supervision of Athenian Stuart' [William, 2nd Lord Bagot, *Memorials of the Bagot Family*, 1824, 146] (*C. Life*, 28 Oct. 1954, fig. 3).

MONUMENTS

ASHLEY CHURCH, STAFFS., William, Lord Chetwynd (d. 1770), 1772 [E. Meteyard, *Life of Wedgwood* ii, 1866, 225].

BRAUGHING CHURCH, HERTS., Ralph Freeman (d. 1772), executed by Thomas Scheemakers [signed by Stuart].

BRISTOL CATHEDRAL, Elizabeth Mason (d. 1767), wife of the poet William Mason, executed by John Bacon [*A.P.S.D.*].

CHISWICK CHURCH, MIDDLESEX, Thomas Bentley, Wedgwood's partner (d. 1780), executed by Thomas Scheemakers, 1781 [E. Meteyard, *Life of Wedgwood* ii, 1866, 460].

EASTNOR CHURCH, HEREFS., monuments to Joseph Cocks (d. 1775), erected 1778, and Mrs. Mary Cocks (d. 1779), executed by Thomas Scheemakers [signed 'J. Stuart inv.'].

EDINBURGH, GREYFRIARS CHURCHYARD, Lady Catherine Drummond (*née* Powlet) (d. 1774), 1776 [*Scots Magazine* xxxviii, 1776, 496].

PRESTON-ON-STOUR CHURCH, WARWICKS., Thomas Steavens (d. 1759), executed by

Thomas Scheemakers, *c.* 1780 [signed 'J. Stuart inv.'] (J. Physick, *Designs for English Sculpture*, 1969, fig. 99).

attributed: SUDBURY CHURCH, DERBYSHIRE, the Hon. Catherine Venables Vernon (d. 1775), daughter of George Venables Vernon and Martha, daughter of the Hon. Simon (later Earl) Harcourt, with epitaph by William Whitehead.

WESTMINSTER ABBEY, the 3rd Viscount Howe (d. 1758), executed by P. Scheemakers [J. P. Neale & E. W. Brayley, *Westminster Abbey* ii, 1823, 237].

WESTMINSTER ABBEY, Admiral Charles Watson (d. 1757), executed by P. Scheemakers [J. P. Neale & E. W. Brayley, *Westminster Abbey* ii, 1823, 214].

WIMPOLE CHURCH, CAMBS., monuments to the 1st Earl of Hardwicke (d. 1764), erected 1766, and Catherine, wife of the Hon. Charles Yorke (d. 1759, erected 1761), executed by Peter Scheemakers [signed 'J. Stuart inv.'; R.C.H.M., *West Cambridgeshire*, 213 and pl. 127].

STUART, ROBERT, *see* MEIKLEHAM, ROBERT STUART

STUDHOLME, ROBERT, is listed as a 'stone mason' of Sutton Coldfield, Warwicks., in Pigot's *Directory* of 1828–9. He was presumably the 'Mr. Studholme of Sutton Coldfield' who is described as the architect of ST. JOHN'S CHURCH, PERRY BARR, nr. BIRMINGHAM, 1831–33, Gothic, in *Gent's Mag.* 1833 (ii), 172.

STURGES, JOHN, appears to have designed LYNDON HALL, RUTLAND, a house built in 1671–3 in a style reminiscent of Thorpe Hall, nr. Peterborough. A notebook kept by the owner, Sir Abel Barker, lists 'varianda de Modello nuper facto per Johannem Sturges', and records that 'Sturges dit the pitch of the roof must be 4–5 pts. of the wideness from outside of wall plate'. [information from Mr. James Lees-Milne; John Cornforth in *C. Life*, 10 Nov. 1966]. There are references to 'Mr. John Sturges' in the accounts for building BELTON HOUSE, LINCS. (1684–8), which indicate that he was employed as a measurer. Accounts at Chatsworth show that in 1686–7 'Mr. Sturgess & Jacson ... came to give directions for the new hall dore' at HARDWICK HALL, DERBYSHIRE, and in 1685 'Mr. Sturgesse the Surveyour' was paid 5 guineas for a 'designe for altering the East side of' CHATSWORTH HOUSE for the 4th Earl of Devonshire. It was not carried out, and Sturges's place as the Earl's architect was taken by William Talman [Francis Thompson, *A History of Chatsworth*, 1949, 34]. Sturges may, however, have had some connection with the latter, for, in August 1688, Talman told Lord Fitzwilliam's steward that the siting of the new

797

office buildings at MILTON HOUSE, NORTHANTS., 'should be according to Mr. Sturges his draughts' [Fitzwilliam papers in Northamptonshire Record Office]. They were built under the direction of Robert Wright (*q.v.*) and bear the date 1690. The 'Mr. Samuel Sturgis' who is several times mentioned in the building accounts of THORESBY HOUSE, NOTTS. (1684–5), appears to have been a steward or estate official rather than a building surveyor [B. M., Egerton MS. 3539, ff. 153–63].

SUMSION, THOMAS (*c.* 1672–1744), of Colerne in Wiltshire, was one of the last English master masons to carry on authentic medieval traditions of design into the early eighteenth century. His earliest recorded work of this kind was the west tower of DURSLEY CHURCH, GLOS. Its predecessor fell on 7 January 1698/9, and it was rebuilt with the aid of a brief in 1708–9. The contractors were 'Barker and Sumsion', who received £500 'for building the Tower'. Its design is based on that of the existing fifteenth-century tower of Colerne, with the addition of openwork battlements and pinnacles in the style of the 'Gloucester coronet'. In 1730 Sumsion provided the very similar design in accordance with which the central tower of SHERSTON CHURCH, WILTS., was rebuilt by Thomas West, mason. He received £1 15s. for his 'draught', and there is a payment in the churchwardens' accounts 'to Moses Rice for his sons goeing to Cullourn to give notice to Thom^s. Sumption to come the second time'.

Although it is these Gothic towers for which Sumsion is chiefly remarkable, he could also design secular works in a contemporary classical style. It is not known whether the design which he made for the old COUNCIL HOUSE at BRISTOL in 1699 was the one carried out in 1701–4, but it would certainly have been classical, not Gothic, in character [W. Ison, *The Georgian Buildings of Bristol*, 1952, 90–1], and in 1717 he designed and executed two urns on the north front of KING'S WESTON HOUSE, GLOS. [Kerry Downes, 'The Kings Weston Book of Drawings', *Architectural History* x, 1967, figs. 13–14]. Another classical building was the lower part of the tower of ALL SAINTS CHURCH, BRISTOL, which Sumsion and another mason called William Paul built in 1712. The work was then suspended until 1716, when 'Sumsion and his man' gave in an estimate for completing it. This was apparently not accepted, as the masons employed were George Townesend and William Paul [MS. churchwardens' accounts]. Accounts at Badminton House show that Sumsion worked there, and he may have been responsible for the *maison de plaisance* at SWANGROVE, a small building of *c.* 1703 elegantly designed in the Cotswold style of the late seventeenth century (*C. Life*, 16 Dec. 1939).

Sumsion died at Colerne on 21 October 1744.

His will was proved on 11 October 1745 by his widow, Joan Sumsion, and is enrolled on the court roll of the manor of Colerne for that date, preserved among the muniments of New College, Oxford. He left goods worth £329, including 'working Tools' in the 'Shop', and a writing desk in the kitchen. His monument in the churchyard bears the inscription 'Thomas Sumsion of this Parish Freemason who died October the 21, 1744, aged 72 years'. Members of the family continued to follow the masons' trade in Colerne until the war of 1939–46 [H. M. Colvin, 'Gothic Survival and Gothick Revival', *Architectural Review*, March 1948].

SURPLICE, WILLIAM, was the eldest son of William Surplice (1771–1831), a builder established at Beeston, nr. Nottingham, and the grandson of Thomas Surplice, a builder of Lenton in the same neighbourhood. The younger William Surplice, who was probably born soon after his father's marriage in 1796, appears to have taken over the goodwill of the building firm established by the Strettons (*q.v.*). He also practised as an architect and surveyor until 1848, when he emigrated to Australia. His only recorded architectural work appears to be ST. JOHN'S CHURCH, CARRINGTON, nr. NOTTINGHAM, built in the lancet style in 1843 [*Builder* i, 1843, 504], but a town-planning project in which he was concerned is described in *Builder* v, 1847, 88. William had two younger brothers who both practised as architects and surveyors, William at Manchester and Samuel at Beeston [information from Mr. M. A. L. Cooke].

SUTER, RICHARD (–1883), began his architectural career as a pupil of D. A. Alexander, whom he succeeded both as Surveyor to Trinity House Corporation and (1822) as Surveyor to the Fishmongers' Company. For the former body he designed some houses that were built by Thomas Cubitt in 1821–3 on sites adjoining Trinity House [Hermione Hobhouse, *Thomas Cubitt*, 1971, 50–2]. For the Fishmongers' Company he designed two classical churches at BANAGHER and BALLYKELLY on their estate in CO. DERRY, exhibiting the designs at the Royal Academy in 1827. He was probably responsible for some other buildings erected by the Company in Ballykelly about the same time, including the Model Farm (1824), the Lancasterian School (1828) and the Dispensary (1829). For the same Company he also designed ST. PETER'S HOSPITAL, WANDSWORTH, SURREY, 1849–51 [exhib. at R.A. 1851], and THE OLD SCHOOLHOUSE, GRESHAM'S SCHOOL, HOLT, NORFOLK, in the Elizabethan style [*An Account of the Reopening of the Gresham Free School*, Holt 1859]. Suter retired in 1867 and died on 1 February 1883. In the 1830s he was in partnership with Annesley Voysey (*q.v.*) [information from Miss Priscilla Metcalf and Mr. Donald Girvan].

SUTTON, THOMAS (1746–), was apprenticed to Jacob Leroux in 1762, and gained an award from the Society of Arts in 1764. He was admitted to the Royal Academy Schools in 1770, and exhibited architectural designs at the Academy in 1771, 1772 and 1773. In 1774 he was appointed District Surveyor of Clerkenwell. He may have been the Thomas Sutton who was later Surveyor to the Corporation of Great Yarmouth and died shortly before 1819. [P.R.O., Town Apprenticeship Register No. 23, Jan. 1762; Society of Arts, *Register of Premiums*; Middlesex County Records, General Orders, no. 10; John Preston, *Picture of Yarmouth*, Yarmouth 1819, 42.]

SWAN, ABRAHAM, was a carpenter and joiner who published several books of architectural designs between 1745 and 1768. Though his external elevations were more or less Palladian in character, his interior designs reflected the contemporary taste for rococo decoration. His books enjoyed considerable popularity in America, and the Philadelphia edition of his *British Architect* was the first architectural book to be printed in that country.

The titles of Swan's publication were: *The British Architect: or the Builder's Treasury of Staircases*, 1745, 1750, 1758, Philadelphia 1775, Boston 1794; *A Collection of Designs in Architecture, containing New Plans and Elevations of Houses, etc.*, 2 vols., 1757 (two editions, the second with 5 extra plates); *One Hundred and Fifty New Designs for Chimney Pieces*, 1758, 1763, 1765 (?), 1768; *Designs in Carpentry*, 1759; and *The Carpenter's Complete Instructor in Several Hundred Designs, consisting of Domes, Trussed Roofs, and Various Cupolas for Churches, Houses and Other Buildings, and a Great Variety of Timber Bridges of Various Dimensions*, 1768. A number of plates from Swan's publications are reproduced in *Interior Decoration of the Eighteenth Century from the Designs of Abraham Swan*, selected by Arthur Stratton, Tiranti 1923.

Very little is known about Swan's career, but in the preface to his *Designs in Architecture* he stated that he had had 'more than thirty years application, and experience in, the Theory and Practice of Architecture'. Four of the engravings in the second volume of his *Collection of Designs in Architecture* represent the front staircase at BLAIR CASTLE, PERTHSHIRE, which he designed for the 2nd Duke of Atholl in 1757 [Arthur Oswald in *C. Life*, 11 Nov. 1949]. The same volume also includes two designs for Chinese bridges constructed in the grounds at Blair, and one for a large timber bridge, 'intended to cross the River Tay at Dunkeld'. Swan also executed the interior

fittings at EDGCOTE HOUSE, NORTHANTS., for Richard Chauncey in *c.* 1750, a total of £1990 10*s.* being paid to 'Abraham Swan and Co. joiners' [H. A. Tipping in *C. Life*, 10 Jan. 1920]. He was subsequently employed at KEDLESTON HALL, DERBYSHIRE, under James Paine, for when Paine was superseded by Robert Adam in 1760, the latter wrote that 'Mr. Swan the great is dismissed and Mr. Wyatt the carpenter now fills his place' [J. Fleming, *Robert Adam and his Circle*, 1962, 368].

SWANSBOROUGH, WILLIAM, an architect and builder of Wisbech, Cambs., designed the OCTAGON CHAPEL at WISBECH, 1826–30; dem. 1953. The original octagonal lantern was replaced in 1846 by a corona of battlements and pinnacles designed by J. C. Buckler [N. Walker & T. Craddock, *History of Wisbech*, 1849, 383–4]. In 1821 J. Pacey and William Swansborough completed WHAPLODE DROVE CHURCH, LINCS., after the original architect, J. Cunnington of Spalding, had proved incompetent [I.C.B.S.]. The chancel was altered in 1907–8.

SWERDFEGER, or **SWORDFEGGER,** THEODORE, appears to have been an architectural draughtsman. A design by him for a triumphal arch dated 29 January 1746/7 is in the Bodleian Library (Gough Maps 44, f. 18), and Vertue says that he drew a perspective view of St. Paul's Cathedral that was engraved by Fourdrinier [*Note Books*, Walpole Soc., iii, 117]. In 1765, when the Board of Works recommended him for the royal charity on Maundy Thursday, he was described as 'a distressed artist now living in the Parish of St. Martin's in the Fields . . . greatly advanced in years', and nearly blind [P.R.O., Works 1/4, p. 42]. In 1769 Sir William Chambers described him as an architect when recommending him for charity to the Royal Academy [Royal Academy, Minutes of Council, vol. i, 15 June 1769].

SWETLAND, JOHN and TIMOTHY, designed and built the brick tower of MINSTEAD CHURCH, HANTS., in 1774. It was agreed 'to take down the old Tower and New Rebuild itt' at a vestry held on 13 September 1770, and on 9 September 1773, 'it was agreed that a Tower should be built according to the Plan and Estimate given in by John and Timothy Swetland' [MS. Vestry Minutes]. A payment of £2 2s. to Timothy Swetland occurs in the churchwardens' accounts of ELLINGHAM, HANTS., in 1752. The firm was no doubt a local one established in Fordingbridge or Ringwood.

SWITHIN, —, is stated to have been the architect of the ASYLUM FOR DEAF AND DUMB CHILDREN, OLD KENT ROAD, SOUTHWARK, 1807–9 [*Gent's Mag.* 1807 (ii), 678].

SYKES, THOMAS, was Surveyor of Bridges to the County of Derby from 1786 to 1816. During his tenure of office he widened or rebuilt many bridges in the county, including that at DUFFIELD. The specification for the new bridge built under his direction at BELPER in 1796–8 is printed in *Derbyshire Arch. Jnl.* xii, 1890, 8–10. His notebook, covering the period 1791–1813, is preserved among the Derbyshire Quarter Sessions Records. [J. C. Cox, *Three Centuries of Derbyshire Annals*, ii, 1890, 224.]

SYMONDS, THOMAS (–1791), was an architect and monumental mason who became a freeman of Hereford in 1753, and worked there until his death in 1791. He was responsible for some excellent monuments, examples of which can be seen in many local churches. The evidence of his architectural practice is less impressive. His signature appears on a rather crude elevation for a building to be erected on the Castle Green at Hereford [Hereford Public Library, 'Herefordshire Scraps' ii, f. 53ᵛ]. In 1778 he made ineffectual attempts to shore up the west tower of HEREFORD CATHEDRAL, and was dismissed by the Dean and Chapter when it collapsed in 1786 [Chapter Act Book 1768–1801, pp. 160, 241, 243]. He probably designed EVESBATCH COURT, HEREFS., for Robert Dobyns in 1757, for he witnessed the building contract [*penes* Mrs. Yate Allen], and later in the century he carried out extensive alterations to THE LODGE, nr. LUDLOW, SALOP., for Theophilus Richard Salwey, giving it 'the air . . . of an Italian villa' [F. Calvert & W. West, *Picturesque Views* of . . . *Shropshire*, 1831, 125]. After his death in March 1791 his business was carried on by his widow, who announced in the local press that she had 'engaged a Person of acknowledged abilities . . . from London' to assist her [*Hereford Jnl*, 16 March and 20 April 1791].

SYMPSON, —, *see* SIMPSON, JOHN (1755–1815)

T

TAIT, JAMES (*c.* 1762–1834), is described as 'Architect' on his monument in St. Cuthbert's Churchyard, Edinburgh. It is known from other sources that he was from Glencorse, Midlothian, and afterwards lived at Belwood and Portobello. He was the father of William Tait, publisher (1793–1864) [notes at N.M.R.S.]. He designed SHANDWICK PLACE, EDINBURGH, 1809 [information from Mr. David Walker].

TAIT, JOHN (*c.* 1787–1856), is buried in the Dean Cemetery at Edinburgh, where an inscription commemorates his death on 3 November

1856 at the age of 69. In 1830–1 he made additions to KERSE HOUSE, STIRLINGSHIRE (dem. *c.* 1958), for the 1st Earl of Zetland, and in 1837 designed the neighbouring church of GRANGEMOUTH (WEST) for the Earl [drawings in Kerse Estate Office, photos at N.M.R.S.]. He also designed a school at DUNBOG, FIFE, 1840 [S.R.O., HR 254/1], and another at FALKIRK, STIRLINGSHIRE, 1845–6 [J. Love, *Schools and Schoolmasters of Falkirk*, Falkirk 1898, 91].

In Edinburgh Tait was employed in 1830–40 to carry out Archibald Elliot's designs of 1819 for RUTLAND PLACE, STREET and SQUARE, but modified them considerably in execution [Edinburgh Sasines]. For the Heriot Trustees he designed CLARENDON CRESCENT, 1850–3, ETON TERRACE, 1855, and OXFORD TERRACE, 1858–9 [Heriot Trust records].

TALMAN, JOHN (1677–1726), eldest son of William Talman (*q.v.*), spent much of his life in foreign travel, partly, as stated in his father's petition to Harley in 1713, 'to view the most famous buildings', and partly to form a remarkable collection of prints and drawings. According to the inscription on his grave-slab he spent 'near 20 years in travels through France, Germany and Italy in which he made a fine collection of the most curious paintings and drawings of the noblest buildings and Curiosities in those Countrys'. Drawings in the R.I.B.A. Collection show that he was in Holland and Germany in 1698, and according to a note in a MS. volume (xiii) in the Marquess of Ailesbury's archives he was in Italy in 1699. By 1702 he was back in England, but his letter-book for the years 1708–12 (Bodleian Library, MS. Eng. Letters e. 34) shows that he made another expedition to Italy in 1709, travelling by sea in company with William Kent. A volume of 'Plans &c taken by Mr. Talman in Italy' in the course of this visit is in the Witt Collection at the Courtauld Institute. The letter-book shows that while in Italy Talman obtained large numbers of drawings for his own and other English collections, and corresponded with connoisseurs such as Richard Topham and Dean Aldrich of Christ Church, Oxford. A letter to his father describes an elaborate entertainment which he gave in Rome in 1711. Those invited were 'all the top virtuosi in Rome both for learning and arts'. The 'best music' was composed for the occasion, and the dinner was held in a room decorated with festoons of myrtle and flowers and painted with twelve heads 'representing Vitruvius, Fabius the painter, Glycon the sculptor; Palladio, Raphael and Bonarota; on another side Inigo Jones, Fuller and Pierce; [and] at the upper part . . . Horace the poet, Rossius the comedian and Ismenia a singer, with abundance of mottos in Latin and Italian &c.' While Talman was in Italy he was employed by the Commissioners for

Building Fifty New Churches to have a statue of Queen Anne made to surmount the proposed column in the Strand. This was never erected, and although the commissioners paid Sir Edward Gould £340 in 1715, 'in order to his remitting the same to Mr. John Talman at Florence towards defraying the charge of making a statue of her late Ma^{ty} Queen Anne in Braswork', it is not known whether the figure ever reached this country [*Arch. Rev.*, March 1950, 191].

Talman returned to England in or about 1716, but he was apparently in Italy again in 1719, for in the Cottonian Collection in Plymouth City Art Gallery there is a drawing of the font in St. Mark's at Venice signed 'I. Talman 1719'. In 1717 he was chosen to be the first Director of the Society of Antiquaries, in which capacity he was responsible for the publication of prints of antiquarian subjects. He himself was a competent draughtsman and made architectural designs as well as drawings of antiquities, etc. His projects, *e.g.* for a new building at All Souls College, Oxford (1708), and for the proposed 'Trianon' at Hampton Court, show his familiarity with Italian baroque architecture and his fondness for opulent interior decoration, but have a somewhat bizarre character which is particularly evident in his scheme for remodelling All Souls Chapel in Italian Gothic. A design for paving the area beneath the dome of St. Paul's Cathedral, initialled 'March 26, 1708 JT', is illustrated in *Wren Society* xiii, pl. 30, and there is a similar pavement design, evidently by Talman, in a volume of engravings in the Gibbs Collection in the Ashmolean Museum. In December 1725 he supplied the Spalding Gentlemen's Society with a design for a Museum 'in the proportion of a double cube'. It was not carried out, but the drawing is still preserved among the Society's archives. No building is known actually to have been built to the younger Talman's designs, and it was not as a practising architect, but as one of the greatest English collectors of his time, 'the most unwearied conservator of all that can be called curious, both of the present and past ages', that he was known to his contemporaries. His taste was in fact remarkably catholic, embracing mosaics and thirteenth-century sculpture as well as most aspects of Italian art and architecture since the Renaissance. In January 1724/5 his collections were described as follows by a member of the Spalding Gentlemen's Society:

At Hinxworth in Hertfordsh^r the Seat of my learned & most Ingenious Frd John Tallman Esqr. I had the pleasure of seeing his Noble & Sumptuous Collection. It is of the greatest Value & Beauty I ever beheld. The drawings are not black & white but every thing in proper Colours & beautyfully Limned by himself, Seignior Grisoni a Florentine & other Eminent & accurate hands, upon the Largest paper as strong as past-board & most things in their full & exact proportion except his Drawing[s] of Buildings wch are done by a Scale but so large that the Vast Volums in wch they are conteined are Four feet high & require 2 men to open & shutt them. This Treasure consists of ab^t 200 volls. distinguished into Different Subjects the Chiefest of wch are

1. Churches, Pallaces, Castles, Monum^{ts}. & Publick Edifices wth the Alterpieces & Processions in them.
2. Statues, Alto Releivo & Basso Releivo Sculpture.
3. Vases. Utensils.
4. The Exact Dimentions Weights Shape & Colour of all the most Valuable & pretious Jewels in the known World. Cameos & Intaglios.
5. The Crowns, Coronetts, Scepters &c of all Sovereigns Princes & States.
6. All parts of the Habitts of the Emperors, Kings, Doges, Popes, ArchBp^s., Cardinals.

Besides all these aboundance of Fine Paintings, & peices of Antiquity, Porphery.

In 1718 John Talman married Frances Cokayne of Hinxworth, Herts., and it was there that he died on 3 November 1726, at the age of 49. By his will, dated 7 March 1719, he had left the greater part of his collection to the Library of Trinity College, Cambridge. But by a codicil, dated 4 August 1726, he directed that all his books, drawings, paintings, and pictures should be sold for the benefit of his children. The sale appears to have taken place in April 1727, and lasted six days, in the course of which over 1600 architectural drawings alone were dispersed. Some of them have since found their way into public collections, where they are in most cases easily distinguished by their elaborate gilt borders and 'triple T' mark.[1]

[*A.P.S.D.*; *D.N.B.*; *Wren Soc.* xvii, 1–6, 19–22, 48; Sir E. B. Brabrook, 'On the Fellows of the Society of Antiquaries who have held the office of Director', *Archaeologia* lxii (i), 1910; J. Nichols, *Literary Anecdotes* vi, 1812, 159–60; J. Nichols, *Literary Illustrations* iv, 1822, 496; Sir H. Ellis, *Original Letters of Eminent Literary Men*, Camden Soc. 1843, 100–2; Madox, *History of the Exchequer*, 1711, supplementary treatise, 63–4 (for a drawing of the Pipe Office at Westminster made by Talman for the author); Minutes of the Spalding Gentlemen's Society; Walpole Society, *Vertue Note Books*, Index vol.,

---

[1] According to a statement in Gwynn, *London Improved*, 1766, 63, and Riou, *The Greek Orders*, 1768, a 'Talman Collection' was sold in Covent Garden in 1766 and deposited in Eton College Library, but nothing is known of its subsequent history.

256; *The Diary of Humphrey Wanley*, ed. C. E. & R. Wright, 1966, 16, 17–18, 22, 25, 123; Hugh Honour, 'John Talman and William Kent in Italy', *Connoisseur*, Aug. 1954; John Harris on a sketch by John Talman for the decoration of a room in *Burl. Mag.* cii, 1960, 535–6 and fig. 33; H. M. Colvin, *Catalogue of Architectural Drawings of the Eighteenth and Nineteenth Centuries in the Library of Worcester College, Oxford*, 1964; S. Rowland Pierce, 'Turris Fortissima: A Baroque Design and Drawing by John Talman', *Antiquaries' Jnl.* xliv, 1964; T. Friedman, 'The English Appreciation of Italian Decoration', *Burlington Mag.*, Dec. 1975.]

DRAWINGS FORMERLY IN
JOHN TALMAN'S COLLECTION

Ashmolean Museum

(1) A volume of cartouches entitled *Cartels Prints and Drawings*: from the collection of James Gibbs.
(2) A volume of prints and drawings entitled *The Five Orders and Ornaments Relating Thereto:* with the bookplate of Christopher Turnor.
(3) A volume of *Architectural Drawings* consisting largely of plans and elevations of churches in Rome.
(4) A volume containing drawings of fountains, bound up with a set of Le Brun's *Recueil de divers Desseins de Fontaines*, etc.: from the collection of James Gibbs.

Victoria and Albert Museum

(1) An album of architectural drawings with a note that it was bought by Francis St. John 'at Mr. Talman's Sale February 2nd 1725/6 [*sic*] cost £7–10' (92 D.46).
(2) A bound volume containing many rough sketches of architectural details and some of mitres and other ecclesiastical subjects (E 79–185. 1940). On the fly-leaf are the following notes: '25 Different Designs by Mr. Hawkesmoor No. 27. 3d. Night Lot 1, A Portefolio with about 300 drawings of Churches etc. in Italy bought by Mr. Tahlman'. The latter was bought by George Vertue and sold when his collection was dispersed on 18 March 1757.
(3) A portfolio of loose drawings (E 186–360. 1940).

Society of Antiquaries

A volume of antiquarian drawings including some of monuments in Norfolk churches made by John Talman in 1705–8, and a design by him for a tower in North Italian baroque style dated 1704.

Royal Institute of British Architects

A collection of architectural designs by William Talman, with some topographical drawings

made by John Talman on the Lower Rhine (one dated 13 August 1698). Presented by J. W. Hiort in 1835.

Sir John Soane's Museum

Some designs for monuments by Edward Pierce (in a folio volume, now disbound, containing designs by Wren, William Talman and other architects).

British Museum (Print Room)

(1) A large folio containing coloured drawings of papal and other Italian vestments, etc., by Grisoni and Talman.
(2) A small folio containing drawings of chalices, pectorals, crosses, etc., by Grisoni and Francesco Bartoli, with annotations by Talman: from the Sloane Collection.
(3) Designs for monuments attributed to Edward Pierce: formerly in the collection of Richard Bull of Ongar.

Courtauld Institute of Art (Witt Collection)

A volume of 'Plans &c. taken by Mr. Talman in Italy', with the bookplate of Richard Bull of Ongar.

Westminster Abbey Library

Fifty-four drawings of architecture, sculpture, ecclesiastical jewellery, etc., mostly made in Italy (some dated 1709), but including St. Edward's Crown (Randall Davies gift, 1939).

TALMAN, WILLIAM (1650–1719), born at West Lavington, Wilts, in 1650, was the second son of William Talman, a gentleman with a small estate in the neighbouring hamlet of Eastcott. When William Talman, senior, died in 1663, he left the Wiltshire property in trust for his elder son Christopher, but William inherited three houses in King Street, Westminster, which his father held on lease from the Dean and Chapter of Westminster. Nothing is known of his early life or of his training as an architect. It would be surprising if so sophisticated an architectural designer had not travelled on the Continent, but when he was petitioning Harley for reinstatement in the Office of Works in 1713, he mentioned only his son's travels, not his own.

In 1678 Talman obtained the office of King's Waiter in the Port of London, worth £52 per annum, which he subsequently served by deputy.[1] For this he must have been indebted to a patron. Dr. Whinney has drawn attention to

---

[1] He surrendered the office in 1711 in favour of his brother-in-law James Tate (*Cal. Treasury Papers 1708–14*, 305).

some indications that that patron might have been the 2nd Earl of Clarendon, who was influential at Court during the 1670s. Talman appears to have shared the customs post with Thomas Apprice, who was a member of Clarendon's household; he was involved with Clarendon financially, for in 1685 judgement was given against Clarendon for a debt of £800 owing to Talman;[1] and in 1689 he designed the Earl's country seat at Swallowfield in Berkshire. It can hardly, however, have been Clarendon who was instrumental in getting Talman appointed Comptroller of Works to King William III in May 1689, for he had withdrawn from Court on James II's deposition in 1688. The post had been vacant since Hugh May's death in 1684, and might not have been filled at all had not someone begged it for Talman. The courtier most likely to have intervened in his favour was the Earl of Portland, who at the same time made him his own deputy in the new Superintendentship of the Royal Gardens which the King created for Portland's benefit. As Portland's deputy Talman was now in effective charge of a department which was laying out very large sums of money on the King's behalf, chiefly at Hampton Court. At the same time he was, as Comptroller, a senior officer of the Royal Works, with a seat on the Board and an official house in Whitehall. His double appointment gave him a degree of independence which he used to undermine Wren's position as Surveyor of the Works. In 1689, when part of the new buildings at Hampton Court collapsed, killing two workmen and injuring eleven others, Talman went out of his way to throw the blame on Wren; in 1699 he not only accused Wren of nepotism in the appointment of a clerk of the works but went so far as to petition the Treasury for the Comptrollership of the Works at Windsor which Wren had held without interruption since 1684. His attitude, in short, was that of a rival rather than a colleague. As an administrator the Surveyor-General was by no means faultless, and these tactics might in the end have brought Talman some preferment at Wren's expense. But it was not only at the Office of Works that he made enemies. One after another he quarrelled with nearly all his private clients. His employment at Chatsworth came to an abrupt end in 1696, when the Duke of Devonshire also dismissed his favourite mason Benjamin Jackson;[2] in 1703 he

demanded such stiff terms from the Duke of Newcastle for building at Welbeck that the Duke abandoned the idea altogether; in the same year he failed in a lawsuit against the Earl of Carlisle, who had refused to pay him more than £40 for visiting Castle Howard and making designs for a new house there; and in 1714 the Duke of Chandos was complaining of his 'ridiculous and extravagant' charges for designing the offices at Cannons. In 1703 Vanbrugh was able to send the Duke of Newcastle an even longer list of those whose employment of Talman had ended in 'vexation and disappointment'. Besides the Duke of Devonshire and Lord Carlisle, it included Lord Normanby, Sir John Germaine, Lady Falkland, Lord Coningsby, Lord Portmore and the Earl of Kingston. Private intransigence led in the end to public disgrace. For when King William died in 1702 it was Carlisle who became Queen Anne's first Lord Treasurer, and in that capacity he made it his business to see that Talman's patent was not renewed. On 20 May Talman was dismissed from the Works, and Vanbrugh was appointed Comptroller in his place. When Vanbrugh was dismissed in turn in 1713, Talman made an attempt to regain the Comptrollership, but it was in vain, and in 1715 Vanbrugh was reinstated.

Despite his loss of office, Talman cannot have been in serious financial difficulties. For he was able to pay for the prolonged and expensive travels of his son John (q.v.), and in 1718 he purchased the manor of Felmingham in Norfolk, where he died on 22 November 1719, aged 69. He left £1500 to his son John 'to clear off the incumberances upon his wife's estate and have likewise given him my chambers in Grays' Inn and also the use of all my collection of drawings prints and books for his life'. He provided annuities for his wife Hannah and his younger children, James, Hannah and Henry. His grave was marked by a black marble slab with a now illegible inscription (given in *Wren. Soc.* xvii, 7) and the device of three interlaced T's which he and his son used as a collector's mark.

It is evident that, before his eclipse by Vanbrugh, Talman enjoyed a considerable reputation as a country-house architect. In fact he was probably the leading Whig architect of the 1680s and 1690s. The evidence for his commissions is unfortunately confined to a small number of drawings (chiefly in the R.I.B.A. Collection) and to scattered references in private archives, supplemented by Vanbrugh's enumeration of his disappointed clients. Though the list of his fully authenticated works is confined to some half a dozen buildings,[1] several more can be assigned

---

[1] This appears from some deeds which in 1908 were in the hands of H. F. Johnson, solicitor to Mr. John Dutton of Oakhanger. Their present whereabouts is unknown, and for information about them I am indebted to Mr. John Harris.

[2] Benjamin Jackson, who was Master Mason of the King's Works from 1701 until his death in 1719, was often employed in works with which Talman was concerned, *e.g.* at Chatsworth (1687–96), Dyrham (1699, inspecting work with Talman) and Drayton (1702).

---

[1] Chatsworth, Swallowfield, Dyrham, Hampton Court Palace, Fetcham, Drayton and the offices at Cannons.

to him with some confidence, and there are others which might be attributed to him on stylistic grounds (notably Hackwood Park, Hants, 1683–8, Blyth Hall, Notts., 1684–5, and Waldershare Park, Kent, c. 1705). Both the buildings listed below and the drawings reveal Talman as a disconcertingly eclectic desig..er whose work shows no consistency of style, nor any obvious chronological development. Thus Stanstead, Uppark and an unexecuted design for a London house for the Duke of Devonshire follow the conventions established by Sir Roger Pratt at Clarendon House. But Dyrham and the Hampton Court 'Trianon' schemes show a familiarity with contemporary French sources, while in the designs for, e.g., Welbeck Abbey, the predominant influence is Italian baroque, studied probably in Rossi's *Studio d'Architettura Civile* of 1702. In the history of English architecture the most important works with which Talman is associated are Thoresby and Chatsworth, the two houses in which the splendours of Stuart palace architecture were first employed to dignify the residence of a Whig nobleman. In the light of recent research Talman's responsibility for Thoresby can no longer be taken for granted. But his authorship of Chatsworth is indisputable. Here the new grandeur is clearly seen in the monumental south front, and in the sumptuous interior, in which all the resources of craftsmanship at the disposal of the Crown were employed for the benefit of a subject. Nowhere else did Talman find so lavish a patron as at Chatsworth, but at Burghley House he probably directed a similar, though purely internal, transformation, and but for his arrogance towards his noble clients he might also have been the architect of great new houses at Castle Howard and Welbeck Abbey. Vanbrugh's reference to Lord Normanby (later Duke of Buckingham) as one of those whose patronage of Talman had ended in vexation has led to the suggestion that he may have played some part in the design of Buckingham House, another highly influential building, of which William Winde was the effective (though possibly not the original) architect. At Hampton Court Talman was largely responsible for the interior of William III's new building as well as for the gardens, and he was the destined architect of the Trianon which the King contemplated building on the other side of the Thames at Ditton. William III's death in 1702 meant the end of Talman's career as an official architect, and Vanbrugh's ascendancy as the leading Whig architect of the reign of Queen Anne was largely achieved at Talman's expense. After 1702 very few commissions are known to have come Talman's way, and the latter part of his life is almost as obscure as its beginning.

Talman was, as his will indicates, a collector and connoisseur as well as a practising architect,

and in the petition which he addressed to Harley in 1713 he stated that he had made 'and is still collecting by his son abroad, the most valuable Collection of Books, Prints, Drawings &c., as is in any one person's hands in Europe, as all the artists in Towne well know'. A fuller account of this collection will be found in the notice of John Talman above. Besides many drawings by Italian masters, it appears to have included the architectural drawings by Inigo Jones and John Webb that afterwards passed to Lord Burlington. In addition, Talman's probate inventory lists a large and impressive collection of pictures, busts, statues, vases, marble tables and the like, which at the time of his death was in Dr. Desaguliers' house in Channel Row, Westminster. In 1700 Talman was elected Steward of the Society of Virtuosi of St. Luke, a body of artists and connoisseurs which met on St. Luke's day to enjoy an annual feast.

A bust of Talman by John Bushnell was in the latter's studio at the time of his death, but it is not known if it is still extant. James West records a small painting of 'Mr. Talman & son with two Ladies' which he saw at John Talman's house in 1733, but this too has disappeared. A small and inferior woodcut in Wornum's edition (1862) of Walpole's *Anecdotes of Painting* purports to represent Talman, but is more probably a portrait of his son. At Freemasons' Hall there is a portrait of an unidentified architect whose unamiable features might well be those of the man who quarrelled with so many of his contemporaries.

[*A.P.S.D.*; *D.N.B.*; *Wren Soc.* xvii, 1–8, 20–43, and xx, 222–3; *History of the King's Works* v; Walpole Society, *Vertue Note Books* i, 129, ii, 8; W. T. Whitley, *Artists and their Friends in England* ii, 1928, 243; *R.I.B.A. Drawings Catalogue: Inigo Jones and John Webb*, 7, and *T–Z*; L. Whistler, *The Imagination of Vanbrugh and his Fellow Artists*, 1954, 35–8; *Cal. Treasury Books* v, 161, 1458; P.C.C. 44 SHALLER (will); P.R.O., Prob 3/19/45 (inventory); M. D. Whinney, 'William Talman', *Journal of the Warburg and Courtauld Institutes* xviii, 1955.]

The following is a chronological list of buildings in whose design William Talman is known to have been involved, and includes abortive as well as executed designs.

THORESBY HOUSE, NOTTS., is stated by Campbell (*Vitruvius Britannicus* i, 1715, 6) to have been 'built *Anno* 1671', the front being 'performed by the same hand that afterwards built Chatsworth'. It has been assumed that by this Cambell meant that William Talman was the architect of Thoresby as well as of Chatsworth. But the date 1671 is certainly wrong, as a large house had already been built at Thoresby in the reign of Charles I, and the Hearth-Tax returns show that there was no change in its assessment of 43 hearths between 1661 and 1678. The accounts of the 4th Earl of Kingston, who succeeded in 1682 and died in 1690, show that in 1685–7 the house was being remodelled (but not rebuilt) by a team of craftsmen that included Benjamin Jackson (master mason), Edward Goudge (plasterer), John Nost and C. G. Cibber (carvers), Antonio Verrio and Louis Laguerre (painters), and René Cousin (guilder) [B. M. Egerton MSS. 3256 and 3539; Nottingham University Library, Pierrepont papers, 4205, 4206, 4210]. There is no mention of Talman, and the only reference to architectural supervision is a payment of 5 guineas to 'Sr. Christopher Wren's man' (presumably Hawksmoor) in June 1686. The existence among Wren's drawings at All Souls of an alternative elevation for Thoresby (*Wren Soc.* vii, pl. 2) is further evidence of the involvement of Wren's office. As for the front being 'performed by the same hand that afterwards built Chatsworth', the word 'performed' is one that Campbell uses elsewhere of masons, not architects,[1] and it would fit Benjamin Jackson, who was master mason both at Thoresby and at Chatsworth. The possibility that Talman was concerned in Thoresby, perhaps at a later date, cannot, however, be ruled out, for Vanbrugh includes 'my Lord Kingston' (*i.e.* the 5th Earl, who succeeded in 1690) in his list of those who had employed Talman and regretted it.

Hawksmoor, writing in 1731, says that Thoresby 'was burnt down as soon as finished', and that the attic storey shown in Campbell's plate 'was added at the refitting the house after the fire, but all the walls remained as the fire had left them' [*Walpole Soc.* xix, 126; cf. *Vertue* vi, 24, 73]. This fire is not mentioned in the accounts, but the attic existed by 1690, for it is visible in a miniature drawing of the house on a map made in that year (Nottingham University Library). Other early views of the house were reproduced by John Harris in *Architectural History* iv, 1961, fig. 4, and vi, 1963, 105. It was finally destroyed by fire in 1745.

LONDON, ST. ANNE'S CHURCH, SOHO: Talman was, with Wren, concerned in the completion of this church in 1685, and provided a design for the steeple in 1714. It is not clear whether he or Wren was responsible for the design of the church (reconstructed 1830–1 and dem. 1953

after war-damage), nor whether the steeple built in 1714 (dem. 1800) was in accordance with his 'draught' [*Survey of London* xxxiii, 256–62].

STANSTEAD PARK, STOUGHTON, SUSSEX, was designed by Talman for the 1st Earl of Scarbrough in 1686, according to J. Dallaway, *Western Division of Sussex* i, 1815, 158–9. The house was remodelled by Joseph Bonomi & James Wyatt in 1786–9 and destroyed by fire in 1900 (J. Kip, *Britannia Illustrata* i, 1714, pl. 36).

CHATSWORTH HOUSE, DERBYSHIRE, rebuilt south and east fronts for the 1st Duke of Devonshire, 1687–96. Talman was dismissed in 1696, and the authorship of the west front, built in 1700–3, is uncertain. The north front (1705–7) is by Archer [Francis Thompson, *A History of Chatsworth*, 1949, chaps. 2–4; contract, etc., printed in *Wren Soc.* xvii, 22–42] (*Vitruvius Britannicus* i, 1715, pls. 72–6; *C. Life*, 5–26 Jan. 1918, 11–25 April, 2 May 1968).

MILTON HOUSE, NORTHANTS., advice about building of offices and proposed rebuilding of house for the 1st Earl Fitzwilliam, 1688. The house was not rebuilt and there is no evidence that the offices (dated 1690) were designed by Talman, though he advised about their siting [Northants. Record Office, Fitzwilliam papers F (M) C 651, 652, and letters from J. Pendleton dated 14 Aug. and 11 Sept. 1688].

BURGHLEY HOUSE, NORTHANTS., probably directed redecoration of interior for the 5th Earl of Exeter, *c.* 1688–90 [several visits by Talman to Burley in August and Sept. 1688 are mentioned incidentally in correspondence among the Fitzwilliam papers in the Northants. Record Office, *e.g.* F (M) C 651, 652]. The Earl's trustees paid him £200 in 1704, probably for services rendered in the 1680s [accounts at Burghley, *ex inf.* Dr. E. R. Till] (*C. Life*, 17 Dec. 1953).

SWALLOWFIELD HOUSE, BERKS., for the 2nd Earl of Clarendon, 1689–91; altered by John James 1720–2, remodelled by W. Atkinson 1820 [*Correspondence of Henry Hyde, Earl of Clarendon*, ed. S. W. Singer, ii, 1828, 273, 285, 288, 309; Constance, Lady Russell, *Swallowfield and its Owners*, 1901] (J. Lees-Milne, *English Country Houses: Baroque 1685–1715*, 1970, fig. 7, reproduces a late eighteenth-century drawing of the front from B. M., *King's Maps* vii, 49*a*).

UPPARK, SUSSEX, was designed by Talman for Forde, Lord Grey, cr. 1st Earl of Tankerville, *c.* 1690, according to J. Dallaway, *Western Division of Sussex* i, 1815, 193. The detached wings are a later addition, and the entrance was remodelled by H. Repton in 1805 (*C. Life*, 14–28 June 1941).

LOWTHER HALL, WESTMORLAND, as rebuilt by

---

[1] Thus St. Paul's Cathedral is 'performed in stone, by those excellent and judicious Artists, Mr. Edward Strong, senior and junior', and Chatsworth itself is 'performed in the best stone'. For pointing out the significance of this word in Campbell's vocabulary I am indebted to Mr. T. P. Connor.

Edward Addison (*q.v.*) for Sir John Lowther, Bart., in 1692–5, may have been derived from a design supplied by Talman, for in a MS. in the Cumbria Record Office (D/Lons.L/Sir John Lowther's MS. Book 1690–7) Lowther wrote that 'for my Hous. after I had directed Mr. Talman the King's Comptroller off his Works to draw me a design such as I thought convenient for me, I had the Correction and approbation off Sir Samuel Morland'. One surviving drawing (D/Lons./L/L1), a design for a double flight of external stairs, can be attributed to Talman, but was not carried out. The house was destroyed by fire in 1718.

CAMBRIDGE, ST. CATHERINE'S COLLEGE; in 1694–5 the College paid 'Mr. Talman Controwler of the King's Works' £1 10s., probably for advice in connection with the building of the Chapel, then in progress [Arthur Oswald in *C. Life*, 29 Oct. 1932, 493].

KIVETON or KEITON PARK, YORKS. (W.R.), was built for the 1st Duke of Leeds, 1698–1704; dem. 1811. A plan 'For ye D. of Leeds at Keiton in Yorkshire' is among Talman's drawings at the R.I.B.A., but does not correspond to the house as built. No architect is mentioned in the contract dated 3 March 1697–8 whereby Daniel Brand of the Minories, London, a carpenter, undertook to erect the main body of the house for the Duke [Yorkshire Archaeological Soc., Duke of Leeds papers, DD5, Box 3; cf. G. Beard, *Georgian Craftsmen*, 1966, 184–5] (Badeslade & Rocque, *Vitruvius Brittanicus* iv, 1739, pls. 11–12).

CASTLE ASHBY, NORTHANTS: in 1695 Talman made an estimate for remodelling the north wing of the house for the 4th Earl of Northampton, but nothing was done [Castle Ashby archives 1084/34]. He may, however, have designed the Greenhouse which was erected on the south side of the churchyard in 1695 and demolished *c.* 1868.

DYRHAM PARK, GLOS., east front, etc., for William Blathwayt, Secretary of State, 1698–1704 [*Vitruvius Britannicus* ii, 1717, pls. 91, 93; letter from Talman printed in *Wren Soc.* iv, 59–60; Mark Girouard in *C. Life*, 15, 22 Feb. 1962].

CASTLE HOWARD, YORKS. (N.R.), unexecuted design for the 3rd Earl of Carlisle, *c.* 1698 [plan in R.I.B.A. Coll.; L. Whistler, *The Imagination of Vanbrugh*, 1954, 31–5].

HAMPTON COURT PALACE, MIDDLESEX, completion of interior of state apartments for King William III, 1699–1702, and layout of gardens, 1689–1702 [*History of the King's Works* v, 163–74].

HAMPTON COURT, MIDDLESEX, unexecuted designs for a 'trianon' for King William III, *c.* 1699 [John Harris, 'The Hampton Court Trianon Designs of William and John Talman', *Jnl. of*

the *Warburg and Courtauld Institutes* xxiii, 1960].

FETCHAM PARK, SURREY, for Arthur Moore, *c.* 1700; remodelled *c.* 1870 [described as 'from the Design of the late Mr. Tallmann' in Bodleian Library, MS. North b. 24, f. 196; cf. MS. Eng. Letters e. 34, p. 83].

DORCHESTER HOUSE, WEYBRIDGE, SURREY, alterations for the 1st Earl of Portmore, *c.* 1700; dem. *c.* 1830 [John Harris, 'Dorchester House, Surrey', in *The Country Seat*, ed. Colvin & Harris, 1970, 72–4].

HERRIARD PARK, HANTS., unexecuted designs for Thomas Jervoise, *c.* 1700 [F. H. J. Jervoise, 'The Jervoises', *The Ancestor* iii, 1902, 7; drawings attributed to Talman among Jervoise papers in Hants. County Record Office].

KIMBERLEY HALL, NORFOLK, designs for Sir John Wodehouse, Bart., *c.* 1700, probably executed soon afterwards; stables built 1720; house altered by T. Prowse and J. Sanderson *c.* 1755–7; quadrants by A. Salvin 1835 [payment of £50 to Talman in Sir John Wodehouse's bank account, *ex inf.* Mr. T. P. Connor; plan by Talman for Kimberley in R.I.B.A. Coll. resembling house as built].

DRAYTON HOUSE, NORTHANTS., rebuilt south front of the hall facing the courtyard, for Sir John Germaine, Bart., 1702, and probably designed the cupolas on the two towers [contract printed by Margaret Whinney in *Archaeological Jnl.* cx, 1953, 189] (*C. Life*, 27 May 1965).

WITHAM PARK, SOMERSET: Talman made designs for remodelling the front of the house for Sir William Wyndham, Bart. *c.* 1702. His proposal for a columnar screen or transparent portico was not carried out, but the idea was taken over by Gibbs in an unexecuted design illustrated by Campbell in *Vitruvius Britanicus* (see p. 344). See also the drawings by Dr. Clarke and others illustrated by H. M. Colvin, *Catalogue of Architectural Drawings . . . in the Library of Worcester College, Oxford*, 1964, pls. 119, 120, 121, which are evidently for Witham, and not for Eastbury as there suggested, p. 45 [J. Harris, 'The Transparent Portico', *Arch. Rev*, cxxviii, 1958, 108–9; *R.I.B.A. Drawings Catalogue: G–K*, 24].

WELBECK ABBEY, NOTTS., unexecuted design for a new house for the 1st Duke of Newcastle, 1703 [*Wren Soc.* xii, pls. 39–40, and xvii, pls. 11–13; letter from Talman to Newcastle printed in *Wren Soc.* xvii, 8; L. Whistler, *Imagination of Vanbrugh*, 1954, 34–9; Margaret Whinney, *Jnl. of the Warburg and Courtauld Institutes* xviii, 1955, 134].

CANNONS HOUSE, MIDDLESEX, added offices (dem.) for the 1st Duke of Chandos, 1713–14, and made unexecuted plans for rebuilding the house [C. H. & M. I. Collins Baker, *The Life of James Brydges, Duke of Chandos*, 1949, 114–15].

ABBOTSTONE, nr. ALRESFORD, HANTS., designs for a house for the 1st Duke of Bolton (d. 1699) attributable to Talman, and represented by drawings in Bodleian, Gough Maps 10, f. 37, and Ashmolean Museum, Gibbs Collection II, 28, the latter with the name 'Talman' crossed out. A house was built at Abbotstone c. 1685 and dem. c. 1760. Talman may be regarded as a possible candidate for the design of HACK-WOOD PARK, HANTS., built by the 1st Duke in 1683–8. A portico was added by Gibbs, but removed c. 1805, when the house was remodelled by Samuel & Lewis Wyatt (C. Life, 17, 24 May 1913, with plan; eighteenth-century view by Sandby in Bodleian, Gough Maps 10, f. 52).

TAPPEN, GEORGE (c. 1771–1830), was probably related to J. Tappen, who was a Warden of the Carpenters' Company in 1793. Nothing is known of his early life beyond the fact that he travelled on the Continent in 1802–3, publishing on his return a *Short Description of a Tour*, 1804, afterwards enlarged as *Professional Observations on the Architecture of the Principal Ancient and Modern Buildings in France and Italy*, 1806. He subsequently practised from London, exhibiting at the Royal Academy from 1802 onwards, and held the office of Surveyor to Dulwich College. His executed works included a house called GLENLEA at DULWICH for C. Druce, 1803–4 [exhibited 1803] (C. Life, 29 Nov. 1962, 1349); a Gothic house at SYDENHAM for R. Shute, exhibited 1806; EASTCOMBE HOUSE, nr. CHARLTON, KENT, for D. Hunter, exhibited 1807; the SCHOOL FOR THE INDIGENT BLIND, ST. GEORGE'S FIELDS, SOUTHWARK, 1811–12, subsequently rebuilt in Gothic style by John Newman [exhibited 1812] (J. Elmes, *Metropolitan Improvements*, 1831, plate); and the Greek Revival ROYAL CALEDONIAN ASYLUM, ISLINGTON, with a portico based on that of Philip of Macedon at Delos, 1827–8, dem. [exhibited 1827; S. Lewis, *History of Islington*, 1842, 345] (J. Elmes, *Metropolitan Improvements*, 1831, plate). His unexecuted designs included one for a 'mansion in the style of an old Norman Castle', exhibited at the R.A. in 1819. In conjunction with J. Narrien he was the author of *A New and More Effectual Method of building Groined Arches in Brickwork*, 1808, and published an article on the same subject in the *Monthly Magazine* xxiv, 1807, 140–3. He died on 1 March 1830, aged 59 [*Gent's Mag.* 1830 (i), 282; *A.P.S.D.*].

TASKER, EDWARD, described himself in 1670 as 'a skilful surveyor and contriver of buildings'. In that year there was litigation between himself and Elizabeth Tyther about the rebuilding of three houses in Love Lane, London, of which Tasker had undertaken the 'surveying, ordering and contrivance'. Other buildings of which he claimed to be the surveyor were a house at Hampton Court and a building in the Inner Temple for Francis Phillips [P.R.O., C 6/289/21 and 34, *ex inf.* Mr. Frank Kelsall]. Tasker had been admitted to the freedom of the Salters' Company by redemption on 1 July 1649, and from 1661 to 1668 held the office of Collector of dues from Leadenhall Market, together with custody of the City's building store-yard in the Greenyard at Leadenhall [*ex inf.* Guildhall Record Office].

TASKER, JOHN (c. 1738–1816), was an architect and builder who belonged to the Catholic Church and who worked chiefly for Catholic clients. He practised in Mortimer Street, Cavendish Square, and exhibited at the Royal Academy in 1782, 1784 and 1814. He retired in 1814 or 1815 to a house that he had designed and built at 8 Baker Street, where he died on 6 March 1816, aged 78. The building side of his business was continued by his nephew, John Tasker II (c. 1769–1817), who was the grandfather of the Catholic architect Francis William Tasker (1848–1904) [*Gent's Mag.* 1816 (i), 373; *Catholic Record Soc.* xii, 1913, 134, 140; information from Mr. D. Evinson].

Tasker was much employed by Thomas Weld, of Lulworth, Dorset, for whom he redecorated the interior of LULWORTH CASTLE in 'Adam' style in about 1780 [*The Weymouth Guide*, 3rd ed. c. 1800, 95; accounts among Weld archives in Dorset County Record Office]. His work was destroyed by fire in 1929, but is illustrated in C. Life, 9 Jan. 1926. In 1786–7 a domed Roman Catholic chapel was built at LULWORTH to Tasker's designs. It is a building of considerable architectural merit in an elegant neo-classical style reminiscent of Wyatt [R.C.H.M., *Dorset* ii (1), 145]. For Thomas Weld Tasker also designed in about 1798 a house at ASTON, nr. STONE, STAFFS., as a residence for his son Joseph [S. Shaw, *History of Staffordshire* i, 1798, 355; drawings in Weld archives, Dorset County Record Office]. In 1811 Tasker designed SPETCHLEY PARK, WORCS., for Robert Berkeley [J. P. Neale, *Views of Seats*, 1st ser., ii, 1819] (C. Life, 8 July 1916), and in 1814 he refronted ACTON BURNELL HALL, SALOP., for Sir Joseph Edward Smythe, Bart. [*V.C.H. Salop.* viii, 8; drawing by Tasker in Salop. Record Office, 1514/2/1222] (J. P. Neale, *Views of Seats*, 2nd ser., ii, 1825). Spetchley and Acton Burnell both have competently designed Greek Revival façades with Ionic porticoes, showing that Tasker was able to adapt his style to changing taste right up to the end of his life.

A book of survey plans made by Tasker of houses on the Portman estate in George Street, Gloucester Place, Lower Berkeley Street and Bedford Street is in the R.I.B.A. Collection, together with two sections of a Gothic chapel among drawings for Milton Abbey, Dorset. Designs for a classical lodge and summer-house by Tasker are in the possession of Sir John Summerson. Drawings for Downside Abbey made in 1814 are referred to in *Downside Review* xxiii, 1914, 143.

TATHAM, CHARLES HEATHCOTE (1772–1842), was born in Duke Street, Westminster, on 8 February 1772. He was the youngest of the five sons of Ralph Tatham, a native of Stockton in Durham, who married the daughter of a wealthy London tradesman. His father, after attempting unsuccessfully to establish himself as a gentleman farmer in Essex, became private secretary to Admiral Rodney, but died suddenly at the age of 50. Tatham was educated in the grammar school at Louth in Lincolnshire. At the age of 16 he was engaged as a clerk by S. P. Cockerell in his London office, but resented the menial duties he was expected to perform, and ran away. For a time he lived with his mother, teaching himself to draw with the help of Chambers's *Treatise*, until he fortunately attracted the attention of Henry Holland, who gave him employment as a draughtsman, and eventually helped him to visit Italy. Tatham arrived in Rome in July 1794, and remained there for two years. During this period he made numerous drawings of architectural details, and acquired for Holland a large number of antique Roman fragments (subsequently bought by Sir John Soane, and now in his Museum). In Italy he became friendly with Antonio Canova, Angelica Kauffmann, Sir William Hamilton, Abbate Carlo Bonomi (brother of Joseph Bonomi, R.A.), the Italian architect Mario Asprucci, and the Spanish architect Isidoro Velasquez, afterwards the designer of the Casa del Labrador at Aranjuez. In Rome he also met the eccentric Earl-Bishop of Derry, who talked of employing him at Ickworth, and the 5th Earl of Carlisle, who was to be one of his principal English patrons. Tatham left Rome in 1796, when Napoleon's first attack on the Papal States was imminent, reluctantly declining the opportunity to buy the Altieri Claudes from their owner, Prince Altieri, who was convinced that if they remained in Rome they would fall into the hands of the French.[1] He returned to England through Vicenza, Dresden, Prague and Berlin, making architectural drawings on the way.

In England Tatham began practice as an architect, exhibiting frequently at the Royal Academy, and entering for such competitions as the proposed naval monument (1799). His unwillingness

to compromise and his severe neo-classical taste did not, however, invite extensive employment, and picture-galleries, mausolea and the like formed a large part of his practice. Of these, the most important were the Sculpture Gallery which he designed for Lord Carlisle at Castle Howard, and the mausoleum for Lord Stafford at Trentham. The latter is a formidable statement of neo-classical principle, almost brutalist in its exaggeratedly simple forms. His other works are listed below. To these should be added two important projects that were never executed: a palace for the Duke of Wellington at Stratfieldsaye, Hants. (illustrated in *C. Life*, 26 Nov. 1948, 1107, and 25 May 1972, 1322), and a design for the Fitzwilliam Museum at Cambridge, made in 1827 (before the competition had been announced) and based on the Library of Hadrian at Athens (illustrated in *C. Life*, 13/20 April 1972, 921].

As Holland's agent in Rome, Tatham made an important contribution to the development of the former's style. His publications were equally important in providing exemplars for neo-classical decoration and furniture. *His Etchings of Ancient Ornamental Architecture drawn from the Originals in Rome and other Parts of Italy during the years 1794, 1795 and 1797* was published in 1799–1800. It was a major source-book, based on the results of the excavations at Pompeii, Herculaneum, Tivoli and Rome, and enjoyed immediate success. There was a second edition in 1803, a third in 1810, and a German translation was published in Weimar in 1805. Tatham's linear engravings followed the style established by Flaxman and Tischbein (whom he had met in Italy), and the technique was copied in turn by Hope in his *Household Furniture* of 1807 (which drew extensively on Tatham's book) and by Percier and Fontaine in their *Recueil de décoration intérieures* of 1812. Tatham himself designed candelabra and other ornamental metalwork of high quality, and through his relation John Linnell and his brother Thomas Tatham, both leading cabinet-makers of their day, he probably had a direct influence on the design of contemporary furniture. A mahogany copy of the Barberini candelabrum at Kenwood is a case in point.

In 1806 Tatham published a further work of the same kind entitled *Etchings representing Fragments of Grecian and Roman Architectural Ornaments*. In 1826 this and the earlier book were republished in one volume as *Etchings representing the Best Examples of Grecian and Roman Architectural Ornament drawn from the Originals, and chiefly collected in Italy, before the late Revolutions in that Country*. He also published *Three Designs for the National Monument proposed to be erected in commemoration of the late glorious victories of the British Navy*, 1802; *Designs for Ornamental Plate*, 1806; *The Gallery at*

---

[1] Tatham wrote an account of this incident which was published in *Gent's Mag.* 1799 (ii), 647–8, and in *Monthly Mag.* viii (1799), 536–7.

Castle Howard, 1811; *The Gallery at Brocklesby*, 1811; *Representations of a Greek Vase in the Possession of C. H. Tatham*, 1811, and a description of *The Mausoleum at Castle Howard* designed by Nicholas Hawksmoor, 1812. He also wrote the descriptions for Coney's *Cathedrals* (1829–31), and for some other works. A proposed *Collection of Designs*, illustrating his executed works, was projected by Tatham, but is represented only by an 'Advertisement' bound into some copies of his book on *Ornamental Plate*. This lists eighteen buildings which were to have been illustrated.

Tatham married in 1801, and built a house for himself in Alpha Road, St. John's Wood. This became a centre of artistic society, for Tatham had many artist friends, including Benjamin Robert Haydon, William Blake and Samuel Palmer. But in the 1830s his practice declined, ill-advised litigation with more than one of his employers got him into financial difficulties, and the house had to be sold, together with Tatham's collection. From this predicament he was rescued by Thomas Grenville, the Duchess of Sutherland and other friends, who in 1837 obtained for him the place of Master of Holy Trinity Hospital, Greenwich. Here 'he ended his days happily and usefully', dying on 10 April 1842, aged 71.

Tatham had four sons and six daughters. His eldest son Frederick (1805–78) became a sculptor and painter. His second daughter, Julia, married George Richmond, R.A., the portrait-painter. A crayon portrait of Tatham by B. R. Haydon is in the Print Room of the British Museum. Another by Haydon dated 1823 is in the possession of Mr. John Harris. A bust by his son is in the Holy Trinity Hospital at Greenwich. A portrait by Thomas Kearsley was, in 1965, in the possession of his great-grandson Sir John Richmond.

Tatham left a MS. autobiography written in 1826. This is believed to have been destroyed by his daughter Julia, and all that survives is a transcript of the first 31 pages, describing his early life and his residence in Rome. A collection of original letters written by Tatham in Rome to Henry Holland, accompanied by drawings, is in the Print Room of the Victoria and Albert Museum (D 1479–1551, 1898). Copies of these letters, together with a number of original drawings, are in Sir John Soane's Museum. Several drawings, including a sketch of himself on a horse, are among the archives of Fetherstonhaugh of Uppark. Six alternative versions of Tatham's design for the Naval Monument are in the Mellon Collection. A design by him for a hunting pavilion dated 1796 is at the Academy of St. Luke at Rome (*I disegni di architettura dell' Archivio storico dell' Accademia di San Luca*, 1974, nos. 2148–9).

[*A.P.S.D.*; *D.N.B.*; *The Farington Diary*, ed. J. Greig, viii, 43; W. T. Whitley, *Artists and their Friends in England* ii, 1928, 225–6; A. M. W. Stirling, *The Richmond Papers*, 1926, 24, 32, 98–9; W. S. Childe-Pemberton, *The Earl Bishop*, ii, 1924, 465; *Gent's Mag.* 1842 (ii), 436; D. Udy, 'The Neo-Classicism of C. H. Tatham', *Connoisseur* clxxvii, 1971; C. Proudfoot & D. Watkin, 'A pioneer of English Neo-classicism', *C. Life*, 13/20 April 1972, and 'The Furniture of C. H. Tatham', *C. Life*, 8 June 1972.]

In the following list of works 'Advertisement' refers to the printed list of contents of a proposed Collection of Tatham's designs, issued *c.* 1808 and bound up with some copies of his book on *Ornamental Plate*.

COWDRAY LODGE (now COWDRAY PARK), EASEBOURNE, SUSSEX, for W. S. Poyntz, *c.* 1800; rebuilt 1876 [exhib. at R.A. 1801].

CASTLE HOWARD, YORKS. (N.R.), THE SCULPTURE GALLERY AND MUSEUM for the 5th Earl of Carlisle, 1800–1 [exhib. at R.A. 1802; C. H. Tatham, *The Gallery at Castle Howard*, 1811].

STOKE EDITH, HEREFS., drawing-room, park gate and cottage for the Hon. Edward Foley, *c.* 1800; house gutted 1927 and since demolished ['Advertisement'].

ALPHA ROAD, ST. JOHN'S WOOD, house (No. 34) for himself soon after 1801; dem. [A. M. W. Stirling, *The Richmond Papers*, 1926, 98–9; sketch-plan among Fetherstonhaugh of Uppark papers].

GREAT MALVERN PRIORY CHURCH, WORCS., survey and estimate for repairs, 1802 [printed *Report of a Survey of the Parish Church of Great Malvern, made by the direction of the Hon. Edward Foley*, May 1802, of which there is a copy in the Bodleian Library, Gough Worcester 1].

CHESHUNT NUNNERY, HERTS., works for William Butt, *c.* 1802 onwards, including an 'American cottage', 'designed to be built' in 1802 [exhib. at R.A.], entrance lodge, Fisherman's Hut, and improvements to house and offices ['Advertisement'].

STOKE EDITH CHURCH, HEREFS., monument to the Hon. Edward Foley (d. 1803), executed by R. Blore [*Gent's Mag.* 1805 (i), 278].

WILTON PARK, nr. BEACONSFIELD, BUCKS., alterations to house, new dairy and greenhouse for James Dupré, 1803–5; dem. 1967 [exhib. at R.A. 1809; 'Advertisement'].

LONDON, CLEVELAND HOUSE, ST. JAMES'S, additions for the 2nd Marquess of Stafford, including Doric portico, park elevation and Picture Gallery, 1803–6; dem. 1840 ['Advertisement'; C. M. Westmacott, *British Galleries of Painting and Sculpture*, 1824, 177].

LONDON, NO. 12 GROSVENOR PLACE, library for the 5th Earl of Carlisle, *c.* 1805 ['Advertisement'].

ROCHE COURT, nr. WINTERSLOW, WILTS., for Francis T. Egerton, *c.* 1805 [J. Britton, *Beauties of England and Wales* xv, 1814, 201].

DROPMORE, BUCKS., greenhouse, dairy, gardener's house 'and other works' for Lady Grenville, c. 1806–9 ['Advertisement']. As Lord Grenville's bank account [B.M., Add. MS. 59454] shows that he paid Tatham over £10,000 between 1806 and 1809, the 'other works' may well have included the enlargement of the house itself (C. Life, 11–18 Oct. 1956).

BALGOWAN, nr. METHVEN, PERTHSHIRE, lodges for Col. Thomas Graham, cr. Lord Lynedoch, before 1807 ['Advertisement'].

BROCKLESBY PARK, LINCS., the PICTURE GALLERY for the 1st Lord Yarborough, 1807; since remodelled [exhib. at R.A. 1807; 'Advertisement'; C. H. Tatham, The Gallery at Brocklesby, 1811].[1]

TRENTHAM PARK, STAFFS., fountain, greenhouse, park-bridges and new lodge for the 2nd Marquess of Stafford, 1807–8 [exhib. at R.A. 1807, 1809; 'Advertisement'].

TRENTHAM, STAFFS., mausoleum for the 2nd Marquess of Stafford, 1807–8 [exhib. at R.A. 1807; 'Advertisement'; engraving in B.M., King's Maps xxxviii, 57 b] (C. Life, 15 Jan. 1968, 180, figs. 11–12).

LYNEDOCH LODGE, PERTHSHIRE, for Col. Thomas Graham, cr. Lord Lynedoch, 1807–9; dem. before 1900 [exhib. at R.A. 1807; 'Advertisement'].

OCHTERTYRE, PERTHSHIRE, park gates and Gothic mausoleum in park for Sir Patrick Murray, Bart., 1809 [exhib. at R.A. 1807; 'Advertisement'] (C. Life, 13/20 April 1970, figs. 9–10).

ALTHORP, NORTHANTS., park entrance for the 2nd Earl Spencer, exhibited at R.A. as 'now building' in 1809, but never completed [original drawing at Althorp].

BROXMORE HOUSE, WHITEPARISH, WILTS., for R. Bristow, c. 1810; dem. [J. Britton, Beauties of England and Wales xv, 1814, 218; exhib. at R.A. 1809, 1818].

COWSFIELD HOUSE, WILTS., enlarged for Sir Arthur Paget, 1814; dem. [J. Britton, Beauties of England and Wales xv, 1814, 216–17].

HENNERTON HOUSE, nr. WARGRAVE, BERKS., for C. F. Johnson, c. 1817 [exhib. at R.A. 1817].

QUIDENHAM HALL, NORFOLK, decorated interior for the 4th Earl of Albemarle, c. 1820 [A. E. Garnier, Chronicles of the Garniers, 1900].

ROOKESBURY, nr. WICKHAM, HANTS., for the Rev. W. Garnier, 1820–5 [exhib. at R.A. 1825; G. F. Prosser, Select Illustrations of Hampshire, 1833].

ROOKESBURY, HANTS., tower on HOLLY HILL for the Rev. W. Garnier, 1826 [exhib. at R.A. 1826].

---

[1] The monument in Godshill Church, Isle of Wight, to Sir Richard Worsley (d. 1805), erected by Lord Yarborough's son the Hon. Charles Pelham, may well have been designed by Tatham.

PAULTONS, nr. ROMSEY, HANTS., alterations, addition of office wing, and bridge for William Sloane-Stanley, 1826–8; dem. 1955 [G. F. Prosser, Select Illustrations of Hampshire, 1833; drawings in R.I.B.A. Coll.] (C. Life, 17 Sept., 1938, 276).

MONREPOS, RUSSIA, monument to memory of the Prince de Broglie and his brother for Baron Nicolay [exhib. at R.A. 1829].

MORESTEAD RECTORY, HANTS., 1835–6 [Bodleian Library, records of Queen Anne's Bounty; Winchester Diocesan Records].

NAWORTH CASTLE, CUMBERLAND, work for the 5th Earl of Carlisle [D.N.B.].

TATTERSALL, GEORGE (1817–1849), was the younger son of Richard Tattersall (d. 1859), the proprietor of the well-known auction mart for horses. Having shown an early talent for drawing, he was placed in an architect's office, and eventually established himself in practice at 52 Pall Mall. Besides working as an architect he had some reputation as a topographical and sporting artist, publishing in 1836 a small illustrated guide-book to the Lakes, and subsequently, under the pseudonym of 'Wildrake', several sets of sporting engravings. His experience in designing stables, including Messrs. Tattersall's at Willesden, led him to publish in 1841 an illustrated treatise entitled Sporting Architecture, dealing with stables, stud-farms, kennels and race-stands. In 1847 he won the first competition for the Army and Navy Club in Pall Mall, but was not successful when the acquisition of a larger site necessitated a second competition. His winning design of 1847 is in the London Museum. He was surveyor to the Brewers' Company and exhibited at the Royal Academy in 1840, 1846 and 1848. His early death, in August 1849, was due to brain-fever [A.P.S.D.; D.N.B.].

WILLESDEN, MIDDLESEX, MESSRS. TATTERSALL'S STABLES, c. 1840 [Sporting Architecture, 1841, plates facing pp. 10, 18, 23].

ISLINGTON, LADY OWEN'S ALMSHOUSES and SCHOOL, for the Brewers' Company, 1840–1, Elizabethan style [W. J. Pinks, History of Clerkenwell, 1881, 477; exhib. at R.A. 1840, 1846].

WYNNSTAY, DENBIGHSHIRE, Kennels and Kennel Lodge for Sir Watkin Williams Wynn, Bart., 1843 [exhib. at R.A. 1846; Peter Howell & T. W. Pritchard in C. Life, 6 April 1972, 853].

LADYKIRK HOUSE, BERWICKSHIRE, stables for David Robertson, c. 1846 [exhib. at R.A. 1846].

TATTERSALL, RICHARD (c. 1803–1844), was born about 1803 at Burnley in Lanchasire, and articled to William Hayley of Manchester, in whose office he remained until about 1830, when he commenced practice on his own. Having won the competition for the County Infirmary at Carlisle, he designed the existing building, with a fine Greek Doric portico. His Unitarian Chapel at Dukinfield was an early example of the 'Second Pointed' style, and explains why his Gothic designs were considered 'far in advance of their time'. He designed many cotton mills, notably those for Peter Dixon & Sons at Carlisle, at that time the largest in the country: they were fireproof, and had a chimney 300 feet high.

Tattersall became stone deaf in 1835. His last work, the 'moral and industrial training schools' at Swinton, proved too great a strain, and he died 'in confinement' in 1844. Shortly before his death he had taken T. Dickon as a partner. Dickon subsequently took W. H. Brakspear into partnership and they finished the schools. J. S. Crowther of Manchester was a pupil until 1843 [*A.P.S.D.*].

CHASELY, nr. PENDLETON, LANCS., for R. Gardner (his first work), *c.* 1830 [*A.P.S.D.*]

CARLISLE, CUMBERLAND, THE COUNTY INFIRMARY, 1830–2 [*A.P.S.D.*].

ASHTON–ON–MERSEY CHURCH, CHESHIRE, restoration, 1835 [*A.P.S.D.*].

CARLISLE, CUMBERLAND, cotton mills (now the Shaddon Works) for Peter Dixon & Sons, 1835–6 [*A.P.S.D.*].

MANCHESTER, THE MANCHESTER AND SALFORD BANK, MOSLEY STREET, 1838; dem. 1860 [*Civil Engineer and Architect's Jnl.* i, 235].

STALYBRIDGE, CHESHIRE, ST. PAUL'S CHURCH, 1839, Gothic [*Companion to the Almanac*, 1839, 221].

GOLBORNE, LANCS., cotton mill for Samuel Brewis, 1839 [*A.P.S.D.*].

DUKINFIELD, CHESHIRE, UNITARIAN CHAPEL, 1840–1, Gothic [*Companion to the Almanac*, 1840, 235–7].

STOCKPORT, CHESHIRE, UNITARIAN CHAPEL, ST. PETER'S GATE, 1841–2, Gothic [*A.P.S.D.*].

MANCHESTER, ST. BARNABAS CHURCH, RODNEY STREET, OLDHAM ROAD, 1842–4 [*Civil Engineer and Architect's Jnl* v, 211].

SWINTON, nr. MANCHESTER, THE MORAL AND INDUSTRIAL TRAINING SCHOOLS, 1842–5, Elizabethan; completed by T. Dickson & W. H. Brakspear [*Civil Engineer and Architect's Jnl.* viii, 129].

MANCHESTER COLLEGIATE CHURCH (now CATHEDRAL), restored DERBY CHAPEL [*A.P.S.D.*].

MANCHESTER, warehouse behind the Royal Infirmary, for George Faulkner [*A.P.S.D.*].

HIGHER BROUGHTON, LANCS., houses for Dr. Radford and Mr. Armstrong [*A.P.S.D.*].

BIRCH, LANCS., parish schools [*A.P.S.D.*].

CHEETHAM, LANCS., ST. LUKE'S RECTORY [*A.P.S.D.*].

TAYLOR, ALEXANDER (–*c.* 1845), practised in Glasgow. Gildard states that he designed CLARENDON PLACE and the somewhat idiosyncratic ROYAL CRESCENT, SAUCHIEHALL STREET, *c.* 1839 [T. Gildard, 'An Old Glasgow Architect on

Some Older Ones', *Trans. Royal Philosophical Soc. of Glasgow* xxvi, 1895, 116; J. Pagan, *Sketch of the History of Glasgow*, 1847, 181; A. Gomme & D. Walker, *Architecture of Glasgow*, 1968, 89].

TAYLOR, BENJAMIN BROOMHEAD, of Sheffield, designed the entrance to the SHEFFIELD BOTANICAL GARDENS in 1836. In 1832 he was the runner-up in the competition for the design of the CUTLERS' HALL, SHEFFIELD, the winner being Samuel Worth (*q.v.*). In the event, however, the building was erected to designs made jointly by Worth and Taylor [R. E. Leader, *Surveyors and Architects of the Past in Sheffield*, 1903; R. E. Leader, *History of the Company of Cutlers in Hallamshire*, Sheffield 1905, i, 191–2]. Taylor also designed DODWORTH CHURCH, YORKS. (W.R.), in the neo-Norman style in 1844 [Port, 166–7]. He appears to have died between 1845 and 1849.

TAYLOR, EDWARD (*c.* 1635–1722), of Newent, Glos., was, as stated on his table-tomb in Newent Churchyard, 'Head Workman in contriving and rebuilding the roof of this Church in the year 1679'. He was a carpenter by trade, and had worked in London under Sir Christopher Wren before retiring to his native town. His part in rebuilding Newent Church is described in a manuscript written by Walter Nourse early in the eighteenth century:[1]

The old church of Newent fell down January 18th. 1673, which was built up again in six years time. ... The first stone [was] laid in the foundation July 31st. 1675 by Francis Jones of Hasfield who was the head workman,[2] likewise three pillars of Freestone were being built answering to the three pilasters. Francis Jones and another were: have for the pillars 25£ each (into 75£). When the pillars were built about halfway some Gentlemen coming in to take a view of the Building (I think Mr. Kyrle of Ross was one) they mightily disliked these pillars and would have them taken down by all means. They said the pillars would take up much room in the church which they thought was too little for so large a parish. Edward Taylor Carpenter of Newent, [now] in the 85th. year of his age 1719, hearing of this came to the Gentlemen and proferred to build the rest of the church and they should take down the pillars. They asked him how he could do it, he told them that when he was at work in London after the Fire he saw at Saint Bride's and at

[1] Printed from a copy of the original made by Edward Conder in 1898.
[2] Elsewhere in the MS. it is stated that the 'head workmen' were Francis Jones of Hasfield and James Hill of Cheltenham, masons, some account of whom will be found in this *Dictionary* under their respective names.

some other places such Blades[1] as would soon run up this Building. The Gentlemen desired to see a draft of it which he drew and they liked it well enough but thought they had better shew it to somebody that understood it. Old Edward desired to send it to his old Master in London who was accounted the best carpenter there.[2] Capt. Woodward when he went to London carried the draft to Edward's master who liked it very well and told Captn. Woodward that he need not fear the building and sent a letter to Edward Taylor to put a double buttiment in every pair of blades and then it would be a firm piece of work. When the walls were built up some way it was time to look after the timber, which they considered must be the best the country could afford and likewise a large quantity. This made a great many repent that they had let the pillars be taken down, the timber was soon found in the Lea Bailey which is the King's Wood. This put the parish in hopes of having it for nothing, to obtain which they made friends to acquaint the King of it. The case was fully drawn out for His Majesty to know that the parish had been at so great an [expense] and was not able to buy the timber.... The King readily acquiesced in their demand and gave them the timber ... Edward Taylor went to look it out and being felled was hauled home with great strength of cattle, he and his workmen got it up that summer. The Blades 7 in number they hauled up with a great cable containing 4 Tons in timber which is accounted 6 Tons in weight. Mr. Greenbank of Worcester was the plumber, the church being leaded with 2 sorts of lead Mendip and Derbyshire. Thomas Careless of this town was Glazier. Jno. Wall made the Iron Work, Nathaniel Seny of Tewkesbury was the joiner, the timbers that made the seats came from that place. Mrs. Elizabeth Rogers gave the pulpit value 5£. Edward Taylor laid the flooring of the seats 2 feet [apart] which saved the parish a great deal of expense.

Taylor's roof appears to have been constructed on the same principle as that of the Sheldonian Theatre at Oxford. It has since been rebuilt. Taylor died on 11 February 1721/2, aged 87, and was buried in Newent Churchyard.

TAYLOR, GEORGE LEDWELL (1788–1873), was born in London on 31 March 1788 and educated at Rawes's Academy at Bromley. In 1804 he was articled to J. T. Parkinson, under whom he supervised the building of Montagu and Bryanston Squares and the neighbouring streets on the Portman estate. In 1816 he undertook a walking tour of England in company with his fellow-pupil, Edward Cresy, and in 1817–19 they travelled, largely on foot, in France, Italy, Greece, Malta and Sicily. In Rome they met John Sanders and his draughtsman, W. Purser, in whose company they discovered the Theban lion at Chaeroneia in June 1818 (see Taylor's account of the discovery in *Builder* xx, 1862, 908). On their return, they published *The Architectural Antiquities of Rome, measured and delineated by G. L. Taylor and E. Cresy*, 2 vols., 1821–2, of which a second edition appeared in 1874. Their interests were not confined to classical architecture, and in 1829 they published *The Architecture of the Middle Ages in Italy illustrated by views ...of the Cathedral, etc. of Pisa*, 1829. They intended a third work on the architecture of the Renaissance, but it was abandoned after the publication of a section dealing with the *Palaces of Genoa* in 1822. Taylor shared an office in Furnival's Inn with Cresy, and lived in London (first at 52 Bedford Square, afterwards in Spring Gardens and later at various addresses in Bayswater. In February 1824 he was appointed Civil Architect to the Navy as successor to Edward Holl. In this capacity he carried out important works in the dockyards at Sheerness, Chatham and Woolwich, and in 1828–32 built the new Clarence Victualling Yard at Gosport. He came into contact with William IV, and claimed that it was his tact which led the King in 1830 to accept 'Trafalgar Square' instead of 'King William IV Square' as the name of the new open space on the site of the King's Mews.

In 1837 Taylor lost his post as a result of a reorganization at the Admiralty, and was obliged to take up general practice. In 1843–8 he laid out much of the Bishop of London's estate in Paddington, including Chester Place and parts of Hyde Park Square and Gloucester Square. In 1848 he succeeded J. T. Parkinson as District Surveyor of Westminster. In 1849 he undertook the extension of the North Kent Railway from Strood, through Chatham and Canterbury, to Dover, but the project fell through, at a personal loss to Taylor of £3000. After this, he appears to have given up professional work and devoted himself to archaeological pursuits. In 1856 he made a second visit to Italy with his wife, in order to collect material for his *Stones of Etruria and Marbles of Ancient Rome*, 1859. He finally returned to England in 1868 and settled at Broadstairs, where he died on 1 May 1873. His last years were spent in writing *The Auto-Biography of an Octogenarian Architect*, 2 vols., 1870–2, a diffuse and incoherent work which consists mainly of sketches and descriptions of places visited during his travels.

Taylor was a member of the Architects' Club founded in 1791, and also of the Architects' and

---

[1] *I.e.* beams.

[2] Perhaps John Longland, master carpenter at St. Paul's, who built the roof of St. Bride's.

Antiquaries' Club founded in 1819, of which he was President in 1822–3. He was a Fellow of the Society of Antiquaries, of the Institute of Civil Engineers, and of the Royal Institute of British Architects. He read several papers to the latter body, one of which, an 'Account of the Methods used in Underpinning at Chatham Dockyard in 1834', was printed in the *Transactions* i, 40, in *Professional Papers of the Corps of Royal Engineers*, ed. Denison, 1844 (i), and also in his *Auto-Biography*. Another on *Gas Works*, read on 7 February 1848, was printed separately. In 1855 he published a *Programme and Plan of the Metropolitan General Junction Railways and Roads*, advocating, *inter alia*, the construction of a new bridge over the Thames to the east of Blackfriars Bridge. As an architect he achieved nothing of great distinction. But in London he was responsible for some agreeable stuccoed architecture in the Nash tradition. Elsewhere his most remarkable work was the 170 foot high Gothic tower of Hadlow Castle – an early Victorian folly rivalling Beckford's Fonthill in vertiginous drama.

Taylor was married three (according to some accounts four) times. By his first, wife, Bella Neufville, he had eleven children. The sketchbook of his tour in Italy and Greece in 1817–18 is in the Victoria & Albert Museum (E 4087–1918). A survey which he made of all the naval dockyards is in the National Maritime Museum (LAD/11). [*D.N.B.*; *A.P.S.D.*; Taylor's *Auto-Biography*, 1870–2; A. T. Bolton, *The Portrait of Sir John Soane*, 270–1.]

SHEERNESS DOCKYARD, KENT, completed works begun by E. Holl (including the Quadrangle, dated 1829), and designed the DOCKYARD CHAPEL, 1828 (damaged by fire 1881) [*Auto-Biography*, 163; *The Watering Places of Great Britain*, 1833, Sheppey, 26–7].

LONDON, SUFFOLK STREET, NOS. 4 and 5, c. 1826 [*Survey of London* xx, 92].

LONDON, THE ADMIRALTY, WHITEHALL, cut openings through the Adam screen, 1827–8; restored 1923 [*Auto-Biography*, 165–6].

CHATHAM, KENT, THE MELVILLE HOSPITAL, 1827; dem. [*Auto-Biography*, 173].

GOSPORT, HANTS., THE CLARENCE VICTUALLING YARD, 1828–32 [*Auto-Biography*, 172].

LONDON, TRAFALGAR SQUARE, block (afterwards Morley's Hotel) on east side, 1830; dem. 1936 [*Auto-Biography*, 177] (*Survey of London* xx, pl. 38).

LEE, KENT, BELMONT HOUSE for himself, 1830 [*Auto-Biography*, 162; F. H. Hart, *History of Lee*, 1882, 20, 33].

BROUGHTON RECTORY, nr. BRIGG, LINCS., for the Rev. Henry de Brett (of Linton, Kent), 1831 [Lincolnshire Record Office, MGA 164].

WOOLWICH, KENT, THE RIVER WALL, 1831 [*A.P.S.D.*; *D.N.B.*].

SHEERNESS, KENT, HOLY TRINITY CHURCH, 1835–6, Gothic [Port, 146–7].

LEE, KENT, THE PROPRIETARY SCHOOL (built of concrete and based on the Propylaea at Athens), 1836 [*Auto-Biography*, 171].

HADLOW CASTLE, KENT, the tower for W. B. May, c. 1840, Gothic [cf. lithograph of the 'projected tower' by G. L. Taylor in Greenwood's *Epitome of County History: Kent*, 1838, 129].[1]

LONDON, PADDINGTON: HYDE PARK SQUARE, the west end and the south side, with the exception of three houses; CHESTER PLACE; GLOUCESTER SQUARE, the south side consisting of thirty houses; ORSETT HOUSE, 1843–8 [*Auto-Biography*, 180–1].

LONDON, WESTBOURNE TERRACE, NO. 140 for himself, 1850 [*Auto-Biography*, 181].

BROADSTAIRS, KENT, THE MAISONETTE, c. 1870, 271; *Auto-Biography*, 162].

BIRCHINGTON–ON–SEA, KENT, bungalows, c. 1870 [Bolton, 271].

ERIDGE CASTLE, SUSSEX, enlarged c. 1820/30, dem. 1939, is stated in *Notes and Queries*, 10th ser., vi, 1906, 371, to have been designed by an architect called Taylor who lived in Bayswater, presumably to be identified as G. L. T. (*C. Life*, 23, 30 Sept. 1965).

TAYLOR, JAMES (c. 1765–1846), was a Roman Catholic architect and builder who lived from 1791 in Greenwich and from 1820 at Weybridge, but operated from an office at 2 York Place, City Road, Islington. Deeds in the Middlesex Land Registry show that in ISLINGTON he developed and presumably designed NEW TERRACE (now NOS. 46–58 DUNCAN TERRACE), 1791–4, and CHARLTON PLACE, 1790–5. In GREENWICH he appears to have built PARK PLACE, dated 1791, which in 1820 he presented to the Greenwich R.C. Mission for the use of the priest [letter of 30 June 1820 in Southwark Diocesan Archives, *ex inf.* Mr. D. Evinson]. He also designed Roman Catholic chapels at GREENWICH (East Street), 1792; SOUTHWARK (London Road, superseded by Pugin's cathedral in 1848), 1793; CHATHAM, 1793 (dem. 1804); and WEYBRIDGE (now the sacristy of the church of St. Charles Borromeo), 1836. His most important works for the Catholic Church were ST. EDMUND'S COLLEGE, OLD HALL GREEN, nr. STANDON, HERTS., 1795–9, and the original (classical) buildings of ST. CUTHBERT'S COLLEGE, USHAW, CO. DURHAM, 1804–8. [B. W. Kelly, *Historical Notes on English Catholic Missions*, 1907, 365, 404, 428; Bernard Ward, *History of St. Edmund's College, Old Hall*, 1893, 147–8, 177; B. Little, *Catholic Churches since 1623*, 1966, 45, 46, 48, 54;

---

[1] The castle itself appears to have been designed by J. B. Bunning, who exhibited his design for the south front at the R.A. in 1821. But see J. Dugdale, above, p. 276.

information from Mr. D. Evinson and Mr. F. Kelsall.]

TAYLOR, JOHN (–*c*.1841), received his architectural training in the Dublin Society's Schools [J. D. Herbert, *Irish Varieties*, 1836, 56]. In 1791 and 1792 he was awarded premiums for architectural drawing [*Proceedings of the Royal Dublin Soc.*, vol. 27, 7 April 1791, vol. 28, 26 April 1792]. By 1815 he was established as an architect in Dublin, where he designed the churches of STS. MICHAEL AND JOHN (R.C.) and ST. MICHAEL AND ALL ANGELS (C. of E.), DUBLIN [Maurice Craig, *Dublin 1660–1860*, 1952, 291], and supervised the erection of the neo-classical Roman Catholic Pro-Cathedral in Marlborough Street, designed 'by an amateur artist residing in Paris' [G. N. Wright, *Historical Guide to Dublin*, 1821, 175; E. McParland, 'Who was P?', *Arch. Rev.*, Feb. 1975, 72]. In about 1820 he became Chief Clerk to J. E. Davis, Surveyor of Revenue Buildings in Ireland, and subsequently succeeded Davis as Surveyor. In that capacity he made designs [P.R.O., MPD 28 and 33] for the CUSTOM HOUSE at WATERFORD (1825, a very unpretentious building dem. 1874) and for a symmetrical row of Revenue Houses at BALTIMORE, CO. CORK.

In 1830 Taylor was transferred from Dublin to London to fill the post of Surveyor of Buildings to H.M. Customs, vacant since the dismissal of David Laing in 1825 [P.R.O., Customs 29/9]. In 1839–40 he designed the Greek Revival CUSTOM HOUSE at GLASGOW [P.R.O., T1/3783; J. M. Leighton, *Strath-Clutha, or the beauties of Clyde*, n.d., 113]. In 1839–40 he collaborated with James Leslie, the local Harbour Engineer, in designing a new CUSTOM HOUSE at DUNDEE. The plan was Leslie's work, but the façade was chiefly Taylor's [London Custom House Records, MS. 160; J. Thomson & J. Maclaren, *History of Dundee*, 1874, 280].

Taylor appears to have died soon after 1840.

TAYLOR, JOHN, was practising as an architect in Southampton in 1830 [Pigot's *Directory* iii, 1830, 468]. He was presumably the J. Taylor who was an honorary exhibitor at the Royal Academy between 1797 and 1800, giving 'At Mr. Plaw's, Southampton' as his address. His exhibits included (1798) the north front of CHESSEL HOUSE, HANTS. (dem.), a view (1798) of BANNISTER LODGE, HANTS., and a design (1799) for a bridge over the R. Itchen at Northam, Hants. He is stated in Brayley & Britton, *Beauties of England and Wales* vi, 1805, 121, to have added a portico to PORTSWOOD HOUSE, HANTS. (dem. *c*. 1850). He may have been related to the 'TAYLOR Mason SOUTHAMPTON', whose name appears on the Heathcote Mausoleum in HURSLEY CHURCHYARD, HANTS., or to the Taylor family of Southampton

who were well known as makers of mechanical equipment for the Navy during the Napoleonic Wars.

TAYLOR, JOHN HENRY (–1867), practised from 22 Parliament Street, London. He exhibited at the Royal Academy between 1827 and 1841. He was President of the Surveyors' Club in 1838 and was one of the founding members of the R.I.B.A. in 1834. In 1825 he repaired the interior of ST. MARGARET'S CHURCH, WESTMINSTER [*A.P.S.D.*], and in 1830–1 in collaboration with Alfred Ainger repaired the City church of ST. AUGUSTINE, OLD CHANGE [Guildhall Library, MSS. 8881, 8898]. He designed ST. JOHN'S CHURCH, WALHAM GREEN, FULHAM, 1827–8, Gothic [*Gent's Mag.* 1830 (i), 577–8; C. J. Fèret, *Fulham Old and New* ii, 1900, 235–7]; ST. ANNE'S SOCIETY SCHOOLS, BRIXTON HILL, 1829 [*A.P.S.D.*]; THE ALBANY (DISSENTERS') CHAPEL, FREDERICK STREET, HAMPSTEAD ROAD, 1835 [exhib. at R.A. 1837]; ALL SAINTS CHURCH, SIDMOUTH, DEVON, 1838–40, Gothic [exhib. at R.A. 1835 and 1838]; premises at 9 LUDGATE HILL for Messrs. John Harvey & Co., linen-drapers, 1841 [exhib. at R.A. 1841 by Taylor's son]; and the INFIRMARY of the INFANT ORPHAN ASYLUM at WANSTEAD, ESSEX, 1854 [*A.P.S.D*]. In 1841 he laid out an estate in the neighbourhood of HACKNEY for J. B. Nichols, designing NICHOLS SQUARE as its principal feature [exhib. at R.A. 1841]. Two sets of unexecuted designs for rebuilding Escot House, Devonshire, in a conventional Grecian style labelled as by 'Mr. Taylor' are probably his work [Devon County Record Office, 961 M/E 29].

Taylor died on 22 March 1867. He was the father of John Taylor, junior, who also practised as an architect and who in 1834 published an engraved 'View of the Remains of St. Stephen's Chapel, on the Morning after the Fire of 16 October 1834, taken from the Roof of the Speaker's Gallery'. One of the latter's principal works was St. Mary's Church, Spring Grove, Hounslow. [*A.P.S.D.*; *Architectural Mag.* ii, 1835, 186–7; *Builder* xiv, 1856, 691–2.]

TAYLOR, Sir ROBERT (1714–1788), was the son of Robert Taylor, a successful master mason and monumental sculptor who was Master of the London Masons' Company in 1733. The elder Taylor settled at Woodford in Essex, where he built himself a villa, and lived beyond his means. His son, Robert Taylor, junior, was born at Woodford in 1714, and at the age of 18 was apprenticed to the sculptor Henry Cheere. When his apprenticeship was over, his father, whose wealth was already somewhat depleted, managed to give him 'just money enough to travel on a plan of frugal study to Rome'. While Robert was in Rome, news reached him of his father's death, and he decided to return home at once. Lacking the passports which were necessary to cross Europe in wartime, Taylor is said to have disguised himself as a Franciscan friar. Having thus 'passed unmolested through the enemy's camp', he found on reaching England that his father had died a bankrupt. In this crisis he received generous aid from his father's friends, the Godfrey family of Woodford,[1] which enabled him to set up in business as a sculptor. His father's death had taken place in 1742, and by 1744 he was sufficiently well known to be commissioned by Parliament to design and erect the monument to Captain Cornewall in Westminster Abbey. That to General Guest (d. 1747) is also his work. In 1744 he was chosen to carve the pediment of the Mansion House in preference to Roubiliac, a commission which he owed to his City connection (like his father he was a member of the Masons' Company) and also perhaps to the fact that his father had been one of the mason-contractors for the building. The composition, intended to typify London's commercial prosperity, is trivial in conception and undistinguished in execution. Though generally competent enough as a sculptor, Taylor was undoubtedly inferior in talent to his principal rivals, Roubiliac, Rysbrack and Scheemakers, and by the time he was 40 he had embarked on a more distinguished career as an architect.

Taylor's success as an architect was due partly to ability as a designer and partly to an exceptional capacity for hard work. It was said that he never remained in bed after 4 o'clock in the morning, and that he made a point of travelling by night in order to save time by sleeping in the coach. Certainly he was an extremely active and business-like man. George Byfield told Joseph Farington that 'Sir Robert Taylor had three rules for growing rich viz: rising early, keeping appointments and regular accounts'. The result was that extensive practice which led Thomas Hardwick, in his *Memoir* of Sir William Chambers, to observe that Taylor and James Paine 'nearly divided the practice of the profession between them till Mr. Robert Adam entered the lists'. City merchants formed the basis of Taylor's clientele, and for them he designed offices in London and villas in the country. As surveyor to the Bank of England he held the principal architectural post in their gift. To this he was appointed in 1764 on the death or retirement of George Sampson. In March 1769 he joined the Office of Works as one of the two Architects of the Works; in 1777 he was appointed Master

Carpenter, and in 1780 Master Mason and Deputy Surveyor. Both these posts were, however, abolished as a result of the reforms of 1782. In February 1788 Taylor was appointed Surveyor of Greenwich Hospital, and at the time of his death he was also surveyor to the Foundling Hospital and Lincoln's Inn. Other estates for which he acted as surveyor were those of the Duke of Grafton and General Pulteney. He was knighted in 1782 on his election as Sheriff of London. He died on 27 September 1788, from a chill caught at the funeral of his friend Sir Charles Asgill, and was buried in the church of St. Martin-in-the-Fields. There is a monument to his memory in the south transept of Westminster Abbey, on which the date of his death is incorrectly given as 26 September, and his age as 70 instead of 74. He left an only son, Michael Angelo Taylor, who was called to the Bar and was well known as a Member of Parliament. The bulk of his fortune of £180,000 was left to the University of Oxford 'for extablishing a foundation for the teaching and improving the European languages'. The will was, however, contested by his son, and it was only after the latter's death in 1834 that the bequest took effect. The result was the Taylorian Institution, designed by C. R. Cockerell, which still forms the centre of modern language studies in Oxford. Two similar half-length portraits of Taylor exist, one at the Taylorian Institution, the other at the R.I.B.A. Neither is signed, but both appear, on the evidence of an engraving in the British Museum, to be by William Miller. There is also an anonymous stipple portrait in the 'Crowle Pennant' in the British Museum (vol. xii, 93).

As one of the most successful architects of his time, Taylor attracted a number of pupils, some of whom were to be among the leading members of the profession in the next generation. They included Charles Beazley, T. Burnell, George Byfield, S. P. Cockerell, C. A. Craig, John Leach, John Nash and William Pilkington.

Taylor was an architect of considerable originality who, as Mr. Binney has shown, was by no means content merely to follow established Palladian prototypes. His villas, with their ingeniously varied plans, represented a new departure in country-house architecture that was calculated to appeal to his clientele of rich merchants and bankers, building relatively compact yet handsome houses on new sites without large estates to support them. At Purbrook House he gave himself a place in the history of the neoclassical revival by designing what was almost certainly the first recreation of a Roman atrium in England. At the Bank of England the side-lit domes and segmental arches of his Reduced Annuities Office formed one of the starting-points of Soane's distinctive style. In the interiors of his earlier works he showed a fondness for

---

[1] On Edward Godfrey's death, Taylor erected a monument to his memory costing £1500. It stands in Woodford Churchyard and consists of a jasper column surmounted by an urn.

decoration of a rococo character, but at Purbrook, the Bank of England and elsewhere he developed an elegant decorative style based on antique sources in a manner comparable to that of Robert Adam. With Chambers and Paine he must therefore be ranked as one of the outstanding English architects of the generation between the Palladians and the School of Adam. But for the unfortunate destruction of nearly all his work at the Bank of England he would have been better known as a major English classical architect. As it is his skill as an architectural designer can still be appreciated in his surviving country houses (notably Sharpham) and in the 32 aquatint plates of his executed designs that were published by Thomas Malton, junior, in 1790–2.[1]

A large volume of Taylor's designs for monuments is in the library of the Taylorian Institution, together with a smaller one containing 12 designs for rococo chimney-pieces and overmantels and a third consisting of 'Problems in Geometry and Mensuration with Diagrams'. The same Institution contains some seventy architectural books from Taylor's library (see *Books from the Library of Sir Robert Taylor in the Library of the Taylor Institution Oxford*, a checklist compiled by D. J. Gilson, 1973).

[*A.P.S.D.; D.N.B.;* obituaries in *Gent's Mag.* 1788 (ii), 842, 930, and *London Mag.* lxiv, 1788, 27–30 Sept., 319; Walpole, *Anecdotes of Painting* v, ed. Hilles & Daghlian, 1937, 190–200 (mostly copied from the *Gent's Mag.* obituary); *The Farington Diary*, 20 May 1797, 20 Aug. 1807, 5 Nov. 1821; S. Perks, *The History of the Mansion House*, 1922, 185; Walpole Soc., *Vertue Note Books* iii, 161; Marcus Binney, 'The Villas of Sir Robert Taylor', *C. Life*, 6–13 July 1967.]

PUBLIC BUILDINGS, ETC.

LONDON BRIDGE, removal of houses, replacement of two central arches by a single arch, and erection of balustrades and parapets, in collaboration with George Dance, senior, 1756–66; dem. 1831 [Dorothy Stroud, *George Dance, Architect*, 1971, 52].

LONDON, NO. 70 LOMBARD STREET, BANKING HOUSE for Sir Charles Asgill, *c.* 1756, afterwards the Pelican Life Assurance Co's offices; dem. [Malton].

LONDON, BANK BUILDINGS, consisting of two facing blocks in Threadneedle Street opposite the Bank of England, 1764–6; dem. 1844 [Marcus Binney in *C. Life*, 13 Nov. 1969, 1247 and figs. 1, 10].

---

[1] A set of these plates can be found in the Ashmolean Museum, Oxford, together with some of Malton's original drawings. There are other sets at the Courtauld Institute of Art and Sir John Soane's Museum.

LONDON, THE BANK OF ENGLAND, extensive additions, including the wings on either side of Sampson's original façade, the Reduced Annuity Office, the Transfer and other offices, the Court and Committee rooms, etc., 1766–88. Some of Taylor's work was replaced by his successor, Sir John Soane: the remainder was destroyed or mutilated in 1921–37, but the Court Room (*c.* 1767–70) survives in reconstructed form [Malton; H. R. Steele & F. R. Yerbury, *The Old Bank of England*, 1930; Marcus Binney, 'Sir Robert Taylor's Bank of England', *C. Life*, 13–20 Nov. 1969].

OXFORD, six minor bridges on the Botley Road, of which Osney Bridge is a survivor, 1767 [*Jackson's Oxford Jnl.*, 13 June 1767].

attributed: SWINFORD BRIDGE, EYNSHAM, OXON. (R. Thames), for the 4th Earl of Abingdon, 1767–9 [stylistic attribution: cf. H. C. D. Cooper in E. de Villiers, *Swinford Bridge*, Eynsham 1969, 27–30].

MAIDENHEAD BRIDGE, BERKS. (R. Thames), 1772–7 [Malton; drawings in Berkshire County Record Office, MAB 4].

LONDON, LINCOLN'S INN, STONE BUILDINGS, begun 1774–80; south wing completed by P. Hardwick 1842–5. For Robert Adam's rival design, see A. T. Bolton in *Arch. Rev.*, June 1917. Those by Brettingham and Paine formerly preserved in the Library of Lincoln's Inn have been lost. A plan in the Ashmolean Museum shows Taylor's original scheme extending the whole length of the Chancery Lane frontage of the Inn [*Records of the Society of Lincoln's Inn: The Black Books* iii, 407, 410, 412, 423 *et seq.*; iv, 5–9, 17, 219, 226].

LONDON, THE SIX CLERKS' AND ENROLMENT OFFICES, CHANCERY LANE, 1775–7 [*A.P.S.D.*; cf. *Records of the Society of Lincoln's Inn: The Black Books* iii, 423–4, etc.].

BELFAST, IRELAND, ASSEMBLY ROOM in OLD EXCHANGE, 1776; exterior altered by C. Lanyon 1845, interior by W. H. Lynn 1895; now offices of Belfast Banking Co. [Malton].

WALLINGFORD, BERKS., ST. PETER'S CHURCH, the Gothic spire, 1776–7. Taylor was also employed to fit up the interior of the church on its completion in 1767, but there is no evidence that he designed the church as a whole [MS. Vestry Minutes; documents in Berks. County Record Office, D/P. 139/6/2–3].

LONG DITTON CHURCH, SURREY, 1778; dem. 1880 [Malton, who shows an alternative Gothic design with a spire resembling the one at Wallingford; drawings in Surrey Archdeaconry Records, now G.L.C. Record Office, DWOP/ 1885/3].

SALISBURY, WILTS., THE GUILDHALL, 1788–95, executed 'with some alterations' by Taylor's pupil W. Pilkington after his death; enlarged by T. Hopper 1829, forming existing portico

[Malton; J. Britton, *Beauties of Wiltshire* i, 1801, 86–9; R.C.H.M., *Salisbury*, forthcoming].

COUNTRY HOUSES, ETC.

BRAXTED PARK, ESSEX, rebuilt for Peter Du Cane, 1753–6; north front rebuilt by J. Johnson 1804–6 [Nancy Briggs in *Essex Jnl.* v, 1970, 98].

CHESTER, THE BISHOP'S PALACE, remodelled for Edmund Keene, Bishop of Chester, 1754–7; dem. 1874 [B. C. Redwood in *Chester Observer*, 9 Dec. 1966, citing payment to Taylor in Cheshire Record Office, EEB 99487, 61, 62; cf. J. H. E. Bennett, 'The Old Bishop's Palace, Chester', in *Jnl. of the Chester and N. Wales Architectural ... Soc.*, N.S. xxxvii, 1948].

HARLEYFORD MANOR, nr. MARLOW, BUCKS., for Sir William Clayton, Bart., 1755 [T. Langley, *Hundred of Desborough*, 1797, 100].

COPTFOLD HALL, MARGARETTING, ESSEX, extensive alterations for Richard Holden, soon after 1755; dem. 1850 [Malton].

THE GROVE, nr. WATFORD, HERTS., alterations for Thomas Villiers, 1st Earl of Clarendon, date uncertain, but 1756 according to *A.P.S.D.* [*Gent's Mag.* 1788 (ii) 930; *A.P.S.D.*].

attributed: BARLASTON HALL, STAFFS., for Thomas Mills, 1756–8 [Andor Gomme in *C. Life*, 18 April 1968].

LONGFORD CASTLE, WILTS., unspecified 'additions' for the 1st Viscount Folkestone, presumably in 1760, when he received a fee and expenses for a professional visit [*Gent's Mag.* 1788 (ii), 930; C. Hussey in *C. Life*, 26 Dec. 1931, 726].

OTTERSHAW PARK, nr. CHERTSEY, SURREY, for Sir Thomas Sewell, soon after 1761; dem. 1908 [*The World*, 7 Dec. 1787, *ex inf.* Mr. P. A. Bezodis] (*C. Life*, 5 Aug. 1965, 349).

DANSON HILL, BEXLEYHEATH, KENT, for (Sir) John Boyd, *c.* 1760–5; interior completed by Sir. W. Chambers [Malton] (*C. Life*, 6 July 1967, figs. 3–6).

ASGILL HOUSE, RICHMOND, SURREY, for Sir Charles Asgill, Bart., probably *c.* 1760–5 [*Vitruvius Britannicus* iv, 1767, pl. 74; Malton] (*C. Life*, 9 June 1944).

TREWITHEN, nr. TRURO, CORNWALL, dining-room and other alterations for Thomas Hawkins, *c.* 1763–4 [Cornwall County Record Office, Hawkins papers, letter from James Heywood to Hawkins, 9 April 1764, mentioning Taylor as architect] (*C. Life*, 2–9 April 1953).

ARNO'S GROVE, SOUTHGATE, MIDDLESEX, library and dining-room for Sir George Colebrooke, Bart., probably *c.* 1765 [Watts's *Views of Seats*, pl. 63, 1784].

KEVINGTON, ST. MARY CRAY, KENT, enlarged for Herman Berens, 1767–9; dem. [photocopy in R.I.B.A. Library of account-book in the possession of Mr. H. C. B. Berens].

attributed: RICHMOND, SURREY, NO. 3 THE TERRACE, for Christopher Blanchard, playing-card manufacturer, 1769 [stylistic attribution; cf. Ely House, London].

PURBROOK HOUSE, PORTSDOWN HILL, HANTS., for Peter Taylor, 1770; dem. 1829 [Malton].

SHARPHAM HOUSE, DEVON, for Capt. Philemon Pownoll, *c.* 1770 [Marcus Binney in *C. Life*, 17–24 April 1969].

ELY, CAMBS., works for Bishop Edmund Keene, who carried out extensive alterations to the Bishop's Palace on his appointment to the see in 1771 [*A.P.S.D.*].

ALTHORP, NORTHANTS., repairs for the 1st Earl Spencer after the fall of part of the roof in 1772 [*A Short History of Althorp and the Spencer Family*, 1949].

THORNCROFT, LEATHERHEAD, SURREY, for Henry Crabb Boulton, 1772 [Brayley, *Topographical History of Surrey* iv, 1841, 431].

PORTERS LODGE, SHENLEY, HERTS. (now part of Shenley Mental Hospital), for the 1st Earl Howe, soon after 1772; altered in 1903 [*Gent's Mag.* 1788 (ii), 930; Howe letters at Althorp, Northants.].

GORHAMBURY, HERTS., for the 3rd Viscount Grimston, 1777–90; alterations by W. Atkinson 1816–17 and 1826–8 and by W. Burn 1847 [Malton; J. C. Rogers, 'The Manor and Houses of Gorhambury', *Trans. St. Albans and Herts. Archaeological Soc.*, 1933] (*C. Life*, 25 Nov. 1933).

HEVENINGHAM HALL, SUFFOLK, for Sir Gerard Vanneck, Bart., 1778–*c.* 1780; completed by James Wyatt [Malton] (*C. Life*, 19–26 Sept. 1925; C. Hussey, *English Country Houses: Mid Georgian*, 1956, 165–76).

SALISBURY, WILTS., THE BISHOP'S PALACE, alterations, including Gothic porch, and doors, windows and chimney-piece of great room, for Bishop Shute Barrington, soon after 1782 [*The Farington Diary*, ed. J. Greig, v, 228; J. Nichols, *Literary Illustrations* v, 1828, 610 n.] (P. Hall, *Picturesque Memorials of Salisbury*, 1834, pl. 16).

attributed: CHUTE LODGE, nr. LUDGERSHALL, WILTS., for John Freeman, probably in the 1760s [stylistic attribution] (*C. Life*, 13 July 1967, 81–2, figs. 8–11).

LONDON HOUSES

CHARING CROSS ROAD, NO. 16, for himself, after 1745; dem. [*Survey of London* xvi, 140].

BISHOPSGATE STREET, NO. 112, for John Gore, *c.* 1750; dem. [*Gent's Mag.* 1788 (ii), 930, 1070].

LINCOLN'S INN FIELDS, NOS. 35 and 36, 1754–5. No. 35 was destroyed by bombing in 1941, No. 36 was rebuilt in 1859 [*Survey of London* iii, 36–47 and pls. 24–41].

GRAFTON HOUSE, PICCADILLY, for the 3rd Duke of

Grafton, c. 1760; afterwards the Turf Club; façade and interior altered 1876; dem. 1966 [*Gent's Mag.* 1788 (ii), 930].

UPPER BROOK STREET, NO. 33, for (Sir) John Boyd, 1767–8 [reference to Taylor in Rate Books in Westminster Public Library, c. 343–7, *ex inf.* Mr. Marcus Binney].

GRAFTON STREET, NOS. 3–6, for the 3rd Duke of Grafton, 1771–3 [Duke of Grafton's papers in West Suffolk Record Office and Vestry Minutes of St. George, Hanover Square, in Westminster Public Library, *ex inf.* Mr. P. A. Bezodis].

SPENCER HOUSE, ST. JAMES'S PLACE, decoration of ceiling of staircase for the 1st Earl Spencer, 1772 [*Survey of London* xxx, 521 and pl. 257a]

ELY HOUSE, NO. 37 DOVER STREET, for Edmund Keene, Bishop of Ely, 1772–6; interior remodelled 1909 [Malton; *Gent's Mag.* 1788 (ii), 930] (C. Hussey, *The Story of Ely House*, 1956).

PHILPOT LANE, NO. 15, date uncertain [*A.P.S.D.*].

SPRING GARDENS, NO. 34, for himself, date uncertain but before 1767; dem. 1885 [*London Chronicle*, 27–30 Sept. 1788, 319] (*Survey of London* xx, pl. 45).

MAUSOLEUM

CHILHAM CHURCH, KENT, domed mausoleum on north side of chancel for Sir Robert Colebrooke, Bart., 1755; dem. 1862 [*Gent's Mag.* 1800 (ii), 825].

TAYLOR, SAMUEL, of Stoke Ferry, Norfolk, appears to have been a gentleman farmer with literary and architectural interests. He was a friend of J. C. Loudon, who published several of his designs in his *Encyclopaedia of Rural Architecture*. In the 1846 edition these include a farmyard built for an iron company in South Wales (pp. 511–12), a farm-house and farm at STARSTON PLACE, nr. HARLESTON, in NORFOLK, for his uncle, Meadows Taylor (pp. 516–19), and a design for a country inn in the Italian style, with an elevation supplied by John Robertson (pp. 678–80).

TAYLOR, THOMAS (c. 1778–1826), was the leading architect practising in Leeds during the Regency, and designed many churches in the industrial towns of the West Riding. According to his own statement, made in the *Leeds Mercury* of 9 September 1811, he had had 'Five Years Practice under Mr. Andrews, a builder of eminence in London', followed by a period of eight years in the office of James Wyatt, for whom 'he was in the Habit of making Plans, Elevations, and Sections, for executing some of the most distinguished Buildings in the Kingdom'. It was from James Wyatt's office that he exhibited his first drawings at the Royal Academy in 1792–3, and he continued to send topographical drawings

and architectural designs to the Academy annually until 1811. By then he was established in Yorkshire, and was employed to make the drawings to illustrate Whitaker's *Loidis and Elmete*, and the same author's new edition of Thoresby's *Ducatus Leodiensis*, both of which were published in 1816. In 1811 he obtained his first important architectural commission, the Leeds Court House, and in the following year he built his first church, Christ Church, Liversedge, for the Rev. Hammond Roberson. This was, for its date, a serious essay in the Gothic style. It had, as Whitaker put it, 'every constituent part of a church of the fifteenth century, tower, nave columns, pointed arches, side aisles, clerestory and choir', and as such it established Taylor's reputation as an ecclesiastical architect at a time when churchbuilding was beginning to be affected by antiquarian influence. The Act for building new churches which was passed in 1818 gave Taylor extensive employment, and in 1825 he stated that he was so preoccupied with ecclesiastical work that he had no time even to compete for a secular building. He died on 25 March 1826, aged 48, after catching cold in the new church of Quarry Hill, and was buried in the crypt of Christ Church, Liversedge.

[Frank Beckwith, *Thomas Taylor, Regency Architect, Leeds*, Thoresby Society's Publications, 1949, upon which the following list of buildings is based.]

SECULAR BUILDINGS

LEEDS, THE COURT HOUSE, 1811–13; altered by R. D. Chantrell 1834; dem. 1901.

LEEDS, THE LANCASTERIAN SCHOOL, 1811–12.

LEEDS, THE NATIONAL SCHOOL, 1812–13.

LEEDS, THE UNION BANK, COMMERCIAL STREET, 1812–13; since rebuilt.

LEEDS, THE CHARITY SCHOOL, 1815–16, Gothic.

SHEFFIELD, THE NATIONAL SCHOOL FOR GIRLS, 1823–4.

CHURCHES (all Gothic)

LIVERSEDGE, YORKS. (W.R.), CHRIST CHURCH, 1812–16.

BRADFORD, YORKS. (W.R.), CHRIST CHURCH, 1813–15; dem. 1878.

COLNE PARISH CHURCH, LANCS., repairs, 1815.

ROCHDALE PARISH CHURCH, LANCS., repairs, 1815–16; obliterated by later restorations.

LUDDENDEN, YORKS. (W. R.), ST. MARY, 1816–17; altered 1866.

SOUTHOWRAM, YORKS. (W.R.), ST ANNE, 1816–19; chancel 1869.

HUDDERSFIELD, YORKS. (W.R.), HOLY TRINITY, 1816–19.

LITTLEBOROUGH, LANCS., HOLY TRINITY, 1818–20; galleries 1823; chancel 1889.

OSSETT PARISH CHURCH, YORKS. (W.R.), addition of a semi-transept on south side, 1821; rebuilt 1865.

PUDSEY, YORKS. (W.R.), ST LAWRENCE*, 1821–4.

SHEFFIELD, YORKS. (W.R.), ST PHLIP*, 1822–8; dem. 1952.

ATTERCLIFFE (SHEFFIELD), YORKS. (W.R.), CHRIST CHURCH*, 1822–6; altered by W. Fawcett 1867, and destroyed by bombing 1940. The original plans are in the Public Library at Sheffield.

LEEDS, ST. MARY'S*, QUARRY HILL, 1823–6; altered 1862.

WOODHOUSE HILL, nr. HUDDERSFIELD, YORKS. (W.R.), CHRIST CHURCH, 1823–4; chancel 1901.

DEWSBURY MOOR, YORKS. (W.R.), ST. JOHN*, 1823–7.

HANGING HEATON, YORKS. (W.R.), ST. PAUL*, 1823–5; east end altered 1894; rebuilt after a fire in 1917.

ROUNDHAY, nr. LEEDS, YORKS. (W.R.), ST. JOHN, 1824–6; altered 1885.

EARLS HEATON, YORKS. (W.R.), ST. PETER*, 1825–7.

RIPON, YORKS. (W.R.), HOLY TRINITY, 1826–7; altered 1876 and 1884.

TAYLOR, THOMAS FISH, was practising from Salisbury Street, Strand, in the late 1820s. He appears to have been the 'J. F. Taylor' of 7 Salisbury Street, whose design for a suspension bridge on the site of the future Holborn Viaduct was exhibited at the Royal Academy in 1830.

TAYLOR, WILLIAM, was a surveyor active in the reigns of Charles II and James II. In 1678 Sir John Banks paid 'Wm. Taylor Surveyor' £10 in connection with the remodelling of his house, THE FRIARS, at AYLESFORD, KENT [Kent County Record Office, U.234. A. 24, Dec. 1678]. The 1st Viscount Weymouth employed Taylor to carry out alterations to LONGLEAT HOUSE, WILTS.. soon after he succeeded to the property in 1682. They included the fitting up of the chapel in the west wing, the formation of the gallery in the east wing, and extensive works in the office-buildings. In March 1682/3 Lord Weymouth wrote to his brother to say that he was 'pulling all downe in the Country, but desiring a little better advice than either my owne, or Mr. Tayler's', he would be grateful for 'Sir Christopher Wren's opinion' [Longleat archives, Thynne papers xxxiv, ff. 103, 109]. A year later Taylor wrote to Lord Weymouth, then in London, to report on the progress of the work [ibid. xxii, f. 75]. In the same letter he refers to an intended visit to Shropshire, and adds that he will not be in London for some weeks, 'as I must be att Sir William Portment's and Sir Haswell's before I come to London'. His engagements in Shropshire included a visit to Minsterley, where a new church was about to be

* Commissioners' church.

built at Lord Weymouth's expense (it was completed in 1689). A design for it is preserved in the library at Longleat, and as Taylor was paid £14 in 1688 'in part of £40 for the Chapell at Minsterly' [Longleat account-book 176], he was presumably the architect of this curious semi-baroque building. Sir William Portman's seat was Orchard Portman, Somerset (dem., but illustrated by Kip as a building probably of the late seventeenth century), and 'Sir Haswell' was Sir Halswell Tynte, whose house at Halswell, Somerset, he was then rebuilding or about to rebuild, for the date 1689 is carved on the north front (C. Life, 21 Nov. 1908). Halswell is quite a sophisticated building whose attribution to Taylor would, if substantiated, establish him as a designer of some importance. Another reference to him occurs in the records of the Pewterers' Company, in connection with the rebuilding of their Hall in Lime Street, London, in 1668–70. For this John Wildgos (q.v.) made three draughts, but 'Mr. Taylor' was paid 'for a later draught' [C. Welch, History of the Pewterers' Company ii, 1902, 137].

TAYLOR, WILLIAM ALEXANDER (– 1839), was articled to J. B. Papworth in 1835 and died on 5 August 1839 [R.I.B.A. Library, list of J.B.P.'s pupils by Wyatt Papworth]. He exhibited a design for a museum at the Royal Academy in 1838 and competed for the Ashmolean Museum at Oxford in 1839. There are two drawings by him in the R.I.B.A. Collection.

TEANBY, WILLIAM, was a bricklayer of Old Street, London. For Francis Cobb, junior, he designed and built COBB'S BREWERY, MARGATE, KENT, in 1807–8, as commemorated by a plaque beneath the pediment.

TEASDALE, JAMES, was born at Greystoke in Cumberland, on the estates of the 11th Duke of Norfolk, and was one of the local artificers who were trained as architects and sculptors at the Duke's expense with the intention of employing them at Arundel Castle. The Duke appears to have been largely his own architect, and Teasdale was his executant. According to the inscription on the corner-stone given in Gent's Mag. 1816 (ii), 32, Teasdale was the architect of the 'Barons' Hall' built between 1806 and 1815. For his brother John, who executed much of the sculpture, see Rupert Gunnis, Dictionary of British Sculptors. [J. Dallaway, West Sussex ii (1), 1832, 188].

TELFORD, THOMAS (1757–1834), born at Glendinning, in the parish of Westerkirk in Dumfriesshire, was the son of a shepherd. After being apprenticed to a country mason, he worked for some time on the building of the New Town

TELFORD, THOMAS

at Edinburgh, before going to London in 1782 to find employment as a journeyman mason at Somerset House. He had by now acquired a considerable knowledge of architecture and surveying, and was employed by William Pulteney, the brother of Sir James Johnstone, Bart., of Westerhall, to make plans for alterations to that house, and to the vicarage of Sudborough, Northants., of which living Pulteney was the patron. In 1784–6 he was engaged in supervising the building of the Commissioner's House at Portsmouth Dockyard to the designs of Samuel Wyatt. Soon afterwards he removed to Shrewsbury in order to fit up the Castle as a residence for Pulteney, who had recently become M.P. for that town. It was probably through Pulteney's influence that he was employed by the County as surveyor of bridges and (in 1787) to superintend the building of the new County Gaol. His abilities received a considerable advertisement in 1788 as a result of the dramatic collapse of the church of St. Chad, soon after he had warned the incredulous churchwardens that it was about to fall; and with Pulteney behind him, he was busy making plans for improvements in the town, rebuilding the County Gaol in accordance with the principles of John Howard, and even designing a country house for a Shropshire gentleman. As a bridge-builder he was not slow to realize the possibilities of iron, already demonstrated by T. F. Pritchard at Coalbrookdale, and his iron bridge at Buildwas was one of the pioneer structures of its kind. The Menai and Conway Suspension Bridges in Wales and the Craigellachie Bridge over the R. Spey in Scotland are the best known of his later iron bridges. Altogether Telford was responsible for well over a thousand bridges of one arch or more, a selection of which is listed below. In 1793 he was appointed surveyor, engineer and architect to the Ellesmere Canal, and from this time onwards his engineering activities left little time for architectural works other than bridges. His achievements as a road-builder and canal-maker, his successes as a drainer of fens and an improver of harbours, fall outside the scope of this *Dictionary*. In 1820 he became the first president of the Institution of Civil Engineers, and the death of John Rennie in the following year left Telford the unchallenged head of a new profession. When he himself died in 1834, architecture and civil engineering were recognized as distinct occupations, and the time has passed when the practice of both could be united in one person.

[*The Life of Thomas Telford, Civil Engineer, written by himself; containing a descriptive narrative of his professional labours*, ed. J. Rickman, 1839; *Atlas to the Life of Thomas Telford, Civil Engineer, containing eighty-three copper plates illustrative of his professional Labours*, 1838;

820

Samuel Smiles, *Lives of the Engineers* ii, 1861; Sir A. Gibb, *The Story of Telford*, 1935; L. T. C. Rolt, *Thomas Telford*, 1958; A. R. B. Haldane, *New Ways through the Glens*, 1962; John Hulbert, 'Thomas Telford: Highland Engineer', *C. Life*, 8 Oct. 1970; obituary by J. C. Loudon in *Architectural Mag.* i, 1834, 320; *D.N.B.*]

The following list comprises Telford's early architectural works, together with a selection of his stone bridges. For a complete list of the canals, docks, bridges, harbours, piers, waterworks, etc., executed under his supervision, see Sir A. Gibb, *The Story of Telford*.

SHREWSBURY CASTLE, alterations for William Pulteney, 1787.

SHREWSBURY COUNTY GAOL, designed by J. H. Haycock, but executed by Telford, with modifications designed to make the building conform to the principles advocated by John Howard, 1787–93.

SHREWSBURY, ST. MARY'S CHURCH, new pulpit, 1788.

BRIDGNORTH, ST. MARY'S CHURCH, 1792–4; chancel by Blomfield 1876, refitted 1889 (*Atlas*, pl. 9.).

CLEOBURY MORTIMER CHURCH, SALOP., emergency buttressing, etc., 1793.

MADELEY CHURCH, SALOP., 1794–6, octagonal; chancel 1910.

CARLISLE, THE COUNTY COURTS were begun by Telford with the assistance of John Chisholme, who was in actual charge of the building. On Chisholme's death in 1808 the work was continued by Peter Nicholson until 1811, when the foundations were found to be defective, and Robert Smirke completed the buildings largely to his own designs.

PULTENEYTOWN, nr. WICK, CAITHNESS, model fishing-town for the British Fisheries Society, 1808 [A. J. Youngson, *After the Forty-five*, 1973, 132].

LONDON, warehouses at ST. KATHERINE'S DOCKS, 1827–8 (plan in *Atlas*, pl. 40).

HIGHLAND CHURCHES

Over thirty churches and manses were built in the Highlands between 1824 and 1834 under a Parliamentary Commission. They were economically erected to uniform designs at a total cost of £54,422. The plans and specifications were made by James Smith of Inverness (*q.v.*) under Telford's direction. See *Atlas* pl. 59, or George Hay, *The Architecture of Scottish Post-Reformation Churches*, 1957, fig. 55, for typical plans.

Argyllshire: ACHARACLE, ARDGOUR, DUROR, IONA, KINLOCKSPELVIE, LOCHGILPHEAD (dem.), OA, PORTNAHAVEN, STRONTIAN, TOBERMORY, ULVA.

Banffshire: TOMINTOUL.

Caithness: BERRIEDALE, KEISS.

Inverness-shire: BERNERA (HARRIS), NORTH BALLA-CHULISH, STENSCHOLL (SKYE), TRUMISGARRY (N. UIST), WATERNISH (SKYE).

Ross-shire: CROICK, CROSS (LEWIS), KINLOCHLUI-CHART, PLOCKTON, POOLEWE, SHIELDAIG, STRATHCONON, UI (LEWIS), ULLAPOOL.

Sutherland: KINLOCHBERVIE, STOER, STRATHY.

Shetland: QUARFF.

SELECT LIST OF BRIDGES

MONTFORD BRIDGE, SALOP. (R. Severn), 1790–2 (*Atlas,* pl. 5).

TERN AQUEDUCT, LONGDON, SALOP., carrying the Shropshire Union Canal over the R. Tern, 1793–4.

BUILDWAS BRIDGE, SALOP. (R. Severn), 1795–6; dem. 1905 (*Atlas,* pl. 6).

BEWDLEY BRIDGE, WORCS. (R. Severn), 1795–9 (*Atlas,* pl. 7).

PONT-Y-CYSYLLTE AQUEDUCT, carrying the Ellesmere Canal over the R. Dee, 1795–1805 (*Atlas,* pl. 14).

CHIRK AQUEDUCT, DENBIGHSHIRE, carrying the Ellesmere Canal over the R. Ceiriog, 1796–1801 (*Atlas,* pl. 13).

WICK BRIDGE, CAITHNESS (Water of Wick), 1805–7 (*Atlas,* pl. 51).

TONGLAND BRIDGE, KIRKCUDBRIGHTSHIRE (R. Dee), 1805–6 (*Atlas,* pl. 8).

DUNKELD BRIDGE, PERTHSHIRE (R. Tay), 1806–8 (*Atlas,* pl. 46).

CONON BRIDGE, ROSS-SHIRE (R. Conon), 1806–9 (*Atlas,* pl. 49).

BALLATER BRIDGE, ABERDEENSHIRE (R. Dee), 1807–9 (*Atlas,* pl. 51).

ALFORD BRIDGE, ABERDEENSHIRE (R. Don), 1810–11 (*Atlas,* pl. 51).

HELMSDALE BRIDGE, SUTHERLAND (R. Helmsdale), 1811–12 (*Atlas,* pl. 48).

LOVAT BRIDGE, INVERNESS–SHIRE (R. Beauly), 1811–14 (*Atlas,* pl. 51).

POTARCH BRIDGE, ABERDEENSHIRE (R. Dee), 1811–15 (*Atlas,* pl. 49).

CRAIGELLACHIE BRIDGE, BANFFSHIRE (R. Spey), 1812–15 (*Atlas,* pl. 47).

BETTWS-Y-COED, CAERNARVONSHIRE, WATERLOO BRIDGE (R. Conway), 1815 (*Atlas,* pl. 69).

BEATTOCK BRIDGE, DUMFRIESSHIRE (Evan Water), 1819; widened 1951 [inscription].

MENAI SUSPENSION BRIDGE, MENAI STRAITS, CAERNARVONSHIRE, 1819–26 (*Atlas,* pls. 70–5).

CARTLAND CRAGS BRIDGE, LANARKSHIRE (Mouse Water), 1821–2 (*Atlas,* pls. 55–7).

CONWAY SUSPENSION BRIDGE, CAERNARVONSHIRE (R. Conway), 1821–6 (*Atlas,* pl. 78).

TEWKESBURY, GLOS., MYTHE BRIDGE (R. Severn), 1823–6 (*Atlas,* pl. 81).

HAMILTON, LANARKS., bridge over R. Avon, 1825 (*Atlas,* pl. 54).

OVER BRIDGE, nr. GLOUCESTER (R. Severn), 1825–8 (*Atlas,* pls. 63, 82).

DON BRIDGE, nr. ABERDEEN (R. Don), 1826–9.

PATHHEAD BRIDGE, MIDLOTHIAN (Tyne Water), 1827–31 (*Atlas,* pl. 64).

EDINBURGH, DEAN BRIDGE (Water of Leith), 1829–31 (*Atlas,* pl. 62).

GLASGOW, BROOMIELAW BRIDGE (R. Clyde), 1833–5; dem. 1899 (*Atlas,* pl. 61)

CHIRK BRIDGE, DENBIGHSHIRE (R. Ceiriog), 1831.

MORPETH BRIDGE, NORTHUMBERLAND (R. Wansbeck), 1831 (*Atlas,* pl. 65).

THIN, JOHN (*c.* 1765–1827), is described as 'Builder and Architect' on the monument in the Calton Hill New Cemetery at Edinburgh which records his death on 10 January 1827 at the age of 62. At Culzean Castle there are two designs for a gateway by him dated 1796 and a design for an octagonal lodge and gateway endorsed 'Mr. Thin's plans 1801' is among the Saltoun Hall plans in the National Library of Scotland (no. 97). In 1805 he was associated with William Sibbald, senior or junior (*q.v.*), in an abortive design for rebuilding Falkirk Church [S.R.O., HR 139/1]. Towards the end of his life he was in 'indifferent circumstances' and was employed by W. H. Playfair as a draughtsman [Edinburgh University Library, W. H. Playfair's letter-book no. 4, p. 239].

THOM, ALEXANDER, 'architectour', was on 9 October 1678 given licence to reside in the burgh of Glasgow, 'and to exerce his imployment and calling in architectorie or in measonrie' until Candlemas 1680. He may have been Alexander Thom, a mason and burgess of Dumfries, who took an apprentice in 1675 [S.R.O., Deeds, Dal. 61, 749, *ex inf.* Mr. J. G. Dunbar]. He was still working in Glasgow in 1684, when he submitted an account for various tasks which he had performed for the city authorities. They included 'cutting the king's armes upon stone', 'cutting the king's arms in timber for the king's seat in the High Kirk, contriving the modells of the frontespiece of the lofts thereof ... taking down and putting up the said lofts' and supplying eight cedar tables [*Extracts from the Records of the Burgh of Glasgow 1663–90,* 259, 363].

THOM, JOHN, was an architect-builder of Oban. He designed a substantial manse (now KILMORE HOUSE) at Kilmore in Argyllshire in 1828, and a simple Gothic church at ARDCHATTAN, completed in 1836 [R.C.A.M., *Argyll* ii, 99, 260].

THOMAS, DANIEL (–1658), was (according to his will) a native of Wainfleet in Lincolnshire. He died in 1658 at Ballymoe, Ireland (Co. Galway), where he was building a fort. In 1657 Henry Cromwell proposed to employ him to build a bridge at PORTUMNA CASTLE, CO. GALWAY, and in the British Museum there is a letter from Thomas to Cromwell dated 14 Oct. 1657, in which he gives the following account of his career as a master builder:

My education and practice from my youth untill this warr hath binn with the best of undertakers for Buildings in London and cann make knowne my former performances before I cam thence. As the buildings of the Inn of Chancery called Furnifall's Inn, Holborne, South Hampton house behinde Gray's Inn, the Lord Grey of Warke in the Charter house yard. The Charter house itself for 20 yeares together untill the warre and severall other good Buildings of my owne undertaking and performinge...I have built within 2 yeares space: the Castle of T...bury: this of Belamor. Coll. Rich. Cootes & Castle Coote: & all at greate distances... [B.M., Lansdowne MS. 822, ff. 212, 218].

Of the London buildings mentioned in this letter, FURNIVAL'S INN, HOLBORN (dem. 1818), is architecturally the most important, having been built in 1640 in a striking 'artisan mannerist' style (see illustration in W. Thornbury, *Old and New London* ii, 570). SOUTHAMPTON HOUSE, HOLBORN, was reported in 1657 to have been 'quite taken down and turned to several private tenements' [Howell, *Londinopolis*, 1657, 344], and it was these tenements upon whose construction Thomas had presumably been engaged. What he did at THE CHARTERHOUSE is not clear, and nothing significant appears to remain of his works in Ireland. But if, as seems likely, Thomas both designed and built Furnival's Inn, he must clearly have been one of the leading architect-builders in London in the reign of Charles I.

Thomas died at Ballymoe in 1658. An abstract of his will in the Genealogical Office at Dublin Castle shows that he left three sons, named Daniel, Philip and Thomas [*Appendix to the 26th Report of the Deputy Keeper of the Public Records in Ireland*, Dublin 1895, 839; information from Dr. Rolf Loeber].

THOMAS, MATTHEW EVAN (1788–1830), became a student at the Royal Academy in 1812 and was awarded the Academy's Gold Medal in 1815. In the following year he went to Italy, where he became a member of the academies of Florence and Rome. He returned to England in 1819, and exhibited architectural drawings at the Royal Academy in 1820–21–22. He died at Hackney on 12 July 1830, aged 42, and was buried in St. John's Wood Chapel. His executed works, if any, appear to be unrecorded [*Gent's Mag.* 1830 (ii), 91; *A.P.S.D.*; *D.N.B*].

THOMAS, WILLIAM (–1800), was the son of William Thomas of Pembroke, in whose obituary (*Gent's Mag.* 1800 (i), 87), he is described as 'architect to his Royal Highness the Duke of Clarence'. He practised in Marylebone, and exhibited at the Royal Academy from 1780 onwards. From 1781 to 1792 he was a member of the Smeatonian Society of Civil Engineers. In 1783 he published a volume entitled *Original Designs in Architecture*, containing designs for villas, temples, a grotto, etc., as well as some executed works. These were all in an elegant neo-classical style derived from Robert Adam. Thomas died on 25 October 1800. His library and architectural drawings were sold by auction in February 1801 (catalogue in Ashmolean Museum, Oxford, Sutherland Coll. 55 (5)). At the R.I.B.A. Drawings Collection there is a portrait of Thomas holding a plan of Willersley Castle [*A.P.S.D.*; *D.N.B.*; Marylebone Parish Register].

Thomas's principal executed works are listed below. Designs illustrated in his book, but apparently not carried out, include a Gothic garden temple for Lord Shelburne and 'the garden front of the west wing of Stackpole Court, Pembrokeshire, for John Campbell' (also exhibited at the R.A. in 1782). In 1794 he exhibited 'the garden front of Eaton Hall, Cheshire, the seat of Lord Grosvenor', at the Royal Academy, and among the drawings sold after his death was a set of designs for Eaton Hall, described as 'highly finished, in colours'. Another unexecuted design was represented by the 'elevation of a villa at Upton, Pembrokeshire', exhibited at the Academy in 1795. His sale included a design for a column at Runnymede 'to the immortal memory of King William III'. For his design for a naval obelisk to be erected on Portsdown Hill, nr. Portsmouth, exhibited at the R.A. in 1799, see *The Banks Letters*, ed. W. R. Dawson, 1958, 808. Among the Ferrers papers in the Leicestershire Record Office there is an undated design by him for a Temple at Chartley Park, Staffs., 'to be dedicated to the Deities that preside over learning, music and oratory'.

LONDON, THE SURREY CHAPEL, BLACKFRIARS ROAD, SOUTHWARK, for the Rev. Rowland Hill, 1782–3; subsequently used as a boxing ring, destroyed by bombing 1940 [*Original Designs*, pls. 20–1] (*Survey of London* xxii, pl. 85).

BROWNSLADE HOUSE, CASTLEMARTIN, PEMBROKESHIRE, for John Mirehouse, before 1783; now in ruins [*Original Designs*, pls. 22–3].

LONDON, GROSVENOR HOUSE, MILLBANK, alterations for the 1st Earl Grosvenor, *c.* 1785; dem. 1809 [design for ceiling in R.I.B.A. Drawings Coll.].

WILLERSLEY CASTLE, nr. MATLOCK, DERBYSHIRE, for Sir Richard Arkwright, 1789–90; interior restored after fire on 8 Aug. 1791 [drawings in Bodleian Library, Gough Maps 41 A, ff. 53–81].

MOUNTSORREL, LEICS., THE MARKET HOUSE, for Sir John Danvers, Bart., 1793 [J. Nichols, *History of Leicestershire* iii (1), 1800, 85 (engraving); *The Copper Plate Magazine* iv, *c.* 1800, text to pl. clxxi] (*C. Life*, 10 Oct. 1947, 735; Pevsner, *Leicestershire*, pl. 38).

THOMAS, WILLIAM (1800–1860), was the elder brother of John Thomas (1813–62), the well-known sculptor, and like him was a native of Chalford nr. Stroud in Gloucestershire. He appears to have begun his career at Birmingham as a pupil or partner of Richard Tutin (*q.v.*), but by 1833 he was established in independent practice at Leamington Spa. He exhibited at the Birmingham Society of Artists in 1827, 1834, 1838 and 1839, and published a book of rather commonplace *Designs for Monuments and Chimney-pieces* in 1843. About the same time he emigrated to Canada, where he died in 1860 after a successful career in the course of which he designed 'some thirty churches, several town halls, gaols, and other public buildings, besides numerous mansions and villas in all the principal cities and towns of the Western Province' [*Illustrated London News*, 30 Aug. 1862, 231]. Among his Canadian works were St. Paul's Anglican Cathedral at London, Ontario, and St. Michael's Roman Catholic Cathedral at Toronto.

LEAMINGTON, WARWICKS., house for W. Phipson, before 1833 [Moncrieff's *Guide to Leamington Spa*, 1833, 72]; houses in WARWICK STREET [design exhibited at Birmingham Society of Artists 1834]; LANSDOWNE CRESCENT and CIRCUS, *c.* 1834, and villas in BRANDON PARADE [R. P. Ross Williamson, 'Leamington Spa', *Arch. Rev.*, May 1942]; BATH TERRACE and VICTORIA PUMP ROOM AND BATHS [exhibited as 'erected' at B.S.A. 1838].

RADFORD SEMELE HALL, WARWICKS., restored and improved for H. Greswold, *c.* 1835 [exhib. at B.S.A. 1839].

HANDSWORTH, nr. BIRMINGHAM, Gothic mansion for J. Russell, 1839 [exhib. at B.S.A. 1839].

BIRMINGHAM, WARWICK HOUSE, NEW STREET, for W. Holliday, a draper, 1839 [exhib. at B.S.A. 1839; water-colour by Thomas in Birmingham Art Gallery dated 1840].

BIRMINGHAM, ST. MATTHEW'S CHURCH, DUDDESTON, 1839–40, Gothic [*Gent's Mag.* 1839 (ii), 641].

THOMPSON, GEORGE, was a builder at Woodbridge in Suffolk, where in 1806 he designed a building known as 'The Castle' as a

club for officers and as a Lodge for the local Freemasons [R. Gunnis, *Dictionary of British Sculptors*, 1968, 312, citing Lockwood, *Woodbridge in the Olden Times*, privately printed 1889]. Pigot's *Directory* shows that he was still in business as a builder in 1830, and he may have been the 'Thompson' whose Doric lodge to THE CHANTRY, SPROUGHTON, SUFFOLK, is mentioned by J. P. Neale, *Views of Seats*, 1st ser., ii, 1819.

THOMPSON, JAMES, probably a local builder, designed ST. JAMES CHAPEL, LEITH, 1805–6; rebuilt 1862 [J. & H. S. Storer, *Views in Edinburgh and its Vicinity*, 1820].

THOMPSON, JAMES ROBERT, was a pupil or assistant of John Britton, the architectural topographer, from whose address he first began to exhibit drawings of ancient buildings at the Royal Academy in 1808. In 1807–8 he was one of those employed to survey Henry VII's Chapel at Westminster in connection with its proposed restoration, and subsequently crossed pens with John Carter in the pages of the *Gentleman's Magazine* (1811 (i), 232, 327, 424). He continued to exhibit at the Royal Academy up to 1843, showing an occasional architectural design (*e.g.* a 'design for a Doric column to the memory of Sir Walter Scott', 1841), but chiefly topographical drawings. In the 1840s he was probably working as an assistant in the office of Lewis Vulliamy, for he exhibited views of buildings designed by the latter in 1841 and 1842.

THOMPSON, JOHN (–1792), was 'an eminent architect' of Wakefield, where in 1791 the terrace of houses known as ST. JOHN'S NORTH was begun to a uniform elevation specified by him [J. Goodchild, *Wakefield Town Trail*, 1975, 2].

THOMPSON, MARK GRAYSTONE, practised as an architect and surveyor from Dedham in Essex. He was a carpenter by trade and described himself as such in 1806 when he advertised in the *Ipswich Journal* (10 May) that he had taken premises near the Wharf in that town. As an architect he enlarged and remodelled ORMESBY HOUSE, NORFOLK, for Sir Edmund Knowles Lacon, Bart., in a 'plain Gothic style' soon after 1810 [J. P. Neale, *Views of Seats* vi, 1823]; designed the ESSEX COUNTY HOSPITAL at COLCHESTER in 1819 [Hospital Minute Books, *ex inf.* Dr. Paul Thompson]; rebuilt LEXDEN CHURCH, ESSEX, in the lancet style (cemented) in 1820–1 [MS. Vestry Minutes]; designed ST. NICHOLAS CHURCH, HARWICH, ESSEX, in 1820–1 in 'Perpendicular' Gothic (brick) [accounts in Essex County Record Office]; enlarged and repewed MANNINGTREE CHURCH, ESSEX, 1821, dem. *c.* 1968 [I.C.B.S.], and rebuilt THORPE HALL, THORPE-LE-SOKEN, ESSEX, for John Martin Leake in 1822–5

[Essex Record Office, D/DH f. T92/77, 1–2, plan and perspective signed by Thompson; cf. F. A. Wood, 'Three Georgian Houses', *Trans. Essex Arch. Soc.* ii, 3rd ser. (2), 1967, 125–9]. Documents in the West Suffolk Record Office show that he made plans for rebuilding BOXFORD and HARTEST RECTORIES in 1818–21 [806/2/3 and 9], and in 1825 he rebuilt DEDHAM VICARAGE [Bodleian Library, records of Queen Anne's Bounty]. He may have been the designer of the Doric lodge at THE CHANTRY, SPROUGHTON, SUFFOLK, mentioned above under George Thompson.

THOMPSON, PETER (*c.* 1800–1874), was an ingenious but dubious character who made a precarious living on the fringes of early Victorian architectural practice. He was born in Norwich and exhibited designs for a mansion and the interior of a palace at the Norwich Society of Artists in 1817. By 1828 he was established in London as a carpenter and builder. He appears to have designed THE ROYAL BAZAAR, ST. ANDREW'S STREET, NORWICH, 1831, dem. [see advt. for tenders in *Norfolk Chronicle*, 20 Aug. 1831, *ex inf.* Mr. D. C. Young]. In 1835 he competed for the new Houses of Parliament, publishing his very indifferent Gothic design (copy in Soane Museum). In the 1840s he turned his attention to prefabricated buildings, erecting several temporary churches in London and manufacturing 'portable houses' for export to the colonies. In the 1850s he was active as an antiquarian forger, producing a number of topographical drawings purporting to be the work of Wenceslas Hollar and of a certain 'Captain John Eyre'. When these were exposed as fraudulent he started a short-lived trade journal, *The Oil and Colourman* (1863), and issued a series of pamphlets about working-class housing. He died in Barnet in 1874 [Ida Darlington, 'Thompson Fecit', *Arch. Rev.* cxxiv, 1958, 187–8].

THOMSON, ALEXANDER, was the author of an unexecuted design for a new Town and County Hall at Forfar in about 1785 [photo at N.M.R.S. of drawing at Forfar]. No other reference to him has so far been found.

THOMSON, JAMES, a mason by trade, designed and built CURRIE CHURCH, MIDLOTHIAN, 1784–5, in an attractive mixture of classical and Gothic styles (see G. Hay, *The Architecture of Scottish Post-Reformation Churches*, 1957, pl. 19*d*) [S.R.O., CH 2/83/7, *ex inf.* Mr. David Walker].

THOMSON, JAMES (*c.* 1784–1832), a native of Edinburgh, practised in Dumfries. He first came to Dumfries in 1815 in order to convert a chapel in Buccleuch Street into a Court-House, settled there, and eventually became Convener of the Trades. In 1823–4 he designed and built an engagingly unsophisticated Gothic church at DUNSCORE, DUMFRIESSHIRE [contract in S.R.O., GD 165, Box 39]. In 1832 he fell a victim to a cholera epidemic which, as a member of the newly formed Board of Health, he was engaged in combating. His son George Thomson, engineer, died at Poonah in 1842, aged 27 [W. McDowall, *Memorials of St. Michael's Churchyard, Dumfries*, Edinburgh 1876, 125].

THORNHILL, SIR JAMES (1675–1734), came of an old Dorsetshire family seated at Thornhill and Woolland in that county. James was the youngest son of Walter Thornhull (as the name was then spelled), himself the youngest (and improverished) son of George Thornhull of Thornhill. At the age of 14 James was sent to London to be apprenticed to Thomas Highmore, the King's Sergeant Painter, who was a distant kinsman. He eventually became the leading English decorative painter of his day, working with great success in the baroque style established by Verrio and Laguerre. In 1718 he was appointed History Painter in Ordinary to George I, and on Highmore's death in 1720 he succeeded him as Sergeant Painter. He was knighted at the same time through the influence of Lord Sunderland. But the latter's death two years later deprived him of his chief patron and protector, and in March 1722 the decoration of the new apartments at Kensington Palace was entrusted to William Kent, although by his patent as Sergeant Painter Thornhill was entitled to expect the commission. Kent's employment was due to the influence of his patron, Lord Burlington, but Vertue believed that the latter was exploiting differences which already existed between Thornhill and the Board of Works. According to Vertue, the 'original cause' of Thornhill's loss of favour was his declared intention of setting himself up as an architect in competition with the existing officers of the King's Works:

> Everybody may remember some years ago . . . when Sr. James Thornhill declar'd he woud practice as an Architect, and certainly had skill and knowledge enough in that branch to practice it. Yet what a clamour! What outcries of invasion! What blending of parties together – against him in all his affairs of painting also, that to this Time [1731] he sensibly feels it and has long been unimployed even in his own way of history painting.

Vertue's account is confirmed by a letter written by Sir John Vanbrugh to the Duke of Newcastle in August 1719, in which he reported that Thornhill was actually seeking to secure the vacant Surveyorship of the King's Works, and that there was a 'great struggle' between him and

Hewitt for the post. He thought it 'a Monstruous project' that 'such a Volatile Gentleman as Thornhill, shou'd turn his thoughts & Application to the duty of a Surveyor's business' (*Works* iv, ed. G. F. Webb, 116–17). But Vanbrugh himself had successfully abandoned play-writing for architecture, and Kent, as 'volatile' as Thornhill in character, and immeasurably his inferior as a painter, was similarly embarking upon an architectural career with Lord Burlington's assistance. At a time when rigid professional barriers did not exist there was, in fact, nothing to prevent a versatile artist such as Thornhill from turning his attention to architecture, and Vertue stated that 'he had much studied architecture and has executed some designs in building and made infinitely more'.

That Vertue was not alone in taking Thornhill's architectural pretensions seriously is shown by the fact that in 1720 both the Radcliffe Trustees and the Commissioners for the rebuilding of St. Martin's-in-the-Fields should have applied to him for designs along with other well-known architects. There is no evidence to show that he accepted the former invitation, but on 20 July he attended the St. Martin's Committee 'about his plans and Estimate and left several others with the Committee'. His original design for the west front of St. Martin's Church is preserved in the R.I.B.A. Drawings Collection. It shows an Ionic portico flanked by two towers, and there is an estimate for £20,000 on the back. Several other architectural drawings by Thornhill are in existence, and according to the French virtuoso Dézallier d'Argenville, who met him in 1728, he practised architecture 'like a professional' ('comme un homme de métier') and had 'built several houses'. The earliest documentary evidence of Thornhill's architectural activities seems to be an unexecuted design for remodelling the screen in the CHAPEL of ALL SOULS COLLEGE, OXFORD, which he was then engaged in redecorating. This is in the Clarke Collection in Worcester College Library and is inscribed 'Half the Skreen of All Souls Chappell as it was first proposd to be alterd, by Mr. Thornhill, 1715'. In the same collection there are several designs by Thornhill for a 'Banquetting Room' or garden house for 'Mr. Berkeley's Terrace' which can be connected with STOKE GIFFORD HOUSE, GLOS., where a banqueting house was built by John Symes Berkeley about this time [H. M. Colvin, *Catalogue of Architectural Drawings in the Library of Worcester College, Oxford*, 1964, pls. 82, 114]. In the Victoria and Albert Museum there is a somewhat similar design by Thornhill for a 'Pleasure room' (D.126–1891, illustrated by E. de N. Mayhew, *Sketches by Thornhill*, 1967, pl. 40), and in the same Museum there are designs by Thornhill for the façade of a small house dated 1721 (D.129A–1891) and for a small town house, endorsed 'Mr.

Tho. Carr over against ye Crown & P . . . in Chancery Lane' (D.91, 92–1891).

A more ambitious design is represented by an elevation in Thornhill's hand for a large country house dated 15 January 1716/17. This is among the Cannons House drawings in the G.L.C. Record Office (Acc 262/71/5) and was reproduced (without identification of its authorship) in *C. Life*, 30 Dec. 1949, fig. 11. The only important building actually known to have been designed by Thornhill is, however, MOOR PARK, HERTS., a mansion often but erroneously attributed to Leoni, despite the fact that 'Sir James Thornhill Arch.' appears beneath the plates in *Vitruvius Britannicus* v, 1771, pls. 50–5. The house was rebuilt *c.* 1720–8 for the South Sea Company profiteer Benjamin Styles, and Thornhill's responsibility for the architectural design (as well as for the internal decoration) is confirmed by the record of a lawsuit, in which Thornhill claimed remuneration not only for painting, but also for acting 'as Chiefe Architect for several years before the undertaking [of] the said Painting as well as during the time of the said Painting in directing the workmen in the buildings done and performed about the said house'. After a long hearing, in the course of which evidence was given by several architects and builders, it was 'proved that Sr. James Thornhill was imployd as Surveyor & designer of that building', and Styles was ordered to pay him £500 and costs [T. P. Hudson, 'Moor Park, Leoni and Sir James Thornhill', *Burlington Mag.*, Nov. 1971]. The house is described in *C. Life*, 6–13 Jan. 1912, Tipping, *English Homes, Period V* (i), 1921, and Hussey, *English Country Houses: Early Georgian*, 1955. The wings (shown in Vertue's sketch-plan of 1730) were removed in 1785.

In 1721 Thornhill again appeared in an architectural role when he gave evidence to a committee of the House of Commons that was considering the building of a bridge across the Thames at Westminster. He said he had measured and bored the river, that the ground was firm and capable of providing a good foundation, and that it would be practicable to build a bridge there [*Commons' Jnls.* xix, 1718–21, 708]. His design for a bridge of nine arches in this position is in the R.I.B.A. Collection. At some date before 1729 Thornhill was giving advice to Lord Chancellor King in connection with proposed alterations to his house at OCKHAM in SURREY, for in February of that year Hawksmoor noted that one of the designs 'was proposed when Sr. James Thornhill was at Occham', and on the back of a design for wainscoting the hall is written what appears to be the signature 'Jacobus T.' [L. Whistler in *C. Life*, 29 Dec. 1950, 2221]. In an album at Hovingham Hall, Yorks., there is a set of plans and a corresponding elevation by Thorn-

825

hill for an institutional building, perhaps a workhouse.

In 1720 Thornhill bought back the family estate at Thornhill, and built a new house there (THORNHILL HOUSE) in which he died on 13 May 1734. In the grounds he erected in 1727 an obelisk in honour of George II's accession. There is a drawing of it by himself in B.M., *King's Maps*, Supplementary volume 124, f. 31. From 1722 to 1734 he sat in Parliament as member for Weymouth and Melcombe Regis, and in 1732 he was one of the Commissioners appointed under the Act for rebuilding the town of Blandford, which had been destroyed by fire on 4 June 1731. This explains how he came to make a plan and elevation of a 'Town Hall, or Genll. Assembly, Market House, etc.' for Blandford, which is now in Sir John Soane's Museum. It is signed and dated 'J. Th. 1733' (*Archaeological Jnl.* civ, 1948, pl. xxiv).

The buildings and designs mentioned above are sufficiently numerous to justify Thornhill's claim to be taken seriously as an architect. But it is unlikely that they tell the full story of his architectural activity, and they scarcely afford enough evidence for a full assessment of his ability as an architectural designer. Moor Park and the Cannons design belong to the English baroque tradition, but Thornhill House and some of the unexecuted drawings (notably the one for Blandford Town Hall) show a degree of Palladian influence that is unexpected in one who as an artist was so consistently baroque in style.

[*A.P.S.D.*; *D.N.B.*; Walpole Society, *Vertue Note Books* i, 100–1, iii, 35, 46, 55, 70, 114, v, 94; Ralph Edwards, 'Sir James Thornhill as an Architect', *C. Life*, 9 Feb. 1935 (correspondence); Arthur Oswald, 'Sir James Thornhill and Dorset', *C. Life*, 27 April 1935 (correspondence); Minutes of the Radcliffe Trustees (Bodleian Library); Minutes of the Commissioners for building St. Martin's Church (Westminster Library); J. S. Corder, 'Extracts from the Diary of Sir James Thornhill May 16–June 7, 1711', *Proceedings of the Suffolk Institute of Archaeology* xiii, 1909, 33–43;[1] Hutchins, *History of Dorset* ii, 1774, 245–6, 451; *Builder* i, 1843, 414–15; 'Sir James Thornhill's Collection', *Burlington Magazine* lxxxii, June 1943; Catalogue of *An Exhibition of Paintings & Drawings by Sir James Thornhill* at the Guildhall Art Gallery, 1958; E. Croft Murray, *Decorative Painting in England* i, 1962, chap. vii; H. M. Colvin, *Catalogue of Architectural Drawings of the Eighteenth and Nineteenth Centuries in the Library of Worcester College, Oxford*, 1964; John Harthan, 'Two Travel Diaries by Sir James Thornhill',

Victoria and Albert Museum Bulletin, vol. ii, no. 3, 1966; E. de N. Mayhew, *Sketches by Thornhill*, H.M.S.O. 1967; John Harris, *Catalogue of British Drawings for Architecture, etc., in American Collections*, 1971; Joan Brocklebank, 'James Thornhill', *Notes and Queries for Somerset and Dorset* xxx, March 1975, 73–82; *History of the King's Works* v, 1976.]

THORNTHWAITE, ANDREW, was no doubt related to the engraver J. Thornthwaite. He began life a an architectural draughtsman but subsequently entered the Army. He was awarded premiums by the Society of Arts in 1763, 1764 and 1765. In 1763 he was described as a pupil of the artist Pars, in 1765 of the architect Boulton Mainwaring [R. Dossie, *Memoirs of Agriculture* iii, 1782, 421]. In 1771 he exhibited at the Society of Artists an elevation of the east end of Henry VII's Chapel at Westminster. He designed the frontispiece to the second edition of William Wrighte's *Grotesque Architecture*, published in 1790.

THORNTON, WILLIAM (*c.* 1670–1721), of York, was a carpenter and joiner by trade. In his *Eboracum*, 1736, p. 260, Francis Drake describes him as a 'Joyner and architect', and says that 'by the ablest judges in the former kind of work, he was look'd upon as the best artist in *England*; and, for architecture, his reparation of Beverleyminster ought to give him a lasting memorial'. At BEVERLEY MINSTER he had, in 1716–20, restored the leaning north face of the north transept to the perpendicular under the direction of Nicholas Hawksmoor. The elaborate timber framing employed in this operation is shown in an engraving published in 1739 (reproduced by C. Hiatt, *Beverley Minster*, 1898, 35). An inscription refers to the framing as being of Thornton's invention, and according to John Loveday, who visited Beverley in 1732, 'Hawksmoor . . . and He had concerted of the Affair between 'em' [*The Diary of a Tour in 1732*, Roxburghe Club 1890, 199–201].

Thornton's employment as a carpenter or joiner is documented at CASTLE HOWARD, YORKS. (N.R.), in 1706–11 [Castle Howard archives, carpenters' book, *ex inf.* Mr. Geoffrey Beard]; at BENINGBOROUGH HALL and WENTWORTH CASTLE, YORKS (W.R.), in 1714 [Strafford papers, B.M., Add. MS. 22238, f. 10]; and at Sir Charles Hotham's house in BEVERLEY in 1720 [accounts in E. Riding Record Office, D D Ho/15/4]. His activity as an architect is less well documented, but in 1700 'Wm. Thornton's Model' for a summer-house at SWINTON PARK, YORK. (N.R.), was approved by Sir Abstrupus Danby [John Cornforth in *C. Life*, 7 April 1966, 790], and drawings by him exist for living accommodation in the stables at LEDSTON HALL, YORKS. (W.R.) [*ex inf.*

---

[1] There are transcripts of this diary in the British Museum (Add. MS. 34788, formerly Phillipps MS. 1777), and the Library of the Society of Antiquaries (187 D., formerly Phillipps MS. 17479).

Mr. Peter Willis]. According to an eighteenth-century list of Yorkshire houses in a copy of *The Builder's Dictionary* (1734) in the Metropolitan Museum at New York, Thornton was the architect of 'Mr. Bourchier's', *i.e.* BENINGBOROUGH HALL, built by John Bourchier and completed in 1716. Independent evidence of Thornton's responsibility for the joinery here has been cited above, and he presumably designed as well as executed the very elaborate interiors in a sophisticated style derived from that of Daniel Marot (*C. Life*, 26 Nov., 3 Dec. 1927; H. A. Tipping, *English Homes, Period IV* (ii), 1928, 221–46).

A tablet in St. Olave's Church, York, records the death of William Thornton, 'Joyner & Architect', on 23 September 1721, at the age of 51 (R.C.H.M., *York* iv, pl. 51). His will indicates that he lived in Marygate and that he left seven children. Nothing is at present known of his origins or training, but it may be noted that a Thomas Thornton was Master of the London Joiners' Company in 1691. William Thornton's business appears to have been carried on by his second son William, who in 1728 subscribed to Gibbs's *Book of Architecture* and in 1732 provided a design for rebuilding the cupola on the roof of BURTON CONSTABLE HOUSE, YORKS. (E.R.) [letter dated from York 16 Sept. 1732 in letter-book in E. Riding Record Office].

THOROLD, WILLIAM (1798–1878), of Norwich, was well known in East Anglia as a farmer, millwright, engineer and surveyor. He also practised as an architect. In 1824 he exhibited a design for a County Hall and Corn Exchange at the Norwich Society of Artists, and in 1835 he submitted plans for the Houses of Parliament (presumably those described in the *Catalogue of Designs* as by 'J. Thorold'). Designs by him for a Norfolk farm-house incorporating a windmill were published by J. C. Loudon in his *Encyclopaedia of Rural Architecture* (1846 ed., 471–3, 544–5), and his executed works appear mostly to have been farm-buildings and Union Workhouses. Six of the latter were erected to his designs in 1836–7 – at THETFORD, PULHAM MARKET, KENNINGHALL, ROCKLAND ALL SAINTS, HINDRINGHAM and GREAT SNORING. [*Minutes of Proceedings of the Institution of Civil Engineers* lv, 1878–9, 321–2; *Norfolk Chronicle*, 19 March, 23 and 30 April, 14 May, 25 June 1836, 4 Feb. 1837, *ex inf.* Mr. D. C. Young.]

THORP, JAMES, of Princes Street, Leicester Square, was the architect in accordance with whose designs the interior of the medieval chapel at STONOR PARK, OXON., was remodelled for Thomas Stonor in 1796–1800. [Arthur Oswald in *C. Life*, 13 Oct. 1950; *V.C.H. Oxon.* viii, 176.]

THORPE, JOHN (*c.* 1565–1655?), born at Kingscliffe in Northamptonshire, was the second son of Thomas Thorpe, a master mason of that parish. As a child, he laid the first stone of Kirby Hall, a house of which his father was presumably the principal mason, but he does not appear to have been brought up to the mason's trade. Instead he joined the Office of Works, serving as a clerk at Richmond, Greenwich, Whitehall and other palaces from 1583 to 1601. In the latter year he left the Office of Works and practised as a land and building surveyor, at first independently, and from 1611 onwards as assistant to Robert Treswell, the Surveyor-General of Woods South of Trent. In this capacity he surveyed numerous royal estates in various parts of the country. He appears to have retired in the 1630s, but to have lived on to an advanced age, dying probably in 1655. For most of his working life he lived in Little Church Street near St. Martins-in-the-Fields, of which he was a vestryman.

Thorpe was primarily an eminent land surveyor of the same sort as John Norden. But his interest in buildings is attested by his book of plans preserved in Sir John Soane's Museum. This contains over 150 plans, mostly of country houses. Some of these are projects for new houses, some are surveys of existing buildings, and others are probably copies of designs by other surveyors. Despite the importance of these plans for the study of Elizabethan and Jacobean architecture, they have so far afforded little direct evidence of Thorpe's activity as a practising architect. Several plans are, however, inscribed with the names of Lincolnshire gentlemen, and DOWSBY HALL, LINCS., built soon after 1610 by Richard Burrell, resembles two of these plans sufficiently closely to justify the conclusion that it was designed by Thorpe or at least based on a plan provided by him [D. L. Roberts, 'John Thorpe's Designs for Dowsby Hall and the Red Hall, Bourne', *Lincolnshire History and Archaeology* viii, 1973]. The only other building of any significance that Thorpe is at present known to have designed is a gallery between the Rosse and Stanton Towers on the south front of BELVOIR CASTLE, LEICS., for which a drawing is preserved in the muniment-room at Belvoir (Map no. 164). As 'surveir of the contractinge' Thorpe was paid £5 by command of the 6th Earl of Rutland for superintending the work in the years 1625–7 [Belvoir Castle MSS., Accounts nos. 144 and 145]. The drawing shows a symmetrical façade of eight bays (3-2-3) with a large balcony linking the two central windows.

In his *Gentleman's Exercise* (1612 edition) Henry Peacham pays a compliment to the learning of his 'especial friend Master John Thorpe', whom he describes as an 'excellent Geometrician and Surveyor', and it is possible that Thorpe was the 'I.T.' who translated Hans Blum's treatise on the orders into English in 1608.

[John Summerson, 'John Thorpe and the

Thorpes of Kingscliffe', *Arch. Rev.*, Nov. 1949; *The Book of Architecture of John Thorpe*, ed. John Summerson, Walpole Soc. vol. xl, 1966.]

TIMBRELL, BENJAMIN (–1754), was one of the leading carpenters and master builders in Georgian London. He was probably the most prominent speculative builder in London between 1720 and 1750, especially in the Mayfair area. He built on the Earl of Scarbrough's land near Hanover Square, on the City of London's Conduit Mead estate, and the Berkeley and Grosvenor estates [information from Mr. Frank Kelsall]. Between 1723 and 1730 he took three building leases on the Harley estate in Marylebone [B.M., Add. MS. 18240, ff. 10–18]. In 1735 he bought Chandos House in St. James's Square, pulled it down, and built three houses on the site [*Survey of London* xxix, 122–3]. His last scheme, the redevelopment of the site of Stafford House, Buckingham Gate, was completed by his executors [deeds in Middlesex Land Register]. For some time Timbrell appears to have been in partnership with another well-known London carpenter, Thomas Phillips (d. 1736),[1] in conjunction with whom he executed the structural woodwork of the church of St. Martin-in-the-Fields in 1722–6 [J. McMaster, *St. Martin-in-the-Fields*, 1916, 79] and built the church of St. Peter, Vere Street, in 1721–4 [B.M., Add. MS. 18238, ff. 37–9]. Though he often built to the designs of others, Timbrell was no doubt capable of being his own architect. Thus it appears that in 1737–8 he designed as well as built NOS. 1–3 CROWN OFFICE ROW, INNER TEMPLE, altered by S. Smirke in 1863–4 and destroyed by bombing in 1941 [*Calendar of Inner Temple Records* iv, 1933, 348, 353, 365, 366–9, 371–2, 373, 391]. In 1743 he was paid 'for supervising the Repairing and fitting up' of LEICESTER HOUSE, LEICESTER SQUARE, for the Prince of Wales [*Survey of London* xxxiv, 447]. In 1730 he was the principal member of the group of 'undertakers' who contracted to build the GROSVENOR CHAPEL in SOUTH AUDLEY STREET, and may possibly have made the design, although there is no direct evidence that this was the case [Vestry Minutes of St. George's, Hanover Square, in Westminster City Library].

Timbrell, who was a vestryman of St. George's, Hanover Square, died in or about January 1754. His will, dated December 1750 [P.C.C. 28 PINFOLD], refers to his purchase of a house in Fulham 'which I have pulled down and am rebuilding'. A codicil shows that he had sold it by November 1753.

TINLEY, —, made designs for rebuilding DITCHLEY HOUSE, OXON., for the 2nd Earl of Lichfield in 1720. They were criticized by Francis Smith of Warwick in a letter to the Earl dated 4 May 1720, and were not adopted. What appears to be Tinley's plan is preserved among the Ditchley papers in the County Record Office at Oxford. It is crudely drawn and bears a note, 'This Plane drawn in imitation of Mr. Wallop's House. But not at all like it.' Mr. Wallop's house was at Hurstbourne Priors, Hants.

TITE, SIR WILLIAM (1798–1873), was the son of Arthur Tite, a wealthy London merchant. He became a pupil of David Laing and assisted him (1817–20) in rebuilding the body of the church of St. Dunstan-in-the-East (of which, according to Eastlake, he was the effective architect). He was admitted to the Royal Academy Schools in 1818, and exhibited at the Academy in 1817 and the following years.[1] After failing in several competitions he obtained the commission to design Mill Hill School in 1825, followed by the National Scotch Church in Regent Square in 1827–8. His most important work was the Royal Exchange. Tite was not among the thirty-eight architects who entered designs for the original competition in 1839, but when the three best designs were set aside on the ground that they could not be built within the prescribed sum, Tite was brought in, first as an adviser and then as a competitor. Ultimately only he and Cockerell were left in the field, and Tite's design was chosen by 13 votes to 7. In the circumstances the propriety of his conduct was questionable, and in the eyes of everyone but the committee his design was markedly inferior to Cockerell's. The building was completed at a cost of £150,000, and was opened by Queen Victoria on 28 October 1844.

Tite's practice was largely concerned with railways. In the 1840s he was extensively engaged in the valuation, purchase and sale of land for railways, and designed a number of railway stations, notably the termini of the London and South-Western Railway Company at Vauxhall (Nine Elms) and Southampton, the Citadel Station at Carlisle, most of the stations on the Caledonian and Scottish Central Railways, including Edinburgh (Caledonian), those on the Exeter and Yeovil Railway, and on the line from Havre to Paris; and the station at Windsor (1850).

After a serious illness, followed by a journey to Italy in 1851–2, Tite gradually withdrew from practice, but his wealth ('I inherited a fortune, I married a fortune, and I have made a fortune', he is reported to have told the Prince of Wales) enabled him to remain active in other capacities.

---

[1] In 1854, after a long absence from the Academy, he showed 'a composition of the works of Inigo Jones' which was evidently intended to be a companion to Cockerell's well-known 'Tribute to Wren' of 1838. This drawing, now in the R.I.B.A. Collection, is illustrated in *R.I.B.A. Jnl.*, July 1965, 342–3.

---

[1] See above, p. 633.

In 1838 he was elected President of the Architectural Society, which was merged with the R.I.B.A. in 1842. He was President of the Institute from 1861 to 1863 and from 1867 to 1870. He was Liberal M.P. for Bath from 1855 until his death, a magistrate for the counties of Middlesex and Somerset, a member of the Metropolitan Board of Works, and chairman of several companies. He was a member of numerous committees, and in 1860 headed a deputation to Lord Palmerston opposing Scott's Italianate Gothic design for the Foreign Office. He was knighted in 1869, and in 1870 was made a Companion of the Bath. Tite was also well known as an antiquary and collector of books, manuscripts and works of art. He was elected a Fellow of the Royal Society in 1835, of the Society of Antiquaries in 1839, and was President of the Cambridge Camden Society in 1866. From 1824 to 1869 he was honorary secretary of the London Institution.

As an architect Tite was eclectic, his works ranging stylistically from Greek Revival (Mill Hill School) and Durandesque neo-classical (Nine Elms Station) to Perpendicular Gothic (the Scotch Church) and neo-Byzantine (church at Gerrards Cross). His most famous building, the Royal Exchange, is a somewhat coarse amalgam of classical sources, chiefly Italian Renaissance and Baroque in origin. Though it inevitably compares unfavourably with the elegant sophistication of C. R. Cockerell's contemporary work, it is by no means inappropriate as the temple of Victorian finance. As a Gothicist Tite is better represented by his railway stations at Carlisle (1847) and Perth (1848) than by the reduced version of York Minister which he built in Regent Square, London (1826–8).

Tite married, in 1832, Emily, daughter of John Curtis, of Herne Hill, Surrey. He died without issue at Torquay on 20 April 1873, and was buried in Norwood Cemetery. His estate was valued for probate at 'under £400,000'. A portrait of Tite by J. P. Knight is at the R.I.B.A. and there is a bust by Theed (1869) at the Guildhall. Ebenezer Trotman and Charles Ferdinand Porden were his principal assistants, and Arthur Baker, Charles Bailey and J. H. Steinmetz were also in his office in various capacities. His nephew Arthur John Green (d. 1855, aged 34) and T. Hayter Lewis were his pupils. E. N. Clifton was for some years his partner.

[*A.P.S.D.*; *D.N.B.*; *Builder* xxxi, 1873, 337–9; *R.I.B.A. Proceedings*, 1873–4, 209–12; S. Redgrave, *Dictionary of Artists of the British School*, 1878, 432; M. S. Briggs, 'Sir William Tite, M.P.', *Builder*, 13–20 Jan. 1950.]

MILL HILL SCHOOL, MIDDLESEX, 1825–7 [N. G. Brett-James, *The History of Mill Hill School*, 1924, 60, 65, 66, 89 (plate)].

LONDON, THE NATIONAL SCOTCH CHURCH, SIDMOUTH STREET, REGENT SQUARE, 1826–8, Gothic; dem. [J. Elmes, *Metropolitan Improvements*, 1829, 151–2 and plate].

LONDON, THE GOLDEN CROSS HOTEL, STRAND, 1832; dem. 1936 [*A.P.S.D.*] (*Survey of London* xx, pl. 36*b*).

LONDON, THE LONDON AND WESTMINSTER BANK, LOTHBURY, in collaboration with C. R. Cockerell, who designed the exterior, 1837–9; dem. 1928 [see Tite's account of the partnership in *R.I.B.A. Trans.*, 1863–4, 24] (measured drawings in *Architect and Building News*, 1 March 1935).

LONDON, THE SOUTH METROPOLITAN CEMETERY, NORWOOD, 1838; Gothic chapels dem. [*A.P.S.D.*].

DOLLAR PARISH CHURCH, CLACKMANNANSHIRE, 1841, Gothic; enlarged 1921 [*N.S.A.* viii, 109].

LONDON, THE ROYAL EXCHANGE, THREADNEEDLE STREET, 1842–44 [*Proceedings connected with the rebuilding of the Royal Exchange 1838–44*, 1845].

BROOKWOOD, SURREY, THE LONDON METROPOLIS CEMETERY, 1853–4 [*A.P.S.D.*].

LONDON, GRESHAM HOUSE, OLD BROAD STREET, 1854–6, with E. N. Clifton; dem. [*A.P.S.D.*].

LONDON, warehouse for Messrs. Tapling & Co., 1–8 GRESHAM STREET, 1857; dem. 1940 [*A.P.S.D.*].

GERRARDS CROSS, BUCKS., ST. JAMES'S CHURCH, 1858–9, in memory of Major-General Reid, Italianate [*Builder* xvii, 1859, 588, 616].

TOD, A—, was employed by Robert Mylne as a clerk from 1801 onwards. He exhibited at the Royal Academy from 1800 to 1805, showing a drawing of the west front of Gosford House, East Lothian, 'a mausoleum near Edinburgh' (1801), a 'Villa at Norwood, in Surrey' (1803), and the 'west front of a house intended to be built in Shropshire' (1805). An elevation of 'Mr. Tassie's House, Leicester Square', signed 'A. Tod, architect 1806', exists in a private collection. The house in question was No. 20 Leicester Square, which was occupied by William Tassie, the modeller, from 1799 to 1837 [*Survey of London* xxxiv, 489].

TOWNESEND, GEORGE (–1719), was one of the sons of John Townesend of Oxford (d. 1728), and a brother of William Townesend (d. 1739). He established himself as a mason and carver in Bristol, and was made free of the city on 8 July 1706, on his marriage to Margaret, the widow of Malachi Harford, a former burgess. There are one or two payments to him in connection with the building of the new TOLSEY or COUNCIL HOUSE in 1701–4, though the principal contractor was a carpenter named Joseph Jones.

THE TOWNESEND FAMILY[1]

JOHN TOWNESEND = Elizabeth Morrell
Mayor of Oxford
1648–1728

GEORGE = Margaret
of Bristol,
d. 1719

WILLIAM = Anne Brian
of Oxford
d. 1739

JOHN
of London
d. 1742

JOHN = Elizabeth   Mary = William Ives
of Oxford,
d. 1746

William

JOHN TOWNESEND = Mary
d. 1784 | d. 1792

STEPHEN
1755–1800

JOHN

Townesend received 9s. 'for a stone chimney piece in the lower room' in 1704, and in January 1709/10 he was paid £12 'for the frontispiece at the Councill House'. The Council House was rebuilt in 1824 [Bristol City Archives; cf. W. Ison, *The Georgian Buildings of Bristol*, 1952, 90]. In 1716 Townesend contracted to complete the tower of ALL SAINTS CHURCH, BRISTOL, and was presumably responsible for the design of the cupola[2] by which it is surmounted. He was associated in this work with William Paul, a mason who had been concerned in rebuilding the lower part of the tower in 1711–12. The new tower was completed in February 1716/17, when a dolphin weather-vane made by Simon Edney was placed in position [MS. churchwardens' accounts].

George Townesend is probably to be identified with the 'Mr. Townesend' who is referred to by Sir John Vanbrugh in one of his letters as the mason 'who did Mr. Southwell's masonry' at KING'S WESTON, nr. BRISTOL. King's Weston was

built by the Hon. Edward Southwell to Vanbrugh's designs in 1711–13, but there exists a 'Book of Designs' made for Southwell by various architects, and in it there is a design for a terminal feature signed by George Townesend and dated 21 May 1717, together with an undertaking to 'do the same for Forty Pounds and twelve pence per Perch for the inside wall' [H. A. Tipping, *English Homes, School of Vanbrugh*, fig. 153; *Architectural History* x, 1967, fig. 23]. Another of the designs in the book is for a fireplace similar to one in Kingston Bagpuize House, Berks., which may have been built by one of the Townesends (*C. Life*, 6–13 Nov. 1942).

There are two monuments in LONG ASHTON CHURCH, SOMERSET, which bear the signature 'Townesend of Bristol'. They commemorate Sir Hugh Smyth (d. 1680, monument erected 1697) and Lady Smith (d. 1715).

By his will, dated 15 March 1718/19, and proved on 14 May 1719, George Townesend ('of Bristol, freemason') left all his plate to his nephew John Townesend, son of his brother William Townesend of Oxford. The remainder of his property was to be divided between his good friend Samuel Child of Henbury, yeoman, and Sarah Evans of the same place, relict of William Evans, shipwright [P.C.C. 92 BROWNING].

TOWNESEND, JOHN (–1742), was one of the sons of John Townesend of Oxford (d. 1728),

[1] These two pedigrees are subject to correction, and many members of the family not mentioned in the text have been omitted.

[2] This was rebuilt in 1807–8 when the tower was repaired by Luke Henwood. A survey drawing made in April 1807 shows that it originally had a different profile in the form of an inverted *cymá recta*, the lower (concave) portion being separated from the upper (convex) by a bold torus moulding.

and a brother of William Townesend (d. 1739). He established himself as a master mason in London, and is probably to be identified with the John Townesend who was made free of the Masons' Company in 1711 as an apprentice of Edward Edwards. He was certainly in London in 1716, when he received a payment from the Radcliffe Trustees on behalf of his brother William 'on Account of work done & to be done at University College at Oxford' [Bodleian Library, Accounts of Radcliffe Trustees, 1714–50, f. 25]. In 1718 the 6th Earl of Westmorland paid him £6 16s. 6d. for carving a coat of arms to be sent to his seat at SHARLSTON, YORKS. (W.R.) [Westmorland family accounts in Northamptonshire Record Office]. In 1731 he examined the tower of the church of ST. OLAVE, HART STREET, and made an 'estimate of the Masons' charge' for 'takeing down 24 Foot of the Church Steeple computed to be to the Lower End of the Windows to the Bells and to new rebuild the same againe the same Heigth, wth Portland Stone £255. And with Bath Stone £230' [Vestry Minutes in Guildhall Library, MS. 858/1]. In February 1732/3 he gave evidence before a committee of the House of Commons about the condition of ST. GEORGE'S CHURCH, SOUTHWARK [*Commons' Jnls.* xxii, 43]. He appears to have been in partnership with Thomas Dunn, whose name appears with his own on the foundation-stone of the Bank of England, the original central block of which they built to the designs of George Sampson in 1732–4 [*Ars Quatuor Coronatorum* xli, 1928, 160 ff.]. In February 1737/8 Dunn and Townesend tendered unsuccessfully for the masonry contract at ST. OLAVE'S, SOUTHWARK [*Builder* ii, 1844, 252–3]. Subsequently, however, he was associated with Christopher Horsenaile and Robert Taylor (senior) in tendering for the masonry of the MANSION HOUSE, Dunn on this occasion being paired with Devall. The contract was given to Townesend, Horsenaile and Taylor, all three of whom were members of the Court of Common Council, a fact which justifiably occasioned charges of corruption against the committee [S. Perks, *The History of the Mansion House*, 1922, 176–8]. His death in 1742 is thus noticed in the *London Magazine*, p. 205 – 'Mr. John Townesend, Mason, one of the Common Council men for Castle-Baynard Ward, and Brother to the late Mr. Townesend of Oxford, well known for his many noble structures in that place'. He is usually referred to as 'of St. Paul's Wharf'.

TOWNESEND, JOHN (–1746), was the son and successor of William Townesend of Oxford (d. 1739). He figures as 'stone-carver' in the list of workmen employed on the Radcliffe Camera given by Gibbs in his *Bibliotheca Radcliviana*, and succeeded his father as one of the principal mason-contractors for that building in 1739. He also took his place as mason to the Dean and Chapter of Christ Church. In 1742, when James Gibbs went to Tetbury, Glos., in order to report on the state of the church, he took with him Mr. John Townesend, 'an eminent master builder from Oxford' [A. T. Lee, *History of Tetbury*, 1857, 104]. He was at that time engaged in building the stone screen in St. John's College Hall to the designs of James Gibbs, and himself submitted alternative schemes for raising the front of the college which were not carried out [St. John's College Archives]. Shortly before his death, he refronted the north side of Corpus Christi College, and in 1748 William Robinson produced an estimate of £335 which 'his late Master, Mr. John Townesend, had made for the mason's work in making the west front of Corpus Christi College in all things agreeable to the north side of the building already done' [Corpus Christi College Archives]. He died in 1746, and the burial of 'Mr. Townesend of St. Michael's' is recorded in the St. Giles' registers on 20 August. His will, dated 9 June 1746, was proved on 20 January 1746/7. The executors were his brother-in-law, William Ives, and William Smith of Warwick. He left a widow, a son William, and three daughters. He left William his 'study of Books, Statues, Mathematical Instruments, Pictures and Plate', and directed that he should be bred up a mason. His property included a farm at Littlemore purchased by his father, houses in St. Michael's parish, Oxford, and leasehold property held from General Tyrrell of Shotover [P.C.C. 25 POTTER]. In 1754 'a large handsome House, late in the Possession of Mr. Townesend, Mason, deceas'd', was advertised to be let with a note that applicants should apply to 'Alderman Ives or Mr. Townesend' [*Jackson's Oxford Jnl.*, 12 Oct. 1754].

The following monuments are signed by John Townesend:

WANTAGE, BERKS., Stamp family, *c.* 1741.
FIGHELDEAN, WILTS., John Clerk (d. 1740).

TOWNESEND, JOHN (–1784), succeeded to the family business after the death of John Townesend II in 1746, although his precise relationship to the latter is at present uncertain. He was a mason-contractor of considerable importance as well as an accomplished carver of monuments. After John Townesend's death he carried out the finishing touches to the masonry of the RADCLIFFE LIBRARY, making in 1751 the fourteen obelisks of Burford stone which surrounded the Library until their removal in the nineteenth century [*Building Accounts of the Radcliffe Camera*, ed. S. G. Gillam, Oxford Hist. Soc. 1958, xxix, etc.]. In 1751 he contracted, with Richard Piddington and Robert Tawney, to build the new OXFORD TOWN HALL to the designs of Isaac Ware

[Bodleian, MS. Top. Oxon. c. 300, f. 154]. In 1757, in conjunction with his partner Edward King, he submitted an 'Estimate for an additional building at Queen's (the benefaction of Mr. Mitchell) joined to that already done on the East side of the South Quadrangle to consist of 3 sets of Rooms on each floor and a staircase' [Bodleian, MS. Rawlinson D.912, f. 534]. This was built between 1757 and 1759, and comprises the greater part of the east side of the front quadrangle of THE QUEEN'S COLLEGE [Queen's College Archives 5 L 11, a–b]. In 1758–9 Townesend built the Gothic fan vault over the CONVOCATION HOUSE beneath the Selden End of the Bodleian Library. This reproduced the pattern of the seventeenth-century plaster vault, which was found to be insecure [I. G. Philip in *Bodleian Library Record* vi, 1958, 416–27]. In 1779 he designed and built the library of EXETER COLLEGE under the supervision of the Rev. William Crowe of New College, an amateur architect: it was destroyed in 1859 to make way for a new building designed by Sir Gilbert Scott [J. Ingram, *Memorials of Oxford* i, 1837, 14]. An elevation of 'St. Mary's spire in Oxford measured by Jno. Townesend 1757' is preserved among the Buckler drawings in the British Museum [Add. MS. 36402, f. 23; see also Add. MS. 36979, f. 71], and in 1758 he rebuilt the spire of SHOTTESBROOKE CHURCH, BERKS., at the expense of Arthur Vansittart. A note in the register made by Vansittart's son William records that 'My Father advertised the steeple to be repaired. A Stone Mason from London engaged to repair it at £900. One from Bath at six hundred. Mr. Townshend from Oxford at £300. His offer was accepted.' The spire was again altered in the course of a restoration by G. E. Street in 1852, but its previous appearance is shown in W. Butterfield's *Elevations, Sections and Details of Shottesbrooke Church, Berks.*, published by the Oxford Architectural Society in 1844. In 1767 Townesend was employed by the Earl of Abingdon to build an inn near Swinford Bridge. On its completion, there was a dispute as to the value of the work performed, each party employing a different surveyor, whose estimates differed by more than £100. Litigation was still in progress at the time of Townesend's death in 1784 [Bodleian, MS. Top. Oxon. c. 388]. One of Townsend's most important contracts was the building of MAIDENHEAD BRIDGE to the designs of Sir Robert Taylor in 1772–7. The contract price (with extras) was £15,741, but according to a memorandum[1] left by Townesend's son Stephen the cost to the contractor was £16,623.[2] This loss of over £880 was

'in a Great measure . . . incur'd by bad weather and flood [and other] unforseen accidents. At the time when the Act where [*sic*] settled the Corporation was willing to give £500 provided Mr. Taylor could say the work was well done by way of a sanction [*i.e.* an *ex gratia* payment], but he wrote a letter to the Corporation when they press'd him for an answer, that they ought to be careful how they gave away the Publick money', and the extra payment was never made. In 1781 or 1782 Townesend contracted to build HENLEY-ON-THAMES BRIDGE to the designs of William Hayward (*q.v.*). It was not completed until 1786, two years after his death on 4 September 1784 [*Jackson's Oxford Jnl.*, 11 Sept. 1784]. He left a widow, Mary, and a son, Stephen, who carried on the business.

In 1771–2 Townesend had bought two large tenements on the north side of Oxford High Street immediately to the west of its junction with Longwall, and including what is now Longwall Place [*Oxford City Properties*, Oxford Historical Society, 311–12]. Here he presumably had his working premises, and here he built a new house which is indicated as such on a plan of the approaches to Magdalen Bridge made soon after his purchase (B.M., *King's Maps* xxxiv, 33, 3 (b), reproduced in *Surveys and Tokens*, Oxford Hist. Soc., lxxv, 1920).

The following monuments are known to have been executed by John Townesend:

OXFORD, ST. JOHN'S COLLEGE CHAPEL, marble shield commemorating Mrs. Holmes, widow of President Holmes, added to the latter's monument in 1757 [College Archives].

OXFORD, NEW COLLEGE CHAPEL, Henry Bowles (d. 1765), *signed*.

OXFORD, ST. MARY'S CHURCH, Henrietta Fermor, Countess of Pomfret (d. 1762), Gothic, *signed*.

SWALCLIFFE CHURCH, OXON., Richard Wykeham and wife (d. 1751, 1768), *signed*.

TOWNESEND, STEPHEN (1755–1800), was the son of John Townesend (d. 1784), and is probably to be identified with the Stephen, son of John Townesend, mason, and Elizabeth his wife, who was baptized in St. Michael's Church on 23 September 1755.[1] In 1780–1 he completed the tower of BENSON CHURCH, OXON., in a plain classical style with battlemented parapet and pinnacles. The original decision to build a new tower had been taken in 1765, but the work was stopped for lack of funds in 1771. The mason employed was called Hart, but a surveyor named Townesend (probably Stephen's father John) was paid

---

[1] In the possession of Messrs. Knowles & Son Ltd., of Oxford, who kindly permitted me to examine the document.

[2] According to the original document in the County

Record Office (M/AB4/12) the contract price was £14,500, afterwards increased to £15,523.

[1] If so, his father married twice, for he left a widow Mary at his death in 1784 [Bodleian, MS. Top. Oxon. c. 388].

a guinea in 1772. In 1779 the Vestry agreed that the tower should be finished 'according to the design made by — of Woodstock', but nothing was done, and in 1780 it was resolved to complete it 'in a plain and decent manner'. Stephen Townesend contracted to finish it for £264 with facings, dressings, cornices and pinnacles of Headington freestone [MS. Vestry Minutes *ex inf.* Canon B. F. L. Clarke]. In 1785 he rebuilt the tower of WOODSTOCK CHURCH, OXON., in accordance with designs which he had submitted to the vestry in December 1784. The medieval tower had been taken down ten years before, and designs for a new one had been made by Sir William Chambers and his pupil John Yenn. These, however, were not adopted, and on 12 December 1784 it was finally decided to build a new tower, 'according to the plan of Mr. Stephen Townesend of Oxford with whom the Committee are desir'd to enter into Contract jointly with Mr. Churchill who is to do the Carpenter's work' [H. M. Colvin, 'The Rebuilding of Woodstock Church Tower 1770–1786', *Oxfordshire Archaeological Society's Report* no. 87, 1949].

In 1793–5, WHEATLEY CHURCH, OXON., was rebuilt by Stephen Townesend and Henry Tawney of Oxford, the latter being a carpenter by trade. An original elevation for this church is preserved in a volume of topographical drawings in the Bodleian Library (MS. Top. Oxon. b. 220, f. 254). It was probably made by Townesend, as the tower resembled that of Woodstock Church. The church was demolished in 1857 [MS. parish records].

At MAGDALEN COLLEGE, Townesend was the builder of the Gothic 'necessary house' known as West's Building, which was erected in 1782 [T. S. R. Boase, 'An Oxford College and the Gothic Revival', *Jnl. of the Warburg and Courtauld Institutes* xviii, 1955, 148].

Townesend lived at Iffley towards the end of his life, apparently in Court Place, the large house near the church. He died on 6 October 1800, aged about 45, according to a memorandum in a notebook kept by Thomas Knowles, who seems to have been Townesend's foreman. His will is P.C.C. 903 ADDERLEY. On 15 March 1799, Knowles announced that, having for 'many years conducted the business of Mr. S. Townesend', he had 'opened a yard near the bottom of Holywell Street where he means to carry on the above business in its various branches'. The site of his yard (seen in the Oxford Almanack for 1844) is now occupied by the New College Memorial Library, but the firm which he founded is still in business on the opposite side of Holywell Street, and has in its possession the ledger which he opened in 1799.

TOWNESEND, WILLIAM (–1739), was the most successful member of a family of master masons who lived and worked in Oxford throughout the eighteenth century and have an important place in its architectural history. He was the son of John Townesend I (1648–1728), who served his apprenticeship under Bartholomew Peisley and became an alderman of Oxford, holding office as Mayor in 1682–3 and 1720–1. Hearne, who disliked both father and son, records that 'This old Townesend is commonly called old Pincher, from his pinching his workmen'. He died of dropsy on 23 May 1728, and was buried in St. Giles' Churchyard, where there is a handsome monument to his memory erected by his son. According to the inscription, he was 'in [re] architectonica magister peritissimus, exactis demum pluribus et ad scientiam et ad universitatis hujusce ornamentum aedificiis'. Little, however, is known of his building activities, except that he was employed at Queen's College from 1688 onwards, and at Blenheim Palace from 'about the latter end of the year 1705 until some time in or about the year 1711' (B.M., Add. MS. 19617, f. 79).

The date of William Townesend's birth is at present unknown, but it is likely to have taken place in about 1668, as he married in 1688. By the second decade of the eighteenth century he was beginning to take his father's place as the leading master mason in Oxford, and it is clear that, like other men of his kind, he was competent to design as well as to build. In the Queen's accounts he is referred to as 'architecto Townesend', whereas the payments to his father were credited to 'Lapicidae Townesend', and it would appear that he was largely responsible for the design of the main quadrangle of that college as well as for its execution. In particular, he modified Hawksmoor's design for the cupola over the entrance-screen. At Magdalen and Christ Church it was Townesend whose practical knowledge and ability as a draughtsman gave actuality to the amateur proposals of the learned Doctors Aldrich and Clarke. From the list given below it will be apparent that Hearne was not exaggerating when he stated that Townesend 'hath a hand in all the Buildings in Oxford, and gets a vast deal of Money that way', for it includes nearly every important building erected in the University between 1720 and 1740. That they should differ widely in style is scarcely surprising, for, while some represented the designs of a competent architect of which Townesend was merely the executant (*e.g.* the Clarendon Building and the Radcliffe Camera), others were conceived in the academic minds of Aldrich and Clarke, and only a minority were entirely of his own invention. A design for All Souls in the Clarke Collection at Worcester College, dated 30 June 1709, and endorsed as 'Young Mr. Townesend's draft', shows the influence of Vanbrugh, under whom he and his father were working at Blenheim; but

Palladian motifs appear in the design for Christ Church Library which he prepared under Dr. Clarke's direction, and at Oriel and University Colleges he erected buildings in a traditional Jacobean style scarcely distinguishable from that of their older neighbours.

Like most eighteenth-century master masons, Townesend was a sculptor as well as a mason, and much carved work, both for decorative and for monumental purposes, must have been executed in his yard. He does not, however, appear to have signed his monuments, and the list of documented works given below cannot represent more than a small fraction of his total output. That he was also a quarry-owner is shown by a letter among the archives of All Souls in which Hawksmoor writes to Dr. Clarke that 'you are in some measure, ty'd by his haveing all the best quarrys of stone in his owne hands'.

Townesend married Anne Brian of Witney, by whom he had at least eight children, of whom six died in infancy. He died in September 1739, being buried in St. Giles' Churchyard on the 22nd of that month. He was survived by his son John, who carried on his business, and by his daughter Elizabeth, who married William Ives, a wealthy mercer of Oxford. His will, proved on 5 October 1739, is P.C.C. 219 HENCHMAN. His apprentices included William King (1704), John Osborne (1706) and Daniel Bowdon (1714). [W. G. Hiscock, 'William Townesend, mason and architect of Oxford', *Arch. Rev.*, Oct. 1945, reprinted in *A Christ Church Miscellany*, 1946; H. M. Colvin, *Catalogue of Architectural Drawings of the Eighteenth and Nineteenth Centuries in the Library of Worcester College, Oxford*, 1964.]

OXFORD

CORPUS CHRISTI COLLEGE, *designed* carving of Hall screen and decorative carving in Chapel, 1701–5 [W. G. Hiscock, *A Christ Church Miscellany*, 1946, 40].

EXETER COLLEGE, *executed* vaulting and carving of new gateway to Turl Street, 1702–3 [College Archives].

CORPUS CHRISTI COLLEGE, *built, and perhaps designed*, THE FELLOWS' BUILDING and CLOISTER, 1706–12, and the GENTLEMEN COMMONERS' BUILDING, 1737 [W. G. Hiscock, *A Christ Church Miscellany*, 1946, 41–2; *V.C.H. Oxon.* iii, 227].

CHRIST CHURCH, *built* PECKWATER QUADRANGLE to the designs of Dean Aldrich, 1706–14 [W. G. Hiscock, *A Christ Church Miscellany*, 1946, 40].

NEW COLLEGE, *built* the north-east block of THE GARDEN QUADRANGLE in 1707 to match the south-east block built by Richard Piddington in 1700 [Willis and Clark, iii, 280 n.].

THE QUEEN'S COLLEGE, *built* THE FRONT QUADRANGLE, including HALL and CHAPEL, under the direction of Dr. George Clarke, 1710–21: in 1733–6 he built the entrance-screen and cupola, for which Hawksmoor had made designs which were modified by Townesend [W. G. Hiscock, *A Christ Church Miscellany*, 1946, 42–4; Kerry Downes, *Hawksmoor*, 1959, 107, n. 14; H. M. Colvin, *Catalogue of Architectural Drawings in . . . Worcester College*, 1964, xviii–xix; building account in Bodleian, MS. Rawlinson D.912, f. 528; letter from Townesend about the cupola in Queen's College MS. 475, ff. 188–9].

THE CLARENDON BUILDING, *built* to the designs of Nicholas Hawksmoor, 1712–15 [*V.C.H. Oxon.* iii, 54–5].

BALLIOL COLLEGE, *built* THE BRISTOL BUILDINGS, 1716–20; refaced 1826 and since heightened; and *built* the south-east portion of the FRONT QUADRANGLE, 1738–9 (completed 1743); dem. 1866 [extracts from bursars' accounts in Bodleian, MS. Top. Oxon. e. 124/12, ff. 13ᵛ, 15–16].

ALL SOULS COLLEGE, *built* (with B. Peisley) THE NORTH QUADRANGLE, HALL, BUTTERY and CODRINGTON LIBRARY to the designs of Nicholas Hawksmoor, 1716–35 [*V.C.H. Oxon.* iii, 190–3]. For Townesend's own rejected design see Colvin, *Catalogue of Architectural Drawings in . . . Worcester College*, 1964, pl. 51.

UNIVERSITY COLLEGE, *built* (with B. Peisley) THE RADCLIFFE QUADRANGLE under the direction of Dr. George Clarke, 1717–19 [*V.C.H. Oxon.* iii, 77–8; H. M. Colvin, *Catalogue of Architectural Drawings in . . . Worcester College*, 1964, xx].

CHRIST CHURCH, *built* THE LIBRARY to the designs of Dr. George Clarke, 1717–38 [W. G. Hiscock, *A Christ Church Miscellany*, 1946, 49–53].

ALL SAINTS CHURCH, *completed* (with B. Peisley) the steeple, 1718–20, to a design which represents a compromise between Aldrich's original proposal and an alternative one submitted by Hawksmoor [H. M. Colvin, 'The Architects of All Saints Church, Oxford', *Oxoniensia* xix, 1954].

ORIEL COLLEGE, *designed and built* THE ROBINSON BUILDINGS, 1719–20, the mouldings and ornaments being 'answerable to the rest of the college' [W. G. Hiscock, *A Christ Church Miscellany*, 1946, 52].

CHRIST CHURCH, *wainscoted* the east end of the Hall (removed 1799) and *designed and built* THE BUTTERY, 1722 [W. G. Hiscock, *A Christ Church Miscellany*, 1946, 54].

NEW COLLEGE, *paved* THE HALL, 1722 [W. G. Hiscock, *A Christ Church Miscellany*, 1946, 54].

BOTANIC GARDEN, *built* GREENHOUSE, 1727 [W. G.

Hiscock, *A Christ Church Miscellany*, 1946, 55].

TRINITY COLLEGE, *rebuilt* north range of DURHAM QUADRANGLE, 1728, to correspond with the north range of the Garden Quadrangle, built to Wren's designs in 1668 [W. G. Hiscock, *A Christ Church Miscellany*, 1946, 55].

attributed: PEMBROKE COLLEGE CHAPEL, 1728–32; interior decorated by C. E. Kempe 1884 [W. G. Hiscock, *A Christ Church Miscellany*, 1946, 55].

ST. JOHN'S COLLEGE, *erected* marble chimney-piece in Hall, 1731 [College Archives].

Completed building of ST. PETER LE BAILEY CHURCH after the death of William Chipps, the original master mason, 1732–40 (the foundation-stone had been laid in Jan. 1728); dem. 1874 [Hearne, *Collections* xi, 114].

MAGDALEN COLLEGE, *drew designs* for THE NEW BUILDINGS on lines prescribed by Dr. George Clarke. Townesend's plans were accepted on 1 Feb. 1730/1 and carried out by Richard Piddington and William King in 1733–4. Only the northern range of what was to have been a new quadrangle was completed, and the returns remained incomplete until 1826, when they were faced in ashlar by Thomas Harrison of Chester. The traditional attribution of the design to Edward Holdsworth is without foundation [H. M. Colvin, *Catalogue of Architectural Drawings in ... Worcester College*, 1964, xxi–xxiii].

WORCESTER COLLEGE, submitted an estimate for completion of Hall, Chapel and Library to designs of Nicholas Hawksmoor and Dr. George Clarke, Jan. 1734/5; he was probably the contracting mason from the commencement of the new buildings in 1720 [W. G. Hiscock, *A Christ Church Miscellany*, 1946, 59].

THE RADCLIFFE LIBRARY, *contracted* (with Francis Smith) to execute the masonry to the designs of James Gibbs, 1737. John Townesend completed the contract after his father's death in 1739 [*The Building Accounts of the Radcliffe Camera*, ed. S. G. Gillam, Oxford Historical Soc. 1958, xiii–xvi].

OTHER WORKS

ABINGDON, ST. HELEN'S CHURCH. In 1706 Thomas Fletcher, carpenter, agreed to build a gallery in Read's Isle, 'the Front to be done with Spanish Oake according to a designe to be given by Mr. Townsend' [MS. Vestry Minutes]. This may, however, have been John Townesend I.

RADLEY HALL, BERKS., *built, and probably designed*, for Sir John Stonehouse, in partnership with Bartholomew Peisley, 1721–5 [V. Hope, 'The Architect of Radley Hall, *C. Life*, 27 Jan. 1950].

BLENHEIM PALACE, OXON., masonry contracts in partnership with Bartholomew Peisley, *c.* 1720–39, including the erection of the Woodstock Gate (1722–3) and the Column of Victory (1727–30) [W. J. Churchill, 'Some Unpublished Letters of Sarah, Duchess of Marlborough, relating to the Building of Blenheim Palace', *Trans. Birmingham and Midland Institute*, 1884–5; Angela Green, 'Letters of Sarah Churchill, Duchess of Marlborough, on the Column of Victory at Blenheim', *Oxoniensia* xxxi, 1966; David Green, *Blenheim Palace*, 1951].

THORNHILL MANOR FARM-HOUSE, CLYFFE PYPARD, WILTS., *enlarged* for Brasenose College, 1723–4 [*V.C.H. Wilts.* ix, 31].

attributed: WOODPERRY HOUSE, OXON., for John Morse, 1728–30; wings added by F. Codd 1879–80 [John Cornforth in *C. Life*, 5–12 Jan. 1961].

EAST STANDEN, ISLE OF WIGHT, *designed* a farmhouse for the Dean and Chapter of Christ Church, 1737 [W. G. Hiscock, *A Christ Church Miscellany*, 1946, 60].

ROUSHAM HOUSE, OXON., *designed and built* 'Townesend's Temple' for Lieut.-Gen. James Dormer, 1738–9 [M. Jourdain, *The Work of William Kent*, 1948, 80, fig. 114].

MONUMENTS

LLANBADARN CHURCH, ABERYSTWYTH, Sir Thomas Powell, 1706 [R. T. Gunther, *Life and Letters of Edward Lhwyd, Early Science in Oxford* xiv, 508–9].

OXFORD CATHEDRAL, James Narborough (d. 1707), for the Dean and Chapter of Christ Church [W. G. Hiscock, *A Christ Church Miscellany*, 1946, 59.].

OXFORD, ST. MARY'S CHURCH, David Gregory (d. 1708) [Bodleian, Ballard MS. xxxv, f. 158, cited by Hiscock, *op. cit.*, 60].

attributed: OXFORD, ST. MARY'S CHURCH, John Wallis (d. 1703) [W. G. Hiscock, *A Christ Church Miscellany*, 1946, 60].

OXFORD CATHEDRAL, Lord Charles Somerset, erected 1713 [W. G. Hiscock, *A Christ Church Miscellany*, 1946, 60.].

OXFORD, ST. GILES' CHURCHYARD, tomb of his father, John Townesend (d. 1728).

TOWSEY, JOSEPH, of Blandford, was primarily a builder, but an inscription on the three-arched bridge over the R. Stour at DURWESTON, DORSET (nr. Blandford), records that it 'was Built by Henry Portman Esq. Anno Domini 1795. Joseph Towsey Architect.' In 1780 Towsey was working at LULWORTH CASTLE, DORSET, where he rebuilt the staircase in Portland stone for Thomas Weld, and where in 1792–3 he built the lodges [contract and bills in Dorset County Record

Office]. In 1788 he built AMMERDOWN PARK, SOMERSET, to the designs of James Wyatt [C. Hussey in *C. Life*, 16 Feb. 1929, 216].

TRACY, CHARLES HANBURY, cr. BARON SUDELEY (1778–1858), was the third son of John Hanbury of Pontypool Park, Monmouthshire, the wealthy owner of the Pontypool Ironworks. He was educated at Rugby and Christ Church, Oxford. In 1798 he married his cousin Henrietta, daughter and heiress of Henry, 8th and last Viscount Tracy, the owner of the mansions and estates of Toddington in Gloucestershire and Gregynog in Montgomeryshire. He thereupon added the name of Tracy to that of Hanbury. He took an active part in public life, serving as High Sheriff of Gloucestershire in 1801 and of Montgomeryshire in 1804, and entering Parliament in 1807 as Whig Member for Tewkesbury. In 1835 he became chairman of the Commissioners appointed to judge the designs submitted for the new Houses of Parliament, and subsequently showed much pertinacity in defending the choice of Charles Barry as architect. His interest in architecture had earlier been manifested in the rebuilding of Toddington, carried out entirely to his own designs between 1820 and 1835 at a cost of £150,000. With details derived (*via* Pugin's *Specimens*, etc.) from Magdalen College Tower, Christ Church cloister, the roof of Crosby Hall, and other well-known medieval buildings, the house represents a serious attempt to adapt Gothic architecture to domestic purposes, and achieves considerable effect as a picturesque composition. In 1834 Hanbury Tracy offered his services to John Arkwright, the owner of the medieval mansion of Hampton Court in Herefordshire, who contemplated extensive alterations there. Though begged by the architect William Atkinson not to 'make Hampton Court a cell to the Abbey of Toddington', Arkwright was induced to adopt Hanbury Tracy's plans, and the south front and other parts of the house were rebuilt under his direction during the years 1835–41.

Toddington and Hampton Court appear to have been Hanbury Tracy's only architectural works, but they are sufficiently remarkable to give him a place in the history of the Gothic Revival alongside the professionals who by then were monopolizing the style. He died at Toddington in February 1858, aged 79, leaving £5000 for the erection of a monument to himself and his wife in the parish church.

[J. M. McCarthy, thesis on Charles Hanbury Tracy, 1964; J. Britton, *Toddington, Graphic Illustrations with Historical and Descriptive Accounts*, 1841; J. Britton, *The History and Description of Cassiobury Park*, 1837, 27; *Country Life*, 9 Oct. 1937 (Toddington), 22 Feb., 1–8 March 1973 (Hampton Court); Arkwright

papers in Hereford County Record Office, A 63; C. Hussey, *English Country Houses: Late Georgian 1800–1840*, 1958, 161–7.]

TREACHER, JOHN (*c.* 1735–1802), a carpenter of Sonning on Thames, was the founder of a firm of builders and surveyors who specialized in work connected with the river. He held the post of surveyor to the Thames Commissioners from 1787 until his death, when his son John Treacher, junior, succeeded to the post. The latter died in about 1835, in which year his son, George Treacher, took over the surveyorship. George died in 1862 at the age of 71, just before the Commissioners were superseded by the Thames Conservancy Board (1866). John Treacher, senior, was responsible for the building of the first pound-locks between 1770 and 1773. Several new locks were constructed by his son in the 1820s, and it was John Treacher, junior, who designed the charming 'Pound Houses' or lock-keeper's cottages, which in many cases still remain. His designs for those at CLIFTON HAMPDEN, SANDFORD, BOULTERS, RAY MILL, ST. JOHN'S BRIDGE, COOKHAM, CLEEVE and MARLOW are preserved in the Treacher Collection in Reading Public Library. John Treacher the younger also held the post of Surveyor of Bridges to the county of Berkshire, and was concerned in the repair or construction of a number of small bridges in that county. In 1810–13 he and his son rebuilt the principal arches of WALLINGFORD BRIDGE, reducing their number from four to three and widening the roadway. They also carried out extensive repairs to CAVERSHAM BRIDGE in 1815 under the direction of W. C. Mylne. The Treacher family papers, covering the period 1773–1862, and containing many plans and drawings connected with the Thames navigation, were bequeathed to the Reading Public Library by Llewellyn, grandson of George Treacher. Some account of the family will be found in F. S. Thacker, *The Thames Highway: A History of the Locks and Weirs*, 1920, 249–50.

TRENDALL, EDWARD W—, practised from various London addresses, exhibiting at the Royal Academy from 1816 to 1836 and at the Society of British Artists in 1827 and 1831. His exhibits included a 'Design for a Public Library and Baths proposed to be built on the East Cliff, Brighton' (1830), and a 'Design for a residence about to be erected on the coast of Normandy' (1836). The only building actually known to have been erected to his designs is the GRAND-STAND on EPSOM RACE-COURSE, 1829–30 [Brayley, *Topographical History of Surrey* iv, 370].

Trendall published several books of designs under the following titles: *Original Designs for Cottages and Villas, in the Grecian, Gothic and Italian styles of Architecture*, 1831; *Examples for*

Interior Finishings, consisting of 24 plates of folding doors, staircases, cornices, french windows, chimney-pieces, etc., 1833; *Examples for Roofs for Stables, Cottages, Schools, etc.*, 1843; *Examples for Exterior and Interior Finishings*, 1848; and *Monuments, Cenotaphs, Tombs, and Tablets*, 1850, 1858.

TREVOR, ROBERT HAMPDEN, 1ST VISCOUNT HAMPDEN and 4TH BARON TREVOR, (1706–1783), was the third son of Thomas, Lord Trevor of Bromham. He was educated at Queen's College, Oxford, and became a Fellow of All Souls in 1725. In 1734 he was appointed secretary to the British legation at the Hague, and rose to be minister plenipotentiary before his recall in 1746. From 1759 to 1765 he was joint postmaster-general. In 1754, on succeeding to the Hampden estates at Great Hampden in Buckinghamshire, he took the additonal name of Hampden, and in 1764 he succeeded his elder brother as Lord Trevor and owner of Bromham in Bedfordshire. He died at Bromham on 22 August 1783 [*D.N.B.*].

Treviour was a man of scholarly tastes whose collection of drawings and prints was regarded as 'one of the choicest in England', He was the author of Latin poems entitled *Britannia, Lathmon* and *Villa Bromhamensis*, and a number of surviving drawings show that he was an amateur architect of some ability. One is a proposal for the Radcliffe Library in Oxford based on the Roman Pantheon [*The Building Accounts of the Radcliffe Camera*, ed. S. G. Gillam, Oxford Historical Soc. 1958, pl. 17]. Others in the R.I.B.A. Collection include an exchange, a house, an obelisk (reproduced by A. Rowan, *Garden Buildings*, 1968, 20), a building in Spring Gardens, London, apparently intended for a society, and an ingenious design for Glynde Church, Sussex (evidently made for his brother, Richard Trevor, Bishop of Durham and owner of Glynde), in the form of interlocking hexagons. Drawings attributable to him among the Hampden papers in the Buckinghamshire Record Office include a design for a Gothic alcove, and for a rotunda for Lord Foley. At West Wycombe Park there is a 'Plan of an Hospitable Nobleman's Kitchen' in Trevor's hand. So far no building erected to his designs has been identified, though he was probably responsible for alterations to Hampden House in the 1750s.

TROLLOPE, or TROLLAP, ROBERT (– 1686), is said to have been 'descended from a line of stone-masons'. He is first found at York, where in 1647, as 'Robert Trollop, freemason', he obtained the freedom of the city by redemption. When, in 1655, the Corporation of Newcastle-on-Tyne decided to build a new Exchange and Guildhall, a committee was appointed for the

purpose, and in May of that year received instructions to 'confer further with the surveyor that came from Yorke about it'. That this surveyor was Trollope is clear from a subsequent minute resolving 'to write to Mr. Trolop to bee surveyor and to intreate him to come, for that the Towne is desireous that the worke may be forthwith taken in hand'. In October the committee reported that 'they conceive that the first modell presented in pastboard is the fittest Modell to be observed', and a contract was made by which Trollope agreed to erect the building for £2000 and to perform the work 'according to the best Authors now in English'. Various modifications were, however, made to the design before it was completed in 1660 at considerably greater cost. The new Exchange was described by Celia Fiennes in 1698 as 'a lofty good building of stone, very uniforme on all sides with stone pillars in the fronts both to the streete and market place and to the water-side'. It was in fact the first building of importance in Newcastle to be built in a classical style. The principal front was rebuilt by Messrs. Newton and Stevenson in 1791–3, and the south front was 'new fronted in a corresponding style' in 1809. [Newcastle Corporation Archives, Common Council Book 1649–59, pp. 260 *et seq.*, contract (18/1/50); E. Mackenzie, *History of Newcastle* i, 1827, 215–16.]

On 25 September 1657 Trollope was admitted a freeman of Newcastle, and he subsequently established himself at Redheugh, in the parish of Gateshead on the other side of the Tyne. In 1663 he undertook to complete the building of CHRISTCHURCH, TYNEMOUTH, to raise and ceil the roof, and to plaster the walls. The church had been begun in 1658 and was eventually consecrated in July 1668. It was reconstructed in 1792 [*History of Northumberland* viii, 1907, 359]. In 1667 Trollope contracted to build CAPHEATON HALL, NORTHUMBERLAND, for Sir John Swinburne, and according to John Hodgson he also designed NETHER WITTON HALL, NORTHUMBERLAND, built in 1672 by Sir John's son-in-law Nicholas Thornton [J. Hodgson, *History of Northumberland* ii (1), 1827, 220–1 (where the Capheaton contract is printed in full), 323] (*C. Life*, 12 Aug. 1965, article on Capheaton). These buildings establish Trollope as the author of a vigorous and individual style of vernacular baroque, 'totally free of academic inhibitions', but of considerable charm. Other Northumbrian buildings in a similar style which may have been designed by Trollope are BOCKENFIELD MANOR HOUSE, nr. Morpeth, *c.* 1670 (*History of Northumberland* vii, 364); the south front of CALLALY CASTLE, dated 1676 (*C. Life*, 12–19 Feb. 1959); and alterations to WIDDRINGTON CASTLE (dem. *c.* 1775) as shown in an engraving by S. & N. Buck. His only other documented works appear, however, to be a small fort built on LINDISFARNE ISLAND in 1675, of which there is a plan in the William Salt Library at Stafford (Dartmouth Collection D 1778/ III 03) [J. Raine, *North Durham*, 1852, 151; *Proc. Soc. Antiquaries of Newcastle on Tyne*, 3rd ser., ii, 1907, 42–4; Peter Orde, *Lindisfarne Castle*, National Trust Guide, 1975], and the font (a gadrooned bowl standing on a twisted column) which he made for SOUTH SHIELDS CHURCH, CO. DURHAM, in the same year [G. B. Hobson, *The Borough of South Shields*, 1903, 241].

In September 1671 Robert Trollop and his son Henry gave evidence on behalf of the Bishop of Carlisle in his suit against Archbishop Sterne of York for the cost of dilapidations at ROSE CASTLE, CUMBERLAND. Their submission was accompanied by 'a platforme for a new building under their hands', but this was never built [J. Wilson, *Rose Castle*, 1912, 239]. In the same year Robert played an important part in obtaining from the Bishop of Durham a charter incorporating the freemasons, carvers, stone-cutters, sculptors, brickmakers, tilers, bricklayers and other building craftsmen of Gateshead. He died in 1686, and was buried on 11 December in Gateshead Churchyard, where he is supposed to have erected the square mausoleum afterwards used by the Green family, by whom it was repaired in 1855–60. No trace now remains of the statue and doggerel inscription (beginning 'Here lies Robert Trollop/who made yon stones roll up') which are said to have formed part of the monument, but of whose existence there appears to be no authentic record.

[R. Surtees, *History of Durham* ii, 1820, 112 n. (d), 120; E. Mackenzie, *History of Newcastle* ii, 1827, 752; *Freemen of York* ii (Surtees Soc. 1899), 106, 136; *Notes and Queries*, 6th ser., xi, 1885, 14; Bruce Allsopp & Ursula Clark, *Historic Architecture of Northumberland*, 1970, 54, 58–9.]

TROTMAN, EBENEZER (*c.* 1810–1865), was the son of a Baptist minister at Tewkesbury. He was educated at Mill Hill School and was subsequently articled to William Wallen. He entered the office of William Tite as a junior clerk and eventually became his principal assistant. All his working life was spent in Tite's office, and his only independent work appears to have been HOLY TRINITY CHURCH, TEWKESBURY, 1837, Gothic [*Tewkesbury Yearly Register* i, 1840, 244, 283]. He was the author of two well-written articles, one on Tudor architecture in Loudon's *Encyclopaedia of Cottage, Farm and Villa Architecture* (1833), the other on 'the Extent to which the elementary forms of Classic Architecture are fixed or arbitrary' in the first volume of Loudon's *Architectural Magazine* (1834). Failing health obliged him to give up his post in Tite's office, and he died at his house in Park Village East on 1 January 1865, in his 56th year [*Builder* xxiii, 1865, 31].

TROUGHT, JOSEPH, exhibited architectural designs at the Free Society of Artists between 1765 and 1769. They included a 'Plan, elevation, and section for an assembly room intended to be built in Chelsea' (1766), a 'Design for a gentleman's villa, intended to be built in the North Riding of Yorkshire' (1767), and a 'Design calculated for a military gentleman, with regular bastions, in the angles of a square' (1767). A house of the latter description was actually built at Sidcup, Kent, by an officer of the Royal Engineers in 1743: it now forms the nucleus of the Council Offices. Another, known as 'The Fort', was built on Hampton Common by a military gentleman, but was burned down in 1845 [Brayley, *Surrey* iv, 438].

TRUBSHAW, CHARLES (–1851), was probably one of the sons of James Trubshaw (d. 1808). He practised at Newcastle-under-Lyme and held the post of County Surveyor at the time of his death in 1851 [W. White, *History, Gazeteer and Directory of Staffordshire*, 1851, 311]. He must have been the 'C. Trubshaw' who was joint architect with James Trubshaw of HOLY TRINITY, NORTHWOOD, nr. STOKE-ON-TRENT, STAFFS., 1847–9 [I.C.B.S.], ST. JAMES'S CHURCH, CONGLETON, CHESHIRE, 1847–9, dem. 1904 [I.C.B.S.], and ST. PETER'S CHURCH, MACCLESFIELD, CHESHIRE, 1849 [Port, 140].

TRUBSHAW, CHARLES COPE (1715–1772), born at Haywood on 13 September 1715, was the eldest and only surviving son of Richard Trubshaw. He was sent to London to learn carving under Peter Scheemakers, and afterwards carried on an extensive business as a sculptor and master mason. His ledgers (now lost) showed that chimney-pieces and monumental sculpture were carved in his yard at Haywood from marble supplied by an agent at Westminster. He executed monuments to various persons, including Christopher Horton (d. 1764) in Croxall Church, Staffs., the husband of Mrs. Talbot of Hoar Cross (1767), and a Mr. Lucas (1770). He made chimney-pieces for Keele Hall, Himley Hall, Tixall Hall, Hoar Cross (Mr. Talbot), and the Raven Inn at Shrewsbury: and he did carving of a decorative character for Sir Lynch Cotton, Madame Boswell (1759) and others, including Mr. Corbett of Sundorn Hall, Salop., whom he supplied with a marble sideboard. He continued the works at TIXALL HALL begun by his father, and built BELLAMOUR HOUSE, nr. RUGELEY; dem. *c.* 1920. He also 'built, or added to, and altered, Acton Chapel [*i.e.* Acton Church, Cheshire], Newborough Chapel (near Lord Bagot's), Darfold Chapel, Gayton Church, Trentham Church, Ellenhall, Sidway Hall, and others'. He rebuilt STONE CHURCH to the designs of William Robin-

THE TRUBSHAW FAMILY

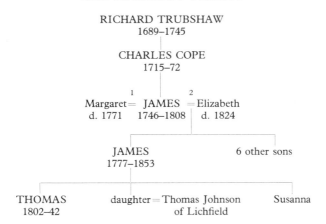

RICHARD TRUBSHAW
1689–1745

CHARLES COPE
1715–72

Margaret = JAMES = Elizabeth
d. 1771   1746–1808   d. 1824
(1)   (2)

JAMES   6 other sons
1777–1853

THOMAS   daughter = Thomas Johnson   Susanna
1802–42   of Lichfield

son of the Board of Works in 1754–8, and in 1764 he erected the TEMPLE OF THE WINDS at SHUGBOROUGH, STAFFS., to the designs of James Stuart. Miss Trubshaw gives the following list of persons for whom he executed work at various times:

Hon. Thos. Anson (of Shugborough)
Hon. J. Barry, Esq.
Sir Thos. Broughton
Hon. Mr. Clifford
Sir Brian Broughton Delves
Lord Kilmorey
Parsonage at Swynnerton, 1760
Hon. Mrs. Talbot (of Hoar Cross)
Geo. Venables Vernon
Geo. Adams
Rev. Mr. Bagot
Sir Wm. Bagot (of Blithfield)
Visct. Chetwynd (of Ingestre)
Thos. Fitzherbert (of Swynnerton)
Sir Ed. Littleton (of Teddesley)
Mainwaring, Esq., Whitmore
Trentham Bridge, 1766
Mr. Talbot – Hoarcross
Mr. Whitby

Trubshaw died at Haywood on 22 December 1772, at the age of 56, and is commemorated by a tablet in Colwich Church, of which he was a warden. His pocket-book for the years 1754–5 is in the National Library of Wales (MS. 16635 B). He left a son James (1746–1808), who carried on the family business. [Susanna Trubshaw, *Family Records*, 1876; 'Stafforda', *Guide and History of Haywood*, 1924, and *Supplement*, 1930.]

TRUBSHAW, JAMES (1746–1808), the son and successor of Charles Cope Trubshaw, was appointed County Surveyor of Staffordshire in January 1793, at a salary of £52 12s. He was 're-quired to attend two days a week to the work

under hand, and also to deliver a report of necessary repairs wanting at every Quarter Sessions'. He lived at first at Mount Pleasant, now Colwich Priory, but getting into difficulties, sold it in 1791 and moved to a smaller house in Haywood village. In 1788 he carried out some alterations to SANDON HALL for Lord Harrowby, but little else is known of his activities as a builder and architect. He died on 13 April 1808, aged 61, leaving seven sons, of whom James, his successor, is noticed below.

TRUBSHAW, JAMES (1777–1853), born on 13 February 1777, was the son of James Trubshaw of Haywood (d. 1808) by his second wife Elizabeth. He attended a school at Rugeley and learned the mason's trade in his father's yard. At the age of 16 he went to London to seek employment through his father's friend, Richard Westmacott (father of Sir Richard). Westmacott sent him to Fonthill Abbey, then in course of erection for William Beckford, and afterwards to Buckingham Palace and Windsor Castle. He married in 1800 and settled in Haywood, but, failing to prosper, set up business on his own at Stone with very slender resources. He was fortunate enough to attract the attention of Mrs. Sneyd, then about to build Ashcombe Hall. 'Struck by his integrity and business-like habits', she insisted on employing him as builder, despite his lack of capital, and helped by timely advances of money. He afterwards said that he 'never built a better house than this, his first formidable undertaking'. On his father's death in 1808, he returned to Haywood to take charge of the family business, which he managed with considerable success. Among the buildings which he erected were Ilam Hall, nr. Ashbourne, to the designs of John Shaw, Weston House, Warwicks., to those of Edward Blore, and Trentham Park, Staffs., to those of Charles Barry. Although he designed several churches and other buildings Trubshaw regarded himself primarily as a builder and civil engineer, and 'as far as possible avoided that which he considered as interfereing with the professional Architect'. As a builder his most celebrated achievement was the construction of the Grosvenor Bridge at Chester to the designs of Thomas Harrison. This consisted of a single arch of 200 feet span, and competent engineers, Telford included, were doubtful whether it could be built. Harrison died in 1829, but the bridge was successfully completed by Trubshaw in 1833 under the direction of Jesse Hartley, C.E. Models of the bridge, showing the method of construction employed, were afterwards presented by Trubshaw to the Institution of Civil Engineers, of which he became a member in 1827. He also built the Exeter Bridge over the R. Derwent at Derby (opened in Oct. 1850), a work of great difficulty owing to sudden floods and quicksands. Another of Trubshaw's engineering achievements was to restore the tower of Wybunbury Church, in Cheshire, to the perpendicular, from which it had declined more than 5 feet. He accomplished this by means of specially constructed gouges, with which he removed the soil from beneath the higher side (see *Architectural Mag.* i, 1834, 209, for an account of the operation). He was for some time engineer to the Trent and Mersey Canal Company, whose works he directed with characteristic competence.

Trubshaw's success as a practical engineer was remarkable in view of his very limited education. He 'seemed to be gifted with an instinctive perception of all great mechanical principles', and a combination of intelligence, integrity and hard work enabled him to surmount problems that to others seemed insuperable. As an architect he does not appear to have designed anything remarkable, his Gothic churches being typical products of their time.

Like his great-grandfather Richard, Trubshaw was a man of exceptional stature and strength. His daughter records that when he was building Ilam Hall he was invited to run against the Watts Russells' family tutor, who was held in repute for swiftness of foot. Trubshaw 'eyeing his man and knowing his own powers, offered to compete with Chantrey[1] on his back, and came off victorious'. He died on 28 October 1853, aged 76, and was buried in Colwich Churchyard. There is a monument to his memory in the church. A posthumous bust was exhibited at the Royal Academy by E. W. Wyon in 1857. Trubshaw had three sons and three daughters. The eldest son, Thomas (1802–42), is noticed below. One of the daughters

married Thomas Johnson (1794–1865), the Lichfield architect, with whom her father appears to have been for a time in partnership.[1] Another daughter, Susanna, who died unmarried, was the author of a volume of *Poems* (1863) and of the *Family Records* (1876) upon which this account of her father is largely based. Several drawings by Trubshaw are in the R.I.B.A. Collection.

[Susanna Trubshaw, *Family Records*, 1876; obituaries in *Gent's Mag.* 1854 (i), 97–100, and *Minutes of Proceedings of the Institution of Civil Engineers* xiv, 1854–5, 142–6; *D.N.B.*; 'Stafforda', *Guide and History of Haywood*, 1924.]

ASHCOMBE PARK, nr. LEEK, STAFFS., for Mrs. Sneyd, *c.* 1808–10 [S. Trubshaw, *Family Records*, 17] (F. O. Morris, *Picturesque Views of Seats* iv, 75). It is not certain that Trubshaw designed as well as built this house.

SWYNNERTON HALL, STAFFS., alterations for Thomas Fitzherbert, including new staircase and columnar screen in hall, *c.* 1810 ['Stafforda', *Haywood*, 86].

KINGLSEY CHURCH, STAFFS., rebuilt (retaining old tower), 1821, Gothic [I.C.B.S.].

WOLSELEY HALL, STAFFS., reconstructed for Sir Charles Wolseley, Bart., 1821, Tudor Gothic; dem. *c.* 1965 ['Stafforda', *Haywood*, 45; P. W. Montague-Smith, letter in *C. Life*, 15 Sept. 1966, 641–2] (J. P. Neale, *Views of Seats* iv, 1821).

WALKERINGHAM VICARAGE, NOTTS., 1823 [Borthwick Institute, York, MGA 1823/5].

CHAPEL CHORLTON CHURCH, STAFFS., rebuilt 1826–7 on the basis of a plan by Trubshaw that was considerably modified in execution, Gothic [I.C.B.S.].

UTTOXETER CHURCH, STAFFS., rebuilt in conjunction with Thomas Johnson (retaining old tower), 1828, Gothic [I.C.B.S.].

GREAT WOLFORD CHURCH, WARWICKS., rebuilt 1833–5, Gothic [I.C.B.S.].

WYBUNBURY CHURCH, CHESHIRE, rebuilt church and restored tower to perpendicular, 1833–4; rebuilt (except tower) 1893 [I.C.B.S.; *Architectural Mag.* i, 1834, 209].

WILLINGTON BRIDGE, DERBYSHIRE (R. Trent), 1839–40 [*Companion to the Almanac*, 1840, 249].

ASTON CHURCH, nr. STONE, STAFFS., 1846; spire added 1870 [*Staffordshire Advertiser*, 18 July 1846].

NORTHWOOD, nr. STOKE-ON-TRENT, STAFFS., HOLY TRINITY CHURCH, 1847–9, Gothic, in collaboration with Charles Trubshaw [I.C.B.S.].

---

[1] The sculptor, who was then at work on the Pike-Watts monument in Ilam Church.

[1] The I.C.B.S. certificate for St. Mary's Church, Uttoxeter (1828), is signed by 'James Trubshaw and Thomas Johnson, surveyors', and Messrs. Trubshaw & Johnson were the contractors for Barry's Royal Manchester Institution in 1829 [Whiffen, *The Architecture of Sir Charles Barry in Manchester*, 1950, 9].

CONGLETON, CHESHIRE, ST. JAMES'S CHURCH, 1847–9, Gothic; dem. 1904, in collaboration with Charles Trubshaw [I.C.B.S.].

MACCLESFIELD, CHESHIRE, ST. PETER'S CHURCH, 1849, Gothic, in collaboration with Charles Trubshaw [Port, 140].

TRUBSHAW, RICHARD (1689–1745), of Haywood, Staffs., was a mason and quarry-owner who established a considerable business as a master builder in the West Midlands in the early eighteenth century. He came of a family of Staffordshire masons,[1] but spent some time in Oxford as a young man, and may perhaps have been employed in the building of Blenheim Palace, for he records that it was at Woodstock that he 'kept company' with his future wife, whom he married in Merton College Chapel on 6 January 1714. Like other members of his family, Trubshaw was a man of fine physique and great strength. His fame as a wrestler is celebrated in a contemporary ballad which relates how he defeated Richard Allen, or Green, of Hucknall, who had 'reign'd Champion of Nottinghamshire, and the Neighbouring Counties for twenty years at least', until he was thrown by Trubshaw in a wrestling-match at Repton. Trubshaw's account-books, which remained until the 1940s in the possession of his descendants, showed that while in Oxford he bought books on architecture, including *Vitruvius Britannicus*. These ledgers (now lost) contained architectural sketches as well as details of Trubshaw's building activities. Some extracts from them were printed by Susanna Trubshaw in her *Family Records* (1876), and they were also made use of by 'Stafforda' (Miss Whitehouse) in writing her *Guide and History of Haywood* (1924) and *Supplement* thereto (1930). It is from these works that the following imperfect list of Trubshaw's works is (unless otherwise stated) taken. In the absence of the original accounts it is difficult in many cases to determine the exact nature of Trubshaw's various commissions, and still more to assess his ability as an architectural designer. However, the demolished Emral Hall, with a reversed Borrominesque pediment over the main doorway, establishes its architect as the author of a vernacular baroque style comparable to that of the Bastards of Blandford, and both family connections and architectural resemblances suggest that Trubshaw was also the designer of Pickhill House, Denbighshire, built by John Puleston c. 1720–30.

[1] The name of 'Edward Trubshaw, Mason, 1655' is carved on the gable of the south-east chapel of Sandon Church, Staffs., and that of 'Thomas Trubshaw' appears on the tower of Armitage Church in the same county, which is dated 1632 [Shaw, *History of Staffordshire* i, 210].

Emral and Pickhill both share distinctive features with Hilton Hall, Staffs. (c. 1720–30), the seat of the Vernon family, for whom Trubshaw is known to have worked, both at Sudbury in 1734 and at Hilton itself in 1743. A case can therefore be made for attributing to Trubshaw an interesting group of provincial baroque houses, but without further evidence in the form of drawings or documents this cannot be regarded as more than tentative.

Trubshaw died at Haywood on 28 April 1745, aged 56, and is commemorated by a tombstone in Colwich Churchyard. He left a son, Charles Trubshaw, to succeed to his business.

LICHFIELD, ST. MARY'S CHURCH: after the fall of part of the spire at Easter 1716, it was agreed that it should be taken down by Thomas Wilkinson, Richard Hollinghurst and Richard Trubshaw. Eventually the whole church was taken down and rebuilt between 1717 and 1721, probably to the designs of William Smith of Tettenhall (q.v.) [T. Harwood, *History of Lichfield*, 1806, 460; *Historical Colls. for Staffs*, 1942–3, p. xl].

TIXALL HALL, STAFFS., much work for the 4th Lord Aston from 1721 onwards, including the erection of a lodge (1721), the repair of the Elizabethan gatehouse, and the rebuilding of the east front (8 April 1729: 'Then began to pluck down the East front of Tixall'). The house was dem. c. 1925.

EMRAL HALL, FLINTS., work for Thomas Puleston in conjunction with Joseph Evans, including addition of wings, 1724–6, and refronting of central block, 1727; damaged by fire 1904, dem. 1936 [National Library of Wales, Puleston papers, no. 776] (*C. Life*, 19 Feb. 1910).

WOLSELEY BRIDGE, STAFFS., repaired or rebuilt 1725; destroyed by a flood 1795.

ASTON HOUSE, nr. STONE, STAFFS., work for Sir Edward Simeon, Bart., 1725; dem. c. 1800. A survey plan of this house in Trubshaw's hand is in the Bodleian Library (MS. d.d. Weld a.1).

GRENDON HALL, WARWICKS., work for Walter Chetwynd, 1725; rebuilt c. 1825; dem. 1932.

BANGOR ISCOED CHURCH, FLINTS., rebuilt tower and south side of church, 1726.

COLWICH CHURCH, STAFFS., repairs and alterations, 1730–3.

KEELE HALL, STAFFS., works for Ralph Sneyd, 1731.

SWYNNERTON, STAFFS., work (perhaps to dower house) for Mrs. Fitzherbert, 1731.

SUDBURY HALL, DERBYSHIRE, work for George Vernon, 1734.

WORTHENBURY CHURCH, FLINTS., 1736–9 [T. H. G. Puleston, *The Story of a Quiet Country Parish*, c. 1895, 174–7].

STAFFORD, work for 'Lord Falconbridge' at his house, 1737.

NORTON-IN-THE-MOORS CHURCH, STAFFS., rebuilt 1737–8; enlarged 1914.

BLITHFIELD HOUSE, STAFFS., work for Sir Walter Bagot, Bart., 1738. A survey plan of the house in Trubshaw's hand is reproduced in *C. Life*, 4 Nov. 1954, fig. 9.

HAUNCH HALL, nr. LICHFIELD, STAFFS., work for 'Esqr. Parkhurst', 1739.

BASWICH CHURCH, STAFFS., rebuilt 1739–40 by Richard Trubshaw and Richard Jackson, masons [William Salt Library, Stafford, Salt MS. 436, pp. 167–8].

MARCHINGTON CHURCH, STAFFS., rebuilt 1742; altered 1903–7 [variant design by Trubshaw in William Salt Library, Stafford, Staffordshire Views, vii, f. 63ᵛ].

Work for Sir Theophilus Biddulph, Bart., presumably at BIRDINGBURY HALL, WARWICKS., 1742.

Work for 'Esqr. Congreve', presumably at STRETTON HALL, STAFFS., 1742.

Work for 'Esqr. Arblaster', presumably at LYSWAYES HALL, LONGDON, STAFFS., 1742.

STAFFORD, ST. CHAD'S CHURCH, repairs including casing exterior in brick, 1743; since restored [William Salt Library, Stafford, Hickin papers 319/40].

HILTON HALL, STAFFS., work for Henry Vernon, 1743.

TRUBSHAW, THOMAS (1802–1842), born on 4 April 1802, was the eldest son of James Trubshaw (d. 1853). His early death on 7 June 1842 cut short a successful practice as an architect and landscape-gardener. Some of his churches – notably Knightly and Salt – display a perverse originality criticized by Professor Pevsner in the Staffordshire volume of his 'Buildings of England'. He was elected a Fellow of the Society of Antiquaries in 1836 [S. Trubshaw, *Family Records*, 1876, 25; *Architectural Mag.* i, 1834, 47].

HILDERSTONE CHURCH, STAFFS., 1827–9, Gothic ['Thomas Trubshaw Architect, 1829' carved on a corbel on south side of nave].

WESTON-ON-TRENT CHURCH, STAFFS., rebuilt upper part of tower and spire, 1830 [A. Scrivener, 'Weston-upon-Trent Church', *Trans. North Staffs. Field Club* xxxix, 1905, 150].

HEATH HOUSE, TEAN, STAFFS., orangery and layout of flower-garden for John Philips, 1830–1 [*Architectural Mag.* i, 1834, 47, but the drawings for the garden are reported to be signed by his father James Trubshaw] (*C. Life*, 10 Jan. 1963).

MANLEY HALL, nr. LICHFIELD, STAFFS., for J. S.

Manley, 1831–6, Tudor style[1] [B. Burke, *Visitation of Seats and Arms*, 2nd ser., ii, 1855, 70, with illustration].

KEELE HALL, STAFFS., three lodges for Ralph Sneyd, 1832 [steward's letters at Keele University, *ex inf.* Mr. Keith Goodway].

BIDDULPH CHURCH, STAFFS., largely rebuilt 1833, Gothic [I.C.B.S.].

BRERETON CHURCH, STAFFS., 1837, Gothic; enlarged 1877–8 [I.C.B.S.].

MORETON CHURCH, STAFFS., 1837–8, neo-Norman [I.C.B.S.].

STAFFORD WORKHOUSE (Fernleigh Hospital), 1837–8 [*N. Staffs. Jnl. of Field Studies* ii, 1962, 97].

UTTOXETER UNION WORKHOUSE, STAFFS., 1838–9, Tudor style.

BAGOTS PARK, STAFFS., woodman's lodge for the 2nd Lord Bagot, 1839 [S. Trubshaw, *Family Records*, 25; *Historical Collections for Staffs: Staffordshire Views*, 1942–3, 24; B.M., Add. MS. 36385, f. 152].

SANDON CHURCH, STAFFS., repaired nave and aisles, 1839 ['TRUBSHAW F.S.A. 1839' carved on west gable of nave; F. E. Coplestone, *Sandon Church Restorations*, 1929].

KNIGHTLEY CHURCH, STAFFS., 1840–1, Gothic [B.M., Add. MS. 36386, f. 146].

SALT CHURCH, STAFFS., 1840–2, Gothic [S. Trubshaw, *Family Records*, 25].

WALTON CHURCH, nr. BASWICH, STAFFS., 1842, Gothic; the stone spire designed by Trubshaw was destroyed by lightning in 1845 and replaced by a wooden spire, of different design [B.M., Add. MS. 36388, ff. 81–3].

GREAT HAYWOOD, STAFFS., ST. STEPHEN'S CHAPEL, c. 1842–5, designed by Trubshaw before his death but altered in execution and subsequently enlarged by H. I. Stevens [S. Trubshaw, *Family Records*, 25; G.R.].

TUCK, WILLIAM, of King's Lynn, was a carpenter by trade. He was probably the William Tuck of Denver, Norfolk, who in 1741 was apprenticed to John Green of West Dereham, carpenter [P.R.O., Apprenticeship Registers]. In 1766–8 the NEW ASSEMBLY ROOMS in the rear of the Guildhall at KING'S LYNN were erected in accordance with plans produced by himself and Thomas King, a bricklayer. He was Town Chamberlain in 1784, and on 17 July it was agreed that the GAOL should be rebuilt of white brick agreeable to his plans [Corporation Minute Books, ff. 118ᵛ, 153, 394ᵛ]. This building, which stands in the market-place opposite St. Margaret's Church, is now used as a police-station.

---

[1] Burke says that 'The interior of the mansion was arranged on Mr. Manley's own plan, and the external architecture was designed by Mr. Thomas Trubshaw, architect, of Great Haywood'.

It has a central feature ornamented with an iron grille and festooned shackles evidently derived from Dance's Newgate Prison in London.

TULLOCH, JOHN, was a builder-architect of Poole in Dorset (though twice in the 1830s described as of the neighbouring town of Wimborne). He designed several local churches in a spiritless Gothic style.

PARKSTONE CHURCH, DORSET, 1833–5, Gothic; rebuilt 1876–1892 [I.C.B.S., East Boldre file] (Sydenham, *History of Poole*, 1839, 461).

LYTCHETT MINSTER CHURCH, DORSET, rebuilt 1833–4, except tower; Gothic [*British Magazine*, Sept. 1833; I.C.B.S.].

HOLT CHURCH, DORSET, 1834, Gothic; chancel 1889 [I.C.B.S.].

BLANDFORD CHURCH, DORSET, inserted galleries in nave, 1836–7; removed 1970 [I.C.B.S.].

POOLE, DORSET, POOLE UNION WORKHOUSE (now St. Mary's Hospital), 1838–9 [R.C.H.M., *Dorset* ii (2), 205–6].

EAST BOLDRE CHURCH, HANTS., 1839, Gothic; chancel 1891 [I.C.B.S.].

BOURNEMOUTH, HANTS., ST. PETER'S CHURCH, 1841–3, Gothic; south aisle added 1851, remainder rebuilt 1854–79 [E. W. Leachman, *St. Peter's Bournemouth*, Bournemouth 1915, 9].

PENNINGTON CHURCH, HANTS., 1843, Gothic; rebuilt *c.* 1865 [I.C.B.S.].

TULLY, GEORGE (–1770), was a carpenter and surveyor at Bristol. A native of Surrey, he was apprenticed at Bristol, first to John Stibbs, a carpenter, and then, on the latter's death, to John Price. Having completed his apprenticeship he was admitted a free burgess of Bristol on 17 May 1715. Soon after 1720 he laid out DOWRY SQUARE and CHAPEL ROW on ground leased to him jointly with Thomas Oldfield. KING SQUARE, laid out shortly before 1740, was probably planned by Tully, who built houses there, one for his own occupation and others for letting. His last important development was the laying out of BRUNSWICK SQUARE and the adjoining streets in 1766. Tully designed DOWRY CHAPEL, 1746 (dem.), the FRIENDS' MEETING HOUSE in THE FRIARS, 1747–9, and probably WESLEY'S CHAPEL in BROADMEAD, as enlarged in 1748. In 1741 he was among those who were invited to submit designs for the Bristol Exchange, but those of John Wood were eventually adopted. He may have been the author of a design for a Palladian country house in the collection of Mr. W. S. Lewis at Farmington, Connecticut, which is signed with the initials GT and the date [17]40. Tully died in 1770, leaving considerable property in Bristol. His son William, a Quaker, had predeceased him in 1763. Little is known about William Tully except that he 'delivered several ingenious plans for rebuilding

Bristol Bridge' and was regarded by the builder-architect John Wallis as one 'whose Knowledge and Experience exceed that of all Mankind'. [W. Ison, *The Georgian Buildings of Bristol*, 1952, 47–9.]

TUNNICLIFFE, RALPH (*c.* 1688–1736), of Dalton, nr. Rotherham, is described as 'architect' in his will, and as 'gentleman' on his memorial brass in Rotherham Church. At the time of his death he was employed at WENTWORTH WOODHOUSE, YORKS. (W.R.), where he appears to have preceded Henry Flitcroft as the 1st Marquess of Rockingham's architect. An engraving of the east front with the inscription 'R. Tunnicliff, Architectus' is *prima facie* evidence that the exterior of the mansion at least was designed by him before Flitcroft came on the scene, for it is dedicated to Rockingham as 'Baron Malton', the title by which he was known from 1728 to 1734, and there is no evidence of Flitcroft's presence at Wentworth Woodhouse before 1736. Further investigation into the respective roles of Tunnicliffe and Flitcroft at Wentworth Woodhouse is, however, needed. [H. A. Tipping in *C. Life*, 27 Sept. 1924; A. Booth, 'The Architects of Wentworth Castle and Wentworth Woodhouse', *R.I.B.A. Jnl.*, 25 Nov. 1933; Hist. MSS. Comm., *Carlisle*, 174; J. D. Potts, *Platt of Rotherham*, Sheffield 1959, 3.]

Some at least of the following references presumably relate to the same person. In 1716 'Mr. Tunicliff' was paid £12 in part for taking down the tower of ST. MARY'S CHURCH, LICHFIELD [MS. churchwardens' accounts, 1683–1726]. In 1720–1 the steeple of ST. PAUL'S CHURCH, SHEFFIELD, was begun by 'Mr. Tunnicliffe' and John Platt, but left unfinished [J. D. Potts, *Platt of Rotherham*, Sheffield 1959, 3]. In 1722 'Mr. Tunnicliffe' was paid £3 3s. by the churchwardens of ALL SAINTS CHURCH, DERBY, 'for drawing a draught of the church and other expenses' [MS. churchwardens' accounts, *ex inf.* Mr. Edward Saunders]. And in 1723 'Mr. Tuniclif' was paid 10s. 6d. for making a 'draft' for steps at CALKE ABBEY, DERBYSHIRE [accounts at Calke Abbey].

The will of 'Ralph Tunnicliffe of Dalton in the County of York Architect', dated 14 April 1736, was proved in July of the same year. He left a wife and three children, Ralph, Mary and Dorothy [Borthwick Institute, York, York Prerogative Wills, July 1736]. The inscription on the brass in Rotherham Church is given by Hunter, *South Yorkshire* ii, 1831, 21.

TURNBULL, ADAM OGILVIE (–*c.* 1834), was a builder-architect of Edinburgh, where he was responsible for designing and building SAXE COBURG PLACE and SAXE COBURG (formerly WEST CLAREMONT) STREET for James Rose's Trustees, *c.* 1825–30 [Edinburgh Sasines].

TURNER, JOHN, was paid 30 guineas in 1739 as a gratuity 'for his care and trouble in surveying and directing the work of the new Town Hall' at Portsmouth, Hants. (dem. 1837) [R. East, *Extracts from the Portsmouth Records*, 1891, 808]. He is said to have assisted in the construction of the NAVAL HOSPITAL at HASLAR in 1745.

TURNER, JOHN (–1827), was one of a family of architects from Whitchurch in Shropshire. When part of the Exchange at Chester was in danger of collapse in 1756, 'Mr. Turner, an architect, was sent for from Whitchurch, to survey it' [J. Hemingway, *History of Chester* ii, 1831, 17]. This Mr. Turner was probably the Samuel Turner, of Whitchurch, builder, who was employed at HAWARDEN CASTLE, FLINTS., in 1750–5, and received a gratuity of £87 'for his inspection and honest dealing' [John Cornforth in *C. Life*, 15 June 1967, 1519]. He was no doubt the father of the William Turner, also an architect of Whitchurch, who married in 1782 [Salop. Record Office, 665], and whose will, made in 1784, shows that he had a brother Samuel living at Whitchurch and a cousin Joseph (*q.v.*) who was in practice as an architect in Chester [Shrewsbury Public Library, 12332–3]. In the 1790s William Turner made a number of preliminary surveys for the Ellesmere Canal, and subsequently assisted Telford in its construction [L. T. C. Rolt, *Thomas Telford*, 1958, 40–6]. The only architectural work by him so far noted is OVER PEOVER CHURCH, CHESHIRE, a poor brick building which he designed and built in 1811 [R. Richards, *Old Cheshire Churches*, 1947, 271].

John Turner was probably the son either of the younger Samuel Turner or of the latter's brother William. In 1814 he was awarded the Silver Medal of the Society of Arts for a design for a church. He held the post of County Surveyor of Flintshire from 1815 until his death in 1827 [M. Bevan-Evans, *Guide to the Flintshire Record Office*, 1955, 23]. He was presumably the 'Mr. Turner' who was employed to furnish the choir of ST. ASAPH CATHEDRAL in 1809–10 [D. R. Thomas, *History of the Diocese of St. Asaph*, 1870, 207]. In 1816 the Dean and Chapter of BANGOR CATHEDRAL employed him to make estimates for the repair of their church and for the enlargement of the choir. Owing to a Chancery suit the work was not carried out until 1824–7, and then under the direction of a different architect, John Hall of Bangor [M. L. Clarke, 'Bangor Cathedral 1700–1828', *Caernarvonshire Historical Soc.'s Trans.* xiii, 1952, 32]. In 1819 John Turner carried out some alterations (since obliterated) to LLANDEGAI CHURCH, CARNARVONSHIRE [*North Wales Gazette*, 7 Jan. 1819]; in 1822 he made designs for altering or rebuilding BENNINGTON RECTORY, LINCS. [Lincolnshire Archives Office, MGA 115]; and shortly before his death

in 1827 he made plans for rebuilding PONTESBURY CHURCH, SALOP., which were completed in 1829 by Samuel Smith of Madeley [*V.C.H. Salop.* viii, 288]. This church is built in an 'Early English' style of unusual competence for its date.

TURNER, JOSEPH (*c.* 1729–1807), was the cousin of William Turner of Whitchurch and therefore probably the uncle of John Turner of the same place (*q.v.*). In the 1760s and early 1770s he was living at Hawarden in Flintshire, but in October 1774 he became a freeman of Chester, and evidently took up residence there, for he subsequently became an alderman of the city and was always referred to as 'Mr. Turner of Chester'. During the last quarter of the eighteenth century he was the leading architect practising in Cheshire and Flintshire, and appears to have been a competent designer in an orthodox late Georgian style. He died in 1807 at the age of 78, and was buried at Hawarden, where there is a tablet to his memory in the parish church. The inscription claims that 'the many Splendid & Publick Works in which he was concern'd in the Counties of Flint, Denbigh, and Chester, will be a lasting Memorial of his Taste and Abilities as an Architect'.

CHIRK CASTLE, DENBIGHSHIRE, internal alterations, including new staircase, for Richard Myddelton, 1766–73 [Steward's MS. commonplace book at Chirk Castle, recording the employment of 'Mr. Turner from Hawarden'; C. Hussey in *C. Life*, 12 Oct. 1951].

GARTHEWIN, DENBIGHSHIRE, remodelled for Robert Wynne, 1767–72 [C. Hussey in *C. Life*, 13 Feb. 1958].

ERDDIG HALL, DENBIGHSHIRE, employed by Philip Yorke, 1772–4, probably to implement designs for alterations by James Wyatt [letters and accounts at Erddig, *ex inf.* Mr. G. Jackson-Stops].

MOLD CHURCH, FLINTS., rebuilt west tower, 1773, Gothic [W. Bell-Jones, *The Story of the Parish Church of St. Mary Mold*, 7].

RUTHIN, DENBIGHSHIRE, THE GAOL, 1775 [inscribed 'J. TURNER, ARCHITECT'].

OULTON HALL, CHESHIRE, entrance lodge for Philip Egerton, *c.* 1775 [*Jnl. of the Chester Archaeological Soc.*, N.S. xxxvii, 1948–9, 216].

DYFFRYN ALED, DENBIGHSHIRE, main body of house for Mrs. Meyrick, 1777; wings and interior by J. Woolfe; dem. *c.* 1920 [W. Angus, *Select Views of Seats*, pl. xlviii, 1797].

CHESTER, THE BRIDGE GATE, 1782 [J. Hemingway, *History of Chester* i, 1839, 369].

FLINT, THE COUNTY GAOL, 1785; dem. *c.* 1965 [inscribed 'J. TURNER, ARCHITECT'].

PENTRE, nr. MOLD, FLINTS., bridge over R. Alyn, 1786 [M. Bevan-Evans, *Guide to the Flintshire Record Office*, 1955, 22].

TURNER, WILLIAM (1789–1862), of Oxford, well known as an artist in water-colours, is known to have designed one building: SHIPTON-ON-CHERWELL CHURCH, OXON., which was rebuilt in 1831–2 at the expense of his uncle, William Turner, who in 1804 had bought the Shipton estate together with the patronage of the living. Correspondence with the elder Turner in the I.C.B.S. records confirms the tradition that his nephew acted as architect for the church, which is competently designed in an early fourteenth-century style. A north-west view of the church by Turner is in the R.I.B.A. Collection. When Turner died in 1862 he was buried at Shipton, where a new screen was erected to his memory in 1896. For his career as an artist, see Luke Herrmann, 'William Turner of Oxford', *Oxoniensia* xxvi–xxvii, 1961–2.

TUTIN, RICHARD, practised as an architect and surveyor in Birmingham from before 1820 until after 1840. William Thomas (d. 1860) (*q.v.*) was his pupil or partner *c.* 1830, and they are credited in a contemporary Directory with the design of the AMPHITHEATRE, BRADFORD STREET, BIRMINGHAM [*ex inf.* Mr. R. Stanley-Morgan].

TWADDELL, THOMAS (*c.* 1707–1762), 'late Deacon of the Squaremen of Dumfries', is commemorated by a tombstone in St. Michael's Churchyard, Dumfries. He was a mason by trade, and in 1744–5 he was, with Alexander Fleck or Affleck, another Dumfries mason, and James Harley, wright, responsible for rebuilding ST. MICHAEL'S CHURCH in a plain classical style. A plan submitted by William Adam was rejected as too expensive, and the design adopted was submitted by the contracting builders themselves [John Paton, *The Book of St. Michael's Church, Dumfries*, Dumfries 1904, 13, 37–8, 60–3]. Alexander Twaddell (*c.* 1735–87), likewise Deacon of the Squaremen, appears to have been Thomas's son.

TYERMAN, THOMAS, was a pupil of Messrs. Bailey & Willshire of Lambeth. He exhibited a design for a museum at the Royal Academy in 1821, competed for the Houses of Parliament in 1835, and for the Royal Berkshire Infirmary at Reading in 1837. He continued to practise from various London addresses until the 1860s. W. J. Gardiner (d. 1896) was his pupil. His designs for PRESTON BISSETT RECTORY, BUCKS., dated 1839, are in the Lincolnshire Archives Office [MGA 244].

TYLER, WILLIAM (–1801), was known chiefly as a sculptor, but practised also as an architect. As he told a City committee in 1762, he was 'the son and grandson of a citizen [of London] and many years student under the late Mr. Roubiliac'. He exhibited with the Society of Artists from its foundation in 1760, becoming one of its directors in 1765. On the foundation of the Royal Academy in 1768 Tyler was one of the original forty members. At a later date he would hardly have been considered eligible for election, and Benjamin West afterwards explained his inclusion on the ground that 'there was not a choice of Artists as at present, and some indifferent artists were admitted'. However, he proved useful as an auditor of the Academy's accounts, and in 1799 was presented with a silver cup in recognition of his services in drawing up a report on the financial position of the Academy in conjunction with George Dance. He exhibited annually at the Academy from 1769 to 1786, and again in 1800. As an architect he enjoyed the patronage of the Duke of Gloucester, who employed him to alter his house at Hampton Court, and to design a villa at Kensington for the Duchess.

As a sculptor Tyler is represented by some thirty-five monuments (listed by Gunnis), which illustrate his progression from a baroque manner derived from Roubiliac to the neo-classical style of the late eighteenth century. His best architectural work, the short-lived Ordnance Office in Westminster, had an elegant façade in the style of Sir William Chambers.

Tyler died at his house in Caroline Street, Bedford Square, on 6 September 1801. There is a portrait by George Dance in the Royal Academy Library.

[*A.P.S.D.*; *D.N.B.*; *The Farington Diary*, ed. J. Greig, ii, 179; R. Gunnis, *Dictionary of British Sculptors*, 1968, 403–4; M. Whinney, *Sculpture in Britain 1530–1830*, 1964, 142.]

WESTMINSTER, ORDNANCE OFFICE, OLD PALACE YARD, 1779–80; dem. 1805 [T. Malton, *Picturesque Tour through the Cities of London and Westminster*, 1792–1801, 7].

MAIDSTONE, KENT, COUNTY GAOL, addition of wing, 1784; dem. in nineteenth century [Kent Record Office, QS Gaol Plans S.1 and QS Papers 213].

DORCHESTER, DORSET, COUNTY GAOL, 1784–5; superseded by new gaol designed by William Blackburn 1789–95 [exhib. at R.A. 1784; Hutchins, *History of Dorset* ii, 1863, 372].

BRIDPORT, DORSET, TOWN HALL, 1785–6 [exhib. at R.A. 1786].

LONDON, THE FREEMASONS' TAVERN, GREAT QUEEN STREET, 1786; dem. 1863 [Britton & Pugin, *The Public Buildings of London* i, 1825, 331 n.; *Survey of London* v, 61–2 and pl. 23].

HAMPTON COURT, MIDDLESEX, enlarged THE PAVILIONS for the Duke of Gloucester, 1792–3 [*History of the King's Works* vi, 332 and pl. 14 A].

LONDON, THE VILLA MARIA, KENSINGTON, for the Duchess of Gloucester, *c.* 1800; dem. [exhib. at R.A. 1800; cf. *Beauties of England and Wales* x (5), 1816, 157].

845

TYRRELL, CHARLES (1795–1832), was the fifth son of Timothy Tyrrell, a solicitor who was an old friend of Sir John Soane. He was articled to Soane in January 1811, and remained in his office for six years [A. T. Bolton, *The Works of Sir John Soane*, 1924, Appendix C, p. xlv]. Tyrrell became a student at the Royal Academy in 1814, and was awarded the Silver Medal in 1815. He was in practice by 1820, when he was commissioned to carry out repairs to ST. ANNE AND ST. AGNES CHURCH, GRESHAM STREET, LONDON [W. McMurray, *A City Church Chronicle*, 1914, 66]. In 1821–2 he travelled in Italy and Sicily, where he made measured drawings in company with a fellow-pupil of Soane, Henry Parke (*q.v.*). Immediately after his return he published (1823), in conjunction with an engineer named William Anderson, a design for rebuilding London Bridge on the old foundations. There is a copy in Sir John Soane's Museum (P.C. 52). In 1828 he was appointed Surveyor for the Eastern District of London. In 1830 he repaired ST. MARY ALDERMANBURY CHURCH in the City [P. C. Carter, *History of St. Mary Aldermanbury*, 1913, 24]. In the same year he made unexecuted designs for enlarging ST. ANNE'S CHURCH, KEW, that are preserved among the Surrey Archdeaconry Records. He died on 23 September 1832, aged 37, and is commemorated by a tablet in Kew Church. His library was sold by Southgate & Co. on 6–11 August 1833 (*Catalogue of a miscellaneous collection of books including the library of an architect deceased*).

U

UNDERWOOD, CHARLES, was originally a builder at Cheltenham. When in 1821 he was declared bankrupt his contracts were taken over and completed by his brother Henry Underwood of London [I.C.B.S., Rugeley file]. Charles subsequently started a new career as an architect in Bristol. Here he designed some Grecian terraces and villas in Clifton [W. Ison, *The Georgian Buildings of Bristol*, 1952, 29], in 1836–40 the Greek Revival buildings of the GENERAL CEMETERY at ARNO'S VALE [*A.P.S.D.*, *s.v.* 'Bristol'], and in 1857 the ROYAL WEST OF ENGLAND ACADEMY at CLIFTON, with a classical façade provided by J. H. Hirst [*Builder* xv, 1857, 531]. He also designed BURLEY CHURCH, HANTS., in the lancet style in 1838–9 [I.C.B.S.].

UNDERWOOD, GEORGE ALLEN (*c.* 1793–1829), was the brother of Charles Underwood (*q.v.*). After a period (1807–15) in the office of Sir John Soane, he started practice on his own in Cheltenham. His first patron was Sir John Coxe Hippisley, a Somerset landowner from whose

seat at Ston Easton he wrote to Soane in 1816, and who recommended him in 1819 to the Catholic community at Downside. Exactly what Underwood did for Hippisley is uncertain, but he appears to have been concerned in the villa which the latter was about to build at Cowes to the designs of John Nash. He became Surveyor to the County of Somerset and (according to Pigot's *London and Provincial Directory* for 1822–3) also of Dorset. In the 1820s he moved to Bath, where he died unmarried on 1 November 1829, aged 36. He designed several minor public buildings in Cheltenham, Bath and the south-western counties in a style which sometimes shows the characteristic influence of Soane. [A. T. Bolton, *The Works of Sir John Soane*, 1929, Appendix C. p. xliv; A. T. Bolton, *The Portrait of Sir John Soane*, 1927, 130–1, 216; *Gent's Mag.* 1829 (ii), 476; P.C.C. Admon. Register, 1830.]

CHELTENHAM, GLOS., THE MONTPELLIER SPA (now Lloyd's Bank) for Henry Thompson, 1817; Rotunda or Pump Room added by J. B. Papworth 1825–6 [*The New Guide to Cheltenham*, 1824, engraving inscribed 'G. A. Underwood Archt.'].

CHELTENHAM, THE SHERBORNE SPA, 1818; dem. 1838 [*The New Guide to Cheltenham*, 1824, engraving signed 'G. A. Underwood Archt.'].

CHELTENHAM, GLOS., THE MASONIC HALL, PORTLAND STREET, 1818–23 [Hugh Casson, 'Masonic Temple, Cheltenham', *Arch. Rev.*, June 1941].

FROME, SOMERSET, HOLY TRINITY CHURCH, 1818, Gothic; altered by Manners & Gill at various dates [I.C.B.S.].

CHELTENHAM, GLOS., HOLY TRINITY CHURCH, 1820–2, Gothic; interior altered 1875–8 [correspondence in Sir John Soane's Museum, Cupboard 2, Div. XV, A 14].

BEAMINSTER MANOR HOUSE, DORSET, enlarged 1822 [R.C.H.M., *Dorset* i, *West*, 23].

MARNHULL, DORSET, KINGS MILL BRIDGE, 1823 [R.C.H.M., *Dorset* iii (2), 156].

BATH, rebuilt the burnt-out LOWER ASSEMBLY ROOMS as the ROYAL LITERARY INSTITUTION, 1823–5, retaining the portico added by Wilkins in 1808–9; dem. 1933 [*A.P.S.D.*, *s.v.* 'Wilkins'] (*C. Life*, 21 Jan. 1933, 76).

ASHWICK CHURCH, SOMERSET, rebuilt (except tower) 1825; remodelled 1876 [I.C.B.S.].

TIMSBURY CHURCH, SOMERSET, rebuilt 1826; chancel and transepts added 1852 [I.C.B.S.].

CHELTENHAM, GLOS., THE PLOUGH HOTEL, HIGH STREET, before 1826 [Griffith's *New Historical Description of Cheltenham* i, 1826, engraving 'drawn by G. A. Underwood Esq. Architect'].

UNDERWOOD, HENRY JONES (1804–1852), was a native of Bristol. He became a pupil of H. H. Seward in London, attended the Royal

Academy Schools, and exhibited at the Academy in 1822 and 1823. He subsequently joined the office of Sir Robert Smirke. In 1830 Smirke sent Underwood to Oxford to supervise the alterations to the interior of the Bodleian Library, and he decided to settle there. Since the death of Thomas Plowman and the departure of Daniel Robertson there had been no London-trained architect in practice in Oxford, and Underwood soon received numerous commissions, especially for ecclesiastical work. Although St. Paul's Church and the Library at the Botanical Gardens showed that he could design in an orthodox Greek Revival style, it was as a Gothic Revivalist that he made a modest reputation. His authentically 'Early English' design for Newman's church at Littlemore was much admired, and the plans were published by the Oxford Architectural Society in 1845 as a model to be imitated elsewhere.[1] Underwood's career was cut short on 22 March 1852, when a nervous breakdown or an attack of insanity culminated in his suicide at the White Hart Hotel in Bath. E. G. Bruton, who was then his assistant, took over his practice. W. J. Hopkins was also a pupil.

[*A.P.S.D.*; *Jackson's Oxford Jnl.*, 27 March 1852.]

OXFORD, ST. JOHN'S CHURCH, SUMMERTOWN, 1831–3, Gothic; chancel added 1854; dem. 1924 [*A.P.S.D.*] (*Oxoniensia* xi–xii, 1946–7, pl. xvi).

OXFORD, EXETER COLLEGE, section of Broad Street front next to Old Ashmolean, 1833–4; remodelled Turl Street front 1834–5, Gothic [*V.C.H. Oxon.* iii, 117].

OXFORD, WOLSEY'S ALMSHOUSES, ST. ALDATE'S (now part of Pembroke College), restoration, 1834 [*V.C.H. Oxon.* iii, 292; Bodleian Library, MS. Top. Oxon. c. 77, f. 79].

OXFORD, BOTANICAL GARDENS, LIBRARY AND LECTURE ROOM (now Magdalen College Bursary), 1835 [*A.P.S.D.*].

LITTLEMORE CHURCH, OXON., for J. H. Newman, 1835–6, Gothic; chancel and tower added by Joseph Clarke 1848 [H. J. Underwood, *Elevations, Sections and Details of Littlemore Church*, 1845; *V.C.H. Oxon.* v, 213; E. A. Greening Lamborn, 'Newman's Church at Littlemore', *Notes and Queries* cxc, 1946, 46–9].

OXFORD, ST. PAUL'S CHURCH, WALTON STREET, 1836; apse added by E. G. Bruton 1853–4 [J. Ingram, *Memorials of Oxford* iii, 1837, 'Parish of St. Thomas', 4].

BUSHEY HEATH CHURCH, HERTS., 1836–7, Gothic; chancel added *c.* 1891, nave rebuilt 1911 [I.C.B.S.; *Gent's Mag.* 1837 (ii), 187].

[1] Withyham Church, Sussex, built in 1839 by a surveyor named W. L. Blaker, junior, was stated by the incumbent to be 'an exact copy of Littlemore' (I.C.B.S. file).

LOWER SWELL VICARAGE, GLOS., 1837, Tudor Gothic [Gloucester Diocesan Records, F4/1].

LITTLEWORTH CHURCH, BERKS., 1838–9, Gothic; chancel added 1876 [*Gent's Mag.* 1839 (ii), 303].

OXFORD, ST. GILES' CHURCH, repairs and internal alterations, 1838–9 [Bodleian Library, MS. Top. Oxon. b. 111].

LATHBURY VICARAGE, BUCKS., alterations and additions, 1839 [Lincolnshire Archives Office, MGA 236].

BRAUNSTON RECTORY, NORTHANTS., 1839 [plans and specifications formerly in the Rectory, *ex inf.* Sir Gyles Isham, Bart.].

LOWER BEEDING CHURCH, SUSSEX, 1840, Gothic; enlarged 1864 [I.C.B.S.].

SIBFORD GOWER CHURCH, OXON., 1840, Gothic [Bodleian Library, MS. Oxf. dioc. papers c. 2172].

CHIPPING NORTON CHURCH, OXON., internal alterations (gallery and pews), 1841; restored by E. G. Bruton 1878 [I.C.B.S.].

LLANGORWEN CHURCH, CARDIGANSHIRE, 1841–2, Gothic; bell-turret and porch by Butterfield added 1848 [building accounts in National Library of Wales, *ex inf.* Mr. Peter Howell & Dr. Paul Thompson].

BROUGHTON RECTORY, OXON., new kitchens, offices and upper coach-house, 1842 [MS. notes in parish chest by C. F. Wyatt, rector].

HANBOROUGH CHURCH, OXON., internal alterations, 1842 [*Oxford Herald*, 16 April 1842].

WHAPLODE VICARAGE, LINCS., altered or rebuilt, 1842 [Lincolnshire Archives Office, MGA 274].

HOOK NORTON CHURCH, OXON., repaired roof, 1845, and probably refitted interior, 1848–9 [Margaret Dickins, *History of Hook Norton*, Banbury 1928, 151–2].

WOODCOTE CHURCH, OXON., rebuilt 1845–6, Norman style [*V.C.H. Oxon.* vii, 109].

SWERFORD CHURCH, OXON., added north aisle, etc., 1846 [I.C.B.S.].

OXFORD, OSENEY, HOLYWELL and ST. SEPULCHRE CEMETERY CHAPELS, 1848, Norman and Gothic; all dem. [H. J. Underwood, *Oxford Parish Burial Ground Chapels*, 1849].

LOWER HEYFORD CHURCH, OXON., reroofed nave and north aisle, 1848 [*V.C.H. Oxon.* vi, 194].

BANBURY, CHRIST CHURCH (UNITARIAN), 1849–50, Gothic [*Gardner's Gazeteer of Oxfordshire*, 1852, 418].

OXFORD, COUNTY GAOL, enlarged 1850–2 [*A.P.S.D.*, *s.v.* 'Oxford'].

DIDCOT RECTORY, BERKS., 1852 (completed by E. G. Bruton) [*A.P.S.D.*].

HORSPATH CHURCH, OXON., rebuilt north wall of nave, added north transept, etc., 1852 (completed by E. G. Bruton) [*V.C.H. Oxon.* v, 187].

UNWIN, ROBERT, *see* ROYLE, THOMAS

See p. 986

UNWIN, WILLIAM, practised in Sheffield as an architect and surveyor from before 1820 until after 1840. From *c.* 1817 to *c.* 1822 he was in partnership with Thomas Hirst (*q.v.*), and he was no doubt the father of Charles Unwin, who took his place in the 1840s and was still in practice in Sheffield in 1868.

UPSDELL, PETER, exhibited a 'Sketch of a section of an intended church' at the Royal Academy in 1792. He became a member of the Surveyors' Club in 1792, and Johnstone's *Commercial Street Directory of London* shows that he was still in practice in 1817.

UPWARD, J— WILLIAM, *see* CHAPMAN, ROBERT

V

VALDRÈ (VALDRATI), VINCENZO (*c.* 1742–1814), was an Italian painter-architect who came to England in the 1770s and subsequently established himself in Ireland. He was born in Faenza and studied painting at Parma and Rome. By 1774 he was in London, where he designed scenery for the Italian operas at the King's Theatre in the Haymarket. Soon afterwards he was employed by the 1st Marquess of Buckingham at STOWE HOUSE, BUCKS., where his principal works were the Pompeian Music Room, the remarkable oval neo-classical Saloon and the State Drawing-Room. In the park the small lodges flanking the Oxford Gate and the base of Lord Cobham's pillar were designed by him, and the Menagerie may also have been his work. While at Stowe he attended a wedding in the neighbourhood and, when the bridegroom failed to appear, chivalrously offered himself as a substitute – and was accepted. In 1787 he accompanied his patron to Ireland when the latter was appointed Lord Lieutenant and eventually settled in Dublin, where he decorated the ceiling of St. Patrick's Hall in the Castle (*C. Life*, 6 Aug. 1970, fig. 7). In 1792 he succeeded Thomas Penrose as architect to the Irish Board of Works, and in that capacity was responsible for reconstructing the House of Commons in the Parliament House after its destruction by fire in February of that year. His circular chamber, completed in 1796, was destroyed in 1804–6 when the building was remodelled for use by the Bank of Ireland. Valdrè, who in Ireland was usually known as Waldré, died in Dublin in August 1814, aged 72.

[Edward Croft-Murray, 'Un Decoratore Faentino in Inghilterra: Vincenzo Valdrati o Valdrè', *Studi Romagnoli* viii, 1957; Michael Gibbon, 'A Forgotten Italian at Stowe', *C. Life*, 4 Aug. 1966; E. Croft-Murray, *Decorative Paint-*

ing in England ii, 1970, 288–9; Michael McCarthy, 'The Rebuilding of Stowe House, 1770–1777', *Huntingdon Library Quarterly* xxxvi, 1973, 275–6; Desmond Fitz-Gerald, 'A History of the Interior of Stowe', *Apollo*, June 1973, 577–8; T. J. Mulvany, *Life of James Gandon*, 1846, 143–8; F. G. Hall, *The Bank of Ireland*, 1949, 450.]

VALENTINE, JOHN, was an Italian architect who specialized in the building of public baths. The *London Gazette* no. 2906 for 14–18 Sept. 1693 contains the following advertisement: 'John Valentine, our Italian, living in the Venetian Coffee-House in the Pall Mall, who built the Royal Bagnio in Newgate Street, and that in Long Acre, is ready to Build any Bagnio, or Hummums, after the best manner, for Persons of Quality, and others, who are desirous to build the same'. The two baths referred to were the one (sometimes known as 'Charles II's Bath') in BATH STREET, NEWGATE STREET, which was built by some Turkey merchants in about 1679, and the KING'S BAGNIO in LONG ACRE, built by Sir William Jennens in 1682. Both were architecturally buildings of some sophistication. The Newgate Street bath was octagonal in plan with a circular brick dome ornamented with plaster coffering and lit by a central oculus. The King's Bagnio was oval in plan. A crude broad-sheet issued by Jennens in 1686 shows a cupola 40 feet high supported by a continuous arcade concentric with the walls and enclosing an oval or circular central bath. The Newgate Street bath was demolished in 1876, but an illustrated account of it by A. W. Hakewill was published in *The Architect and Building Gazette* ii, 1850, 483–4. See also *A.P.S.D.*, *s.v.* 'Bath-House', and Wheatley & Cunningham, *London Past and Present* i, 1891, 89–90.

VANBRUGH, Sir JOHN (1664–1726), was born in January 1664. His father, Giles Vanbrugh, was the son of Giles van Brugg, a merchant from Haarlem whose parents had left Flanders as Protestant refugees. His mother was Elizabeth, the youngest daughter of Sir Dudley Carleton of Imber Court in Surrey. John Vanbrugh, the fourth of their nineteen children, was born in London, but before he was three years old the family moved to Chester, perhaps as a result of the Great Plague of 1665. Here Vanbrugh may have been educated, but nothing is known of his early life until 1681, when he was working for his cousin William Matthews in the wine trade in London. In January 1686 he received a commission in the regiment of foot commanded by the Earl of Huntingdon, to whom he claimed to be related. This he resigned soon afterwards, in order to escape the tedious duty of garrisoning Guernsey for life. Instead, he succeeded in getting himself arrested in France in September 1688, 'accus'd of speaking something in favour of [William of Orange]'. For over four years he was imprisoned, first at Calais, then at Vincennes, and finally in the Bastille. After his release he obtained a captain's commission in the marines, and served until his regiment was disbanded in 1698. He subsequently resumed his connection with the Earl of Huntingdon's regiment, resigning a new commission in 1702 on his appointment as Comptroller of the Works. In 1702 he also relinquished a sinecure auditorship in the Duchy of Lancaster whose profits he had enjoyed since 1693.

In the meantime 'Captain Vanbrugh' had abandoned the profession of soldiering for that of playwriting. The production of Cibber's *Love's Last Shift* at the Theatre Royal in January 1695/6 inspired Vanbrugh with the idea of writing a sequel: the result was *The Relapse, or Virtue in Danger*, a comedy 'Got, Conceiv'd, and Born (according to the Prologue) in six weeks' space'. Its performance on Boxing Day 1696 was an unqualified success, which Vanbrugh followed up by *Aesop*, a free translation of a French play by Boursault. This, containing as it did:

No Hero, no Romance, no Plot, no Show,
No Rape, no Bawdy, no Intrigue, no Beau,

did little to enhance Vanbrugh's reputation as a dramatist. But almost all these ingredients of a popular play were present in *The Provok'd Wife*, which was performed at Lincoln's Inn Fields in May 1697, with Betterton as Sir John Brute. Its indecencies did not escape the notice of Jeremy Collier, and both *The Relapse* and *The Provok'd Wife* figured prominently in his *Short View of the Immorality and Profaneness of the English Stage*, published in March 1698. Vanbrugh replied in June with *A Short Vindication of The Relapse and The Provok'd Wife from Immorality and Profaneness*. But puritanism prevailed, and Vanbrugh's witty but improper comedies were to be among the last of their type. None of his subsequent plays achieved quite the success of the first two, perhaps because he never again offered the public a comedy entirely of his own invention. For *The Pilgrim*, which was performed at Drury Lane early in 1700 to celebrate the advent of 'a new century', was a prose adaptation of Beaumont and Fletcher's play of the same name, while *The Country House* (1698), *The False Friend* (1702), *The Confederacy* (1705), and *The Mistake* (1705), were all based on French comedies. Nevertheless, Vanbrugh's plays maintained their popularity throughout the eighteenth century, and his unfinished *Journey to London*, completed by Cibber and produced by him as *The Provok'd Husband* in 1728, long remained a favourite with the play-going public.

In 1704 Vanbrugh involved himself more closely in the dramatic world by building his own theatre. The Queen's Theatre or Italian Opera House in the Haymarket enjoyed only a moderate degree of success. The enterprise was supported by thirty shareholders at £100 each, but Vanbrugh was the legal proprietor, and although he disposed of the management to Owen Swiney in 1708 it is doubtful whether he ever recovered all the capital that he had invested in this theatrical speculation.

Meanwhile playwriting had been superseded by architecture as Vanbrugh's ruling interest. How and when the ambition to be an architect first entered his mind will probably never be known: but the transformation was sufficiently abrupt for even a contemporary (Swift) to remark how

Van's genius, without thought or lecture,
is hugely turn'd to architecture.

All that is certainly known is that in 1699 he made designs for Castle Howard, the Earl of Carlisle's great house in Yorkshire, which began to be carried into effect in the following year with the assistance of Nicholas Hawksmoor. Whatever indications of immaturity may be detected in Castle Howard, and however considerable may have been Hawksmoor's contribution as draughtsman and clerk of the works, the conception of this great design remains a remarkable achievement for one whose architectural experience was as slight as Vanbrugh's appears to have been. Moreover, in thus becoming Lord Carlisle's architect, Vanbrugh had superseded no less a person than William Talman, the Comptroller of His Majesty's Works, who had made designs for Castle Howard for which he charged more than Lord Carlisle thought reasonable. Talman's discredit was Vanbrugh's opportunity, for Lord Carlisle was First Lord of the Treasury and in a position to make and unmake the officers of the King's Works. Thus it came about that, in June 1702, Vanbrugh displaced Talman as Comptroller and so became Wren's principal colleague on the Board of Works. Having secured Talman's post, Vanbrugh succeeded in the course of the next few years in supplanting him as the architect chiefly employed by the Whig aristocracy: and a letter from the new Comptroller to the Duke of Newcastle shows that he lost no opportunity of calling attention to the 'vexations and disappointments' which were the lot of those who were so ill-advised as to employ his rival.

For ten years Vanbrugh enjoyed the authority and perquisites of a Comptroller of Her Majesty's Works: but in 1713 an indiscreet letter to the Mayor of Woodstock provided the pretext for his dismissal at the hands of a Tory government, and on 16 April his patent was revoked. But no successor was appointed, and when Queen Anne died and the Whigs returned to power in the following year, Vanbrugh was first knighted (19 Sept. 1714), and then restored to the comptrollership (24 Jan. 1714/15). In the following June, he became the first holder of the newly created surveyorship of Gardens and Waters, which brought him an additional salary of £400 a year, and for the next few years he was the dominant figure in the Office of Works. According to his own account, the Surveyor's post itself was within his grasp, but – as he afterwards told Jacob Tonson – he refused it, 'out of Tenderness to Sir Chr. Wren'. It was an act of self-denial which he had reason to regret when, in 1718, Wren was superseded by William Benson, and Vanbrugh saw Hawksmoor dismissed from his post as Secretary to the Board to make way for the new Surveyor's brother. He himself contrived to retain his post as Comptroller until his death. But during his last years the Office of Works became increasingly influenced by the Palladian protégés of Lord Burlington, and by the time of his death his own highly individual baroque style was already outmoded. In 1703 Vanbrugh was appointed a member of the Board of Directors of Greenwich Hospital, and the minutes of its meetings show that he played an increasingly important part in the affairs of the hospital until in 1716 he took Wren's place as the surveyor in charge. By then the general plan of the Hospital had already been determined, and his own contribution to its design appears to have been small, though he may have encouraged Hawksmoor in some of the grandiose schemes for its further embellishment for which the latter was responsible.

Already a soldier, a playwright and an architect, Vanbrugh became in 1704 a herald, being created Clarenceux King of Arms in March of that year. He owed this profitable appointment to his friend the Earl of Carlisle, who was acting as Earl Marshal during the incapacity of the Duke of Norfolk. The choice of one who was 'totally ignorant of the profession of heraldry and genealogy', who had, moreover, ridiculed it in public in his plays, caused great indignation in the College of Heralds, above all to Gregory King, the senior pursuivant, who had hoped for the office himself. He 'persuaded some other heralds to join with him in a petition against the Lord Marshall's power', but their objections were overruled by the Council, and Vanbrugh was installed on 29 March 1704, having previously been appointed Carlisle Herald Extraordinary in order to satisfy a rule of the College that a King of Arms should have passed through the grade of herald. In later years there was further rivalry and recrimination over the office of Garter King of Arms, for which both Vanbrugh and John Anstis were angling. Anstis finally secured the reversion when Vanbrugh fell into disfavour with the Queen in 1714. But when the office was

vacant in the following year, Anstis found himself in prison as a Jacobite, and it was granted to Vanbrugh for the time being. In 1717, however, Anstis renewed his claim, and in April 1718 a decision was reached in his favour.

It was in the winter of 1704–5 that Vanbrugh obtained what was to be his greatest architectural commission – the designing of Blenheim Palace, near Woodstock. This vast mansion was intended as a mark of royal gratitude to the Duke of Marlborough for his victories over Louis XIV. For Vanbrugh it was a unique opportunity to build on an heroic scale, uninhibited by considerations of economy. Unfortunately, there was no written agreement between the Duke and his Queen: even Vanbrugh's position as architect depended upon an ambiguous document in the name of Lord Treasurer Godolphin declaring that whereas the Duke had 'resolv'd to erect a large Fabrik ... at Woodstock', he, Godolphin, had, 'at the request and desire of the said Duke', appointed 'John Vanbrugh, Esq., to be Surveyor of all the Works and Buildings so intended to be erected ...', and had authorized him to make contracts and to engage labourers as required. A model was made for the Queen's approval, Wren estimated the cost at £100,000, and building started in 1705 with the aid of liberal grants from the Treasury. Their continuance depended entirely upon royal favour, and when that was diverted from the Duchess to Mrs. Masham, Treasury payments for the building of Blenheim began to dwindle and finally ceased. The masons and others whose wages were in arrear sued the Duke, who understandably 'resented and resisted the notion of having to pay for his own reward'. For four years all work at Blenheim was at a standstill, but with the accession of George I in 1714 the Duke and Duchess were restored to favour, and in the summer of 1716 work on the unfinished palace was resumed. By this time, however, the masterful Duchess and her ever-sanguine architect were already confirmed in opposition to one another: 'I made Mr. Vanbrugh my enemy by the constant disputes I had with him to prevent his extravagance', wrote the Duchess, and now that money was short, and the Duke approaching his end, their disagreements became continually more bitter. The final breach came in November 1716, when the Duchess formally accused him of mismanagement in such terms that, as he wrote, he

shou'd put a very great affront upon your understanding if I suppos'd it possible you cou'd mean any thing in earnest by them; but to put a Stop to my troubling you any more. You have your end Madam, for I will never trouble you more Unless the Duke of Marlborough recovers so far, to shelter me from such intolerable Treatment.

I shall in the mean time have only this Concern on his account (for whom I shall ever retain the greatest Veneration) That your Grace having like the Queen thought fit to get rid of a faithful servant, the Torys will have the pleasure to see your Glassmaker, Moor, make just such an end of the Dukes Building as her Minister Harley did of his Victories for which it was erected.

It was, in fact, under the direction of the cabinet-maker James Moore that work proceeded during the next five years, and it was not until after the Duke's death in 1722 that Hawksmoor was recalled to design the Woodstock Gateway and other outworks. Vanbrugh himself remained 'in permanent and irretrievable disgrace', and in 1725, when, with the Earl of Carlisle and his party, he and Lady Vanbrugh came to see the finished palace, they were refused admittance even to the park.

Though Vanbrugh could communicate architectural ideas by means of eloquent freehand sketches, there is no evidence that he ever troubled to learn the tedious discipline of formal architectural draughtsmanship. For that he had recourse sometimes to an unidentified draughtsman whom he called 'Arthur', and more often to Nicholas Hawksmoor, upon whose professional expertise he relied for the realization of all his major buildings from Castle Howard onwards. But Hawksmoor, a distinguished designer in his own right, was never merely Vanbrugh's architectural amanuensis, and in the last resort Vanbrugh's country houses must be seen as a work of collaboration between two gifted men who between them created an architectural style that has no exact parallel in the history of European architecture, though it drew on French, English and Italian sources. Its character was baroque in the sense that it aimed at effects of 'movement', but it achieved them by the grouping of masses and the skilful handling of recession and projection rather than by the mere manipulation of the conventional apparatus of classical architecture. In achieving these effects Vanbrugh drew inspiration from the medieval and Elizabethan past as well as from the English baroque of Talman and Wren. But his evocation of medieval towers or Elizabethan turrets was no more deferential to the past than his use of the classical orders. The desire to give his buildings 'something of the Castle Air' was achieved without the actual use of Gothic forms, but is none the less apparent in the composition of such houses as Eastbury and Seaton Delaval. The result was the 'heroic architecture' with which, at Blenheim, Vanbrugh so well expressed a nation's gratitude to its victorious general, and which, on a smaller scale, found so appropriate an outlet in the buildings which he appears to have designed for the Board

of Ordnance.[1] His 'massive and masculine style' was most successful when deployed on the largest scale, and it was Vanbrugh's good fortune to live in an age when great men had both the desire and the means to house themselves with appropriate magnificence. Despite their formal settings and strictly symmetrical ground-plans,[2] Vanbrugh's mansions show a strong sense of the picturesque. The 'painter-like' quality of his architectural composition was indeed recognized by Sir Joshua Reynolds, and Vanbrugh's attempt to preserve the remains of Woodstock Manor is evidence that he was fully conscious of the value of ruins in a landscape. Though never himself a professed landscape-gardner, Vanbrugh was involved in the planning of two famous gardens at Stowe and Castle Howard, and must be regarded as one of the pioneers of the Picturesque landscape.

In 1711 Vanbrugh was put on the Commission for building Fifty New Churches in the suburbs of London. The designs which he submitted to his fellow-Commissioners for St. Mary-le-Strand (1714) and St. George, Bloomsbury (1715) were not carried out, but the memorandum on church-building which he drew up in 1712 was not without its influence. Like Wren, he emphasized the importance of open or detached sites, condemned intramural burial, and deprecated the internal clutter of too many pews. But unlike Wren he urged that the new churches should be envisaged as 'monuments to posterity ... ornaments to the Town, and a credit to the Nation'. His plea for architectural grandeur, though coming from a Whig, coincided with the inclination of the predominantly Tory commissioners, and most of the new churches were in fact designed in a manner which fully satisfied the spirit of Vanbrugh's 'Proposals'.

In private life, Vanbrugh was a witty and convivial companion, the friend of Tonson and Congreve, and one of the forty-eight members of the Kit-Cat Club which met at the former's house at Barn Elms. He lived on terms of easy familiarity with the great men who were his clients,

---

[1] The Duke of Marlborough was Master of the Ordnance, and it was probably due to his influence that in 1716 Vanbrugh was apparently asked to provide designs for the Royal Arsenal at Woolwich. Such military buildings were peculiarly suited to his bold, masculine style of architecture, and at Chatham, Upnor, Plymouth, Berwick and elsewhere, barracks, storehouses and gateways were built at about the same time which, if not designed by Vanbrugh himself, exhibit all the characteristics of his manner.

[2] Vanbrugh Castle became asymmetrical by accretion, but it was originally symmetrical, and only the eastern extension appears to have been of Vanbrugh's own building (see the plan published by G. F. Webb in *Burlington Mag.* xlvii, 1925, 226). In the album of Vanbrugh's drawings at Elton Hall there is, however, one sketch for a small house in which he has allowed himself to envisage a deliberately asymmetrical building.

and he was a close friend of the Earl of Carlisle to whose patronage he owed so much.

The author of *The Provok'd Wife* did not escape insinuations of personal immorality: but there is nothing to suggest that he was a rake, and his married life appears to have been entirely happy, though short. For it was not until January 1719, that, at the age of 54, Vanbrugh married Henrietta Maria, the daughter of Colonel Yarburgh of Heslington Hall in Yorkshire. By her he had two sons, of whom the younger died in infancy. Charles, the survivor (b. 1720), obtained an ensigncy in the Coldstream Guards and was killed at the Battle of Fontenoy in 1745. Vanbrugh himself died at his house in Whitehall on 26 March 1726, and was buried in the Vanbrugh vault in the north aisle of the church of St. Stephen, Walbrook. He had previously disposed of his place as Clarenceux King of Arms to Knox Ward for £2500. His will (P.C.C. 84 PLYMOUTH) was proved on 22 April. Lady Vanbrugh lived to the age of 82, dying at Greenwich on 26 April 1776.

The best-known portrait of Vanbrugh is the Kit-Cat by Kneller, painted when he was about 40, and now in the National Portrait Gallery. There is another in the same Gallery, formerly attributed to Closterman and now to Murray. A third, painted by J. Richardson in 1725, is at the College of Heralds.

The first collected edition of Vanbrugh's plays was published in 1719: the best is the Nonesuch edition of 1927–8, in four volumes, of which the fourth contains Vanbrugh's letters, edited by G. F. Webb. Twenty-five additional letters were printed by Laurence Whistler as an appendix to his *Imagination of Vanbrugh*, 1954.[1] A 'Journal of Receipts and Payments' kept by Vanbrugh from January 1715 until his death, and continued by Lady Vanbrugh, is among papers from Heslington Hall now in the Borthwick Institute of Historical Research at York. The principal collections of Vanbrugh's drawings are at Elton Hall, Hunts., and in the Victoria and Albert Museum. The former collection was edited by H. Colvin & M. Craig for the Roxburghe Club in 1964 as *Architectural Drawings in the Library of Elton Hall by Sir John Vanbrugh and Sir Edward Lovett Pearce*. Other drawings, from various sources, are reproduced in the Wren Society's volumes and in Laurence Whistler's book.

[*A.P.S.D.*; *D.N.B.*; *Wren Soc.*, *passim*;

---

[1] The following additional letters, not printed by Webb or Whistler, may be noted: to his mother from prison in Vincennes, 9 Nov. 1691 (Hist. MSS. Comm., *Finch* iii, 293–4); to Walpole, 1715 (Cambridge University Library, Walpole (Cholmondeley) papers, 759); to an unidentified lady, 30 April 1717 (B.M., Add. MS. 32686, ff. 104–5); to the Duke of Ancaster, 13 Feb. 1721/2 (Sotheby's 28 March 1972, lot 330).

Christian Barman, *Sir John Vanbrugh*, 1924; K. A. Esdaile, 'Sir John Vanbrugh: Some New Historical Facts', *Architect and Building News*, 26 March 1926; H. A. Tipping, *English Homes*, IV (ii), *The Works of Sir John Vanbrugh and his School, 1699–1736*, 1928; Laurence Whistler, *Sir John Vanbrugh*, 1938; Laurence Whistler, *The Imagination of Vanbrugh and his Fellow Artists* 1954; Albert Rosenberg, 'New Light on Vanbrugh' (eight unpublished letters), *Philological Quarterly* xlv, 1966, 603–13; *The History of the King's Works* v, 1976; Kerry Downes, *Vanbrugh*, 1977.]

AUTHENTICATED WORKS

CASTLE HOWARD, YORKS. (N.R.), for the 3rd Earl of Carlisle, 1700–26. The original design engraved in *Vitruvius Britannicus* i, 1715, pls. 63–71, and iii, 1725, pls. 5–6, was never completed, and the west wing is the work of Sir Thomas Robinson, 1753–9. The centre and east wing were seriously damaged by fire in 1940. Vanbrugh also designed the Obelisk, 1714, the Pyramid Gate, 1719, and the Belvedere Temple, 1725–8 [H. A. Tipping, *English Homes*, IV (ii), 1928, 1–62; Whistler, *Imagination*, 1954, 26–82].

LONDON, 'GOOSE-PIE HOUSE', WHITEHALL, for himself, 1700–1; dem. 1898 [*Wren Soc.* iv, 74–5; *Survey of London* xvi, 168–71; Whistler, *Imagination*, 1954, 197–9].

KENSINGTON PALACE, revised the design for the ORANGERY, probably basically the work of Hawksmoor, 1704 [*History of the King's Works* v, 193–4].

LONDON, THE QUEEN'S THEATRE, HAYMARKET, 1704–5; refitted 1778; destroyed by fire 1789 [*The Complete Works of Sir John Vanbrugh*, ed. Dobrée, i, 1927, xxi–xxiii] (K. Downes, *English Baroque Architecture*, 1966, pl. 497).

BLENHEIM PALACE, OXON., for the 1st Duke of Marlborough, 1705–16, completed by Hawksmoor, 1722–5; also the Grand Bridge, begun 1708 [David Green, *Blenheim Palace*, 1951; Whistler, *Imagination*, 1954, 83–123].

KIMBOLTON CASTLE, HUNTS., remodelled for the 1st Duke of Manchester, 1707–10. The Doric portico on the east front is by Alessandro Galilei, 1718–19 [Tipping, *English Homes*, IV (ii), 113–18; Whistler, *Imagination*, 1954, 131–43; Arthur Oswald in *C. Life*, 5, 12, 19, 26 Dec. 1968].

AUDLEY END, ESSEX, alterations for the Earl of Bindon, afterwards 6th Earl of Suffolk, 1708. Vanbrugh appears to have been responsible for the demolition of the decayed outer court and for designing the staircase and screen in the hall [*Letters*, 24–5; Bodleian Library, MS. Rawlinson C.335; Horace Walpole, 'Visits to Country Seats', *Walpole Soc.* xvi, 33] (Tipping, *English Homes*, III (ii), fig. 325).

ESHER, SURREY, house (known as CHARGATE) for himself, 1709–10; subsequently incorporated in Claremont (see below) [Whistler, *Imagination*, 144–6].

ROBIN HOOD'S WELL, SKELBROOKE, nr. DONCASTER, YORKS. (W.R.), for the 3rd Earl of Carlisle, *c.* 1710 [Hist. MSS. Comm., *Portland* vi, 90; *Family Memoirs of the Rev. William Stukeley*, Surtees Soc., iii, 1887, 373] (J. Hunter, *South Yorkshire* ii, 1831, 488; Downes, *English Baroque Architecture*, 1966, pl. 496).

KINGS WESTON, nr. BRISTOL, GLOS., for Edward Southwell, 1712–14; interior altered by Robert Mylne, who also designed the stables, 1763–8 [*Vitruvius Britannicus* i, 1715, pls. 47–8; Tipping, *English Homes*, IV (ii), 141–56; 'The Kings Weston Book of Drawings', ed. K. Downes, *Architectural History* x, 1967].

MORPETH, NORTHUMBERLAND, THE TOWN HALL, for the 3rd Earl of Carlisle, 1714; reconstructed to the original design after a fire *c.* 1875 [stated by Sir John Clerk of Penicuik to be 'of the architecture of Sir John Vanbrook' in 1724: S.R.O., GD 18/2106; S. Lewis, *Topographical Dictionary of England* iii, 1848, 347] (measured drawings by B. Ferrey in R.I.B.A. Coll.).

LONDON, NEWCASTLE HOUSE, NOS. 66–67 LINCOLN'S INN FIELDS, internal alterations for the 1st Duke of Newcastle, 1714–17; rebuilt 1930–1 [*Letters*, 61, 88; joiner's account in B.M., Add. MS. 33442] (*Survey of London* iii, 110–13).

CLAREMONT, ESHER, SURREY, for the 1st Duke of Newcastle, 1715–20, incorporating the house previously built by Vanbrugh for himself, which he sold to the duke in 1714; dem. *c.* 1763 except the Belvedere tower and the White Cottage [Tipping, *English Homes*, IV (ii), 167–74; Whistler, *Imagination*, 144–55; joiner's account in B.M., Add. MS. 33442; inscription on obelisk in *Notes and Queries* clxxvii, 1939, 279].

WALPOLE HOUSE, CHELSEA HOSPITAL, alterations for Sir Robert Walpole, cr. 1st Earl of Orford, 1715–16; converted into infirmary 1809; dem. 1941 [C. G. T. Dean, *The Royal Hospital Chelsea*, 1950, 202–3; Walpole (Cholmondeley) papers, letter 759].

HAMPTON COURT PALACE, completion of interiors of Prince's (now Queen's) Guard Chamber, Presence Chamber, etc., at north end of east front, for George, Prince of Wales, 1716–18 [*History of the King's Works* v, 176–8].

GREENWICH, VANBRUGH CASTLE, MINCE-PIE HOUSE, THE NUNNERY (later Sherwood), two WHITE TOWERS, etc., for himself and his brothers and sisters, 1718 onwards; all dem. except Vanbrugh Castle [H. G. Lovegrove in *London Topographical Record* iv, 1907; *Trans. Greenwich Antiquarian Soc.* i (3), 1910–11; Tipping,

English Homes, IV (ii), 187–92; Whistler, *Imagination*, 200–6; *Architectural Drawings at Elton Hall*, pls. xvii, xxv, xxvi].

EASTBURY PARK, DORSET, begun 1718 for George Dodington (d. 1720), and continued for his nephew George Bubb Dodington, cr. Lord Melcombe; completed by Roger Morris *c.* 1733–8; dem. 1775 except one wing and gateway [*Vitruvius Britannicus* ii, 1717, pls. 52–3, iii, 1725, pls. 15–17; Tipping, *English Homes*, IV (ii), 175–186; Whistler, *Imagination*, 156–77].

NOTTINGHAM CASTLE, internal alterations for the 1st Duke of Newcastle, 1719; interior destroyed by fire 1831 and rebuilt as a museum 1878 [*Letters*, 105–6, 110, 112; joiner's account in B.M., Add. MS. 33442].

STOWE, BUCKS., additions to house, perhaps including north portico, and garden buildings for the 1st Visct. Cobham, *c.* 1719–24. The principal garden buildings designed by Vanbrugh were THE LAKE PAVILIONS (altered), THE ROTONDO (altered), THE TEMPLE OF BACCHUS (dem.), THE TEMPLE OF SLEEP (dem.), NELSON'S SEAT (dem.), THE COLD BATH (dem.) and THE PYRAMID (dem.) [L. Whistler, 'The Authorship of the Stowe Temples', *C. Life*, 29 Sept. 1950 and 12 Jan. 1951, 119; *Imagination*, 178–93; 'Stowe in the Making', *C. Life*, 11 July 1957. A MS. tour of country seats made in 1724 (Yorkshire Archaeological Society's Library MS. 328) describes Stowe as 'an house of 13 windows in front, with offices at both ends built by Sir John Vanbrugh'].

SEATON DELAVAL, NORTHUMBERLAND, for Admiral George Delaval, 1720–8; interior of centre block destroyed by fire 1822 [*Vitruvius Britannicus* iii, 1725, 20–1; Tipping, *English Homes*, IV (ii), 271–90].

LUMLEY CASTLE, CO. DURHAM, remodelled entrance front and altered interior for the 2nd Earl of Scarbrough, 1722 [*Letters*, 137, 138, 142; Tipping, *English Homes*, IV (ii), 291–4].

KENSINGTON PALACE, THE WATER TOWER on THE PALACE GREEN, 1722–4; dem. [*History of the King's Works* v, 195 n. 2 and pl. 19 A].

GRIMSTHORPE CASTLE, LINCS., rebuilt north front for the 1st Duke of Ancaster, 1722–6 [*Vitruvius Britannicus* iii, 1725, pls. 11–14, showing the unexecuted design for the south front; Tipping, *English Homes*, IV (ii), 295–322; H. Colvin, 'Grimsthorpe Castle, the North Front', in *The Country Seat*, ed. Colvin & Harris, 1970; T. P. Connor, note with dated plan in *Archaeological Jnl.* cxxxi, 1974, 330–3].

ESHER CHURCH, SURREY, THE NEWCASTLE PEW, for the 1st Duke of Newcastle, 1723 [*Letters*, 83, no. 69, dated 1723 by an endorsement] (Downes, *English Baroque Architecture*, 1966, pl. 286).

853

BARN ELMS, SURREY, alterations for Jacob Tonson, 1703; dem. [*Letters*, 7, refers to alterations here which were apparently under Vanbrugh's direction].

CHOLMONDELEY HALL, CHESHIRE, advice about the remodelling of the house for the 1st Earl of Cholmondeley, 1713 [letter printed by Whistler, *Imagination*, 242]. This house had been in process of reconstruction by Francis Smith since 1704. Vanbrugh's advice probably related to the north front, and the engravings in *Vitruvius Britannicus* ii, 1717, pls. 31–2, probably represent his proposal. A drawing made before the demolition of the house in 1801 shows that it was not carried out [Gervase Jackson-Stops in *C. Life*, 19 July 1973].

KENSINGTON, Henry Wise's house, on the site of the Victoria and Albert Museum, was a small house in the Vanbrugh manner [*Survey of London* xxxviii, 6–7].

KINGSTON, SURREY, a house formerly standing 'near the Free Grammar School' on the Wandsworth Road, and described as 'a residence of peculiar character (formerly inhabited by Massy Dawson, Esq., M.P. for Clonmel), one of the latest productions of Sir John Vanbrugh. It is of brick, and strongly built. Its stack of chimneys forms a turret in the centre of the roof' [Brayley, *Surrey*, ed. Walford, ii, 1878, 237].

LONDON, ST. JAMES'S PALACE, the kitchen built in 1716–19 may be attributed to Vanbrugh [*History of the King's Works* v, 240–1].

MIDDLETON PARK, MIDDLETON STONEY, OXON., alterations probably for Henry Boyle, cr. Lord Carleton, *c.* 1715; destroyed by fire 1755. In a letter of 3 Sept. 1734 (at Woburn Abbey) to her daughter Diana, Duchess of Bedford, Sarah, Duchess of Marlborough, says the house was 'fancifi'd in a very whimsical rediculous manner by Sir John Vanbrugh', and an estate map of 1736 in the Oxon. County Record Office (J. 1a/24) shows a house with a plan of Vanbrughian character.

ORDNANCE BUILDINGS. Though no evidence of Vanbrugh's responsibility for their design has been found, the Ordnance buildings at Woolwich Arsenal (1716–19), Berwick-on-Tweed (1717–19) Chatham (Great Store 1717 and gateway 1720) and elsewhere are close to his style and may have been designed by him or under his influence [Whistler, *Imagination*, 216–26; see also Whistler, 'Hawksmoor and the Ordnance', *Arch. Rev.*, Oct. 1955].

PECKHAM, SURREY, HANOVER HOUSE, may confidently be attributed to Vanbrugh on stylistic grounds: see *Architectural Drawings at Elton Hall*, p. xxxvi and pl. xxxi.

SACOMBE PARK, HERTS., belonged to Edward Rolt

(d. 1722), who laid out the gardens and intended to build a house. The walling of the Kitchen Garden is described by Salmon in his *History of Hertfordshire* (1728), 225, as 'equal to that of Blenheim, with Houses of Pleasure ... at the Corners'. A plan of the estate in the Bodleian Library (MS. Gough Drawings a. 4, f. 64) shows the bastioned garden together with the outline of a Vanbrughian house that was never built. For Gibbs's unexecuted design see p. 344.

SOMERSBY HALL, LINCS., built by Robert Burton in 1722, is a small house which could unhesitatingly be ascribed to Vanbrugh on stylistic grounds, but see p. 65 for evidence that it was designed by Robert Alfray.

SWINSTEAD, LINCS., on the Ancaster estate, has a Summer House attributed to Vanbrugh by J. Harris, *Arch. Rev.*, Feb. 1961. Cf. a sketch by Buck in Bodleian, Gough Maps 16, f. 53^v.

THE VINE, SEVENOAKS, KENT, is said to have been designed by Vanbrugh for Col. Lambert in the diary of William Freeman in Sir John Soane's Museum (p. 97, under the year 1743). Designs for this house exist in the Elton Album and the Victoria and Albert Museum. Photographs show a simpler building (dem.) which may have been designed by Vanbrugh [*Architectural Drawings at Elton Hall*, 23–4 and pl. xxx].

WINDSOR PARK, PUMP HOUSE, 1718, probably designed by Vanbrugh: see *History of the King's Works* v, 335.

VARDY, JOHN (–1765), had a long career in the Georgian Office of Works, being successively Clerk of the Works at Greenwich (May 1736–1744), Hampton Court (Jan. 1745–1746), Whitehall, Westminster and St. James's (Dec. 1746–1754) and Kensington (July 1754–1761). In 1756 he was in addition appointed Clerk of the Works at Chelsea Hospital, and from 1749 to 1763 he was also Surveyor to the Royal Mint. Of Vardy's origins and early life nothing is at present known, but his surname is associated with Durham, and that may have been his native city.

Vardy had close connections with William Kent, who was his senior colleague at the Office of Works, and whose style he imitated. If not actually a pupil of Kent in the strict sense, he was certainly one of his most faithful disciples. It was he who in 1744 published the volume of engravings entitled *Some Designs of Mr. Inigo Jones and Mr. William Kent*, and he also drew and engraved Kent's design for the pulpit erected in York Minster in 1741 and a view of the interior of the Great Hall at Hampton Court, based on a drawing by Kent (1749). After Kent's death in 1748 Vardy and William Robinson were the clerks of works jointly responsible for building the Horse Guards in Whitehall to his designs, and in 1751–3 Vardy published plans and elevations of the building. Many of the drawings for the projected Houses of Parliament were made by Vardy under Kent's direction, and it was he who was chiefly responsible for the 'New Stone Building' in St. Margaret's Lane for the records of the Court of King's Bench whose erection in 1755–8 represented a fragmentary realization of the great scheme.

As a private architect, Vardy's most important work was SPENCER HOUSE, GREEN PARK, LONDON, built to his designs by the 1st Earl Spencer in 1756–65. Colonel George Gray, a member of the Society of Dilettanti, acted in a supervisory capacity, and several of Vardy's drawings for interior features of the house bear endorsements recording Gray's approval (Soane Museum and R.I.B.A. Collection). Designs for Spencer House were exhibited by Vardy at the Society of Artists in 1763, and an elevation of the west front 'as Designed and Executed by J. Vardy Architect in 1759' is in the Victoria and Albert Museum, together with a section from east to west signed 'J. Vardy Inv.' (3321–2). The house is illustrated in *Vitruvius Britannicus* iv, 1767, pls. 37–40, and *Country Life*, 30 Oct., 6 Nov. 1926. According to the late Lord Spencer's *Short History of Althorp*, Northampton 1949, Vardy also designed some chimney-pieces at ALTHORP, NORTHANTS.

Other private commissions were the monument in Fulham Churchyard to Bishop Thomas Sherlock (d. 1761), which bears Vardy's signature; alterations to HACKWOOD PARK, HANTS., for the 5th Duke of Bolton, 1761–3 [see Vardy's account in Hants. Record Office, 11. M. 49, drawings for garden buildings, etc., at Hackwood, and the engraving in Sandby's *Select Views*, 1783, pl. xix, showing the house with features since removed but attributable to Vardy];[1] 'plans and planning' at DURHAM YARD, STRAND, for which he was paid 12 guineas by the 3rd Duke of St. Albans in 1763 [Duke's account at Drummond's Bank]; and STANMORE HOUSE or PARK, MIDDLESEX, for Andrew Drummond, 1763–5, completed by Sir William Chambers after Vardy's death and since demolished [John Harris, *Chambers*, 1970, 247] (*Beauties of England and Wales* x (4), 1816, 630).

Drawings in the R.I.B.A. Collection show that in 1754 Vardy made designs (perhaps unexecuted) for internal alterations to LEES COURT, KENT (destroyed by fire *c.* 1913), for Lewis Watson (afterwards 1st Lord Sondes), and *c.* 1755 alternative classical and Gothic designs (both unexecuted) for a new house at MILTON ABBEY, DORSET, for the 1st Lord Milton (reproduced by John Harris, *Georgian Country Houses*, 1968, 29).

---

[1] See also A. Coleridge, 'John Vardy and the Hackwood Suite', *Connoisseur* cxlix, 1962, 12–17, for furniture at Hackwood designed by Vardy.

Shortly before his death Vardy was employed by the same nobleman to alter his London house in PARK LANE (dem. 1851), but the work was left to be completed by Chambers [Harris, *Chambers*, 74–5, 225]. Among Vardy's drawings in the Victoria and Albert Museum there are plans and elevations for the 'Duke of Rutland's House at Knightsbridge' dated 1763, 'A Design for S.ʳ Tho.ˢ Hayles at Howletts in Kent 1755', and a design for a house endorsed 'J.V. 1746 for Mr. Arundell' (presumably Richard Arundell, Surveyor of the King's Works from 1726 to 1737). An elaborate map of Windsor Great Park by him, with elevations of the buildings, dated 1750, is in the P.R.O. (MR 280).

Vardy exhibited at the Society of Artists from 1761 to 1764, sending in 1761 'A design for a building for the Society of Dilettanti, anno 1751' (intended for a site on the north side of Cavendish Square); a 'Design for a building for the British Museum, by order of the trustees, anno 1754' (probably the drawing in the collection of the late Sir Albert Richardson reproduced in *Arch. Rev.*, July 1967, 5, and in J. M. Crook, *The British Museum*, 1972, fig. 15); a 'Design for a royal palace at Whitehall, fronting the park, just before the new building of the Horse-guards was begun, when Clerk of the Works to Whitehall 1748'; and a 'Design for the north front of St. James's, when the old buildings were taken away next Marlborough House, anno 1748, when Clerk of the Works to that palace' (cf. *History of the King's Works* v, 244). In 1762 his exhibits included the designs for the 'New Stone Building' in St. Margaret's Lane already mentioned, and 'A coloured view of the gothick hall at Hampton Court, from a drawing made on the spot, and engraved by Mr. Vardy when Clerk of the Works of that palace'. In 1764 he showed 'A design for a nobleman's stable and terrace to the garden near Hyde Park', identified by Horace Walpole (*Walpole Soc.* xxvii, 80) as a design for Lord Milton's house in Park Lane, 'The inside view of a bath design'd for a gentleman in Suffolk', and 'The North-East front, and one pair of stairs plan of Colonel Wade's house at Whitehall'.

Vardy was a highly professional draughtsman and a very competent designer. He worked chiefly in the Anglo-Palladian manner in which he had been trained, but also designed interior features in the rococo style of the mid eighteenth century. It is, however, as a faithful follower of William Kent rather than as a man capable of making an individual contribution of his own that he figures in English architectural history.

Vardy died on 17 May 1765. His will, dated 13 April 1762, mentions his brother Thomas, a carver of Park Street, Grosvenor Square, and his son John, to whom he left 'all my books, drawings, instruments and matters relating to architecture' [P.C.C. 239 RUSHWORTH]. [*A.P.S.D.*; *D.N.B.*]

VARDY, JOHN, junior, was the son of John Vardy (d. 1765), and succeeded him as Surveyor to the Royal Mint, retiring in 1793. His only recorded architectural work appears to be the alteration and enlargement of Leoni's Queensberry House, Burlington Gardens, London, for the 1st Earl of Uxbridge in 1785–9. His skilful adaptation of what thereafter became known as UXBRIDGE HOUSE (now the Royal Bank of Scotland) is fully described and illustrated in *Survey of London* xxxii, 461–4. The G. Vardy who exhibited architectural designs at the Royal Academy from an address in Knightsbridge in 1800 and 1818 may perhaps have been his son.

VARNHAM, HENRY (*c.* 1781–1823), practised as an architect and surveyor in Tooley Street, Southwark, and was Surveyor to the Grocers' Company at the time of his death on 2 October 1823, aged 42 [*Gent's Mag.* 1823 (ii), 380]. He was responsible for taking down the steeple of ST. MARY MAGDALENE CHURCH, BERMONDSEY, in 1811 [Vestry Minutes, *ex inf.* Canon B. F. L. Clarke].

VASS, NICHOLAS, of Portsea, Hampshire, was a carpenter by trade [deed of 1744 in Portsmouth Record Office, 95A/1/1/12]. In 1753–4 he was employed to 'oversee the workmanship and materials' for the building of ST. GEORGE'S CHURCH, PORTSEA [Vestry Minutes in Portsmouth Record Office, f. 7], and in 1787–9 ST. JOHN'S CHAPEL, PORTSEA (dem. 1941), was built under his inspection [B. F. L. Clarke, *The Building of the Eighteenth-Century Church*, 1963, 105]. Both churches were attractive examples of Georgian vernacular architecture which Vass may well have designed himself [R. Hubbuck, *Portsea Island Churches*, 1969, 6–7].

VILET, or **VILETT**, J—, signs a design for an entrance archway dated 1763 in the Yorkshire Archaeological Society's Library (MD 290/9). It is competently drawn in a style resembling that of James Paine. At Syon House, Middlesex, there is a design by him for a Gothic 'necessary house' dated 1771.

VINER, CHARLES, of Bath, may have been a son of Richard Viner, a carpenter and joiner of that place. In 1821–2 he competed for the Cambridge Observatory and in 1838 he exhibited a design for a triumphal monument at the Royal Academy. In the Hunt Collection in the Reference Library at Bath there is an unexecuted design by him for a colonnade through Gay Street to Gravel Walks.

856

VINING, ROBERT, described in Pigot's *Directory* (1830) as a builder of Weymouth, designed the octagonal NOTTINGTON SPA at BROADWEY, nr. WEYMOUTH, DORSET, in 1830 [R.C.H.M., *Dorset* ii (2), 360].

VOKINS, CHARLES, of Wilton Road, Pimlico, was a pupil or assistant of Charles Bacon (*q.v.*). He completed OAKLANDS, nr. OKEHAMPTON, DEVON, for Albany Savile after Bacon's death in 1820. There is a plan of this Greek Revival mansion in Loudon's *Encyclopaedia of Rural Architecture*, 1846, 915, and a view of it, dated 1831, is given in *Devonshire illustrated from Original Drawings by Thomas Allom and W. H. Bartlett*. Loudon also gives (p. 919) a design by Vokins for a castellated villa. In the 1840s Vokins appears to have given up practice and become a coalmerchant in Pimlico.

VOYSEY, ANNESLEY (*c.* 1794–1839), practised as an architect and surveyor in London in the early nineteenth century. In 1811 he exhibited a design for a bridge over the Thames at Vauxhall at the Royal Academy. According to Edward I'Anson he was responsible for the first building in London to be designed exclusively for use as offices. It stood at the Lombard Street end of Clement's Lane and was built in about 1823 [*R.I.B.A. Trans.*, 1864–5, 25]. In the early 1830s Voysey was in partnership with Richard Suter (*q.v.*), but he subsequently emigrated to Jamaica, where he died of fever on 5 August 1839, aged 45 [*Gent's Mag.* 1839 (ii), 667]. His son, the Rev. Charles Voysey, was the father of the well-known architect Charles Francis Annesley Voysey (1857–1941).

VULLIAMY, LEWIS (1791–1871), born on 15 March 1791, was the son of Benjamin Vulliamy, the celebrated clockmaker. He was articled to Sir Robert Smirke, and became a student at the Royal Academy in 1809, winning the Silver Medal in 1810 and the Gold Medal in 1813. In 1818 he was awarded the Academy's travelling scholarship, which enabled him to spend four years abroad, chiefly in Italy. On his return he began to exhibit at the Royal Academy, and soon obtained a considerable practice, especially for churches of the Commissioners' sort. In London he designed the Greek Revival Law Institution in Chancery Lane, gave the Royal Institution in Albemarle Street a handsome new Corinthian front, and provided urbane elevations for speculative builders in Bloomsbury. His principal patron was R. S. Holford, a millionaire who employed him to design a prestigious town house in Park Lane and a large country house at Westonbirt in Gloucestershire. The former was in the Italianate, the latter in the Elizabethan, style; but Vulliamy could also design Grecian façades in the manner of his master (*e.g.* the Law Institution) and his churches show equal facility in Romanesque and Gothic. He was in fact an eclectic designer who could turn his hand to any style that early Victorian taste might demand. To his contemporaries he was not quite in the first rank of metropolitan architects, and posterity has not sought to alter his standing as a highly competent practitioner of the second rank. His churches were mostly routine productions of their time, but his houses were buildings of greater pretensions. Dorchester House was a dexterous synthesis of motifs from the Italian Renaissance rendered splendid by the sculpture of Alfred Stevens. Westonbirt is externally a magnificent amalgam of Wollaton and Bramshill with a sumptuous Renaissance interior and elaborate formal gardens. Technically Vulliamy was a thoroughly professional architect who prided himself on the accuracy of his estimates and the efficiency of his office. He was, however, 'known to be peculiar in his notions' and his eccentricities are said to have occasioned 'many odd anecdotes'.

Vulliamy remained in practice until the day of his death, and left a considerable fortune. He died at his house on Clapham Common on 4 January 1871. In 1838 he had married Elizabeth Papendiek, only daughter of the Rev. Frederick Papendiek, vicar of Morden in Surrey, whom he is said to have met in Wales while designing Glasbury Church. They had four sons, with all of whom Vulliamy quarrelled. He published two works early in life: *The Bridge of the Sta. Trinita at Florence*, 1822, and *Examples of Ornamental Sculpture in Architecture, drawn from the originals in Greece, Asia Minor, and Italy in the years 1818, 1819, 1820, 1821*, 1823, 2nd ed. 1828(?). He also made the drawings of the Castle at Newcastle which were published in *Vetusta Monumenta* v, 1835, pls. 10–18. His pupils included Owen Jones, C. F. Maltby, F. W. Porter, R. H. Shout, J. Williams and W. Wright. Talbot Bury, John Johnson and Edward Walters were assistants. His nephew George John Vulliamy (1817–86) was in his office for some years, but left in 1861, 'being dissatisfied with his uncle's treatment' of him, and became Superintending Architect to the Metropolitan Board of Works. A quantity of drawings from Vulliamy's office remained in the possession of his family until about 1950, when they were dispersed. A number of drawings and letters, etc., including those relating to Westonbirt House, are in the R.I.B.A. Collection. An elaborate list of his works, drawn up by himself, is printed in *Builder* xxix, 1871, together with a short memoir.

[*A.P.S.D.*; *D.N.B.*; *Builder* xxix, 1871, 142; private information.]

Unless otherwise stated, the following list is based on the one printed in *Builder* xxix, 1871.

PUBLIC BUILDINGS, INCLUDING CHURCHES

ST. BARTHOLOMEW'S CHURCH, WEST HILL, SYDENHAM, KENT, 1826–31, Gothic; chancel by E. Nash 1857.

WOLVERHAMPTON, STAFFS., THE RACECOURSE GRANDSTAND, 1828.

BISHOP'S STORTFORD, HERTS., THE CORN EXCHANGE, 1828.

LONDON, ST. BARNABAS CHURCH, ADDISON ROAD, KENSINGTON, 1828–9, Gothic; chancel 1861.

LONDON, ST. JAMES'S CHURCH, PARK HILL, CLAPHAM COMMON, 1828–9; enlarged 1870–1; destroyed by bombing 1940 (E. E. F. Smith, *Clapham*, 1975, 86–7).

BURSLEM, STAFFS., ST. PAUL'S CHURCH, 1828–30, Gothic; dem. *c*. 1975.

LONDON, THE LAW SOCIETY'S HALL, CHANCERY LANE, 1828–32, completed 1849 and 1857; enlarged by P. C. Hardwick 1864–70 [P. W. Chandler, 'The Site of the Law Society's Hall', *Trans. London and Middlesex Arch. Soc.*, N.S. vi, 1929–32].

WOLVERHAMPTON, STAFFS., THE ASSEMBLY ROOMS (now COUNTY COURT), QUEEN STREET, addition of upper (Ionic) storey to façade, 1829 (J. S. Roper, *Historic Buildings of Wolverhampton*, 1957, 44).

WORDSLEY, STAFFS., HOLY TRINITY CHURCH, 1830–1, Gothic; chancel 1887.

RICHMOND, SURREY, ST. JOHN'S CHURCH, 1830–1, Gothic; chancel 1905.

TODMORDEN, YORKS. (W.R.), CHRIST CHURCH, 1830–1, Gothic; chancel 1885.

LONDON, ST. MICHAEL'S CHURCH, HIGHGATE, 1830–2, Gothic; chancel 1881.

LONDON, CHRISTCHURCH, WOBURN SQUARE, 1831–3, Gothic.

WUERDLE (SMALLBRIDGE), LANCS., ST. JOHN'S CHURCH, 1831–3, Gothic.

SPOTLAND, LANCS., ST. CLEMENT'S CHURCH, 1832–4, Gothic.

RICHMOND, SURREY, HICKEY'S ALMSHOUSES, SHEEN ROAD, 1834, Tudor.

WORSTHORNE, LANCS., ST. JOHN'S CHURCH, 1834–5, Gothic; chancel 1894, tower 1903.

BURNLEY, LANCS, HOLY TRINITY CHURCH, ACCRINGTON ROAD, 1835–6, Gothic.

HABERGHAM EAVES, LANCS., HOLY TRINITY CHURCH, 1835–6, Gothic.

BRIERLY HILL CHAPEL, nr. STOURBRIDGE, STAFFS., enlargement at east end, 1836–7 [I.C.B.S.].

GLASBURY CHURCH, BRECKNOCKSHIRE, 1836–7, Norman.

KNOWLE ST. GILES CHURCH, SOMERSET, 1837–40, Gothic.

STURMINSTER UNION WORKHOUSE (now Stour View House), STURMINSTER NEWTON, DORSET, 1838.

BRENTFORD UNION WORKHOUSE, MIDDLESEX, 1838.

LONDON, ST. JAMES'S CHURCH, CURTAIN ROAD, SHOREDITCH, 1838–9, Gothic; altered 1872; dem. 1937.

LONDON, THE ROYAL INSTITUTION, ALBEMARLE STREET, refronted with façade of Corinthian half-columns, 1838.

STONEGATE CHAPEL, TICEHURST, SUSSEX, for Mrs. Courthope, 1838; Gothic; rebuilt 1904.

LONDON, CHRIST CHURCH, JAMAICA ROAD, ROTHERHITHE, 1838–9, Gothic.

COBRIDGE, nr. BURSLEM, STAFFS., CHRIST CHURCH, 1838–41, Gothic; chancel 1899.

WINTERBORNE CLENSTON CHURCH, DORSET, 1839–40, Gothic.

ROSEDALE CHURCH, YORKS. (N.R.), 1839–40, Gothic.

RAYNE CHURCH, ESSEX, rebuilt (except Tudor tower), 1840.

ROYDON CHURCH, NORFOLK, south porch, 1840, Gothic; removed to different position 1864.

LONDON, ST. PETER'S CHURCH, BETHNAL GREEN, 1840–1, Norman; also the Rectory.

LONDON, ST. JAMES THE LESS CHURCH, BETHNAL GREEN, 1840–2, Norman; reconstructed after war-damage in 1940; also the Rectory.

LONDON, THE SMALL-POX HOSPITAL, UPPER HOLLOWAY, HIGHGATE, alterations, 1841.

WING RECTORY, NORTHANTS., alterations, 1841 [Northants. Record Office, Peterborough Diocesan Records].

ROCHESTER, KENT, KING'S SCHOOL, 1842, Tudor; enlarged 1911.

LONDON, THE LOCK HOSPITAL, CHAPEL and ASYLUM, HARROW ROAD, PADDINGTON, 1842–3 and 1845–9.

HAWKESBURY UPTON, GLOS., MONUMENTAL TOWER in memory of Lord Edward Somerset, 1843–8 (drawings in Mellon Collection).

CHINGFORD, ESSEX, ST. PETER AND ST. PAUL CHURCH, 1844, Gothic; enlarged 1903.

BEVERSTON CHURCH, GLOS., rebuilt south aisle and porch for R. S. Holford, 1844, Gothic.

LONDON, THE LONDON AND WESTMINSTER BANK (WEST END BRANCH), NO. 1 ST. JAMES'S SQUARE, conversion of mansion for bank premises, 1844–5, and subsequent alterations in 1858, 1864 and 1867; dem. 1955–6 (*Survey of London* xxix, 81–2).

LONDON, ST. JAMES'S CHURCH, NORLAND SQUARE, 1844–5, Gothic; enlarged 1876.

ROCHESTER CATHEDRAL, KENT, alterations, 1845.

LONDON, ALL SAINTS CHURCH, ENNISMORE GARDENS, WESTMINSTER, 1848–9, Italianate.

LONDON, ST. THOMAS'S CHURCH, BETHNAL GREEN, 1849–50; dem. 1954.

THORLEY CHURCH, HERTS., restoration, 1855 [J. E. Cussans, *History of Hertfordshire* i, 1870–3, 104].

LASBOROUGH CHURCH, GLOS., rebuilt for R. S. Holford, 1861–2, Gothic [Kelly's *Directory of Gloucestershire*].

DOMESTIC ARCHITECTURE

SYSTON HALL, LINCS., new library and other additions and alterations for Sir J. H. Thorold, Bart., 1822–4; dem. *c.* 1935.

LONDON, LIMEHOUSE, alterations to house for T. Thornwaite, 1823.

BOOTHBY PAGNELL HALL, LINCS., for J. Litchford, 1825, Tudor.

LONDON, TAVISTOCK SQUARE, houses on north and west sides for the speculative builders G. Anstey and J. A. Frampton, 1827 (Hermione Hobhouse, *Thomas Cubitt*, 1971, pl. 12).

LONDON, GORDON (now ENDSLEIGH) PLACE, BLOOMSBURY, houses for James Humphries, builder, 1827 (Humphries, like Anstey and Frampton, must have been a 'taker' under Cubitt: see Hermione Hobhouse, *Thomas Cubitt*, 1971, 71).

LEADENHAM HOUSE, LINCS., alterations for General John Reeve, 1829 (*C. Life*, 17, 24 June 1965).

ASHBURNHAM PLACE, SUSSEX, alterations for the 3rd Earl of Ashburnham, 1829.[1]

NORTON PLACE, LINCS., alterations for Sir Montague Cholmeley, Bart., 1830.

EDITH WESTON HALL, RUTLAND, for the Rev. R. Lucas, 1830, Tudor; dem. *c.* 1960.

BLOXHOLM HALL, LINCS., alterations for G. Manners, 1830–6; dem. 1954.

ROCKHILL HOUSE, SYDENHAM, KENT, alterations for — Nix, 1832.

LEIGH PARK, HAVANT, HANTS., lodges, octagonal Gothic Library, etc., for Sir G. T. Staunton, Bart., 1832–3; dem. (G. F. Prosser, *Select Illustrations of Hampshire*, 1833, plate and description).

CARLTON LODGE, GREAT CARLTON, LINCS., for S. Forster, 1833–6, Elizabethan; dem.

RICHMOND, SURREY, alterations to house for Samuel Painter, 1834.

EMO PARK, CO. LEIX, IRELAND, alterations for the 2nd Earl of Portarlington, 1834–6 (*C. Life*, 23, 30 May 1974).

TWICKENHAM, MIDDLESEX, CAMBRIDGE HOUSE, alterations for Henry Bevan, 1835.

RICHMOND, SURREY, QUEENSBERRY VILLA, alterations for Sir William Dundas, Bart., 1835; dem.

TWYFORD HOUSE, HOCKERILL, HERTS., stables, etc., for G. Frere, 1835.

WHILIGH HOUSE, TICEHURST, SUSSEX, alterations for G. Courthope, 1836.

TWICKENHAM, MIDDLESEX, alterations to villa for J. Weld, 1836.

RICHMOND GREEN, SURREY, alterations to house for J. Ward, 1836.

---

[1] This is the date given in Vulliamy's list of his commissions, but cf. *The Ashburnham Archives*, ed. F. W. Steer, Lewes 1958, 45–6.

DOWNHAM HALL, SANTON DOWNHAM, SUFFOLK, alterations for Lord William Powlett, 1836; dem.

MEREWORTH CASTLE, KENT, alterations for Lady le Despencer, 1836.

LONDON, NO. 51 GROSVENOR STREET, alterations for — Mansfield, 1836.

MUCKROSS ABBEY, KILLARNEY, IRELAND, alterations for Henry Herbert, 1836–7.

WORDSLEY RECTORY, STAFFS., for the Rev. Dr. Penfold, 1837.

LONDON, HIGHGATE, house for — Snow, 1838.

SOUTHEND, LEWISHAM, KENT, alterations for S. Forster, 1839; dem.

WINDHILL HOUSE, BISHOP'S STORTFORD, HERTS., for J. Fairman, 1839.

WESTONBIRT HOUSE, TETBURY, GLOS., extensive alterations and additions to the old house for R. S. Holford, 1839; subsequently rebuilt by Vulliamy (see below).

HILL PARK, WESTERHAM, KENT, cottages, conservatory, stables, etc., for David Baillie, 1839; house dem.

BURSTON RECTORY, NORFOLK, for the Rev. Temple Frere, 1840; enlarged 1862.

FRIDAY HILL HOUSE, CHINGFORD, ESSEX, for the Rev. R. B. Heathcote, 1839–40, Tudor.

HIGHNAM COURT, GLOS., alterations for Thomas Gambier Parry, c. 1840 (C. Life, 12, 19 May 1950).

DULLINGHAM, CAMBS., farm buildings, 1841.

COTTENHAM RECTORY, CAMBS., alterations for the Rev. John Frere, 1842.

TREGOTHNAN HOUSE, CORNWALL, enlarged house and designed Nansawn Lodge for the 2nd Earl of Falmouth, 1842–8 (C. Life, 17, 24 May 1956).

LONDON, NO. 26 ST. JAMES'S PLACE, alterations for the Dowager Lady Arden, 1843; destroyed by bombing 1939–45 (Survey of London xxx, 518).

LONDON, NO. 15 CHARLES STREET, alterations for General J. Humphry, 1843.

NORK HOUSE, BANSTEAD, SURREY, alterations for the Dowager Lady Arden, 1844; dem. c. 1930.

ROCHESTER, KENT, CANON'S HOUSE, for the Rev. John Griffith, 1844.

NESLEY FARM, BEVERSTON, GLOS., alterations for R. S. Holford, 1844.

SEWARDSTONE MANOR HOUSE, HIGH BEECH, ESSEX, alterations for Admiral Charles Sotheby, 1845.

DINGESTOW COURT, MONMOUTHSHIRE, rebuilt south front for S. Bosanquet, 1845–6, Elizabethan.

NEWTON HOUSE, nr. BEDALE, YORKS. (N.R.), alterations for the Dowager Duchess of Cleveland, 1846; dem. 1956.

BABDOWN FARM-HOUSE, WESTONBIRT, GLOS., for R. S. Holford, 1846.

GREAT BRIDDLESFORD FARM, WOOTTON, ISLE OF WIGHT, alterations for R. S. Holford, 1846.

CHESTAL HOUSE, DURSLEY, GLOS., for James Phelps, 1848, Jacobethan.

WOOLHAMPTON HOUSE, BERKS., alterations for the 2nd Earl of Falmouth, 1848.

LAMORRAN RECTORY, CORNWALL, for the 2nd Earl of Falmouth, 1848.

DOWN FARM, WESTONBIRT, GLOS., for R. S. Holford, 1848.

ELMSTREE FARM, WESTONBIRT, GLOS., for R. S. Holford, 1848.

WANLIP HALL, LEICS., alterations and conservatory for Sir Geoffrey Palmer, Bart., 1849; dem. 1938.

TETBURY, GLOS., THE WHITE HART INN., for R. S. Holford, 1849, Jacobean.

PALMER'S FARM, WOOTTON, ISLE OF WIGHT, for R. S. Holford, 1849.

LONDON, DORCHESTER HOUSE, PARK LANE, for R. S. Holford, 1850–63; dem. 1929 (Builder x, 1852, 550–1; C. Life, 5, 12 May 1928; R.I.B.A. Jnl., 3rd ser., xxxv, 1928, 623, 667; measured drawings in Architect and Building News, 4 July, 1 Aug., 5 Sept., 3 Oct. 1930).

ISLEWORTH, MIDDLESEX, ST. MARGARET'S HOUSE (afterwards the Royal Naval Female School, now Kilmorey House), for the 2nd Earl of Kilmorey, 1852–3 (Builder x, 1852, 424–5).

SHERNFOLD PARK, FRANT, SUSSEX, for the Hon. P. Ashburnham, 1853.

BRAMSHOTT GRANGE, HANTS., for Sir William Erle, 1855.

LONDON, NOS. 20–21 BERKELEY SQUARE, alterations for Lord Lindsay, 1856.

WESTONBIRT HOUSE, GLOS., for R. S. Holford, 1863–70, Elizabethan (C. Life, 18, 25 May 1972).

W

WADMAN, WILLIAM, 'Surveyor and Architect' of Martock, Somerset, designed the Tudor Gothic south aisle that was added to WEST COKER CHURCH, SOMERSET, in 1834 [I.C.B.S.].

WAGSTAFF, JOHN (–1784), was a carpenter and joiner at Daventry in Northamptonshire. In 1735–6 he was working at Brogyntyn in Shropshire under Francis Smith [National Library of Wales, Brogyntyn papers, 2008]. An 'Elevation of a House design'd for Thos. Langton Esqr. at Teeton per Tho. Wagstaff', shows that he designed TEETON HALL, NORTHANTS., a small Georgian mansion of c. 1750, remodelled 1879 [Langton-Lockton papers]. Either he or his son John Wagstaff (d. 1802) built EAST HADDON HALL, NORTHANTS., for Henry Sawbridge in 1780–3, perhaps to the designs of John Johnson (q.v.) [Sir Gyles Isham in Reports and Papers of the Northants. Antiquarian Soc. lxiv, 1962–3, 37]. The elder Wagstaff was bailiff (*i.e.* mayor) of Daventry in 1764, the younger in 1781 and 1799. [Information from the late Sir Gyles Isham.]

WAINWRIGHT, JOHN (1762–1828), was apprenticed to Charles Rawlinson of Lostwithiel (*q.v.*) in 1774, and was described as 'architect' in 1790 when he married Elizabeth Westlake of Lostwithiel. He subsequently moved to Bruton in Somerset and later to Shepton Mallet, where he died in 1828. His business as an architect and builder was continued by his elder son Charles Rawlinson Wainwright (1790–1852), who became surveyor to the Dean and Chapter of Wells. The latter's architectural work included a gallery in PILTON CHURCH, SOMERSET, 1825 [I.C.B.S.]; additional pewing in CROSCOMBE CHURCH, SOMERSET, 1830–1 [I.C.B.S.]; and rebuilding the aisles of SHEPTON MALLET CHURCH in 1837 [J. E. Farbrother, *Shepton Mallet*, 1859, 53]. He died at Christon Court in 1852, leaving a son Charles Rawlinson Wainwright II (1823–92), who was a pupil of G. P. Manners of Bath and practised as an architect and surveyor at Shepton Mallet. John Wainwright's younger son John Westlake Wainwright (born 1793) enlarged CHILTON POLDEN CHURCH, SOMERSET, in 1829 [I.C.B.S.]. Other buildings for which the family were responsible were PYLLE RECTORY, the north front of CROSCOMBE RECTORY, Union Workhouses at WELLS and SHEPTON MALLET and the POLICE STATION at SHEPTON MALLET. [Information from Mr. David Wainwright, A.R.I.C.S.]

WAKEFIELD, WILLIAM (–1730), of Huby Hall, nr. Easingwold in Yorkshire, was a gentleman who enjoyed a considerable reputation as an architect in his native county. Francis Drake, noting in 1736 that he was buried ('as yet without any memorial') in the church of St. Michael-le-Belfry at York, speaks of him as 'that worthy gentleman William Wakefield esquire, whose great skill in architecture will always be commended, as long as the houses of Duncombe Park and Gilling Castle shall stand'. Sir Thomas Robinson, writing to Lord Carlisle in December 1730, thought it 'but doing a justice to my late dear friend Mr. Wakefield' to believe that had he lived he would have made plans for the York Assembly Rooms 'full as convenient as' Lord Burlington's, and certainly cheaper, 'tho' perhaps [with] not so many Palladian strokes in 'em'. He would, he said, make 'this distinction between them', that he would 'chuse to follow the plan of a house from the one and that for a publick building from the other, for examine all Mr. Wakefield's designs and the many alterations he has made in the old houses of his friends, we shall always find state [and] conveniency with good economy inseparable companions ...'

What little is known of Wakefield's architec-

tural activities is set out below. The massing of Duncombe, and above all the external expression of its twin staircase towers, shows that he was strongly influenced by Vanbrugh, and his other designs confirm his status as a provincial member of the English baroque school. Of the many old houses that he is said to have altered, Gilling and Holme are the only ones so far identified, but at Newburgh Priory there is a pulvinated gateway closely resembling one at Gilling, and it has more than once been noted that the undocumented Debtors' Prison at York (1701–5) is a building which he could well have designed.

Wakefield died in April 1730, and was buried at St. Michael-le-Belfry on 28 April of that year. F. Drake, *Eboracum*, 1736, 341 n. *c.*; T. Gill, *Vallis Eboracensis*, 1852, 410–11; *Walpole Soc.* xix, 132; *Registers of St. Michael le Belfry, York*, York Parish Register Soc. 1901, 236, 245; Kerry Downes, *English Baroque Architecture*, 1966, 92, 111.]

DUNCOMBE PARK, YORKS. (N.R.), for Thomas Duncombe, 1713; wings added by Sir Charles Barry 1843–6; gutted by fire 1879 and reconstructed in the 1890s with modifications to east front [*Vitruvius Britannicus* iii, pls. 85–6] (H. A. Tipping, *English Homes, Period IV* (ii), 193–200).

HOLME HALL, YORKS. (E.R.), enlarged for the 4th Lord Langdale, 1720–3; remodelled *c.* 1840 [E. Riding Record Office, DD HA 14/25–6; letter from Lord Langdale's agent 6 July 1720: 'Mr. Wakefield hath been here att Hoome setting out the Foundation for the New Building and giveing his Directions to the Bricklayers and Carpanders ...'].

ATHERTON HALL, LANCS., for Richard Atherton, 1723–43; dem. 1825 [*Vitruvius Britannicus* iii, pl. 89; J. Rose, *Leigh in the Eighteenth Century*, 1882, 78, records the inscription on the foundation-stone as 'Marcij 28 1723, Rics. Atherton Ar[miger], W.W: Ar[miger] Arch[i-tectu]s'].

ROKEBY HALL, YORKS. (N.R.), unexecuted design for Sir Thomas Robinson, Bart., 1724, illustrated in *Vitruvius Britannicus* iii, pl. 90.

GILLING CASTLE, YORKS. (N.R.), design attributed to Wakefield by F. Drake, *Eboracum*, 1736, 341. The remodelling of Gilling was probably begun by the 8th Viscount Fairfax soon after his succession in 1719 and completed by the 9th Viscount after his death in 1738, for Fairfax documents in York Archaeological Society's library show that the 'new building' was still in progress in 1738 and that the gallery was not complete until *c.* 1740 [*ex inf.* Fr. James Forbes] (H. A. Tipping, *English Homes, Period IV* (ii), 201–10). The arched features on coupled columns in the hall resemble the main doorway in Wakefield's design for Rokeby, and the plan of the wings should be compared with Vanbrugh's unexecuted scheme for Hampton Court Palace of *c.* 1716 (*History of the King's Works* v, pl. 14 and fig. 6).

WALE, JAMES, of Leicester, was a carpenter and builder by trade, but is also described as an architect and surveyor. He either died or left Leicester in or about 1833 [J. D. Bennett, *Leicestershire Architects 1700–1850*, Leicester Museums 1968].

WALFORD, WILLIAM, probably a local builder, designed the MECHANICS' INSTITUTE (now Recruiting Office), QUEEN STREET, WOLVERHAMPTON, in *c.* 1835–6 [J. S. Roper, *Historic Buildings of Wolverhampton*, 1957, 61]. Obadiah Walford was a builder in Wolverhampton in 1802 [J. S. Roper, *Trades and Professions in Wolverhampton in 1802*, Wolverhampton 1969, 10], and William Walford was a timber merchant in 1851 [W. White's *Directory of Staffordshire*, 1851, 135].

WALKER, JOSEPH, practised from 21 Earl Street, Blackfriars, in the 1820s. He may have been the J. Walker who exhibited a design for an academy at the Royal Academy in 1834 from 105 Stamford Street. W. H. Newnham was his pupil or assistant.

WALKER, ROBERT (*c.* 1771–   ), a pupil of Thomas Leverton, was admitted to the Royal Academy Schools in 1792 at the age of 21. He exhibited drawings at the Academy between 1793 and 1813. They included 'Chedburgh Hall' (1813), perhaps an unexecuted design for a house at Chedburgh in Suffolk, and 'the seat of the Earl of Harrington' (1813), *i.e.* ELVASTON HALL, DERBYSHIRE, which Walker rebuilt to the designs of James Wyatt after the latter's death in 1813 [J. P. Neale, *Views of Seats* vi, 1823].

WALKER, WILLIAM, practised as a surveyor in Chertsey, Surrey, during the first quarter of the nineteenth century. The churches at ASHFORD and FELTHAM in MIDDLESEX were rebuilt to his designs in 1796 and 1802, respectively [faculties in London Diocesan Records, *ex inf.* Canon B. F. L. Clarke]. Pigot's *Directory* shows that he was still in practice in 1827–8.

WALKER, WILLIAM, of Stratford-on-Avon, designed undistinguished Gothic churches at NEWBOLD-ON-STOUR, WARWICKS., 1835 [I.C.B.S.], ALVESTON, WARWICKS., 1839 [I.C.B.S.], and LONG LAWFORD, WARWICKS., 1839 [G.R.], and enlarged GREAT ALNE CHURCH, WARWICKS., in 1837 [I.C.B.S.].

WALKER, WILLIAM, of Shaftesbury, designed an unconvincing neo-Norman church with two west towers at CHARLTON, nr. DONHEAD ST. MARY, WILTS., 1839 [I.C.B.S.]; rebuilt CANN CHURCH, DORSET, in the lancet style in 1840 [I.C.B.S.]; and rebuilt NORTON BAVANT CHURCH, WILTS. (except the tower), in 1840 [I.C.B.S.]. In 1837 his designs for rebuilding Gillingham Church were rejected in favour of those submitted by Henry Malpas [*Somerset and Dorset Notes and Queries* xv, 1917, 26, 33, 40, 80].

WALLACE, LEWIS ALEXANDER (*c.* 1789–1861), was the son of William Wallace, an Edinburgh builder. He was admitted a burgess of Edinburgh in 1815 [*Roll of Edinburgh Burgesses 1761–1841*, 164], and died on 23 November 1861, aged 72 [H.M. New Register House, Edinburgh Death Register]. *The Report on the Burgh of Portobello* of 1832 shows that in 1815–16 he had been responsible for the layout of REGENT STREET, WELLINGTON (now MARLBOROUGH) STREET, and STRAITON PLACE, PORTOBELLO. A plan and elevation by him for a small house at HYVOT'S MILL, EDINBURGH 1818, are in S.R.O., RHP 6012.

WALLACE, ROBERT (*c.* 1790–1874), was evidently of Scottish origin, but lived and practised in London. He became a pupil of J. H. Good, was admitted to the Royal Academy Schools in 1813 at the age of 23, and exhibited at the Academy between 1809 and 1838. In 1824 his designs for the National Scotch Church in Regent Square, London, were selected in competition, but were eventually turned down in favour of those of William Tite. Wallace published *A Letter* protesting against his treatment. In 1823 he competed unsuccessfully for the new buildings at King's College, Cambridge, and in 1835 for the Houses of Parliament; but in 1837 he won the competition for the new Athenaeum and adjoining public buildings at Derby. This was a comprehensive development comparable to Foulston's at Plymouth. Besides the Athenaeum it included a hotel, a Post Office and a bank, treated as a single architectural composition. The whole scheme cost the then considerable sum of £20,000, and constituted Wallace's most important work. His Romanesque remodelling of the Scotch Church in Crown Court (1842) was praised in the *Builder*, and showed considerable ingenuity.

Wallace retired in about 1849, and went to live at Tunbridge Wells, where he died on 11 February 1874 [*A.P.S.D.*; Principal Probate Registry, Calendar of Probates]. His unexecuted design of 1824 for enlarging the Castle Prison at York in the Romanesque style is described in R.C.H.M., *York* ii, 65. At Blairquhan, Ayrshire, there are unexecuted designs by him for that house, made in 1818. John Blore was a pupil.

CLONCAIRD CASTLE, nr. MAYBOLE, AYRSHIRE, entrance gateway and lodge for Robert Cunynghame, 1819 [exhib. at R.A.].

AUCHANS, AYRSHIRE, designs for a mansion 'proposed to be erected' for C. Monteaulieu Burgess of Colesfield, exhibited at R.A. 1819.

AYR, THE COUNTY BUILDINGS, WELLINGTON SQUARE, c. 1820 [N.S.A. v, 22].

ORE PLACE, SUSSEX, designs for a 'residence in the villa style', proposed to be erected for Sir Howard Elphinstone, Bart., exhibited at R.A. 1827.

CROYDON, SURREY, ST. JAMES'S CHURCH, 1827–9, Gothic; chancel 1881 [exhib. at R.A.].

SOUTHWARK, ST. SAVIOUR'S CHURCH (now CATHEDRAL), restored transepts and stone reredos, 1829–30 [W. Taylor, *Annals of St. Mary Overy*, 1833, 50–1, 58–60].

PENTON MEWSEY RECTORY, HANTS., 1833 [Winchester Diocesan Records].

DERBY, THE ATHENAEUM, ROYAL HOTEL, POST OFFICE and DERBY AND DERBYSHIRE BANK, 1837–9. The bank was altered by James Thomson in 1850 [*Companion to the Almanac*, 1839, 240–3; *Civil Engineer and Architect's Jnl.* ii, 1839, 31–2].

LONDON, remodelled the NATIONAL SCOTCH CHURCH, CROWN COURT, COVENT GARDEN, 1842, Romanesque; enlarged by H. Roberts 1848; rebuilt 1905 [*Builder* i, 1843, 267; *Civil Engineer and Architect's Jnl.* v, 1842, 33].

GLASGOW NECROPOLIS, Gothic monument to his sister, Mrs. Mary Anne Lockhart (d. 1842) [G. Blair, *Sketches of Glasgow Necropolis*, 1857, 57].

WALLACE, WILLIAM (–1631), held the post of Master Mason to the Scottish Crown from 18 April 1617 until his death in October 1631. Shortly before this appointment he was employed as a carver at Edinburgh Castle, where he stood first in the list of masons and was in addition paid for making moulds for the plasterers. He appears to have lived at Musselburgh, for in 1618–19 there are payments for his travelling expenses from there to the royal works then in progress at Linlithgow and Stirling. In 1621 Wallace was admitted a burgess of Edinburgh, and was subsequently Deacon of the masons' lodge there. From 1628 until his death he was engaged in building HERIOT'S HOSPITAL, EDINBURGH. After his death his widow, in petitioning the governors for help for herself and her 'small bairns', drew attention to the 'extraordinar panes and cair my said umquhile spous paid and tuik upone the said wark thir divers yeiris bygane, and at the begynning thairof upone the modell and fram thairof'. The governors agreed to assist her, and asked her to let them have the 'haill muildis and drauchtis' which her husband had left. There can therefore be no doubt that Wallace was the

effective designer of this important building, and in particular of its exuberant Anglo-Flemish mannerist decoration. As he was responsible for work of a similar character in the KING'S LODGING at EDINBURGH CASTLE (1615–17) and at LINLITHGOW PALACE, WEST LOTHIAN (the 'new wark' on the north side, 1618–20), it is clear that Wallace was 'a key figure in the popularisation of the Anglo-Flemish style' in Scotland (Dunbar). Though there are several buildings (*e.g.* Pinkie House, Midlothian, and the original design for Drumlanrig Castle, Dumfriesshire) which have been attributed to Wallace on stylistic grounds, the only other one with which he can be connected by documentary evidence is WINTOUN CASTLE, EAST LOTHIAN, which was rebuilt by the 3rd Earl of Wintoun *c.* 1620 onwards. After Wallace's death 500 merks were found to be due to his estate 'in acknowledgment of his panes in his Lordship's works'. Though traditional in plan, this house is stylistically akin to Heriot's Hospital and the royal works with which Wallace was associated.

Wallace's testament shows that he was also responsible for making the monument to John Byres of Coates (d. 1629) in the Greyfriars Cemetery at Edinburgh, for which 500 merks were still owed by Byres's widow. This large monument, plentifully decorated with strapwork, is illustrated by James Brown, *Epitaphs ... in Greyfriars Churchyard*, Edinburgh 1867, 81. Another monument made by Wallace was that (apparently no longer extant) of his colleague Arthur Hamilton, Master Wright to Charles I. The epitaph was composed by the Principal of Edinburgh College, 'at the desire of William Wallace, Master Mason, Cutter of the Stone' [*The Works of Alexander Pennecuick*, Leith 1815, 366].

[*Builder* ix, 1851, 770; R. S. Mylne, *The Master Masons to the Crown of Scotland*, 1893, 70–8; D. MacGibbon & T. Ross, *The Castellated and Domestic Architecture of Scotland*, 1887–92, ii, 520–9, iv, 144, v, 559–60; J. G. Dunbar, *The Historic Architecture of Scotland*, 1966, 54–5; Alistair Rowan, 'George Heriot's Hospital, Edinburgh', *C. Life*, 6 March 1975; testament in S.R.O., CC 8/8/56, ff. 39ᵛ–40ᵛ.]

WALLEN, JOHN (1785–1865), was a pupil of D. A. Alexander. Until about 1826 he was in partnership with George Ferry (*q.v.*) in Spitalfields. In 1818 they designed MYDDELTON HOUSE, ENFIELD, MIDDLESEX, for H. C. Bowles [W. Robinson, *History of Enfield* i, 1823, 269–70]. Though largely employed as a quantity surveyor, Wallen also designed several warehouses in the City of London, such as one in Milton Street, Cripplegate, for Messrs. Morrison. His later works included a block of buildings in Cateaton (later Gresham) Street for Morley & Co., destroyed by bombing in 1940/1; a warehouse in

Wood Street for Dent & Co., 1850, and ST. MARK'S HOSPITAL, CITY ROAD, 1852. He repaired the UNITARIAN CHAPEL, SOUTH PLACE, FINSBURY CIRCUS, in 1843, the CHURCH OF ST. ANNE AND ST. AGNES, GRESHAM STREET, in 1847–50, and the GREAT SYNAGOGUE, DUKE'S PLACE, ALDGATE, in 1852. Sir Horace Jones was among his many pupils. He died on 13 February 1865, aged 80 [A.P.S.D.]. His elder brother, William Wallen, was also well known as a surveyor. In 1822 the latter designed a Nonconformist chapel at Newbury in Berkshire [plans and specification among Nash, Son & Rowley's papers in County Record Office, Cambridge].

WALLIS, CHARLES, of Dorchester, designed the following churches in Dorset: DORCHESTER, HOLY TRINITY, 1824, Gothic, rebuilt 1876 [I.C.B.S.]; ALLINGTON, nr. BRIDPORT, with Tuscan portico and cupola, 1826–7 [I.C.B.S.]; and LANGTON MALTRAVERS, 1828, rebuilt 1876 [I.C.B.S.]. In 1825 he designed BATHS at SWANAGE, now converted into the houses known as 'Marine Villas' [R.C.H.M., Dorset ii (2), 294], and in 1836–8 the UNION WORKHOUSE at CERNE ABBAS [Elizabeth Cockburn, 'The Cerne Abbas Union Workhouse', Dorset Natural History and Archaeological Soc.'s Proceedings xciv, 1972].

WALLIS, JAMES (c. 1748–1824), was apprenticed to Christopher Staveley of Melton Mowbray in 1761 [P.R.O., Apprenticeship Register 22/203]. He subsequently established himself as a builder and monumental mason in Newark, where he is said to have designed several houses. He died on 6 January 1824, aged 76, and is described as 'Architect' in a monumental inscription now in the north transept of Newark Church. For his work as a monumental mason see Gunnis, Dictionary of British Sculptors.

WALLIS, JOHN (–1777), was apprenticed to Samuel Sage of Bristol, carpenter, in 1724 [P.R.O., Apprenticeship Register 48/135]. He was described as 'late an eminent architect of this city' when he died on 30 October 1777. He erected 'Wallis's Wall' along the edge of the great ravine on Durdham Down, and in about 1758 designed and built a large building known as 'The Circular Stables' which was situated between Stokes Croft and Wilder Street. He was one of the principal opponents of James Bridges in the Bristol Bridge controversy, and 'appears to have held considerable influence in civic affairs' [W. Ison, The Georgian Buildings of Bristol, 1952, 49].

WALLIS, JOHN, exhibited at the Royal Academy in 1808–10 and again in 1825. His exhibits included the 'elevation of a villa erected for Mr. Robinson' (1808), and the 'elevation for a villa at Ingress near Gravesend for the late Sir H. D.

Roebuck, Bt.' (1810). Ingress was the property which afterwards passed to James Harmer, who in the 1830s employed Charles Moreing to design a new house for him known as Ingress Abbey or Park [Architectural Mag. i, 1834, 47].

WALLIS, N—, 'architect', was the author of three pattern-books – A Book of Ornaments in the Palmyrene Taste, containing upwards of Sixty New Designs for Ceilings, Pannels, Pateras and Mouldings, 1771; The Complete Modern Joiner, or a Collection of Original Designs in the Present Taste, for Chimney-Pieces and Door-Cases, 1772; and The Carpenter's Treasure, a Collection of Designs for Temples, etc., in the Gothic Taste, 1773. Though both the Modern Joiner and the Carpenter's Treasure were twice reissued, the standard of Wallis's designs was not high, and they were not among the more influential pattern-books of their time.

WALMSLEY, JOHN (c. 1765–1812), was the son of Isaac Walmsley, a mason of Liverpool. He had a considerable business as a builder and statuary mason, owning his own quarries of stone and marble at Toxteth Park, nr. Liverpool, and at Kilkenny in Ireland. Picton says the he was 'a man of considerable taste' and records that in 1798 he designed and built handsome new premises for himself in Berry Street. 'The wings were faced with pediments and pilasters, and the centre set back, with an open quadrangle, in which the business was carried on'. He also designed an octagonal Unitarian Chapel in Paradise Street, built in 1791 (engraving in Lancashire Illustrated, 1831). He was the father of Sir Joshua Walmsley, M.P. [J. A. Picton, Memorials of Liverpool ii, 1875, 280; information from Mr. S. A. Harris and Mr. Andrew Wells].

WALTER, JAMES, was a minor architect practising in CAMBRIDGE, where he superintended the execution of William Wilkins's new buildings at CORPUS CHRISTI COLLEGE in 1825, enlarged the UNIVERSITY PRESS in 1826–7, added two wards to ADDENBROOKE'S HOSPITAL in 1833, and designed NOS. 21–22 BRIDGE STREET in 1835. He competed unsuccessfully for the Fitzwilliam Museum in 1835 [Willis & Clark, iii, 135, 204; R.C.H.M., Cambridge, 24, 57, 312, 337]. The records of the Incorporated Church Building Society show that he repewed BARRINGTON CHURCH, CAMBS, in 1840, and GREAT WILBRAHAM CHURCH, CAMBS., in 1846. He was still in practice in 1851.

WALTERS, JOHN (1782–1821), was educated at the Grammar School at Bishop's Waltham, Hants., of which two of his relations were successively headmasters. For his architectural education he was indebted to D. A. Alexander. He lived and practised in Fenchurch Buildings, London.

He was an able architect whose principal works were the Palladian AUCTION MART, BARTHOLOMEW LANE, LONDON, 1808–9, dem. 1865 [R. Ackermann, *Repository of Arts* vi, 1811, 93–6, and *Beauties of England and Wales* x (3), 1815, 235]; the Perpendicular Gothic ST. PHILIP'S CHAPEL, TURNER STREET, STEPNEY, 1818–20, dem. 1888 [specification in Soane Museum, P.C. 93, description in *Gent's Mag.* 1823 (i), 7, and engraving in Shepherd, *Metropolitan Improvements*, 1831]; and the classical ST. PAUL'S CHURCH, SHADWELL, 1820–1, with a well-composed steeple rising from a Greek Revival body [*Gent's Mag.* 1823 (i), 201 and lithograph]. In 1808 the porch of BROWNE'S HOSPITAL, STAMFORD, was rebuilt under Walters' direction [R.C.H.M., *Stamford*, forthcoming]. In 1811 his plans for enlarging LEYTON PARISH CHURCH, ESSEX, were accepted, but not executed [J. Kennedy, *History of Leyton*, 1894, 53–4].

Walters was much interested in naval architecture and invented a diagonal truss with metal braces, of which he published a description in the *Philosophical Magazine* xlv, 1815, 280. 'Enthusiastically devoted to his profession, he pursued with indefatigable ardour the various studies connected with it', and it was to the consequences of over-work that his early death was attributed. He died at Brighton on 4 October 1821, aged 39. He married the sister of Edward I'Anson, senior, and left a son Edward (1808–72) who had a successful practice in Manchester. [*A.P.S.D.*; *Gent's Mag.* 1821 (ii), 374; *Civil Engineer and Architect's Jnl.* x, 1847, 381.]

WARD, JOHN, was a pupil of James Paine, to whom he was apprenticed in 1767 [P.R.O., Apprenticeship Registers]. He was among the District Surveyors for London appointed under the Act of 1774. As 'John Ward, Architect', he subscribed to George Richardson's *Five Orders*, 1787, and to his *New Designs in Architecture*, 1792.

WARDLE, JOHN (–*c.* 1868), was an architect who played what may have been an important part in designing the new streets and other buildings erected in Newcastle-on-Tyne by Thomas Grainger (*q.v.*) in the 1830s. In the *Newcastle Journal* of 3 June 1837, it was stated that the central part of Grey Street, the western half of Market Street, and Grainger Street were 'entirely designed in Mr. Grainger's office by Mr. Wardle under Mr. Grainger's immediate directions'. In addition Wardle is said in the same article to have designed the south side of Shakespeare Street, and according to a letter published in the *Newcastle Daily Chronicle* in 1868, the Central Exchange 'was not Mr. Dobson's design but Mr. Wardle's assisted by Mr. George

Walker'. Wardle appears in fact to have been Grainger's principal architectural designer, but of his earlier or subsequent career nothing is at present known. He died in or about 1868. [L. Wilkes and Gordon Dodds, *Tyneside Classical*, 1964, 97, 99–101.]

WARE, ISAAC (–1766), was the son of Isaac Ware, a London cordwainer, and was apprenticed to Thomas Ripley (*q.v.*) for seven years on 1 August 1721. Since apprenticeship normally took place at the age of 14, it is likely that he was born in about 1707. Ripley was an official of the Royal Works, and was no doubt instrumental in obtaining for his pupil the post of Clerk Itinerant and Draughtsman (April 1728). Later in the same year Ware was appointed Purveyor, holding the post in trust for the two sons of his predecessor, Robert Hardy. What this meant was that a deduction was made from Ware's salary for the support of the Hardy children. A year later, on 14 October 1729, he was given the Clerkship of the Works at Windsor Castle. In 1733 he moved to the equivalent post at Greenwich. Finally, on 24 May 1736, he was appointed Secretary to the Board, retaining his posts as Purveyor and Clerk Itinerant, but resigning the Clerk's place at Greenwich. For over thirty years Ware was thus a senior official of the Works, though never a member of the Board, which he attended only in the capacity of Secretary.

The recorded facts of Ware's early life throw some doubt on the well-known story that he began life as a chimney-sweeper's boy, and owed his career as an architect to a benevolent gentleman who, walking down Whitehall, found him sketching an elevation of the Banqueting House with a piece of chalk. This unknown benefactor, reputed to have been Lord Burlington himself, is said to have given him 'an excellent education; then sent him to Italy; and upon his return, employed him and introduced him to his friends as an architect'. This story, said to have been told by Ware himself to Roubiliac while sitting for his bust, can hardly be true as it stands. But as a young man Ware did undoubtedly have close connections with Lord Burlington's circle, and his career may well have benefited in some way from Burlington's patronage. In 1727 his name appears among the subscribers to Kent's *Designs of Inigo Jones*, whose publication was sponsored by Burlington, and his own translation of Palladio (1738) is dedicated to the Earl, whose assistance is acknowledged in the preface. The ability to translate Palladio was, moreover, something that Ware could not have learned from Ripley, and references to ancient Roman buildings in Ware's publications suggest that he had visited Italy in person. Burlington's benevolence would hardly have led to the boy's apprenticeship to the unscholarly Ripley, but it might well have made it possible for him to make an all-important visit to Italy as a young man.

By 1733 Ware had obtained his first recorded commission, the conversion of a London mansion into a hospital, and about the same time he published a small volume entitled *Designs of Inigo Jones and Others*, containing designs for chimney-pieces, etc., by Inigo Jones, Lord Burlington and William Kent. The first edition is undated, but not later than 1733. There were later editions in 1743 and 1756. The original drawings are in Sir John Soane's Museum. This was followed in 1735 by *The Plans, Elevations and Sections of Houghton in Norfolk* (the great house designed by Campbell and Kent whose erection had been superintended by Ripley), and in 1738 by the translation of Palladio's *Four Books of Architecture*. In 1741 Ware drew and engraved two views of Rokeby House, Yorks., the seat of Sir Thomas Robinson (*q.v.*), and in 1756 he published *A Complete Body of Architecture* (several later editions) and a translation of Sirigatti's *La Pratica di Prospettiva* (Venice 1596), entitled *The Practice of Perspective, from the Original Italian of Lorenzo Sirigatti, with the figures engraved by Isaac Ware, Esq*. The *Palladio* was a careful and scholarly work in which 'particular care' was taken 'to preserve the Proportions and Measures from the Original, all the plates being Engraved by the Author's own hand'. It was in fact (and still remains) the best and most reliable English translation of Palladio. The *Complete Body* is a massive work of 748 folio pages, providing a comprehensive statement of Georgian architectural theory and practice which held the field until superseded by Chambers's *Treatise*.

As a practising architect Ware's principal works were Lord Chesterfield's town house in South Audley Street, the former Town Hall at Oxford, and some half a dozen country houses listed below. Like many other Georgian architects he engaged in speculative building. In 1738 he was involved in the development of Long Alley on the north side of the Strand, and in 1736–7 of some property in Kensington [*Survey of London* xxxvi, 264; xxxvii, 39]. In 1739 he was co-lessee with John Phillips (*q.v.*) of No. 23 Bruton Street, a house subsequently occupied by the Mr. Pitt whose chimney-piece is illustrated in plate 90 of the *Complete Body*; and other houses in this area can probably be attributed to him on the strength of chimney-pieces designed for Earl Poulett and Admiral Byng, who occupied adjoining houses on the west side of Berkeley Square.

In 1742 Ware purchased a small estate at Westbourne Green, Paddington, upon which he built himself a house that was later occupied by S.P. Cockerell. It is said to have been built partly of materials taken from the old house in South Audley Street which Ware rebuilt for Lord Chesterfield in 1748–9. In 1764 he sold Westbourne House to Sir William Yorke, and moved to Frognall Hall, Hampstead, where he died on 6 January 1766. He was buried in the chancel of the old church at Paddington. According to J. T. Smith he also occupied the house on the west side of Bloomsbury Square which was afterwards the house of Isaac Disraeli, but W. L. Rutton showed that there is no evidence to support Smith's statement. Park, in his *Topography of Hampstead*, states erroneously that Ware's death occurred 'at his house in Kensington Gravel Pits' and that he was in depressed circumstances at the time. There is no suggestion that this was the case in Ware's will (P.C.C. 41 TYNDALE), but it is true that after his death his younger daughter Mary received some financial assistance from the Royal Academy [W. T. Whitley, *Artists and their Friends in England* i, 1928, 318]. Ware married twice. His first wife was Elizabeth, the daughter of James Richards, Master Carver in the Office of Works. By her he had a son, Walter James Ware. By his second wife Mary Bolton he had two daughters. A portrait of Ware by Andrea Soldi is in the R.I.B.A. Collection. He is depicted with a drawing of Wrotham Park, the most important of his country houses. A bust of Ware by Roubiliac, formerly at Buckland House, Berks., is now in the National Portrait Gallery.

Ware was a Warden of the Carpenters' Company in 1761–2 and served as Master in 1763. The Company's records show that the following were his apprentices: George Shakespear (1739), Thomas (son of Leonard) Phillips (1745), Abraham Roumieu (*q.v.*) (1748), Thomas Fulling (1755) and William Fisum (1763). Charles Cameron (*q.v.*) was also his pupil.

Although Ware was probably a protégé and certainly an associate of Lord Burlington, his conformity to Palladian orthodoxy was by no means complete. Externally his houses were, like his Mansion House design of 1735 (S. Perks, *The Mansion House*, Cambridge 1922, pls. 33–6), conformist enough, but Chesterfield House contained several rooms decorated in an elaborate French rococo style, and Ware illustrated a ceiling of this sort in the *Complete Body* (pls. 81–2). He is known, moreover, to have been a prominent member of the St. Martin's Lane Academy, where Hogarth, Roubiliac, Hayman and others were busy undermining the Palladian establishment to which Ware nominally belonged. The extent of Ware's deviation from strict Palladian principle is apparent from a careful reading of the *Complete Body*, which allows a considerable degree of latitude in the interpretation of the Palladian canon. Ware was, therefore, more than a mere disciple of Lord Burlington. Having thoroughly assimilated Palladian theory, he looked beyond it, and in the 1740s himself helped to dissolve the dictatorship of taste that Burlington imposed in the 1720s.

[*A.P.S.D.*; *D.N.B.*; records of the Carpenters' Company in Guildhall Library; Walpole Soc., *Vertue Note Books* vi, 170; J. T. Smith, *Nollekens and his Times* ii, 1828, 206–8; W. L. Rutton, 'Bloomsbury Square: Isaac Ware and Isaac D'Israeili, Residents', *Home Counties Mag.* iv, 1902; B. H. Johnson, *Berkeley Square to Bond Street*, 1952, 178–80; H. M. Colvin, 'Roubiliac's Bust of Isaac Ware', *Burlington Mag.*, May 1955, 151; Mark Girouard, 'English Art and the Rococo', *C. Life*, 13 Jan. 1966; R. Wittkower, *Palladio and English Palladianism* 1974, 88–9; information from Mr. Frank Kelsall and Mr. Roger White.]

AUTHENTICATED WORKS

LONDON, conversion of Lanesborough House into ST. GEORGE'S HOSPITAL, HYDE PARK CORNER, 1733; rebuilt by W. Wilkins 1828–9 [B.M., Crace Views, portfolio x, 29, engraving signed by Ware as architect].

BRISTOL, CLIFTON HILL HOUSE, for Paul Fisher, 1746–50 [Ware, *Complete Body*, pl. 40; W. Ison, *The Georgian Buildings of Bristol*, 1952, 177–81].

LONDON, CHESTERFIELD HOUSE, SOUTH AUDLEY STREET, for the 4th Earl of Chesterfield, 1748–9 (incorporating staircase from Cannons House, Middlesex); dem. 1937 [Ware, *Complete Body*, pls. 60, 61, 81–3, 85, 88; *Vitruvius Britannicus* iv, pl. 46; original drawings in Soane Museum, xliii, 2] (*C. Life*, 25 Feb., 4 March 1922).

LONDON, WESTBOURNE HOUSE, WESTBOURNE GREEN, PADDINGTON, for himself, *c.* 1750; dem. 1846 (plan by C. R. Cockerell in *Architectural History* xiv, 1971, fig. 14b, views in B.M., Crace Views, portfolio xxx, 23–4).

CHICKSANDS PRIORY, BEDS., altered or rebuilt south and east fronts for Sir Danvers Osborn, Bart., 1750, Gothic; further altered by James Wyatt 1813–14 [I. D. Parry, *Select Illustrations of Bedfordshire*, 1827, 116; J. P. Neale, *Views of Seats*, 2nd ser., v, 1829] (W. Watts, *Seats of the Nobility and Gentry*, engraving dated 1781).

OXFORD, THE TOWN HALL, 1751–2; dem. 1893 [Ware, *Complete Body*, pl. 48] (J. Ingram, *Memorials of Oxford* iii, 1837, plate).

WROTHAM PARK, MIDDLESEX, for Admiral John Byng, 1754; wings raised 1811 [Ware, *Complete Body*, pls. 52–3; *Vitruvius Britannicus* iv, pl. 46; what appear to be Ware's original drawings are in B.M., *King's Maps* xxxiv, 32 *b*, *c*] (*C. Life*, 9, 23 Nov. 1918).

EYTHROP HOUSE, BUCKS., stables and garden buildings for Sir William Stanhope, *c.* 1750; house and stables dem. 1810–11; Gothic eye-catcher known as 'Winchendon Castle' dem.

1916 [Ware, *Complete Body*, pls. 104, 105, 107; H. M. Colvin, 'Eythrop House and its Demolition in 1810–11', *Records of Bucks.* xvii, 1964].

AMISFIELD HOUSE, EAST LOTHIAN, SCOTLAND, for Francis Charteris, 1756–9; wings added by J. Henderson 1785; dem. *c.* 1928 [Ware, *Complete Body*, pls. 39, 45] (engraving by Henderson in *Archaeologia Scotica* i, 1792, 46; photo in J. Small, *Castles and Mansions of the Lothians* i, 1883).

DANBURY PLACE, ESSEX, chimney-piece for Thomas Ffytche; house rebuilt 1832 [Ware, *Complete Body*, pl. 94].

CALDECOTE, nr. BIGGLESWADE, BEDS., farm-house [Ware, *Complete Body*, pl. 36].

LONDON, houses in which Ware illustrates chimney-pieces, etc., presumably designed by himself: James Lumley in SOUTH AUDLEY STREET (pl. 86); Mr. Pitt at 23 BRUTON STREET (pl. 90); John de Pesters in HANOVER SQUARE (pl. 91); Henry Fox, afterwards Lord Holland, in ALBEMARLE STREET (pl. 95); William Bristow in DOVER STREET (pl. 95); Admiral John Byng at 41 BERKELEY SQUARE (pl. 96); the 2nd Earl Poulett at 40 BERKELEY HOUSE (pl. 65); Richard Chandler at 3 BURLINGTON GARDENS (pl. 69); Sir William Stanhope in DOVER STREET (staircase, pl. 74); and the 1st Earl Cornwallis in DOVER STREET (pl. 7 b).

DOUBTFUL AND ATTRIBUTED WORKS

BELVEDERE HOUSE, nr. ERITH, KENT, addition of Great Room for Sampson Gideon, after 1751; dem. 1960 [stylistic attribution, based on the combination of Palladian exterior and rococo interior] (*London and its Environs Described*, R. & J. Dodsley, i, 1761, 270, engraving).

BLACKHEATH, KENT, RANGER'S (formerly CHESTERFIELD) HOUSE, addition of gallery for the 4th Earl of Chesterfield, 1749–51 [Ware was simultaneously building Chesterfield House, London, for the same nobleman].

CARNSALLOCH, KIRKMAHOE, DUMFRIESSHIRE, for Alexander Johnstone, *c.* 1754 [in his *Complete Body*, pls. 54–5, Ware illustrates a 'House built for Alexander Johnston, Esq., in Scotland'. The design does not correspond to any house known to have been built in Scotland at this date, but Alexander Johnstone was the builder of Carnsalloch, a Palladian mansion with features for which Ware might well have been responsible] (*Scottish Field*, April 1957).

FOOTS CRAY PLACE, KENT, is said to have been designed by Ware for Bourchier Cleeve, *c.* 1754, in a 'Chronological Lists of Works of Architects who died in the 18th and 19th centuries', published by W. H. Leeds in *Civil Engineer and Architect's Jnl.*, 1840. There seems to be no evidence that this Palladian villa was designed by Ware, but the attribution is acceptable on stylistic grounds. The house was dem. after a fire in 1949. (*Vitruvius Britannicus* iv, pls. 8, 9, 10).

LONDON, NO. 17 BRUTON STREET, *c.* 1740; dem. 1937 [stylistic attribution, based on the combination of Palladian exterior in Ware's manner and rococo ceilings: C. Hussey in *C. Life*, 31 July 1937, 122, and B. H. Johnson, *Berkeley Square to Bond Street*, 1952, 180 with illustration].

LONDON, NOS. 6–7 OLD PALACE YARD, WESTMINSTER, 1755–6 [attribution based on the existence of the original elevation in a collection of drawings attributed to Ware by John Harris, *Catalogue of British Drawings for Architecture, etc., in American Collections*, 1970, 267; cf. *History of the King's Works* v, 411. Although this attribution may well be correct, it is now clear that not all the drawings in the collection are by Ware, and the two houses in question could have been designed by some other member of the Office of Works].

WOODCOTE PARK, EPSOM, SURREY, for the 6th Lord Baltimore, *c.* 1755; reconstructed after fire in 1934; Drawing-Room removed to Boston Museum of Fine Arts 1911 [stylistic attribution based on the combination of a Palladian exterior with rococo interiors, and supported by an elevation in the collection of drawings referred to under London, Nos. 6–7 Old Palace Yard, above [John Harris, 'Clues to the Frenchness of Woodcote Park', *Connoisseur*, May 1961].

WARE, SAMUEL (1781–1860), was the son of a prosperous London leather-merchant. He was articled to James Carr (*q.v.*), became a student at the Royal Academy in 1800, and exhibited there between 1799 and 1814. According to James Elmes he was 'architect to many excellent buildings in Ireland' and was responsible for 'the splendid alterations at Chatsworth, at Northumberland House, and other places for the Dukes of Devonshire and Northumberland'. He is known to have been employed at Chatsworth in 1813, and in 1814 he exhibited at the Academy a 'view of Lismore Castle, Ireland, a seat of the Duke of Devonshire' (then recently altered and repaired by William Atkinson, *q.v.*). For Lord George Cavendish he altered the interior of BURLINGTON HOUSE, PICCADILLY, between 1815 and 1818, and remodelled the north elevation [*Survey of London* xxxii, 407–12 and plates]. At the same time he designed the BURLINGTON ARCADE, PICCADILLY, containing some seventy shops. The Piccadilly entrance was rebuilt in 1911 to the designs of Beresford Pite, but Ware's original elevation is illustrated in *Metropolitan Improvements*, 1831 [*Survey of London* xxxii, chap. xxiv]. For the 3rd Duke of Northumberland he is said to have carried out alterations to

NORTHUMBERLAND HOUSE, STRAND (dem. 1874), in 1824, and for the 4th Duke of Portland (whose London estate he managed) he designed stabling in the rear of HARCOURT HOUSE, CAVENDISH SQUARE (dem. 1906). He also designed the MIDDLESEX HOUSE OF DETENTION at CLERKENWELL, 1816–18, rebuilt by William Moseley, 1845–6 [Parliamentary Papers, *Report on the Police of the Metropolis*, 5 June 1818, 423] and the RECTORY of HOLY TRINITY AND ST. MARY, GUILDFORD, SURREY, 1826 [Surrey Record Office, Q.A.B. Records 1056/869].

Ware published *Remarks on Theatres, and on the propriety of vaulting them with brick and stone, with an Appendix on the construction of Gothic vaulting*, 1809, 1822; a *Treatise on the Properties of Arches*, 1809; and *Tracts on Vaults and Bridges*, 1822. He was elected a Fellow of the Society of Antiquaries in 1816, and contributed papers to *Archaeologia* on vaults (xvii, 1812, 40), 'the Origin of Features in Decorative Architecture' (xviii, 1817, 336), and on celts found at Postlingford, Suffolk (xxxi, 1846, 497).

Ware was a good business-man, and by industry and skilful investment accumulated a large fortune. By the 1840s, when he retired, he had a town house in Portland Place and a country seat at Hendon Hall in Middlesex (which he appears largely to have rebuilt). His practice was continued by his nephew C. N. Cumberlege, to whom he bequeathed the bulk of his property when he died in December 1860. Henry Baker, F.R.I.B.A., was a pupil.

[*A.P.S.D.*; James Elmes, *Metropolitan Improvements*, 1831, 141; *Builder* i, 1843, 24, xxiii, 1865, 372, xxviii, 1870, 1024; W. J. Pinks, *History of Clerkenwell*, 1881, 268; William Keane, *The Beauties of Middlesex*, 1850, 237–8; Sotheby & Co., *Catalogue of MSS.*, 6 June 1966, lot 2294.]

WARREN, HUGH (–1728), was Surveyor of Chelsea Hospital and of the Horse Guards building in Whitehall from 1710 until his death in 1728. In 1719 he was concerned in the building of the BURLINGTON SCHOOL FOR GIRLS in BOYLE STREET, WESTMINSTER [*Survey of London* xxxii, 541].

WATSON, CHARLES (*c.* 1770–1836), practised in Yorkshire from *c.* 1790, first in Wakefield and later in York. He was probably the son of John Watson (d. 1771) and the grandson of John Watson (d. 1757), who both lived in Wakefield and were successively surveyors of bridges to the West Riding of Yorkshire from 1743 onwards.[1]

[1] The West Riding Quarter Sessions Records show that John Watson the elder was appointed jointly with Robert Carr in 1743. In 1757 John Watson, junior, succeeded his late father, and in 1761 Robert Carr (d. 1760) was replaced by his son John. When John Watson died in 1771 his place was taken by J. Billington.

The Watson who designed the Foundling Hospital (later Quaker) SCHOOL at ACKWORTH, YORKS. (W.R.), in 1759–63 [H. Thompson, *History of Ackworth School*, 1879, 2–3] was presumably John Watson II. Among the plans for Campsall House, Yorks. (W.R.) in the R.I.B.A. Drawings Collection there is one 'drawn by John Watson Junr.' in 1752, and another described as 'Mr. Paine's Plan, as proposed to be altered per Mr. Watson 1752'.

Charles Watson lived in Wakefield until 1807, when he moved to York. In the 1790s he was in partnership with William Lindley of Doncaster (*q.v.*), and from 1813 to 1831 with J. P. Pritchett of York (*q.v.*). In about 1825 Charles Watson's son William joined the partnership, which then became 'Watson, Pritchett and Watson', but he died in 1829 in his 25th year, and in 1831 his father retired.

During the first decade of the nineteenth century Watson was the leading architect in Yorkshire. His two partnerships make it difficult to isolate his personal style, but the Court Houses at Beverley, Wakefield, Pontefract and Sheffield were his independent work, and show him as a competent purveyor of public buildings in the Grecian style of the period. All his Gothic buildings were designed in partnership with Pritchett.

[R.C.H.M., *York* iii, 64; *Yorkshire Gazette*, 5 Dec. 1829, 3 Dec. 1836.]

†WAKEFIELD, YORKS. (W.R.), ST. JOHN'S CHURCH, 1791–5 [engraving by Malton in Soane Museum, drawer lix, inscribed 'Lindley & Watson Archts.'].

†WATH-UPON-DEARNE VICARAGE, YORKS. (W.R.), 1793 [Borthwick Institute, York, MGA 1793/1].

†WAKEFIELD, YORKS. (W.R.), ALL SAINTS CHURCH (now Cathedral), surveyed spire 1796 [J. W. Walker, *Wakefield*, 1939, 260].

SHEFFIELD, YORKS. (W.R.), ST. PETER'S CHURCH (now Cathedral), alterations 1802 onwards [R. E. Leader, *Surveyors and Architects of the Past in Sheffield*, 1903, 31].

BEVERLEY, YORKS. (E.R.), THE COURT HOUSE and GAOL, 1804–14 [G. Poulson, *Beverlac* i, 1829, 426].

WILLOW HALL, nr. HALIFAX, YORKS. (W.R.), for Mr. Dyson, 1805 [letter from Watson in archives at Nostell Priory, C 3/2/4/5].

OUSLETHWAITE HALL, nr. BARNSLEY, YORKS. (W.R.), farm buildings for William Elmhirst, 1805 [drawing in Sheffield City Library, EM 1753].

WAKEFIELD, YORKS. (W.R.), THE COURT HOUSE, 1807–10; enlarged 1849–50 [J. W. Walker, *Wakefield*, 1939, 555].

PONTEFRACT, YORKS. (W.R.), THE COURT HOUSE,

1807–8 [West Riding Quarter Sessions Order Book 1807–9, p. 51].

SHEFFIELD, YORKS. (W.R.), THE TOWN HALL (later Court House), 1807–8 [J. D. Leader, *Burgery of Sheffield*, 1897, 405, 411, 413, 418].

CASTLEFORD RECTORY, YORKS. (W.R.), repairs, 1810 [Borthwick Institute, York, MGA 1810/1].

PARLINGTON HALL, YORKS. (W.R.), alterations for R. O. Gascoigne, 1811–12; dem. [Angus Taylor in *Leeds Arts Calendar*, no. 77, 1975, 25].

*WOOLLEY PARK, YORKS. (W.R.), lodge and gateway for Godfrey Wentworth, 1814 [D. Linstrum in *Leeds Arts Calendar* lxviii, 1971, 11].

*BURGHWALLIS RECTORY, YORKS. (W.R.), rebuilt 1815 [Borthwick Institute, York, MGA 1815/2].

attributed: RISE PARK, YORKS. (E.R.), for Richard Bethell, 1815–20 [design for Doric lodge at Rise in album at Stoneleigh Park, Warwicks., signed 'Watson & Pritchett 1818'].

*YORK, LENDAL INDEPENDENT CHAPEL, 1816; now a department store [*A.P.S.D.*; *s.v.* 'Pritchett'].

*NORTON CHURCH, YORKS. (E.R.), rebuilt 1816; dem. 1899; classical (T-shaped plan) [Borthwick Institute, York, Fac. 1814/2].

*WAKEFIELD, THE WEST RIDING LUNATIC ASYLUM, 1816–18 [*Plans, etc., of the Pauper Lunatic Asylum lately erected at Wakefield*, York 1819].

*YORK, THE FRIENDS' MEETING HOUSE, 1816–19 [plans, etc., in W. Alexander, *Observations on the Construction of Meeting Houses*, York 1820].

*BRAFFERTON VICARAGE, YORKS. (N.R.), enlarged 1818 [Borthwick Institute, York, MGA 1818/3].

*SLEDMERE HOUSE, YORKS. (E.R.), gates to main road for Sir Mark Sykes, Bart., 1818 [drawings at Sledmere].

*WAKEFIELD, YORKS. (W.R.), library etc. (now Museum), 1820–1 [Yorkshire Archl. Soc. MS. 1142, *ex inf.* Dr. D. Linstrum].

*HUDDERSFIELD, YORKS. (W.R.), THE RAMSDEN STREET NONCONFORMIST CHAPEL, 1824; dem. 1936 [G. H. Broadbent in *Studies in Architectural History*, ed. Singleton, ii, 1956, 110, citing Sykes, *History of the Ramsden Street Chapel*].

*SALTMARSHE HALL, YORKS. (E.R.), for Philip Saltmarshe, 1825 [drawings in the possession of Mr. J. E. Scott of Huyton, 1971].

*GREASBROUGH CHURCH, YORKS. (W.R.), rebuilt 1826–8, Gothic [Port, 166–7].

*SHEFFIELD, NETHER CHAPEL (INDEPENDENT), 1827; altered 1878 [R. E. Leader, *Surveyors and Architects of the Past in Sheffield*, 1903].

*YORK, ASSEMBLY ROOMS, new façade and portico, 1828 [*A.P.S.D.*, *s.v.* 'Pritchett'].

*LOTHERTON HALL, YORKS. (W.R.), alterations, including existing drawing-room, for R. O.

---

† Designed in partnership with William Lindley.

* Designed in partnership with J. P. Pritchett.

Gascoigne, c. 1828 [Angus Taylor in *Leeds Arts Calendar*, no. 77, 1975, 28].

*NOSTELL PRIORY, YORKS. (W.R.), north and east sides of stable block for C. W. Winn, 1828–9, adopting Robert Adam's design (1776) for the cupola [drawings at Nostell].

*YORK, ST. PETER'S SCHOOL (now Choir School), MINSTER YARD, 1829, Tudor Gothic [*A.P.S.D.*, *s.v.* 'Pritchett'].

*YORK, THE SAVINGS BANK, ST. HELEN'S SQUARE, 1829–30 [W. Camidge, *History of the York Savings Bank*, 1886, 49–51].

*NETHER HOYLAND CHURCH, YORKS. (W.R.), 1830, Gothic [Port, 168–9].

WATSON, JOHN (–1707), is described as 'architect of Glashampton' on his tombstone in Astley Church, Worcs. GLASHAMPTON HOUSE, ASTLEY, was built by a member of the Winford family (probably Thomas Cookes Winford) c. 1705, and was destroyed by fire in 1810. An engraving in Nash's *History of Worcestershire* shows a large rectangular mansion of the sort associated with the Smiths of Warwick. Watson died intestate on 26 October 1707 and was buried at Astley on 28 October [P.C.C., Admon. Act Book 1707; Astley Parish Register].

It is possible, but by no means certain, that this John Watson is to be identified with an architect or architects of this surname who were employed at WROXTON ABBEY, OXON., in 1680–5 and at MELBURY HOUSE, DORSET, in 1692. A portrait inscribed 'Mr. Watson, architect to Thos. Strangways senr. esqr. who enlarged & adorned this house 1692' is preserved at Melbury. Horace Walpole refers to these alterations in his *Journal of Visits to Country Seats* (Walpole Soc. xvi, 47), but ascribes them to 'Thomas Sutton, styling himself Architect to Thomas Strangways esq.' – a statement which must have been due to a faulty recollection of the inscription on Watson's portrait. The house is described in R.C.H.M., *Dorset* i, 164–7.

The alterations at Wroxton were due to Francis North, 1st Lord Guilford (d. 1685). Roger North (*q.v.*) wrote that his brother 'had a plain man to put out his work, and see to the executory part, one Watson, very fitt for the business, ... but I took upon me the honor of being prime architect'. [B.M., Add. MS. 32510, ff. 137–9; cf. *V.C.H. Oxon.* ix, 172–3.]

WATSON, JOHN BURGES (1803–1881), was the son of Joseph Burges Watson of Surbiton Hill House, nr. Kingston, Surrey. He was a pupil of William Atkinson, became a student at the Royal Academy Schools in 1823 and gained medals at the Society of Arts in 1824 for a perspective drawing of a crane and for a design for houses

in Grecian architecture. He exhibited at the Royal Academy from 1824 to 1838, and competed for the Houses of Parliament (1835), the Royal Berkshire Infirmary (1837), and the Surrey Lunatic Asylum (1839). He was for forty years surveyor to the Pentonville Estate. Having considerable knowledge of trees, he also practised as a landscape-gardener. T. W. Fletcher, who was his pupil in the 1850s, describes him as a bald, florid man with a fondness for music and a fund of smutty stories. He was three times Master of the Farriers' Company. He died at Carondolet, Hornsey, on 10 April 1881, aged 78. One of his sons, Thomas Henry Watson, also practised as an architect. [*A.P.S.D.*; *The Architects, Engineers and Building Trades Directory*, 1868, 142; 'The Autobiography of Thomas Wayland Fletcher', ed. M. H. Port, *East London Papers* xi, 1968, 27.]

CHURCHES, PARSONAGES AND SCHOOLS

STAINES CHURCH, MIDDLESEX, rebuilt 1828–9, Gothic; chancel extended 1885 [*Gent's Mag.* 1828 (ii), 393, with engraving].

EAST BEDFONT CHURCH, MIDDLESEX, added north transept, 1828–9 [I.C.B.S.].

NORTON VICARAGE, HERTS., for the Rev. Joseph Burges Watson, 1831 [exhib. at R.A. 1831].

HOLMWOOD CHURCH, SURREY, 1837–8, Norman; rebuilt at various dates [*Architectural Mag.* iv, 499]; also PARSONAGE, 1839 [Surrey County Record Office, 1079/3].

HOOK CHURCH, SURREY, 1837–8, Gothic; rebuilt 1881 [*Architectural Mag.* iv, 499; exhib. at R.A. 1838]; also PARSONAGE [*The Architects ... Directory*].

HAM PARSONAGE, SURREY, 1838–9 [Surrey County Record Office, 1079/1].

MESSING CHURCH, ESSEX, enlarged by addition of transepts, 1840 [I.C.B.S.].

LAYER BRETON RECTORY, ESSEX, c. 1840 [*The Architects ... Directory*].

LAPLEY VICARAGE, STAFFS., c. 1840 [*The Architects ... Directory*].

BRANSGORE PARSONAGE, HANTS., 1843–4 [*The Architects ... Directory*].

SCHOOLS at HAM, KINGSTON and SYDENHAM [*The Architects ... Directory*].

OTHER WORKS

LONDON, houses in HYDE PARK GARDENS and SUSSEX SQUARE, PADDINGTON, c. 1837 onwards [*The Architects ... Directory*].

LONDON, NO. 21 PARK LANE, for the 2nd Marquess of Breadalbane [*The Architects ... Directory*].

LONDON, ST. JAMES'S PARK, cottage for the Ornithological Society, 1840 [*A.P.S.D.*].

LONDON, THE NATIONAL PROVINCIAL BANK, NO.

---

* Designed in partnership with J. P. Pritchett.

112 BISHOPSGATE, *c.* 1840; rebuilt 1864 [*A.P.S.D.*].

ASHLEY PARK, SURREY, alterations for Sir Henry Fletcher, Bart.; dem. [*The Architects . . . Directory*].

RAY MEAD, HAMPSTEAD MARSHALL, BERKS., additions for Albert Ricardo, 1858 [*A.P.S.D.*].

WATSON, WILLIAM (*c.* 1805–1829), *see* WATSON, CHARLES

WATT, JAMES (–1832), was an architect practising in Glasgow, where he was a member of the Philosophical and Dilettante Societies [T. Gildard, 'An Old Glasgow Architect on Some Older Ones', *Trans. Royal Philosophical Soc. of Glasgow* xxvi, 1895, 121]. He died on 12 Sept. 1832 [*Glasgow Courier*, 1832, *ex inf.* Mr. J. Stevens Curl].

WEBB, JOHN (1611–1672), was born in London in 1611, and educated at Merchant Taylors' School, where he remained three years (1625–8). He came of a Somerset family, but nothing is known of his parentage, or of the circumstances in which, in 1628, he became a pupil of Inigo Jones. According to his own statement, made in 1660, he was 'brought up by his Unckle Mr. Inigo Jones upon his late Maiestyes command in the study of Architecture, as well that wch relates to building as for masques Tryumphs and the like'. Webb was Jones's 'nephew' by marriage, his wife, Anne Jones, being a near relation of Inigo (perhaps a niece in the strict sense, but equally likely an illegitimate daughter known officially as a 'niece'). As Jones's pupil, Webb received a thorough training in classical architecture based on a careful study of the works of Serlio, Palladio, Scamozzi and other Italian masters. There is no evidence that he ever visited Italy,[1] but his drawings show 'a high degree of technical competence' and 'an exact knowledge of Italian detail'. His earliest datable drawings belong to the 1630s, when he was assisting Jones in the repair of St. Paul's Cathedral and the building of the Barber-Surgeons' Theatre. Drawings for a lodge or villa at Hale in Hampshire and for a stable for a Mr. Fetherstone (probably at Hassenbrook in Essex), both dated 1638, may represent Webb's first wholly independent commissions, though neither is known to have been carried out. It was probably at this period too that under Jones's supervision he made the first of the many surviving drawings for a new Whitehall Palace in the Palladian style already exemplified by the Banqueting House; and in 1638, again under Jones's direction, he made designs of similar character for a proposed extension of Somerset House for the Queen.

With the outbreak of the Civil War in 1642 these projects had to be laid aside together with the masques to whose production Jones and his pupil had devoted so much of their time. Jones himself went north with the King, leaving Webb as his deputy in charge of the Royal Works until in 1643 they were both displaced by Edward Carter (*q.v.*). Thus deprived of his official employment, Webb appears to have acted as a royal agent, for, according to his own account, he 'sent to the King at Oxford the designs of all the fortifications about London, their proportions, the number of guns mounted on them, how many soldiers would man them, how they might be attempted and carried and all particulars relating thereto in writing'. Moreover, he carried £500 to the King 'sew'd up in his waistcoat through all the enemy's quarters unto Beverley in Yorkshire, which being afterwards discovered, Mr. Webb was plundered to the purpose, and a long time kept in prison being close prisoner for a month'. But apart from this confinement, Webb appears to have suffered little for his royalist sympathies, and he was even allowed to 'attend his Majesty . . . at Hampton Court and at the Isle of Wight, where he received his majesty's command to design a palace for Whitehall,[1] which he did until his majesty's unfortunate calamity caused him to desist'. The King's death in 1649 did not, however, prevent Webb from practising as an architect, for during that year he was engaged in reconstructing the interior of Wilton House for the Earl of Pembroke after a fire, and in designing a proposed new house for him in the Strand. When Jones made his will in 1650 he named Webb as his executor, and his 'kinswoman Anne Jones', Webb's wife, was his principal legatee.

Jones's death in 1652 left his pupil almost without a rival in the field of architectural design, and during the next few years 'Inigo Jones's man' had no lack of employment. He was working for the Earl of Rutland at Belvoir, for the Earl of Peterborough at Drayton, for Lord Dacre at Chevening in Kent, and for Sir Justinian Isham at Lamport in Northants. The fortunate survival of his letters to the latter show, moreover, that he was still living in Scotland Yard, where the officers of the Works had their quarters,[2] though there appears to be no evidence that he was in

---

[1] He may, however, have visited France, for in July 1656 the Protector granted a warrant for John Webb (presumably but not certainly the architect) to have a pass to go to that country (*Cal. State Papers Domestic 1656–7*, 58).

[1] This refers to the 'taken' design of 1647 which Webb submitted to Charles II at the Restoration.

[2] Webb appears as the occupant of Jones's house in Whitehall in a survey made in 1650, but Jones himself reappears in 1651 and presumably remained in occupation until his death in 1652 (E. S. de Beer, 'Notes on Inigo Jones', *Notes and Queries*, 178, 27 April 1940, 292.)

official employment.[1] For this, he must wait for the restoration of King Charles II, when, as Jones's pupil and deputy, he hoped to take his rightful place as Surveyor of His Majesty's Works. With that object, he petitioned the King in May 1660. But there were others – including Hugh May and John Denham – who claimed the post, and it was in vain that Webb represented that he 'was by the especiall command of y^r Maties Royall Father of ever blessed memory, brought up by Inigo Jones Esqr., Y^r Maties late Surveyor of the Works in ye study of Architecture, for enabling him to do y^{or} Royall Father and y^r Matie service in ye said office', that there were arrears of salary due to him, both on his own account and as Jones's executor, that 'Mr. Denham may possibly, as most gentry in England at this day, have some knowledge in the Theory of Architecture; but nothing of ye practique soe that he must of necessity have another at his Maties charges to doe his business; whereas Mr. Webb himself designes, orders, and directs … without any other man's assistance. His Matie may please to grant some other place more proper for Mr. Denham's abilityes and confirme unto Mr. Webb the Surveyor's place wherein he hath consumed 30 years study, there being scarce any of the greate Nobility or eminent gentry of England but he hath done service for in matter of building, ordering of medalls, statues and the like.' Denham was appointed Surveyor in June 1660, and Webb had to content himself with a promise of the reversion of the surveyorship, for which he obtained a warrant in June 1660. But even this proved abortive, for Denham, fearing that it would prevent him from selling his place at some future date, stopped it from passing the Great Seal.[2]

But Webb's services were too valuable to be dispensed with altogether, and in 1663 he was recalled in order to design the King Charles block at Greenwich Palace, to superintend the fortification of Woolwich Dockyard, and to initiate others in the mysteries of 'the Scenicall Art, which to others than himselfe was before muche un-

knowne'. It was, in fact, Webb who designed the setting for *The Tragedy of Mustapha*, given by D'Avenant's company at Whitehall in October 1666, and Mr. Grant Keith has shown how Webb 'carried on the traditions of stagecraft of Inigo Jones, as it had been left to him to carry on the traditions of his architecture'. In November 1666 he was formally placed in charge of the works at Greenwich, 'to execute, act and proceed there, according to your best skill and judgment in Architecture, as our Surveyor Assistant unto Sir John Denham'. The salary was £200 a year, with travelling expenses, and was to be paid as from January 1664. But even this belated remuneration was allowed to fall into arrears, and in 1669, when Denham lay dying, a new rival appeared in the person of Dr. Christopher Wren. Webb now made a last effort to gain office, reminding the King of his past services, of his promised reversion of the Surveyorship, and of his inadequate remuneration. He had, he said, 'acted under S^r. John Denham, a person of Honour', but he 'conceived it much beneath him, to doe ye like under one, who in whatever respects is his inferior by farr. May Y^{or} Majestie please if not to confirm y^{or} Petitioner's Grant as in the honor of a King you appear to bee obliged, then to Joyne him in Patent with Mr. Wren and he shalbee ready to instruct him in the course of the office of y^{or} works, whereof hee professeth to bee wholy ignorant, and y^{or} Petitioner, if you vouchsafe, may take care of your Majesties works at Greenwich, or elsewhere as hitherto hee hath done.' But once more Webb's claims were passed over, and it was Wren who took Denham's place as Surveyor-General. Webb himself had only three more years to live; he died at Butleigh on 30 October 1672, and was buried in the aisle of the parish church. He left three sons and four daughters. One of the latter married Dr. John Westley (d. 1687), a lawyer who also practised architecture, chiefly, perhaps exclusively, in Ireland.[1]

By his will (P.C.C. 145 EURE), dated 24 October 1672, Webb left his library and all his 'Prints and Cutts and drawings of Architecture of what nature or kind soever' to his son William, with instructions to 'keepe them intire together without selling or imbezzling any of them'. But William Webb did not long survive his father, and his widow disregarded her father-in-law's last wishes. Some of Webb's books were already on sale in London in 1675 (see Hooke's *Diary*, 2 April and 22 June), and by the 1680s many of the drawings had already passed into the possession of John Oliver (*q.v.*). Their subsequent acquisition by Lord Burlington and Dr. George

---

[1] But he was not prepared to refuse it if the opportunity arose, for, in April 1657, he wrote to Sir Christopher Hatton to say that his name had been put forward for nomination as a Commissioner under the Act for regulating building in London, and that although he 'would not seeme to seeke after so troublous emploiment yett I think it improper to neglect so faire opportunity whereby I may bee further enabled to expresse my selfe' (B.M., Add. MS. 29550, f. 297). For this 'Act for preventing multiplicity of Buildings in and about the Suburbs of London', which was passed on 26 June 1657, see *Acts and Ordinances of the Interregnum*, ed. Firth and Rait, i, 1223–34.

[2] The original document, lacking only the Great Seal, is among the Butleigh deeds in the Somerset County Record Office.

[1] See Bodleian, Carte MS. 31, ff. 440–1, and B.M., Add. MS. 15893, ff. 243, 245, 247. For information about Westley I am indebted to Dr. Rolf Loeber.

Clarke, and their ultimate division between the R.I.B.A. Drawings Collection and Worcester College, Oxford, is described above (p. 470). Many of the drawings in Lord Burlington's collection were published by William Kent in 1727 as *The Designs of Inigo Jones*, though the selection was in fact almost entirely from Webb's drawings, and it was not until 1911 that Mr. J. A. Gotch demonstrated that these and other drawings hitherto attributed to Inigo Jones were in reality from the hand of his pupil. Apart from the two collections already mentioned, the only other drawings known to be by Webb are several at Lamport Hall, one at Belvoir, another at Alnwick, and two in the Victoria and Albert Museum. Webb's somewhat hard and meticulous hand is, in fact, easily distinguishable from that of his master, which has a spontaneous quality lacking in the more studied work of the pupil. Webb was nevertheless an accomplished draughtsman, and some of his later drawings (*e.g.* for Lamport) show something of the ease and freedom which are lacking in his earlier studies.

Webb's achievement as a practising architect was curtailed by war and misfortune. Many of the buildings for which he made designs never materialized, and the list given below contains less than a dozen works of any consequence. Some of these, however, were buildings of crucial importance in the history of English architecture; the famous interiors at Wilton, the first country-house portico at The Vyne, one of the outstanding houses of the Restoration period at Amesbury, and the King Charles Block of Greenwich Palace. The last demonstrates, moreover, that Webb was something more than just a faithful disciple of Inigo Jones, who never deviated from the manner that he had learned from his master. For it shows that in the ten years after Inigo Jones's death, Webb had learned to handle such baroque devices as the giant order and the impendent keystone, while the Whitehall drawings, as analysed by Dr. Whinney, can now be seen to 'bridge the gap, in style as well as in time, between the school of Inigo Jones and that of Wren'.

In 1655 Webb published an account of *The Most Notable Antiquity called Stone-Heng*, based on notes left by Inigo Jones, in which he endeavoured to show that it was of Roman origin. Dr. William Charleton, in his *Chorea Gigantum* (1663), was equally emphatic in attributing the monument to the Danes, and in 1665 Webb replied in *A Vindication of Stone-Heng Restored* (2nd ed. 1725). He also published in 1669 a curious work entitled *An Historical Essay endeavouring a Probability that the Language of the Empire of China is the Primitive Language*, with a dedication to Charles II. An intended treatise on architecture is represented only by many drawings at Worcester College that were evi-

dently prepared with such a publication in mind. Among Webb's drawings there is his design for the architectural title-page of B. Walton's *Biblia Polyglotta*, engraved by Hollar and published in 1657.

[*A.P.S.D.*; *D.N.B.*; Wood, *Athenae Oxonienses*, ed. Bliss, iv, 1820, 754; *Register of Merchant Taylors' School*, ed. C. J. Robinson, i, 1882, 114; Walpole Soc., *Vertue Note Books* i, 49; Hist. MSS. Comm., *Seventh Report*, 88a (note); *Wren Soc.* xviii, 154–7; will, P.C.C. 145 EURE; W. G. Keith, 'John Webb and the Court Theatre of Charles II', *Arch. Rev.* lvii, Feb. 1925; W. G. Keith, 'John Webb and the Marshalls', *R.I.B.A. Jnl.*, 3rd ser., xl, 1933, 732; Margaret Whinney, 'Some Church Designs by John Webb', *Jnl. of the Warburg and Courtauld Institutes* vi, 1943; Margaret Whinney, 'John Webb's Drawings for Whitehall Palace', *Walpole Soc.* xxxi for 1942–3, 1946; *Catalogue of the R.I.B.A. Drawings Collection: Inigo Jones & John Webb*, by John Harris, 1972; *History of the King's Works* v, 1976, *passim*; John Harris & A. A. Tait, forthcoming *Catalogue of Seventeenth-Century Architectural Drawings in the Library of Worcester College, Oxford*; see also the bibliography for Inigo Jones, above p. 471.]

HALE PARK, HANTS., design, apparently unexecuted, for a 'lodge' or villa for John Penruddock, 1638 [R.I.B.A.D.].

HASSENBROOK HALL, ESSEX, design, probably unexecuted, for a stable for Henry Fetherstone, 1638 [R.I.B.A.D.].

NEW MEAD, MAIDEN BRADLEY, WILTS., design for a house for 'Colonel Ludlow at Mayden Bradley, Wiltshire' (Worcester Coll.), presumably before 1650, when Col. Edmund Ludlow was promoted to the rank of Lieut. General by Cromwell. It is very doubtful whether this was built, as Aubrey says (1671) 'there was a handsome well-built house, built by Sir Henry Ludlowe [Edmund's father] or his ancestors, now dilapidated since the late warres' (*Wiltshire Collections*, ed. J. E. Jackson, 1862, 383–4). A house on the site was dem. *c.* 1881 to make way for a farm.

WILTON HOUSE, WILTS., reconstruction of interior after fire of 1647/8, for the 4th Earl of Pembroke, 1648–50 [H. M. Colvin, 'The South Front of Wilton House', *Archaeological Jnl.* cxi, 1955, 187–9] (Oliver Hill & John Cornforth, *English Country Houses: Caroline*, 1966, 75–87).

LONDON, DURHAM HOUSE, STRAND, unexecuted designs for a new house for the 4th Earl of Pembroke, 1649 [Worcester Coll.].

COLESHILL HOUSE, BERKS., designs for chimneypiece, etc., for Sir George Pratt, Bart., *c.* 1650 [R.I.B.A.D. and Chatsworth 'Book of Capitals']. For this house see above, pp. 658–9.

LONDON, THE ROYAL COLLEGE OF PHYSICIANS, library and repository, 1651–3; destroyed by fire 1666 [Worcester Coll. and Chatsworth 'Book of Capitals'; see C. E. Newman, 'The First Library of the Royal College of Physicians', *Jnl. of the Royal College of Physicians* iii (3), 1969].

DRAYTON HOUSE, NORTHANTS., designs for chimney-pieces for the 2nd Earl of Peterborough, 1653 [R.I.B.A.D.]. One of Webb's chimney-pieces still exists in the State Bedchamber (H. A. Tipping, *English Homes, Period IV* (i), 1929, figs. 343–4).

THE VYNE, HANTS., altered the interior and designed the portico for Chaloner Chute, 1654–6 [there are two designs for capitals by Webb for 'Mr. Chute at the Vine', one dated 1654, in the Chatsworth 'Book of Capitals': for other evidence pointing to Webb as the architect see W. G. Keith in *R.I.B.A. Jnl.*, 3rd ser., xl, 1933, 732; Edward Marshall's contract to build the portico, dated 4 March 1654, is now in the Hants. Record Office] (*C. Life*, 14–21 May 1921, 3 Jan. 1957).

CHEVENING HOUSE, KENT, work for the 14th Lord Dacre, 1655. On 16 April 1655 Webb wrote to Sir Justinian Isham of Lamport that he was designing 'ornaments of wainscott for a roome in Kent for my Lo: Dacres wch is 31 fo: long 22 broad & 24 fo: high', and in the Chatsworth 'Book of Capitals' there is a drawing of a capital by Webb which is inscribed 'Lo. Dacre's at Chevening'. The room in question may have been the existing Saloon, but the dimensions do not correspond exactly with those given by Webb. See *Vitruvius Britannicus* ii, 1717, pl. 85, for plans and elevation of the house as existing in 1717, and Oliver Hill & John Cornforth, *English Country Houses: Caroline*, 1966, 25–6, and John Newman, *West Kent and the Weald* (Buildings of England, 1976), for the problems connected with its architectural history.

LUDLOW, SALOP., corresponded with Col. Edward Harley about a projected building there, 1655 [*Wren Soc.* xviii, 154–5].

LAMPORT HALL, NORTHANTS., for Sir Justinian Isham, Bart., 1655–7; wings added by Francis and William Smith 1732–40, ceiling of Music Hall remodelled 1738 [J. A. Gotch, 'Some Newly-found Drawings and Letters of John Webb', *R.I.B.A. Jnl.*, 3rd ser., xxviii, 1921; Sir Gyles Isham, 'The Architectural History of Lamport', *Reports of the Northants. Architectural and Archaeological Soc.* lvii, 1951] (*C. Life*, 26 Sept., 3, 10 Oct. 1952).

BELVOIR CASTLE, LEICS., reconstruction after 'slighting' by Parliamentary forces in 1649, for the 8th Earl of Rutland, 1655–68; remodelled 1800 onwards. Webb visited Belvoir in 1654 [letter of 20 July 1654 to Sir Justinian Isham of Lamport], and a working drawing in his hand for 'The Architrave freese and cornice that goes about the roome 1667' is preserved in the Belvoir archives [Map 127]. A summary of the building accounts [Belvoir archives, Misc. MS. 67] shows that £11,730 was spent between 1655 and 1668. Unexecuted designs by Webb for a much grander house are in R.I.B.A.D. The castle as rebuilt in 1655–68 is shown in an engraving by Badeslade & Rocque in *Vitruvius Brittanicus* iv, 1739, and by a model made in 1799 and preserved at Belvoir.

SYON HOUSE, ISLEWORTH, MIDDLESEX, work for the 10th Earl of Northumberland, 1656 [Percy archives at Alnwick Castle, U.III.5, including a survey by Edward Marshall and others dated 21 Jan. 1655, 'Mr. Webb's estimate of vaultinge the sellar att Syon & making chymneys on my Lord's lodgings', and a drawing by Webb dated 1656 for a modillion cornice 'to goe round his Lopp⁵. House at Sion']. The cornice was not executed, and nothing recognizable appears to remain of these alterations.

LONDON, NORTHUMBERLAND HOUSE, STRAND, internal alterations for the 10th Earl of Northumberland, 1657–60; dem. 1874 [R.I.B.A.D., drawings by Webb for chimney-pieces in the dining-room (1657) and withdrawing-room (1660); letter at Chatsworth from Webb to Edward Marshall dated 17 Oct. 1658 about modelling a pedestal for the Earl of Northumberland, printed by W. G. Keith in *R.I.B.A. Jnl.*, 3rd ser., xl, 1933, 733; Percy archives at Alnwick Castle, U.III.3, account of Edward Marshall for mason's work performed in 1655–7 totalling £899, including the great stone stairs from the dining-room down to the terrace (£200), and 'the greate carved Pedestall and bringing it from Fetter Lane to Northumberland Garden' (£9)]. For an engraving showing the 'great stone stairs' see Dodsley's *London and its Environs* v, 1761, 59.

GUNNERSBURY HOUSE, MIDDLESEX, for Sir John Maynard, c. 1658–63; dem. 1801 [R.I.B.A.D., design by Webb for chimney-piece in 'the little Parlor, Gunnersbury', and designs for capitals 'for Serjeant Maynard Gunnersbury' in the Chatsworth 'Book of Capitals'. In a letter at Chatsworth printed by W. G. Keith in *R.I.B.A. Jnl.*, 3rd ser., xl, 1933, 733, Webb writes to tell Edward Marshall that he is about to 'measure off the worke at Gunnersbury', 17 Oct. 1658; the date 1663 is that given by Campbell (plan and elevation in *Vitruvius Britannicus* i, 1715, pls. 18–19; engraving in Dodsley's *London and its Environs* iii, 1761, 110).

AMESBURY HOUSE, WILTS., for William Seymour, 1st Marquess of Hertford (1640) and 2nd Duke of Somerset (1660), begun before 1660, perhaps completed 1661 (the date given by Campbell); rebuilt 1834–40 [drawing by Webb at Chatsworth (vol. 24, no. 13) for a capital in-

scribed 'Ambresbury for Marquess Hertford';
cf. Walpole Soc., *Vertue Note Books* ii, 32]
(*Vitruvius Britannicus* iii, 1725, pl. 7; W. Kent,
Designs of Inigo Jones ii, 1727, pls. 8–9;
sketches by C. R. Cockerell in *Architectural
History* xiv, 1971, fig. 1 A; measured drawings
by Wyatt Papworth in R.I.B.A.D.; detail of
staircase in *Builder* ii, 1844, 563).
GREENWICH, THE QUEEN'S HOUSE, alterations, including addition of the east and west bridges,
1661–2 [G. H. Chettle, *The Queen's House*,
1937, 39–40, 84; *History of the King's Works*
v, 144–7].
attributed: LONDON, SOMERSET HOUSE, STRAND,
THE GALLERY for the Queen Mother Henrietta
Maria, 1662–3; dem. 1776 [*History of the
King's Works* v, 255–6 and pl. 32] (inaccurate
engraving in *Vitruvius Britannicus* i, 1715, pl.
16).
GREENWICH PALACE (now HOSPITAL), THE KING
CHARLES II BLOCK, 1664–9, designed as part of
a new palace that was not completed [*History
of the King's Works* v, 147–51; for the complete
plan see figs. 2 and 3] (*Vitruvius Britannicus*
i, 1715, pls. 88–9).
LONDON, WHITEHALL PALACE, probably remodelled the COCKPIT THEATRE for King Charles
II, *c.* 1665; dem. [W. G. Keith, 'John Webb
and the Court Theatre of Charles II', *Arch.
Rev.* lvii, 1925].
attributed: LONDON, ASHBURNHAM HOUSE, WEST-
MINSTER, which was apparently built by
William Ashburnham before 1662. His descendant John, 1st Earl of Ashburnham, told
Batty Langley that Webb was the architect
employed [B. Langley, *Ancient Masonry* i,
1736, 391] (H. Sirr, 'Ashburnham House',
R.I.B.A. Jnl., 3rd ser., xvii, 1910; *C. Life*, 3
Sept. 1943; plan and section of staircase in
Isaac Ware's *Designs of Inigo Jones*, pls. 6–7).

WEBB, JOHN (*c.* 1754–1828), was an architect
and landscape-gardener who lived at Lee Hall in
the village of Armitage, nr. Lichfield. By 1805 his
practice as a landscape-gardener was reported to
be 'all over England', and in the course of that
year he is known to have been consulted at Eaton
Hall, Cheshire, Sandon Hall, Staffs., Ashridge
Park, Herts., and Cassiobury Park, Herts. [corres-
pondence in Harrowby and Grosvenor
archives]. In Cheshire he laid out the grounds at
Cholmondeley Hall, Bradwell Manor (Sand-
bach), Poole Hall (Nantwich), Oulton Park,
Somerford Park and Tatton Park [see Ormerod,
History of Cheshire, ed. Helsby, i, 444, ii, 219, iii,
114, 352, 560, and Loudon's *Encyclopaedia of
Gardening*, 1828, 1081]. Elsewhere he is known
to have been consulted about landscaping at Astley Hall, Lancs., Campsmount (Campsall),
Yorks. (1802), Grove Park, Warwicks. (1804),

Holkham Hall, Norfolk (1801–3), Lowther
Castle, Westmorland (1807), Quernmore Park,
Lancs., Serlby Hall, Notts., Shugborough,
Staffs. (1804), Weston Hall, Staffs. (1827–8), and
Woolley Park, Yorks. (1811). According to
Ormerod he was a pupil of William Eames (d.
1803), a landscape-gardener himself said to have
been 'an élève of the great Brown'.

In Neale's *Seats* (2nd ser., iii, 1826) it is stated
that Webb designed WANSTEAD GROVE, ESSEX, for
the Hon. Anne Rushout, and he no doubt laid
out the 'extensive Pleasure Grounds'. The house,
which was built in 1821–3, was demolished later
in the nineteenth century. In her diaries (in private possession) Miss Rushout refers on several
occasions to 'my friend Mr. Webbe', and mentions his employment as an architect at APLEY
PARK, SALOP., a castellated Gothic mansion built
by Thomas Whitmore in 1811 (F. Calvert & W.
West, *Picturesque Views in Staffs. and Salop.* ii,
1831, 131; *C. Life*, 25 May 1907, 738), and at
THRYBERGH PARK, YORKS. (W.R.), which he rebuilt
for Col. J. Fullerton in *c.* 1820. He also designed
WARLEIGH HOUSE, SOMERSET, for Henry Skrine in
the Tudor Gothic style in 1814, as recorded in
Neale's *Seats*, 2nd ser., i, 1824, and carried out
alterations to SOMERFORD BOOTHS HALL, CHESHIRE,
for Clement Swetenham in 1817 [Ormerod, iii,
560] (Neale, 2nd ser., i, 1824). He was doubtless
the 'Mr. Webb' who remodelled the exterior of
OMBERSLEY COURT, WORCS., for the Marchioness
of Downshire in 1812–14 and designed the
stables [Arthur Oswald in *C. Life*, 16 Jan. 1953].
Unexecuted designs by Webb include one for a
Gothic lodge preserved at Alscot Park, Warwicks. (1810), and a Gothic scheme for the reconstruction of ETTINGTON PARK, WARWICKS. (1814),
now among the Shirley papers in the County
Record Office at Warwick.

Webb died at Lee Hall on 25 May 1828, aged
74, and was buried in Armitage Churchyard
[*Gent's Mag.* 1828 (i), 573; P.C.C. 565 SUTTON].

WEBB, THOMAS, of Middlewich in Cheshire,
'freemason', designed ERDDIG PARK, DENBIGH-
SHIRE, for Joshua Edisbury in 1683. In November
of that year, he agreed to 'entertake and perform
the care & oversight of the contriving building
& finishing of a case or body of a new house ffor
the said Joshua Edsbury att Erthigge aforesaid
... according to the designs, compass, manner &
methode of draughts already given by the said
Thomas Webb'. Contracts were made in March
1684 with Edward Price, mason, and William
Carter of Chester, bricklayer, and the house was
completed in about three years. [Lady Cust (Mrs.
Wherry), *Chronicles of Erthig on the Dyke*, 1914;
C. Life, 16–23 Aug. 1930.]

In 1696 Webb is named as measurer in a contract between Sir Willoughby Aston and Edward
Nixon of Chester, mason, for building the

874

chancel of the church of ASTON-BY-SUTTON, CHESHIRE [B.M., Add. MS. 36919, ff. 249–50].

WEBSTER, GEORGE (1797–1864), of Kendal in Westmorland, was the son of Francis Webster (1767–1827), builder and architect of the same town. Francis Webster was the son of a mason at Quarry Flat, nr. Cartmel. As a young man he moved to Kendal, where he entered into partnership with a mason called William Holme. Here he developed a highly successful business as a builder, specializing in the production of monuments and marble chimney-pieces. In 1788 he was the first to polish Kendal Fell limestone for making into chimney-pieces, and in 1800 he devised water-powered machinery for sawing and polishing marble, and eventually for accurately cutting both classical and Gothic mouldings. Although primarily a builder and marble-mason, Francis Webster also acted as an architect, designing such buildings as workhouses, warehouses, bridges and the firm's own offices and showrooms in Kendal. Between 1796 and 1802 he was responsible for an abortive scheme to rehabilitate the gutted Lowther Hall for the 1st Earl of Lonsdale, who eventually employed Robert Smirke to design an entirely new house. In about 1820 he took his son George into partnership, and began to extend the architectural side of the firm of 'Francis Webster and Sons'. Although some highly finished sets of drawings of this period bear Francis's name he was probably not their author but signed as the senior partner. By 1818 Francis was sufficiently prosperous to buy an estate at Eller How, nr. Lindale, where he enlarged a cottage into a small country house. He was a prominent figure in the public life of Kendal, and served as Mayor in 1823–4. He died at Eller How on 10 October 1827, and is commemorated both by a tombstone in Kendal Churchyard and by a tablet at Lindale.

George Webster, born on 3 May 1797, must have had a professional training in an architect's office. As he did not attend the Royal Academy Schools in London it seems likely that he was apprenticed to some northern architect such as Harrison of Chester or Foster of Liverpool. After his father's death in 1827 he devoted his time entirely to architecture, leaving the management of the marble works to his brother Francis. In 1845 Miles Thompson, who had been employed as a draughtsman since the 1820s, was taken into partnership, and the firm became 'Webster and Thompson'. George Webster was Mayor of Kendal in 1829–30. He visited Italy more than once in middle life, and made a collection of Roman coins, medals and other antiquities. He died on 16 April 1864, and was buried in a vault which he had built in Lindale Churchyard. As an architect he had a considerable practice in

north-west England in the 1820s and 1830s. His classical public buildings and Gothic churches were standard products of their time, but at Eshton and Underley he designed two of the earliest country houses in the revived Jacobean style which became his speciality. These are contemporary with William Burn's earliest experiments with the same style in Scotland, and were (with Salvin's Moreby and Harlaxton) singled out for commendation in the preface to Shaw's *Details of Elizabethan Architecture*. Several other houses in the same style (notably Whittington Hall, nr. Kirkby Lonsdale, 1831) can be attributed to Webster, who must be regarded as a remarkably able and precocious pioneer of the Jacobethan revival.

[Jeffrey P. Haworth & Angus C. Taylor, *The Websters of Kendal*, catalogue of exhibition at Abbot Hall, Kendal, 1973; C. Nicholson, *Annals of Kendal*, 1861; monumental inscriptions at Cartmel, Kendal and Lindale.]

PUBLIC BUILDINGS, ETC.

KENDAL, WESTMORLAND, ASSEMBLY ROOMS (now TOWN HALL), HIGHGATE, 1825–7; addition of Clock Tower by G. K. when converted to Town Hall 1859; enlarged 1893 [C. Nicholson, *Annals of Kendal*, 1861, 151–2].

SETTLE, YORKS. (W.R.), PUBLIC ROOMS (now TOWN HALL), MARKET PLACE, 1832, Jacobean [*The Websters of Kendal*, no. 65].

KENDAL, WESTMORLAND, DOWKER'S HOSPITAL, HIGHGATE, 1833, Tudor; dem. 1965 [C. Nicholson, *Annals of Kendal*, 1861, 228].

KENDAL, WESTMORLAND, THE BANK OF WESTMORLAND (now Midland Bank), HIGHGATE, 1834–5 [C. Nicholson, *Annals of Kendal*, 1861, 153].

BOWNESS-ON-WINDERMERE SCHOOL, WESTMORLAND, 1836, Tudor; dem. 1973 [signed tablet formerly on school].

ULVERSTON, LANCS., THE TRUSTEE SAVINGS BANK, 1837–8; clock-tower added 1844; interior of ground floor rebuilt 1850 [Angus Taylor, 'Ulverston Trustee Savings Bank', *Trans. Cumberland and Westmorland A. and A. Soc.* lxxiv, 1974].

BOWNESS-ON-WINDERMERE, WESTMORLAND, THE ROYAL HOTEL, c. 1839, Italianate [engraving endorsed by Webster as built 'under my direction', *ex inf.* Mr. Angus Taylor].

RIGGS (now WINDERMERE) HOTEL, WINDERMERE, WESTMORLAND, 1845 [*Westmorland Gazette*, 8 Nov. 1845, *ex inf.* Mr. Angus Taylor].

KIRKBY LONSDALE, WESTMORLAND, THE TRUSTEE SAVINGS BANK, MARKET PLACE, 1847 [Minute Books of the Bank, *ex inf.* Mr. Angus Taylor].

KENDAL, WESTMORLAND, THE MARKET HALL, 1855; converted into public library 1892, when façade was re-erected in Sandes Avenue [C. Nicholson, *Annals of Kendal*, 1861, 157–8].

CHURCHES

BURNSIDE, WESTMORLAND, rebuilt 1823–6, Gothic; rebuilt 1880 [I.C.B.S.].

RYDAL, WESTMORLAND, 1824–5, Gothic [specification in Cumbria Record Office, Kendal, *ex inf.* Mr. Angus Taylor].

NATLAND, WESTMORLAND, rebuilt 1825–6, Gothic; rebuilt 1909 [I.C.B.S.]

LINDALE, LANCS., 1828–9, Gothic; north aisle 1912 [I.C.B.S.].

NEW HUTTON, WESTMORLAND, rebuilt 1828–9, Gothic [I.C.B.S.].

KENDAL, WESTMORLAND, HOLY TRINITY (R.C.), 1835–7, Gothic [*Civil Engineer and Architect's Jnl.* i, 1837–8, 57].

attributed: MILNTHORPE, WESTMORLAND, rebuilt 1835–7, Gothic; remodelled 1882–3 [stylistic attribution].

KENDAL, WESTMORLAND, ST. THOMAS, 1835–7, Gothic [C. Nicholson, *Annals of Kendal*, 1861, 76–7].

GRAYRIGG, WESTMORLAND, rebuilt 1838, Gothic; west tower 1869 [I.C.B.S.].

KENDAL, WESTMORLAND, ST. GEORGE, 1839–41, Gothic; chancel 1910–11; west towers truncated 1940 [C. Nicholson, *Annals of Kendal*, 1861, 77].

GRASMERE, WESTMORLAND, alterations, 1840 [*The Websters of Kendal*, no. 96].

CLEATOR, CUMBERLAND, 1841–2, Gothic [I.C.B.S.].

BARDSEA, LANCS., 1843–53, Gothic [*Westmorland Gazette*, 9 Sept. 1843, *ex inf.* Mr. Angus Taylor].

DOMESTIC ARCHITECTURE

READ HALL, nr. WHALLEY, LANCS., for John Fort, 1818–25 [T. D. Whitaker, *History of Whalley* ii, 1876, 40].

KENDAL, WESTMORLAND, houses on THORNY HILLS, including No. 4 for himself, 1823 onwards [*The Websters of Kendal*, no. 44].

HELME LODGE, nr. KENDAL, WESTMORLAND, for W. D. Crewdson, 1824 [*The Websters of Kendal*, no. 9].

RIGMADEN, nr. KIRKBY LONSDALE, WESTMORLAND, for Christopher Wilson, 1825; now in ruins [*The Websters of Kendal*, no. 10].

UNDERLEY HALL, nr. KIRKBY LONSDALE, WESTMORLAND, for Alexander Nowell, 1825–8, Jacobean; tower, etc., added 1872 [exhib. at R.A. 1826; *Local Chronology, being notes of the Principal Events published in the Kendal Newspapers*, 1865, 61] (*The Websters of Kendal*, plate showing original design and house before alteration).

ESHTON HALL, GARGRAVE, YORKS. (W.R.), for Matthew Wilson, 1825–7, Jacobean [J. P. Neale, *Views of Seats*, 2nd ser., v, 1829].

DALLAM TOWER, BEETHAM, WESTMORLAND, remodelled for George Wilson, 1826 [*The Websters of Kendal*, no. 13].

HUTTON-IN-THE-FOREST, CUMBERLAND, south-east tower for Francis Vane, 1826, perhaps in collaboration with A. Salvin [John Cornforth in *C. Life*, 4, 11 and 18 Feb. 1965; *The Websters of Kendal*, no. 14].

ELLER HOW, LINDALE, LANCS., enlarged first by Francis Webster, *c.* 1818, and then by G. Webster, 1828, *cottage orné* style [Twycross, *Mansions of England and Wales: Lancashire* ii, 1847, 31].

THURLAND CASTLE, TUNSTALL, LANCS., new drawing-room, etc., for R. T. North, *c.* 1827–9; altered after fire in 1879 [*V.C.H. Lancs.* viii, 236; cf. D. Linstrum, *Wyatville*, 249].

MORETON HALL, WHALLEY, LANCS., for John Taylor, 1829, Jacobethan; dem. 1955 [T. D. Whitaker, *History of Whalley* ii, 1876, 41] (E. Baines, *History of Lancashire* iii, 1836, 192, engraving).

PENWORTHAM PRIORY, nr. PRESTON, LANCS., remodelled for Lt. Col. Lawrence Rawstorne, 1832, Jacobethan; dem. *c.* 1922 [*The Websters of Kendal*, no. 22].

ORMEROD HOUSE, nr. BURNLEY, LANCS., west porch, etc., for Col. John Hargeaves, 1833–4, Jacobean; dem. *c.* 1950 [T. D. Whitaker, *History of Whalley*, 4th ed., ii, 1876, 221, n. 1].

DOWNHAM HALL, CLITHEROE, LANCS., remodelled for William Assheton, 1834–5 [*The Websters of Kendal*, no. 25].

BROUGHTON HALL, nr. SKIPTON, YORKS. (W.R.), alterations and additions, including refacing of north front, addition of portico and clock-tower and White Drawing-Room, for Sir Charles Tempest, Bart., 1838–41 [C. Hussey in *C. Life*, 31 March–14 April 1950; *The Websters of Kendal*, no. 30].

EDEN GROVE, BOLTON, WESTMORLAND, for Richard Tinkler, *c.* 1840, Tudor [stated to be 'by the late Mr. Webster of Kendal' in sale catalogue of 1872 in Kendal Library].

HOLKER HALL, nr. CARTMEL, LANCS., remodelled for the 2nd Earl of Burlington (d. 1891), *c.* 1840, Elizabethan; partly rebuilt after a fire in 1871 [*V.C.H. Lancs.* viii, 272, n. 33].

HEYSHAM HALL, LANCS., for Thomas Rawstorne, *c.* 1840; mutilated [letter from Rawstorne in Cumbria Record Office, Kendal, 6 July 1840, *ex inf.* Mr. Angus Taylor].

BLACK ROCK VILLA, GRANGE-OVER-SANDS, LANCS., for himself, 1840–1, and alterations, 1851; mutilated [*The Websters of Kendal*, no. 47].

WEBSTER, THOMAS (1773–1844), was a native of the Orkneys. He was admitted to the Royal Academy Schools as an architectural student in 1793, and appears to have been a pupil of Robert Mitchell, at whose address in Newman

Street he was living in 1796. His professional card in the R.I.B.A. Collection (E4/114) shows that he subsequently described himself as a 'Teacher of Architecture, Perspective, etc.', and offered to give instruction in 'Geometry, Mensuration, Land Surveying, Architecture, The doctrine of Light & Shadow, Perspective, Landscape & the Elements of Natural Philosophy'. In 1800 he assisted Count Rumford in the design of the Lecture Theatre, Library and Repository of the ROYAL INSTITUTION in ALBEMARLE STREET, LONDON, though their plans were subsequently revised by James Spiller (*q.v.*) [*Architects' Jnl.*, 23 Oct. 1941, 269–70]. His only recorded work as an architect appears to be THE OBSERVATORY at GLASGOW, built in 1810 to the designs of 'Mr. Webster of London' [R. Chapman, *Picture of Glasgow*, 1822, 166]. By 1814 he had abandoned architecture and embarked on a distinguished career as a geologist, ending with a chair at University College, London. He died in London on 26 December 1844, aged 72 [*D.N.B.*].

WEIR, JAMES, of Tolcross, Edinburgh, variously described as 'wright' and 'architect', contracted in October 1773 to complete the structure of ST. CUTHBERT'S CHURCH, EDINBURGH, on foundations already laid, but to modified designs whose authorship is unknown [S.R.O., GD 69/210]. The attribution to Weir of the steeple added in 1789 is without authority: its authorship is not mentioned in the Heritors' minutes [S.R.O., HR 152/2], but it may have been designed by Alexander Stevens (*q.v.*).

WEIR, JOHN, was described as 'architect' when he was admitted to the Incorporation of Wrights of Glasgow in 1814 [*The Incorporation of Wrights in Glasgow*, 1880, 68]. His only known work appears to be the façades of LONDON STREET, GLASGOW, 1824; dem. [T. Gildard in *Trans. Royal Philosophical Soc. of Glasgow* xxvi, 1895, 122; A. Gomme & D. Walker, *Architecture of Glasgow*, 1968, 72]. James Wylson (1811–70) was his pupil [*A.P.S.D.*, s.v. 'Wylson, James'].

WELCH, EDWARD (1806–1868), was born at Overton in Flintshire in 1806. He became a pupil or assistant of John Oates of Halifax and in 1828 entered into partnership with Joseph Aloysius Hansom (1803–82), who was also in Oates's office. They established themselves first in York and then in Liverpool, and designed several churches and other buildings in Yorkshire, Lancashire and North Wales. In 1830 they won the important competition for the Town Hall at Birmingham, defeating, among others, Barry, Beazley, Goodwin and Rickman. The successful design was Hansom's, but a modification of the clients' requirements led ultimately to the adoption of a different design for which Welch

claimed some share of credit. The result was a large peripteral temple of the Corinthian order standing on a high rusticated basement and enclosing a spacious galleried hall. As an architectural concept it was simple and dignified, though much less sophisticated than H. L. Elmes's Liverpool hall of ten years later. The building was to be faced with a hard stone from Anglesey recommended by the architects. Doubts were expressed about the contractors' ability to perform the work for the agreed sum, and the architects unwisely stood surety for the builders. The cost of quarrying, transporting and working the Anglesey stone proved to be far greater than the two young architects had supposed: all their financial resources were soon exhausted, and bankruptcy ensued in 1834. John Foster of Liverpool was then brought in to supervise the work, but the building was eventually completed in 1849 under the direction of Charles Edge (*q.v.*).

After this catastrophe the two architects parted company. Hansom took up business management (incidentally founding the *Builder* and inventing the 'Hansom cab') before resuming an architectural practice which lasted until 1879.[1] Welch returned to Liverpool, where he practised from 1837 to 1849. Of the latter years of his life little is known, but he appears to have devoted his attention chiefly to the heating and ventilation of houses, for which he took out patents in 1850 and 1865. He died in Southampton Row, London, on 3 August 1868. According to the *Builder* he was 'a man of liberal and expansive ideas, and generously open to the merits and abilities of others, while modestly undervaluing his own'.

[*Builder* xxvi, 1868, 863, xliii, 1882, 43–4; *D.N.B.*, *s.v.* 'Hansom, J. A.'; *Architectural Mag.* ii, 1835, 16–27, 237–9, 325–6.]

BUILDINGS BY HANSOM & WELCH

COLLINGHAM VICARAGE, YORKS. (W.R.), enlarged 1828 [Borthwick Institute, York, MGA 1828/3].

BEAUMARIS GAOL, ANGLESEY, 1828–9 [*Builder* xxvi, 1868, 863; *N. Wales Chronicle*, 17 Jan. 1828].

MIDDLEHAM, YORKS. (N.R.), SUSPENSION BRIDGE (R. Ure), 1829 [inscription].

YORK, THE DISPENSARY, NEW STREET, 1829; dem. 1899 [*V.C.H. Yorks., City of York*, 470–1].

---

[1] Among Hansom's early architectural works were THE TOWN HALL at LUTTERWORTH, LEICS., 1836 [*Architectural Mag.* iii, 1836, 569–73, iv, 405–7]; the DOMINICAN CONVENT at ATHERSTONE, WARWICKS., 1837–41 [*Gent's Mag.* 1837 (ii), 644]; parts of the BENEDICTINE PRIORY at PRINCETHORPE, WARWICKS., 1837–50 [*Catholic Annual Register*, 1850, 116]; and the NONCONFORMIST PROPRIETARY SCHOOL, now THE MUSEUM, LEICESTER, 1837 [*V.C.H. Leics.* iv, 335].

HULL, YORKS. (E.R.), ST. JAMES'S CHURCH, MYTON, 1829–31; dem. 1957, Gothic [*V.C.H. Yorks.*, *E.R.* i, 293].

ACOMB CHURCH, YORKS. (W.R.), rebuilt 1830–1, Gothic [I.C.B.S.].

LIVERPOOL, ST. JOHN'S CHURCH, TOXTETH PARK, 1830–2, Gothic [*Builder* xxvi, 1868, 863].

KING WILLIAM'S COLLEGE, ISLE OF MAN, 1830–3, Gothic; gutted by fire 1844 and rebuilt [*Builder* ii, 1844, 41].

BEAUMARIS, ANGLESEY, VICTORIA TERRACE, 1830–5 [*Builder* xxvi, 1868, 863] (*Shell Guide to North Wales*, 1971, 68).

BEAUMARIS, ANGLESEY, THE BULKELEY ARMS HOTEL, 1831–5 [*Builder* xxvi, 1868, 863].

BODELWYDDAN HALL, FLINTS., for Sir John Williams, Bart., *c.* 1830–40, castellated [*Builder* xliii, 1882, 43–4; cf. Lewis's *Topographical Dictionary of Wales* i, 1842, *s.v.* 'St. Asaph'].

DOUGLAS, ISLE OF MAN, ST. BARNABAS'S CHURCH, 1832, Gothic [L. D. Butler, *An Architectural History of the Churches in the Isle of Man*, typescript 1970, 9].

NEW BALLAUGH CHURCH, ISLE OF MAN, 1832, Gothic; altered 1893 [L. D. Butler, *op. cit.*, 10].

BIRMINGHAM, THE TOWN HALL, 1832–4, completed by Charles Edge (*q.v.*) [*Architectural Mag.* ii, 1835, 16–27, 237–9, 325–6; iii, 1836, 430–4].

ONCHAN CHURCH, ISLE OF MAN, 1833, Gothic; altered 1885 and 1933 [L. D. Butler, *op. cit.*, 10].

LONAN NEW CHURCH, ISLE OF MAN, 1833–4, Gothic [L. D. Butler, *op. cit.*, 10].

BIRMINGHAM, THE OPERATIVE BUILDERS' GUILD-HALL, SHADWELL STREET, 1833–4; dem. [*The Pioneer; or Trades Union Magazine*, 7 Dec. 1833, 107].

BUILDINGS BY EDWARD WELCH

LIVERPOOL, THE NORTHERN HOSPITAL, GREAT HOWARD STREET, 1834, Tudor; rebuilt [*Builder* xxvi, 1868, 863].

RHOS-Y-MEDRE CHURCH, nr. RUABON, DENBIGH-SHIRE, 1836–7, Gothic [I.C.B.S.].

YSGEIVIOG CHURCH, FLINTS., 1836–7, Gothic [D. R. Thomas, *History of the Diocese of St. Asaph*, 1870, 495].

BOLTON, LANCS., EMMANUEL CHURCH, CANNON STREET, 1837–9; chancel 1848; Gothic [G.R.].

ADLINGTON, LANCS., CHRIST CHURCH, 1838, neo-Norman [Port, 146–7].

HARPURHEY, nr. MANCHESTER, LANCS., CHRIST CHURCH, 1838–41, Gothic [*Christ Church Harpurhey, Centenary Souvenir*, 1938, 10, engraving with Welch's name].

SOWERBY, YORKS. (W.R.), ST. GEORGE'S CHURCH, QUARRY HILL, 1839–40, neo-Norman [account in Sowerby Parish Records, Leeds City Library Archives Dept.].

878

BARTON-UPON-IRWELL, LANCS., ST. CATHERINE'S CHURCH, 1843; chancel 1893; Gothic [G.R.].

WEST DERBY CHURCH, LANCS., ST. JAMES'S CHURCH, 1845–6; chancel 1876–9, Gothic [G.R.].

BIRKENHEAD, CHESHIRE, THE MONKS' FERRY HOTEL, *c.* 1845; dem. [*Builder* xxvi, 1868, 863].

BIRKENHEAD, CHESHIRE, ASSEMBLY ROOMS, MARKET STREET, 1846 [*Builder* iv, 1846, 200].

WELCH, JOHN (1810–), was Edward Welch's younger brother, and was born at Overton in Flintshire on 7 May 1810. Nothing certain is known about his early life, and his career as an architect appears to have begun when he arrived in the Isle of Man in about 1830. Here he was for a short time in partnership with a builder's merchant called John Moore, and may have superintended the erection of the buildings designed by his brother and Joseph Hansom. He was certainly involved in their financial disaster in 1834–5, but escaped bankruptcy and in 1836 advertised his services as 'architect, civil engineer and general surveyor'. By 1838, however, he had migrated to North Wales, where from 1839 he was established in St. Asaph. Later he moved to Preston in Lancashire, where he died before 1857. He designed a number of churches and other buildings in the Isle of Man, North Wales and Preston. According to W. Cubbon's *Bibliography of the Isle of Man*, 1939, he was the author of the anonymous *Six Days' Tour through the Isle of Man* published in 1836. [L. D. Butler, *An Architectural History of the Churches of the Isle of Man*, typescript 1970, 8–9.]

DOUGLAS, ISLE OF MAN, THE TOWER OF REFUGE, 1832, castellated [Butler, *op. cit.*].

MICHAEL CHURCH, ISLE OF MAN, 1835, Gothic [Butler, *op. cit.*].

LEZAYRE CHURCH, ISLE OF MAN, 1835, Gothic [Butler, *op. cit.*].

CASTLETOWN, ISLE OF MAN, THE SMELT COLUMN, 1836 [Butler, *op. cit.*].

FLINT TOWN HALL, 1837–9 [National Library of Wales, MSS. 6277–8].

BAGILLT CHURCH, FLINTS., 1837–9, Gothic [National Library of Wales, MS. 2590 E].

HOLYWELL, FLINTS., unexecuted design for Baths, 1837 [National Library of Wales, MS. 6293 E].

HOLYWELL, FLINTS., SAVINGS BANK, 1838 [Butler, *op. cit.*].

LLANBEDROG RECTORY, CAERNARVONSHIRE, alterations, 1838 [Butler, *op. cit.*].

ST. ASAPH UNION WORKHOUSE, FLINTS., 1838 [Butler, *op. cit.*].

BETTWS YN ROS CHURCH, DENBIGHSHIRE, 1838, Gothic [D. R. Thomas, *History of the Diocese of St. Asaph*, 1870, 356] (*Shell Guide to N. Wales*, 1971, 100).

LLANSANTFFRAID GLAN CONWAY CHURCH, DEN-

BIGHSHIRE, rebuilt 1839, Romanesque [I.C.B.S.].

LLANDUDNO CHURCH, CAERNARVONSHIRE, 1840, Gothic [I.C.B.S.].

LLANDEGWNING CHURCH, CAERNARVONSHIRE, 1840, Gothic [I.C.B.S.].

ABERDARON NEW CHURCH, CAERNARVONSHIRE, 1840–1, Romanesque [I.C.B.S.].

LLANFFINAN CHURCH, ANGLESEY, 1841, Romanesque [I.C.B.S.].

LLANIDAN NEW CHURCH, ANGLESEY, 1843, Gothic [I.C.B.S.].

PRESTON, LANCS., THE LITERARY AND PHILOSOPHICAL INSTITUTION, 1844–5, Gothic [C. Hardwick, *History of Preston*, 1857, 451–2].

PRESTON, LANCS., THE INSTITUTION FOR THE DIFFUSION OF USEFUL KNOWLEDGE, Grecian, 1846–9 [C. Hardwick, *History of Preston*, 1857, 449–50].

WELLS, JOHN, was a carpenter who became a freeman of Norwich in 1820. He exhibited twice at the Norwich Society of Artists, showing 'Three Cottages and a Dwelling House at Mile End' in 1824, and a 'Design for a Gothic Mansion in the style of the Fourteenth Century' in 1825 [*ex inf.* Mr. A. P. Baggs].

WENTWORTH, WILLIAM, 2ND EARL OF STRAFFORD (1722–1791), who succeeded his father in 1739, had some skill as an amateur architect. At his Yorkshire seat, WENTWORTH CASTLE, he built the Palladian south-east wing to his own designs in 1759–64, with John Platt (*q.v.*) as master mason, and Charles Ross (*q.v.*) as executant architect. Lord Verulam wrote in 1768 that 'Lord Strafford himself is his own architect and contriver in everything', and this is confirmed both by Horace Walpole and by William Bray. Lord Strafford employed Matthew Brettingham (*q.v.*) to design his London house, NO. 5 ST. JAMES'S SQUARE, in 1748–9, but Horace Walpole tells us that he 'chose all the ornaments himself'. His only other recorded architectural work appears to have been an obelisk at BOUGHTON HALL, NORTHANTS. [G.E.C., *Complete Peerage*; Horace Walpole, 'Journals of Visits to Country Seats', *Walpole Soc.* xvi, 65; Walpole, *Anecdotes of Painting* v, ed. Hilles & Daghlian, 161; Hist. MSS. Comm., *Verulam*, 239; W. Bray, *Sketch of a Tour into Derbyshire and Yorkshire*, 2nd ed. 1783, 249; *Letters and Journals of Lady Mary Coke*, ed. J. A. Home, 1889–96, i, 36, ii, 276, 326, 339, iii, 2.]

WEST, ROBERT, received payment in March 1738/9 'for plans and Elevations for the building a house at Garn' [*Chirk Castle Accounts 1666–1753*, ed. W. M. Myddleton, 1931, 502]. Garn, in the parish of Henllan, Denbighshire, was the seat of John Griffith, and had recently been burned down. It was rebuilt in 1739, presumably to West's designs.

WEST, THOMAS, was an architect of Wisbech, Cambs., where he designed the SESSION HOUSE erected in 1807 [N. Walker & T. Craddock, *History of Wisbech and the Fens*, 1849, 426]. His designs for stables, a gardener's house, and other buildings on the estate at WIMPOLE, CAMBS., made in 1805, are among the Hardwicke papers in the British Museum (Add. MS. 36278, K.1–4, M.2).

WESTBROOK, SAMUEL, was a mason at Abingdon in Berkshire. In 1718–20 he and Charles Etty, a carpenter of Abingdon, built the BRICK ALLEY ALMSHOUSES at ABINGDON, perhaps to their own designs, since no architect is mentioned in the accounts [A. E. Preston, *Christ's Hospital, Abingdon*, 1929, 59–60]. In 1731 they contracted to build the COUNCIL CHAMBER at ABINGDON, apparently to designs made by John Stevens of Wantage (*q.v.*). In 1740 Westbrook made a plan of premises in Boar Street, Abingdon, belonging to the Feoffees of Sunningwell [*The Chirograph*, no. 9, Jan. 1940, p. 2].

WESTCOTT, JAMES, 'Architect, Builder, sworn Timber Measurer, Appraiser, and Auctioneer', issued a printed circular in November 1819, announcing that he had removed from Lydney to Ailburton in Gloucestershire, where he would continue to practise those professions [Monmouthshire County Records, C. Bu. 0003]. In 1825 he altered the MARKET HOUSE at ABERGAVENNY designed by John Nash in 1794–5 and since demolished [John Summerson, *John Nash*, 1935, 43].

WESTLEY, JOHN (–1644), was a master builder of some standing at Cambridge in the reign of Charles I. He first appears as the contractor for the BRICK BUILDING erected at EMMANUEL COLLEGE in 1633–4. In 1637 he extended the CHAPEL of GONVILLE AND CAIUS COLLEGE eastwards, and in 1638 he began the rebuilding of CLARE COLLEGE, of which he erected the east and south ranges before work was suspended in 1642 owing to the outbreak of the Civil War. He himself died in December 1644 and was buried in St. Benedict's Church. Although there is no evidence that Westley designed any of the buildings that he erected, it is very likely that he did so. [Willis & Clark, i, 34, 94, 193, 531 n., 620; ii, 695; iii, 531.]

WESTLEY, JOHN (1702–1769), of Leicester, was a carpenter and joiner by trade, and described himself as 'master builder' in his will. He is believed to have been a native of Mountsorrel or Woodhouse, and was admitted a freeman of Leicester in 1723. He was elected Chamberlain in 1746, and held office as Mayor in 1760–1 and 1768–9. He died on 4 February 1769, and was buried in St. Martin's Church, where there is a tablet to his memory. [Hartopp, *Leicester Freemen* i, 312, 539; J. D. Bennett, *Leicestershire Architects 1700–1850*, 1968; will in Leicester Record Office.]

As an architect Westley is recorded to have designed BEAUMANOR PARK, LEICS., for William Herrick, 1725–7, rebuilt 1845–6 [J. Nichols, *History of Leicestershire* iii (1), 1800, 147 and pl. xxvi; contract, with Westley's drawing attached, in Leicestershire Record Office, DG9/2135]; THE SHAMBLES, LEICESTER, 1726 [*Records of the Borough of Leicester* v, 106]; THE CORN EXCHANGE, MARKET PLACE, LEICESTER, 1747–8, rebuilt 1851 [*V.C.H. Leics.* iv, 364]; GOPSALL HALL, LEICS., for Charles Jennens, *c.* 1750, but after a 'misunderstanding' between the owner and his architect the stables and probably the interior were completed by William and David Hiorn (*q.v.*); dem. 1951 [J. Throsby, *Select Views in Leicestershire* i, 1789, 280] (L. G. G. Ramsay, 'Gopsal Hall', *Connoisseur*, vol. 128, 1951); and an altar-piece (since removed) in CARLTON CURLIEU CHURCH, LEICS., *c.* 1767 [Throsby, *op. cit.* ii, 48]. Beaumanor was a compact rectangular house with an order of pilasters, Gopsall a more pretentious one with a large portico awkwardly related to a pedimented centre.

WESTMACOTT, JOHN, *see* WESTMACOTT, WILLIAM

WESTMACOTT, THOMAS, *see* WESTMACOTT, WILLIAM

WESTMACOTT, WILLIAM, appears to have been the youngest son of Richard Westmacott the elder (1748–1808), sculptor and statuary mason. Richard Westmacott and his wife Sarah (the daughter of the carver Thomas Vardy, and not, as often stated, of his brother John, the architect) had a large family. Their eldest son Richard (1775–1856) had a very successful career as a sculptor and was knighted in 1837. Three of his brothers, Thomas, John and William, were brought up as architects. Thomas and John both became pupils of James Wyatt, an architect with whom their father was often associated professionally. But Thomas died in 1798 at the age of 19, two weeks after winning the Royal Academy's Silver Medal, while John, who won the same Medal in 1802, may also have died young, since no trace of him has been found after 1806, when he exhibited a design 'for an intended alteration at Drakelow, Derbyshire, the seat of Sir Nigel Gresley'.

At the time of his father's death in 1808

William was evidently still under age, for his upbringing is provided for in the former's will [P.C.C. 621 ELY]. Nothing is known of his architectural training, but he was presumably the Westmacott mentioned by Farington as Robert Smirke's clerk in 1819 [Diary, 19 Sept. 1819]. He exhibited at the Royal Academy from time to time between 1816 and 1848. His exhibited designs included a mausoleum to the memory of the poet James Thomson (1816), a cottage 'designed to be erected in Devonshire' (1817), a 'residence designed for a Russian nobleman' (1822), and 'Basket Lodge, a proposed residence for a gentleman in Hampshire' (1828). In 1839 he was among the competitors for the Ashmolean Museum at Oxford and for the Nelson Monument in Trafalgar Square. His principal executed works appear to have been THE ROYAL VICTORIA ARCADE at RYDE, ISLE OF WIGHT, 1835–6, entrance altered 1856 [*Hampshire Advertiser*, 30 May 1835, and *Freemasons' Quarterly Review*, 1836, *ex inf.* Mr. R. F. Brinton; *Arch. Rev.*, April 1972, 258], and ST. MARTIN'S MUSIC HALL, NO. 89 LONG ACRE, LONDON, for John Hullah, 1847–50 [exhib. at R.A. 1846; *Builder* viii, 1850, 73] (H. R. Hitchcock, *Early Victorian Architecture in Britain*, 1954, ii, X 32). The former is classical in style, the latter Jacobean. In the R.I.B.A. Drawings Collection there are seven sketch-books containing drawings by various members of the Westmacott family, including Richard (junior), William, and William B. Westmacott, who may have been the latter's son.

WESTON, WILLIAM, practised as an architect and builder at Gainsborough, where he is said to have designed the bridge over the R. Trent erected under an Act of 1787 and completed in 1791, though he is not mentioned in the incomplete minutes of the responsible committee in Nottingham University Library [Ne C.4, 339, 358–9]. According to C. Moor's *History of Gainsborough*, 1904, 172, he was 'a man of great capacity', and later went to America, where he carried out important works for the government. He eventually returned to England, and lived in retirement at Lea, nr. Gainsborough. In his copy of the *Beauties of England and Wales*, now in the Library of the Society of Antiquaries, E. J. Willson noted that, besides designing the bridge, Weston 'also built two elegant small villas at Morton near Gainsborough'.

WETTEN, ROBERT GUNTER (–1868), was a pupil of P. F. Robinson. He exhibited occasionally at the Royal Academy and competed for the Houses of Parliament in 1835, submitting a Gothic design with a House of Lords resembling King's College Chapel at Cambridge. In 1829–30 he published *Designs for Villas in the Italian Style of Architecture, comprising designs for 6 dif-*

ferent houses with descriptive text. His only recorded building appears to be PARHAM NEW HALL, SUFFOLK, for F. Corrance, 1851–2, which he exhibited at the R.A. in 1852. He practised in Westminster and died at Hanover Lodge, Kew Bridge, on 29 February 1868 [Principal Probate Registry, Calendar of Probates].

WHARTON, SAMUEL, of Gray's Inn Square, London, was primarily a land surveyor. He was an 'honorary exhibitor' at the Royal Academy between 1810 and 1814. His designs included one for 'A National Edifice, extending from Carlton House to the site of St. James's Palace'.

WHEELER, JOHN, of Gloucester, was County Surveyor in the 1790s, and in that capacity completed the COUNTY GAOL at GLOUCESTER after the death of William Blackburn in 1790. He designed the BLUE COAT HOSPITAL, GLOUCESTER, a fine building erected in 1807 and demolished in 1889 [*A.P.S.D., s.v.* 'Gloucester']. Wheeler also practised as a landscape-gardener, *e.g.* at THE MYNDE PARK, HEREFS., where he laid out the grounds for Thomas Symons in 1798 [National Library of Wales, Mynde Park documents, 2473].

WHEELER, JOSEPH (*c.* 1775–1832), practised as an architect and surveyor in Cardiff. He died at his daughter's house in Gloucester on 5 January 1856, aged either 56 or 58, and was buried in St. Mary le Crypt Churchyard, where there is a tombstone to his memory [*Gloucester Jnl.*, 21 Jan. 1832].

WHETTEN, THOMAS (1754–1836), was a pupil of Sir William Chambers. He entered the Royal Academy Schools in 1771, was awarded the Silver Medal in 1771 and the Gold Medal in 1774. He exhibited at the Academy from 1774 to 1786. According to *A.P.S.D.* he rebuilt the premises on the east side of Berkeley Square occupied by Gunters the confectioners from about 1760 onwards. In 1788 he was paid 30 guineas for designs for the Council Room at the Liverpool Exchange, but they do not appear to have been executed [J. A. Picton, *Liverpool Municipal Records* ii, 1886, 265–6]. According to Redgrave's *Dictionary of Artists* (1878), he 'was allured from his profession by inheriting an ample fortune'. For many years he lived at Sunninghill in Berkshire, where he died on 18 July 1836, in his 83rd year.

WHICHCORD, JOHN (1790–1860), was born at Devizes, where his father practised as a surveyor. He was articled in 1806 to C. H. Masters of Bath, and subsequently entered the office of D. A. Alexander of London, who employed him at the London docks and at Maidstone Gaol, and to much of whose practice Whichcord eventually

succeeded. Early in the 1820s he settled in Maidstone, where he became Surveyor to the County of Kent and also to the Medway Navigation Company, for whom he executed extensive hydraulic works, some tidal locks, and a number of bridges. For a time he was in partnership with an architect called Walker, but from about 1845 he was assisted by his son John Whichcord, junior (1823–85), Fellow and in 1879–81 President of the R.I.B.A. He died at Maidstone on 10 June 1860, aged 70. A cast of a bust by E. W. Wyon is in the Maidstone Museum.

Whichcord was a competent architect but designed nothing of great distinction. His Holy Trinity Church at Maidstone (1826–8) is a dull classical building reminiscent of Smirke, but his later churches are mostly in a perfunctory Gothic style that betrays no sympathy with the ecclesiologists. His Royal Insurance Offices of 1827 have a handsome Italianate façade of considerable merit. His finest work is the grandly conceived Oakwood Hospital (1830), in a formal classical style.

[*A.P.S.D.; D.N.B.;* obituary in *Builder* xviii, 1860, 383; J. Newman, *The Buildings of Kent*, 1969, 106–7.]

WATERINGBURY CHURCH, KENT, enlarged north side, 1824–5, Gothic; rebuilt 1883–4 [I.C.B.S.].

MAIDSTONE, KENT, THE MARKETS and MITRE INN, *c.* 1825 [*Topography of Maidstone*, Maidstone 1839, 22].

MAIDSTONE, KENT, HOLY TRINITY CHURCH, 1826–8, classical; altered 1878 [I.C.B.S.].

MAIDSTONE, KENT, THE KENT FIRE (now Royal Insurance) OFFICES, HIGH STREET, 1827 [*A.P.S.D.*].

MAIDSTONE, KENT, OAKWOOD HOSPITAL, 1830 [*Archaeologia Cantiana* lxxvii, 1962, 206].

MAIDSTONE, KENT, THE COUNTY LUNATIC ASYLUM, BARMING HEATH, 1830–3 [*A.P.S.D.*].

MAIDSTONE, KENT, THE WEST KENT INFIRMARY, MARSHAM STREET, 1832; since enlarged and altered [*Archaeologia Cantiana* lxxvii, 1962, 206].

MAIDSTONE, KENT, ROCKY HILL TERRACE, for the 2nd Earl of Romney, *c.* 1834 [*Topography of Maidstone*, Maidstone 1839, 102].

MAIDSTONE, KENT, THE CORN EXCHANGE, 1835 [*A.P.S.D.*; drawings in Maidstone Museum].

MAIDSTONE, KENT, ST. PETER'S CHAPEL, restored and enlarged, 1836–7, Gothic [F. Haslewood, *Memorials of Smarden*, Ipswich 1886, 61].

COWDEN CHURCH, KENT, added north aisle, 1837, Gothic [I.C.B.S.].

SEVENOAKS WEALD CHAPEL, KENT, enlarged 1839, Gothic [Kent Record Office, Herries MSS. U543/E11, *ex inf.* Mr. John Newman].

TOVIL CHURCH, KENT, 1839–41, Gothic [engraving in B.M., Add. MS. 32367].

DUNKIRK CHURCH, KENT, 1840, Gothic [I.C.B.S.].

PLATT CHURCH, KENT, with Walker, 1841-2, Gothic [*Civil Engineer and Architect's Jnl.* iv, 1841, 439].

BLINDLEY HEATH CHURCH, SURREY, with Walker, 1842, Gothic; chancel 1882 [Brayley, *History of Surrey* iv, 144].

EAST PECKHAM, KENT, HOLY TRINITY CHURCH, with Walker, 1842, Gothic [I.C.B.S.].

SISSINGHURST VICARAGE, KENT, with Walker, 1843 [C. C. R. Pile, *Cranbrook*, 1955, 97].

AYLESFORD, KENT, half-timbered houses for Charles Milner, with J. Whichcord, junior, 1846 [exhib. at R.A. 1846].

WEST WICKHAM CHURCH, KENT, restoration, with J. Whichcord, junior, 1847 [exhib. at R.A. 1847].

Numerous UNION WORKHOUSES in various parts of the country [*A.P.S.D.*].

WHITE, BENONI (*c.* 1784–1833), was an architect of Devizes, where his father, Benoni White, senior, was in business as a builder. He died on 28 July 1833, aged 49, surviving his father by only a month [*Gent's Mag.* 1833 (ii), 189]. A third generation is represented by Benoni Thomas White (*c.* 1808–51), to whom there is an inscription in St. James's Churchyard, Devizes. He too appears to have been an architect. Benoni White (d. 1833) was the surveyor in charge of the repewing of ALL CANNINGS CHURCH, WILTS., in 1829 [I.C.B.S.]. His designs for the vicarage at WEST or BISHOP'S LAVINGTON, WILTS., 1830, are in the Salisbury Diocesan Records. Shortly before his death he made designs for rebuilding the body of ST. JAMES'S CHURCH, DEVIZES, which were carried out after his death by John Peniston of Salisbury (*q.v.*).

WHITE, CHARLES, an architect employed by the Board of Ordnance, exhibited at the Society of Artists in 1765, and at the Free Society of Artists between 1768 and 1783. The majority of his exhibits were of a topographical character, but they included a 'design for a town house for a person of distinction' (1769). In 1783 he showed 'a drawing of the entrance of the Dockyard at Portsmouth' and when Mrs. Lybbe Powys visited Portsmouth in 1792 with Lady Parker, it was 'Mr. White, Master of the Works', who showed them round [*Passages from the Diaries of Mrs. Lybbe Powys*, ed. Climenson, 1899, 267].

WHITE, EDWARD, was a builder, surveyor and architect at Margate, Kent, where he designed the Town Hall and Market Place in 1821 [Kidd's *Companion to the Isle of Thanet, c.* 1830].

WHITE, FULLER, must have been related to a Georgian silversmith of the same name. He

himself was a carpenter by trade. Early in the 1760s he was being employed by the Earl of Lincoln at OATLANDS, SURREY, and CLUMBER, NOTTS. [Newcastle papers in Nottingham University Library]. In 1771 he submitted designs for a wooden bridge across the Thames at Maidenhead [J. W. Walker, *History of Maidenhead*, 1931, 13–14], and he may have been the 'White of Weybridge' who is said to have designed and built the wooden bridge at HAMPTON COURT, 1751–3 [H. Ripley, *History of Hampton*, 1884, 82]. In 1770 Fuller White received £210 for the 'repair' and 'adornment' of the churchyard at NEWBURY, BERKS. This probably included the erection of the two Gothic gateways, but the parish records do not indicate whether White designed them himself [H. Clifford Smith in *C. Life*, 24 March 1950, correspondence; *Berkshire Archaeological Jnl.* liv, 1954–5, 65–6].

WHITE, JOHN, was a baillie of Paisley, where he lived in Townhead. He held the office of Stampmaster and was founder and fourth president of the local Society for Reform of Manners. Among other buildings in Paisley he designed the HOSPITAL in HIGH STREET (dem.) and the TOLBOOTH, 1757 ['Semplis Scraps' in Paisley Library, *ex inf.* Mr. David Walker; W. M. Metcalfe, *History of Paisley*, 1909, 316, with illustration of Tolbooth]. The Tolbooth was rebuilt in 1821 and its steeple was demolished in 1870. White also designed the HIGH CHURCH, 1750–4, and its tower, 1770 [Robert Brown, *History of the High Church, Paisley*, Paisley 1880, 5–6, 11, 14; drawings of the roof construction among plans at Inveraray Castle].

WHITE, JOHN (*c.* 1747–1813), was an able and successful surveyor who made a fortune out of property development in London. As surveyor to the Duke of Portland he was employed to lay out the Portland estate in Marylebone from about 1787 onwards. He himself was one of the principal speculators, and a survey of the estate made by him in 1797–9 (reproduced by A. T. Bolton in *The Architecture of R. and J. Adam* ii, 102) shows that he was personally responsible for the erection of the houses on the west side of Harley Street between Weymouth Street and New Cavendish Street. Later he was concerned in the plans for the development of Marylebone Park, the greater part of which, leased to the Duke of Portland, was due to revert to the Crown in 1811. He submitted three plans for the layout of the park to John Fordyce, the Surveyor-General of Land Revenues, one of which (made in 1809) he published in 1813 together with an *Explanation of a Plan for the Improvement of Mary-le-bone Park*. One of its principal features was to be a 'Grand Crescent' approached by a continuation of Harley Street, with a new parish church designed by his son in the middle of the semi-circle. Beyond there was to be a landscaped park surrounded by detached villas. White's proposals were set aside in favour of others by Nash, but his conception of a residential park (as opposed to a mere extension of urban London) was one which Nash took over and developed into the present Regent's Park.

White also had a considerable business as a builder and architect. A volume of drawings in the R.I.B.A. Collection shows that he designed and built at least one large country house (Glevering Hall), and a list of other buildings with which he was concerned is given below. He occupied a house of his own erection in Marylebone, where he was active in local affairs, and built a country house for himself at Two Waters, nr. Hemel Hempstead in Hertfordshire. He married the daughter of Thomas Farnolls Pritchard, the Shrewsbury architect (q.v.), by whom he had two sons, John (q.v.) and Henry. He died in Marylebone on 21 November 1813, in his 67th year. His portrait in the R.I.B.A. Collection is illustrated in *R.I.B.A. Jnl.* xlix, 1942, 109. [*A.P.S.D.; Gent's Mag.* 1813 (ii), 510; John Summerson, *John Nash*, 1935, 104, 109, 111, 118; Ann Saunders, *Regent's Park*, 1969, *passim.*]

LONDON, MARYLEBONE PARISH WORKHOUSE, 1775, and the attached INFIRMARY, 1796–7 [Thomas Smith, *Parish of St. Marylebone*, 1833, 271–3; R.I.B.A.D.].

CHISWICK HOUSE, MIDDLESEX, addition of wings for the 5th Duke of Devonshire, 1788; dem. 1952. Although the wings are generally attributed to James Wyatt, *e.g.* by Neale, *Seats*, 2nd ser., v, 1829, there are drawings for them by White in R.I.B.A.D., and in 1837 the (R.)I.B.A. was told that 'the wings ... were not added by Wyatt, as generally supposed, but by Mr. White' [*Gent's Mag.* 1837 (ii), 1781].[1]

LONDON, MARYLEBONE, house for himself in New Road, opposite north end of Devonshire Place, 1791; dem. 1820 (drawing by Grimm in B.M., Add. MS. 15542, f. 139).

WOOLBEDING, nr. MIDHURST, SUSSEX, alterations for Lord Robert Spencer, 1791 [Arthur Oswald in *C. Life*, 15 Aug. 1947].

GLEVERING HALL, SUFFOLK, for Chaloner Arcedekne, 1792–4; enlarged by D. Burton 1834–5 [H. Davy, *Views of the Seats of Noblemen and Gentlemen in Suffolk*, 1827; R.I.B.A.D.].

FENGATE HOUSE, WEETING, NORFOLK, proposed alterations to farm-buildings, etc., 1801 [Norfolk Record Office, 13733].

WESTON PARK, STAFFS., repairs and improvements for the 2nd Lord (1st Earl of) Bradford, 1802–

8 [Weston muniments 3/13] (*C. Life*, 9, 16, 23 Nov. 1945).

BUXTON, DERBYSHIRE, ST. JOHN'S CHURCH, 1811–12 [drawings in B.M., Add. MS. 31323, I & J. signed 'John White & Son 1802 & 1811'].

LONDON, NO. 3 SLOANE TERRACE, work for David Thomas [R.I.B.A.D., bills ff. 215 *et seq.*].

TWO WATERS, nr. HEMEL HEMPSTEAD, HERTS., for himself; dem.

Works for Lady Bute 'at her New Offices, Green & Hot Houses, Garden, etc.', probably at BUTE HOUSE, PETERSHAM, SURREY (dem.) [R.I.B.A.D., f. 201].

WHITE, JOHN (–1850), son of John White (d. 1813), was educated at Roy's Academy in Burlington Street, and afterwards assisted his father as surveyor to the Duke of Portland. He made a design for a double church 'upon a new principle accommodating a large number of persons', which he presented to the Marylebone vestry in 1812. It is illustrated in his pamphlet on the plans for Regent's Park. In 1807 he was appointed District Surveyor for St. Marylebone parish, a position which he retained for the remainder of his life. In 1845 he became the first chairman of the newly formed Association of District Surveyors. He was also a Commissioner of the Property Tax and on the Commission of Sewers for Westminster. After his father's death, White carried on his architectural practice, designing, in 1820, the premises of Smith's, the coachmakers, at 210 REGENT STREET [John Summerson, *John Nash*, 1935, 224]. He also designed the EYRE ARMS TAVERN and ASSEMBLY ROOMS at ST. JOHN'S WOOD, and competed for London Bridge (1823) and the Houses of Parliament (1835). He published his designs for the former in a pamphlet *On Cementitious Architecture as applicable to the Construction of Bridges*, with an account of the first iron bridge designed by his grandfather, T. F. Pritchard, in 1775. In 1824 he took out a patent for a floating breakwater, of which he published an account entitled *An Essay on the Formation of Harbours of Refuge . . . by the Adoption of Moored Floating Constructions as Breakwaters*, 1840. He also published *Some Account of the Proposed Improvements of the Western Part of London by the Formation of the Regent's Park, etc.* (1814, 2nd ed. 1815), in which he described and illustrated the rival plans for the new park, including that made by his father in 1809. A letter illustrating the method suggested by him for lighting Benjamin West's picture gallery in Newman Street was printed in the *Builder* iii, 1845, 367. White married in 1805, and built himself a small house called Bridge House, on the north side of the canal at Westbourne Green, Paddington. He died in 1850, leaving a son, John Alfred White, who succeeded to his post as District Surveyor. [*A.P.S.D.*; W. L. Rutton, 'Westbourne Green',

---

[1] There is, however, a design for a ceiling at Chiswick in the Wyatt album in the Metropolitan Museum at New York.

Home Counties Magazine ii, 1900, 277–8; R. M. Robbins, 'Some Designs for St. Marylebone Church', *London Topographical Record* xxiii, 1972.]

WHITE, THOMAS (*c.* 1674–1748), of Worcester, was a carver and monumental mason whose claim to be considered as an architect rests on a passage in Nash's *History of Worcestershire* (1782). According to Nash, White was a native of Worcester and was apprenticed to 'a statuary and stonecutter in Piccadilly near Hyde Park Corner', after which 'Sir Chr.' Wren took him with him to Rome, and placed him with a statuary there; in the intervals of his business, he by stealth made admeasurements of all the component parts of St. Peter's Church, and assisted Sir Chr. in modelling that of St. Paul's, London. At his return to England, Wren would have retained him for his foreman, to superintend the building of St. Paul's, but Mr. White having an estate in houses at Sidbury in Worcester, chose rather to retire to his native city, where he lived in great reputation as a master-builder and architect. He also occasionally exercised the art of sculpture, for he wrought the statue of Queen Anne which originally stood on a pedestal before the town hall, and is now placed in a nich over the door of the modern building, for which the City of Worcester gave him his freedom. A better specimen of his skill was the Britannia in the tything of Whiston's; he also carved the bust of bishop Hough, in the east end of All Saints Church, and the bust of King George, over the gateway of Edgar's Tower, for which he is said to have taken only a promise to be invited yearly to the audit dinner. He is believed to have been the architect to several of the new churches, and at length at the request of the corporation he undertook to rebuild the town hall, which he performed so much to their satisfaction that they settled upon him a yearly pension for life of £30 a year. He never married, lived in easy circumstances, and died about the year 1738.'

Little of this account can be substantiated by documentary evidence, and parts of it are demonstrably inaccurate. Sir Christopher Wren was never in Italy, and there is no evidence that he employed White at St. Paul's or elsewhere.[1] White's will (P.C.C. 282 STRAHAN) shows that he died in 1748, not in 1738, and the *Worcester Postman* for 1713–14 proves that Nash was wrong in supposing that he never married, for it contains an advertisement in the name of 'Thomas White

of the City of Worcester, Carver', disowning debts incurred by his wife Elinor.

That White was admitted a freeman of Worcester in return for making the statue of Queen Anne is, however, confirmed by a resolution of the City Chamber in 1709, 'that Thomas White be and is admitted a Freeman of this City making a handsome effigie of the Queen to the well likeing of the Mayor and Aldermen for the time being but that he be not sworne before the Effigie be done'. There is, moreover, evidence that he was responsible for the elaborate carving which is the most striking feature of the Worcester Guildhall, for the great trophy in the pediment is signed by him and dated 1722. The Corporation records throw no light on the identity of the architect. In 1717 a committee was appointed to ascertain 'what the charge may be of building the Town Hall according to the modell now produced by Mr. Alderman Hughes, or any other modell'. The author of the plan finally adopted is not stated, but according to Green (*History of Worcester* ii, 1796, 6), designs for the building were handed in by White in 1718. The work was begun in 1721 and completed in 1723 or 1724. The only payments to White were £5 in 1721, and £1. 1s. in 1925 'for mending the statues'. In 1724, however, the committee was directed 'to treat with Mr. Thomas White and make a report what annuity for his life, or what ready money he insists upon for his work done at the said Hall'. The Corporation then agreed to settle upon him an annuity of £30, 'provided that the said Mr. White give security to finish all the work that shall be done about the said Hall by a stone-cutter, and that he put up the effigies of King Charles I and II and beautify the same'. That this annuity was accepted by White in payment for his work is shown by a codicil to his will, dated 23 August 1748, by which he left to Worcester Infirmary 'all and every such ... sums of money that shall appear to be due to me at the time of my decease from the Corporation of the City of Worcester for and on account of an annuity due to me from them'.

The 'new churches' of which (according to Nash) White was 'believed to have been the architect' were those of St. Nicholas (1730–5), St. Swithin (1734–6), and All Saints (1738–42). St. Swithin's was designed and built by Thomas & Edward Woodward of Chipping Campden, but in the case of the two other churches there is unfortunately no documentary evidence by which Nash's statement can be tested. No contemporary parish records survive at All Saints and those at St. Nicholas relate only to the completion of the tower in 1735,[1] the church itself having

---

[1] Nash's statement may have been due to a confusion with another White who died on 13 Dec. 1764, aged 'near 90', and who is said to have 'conducted the curious woodwork in the dome of St. Paul's, a large part of Greenwich Hospital, and many other public buildings' [*Gent's Mag.*, 1764, 603].

[1] Its builder was Humphry Hollins, but it is not stated who made the design, which is based on one of the plates in James Gibbs's *Book of Architecture*, 1728.

been built by trustees whose minute books have been lost. The identity of the builders of All Saints Church is, however, revealed by an inscription on the tower which gives their names as Richard Squire and William Davis. Davis was a carpenter by trade, Squire a master mason who carved monuments and acted as surveyor at the rebuilding of Upton-on-Severn Church in 1755–7. In 1737 he appeared before the House of Commons to testify that All Saints required rebuilding, but this does not prove that he made the designs, although he may well have done so.

Of the works of sculpture attributed to White by Nash, the 'Britannia' forms the distinguishing ornament of Britannia House, now the Alice Ottley School, while the bust of Bishop Hough (d. 1743) still occupies its niche in the east wall of All Saints Church. Hough, who became Bishop of Worcester in 1717, had the Bishop's Palace refronted in a style which invites comparison with the Guildhall and the two churches already mentioned. Another work which might be attributed to White on stylistic grounds is the Triumphal Arch which was erected in honour of Robert Tracy, Esq., by the Worcester Constitution Club on 11 June 1748. An engraving in the Bodleian Library (Gough Maps 33, f. 53ᵛ) shows that it was liberally ornamented with allegorical reliefs in the manner of those on the façade of the Guildhall.

Outside Worcester the only building with which White can be associated is CASTLE BROMWICH CHURCH, WARWICKS., which was remodelled at the expense of Sir John Bridgeman between 1726 and 1731. Among the Bridgeman papers at Weston Hall, Staffs., is the contract, dated 18 January 1724/5, whereby Thomas Clear *alias* Smith, of Castle Bromwich, mason, undertook to rebuild the tower of the church 'according to the form and module hereunto annexed' – that is to say, in accordance with a crude elevation still attached to the document. The tower is surmounted by a panelled parapet with urns at the angles, and the contract specifies that the 'Battlements' 'are to be made and built of Stone so much as Mr. White of the City of Worcester, carver, shall think and say he reasonably deserves for the finishing the same' [G. W. Beard in *C. Life*, 20 July 1951]. This by no means proves that the church was designed by White, and it is significant that the clause in which his name appears is concerned solely with the value of ornamental masonry. The crude drawing is, moreover, in marked contrast to the very competent draughtsmanship of White's designs for two monuments in Blodwell Church, Shropshire, which survive in the muniments at Weston Hall. These drawings are signed 'T. White, Worcester', but the monuments themselves (to Ursula, wife of Sir John Bridgeman, and her father Roger Mathews) are signed 'T. White, Salop.', which appears to

indicate that the sculptor also had a yard at Shrewsbury. For a list of other monuments signed by White, see Gunnis's *Dictionary of British Sculptors*.

White died at Worcester in August 1748, and was buried at Kempsey, nr. Worcester, on the 26th of that month. According to a manuscript note in the Birmingham Reference Library copy of Green's *History of Worcester*, he was 74 years of age. In his will, dated 23 August 1748, he is described as 'Thomas White of the parish of St. Peter in the City of Worcester Statuary'. He left most of his property, which included a tenement in Prince Street, Westminster, to his servant, Mary Rudsbey.[1]

[T. R. Nash, *History of Worcestershire* ii, 1782, Appendix, p. cxvi; V. Green, *History of Worcester* ii, 1796, 89–90; J. Chambers, *Biographical Illustrations of Worcester*, 1820, 344–6; J. Noake, 'The History of the Guildhall Worcester', *Associated Architectural Societies' Reports and Papers* xv, 1879–80; W. R. Buchanan-Dunlop, 'Thomas White of Worcester, Sculptor and Architect', *Trans. Worcestershire Arch. Soc.*, N.S. xx, 1943, N.S. xxi, 1944, 64–5; Marcus Whiffen, 'A Note on Thomas White of Worcester', *Burlington Mag.* lxxxiv, May 1944, and lxxxviii, 1946, 76; Marcus Whiffen, 'White of Worcester', *C. Life*, 7 Dec. 1945; *Wren Soc.* iv, 17, xviii, 188–9, 203–4; information from Mr. B. Brotherton and Mr. D. A. Whitehead.]

WHITING, —, designed BREWERS' HALL, ADDLE LANE, LONDON, which was built in 1670–3 by John Caine, bricklayer (*q.v.*), 'according to the designe drawne by Mr. Whiting the Surveyor'. Whiting's 'Platforme of the Hall front' is preserved with the building accounts in the Guildhall Library (MS. 5502). The Hall is illustrated by R.C.H.M., *London* iv, 1929, 93–5. According to H. A. Tipping, *Grinling Gibbons and the Woodwork of his Age*, 1914, 43, Whiting's Christian name was William.

WHITING, JOHN, a carpenter, set up business in Ipswich in 1804, when he advertised his willingness to make designs and estimates for houses [*Ipswich Jnl.*, 12 May 1804, *ex inf.* Mr. J. Bensusan-Butt]. In Pigot's *Directory* of 1830 he is listed as an 'architect'.

WHITLING, HENRY JOHN, lived in London, but appears to have practised chiefly in the West of England. In 1835 he was successful in the competition for the new GUILDHALL AND MARKET HOUSE at PENZANCE, CORNWALL, which was

---

[1] The architectural models found in Sidbury in *c.* 1915 and once attributed to White are now known to have been connected with the architect Thomas Johnson (see p. 466).

erected to his designs in that and the following year [Penzance Corporation Archives; *Architectural Mag.* ii, 1835, 138].[1] He also designed WORKHOUSES at BEAMINSTER and BRIDPORT in 1836 [*Architectural Mag.* iii, 1836, 532], and competed unsuccessfully for one at BIDEFORD [*Trans. Devonshire Association*, vol. 50, 552]. He was the author of *A Series of Original Designs for Shop Fronts*, 1834.

WHITMORE, Sir GEORGE (1775–1862), was the son of George Whitmore of Lower Slaughter Manor in Gloucestershire, and himself succeeded to the property on his father's death in 1794. In 1789 he entered the Royal Military Academy at Woolwich as a Gentleman Cadet, and in 1794 joined the Royal Engineers, in which he eventually rose to the rank of General. As a young officer he served at Gibraltar, and from 1811 to 1829 was Commanding Officer of the Royal Engineers in Malta. He died in England on 2 April 1862, aged 87.

While in Malta Whitmore went to Corfu at the behest of Sir Thomas Maitland, the governor of Malta and high commissioner of the Ionian Islands, and there designed and built the PALACE OF ST. MICHAEL AND ST. GEORGE, 1819–24, and the circular temple known as SIR THOMAS MAITLAND'S MONUMENT, dated 1816 but not in fact built until 1821. These were notable as the first Greek Revival buildings on Greek territory, and show considerable scholarship and architectural ability. In 1822 Whitmore supervised the excavation of the archaic Greek temple at Cadacchio in Corfu, and supplied an account of it for inclusion in the supplementary volume of the *Antiquities of Athens* published in 1830.

[J. E. Dimacopoulos, 'Neo-classical preludes in Greece: George Whitmore's Architecture in Corfu', thesis submitted for the Diploma in Conservation Studies, York, 1975; Stelio Hourmouzios, 'An English Palace in Corfu', *C. Life*, 26 April 1962; Burke's *Landed Gentry*, *s. v.* 'Whitmore of Orsett Hall and Gumley'; monumental inscription in Lower Slaughter Church.]

WHITTAKER, the Rev. JOHN WILLIAM (?1790–1854), was a learned clergyman who had considerable knowledge in the fields of philology, geology and astronomy. He was vicar of Blackburn from 1822 until his death, and in 1825 married the eldest daughter of William Feilden of Feniscowles in Lancashire [*D.N.B.*]. The records of the Incorporated Church Building Society show that it was he who designed IMMANUEL CHURCH at FENISCOWLES in 1835–6 in

a competent Gothic style. No other evidence of his architectural activities has so far come to light.

WHITTICKE, or **WHITTRICKE,** —, was employed by George Vernon in connection with the building of SUDBURY HALL, DERBYSHIRE, between 1660 and 1690. Vernon's account-book shows that in 1668 'Mr. Whitticke' was paid £100 for unspecified work or services, and that in September 1671 'Mr. Whittricke, surveyor' received the final instalment of a further payment of £11, but it is not clear what part, if any, he played in designing the house (illustrated in *C. Life*, 15–29 June 1935 and 10 June 1971).

WHITWELL, THOMAS STEDMAN (– 1840), was a native of Coventry. He was in London by 1806, when he began to exhibit at the Royal Academy, and in 1811 gave his address as the Architect's Office at the London Docks, where he was presumably employed as an assistant under D. A. Alexander. He attended Soane's lectures at the Royal Academy, and in 1813 offered his help in making the illustrative drawings and diagrams which accompanied them. This offer does not appear to have been accepted, and Whitwell was subsequently suspected of being the author of an attack on Soane which was printed in the *Guardian* of 20 May 1821, and also of the amusing but offensive article on 'The Sixth or Boeotian Order of Architecture', whose appearance in *Knight's Quarterly Magazine* for 1824 led Soane to institute legal proceedings against the publishers.

Whitwell's practice was chiefly in Birmingham and Coventry, where he designed a number of minor public buildings which have nearly all been demolished. In 1819 he made designs for some new buildings at Southville, Leamington Spa, of which a sketch was exhibited at the Royal Academy by W. Finley. The scheme included a church known as be 'in dimension and external style, a facsimile of the Parthenon'. In 1825–6 Whitwell was involved in another utopian project, Robert Owen's Socialist community at New Harmony in Indiana, of which he made a bird's eye view now in the National Library of Wales at Aberystwyth. His professional career was marred, if not ruined, by the collapse of the Brunswick Theatre in Whitechapel, whose iron roof fell only three days after its completion, with considerable loss of life. According, however, to the architect, the accident was due to 'an improper suspension of machinery and other heavy weights upon the tie-beams' rather than to any inherent defect in the construction. Whitwell died in Gray's Inn in May 1840. He had made a large collection of notes and sketches for a book to be called *Architectural Absurdities*, but it was not published and the MS. has been lost. He did, however, publish a tract *On warming and ventilat-*

¹ This building is erroneously ascribed to William Harris of Bristol by A. E. Richardson & C. L. Gill, *Regional Architecture of the West of England*, 1924, 137, 178.

886

ing houses and buildings by means of large volumes of attempered air, as applied to some of the public edifices of the University of Cambridge; and illustrated by the case of the new fever-wards of Addenbrooke's Hospital in that town, Cambridge 1834. The Gothic ticket of admission to Fonthill Abbey which he designed for the sale of 1823 is illustrated in C. Life, 25 April 1968.

[A.P.S.D.; B. Poole, Coventry, its History and Antiquities, 1870, 134; Gent's Mag. 1840 (ii), 107; A. T. Bolton, The Portrait of Sir John Soane, 1927, 143–4, 250, 374–81; S. Redgrave, Dictionary of Artists of the English School, 1878, 469.]

BEECH HOUSE, BRANSGORE, HANTS., remodelled for J. P. Anderdon, 1816 [Beauties of England and Wales, Appendix to Introduction, 600].

BIRMINGHAM, THE NEW INDEPENDENT MEETING HOUSE, CARR'S LANE, 1819–20; refronted 1876 [exhib. at R.A. 1821].

COVENTRY, THE WEST ORCHARD CONGREGATIONAL CHAPEL, 1820; destroyed by bombing 1940 [V.C.H. Warwicks. viii, 389].

COVENTRY, ST. MICHAEL'S CHURCH, abortive scheme for refitting interior, 1820 [B. Poole, Coventry, its History and Antiquities, 1870, 134].

BIRMINGHAM, THE NEW LIBRARY (afterwards the Birmingham Joint Stock Bank), TEMPLE ROW WEST, 1820–1, Italianate [exhib. at R.A. 1820, 1821].

BRAMPTON PARK, HUNTS., for Lady Olivia Sparrow, 1821–2, Gothic; destroyed by fire 1907 [A.P.S.D.].

BIRMINGHAM, THE PANTECHNETHECA, NEW STREET (show-rooms), for Charles Jones, 1823 [correspondence in the Birmingham Chronicle and The Bazaar, 1823].

BIRMINGHAM, JONES'S GOLD AND SILVER MANUFACTORY, NEW STREET, 1823–4 [Birmingham Reference Library, 398204, f. 75].

COVENTRY, ST. MARY'S HALL, restoration, 1824 [V.C.H. Warwicks. viii, 143].

LONDON, THE BRUNSWICK THEATRE, GOODMAN'S FIELDS, 1827–8; collapsed 1828 [Companion to the Almanac, 1828, 174].

COVENTRY, THE GAOL, c. 1831; dem. 1860 [V.C.H. Warwicks. viii, 144].

WARWICK, THE INDEPENDENT CHAPEL, COW LANE (now Brook Street), enlarged [J. N. Brewer, The Warwick Guide, n.d., 82].

WHITWORTH, JOHN (–1863), practised in Barnsley, where he died on 27 January 1863 [Principal Probate Registry, Calendar of Probates]. A new south aisle and chancel were added to CAWTHORNE CHURCH, YORKS. (W.R.), to his designs in 1829 [I.C.B.S.]. The church was largely rebuilt by G. F. Bodley at the end of the nineteenth century.

WHYTE, DAVID A— (–1830), was a builder-architect living at Templeton, nr. Newtyle in Angus. Advertisements for contracts in the Dundee Advertiser show that he built a number of farm-houses in the neighbourhood between 1810 and 1830. His more important works were BANDIRRAN HOUSE, PERTHSHIRE, 1811, dem. c. 1957; offices at AIRLIE CASTLE, ANGUS, for the 7th Earl of Airlie, 1813; GLENISLA MANSE, ANGUS, 1813 [S.R.O., HR 338/4]; KEITHICK HOUSE, nr. COUPAR ANGUS, PERTHSHIRE, for Dr. Wood, 1818–23, altered by D. Bryce 1839 [accounts at Keithick]; GLENISLA CHURCH, ANGUS, 1821 [S.R.O., RHP 7724]; and BALNABOTH HOUSE, ANGUS, reconstruction and offices, for the Hon. Donald Ogilvy, 1824–5 [S.R.O., GD 16/27/311]. [Information from Mr. David Walker].

WICKHAM, WILLIAM (c. 1750–), was a pupil of Edward Stevens, to whom he was apprenticed in 1767 [P.R.O., Apprenticeship Registers]. He was admitted to the Royal Academy Schools in 1770 at the age of 20, and was awarded the Silver Medal the same year. He exhibited at the Academy from 1772 to 1787, at first (1772) from Putney, then from various London addresses, and finally (1787) from Walworth. A set of designs by him for additions to Giles Hudson's house at Putney is in the Mellon Collection.

WICKINGS, WILLIAM (c. 1757–1841), was Surveyor to the County of Middlesex from 1805 to 1815. He designed the CHAPEL OF ST. MARY MAGDALENE, HOLLOWAY ROAD, ISLINGTON, an undistinguished classical building erected in 1812–14 [S. Lewis, History of Islington, 1842, 254]. Wickings was President of the Surveyors' Club in 1807 and again in 1828, and gave the President's chain and badge in 1823. He died in Barnsbury Place, Islington, on 26 November 1841, aged 84 [Gent's Mag. 1842 (i), 112].

WIDDOWS, JOHN, designed the brick upper part of the tower of ST. OLAVE'S CHURCH, HART STREET, LONDON. On 10 March 1731/2, 'the Plan of Mr. John Widdows was approved off by the Gentlemen in Vestry', and on the completion of the work in 1732, it 'was agreed to make him a present of 20 guineas' for his 'care pains and trouble in attending from time to time as Surveyor during the Rebuilding of the Church Steeple' [Vestry Minutes in Guildhall Library, MS. 858/1].

WIGG, FRANCIS (–1868), was the son and successor of Joseph Wigg (c. 1752–1824), Surveyor to the Inner Temple and Master of the Tylers' and Bricklayers' Company in 1819–20. The firm of Wigg & Mansfield, subsequently Wigg, Mansfield & Wigg, and eventually Wigg

& Pownall, builders, surveyors, and ultimately architects, had premises first at 10 North Place, Gray's Inn Lane, and later at 7 Bedford Row. Drawings exhibited at the Royal Academy by Francis Wigg and George Pownall in 1840–5 show that they competed for the Royal Exchange and the Liverpool Assize Courts and were employed by the Society of GRAY'S INN, HOLBORN, for whom they designed the Italianate Library of 1841 (gutted 1941) and the Jacobean STAPLE INN BUILDINGS of 1842–3 (damaged 1941), together with the lodge and gates between Staple Inn and Southampton Buildings [G. Timbs, *The Curiosities of London*, 1867, 471, 475; *Builder* i, 1843, 171]. Under the names of 'Wigg, Son and Oliver' and 'Wigg, Oliver and Hudson', the firm continued at 7 Bedford Row up to the end of the century. It was evidently a successful one, for the elder Wigg left considerable property in Hertfordshire, including a country house at Frogmore in the parish of Aston, and the son's estate was valued at some £60,000 when he died on 26 February 1868. In 1852 he had founded almshouses at St. Stephen's near St. Albans, and it was presumably he who built the existing Victorian Gothic house at Frogmore.

[*Gent's Mag.* 1824 (ii), 571; *V.C.H. Herts.* ii, 431–2; P.C.C. 698 ERSKINE; Principal Probate Registry, Calendar of Probates.]

WIGGENS, THOMAS, of Greenwich, won a premium from the Society of Arts in 1761 for his designs for a 'Temple of Fame' [Dossie, *Memoirs of Agriculture* iii, 1782, 420]. As he was then under 25 years of age he was probably a son of the Thomas Wiggens of Greenwich who in 1755 had been employed to survey the estates of Thomas Steavens in the Isle of Sheppey [*The Chirograph*, no. 9, Jan. 1940, 5]. In 1764 either he or his father designed the GREENWICH PARISH WORKHOUSE [Greenwich Vestry Minutes, 14 Dec. 1764, *ex inf.* Mr. Frank Kelsall]. In 1769 Thomas Wiggins of London competed for the Royal Exchange at Dublin [*Builder* xxvii, 1869, 781]. With George Gibson, he surveyed and condemned the old parish church of Lewisham, Kent, in 1773 [L. L. Duncan, *The Parish Church of St. Mary, Lewisham*, 1892, 12–16].

WIGHTWICK, GEORGE (1802–1872), was the only son of a country gentleman who lived first at Albrighton in Salop. and then at Alyn-Bank, nr. Mold in Flintshire, where George was born on 26 August 1802. His father was accidentally drowned in 1811. Four years later his mother married again and moved with her husband, a Mr. Damant, to London. George, who had begun his education at Wolverhampton Grammar School, was now sent to Lord's School at Tooting. In 1818 he was articled to Edward Lapidge but failed to secure admission to the Royal Academy Schools. On the termination of

his pupilage in 1823, he obtained some desultory work by writing for a topographical dictionary and making drawings for Britton & Pugin's *Public Buildings of London*. Seeing no prospect of regular employment, he thought of abandoning architecture for the stage, but in 1825 his stepfather came to the rescue and gave him £100 to visit Italy. Here he worked industriously, making drawings which were to form the basis of his future publications. On his return in the following year he applied to Sir John Soane for employment, and for several months fulfilled the exacting duties of amanuensis and companion to the eccentric old gentleman, of whose person and dwelling he afterwards wrote a lively description (reprinted by A. T. Bolton in *The Portrait of Sir John Soane*, 395–410). But permanent employment still eluded him, and in 1827, with the aid of a friendly loan, he published a volume of *Select Views of Roman Antiquities* in the hope of attracting prospective clients. This made a small profit, but failed to bring its author any commissions. It was followed by an unpublished play, and a volume of essays entitled *The Life and Remains of Wilmot Warwick*, which the *Examiner* acknowledged as good enough for 'lassitude and a sofa'. In 1829, seeing no hope of establishing himself in London, Wightwick moved to Plymouth, where he soon built up a considerable local practice. He was invited by John Foulston, then about to retire, to enter into partnership with him, and in due course took his place as the leading architect in the western counties. In his own words:

Houses, shops, terrace-rows, and other buildings in Plymouth, were committed to my superintendence: the stewards of the manor of Stoke Damerel (the late Mr. Cole and E. St. Aubyn, Esq.) retained me as architect to Devonport and its spreading suburb; and I made my entry into Cornwall as designer of a large residence, in the *then* Tudor style, at Liskeard. My friend, Dr. E. M., had put into my hands the first of my more important Plymouth works; and soon after its completion I removed into No. 3 Athenaeum Terrace, the 'important work' aforesaid. . . . Befriended also by the Rev. T. Phillpotts, my clerical connection so increased, that I had soon a half-dozen chapels, as many schools, and twice as many parsonage houses in hand. Then came the county 'great ones' and gentry, with their profitable requirements; and I was shortly busy, either in the construction of new, or the improvement of existing, buildings, varying in importance from the second-rate mansion to the lodge or cottage. . . . This indeed was my 'golden period', my clear receipts, before the establishment of income tax, averaging £1000 a year and in one year reaching £1800.

Like Foulston, Wightwick was eclectic in his choice of styles, and designed Gothic churches as well as classical public buildings and Italianate terraces. But his interest in ecclesiology was not sufficient to satisfy the High Church party which dominated the diocese of Exeter in the 1840s, and soon he began to lose his ecclesiastical patronage:

> My obstinate adherence to the principle of a peculiar form for the *auditorium* of a Protestant church, and to the necessity for modifying old Gothic design so as to adapt it to modern purposes,[1] lost me all prestige with my kind clerical employers.... Others were soon in the place which had very likely remained mine had I consented to be the mere draughtsman of the Diocesan Architectural Society; and from this time I declined as the leading practitioner in the south-western counties.

In 1851, seeing no prospect of recovering his former position, he gave up practice and retired to Clifton. In 1855 he moved to Portishead in Somerset, where he died on 9 July 1872. His first wife, the daughter of his stepfather by a former marriage, died in 1867, and in the following year he married Isabella, the daughter of Samuel Jackson, a water-colour painter of Clifton.

Wightwick is described as 'a man much sought after as a fine-talker, a good story teller, and one of the best readers of Shakespeare's plays that ever read to the public ... and much sought after as an entertainer of guests at ... parties at country houses'. 'He possessed brilliant powers of conversation, with an unusual amount of wit, which made him a great favourite in society.' Writing came almost as naturally to him as drawing. In fact he may probably be regarded as the first English architectural journalist, contributing lightweight articles to *Fraser's Magazine* and the *New Monthly Magazine* as well as writing serious architectural criticism in *The Library of the Fine Arts* or Weale's *Quarterly Papers*. His first publication of 1827 was followed by 'Sketches by a Travelling Architect', published in *The Library of the Fine Arts* i–iv, 1831–2; *Remarks on Theatres*, 1832; *Nettleton's Guide to Plymouth, Stonehouse, Devonport and the Neighbouring Country*, 1836; *Sketches of a Practising Architect: A Selection of Vases, Chairs, Altars and Fragments from the Vatican*, 1837; an essay on the use of iron in architecture, printed in Loudon's *Architectural Magazine* iv, 1837; *The Palace of Architecture: a Romance of Art and History*, an elaborately illustrated survey of the historical styles aimed 'at the boudoir of the ladies' and designed 'to promote a just appreciation of Architecture in the minds of all who are susceptible of the Beautiful, the Poetical and the

---

[1] See Wightwick's letter on the subject in *Builder* iii, 1845, 16.

Romantic'; 'Ancient and Modern English Gothic Architecture', in Weale's *Quarterly Papers on Architecture* iii, 1845; *Hints to Young Architects*, 1846, 1847, 2nd ed. 1860, new ed. by Guillaume 1875, 1880; critical comments on Ruskin's *Seven Lamps of Architecture* in *The Architect and Building Operative*, 1849, 482 *et seq.*; and 'The Principles and Practice of Architectural Design', in the *Detached Essays* of the Architectural Publication Society, 1853. In 1858 he was awarded the Essay Medal of the R.I.B.A. for a 'Critical Study on the Architecture and Genius of Sir Christopher Wren'. His terms of employment were printed in *The Architect* ii, 1850, 28, and reprinted in *R.I.B.A. Jnl.*, 1891, 61. His autobiography was published serially as 'The Life of an Architect', in *Bentley's Miscellany* xxxi–xxxv, 1852–4; xlii–xliii, 1857–8. He left his MS. lectures and a large collection of his drawings to the R.I.B.A. Library.

[*A.P.S.D.*; *D.N.B.*; A. T. Bolton, *The Portrait of Sir John Soane*, 1927, 393–413; J. Mordaunt Crook, 'Regency Architecture in the West Country', in *Journal of the Royal Society of Arts* cxix, 1971, 438–51.]

Drawings for nearly all the works listed below exist in the six volumes of Wightwick's drawings in the R.I.B.A. Collection, which appear to constitute a complete record of his work. If no other source is stated, it may be assumed that it is a drawing or drawings in the R.I.B.A. Collection.

PLYMOUTH AND DEVONPORT

ATHENAEUM TERRACE, 1832–4.

THE CRESCENT, for John Marshall, *c.* 1833.

SUSSEX PLACE, 1833–6.

THE INDEPENDENT CHAPEL, MORLEY STREET, 1834; dem.

THE DEVON AND CORNWALL FEMALE ORPHANAGE, LOCKYER STREET, 1834.

THE SOUTH DEVON AND EAST CORNWALL HOSPITAL, 1835–6 (*Architectural Mag.* iii, 1836, 566–9).

THE ESPLANADE, 1836.

THE TOWN HALL, 1839–40; dem. [*Civil Engineer and Architect's Jnl.* ii, 1839, 397].

HOLY TRINITY CHURCH, 1840–2, classical; dem.

THE BAPTIST CHURCH, GEORGE STREET, 1845, classical.

GEORGE STREET, shops, *c.* 1845 [*Companion to the Almanac*, 1847, 248].

THE ROYAL BRITISH FEMALE ORPHAN ASYLUM, STOKE DAMEREL, 1845–6.

CHRIST CHURCH, ETON PLACE, 1845–6; dem.

THE PUBLIC CEMETERY, 1847–8.

CONGREGATIONAL CHAPEL, COURTENAY STREET, façade in 'Anglo-Norman' style, *c.* 1847–8 (*Builder* vi, 1848, 499).

THE PUBLIC AND COTTONIAN LIBRARIES, enlarged and refronted, 1850; dem. (*Civil Engineer and*

Architect's Jnl. xiii, 1850, 316; *The Architect and Building Gazette* ii, 1850, 426–7).

THE POST OFFICE, DEVONPORT, 1850 [*Architect and Building Gazette* ii, 1850, 223, 566–7, with plan and elevation].

THE MECHANICS' INSTITUTE, designed the interior, 1850 [*Architect and Building Gazette* ii, 1850, 318, with plan].

DEVON AND CORNWALL

LUXSTOWE, nr. LISKEARD, CORNWALL (now Council Offices), for William Glencross, 1831–2 (E. Twycross, *Mansions of England and Wales: Cornwall,* 1846).

CALLINGTON, CORNWALL, MARKET HOUSE and INN, for Alexander Baring, 1832–3; dem.

FALMOUTH, CORNWALL, ROYAL CORNWALL POLYTECHNIC HALL, 1833.

HAZELDON, nr. TAVISTOCK, DEVON, for C. V. Bridgman, 1833–4, Tudor Gothic.

HELSTON, CORNWALL, THE GUILDHALL, 1834 [*Architectural Mag.* ii, 1835, 44; drawings in Cornwall County Record Office].

HELSTON, CORNWALL, THE GRAMMAR SCHOOL, 1834.

HELSTON, CORNWALL, MONUMENT to H. M. Grylls, 1834, in form of Tudor Gothic gateway.

BRIXTON HOUSE, DEVON, new front, etc., for Henry Collins-Splatt, 1834.

BUDE CHURCH, CORNWALL, for Sir T. D. Acland, 1834–5, Gothic; enlarged 1876–7 (*Architectural Mag.* ii, 1835, 345–8).

HELSTON CHURCH, CORNWALL, restoration, 1837–8 [I.C.B.S.].

CREDITON CHURCH, DEVON, 'refitted and improved', 1838 [*Civil Engineer and Architect's Jnl.* i, 1837–8, 264].

TREVARNO, nr. HELSTON, CORNWALL, for C. W. Popham, 1839.

LAUNCESTON, CORNWALL, THE MARKETS, *c.* 1840.

LANNER CHURCH, CORNWALL, 1840, Italianate.

LUPTON HOUSE, nr. BRIXHAM, DEVON, alterations for Sir J. B. Yarde Buller, Bart., *c.* 1840.

MOUNT EDGCUMBE, CORNWALL, alterations and additions for the 3rd Earl of Mount Edgcumbe, *c.* 1840–4; little of Wightwick's work survived the bombing of 1941 and subsequent restoration (*C. Life,* 8 March 1902, 22–29 Dec. 1960).

PENDARVES, nr. CAMBORNE, CORNWALL, alterations to dining-room for E. W. W. Pendarves, 1841; dem. *c.* 1955.

PORTREATH CHURCH, CORNWALL, 1841, Gothic.

FLUSHING CHURCH, CORNWALL, 1841–2, 'Anglo-Norman'.

TRESLOTHAN CHURCH, CORNWALL, 1842, Gothic.

BODMIN, CORNWALL, COUNTY LUNATIC ASYLUM, additions, 1842 and 1847–8 [J. MacLean, *Deanery of Trigg Minor* i, 1873, 105].

BROWNSTON CHURCH, DEVON, 1844, Gothic.

CALVERLEIGH COURT, DEVON, for Joseph Chichester Nagle, 1844–5.

TREGREHAN HOUSE, ST. BLAZEY, CORNWALL, alterations for Col. Edward Carlyon, *c.* 1840–5 (E. Twycross, *Mansions of England and Wales: Cornwall,* 1846).

TREGENNA CASTLE, nr. ST. IVES, CORNWALL, enlarged for H. L. Stevens, 1845.

WATERMOUTH CASTLE, nr. ILFRACOMBE, DEVON, completion of interior and alterations to north front, for Arthur Basset, *c.* 1845, Gothic.

PENQUITE, GOLANT, CORNWALL, for Thomas Graham, 1848–50.

PARSONAGES

Designs were made by Wightwick for the following Cornish parsonages, not all of which were necessarily built: GWENNAP, Tudor Gothic; LANREATH; LISKEARD, Tudor Gothic; MORVAH; PELYNT, Gothic; PROBUS, Tudor Gothic; ST. DOMINIC, Tudor Gothic; ST. IVES; SITHREY; WENDRON.

WILCOX, EDWARD, was the son of Jonathan Wilcox (d. 1687), a master carpenter employed in building Wren's church of St. Vedast, Foster Lane, in 1670–3, and at Combe Abbey in Warwickshire under William Winde in 1683. Winde's correspondence (Bodleian, MS. Gough Warwicks. 1) shows that Edward was left in charge of the business during his father's absence in Warwickshire. Both father and son were concerned in the building of ST. JAMES'S CHURCH, PICCADILLY, and in 1686 it was a design for the spire submitted by 'Mr. Wilcox' (probably the father) that was adopted by the Vestry in preference to one provided by Wren. This spire, a simple structure of wood covered with lead, was erected by Edward Wilcox in 1687, but had almost immediately to be dismantled owing to the appearance of cracks in the tower. Twelve years later, when the tower had been stabilized, it was decided to construct a new spire. Wilcox was asked to 'prepare some pretty design', but it is not clear whether the spire actually built (which survived until 1940) was his design or Wren's [*Survey of London* xxix, 32–8].

In 1689 Edward Wilcox contracted to perform the carpenter's work of the new stables and guard-house at Kensington Palace, and he was also employed in Hampton Court Gardens and at Dyrham Park, Glos., by William Talman. He was no doubt the 'Mr. Wilcocks' whose somewhat old-fashioned design for a new building at ALL SOULS COLLEGE, OXFORD, *c.* 1710, is in the Clarke Collection at Worcester College [H. M. Colvin, *Catalogue of Architectural Drawings … in the Library of Worcester College,* 1964, pl. 52].
In 1721 the Duke of Chandos asked Wilcox to

'look over' the plans for his projected house in CAVENDISH SQUARE, LONDON, in order 'to reduce them into a less expensive compass', and invited him to 'undertake the whole care & conduct of the structure'. In the event the house was never built, but in *c.* 1725 Wilcox built another house in the same square for the 1st Visct. Harcourt. The architect was Thomas Archer, but Wilcox modified his designs in execution, for there is an engraving by Rocque of the principal elevation, 'as it was drawn by Mr. Archer, but Built & Altered to what it now is by Edward Wilcox, Esq.' (see above, p. 69, and C. H. & M. I. Baker, *The Life and Circumstances of James Brydges, Duke of Chandos,* 1949, 267–8).

[*Wren Soc.* xx, 245; *Cal. Treas. Books and Papers 1702–14, passim.*]

WILDGOS, JOHN (–1672), was a member of the London Carpenters' Company, serving as a Warden in 1652, 1656 and 1658, and as Master in 1660. He was appointed one of the two City Viewers in 1655, and was among the 'former viewers of this Citty' who signed surveys made by Hooke, Mills and Oliver after the Great Fire. In 1664 his designs for the new Court Room at CARPENTERS' HALL were ordered to be executed, 'as best approved of by the Committee', and he himself advanced £600 to complete the work. In 1671 it was 'ordered upon vote that the window worke in the Hall be altered and be otherwise done according to Deputy Wildgos his design and proposal'. These windows, with 'round or ovall frames at the topp and no transum', survived in part until 1848. The Hall, as a whole, was demolished in 1876 [E. B. Jupp & W. W. Pocock, *Historical Account of the Company of Carpenters,* 1887, 229–32].

After the Great Fire of 1666 Wildgos was involved in rebuilding the Halls of several of the City Companies. In 1666–8 he was responsible for the rebuilding of SALTERS' HALL (dem. 1823) [J. Steven Watson, *A History of the Salters' Company,* 1963, 81–2]; in 1668 he made a 'draught or modell' for rebuilding the HALL OF THE COOPERS' COMPANY (dem. 1865), for which he was rewarded with a gift of five gold pieces [W. Foster, *Short History of the Coopers' Company,* Cambridge 1944, 76]; and in 1668–70 he rebuilt the HALL OF THE PEWTERERS' COMPANY (dem. 1840), for which he made several 'draughts' [C. Welch, *History of the Pewterers' Company* ii, 1902, 137; accounts in Guildhall Library, MS. 7086/4].

Wildgos died in May 1672, leaving considerable property to his family. His yard in Petticoat Lane went to his son John Wildgos, junior [P.C.C. 68 EURE].

WILDS, AMON (*c.* 1762–1833), originally established at Lewes, moved to Brighton with his

son, A. H. Wilds, in *c.* 1815, and for some years carried on business as a builder in both towns simultaneously. He sold the Lewes business in about 1820, and entered into partnership with the architect C. A. Busby, in conjunction with whom he carried on extensive building in Brighton. He acted as Surveyor to the Town Commissioners of Brighton from 1825 to 1828, and was himself a Commissioner in 1832–3. He died in the latter year, and was buried in St. Nicholas Churchyard. The inscription on his tomb is given in J. A. Erredge's *History of Brightelmston,* 1862, 107.

At Lewes, Wilds rebuilt the nave of ALL SAINTS CHURCH in 1806, and soon afterwards designed and built NOS. 1–4 CASTLE PLACE. Nos. 2–3 were bought by Dr. Gideon Mantell, the geologist, and converted into a single house, whose porch has capitals designed in the form of the fossil Ammonite. The 'Ammonite' capital was adopted by the firm, and occurs on several buildings in Brighton designed by A. H. Wilds. He also designed the FIRE ENGINE HOUSE in the yard of the Star Inn in Fisher Street, 1817–18, demolished 1893 [W. H. Godfrey in *Sussex Notes and Queries* xv, May 1958, 4–6].

In Brighton Wilds's principal works were carried out in partnership with Busby, to whom – or to A. H. Wilds – their design can, in most cases, be attributed. Before 1822, however, Amon Wilds appears to have been his own architect, and to this period belong WESTERN LODGE, which he erected for Mrs. Ann Sober *c.* 1817, and RICHMOND TERRACE, which he built as a speculation in 1818. The CONGREGATIONAL CHAPEL or ELIM FREE CHURCH in UNION STREET, which he built in 1820, is also said to have been of his own design. A list of buildings erected in partnership with Busby will be found under the latter's name. [A. Dale, *Fashionable Brighton,* 1947, *passim.*]

WILDS, AMON HENRY, was the son and at first the partner of Amon Wilds (d. 1833) of Lewes and Brighton. From about 1822, however, when his father entered into partnership with C. A. Busby, he practised independently, exhibiting at the Royal Academy in 1830 and 1831 under his own name. He continued, however, to live in Brighton, occupying a miniature Pavilion which he had built for himself in Western Terrace, and taking an active part in the development of the town, which he embellished with numerous stuccoed crescents and terraces in the manner of John Nash. His father appears to have employed him in connection with the building of Kemp Town, for, according to the *Watering Places of Great Britain and Fashionable Directory* of 1833, 'the general style of the architecture ... was under the direction of Mr. H. Wilds'. In 1827 the *Brighton Gazette* announced that he was about to undertake extensive work at Chepstow on 'property belonging to the Duke of Beaufort, Mr. Jenkins and Mr. Stoke', and in 1829 that he had just returned from Limerick, where he was engaged upon 'some plans for the improvement and embellishment of that city' and a house for Sir Aubrey Hunter. Nine months later the same paper stated that he was 'shortly to commence large works in Wales and elsewhere'. In 1830 he was engaged in laying out a 'new town' on the Milton Park estate, nr. Gravesend, of which he exhibited a 'general view' at the Royal Academy. In 1834 he was associated with an abortive plan to widen the esplanade at Brighton from the Battery to Brunswick Terrace and to construct beneath it a piazza containing 112 shops. He was Town Commissioner for Brighton from 1845 to 1848. The date of his death is not known. [A. Dale, *Fashionable Brighton*, 1947, *passim*.]

Unless otherwise stated the following list of works is based on Mr. Dale's book cited above.

BRIGHTON

HOLY TRINITY CHAPEL, for Thomas Read Kemp, 1817; since altered and enlarged [*The Watering-Places of Great Britain and Fashionable Directory*, 1933, 30].

THE ROYAL PAVILION HOTEL, CASTLE SQUARE, alterations, 1820.

attributed: THE UNITARIAN CHAPEL, NEW ROAD, 1820.

attributed: NOS. 53–56 MONTPELIER ROAD.

Houses in KING'S ROAD between Middle Street and West Street, opened 1822.

ORIENTAL PLACE AND TERRACE, WEST CLIFF, 1825.

THE ROYAL NEWBURGH ASSEMBLY ROOMS, NO. 31 CANNON PLACE (now flats), *c.* 1825–33.

SILLWOOD PLACE, 1827.

SILLWOOD HOUSE (now Hotel), WEST CLIFF, for Sir David Scott, 1827–8.

ST. MARY'S CHAPEL, ROCK GARDENS, completed *c.* 1827; dem. *c.* 1878. 'The first architect and designer was Mr. Clarke; it was subsequently completed under the direction of Mr. Wilds' [*The Watering-Places of Great Britain and Fashionable Directory*, 1833, 30].

WESTERN TERRACE (including his own house, Western Pavilion), *c.* 1827.

HANOVER CRESCENT, *c.* 1827.

ST. ALBAN'S HOUSE, REGENCY SQUARE, 1828–9.

PARK CRESCENT, 1829.

MONTPELIER CRESCENT, 1843–7.

VICTORIA TERRACE, HOVE (incomplete).

NO. 26 THE STEYNE.

THE VICTORIA FOUNTAIN on THE STEINE, 1846.

ELSEWHERE

CHEPSTOW, MONMOUTHSHIRE, works for the 6th Duke of Beaufort, Mr. Jenkins and Mr. Stoke, *c.* 1827.

LIMERICK, IRELAND, a house for Sir Aubrey Hunter, 1829.

WORTHING, SUSSEX, PARK CRESCENT, *c.* 1830 [exhib. at R.A. 1830–1].

CLANDON REGIS (dower house), CLANDON, SURREY, for the 3rd Earl of Onslow, *c.* 1830; rebuilt by Basil Champneys *c.* 1890 [exhib. at R.A. 1830].

GRAVESEND, KENT, laid out MILTON PARK ESTATE (*i.e.* Berkeley Crescent, Harmer Street, etc.), *c.* 1830.

GRAVESEND, KENT, THE BATHS, 1835, 'Moorish style' [*Gent's Mag.* 1836 (i), 654].

GRAVESEND, KENT, refronted the TOWN HALL, 1836 [R. P. Cruden, *History of Gravesend*, 1843, 425].

WILKIE, ALEXANDER (*c.* 1744–1811), 'Wright and Architect in this Burgh', is commemorated in Pittenweem Churchyard, Fife. He died on 18 June 1811, aged 67.

WILKINS, WILLIAM (1751–1815), born in Norwich in 1751, was the son of William Wilkins, a plasterer and stucco worker of St. Benedict's parish. He was brought up to his father's trade, but acquired sufficient ability in draughtsmanship to practise as an architect. Sir John Soane, who early in his career had carried out alterations to Norwich Castle of which Wilkins disapproved, wrote of him as 'an able stuccatore who ... had acquired some facility in drawing, and a smattering of Gothic lore, fancying himself an Architect' (*Professional Memoirs*, 1835, 20). One of his earliest architectural works was a mausoleum designed for Thomas Wale of Shelford, Cambridgeshire, in 1775. In 1783 he advertised in the *Ipswich Journal* that, besides executing stucco-work and plastering 'in the very best manner', he also made 'Designs in Architecture ... with Drawings of Buildings in Section, Elevation and Perspective'. Many of his architectural commissions were due to his friend Humphry Repton, who introduced him to prospective clients such as Lord Moira and Bartlett Gurney of Northrepps (for whom he designed a new house which was never built but is shown in Repton's Northrepps 'Red Book'). Repton's son, John Adey Repton, afterwards became his pupil.

In 1799 or 1800 Wilkins took a lease of the Norwich Theatre, of which he (and apparently his father before him) had for some years been one of the proprietors. He completely refitted the interior and added a colonnade at the east end before reopening the theatre, which, with its circuit, remained under his management until his death.

Wilkins was a Fellow of the Society of Antiquaries and had strong antiquarian interests. He wrote a number of papers on antiquarian and astronomical topics, including an 'Essay towards a History of the Venta Icenorum of the Romans and of Norwich Castle, with Remarks on the Architecture of the Anglo-Saxons and Normans', which was printed in *Archaeologia* xii, 1796, 132–80. Between 1782 and 1787 he exhibited at the Royal Academy several drawings and views of Norwich Cathedral, and between 1798 and 1800 John Adey Repton made, under his direction, an elaborate series of drawings of the Cathedral that was bought by the Society of Antiquaries and eventually published in facsimile in 1965.

As a classical architect Wilkins designed nothing outstanding, but the fruits of his antiquarian studies are apparent in the Gothick fancies of Donington Hall, and at Stanfield Hall where, as early as 1792, he enlarged an old sixteenth-century mansion in what (to judge by Neale's engraving of 1819) was a remarkably convincing Elizabethan style.

Towards the end of his life Wilkins moved to Cambridge, where he built himself a house. He died in London on 22 April 1815, in his 64th year. There is a marble tablet to his memory in St. Giles's Church, Cambridge. He had a very large family (thirty children altogether, according to William Daniell, though many died in infancy), the eldest of whom, William Wilkins, R.A., is noticed below. Another son, George, had a successful career in the Church, and a third, Henry, established himself as a builder at Bury St. Edmunds.

[*A.P.S.D.*; J. Chambers, *Norfolk Tour* ii, 1826, 1160—1; S. J. Wearing, *Georgian Norwich; its Builders*, 1926, 42–51; Dorothy Stroud, *Humphry Repton*, 1962, 38–9; Farington's Diary, 11 May 1808; *Gent's Mag.* 1815 (i), 474.]

SHELFORD, CAMBS., MAUSOLEUM in THE CAMPING CLOSE for Thomas Wale, 1775; dem. 1845 [H. J. Wale, *My Grandfather's Pocket Book*, 1883, 5, 176, 179].

DONINGTON HALL, LEICS., for the 2nd Earl of Moira (afterwards Marquess of Hastings), 1790–3, externally Gothic [G. Richardson, *New Vitruvius Britannicus* ii, 1808, pls. 31–5].

STANFIELD HALL, NORFOLK, altered and enlarged for the Rev. George Preston, 1792, Elizabethan style; altered 1830–5 [J. P. Neale, *Views of Seats*, 1st ser., ii, 1819].

STOKE EDITH, HEREFS., lodges at Hereford and Ledbury entrances to park and cottages in village, for Edward Foley, 1792 [drawings in Hereford County Record Office, B 30/1, nos. 11–12, etc.].

NORWICH CASTLE, restoration, 1792–3 [*A.P.S.D.*].

BRACONDALE, nr. NORWICH, NORFOLK, for Philip Martineau, *c.* 1795 [D. Stroud, *Humphry Repton*, 1962, 66–7].

CAMBRIDGE, GONVILLE AND CAIUS COLLEGE, enlarged THE MASTER'S LODGE, 1795 [Willis & Clark, i, 202].

CAMBRIDGE, NO. 38 NEWMARKET ROAD, for himself, *c.* 1795 [R.C.H.M., *Cambridge*, 369].

HIGH LEGH HALL, CHESHIRE, stables, coach-house, etc., for G. J. Legh, 1795–7 [John Rylands Library, Manchester, correspondence among Legh muniments].

CAMBRIDGE, KING'S COLLEGE CHAPEL, minor repairs, 1798–1802 and 1811–12 [Willis & Clark, i, 531–2].

MILTON HOUSE, NORTHANTS., Gothic lodge for the 4th Earl Fitzwilliam, *c.* 1800 [*Gent's Mag.* 1801 (ii), 707].

CAMBRIDGE, NEWNHAM COTTAGE, QUEEN'S ROAD, for himself, *c.* 1800 [R.C.H.M., *Cambridge*, 375–6].

NORWICH, THE THEATRE, reconstructed 1800; dem. [S. J. Wearing, *Georgian Norwich: its Builders*, 1926, 44–51].

THORESBY PARK, NOTTS., bridge for Lord Newark, *c.* 1800 [J. H. Hodson, 'The building and alteration of the second Thoresby House, 1767–1804', *Thoroton Soc. Record Series* xxi, 1962, 18].

SOUTHWELL MINSTER, NOTTS., repaved choir and reroofed Chapter House, 1803; again reroofed 1880 [N. Summers, *A Prospect of Southwell*, 1974, 45].

CALKE ABBEY, DERBYSHIRE, lodges for Sir Henry Harpur, Bart., 1804, and *attributed*: addition of portico to house, probably *c.* 1790 [documents at Calke Abbey].

PRESTWOLD HALL, LEICS., alterations for C. J. Packe, 1805 [C. Hussey in *C. Life*, 23 April 1959].

NORWICH CATHEDRAL, repaired interior after fire, 1806 [Wearing, *op. cit.*, 44].

COLCHESTER, ESSEX, THE NEW THEATRE, QUEEN STREET, 1812; destroyed by fire 1918 [Wearing, *op. cit.*, 51].

WILKINS, WILLIAM (1778–1839), the eldest son of William Wilkins (*q.v.*), was born in Norwich on 31 August 1778. After receiving his early education at Norwich Grammar School, he entered Caius College, Cambridge, as a scholar in 1796, graduating B.A. as sixth wrangler in 1800. In the following year he was given a travelling scholarship which enabled him to spend four years in Greece, Asia Minor and Italy. During his absence he was elected (1803) a Fellow of Caius, and from 1804 to 1806 was Master of the Perse School. His fellowship terminated on his marriage in 1811.

Simultaneously with his academic education Wilkins was being brought up by his father as an architect. While still an undergraduate he made measured drawings (now at Columbia University) of King's College Chapel which show his precocious ability as a draughtsman, and in 1799 he exhibited two drawings at the Royal Academy, one a view of the Gate of Honour at his own college, the other a 'Design for improving the seat of a nobleman in Nottinghamshire'. On his return from the Mediterranean in 1804 he immediately started practice in Cambridge, where he remained until about 1809, when he established an office in London (at first in Bedford Place, later in Weymouth Street).

Wilkins soon established himself as a leading protagonist of the Greek Revival. His earliest recorded work, Osberton House in Nottinghamshire, is notable for its Greek Doric portico, 'the first full-scale, pure Grecian portico in British domestic architecture'. This was followed by Downing College, where Wilkins's uncompromisingly Grecian design, backed by Thomas Hope, triumphed over James Wyatt's more old-fashioned neo-classicism. At the same time his similar design for Haileybury College was chosen by the Directors of the East India Company in preference to submitted by their own surveyor, Henry Holland. Other major buildings designed by Wilkins in the Grecian style were University College, London, the Museum at York and the National Gallery in Trafalgar Square. In his domestic (as in most of his collegiate) work Wilkins bowed to the current fashion for Tudor Gothic, and only at Grange Park, Hampshire, was he able to persuade his client that a Greek temple could form a suitable residence for an English gentleman.

Like every architect of his time who sought for important commissions, Wilkins was obliged to enter for public competitions. In 1817, in conjunction with J. P. Gandy, he obtained the premium for the 'Waterloo Monument', with a design for an ornamental tower of three orders surrounded by a colonnade based on the Temple of the Sybils at Tivoli. This 'national monument', for which the estimate was £200,000, was to have stood at the north end of Portland Place, but was never built [Gent's Mag. 1817 (i), 624; The Farington Diary, ed. J. Greig, viii, 127]. In 1834 he competed for the Duke of York's column in Waterloo Place, and in 1835 for the Houses of Parliament. After the latter competition, he wrote a pamphlet entitled An Apology for the Design of the New Houses of Parliament marked Phil. Archimedes, in which he criticized the plans of his rivals and attacked the decision of the committee. At Cambridge he had, in 1822, obtained the second prize for a design for the new Observatory, and in 1825, when the Fellows of St. John's College 'agreed to apply to Mr. Wilkins, Mr. Browne and Mr. Rickman' for designs for their new Court, it was the last-named whose plans they eventually adopted. In 1829, Wilkins was one of the four architects who were invited to submit designs for the proposed extension of the University Library. None was, however, adopted, and fresh designs were solicited from the same architects in the following year. Once more there was no agreement as to whose was the best design, and pamphlets were published in favour of those submitted by C. R. Cockerell and Messrs. Rickman & Hutchinson. Wilkins's design met with little favour, but he endeavoured to gain support by publishing an Appeal to the Senate in April 1831. In 1836, when the competition at last terminated in Cockerell's favour, none of the sixty-nine votes cast was in favour of Wilkins. Wilkins also competed without success for the Fitzwilliam Museum in 1835.

The circumstances in which Wilkins was chosen to be architect of the National Gallery are difficult to elucidate. Designs were also submitted by John Nash and C. R. Cockerell, but there was no formal competition, and the whole affair was denounced as a 'job' in the Spectator and the Literary Gazette. Wilkins himself claimed at the Royal Academy banquet of 1832 that he had been the first to suggest that the site of the former Royal Mews should be used for the erection of a National Gallery. This was in 1831, when it was proposed to demolish the Mews and build shops on their site. Wilkins at once made designs for adapting the existing buildings for the purposes of a gallery. His scheme was brought to the notice of Lord Grey, the Prime Minister, who appointed a committee to consider it. The idea ultimately met with approval, and in March 1833 Parliament voted £50,000 for the erection of a new building to house both the Royal Academy, the Public Records, and the national collection of pictures. The story that Nash and Cockerell submitted their designs in good time, but that Wilkins did not complete his until the last moment, when, urged by Samuel Rogers (a member of the committee), he 'sat up all night [and] sent one in [which was] instantly accepted against Cockerell and Nash', appears to be ben trovato.

Wilkins was an architect for whom scholarship was in some danger of inhibiting invention. Though his knowledge of antique sources was probably as wide as Cockerell's he lacked the latter's ability to assimilate and to synthesize. His was an architecture based essentially on archaeological investigation. It was a style more suited for public than for private buildings, and it was fortunate for Wilkins that the period after Waterloo was one of great public works which provided many opportunities for monumental architecture. In his handling of the Greek orders Wilkins showed more scholarship than Nash or Burton, and more sensibility than Smirke or Burn. But his architecture is effective in detail rather than in mass, and the National Gallery illustrates his characteristic inability to subordinate the parts to the whole. As a Gothic architect he has not been much studied, but Dalmeny House (with details derived from East Anglian manor-houses such as East Barsham) had its imitators in Scotland, and the King's College screen is an ingenious and effective architectural impropriety that shows what Wilkins could do when he was released from the shackles of classical scholarship.

Wilkins was elected to membership of the Society of Dilettanti in 1809. He was elected A.R.A. in 1824, R.A. in 1826, and F.R.S. in 1831. In May 1837 he was appointed Professor of Architecture in succession to Sir John Soane, but did not live to deliver any lectures. In 1824 he succeeded S. P. Cockerell as Surveyor to the East India Company. From his father Wilkins inherited the management of the Theatre Royal at Norwich (which he rebuilt), and he had a controlling interest in the theatres at Bury St. Edmunds, Cambridge, Colchester, Ipswich and Yarmouth. He was an enthusiastic patron of the theatre, and a portrait of him and his family in theatrical dress is reproduced in *R.I.B.A. Journal* xlvi, 1939, 914.

Very much a scholar, Wilkins was the author of several learned works on classical architecture, and as a commentator on Vitruvius he had the distinction of being the first to interpret the passage in Book V concerning *scamilli impares* in terms of a device for the correction of optical illusions in architecture (cf. *R.I.B.A. Journal*, 27 Aug. 1891, 424). His published works were 'An Account of the Prior's Chapel at Ely', in *Archaeologia* xiv, 1801; *The Antiquities of Magna Graecia*, Cambridge 1807, containing drawings of the temples at Syracuse, Agrigentum, Ægesta and Paestum; 'John of Padua and Porta Honoris', in *Vetusta Monumenta* iv, 1809; *Atheniensia, or Remarks on the Topography and Buildings of Athens*, 1816; *The Civil Architecture of Vitruvius*, a translation with 41 plates, prefaced by a 'History of the Rise and Progress of Grecian Architecture', 1812; and *Prolusiones Architectionicae*, essays on Greek and Roman architecture, 1837. He was also the author of *A Letter to Lord Viscount Goderich on the Patronage of the Arts by the English Government*, 1832, which was reprinted in the *Library of the Fine Arts* later the same year.

Wilkins died on 31 August 1839 at his house in Lensfield Road, Cambridge. He was buried in the crypt of Corpus Christi College Chapel. A bust by E. H. Baily dated 1830 belongs to Trinity College, Cambridge, and is at present on loan to the Fitzwilliam Museum. John Hargrave Stevens was his pupil and Benjamin Ferrey was in his office for a time. Several drawings by him are in the collection of Mr. Paul Mellon.

[*A.P.S.D.; D.N.B.*; *Gent's Mag.* 1839 (ii), 426–7; *Civil Engineer and Architect's Jnl.* ii, 1839, 388; *The Architect*, 1866, 138–9; A. Beresford Pite, 'The Work of William Wilkins, R.A.', *R.I.B.A. Jnl.*, 3rd ser., xl, 24 Dec. 1932; Gavin Walkley, 'William Wilkins', *C. Life*, 30 Dec. 1939; J. Mordaunt Crook, 'Haileybury and the Greek Revival. The Architecture of William Wilkins, R.A.', *The Haileyburian and I.S.C.*

Chronicle, 1964; David Watkin, *Thomas Hope*, 1968; J. A. Venn, *Alumni Cantabrigienses*; Willis & Clark, ii, 278, iii, 97–117, 195; *History of the King's Works* vi, 1973, 461–70; John Harris, *Catalogue of British Drawings for Architecture, etc., in American Collections*, 1971, 276–8.]

PUBLIC BUILDINGS

THE EAST INDIA (now HAILEYBURY) COLLEGE, HERTS., 1806–9; enlarged 1874–5 [J. Mordaunt Crook, 'Haileybury and the Greek Revival', *The Haileyburian and I.S.C. Chronicle*, 1964].

GREAT YARMOUTH, NORFOLK, ST. NICHOLAS CHURCH, new spire, 1807; since removed [J. Preston, *Picture of Yarmouth*, Yarmouth 1819, 39].

CAMBRIDGE, DOWNING COLLEGE, 1807–20 [Willis & Clark, ii, 761; G. Walkley, 'Designs for Downing College', *R.I.B.A. Jnl.* xlv, 17 Oct. 1938, 1014].

BATH, LOWER ASSEMBLY ROOMS, added Doric portico, 1808–9; rooms rebuilt by G. A. Underwood 1823–5, retaining the portico; dem. 1933 [exhib. at R.A. 1809] (*C. Life*, 21 Jan. 1933, 76).

DUBLIN, THE NELSON PILLAR, SACKVILLE (now O'CONNELL) STREET, 1808–9; dem. 1966 [exhib. at R.A. 1809].

CAMBRIDGE, THE PERSE SCHOOL, alterations to accommodate Fitzwilliam Collection, 1816; dem. 1868 [Willis & Clark, iii, 199].

GREAT YARMOUTH, NORFOLK, THE NELSON COLUMN, 1817–20 [exhib. at R.A. 1821]. See S. D. Kitson, *J. S. Cotman*, 1937, fig. 80, for Wilkins's original design for a column surmounted by a trireme supported by caryatides.

BATH, THE FREEMASONS' HALL (now Friends' Meeting House), YORK STREET, 1817–19 [W. Ison, *The Georgian Buildings of Bath*, 1948, 83–4].

CAMBRIDGE, KING'S COLLEGE, THE BRIDGE, 1819 [Willis & Clark, i, 573–4].

BURY ST. EDMUNDS, SUFFOLK, THE THEATRE, WEST GATE STREET, 1819 [S. Tymms, *Handbook to Bury St. Edmunds*, 1872, 83].

BURY ST. EDMUNDS, SUFFOLK, THE COUNTY GAOL, alterations in collaboration with John Orridge, the Governor, *c.* 1819 [J. Orridge, *Description of the Gaol at Bury St. Edmunds*, 1819, p. viii].

NOTTINGHAM, ST. PAUL'S CHURCH, 1821–2; dem. 1922 [exhib. at R.A. 1821; J. Orange, *History of Nottingham* ii, 1840, 881].

CAMBRIDGE, TRINITY COLLEGE, THE NEW (KING'S) COURT, 1821–3, Tudor Gothic [Willis & Clark, ii, 652–9].

NORWICH, THE SHIRE HALL, 1822–3, Tudor Gothic; refaced 1913 [G. K. Blyth, *The Norwich Guide*, 1843, 82].

LONDON, THE UNITED UNIVERSITY CLUB, PALL MALL EAST, with J. P. Gandy, 1822–6; attic storey added 1850–1; dem. 1902 [Britton & Pugin, *The Public Buildings of London* ii, 1828, 130–4].

CAMBRIDGE, CORPUS CHRISTI COLLEGE, NEW QUADRANGLE, 1823–7, Gothic [Willis & Clark, i, 302–4].

CAMBRIDGE, KING'S COLLEGE, NEW BUILDINGS and ENTRANCE SCREEN, 1824–8, Gothic [Willis & Clark, i, 564–5; for the competition, see the catalogue of the *Exhibition of Designs for completing King's College, Cambridge*, 1823, and *Architect and Building News*, 23 June 1933].

NORWICH, THE NEW NORFOLK GAOL, 1824–8 [Norfolk Record Office, QS Order Book C/S4/4].

ADDISCOMBE, SURREY, THE MILITARY SEMINARY, dining-room, barracks and other buildings, 1825–8; dem. 1861 [H. M. Vibart, *Addiscombe*, 1894, 29].

NORWICH, THE THEATRE, 1826; burnt 1934 [J. Chambers, *Norfolk Tour* iii, 1829, 1124–5].

HUNTINGDON, THE COUNTY GAOL, 1826–8 [J. Harris, *Catalogue of British Drawings for Architecture, etc., in American Collections*, 1971, 276; J. Gallier, *Autobiography of James Gallier*, Paris 1864, 15, 16].

LONDON, UNIVERSITY COLLEGE, GOWER STREET, assisted by J. P. Gandy, 1827–8 [exhib. at R.A. 1827, 1828; W. H. Leeds, *Supplement* to Britton & Pugin's *Public Buildings of London*, 1838, 77–88]. The library was designed by Prof. T. L. Donaldson, 1848–9, and the wings were completed later to the designs of Prof. T. Hayter Lewis and others. Wilkins's original scheme, with wings terminating in pavilions, is illustrated in *R.I.B.A. Jnl.*, 3rd ser., xl, 14 Jan. 1933, frontispiece.

YORK, THE PHILOSOPHICAL SOCIETY'S MUSEUM, 1827–30, executed under the superintendence of R. H. Sharp (*q.v.*) [*Gent's Mag.* 1827 (ii), 457; *Library of the Fine Arts* i, 1831, 172–3].

LONDON, ST. GEORGE'S HOSPITAL, HYDE PARK CORNER, 1828–9; enlarged 1859, 1868, etc. [W. H. Leeds, *Supplement* to Britton & Pugin's *Public Buildings of London*, 1838, 41–9].

LONDON, EAST INDIA HOUSE, LEADENHALL STREET, alterations, 1828; dem. 1861–2 [Britton & Pugin's *Public Buildings of London*, ed. Leeds, ii, 1838, 36].

LONDON, THE NATIONAL GALLERY, TRAFALGAR SQUARE, 1834–8 [W. H. Leeds, *Supplement* to Britton & Pugin's *Public Buildings of Leadon*, 1838, 56–76].

DOMESTIC ARCHITECTURE

OSBERTON HOUSE, NOTTS., for F. F. Foljambe, *c.* 1805; altered 1847–8 and 1872–80 [G. Richardson, *New Vitruvius Britannicus* ii, 1808, pls. 60–1].

GRANGE PARK, HANTS., remodelled for Henry Drummond, 1805–9; enlarged by C. R. Cock-

erell 1823–5 [J. Mordaunt Crook, 'Grange Park Transformed', in *The Country Seat*, ed. Colvin & Harris, 1970, 220–8; J. Redmill in *C. Life*, 1 May 1975].

NORTH BERWICK, EAST LOTHIAN, villa for Sir Hew Dalrymple, exhibited at R.A. 1808, apparently not built.

PENTILLIE CASTLE, CORNWALL, for J. T. Coryton, *c.* 1811, Tudor Gothic; dem. 1968 [*Cornwall Illustrated*, with text by J. Britton & E. W. Brayley, 1831, 16] (W. P. Wilkins, 'Pentillie Castle', *Arch. Rev.*, June 1968).

DALMENY HOUSE, WEST LOTHIAN, for the 4th Earl of Rosebery, 1814–17, Tudor Gothic [exhib. at R.A. 1817; J. P. Neale, *Views of Seats*, 1st ser., ii, 1819].

CAMBRIDGE, house in LENSFIELD ROAD, additions, including portico, for himself, *c.* 1815; dem. 1955.

STOURHEAD, WILTS., Grecian lodge for Sir R. Colt Hoare, 1816–17 [exhib. at R.A. 1817; payment in Stourhead archives, 1815].

TREGOTHNAN, nr. TRURO, CORNWALL, for the 4th Viscount Falmouth, 1816–18, Tudor Gothic; enlarged by L. Vulliamy, 1842–6 [exhib. at R.A. 1817] (*C. Life*, 17–24 May 1956).

KESWICK HALL, NORFOLK, for Hudson Gurney, 1817–19; enlarged by Wilkins for Gurney, 1837; enlarged as Training College 1951 [C. H. Barham Johnson, *Keswick Hall*, Norwich 1957, 11–14; B.M., Add. MS. 23033, f. 87, engraving of house 'as altered by Wilkins in 1837'.]

DUNMORE PARK, STIRLINGSHIRE, for the 2nd Earl of Dunmore, 1820–2, Tudor Gothic; dem. 1972 [exhib. at R.A. 1821; J. P. Neale, *Views of Seats*, 2nd ser., iii, 1826].

BYLAUGH HALL, NORFOLK, unexecuted design, 1822, Elizabethan style [R. W. Liscombe, 'Designs by William Wilkins for Bylaugh Hall, Norfolk', *Burlington Mag.* xvi, July 1974].

KINGWESTON HOUSE, SOMERSET, portico for W. Dickinson, before 1828 [J. Britton, *Bath and Bristol*, 1829, 73; J. P. Neale, *Views of Seats*, 2nd ser., iv, 1828].

BROOKE HALL, NORFOLK, for the Rev. J. Holmes, 1827–30; dem. [contemporary statement in author's possession].

WILKINSON, GEORGE (1814–1890), was the son of W. A. Wilkinson, a carpenter and builder of Witney in Oxfordshire, and the elder brother of the Oxford architect William Wilkinson (1819–1901). In 1835 he won the competition for the workhouse at THAME, OXON. (now the Ryecotewood College), and subsequently designed many other workhouses, including those at WITNEY and CHIPPING NORTON whose main blocks are built in the form of a cross, with a central lantern. He also designed the modest Italianate TOWN HALL at BAMPTON, OXON., in 1838. In about 1840 he went out to Ireland as the chosen architect of the Poor Law Commissioners. There, besides many more workhouses, he designed the classical HARCOURT STREET RAILWAY STATION at DUBLIN, 1858–9, and made large additions to the COURTHOUSE at CASTLEBAR, CO. MAYO, 1860. He was the author of *Practical Geology and Ancient Architecture of Ireland*, 1845. He returned to England in about 1888, and died at Ryde House, Twickenham, on 4 October 1890. [Andrew Saint, 'Three Oxford Architects', *Oxoniensia* xxxv, 1970, 55–6; Witney Parish Register; Principal Probate Registry, Calendar of Probates.]

WILKINSON, NATHANIEL (–1764), was the best-known member of a family of master masons of Worcester. In 1713 the churchwardens of RIPPLE, WORCS., contracted with Thomas Wilkinson, of the parish of St. Helen's in Worcester, to take down the spire and part of the tower of their church and to rebuild the latter with 'rails and balisters, flower potts, fannes, and other handsome ornaments', some of which survived until 1937 [contract in Worcester County Record Office]. In 1716 Thomas Wilkinson was employed to take down the spire of ST. MARY'S CHURCH, LICHFIELD, STAFFS., as far as the battlements [MS. churchwardens' accounts]. He died in 1716, and was succeeded by his son Thomas, who was regularly employed on repairing the stonework of WORCESTER CATHEDRAL until his death on 25 November 1736. His place as cathedral mason was then taken by his son Nathaniel, who between 1748 and 1751 virtually rebuilt the north end of the north transept and paved the church with Painswick stone. He was well known as a 'spire-mender', and in 1751 built the exceptionally slender spire of ST. ANDREW'S CHURCH, which is one of the principal landmarks of Worcester. It stands on a tower 90 feet high, and its apex is 245 feet from the ground. A measured drawing made by C. R. Cockerell in 1818 is in the Victoria and Albert Museum (E. 3015-1909); there is a view in *Associated Architectural Societies' Reports and Papers* for 1856–7, 330. The celebrated spire of ROSS CHURCH, HEREFS., was built or rebuilt by Wilkinson in 1743, and he also constructed those of LEDBURY, in the same county (1732), MICHELDEAN, GLOS. (? *c.* 1760), and MONMOUTH. He died intestate on 28 September 1764, and was buried in St. Peter's Church, Worcester. His son, who bore the same name, followed his father's trade. [J. Chambers, *Biographical Illustrations of Worcester*, 1820, 352–3; J. Chambers, *General History of Worcester*, 1819, 131; J. Noake, *Notes and Queries for Worcestershire*, 1856, 41; J. Noake, *Worcestershire Scraps*, no. 8, p. 19; J. Noake, *The Monastery and Cathedral of Worcester*, 1866; C. Heath, *History of Monmouth*, 1804; information from Mr. D. A. Whitehead.]

WILKINSON, WILLIAM, of Mansfield Woodhouse, Notts., practised as an architect there during the second and third decades of the nineteenth century. He was the author of a fantastic Gothic design for a 'National Mausoleum', presented to the Prince Regent in 1814, which is now in the Royal Library at Windsor. He designed BARLOW VICARAGE, DERBYSHIRE, in 1819 [Bodleian Library, records of Queen Anne's Bounty], and in 1817 made a report on the steeple of CHESTERFIELD CHURCH which is printed in G. Hall's *History of Chesterfield*, 1839, 56–7.

WILLCOX, GEORGE H—, practised in Northampton, where he designed the classical NORTHAMPTON BATHS in ALBION PLACE (later the Victoria Dispensary and now the City Housing Department), 1836, and the Gothic ST. KATHARINE'S CHURCH, 1838–9, demolished 1950 [*Northampton Mercury*, 16 July 1836 and 12 Aug. 1837, *ex inf.* Mr. V. A. Hatley].

WILLDIG, JOHN, one of the 'trustees and managers' for rebuilding the church of GREAT BOLAS, SALOP., *c.* 1726–9, was paid £15 15s. 'for his trouble in buying timber, and measuring the Joyner and Carpenters work, and drawing Draughts; and attending on the work and workmen even from the beginning to the end' [W. G. D. Fletcher, 'The Building of the Church of Great Bolas, 1726-9', *Trans. Shropshire Archaeological Society*, 4th ser., x, 1925–6, 222–32].

WILLIAMS, ARTHUR Y— and GEORGE, were in partnership as architects in Liverpool from about 1838 onwards. A. Y. Williams had previously been in partnership with Stephen Lane Edwards, in conjunction with whom he designed the LIVERPOOL MECHANICS' INSTITUTE in 1835–7, ST. JOHN'S CHURCH, KNOTTY ASH, LANCS., in 1836–7, and CHRIST CHURCH, ACCRINGTON, LANCS., in 1837–8 [above, p. 283]. Most of the Williamses' buildings in Lancashire have been demolished, but their handsome Athenaeum at Carlisle survives as a bank.

DINGLE COTTAGE, LANCS., for James Yates (?), 1838 [E. Twycross, *The Mansions of England: Lancashire* iii, 1847, 55].

ST. HELEN'S, LANCS., THE TOWN HALL, 1839–40; dem. [*Civil Engineer and Architect's Jnl.* i, 1837–8, 296; T. C. Barker & J. R. Harris, *A Merseyside Town in the Industrial Revolution*, 1954].

ST. HELEN'S, LANCS., ST. THOMAS'S CHURCH, 1839–40, Gothic; rebuilt 1890–1 and 1910 [*Civil Engineer and Architect's Jnl.* i, 1837–8, 296; *Gent's Mag.* 1840 (i), 82].

WATERLOO, LANCS., CHRIST CHURCH, 1839–41; rebuilt 1891–4 [*Civil Engineer and Architect's Jnl.* i, 1837–8, 88].

LIVERPOOL, ST. BARNABAS' CHURCH, 1840; dem. [*Civil Engineer and Architect's Jnl.* iii, 1840, 71].

CARLISLE, CUMBERLAND, THE ATHENAEUM (now Savings Bank), LOWTHER STREET, 1840 [Mannix & Whellan, *History, Gazeteer and Directory of Cumberland*, 1847, 140].

NEW BRIGHTON, WALLASEY, CHESHIRE, villa for J. C. Ewart, *c.* 1842 [exhib. at Liverpool Society of Artists, 1842].

LIVERPOOL, PRINCE'S PARK, supervision of works under general direction of Sir Joseph Paxton, 1842–4 [S. Lewis, *Topographical Dictionary of England* iv, 1848, 386; G. F. Chadwick, *The Works of Sir Joseph Paxton*, 1961, 47].

LIVERPOOL, BRUNSWICK BUILDINGS, BRUNSWICK STREET, for J. C. Ewart, 1843, Italianate; dem. [*Companion to the Almanac*, 1843, 254–6, with illustration].

WILLIAMS, J—, exhibited a 'Design for a stable proposed to be built for J. Cholmondeley, Esq., M.P.', at the Royal Academy in 1807. His address (4 Marshall Street, London Road) differed from that of John Williams (*q.v.*).

WILLIAMS, JOHN (–1817), was a pupil of Thomas Hardwick. All that is known of his works is derived from the designs which he exhibited at the Royal Academy between 1799 and 1810. They included 'a villa intended to be erected in Carmarthenshire' (1802), another 'designed to be erected for the Duchess of Devonshire' (1803), and a third 'intended to be erected on Sydenham Common' (1804). He also made unexecuted designs 'for the village church at Bunney, Notts.' (1805), and for a chapel 'proposed to be erected on Sydenham Common' (1807). In 1812 he was awarded the first premium of £200 for a design for the penitentiary at Millbank, but it was not built in accordance with his designs. He died at his house in Jermyn Street, London, on 22 April 1817. [*A.P.S.D.*; *Builder* xxvi, 1868, 181; *Gent's Mag.* 1817 (i), 474.]

WILLIAMSON, COLIN, was the author of a plan of MOY HOUSE, MORAYSHIRE, with proposed additions to the offices, now in the Scottish Record Office [RHP 9060] and said to have been made in 1761–2.

WILLOUGHBY, JOHN RIVIS, held the post of Surveyor to the Corporation of York from 1833 until 1838, when he resigned [York Council Minutes, *ex inf.* Dr. E. A. Gee]. He was presumably the father of George Rivis Willoughby, who practised in Louth from the 1840s onwards and who designed, *inter alia*, the church at HAUGHAM, LINCS., with a steeple imitating that of Louth, 1840–1 [S. Lewis, *Topographical Dictionary of England*, 1848, ii, 443–4].

WILLSHIRE, RAYMOND (–1857), was first (1802–6) a pupil of Messrs. Middleton & Bailey of Lambeth, and later (*c.* 1820-50) the partner of the latter. After Bailey's death in 1850 Willshire continued the practice in partnership with R. Parris. He died on 10 December 1857 [*Gent's Mag.* 1858 (i), 118]. In 1833 he was responsible for alterations to TEDDINGTON CHURCH, MIDDLESEXX, including the addition of the chancel [I.C.B.S.].

WILLSON, ALEXANDER, is known only as the author of a rare publication entitled *The Antique and Modern Embellisher*, 1761, consisting of 40 plates of engraved designs for architectural ornament, on the title-page of which he is described as 'Architect, and Professor of Ornament'.

WILLSON, EDWARD JAMES (1787–1854), was born at Lincoln on 21 June 1787. His father, William Willson (1745–1827), was a cabinet-maker and joiner by trade, but also described himself as a 'master-builder', and is said to have had an 'unusual knowledge of theoretical construction'.[1] The son had no regular architectural training, but worked for some time in his father's yard, and, by studying the cathedral and other ancient buildings in the city, acquired a considerable knowledge of Gothic architecture. This led to his employment by Dr. Bayley, the Archdeacon of Stow, for whom he rebuilt Messingham Church, and through whose influence he obtained a number of similar commissions in the diocese. In 1833 he was appointed County Surveyor, and in that capacity restored the keep and walls of the Castle. For many years he was a member of the Lincoln City Council, and served as Mayor in 1851–2.

Willson was an enthusiastic antiquary, with a wide knowledge of medieval English architecture and archaeology. He was the friend and collaborator of John Britton, whom he assisted in his *Architectural Antiquities* (1807–10) by writing the accounts of Boston and Barton-on-Humber Churches and of Beverley and Lincoln Ministers. Britton's *Cathedral Antiquities* (1814–35) and *Picturesque Antiquities of English Cities* (1830) also incorporate material supplied by Willson. He wrote the letterpress for the elder Pugin's *Specimens of Gothic Architecture* (1820–5) and for his *Examples of Gothic Architecture* (1831–6), compiling for the former the pioneer 'Glossary

[1] In Nov. 1729, Thomas Wilson, mason, contracted to rebuild Revesby Church, Lincs., for Joseph Banks [Banks papers in possession of Sir Francis Hill of Lincoln]. The original plan, section and elevation are preserved in the Banks Collection of drawings now in the Public Library at Lincoln (iii, 205). They are in the best style of eighteenth-century architectural draughtsmanship and were probably made by a London architect.

of Medieval Technical Terms'. He made extensive topographical collections relating chiefly to Lincolnshire, and in 1841 delivered the opening address 'On Topography' which was published in the only volume of the *Trans. of the Lincolnshire Topographical Society*, 1843. He also took a prominent part in the Lincoln meeting of the Royal Archaeological Institute in 1848, contributing a paper on the bishop's palace which was printed in the volume of *Proceedings*. His library was sold at Lincoln on 21–23 November 1854, but his Lincolnshire collections are now in the Library of the Society of Antiquaries of London, of which he was a Fellow.

Willson was, for his time, a relatively careful and scholarly restorer of churches. In his own Gothic churches (usually built of yellow brick) he failed to translate antiquarian knowledge into effective design, but his classical R.C. chapel at Grantham has modest charm.

Willson died at Lincoln on 8 September 1854, aged 67, and was buried at Hainton. Like his parents, he was a Roman Catholic. He left two sons, one of whom, Thomas John Willson (1824–1903), became an architect and a Fellow of the Royal Institute of British Architects. There is a portrait of Willson in the Public Library at Lincoln. [*A.P.S.D.; D.N.B.*; obituaries in *Builder* xiii, 1855, 4–5 (by John Brittòn), and *Gent's Mag.* 1855 (i), 321; Society of Antiquaries, Willson Collection, vol. iv.]

Unless otherwise stated the following list of works is based on the *D.N.B.* article, which incorporated information supplied by Willson's son.

MESSINGHAM CHURCH, LINCS., reconstructed for Archdeacon Bayley, 1817–18 [W. B. Stonehouse, *A Stow Visitation*, ed. N. S. Harding, 1940, 7–8, 52].

SAUNDBY CHURCH, NOTTS., repair or restoration, 1823; rebuilt by J. L. Pearson 1886–91.

BLANKNEY HALL, LINCS., stables and offices for Charles Chaplin, 1825 [Lincolnshire Record Office, Heneage 8/2/5].

LOUTH CHURCH, LINCS., reroofed nave and aisles and rebuilt north porch, 1825–7 [R. W. Goulding, *Louth Parish Church*, 1916, 19].

NOTTINGHAM, ST. JOHN'S CHURCH (R.C.), for his brother, the Rev. R. W. Willson, afterwards Bishop of Hobart, c. 1825–8; now secularized.

LINCOLN CATHEDRAL, the organ case, 1826, Gothic.

WEST RASEN CURCH, LINCS., repairs, 1828–9.

MOORGATE CHURCH, nr. EAST RETFORD, NOTTS., 1828–9, Gothic [I.C.B.S.].

GRANTHAM, LINCS., ST. MARY'S CHURCH (R.C.), 1832.

LEADENHAM HOUSE, LINCS., stables for Genl. John Reeve, 1833 [Lincolnshire Record Office, Heneage 8/2/5].

LOUTH, LINCS., ST. MARY'S CHAPEL (R.C.), 1833; since enlarged.

BUSLINGTHORPE CHURCH, LINCS., rebuilt 1835 [Kelly's *Directory of Lincolnshire*, 1885, 346].

LINCOLN CASTLE, restoration of keep, towers and walls, 1835–45 (see his *Report on the present state of the outward walls ... of the Castle*, presented 1 Jan. 1835).

HAINTON, LINCS., R.C. CHAPEL, for C. F. Heneage, 1836, Gothic.

MELTON MOWBRAY, LEICS., ST. JOHN'S CHURCH (R.C.), THORPE END, 1840, Gothic.

CABOURN, LINCS., THE PELHAM COLUMN, for the 1st Earl of Yarborough, 1843–9.

HAINTON, LINCS., SCHOOL, 1846–7; enlarged 1886 [Lincolnshire Record Office, 3 Hen 3/40].

HAINTON CHURCH, LINCS., reconstructed 1848 [*Ecclesiologist* ix, 1849, 138–9].

STAUNTON CHURCH, NOTTS., restoration, 1853.

WILLSON, THOMAS (c. 1780–), was admitted to the Royal Academy Schools in 1800 at the age of 20. He obtained the Gold Medal the following year. His exhibits at the Royal Academy (1799–1831) included 'the principal building of a Royal Military College, designed for the Emperor of Russia' (1805), 'a gentleman's house now building at Stockwell' (1805), and 'a marine villa intended for Greenpoint, near Cape Town' (1824). In 1824 he exhibited designs for a 'Pyramid Cemetery for the Metropolis', the base of which was to cover eighteen acres, 'which being multiplied by the several stages to be erected one above the other will generate nearly 1,000 acres, self-created out of the void space overhead as the building progresses above the earth'. An engraved version of his design for the Pyramid Cemetery is in the Royal Library at Windsor, bound up with C. H. Tatham's designs for a Naval Monument. Willson was among the competitors for the Houses of Parliament in 1835.

WILSFORD, THOMAS, was the author of an early surveyor's manual entitled *Architectonice, the Art of Building: or an Introduction to all Young Surveyors in Common Structures*, 1659.

WILSON, JOHN (–1764/5), was a master mason living at or near Sowerby in the West Riding of Yorkshire. Minutes in the Leeds Library Archives Department show that he designed and built SOWERBY CHURCH in 1761–3. It is a handsome classical building with a southern façade resembling that of Etty's Holy Trinity Church, Leeds. A payment in 1765 to Wilson's widow indicates that he died in that or the previous year.

WILSON, JOHN, was from 1815 to 1830 the leading architect in Guernsey, and during these years he designed a number of important buildings on the island, including the Greek Revival Church of St. James in St. Peter Port and the Tudor Gothic Elizabeth College. In 1828 he was appointed Surveyor to the Guernsey Board of Works. There is no record of his origins, unless he was the 'J. Wilson, junior', who exhibited architectural designs at the Royal Academy from London addresses in 1794–6, nor is it known why he left Guernsey soon after 1830. Besides the documented buildings listed below, several other houses in Guernsey (e.g. Bonamy, 1826, Summerland, Mount Durand, ?1828, Castle Carey, ?1829, and Grange Lodge, ?1830) can probably be attributed to him on stylistic grounds.

Several maps and plans made by Wilson while working in the Channel Islands are in the Public Record Office (MPD 22, MR 1363 and MPH 722). MPH 722 is a design for a Place d'Armes in Alderney in the distinctive style of draughtsmanship of an architect trained by the Royal Engineers. This suggests that Wilson may have been the John Wilson who was Clerk of Works at the Royal Arsenal, Woolwich, from 1839 until 1845, when he retired. This John Wilson, who died at Cardew Villa, Shirley, Milbrook, Hants., in January 1866, was a native of Cumberland, and left some £12,000, to be laid out ultimately on the purchase of an estate in Cumberland for the benefit of a great-nephew of the same name.

[John Jacob, *Annals of Some of the British Norman Isles*, Paris 1830; B. Little, *St. Peter Port*, 1963; C. E. B. Brett, *Buildings in the Town and Parish of St. Peter Port*, National Trust of Guernsey 1975; O. F. G. Hogg, *The Royal Arsenal* ii, 1963, 1107, 1228–9; Principal Probate Registry, will of John Wilson 1866.]

GUERNSEY

TORTEVAL CHURCH, 1816–17 [*Gazette de Guernsey*, 4 Mai 1816; *Guernsey and Jersey Magazine* v, 1838, 275].

ST. PETER PORT, ST. JAMES'S CHURCH, 1817–18 [Brett, 42, no. 31].

ST. PETER PORT, THE MARKET HALL, 1822 [signed; Brett, 32, no. 8b].

ST. PETER PORT, THE ROYAL COURT HOUSE, alterations, 1822 [Brett, 36, no. 15].

ST. PETER PORT, THE TOWN CHURCH, alterations, 1823–6 [Brett, 25, no. 3].

ST. PETER PORT, SPRINGFIELD HOUSE, for Thomas Gosselin, c. 1826–7 [Brett, 60, no. 49m].

ST. PETER PORT, ELIZABETH COLLEGE, 1826–9, Tudor Gothic [Brett, 44, no. 33].

ST. PETER PORT, LES ARCADES (former FISH MARKET), 1830 [Brett, 32, no. 8c].

ST. PETER PORT, FOUNTAIN STREET, c. 1830 [Brett, 33, no. 6f].

WILSON, Sir WILLIAM (1641–1710), was a native of Leicester, and can probably be identi-

fied with William, son of William Willson, baker, who was baptized in St. Nicholas Church, Leicester, on 16 May 1641. He appears to have served his apprenticeship with a statuary mason, and is said to have carved the statue of King Charles II which was set up on the west front of Lichfield Cathedral shortly before 1669, when Bishop Hacket's restoration was completed.[1] In 1670 he was employed as a carver at SUDBURY HALL, DERBYSHIRE, then being rebuilt by George Vernon, and executed, among other works, the elaborate sculpture of the entrance porch [C. Hussey in *C. Life*, 15, 22, 29 June 1935]. In or about 1671, he executed the Wilbraham family monuments in WESTON CHURCH, STAFFS., for Lady Elizabeth Wilbraham, who recorded her bargain with the sculptor in her copy of Palladio's *First Book of Architecture* (trans. Godfrey Richards, 1663), preserved in the library at Weston Park [C. Hussey in *C. Life*, 9 Nov. 1945, 819]. He is also stated by Charles Deering, in his *Nottinghamia Vetus et Nova, or an Historical Account of Nottingham*, 1751, 186–7, to have carved the equestrian statue of William, Duke of Newcastle (d. 1676), on the north-east front of Nottingham Castle, which was completed in 1679. Soon afterwards, according to Deering, 'he was for a time spoiled for a statuary, because a Leicestershire [really a Warwickshire] widow lady, the Lady Pudsey, who was possessed of a very large jointure falling deeply in love with him, got him knighted and married him'. Jane Pudsey was the widow of Henry Pudsey of Langley, nr. Sutton Coldfield, Warwicks., who had died in 1677, and it has been plausibly suggested that his monument in Sutton Coldfield Church was executed by Wilson. The date of the marriage has not been established, but Wilson was knighted at Whitehall on 8 March 1681/2. An entry in Ashmole's diary shows that two days later he was 'admitted into the Fellowship of Freemasons' at Masons' Hall, London.

Between 1693 and 1697 Wilson supervised the erection of the FREE SCHOOL at APPLEBY, LEICS., for Sir John Moore. Moore was an Alderman of London and it was at his expense that the Writing School at Christ's Hospital was then in course of erection to the designs of Hawksmoor and Wren. Wren also prepared plans for Appleby School, which are among his drawings at All Souls College, Oxford (*Wren Soc.* xi, pls. liii–liv). They were to have been executed under the direction of Thomas Woodstock, a carpenter whom Wren had employed on many of the City churches. Wilson also offered his services as surveyor, but Moore hesitated to disoblige Wren by not employing Woodstock, although he believed

---

[1] The statue was taken down in 1877 and is now in the north-west tower; it is illustrated in *Wren Soc.* xi, pl. lix.

Wilson 'to be an ingenious gentleman', whose advice would be valuable. When Woodstock died in 1694, Wilson at once took his place as surveyor in charge and proposed drastic alterations to Wren's design. Moore summoned him to London and (according to Wilson's own account) arranged an interview with Wren 'and shewed him my draughts of the Schoole, and asked his opinion of them. Sir Christopher Wren did aprove of mine rather than his own.' The result was a building which, while it conformed to Wren's general plan, had, with its mullioned and transomed windows, the appearance of a Jacobean structure of the first half of the seventeenth century (*Wren Soc.* xi, pl. lv). In the end, Moore found that the school cost more than he had anticipated, and Wilson had some difficulty in obtaining payment for his trouble as surveyor and for the statue of the founder which he had executed and set up in a pedimented niche in the main schoolroom [*Wren Soc.* xi, 84–107].

Both Wren and Wilson were concerned in the rebuilding of ST. MARY'S CHURCH at WARWICK after the fire of 1694, but the former's designs (*Wren Soc.* x, pls. 15–18) were not adopted, and it was under Wilson's direction that the rebuilding of the church was begun by William and Francis Smith in 1698. The tower was originally intended to stand on the four piers inside the west end of the nave, but the following entry in the accounts shows that they proved inadequate to support its weight:

Sir William Wilson's tower y^t failed which should have been 98 feet high with 4 Pinnacles, Particularly

The Hight to ye Nave	45 foot
The part built and pulled down again	29
The part left unbuilt	24
	98

The present tower, 117 feet in height, was then built on new foundations outside the west wall of the nave. Although the minutes of the Commissioners for rebuilding the church do not say who was responsible for the design, there is no reason to suppose that it was made by anyone but Wilson, and an abstract of the accounts survives in which it is specifically stated that the new tower was built 'according to Sir Wm. Wilson's directions' [B.M., copy of Dugdale's *Warwickshire* annotated by Hamper, p. 319]. Like the rest of the church, it exhibits a curious and rather awkward mixture of Gothic and classical motives.

Another building in which both Wren and Wilson were concerned was the stable at ARBURY HALL, WARWICKS., which was built by Richard Newdigate in *c.* 1675. Wren was consulted, made a design for a 'porch' or doorway

which is still preserved, and was presented with a pair of silver candlesticks costing £11 9s. But his design does not correspond to the doorway as built, and as Sir William Wilson was also paid £1 for a 'draught' of the porch, its ultimate form may have been due to him [*Wren Soc.* xii, 21 and and pl. xlix; Gordon Nares in *C. Life*, 8 Oct. 1953].

Soon after 1696 Wilson is said to have designed FOUR OAKS HALL, nr. SUTTON COLDFIELD, WARWICKS. (remodelled in the eighteenth century and dem. *c.* 1900), for Lord Folliot of Ballyshannon, who had married Elizabeth, daughter and coheir of Henry Pudsey. This house, which had a rather old-fashioned roofline of curved and scrolled gables, is illustrated in *Wren Soc.* xi, pls. lxi–lxii. Two other buildings in Sutton Coldfield are attributed to Wilson because he is believed to have owned or occupied them both: the stables at LANGLEY HALL, *c.* 1685, and MOAT HOUSE, a handsome house which he probably built for himself after his wife's death in 1697.

Wilson's later works as a sculptor included the allegorical statues over the porch of CASTLE BROMWICH HALL, WARWICKS., 1697 [G. W. Beard in *C. Life*, 18 March 1954, 780], the monument to Sir Thomas Gresley (d. 1699) in CHURCH GRESLEY CHURCH, DERBYSHIRE [F. Madan, *The Gresleys of Drakelowe*, 1899, 180–1], and a statue of King Edward VI (destroyed 1833) for the BIRMINGHAM GRAMMAR SCHOOL [N. Carlisle, *Endowed Grammar Schools* ii, 1818, 644]. None of these suggest that he was a sculptor of more than second-rate ability.

Lady Wilson died in 1697 and was buried at Sutton Coldfield. Her husband died there, at the age of 69, on 3 June 1710 and is commemorated by a monument now in the vestry. In his will he provided for a benefaction to the poor of St. Nicholas parish, Leicester. A portrait of him is reproduced in *Wren Soc.* xi, pl. lviii.

[*A.P.S.D.*; 'A Biographical Note on Sir William Wilson', *Wren Soc.* xi, 108–13; *History of the Forest and Chase of Sutton Coldfield*, 1860, 90, 101; R. Gunnis, *Dictionary of British Sculptors*, 1968; Warwick County Record Office, Minutes of the Commissioners for rebuilding the town of Warwick.]

WINCKWORTH, JOHN (*c.* 1790–), was a pupil of Henry Hakewill. He entered the Royal Academy Schools in 1812 at the age of 22. In 1816 he was awarded a Silver Medal by the Society of Arts. Drawings in the Warwickshire Record Office made for Edward Willes show that in the 1820s he was living at Beaconsfield in Buckinghamshire. One, dated 1821, is for the interior of a library at NEWBOLD COMYN, WARWICKS.; another, dated 1826, is for alterations to SHINFIELD HOUSE, BERKS. [CR 1247/40 and 47].

WINDE, WILLIAM (–1722), was an architect of gentle birth, whose family had held lands at South Wootton in Norfolk since the sixteenth century. His grandfather, Sir Robert Winde, had been knighted by James I, and was Gentleman of the Privy Chamber to Charles I. He was with the King at Oxford during the siege of 1646, and forfeited part of his estate on account of his loyalty. He died in December 1652, and was buried in the church of St. Martin-in-the-Fields, London. Like so many royalists, his son Henry found refuge in Holland, and it was stated in 1655 that he was then 'resident at Bergen-op-Zoom in Brabant and hath been constantly there in residence since 1647'. He 'died a Lieut.-Colonel in the service of the States of Holland' on 1 August 1658, and was buried in the Great Church at Bergen. According to George Vertue it was at Bergen-op-Zoom that his son William, the architect, was born, though the exact date of the event is unknown. It must, however, have taken place some years before 1647, for among the Montagu manuscripts there is a letter dated 8 April 1658, which shows that at that date Winde was already an Ensign in command of English troops at Bergen-op-Zoom. At the Restoration he evidently came to England to claim his patrimony, for it was on 15 August 1660 that he obtained the administration of his grandfather's estate. In 1661 he was made gentleman usher to Elizabeth, Queen of Bohemia (daughter of James I), and in September 1667 he bought a Cornet's commission in the King's Troop of the Royal Regiment of Horse. Although a cavalry officer, he evidently had some knowledge of military architecture, for in July 1667, when a squadron of Dutch ships lay in the Thames, he assisted in the fortification of Gravesend Reach. In his own words:

Sir Godfrey Floyd being employed to fortify both the sides of the River at Gravesend and Tilbury: But he staying but one night Prince Rupert sending for him to Sheerness I was then left to fortify those Places on Gravesend and Tilbury side: I raised a new Platforme on the old Blockhouse which stands firm still, as also another on the top of the Leads for small Guns. His late Majesty and Sir Godfrey Floyd coming afterward to see these works were extreamly satisfied with them. . . .

In July 1676 Winde was promoted Lieutenant, and early in 1678 he was given the rank of Captain and sent to Jersey in command of his own troop of horse. He made a map of the island which, with 'several other Draughts', he sent to the King. According to his own account, he was to have superintended the fortification of the Channel Islands, but nothing was done owing to the death of the Governor, Sir Thomas Morgan, in 1679. In July Winde's troop was disbanded and he was recalled to England. He brought with

him some additions to the map which he had made, and presented the King with a book 'with all the Castles, Landing-places and several views of the island set forth in Colours, and all done by my own hand, upon which his Majestie was pleased to say He never understood the Place till then and expressed great satisfaction'.[1] He was rewarded by a grant of the reversion of Major Martin Beckman's post of Second Engineer to the Ordnance (25 Sept. 1679). In 1680 he was ordered by the Commissioners of the Ordnance and Sir Bernard de Gomme, then Principal Engineer, 'to go to Portsmouth to look over the Fortifications, there having the year before been some failure in those works, which I readily undertook. But before I had received full instructions for that business, I was again sent for and ordered to go to Tangier as Comptroller of the Train of Artillery ... but a Truce being made between that Garrison and the Enemy I went not.' Thus deprived once more of the opportunity of distinguishing himself as a military engineer, 'Captain' Winde (as he remained for the rest of his life) returned to the duties of a Lieutenant in the King's Troop. As such he took part in the Battle of Sedgemoor in June 1685, when 'he charged with the said Troop the Green Regiment of the Rebells and totally routed them taking a Colonel's Colours besides a Horse Colours'. But promotion still eluded him, despite the fact that he had the King's promise of preferment 'by the Rt. Honble the Marquis of Powis and the Earl of Craven' (who was his godfather),[2] and in 1685 and again in 1688 he addressed memorials to the King representing that he was the oldest officer of his rank in the Regiment and had more than once been passed over in favour of others with less service to their credit.

The Revolution of 1688 must finally have extinguished Winde's hopes of military preferment, and for the remainder of his life he practised as an architect, designing country houses instead of fortifications, and directing masons and carpenters where before he had commanded troopers. It is possible that for his architectural training he was in some measure indebted to Sir Balthazar Gerbier, for it was to 'Master William Wine' that Gerbier addressed the last of the forty dedications with which he prefaced his *Counsel and Advise to All Builders*, 1663, and in it he refers to the study of military architecture upon which Winde had already embarked. When Gerbier died soon afterwards, it was Winde who took his place as architect of Lord Craven's new house at Hampstead Marshall in Berkshire. The

---

[1] Winde's description of Jersey is probably to be identified with B.M., King's MS. 49.

[2] See Craven's will, in which he leaves £100 to 'Capt. William Winde Esqr. my Godson'.

original drawings, now in the Bodleian Library, show that work had started at least as early as 1662 and that the decoration of the interior was still in progress as late as 1688. The drawings are by several hands, and the formula 'This Draught allowed of by me, William Winde', shows that, like other architects of his time, Winde relied on his skilled artificers to submit their own designs for plaster-work, sculpture and joinery. Winde's correspondence with Lord Ashburnham and Lady Bridgeman shows that he was willing to bespeak pictures and other works of art for his clients, and there is evidence that he counted formal landscape-gardening among his accomplishments, for in one letter he recalled that 'When I was quartered in Kent and imployed in altering the Earle of Winchelsea's house of Eastwell ... I transplanted trees of a considerable bigeness wch did very well & the same I did at Sr Charles Kemishe orchard at Rupera in Wales'.

The 'learned and ingenious Captain Wynne', as Colen Campbell calls him, must have been a figure of some importance in the artistic world of his day. He was a friend of Samuel Pepys, who left him a mourning ring in his will, and George Vertue gives details of pictures in his possession. He corresponded with Sir Hans Sloane, and there is evidence that he was acquainted with Wren, for it was at the latter's house that Robert Hooke heard him talk of Dutch methods of walking on ice and of fortifications made of straw 'frozen together in a night or two by water thrown on them . . . and . . . secured from scaling by freezing the out sides in the same manner, and making them slippery'. In 1662 he became a Fellow of the Royal Society, but was expelled in 1685, apparently for failure to pay his subscription. He was the author of an unpublished *Cursus Mathematicus* in two volumes, of which the manuscript is now in the British Museum (King's MSS. 266–7). It includes sections on Arithmetic, Geometry, Military Architecture, Cartography, Perspective, etc., and is dated 1688 on the title-page. Another manuscript containing mathematical and architectural notes by Winde is in the Inner Temple Library.

Although his recorded works are not numerous, Winde ranks with Hooke, May, Pratt and Talman as one of the principal English country-house architects of the late seventeenth century. At Hampstead Marshall he was completing another's work, and his share in a building destroyed as long ago as 1718 is not easy to determine. But at Combe Abbey, apparently his first independent work, he followed the pattern of Pratt's Clarendon House. At Belton House (whose attribution to Winde is argued below) he did the same. At Ampthill (a similar house) he appears merely to have been consulted about the interior decoration after the shell had been completed. Cliveden and Buckingham House were houses of a different and architecturally a more advanced character, in which the hipped roof has given way to the balustraded attic. If Winde designed these two houses, then he was one of the originators of an architectural formula that was to be much employed in the early eighteenth century. Buckingham House, in particular, was the prototype of many country houses with quadrant colonnades and flanking wings that were consciously modelled on the Duke of Buckingham's well-known London mansion.[1] But the attribution of Cliveden to Winde rests solely on a muddled statement by George Vertue that may well be incorrect, and it is possible that at Buckingham House Talman had preceded Winde as architect (below, p. 904). Other buildings by Winde remain to be identified. In May 1701 he told Lady Bridgeman that he intended shortly to visit an unnamed 'Building under my inspection in the Country', and the volume in the Inner Temple Library contains the dimensions of a proposed house for Major Knatchbull that has not been identified and was probably never built. The interiors of Winde's houses were handsomely fitted up with the help of the best contemporary craftsmen. Among those whom Winde regularly employed were Edward Pierce, the sculptor, Edward Goudge, the plasterer, and Jonathan and Edward Wilcox, carpenters. In 1688 he told Lady Bridgeman that Goudge had been 'imployed by mee this 6 or 7 yeares, is an excelent draufftsman and mackes all his desines hime sellfe'.

Winde married Magdalen, daughter of Sir James Bridgeman and elder sister of Lady Howard of Escrick. 'Mrs. Magdalen Wind of the parish of St. Martin' was buried in Richmond Church, Surrey, on 8 January 1708/9, is commemorated by an inscription on her sister's ledger-stone.[2] Her husband died in 1722 and was buried at St. Martin-in-the-Fields on 28 April. He left a son William, to whom administration was granted on 9 May. This son lived at Bexley in Kent, and held the post of Chamberlain to Princess Sophia. When he died intestate in 1741, there was a sale of prints and drawings belonging to his father which was attended by George Vertue.[3] Vertue's account of the architectural drawings enables them to be identified as those now in the Bodleian Library (MSS. Gough Drawings a. 2–3). In the same library there is a volume (MS. Rawlinson B.143) containing a

---

[1] *E.g.* Wotton House, Bucks.; Gregories, nr. Beaconsfield; and Dunton Hall, Tydd St. Giles, Cambs. (dem. *c.* 1755).

[2] 'In this Church also Lyes Buried Mrs. MAGDELEN WINDE, Eldest Sister of the said Lady Howard, with two of her children JOHN & MAGDELEN WINDE.'

[3] There is a copy of the Sale Catalogue in the B.M. (S.C. 266 (4)).

transcript of legal and other documents relating to the Winde family and its property, including William Winde's petitions to James II, and a pedigree giving details of his father's death at Bergen-op-Zoom.

[J. Challenor-Smith, 'Captain William Winde, the Architect', *Genealogist*, N.S. xxxi, 1914–15, 243–4; C. Dalton, *English Army Lists and Commission Registers* i, 92, 190, 226, ii, 4, 120; *The Diary of Robert Hooke*, ed. H. W. Robinson & W. Adams, 1935, 113, 206, 401; Hist. MSS. Comm., *Manuscripts of Lord Montagu of Beaulieu, passim;* Walpole Society, *Vertue Note Books* i, 11, 84, 89, 91, 127, ii, 88, iv, 11, 111, 196; British Museum, Add. MSS. 4063, ff. 56, 88, 129–30, 29557, ff. 43, 65; E. S. de Beer, 'The Earliest Fellows of the Royal Society', *Notes and Records of the Royal Society* vii, no. 2, 1950, 189.]

HAMPSTEAD MARSHALL, BERKS., completed house for the 1st Earl of Craven after the death of Sir Balthazar Gerbier, *c.* 1663–*c.* 1688;[1] destroyed by fire 1718 (Thomas Story, mason; Edward Pierce, carver, Edward Goudge, plasterer) [original designs in Bodleian Library, MS. Gough Drawings a. 2; British Museum Print Room 1881-6-11-154; and Soane Museum, case 24, no. 68 (*Wren Soc.* xvii, pl. xxvii)]. (Surviving gate-piers are illustrated in *Arch. Rev.* xix, 1906, 155–64 and *C. Life*, 29 March 1913.)

CLIVEDEN HOUSE, BUCKS., for George Villiers, 2nd Duke of Buckingham (d. 1687), *c.* 1674–7; wings added by Thomas Archer probably *c.* 1705; house destroyed by fire 1795 [Walpole Soc., *Vertue Note Books* iv, 11, a source questioned by K. Downes, *English Baroque Architecture*, 1966, 69, but accepted by G. Jackson-Stops, 'The Cliveden Album', *Architectural History* xix, 1976, 5–6] (*Vitruvius Britannicus* ii, 1717, pls. 70–4).

COMBE ABBEY, WARWICKS., rebuilt centre and north wing for the 1st Earl of Craven, 1682–5; north wing dem. probably in 1925 (William Cooles, mason; Jonathan Wilcox, carpenter; Edward Pierce, carver; Edward Goudge, plasterer) [original designs in Bodleian Library, MS. Gough Drawings a. 3; correspondence in MS. Gough Warwicks. 1.] (H. A. Tipping, *English Homes, Period IV* (i), 155–78.)

LONDON, POWIS (afterwards NEWCASTLE) HOUSE, LINCOLN'S INN FIELDS, for the 1st Marquess of Powis, 1684–9; fitted up as the offices of the Great Seal after the Marquess's outlawry in 1690; refitted for the Duke of Newcastle 1715–

17; divided 1771; rebuilt by Sir Edwin Lutyens 1930–1 [Walpole Soc., *Vertue Note Books* i, 127] (*Survey of London* iii, 110–18).

attributed: BELTON HOUSE, LINCS., for Sir John Brownlow, Bart., 1685–8 [stylistic attribution, based on close resemblance to Combe Abbey, and supported by the employment of Edward Goudge and Edward Wilcox]. In Feb. 1689/90 Winde told Lady Bridgeman that Goudge 'is now looked on as the beste master in Ingland in his profession, as his worke at Coombe, Hampsted, & Sr. John Brownloe's will evidence'. Accounts at Belton do not mention the architect, but name the mason as William Stanton and the carpenter as Edward Wilcox. (H. A. Tipping, *English Homes*, IV (i), 225–8; *C. Life*, 3, 10, 17 Sept. 1964; Oliver Hill & John Cornforth, *English Country Houses: Caroline*, 1966, 192–202).

CASTLE BROMWICH HALL, WARWICKS., alterations to interior of house for Sir John and Lady Bridgeman, 1685–90 (Edward Pierce, carver; Edward Goudge, plasterer) [G. W. Beard in *C. Life*, 9 May 1952].

EASTWELL PARK, KENT, alterations for the (2nd?) Earl of Winchilsea, probably *c.* 1685 [mentioned in an undated letter from Winde to Lady Bridgeman].

LONDON, BUCKINGHAM HOUSE, ST. JAMES'S, for John Sheffield, 1st Duke of Buckingham, 1702–5; bought in 1762 by King George III, for whom the house was altered and enlarged by Sir William Chambers 1762–9; incorporated in the structure of Buckingham Palace, 1825–30 (a summary of the cost in London University MS. 533, ff. 9–11, shows that John Fitch built the main structure by contract for £7000). Campbell says that this house was 'conducted by the learned and ingenious Capt. Wynne'. Elsewhere he uses the word 'conducted' in a sense different from 'designed'. Thus the Queen's gallery at Somerset House was 'taken from a Design of Inigo Jones, but conducted by another Hand', and 'Mr. Hudson's house at Sunbury was 'designed and conducted by Mr. Fort'. Winde may therefore have been carrying out another architect's design at Buckingham House, and if so that architect was probably William Talman (above, p. 804) [*Vitruvius Britannicus* i, 1715, pls. 43–4; *History of the King's Works* v, 133–8; John Cornforth in *C. Life*, 12 July 1962].

AMPTHILL PARK, BEDS., advised the 1st Lord Ashburnham on interior decoration (by Laguerre), iron work (by Tijou), and statues, 1706 [letter-book of Lord Ashburnham in West Sussex Record Office].

Note: On 17 Dec. 1689, Winde apologized to Lady Bridgeman for delay in answering a letter

---

[1] The earliest of the Hampstead Marshall drawings is dated 1662, the latest 1688. One of them bears a note to the effect that the first floor was begun on 27 July 1664. Among the Montagu papers there is a pass, dated 17 July 1665, authorizing Winde to proceed to Hampstead Marshall in time of plague.

because of the arrival of Lord Craven's steward with workmen's bills 'from severall places, where his Lordship has buillte'. In addition to Hampstead Marshall and Combe Abbey, Lord Craven then owned Ashdown House, Berks., and Drury House, Drury Lane, London (dem. 1809). In August 1688 Winde refers in a letter to Goudge's work 'in a late building at Drury House'. It is likely that this was done under his supervision, as his address at this time was 'over against the Earl of Craven's house in Drury Lane'. In December 1697 Winde wrote that in the spring he was engaged 'to waite on the Duchess of Norfolk to Drayden in Northamptonshire and from thence withe the D. of Powis to the Read Castel', *i.e.* Powis Castle, Montgomeryshire, where there is a fine staircase decorated by Lanscroon, for which Winde could well have been responsible (*C. Life*, 20 June 1936).

WING, EDWARD, was a carpenter and master builder of Aynho in Northants. An account-book from Aynho Park now in the County Record Office shows that he was employed to rebuild the parish church of AYNHO in 1723–5, retaining the medieval tower. In November 1733 he was paid 1 guinea for making a 'draught', showing the plan of the existing church superimposed on that of the former one. This plan, signed 'Ed. Wing, Architect', is also among the Aynho papers. The building is chiefly remarkable as a rustic attempt to build something after the style of the churches erected in London under the 'Fifty New Churches' Act of 1711. Wing's designs, described as 'all of his own drawing', are preserved in the Diocesan Records. What is evidently another of Wing's 'draughts' is preserved among Browne Willis's manuscripts in the Bodleian Library (MS. Willis 34, f. 289). It corresponds with the church as built, except that the north and south doors are treated in a different manner.

Between 1724 and 1730, Wing was employed by Browne Willis to rebuild ST. MARTIN'S CHAPEL at FENNY STRATFORD, BUCKS. An engraving of the chapel, signed 'Ed. Wing de Aynhoe desig.', is preserved in the Bodleian Library. The traditional character of the design was, however, due to Browne Willis's antiquarian tastes. The brickwork was executed by Daniel Estment, while Wing and a joiner named Round, with whom he appears to have been in partnership, were responsible for the roof, gallery and other woodwork. In 1728 there was a dispute as a result of which Wing gave up the job, his place being taken by a joiner named John Simmonds, who strongly criticized his predecessor's workmanship. A south aisle was added in 1823, and in 1866 a new nave and chancel were built, the nave of Willis's chapel being retained as a north aisle. [Bodleian Library, MS. Willis 52; H. Roundell, 'Notes on the Life of Browne Willis', *Records of Bucks.* ii, 1870, 8.]

WING, JOHN (1728–1794), was the eldest son of John Wing of North Luffenham in Rutland and his first wife Elizabeth. Both his father, who died in 1752, and his grandfather Aaron Wing, who died in 1751 at the age of 85, were masons by trade. Aaron Wing was a nephew of Vincent Wing (1619–68), the astronomer and land surveyor, who also lived at North Luffenham, and a cousin of Tycho Wing (1696–1750) of Pickworth, the astrologer. Their common ancestor Jasper Wing, who died at North Luffenham in 1620, may well have been a mason also, since he mentions his tools in his will. He himself had come to North Luffenham from Great Ponton in Lincolnshire towards the end of the sixteenth century, and his Christian name seems to confirm the statement made by Vincent Wing's biographer that the family was of Welsh origin.

John must have begun to assist his father at an early age, for a note in the parish register records that in March 1739/40 the dove-house over the porch of the rectory barn 'was made by John Wing Sen.ʳ assisted by J. Wing Junʳ.' Subsequently he left North Luffenham for Hallaton in Leicestershire, a village with which his father had some connection, for in his will he had left a cottage there to his second wife Dorothy. In 1755 John Wing and Elizabeth Gibbins, 'both of this parish', were married at Hallaton, and Wing lived there for the greater part of his life. For the next quarter of a century he was the leading architect and stone-mason in Leicestershire and designed two remarkable Gothic churches in that neighbourhood. As early as 1741 his father had rebuilt the tower and nave of GALBY CHURCH, LEICS., in a somewhat bizarre Gothic of his own devising, as recorded by J. Throsby in his *Select Views in Leicestershire* ii, 1790, 137. This was done at the expense of William Fortrey, a local squire, who in 1757 obtained a faculty to rebuild KING'S NORTON CHURCH, LEICS., to the designs of the younger Wing. Work began in 1760 and was completed in 1775.[1] The church is rectangular in plan, with closely spaced buttresses separating tall windows containing elaborate tracery of correct 'Early Decorated' character. The west tower was originally surmounted by a spire which was destroyed by lightning in 1850. Outside the east end of the church there is a handsome monument to Fortrey, who died in 1783. In 1788 Wing designed EAST CARLTON CHURCH, NORTHANTS., in a similar Gothic style for Sir John Palmer [J. P. Neale, *Views of Seats*, 1st ser., vi, 1823]. In 1772 he repaired 'the four middle windows in the spire' of ST. MARTIN'S CHURCH, LEICESTER [T. North,

[1] Dates recorded at the Archdeacon's Visitation in 1776 (Leicestershire Archdeaconry Records). A drawing of the tower and spire signed by Wing is in the Local Collection in Northampton Public Library. See also Throsby, *Select Views in Leicestershire* ii, 1790, 139.

Accounts of the Churchwardens of St. Martin's Leicester, 1884, 225], and in 1774 he was paid £65 for repairing the steeple of BILLESDON CHURCH, LEICS. [*V.C.H. Leics.* v, 13].

Evidence for Wing's other architectural works comes chiefly from his pocket-books for the years 1775 and 1780, now in the County Record Office at Bedford [X 106/79–80]. Entries in the later pocket-book show that in 1780 he was building a bridge at Sandy in Bedfordshire, and in 1781 he took a lease of a stone-quarry at Totternhoe in that county. Some time within the next few years he moved from Hallaton to Leicester, but eventually he left Leicestershire for Bedford, where he died on 24 June 1794, aged 65, and is commemorated by a tablet in the south aisle of St. Mary's Church. At Bedford Wing's business as an architect and mason was carried on by his eldest son John Wing (*q.v.*). His second son Moses (b. 1761) started business as a mason in Leicester in 1782, but died three years later at the age of 25. His third son Vincent (1763–1843) was apprenticed to a grocer in Melton Mowbray, and was the father of Vincent Wing (1803–79), also a grocer by trade, who inherited his grandfather's interest in Gothic architecture and contributed a number of papers on that subject to the first four volumes of the Leicestershire Archaeological Society's *Transactions*.

[*The Registers of North Luffenham*, ed. P. G. Dennis (Parish Register Soc., 1896); parish registers of Hallaton; wills in Peterborough Probate Registry; J. Gadbury, *A Brief Relation of the Life and Death of Mr. Vincent Wing*, 1670, 2; *A Pedigree of the Family of Wing* compiled by E. Green, 1886; W. Hartopp, *Register of the Freemen of Leicester 1770–1930*, 1933, 454; John Wing's pocket-books and other papers in the Bedfordshire County Record Office; *Trans. Leicestershire Arch. Soc.* v, 1882, 226; information from Mrs. F. E. Skillington.]

WING, JOHN (1756–1826), was the eldest son of John Wing (*q.v.*) of Hallaton in Leicestershire, where he was born in July 1756. Early in the 1780s he moved from Leicestershire to Bedfordshire, where his father had recently acquired a stone-quarry at Totternhoe. He settled at Bedford, took over the quarry, and soon became the leading architect and builder in the county. He frequently acted as surveyor of bridges for the county, and designed and built most of the public buildings in Bedford. He also made monuments, examples of which can be seen in the churches of Bedford, Flitton, Henlow, Great Bowden (Leics.), Sandy, Aspley Guise, and Irthlingborough (Northants.).

Having in 1792 been admitted a burgess of Bedford, Wing became a prominent member of the corporation, and held the office of Mayor on three occasions (in 1793, 1808 and 1817). In 1799

he married Elizabeth Tacy, by whom he had five sons. John (b. 1802) entered the Church and became vicar of St. Mary's Leicester. William Henry (b. 1803) died young. James Tacy (b. 1805) practised as an architect in Bedford and died at Sharnbrook in 1880.[1] Vincent (b. 1808) was apprenticed to an ironmonger at Melton Mowbray. Samuel (1812–65) became a solicitor in Bedford. John Wing died at Bedford on 2 December 1826, aged 70, and was buried in St. Mary's Church, where there is an inscription to his memory in the south aisle. [Wing family records in Bedford County Record Office; W. Hartopp, *Register of the Freemen of Leicester 1770–1930*, 581; L. N. Cottingham, *Plans etc. of King Henry VII's Chapel*, 1822, 11.]

BEDFORD

THE HOUSE OF INDUSTRY, 1795–6 [Bedford County Records, X 67/110] (engraved plan and elevation in Bodleian, Gough Maps 1, f. 3).

THE COUNTY GAOL, 1801 [*Report from the Committee of Aldermen appointed to visit Several Gaols in England*, 1816, 32].

THE INFIRMARY, 1802–3; rebuilt 1899 [infirmary minutes in Bedford County Record Office].

THE LUNATIC ASYLUM, 1809–12 [J. H. Matthiason, *Bedford and its Environs*, 1831, 119].

THE BRIDGE, 1811–13, widened 1938–40 ['Designed and executed by John Wing of Bedford', as recorded by an inscription on the parapet].

ELSEWHERE

AVENUE HOUSE, AMPTHILL, BEDS., the COACH-HOUSE for John Morris, 1801 [Morris's House-Book, Sir Albert Richardson's Collection].

WINKS, CHARLES, was a builder and architect of Trentham in Staffordshire. He designed and built two Staffordshire churches, at FULFORD, 1825, Gothic [I.C.B.S.], and HANFORD, 1827–8, rebuilt 1868 [I.C.B.S.]. He was also responsible for rebuilding CHAPEL CHORLTON CHURCH, STAFFS., in 1826–7, modifying plans originally made by James Trubshaw, junior [I.C.B.S.]. He designed the column erected at TRENTHAM PARK in 1836 to the memory of the 1st Duke of Sutherland (d. 1833) [Staffordshire Record Office, Gower papers, D 593/H/13/40].

WINTER, JAMES, was a Scottish architect and master mason. In 1743–4 he was employed by the 2nd Duke of Atholl to build a new stable-block at BLAIR CASTLE, PERTHSHIRE, and in 1747–58 to re-

---

[1] His works included Pulloxhill Church, Beds., 1845–6, the village school at Tingrith, and the restoration of Aspley Guise Church.

model the castle itself. His alterations to the exterior of the castle were destroyed in 1869, when the building was recastellated by David Bryce, and the interior was not his responsibility [Arthur Oswald in *C. Life*, 11 Nov. 1949]. A set of designs for remodelling the castle, marked 'By Mr. Winter 1743', remains at Blair, together with a design by him for an intended addition to Dunkeld House, Perthshire, dated 1744 [D.2.14 (9–12) and D.1.26]. In about 1750 Winter contracted for the masonry of STEWARTFIELD HOUSE, ROXBURGHSHIRE, for John Scot (designer unknown) [S.R.O., GD 237/213/3]. In 1756 he was named as arbitrator by Joseph Dodds (*q.v.*) in connection with his dispute over the erection of the Town Hall at Berwick [Berwick Guild-Books, 14 Jan. 1756].

James was probably related to Thomas Winter, a foreman mason employed by William Adam at Floors Castle in 1726 [accounts at Floors] and at Aberuthven mausoleum in 1735 [S.R.O., GD 220/6, Misc. 1684–1742, i], but Thomas Winter, a land surveyor and landscape-gardener active in Scotland in the 1730s and 1740s, was an Englishman brought from Norfolk in 1726 by Sir Archibald Grant of Monymusk [*Monymusk Papers*, ed. H. Hamilton, Scottish Historical Soc. 1945].

WINTER, THOMAS, of Nottingham, is described as a 'builder' in White's 1832 Directory. With the exception of the tower, WIDMERPOOL CHURCH, NOTTS., was rebuilt to his designs in 1831–2; again rebuilt 1888–95 [I.C.B.S.]. In 1835 he made Gothic designs for rebuilding the church of OLD DALBY or DALBY-ON-THE WOLDS, LEICS., which were presumably those carried out in that or the following year [I.C.B.S.]. A design by him for refronting WESTON COTTAGE, WESTON UNDERWOOD, DERBYSHIRE, dated 1831, is among the muniments at Kedleston Hall.

WINTON, GEORGE (*c.* 1759–1822), is described as 'architect' on a large monument in St. Cuthbert's Churchyard, Edinburgh. He was a mason by trade, and was concerned in the building of houses in ALBANY STREET, ABERCROMBY PLACE, DUBLIN STREET and NORTHUMBERLAND STREET during the first decade of the nineteenth century [S.R.O., Edinburgh Sasines]. He died on 30 November 1822, aged 63.

WISHART, J—, exhibited at the Royal Academy between 1798 and 1808. From 1801 to 1808 his address was at the London Dock Office. His exhibits included a 'Design for a town hall and market place' (1799), 'A view of Sir G. Buggan's villa, and a remarkable rock, on Rustall Common, near Tunbridge Wells' (1802), 'The entrance from the River Thames into the London

Docks at Bell-Dock' (1802), a 'design for a villa' (1804), and a 'design for a royal hospital' (1805).

WISHLADE, BENJAMIN, was born in Devonshire, but moved to Kington in Herefordshire in 1806, and established himself there as a builder and surveyor. In KINGTON he built the TOWN HALL in a provincial Greek Revival style in 1820, the WORKHOUSE (now Kingswood House) in 1837, the NATIONAL SCHOOL, THE RAILWAY STATION, and 'many gentlemen's residences in the neighbourhood', including GRAVEL HILL VILLA for Morris Sayce, and PORTWAY VILLA for William Sayce in a Tudor Gothic style, 1833. The parish church was enlarged by him on the north side in 1829 [I.C.B.S.]. In Radnorshire he was responsible for the GAOL at PRESTEIGN and for the suspension bridge over the R. Ithon at PENY-BONT. [Parry, *History of Kington*, 23, 225, 226.]

WITHENBURY, JAMES, was a mason of Worcester. The crudely drawn design which he made for HANBURY HALL, WORCS., in about 1700 is illustrated in *Country Life*, 4 January 1968, fig. 7. The marble monument to Bishop Lloyd in Fladbury Church which Withenbury made in 1718 has been dismembered [A. Tindal Hart, *William Lloyd 1627–1717*, 1952, 258].

WOLFE, JOHN LEWIS (–1881), was a pupil of Joseph Gwilt and the lifelong friend of Sir Charles Barry, whom he met in Rome in 1820 and subsequently accompanied on his travels in Italy. He was 'almost the only person' who knew Barry intimately, and to him the Rev. A. Barry was indebted for much of the information contained in the *Life* of his father. In 1818 Wolfe exhibited a design for a museum at the Royal Academy, and in 1823 he competed for the new buildings at King's College, Cambridge. He eventually gave up architecture, and died a wealthy man on 6 October 1881. Fourteen of his notebooks and two sketch-books are in the R.I.B.A. Library [A. Barry, *Life and Works of Sir Charles Barry*, 1867, pp. v, 46–7].

WOOD, —, was the architect (otherwise unknown) to whose designs THORPE MARKET CHURCH, NORFOLK, was rebuilt in 1796 at the expense of the 1st Lord Suffield. It is a small Gothic building of flint with stone dressings [E. Bartell, *Observations on Cromer as a Watering Place*, 1800, 43].

WOOD, FREDERICK, exhibited at the Royal Academy between 1817 and 1839 and practised as an architect and surveyor from 28 Queen Street, Brompton, until soon after 1840. In 1838 he showed 'a view of a mansion lately built for a gentleman in the neighbourhood of London'. He competed for the Houses of Parliament in

1835, and for the Royal Exchange in 1839. Drawings in the estate office at Grimsthorpe show that he altered the kitchens of GRIMSTHORPE CASTLE, LINCS., in 1831.

WOOD, HENRY, was described as 'architect and statuary of London' when, in 1801, he bought the yard and business of William Paty of Bristol (*q.v.*). It was chiefly as a statuary mason that he worked in Bristol for the next thirty years, but in 1806–8 he designed and built MERTHYR MAWR, a small country house in GLAMORGAN-SHIRE, for Sir John Nicholl. [R. Gunnis, *Dictionary of British Sculptors*, 1968, 439; Hilary M. Thomas, *Merthyr Mawr House*, Glamorgan Archives Service, 1976.]

WOOD, HENRY MOSES (–1867), practised in Nottingham from about 1810 onwards. His recorded works include ST. PETER'S CHURCH, RADFORD, NOTTS., 1810–12, in elementary Gothic [J. F. Sutton, *The Date Book for Nottingham*, 1852, 144]; DARLEY ABBEY CHURCH, DERBYSHIRE, 1818–19, a Gothic building of the Commissioners' type [S. Glover, *History of Derbyshire* ii (1), 1833, 350]; parsonages at SAWLEY, DERBYSHIRE, 1822–4 [Bodleian Library, records of Queen Anne's Bounty], RADCLIFFE-ON-TRENT, NOTTS., 1827 [Borthwick Institute, York, MGA 1827], CLIFTON, NOTTS., enlarged 1830 [*ibid.*, 1830/1], and COLSTON BASSETT, NOTTS., 1834 [*ibid.*, 1834/1]; the enlargement of DENTON HOUSE, nr. GRANTHAM, LINCS., for Sir W. Earle Welby, Bart., 1815 [plans reported to be in estate office] (J. P. Neale, *Views of Seats*, 1st ser., iii, 1820), and additions, including a new dining-room with Greek Revival façade to the street, to the JUDGES' LODGINGS or COUNTY HOUSE (now Record Office), HIGH PAVEMENT, NOTTINGHAM, 1833 [A. Henstock, 'County House, High Pavement, Nottingham', *Thoroton Society's Trans.* lxxviii, 1974, 63]. Wood was active as a land surveyor and was the author of a map of Nottingham, published in 1830. He died at Buxton on 28 September 1867, leaving two sons, Henry Walker Wood, who continued his practice in Nottingham, and Arthur Augustus Wood, a playwright [Principal Probate Registry, Calendar of Probates].

WOOD, JOHN (1704–1754), was born in Bath in 1704, baptized in St. James's Church on 26 August, and educated at the Blue Coat School. His father, George Wood, was a local builder of whom nothing is known beyond the fact that he was still working in Bath as late as 1727. John Wood's early life is obscure, but there is evidence that he was living in London in 1725–7, and that he was working in Yorkshire during the same period. He himself refers to 'engagements in London' which came to an end in the spring of 1727, and the St. Marylebone rate-books show

908

that a John Wood was resident in Oxford Street between 1725 and 1727. He was, in fact, one of the principal builders on the Cavendish-Harley estate, then being laid out by the Earl of Oxford, to whom Wood was afterwards to dedicate his book on Stonehenge. The register of building leases (B.M., Add. MS. 18240) shows that between March 1723 and July 1730 he undertook to build five houses in Oxford Street, one in Margaret Street, and several more in Edward Street. He was also engaged in building in Cavendish Square, both for the Duke of Chandos and for Lord Bingley. The latter was erecting a large house on the west side of the Square, and Wood appears to have been acting as his surveyor. Lord Bingley had recently completed his country seat at Bramham Park in Yorkshire, and here Wood seems to have been employed in laying out the grounds, for there exists an engraved plan of the park signed 'Jo: Wood', and the volume of Wood's designs in Bath Reference Library contains a design for an aqueduct at Bramham. In his *Description of Bath*, published in 1742, Wood says that he was at Bramham Park 'about eighteen years ago', *i.e. c.* 1724; he also states that it was while he was in Yorkshire in the summer of 1725 that he first began to plan the improvement of Bath, and that in the following year business 'called me twice into the North of England'. Further evidence of Wood's activity in the North comes in a letter written from Bath in 1749 by a Liverpool lady who reported (probably wrongly) that he had designed a house at Capesthorne in Cheshire early in the 1730s.[1]

By 1727, therefore, Wood had already gained an unusually wide experience of building operations for one still only in his 23rd year. In Marylebone he had seen how the speculative builder could be made to conform to a regular architectural scheme planned in advance, and he had been employed at at least one country house besides acting the parts of both builder and surveyor in London.

It was natural that Wood should sooner or later turn his attention to the improvement of his native city of Bath, then on the threshold of its Georgian prosperity. Acts had already been obtained to improve the roads leading to the city, 'to pave, clean and light' its streets, and to make the Avon navigable to Bristol; and so (to quote Wood's own account) 'when I found the Work was likely to go on, I began to turn my Thoughts towards the Improvement of the City by Building, and for this Purpose I procured a Plan of the Town, which was sent me into Yorkshire, in the summer of the year 1725, where I, at my leisure Hours, formed one Design for the Ground, at the North West Corner of the City', belonging to Robert Gay, an eminent London surgeon who had been M.P. for Bath, and 'another for the Land on the North East side of the Town and River' on the Earl of Essex's estate. These were alternative designs, for both included 'a grand Place of Assembly, to be called the Royal Forum of Bath; another Place, no less magnificent, for the Exhibition of Sports, to be called the Grand Circus; and a third Place, of equal State with either of the former, for the Practice of medicinal Exercises, to be called the Imperial Gymnasium of the City, from a Work of that kind, taking its Rise at first in Bath, during the Time of the Roman Emperors'. On his return to London, Wood immediately communicated these ambitious proposals to the proprietors of the lands in question. They lay under consideration for a year, while Wood completed his business in the North of England. But in November 1726 he became Gay's agent, with authority to enter into agreements with anyone willing to build a new street of houses known at first as Barton, but eventually as Gay, Street. In the following January he contracted with the Duke of Chandos to build a 'court of houses' on the site of St. John's Hospital, of which the Duke had acquired the lease, and on 10 March he undertook the execution of the Avon navigation scheme. Finding that the local builders were inefficient and antiquated in their methods, he procured masons from Yorkshire and carpenters, joiners and plasteres from London and elsewhere, 'and from time to time sent such as were necessary down to Bath to carry on the Buildings I had undertaken'. For the 'better execution' of the Avon scheme he employed labourers who had been engaged on the Chelsea waterworks, with the result that the cost of excavation was cut by a third.

In May 1727, having completed his engagements in London, Wood took up permanent residence in Bath, where he was soon engaged in further schemes of building for Ralph Allen and Humphrey Thayer, the treasurers of the General Hospital. The death of George I in June 1727 caused a temporary set-back to his building activities, for with the prospect of a general election Gay bowed to opinion in the city which was hostile to the creation of a New Town and withdrew his support for the continuation of Barton Street. Wood now produced a plan which put the rebuilding of the old town first, but this was rejected by the Corporation as 'chimerical'. Faced with the total failure of his scheme for erecting a new Bath, Wood decided on the bold step of becoming 'sole contractor' for a great residential square which was to be erected under his supervision and at his own risk. With this object he secured from Gay a ninety-nine years' lease of sufficient land upon which to build the east

side of the Square. Further leases were granted between 1728 and 1734, and in 1736 Queen Square was completed as the first instalment of Wood's plan for a new Bath. Both in its design and in its mode of erection, the Square followed London precedent. Having marked out the site of the individual houses, Wood sub-leased them to owner-builders or building-tradesmen, who were bound by their leases to follow his elevations, but left to plan and decorate the interiors as they chose. The effect (as in Cavendish and Grosvenor Squares) was 'to group ordinary town houses in such as way as to gain the effect of a single palace', and the existence of the local quarries enabled Wood's handsome Palladian façades to be carried out entirely in stone at reasonable cost. Encouraged by the success of the Square, Wood revived his schemes for a Circus and a Forum. The latter was actually begun in 1739 on the site of the Abbey Orchard, but the Parades and their connecting streets were the only portion of 'the Grand Place of Assembly to be called the Royal Forum of Bath' which was realized. The Circus, owing to the opposition of interested parties, was not begun until February 1754, within three months of Wood's death, and the greater part of it was erected under the superintendence of his son, John Wood the younger. As a residential unit it bore little resemblance to the 'Grand Circus for the exhibition of sports' of which Wood had dreamed in 1725, but it possessed the form, if not the function, of a Roman amphitheatre, and its façade was recognizable as that of a miniature Colosseum turned inside out. Archaeologically, it was indefensible, but architecturally it was highly effective, and the circus became a permanent feature of the English town-planning tradition.

As Bath became a place of fashionable resort, so the celebrity of its architect spread, and Wood was invited to design public buildings in Bristol and Liverpool, as well as country houses in the neighbourhood of Bath itself. The most celebrated of these was Ralph Allen's great mansion at Prior Park, which he began in 1735. Owing to a quarrel with the owner, its completion was entrusted to Richard Jones, Allen's clerk of the works, who altered the east wing in execution, destroying the symmetrical balance of Wood's design.

In 1741 Wood published a curious work entitled *The Origin of Building, or the Plagiarism of the Heathens Detected*, in which he endeavoured to prove that the development of classical architecture was anticipated in Biblical times and that the three primary orders had been divinely revealed to the Jews and exemplified in the Temple at Jerusalem. This thesis, which had first been put forward by G. B. Villalpanda in his Commentaries on Ezekiel, published in 1604, was apparently intended to vindicate classical architecture from the stigma of a pagan origin and thereby to justify its employment on religious as well as aesthetic grounds. In the following year, Wood published *An Essay towards a Description of Bath* (2nd ed. 1749; reissued 1765), in which he allowed his imagination full scope, identifying the city of Bladud as the ancient seat of Apollo and establishing a Druidic University at Stanton Drew. This historical romanticism serves as an introduction to Wood's own account of the Georgian improvements in which he had played so prominent a part. He also took the opportunity to attack those who had opposed his schemes, and to denounce the 'piratical' architecture of those master builders who did not submit themselves to his architectural direction. Wood's other works were *A Description of the Exchange of Bristol*, 1745, *Choir Gaure, vulgarly called Stonehenge, described, restored and explained*, 1747, and a *Dissertation Upon the Orders of Columns and their Appendages*, 1750. The work on Stonehenge was based on a survey which Wood had made for Lord Oxford in 1740 (now B.M., Harleian MSS. 7354, 7355). Its object was to demonstrate that the Wiltshire monument was 'a temple of the British Druids', and that the stone circles at Stanton Drew were its prototype. What connection there may have been between Wood's antiquarian researches and his architectural projects is a subject that deserves investigation.

Wood died at his house on the south side of Queen Square on 23 May 1754, after 'a long and tedious illness', and was buried at Swainswick. He was in his 50th year. His speculations had been financially successful, and he left substantial property to his wife Jane (who died in 1766), subject to annuities for his sons, John and Thayer Allen Wood, and his daughters, Jane and Elizabeth [P.C.C. 186 PINFOLD]. A volume containing some 80 architectural drawings by Wood is in the Bath Reference Library. It includes the plan of an unexecuted design for the Ranger's Lodge (later Viceregal Lodge) in Phoenix Park, Dublin.

[*A.P.S.D.*; *D.N.B.*; *Builder*, 1856, 386; 'Some Original Drawings by John Wood', *Architect and Building News*, 4 Nov. 1927; R. Wittkower, 'Federico Zuccari and John Wood of Bath', *Journal of the Warburg and Courtauld Institutes* v, 1943; W. Ison, *The Georgian Buildings of Bath*, 1948; John Summerson, 'John Wood and the English Town-Planning Tradition', in *Heavenly Mansions*, 1949; C. H. & M. I. Collins Baker, *The Life of James Brydges, Duke of Chandos*, 1949, chaps. 12–13; W. S. Dakers, *John Wood and his Times* (a pamphlet, Bath 1954); B.M., Egerton MS. 3647, ff. 91, 105, etc. (Duke of Kingston's Bath estate records); Nottingham University Library, Manvers MS. 4184 (Bath lease book); plan of Bath layout in Monson MS. XLIII

(Kingston executorship papers); B.M., Add. MSS. 18239–40 (Harley Estate records).]

BUILDINGS IN BATH

ST. JOHN'S HOSPITAL, CHAPEL COURT HOUSE and CHANDOS BUILDINGS, for the 1st Duke of Chandos, 1727–30 [Baker, *op. cit.*, chap. 13].

LILLIPUT ALLEY, enlarged house for Ralph Allen, 1727–8 [described by Wood in his *Essay* as 'a sample for the greatest Magnificence that was ever proposed by me for our City Houses', but not accepted by Ison as Wood's own work].

LINDSEY'S (later WILTSHIRE'S) ASSEMBLY ROOMS, for Humphrey Thayer, 1728–30; dem. *c.* 1820 [Ison, *op. cit.*, 50 and pl. 7].

QUEEN SQUARE and houses in WOOD STREET, JOHN STREET and OLD KING STREET, 1729–36 [Ison, 127–33].

ST. MARY'S CHAPEL, QUEEN SQUARE, 1732–4; dem. *c.* 1875 [Ison, 72 and fig. 10; plan and elevation by Wood in Bath City Art Gallery].

THE GENERAL (now ROYAL MINERAL WATER) HOSPITAL, 1738–42; attic storey added by J. Palmer *c.* 1793; extensions by Manners & Gill 1850–60 [Ison, 88–91].

THE NORTH and SOUTH PARADES, with PIERREPONT and DUKE STREETS, 1740–3 [Ison, 145–8].

GAY STREET, *c.* 1750 onwards [Ison, 133].

THE CIRCUS, began 1754, completed by John Wood, junior [Ison, 150–1].

BUILDINGS ELSEWHERE

BRAMHAM PARK, YORKS. (W.R.), work for the 1st Lord Bingley, 1722–4, probably in connection with the formal garden layout, of which Wood published an engraved plan (B.M., *King's Maps* xlv, 16, and York Minster Library, Hailstone Collection). The dates are established by payments to Wood in Bingley's account at Hoare's bank published by G. W. Beard in *C. Life*, 11 Dec. 1958, 1421 (*C. Life*, 12 June 1958).

TIBERTON COURT, HEREFS., for William Brydges, 1728; dem. 1952 [Baker, *op. cit.*, 308, 319; W. S. Dakers, *op. cit.*, 13].

TIBERTON CHURCH, HEREFS., reredos for William Brydges, 1728 [W. S. Dakers, *op. cit.*, 13; B. A. Bailey, 'William Brydges and the rebuilding of Tyberton Church', *Trans. Woolhope Field Club* xxxvii, 1962].

BELCOMBE COURT, nr. BRADFORD-ON-AVON, WILTS., for Francis Yerbury, 1734 [J. Wood, *Essay towards a Description of Bath*, 1749, 237–9] (*C. Life*, 22 Dec. 1950).

LLANDAFF CATHEDRAL, GLAMORGANSHIRE, constructed classical church within the ruined nave, 1734–52; dem. *c.* 1850 [*Some Account of the Condition of the Fabric of Llandaff Cathedral from 1575 to the Present Time*, by the

Bishop of Llandaff, 1860; N. Pevsner, 'John Wood at Llandaff', *Arch. Rev.*, June 1954; E. T. Davies, 'John Wood's Italianate Temple', *Jnl. of the Historical Soc. of the Church in Wales* vi, 1956; D. R. Buttress, 'Llandaff Cathedral in the 18th and 19th Centuries', *ibid.* xvi, 1966].

PRIOR PARK, nr. BATH, for Ralph Allen, 1735–48. The east wing was completed by Richard Jones to a different design. In 1829 the mansion became a Roman Catholic college, and the wings were remodelled by H. E. Goodridge. There was a fire in 1836, after which the interior of the main building was rebuilt by the same architect. The west pavilion was dem. in 1844 to make way for the chapel designed by J. J. Scoles [W. Ison, *The Georgian Buildings of Bath*, 1948, 135–44; drawings by Wood in volume in Bath Reference Library, ff. 43–56].

LILLIPUT CASTLE, LANSDOWN, nr. BATH, for Jeremiah Pierce, 1738; incorporated in Battlefields, 1802 [J. Wood, *op. cit.*, 234–7; drawings by Wood in volume in Bath Reference Library, ff. 23–4].

BRISTOL, THE EXCHANGE and MARKET, CORN STREET, 1741–3 [J. Wood, *A Description of the Exchange of Bristol*, 1745; W. Ison, *The Georgian Buildings of Bristol*, 1952, 95–105].

BATHFORD, SOMERSET, THE SPA, 1746; dem. [J. Wood, *Essay towards a Description of Bath*, 1749, 70].

TITANBARROW LOGIA (now WHITEHAVEN), KINGSDOWN ROAD, BATHFORD, nr. BATH, for Southwell Pigott, 1748–9 [J. Wood, *Essay towards a Description of Bath*, 1749, 239–40; contract and drawings by Wood in volume in Bath Reference Library, ff. 1–6].

LIVERPOOL, THE EXCHANGE (now TOWN HALL), 1749–54; interior destroyed by fire 1795 and rebuilt by J. Foster; dome and cupola added 1802, portico 1811 [J. A. Picton, *Liverpool Municipal Records, 1700–1835*, 1886, 158–9, 269–72] (*C. Life*, 23 July 1927).

WOOD, JOHN (1728–1781), the younger, son of John Wood of Bath, was christened in Bath Abbey on 25 February 1727/8. As a young man he evidently acted as his father's assistant, for in 1749, when the elder Wood designed the Exchange at Liverpool, he agreed 'to leave his son Mr. John Wood at Liverpoole during the summer season to superintend and carry on the said building', and a house in Liverpool was rented in the name of John Wood between 1750 and 1753. In July 1749 both he and his father were admitted freemen of Liverpool, and in 1751 he was elected a member of the Ugly Face Clubbe in that town. In the Club's minute-book his qualifications for membership are recorded in architectural terms. They read 'A stone colour'd complexion, a dimple in his Attick Story. The

Pillasters of his face fluted. Tortoise-ey'd, a prominent nose. Wild grin, and face altogether resembling a badger, and finer tho' smaller than Sir Christopher Wren or Inigo Jones's.' After his father's death in 1754, Wood took his place as the leading architect in Bath, completing the building of the Circus, and adding the Royal Crescent as the culmination of the great sequence of residential buildings begun by his father in 1727. Completed in 1775, the Crescent was the first (as well as the largest and grandest) of its kind, and was destined to find more imitators even than the neighbouring Circus. Wood's second masterpiece, the New Assembly Rooms, provided the city with a public building worthy of its domestic architecture, while his Hot Bath, built for the Corporation between 1773 and 1777, showed that its architect could design a small but complicated structure with as much success as the monumental Royal Crescent. The work of the younger Wood represents the climax of the Palladian tradition in Bath, and after his death the architectural initiative passed to those who, like Thomas Baldwin, looked for their inspiration to Robert Adam rather than to Palladio. John Wood died at Batheaston on 16 June 1781, and was buried in the family vault in Swainswick Church. He had been for many years a Justice of the Peace for the County of Somerset. He published *A Series of Plans, for Cottages or Habitations of the Labourer*, 1781, 2nd ed. 1792, 3rd ed. 1806, reprinted 1837, which shows a serious interest in working-class housing.

[*A.P.S.D.*; *D.N.B.*; *Registers of Bath Abbey*, Harleian Soc. i, 101; *Gent's Mag.* 1781, 295; J. A. Picton, *Liverpool Municipal Records, 1700–1835*, 1886, 158–9; S. A. Harris, 'Sarah Clayton's Letter and John Wood of Bath', *Trans. Historic Soc. of Lancs. and Cheshire*, c, 1948, 59, n. 3; W. Ison, *The Georgian Buildings of Bath*, 1948; John Summerson, 'John Wood and the English Town Planning Tradition', in *Heavenly Mansions*, 1949.]

BATH

THE ROYAL CRESCENT, 1767–75 [Ison, *op. cit.*, 154–6].

BROCK STREET, *c.* 1767 [Ison, *op. cit.*, 153–4].

RIVERS STREET, *c.* 1770 [Ison, *op. cit.*, 34].

CATHERINE PLACE, *c.* 1780 [Ison, *op. cit.*, 34].

THE NEW ASSEMBLY ROOMS, 1769–71; interior restored after destruction by bombing 1942 [Ison, *op. cit.*, 50–4].

attributed: ALFRED STREET, BENNETT STREET and RUSSELL STREET, 1772–6 [Ison, *op. cit.*, 159–60].

MARGARET CHAPEL, BROCK STREET, for Cornelius Norton, *c.* 1773, Gothic; secularized in the nineteenth century, and damaged by bombing 1942 [Ison, *op. cit.*, 76].

THE HOT BATH (now THE OLD ROYAL BATHS), 1773–7 [Ison, *op. cit.*, 55–7].

BUCKLAND HOUSE, BERKS., for Sir Robert Throckmorton, 1755–7; enlarged by Romaine Walker
1910 [*Vitruvius Britannicus*, iv, 1767, pls. 90–
3] (*C. Life*, 15–22 May 1915).

BITTON CHURCH, GLOS., designed reredos, etc.,
1760–1 [H. T. Ellacombe, *History of the Parish
of Bitton*, 1881, 5].

STANDLYNCH, now TRAFALGAR HOUSE, WILTS.,
added the wings for Henry Dawkins, 1766
[*Vitruvius Britannicus* v, 1771, pls. 78–81] (*C.
Life*, 13–20 July 1945).

SALISBURY, WILTS., THE INFIRMARY, 1767–71
[*V.C.H. Wilts.* vi, 183].

TREGENNA CASTLE, nr. ST. IVES, CORNWALL, for
Samuel Stephens, 1773–4, castellated;
enlarged by G. Wightwick 1845 [Lake's
Parochial History of Cornwall ii, 1868, 262].

HARDENHUISH CHURCH, WILTS., for Benjamin Colbourne of Bath, consecrated 1779[1] [J. Britton,
Beauties of Wiltshire iii, 1825, 162].

ST. IVES, CORNWALL, almshouses, before 1781 [J.
Wood, *Plans for Labourers' Cottages*, 1792 ed.,
24, 26, pl. iv].

WOOD, THOMAS (*c.* 1644–1695), was a leading Oxford master mason and sculptor. He was
the son of Richard Wood of Charlbury in
Oxfordshire and was apprenticed at the age of 12
to William Byrd (*q.v.*). He was working on his
own by 1675–6, when he was paid £4 14s. 4d.
'for carving of anticks etc.' in Adam de Brome's
Chapel in St. Mary's Church, and £87 19s. 2d.
for laying the marble paving in the chancel [T.
G. Jackson, *Church of St. Mary the Virgin,
Oxford*, 1897, 134–5]. In 1679 he undertook to
perform the stonework of the BISHOP'S PALACE at
CUDDESDON, OXON., as sub-contractor to Richard
Frogley, a master carpenter to whom Bishop Fell
had 'set the whole work by the great'. In
November of the following year, Wood began a
suit against Frogley in the Vice-Chancellor's
Court, from which it appears that the latter had
also commissioned him to erect a chimney-piece
'of Burford stone handsomely wrought' at
Esquire Lenthall's house at Haseley, and to work
230 feet of 'cornish' at Newington.[2] Wood alleged
that in spite of repeated applications for
payment, Frogley had 'utterly refused or at least
delayed more than is just'. In April 1681 Frogley
began a counter-suit, claiming that in 1678 Wood
had employed him to build a new stable 'by the
Lady's Chappell or Round House by Smith Gate

[1] Wood is said also to have designed Woolley Church,
Somerset (1761), for Mrs. Elizabeth Parkins, but
definite evidence appears to be lacking.
[2] Presumably Newington Hall, 10 miles south-east of
Oxford, which was built by one of the Dunch family
(*Gent's Mag.* 1796 (ii), 809).

in Oxford',[2] and to execute some work 'in the said
Thomas Wood's rackett courts', but that Wood
refused to pay him either for his workmanship
or for some cedar wood which he had commissioned him to buy. Wood replied that Frogley
had charged excessively for his work; that he had
commissioned Frogley to buy 60 feet of cedar for
the Chapel of Corpus Christi College[2] to match
a pattern, but that only 9 feet matched the pattern
in colour and that the rest was useless. Judgement
was eventually given in favour of Wood, but
Frogley appealed and the final result is unknown
[Mrs. J. C. Cole, 'The Building of the Second
Palace at Cuddesdon', *Oxoniensia* xxiv, 1959].

In 1678 Wood carved the monument to
Francis Junius in St. George's Chapel, Windsor,
which was erected at the expense of the University of Oxford, and in 1679–83 he was the
master mason chosen to build the OLD ASHMO-
LEAN MUSEUM. A contemporary print by M.
Burghers has the inscription 'T. Wood Archt.',
and as the building accounts contain no payments
for designs to anyone else, it is safe to assume that
they were made by Wood himself [C. E. Mallet,
History of the University of Oxford ii, 1924, 435–
6]. There are measured drawings of the building
in *Details*, ed. R. R. Philips, i, 1909, 230–34.

In 1682 Wood designed a new parsonage house
at Kingham, Oxon., for the rector, the Rev.
William Dowdeswell, but his plans were rejected
as too ambitious, and another master builder was
employed to erect the existing rectory. Wood
subsequently sued Dowdeswell for the value of
his drawings, some of which were produced in
evidence, and are preserved among the records
of the Vice-Chancellor's Court [University
Archives, Vice-Chancellor's Court, 1688/9,
Easter Term, 54].

In 1683–5 Wood rebuilt the west tower of
DEDDINGTON CHURCH, OXON., in traditional
Gothic style with battlements and pinnacles. It
had fallen in 1634 and had been partly rebuilt
during the next two years. But nothing more was
done owing to the Civil War, and it was not until
1683 that the parishioners decided to complete
the rebuilding. Wood contracted to perform
work for five or six hundred pounds [H. M. Colvin, *History of Deddington*, 1963, 105].

In October 1685 Wood was sent for by the
Dean and Canons of WELLS CATHEDRAL to repair
the roof of the nave of their church, which was
'in very great decay', and undertook to perform
the necessary work for between £400 and £500
[Hist. MSS. Comm., *Wells* ii, 460–1].

Wood was an able provincial sculptor, and the
Old Ashmolean Museum shows that he had some
understanding of classical architecture. He died

[1] *I.e.* the octagonal Chapel of St. Mary, which is now
the Junior Common Room of Hertford College.
[2] Refitted in 1676.

on 22 February 1694/5, in his 52nd year, and was buried in St. Michael's Church, Oxford, where there is a floor-slab to his memory. According to the inscription he 'was esteemed sufficiently qualified for better employments than those he was bound to by his education'.

[A. Wood, *Life and Times*, ed. Clark, iv, 75, 78; *Wren Soc.* xix, 94 n.; R. Gunnis, *Dictionary of British Sculptors*, 1968, 440; Mrs. J. C. Cole in *Oxoniensia* xiv, 1949, 68–9, xvii–xviii, 1952–3, 198, and xxix–xxx, 1964–5, 149; D. G. Vaisey, 'Thomas Wood and his Workshop', *Oxoniensia* xxxvi, 1971.]

WOOD, WILLIAM (*c.* 1745–1818), of Truro, began his career as the apprentice or foreman of John Bland, a builder of that town. He eventually became the leading architect and builder in Truro, and acted as surveyor for the Lemon estate there. He was declared bankrupt in 1783 and died in January 1818, aged 73 [*Gent's Mag.* 1783, 455; *West Briton and Cornwall Advertiser*, 9 Jan. 1818; Taunton MSS. at Royal Cornwall Institution].

WOODHEAD, JOHN (–*c.* 1838), practised in Doncaster, where he was the partner first of William Lindley (*q.v.*) and then of William Hurst (*q.v.*).

WOODROFFE, EDWARD (*c.* 1622–1675), held the post of Surveyor to the Dean and Chapter of Westminster from 22 October 1662 until his death in 1675.[1] After the Great Fire he was one of the three surveyors appointed to rebuild the City churches, the others being Sir Christopher Wren and Robert Hooke. There are several references to him in the parish records,[2] but he remains a somewhat obscure figure in comparison with his more celebrated colleagues. Woodroffe also held the post of Assistant Surveyor of St. Paul's Cathdral, and there are payments to him in the accounts for assisting Wren in the preparation of drawings, making contracts, measuring masons' work, etc., from 1668 onwards.[3] In 1670 he designed the houses

[1] The appointment of Edward Woodroffe as Surveyor is recorded in the Chapter Books on 22 Oct. 1662, but the payments in the Treasurer's Accounts from 1663 to 1671 are to *Robert* Woodroffe. Edward Woodroffe then appears in the accounts from 1672 until his death in 1675. There is no record of any fresh appointment in 1672.

[2] *E.g.* at St. George Botolph Lane, where, in 1672, 9s. 8d. was accounted for the expenses of 'the Doctor and Mr. Woodrufe and Mr. Hooke, the three Surveyors' (*Wren Soc.* xix, 20).

[3] In Sept. 1673 a correspondent of Dean Sancroft wrote that 'Dr. Wren and Mr. Woodroof have been the week last past in the Convocation House, drawing the Lines of the Designe of the church upon the Table there, for the Joyner's Directions for making the new Modell' (*Wren Soc.* xiii, 51).

for the three Residentiary Canons in Amen Court. In conjunction with John Oliver, he also reported on the cost of building the new Deanery in 1669, and in 1672 signed the contract on behalf of Dean Sancroft [*Wren Soc.* xiii, 52–6]. He died on 16 November 1675, in his 54th year, and was buried in the Cloisters of Westminster Abbey, where there was formerly a slab to his memory. In his will he is described as 'of St. Andrew's, Holborn, gentleman'. He may have been related to John Woodruff, a master mason of Windsor, who died in 1728 at the age of 58 [Westminster Abbey Muniments; J. Chester, *Westminster Abbey Registers* (Harleian Soc.), 163, 188; *Wren Soc.* xx, 252; J. Crull, *Antiquities of Westminster Abbey* ii, 1722, 185; J. Dart, *Westminster Abbey* ii, 1723, 138].

WOODS, JOSEPH (1776–1864), born at Stoke Newington on 24 August 1776, was the second son of Joseph Woods, a member of the Society of Friends. Owing to delicate health he left school early, but nevertheless became proficient in Latin, Greek, Hebrew, French and Italian. At the age of 16 he was articled to a business at Dover, but, preferring architecture, became a pupil of D. A. Alexander. He obtained admission to the Royal Academy Schools in 1798, and exhibited at the Academy between 1801 and 1815. Some of his exhibited designs were of a visionary character. In 1802 he showed a project for a stone bridge of a single span 600 feet wide over the Thames at London, of which he published an account in the *Monthly Magazine*, July 1802, 545–7, and in 1814 a design for a palace and public buildings extending continuously from Charing Cross to Westminster Bridge, a distance of 2500 feet. In 1803 he obtained the third premium in the competition for the conversion of the Parliament House at Dublin into a bank.

Wood's abilities lay in literary and scholarly pursuits rather than in practical architectural work, and as a practising architect he was not very successful. For his maternal uncle, Jonathan Hoare, he designed CLISSOLD HOUSE, CLISSOLD PARK, STOKE NEWINGTON, a severe neo-classical villa with a Greek Doric veranda (Pevsner, *London except the Cities of London and Westminster*, 1952, pl. 45A). In 1811–12 he designed THE LONDON COMMERCIAL SALE ROOMS in MINCING LANE (dem.). The façade, in which he employed the order of the temple of Minerva Polias at Priene, is illustrated in Ackermann's *Repository of Arts*, 1813, 300. Owing to a miscalculation of the strength of some iron trusses there was a failure in the floor, which Woods was obliged to make good at his own expense, and soon afterwards he gave up architectural practice.

In 1806 Woods founded the London Architectural Society, of which he became the first president, and contributed papers on 'The Situation and Arrangement of Villas', 'Dilapidations' and 'Modern Theories of Taste' to the Society's *Essays* (1808–10). Having been invited to edit the remainder of James Stuart's drawings of Grecian architecture, he issued the fourth or supplementary volume of the *Antiquities of Athens* in 1816. During the years 1816–19 he travelled in France, Italy and Greece, and in 1825–6 he again visited the Continent, publishing in 1828 *Letters of an Architect from France, Italy, and Greece*, 2 vols. Having independent means he was able in 1833 to retire to Lewes in Sussex. Here he devoted himself to botany, to which he made important contributions, publishing in 1850 his well-known *Tourists' Flora: A Descriptive Catalogue of the Flowering Plants and Ferns of the British Islands, France, Germany, Switzerland, Italy, and the Italian Islands*. He was a Fellow of the Linnean, Geological and Antiquarian Societies. He died at his home in Southover Crescent, Lewes, on 9 January 1864. There is an engraved portrait by Cotman, the original of which is in the Victoria and Albert Museum.

[*Builder* xxi, 1863, 86, 112–13, xxii, 1864, 56; *R.I.B.A. Trans.* xv, 1863–4; *A.P.S.D.*; *D.N.B.*; M. A. Lower, *The Worthies of Sussex*, 1865, 312–14.]

WOODS, RICHARD (–1793), was primarily a land surveyor and landscape-gardener. A list of grounds improved by him is given by Hugh Prince, *Parks in England* (1967). See also B. E. Coates, 'The Work of Richard Woods in the West Riding of Yorkshire', *Trans. Hunter Archaeological Soc.* viii, 1963, 297–306. He occasionally acted as an architect, notably at WARDOUR CASTLE, WILTS., where he designed various garden buildings for the 8th Lord Arundell *c.* 1766–71, and at IRNHAM HALL, LINCS., where he designed the stables for the same nobleman in 1769–70. His unexecuted designs for a Palladian mansion at Wardour are among the archives of Mr. R. J. R. Arundell, together with evidence of his activities as an architect and landscape-gardener at both Wardour and Irnham. In the 1750s Woods was living at Chertsey in Surrey, but later he moved to North Ockendon in Essex and ultimately to Ingrave in the same county.

WOODSTOCK, THOMAS (–1694), was a master carpenter who was extensively employed by Sir Christopher Wren in rebuilding St. Paul's Cathedral and the City churches (see *Wren Soc.* x, 46–55, for details). According to Sir John Moore, to whom Woodstock had been recommended by Wren as a proper person to supervise the erection of his new School at Appleby, Leics., the Surveyor-General made 'use of Mr. Woodstock to oversee his workes and buildings in most places' [*Wren Soc.* xi, 87–9]. In 1677 Woodstock was consulted by Thomas Papillon, for whom he

914

made a 'draft' for altering or rebuilding Acrise Place, Kent, which Papillon considered to be 'handsome' but unduly expensive [Arthur Oswald in *C. Life*, 8 Aug. 1957, 261]. In 1694 he was engaged as the architect of the proposed Danish Church in Wellclose Square, but his death in the summer of that year resulted in the commission being given to C. G. Cibber [H. Faber, *C. G. Cibber*, 1926, 63–4]. The contract whereby, on 15 December 1670, Thomas Woodstock and Nicholas Stapell contracted with George Ligoe to build on Fish Street Hill two houses 'of the third sort of building mentioned in the late Act of Parliament for the Rebuilding of the City of London' is preserved among the Guildhall Records [Deeds 94, 3].

WOODWARD, EDWARD (*c.* 1697–1766), and his brother THOMAS were master masons and quarry-owners of Chipping Campden in Gloucestershire. They were the sons of Thomas Woodward, who in 1719 took a lease of Westington Quarries for the lives of himself, his wife Mary and his third son Robert.[1] The only recorded works of Thomas Woodward the elder, who died in 1748 at the age of 76, are the repair of the spire of QUINTON CHURCH, WARWICKS., in 1712 [Warwick Record Office, DR 468/21] and the rebuilding of the tower of BLOCKLEY CHURCH, WORCS., in 1725–7. The original contract, with Woodward's plan and elevation attached, is among the documents from Northwick Park now in the County Record Office at Worcester [bundle 31/1]. The tower is medieval in outline, with Gothic belfry windows copied from those of Chipping Campden Church.

Edward and Thomas Woodward worked in partnership in the 1730s. In March 1729/30 they contracted to rebuild ALCESTER CHURCH, WARWICKS., in accordance with a design formerly attached to the contract but now lost. They were to employ Alcester workmen, and throughout were to 'be under the advise direccion and Government ... of Mr. Francis Smith [of Warwick] so as to do alter or amend anything of the said worke which hee shall think fitt to have done or altered'. It is probable, however, that they supplied the design themselves, and that Smith's functions were merely of a supervisory character. The church combines a classical interior with a Gothic exterior; its windows were remodelled in 1870–1, but their original form can be seen from the lithograph in *Notices of the Churches of Warwickshire* ii, 1858; the medieval tower was

[1] Thomas (d. 1748) was the son of Thomas Woodward of Aston-sub-Edge, mason (d. 1 May 1716, aged 71), who was the son of Edward Woodward of Campden, mason (d. 13 May 1692). The first Thomas, disapproving of his son's second marriage, cut him off with a shilling, and left his property in Aston-sub-Edge to his grandson Edward.

retained. The Woodwards' next contract was the rebuilding of the church of ST. JOHN THE BAPTIST at GLOUCESTER in 1732–4. Here there is no doubt that they were the designers as well as the builders, for in 1729 the churchwardens 'Payd the two Mr. Woodwards, for surveying, giving in an Estimation and draught of our church 10s. 6d.' The result was a handsome but rather unsophisticated classical building. St. John's was scarcely completed before the Woodwards had undertaken the rebuilding of ST. SWITHIN'S CHURCH, WORCESTER, a contract which necessitated their becoming freemen of the city in January 1734/5, on payment of a fine of £20. A brass plate over the west door records that 'This church was rebuilt by Ed. and Tho. Woodward in the year of our Lord 1736. Tho. Hoskyns, Tho. Wakeman, churchwardens.' The east front closely resembles that of St. John's, Gloucester, while the tower has ogee surrounds to the belfry windows which are derived from similar features on the tower of Chipping Camden Church. At about the same time they reconstructed the nave of LLANDAFF CATHEDRAL in classical style to the designs of John Wood of Bath and carried out repairs to the bishop's palace at MATHERN in MONMOUTHSHIRE [D. R. Buttress, 'Llandaff Cathedral in the 18th and 19th Centuries', *Jnl. of the Historical Soc. of the Church in Wales* xvi, 1966].

Thomas Woodward appears to have settled in Worcester, for he is described as 'of Worcester' in several subsequent documents. In 1739 he rebuilt the nave of ST. MARY'S CHURCH, SWANSEA (dem. 1897) [D. G. Walker, *A Short History of the Parish Church of Swansea*, 1959, 12], and in 1745 he and Thomas Cook of Bewdley, joiner, undertook to build ST. ANNE'S CHURCH, BEWDLEY, in a classical style very similar to the Woodwards' other churches [Society of Antiquaries, Prattinton Miscellanea II/xiii]. A stone dislodged in 1950 was found to bear the name of 'Ric. Woodward Campden in Glos. 1745' – that is of Edward's son Richard (died 1755, aged 32), who was evidently working with his uncle at the time.

Between 1750 and 1764[1] Edward Woodward was employed by the antiquary James West to reconstruct his house at ALSCOT, WARWICKS., and to remodel the neighbouring church of PRESTON-ON-STOUR (both illustrated in *C. Life*, 15, 22 and 29 May 1958). Letters and drawings preserved at Alscot Park show that in 1752 Woodward submitted designs for rebuilding the church in an elaborate Gothic style, with embattled parapets and crocketed pinnacles crowned by metal vanes.[2] The buttresses were to be ornamented by

a series of shallow niches, and the tower was to be surmounted by a spire supported on flying buttresses, like that of St. Nicholas, Newcastle. In the event Woodward was merely allowed to remodel the existing church piecemeal, beginning with the chancel, which was rebuilt to the same dimensions as before, with three 'gothick' windows costing £90. The tower was strengthened by building up the staircase, and the nave was reconstructed with more Gothic windows, 'like the great one' in the chancel. The result was much less elaborate than his original proposals, but it is none the less remarkable as one of the earliest eighteenth-century Gothic churches, and the only one of its kind known to have been designed by a mason with a traditional background and not by an architect like Henry Keene or by an amateur like Sanderson Miller.

The rebuilding of Alscot Park was also carried out in the Gothic style, but here Woodward was working under the direction of Messrs. Shakespear & Phillips, London surveyors who provided drawings of a more sophisticated character than the rough 'draughts' of the Costwold mason. Woodward did, however, submit designs of his own for various garden-buildings, including an octagonal Gothic tower and an obelisk 70 feet high. The latter was apparently erected by him in 1757, but has since been destroyed.

In the churchyard at ILMINGTON, WARWICKS., four miles north-east of Chipping Campden, there is an elaborate Gothic monument which can hardly have been designed by anyone but Edward Woodward. It commemorates Samuel Sansom (d. 1750), and consists of a buttressed tomb-chest surmounted by a miniature tower and spire, complete with pinnacles and battlements very similar in character to those shown in Woodward's design for Preston Church. Other more conventional monumental tablets bearing the signature of Edward Woodward can be seen in several Cotswold churches, *e.g.* at Mickleton (Graves monument, 1721), Pebworth (Robert Martin, d. 1720), Alcester (John Brandis, d. 1724) and Blockley (Edward Croft and wife). The monument to his grandparents at Mickleton bears an inscription to the effect that it 'was made and erected by their Grandson Edwd. Woodward', and the family tomb in Chipping Campden Churchyard was also 'built by him'. He himself died on 24 March 1766, aged 69, leaving a widow and three sons. Thomas (apparently his eldest son) was cut off with a shilling; Charles received a legacy of £50, leaving Edward as his principal legatee [P.C.C. 165 TYNDALL].

The account-book of the Hon. George Shirley of Ettington Park, Warwicks., contains a memorandum, dated 27 July 1766, to the effect that 'Mr. Woodward promised to be at work at Eatington the 4th of Augt and to finish the Venetian Windows, viz. the window in the Drawing

---

[1] The church was rebuilt between 1753 and 1757; work on the house began in about 1750 and was still in progress in 1764.

[2] Such metal vanes can actually be seen in the 1858 lithograph of Alcester Church, crowning the pinnacles of the nave as well as of the tower.

room and the window in the Bed-chamber over it, which he proposes to finish in less than 3 weeks from that time'. This was presumably Edward Woodward, junior, of whom nothing more is known except that he was declared bankrupt in January 1777. It should be added that Rushen, in his *History of Campden*, states that the Woodwards are 'believed' to have built Bedfont House, an early eighteenth-century residence in the main street of their native town.

[P. C. Rushen, *History of Campden*, 1911, 38, 93–4, 136, 141; J. H. Bloom, *History of Preston-upon-Stour*, 1896; H. M. Colvin, 'Gothic Survival and Gothick Revival', *Arch. Rev.*, March 1948; G. W. Beard & J. A. Piper, 'An Architectural Discovery', *C. Life*, 9 March 1951; *Gent's Mag.* 1777, 48; wills in Gloucester Probate Registry.]

WOOLER, JOHN, was an engineer and architect who was active in North Yorkshire and County Durham in the latter part of the eighteenth century. In 1763, when he was consulted about the harbour at Sunderland, he was described as 'Engineer at Whitby'. In 1768 he was paid 5 guineas by the Dean and Chapter of Durham for a plan of South Shields Market, and in 1777 he was invited to survey the Cathedral Church of Durham and make an estimate of the cost of repairing and beautifying it. In 1777 he also repaired the steeple of St. Nicholas's Church (now the Cathedral) at Newcastle.

In 1772 Wooler was the joint author with John Smeaton of a printed *Report relative to Tyne Bridge* in which they considered the state of the old Tyne Bridge at Newcastle, and in 1775–81 he was associated with Robert Mylne in building the new Tyne Bridge which stood until 1873. Responsibility for the bridge was shared between the Bishop of Durham and the Corporation of Newcastle. Mylne was employed by the former, Wooler by the latter. In 1775 Wooler was employed to consider the building of a new bridge across the Tyne at Hexham to replace one destroyed by a flood in 1771, but wisely concluded that 'whoever meddled with a bridge there, would burn their fingers', as indeed proved to be the case when the bridge designed by Smeaton was swept away in 1782.

[Durham Cathedral Chapter Acts; J. Sykes, *Local Records*, Newcastle 1865, i, 294, 300, 311; *Reports of the late John Smeaton*, 1812, i, 230, ii, 163, 252–60, iii, 267 *et seq.*; information from Prof. A. W. Skempton.]

WOOLFE, JOHN (–1793), was an Irishman, 'of a family of high respectability in the county of Kildare'. He was employed by James Paine as his clerk in the 1750s, and it was perhaps through Paine's agency that he obtained a post in the

Office of Works as a 'labourer in trust'. In 1774 he was given the Clerkship of the Works at the Mews at Charing Cross. In the following year he was promoted to be Clerk of the Works at Whitehall, Westminster and St. James's, and in 1790 he succeeded Kenton Couse in the senior post of Examining Clerk.

Woolfe is best known as the joint author with James Gandon of the fourth and fifth volumes of *Vitruvius Britannicus*, which appeared under their names in 1767 and 1771, and constituted a valuable record of English architectural activity since the appearance of Colen Campbell's three volumes in the reign of George I. According to Gandon's biographer, Woolfe 'was not of very active habits; hence the whole labour of preparing and bringing out the book rested with Mr. Gandon'. But as 84 of the plates were engraved from drawings by Woolfe and only 60 from drawings by Gandon, this statement is open to question.

As a practising architect Woolfe appears to have accomplished relatively little. Not a single work of his own is illustrated in *Vitruvius Britannicus*, and only two buildings can be ascribed to him. Angus's *Select Views of Seats*, pl. xlviii, dated 1797, records that he designed the wings and interior of DYFFRYN ALED, DENBIGHSHIRE, a house erected by J. Turner of Chester in 1777 for Mrs. Meyrick, widow of R. O. Meyrick of Bodorgan and demolished *c.* 1920. A payment of £63 to 'Mr. Woolfe, architect' in 1779 probably relates to this commission [Meyrick papers in Bangor University Library]. According to C. R. Cockerell's diary (25 Dec. 1821) he was responsible for the staircase and other alterations to NORTHWICK PARK, GLOS., probably in the 1770s, and among the Northwick papers in the Worcestershire Record Office there are (67) two plans for remodelling the house endorsed 'Mr. Woolfe's plan for a house not executed'.

Woolfe died at his house in Whitehall on 13 November 1793. His son John Woolfe, junior, had an architectural training and occupied a post as labourer in trust at Whitehall from 1787 until his death in 1806, but does not appear to have practised outside the Office of Works.

[*A.P.S.D.*; *D.N.B.*; *Gent's Mag.* 1793 (ii), 1060; T. Mulvany, *Life of James Gandon*, 1846, 18; *History of the King's Works* vi, 59, 673–4.]

WOOLLEY, JOHN (–1849), was the son of George Outram Woolley. He exhibited at the Royal Academy between 1829 and 1831. In recording his 'premature death' in 1849, the *Builder* expressed the belief that 'had he been led to practise (his circumstances rendered it unnecessary), he would have distinguished himself in his art'. Woolley was on the Council of the Institute of British Architects. [*Builder* vii, 1849, 451; *Gent's Mag.* 1849 (ii), 551.]

WORRALL, SAMUEL and JOHN, both of London, received £31 10s. in 1754 'for drawing three Plans, two Elevations and one Section for the new Town house and Steeple' at BERWICK-ON-TWEED, which was built by Joseph Dods between 1750 and 1755. It is Dods's name which appears on the building as 'Architect', but it seems clear that the design was supplied by the Worralls [J. Scott, *Berwick-on-Tweed*, 1887, 227; Corporation Guild-Books 1752–60, 73].

There were two London builders named Samuel Worrall. One, a mason, was Master of the Masons' Company in 1739. The other, a carpenter, played an important part in the Georgian development of Spitalfields, where he had his yard. They were evidently related, for in 1735 the lease of a house in Spitalfields built by Samuel Worrall, carpenter, was assigned by Samuel Worrall, 'citizen and mason of London', to John Worrall of Spitalfields, carpenter [*Survey of London* xxvii, 182–3].

WORSLEY, THOMAS (1710–1778), of Hovingham Hall in Yorkshire, was a landowner, horse-breeder and amateur architect who was Surveyor of the Office of Works from 1760 until his death. He was educated at Eton, made the Grand Tour in 1735–7, and succeeded his father as the owner of Hovingham in 1750. Horses and architecture were his great interests in life. Horace Walpole calls him 'a creature of Lord Bute, and a kind of riding-master to the King'. It was Bute and George III who gave him the Surveyorship in 1760, and in the following year he was returned as M.P. for the Treasury borough of Orford. By 1760 the Surveyorship of the Works was essentially a political sinecure, and the day-to-day administration fell on William Chambers as Comptroller, but until his health broke down in about 1770 Worsley kept himself well informed about the affairs of the Office over which he presided.

Worsley's interest in architecture went back to his boyhood, for among his drawings at Hovingham there is one of a Doric order made by him at Eton in 1728. Together with his friend Ralph Knight of Langold Park he made many architectural designs for his amusement, and was quite a competent draughtsman, but HOVINGHAM HALL itself, which he rebuilt in the 1750s, appears to have been his only executed work of importance. The plan, by giving the manège, or riding-school, pride of place, pays tribute to Worsley's equestrian interests, but the elevations show that he was an excellent Palladian architect (*C. Life*, 10, 17 Dec. 1927, 15 June 1961). Among his drawings at Hovingham there is a plan of an unidentified house inscribed 'These rooms are executed but in a different disposition for the sake of the prospects'. At Wallington, Northumberland, there is a design by Worsley for a gardener's

house dated 1764. A design by him for a country house in the Avery Library at Columbia University is illustrated by John Harris, *Catalogue of British Drawings for Architecture, etc., in American Collections*, 1971, 278–9.

[Namier & Brooke, *The House of Commons 1754–70* iii, 1964, 659–61; *History of the King's Works* v, 76–7; J. Hunter, *South Yorkshire* i, 1828, 299.]

WORTH, SAMUEL (1779–1870), was taken into partnership by Joseph Botham of Sheffield in 1826. Two years later he entered into a brief partnership with James Harrison (*q.v.*), in conjunction with whom he designed the MEDICAL SOCIETY's buildings or SURGEONS' HALL in SURREY STREET, 1829 [S. Lewis, *Topographical Dictionary of England* iv, 1848, 62]. In 1832 he won the competition for the CUTLERS' HALL. The runner-up was B. B. Taylor (*q.v.*), who collaborated with him in designing the existing Grecian building in Church Street, enlarged in 1888. Worth's other principal works in Sheffield were the FREE WRITING-SCHOOL in TOWNHEAD STREET, 1827–8, and the Doric Chapel, etc., for the GENERAL CEMETERY, 1836. In about 1840 Worth took John Frith into partnership. J. B. Mitchell-Withers (1837–94) was his pupil. [R. E. Leader, *Surveyors and Architects of the Past in Sheffield*, 1903; *Architectural Mag.* iv, 1837, 81–2.]

WREN, Sir CHRISTOPHER (1632–1723), was born at East Knoyle in Wiltshire on 20 October 1632. His father, the Rev. Christopher Wren, was Rector of Knoyle and a former Fellow of St. John's College, Oxford. He later became Dean of Windsor in succession to his brother Matthew, who had been consecrated Bishop of Hereford in 1634, was soon afterwards translated to Norwich, and died Bishop of Ely. Both Wren's father and his uncle were pillars of the High Church tradition, and it was in the atmosphere of conservative churchmanship that he was brought up. His first tutor was a clergyman, but later he was sent to Westminster School, where he became one of Dr. Busby's earliest pupils. After leaving Westminster in 1646, he spent some three years in London before going up to Wadham College, Oxford, as a Gentleman Commoner, probably in 1649. Meanwhile the outbreak of civil war had brought trouble to his family. His father's deanery was pillaged on two occasions, and his uncle, the Bishop of Ely, who had incurred the hostility of the extreme Puritan party, was imprisoned in the Tower. His father took refuge at Bletchingdon, nr. Oxford, where his son-in-law, William Holder, held the rectory. Holder, formerly a Fellow of Pembroke College, Cambridge, was a young man of considerable intellectual attainments, and according to Aubrey he was

917

'very helpful in the education of his brother-in-law ... of whom he was as tender as if he had been his own child, whom he instructed first in geometrie and arithmetique'. At Oxford, Wren came into contact with Dr. Charles Scarburgh, an eminent anatomist and mathematician, whom he assisted in his work, and with the group of scientific scholars who later formed the nucleus of the Royal Society. They included John Wilkins, the Warden of Wadham, Wallis, the mathematician, Boyle, the physicist, and Lawrence Rooke, the astronomer. In company with these eminent men, Wren made rapid progress in the new, experimental, learning of which they were the pioneers. He assisted Scarburgh in his dissections, and made pasteboard models demonstrating the working of the muscles in order to illustrate his friend's lectures at Surgeons' Hall. Scarburgh was a disciple of Harvey, the discoverer of the circulation of the blood, and later on Wren carried out an important experiment to show that fluids could be injected directly into the bloodstream of animals. He also made drawings of the brain which were published in Willis's *Cerebri Anatome* of 1664, and constructed a model of the human eye.

But anatomy was only one of Wren's scientific interests. At the age of 15 or 16 he had translated into Latin the passage on dialling in William Oughtred's *Clavis Mathematica*. Dialling was one of his father's hobbies, and it was probably through the sun-dial that Wren came to be interested in astronomy. Astronomy was to be his principal scientific occupation until the time when, as Surveyor of the King's Works and architect of St. Paul's, his energies were to be largely absorbed by his architectural work. His first recorded invention was a *Panorganum Astronomicum*, or model showing the earth, sun and moon in their periodic relationships. At Oxford he received further encouragement from Seth Ward, then Professor of Astronomy, and from Sir Paul Neille, a wealthy amateur, who assisted him in his study of the planet Saturn. In addition to this strictly astronomical work, Wren concerned himself with related sciences such as physics and meteorology. In all these fields of 'philosophical' enquiry he distinguished himself by his skill in scientific demonstration and in devising appropriate apparatus to test his own and his friends' theories. Some of his inventions, like the transparent bee-hives 'built like castles and palaces' which he showed to Evelyn in 1654, were perhaps more ingenious than useful; but there were others which played an important part in the study of physics and astronomy, and it was this early interest in models and diagrams which was to give the experimental scientist his later facility in architectural design.

Wren took his B.A. degree on 18 March 1650/1, and his M.A. on 11 December 1653. In the latter year he became a Fellow of All Souls, where he continued his scientific studies until 1657, when he resigned to become Professor of Astronomy at Gresham College, London, in succession to Lawrence Rooke. In 1661 he returned to Oxford as Savilian Professor of Astronomy, and received the degree of D.C.L. He was now, though only in his 29th year, at the height of his scientific fame: in the opinion of Robert Hooke, himself a brilliant experimentalist, 'there scarce ever met in one man, in so great a perfection, such a Mechanical Hand, and so Philosophical a Mind' (*Micrographia*, 1665). In 1660 the trials of his family had been terminated by the Restoration of Charles II, and the 'experimental philosophical clubbe' which had met in his rooms at Gresham College was about to be elevated into the Royal Society. The King himself was taking a personal interest in his scientific work and soon after the acquisition of Tangier in 1661 invited him to supervise its fortification, offering him at the same time the reversion of Sir John Denham's post as Surveyor-General of the Royal Works. This offer Wren declined on grounds of health, but there are indications that, in the intervals of scientific work, he was already turning his attention to architectural matters. In 1660 his exhibits at a scientific meeting included certain 'new designs tending to strength, convenience and beauty in building', and in 1663 he was consulted by the Commission for repairing St. Paul's Cathedral. Such activities – though they might take up more of the Savilian Professor's time than was thought fitting at Oxford – were in no way exceptional: architecture in the seventeenth century was not yet a profession, and several of Wren's acquaintances counted it among their intellectual diversions. For Evelyn it was 'the flower and crown as it were of all the sciences mathematical', and Wren, with his skill as a draughtsman and his fondness for model-making, was bound sooner or later to add it to his other accomplishments. His academic training gave him a ready understanding of the conventions of the Roman orders, and in 1663, when his uncle, the aged Bishop of Ely, asked him to design the new chapel of Pembroke College, Cambridge, the result was an entirely competent, if somewhat unimaginative, essay in classical architecture. His second building of importance, the Sheldonian Theatre at Oxford, is equally academic in design, the prototype being an antique theatre of the kind represented in the Italian architectural treatises: but the novel construction of its roof attracted a great deal of attention, and added much to Wren's reputation as an architect. For Roman theatres were open to the sky, and the difficulty of covering his English reproduction without the inappropriate support of columns set Wren a problem in carpentry which he solved by means of an ingenious timber truss based on the researches of his friend and colleague Dr. Wallis, the Professor of Geometry.

The Sheldonian Theatre was followed by a new building for Trinity College, Oxford, and in 1665, when Wren made his only visit abroad, his purpose was not only to add to his scientific experience, but also 'to survey the most esteem'd Fabricks of Paris', and to observe the achievements of contemporary French artists and architects. Back in England, he applied himself once more to the problem of restoring St. Paul's, and had actually prepared an elaborate scheme for its repair, when the Great Fire of London at once placed the old cathedral beyond hope of redemption, and gave Wren a unique opportunity of exercising his talents as an architect. Within a few days of the disaster, he had presented the King with a scheme for rebuilding the City in accordance with a regular plan. It soon became evident, however, that this was a Utopian project, for the survival of London as a commercial capital depended upon its immediate reconstruction, and this could only be done on the lines of the existing streets. Much could, however, be done to improve the City by replanning in detail, and in October 1666 the King appointed Wren, Pratt and May as his 'Commissioners' to join with three nominees of the City in order to make a survey of the destroyed area and to consider how it should best be rebuilt.[1] To this committee was due the drafting of the Rebuilding Act which was passed by Parliament in 1667, but the design of individual buildings was beyond its terms of reference, and the statement in *Parentalia* that Wren was appointed 'Surveyor-general and principal Architect for rebuilding the whole city' is incorrect. Indeed, it has been stated that the scheme for the Fleet Canal is the only part of 'the general secular rebuilding which can indisputably be attributed to Wren', and it is uncertain whether even the Monument can be regarded as his own design. But for the City churches, Wren's responsibility is indisputable. They were to be rebuilt out of a tax on the import of coal to London, and Wren, assisted by Robert Hooke and Edward Woodroffe, was the surveyor in charge. Thus the fifty-two City churches (upon which work began in earnest after the second Rebuilding Act of 1670) form the major part of Wren's early work as an architect, and the necessity of adapting the medieval irregularity of their sites to the needs of Protestant worship provided him with a series of problems in planning and internal composition which he solved with characteristic ingenuity. The coal money paid only for the fabrics of the new churches: for their internal fittings and decoration the parishes were

individually responsible, and although Wren's advice was often asked, the designs for galleries, altar-pieces and the like were submitted by the craftsmen concerned and selected by the vestrymen on their own authority. The towers, on the other hand, were in every case a product of Wren's office, and display an astonishing variety of invention which is among his chief claims to greatness as an architect. Few of them were completed until the 1690s or even later, and they show an assurance in design which is often absent from the churches themselves.

The rebuilding of St. Paul's Cathedral was financed in the same way as that of the City churches. But the latter had first call on the Coal Money, and it was not until 1675 that work was actually begun on the new cathedral, with Wren as architect in charge. The design had, however, been under consideration ever since it became apparent (in 1668) that Old St. Paul's was incapable of repair. Wren himself favoured a centrally planned church of the type represented by the 'Great Model' of 1673. This indeed 'pleased persons of distinction, skilled in antiquity and architecture': but it did not find favour in ecclesiastical circles and suffered, moreover, from the disadvantage that it could not be built in stages. Wren, therefore, 'turned his thoughts to a cathedral form, as they called it, but so rectified as to reconcile the Gothick to a better manner of architecture'. The result was the 'Warrant Design' of 1675, in which the medieval plan was preserved beneath a classical dress. The design of the western portico and towers, and of the dome which took the place of a central tower, underwent many modifications as the work progressed, and in their final form the towers have a baroque character which owed something to the influence of Roman churches which Wren was able to study in engravings.

In March 1668/9, Wren became Surveyor-General of the King's Works in succession to Sir John Denham. Both John Webb and Hugh May had strong claims to this coveted post, and Wren's appointment was apparently due to the personal favour of Charles II. The parallel post of Comptroller at Windsor was, however, given to May, and as Webb was already in charge of the new Palace at Greenwich, the two most important works undertaken by Wren's department during the early years of his tenure of office were designed by others. But the Surveyorship brought with it administrative responsibilities which were hardly compatible with academic routine, and in 1673 Wren resigned his professorship at Oxford. On 14 November the same year he received the honour of knighthood. In 1684, on the death of Hugh May, he succeeded to the latter's post at Windsor, and in 1696, when it was decided to complete Greenwich Palace as a Naval Hospital, Wren was appointed Surveyor. He was

---

[1] For Wren's share in the rebuilding of London, see T. F. Reddaway, *The Rebuilding of London after the Great Fire*, 1940.

also one of the chief promoters of the Military Hospital at Chelsea, as well as being the architect of its buildings. In 1699 he was placed in charge of the repair of Westminster Abbey, for which money had been voted by Parliament, and made designs for a central tower which were not, however, executed. In addition to discharging these official duties, Wren was an active member of the Royal Society, of which he was President for two years (1681–3), a member of the Council of the Hudson's Bay Company, and on two occasions a member of Parliament, representing Plympton in 1685–7 and Weymouth in 1701–2. He was also one of the Commissioners for Building Fifty New Churches in London under the Act of 1711, and took an active part in its proceedings until the original commission was dissolved in 1715.

Despite his Tory connections, Wren survived the Whig Revolution of 1688 without loss of office. But his management of the Office of Works during his later years was somewhat lax, and in 1714 reforms were introduced by Lord Halifax, the First Lord of the Treasury. Wren retained the title of Surveyor, but authority was vested in a body of Commissioners, of whom he was one, and Vanbrugh as Comptroller became the leading figure in the Office. In 1718 this civilized arrangement was upset in order to provide a place of profit for William Benson (q.v.). Wren was dismissed and went into retirement at Hampton Court, where he had been allowed by Queen Anne to acquire a lease for life of the Surveyor's official residence on the Green. He had already given up the Surveyorship of Greenwich Hospital in 1716, and his Comptrollership at Windsor had come to an end the same year when the nominally separate organization there was united with the Office of Works in London. Only the Surveyorships of St. Paul's Cathedral and Westminster Abbey remained in his possession when, 'having', in his own words, 'worn out (by God's Mercy) a long life in the Royal Service, and having made some Figure in the world', Wren died on 25 February 1723, at the age of 90. He was buried in the crypt of St. Paul's Cathedral, where a monument was later erected to his memory.

Wren's achievement as an architect cannot adequately be summarized within the compass of a dictionary. For forty years he was the acknowledged arbiter of English architectural taste, and his own output of buildings was greater than that of any other English architect of his time. Being a self-taught architect, his education as a designer was a continuing process, and in the course of his long life he was receptive to many ideas, native and foreign. French and Dutch architecture provided the main influences on his style in its formative years, but his approach to design was essentially empirical, and he showed his familiarity both with classical antiquity (as represented by Serlio, Palladio and others) and with Italian baroque buildings studied in engravings. His own works, ranging from the simple Renaissance classicism of Pembroke College Chapel to the Borrominesque spire of St. Vedast's Church, epitomize the whole history of English architecture during the fifty years after the Restoration. Even Gothic had its place in Wren's architectural vocabulary, to be used in situations (as at Christ Church, Oxford) where conformity to existing work authorized its use. His capacity for brilliant improvisation is no less apparent in Tom Tower than it is in many of the London churches, where he ingeniously fitted an infinite variety of classical interiors into the awkwardly constricted spaces afforded by the irregular medieval sites. In the steeples he displayed his powers to the full, creating a classical equivalent of the traditional medieval spire that was to become a characteristic feature of English church architecture until the nineteenth century. If the city churches were triumphs of improvisation, St. Paul's Cathedral was a long-meditated masterpiece. Though the final result is a major architectural achievement, the insistence of the clergy on a traditional cruciform plan robbed Wren of the opportunity to design a building in which the logic of classical design could be clearly and uncompromisingly expressed. St. Paul's is therefore in some ways a disappointing building. The dome and west towers compose splendidly from afar, but at close quarters the former is seen to be less satisfactorily related to the body of the building. Within, there is much to admire in detail, but all Wren's ingenuity could not conceal an awkward inequality in the arches supporting the dome, and the interior as a whole lacks either the mystery latent in its Gothic plan or the baroque drama promised by its west front.

As a secular architect Wren's services were almost entirely monopolized by his royal masters. But circumstances proved fatal to all his major schemes for Winchester, Hampton Court, Greenwich and Whitehall, and it is only on paper that Wren's potentiality as a designer of palaces can be fully appreciated. At Winchester he envisaged, and almost completed, a building with a recessed centre like Le Vau's Versailles. Formally aligned on the west front of the Cathedral, it would have been a major monument of Anglo-French taste. At Greenwich the necessity of retaining the Queen's House frustrated a more elaborate design of the same sort, and left Wren dexterously to dignify an unresolved duality by means of two answering domes. The Whitehall scheme went through several revisions, but emerged at last as a vast and grandiose palace, linked by a long processional colonnade to a new Parliament House sharply distinguished by its antique Roman dress from the baroque splendour of the Court.

Compared with these visions of grandeur, Wren's actual achievements at Chelsea Hospital, Whitehall Palace, Hampton Court and Kensington were relatively modest, and his share in the great country houses of the period was minimal. But his unrealized designs were not without their influence. Just as Winchester Palace was a child of Versailles, so the unfinished Winchester had its architectural progeny in the Garden Quadrangle of New College, Oxford (above, p. 178). More importantly, it is in Wren's first design for Greenwich Hospital, with quadrant colonnades linking the wings to a domed central block, that the genesis of Vanbrugh's Castle Howard must be sought, and incidentally it is to Wren's twin domes that Gandon's Dublin Custom House owes the form of its principal ornament. And many details of Wren's works, both secular and ecclesiastical, were of course imitated by the craftsmen who worked for him both in the Royal Works and in the City churches. Together with Hawksmoor and Dickinson, his personal assistants, these were the men who assimilated his ideas and reproduced them in their own buildings. If the conception of a 'school of Wren' has any validity, it is to be found in the work of men such as Matthew Banckes and Christopher Kempster (qq.v.), rather than in that of Wren's colleagues May, Pratt, Talman and Vanbrugh, each of whom had a distinctive style of his own. This 'school' survived until the 1720s, when the Palladian group, led by Lord Burlington, captured the Office of Works and spread a new doctrine of classical correctitude which supplanted the pragmatic English baroque of Wren and his disciples.

In 1669 Wren married Faith, the daughter of Sir John Coghill of Bletchingdon, the Oxfordshire village where he spent much of his early life. There were two sons of the marriage, Gilbert, who died in infancy, and Christopher, who was born in February 1675, only a few months before his mother's death the following September. In 1677 Wren married again, his second wife being Jane, daughter of Lord Fitzwilliam of Lifford. By her he had a daughter Jane, who died unmarried in 1702, aged 26, and a son William, who survived his father, dying in 1738. Christopher Wren, junior (1675–1747), held the post of Chief Clerk of the King's Works from 1702 until 1716, when he was dismissed as a result of Lord Halifax's reforms. Although in *Vitruvius Britannicus* he is given the credit for having designed Marlborough House, he appears merely to have assisted his father, and nothing suggests that he had any genuine ability as an architect.[1] He made

the collection of family documents which, as *Parentalia, or Memoirs of the Family of the Wrens*, was published by his son Stephen in 1750.[1] In 1715 he married, as his second wife, the widow of a Warwickshire gentleman, from whose family his father had purchased for him the estate of Wroxall Abbey in that county.[2] His death in 1747 resulted in the sale of his father's architectural drawings, the majority of which came eventually into the possession of All Souls College, Oxford. Others, purchased by the 3rd Duke of Argyll, and subsequently in the Bute Collection, were dispersed by auction at Sotheby's in May 1951.

Of the numerous portraits of Wren in existence, the most authentic are: (i) the marble bust by Edward Pierce in the Ashmolean Museum, Oxford, dating probably from the 1670s; (ii) the portrait in the possession of the Royal Society by Closterman (*c.* 1695); (iii) that in the Sheldonian Theatre at Oxford begun by Verrio (d. 1707) and completed by Thornhill and Kneller; (iv) the portrait in the National Portrait Gallery by Kneller, which is dated 1711; (v) an ivory plaque of Wren in old age attributed to Le Marchand and also in the National Portrait Gallery.

The chief sources for Wren's life and works are: (i) the family records published in *Parentalia*; (ii) the *Diary* of his friend and colleague Robert Hooke (*q.v.*); (iii) the records of the Royal Society; (iv) the official records of the Office of Works; (v) the *Calendars of Treasury Books* and *Papers*; and (vi) his own drawings, of which a catalogue is given in *Wren Soc.* xx.[3]

There are several biographies of Wren, but the older lives (*e.g.* those by James Elmes, L. Phillimore, L. Milman and Sir Lawrence Weaver) have been rendered obsolete by the enterprise of the *Wren Society* (20 vols. 1924–43) in documenting Wren's works and in publishing his drawings and those of his contemporaries. The best modern studies of Wren are those by G. F. Webb

---

[1] Mr. Hugh Scrutton has in his possession a model for the east end of a church, inscribed in a contemporary hand, 'St. Paul Basilica. Submitted & rejected. Christopher Wren Esq.' This probably represents a design

submitted by the younger Wren to the Commissioners for Building Fifty New Churches under the Act of 1711.

[1] There are three manuscripts of this work, one in B.M., Add. MS. 25071 dated 1719, another at All Souls College (MS. 313) dated 1728 but containing later material, and a third at the Royal Society dated 1741 but probably begun earlier. For the 'heirloom' copy of the book in the R.I.B.A. Library, containing MS. additions, see L. Weaver in *R.I.B.A. Jnl.* xviii, 1911, 569.

[2] The conveyance, as enrolled in Chancery (P.R.O., C 54/5045, no. 3), shows that Wren paid £19,600 for the estate in August 1713. For this information I am indebted to Mr. Frank Kelsall.

[3] This does not include the drawings from the Bute Collection sold in 1951. The greater part were purchased by the National Art Collections Fund and divided between St. Paul's Cathedral Library, the R.I.B.A. Collection (drawings of St. Stephen's Wallbrook and other City churches), All Souls College, Oxford (elevation of design for Whitehall Palace), and the Victoria and Albert Museum (miscellaneous drawings).

(1937), John Summerson (1953), E. F. Sekler (1956), Margaret Whinney (1971) and Kerry Downes (1971).

With the possible exception of Inigo Jones, no English architect has been the victim of more reckless and ill-informed attributions than Wren. The number of his authenticated works, large as it is, has been swollen by the addition of many buildings whose claim to be designed by Wren rests in most cases on nothing more than a superficial resemblance to what is popularly supposed to have been his 'style'. The list drawn up by his son, and now in the British Museum (Lansdowne MS. 698), though initialled by Wren about a year before his death, is imperfect and inaccurate, while that in *A.P.S.D.*, compiled by Wyatt Papworth, contains many attributions which subsequent research has shown to be unacceptable. In recent years, the publication of original drawings and documents by the Wren Society has done much to establish Wren's authentic works. Unhappily, however, even the editors of the Wren Society at times allowed speculation to take the place of scholarship, and included in their volumes more than one building whose ascription to Wren is unwarranted by the evidence of either drawings or documents.[1] In the following list these have been silently omitted, and in doubtful cases the evidence upon which the attribution rests has been briefly indicated.

SELECT BIBLIOGRAPHY

J. A. Bennett, 'Christopher Wren: the natural causes of beauty', *Architectural History* xv, 1972.

J. A. Bennett, 'A Study of Parentalia, with two unpublished letters of Sir Christopher Wren', *Annals of Science* xxx, 1973.

J. A. Bennett, 'Studies in the Life and Work of Sir Christopher Wren' (mainly a study of Wren's scientific work), unpublished Cambridge Ph.D. thesis, 1974.

J. A. Bennett, 'Christopher Wren: Astronomy, Architecture and the Mathematical Sciences', *Journal for the History of Astronomy* vi, 1975.

H. M. Colvin, 'Roger North and Sir Christopher Wren', *Architectural Review*, Oct. 1951.

H. M. Colvin, J. Mordaunt Crook, Kerry Downes & John Newman, *The History of the King's Works* v, 1976.

Kerry Downes, 'Wren and Whitehall in 1664', *Burlington Mag.*, Feb. 1971.

Kerry Downes, *Christopher Wren*, 1971.

V. Fürst, *The Architecture of Sir Christopher Wren*, 1956.

S. B. Hamilton, 'The Place of Sir Christopher Wren in the History of Structural Engineer-

ing', *Newcomen Society's Transactions* xiv, 1933–4.

P. D. Harvey, 'A Signed Plan by Sir Christopher Wren', *British Museum Quarterly* xxv, 1963.

G. H. Huxley, 'The Geometrical Work of Sir Christopher Wren', *Scripta Mathematica* xxv, 1960.

H. W. Jones, 'Sir Christopher Wren and Natural Philosophy: with a check list of his scientific activities', *Notes and Records of the Royal Society* xiii, 1958.

F. Kimball, 'Wren: some of his sources', *Arch. Rev.* lv, 1924.

W. T. Law, 'Notes on the Wren Pedigree', *Genealogist*, N.S. vi, 1889, 168–71.

Jane Lang, *Rebuilding St. Paul's after the Great Fire of London*, 1956.

T. F. Reddaway, *The Rebuilding of London after the Great Fire*, 1940.

J. W. Ryland, *Records of Wroxall Abbey and Manor*, 1903.

Sale Catalogues of Libraries of Eminent Persons, vol. iv, *Architects*, ed. D. J. Watkin, 1972, 1–43.

E. F. Sekler, *Wren and his Place in European Architecture*, 1956.

H. S. Smith, 'Pedigree of Wren', *Genealogist*, N.S. i, 1884, 262–6.

Sotheby & Co., *Catalogue of Architectural Drawings ... by Sir Christopher Wren*, 23 May 1951.

John Summerson, 'The Mind of Wren', in *Heavenly Mansions and Other Essays on Architecture*, 1949.

John Summerson, *Sir Christopher Wren*, 1953.

John Summerson, 'Sir Christopher Wren, P.R.S.', *Notes and Records of the Royal Society* xv, 1960.

John Summerson, 'Drawings of London Churches in the Bute Collection: a catalogue', *Architectural History* xiii, 1970.

Geoffrey Webb, *Wren*, 1937.

Margaret Whinney, *Wren*, 1971.

Stephen Wren, *Parentalia, or Memoirs of the Family of the Wrens*, 1750 (reprinted by the Gregg Press, 1965).

The Wren Memorial Volume, published by the R.I.B.A. 1923.

The Wren Society, 20 vols. 1924–43.

UNIVERSITY BUILDINGS

attributed: PEMBROKE COLLEGE CHAPEL, CAMBRIDGE, for his uncle Matthew Wren, Bishop of Ely, 1663–5; east end extended 1880 [Willis & Clark, i, 147; *Wren Soc.* v, 27–9, pl. xi] (R.C.H.M., *Cambridge*, 153–4).

THE SHELDONIAN THEATRE, OXFORD, 1664–9; roof reconstructed by G. Saunders 1802, cupola rebuilt by E. Blore 1838, restoration of stonework, etc., by W. Godfrey Allen 1959–60 [*Wren Soc.* v, pls. ii–iii; xix, 91–9; engravings

---

[1] *E.g.* Temple Bar, Farley Hospital, Fawley Court, All Saints, Northampton, and Morden College.

of roof in R. Plot, *Natural History of Oxford-shire*, 1677, and S. Wren, *Parentalia*, 1750, 334–5; John Summerson, *The Sheldonian in its Time*, 1964; H. M. Colvin, *The Sheldonian Theatre and the Divinity School*, 1964, 2nd ed. 1974].

ALL SOULS COLLEGE, OXFORD, SCREEN in CHAPEL, 1664 (the gift of Sir William Portman). One of Wren's designs for this work is illustrated in *Wren Soc.* v, pl. vii, but it does not represent the screen as executed (see elevation of 'Half the screen as made by S.ʳ W.ᵐ Portman, before the whole was pulled down A.D. 1716' in Clarke Collection, Worcester College). In 1716 the screen was remodelled by Sir James Thornhill, who entirely altered the part above the cornice, and converted Wren's pedimented doorway into an open archway [All Souls College Archives].

EMMANUEL COLLEGE, CAMBRIDGE, THE CHAPEL and GALLERY, 1668–73 [Willis & Clark, ii, 703–9; *Wren Soc.* v, 29–31, pl. xii] (R.C.H.M., *Cambridge*, 64–6).

TRINITY COLLEGE, OXFORD, THE GARDEN QUAD-RANGLE, built in three stages:

(1) North wing, 1668 (Thomas Strong, mason; Robert Minchin, carpenter).

(2) West wing, 1682.

(3) South wing,[1] 1728 (William Towne-send, mason).

In 1802 the walls were raised to create an attic storey and the original mansard roofs were re-moved. When the building was refaced in 1958–65 the proportions of the attic windows were altered and improved [*Wren Soc.* v, 14–16, pls. iv–v].

In 1692 Wren was shown the designs for the CHAPEL (possibly by Dean Aldrich), and wrote to the President that he had 'considered the designe you sent me of your chapel, which in the maine is very well, and I believe your worke is too far advanced to admitt of any advice: however, I have sent my thoughts which will be of use to the mason to form his mouldings' [*Wren Soc.* v, 15]. The Bursar's Accounts for 1692 (B.M., MS. Lansdowne 718) contain a payment of £2 3s. 'to Sir Christopher Wren's servant'.

ST. JOHN'S COLLEGE, OXFORD, SCREEN in CHAPEL, c. 1670; destroyed 1843, when two Corinthian columns were incorporated in the staircase at Painswick House, Glos. [*Wren Soc.* ix, pl. 39; x, 129 n.].

MERTON COLLEGE, OXFORD, SCREEN in CHAPEL, 1671–3; dismantled c. 1850, partly restored 1960 [J. R. L. Highfield, 'Alexander Fisher, Sir Christopher Wren and Merton College Chapel', *Oxoniensia* xxiv, 1959].

THE QUEEN'S COLLEGE, OXFORD, THE WILLIAMSON

BUILDING, 1671–4; upper storey added c. 1730 [*Cal. of State Papers, Domestic, 1671*, 4, 122; ibid., *1671–2*, 369] (*V.C.H. Oxon.* iii, 125, plate).

TRINITY COLLEGE, CAMBRIDGE, THE LIBRARY, 1676–84 [Willis & Clark, ii, 533–51; *Wren Soc.* v, 32–44, pls. xv–xxvi; H. M. Fletcher, 'Sir Christopher Wren's Carpentry; a Note on the Library at Trinity College, Cambridge', *R.I.B.A. Jnl.*, 3rd ser., xxx, 1923, 388] (R.C.H.M., *Cambridge*, 236–41).

CHRIST CHURCH, OXFORD, TOM TOWER, 1681–2, Gothic [*Wren Soc.* v, 17–23, pl. viii; xix, pls. liv–lvi; W. D. Caröe, *Tom Tower, Christ Church, Oxford*, 1923].

BODLEIAN LIBRARY, OXFORD, repaired Divinity School and designed buttresses (removed 1960) on south side of Duke Humphrey's Library, 1701–3 [John Walker, *Oxoniana* iii, 1809, 16–27 (for Wren's letters); E. P. Warren, 'Sir Christopher Wren's Repair of the Divinity School and Duke Humphrey's Library', *Wren Memorial Volume*, 1923, 233–8; J. N. L. Myres, 'Recent Discoveries in the Bodleian Library', *Archaeologia* ci, 1967].

ROYAL PALACES, ETC.

ST. JAMES'S PALACE, repairs and alterations to the Queen's Catholic Chapel, for Queen Catherine of Braganza, 1682–4 [*History of the King's Works* v, 249–53].

WINCHESTER PALACE, for King Charles II, 1683–5; left unfinished at the King's death; used for the reception of French prisoners of war 1757–64 and 1778–85; occupied by French refugee clergy 1792–6; converted into barracks 1810; destroyed by fire 1894 [*Wren Soc.* vii, 11–69, pls. i–iv; *History of the King's Works* v, 304–13].

WINDSOR CASTLE, THE GUARD-HOUSE, 1685; dem. [*Wren Soc.* viii, 13–15; *History of the King's Works* v, 329].

WHITEHALL PALACE, new range containing CATH-OLIC CHAPEL, COUNCIL CHAMBER and PRIVY GALLERY, for King James II, 1685–7; de-stroyed by fire 1698; THE QUEEN'S APARTMENT and TERRACE GARDEN, begun for Queen Mary of Modena, completed for Queen Mary II, 1688–93; destroyed by fire 1698 [*Wren Soc.* vii, 71–9, pls. vii, xiii–xxi; *History of the King's Works* v, 285–97]. Wren's unexecuted designs for a new palace after the fire of 1698 are illu-strated in *Wren Soc.* viii.

HAMPTON COURT PALACE, rebuilt south and east ranges for King William III and Queen Mary II, 1689–94; interior of King's Apartment completed by W. Talman 1699 [*Wren Soc.* iv; *History of the King's Works* v, 156–65].

KENSINGTON PALACE, reconstructed for King William III and Queen Mary II, 1689–96

---

[1] *I.e.* the north range of the Durham Quadrangle.

[*Wren Soc.* vii, 135–96 and plates; G. H. Chettle & P. A. Faulkner, 'Sir Christopher Wren and Kensington Palace', *Jnl. of the British Archaeological Assn.*, 3rd ser., xiv, 1951; *History of the King's Works* v, 183–91].

WESTMINSTER PALACE, refitted interior of HOUSE OF COMMONS, 1692, widened galleries 1707 to accommodate Scottish members; altered by James Wyatt 1800, destroyed by fire 1834. For this, and other minor alterations to the palace for which Wren was responsible, see *History of the King's Works* v, 385–418.

ST. JAMES'S PALACE, range of STATE APARTMENTS for Queen Anne, 1703 [*History of the King's Works* v, 237–9].

PUBLIC BUILDINGS, ETC.

LONDON, THE CUSTOM HOUSE, 1669–71; reconstructed by Thomas Ripley 1718–25; destroyed by fire 1814 [*History of the King's Works* v, 345–8].

LONDON, THE MONUMENT (to the Fire of 1666), FISH STREET HILL, 1671–6. Hooke was actively concerned in the erection of the Column, and according to Aubrey's *Brief Lives*, he was its architect: but it is impossible to give either Hooke or Wren the sole credit for what seems to have been a work of collaboration. A drawing of the scaffolding used is given in *Civil Engineer and Architect's Jnl.* i, 267. [C. Welch, *The History of the Monument*, 1893; *Wren Soc.* v, 45–51, pls. xxxiv–xxxvii; xviii, 190–1, pls. xvii–xviii; M. I. Batten, 'The Architecture of Robert Hooke', *Walpole Soc.* xxv, 84; T. F. Reddaway, *The Rebuilding of London after the Great Fire*, 1940, 216 n.; and unpublished documents in Bodleian Library, MS. Rawlinson B.363.]

LONDON, DRURY LANE THEATRE, for Thomas Killigrew, 1672–4; remodelled by R. Adam 1775–6, rebuilt by H. Holland 1791–4 [R. Leacroft, 'Wren's Drury Lane', *Arch. Rev.*, July 1950; *Wren Soc.* xii, pl. xxiii].

LINCOLN CATHEDRAL LIBRARY, built for Dean Honywood, 1674–5, according to Wren's 'directions' and 'Mr. Tompson's modell' [*Wren Soc.* xvii, 76–7, pls. lxv–lxvi] (measured drawings in *Builder* lxii, 1892, 259–63). Mr. Tompson was probably the London mason John Thompson (d. 1700), who worked under Wren at St. Paul's and elsewhere.

GREENWICH, THE ROYAL OBSERVATORY, 1675–6; new buildings added 1813–44 [*Wren Soc.* xix, 113–15, pls. lxviii–lxix].

? ABINGDON TOWN HALL, BERKS., 1678–80. There is no documentary evidence that this building was designed by Wren, but the attribution is possible on stylistic grounds, and in 1681, when recommending Christopher Kempster, the master mason, as one whom he had 'used

in good workes', Wren mentioned that he 'wrought the Town-house at Abbington'. The fact that John Scarborough (*q.v.*) was employed as a measurer is also in favour of Wren's authorship [*Wren Soc.* v, 18, xix, 100–2; accounts in B.M., Add. MS. 28666, ff. 338–9] (measured drawings in *Details*, ed. R. R. Phillips, i, 1909, 69–71).

LONDON, MIDDLE TEMPLE, THE CLOISTERS in PUMP COURT, 1680–1; destroyed by bombing 1940–1. Nicholas Barbon prepared a 'model' for this building in 1679, but it was rejected in favour of 'a model drawn by Sir C. Wren', and when the work was completed, John Foltrop the builder claimed £250 from the Society 'for his loss in materials about the foundations and for extraordinary charges in building the Cloisters according to Sir Christopher Wren's model and directions, over and above his agreement with Dr. Barbon' [*Middle Temple Records*, ed. C. H. Hopwood, iii, 1905, 1334–8]. Wren's original design (illustrated in *C. Life*, 28 May 1948, 1073) showed a cloister of seven arches, but this was increased in execution to eight.

LONDON, THE NAVY OFFICE, SEETHING LANE, 1682–3; dem. [T. F. Reddaway, 'Sir Christopher Wren's Navy Office', *Bulletin of the Institute of Historical Research* xxx, 1957].

CHELSEA, THE ROYAL HOSPITAL, 1682–92 [*Wren Soc.* xix, 61–86, pls. xxx–xlvii; C. G. T. Dean, *The Royal Hospital, Chelsea*, 1950].

WINDSOR, BERKS., THE COURT HOUSE, supervised completion after the death of its builder, Sir Thomas Fitch (*q.v.*), in 1688 [Tighe & Davis, *Annals of Windsor* ii, 1858, 423]. The statue of Prince George of Denmark was presented by Wren's son Christopher in 1713, when he was elected M.P. for the borough.

CHRIST'S HOSPITAL, LONDON. In 1692 Wren 'presented the draught of the New intended Writing Schoole', but there is evidence that the drawings were made by Hawksmoor, and those which are preserved in the All Souls Collection are in his hand. Sir John Moore's Writing School (1693–5; dem. 1902) may therefore be regarded either as a design by Wren worked out by Hawksmoor, or as an early work of the latter carried out under Wren's directions. There appears to be no evidence that Wren designed the Mathematical School (1682–3; dem. 1902), which seems to have been designed by Hooke or Oliver. [*Wren Soc.* xi, 60–80, pls. xliv–li; xvii, pl. xlvii; E. H. Pearce, *Christ's Hospital*, 1908, 151.]

APPLEBY, LEICS., SIR JOHN MOORE'S SCHOOL, 1693–7. The original designs were made by Wren, but they were carried out by Sir William Wilson, who completely altered their character in execution [*Wren Soc.* xi, 84 *et seq.*, pls. liii–liv].

? WILLIAMSBURG, VIRGINIA, U.S.A., WILLIAM AND MARY COLLEGE, 1695. According to Hugh

Jones, *Present State of Virginia*, 1724, 26, the College was 'first modelled by Sir Christopher Wren, adapted to the Nature of the Country by the Gentlemen there'. The accounts show that workmen and materials were brought from England, and that Thomas Hadley was the surveyor in charge. There was a fire in 1705, after which the College was rebuilt [*Wren Soc.* xix, p. xiv].

GREENWICH, THE ROYAL HOSPITAL FOR SEAMEN, 1696 onwards. As Surveyor in charge from 1696 to 1716, Wren was responsible for the general layout, and personally designed the base wing on the west side of King Charles's Court (subsequently remodelled), the Great Hall, the twin domes and the colonnades. Though they were erected during his surveyorship, his responsibility for the design of the east range of Queen Anne's Court and the West and South Dormitories in King William's Court is doubtful. [*Wren Soc.* vi; J. H. V. Davies, 'The Dating of the Buildings of the Royal Hospital at Greenwich', *Archaeological Jnl.* cxiii, 1956.]

LONDON, THE ROYAL SOCIETY'S REPOSITORY, CRANE COURT, FLEET STREET, 1711–12; dem. *c.* 1782 [J. A. Bennett, 'Wren's Last Building?', *Notes and Records of the Royal Society* xxvii, 1973].

DOMESTIC ARCHITECTURE

LONGLEAT HOUSE, WILTS., principal doorway for Sir James Thynne (d. 1670); replaced 1705 by the existing doorway apparently designed by the French sculptor Claude David, and re-erected, with only one pair of columns instead of two, at the School House built by Lord Weymouth at WARMINSTER, WILTS., in 1707. Lord Weymouth himself consulted Wren when altering Longleat in 1683 [Longleat archives, Book 179 B, and Thynne Papers xxxiv, ff. 103, 109; R. Hope, 'Doorway by Wren', *Arch. Rev.*, June 1966, 478–9].

TRING MANOR HOUSE, HERTS., for Henry Guy, Gentleman of the Privy Chamber to King Charles II, *c.* 1670; dem. in nineteenth century. This house is stated by Roger North to have been 'built by Sʳ Chr. Wren' in his MS. treatise 'Of Building' [B.M., Add. MS. 32540, f. 48ᵛ]. The engraving in Chauncy's *Historical Antiquities of Hertfordshire*, 1700, is dedicated to Guy by John Oliver, who in 1675 became Assistant Surveyor of St. Paul's; cf. *Wren Soc.* xii, 23; xix, 152, pl. lxxiii.

ARBURY HALL, WARWICKS., design for a stable doorway for Richard Newdigate, 1674, either not executed, or modified in execution by Sir William Wilson [above, p. 901].

THORESBY HOUSE, NOTTS., for Wren's involvement in the remodelling of 1685–7 see above, p. 805.

EASTON NESTON, NORTHANTS. The house built for Sir William Fermor, Bart. (cr. Baron Leominster 1692), *c.* 1685–95, appears to have been designed in Wren's office. Two letters from Wren to Fermor about Easton Neston survive (one printed in *Wren Soc.* xii, 23, the other unpublished at Easton Neston): in 1708 John Lumley (*q.v.*) told Lord Nottingham that the 'noble staires' at Easton Neston were designed by 'Sir Christopher Renn and Mr. Hawkesmoore' [Pearl Finch, *Burley on the Hill* i, 1904, 110], and John Bridges (d. 1724) stated in his *History of Northants.* i, 1791, 289, that the wings (one of which survives) were designed by Wren. In *c.* 1700–2 the exterior was remodelled by Hawksmoor in its present form. The model in the R.I.B.A. Drawings Collection may represent either a version of the design adopted *c.* 1685 or an alternative design for remodelling the exterior *c.* 1700. [H. M. Colvin, 'Easton Neston Reconsidered', *C. Life*, 15 Oct. 1970, and other references cited above, p. 403.]

LONDON, BRIDGEWATER SQUARE, BARBICAN, was built as a personal speculation by Wren and George Jackson of Chipping Warden on the site of Bridgewater House, which was destroyed by fire in 1687. They bought the site for £4400 in 1688. Those who took building plots included Nicholas Hawksmoor, William Emmett (bricklayer), Samuel Fulkes (mason), Henry Doogood (plasterer), Edward Strong (mason), John Smallwell (joiner), Thomas Hill (mason), Nicholas Goodwin (brickmaker), Richard Billinghurst (bricklayer) and Samuel Wing (ironmonger) [Guildhall Library, MS. 2461]. An earlier scheme for laying out the site for building had been made by Wren in 1673 on behalf of the Earl of Bridgewater, but was not carried out. The Royal Warrant [P.R.O., C 82/2441], dated 30 June 1673, states that Wren 'hath ... made and framed a Draught mapp or chart of the Whole Designe'. The plan referred to is now P.R.O., MPA 22. The original houses in Bridgewater Square have all been demolished or rebuilt.

WINSLOW HALL, BUCKS., was probably designed by Wren for William Lowndes, Secretary of the Treasury, 1699–1702, as he examined and passed the workmen's bills, but the fact that he performed this service does not prove that he was the architect [*Wren Soc.* xvii, 54–75, pls. lviii–lxiv] (*C. Life*, 24 Aug. 1951).

LONDON, MARLBOROUGH HOUSE, ST. JAMES'S, for the 1st Duke of Marlborough, 1709–11. Although Christopher Wren, junior, is credited with the design by Campbell, *Vitruvius Britannicus* i, 1715, pls. 39–40, it is clear that he was merely assisting his father. There have been numerous alterations, including the addition of a low attic storey in 1771–3. A new entrance hall was added on the north side in 1850 when the house became the official residence of the Prince of Wales, and the attic storey was raised in 1865–70 [*Wren Soc.* vii, 225–9; David Green, *Blenheim Palace*, 1951, 248–9] (R.C.H.M., *London (West)*, 132–4).

CHURCHES

(excluding the churches in the City of London rebuilt after the Great Fire)

SALISBURY CATHEDRAL, WILTS., report for Dr. Seth Ward, Bishop of Salisbury, 1668: printed in *Wren Soc.* xi, 21–6, from *Parentalia*, 303–6; see also R. Rawlinson, *History of the Cathedral Church of Salisbury*, 1719, 1–21; designed bishop's throne and furniture for choir, 1671–3 [G. J. Elkington, 'Alexander Fort and Salisbury Cathedral', *Wilts. Archaeological Mag.* lvii, 1958, 56–63].

WESTMINSTER, ST. MARTIN-IN-THE-FIELDS CHURCH, designed cupola to surmount tower in 1672; dem. 1722 [*Survey of London* xx, 23 n., pls. 8–9].

INGESTRE CHURCH, STAFFS., may have been designed by Wren for Walter Chetwnd, who, like himself, was a Fellow of the Royal Society, 1673–6. The attribution is supported by an elevation for a lantern on a tower, inscribed 'Mr. Chetwin's Tower', which was sold with other Wren drawings in the Bute sale of 1951. The lantern was not, however, built, and the church could have been designed by someone else closely connected with Wren's office. (*Wren Soc.* xix, 57, pls. xv–xxiv).

ST. PAUL'S CATHEDRAL, LONDON, 1675–1710. Wren's designs are illustrated in *Wren Soc.* i–iii and xiii–xiv. For others in the Bute sale of 1951 see Sotheby's *Catalogue* (23 May 1951). An important drawing corresponding to the first model is described by Norbert Lynton in *Burlington Mag.* xcvii, 1955, 40–4. The transition from the 'Warrant' design to the executed structure is discussed by John Summerson in 'The Penultimate Design for St. Paul's Cathedral', *Burlington Mag.*, March 1961. Jane Lang, *Rebuilding St. Paul's*, 1956, is a fully documented history of Wren's cathedral. A. F. E. Poley, *St. Paul's Cathedral*, 1927, contains a magnificent set of measured drawings.

WESTMINSTER, ST. JAMES'S CHURCH, PICCADILLY, 1676–84; wooden spire (perhaps designed by Edward Wilcox, *q.v.*) added 1687; church seriously damaged by bombing 1940 but restored by Sir Albert Richardson 1947–54 [*Survey of London* xxix, chap. iii and plates] (measured drawings in *Wren Soc.* ix, 30–2).

WESTMINSTER, ST. ANNE'S CHURCH, SOHO: Wren was one of the commissioners appointed to complete this church in 1685, and may have designed it when work began in 1677. But Talman was also concerned in 1685, and the

authorship of the design remains uncertain. The church was reconstructed in 1830–1 and dem. 1953 after war-damage [*Survey of London* xxxiii, chap. x and plates].

WESTMINSTER, ST. CLEMENT DANES, STRAND, 1680–2; upper stage of tower added by James Gibbs 1719–20; semi-circular porch on south side removed in nineteenth century; interior destroyed by bombing 1941 and restored by W. A. S. Lloyd 1957–8 [*Wren Soc.* ix, 21–2; x, 23–4, 108–11].

WINDSOR, ST. GEORGE'S CHAPEL, survey and repairs, 1681–2 [W. H. St. J. Hope, *History of Windsor Castle* ii, 386].

WESTMINSTER, ST. MARGARET'S CHURCH, advice in connection with erection of a gallery in the south aisle in 1682; destroyed 1877–82 [Vestry Minutes in Westminster City Library, 13 Jan. 1681/2: 'Sir Christopher Wren being this day present, at the desire of the Gentlemen of the Vestry, will assist them with his Advice, concerning the New Gallery designed to be Erected in the parish Church, and will Agree with the Artificers touching the same at as reasonable Rates as he can. And the Churchwardens are desired to attend the said Sʳ Christopher from time to time with the Artificers viz. – Noell Ansell Joyner and Bernard Angier Carpenter.']

LONDON, THE TEMPLE CHURCH, repaired fabric and refitted interior, 1682–3. Wren's altarpiece was removed in 1840 but replaced in 1954 [*Wren Soc.* x, (58)–(60)].

LONDON, THE FRENCH PROTESTANT CHURCH in THE SAVOY, enlarged 1686; dem. An engraved plan and elevation, accompanied by a licence, dated 24 Feb. 1685/6, to enlarge the church 'according to the Draught thereof made by our said Surveyor General', is in the P.R.O. (MPA 41) and is reproduced by R. Somerville, *The Savoy*, 1960, 66 [*History of the King's Works* v, 361].

AMPTHILL CHURCH, BEDS., approved design of a family pew for Lord Ashburnham, 1696; erected by Alexander Fort, joiner; dem. 1877 [R. Gunnis, 'A Storm about a Pew', *Bedfordshire Magazine* ii, no. 15, 1950–1; Lincoln Diocesan Registry, Fac. 9/3 and 17].

WESTMINSTER ABBEY, extensive repairs, 1698–1722 [*Wren Soc.* xi, 12–20, 27–32, pls. i–vi; E. Beresford Chancellor, 'Wren's Restoration of Westminster Abbey', *Connoisseur* lxxviii, 1927, 145]. In addition to the accounts summarized in *Wren Soc.* xi, 13–14, there is in the Bodleian Library a volume recording payments authorized by Wren from 1698 to 1713 (MS. Gough Westminster 1).

WARWICK, ST. MARY'S CHURCH. Wren was consulted after the fire of 1694, and made designs (*Wren Soc.* x, pls. 15–18) for rebuilding the church, which were not executed. But, accord-

926

ing to *Parentalia*, he was concerned in the erection of the tower 'after an unsuccessful attempt in Execution of a defective Design by other Hands'. This refers to Sir William Wilson's tower, which proved to be defective and had to be taken down before it was completed. It has been claimed[1] that undated payments 'to S^r· C^{hr}· Wren for ye Church £10–0–0' and 'to S^r· C^{hr}· Renns man for Ch: Work £11–0–0' confirm that Wren was consulted after the failure, but there is no evidence of this in the minutes and accounts of the Commissioners for rebuilding the town and church [Warwickshire County Record Office, formerly P.R.O., C 104/7]. There is, moreover, reason to think that the payments in question were made in 1697, when Hawksmoor acknowledged the receipt of 10 guineas 'as a Gratuity for Coppy designes and Papers by S^r· C^{hr}: Wrens order for ye use of Warwick Church', and that they therefore relate to the unexecuted designs already referred to. The failure did not occur until the winter of 1699/1700, and a contemporary document states that the tower was then rebuilt 'according to Sir William Wilson's directions' (above, p. 901). The statement in *Parentalia* is therefore almost certainly mistaken.

ELY CATHEDRAL, advice in connection with repairs to north transept in 1699–1702 [*Wren Soc.*, xix, 148]. The doorway to the north transept was designed either by Wren or by Robert Grumbold, the contracting mason, who is known to have submitted a design.

THE LONDON CITY CHURCHES

The City churches destroyed in the Great Fire of 1666 were rebuilt under the joint direction of Wren, Hooke and Woodroffe (d. 1675). Much of the designing and supervision must have been delegated by Wren to his two colleagues, but he appears to have retained ultimate control. Thus a drawing for the west front of St. Edmund, Lombard Street (*Wren Soc.* ix, pl. 15), is in Hooke's hand, but bears the initials C W in the pediment to show that Wren had approved it. All the fifty-two churches listed below may therefore be included in the catalogue of Wren's works, but it must be emphasized that in most cases the fittings, and sometimes even the architectural details, were designed by the craftsmen employed, and that Wren often exercised only a very loose control over their execution. For this reason, the names of the principal craftsmen have been given in the following list whenever they are known. The building accounts in the Bodleian

---

[1] By P. B. Chatwin, 'The Great Fire of Warwick', *Trans. Birmingham Arch. Soc.* lxvii, 1947–8, 39–40. See also Kerry Downes, *English Baroque Architecture*, 1966, 122–3.

Library (MSS. Rawlinson B.387–9) are summarized in *Wren Soc.* x, and extracts from the parish records are printed in vol. xix; in one or two cases it has been possible to supplement the information there given from parish records which were not available to the editors of the Wren Society. A large number of Wren's original designs for the City churches have been published by the Wren Society, but over fifty more drawings were sold at Sotheby's on 23 May 1951. For these see John Summerson, 'Drawings for the London City Churches', *R.I.B.A. Jnl.*, Feb. 1952, and 'Drawings of London Churches in the Bute Collection: a catalogue', in *Architectural History* xiii, 1970.

In 1848–9 measured drawings of all but four of the churches then still in existence were published by John Clayton as *Plans Elevations and Sections of the Parochial Churches of Sir Chr. Wren*. The 60 plates comprised in this now rare work were reproduced in vol. ix of the *Wren Society*. *The Churches of London* by George Godwin, 2 vols., 1838–9, contains engravings by Le Keux showing many of the churches and their interiors before alteration or destruction. The valuable contemporary descriptions given by E. Hatton, *A New View of London*, 2 vols., 1708, are reprinted in *Wren Soc.* x, 15–44. Other works dealing wholly or in part with Wren's City churches are A. T. Taylor, *The Towers and Steeples designed by Sir Christopher Wren*, 1881; W. Niven, *London City Churches destroyed since 1800, or now threatened*, privately printed, 1887; G. H. Birch, *London Churches of the Seventeenth and Eighteenth Centuries*, 1896 (with superb photogravure plates); Philip Norman, *The London City Churches*, published by the London Society, 2nd ed. 1929; The Royal Commission on Historical Monuments' *Report* on London, vol. iv, *The City*, 1929; Miss E. Jeffries Davis, 'The Parish Churches of the City of London', *Jnl. of the Royal Society of Arts* lxxxiii, 9 Aug. 1935; Gerald Cobb, *The Old Churches of London*, 3rd ed. 1948; Elizabeth & Wayland Young, *Old London Churches*, 1956; and B. F. L. Clarke, *Parish Churches of London*, 1966.

ST. ALBAN, WOOD STREET, 1682–5; apse added and interior refitted by Sir Gilbert Scott 1859; destroyed by bombing 1940 except for tower. Sam Fulkes, mason; Matthew Banckes, carpenter; William Cleer, joiner; John Grove and H. Doogood, plasterers. Much of the medieval fabric had survived the alterations of 1633–4 and the fire of 1666 and was incorporated by Wren in his rebuilding, which was Gothic in style.

ALL HALLOWS, LOMBARD STREET, 1686–94; repaired 1824 and 1871; internal alterations 1888; dem. 1939. John Thompson, mason; Charles King and John Evans, bricklayers;

Thos. Woodstock, carpenter; William Cleer, Thomas Powell, William Grey and John Mitchell, joiners; John Miller and Saunders, carvers; H. Doogood, plasterer. The tower was re-erected as part of All Hallows, Twickenham (consecrated 1940), which contains the organ, monuments and other fittings.

ALL HALLOWS THE GREAT, UPPER THAMES STREET, 1677–83; the tower was rebuilt in 1876–7; dem. 1893–4. William Hammond, mason; Thos. Horn, bricklayer; Robert Day, carpenter; Thos. Powell and William Cleer, joiners; H. Doogood, John Grove and John Sherwood, plasterers. The fittings are now distributed between St. Margaret, Lothbury (screen and sounding-board), St. Michael, Paternoster Royal (candelabrum, etc.), All Hallows, Gospel Oak (communion table), and St. Paul's, Hammersmith (pulpit).

ALL HALLOWS, WATLING STREET, 1677–84; steeple completed 1697; dem. 1876–7. Sam Fulkes, mason; John Longland, carpenter; William Cleer, joiner; H. Doogood and John Grove, plasterers. Some of the fittings were placed in the church of All Hallows, London Docks.

ST. ANDREW BY THE WARDROBE, 1685–93; west gallery inserted 1774; repaired by S. S. Teulon 1838; south front and tower altered by T. Garner c. 1875; gutted by bombing 1940, restored by Marshall Sisson 1959–61. Nicholas Young, mason; Thomas Horn, bricklayer; John Longland and Israel Knowles, carpenters; Roger Davis, William Cleer and William Smith, joiners; Jonathan Maine, wood-carver; H. Doogood, plasterer.

ST. ANDREW, HOLBORN, 1684–90; tower completed 1703; internal alterations by J. H. Good, 1818, and in 1872 by S. S. Teulon, who exposed medieval features in lower part of tower, etc.; gutted by bombing 1941, restored by Mottistone & Paget, 1960. Edward Pierce and William Stanton, masons; John Longland, carpenter; Valentine Houseman, joiner; Edward Pierce, wood carver; Robert Dyer, plasterer.

ST. ANNE AND ST. AGNES, GRESHAM STREET, 1677–80; steeple added later c. 1714; exterior rendered in cement by Charles Tyrrell 1820–1; alterations to interior by W. M. Brooks 1838–9, and by E. Christian 1888–9; damaged by bombing 1940 and subsequently restored. R. Walters and Wm. Hammond, masons; John Fitch, bricklayer; Ralph Cadman and Messrs. Cheltenham, Fuller and Page, joiners; John Sherwood, plasterer.

ST. ANTHOLIN, WATLING STREET, 1678–82; tower completed 1688; dem. 1875. Thos. Cartwright, mason; Edward Elder and Thomas Horn, bricklayers; John Longland and William Atwell, carpenters; William Cleer and William Grey, joiners; Jonathan Maine,

carver; H. Doogood and John Grove, plasterers. The upper part of the spire, renewed c. 1825, is preserved in a private garden at Forest Hill (C. Life, 26 Aug. 1939, 214). The reredos was removed to St. Antholin, Nunhead Row, Camberwell; the pulpit is in Blandford Church, Dorset.

ST. AUGUSTINE, WATLING STREET, 1680–3, spire completed 1695; interior altered by Sir A. Blomfield 1878; spire and most of church destroyed by bombing 1941; tower and restored spire remain incorporated in St. Paul's Cathedral choir school. Edward Strong, mason; Israel Knowles, carpenter; William Draper, joiner; Jonathan Maine, carver; John Combes, plasterer.

ST. BARTHOLOMEW, EXCHANGE, 1674–9; dem. 1840–1 for site of the Royal Exchange and 'Sun' Fire Office. John Thompson, mason; Robert Brown, bricklayer; Matthew Banckes, carpenter; William Cleer and T. Poultney, joiners; Henry Doogood and John Grove, plasterers. The new church of St. Bartholomew, Moor Lane, by C. R. Cockerell was 'in the style of the old one' and incorporated its fittings and some of its carved stonework. On its demolition in 1902 the reredos and carved door-cases were removed to a chapel in St. Giles', Cripplegate, where they were destroyed by bombing in 1940–1. Some panelling is at St. John's, Hendon.

ST. BENET, GRACECHURCH STREET, 1681–6; dem. 1867–8. Thos. Wise, mason; John Longland, carpenter; William Cleer and John Mitchell, joiners; H. Doogood and John Grove, plasterers. The pulpit is now in St. Olave, Hart Street.

ST. BENET, PAUL'S WHARF, 1677–83 (now the Welsh Church). Thomas and Edward Strong, masons; Israel Knowles, carpenter; William Cleer, joiner; H. Doogood and John Grove, plasterers.

ST. BENET FINK, THREADNEEDLE STREET, 1670–3; dem. 1842–4 for site of the Royal Exchange. Thos. Cartwright, mason; Nicholas Wood, bricklayer; Henry Blowes, carpenter; William Cleer and William Gray, joiners; Edward Pierce, carver; John Grove, plasterer. The organ (1714) is now in Malmesbury Abbey Church, the reredos and pulpit in Emanuel School Chapel, and a door-case in Lytes Cary House, Somerset.

ST. BRIDE, FLEET STREET, 1671–8; steeple 1701–3; interior destroyed by bombing 1940, and restored by W. Godfrey Allen 1955–7. Joshua Marshall and Sam. Fulkes, masons; Benjamin Leach, bricklayer; John Longland, carpenter; William Cleer and William Grey, joiners; William Emmett, wood carver; John Grove, plasterer. The spire was struck by lightning in 1764, after which the upper 84 feet were rebuilt by William Staines; it was again damaged by lightning in 1803. (W. H. Godfrey, *The Church of St. Bride, Fleet Street*, London Survey Monograph no. 15, 1944.)

CHRIST CHURCH, NEWGATE STREET, 1677–87; steeple completed 1704: the urns which formerly surmounted the colonnaded storey were removed before 1814, but restored in 1960; interior 'repaired and beautified' in 1834, and again in 1880; body of church destroyed by bombing 1940. John Shorthose and Richard Crooke, masons; Edward Elder and John Horn, bricklayers; John Longland, carpenter; Matthew Williams, joiner; H. Doogood, plasterer.

ST. CHRISTOPHER LE STOCKS, THREADNEEDLE STREET, 1670–1 (incorporating much of the medieval fabric); dem. 1781 for site of Bank of England. John Thompson, mason; Matthew Banckes, carpenter; William Gray, joiner; William Emmett, wood carver; John Grove, plasterer. The figures of Moses and Aaron from the altar-piece of this church are now in St. Margaret, Lothbury, the reredos in Great Bearsted Church, Essex, the pulpit in Canewdon Church, Essex.

ST. CLEMENT, EASTCHEAP, 1683–7; interior rearranged by Butterfield in 1872 and again in 1889; roof rebuilt 1925. Edward Strong, mason; Israel Knowles and William Gray, carpenters; T. Poultney, joiner; Jonathan Maine, carver; John Grove and H. Doogood, plasterers.

ST. DIONIS BACKCHURCH, FENCHURCH STREET, 1670–4; steeple completed 1684; dem. 1878–9. John Thompson, mason; William Taylour, Richard Reading, William Atwell, John Longland, carpenters; William Cleer and William Gray, joiners; H. Doogood and John Grove, plasterers. The altar, pulpit, font and other fittings are in St. Dionis, Fulham; the royal arms and some panelling in St. Dionis Hall, Lime Street. The monument to Sir Thomas Rawlinson was re-erected in Hawkshead Church, Westmorland.

ST. DUNSTAN IN THE EAST, 1670–1 (incorporating shell of the old church); Gothic steeple 1697–9; nave and chancel rebuilt by D. Laing and W. Tite 1817–21; destroyed by bombing 1941 except steeple. James Flory, mason (of church); Ephraim Beauchamp, mason (of steeple); Thomas Lane, joiner.

ST. EDMUND KING AND MARTYR, LOMBARD STREET 1670–9; spire completed after 1708; repaired 1833; urns removed from steeple *c.* 1908; damaged by bombing 1917. Abraham Story, mason; Maurice Emmett, bricklayer; Geo. Choby and Henry Wilkins, carpenters; Thos. Whiting and Thos. Creecher, joiners; Daniel Morrice and John Sherwood, plasterers.

ST. GEORGE, BOTOLPH LANE, 1671–4; dem. 1903–

4. Nicholas Young, mason; Thos. Horn, bricklayer; Robert Day, carpenter; Wm. Cleer, joiner; Simon Audrey, carver; John Grove and Henry Doogood, plasterers. The organ is now at St. George's Church, Southall, Middlesex, the royal arms at St. Mary-at-Hill, and the altar-table at St. Silas, Pentonville.

ST. JAMES, GARLICK HILL, 1676–83; spire 1713–17; repaired 1838, when three windows on north side were blocked and four others opened at east end; decorated by B. Champneys 1886. Chr. Kempster, mason; Thos. Warren, bricklayer; Israel Knowles, carpenter; Wm. Cleer and J. Fuller, joiners; William Newman, carvers; John Grove and H. Doogood, plasterers.

ST. LAWRENCE, JEWRY, 1671–7; north gallery removed by Sir A. Blomfield 1866–7; roof repaired 1892; gutted by bombing 1940; restored by Cecil Brown 1954–7. Edward Pierce, mason; Thomas Newman, bricklayer; John Longland, carpenter; Wm. Cleer and Richard Kedge, joiners; Thos. Mead, plasterer; Edward Pierce, wood carver.

ST. MAGNUS MARTYR, LOWER THAMES STREET, 1671–6; steeple completed 1705; damaged by fire 1760; in *c.* 1765 the west ends of the north and south aisles were set back and a passageway made through the tower in order to improve the approach to Old London Bridge; later the windows of the north aisle were reduced to circular form, and the south aisle was partially rebuilt; there were internal alterations by E. I'Anson in 1893 and by Martin Travers in 1924. George Dowdeswell and John Thompson, masons; Robert Brown, bricklayer; Matthew Banckes, carpenter; Wm. Cleer, Wm. Gray and — Massey, joiners; John Grove and H. Doogood, plasterers.

ST. MARGARET, LOTHBURY, 1686–90; alterations by Bodley and Garner 1890–1. Sam Fulkes, mason; John Longland, carpenter; Wm. Cleer, joiner; H. Doogood, plasterer.

ST. MARGARET PATTENS, 1684–7; spire 1699–1703; the lead vases which formerly decorated the spire have been removed. Sam Fulkes, mason; John Evans, bricklayer; Thos. Woodstock, carpenter; Wm. Cleer, joiner; John Grove and H. Doogood, plasterers.

ST. MARTIN, LUDGATE, 1677–84. Nicholas Young, mason; Allan Garway and Thos. Horn, bricklayers; Henry Blowes, Robert Day, and Matthew Banckes, carpenters; Messrs. Poulden and Athey, William Gray, joiners; Wm. Emmett, carver; H. Doogood and John Grove, plasterers.

ST. MARY ABCHURCH, 1681–6; damaged by bombing 1940 and restored by W. Godfrey Allen. Chr. Kempster, mason; John Bridges and John Evans, bricklayers; Thos. Woodstock, carpenter; Thos. Creecher and Wm. Grey, joiners; Grinling Gibbons, carver (of altar-piece);[1] William Emmett, carver (of gallery, etc.); H. Doogood and John Grove, plasterers.

ST. MARY, ALDERMANBURY, 1670–6; repaired by W. Hillier 1777, when windows on north side were partly bricked up; re-roofed 1808–10; repaired by Chas. Tyrrell 1830; tracery inserted in windows and other alterations by Woodthorpe 1864; further alterations 1923; interior destroyed by bombing 1940; church demolished and re-erected at Westminster College, Fulton, Missouri, U.S.A., 1964–5. Joshua Marshall, mason; Matthew Banckes, carpenter; Wm. Cleer, joiner; Thos. Turnly and Richard Kedge, carvers; John Grove, plasterer.

ST. MARY ALDERMARY, BOW LANE, WATLING STREET, 1681–2, Gothic; tower completed 1702–4; repaired by Samuel Ainger 1823; interior altered by Tress and Innes 1876. Edward Strong, mason (of church); — Clark, mason (of tower); John Longland, carpenter; Thos. Creecher, joiner.

ST. MARY MAGDALENE, OLD FISH STREET, 1683–5; gutted by fire 1886 and dem. 1887. Edward Strong, mason; Israel Knowles, carpenter; Richard Kedge, joiner; Jonathan Maine, carver; H. Doogood, plasterer.

ST. MARY AT HILL, THAMES STREET, 1670–6; in 1787–8 the tower and west end were rebuilt in brick to the designs of George Gwilt; in 1827–8 the body of the church was repaired and partly rebuilt by James Savage, who in 1848–9 refitted the interior after a fire, employing W. Gibbs Rogers to execute the wood-carving in seventeenth-century style. Joshua Marshall, mason; Thos. Lock, carpenter; Wm. Cleer, joiner; John Grove, plasterer.

ST. MARY SOMERSET, THAMES STREET, 1686–95; dem., except tower, 1871. Chr. Kempster, mason; John Evans, bricklayer; James Groves, carpenter; Chas. Hopson and Wm. Cleer, joiners; H. Doogood, plasterer. The fittings were removed to St. Mary's, Britannia Street, Hoxton, where they were destroyed by bombing in 1940/1.

ST. MARY LE BOW, CHEAPSIDE, 1671–3; steeple completed 1680; the upper part of the steeple was rebuilt by George Gwilt, junior, in 1818–20, when the upper columns were renewed in Aberdeen granite and the terminal feature reduced in height; the church was severely damaged by bombing in 1941, and restored by L. King, 1956–64. Thos. Cartwright, mason (of church); Thos. Cartwright and J. Thompson, masons (of steeple); Antony Tanner,

bricklayer; Matthew Banckes, carpenter; Wm. Cleer and T. Whiting, joiners; John Grove and H. Doogood, plasterers.

ST. MARY, WOOLNOTH, repaired 1670–7; rebuilt by N. Hawksmoor 1716–27.

ST. MATTHEW, FRIDAY STREET, 1681–5; dem. 1881. Edward Pierce, mason; Thos. Horn, bricklayer; John Longland, carpenter; Wm. Cleer and Richard Kedge, joiners; Edward Pierce, carver; H. Doogood and John Grove, plasterers. The altar-piece and doorcases are now in the hall of Polesden Lacey House, Surrey: the font and furniture are at St. Clement's, Fulham, and the pulpit at St. Peter's, Fulham.

ST. MICHAEL, BASSISHAW, 1676–9; dem. 1899. John Fitch and James Flory, masons; Edward Dale, carpenter; John Blinco, Robert Christmas and Francis Ragg, joiners; John Sherwood, plasterer. For the sale of the fittings, see N. and Q., 9th series, v, 1900, 6: the plaster royal arms are now in the Museum of London.

ST. MICHAEL, CORNHILL, 1670–2; Gothic tower begun by Wren's office in 1715–17, but building suspended owing to lack of funds, and completed by N. Hawksmoor to his own designs 1718–22; in 1790 the windows of the south aisle were reduced to circular form; in 1858–60 Sir Gilbert Scott inserted tracery in the windows, refitted the interior with carving by W. Gibbs Rogers, and added a Gothic porch to the tower, 'in an attempt to give tone to the existing classic architecture'; in 1867–8 the transformation was completed by polychromatic decoration and a tiled floor. Nicholas Young, mason; Antony Tanner, bricklayer; Thos. Gammon and — Miller, carpenters; Wm. Cleer, joiner; John Grove, plasterer.

ST. MICHAEL, CROOKED LANE, 1684–8; tower completed 1698; dem. 1831 to make way for approaches to London Bridge. Wm. Hammond, mason; John Evans, bricklayer; Matthew Banckes and Robert Day, carpenters; Wm. Cleer, John Mitchell and Thos. Creecher, joiners; H. Doogood and John Grove, plasterers. The pulpit, altar-piece, communion railing, and other fittings were offered for sale to the Commissioners for Building New Churches in 1832 (Church Commissioners, File 21744, 41/27 (Part 6)). Their fate is unknown.

ST. MICHAEL, PATERNOSTER ROYAL, COLLEGE HILL, 1686–94; steeple completed 1713; internal repairs by J. Elmes 1820; alterations by Butterfield 1866; damaged by bombing 1944, and restored by E. Davies. Edward Strong, mason; Thos. Denning, carpenter; Wm. Cleer, joiner; H. Doogood, plasterer.

ST. MICHAEL, QUEENHITHE, 1676–87; dem. 1876. James Flory and Sam. Fulkes, masons; Thos.

---

[1] For documentary evidence that Grinling Gibbons was the carver of the altar-piece, see R. M. La Porte-Payne, *A Short History of St. Mary Abchurch*, 1946, Appendix IV.

Warren, bricklayer; Matthew Banckes, carpenter; Robert Layton, joiner; Jonathan Maine and William Newman, carvers; H. Doogood and John Grove, plasterers. Some of the fittings, including the pulpit, were removed to St. James, Garlick Hill; the organ is now in Christchurch, Chelsea.

ST. MICHAEL, WOOD STREET, 1670–5; repaired by W. M. Brooks in 1831, when the tower 'was thrown open to the body of the church'; interior altered 1888; dem. 1894. Thos. Wise, mason; Rich. Cobbett, bricklayer; Saml. Lime, carpenter; Gerrard Lens, joiner; Sherwood and Morrice, plasterers. The pulpit is now in St. Mark's, Kennington.

ST. MILDRED, BREAD STREET, 1681–7; destroyed by bombing 1941. Edward Strong, mason; Thos. Horn, bricklayer; Israel Knowles, carpenter; Wm. Cleer and Roger Davis, joiners; H. Doogood and John Grove, plasterers.

ST. MILDRED, POULTRY, 1670–6, tower not completed until early eighteenth century, when parish asked for assistance from Fifty New Churches Fund; dem. 1872. Jasper Latham, mason; Morrice Emmett, bricklayer; Thos. Lock, carpenter; Wm. Cleer, joiner; H. Doogood and John Grove, plasterers. Some of the fittings were removed to St. Paul's, Clerkenwell, where they were destroyed by bombing in 1940/1.

ST. NICHOLAS, COLE ABBEY, 1671–7; interior rearranged 1873, but partially restored to its original state 1928–9; gutted by bombing 1941 and restored by Arthur Bailey. Thos. Wise, mason; Henry Blowes, carpenter; Wm. Cleer and Richard Kedge, joiners; John Sherwood and Edw. Martin, plasterers.

ST. OLAVE, OLD JEWRY, 1670–6; dem., except the tower, 1888–9. John Shorthose, mason; Matthew Banckes and Robert Day, carpenters; Thos. Whiting and Valentine Houseman, joiners; Richard Cleere, carver; John Grove, plasterer. The pulpit and font are at the church of St. Olave, Woodberry Down, the other fittings at St. Margaret, Lothbury.

ST. PETER, CORNHILL, 1675–81; internal alterations by J. D. Wyatt 1872. Joshua Marshall and Abraham Story, masons; Thos. Warren, bricklayer; Thos. Woodstock, carpenter; Wm. Cleer, Thomas Poultney and Thomas Athew, joiners; Edward Freeman and Richard Howes, carvers; H. Doogood and John Grove, plasterers.

ST. SEPULCHRE, HOLBORN, reconstructed c. 1668–1680, incorporating most of the surviving fabric of the medieval church, including the outer walls, south porch and west tower. The medieval windows and battlements survived until 1789, when classical windows and a plain parapet were substituted; they were restored in 1879–80, when the seventeenth-century gal-

leries and pews were removed. The roof was reconstructed c. 1835. Joshua Marshall, mason; — Hodgkins, carpenter; — Blount, plasterer.

ST. STEPHEN, COLEMAN STREET, 1674–6; much altered at various dates; dem. after damage by bombing 1940. Joshua Marshall, mason; Jos. Lemm and Ab. Williams, bricklayers; Robert Horton, carpenter; Wm. Cleer and Thos. Creecher, joiners; Wm. Newman, carver; Robert Horton and Burton, plasterers.

ST. STEPHEN, WALBROOK, 1672–9; repaired by James Peacock 1830–4; pews removed, octagonal pedestals of columns made square, and mosaic floor inserted by F. C. Penrose 18–; damaged by bombing 1941, restored 1951–4; Thomas Strong and Chr. Kempster, masons; John Longland, carpenter; Roger Davis, Stephen College and Thos. Creecher, joiners; Jonathan Maine and William Newman, carvers; H. Doogood and John Grove, plasterers.

ST. SWITHIN, CANNON STREET, 1677–85; Italianate tracery inserted in windows by E. Woodthorpe 1869; dem. after damage by bombing 1941. Joshua Marshall and Sam. Fulkes, masons; John Longland, carpenter; Wm. Cleer, joiner; Richard Cleere, wood carver; Edward Pierce, carver (of dial); H. Doogood and John Grove, plasterers.

ST. VEDAST, FOSTER LANE, 1670–3; tower 1694–7; gutted by bombing 1940; restored by S. E. Dykes Bower 1960–3. John Thompson, mason, Jonathan Wilcox, carpenter, and Christopher Russell, bricklayer, contractors for church; Edward Strong and William Collins, masons (of tower).

WRIGHT, NATHANIEL (–1821) was a builder-architect in the City of London. He was a carpenter by trade, and was Master of the Carpenters' Company in 1800. He served as a member of the City Lands Committee in 1778, and held the post of District Surveyor for the Northern District of the City of London from 1782 onwards. As a builder he was active in the development of Finsbury in the 1770s. As an architect he was responsible for the virtual rebuilding of ST. BOTOLPH'S CHURCH, ALDERSGATE, in 1789–91, in a style closely modelled on Dance's All Hallows, London Wall. The east front to Aldersgate Street dates, however, from 1830, when it was executed in Roman cement by Messrs. John Ward & Son, builders, of Jewin Street [Vestry Minutes and accounts in Guildhall Library, 3863/1–2 and 1455/6]. Wright's will showed that he died possessed of considerable property. He lived for most of his life in Hatton Garden, but had a country retreat at Godstone and died in Sloane Street on 24 April 1821. Samuel Acton (*q.v.*) was his nephew and pupil.

[Dorothy Stroud, *George Dance*, 1971, 129; *Gent's Mag.* 1821 (i), 476; P.C.C. 309 MANS-FIELD.]

WRIGHT, ROBERT (*c.* 1661–1736), of Castor in Northamptonshire, was a successful master carpenter who also acted as an architect and became Surveyor to the Dean and Chapter of Peterborough. He was much employed at Milton House, Northants., and is often mentioned in letters to the 1st Earl Fitzwilliam from his steward [Northants. Record Office, F(M) C, 637, 658, 712, etc.]. In 1688 he was reported to be putting the wooden balustrade on the roof of Uffington House, nr. Stamford, for Charles Bertie, and the steward considered him, though 'very young', to be 'a very prettie ingenious workman and one that understands all things belonging to any building'. He had recently 'been at a seat of Lord Danby's [afterwards 1st Duke of Leeds] near Scarborough in Yorkshire,[1] where hee has drawn his lordship the draught of a fine new house, it is a treble house & in the shell not unlike Thorp house'. At MILTON Wright undertook in 1689 to build the new stable wing. The original design appears to have been made by John Sturges (*q.v.*), but was subsequently modified by someone else (possibly Wright himself), for an anonymous account dated 1692 contains charges for 'drawing a new draught for the wing building' as well as for 'a draught drawn in prospecttive of the great house with the rest of the building adjacent to it'.[2] Two later drawings by him survive among the Fitzwilliam papers. One (map 1966) is a plan of a large new house for Milton on Palladian lines signed and dated 1723, the other (plan 150) is a 'Draft of a wing for Milton House to be joyned to the great House on the East side of the Great Garden' dated 1725, and shows a plain two-storey range that was not built. He also made an undated 'Draught of the Roof' of the church of MARHOLM CHURCH, NORTHANTS., which is in the same collection (plan 56). In 1719 he made designs for rebuilding a house at THURLBY, nr. BOURNE, LINCS., apparently for a Mr. Denshire. His drawings and estimate for £269 4s. 6d. are among the Ancaster papers in the Lincolnshire Record Office (Ancaster 3/24/8/62].

In 1720 Wright contracted to build Blather-wycke Hall, Northants, for Henry O'Brien to the designs of Thomas Ripley for £3000 [North-

---

[1] This house was not built, and its intended site is uncertain. Lord Danby (formerly Sir Thomas Osborne) had land in several parts of Yorkshire. In 1673 he was described as 'of Wickmore' in the parish of Brafferton in the North Riding.
[2] Milton House plan 19 is a perspective of the new stables which may be by Wright. The building is illustrated in *C. Life*, 18 May 1961, where it is wrongly attributed to William Talman.

ants. Record Office, OBB 12]. In the contract he is described as 'timber-merchant', and in 1715 he had bought all the timber in Blatherwycke and Bulwick woods for £7420 [Northants. Record Office, XYZ 1247]. In 1726 he was one of the contractors who undertook to make the R. Nene navigable under an Act of 11 George I, cap. xix. The work had been completed up to Oundle by 1730 [*Nene Valley Drainage & Navigation, Statement of Facts*, London 1891, 4]. In 1734, as surveyor to the Dean and Chapter of Peterborough, Wright was directed to make a general survey of the fabric of the cathedral and other buildings [Peterborough Chapter Act Book 1704–1814, f. 83d.].

During the latter part of his life Wright lived at Castor, nr. Peterborough, where he died on 6 December 1736, aged 75. A monument at the west end of the church commemorates him as 'a Person that with an Honest Industry Purchased a Plentifull Fortune with a Fair Character'. His will is P.C.C. 284 DERBY.

WRIGHT, ROBERT, practised in Edinburgh, where he laid out MORNINGSIDE PLACE in 1823–4 and designed 1–4 CASTLE TERRACE in conjunction with Thomas Hamilton in 1826 [S.R.O., Edinburgh Sasines]. 'Robert Wright & Son' are listed among the Edinburgh architects in Pigot's *Directory* of 1837.

WRIGHT, STEPHEN (–1780), entered the employment of the Office of Works in December 1746, when he became Clerk of the Works at Hampton Court. He appears to have been a clerk or assistant of William Kent, for the latter's will, dated 1748, contains a clause bequeathing 'unto Stephen Wright fifty pounds, and unto my servant who shall be living with me at the time of my decease ten pounds'. He is probably the 'Stephen' referred to in letters written by Kent to Lord Burlington in 1738–9 [*Arch. Rev.* lxiii, 1928, 180], and in 1749 he had in his possession a number of Kent's designs for public buildings which he offered to the Board of Works for £80. At what date he became a protégé of the Duke of Newcastle is uncertain, but there is abundant evidence that he enjoyed the Duke's patronage. When Thomas Ripley, the Comptroller of the Works, was reported to be dying in 1758, Wright at once wrote to Newcastle to beg for his post. Ripley's successor was Henry Flitcroft, but it was by Newcastle's 'immediate appointment' that Wright was preferred to the posts of Master Mason and Deputy Surveyor vacated by the new Comptroller. When Flitcroft fell ill in his turn in 1766, Wright again solicited the Duke's favour on his behalf, though on this occasion his application was premature, as Flitcroft lived until 1769, and Wright remained Master Mason for the remainder of his life. Newcastle employed Wright as his architect at Claremont, and in 1754 when, as Chancellor of Cambridge University, he gave £500 towards building a new front to the University Library, it was Wright's design which he forced on the unwilling Syndics.

Wright was, as might be expected from his association with Kent, essentially a Palladian architect, and his University Library façade at Cambridge is a most elegant composition in that style. His work at Milton Hall shows that, like Kent, he could also make attractive Gothic designs if called upon to do so – in this case by a Catholic client apparently anxious to emphasize the medieval associations of his religion.

Wright died on 28 September 1780, after 'a lingering tho' not very painful illness', and was buried in the churchyard at Hampton in Middlesex. By his will he left £20 to the poor at Oxburgh, Norfolk, which may have been his native village. [*A.P.S.D.*; *History of the King's Works* v, 89–90, 424 n.; P.C.C. 498 COLLINS.]

LONDON, NO. 22 ARLINGTON STREET, completed house for the Hon. Henry Pelham after William Kent's death in 1748 [R.I.B.A. Drawings Coll., MS. 'Expences relating to Building in Arlington Street'].

SUNBURY CHURCH, MIDDLESEX, 1751–2; remodelled in neo-Byzantine style by S. S. Teulon 1856 [a contemporary entry in the Parish Register records that 'The Designer and Surveyor was Mr. Wright of the Board of Works at Hampton Court; and the Builder Richard Jupp, City Builder'].

THE WHITE LODGE, RICHMOND NEW PARK, repairs and redecoration for Princess Amelia, 1751–2; addition of wings for Princess Amelia, before 1761 [*Vitruvius Britannicus* iv, 1767, pls. 1–4; *History of the King's Works* v, 232].

CLAREMONT HOUSE, SURREY, work for the 1st Duke of Newcastle, 1752; dem. [MS. account-book of William Farmer, a plumber, among the parish records of Kingston-on-Thames, shows that his work at Claremont in this year was valued by 'Mr. Wright of Hampton Court'. Farmer also did a good deal of work for the Earl of Lincoln (afterwards 2nd Duke of Newcastle) 'by order of Mr. Wright'].

CAMBRIDGE, THE UNIVERSITY LIBRARY, 1754–8 [Willis & Clark, iii, 63–8; original drawing illustrated in *Builder*, 28 Sept. 1907] (R.C.H.M., *Cambridge*, pl. 71 and plan, p. 13).

ASHBURNHAM PLACE, SUSSEX, measured work for the 2nd Earl of Ashburnham, and may have been concerned in design of new front, 1760–1; remodelled 1813–17; refaced 1853; dem. 1959 [C. Hussey in *C. Life*, 23 April 1953].

MILTON HALL, nr. STEVENTON, BERKS., Gothic chapel and library for Bryant Barrett, 1764–72 [Arthur Oswald in *C. Life*, 24 Dec. 1948].

CLUMBER HOUSE, NOTTS., for the 2nd Duke of Newcastle, 1768–78; centre rebuilt after a fire in 1879; dem. 1938. Wright also designed the bridge over the lake and various buildings on the estate [accounts in Nottingham University Library, Newcastle papers; Watts, *Seats of the Nobility & Gentry*, pl. xxix, 1781; original drawing for south front illustrated in Sotheby's Catalogue, 1951, lot 101] (*C. Life*, 12–19 Sept. 1908; survey plans in R.I.B.A. Drawings Coll.).

NEWARK BRIDGE, NOTTS. (R. Trent), for the 2nd Duke of Newcastle, 1775; footpaths added 1848 [accounts in Nottingham University Library, Newcastle papers].

NOTTINGHAM, THE BLACKAMOOR'S HEAD INN, enlarged for the 2nd Duke of Newcastle, 1775 [*ibid.*].

BUSHEY VILLA, TEDDINGTON, MIDDLESEX (dem.), is stated by W. Keane, *Beauties of Middlesex*, 1850, 103, to have been designed 'by Wright'.

WRIGHT, THOMAS (1711 – 1786), astronomer, landscape-gardener and architect, was born at Byers Green, nr. Bishop Auckland in Durham, where his father was a carpenter. By the age of 14 he was, in his own words, 'much in love with Mathematicks' and 'very much given to the Amusements of Drawing, Planning of Maps and Buildings'. After four unhappy years as a clockmaker's apprentice, he tried without much success to make a living by teaching mathematics and publishing almanacs. The Earl of Scarbrough's patronage eventually enabled him to gain some reputation as a writer on astronomy. In 1737 he published *Universal Vicissitudes of the Seasons*, in 1740 *The Use of the Globes* (commissioned by John Senex), in 1742 *Clavis Coelestis*, and in 1750 his best-known book, *An Original Theory or New Hypothesis of the Universe*, an ingeniously speculative work of little real scientific value. A visit to Ireland in 1746–7 resulted in *Louthiana, or an Introduction to the Antiquities of Ireland*, 1748. This was a pioneer work on its subject, and a product of the antiquarian interests which Wright pursued alongside astronomy.

As an architect and landscape-gardener Wright owed his commissions largely to a small circle of aristocratic friends and patrons, which included the Dukes of Kent and Portland, Viscount Midleton, the Earl of Essex, Lord Limerick, and the Ansons of Shugborough. Among the grounds which he embellished were those at Badminton, Beckett Park (Berks.), Culford, Oatlands, Stoke Gifford, Shugborough and Wallington. In 1755 and 1758 he published two sets of engravings entitled *Six Original Designs of Arbours* and *Six Original Designs of Grottos*. These were the first and only instalments of a projected *Universal Architecture*. They are notable both for the elegance of the engravings, and for showing the buildings (for the first time in a work of this kind) in a natural setting. Many of Wright's executed works were mock castles, Gothick arbours, ruined grottoes and such-like follies. Though basically a Palladian, he favoured a rococo style which found expression in elaborately decorated interiors and in projecting bows and other deviations from the correct Palladian canon. Nuthall Temple, his most important work, was a much enlarged and elaborated version of Scamozzi's Rocca Pisana.

In 1762 Wright retired to Byers Green, where he built himself a small villa and decorated its interior with elaborate sequences of prints illustrating the faculties of human knowledge, human passions, etc. On a neighbouring hill he began the erection of an observatory in the form of a round tower, but died in 1786 before it was finished. In 1793 the *Gentleman's Magazine* published a memoir illustrated by an engraved portrait, and the recent research of Dr. Eileen Harris is summarized in three articles in *Country Life*, 26 Aug., 2 and 9 Sept. 1971[1]. Wright's journals are in the British Museum (Add. MSS. 15627–8). A design by him for a royal palace, submitted to King George III in 1766, is in the Royal Library at Windsor. A sketch-book is in the Avery Library at Columbia University. Another is in a private collection in England.

OLD WINDSOR, BERKS., house (later BEAUMONT LODGE) for the dowager Duchess of Kent, 1743; altered by Henry Emlyn *c.* 1790 [Eileen Harris in *C. Life*, 26 Aug. 1971, 494].

attributed: SHUGBOROUGH, STAFFS., addition of wings for Thomas Anson, 1748, and garden buildings, including the SHEPHERD'S MONUMENT [Eileen Harris in *C. Life*, 2 Sept. 1971, 546–8].

BADMINTON HOUSE, GLOS., picturesque buildings in the park for the 4th Duke of Beaufort, including the Ragged Castle, Castle Barn, Root House and thatched cottages, 1748–56 [Eileen Harris in *C. Life*, 9 Sept. 1971, 613–14].

STOKE GIFFORD, GLOS., remodelled exterior in castellated style for Norborne Berkeley, cr. Lord Botetourt, *c.* 1750–60 ['Mr. Wright' is stated to have been the architect of Stoke Gifford in the eighteenth-century list of country houses in Alnwick Castle Library, and in Nov. 1755 Lady Anson wrote to Marchioness Grey to say that she had dined at Stoke Gifford 'in an Octagon Room with 4 windows (built by *your* Mr. Wright)'].

NUTHALL TEMPLE, NOTTS., for Sir Charles Sedley, Bart., 1754–7; interior of hall stuccoed by Thomas Roberts of Oxford to his own designs 1769 [Bucks. Record Office, D/LE/11/2]; din-

ing-room redecorated and garden front altered *c.* 1780; dem. 1929 [*Vitruvius Britannicus* iv, 1767, pls. 56–7] (*C. Life*, 28 April, 5 May 1923).

BYERS GREEN, nr. BISHOP AUCKLAND, CO. DURHAM, house for himself, 1756–7; dem. [accounts in B.M., Add. MS. 15627].

HORTON HOUSE, NORTHANTS., remodelled east front for the 2nd Earl of Halifax (d. 1772), *c.* 1760; dem. 1936; and *attributed*: THE MENAGERY [Wright's employment here is mentioned by Walpole, 'Visits to Country Seats', *Walpole Soc.* xvi, 52 (1763), and discussed by Eileen Harris in *C. Life*, 26 Aug. 1971, 495].

CODGER CASTLE (a folly), ROTHLEY, NORTHUMBERLAND, for Sir Walter Blackett of Wallington, 1769 [drawing at Wallington, reproduced by Eileen Harris, *C. Life*, 9 Sept. 1971, 615].

WESTERTON HILL, nr. BISHOP AUCKLAND, CO. DURHAM, Observatory for himself, *c.* 1785 [Eileen Harris in *C. Life*, 26 Aug. 1971, 493].

IRELAND, probably designed garden buildings for Lord Limerick (later 3rd Earl of Clanbrassil, at DUNDALK, 1746–7. At BELVEDERE HOUSE, CO. WESTMEATH, there is a folly derived from one of Wright's engraved designs for grottoes [Eileen Harris in *C. Life*, 9 Sept. 1971, 615].

WRIGHT, THOMAS, practised in Salford (Manchester). In 1818 he won the competition for the BLACKFRIARS BRIDGE over the R. Irwell at MANCHESTER, completed in 1820 [Thomas Rickman's diary, 13 May 1818]. He was the architect of the COUNTY GAOL at KIRKDALE, nr. LIVERPOOL, designed on the panopticon principle, and erected in 1821–2 [J. A. Picton, *Memorials of Liverpool* ii, 1875, 409; *Lancashire illustrated in a Series of Views by R. Wallis*, 1829, 54–5]. He also designed the (classical) church of CHRIST CHURCH, SALFORD, 1830–1; steeple added by E. H. Shellard 1846; dem. 1958 [*Manchester Herald*, 6 May 1830].

WRIGHTE, WILLIAM, 'Architect', was the author of *Grotesque Architecture or Rural Amusement, consisting of Plans, Elevations and Sections for Huts, Retreats, Summer and Winter Hermitages, Terminaries, Chinese, Gothic and Natural Grottos, Cascades, Mosques, Moresque Pavilions, Grotesque and Rustic Seats, Greenhouses, etc., many of which may be executed with Flints, Irregular Stones, Rude Branches and Roots of Trees*, 1767, 2nd ed. 1790.

WYATT, BENJAMIN (1709–1772), was the founder of the Wyatt building business in Staffordshire, and the father of Samuel and James Wyatt (*qq.v.*). His family had long been yeoman farmers in the parish of Weeford, nr. Lichfield. He was one of the eight sons of John Wyatt of Thickbroom in that parish. His elder brother

---

[1] See also an article by Dr. Harris in *Arte Illustrata*, Dec. 1973.

THE WYATT FAMILY

showing the relationship of the principal members engaged in architecture and the allied trades

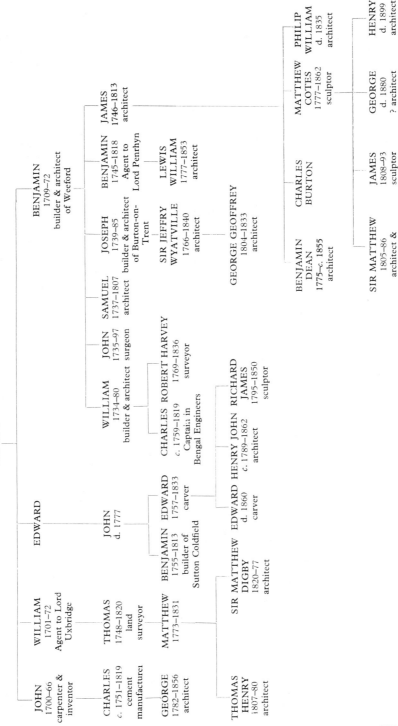

JOHN WYATT
1675–1742

JOHN
1700–66
carpenter &
inventor

WILLIAM
1701–72
Agent to Lord
Uxbridge

EDWARD

BENJAMIN
1709–72
builder & architect
of Weeford

CHARLES
c. 1751–1819
cement
manufacturer

THOMAS
1748–1820
land
surveyor

JOHN
d. 1777

WILLIAM
1734–80
builder & architect

JOHN
1735–97
surgeon

SAMUEL
1737–1807
architect

JOSEPH
1739–85
builder & architect
of Burton-on-
Trent

BENJAMIN
1745–1818
Agent to
Lord Penrhyn

JAMES
1746–1813
architect

GEORGE
1782–1856
architect

MATTHEW
1773–1831

BENJAMIN
1755–1813
builder of
Sutton Coldfield

EDWARD
1757–1833
carver

CHARLES
c. 1759–1819
Captain in
Bengal Engineers

ROBERT HARVEY
1769–1836
surveyor

SIR JEFFRY
WYATTVILLE
1766–1840
architect

LEWIS
WILLIAM
1777–1853
architect

THOMAS
HENRY
1807–80
architect

SIR MATTHEW
DIGBY
1820–77
architect

EDWARD
d. 1860
carver

HENRY JOHN
c. 1789–1862
architect

RICHARD
JAMES
1795–1850
sculptor

GEORGE GEOFFREY
1804–1833
architect

BENJAMIN
DEAN
1775–c. 1855
architect

CHARLES
BURTON

MATTHEW
COTES
1777–1862
sculptor

PHILIP
WILLIAM
d. 1835
architect

SIR MATTHEW
1805–86
architect &
builder

JAMES
1808–93
sculptor

GEORGE
d. 1880
? architect

HENRY
d. 1899
architect

935

John (1700–66) was a master carpenter who submitted a design for rebuilding Westminster Bridge in 1737, but was best known as an inventor of spinning machinery. Another brother, Job, patented a machine for making screws, while a third, William, became agent to the Paget family at Beaudesert. Benjamin himself was a farmer and timber merchant who developed a successful business as a builder and architect. He was assisted by several of his seven sons, especially the eldest, William, who appears to have designed most of the buildings erected by 'Benjamin Wyatt and Sons' in the 1750s and 1760s.

The building which is said to have 'first brought Benjamin Wyatt and his family into repute' as architects and builders was SWINFEN HALL, STAFFS., built for Samuel Swynfen in 1755 in a somewhat unsophisticated classical style [S. Shaw, *History of Staffordshire* ii, 1801, 30*]. In 1758–61 Benjamin and his sons rebuilt EGGINTON HALL, DERBYSHIRE (subsequently altered, and dem. 1955), for Sir John Every, Bart., either to their own designs or to designs made a few years earlier by William Baker (*q.v.*) [Edward Saunders, 'Egginton Hall', *Derbyshire Life*, March 1974, 66]. One of their most important works was the construction of the SOHO MANUFACTORY at BIRMINGHAM (1765–6) for Matthew Boulton, who also employed them to complete his house at Soho, and did much to assist the younger members of the family in their subsequent careers [J. M. Robinson, article cited below]. It was through Boulton that in 1766 William Wyatt began to make designs for the newly established GENERAL INFIRMARY at STAFFORD, which was built by the firm in 1769–72. William's 'plain and useful design' is represented in an engraving signed 'Benjamin Wyatt & Sons. Archit.' [B.M., *King's Maps* xxxviii, 46a]. In 1768–70 LEICESTER INFIRMARY was built by William Henderson (*q.v.*) under the direction of Benjamin Wyatt [see p. 413]. For the 9th Lord Paget (afterwards 1st Earl of Uxbridge) the Wyatts in 1770–2 built BURTON–ON–TRENT TOWN HALL, dem. 1883 (illustration in C. H. Underhill, *History of Burton on Trent*, 1941, 68), and in 1771–2 remodelled the interior of BEAUDESERT, STAFFS., dem. *c*. 1925 [accounts in Staffs. Record Office, *ex inf.* Mr. J. M. Frew]. For the design of the last work, which was partly in the Gothic style, the young James Wyatt was responsible, and his help may also explain the neo-classical influence apparent in the town hall at Burton.

In the R.I.B.A. Collection there is a design for a farm-house for the Earl of Suffolk and Berkshire at Elford in Staffordshire, dated 1767 and signed 'Benj. Wyatt & Sons'.

Benjamin Wyatt died at Blackbrook Farm, Weeford, in July 1772. By his wife Mary Wright he had seven sons. William, the eldest, succeeded to his business, but died in 1780; John practised

as a surgeon in London; Samuel, Joseph, Benjamin and James are all noticed separately below; Charles, the youngest, died in infancy. [*A.P.S.D.*; *John Wyatt, Master Carpenter and Inventor*, 1885 (published anonymously, but by Laurence Jacob); *Weeford Parish Register* (Staffs. Parish Record Soc. 1955); D. Linstrum, *The Wyatt Family*, R.I.B.A. Drawings Catalogue, 1973, 7–8; J. M. Robinson, 'A Great Architectural Family', *C. Life*, 13 Dec. 1973.]

WYATT, BENJAMIN (1745–1818), the fifth son of Benjamin Wyatt of Weeford, was born on 14 January 1744/5. According to the inscription on his monument, he was 'for upwards of thirty years Chief Agent to the Penrhyn Estates' in North Wales. The first Lord Penrhyn was an enterprising landowner who made a fortune out of the Penrhyn slate quarries. Wyatt was concerned in several of his projects, including the building of Port Penrhyn and the construction of the railway from the quarries to the port. He was also responsible for a good deal of architectural work on the estate. An obituary in the *North Wales Gazette* mentions as 'monuments of his well-cultivated taste' the MARINE BATHS at PENRHYN, a villa for Lord Penrhyn at OGWEN PARK, and 'the characteristic order and embellishments of the Dairy Farm at Penanisarnant'. At BANGOR he designed a building for the CARNARVONSHIRE AND ANGLESEY DISPENSARY (1809–10), now a private house, and the PENRHYN ARMS HOTEL, later the first home of the University College, but now demolished. Elsewhere he designed an inn at CAPEL CURIG and carried out alterations to ST. MARY'S CHAPEL, CAERNARVON, 1810–14.

Benjamin Wyatt lived at Lime Grove, nr. Bangor, in a house designed for him by his brother Samuel. He died on 5 January 1818, aged 73, and was buried in Llandegai Churchyard beneath a pyramid of slate. He left five sons, among whom were Lewis William (1777–1853), architect (*q.v.*), and James (1795–1882), of Bryngwynant, Beddgelert, who succeeded him as agent to Lord Penrhyn. [*Gent's Mag.* 1818 (i), 89; L. W. Wyatt, *A Collection of Architectural Designs … executed upon the Estates of Lord Penrhyn*, 1880–1; W. Bingley, *North Wales*, 2nd ed. 1814, 106, 112, 293; *Cambria Depicta*, 1816, 111; P. B. Williams, *Tourist's Guide through the County of Caernarvon*, 1821, 32–8; R. Fenton, *Tours in Wales*, 1917, 237–40; *Trans. Caernarvonshire Hist. Soc.* xi, 1950, 61; will (P.C.C. 102 CRESSWELL); information from Prof. M. L. Clarke.]

WYATT, BENJAMIN (1755–1813), was the second son of John Wyatt (d. 1777) and a second cousin of Samuel and James Wyatt. He established himself at Sutton Coldfield in Warwickshire, where he died on 29 November 1813, aged

59. Although sometimes described as an architect in contemporary documents, he was mainly a builder, who appears generally to have relied on his architect relations for designs. Thus in 1803–5 he was obtaining drawing from Lewis Wyatt (then in James Wyatt's office) for alterations at Patshull House and for a house that he was building for Sir Charles Clarke at Wigginton, nr. Tamworth. It was he who rebuilt Weeford Church to James Wyatt's designs in 1803–4. [*Gent's Mag.* 1795 (ii), 877, 1814 (i), 304; Birmingham Probate Registry, Register of Administrations, 25 Feb. 1814; William Salt Library, Stafford, M96.]

WYATT, BENJAMIN DEAN (1775–*c.* 1855), the eldest son of James Wyatt, was born in London and educated at Westminster School. He matriculated at Christ Church, Oxford, in April 1795, but got into debt and went down in 1797 without taking a degree. In 1797 he went out to India to take up a secretarial appointment in the office of the East India India Company at Calcutta, but finding his duties both more onerous and less remunerative than he had expected, resigned his post (18 Feb. 1802) and returned to England. In Calcutta he had worked for a time in the office of the Governor-General, Lord Wellesley, and it was this contact with the Wellesley family that led in 1807 to his appointment as secretary to Wellesley's younger brother Arthur, when the latter went to Dublin as Chief Secretary of Ireland in 1807. Two years later Wyatt returned to London and soon after began to practise as an architect from 22 Foley Place.

Although it was apparently not until 1809 that Wyatt decided to take up architecture as a career, he pursued it with such success that in 1811 he won the competition for rebuilding Drury Lane Theatre. When Joseph Farington asked Jeffry Wyatville 'how Benjamin Wyatt had acquired sufficient knowledge of Architecture to qualify him for such an undertaking', he was told that, after spending a period in his father's office, Benjamin 'had devoted his attention particularly to the study of a Theatre', and that, contrary to the general belief, he had received no assistance from his father: 'on the contrary, Wyatt was much displeased with Benjamin for offering a design as his younger brother Philip Wyatt had [also competed] for it', and had refused to have anything more to do with him when he won the commission. In 1811 Benjamin Wyatt published *Observations on the Principles of the Design for the Theatre now building in Drury Lane*, reissued in 1813 as *Observations on the Design for the Theatre Royal, Drury Lane, as executed in the year 1812*. The second edition was intended to refute 'a most unfounded and scandalous insinuation which appeared . . . in one of the weekly newspapers', that 'the design of the theatre was

not his own, but had been copied without acknowledgement from one made by his cousin George Wyatt' (*q.v.*). Wyatt also exhibited a model of a 'superior design' at his house (Ackermann, *Repository of Arts* viii, 1812, 287).

In 1813 Benjamin Wyatt succeeded his father as Surveyor of Westminster Abbey, and for some years he enjoyed a successful London practice. In 1815–16 he made designs for a vast palace for Arthur Wellesley, now victor of Waterloo and Duke of Wellington. Conceived as a neo-classical Blenheim, this was never built, for the Duke decided to live at Stratfieldsaye instead. The numerous surviving drawings show a grand but somewhat arid exterior of a familiar Wyatt type, but (as at Covent Garden) the interiors were to be handsomely decorated in a rich neo-classical style. It is the interiors rather than the exteriors of Wyatt's later buildings that are of most interest and merit, for at Crockford's Club and the three great London houses which he designed in collaboration with his brother Philip he achieved strikingly effective recreations of the French rococo style of the period of Louis XIV. Although Wyatt had visited France in 1815, the means by which he achieved this mastery of an intricate foreign style are by no means clear. All the drawings were, however, made in his office either by himself or his brother and their assistants (all of whom appear to have been of English nationality), and Wyatt's correspondence with the Duke of Sutherland shows that he was fully conversant with the techniques involved in fashioning *boiseries* and gilded stucco ornamentation in the French manner.

Wyatt's last recorded commission was the Duke of York's Column (1831–4). In 1827 he had resigned the surveyorship of Westminster Abbey, and in 1833 he was declared bankrupt. For the rest of his life he appears to have been without architectural employment, and how he supported himself is unknown. In 1836 a false announcement of his death appeared in the *Companion to the Almanac*, but his will is dated 1850 and was proved in 1855. It shows that in the former year he was living in Camden Town, and that he left all his worldly goods to his 'good and faithful servant' Martha Turner. A portrait of Wyatt by S. Drummond, A.R.A., was engraved by T. Blood for the *European Magazine* of October 1812. W. G. Colman, A. D. Gough, John Harper, J. D. Paine and R. L. Roumieu were his pupils or assistants. A number of his drawings are in the R.I.B.A. Collection.

[*A.P.S.D.*; *London Gazette*, 1833 (i), 1032 (bankruptcy); P.R.O., P.C.C. 1855 register, f. 882 (will); *The Farington Diary*, ed. J. Greig, iv, 33, vii, 12, 130; *The Diary of Frances, Lady Shelley*, ed. R. Edgcumbe, ii, 1913; G. F. R. Barker & A. H. Stenning, *The Record of Old Westminsters* ii, 1928, 1028; R. Stanley-Morgan, 'Benjamin Wyatt and his Noble Clients', *Arch. Rev.* cxlv, Feb. 1969; D. Linstrum, *The Wyatt Family* (R.I.B.A. Drawings Catalogue), 1973; D. Linstrum, 'The Waterloo Palace', *Arch. Rev.* clv, April 1974.]

LONDON, THE THEATRE ROYAL, DRURY LANE, 1811–12; auditorium reconstructed by S. Beazley 1822, portico added 1831 [Britton & Pugin, *Public Buildings of London* i, 1825, 227–61; *Gent's Mag.* 1811 (ii), 478; *European Mag.*, Oct. 1812, 260–4; *Builder* xiii, 1855, 437, 470; R. Carter, 'The Drury Lane Theatres of Henry Holland and B. D. Wyatt', *Journal of the Society of Architectural Historians* [of America] xxvi, 1967; Marcus Binney, 'The Theatre Royal, Drury Lane', *C. Life*, 10 Dec. 1970].

DEVIZES, WILTS., THE MARKET CROSS, for the 1st Viscount Sidmouth, 1814, Gothic [J. Waylen, *Chronicles of the Devizes*, 1839, 316].

WESTMINSTER ABBEY, restoration of rose window of south transept, 1814; rearrangement of choir, etc., 1822–3 [J. P. Neale & E. W. Brayley, *Westminster Abbey* ii, 1823, 15, 270–1].

MARESFIELD PARK, SUSSEX, remodelled for Sir John Shelley, Bart., 1816, Jacobean style; dem. after fire in 1921 [*The Diary of Frances Lady Shelley*, ed. R. Edgcumbe, ii, 1913, 67; T. W. Horsfield, *History of Sussex* i, 1835, 375–6].

WESTPORT, CO. MAYO, IRELAND, added wing containing library and gallery for the 2nd Marquess of Sligo, 1819; destroyed by fire 1826 [drawings at Westport;[1] Mark Girouard in *C. Life*, 6 May 1965].

STRATFIELD SAYE, HANTS., minor repairs and redecoration for the 1st Duke of Wellington, 1822 [John Cornforth in *C. Life*, 10 April 1975]. Wyatt appears also to have designed the porch and conservatory added in 1838.

BELVOIR CASTLE, LEICS., interior decoration of principal rooms and Romanesque Mausoleum in grounds, for the 5th Duke of Rutland, in collaboration with M. C. Wyatt, *c.* 1825–30 [T. F. Dibdin, *Northern Tour* i, 1838, 73; I. Eller, *History of Belvoir Castle*, 1841, 349–53; C. Hussey in *C. Life*, 6, 13, 20, 27 Dec. 1956; C. Hussey, *English Country Houses: Late Georgian*, 1958, 122–39].

LONDON, YORK (afterwards STAFFORD, now LANCASTER) HOUSE, ST. JAMES'S, for Frederick Augustus, Duke of York, in collaboration with Philip Wyatt, 1825–7. This mansion was begun by R. Smirke in 1820, but he was dismissed in 1825, when the building was up to ground level, and fresh designs were made by Wyatt and put into execution. On the Duke's death in 1827 the incomplete shell was bought by the 2nd Marquess of Stafford (cr. Duke of Sutherland in 1833), whose son, on succeeding as 2nd Duke in 1833, added an attic storey and completed the interior. Wyatt made the designs, but the Duke and his agent evidently mistrusted him, for they insisted on employing Smirke as executant architect. The house was more or less complete by 1838, when Wyatt and the Duke fell out, and Charles Barry was employed to redesign the lantern and to decorate the staircase. [H. M. Colvin, 'The Architects of Stafford House', *Architectural History* i, 1958; John Cornforth, 'Stafford House Revisited', *C. Life*, 7–14 Nov. 1968.]

LONDON, LONDONDERRY (formerly HOLDERNESSE) HOUSE, PARK LANE, reconstructed for the 3rd Marquess of Londonderry, in collaboration with Philip Wyatt, 1825–8; dem. 1964 [*A.P.S.D.*; Arthur Oswald in *C. Life*, 10 July 1937].

LONDON, CROCKFORD'S CLUBHOUSE, NO. 50–53 ST. JAMES'S STREET, in collaboration with Philip Wyatt, 1827; altered internally 1849 and refaced 1870–5 [J. Elmes, *Metropolitan Improvements*, 1831, 140–1].

LONDON, THE ORIENTAL CLUB, NO. 18 HANOVER SQUARE, in collaboration with Philip Wyatt, 1827–8; enlarged by D. Burton 1852–4; dem. 1962 [*A.P.S.D.*; *A New Survey of London*, John Weale 1853, i, 304–5, with plan].

LONDON, APSLEY HOUSE, PICCADILLY, remodelled for the 1st Duke of Wellington, in collaboration with Philip Wyatt, 1828–9 [*A.P.S.D.*]. Wyatt cased the house in Bath stone, added the Corinthian portico, and constructed the gallery in which the Waterloo Banquets were held until 1852.

LONDON, SPRING GARDENS, proposed alterations to basement of house for Lord Dover, 1831; dem. [P.R.O., MPE 839].

LONDON, CARLTON HOUSE TERRACE, house (No. 6) for the Marquess of Tavistock, 1831 [*A.P.S.D.*].

LONDON, THE DUKE OF YORK'S COLUMN, CARLTON GARDENS, 1831–4 [*Architectural Mag.* i, 1834, 192–201].

WYATT, CHARLES (*c.* 1751–1819), of Bedford Row, London, was a son of John Wyatt (1700–66), the inventor, by his second wife Marabella. He was one of the original partners in the firm of Parker & Wyatt, manufacturers of the composition known at first as Parker's, sometimes as Wyatt's, and often as 'Roman' cement. It was patented in 1796 by James Parker of Northfleet, who obtained the raw material for its manufacture in the neighbourhood of the Isle of Sheppey. It had the property of hardening under water, and was extensively used in hydraulic works. It was also used as a stucco. After Charles

---

[1] These include an unexecuted design for a theatre at Westport by B. D. Wyatt, dated 1812 (illustrated by John Harris, 'The Wyatts at Westport', *Connoisseur* clxii, 1966, 224–7).

Wyatt's death on 11 June 1819, in his 69th year, the manufacture was continued first by his son James (1779–1854), and then by the latter's cousin Walter Henry Wyatt (1781–1849). When he died, the firm came to an end. A *Catalogue of Statues, Furniture, Vases, etc.* was published by 'Wyatt, Parker & Co.' in 1841. [*Gent's Mag.* 1819 (i), 589; G. R. Clarke, *History and Description of Ipswich*, 1830, 393; *A.P.S.D.*, *s.v.* 'Parker's Cement', 'Roman Cement' and 'Wyatt's Cement.']

WYATT, CHARLES (*c.* 1759–1819), was the son of James Wyatt's eldest brother William. He obtained a commission in the Bengal Engineers, and rose to the rank of Captain. From 1798 onwards he was employed by the Marquess Wellesley as Governor-General of India to carry out various public works in Calcutta, and in that year it was his designs for the palatial Government House (1799–1804) that were preferred to those submitted by Edward Tiretta, architect to the East India Company. Wyatt's plans were based on James Paine's designs for Kedleston Hall, but with neo-classical detailing and other alterations which give the building a late rather than mid-Georgian character. Wyatt returned to England in 1804 and became M.P. for Sudbury, which he represented in two successive parliaments. After James Wyatt's death in 1813 Charles took over his house in Foley Place, where he died on 13 March 1819, aged 60. [S. Nilsson, *European Architecture in India 1750–1850*, 1968, 101–9, 110; *Gent's Mag.* 1819 (i), 377; correspondence in *C. Life*, 7 Jan. 1949, 1 Nov. 1956; will, P.C.C. ELLENBOROUGH, 2 April 1819.]

WYATT, GEORGE (–1790), may have been a member of the Wyatt family whose pedigree is set out on page 935, but his parentage has not so far been ascertained. The statement in the *Gentleman's Magazine* for 1790 that he was a brother of James Wyatt cannot be substantiated. He was a very successful builder in London, was Surveyor of Paving in the City in the 1770s, and for several years a Common Councillor for the ward of Farringdon Without. He was one of the proprietors of the Albion Mills built by Samuel Wyatt, and lived in the adjoining Albion Place. His niece, Elizabeth Smith, was the wife of Sir John Soane, and it was to the Soanes that Wyatt left all his considerable real property when he died on 23 February 1790. His business was carried on by Thomas Shepherd, his clerk, who died in 1792. [*Gent's Mag.* 1790 (i), 186, 1792 (i), 286; P.C.C. 111 BISHOP.]

WYATT, GEORGE (1782–1856), was the son of Charles Wyatt (d. 1819), the cement manufacturer. He became a pupil of James Wyatt, from whose office he exhibited student's work at the

Royal Acadmy in 1798, 1799 and 1800. He subsequently practised as an architect, at first from Albany, Piccadilly,[1] and later from his father's house in Bedford Row. In 1812 he published *A Compendious Description of a Design for . . . erecting a Third Theatre in the Metropolis*. It was afterwards alleged in the press that Benjamin Dean Wyatt's plans for Drury Lane Theatre were based on these designs of George Wyatt's, an insinuation which Benjamin was at pains to deny in print (above, p. 937). The list of buildings given below show that George Wyatt was a competent designer in both neo-classical and Gothic styles, but he appears to have given up practice early to live in retirement on the profits of the family cement-works.

CULFORD HALL, SUFFOLK, curved Doric portico on entrance front for the 2nd Marquess Cornwallis, 1806–8; since removed [signed drawing dated 1806 belonging to Lord Cadogan, *ex inf.* Mr. J. M. Robinson].

HOWICK HALL, NORTHUMBERLAND, remodelled north front for the 2nd Earl Grey, 1808–9 [exhib. at R.A. 1809; Grey of Howick papers, Prior's Kitchen, Durham].

ROWTON CASTLE, SALOP., remodelled for Col. Richard Lyster, 1810–12, castellated [exhib. at R.A. as 'about to be' carried out in 1809, and as 'lately executed' in 1812].

DEVIZES, WILTS., castellated toll house on Bath Road, 1812 [exhib. at R.A. 1812].

TWIZELL HOUSE, nr. BELFORD, NORTHUMBERLAND, proposed alterations for P. J. Selby, exhibited at R.A. 1812; these probably included the Ionic portico; dem. *c.* 1969.

BROME HALL, SUFFOLK, alterations for the 2nd Marquess Cornwallis, 1815 [letters in the Fytch Collection, Hartismere volume, Ipswich Public Library, *ex inf.* Mr. J. M. Robinson].

WYATT, HENRY JOHN (*c.* 1789–1862), was one of the sons of Edward Wyatt (1757–1833), a second cousin of Samuel and James Wyatt. Edward was a successful carver and gilder with a shop in Oxford Street, and his younger son Richard James Wyatt (1795–1850) became a well-known sculptor. Henry John became a pupil of James Wyatt, attended the Royal Academy Schools, and won the Silver Medal in 1809. He exhibited at the Academy from 1806 to 1828, and was still in practice in London in the 1840s in Sloane Terrace and later in Osnaburgh Street. Having retired to Sussex, he died on 20 July 1862, aged 73, and was buried in the family vault

---

[1] He was at 2 Albany Court Yard from *c.* 1809 to 1812. Lewis Wyatt succeeded him at the same address in 1813 and remained there until 1823. Although George and Lewis were evidently on friendly terms, their successive occupancy of the same premises affords no evidence that they were in practice together.

on the south side of the chancel of Merton Church, Surrey. His few recorded architectural works comprise ST. MARY'S CHURCH, HAMMER-SMITH, 1812–13, remodelled 1883, dem. 1944 [exhib. at R.A. 1812]; a farm-house at BARCOMBE, SUSSEX, exhibited at the R.A. in 1823; and the houses (dem.) at the corner of GREAT GEORGE and DELAHAY STREETS, WESTMINSTER [*A.P.S.D.*].

Henry John Wyatt must not be confused with Henry Wyatt (d. 1899), fourth son of Matthew Cotes Wyatt, the sculptor. His practice was chiefly in Yorkshire, where he enlarged ALDBY PARK (E.R.), 1847–9, rebuilt NEWBY WISKE HALL, *c.* 1850, and was responsible for a number of buildings in SCARBOROUGH, including the castellated SPA, 1837–9, destroyed by fire 1876. [Theakston's *Guide to Scarborough*, 1856; information from the late Miss Emily Wyatt; Aldby Park papers at Borthwick Institute, York.]

WYATT, JAMES (1746–1813), was the sixth son of Benjamin Wyatt of Weeford (*q.v.*). Very little is known about his boyhood, but some early signs of artistic ability must have led to the decision to send him to Italy. A member of the Bagot family of Blithfield who was secretary to the Earl of Northampton's embassy to the Venetian Republic appears to have offered or agreed to take James with him, and if so 1762 will have been the year of his arrival in Venice. There he became a pupil of Antonio Visentini (d. 1782), under whom he made rapid progress as an architectural draughtsman. After two years in Venice, Wyatt moved to Rome, where he is said to have caused some excitement by the intrepidity with which he made measured drawings of the dome of St. Peter's, 'lying on his back on a ladder slung horizontally, without cradle or side-rail, over a frightful void of 300 feet'.

Wyatt returned to England in or about 1768, and for the next few years worked in close association with the family firm, and in particular with his elder brother Samuel. Although he bought with him a first-hand knowledge of both antique and renaissance architecture, the elegant neo-classical style displayed in nearly all the buildings which he designed in the course of the next few years owed much to that of Robert and James Adam, which he was probably able to study at first-hand at Kedleston, where Samuel was master carpenter. Indeed a design by James for a large country house dated 1771 is clearly indebted to the south front of Kedleston, for it features the central bow originally envisaged by Paine with the simpler neo-classical treatment of the elevation substituted by Adam. Heaton Hall, Wyatt's first important country house, was also an elegant simplification of Paine's Kedleston. The building which made Wyatt's reputation was, however, not a country house but the Pantheon in Oxford Street, London. His brother

John, a surgeon, was one of the shareholders, but the choice of a young and almost unknown architect appears to have been due to P. E. Turst, the owner of the site and the principal promoter of the project for a 'Winter Ranelagh'. When the Pantheon was opened in 1772 Turst's choice was endorsed by the fashionable public, and in a moment of enthusiasm Horace Walpole pronounced it to be 'the most beautiful edifice in England'. Externally it presented a conventional Palladian façade to the street, but the basilica-like hall, with its coffered dome, colonnaded aisles and apsidal ends, was something new in assembly rooms, and brought its architect immediate celebrity. The design was exhibited at the Royal Academy, private commissions followed, and at the age of 26 Wyatt found himself a fashionable domestic architect and an Associate of the Royal Academy.

Though the conception of the Pantheon was no doubt entirely due to James Wyatt, its realization was a joint enterprise with his brother Samuel. From 1774 onwards, however, they conducted independent practices, and James soon outstripped his brother in celebrity, becoming in 1776 Surveyor to Westminster Abbey, in 1782 or 1783 Architect to the Board of Ordnance, and in 1796 Surveyor-General and Comptroller of the Office of Works. The royal favour to which Wyatt owed the last appointment dated from 1792–5, when he had rebuilt Frogmore House for Queen Charlotte. In 1793 Farington reported that George III had promised Wyatt the reversion of the surveyorship, and when Sir William Chambers died in 1796 Wyatt was duly given the post. As a royal architect he continued to give satisfaction by his works at Windsor and Kew, while his polished manners and polite accomplishments made him always welcome at Court. But as an administrator he was dilatory, negligent and irresponsible. Persistent neglect of his duties led in 1805 to his dismissal from the post of Deputy Surveyor of the Office of Woods and Forests, which he had held in plurality with the Works since 1799, and only royal favour can have prevented the Treasury from threatening him with dismissal from the Surveyor-General-ship itself. During the last decade of his regime the Office of Works was in a state of disarray, and from 1806 onwards various government enquiries were under way which, but for Wyatt's death, would inevitably have resulted in public disgrace. As it was, the Commissioners of Military Inquiry who investigated the confusion which he left behind him condemned not only the man but also the system which had permitted him to mismanage the royal works for seventeen years. The reforms of 1814 were a direct consequence of Wyatt's incompetence: as Jeffry Wyatt later admitted, his uncle's 'neglect [had] destroyed the Office of Works as it was'.

The unbusinesslike habits which unfitted Wyatt for public office also bedevilled his private practice. At Rome he left the reputation of being an exceptionally talented student who 'did not apply sufficiently to his profession'. In England his early success brought him far more commissions than he could properly attend to. Between 1769 and 1813 he designed or altered several royal palaces, five cathedrals, seventeen other churches, eight colleges and well over a hundred country houses in England, Wales and Ireland.[1] It was more than even a well-organized office could easily manage, and Wyatt, despite numerous pupils and the delegation of some commissions to provincial architects like Potter of Lichfield, could not keep abreast of all the work he undertook. Already in 1776 reported to be 'as difficult of access as a Prime Minister', he became as time went on more and more capricious and inaccessible. When approached by a new client, he would at first take the keenest interest in the commission, but when the work was about to begin he would lose interest in it and 'employ himself upon trifling professional matters which others could do'. This sort of conduct, so Jeffry Wyatt told Farington in 1806, had lost him his uncle 'many great commissions'. Although he endeavoured to supplement his professional income by speculative building in London and by contracting for some of the country houses which he designed (notably Ragley), Wyatt's unbusiness-like methods were not calculated to make a success of such enterprises, and in 1806 William Porden told Farington that Wyatt lost two to three thousand pounds a year 'from mere neglect in respect of order in his accounts'. When he died (intestate) in 1813 he owed £900 to his principal draughtsman, John Dixon, and £2000 to the plasterer Bartolini. His house in Foley Place was mortgaged to the utmost, and his widow, left without means of support, depended for the rest of her life on a pension of £100 granted by Lord Liverpool.

Wyatt was a brilliant but facile designer whose work lacks the consistency of a man dedicated to some definite aesthetic creed. He had, as Porden put it, 'no principles in his own Art', but drew on a wide variety of sources to produce a neoclassical architecture that began in the late Palladian tradition and ended with some acknowledgements to the Greek Revival. What he himself told George III was that 'there had been no regular architecture since Sir William Chambers – that when he came from Italy he

found the public taste corrupted by the Adams, and he was obliged to comply with it'. Indeed he became almost as adept a purveyor of the Adam decorative style as the Adams themselves, and in 1773, when the Adams complained of imitators in the preface to their *Works*, Horace Walpole was quick to detect a hostile reference to Wyatt. Wyatt's decorative repertoire awaits detailed study, but in general his walls and ceilings are apt to be rather more sparsely ornamented than those designed by his rivals. Spatially, the Pantheon was undoubtedly his finest classical interior, but the ceiling of the hall at Heveningham is a brilliant exercise in interpenetrating forms which has no parallel in the Adams' work. Externally, the one consistent feature of Wyatt's domestic style is the prominent bow, often domed, which first appears in his drawing of 1771 and recurs in most of his classical houses. Like his brother Samuel he favoured crisp, clear-cut masonry with the minimum of ornamentation, but unlike Samuel, who preferred astylar façades, he often used an order to accentuate the central feature. The surviving houses that best exemplify these characteristics are Heaton, Bowden, Aston, Castle Coole and Dodington.

Despite his seventeen-year tenure of office as Surveyor of the Works, Wyatt had relatively few opportunities for public works on a large scale. His career as a government architect coincided with the Napoleonic Wars, and his death deprived him of participation in the metropolitan improvements of the Regency period. At Oxford (where he was the favoured architect from the 1770s onwards) there was no major commission to offer him, and at Cambridge his design for Downing College was defeated by a more doctrinaire neo-classicism than he was prepared to conform to.

It was, however, as a Gothic architect that Wyatt enjoyed a special celebrity. Every Georgian architect was called upon from time to time to produce designs in the medieval style, and Wyatt was by no means the first in the field. His success as a Gothicist was due partly to a better knowledge of authentic medieval prototypes than any of his predecessors had displayed, and partly to his success in recapturing the picturesque irregularity which was now seen to be an attractive and characteristic feature of medieval architecture. Of his earliest Gothic work at Beaudesert there appears to be no visual record. But at Sheffield Place, Sandleford Priory and Lee Priory, Wyatt displayed those qualities which were to win him the enthusiastic support of Horace Walpole. Here was something more convincing than the rococo Gothic of the previous generation, something that to Walpole's contemporaries seemed effectively to 'revive the long-forgotten beauties of Gothic architecture'. Soon Wyatt was the acknowledged expert in Gothic design. Shute

---

[1] Wyatt had a hand in several Irish houses in the 1770s, but his first recorded visit to Ireland was in 1785 (see *C. Life*, 21 Feb. 1963, 368, and a letter of 18 Sept. 1785 from Wyatt mentioning his impending journey to Ireland in an extra-illustrated copy of Lysons' *Environs* in the Mellon Collection, vi, f. 596).

Barrington, Bishop successively of Salisbury and Durham, gave him important ecclesiastical commissions, and the millionaire William Beckford employed him to design the fabulous Fonthill Abbey in Wiltshire. At Fonthill Wyatt attempted the sublime, and perhaps achieved it. Fonthill was a rich man's folly that stood alone, but it ranks as the supreme example of ecclesiastical Gothic applied to secular purposes. Wycombe, Ashridge and Wilton were other works in the 'abbey' style, while Belvoir, Norris and Kew were experiments in the 'castle' style. At Belvoir a multiplicity of oriels, towers and turrets ensured a highly picturesque composition, but at Norris the same effect was achieved by the skilful use of simple castellated forms designed to be seen in silhouette, while at Kew Wyatt provided the prototype for a type of symmetrical castle that was to be taken up later by Smirke at Lowther and Eastnor. All these buildings were highly influential in the next generation, and establish Wyatt as a major figure in the history of the Picturesque.

As a restorer and improver of cathedrals, Wyatt's activities were, even in his own day, highly controversial. Here he was actuated by an essentially rationalist approach (akin to that expounded by Laugier) which saw merit in Gothic architecture, but sought to improve it by removing those accidental excrescences which are so characteristic of ancient buildings. Hence his advice, at Salisbury, to emphasize the unity of the thirteenth-century church by removing both external and internal obstructions and by levelling the Close; at Hereford to reduce the nave by one bay in order to give the central tower more centrality; and at Durham to pull the exterior together by demolishing the Galilee and crowning the central tower by a lantern and spire. At all three cathedrals Bishop and Chapter were generally sympathetic to Wyatt's proposals, but his programmes of 'improvement' were bitterly criticized by Richard Gough and John Carter in the *Gentleman's Magazine,* and the antiquarian opposition which they mobilized was instrumental in saving the Durham Galilee and the Neville screen. It was due in large measure to their persistent denunciations that in 1797 Wyatt experienced some difficulty in obtaining election to the Society of Antiquaries (black-balled in September, he was eventually admitted in December). The nineteenth century did not, however, forgive what the eighteenth had condoned, and Wyatt's reputation as the 'Destroyer' has lived on in antiquarian and ecclesiological circles almost to the present day. Although a better understanding of current aesthetic ideas helps to explain Wyatt's proposals, it is still difficult to regard his activities at Lichfield, Hereford, Salisbury and Durham otherwise than as those of an irresponsible meddler.

Wyatt became a full R.A. in 1785, and took an active part in the politics of the Academy. In 1803–4 he was the leader of an opposition party which eventually forced Benjamin West to resign the Presidency. But the rebels had mistaken their man. Wyatt's ambitions were satisfied by his own election as President (1805) and he did nothing to implement the reforms which his party expected. 'He slept in committee, mumbled his speeches, and infuriated political patrons by his "old habits of delay". Within a year West was back in office. Wyatt had merely succeeded in making almost as many enemies in the Royal Academy as he had in the Society of Antiquaries.' He was one of the original members of the Architects' Club founded in 1791, and sometimes presided over its meetings at the Thatched House Tavern.

Wyatt died on 4 September 1813. He was travelling over the Marlborough Downs with his friend and patron Christopher Codrington of Dodington Park, when their carriage was involved in an accident. Wyatt's head struck the roof with great violence and he was killed instantaneously. His body was buried in Westminster Abbey. He left a widow and four sons, of whom the eldest, Benjamin Dean, and the youngest, Philip, are noticed separately. Matthew Cotes (1777–1862), the third son, became a well-known sculptor, whose best work is the bronze statue of George III in Cockspur Street. He was the father of Sir Matthew Wyatt, Lieutenant of the Queen's Gentlemen at Arms, of James Wyatt (d. 1893), a sculptor, and of Henry Wyatt (d. 1899), an architect who practised in Scarborough. Charles Burton, the second son, had a brief career as Surveyor-General of Crown Lands in Canada before he quarrelled with the Governor and was recalled to England, where he eventually entered the wine trade.

Wyatt's first London address was in Great Newport Street. In 1774 he moved to Newman Street, where he remained until 1783, when he took up residence at No. 69 Anne Street East (later 1 Foley Place), which he had built for himself. He also had a country house at Hanworth in Middlesex.

The best portrait of Wyatt is that by Sir William Beechey at the Royal Academy. One by Ozias Humphrey, painted in 1793, and exhibited at the Royal Academy in 1795, was engraved by Singleton in 1796. One by his son Matthew Cotes, which was also engraved, now belongs to his descendants. The National Portrait Gallery has a bronze bust by Rossi, and there is a pencil portrait by George Dance in the Royal Academy Library. There is also a Wedgwood portrait medallion (example in Brooklyn Museum, U.S.A.). Wyatt's principal draughtsman was John Dixon (*q.v.*), who, according to Farington, had been with him from the time of the building of the Pantheon. He had many pupils, of whom the following is an incomplete list: Joseph Badger, junior, William Blogg, Henry Brown, J. M. Gandy, J. P. Gandy, George Hadfield, Charles Humfrey, Henry Kitchen, William Newham, James Parlby, J. Percy, Charles and William Porden, John Rawstorne, J. W. Sanderson, Richard Smith, James Spiller, Thomas Taylor, Thomas and John Westmacott, Michael Wynn, and his own sons Benjamin and Philip Wyatt.

There is no *corpus* of drawings by Wyatt, but a number, from various sources, are in the R.I.B.A. Collection (see the *Catalogue* of Wyatt drawings by D. Linstrum, 1973). There is an album of designs for ceilings in the Metropolitan Museum at New York (see J. Harris, *Catalogue of British Drawings for Architecture, etc., in American Collections*, 1971) and another album of miscellaneous drawings is in the Victoria and Albert Museum. A third album is in the possession of the Vicomte de Noailles (see *C. Life*, 5 Dec. 1947 and 2 July 1948).[1] For other drawings for particular buildings see Appendix A to D. Linstrum's *Catalogue* and the list of Wyatt's works in this *Dictionary*.

Miscellaneous letters and papers of James Wyatt are in the R.I.B.A. Collection (WY.1), the British Museum (Egerton MS. 3515), the Victoria and Albert Museum (MS. 86ZZ.170), and Edinburgh University Library (La. II. 426/529).

[*A.P.S.D.*; *D.N.B.*; *Gent's Mag.* 1813 (ii), 296–7; *Universal Mag.* xx, 1813, 342–3; *The Farington Diary*, ed. J. Greig, *passim*; biographical note in T. F. Hunt, *Architettura Campestre*, 1827, xiii–xvi; A. Dale, *James Wyatt*, 1936; A. Dale, 'James Wyatt and his Sons', *Architect and Building News* cxciii, 26 March 1948, 294–6; R. Turnor, *James Wyatt*, 1950 (a slight work); A. Dale, *James Wyatt*, 1956 (a revised version of the book published in 1936); John Summerson, 'The Classical Country House in 18th-Century England', *Journal of the Royal Society of Arts* cvii, July 1959, 564–6; David Watkin, *Thomas Hope and the Neo-Classical Ideal*, 1968, 61, 245–7, 277; C. L. Eastlake, *A History of the Gothic Revival*, ed. J. M. Crook, 1970, introduction, 52–3; J. M. Crook, *The Greek Revival*, 1972, 75–6, 79, 132; Derek Linstrum, Introduction to *The Wyatt Family* (R.I.B.A. Drawings Catalogue), 1973; J. M. Robinson, 'The Evolution of the Wyatt Style', *C. Life*, 20 Dec. 1973.]

PUBLIC BUILDINGS, ETC.

LONDON, THE PANTHEON, OXFORD STREET, 1769–72; altered by Wyatt as a theatre for the Italian Opera 1790–1; destroyed by fire Jan. 1792;

rebuilt to serve its original purpose as a 'Winter Ranelagh' in 1794–5, retaining Wyatt's original entrance-fronts to Oxford and Poland Streets; reconstructed by N. W. Cundy as the Pantheon Theatre 1811–12; remodelled by S. Smirke as the Pantheon Bazaar, 1833–4; closed 1867 and converted into a wine-store; dem. 1937 [A. T. Bolton, 'The Pantheon', *London Topographical Record* xiii, 1923; *Survey of London* xxxi, chap. xiii].

EXETER, DEVON, THE SESSIONS HOUSE: Wyatt revised a design for the façade submitted by Messrs. Stowey & Jones (*q.v.*), eliminating the proposed pilasters and entablature and altering the proportions, 1773 [Devon County Records, File A5/166/22] (A. E. Richardson & C. L. Gill, *Regional Architecture of the West of England*, 1924, 100).

OXFORD, CHRIST CHURCH: CANTERBURY QUADRANGLE and GATEWAY, 1773–83; alterations to HALL, including staircase and panelling, 1801–4, Gothic; restoration of rooms in south-east corner of TOM QUADRANGLE after fire in March 1809 [R. Ackermann, *History of the University of Oxford* ii, 1814, 79; W. G. Hiscock, *A Christ Church Miscellany*, 1946, 204, 208–9].

OXFORD, WORCESTER COLLEGE, completed interior of HALL and CHAPEL after death of Henry Keene in 1776. The Hall was completed in 1784, the Chapel *c.* 1790. W. Burges redecorated the Chapel in 1863–4, the Hall in 1877, but Wyatt's decoration in the latter was restored in 1966 [*V.C.H. Oxon.* iii, 308; H. M. Colvin, *Catalogue of Architectural Drawings . . . in the Library of Worcester College, Oxford*, 1964, 62].

OXFORD, THE RADCLIFFE OBSERVATORY, completion after death of Henry Keene, 1776–94. In 1773 the Trustees had ordered Keene to follow 'another Elevation' which was probably Wyatt's, and after his death they directed Keene's son to complete the building 'under the direction of Mr. Wyatt'. The globe surmounting the building bears an inscription giving the names of 'James Wyatt, Esq. R.A. Architect, James Pears Esq. Mayor of Oxford Builder & John Bacon Esq. R.A. Sculptor' [C. Hussey, 'The Radcliffe Observatory', *C. Life*, 10 May 1930].

OXFORD, NEW COLLEGE: remodelled UPPER LIBRARY, 1778; re-roofed and ceiled HALL, 1786 (re-roofed by Sir Gilbert Scott 1865–6); re-roofed and refitted CHAPEL in Gothic style, 1789–94 (re-roofed and refitted by Scott 1877–81) [*V.C.H. Oxon.* iii, 147–9].

OXFORD, BRASENOSE COLLEGE, remodelled interior of LIBRARY, 1779–80 [*Brasenose Quatercentenary Monographs* iii, 1909, 34–5].

OXFORD, THE MUSIC SCHOOL, HOLYWELL, rearranged interior, 1780 [*The Magdalen College Register*, ed. Bloxam, ii, 1857, 222].

[1] A microfilm of the album is at the R.I.B.A. Drawings Collection.

CHICHESTER, SUSSEX, interior of ASSEMBLY ROOMS at rear of Council Chamber, 1781–3 [J. Dallaway, *Western Division of Sussex* i, 1815, 170].

PETWORTH, SUSSEX, THE COUNTY BRIDEWELL, 1785–8; altered by G. Moneypenny 1816; dem. 1835 [J. Dallaway, *Western Division of Sussex*, ed. Cartwright, ii (i), 1832, vii–x and plate].

ROMFORD, ESSEX, THE WORKHOUSE, 1786; dem. [Essex Record Office, D/DQ 75].

OXFORD, BODLEIAN LIBRARY, fitted up the room known as the AUCTARIUM, 1787; altered 1953 [Minutes of the Curators of the Bodleian Library, 1786–7].

attributed: LONDON, WHITE'S CLUB, ST. JAMES'S STREET, 1787–8; façade altered 1850 [*Survey of London* xxx, 452–3].

OXFORD, ORIEL COLLEGE, LIBRARY and COMMON ROOM, 1788–9 [J. Ingram, *Memorials of Oxford* i, 1837, 'Oriel College', 14].

LIVERPOOL, THE EXCHANGE (now TOWN HALL), enlarged by John Foster to Wyatt's designs, 1789–92; in 1795 the interior was destroyed by fire and rebuilt by Foster under Wyatt's direction. The dome and cupola were added in 1802, the portico in 1811 [J. A. Picton, *Liverpool Municipal Records 1700–1835*, 1886, 265–72] (*C. Life*, 23 July 1927).

OXFORD, MERTON COLLEGE, remodelled HALL in Gothic style, 1790–1; remodelled by Sir Gilbert Scott 1872–4 [J. Ingram, *Memorials of Oxford* i, 1837, 'Merton College', 12–13].

OXFORD, MAGDALEN COLLEGE, re-roofed CHAPEL, 1790–3 (altered by Cottingham 1830–2), and inserted plaster vault in HALL, 1790–5 (removed 1903) [*The Magdalen College Register*, ed. Bloxam, ii, 1857, clxxxvi–clxxxix, cxcv–ccii; T. S. R. Boase, 'An Oxford College and the Gothic Revival', *Jnl. of the Warburg and Courtauld Institutes* xviii, 1955].

BRISTOL, design for CRESCENT in TYNDALL'S PARK, begun 1793 but never completed [W. Ison, *The Georgian Buildings of Bristol*, 1952, 26–7].

OXFORD, BALLIOL COLLEGE, altered HALL and refitted LIBRARY with plaster Gothic vault, 1792–4 [*V.C.H. Oxon*, iii, 92–3].

LONDON, WEEKS'S MUSEUM, TICHBORNE STREET, for Thomas Weeks, *c.* 1795; dem. 1885 [by 'Wyatt': *Survey of London* xxxi, 54–5].

BIRMINGHAM, THE HEN AND CHICKENS HOTEL, NEW STREET, 1798; dem. [*Aris's Birmingham Gazette*, 26 March 1798].

RIPON, YORKS. (W.R.), THE TOWN HALL, 1798–9 [anon. *History of Ripon*, 1801, 58].

WESTMINSTER PALACE: cut away walls of HOUSE OF COMMONS to provide extra accommodation for the Irish members, 1800–1; fitted up Court of Requests for accommodation of HOUSE OF LORDS, 1800–1; reconstructed SPEAKER'S HOUSE, 1802–8; and constructed Gothic façade to offices on east side of OLD PALACE YARD; all

destroyed by fire 1834 except Speaker's House, which was dem. 1842 [*History of the King's Works* vi, 517–19, 526, 532–4].

THE LAZARETTO, CHETNEY HILL, IWADE, KENT, 1800–6; dem. 1820 [*History of the King's Works* vi, 448–51].

ROYAL MILITARY ACADEMY, WOOLWICH, *c.* 1800–6, castellated; damaged by fire 1873 [D. Lysons, *Environs of London* i (2), 1811, 596].

WOOLWICH, THE ROYAL ARTILLERY BARRACKS, additional BARRACKS and RIDING SCHOOL, 1802–8 [*A.P.S.D.*].

LIVERPOOL, LANCS., THE NEW EXCHANGE: Wyatt may have had some share in the design of this building by John Foster, 1803–9; dem. *c.* 1863 [above, p. 316].

DERBY, THE ORDNANCE DEPOT (later used as a factory), 1804–5; dem. [R. Simpson, *Collection of Fragments illustrative of the History of Derby* i, 1826, 530].

LONDON, DORSET HOUSE, WHITEHALL, alterations to government offices, 1804–8; dem. 1845–6 [*History of the King's Works* vi, 550–1].

GREAT YARMOUTH, NORFOLK, THE NAVAL ARSENAL, 1806 [J. Chambers, *Norfolk Tour* i, 1829, 276].

SHREWSBURY, THE ARMOURY, 1806 [S. Lewis, *Topographical Dictionary of England* iv, 1831, 71].

LONDON, THE BANQUETTING HOUSE (then CHAPEL ROYAL), WHITEHALL, added staircase at north end, 1808–9 [*History of the King's Works* vi, 545–6].

BADBY SCHOOL, NORTHANTS., for the Dowager Lady Knightley, *c.* 1812, Gothic [G. Baker, *History of Northants* i, 1822, 257].

ECCLESIASTICAL WORKS

BURTON–ON–TRENT CHURCH, STAFFS., organ-case, 1771; altered 1902 [signed drawing in R.I.B.A.D.].

LONDON, KENTISH TOWN EPISCOPAL CHAPEL (now PARISH CHURCH), LOWER CRAVEN PLACE, 1784–5; remodelled by J. H. Hakewill 1843–5 [T. Hope, *Observations on the Plans and Elevations by James Wyatt for Downing College, Cambridge*, 1804, 34; unsigned drawings in Hampstead Public Library, Heal Collection, A.5, 31, 32, 37].

LICHFIELD CATHEDRAL, STAFFS., survey, 1787, followed by repairs and improvements, 1788–93, including replacement of five divisions of vaulting in nave with plaster, rearrangement and refitting of choir, etc. The work was carried out by Joseph Potter (*q.v.*). It was all undone by Sir Gilbert Scott from 1856 onwards [J. Britton, *History of the Cathedral Church of Lichfield*, 1820; drawings by Wyatt in William Salt Library, Stafford, Staffordshire Views, vi, 102, 104, 105].

SALISBURY CATHEDRAL, WILTS., survey, 1787, and alterations to Cathedral, 1789–92, including destruction of north and south porches to transepts and of Hungerford and Beauchamp Chantries, rearrangement of interior, levelling of Close and demolition of detached belfry [W. Dodsworth, *A Guide to the Cathedral Church of Salisbury, with a particular account of the late Great Improvements made therein under the direction of James Wyatt, Esq.*, 1792; *Gent's Mag.* 1789 (ii), 873–4, 1042, 1064–6, 1194–6].

MANCHESTER, ST. PETER'S CHURCH, MOSLEY STREET, 1788–94; tower and spire added by F. Goodwin 1824; dem. 1906–7 [W. E. A. Axon, *Annals of Manchester*, 1886, 115–16].

HEREFORD CATHEDRAL, repairs following the collapse of the west tower and west end of the nave in 1786–7. Between 1788 and 1796 Wyatt rebuilt the west end of the nave, which was shortened by one bay, together with the whole of the nave triforium, clerestorey and vault. He also remodelled the central tower. The west front was again rebuilt by J. O. Scott in 1904–8 [J. Britton, *History of the Cathedral Church of Hereford*, 1831; G. Marshall, *Hereford Cathedral*, Worcester *c*. 1950].

MARCHWIEL CHURCH, DENBIGHSHIRE, steeple built at expense of Philip Yorke of Erddig, 1789 [John Jones, *Wrexham and its Neighbourhood*, 1868, 66; Erddig archives, payment of 15 gns. to 'Wyat' for 'plan of Church and monument' 1788, *ex inf*. Mr. Gervase Jackson-Stops].

EAST GRINSTEAD CHURCH, SUSSEX, 1789, Gothic; tower completed 1811–13 by J. T. Groves (*q.v.*) [W. H. Wills, *History of East Grinstead*, 1906, 66–7].

MILTON ABBAS, DORSET, restoration of ABBEY CHURCH for the 1st Lord Milton, 1789–91 [J. Hutchins, *History of Dorset* iv, 1873, 405; *Diary and Letters of Fanny Burney*, ed. Dobson, v, 1904–5, 14] (R.C.H.M., *Dorset* iii (2), 184–9).

attributed: MONGEWELL CHURCH, OXON., remodelled for Shute Barrington, Bishop of Durham, 1791, Gothic; altered 1880, now ruinous [Barrington was one of Wyatt's principal patrons, employing him at Salisbury, Durham and Bishop Auckland].

COVENTRY, WARWICKS., ST. MICHAEL'S CHURCH, repair of tower, carried out by Joseph Potter (*q.v.*), 1794 [T. Sharpe, *Illustrations of the History of St. Michael's Church, Coventry*, 1818, 48–9].

LONDON, LINCOLN'S INN CHAPEL, renewed roof and east window, 1795–6, Gothic [*The Black Books of Lincoln's Inn* iv, 53, 55–6, 58–60, 65; *The Farington Diary*, ed. J. Greig, i, 213].

DURHAM CATHEDRAL, survey, 1795, followed by repair of east end of Cathedral, 1797–1805, and controversial proposals for rearrangement of choir, demolition of Galilee, new central spire, etc., which were not carried out [R. A. Cordingley, 'Cathedral Innovations: James Wyatt at Durham Cathedral 1795–7', *Ancient Monuments Society's Trans.*, N.S. iii, 1955].

BISHOP AUCKLAND, DURHAM, ST. ANNE'S CHAPEL in Market Place: the Gothic west tower built *c*. 1800 by W. Atkinson (*q.v.*) and dem. 1847 with the rest of the chapel was probably based on a design made by Wyatt in 1796 [signed drawing at Auckland Castle, *ex inf*. Mr. J. M. Frew].

AMLWCH CHURCH, ANGLESEY, Gothic, was probably based on a design made by Wyatt *c*. 1790 but not carried out until 1800 owing to obstruction by the bishop [*A Letter to the Right Rev. Dr. Warren by Shôn Gwialan*, 1796, 61 *et seq.*, *ex inf*. Prof. M. L. Clarke].

ELY CATHEDRAL, CAMBS., repairs in association with J. T. Groves (*q.v.*), 1800–2 [above, p. 367; for Wyatt's report of 1796 see A. Gibbons, *Calendar of the Episcopal Records . . . at Ely*, 1891, 113].

WINDSOR, BERKS., ST. GEORGE'S CHAPEL, repairs to TOMB HOUSE (now ALBERT MEMORIAL CHAPEL), 1800–4, and formation of royal burial vault, 1804–10 [W. H. St. J. Hope, *Architectural History of Windsor Castle*, 1913, 408, 486, 489; *History of the King's Works* vi, 379].

ST. KEA CHURCH, CORNWALL, 1802, Gothic; dem. 1895 [W. Paraluna, *The Circle, or Historical Survey of Sixty Parishes in Cornwall*, 1819; Lake's *Parochial History of Cornwall*, 1867–73, ii, 318].

EGLWYS NEWYDD, HAFOD, CADIGANSHIRE, for Thomas Johnes, 1803, Gothic; badly damaged by fire 1932 [B. H. Malkin, *The Scenery, etc., of S. Wales*, 1804; S. R. Meyrick, *History and Antiquities of the County of Cardigan*, 1810, 347].

WEEFORD CHURCH, STAFFS., 1803–4; Gothic; chancel rebuilt 1876 [correspondence about erection of church in William Salt Library, Stafford, MS. M. 96; variant drawings signed 'J.W.' 1803 and 1805 in Vestry].

WESTMINSTER ABBEY, arrangements for Handel Festival, 1784 [*Gent's Mag.* 1784 (i), 391–2]; rebuilt vault of central tower in Bernasconi's composition after fire of July 1803, destroyed by bombing 1941; directed refacing of Henry VII's Chapel by Thomas Gayfere (*q.v.*), 1809 onwards [J. P. Neale & E. W. Brayley, *Westminster Abbey* i, 1818, 'Henry VII's Chapel', 21–7, ii, 1823, 148].

DODINGTON CHURCH, GLOS., for Christopher Codrington, *c*. 1800–5 [forms part of the outbuildings of Dodington Park, for which see below, p. 950].

HANWORTH CHURCH, MIDDLESEX, designed 1808, built 1815–16 under the direction of B. D. Wyatt, Gothic; rebuilt by S. S. Teulon 1865 [Trustees' Minutes in G.L.C. Record Office, DRO 18/B3/1].

945

COUNTRY HOUSES, ETC.

GADDESDEN PLACE, GREAT GADDESDEN, HERTS., for Thomas Halsey, 1768–74; interior rebuilt after fire in 1903; wings dem. 1960 [J. E. Cussans, *History of Hertfordshire* iii, 1879, 121, and designs for ceilings in the Wyatt album in the Metropolitan Museum]. Cussans says the house was completed in 1774, and the date 1768 is scratched on a wall. The conventional Palladian detailing should be compared with the exterior of the Pantheon as illustrated in *Survey of London* xxxii, pl. 20a.

GUNTON HALL, NORFOLK, enlarged house and designed offices for Harbord Harbord, cr. Lord Suffield, soon after 1770 [Anon., *History of Norfolk* iii, 1781, 66; J. P. Neale, *Views of Seats*, 1st ser., iii, 1820].

FAWLEY COURT, BUCKS., interior decoration and ISLAND TEMPLE for Sambrook Freeman, 1771 [*Passages from the Diary of Mrs. Lybbe Powys*, ed. Climenson, 1899, 145–8].

HAGLEY HALL, STAFFS., octagonal drawing-room for Assheton Curzon, 1771; dem. *c.* 1932 [ceiling exhib. at R.A. 1771; G. Beard, *Decorative Plasterwork in Great Britain*, 1975, 244].

BEAUDESERT, STAFFS., remodelling of interior for the 1st Earl of Uxbridge, executed by Benjamin Wyatt & Sons, 1771–2, partly Gothic; Gothic hall altered by Joseph Potter 1826–31; dem. *c.* 1925 [accounts in Staffs. Record Office, *ex inf.* Mr. J. M. Frew; unsigned plan dated 1771 in William Salt Library, Stafford, Staffordshire Views, i, 154; G. Beard, *Decorative Plasterwork in Great Britain*, 1975, 239, for references to 'Mr. Wyatt's design 1771' in sketch-book of the plasterer Joseph Rose].

HEATON HOUSE, LANCS., rebuilt for Sir Thomas Egerton, Bart., cr. Earl of Wilton, *c.* 1772 [exhib. at R.A. 1772] (*C. Life*, 29 Aug., 5 Sept. 1925; H. A. Tipping, *English Homes*, V (ii), 199–218; *Heaton Hall, Manchester: Bicentenary Exhibition*, 1972).

ERDDIG PARK, DENBIGHSHIRE, was consulted about the alterations carried out for Philip Yorke in 1773–4 [Erddig archives, *ex inf.* Mr. G. Jackson-Stops], and is credited with responsibility for them by J. Evans, *Beauties of England and Wales* xvii (i), 1812, 589, and *Cambrian Traveller's Guide*, 1813, 1161 (*C. Life*, 16–23 Aug. 1930).

ALDWARK HALL, YORKS. (W.R.), designs for ceilings for Francis Foljambe, 1773–5; dem. 1899 [drawings in R.I.B.A. Collection (dated 1775), Wyatt Album in Metropolitan Museum (undated), and Pierpont Morgan Library (dated 1773)].

ABBEYLEIX, CO. LEIX, IRELAND, for the 2nd Lord Knapton, 1773–6; exterior refaced by T. H. Wyatt in nineteenth century [drawings by Wyatt in National Library of Ireland, LR

72884, and Metropolitan Museum, New York, Wyatt Album, no. 43] (T. U. Sadleir & P. L. Dickinson, *Georgian Mansions in Ireland*, 1915, 10–16 and pl. 1; D. Guinness & W. Ryan, *Irish Houses and Castles*, 1971, 225–32).

AUBREY HOUSE, NOTTING HILL, nr. LONDON, redecorated drawing-room for Lady Mary Coke, 1774 [*Letters and Journals of Lady Mary Coke* iv, 1896, 398–9, 438–9, 446] (*C. Life*, 2–9 May 1957).

COPPED HALL, ESSEX, internal alterations and redecoration for John Conyers, 1775–7; damaged by fire 1917 [drawings by Wyatt in Essex Record Office, D/DWE. 38–9; Brayley & Britton, *Beauties of England and Wales* v, 1803, 431] (*C. Life*, 29 Oct., 5 Nov. 1910).

attributed: WINNINGTON HALL, CHESHIRE, enlargement for Richard Pennant, cr. Lord Penrhyn, *c.* 1775 [C. Hussey in *C. Life*, 8 Sept. 1923; A. S. Irvine, *A History of Winnington Hall*, I.C.I. 1951, 23].

SHARDELOES, nr. AMERSHAM, BUCKS., decoration of walls of library (with paintings by Rebecca), *c.* 1775, and garden pavilion, 1785–6, for William Drake [Bucks. Record Office, Shardeloes papers D/Dr. 5/43, 61, 69a; G. Eland, *Shardeloes Papers*, 1937, 135; John Harris in *Connoisseur* cxlviii, 1961, 269–75].

MILTON ABBEY, DORSET, decoration of rooms on first floor and bookcases in library for 1st Lord Milton, 1775–6 [drawings in R.I.B.A. Coll.; Arthur Oswald in *C. Life*, 28 July 1966].

BELTON HOUSE, LINCS., removed cupola and balustrade from roof (both restored 1872–93) and designed interiors of drawing-room (now library) and boudoir for the 1st Lord Brownlow, 1776 [J. Britton, *Beauties of England and Wales* ix, 1807, 772] (*C. Life*, 17 Sept. 1964).

BURTON CONSTABLE, YORKS. (E.R.), interior of drawing-room, 1776, and the castellated Old Lodge, 1785–6, for William Constable [drawings at Burton Constable, nos. 9 and 12; G. Poulson, *History of Holderness* ii, 1841, 242; Geoffrey Webb in *C. Life*, 27 Aug., 3 Sept. 1932].

ARDBRACCAN HOUSE, CO. MEATH, IRELAND: Wyatt is credited by J. N. Brewer, *The Beauties of Ireland* ii, 1826, 189, with the design of the central block for Henry Maxwell, Bishop of Meath, 1776. Brewer says that the building was erected under the direction of the amateur architect, the Rev. Daniel Augustus Beaufort. Beaufort's surviving drawings suggest that he rather than Wyatt was the effective architect [C. C. Ellison, 'Remembering Dr. Beaufort', Irish Georgian Society's *Bulletin* xviii, no. 1, 1975, 13–14].

DOWNHILL, CO. LONDONDERRY, IRELAND, is said to have been built *c.* 1776–9 for Frederick Hervey, Bishop of Derry, by the Irish architect Michael Shanahan in accordance with a plan 'first made by Mr. James Wyatt of London'. That Wyatt had some share in the design is confirmed by references in the Hervey papers in the West Suffolk Record Office. The house was damaged by fire in 1851 and unroofed in 1950 [P. Rankin, *Irish Building Ventures of the Earl Bishop of Derry*, Ulster Architectural Heritage Soc. 1972, 15–17, and in *C. Life*, 8–15 July 1971].

SHEFFIELD PLACE, SUSSEX, remodelled for J. B. Holroyd, cr. Earl of Sheffield, *c.* 1776–7, and further alterations, especially to south front, *c.* 1780–90; Gothic [Holroyd papers in East Sussex Record Office, 5440/55, 58 and 63, *ex inf.* Mr. J. M. Frew; engraving dated 1779 in W. Watts, *Seats of the Nobility and Gentry*, showing first stage of work complete; W. Angus, *Seats of the Nobility and Gentry*, pl. xxvi, 1791, showing further additions].

HOTHFIELD PLACE, KENT, for the 8th Earl of Thanet, 1776–80; dem. 1954 [design for a ceiling by Wyatt dated 1776 in Victoria and Albert Museum; A. Dale, *James Wyatt*, 1956, 43].

ROEHAMPTON GROVE (now Froebel Institute), PUTNEY, SURREY, for Sir Joshua Vanneck, 1777; enlarged by W. Burn 1851 [J. P. Neale, *Views of Seats*, 2nd ser., iii, 1826].

NUTHALL TEMPLE, NOTTS., interior decoration for Sir Charles Sedley, Bart., before 1778; dem. 1929 [three designs for ceilings inscribed 'Sir Charles Sedley' in Wyatt album, Metropolitan Museum; cf. *C. Life*, 25 April 1923, figs. 7, 9, 11].

BROOME PARK, KENT, internal decoration of saloon, etc., for Sir Henry Oxenden, Bart., 1778 [W. Angus, *Seats of the Nobility and Gentry*, pl. xviii, 1789; H. A. Tipping in *C. Life*, 6 July 1907].

BRYANSTON HOUSE, nr. BLANDFORD, DORSET, for H. W. B. Portman, 1778; rebuilt by Norman Shaw 1890 [W. Watts, *Seats of the Nobility and Gentry*, pl. lxxxiii, 1786].

KELMARSH HALL, NORTHANTS., design for interior decoration for William Hanbury, *c.* 1778. A design for a dining-room ceiling by Wyatt is in the album in the Metropolitan Museum, but it is not known whether it was executed, as the interior of the house was entirely redecorated in 1928–9 (see *C. Life*, 25 Feb. 1933). Wyatt's design for gate-lodges, dated 1778, was carried out in 1965 by Col. C. Lancaster (see *Northants. Past and Present* iv, 1966–7, 16).

CHELSEA FARM (CREMORNE HOUSE), CHELSEA, MIDDLESEX, enlarged for the 1st Viscount Cremorne, soon after 1778; dem. 1878 [T. Faulkner, *Chelsea* i, 1829, 65].

CURRAGHMORE, CO. WATERFORD, IRELAND, interiors of dining-room, staircase, library, etc., for the 1st Marquess of Waterford, *c.* 1778–80 [drawings in Wyatt album, Metropolitan

Museum; Mark Girouard in *C. Life*, 14–21 Feb. 1963; for the date of Wyatt's work see diary of Rev. Daniel Augustus Beaufort quoted in Irish Georgian Society's *Bulletin* xviii (i), 1975, 28].

BLAGDON, NORTHUMBERLAND, stables and interior of dining-room, etc., for Sir Matthew White Ridley, Bart., 1778–91 [C. Hussey in *C. Life*, 18–25 July 1952].

BADGER HALL, SALOP., remodelled for Isaac Hawkins Browne, 1779–83; dem. 1952 [R.I.B.A.D.]. A classical 'pigeon house' designed by Wyatt after the Tower of the Winds at Athens survives.

RAGLEY HALL, WARWICKS., altered house and designed stable-court for the 1st Marquess of Hertford, 1779–1797 [Ragley papers, Warwick County Record Office, CR 114 A/194, 202, 203, 220/17–20, 195, 196, 197; B.M., Egerton MS. 3515, f. 13]. The date of the portico is not clear, but it presumably formed part of Wyatt's works. (*C. Life*, 22–29 March 1924, 1–8 May 1958).

NORTON PRIORY, CHESHIRE, remodelled for Sir Richard Brooke, Bart. (d. 1781) 'in his latter years'; dem. 1928 [B. Burke, *Visitation of Seats and Arms* ii, 1853, 171–2; H. W. Thompson in *Archaeological Jnl.* cxxiii, 1966, 62–8].

HARTWELL HOUSE, BUCKS., completed the bridge (dem.) designed by Henry Keene (*q.v.*) and made designs for offices for Sir William Lee, Bart., 1780 [W. H. Smyth, *Addenda to the Ædes Hartwellianae*, 1864, 21; designs for offices in Bodleian, MS. Top. Gen. b.55].

NEW (ROUNDWAY) PARK, nr. DEVIZES, WILTS., for James Sutton, *c.* 1780; dem. 1955 [exhib. at R.A. in 1784 by Wyatt's draughtsman Dixon as 'lately built by Mr. Wyatt'; J. P. Neale, *Views of Seats*, 1st ser., v, 1822].

HEVENINGHAM HALL, SUFFOLK, completed interior for Sir Gerard Vanneck, Bart., after dismissal of Sir Robert Taylor (*q.v.*), *c.* 1780–4 [F. Shoberl, *Beauties of England and Wales* xiv, 1813, 360; C. Hussey, *English Country Houses: Mid Georgian*, 1956, 165—76].

HURSTBOURNE PARK, HANTS., for the 2nd Earl of Portsmouth, *c.* 1780–5; destroyed by fire 1870 [Harrison's *Views of Seats*, 1787, where it is stated to have been executed to Wyatt's designs by John Meadows, *q.v.*].

SANDLEFORD PRIORY, nr. NEWBURY, BERKS., remodelled for Mrs. Elizabeth Montagu, 1780–9, Gothic [S. Lysons, *Magna Britannia* i, 1806, 353; *Mrs. Montagu: her letters and friendships*, ed. R. Blunt, ii, 1923, 104, 108–9, 177, 201, 292].

WESTPORT, CO. MAYO, IRELAND, interior of dining-room, 1781, and design for greenhouse, 1796, for the 1st Marquess of Sligo [Mark Girouard in *C. Life*, 29 April, 6 May 1965].

PISHIOBURY PARK, HERTS., remodelled for Jeremiah Milles, 1782–4, externally Gothic [J. P. Neale, *Views of Seats*, 1st ser., iv, 1821; J. Cussans, *History of Hertfordshire* i, 1870–3, 80].

MOUNT KENNEDY, CO. WICKLOW, IRELAND, for General Robert Cunninghame, cr. Lord Rossmore, built by T. Cooley *c.* 1782 in accordance with designs made by Wyatt in 1772 [drawings in National Library of Ireland, LR 72884; J. Cornforth in *C. Life*, 28 Oct., 11 Nov. 1965].

MOUNT STEWART, CO. DOWN, IRELAND, designs for house and stables for the 1st Marquess of Londonderry, 1783, probably not executed [Londonderry papers in P.R.O. N. Ireland at Belfast, D 654/H 1/1, p. 39, and drawings for stables in D 671/M71/4, *ex inf.* Dr. Alistair Rowan]. The existing house was built in the 1840s.

attributed: WETHERBY (or MICKLETHWAITE) GRANGE, YORKS. (W.R.), for Beilby Thompson, *c.* 1784; dem. *c.* 1962 [stylistic attribution, supported by a letter from John Carr to Beilby Thompson dated 9 Feb. 1784 about 'the alterations you have made to the great Mr. Wyatt's plan' (Leeds City Library archives dept., Lane-Fox deeds cxviii, 18). Alternative designs by Carr dated 1772 and 1783 exist in the same collection, but they were not adopted, and the house as built was a characteristic Wyatt design (H. Speight, *Lower Wharfedale*, 1902, 439).

THIRKLEBY PARK, YORKS. (N.R.), for Sir Thomas Frankland, Bart., *c.* 1785–7; dem. 1927 [J. P. Neale, *Views of Seats*, 1st ser., v, 1822; design for ceiling in Wyatt album, Metropolitan Museum].

SUDBOURNE HALL, SUFFOLK, for the 1st Marquess of Hertford, *c.* 1784; refaced in brick 1872–3; remodelled internally *c.* 1905; dem. 1953 [F. Shoberl, *Beauties of England and Wales* xiv, 1813, 326] (*C. Life*, 23 Feb. 1901).

WYNNSTAY, DENBIGHSHIRE, alterations to south front begun for Sir Watkin Williams-Wynn, Bart., *c.* 1785–9, but not completed owing to Wynn's death (1789); destroyed by fire 1858; also column in park to Wynn's memory, *c.* 1790 [Peter Howell & T. W. Pritchard in *C. Life*, 30 March, 6 April 1972].

SLANE CASTLE, CO. MEATH, IRELAND, for the 2nd Lord Conyngham, 1785–6, castellated [A. Rowan, 'Georgian Castles in Ireland', *Bulletin of the Irish Georgian Soc.* vii (i), 1964, 16–17].

FORNHAM HALL, SUFFOLK, for Sir Charles Kent, Bart., *c.* 1785; dem. *c.* 1951 [drawings by Wyatt in Victoria and Albert Museum and Wyatt album, Metropolitan Museum] (H. Davy, *Views of Seats in Suffolk*, 1827; H. R. Barker, *West Suffolk Illustrated*, 1907, 143–4).

LEE PRIORY, ICKHAM, KENT, remodelled for Thomas Barrett, *c.* 1785–90, Gothic; altered by Sir Gilbert Scott *c.* 1865; dem. 1955 (por-

tion of interior re-erected in Victoria and Albert Museum) [E. Hasted, *History of Kent* iii, 1790, 665; exhibited at R.A. 1785 by Dixon, Wyatt's draughtsman, as 'built from the designs of James Wyatt'; working drawings in Victoria and Albert Museum, 93 D.59] (*C. Life*, 30 May 1952, 1665–6).

STANSTEAD HOUSE, SUSSEX, remodelled, with Joseph Bonomi, for Richard Barwell, 1786–91; destroyed by fire 1900 [J. Dallaway, *Western Division of Sussex* ii, 1815, 159].

CHEVENING HOUSE, KENT, refronted with pilasters and mathematical tiles for the 3rd Earl Stanhope, 1786–96; tiles removed *c.* 1970 [Stanhope papers at Chevening, 1042, accounts of A. Penberthey, 'Mr. Wyatt's building surveyor'] (*C. Life*, 17, 24 April, 1 May 1920, 11 June 1959).

GOODWOOD HOUSE, SUSSEX, works for the 3rd Duke of Richmond, 1787 onwards, including the Kennels, 1787, the enlargement of the house, and various other buildings, including the dower house known as Molecombe, *c.* 1790–1806 [F. Shoberl, *The Beauties of England and Wales* xiv, 1813, 69; W. H. Mason, *Goodwood*, 1839, 168] (*C. Life*, 9–16 July 1932).

GIDEA HALL, ESSEX, bridge in park and 'temple for a cold-bath' for Richard Benyon, before 1788 [*Picturesque Views of Seats*, Harrison & Co., 1788]. The bridge survives in Raphael Park, Romford.

AMMERDOWN HOUSE, SOMERSET, for T. S. Jolliffe, 1788; enlarged 1857, 1877 and 1901 [C. Hussey in *C. Life*, 16 Feb., 2–9 March 1929].

GREAT MILTON HOUSE, OXON., enlarged for Sir John Skynner, 1788 (or for the Hon. Richard Ryder, *c.* 1806?) [Thomas Ellis, *Some Account of Great Milton*, Oxford 1819, 18; rainwater heads dated 1788].

BELMONT HOUSE, CLEHONGER, HEREFS., for John Matthews, 1788–90; dem. in nineteenth century [J. Price, *Historical Account of the City of Hereford*, 1796, 191; E. W. Brayley & J. Britton, *Beauties of England and Wales* vi, 1805, 586].

COBHAM HALL, KENT, works for the 4th Earl of Darnley, including stables, 1789–90, pilasters, etc., in Gilt Hall, 1791–3, Gothic dairy, 1794–5, alterations to north wing, 1802–4, interiors of picture gallery and dining-room, 1805–10 [Darnley papers in Kent Record Office, *ex inf.* Mr. J. M. Frew; drawings in Cambridge University School of Architecture]. There is no evidence of Wyatt's employment at Cobham before the early 1780s, when he designed the Mausoleum (below, p. 952). He appears to have been first employed by the 4th Earl, who inherited in 1781, succeeding William Chambers and George Shakespear, the architects employed by the 3rd Earl in the 1760s and

1770s (cf. E. Wingfield-Stratford, *The Lords of Cobham Hall*, 1959, 259–60).

SYON HOUSE, MIDDLESEX, castellated stables, 1789–90, and iron bridge in park, 1790, for the 2nd Duke of Northumberland [accounts for stables in Percy archives, Alnwick, U.III. 5(28), signed drawings for stables and bridge at Syon].

STRAWBERRY HILL, TWICKENHAM, MIDDLESEX, the Offices for Horace Walpole, 1790, Gothic, following a design made by James Essex (d. 1784) [W. D. Lewis, 'The Genesis of Strawberry Hill', *Metropolitan Museum Studies* v (i), 1934, 82 and fig. 29].

ASTON HALL, nr. OSWESTRY, SALOP., for the Rev. J. R. Lloyd, 1789–93 [National Library of Wales, Aston Hall papers nos. 5234–5, Wyatt's account for drawings; N.M.R., photos of drawings by Wyatt sold in 1969].

LITTLE ASTON HALL, SHENSTONE, STAFFS., alterations and additions for William Tennant, probably *c.* 1790; rebuilt 1857–9 [S. Shaw, *History of Staffordshire* ii, 1801, 52, with engraving].

GRESFORD LODGE, nr. WREXHAM, DENBIGHSHIRE, for John Parry, *c.* 1790; dem. 1955–60 [J. Aikin, *Description of Country round Manchester*, 1795, 401].[1]

SUFTON COURT, HEREFS., built for James Hereford, *c.* 1790, is said to have been designed by Wyatt by W. H. Cooke, *Collections towards the History of Herefordshire* iii, 1882, 73.

BIDBOROUGH RECTORY (now 'WYATTS'), KENT, *c.* 1790 ['after a design of Mr. Wyatt's': E. Hasted, *History of Kent*, 2nd ed., v, 275].

HARTHAM PARK, PICKWICK, WILTS., for Lady James, 1790–5; enlarged 1858 and 1888 [J. Britton, *Beauties of Wiltshire* iii, 1825, 184, with engraving].

CASTLE COOLE, CO. FERMANAGH, IRELAND, for the 1st Earl Belmore, 1790–7; offices added 1823 [G. Richardson, *New Vitruvius Britannicus* ii, 1808, pls. 65–70] (*C. Life*, 19–26 Dec. 1936).

attributed: DURHAM CASTLE, remodelling of gatehouse for Bishop Shute Barrington, 1791 [Barrington had recently employed Wyatt at Salisbury Cathedral and was soon to do so at Durham Cathedral].

FELBRIGG HALL, NORFOLK: Wyatt was employed by William Windham to carry out alterations between 1791 and 1804, but apparently did little except exasperate his client [*The Windham Papers*, ed. Earl of Rosebery, 1913, i, 182–3; ii, 229–30].

BROKE HALL, NACTON, SUFFOLK, rebuilt for Philip Broke, 1791–2, castellated [H. Repton, *Sketches and Hints on Landscape Gardening*,

---

[1] According to S. Lewis, *Topographical Dictionary of Wales* ii, 1844, 363, this house was designed by Sir Jeffry Wyatville.

1795, 18; drawings in E. Suffolk Record Office, HA 93/722/240, *ex inf.* Mr. J. M. Frew] (J. P. Neale, *Views of Seats*, 1st ser., v, 1821; *C. Life*, 8 Aug. 1936, 158).

WORSTEAD HALL, NORFOLK, for Sir Berney Brograve, Bart., probably *c.* 1791–7; dem. [J. P. Neale, *Views of Seats*, 1st ser., ii, 1819].

FROGMORE HOUSE, nr. WINDSOR, BERKS., rebuilt for Queen Charlotte, 1792–5; wings enlarged in nineteenth century [R. Ackermann, *Repository of Arts*, 3rd ser., i, 125–8; J. Hakewill, *History of Windsor*, 1813, 299–302; *History of the King's Works* vi, 326].

NEW HALL, NUNTON, WILTS., enlarged for J. T. Batt, 1792; rebuilt [J. Britton, *Beauties of Wiltshire* i, 1801, 114; B. Burke, *Visitation of Seats and Arms*, 2nd ser., ii, 1855, 127].

STOKE PARK, STOKE POGES, BUCKS., completed house for John Penn after death of R. Nasmith (*q.v.*), *c.* 1793–8 [J. Penn, *An Historical and Descriptive Account of Stoke Park*, 1813, 60–1; drawings by Wyatt in B.M., Add. MS. 32450, E–H].

SWINTON PARK, YORKS. (W.R.), decoration of drawing-room for William Danby, *c.* 1793–4 [J. P. Neale, *Views of Seats*, 2nd ser., iv, 1828; J. Cornforth in *C. Life*, 14 April 1966].

HENHAM HALL, SUFFOLK, for Sir John Rous, Bart., cr. Earl of Stradbroke, 1793–7; remodelled by E. M. Barry; dem. 1953 [H. Davy, *Views of Seats in Suffolk*, 1827; J. P. Neale, *Views of Seats*, 1st ser., iii, 1820; drawings in East Suffolk Record Office].

BULBRIDGE HOUSE, WILTON, WILTS., remodelled for Lieut. Gen. Philip Goldsworthy, 1794 [C. Hussey in *C. Life*, 28 Feb., 7 March 1963].

LASBOROUGH PARK, nr. TETBURY, GLOS., for Edmund Estcourt, 1794, castellated [drawings by Wyatt preserved in house: see *C. Life*, 11 Feb. 1960, 279] (T. D. Fosbroke, *History of Gloucestershire* i, 1807, 410).

CROOME COURT, WORCS., ornamental buildings in grounds for the 6th Earl of Coventry, 1794–1801, including the Panorama Temple (1801), a Gothic ruin in the woods, and the Doric lodge at the west entrance to the park [drawings by Wyatt in Estate Office, Croome, 1954].

BROADWAY, WORCS., the 'Saxon' tower on Broadway Hill for the 6th Earl of Coventry, 1794 [drawings by Wyatt in Estate Office, Croome, 1954].

ESCOT HOUSE, nr. HONITON, DEVON, alterations for Sir John Kennaway, Bart., *c.* 1795; destroyed by fire 1808 [J. Britton & E. W. Brayley, *Beauties of England and Wales* iv, 1803, 301].

POWDERHAM CASTLE, DEVON, extensive alterations, including the Music Room, for the 3rd Viscount Courtenay, 1794–6 [Mark Girouard in *C. Life*, 18 July 1963].

PLAS NEWYDD, ANGLESEY, remodelled for the 1st Earl of Uxbridge, 1795 onwards, Gothic. The transformation of Plas Newydd was a long process, initiated by Wyatt in the 1790s, but not completed (by Joseph Potter, *q.v.*) until the 1820s [C. Hussey in *C. Life*, 24 Nov., 1 Dec. 1955; R.I.B.A.D.].

ALLESTREE HALL, DERBYSHIRE, for Bache Thornhill, 1795 [described as 'after a very clever plan of Wyatt's' by William Holbech of Farnborough, Warwicks., who visited the house in 1795 (MS. diary at Farnborough); plan signed by Wyatt and dated 1795 in Derbyshire County Museum Service, D.165].

CANWELL HALL, STAFFS., remodelled interior and added wings for Sir Robert Lawley, Bart., cr. Lord Wenlock, *c.* 1795; dem. [S. Shaw, *History of Staffordshire* ii, 1801, 22*].

BISHOP AUCKLAND CASTLE, CO. DURHAM, extensive alterations for Bishop Shute Barrington, including Gothic screen and inner gateway and remodelling of principal rooms in Gothic style, *c.* 1795 [drawings at Auckland Castle dated 1795; E. W. Brayley & J. Britton, *Beauties of England and Wales* v, 1803, 220–1; J. Cornforth in *C. Life*, 27 Jan., 3, 10 Feb. 1972].

BOWDEN HOUSE, nr. LACOCK, WILTS., for B. Dickinson, 1796 [exhib. at R.A. 1796; G. Richardson, *New Vitruvius Britannicus* i, 1802, pls. 1–2] (Ralph Edwards, 'Bowden Park', *Connoisseur*, April 1961).

LONGFORD CASTLE, WILTS., designs and model for additional towers for the 2nd Earl of Radnor, 1796 [accounts at Longford]. This was the beginning of the project for enlarging the house, afterwards carried out by D. A. Alexander in 1802–17 (*C. Life*, 12, 19, 26 Dec. 1931).

FONTHILL ABBEY, WILTS., for William Beckford, 1796–1812, Gothic; tower collapsed 1825; remainder of house subsequently dem. except part of north wing [J. Rutter, *Delineations of Fonthill and its Abbey*, 1823; J. Britton, *Illustrations of Fonthill Abbey*, 1823; Boyd Alexander, *Life at Fonthill 1807–1822*, 1957; J. Wilton-Ely in *William Beckford Exhibition*, 1976, 35–57].

ACTON PARK, nr. WREXHAM, DENBIGHSHIRE, alterations for Sir Foster Cunliffe, Bart., completed 1797 [Madame D'Arblay, *Memoirs of Dr. Burney* iii, 1832, 247] (J. P. Neale, *Views of Seats*, 2nd ser., v, 1829).

TRENTHAM HALL, STAFFS., said in 1797 to have been 'lately altered and enlarged by Wyatt' for the 1st Marquess of Stafford; remodelled by Sir C. Barry 1834 onwards; dem. 1910 [*Diary and Letters of Madame D'Arblay*, ed. A. Dobson, v, 1905, 338].

SOHO HOUSE, HANDSWORTH, BIRMINGHAM, additions for Matthew Boulton, 1796–8, completed by Samuel Wyatt [Tew MSS., Assay Office, Birmingham, *ex inf.* Mr. J. M. Robinson].

PEPER HAROW, SURREY, conservatory for the 4th Viscount Midleton, 1797; dem. probably in

1913 [E. W. Brayley, *History of Surrey* v, 1848, 232; drawing by Wyatt dated 1795 in collection of the late Sir Albert Richardson].

DODINGTON PARK, GLOS., for Christopher Codrington, 1798–1813 [exhib. at R.A. 1798; C. Hussey in *C. Life*, 22, 29 Nov. 1956; C. Hussey, *English Country Houses: Late Georgian*, 1958, 41–54].

NORRIS CASTLE, EAST COWES, ISLE OF WIGHT, for Lord Henry Seymour, 1799, castellated [E. W. Brayley & J. Britton, *Beauties of England and Wales* vi, 1805, 391; W. Cooke, *New Picture of the Isle of Wight*, 1808, 143; B. Burke, *Visitation of Seats* i (2), 1853, 89].

PENNSYLVANIA CASTLE, PORTLAND, DORSET, for John Penn, 1800, castellated [*D.N.B.*, *s.v.* 'Penn'; *Dorset Arch. Soc. Trans.* xxxvii, 1916, 248–51].

OTTERSHAW PARK, SURREY, entrance lodges for Edward Boehm, *c.* 1800 [G. F. Prosser, *Illustrations of the County of Surrey*, 1828].

PURLEY HOUSE, BERKS., for the executors of Anthony Storer (d. 1799), who provided for its erection in his will, *c.* 1800 [*Gent's Mag.* 1799 (ii), 626; D. & S. Lysons, *Magna Britannia* i, 1806, 325].

HANWORTH FARM, MIDDLESEX, for himself, *c.* 1800. Cary's *New Itinerary* of 1812 refers to Wyatt's country seat as 'Hanworth House', but it appears generally to have been known as 'Hanworth Farm', and stood about half a mile north-east of Hanworth Park.

BICTON LODGE, DEVON, completed house for the 1st Lord Rolle (who succeeded to the property in 1797), *c.* 1800; remodelled by W. Tapper 1908–9 [*The Copper-Plate Magazine* v, pl. ccx, 1800].

HINTON ST. GEORGE, SOMERSET, alterations and additions for the 4th Earl Poulett, *c.* 1800–5, Gothic [J. Soane, *Professional Memoirs*, 1835, 24; drawings by Wyatt in Mellon Collection dated 1801 and 1804] (J. P. Neale, *Views of Seats*, 2nd ser., iv, 1828).

CASSIOBURY PARK, HERTS., remodelled for the 5th Earl of Essex, *c.* 1800–5, castellated; dem. 1922 [J. Britton, *History ... of Cassiobury Park*, 1837, 27] (*C. Life*, 17 Sept. 1910).

attributed: ITCHENOR HOUSE, WEST ITCHENOR, SUSSEX, for the 3rd Duke of Richmond, 1787 [attributed to Wyatt because of his employment by the Duke at Goodwood, and similarity to the dower house which he designed there].

WINDSOR CASTLE, BERKS., remodelled royal apartments in Upper Ward for King George III, 1800–13, castellated Gothic; largely remodelled by Sir Jeffry Wyatville 1824–40 [W. H. St. J. Hope, *Architectural History of Windsor Castle*, 1913, 348–55; *History of the King's Works* vi, 375–9].

WILTON HOUSE, WILTS., restoration and additions for the 11th Earl of Pembroke, including rebuilding of north and west fronts and erection of cloister, 1801–11, Gothic; north front remodelled by E. Warre 1914–18 [drawings at Wilton; J. Britton, *Beauties of England and Wales* xv, 1814, 336–7] (*C. Life*, 8 Aug. 1963 and 22 Aug., p. 439).

KEW PALACE, SURREY, for King George III, 1801–11, castellated Gothic; dem. 1827–8 [*History of the King's Works* vi, 356–8, fig. 7 and pl. 15].

THE WHITE LODGE, RICHMOND PARK, SURREY, alterations for benefit of the 1st Viscount Sidmouth, 1801–6 [*History of the King's Works* vi, 355].

BELVOIR CASTLE, LEICS., remodelled for the 5th Duke of Rutland, 1801–13, castellated Gothic; seriously damaged by fire 1816, after which the castle was restored under the direction of the amateur architect the Rev. J. Thoroton (d. 1820).[1] The north-east and north-west fronts are Thoroton's work, the south-east and south-west fronts Wyatt's [drawings in Belvoir muniments, maps 129, 130, 132; I. Eller, *History of Belvoir Castle*, 1841] (*C. Life*, 6, 13, 20, 27 Dec. 1956).

STOKE POGES VICARAGE, BUCKS., for John Penn, 1802–4, Gothic [J. Penn, *An Historical and Descriptive Account of Stoke Park*, 1813, 68].

WYCOMBE ABBEY, BUCKS., reconstructed for the 1st Lord Carrington, *c.* 1803–4, Gothic [D. & S. Lysons, *Magna Britannia* i, 1806, 676; *Passages from the Diaries of Mrs. Lybbe-Powys*, ed. Climenson, 1899, 356].

CRANBOURNE LODGE, WINDSOR, BERKS., remodelled for King George III, 1804–8; dem. 1830 [*History of the King's Works* vi, 394–5].

WEST DEAN PARK, SUSSEX, rebuilt for Sir James Peachey, Bart., cr. 1st Lord Selsey (d. 1808), *c.* 1804–8, Gothic; completed by F. Sandys (*q.v.*); rebuilt 1893 [R. Ackermann, *Views of Seats* ii, 1830, 36–7] (J. P. Neale, *Views of Seats*, 1st ser., iv, 1821; T. W. Horsfield, *History of Sussex* ii, 1835, 82).

SUNNINGHILL PARK, BERKS., alterations for G. H. Crutchley, probably soon after 1805; dem. [J. P. Neale, *Views of Seats*, 1st ser., iii, 1820].

BULSTRODE PARK, BUCKS., began reconstruction of west wing for 3rd Duke of Portland, *c.* 1806–9, Gothic; not completed after Duke's death in 1809; rebuilt by B. Ferrey 1862 [*The Farington Diary*, ed. J. Greig, vii, 34; J. Harris, 'Bulstrode', *Arch. Rev.*, Nov. 1958].

ASHRIDGE PARK, HERTS., for the 7th Earl of Bridgewater, 1808–13, completed by Sir Jeffry Wyat-

---

[1] 'Of His architectural talents the new buildings erected at Belvoir Castle will be a lasting monument, for he participated in every plan connected with them, from their commencement in the year 1801, and during the latter years of his life he had the chief direction both in the design and execution of them' (inscription on monument in Bottesford Church).

ville 1813 onwards; Gothic [R.I.B.A.D.; inscription on brass plate in hall] (H. A. Tipping, *English Homes, VI* (i), 339–46).

STREATHAM, SURREY, house for the Dowager Countess of Coventry, 1810; dem. [Coventry archives in Estate Office, Croome; Manning & Bray, *History of Surrey* iii, 1814, 382].

NEWARK PARK, nr. WOTTON-UNDER-EDGE, GLOS., alterations, including south front, for Lewis Clutterbuck, *c.* 1810, Gothic [J. & H. S. Storer, *Delineations of the County of Gloucester*, 1824].

attributed: ALTON ABBEY (later TOWERS), STAFFS., remodelling for 15th Earl of Shrewsbury, 1811–13, Gothic; continued by William Hollins, Thomas Allason, A. W. N. Pugin and others [stylistic attribution; accounts in the Staffordshire Record Office show that work started in 1811, but no architect is named until Hollins in 1817, *ex inf.* Mr. J. M. Frew] (J. P. Neale, *Views of Seats* iii, 1829).

CHICKSANDS PRIORY, BEDS., alterations for Sir George Osborn, Bart., 1813, Gothic [I. D. Parry, *Select Illustrations of Bedfordshire*, 1827, 117; J. P. Neale, *Views of Seats*, 2nd ser., v, 1829].

ELVASTON HALL, DERBYSHIRE, rebuilt for the 3rd Earl of Harrington, *c.* 1815–19, by R. Walker (*q.v.*), to Gothic designs said to have been made by James Wyatt before his death [J. P. Neale, *Views of Seats*, 1st ser., vi, 1823].

SOPHIA LODGE, CLEWER, BERKS., remodelled for William Dawson, date uncertain, Gothic [R. Ackermann, *Repository of Arts*, 3rd ser., ii, 1823, 249–50].

LONDON HOUSES

GROSVENOR SQUARE, NO. 16, alterations for William Drake, *c.* 1773–5, and new back staircase, 1789; dem. [Drake papers, Bucks. Record Office, D/Dr. 5/69, 71; 12/61] (*C. Life*, 2 July 1948).

PORTMAN SQUARE, NOS. 11–15 (north side), 1773–84, as a personal speculation [A. T. Bolton, *The Works of R. and J. Adam* ii, 1922, 81, 91].

DEVONSHIRE HOUSE, PICCADILLY, repairs and decoration for the 5th Duke of Devonshire, 1776–90; dem. 1924–5 [household accounts at Chatsworth, *ex inf.* Mr. J. M. Robinson].

GROSVENOR SQUARE, NO. 36 (later 41), for Peter Delmé, 1778–9; dem. [*A.P.S.D.*; designs for ceilings in Wyatt album, Metropolitan Museum].

CONDUIT STREET, NO. 9, for Robert Vyner, 1779 [*A.P.S.D.*].

FOLEY PLACE (formerly QUEEN ANNE STREET EAST), NO. 1, for himself, *c.* 1780–3; dem. *c.* 1928 [A. Dale, *James Wyatt*, 1956, 15–16] (A. E. Richardson & C. L. Gill, *London Houses 1660–1720*, 1911, pl. lxxii).

RICHMOND HOUSE, WHITEHALL, added staircase

and two rooms for the 3rd Duke of Richmond, 1782; destroyed by fire 1791 [H. Walpole, *Anecdotes of Painting* v, ed. F. W. Hilles & P. B. Daghlian, 1939, 161]; temporary theatre 1787 [Hist. MSS. Comm., *XVth Report*, Appendix, part vii, 281].

DOWNSHIRE HOUSE, NO. 20 HANOVER SQUARE, interior decoration for the 1st Marquess of Downshire, *c.* 1789; since destroyed [design for ceiling for 'Lord Fairford now Marquis of Down' in Wyatt album, Metropolitan Museum].

BUCKINGHAM HOUSE, ST. JAMES'S, principal staircase for King George III, *c.* 1800; dem. 1825 [*History of the King's Works* vi, 261].

ST. JAMES'S PLACE, NO. 22, for Samuel Rogers, 1802–3; destroyed by bombing 1940 [*A.P.S.D.*; *Survey of London* xxx, 536–8].

CARLTON HOUSE, PALL MALL, repairs and redecoration of rooms in basement of garden front for the Prince of Wales, 1804–5; fitting up of additional library and strong room, 1812–13; dem. 1826 [*History of the King's Works* vi, 312–13, 315].

HOUSES ELSEWHERE

DUBLIN, LEINSTER HOUSE, decoration of picture gallery (now Senate Chamber) for the 2nd Duke of Leinster, before 1794 [C. P. Curran, *Dublin Decorative Plasterwork*, 1967, 85 and pls. 171–2].

LEIDEN, HOLLAND, NO. 19 RAPENBERG, ceiling for Johannes Meerman, 1788 [J. Harris, *Catalogue of British Drawings for Architecture, etc., in American Collections*, 1971, 300].

OXFORD, PHYSIC (BOTANICAL) GARDEN, conversion of greenhouse into library and residence for Professor of Botany, 1789; enlarged by H. J. Underwood 1834 [T. W. M. Jaine in *Oxoniensia* xxxvi, 1971, 70].

MAUSOLEA AND MONUMENTS, ETC.

DARTREY (DAWSON'S GROVE), CO. MONAGHAN, Mausoleum for Thomas Dawson, 1st Viscount Cremorne, 1770 [drawing in National Library of Ireland].

CHELTENHAM PARISH CHURCH, GLOS., tablet to Katherine A'Court, d. 1776, executed by R. Westmacott [*The Torrington Diaries*, ed. C. B. Andrews, i, 1934, 123].

LICHFIELD CATHEDRAL, STAFFS., monument to David Garrick, d. 1779 [F. Calvert & W. West, *Picturesque Views of Staffordshire*, 1830, 3].

COBHAM HALL, KENT, Mausoleum for the 4th Earl of Darnley, *c.* 1783–4 [exhib. at R.A. 1783; drawings in Soane Museum].

BROCKLESBY PARK, LINCS., Mausoleum for the 1st Lord Yarborough, 1787–94 [signed 'J. WYATT ESQR. ARCHT.'; exhib. at R.A. 1795] (*C. Life*, 3 March 1934).

SHRIVENHAM CHURCH, BERKS., monument to the 2nd Viscount Barrington, d. 1793 [signed by Wyatt as architect and R. Westmacott as sculptor].

WILTON CHURCH, WILTS., monument to the 10th Earl of Pembroke, d. 1794 [signed by Wyatt as architect and R. Westmacott as sculptor].

HALE CHURCH, HANTS., monument to Joseph May, d. 1796 [signed by Wyatt as architect and R. Westmacott as sculptor].

STOKE POGES CHURCHYARD, BUCKS., monument to Thomas Gray, erected 1799 [J. Penn, *An Historical and Descriptive Account of Stoke Park*, 1813, 61].

STOKE POGES PARK, BUCKS., column in memory of Sir Edward Coke, with statue by Rossi, 1800 [J. Penn, *An Historical and Descriptive Account of Stoke Park*, 1813, 61–2].

HAVERING CHURCH, ESSEX, monument to Sir John Smith Burges, Bart., d. 1803 [E. W. Brayley & J. Britton, *Beauties of England and Wales* v, 1803, 476].

WYATT, JEFFRY, *see* WYATVILLE

WYATT, JOSEPH (1739–1785), the fourth son of Benjamin Wyatt of Weeford, was born on 9 October 1739. He practised as a mason and architect in Burton-on-Trent. In 1783 he made designs for rebuilding the church of BREEDON-ON-THE-HILL, LEICS., which was in disrepair, but it proved impossible to raise sufficient money to carry them out [B.M., Church Briefs, B. XXIV, 4]. The same difficulty prevented the execution of his designs for rebuilding GRESLEY CHURCH, DERBYSHIRE, for which a Brief was obtained in 1786, and his plans are still preserved among the Quarter Session Records at Derby [J. C. Cox, *Churches of Derbyshire* iii, 1877, 373 n.]. Wyatt, who died in 1785, was the father of Sir Jeffry Wyatville. He had the reputation of being a 'clever, but indolent' architect [*A.P.S.D.*]. A competently drawn design by him for a greenhouse for Sir Robert Wilmot of Osmaston Hall, nr. Derby, is among the Wilmot-Horton papers in the Derbyshire Record Office.

WYATT, LEWIS WILLIAM (1777–1853), was one of the sons of Benjamin Wyatt (d. 1818), agent to Lord Penrhyn. He was apprenticed first to his uncle Samuel, and then to his uncle James, and began practice on his own in about 1805. For some years, however, he continued to assist James Wyatt in his work as Surveyor of the Ordnance. In 1800 James gave him a place in the Office of Works as Labourer in Trust at Carlton House. In 1818 he was promoted to the Clerkship of the Works at the Tower of London, Somerset House, etc., and in 1829 was transferred to Hampton Court, but lost his post when the Office was reorganized in 1832.

Lewis Wyatt began to exhibit at the Royal Academy in 1797, showing in that year views of various buildings erected on the Penrhyn estates by his father and his uncle Samuel. These were published in 1800–1 as '*A Collection of Architectural Designs, rural and ornamental, executed upon the Estates of the Right Hon. Lord Penrhyn in Caernarvonshire and Cheshire*, delineated by L. W. Wyatt'. Lewis's earliest recorded works were designed in James Wyatt's office for execution by another member of the family who continued the family building business in Staffordshire (see below). When Samuel Wyatt died in 1807, Lewis completed two of his country-house commissions, and succeeded to his practice in Cheshire.

Wyatt was primarily a country-house architect, his only public buildings of any consequence being the parish church at Stockport and the town hall at Basingstoke. In 1805 he was one of those who submitted designs for Downing College, Cambridge. Plans by James Wyatt were already under consideration, but had been severely criticized by Thomas Hope, and it is possible that Lewis Wyatt's entry was an attempt to salvage the commission for the Wyatt family. It was, however, the Greek Revival designs of William Wilkins that were selected by the judges. In 1816 Wyatt published a *Prospectus of a Design for Various Improvements in the Metropolis*, in which he insisted on the need for a 'pre-arranged and well-organised plan' for the development of London, and advocated certain specific 'improvements', including the replanning of the West End so as to 'converge to a natural and appropriate focus in a palace for the sovereign'. This was to be on the site of Carlton House in St. James's Park. Other proposals were for a crescent on the site of the present Trafalgar Square, facing a 'College of Arts and Sciences', and for a Thames embankment from Waterloo Bridge to Westminster. In 1827 he competed for St. George's Hospital, and in 1835 for the Houses of Parliament. His plans for the latter envisaged retaining as many of the buildings as had escaped the fire, and replacing those that had been destroyed in appropriate historical styles: 'Saxon' for the Painted Chamber, the 'Gothic of Edward III' for St. Stephen's Chapel, 'Plantagenet' for the two Houses, and 'Elizabethan' for the Speaker's house.

In his executed works Wyatt was eclectic in style. His best designs were in the neo-classical manner of his uncles Samuel and James (cf. Willey Hall and James Wyatt's Dodington Hall), but at Cranage Hall he tried the Tudor style, at Eaton Hall the Jacobean, and at Sherborne he reproduced the principal features of a sixteenth-century house with superimposed orders like Longleat. At Hackwood and Lyme his skill in incorporating and adapting earlier panelling and carving makes it difficult to decide precisely what

is his and what is original, and at Hawkstone he showed the same expertise as his cousins Benjamin and Philip in recreating the *décor* of the age of Louis XIV. He had had the opportunity to study it on the spot, for he visited Paris in 1815 and again in 1825, when he was sent there to supervise repairs to the British Embassy. In 1820 he was given six months' leave by the Board of Works in order to visit Italy.

Wyatt appears to have given up practice in about 1835. He retired to Cliff Cottage, Puckpool, nr. Ryde in the Isle of Wight, where he died on 14 February 1853, aged 75. He left all his architectural drawings to his nephew Benjamin Wyatt Greenfield of Shirley, Hants. His excellent library and his small collection of Italian paintings were sold at Christie's on 1 June. Among the latter were several pictures 'purchased at Bologna, from the gallery of Count Marescalchi'. D. Harrison was a pupil.

[*A.P.S.D.*; *Gent's Mag.* 1853 (i), 670; *History of the King's Works* vi, 119, 633, 677; G. Walkley, 'A Recently Found James Wyatt Design', *R.I.B.A. Jnl.*, 12 Sept. 1938; will in P.C.C. 1853, f. 241].

PATSHULL HOUSE, STAFFS., supplied designs for alterations carried out by Benjamin Wyatt of Sutton Coldfield for Sir George Pigott, Bart., 1803–5 [William Salt Library, Stafford, Wyatt correspondence (M.96)].

WIGGINTON LODGE, nr. TAMWORTH, STAFFS., supplied designs for new house to be carried out by Benjamin Wyatt of Sutton Coldfield for Sir Charles Clarke, Bart., M.D., 1804 [William Salt Library, Stafford, Wyatt correspondence (M.96)].

HEATON HALL, LANCS., probably designed orangery, north front of house, library, chimney-stacks and lodges for the 1st Earl of Wilton, 1806–24 [*Heaton Hall, Manchester, Bicentenary Exhibition Catalogue*, 1972, 86].

TATTON PARK, CHESHIRE, completion for Wilbraham Egerton of house begun by Samuel Wyatt (d. 1807) for William Egerton (d. 1806), 1807–13, including entrance to park from Knutsford and conservatory [exhib. at R.A. 1811 and 1812; Arthur Oswald in *C. Life*, 16, 23, 30 July 1964].

HACKWOOD PARK, HANTS., completion for the 2nd Lord Bolton of remodelling begun by Samuel Wyatt (d. 1807) for the 1st Lord Bolton (d. 1807), 1807–13 and later [exhib. at R.A. 1810; R. Ackermann, *Repository of Arts*, 3rd ser., vi, 1825, 125–6] (*C. Life*, 17–24 May 1913).

WEMYSS CASTLE, FIFE, Gothic gateway and lodge for William Wemyss, exhibited at R.A. 1808, but apparently not executed.

WONHAM MANOR, BETCHWORTH, SURREY, alterations for the 1st Viscount Templeton, c. 1805–10, Gothic; dem. [exhib. at R.A. 1810] (R.

Ackermann, *Views of Country Seats* ii, 1830, 48).

MOUNT SHANNON, CO. LIMERICK, IRELAND, added portico for the 2nd Earl of Clare, 1809; destroyed by fire 1922 [C. FitzGibbon in *Quarterly Bulletin of the Irish Georgian Soc.* xix, 1976, 14–19].

RODE HALL, CHESHIRE, alterations, including new dining-room, for Randle Wilbraham, 1810–12 [accounts at Rode Hall, *ex inf.* Mr. J. M. Robinson].

STOKE HALL, NOTTS., enlarged for Sir Robert Bromley, Bart., 1812; altered 1923 [*A.P.S.D.*; A. Graves, *The Royal Academy of Arts* viii, 1905, 377. Both sources refer to a drawing, said to have been exhibited at the R.A. in 1812, which cannot, however, be found in the original R.A. catalogue for this year].

WILLEY HALL, SALOP., for Cecil Weld-Forester, cr. Lord Forester, 1813–15 [signed drawings in Shropshire Record Office and Avery Library, Columbia University, U.S.A.; J. P. Neale, *Views of Seats*, 2nd ser., ii, 1825; C. Hussey, *English Country Houses: Late Georgian*, 1958, 115–21].

STOCKPORT PARISH CHURCH, CHESHIRE, rebuilt 1813–17, incorporating medieval chancel, Gothic [H. Heginbotham, *Stockport, Ancient and Modern* i, 1882, 217; exhib. at R.A. 1814; drawings in Soane Museum, xlvii, 10, 1–11].

LYME PARK, CHESHIRE, alterations for Thomas Legh, 1814–17, including addition of tower behind pediment on south front and remodelling of rooms on east front [exhib. at R.A. 1816; J. P. Neale, *Views of Seats*, 2nd ser., i, 1824; John Cornforth in *C. Life*, 26 Dec. 1974].

CUERDEN HALL, LANCS., enlarged for Robert Townley Parker, 1815 [E. Twycross, *The Mansions of England and Wales: Lancashire* i, 1847, 42].

ROSTHERNE, CHESHIRE, school for Wilbraham Egerton, 1815, and addition of *cottage orné*, 1826 [drawings at Tatton Park, *ex inf.* Mr. J. M. Robinson].

CHESTER, MESSRS. HUGHES, WILLIAMS & CO.'S (now LLOYD'S) BANK, FOREGATE STREET, c. 1815 [by 'Wyatt': J. Broster, *A Walk round the Walls and City of Chester*, 1821].

WINSLADE CHURCH, HANTS., extensive repairs for the 2nd Lord Bolton, 1816–17 [Hants. Record Office, A/X b/5/3, *ex inf.* Mr. J. M. Robinson].

OULTON HALL, CHESHIRE, altered interior, added terrace and designed stables for Sir John Grey-Egerton, Bart., c. 1816–26; gutted by fire 1926 and since dem. [G. Ormerod, *History of Cheshire*, ed. Helsby, ii, 1882, 219].

WINSTANLEY HALL, LANCS., alterations for Meyrick Banckes, 1818–19 [drawings in Lancashire Record Office].

RADCLIFFE CHAPEL, nr. BURY, LANCS., for Countess

Grosvenor, 1818–19, Gothic; rebuilt 1864–5 [by 'Mr. Wyatt': *Gent's Mag.* 1818 (i), 633].

ST. ASAPH CATHEDRAL, FLINTSHIRE, ceiled nave and aisles with stucco, c. 1822; removed 1865 [D. R. Thomas, *History of the Diocese of St. Asaph*, 1870, 207].

LONDON, NOS. 12–17 SUFFOLK STREET, c. 1822–3. Wyatt built Nos. 12–14 as a personal speculation and lived in No. 13 from 1823 to 1829; Nos. 15–17 were built to his designs for John Holroyd [*Survey of London* xx, 93].

BOLTON HALL, YORKS. (N.R.), repairs and alterations for the 2nd Lord Bolton, c. 1823–4; gutted by fire 1902 [plans, *ex inf.* National Register of Archives, list 8638].

BAKEWELL CHURCH, DERBYSHIRE, report on spire with Joseph Potter, 1824 [parish records].

ELSTREE CHURCH, HERTS., enlarged 1824; rebuilt 1853 by P. C. Hardwick [I.C.B.S.].

FLINTHAM HALL, NOTTS., library, offices and conservatory for Col. T. B. Hildyard, 1829; remodelled by T. Hine c. 1850 [drawings at Flintham Hall].

CRANAGE HALL, CHESHIRE, for Lawrence Armistead, 1828–9, Tudor [Ormerod, *History of Cheshire*, ed. Helsby, iii, 1882, 129].

EATON HALL, nr. CONGLETON, CHESHIRE, for G. C. Antrobus, 1829, Jacobean; dem. 1975 [drawings at Manchester School of Architecture, *ex inf.* Mr. J. M. Robinson].

SHERBORNE HOUSE, GLOS., rebuilt for the 2nd Lord Sherborne, 1829–34, reproducing the style of the seventeenth-century house [Dutton papers in Gloucestershire Record Office, which show that soon after the completion of the work serious defects were discovered which led to an arbitrators' award of £996 against Wyatt for negligence] (*Connoisseur* xxx, 1911).

BIBURY COURT, GLOS., minor alterations for the 2nd Lord Sherborne, 1830 [account for drawings in Glos. Record Office, D 678, Family 322, *ex inf.* Mr. J. M. Robinson].

LONDON, NO. 53 LOWER GROSVENOR STREET, alterations for the 2nd Lord Sherborne, 1831 [account for drawings in Glos. Record Office, D 678, Family 322, *ex inf.* Mr. J. M. Robinson].

HAWKSTONE HALL, SALOP., drawing-room and other additions for Sir Rowland Hill, Bart., 1832–4 [Arthur Oswald in *C. Life*, 3 April 1958].

BASINGSTOKE TOWN HALL, HANTS., 1833 [S. Lewis, *Topographical Dictionary of England* i, 1848, 169].

WYATT, Sir MATTHEW (1805–1886), was the eldest son of Matthew Cotes Wyatt (1777–1862), the sculptor. During the earlier part of his life he was active as an architect and speculative builder in London. In 1837 he designed and built VICTORIA SQUARE, PIMLICO. He then moved to

Paddington, where he erected houses in STAN-HOPE TERRACE, WESTBOURNE and BATHURST STREETS, and the triangle of land bounded by CONNAUGHT STREET, SOUTHWICK STREET, HYDE PARK STREET and HYDE PARK SQUARE. He also built smaller houses, now demolished, in HOWLEY PLACE and PORTEUS ROAD on the Bishop of London's Paddington estate. Many of his houses were built in partnership with his brother George Wyatt (d. 1880).

By the late 1840s Wyatt was living in affluence in Hyde Park Square and gave up active participation in building. He was knighted in 1848 on becoming an officer of the Honourable Corps of Gentlemen at Arms. [Middlesex Land Register, Grosvenor Estate archives and Church Commissioners' archives, *ex inf.* Mr. Frank Kelsall.]

WYATT, PHILIP WILLIAM (-1835), was the fourth and youngest son of James Wyatt. He was educated by the Rev. John Owen of Fulham, who appears to have run a small private school there, and afterwards became a pupil in his father's office. Feckless and improvident, he failed to make the most of his opportunities, and was frequently in financial difficulties, culminating in his imprisonment for debt in 1833. Throughout his life he was destined to be overshadowed by his elder brother Benjamin. In 1811, encouraged by his father, he competed for the Drury Lane Theatre, only to be defeated by Benjamin's rival plan. In 1813 he seized the opportunity of his brother's absence in Ireland to ride to Ragley in Warwickshire to announce his father's death to the Prince Regent at 3 o'clock in the morning, and to solicit his patronage, but the Prince merely 'returned a civil answer in a general way', and Philip failed to secure any of his father's posts. In 1814, no doubt hoping to attract clients, he exhibited a drawing at the Royal Academy, but relatively few commissions appear to have come his way, and in the 1820s he was acting as Benjamin's assistant or junior partner. As such he participated in the design of some important works, including York, Londonderry and Apsley Houses.

As an independent architect Philip's principal works were the classical Wynyard Park and the picturesque Gothic Conishead Priory, both buildings of some size and importance in their respective styles. Red Hall is or was a 'many-gabled mansion' designed by Wyatt 'upon the spot and on the spur of the moment', and subsequently carried out 'without any material alteration'.

No portrait of Philip Wyatt is recorded, but William Beckford described him in 1819 as 'more hirsute, bearded and baboon-like than the fantastic faces one can see on coconuts'.

[B.M., Add. MSS. 38256, ff. 14–19, 38265, ff. 194–5; P.R.O., PRIS/4/43, p. 11; *The Farington*

Diary, ed. J. Greig, vii, 130, 205; Boyd Alexander, *Life at Fonthill*, 1957, 295–6.]

GREAT YARMOUTH, NORFOLK, ST. NICHOLAS CHURCH, repairs, *c.* 1813 [Birmingham Reference Library, Tew MSS., M. Yatman to M. Boulton, 25 April 1814, *ex inf.* Mr. J. M. Robinson; cf. J. Preston, *Picture of Yarmouth*, Yarmouth 1819, 39, 42].

LONDON, NO. 40 UPPER BROOK STREET, redecorated for E. H. Ball Hughes, 1819 [Boyd Alexander, *Life at Fonthill*, 1957, 296; *Reminiscences of Capt. Gronow*, ed. J. Raymond, 1964, 262].

LONDON, NO. 10 ST. JAMES'S SQUARE, interior decoration for the Earl of Blessington, in collaboration with M. C. Wyatt, 1821 [B.M., Egerton MS. 3515] (*Survey of London* xxix, 123, 130–2).

CONISHEAD PRIORY, LANCS., for T. R. Gale Braddyll, 1821–36, Gothic [*Lancashire Illustrated ... by R. Wallis*, 1829, 96].

WYNYARD PARK, CO. DURHAM, for the 3rd Marquess of Londonderry, 1822–30; interior destroyed by fire 1841 and restored by I. Bonomi & J. A. Cory 1842–4 [W. Fordyce, *History of Durham* ii, 1855, 322].

BISHOPWEARMOUTH, SUNDERLAND, CO. DURHAM, ST. THOMAS'S CHURCH, 1827–9, Gothic; dem. [W. Fordyce, *History of Durham* ii, 1855, 436].

SEAHAM HALL, CO. DURHAM, alterations and lodges for the 3rd Marquess of Londonderry, 1828 [accounts and sketch of lodges in Londonderry papers, Durham County Record Office, *ex inf.* Mr. J. M. Robinson].

RED HALL, HAUGHTON-LE-SKERNE, CO. DURHAM, for Capt. Robert Colling, 1830 [B. Burke, *A Visitation of Seats and Arms* i, 1852, 116].

WEYMOUTH, DORSET, HOLY TRINITY CHURCH, 1834–6, Gothic, completed after Wyatt's death by his nephew Matthew Wyatt [R.C.H.M., *Dorset* ii (2), 334].

WYATT, SAMUEL (1737–1807), born on 8 September 1737, at Blackbrook Farm, Weeford, Staffs., was the third son of Benjamin Wyatt, builder and architect (*q.v.*). He was trained as a carpenter, and worked at first as a member of the family firm. In 1759 he was engaged first as master carpenter and then as clerk of the works at Kedleston Hall by Robert Adam. This appointment was to be of great importance in his career, for it brought him into contact with the leading neo-classical architect of the time, and gave him practical experience in the designing and construction of a major building. It was also at Kedleston that he met and in 1765 married Ann Sherwin, the daughter of Lord Scarsdale's land agent. In about 1768 he returned to Weeford, and in the following year he obtained his first architectural commission, a new drawing-room at Blithfield Hall, the seat of Sir William

Bagot. Between 1769 and 1771 he was closely associated with his younger brother James in the design and construction of the Pantheon in Oxford Street, to whose complicated carpentry he applied the experience he had gained in executing the 'circular roofing' over the saloon at Kedleston, and it was almost certainly James's designs that he and his brother William carried out when they remodelled the interior of Beaudesert in 1771–3. The death in 1772 of Benjamin Wyatt led to the break-up of the family firm, and in 1774 Samuel settled permanently in London. From the Duke of Portland he obtained the lease of a large house and timber-yard in Berwick Street, from which for the next thirty years he was to conduct a highly successful business as architect, builder and timber-merchant.

As an architect Samuel Wyatt specialized in the designing of medium-sized country houses in an elegant and restrained neo-classical manner. Characteristic features of his houses were astylar elevations with prominent bowed projections, either domed (as at Doddington and Delamere) or duplicated (as at Belmont and Hurstmonceaux); oval or circular rooms ingeniously fitted into the plan; overarched tripartite windows; and the sparing use of Coade stone plaques as external decoration. Unlike his brother James he deviated little from his chosen neo-classical formulae, rarely using the Gothic style, and then only in exceptional circumstances (e.g. at Penrhyn).

Wyatt's spare neo-classical style was well adapted to utilitarian buildings, and he enjoyed a considerable reputation as a designer of model farm-buildings for improving landlords – notably at Holkham, where between 1780 and 1807 he built nearly fifty farms, barns, lodges, cottages, etc., for 'Coke of Norfolk'. A strong practical interest in building techniques led him to make extensive use of slate (from the Penrhyn quarries in North Wales managed by his brother Benjamin) for cladding and other purposes, and to experiment with cast-iron construction. It was he who in 1783–6 built the celebrated Albion Mills at Blackfriars. This was the first mill to be designed from the start to be powered by steam, and contained two of Boulton and Watt's double-acting rotative engines, each of 50 h.p. It was also one of the first large buildings to be founded on a structural raft. Its destruction by fire in March 1791 was a disaster which does nothing to impair Wyatt's credit as a structural innovator. In 1799 he was consulted about the scheme for a Thames Tunnel, and in 1800 he took out a patent for building cast-iron bridges, warehouses, etc. He was also the inventor of a 'sympathetic hinge', a device whereby both leaves of a double door are made to open simultaneously. He thought of himself as an engineer-architect rather than as an artist-architect like his brother James, and it is significant that he became a member of the

956

Society for the Promotion of Arts, Manufactures and Commerce, and of the Smeatonian Society of Civil Engineers, but never exhibited at the Royal Academy, nor sought election to that body.

In 1792 Wyatt was appointed to his two principal public offices – the Surveyorship of Trinity House (Feb.) and the Clerkship of the Works at Chelsea Hospital (March). In October 1793 he succeeded John Vardy, junior, as Surveyor to the Mint, but was dismissed in December of the following year for inattention to his duties. His energies had perhaps been too much diverted to Ramsgate Harbour, of which he became Surveyor and Civil Engineer in March 1794. He died suddenly at Chelsea on 8 February 1807 at the age of 70, and was buried in the Hospital cemetery. He left no children. A portrait by Lemuel Abbott is in the Baker Museum of Furniture, Holland, Michigan, U.S.A. It shows him with four notebooks, inscribed 'Marston House', 'Pantheon 1772', 'Berechurch Hall' and 'Spring Gardens'. The group portrait of the Elder Brethren of Trinity House, painted by Gainsborough Dupont in 1793, shows Wyatt submitting his design for their building to the brethren (*Burlington Mag.*, July 1964, fig. 217). John Harvey (*q.v.*) and his nephew L. W. Wyatt (*q.v.*) were his principal pupils. Others were W. Atkinson (not the well-known architect of this name), R. Moreton (who was 'a relation of Mr. Godwin of Coalbrookdale') and W. Vierpyl (*q.v.*).

[J. M. Robinson, 'Samuel Wyatt, Architect', unpublished D.Phil. thesis, Oxford, 1973; J. M. Robinson, 'A Great Architectural Family', *C. Life*, 13–20 Dec. 1973; A. W. Skempton, 'Early Members of the Smeatonian Society of Civil Engineers', *Trans. Newcomen Soc.* xliv, 1971–2, 35; *Survey of London* xxxi, 233.]

In the following list sources marked 'J.M.R.' are due to Mr. J. M. Robinson.

COUNTRY HOUSES, ETC.

BLITHFIELD HOUSE, STAFFS., additions and alterations, including drawing-room for the 1st Lord Bagot, 1769–70; remodelled in Gothic style c. 1820–22 [Bagot papers in Staffordshire Record Office; J.M.R.] (*C. Life*, 28 Oct., 4–11 Nov. 1954).

BERECHURCH HALL, ESSEX, alterations and additions for Sir Robert Smythe, Bart., c. 1770; rebuilt 1881–2; dem. c. 1960 [one of the books in Wyatt's portrait is labelled 'Berechurch Hall'].

attributed: DORFOLD HALL, CHESHIRE, alterations, including library, for James Tomkinson, 1771 [stylistic attribution, supported by a sheet of paper inscribed 'Henry Tomkinson Esq. Dorfold Hall' (*sic*) among Samuel Wyatt's drawings at Tatton Park] (*C. Life*, 31 Oct. 1908).

KEDLESTON RECTORY, DERBYSHIRE, rebuilt on new site, 1771, retaining façade of 1761 [Kedleston archives; J.M.R.].

BOSTOCK HALL, CHESHIRE, probably completed interior for Edward Tomkinson, c. 1775 [house said to be by 'Wyatt' by E. Twycross, *The Mansions of England* iv, 1850, 138].

MARSTON HOUSE, MARSTON BIGOT, SOMERSET, added wings for the 7th Earl of Cork & Orrery, 1776; interior of west wing remodelled 1868 [one of the books in Wyatt's portrait is labelled 'Marston House'; cf. M. McGarvie, 'Marston House', *Proceedings of the Somerset Archaeological and N.H. Soc.* cxviii, 1974, 19].

BARON HILL, ANGLESEY, remodelled for the 7th Viscount Bulkeley, 1776–9; gutted by fire 1836, now ruinous [drawings in Bodleian, MS. Top. Anglesey a.2] (W. Watts, *Views of Seats*, pl. xi, 1779).

DODDINGTON HALL, CHESHIRE, for Sir Thomas Broughton, Bart., 1777–98 [G. Richardson, *New Vitruvius Britannicus* i, 1802, pls. 57–60] (*C. Life*, 6–13 Feb. 1953). Wyatt also designed the Demesne Farm, for which his design is in the Cheshire Record Office [DDB/Q/3].

HERSTMONCEAUX PLACE, SUSSEX, additions for Francis Nayler, including south and east fronts, 1777 [J. Dallaway, *Discourses upon Architecture*, 1833, 330].

SANDON HALL, STAFFS., alterations to house for the 1st Lord Harrowby, 1777–84; rebuilt by W. Burn 1851–55; office court, and farm in park [*Autobiography of Dudley, 1st Earl of Harrowby*, 1891, 12–13; Harrowby archives].

THORNDON HALL, ESSEX, completed interior for the 9th Lord Petre, 1777–1801; destroyed by fire 1878; also Hatch Farm in the park [Petre archives in Essex Record Office; J.M.R.].

HOOTON HALL, CHESHIRE, for Sir William Stanley, Bart., 1778–88; remodelled in nineteenth century, dem. c. 1935 [W. Watts, *Views of Seats*, pl. xxiii, 1780]. The fine lodges by Wyatt survive near the church at Childer Thornton.

TIXALL HALL, STAFFS., interior of south wing for the Hon. Thomas Clifford, c. 1780–2; dem. 1927 [Sir T. & A. Clifford, *Description of Tixall*, 1817, 92].

HOLKHAM HALL, NORFOLK, numerous lodges, farm-houses, barns, cottages and other estate buildings for the 1st Earl of Leicester, 1780–1807 [J. M. Robinson, 'Estate Buildings at Holkham', *C. Life*, 21–28 Nov. 1974].

MARBLE HILL HOUSE, TWICKENHAM, MIDDLESEX, repairs for the 2nd Earl of Buckinghamshire, 1781 [M. P. G. Draper, *Marble Hill House*, 1970, 50].

EGGINTON HALL, DERBYSHIRE, alterations, including addition of central bow, for Sir Edward Every, Bart., 1782–3; dem. 1955 [payments to 'Mr. Wyatt' cited by Edward Saunders, 'Egginton Hall', *Derbyshire Life*, March 1974].

PENRHYN CASTLE, CAERNARVONSHIRE, remodelled for Richard Pennant, cr. 1st Lord Penrhyn, 1782 onwards, Gothic; rebuilt by T. Hopper c. 1825–44 [D. B. Hague in *C. Life*, 14 July, 1955, and *Caernarvonshire Archaeological Soc.'s Trans.* xx, 1959].

attributed: WINNINGTON HALL, CHESHIRE, the POULTRY HOUSE for Richard Pennant, cr. 1st Lord Penrhyn, c. 1782–5; dem. [stylistic attribution] (A. S. Irvine, *History of Winnington Hall*, I.C.I. 1951, 46–7).

DELAMERE HOUSE, CHESHIRE, for George Wilbraham, 1784; dem. 1939 [by 'Wyatt' according to Ormerod, *History of Cheshire*, ed. Helsby, ii, 1882, 137] (E. Twycross, *The Mansions of England* iv, 1850, 112).

PORTSMOUTH DOCKYARD, HANTS., THE COMMISSIONER'S HOUSE, 1784–5 [G. Richardson, *New Vitruvius Britannicus* ii, 1808, pls. 17–22] (*C. Life*, 2–9 April 1964).

attributed: COTON HOUSE, CHURCHOVER, WARWICKS., for Abraham Grimes, c. 1785 [stylistic attribution, combined with evidence that Wyatt visited a Mr. Grimes in Warwickshire in 1784; J.M.R.].

TATTON PARK, CHESHIRE, for William Egerton, 1785–91; subsequently completed by L. W. Wyatt for Wilbraham Egerton [Ormerod, *History of Cheshire*, ed. Helsby, i, 1882, 445] (*C. Life*, 16, 23 and 30 July 1964).

SOHO HOUSE, HANDSWORTH, BIRMINHAM, enlarged for Matthew Boulton, 1787–8, and completion of additions by James Wyatt, 1798; dem. [Tew MSS., Assay Office, Birmingham; J.M.R.].

HEATHFIELD HOUSE, HANDSWORTH, STAFFS., for James Watt, 1789–90; dem. 1927 [H. W. Dickinson, *James Watt*, 1936, 13; G. W. Beard, letter in *C. Life*, 6 March 1953, 667].

HEATON HOUSE, LANCS., alterations, including Music Room, for Sir Thomas Egerton, Bart., cr. Earl of Wilton, 1790. The stables (1777) may also be attributed to Wyatt [frieze in Music Room identical to that in Drawing-Room at Tatton and organ case similar to Wyatt's unexecuted design for one at Tatton] (*C. Life*, 29 Aug., 5 Sept. 1925; *Heaton Hall Manchester: Bicentenary Exhibition 1772–1972*).

TEMPLE HOUSE, HURLEY, BERKS., for Thomas Williams, c. 1790; dem. c. 1930 [*The Farington Diary*, ed. J. Greig, iii, 103].

LIME GROVE, nr. BANGOR, CAERNARVONSHIRE, for his brother Benjamin Wyatt (*q.v.*), probably c. 1790 [L. W. Wyatt, *A Collection of Designs … executed upon the Estates of Lord Penrhyn*, 1800–1; P. B. Williams, *Guide to North Wales*, 1821, 38].

CULFORD HALL, SUFFOLK, remodelled for the 1st Marquess Cornwallis, 1790–6; enlarged and altered 1894 [Wyatt is mentioned as architect in Repton's 'Red Book' of 1791–2, now in the

Morton Arboretum Library, Lisle, Illinois, U.S.A.] (J. P. Neale, *Views of Seats*, 1st ser., vi, 1823).

SHUGBOROUGH, STAFFS., remodelled for Thomas Anson, cr. 1st Viscount Anson, 1790–8; also lodges, enlargement of stables and home farm, conversion of Tower of the Winds into a dairy, and two groups of cottages (one, known as 'The Ring', dem. *c.* 1965), 1803–6 [accounts among Anson records in Staffs. Record Office; W. Pitt, *Topographical History of Staffordshire*, 1817, 90–1] (*C. Life*, 25 Feb., 11 March, 15–22 April 1954).

KINMEL PARK, DENBIGHSHIRE, for the Rev. Edward Hughes, 1790–1810; destroyed by fire 1841 [Kinmel MSS. in Bangor University Library; J.M.R.].

BELMONT PARK, KENT, reconstruction for General Lord Harris, 1787–92 [drawings from S. Wyatt's office, one inscribed in his hand; C. Hussey in *C. Life*, 27 Jan.–3 Feb. 1955].

DROPMORE, BUCKS., new façade with two bows for Lord Grenville, 1792–4 [accounts in Fortescue papers, Cornwall County Record Office; J.M.R.] (*C. Life*, 11–18 Oct. 1956).

SOMERLEY, nr. RINGWOOD, HANTS., for Daniel Hobson, 1792–5; additions by W. Burn & J. McVicar Anderson 1869–74 [C. Hussey in *C. Life*, 16, 23 and 30 Jan. 1958].

attributed: LIVERMERE PARK, SUFFOLK, addition of wings, etc., for N. Lee Acton, 1795–6; dem. 1887 [stylistic attribution] (J. P. Neale, *Views of Seats* vi, 1823).

SUNDRIDGE PARK, nr. BROMLEY, KENT, completion of house designed by John Nash and Humphry Repton for Sir Claude Scott, Bart., *c.* 1800. Wyatt was responsible for the interior and the stables [S. Shaw, *History of Staffordshire* ii, 1801, Addenda, 16 and references cited on p. 583].

IGHTHAM COURT, KENT, repairs and alterations for Col. Richard James, 1801–7 [payment to Wyatt in James papers, Kent Record Office; Mark Girouard in *C. Life*, 26 June 1958].

WROTHAM RECTORY (now Court Lodge), KENT, for the Rev. George Moore, 1801–2 [C. Greenwood, *Epitome of County History: Kent*, 1838, 136].

LUTTERWORTH RECTORY, LEICS., for the Hon. and Rev. Henry Ryder, 1803 [drawings in Lincolnshire Record Office, MGA 39].

HURTS HALL, SAXMUNDHAM, SUFFOLK, for Charles Long, 1803; rebuilt 1893 [H. Davy, *Views of the Seats of Noblemen and Gentlemen in Suffolk*, 1827].

BUCKENHAM HALL, NORFOLK, alterations for the 9th Lord Petre, 1803; dem. except the stables [Petre archives, Essex Record Office; J.M.R.].

HACKWOOD PARK, HANTS., remodelled for the 1st Lord Bolton, 1805–7; completed by L. W.

Wyatt [Bolton papers in Hants. Record Office; J.M.R.] (*C. Life* 17–24 May 1913).

PANSHANGER, HERTS., additions for the 5th Earl Cowper, 1806–7, completed by W. Atkinson, who Gothicized Wyatt's addition; dem. 1953 [Cowper papers, Herts. County Record Office; J.M.R.] (*C. Life*, 11–18 Jan. 1936).

DIGSWELL HOUSE, HERTS., for the Hon. Spencer Cowper, *c.* 1807 [Farington's Diary, 13 Feb. 1807].

LONDON: DOMESTIC ARCHITECTURE

PARK STREET, NO. 113 (later 13), internal alterations for the 1st Lord Harrowby, 1774–6 [Harrowby archives, Sandon Hall; J.M.R.].

SPRING GARDENS, nr. CHARING CROSS, unidentified work, probably *c.* 1775; dem. [one of the books in Wyatt's portrait is labelled 'Spring Gardens'].

ALBION PLACE, BLACKFRIARS, 1784–6; dem. [see Albion Mill, below].

attributed: OLD BURLINGTON STREET, NO. 29, alterations, including porch, for Sir John Call, *c.* 1785; dem. 1935 [*Survey of London* xxxii, 502 and pl. 80 b].

UPPER BROOK STREET, No. 6, probably altered interior for William Weddell, *c.* 1787–90; dem. *c.* 1934 [design for Mrs. Weddell's dressing-room signed 'S. W.' among Newby drawings in Pennington-Ramsden papers in Cumbria Record Office, and sketch of a sash fastener 'At Mr. Weddell's in Brook Street from Sam. Wyatt' in Yorkshire Arch. Soc's Library, Sir Thos. Frankland's notebook, Paine-Gallwey PD94, Box 2].

ST. JAMES'S SQUARE, NO. 15 (LICHFIELD HOUSE), remodelled interior for Thomas Anson, cr. 1st Viscount Anson, 1791–4 [*Survey of London* xxix, 148–53].

CLEVELAND ROW, NO. 4, for Lord Grenville, 1794–6 [G. L. C. Record Office, Stowe MS. 528; Cornwall Record Office, Fortescue MSS. DDF 259; J.M.R.].

GROSVENOR SQUARE, NO. 10, repairs and alterations for the Dowager Lady Petre, 1801–3; dem. [Petre archives, Essex Record Office; J.M.R.].

GROSVENOR SQUARE, NO. 40 (later 45) (PETRE HOUSE), reconstructed for the 10th Lord Petre, 1801–6; dem. [Petre archives, Essex Record Office; J.M.R.].

ST. JAMES'S SQUARE, NO. 3, alterations for the 3rd Earl of Hardwicke, 1806; dem. 1930 [correspondence sold at Sotheby's, 6 June 1966[1]] (*Survey of London* xxix, 83–8).

---

[1] Wrongly attributed in the Catalogue to James Wyatt.

PUBLIC AND INDUSTRIAL BUILDINGS

AMERSHAM CHURCH, BUCKS., repaired and refitted for William Drake, 1778–85; altered 1890 [Drake papers, Bucks. Record Office, D/DR/ 12/60–1].

BANGOR CATHEDRAL, probably the 'Mr. Wyatt' who rebuilt upper storey of Chapter House as library and registry, Gothic; dem. [M. L. Clarke, 'Bangor Cathedral 1700–1828', *Caernarvonshire Hist. Soc.'s Trans.* xiii, 1952, 29].

BIRMINGHAM, THEATRE ROYAL, NEW STREET, new façade, 1780–2; dem. 1902 [signed drawing in B.M., *King's Maps* xlii, 82 1; minutes of proprietors in Birmingham Reference Library] (*C. Life*, 11 Dec. 1915, 820).

SANDON CHURCH, STAFFS., refitted chancel for the 1st Lord Harrowby, 1782; altered 1928 [F. E. Copleston, *Sandon Church Restorations*, 1929].

DEPTFORD, KENT, THE VICTUALLING YARD, 1782; dem. [P.R.O., Adm. 111/89].

LONDON, THE ALBION MILL, BLACKFRIARS, 1783–6; destroyed by fire 1791 [A. W. Skempton, 'Samuel Wyatt and the Albion Mill', *Architectural History* xiv, 1971].

BIRMINGHAM, remodelled warehouse in Livery Street for Matthew Boulton, 1787–8; dem. 1950 [correspondence in Birmingham Assay Office, Tew MSS; J.M.R.].

LONDON, ST. MARY'S CHURCH, LAMBETH, alterations, 1786–7; altered 1851–2 [G.L.C. Record Office, Surrey Archdeaconry Records].

DUNGENESS, KENT, LIGHTHOUSE for T. W. Coke of Holkham, 1792 [accounts at Holkham Hall; J.M.R.].

LONGSHIPS LIGHTHOUSE, CORNWALL, for Trinity House, 1792 [Trinity House records; J.M.R.].

STAFFORD, SHIRE HALL, joint design with John Harvey, 1794 [see p. 399].

LONDON, TRINITY HOUSE, TOWER HILL, 1793–6; gutted by bombing 1940, restored by A. E. Richardson 1953 [G. Richardson, *New Vitruvius Britannicus* i, 1802, pls. 22–3] (*C. Life*, 18 Jan. 1941, 22 Oct. 1953).

RAMSGATE HARBOUR, KENT, lighthouse, storehouse, harbour-master's house, gate-lodge, board room or pier house, etc., 1794–1805; all dem. [J. M. Robinson, 'Samuel Wyatt at Ramsgate', *Architectural History* xvi, 1973].

ST. AGNES LIGHTHOUSE, SCILLY ISLES, partially rebuilt to new design, 1806 [Trinity House records; J.M.R.].

FLAMBOROUGH HEAD LIGHTHOUSE, YORKS. (E.R.), for Trinity House, 1806 [Trinity House records; J.M.R.].

LONDON, TRINITY ALMSHOUSES, MILE END ROAD, new Quadrangle, 1806; dem. *c.* 1941 [Trinity Hospital records; J.M.R.] (C. R. Ashbee, *Trinity Hospital*, 1888).

MARLOW, BUCKS., THE MARKET HOUSE (later Crown Inn) for Thomas Williams, 1807 [H. M. Col-

vin, 'The Architectural History of Marlow', *Records of Bucks.* xv, 1947, 11].

WYATT, WILLIAM (1734–1780), *see* WYATT, BENJAMIN (1709–1772).

WYATVILLE, Sir JEFFRY (1766–1840), son of Joseph Wyatt of Burton-on-Trent, was born there on 3 August 1766. His mother died soon after his birth, and his 'clever but indolent' father married again. The result was an unhappy childhood from which Jeffry tried unsuccessfully to escape by running away to sea. Eventually, however, he was apprenticed to his uncle Samuel Wyatt (*q.v.*), in whose London office he worked from 1784 or 1785 to 1791 or 1792. From 1786 onwards he exhibited regularly at the Royal Academy, and surviving drawings show that he had acquired considerable skill in architectural composition. In 1792 he transferred to the office of his more celebrated uncle James Wyatt, with whom he remained until 1799, when he entered into partnership with John Armstrong (d. 1803), a carpenter and building contractor with a successful business in Pimlico. This link with the building trade gave him a steady income while at the same time permitting him to develop a personal architectural practice. He soon became well known as a country-house architect with a large clientele among the Whig aristocracy. Unlike his uncle James he was efficient, methodical and dependable, with a large and well-organized office in which by 1812 he was employing as many as ten clerks. When James died in 1813 Jeffry inherited some of his commissions (*e.g.* Bretby and Ashridge), and took his place as the principal representative of the Wyatt dynasty.

By the 1820s Jeffry Wyatt was one of the half-dozen leading English architects. On the back of a portrait painted about this time he complacently listed his principal employers, giving the names of four dukes, one marquess, seven earls and thirteen other landowners whose houses he had altered or rebuilt. In 1824 he was able to claim the supreme honour of royal patronage when he began the transformation of Windsor Castle for King George IV. Although extensively altered by Charles II, the Castle had, by the nineteenth century, become quite unfitted for residence of the Sovereign, and in 1824 the sum of £150,000 was voted by the House of Commons for its improvement. A brief was drawn up by Sir Charles Long, the King's principal artistic adviser, and Jeffry Wyatt was invited to submit designs in company with the three architects of the Office of Works – Soane, Smirke and Nash. Wyatt's inclusion in this limited competition showed that he was highly regarded by the King and his mentor Long, and it was his designs – closely following Long's extremely detailed and specific brief – that were chosen. On 12 August

959

1824 the first stone was laid by George IV, who on the same day authorized the architect to call himself 'Wyatville' and to adopt the word 'Windsor' as his motto.[1] In 1828, on the completion of the royal apartments, Wyatville was knighted and granted a residence in the Winchester Tower, a privilege afterwards confirmed by William IV and Queen Victoria. As the work progressed, the original estimates were far exceeded, and in 1830, when no less than £527,000 had been advanced, a select committee was appointed to enquire into the cost of completion. The committee found 'no reason to attribute the error of the original estimate to any want of due precaution on the part of the architect', and with the aid of further grants, totalling well over half a million pounds, the reconstruction of the Castle was finally completed soon after the accession of Queen Victoria in 1837. The Upper Ward was almost completely rebuilt on a large scale with a new 'George IV Gateway' forming a grand entrance on the south side. The State Apartments on the north side were reconstructed round a new Grand Staircase (subsequently replaced in 1866 by a new staircase designed by Salvin) and new and more convenient royal apartments were created on the east side facing the gardens. Externally Wyatville (following Long's directive) added greatly to the picturesque outline of the Castle by raising the Round Tower 33 feet, and so making of it a dominant feature round which to group the newly battlemented and machicolated towers. Wyatville's rehabilitation of Windsor Castle was not effected without much destruction of older buildings, including Hugh May's magnificently decorated State Apartments and the old royal chapel which had stood to the west of St. George's Hall since the twelfth century. But it fully achieved its main purpose in converting the old, scarcely habitable fortress into what the select committee of 1830 described as 'in all respects a fit residence for the Sovereign of this country'. At the command of George IV, Wyatville prepared a full account of the works carried out under his direction, which was eventually published in 1841 as *Illustrations of Windsor Castle by the late Sir Jeffry Wyatville, R.A.*, edited by his pupil Henry Ashton.

Wyatville was an able architect, but scarcely a designer of genius. Best known as an expert purveyor of the picturesque country house, usually in a Tudor Gothic or 'Elizabethan' dress, he could also offer unexceptionable 'Grecian' elevations if required. But the latter contributed noth-

ing significant to the development of English neo-classical architecture, while only a readiness to advance stylistically into the sixteenth century distinguishes his Gothic houses from those of his uncle James. The general form of his greatest work – Windsor Castle – was to a large extent dictated by the detailed brief drawn up by Sir Charles Long, which Wyatville carried out in a workmanlike but not over-sensitive manner. The result was 'a masterpiece of Picturesque architecture that composes magnificently from almost any point of view, but does not bear inspection at close quarters, when Wyatville's coarse detailing and ubiquitous black ash mortar show a marked insensitivity to those variations in texture and profile that give life and interest to an ancient building'.

Wyatville was elected A.R.A. in 1822 and R.A. in 1824. He had sought admission as an Associate as early as 1800, but there were objections to the election of an architect who was also in business as a builder, and he was allowed to remain a candidate for over twenty years before he was finally elected in 1822 at the age of 56. He was a Fellow of the Royal and Antiquarian Societies, and a member of the Saxon Ernestine Order, the Grand Cross of which was granted him by Queen Adelaide's brother, the Duke of Saxe-Meiningen, for whom he gave advice about the design of the castle at Landsberg and planned a ducal residence at Meiningen that was never built. His office and town residence were at 49 (now 39) Lower Brook Street, where he died on 18 February 1840 at the age of 73. He was buried in a vault at the east end of St. George's Chapel, Windsor. By his wife Sophia Powell (who died in 1810), he had two daughters and one son, George Geoffrey, who intended to follow his father's profession, but died in 1833 at the age of 29. Among his pupils or assistants were Henry Ashton, C. H. Basnett, Benjamin Baud, R. Carver, C. Chalkley, P. B. Cotes, W. J. Donthorn, J. Foster, W. Harris, Edward Haycock, H. Lester, Charles Parker, J. Sanderson and J. T. Wood. Michael Gandy was in his office from 1807 to 1840.

Wyatville is described as being 'of low stature and inelegant personal form' which was, however, redeemed by a lively expression. Throughout his life he retained a characteristic Midland accent and an engaging simplicity of manner. He got on well with royalty, but the fastidious C. R. Cockerell thought him, though 'good natured', 'no gentleman, vulgar minded ... [and] a great boaster'. A list of portraits is given in Dr. Linstrum's book. The most important are the one by Sir Thomas Lawrence painted in 1827–8 and the bust by Chantrey carved *c.* 1835, both at Windsor Castle.

[Obituary in *Gent's Mag.* 1840 (i), 545–9; *A.P.S.D.*; *D.N.B.*; D. Linstrum, *Sir Jeffry*

---

[1] According to *Gent's Mag.*, this was intended 'not merely as a personal compliment' but was done 'for the purpose of distinguishing and separating the Wyatt of that reign from his uncle, Mr. James Wyatt', who had been employed at Windsor in the preceding reign.

Wyatville, 1972; D. Linstrum, *The Wyatt Family* (R.I.B.A. Drawings Catalogue, 1974.]

The following list of executed works may be supplemented by reference to the more elaborate 'Catalogue of Work' in Dr. Linstrum's biography, which gives additional references and includes some doubtful and unexecuted works not listed below. Illustrations of all Wyatville's principal buildings will be found in the same book.

WOOLLEY PARK, BERKS., remodelled for the Rev. P. Wroughton, *c.* 1799; wings added *c.* 1860 [G. Richardson, *New Vitruvius Britannicus* ii, 1808, pls. 36–8; exhib. at R.A. 1799].

BLADON CASTLE, NEWTON SOLNEY, DERBYSHIRE, for Abraham Hoskins, 1801–5, castellated [apparently the building exhibited at the R.A. in 1799 as a 'villa at Bladon Hill ... seat of Abraham Hoskins', and enlarged into a castellated house].

HILLFIELD LODGE (now CASTLE), nr. WATFORD, HERTS., for the Hon. George Villiers, *c.* 1800–5, castellated [exhib. at R.A. 1805].

WOLLATON HALL, NOTTS., alterations and extensions for the 6th Lord Middleton, *c.* 1801 and 1823; Beeston and Lenton gateways to park, 1823–4; Elizabethan style [exhib. at R.A. 1804 and 1824; Linstrum, 255].

LONDON, HOLDERNESSE (later LONDONDERRY) HOUSE, HERTFORD STREET, alterations for the 6th Lord Middleton, 1802; remodelled by B. D. Wyatt 1825–8; dem. 1964 [Linstrum, 241].

NONSUCH PARK, SURREY, for Samuel Farmer, 1802–6, Tudor style; altered 1845 [exhib. at R.A. 1802–3].

GREATHAM HOSPITAL, CO. DURHAM, rebuilt at the expense of the 7th Earl of Bridgewater, 1803–4, Tudor style [J. Dugdale, *The British Traveller* ii, 1819, 305].

BROWSHOLME HALL, YORKS. (W.R.), decoration of new gallery or drawing-room for T. L. Parker, 1805 [T. L. Parker, *A Description of Browsholme Hall*, 1815, 8] (*C. Life*, 13 July 1935).

HYDE HALL (now Royal Wanstead School), nr. SAWBRIDGEWORTH, HERTS., remodelled for the 2nd Earl of Roden, 1806–7; lodges to drive [Linstrum, 238].

LONGLEAT HOUSE, WILTS., alterations for the 2nd Marquess of Bath, 1806–13, including reconstruction of north front, addition of Stable Court, a new principal staircase, and extensive internal alterations, chiefly in Elizabethan style; also Horningsham Lodge and estate buildings [Linstrum, 244–5] (*C. Life*, 29 April 1949).

ROCHE COURT, HANTS., castellated lodge for Sir J. S. W. Gardiner, Bart., 1808 [exhib. at R.A. 1808].

ROOD ASHTON HOUSE nr. TROWBRIDGE, WILTS., enlarged for R. G. Long, 1808, Tudor style;

altered by T. Hopper 1836 [exhib. at R.A. 1808].

LYPIATT PARK, GLOS., alterations and additions for Paul Wathen (later Sir Paul Baghot), 1809, Tudor Gothic; enlarged by T. H. Wyatt 1876 [exhib. at R.A. 1809].

THURLAND CASTLE, LANCS., design for chapel and entrance court for R. T. North, exhibited at R.A. 1809 and probably carried out as part of a general renovation; new drawing-room, etc., by G. Webster of Kendal, *c.* 1827–9; extensive alterations after fire in 1879 [Linstrum, 249, where the reference to a design by Robert Walker is due to a mistake in Graves's catalogue of Royal Academy exhibitors, viii, 108].

BADMINTON HOUSE, GLOS., work for the 6th Duke of Beaufort, including remodelling of interiors of drawing-room and library, new top light to staircase and conservatory, 1809–11 [exhib. at R.A. 1811; accounts at Badminton] (*C. Life*, 2 Dec. 1939).

ENDSLEIGH, nr. MILTON ABBOT, DEVON, *cottage orné* for the 6th Duke of Bedford, 1810 [exhib. at R.A. 1811; other references in Linstrum, 236] (*C. Life*, 3–10 Aug. 1961).

WYNNSTAY, DENBIGHSHIRE, round tower at Nant-y-Belan intended as cenotaph in memory of officers killed in Irish Rebellion of 1798, for Sir Watkin Williams-Wynn, Bart., *c.* 1810 [S. Lewis, *Topographical Dictionary of Wales* ii, 1849, 372] (*C. Life*, 6 April 1972, 852, fig. 6).

BELTON HOUSE, LINCS., minor alterations to house, conservatory and dairy for the 1st Earl Brownlow, *c.* 1810 [exhib. at R.A. 1811; cf. Linstrum, 230 for drawings at Belton] (*C. Life*, 17 Sept. 1964).

ABINGDON, BERKS., COUNTY BRIDEWELL (now recreation centre), 1805–11, built by Daniel Harris (*q.v.*) to Wyatville's designs [payment to Wyatville cited by Linstrum, 258; unsigned drawings in Berkshire Record Office, Q/AG/2/1; for Harris see *Report from the Committee of Aldermen appointed to visit Several Gaols in England*, 1816, 25].

LONDON, CHESTERFIELD HOUSE, SOUTH AUDLEY STREET, repairs costing £15,264 for the 5th Earl of Chesterfield, 1811–13; dem. 1937 [account in Guildhall Library, MS. 3070 A].

CASSIOBURY PARK, HERTS., employed by 5th Earl of Essex after death of James Wyatt (1813), but uncertain precisely what he designed; house dem. 1922 [Linstrum, 234] (J. Britton, *Cassiobury Park*, 1837; *C. Life*, 17 Sept. 1910).

STUBTON HALL, LINCS., for Sir Robert Heron, Bart., 1813–14; portico and porch are later additions [inscription in house; exhib. at R.A. 1816].

BRETBY HALL, DERBYSHIRE, for the 5th Earl of Chesterfield, *c.* 1813–15, castellated. Designs had been made by James Wyatt before his death in 1813, but they were probably superseded by the designs for which Jeffry Wyatt was paid £408 2s. in 1819, some of which he exhibited at the R.A. in 1812 and 1813. According to J. Glover, *History of the County of Derby* ii, 1833, 163, the house 'was designed by Sir Jeffry Wyatville and Mr. Martin, the Earl's architect, and built under the direction of the latter', but was left unfinished after the Earl's death in 1815 [executors' accounts, formerly at Ettington Hall, now in Warwickshire Record Office; cf. Linstrum, 231].

HINTON ST. GEORGE, SOMERSET, Gothic entrance and perhaps other works for the 4th Earl Poulett, 1814 [exhib. at R.A. 1814].

FROME, SOMERSET, ST. JOHN'S CHURCH, designed Gothic screen to forecourt, and cased west front in ashlar, 1814; west front rebuilt 1862–4 [W. J. E. Bennett, *History of the Church of St. John of Frome*, 1866, 46–8].

ASHRIDGE PARK, HERTS., completion of and additions to the house (Gothic), lodges, etc., for the 7th Earl of Bridgewater, *c.* 1814–17; the Bridgewater Column 1831–2 [inscription on brass plate in hall; exhib. at R.A. 1816–17; Linstrum, 228–9] (H. A. Tipping, *English Homes*, VI (i), 339–46).

DINTON HOUSE, nr. SALISBURY, WILTS., for William Wyndham, 1814–17 [drawings in R.I.B.A. Coll.] (*C. Life*, 17 Dec. 1943).

TREBARTHA HALL, NORTHILL, CORNWALL, alterations and additions for F. H. Rodd, 1815; dem. 1948 [plan in R.I.B.A. Coll.] (E. Twycross, *The Mansions of England: Cornwall*, 1846, 62; plans (not seen) in Cornwall Record Office, 49/1/131/1–10).

DENFORD HOUSE, BERKS., for William Hallett, *c.* 1815; alterations by J. B. Papworth 1827–8; wings added 1939 [included in the list of Wyatville's works given by Ashton in his *Illustrations of Windsor Castle*].

BRETTON HALL, YORKS. (W.R.), enlarged and altered house and designed aviary, etc., for Col. T. R. Beaumont, *c.* 1815 [exhib. at R.A. 1815; Arthur Oswald in *C. Life*, 21–28 May 1938; D. Linstrum, 'Two Wentworth Houses', *Leeds Arts Calendar*, no. 68, 1971].

BELTON CHURCH, LINCS., mortuary chapel for the 1st Earl Brownlow, 1816 [exhib. at R.A. 1816].

MARSTON HOUSE, MARSTON BIGOT, SOMERSET, Ionic loggia for the 8th Earl of Cork and Orrery, probably *c.* 1817 when Wyatville wrote of going to Lord Cork's [Lord Cork is named as one of Wyatville's employers on the back of the portrait preserved in his family; M. McGarvie, 'Marston House', *Proceedings of the Somerset Archaeological and N.H. Soc.* cxviii, 1974, 20].

WOBURN ABBEY, BEDS., conversion of conservatory into sculpture gallery and addition of Temple of the Graces to contain group of 'The Graces' by Canova, for the 6th Duke of Bedford, *c.*

1816–18 [exhib. at R.A. 1818] (*C. Life*, 15 July 1965); Botanical House 1837 (dem.) and Araucaria House [Linstrum, 255; *History and Description of Woburn Abbey*, 1845, 180–1].

TOWNELEY HALL, LANCS., alterations for Peregrine Towneley, 1817–19, Gothic [drawings at Towneley Hall Museum] (*C. Life*, 16 Aug. 1913).

BANNER CROSS, ECCLESALL, nr. SHEFFIELD, YORKS. (W.R.), for General William Murray, 1817–21, castellated [Linstrum, 229].

LITTLE GADDESDEN CHURCH, HERTS., added south chapel to chancel, 1819, and probably designed south aisle, for the executors of the 8th Earl of Bridgewater, 1830 [Linstrum, 240].

GOPSALL HALL, HERTS., entrance archway and probable alterations to house for the Hon. R. W. P. Curzon (later 1st Earl Howe), 1819; dem. 1951 [exhib. at R.A. 1819] (*Connoisseur* cxxviii, 1951).

TREBURSEY HOUSE nr. LAUNCESTON, CORNWALL, for the Hon. William Eliot (later 2nd Earl of St. Germans), before 1820, Gothic [included in the list of Wyatville's works given by Ashton in his *Illustrations of Windsor Castle*; described as 'recently erected' by C. S. Gilbert, *Topography of Cornwall*, 1820, 492].

CHATSWORTH HOUSE, DERBYSHIRE, alterations and additions for the 6th Duke of Devonshire, 1820–41, including the library, the north wing and tower, the north entrance archway, lodges and estate buildings [Francis Thompson, *A History of Chatsworth*, 1949; J. Cornforth in *C. Life*, 25 July, 1 Aug. 1968].

GREAT BERKHAMSTED CHURCH, HERTS., restorations, 1820 [*V.C.H. Herts.* ii, 174].

WOOLLEY PARK, YORKS. (W.R.), lodge and gateway to Sheffield road, for Godfrey Wentworth, 1820 [Linstrum, 255–6].

BISHOPS WOOD HOUSE, HEREFS., for John Partridge, *c.* 1820, Gothic; destroyed by fire 1873 [Linstrum, 230–1].

CLAVERTON HOUSE, nr. BATH, SOMERSET, for John Vivian, *c.* 1820 [included in the list of Wyatville's works given by Ashton in his *Illustrations of Windsor Castle*].

CAMBRIDGE, SIDNEY SUSSEX COLLEGE, remodelled 1821–2, in Tudor Gothic style [exhib. at R.A. 1822 and 1832; Willis & Clark, ii, 741, 747–9] (R.C.H.M., *Cambridge* ii, 203 *et seq.*).

LONDON, NO. 49 (later 50, now 39) LOWER BROOK STREET, remodelled for himself, 1821–3 [Linstrum, 23, 242–3].

STACKPOLE COURT, PEMBROKESHIRE, remodelled for the 1st Earl of Cawdor, after 1821; dem. 1961 [S. Lewis, *Topographical Dictionary of Wales* ii, 1849, 373]; bridge 1832 [Linstrum, 248]. The stables bore the date 1844.

MARBURY CHURCH, CHESHIRE, rebuilt chancel for the 7th Earl of Bridgewater, 1822; altered 1891–2 [Linstrum, 245].

SANS SOUCI, LYTCHETT MINSTER, DORSET, green-house for Sir Claude Scott, Bart., 1822; dem. [exhib. at R.A. 1822].

WHITELEY WOOD HALL, nr. SHEFFIELD, YORKS. (W.R.), enlarged for William Silcock, 1822; dem. 1959 [exhib. at R.A. 1822; Linstrum, 251].

ALLENDALE HOUSE, WIMBORNE MINSTER, DORSET, for William Castleman, 1823 [included in the list of Wyatville's works given by Ashton in his *Illustrations of Windsor Castle*].

LONDON, BEDFORD LODGE, CAMPDEN HILL, altera-tions and additions for the 6th Duke of Bed-ford, 1823 and 1835–6; dem. [drawings by Wyatville in Woburn Abbey MS. 178; Lin-strum, 240].

WINDSOR GREAT PARK, ROYAL LODGE, alterations and additions for King George IV, 1823–30, Gothic; dem. 1830 except conservatory and dining-room, which form the nucleus of the existing building [Sir O. Morshead, *George IV and Royal Lodge*, Brighton 1965; *History of the King's Works* vi, 399–401] (*C. Life*, 1 July 1939).

WINDSOR CASTLE, BERKS., remodelled Upper Ward and Round Tower for King George IV and King William IV, 1824–40 [H. Ashton, *Illustrations of Windsor Castle*, 1841; M. Gandy & B. Baud, *Architectural Illustrations of Windsor Castle*, 1842; Sir O. Morshead, *Windsor Castle*, 1957; *History of the King's Works* vi, 373–94; Linstrum, 252–3].

HASTINGS, SUSSEX, NO. 14 MARINE PARADE, un-specified work for the Comte de Vandes, 1824 [*A.P.S.D.*; Linstrum, 237].

YESTER HOUSE, EAST LOTHIAN, keeper's lodge for the 8th Marquess of Tweeddale, 1824 [exhib. at R.A. 1824].

SOMERHILL, nr. TONBRIDGE, KENT, interior of library in Jacobean style for James Alexander, *c.* 1824; altered by Sir Herbert Baker in the 1930s [J. Britton, *Descriptive Sketches of Tun-bridge Wells*, 1832, 121]. Further alterations to the house were carried out by Salvin in 1828–33 (below, p. 971).

LONDON, NO. 74 GROSVENOR SQUARE, alterations for the 2nd Lord (later 1st Earl of Cawdor, *c.* 1824 [Linstrum, 241].

LONDON, SCOTT'S (now Westminster) BANK, NO. 2 CAVENDISH SQUARE, new banking hall, etc., 1825; since altered [*A.P.S.D.*; Linstrum, 241].

WINDSOR GREAT PARK, rebuilt bridge over Vir-ginia Water and constructed ornamental ruin known as 'Temple of Augustus', formed from classical fragments from Lepcis Magna, North Africa, 1826–9 [*History of the King's Works* vi, 396–7; G. E. Chambers, 'The Ruins at Virginia Water', *Berkshire Arch. Jnl.* liv, 1954–5].

LILLESHALL HALL, SALOP., for Lord Gower (later 2nd Duke of Sutherland), 1826–30, Eliza-bethan style [exhib. at R.A. 1829; Linstrum, 240].

GOLDEN GROVE, CARMARTHENSHIRE, for the 2nd Lord (later 1st Earl of) Cawdor, 1826–37, Elizabethan style [exhib. at R.A. 1829; Lin-strum, 236–7].

FORT BELVEDERE, WINDSOR GREAT PARK, altera-tions and additions for King George IV, 1828–9, castellated [*History of the King's Works* vi, 397: C. Hussey in *C. Life*, 19–26 Nov. 1959].

CHILLINGHAM CASTLE, NORTHUMBERLAND, work for the 5th Earl of Tankerville, probably in-cluding alterations to hall and south wing and design of Village Lodge, *c.* 1825–8 [*History of Northumberland* xiv, p. 336 *et seq.*; Tankerville papers in Northumberland Record Office; Linstrum, 234–5] (*C. Life*, 8 March 1913).

COBHAM HALL, KENT, repaired interior of north wing and designed Gothic entrance thereto, for the 5th Earl of Darnley, who succeeded in 1831 and died in 1835 [C. Greenwood, *Epitome of County History: Kent*, 1838, 215].

KENSINGTON PALACE, LONDON, internal altera-tions, 1833 and 1835, including conversion of former kitchen into chapel [*History of the King's Works* vi, 347–8].

KEW GARDENS, SURREY, THE PANTHEON or KING WILLIAM'S TEMPLE, 1836–7 [Linstrum, 239; *History of the King's Works* vi, 441].

CADLAND, nr. SOUTHAMPTON, HANTS., enlarged and remodelled for A. R. Drummond, 1837–8; dem. 1953 [Linstrum, 137–40, 232–3].

RANGER'S LODGE, BUSHY PARK, MIDDLESEX, altera-tions, probably including conservatory, for Queen Adelaide, 1837–8 [Linstrum, 232].

KEW CHURCH, SURREY, enlarged at expense of King William IV, 1837–8 [E. W. Brayley, *Topographical History of Surrey*, 1841–8, iii, 153].

EASTBURY HOUSE, COMPTON, SURREY, additions for the Rev. Edward Fulham, who succeeded to the property in 1777 and died in 1832 [E. W. Brayley, *Topographical History of Surrey*, 1841–8, v, 225].

LEXHAM HALL, NORFOLK, additions for Col. F. W. Keppel; partly dem. after fire *c.* 1950 [Lin-strum, 240].

UNEXECUTED

Wyatville's most important unexecuted designs were for a PARLIAMENT HOUSE at QUEBEC, CANADA, 1812; a palatial mansion for the 2nd Lord (later 1st Earl) Yarborough at BROCKLESBY, LINCS., 1820; a mansion at TOTTENHAM PARK, WILTS., for 1st Marquess of Ailesbury, 1821; remodelling ST. JAMES'S PALACE, LONDON, for King William IV, 1831–5, and for a Royal Villa at MEININGEN, Ger-many, for the Duke of Saxe-Meiningen, 1835. The designs for Tottenham are in a bound volume among the Ailesbury muniments: all the others are described and illustrated by Linstrum.

WYNNE, JOHN, exhibited architectural designs at the Royal Academy in 1812–13 from 45 Paternoster Row, London. He was presumably the John Wynn whose designs for GREAT BERKHAMSTED RECTORY, HERTS., dated 1811, are in the Lincolnshire Record Office [MGA 63].

Y

YELLOWLEY, JOSEPH (–1828), was presumably a carpenter by trade, as he was Master of the Carpenters' Company in 1799 and again in the year of his death. He is described as an architect or surveyor in contemporary directories, and was President of the Surveyors' Club in 1810. He was employed by Whitbread's brewery and in 1812 planned docks in the Isle of Dogs [Middlesex County Records, D.P. 80, *ex inf.* Mr. M. H. Port].

YEMANS, or **YEOMANS, JOHN,** was a master bricklayer of Hampton-on-Thames, Middlesex. On 1 February 1699/1700, he contracted with William Lowndes to 'performe the workmanship of all the Brickwork and Tyling of an House intended to be forthwith built for the said Wm. Lowndes at Winslowe in the County of Bucks.' The excellent brickwork of this house, which may have been designed by Wren, shows that Yemans was a highly competent workman [*Wren Soc.* xvii, 62–3.] In 1708 Yemans rebuilt the central tower of KINGSTON ON THAMES CHURCH, SURREY, 'according to the modell or Scheme drawn by him'. The former tower had been so badly damaged in the great storm of 1703 that it had had to be taken down soon afterwards [MS. Vestry Minutes]. Yemans's ledger, covering the years 1698–1711, is preserved among the Kingston Borough Records (D. IV, d. i). It shows that he lived at Hampton Wick, and that he held office as churchwarden in 1699. In that year he carried out some minor alterations to the Earl of Rochester's house at Petersham, and in 1703–4 he did a good deal of work in connection with Mr. Hill's 'new building at Richmond', *i.e.* TRUMPETERS' HOUSE.

YENN, JOHN (1750–1821), the son of a City barber and wig-maker, was born on 8 March 1750. In 1764 he became a pupil of Sir William Chambers, and in 1769 was one of the first students admitted to the newly formed Royal Academy Schools. He was awarded the Gold Medal in 1771 for his design for a nobleman's villa (now in the R.I.B.A. Drawings Collection). Chambers employed him as a clerk of works at Somerset House from 1776 onwards, and was no doubt instrumental in obtaining for him the post of a labourer in trust in the Office of Works in 1777. In 1780 he became Clerk of the Works at Richmond New Park Lodge, and in 1782 was promoted to be Clerk of the Works at Buckingham House, Kensington Palace and the Royal Mews. In 1788 he succeeded Sir Robert Taylor as Surveyor of Greenwich Hospital.

Yenn was elected A.R.A. in 1774, and became a full academician in 1791. In 1796 he succeeded Chambers as Treasurer. He played an active part in Royal Academy politics and caused much trouble in 1803 by demanding an increase in the Treasurer's stipend. He incurred the dislike of Benjamin West, who told Farington that Yenn's 'watery eye' was a sure sign of treacherous character. Yenn was also a member of the Architects' Club from its foundation in 1791. He retired from the Office of Works in 1819 and died in Gloucester Place on 1 March 1821. His library was sold at Sotheby's on 30 April 1835 (B.M., SC.S 203(8)). A portrait in oils by J. F. Rigaud, painted in 1785, is at the Royal Academy, where there is also a pencil portrait by George Dance. The former portrait was engraved by J. K. Sherwin. J. Fidler, George Meredith and Henry Hakewill were pupils.

Yenn's private practice was on a modest scale, and his executed buildings show him as a faithful disciple of his master Chambers.[1] His correct neo-classical style is best seen at Greenwich, where in 1811–14 he and H. H. Seward together rebuilt the west front of the King Charles block. His real distinction lay, however, in his brilliant architectural draughtsmanship. His exquisite coloured drawings, based on techniques of presentation learned in Chambers's office, are probably the finest made by any English architect of the eighteenth century. They show 'none of the leaning towards austerity that usually characterises neo-classicism'. On the contrary Yenn used his neo-classical repertoire with a lavish abandon that would have been more appropriate in the age of rococo. The principal collection of his drawings was given to the Royal Academy in 1865 by his daughter, Mrs. Thackeray. Other (though generally less spectacular) examples of Yenn's draughtsmanship are to be seen in the Victoria and Albert Museum, R.I.B.A. Drawings Collection, Minet Library at Camberwell, the Mellon Collection and the Memorial Library of the University of Delaware.

[*A.P.S.D.*; *The Farington Diary*, ed. J. Greig, i, 79, 80, 176, ii, 184, and unpublished MS., 7 May 1795; P.R.O., Apprenticeship Registers, 1764; *History of the King's Works* vi; J. Harris, *Catalogue of British Drawings for Architecture,*

---

[1] In 1774, Chambers described Yenn as 'an ingenious faithful intelligent servant' who had lived with him for the past ten years, and who 'for two or three years past has managed a great part of my extensive business very much to my satisfaction' [B.M., Add. MS. 41135, f. 26].

etc., in American Collections, 1970, 310–17; R.I.B.A. Drawings Catalogue, forthcoming; John Yenn, Draughtsman Extraordinary (catalogue of exhibition at R.I.B.A. Drawings Coll.), 1973; Marcus Binney, 'A Forgotten Pupil of Chambers', C. Life, 13 Sept. 1973.]

HADZOR HOUSE, nr. DROITWICH, WORCS., for Richard Amphlett, 1779; rebuilt 1827 [exhib. at R.A. as 'now building' 1779].

EALING GROVE, MIDDLESEX, alterations and entrance lodges for the 4th Duke of Marlborough, c. 1780; dem. [exhib. at R.A. 1780; drawings in Delaware University Library].

LONDON, MARLBOROUGH HOUSE, ST. JAMES'S, decorations, etc., for the 4th Duke of Marlborough, c. 1780–90 [drawings in Delaware University Library].

LONDON, GRANTHAM HOUSE, WHITEHALL, alterations for the 2nd Lord Grantham, probably c. 1780; dem. c. 1896 [drawings in Delaware University Library] (Survey of London xiii, 160–1).

BLENHEIM PALACE, OXON., THE DITCHLEY GATE LODGE, 1781, THE TEMPLE OF HEALTH, 1789, and other minor works for the 4th Duke of Marlborough [Temple exhib. at R.A. 1791; drawings for Temple and lodges in Delaware University Library; drawings for pier-glasses, fireplaces, etc., in Bodleian Library, MS. Top. Oxon. a. 37, ff. 143–7; other drawings, including unexecuted design for Rosamund's Well, in Royal Academy Library].

NORTH ASTON HALL, OXON., alterations for Oldfield Bowles, 1781–2; remodelled c. 1850 [south front exhib. at R.A. 1782; drawings in Delaware University Library; working drawings in Bodleian Library, MS. Top. Oxon. a. 37, ff. 58–64].

WOODSTOCK CHURCH, OXON., rebuilt north aisle, 1783, Gothic; rebuilt by Sir A. W. Blomfield 1878. Yenn also made designs for rebuilding the tower which were not executed, but are preserved among the Oxford Diocesan Records in the Bodleian Library. [H. M. Colvin, 'The Rebuilding of Woodstock Church Tower, 1770–1786', Oxfordshire Archaeological Soc.'s Report, no. 87, 1949; drawings in Delaware University Library.]

LLANFYLLIN, MONTGOMERYSHIRE, THE TOWN HALL, c. 1790; dem. 1960 [exhib. at R.A. 1791 as 'to be built', but said to have been built in 1789].

WARGRAVE HILL (now MANOR), WARGRAVE, BERKS., for Joseph Hill, c. 1780–90; since enlarged [plans at Royal Academy] (E. B. Pope, History of Wargrave, Hitchin 1929, 59).

PUTNEY HEATH, SURREY, alterations to villa for Lady Polwarth, 1791–3 [Bedfordshire Record Office, L 31/282–4, and drawings in Minet Library, Camberwell].

PUTNEY HEATH, SURREY, alterations to Lady Grantham's house, 1792–3 [drawings in Minet Library, Camberwell].

WINDSOR CASTLE, BERKS., music room and dining-room in east range of Upper Ward for King George III, 1795; dem. c. 1825 [History of the King's Works vi, 374–5].

KENSINGTON PALACE, LONDON, alterations to the apartments of Edward, Duke of Kent, c. 1800–10 [History of the King's Works vi, 340–1].

NEW YORK, AMERICA, design for a four-storey house made for a gentleman who intended to build a house in the city, but changed his mind, whereupon Yenn's designs were advertised for sale in the New York newspapers in 1804 [R. S. Gottesman, The Arts and Crafts in New York, 1800–1804, New York Historical Soc. 1965, 179].

LONDON, MELBOURNE, now DOVER, HOUSE, WHITEHALL, internal alterations for the 1st Viscount Melbourne, 1805 [drawings at Royal Academy] (Survey of London xiv, chap. vi).

GREENWICH HOSPITAL, KENT, rebuilt west façade of King Charles Block, in association with H. H. Seward, 1811–14 [Hasted's History of Kent: Hundred of Blackheath, ed. Drake, 1886, 69].

YOUNG, JOHN, was a prominent London master mason of the seventeenth century. Having been made 'sinisterly free' of the Weavers' Company, he regularized his position by transferring to the Masons' Company in 1637, and subsequently served as Warden and Master (1657). From 1638 onwards he did a good deal of work at the INNER TEMPLE [F. Inderwick, Calendar of Inner Temple Records ii, 246–7, 258, 263, 312–13, 321]. In 1638–40 he was, with Edmund Kinsman (q.v.) and James Holmes, one of the three London masons who contracted to build the tower of GOUDHURST CHURCH, KENT [Archaeologia Cantiana xxviii, 10–13]. In March 1649/50, as John Young, 'freemason in Blackfriars', he contracted to build the new church at BERWICK-ON-TWEED, 'conforme to his Moddell or draught', and performed his task to the satisfaction of three Scottish and three English masons who were employed to inspect the completed building in February 1652/3 [Berwick-on-Tweed Guild-books]. It was designed by Young in a mixture of Gothic and classical motives somewhat reminiscent of the London church of St. Katherine Cree (1628–31). In the reign of Charles II, Young was employed as a mason at Greenwich Hospital, Mercers' Hall, Apothecaries' Hall and elsewhere. At APOTHECARIES' HALL, BLACKFRIARS LANE, he supplied in 1670 a 'draught' of the doorcase to the hall incorporating the Company's arms, and built the stone stairs in the courtyard at his own cost in discharge of unpaid rent for the riverside premises (destroyed in the Great Fire) whose site he leased from the Company [Arthur Oswald in *C. Life*, 10 Oct. 1947]. His account-book in the Bodleian Library (MS. Rawlinson C.495) shows that he was also a monumental sculptor. In January 1656/7 he agreed to make a marble monument for Lady St. John to cost £70, and in November 1657 he agreed with Mr. St. John of Woodford, Northants., to make a monument of black and white marble 'like to Mr. Seldens in the Temple Church' for £40.

Young appears to have died in about 1680, leaving two sons, Nicholas and John, both of whom followed their father's craft. Nicholas Young, who had several contracts for building Wren's City Churches, was Master of the Masons' Company in 1682. The date of his death has not been established, but he was still alive in 1700. His portrait is in Mr. Derek Sherborne's collection. John Young, junior, was Master of the Company in 1695 and died during his term of office.

[D. Knoop & G. P. Jones, *The London Mason in the Seventeenth Century*, 1935, 31; R. Gunnis, *Dictionary of British Sculptors*, 1968, 451–2; *Middle Temple Records*, ed. C. H. Hopwood, iii, 1460.]

YOUNG, JOHN (–1801), of Edinburgh, was a wright by trade, but is often described as 'architect' in contemporary sources. He was prominent among the builders of the New Town, taking five feus in 1767, and seventeen more between 1776 and 1795. Several houses in St. Andrew Square were built by him, and he was the builder of Young Street in 1779–90. He was a member of the Town Council in 1790 and again in 1792 and 1793. He died on 26 July 1801. [A. J. Youngson,

The Making of Classical Edinburgh, 1966, 84, 91, 101, 205; Town Council Minutes, 11 Aug. 1779 and 16 June 1806; *Scots Mag.*, 1801, 516.]

YOUNG, JOHN (*c.* 1798–1877), was born in Suffolk, came to London in his 23rd year and became a pupil of William Porden. He subsequently worked for Decimus Burton and Thomas Cubitt before becoming assistant to William Mountague, the City Surveyor, and eventually had a considerable practice in the 1850s and 1860s. From 1853 until his death on 23 March 1877 he was District Surveyor of the Eastern Division of the City of London. His works included LAUGHTON LODGE, SUSSEX, for Sir James Duke, Bart., many buildings in the City, and the restoration of several churches in his native Suffolk. In 1828 he published *A Series of Designs for Shop Fronts, Porticoes and Entrances to Buildings Public and Private*, of which there was another edition in 1835. [*Builder* xxxv, 1877, 328.]

YOXALL, WILLIAM (–1770), was an architect of Nantwich in Cheshire. In 1731 he designed an altar-piece for NANTWICH CHURCH which was removed in 1855, and in 1742 he made a drawing of CREWE HALL, CHESHIRE, which was engraved [J. Partridge, *History of Nantwich*, 1774, 25; J. Hall, *History of Nantwich*, 1883, 219]. In 1762–3 he was employed to refit some of the rooms at CHIRK CASTLE, DENBIGHSHIRE, for Richard Myddleton. He proposed to ornament both the Drawing and Dining Rooms with a 'neat ornamental Gothick cornish', etc. [National Library of Wales, Myddleton papers, F.7375 and Steward's Commonplace book, 1762–3.]

Appendices

Appendix A

SOME BUILDINGS ERECTED BEFORE 1840
TO THE DESIGNS OF VICTORIAN ARCHITECTS
NOT INCLUDED IN THIS DICTIONARY

As one of the functions of this Dictionary is to serve as a work of reference for buildings erected between 1600 and 1840, it has seemed worth while to list below the earlier works of some Victorian architects who do not qualify for biographical treatment. No attempt has, however, been made to list every such building.

BUNNING, JAMES BUNSTONE (1802–1863)
>LONDON, ROYAL HUMANE SOCIETY'S RECEIVING HOUSE, HYDE PARK, 1834; dem. [exhib. at R.A. 1834–5].
>LONDON, THE CITY OF LONDON SCHOOL, CHEAPSIDE, 1835–7, Gothic; dem. 1882 [exhib. at R.A. 1836] (W. Thornbury, *Old and New London* i, n.d., 379).

BURT, HENRY, of Launceston (–1884)
>BODMIN, CORNWALL, THE ASSIZE COURT, 1837–8 [J. Maclean, *Deanery of Trigg Minor* i, 1873, 109].

HENDERSON, JOHN, of Edinburgh (1804–1862)
>ARBROATH CHURCH, ANGUS, steeple, 1831 [*N.S.A.* xi, 81].
>GLASGOW, CHRIST CHURCH (Episcopal), BROOK STREET, 1835 [*The Scottish Episcopal Church Year Book*, 1973–4, 206].
>DUMFRIES, ST. MARY'S CHAPEL, 1837–8, Gothic [*A.P.S.D.*] (W. Fraser, *The Kirk and the Manse*, 1857, 180).
>MONTROSE, ANGUS, THE MUSEUM, PANMURE PLACE, 1837 [*A.P.S.D.*].
>EDINBURGH, MORNINGSIDE PARISH CHURCH, 1838, Romanesque; transepts added 1869 [*A.P.S.D.*].
>BRECHIN, ANGUS, THE MECHANICS' INSTITUTE, 1838–9, Tudor Gothic [D. D. Black, *History of Dundee*, 1867, 211].
>EDINBURGH, TRINITY EPISCOPAL CHAPEL, DEAN BRIDGE, 1838–9, Gothic; sanctuary 1900 [*A.P.S.D.*].
>PANMURE, ANGUS, tower on Camustane Hill in honour of Lord Panmure, 1839 [*Forfarshire Illustrated*, 1843, 48].

HINDLE, WILLIAM JAMES, of Barnsley (–1884)
>BARNSLEY, THE ODDFELLOWS' (now TEMPERANCE) HALL, PITT STREET, 1836–7 [R. Jackson, *History of Barnsley*, 1858, 136].
>BARNSLEY, THE COMMERCIAL BUILDINGS, 1837 [Jackson, *op. cit.*, 137].

JOHNSON, THOMAS, of Lichfield (1794–1865)
>STOKE-ON-TRENT, STAFFS., ST. PETER'S CHURCH, 1826–9, Gothic [I.C.B.S.].
>NORTON CANES CHURCH, STAFFS., rebuilt 1832, Gothic; reconstructed 1888 [I.C.B.S.].
>LONGTON, STAFFS., ST. JAMES'S CHURCH, LANE END, 1832–4, Gothic [Port, 160–1].

HEATH HOUSE, TEAN, STAFFS., for J. B. Philips, 1836–40, Gothic [J. Cornforth in *C. Life*, 3 Jan. 1963].

CHESTERFIELD, DERBYSHIRE, HOLY TRINITY CHURCH, 1837–8, Gothic; remodelled 1889 [G. Hall, *History of Chesterfield*, 1839, 267–9].

SMETHWICK, STAFFS., HOLY TRINITY CHURCH, 1838, Gothic; rebuilt 1887–8 [Birmingham City Library, Edge drawings nos. 186–9].

LAMB, EDWARD BUCKTON (1806–1869)

LONDON, ST. PHILIP'S CHURCH, CLERKENWELL, 1831–2, Gothic; dem. 1938 [Port, 152–3].

MAIR, GEORGE JAMES JOHN (c. 1809–1889)

NORTHWOOD HOUSE, WEST COWES, ISLE OF WIGHT, remodelled for George Henry Ward, 1838 onwards [exhib. at R.A. 1838, 1839, 1841, 1843, 1846; drawings in B.M., Add. MSS. 18157–8].

WELCOMBE HOUSE, nr. STRATFORD-ON-AVON, WARWICKS., for C. T. Warde, 1838; rebuilt 1869 [exhib. at R.A. 1838; plans in B.M., Add. MS. 18159, f. 18].

MOREING, CHARLES (–1885)

INGRESS ABBEY, GREENHITHE, KENT, for James Harmer, c. 1832–4, Elizabethan [J. C. Loudon, *Architectural Mag.* i, 1834, 47; exhib. at R.A. 1832 and 1845] (C. Greenwood, *Epitome of County History: Kent*, 1838, 76).

NICHOLSON, WILLIAM ADAMS (1803–1853)

MANSFIELD, NOTTS., THE TOWN HALL, 1836 [*Builder* xi, 1853, 262].

BRATTLEBY HALL, LINCS., remodelled for Edward Wright, 1838–9 [Lincs. Record Office, Misc. Dep. 118/1/2/4].

WRAGBY CHURCH, LINCS., rebuilt 1839, Gothic [*Builder* xi, 1853, 262].

SCAWBY CHURCH, LINCS., rebuilt 1839–40, Gothic [Lincs. Record Office, Cor. B.5/4/124/4; C. Anderson, *Ancient Models, or Hints on Church Building*, 2nd ed. 1841, 189–91].

PENNETHORNE, Sir JAMES (1801–1871)

SWITHLAND HALL, LEICS., for the 4th Earl of Lanesborough, 1834 [*A.P.S.D.*].

LONDON, CHRIST CHURCH, ALBANY STREET, ST. PANCRAS, 1836–7; altered by Butterfield 1866–85 [*Companion to the Almanac*, 1838, 219].

LONDON, HOLY TRINITY CHURCH, GRAY'S INN ROAD, HOLBORN, 1837–8; dem. 1928 [*Companion to the Almanac*, 1838, 219; Port, 152–3].

DILLINGTON HOUSE, nr. ILMINSTER, SOMERSET, remodelled for J. Lee Lee, 1838 [*A.P.S.D.*].

PUGIN, AUGUSTUS WELBY (1812–1852)

all from Phoebe Stanton, *Pugin*, 1971, 196–7.

ST. MARIE'S GRANGE, ALDERBURY, WILTS., for himself, 1835, Gothic; altered c. 1875.

ALTON TOWERS, STAFFS., additions for the 16th Earl of Shrewsbury, 1837 onwards, Gothic.

DERBY, ST. MARY'S CHURCH (R.C.), 1837–9, Gothic.

DUDLEY, WORCS., R.C. CHURCH, 1838–9, Gothic.

KEIGHLEY, YORKS. (W.R.), ST. ANNE'S CHURCH (R.C.), 1838, Gothic.

MACCLESFIELD, CHESHIRE, ST. ALBAN'S CHURCH (R.C.), 1839–41, Gothic.

NEWPORT CHURCH, SALOP., repairs for the 16th Earl of Shrewsbury, 1838.

SCARISBRICK HALL, LANCS., remodelled for Charles Scarisbrick, 1837–45, Gothic (*C. Life*, 13–20 March 1958).

READING, BERKS., ST. JAMES'S CHURCH (R.C.), 1837–40, Norman; much altered.

SOLIHULL, WARWICKS., ST. AUGUSTINE'S CHURCH (R.C.), 1838– .

SOUTHPORT, LANCS., ST. MARIE'S CHURCH (R.C.), 1838–40, Gothic; much altered.

UTTOXETER, STAFFS., ST. MARY'S CHURCH (R.C.), 1838–9, Gothic; since remodelled.

SALVIN, ANTHONY (1799–1881)

NORTHALLERTON VICARAGE, YORKS. (N.R.), 1827–8, Tudor [Borthwick Institute, York, MGA 1827/ 1; exhib. at R.A. 1829].

SOMERHILL, nr. TONBRIDGE, KENT, alterations for James Alexander, 1828–33 [*Builder* xli, 1881, 810; J. Britton, *Descriptive Sketches of Tunbridge Wells*, 1832, 121; C. Greenwood, *Epitome of County History: Kent*, 1838, 126].

MOREBY HALL, YORKS. (E.R.), for Henry Preston, 1828–33, Tudor [R.I.B.A.D.; *Builder* xli, 1881, 810; exhib. at R.A. 1828] (*C. Life*, 16 Feb. 1907).

MAMHEAD, DEVON, rebuilt for R. W. Newman, 1828–38, Tudor [R.I.B.A.D.; *Builder* xli, 1881, 810; exhib. at R.A. 1830] (*C. Life*, 26 May, 2 June 1955; C. Hussey, *English Country Houses: Late Georgian*, 1958, 193–205).

BRANCEPETH CASTLE, CO. DURHAM, alterations to hall, etc., for W. Russell, 1829 [*Builder* xli, 1881, 810].

ULVERSTON, LANCS., HOLY TRINITY CHURCH, 1829–31, Gothic [Port, 150–1].

WROXHAM CHURCHYARD, NORFOLK, TRAFFORD MAUSOLEUM, 1830–1, Gothic [exhib. at R.A. 1830].

METHLEY HALL, YORKS. (W.R.), remodelled for the 3rd Earl of Mexborough, 1830–6, Elizabethan; dem. *c.* 1960 [R.I.B.A.D.; *Builder* xli, 1881, 810; exhib. at R.A. 1831] (*C. Life*, 18 May 1907).

LEVEN GROVE, now SKUTTERSKELFE HOUSE, RUDBY-IN-CLEVELAND, YORKS. (N.R.), for the 10th Viscount Falkland, 1831, classical [*Builder* xli, 1881, 810, where date is given as 1838].

NORTH SUNDERLAND CHURCH, NORTHUMBERLAND, 1831–4, Norman [*Builder* xli, 1881, 810].

HARLAXTON MANOR, LINCS., for Gregory de Ligne Gregory, 1831–7; completed by William Burn 1838 onwards; Elizabethan [R.I.B.A.D.; *Builder* xli 1881, 810; *Civil Engineer and Architect's Jnl.* ii, 1839, 39] (*C. Life*, 11–18 April 1957; C. Hussey, *English Country Houses: Late Georgian*, 1958, 242; Arthur Grogan in *Archaeological Jnl.* cxxxi, 1974, 324–9, with plans).

SLALEY CHURCH, NORTHUMBERLAND, 1832, Gothic [I.C.B.S.].

COWESBY HALL, YORKS. (N.R.), for G. Lloyd, 1832, Elizabethan; rebuilt 1949 [T. Whellan, *History and Topography of York and the N. Riding* ii, 1859, 648; *Builder* xli, 1881, 810, where the date is given as 1836] (*V.C.H. N. Riding* ii, 6).

PARHAM HOUSE, SUSSEX, restoration for the Hon. Robert Curzon, 1832–6 [R.I.B.A.D.; *Builder* xli, 1881, 810] (*C. Life*, 19 April 1902, 1, 8, 15 June 1951; J. W. Fitzwilliam, *Parham in Sussex*, 1947).

SHILDON CHURCH, DURHAM, 1833, Gothic; enlarged 1881–2, tower 1900 [I.C.B.S.].

STOKE GREEN HOUSE, STOKE, nr. COVENTRY, WARWICKS., for Lt. Col. Rolfe, 1833; dem.

SOUTH SHIELDS, DURHAM, HOLY TRINITY CHURCH, 1833–4, Gothic [G. B. Hobson, *The Borough of South Shields*, 1903, 257].

RUNCTON HALL, NORTH RUNCTON, NORFOLK, for Daniel Gurney, 1834–5; enlarged by Salvin 1853 [*Builder* xli, 1881, 810].

NORWICH CASTLE, restoration, 1834–9 [C. Mackie, *Norfolk Annals* i, 1901, 420–1].

KIMBERLEY HALL, NORFOLK, added quadrants connecting main house to wings, for the 2nd Lord Kimberley, 1835 [drawings in R.I.B.A. Coll.].

BURWARTON HALL, SALOP., for the Hon. G. F. Hamilton, 1835–9; enlarged by Salvin 1876–7, plain Italianate; altered *c.* 1900; reduced in size 1956–7 [*Builder* xli, 1881, 810] (F. Leach, *The County Seats of Shropshire*, 1891, 225; *C. Life*, 17 March 1960).

CHALFONT HOUSE, BUCKS., alterations for John Hibbert, 1836, Gothic [*Builder* xli, 1881, 810].

WOODLANDS, KENN, DEVONSHIRE, for W. Ley, 1836 [*Builder* xli, 1881, 810].

DARLINGTON, CO. DURHAM, HOLY TRINITY CHURCH, 1836–8, Gothic; chancel added 1867; altered 1883 and 1890 [I.C.B.S.].

DANESFIELD HOUSE, MARLOW, BUCKS., for C. Scott Murray, 1837–41, irregular classical style; rebuilt 1899–1901 [*Builder* xli, 1881, 810] (F. O. Morris, *Picturesque Views of Seats* v, 1880, 77).

SEATON CAREW PARSONAGE, CO. DURHAM, 1837 [*Builder* xli, 1881, 810].

SCOTNEY CASTLE, KENT, for Edward Hussey, 1837–43, Elizabethan [R.I.B.A.D.; exhib. at R.A. 1838; C. Hussey in *C. Life*, 6, 13 Sept. 1956; C. Hussey, *English Country Houses: Late Georgian*, 1958, 220–9].

971

BELTON, LINCS., Village Cross, 1838 [R.I.B.A.D.].

KESWICK CHURCH, CUMBERLAND, 1838–9, Gothic; aisles added 1862 and 1882; chancel lengthened 1889 [*Builder* xli, 1881, 810].

BURTONFIELD HOUSE, STAMFORDBRIDGE, YORKS. (E.R.), for C. A. Darley, 1838–40 [*Builder* xli, 1881, 810].

SAND HUTTON PARK, YORKS. (N.R.), altered or remodelled for J. Walker, 1839–41; enlarged 1851–2; dem. 1971 [*Builder* xli, 1881, 810].

SAND HUTTON CHURCH, YORKS. (N.R.), at expense of J. Walker, 1839–40, Gothic; remodelled 1885–6 [G.R.].

RUFFORD ABBEY, NOTTS., internal alterations for the 8th Earl of Scarbrough, 1839–42; dem. *c.* 1950 [R.I.B.A.D.; *Builder* xli, 1881, 810] (*C. Life*, 7 Nov. 1903).

SMIRKE, SYDNEY (1797–1877)

OAKLEY PARK, nr. EYE, SUFFOLK, for Sir Edward Kerrison, Bart., *c.* 1830; dem. *c.* 1930 [*A.P.S.D.*] (*C. Life*, 4 Jan. 1908).

GUNNERSBURY HOUSE, MIDDLESEX, remodelled for Baroness Rothschild, *c.* 1834 [*A.P.S.D.*].

THORNHAM HALL, SUFFOLK, for the 4th Lord Henniker, *c.* 1837, Jacobean; dem. 1934 [*A.P.S.D.*] (H. R. Barker, *East Suffolk Illustrated*, 1908–9, 474).

CUSTOM HOUSES at BRISTOL, GLOUCESTER, NEWCASTLE and SHOREHAM, SUSSEX, *c.* 1830–40 [J. M. Crook in *Seven Victorian Architects*, ed. Fawcett, 1976, 152].

SPENCE, WILLIAM, of Glasgow (*c.* 1806–1883)

COULTERMAINS, LANARKSHIRE, for Adam Sim, 1838 [W. Hunter, *Biggar and the House of Fleming*, 1867, 588].

VARDEN, RICHARD, of Worcester (1812–1873)

DITCHLEY HOUSE, OXON., colonnaded conservatory behind west quadrant-wall, for the 14th Viscount Dillon, 1837 [*Architectural Mag.* iv, 1837, 548–9].

WILD, JAMES WILLIAM (1814–1892)

GREENWICH, KENT, HOLY TRINITY CHURCH, 1838–9, Gothic [Port, 152–3].

WYATT, THOMAS HENRY (1807–1880)

LLANTARNAM ABBEY, MONMOUTHSHIRE, rebuilt for R. S. Blewitt, 1835, Elizabethan [exhib. at R.A. 1835].

NEWPORT, MONMOUTHSHIRE, ST. PAUL'S CHURCH, 1835, Gothic [exhib. at R.A. 1835].

MALPAS COURT, nr. NEWPORT, MONMOUTHSHIRE, for Thomas Prothero, 1836–8, Gothic [exhib. at R.A. 1838] (T. Nicholas, *The County Families of Wales* ii, 1875, 721).

Appendix B

ARCHITECTS INCLUDED IN
A BIOGRAPHICAL DICTIONARY OF
ENGLISH ARCHITECTS 1660–1840,
BUT EXCLUDED FROM THE PRESENT WORK

C   omitted as a craftsman only
I   omitted as an architect practising in Ireland
O   omitted as too obscure or unimportant for inclusion
V   omitted as a Victorian architect, the bulk of whose practice was after 1840
X   included in *B.D.E.A. 1660–1840* in error.

Acres, Jonathan O
Adams, George O
Ainger, Samuel O
Akerman, John O
Alcock, J— O
Alderson, James O
Allin, Nathaniel O
Allingham, W— O
Anderson, Robert O
Andrews, George
  Townsend V
Apsdell, — O
Arnold, or Arnoll, — O
Ashworth, Robert Holden O
Atkey, W— O
Atkinson, G— O
Atkinson, James X
Atkinson, William Lynn O
Austin O
Avis, Joseph C
Baber, J— O
Baker, Robert O
Ball, John O
Ball, John O
Ballard, R— V
Balls, Samuel Charles X
Banckes, Henry C
Banks, Mark O
Barker, Robert C
Barlow, Edward O
Barlow, Henry Clark X
Barnard, William O
Barnes, T— O
Barnes, William V
Barr, James V
Bartell, Edmund X
Bartells, T— O
Barton, T— O

Basill, Simon O
Bateman, Thomas O
Baxter, J— O
Bayles, James O
Beadel, James O
Beadnell, G— O
Beatson, W— V
Beaumont, Alfred V
Bell, J— A— V
Bell, John O
Bell, W— O
Belling, Lewis O
Bennett, Alexander O
Bennett, John O
Bennett, Joseph B— H— O
Best, G— O
Bevan, R—, and J— O
Biers, H— O
Birch, J— R— O
Bird, W— S— O
Bishop, E— W— O
Bishop, John O
Blackburn, C— V
Bland, John C
Blunt, Henry V
Bower, G— T— O
Bowerbank, Thomas O
Brain, H— X
Brewer, Peter O
Bridge, Thomas O
Bridger, James O
Brock, G— R— O
Brooks, S— H— V
Brough, Benjamin O
Brown, Henry O
Brown, William V
Browne, James O
Bubb, W— O

Buck, Peter O
Buddle, Richard O
Burcham, Samuel O
Burgess, Henry O .
Burgess, Thomas O
Burnett, William
  Suckling O
Butcher, Thomas O
Buxton, John O
Carr, R— O
Cartwright, U— O
Cass, Christopher C
Chambers, John O
Chambers, T— O
Chapman, R— O
Child, Anthony O
Churchill, John C
Clark, John O
Clark, Richard O
Clark, R— G— O
Cleare, Samuel O
Clemence, J— O
Cobden, T— I
Coley, Benjamin O
Collard, Richard O
Comins, — O
Cooper, B— O
Cooper, Henry O
Corlass, Thomas O
Couldery, W— E— O
Courtney, H— F— T— V
Cox, J— O
Cox, Peter O
Crabtree, Samuel O
Creighton, J— O
Croshaw, C— W— V
Crouch, E— O
Crowe, J— O

Cumber, J— O
Curtis, Abraham O
Dade, Thomas O
Danvers, Samuel X
Davenport, John C
Davis, William C
Dean, W— O
Deane, Anthony C
D'Egville, James O
Delamaine, Edmund O
Denham, William C
Devall, John C
Dickinson, William (d. 1702) O
Docker, John O
Donne, J— O
Driffield, Robert O
Driffield, Thomas O
Dubisson, Thomas O
Duncombe, Nicholas O
Durant, Eustace C
Edwards, Henry O
Egenolf, G— O
Elland, R— O
Elmes, H— J— O
England, J— O
England, W— O
Farmer, John O
Fellow, John O
Fenning, H— O
Fentiman, — O
Fetherston, Thomas C
Field, T— O
Fieldwick, — O
Filer, Martin O
Flemming, John O
Foster, B— O
Fox, B— O
Foyster, H— S— O
Fradgley, — V
Francis, Frederick John V
Freeman, Thomas O
Fulling, Thomas O
Gammon, Leonard O
Gammon, Richard O
Gansel, David O
Garnett, R— O
Garrett, John O
Garrod, Thomas O
Gatton, Francis O
Gautrey, J— O
Gay, Robert O
Gayfere, Thomas (d. 1812) C
Gethin, John O
Gittos, J— B— O
Glegg, T— O
Goodman, Francis O
Goodwin, John O
Grantham, William O
Gray, Edward O

Gray, Thomas C
Green, F— G— O
Grix, Henry O
Groom, A— J— O
Hague, T— O
Halford, Edward O
Hambley, — V
Hance, J— W— O
Hanson, John V
Harcourt, C— F— O
Harding, — X
Harding, Thomas O
Harowfield, J— X
Harrison, B— R— O
Harrison, D— O
Harrison, Gregory O
Harrison, James O
Harvey, Daniel C
Harvey, John O
Haughton, Charles O
Hawkins, Edward O
Hawkins, George O
Healy, T— O
Heaton, William Draper O
Hele, John O
Hellis, Edward O
Heming, — O
Henman, Charles V
Herron, George O
Hewlett, Samuel O
Hicks, Jonathan C
Hicks, William O
Hilliar, J— O
Hinton, Thomas O
Hitchens, J— O
Hoare, George C
Hobbes, Thomas O
Hodgson, C— X
Hodskinson, J— X
Holden, Strickland O
Hollingsworth, Richard M— O
Hollins, Humphry C
Hooley, Thomas O
Hooper, Thomas C
Hopson, Sir Charles C
Horsenaile, Christopher C
Hughes, R— X
Hunt, Henry O
Hunt, John C
Hurdis, James O
Hurst, John C
Hutchins, S— or T— O
Inskipp, Walter O
Ives, G— E— O
Jackson, Benjamin C
Jackson, T— J— R— O
Jackson, William C
Jacques, John V
Jagger, John O
James, Richard C
Jennings, Richard C

Johnston, John X
Jones, Henry C
Jones, John O
Judge, George V
Kendall, George C
Kerison, Henry O
Kidd, Robert Charles O
Killock, — O
Kilpin, William O
Kimber, — O
King, John William Pusey O
Knight, John O
Knight, Thomas C
Kyffin, Alexander O
Kynaston, Thomas O
Langridge, William O
Lawrence, — O
Leach, George O
Lee, Abraham O
Lee, Christopher O
Lee, Henry C
Lee, John C
Legg, George V
Leicester, G— O— V
Leigh, William O
Lester, H— O
Lever, G— O
Lewington, John O
Lindegren, Nathaniel O
Lloyd, T— O
Loader, Thomas O
Lomas, W— O
Long, T— O
Lotan, J— O
Lovel, James O
Mair, George James John V
Mallison, F— O
Markes, A— O
Martin, Albinus X
Martin, John C
Maskrey, William and Bartholomew C
Matthews, John O
May, B— O
Meakin, — V
Mill, J— O
Miller, J— O
Mills, Charles O
Mills, Richard O
Mitchell, George O
Mole, William C
Monday, Thomas C
Money, J— O
Moreing, Charles V
Morfitt, John C
Morris, Thomas O
Morrison, Robert X
Morton, R— O
Mulholland, John O
Muschamp, John C

Muspratt, Thomas C
Mutleo, Robert C
Naish, James X
Naish, Thomas O
Neagle, John O
Negus, Francis O
Neill, Thomas O
Nevill, Thomas O
Newcombe, — C
Newling, — C
Newman, Robert C
Newman, William O
Nicholson, Samuel O
Nicholson, William
  Adams V
Norman, William O
Olliphant, James C
Pain, Ambrose O
Palmer, G— H— O
Parish, C— V
Park, J— O
Parker, R— O
Parlby, James O
Parrish, J— O
Parry, H— B— O
Pearce, Edmund V
Pepper, C— O
Percy, Thomas V
Phillips, John O
Pilkington, Thomas V
Pilling, William O
Pink, James C
Piper, Frederick Magnus O
Pitt, Charles O
Plucknett, Thomas O
Plumridge, W— O
Pollden, R— O
Ponder, S— O
Ponsford, John O
Porden, Charles O
Poultney, Joseph O
Powell, Richard C
Pratt, G— O
Pratt, J— O
Proctor, J— O
Provis, W— A— X
Pullen, T— W— O
Quick, Samuel O
Rampling, R— B— V
Randle, Ephraim O
Rawlinson, S— S— V
Reed, John C
Restall, W— O
Richardson, W— H— O
Riches, J— O
Richley, Richard O
Ride, John O
Ridley, W— J— O
Roberts, E— O

Robertson, W— I
Robinson, George O
Robinson, George James O
Robinson, John O
Robinson, John O
Rogers, William V
Rose, William O
Rotherham, Thomas O
Rowe, James O
Ruck, T— O
Russell, F— B— O
Russell, George O
Sadleir, Richard O
Sanders, John O
Sanderson, — C
Santler, G— O
Saunders, John O
Scott, John O
See, Thomas see Gee
Seed, Brice C
Shannon, M— O
Sharp, John O
Sheasby, Thomas O
Shelston, J— O
Shirley, Thomas O
Short, William J— V
Showbridge, John O
Shrugg, James C
Simes, Charles O
Simmons, A— O
Simmons, Henry O
Sisson, Jeremiah O
Slightholme, Thomas O
Slingsby, Joseph O
Smallwell, John C
Smith, Richard O
Smith, S— X
Smith, William Alwell O
Spray, Matthew C
Spurrell, B— O
Squirhill, David or
  Daniel V
Stacey, — C
Stakes, W— O
Stallard, Henry O
Stallwood, N— O
Stanford, R— O
Stanley, G— X
Starkey, J— O
Stayner, Thomas C
Stead, Joseph C
Stebbing, J— L— O
Stokes, William O
Story, Abraham C
Stow, or Stowe, W— C— V
Straphen, John C
Stringer, James O
Stutely, Martin Joseph V
Swaine, George O

Sword, Thomas O
Tarte, J— O
Tawney, — C
Tayier, Thomas O
Taylor, Edward O
Taylor, Thomas O
Temple, J— O
Thomas, Josiah O
Thomas, M— O
Thomas, William O
Thompson, Henry
  Augustus O
Thompson, Richard C
Thomson, James William O
Tildesley, Thomas O
Tress, William V
Tufnell, Capt. Edward C
Tufnell, Samuel C
Tufnell, William C
Varden, Richard V
Vierpyl, W— O
Vyvyan, J— I
Wadeson, Edward O
Walker, Samuel D— V
Walsh, Frederick O
Waring, F— O
Waterman, J— O
Watson, T— O
Watts, G— O
Webb, E— O
Webb, Thomas C
Webb, West O
Webb, William O
Wells, J— S— O
West, S— O
White, S— O
Whitehead, T— O
Willoughby, Nicholas C
Wilmot, John O
Wilson, H— O
Wilson, J— O
Wilson, J— O
Wise, Thomas C
Wood, J— T— O
Woodeson, Leonard O
Woodgate, Robert I
Woodward, R— O
Woolcott, D— E— O
Woolley, Samuel O
Wright, C— X
Wright, W— O
Wyatt, Robert Harvey O
Wyatt, Thomas O
Wyatt, William O
Wyatville, George
  Geoffrey O
Wynn, M— O

Appendix C

PUBLIC OFFICES HELD BY ARCHITECTS
1600–1840

d. = died   r. = retired or resigned

ENGLAND

THE ADMIRALTY

Inspector of Repairs to the Admiralty and Surveyor of Works to the Victualling Office
The salary was £30. The office was abolished in 1800 (J. C. Sainty, *Admiralty Officials 1660–1870*, 1975, 76).

Benjamin Glanville	1731–1774 (d.)
James Arrow	1774–1785
S. P. Cockerell	1785–1800

Architect and Engineer to the Naval Works Department
This office was established in 1796 at a salary of £400. In 1807 it was transferred from the Admiralty to the Navy Board and renamed Assistant Civil Architect and Engineer to the Navy (J. C. Sainty, *Admiralty Officials 1660–1870*, 1975, 91).

Samuel Bunce	1796–1802 (d.)
Edward Holl	1804–1824 (d.)
G. L. Taylor	1824–1837 (r.)
Capt. H. R. Brandreth, R.E.	1836–1846 (r.)

THE BANK OF ENGLAND

Architects

George Sampson	1732–1765
Sir Robert Taylor	1765–1788 (d.)
Sir John Soane	1788–1833 (r.)
C. R. Cockerell	1833–1855 (r.)

BETHLEHEM HOSPITAL

Surveyors

Strickland Holden	–1765 (d.)
— Williams	*c.* 1765–*c.* 1780
William Hillyer	*c.* 1780–1782 (d.)
Henry Holland	1782–1793 (r.)
James Lewis	1793–1816 (r.)
Philip Hardwick	1816–1837 (r.)
Sydney Smirke	1837–1861 (r.)

CHELSEA HOSPITAL

Clerks of the Works

A salary of £200 p.a. was paid from 1793 onwards (C. G. T. Dean, *The Royal Hospital, Chelsea*, 1950, 121, 316). The office was abolished in 1837.

Roger Hewitt	1691–1698 (r.)
Sir Charles Hopson	1698–1710 (d.)
Hugh Warren	1710–1728 (d.)
John Lane	1729–1753 (d.)
George Leach	1753–1755 (d.)
John Vardy	1756–1765 (d.)
Robert Adam	1765–1792 (d.)
Samuel Wyatt	1792–1807 (d.)
Sir John Soane	1807–1837 (d.)

COMMISSIONERS FOR BUILDING FIFTY NEW CHURCHES

Surveyors

Two Surveyors were appointed under the Act of 1711 at a salary of £200 each: Nicholas Hawksmoor and William Dickinson. Dickinson resigned in 1713, his place being taken by James Gibbs, who was superseded in 1715 by John James. Hawksmoor and James continued in charge until Midsummer 1733, when their appointments officially terminated, though both were paid 'for carrying on and finishing the works under their care' for some time afterwards.

COMMISSIONERS FOR BUILDING NEW CHURCHES
(UNDER THE ACT OF 1818)

Architects

At first the Commissioners relied upon the three architects attached to H.M. Office of Works to examine and report upon the plans and estimates submitted, but in 1821 they were obliged, by increasing pressure of business, to appoint their own architect. The office was abolished on 1 Jan. 1857.

Edward Mawley	1821–1826 (d.)
J. H. Good	1826–1857

H.M. CUSTOMS

Surveyors of Buildings

The salary was £40 p.a. in the eighteenth century.

William Robinson	occurs 1752 onwards
William Rice	1768–1781 (r.)
William Pilkington	1781–1810 (r.)
David Laing	1810–1825 (dismissed)
vacant	1825–1830
John Taylor	1830–*c.* 1841

EAST INDIA COMPANY

Surveyors

In 1752 the Company resolved to appoint a surveyor to supervise 'the work necessary to be done at this House and the Company's several warehouses'. At first the salary was £30 p.a. with a percentage for architectural work carried out under the Surveyor's direction, but it was increased to £60 in 1779, and Cockerell and Wilkins both received £500 p.a.

William Jones	1752–1757 (d.)
William Robinson	1757–1767 (d.)
Richard Jupp	1768–1799 (d.)
Henry Holland	1799–1806 (d.)
S. P. Cockerell	1806–1824 (r.)
William Wilkins	1824–1837 (r.)

Clerks of the Works

George Harrison	1837–*c.* 1850
Arthur J. Green	*c.* 1850–1855 (d.)

GREENWICH HOSPITAL

Surveyors

The salary was £200 a year. In 1821 the offices of Surveyor and Clerk of the Works were combined.

Sir Christopher Wren	1696–1716 (r.)
Sir John Vanbrugh	1716–1726 (d.)
Colen Campbell	1726–1729 (d.)
Thomas Ripley	1729–1758 (d.)
James Stuart	1758–1788 (d.)
Sir Robert Taylor	Feb.–Sept. 1788 (d.)
John Yenn	1788–1821 (d.)
H. H. Seward	1821–1823 (r.)

Clerks of the Works

John Scarborough	May–Nov. 1696 (d.)
Henry Symmonds	1696–1698 (d.)
Nicholas Hawksmoor[1]	1698–1735
John James[1]	1718–1746 (d.)
William Robinson	1746–1775 (d.)
Robert Mylne	1775–1782 (dismissed)
William Newton	1782–1790 (d.)
George Knight	1790–1810 (r.)
H. H. Seward	1810–1823 (r.)
Joseph Kay	1823–1847 (d.)

[1] Hawksmoor and James acted jointly from 1718 onwards (*Wren Soc.* vi, 31).

THE CITY OF LONDON

Clerks of the Works

The appointment was held by purchase, each Clerk of the Works having the right to nominate his successor in return for a substantial payment. He had no staff, but gave directions to the City Artificers, who had a monopoly of building work carried out for the Corporation. George Dance the elder discharged his duties in this regard by 'having all the artificers to meet him on a stated day once a week at the Moorgate Coffee-house, to receive his orders and instructions'. In 1771 his son obtained leave to appoint an Assistant Clerk of Works at his own expense, and nominated James Peacock, who was succeeded in 1814 by William Mountague. In 1848 the title was changed from 'Clerk of the City Works' to 'Architect of the City of London'. The following list gives the holders of the office from the Restoration onwards.

James Hayton	–1662 (r.)
Nicholas Duncomb	1662–1676 (r.)
Thomas Aylward	1676–1691 (r.)
John Noyes	1691–1692 (r.)
James Fell	1692–1693 (r.)
John Olley	1693–1711 (r.)
Isaac Olley	1711–1724 (d.)
George Smith	1724–1734 (dismissed)
George Dance, senior	1735–1768 (r.)
George Dance, junior	1768–1815 (r.)
William Mountague	1816–1843 (d.)

THE ROYAL MINT

Surveyors

The office was abolished in 1815, when the maintenance of the Mint was taken over by the Office of Works.

John Vardy	1749–1763 (r.)
John Vardy, junior	1763–1793 (r.)
Samuel Wyatt	1793–1794 (dismissed)
James Johnson	–1807 (d.)
Robert Smirke	1807–1815

THE ORDNANCE

The post of *Architect of the Ordnance* was created in 1719, at a time when the Ordnance Office was engaged in building forts in Scotland after the rebellion of 1715. It subsequently became more or less of a sinecure, and as such was held from 1762 to 1782 by the sons of Sir Charles Frederick, then Surveyor-General of the Ordnance. The salary was £120 p.a. The post was abolished in 1829. The following list of its occupants is based on the Ordnance records in the P.R.O., chiefly WO 48/ 68 and WO 54/203, 210, 212.

Andrews Jelfe	1719–1727
James Gibbs	1727–1754 (d.)
Capt. J. P. Desmaretz	1754–1762
Charles Frederick	1762–1777
Edward Boscawen Frederick	1778–1782
James Wyatt	1782–1813 (d.)
William Atkinson	1813–1829

THE ROYAL ACADEMY

Professors of Architecture

The Rules of the Royal Academy, drawn up at its foundation in 1768, provided that there should be a Professor of Architecture, 'who shall read annually Six Public Lectures, calculated to form the taste of the Students; to instruct them in the laws and principles of composition; and to point out to them the beauties and faults of celebrated productions'. His salary was to be £30 a year, and he was to 'continue in office during the King's pleasure'.

Thomas Sandby	1768–1798 (d.)
George Dance	1798–1805 (r.)
Sir John Soane	1806–1837 (d.)
William Wilkins	1837–1839 (d.)
C. R. Cockerell	1839–1857 (r.)

ST. PAUL'S CATHEDRAL

Surveyors

This post was in the gift of the Archbishop of Canterbury, the Bishop of London and the Lord Mayor. It is described by Farington (*Diary*, ed. J. Greig, vi, 268) as 'a place of honour, the salary only £70 a year', and should not be confused with the post of Surveyor to the Dean and Chapter of St. Paul's.

Sir Christopher Wren	1675–1723 (d.)
John James	1724–1746 (d.)
Henry Flitcroft	1746–1756
Stiff Leadbetter	1756–1766 (d.)
Robert Mylne	1766–1811 (d.)
S. P. Cockerell	1811–1819
C. R. Cockerell	1819–1852 (r.)

Assistant Surveyor

This post became redundant after the completion of the cathedral, and ceased to exist when John James succeeded Wren as Surveyor.

Edward Woodroffe	1668–1675 (d.)
John Oliver	1675–1701 (d.)
Thomas Bateman	1701–1715
John James	1715–1724 (promoted)

WESTMINSTER ABBEY

The Dean and Chapter of Westminster appointed an official, known as the 'College Surveyor', who looked after their urban property and made plans and surveys of their other estates when required. Until 1698, he was also in charge of the buildings of Westminster Abbey, but in that year Parliament granted an annual sum of money towards the repair and completion of the Abbey Church, and a new post of 'Surveyor to the Fabric' was created, together with a subordinate under-surveyorship. The under-surveyorship came to an end when Thomas Hinton became 'College Surveyor' in 1746, and in 1752 the latter office was merged with that of 'Surveyor to the Fabric'.

College Surveyors

William Mann	1598–1635 (d.)
William Ireland	1636–1638 (d.)
Adam Browne	1639–1655

John Sherman	1655–1660
Drew Sterrill	c. 1660–1662 (d.)
Robert Woodroffe	1662–1671
Edward Woodroffe	1672–1675 (d.)
Thomas Plucknett	1675–1690
Robert Hooke	1691–
James Broughton	1697–1711 (d.)
William Dickinson	1711–1725 (d.)
John James	1725–1746 (d.)
Thomas Hinton	May–Aug. 1746 (d.)
Henry Keene	1746–1776 (d.)

Surveyors to the Fabric

Sir Christopher Wren	1699–1723 (d.)
Nicholas Hawksmoor	1723–1736 (d.)
John James	1736–1746 (d.)
James Horne	1746–1752 (r.)
Henry Keene	1752–1776 (d.)
James Wyatt	1776–1813 (d.)
Benjamin Dean Wyatt	1813–1827 (r.)
Edward Blore	1827–1849 (r.)

Under-Surveyors

James Broughton	1699–1711 (d.)
William Dickinson	1711–1725 (d.)
Thomas Hinton	1725–1746 (appointed College Surveyor)

H.M. OFFICE OF WOODS AND FORESTS

In 1795 the Treasury was persuaded that it would be advantageous if 'an experienced Architect should be appointed *Deputy Surveyor of His Majesty's Woods and Forests* for the purpose of preparing Plans & Estimates for Buildings & Repairs within the Department of the Surveyor General of H.M.'s Woods & Forests' (P.R.O., T 25/2, p. 387). The salary was £200 p.a. The office was abolished in 1815.

John Soane	1795–1799 (r.)
James Wyatt	1799–1805 (dismissed)
John Harvey	1805–1806 (dismissed)
John Nash James Morgan }	1806–1815

H.M. OFFICE OF WORKS

For the history and constitution of the Office of Works see *The History of the King's Works*, ed. Colvin, in which full lists of officials will be found. Only the principal posts held by architects are given below.

Surveyors-General of the King's Works

William Spicer	1597–1604 (d.)
Sir David Cuningham	1604–1606
Simon Basil	1606–1615 (d.)
Inigo Jones	1615–1643 (ejected)
Edward Carter	1643–1653
(John Embree)	1653–1660 (ejected)

Sir John Denham	1660–1669 (d.)
Sir Christopher Wren	1669–1718 (dismissed)
William Benson	1718–1719 (dismissed)
Sir Thomas Hewett	1719–1726 (d.)
Hon. Richard Arundell, M.P.	1726–1737 (r.)
Hon. Henry Fox, M.P.	1737–1743 (r.)
Hon. Henry Finch, M.P.	1743–1760 (r.)
Thomas Worsley, M.P.	1760–1778 (d.)
Col. James Whitshed Keene, M.P.	1779–1782

Comptrollers of the King's Works

Simon Basil	1597–1606 (promoted)
Thomas Baldwin	1606–1641 (d.)
Francis Wethered	1641–1668 (d.)
Hugh May	1668–1684 (d.)
vacant	1684–1689
William Talman	1689–1702 (dismissed)
Sir John Vanbrugh	1702–1726 (d.)
Thomas Ripley	1726–1758 (d.)
Henry Flitcroft	1758–1769 (d.)
Sir William Chambers	1769–1782 (promoted)

Surveyors-General and Comptrollers of the King's Works

| Sir William Chambers | 1782–1796 (d.) |
| James Wyatt | 1796–1813 (d.) |

After Wyatt's death the Office of Works was reorganized with a non-professional *Surveyor-General of Works and Public Buildings*, Col. B. C. Stephenson, assisted by three 'Attached Architects' (John Nash, John Soane and Robert Smirke), who received a retaining fee and a percentage on work carried out under their direction. Stephenson had as his subordinate an *Assistant Surveyor and Cashier* (Robert Browne, 1814–1823, H. H. Seward, 1823–1832). This arrangement came to an end in 1832, when the Office of Works and the Office of Woods and Forests were combined under a body of Commissioners, with Seward as *Surveyor of Works and Buildings*. It was not until 1851 that the Office of Works became once more an independent institution, the ancestor of the modern Ministry of Works (now merged in the Department of the Environment).

Deputy Surveyors

Colen Campbell	1718–1719 (dismissed)
Westby Gill	1719–1735 (promoted)
William Kent	1735–1748 (d.)
Henry Flitcroft	1748–1758 (promoted)
Stephen Wright	1758–1780 (d.)
Sir Robert Taylor	1780–1782

Architects of the Works

Sir William Chambers	1761–1769 (promoted)
Robert Adam	1761–1769 (r.)
Sir Robert Taylor	1769–1777 (promoted)
James Adam	1769–1782
Thomas Sandby	1777–1780 (promoted)
James Paine	1780–1782

Secretaries to the Board of Works

Nicholas Hawksmoor	1715–1718 (dismissed)
Benjamin Benson	1718–1719 (dismissed)
John Hallam	1719–1726 (dismissed)
Nicholas Hawksmoor	1726–1736 (d.)
Isaac Ware	1736–1766 (d.)
William Robinson	1766–1775 (d.)
Kenton Couse	1775–1782

Master Masons

William Cure	1605–1632 (d.)
Nicholas Stone	1632–after 1640
Edward Marshall	1660–1673 (r.)
Joshua Marshall	1673–1678 (d.)
Thomas Wise	1678–1685 (d.)
John Oliver	1686–1701 (d.)
Benjamin Jackson	1701–1719 (d.)
Nicholas Dubois	1719–1735 (d.)
William Kent	1735–1748 (d.)
Henry Flitcroft	1748–1758 (promoted)
Stephen Wright	1758–1780 (d.)
Sir Robert Taylor	1780–1782

Master Carpenters

William Portington	1579–1629 (d.)
Richard Binding	1604–1611
Ralph Brice	–after 1640
John Davenport	1660–1668 (d.)
Richard Ryder	1668–1683 (d.)
Matthew Bancks, junior	1683–1706 (d.)
John Churchill	1706–1715 (d.)
Robert Barker	1718–1719 (dismissed)
Grinling Gibbons	1719–1721 (d.)
Thomas Ripley	1721–1726 (promoted)
William Kent	1726–1735 (promoted)
Westby Gill	1735–1746 (d.)
Henry Flitcroft	1746–1748 (promoted)
William Oram	1748–1777 (d.)
Sir Robert Taylor	1777–1780 (promoted)
Thomas Sandby	1780–1782

Comptrollers of the Works at Windsor Castle (from 1660)

Hartgill Baron	1660–1673 (d.)
Hugh May	1674–1684 (d.)
Sir Christopher Wren	1684–1716

SCOTLAND

THE SCOTTISH ROYAL WORKS

Until the Union (1707) the Scottish Master of Work was the equivalent of the English Surveyor-General of Works, and at least two holders of the post (Sir William Bruce and James Smith) were practising architects as well as administrators. But after the Union the absence of a resident sovereign meant that there were few works to supervise, and the office became a sinecure (worth £400 p.a.). This situation lasted until the early nineteenth century. In 1808 the Edinburgh architect Robert Reid (*q.v.*) obtained a commission authorizing him to use the title of 'Architect and Surveyor to the King in Scotland', without any salary. When the then Master of Work, James Brodie, died in 1824, Reid succeeded in getting his office merged with his own, and in 1827 he became the head of a properly constituted Scottish Office of Works with a salary of £500 p.a. and a small staff. In 1831, however, Reid's department was made subordinate to the English Office of Works, and in 1840, when he retired, his post was abolished.

Masters of Work

David Cunningham of Robertland	1602–1607 (d.)
Sir James Murray of Kilbaberton	1607–1634 (d.)
Sir Anthony Alexander	1629–1637 (d.)
Henry Alexander (later 3rd Earl of Stirling)	1637–1641
Sir John Veitch of Dawyck	1641–
John Carmichael	1643–1644 (d.)
Sir Daniel Carmichael of Hyndford	1645–1649 (r.)
Sir Robert Montgomery	1649–
Sir William Moray of Dreghorn	1660–1668
vacant	1669–1670
Sir William Bruce of Balcaskie	1671–1678
David Maitland (acting)	1678–1682
James Smith	1683–1688
Sir Archibald Murray of Blackbarony	1689–1700 (d.)
James Scott of Logie, junior	1700–1704
Sir Francis Scott of Thirlestane	1704–1705
John Urquhart of Meldrum } John Campbell of Mamor }	{ 1705–1714 1717
Sir John Anstruther of Anstruther	1717–1743
George Dundas	1743–1761
William Stewart of Hartwood	1761–1764
James Duff	1765–1768
Lt. Col. James Pringle	1768–1809 (d.)
James Brodie of Brodie	1809–1824 (d.)
Robert Reid	1824–1840 (r.)

THE CITY OF EDINBURGH

In 1720 Alexander McGill was appointed to the newly constituted post of City Architect at a salary of £50 p.a., but this was discontinued in 1725 as a measure of economy. An Overseer of Public Works was one of the City officials from at least the early eighteenth century until the office was discontinued in 1758, but its holders were clerks of the works rather than architects. The office of *Superintendent of Public Works* can be traced from 1786 onwards and was held by the following:

James Gordon	1786–1789 (r.)
William Sibbald	1790–1809 (d.)
John Paterson[1]	May–Dec. 1809
Thomas Bonnar	1809–1818 (dismissed)
Thomas Brown	1819–1847 (r.)

HERIOT'S HOSPITAL

George Heriot's Hospital was a major landowner in Edinburgh and appointed a *Superintendent of Property, Plans and Works*. The following holders of the office are given by William Stevens, *History of George Heriot's Hospital*, ed. Bedford, 1859, 311:

John Paterson[1]	1809–1810 (r.)
Thomas Bonnar	1810–*c.* 1832 (d.)
Alexander Black	1833[2]–1858 (d.)

[1] This was John Paterson, civil engineer of Leith (d. 1823), not the architect of the same name.
[2] Stevens gives the date of his appointment as 1836, but in the *Edinburgh Almanac* he is listed as Superintendent from 1833 onwards.

Addenda (not indexed)

p. 55   ADAM, ROBERT
MAUSOLEA AND MONUMENTS
    WESTMINSTER ABBEY, monuments to Lt. Col. Roger Townshend (d. 1759); James Thomson (d. 1748, erected 1762); Mary Hope (d. 1767), Elizabeth, Duchess of Northumberland (d. 1776); Major John André (d. 1780).
    KING'S LYNN, NORFOLK, ST. NICHOLAS' CHAPEL, monument to Sir Benjamin Keene (d. 1758, erected 1762) [Soane Museum xix, 61; *Gent's Mag.* 1762, 503].

p. 70   ARMSTRONG, WILLIAM
    BRISTOL, CONGREGATIONAL CHAPEL, BRUNSWICK SQUARE, 1835 [W. Ison, *The Georgian Buildings of Bristol*, 1952, 205].

p. 305   FENTON, JAMES
    WIVENHOE, ESSEX, CONGREGATIONAL CHAPEL, 1847 [*Congregational Year Book*, 1847, 166].

p. 316   FOSTER, JAMES
    RODBOROUGH CHURCH, GLOS., rebuilt nave 1842–3, Gothic [*V. C. H. Glos*, xi, 232].

p. 357   GRAHAM, JAMES GILLESPIE
    CHANNELKIRK CHURCH, BERWICKS., 1817, Gothic [S.R.O., HR 313/2].

p. 591   NEWTON, WILLIAM (1730–1798)
    DISSINGTON HALL, NORTHUMBERLAND, for Edward Collingwood, *c.* 1795–7 [signed drawings dated 1794 on sale in London, 1977].

p. 696   ROBERTS, HENRY
    WIGTOWN CHURCH, WIGTOWNSHIRE, 1851–3, Gothic [S.R.O., HR 355/1 & 4].

p. 760   SMITH, JOHN (*c.* 1748–1815)
    Other buildings designed and built by the Smiths included MELROSE PARISH CHURCH, a simple classical building erected in 1809–10 [S.R.O., HR 233/3]; GALASHIELS CHURCH in a 'semi-Gothic' style in 1812–13 [Robert Hall, *History of Galashiels*, 1898, 208–9]; DARNLEE, DARNICK (the younger John Smith's own house), 1816; HOLYLEE, PEEBLES-SHIRE, 1825–7 [National Library of Scotland, MS. 8499] (R.C.A.M. *Peeblesshire*, fig. 275 and pl. 69); GATTONSIDE HOUSE, nr. MELROSE, 1826 [*ibid.*]; and the ETTRICK MILLS at SELKIRK, 1850 [*ibid.*].

p. 784   STOKES, ROBERT
    AMBERLEY CHURCH, GLOS., 1836, Gothic [*V.C.H. Glos.* xi, 204].

p. 847   UNDERWOOD, HENRY JONES
    BOOTLE CHURCH, CUMBERLAND, enlarged 1837 [I.C.B.S.].
    OXFORD, HOLY TRINITY CHURCH, 1845, Gothic; dem. 1957 [Gardner's *Gazetteer of Oxfordshire*, 1852, 302].

Index of Persons

Abbot, Charles, *see* Colchester, 1st Lord
Abercorn, 8th Earl, 207, 780, 781
Abercorn, 1st Marquess, 148, 744, 769 (*bis*), 771
Abercrombie, Genl., 398
Abercromby, Arthur, 737
Abercromby, 2nd Lord, 784
Abercromby, Sir Ralph, 762
Abercromby, Sir Robert, 784
Aberdeen, 2nd Earl, 58, 99, 220
Aberdeen, 3rd Earl, 100
Aberdeen, 4th Earl, 737, 762, 784
Abingdon, 4th Earl, 816, 832
Abingdon, 5th Earl, 245
Abraham, H. R., 43, 564, 728
Ackermann, R., 619, 667
Ackers, G. H., 118
Acland, Sir Thomas, 463
Acland, Sir Thomas Dyke, 226, 890
A'Court, Katherine, 952
Acraman, D. W., 480
Acton, Edward, 84
Acton, N. Lee, 958
Acton, Sir Richard, 83, 663
Acton, Sir Whitmore, 663
Adam, William (d. 1822), 49, 697
Adam, William (d. 1839), 45, 149
Adams, Francis, 770
Adams, George, 839
Adams, Robert, 95
Adderley, C. B. (d. 1826), 635
Adderley, C. B. (d. 1905), 71
Addington, Henry, 715
Addison, John, 60
Addison, Robert, 60
Adeane, H. J., 387
Adelaide, Queen, 722, 963
Adey, D. G., 527
Adie, Robert, 587
Affleck, Alexander, 845
Agar, Col. E., 671
Agnew, E. J., 583
Agnew, R. V., 525
Ailesbury, 1st Earl, 368, 710, 769
Ailesbury, 2nd Earl, 275
Ailesbury, 3rd Earl, *see* Bruce, Charles Lord
Ailesbury, 1st Marquess, 246 (*bis*), 963
Ainger, Canon Alfred, 61
Ainger, Samuel, 61
Airlie, 7th Earl, 887
Airlie, 8th Earl, 260, 623
Aislabie, John, 185 (*bis*)
Akers, Aretas, 174
Albemarle, 1st Duke, 151, 494
Albemarle, 3rd Earl, 612
Albemarle, 4th Earl, 810
Albert, Prince Consort, 244, 695
Aldborough, 1st Earl, 286

Aldborough, 2nd Earl, 186
Aldworth, Charles, 709
Alemoor, Lord, 46
Alexander I, Emperor of Russia, 181
Alexander, Cosmo, 338
Alexander, Fulton, 594
Alexander, George, 43
Alexander, H. B., 94
Alexander, James, 963, 971
Alexander, John, 93, 94
Alexander, William, 257
Alford, Rev. H., 375
Alington, 1st Lord, 659
Alison, —, 587
Aiken, Sefferin, 71
Allan, Thomas, 163
Allan, William, 647
Allen, J. M., 320
Allen, Ralph, 146, 475, 550, 909, 910, 911
Allen, William, 150
Alley, P. B., 502
Allgood, Lancelot, 333
Allgood, R. L., 122, 267
Allison, —, 610
Allnutt, F., 173
Allnutt, John, 618
Allom, Thomas, 353
Alvanley, 3rd Lord, 166
Amcotts, Sir Wharton, 495
Amelia, Princess, 934
Amherst, 1st Earl, 77, 246
Amiconi, Giacomo, 343
Amory, William, 617
Amos, J., 667
Amphlett, Richard, 965
Ancaster, 1st Duke, 853
Ancaster, 3rd Duke, 431
Anderson, Alexander, 645
Anderson, J. MacVicar, 159
Anderson, Sir John, 463
Anderson, Major, 267
Anderson, Robert, 762
Anderson, William, 846
Anderton, William, 67
Andrew, Robert, 682
Andrews, J. P., 214
Angerstein, James, 394
Angerstein, John Julius, 345
Angier, Bernard, 926
Anglesey, 1st Marquess, 655 (*ter*), 729; *and see* Uxbridge, 2nd Earl
Anguish, Miss, 771
Annandale, 2nd Earl, 154
Annandale, 1st Marquess, 283, 530
Annandale, 2nd Marquess, 56
Annandale, Marchioness, 56
Anne, Queen, 924; statue of, 801
Anne of Denmark, Queen, 256, 468, 472, 473
Annesley, Arthur, 518

Annesley, Francis, Master of Downing Coll., 432
Annesley, Rev. Francis, 518
Annesley, 4th Earl, 166
Ansell, Noel, 926
Ansley, John, 372
Anson, 1st Visct., 958 (*bis*)
Anson, George, Lord, 136
Anson, Thomas, 137, 261, 796 (*bis*), 839
Anstey, G., 858
Anstis, John, 850
Anstruther, James, 152 n.
Anstruther, Sir John, 58
Anstruther, Col. Sir Philip, 59
Anstruther, Sir Ralph, 163
Antonie, Lee, 685
Antrobus, Edward, 244
Antrobus, G. C., 954
Arabin, Richard, 103
Arblaster, —, 842
Arbuthnot, Charles, 80, 421
Arbuthnot, James C., 163
Arbuthnot, Sir Robert, 585
Arbuthnott, 8th Visct., 261
Arcedekne, A., 173
Arcedekne, Chaloner, 883
Archdale, Thomas, 105
Archer, Andrew, 69, 70, 749
Archer, Elizabeth, 70
Archer, John, 674
Archer, Lady, 72
Archer, Lady Elizabeth, 425
Archer, Thomas (d. 1685), 68, 70
Arden, 2nd Lord, 200, 638 (*bis*)
Arden, Lady, 859 (*bis*)
Argyll, 2nd Duke, 58, 338, 343, 344, 531, 560, 561
Argyll, 3rd Duke, 46, 59, 186, 562
Argyll, 4th Duke, 561
Argyll, 5th Duke, 125, 574, 575 (*bis*), 576, 577, 586
Argyll, 6th Duke, 125
Arkly, Peter, 359
Arkwright, John, 77, 836
Arkwright, Peter, 118
Arkwright, Sir Richard (d. 1792), 788-9, 823
Arkwright, Richard (d. 1843), 332
Arlington, 1st Earl, 712
Armistead, Lawrence, 954
Armstead, —, 811
Armstrong, John, 959
Armstrong, Sir W. G., 268
Armytage, Sir George, 521
Arniston, Lord, *see* Dundas, Robert
Arnold, Miss, 701
Arran, 3rd Earl, 730
Artari, Albert, 751
Artari, Guiseppe, 338
Arundel, 14th Earl, 468, 472
Arundell, 8th Lord, 179, 612, 769, 914

Arundell, Hon. Richard, 607, 855
Asgill, Sir Charles, 484, 816, 817
Ashburnham, 1st Lord, 314, 904, 926
Ashburnham, 3rd Lord, see 1st Earl
Ashburnham, 1st Earl, 147, 403
Ashburnham, 2nd Earl, 51, 54, 933
Ashburnham, 3rd Earl, 252, 858
Ashburnham, Hon. P., 859
Ashburnham, William, 874
Ashburton, Lady (Anne), 527
Ashburton, Lady (Elizabeth), 583
Ashburton, 1st Lord, 174, 225, 394; and see Baring, Alexander
Ashby, John, 663
Ashford, William, 327
Ashley, John, 552
Ashpitel, Arthur, 71
Ashton, A. F., 307
Ashton, Henry, 351, 960
Ashton, Nicholas, 54
Ashton, Thomas, 92
Ashurst, Sir Henry, 602
Ashurst, Sir W. H., 228
Askew, H. W., 359
Asprucci, Mario, 718
Assheton, William, 876
Astell, William, 770
Astley, Sir Edward, 448
Astley, Francis Dugdale, 558
Astley, Sir Jacob, 266
Astley, Sir John, 84, 340, 343
Astley, Rev. William, 84 (bis)
Aston, 4th Lord, 841
Aston, 5th Lord, 84
Aston, Sir Willoughby, 874
Atherton, Richard, 860
Athew (Athey), Thomas, 929, 931
Atholl, 1st Marquess, 154, 283
Atholl, 2nd Marquess, 283
Atholl, 2nd Duke, 272, 906
Atholl, 3rd Duke, 780
Atholl, 4th Duke, 288, 435, 780 (bis)
Atholl, 6th Duke, 260, 261
Athorpe, Henry, 610
Atkins, A. E. M., 605
Atkinson, Charles, 75
Atkinson, Henry George, 76
Atkinson, John Bownas, 71, 72
Atkinson, Ralph, 267
Atkinson, W., 956
Atkinson, William (d. 1886), 72
Attree, Thomas, 92
Attwood, John, 619
Atwell, William, 928, 929
Audrey, Simon, 929
Augusta, Princess of Wales, 206
Aust, George, 177
Austen, Jane, 124
Austin, Cornelius, 601
Austin, H. G., 78
Avery, —, 280
Awsiter, Dr., 349
Aylesford, 3rd Earl, 137, 235, 421
Aylesford, 4th Earl, 124, 125, 167
Aylesford, 5th Earl, 376
Aylesford, 6th Earl, 167
Aylmer, G. W., 377
Aytoun, Mrs. M. A., 166

Backhouse, Benjamin, 79
Backhouse, Elisha, 79
Backhouse, John, 79
Backhouse, William, 79

Backwell, Barnaby, 343
Bacon, Anthony, 592
Bacon, Basil, 612
Bacon, John, 79, 797, 943
Bacon, Rev. John, 612
Bacon, Sir Nicholas, 455
Baghot, Sir Paul, 961
Bagot, Rev. —, 839
Bagot, 1st Lord, 797, 956
Bagot, 2nd Lord, 156, 369, 842
Bagot, 3rd Lord, 167
Bagot, Sir Walter, 842
Bagot, Sir William, 839
Bagshawe, Sir W. C., 80, 522
Bagshawe, W. J., 441
Bagutti, Giovanni, 338
Bailey, Charles, 829
Bailey, Joseph, 527
Bailey, Thomas, 81
Baillie, David, 89, 859
Baillie, George I, 57
Baillie, George II, 53
Baillie, Col. Hugh Duncan, 165
Baillie, Col. John, 103
Baily, E. H., 362, 670, 742, 895
Baird, Alexander, 82
Baird, David, 288
Baird, Sir David, 783
Baird, Dr. John, 602
Baird, John (d. 1893), 81, 308, 593
Baker, Rev. Mr., 393
Baker, Arthur, 829
Baker, A. St. John, 293
Baker, Charles, 309
Baker, H. A., 326
Baker, Henry, 867
Baker, T. J. Lloyd, 745
Baker, W., 82
Baker, William, 63
Balcarres, Countess, 355
Baldwin, Martin, 750
Balfour, B. T., 645
Balfour, James, 163 (bis), 394, 745
Balfour, Genl. Robert, 241, 260, 394
Balgonie, Lord, 87
Ballantyne, Alexander, 684
Balmerino, Master of, 283
Baltimore, 4th Lord, 133
Baltimore, 6th Lord, 133, 867
Bampfylde, Sir Charles, 464
Banckes, Meyrick, 954
Bankes, Sir Ralph, 308, 659
Bankes, W. J., 92
Banks, — (of Haddington), 158
Banks, — (of Leyton), 649
Banks, George, 215
Banks, Sir John, 819
Banks, Lady, 770
Banks, R. R., 76, 91
Bannatyne, Thomas, 567
Bannerman, Alexander, 737
Bannerman, John, 167
Barbon, Nicholas, 597, 924
Barclay, A. K., 173
Barclay, Charles, 173, 632
Barclay, George, 87
Barclay, J. R., 784
Barclay, James, 87
Barclay, Robert, 645
Barham, 1st Lord, 507
Barham, Rev. C. H., 393
Baring, Alexander, 745, 890; and see Ashburton, 1st Lord
Baring, Sir Francis, 251, 252 (bis)
Baring, Henry, 394, 745
Barker, —, 554

Barker, Sir Abel, 797
Barker, Andrew, 791
Barker, J. R., 769
Barker, Genl. Sir Robert, 242
Barker, Thomas (of Bath), 329
Barker, Thomas (of Derbyshire), 89
Barkley, William, 266
Barlow, H. C., 218, 753
Barnaby, J., 177
Barnard, Lord, 340, 341, 344, 345
Barnard, H. B., 376
Barnardiston, N., 527
Barneby, Bartholomew, 663
Barnes, John, 619
Barnes, W., 753
Barr, James, 753
Barras, George, 266
Barrett, Bryant, 933
Barrett, E. M., 525
Barrett, Thomas, 948
Barrington, John, 717
Barrington, Sir John, 653
Barrington, Matthew, 88
Barrington, Shute, Bp. of Salisbury & Durham, 75, 122, 519, 817, 945, 949, 951
Barrington, 2nd Visct., 306, 551, 793, 952
Barrington, 5th Visct., 519
Barrington, 6th Visct., 77, 219, 519
Barrington, Sir William, 685
Barrodale, William, 309
Barrow, R. J., 524
Barry, E. M., 66, 90, 91, 92, 94, 118, 184, 224
Barry, Hon. J., 839
Barrymore, 7th Earl, 598
Bartoli, Francesco, 598
Bartolini, —, 941
Barton, John, 87
Barton, R. A., 172
Barwell, Richard, 125, 147, 425, 948
Basevi, J. P., 93–4
Basevi, Nathaniel, 95
Basil, Simon (d. 1663), 95
Basset, Arthur, 890
Basset, Sir Francis, 280
Basset, J. F., 167
Basset, J. P., 285
Bassett, George, 95
Bastard, E. P., 679
Bate-Dudley, Rev. Sir Henry, 463
Bateman, 1st Lord, 407 (bis)
Bateman, 2nd Visct., 109, 312
Bateman, —, 629
Bateman, Sir James, 69
Bateman, John Jones, 98
Bateman, Richard, 109, 566
Bateman, Thomas, 452
Bates, Ralph, 624
Bath, 1st Earl, 132, 436, 513, 663
Bath, 1st Marquess, 139
Bath, 2nd Marquess, 961
Bath & Wells, Bishop of, see Law, G. H.
Bathurst, 2nd Earl, 51
Bathurst, 3rd Earl, 744
Bathurst, Sir Frederick Henry, 630
Bathurst, Dr. Ralph, 64
Bathurst, Hon. Seymour, 174
Batt, J. T., 949
Battersby, Mrs. H., 226
Baugh, Isaac, 508
Bax, Marcel, 455
Baxter, John, 587

Baxter, Robert, 398
Bayley, —, 527
Bayley, Daniel, 770
Bayley, Archdeacon H. V., 321, 898, 899
Baynes, John, 311
Baynton, Sir Edward, 781
Beach, Michael Hicks, 605, 769 (bis)
Beachcroft, Samuel, 769
Bearcroft, E. H., 374
Beauchamp, Ephraim, 792, 929
Beauchamp, 1st Earl, 177
Beauchamp-Proctor, Sir Thomas, 768
Beauclerc, Lord Vere, 549
Beauclerk, Charles, G., 464
Beaufort, 2nd Duke, 87
Beaufort, 3rd Duke, 344, 493
Beaufort, 4th Duke, 934
Beaufort, 5th Duke, 301
Beaufort, 6th Duke, 891, 961 (bis)
Beaufort, Rev. Daniel Augustus, 946
Beaufort, Capt. Francis, 221
Beaumont, Sir George, 252, 644
Beaumont, Richard, 610
Beaumont, Col. T. R., 76, 196, 267, 591, 962
Beaumont, T. W., 95 (bis)
Beckett, Christopher, 216
Beckford, F. L., 679
Beckford, William (d. 1770), 52, 422, 769
Beckford, William (d. 1844), 352, 950
Beckman, Sir Martin, 902
Bective, 1st Earl, 53, 209
Bedford, 4th Earl, 197, 256, 472 (bis)
Bedford, 5th Earl, 526, 710
Bedford, 2nd Duke, 209
Bedford, 3rd Duke, 716
Bedford, 4th Duke, 207, 312 (bis), 716
Bedford, 5th Duke, 425 (passim), 426, 649, 711
Bedford, 6th Duke, 116 (bis), 119, 320 (bis), 962, 963
Bedford, Rev. W. R., 692
Beech, John, 534
Beechey, Sir William, 228
Beek, James, 65
Beeston, F. R., 102
Belcher, A. B., 173
Belhaven, 4th Lord, 59
Belhaven, 8th Lord, 167, 359
Bell, J. A., 689
Bell, John (of Gateshead), 106
Bell, Matthew (of Bourne), 730
Bell, Matthew (of Woolsington), 267
Bell, Ralph, 195
Bellamont, 1st Earl, 772
Bellamy, T., 500
Bellew, Sir Patrick, 762, 763
Bellhouse, F. T., 75
Belli, Mrs., 225
Belli, Rev. C. A., 377
Belling, Lewis, 526
Bellingham, Sir Alan Edward, 763
Bellucci, Antonio, 341
Belmore, 1st Earl, 949
Belper, 1st Lord, 118
Belshes, Col. J. H., 159, 500, 594
Benefiale, Cav. Marco, 683
Benett, Thomas, 107

Bennet, Rev. —, 605
Bennet, Squire, 475
Bentham, Jeremy, 683
Bentham, Genl. Sir Samuel, 60
Bentley, Michael, 62
Bentley, Thomas, 797
Benyon, Mrs., 771
Benyon, Richard (d. 1796), 948
Benyon, Richard (d. 1854), 770, 771
Berens, Messrs., 437
Berens, Rev. —, 605
Berens, Herman, 817
Beresford, Rev. J. I., 164
Beresford, John, 326, 327
Berkeley, Charles, 447
Berkeley, John Symes, 825
Berkeley, Robert, 177, 807
Berkeley, 3rd Earl, 228
Berkeley, 5th Earl, 102
Berkeley, 1st Lord, 544
Berkeley, 14th Lord, 309
Berkshire, 4th Earl, 752
Bernard, Francis, 717
Bernard, Thomas, 103
Berners, Charles (d. 1815), 577
Berners, Charles (d. 1831), 435
Berners, Henry, 576, 577
Berners, William, 463
Berrarese, Vincenzo, 517
Berry, Elizabeth, 577
Berry, William, 754
Bertie, Charles, 710, 932
Bertram & Spencer, Messrs., 602
Berwick, 1st Lord, 780
Berwick, 2nd Lord, 142, 584, 682, 771
Berwick, 3rd Lord, 439
Bessborough, 2nd Earl, 207
Best, Rev. Thomas, 165
Bethell, Richard, 665, 868
Bethune, Sir Henry, 164
Betts, J. T., 618
Bevan, Henry, 858
Bevan, Silvanus, 517
Bexley, 1st Lord, 376, 421
Bibby, John, 692
Bickerton, —, 110
Biddulph, John, 96
Biddulph, Richard, 514
Biddulph, Robert, 177
Biddulph, Sir Theophilus, 842
Bidleson, R., 111
Bigge, Charles William, 554
Bill, C., 331
Billinghurst, Richard, 925
Billings, R. W., 82, 594
Bindley, —, 576
Bindon, Lord, 852
Bingley, Lord (d. 1773), 196 (bis), 611
Birt, Peter, 54
Biscoe, J. I., 95
Bishop, John, 80
Bisset, William, 737
Bisshopp, Sir Cecil, 683
Blachford, B. P., 653
Black, Capt., 587
Blackburne, John, 583
Blackerby, Nathaniel, 401–2, 503
Blackett, Sir Edward (d. 1718), 300
Blackett, Sir Edward (d. 1885), 267, 692
Blackett, W., 268
Blackett, Walter (architect), 664
Blackett, Sir Walter, 333, 934
Blades, John, 616, 618, 619, 706

Blair, Dr. Hugh, 238
Blair, Robert, 100
Blair, Hunter, see Hunter Blair
Blake, Sir Francis, 595 (bis)
Blake, William, 809
Blaker, W. L., 847n.
Blakeway, Rev. John B., 188
Blakeway, Joshua, 780
Blanchard, Christopher, 817
Bland, Genl. Humphry, 52
Bland, John, 285
Bland, Sir John, 334
Bland, N., 669
Blandford, Marquess, 617
Blantyre, 11th Lord, 168, 745
Blashfield, J. M., 307
Blathwayt, William, 806
Blayds, John, 215, 691, 745
Blencowe, J. G., 174
Blencowe, R. W., 173
Blessington, Earl, 541, 955
Blewitt, R. S., 972
Blicke, C. T., 585
Blinco, John, 930
Blore, John, 861
Blount, — (plasterer), 931
Blount, Sir Edward, 83, 752
Blount, Sir Henry, 551
Blount, William, Governor of Tennessee, 140
Blowes, Henry, 928, 929, 931
Blundell, Henry, 303, 329, 431
Blundell, Robert, 726
Blundell, Thomas Weld, 724
Blundell, William, 527
Blunt, E. W., 487
Blunt, Rev. Walter, 200
Blunt, Governor, see Blount
Bodenham, Charles, 343
Boddington, Samuel, 769, 771
Bodley, Sir Thomas, 62
Boehm, Edward, 950
Boehm, Roger, 769
Bold, Peter, 513
Bolingbroke, 1st Visct., 341
Bolton, John, 329 (bis)
Bolton, Rev. Robert, 455
Bolton, Sir Robert, 329
Bolton, 1st Lord, 958
Bolton, 2nd Lord, 953, 954 (bis)
Bolton, 1st Duke, 342, 807
Bolton, 5th Duke, 855
Bonar, John, 163
Bonar, Thomson, 251
Bond, Dennis, 201
Bonelli, A., 704
Bonnar, Thomas, 159
Bonneval, Marquis, 186
Bonomi, Joseph (d. 1878), 122, 124
Bonsor, Joseph, 244
Boone, Tatnal, 218
Booth, Henry Gore, 354
Booth, J. G., 618
Booth, Sir Robert Gore, 354
Bootle, Sir Thomas, 514
Borett, T., 128
Boringdon, Lord, 51, 53, 704
Bosanquet, Charles, 268
Bosanquet, Claude, 772
Bosanquet, Samuel (d. 1806), 772
Bosanquet, Samuel (d. 1882), 859
Boscawen, Adml. Edward, 52, 55
Boston, 2nd Lord, 208
Bosvile, Godfrey, 565
Boswell, Claud, 100
Boswell, Madame, 838
Botetourt, 1st Lord, 934

Botfield, Thomas, 584
Botfield, William, 187
Boucher, W., 631
Boughey, Sir John F., 584
Boughton, Sir Edward, 207
Boulton, Henry Crabb, 817
Boulton, Matthew, 261, 427, 520, 677, 936, 950, 957, 959
Boulton, Matthew Robinson, 692
Bourchier, Charles, 236
Bourchier, John, 827
Bourgeois, Sir Francis, 771
Bourke, Hon. Joseph Dean, 327 (bis)
Boutcher, William, 701
Bouverie, C. H., 245
Bouverie, Sir Jacob, 450
Bouverie, Hon. W. H., 637
Bovey, Katherine, 344
Bowdon, Daniel, 834
Bowen, James. 43
Bower, G. T., 523
Bowes, George, 301, 333, 611, 612
Bowes, Mrs. George, 612
Bowes, John, 363
Bowles, H. C., 306, 862
Bowles, Henry, 832
Bowles, Oldfield, 965
Bowman, R., 507
Bowyer, Major Atkins, 244
Boyd, George, 606
Boyd, Sir John, 208, 817, 818
Boyle, Lord, 717
Boyle, Hon. & Rev. R. C., 254
Boys, Thomas Shotter, 656
Braddyll, T. R. Gale, 955
Bradford, 1st Earl, 883
Bradford, 2nd Earl, 692
Bradford, 3rd Earl, 167
Bradney, Thomas, 83
Bradshaw, —, 75
Bradstreet, R., 168
Bragg, Rev. —, 303
Bragge, John, 463
Braham, John, 103
Braine, F. E., 132
Braithwaite, John, 619
Bramston-Stane, Rev. John, 464
Brand, Daniel, 806
Brand, Thomas (of The Hyde), 207
Brand-Hollis, Thomas, see Brand, Thomas (of The Hyde)
Brandling, Charles, 611
Brandon, —, 391
Brandon, David, 753
Brandon, Raphael, 621
Brandram, Thomas, 372 (bis)
Branthwayt, M. S., 768
Bray, Reginald, 95
Braybrooke, 2nd Lord, 715
Braybrooke, 3rd Lord, 393
Breadalbane, 2nd Earl, 272
Breadalbane, 3rd Earl, 58, 84, 732
Breadalbane, 4th Earl (1st Marquess), 76, 288 (bis), 586, 624, 771
Breadalbane, 2nd Marquess, 359, 869
Brebner, —, 762
Breedon, Rev. J. S., 444
Breton, W., 653
Brett, Rev. Henry de, 813
Brettingham, Matthew (d. 1826), 136
Brewster, John, 258
Briant, Nathaniel, 140
Briant, W. N., 140

Bridge, John, 226
Bridgeman, Sir Henry, 609, 611
Bridgeman, Sir John (d. 1710), 345, 904
Bridgeman, Sir John (d. 1747), 885
Bridgeman, Ursula, 885
Bridger, H., 674
Bridger, Sir John, 558
Bridges, Sir Brook, 576
Bridges, Rev. E. T., 642
Bridges, Henry, 546
Bridges, John, 929
Bridges, Thomas, 483
Bridgewater, 2nd Earl, 925
Bridgewater, 7th Earl, 951, 961, 962 (bis)
Bridgewater, 8th Earl, 962
Bridgewater, 1st Duke, 275
Bridgewater, 3rd Duke, 518 (bis)
Bridgman, C. V., 890
Bridport, 1st Visct., 768, 772
Bright, Rev. J. B., 187
Brisco, Musgrave, 173
Briscoe, —, 575
Bristol, 1st Earl, 561
Bristol, 4th Earl (Bishop), 231, 306, 412, 718, 765, 808, 946
Bristol, 5th Earl, 306
Bristol, 1st Marquess, 488, 718
Bristow, R., 810
Bristow, William, 866
Britton, John, 99, 115, 510, 667, 898
Broadbent, Thomas, 641
Broadwood, Thomas, 284
Brocas, Anne, 372
Brocas, Mrs., 767, 769, 771
Brockedon, William, 71
Broderip, William, 682
Brodie, James, 674
Brodie, William, 163
Brodribb, —, 83
Broglie, Prince de, 810
Brograve, Sir Berney, 949
Broke, Philip, 596, 949
Bromley, R., 319
Bromley, Sir Robert, 954
Bromley, Rev. Thomas, 526
Bromley, William, 750
Brooke, 4th Lord, 440
Brooke, Sir Richard, 947
Brooks, C. W. Shirley, 143
Brooks, J., 121
Brooks, William, 379
Brooksbank, Stamp, 185
Broom, James, 613
Broome, R., 605
Broster, —, 650
Brotherton, Lt. Col. Sir Thomas, 394
Brougham, 1st Lord, 234
Broughton, Lady, 398
Broughton, Sir Thomas, 839, 957
Brouncker, Henry, 302
Brown, Dr., 676
Brown, Edward, 89
Brown, George, 144
Brown, Henry, 943
Brown, J., 605
Brown, James, 358
Brown, John, 78
Brown, John Henry, 144
Brown, Patrick, 106
Brown, Robert (bricklayer), 928, 929
Brown, Robert (d. 1860), 148
Brown, Thomas, 54

Brown, William, 173
Browne, Isaac Hawkins, 947
Browne, Capt. S., 353
Browning, Edward (d. 1882), 151
Brownlow, Sir John, 904
Brownlow, William, 647
Brownlow, 1st Lord, 946
Brownlow, 1st Earl, 746, 961, 962
Braco, Lord, 57, 58 (bis)
Bruce, C. L. Cumming, 647
Bruce, Charles, 267
Bruce, Charles Lord (afterwards 3rd Earl of Ailesbury), 108, 130, 131
Bruce, James, 784
Bruce, Lady, 312
Bruce, Lord, 769
Bruce, Sir Michael, 164, 737
Bruce, P. C., 532
Bruce, Robert, 397
Brunias, Agostino, 48
Brunswick, Duchess, 524
Bruton, E. G., 847
Bryant, Dr. Walter, 167
Bryce, David, 55, 57, 155, 159, 160, 161, 162, 165, 166, 220, 359, 385, 644, 646, 675, 887, 907
Bryce, William, 155
Brydges, Sir Samuel Egerton, 127
Brydges, William, 910 (bis)
Buccleuch, 2nd Duke, 59, 220
Buccleuch, 3rd Duke, 49, 55, 207, 208, 644
Buccleuch, 4th Duke, 289
Buccleuch, 5th Duke, 76, 77, 162 (passim), 163 (bis), 164, 165 (bis), 167, 168, 363, 759, 760
Buccleuch, Anne Duchess, 758
Buchan, 6th Earl, 124
Buchan, James, 164, 761
Buchanan, —, 594
Buchanan, (Col.) Hector Macdonald, 358 (bis)
Buchanan, John, 526, 527, 725
Buchanan, Countess, 472
Buckingham, 1st Duke (d. 1628), 335–6, 473
Buckingham, 2nd Duke (d. 1687), 300, 543, 904
Buckingham, 1st Duke (d. 1721), 804, 904
Buckingham, 1st Duke (d. 1839), 621
Buckingham, Marquess, 472; and see 1st Duke (d. 1628)
Buckingham, 1st Marquess (d. 1813), 139, 140, 770 (bis), 771
Buckinghamshire, 1st Earl, 137
Buckinghamshire, 2nd Earl, 125, 448, 957
Buckinghamshire, 3rd Earl, 51
Buckinghamshire, 4th Earl, 517
Budd, Henry, 255
Buddicum, R. P., 693
Buggan, Sir G., 907
Bulfinch, Charles, 126
Bulkeley, Henry, 582
Bulkeley, 7th Visct., 957
Bull, David, 53
Buller, James, 201
Buller, Sir J. B. Yarde, 890
Bullock, George, 140, 328
Bullock, John, 262
Bullock, William, 616, 619, 700
Bulteel, H. B., 308
Bunbury, Sir Charles, 207
Bund, Thomas, 177, 634

Bunning, J. B., 276, 969
Burdett, Sir Robert, 421
Burdon, John, 610 (bis)
Burdon, Richard, 267
Burdon, Rowland, 76, 590
Burdon, Sir Thomas, 267
Burdon, William, 785
Burges, H., 767
Burges, Sir John Smith, 952
Burges, William, 116
Burgess, C. Monteaulieu, 862
Burgoyne, Genl. John, 51
Burgoyne, Sir Montagu, 518
Burlington, 1st Earl, 430, 544
Burlington, 2nd Earl (later 7th
    Duke of Devonshire), 876
Burmester, H., 617
Burn, G. A., 433
Burnett, John, 761
Burns, Robert, 346
Burrard-Neale, Adml. Sir H., 274
Burrell, Sir Charles, 432, 584
Burrell, Sir Peter, 125
Burrell, Richard, 827
Burrell, Walter, 584
Burrell, William, 267
Burroughs, Rev. Lynch, 744
Burt, Henry, 969
Burton, —, 622
Burton, — (plasterer), 931
Burton, Henry Marley, 170
Burton, Robert (of Longner), 583
Burton, Robert (of Somersby), 65,
    854
Bury, Thomas Talbot, 71, 667,
    857
Busby, Dr. Richard, 428, 431, 917
Butcher, Francis, 748, 751
Bute, 2nd Earl, 531
Bute, 3rd Earl, 51, 53, 181, 204,
    238, 496
Bute, Lady, 641
Bute, 1st Marquess, 577
Bute, 2nd Marquess, 162, 330,
    745 (bis)
Butler, —, 457
Butler, Alexander, 193
Butler, J. F., 614
Butler, Joseph, Bp. of Durham,
    550
Butler, Dr. Samuel, 408
Butler, Rev. Dr. Weeden, 173
Butt, William, 809
Butterworth, Joseph, 619
Button, Zacharias, 456
Buxton, Isaac, 242
Buxton, John, 137
Buxton, Sir R. J., 118
Buxton, T. F., 603
Byng, Adml. John, 866 (bis)
Byng, Hon. John, 681
Byres, John (of Coates), 862
Byres, Genl. Patrick, 761

Cadman, Ralph, 928
Cadogan, 2nd Lord, 360
Caithness, 12th Earl, 162
Calcraft, John, 208 (bis)
Caldwell, George, 396
Caledon, 2nd Earl, 584
Call, Sir John, 958
Callender, Sir John, 554
Callow, William, 419
Calman, —, 587
Calthorpe, 3rd Lord, 696
Calthorpe, 4th Lord, 92
Calverley, Thomas, 497
Calvert, Benedict L., 133

Calvert, Charles, 387
Calvert, Nicolson, 508
Camden, 1st Earl, 249, 251
Camden, 2nd Earl, 252
Camden, 1st Marquess, 246, 480
Camden, 2nd Marquess, 172
Camelford, 2nd Lord, 640, 650
Cameron, Donald, 358
Cameron, Walter, 180–1
Campbell, Col. (of Blythswood),
    238
Campbell, Genl. Alexander, 624,
    784
Campbell, Sir Alexander, 645
Campbell, Major Archibald, 358
Campbell, Sir Archibald (of
    Succoth), 163
Campbell, Genl. Sir Archibald,
    411
Campbell, Colin (of Colgrain),
    383
Campbell, Colin (of Everton), 692
Campbell, Colin (of Jura), 165,
    168
Campbell, Daniel, 184
Campbell, Lt. Gen. Duncan, 288–
    9
Campbell, Sir Duncan, 467
Campbell, Lord Frederick, 49,
    200, 576
Campbell, Sir H. P. Hume, 164
Campbell, Sir Hugh, 182
Campbell, J. A., 164
Campbell, Genl. J. F., 159
Campbell, James, 647
Campbell, Sir James (of
    Ardkinglas), 112
Campbell, Sir James (of
    Glasgow), 81, 82
Campbell, Sir James (of Lawers),
    57
Campbell, Jane, 183
Campbell, John (of Barmore), 647
Campbell, John (of Cawdor), 822
Campbell, Col. John (later 4th
    Duke of Argyll), 561
Campbell, P., 525
Campbell, Richard, 165
Campbell, Thomas, 160, 741, 742
Campbell, W. F., 647
Camperdown, 1st Earl, 162
Camplin, Rev. Dr., 627
Canning, George, 770
Cannison, James, 54
Capel, Capt. Daniel, 618
Capell, Sir Henry, 544
Carabelli, Donato, 324n.
Carabelli, Francesco, 324n.
Carbonell, J., 43
Cardigan, 4th Earl, 312
Cardigan, 7th Earl, 239
Careless, Thomas, 812
Carew, Thomas, 447, 620
Carew, Sir William, 341, 565
Carew, 1st Lord, 698
Carey, William, Bp. of St. Asaph,
    117
Carfrae, Col. J., 164
Carleton, Lord, 854
Carline, Thomas, 187
Carlini, Agostino, 55
Carlisle, Nicholas, 755
Carlisle, 3rd Earl, 301, 333, 404,
    702, 703, 803, 806, 849, 850,
    852, 853 (bis)
Carlisle, 4th Earl, 333
Carlisle, 5th Earl, 195, 208, 209,
    808, 809, 810

Carlyon, Col. Edward, 890
Carmichael, James, 220
Carnarvon, 1st Earl (d. 1643), 473
Carnarvon, 3rd Earl, 92
Carnegie, Sir David, 644
Caroline, Queen, 490, 492, 493
Carr, Maj. G. D., 464
Carr, John (d. 1736), 188
Carr, Robert, 189
Carrington, 1st Lord, 245, 771,
    951
Carruthers, J., 173
Cart, James, 654
Carter, Benjamin, 198, 482
Carter, Dr. H. W., 173
Carter, Rev. Robert, 528
Carter, Thomas, 181, 214
Carter, William, 198
Carter, William (bricklayer), 874
Carteret, 1st Lord, 518
Cartwright, John, 539
Cartwright, Samuel, 721
Cartwright, Thomas, 69, 536
Cartwright, Thomas (mason), 928,
    930
Cartwright, W. R., 770
Carver, David, 201
Carver, John (d. 1896), 201
Cary, S., 679
Carysfort, 1st Earl, 199, 394
Cass, Christopher, 456, 792
Cass, Frederick, 618, 619
Cassilis, 7th Earl, 152
Cassilis, 10th Earl, 54
Cassilis, 12th Earl, 527 (bis)
Castleman, William, 963
Catherine, Empress of Russia, 181
Catherine of Aragon, Queen, 299
Catherine of Braganza, Queen,
    430, 923
Cator, John (of Beckenham), 454
Cator, John (of Woodbastwick),
    754
Cave, Sir Francis, 749
Cave, Mrs. Otway, 542
Cave, Sir Thomas, 301, 751, 763
Cave, Sir Verney, 749, 751
Cavendish, Hon. Charles C., 117,
    119
Cavendish, Sir Charles (d. 1617),
    764
Cavendish, Sir Charles (d. 1654),
    764
Cavendish, Sir Henry, 331
Cavendish, Lord John, 195
Cavendish, Sir William, 764
Cawdor, 1st Earl, 962, 963 (bis)
Cawthorne, J. F., 55
Caygill, John, 194
Cecil, Sir Edward, 472
Chafin, George, 69
Chalk, A. R., 656
Chalmers, David, 737
Chamberlayne, Thomas, 618
Chambers, Mrs., 657
Champernowne, Arthur, 719
Chandler, Richard, 866
Chandler, Richard (d. 1810), 684
Chandos, 1st Duke, 108, 314, 341,
    428, 453, 454, 489, 660, 694,
    732 (passim), 750, 806, 890–1,
    909, 910
Chandos, 3rd Duke, 51
Chantrell, John Boham, 209
Chantrey, Sir Francis, 65, 168,
    738, 772, 840, 960
Chaplin, Charles, 899
Chapman, Rev. C. J., 150

Chapman, George, 472–3
Chapman, William, 107
Chapman, R., 351
Charlemont, 1st Earl, 207 (bis), 209, 326, 327, 566, 572, 794
Charles II, King, 153, 712, 874, 923; coronation, 336–7, 552; statue, 900
Charleton, Dr. William, 872
Charleville, Earl, 179
Charlotte, Princess of Wales, 80, 421, 617
Charlotte, Queen, 51, 208, 949
Charlton, Sir Francis, 663
Charlton, St. John, 142
Charlton, W. H., 123
Charlton, William, 591
Charteris, Francis, 575, 866
Charteris-Wemyss, Hon. Francis, 412
Châteauneuf, Alexis de, 546
Chatham, 1st Earl, 146
Chatham, 2nd Earl, 394
Chauncey, Richard, 476, 764, 799
Chauvett, Lewis, 592
Chaytor, Sir William, 123 (bis)
Cheape family, 86
Cheape, Henry, 623
Cheere, C. M., 177
Cheere, Sir Henry, 347, 814
Cheese, Edmund, 553
Cheetham, David, 75, 557
Cheltenham, —, 928
Cherry, G. H., 618 (bis)
Cheselden, Dr. William, 633, 660, 694
Chesham, 1st Lord, see Cavendish, C. C.
Cheshire, Sir John, 342
Chester, Sir John, 311, 489, 750
Chester, William B., 688
Chesterfield, 4th Earl, 866 (bis)
Chesterfield, 5th Earl, 961 (bis)
Chesterfield, Countess, 103
Chetwynd, Sir George, 655
Chetwynd, 2nd Visct., 549, 839
Chetwynd, 3rd Visct., 797
Chetwynd, Walter (of Grendon), 841
Chetwynd, Walter (of Ingestre), 926
Chichester, 2nd Earl, 480
Chichester, Col. J. P., 510
Chichester, Robert, 387
Chichester, Lord Spencer, 617
Child, Charles (d. 1862), 213
Child, Francis, 52n.
Child, Henry Paul, 213
Child, Sir Richard, see Tylney
Child, Robert, 52, 55
Child, W. H., 168
Childe, William Lacon, 751
Childers, J. W., 522
Chipps, William, 835
Chiswell, R. M. T., 199–200, 426 (bis)
Chivers, Elizabeth, 192
Choby, George, 929
Cholmeley, Francis, 74
Cholmeley, Sir Montague, 858
Cholmondeley, 1st Earl, 88, 475, 750, 854
Cholmondeley, 2nd Marquess, 745
Cholmondeley, Rev. H., 173
Cholmondeley, J., 898
Christian IV, King of Denmark, 206

Christian V, King of Denmark, 214
Christian, Ewan (d. 1719), 60
Christian, Ewan (d. 1895), 144, 374
Christian, John, 751
Christie, Robert, 163
Christmas, Robert, 930
Christopher, Henry, 332
Churchill, Charles (of Chalfont), 213
Churchill, Charles (satirist), 572
Churchill, John (carpenter), 86, 474, 708
Churchill, John (mason), 775
Churchill, Lady Mary, 109, 213
Churchill, 1st Lord, 377
Chute, Chaloner, 214, 873
Chute, W. L. Wiggett, 270
Clancarty, 2nd Earl, 246, 367
Clanrickarde, 11th Earl, 137
Clare, 2nd Earl, 954
Clarence, Duke, 255, 582, 770
Clarendon, 1st Earl (d. 1674), 544, 659, 791
Clarendon, 2nd Earl (d. 1700), 803, 805
Clarendon, 1st Earl (d. 1786), 817
Clarendon, 4th Earl (d. 1870), 118
Clark, — (mason), 930
Clark, J. M., 523
Clark, John, 196
Clark, Thomas, 96
Clark, Thomas (mason), 272
Clark, Sir Thomas, 312
Clark, William, 267
Clark, William (carpenter), 155
Clarke family, 663
Clarke, Bartholomew, 343
Clarke, Sir Charles, 937, 953
Clarke, E., 701
Clarke, George Somers, 90, 91
Clarke, Rev. H. D., 363
Clarke, Isaac, 216
Clarke, Rev. J. S., 488
Clarke, Jervoise, 181
Clarke, John, 539
Clarke, Capt. W. S., 173
Clarke-Jervoise, Sir J., 166
Clarkson & Turner, Messrs., 619
Clavering, Sir John, 267
Clavering, Sir Thomas, 611
Clayhills, —, 587
Clayhills, Alexander, 165
Clayton, John, 267, 359–60
Clayton, Sir William, 817
Cleaver, Rev. —, 605
Cleer, William, 927, 928, 929, 930, 931
Cleere, Richard, 931
Cleeve, Bourchier, 866
Cleland, D. S., 676
Clemence, J. L., 223n.
Clennell, T. F., 267
Clephan, William, 219
Clérisseau, Charles-Louis, 44, 47, 124, 180, 204, 261
Clerk, Sir James, 220
Clerk, John, 831
Clerk, John (of Eldin), 56
Clerk, Genl. Robert, 51
Clermont, 1st Earl, 638
Cleveland, 2nd Duke, 165, 334 (bis), 562, 609
Cleveland, Duchess, 859
Clifden, 3rd Visct., 118
Clifford, Hon. —, 839

Clifford of Chudleigh, 4th Lord, 52
Clifford of Chudleigh, 6th Lord, 446
Clifford, Lord de (d. 1777), 575
Clifford, Lord de (d. 1832), 172
Clifford, Hon. Thomas, 74, 957
Clifford, Capt. W. A., 225
Clifton, E. N., 445, 829
Clifton, 1st Lord, 513
Clifton, Sir Gervase, 195
Clifton, Sir Robert, 132, 195
Clifton, Thomas, 193
Clinton, Lord, see Fortescue, 1st Lord
Clive, 1st Lord, 147, 207 (bis), 208, 425
Clive, Lord (d. 1839), 178n.
Clive, Hon. R. H., 225
Clive, Hon. Robert, 142
Close, Maxwell, 647
Clowes, Charles, 519
Cludde, William, 407
Clutterbuck, Lewis, 951
Clutterbuck, Richard, 788
Clutterbuck, Thomas, 770
Clutton, Col., 168
Clutton, Henry, 116
Clutton, Thomas, 177
Cobb, Francis, 819
Cobbett, Richard, 931
Cobbett, William, 482
Cobden, Thomas A., 717
Cobham, 1st Viscount, 145–6, 311, 343, 492, 514, 853
Cochrane, William, 382
Cockburn, George, 99
Cockburn, Henry Thomas (Lord), 647
Cockerell, Sir Charles, 224, 225 (ter), 228
Cockerell, F. P., 222, 225
Cockerell, Rev. Henry, 225
Cockerell, John, 225, 226
Cocks, Joseph, 797
Cocks, Mary, 797
Cockshutt, Stephen, 192
Codrington, Christopher, 945, 950
Coke, Sir Edward, 952
Coke, G. L., 228n., 764
Coke, Lady Mary, 946
Coke, Thomas, 228, 749
Coke, Thomas William, see Leicester, 1st Earl
Coke, Wenman, 635
Colbourne, Benjamin, 912
Colby, John, 582
Colby, Sir Thomas, 403
Colchester, 1st Lord, 252, 715
Colchester, Maynard, 735
Cole, Nathaniel, 544
Cole, Rev. William, 299
Colebrooke, Sir Edward (d. 1838), 78
Colebrooke, Sir Edward (d. 1896), 167
Colebrooke, Sir George, 817
Colebrooke, Sir Robert, 818
Colenso, Rev. J. W., 173
Colhoun, William, 769
Colingridge, J., 671
Collard, R., 218
Collard & Co., 619
College, Stephen, 931
Collenguin, J. S., 671
Colling, J. K., 144
Colling, Capt. Robert, 955
Collinge, Messrs., 619

Collingwood, Admiral Lord, 226
Collingwood, E. J., 267
Collingwood, H. J. W., 267
Collingwood, Henry, 267
Collins, John, 667
Collins, Robert, 324
Collins, Thomas, 208, 482, 782
Collins, William, 931
Collins-Splatt, Henry, 890
Collyer, Charles, 769
Colman, W. G., 937
Colonna, —, 376
Colquhoun, James, 707
Colquhoun, Sir James, 148, 220
Colson, John, 144
Colston, Edward, 345, 735
Colston, E., 605
Colt, Robert, 642
Combe, Henry, 788
Combe, James, 124n.
Combermere, 1st Visct., 118
Combes, John, 928
Compton, Sir Spencer, see
   Wilmington, 1st Earl
Compton, Sir Thomas, 472
Coney, John, 176
Congreve, —, 842
Coningsby, 1st Lord, 803
Conolly, Thomas, 207
Conolly, William, 324
Constable, Rev. Charles, 245
Constable, Edward, 74
Constable, Sir George Clifford,
   446
Constable, Sir Thomas Clifford,
   446
Constable, William, 74, 147, 946
Constable-Maxwell, William, 391
Constable-Maxwell, William H.,
   74, 193
Conway, 1st Lord, 752
Conway, 1st Earl, 431, 440, 474
Conway, Genl. H. S., 550, 639
Conyers, John (d. 1775), 588, 666,
   716
Conyers, John (d. 1818), 946
Conyngham, 2nd Lord, 948
Conyngham, 1st Visct., 147
Conyngham, 1st Marquess, 434,
   439
Conyngham, Marchioness, 755
Cook, A. G., 198n.
Cook, Charles, 266
Cook, Thomas, 915
Cooke, Bryan, 522, 653
Cooke, Charles, 374
Cooke, E. W., 172
Cooke, Sir H. F., 172
Cooke, Thomas, 638
Cooke, William, 768
Cookson, Isaac, 267
Cookson, J. S., 267
Cooles, William, 904
Cooley, Thomas, 573
Cooper, E. J., 354, 372
Cooper, George, 232
Cooper, W. H., 172, 173
Coote, Sir Eyre, 274
Coote, Col. Richard, 822
Cope, Sir Jonathan, 83
Copland, Edward, 305
Copland, John, 305
Copley, Godfrey, 610
Copley, Sir Godfrey, 300
Corbet, Andrew, 407
Corbet, Sir Andrew, 408
Corbet, Sir Corbet, 187
Corbet, John, 576

Corbet, Philip, 187
Corbett, Panton, 407
Cordwell, John, 559
Corehouse, Lord, 116–17
Cork, 1st Earl, 256
Cork & Orrery, 7th Earl, 957
Cork & Orrery, 8th Earl, 962
Cornewall, Sir George, 481, 583
Cornewall, Capt. James, 815
Cornwall, Genl. Henry, 341
Cornwall, John, 769
Cornwallis, 1st Earl, 866
Cornwallis, 5th Earl, 244
Cornwallis, 1st Marquess, 255,
   957
Cornwallis, 2nd Marquess, 939
   (bis)
Cornwallis, the Ladies, 394
Corrance, F., 881
Cory, J. A., 122, 123n.
Coryton, J. T., 896
Cossins, John, 378, 787–8
Cosway, Sir Richard, 232
Cotterell, Charles, 335
Cotterell, Sir J. G., 76
Cottingham, N. J., 235
Cotton, Mrs. Holford, 746
Cotton, John, 341
Cotton, Sir John Hynde, 299
Cotton, Lady, 472
Cotton, Sir Lynch, 838
Cotton, Sir Rowland, 472
Cotton, William (of Leatherhead),
   240
Cotton, William (of Wallwood),
   329
Coulson, Maj. J. B., 267
Coulter, —, 382
Courtenay, 3rd Visct., 949
Courtenay, William, 320
Courtenay, Sir William (d. 1736),
   565
Courtenay, Sir William (d. 1762),
   334
Courthope, G., 858
Courthope, Mrs., 858
Cousin, David, 148, 645
Cousin, René, 805
Coutts, Mrs. Harriet, 618
Coutts, James, 609, 612
Coutts, Thomas, 609
Coventry, 4th Earl, 750
Coventry, 6th Earl, 49, 51, 52,
   146 (bis), 550, 949 (bis)
Coventry, 7th Earl, 79, 245
Coventry, Countess, 951
Cowan, Alexander, 237
Cowan, Rev. Dr., 268
Cowper, —, 56n.
Cowper, Henry, 367
Cowper, Hon. Spencer, 958
Cowper, 2nd Earl, 249
Cowper, 3rd Earl, 280
Cowper, 5th Earl, 76, 958
Cowper, Sir W. H., 117
Cox, Laurence, 242
Cox, Samuel, 177
Coxe, Dr. William, 769
Crabb, John, 464
Crace, J. G., 445
Cracroft, J., 518
Cragg, John, 689, 690 (ter)
Craggs, James, 344
Craig, John (d. 1783), 239
Craig, William, 239
Craig, Sir William Gibson, 162
Craigie, —, 737
Crake, Michael, 239

Cram, David, 268
Cramer, T., 667
Crane, Sir Francis, 473
Cranfield, Lionel, 472; and see
   Middlesex, 1st Earl
Cranstoun, George, 116–17
Craven, 1st Earl, 336, 636, 902,
   904 (bis)
Craven, 2nd Earl, 234
Craven, 3rd Lord, 342
Craven, 6th Lord, 139, 147
Craven, William, 312
Crawford, Lady Mary Lindsay,
   358, 382
Crawford, Mary E., 125
Crawfurd, Lt.-Col. Henry, 777
Crawfurd, Hew, 57
Crawhall, Thomas, 267
Crawley-Boevey, Thomas, 481
Crawshaw, William, 240
Crawshay, William, 526, 527
Creecher, Thomas, 929, 930, 931
Cregoe, Capt. F., 618
Cremorne, Lord, see Dartrey, 1st
   Earl
Cremorne, 1st Visct., 947, 952
Crespigny, —, 236
Cressett, Edward, 662
Cresswell, A. J. B., 729
Crewdson, W. D., 876
Crewe, John, 576
Crewe, Rev. Joseph, 84
Crewe, 3rd Lord, 118
Crichton, James, 240
Cripps, Thomas, 379
Critchlow, —, 374
Croft, Edward, 419
Croker, J. W., 173, 174, 745
Crombie, Alexander, 761
Crompton, Elizabeth, 304
Cromwell, Elizabeth, 712
Cromwell, Henry, 822
Crooke, —, 771
Crooke, Richard, 929
Crow, George, 618
Crowe, James, 137
Crowther, J. S., 811
Cruddace, William, 268
Cruickshanks, Alexander, 737
Crutchley, G. H., 951
Cryder, J., 619
Cubitt, Jonathan, 243
Cubitt, Mrs., 680
Cuitt, George, 395
Cullen, —, 142
Cullum, Sir Thomas, 375
Cumberland, Duke (d. 1765), 310,
   312, 493, 705, 713, 714
Cumberland, Duke (d. 1790), 51,
   713
Cumberlege, C. N., 867
Cuningham, Sir David, 95
Cunlliffe, —, 83
Cunliffe, Sir Ellis, 53
Cunliffe, Sir Foster, 476, 950
Cunningham, David, 567
Cunningham, Sir David, 787
Cunningham, Rev. J. M., 143
Cunningham, John, 527
Cunningham, W., 385
Cunynghame, Robert, 862
Cure, Capel, 95
Cure, William, 786
Currey, Henry, 170
Currie, William, 92, 125, 527
Curteis, Rev. Thomas, 173
Curtis, Mrs. Susanna, 349
Curtois, Rev. P., 95

Curwen, Henry, 195
Curwen, John Christian, 195
Curzon, Assheton, 946
Curzon, Sir John, 344
Curzon, Sir Nathaniel (d. 1718), 749
Curzon, Sir Nathaniel (d. 1758), 55
Curzon, Sir Nathaniel (d. 1804), *see* Scarsdale, 1st Lord
Curzon, Hon. Robert, 971
Cuthbert, William, 267

Dacre, 14th Lord, 873
Dacre, 17th Lord, 550
Daer, Lord, 59
Dain, M. J., 622
Dalbiac, Charles, 592 (*bis*)
Dale, Edward, 930
Dalgety, F. G., 167
Dalhousie, 8th Earl, 623
Dalhousie, 9th Earl, 163
Dalison, —, 456
Dalrymple, George, 57
Dalrymple, Sir Hew (d. 1800), 628
Dalrymple, Sir Hew (d. 1834), 896
Dalrymple, Sir John, 54
Dalrymple, Miss, 239
Dalrymple-Hamilton, *see* Dalrymple, Sir Hew
Dalton, James, 174
Dalzell, Robert, 128
Damer, Anne, 410
Damer, John, 201
Danby, Sir Abstrupus, 826
Danby, 1st Earl, 786 (*bis*), 789
Danby, Lord, *see* Leeds, 1st Duke
Danby, William (d. 1781), 194
Danby, William (d. 1833), 315, 527, 949
Dance, Giles, 248
Dance, James, 248
Dance-Holland, Sir Nathaniel, 248, 249, 252
Dandervall, Martha, 379
Daniell, Lady Duckenfield, 72
Daniell, Thomas (painter), 228
Daniell, Thomas (of Trelissick), 701
Daniell, Thomas (of Truro), 285
Daniell, William, 250, 251
Danvers, Sir John, 823
Darby, Abraham, 662
Darbyshire, Alfred, 502
D'Arcy, Sir Conyers, 492
Darell family, 739
Darley, C. A., 972
Darley, John, 253
Darlington, 1st Earl, 610
Darlington, 2nd Earl, 194
Darlington, 3rd Earl, 638
Darnley, 3rd Earl, 207
Darnley, 4th Earl, 653, 679 (*bis*), 682, 948, 952
Darnley, 5th Earl, 963
Dartmouth, 1st Earl, 750
Dartmouth, 2nd Earl, 137
Dartmouth, 4th Earl, 692
Dartmouth, 5th Earl, 167
Dartrey, 1st Earl, 165
Dash, Mrs. Ann, 378
Dashwood, Charles Vere, 413
Dashwood, Sir Francis, 270; *and see* Despenser, Lord le
Dashwood, Sir George, 435

Dashwood, Sir James, 333, 344, 716, 763
Daubeny, Archdeacon C., 352
Daukes, S. W., 664
Davenport, E. D., 118
Davenport, Henry, 751
David, Claude, 925
Davidson, James, 587
Davies, —, 439
Davies, Dr., 225
Davis, —, 263
Davis, C. E., 85, 254
Davis, Peter, 98
Davis, Roger, 928, 931
Davis, W. H., 700
Davis, William, 773, 885
Davison, Barbara, 84
Davison, Robert, 84
Davison, Samuel (of Durham), 505
Davison, Samuel (of Salop), 84
Davison, Thomas, 267
Dawe, George, 60
Dawes, Richard, 248
Dawes, William, 408
Dawkins, Henry, 684, 912
Dawkins, James, 126, 684, 794
Dawkins, James, jnr., 684
Dawson, Edward (d. 1815), 464
Dawson, Edward (d. 1859), 670, 692
Dawson, Dr. James, 520
Dawson, Massy, 854
Dawson, William, 951
Day, E. A., 255
Day, Henry, 255
Day, John, 350
Day, Robert, 928, 929, 930, 931
Deacon, Col., 714
Deacon, John, 171, 173
Dealtry, Miss, 174
Deane, Anthony, 255, 544
Deards, John, 374
Deare, John, 615
De Carle family, 136
De Caux, Salomon, 256
Decker, Sir Matthew, 320
De Dunstanville, Lady, 394
Deedes, W., 125
Deering, Henry, 329
D'Egville, James, 541, 667
Delamere, 1st Lord, 117
Delaval, Edward Hussey, 200
Delaval, Adml. George, 853
Delaval, Sir John Hussey, 51–2, 262, 528 (*bis*), 595, 668
Delaval, 1st Lord, 54, 346; *and see* Delaval, Sir John Hussey
De La Warr, 5th Earl, 682 (*bis*)
Delmé, Peter, 951
Delvaux, Laurent, 716
Delves, Sir Brian Broughton, 839
Denbigh, 5th Earl, 145
Denbigh, 6th Earl, 145
Denholm, James, 647
Denison, Robert, 191
Denison, William, 521
Denning, Thomas, 930
Denshire, —, 932
Dent & Co., 863
Derby, 6th Earl, 783
Derby, 11th Earl, 333
Derby, 12th Earl, 51, 54, 318, 723
Derby, 13th Earl, 165
Dering, Sir Edward, 166
Derry, Bishop of, *see* Bristol, 4th Earl
Desaguliers, J. T., 804

Deskford, Lord, 46
Despencer, Lady le, 859
Despenser, Lord le, 51, 77, 684
Devall, John (mason), 831
Devall, John (plumber), 482
Deverell, John, 226
Devon, 10th Earl, 320, 321 (*bis*)
Devonport, J., 292
Devonshire, 4th Earl, 797
Devonshire, Countess, 764
Devonshire, 1st Duke, 68, 69, 803, 805
Devonshire, 2nd Duke, 88
Devonshire, 3rd Duke, 492
Devonshire, 4th Duke, 611
Devonshire, 5th Duke, 191, 196, 883, 951
Devonshire, 6th Duke, 76, 172, 173 (*ter*), 488, 698, 867, 962
Devonshire, 7th Duke, 172 (*bis*)
Devonshire, Duchess (d. 1806), 898
Devonshire, Duchess (d. 1824), 140
Dewes, —, 465
Dewez, Laurent-Benoit, 48
Deykes, Samuel, 259
Diaper, Frederick, 203
Dibdin, Charles, 515
Dick, Prof. John, 113
Dick, Sir John, 231
Dickens, C. S., 118
Dicker, Samuel, 300
Dickinson, B., 951
Dickinson, William (d. 1806), 426
Dickinson, William (d. 1837), 896
Dickson, James, 595
Dickson, T., 811
Digges, Sir Dudley, 786
Dillingham, B. G., 768
Dillon, 14th Visct., 972
Dimsdale, Baron, 762
Dingwall, John, 761
Dinorben, Lady, 476
Dinorben, Lord, 435
Dinwiddie, Lawrence, 382
Dirdoe, John, 96
D'Israeli, Isaac, 93
Dixon, Abraham, 611
Dixon, Charles, 435
Dixon, Dixon, 266
Dixon, J—, 192
Dixon, Jeremiah, 192n., 194
Dixon, John, 268
Dixon, Joseph, 53
Dixon, Peter, 267
Dixon, Peter, & Sons, 811
Dixon, Richard, 53, 262–3
Dixon, S., 175
Dixon, Thomas, 369
Dobson, Alexander, 264
Dobyns, Robert, 800
Dodd, George, 121, 395, 677
Dodington, George, 853
Dodington, George Bubb, 561, 562, 727, 853
Dodson, Richard, 188
Dollman, F. T., 93, 94, 667
Dominiceti, Dr. Bartholomew de, 208
Don, Sir Alexander, 745
Donegall, 1st Marquess, 147
Donegall, ?2nd Marquess, 125
Donkin, Armorer, 267
Donkin, Bryan, 360
Doogood, Henry, 925, 927–31 (*passim*)
Dore, Peter, 642

Dormer, Genl. James, 493, 835
Dormer, 11th Lord, 746
Dorrien, George, 617, 619
Dorrien, Thomas, 617, 619
Dorrien, Magens & Co., 619
Dougal, John, 737
Dougherty, Miss, 617
Doughty, —, 136
Doughty, J., 293
Douglas, —, 761
Douglas, Archibald, 644 (bis)
Douglas, Duke, 46, 623
Douglas, Marquess, 501
Douglas, Sir John James, 359
Douglas, R., 535
Douglas, Sir William, 241
Douglas, Hon. Mrs., 163
Dover, Lord, 938
Dowdeswell, Rev. E. C., 117, 120
Dowdeswell, George, 692
Downe, 3rd Visct., 610
Downe, 5th Visct., 125
Downing, Francis, 510
Downshire, 1st Marquess, 952
Downshire, 2nd Marquess, 140 (bis)
Downshire, 3rd Marquess, 501, 667, 717
Downshire, Marchioness, 110, 691, 874
Doyne, Robert, 698
Drake, Montague, 345
Drake, Montague Garrard, 514, 751
Drake, William, 52, 509, 946, 951, 959
Draper, William, 403, 792
Draper, William (joiner), 928
Dredge, William, 566
Drew, T. R., 275
Driver, G. N., 275
Driver, S. T., 275
Druce, C., 807
Drummond, Genl. A. J., 358
Drummond, A. R., 963
Drummond, Adml. Sir Adam, 533
Drummond, Andrew, 207, 855
Drummond, Lady Catherine, 797
Drummond, George (of Blair Drummond), 530
Drummond, George (of Stanmore), 425
Drummond, George Harley, 358
Drummond, H. H., 701
Drummond, Henry, 143 (bis), 377, 896
Drummond, Henry Home, 261
Drummond, J. G. Home, 260
Drummond, John (of Quarrell), 343
Drummond, John (of Stanmore), 207
Drummond, R. H., Archbishop of York, 74 (bis)
Drummond, Hon. Robert, 147, 425, 711
Drummond, Messrs., 51
Drummond, Mrs., 172
Drummond-Stewart, Sir John A., 359
Dryden, John, 344
Dryhurst, Thomas, 482
Duberley, J., 177
Dubourgay, Charles, 275
Du Cane, Peter (d. 1803), 817
Du Cane, Peter (d. 1822), 464
Du Cane, Peter (d. 1841), 393

Ducie, 1st Earl, 619, 682
Ducie, 2nd Earl, 244
Duckett, William, 717
Dudgeon, Patrick, 164
Dudley, 1st Earl, 510
Dudley & Ward, 1st Viscount, 77
Duff, Richard Wharton, 699
Duff, Col. Robert William, 624
Duff, William, 341
Dufferin, 1st Earl, 167
Dufour, C., 270
Dugdale, W. S., 118
Dugdale, Sir William, 588
Duke, Sir James, 966
Dumfries, 4th Earl, 46
Dummer, Thomas, 251
Dun, Lord, 57
Dunbar, Sir Archibald, 699
Dunbar, Sir James, 737
Duncan, —, 383
Duncan, Mrs., 617
Duncan, Lady Mary, 576
Duncan, Sir William, 577
Duncombe, Hon. & Rev. A., 166
Duncombe, Sir John, 544
Duncombe, Thomas, 860
Dundas, Sir David, 166
Dundas, James, 162
Dundas, Sir Lawrence, 46, 51, 52, 147, 179, 194, 209, 395, 687
Dundas, Robert (Lord Arniston), 46, 57, 220
Dundas, Sir Robert, 734
Dundas, Sir Thomas (1st Lord Dundas), 122, 425
Dundas, Sir William, 858
Dunfermline, 1st Lord, 647
Dungannon, 2nd Visct., 649
Dunlop, Alexander, 82
Dunlop, Allan C., 737
Dunlop, Sir James, 383
Dunmore, 2nd Earl, 896
Dunn, Thomas, 831
Dunning, Charles, 417
Dunnington-Jefferson, Rev. J., 118
Dunraven, 2nd Earl, 234
Dunston, Robinson & Flanders, Messrs., 632
Duppa, B. D., 102
Duppa & Collins, 619
Dupper, Mr., 472
Dupré, James, 809
Dupré, Josias, 478
Durand, —, 577
Durham, 1st Earl, 122 (bis), 123, 363
Durham, 2nd Earl, 268
Duroure, Alexander, 252
Duroure, Scipio, 252
Dutton, —, 619
Dutton, John, 791
Dutton, Capt. John, 267
Dutton, Sir John, 492
Dyer, Robert, 928
Dyott, Genl. William, 655
Dysart, 6th Earl, 583
Dysart, Countess, 154
Dyson, —, 868
Dyson, R. R., 600

Eamer, Sir John, 649
Earle, Col., 136
Earle, Sir Hardman, 291
Earle, T. H., 770
Earle, William, 290
Easthope, Sir John, 619
Eastlake, C. L., 89, 495

Eayre, Joseph, 279
Eboral, Thomas, 748, 751
Ebury, 1st Lord, 166
Eden, Sir Robert J., 123
Edge, Edward, 391
Edge, T. W., 332
Edisbury, Joshua, 874
Edmonds, C. W. C., 282
Edmunds, Francis, 641
Edney, Simon, 830
Edridge, William, 725
Edwards, Charles, 617
Edwards, Edward, 831
Edwards, Evan, 467
Edwards, John (of Pye Nest), 194
Edwards, John (of Rheola), 584, 585
Effingham, 2nd Earl, 167
Effingham, 3rd Earl, 641
Effingham, Countess, 276
Egerton, Francis T., 809
Egerton, Lord Francis, 118 (bis)
Egerton, John, Bishop of Durham, 194
Egerton, Philip, 842
Egerton, Wilbraham, 229, 377, 953, 954
Egerton, William, 957
Eglinton, 9th Earl, 59
Eglinton, 10th Earl, 575
Eglinton, 11th Earl, 51, 100
Eglinton, 12th Earl, 624 (bis)
Egremont, 1st Earl, 137
Egremont, 2nd Earl, 137, 138
Egremont, 4th Earl, 91
Eizatt, Alexander, see Izit
Eld, —, 84
Elder, Edward, 928, 929
Eldon, 1st Earl, 679
Elgin, 5th Earl, 46
Elgin, 7th Earl, 329, 397, 467, 653, 777
Eliot, Hon. E. J., 367
Eliot, Hon. John, 770
Eliot, 1st Lord, 672
Eliot, 2nd Lord, 770, 771
Elland, R., 328
Ellesmere, 1st Earl, 92
Elliott, Sir Gilbert, 58 (bis)
Elliott, Rev. H. V., 94
Elliott, John, 719
Elliott, Thomas, 789
Elliott, Col. William, 421
Elliott, Sir William, 55
Ellis, Alexander, 760
Ellis, Daniel, 647
Ellis, James, 69
Ellis, John, 177
Ellison, Cuthbert, 172, 267
Ellison, Henry, 341
Ellison, Richard, 268
Elliston, —, 102
Elmhirst, William, 868
Elphinstone, Sir Howard, 862
Elton, Sir Edward M., 679
Elvill, Sir John, 509
Elwes, J. M., 253
Elwes, R. C., 377
Emery, J., 501
English, Thomas, 642
Enys, J. S., 393
Erle, Sir William, 859
Erne, 3rd Earl, 118
Errington, Henry, 208
Errington, J., 266
Errington, John (of Chesters), 194
Errington, John (of High Warden), 267

Errington, Sir Rowland, 268
Errol, 17th Earl, 762
Erskine, Charles, 58, 220
Erskine, David (of Cardross), 784
Erskine, David (of Dun), 57
Erskine, Lord, 338
Erskine, Thomas, 784
Erskine, Sir William, 717
Esdaile, E. J., 541
Esdaile, Sir James, 612
Essex, 1st Earl, 545
Essex, 3rd Earl, 276
Essex, 5th Earl, 667, 701, 950, 961
Estcourt, Edmund, 949
Estcourt, Thomas, 269
Estment, Daniel, 905
Etty, Charles, 782, 879
Evans, George, 302
Evans, George F., 252, 682
Evans, John, 927, 929, 930
Evans, Joseph, 841
Evans, Thomas, 293
Evelyn, George, 303
Evelyn, Sir George S., 228
Evelyn, James, 772
Evelyn, Sir John, 493
Evelyn, W. J., 284
Everard, Rev. E., 91
Every, Sir Edward, 957
Every, Sir John, 84, 936
Ewart, J. C., 898
Ewart, D. R. W., 241
Ewing, James, 383
Ewing, James (d. 1853), 82
Exeter, 5th Earl, 805
Exeter, 8th Earl, 654
Exeter, 9th Earl, 146, 528
Exeter, 1st Marquess, 511
Exeter, 2nd Marquess, 151
Exeter, Countess, 710
Exmouth, 2nd Visct., 78
Eyre, —, 583
Eyre, Anthony, 193
Eyre, Rev. C. W., 166
Eyre, Francis, 446
Eyre, H. S., 729
Eyre, James, 148
Eyre, Sir James, 54

Fagg, Sir Robert, 344
Fairfax, Charles, 64
Fairfax, 8th Visct., 860
Fairfax, 9th Visct., 193, 194
Fairman, J., 859
Falconbridge, Lord, 842
Falkland, 5th Visct., 297
Falkland, 10th Visct., 971
Falkland, Lady, 803
Falmouth, 2nd Earl, 859 (ter)
Falmouth, 4th Visct., 896
Fane, Hon. John, see Westmorland, 7th Earl
Fardell, Rev. Mr., 394
Farington, Joseph, 643
Farington, Rev. Robert, 252
Farmer, —, 650
Farmer, Mrs., 740
Farmer, Samuel, 961
Farnborough, Lord, see Long, Sir Charles
Farquharson, James John, 225, 383
Farr, Thomas, 575
Farrer, James, 76
Fauconberg, 2nd Earl, 74, 209
Faulkner, George, 811
Faulkner, Thomas, 87

Fauntleroy, H., 173
Fausett, Bryan, 258
Fawcett, Thomas, 506
Fawkes, W. H., 196
Fellowes, Edward, 118 (bis)
Fellowes, H., 770
Fellowes, Sir John, 477
Fellowes, Hon. Newton, 510
Fellowes, R., 768
Fellows, —, 592
Fellows, Thomas, 617
Fenwick, John, 267
Fenwick, John (of Bywell), 199
Fenwick, Nicholas, 591
Fenwick, P., 266
Fenwick, Robert, 640
Fenwick, Thomas, 267
Fenwick, William, 611
Fereday, J., 510
Ferguson, Alexander, 57
Ferguson, C. J., 122
Ferguson, Capt. George, 762
Ferguson, Robert, 647
Ferguson, William, 644
Ferguson-Davie, Col. Sir H., 166
Ferguson, Sir James, 358
Fermor, William, 576
Fermor, Sir William, 403, 925
Fernier, R., 724
Ferrand, Benjamin, 611
Ferrey, Benjamin, 71, 202, 265, 667, 668, 692, 895
Fetherstone, Henry, 872
Fetherston, William, 726
Fetherstonhaugh, Sir Harry, 680, 682
Fetherstonhaugh, Sir Matthew, 484, 609
Feuchères, Baroness de, 253, 271
Feversham, 2nd Lord, 92
Fewster, Thomas, 293
Ffolkes, Sir William Browne, 270
Ffytche, Thomas, 866
Fiddian, F. W., 589
Field, John, 234
Field, Robert, 66
Fife, 1st Earl, 58
Fife, 2nd Earl, 51
Fife, 4th Earl, 738
Fife, Sir John, 267
Finch, Heneage, 272n.
Finch, Rev. Heneage, 393
Finch, Lady Isabella, 493
Finch, Rev. Robert, 657
Finch, Rev. William, 394
Findlater, 7th Earl, 644, 645
Finlay, Kirkman, 382
Finlayson, —, 330
Finley, W., 886
Fish, J., 705
Fisher, Henry, 457
Fisher, J. J., 173
Fisher, Paul, 866
Fisher, R. B., 155
Fisher, Messrs., 253
Fisum, William, 865
Fitch, John (mason), 309, 930
Fitzgerald, Lord Henry, 685
Fitzherbert, Mrs. (wife of George IV), 425, 653
Fitzherbert, Mrs. (of Swynnerton), 841
Fitzherbert, Thomas (d. 1765), 83, 752
Fitzherbert, Thomas (d. 1778), 839
Fitzherbert, Thomas (d. 1857), 840

Fitzmaurice, Hon. Thomas, 609 (bis), 714
Fitzwalter, 1st Earl, 512, 513
Fitzwilliam, 1st Earl, 805
Fitzwilliam, 2nd Earl, 344
Fitzwilliam, 3rd Earl, 312
Fitzwilliam, 4th Earl, 193, 196 (bis), 208 (bis), 521, 893
Flaxman, John, 157, 225, 276, 432
Fleming, J. W., 434
Fleming, W. H., 253
Fletcher, —, 83
Fletcher, Andrew, 162
Fletcher, Andrew (Lord Milton), 46, 531
Fletcher, Sir George, 60
Fletcher, Sir Henry (d. 1645), 650
Fletcher, Sir Henry (d. 1851), 870
Fletcher, Jacob, 398
Fletcher, T. W., 869
Fletcher, Thomas, 835
Fletcher, Sir Thomas, 584
Flight & Barr, Messrs., 374
Flory, James, 929, 930
Flower, H., 43
Flower, W., 618
Floyd, Sir Godfrey, 902
Fludyer, George, 511, 718
Foley, Hon. Edward, 809, 893
Foley, H. H., 701 (bis)
Foley, J. H., 90
Foley, Lord, 837
Foley, 2nd Lord, 312, 341, 508
Foley, 3rd Lord, 583
Foley, Richard, 582
Foley, Thomas, 311
Foljambe, Francis F., 657, 896, 946
Foljambe, George Savile, 652
Folkestone, 1st Visct., 562, 817
Folliot, Lord, 901
Fontana, Carlo, 337
Forbes, Sir Charles, 737
Forbes, Sir David, 219
Forbes, Sir John, 160, 761
Forbes, William (of Callendar, d. 1815), 133, 238, 288
Forbes, William (of Callendar, d. 1855), 383
Forbes, William (of Dunecht), 761
Forbes, Sir William (d. 1806), 241, 394
Forbes, Sir William (d. 1828), 163
Forbes, 17th Lord, 737
Forbes-Mitchell, Duncan, 737
Fordyce, John, 882
Fordyce, Sir William, 137
Forester, James, 402
Forester, 1st Lord, 954
Forster, S., 488
Forster, Samuel, 858, 859
Forster, Thomas, 162
Forsyth, James (?), 228
Fort, John, 876
Fort, Thomas (mason), 710
Fortescue, 1st Lord, 131, 414, 561
Fortescue, 1st Earl, 771
Fortescue, 2nd Earl, 118
Fortescue, 3rd Earl, 168
Fortescue, J. I., 361
Fortrey, William, 905
Foster, James, 746
Foster, Thomas, 315
Foulis, Rev. H., 173
Fountayne, Rev. John, 610, 611
Fournereau, T. G., 174
Fowler, James, 654

Fownes, Henry, 613
Fox, Charles Richard, 92
Fox, Devereux, 482
Fox, George, 758
Fox, Henry, 109
Fox, Sir Stephen, 314, 545
Foy, Fitz, 207
Frampton, J. A., 858
Frampton, James, 383
Francis, F. J., 433
Frank, Dr. Richard, 324
Frankland, Sir Thomas, 948
Franks, J. H., 488
Franks, Moses, 207
Fraser, Rev. H., 617
Fraser, J., 244
Fraser, Miss Eliza, 179
Fraser, Mrs., 761
Frayer, —, 408
Frazer, James, 58
Frederick, Prince of Wales, 209, 491n., 492, 494, 726
Freeman, Edward, 931
Freeman, John (of Chute Lodge), 817
Freeman, John (of Gaines), 663
Freeman, Ralph, 797
Freeman, Sambrook, 946
Freeman, Strickland, 196
Freeman, Thomas, 331
Freind, Dr. John, 344
Freind, Dr. Robert, 259
Fremantle, Sir Thomas, 167
Fremeaux, James, 463
Frere, G., 858
Frere, Rev. John, 859
Frere, Rev. Temple, 859
Fricker, Charles, 198
Fripp, E. B., 692
Fripp, S. C., 689
Frisbey, Sampson, 552
Frith, John, 917
Frogley, Richard, 912
Fryer, John, 139
Fulger, —, 592
Fulham, Rev. Edward, 964
Fulkes, Samuel, 925, 927, 928, 929, 930, 931
Fullarton, Col. William, 55
Fuller, —, 928
Fuller, J., 929
Fuller, J. G., 617
Fuller, John, 744
Fuller, Trayton, 507
Fullerton, Col. John, 874
Fulling, Thomas, 865
Fulljames, Thomas, 689
Furnese, Sir Robert, 130
Furs, Michael Savary, 134, 139
Fydell, Samuel, 198
Fydell, Thomas, 198
Fyfe, James, 781

Gace, Joseph, 403
Gage, Robert Harvey, 605
Gage, 3rd Visct., 685
Gainsborough, 1st Earl, 696
Galen, Alexander, 737
Gallini, Sir John, 286
Galloway, 7th Earl, 464
Galloway, 9th Earl, 165
Galloway, Messrs., 618
Galloway, Alexander, 619 (ter)
Galloway, Thomas, 618
Galton, Hubert, 527
Galton, J. H., 374, 375, 487
Galton, Samuel, 527
Galway, 2nd Visct., 611

Galway, 5th Visct., 522
Gambier, W., 218
Gammon, Thomas, 930
Garbett, Edward Lacy, 331
Gardenstone, Lord, 586
Gardiner, Sir J. S. W., 961
Gardiner, Samuel, 715
Gardner, Sir Alan, 771
Gardner, R., 811
Garforth, Rev. Edmund, 193
Garforth, W., 192
Garforth, William, 196
Garlies, Lord, 99, 220, 272, 575
Garnier, Rev. W., 810 (bis)
Garrard, Col. Drake, 324
Garrick, David, 54, 952
Garstin, Rev. Anthony, 763
Garway, Allan, 929
Gascoigne, Sir Edward, 325
Gascoigne, R. O., 666, 868–9 (bis)
Gascoigne, Sir Thomas, 517
Gascoyne, Bamber, 418, 583
Gascoyne, Genl. Isaac, 79
Gaunt, J., 293
Gay, Robert, 909
Gedd, James, 453
Gedd, William, 453
Gedges, Messrs., 605
Gee, Mrs. A. P., 65
Gee, Col. William, 132
Gell, Sir Phillip, 88
Gell, Sir William, 103, 329, 554
George I, King, 414, 490, 494, 561
George II, King, 414, 561
George III, King, 50, 151, 204, 206, 208 (ter), 209, 294, 496, 950, 951 (bis), 952, 965; coronation, 602
George IV, King, 151, 580, 959–60, 963; coronation, 421
George, Prince of Wales (afterwards George II), 183, 184, 276, 853
George, Prince of Wales (afterwards George IV), 425 (bis), 434, 584 (ter), 653, 680, 955
Gerard, Sir John, 318
Germain, Lady Betty, 228
Germaine, Sir John, 803, 806
Gibb, Alexander, 762
Gibbeson, Alderman, 528
Gibbon, Edward, 178
Gibbons, Grinling, 300, 543, 544, 757, 930
Gibbs, —, 418
Gibbs, H. S., 692
Gibson, John (architect), 90
Gibson, John (Scottish architect), 106
Gibson, John (sculptor), 318
Gibson, Sir John, 570
Gibson, Walter, 155
Gibson, William, 327
Gideon, Sir Sampson, 796, 866
Giffard, Peter, 752
Giffard, Thomas (d. 1775), 146, 612
Giffard, Thomas (d. 1823), 768
Gifford, Miss, 369
Gifford, Sir William, 453n.
Giles, C. E., 202
Giles, Daniel, 592
Giles, James, 736
Giles, Nicholas, 346
Gill, J. E., 536–7
Gilliam, John, 69

Gillies, Robert, 127
Gilpin, J., 268
Giorgioli, Agostino, 391
Gisborne, John, 683
Gist, Josiah, 377
Glanville, Mrs., 672
Glasgow, Countess, 644
Glegg, E. H., 247
Glencairn, 13th Earl, 272
Glencross, William, 890
Glengall, 2nd Earl, 103
Glenorchy, Lord, 272
Gloucester, Duke (d. 1805), 845
Gloucester, Duke (d. 1834), 225
Gloucester, Duchess, 845
Glyn, Sir Richard Carr, 302
Glynn, Lady, 394
Glynne, Sir Stephen, 245
Goddard, Edward, 603
Goddard, Richard, 667
Godeffroy, R., 546
Godfrey, Edward, 815n.
Godfrey & Cooke, Messrs., 534
Goding, Messrs., 284
Goding, Thomas, 284 (bis)
Godolphin, Francis, 455, 508
Godolphin, Dr. Henry, 708
Godolphin, Sidney, 303
Godwin, William, 683
Goldie-Taubman, Genl., 638
Goldsmid, Abraham, 367
Goldsmid, Baron de, 92, 657
Goldsmid, Benjamin, 773
Goldsmid, Sir Isaac Lyon, 172, 173
Goldsworthy, Lt. Gen. Philip, 949
Gompertz, Ephraim, 501
Gompertz, S., 253
Gooch, Rev. J., 768
Gooch, Sir Thomas, 137
Good, —, 662
Goodchild, J. E., 223
Goodenough, Rev. —, 605
Goodman, Joseph, 173
Goodricke, Sir F. L. H., 103
Goodricke, Sir John, 195
Goodwin, John, 262n.
Goodwin, Nicholas, 925
Goodwin, Robert, 637
Goodwin, Mrs. S., 133
Gordon, —, 54
Gordon, —, 737
Gordon, Col. Sir Alexander, 616, 617
Gordon, Arthur, 58
Gordon, Charles (of Cairness), 158, 645, 769
Gordon, Charles (of Cluny), 158
Gordon, Genl. J. W., 517
Gordon, James (of Manar), 762
Gordon, James (of Moor Place), 554
Gordon, Sir Jenison, 488
Gordon, John, 382, 383
Gordon, Lt. Col. John, 762
Gordon, R. T., 653
Gordon, Robert, 701
Gordon, Sir Robert (d. 1776), 100
Gordon, Sir Robert (d. 1847), 762
Gordon, 4th Duke, 100 (bis), 101 (bis), 642, 707, 711, 737
Gordon, 5th Duke, 150, 736
Gordon, Duchess (d. 1760), 59
Gordon, Duchess (d. 1812), 714
Gordon, Duchess (d. 1864), 736, 737
Gordon, William, 745

Gordon, Genl. William Cumming Skene, 737
Gore, John, 817
Gore, William (of Brogyntyn), 369
Gore, William (of Tring), 343
Goreing, Lord, *see* Goring, Sir Charles
Goring, Charles, 118
Goring, Sir Charles, 186
Gosford, 2nd Earl, 435
Gosling, J., 753
Gosselin, Thomas, 900
Gostling, Francis, 150
Gostling, Robert, 118
Gott, Benjamin, 354, 745
Goudge, Edward, 805, 903, 904 (*passim*)
Gough, A. D., 91, 937
Gough, Sir Henry, 420
Gough, Richard, 298, 300, 942
Gould, R. D., 387
Goupy, Lewis, 793
Gourlay, Bailie, 308
Goverson, Arnold, 70
Goverson, William, 70
Gower, A. A., 658
Gower, 1st Earl, 137
Gower, 2nd Earl, 147, 208, 425, 635
Gower, 1st Lord, 750
Gower, 2nd Lord, 311
Grafton, 2nd Duke, 131, 136, 137, 490, 493 (*bis*)
Grafton, 3rd Duke, 637, 815, 817–18
Graham, James, 59
Graham, Sir James, 164
Graham, Rev. John, 728
Graham, Lord, 644 (*bis*)
Graham, Nicol, 59
Graham, Richard, 498
Graham, Robert, 100
Graham, Thomas (of Balgowan), 644 (*bis*), 646, 647, 771, 810 (*bis*)
Graham, Thomas (of Edmond Castle), 745
Graham, Thomas (of Penquite), 890
Graham, William Stirling, 163
Gram, A., 293
Grant, Alexander (of Aberlour), 699
Grant, Alexander (of Druminnor), 737
Grant, Capt. Alexander, 737
Grant, Sir Alexander, 745
Grant, Sir Archibald, 451, 907
Grant, Charles, 699 (*bis*)
Grant, Col. F. W., 699
Grant, Forsyth, 352
Grant, Henrietta, 183
Grant, James, 46, 701
Grant, John (Baron), 51
Grant, Abbé Peter, 180
Grant, W. C., 103
Grant, William, 557
Grantham, 1st Lord, 207, 208
Grantham, 2nd Lord, 107, 703, 965
Grantham, Lady, 965
Grantham, R., 667
Grantley, 3rd Lord, 280
Graves, —, 671
Gray, —, 587
Gray, Charles, 255
Gray, Sir James, 684, 794

Gray, John, 273
Gray, Joseph, 145
Gray, 15th Lord, 745
Gray, Robert, 378
Gray, Thomas, 952
Gray, Walker, 583
Gray, William, 268
Greame, John, 466
Green, —, 194
Green, Arthur John, 829
Green, J., 400
Green, John, 842
Green, Richard, 195
Green, T. A., 770
Greenbank, —, 812
Greene, G. T., 722
Greene, William, 43
Greening, Robert, 686
Greenough, G. B., 172
Greenwood, Charles, 527
Gregan, J. E., 75
Gregor, C. W. F., 393
Gregory, Arthur, 312
Gregory, David, 835
Gregory, Gregory de L., 117, 165, 971
Gregory, Robert, 518
Grenfell, C. Pascoe, 167
Grenville, George, 550
Grenville, Henry, 111
Grenville, Lady, 810
Grenville, Lord, 958 (*bis*)
Grenville, Thomas, 809
Gresley, Sir Nigel, 880
Gresley, Sir Thomas, 901
Greswold, H., 823
Greville, Hon. Charles, 464
Greville, Fulk, 118
Greville, Sir Fulk, 473
Greville, Richard, 726
Grey, Amabel, Countess de, 365
Grey, Lady Amabell de, 732
Grey, Jemima, Marchioness de, 177
Grey, 2nd Earl, 385, 939
Grey, Sir Charles, 619
Grey, Sir George, 266
Grey, Sir Henry, 591
Grey, R. W., 591
Grey, William, 928, 929
Grey de Ruthin, 19th Lord, 527
Grey of Warke, Lord, 822
Grey-Egerton, Sir John, 954
Gribble, E. W., 318
Grieve, D. R., 190
Griffin, —, 145
Griffin, Sir Edward, 545
Griffin, Sir John, 51, 52, 423; *and see* Howard de Walden, Lord
Griffith, Christopher, 423
Griffith, Rev. John, 859
Griffith, Thomas, 476
Griffiths, Henry, 294
Griffiths, Joseph, 133
Grimes, Abraham, 957
Grimston, John, 194
Grimston, Thomas, 194, 196, 278
Grimston, 3rd Visct., 817
Grissell & Peto, Messrs., 92
Grose, Francis, 326
Grosvenor, Richard Erle Drax, 584
Grosvenor, 1st Earl, 822
Grosvenor, 2nd Earl, 156, 369 (*ter*), 653 (*quater*)
Grosvenor, Countess, 954
Grosvenor, Sir Robert, 732
Grosvenor, Genl. Thomas, 546

Grosvenor, Sir Thomas, 712
Grote, Prescott & Grote, 771
Grove, James, 69
Grove, John (plasterer), 86, 927–31 (*passim*)
Groves, James, 930
Grylls, H. M., 890
Guelfi, G. B., 128, 494
Guest, Sir John, 92 (*bis*)
Guest, Genl. Joshua, 815
Guilford, 1st Lord, 597, 869
Guilford, 1st Earl, 549 (*bis*), 707
Guilford, 2nd Earl, *see* North, Lord
Guilford, 3rd Earl, 140
Guilford, Countess, 745
Guillaume, George, 617
Guise, Genl. (Col.), John, 256, 661
Gulston, Joseph, 483
Gumley, John, 342
Gunning & Tanner, 302
Gunters, Messrs., 881
Gurnell, Thomas, 251
Gurney, Daniel, 971
Gurney, Hudson, 896
Guy, Henry, 925
Guy, Thomas, 252
Gwydyr, 1st Lord, 125
Gwydyr, 2nd Lord, 332, 606

Hacket, John, Bp. of Lichfield, 900
Haddington, 8th Earl, 624
Hadfield, M. E., 441
Hadley, Thomas, 925
Hagart, —, 382
Haies, John, 621
Haines, Alfred, 394
Haldane, Robert, 55
Haldimand, George, 93, 94, 95, 243
Haldimand, William, 93, 94, 95, 243
Hales, Sir Edward, 559
Haliburton, James, jr., 174
Haliburton, William, 174
Halifax, Earl (d. 1739), 334
Halifax, Earl (d. 1771), 481, 484 (*bis*), 934
Hall, Sir Benjamin, 435
Hall, Edward, 75
Hall, Sir James, 115, 178, 241, 586
Hall, John, 769
Hall, Rev. Robert, 120
Haller von Hallenstein, Baron, 66, 221, 222, 317
Hallett, William, 962
Halliday, Simon, 349
Hallifax, Thomas, 387
Halsey, Thomas, 946
Hambrough, John, 279, 715
Hamey, Baldwin, 636
Hamilton, 3rd Duke, 79, 87, 152, 758 (*bis*)
Hamilton, 5th Duke, 58, 59
Hamilton, 6th Duke, 272
Hamilton, 10th Duke, 352, 359, 383
Hamilton, 11th Duke, 167, 168
Hamilton, Lord Archibald, 635
Hamilton, Arthur, 862
Hamilton, Hon. Charles, 478
Hamilton, Hon. G. F., 971
Hamilton, Gavin, 794
Hamilton, J. B., 166
Hamilton, J. F., 165

Hamilton, Rev. James, 619
Hamilton, Col. John, 624
Hamilton, Thomas, 58
Hammet, J., 771
Hammond, —, 693
Hammond, Anthony, 270
Hammond, Peter, 612
Hammond, William, 928, 930
Hampden, John, 732
Hampden, 3rd. Visct., 394
Hanbury, —, 293
Hanbury, William (d. 1768), 342
Hanbury, William (d. 1800), 947
Hanbury, Rev. William, 659
Hancock & Rixon, Messrs., 685
Hands, James, 69
Hankey, J. A., 94
Hankey, Thomas, 596
Hanmer, Col. Henry, 173
Hanmer, Humphrey, 84
Hannay, Sir Samuel, 54
Hannen, James, 618
Hannes, Sir Edward, 63
Hanson, John, 527
Hanway, Jonas, 261
Harbord, Sir William, 50, 136
Harborough, 4th Earl, 687, 777
Harcourt, Edward Vernon, Abp.
    of York, 745
Harcourt, 1st Earl, 69, 418, 508,
    796
Harcourt, 2nd Earl, 147, 425
Harcourt, 1st Visct., 69, 217, 891
Hardenburg, Prince, 681
Hardinge, George, 574
Hardinge, Nicholas, 109
Hardwick, P. C., 177, 387–8, 954
Hardwicke, 1st Earl, 311 (bis),
    549, 759, 797
Hardwicke, 2nd Earl, 147, 207,
    237, 299, 781
Hardwicke, 3rd Earl, 464, 769,
    958
Hardwicke, 4th Earl, 488, 771
Hardy, Henry, 754
Hardy, Col. Joseph, 617
Hardy, Robert, 864
Harewood, Lord, 52, 193, 209
Harewood, 1st Earl, 72, 606
Harewood, 3rd Earl, 92
Harford, J. S., 226, 584, 627
Hargrave, John, 396
Hargreaves, Col. John, 876
Harley, see Oxford, Earl
Harley, Col. Edward, 873
Harley, James, 241, 845
Harley, Hon. Thomas, 425
Harman, John, 680
Harmer, James, 863, 970
Harper, G., 228
Harpur, Sir Henry, 893
Harpur, Sir John, 341, 347
Harpur-Crewe, Sir Henry, 535
Harrington, 1st Earl, 131, 732
Harrington, 3rd Earl, 951
Harrington, 4th Earl, 234
Harris, Joseph, 422
Harris, Josias, 496
Harris, Genl. Lord, 958
Harris, Thomas, 426
Harrison, —, 617
Harrison, Catherine, 693
Harrison, Charles, 394
Harrison, Frederick, 394
Harrison, George, 688
Harrison, H., 268
Harrison, Isaac, 112
Harrison, John (of Norton), 195

Harrison, John (of Snelston), 234
Harrison, Sir John, 787
Harrison, Miss, 617
Harrison, William, 75n.
Harrowby, 2nd Earl, 166
Harrowby, 1st Lord, 465, 839,
    957, 958, 959
Hart, Thomas, 331
Hart-Dyke, Sir Percival, 393
Hartley, David, 252, 424
Hartley, George, 195
Hartley, H. R., 372
Hartley, Jesse, 395, 397, 398,
    840
Hartopp, E. B., 269
Harvey, J., 268
Harvey, John & Co., 814
Harvey, Sir R. Bateson, 293
Hase, Henry, 771
Hastings, Lady Elizabeth, 108
Hastings, 1st Marquess, 288
Hastings, Warren, 228
Haswell, George, 144
Hatch, James, 345
Hatchard, Thomas, 126
Hatherton, 1st Lord, 354
Hatton, George Finch, 125
Hawkesbury, Lord, see Liverpool,
    2nd Earl
Hawkins, Christopher, 413
Hawkins, Sir Christopher, 114
Hawkins, John, 393
Hawkins, Philip, 285, 344
Hawkins, Thomas, 817
Hawtrey, Rev. Stephen, 268
Hay, —, 164
Hay, Capt., 158
Hay, Lt. Col. Alexander, 359
Hay, John, 737
Hay, Robert (of Duns), 100
Hay, Robert (of Linplum), 71,
    200
Hay, William, 358
Hay, Lord William, 59
Hayles, Sir Thomas, 855
Hayley, Thomas, 733
Hayley, William, 157
Hayman, Francis, 608, 865
Hays, W. B., 66
Hayward, C., 301
Hayward, James, 706
Hayward, John, 240
Hayward, W., 372
Head, Charles, 268
Headfort, 1st Marquess, 714
Headlam, T. E., 267
Healey, Thomas, 209
Heals, John, 717
Heathcote, Sir Gilbert, 236 (bis),
    245
Heathcote, J. E., 331
Heathcote, J. M., 118
Heathcote, Sir John, 477
Heathcote, Rev. R. B., 859
Heathcote, Robert, 245
Heathcote, Sir William (d. 1751),
    312, 454
Heathcote, Sir William (d. 1881),
    679
Heathfield, 2nd Lord, 228
Heber, Bishop, 406
Heberden, Dr. William, 609
Hedger, James, 249
Hedworth, John, 184
Heelis, —, 75
Hefford, Thomas, 482
Heginbottom, Samuel, 237
Heinz, D., 135, 136

Hellier, Samuel, 84
Hellier, Sir Samuel, 327
Hellier, Rev. Shaw, 643
Helmes, —, 674
Henderson, —, 164
Henderson, John (d. 1862), 384,
    413, 969
Hendrie, —, 282
Heneage, C. F., 899
Heneage, George, 72
Henley, Sir Robert, 712
Henman, Charles, 563
Henniker, 4th Lord, 972
Henrietta Maria, Queen, 472, 473,
    874
Henry, Prince of Wales, 197, 256,
    468
Hepburn, —, 76
Hepburn, John, 784
Herbert, H. A., 165
Herbert, Henry, 859
Herbert, Jacob, 604
Herbert, Hon. Robert, 415
Herbert of Chirbury, 1st Lord,
    722
Herbert, William, 407
Hereford, James, 949
Heron, Major, 324
Heron, Sir Robert, 961
Heron, Thomas, 147
Herrick, W. P., 670
Herrick, William, 880
Herries, Robert, 617
Herron, G., 371
Hertford, 1st Earl, 343
Hertford, 1st Marquess, 873, 947,
    948
Hertford, 3rd Marquess, 172, 745
Hervey, Frederick, Bp. of Derry,
    see Bristol, 4th Earl
Hervey, John, 430 (bis)
Hervey, Lady, 312
Hervey, William, 76, 605 (bis)
Heseltine, William, 618
Hesketh, L. B., 175, 692
Hesketh-Fleetwood, Sir Peter,
    171–2, 172
Hewett, Thomas, 275
Hewitt, James, 188
Hewitt, Lady, 710
Hewlett, Richard, 613
Hext, Sir Edward, 70
Hibbert & Co., 172
Hibbert, John, 971
Hibbert, Thomas, 583
Hibbert-Ware, Dr. S., 614
Hicks, Rev. W., 605
Hicks Beach, see Beach
Higgs, —, 111
Highmore, Thomas, 824
Hildyard, Sir Robert, 194
Hildyard, Sir Robert D'Arcy, 194,
    315
Hildyard, Col. T. B., 954
Hill, Sir John, 188
Hill, Joseph, 965
Hill, Noel, 410, 576
Hill, Richard, 228
Hill, Richard (of Richmond), 964
Hill, Hon. & Rev. Richard Noel,
    142
Hill, Sir Roger, 774
Hill, Rev. Rowland, 822
Hill, Sir Rowland, 398, 954
Hill, Thomas, 663
Hill, Thomas (mason), 925
Hill, 1st Visct. (Genl.), 398;
    Column to, 187, 397, 405

Hill, Hon. W. Noel, 439
Hills, Philip, 769
Hillsborough, 1st Earl, 425
Hillsborough, 1st Visct., 378
Hilton, William, 120
Hinchcliffe, Sarah, 190
Hinckes, Miss, 692
Hinde, J. H., 268
Hindle, W. J., 969
Hine, T. C., 626
Hinton, Thomas, 481
Hinxman, John, 701
Hippisley, Henry, 269
Hippisley, J. H., 269
Hippisley, Sir John Coxe, 585, 846
Hirst, J. H., 846
Hitchcox, William, 549
Hives, John, 216
Hives & Anderson, Messrs., 215
Hoare, Benjamin, 311, 732
Hoare, Charles, 583
Hoare, George, 177
Hoare, Henry (d. 1725), 109, 184, 446
Hoare, Henry (d. 1785), 109, 201, 312 (bis)
Hoare, Henry (d. 1866), 307
Hoare, Sir Hugh, 620
Hoare, Jonathan, 913
Hoare, Sir Richard Colt, 155, 156, 200, 638, 896
Hobart, George, 51
Hobart, Sir Henry, 281, 511
Hobart, Lord, 671
Hobbs, John, 787
Hoblyn, Robert, 285
Hobson, Daniel, 958
Hobson, William, 113
Hodgkins, —, 931
Hodgson, —, 617
Hodgson, Christopher, 595, 603
Hodgson, John, 785
Hodgson, Rev. T. D., 393
Hodgson, William, 594
Hodgson-Cadogan, Major William, 267
Hofland, T. C., 615
Hogarth, William, 489, 496, 865
Hogg, Thomas, 54–5
Holbech, William, 376
Holcroft, Thomas, 683
Holden, Richard, 817
Holden, Robert, 635
Holden, Strickland, 423
Holder, Col., 394
Holder, Rev. William, 917–18
Holderness, 4th Earl, 109, 195, 514, 796
Holdsworth, Edward, 835
Holford, Sir James, 172
Holford, R. S., 856, 858 (bis), 859 (passim)
Holland, Edward, 679
Holland, H. L., 508
Holland, 1st Earl, 85
Holland, 1st Lord, 866
Holland, 3rd Lord, 147, 172, 714
Holley, J. H., 679
Holliday, W., 823
Hollinghurst, Richard, 841
Hollingsworth, Rev. N. H., 267
Hollins, Humphry, 884n.
Hollist, Hasler, 118
Holme, A. H., 283, 689
Holme, William, 875
Holmes, —, 459n., 473
Holmes, Rev. Gervase, 709

Holmes, Rev. J., 896
Holmes, James, 965
Holmes, Sarah, 832
Holmes, Thomas, 714
Holroyd, J. B., 507
Holt, Richard, 695
Holt, Rowland, 146
Holzendorf, Charles, 121
Home, Countess (widow of 2nd Earl), 256
Home, Countess (widow of 8th Earl), 51
Home, 8th Earl, 59
Home, 11th Earl, 166
Home, George, 676
Home, John, 53
Home, Patrick, 53
Honywood, Sir John, 649
Honywood, Michael, Dean of Lincoln, 924
Hood, 1st Visct., 770
Hook, Henry, 430
Hook, Mrs., 101
Hookey, John, 683
Hooper, Dr., 715
Hope, Sir Archibald, 101
Hope, Hon. Charles, 47
Hope, Major John, 148
Hope, Sir John, 163
Hope, Samuel & J., 431n.
Hope, Thomas, 76 (bis)
Hope, Sir Thomas, 153
Hope, Sir William, 154
Hope-Edwardes, T. H., 407
Hopetoun, 1st Earl, 57, 154 (bis), 283
Hopetoun, 2nd Earl, 46, 57
Hopetoun, 3rd Earl, 781
Hopgood, James, 415
Hopkins, Benjamin B., 478
Hopkins, R., 282
Hopkins, W. J., 846
Hopkinson, Robert, 610
Hopson, Charles, 930
Hopson, Richard, 474
Hopton, Richard Cope, 481
Hordern, Henry, 354
Horn, John, 929
Horn, Thomas, 928. 929, 930, 931
Hornby, Joseph, 291
Hornby, Rev. J. J., 394
Horner, H. P., 520
Horner, Thomas, 447
Horner, Col. Thomas, 770, 773
Hornor, Thomas, 171, 689, 701
Horsenaile, Christopher, 775, 831
Horsley, George, 421
Horton, Christopher, 344, 763, 838
Horton, Robert, 931
Hoskins, Abraham, 961
Hotham, Beaumont, 74
Hotham, Sir Charles, 184, 826
Hotham, Rev. Sir John, 464
Houblon, Jacob, 674
Houblon, John Archer, 435, 463, 464
Hough, John, Bp. of Worcester, 884, 885
Houseman, Valentine, 928, 931
How, Thomas, 751
Howard, Edward, 276
Howard, Lady Elizabeth, 197
Howard, Frank, 178
Howard, Henrietta, see Suffolk, Countess
Howard, Henry (of Corby), 594

Howard, Henry (afterwards 6th Duke of Norfolk), 303
Howard, J., 789
Howard, John, 113, 249, 407, 820
Howard, Richard, 125
Howard de Walden, 4th Lord, 52, 139, 231, 423; and see Griffin, Sir John
Howden, 2nd Lord, 174
Howe, 1st Earl, 116, 117, 817, 962
Howe, 3rd Visct., 797
Howell, John, 619
Howes, Richard, 931
Howland, Sir Robert, 686
Howley, William, Bp. of London, 225, 228 (bis), Abp. of Canterbury, 117, 119–20, 393
Howth, 3rd Earl, 172
Hoyland, Maj., 693
Hudson, Charles Grave, 596
Hudson, George, 244, 265, 362
Hudson, Giles, 887
Hudson, Harrington, 245
Hues, Thomas, 69
Hughes, —, Alderman of Worcester, 884
Hughes, E. H. Ball, 955
Hughes, Rev. Edward, 958
Hughes, H. R., 166
Hughes, Michael, 394
Hullah, John, 880
Hume, Sir Abraham, 51, 54, 576 (bis)
Hume, David, 55
Hume, Elizabeth, 165
Hume, Rev. James, 340
Humphery, John, 66
Humphries, James, 858
Humphry, Genl. J., 859
Hungerford, H. H., 349, 377
Hunloke, Sir Henry, 84
Hunloke, Thomas Winsor, 752
Hunt, Henry, 429
Hunt, J. H., 306–7
Hunt, Leigh, 733
Hunt, W. O., 173
Hunt, William, 516
Hunter, —, 737
Hunter, Sir Aubrey, 892
Hunter, D., 807
Hunter, James, 71
Hunter, Capt. James, 164
Hunter, Genl. Sir Michael, 164
Hunter, Thomas, 55
Hunter, Thomas Orby, 185, 717
Hunter, Dr. William, 576
Hunter Blair, Sir David, 162
Huntingdon, 9th Earl, 494
Huntington, John, 712
Huntly, Marquess (afterwards 5th Duke of Gordon), 618, 642–3
Huntly, 9th Marquess, 164
Hurd, Richard, Bp. of Worcester, 632
Husband, —, 721
Hussey, Edward, 971
Hussey, R. C., 689, 690
Hutchins, Jeremiah, 482
Hutchins, S., 433
Hutchinson, Edmund, 718
Hutchinson, William (surveyor), 73
Hutchinson, William, 122
Hutton, R., 173
Hutton, Thomas, 641
Hutton, Timothy, 315
Hyde, —, 200

Hyett, W. H., 95
Hyndford, 5th Earl, 55

Ibbetson, Sir James, 191, 194
Ilay, Earl of, 343, 344, 561, 562
Ilchester, 1st Earl, 312, 447
Inge, William, 332
Ingham, L., 466
Inglis, —, 105
Inglis, Alexander, 58
Inglis, John, 154
Inglis, Sir Patrick, 54
Ingram, Arthur, 301
Ingram, William, 135
Inman, William, 247
Innes, John, 737
Innes, W. Mitchell, 359
Innes, William, 761
Irlam, William, 291
Irvine, J., 619
Irwin, 2nd Visct., 300
Irwin, 4th Visct., 301
Irwin, Anne Viscountess, 404
Irwin, Frances Viscountess, 466
Iselin, J. F., 769
Isham, Sir Charles, 167
Isham, Sir Justinian (d. 1674), 615, 873
Isham, Sir Justinian (d. 1737), 751
Isham, Sir Justinian (d. 1845), 377
Isted, Ambrose, 551
Izit (Eizatt), Alexander, 283

Jackson, Benjamin, 803, 805
Jackson, George, 925
Jackson, Richard, 842
Jackson, Robert, 112
Jackson, T. J. R., 139
Jackson, W. A., Peters & Co., 771
Jackson, William, 394
Jagger, J., 424
Jalland, B. M., 219
Jalland, W. E., 219
James I & VI, King, 197, 469, 568, 787
James II, King, 757, 923
James, J., 268
James, Lady, 949
James, Col. Richard, 958
James, Sir Walter, 255
James, Sir William, 478
Jamieson, Patrick, 305
Jamieson, Thomas, 594
Janssen, Sir Theodore, 184
Jarrett, John, 679
Jebb, Major Joshua, 91
Jebb, Sir Richard, 208
Jeffrey, Francis (Lord), 647, 648
Jeffrey, William, 751
Jekyll, Sir Joseph, 184, 752
Jelfes, Robert, 70
Jelly, John, 302, 614
Jenkins, —, 892
Jenkins, Thomas, 599
Jenkinson, —, 773
Jennens, Charles, 421, 611, 880
Jennens, Robert, 340
Jennens, Sir William, 848
Jennings, Joseph, 621
Jennings, Richard, 452, 458
Jephson, D., 118
Jepson, William, 528
Jerdan, William, 439
Jerman, Anthony, 459n., 473
Jerningham, Sir George, 461
Jerningham, Sir William, 768

Jersey, 3rd Earl, 549
Jersey, 5th Earl, 117, 245, 246, 613
Jervas, Charles, 490
Jervis, John, 84
Jervoise, Thomas, 454, 806
Jessop, J. S., 173
Jessop, William, 677
Johnes, John, 582
Johnes, Thomas, senior, 582, 663
Johnes, Thomas, 86, 579, 582, 649, 945
Johnson, A., 435
Johnson, C. F., 810
Johnson, Godschall, 231
Johnson, James, Bishop of Worcester, 55, 509
Johnson, John (architect), 857
Johnson, John (Lord Mayor of London), 421
Johnson, Rev. John, 528
Johnson, Maurice, 717
Johnson, Peter, 193
Johnson, Dr. Samuel, 369, 372, 572
Johnson, Thomas, 654, 729, 839, 840, 970
Johnson, Dr. William, 440
Johnston, James (Secretary), 296, 343, 454
Johnstone, Alexander, 866
Johnstone, Miss Elizabeth, 772
Johnstone, James (of Alva), 784
Johnstone, Sir James, 55
Johnstone, John (of Alva), 54, 55
Johnstone, John James Hope, 164
Johnstone, Sir R. V. B., 72 (bis)
Jolliffe, T. S., 477, 948
Jolliffe, William, 79
Jones, Griffith, 501
Jones, Sir Horace, 863
Jones, John, 225
Jones, Sir John Tyrwhit, 740
Jones, Joseph, 829
Jones, Owen, 857
Jones, Thomas, 388
Jones, William, 617
Jones, Sir William, 431
Jones, William (of Clytha), 582
Jones-Brydges, Sir Harford, 744
Jonson, Ben, 344, 468
Joyce, Jeremiah, 451
Judd, John, 464
Judge, George, 67
Julian, George, 692
Junius, Francis, 912

Kavanagh, Mrs. 585
Kay, Robert, 322
Kaygill, Thomas, 642
Kay-Shuttleworth, Sir James, 92
Keats, —, 704
Keay, James, 163
Kedge, Richard, 929, 930, 931
Keene, Rev. C. E. R., 393
Keene, Edmund, Bp. of Chester & Ely, 817 (bis), 818
Keepe, Edward, 702
Keith, Viscount, 76
Keith, Capt. William, 164
Kekewich, S. T., 679
Kelly, Arthur, 709
Kemeys, Sir Charles, 903
Kemp, C. J., 706
Kemp, T. R., 176 (bis), 244, 488, 892
Kempe, Samuel, 285
Kendall, Henry, 516

Kennaway, Sir John (d. 1836), 949
Kennaway, Sir John (d. 1873), 696 (bis)
Kennedy, Thomas, 54
Kent, Sir Charles, 948
Kent, Duke (d. 1740), 512, 514, 732 (bis)
Kent, Duke (d. 1820), 965
Kent, Duchess, 934
Kent, 11th Earl, 368
Kenyon, 2nd Lord, 397
Kenyon, Hon. Thomas, 187, 408
Keppel, Col. F. W., 964
Kerr, Robert, 174, 760
Kerrich, Rev. Thomas, 105, 298
Kerrison, Sir Edward, 972
Keyser, Hendrik de, 786
Keyte, J., 280
Kiallmarll, George, 150
Kidd, R. C., 151
Kidwell, Robert, 283
Kidwell, William, 636
Kielmansegg, Baron, 325
Kilby, Thomas, 626
Kilderbee, Rev. Samuel, 324
Killigrew, Thomas, 924
Kilmorey, 2nd Earl, 859
Kilmorey, 9th Visct., 839
Kimberley, James, 589
Kimberley, 2nd Lord, 971
Kincaid, —, 382
Kincaid, Provost, 238
King, C., 542
King, Charles (bricklayer), 927
King, Edward, 832
King, J. J., 78
King, Lord, 244
King, Peter, Ld. Chancellor, 404, 825
King, Thomas, 626
King, W. B., 364
King, William, 834, 835
Kingston, 1st Duke, 314
Kingston, 2nd Duke, 194
Kingston, 4th Earl, 805
Kingston, 5th Earl, 803
Kingston, Rev. Robert, 446–7
Kinnaird, 8th Lord, 76
Kinnaird, W., 89
Kinnoull, 6th Earl, 758
Kinnoull, 7th Earl, 337n., 758
Kinnoull, 8th Earl, 639
Kinnoull, 9th Earl, 644
Kinnoull, 10th Earl, 164, 394 (bis), 784
Kintore, Earl, 762
Kinward, Thomas, 314
Kirkby, William, 726
Kirkland, Alexander, 155
Kirkland, Sir John, 172
Kirsopp, William, 268
Knapp, George, 198
Knapton, George, 130
Knapton, 2nd Lord, 946
Knatchbull, Maj. 902
Knatchbull, Sir Wyndham, 52, 572, 573
Knight, —, 771
Knight, Charles, 657
Knight, Edward, 166
Knight, Henry Gally, 441 (bis)
Knight, J., 200
Knight, J. P., 90
Knight, Ralph, 917
Knight, Richard Payne, 579, 663
Knight, Robert, 125, 771
Knight, William, 156

Knightley, Charles, 246
Knightley, Lady, 944
Knights, P. J., 150
Knowles, Adml. Charles, 538
Knowles, Israel, 928, 929, 930, 931
Knowles, James, 761
Knyff, Leonard, 283
Kynaston, Thomas, 711
Kynnersley, Anthony, 408
Kyrle, John, 811
Kyte, Richard, 419

Labouchère, P. C., 76
Lacon, Sir Edmund Knowles, 823
Laguerre, Louis, 805
Laidlaw, John, 595
Laird, Adml., 587
Laird, William, 359
Lamb, Edward Buckton, 970
Lamb, Matthew, 610
Lamb, (Sir) Matthew, 611
Lamb, Sir Peniston, 611
Lambert, Col., 854
Lambton, Genl. John, 268
Lambton, J. G., 122 (bis)
Lambton, W. H., 125
Lamplugh family, 60
Lancaster, Col. C., 947
Lane, John, 609
Lane, John (builder), 139
Lane, Thomas, 642
Lane, Thomas (joiner), 929
Lanesborough, 4th Earl, 970
Langdale, Hon. Charles, 446
Langdale, 4th Lord, 301, 860
Langdale, Philip, 74
Langham, Sir James (d. 1795), 554
Langham, Sir James (d. 1833), 584
Langham, Sir John (d. 1671), 201
Langham, Sir John (d. 1747), 752
Langhorne, Katherine, 65
Langley, Euclid, 482, 504
Langley, Thomas, 584
Langston, J. H., 679 (bis)
Langton, Joseph, 509
Langton, Thomas, 859
Lankersheer, Richard, 722
Lanscroon, Gerard, 905
Lansdown, James, 700
Lansdowne, 1st Marquess, 51, 252 (bis)
Lansdowne, 2nd Marquess, 121
Lansdowne, 3rd Marquess, 91, 92, 225, 745 (bis)
Lanyon, Sir Charles, 603
Lanza, Sig. Gesualdo, 335
Lapsley, Margaret, 79
Larking, John, 725
Larpent, Seymour, 393
Lascelles, Daniel, 193
Lascelles, Edwin, 52
Lascelles, Rose, 188
Latham, Jasper, 931
Latter, Thomas, 617
Laud, William, Abp. of Canterbury, 149–50, 470
Lauder, Sir Thomas Dick, 647
Lauderdale, Duke, 152, 153, 154 (bis), 571, 712
Lauderdale, Duchess, 154, 712
Lauderdale, 8th Earl, 49, 55
Lauderdale, 9th Earl, 165
Laurell, James, 507
Laurence, Charles, 701

Laurence, Edward, 560
Law, G. H., Bishop of Bath & Wells, 156
Law, Col. John, 166
Lawley, Sir Robert, 950
Lawrence, G. H., 291
Lawrence, Sir Thomas, 741
Lawson, —, 266
Lawson, Sir John, 74, 315
Lawson, William 267
Lawson, William (of Netherurd), 158, 533
Lawson, Sir William, 123
Layland, John, 693
Layton, Robert, 931
Lea, —, 75
Lea, —, 752
Leach, Benjamin, 928
Leach, V., 352
Leadbitter, R., 268
Leader, William, 729
Leaf, William, 618
Leake, John Martin, 823
Leclère, A., 349
Lee, Capt., 770
Lee, Christopher, 559
Lee, Lancelot, 664
Lee, Sir Thomas, 342
Lee, Sir William, 483 (bis), 947
Leech, John, 632
Leeds, 1st Duke, 806, 932
Leeds, 4th Duke, 344
Leeds, 5th Duke, 139, 770, 771
Leeke, Ralph, 125
Lefevre, see Shaw Lefevre
Lefroy, Anthony, 698
Legard, Sir F. D., 167
Legard, Sir John, 328
Legh, George C., 377
Legh, George J., 583, 893
Legh, Henry C., 431
Legh, Peter, 513, 640
Legh, Thomas, 954
Leicester, Sir John F. (afterwards Lord de Tabley), 245, 397, 555
Leicester, Sir Peter, 193
Leicester, Earl (d. 1759), 131 (bis), 135, 136, 137, 489, 492
Leicester, 1st Earl (d. 1842), 245, 271, 957, 959
Leicester, 2nd Earl, 166
Leigh, Hon. Charles, 342
Leigh, James, 550
Leigh, James Henry, 678, 746
Leigh, 3rd Lord (d. 1738), 750 (bis)
Leigh, 5th Lord (d. 1786), 520
Leigh, 1st Lord (d. 1850), 746
Leigh, 2nd Lord (d. 1905), 166
Leigh, Rev. W., 354
Leighton, Anna Maria, 576
Leighton, Sir Baldwin, 406, 476
Leighton, Sir Charlton, 576
Leighton, Elizabeth, 84
Leinster, 1st Duke, 209
Leinster, 2nd Duke, 952
Leith, Col. J. J. F., 762
Lejolivet, Anne, 716
Lely, Sir Peter, 428, 543–4
Lemm, Joseph, 931
Lemon, Sir Charles, 393
Lemon, William, 285
Lennard, Col. Farnaby, 167
Lennard, T. B., 225
Lennox, J. Kincaid, 383
Lens, Gerrard, 931
Lenthall, —, 912

Leominster, 1st Lord, 403, 925
Leopold, Prince of Saxe-Coburg, 617
Leslie, —, 762
Leslie, Archibald Y., 699
Leslie, Hugh, 451
Leslie, John, 541
Leslie, W., 92
Lester, H., 960
L'Estrange, Sir Hamon, 281
Lethieullier, Smart, 322
Lever, Sir Darcy, 514
Levinge, Sir R., 535
Lewes, Col., 582
Lewis, —, 302
Lewis, —, 592
Lewis, Major, 582
Lewis, Frankland, 583
Lewis, Henry Greswold, 768
Lewis, T. Hayter, 307, 621, 829, 896
Lewis, Thomas, 769, 771
Lewis, W., 168
Lewys, Sir John, 201
Ley, J. H., 78
Ley, W., 971
Leycester, Ralph, 696
Liardet, —, 49
Lichfield, 2nd Earl, 311, 341, 750, 828
Lichfield, 3rd Earl, 484
Liebenrood, J. E., 715
Ligoe, George, 914
Lilly, Rev. J., 727
Lillyman, John, 751
Lime, Samuel, 931
Limerick, Lord, 934
Linckh, J., 221, 317
Lincoln, Earl (d. 1778), 882
Lincoln, 9th Earl, 132, 493; and see Newcastle-under-Lyme, 1st Duke
Lindsay, Col. James, 165
Lindsay, Lord, 859
Linell, Henry, 187
Linnaeus, Sir Charles, 55
Linnell, John, 808
Linton, Rev. J., 174
Linwood, Mary, 606
Lisburne, 1st Earl, 53
Lisburne, 4th Visct., 53
Lismore, 1st Visct., 585
Lister, Anne, 391
Liston, Sir Robert, 386
Litchford, J., 858
Little, Thomas, 43
Littlejohn, Ann, 71
Littleton, E. J., 655
Littleton, Sir Edward, 84, 521, 839
Liverpool, 2nd Earl, 771, 772
Livesay, A. F., 59
Llewellyn, —, 551
Lloyd, Bevis, 708
Lloyd, G., 971
Lloyd, J. A., 407
Lloyd, Rev. J. R., 949
Lloyd, T., 433
Lloyd, William, 483
Lloyd, William, Bp. of Worcester, 907
Lock, Thomas, 930, 931
Lock, William, 124
Locke, William, 489
Lockhart, Sir Charles, 358
Lockhart, Mary Anne, 862
Lockhart, Robert, 358
Lockhart-Ross, Sir Charles, 359

Lockwood, H. F., 700
Lockyer, J., 43
Lodder, William, 767
Loftus, 4th Visct., 208
Logan, R. H., 435
Londesborough, 1st Lord, 762
Londonderry, 1st Marquess, 797, 948
Londonderry, 3rd Marquess, 123, 265, 938, 955 (bis)
Long, Rev. C. M., 268
Long, Charles, 958
Long, Sir Charles (afterwards Lord Farnborough), 701, 745, 959–60
Long, Sir Philip Parker, 342
Long, R. G., 961
Long, Walter (of Rood Ashton), 435
Long, Walter (of Preshaw), 584
Longford, Earl, 545
Longland, John, 368, 812, 928, 929, 930, 931
Lonsdale, 1st Earl, 45, 744
Lonsdale, 3rd Visct., 344
Lonsdale, James, 291
Lopes, Sir Ralph, 321 (bis)
Lopez, Sir Manasseh, 147
Loraine, Sir William, 145
Lorton, 1st Visct., 584
Losh, James, 267
Lotan, J., 516
Lothian, 1st Earl, 570
Lothian, 4th Earl, 757
Lothian, 7th Marquess, 117, 120
Lothian, 8th Marquess, 167
Loudoun, 3rd Earl, 283, 343
Loudoun, Countess, 288
Loughborough, 1st Lord, 516
Louisa, Queen of Sweden, 209
Loutherbourg, P. J. de, 772
Lovat, 12th Lord, 46, 59
Lovat, Lord (d. 1875), 761
Lovden, E. Lovden, 605
Lovelace, 1st Earl, 92, 244
Lovell, Dr., 682
Lovell, Robert, 345
Lovett, J. H., 693
Low, George, 753
Lowndes, William, 925, 964
Lowther, Sir James, 53, 137
Lowther, Sir John, 60, 314, 430, 650
Lowther, Sir John (of Wilton Castle), 744
Lowther, Lord, 254
Lubbock, Sir John, 517
Lucan, 2nd Earl, 517, 617
Lucan, 3rd Earl, 619
Lucas, Rev. R., 858
Lucas, Thomas (bricklayer), 69
Lucas, Thomas, 478
Lucy, Rev. John, 690
Ludford, John, 207
Ludlow, Col. Edmund, 872
Lumley, James, 866
Lumley, William, 734
Lund, J., 535
Lundin, Capt., 443
Luttrell, George, 71
Luxmoore, John, Bp. of St. Asaph, 476
Lyde, Sir Lionel, 684
Lymington, 1st Visct., 69
Lynedoch, Lord, see Graham, Thomas (of Balgowan)
Lyon, David, 92, 167, 171
Lyon, J. S., 164

Lyon, William, 644
Lyster, Col. Richard, 939
Lyttelton, Charles, Bp. of Carlisle, 639
Lyttelton, Hon. G. F., 770
Lyttelton, 1st Lord, 213, 549, 550 (bis), 639, 796
Lyttelton, Lucy Lady, 322
Lyttelton, Sir Richard, 137, 639 (bis)
Lyttelton, Sir Thomas, 550
Lytton, Mrs. Bulwer, 617, 674

McAdam, J. L., 254
MacAlister, Genl. Keith, 358
MacAlister, Col. Matthew, 358
McCombie, William, 761
McConnell, John, 501
Macculloch, —, 501
McCulloch, John, 54
MacDonald, Messrs. J. & D., 82
Macdonald, Sir James (d. 1766), 179
Macdonald, Sir James (d. 1832), 701
Macdonald, 2nd Lord, 355, 358
MacDougall, Dugald, 162
McDowall, —, 699
Macdowall, D., 55
McDowall, John, 58
McGregor, Genl. A. M., 173
McInerheny, William, 527
McInroy, J. P., 165
Mackay, Robert, 198
Mackenzie, Alexander (of Castle Fraser), 624
Mackenzie, Alexander (of Seton), 55
Mackenzie, Henry, 58n.
Mackenzie, Humberstone (Lord Seaforth), 642
Mackenzie, Thomas (of Elgin), 532, 736, 760
Mackenzie, Thomas (Lord), 647
Mackintosh, T., 43
McKirdy, J. G., 82
McLaren, Donald, 165
Maclean, Hugh, 163
MacLeod, Norman, 148
Maconochie, Alexander, 647
Macpherson, James, 55
Macquarie, Lachlan, 364
Macrae, Walter Ewing, 671
McVicar, Rev. —, 587
MacVicar, John, 165
Macclesfield, 1st Earl, 416
Macclesfield, 2nd Earl, 347
Macclesfield, 5th Earl, 92
Macclesfield, 6th Earl, 167
Machell, Hugh, 532
Mackworth, Bulkeley, 750
Mackworth, Sir Herbert, 462, 463
Madderty, David Lord, 322
Maddox, Isaac, Bp. of Worcester, 483
Maffei, Scipione, 129
Maher, John, 698
Maine, Jonathan, 928, 929, 930, 931
Mainwaring, Edward, 84, 839
Mair, George James John, 170, 585, 970
Maister, H. W., 584
Maister, Henry, 606
Maitland, Adam, 385
Maitland, F., 700

Maitland, Adml. Sir Frederick, 358
Maitland, J—, 80
Maitland, Thomas, 647
Makdougal, —, 59
Malcolm, —, 729
Malcolm, Genl. Sir John, 746
Malcolm, Neill, 166
Malmesbury, 1st Earl, 426
Maltby, C. F., 857
Maltby, Messrs., 706
Malton, 1st Earl, 110, 311, 312, 344, 843
Manby, Thomas, 636
Manchester, 1st Duke, 325, 852
Manchester, 4th Duke, 52
Manchester, 6th Duke, 696
Manchester, 7th Duke, 167
Manchester, Duchess, 312
Manchester, 4th Earl, 230
Manley, Isaac George, 391
Manley, John Shawe, 842
Mann, Galfridus, 109
Manners, George, 858
Manners, Lord George, 168
Manners, Lady Louisa, 771
Manners, Sir William, 721
Mansfield, —, 859
Mansfield, 1st Earl, 49, 53, 462
Mansfield, 2nd Earl, 719
Mansfield, 3rd Earl, 76, 524
Mansfield, Isaac, 403
Mantell, Dr. Gideon, 891
Mantun, John, 287
Manvers, 1st Earl, see Newark, Viscount
Manvers, 2nd Earl, 745
Mar, 9th Earl, 68
March, 3rd Earl, 137, 262
March, Lord, 463
Marchant, Sir Denis le, 619
Marchmont, 3rd Earl, 346, 499
March-Phillipps, Ambrose Lisle, 669
March-Phillipps, Charles, 669
Marescalchi, Count, 953
Marjoribanks, Alexander, 55
Marjoribanks, Stewart, 95
Markham, Sir George, 324
Markham, William, 521
Marks, J., 374
Marlborough, 1st Duke, 228, 494, 850, 852, 925
Marlborough, 3rd Duke, 508
Marlborough, 4th Duke, 78, 146, 206, 207, 208, 373, 376, 965 (bis)
Marlborough, 6th Duke, 66
Marlborough, Sarah Duchess, 312, 403, 414, 415, 461 (bis), 748, 751, 792, 850–1
Marrable, Frederick, 116
Marsac, Col., 81
Marshall, Beaumont, 523
Marsham, Rev. R. B., 226
Marsland, Peter, 397–8
Martin, David, 587
Martin, Edward, 931
Martin, James, 665
Martin, John, 481
Martin, Rev. R., 670
Martin, Thomas, 349
Martin, W. B., 227
Martindale, John, 328
Martineau, Philip, 893
Mary II, Queen, 923 (bis)
Mary of Modena, Queen, 923
Mason, Elizabeth, 797

Mason, G., 753
Mason, Capt. H. B., 618
Mason, Rev. J., 650
Mason, William, 116
Mason, Rev. William, 195, 206
Massey, —, 929
Massey, Edward, 724
Massingberd, Burrell, 489
Massingberd, Charles Burrell, 72
Massingberd, William Burrell, 610
Masterman, John, 174
Masters, Rev. Robert, 297-8
Mathews, Charles, 541, 667
Mathews, R., 656
Mathews, Roger, 885
Matthews, James, 532, 736
Matthews, Col. John, 411n., 948
Maude, Francis, 156
Maule, Henry, 282, 530
Mauleverer, Thomas, 192
Mauley, Lord de, 117
Mawbey, Sir Joseph, 236
Maxtone, Anthony, 745
Maxwell, A. H., 165
Maxwell, Henry, Bp. of Meath, 946
Maxwell, Sir John, 59
Maxwell, John Clerk, 588
Maxwell, Wellwood, 692
May, B., 540
May, E. J., 170
May, Edward, 618
May, John, 527
May, Joseph, 952
May, Walter Barton, 276, 813
May, William, 293
Mayhew, G. W., 307
Maynard, —, 603
Maynard, Sir John, 873
Maynard, 3rd Visct., 435
Mayo, Rev. Charles, 378
Mead, Dr. Richard, 129, 342
Mead, Thomas, 929
Meadowbank, Lord, see Maconochie, Alexander
Mear, Stephen, 546
Meard, John, 69
Meason, Gilbert, 209
Meason, Gilbert Lang, 288
Meath, 10th Earl, 698
Meath, 11th Earl, 166
Medina, Sir John, 153
Medland, James, 664
Medlicote, Hon. Mrs. Cockayne, 622
Medlycott, James, 447
Medlycott, Sir W., 173
Meerman, Johannes, 952
Melbourne, 1st Lord (later 1st Visct.), 209, 609 (bis), 965
Mellish, Samuel, 400
Mellish, William, 195
Melville, 1st Earl, 758
Melville, 1st Visct., 359, 426, 644, 784
Melville, 2nd Visct., 784
Menzies, Sir Niel, 165
Mercer, George, 456, 482
Mercer, J. D., 256
Metcalfe, Edward, 268
Metcalfe, John, 106
Metcalfe, Philip, 246
Methuen, Paul, 146
Methuen, Paul Cobb, 583, 682
Methuen, Peter, 483
Mexborough, 1st Earl, 195
Mexborough, 3rd Earl, 971

Meyer, Frederick, 767
Meyer, Jeremiah, 252
Meynell, Godfrey, 354
Meyrick family, 232
Meyrick, Col. Augustus, 393 (bis), 394
Meyrick, John, 441
Meyrick, Mrs., 842, 916
Meyrick, O. P., 257
Meyrick, Sir S. R., 117
Middlesex, 1st Earl, 495, 787; and see Cranfield, Lionel
Middleton, George, 559, 562
Middleton, H. N., 172
Middleton, John, 664
Middleton, John Henry, 664
Middleton, Nathaniel, 517
Middleton, Sir W. F., 92, 330
Middleton, William, 611
Middleton, 6th Lord, 600, 961 (bis)
Midleton, 3rd Visct., 207
Midleton, 4th Visct., 207, 950
Midleton, 5th Visct., 172, 226
Milbanke, Mark, 315
Mildmay, C. H., 96
Mildmay, Sir Henry St. John (d. 1808), 278
Mildmay, Sir Henry St. John (d. 1902), 167
Mildmay, Humphrey St. John, 117
Miles, P. J., 434
Millar, Andrew, 51
Millar, James, 106
Miller, — (carpenter), 930
Miller, J., 433
Miller, John (carver), 928
Miller, Thomas, 587
Miller, Tobias, 280
Miller, Sir William, 382
Milles, Hon. G. J., 270
Milles, Jeremiah, 947-8
Milles, R., 769
Milles, Thomas, Bp. of Waterford, 322
Millican, William, 309
Milligan, Robert, 216
Mills, Charles, 771
Mills, J. F., 501
Mills, Thomas (of Barlaston), 817
Mills, Thomas (of Great Saxham), 625
Milne, Adml. Sir David, 358
Milne, Patrick, 761
Milner, Charles, 882
Milner, Rev. John, 199
Milnes, James, 195
Milton, Lady, 55
Milton, Lord (Fletcher), 46, 531
Milton, 1st Lord, 147, 208, 855, 945, 946
Minchin, Robert, 923
Minto, Lord, 58 (bis)
Minto, 1st Earl, 288
Minto, 2nd Earl, 647
Mirehouse, John, 822
Mitchell, A., 172
Mitchell, Capt. Charles William, 585
Mitchell, Edmund, 449
Mitchell, J., 193
Mitchell, John (joiner), 928, 930
Mitchell-Withers, J. B., 917
Mitford, B. O., 267
Mitford, D., 192
Mitford, William, 769
Mocatta, David, 767

Moffat, W., 683, 770
Moffatt, W. B., 282
Moir, William, 737
Moira, 2nd Earl, 288, 893
Molesworth, John, 275, 324
Molesworth, 1st Lord, 324
Monck, George, see Albemarle, 1st Duke
Moncreiffe, Sir David, 784
Moncreiffe, Thomas, 154
Money, Col. James, 463
Monkhouse, William, 395
Monins, Rev. John, 770
Monmouth, Duke, 314, 545
Monson, 2nd Lord, 612
Montagu, 1st Duke, 430, 655-6
Montagu, 2nd Duke, 279, 312
Montagu, Edward Wortley, 136, 514, 641 (bis)
Montagu, Mrs. Elizabeth, 51, 125, 795, 797, 947
Montagu, Lord, 76
Monteath, James, 82, 383
Monteith, Henry, 162
Montgomerie, Matthew, 172
Montefiore, Joseph, 173
Montefiore, Sir Moses, 173
Montgomery, Hugh, 118
Montgomery, James (poet), 313
Montgomery, Sir James, 288
Montresor, Col. John, 642
Montrose, 1st Duke, 57, 59, 530
Montrose, 2nd Duke, 46
Montrose, 4th Duke, 166
Monypenny, David, 86
Moore, A. J., 363
Moore, Arthur, 806
Moore, George Belton, 71, 667
Moore, Rev. George, 958
Moore, John, 878
Moore, Sir John (d. 1702), 900-1, 924
Moore, Sir John (d. 1809), 438
Moore, Thomas, 778
Morant, George, 619 (bis)
Morant, John, 642
Moray, 6th Earl, 531 (bis)
Moray, 8th Earl, 500 (bis), 784
Moray, 10th Earl, 357, 359
Moray, James (fl. 1735-60), 272, 322
Moray, James (d. 1840), 241, 260
Moray, William, 241, 260
Mordaunt, Sir Charles, 376
Mordwinoff, Adml. Count, 400
More family, 780
More, George, 116
More, Robert, 477
Moreing, Charles, 863, 972
Moreton, R., 956
Morewood, Rowland, 751
Morgan, Charles, 389
Morgan, Sir Charles, 564
Morgan, Francis, 105
Morgan, H. K. G., 698
Morgan, John, 302
Morgan, William, 757
Morhall, Richard, 576
Morier, John, 156
Morison, Alexander, 762
Morison, Rev. George, 761
Morland, William, 769
Morley & Co., 862
Morley, 1st Earl, 319
Mornington, 2nd Earl, 771
Morpeth, William, 593
Morrice, Daniel, 929, 931
Morrice, F. E., 527

Morris, John, 906
Morris, Sir John (d. 1819), 463
Morris, Sir John (d. 1855), 460
Morris, Robert, 618
Morris, Thomas, 309
Morrison, James (of Fonthill), 617, 618 (bis), 619
Morrison, James (of Newcastle), 268
Morrison, Sir Richard, 326, 389
Morrison, Robert, 767
Morrison & Co., 619 (bis), 862
Morritt, J. S., 191
Morse, John, 835
Mortimer, J. H., 327
Morton, 15th Earl, 220
Morton, 16th Earl, 85, 575 (bis)
Mosley, Sir Oswald, 331
Mossman, William, 381
Mostyn, Hon. Edward M. L., 657
Mostyn, Sir Piers, 476
Mostyn-Owen, William, 576
Mott, John Thruston, 682
Moulson, —, 649
Mounsey, Robert, 594, 676
Mount, John, 423
Mount Edgcumbe, 2nd Earl, 59
Mount Edgcumbe, 3rd Earl, 890
Mount Stuart, Lord, 147, 425
Mountrath, 6th Earl, 130, 209
Moyes, James, 638
Moysey, Rev. —, 605
Mozley, Rev. T., 174
Mulgrave, 1st Earl, 75, 76
Mulgrave, 2nd Lord, 768
Mullings, J. R., 455
Mulready, William, 66
Muncaster, 3rd Lord, 701
Mure, Hutchison, 54
Mure, William, 53
Murray, Alexander (d. 1750), 59
Murray, Alexander (fl. 1835), 618 (ter)
Murray, C. Scott, 971
Murray, Mrs. Emma, 618
Murray, Hon. George, Bp. of Sodor & Man, 141
Murray, Lord Henry, 780-1
Murray, James, 128, 575
Murray, Genl. James, 769
Murray, Col. John, 167
Murray, Patrick, 164 (bis)
Murray, Sir Patrick, 810
Murray, Genl. William, 962
Musgrave, Sir Christopher, 710
Musgrave, Sir James, 481, 583, 605
Musgrave, Sir Philip, 745
Muskett, J. S., 150
Musso, Boniface, 263
Musters, John, 195
Muter, Rev. Robert, 779
Myddelton, Sir Hugh, 577
Myddelton, Richard (d. 1795), 844, 966
Myddelton, Richard (d. 1796), 232
Myddelton-Biddulph, Robert (d. 1843), 398
Myddelton-Biddulph, Robert (d. 1872), 369
Myers, Graham, 206
Mytton, Henry, 664
Mytton, John, 576
Mytton, R. 525
Mytton, Thomas, 664

Nagle, Joseph Chichester, 890
Nairn, 2nd Lord, 154, 530
Naish, Thomas, 348
Namur, Bishop of, 297n.
Naper, J. L., 225
Napier, Sir George, 239
Napier, Margaret, 239
Narborough, James, 835
Narrien, J., 807
Nash, Charles, 585
Nash, Edwin, 534, 702
Nash, Frederick, 254
Nash, Joseph, 667
Nash, Dr. T. R., 481
Nasmith, —, 53
Nasmyth, Alexander, 240
Nasmyth, Sir John, 164
Nayler, Francis, 957
Neave, James, 768
Neave, Sir Richard, 345
Neave, Thomas, 345
Needham, Joshua, 748, 751
Needham, Dr. Peter, 168
Needham, Thomas, 324
Neille, Sir Paul, 918
Neilson, Daniel, 291
Nelson, C. C., 742
Nelson, Adml. Visct., 150, 367, 632, 670
Nelson, Matthew, 112
Nesbit, Alexander, 570
Nesfield, W. E., 160
Nevill, Charles, 618
New, George, 102
Newark, Visct. (afterwards 1st Earl Manvers), 196, 893
Newbery, —, 198
Newborough, 3rd Lord, 407
Newburgh, Earl, 446
Newcastle-on-Tyne, 1st Duke (Cavendish, d. 1676), 538, 764, 900
Newcastle-on-Tyne, 1st Duke (Holles, d. 1711), 344, 803, 806
Newcastle-under-Lyme, 1st Duke (Pelham, d. 1768), 169, 324, 492, 853 (passim), 932, 933; and see Lincoln, 9th Earl
Newcastle, 2nd Duke, 345, 933 (ter)
Newcastle, 4th Duke, 329, 744, 746
Newcastle, 5th Duke, 168
Newcomen, Sir William, 9, 327
Newdigate, Richard, 901, 925
Newenham, W. H., 246
Newland, Abraham, 772
Newman, J. H., 847
Newman, R. W., 971
Newman, Thomas, 929
Newman, William, 929, 931
Newport, John, 663 (passim), 664
Newton, Sir Isaac, 168, 494
Newton, Sir John, 775
Newton, Sir Michael, 559, 561 (bis)
Newton, W., 535
Nicholas, J. F., 527
Nicholl, Sir John, 908
Nicholl, S. J., 723
Nicholl, W. G., 225, 226
Nicholls, Walter, 177
Nichols, J. B., 814
Nichols, T., 753
Nicholson, J., 266
Nicholson, Otho, 215
Nicholson, Thomas, 215

Nicholson, Thomas (surveyor), 67n.
Nicholson, W., 363
Nicholson, W. A., 617, 970
Nicol, —, 762
Nicolay, Baron, 810
Nisbet, W. H., 76
Nisbet, William (of Archerfield), 55
Nisbet, William (of Marlefield), 623
Nisbett, G. M., 82
Nix, —, 858
Nixon, Edward, 874
Nixon, Samuel, 485
Noble, —, 617
Noel, Sir Gerard, 121
Nollekens, Joseph, 55, 188, 687
Norfolk, 8th Duke, 774
Norfolk, 9th Duke, 74, 126, 137, 344, 608, 611
Norfolk, 11th Duke, 80, 418, 419, 819
Norfolk, 12th Duke, 43, 44
Norfolk, 13th Duke, 43, 44, 166
Norfolk, Duchess (née Mordaunt), 905
Norfolk, Duchess (née Shirburne), 341, 342
Norman, John, 319
Normanby, Lord, 803, 804; and see Buckingham, 1st Duke (d. 1721)
Normanton, 2nd Earl, 631
Normanton, 3rd Earl, 168
North, Dudley, 399
North, Frederick, 480
North, Hon. Frederick, 221
North, Lord (2nd Earl of Guilford), 138
North, R. T., 876, 961
Northampton, 1st Earl, 455
Northampton, 4th Earl, 806
Northampton, 8th Earl, 146
Northampton, 1st Marquess, 120
Northampton, Dowager Marchioness, 701
Northcote, Sir Stafford Henry, 657
Northesk, 4th Earl, 283
Northumberland, 1st Duke, 51, 52, 53, 334, 493, 591, 609, 610, 611, 732
Northumberland, 2nd Duke, 389, 466, 949
Northumberland, 3rd Duke, 225, 246 (bis), 320, 867
Northumberland, 4th Duke, 173, 174
Northumberland, 10th Earl, 197, 710, 873 (bis)
Northwick, 1st Lord, 729
Northwick, 2nd Lord, 438
Norton, Christopher, 178
Norton, Cornelius, 911
Nost, John, 805
Nott, John, 751
Nottingham, 2nd Earl, 271, 309, 529
Nouaille, —, 592
Nowell, Alexander, 876
Nugent, 1st Lord, 550
Nugent, N. H., 254
Nunn, W., 175

Oakeley, John, 408
Oakes, James, 772
Oakley, Benjamin, 173, 243

Oakley, Rev. Herbert, 408
O'Brien, Sir Edward, 434
O'Brien, Henry, 695, 932
O'Brien, Percy W., see Thomond, Earl (d. 1774)
Ogilvie, James, 587
Ogilvie, Thos. Elliot, 289
Ogilvy, Hon. Donald, 887
Oglander, Sir William, 584
Ogle, Sir Chaloner, 343
Ogle, Sir Charles, 284, 745
O'Keefe, —, 645
Okely, William I., 315
Okeover, H. F., 655
Okeover, Leak, 717
Okey, C. H., 173
Okill, John, 527, 692
Oldfield, Thomas, 842
Oliphant, Laurence, 241
Olive, J—, 76
Oliver, Silver, 518
Oliver, Thomas, 53
O'Neil, 2nd Visct., 434–5n., 584
Onley, C. S., 377, 631
Onley, Samuel, 628
Onslow, Arthur, 703
Onslow, 1st Earl, 147
Onslow, 3rd Earl, 445
Onslow, 2nd Lord, 513
Onslow, Serjeant, 616
Ord, William (d. 1768), 333
Ord, William (d. 1789), 591 (bis)
Orde, Robert (Baron), 52
Orde, William, 267
O'Reilly, Col. W. F., 172
Orford, Earl (d. 1727), 69
Orford, 1st Earl, 184, 342, 415, 492, 695, 853
Orford, 3rd Earl, 679
Orford, 4th Earl, see Walpole, Horace
Orger, Rev. William, 679
Orkney, 1st Earl, 69, 513, 514
Orkney, Countess, 594
Orme, Edward, 232
Ormerod, George, 745
Ormonde, 1st Duke, 545
Ormonde, 2nd Duke, 474
Ormsby, Mary Jane, 369
Orr, William, 382
Osbaldeston, G., 700
Osborn, Sir Danvers, 866
Osborn, Sir George, 951
Osborne, John, 834
Osmond, John, 535
Oswald, Miss Elizabeth, 383
Oswald, Richard, 53
Ouseley, Sir Gore, 225
Ouvry, —, 592
Owen, Sir Arthur Davies, 142
Owen, Rev. C. G., 394
Owen, William, 751
Oxenden, Sir Henry, 947
Oxford, 20th Earl (Vere), 430
Oxford, 1st Earl, 337
Oxford, 2nd Earl, 338, 339, 340, 342, 343, 661, 908, 910
Oxford, 5th Earl, 744 (bis)
Oxford, Henrietta Countess, 455, 661n.

Pack, Genl. Count, 456
Packe, C. J., 893
Packe, C. W., 165, 166
Packe, Col. G. H., 622
Padwick, William, 44
Page, —, 928
Page, Sir Gregory, 454

Page, Richard, 583
Paget, Sir Arthur, 810
Painter, Samuel, 858
Paisley, Lord, 504
Pakington, J. S. Russell, 387
Palk, Sir Lawrence, 399
Palliser, Sir Hugh, 464
Palmer, Sir Geoffrey, 859
Palmer, George, 268
Palmer, Sir John, 463, 905
Palmer, Robert (bricklayer), 186
Palmer, Robert, 376
Palmer, Sir Roger, 619
Palmer, Samuel, 809
Palmer, William, 518
Palmerston, 2nd Visct., 146, 425
Panmure, 2nd Earl, 570
Panmure, 3rd Earl, 154
Panmure, 4th Earl, 282, 283
Panmure, 6th Earl, 969
Panmure, 1st Lord, 158, 500
Papillon, Thomas, 914
Papworth, R., 433
Pardoe, —, 83
Parfect, George, 278
Park, Patric, 381
Park, R., 91
Parker, Sir Hyde, 324
Parker, James, 938
Parker, John, see Boringdon
Parker, Matthew, Abp. of Canterbury, 637
Parker, Sir Peter, 177
Parker, R., 444
Parker, Robert Townley, 954
Parker, T. L., 155, 961
Parker, T. N., 408
Parker, Sir William, 434
Parkhurst, —, 842
Parkin, Elizabeth, 191, 193
Parkinson, F. C. J., 621
Parkinson, James, 174
Parkinson, Samuel, 101
Parlby, James, 943
Parris, Robert, 81, 898
Parry, Caleb H., 302
Parry, H. B., 523
Parry, John, 949
Parry, Thomas Gambier, 859
Pars, William, 684
Parsons, Robert, 475
Partridge, John, 962
Partridge, Rev. S., 198
Pasquali, Francis, 598
Paterson family, 86
Paterson, James, 105
Paterson, R., 618
Paterson, Samuel, 253
Patten, Thomas, 341
Patterson, John, 772
Patterson, T., 575
Pattison, —, 137
Paton, James, 289
Paul, Emperor of Russia, 181
Paul, Sir G. O., 481
Paul, Sir J. D., 487
Paul, William, 798, 830
Pawson, W. J. H., 268
Paxton, Sir Joseph, 173, 698, 898
Paxton, Sir William, 228
Payne, George, 242
Payne, René, 769
Payne, William, 682
Peacham, Henry, 827
Pearce, Rev. Mr., 393
Pearse, John, 637, 771
Pearson, J. L., 122
Pease, J. R., 564

Peat & Badder, Messrs., 713
Pécheux, Laurent, 204
Peck, Richard, 394
Peddie, James, 148
Pedley, Joseph, 69
Peek, Dr., 137
Peek, William, 605
Peel, Edmund, 271
Peel, Sir Robert, 741, 745 (bis)
Peers, Charles, 273
Pelham, Hon. Charles, 810
Pelham, Henry (of Stanmer), 276
Pelham, Hon. Henry, 492, 493, 933
Pelham, Thomas, 276
Pellew, Hon. Capt. P. B., 78
Pemberton, Rev. C. L., 174
Pemberton, Dr. C. R., 771
Pemberton, Rev. R. A., 407
Pembroke, 4th Earl, 256, 474, 872 (bis)
Pembroke, 10th Earl, 206, 208, 301, 952
Pembroke, 11th Earl, 950
Pembroke, Countess (d. 1621), 473
Pembroke, Countess (d. 1831), 769
Pendarves, E. W. W., 393, 890
Pendegrass, Capt., 745
Penfold, Rev. Dr., 859
Penn, John, 949, 950, 951
Penn, Thomas, 509
Pennant, Caroline, 693
Pennant, G. H. D., 435
Pennethorne, Sir James, 206, 244, 580, 585, 617, 667, 685, 970
Pennington, Sir Joseph, 74
Pennyman, Sir James, 195
Penrhyn, 1st Lord, 936, 946, 957 (bis)
Penrice, Thomas, 377
Penrose, F. C., 116
Penruddock, John, 872
Peploe, Samuel, 583
Percy, Earl, 591
Percy, Hugh, Bp. of Carlisle, 692
Perkin, William, 79
Perkins, A. E., 689
Perkins, Rev. John, 752
Perrin, John, 513
Perritt, William, 559
Perrot, James, 486
Perrott, George, 177
Perry, John, 656
Perry, Hon. Mrs., 770
Pesters, John de, 866
Peterborough, 2nd Earl, 708, 873
Peters, Henry, 770, 771
Peters, Mrs., 771
Peto, Henry, 720
Petre, Hon. Edward, 218
Petre, Lady, 958
Petre, 8th Lord, 513
Petre, 9th Lord, 305, 609, 611, 957, 958
Petre, 10th Lord, 958
Pettiward, Roger, 718
Peyto, Sir Edward, 785
Phelips, Sir Edward, 70
Phelps, James, 859
Phelps, Richard, 572
Philips, Sir George, 117
Philips, John, 842
Philips, R. E., 43
Phillimore, Rev. —, 605
Phillimore, Capt. R. W., 95
Phillimore, W., 700

Phillipps, Robert, 481
Phillips, Francis, 807
Phillips, Henry, 314
Phillips, John, 729
Phillips, Richard, 343
Phillips, Thomas, 865
Phillips, Rev. W. Spencer, 618
Phillips, William, 582
Phillpotts, Dr. Henry, 122
Phillpotts, John, 745
Phillpotts, Rev. T., 888
Pickersgill, Henry W., 71, 615
Picton, J. A., 782
Picton, Sir Thomas, 168
Piddington, Richard, 831, 834, 835
Pierce, Jeremiah, 911
Pierene, John, 513
Pierrepont, William, 539
Piggott family, 514
Pigot, Charles, 84
Pigott, Sir George, 953
Pigott, H. Smith, 156
Pigott, Southwell, 911
Pigott, Rev. William, 577
Pigou, C. E., 102
Pigou, W. H., 683
Pilkington, Sir Thomas, 672
Pilkington, Sir William, 434, 435
Pinches, —, 497
Pink, James, 299
Pinneger, P., 605
Pinney, John P., 627
Piozzi, Gabriel, 545
Piranesi, J. B., 572, 588–9
Pitcairn, J., 163
Pite, A. R., 374
Pitmilly, Lord, 86
Pitt, —, 866
Pitt, Joseph, 313
Pitt, Thomas (d. 1726), 276, 454, 565
Pitt, William, 765, 769
Pitter, J., 245
Place, G. G., 445
Place, Lionel, 528
Plant, Frederick, 622
Plater, Rev. C., 218
Player, George, 715
Playfair, Prof. John, 643, 645, 647
Plestow, Charles B., 270
Pleydell, Sir Mark, 131, 658
Plumptre, John, 185, 713
Plumridge, W., 424
Plymouth, 2nd Earl, 752
Plymouth, 6th Earl, 245, 246
Pocock, George, 649n.
Pococke, Richard, Bp. of Ossory, 550
Pole, Charles, 638
Pole, German, 763
Pole-Carew, Sir Reginald, 231
Pollard, W. D., 225
Pollard-Urquhart, William, 672
Polwarth, Lady, 965
Polwarth, Lord, 165
Pomfret, 1st Earl, 492
Pomfret, 3rd Earl, 669
Pomfret, Countess, 550, 832
Poniatowski, Prince, 566
Ponsonby, William, 117
Poole, Edward, 744
Pope, Alexander, 343, 492, 694
Popham, C. W., 890
Popham, Genl. E. W., 605
Porcher, J. D., 497
Portal, Henry, 125

Portarlington, 1st Earl, 326, 327 (bis)
Portarlington, 2nd Earl, 858
Porter, F. W., 857
Porter, Sir James, 794
Porter, Walsh, 434
Portland, 3rd Duke, 191, 193–4, 574, 951
Portland, 4th Duke, 456, 867
Portman, Henry Seymour, 98
Portman, Henry W. B., 835, 947
Portman, Sir William, 819, 923
Portmore, 1st Earl, 803, 806
Portsmouth, 1st Earl, 69 (bis)
Portsmouth, 2nd Earl, 947
Portsmouth, Lady, 633
Pott, A., 173
Potter, Mary, 285
Potter, Sir Thomas, 92
Potts, Henry, 397, 398
Potts, William, 112
Poulden, —, see Poultney, Thomas
Poulett, 2nd Earl, 137, 866
Poulett, 4th Earl, 950, 962
Poultney, Thomas, 929, 931
Powel, W. E., 407
Powell, —, 649
Powell, Sir Christopher, 70n.
Powell, Pryse, 700
Powell, Thomas, 928
Powell, Sir Thomas, 835
Powell, William (actor), 612
Powell, William (sculptor), 70
Powerscourt, 6th Visct., 698
Powerscourt, 7th Visct., 167
Powis, 1st Earl, 83 (bis), 142, 407, 745 (ter)
Powis, 2nd Earl, 664
Powis, 1st Marquess, 904
Powis, 2nd Marquess (titular Duke), 905
Powlett, Lord William, 859
Pownall, George, 888
Pownoll, Capt. Philemon, 817
Powys, Henry, 663
Powys, Mrs., 467
Powys, Thomas (of Berwick), 752
Powys, Thomas (of Lilford), 311
Powys, Thomas Jelf, 577
Poynton, Edward, 748, 751
Poyntz, Hon. Stephen, 311
Poyntz, W. S., 119, 809
Praed, William, 769, 771
Praed, William Mackworth, 95
Pratt, Edward, 768
Pratt, Sir George, 658–9, 872
Pratt, Sir Henry, 658
Pratt, J., 482
Prescott, H. J., 226
Preston, Rev. George, 893
Preston, Henry, 971
Preston, 1st Visct., 308
Price, Rev. —, 605
Price, Edward, 874
Price, Francis, 690
Price, Joshua, 341
Price, R. Thelwall, 692
Price, Sir Rose, 252
Price, Sir Uvedale, 579, 582
Price, W. Lake, 667
Prickard, N. S., 421
Priestley, John, 193
Prime, Richard, 745
Pringle, Andrew, 46
Pringle, John, 289
Pringle, Robert, 338
Prior, Matthew, 344 (bis)

Pritchard, Mrs. —, 111
Proby, Sarah, 612
Proby, Sir Thomas, 707
Proctor, Sir William Beauchamp, 136
Proger, Edward, 712
Prothero, Thomas, 972
Proudlove, John, 717
Prowse, Abigail, 447
Prudhoe, Lord, 173, 692
Pryce, Richard, 408
Puckering, Sir Thomas, 787
Pückler-Muskau, Prince, 681
Pudsey, Henry, 900, 901
Pudsey, Jane, 900
Pugin, A. W. N., 90, 356, 357 (bis), 374, 655, 668, 692, 723, 739, 970
Puleston, John, 841
Puleston, Thomas, 841
Pulteney, Daniel, 514
Pulteney, Genl. Harry, 815
Pulteney, Joseph, 244
Pulteney, Lady, 226
Pulteney, William (d. 1764), see Bath, 1st Earl
Pulteney, Sir William (Johnstone) (d. 1805), 49, 50, 228, 820
Purves, John, 595
Pusey, John Allen, 716
Pybus, John, 464
Pye, Charles, 793
Pye, Sir Charles, 259, 750
Pyne, W. H., 615
Pytts, Edmund, 420
Pytts, Sir Edward, 62n., 197, 726, 783
Pytts, Jonathan, 664

Queensberry, 1st Duke, 152, 757, 758
Queensberry, 3rd Duke, 55, 130, 311, 513
Queensberry, 4th Duke, 137
Queensberry, Duchess, 208
Queensberry, 5th Marquess, 744

Radcliff, J., 147
Radcliffe, Sir Francis, 462
Radcliffe, John, 53
Radcliffe, Sir Joseph, 210
Radcliffe, Rev. Walter, 319
Radcliffe, William, 610
Radford, Dr., 811
Radnor, 2nd Earl, 65 (ter), 637 (bis), 951
Radnor, 3rd Earl, 172, 480
Ragg, Francis, 930
Raggett, Henry, 619
Raikes, Richard, 693
Raikes, Thomas, 711
Railton, William A., 669
Raincock, H. D., 127
Rainsford, John N., 763
Rait, John, 644
Rake, George, 604
Raleigh, Sir Walter, 95
Ralph, James, 503
Ramsay, Sir Alexander, 59
Ramsay, B. Wardlaw, 165
Ramsay, George, 55
Ramsay, Sir James, 165
Ramsay, William R., 382
Ramsden, Sir John, 54, 194
Rancliffe, 2nd Lord, 151
Randall, John, 299
Ranfurly, Lord, 762

Ransome, Morland &
 Hammersley, Messrs., 771
Raphael, Alexander, 620
Rashleigh, Sir Colman, 393
Ravensworth, 1st Lord, 137, 266,
 519, 584, 611
Rawlinson, Edmund, 482
Rawlinson, Robert, 290, 291
Rawstorne, Lt. Col. Lawrence,
 876
Rawstorne, Thomas, 876
Ray, James, 622
Ray, Rev. P. W., 173
Raymond, J., 507
Raymond, Sir Robert, 347
Read, John, 206
Read, William, 196
Reading, John, 748, 751
Reading, Richard, 929
Rebow, Isaac, 685
Rebow, J. G., 435
Redfern, W., 437
Reed, John, 267
Rees, Dr. Abraham, 60, 102
Reeve, Genl. John, 858, 899
Reeve, William, 777
Reeves, J. F., 156
Reid, Maj.-Genl. Alexander, 829
Reid, Dr. David Boswell, 90
Reid, James, 587
Rendel, J. M., 546
Rendlesham, 5th Lord, 167
Repton, Rev. Edward, 679
Retburgh, J., 501
Reynolds, Sir Joshua, 124, 205,
 208, 609
Reynolds, T. F., 557
Ricardo, Albert, 870
Ricardo, David, 95
Ricardo, Mortimer, 92
Ricardo, Osman, 95
Ricardo, Sampson, 95
Rice, Hon. & Rev. Dr. Edward,
 605
Rice, Rev. H., 143
Rich, Sir Robert, 185
Richards, —, 603
Richards, Rev. —, 772
Richards, James, 865
Richards, John, 718
Richards, Roland, 606
Richardson, C. J., 767
Richardson, J., 216
Richardson, John (of Kirklands),
 117
Richardson, John (of Pitfour), 54
Richardson, Sir John Stewart, 163
Richardson, Dr. Richard, 191
Richardson, Capt. Thomas, 563
Richmond, —, 617
Richmond, George, 809
Richmond, 2nd Duke, 131 (bis),
 132, 185, 562
Richmond, 3rd Duke, 207, 208,
 552, 693, 948, 950, 952
Richmond, 5th Duke, 289
Ricketts, C. S., 377
Riddell, Ralph, 267
Riddell, Thomas, 268
Rideing, Richard, 540
Ridgway, Joseph, 140
Ridley, Sir Matthew White
 (d. 1813), 591, 947
Ridley, Sir Matthew White
 (d. 1836), 122 (bis)
Rigby, Richard, 50, 54
Riland, Rev. John, 749
Ripley, Horatio, 111

Ripley, Richard, 206
Ripon, 1st Earl, 731
Rippon, R., 266
Ritchie, Alexander Handyside,
 486
Rivers, 1st Lord, 639
Rix, Nathaniel, 768
Robarts & Curtis, Messrs., 517
Roberts, Joseph, 792
Roberts, Thomas (plasterer), 934
Robertson, —, 647
Robertson, —, 762
Robertson, David, 166, 810
Robertson, George, 702
Robertson, Mary, 56
Robertson, Thomas, 154
Robertson, William (of Gladney),
 56
Robertson, William (of Kilkenny),
 585, 698
Robertson, William (of Ladykirk),
 289
Robertson, William (of Viewpark),
 82
Robins, John, 770, 771 (bis)
Robinson, —, 863
Robinson, G. J., 433
Robinson, John, 54
Robinson, John (carpenter), 106
Robinson, Joseph, 511
Robinson, Richard, Abp. of
 Armagh, 196
Robinson, Robert, 305
Robinson, William (mason), 831
Robinson, Sir William (of
 Newby), 184, 300
Robinson, Sir William (Surveyor-
 General of Ireland), 545
Robison, Sir John, 553
Robson, —, 325
Robson, Michael, 267
Rocheid, James, 412
Rochester, 1st Earl (d. 1711), 87,
 474, 964
Rockingham, 1st Marquess, 843;
 and see Malton, 1st Earl
Rockingham, 2nd Marquess, 193,
 196, 794, 796
Rodd, F. H., 962
Roden, 2nd Earl, 961
Roe, H. R., 112
Roebuck, Henry Disney, 199,
 863
Rogers, Charles, 682
Rogers, Mrs. Elizabeth, 812
Rogers, Mrs. Hester, 628
Rogers, Rev. James, 86
Rogers, Rev. John, 407
Rogers, Samuel, 894, 952
Rogers, William, 102
Rolfe, Lt. Col., 971
Rolle, 1st Lord, 950
Rollo, 8th Lord, 165
Rolls, John, 534, 669
Rolls, John E. W., 534
Rolt, Edward, 344, 854
Romney, 1st Earl, 65, 588
Romney, George, 157
Rook, John, 324
Rooke, Lawrence, 918
Rose, George, 769
Rose, Rev. H. J., 393
Rose, James, 843
Rose, Joseph, 48, 946
Rose, W. S., 349
Rosebery, 4th Earl, 896
Ross, Hercules, 241
Ross, Adml. Sir J. Lockhart, 101

Ross, Master of, 99
Rossi, G. I., 726
Rossi, J. C. F., 226 (ter), 250,
 581, 952
Rossmore, 1st Lord, 948
Rothes, 1st Duke, 154, 570
Rothschild, Baroness, 972
Rothschild, Solomon, 253
Rotier, M., 297n.
Roubiliac, L. F., 322, 523, 845,
 864, 865
Roughead, —, 158
Roumieu, R. L., 91
Round, C. G., 435
Round, John, 435
Roundell, Richard, 194
Roundell, Rev. William, 194
Rous, Lady Frances, 70
Rous, Sir Francis, 70
Rousseau, Jacques, 656
Routh, William, 582
Rowden, Philip, 592
Rowles, Henry, 424
Rowley, Hercules, 52
Rowley, Sir Joshua, 768
Rowney, Thomas, 630
Roxburghe, 1st Duke, 57, 59
Roxburghe, 3rd Duke, 51, 711
Roxburghe, 6th Duke, 647
Roxburghe, Duchess, 172
Royds, John, 194
Rubens, P. P., 335, 337
Ruck, T., 705
Rucker, J. A., 345
Rumbold, Sir Thomas, 516
Rumford, Count, 877
Runciman, Alexander, 99, 100
Runciman, John, 100
Rundell, Bridge & Rundell,
 Messrs., 545
Ruppel, E., 366
Rush, Sir Wm. Beaumaris, 464
 (bis)
Rushout, Hon. Anne, 874
Rushout, Sir John (d. 1775), 131
Rushout, Sir John (d. 1800), 582
Russell, Christopher, 931
Russell, Adml. Edward, 69
Russell, F. B., 445
Russell, Sir George, 685
Russell, Sir Henry, 77
Russell, J., 823
Russell, James, 762
Russell, Jesse Watts, 729
Russell, Matthew, 624
Russell, R. Greenhill, 77
Russell, Major V., 176
Russell, William, 971
Rutherford, Andrew, 646, 647
Rutherford, Sophia, 646, 648
Ruthven, 6th Lord, 117
Rutland, 5th Earl, 468
Rutland, 6th Earl, 827
Rutland, 8th Earl, 873
Rutland, 1st Duke, 88
Rutland, 3rd Duke, 88, 855
Rutland, 5th Duke, 938, 951
Rutland, 6th Duke, 167
Rutten, Isaac, 102
Ryan, Daniel, 294
Ryder, Hon. & Rev. Henry, 958
Ryder, Hon. Richard, 948
Rysbrack, J. M., 55, 109, 339,
 343, 416, 419, 494, 735, 788

Sackville, Visct., 686
St. Albans, —, 617
St. Albans, 1st Duke, 323

St. Albans, 3rd Duke, 855
St. Aubyn, E., 888
St. Aubyn, Lady, 576 (bis), 672
St. Aubyn, Sir J., 82
St. David's, Bishop of, 225
St. Germans, 1st Earl, 771
St. Germans, 2nd Earl, 393, 962
St. John, —, 966
St. John, H., 400
St. John, Lady, 966
St. John, Maj.-Genl., 583
St. John, Oliver, 552 (bis)
St. John, 14th Lord, 332
St. John, 2nd Visct., 562
St. Quintin, W. T., 517
St. Quintin, Sir William, 147
Salisbury, 1st Earl, 70, 95, 473,
    511
Salisbury, 2nd Earl, 197, 709, 710
Salisbury, 6th Earl, 609
Salisbury, H., 392
Salmon, James, 113, 133
Salomons, David, 173 (bis)
Salt, William, 156
Saltmarshe, Philip, 666, 868
Salusbury, Rev. Thelwall, 744
Salvin, Anthony, 53, 71, 84, 117,
    118, 195, 244, 343, 507, 581,
    785, 806, 970
Salvin, B. J., 122
Salwey, T. R., 800
Sambrook, Jeremy, 342
Sandberg, David, 208
Sancroft, William, Abp. of
    Canterbury, 636, 637
Sanderson, R. B., 267
Sandford, W. A., 510
Sandford, William, 532
Sandwich, 7th Earl, 117
Sandys, Samuel, 750
Sanford family, 80
Sansom, Samuel, 915
Santler, G., 230
Sargent, —, 237
Sargent, John, 518
Saul, George, 692
Saunders, — (carver), 928
Saunders, Mrs., 770
Saunders, Dr. William, 65
Savile, Albany, 80, 856
Savile, Lord, 61
Savile, Sir George (d. 1743), 342,
    380
Savile, Sir George (d. 1784), 354
Savile, Sir Henry, 61, 62
Savile, Sir John (d. 1607), 61
Savile, Sir John (d. 1630), 61
Savill, Samuel, 129
Savory, Capt. Thomas, 757
Sawbridge, Henry, 464, 859
Sawyer, Sir Robert, 415
Saxe-Meiningen, Duke, 960, 963
Sayce, Morris, 907
Scarbrough, 1st Earl, 89, 275, 805
Scarbrough, 2nd Earl, 853
Scarbrough, 4th Earl, 609, 610, 611
Scarbrough, 6th Earl, 79
Scarbrough, 8th Earl, 972
Scarbrough, 9th Earl, 167
Scarburgh, Dr. William, 918
Scarisbrick, Charles, 970
Scarisbrick, Thomas, 689, 692,
    739
Scarsdale, 4th Earl, 750, 751
Scarsdale, 1st Lord, 52, 136, 611
Scawen, Thomas, 504, 513
Scawen, Sir Thomas, 513
Schaw, William, 725

Scheemakers, Peter, 70n., 494,
    797, 838
Scheemakers, Thomas, 797
Scone, Lord, 568
Scot, John, 907
Scott, Sir Claude, 583, 958, 963
Scott, David, 645
Scott, Hercules, 283
Scott, Sir Gilbert, 254, 282, 534,
    696
Scott, J. R. Hope, 166
Scott, James, 621
Scott, Genl. John, 144
Scott, Joseph, 583
Scott, Sir Walter, 76, 115, 116,
    759, 760n., 823
Scott, William, 164
Scott, Sir William, 154
Scovell, Messrs., 66
Scrivenor, Arthur, 753
Scutt, Rev. T., 176
Scrope, Thomas, 207
Scudamore, John, 582
Scudamore, 1st Visct., 43, 544
Scudamore, 3rd Visct., 671
Seafield family, 647
Seafield, 2nd Earl, 59
Seafield, 3rd Earl, 44, 46
Sebright, Sir John, 140, 245, 771
Sebright, Sir Thomas (d. 1736),
    561
Sebright, Sir Thomas (d. 1761),
    109
Sebright, Sir Thomas (d. 1864),
    166
Seddon, Messrs. G. & T., 619
Sederbach, V. A., 550
Sedley, Sir Charles, 934, 947
Seel, Thomas, 778
Sefton, 1st Earl, 112
Sefton, 3rd Earl, 387
Selby, Henry Collingwood, 265,
    267
Selby, N., 706
Selby, P. J., 939
Selby, Walter, 267
Selsey, 1st Lord, 951
Selsey, 2nd Lord, 718
Seny, Nathaniel, 812
Sergison, Warden, 271
Seward, Rev. E., 126
Sewell & Cross, Messrs., 619
Sewell, Sir Thomas, 817
Seymour, Sir Edward (d. 1688),
    440
Seymour, Sir Edward (d. 1708),
    345
Seymour, Lord Henry, 950
Shaftesbury, 1st Earl, 348
Shaftesbury, 3rd Earl, 63
Shaftesbury, 4th Earl, 311
Shaftesbury, 6th Earl, 246
Shairp-Erskine, Mrs., 261
Shakerley, C. W. S., 699
Shakespear, George, 633, 865,
    948
Shakespeare, William, 494
Shanahan, Michael, 946
Shand, William, 762
Shannon, 2nd Visct., 514, 629
Sharp, John, Abp. of York, 258
Sharpe, Hercules, 173
Sharpe, Genl. Matthew, 163
Shaw, Capt. 587
Shaw, J. R., 247
Shaw, Sir John (of Eltham), 544
Shaw, Sir John (of Greenock),
    283

Shaw, Sir John (of Staplefield),
    721
Shaw, Norman, 160
Shaw, T., 210
Shaw Lefevre, Charles, 119
Shaw-Stewart, Sir John, 180
Shaw-Stewart, Sir Michael, 164
Shawe, Richard, 583
Shee, Martin Archer, 73
Sheeres, Sir Henry, 272n.
Sheffield, 1st Earl, 652, 947
Sheffield, Sir Robert, 745
Shelburne, 1st Earl, 55, 483 (bis)
Shelburne, 2nd Earl, 52, 822
Sheldon, Ralph, 460
Shelley, Sir Bysshe, 674
Shelley, Sir John, 938
Shenton, Henry, 309
Shepherd, —, 81
Shepherd, Francis, 457
Shepherd, Thomas, 939
Sheppard, Edward, 679
Sheppard, Thomas, 271
Sherborne, 1st Lord, 605
Sherborne, 2nd Lord, 952 (ter)
Shergold, Mrs., 242
Sheridan, R. B., 426
Sherlock, Thomas, Bp. of
    Salisbury & London, 659,
    855
Sherwood, John, 928, 929, 930,
    931
Shipdem, John, 294
Shireburn, Sir Nicholas, 276, 540
Shirley, Evelyn, 465
Shirley, Evelyn John, 302, 692
    (bis)
Shirley, Hon. George, 915
Shirley, Sir Robert, 732
Shoolbred, Dr. John, 618
Shorey, Mrs., 367
Shorthose, John, 636, 929, 931
Shortridge, Robert, 268
Shout, R. H., 734, 857
Shrewsbury, Duke, 69, 750
Shrewsbury, 14th Earl, 342
Shrewsbury, 15th Earl, 43, 66,
    427, 434, 617, 951
Shrewsbury, 16th Earl, 446, 970
    (bis)
Shute, R., 807
Shutte, Baron, 259
Shuttleworth, James, 611
Shuttleworth, Richard, 333
Sibbald, Sir James, 554
Sibbald, Sir Robert, 283
Sidmouth, 1st Visct., 938, 951
Sidney, Sir John Shelley, 674 (bis)
Silcock, William, 963
Sillitoe, Purney, 187, 770
Silverside, George, 369
Silvertop, Charles, 266
Silvester, John, 717
Sim, Adam, 972
Simcox, George, 692
Simeon, Edward, 767
Simeon, Sir Edward, 841
Simmonds, John, 905
Simon, Peter, 421
Simpson, David, 158
Simpson, H. Bridgman, 166
Simpson, Rev. John, 126
Simpson, Mrs., 618
Simpson, Joseph, 395
Sinclair, Mrs., 385
Sinclair, Sir John (d. 1835), 164
Sitwell, Francis, 624
Sitwell, Francis Hurt, 80, 641

Sitwell, Sir Sitwell, 80
Skeet, Dr. Denham, 302
Skene, George, 644
Skene, Genl. Philip, 576
Skipwith, Sir Thomas, 296
Skrine, Henry, 874
Skynner, Sir John, 948
Slack, John, 502
Slaney, Plowden, 663
Slaney, R. A., 407
Slater, —, 75
Sleep, J. T., 66
Sleter, Francis, 512n.
Sligo, George, 165
Sligo, John, 164
Sligo, 1st Marquess, 426, 700, 947
Sligo, 2nd Marquess, 619, 938
Slingsby, Sir Henry, 301
Sloane, Sir Hans, 283, 712, 903
Sloane-Stanley, Hans, 489
Sloane-Stanley, William, 810
Sloper, Dr. Charles, 96
Small, Rev. J. A., 376
Small, Robert, 634
Small, William, 587
Smallwell, John, 925
Smart, J., 267
Smeaton, John, 89, 373, 411, 507, 572, 573, 634
Smirke, Robert (d. 1845), 263, 740
Smirke, Sydney, 53, 94, 95, 172, 264, 268, 720, 721, 742, 744, 970
Smith, Erasmus, 601
Smith, George, 248
Smith, George (of Piercefield), 768 (bis)
Smith, Gilbert (mason), 757
Smith, Gilbert (of Ryde), 167
Smith, H., 488
Smith, Humphrey, 716
Smith, James (of Craigend), 670, 759
Smith, James (architect, d. 1863), 381
Smith, John (d. 1718), 344
Smith, John (architect of Cambridge), 689
Smith, John (of Blendon Hall), 729
Smith, Joseph (Consul), 794
Smith, Joshua, 132, 780
Smith, Richard, 943
Smith, S. Pountney, 740
Smith, Samuel, 413, 789
Smith, Seth, 477
Smith, Rev. Sydney, 73
Smith, Thomas, 480
Smith, Adml. Thomas, 550
Smith, W. J., 92
Smith, William (of Camer Court), 65
Smith, William (of Carbeth Guthrie), 82
Smith, William (of Haughton Castle), 268
Smith, William (joiner), 928
Smith & Baber, Messrs., 649
Smith-Barry, Hon. John, 343
Smithson, Sir Hugh, see Northumberland, 1st Duke
Smyth, Sir Hugh, 830
Smyth, J. P., 518
Smyth, John (of Balhary), 201
Smyth, John (of Heath), 192
Smythe, Sir Edward, 84
Smythe, Sir Joseph Edward, 807

Smythe, Robert, 784
Smythe, Sir Robert, 956
Smythies, Francis, 527
Snell, Edward, 619
Snell, Nathaniel, 527, 653
Snell, William, 619 (bis)
Sneyd, Mrs., 839, 840
Sneyd, Ralph (d. 1733), 841
Sneyd, Ralph (d. 1793), 84
Sneyd, Ralph (d. 1870), 117, 842
Snooke, W., 307
Snow, —, 859
Soane, Mrs., 772
Sober, Mrs. Anne, 891
Somers, 2nd Lord, 744
Somerset, 2nd Duke, 873
Somerset, 6th Duke, 255, 722
Somerset, 7th Duke, 334, 659
Somerset, Lord Charles, 835
Somerset, Lord Edward, 858
Somervell, Bartholomew, 570
Somerville, Sir William, 755
Somerville, 7th Lord, 567
Somerville, 13th Lord, 57
Sondes, Lady, 612
Sondes, 1st Lord, 855
Soot, James, 587
Sophia of Gloucester, Princess, 618
Sorocold, George, 757
Sorsbie, Mr., 264
Sotheby, Adml. Charles, 859
Souter, James, 587
Southcote, Philip, 131
Southampton, 2nd Lord, 167
Southesk, 4th Earl, 154, 282, 283
Southwell, Edward, 853
Southwell, Sir Robert, 430
Sowerby family, 136
Spackman, Charles, 613
Sparke, Rev. E. P., 393
Sparrow, Messrs. F. & R., 619
Sparrow, J. G., 293
Sparrow, Lady Olivia, 375, 617, 618 (bis)
Sparrow, Robert, 718
Spence, —, 103
Spence, William, 972
Spencer, 1st Earl, 360, 796, 797, 817, 818, 855
Spencer, 2nd Earl, 119, 246, 419, 425 (bis), 426, 810
Spencer, 3rd Earl, 322
Spencer, 4th Earl, 103
Spencer, John, 195
Spencer, Lord Robert, 883
Spencer-Stanhope, Walter, 195
Sperling, —, 507
Spicer, J. W. G., 167
Spottiswoode, John, 164
Sprignell, Robert, 551
Springbett, E. H., 282
Sprot, James, 164
Sprott, Mark, 382
Squire, Joseph, 65
Stafford, 1st Marquess, 950
Stafford, 2nd Marquess, 809, 810 (bis)
Stair, 2nd Earl, 56, 57, 59
Stair, 8th Earl, 165
Stamford, 4th Earl, 83, 549
Stamford, 5th Earl, 209, 431
Stamford, 6th Earl, 729
Stamp family, 831
Stanhope, 1st Earl, 276, 314, 325, 494, 514
Stanhope, 3rd Earl, 948
Stanhope, Countess, 276

Stanhope, Edward Spencer, 66
Stanhope, Grizel Lady, 276
Stanhope, J. Banks, 165
Stanhope, John Spencer, 66
Stanhope, Sir William, 866 (bis)
Stanley, Edward, 612
Stanley, Hon. Hans, 137
Stanley, Lord, 51, 54
Stanley, Lady, 257
Stanley, Sir William, 957
Stannard, —, 137
Stanton, T., 614
Stapell, Nicholas, 914
Staples, Rev. John, 583
Staples, S., 306
Stapleton, Thomas, 74
Stark, Sarah, 239
Starkey, J., 542
Staunton, Sir G. T., 858
Steavens, Thomas, 797, 888
Steinmetz, John, 656
Steinmetz, John Henry, 829
Stephens, J. L., 203
Stephens, Rev. Richard, 755
Stephens, S. Lyne, 166, 167, 168
Stephens, Samuel, 912
Stephenson, Edward, 518
Stephenson, Rowland, 518
Steuart, Sir Henry, 358
Stevens, H. L., 890
Stevens, J. H., 782, 895
Stevenson, J. E. B., 619
Stevenson, John Hall, 208
Stevenson, Robert, 524, 587
Stevenson, W., 150
Stewart, —, 383
Stewart, Alston, 164
Stewart, Rev. C. A., 279
Stewart, Dugald, 647
Stewart, Capt. Houston, 164
Stewart, Col. James, 59
Stewart, Adml. Keith, 54
Stewart, Col. William, 583
Stibbs, John, 843
Stirling, Andrew, 239
Stirling, Archibald, 382
Stirling, Charles, 382 (bis)
Stirling, Col. Charles Moray, 241
Stirling, Sir Gilbert, 383
Stirling, Genl. Graham, 148
Stirling, John (of Kippenross), 645, 784
Stirling, John (of Tullichewan), 527
Stirling, T. G., 382
Stirling, Sir Thomas, 784
Stirling, Sir Walter, 128
Stirling, William Moray, 784
Stoke, —, 892
Stokes, G. H., 617
Stokes, J. G., 212
Stone, Henry, 715
Stonehouse, Sir John, 630, 835
Stones, Thomas, 614, 691
Stones, William, 789
Stonor, Thomas (d. 1772), 61
Stonor, Thomas (d. 1831), 827
Stonor, Thomas (Ld. Camoys), 541
Storace, Anna, 772
Storer, Anthony, 950
Storey, R., 507
Stormont, Viscount, 49
Story, Abraham, 929, 931
Story, Thomas, 904
Stow, John, 419
Strachan, Lieut., 89
Strachan, William, 488
Stradbroke, 1st Earl, 179, 949

Strafford, 1st Earl, 108, 121, 343, 674
Strafford, 2nd Earl, 109, 137, 706, 707
Strangways, Thomas, 869
Stratford, Hon. Edward, 286
Strathallan, 1st Lord, 745
Strathavon, Lord, 755
Strathmore, 4th Earl, 283
Strathmore, 9th Earl, 639
Strathmore, 10th Earl, 346
Strathmore, 12th Earl, 268
Straton, William, 587
Streatfield, Henry (d. 1829), 76
Streatfield, Henry (d. 1852), 488
Streeter, Robert, 710
Strickland, Mrs., 230
Strickland, Sir George, 194
Strickland, Sir William, 131
Strickson, John, 752
Stringer, Catherine, 494
Stringer, Thomas, 494
Strode, Sir John, 556
Strong, Rev. William, 271
Strutt, Col. J. H., 435
Strutt, John, 463
Strutt, W., 702
Stuart, Genl. Sir Charles, 770
Stuart, Sir John, 770
Stuart, Robert, 345
Stuart de Rothesay, Lord, 172
Stubbs, Beaumont, 716
Stukeley, Dr. William, 279, 312–13, 413, 555, 654, 685
Sturt, H. C., 302, 435
Sturt, H. G., 167
Stutely, M. J., 43
Styles, Benjamin, 343, 825
Sudeley, 1st Lord, see Tracy, C. H.
Suffield, 1st Lord, 538, 907, 946
Suffolk, 1st Earl, 455
Suffolk, 6th Earl, 852
Suffolk, 12th Earl, 138, 936
Suffolk, Countess, 109, 136, 414, 561
Sullivan, C. P., 618
Sumner, W. B., 125
Sunderland, 2nd Earl, 289
Sunderland, 3rd Earl, 380, 416
Sunderland, 5th Earl, 561
Surman, —, 103
Surtees, Robert, 120
Sutherland, 1st Duke, 168, 383, 906, 938
Sutherland, 2nd Duke, 91, 92 (passim), 118, 746, 963
Sutherland, Duchess, 92, 162, 809
Sutherland, 15th Earl, 757n.
Sutherland, 17th Earl, 46
Sutherland, S. H., 387
Suttie, E. Grant, 647
Suttie, Sir G. Grant, 647
Sutton, James, 947
Sutton, Sir John, 321
Sutton, Sir Richard, 225, 533
Sutton, Thomas (architect), 869
Sutton, Thomas (d. 1611), 495
Swain, George, 727–8
Swainson, Isaac, 554
Swan & Edgar, Messrs., 416
Swetenham, Clement, 874
Swinburne, Sir John (d. 1706), 837
Swinburne, Sir John (d. 1860), 591
Swinburne, Robert, 268
Swindon, —, 725
Swinnerton, Thomas, 523, 770

Swinton, Archibald, 346
Swinton, John, 382
Swire, —, 75
Sword, Thomas, 767
Swynfen, Samuel, 936
Sydney, Lord, 92
Sykes, Sir Christopher, 232
Sykes, D., 668
Sykes, Sir Francis, 195
Sykes, Sir Mark, 666, 868
Symm, J. R., 301, 302
Symmons, John, 180
Symonds, John, 53
Symons, Thomas, 881
Synge, Rev. Dr., 517

Tabley, 1st Lord de, see Leicester, Sir John F.
Talbot, C. R. Mansel, 435
Talbot, Hon. Charles, 838, 839
Talbot, Charles, Ld. Chancellor, 477
Talbot, Sir Charles, 71
Talbot, 2nd Earl, 584
Talbot, Henry, 550
Talbot, Ivory, 659
Talbot, John Ivory, 550
Talbot, Mrs., 838, 839
Talbot, Robert, 377
Talbot, Thomas Mansel, 481 (bis)
Talbot, Rev. William, 550
Tamworth, Visct., 211
Tankerville, 1st Earl, 276, 805
Tankerville, 2nd Earl, 459
Tankerville, 4th Earl, 615, 624
Tankerville, 5th Earl, 92, 963
Tanner, Antony, 930
Tanner, John, 459
Tapling & Co., 829
Tarring, John, 148
Tasker, Rev. H., 692
Tassie, William, 829
Taswell, William, 618
Tate, Benjamin, 156
Tate, George, 252
Tate, George (of Mitcham), 156
Tatham, Edward, 484
Tatham, Rev. W., 692
Tatham & Bailey, Messrs., 121
Tavistock, Marquess (d. 1767), 207
Tavistock, Marquess (afterwards 7th Duke of Bedford), 938
Tawney, Henry, 833
Tawney, Robert, 831
Tayler, Thomas, 444
Taylor, —, 242
Taylor, Sir Charles, 583
Taylor, George Watson, 350
Taylor, Genl. Sir Herbert, 649
Taylor, J., 641
Taylor, John (of Moreton Hall), 876
Taylor, John (of Strensham Court), 534
Taylor, Genl. Sir John, 501
Taylor, Rev. John, 635
Taylor, Josiah, 700
Taylor, Meadows, 818
Taylor, Peter, 817
Taylor, Robert, 773
Taylor, Thomas, 230
Taylor, William (of Doxford Hall), 267
Taylor, William (of Worcester Park), 585
Taylour, William, 929

Teissier, Stephen, 501
Tempest, Sir Charles, 876
Tempest, Sir George, 731
Tempest, Maj. John, 641
Tempest, Stephen, 76
Temple, 1st Earl, 53, 115, 127, 639
Temple, J., 652
Temple, William, 638
Templer, James, 389
Templeton, 1st Visct., 953
Templetown, 1st Lord, 54, 117
Templetown, 2nd Lord, 54
Tenison, Edward, 453
Tenison, Thomas, Abp. of Canterbury, 404
Tennant, William, 949
Tennyson, George, 668
Teodoli, Marchese, 124
Ternouth, John, 116, 433
Terrick, Richard, Bp. of London, 509
Tessé, Marquis de, 296
Teulon, S. S., 486, 653
Thackeray, W. M., 416
Thanet, 3rd Earl, 531
Thanet, 6th Earl, 532
Thanet, 8th Earl, 51, 947
Tharp, John, 718
Thayer, Humphrey, 909, 910
Thellusson, Charles, 771
Thellusson, Peter, 516, 771
Thellusson, Peter Isaac, 376
Thelwall, R. P., 518
Thelwall, Rev. Robert Carter, 195
Thistlethwayte, Thomas, 437
Thomas, David, 883
Thomas, E., 507
Thomas, Sir George, 124
Thomas, Susannah, 70
Thomason, Yeoville, 280
Thomond, Earl (d. 1774), 136, 137
Thomond, 2nd Marquess, 95
Thompson, Mrs. Anna, 225
Thompson, Beilby, 193, 653, 948
Thompson, Adml. Sir Charles, 577
Thompson, George, 732
Thompson, Henry (of Cheltenham), 456, 846
Thompson, Henry (of Kirby Hall), 131n.
Thompson, John, 924, 927, 928, 929, 930, 931
Thompson, Mary, 192
Thompson, Miles, 875
Thompson, Pearson, 618
Thompson, Sir Peter, 96
Thompson, R. J., 527, 618
Thompson, S. H., 291
Thompson, Stephen, 131, 192, 562, 565
Thompson, William, 184
Thompson & Fearon & Co., 619
Thomson, Alexander (architect), 81, 313
Thomson, Alexander (of Banchory), 762
Thomson, George, 567
Thomson, James (architect, d. 1883), 617, 862
Thomson, James (architect, d. 1905), 81
Thomson, James (poet), 237–8, 880
Thomson, James (of Wester Bogie), 359

Thomson, John, 770
Thomson, John Anstruther, 164
Thornhill family, 480
Thornhill, Bache, 522, 950
Thornton, C. G., 770
Thornton, James, 559
Thornton, Nicholas, 837
Thornton, Samuel, 770, 771
Thornton, Stephen, 770, 771
Thornton, Col. Thomas, 642
Thornwaite, T., 858
Thorold, Sir John, 505
Thorold, Sir John Hayford, 858
Thorpe, Thomas, 281
Thoyte, M. G., 66
Thrale, Henry, 369
Throckmorton, Sir Robert (d. 1720), 344
Throckmorton, Sir Robert (d. 1791), 912
Thrupp, J., 157
Thurburn, John, 737
Thurloe, John, 551, 552
Thurlow, 1st Lord, 425
Thurlow, Rev. Thomas, 692
Thursby, J. H., 752
Thynne, H. F., 51
Thynne, Sir James, 791, 925
Tilley, John, 187
Times, N. G., 557
Tinkler, —, 444
Tinkler, Richard, 876
Tippetts, Sir John, 276–7
Tiretta, Edward, 939
Tod, John, 385
Todd, George, 621
Todd, John, 446
Todd, Joseph, 523
Todd, Thomas, 618
Todd, William, 268
Todrick, —, 158
Toll, H. L., 177
Tollemache, 1st Lord, 507
Tollemache, Hon. Wilbraham, 768, 770
Tomkins, Uvedall, 467
Tomkinson, Edward, 957
Tomkinson, James, 84, 956
Tomkinson, Rev. James, 118
Tomline, George, 166
Tonson, Jacob, 850, 851, 854
Tooker, Samuel, 641
Topham, A., 268
Topham, George, 523
Topham, Richard, 800
Toplis, —, 321
Tournay, William, 120
Tower, Christopher, 54
Towgood, William, 682
Towneley, Charles, 125, 178
Towneley, Peregrine, 962
Townley, George, 422
Townsend, Joseph, 323, 476, 549
Townshend, Mrs. Henrietta, 136
Townshend, Sir Roger, 281
Townshend, 2nd Visct., 492
Townshend, Viscountess, 79
Tracy, Charles Hanbury, 102
Tracy, Robert, 885
Trafford, Trafford, 397
Trail, Henry, 225
Traill, James, 173
Traquair, 4th Earl, 758
Trecothick, Barlow, 576, 577
Trécourt, J. P., 424
Tredcroft, Henry, 394
Tredgold, Thomas, 76
Tregonwell, L. D. G., 302

Tremayne, J. H., 393
Trench, Henry, 416
Trench, Michael F., 327
Tresham, Henry, 643
Tresham, Sir Thomas, 186, 367, 783
Trevanion, J. B., 584
Trevelyan, Sir Walter, 268
Trevisani, Mgr., Bp. of Verona, 129
Trevor, Richard, Bp. of Durham, 109, 194, 558, 703, 837
Tritton, George, 617
Trollope, Sir Thomas, 511
Trotman family, 551
Trotter, Alexander, 288
Trumbull, William, 197
Trumbull, Sir William, 630
Tryon, Thomas, 511
Tucker, —, 534
Tufnell, Capt. Edward, 69, 260, 792
Tufnell, J. J., 225
Tufnell, Samuel, 457, 498, 654
Tufnell, William, 69
Tulk, C. A., 669
Tunstall, Robert, 609
Turbutt, William, 522, 635
Turner, Charles, 105
Turner, Sir Charles, 193, 194, 207, 209
Turner, Cholmondely, 340, 344
Turner, Christopher, 161, 165, 168
Turner, Sir Edward, 275, 549
Turner, Col. George, 762
Turner, Jane, 233
Turner, John, 376
Turner, Sir John, 105
Turner, Thomas, 696
Turnly, Thomas, 930
Turnor, Edmund, 195, 312
Turnour, Edward, 778
Turton, Dr. John, 54
Turville, F. F., 125
Tweeddale, 2nd Earl, 152, 155
Tweeddale, 1st Marquess, 757
Tweeddale, 2nd Marquess, 758 (bis)
Tweeddale, 4th Marquess, 46, 58 (bis)
Tweeddale, 7th Marquess, 54
Tweeddale, 8th Marquess, 148, 963
Twell, —, 774
Tylney, 1st Earl, 184, 489
Tyndall, Thomas, 141
Tyndall-Bruce, O., 165
Tynte, Sir Charles Kemeys, 53, 463
Tynte, Sir Halswell, 819
Tyronnel, 4th Earl, 700
Tyrrell, Col. (Genl.) James, 492, 831
Tyrell, Col. (later Sir) John, 435, 464 (bis)
Tyson, W. G. D., 282
Tytler, James, 486

Udny, Robert F., 55
Udny, William, 464
Underhill, William, 603
Unett, J. W., 280
Upcher, Abbot, 682
Upper Ossory, 2nd Earl, 208
Upton, Arthur, 55
Upward, J. W., 211

Urquhart, B. C., 737
Utterson, E. V., 715
Uxbridge, 1st Earl, 124, 232, 936, 946, 949
Uxbridge, 2nd Earl, 729; and see Anglesey, 1st Marquess

Vachell, Col., 457
Vandes, Comte de, 963
Vane, Francis, 876
Van Gelder, P. M., 55
Vanneck, Sir Gerard, 817, 947
Vanneck, Sir Joshua, 947
Vansittart, Arthur, 653, 832
Vansittart, Henry, 123
Vansittart, Robert, 550
Van Spanger, —, 340
Varden, Richard, 632, 972
Varley, John, 263, 615
Vassalli, Francesco, see Vessali, Francis
Vaughan, John, 582
Vaughan, Sir John, Baron of the Exchequer, 332
Vaughan, Richard, 431
Vaughan, Sir Robert, 142
Veitch, James, 364
Velasquez, Isidoro, 808
Vereker, Hon. Charles, 584
Verelst, C., 43
Verney, 2nd Earl, 269
Verney, Sir Harry, 224, 696
Verney, 2nd Lord, 703
Verney, Sir Ralph, 544
Vernon, —, 110
Vernon, Hon. Catherine Venables, 797
Vernon, George, 841, 900
Vernon, George Venables, 839
Vernon, Henry, 842
Vernon, 1st Lord, 332
Verrio, Antonio, 805
Verulam, 1st Earl, 76
Verulam, 2nd Earl, 166
Vesey, Agmondesham, 208
Vessali, Francis, 751
Victoria, Queen, 118, 244, 762
Vilion, —, 592
Villebois, Henry, 270
Villiers, Hon. George, 961
Vine, James, 527
Viner, J. Ellis, 692
Visentini, Antonio, 940
Visme, Gerard de, 441
Vivian, J. H., 701
Vivian, John, 962
Vivian, W. G., 460
Vose, G., 689
Voysey, Abraham, 686
Vyner, Robert, 522, 951
Vyse, R., 721

Wade, Col. 855
Wade, Genl. George, 130
Wade, Walter, 610
Waddington, Rev. Thomas, 769
Wadham, Dorothy, 70
Wadham, John, 651
Wadham, Nicholas, 70
Wainwright, John, 493
Wainwright, Thomas, 493
Wainwright, Thomas (builder), 431
Waistell, Charles, 477
Waite, Moses, 369
Waithman, Robert, 292
Wake, Sir William, 721

Wakeman, Henry, 177
Walcot, Charles, 663
Waldegrave, Dowager Countess, 714
Waldo, Mrs., 701
Wale, Capt. R. G., 271
Wale, Samuel, 372, 374, 608
Wale, Thomas, 893
Walford, Francis, 583
Walker, —, 881–2
Walker, Genl. Alexander, 358
Walker, Maj. Charles, 398
Walker, Genl. Foster, 120
Walker, Sir Francis, 359
Walker, George, 360, 864
Walker, Hay, 158
Walker, J., 972 (bis)
Walker, Jonathan, 641
Walker, Joseph, 196
Walker, Joshua, 196
Walker, Richard, 177
Walker, Samuel, 641 (bis)
Walker, T. L., 667, 668
Walker, William, 740
Walker, William (of Crownest), 132
Wall, C. B., 117, 393
Wall, John, 812
Waller, Capt., 700
Waller, Edmund, 185
Waller, John, 553
Wallinger, J. A., 612
Wallis, Maj.-Genl. B., 700
Wallis, John, 835, 918, 919
Walls, Albert, 150
Walmsley, —, 75
Walmsley, George, 229
Walpole, Sir Edward, 602, 695
Walpole, Capt. Galfridus, 414
Walpole, Horace, 52, 109, 206, 213–14, 299, 566, 949
Walpole, 1st Lord, 695
Walpole, Robert, see Orford, 1st Earl
Walsh, John, 702
Walsingham, 4th Lord, 117
Walsingham, 5th Lord, 117
Walter, John (d. 1847), 715
Walter, John (d. 1894), 174
Walters, Edward, 857
Walters, R., 928
Wane, J., 605
Wansey, William, 348
Wapshott, Thomas, 615
Warburton, —, 304
Warburton, R. E., 507
Warburton, William, Bp. of Gloucester, 475
Ward, Sir Edward, 176
Ward, George, 526, 585
Ward, George Henry, 970
Ward, J., 858
Ward, James, 615, 617
Ward, John (of Holwood Ho.), 172, 173
Ward, John (of Capesthorne), 750, 751
Ward, John & Sons, 366, 931
Ward, R. E., 166
Ward, S. N., 173
Ward, Seth, Bp. of Salisbury, 348, 918, 926
Warde, C. T., 970
Warford, —, 592
Wark, David, 49
Warner, E., 649
Warner, Henry, 649
Warner, Richard, 708

Warren, Hugh, 474
Warren, Adml. Sir John Borlase, 332, 592 (bis)
Warren, Thomas, 929, 930–1
Warrender, Sir George, 162, 163
Warriner, E., 444
Warrington, 2nd Earl, 596
Warwick, 1st Earl, 146, 419, 521, 574
Warwick, 3rd Earl, 657
Warwick, J., 266
Warwick, Sir Philip, 294
Wastell, Rev. H., 267
Waterford, 1st Marquess, 947
Waterhouse, Alfred, 502
Wathen, Paul, 961
Watson, —, 84
Watson, Adml. Charles, 797
Watson, Henry, 110
Watson, James, 59
Watson, L. T., 768
Watson, Lewis, 855
Watson, Hon. R., 118
Watson-Wentworth, Thomas, see Malton, 1st Earl
Watt, —, 587
Watt, Isaac, 587
Watt, James, 140–1, 652, 677, 957
Watts, Banister, 270
Wauchope, Andrew, 58
Wauchope, Col. John, 164
Wauchope, Col. William, 162
Waynflete, William, Bp. of Winchester, 156
Wealands, C., 267
Weaver, Arthur, 83
Webb, —, 251
Webb, Henry, 622
Webster, David, 644
Webster, Godfrey, 483
Webster, James, 587
Webster, Thomas, 773
Webster, Sir Thomas, 276
Weddell, William, 53, 107, 365, 958
Wedderburn, Sir David, 617
Wedgwood, Josiah, 635, 795
Wehnert, F., 649
Weightman, J. G., 441
Welby, Sir W. Earle, 908
Weld, Edward, 96
Weld, George, 706
Weld, J., 858
Weld, Joseph, 807
Weld, Thomas, 807, 835
Wellesley, Marquess, 937, 939
Wellington, 1st Duke, 222, 226, 510, 808, 937, 938 (bis)
Wells, Capt., 394
Wells, John, 576, 744
Welman, C. N., 696
Wemyss, 2nd Earl, 570
Wemyss, 6th Earl, 99, 412
Wemyss, 7th Earl, 55, 164
Wemyss, 8th Earl, 167
Wemyss, John, 154
Wemyss, William, 953
Wenlock, 1st Lord (d. 1852), 117, 950
Wenlock, 2nd Lord, 394
Wenman, Baroness, 44
Wenman, 6th Visct., 764
Wentworth, Godfrey (d. 1789), 111, 610
Wentworth, Godfrey (d. 1834), 665, 868, 962
Wentworth, Sir John, 290
Wentworth, Thomas Watson, 494

Wentworth, Sir William, 489, 565
West, Benjamin, 581, 671, 883, 942, 964
West, James, 56n., 63n., 633
West, James Roberts, 434
West, Samuel, 617
West, Thomas, 798
West, William, 527
Westbury, 1st Lord, 43
Westcombe, N., 464
Westenra, H. R., 349
Westley, Dr. John, 871
Westmacott, Richard, 125, 641, 839, 880, 952
Westmacott, Sir Richard, 405, 880
Westminster, 1st Marquess, 246, 476
Westminster, 2nd Marquess, 166, 167
Westmorland, 6th Earl, 529, 831
Westmorland, 7th Earl, 184, 562
Weston, J. Webbe, 125
Wetherid, Francis, 85
Wetten, Luke, 637, 700
Wettenhall, —, 84
Weyland, John, 769
Weymouth, 1st Visct., 819
Weymouth, 3rd Visct., 146, 208, 341
Wharncliffe, 1st Earl, 167
Wharncliffe, 1st Lord, 72, 641
Wharton, John, 125, 769
Whatton, W. R., 614
Wheat, James, 313
Wheatley, —, 448
Wheeler, Maurice, 63
Wheler, Granville H., 637
Whellan, W., 271
Whichcote, Sir Thomas, 119, 488
Whipham, Thomas, 676
Whitaker, F., 667
Whitaker, Dr. T. D., 156
Whitaker, W. W., 176
Whitbread, Samuel, 426, 685
Whitby, —, 839
White, John, 697
White, Sir Matthew, 610
White, Simon, 449
Whitefoord, Allan, 46
Whitefoord, Sir John, 576
Whitehead, Paul, 77
Whitehurst, John, 635
Whitfield, G., 729
Whiting, Thomas, 929, 930, 931
Whitmore, Richard, 791
Whitmore, Thomas, 874
Whitmore, W. W., 740
Whitmore, William, 598
Whitworth, Robert, 693
Whyte-Melville, John, 358
Wicklow, 1st Visct., 138
Widdrington, 4th Lord, 345
Wigtown, Earl, 58
Wilbraham, Lady Elizabeth, 900
Wilbraham, George, 957
Wilbraham, Randle, 431, 954
Wilbraham, Roger, 178n.
Wild, James William, 972
Wilde, Capt. de, 296
Wilder, John, 434
Wildman family, 649
Wildman, James B., 729
Wildman, Col. Thomas, 729
Wilhelm I, King of Württemberg, 616
Wilkins, —, 302
Wilkins, —, 617
Wilkins, Charles, 254

Wilkins, Rev. David, 496
Wilkins, Henry, 929
Wilkins, Walter, 527
Wilkinson, John, 215
Wilkinson, Thomas, 841
Wilkinson, William, 725
Wilkinson & Prince, Messrs., 191
Wilks, John, 751
Willan, Thomas, 76, 77
Willan, W., 617
Willes, Edward, 585, 700, 701 (bis), 709, 901
Willes, J., 625
Willes, Rev. W. S., 770
Willett, Ralph, 583
William III, King, 405, 806 (bis), 923
William IV, King, 964; statue of, 485
Williams, Abraham, 931
Williams, Edward, 517
Williams, G. B., 753
Williams, Gregory, 789
Williams, H. W. ('Grecian'), 646
Williams, Herbert, 67
Williams, J., 857
Williams, J. Lloyd, 225
Williams, John, 551
Williams, Matthew, 929
Williams, Mrs., 180
Williams, Robert, 701
Williams, Thomas, 767
Williams, Thomas (of Temple Ho.), 957, 959
Williams–Bulkeley, Sir Richard, 393
Williams-Wynn, Sir Watkin (d. 1749), 751
Williams-Wynn, Sir Watkin (d. 1789), 51, 147, 179, 327, 663 (bis), 948, 961
Williams-Wynn, Sir Watkin (d. 1840), 225, 369
Williams-Wynn, Sir Watkin (d. 1885), 810
Williamson, Alexander, 45
Williamson, Miss Alison, 165
Williamson, Sir Hedworth, 268
Williamson, Sir Joseph, 531
Willis, Browne, 905
Willis, Dr. John, 746
Willis, Richard, 769
Willmer, Henry, 649, 650 (bis)
Willoughby, Hon. Henry, 464
Willoughby, Thomas, 773
Willoughby de Broke, 5th Lord, 341
Willoughby de Broke, 6th Lord, 52, 147, 287
Willoughby de Eresby, 19th Lord, 332, 606
Wills, John, 120
Willson, Anthony, 165
Willson, Rev. R. W., 899
Willson, T. J., 723
Wilmington, 1st Earl, 185
Wilmot, Sir Robert, 952
Wilshere, William, 118
Wilson, Christopher, 876
Wilson, Ford, 173
Wilson, George, 876
Wilson, Col. George, 193
Wilson, J., 267
Wilson, Col. James, 441 (bis)
Wilson, John, 375

Wilson, Matthew, 876
Wilson, Sir T. Maryon, 371
Wilson, Thomas, 898n.
Wilson, Rev. W. Carus, 522
Wilton, 1st Earl, 946, 953, 957
Wilton, Joseph, 207, 208 (bis)
Winchester, 14th Marquess, 167
Winchilsea, 2nd Earl, 904
Winchilsea, 8th Earl, 464, 644 (bis)
Winchilsea, 9th Earl, 166
Windham, William (d. 1689), 712
Windham, William (d. 1761), 610
Windham, William (d. 1810), 139, 680, 949
Windham, Adml. William (d. 1833), 270
Windle, William, 621
Winford, Thomas Cookes, 869
Wing, Samuel, 925
Wingfield, John, 406
Winn, C. W., 666, 869
Winn, Sir Rowland, 50, 52, 111, 565, 609
Winnington, Sir Edward, 581, 706
Winter, John, 770
Winter, R., 769
Wintoun, 3rd Earl, 862
Wire, Alderman, 345
Wise, Edward, 98
Wise, Henry, 228, 474, 854
Wise, Matthew, 377
Wise, Thomas, 545, 928, 931
Witton, Richard, 731
Wodehouse, Sir Armine, 667, 716
Wodehouse, John, 716
Wodehouse, Sir John, 806
Wolff, Jens, 744
Wolryche, Sir Thomas, 751
Wolseley, Sir Charles (d. 1714), 636
Wolseley, Sir Charles (d. 1846), 840
Wood, Dr., 887
Wood, Capt. Charles, 195
Wood, J. T., 960
Wood, Sir Mark, 125
Wood, Nicholas, 928
Wood, Robert, 126, 794
Woolley, J., 43
Woolley, S., 139
Woodcock, J., 700
Wood-Craster, Thomas, 268
Woodfall, H. S., 575
Woodhouse, Samuel, 218
Woodmason, J., 328
Woods, Miss, 289
Woodward, Capt., 812
Woody, Dr., 617
Woolcott & Browning, Messrs., 534
Woolley, John, 699
Wordsworth, Josias, 610
Wormald, Smith, 701
Woronzow, Count Michael, 398
Woronzow, Prince Michael, 118
Worsley, Henry, 514
Worsley, John, 521
Worsley, Sir Richard, 269, 682–3, 810n.
Worsley, Sir Robert, 454
Wortley, J. A. Stuart, 72, 641
Wren, Christopher, Dean of Windsor, 917

Wren, Christopher, junior, 921
Wren, Matthew, Bp. of Ely, 917, 922
Wrey, Sir Bourchier, 769
Wright, Daniel, 572
Wright, Edward, 970
Wright, Sir James, 617
Wright, John, 763–4
Wright, Joseph, 635
Wright, Michael, 153
Wright, Thomas, 270
Wright, W., 857
Wrightson, William, 610, 640
Wroughton, Rev. P., 961
Wyatt, Matthew Cotes, 615, 938, 942
Wyatt, Thomas, 618
Wyatt, Mrs. T., 619
Wyatt, Thomas Henry, 103, 935, 972
Wykeham, Richard, 832
Wylson, James, 144
Wyndham, George T., 270
Wyndham, H. P., 228
Wyndham, Smith, 701
Wyndham, Thomas, 561
Wyndham, William (of Dinton), 962
Wyndham, William (of Earsham), 768
Wyndham, Sir William, 344, 806
Wynn, Lady, 769
Wynn, Michael, 943
Wynn, Sir Watkin Williams, see Williams-Wynn
Wynne, John, 467
Wynne, Robert, 844
Wyon, E. W., 881
Wythe, Thomas, 413
Wyvill, Sir Marmaduke, 193

Ximenes, M., 281

Yarborough, George Cooke, 522
Yarborough, 1st Earl, 963
Yarborough, 3rd Earl, 167
Yarborough, 1st Lord, 147, 810, 952
Yarborough, Thomas, 192
Yate, Robert Dobyns, 788
Yates, J. B., 173
Yates, James, 897
Yates, Mrs., 618
Yeoman, James, 645
Yerbury, Francis, 910
Yoget, C., 374
Yonge, Sir Walter, 429
Yonge, William, 200
York, Duke (d. 1767), 137, 209
York, Duke (d. 1827), 187, 200, 425 (bis), 426, 700
Yorke, Catherine, 797
Yorke, Hon. Philip, 768, 770
Yorke, Philip (of Erddig), 844, 945, 946
Yorke, Simon, 435
Yorke, Hon. Mrs., 768, 769
Yorke, Sir William, 865
Young, Hitch, 343

Zandt, Baroness von, 564
Zetland, 1st Earl, 744, 800
Zubov, Prince Platon, 400
Zucchi, Antonio, 48
Zugheer, ––, 689

Index of Places

I BRITISH ISLES

Abbeville, Ireland, 327
Abbey Dore, Herefs., Ch., 43
Abbeyleix, Ireland, 946
Abbot Hall, Westmld., 193
Abbots Bromley, Staffs., Ch., 752
Abbots Langley, Herts.
  Ch., mont., 347
  ho., 501
Abbotsford, Roxb., 76, 115, 116, 166, 759
Abbotstone, Hants., 342, 807
Abdie, Fife, Ch., 162, 443
Aberavon Bridge, Glam., 286
Aberayron, Card., Ch., 406
Abercairny Abbey (Ho.), Perthshire, 241, 260, 272, 322, 624
Abercorn, W. Lothian
  Ch., 154
  ho., 79
Abercrombie, Fife, St. Monans' Ch., 162
Aberdalgie, Perths., Manse, 164
Aberdaron, Caern., New Ch., 879
Aberdeen
  Aberdeen Bank, 158
  Advocates' Hall, 760
  Assembly Rooms, 213, 736
  Asylum for blind, 230, 760
  Athenæum Reading Room, 736
  Bon-accord Crescent, 737
  Bon-accord Square, 737
  Bridge of Dee, 760
  Bridge of Don, 760
  Bridewell, 158
  Commercial Bank, 356
  Crimonmogate Ho., 761
  Court Ho., 760
  Dr. Bell's School, 736
  East prison, 760
  Holburn U.P. Ch., 322
  Infant School, 736
  John Knox's Churchyard, 322
  King's Coll., 179, 760
  Lunatic Asylum, 736
  Marine Terrace, Ferryhill, 737
  Marischal College, 736
  Meal Market, 456
  Mechanics' Institute, 736
  Medico-Chirurgical Society's Hall, 736
  Mercat Cross, 556
  Mrs. Elmslie's Institution, 736
  New market, 736
  North Ch., 761
  North of Scotland Bank, 736
  Northern Assurance Company, 736
  Old Aberdeen Free Ch., 737
  Post Office, 736
  Powis Ho., 322, 451
  quarries, 45, 47n.
  Record Office, 760

Aberdeen—contd.
  Robert Gordon's Hospital, 57, 760
  Royal Infirmary, 736
  St. Andrew's Episcopal Ch. (Cathedral), 736
  St. Clement's Ch., 761
  St. Machar's Cathedral, mont., 556
  St. Nicholas Ch. East, 737
  St. Nicholas Ch. West, 340
  St. Nicholas churchyard screen, 171, 760
  St. Peter's Ch., 541
  South Ch., 761
  Theatre, 426
  Tolbooth, steeple, 568–9; and see Town House
  Town and County Bank, 736
  Town Hall, Old Aberdeen, 451
  Town Ho., 57, 760; and see Tolbooth
  Town's schools, 760
  Trinity Hall, 761
  Union Bridge, 158, 213
  Union Buildings, 737
  Union St., 213; ho., 737
  Union United Free Ch., 761
  United Free Ch., 737
  West Parish Church School, 736
  Westburn Ho., 737
  Woodside Chapel, 736
  Woodside Ch. of Scotland, 737
Aberdour, Aberdeens., Manse, 500
Aberdour Ho., Fife, 220
Aberfeldy, Perths., bridge, 57
Abergavenny, Mon., Market Ho., 581, 879
Aberglaslyn Bridge, Caern., 257
Abergwili Palace, Carm., 225, 315
Aberlour, Banffs.
  Blairshannock, 699
  Ch., 699
  Ho., 699
Abernyte, Perths.
  Ch., 740
  School, 587
Aberuthven, Perths., mausoleum, 57, 907
Aberyschan, Mon.
  Ch., 406
  ironworks, 171
Aberystwyth, Card.
  Assembly Rooms, 679
  bridge, 581
  Castle Ho., 582
  St. Michael's Ch., 406
Abingdon, Berks.
  Brick Alley Almshouses, 879
  Council Chamber, 782, 793, 879
  County Bridewell, 391, 961

Abingdon, Berks.—contd.
  hos., 198
  St. Helen's Ch., 198, 835
  Town Hall, 486, 722, 794
  Workhouse, 486, 487
Abington, Cambs., ho., 457
Abington, Northants.
  Ch., 773
  Hall, 752
Aboyne, Aberdeens.
  Castle, 164
  Ch., 761
Abram, Lancs., St. John's Ch., 614
Accrington, Lancs.
  Ch., 283
  Christ Ch., 897
Acharacle, Argylls., Ch., 820
Achnacarry, Inverness., 358
Ackworth, Yorks.
  Friends' Meeting Ho., 665
  School, 521, 868
Acomb, Yorks., Ch., 878
Acrise Place, Kent, 914
Acton, Cheshire, Ch., 84, 838
Acton, Middlx.
  Goldsmiths' Almshouses, 102
  Horn Lane, villa, 706
Acton Burnell Hall, Salop., 84, 807
Acton Park, Denbighs., 950
Acton Place, Suffolk, 340
Acton Reynald Hall, Salop., 408
Acton Round, Salop., chapel & mont., 663, 664
Acton Scott, Salop., mont., 84
Adamton, Ayrshire, 587
Adare Manor, Ireland, 234
Adderbury, Oxon.
  Ch., 213, 648
  Ho., 207, 344, 561
  ho., 746
  Rectory, 120
Adderley, Salop.
  Ch., 83
  Hall, 187
Adderstone Hall, Northumb., 162
Addington, Surrey
  Ch., 119–20; mont., 577
  Lodge, Park or Place, 393, 576
Addiscombe Ho. (later Military Seminary), Surrey, 403, 792, 896
Addiston Ho., Midlothian, 570
Addlestone, Surrey
  Cottage, 212
  St. Paul's Ch., 721
Adel, Yorks., Ch., 210
Aden Ho., Aberdeens., 762
Adlestrop, Glos.
  Ch., 550
  Ho. (Park), 275, 550
Adlingfleet, Yorks., Ch., 321

Adlington, Lancs., Christ Ch., 878
Aigburth, Lancs., St. Anne's Ch., 247
Aikenhead, Renfrews., 54
Ainsworth, Lancs., Ch., 258
Airdrie, Fife, 59
Airedale College, Yorks., 215
Airlie Castle, Angus, 887
Airth, Stirlings.
  Castle, 382
  Ho., 59
  North Ch., 783
Airthrey Castle, Stirlings., 55, 784
Akingford, Essex, bridge, 464
Alberbury, Salop., mont., 664
Albrighton, Salop., Ch., 188
Albury, Surrey
  Ch., 143
  Catholic Apostolic Ch., 143
  Park, 272n., 303, 309, 377, 770
Alcester, Warwicks., Ch., 914; mont., 915
Aldborough, Norfolk, Ch., 145
Aldborough, Yorks., farmho., 692
Aldbourne, Wilts., Vicarage, 277
Aldbury Grove, Herts., 173
Aldby Park, Yorks., 258, 940
Aldenham, Herts.
  Grammar School, 650
  Lodge, 753
Aldenham Ho., Salop., 83
Alderbury, Wilts., St. Marie's Grange, 970
Alderley, Glos., Poorhouse, 455
Alderney, C.I., Place d'Armes, 899
Alderton, Suffolk, Rectory, 324
Aldwark Hall, Yorks., 652, 946
Alford Bridge, Aberdeens., 821
Alfreton Hall, Derbys., 751
Alkrington Hall, Lancs., 514
All Cannings, Wilts., Ch., 882
Allanton Castle, Lanarks., 358
Allendale Ho., Dorset, 963
Allensmore Ho., Herefs., 480
Allerton, Lancs.
  Grove Ho., 398
  Tower, 291
Allerton Mauleverer, Yorks., 425, 642
Allestree Hall, Derbys., 950
Allington, Dorset, Ch. 863
Alloa, Clack.
  Ch., 79, 357, 531
  Ch. (Episcopal), 68
  Ch. (R.C.), 68
  Cross, 79
  Ho., 68, 296, 337n., 531
  ho., 79
Alloway, Ayrshire, Burns Mont., 384, 386
Almer, Dorset
  Ch., 96
  School, 477
Alnwick, Northumb.
  Bridge, 53, 144
  Brizlee Tower, 53
  Castle, 53, 105, 610–11, 732
  Ch., 265, 732
  Clayport, ho., 591
  Column, 780
  farmhos., 779–80
  Hulne Abbey, 53
  Hulne Park, bridge, 780
  Ratcheugh Crag, 53
  St. Mary's Chapel (R.C.), 363

Alscot Ho. (Park), Warwicks., 434, 438, 633, 773, 915
Alston, Cumb., Ch., 266
Althorp Ho.,Northants., 246, 289, 425, 497, 810, 817; Stables, 419, 561
Alton, Dumfriess., farmho., 588
Alton Abbey or Towers, Staffs., 43, 66, 427, 434, 617, 951, 970
Alva, Clack.
  Ho., 54, 784
  mausoleum, 55
Alverbank, Hants., 174
Alverstoke, Hants., Ch., 604
Alverthorpe, Yorks., Ch., 73
Alveston, Warwicks., Ch., 861
Alwalton, Hunts., parsonage, 151
Alyth, Perths., Ch., 385
Ambrosden Ho., Oxon., 549
Amersham, Bucks., Ch., 959; mont., 345
Amesbury, Wilts.
  Abbey or Ho., 108, 311, 435, 873; temple, 208
  parsonage, 313
Amisfield Ho., E. Lothian, 99, 412, 623, 866
Amlwch, Anglesey, Ch., 945
Ammerdown Ho. (Park), Som., 836, 948; column, 477
Ampfield, Hants., Ch., 200
Amport Ho., Hants., 167
Ampthill, Beds.
  Avenue Ho., 906
  Cedars (The), 219
  Ch., 314, 926
  Cross, 299
  Great Park Ho., 208, 275, 368, 529, 710, 904
  Workhouse, 219
Ampton, Suffolk, pavilion, 151
Amwell (Great), Herts.
  Flint Ho., 578
  Grove (The), 577
  mausoleum, 577
  urn, 577
Andover, Hants., Guildhall, 503
Angerton Hall, Northumb., 267
Angley, Kent, 255
Annfield, Angus, villa, 587
Anniston Ho., Angus, 644
Ansley Hall, Warwicks., 207
Anstey, Leics., School, 497
Anstey Pastures Hall, Leics., 670
Antons Hill, Berwicks., 164
Antony Ho., Cornwall, 231, 341, 565
Apethorpe, Northants, 151, 562
Apley Castle, Salop., 142
Apley Park, Salop., 874
Apperley Bridge, Yorks., ho., 216
Apperley Court, Glos., 230
Appleby, Leics., School, 900–1, 924
Appleby, Lincs.
  Ch., 321
  Hall, 321
Appleby, Westmld.
  Castle, 532
  Ch., 531–2
  ho., 106
  Market Ho., 743
Appleshaw, Hants., Ch., 734
Apps Court, Surrey, 351
Appuldurcombe Ho., I. of W., 269, 454
Aqualate Hall, Staffs., 584

Arbroath, Angus
  Academy, 113
  Ch., 969
  High School, 113
  Infirmary, 747
  St. Thomas's Ch. (R.C.), 542
  Sheriff Court Ho., 417
  Town Hall, 524, 747
  Trades Hall, 417
Arbury Hall, Warwicks., 149, 235, 420, 483, 550, 588, 901, 925
Arbuthnott Ho., Kinc., 261
Archerfield Ho., E. Lothian, 55
Ardanaiseig Ho., Argylls., 164
Ardbraccan Ho., Ireland, 946
Ardchattan, Argylls., Ch., 821
Arddarroch Ho., Dunb., 165
Ardglass, Ireland, harbour, 524
Ardgour, Argylls., Ch., 820
Ardgowan Ho., Renfrews., 164, 180, 218
Ardincaple Castle, Dunb., 576
Ardkinglas(s) Ho., Argylls., 112, 185, 645
Ardmaddy Castle, Argylls., 359
Ardnamurchan, Argylls., Ch., 162
Ardoch Castle, Dunb., 526
Ardoch Ho., Perths., 784
Ardrossan, Ayrshire, 593
Ardsley, Yorks., Christ Ch., 442
Arley Hall, Cheshire, 507
Arlington Court, Devon, 510, 546
Armadale Castle, Skye, 358
Armagh, Ireland
  Cathedral, 234
  Obelisk, 196
Armitage, Staffs.
  Ch., 841n.
  High Bridge, 655
Armitage Bridge, Yorks., Ch., 211
Armley Ho., Yorks., 680n., 745
Armthorpe, Yorks, Ch., 441
Arncliffe Hall, Yorks., 192
Arndilly Ho., Banffs., 699
Arngask, Perths., Manse, 533
Arniston, Midlothian, 46, 57, 220
Arno's Grove, Middlx., 817
Aros Ho., Argylls., 163
Arrowe Hall, Cheshire, 247
Arthurstone Ho., Perths., 164
Arundel, Sussex
  Castle, 43, 166, 344, 418, 819
  Congregational Ch., 44
  Tower in Park, 419
  Town Hall, 44
Ascog, Bute, Free Ch., 382
Ascot, Berks., Race-stand, 417, 581
Ascott Ho., Bucks., 473
Asfordby, Leics., Railway Station, 622
Ash, Som., Ch., 487
Ash Grove, Kent, 95
Ashbourne, Derbys.
  Ch., 234
  Mansion (The), 635
Ashburnham Place, Sussex, 54, 147, 252, 558, 858, 933
Ashby-de-la-Zouche, Leics.
  Ch., mont., 494
  Hastings (Royal) Hotel, 211
  Ivanhoe Baths, 211
  Rawdon Terrace, 211
Ashcombe Park, Staffs., 839, 840
Ashcott, Som., Ch., 101

Ashdown Ho., Berks., 905
Ashdown Ho., Sussex, 507
Ashford, Kent
  Ch., 232
  housing, 103
Ashford, Middlx., Ch., 861
Ashiesteel, Selkirks., bridge, 760
Ashley Park, Surrey, 629, 870
Ashley, Staffs., mont., 797
Ashridge Park, Herts., 874, 951,
  962; Column, 962
Ashtead Park, Surrey, 125
Ashton-under-Lyne, Lancs.
  Ch., 74
  ho., 75
  St. Peter's Ch., 353
Ashton-in-Makerfield, Lancs.,
  Holy Trinity Ch., 614
Ashton-on-Mersey, Cheshire, Ch.,
  811
Ashton-by-Sutton, Cheshire, Ch.,
  693
Ashurst Lodge, Surrey, 488
Ashwell, Herts., Vicarage, 600
Ashwick, Som., Ch., 846
Aske Hall, Yorks., 147, 194;
  Temple, 333, 492
Askham, Westmld., Ch., 744
Askham Hall, Yorks., 192
Askham Richard, Yorks., mont.,
  577
Askrigg, Yorks., Ch., 778
Aspley Guise, Beds., Ch., 906n.;
  mont., 906
Astbury, Cheshire, rectory, 84
Astley, Warwicks., Ch., 484
Astley Hall, Lancs., 874
Aston, Staffs.
  Ch., 840
  Ho., 807, 841
Aston Hall, Salop., 949
Aston, Warwicks.
  Ch., 213, 287; mont., 345
  Hall, 140–1
Aston, Yorks.
  Hall, 109, 195, 641
  Rectory, 195
Aston Sandford, Bucks., Rectory,
  375
Aston Subedge, Glos., Ch., 465
Aston-by-Sutton, Cheshire, Ch.,
  875
Astrop Park, Northants., 770
Aswarby, Lincs.
  Ch., 119
  Park, 488
Atcham, Salop.
  Bridges, 373, 410
  Workhouse, 407
Atherstone, Warwicks.
  Ch., 235
  Dominican Convent, 877n.
Atherton Hall, Lancs., 860
Attingham Hall (Park), Salop.,
  583, 682, 780
Attwaters, Kent, 256
Atworth, Wilts., Ch., 352
Auberies, Essex, 393
Auchans, Ayrshire, ho., 862
Auchencruive Ho., Ayrshire, 53
Auchindinny, Midlothian, 154
Auchinraith, Lanarks., 382
Auchmacoy Ho., Aberdeens., 164,
  761
Auchmore Ho., Perths., 288
Auchterarder Ho., Perths., 164
Auchtergaven, Perths., Ch., 782
Auchtertool, Fife, Manse, 358

Audley End, Essex, 52, 231, 276,
  294, 368, 393, 422–3, 448,
  455, 633, 730, 852; lodge,
  693; temple, 139
Aughton Hospital, Yorks., 195
Ault Hucknall, Derbys., mont.,
  764
Averham, Notts., Rectory, 626
Avington, Hants., Rectory, 351
Avontown Ho., W. Lothian, 100
Awbridge Danes Water, Hants.,
  boat-ho., 331
Aylesbury, Bucks.
  Ch., 648
  County Hall, 391
Aylesford, Kent
  Friars (The), 819
  hos., 882
Aylestone, Leics., Rectory, 308,
  622
Aylsham, Norfolk, workhouse,
  271
Aynho, Northants.
  Ch., 539, 905
  Park, 69, 529, 539, 770
Ayot St. Lawrence, Herts., Ch.,
  684
Ayr
  Academy, 698
  Assembly Rooms, 624, 698
  Bridge, 781
  Ch., 698
  Ch. (New), 382
  County Buildings, 862
  ho., 781
  Market, 698
  Municipal Buildings, 385
  square (projected), 781
  Tontine Inn, 624
  Wallace Tower, 385
Ayston Hall, Rutland, 511, 718
Ayton, Yorks., bridge, 192
Ayton Ho., Berwicks., 359
Aytoun Ho., Perths., 163
Axwell Park, Durham, 105, 267,
  611

Baberton Ho., Midlothian, 567
Babraham Ho., Cambs., 387
Baburgh, Norfolk, bridge, 785
Backford Hall, Cheshire, 247
Backworth Hall, Northumb.,
  591
Badby, Northants.
  School, 944
  Vicarage, 377
Badentoy Ho., Aberdeens., 762
Badger Hall, Salop., 947
Badgeworth Court, Glos., 692
Badminton, Glos.
  Ch., 301
  Ho., 344, 493, 798, 934, 961
  Swangrove, 798
  Worcester Lodge, 493
Badsworth, Yorks.
  Hall, 196
  Rectory, 456
Bagden Lodge, Wilts., 769
Bagillt, Flints., Ch., 878
Baginton Hall, Warwicks., 750
Bagots Park, Staffs., lodge, 842
Bagshot, Surrey
  Park, 612, 770; lodge, 472
  St. Anne's Chapel, 621
Bailbrook Ho., Som., 682
Bakewell, Derbys., Ch., 313, 655,
  954

Bala, Merioneths., Workhouse,
  476
Balavil Ho., Inverness., 55
Balbardie Ho., W. Lothian, 55
Balbirnie, Fife
  Ho., 87, 241, 260, 701
  Manse, 87
Balcarres Ho., Fife, 165
Balcaskie Ho., Fife, 154, 163
Baldersby Park, Yorks., 107, 184,
  207, 301
Baldornie Tower, I. of W., 715
Baldovan Ho., Angus, 532
Baldovie, Angus, 645
Balfron, Stirlings., Ch., 416
Balgowan, Perths., 810
Balgregan Ho., Wigtowns., 58
Balham Hill, Surrey, ho., 617
Balhary Ho., Perths., 201
Balhazy, Kirkcud., 54
Balintore Castle, Angus, 167
Ballater Bridge, Aberdeens., 821
Balliad, Perths., 525
Ballinkeel Ho., Ireland, 698
Balloch Castle, Dunb., 526
Ballochmyle Ho., Ayrshire, 46
Balls Park, Herts., 79, 787
Ballydrain, Ireland, 118
Ballykelly, Ireland
  Ch., 798
  Dispensary, 798
  Model Farm, 798
  School, 798
Ballymahon, Ireland, villa, 501
Ballymoe, Ireland, fort, 822
Ballymote, Ireland, market-ho.,
  etc., 609
Ballyscullion, Ireland, 718
Balmoral, Aberdeens., 762
Balmuto Ho., Fife, 100
Balnaboth Ho., Angus, 887
Balnamoon Ho., Angus, 163
Balruddery Ho., Angus, 587
Balveny Ho., Banffs., 58, 341
Bamburgh, Castle, Northumb.,
  268
Bamff Ho., Perths., 165
Bampton, Oxon.
  parsonage, 391
  Town Hall, 896
Bampton, Westmld., Ch., 60
Bampton Aston, Oxon., Ch., 363
Banagher, Ireland, Ch., 798
Banbury, Oxon.
  Ch., 223, 227, 273; mont., 372
  Christ Ch., 847
  Wesleyan Chapel, 110
  Workhouse, 487
Banchory Ho., Aberdeens., 762
Bandirran Ho., Perths., 887
Banff
  Academy, 699
  Castle, 46
  North of Scotland Bank, 736
  St. Andrew's Episcopal Ch.,
    737
  Tolbooth, 46
  Trinity & Alvah Ch., 669
Bangor, Caern.
  Castle, 166
  Cathedral, 318, 380, 390, 844,
    959; mont., 693
  Dispensary, 936
  National School, 380
  Penrhyn Arms Hotel, 936
  St Mary's Ch. (R.C.), 723
  Town Hall, 166
Bangor Iscoed, Flints., Ch., 841

Bank Ho., Newbiggin, Durham, 268
Banks Hall, Cumb., 500
Bannatyne Ho., Angus, 567
Banner Cross, Yorks., 967
Bannister Lodge, Hants., 814
Bantry, Ireland, Ch., 488
Barcombe, nr. Paignton, Devon, 254
Barcombe, Sussex
   farmho., 940
   Sutton Hurst, 563
Bardsea, Lancs., Ch. 876
Barham Court, Kent, 507
Barholm, Kirkcud., 54
Barkby, Leics., Ch., 497
Barking, Essex, Ho. of Correction, 463
Barkingside, Essex, Holy Trinity Ch., 119
Barkston, Lincs., Rectory, 505
   (bis)
Barlaston, Staffs.
   Ch., 383
   Hall, 817
Barlow, Derbys., Vicarage, 897
Barmeath, Ireland, 763
Barming, Kent, Rectory, 393
Barmoor Castle, Northumb., 624
Barmore, Argylls., 647
Barmouth, Merioneths.
   Ch., 406
   School, 476
Barn Elms, Surrey, ho., 536, 539, 854
Barnbarrow, Wigtowns., 525
Barnes, Surrey
   Castelnau estate, 508
   ho., 72
   Manor Ho. Hotel, 237
   Workhouse, 237
Barnet, Herts., Leathersellers' Almshouses, 417
Barney, Norfolk, bridge, 785
Barningham Hall, Norfolk, 682
Barnoldswick, Yorks., St. James's Ch., 67
Barns Ho., Peebles., 586n.
Barnsley, Yorks.
   Ch., 74
   Commercial Bldngs., 969
   Methodist Chapel, 738
   New Lodge, 196
   Oddfellows' Hall, 969
   St. George's Ch., 690
   St. Mary's Ch., 690
   Shambles, 642
Barnsley Park, Glos., 481, 583
Barnstaple, Devon, Guildhall, 510
Barnton Castle, Midlothian, 55, 59, 382
Baron Hill, Anglesey, 393, 957
Baron's Court, Ireland, 769, 781
Barr Hall, Staffs., 583
Barr Ho., Argylls., 358
Barrells, Warwicks., 125
Barrington, Cambs., Ch., 863
Barrington Hall, Essex, 685, 717
Barrington Park, Glos., 477
Barrogill Castle, Caithness, 162
Barrowby Hall, Yorks., 301
Barskimming, Ayrshire, 382
Barston, Warwicks., bridge, 592
Bartley Green, Worcs., Ch., 589
Barton, Yorks., Ch., 123
Barton Hall, Suffolk, 207
Barton-on-Humber, Lincs., Prospect Place, 588

Barton-upon-Irwell, Lancs., St. Catherine's Ch., 878
Barwick-in-Elmet, Yorks., Ch., 325
Basildon Ho. (Park), Berks., 195, 618
Basingstoke, Hants., Town Hall, 954
Basket Lodge, Hants., 880
Bass Rock, 152
Bassingbourne Hall, Essex, 177, 717
Bassingham, Lincs., Ch., 106
Baston Ho., Kent, 173
Baswich, Staffs., Ch., 842
Bath
   Abbey Cemetery Chapel, 537
   Abbey Ch., 119, 254, 330, 536; Birde's Oratory, 157
   Abbey Church Yard, ho., 364
   Abbey St., 457
   Alfred St., 911
   All Saints' Chapel, Lansdown, 614
   Argyle Bldngs., 85
   Argyle Chapel, 86, 351
   Argyle Church Schools, 352
   Argyle St., 85
   Assembly Rooms (Lindsey's), 910
   Assembly Rooms (Lower), 306, 475, 494, 846, 895
   Assembly Rooms (New), 911
   Avon St., 787
   Bath St., 86
   Baths, 261, 536, 911
   Bathwick Grange, 352
   Bathwick St., 85
   Beauford Sq., 787
   Beaufort Bldngs., London Rd., 302
   Bennett St., 911
   Bloomfield Crescent, 541
   Bluecoat School, 494, 537
   Bridge (old), 475
   Brock St., 911
   Camden Crescent, 302
   Casa Bianca, 352
   Catherine Place, 911
   Catholic Apostolic Ch., 537
   Cavendish Crescent, 638
   Cavendish Place, 638
   Cheap St., 86
   Christ Church, Montpelier Row, 614
   Circus, 910
   Cleveland Bridge, 352
   Congregational Chapel, 352
   Corn Market, 537
   Corridor (The), 352
   Cottage Crescent, 541
   Countess of Huntingdon's Schools, 537
   Cross Bath, 85
   Cross Bath Pump Room, 85
   'Doric Ho.', 329
   Duke St., 910
   Eastern Dispensary, 352
   Entry Hill, 254
   'Fiesole', 352
   Freemasons' Hall, 895
   Gas Works, 537
   Gay St., 910
   Great Pulteney St., 85
   Green Pk. Bldngs., 613
   Grosvenor Place, 302
   Guildhall, 77, 85, 494
   Holburne Museum, 541

Bath—contd.
   Holy Trinity Ch., 526
   Hospital, 910
   Independent Chapel, 352
   Jewish Synagogue, 352
   John St., 910
   Kensington Chapel, 614
   King Edward's Grammar School, 457
   King's Bath Spring, 85
   Kingsmead Square, 787
   Kingsmead St., 787
   Kingston Baths, 457
   Lambridge Place, 302
   Lansdown Cemetery, 352
   Lansdown Crescent, 613; no. 19, 352
   Lansdown Tower, 352
   Laura Chapel, 86
   Laura Place, 85
   Lilliput Alley, 910
   Margaret Chapel, 911
   Milsom St., 457
   Monmouth St., 787
   'Montebello', 352
   National School, 526
   New Bond St., 614
   New Private Baths, 85
   New Sydney Place, 638
   North Parade, 911
   North Parade Bldngs., 457
   Northumberland Bldngs., 85
   Octagon Chapel, 521
   Old King St., 910
   Orchard St. Theatre, 613
   Oxford Row, 77
   Paragon Crescent, 77
   Partis' College, 606
   Pierrepont St., 910
   Prior Park, q.v.
   Prison, 77
   Prison (New), 537
   Pulteney Bridge, 50
   Pump Rooms, 86, 399, 683
   Pump Room Colonnade, 85
   Queen Square, 638, 910
   Rivers St., 911
   Royal Crescent, 911
   Royal Literary Institution, 846
   Royal Mineral Water Hospital, 537, 614
   Royal United Hospital, 537, 638
   Russell St., 911
   St. Catherine's Hermitage, 302
   St. Catherine's Hospital, 536
   St. James's Ch., 537, 613
   St. James's Sq., 613
   St. James's St. South, 494
   St. John's Court, 364
   St. John's Hospital, 910
   St. Mark's Ch., Lyncombe, 536
   St. Mary's Chapel, 910
   St. Mary's Ch., Bathwick, 638
   St. Mary's Schools, 537
   St. Matthew's Ch., Widcombe, 537
   St. Michael's Ch., 536
   St. Michael-extra-Muros, 399
   St. Michael's Cemetery Chapels, 537
   St. Saviour's Ch., 638
   St. Swithin's Ch., Walcot, 613
   Seymour St., 613
   Sham Castle, 475, 550
   Sion Hill Place, 638
   Sion Row, Camden Rd., 302
   Somerset Place, 302

Bath—*contd.*
Somersetshire Bldngs., 85
South Parade, 910
Stall St., 86
Summer Hill Place, 302
Sydney Gardens, 541
Sydney Hotel, 541, 638
Sydney Place, 85
Technical College, 537
Tepid Swimming Bath, 171
Theatre Royal, 186, 251, 614
Town Hall, 104, 520
Trim St., 364
Union St., 86
Victoria Park, 254; obelisk, 536
Walcot Methodist Chapel, 458
West of England Club, 306
Weymouth Ho., 494
Wood St., 910
Workhouse, 487
Bathampton, Som., Ch., 475
Batheaston, Som., Bailbrook
Lodge, 302
Bathford, Som.
Ch., 519
Spa, 911
Titanbarow Logia
(Whitehaven), 911
Bathgate, W. Lothian, Academy,
260
Batley Carr, Yorks.
Ch., 210
parsonage, 216
Battle Bridge, Essex, 464
Battlefield(s) Ho., nr. Bath, 277,
541, 911
Battlesden Ho., Beds., 544
Battyford, Yorks., Christ Ch., 123
Baverstock, Wilts.
Ch., 691
Rectory, 648
Bawdeswell, Norfolk, Ch., 145
Bay Ho., Hants., 174
Bayfordbury, Herts., 63
Bayham Abbey, Sussex, 246, 682
Baylies Ho., Bucks., 455, 508, 708
Baynards Park, Surrey, 692
Baystonhill, Salop., Ch., 406
Baythorn Bridge, Essex, 464
Beachborough Ho., Kent, 782
Beachley, Glos., Ch., 315
Beam Bridge Aqueduct, Devon,
361
Beaminster, Dorset
Holy Trinity Ch., 202
Manor Ho., 846
Workhouse, 886
Bear Place, Berks., 281
Bearwood, Berks., 174, 715
Beath, Fife, Ch., 530
Beattock Bridge, Dumfriess., 821
Beaudesert, Staffs., 655, 729, 936,
946
Beaufront Castle, Northumb.,
267; estate, 862
Beaulieu Lodge, Middlx., 619
Beaumanor Park, Leics., 556, 670,
880
Beaumaris, Anglesey
Ch., 380
Gaol, 877
Green, terrace, 380
Victoria Terrace, 878
Beaumont Lodge, Berks., 294,
341, 934
Beauport, Sussex, 769
Beaver Hall, Middlx., 625
Becca Hall, Yorks., 521

Beccles, Suffolk
Assembly Rooms, 324
Independent Chapel, 305
Theatre, 324
Beckenham, Kent
Place, 454
villa, 173
Beckett Park, Berks., 77, 219, 306,
519, 550–1, 793, 933
Beckett Park College, Yorks., 610
Beddington, Surrey
Ho. (Park), 65 and n., 323, 546
Rectory, 145, 619
Schools, 145
Bedford
Barham estate, 103
Bridge, 906
Gaol (County), 906
Gaol (New), 292
Harpur School, 287
Holy Trinity Ch., 145
House of Industry, 906
Infirmary, 906
Lunatic Asylum, 906
School, 116
Swan Hotel, 426
Bedwas, Mon., bridge, 286
Beech Hill Ho., Essex, 103
Beech Ho., Hants., 887
Beechwood, Midlothian, 734
Beechwood Park, Herts., 109, 166,
245, 499, 561, 562
Beenham, Berks., Vicarage, 111
Belan Ho., Ireland, 186
Belcombe Court, Wilts., 910
Belfast
Academical Institution, 767
Assembly Room, 816
College, 353
St. Anne's Ch., 419
Belfield, Dorset, 242
Belford, Northumb.
Ch., 265
Hall, 267, 611
Belgrave Bridge, Leics., 622
Belhaven Ho., E. Lothian, 59
Belhus Hall, Essex, 520, 550
Bell Rock lighthouse, 524
Bellamont Forest, Ireland, 629
Bellamour Hall, Staffs., 838
Belle Isle, Westmld., 642
Belleville Ho., Inverness., 55, 456
Bellevue, Co. Wicklow, Ireland, 718
Bellingham, Northumb.
bridge, 362
Ch. (R.C.), 265
Belmont, Hants., ho., 137
Belmont, Kent
cottages ('New York'), 642
Park, 958
Belmont, Midlothian, 647
Belmont Castle, Essex, 456
Belmont Ho., Herefs., 411n., 948
Belper, Derbys.
bridge, 800
St. Peter's Ch., 374
Belsay, Northumb.
Castle, 554
village, 554
School, 554
Belton, Lincs.
Ch., 962
Cross, 972
Ho., 539, 774, 797, 904, 946,
961
Belvedere, Kent, 733, 796–7, 866
Belvedere Ho., Ireland, 934
Belvidere Ho., Midlothian, 57

Belvil Ho., Inverness., *see*
Belleville Ho.
Belvoir Castle, Leics., 88, 539,
827, 873, 938, 951
Bembridge, I. of W., Ch., 582,
603
Bemerton, Wilts., Rectory, 769
Ben Bhragie, Sutherld., statue,
168
Benacre Hall, Suffolk, 137, 138
Benfieldside, Durham, Ch., 266
Benhall Lodge, Suffolk, 324, 464
Benham Place, Berks., 139, 147,
425, 534
Beningborough Hall, Yorks., 826–
7
Bennington, Lincs., Rectory, 844
Bensford Bridge, Leics., 496
Benson, Oxon., Ch., 648, 832–3
Bentham Hill, Kent, 173
Bentley, Hants., Ch., 278
Bentley Priory, Middlx., 744, 769
Benton Ho., Northumb., 687
Benwell, Northumb.
Grove, 266
St. James's Ch., 265
Tower, 267
Beoley Hall, Worcs., 714
Berechurch Hall, Essex, 956
Bergh Apton, Norfolk, Ch., 145
Berkeley, Glos., Ch., 215
Berkley Ho., Som., 447, 666
Bernera, Harris, Ch., 821
Bernera, Inverness., barracks, 457,
705
Berriedale, Caithness, Ch., 821
Berrington, Salop.
Hospital, 407
Rectory (Hall), 142
Berrington Hall, Herefs., 425
Berrow, Som., Ch., 537
Berry Hill, Glos., Ch., 650
Berrymede Priory, Middlx., 168,
724
Berwick Ho., Salop., 467, 577,
752
Berwick Place, Essex, 435
Berwick-on-Tweed
Barracks, 854
Ch., 965
Palace, 300
Townhouse, 268, 907, 917
Besford Court, Worcs., 706
Bessingby Hall, Yorks., 245, 246
Betchworth, Surrey
Bridge, 506
Castle, 770
Ch., 773
Ho., 245
Bethelnie, Aberdeens., Ch., 761
Betley Court, Staffs., 584
Betteshanger Ho., Kent, 527
Bettws Bridge, Glam., 286
Bettws-y-Coed, Caern., Waterloo
Bridge, 821
Bettws yn Ros, Denbighs., Ch.,
878
Bevere Ho., Worcs., 83, 481
Beverley, Yorks.
Assembly Rooms, 190
Beverley Arms Hotel, 548
Charity School, 731
Court Ho., 107, 868
Eastgate, ho., 184, 826
Gaol, 107
Guildhall, 548, 564
Lairgate, nos. 72–4, 548
Market Cross, 731

Beverley, Yorks.—contd.
  Minster, 404, 565, 691, 826
  North Bar Within, no. 40, 548
  North Bar Without, no. 39, 548
  Register Ho., 107
  Routh's Hospital, 565
Beverston, Glos.
  Ch., 858
  Nesley Farm, 859
Bewdley, Worcs.
  Bridge, 738, 821
  St. Anne's Ch., 915
  Town Hall, 738
Bexhill, Sussex, Rectory, 393
Bibury, Glos.
  Court, 954
  Race-stand, 605
Bicester, Oxon., Workhouse, 648
Bickleigh, Devon, Ch., 321
Bickley Place, Kent, 576, 744
Bicton Heath, Salop., Lunatic
  Asylum, 405
Bicton Lodge, Devon, 950
Bidborough, Kent, Rectory
  ('Wyatts'), 949
Biddlestone, Northumb., 267
Biddulph, Staffs., Ch., 842
Bideford, Devon, Workhouse, 219
Bidford, Warwicks., Ch., 507
Bidston Hill, Cheshire, signal ho.,
  521
Biel, E. Lothian, 76
Bierly, Yorks., Ch., 191
Bifrons, Essex, 418
Bifrons Ho., Kent, 439, 755
Bignor Park, Sussex, 393
Bilham Hall, Yorks., 673
Billericay, Essex, Independent
  Chapel, 305
Billesdon, Leics., Ch., 906
Bill Hill, Berks., 137
Billing Hall, Northants., 195, 377
Billingbear, Berks., 715
Bilsdean Bridge, E. Lothian, 157
Bilsington, Kent, obelisk, 232
Bilston, Staffs.
  Parsonage, 354
  St. Leonard's Ch., 354
  St. Mary's Ch., 354
Bineham, Sussex, 174
Binfield, Berks.
  Lodge, 639
  Rectory, 331
Bingley, Yorks., Ch., 673
Birch, Lancs.
  St. Mary's Ch., 670
  Schools, 811
Birch Hall, Essex, 435
Birchington-on-Sea, Kent,
  bungalows, 813
Birdforth, Yorks., bridge, 192
Birdingbury Hall, Warwicks., 842
Birdsall, Yorks., Ch., 600
Birkenhead, Cheshire
  Assembly Rooms, 878
  Baptist Chapel, 230
  Christ Ch., Claughton, 456
  Congregational Ch., 230
  Hamilton Square, 359
  Holy Trinity Ch., 247
  Magistrates' Offices, 670
  Monks' Ferry Hotel, 878
  Raby Hall, Rock Ferry, 291
  St. Anne's Ch., 230
  St. Mary's Ch., 690
  St. Peter's Ch., 442
  Town Hall, 670
Birkenshaw, Yorks., Ch., 73

Birkwood Ho., Lanarks., 82
Birmingham
  All Saints Ch., Nineveh, 691
  Amphitheatre, 845
  Assembly Rooms, 719
  Aston Waterworks, 281
  Athenaeum, 427
  Bank of Birmingham, 281
  Birmingham Banking Co., 692
  Birmingham & Midland Bank,
    281
  Bishop Ryder's Ch., 691
  Blue Coat School, 672
  Builders' Guildhall, 878
  Bull Ring Pump, 427
  Cavalry Barracks, 672
  Cemetery, 281
  Christ Ch., 598, 774
  Crescent (The), 672
  Curzon St. Station, 387
  Deaf & Dumb Asylum, 692
  Dispensary, 427
  Exhibition Room, 692
  Grammar School, 901
  Gunbarrel Proof Ho., 436
  Hen & Chickens Hotel, 944
  Holy Trinity Ch., Bordesley,
    353
  Holy Trinity School, Bordesley,
    692
  Islington Row, no. 12, 692
  Jones's Manufactory, 887
  King Edward's School, 91, 217,
    353, 420
  lead works, 415
  Library (New), 887
  Library (Old), 427
  Livery St., warehouse, 959
  Market Hall, 281
  Mechanics' Institute, 304
  Meeting Ho., 887
  Midland Bank, 692
  National Provincial Bank, 281
  News Room, 692
  Norwich Union Office, 281
  Pantechnetheca, 887
  Post Office, 281
  Public Office, 281, 427
  Queen's College, 98
  Queen's Hospital, 98
  St. Bartholomew's Ch., 420
  St. George's Ch., 690
  St. George's Ch., Edgbaston,
    281, 723–4
  St. Martin's Ch., 213, 388, 420
  St. Mary's Ch., 304, 635
  St. Matthew's Ch., Duddeston,
    823
  St. Paul's Ch., 304, 354
  St. Peter's Ch., Dale End, 281,
    691
  St. Philip's Church, 69
  St. Thomas's Ch., 691
  Society of Artists, 692
  Theatre Royal, 102, 133, 180,
    262, 427, 598, 719, 959
  Town Hall, 281, 304, 689, 877,
    878
  Warwick Ho., New St., 823
  Wellington Rd., villa, 589
Birstall, Leics., Ch., 622
Birtley, Durham
  Ch. (R.C.), 266
  Hall, 266
Bisham, Berks., Ch., 503
Bishop Auckland, Durham
  Castle, 109, 194, 236, 503, 703,
    950

Bishop Auckland, Durham—
  contd.
  St. Anne's Chapel, 77, 945
Bishop Burton, Yorks., 132
Bishop Middleham, Durham,
  mont., 120
Bishop Thornton, Yorks., Ch.,
  600
Bishops Castle, Salop., Town
  Hall, 83
Bishop's Cleeve, Glos., Ch., 418
Bishop's Hull, Som., Ch., 202
Bishop's Lavington, Wilts., Ch.,
  882
Bishop's Stortford, Herts.
  Corn Exchange, 857
  Workhouse, 487
Bishops Wood Ho., Herefs.,
  962
Bishopscourt, Isle of Man, 141
Bishopstone, Hants., Rectory
  (Ho.), 526
Bishopstrow Ho., Wilts., 638
Bishopswood, Herefs., Ch., 648
Bishopthorpe, Yorks.
  Ch., 74
  Palace, 74, 258
Bishopton, Warwicks., Ch., 507
Bishopwearmouth, Durham
  Ch., 266
  Rectory, 268
  St. Thomas's Ch., 955
  School, 265
Bistre, Flints., Emmanuel Ch.,
  522
Bitterley Court, Salop., 663
Bitteswell, Leics., Almshouses,
  622
Bitton, Glos., Ch., 912
Bixley Hall, Norfolk, 176
Black Bourton, Oxon., Vicarage,
  364
Black Rock Villa, Lancs., 876
Blackadder Ho., Berwicks., 346,
  645, 781
Blackadder Mount, Berwicks.,
  220n.
Blackburn, Lancs.
  St. Mary's Ch. (Cathedral),
    614, 691
  St. Peter's Chapel, 614
Blackford, Som., Ch., 202
Blackheath, Kent
  'Brooklands', Blackheath Park,
    753
  Brunswick Ho., 524
  Chesterfield Ho., 866
  Colonnade Ho., 725
  cottage orné, 649
  Dartmouth Hill, ho., 400
  ho., 173
  landscape-gardening, 618
  Morden Coll., 485, 792, 922n.
  Paragon (The), 725
  Ranger's Ho., 866
  St. Michael & All Angels
    Chapel, 754
  Westcombe Ho., 413, 561
  Wricklemarsh, 454
Blacktoft, Yorks.
  Ch., 391
  Vicarage, 449
Blackwell, Derbys., Ch., 423
Blackwell Bridge, Durham, 362
Bladon Castle, Derbys., 961
Blagdon (Hall), Northumb., 122,
  610, 947
Blair Adam, Kinross., 45, 56, 149

Blair Atholl, Perths.
'Atholl Arms' Hotel, 260
Blair Cottages, 261
Castle, 272, 562, 707, 780, 799, 906
Ch., 288
Blair Crambeth, Kinross., 56
Blair Drummond, Perths., 261, 296, 530; Corner, 241; toll-ho., 701
Blairquhan, Ayrshire, 162, 861
Blairs Ho., Kinc., 325
Blaise Castle, see Bristol
Blaise Hamlet, Glos., 584
Blake Hall, Essex, 95
Blandford Forum, Dorset
Ch., 96, 843
East St., no. 75, 96
Greyhound Inn, 96
Pump-house, 96
Red Lion Inn, 96
Town Hall, 96, 826
Blandford St. Mary, Dorset, mont., 201
Blanerne, Berwicks., 163
Blankney Hall, Lincs., 899
Blatherwycke Hall, Northants., 695, 932
Bleasdale, Lancs., Ch., 258
Bledlow, Bucks., Ch., 374
Bledlow Ridge, Bucks., Chapel, 111
Blendon Hall, Kent, 729
Blendworth Lodge, Hants., 351
Blenheim Palace, Oxon., 66, 78, 87, 403–4, 477, 792, 833, 835, 850–1, 852, 965; Aviary, 376; Bladon Bridge, 207; Grand Bridge, 630, 852; Chapel, mont., 494; Column, 310, 404, 414, 561, 835; Ditchley Gate, 965; garden bldngs., 207; High Lodge, 146; Park Farm, 146; Temples, 207, 965; Woodstock Gate, 231, 404, 630, 835
Blenkinsopp, Northumb., 267
Bletchingdon Ho., Oxon., 518
Bletchingley, Surrey, Pendrell Ho., 457
Bletchley, Bucks.
Ch., 284
Rectory, 393
Blickling, Norfolk
Ch., mont., 120
Hall, 137, 167, 281, 448, 511
mausoleum, 125
Blindley Heath, Surrey, Ch., 882
Blithfield Ho., Staffs., 167, 797, 839, 842, 956
Blockley, Worcs., Ch., 438, 914; mont., 915
Bloxham, Oxon., Ch., 227
Bloxholm Hall, Lincs., 858
Blundeston, Suffolk
Ch., 724
Ho., 768
Blyth Hall, Notts., 195, 804
Blythswood Ho., Renfrews., 358
Boath Ho., Nairns., 737
Bobbingworth, Essex, Ch., 171
Bockenfield Manor Ho., Northumb., 837
Boconnoc, Cornwall, 127, 565, 639, 640, 672, 768
Bodecton Park, Sussex, see Burton Park
Bodelwyddan Hall, Flints., 878

Bodicote, Oxon., Ch., 648
Bodmin, Cornwall
Assize Court, 969
Judges' Lodgings, 622
Lunatic Asylum, 319, 890
Market Ho., 392
Bodnant, Denbighs., garden ho., 788
Bodorgan, Anglesey, 232, 257
Bognor Regis, Sussex
Clarence Hotel, 103
Crescent, 103
Sudley Lodge, 730
Boharm, Banffs.
Ch., 699
School, 699
Bold Hall, Lancs., 513
Bolesworth Castle, Cheshire, 229, 576
Bolling Hall, Yorks., 195
Bollington, nr. Macclesfield, Cheshire
St. Gregory's Ch. (R.C.), 318
St. John's Ch., 408
Bolnore Ho., Sussex, 174
Bolsover, Derbys.
Castle, 538, 764
Ch.; mont., 345
Bolton, Lancs.
Emmanuel Ch., 878
'Gallery of Arts', 535
Holy Trinity Ch., 390
Bolton, Westmld., bridge, 743
Bolton Hall, Yorks. (N.R.), 954
Bolton Hall, Yorks. (W.R.), 329
Bonaly Tower, Midlothian, 647
Bonar Bridge, Sutherland, 738
Bonhill, Dunb., Ch., 82
Bonnington Ho., Lanarks., 359
Boothby Pagnell Hall, Lincs., 858
Boreham Ho., Essex, 311, 355, 435, 464, 732
Boreton Farmhouse, Salop., 187
Boscombe, Wilts., Rectory, 734
Bossall, Yorks., Vicarage, 666
Bossington Ho., Hants., 253
Bostock Hall, Cheshire, 957
Boston, Lincs.
Bridge, 678
Ch., 733
South End, hos., 198
Bosworth Hall, Leics., 125
Bothwell, Lanarks.
Castle, 623, 644
Ch., 382; mont., 758
Botleys, Surrey, 118, 236
Bottesford, Leics., bridge, 622
Bottle End, Essex, Ch., 323
Boturich Castle, Dunb., 527, 725
Boughton Hall, Northants., 497, 879
Boughton Ho., Northants., 279, 555
Boughton Monchelsea, Kent, mont., 70n.
Boulters Lock, Berks., 836
Boultibrooke, Radnors., 744
Bourn Hall, Cambs., 682
Bourne, Lincs., Sessions Ho., 151
Bourne Park, Kent, 730
Bournemouth, Hants.
Gervis estate, 172
Portman Lodge, 302
St. Peter's Ch., 843
Bourton-on-the-Water, Glos., Ch., 539
Boveridge Ho., Dorset, 302
Bow Bridge, Yorks., 192

Bowden Hall, Derbys., 502
Bowden Ho., Wilts., 950
Bowdendale, Wilts., 605
Bower Ho., Essex, 311
Bowerhouse, E. Lothian, 164
Bowhill, Selkirks., 76, 164, 759
Bowland, Midlothian, 358
Bowling, Yorks., Ch., 728
Bowness, Westmld.
Royal Hotel, 875
School, 875
Bowood Ho., Wilts., 52, 92, 225, 252, 483, 745; mausoleum, 52, 55
Box, Wilts., Ch., 253
Boxford, Suffolk, Rectory, 824
Boxmoor, Herts., Ch., 366
Boyles Court, Essex, 516
Boynton, Yorks.
Ch., 191
Hall, 131, 194
Bracondale, Norfolk, 893
Bradfield, Berks., Workhouse, 487
Bradford, Yorks.
Airedale Coll. Chapel, 665
Christ Ch., 818
Court Ho., 686
Dispensary, 73
Eastbrook Wesleyan Chapel, 127
Exchange Buildings, 353
Field Ho., 686
Grammar School, 73
Infirmary, 673
Library, 73
Market Ho., 686
Post Office Chambers, 353
Public Rooms, 353
St. James's Ch., 673
St. John's Ch., 728
St. Peter's Ch. (Cathedral), 215
Westgate Chapel, 665
Bradford-on-Avon, Wilts.
Christ Ch., 537
Vicarage, 651
Bradford Peverell, Dorset, Ch., 172
Bradley Hall, Durham, 266
Bradley Hall, Yorks., 61
Bradmore, Notts., Rancliffe Farm, 622
Bradshaw, Yorks., Ch., 213
Bradwell Lodge, Essex, 463
Bradwell Manor, Cheshire, 874
Braemar, Aberdeens.
Ch., 322
Chapel (R.C.), 526
Brafferton, Durham, Manor Ho., 505
Brafferton, Yorks.
Ch., 665
Vicarage, 665, 868
Braganstown Ho., Ireland, 763
Bramham, Yorks.
Biggin, 610
Park, 108, 910; Gothic Octagon, 504; Stables, 196, 611; Temple (Chapel), 611
Bramley, Hants., Ch., 767
Bramley, Yorks.
Ch., 210
parsonage, 210
Brampton, Hunts.,
Cottages, 375
Park, 617, 887
Schools, 618
Brampton Bierlow, Yorks., Ch., 665

Bramshaw, Hants.
  Ch., 630
  Warrens (The), 583
Bramshott, Hants.
  Ch., 386
  Grange, 859
Brancepeth Castle, Durham, 624, 971
Brand Hall, Salop., 84
Brandesbury, Middlx., 680n.
Brandeston Hall, Suffolk, 684
Brandiston, Norfolk, Ch., 120
Brandon, Suffolk, parsonage, 670
Brandon Cottage (Hotel), Warwicks., 527
Brandon Creek, Norfolk, bridge, 785
Brandsby, Yorks., Ch., 74
Branksome Tower, Dorset, 166
Brannas Lodge, Merioneths., 142
Bransgore, Hants.
  Ch., 386
  parsonage, 869
Branxholm Castle, Roxb., 165
Brasted Place, Kent, 54
Brattleby Hall, Lincs., 970
Braughing, Herts., mont., 797
Braunston, Northants., Rectory, 847
Braunstone Hall, Leics., 601
Brawl Castle, Caithness, 167
Braxted Park, Essex, 393, 464, 817
Bray, Berks.
  ho., 111
  Jesus Hospital, 85
Braziers, Oxon, 391
Brearton, Yorks., Ch., 665
Brechin, Angus
  Castle, 282, 500; Image Bridge, 158
  Mechanics' Institute, 969
Brecon, Market Ho., 43
Bredfield, Suffolk, rectory, 111
Breedon-on-the-Hill, Leics., Ch., 952
Brenchley, Kent, Ch., 556
Brentford, Middlx.
  Bridge, 499, 538
  St. George's Chapel, 496
  St. Laurence's Ch., 388
  Schools, 66, 563
  Workhouse, 857
Brentwood, Essex
  Schools, 721
  St. Thomas's Ch., 721
Brenty Hill, Glos., 682
Brereton, Staffs., Ch., 842
Bretby Hall (Park), Derbys., 103, 961–2
Bretton Hall, Yorks., 76, 95, 196, 296, 565, 962
Bridehead, Dorset, 701
Bridge of Allan, Stirlings.
  Bellmoir Ho., 230
  Inn, 784
Bridge of Earn, Perths., village, 168
Bridgnorth, Salop.
  Almshouses, 632
  Bridge, 632, 740
  St. Mary's Ch., 820
  Theatre, 740
Bridgwater, Som.
  Baptist Ch., 274
  Baths, 542
  Castle Street, 314, 428
  Chandos Street, 428

Bridgwater, Som.—contd.
  Holy Trinity Ch., 202
  Lions (The), 428
  Market Hall, 127, 411
  St. John's Ch., 145
Bridlington, Yorks.
  Baths, 542
  Harbour, 107
Bridport, Dorset
  Town Hall, 845
  Workhouse, 886
Brierly Hill, Staffs., Chapel, 857
Brigg, Lincs., hos., 564
Brightling Park, Sussex, 744
Brightlingsea, Essex, St. James's Ch., 540
Brighton
  All Souls Ch., 547
  Arundel Terrace, 176
  Baths, 349, 836
  Bedford Hotel, 232
  Brunswick Town, 221
  Castle Hotel, 242
  Cemetery, 226
  Chapel, 232
  Chapel Royal, 242
  Chichester Terrace, 176; no. 12, 488
  Christ Church, 212
  Congregational Chapel, 891
  crescent, 177
  esplanade, 892
  Furze Hill Villa, 173
  Gothic House, 176
  Hanover Crescent, 892
  Holy Trinity Chapel, 892
  ho. (Mrs. Fitzherbert), 653
  Hospital, 91
  Kemp Town, 176, 244, 488, 891
  Lewes Crescent, 176
  King's Rd., hos., 892
  Library, 836
  London Road Chapel, 738
  Montpelier Crescent, 892
  Montpelier Rd., nos. 53–56, 892
  New St., 114
  Old Ship Tavern, 349
  Oriental Place, 892
  Oriental Terrace, 892
  Park Crescent, 892
  Portland Place, 176
  Priory Lodge, 176
  Queen Adelaide Crescent, 172
  Richmond Terrace, 891
  Royal Newburgh Assembly Rooms, 892
  Royal Pavilion, 351, 425, 584, 653
  Royal Pavilion Hotel, 892
  St. Alban's Ho., 892
  St. George's Chapel, 176
  St. John the Evangelist Ch., 212
  St. Margaret's Ch., 216
  St. Mary's Chapel, 216, 892
  St. Peter's Ch., 91
  School, Church St., 547
  Silwood House, 892
  Silwood Place, 892
  Steyne (The), no. 26, 892; Victoria Fountain, 892
  Sussex Sq., 176; nos. 19–20, 488
  Town Hall, 232
  Unitarian Chapel, New Rd., 892

Brighton—contd.
  Victoria Terrace, 892
  villa, 173
  Western Lodge, 891
  Western Terrace, no. 1, 176, 892
Brinkburn Priory, Northumb., 267
Bristol
  All Saints Ch., 413, 627, 798, 830; monts., 345, 735
  Arcades, 315
  Arno's Court, 626
  Assembly Rooms, 379
  Assembly Rooms, Clifton, 364
  Athenaeum, 315
  Bank of England, 224
  Baptist College, 65, 348
  Bath St., 626
  Baths, etc., Clifton, 727
  Bell Lane, hos., 651
  Berkeley Crescent, 626
  Berkeley Sq., 626
  Bishop's Coll., 277
  Blaise Castle, 226, 575, 627
  Blind Asylum, 692
  Bridewell, 651
  Bridge, 141, 627, 788, 843
  Bridge St., 626
  Broad St., shops, 743
  Brunel Ho., 651
  Brunswick Sq., 843
  Buckingham Baptist Ch., 651
  Caledonia Place, Clifton, 315
  Camp Ho., Clifton, 277
  Cathedral, monts., 612, 797
  Cattle Market, 651
  Cemetery, 846
  Chapel Row, 843
  Charlotte St., 626
  Christ Ch., 627
  Christ Ch., Clifton, 278
  Circular Stables, 863
  City Hotel, 315
  Clare St., 626
  Clifton Bridge, 70
  Clifton Court, 379
  Clifton Hill Ho., 626, 866
  Clifton, terraces, etc., 846
  Clifton Vale, 315
  College St., 627
  Colston Hall, 315
  Colston's School, 174
  Commercial Rooms, 175
  Congregational Chapel, 70
  Coopers' Hall, 378
  Cornwallis Crescent, 364
  Council Ho., 278, 743, 798, 829–30
  County Bridewell, 114
  Court of Justice, 278, 651
  Custom Ho., 972
  Deanery, 475
  Dr. White's Hospital, 141
  Dowry Chapel, 843
  Dowry Sq., 843
  Exchange, 258, 364, 378, 626, 843, 911
  Excise Office, 415
  Female Orphan Asylum, 144, 277
  Foster's Almshouses, 315
  Friends' Meeting Ho., 843
  Gaol, 651, 727
  Goldney Ho., Clifton, 626
  Great George St., 626; no. 7, 627
  Guildhall, 651
  High St., 626
  Holy Trinity Ch., 691

Bristol—contd.
Holy Trinity Ch., Hotwells, 224
Hotel, Clifton, 364
Independent Chapel, Clifton, 392
King Sq., 843
Literary & Philosophical Inst., 224
Litfield Ho., Clifton, 277
Lodge St., 626
Lower Park Row, ho., 651
Mall (The), 302
Mall Assembly Rooms, Clifton, 364, 480
Markets, 348
Meat Market, 651
Merchants' Hall, 627
New Mall, Clifton, 316
Orphan Houses, 315
Oyster Market, 627n.
Park St., 626
Police Station, 651
Portland Sq., 376
Post Office, 348
Prince St., no. 40, 379
Pro-Cathedral (R.C.), 352
Queen Elizabeth's Hospital School, 316
Queen Sq., 709
Red Maids' School, 316
Redland Court, 258, 787
Redland Chapel, 378–9, 626, 788
Royal Fort, 141, 626, 680n.
Royal Infirmary, 376, 627
Royal West of England Academy, 846
Royal Western Hotel, 651
St. Andrews Ch., Clifton, 315
St. Augustine's Ch., 627
St. Barnabas parsonage, 670
St. George's Ch., see Kingswood
St. George's Ch., Brandon Hill, 744
St. James's Market, 627
St. Mark's Ch., Easton, 278
St. Mary-on-the-Quay Ch., 651
St. Mary Redcliffe Ch., 788
St. Matthew's Ch., Kingsdown, 691
St. Michael's Ch., 627
St. Nicholas Ch., 141, 627
St. Paul's Church, 66, 376
St. Paul's Ch., Bedminster, 277
St. Philip & St. Jacob's Ch., 70
St. Thomas's Ch., 66
St. Werburgh's Ch., 627
Salvation Army Home, 144, 277
Savile Place, Clifton, 277
Savings Bank, Clifton, 278
Stapleton Ho., 174
Stokes Croft, ho., 348
Theatre Royal, 626
Tolsey, see Council Ho.
Trinity Almshouses, 315
Tyndall's Park, 278, 944
Union St., 626
Unitarian Chapel, 114
Upper Berkeley Place, 626
Victoria Rooms, 277
Victoria St., 651
Wallis's Wall, 863
Wesley's Chapel, 843
Windsor Terrace, 302
Brixton, Devon, 890
Brixton Lodge, Surrey, 245
Brixworth Ho., Northants., 763
Broad Campden, Glos., hos., 438
Broadfield Hall, Herts., 402

Broadlands, Hants., 146–7, 425
Broadlease, Wilts., 605
Broadmeadows Ho., Berwicks., 346, 382
Broadstairs, Kent
Holy Trinity Ch., 89
Library, 89
Maisonette, 813
Broadway, Worcs., tower, 949
Broadwell, Glos.
Ch., 605
ho., 605
Broadwell Grove, Oxon., 76, 605
Broadwindsor, Dorset, Vicarage, 351
Brockenhurst Ho. (Park), Hants., 642, 687
Brocket Hall, Herts., 611, 612
Brockhampton, nr. Bromyard, Herefs.
Chapel, 177
Hall, 663
Brocklesby Park, Lincs., 147, 167, 810, 963; mausoleum, 952
Brodick Castle, Arran, 167, 359
Brodie Castle, Morays., 163
Brogyntyn, Salop., 369, 751, 859
Broke Hall, Suffolk, 596, 949
Brome Hall, Suffolk, 939
Bromham, Wilts., Ch., 537
Bromley, Kent
Ch., 754
Hill Ho., 701
Holy Trinity Ch., 434
Plaistow Lodge, 516
Quernmore School, 516
Redwood Ho., 295
Workhouse, 295
Bromsberrow, Glos.
Ho., 788
Place, 95
Brook, Kent, 218
Brooke, Norfolk
Ch., 145
Hall, 896
Brooklands, Surrey, 242
Brooksby, Leics.
Hall, 644
Railway Station, 622
Brookwood Cemetery, Surrey, 829
Broom Hill, Kent, 173
Broome Park, Kent, 947
Broome Park, Northumb., 267
Broomfield Lodge, Essex, 464
Broomhall, Fife, 46, 329, 397, 467, 653, 777
Broseley, Salop.
Ch.; mont., 304
Lawns (The), 664
Brough Hall, Yorks., 74, 315; Chapel (R.C.), 123
Brougham Hall, Westmld., 234
Broughton, Lancs., Ch., 706
Broughton, Lincs., Rectory, 813
Broughton, Oxon., Rectory, 228, 847
Broughton Hall, Yorks., 76, 876
Broughton Poggs, Oxon., Rectory, 605
Brownlow Ho., Ireland, 647
Brownslade Ho., Pemb., 822
Brownston, Devon, Ch., 890
Browsholme Hall, Yorks., 62, 961
Broxbourne, Herts., Vicarage, 721
Broxmore Ho., Wilts., 810
Broxmouth Ho., E. Lothian, 59, 595
Bruckley Castle, Aberdeens., 761

Brunstane Ho., Midlothian, 154, 531
Brunstock Ho., Cumb., 692
Bruton, Som., Ch., 447
Bryanston Ho., Dorset, 631, 947
Brymbo, Denbighs., St. Mary's Ch., 522
Brynbella, Denbighs., 545
Bryngwyn Hall, Montgom., 576
Buchanan Ho., Stirlings., 46, 56, 59, 166, 644
Buchanness Lodge, Aberdeens., 762
Buckden, Hunts.
Ch., 693
Vicarage, 515
Buckenham Hall, Norfolk, 958
Buckhaven, Fife, Ch., 161
Buckhold, Berks., Ch., 487
Buckhurst Park, Sussex, 682; and see Stonelands
Buckie, Banffs., Chapel, 699
Buckland Ho., Berks., 912
Buckland Filleigh Ho., Devon, 361
Buckley, Flints., Ch., 600
Buckminster Park, Leics., 721
Bude, Cornwall, Ch., 890
Bugbrook, Northants., Ch., 773
Buglawton, Cheshire, Ch., 670
Buildwas, Salop., Bridge, 821
Buile Hill, Lancs., 92
Bulbridge Ho., Wilts., 949
Bulchamp, Suffolk, Workhouse, 324
Bulstrode Park, Bucks., 951
Bulwell, Notts., Ch., 697
Bulwick Hall, Northants., 511
Bungay, Norfolk, bridge, 273
Bunny, Notts.
Almshouses, 621
Ch., 898; mont., 621
Hall (Park), 151, 621
School, 621
Vicarage, 621
Buntingford, Herts., Almshouses, 429
Buntingsdale Hall, Salop., 750
Burbage, Leics., Ch., 375
Bure Homage, Hants., 253, 271
Burfield Lodge, Som., 692
Burford, Oxon., Ch., 605
Burgh Castle, Suffolk, Ch., 724
Burgh Hall, Norfolk, 679
Burgh-upon-Bain, Lincs., vicarage, 196
Burgh-on-Sands, Cumb., Column, 505n.
Burghfield, Berks., cottage, 446
Burghley Ho., Northants., 145, 151, 262, 511, 654, 805
Burghwallis, Yorks., Rectory, 665, 868
Burley, Hants., Ch., 846
Burley-on-the-Hill, Rutland, 271, 346, 464, 529, 644
Burley-in-Wharfedale, Yorks.
Ch., 673
Chapel, 665
Burn Hall, Durham, 122, 768
Burnham Market, Norfolk, ho. (proposed), 150
Burnham Westgate Hall, Norfolk, 768
Burnley, Lancs.
Holy Trinity Ch., 857
St. Paul's Ch., 673
Burnside, Westmld., School, 876
Burntwood, Staffs., Ch., 655

Burrow Hall, Lancs., 347, 640
Burrowbridge, Som., Ch., 202
Burrswood Ho., Kent, 173
Burscough Bridge, Lancs., St.
    John's Ch., 782
Burslem, Staffs., St. Paul's Ch.,
    857
Burston, Norfolk, Rectory, 859
Burtle, Som., Ch., 202
Burton Agnes, Yorks.
    Ch., 301
    Hall, 301
Burton Constable, Yorks., 74,
    147, 520, 827, 946
Burton Hall, Lincs., 246, 612
Burton Leonard, Yorks., Ch.,
    107
Burton Overy, Leics., Ch., 272
Burton Park, Sussex, 96, 514
Burton Pedwardine, Lincs., ho.,
    717
Burton Pynsent, Som., Column,
    146
Burton-on-Trent, Staffs.
    Burton & Uttoxeter Bank, 247
    Ch., 347, 752, 944
    Holy Trinity Ch., 354
    Town Hall, 936
Burtonfield Ho., Yorks., 972
Burwarton Hall, Salop., 971
Bury, Hunts., ho., 692
Bury, Lancs.
    Rowlands Methodist Chapel,
        738
    St. Marie's Ch. (R.C.), 391
Bury (The), Herts., see St. Paul's
    Walden Bury
Bury Hill, Surrey, 173, 632
Bury St. Edmunds, Suffolk
    Assembly Rooms, 718
    Athenaeum, 718
    Corn Exchange, 79
    Gaol, 150, 177, 603, 895
    Guildhall St., no. 81, 772
    Manor Ho., 170
    Market Hall, 50
    Norman Gateway, 234
    St. Edmund's Ch. (R.C.), 255
    St. Mary's Ch., 234
    Savings Bank, 234
    Shire Hall, 143
    Theatre, 50, 895
    Town Hall, 50
Busby Hall, Yorks., 190, 233
Bushbury, Staffs., Ch., 557
Bushey, Herts.
    Grove, 95
    villa, 121
Bushey Heath, Herts., Ch., 847
Bushley, Worcs., Ch., 120
Bushridge, Surrey, 242
Bushy Ho., Middlx., 712, 963
Buslingthorpe, Lincs., Ch., 899
Butleigh, Som.
    Court, 156, 627
    Hood Mont., 352
Buttershaw, Yorks., Ch., 673
Butterton, Staffs.
    Butterton Grange Farmho., 770
    Ch., 434
    Hall, 435, 523
Buxted Park, Sussex, 228
Buxton, Derbys.
    Assembly Rooms, 191
    Baths, 88
    Crescent, 196
    St. John's Ch., 883
    Stables, 126, 196

Buxton Hill Ho., Wilts., 226
Byers Green, Durham, 934
Byfleet, Surrey
    Ho., 473
    ho., 341
Bylaugh Hall, Norfolk, 896
Byram Hall, Yorks., 54, 194
Bywell Hall, Northumb., 199, 611
Bywell St. Peter, Northumb., Ch.,
    266

Cabourn, Lincs., Pelham Column,
    899
Cadder Ho., Lanarks., 382
Caddington, Beds., Vicarage, 661
Cadland, Hants., 147, 425, 963
Cadoxton, Glam., ho., 180
Caen Wood Ho., Middlx., see
    Kenwood
Caenby Hall, Lincs., 321
Caerhays Castle, Cornwall, 584
Caernarvon
    Assembly Rooms, 655
    Baths, 655
    County Gaol, 631
    Market Hall, 522
    St. Mary's Chapel, 936
Caerphilly, Glam., Ch., 406
Cahir Castle, Ireland, 103
Cainscross, Glos., Ch., 82
Cairness Ho., Aberdeens., 158,
    645, 769
Cairnhill Ho., Ayrshire, 165
Cairnhill Ho., Lanarks., 82
Caldecote, Beds., farmho., 866
Caldwell Ho., Ayrshire, 53
Caledon, Ireland, 584
Caledonian Canal, 738
Calehill Ho., Kent, 739
Calke Abbey, Derbys., 341, 347,
    466, 751, 843, 893
Callaly Castle, Northumb., 837
Callander, Perths., Ch., 100
Callendar Ho. (Park), Stirlings.,
    133, 238, 383; mausoleum,
    288
Callington, Cornwall, Market Ho.,
    890
Callton Mor, Argylls., 166
Cally Ho., Kirkcud., 59, 128, 575,
    618, 671
Calne, Wilts., Castle Ho., 53
Calstock, Cornwall, Rectory, 174
Calverleigh Court, Devon, 890
Calverton, Bucks.
    Ch., 638
    Ho., 638
Calwich Abbey, Staffs., 166
Camberwell, Surrey
    Collegiate School, 696
    Grove Chapel, 706
Cambo, Northumb., Ch., 363
Camborne, Cornwall, Rectory,
    274
Cambridge
    Addenbrooke's Hospital, 439,
        863
    Anatomical Museum, 439
    Botanic Garden, 132, 138
    Bridge St., nos. 21–22, 863
    Caius Coll., see Gonville &
        Caius Coll.
    Christ Ch., 657
    Christ's Coll., 299, 368
    Civil Law School, 368
    Clare Coll. (Hall), 170, 299,
        367, 368, 448
    Clarendon Ho., 439

Cambridge—contd.
    Corpus Christi Coll., 170, 863,
        896
    Doll's Close, 438
    Downing Coll., 81, 176, 432,
        652, 895, 953
    Emmanuel Coll., 150, 169, 299,
        368, 438, 601, 636, 879,
        923; Westmorland Bldng.,
        368, 529
    Fair St., 438
    Fitzwilliam Museum, 224;
        competition, 87, 93, 94,
        212, 422, 444, 506, 689,
        808, 863, 894
    Fitzwilliam St., no. 15, 439
    Gaol (County), 177
    Gaol (Town), 143
    Garret Hostel Bridge, 299, 578
    Gonville & Caius Coll., 169,
        453, 767, 879, 893
    Great (Magdalene) Bridge, 150,
        299
    Great St. Mary's Ch., 170, 299,
        340, 367
    Grove (The), 247
    Guildhall, 300
    hos., 150
    Jesus Coll., 299, 368
    Kenmare, Trumpington St.,
        299
    King's College, 299, 339, 367,
        405, 411, 774, 893, 895,
        896; competition (1823),
        349, 353, 444, 458, 506,
        545, 648, 689, 861, 907
    Lensfield Rd., ho., 896
    Magdalene Coll., 429
    Maid's Causeway, 438
    Miller Lane, mews, 439
    Newmarket Rd., no. 38, 893
    Newnham Cottage, 893
    Observatory, 545; competition,
        349, 705, 856, 894
    Pemberton's Grove Lodge, 247
    Pembroke Coll., 448, 552, 922
    Perse School, 895
    Peterhouse, 143, 170, 368
    Philosophical Soc., 439
    Physic Garden, 368
    Printing Ho. (Pitt Press), 116,
        368, 863
    Queens' Coll., 169, 299; bridge,
        297, 299, 300
    Randall Ho., Trumpington St.,
        299
    Regent Ho., 368
    St. Andrew the Great's Ch.,
        657
    St. Andrew's Hill, nos. 9–10,
        439
    St. Catherine's Coll. (Hall),
        287, 299, 368, 806
    St. Clement's Ch., 439, 657
    St. John's Coll., 299, 367, 368,
        508, 545; Gothic bridge,
        442; New Court, 691
    St. Paul's Ch., 657
    Senate Ho., 169, 299, 339, 453
    Short St., 438
    Sidney Sussex Coll., 170, 299,
        438, 962
    Tennis Court Rd., nos. 4–12,
        439
    Trinity Coll., 119, 197, 299,
        439, 895; Fountain, 368;
        Library, 87, 368, 923;
        Master's Lodge, 368;

Cambridge—*contd.*
Trinity Coll.—*contd.*
Nevile's Court, 299, 368;
'Tribunal', 368
Trinity Hall, 170
University Library, 224, 299,
933
Willow Walk, 438
Cambusnethan Ho., Lanarks., 358
Camden Place, Kent, 251
Came Ho., Dorset, 201
Camer Court, Kent, 65
Camerton, Som.
Ch., 638
Court, 679
Camisekan Ho., Dunb., 383
Cammo, Midlothian, 219
Campbeltown, Argylls.
Castlehill Ch., 144, 400
Gaelic Ch., 257
Town Ho., 144
Camperdown Ho., Angus, 162
Campsall Hall, Yorks., 868
Campsey Ash, Suffolk, Rectory,
324
Campsmount, Yorks., 192, 522,
874
Cams Hall, Hants., 514–15
Candacraig, Aberdeens., 762
Candlesby, Lincs., Ch., 670
Canford Magna, Dorset, Ch., 119
Canford Manor, Dorset, 92, 117
Canklow Hall, Yorks., 641
Cann, Dorset, Ch., 861
Cannam Heath, Hants., 342
Cannington, Som., Ch., 202
Cannington Priory, Som., Chapel
(R.C.), 630
Cannon Hall, Yorks., 195
Can(n)ons Ho., Middlx., 314, 323,
341, 454, 489, 600, 732,
792, 806, 825, 866
Canon Frome Court, Herefs., 481
Canonbie, Dumfriess., Ch., 77
Canonteign Ho., Devon, 78
Canterbury
Cathedral, 78, 299, 404, 434;
altarpiece, 169; choir, 199,
429; tower (N.W.), 691;
transept, 249
County Gaol, 177
Infirmary, 683
Market-place, 375
Methodist Chapel, 458
Cantley, Yorks.
Hall, 522
Vicarage, 522
Canwell Hall, Staffs., 261, 950
Capel Curig, Caern., Inn, 936
Capesthorne Hall, Cheshire, 118,
538, 750, 751, 908
Capheaton Hall, Northumb., 591,
837
Carbeth Guthrie, Stirlings., 82
Carclew, Cornwall, 285, 393
Cardean, Perthshire, ho., 164
Cardiff, Glam.
Castle, 147, 425, 745
Gaol, 460
St. David's Ch. (R.C.), 724
St. Mary's Ch., 316
Cardigan
County Gaol, 581
Priory, 582
War Memorial Hospital, 582
Cardrona Ho., Peebles., 165
Cardross Ho., Perths., 784
Cargill, Perths., Ch., 533

Carisbrooke, I. of W., St. John's
parsonage, 670
Carlisle, Cumb.
Athenaeum, 898
Barclay's Bank, 692
Cathedral, 639, 744
Christ Ch., 691
Citadel Station, 828
cotton mills, 811
County Court Ho., 213, 261,
593, 743, 820
Eden Bridge, 128, 743
Gaol, 595, 603, 676
Holy Trinity Ch., 691
Infirmary, 811
Library, 692
London Road Railway Station,
265
Newsroom, 692
Shaddon Works, 811
Carlton Curlieu, Leics., Ch., 271,
880
Carlton Ferry Bridge, Yorks., 192
Carlton Hall, Northants., 463
Carlton Hall (Towers), Yorks.,
74
Carlton Lodge, Lincs., 858
Carlton-in-Craven, Yorks.,
Rectory, 67
Carluke, Lanarks., Ch., 105
Carmarthen
Ch., 581
County Gaol, 581
Nolton Ho., 582
Picton Mont., 582
St. David's Ch., 406
'Six Bells' Inn, 581
Carmyle Ho. (Cottage), Lanarks.,
164
Carnaby Temple, Yorks., 194
Carnousie Ho., Banffs., 58, 737
Carnsalloch, Dumfriess., 866
Caroline Park, Midlothian, 58
Carpow Ho., Perths., 86
Carradale Ho., Argylls., 165
Carriglas, Ireland, 327, 698
Carrington, Midlothian, Ch., 149
Carrington, Notts., St. John's
Ch., 798
Carshalton, Surrey
Ho., 477
Little Woodcote, 577
Park, 513
Carstairs Ho., Lanarks., 162, 593
Cartland Crags Bridge, Lanarks.,
821
Casewick Ho., Lincs., 511
Cashel Palace, Ireland, 629
Cassiobury Park, Herts., 545, 701,
874, 950, 961
Casterton, Westmld., Ch., 522
Castle Ashby, Northants.
Ch.; mont., 120
Ho., 146, 469, 806
Castle Bellingham, Ireland, 763
Castle Bernard, Ireland, 103
Castle Bromwich, Warwicks.
Ch., 885
Hall, 693, 901, 904
Castle Coole, Ireland, 949
Castle Coote, Ireland, 822
Castle Dounie, Inverness., 59
Castle Eden, Durham, 76, 590
Castle Forbes, Aberdeens., 624,
737
Castle Fraser, Aberdeens., 624
Castle Goring, Sussex, 674
Castle Grant, Morays., 46, 701

Castle Hedingham, Essex, Chapel,
305
Castle Hill, Devon, 118, 131, 413,
561
Castle Hill, Dorset, 207
Castle Howard, Yorks., 194, 208,
209, 301, 404, 703, 733,
806, 809, 826, 852;
Mausoleum, 333, 404
Castle Kennedy, Wigtowns., 59
Castle Maelgwyn, Pembs., 658
Castle Menzies, Perths., 165
Castle Mona, Isle of Man, 287,
780
Castle Newe, Aberdeens., 737
Castle Rushen, Isle of Man, 141
Castle Taylor, Ireland, 501
Castle Toward, Argylls., 382
Castle Upton, Ireland, 54, 117;
mausoleum, 55
Castle William, Notts., 196
Castlebar, Ireland
Courthouse, 897
farmyard, etc., 618
Castleboro Ho., Ireland, 698
Castleford, Yorks.
bridge, 354, 398
Rectory, 868
Castleton, Dorset, mont., 98
Castletown Ho., Cumb., 594, 676
Castletown Ho., Ireland, 207, 324
Castletown, Isle of Man
St. Mary's Ch., 141
Smelt Column, 878
Castlewellan, Ireland, 166
Catchfrench, Cornwall, 672
Cathcart, Renfrews., Ch., 257
Cathkin, Lanarks., 671
Catterick, Yorks., bridge, 192
Catton, Norfolk, ho., 324
Catton Hall, Derbys., 344, 763
Cavan, Ireland, County Prison,
293
Cave Castle, Yorks., 376
Cavendish Bridge, Derbys., 609
Caversfield Ho., Oxon., 226
Caversham, Oxon.
Bridge, 578, 836
Grove, 576
Park, 81, 240, 360
Cawthorne, Yorks., Ch., 466, 887
Caythorpe, Lincs.
Ch., 321
Hall, 622
Ceres, Fife., Ch., 234
Cerne Abbas, Dorset, Workhouse,
863
Chadacre Hall, Suffolk, 387
Chaddesley Corbett, Worcs., Ch.,
706
Chalfont Ho., Bucks., 109, 213,
583, 971
Chalfont St. Peter, Bucks.
Hill Ho., 44
parsonage, 715n.
Channons Hall, Norfolk, 176
Chantmarle, Dorset, 556
Chapel Allerton, Yorks.
Ch., 248
Hospital, 216
Chapel Chorlton, Staffs., Ch.,
840, 906
Chapel-en-le-Frith, Derbys., Ch.,
640
Chapel Hill, Lincs., Chapel, 605
Chapel Lawn, Salop., Ch., 406
Charborough Park, Dorset, 584
Chargate, *see* Esher

Charlecote, Warwicks., bridge, 421, 774
Charleton Ho., Fife, 164
Charleville Forest, Ireland, 179
Charlton, Kent, St. Thomas's Ch., 372
Charlton, Wilts., Ch., 861
Charlton Ho., Wilts., 138, 253
Charlton Marshall, Dorset, Ch., 96
Charlton Musgrove, Som., 70
Charmouth, Dorset, Ch., 321
Chart Park, Surrey, 71, 550
Chart Sutton, Kent, Ch., 425
Chartley Park, Staffs., Temple, 822
Chasely, Lancs., 811
Chasewater, Cornwall, Ch., 442
Chatelherault, Lanarks., 58
Chatham, Kent
  Chapel (R.C.), 813
  Ch., 600; mont., 612
  Dockyard Chapel, 423
  Melville Hospital, 813
  Ordnance bldngs., 854
  St. John's Ch., 744
  Store-house, 705
Chatsworth Ho., Derbys., 69, 88, 214, 309, 314, 380, 797, 805, 867, 962; bridge, 611; Cascade Ho., 69; Conservatory, 173; estate, 442; Home Farm, 173; office wing, 611; Stables, 126, 611
Chatton, Northumb.
  Ch., 266
  Vicarage, 267
Chawton, Hants.
  Ch., 278
  Rectory, 278
Cheadle, Staffs., Ch., 665
Cheam, Surrey, Ch., 716
Chedburgh Hall, Suffolk, 861
Chedington, Som., Ch., 202
Cheeseburn Grange, Northumb., 267
Cheetham, Lancs., St. Luke's Rectory, 811
Chelmsford, Essex
  Baptist Chapel, 305
  Ch. (R.C.), 724
  Club, 305
  conduit, 463
  County Gaol, 418, 434, 463
  Duke St., 355
  Grammar School, 463
  House of Correction, 463
  Independent Chapel, 305
  'Laurel Grove', 305
  Moulsham Bridge, 464
  New London Rd., 305
  Nonconformist Cemetery, 305
  St. Mary's Ch. (Cathedral), 413, 463
  Shire Hall, 463; design for, 418
Chelsea, see London
Chelsea Farm, Middlx., 947
Cheltenham, Glos.
  Berkeley Street Chapel, 618
  Cemetery Chapel, 628
  Charlton Ho., 618
  Christ Ch., 456
  Ch., 418; mont., 952
  Columbia Place, 455
  Evesham Rd., nos. 2–34, 455
  Female Orphan Asylum, 784
  Lansdowne Court, 456

Cheltenham, Glos.—contd.
  Lansdowne Crescent, 456, 618
  Lansdowne Parade, 456
  Lansdowne Place, 618
  Literary & Philosophical Inst., 456
  Masonic Hall, 846
  Montpellier Gardens, 618
  Montpellier Pump Room, 618
  Montpellier Spa, 846
  Pittville Parade, 455
  Pittville Pump Room, 313
  Plough Hotel, 846
  Queen's Hotel, 456
  St. James's Ch., 458, 618
  St. John's Ch., 618
  St. Paul's Ch., 313
  Sherborne Spa, 846
Chenies, Bucks.
  Ch.; mont., 209
  inn, 755
Chepstow, Mon.
  Bridge, 678
  Ch., 392
  development, 891–2
  Wyelands estate, 527
Chequers, Bucks., 77, 685
Chertsey, Surrey
  Abbey Lodge, 67
  Bridge, 111, 609
  Ch., 212, 292, 293
  Workhouse, 487
Cheshunt, Herts.
  cottage, 701
  ho., 592
  Great Ho., 379
  Nunnery, 809
Chessel Ho., Hants., 489, 814
Chestal Ho., Glos., 859
Chester
  Bank, 954
  Bishop's Palace, 817
  Bridge Gate, 844
  Castle, 396, 728
  Cathedral, 397, 688; mont., 493
  Christ Church, Newtown, 476
  Deva Hospital, 229
  Eastgate, 408
  Exchange, 844
  Grosvenor Bridge, 229, 395, 397, 840
  Holy Trinity Ch., 397
  Infirmary, 230
  Lunatic Asylum, 229
  Methodist Chapels, 230, 397
  News-Room, 397
  North Gate, 397
  Old Dee Bridge, 397
  St. Bridget's Ch., 229
  St. Martin's Lodge, 398
  St. Oswald's Ch., 229
  St. Paul's Ch., 230
  St. Peter's Ch., 397
  Watergate Ho., 398
Chesterfield, Derbys.
  Ch., 423, 556, 897
  Holy Trinity Ch., 970
  Methodist Chapel, 423
  Town Hall, 191
Chester-le-Street, Durham
  Ch., 123
  ho., 184
Chesters, Northumb., 194–5, 267
Chesters Ho., Roxb., 289
Chesterton, Hunts., Rectory, 271
Chesterton, Warwicks.
  Ch., monts., 786
  Ho., 785

Chettle Ho., Dorset, 69
Chetton, Salop., Ch., 740
Chetwynd Bridge, Staffs., 655
Cheveley Park, Cambs., 167
Chevening Ho., Kent, 276, 314, 469, 873, 948
Chevet Hall, Yorks., 673
Chicheley Hall, Bucks., 311, 750
Chichester, Sussex
  Assembly Rooms, 944
  Cathedral, 292, 693; mont., 289
  Corn Exchange, 289
  Council Ho., 132, 561
  Infirmary, 274
  King's Holme, 292
  Market Cross, 693
  Market Ho., 581
  St. Bartholomew Without, 274
  St. John's Chapel, 292, 400
  St. Pancras Ch., 693
Chicklade, Wilts., Ch., 618
Chicksands Priory, Beds., 866, 951
Chiddingstone Castle, Kent, 76, 488
Chiefswood, Roxb., 759
Chigwell, Essex
  hos., 617
  Vicarage, 271
  villa, 705
Chigwell Row, Essex, villa, 617
Chilcompton, Som., Ch., 330
Childwall, Lancs.
  Ch., 690
  Hall, 583
Chilham, Kent
  Castle, 147, 729
  Ch., 786
  mausoleum, 818
Chillingham, Northumb.
  Castle, 241, 624, 963
  Ch., 241
Chillington Hall, Staffs., 612, 752, 768; bridge, 146
Chilmark, Wilts., parsonage, 308
Chilton Foliat, Wilts., mausoleum, 637
Chilton Lodge, Berks., 637, 769
Chilton Polden, Som., Ch., 860
Chilvers Coton, Warwicks., Ch., 98
Chingford, Essex, SS. Peter & Paul Ch., 858
Chinnor, Oxon., Rectory, 605
Chipchase Castle, Northumb., 267, 268
Chippenham Park, Cambs., 718
Chipping Campden, Glos.
  Bedfont Ho., 916
  Ch., mont., 915
  Town Hall, 439
Chipping Norton, Oxon.
  Ch., 438, 847
  Town Hall, 679
Chirk, Denbighs.
  Aqueduct, 738, 821
  Bridge, 821
  Castle, 232, 369, 398, 844, 966
Chiselhampton, Oxon.
  Ch., 273n.
  Ho., 273
Chiswick, Middlx.
  Ch, monts., 772, 797
  Corney Ho., 341
  Grove (The), 173
  Ho., 130 (bis), 173, 491, 509, 883
  hos., 545 (Sir S. Fox), 575 (Earl of Morton)

Chiswick, Middlx.—*contd.*
Royal Horticultural Soc., 61, 77
Sutton Court, 173
Chobham Lodge, Surrey, 619
Chollerton, Northumb., school, 265
Cholmondeley, Cheshire
Castle (Hall), 475, 745, 747, 750, 854, 874
Chapel, 88
Chorley, Lancs., St. George's Ch., 690
Chorley Wood, Herts., 619
Chorlton-on-Medlock, Lancs.
St. Saviour's Ch., 408
Town Hall, 502
Christchurch, Hants., Priory Ch., 331, 422, 456
Church Gresley, Staffs., Ch., 331, 952; mont., 901
Church Langton, Leics., coll., 659
Church Oakley, Hants., Parsonage, 324
Churchill, Oxon., Ch., 648
Churchstoke, Montgom.
Ch., 142
Vicarage, 407
Churchstow, Devon, parsonage, 670
Chute, Wilts., Ch., 631
Chute Lodge, Wilts., 817
Cilcain, Flints., Ch., 657
Cinderford, Glos., Ch., 120
Cirencester, Glos.
Park, 744
Watermoor Ho., 455
Clachan Bridge, Argylls., 575
Clackmannan, Ch., 357
Claines, Worcs., St. George's Chapel, 526
Clandeboye, Ireland, Helen's Tower, 167
Clandon Park, Surrey, 147, 445, 513
Clandon Regis, Surrey, 892
Clandown, Som., Ch., 537
Clapham, Surrey
All Saints Ch., 416
Broomfield Lodge, 367
Holy Trinity Ch., 236, 423, 440, 616, 618
hos., 312 (Hoare), 618 (Allnutt), 618 (Betts), 644 (Webster), 770 (Green)
Nightingale Cottage, 175
Park, 244
St. Paul's Ch., 282
Clapham Lodge, Yorks., 76
Clapton, Middlx., garden, 617
Clare Ho., Kent, 725
Claremont Ho., Surrey, 147, 212, 421, 425, 492, 617, 853, 933
Clarendon Park, Wilts., 630
Clasmont, Glam., 463
Clatto, Fife, 166
Claverdon, Warwicks., Ch., 390
Clavering, Essex, Vicarage, 519
Claverton, Som.
Ch., 475, 537; mont., 475
Ho., 475, 962
Clay Hill, Herts., 753
Claybury Hall, Essex, 345, 680n.
Claydon Ho., Bucks., 204, 269, 696, 703, 715n.
Claygate, Surrey, Ch., 488
Clayton-le-Moors, Lancs., Ch., 391

Cleadon Cottage, Durham, 268
Cleadon Meadow, Durham, 268
Clearwell, Glos.
Castle, 561
Ch., 534
Cleatham Hall, Lincs., 321
Cleator, Cumb., Ch., 876
Cleckheaton, Yorks., Ch., 73
Cleeve, Bucks., lock, 836
Cleeve, Som., Ch., 536
Clehonger, Herefs., lodge, 411
Cleobury Mortimer, Salop., Ch., 820
Clermont Hall, Norfolk, 637
Clervaux Castle, Yorks., 123
Clevedon, Som., Christ Ch., 691
Cliefden Ho., Bucks., *see* Cliveden
Cliffhill Copse, Wilts., 603
Clifton, Notts.
Belvedere, 132
Ch., 234
Hall, 195, 765
parsonage, 908
Clifton Campville Hall, Staffs., 259, 750
Clifton Castle, Yorks., 315
Clifton Hall, Yorks., 641
Clifton Hampden, Oxon., lock, 836
Climping, Sussex, Vicarage, 650
Clints Hall, Yorks., 193
Clipston, Northants., School & Hospital, 229
Clitheroe, Lancs.
Castle, 555
St. Mary Magdalene's Ch., 691
Town Hall, 691
Cliveden, Bucks., 69, 92, 163, 269, 513, 514, 594n., 904; Tea Room, 594
Clober Ho., Dunb., 82
Cloncaird Castle, Ayrshire, 862
Clophill, Beds., Ch., 763
Clowance, Cornwall, 576; mausoleum, 577
Clumber Ho. (Park), Notts., 329, 746, 882, 933
Clune Cottage, Morays., 698
Clunie, Perths., Ch., 533
Cluny, Aberdeens.
Castle, 762
mausoleum, 179
School, 761
Clyne Castle, Glam., 460
Clytha, Mon.
Castle, 582
Court, 407
Coalbrookdale, Salop., Iron Bridge, 664
Coates, Glos., Bledisloe Lodge, 635
Coberley, Glos., Rectory, 605
Cobh, Ireland, sea-wall, etc., 172
Cobham, Surrey
Bridge, 370
Ch., 632
Lodge, 618
Cobham Hall, Kent, 207, 552, 679, 682, 948, 963; Mausoleum, 952; Temple, 208
Cobridge, Staffs.
Christ Ch., 858
St. Peter's Chapel (R.C.), 248
Cockburnspath, Berwicks., bridge near, 412
Cockenzie, E. Lothian, harbour, 757

Cockfosters, Middlx., Christ Ch., 488
Cockpen, Midlothian, Ch., 260, 288
Coddington, Cheshire, Ch., 72
Codger Castle, Northumb., 934
Coed-Cwnwr, Mon., Almshouses, 406
Cofton, Devon, Chapel, 321
Cofton Hall, Worcs., 177
Coghurst, Sussex, 173
Coilsfield Ho., Ayrshire, 624
Coker Court, Som., 262
Cokethorpe Ho., Oxon., 217
Colchester
Arthur St., 631
Baptist Meeting Ho., 631
Baths., 631
Corn Exchange, 501
Cross St., 631
Forster St., 631
Hollytrees Ho., 255
Hospital, 823
Osborn St., 631
Royal Eastern Counties Institution, 243
St. Botolph's Ch., 540
St. James's Ch., 724
St. Mary-at-the-Walls Ch., 659
Theatre, 448, 893
Turrets (The), 527
Victoria Hotel, 243
Workhouse, 145
Coldingham, Berwicks., Ch., 570
Coldstream, Berwicks., Manse, 385
Colebrook Park, Kent, 78
Coleby Hall, Lincs., Temple, 207
Coleford, Glos., Ch., 455, 650
Coleford, Som., Ch., 772
Colemore, Hants., Ch., 200
Coleorton Hall, Leics., 252
Coleraine, Ireland, Market Ho., 249
Coleshill Ho., Berks., 65, 131, 658-9, 793, 872
Coley, Yorks., Ch., 132
Coley Park, Berks., 501
Colinton, Midlothian
Ch., 698
Ho., 241, 394, 647
Redhall Ho., 698
Collessie, Fife, Ch., 260
Collierly, Durham, Ch., 449
Collingham, Yorks., Vicarage, 877
Coln St. Dennis, Glos., Rectory, 605
Colne, Lancs., Ch., 818
Colne Park, Essex, column, 769
Colney (Chapel) Ho., Herts., 236
Colney Lodge, Herts., 753
Colonsay, Argylls., Ch., 188
Colquhalzie, Perths., 784
Colston Bassett, Notts., parsonage, 908
Colwich, Staffs.
Ch., 841
St. Mary's Abbey, 211
Colwick, Notts.
Hall, 195
Rectory, 789
Colworth Ho., Beds., 685
Combe Abbey, Warwicks, 234, 636, 890, 904
Combe Bank, Kent, 65, 561
Combe Down, Som., Ch., 352
Combermere Abbey, Cheshire, 118

Combroke, Warwicks., Ch., 592
Compstone Ho., Kirkcud., 385, 647
Compton Abbas, Dorset, Ch., 302
Compton Castle, Compton Pauncefoot, Som., 306–7
Compton Place, Sussex, 185
Compton Verney, Warwicks., 52, 287, 341; Bridge, 147; Chapel, 147
Comrie, Perths.
  Ch., 782
  Lodge, 784
  Manse, 784
  Tullichettle Ho., 784
Condover Hall, Salop., 575–6, 664
Congleton, Cheshire
  Guildhall, 227
  St. James's Ch., 838, 841
Conishead Priory, Lancs., 955
Coniston Cold Bridge, Yorks., 192
Connington, Hunts.
  Castle, 118
  Ch., 119
Conock Ho., Wilts., 444
Conon Bridge, Ross, 821
Constable Burton, Yorks., 193
Conway, Caern., Suspension Bridge, 821
Cookham, Berks., lock, 836
Coolattin Park, Ireland, 196
Coole Ho., Ireland, 518
Coolbanagher, Ireland
  Ch., 327
  Mausoleum, 327
Coolhurst, Sussex, 118, 701
Coolmore, Ireland, 246
Coombe Ho., Surrey, 768, 770
Coombe Lodge, Oxon., 715
Coombe Lodge, Surrey, 173
Coombe Place, Sussex, 558
Coopersale, Essex, 674
Copped Hall, Essex, see Copt Hall
Copt (Copped) Hall, Essex, 495, 588, 666, 716, 787, 946
Copt Oak, Leics., Ch., 669
Coptfold Hall, Essex, 817
Copthorne, Sussex, Newlands, 754
Copythorne, Hants., Ch., 107
Corby Castle, Cumb., 594
Corehouse, Lanarks., 116–17
Cork, Ireland, villa, 518
Cornbury Ho. (Park), Oxon., 303, 377, 544, 786, 789, 791
Cornhill, Northumb., Ch., 123
Cornish Hall End, Essex, St. John's Ch., 557
Cornworthy, Devon, Vicarage, 708
Corringham, Lincs., parsonage, 670
Corsham Court, Wilts., 146, 483, 583, 682
Corsindae Ho., Aberdeens., 762
Corsley, Wilts., Ch., 508
Corstorphine, Midlothian
  Ch., 162
  Hanley Lodge, 164
Cortachy, Angus
  Castle, 260
  Ch., 623
Coseley, Staffs., Christ Ch., 383, 510
Cossey (Costessy), Norfolk
  Hall, 156, 461, 768
  Well, 150

Costock, Notts., Highfields Farm, 622
Cote (Cotham) Bank, Glos., 682
Cothelstone Ho., Som., 541
Coton Hall, Salop., 664
Coton Ho., Warwicks., 957
Cottenham, Cambs., Rectory, 859
Cottesbrooke, Northants.
  Ch., mont., 201
  Hall, 554, 752
Cottingham, Northants., Bury Ho., 622
Cottingham, Yorks., Chapel, 107
Cound Hall, Salop., 662
Coultermains, Lanarks., 972
Courteenhall, Northants., 721
Cove, Ireland,
  Custom House, 79
  dock, 79
  Exchange, 79
Coventry, Warwicks.
  Bablake School, 692
  Bond's Hospital, 692
  Christ Ch., 691
  Congregational Chapel, 887
  County Hall, 287
  Drapers' Hall, 235, 692
  Gaol, 887
  Holy Trinity Ch., 213, 287, 420, 635, 691, 726
  St. Mary's Hall, 887
  St. Michael's Ch., 420, 654, 887, 945
  St. Peter's Ch., 280
Cowden, Kent, Ch., 881
Cowdray Lodge (Park), Sussex, 809
Cowes, I. of W., see East Cowes, West Cowes
Cowesby Hall, Yorks., 971
Cowick Hall, Yorks., 125, 610
Cowley Bridge, Devon, 361
Cowpen, Northumb., R.C. Ch., 266
Cowsfield Ho., Wilts., 810
Coxhoe Hall, Durham, 610
Coxley, Som., Ch., 202
Coxwell, Berks., Rectory, 605
Coxwold, Yorks., Ch., 74
Crackenthorpe Hall, Westmld., 532
Cragg, Yorks., Ch., 213
Craig Ho., Aberdeens., 737
Craig Ho., Angus, 623
Craigcrook Castle, Midlothian, 647
Craigdarroch, Dumfriess., 57
Craigellachie, Banffs., Bridge, 738, 821
Craigellie Ho., Aberdeens., 762
Craigend Castle, Stirlings., 670–1, 759
Craighall, Fife, 154
Craighall Rattray, Perths., mont., 570
Craigiehall Ho., W. Lothian, 78, 154, 530
Craigston Castle, Aberdeens., 56, 762
Crail, Fife
  Ch., 86, 511
  Manse, 511
Crailing Ho., Roxb., 289
Crakaig, Sutherld., 118
Crakehall, Yorks., Ch., 391
Crambe, Yorks., Vicarage, 728
Crambeck, Yorks., bridge, 192

Cramlington Hall, Northumb., 266
Cramond, Midlothian
  Bridge, 678
  Ch., 162
Cranage, Cheshire
  bridge, 397
  Hall, 954
Cranborne House, Dorset, 70, 709–10
Cranbourn(e) Lodge, Berks., 474, 951
Cranbrook, Kent
  Ch., 255
  School, 305
Cranbury Park, Hants., 251, 618
Cranford Ho. (Park), Middlx., 102, 228–9, 309
Cranleigh, Surrey, School, 487
Craster Tower, Northumb., 267–8
Crathie, Aberdeens., Ch., 221
Crawford Priory, Fife, 358, 382
Craycombe Ho., Worcs., 177
Crazies Hill, Berks., ho., 132
Crediton, Devon, Ch., 890
Creech Grange, Dorset, 201
Creedy Park, Devon, 166
Creich, Fife, Ch., 783
Cressage, Salop., Ch., 406
Cresswell Hall, Northumb., 729
Crewe, Cheshire, railway station, 247
Crewe Hall, Cheshire, 118, 966
Crichel Ho., Dorset, 167, 302, 435
Crick, Northants., Rectory, 698
Cricket Lodge, Som., 768
Cricket St. Thomas, Som., mont., 772
Crieff, Perths., Ch., 783
Crimonmogate, Aberdeens., 737
Croft, Lancs.
  Christ Ch., 119
  Ho., 237
Croft, Yorks., bridge, 192
Croft Castle, Herefs., 663
Croft Spa Hotel, Yorks., 123
Crofton Grange, Herts., 768
Croick, Ross, Ch., 821
Crom Castle, Ireland, 118
Cromer Hall, Norfolk, 270
Cronkhill, Salop., 583
Crook, Durham, Ch., 124
Crookham, Hants., Ch., 386
Croome D'Abitot, Worcs.
  Ch., 50, 146
  Court, 52, 146, 550, 949; Chinese bridge, 379; stables, 750
Croome Ho., Surrey, 729
Crosby Hall, Lancs., 527
Croscombe, Som.
  Ch., 860
  Rectory, 860
Cross, I. of Lewis, Ch., 821
Crossens, Lancs., Ch., 507
Crostwick, Norfolk, bridge, 785
Crouch End, Middlx.
  cottage, 110
  pavilion, 618
Crowan, Cornwall, Ch., 82
Crowcombe, Som.
  Ch., 620
  Court, 447, 620
Crowland, Lincs., Ch., 718
Crowell, Oxon., Rectory, 674
Crownest Ho., Yorks., 132

Croxall, Staffs., mont., 838
Croydon, Surrey
  Court Ho., 773
  Palace, 150, 452–3
  St. James's Ch., 862
  villa, 127
Cruckton, Salop., Ch., 406
Cruden, Aberdeens.
  Ch., 761
  School, 761
Crum Castle, Ireland, 118
Cruxton, Lanarks., cottage, 594
Cublington, Bucks.
  ho., 391
  Rectory, 648
Cuckfield Park, Sussex, 271
Cuddesdon, Oxon., Bishop's
    Palace, 912
Cuerden Hall, Lancs., 954
Cuffnells, Hants., 769
Culdees Castle, Perths., 358
Culford Hall, Suffolk, 516, 933,
    939, 957
Culham, Oxon.
  Ho., 633
  parsonage, 438
Cullamore, Ireland, 354
Cullen, Banffs.
  Ho., 44, 46, 530, 531; bridge,
    59; Temple, 644
  Post Office, 699
  Seafield Hotel, 699
  Town Hall, 699
Cullompton, Devon, Vicarage,
    157
Cultoquhey Ho., Perths., 745
Cults, Aberdeens., bridge, 761
Culverhouse, Devon, 755
Culverthorpe Hall, Lincs., 400,
    559, 561, 775
Culzean Castle, Ayrshire, 54, 268,
    527
Cumbernauld Ho., Dunb., 58
Cumnock Ch., Ayrshire, 44
Cunmont Ho., Angus, 541
Cupar, Fife
  Ch., 443
  County Bldngs., 161, 356
  County Prison, 356
  hos., 623
  Town Hall, 443
Curraghmore, Ireland, 947;
    cottages, 354
Currie, Midlothian
  Ch., 824
  School, 161
Cusworth Hall, Yorks., 610, 640,
    673
Cwmaman, Carm., Christ Ch.,
    280
Cwmcynfelin, Card., 225, 263
Cyfarthfa Castle, Glam., 527

Dagenham, Essex
  Ch., 540
  School, 613
Dagnam Park, Essex, 345
Dalby Hall, Leics., 269
Dalby (Old), Leics., Ch., 907
Dalcrue, Perths.
  bridge, 646
  farmho., 647
Daldawn Ho., Kirkcud., 268
Dale Park, Sussex, 124
Dalgety, Fife, Ch., 357
Dalguise, Perths., ho., 624
Dalhousie Castle, Midlothian,
    163, 623

Dalkeith, Midlothian
  Ho. (Palace), 59, 163, 209, 238,
    485, 644, 758; Montagu
    Bridge, 55
  railway viaduct, 363
  St. Mary's Episcopal Ch., 162
  St. Nicholas (East) Ch., 162
  West Ch., 162
Dallam Tower, Westmld., 876
Dallinghoo, Suffolk, parsonage,
    111
Dallington Hall, Northants., 752
Dalmahoy Ho., Midlothian, 57
Dalmeny Ho., W. Lothian, 896
Dalnacardoch Inn, Perths., 100
Dalquharran Castle, Ayrshire, 55
Dalton, Northumb., Holy Trinity
    Ch., 363
Danbury Place, Essex, 435, 866
Danby Wiske, Yorks., bridge, 192
Dancers Hill, Middlx., 605
Dane Hill, Sussex, Ch., 237
Danehurst, Sussex, 439
Danesfield Ho., Bucks., 971
Danson Hill, Kent, 208, 817
Darlaston, Staffs.
  bridge, 678
  Hall, 84
Darley Abbey, Derbys.
  Abbey, 635
  Ch., 908
Darlington, Durham
  Holy Trinity Ch., 971
  ho., 267
  Methodist Chapel, 458
  St. Augustine's Ch. (R.C.), 123
Darnaway Castle, Morays., 500
Darnick Tower, Roxb., 760
Dartford, Kent
  Bridge, 739
  Ch., 240, 725
  Gasworks, 240
  West Hill Hospital, 721
  Workhouse, 721
Dartington Hall, Devon, 719
Dartmoor Prison, Devon, 65
Dartmouth, Devon, St. Petrock's
    Chapel, 520
Dartrey, Ireland, 165;
    mausoleum, 952
Darwen, Lancs., Holy Trinity
    Ch., 691
Datchet, Bucks., bridge, 151
Davenham, Cheshire, Ch., 506
Davenport Hall, Salop., 751
Daventry, Northants., Ch., 420
Dawley Ho., Middlx., 276, 341
Dawlish, Devon, Ch., 625
Dawson Court, Ireland, 327
Dawson's Grove, Ireland,
    mausoleum, 952
Dawyck Ho., Peebles., 164
Daylesford Ho., Glos., 212, 228
Dderw, Radnors., 421
Deal, Kent
  Naval Hospital, 634
  St. Andrew's Ch., 657
  St. George's Ch., 453, 673, 735
  St. Leonard's Ch., 673
Debden, Essex
  Ch., 199, 300, 426–7
  Hall, 426, 427
Deddington, Oxon., Ch., 912
Dedham, Essex
  Bridge, 464
  cottage, 527
  ho., 501
  Vicarage, 824

Dee Hills, Cheshire, 398
Deene Park, Northants., 239
Deepdene (The), Surrey, 76, 432
Deeping St. James, Lincs.,
    parsonage, 151
Delaford Park, Bucks., 519
Delamere, Cheshire
  Ch., 369
  Ho., 957
Dell (The), Berks., 349
Denbies, Surrey, 244
Denbigh, St. David's Ch., 631
Denford, Berks.
  Ch., 618
  Ho., 618, 962
Denham Mount, Bucks., 527
Denham Place, Bucks., 774
Denne Hill, Kent, 617
Denton, Durham, Ch., 123
Denton, Northants., Ch., 773
Denton, Yorks., Ch., 191
Denton Court, Kent, 127
Denton Ho., Lincs., 908
Denton Park, Yorks., 194
Deptford, Kent
  Deptford Creek Bridge Co., 66
  Dockyard, 722
  Evelyn estate, 284
  Goldsmiths' College, 730
  Royal Naval Coll., 730
  Royal Victualling Yard, 71
  St. Nicholas Ch., 776
  St. Paul's Ch., 69, 792
  Trinity Hospital, 775
  Union Place, 725
  Victualling Yard, 959
Derby
  All Saints Ch. (Cathedral), 340,
    753, 843
  Arboretum, 525
  Assembly Rooms, 50, 635, 733
  Athenaeum, 861–2
  Bank, 861–2
  Baptist Chapel, 305
  Christ Ch. (Bp. Ryder's Ch.),
    375
  County Courts, 374
  County Gaol, 353, 421, 540
  County Hall, 278
  Exeter Bridge, 840
  Friargate, no. 41, 635
  Liversage Almshouses, 540
  Methodist Chapel, 738
  Ordnance Depot, 944
  Post Office, 861–2
  Royal Hotel, 861–2
  St. John's Ch., 354
  St. Mary's Bridge, 396
  St. Mary's Ch. (R.C.), 970
  Town Hall, 374
Derry Ormond, Card., 225
Devil's Bit, Ireland, cottage, 293
Devizes, Wilts.
  Bridewell, 685
  Castle, 352
  County Gaol, 443
  Market Cross, 938
  St. James's Ch., 631, 882
  toll-house, 939
  Town Hall, 86
Devonport, Devon
  Column, 319, 503
  Dispensary, 59
  Dockyard Chapel, 423
  Keyham Dockyard, 722
  Mount Zion Baptist Chapel,
    319
  Post Office, 890

Devonport, Devon—*contd.*
  Royal Naval Factory, 92
  St. Aubyn's Chapel, 672
  Town Hall, 319, 503
Dewsbury, Yorks.
  Ch., 191
  St. Matthew's Ch., 123
Dewsbury Moor, Yorks., St.
    John's Ch., 819
Didcot, Berks., Rectory, 847
Digswell Ho., Herts., 958
Dillington Ho., Som., 970
Dilston Hall, Northumb., 462
Dingestow Court, Mon., 859
Dingle Cottage, Lancs., 897
Dingley Hall, Northants., 349,
    377, 545
Dingwall, Ross & Cromarty,
    Bank, 699
Dinnington Hall, Yorks., 610
Dinsdale Park Hotel, Durham,
    122
Dinton, Bucks., Ch., 698
Dinton Ho., Wilts., 962
Diseworth, Leics., Vicarage, 622
Disley, Cheshire, Ch., 510
Ditchingham Dam, Norfolk,
    bridge, 273
Ditchley Ho., Oxon., 311, 750,
    828, 972; Temple, 341
Ditton, Bucks.
  Chapel, 77
  Park, 76
Ditton Priors, Salop., Vicarage,
    740
Dochfour Ho., Inverness., 699
Docking, Norfolk, workhouse,
    145
Dodbrooke, Devon, Rectory, 394
Doddington, Cheshire
  Ch., 506
  Hall, 957
Doddington, Lincs.
  Ch., 528
  Hall, 262, 528
Doddington, Northumb., Ch.,
    123
Dodington, Glos.
  Ch., 945
  Park, 950
Dodworth, Yorks., Ch., 811
Dogmersfield, Hants.
  Ch., 278
  Park, 167
Dogs, Isle of, 964
Dolaucothi, Carm., 582
Dollar, Clack.
  Academy, 646
  Ch., 829
Don Bridge, Aberdeens., 821
Donaghadee, Ireland, harbour,
    524
Doncaster, Yorks.
  Ch., 642
  Christ Ch., 441
  Corn Market, 442
  Green Inn, 642
  hos., 522
  Infirmary, 215, 522
  Mansion Ho., 441, 522, 608
  Market Cross, 442
  Methodist Chapel, 441
  Race-stand, 191, 441, 522
  South Parade, nos. 15, 19–21,
    522
  Theatre, 521
  Town Hall, 521
  Vicarage, 521

Donibristle, Fife
  Chapel, 531
  Ho., 531
Donington Hall, Leics., 893
Donnington Grove, Berks., 213,
    422
Dorchester, Dorset
  County Gaol, 114, 845
  Holy Trinity Ch., 863
  Shire Hall, 98, 389
Dorchester, Oxon., Bridge, 719
Dorchester Ho., Surrey, 806
Dore, Derbys., Ch., 324, 509
Dorfold, Cheshire
  Chapel, 838
  Hall, 84, 118, 956
Dorking, Surrey
  Ch., 143
  Independent Chapel, 435, 730
  Workhouse, 730
Dornoch, Sutherld., Ch., 162
Dorrington, Salop., Ch., 406
Dorton Ho., Kent, 252
Dorton Spa, Bucks., 377
Douglas, Isle of Man
  Courthouse, 780
  Lighthouse, 780
  Red Pier, 780
  St. Barnabas' Ch., 878
  Tower of Refuge, 878
Douglas, Lanarks.
  Castle, 46, 287, 645
  Manse, 359
Doune, Perths., Ch., 357
Doune Lodge, Perths., 784
Dover, Kent
  Baptist Chapel, 673
  Castle Hill, 103
  Gaol, 293
  Harbour, 204, 783
  Holy Trinity Ch., 282
  Lord Warden Hotel, 103
  Maison Dieu estate, 618
  pavilion, 282
  pier, 350
  Pilot House, 103
  Round Ho., 293
  St. Mary's Ch., 204
  Unitarian Chapel, 673
  Waterloo Crescent, 387
Doveridge Hall, Derbys., 331,
    781–2
Dowdeswell Court, Glos., 628
Dowlais, Glam.
  Market Hall, 406
  St. Illtyd's Ch. (R.C.), 724
  Schools, 92
Down Ampney Ho., Glos., 770
Down Hall, Essex, 344
Down Ho., Glos., 692
Downend, Glos., Ch., 364
Downham Hall, Lancs., 876
Downham Hall, Suffolk, 859
Downham Market, Norfolk,
    workhouse, 271
Downhill, Ireland, 231, 412, 765,
    946–7
Downholme, Yorks., bridge, 192
Downpatrick, Ireland
  Cathedral, 139
  Gaol, 139, 675
Downside, Som.
  Abbey, 352
  Christ Ch., 638
Downton, Wilts., Ch., 65
Downton Castle, Herefs., 663
Dowsby Hall, Lincs., 827
Doxford Hall, Northumb., 267

Drakelow Hall, Derbys., 880
Draperstown, Ireland, 126
Drayton Ho., Northants., 228,
    686, 708, 806, 873, 905
Drayton Manor, Staffs., 745
Dreghorn Castle, Midlothian, 288
Dromoland Castle, Ireland, 434
Dron, Perths.
  Ch., 783
  Manse, 533
Dropmore, Bucks., 810, 958
Drum (The), Midlothian, 57, 567
Drumbanagher Ho., Ireland, 647
Drumfinn, Argylls., 163
Druminnor Ho., Aberdeens., 737
Drumlanrig Castle, Dumfries.,
    163, 220, 289, 296, 757
Drummond Castle, Perths., 569
Drumoak, Aberdeens., Ch., 737
Drumpellier Ho., Lanarks., 239
Drumtochty Castle, Kinc., 358
Dryburgh, Berwicks,
  Chain Bridge, 759–60
  Wallace statue, 760
Drypool, Yorks., Ch., 442
Dublin
  Bank of Ireland, 318, 327, 350
  Baths, 353
  Carlisle Bridge, 327
  Castle, 629, 848
  Charlemont Ho., 209, 327
  Custom Ho., 327
  Four Courts, 327, 603
  Harcourt St. Rly. Station, 897
  King's Inns, 603
  Langford Ho., 52
  Leinster Ho., 209, 952
  Library, 632
  Military Infirmary, 327
  Nelson Pillar, 895
  Newgate Gaol, 114
  Ormonde Bridge, 719
  Parliament Ho., 327, 629, 848
  Phoenix Park, 171
  Pro-Cathedral (R.C.), 814
  Richmond Bridge, 721
  Roslyn Park, 327
  Rotunda Assembly Rooms, 327
  Royal Exchange, competition
    for, 113, 286, 326, 458,
    514, 520, 586, 591–2, 671,
    694, 705, 714, 781, 888
  St. Catherine's Ch., mont., 577
  St. Mathias Chapel, 698
  St. Michael & All Angels Ch.,
    814
  Sts. Michael & John Ch.
    (R.C.), 814
  Sandymount, villa, 327
  Sarah Bridge, 781
  Theatre Royal, 102
  Trinity College, 206, 450, 483,
    716
  Viceregal Lodge, Phoenix Park,
    910
  Water Works, 578
  Wellington Monument, 381,
    743
  Whitworth Bridge, 497
Duddestone Ho., Warwicks., 527
Duddingston Ho., Midlothian,
    207
Duddo, Northumb., Ch., 123
Duddon, Cheshire, Ch., 669
Dudley, Worcs.
  Ch. (R.C.), 970
  Priory Hall, 510
  St. Thomas's Ch., 120, 143

Dudmaston Hall, Salop., 740, 751–2
Duff Ho., Banffs., 58
Duffield, Derbys., bridge, 800
Duffus Ho., Morays., 699
Dukinfield, Cheshire
  Lodge, 72
  Unitarian Chapel, 811
Dull, Perths., Ch., 735
Dullingham, Cambs., farm bldngs., 859
Dulwich, Surrey
  Brockwell estate, 618
  Brockwell Hall, 618, 706
  Brockwell Lodge, 618
  Brockwell Terrace, 618
  Casina, Denmark Hill, 583
  College, 91, 340
  Gallery & Mausoleum, 767
  Glenlea, 807
  Grammar School, 92
  ho., 168
  stables, etc., 618
  villa, 625
Dumbleton Hall, Glos., 679
Dumfries
  Bridge, 128
  Burns Mausoleum, 439
  Butcher Market, 241
  Court Ho., 824
  Crichton Royal Lunatic Asylum, 161
  Episcopal Ch. (Old), 439
  Moorhead's Hospital, 241
  Museum, 588
  New Ch., 531
  Observatory, 588
  Queensberry Column, 55
  St. Mary's Chapel, 969
  St. Michael's Ch., 845; monts., 586
  Theatre, 128
  Town Hall & Steeple, 79, 554
  Trades' Hall, 128
  Wesleyan Ch., 439
Dumfries Ho., Ayrshire, 46, 330
Dummer, Hants., Rectory, 271
Dumphail Ho., Morays., 647
Dun, Bridge of, Angus, 781
Dun Ho., Angus, 57, 296
Dunbar, E. Lothian
  Barracks, 55
  Castle, 55
  Ch., 357
  Free Ch., 385
Dunbeath Castle, Caithness, 385
Dunblane, Perths.
  Cathedral, 357
  Holmehill Ho., 784
  Manse, 784
Dunbog, Fife, School, 800
Dunchurch, Warwicks., School, 750
Duncombe Park, Yorks., 92, 860
Duncrub Park, Perths., 165
Dundalk, Ireland
  garden bldngs., 934
  Infirmary, 763
Dundas Aqueduct, Wilts., 678
Dundas Castle, W. Lothian, 162
Dundee
  Bank of Scotland, 161
  Beach Cottage, 542
  Binrock, ho., 587
  Bonnybank, ho., 587
  Bridewell, 67
  Cemetery, 140, 307
  Chapelshade Ch., 587

Dundee—contd.
  Chapelshade, cottage, 587
  Chapelshade grounds, 532
  Charles St., 113
  Commercial St., 113
  Congregational Chapel, 746
  Constitution Brae, 307
  Court Ho., 532
  Craig St., 113
  Croft of Blairgowrie, new street, 542
  Cunmont House, Newbigging, 541
  Custom Ho., 515, 814
  Dock St., 113, 587
  Dudhope Ch., 542
  East Ch., 162
  Elm Lodge, 542
  Episcopal Chapel (English), 106
  Euclid Crescent, 140
  Exchange Coffee Room, 754
  Exchange St., 587; nos. 8–11, 754
  Ferry Rd., 587
  Fleuchar Craig, 532
  Gaols, 67, 140
  Harbour, 524, 567
  High School, 67
  Howff (The), gateway, 113
  Infirmary, 587, 624
  Lindsay St., 113
  Logie St., 587
  Lunatic Asylum, 161, 542, 587, 623, 777
  Magdalen Yard Rd., hos., 587
  Mains school, 542
  Market cross, 567
  Milnbank, ho., 587
  Nethergate, nos. 92–96, 113; no. 166, 587
  New Bank, 586
  Orchestral Centre, 113
  Packhouses, 699
  Panmure St., 113
  Park Place, ho., 587
  Perth Road, ho., 587
  Reform St., 68
  Royal Bank, 161
  Sailors' Hall, 106
  St. Aidan's Ch., 113, 411
  St. Andrew's Ch., 106
  St. Andrew's Ch. (R.C.), 541
  St. Clement's Ch., 106
  St. David's Ch., 378, 587
  St. David's Free Church, 542
  St. David's parish school, 542
  St. George's Ch., 113
  St. Luke's U.P. Ch., 676
  St. Mary's Ch. (R.C.), 542
  St. Peter's Free Ch., 411
  Seagate, ho., 587
  Seminaries, 67, 140, 532
  Somerville Place, 113
  South Ch., 162
  South Tay St., nos. 1–27, 587
  South Union St., 113
  Tabernacle (The), 378, 587
  Tay Square U.P. Ch., 532
  Theatre Royal, 106
  Thistle Hall, 587
  Town Ho., 57, 740
  Town's Churches, 161, 569
  Town's Mills, 699
  Trades' Hall, 106
  Trinity Ho., 106
  Union Bank, 161
  Union Hall, 106
  Union Mount, Perth Rd., 587

Dundee—contd.
  Union St., 168, 542, 587
  U.P. Ch., 113
  Victoria Rd. School, 587
  Wallacetown Ch., 542
  Ward Chapel, 140
  Watt Institution, 68, 623
  Weavers' Hall, 676
  West Dock St., 113
  Western Cemetery, 307
  Windmill, 699
  Y.M.C.A., 68
Dundrum, Ireland, Criminal Lunatic Asylum, 603
Dunecht Ho., Aberdeens., Ch., 761
Dunfermline, Fife
  Abbey Ch., 161, 777; mont., 625
  County Bldngs., 286
Dungeness, Kent, lighthouse, 959
Dunglass, E. Lothian, 241, 586
Dunham Massey, Cheshire, 431, 596, 729
Dunimarle Castle, Fife, 261
Dunino, Fife, Ch., 357
Dunipace, Stirlings., Ch., 783
Dunira, Perths., 166, 426, 784; mont., 359
Dunkeld, Perths.
  Bridge, 738, 821
  Cathedral, 288; mont., 283
  Ho., 154, 288, 435, 780, 907
  School, 260
  town (projected), 676
Dunkirk, Kent, Ch., 882
Dunlop Ho., Ayrshire, 383
Dunlugas, Banffs., 762
Dunmore Park, Stirlings., 896
Dunninald Ho., Angus, 359, 645
Dunning, Perths., Ch., 127
Dunoon, Argylls.
  Castle Ho., 383
  Ch., 357, 382
Dunrobin Castle, Sutherld., 46, 92, 531
Duns, Berwicks.
  Castle, 100, 358
  Manse, 760
  Market Ho., 357
Dunscore, Dumfriess., Ch., 824
Dunskey Ho., Wigtowns., 163
Dunsley Manor, Staffs., 601
Dunstall Lodge, Staffs., 354
Dunstall Priory, Kent, 527
Dunster Castle, Som., 71
Dunston, Lincs.
  lodge, 528
  vicarage, 730
Duntish Court, Dorset, 207
Duntrune, Angus, 163
Dunvegan Castle, Skye, 148
Dunwich, Suffolk, St. James's Ch., 68
Dupplin Castle, Perths., 163, 337n., 644, 758, 784
Durdans, Surrey, 592
Durham
  Almshouses, 504
  Bishop's Palace, 236
  Castle, 122, 550, 949
  Cathedral, 77, 123, 280, 593, 916, 945; mont., 693
  County Courthouse, 122, 719
  County Gaol, 122
  County Hall (1664), 504–5
  Deanery, 122
  Freemasons' Lodge, 280

Durham—contd.
  Library, Palace Green, 505
  Prebends' Bridge, 593
  St. Cuthbert's Ch. (R.C.), 123
  St. Mary the Less Ch., 593
  St. Oswald's Ch., Elvet, 123
  School, 504
Durisdeer, Dumfriess.,
    mausoleum, 758
Duror, Argylls., Ch., 820
Durris Ho., Kinc., 737
Dursley, Glos.
  Ch., 798
  Workhouse, 481
Durweston, Dorset, bridge, 835
Duthil, Inverness., mausoleum,
    647
Dyce, Aberdeens.
  Bridge, 158
  School, 761
Dyffryn Aled, Denbighs., 844,
    916
Dyrham Park, Glos., 400, 806, 890
Dysart, Fife, Ch., 500

Ealing, Middlx.
  London Style Ho., 637
  Pitzhanger Manor, 251, 770
  St. Mary's Ch., 436
  villa, 66
Ealing Grove, Middlx., 483, 965
Eamond Bridge, Cumb., ho., 60
Earl Sterndale, Derbys., Ch., 383
Earl Stoke, Wilts., see Stoke Park
Earls Heaton, Yorks., St. Peter's
    Ch., 819
Earn, Bridge of, Perths., 678
Earnshill, Som., 788
Earsdon, Northumb., Ch., 266,
    363
Earsham Hall, Norfolk, 176, 768
Easebourne, Sussex, Ch., 119
Easington, Yorks., Rectory, 122
East Barnet, Herts.
  Ch., 485
  Little Grove, 341
  New Place, 341
East Bedfont, Middlx., Ch., 869
East Bilney, Norfolk, Rectory, 271
East Boldon Ho., Durham, 268
East Boldre, Hants., Ch., 843
East Bridgford, Notts., Ch., 556,
    697
East Carlton, Northants., Ch., 905
East Cowes, I. of W.
  Castle, 583
  Ch., 582
East Dene, I. of W., 103
East Donyland, Essex, Ch., 540
East Grinstead, Sussex, Ch., 367,
    445, 945
East Haddon Hall, Northants.,
    464, 859
East Ham, Essex, vicarage, 143
East Hendred, Berks., parsonage,
    438
East Horrington, Som., Ch., 202
East Huntspill, Som., Ch., 536
East Knoyle, Hants., Ch., 630
East Leake, Notts., Manor Ho.,
    621
East Moulsey, Surrey, Walnut
    Tree Lodge, 168
East Peckham, Kent, Holy
    Trinity Ch., 882
East Retford, Notts.
  Ch.; monts., 495, 523
  School, 171

East Row Bridge, Yorks., 192
East Standen, I. of W., farmho.,
    835
East Stoke, Dorset, Ch., 604
East Stratton, Hants., Ch., 251
East Teignmouth, Devon
  Public Rooms, 625
  St. Michael's Ch., 625
East Witton, Yorks., Ch., 727
East Woodhay, Hants.
  Ch., 111
  Rectory, 393
Eastbourne, Sussex
  Devonshire estate, 172
  Holy Trinity Ch., 171
  Mill Ho., 327
Eastbury Ho., Essex, 217
Eastbury Ho., Surrey, 963
Eastbury Park, Dorset, 561, 853
Eastcombe Ho., Kent, 807
Easter Skene, Aberdeens., 761
Easter Elchies, Morays., 645
Eastham, Worcs., Ch., 497
Easthampstead Park, Berks.
  cottages, 501
  gallery, 630
  Lodge, 197
Eastnor, Herefs.
  Castle, 744
  Ch.; monts., 797
Easton Lodge, Essex, 435
Easton (St. Paul), Som., Ch., 202
Easton-in-Gordano, Som., Ch.,
    141
Easton Grey, Wilts., Ch., 455
Easton Neston, Northants., 403,
    492, 925; Chain Gate, 669
Eastwell Park, Kent, 125, 166,
    904
Eastwell, Leics., Rectory, 586
Eastwick Park, Surrey, 276
Eastwood, Ireland, cottage, 527
Eaton Constantine, Salop., Ch.,
    762
Eaton Hall, nr. Congleton,
    Cheshire, 954
Eaton Hall, Cheshire, 166, 368,
    369, 476, 479, 616, 653,
    712, 822, 874
Eau Brink Cut, 573, 578
Ebberston Lodge, Yorks., 184,
    700
Ecclesall Bierlow, Yorks.
  Ch., 80
  Court Ho., 521
Ecclesgreig Ho., Kinc., 352
Eccleshill, Yorks., Ch., 673
Eccleston, Cheshire, Ch., 653
Echt, Aberdeens., Ch., 221
Eckford, Roxb., Ch., 760
Eckington, Derbys., Ch., 642
Ecton Hall, Northants., 551
Eden Grove, Westmld., 876
Eden Hall, Cumb., 745
Eden Park, Kent, 699
Edensor, Derbys., village, 698
Edgbaston Hall, Warwicks., 92,
    420
Edgcote Ho., Northants., 476,
    764, 799
Edgehill, Warwicks.
  cottage, 549
  tower, 549
Edgmond, Salop., Rectory, 577
Edinburgh
  Abercromby Place, 676, 907
  Academy, 161
  Advocates' Library, 646, 675

Edinburgh—contd.
  Ainslie Place, 359
  Albany St., 907
  Albany Street Independent
    Chapel, 739
  Albyn Place, 359; Highland
    Soc.'s premises, 646
  Alva St., 359
  Annandale St., 148
  Archers' Hall, 500, 623
  Arthur Lodge, 385
  Assembly Rooms, 161, 412
  Atholl Crescent, 122
  Atholl Place, 122
  Bank of Scotland, 241, 675, 734
  Baths, Hill St., 67
  Baths, Portobello, 734
  Baxter's Place, 101
  Bellevue Crescent, 121
  Bellfield St., 148
  Blacket Place, 359
  Blenheim Place, 647
  Botanical Gardens, 55
  Brandon St., 148
  Bridewell Prison, 50
  Broughton Place Ch., 288
  Broughton St., 159
  Brown Sq., 144
  Brunswick St., 647
  Brunton Place, 647
  Buccleuch Place, 144
  Burgher Ch., 148
  Burns Monument, 386
  Caledonian Railway Station,
    828
  Calton Bridge, 240
  Calton Convening Rooms, 288
  Calton Hill, 239, 240, 586, 645,
    646–7, 676, 776
  Calton Old Burial Ground,
    mont., 386
  Canongate, ho. for Lord
    Milton, 46; no. 53, 576
  Canongate Ch., 757
  Carlton St., 553
  Carlton Terrace, 647
  Castle, 152, 185, 571, 862
  Castle Terrace, 385, 932
  Charles St., 144
  Charlotte Sq., 52; nos. 33–46,
    676
  Circus Gardens, 647
  Circus Place, 148, 647
  Cisterns, 571
  City Chambers, 46, 305
  Claremont Crescent, 168
  Claremont St., 122
  Claremont St. Chapel, 553
  Clarence St., 148
  Clarendon Crescent, 800
  College, 570
  Coll. of Physicians, 179
  Comely Bank, 149
  Commercial Bank, 356
  Congregational Ch., Albany St.,
    739
  County Hall, 288
  Cowgate Bridge, 144
  Crichton Place, 144
  Cumberland St., 149, 676
  Danube St., 553
  Darnaway St., 359
  Deaf & Dumb Institute, 357
  Dean Bridge, 821
  Dean Cemetery, monts., 648
  Dean Orphanage, 385
  Dean Terrace, 553
  Deanhaugh St., 553

Edinburgh—contd.
Debtor's Prison, Calton Hill, 148
Dr. Guthrie's Ch., 385
Dr. Jamieson's Chapel, 357
Donaldson's Hospital, 381, 646
Doune Terrace, 359
Drawing Academy, 67
Drummond Place, 121, 144, 676
Drumsheugh Ho., 500
Dublin St., 676, 907
Duchess of Gordon's School, 736
Dundas Ho., 179, 209, 687
Dundas St., 168, 676
Dundonald St., 676
Earl Grey Pavilion, 385
East Brighton Crescent, Portobello, 101
Edinburgh & Glasgow Bank, 161
Edinburgh Life Assurance Office, 161
Elm Row, 647
Eton Crescent, 800
Exchange, 46, 154, 305
Excise Office, 144
Eyre Place, 148
Fettes Place, 149
Fettes Row, 676
Fife Ho., 58n.
Forbes' Bank, 161
Forres St., 359
Forth St., 159
Free Church Coll., 646
Gardner's Crescent, 261
Gasworks, 161
Gayfield Place, 104
Gayfield Sq., 104, 180
George IV Bridge, 385
George Sq., 144
George St., no. 93, 385; ho., 355
George Watson's Hospital, 57, 161
Gillespie's Hospital, 159
Glenfinlas St., 359
Gloucester Place, 122, 676
Great Colme St., 359
Great King St., 676
Great Stuart St., 359
Greenside Ch., 357
Greenside Well, 101
Greyfriars Ch., 531, 570
Greyfriars Churchyard, 46, 57, 238, 569, 571, 797, 862
Haddington Place, 148
Halkerston's Wynd, 571
Hamilton Place, 148
Hart Close, High St., 571
Hawkhill Villa, S. Leith, 46
Henderson Row, 148, 168
Heriot's Hospital, 46, 78, 121, 569–70, 571, 646, 647, 862; Chapel, 357
Heriot Row, 676
High School, Infirmary St., 500
High St., no. 14, 58; no. 142, 356; ho., 46
Hillside Crescent, 647
Holyroodhouse, 58 (bis), 78, 152, 153, 272, 569, 570, 571, 675, 787; Abbey Ch., 757; mont., 757
Hope Park Chapel, 148
Hopetoun Crescent, 148
Hopetoun Rooms, 384, 385
Howard Place, 359

Edinburgh—contd.
Howe St., 557
Hunter Sq., 480
Huntley St., 148
Hyvot's Mill, ho., 861
India St., 676
Infirmary St. U.P. Ch., 149
Inverleith Ho., 412
Inverleith Place, 149; no. 20, 647
Inverleith Row, 149; no. 8, 647
John Knox's Ch., 384
King's Bridge, 385
Lady Yester's Ch., 734
Law Courts, 675
Leith St., nos. 141–171, 158
Leopold Place, 647
London St., 122
Lothian Rd., 168; nos. 37–65, 754
Lothian Rd. U.P. Ch., 162
Lunatic Asylum, 161, 675
Lynedoch Place, 553
Maitland St. West, 378
Manor Place, 148
Mansfield Place, 676
Market Cross, 568
Marlborough St., Portobello, 861
Masonic Lodge, 67
Melbourne Place, nos. 1–12, 754
Melville Crescent, 148
Melville Monument, 168
Melville St., 148, 359
Merchant Maiden Hospital, 160, 240, 676
Merchants' Hall, 101
Military Academy, 289
Milne's Court, 571
Milne's Land, 571
Minto Ho., 58
Montgomery St., 647
Moray estate, 359
Moray Place, 359
Morningside Ch., 969
Morningside Place, 932
Morrison St., 168, 261, 378
Mound (The), bridge, 586
Mylne's Square, 571
National Gallery of Scotland, 646
National Monument, 222, 223, 224, 646
'National Monumental Church', 676
Nelson Monument, 159, 586
Nelson St., 676
Netherbow Port, 568
New Club, 161
New North Ch., 385
New Prisons, Calton Hill, 288
New Town, 237–8
Newington Place West, 149
Newington & St. Leonard's Ch., 148
Nicholson St. Chapel, 357
Normal School, Johnston Terrace, 754
North Bridge, 296, 412, 578; shops, 260
North British Assurance Office, 161
North St. Andrew St., no. 7, 385; nos. 15–19, 626
Northumberland St., 676, 907
Norwich Insurance Co., 385
Observatory, 646

Edinburgh—contd.
Old Calton Burying Ground; mont., 55
Old Observatory, Calton Hill, 238
Orphans' Hospital, 57
Oxford Terrace, 800
Paisley's Close, 758
Parliament Ho., 288, 567
Parliament Square, 675
Perth St., 168
Physicians' Hall, 238
Picardy Place, 159, 356
Picardy Village, 100, 531
Pitt St., 148
Pittville St., 148
Playfair Monument, 647
Police Office, High St., 595
Portobello Ch., 101, 734
Post Office, Waterloo Place, 480
Preston St. West, 149
Public Dispensary, 158
Quality St., 359
Queen St., no. 8, 52; no. 22, 755
Queen St. Gardens, 122
Queensferry St., 359
Randolph Cliff, 359
Randolph Crescent, 359; ho., 553
Randolph Place, 359
Record Office, 85
Regent Bridge, 288
Regent St., Portobello, 861
Regent Terrace, 647
Register Ho., 50, 675, 710
Riding School, York St., 50
Rosefield Avenue, Portobello, 101
Rosefield Place, Portobello, 101
Ross Ho., 58n.
Royal Bank of Scotland, High St., 57, 159
Royal Bank of Scotland, St. Andrews Sq., 209, 289
Royal Blind Asylum, 159
Royal Circus, 647
Royal Coll. of Physicians, 385
Royal Crescent, 149, 676
Royal High School, 385
Royal Infirmary, 57
Royal Institution, 646
Royal Scottish Academy, 384, 646
Royal Society, 161
Royal Terrace, 647
Rutland Place, 289, 800
Rutland Sq., 289, 800
Rutland St., 289, 800
St. Andrew's Ch., 322, 480, 734
St. Andrew's Sq., no. 26, 209
St. Anthony's Place, 168
St. Bernard's Ch., 553
St. Bernard's Crescent, 553
St. Bernard's Well, 586
St. Cecilia's Hall, 575, 623
St. Columba's Free Ch., 385
St. Cuthbert's Ch., 144, 158, 781, 877
St. Cuthbert's Manse, 144, 734, 781
St. George's Chapel (Episcopal), 44–5, 50
St. George's Ch., 675
St. Giles' Cathedral, 149, 158, 162, 203, 238, 570
St. James Sq., 238
St. John's Ch. (Episcopal), 161

Edinburgh—*contd.*
St. John's Free Ch., 385
St. John's Ch. of Scotland, 754
St. Luke's Free Ch., 162
St. Margaret's Convent Chapel, 357
St. Mary's Ch., Bellevue Crescent, 149
St. Mary's R.C. Ch. (Cathedral), 357
St. Paul's Episcopal Ch., 288
St. Peter's Episcopal Chapel, 644
St. Stephen's Ch., 646
St. Stephen St., 148
Salisbury Cottage, 385
Sandyford Gardens, Portobello, 101
Saxe Coburg Place, 553, 843
Saxe Coburg St., 843
Scotland St., 676
Scott Monument, 485, 689
Shandwick Place, 800
Signet Library, 148, 161, 646, 675, 777
Simpson's Close, 571
Smith's Land, 758
South Bridge, 296, 500
South Bridge St., 480
Stewart (Dugald) Monument, 647
Stockbridge Market, 724
Straiton Place, Portobello, 861
Surgeons' Hall, 646, 758
Tanfield Hall, 161
Theatre Royal, 161
Tolbooth St. John's Ch., 357, 595
Torphichen St., 122, 378
Town Ho., 220
Trinity Episcopal Chapel, 969
Tron Ch., 101, 260, 569
Tweeddale Court, 155
Tweeddale Lodging, High St., 46, 58
Tweeddale's Close, 757
Union St., 159
University, 50, 180, 557, 646, 676
Veterinary Coll., 260
Victoria Hall, 357
Victoria St., shops, etc., 754
Walker St., 148, 359
Waterloo Place, 289
Watson's Hospital, *see* George Watson's Hospital
Weir's Land, 571
Wellington St., Portobello, 861
Wemyss Place, 359
West Bow, no. 87, 755; shop, 577
West Brighton Crescent, Portobello, 101
Whiteford Ho., 576
Windmill St., 144
Windsor St., 647
Writer's Court, High St., 571
York Place, nos. 1–3, 626
Young St., 966
Edington Priory, Wilts., 71
Edith Weston Hall, Rutland, 858
Edmond Castle, Cumb., 745
Edmonstone Castle, Lanarks., 358
Edmonstone Ho., Midlothian, 164
Edmonton, Middlx.
Congregational Ch., 656
Edwinsford, Carm., bridge, 286
Edzell, Angus, Ch., 587

Eggesford, Devon
Ho., 510
Rectory, 546
Egginton Hall, Derbys., 84, 936, 957
Eggleston Hall, Durham, 122
Egham, Surrey, Ch., 685
Eglingham, Northumb., Ch., 363
Eglinton, Ireland, Market Ho., 593
Eglinton Castle, Ayrshire, 59, 100, 624
Eglwysfach, Card., Ch., 221
Egremont, Cheshire, *see* Wallasey
Egton, Yorks., bridge, 734
Eildon Hall, Roxb., 167
Eland Hall, Northumb., 266
Elcho Castle, Perths., farmho., 533
Elford, Staffs.
farmho., 936
Hall, 752
Elgin, Morays.
Anderson Institution, 736
Court Ho., 699
Elgin Institution, 736
Episcopal Ch., 699
Gray's Hospital, 357
Parsonage (Episcopal), 699
St. Giles Ch., 736
Trinity Lodge, 161
Elie Ho., Fife, 58, 221
Ellenhall, Staffs.
Ch., 84
ho., 838
Eller How, Lancs., 876
Ellerbeck Bridge, Yorks., 192
Ellesmere Canal, 820, 844
Ellingham, Hants., Ch., 659, 799
Ellon, Aberdeens.
Castle, 100
Ch., 761
Ellows (The), Staffs., 510
Elmham Hall, Norfolk, 270
Elmley Lovett, Worcs., Ch., 551
Elson, Hants., St. Thomas's Ch., 59
Elstree, Herts., Ch., 954
Elswick Hall, Northumb., 785
Eltham Court Farm, Kent, 428
Eltham Lodge, Kent, 544
Elton Hall, Hunts., 199, 708
Elton, Lancs., All Saints Ch., 391
Elvaston Castle, Derbys., 234, 861, 951
Elvetham, Hants., Ch., 696
Elvills, Surrey, 509
Ely, Cambs.
Bishop's Palace, 817
Cathedral, 80, 119, 299, 367, 368, 927, 945; mont., 716
Gaol, 94, 439
Parson's Almshouses, 94
Shire Hall, 439
Workhouse, 271
Emberton, Bucks., cottages, 535
Embleton, Northumb., Ch., 266
Emo Park, Ireland, 327, 858
Emral Hall, Flints., 841
Emsworth, Ireland, 328
Encombe, Dorset, 639
Endsleigh, Devon, 961
Endsleigh School, Essex, 501
Enfield, Middlx.
Ch., 517, 523
hos., 88
Jesus Ch., 72
Myddelton Ho., 306, 862

Enfield Chase, Middlx., Great Lodge, 732
Enfield Highway, Middlx., St. James's Ch., 523
Enford, Wilts., Ch., 387
Englefield Ho., Berks., 770
Englishcombe, Som., ho., 302
Enstone, Oxon., Vicarage, 225
Enville Hall, Staffs., 83, 209, 431, 549
Enys, Cornwall, 393
Epping, Essex
St. John's Ch., 434, 437
Workhouse, 487
Eppleworth, Yorks., ho., 668
Epsom, Surrey
Ch., 400
Christ Ch., 143
Grand-stand, 836
Vicarage, 143
Workhouse, 540
Erddig Hall (Park), Denbighs., 435, 844, 874, 946
Erdington, Warwicks., St. Barnabas Ch., 690
Eridge, Kent
Castle, 813
estate, 556
Errol, Perths., Ch., 357
Erskine, Renfrews.
Ch., 382
Ho., 745; obelisk, 168
Escot, Devon
Ch., 696
Ho., 429, 696, 814, 949
Escrick Park, Yorks., 117, 193
Esher, Surrey
Chargate, 853
Ch., 853
Claremont, *see* Claremont Place, 492, 506
West End Lodge, 723
Eshton Hall, Yorks., 876
Estcourt Park, Glos., 269
Etherley, Durham, Ch., 671
Eton College, Bucks.
Chapel, 87, 730
Cloister Court, 509
Library, 87, 708
Weston's Yard, 730
Etruria Hall, Staffs., 635
Etruria Works, Staffs., 635
Ettingshall, Staffs.
Ch., 279
Parsonage, 279
Schools, 279
Ettington, Warwicks.
Ch., 235, 465
Hall (Park), 302, 692, 874, 915–16
Ettrick Bridge, Selkirks., Ch., 162
Euston, Suffolk
bridge, 131
Ch., 105
Hall, 136, 712
Temple, 493
Evercreech, Som., Ch., 330
Everingham Park, Yorks., 193; Chapel (R.C.), 391
Everley, Wilts., Ch., 558
Everton, Beds.
Ch., 387
Ho., 770
Everton, Lancs., stables, 692
Evesbatch Court, Herefs., 800
Evington, Leics., Vicarage, 622
Evington Place, Kent, 649
Ewanrigg, Cumb., 60

Ewell, Surrey
  Bourne Hall, 592
  Ch., 497
  Garbrand Hall, 592
  Ho. (Castle), 497
Ewhurst, Surrey
  Ch., 279
  Rectory, 279
Exeter
  Barnfield Crescent, 598
  Baths, Southernhay, 515
  Bedford Circus, 789
  Bridge, 262
  Cathedral, 200, 293, 488
  City Prison, 234
  Close (The), no. 14, 320
  Colleton Crescent, 598
  County Gaol, 114
  County Ho. of Correction, 555
  Dix's Field, 598
  Fire Assurance Office, 625
  Higher Market, 278, 320–1
  Holy Trinity Ch., 233
  Hospital, 686
  Lower Market, 320
  Lunatic Asylum, 321
  Mint Methodist Chapel, 458
  New London Inn, 598
  Pennsylvania Park, 708
  Royal Public Rooms, 157
  St. David's Ch., 361
  St. Edmund's Ch., 233
  St. John's Hospital, Master's
    ho., 787
  St. Leonard's Ch., 625
  St. Pancras' Ch., 234
  St. Petrock's Ch., 411
  St. Stephen's Ch., 708
  St. Sidwell's Ch., 157
  St. Thomas's Ch., 625
  Sessions Ho., 787, 943
  Southernhay, 598
Exmouth, Devon, Holy Trinity
    Ch., 516
Exning Ho., Suffolk, 457
Exton Hall, Rutland, 121, 696
Eyam, Derbys., Rectory, 126
Eydon Lodge, Northants., 518
Eye, Northants., Ch., 94
Eye, Suffolk
  ho., 413
  Workhouse, 540
Eyemouth, Berwicks., Gunsgreen
    Ho., 44
Eynsham, Oxon., mill, 391
Eynsham Hall, Oxon., 92
Eythrope Ho., Bucks., 392, 866
Eyton Turret, Salop., 663
Eywood, Herefs., 744

Fairford, Glos.
  Croft Ho., 605
  Ho. (Park), 769, 791
Fairlawn, Kent, 341
Fairlight, Sussex, Rectory, 393
Fairnilie, Selkirks., 578
Fakenham, Norfolk
  bridge, 785
  Corn Hall, 145
Fala Ho., Midlothian, 58
Falkirk, Stirlings.
  Ch., 180, 357, 734, 821
  Red Lion Inn, 784
  School, 800
  Town Steeple, 381
Falkland, Fife
  Ch., 568
  Ho., 165

Falkland, Fife—contd.
  Manse, 87
  Palace, 283
  Town Ho., 87
Falloden Hall, Northumb., 266
Falmouth, Cornwall, Polytechnic
    Hall, 890
Falstone, Northumb., Ch., 363
Fan Grove (Court), Surrey, 649
Fangfoss, Yorks., Ch., 211
Fareham, Hants.
  Ch.; mont., 577
  Holy Trinity Ch., 604
Faringdon, Berks., Chapel, 306
Farley, Wilts.
  Almshouses (Hospital), 314,
    922n.
  Ch., 314
Farley Hall, Staffs., 331
Farley Hill Castle, Berks., 305
Farnborough Hall, Warwicks.,
    376
Farne Islands, lighthouse, 65
Farnell, Angus, Ch., 644
Farnley Hall, Yorks., 196
Farnworth, Lancs., St. John's
    Ch., 390
Farringdon Hall, Devon (?), 307
Farrington Gurney, Som., Ch.,
    638
Faskally, Perths., 163
Fasque Castle, Kinc., 59, 624
Fauldhope, Selkirks., bridge, 760
Faversham, Kent, Ch., 102, 249
Fawley, Bucks.
  Ch., 323, 341; Mausoleum, 323
  Court, 196, 922n., 946
Fawsley Park, Northants., 246
Fearn Abbey, Ross, mont., 101
Felbridge Place, Surrey, column,
    772
Felbrigg Hall, Norfolk, 139, 270,
    610, 712, 949
Felling, Durham, R.C. Ch., 266
Felpham, Sussex, The Turret,
    157
Felsted School, Essex, 463
Feltham, Middlx.
  Ch., 861
  watermill, 392
Feltwell, Norfolk, Rectory, 393
Fengate Ho., Norfolk, 883
Fenham Hall, Northumb., 333,
    591
Feniscowles, Lancs., Immanuel
    Ch., 886
Fenny Stratford, Bucks., St.
    Martin's Chapel, 905
Fernacres, Bucks., 700
Ferney Hall, Salop., 680n.
Ferns Palace, Ireland, 327
Ferrybridge, Yorks., bridge, 192,
    354, 398
Ferryhill, Durham, St. Luke's
    Ch., 123
Fetcham Park, Surrey, 596, 806
Fettercairn, Kinc., 163
Fetteresso, Kinc.
  Castle, 624
  Ch., 624
Fetternear Ho., Aberdeens., 541
Ffestiniog, Merioneths., St.
    David's Ch., 476
Ffynone, Pembs., 582
Figheldean, Wilts., mont., 831
Filey, Yorks., Crescent, 280
Filkins Hall, Oxon., 605
Fillbrook Lodge, Surrey, 451

Finborough Hall, Suffolk, 292,
    718
Fincham, Norfolk, Rectory, 271
Finchley, Middlx.
  cottage, 306
  villa, 754
Fingringhoe, Essex, Bridge, 527
Finlayston Ho., Renfrews., 272
Finnart Ho., Perthshire, 165
Fintray, Aberdeens.
  Ch., 761
  Ho., 761
Firbeck, Yorks.
  Chapel, 441
  Park, 441
Firle Place, Sussex, 558, 685
Fishbourne, Sussex, Ch., 274
Fisherrow, Midlothian, ho., 577
Fisherwick Park, Staffs., 125, 147,
    617
Fishtoft, Leics., Rectory, 488
Fladbury, Worcs., mont., 907
Flambards, Middlx., 729
Flamborough Head, Yorks.,
    lighthouse, 542, 959
Flatt Hall, Cumb., see
    Whitehaven Castle
Flaxley Abbey, Glos., 481
Fleetwood, Lancs.,
  Ch., 171–2
  Custom Ho., 172
  lighthouses, 172
  North Euston Hotel, 172
  Queen's Terrace, 172
Fletton, Hunts., parsonage, 151
Flimwell, Sussex, Ch., 171
Flint
  County Gaol, 844
  St. Mary's Ch., 657
  Town Hall, 878
Flintham Hall, Notts., 954
Flitton, Beds., Ch.; monts., 732,
    906
Flookburgh, Lancs., Chapel, 422
Floors Castle, Roxb., 57, 647, 907
Flore, Northants., parsonage, 391
Flotterton Ho., Northumb., 267
Flushing, Cornwall, Ch., 890
Fochabers, Morays.
  Bellie Ch., 101
  Episcopal Chapel, 737
  New Town, 101
  Spey Bridge, 157, 736
Foley Ho., Kent, 282
Folkestone, Kent
  Gaol, 637
  Radnor estate, 172, 480
Folkingham, Lincs., Ho. of
    Correction, 151
Folkington Place, Sussex, 271
Follaton Ho., Devon, 679
Fonthill Abbey, Wilts., 950
Fonthill Ho., Wilts., 167, 422,
    618, 769
Fontmell Magna, Dorset
  Ch., 302
  Rectory, 271
Foots Cray, Kent, ho., 76
Foots Cray Place, Kent, 376, 421,
    866
Forcett Hall, Yorks., 333, 611
Ford, Northumb.
  Castle, 346, 595, 669
  Ch., 266
Fordoun, Kinc., Ch., 761
Foremark Hall, Derbys., 421
Forest Hall, Essex, 464
Forest Hill, Oxon., parsonage, 438

Forest Row, Sussex, Ch., 563
Forfar, Angus
  Academy, 523
  County Bldngs., 587
  High St., nos. 20–26, 532
  Manse, 113
  St. James's Ch., 140
  Town & County Hall, 346, 644,
    824
Forglen Ho., Banffs., 762
Fornham Hall, Suffolk, 43, 948
Forres, Morays.
  Assembly Rooms, 736
  Masonic Lodge, 736
  Nelson Mont., 240, 793
  Town Ho., 699
Fort Augustus, Inverness., 705,
  713
Fort Charlotte, Shetland, 570
Fort George, Inverness., 45, 705,
  739
Fort William, Inverness., 185, 705
Forteviot, Perths., Manse, 784
Forton, Hants., St. John's Ch.,
  603, 604
Forty Hill, Middlx., Jesus Ch., 72
Fosdyke Bridge, Lincs., 678
Foston, Leics., Rectory, 685
Foston, Yorks., Rectory, 73
Fotheringhay, Northants., bridge,
  367, 654
Four Oaks Hall, Warwicks., 901
Fowberry Tower, Northumb.,
  595
Fowey, Cornwall, almshouses,
  127
Fowlis Easter, Angus, mausoleum,
  113
Foxhall, Charlton, Sussex, 131
Foxhills, Surrey, 95
Foxlydiate Ho., Worcs., 304
Frampton Ho., Glos., 788
Frant, Sussex, Ch., 556
Freckleton, Lancs., Ch., 507
Freeford Hall, Staffs., 655
Freeland Ho., Perths., 116,
  163
Fremington, Devon, Vicarage,
  233–4
Frenchay, Glos., Ch., 709
Friday Hill Ho., Essex, 859
Frimley, Surrey
  Ch., 621
  Park, 507
Fringford, Oxon., Rectory, 625
Frisby, Leics., Railway Station,
  622
Frogmore, Herts., 888
Frogmore Ho., Berks., 709, 949
Frome, Som.
  Christ Ch., 537
  Holy Trinity Ch., 352, 846
  St. John's Ch., 962
Froyle, Hants., Ch., 386
Fryern Court, Hants., 631
Frythe (The), Herts., 118
Fulford, Staffs., Ch., 906
Fulham, Middlx.
  Bridge, 378, 633, 643, 660, 694
  Ch., 506; mont., 855
  Colehill Ho., 426
  Craven Cottage, 434
  Palace, 228, 509
  Peterborough Ho., 441
Fullarton Castle, Ayrshire, 55
Fyfield, Essex
  Ch., 617
  Ho., 617

Gaddesden Place, Herts., 946
Gaines, Herefs., 663
Gainsborough, Lincs.
  Bridge, 738, 880
  Ch., 110, 408, 753
  Rectory, 110
Galby, Leics.
  Ch., 905
  Rectory, 622
Gallanach Ho., Argylls., 162
Galloway Ho., Wigtowns., 99,
  165, 220, 272, 575
Galston, Ayrshire, Old Ch.,
  133
Galway, Ireland, Gaol, 389
Ganton Hall, Yorks., 167
Garbally Park, Ireland, 246;
  obelisk, 367
Garden Ho., Stirlings., 784
Garendon Park, Leics., 632–3,
  669, 717
Garforth, Yorks., rectory, 79
Garn, Denbighs., 879
Garnkirk Ho., Lanarks., 382
Garnons, Herefs., 76
Garnstone Castle, Herefs., 583
Garryside, Perths., village, 261
Garscadden Ho., Dunb., 707
Garscube, Dunb., 163
Garstang, Lancs., St. Thomas's
  Chapel, 347
Garswood New Hall, Lancs.,
  318
Gart (The), Perths., 164
Gartchonzie Bridge, Perths.,
  101
Garth, Montgom., 525
Garth Ho., Perths., 411
Garthewin, Denbighs., 844
Gartmore Ho., Perths., 59, 100
Gask, Perths.
  Chapel (Episcopal), 358
  Ho., 241
Gatcombe Park, Glos., 95
Gate Burton Hall, Lincs., 321,
  641
Gate Helmsley, Yorks., The
  Retreat, 665
Gateacre, Lancs., ho., 692
Gateshead, Durham
  Ch. (St. Mary), 203, 266;
    mausoleum, 838
  Holy Trinity Chapel, 265
  Park Ho., 341
  Railway Station, 265
  St. Cuthbert's Ch., Bensham,
    266
  Viaduct, 265
  Warehouses, 602
Gateshead Fell, Durham, Ch.,
  445
Gatestack, Dumfriess., farmho.,
  588
Gatton Park, Surrey, 535
Gaunt's Ho., Dorset, 302
Gautby Hall, Lincs., 522
Gawdy Hall, Norfolk, 769
Gawthorpe Hall, Lancs., 92
Gaynes Hall, Hunts., 177
Gaynes Park, Essex, 612
Gayton, Norfolk, Workhouse,
  271
Gayton, Staffs., Ch., 838
Gayton-le-Marsh, Lincs.,
  Vicarage, 196
Gelly Dêg, Carm., 459
Gelston Castle, Kirkcud., 241
Germiston Ho., Lanarks., 382

Gerrards Cross, Bucks., St.
  James's Ch., 829
Gibside, Durham, 268, 301, 333,
  346, 611; Chapel, 611
Gidea Hall, Essex, 948
Gifford, E. Lothian, Ch., 758
Gilling, Yorks.
  Castle, 193, 261, 860
  Ch., 123
Gillingham, Dorset, Ch., 535,
  861; mont., 96
Gilmerton Ho., E. Lothian, 163
Gladsmuir, E. Lothian, Ch., 162
Glamis Castle, Angus, 190
Glansevern, Montgom., 142
Glanton Hall, Northumb., 267
Glanusk Park, Brecons., 527
Glan-yr-Afon, Flints., 397
Glasbury, Brecons., Ch., 857
Glasbury Bridge, Radnors., 286
Glasgow
  Adam's Court, 45
  Adelaide Place, 113
  Aitkenhead Ho., 382, 383
  Andersonian Institution, 239,
    759, 762
  Argyle Arcade, 81
  Argyll St., 436
  Ashley St., 155
  Assembly Rooms, 44, 50, 426
  Bank of Scotland, 161
  Barony Ch., 44, 698
  Bazaar, 219
  Blythswood Sq., 133
  Bothwell St., 155
  Bridewell, 416, 436, 624
  bridge (timber), 594
  Bridge St. Railway Station, 230
  Brisby Memorial Ch., 82
  British Linen Co.'s Bank, 382
  Broomielaw Bridge, 821
  Caledonian Railway Station,
    159n.
  Calton Green, 381
  Cambridge St. Ch., 82
  Carlton Place, 594
  Cathedral, 120, 382, 416, 485,
    776, 821
  Central Ch., 133
  Christ Ch. (Episcopal), 969
  City of Glasgow Bank, 113
  City Hall, 567
  Claremont Ho., 81
  Claremont Terrace, 81
  Clarendon Place, 811
  Cleland Testimonial Bldng.,
    381
  Clyde St., ho., 274
  Clydesdale Bank, Queen St.,
    381
  College St., 451
  College of Weaving, 168
  Court Ho. & Public Offices, 776
  Custom Ho., 265
  Duke of Montrose's ho., 530–1
  Dundas Vale School, see
    Normal School
  Erskine U.P. Ch., 82
  Exchange Place, 313
  Fever Hospital, 567
  Free Normal Seminary, 168
  Free Tron Ch., 779
  George St., Ind. Ch., 357
  Gibson's Land, 155
  Glasgow and Ship (later Union)
    Bank, 382
  Gorbals Ch., 382
  Grammar School, 239

Glasgow—*contd.*
Greyfriars U.P. Ch., 82
High Ch. (Kirk), *see* Cathedral
High School, 219
High St., 52
Horn's Court, 436
Hunterian Museum, 776
Hutcheson's Boys' School, 381
Hutcheson's Hospital, 381
Infirmary, 44, 50
John Knox Ch., *see* Gorbals Ch.
Kelvinside estate, 172
London St., 877
Lunatic Asylum, 776
Lyceum (The), 149
Lynedoch Crescent, 754
Lynedoch St., 754
McLellan Arch, 50
McMillan Calton Ch., 133
Magdalen Asylum, 219
Meadowflatt, 238
Mechanics' Institution, 113
Mosesfield Ho., 383
Necropolis, 82, 113, 155, 779, 862; Bridge of Sighs, 381; Knox Mont., 386
Nelson Mont., 381
New (Jamaica) Bridge, 45, 574, 578
Newton Place, 754
Normal School, 381
Observatory, 567, 877
Old Bridge, 574
Oxford St., bldngs., 308
Petershill Ho., 45
Police Offices, 725
Post Office, 161, 219
Prince of Wales' Bldngs., 81
Queen's Crescent, 155
Queen's Terrace, 158
Ramshorn Ch., *see* St. David's Ch.
Reformatory, 155
Royal Bank of Scotland, 289
Royal Crescent, 811
Royal Exchange, 381, 416
St. Andrew's Ch., 274
St. Andrew's R.C. Chapel (Cathedral), 357
St. Andrew's Square, 386
St. Columba's Ch., 416
St. David's Ch., 416, 691, 717
St. Enoch's Ch., 382, 451
St. George's Ch., 776
St. John's Ch., Bell St., 382
St. Jude's Ch. (Episcopal), 779
St. Mary's Episcopal Chapel, 725
St. Paul's Ch., 382
Shamrock St. U.P. Ch., 82
Shawfield Mansion, 184
Sighthill Cemetery, 779
Somerset Place, 81
Surgeons' Hall, 239
Theatre Royal, 381
Tolbooth, 219, 381
Tolcross Relief Ch., 133
Tontine Hotel, 274, 386
Town Hall, 274
Trades House, 50, 381, 451
Tron Ch., 44, 50
University, 133, 238; Hamilton Bldng., 594; Library, 57, 274
Warehouses, 82, 676
Wellington Arcade, 81
Wellington St. U.P. Ch., 82

Glasgow—*cont.*
West Nile St., premises, 82
West Princes St., 155
Western Bank, 161, 381
Western Club, 381
Woodlands Hill, 754
Woodlands Terrace, 82
Woodside Crescent, 754
Woodside Place, 754
Woodside Terrace, 754
Glashampton Ho., Worcs., 869
Glassaugh Ho., Banffs., 737
Glasserton, Wigtowns.
Ch., 618
Ho., 54
Glastonbury, Som.
Priory, 156
Town Hall, 101
Gledhow Grove, Yorks., 216
Gledhow Hall, Yorks., 194
Gledstone Hall, Yorks., 194
Glen Ho., Peebles., 647
Glenae, Dumfriess., 128
Glenbarr Abbey, Argylls., 358
Glencairn, Dumfriess.
Ch., 529
Manse, 588
Glencarse Ho., Perths., 55
Glenferness, Nairns., 737
Glenfiddich (Glenfiddoch) Lodge, Banffs., 100, 642
Glengunnery, Morays., 698
Glenisla, Angus
Ch., 887
Manse, 887
Glenlair, Kirkcud., 588
Glenlee, Kirkcud., 527
Glenorchy, Argylls., Ch., 288
Glenstal Castle, Ireland, 88
Glentworth Ho., Lincs., 610
Glevering Hall, Suffolk, 173, 883
Glossop, Derbys., Ch., 210
Gloucester
Bishop's Palace, 475
Blue Coat Hospital, 881
Cathedral: altar-screen, 743; choir-screen, 366, 493; mont., 693
Christ Ch., Brunswick Sq., 690
Council Ho., 697
County Gaol, 114, 231, 881
Custom Ho., 972
Debtors' Prison, 230
Eastgate Ho., 688
Horton Road Hospital, 230
Infirmary, 509, 691, 738–9
Judges' Lodgings, 745
Lunatic Asylum, 230, 777
Markets, 481, 661
St. Bartholomew's Hospital, 661
St. James's Ch., Barton, 487
St. John Baptist Ch., 232, 915
St. Mary de Lode Ch., 232
St. Nicholas Ch., 155, 688
Shire Hall, 743
Somerset Ho., 745
Tolsey, 697
Triumphal Arch (1777), 688
Westgate Bridge, 743
Gloucester & Berkeley Ship Canal, 573, 578
Glynde, Sussex
Ch., 558, 703, 837
Place, 558, 703
Glynlliffon, Caern., 407
Gnaton Hall, Devon, 112
Gnoll Castle, Glam., 463

Gobions, Herts., 342
Godalming, Surrey
bridge, 370
Ch., 632
Town Hall, 632
Godmanchester, Hunts., Chinese Bridge, 325
Godmersham Park, Kent, 166
Godney, Som., Ch., 536
Godshill, I. of W., mont., 810n.
Godstow, Oxon., lock, 391
Gogar, Midlothian, mont., 386
Golborne, Lancs., cotton mill, 811
Golcar, Yorks., Ch., 73, 210
Gold Hill, Kent, 527
Golden Grove, Carm., 582, 963
Goldsbrough Hall, Yorks., 193
Golspie, Sutherld., fountain, 92
Goodmanham, Yorks.,
Hall Garth, 564
Rectory, 564
Goodnestone, Kent
Ch., 691
Park, 576
Goodrich Court, Herefs., 117, 393
Goodwin Sands, lighthouse, 613
Goodwood Ho., Sussex, 185, 207, 289, 559, 948; Carné's Seat, 562; Race-stand, 274
Goole, Yorks.
Ch., 442
town, 441
Gopsall Hall, Leics., 117, 421, 611, 880, 962
Gordon Castle, Moray, 100, 650, 707, 737
Gordonstoun Ho., Moray, 100
Gore Court, Kent, 228
Gorhambury Ho., Herts., 76, 166, 710, 817
Goring, Sussex
Ch., 171
Ho., 92
Gortanloisk, Argylls., 267
Gosfield Hall, Essex, 550
Gosfield Place, Essex, 293
Gosford Castle, Ireland, 435
Gosford Ho., E. Lothian, 55, 164, 671, 676, 829
Gosforth, Northumb.
Ch., 265, 268
Ho., 611
Gosport, Hants.
Clarence Victualling Yard, 813
Grammar School, 174
Holy Trinity Ch., 604
Naval Hospital, 436, 450, 844
Goudhurst, Kent, Ch., 495, 965
Gough Park, Middlx., 300
Govan, Lanarks., Ch., 759
Grace-Dieu Manor, Leics., 669
Gracefield Lodge, Ireland, 585
Grafham, Hunts., School, 618
Grange, Banffs., Manse, 699
Grange (The), Yorks., 610
Grange Bridge, Roxb., 781
Grange Ho., nr. Edinburgh, 647
Grange Park, Hants., 225, 712, 745, 896
Grangemouth, Stirlings., 425
Grangemouth (West), Stirlings., Ch., 800
Gransden Magna, Hunts., Vicarage, 438
Grant Lodge, Morays., 624
Grantham, Lincs.
Ch.; monts., 777
Prison, 505

Grantham, Lincs.—*contd.*
St. Mary's Ch. (R.C.), 899
Vicarage, 505
Granton, Midlothian, 168
Grasmere, Westmld., Ch., 876
Gravesend, Kent
Baths, 892
building estate, 172
Chapel, 459
cottage, 150
Market, 320
Milton Park estate, 892
St. George's Ch., 739
School, 546
Town Hall, 739, 892
Town Quay, 706
Grayrigg, Westmld., Ch., 876
Greasbrough, Yorks., Ch., 665, 868
Great Alne, Warwicks., Ch., 861
Great Berkhamsted, Herts.
Ch., 962; mont., 85
Rectory, 964
Great Bolas, Salop., Ch., 897
Great Bowden, Leics., mont., 906
Great Brickhill, Bucks., Rectory, 173
Great Briddlesford Farm, I. of W., 859
Great Brington, Northants., Ch., 119
Great Chesterford, Essex, Ch., 234
Great Cressingham, Norfolk, bridge, 785
Great Crosby, Lancs., Ch., 303
Great Culverden Ho., Kent, 173
Great Doods, Surrey, 634
Great Glen, Leics., Vicarage, 497
Great Hallingbury, Essex, Ch., 463
Great Hampden, Bucks., Rectory, 393
Great Haywood, Staffs.
R.C. Chapel, 446
St. Stephen's Chapel, 842
Great Holland, Essex, Rectory, 143
Great Houghton, Northants., Ch., 421
Great Malvern, Worcs.
Assembly Rooms, 259
Barclays Bank, 259
Baths, 259
Circulating Library, 259
Foley Arms Hotel, 259n.
Priory Ch., 809
Great Marlow, Bucks.
Bridge, 132, 139
Ch., 444, 721
Congregational Chapel, 305
lock cottage, 836
Market Ho., 959
Place, 69
Great Milton Ho., Oxon., 948
Great Oakley, Essex, Rectory, 692
Great Packington, Warwicks., Ch., 125
Great Ponton, Lincs., parsonage, 505
Great Saxham Hall, Suffolk, 54, 625
Great Snoring, Norfolk, workhouse, 827
Great Stanmore, *see* Stanmore
Great Tew, Oxon.
Ch., 691
cottage, 419

Great Tew, Oxon.—*contd.*
farm, 524
Park, 682
village, 692
Great Waltham, Essex, School, 278
Great Wilbraham, Cambs., Ch., 863
Great Witcombe, Glos., Ch., 155, 215
Great Witley, Worcs., *see* Witley
Great Wolford, Warwicks., Ch., 840
Great Woolstone, Bucks., parsonage, 173
Great Yarmouth, Norfolk
Bridge, 133
Harbour, 499, 573
ho., 377
Market Ho., 147
Naval Arsenal, 944
Nelson Column, 895
Paston Grammar School, 361
Royal Naval Hospital, 423, 637
St. George's Ch., 660
St. Mary's Chapel, 723
St. Mary's Ch. (R.C.), 724
St. Nicholas Ch., 723, 895, 955
St. Nicholas' Hospital, 423
St. Peter's Ch., 723
School, 145
Suspension Bridge, 723
Theatre, 324
Town Hall, 660
Greatford, Lincs., parsonage, 151
Greatham Hospital, Durham, 961
Grebten (Gribton), Dumfriess., 588
Gredington, Flints., 397
Greenhead, Northumb., Ch., 265
Greenlaw, Berwicks., Court Ho., 247
Greenmount, Ireland, 225
Greenock, Renfrews.
Assembly Rooms, 160
Bank of Scotland, 161
Blackhall St. Chapel, 257
Ch., 534
Congregational Ch., 82
Custom Ho., 160
Episcopal Chapel, 257
Exchange Buildings, 160
Infirmary, 61
Middle Ch.; mont., 777
School, 777
Watt Institution, 116
Greens Norton, Northants., Ch., 529
Greenstead, Essex, parsonage, 173
Greenwich, Kent
Chapel (R.C.), 813
Christ Ch., 145
Crown & Sceptre Tavern, 755
Gloucester Circus, 725
Holy Trinity Ch., 972
Hospital, 98, 403, 405, 792, 925, 965; Boys' School, 592; Chapel, 591–2, 695, 797; Infirmary, 704, 796; King Charles Block, 727; Queen Mary Block, 695
Macartney Ho., 770
Market, 480
Mince-Pie Ho., 853
Nelson St., 480
Nunnery (The), 853
Observatory, 924
Palace, 257, 258, 472, 874

Greenwich, Kent—*contd.*
Park Hall, 454
Park Place, 813
Queen's Ho., 65, 472, 874
Royal Naval Asylum, 65
St. Alphege's Ch., 404, 454
St. Mary's Ch., 94
Ship Torbay Tavern, 307
Vanbrugh Castle, 853
White Towers, 853
Woodlands Ho., 345
Workhouse, 888
Greenwood, Hants., 268
Gregories, Bucks., 553, 903n.
Grendon, Warwicks.
Ch., 655, 738
Hall, 655, 841
Gresford Lodge, Denbighs., 949
Gresley, Derbys., *see* Church Gresley
Greta Bridge, Yorks., 192, 703
Greystead, Northumb.
Ch., 727
Parsonage, 727
Grimsthorpe Castle, Lincs., 332, 606, 853, 908
Grimston Garth, Yorks., 196, 278
Grimston Park, Yorks., 174
Grinshill, Salop., Ch., 188
Grinton, Yorks., bridge, 192
Grittleton, Wilts., Ch., 638
Grosmont, Yorks., Ch., 442
Grove (The), Berks., 253
Grove (The), Herts., 118, 817
Grove (The), Kirkcud., 692
Grove (The), Surrey, 173
Grove Hall, Notts., 193
Grove Park, Warwicks., 746, 874
Gubbins, Herts., 342
Guernsey
hos., 900
villa, 501
Guildford, Surrey
Bridge, 653
Corn Market, 332
Holy Trinity Ch., 436
Quaker Meeting Ho., 110
Rectory, 867
St. Nicholas Ch., 279
Gundimore, Hants., 349
Gunley Hall, Mon., 408
Gunnersbury Ho. (later Park), Middlx., 233, 539, 873, 972
Gunnersbury Ho., Middlx., 650
Gunthorpe Hall, Norfolk, 769
Gunthwaite, Yorks., ho., 565
Gunton, Norfolk
Ch., 50
Hall, 136, 946
Guy's Cliff Ho., Warwicks., 467
Gwennap, Cornwall, parsonage, 890
Gwernafield, Flints., Holy Trinity Ch., 522
Gwersyllt, Denbighs., Holy Trinity Ch., 631
Gwlith-faes, Brecons., 527
Gwrych Castle, Denbighs., 175, 692
Gwydir Castle, N. Wales, 431
Gwynne Ho., Essex, 617

Habergham Eaves, Lancs., Holy Trinity Ch., 857
Haccombe, Devon, Ch., 489
Haceby, Lincs., parsonage, 505
Hackness Hall, Yorks., 72
Hackney, *see* London

Hackthorn Ho., Lincs., 518
Hackwood Ho., Northumb., 268
Hackwood Park, Hants., 342, 585, 804, 807, 855, 953, 958
Haddington, E. Lothian
  Ch., 158
  Court Ho., 161
  Fleshmarket, 158
  hos., 158
  Town Ho., 57, 357
Haddo Ho., Aberdeens., 58, 99, 220, 737
Hadleigh, Suffolk
  Ch., 496
  Deanery, 393
  villa, 518
Hadley, Salop., Ch., 604
Hadlow Castle, Kent, 276, 813
Hadlow Down, Sussex, Ch., 563
Hadzor, Worcs.
  Ch., 375
  farmho., 375
  Ho., 374, 965
  lodge, 487
Haffield Ho., Herefs., 745
Hafod, Card.
  Ch. (Eglwys Newydd), 945
  Ho., 86, 582, 649
Haggs, Stirlings., Ch., 416
Hagley, Worcs.
  Ch., 550, 691; mont., 322
  Ho., 213, 482, 550, 639; Castle, 549; Palladian Bridge, 639, 717; Temple, 796
  Rockingham Hall, 550
Hagley Hall, Staffs., 946
Haigh with Aspull, Lancs., Ch., 691
Hailes Ho., Midlothian, 220
Haileybury Coll., Herts., 895
Haines Hill, Berks., 321
Hainford, Norfolk, All Saints Ch., 145
Haining (The), Selkirks., 288
Hainton, Lincs.
  Chapel (R.C.), 899
  Ch., 899
  Hall, 72
  School, 899
Hale, Hants.
  Ch., 70, 473; monts., 70, 952
  Ho. (Park), 68, 69, 425, 872
Hale Hall, Lancs., 583
Halesowen, Worcs., Ch., 691
Halesworth, Suffolk, Chapel, 305
Halifax, Yorks.
  Assembly Rooms, 599
  ho., etc., 194
  Holy Trinity Ch., 466
  Lit. & Phil. Soc.'s Hall, 360
  Odd-Fellows' Hall, 213
  Piece Hall, 431
  Rawson's Bank, 194
  St. James's Ch., 600
  St. John's Ch., 210
  St. Paul's Ch., 210
  Town Hall, 92, 784
Halkin Castle, Flints., 156, 369
Halkin Mountain, Flints., 369
Hall, Devon, 387
Hall Barn, Bucks., 185
Hallaton, Leics., Rectory, 271
Hallhead Ho. (Castle), Aberdeens., 100
Hallingbury Place, Essex, 464, 674
Hallow, Worcs., Ch., 526
Halsham, Yorks., mausoleum, 74

Halsnead Hall, Lancs., 769
Halson Wood Villa, Devon, 394
Halstead, Essex
  Ho. of Correction, 418, 463
  Sloe Farm, 293
Halston Hall, Salop., 576
Halstone, Dumfriess., farmho., 588
Halswell Park, Som., 53, 463, 819
Halton, Bucks., Ch., 685
Halton, Lancs., Rectory, 236
Halton, Sussex, Ch., 203
Halton Place, Yorks., 242
Haltwhistle, Northumb., ho., 267
Ham, Surrey
  Ho., 154, 571, 712
  parsonage, 869
  St. Andrew's Chapel, 506
  School, 869
Ham Court, Worcs., 481
Ham Frith, Essex, ho., 495
Ham Manor, Sussex, 393
Hambleton, Rutland, Vicarage, 411
Hamels, Herts., 768
Hamilton, Lanarks.
  Bridge, 821
  Ch., 57
  Collegiate Ch.; mont., 758
  Mausoleum, 352
  Palace, 59, 79, 87, 282, 283, 352, 383, 758
Hamilton Hall, Midlothian, 58
Hammersmith, Middlx.
  Brandenburg Ho., 562, 727
  British School, 350
  Cockburn Ho., 350
  Convent of Good Shepherd, 724
  hos., 168, 441
  North End, 617
  St. Mary's Ch., 940
  St. Peter's Ch., 506
Hammerwood Lodge, Sussex, 507
Hampden Ho., Bucks., 732, 837
Hampstead, see London
Hampstead Marshall, Berks., 336, 342, 636, 791, 904
Hampton, Middlx.
  Ch., 309, 506; monts., 70, 226
  Fort (The), 838
  Garrick's ho., 54
  ho. (Coutts), 612
Hampton Court, Herefs., 77, 836
Hampton Court Palace, Middlx., 118, 214, 314, 493, 806, 853, 855, 923; bridge, 882; ho., 807; Pavilions, 845; 'Trianon' (projected), 804, 806
Hampton Lodge, Surrey, 653
Hampton Lucy, Warwicks.
  Ch., 690; mont., 693
  Rectory, 750
Hampton Wick, Middlx., St. John's Ch., 506
Hamptons, Kent, 456
Hams Hall, Warwicks., 71, 635
Hamstead Farm, I. of W., 583
Hamworthy, Dorset, Ch., 422
Hanborough, Oxon., Ch., 847
Hanbury, Staffs.
  Ch., 690
  Vicarage, 654
Hanbury, Worcs.
  Ch., 465
  Hall, 212, 709, 907

Handsworth, Staffs.
  Ch., 427, 654; Watt Chapel, 691
  ho., 823
  St. James's Ch., 279
Hanford, Staffs., Ch., 906
Hanging Heaton, Yorks., St. Paul's Ch., 819
Hanham Ch., Glos., 316
Hankelow Hall, Cheshire, 84
Hanley, Staffs., Bank, 75
Hanley Lodge, Midlothian, 164
Hanmer Hall, Flints., 84
Hannayfield, Dumfriess., 588
Hanwell, Middlx.
  Ch., 388
  ho. (Berners), 576
  Lunatic Asylum, 62, 563, 734; competition for, 349, 353, 376
Hanworth, Middlx.
  Ch., 625, 945
  Farm, 950
  Ho., 549
  Park, 246
Hanworth Hall, Norfolk, 136
Harborne, Warwicks.
  Ch., 691
  ho., 692
Harbottle Ho., Northumb., 267
Harden Ho., Berwicks., 79, 154, 165
Hardenhuish, Wilts.
  Ch., 912
  Ho., 770
Hardingham, Norfolk, Rectory, 271
Hardwick, Durham, 610
Hardwick Grange, Salop., 398
Hardwick Hall, Derbys., 764, 797
Hardwick Ho., Suffolk, 375
Hardwicke Court, Glos., 745
Hare Hall, Essex, 612
Hare Hatch, Berks., 111
Hare Park, Cambs., 546, 653
Harefield, Middlx.
  Ch., 484, 588
  Grove, 618
  Ho., 235
Harefield Ho., Cheshire, 247
Harefield Ho., Devon, 157
Haresfoot, Herts., 617, 642
Harewood, Yorks.
  Bridge, 192
  Ho., 52, 92, 106, 193, 209; gateway, 72; stables, 193
  village, 193
Harlaxton Manor, Lincs., 117, 165, 971
Harlech, Merioneths., Ch., 476
Harlestone Ho., Northants., 682
Harleyford Manor, Bucks., 817
Harlow, Essex, School, 44
Harpole, Northants.
  Ch., 773
  Rectory, 578
Harpton Court, Radnors., 583
Harptree Court, Som., 541
Harpurhey, Lancs., Christ Ch., 878
Harrogate, Yorks.
  Assembly Room, 643
  Christ Ch., 600
  Royal Chalybeate Spa, 215
  St. Mary's Ch., 211
  Victoria Baths, 215

Harrold, Beds.
  farmho., 218
  Ho., 367
Harrow, Middlx.
  hos., 143, 173
  Park (The), 583
  School, 223, 224; Headmaster's
    Ho., 174
Harston, Leics., Ch., 505
Hartburn, Northumb., Ch., 265
Hartest, Suffolk, Rectory, 824
Hartford Hall, Northumb., 785
Hartford Lodge (Whitehall),
  Cheshire, 273
Hartham Park, Wilts., 949
Harting, Sussex
  Ch., 689n.
  Down Cottage (Place), 650
Hartland Abbey, Devon, 546
Hartlebury, Worcs.
  Castle, 142, 483, 509, 758-9
  Ch., 497, 691; mont., 632
Hartlepool, Durham, cemetery,
  266
Hartsheath Hall, Flints., 541
Hartwell, Bucks.
  Ch., 483
  Ho., 342, 483, 947
  Schools, 124n.
  Spring, 124n.
Harviestoun Castle, Clack., 624
Harwich, Essex
  lighthouse, 65
  St. Nicholas Ch., 823
Haselbury Plucknett, Som., Ch.,
  487
Haseley, Oxon., ho., 912
Haslar, Hants., see Gosport
Hassenbrook Hall, Essex, 872
Hassop, Derbys., R.C. Chapel,
  446
Hastings, Sussex
  Ch. (R.C.), 620
  ho. (North), 480
  Marine Parade, no. 14, 963
  Pelham Crescent, 480
  St. Mary-in-the-Castle Ch., 480
Hatch Court, Kent, see Mersham
  Hatch
Hatch Court, Som., 667
Hatchford, Surrey, 118
Hatchlands, Surrey, 52, 125,
  680n.
Hatfield, Herts.
  Church, Salisbury Chapel, 197
  Ho., 95, 270, 473, 511
Hatfield Peverel, Essex, Ch., 434
Hatfield Place, Essex, 464
Hathern, Leics., Rectory, 395
Hatherop, Glos., Rectory
  (Severalls), 605
Hathersage, Derbys., Ch., 640
Hatton, Warwicks., parsonage,
  622
Hatton Grange, Salop., 663
Haugham, Lincs., Ch., 898
Haughton Castle, Northumb.,
  268
Haunch Hall, Staffs., 842
Havant, Hants., Ch., 604
Haverfordwest, Pemb., Foley Ho.,
  582
Haverholme Priory, Lincs., 488
Havering, Essex, mont., 952
Haveringland Hall, Norfolk, 118
Havra, Shetland, 164
Hawarden Castle, Flints., 245,
  246, 844

Hawick, Roxb., East Bank Ch.,
  162
Hawkhead Park, Renfrews., 99,
  644
Hawkley, Hants., Ch., 278
Hawkstone, Salop.
  Citadel (The), 398
  Hall, 954
Hawley, Hants., Ch., 279
Hawnby, Yorks., bridge, 192
Hawkesbury Upton, Glos., tower,
  858
Hawkesbury, Warwicks., bridge,
  738
Hawnes, Beds., 518
Hawstead Place, Sussex, 246
Hawthorn Dene Ho., Durham,
  267
Hawthorn Tower, Durham, 267
Hay, Brecons., Ch., 406
Hay Hole Docks, Northumb., 265
Haydon Hill, Herts., 174
Hayling Island, Hants., 44, 218,
  416
Haynes, Beds., 518
Hazeldon, Devon, 890
Hazelhead Ho., Aberdeens., 762
Hazlegrove Ho., Som., 96
Headbourne Worthy, Hants., ho.,
  391
Headfort Ho., Ireland, 53, 209
Headingley, Yorks.
  Grange (The), 610
  St. Michael's Ch. 210
Headley, Surrey, 660
Heanton Punchardon, Devon,
  parsonage, 234
Heath, Yorks. (nr. Halifax),
  School, 61
Heath, Yorks. (nr. Wakefield)
  Hall, 192, 731n.
  Ho., 610
Heath Ho., Staffs., 729, 842, 970
Heath & Reach, Beds., Ch., 595
Heathcot, Kinc., 737
Heatherden Ho., Sussex, 114
Heatherton Park, Som., 114
Heathfield Ho., Staffs., 957
Heathfield Lodge, Middlx., 770
Heaton Hall, Northumb., 591
Heaton Ho., Lancs., 946, 953,
  957
Hebburn Hall, Durham, 267
Hebden, Yorks., Bridge, 354
Hebden Bridge, Yorks., Ch., 600
Heckfield Place, Hants., 119
Heckmondwike, Yorks., Ch., 73
Hedsor Lodge, Bucks., 208
Heligan, Cornwall, 393
Helme Lodge, nr. Kendal, 876
Helmingham Hall, Suffolk, 583
Helmsdale Bridge, Sutherld., 821
Helmsley (Castle), Yorks., 300
Helston, Cornwall
  Baptist Chapel, 711
  Ch., 285, 890
  Coinage Hall, 687
  Grammar School, 890
  Guildhall, 890
  Market Ho., 392
  Monument (Grylls), 890
Hemingford Abbots, Hunts., ho.,
  174
Hempstead, ? Norfolk, parsonage,
  271
Henbury, Cheshire, Ch., 502
Henbury, Glos., Ch., 691; mont.,
  226

Hendon, Durham
  Ch., 266
  Rectory, 268
  School, 265
Hendon, Middlx.
  Ch.; mont., 478
  Hall, 867
  ho. (Morant), 619
Hendre (The), Mon., 534
Henham Hall, Suffolk, 179, 949
Henley-on-Thames, Oxon.
  Bridge, 410, 832
  Congregational Ch., 455
  Town Hall, 132
Henlow, Beds., mont., 906
Hennerton Ho., Berks., 810
Hensol, Kirkcud., 527
Heppington Ho., Kent, 258
Hereford
  Bishop's Palace, 387
  Castle Green, 800
  Cathedral, 188, 234, 800, 945
  College of Vicars Choral, 83
  County Gaol, 581
  Fosse (The), 745
  Infirmary, 621
  Market Hall, 43
  Nelson Column, 389
  Pool Cottage, 745
  St. Francis Xavier (R.C.) Ch.,
    255, 724
  St. Martin's Ch., 456
  St. Peter's Ch., 411
  Shire Hall, 743
  Swan Inn, 621
  Theatre, 621
Hermitage (The), Northumb., 267
Hermitage of Braid, Midlothian,
  158
Hermitage Water, Liddesdale,
  bridge, 760
Herne Bay, Kent
  Christ Ch., 218
  Clock Tower, 253
  promenade, 375
Herne Hill, Surrey, ho., 618
Heron Court, Hants., 331
Heronden Hall, Kent, 271
Herriard Park, Hants., 405, 454,
  806
Herringston, Dorset, 517
Hersham, Surrey, School, 730
Herstmonceaux Place, Sussex, 957
Hertford
  All Saints Ch., 763
  Castle, 110, 426
  Christ's Hospital Girls' School,
    518, 601
  County Gaol, 198, 418, 614,
    763
  Hospital, 763
  Shire Hall, 44, 50, 596
  Town Hall, 44, 50
Hesleyside, Northumb., 123, 591
Hessenford, Cornwall, Ch., 393
Hestercombe Ho., Som., 86
Hessle, Yorks., Hesslewood, 564
Heston, Middlx., Ch.; mont., 55
Hethersett, Norfolk, 769
Hetton-le-Hole, Durham, Ch., 67
Hever Castle, Kent, 701
Heveningham Hall, Suffolk, 817,
  947
Hewell Grange, Worcs., 245, 752
Heworth, Durham, Ch., 785
Hexham, Northumb.
  Abbey Ho., 267, 591
  Bridge, 354, 575, 634, 916

Hexham, Northumb.—*contd.*
Priory Ch., 265, 266
Heydon Hall, Norfolk, 136, 629
Heysham Hall, Lancs., 876
Heythrop Ho., Oxon., 69, 750
Heytesbury Hospital, Wilts., 685
Heywood, Ireland, 327
Hickleton Hall, Yorks., 111, 610
High Beech, Essex, Ch., 437
High Cross, Northumb., 268
High Hall, Dorset, 309
High Hatton, Salop., 664
High Legh, Cheshire
Hall, 431, 583, 893; lodge, 377
West Hall, Chapel, 397
High Littleton, Som., Ch., 330
High Melton Hall, Yorks., 611
High Ongar, Essex, bridge, 464
High Warden, Northumb., 267
High Wycombe, Bucks.
Butter Market, 50
Ch., 483
Guildhall, 483
Shambles, 50
Higham-on-the-Hill, Leics., Ch., 235
Higham Hills, Essex, 680
Highams, Essex, 592
Highams, Surrey, 174
Highclere, Hants.
Castle, 92
Ch.; mont., 322
Ionic Temple, 415
Jackdaw's Castle, 415
Milford Lake Ho., 415
Highcliffe Ho., Hants., 53
Highcliffe Castle, Hants., 271
Higher Broughton, Lancs., hos., 811
Highfields, Cheshire, 83
Highnam Court, Glos., 197, 859
Highwoods, Berks., 167
Hildersham Hall, Cambs., 506
Hilderstone, Staffs., Ch., 842
Hilfield, Hants., 618
Hilgay, Norfolk, bridge, 785
Hill Court, Herefs., 663
Hill Hall, Essex, 680n.
Hill Ho., Glos., 481
Hill Park, Kent, 425, 859
Hill of Howth, Ireland, 172
Hill of Tarvit, Fife, 154–5
Hillbeck Hall, Westmld., 106
Hillersdon Ho., Devon, 103
Hillfield Lodge (Castle), Herts., 961
Hillingdon Ho., Middlx., 497
Hillington Hall, Norfolk, 270
Hillsborough Ho., Ireland, 139–40, 717; Horse Barracks, 378
Hilmarton, Wilts., Ch., 730
Hilton Hall, Staffs., 841, 842
Himley Hall, Staffs., 838
Hinchinbrooke, Hunts., 117
Hinchwick Farm (Manor), Glos., 225
Hinckley, Leics.
Ch., 213
National School, 622
R.C. Chapel, 446
Hindley, Lancs., Chapel, 693
Hindon, Wilts., Ch., 355
Hindringham, Norfolk, Workhouse, 827
Hingham, Norfolk, Ch., 767
Hinton Ho., Som., 537
Hinton Parva, Dorset, Ch., 302

Hinton St. George, Som., 67, 137, 950, 962
Hinxton Grange, Cambs., 585
Hirsel (The), Berwicks., 59, 166
Hitchin Priory, Herts., 53, 263
Hoar Cross, Staffs., 838, 839
Hoarwithy, Herefs., bridge, 372
Hockerill, Herts., ho., 769
Hoddam Castle, Dumfriess., 163
Hoddesdon, Herts.
Clock Tower, 763
Friends' Meeting Ho., 62
ho., 212
School, 212
Hodnet, Salop.
Hall, 142
Rectory, 406
Hodsock Priory, Notts., 657
Holbeach, Lincs., St. John's Ch., 290
Holbeck, Yorks., Ch., 210
Holdenby Ho., Northants., 118
Holdenhurst, Dorset, Ch., 302
Holderness Ho., Yorks., 219
Holders Hill Cottage, Middlx., 527
Holeyn Hall, Northumb., 268
Holker Hall, Lancs., 876
Holkham Hall, Norfolk, 131, 135, 136, 138, 166, 492, 874, 957; Leicester Monument, 271
Hollingbourne Ho., Kent, 102
Hollycombe, Sussex, 583
Holmbush, Sussex, 284
Holme Eden, Cumb., 267
Holme Hale, Norfolk, Rectory, 271
Holme Hall, Yorks., 301, 860
Holme Lacy Ho., Herefs., 544
Holme Park, Berks., 376
Holmebridge, Yorks., Ch., 210
Holmewood, Kent, 173
Holmwood, Surrey, Ch., 869
Holmwood (The), Surrey, 701
Holt (The), Devon, 394
Holt, Dorset, Ch., 843
Holt, Norfolk, Gresham's School, 798
Holtye Common, Sussex, Ch., 563
Holwood Ho., Kent, 173, 769
Holy Island, Northumb., cross, 265
Holyhead, Anglesey, Memorial Arch, 397
Holywell, Flints.
Baths, 878
Savings Bank, 878
St. Winifrede's Ch. (R.C.), 723
Holywell, Northants., Ch., 487
Homend (The), Herefs., 744
Honing Hall, Norfolk, 680
Honingham Hall, Norfolk, 136, 491n.; bridge, 785
Honington Hall, Warwicks., 323, 476, 549
Honiton, Devon, Ch., 321
Honley, Yorks., Ch., 210
Hoo (The), Herts., 207
Hoober Stand, Yorks., 311
Hook, Surrey, Ch., 869
Hook, Yorks., Ch., 442
Hook Norton, Oxon., Ch., 847
Hooke (The), Sussex, 173
Hoole Ho., Cheshire, 398
Hooton Hall, Cheshire, 680n., 957
Hope, Salop., Ch., 406

Hope End, Herefs., 525
Hopetoun Ho., W. Lothian, 46, 57, 79, 154, 283; mausoleum, 168
Hopton Court, Salop., 584
Hopton Hall, Derbys., 88
Hopes, E. Lothian, 158
Horbury, Yorks.
Ch., 192
School, 728
Hordle, Hants., Ch., 604
Horkesley Park, Essex, 418
Hornby, Yorks.
Castle, 109, 535
Vicarage, 271
Horningsheath, Suffolk, Ch., 234
Hornsey, Middlx.
Ch., 754
Priory, 649
villas, 366
Horringer, Suffolk, Ch., 234
Horseheath Hall, Cambs., 635, 659
Horsham, Sussex
Gaol, 693
Grammar School, 755
St. Mark's Ch., 563
Horsley, Glos.
Ch., 691
Ho. of Correction, 114
Horsley, Northumb., Ch., 363
Horsley Place (Towers), Surrey, 92, 125, 527
Horspath, Oxon., Ch., 847
Horton, Dorset, Ch., 211
Horton Ho., Northants., 334, 934
Horton Kirby, Kent
Ch., 753
School, 240
Horwich, Lancs., Ch., 104
Hothfield Place, Kent, 947
Hough Hill Priory, Lancs., 75
Houghton, Lancs., Holy Trinity Ch., 706
Houghton Conquest, Beds., inn, 426
Houghton Cottage, Hunts., 372
Houghton Hall, Norfolk, 184, 342, 492, 695; Water Ho., 415
Houghton Hall, Yorks., 74; R.C. Chapel, 446
Houghton Ho., Beds., 207, 473, 494
Houghton Ho., Cumb., 594
Houghton-le-Spring, Durham
Ch., 266
Ch. (R.C.), 123
Hounslow, Middlx.
Holy Trinity Ch., 543
St. Mary's Ch., 814
Hove, Sussex
Brunswick Chapel, 91
Brunswick Sq., 176
Brunswick Town, 176
Ch., 94
Lansdowne Place, 176
Lansdowne Terrace, 176
St. Andrew's Ch., 91
St. Mary's Hall School, 94
Hovingham Hall, Yorks., 733, 917
How Hatch, Essex, 617
Howden, Yorks., Ch., 728
Howgill Castle, Westmld., 532
Howick Hall, Northumb., 591, 939
Howletts, Kent, 508, 855
Howley Hall, Yorks., 61, 62

Huddersfield, Yorks.
Coll., 665
Holy Trinity Ch., 818
Infirmary, 599
Railway Station, 665
Ramsden St. Chapel, 665, 868
St. Paul's Ch., 600
St. Peter's Ch., 665
Hull, Yorks.
Assembly Room, 278, 728
Blaydes Ho., 606
Carroll Place, 564
Charlotte St., no. 8, 693; ho.,
564
Charterhouse Chapel, 390
Christ Ch., Sculcoates, 442
College, 461
Custom House Bldngs., 668
Etherington Ho., 606
Ferries' Hospital, 278
Gaols, 278, 668
George St., 564
Hanover St., 668
ho., 107
Infirmary, 668
Maisters Ho., 606
Master Mariners' Almshouses,
564
Meat Market, 564
Mechanics' Institute, 564
Merchant Seamen's Hospital,
693
Methodist Chapel, 458
Myton Place, 564
Neptune Inn, 668
North St., 564
Paradise Row, 564
Pilot Office, 278
Public Rooms, 564
Savings Bank, 449
St. Charles Ch. (R.C.), 278, 723
St. James's Ch., Myton, 878
St. John's Ch., Newland, 442
Smith's Bank, 564
Subscription Library, 390
Trinity Almshouse, 564
Trinity Ho., 390, 606; Chapel,
206
Trinity Ho. Navigation School,
564
Theatre Royal, 564
Whitefriar Gate, 564
Hulland, Derbys., Ch., 540
Hulne Abbey, Northumb., 53
Hulswood Villa, Kent, 240
Humshaugh, Northumb.
Ch., 727
parsonage, 727
Hungerford, Berks.
Ch., 293, 614, 638, 650, 705
Hungerford Park, Berks., 592
Hunsdon Ho., Herts., 508
Hunsley, Yorks., Ch., 210
Hunstanton Hall, Norfolk, 281
Huntingdon
County Gaol, 325, 763, 896
Infirmary, 763
Huntly, Aberdeens.
Ch., 500
Court Ho., 618
Gordon Schools, 736
North of Scotland Bank, 736
Hurdsfield, Cheshire, Ch., 739
Hurlingham Ho., Middlx., 177
Hursley, Hants.
Ch., 679; mausoleum, 814;
mont., 712
Lodge (Park), 454, 679

Hurst, Hants., lighthouse, 65
Hurstbourne Park, Hants., 69,
545, 947
Hurstpierpoint, Sussex, Ch., 91
Hurts Hall, Suffolk, 958
Huthwaite Hall, Yorks., 192
Hutton Bushell, Yorks., 700
Hutton-in-the-Forest, Cumb., 60,
650, 876
Hyde, Cheshire, Ch., 75
Hyde (The), Essex, 207
Hyde Hall, Herts., 961
Hylands, Essex, 76, 619
Hyndford Bridge, Lanarks., 781
Hythe, Hants., Villa Amalthaea,
485

Ibsley, Wilts., Ch., 631
Ickleton, Cambs., Vicarage, 585
Ickworth, Suffolk, 306, 324, 718
Idle, Yorks., Holy Trinity Ch.,
600
Idsworth Ho., Hants., 166
Idvies, Angus, cottage, 587
Ightham Court, Kent, 958
Ilam Hall, Staffs., 729, 839
Ilford, Essex
Ho. of Correction, 434
St. Mary's Ch., 721
Schools, 721
Ilfracombe, Devon, Assembly
Rooms, 721
Ilmington, Warwicks., mont.,
915
Ilminster, Som., Ch., 157
Ince Blundell, Lancs.
Chapel (R.C.), 724
Hall, 303, 329, 431, 724, 726
School, 724
Inchdairnie, Fife, 165–6
Inchmurrin, Loch Lomond,
tower, 644
Inchmarlo, Kinc., 761
Inchture, Perths., Ch., 532
Ingatestone, Essex, Chapel, 305
Ingestre, Staffs.
Ch., 926
Hall (Park), 405, 549, 584
Ingleborough Hall, Yorks., 76
Inglestone, Dumfriess., farmho.,
588
Inglethorpe Hall, Norfolk, 268
Ingleton, Durham, Ch., 123
Ingress Abbey (Park), Kent, 208,
863, 970
Ingrow, Yorks., Ch., 673
Innerpeffray, Perths., Library,
322
Innes Ho., Morays., 78
Intwood Hall, Norfolk, 150
Inveraray, Argylls.
Aray Bridge, 574
Arkland, 576
Bee-hive Cottage, 586
Castle, 59, 125, 186, 188, 400,
531 (bis), 562, 576, 578
Cherry Park, 46
Ch., 180, 575
Court Ho., 46, 357, 676
Dubh Loch Bridge, 574
Fisherland Barn, 576
Frew's Bridge, 46
Garden Bridge, 46
Garron Bridge, 562
Garron Lodge, 576
Gothic Bridge, 46
Maam Steading, 576
Maltland Court, 576

Inveraray, Argylls.—contd.
Relief Land, 576
Town Ho., 46
Inverarity, Angus, School, 542
Inverawe (New), Argylls., 164
Inverbrothock, Angus, Chapel,
736
Inveresk, Midlothian
Ch., 595, 734; mont., 101
ho., 577
Invergowrie, Angus
Ho., 165
Toll Ho., 532
Inverkeithing, Fife, Ch., 203, 357
Invermay, Perths., 159, 500, 594
Inverness
Bridge, 757
Castle, 161
Ch., 82
County Hall, 161
County Prison, 148
Hotel, 699
Tolbooth, 500
Inversnaid, Stirlings., barracks,
457, 705
Inverurie, Aberdeens., Ch., 761
Iona, Argylls., Ch., 820
Iping, Sussex
Ch., 364
Rectory (Hammerwood Ho.),
363
Ipswich, Suffolk
Assembly Rooms, 149, 540
Corn Exchange, 351
County Courts, 143
County Gaol, 114
Handford Bridge, 149
Holy Trinity Ch., 399
Hospital, 686
hos., 293
Lower Brook St., 149
Market Place, 149, 203
Northgate Ho., 149
Town Hall, 203
villa, 157
Workhouse, 540
Irnham Hall, Lincs., 914; R.C.
Chapel, 446
Ironbridge, Salop., St. Luke's
Ch., 762
Irthlingborough, Northants.,
mont., 906
Irvine, Ayrshire
Academy, 381
Manse, 467
Irvine Ho., Dumfriess, 426
Irvine Ho., Perths., 165
Islay Ho., Hebrides, 647
Isleworth, Middlx.
Ch., 660; monts., 95, 379
Gordon Ho., 52
Gumley Ho., 342
Ho., 117
St. Margaret's, 527, 859
Seaton Ho., 52
Shrewsbury Ho., 342
Smallberry Green, ho., 592
Somerset Ho., 342
Wyke Ho., 54
Isley Walton, Leics., Ch., 395
Itchenor Ho., Sussex, 950

Jedburgh, Roxb.
Abbey Ch., 569
Prison, 288
Jersey, villa, 501
Jerviston Ho., Lanarks., 54
Johnstown Castle, Ireland, 698

Jordanhill, nr. Glasgow, 759
Juniper Hill, Surrey, 773
Jura Ho., Argylls., 165

Keavil Ho., Fife, 784
Kedleston, Derbys.
  Ch.; mont., 55
  Hall, 52, 136, 344, 611, 687,
    749, 799, 955
  Rectory, 957
Keele Hall, Staffs., 84, 117, 589,
  838, 841, 842
Keig, Aberdeens., Ch., 761
Keighley, Yorks.
  Ch., 210–11
  St. Anne's Ch. (R.C.), 970
Keilder Castle, Northumb., 591
Keir, Perths., 387
Keiss, Caithness, Ch., 821
Keith, Banffs., Chapel (R.C.), 526
Keithhall Ho., Aberdeens., 762
Keithick Ho., Perths., 887
Kelham Hall, Notts., 716
Kellie Castle, Angus, 282–3, 530
Kelly Ho., Devon, 709
Kelmarsh Hall, Northants., 342,
  407, 947
Kelshall, Norfolk, Rectory, 769
Kelso, Roxb.
  Bridge, 678
  Ch., 144, 289, 595
  Ednam Ho., 595
  Mont., 647
  Race-stand, 190
  School, 760
  Teviot Bridge, 289
Kemble Ho., Glos., 701
Kemnay Ho., Aberdeens., 761
Kempshott Ho., Hants., 487
Kempton Park, Middlx., 705
Ken Bridge, Kirkcud., 678
Kendal, Westmld.
  Abbot Hall, 193
  Assembly Rooms, 875
  Bank, 875
  Dowker's Hospital, 875
  Holy Trinity Ch. (R.C.), 876
  Market Hall, 875
  St. George's Ch., 876
  St. Thomas's Ch., 876
  School, 688
  Stramongate Bridge, 396
  Theatre, 688
  Thorny Hill, hos., 876
  Town Hall, 875
  White Hart Hotel, 688
Kenmare, Ireland, Market Ho.,
  91
Kenmore, Perths.
  Bridge, 100
  Ch., 84
Kenmure Castle, Kirkcud., 59
Kenmure Ho., Lanarks., 382
Kenn, Devon, Ch., 334
Kennet Ho., Clack., 397
Kennet & Avon Canal, 71
Kenninghall, Norfolk,
  Workhouse, 827
Kennington, Berks., Ch., 698
Kennington Place, Kent, 173
Kennoway, Fife
  Ch., 385
  Manse, 443
Kentchurch Court, Herefs., 582
Kentisbury, Devon, Rectory, 708
Kentwell Hall, Suffolk, 435
Kenwood Ho., Middlx., 53, 719
Kerse, Stirlings., 46, 800

Keston, Kent, ho., 242n.
Keswick, Cumb., Ch., 972
Keswick Hall, Norfolk, 896
Kettins, Angus, Ch., 533
Kettlethorpe Hall, Yorks., 121n.
Kettlewell, Yorks., Ch., 67
Ketton, Rutland, 70
Kevington, Kent, 817
Kew, Surrey
  Bridge, 89, 609
  Ch., 151, 390, 496, 701, 846,
    963; monts., 352, 700
  Gardens, 171, 206–7, 614
  Ho. (White Ho.), 208, 492, 727
  Orangery, 206
  Pagoda, 207
  Palace, 951; lodges, 390
  Palm Ho., 171
  Priory, 617
  Temples, etc., 206–7, 566, 963
Keyham, Devon, see Devonport
Keyham Bridge, Leics., 622
Kibworth, Leics., Ch., 309
Kidbrooke Park, Sussex, 252, 715
Kidderminster, Worcs.
  Ch., 465
  St. George's Ch., 353, 495, 497
Kiddington Hall (Park), Oxon.,
  92, 145
Kilbaberton, Midlothian, see
  Baberton
Kilbarchan, Renfrews., Ch., 81
Kilconquhar, Fife
  Castle, 164
  Ch., 260
Kildonan, Sutherld., Ch., 120
Kilduff, E. Lothian, 53
Kiliwhimen, Inverness., barracks,
  457, 705
Kilkenny, Ireland
  Castle, 545
  Cathedral, 550
Kilkerran Ho., Ayrshire, 358
Killaloe Deanery, Ireland, 327
Killearn, Stirlings., Buchanan
  Monument, 238
Killearnadale, Argylls.,
  mausoleum, 168
Killerton Park, Devon, 463;
  Chapel, 226
Killibegs, Ireland, 618
Killin, Perths., Ch., 272
Killymoon Castle, Ireland, 583
Kilmacolm, Renfrews., Ch., 257
Kilmarnock, Ayrshire, U.P. Ch.,
  467
Kilmaron Castle, Fife, 358
Kilmartin, Argylls., Ch., 254
Kilmaurs, Ayrshire, mont., 725
Kilmore, Argylls., Manse
  (Kilmore Ho.), 821
Kilmuir, Skye, Ch., 357
Kilmun, Argylls., Ch., 168
Kilnwick Hall, Yorks., 194
Kilnwick Percy, Yorks., Vicarage,
  763
Kilrea, Ireland, Ch., 754
Kilrenny, Fife, Ch., 515
Kilruddery Ho., Ireland, 166,
  698
Kilspindie, Perths.
  Ch., 587
  School, 65
Kilvington, Yorks., bridge, 192
Kilwaughter Castle, Ireland, 584
Kimberley Hall, Norfolk, 596,
  667, 716, 806, 971
Kimberworth, Yorks., Ch., 375

Kimbolton Castle, Hunts., 52,
  105, 167, 230, 325, 696,
  852
Kimmerghame Ho., Berwicks.,
  346, 754
Kimpton, Hants., Ch., 620
Kincaid Ho., Stirlings., 382
Kincardine, Perths.
  Ch., 241
  Manse, 784
  School, 260, 530
Kineton, Warwicks., Ch., 550
Kinfauns, Perths.
  Castle, 745
  Ch. (Old), 533
  Manse, 533
  School, 533
King William's Coll., Isle of Man,
  141, 878
Kingarth, Bute, Ch., 161
Kingham, Oxon., Rectory, 912
Kinghorn, Fife
  School, 385
  Town Ho., 385
Kingmoor, Cumb., ho., 361
Kingoldrum, Angus, Ch., 532
King's Langley, Herts., mont.,
  125
King's Lynn, Norfolk
  Assembly Rooms, 842
  Customs Ho., 105
  Duke's Head Inn, 105
  Exchange, 105
  Gaol, 842
  Market Cross, 105
  St. James's Chapel, 105
  St. Margaret's Ch., 105, 137,
    353
  St. Nicholas' Ch., 105
  Theatre, 101, 589
  Wesleyan Chapel, 589
King's Norton, Leics., Ch., 905
King's Norton, Worcs., mont.,
  693
King's Nympton Park, Devon,
  201
Kings Weston, Glos., 575, 660,
  798, 830, 853
Kingsbarns, Fife
  Ch., 86, 234
  Ho., 234
  Manse, 511, 623
  School, 234
Kingsey, Bucks., Vicarage, 393
Kingsley, Staffs., Ch., 840
Kingsteignton, Devon, Vicarage,
  676
Kingsthorpe Hall, Northants., 463
Kingston, Dorset, Chapel, 679
Kingston Bagpuize, Berks.
  Ch., 306
  Ho., 830
  Rectory, 217
Kingston Deverill, Wilts.
  Ch., 447, 537
  Rectory, 537
Kingston Grange, Midlothian, 54
Kingston Hall, Notts., 118
Kingston-upon-Hull, see Hull
Kingston Lacy, Dorset, 92, 308,
  440, 659
Kingston Lisle, Berks., 605
Kingston-on-Soar, Notts., Ch.,
  375
Kingston-on-Thames, Surrey
  Bank Farm, 583
  Bridge, 506
  Ch., 212, 632, 964

Kingston-on-Thames—*contd.*
  ho., 854
  Point Pleasant, 583
  School, 869
  steeple (false), 109
Kingswells, Aberdeens., 451
Kingswood, Glos.
  Holy Trinity Ch., 315
  St. George's Ch., 348, 733
Kingswood, Surrey, Ch., 506
Kington, Herefs.
  Ch., 907
  Grammar School, 43
  Gravel Hill Villa, 907
  Kingswood Ho., 907
  Market Ho., 43
  National School, 907
  Portway Villa, 907
  Railway Station, 907
  Town Hall, 907
  Workhouse, 907
Kingweston Ho., Som., 426, 896
Kininvie Ho., Banffs., 699
Kinlet Hall, Salop., 751
Kinlochbervie, Sutherld., Ch., 821
Kinlochluichart, Ross, Ch., 821
Kinlochmoidart, Inverness., 358
Kinlockspelvie, Argylls., Ch., 820
Kinmel, Denbighs.
  Park, 166, 435, 958
  St. George's Ch.; mausoleum,
    476
Kinmount, Dumfriess., 744
Kinnaird, Perths.
  Manse, 533
  School, 533
Kinnaird Castle, Angus, 154, 282,
  644
Kinnaird Ho., Stirlings., 784
Kinnerley, Salop., Ch., 663
Kinnersley Castle, Herefs., 177
Kinnettles, Angus, Ch., 106
Kinnoul, Perths., Ch., 161
Kinrara Ho., Inverness., 624,
  714
Kinross, Fife
  Ch., 68
  County Bldngs., 50
  Ho., 79, 126, 154, 282
  S. Queich Bridge, 154
Kinsham Court, Herefs., 664
Kintore, Aberdeens.
  Ch., 736
  Manse, 736
Kinturk, Ireland, 225
Kiplin Hall, Yorks., 700
Kippax Park, Yorks., 334
Kippen, Stirlings., Ch., 783
Kippenross, Perths., 784
Kirby Hall, Northants., 787, 827
Kirby Hall, Yorks., 131, 192, 527,
  562, 565, 618, 795n.
Kirby Underdale, Yorks.,
  Rectory, 728
Kirk Braddan, Isle of Man,
  obelisk, 780
Kirk Yetholm, Roxb., Ch., 148
Kirkbean, Kirkcud., Ch., 588
Kirkby Lonsdale, Westmld.,
  Savings Bank, 875
Kirkby Thore, Westmld., 60
Kirkcaldy, Fife
  Bank of Scotland, 161
  Ch., 569
  Ch. (Old), 288
  St. Peter's Ch. (Episcopal), 82
  Town Ho., 161
Kirkcudbright, Ch., 162

Kirkdale, Lancs., County Gaol,
  934
Kirkdale Ho., Kirkcud., 54
Kirkham, Lancs., Ch., 706
Kirkharle, Northumb., 145
Kirkhill Ho., Midlothian, 385
Kirkland Hall, Lancs., 193
Kirklands, Roxb., 117
Kirkleatham, Yorks.
  Ch., 191, 233, 340
  Hall, 123, 194, 207, 344
  Hospital, 233, 340
Kirklees Park, Yorks., 521
Kirkmahoe, Dumfriess., Ch., 588
Kirkmichael, Ross., Ch., 120
Kirkmichael Ho., Dumfriess., 164
Kirknewton, Northumb., Ch., 266
Kirkstall, Yorks., Ch., 210
Kirkthorpe, Yorks., mont., 494
Kirkton Ho., Aberdeens., 761
Kirkville Ho., Aberdeens., 761
Kirriemuir, Angus
  Bank, 68
  Ch., 644
  Seminary, 140
Kirtling Hall, Cambs., 707
Kirtlington Park, Oxon., 333, 344,
  435, 565n., 716, 763
Kirton-in-Holland, Lincs.
  Ch., 410
  villa, 198
Kislingbury, Northants., Rectory,
  752
Kitley Ho., Devon, 679
Kiveton Ho. (Park), Yorks., 309,
  344, 806
Knebworth, Herts.
  Ho., 487n., 674
  mausoleum, 617
Kneller Hall, Middlx., 387
Knells (The), Cumb., 268
Knepp Castle, Sussex, 584
Knightley, Staffs., Ch., 842
Knight's Hill, Surrey, 425
Knipton, Leics., parsonage, 505
Knockdrin Castle, Ireland, 535
Knotty Ash, Lancs., St. John's
  Ch., 283, 897
Knowes (The), Roxb., 158, 164
Knowle St. Giles, Som., Ch., 857
Knowsley Hall, Lancs., 165, 318,
  723, 726
Knutsford, Cheshire
  Ch., 332
  Sessions Ho., 398, 555
Kymin Temple, Mon., 306
Kyre Park, Worcs., 62, 420, 664,
  726
Kyte's Nest, Warwicks., 419

Lacock Abbey, Wilts., 550, 659
Ladyfield West Ho., Dumfriess.,
  588
Ladykirk Ho., Berwicks., 166,
  289, 810
Ladyland, Ayrshire, 382
Laleham, Middlx.
  Ch., 661
  Park, 617
Lambourne Place, Berks., 269
Lambton Castle (Hall), Durham,
  122, 125, 268 (*bis*)
Lamer, Herts., 324
Lamorbey Park, Kent, 729
Lamorran, Cornwall, Rectory, 859
Lampeter, Card.
  St. David's Coll., 224
  Town Hall, etc., 700

Lamport, Northants.
  Ch., 763
  Hall, 167, 271, 377, 615, 708,
    726, 751, 873
  Rectory, 751
Lancaster
  Bath, 329
  Castle, 328, 396
  Courts, 328
  Custom Ho., 347
  Gaol, 328
  Lunatic Asylum, 774
  Moor Hospital, 774
  St. John's Chapel, 396
  Skerton Bridge, 396
  Town Hall, 396, 455
Landford Ho., Wilts., 631
Langdown Ho., Hants., 252
Langford, Oxon., Ch., 605
Langford Grove, Essex, 464
Langford Hall, Notts., 196
Langholm, Dumfriess.
  Ch., 162
  Lodge, 644
Langley Hall (Park), Norfolk, 136,
  768
Langley Marish, Bucks., Ch., 293
Langley Park, Bucks., 508
Langley Park, Kent, 125, 680n.
Langleys, Essex, 225
Langport, Som., Bridge, 360
Langside, Renfrews., 54
Langton Ho., Dorset, 225, 383
Langton Maltravers, Dorset, Ch.,
  863
Langton-by-Spilsby, Lincs., Ch.,
  442
Lanner, Cornwall, Ch., 890
Lanreath, Cornwall, parsonage,
  890
Lapley, Staffs., Vicarage, 869
Larbert, Stirlings.
  Ch., 382
  Ho., 383
Largo, Fife
  Ch., 515
  Wood's Hospital, 515
Largs, Ayrshire
  Broomfield Ho., 676
  St. Fillan's Villa, 383
Lasborough, Glos.
  Ch., 858
  Park, 949
Lathallan Ho., Stirlings., 385
Lathbury, Bucks., Vicarage, 847
Lathom Ho., Lancs., 514
Latimer, Bucks., Chapel, 119
Latimers, Bucks., 117
Lauder, Berwicks., Ch., 153
Laughton Lodge, Sussex, 966
Launceston, Cornwall
  Ch., 172
  Markets, 890
Launde Abbey, Leics., 670, 692
Launton, Oxon., Rectory, 648
Laurence Park Ho., Stirlings., 385
Lauriston Castle, Midlothian, 163,
  647
Lavender Hill, Surrey, villa, 501
Laverstoke Park, Hants., 125
Lavington Ho., Sussex, 518
Lawers Ho., Perths., 57, 241, 711
Laxton Hall, Northants., 252, 682
Layer Breton, Essex, Rectory,
  869
Lazaretto, Kent, 944
Lea Castle, Worcs., 200
Lea Park, Surrey, 632

Leadenham, Lincs.
  Ho., 777, 858, 899
  Rectory, 321
Leaderfoot Bridge, Roxb., 781
Leagram Hall, Lancs., 706
Leamington Spa, Warwicks.
  All Saints Ch., 449
  Assembly Rooms, 102
  Baths, 648
  Bath Terrace, 823
  Beauchamp Sq., 236
  Binswood Cottage, 701
  Brandon Parade, 823
  Christ Ch., 701
  Congregational Ch., 709
  Copp's Royal Hotel, 701
  County Library, etc., 102
  Episcopal Chapel, 449
  Jephson Gardens, 449
  Lansdowne Circus, 823
  Lansdowne Crescent, 823
  Regent Hotel, 746
  Royal Baths & Pump Room,
    746
  St. Mary's Ch., 449
  St. Peter's Ch., 709
  Southville, 886
  Tennis Courts, 449
  town-planning, 585
  Victoria Pump Room & Baths,
    823
  Vittoria Place, 98
  Warneford Hospital, 98
  Warwick St., 236, 823
Learney Ho., Aberdeens., 762
Leask Ho., Aberdeens., 737
Leasowe Castle, Cheshire, 317
Leatherhead, Surrey
  Bridge, 370
  Elm Bank, 173
  Priory (The), 240
  Thorncroft, 817
Leaton Knolls, Salop., 407
Leavenheath, Suffolk, Ch., 323
Leazes (The), Northumb., 268
Lechlade, Glos.
  Ch., 605
  Rectory, 605
Leckhamstead, Bucks., Rectory,
  763
Lecropt, Perths.
  Ch., 783
  Manse, 784
  School, 783
Ledbury, Herefs.
  Ch., 897
  Park, 727
  St. Katherine's Hospital, 743
Ledsham, Yorks.
  Ch.; mont., 201
  Vicarage, 398
Ledston Hall, Yorks., 108, 826
Lee, Kent
  Belmont Ho., 813
  Cedars (The), 372
  cottage, 372
  Grove, 372
  Manor Ho., 478
  Merchant Taylors' Almshouses,
    479
  St. Margaret's Ch., 145, 372
  School, 813
Lee Hall, Lancs., 527, 692
Lee Place, Lanarks., 358
Lee Priory, Kent, 948
Leeds, Yorks.
  Borough Gaol, 442
  Bridge End, ho., 194

Leeds, Yorks—*contd.*
  Brunswick Methodist Chapel,
    738
  Cemetery, 112
  Central Market, 353
  Chapel (R.C.), 466
  Charity School, 818
  Christ Church, 210
  Ch., 260
  Commercial Bldngs., 215
  Conservative Pavilion, 210
  Corn Exchange, 211
  Court Ho., 210, 818
  Hanover Place Chapel, 738
  Holy Trinity Ch., 210, 301,
    378
  ho., 215
  Independent Chapel, 447
  Infirmary, 191
  Lady Lane Chapel, 738
  Lancasterian School, 813
  Library, 466
  mills, 215
  Mixed Cloth Hall, 564
  National School, 818
  Oxford Place Chapel, 738
  Philosophical Hall, 210
  Public Baths, 210
  Railway Station, 666
  Richmond Hill Chapel, 738
  St. Anne's Ch. (R.C.), 213
  St. George's Ch., 215
  St. John's Ch., 215
  St. Mary's Ch., Quarry Hill,
    819
  St. Patrick's Ch. (R.C.), 213
  St. Paul's Ch., 466
  St. Peter's Ch., 210
  St. Peter's St. Chapel, 738
  St. Philip's Ch., 210
  South Market, 209, 210
  Station Hotel, 265
  Temple Mills, 124n.
  Theatre, 98
  Trustee Savings Bank, 215
  Union Bank, 818
  warehouse, 441
  Wellington Bridge, 678
  Wesley Chapel, 738
  White Cloth Hall, 466
  Woodhouse Cemetery, 215
  Woodhouse Moor, almshouses,
    215
  Yorkshire District Bank, 215
Leek, Staffs., Workhouse, 98
Leek Wootton, Warwicks., Ch.,
  287, 449
Leeming, Yorks., St. John's Ch.,
  123
Lees Court, Kent, 768, 855
Legertlaw, Perths., steading, 201
Leicester
  Alderman Newton's School,
    601
  Assembly Rooms, 395
  Baptist Chapel, 232
  Borough Gaol, 463
  Bowling Green Ho., 601
  Brunswick Sq., 464
  Castle Hall, 622
  Chapel (R.C.), 446
  Christ Ch., 622
  Consanguinitarium, 463
  Corah's Warehouse, 309
  Corn Exchange, 880
  County Gaol, 398, 555, 601,
    622
  County Rooms, 463

Leicester—*contd.*
  Ho. of Correction, 395, 496,
    601
  Infirmary, 232, 413, 496, 936
  Lunatic Asylum, 307, 398, 413,
    622
  Methodist Chapel, 458
  Midland Railway Station, 309
  Museum, 877n.
  New Hall, Wellington St., 309
  New Market, 307
  New West Bridge, 309
  News Room, 309, 633
  Phoenix Insurance Bldng., 309
  Race-stand, 601
  Recorder's Ho., 601
  St. George's Ch., 622
  St. Margaret's Vicarage, 622
  St. Martin's Ch., 905
  St. Mary's Ch., 213, 309
  St. Nicholas Ch., 232
  School (Nonconformist), 877n.
  Shambles, 880
  Theatre, 103, 463
  Trinity Hospital, 635
  warehouse, 309
  Workhouse, 309
  Wyggeston's Hospital, 232
Leigh Court, Som., 434
Leigh Park, Hants., 489, 858
Leighton, Salop., Ch., 304;
  mont., 84
Leighton (Buzzard) Ho., Beds.,
  342
Leighton Hall, Lancs., 422
Leith, Midlothian
  Academy, 159
  Assembly Rooms, 149
  Associate Burgher (St. Ninian's)
    Ch., N. Leith, 149
  Bernard St., 501
  bridge, 613
  Claremont Park, 385
  Constitution St., nos. 30–34,
    501
  Custom Ho., 46, 161, 675
  Drawbridge, 781n.
  Exchange Bldngs., 149
  fortifications, 570
  Grammar School, 159
  Gun-battery, 238
  Hermitage Place, 121
  Junction Rd. Ch., 106
  Leith Bank, 624
  National Commercial Bank,
    624
  North Leith Ch., 161
  Prison, 149
  St. Andrew's Place U.P. Ch.,
    67, 106
  St. James Chapel, 823
  St. Mary's Ch., S. Leith, 385,
    571
  Seafield Baths, 624
  Shore, hos., 571
  Tolbooth (Gaol), 357
  Town Hall, 260
  Trinity Ho., 149
  Vanbrugh Place, 501
Leith Head, Midlothian, 671
Lemington, Northumb.
  Column, 772
  Hall, 591
Lennel Ho., Berwicks., 624
Lennox Castle, Stirlings., 383
Lennoxlove, E. Lothian, 154
Lennoxtown, Stirlings., Campsie
  High Ch., 382

Lenton Priory, nr. Nottingham, 789
Lenwade Bridge, Norfolk, 137
Leny Ho., Perths., 166
Leominster, Herefs.
  Grange Court, 43
  Market Ho., 43
Lerwick, Shetland, Union Bank of Scotland, 736
Leslie Ho., Fife, 154, 570
Lesmahagow, Lanarks., hos., 82
Lessendrum Ho., Aberdeens., 737
Letchworth, Herts., Rectory, 763
Letham Grange, Angus, 737
Lethington, E. Lothian, 154
Letterfourie Ho., Banffs., 54
Letton Hall, Norfolk, 768
Leuchars, Fife, Ch., 86
Leuchie Ho., E. Lothian, 628
Leven, Yorks., Ch., 210
Leven Grove, Yorks., 971
Levens Hall, Westmld., 236
Leventhorpe Hall, Yorks., 195
Levington Ho., Suffolk, 398
Lewes, Sussex
  All Saints Ch., 891
  Bridge, 276
  Castle Place, nos. 1–4, 891
  County Hall, 463
  Fire Engine Ho., 891
  Ho. of Correction, 114, 423
  St. John sub Castro Ch., 212
  Theatre, 529
  Town Hall, 558
Lewisham, Kent
  Colfe's Almshouses, 552
  St. John's Ch., 428
  St. Mary's Ch., 345
  Southend, 859
  Stone Ho., 345
  villa, 218
Lexden, Essex, Ch., 823
Lexden Park Ho., Essex, 501
Lexham Hall, Norfolk, 963
Leyland, Lancs., Ch., 524
Leys (The), Herefs., 167
Leys Castle, Inverness., 103
Leyton, Essex
  Ch., 345, 729, 864; mont., 649
  Great Ho., 53
  ho. (Banks), 649
  villa, 306
Leytonstone, Essex
  Ch.; mont., 772
  Dissenting Chapel, 282
  ho., 329
  St. John's Ch., 119
Lezayre, Isle of Man, Ch., 878
Liberton, Midlothian, Ch., 357
Lichfield, Staffs.
  Bishop's Palace, 636
  Cathedral, 654, 900, 944; mont., 952
  Holy Cross Ch. (R.C.), 655
  Newton's Coll., 654
  St. Mary's Ch., 752, 841, 843, 897
Lidlington, Beds., Ch., 595
Liff & Benvie, Angus
  Ch., 553
  School, 587
Lighthorne, Warwicks., Ch., 287
Lilburn Tower, Northumb, 267
Lilford Hall, Northants., 311
Lilleshall, Salop.
  Hall, 963
  obelisk, 383
Lillington, Warwicks., Ch., 450

Lilliput Castle, nr. Bath, 911
Lime Grove, Caern., 936, 957
Limerick, Ireland
  Cathedral, 88
  Gaol, 114
  ho., 892
  Market Ho., 518
  Theatre, 518
Lincoln
  Bishop's College Hospital, 191
  Blue Coat School, 528
  Butcher's Shambles, 262
  Castle, 743, 899
  Cathedral, 299, 340, 410, 454, 528, 721, 899; mont., 120; Library, 924
  Cathedral School, 166
  City Gaol & Sessions Ho., 410
  County Courts, 743
  County Gaol, 505, 528
  County Hospital, 191
  Deanery, 166
  Disney Place, 408
  Gowts Bridge, 411
  High Bridge (obelisk), 262
  ho., 528
  Independent Chapel, 305
  Judges' Lodgings, 410–11
  Lunatic Asylum, 444
  St. Martin's Ch., 410
  St. Mary's Bridge, 410
  St. Peter at Arches Ch., 408, 752
  St. Swithin's Ch., 410
  Shire Hall, 410
  Subdeanery, 321
Lindale, Lancs., Ch., 876
Linden Ho., Northumb., 554
Lindertis Ho., Angus, 288
Lindisfarne, Northumb., fort, 837
Lindley, Yorks., St. Stephen's Ch., 600
Linethwaite, Cumb., 268
Lingwood, Norfolk, workhouse, 145
Linlathen Ho., Angus, 784
Linley Hall, Salop., 477
Linlithgow, W. Lothian
  Ch., 357
  Fountain, 378
  Palace, 862
  School, 759
  Tolbooth, 570, 759
Linthwaite, Yorks., Ch., 73
Linton, Kent
  Ch., 109
  Park, 244
Linton Ho., Aberdeens., 737
Lintrathen, Angus, Bottom Steading, 623
Lintzford, Durham, bridge, 362
Liskeard, Cornwall, parsonage, 890
Lislee, Ireland, villa, 517
Lismore Castle, Ireland, 76, 867
Lismore Cathedral, Ireland; mont., 693
Lissadell Court, Ireland, 354
Lissan, Ireland, Rectory, 583
Litchborough Ho., Northants., 557
Little Aston Hall, Staffs., 949
Little Carlton, Lincs., Vicarage, 196
Little Dunkeld, Perths., Ch., 782
Little Gaddesden, Herts., Ch., 962
Little Glemham Hall, Suffolk, 399
Little Green, Sussex, 680n.
Little Grove, Herts., 618

Little Hill Court, Herts., 770
Little Hinton, Wilts., Rectory, 605
Little Kineton, Warwicks., 228
Little Marlow, Bucks., villa, 592
Little Plumstead, Norfolk, ho., 150
Little Sodbury, Glos., Ch., 455
Little Willenham, Staffs., 426
Littleborough, Lancs., Holy Trinity Ch., 818
Littlecote Ho. (Park), Wilts., 605, 704
Littledean, Glos., Ho. of Correction, 114
Littlehampton, Sussex, St. Mary's Ch., 274
Littlemore, Oxon., Ch., 847
Littleton, Cheshire, 369
Littleworth, Berks., Ch., 847
Livermere Park, Suffolk, 959
Liverpool
  Aintree race-stand, 317
  Apothecaries' Hall, 247
  Assize Courts, 364, 503, 520, 888
  Athenaeum, 316, 398
  Bank Chambers, 225
  Bank of England, 224
  Baths, 317
  Berry St., premises, 863
  Bold St., shops, 60
  Borough Gaol, 316
  Brooks St., 143
  Brunswick Bldngs., 898
  Brunswick Chapel, 179
  building estate, 172
  Chapel (Unitarian), 863
  Collegiate Institution, 291
  Commercial Bank, 247
  Corn Exchange, 316
  Crescent Congregational Chapel, 322
  Custom Ho., 265, 317, 637, 695
  Dispensary, 316
  Dock Traffic Office, 387
  Docks, 778
  Everton, ho., 179
  Exchange, 143, 316, 431, 726, 881, 911, 944
  Fish Hall, 670
  fortifications, 350
  Gaol, 114
  Great George St. Chapel, 322
  Hanover St., hos., 83, 778
  Huskisson mont., 318
  Jewish Synagogue, 395
  Lime St. Railway Station, 317
  Liverpool Arms Hotel, 329
  Liverpool & London Insurance Co.'s Offices, 225
  Liverpool & Manchester Railway, arch, 317
  Liverpool Royal Institution, 60
  Lord St., 317
  Lunatic Asylum, 317
  Lyceum, 396
  Mechanics' Institute, 283, 897
  Medical Institution, 670
  Music Hall, 304
  Necropolis Cemetery Chapel, 317
  New Exchange, 316, 944
  Northern Dispensary, 708
  Northern Hospital, 878
  Observatory, 303
  Octagon Chapel, 307
  Old Ropery Theatre, 778
  Orphans' Asylum, 247

Liverpool—*contd.*
Paradise St., 691, 778
Pembroke Baptist Chapel, 322
Philharmonic Hall, 247
Prince's Park, 898
Queen Insurance Bldngs., 708
Riding School, 691
Rock Lighthouse, 317
Rotunda, 329
Royal Bank, 708
Royal Exchange Insurance
  Bldng., 365
Royal Infirmary, 317
Sailors' Home, 247
St. Andrew's Scottish Ch.,
  317
St. Anne's Ch., Aigburth, 247
St. Anthony's Ch. (R.C.), 142
St. Augustine's Ch., 142
St. Barnabas Ch., 898
St. Bride's Ch., 708
St. Catherine's Ch., 317
St. David's Welsh Ch., 317
St. Francis Xavier's Ch., 724
St. George's Ch., 317, 726,
  779
St. George's Ch., Everton, 690;
  mont., 693
St. George's Crescent, 317
St. George's Hall, 225, 290,
  291
St. James's Cemetery, 317
St. James's Ch., Toxteth Park,
  112
St. John's Ch., 521
St. John's Ch., Toxteth Park,
  878
St. John's Market, 317
St. Jude's Ch., 691
St. Luke's Ch., 283, 316
St. Martin's Ch., 317
St. Mary's Ch., 303, 317, 726
St. Matthias' Ch., 782
St. Michael's Ch., 317
St. Michael's Ch., Toxteth
  Park, 690

Liverpool—*contd.*
St. Nicholas Ch., 143, 335, 397,
  431, 726
St. Nicholas (R.C.) Ch., 112
St. Patrick's Ch. (R.C.), 739
St. Paul's Ch., 397, 520
St. Peter's (Scotch) Ch., 247
St. Philip's Ch., Hardman St.,
  690
St. Thomas's Ch., 304, 726
Scotch Presbyterian Ch., 708
Theatre Royal, 206, 316
Town Hall, *see* Exchange
Toxteth Park, 112
Union Bank, 247
Union Newsroom, 316
Unitarian Chapel, 179
warehouses, 265
Wellington Assembly Rooms,
  60
West Dingle, ho., 173
Workhouse, 143
Liversedge, Yorks., Christ Ch.,
  818
Llanarmon, Denbighs., Ch., 476
Llanayron, Card., 582
Llanbadarn, nr. Aberystwyth,
  Ch.; mont., 835
Llanbedrog, Caern., Rectory, 878
Llandaff Cathedral, Glam., 232,
  910, 916
Llandegai, Caern., Ch., 844
Llandegwning, Caern., Ch., 879
Llandevaud, Mon., Ch., 406
Llandilo, Carm.
  Bridge, 286
  Ch., 254
Llandovery, Carm.
  Bridge, 286
  Market Ho., 221
Llandudno, Caern., Ch., 879
Llanfairpwll, Anglesey, Anglesey
  Column, 397
Llanffinan, Anglesey, Ch., 879
Llanfyllin, Montgom., Town
  Hall, 965

Llanfynydd, Flints., Christ Ch.,
  522
Llangelynen, Caern., Ch., 476
Llangorwen, Card., Ch., 847
Llanhedrick, Salop., farmho., 762
Llanidan, Anglesey, New Ch.,
  879
Llanon, Carm., Ch., 406
Llanover Ho., Mon., 435
Llanrhaiadr Hall, Denbighs., 632
Llansantffraid Glan Conway,
  Denbighs., Ch., 878–9
Llantarnam Abbey, Mon., 972
Llanwddyn, Montgom., Ch., 406
Llanymynech, Salop.
  bridge, 631
  Ch., 631
Lleweni, Denbighs., bleach-
  works, 713
Lleweny Hall, Denbighs., 112
Llysnewydd, Card., 582
Lochee, Angus, St. Ninian's
  Chapel, 587
Lochend Ho., E. Lothian, 162
Lochgilphead, Argylls., Ch., 820
Lochnell Castle (Ho.), Argylls.,
  288, 467
Lockerley Hall, Hants., 167
Locko Park, Derbys., 279
Lock's Bottom, Kent, Workhouse,
  721
Lockwood, Yorks., Ch., 210
Lodge (The), Salop., 800
Lodore, Cumb., villa, 518
Lodsworth Ho., Sussex, 118
Lofthouse-in-Cleveland, Yorks.
  Church, 123
  Rectory, 123
Logie, Stirlings., Ch., 79, 783
Logierait, Perths.
  Ch., 782
  School, 260
Lonan, Isle of Man, New Ch.,
  878
Londesbrough Ho., Yorks., 132,
  430

LONDON

Abney Park Cemetery, 437
Academy Court, 619
Adam St., no. 7, 51
Adams Place, Southwark, shops, etc., 770
Addison Rd., ho., 92
Adelphi Bldngs., Strand, 48, 51, 633
Adelphi Theatre, 103
Admiralty (The), 50, 695, 813
Admiralty Ho., Whitehall, 227
Adult Orphan Asylum, 582
Ailesbury Ho., Leicester Sq., 275
Albany, Piccadilly, 426, 609
Albany Cottage, 225
Albemarle St., no. 6, 345; hos., 89, 538, 866
Albert Gate, 243
Albion Club Ho., 227
Albion Fire Office, Blackfriars, 706
Albion Mills, 677, 939, 956, 959
Albion Place, 576, 958
Aldersgate St., no. 165, 210; ho., 256
Aldridge's Cattle Auction Rooms, 400
Alexander Ho., S. Kensington, 650

Alexander Sq., 94
Alfred Club, 394
Alfred Place, 249
Alhambra Palace, Leicester Sq., 307
Alliance Fire Office, 66
Almack's Club, 262, 575
Alpha Road, St. John's Wood, no. 34, 809
America Circus, Minories, 249
America Crescent, Minories, 249
America Sq., Minories, 249
Amicable Life Assurance Office, Fleet St., 103
Amicable Life Assurance Office, Serjeants' Inn, 257
Amwell St., Clerkenwell, 578
Annett's Crescent, Islington, 438
Apothecaries' Hall, 523, 710, 965
Apsley Ho., Piccadilly, 51, 938
Argyll Ho., Argyll St., 562, 575
Argyll Rooms, Regent St., 581
Argyll Rooms (Old), 376
Argyll St., 559; no. 30, 413
Arlington St., no. 16, 342; no. 19, 51; no. 21, 208;
  no. 22, 168, 493, 933

LONDON

Armourers' & Braziers' Hall, 351
Armoury Ho., Finsbury, 782
Arthur's (now Carlton) Club, 434
Arundel Ho., 472
Ashburnham Ho., Dover St., 51
Ashburnham Ho., Westminster, 874
Ashburton Ho., 398 (and see Bath Ho.)
Aske's Hospital, Hoxton, 430
Asylum (The), 461
Asylum for Deaf & Dumb Children, 799
Asylum for Female Orphans, 523
Athenaeum Club, 171
Atlas Fire Office, 434
Aubrey Ho., Notting Hill, 633, 946
Auction Mart, 864
Bakers' Hall, 292
Baker St., no. 8, 807; ho., 139
Bank Bldngs., 816
Bank of England, 224, 450, 711, 767, 816, 831
Bankruptcy Courts, 320
Banqueting Ho., Whitehall, 256, 472, 709, 744, 768, 787, 944
Banqueting Ho., Whitehall (dem. 1619), 474
Baptist Coll., Stepney, 721
Barber-Surgeons' Hall, 129, 460, 473
Barlow Place (Mews), 89
Barnett, Hoares & Co.'s Bank, 487
Barnsbury Park, villas, 243
Barrymore Ho., 745
Bartholomew Close, obelisk, 292
Bath, Bath St., 848
Bath Ho., 394, 513 (and see Ashburton Ho.)
Bathurst St., 955
Battersea, ho., 613
Battersea Bridge, 425, 633
Battersea Park, 244
Battle Bridge estate, 632, 671
Beaufort Ho., Chelsea, 87, 129, 472, 712
Bedford Estate Office, 778
Bedford Ho., 312, 425, 710
Bedford Lodge, 963
Bedford Sq., 124, 516
Belgrave Place, no. 30, 772
Belgrave Rd., workshop, 619
Belgrave Sq., 94, 243; no. 10, 172; no. 12, 746; no. 24, 488; no. 37, 387
Bengal Warehouse, 478
Berkeley Ho., Piccadilly, 544
Berkeley Sq., no. 9, 140; nos. 20–21, 859; no. 24, 140, 619; no. 27, 394; no. 41, 866; no 44, 493; no. 45, 208, 745; no. 48, 394; ho., 770; premises, 881
Berners estate, 44
Berners St., 208
Bethlehem Hospital, Moorfields, 215, 309, 430
Bethlehem Hospital, Southwark, 519; competition for, 272, 329, 350, 435, 443, 481, 523, 681
Beulah Spa, 171
Billingsgate Market, 251
Bishopsgate Gate, 455
Bishopsgate St., no. 112, 817, 869–70
Blackfriars Bridge, 84–5, 262, 572, 574; designs for, 89, 209, 273, 279, 373, 572, 599, 633
Blenheim St., museum, 121
Blind School, St. John's Wood, 488
Blind School, Southwark, 590, 807
Bloomsbury Sq., nos. 5–6, 312; no. 17, 582
Board of Trade Offices, Whitehall, 92, 768
Bolsover St., hos., 312
Bond St., 321; hos., 89
Boodle's Club, 242, 619
Bookbinders' Almshouses, 416
Borough Compter, Southwark, 251
Borough Market, Southwark, 706
Boyle St., stables, 729
Branch Bank of England, Burlington Gardens, 388
Branch Hill Lodge, Hampstead, 312, 345

Breadalbane Ho., 76
Brewer St., ho., 275
Brewers' Hall, 180, 650, 885
Brewers' Quay, warehouses, 553
brewery (Knightsbridge), 177
Bricklayers' Arms Station, 243
Bridewell Hospital, 519
Bridge Ho., Paddington, 883
Bridge Ho., Southwark, 251
Bridge Ho. Hotel, 743
Bridge Ho. Yard, warehouses, 251
Bridgewater Ho., 92, 746
Bridgewater Sq., 925
British Coffee Ho., 51
British & Foreign School, Southwark, 306, 702
British Institution's Galleries, 88
British Museum, 261, 466, 742, 743; design for (1754), 855; Library, 437; Townley Gallery, 719
Brixton Prison, 212
Broad Street, bank, 563; offices, 345
Broadwood's Manufactory, 284
Brompton Cemetery, 99
Brompton Crescent, 94, 598
Brook St., no. 33, 225; no. 47, 575; nos. 76, 78, 185; ho., 619
Brooks's Club, 425
Brunswick Dock, 656
Brunswick Theatre, 887
Bruton St., no. 17, 867; no. 23, 866
Bryanston Sq., 621
Buckingham Ho., Pall Mall, 139, 771
Buckingham Ho. (later Palace), 50, 51, 208, 309, 904
Buckingham Palace, 117, 208, 244, 365, 580, 582; archway, 171
Budge Row, hos., 553
'Bull & Mouth' Inn, 721
Burlington Arcade, 867
Burlington Gardens, no. 3, 866; no. 7, 130; no. 34, 77
Burlington Ho., 75, 130, 184, 194, 258, 342, 491, 544, 710, 867
Burlington Girls' School, 184, 867
Burton Crescent, 174
Burton St., 174
Cadogan Place, 425
Cambridge Ho., 137
Cambridge Sq., no. 7, 394
Camden High St., 249
Camelford Ho., 639
Campden Hill, villa, 700
Canada Ho., 742
Cannon Brewery, Knightsbridge, 284
Cannon St., no. 14, 253; premises, 437
Canonbury Sq., 514
Cardigan Place, Kennington, 293
Carlton Club, 223, 433, 743
Carlton Gardens, nos. 5 & 6, 745
Carlton Ho., 425, 434, 438, 499, 547, 584, 700, 711
Carlton Ho. Terrace, 585; no. 3, 172; no. 4, 172; no. 6, 938; no. 10, 122; no. 14, 394; no. 18, 168
Carpenters' Hall, 479, 591, 651, 891
Carrington Ho., 208, 771
Cartwright Crescent, 174
Casino, Leicester Sq., 103
Castle St., Holborn, 552
Castle St., Marylebone, 312
Cateaton St., 862
Catholic Charities School, 348
Cavendish Square, no. 1, 69; no. 2 (Bank), 963; nos. 17–18, 483; ho. (Benson), 108; ho. (Chandos), 891; hos., 732
Chalcots estate, Chalk Farm, 730
Chancery Lane, hos., 184, 354
Chandos Ho., Portland Place, 51
Chandos Ho., St. James's Sq., 323, 828
Charing Cross Hospital, 171

LONDON

Charing Cross Rd., no. 16, 817
Charles St., Berkeley Sq., 633; no. 10, 394; no. 15, 859
Charles St., Drury Lane, schools, 724
Charles St., St. James's Sq., no. 19, 464
Charles St., no. 10, 619
Charlotte (now Hallam) St., no. 38, mausoleum, 771
Charlton Place, Islington, 813
Charterhouse, 116, 495, 637 (bis), 822; Chapel, 197
Chatham Place, 576
Cheapside, shop-front, 619
Chelsea Dispensary, 650
Chelsea Hospital, 50, 226, 294, 517, 767, 924; Commissioners' Room, Scotland Yard, 50
Chelsea Schools, 721
Chester Place, 813
Chester Terrace, 505
Chesterfield Ho., 866, 961
Cheyne Walk, no. 6, 208, 212
Christ Ch. Schools, Stepney, 754
Christian Union Almshouses, 377
Christ's Hospital, 403, 430, 518, 553, 601, 729, 730, 924

Churches and Chapels
Albany Chapel, 814
Albion Chapel, 455
All Hallows, Barking, 65
All Hallows, Lombard St., 927
All Hallows, London Wall, 250, 251, 273; mont., 626
All Hallows the Great, 928
All Hallows, Watling St., 928
All Saints, Ennismore Gardens, 858
All Saints, Poplar, 427
All Saints, Rotherhithe, 487
All Saints, Skinner St., 547
All Souls, Langham Place, 582
Archbishop Tenison's Chapel, 224, 390
Baptist Ch., Coldharbour Lane, 168
Bavarian Embassy Chapel, 125
Bayswater Chapel, 232
Bedford Chapel, 488
Belgrave Chapel, 744
Brompton Oratory, 724
Camden Chapel, Camberwell, 370
Camden Chapel, Camden Town, 445
Christ Ch., Albany St., 970
Christ Ch., Bermondsey, 66
Christ Ch., Broadway, 657
Christ Ch., Chelsea, 119
Christ Ch., Hoxton, 119
Christ Ch., Lisson Grove, 390
Christ Ch., Newgate St., 792, 929; mont., 642
Christ Ch., Rotherhithe, 858
Christ Ch., Spitalfields, 404
Christ Ch., Stepney, 730
Christchurch, Southwark, 436
Congregational Chapel, Camden Town, 254
Connaught Chapel, Paddington, 227
Craven Chapel, 43
Danish Ch., Wellclose Sq., 214, 914
Ebury Chapel, Chelsea, 652
Episcopal Jews' Chapel, Bethnal Green, 175, 535
Foley Chapel, 509
French Ch., Savoy, 926
French Protestant Ch., Bloomsbury, 657
French Protestant Ch., St. Martin-le-Grand, 604
German Lutheran Ch., 206
Greek Ch., London Wall, 604
Grosvenor Chapel, Grosvenor Place, 744
Grosvenor Chapel, S. Audley St., 828
Hampstead Parish Ch., 310
Hanover Chapel, Regent St., 224
Holy Trinity, Brompton, 269
Holy Trinity, Cloudesley Sq., 91
Holy Trinity, Gough Sq., 730
Holy Trinity, Gray's Inn Rd., 970

Churches and Chapels—contd.
Holy Trinity, Hoxton, 670
Holy Trinity, Lambeth, 119
Holy Trinity, Little Queen St., 104
Holy Trinity, Marylebone, 768
Holy Trinity, Newington, 104
Holy Trinity, Paddington, 247
Holy Trinity, Rotherhithe, 487
Holy Trinity, Sloane St., 721
Immaculate Conception, Farm St. (R.C.), 724
Kentish Town Episcopal Chapel, 93, 944
Lambeth Parish Ch., 959; mont., 772
Methodist Chapel, Gt. Queen St., 458 (bis)
Methodist Chapel, Hinde St., 458
Methodist Chapel, Lambeth, 458
Methodist Chapel, New Rd., 417
Methodist Chapels, Southwark, 306, 458
Northampton Tabernacle, Clerkenwell, 120
Our Lady (R.C.), St. John's Wood, 723
Portland Chapel, 509
Presbyterian Chapel, Jewin St., 60, 102
Presbyterian Chapel, Soho, 102
Ranelagh Chapel, 649
R.C. Chapel, Horseferry Rd., 446
R.C. Chapel, Romney Terrace, 321
R.C. Chapel, Southwark, 813
St. Alban, Wood St., 86n., 495, 927
St. Alphege, London Wall, 418, 591, 592
St. Andrew, Holborn, 351, 636, 774, 928
St. Andrew by the Wardrobe, 928
St. Anne & St. Agnes, Gresham St., 143, 309, 628, 846, 863, 928
St. Anne, Limehouse, 388, 404, 792
St. Anne, Soho, 227, 805, 926
St. Antholin, 201, 928
St. Augustine, Old Change, Watling St., 61, 791, 814, 928
St. Barnabas, Addison Rd., 857
St. Barnabas, King Sq., 390
St. Barnabas, Pimlico, 247
St. Bartholomew, Bethnal Green, 670
St. Bartholomew, Exchange, 928
St. Bartholomew the Great, Smithfield, 120, 389
St. Bartholomew-the-Less, 251, 390
St. Bartholomew, Moor Lane, 224
St. Benet Fink, 201, 928
St. Benet, Gracechurch St., 928
St. Benet, Paul's Wharf, 791, 928
St. Botolph, Aldgate, 248, 348, 366, 931
St. Botolph, Bishopsgate, 248, 355
St. Bride, Fleet St., 259, 730, 811, 928
St. Christopher le Stocks, 929
St. Clement Danes, 340, 636, 926
St. Clement, Eastcheap, 791, 929
St. Dionis Backchurch, 929
St. Dunstan-in-the-East, 501, 828, 929
St. Dunstan, Fleet St., 730
St. Edmund, Lombard St., 428, 929
St. Ethelburga, Bishopsgate, 364
St. Gabriel, Warwick Sq., 247
St. George, Battersea, 119
St. George, Bloomsbury, 404, 792
St. George, Botolph Lane, 929
St. George, Camberwell, 104
St. George, Hanover Sq., 453–4
St. George-in-the-East, 404, 792
St. George, Queen Sq., 404
St. George, Southwark, 228, 411, 660, 831
St. Giles-in-the-Fields, 310, 405, 472, 600
St. Gregory, 470
St. Helen, Bishopsgate, 211
St. James, Bermondsey, 66, 720
St. James, Bethnal Green, 119, 858
St. James, Clapham Common, 857
St. James, Clerkenwell, 188
St. James, Garlick Hill (Garlickhythe), 486, 792, 929

Churches and Chapels—*contd.*
St. James, Hampstead Rd., 389
St. James, Holloway, 445
St. James, Norland Sq., 858
St. James, Paddington, 349, 369
St. James, Pentonville, 440
St. James, Piccadilly, 389, 706, 744, 890, 926
St. James, Ratcliff, 506
St. James, Shoreditch, 858
St. James, W. Hackney, 744
St. John, Bethnal Green, 768
St. John, Hackney, 661, 773
St. John, Hampstead, 716
St. John, Horselydown, 404, 454
St. John Baptist, Hoxton, 284
St. John (R.C.), Islington, 724
St. John, Marylebone, 209, 344, 502, 661
St. John, Oxford Sq., 320
St. John, St. John's Wood, 389
St. John, S. Hackney, 71
St. John, Upper Holloway, 91
St. John, Walham Green, 814
St. John, Wapping, 461
St. John, Waterloo Rd., 104
St. John, Westminster, 69, 132, 436, 445, 792
St. Jude, Chelsea, 94
St. Katherine Coleman, 233, 436, 661, 782
St. Katherine Cree, 495
St. Katherine's Hospital Chapel, 657
St. Katherine by the Tower, 231
St. Lawrence, Jewry, 636, 929
St. Leonard, Shoreditch, 248
St. Luke, Berwick St., 119
St. Luke, Chelsea, 374, 720
St. Luke, Old St., 404, 454
St. Luke, W. Norwood, 104
St. Magnus Martyr, 523, 929
St. Margaret, Lothbury, 929
St. Margaret Pattens, 929
St. Margaret, Westminster, 227, 236, 368, 454,
    814, 926; mont., 345
St. Mark, Hamilton Terrace, 247
St. Mark, Kennington, 218, 705–6
St. Mark, Myddleton Sq., 578
St. Mark, N. Audley St., 330
St. Martin-in-the-Fields, 276, 340, 453, 495, 539,
    633, 710, 712, 825, 828, 926
St. Martin, Ludgate, 929
St. Martin Orgar, 188, 253
St. Martin Outwich, 91, 227
St. Mary Abchurch, 486, 929
St. Mary Abbots, Kensington, 390; mont., 772
St. Mary, Aldermanbury, 211, 418, 846, 930
St. Mary Aldermary, 260, 791, 930
St. Mary, Battersea, 263, 591, 592
St. Mary le Bow, 201, 370, 495, 636, 721, 930;
    mont., 654
St. Mary's, Bromley St. Leonard's, 670
St. Mary, Haggerston, 582
St. Mary at Hill, 370, 523, 720, 930
St. Mary, Islington, 273
St. Mary, Lambeth, 959; mont., 772
St. Mary the Less, Lambeth, 104
St. Mary, Newington, 440
St. Mary (R.C.), Moorfields, 590
St. Mary, Paddington, 642
St. Mary, Rotherhithe, 273, 347
St. Mary's Chapel, Somers Town, 445
St. Mary Somerset, 486, 930
St. Mary, Stoke Newington, 91
St. Mary le Strand, 259, 340
St. Mary, Vincent Sq., 119
St. Mary Woolnoth, 404, 602, 930
St. Mary, Wyndham Place, 744
St. Mary Magdalene, Bermondsey, 653, 776, 856
St. Mary Magdalene, Islington, 887
St. Mary Magdalene, Old Fish St., 753, 791, 930

Churches and Chapels—*contd.*
St. Marylebone New Ch., 389
St. Matthew, Bethnal Green, 249
St. Matthew, Brixton, 652; mont., 255
St. Matthew, Friday St., 636, 930
St. Michael Bassishaw, 625, 930
St. Michael, Burleigh St., 721
St. Michael, Chester Sq., 247
St. Michael, Cornhill, 260, 404, 792, 930
St. Michael, Crooked Lane, 930
St. Michael, Highgate, 857
St. Michael, Paternoster Royal, College Hill, 292,
    791, 792, 930
St. Michael, Queenhithe, 753, 930
St. Michael le Querne, 459, 473, 551
St. Michael, Wood St., 143, 931
St. Mildred, Bread St., 791, 931
St. Mildred, Poultry, 523, 931
St. Nicholas, Cole Abbey, 931
St. Olave, Hart St., 331, 831, 887
St. Olave, Old Jewry, 931
St. Olave, Southwark, 66, 310, 831
St. Pancras, 652
St. Pancras New Ch., 445
St. Paul, Balls Pond, 91
St. Paul's Cathedral, 60, 197, 224, 259, 295, 372,
    405, 472, 486, 495, 539, 575, 629, 636, 791–2,
    801, 926; mont. to Wren, 577
St. Paul, Covent Garden, 129, 197, 389, 472
St. Paul's Chapel, Great Portland St., 509
St. Paul, Kilburn, 320
St. Paul, Onslow Sq., 281
St. Paul's Ch. for Seamen, 696
St. Paul, Shadwell, 864
St. Paul, Wilton Place, 247
St. Peter, Bankside, 282
St. Peter, Bethnal Green, 858
St. Peter, Cornhill, 931
St. Peter, Eaton Sq., 273, 377, 411
St. Peter, Hackney, 523
St. Peter, Islington, 91
St. Peter-le-Poer, 345
St. Peter, Regent Sq., 445
St. Peter, Saffron Hill, 91
St. Peter, Stepney, 119
St. Peter, Vere St., 340, 633, 828
St. Peter, Walworth, 768
St. Philip, Clerkenwell, 970
St. Philip, Regent St., 679
St. Philip, Stepney, 352, 864
St. Saviour, Chelsea, 94
St. Saviour, Pimlico, 247
St. Sepulchre, Holborn, 931
St. Stephen, Camden Town, 445
St. Stephen, Coleman St.; 931; mont., 772
St. Stephen, Islington, 445
St. Stephen, Walbrook, 486, 535, 628, 791, 792,
    931
St. Swithin, Cannon St., 931
St. Thomas, Bethnal Green, 858
St. Thomas, Chancery Lane, 254
St. Thomas, Charterhouse Gardens, 119
St. Thomas, Clapton Common, 372
St. Thomas, Old Kent Rd., 67
St. Thomas, Regent St., 224
St. Thomas, Southwark, 201
St. Thomas, Stepney, 754
St. Vedast, Foster Lane, 67, 255, 791, 792, 890,
    931
Savoy Chapel, 120, 744
Scotch Ch., Crown Court, 696, 862
Scotch Ch., Regent Sq., 829, 861
Scottish Presbyterian Ch., 517
Southwark Cathedral, 370, 371, 706, 862; mcnt.,
    772
Spanish Chapel, Manchester Sq., 125, 620
Stamford Hill Chapel, 372

LONDON

Churches and Chapels—*contd.*
Surrey Chapel, 255, 822
Swedenborg Chapel, 433
Tavistock Chapel, 269
Temple Ch., 172, 294, 721, 744, 926
Trinity Independent Chapel, Poplar, 437
Unitarian Chapel, Essex St., 671
Unitarian Chapel, South Place, 143–4, 863
Unitarian Chapel, Stamford St., 678n.
Wesleyan Chapel, Jewin St., 102
Wesleyan Chapel, Kensington, 650
Wesleyan Chapel, Stepney, 754
Westminster Abbey, 120, 144, 149, 204, 259, 405,
    454, 484, 926, 938, 945; Handel commem.,
    652n., 945; Henry VII's Chapel, 121, 334,
    823, 826, 945; monts., 209, 252, 344, 494, 514,
    797, 815, 986
Whitfield's Tabernacle, 629
Church Lane, Kensington, ho., 618
Church Missionary College, Islington, 144
City Bank, Threadneedle St., 563
City Club, 387
City Library, 563
City of London Literary Inst., 120
City of London School, 969
City of London Theatre, 103
Clapham Road, Brixton, nos. 17–25, 546
Clapton, 71
Clarence Ho., 582
Clarendon Ho., 659, 710
Clarendon Sq., 514
Clements Inn, 725
Clement's Lane, offices, 856
Clerkenwell Prison, *see* Middlesex Ho. of Detention
Clerkenwell Schools, 578
Clerkenwell Sunday School, 525
Cleveland Ho., 518, 809
Cleveland Row, no. 4, 958; ho., 208
Cleveland Sq., no. 1, 92
Clifford's Inn, 171
Clissold Ho., Stoke Newington, 913
Clothworkers' Hall, 67
Club Chambers, Lower Regent St., 171
Colby Ho., Kensington, 403
Coll. of Arms (Heralds), 44, 294
Coll. of Physicians, 309
Coll. of Surgeons, 671
Colosseum, 171, 701
Commercial Benevolent Coll., 306
Commercial Sale Rooms, 913
Compton Terrace, 514
Concert Room, Tottenham Court Rd., 598
Conduit Mead estate, 828
Conduit St., 321; no. 9, 951
Connaught St., 955
Conservative Club, 94, 433
Constitution Hill, lodge, 767
Coopers' Hall, 891
Cordwainers' Hall, 380
Corn Exchange, Mark Lane, 218, 753–4
Corn Market, Mark Lane, 249
Cornwall Place, Islington, 649n.
Coronation arches (1661), 336–7, 552
County Fire Office, Regent St., 43
Coutts's Bank, Strand, 434, 609
Covent Garden, 197, 254, 256, 472, 626
Covent Garden Market, 320
Covent Garden Theatre, 426, 732, 742
Coventry Ho., Piccadilly, 51, 245
Coventry St., no. 17, 619; stabling, 212
Cowper's Court, Smithfield, 248
Cox's Hotel, 686
Craven St., 312
Cremorne Ho., Chelsea, 947
Crockford's Club, 938
Cromwell Ho., Highgate, 551
Crosby Hall, 117, 253, 254

Cumberland Ho., Pall Mall, 51, 137
Cure's College, Southwark, 371
Curzon St., no. 19, 140, 771; no. 30, 51; ho., 499
Custom Ho., 501, 695, 743, 924
Davis's Wharf, 254
Dean St., Mayfair, 771
De Beauvoir Sq., Hackney, 523
Debtors' Prison, Whitecross St., 563
Delahay St., 940
Denmark Hill, no. 154, 114
Derby Ho., Grosvenor Sq., 51
Devonshire Ho., 172, 492, 951
Diorama (The), 557, 667
Docks, 907
Dr. Williams's Library, 269
Dorchester Ho., 746, 859
Dorset Ho., Whitehall, 944
Dorset Sq., 255
Dover Ho., 425, 609, 965
Dover St., no. 19, 51; no. 29, 583; no. 38, 637; no.
    46, 374; hos., 137, 312, 866
Dowgate Hill, hos., 775
Downing St., no. 10, 236, 772; no. 11, 772; ho,
    237
Downshire Ho., 488
D'Oyley's Warehouse, 103
Drapers' Hall, 201, 354, 460, 687
Drummond's Bank, 51
Drury Ho., 905
Drury Lane Theatre, 50, 102, 179, 186, 426, 924,
    938, 939
Duchess St., ho., 51, 76, 432
Duchy of Lancaster Offices, Strand, 742
Dudley Ho., 77
Duke St., Southwark, 590
Duke St., Westminster, coach-ho., 320
Duke of York's Barracks, Chelsea, 714
Duke of York's Column, 938
Duncan Terrace, Islington, 813
Dunraven St., no. 22, 771
Durham Ho., 872
Durham Yard, Strand, 855
Dutch Almshouses, Finsbury, 653
Dyers' Hall, 277, 478
East India Ho., 227, 426, 450, 454, 476, 478–9, 896
East London Theatre, 261
Eaton Sq., 243; ho., 225
Eccleston Sq., 332
Edward St., 908
Egerton Crescent, 94
Egremont Ho., 137
Egyptian Hall, Piccadilly, 619, 700
Ely Ho., Dover St., 818
Ely Place, Holborn, 229, 354
Emanuel Almshouses, 602
Endsleigh Place, 858
Endsleigh St., 243
Ennismore Gardens, 291
Equitable Assurance Co., 743
Euston Sq., 243
Euston Station, 387
Excise Office, 415, 704
Exeter Hall, Strand, 330, 557
Eyre Arms Tavern, 883
Falmouth Rd., Southwark, 481
Farringdon Market, 563
Farringdon St., obelisk, 292
Fenchurch St., no. 27, 771
Ferns (The), Kensington, 172
Fetherstonhaugh Ho., 425
Fife Ho., Whitehall, 51, 771
Finch Lane, premises, 619
Finsbury Circus, 249, 563
Finsbury Savings Bank, 93
Finsbury Sq., 249
Fire-station (Chandos St.), 150
Fish Street Hill, hos., 914

LONDON

Fishmongers' Hall, 125, 306, 349, 387, 460, 523, 524, 696
Fitzroy Sq., 52
Fleet Ditch, 308
Fleet Market, 248
Fleet St., no. 43, 619; no. 189, 771
Floor Cloth Factory, 372
Foley Ho., 508
Foley Place, no. 1, 951
Fore St., premises, 619
Foundling Hospital, 436, 450; estate, 226
Fountain Court, Aldermanbury, 771
Frederick's Place, 51, 771
Freemasons' Hall, 714, 768
Freemasons' School, 198
Freemasons' Tavern, 845
Frith St., 323; shop-front, 619
Frognal Grove, Hampstead, 312
Furnival St., Holborn, 552
Furnival's Inn, Holborn, 822
Gas Works, 254, 284, 364
General Post Office, 157, 743; competition for, 349, 433, 480, 520
George St., Bloomsbury, 697
George St., Hanover Sq., see St. George St.
George's Place, Islington, 649n.
Giltspur St. Compter, 251
Globe Insurance Co., 387
Gloucester Ho., 225
Gloucester Place, 255
Gloucester Rd., 96
Gloucester Sq., 813
Gold (Gould) Sq., 355
Golden Cross Hotel, 829
Goldsmiths' Hall, 387, 459n., 460, 786
Goodman's Fields Theatre, 732
Goose-Pie Ho., Whitehall, 852
Gordon Place, 858
Gordon Sq., 243
Gower Ho., 208
Grafton Ho., 817–18
Grafton St., nos. 3–6, 818
Grantham Ho., 208, 965
Granville Sq., 126
Gray's Inn, 354, 483, 538, 693, 888
Gray's Inn Rd., 243; workshops, 619
Great Burlington St., see Old Burlington St.
Great Coram St., no. 57, 619
Great George St., hos., 421, 940
Great Ormond St., no. 49, 342; hos., 518
Great Pulteney St., ho., 228
Great Queen St., hos., 552
Great Russell St., nos. 66–71, 582
Great Stanhope St., no. 6, 172
Great Surrey St., ho., 577
Great Windmill St., no. 16, 576
Green Park, fireworks (1749), 726
Green Park Lodge, 51, 642
Green St., Grosvenor Sq., no. 58, 394; no 61, 394, 561
Gresham Coll., 754
Gresham Ho., 829
Gresham St., nos. 1–8, 829
Grocers' Hall, 372, 517
Grosvenor estate, 89, 695n., 697
Grosvenor Ho., Millbank, 822
Grosvenor Ho., Upper Grosvenor St., 246, 653
Grosvenor Place, 460, 598; no. 7, 168; no. 12, 809; ho., 780
Grosvenor Sq., 89, 185, 735; no. 3, 394; no. 4, 312; no. 10, 958; no. 13, 771; no. 16, 951; no. 17 (18), 168; nos. 18–21, 732; no. 18 (19), 51; no. 20, 208; no. 22 (25), 771; no. 23 (26), 51; no. 29 (34), 644; no. 34 (39), 771; no. 36 (41), 951; no. 37 (42), 394; no. 40 (45), 958; no. 44 (49), 771; no. 51, 209; no. 74, 963
Grosvenor St., no. 18, 172; no. 51, 394, 859

Grove End, Paddington, 75, 76
Guards' Club, Pall Mall, 394
Guards' Club, St. James's St., 394
Guildhall, 251, 563, 636, 651
Guy's Hospital, 110, 114, 252, 478
Gwydyr Ho., Whitehall, 538
Haberdashers' (Aske's) Almshouses, 706
Haberdashers' Hall, 201
Hackney Church of England Grammar School, 143
Hackney Grammar School, 281
Hackney, Stamp Brooksbank's ho., 185
Half Moon St., ho., 637
Hallam St., see Charlotte St.
Hamilton Ho., Portman Sq., 383
Hamilton Place, 517
Hammersley's Bank, Pall Mall, 533
Hampstead: Belsize Lane, villa, 621; Frognal, hos., 618; ho (Bayley), 770; ho. (Husband), 721
Hanover Sq., 89, 275, 866; no. 18, 51; hos., 51, 181, 291; Concert Rooms, 286
Hans Place, 425
Hans Town, 425; Assembly Rooms, 700
Harcourt Ho., Cavendish Sq., 69, 891
Harcourt (ex-Bingley) Ho., Cavendish Sq., 69n., 867
Harewood Ho., Hanover Sq., 51, 606
Harley estate, 661
Harley St., ball-room, 704; no. 13, 228; no. 27 (68), 464; no. 43 (63), 464; no. 57, 619; hos., 882
Haverstock Lodge, 535
Haymarket, stabling, 212, 686
Haymarket Opera Ho. (alias King's or Queen's Theatre), 494, 517, 581, 598, 679, 852
Haymarket Theatre, 581
Heath Lodge, Hampstead, 542
Henrietta St., 343
Henry Wood Hall, 104
Heralds' Coll., see Coll. of Arms
Hertford St., no. 10, 51; hos., 640
High Holborn, shop-front, 534
Highbury Coll., 253
Highbury Hill, ho., 65
Highbury Park, 243
Highbury Place, 772
Highgate: Archway, 581; Beechwood, 95; Cemetery, 335; Holly Lodge, 618; Little Priory, 650; hos., etc., 96, 150, 366, 575, 859
Hill St., no. 17, 51, 576; no. 22, 245; no. 23, 771; no. 24, 245; no. 33, 252; Mrs. Montagu's ho., 51
Hoare's Bank, Fleet St., 620
Holborn, no. 69, 619
Holborn Hill, no. 94, 619
Holborn National School, 351
Holborn Union Workhouse, 332
Holborn Viaduct, 661, 819
Holderness Ho., 796, 961
Holland Ho., 85, 109, 147, 172, 714
Holland Park Avenue, 186
Home House, Portman Sq., 51
Homerton, St. Barnabas' School, 281
Honey Lane Market, 251
Horse Guards, 493, 704, 854–5
Ho. of Occupations, Lambeth, 387
Howley Place, 955
Hoxton, Gas Works, 284
Hungerford Market, 320
Hyde Park: barracks, 276; Cumberland Gate, 767; Ionic entrance-screen, 171, 473; lodges, 171; military store-house, 171; Receiving Ho. of Royal Humane Soc., 969; Serpentine Lake, 436; triumphal arches, 495, 514, 703
Hyde Park Gardens, 239, 869; no. 18, 172
Hyde Park Sq., 813, 955
Hyde Park St., 955
Imperial Plate Glass Factory, 566

LONDON

Incorporated Society of Artists' Exhibition Rooms, Strand, 609
Inglebert St., Clerkenwell, 578
Inner Temple, 197, 742, 807, 828, 965
Insolvent Debtors' Court, 768
Ironmongers' Hall, 423
Isle of Dogs, warehouses, 370
Islington: Gas Works, 364; Orphan School, 592; Parochial Schools, 366; Proprietary School, 590; St. John's Schools, 91; Thornhill estate, 480; villas, 366
Ivy Cottage, Kentish Town, 667
James St., 51
Jermyn St., nos. 53–55, 212; ho., 276
Jewish School, Stepney, 782
John St., 51
Jones & Loyd's Bank, Lothbury, 534
Junior United Service Club, 171
Kemble Tavern, 231
Kennington Lane, no. 363, 329
Kennington Park, lodges, 697
Kennington Rd., no. 317, 725
Kennington, St. Mark's School, 81
Kensal Green Cemetery, 487, 667; monts., 94, 120, 226, 619, 647
Kensal Ho., Harrow Rd., 394
Kensington Charity School, 403
Kensington, Henry Wise's ho., 854
Kensington Palace, 109, 183, 294, 493, 963, 965; Orangery, 403, 852; Water Tower, 853
Kensington Palace Gardens, no. 10, 387; no. 12, 92; no. 14, 244; nos. 18, 19 & 20, 92; proposed ho., 307
Kensington Palace Green, no. 2, 416
Kentish Town, villas, 366
King St., Covent Garden, no. 37, 609; no. 43, 69; Westminster Fire Office, 545
King St., Westminster, 633
King William St., 743
King's Bagnio, 848
King's Coll., 743
King's Cross, Battle Bridge, 335
King's Cross Station, 243
King's Theatre, Haymarket, see Haymarket Opera Ho.
Knightsbridge: factories, 590, 649; hos., 208, 855
Ladbroke estate, 66
Ladbroke Terrace, 186
Lady Owen's Almshouses, 810
Lambeth Palace, 117, 149, 452–3
Lamb's Chapel & Almshouses, 67
Lamb's Conduit, Holborn, 249
Lancaster Ho., 92, 534, 746, 938
Lancaster Place, 742
Land Revenue Office, Scotland Yard, 509
Langham Ho., 584
Langham Place, 584
Lansdowne Ho., 51, 125, 252, 744
Law Life Assurance Office, 730
Law Society's Hall, 857
Leadenhall Market, 251
Leather Lane, 507
Leathersellers' Hall, 649
Legal & General Life Office, 434
Leicester Ho., 184, 276, 828
Leicester Sq.: Ailesbury Ho., 275; no. 1 (Gedges), 605; nos. 5–6 (Savile Ho.), 342, 606; no. 20, 829; no. 25, 342; no. 47, 609, 619; proposed gallery, 671
Leman Sq., 252
Leverian Museum, 174
Licensed Victuallers' Asylum, 706
Licensed Victuallers' School, 706
Lichfield Ho., 796
Light Horse Volunteers' stables, 227
Limehouse, ho., 858

Lincoln's Inn, 138, 387; Chapel, 215, 945; Stone Bldngs., 816
Lincoln's Inn Fields: no. 12, 771; no. 13, 495, 766, 771; no. 14, 771; nos. 35–36, 817; no. 51, 771; nos. 57–58, 477, 771; nos. 59–60 (Lindsey Ho.), 787; no. 65, 516; proposed Ch., 185; proposed Law Courts, 672
Linden Grove, no. 1, 66
Lindsey Ho., Lincoln's Inn Fields, 787
Lion Brewery, Golden Sq., 284
Lion Brewery, Lambeth, 284
Little Court, Castle St., 609
Little Theatre, Haymarket, 654
Lloyd-Baker St., 126
Lloyd Sq., 126
Lock Hospital, 461n., 858
Lombard St.: no. 15 (Robarts & Curtis's Bank), 517; no. 19 (Phoenix Fire Office), 505–6; no. 24, 742; no. 62, 487; no. 68, 251; no. 70, 816
London Assurance Co.'s office, 782
London Bridge (dem. 1831), 65, 249, 497, 499, 816
London Bridge (dem. 1967), 573, 678; approaches, 66, 743; competition for (1823), 125, 320, 686, 720, 883
London Bridge Station, 103, 696, 754
London Dock Co., 64, 65
London Fever Hospital, 321
London Hospital, 461, 534, 773
London Institution, 143, 243
London Leather Co., Bermondsey, 653
London Nautical Coll., 678n.
London & Provincial Assurance Co., 730
London School of Printing, 563
London Tavern, Bishopsgate St., 479, 592
London & Westminster Bank, Lothbury, 224, 829
London & Westminster Bank, St. James's Sq., 858
Londonderry Ho., 796, 938
Long Acre, premises, 645
Long Alley, Strand, 865
Lothbury, banks, 224, 534, 829
Lower Brook St., no. 39, 633n., 962
Lower Gower St., no. 34, 771
Lower Grosvenor St., no. 20, 394; no. 53, 954
Lowndes Sq., 243
Lowther Arcade, 415, 582
Ludgate Hill: no. 5, 619; no. 8, 619; no. 9, 814; no. 32 (Rundell, Bridge & Rundell), 545
Lumley Ho., 609
Lyceum Theatre, 102
Lying-in Hospital, City, 575
Lying-in Hospital, Lambeth, 394
Magdalen Hospital, 261, 461
Maida Vale, nos. 120–122, 649n.
Mansfield St., 51; no. 12, 771; ho. (Sligo), 619
Mansion Ho., 248, 251, 273, 563, 743, 815, 831; competition for, 256, 344, 453, 503, 514
Marble Arch, 582
Margaret St., 908
Marine Insurance Office, Cornhill, 253
Mark Lane, no. 17, 771; no. 48, 65
Marlborough Ho., 208–9, 792, 925, 965
Marshalsea Prison, 473
Martin's Bank, Lombard St., 251
Marx Memorial Library, 778
Mary Brewery, 507
Marylebone Manor Ho., 661
Marylebone Park, 882
Marylebone Workhouse, 883
Matson Terrace, Shoreditch, 542
Mecklenburgh Sq., 151, 479
Melbourne Ho., Piccadilly, 209, 426, 609
Melbourne Ho., Whitehall, 425, 609, 965
Mercers' Hall, 201, 460, 601, 753
Mercers' School, 754
Merchant Taylors' Hall, 430
Merchant Taylors' School, 430
Meux's Brewery, 507

LONDON

Michael's Grove, Kensington, 598
Michael's Place, Kensington, 598
Middle Temple, 377, 543, 597, 721, 924; Gateway, 597; Hall, 295
Middlesex Hospital, 94, 98, 608
Middlesex Ho. of Correction, Clerkenwell, 515, 547–8, 563
Middlesex Ho. of Detention, Clerkenwell, 563, 867
Middlesex Sessions Ho., Clerkenwell, 705
Military Depot, Tooley St., 742
Militia Headquarters, 650
Millbank, hos., 613
Millbank Penitentiary, 389, 399, 742, 898
Milton Ho., Park Lane, 855
Milton St., Cripplegate, warehouses, 619, 862
Minerva Insurance Office, 318
Mines Royal, Dowgate Hill, 628
Minories, 249
Monmouth Ho., 69, 314, 323
Montagu Grove, Hampstead, 312
Montagu Ho., Bloomsbury, 309, 430, 655–6
Montagu Ho., Whitehall, 168, 312
Montagu (Portman) Ho., 796
Montagu Sq., 621
Montague Place, 771
Monument (The), 214, 430, 539, 924
Moorgate, 201
Moorgate St., 743
Mortimer Ho., 744
Mount Pleasant, cottage, 400
Mount Row, 459
Mount St., nos. 13–14, 121
Myddelton Sq., 578
National Debt Redemption Office, 224, 767
National Gallery, 746, 896; competition for, 223, 894
Naval & Military Club, 137
Navy Office, 924
Nelson Square, Southwark, 228
Nelson's Column, 433, 670; designs for, 349, 746
New Bank Bldngs., 771
New Bond St., no. 88, 619
New Bridge St., 576
New Burlington St., no. 4, 314; no. 5, 404; no. 10, 51, 423
New Cavendish St., no. 1 (63), 770; no. 7, 231; nos. 61, 63, 464
New Cross, villa, 669
New Exchange, Strand, 95, 198, 468
New Norfolk St., no. 22, 771
New Rd., ho. 883
New Terrace, Islington, 813
Newcastle Ho., Lincoln's Inn Fields, 853, 904
Newcastle Place, Clerkenwell, 188
Newgate Prison, 250, 251, 476
Newington, hos., 440
Newman St., no. 14 (picture-gallery), 581, 883; no. 85, 208
Newport St., 710
Nichols Sq., 814
Noel Ho., Kensington Gore, 177
Norfolk Ho., 43, 126, 137
North London Hospital, 61
North Terrace, Peckham Rd., 103
North Villa, 225
Northumberland Ho., Strand, 51, 197, 225, 246, 334, 455, 539, 609, 710, 867, 873
Norwood Cemetery, 829
Notting Hill, 66
Old Bond St. (City), 771
Old Bond St., no. 22, 444
Old Burlington St., no 15 (Dubois), 275; no. 29, 130, 958; no. 30, 130, 561; nos. 31–34, 184; no. 34, 421
Old Jewry Chambers, 277
Old Kent Rd., no. 155, 726
Old Vic Theatre, 180
Opera Ho., *see* Haymarket Opera Ho.

Ophthalmic Infirmary, 742
Ophthalmic Institution, 581
Ordnance Office, Old Palace Yard, 845
Ordnance Office, Pall Mall, 77
Oriental Club, 171, 938
Ormonde Ho., 323
Orphan Asylum, Clapton, 444
Orsett Ho., 813
Oxford & Cambridge Club, 743
Oxford Market, 339
Oxford Sq., no. 22, 394
Oxford St., 44, 908; no. 314, 619
Paddington: almshouses, 227; cottage, 704; Charity Schools, 489
Pall Mall: nos. 16–17, 92; no. 25, 51; no. 49, 224, 697–8; no. 52, 88; no. 56, 771; no. 69, 534; no. 71, 695; no. 79, 609; no. 80, 172; no. 86, 51, 137; no. 91, 139; no. 103, 771; no. 104, 771; no. 105, 425, 609; hos., 262, 464, 633; premises, 685; proposed opera-ho., 518
Pall Mall East, no. 1, 77; no. 8, 172; ho. & shops, 172
Panharmonium Theatre, 335
Pantechnicon, 477
Pantheon (The), 245, 533, 631, 940, 943, 956
Pantheon Library, 103n.
Paragon (The), New Kent Rd., 725
Park Lane; no. 21, 869; no. 22, 771; no. 50/51, 771; nos. 98, 99, 349; no. 100, 77; hos., 609, 657, 771
Park St., nos. 31–32, 62, 394; no. 113, 958
Parliament, Houses of, 91, 108–9, 366, 399, 746; competition for, 62, 87, 90, 99, 107, 133, 156, 157, 168, 215, 222n., 223, 235, 244, 258, 315, 323, 351, 353, 356, 377, 380, 390, 392n., 433 (*bis*), 444, 456, 506, 509, 519, 526, 557, 669, 681, 689, 700, 709, 711, 720, 824, 827, 836, 845, 869, 880, 883, 894, 899, 907–8, 953; House of Commons, 743, 768, 924, 944; designs for (1833), 93, 329, 353, 509; House of Lords, 472, 743, 768, 944; Painted Chamber, 187, 241, 310; Speaker's Ho., 944; Stone Building, 236, 855
Parliamentary Agency Offices, 292
Parliamentary Mews, 171
Parthenon Club, 103
Paternoster Row, no. 66, 650
Paymaster-General's Office, Whitehall, 502
Pelham Crescent, 94
Pelham Place, 94
Pembroke Ho., Whitehall, 184, 208, 260, 301, 413, 559, 561
Pentonville, hos., 203; Lower Rd., 697
Pentonville Prison, 91
Petty France, 275
Pewterers' Hall, 891
Phillimore Place, 652
Philpot Lane, no. 15, 771, 818
Phoenix & Pelican Insurance Office, 329
Phoenix Fire-Engine Ho., Charing Cross, 517
Phoenix Fire Office, 517
Physic Garden, Chelsea, 599
Piccadilly, no. 29 (106), 51, 245; no. 79, 51, 208, 575; no. 80, 137; no. 82, 394, 398, 513; no. 94, 137; no. 105, 598, 745; nos. 138–139, 137, 262; no. 143, 252; no. 144, 95, 228; no. 145, 228; no. 148, 770; hos., 598; Lord Sunderland's library, 380, 416; shop-fronts, 619
Pickett St., 249
Pilgrim St., printing offices, 754
Pimlico Literary Institution, 330
Pitt estate, Kensington, 66
Pollen estate, 66
Polygon, Somers Town, 514
Pomfret Ho., 550
Porchester Terrace, nos. 3 & 5, 525
Porteus Rd., 955

LONDON

Portland Place, 44, 49, 51; no. 25 (70), 771; no. 56, 619
Portman Ho., 125
Portman Square, no. 1, 619; no. 9, 464; no. 10, 464; nos. 11–15, 951; no. 12 (15), 383; no. 13, 745; no. 20, 51
Portugal Row, 671
Powis Ho., Lincoln's Inn Fields, 904
Primrose Hill, botanical garden, 217; proposed cemetery, 353
Prince's Gate, 287, 291
Princes Place, Lambeth, 725
Privy Council Offices, Whitehall, 92, 509, 768
Privy Gardens, Whitehall, 137, 343, 430
Protestant Dissenters' Coll., 702
'Public Porter' Brewhouse, 400
Pulteney estate, 252
Purday's Warehouses, 65
Quays, 628
Queen Anne's Gate, nos. 6–12, 292; ho., 657
Queen's Theatre, Haymarket, see Haymarket Opera Ho.
Queen's Theatre, Tottenham Court Rd., 598
Queensberry Ho., 130, 513
Rainbow Coffee-Ho., 249
Ramillies St., see Blenheim St.
Ranelagh Gardens, 186, 702; Rotunda, 476
Ranelagh Ho., Chelsea, 474
Ransom & Co.'s Bank, 77
Rathbone Place, 671
Reform Club, 91, 254; competition for, 223
Regent St., 174, 705; nos. 156–172, 177; nos. 176–186, 43; no. 210, 883; no. 326, 557; nos. 579–580, 585; County Fire Office, 43; shop, 416
Regent's Park, 212, 516, 579, 585, 883; Archers' Lodge, 557; Botanic Gardens, 171; Cambridge Terrace, 585; Chester Terrace, 505, 585; Clarence Terrace, 170, 585; Cornwall Terrace, 170, 585; Cumberland Gate, 585; Cumberland Terrace, 585; Gloucester Gate, 505, 585, 723; Gloucester Lodge, 619; Gloucester Terrace, 619, 723; Grove Ho., 172; Hanover Lodge, 585; Hanover Terrace, 585; Holford Ho., 172; Holme (The), 172, 174; Kent Terrace, 585; Macclesfield Bridge, 557; Park Sq., 585; Park Villages, 585; St. Andrew's Terrace, 585; St. Dunstan's Lodge, 172; St. John's Lodge, 92, 657, 669; South Villa, 172; Stratherne Villa, 505; Sussex Place, 585; Ulster Terrace, 585; York Gate, 585; York Terrace, 585; Zoological Gardens, 171
Richmond Gardens, Whitehall, 619
Richmond Ho., Whitehall, 131, 208, 951–2
Richmond Terrace, Whitehall, 212, 394
River St., Clerkenwell, 578
Robert St., 51
Rolls estate, Bermondsey, 725
Rolls Ho., 184
Romney Ho., Hampstead, 157
Rotunda, Leicester Sq., 554
Roxburghe Ho., Hanover Sq., 51
Royal Botanic Soc.'s Gardens, 171
Royal Caledonian Asylum, Islington, 436, 807
Royal Circus Theatre, 179
Royal Coburg Theatre, 180
Royal Coll. of Physicians, Amen Corner, 873
Royal Coll. of Physicians, Trafalgar Sq., 742
Royal Coll. of Physicians, Warwick Lane, 430
Royal Coll. of Surgeons, Lincoln's Inn Fields, 91, 251, 519
Royal Crescent, 186
Royal Exchange (dem. 1838), 201, 214, 459–60, 704, 753
Royal Exchange, 563, 746, 829; competition for, 223, 349, 364, 371, 546, 613, 828, 888, 908
Royal Infirmary for Children, 501

Royal Institution, 773, 858, 877
Royal Mews, Charing Cross, 493, 712
Royal Mews, Pimlico, 582
Royal Military Asylum, Chelsea, 714
Royal Mint, 461, 742
Royal Naval Club, 171
Royal Opera Ho., see Haymarket Opera Ho.
Royal Panopticon, Leicester Sq., 307
Royal Pharmaceutical Soc., 582
Royal Soc. of Arts, 50
Royal Soc. of Literature, 171
Royal Soc. of Musicians, 434
Royal Society's Repository, 925
Royal Soho Theatre, 103
Royal Worcester Porcelain Warehouse, 374
Royalty Theatre, Wellclose Sq., 232, 261–2
Russell Ho., Covent Garden, 69
Russell Institution, 174, 729
Russell Sq., 174
Russell St., hos., 710
Ryder's Court, 710
Ryder St., 710
Sackville St., 633; no. 28, 609; no. 29, 51; no. 36, 312
Saddlers' Co., 67, 345
Sailors' Home, 696
St. Alban's St., stabling, 771
St. Andrew's Holborn; Vestry Hall, 351; Workhouse, 351
St. Anne, Soho; Rectory, 693; Workhouse, 608–9
St. Anne's Schools, Brixton Hill, 814
St. Bartholomew's Hospital, 251, 339, 388, 390, 792
St. Bartholomew's Schools, Bethnal Green, 670
St. Bride's Avenue, 619
St. Dunstan's School, 730
St. George-in-the-East Rectory, 252
St. George St., Hanover Sq., no. 15, 209, 275; no. 24, 771
St. George's Circus, 249
St. George's Hospital, 547, 866, 896
St. George's Place, no. 12, 284
St. Giles' Burial Ground, mont., 772
St. James's Club, Piccadilly, 51
St. James's Palace, 380, 403, 472, 493, 743, 854, 855, 923, 924, 963
St. James's Park, 212, 581, 686; guard-ho., 276; Ornithological Soc.'s cottage, 869
St. James's Piccadilly; Vestry Hall, 389; Workhouse, 390
St. James's Place, no. 16, 493; no. 23, 517; no. 25, 312; no. 26, 859
St. James's Schools, Bermondsey, 653
St. James's Sq., 695; no. 1, 858; no. 3, 403, 771, 958; no. 4, 177, 732; no. 5, 137, 706, 879; no. 6, 306, 430, 561; no. 7, 425, 430; no. 10, 312, 955; no. 11, 51; no. 12, 244; no. 13, 137; no. 15, 261, 796, 958; no. 17, 609; no. 19, 334, 562, 609; no. 20, 51; no. 21, 139, 394, 771; no. 22, 208, 771; no. 23, 394; no. 32, 225, 228; no. 33, 51, 771; St. Albans Ho., 323
St. James's St., no. 85, 227
St. James's Theatre, 103, 582
St. John's Wood, no., 618
St. Katherine's Docks, 61, 387; Warehouses, 820
St. Katherine's Hospital, 657
St. Luke's Hospital, 249, 251
St. Magnus Martyr Rectory, 743
St. Mark's Coll., Chelsea, 116
St. Mark's Hospital, 863
St. Martin's Almshouses, Camden Town, 727
St. Martin's-in-the-Fields, Vestry Hall, Vicarage & Schools, 582
St. Martin's Lane, no. 76, 609
St. Martin's Music Hall, 880
St. Martin Orgar Rectory, 253
St. Mary-at-Hill Rectory, 721
St. Mary Woolnoth Rectory, 743

1055

LONDON

St. Mary's Hospital, Paddington, 434
St. Pancras Collegiate School, 335
St. Pancras Court Ho., 507
St. Pancras National Schools, 444
St. Pancras Workhouse, 389
St. Paul's Churchyard, no. 16, 321
St. Paul's School, 753
St. Saviour's Warehouse, Southwark, 370
St. Swithin's Lane, offices, 253
St. Thomas's Hospital, 201, 306, 702
Salisbury Ho., 95
Salisbury St., 609
Salters' Hall, 188, 348, 545, 891
Salvation Army Congress Hall, 444
Saunder's Chocolate Ho., 227
Savile Ho., 342, 606
Savile Row, no. 18, 770
Savoir Vivre Club, 242
Schomberg Ho., 72
School for Indigent Blind, Southwark, 590, 807
Seamore Place, no. 2, 619
Serjeants' Inn, 257, 452, 743
Sessions Ho., Old Bailey, 251
Seven Dials, pillar, 636
Shakespeare Gallery, 251
Shepherd's Market, 732
Sherwood Lodge, Battersea, 744
Shot Tower, Lambeth, 218, 705-6
Six Clerks' & Enrolment Offices, 816
Skinner St., 249
Skinners' Hall, 248, 269, 479, 601
Sloane Place, 425
Sloane St., 425
Sloane Terrace, no. 3, 883
Small-pox Hospital, 858
Smithfield Market, 564
Smithfield, proposed obelisk, 778
Smith's Charity estate, 94
Snow Hill, Assembly Room, 592
Soane Museum, *see* Lincoln's Inn Fields, no. 13
Society of Arts, 206
Society of British Artists, Suffolk St., 292
Soho Square, no. 20, 51; hos., 308, 605
Someries Ho., 582
Somerset Ho., 206, 256, 430, 742
Somerset Ho. (Old), 472, 874
South Audley St., no. 6, 771; no. 56, 771; nos. 71-
  75, 732; hos., 325, 609, 866
South Sea Ho., 248, 355, 475
South St., Park Lane, 325, 330
Southampton estate, 96
Southampton Ho., Holborn, 822
Southampton St., hos., 89; shop-front, 534
Southwark
  Bridge, 497, 678; approaches, 372
  Court Ho., Tooley St., 251
  New London Bridge Tavern, 66
  St. George's Rd., ho., 547
  St. John's Girls' School, 66
  St. Olave's Girls' School, 590
  St. Olave's Grammar School, Bermondsey St.,
    306
  St. Olave's Grammar School, Magdalen St., 702
  St. Patrick's Society Schools (now London School
    of Printing), 563
  Surrey County Sessions Ho., etc., 306, 370, 506
  Warehouses, 65, 66
  Wharves, 66
  Workhouse, 66
Southwick St., 955
Spencer Ho., 360, 425, 796, 818, 855
Spitalfields, ho., 592
Spring Gardens, 137, 172, 430, 483, 484, 818, 837,
  938, 958
Stafford Ho. (1725), 784
Stafford Ho., *see* Lancaster Ho.
Stag Brewery, 719

Stanhope Street, no. 13, 714
Stanhope Terrace, 955
Staple Bldngs., 888
State Paper Office, 768
Stationers' Hall, 575, 578
Steel-Yard, 214
Stepney, National Schools, 776
Stock Exchange, 66, 628
Stockwell; Grammar School, 253, 306; ho., 899;
  Trinity Homes, 81
Stoke Newington, villas, 243
Strand: no. 59, 562; no. 101, 619; hos., 430, 472,
  473; shop-front, 534; West Strand
  Improvements, 415, 582; Warehouse, 103
Stratford Place, 286, 685
Stratton St., no. 1, 51, 208, 575; no. 12, 771
Streatham St., Bloomsbury, 697
Suffolk St., nos. 4 & 5, 813; no. 6, 240; nos. 12-17,
  954; hos., 710; British Artists' Gallery, 292,
  582
Sun Fire Office, 224
Surgeons' Hall, Old Bailey, 249
Surrey Chapel Almshouses, Southwark, 706
Surrey County Bridewell, Southwark, 370
Surrey County Gaol, Southwark, 370
Surrey County Sessions Ho., Southwark, 306, 370,
  506
Surrey Institution, 174, 621
Surrey Place, Southwark, 725
Surrey Sq., Southwark, 726
Surrey Theatre, 179, 269
Sussex Sq., 869
Swiss Cottage, Regent St., 701
Synagogues: Cree Church Lane, 651; Great,
  Aldgate, 249, 773, 863; New, Great St.
  Helen's, 253; Spanish & Portuguese, Bevis
  Marks, 331; Western, St. Alban's Place, 44
Tallow-Chandlers' Hall, 180, 201
Tart Hall, 787
Tavistock Place, shop-front, 534
Tavistock Sq., 174, 243, 858
Temple Bar, 539, 922n.
Temple Printing Office, 638
Thanksgiving Bldng., 697
Threadneedle St., no. 62, 771
Thurloe estate, 94
Thurloe Sq., 94
Tom's Coffee-Ho., 249
Tower of London, 77, 185, 360-1, 720; Great
  Storehouse, 308
Trafalgar Sq., 91, 700, 813
Transport Office, Cannon Row, 638
Travellers' Club, 49 Pall Mall, 224, 697-8
Travellers' Club, 105-107 Pall Mall, 91
Treasury, Whitehall, 493, 633
Trevor Place, 649
Trevor Terrace, 649
Trinity Almshouses, Mile End, 600, 959
Trinity Ho., 959
Triumphal arches (1661), 336-7, 552
Turret Ho., S. Lambeth, 618
Twining's Coffee Ho., Strand, 543
Tylers & Bricklayers' Almshouses, Islington, 365
Union Almshouses, Edgware Rd., 377
Union Bank, Fleet St., 61
Union Bank, Pall Mall, 61
Union Brewery, Wapping, 507
Union Club, 171, 742-3
Union St., Southwark, hos., 370
United Service Club, 171, 366, 582, 742
United University Club, 330, 895
University Coll., 225, 268, 329, 746, 896
University Coll. Hospital, 61
University Hall, 268
Upper Brook St., no. 6, 958; no. 11, 394; no. 33,
  818; no. 40, 955; ho., 124
Upper George St., hos., 307

LONDON

Upper Grosvenor St.: no. 1, 225, 771; nos. 10–11, 394; no. 14, 771; no. 28, 330; no. 30, 301; no. 46, 394
Uxbridge Ho., 124, 729, 856
Vauxhall, distillery, 284; gas works, 254; villa, 642
Vauxhall Railway Station, 828
Vauxhall Road, 329
Victoria Sq., 954
Victoria St., 88
Villa Maria, Kensington, 845
Vintners' Hall, 460
Walham Green, School, 150
Walpole Ho., Chelsea, 853
Walton Place, 94
Wandsworth Rd., nos. 238–246, 329
Wapping, warehouses, 64
Warehouses (East India Co.), 426; (Southwark), 66
Warwick Ho., 130–1, 294
Warwick Lane, statue, 259
Waterloo Bridge, 121, 395, 678
Waterloo Place, 174
Watermen's Hall, 114
Wax Chandlers' Hall, 321, 460
Weavers' Hall, 201, 460
Weeks's Museum, 944
Wellington Sq., Chelsea, 284
Wells St., theatre, 186
Welsh Charity School, Clerkenwell, 778
Welsh Charity School, Grays Inn Lane, 519
Wesleyan Centenary Hall, 650
West India Docks, 370
West London Cemetery, 99
Westbourne Ho., Paddington, 227, 866
Westbourne St., 955
Westbourne Terrace, 784, 813
Western Grammar School, 650
Western National School, 743
Westminster
  Abbey, see under Churches
  Bridewell, 44
  Bridge, 300, 405, 457, 498–9; competition for, 150, 185, 453, 494–5, 498, 503, 599, 660, 694, 735, 825
  Bridge Rd., shop-front, 619
  Bridge St., 457
  Dean's Yard, 116, 177
  Flesh Market, 482

Westminster—contd.
  Guildhall, 227
  Hall, 334, 403, 493, 494, 602, 743
  Hospital, 445
  Jewel Tower, 403
  Law Courts, 493, 767
  Little Dean's Yard, 139
  Lying-in Hospital, 262
  New Palace Yard, 562
  Old Palace Yard, nos. 6–7, 867
  Palace, see Parliament, Hos. of
  Palace Hotel, 563
  Parliament Stairs, 503; no. (Delaval), 200
  School, 225, 796; Dormitory, 130, 259, 310, 775
  town-planning projects, 87–8, 270
Westminster Life & British Fire Office, 224
Weymouth St., no. 41, 619
Whitecross St., stables, etc., 251
Whitehall Gardens, no. 4, 745; no. 5, 745; no. 6, 172, 745
Whitehall Palace, 295, 303, 472, 588; designs for rebuilding, 121, 325, 469, 870, 920, 923; Banqueting Ho., q.v.; Catholic Chapel, 923; Cockpit Theatre, 874; Council Chamber, 923; Holbein Gateway, 713; Horse Guards, q.v.; Privy Gallery, 923; Privy Gardens, q.v.; Queen's Apartment, 923; Theatre, 710
Whitehall Place, 517
Whitehall Yard, no. 4, 514
White's Club, 350, 619, 944
Whitmore's Bank, 742
Whittington's Almshouses, 753
Widows' Almshouses, Hackney, 702
William St., 51
Willis's Rooms, 575
Wimpole St., ho., 770
Winchester Ho., 139
Winchester Place, Islington, 441
Woburn Lodge, 445
Woburn Place, 243
Wood St., warehouse, 863
York Hotel, Southwark, 577
York Ho., Pall Mall, 51, 137, 209
York Ho., St. James's, see Lancaster Ho.
York Ho., Strand, 336; Watergate, 336, 619, 787
York Ho., Whitehall, 425, 609, 965
Zoological Soc., 171

London Colney, Herts., Ch., 753
Londonderry, Ireland, bridge, 613
Lonesome Lodge, Surrey, 451
Long Ashton, Som., Ch.; monts., 830
Long Benton, Northumb., Ch., 268
Long Ditton, Surrey, Ch., 816
Long Horsley, Northumb., R.C. Ch., 266
Long Lawford, Warwicks., Ch. 861
Long Stratton, Norfolk, Ch., 145
Long Wittenham, Berks., Vicarage, 648
Longborough, Glos., Ch., 224
Longcot, Berks., Ch., 793
Longdon, Worcs., Ch., 540
Longfleet, Dorset, Ch., 119
Longford Castle, Wilts., 65, 450, 480, 562, 817, 950
Longford Hall, Derbys., 635
Longford Hall, Salop., 125
Longforgan, Perths., Manse, 587
Longham, Dorset, Chapel, 305

Longhills Hall, Lincs., 95
Longhirst Ho., Northumb., 267
Longleat, Wilts., 139, 146, 296, 518, 558, 791, 819, 925, 961
Longner Hall, Salop., 583, 664
Longnor Hall, Salop., 407
Longparish, Wilts., Vicarage, 355
Longships Lighthouse, Cornwall, 959
Longside, Aberdeens., Ch., 761
Longton, Staffs.
  Hall, 331
  St. James's Ch., 969
Longworth Hall, Herefs., 481
Lonmay, Aberdeens., 58
Lopen, Som., Ch., 623
Lothersdale, Yorks., Ch., 210
Lotherton Hall, Yorks., 666, 868
Loton Park, Salop., 406, 476, 576, 664
Loudoun Castle, Ayrshire, 288
Lough Cutra Castle, Ireland, 584; casino, 518
Lough Crew, Ireland, 225

Lough Fea Ho., Ireland, 692
Loughborough, Leics.
  Ch., 777
  Emmanuel Ch., 691
  Rectory, 777
Loughton, Essex, bridge, 464
Lount Lodge, Leics., 622
Louth, Lincs.
  Ch., 197, 234, 297, 724, 899
  Ho. of Correction, 488
  Priory Cottage, 297
  St. Mary's Chapel (R.C.), 899
  Town Hall, 297
  Vicarage, 196
Lovat Bridge, Inverness., 157–8, 821
Low Bourn Bridge, Yorks., 192
Lowbridge Ho., Westmld., 318
Lower Beeding, Sussex, Ch., 847
Lower Brixham, Devon, All Saints Ch., 519
Lower Hardres, Kent, Ch., 691
Lower Heyford, Oxon., Ch., 847
Lower Slaughter Manor Ho., Glos., 791

Lower Swell, Glos., Vicarage, 847
Lowestoft, Suffolk, St. Peter's Ch., 145
Lowick, Northumb., Ch., 562
Lowood, Roxb., 674
Lowther, Westmld.
  Ch., 430
  Hall (Castle), 45, 60, 137, 185, 252, 314, 344, 430, 650, 744, 805–6, 874
  village, 53
Lucan Ho., Ireland, 208
Luddenden, Yorks., St. Mary's Ch., 818
Luddenham, Kent, Ch., 563
Lude, Perths., 165
Ludford, Salop.
  Ch.; mont., 664
  Ho., 663
Ludlow, Salop.
  Broad St., no. 27, 664
  building (projected), 873
  Butter Cross, 83
  Castle, 78, 745
  Gaolford Tower, 663
  Guildhall, 663
  Hosyer's Almshouses, 83, 663
Ludstone Hall, Salop., 740
Lugwardine, Herefs., New Court, 727
Lullingstone Castle, Kent, 393
Lulworth, Dorset
  Castle, 96, 807, 835
  Chapel (R.C.), 807
Lumley Castle, Durham, 853
Lund, Lancs., Chapel, 706
Lund, Yorks., Ch., 210
Lundie, Angus, mausoleum, 577
Lundy Island
  lighthouse, 65
  villa, 592
Lune Aqueduct, Lancs., 678, 781
Lupset Hall, Yorks., 731n.
Lupton Ho., Devon, 890
Lurgan Ho., Ireland, 647
Luscombe Castle, Devon, 583
Lushill Ho., Wilts., 605
Lutterworth, Leics.
  Rectory, 958
  Town Hall, 877n.
Luton, Beds., ho., 721
Luton Hoo, Beds., 53, 745; Chapel, 744
Luxstowe, Cornwall, 890
Lydiard Tregose Ho., Wilts., 562
Lydiate, Lancs., Our Lady's Ch. (R.C.), 724
Lyme Park, Cheshire, 513, 639, 954
Lyme Regis, Dorset, St. Michael's Ch. (R.C.), 352
Lymington, Hants.
  Ch., 547
  cottage orné, 642
  obelisk, 274
  Solent Sea Baths, 93
Lymm, Cheshire
  Ch., 266
  School, 265
Lyndon Hall, Rutland, 797
Lynedoch Lodge, Perths., 644, 647, 810
Lynford Hall, Norfolk, 167, 225
Lynn, see King's Lynn
Lynton, Devon, parsonage, 234
Lypiatt Park, Glos., 961
Lyswayes Hall, Staffs., 842

Lytchett Minster, Dorset, Ch., 843
Lytham, Lancs.
  Ch., 423
  Hall, 193
Lythwood Hall, Salop., 780
Lyveden, Northants., New Bldng., 186, 367, 494, 783

Mabledon Park, Kent, 173, 621
Macbiehall Ho., Perths., 164
Macclesfield, Cheshire
  St. Alban's Ch. (R.C.), 970
  St. Paul's Ch., 408
  St. Peter's Ch., 838, 841
  Sunday School, 365
  Town Hall, 353
Machynlleth, Montgom., Ch., 406
Madeley, Salop., Ch. 820
Madingley Hall, Cambs., 299
Madresfield Court, Worcs., 177
Maeslwch Castle, Radnors., 527
Maiden Bradley, Wilts.
  Ch., mont., 345
  Ho., 440
  New Mead, 872
Maidenhead, Berks.
  Bridge, 508, 816, 832
  St. Mary's Ch., 176
  Town Hall, 484
Maidstone, Kent
  Corn Exchange, 881
  County Gaol, 65, 739, 743, 845
  Court Ho., 422
  Holy Trinity Ch., 881
  Infirmary, 881
  Insurance offices, 881
  Lunatic Asylum, 881
  Markets, 881
  Mitre Inn, 881
  Oakwood Hospital, 881
  Rocky Hill Terrace, 881
  St Peter's Chapel, 881
  Sessions Ho., 743
  Town Hall, 422
  triumphal arch, 102
Makerstoun Ho., Roxb., 59, 531
Mallow Castle, Ireland, 118
Malmesbury, Wilts., Abbey Ch., 253, 352
Malpas, Cheshire, Ch., 280, 506
Malpas Court, Mon., 972
Malton Ho., Ireland, 196
Malton (New), Yorks.
  St. Michael's Ch., 211
  Vicarage, 666
Malvern Hall, Warwicks., 768
Mamble, Worcs., mont., 664
Mamhead Ho., Devon, 53, 464, 971
Man, Isle of, St. John's Ch., 503
Manaton, Devon, Rectory, 411
Manar Ho., Aberdeens., 762
Manchester
  All Souls Ch., Ancoats, 408
  Ardwick Cemetery, mont., 503
  Art Gallery, 91
  Athenaeum, 91
  Bank of England, 224
  Blackfriars Bridge, 934
  Blind Asylum, 502
  Bridgewater Trust's offices, 116
  Collegiate Ch. (Cathedral), 614, 811
  Concert Hall, 502
  Corn Exchange, 502
  Cunliffe & Brookes's Bank, 709
  Exchange, 397

Manchester—contd.
  Friends' Meeting-Ho., 502
  Grosvenor Square Chapel, 696
  Lloyd's Bank, 396
  Manchester & Liverpool Bank, 75
  Manchester & Salford Bank, 811
  Mosley St., ho., 564
  Portico Library, 396
  Post Office, 408
  Royal Infirmary, 502
  Royal Institution of Fine Arts, 91
  St. Andrew's Ch., 73
  St. Anne's Ch., 88
  St. Augustine's Chapel (R.C.), 614
  St. Barnabas' Ch., 811
  St. George's Ch., Hulme, 354
  St. Luke's Ch., Cheetham Hill, 75
  St Mary's Ch., 520
  St. Matthew's Ch., Campfield, 91
  St. Peter's Ch., 354, 945
  St. Thomas's Ch., Ardwick Green, 408
  Theatre Royal, 397
  Town Hall, 353
  Union Club, 502
  Unitarian Chapel, 91
  Victoria Park, 502
  warehouse, 811
  Welsh Baptist Ch., 91
Mangotsfield, Glos., Ch., 315
Manley Hall, Staffs., 842
Manningtree, Essex, Ch., 823
Manningham, Yorks., St. Jude's Ch., 673
Mansfield, Notts., Town Hall, 970
Manton, Lincs., Ch., 321
Marble Hill, Middx., see Twickenham
Marbury, Cheshire
  Ch., 962
  Hall, 342
Marcham, Berks., Ch., 308
Marchington, Staffs., Ch., 842
Marchmont, Berwicks, 164, 346
Marchwiel, Denbighs., Ch., 945
Marden Hill, Herts., 198, 770
Maresfield, Sussex, ho., 387
Maresfield Park, Sussex, 938
Marfleet, Yorks., Ch., 668
Margam Abbey, Glam., 435, 481
Margate, Kent
  Ch., 203
  Cobb's Brewery, 819
  Holy Trinity Ch., 282
  Lighthouse, 282
  Market Place, 882
  Pier Co.'s offices, 282
  Sea-bathing Infirmary, 661
  Town Hall, 882
Marham Ho., Norfolk, 270
Marholm, Lincs., Ch., 932
Marino, Glam., 460
Marino, Ireland
  Casino, 207
  Ho., 207, 566
Maristow, Devon, 147, 321
Market Bosworth, Leics., School, 232
Market Harborough, Leics.
  Independent Chapel, 309
  St. Mary in Arden, 271

Market Lavington, Wilts.,
  Vicarage, 364
Market Weston, Suffolk, Ch., 234
Markfield, Leics., Ch., 497
Markham Clinton, Notts.
  Ch. & mausoleum, 744
  Vicarage, 746
Markinch, Fife, Ch., 87
Markree Castle, Ireland, 354, 372
Markyate Cell, Herts., 527
Markyate Street, Herts, Ch., 366
Marlborough, Wilts.
  Castle, 255
  College, 116, 255
  St. Peter's Rectory, 393
Marle Bridge, Yorks., 192
Marlfield Ho., Roxb., 623
Marlow, Bucks., see Great
  Marlow
Marnhull, Dorset, Kings Mill
  Bridge, 846
Marston Bigot, Som., Ch., 254
Marston (Bigot) Ho., Som., 957,
  962
Marston Moretain, Beds.,
  parsonage, 126
Martlesham, Suffolk, parsonage,
  111
Marwood Park, Durham, 60
Masbrough Hall, Yorks., 641
Matfen Hall, Northumb., 267,
  692
Mathern, Mon., Bishop's Palace,
  915
Mauchline, Ayrshire, Ch., 257
Mauldsley Castle, Lanarks., 55
Mavisbank Ho., Midlothian, 57,
  99, 219–20
Mawley Hall, Salop., 83, 752
Maybole, Ayrshire, West Ch., 486
Mayshade Ho., Midlothian, 99
Meadowbank Ho., Midlothian,
  647
Meanwood, Yorks.
  Hall (Hospital), 216
  Holy Trinity Ch., 670
Medburn Bridge, Herts., 754
Medmenham, Bucks., Ch., 679
Meeth, Devon, Rectory, 157
Megginch Castle, Perths., 533
Meigle, Perths.
  Carverfield, 201
  Ho., 164
Melbourne Hall, Derbys., 228–9,
  347, 749, 764
Melbury Abbas, Dorset, Ch., 302
Melbury Ho., Dorset, 869
Melchbourne Park, Beds., 332
Meldon Park, Northumb., 267
Meldrum Ho., Aberdeens., 737
Melksham, Wilts., Workhouse,
  488
Mellerstain, Berwicks., 53, 57
Melford Hall, Suffolk, 434
Melling, Lancs., Ch., 202
Mellor, Lancs., Ch., 691
Mellor Brook, Lancs., Chapel,
  691
Mells Park, Som., 447, 770, 773
Melsonby, Yorks., farmho., 692
Meltham, Yorks., Ch., 665
Meltham Mills, Yorks., Ch., 665
Melton Mowbray, Leics.
  Bridge, 496
  Railway Station, 622
  St. John's Ch. (R.C.), 899
Melville Castle, Midlothian, 644
Melville Ho., Fife, 282, 758

Menai Bridge, Caern., 399, 821
Menie, Aberdeens., 762
Menmuir, Angus, Ch., 746–7
Mere, Wilts., Ch., 784
Mere Hall, Worcs., 374
Merevale Hall, Warwicks., 118
Mereworth, Kent
  Castle, 184, 562, 859
  Ch., 562
  ho., 77
Meriden, Warwicks.
  Ch., 132
  Forest Hall, 125
  Hall, 750
Merly Ho., Dorset, 583
Mersham Hatch, Kent, 52, 574
Merstham, Surrey, Ch., 79
Merthyr Mawr, Glam., 908
Merton, Oxon., Ch., 391
Merton Grove (Place), Surrey,
  671
Merton Hall, Norfolk, 117
Mertoun Ho., Berwicks., 79, 154,
  165
Messing, Essex, Ch., 869
Messingham, Lincs.
  Ch., 899
  Vicarage, 321
Metheringham, Lincs., Vicarage,
  410
Methley, Yorks.
  Bridge, 354
  Hall, 61, 195, 971
Methven, Perths.
  Castle, 784
  Ch., 533; mausoleum, 643, 644
Mey, Castle of, Caithness, 162
Meynell Langley, Derbys., 354
Michael Church, Isle of Man, 878
Michel Grove, Sussex, 177
Micheldean, Glos., Ch., 897
Micheldever, Hants., Ch., 251
Mickleham, Surrey, Ch., 701, 730
Micklethwaite Grange, Yorks., 948
Mickleton, Glos., mont., 915
Middle Claydon, Bucks., School,
  224
Middleham, Yorks., suspension
  bridge, 877
Middlesbrough, Yorks.
  Ch., 363
  Custom Ho., 157
  Exchange, 157
  Freemasons' Lodge, 265
  ho., 268
Middlesex Lunatic Asylum, see
  Hanwell
Middleton, Yorks., Ch., 211
Middleton in Chirbury, Salop.,
  Ch., 406
Middleton Hall, Carm., 228;
  tower, 228
Middleton Lodge, Yorks., 195
Middleton Park, Oxon., 117, 245,
  549, 854
Middleton Stoney, Oxon.,
  Rectory, 246
Middleton-in-Teesdale, Durham,
  cottages, 122
Midford Castle, Som., 199
Midgham Ho., Berks., 311
Midsomer Norton, Som., Ch.,
  638
Milbourne Hall, Northumb., 624
Milburn, Surrey, 54
Milcote Ho., Warwicks., 787
Mildenhall, Wilts., School, 43
Mill Bank, Lancs., villas, 670

Mill Hill, Middlx.
  Belmont, 612
  Holcombe Ho., 463
  St. Mary's Abbey, 463
  St. Paul's Ch., 606
  School, 829
Millbrook, Cornwall, Ch., 442
Millbrook, Hants., Ch., 274
Millearne, Perths., 260
Millfield Cottage, Surrey, 700
Millichope Park, Salop., 407, 780
Milne Graden, Berwicks., 358
Milnsbridge Ho., Yorks., 610, 699
Milnthorpe, Westmld., Ch., 876
Milton, Hants., Ch., 422
Milton, Kent, Ch., 282
Milton Abbas, Dorset
  Abbey Ch., 945; mont., 55
  Abbey Ho., 208, 855, 946
  Village, 147
Milton Bryant, Beds., Ch., 234
Milton Ernest, Beds., vicarage,
  197
Milton Ford, E. Lothian, bridge,
  158
Milton Hall, Berks., 933
Milton Ho., Northants., 196, 208,
  312, 344, 562, 664n., 728,
  798, 805, 893, 932
Milton Lockhart, Lanarks., 163
Milton Lodge, Cambs., 299
Milverton, Som., School, 202
Minard Castle, Argylls., 359
Minchinhampton, Glos., Ch., 316
Minnigaff, Kirkcud., Ch., 162
Minstead, Hants., Ch., 799
Minsteracres, Northumb., 266;
  Chapel (R.C.), 265
Minsterley, Salop., Ch., 819
Minting, Lincs., Rectory, 145
Minto, Roxb.
  Ch., 646
  Ho., 58, 288, 647
  Manse, 647
Mirfield, Yorks., see Battyford
Misterton, Som., Ch., 487
Misterton Ho., Leics., 488
Mistley, Essex
  Ch., 50
  Hall, 54
Mitcham, Surrey
  Baron Ho., 307
  Ch., 156,753
  London Rd., 307
  Tate's Almshouses, 156
Mitchells, Kent, 173
Mitford Castle, Northumb., 267
Moccas Court, Herefs., 481;
  lodges, 583
Modney Creek, Norfolk, bridge,
  785
Moel Fammau, Denbighs.,
  obelisk, 397
Moffat Ho., Dumfriess., 46
Moggerhanger Ho., Beds., 770
Mold, Flints.
  Ch., 844
  County Hall, 476
Molesey Hurst, Surrey, ho., 644
Monaghan, Ireland, gaol, 292
Moncreiffe, Perths.
  Ho., 154, 784
  Inn, 784
Moneymore, Ireland, Ch., 126
Monimail, Fife, Ch., 87, 357
Monk Bretton, Yorks.. Ch., 112
Monkrigg, E. Lothian, 164
Monks Hall, Lincs., 717

Monkton Ho., Ayrshire, 587
Monkwearmouth, Durham
  All Saints Ch., 266
  Scotch Ch., 265
Monmouth
  County Gaol, 114
  Independent Chapel, 70
  New Market, 534
  St Mary's Ch., 753, 897
  Shire Hall, 307, 406
Monney Hill Ho., Herts., 617
Monnington-on-Wye, Herefs.,
    Ch., 467
Montacute Ho., Som., 70
Montblairy, Banffs., 762
Montfort, Salop.
  Bridge, 187, 821
  Ch., 233
Montgomerie Ho., Ayrshire, 624
Montgomery
  Castle, 722
  Market Hall, 83
Montreal, Kent, 77, 246
Montrose, Angus
  Academy, 523
  Bank of Scotland, 161
  Ch., 357, 523
  Dorward Ho., 140
  High St., ho., 89
  Museum, 969
  Royal Infirmary, 230
  St. John's Free Ch., 764
  Town Hall, 442, 764
Monymusk, Aberdeens.
  Ho., 451
  School, 761
Monzie, Perths.
  Ch., 783
  Ho., 624, 784
Mongewell, Oxon., Ch., 945
Monifieth, Angus
  Ch., 106
  Linlathen School, 542
  Manse, 532
  School, 532
  South Grange Ho., 113
Monikie, Angus, Ch., 587
Moor Park, Herts., 52, 136, 166,
    246, 314, 343, 545, 825
Moor Park, Surrey, 612
Moore Park, Lanarks., 382
Moore Place, Herts., 554
Moorgate, Notts., Ch., 899
Moorgate Hall, Yorks., 641
Moorlands Hospital, Staffs., 98
Morden, Surrey
  ho., 367
  stabling, 619
Moreby Hall, Yorks., 971
Moresby Hall, Cumb., 60
Morestead, Hants., Rectory, 810
Moreton, Cheshire, Ch., 247
Moreton, Dorset, obelisk, 383
Moreton, Essex, bridge, 464
Moreton, Staffs., Ch., 842
Moreton Corbet, Salop.
  Castle, 407
  Ch.; mont., 664
Moreton Hall, Cheshire, 118
Moreton Hall, Lancs., 876
Moreton Hall, Suffolk, 53
Morkeu, Kinc., 737
Morley, Yorks., Ch., 210
Morpeth, Northumb.
  Bridge, 265, 821
  Gaol & Sessions Ho., 265
  Town Hall, 853
Mortlake, Surrey, Ch., 101

Morton, Dumfriess., Ch., 162
Morton, nr. Gainsborough, 880
Morton on Swale, Yorks., bridge,
    192
Mortonhall Ho., Midlothian, 100
Morvah, Cornwall, parsonage, 890
Morville Hall, Salop., 83
Moseley, Worcs.
  Ch., 690
  Hall, 672
Mostyn Hall, Flints., 657
Mostyn Quay, Flints., Christ Ch.,
    657
Mote (The), Kent, 65; temple,
    588
Moulsham Hall, Essex, 355, 513
Moulton Chapel, Lincs., 717
Moulton St. Michael, Norfolk,
    Rectory, 271
Mount Clare, Surrey, 231
Mount Edgcumbe Ho., Cornwall,
    59, 890
Mount Felix, Surrey, 92
Mount Kennedy, Ireland, 948
Mount Mascall, Kent, 308
Mount Melville, Fife, 358
Mount Pavilion, Staffs., 211
Mount Pleasant, Yorks., 641
Mount Shannon, Ireland, 954
Mount Stewart, Ireland, 797, 948
Mount Stuart, Bute, 58, 162, 238,
    531
Mounteviot, Roxb., 117
Mountjoy Forest, Ireland, 541
Mountjoy Prison, Ireland, 603
Mountquhanie Ho., Fife, 238
Mountsorrel, Leics., Market Ho.,
    823
Mousehold Ho., nr. Norwich, 546
Moy Ho., Morays., 46, 898
Much Birch, Herefs., Ch., 315
Much Hadham, Herts., hos., 557
Muckhart, Perths., Manse, 784
Muckross Abbey, Ireland, 165,
    859
Muirkirk, Ayrshire, Ch., 777
Mulgrave Castle, Yorks., 76, 768
Mumbles Lighthouse, Glam., 460
Murdostoun Castle, Lanarks., 58
Murie, Perths., 645
Murthly, Perths.
  Ho., 359
  St. Anthony's Chapel, 357
Murtle Ho., Aberdeens., 737
Musselburgh Bridge, Midlothian,
    678
Muswell Hill, Middlx.
  St. James's Ch., 67
  St. James's parsonage, 670
Muthill, Perths.
  Ch., 357
  Ch. (Episcopal), 260
Myddle, Salop., Ch., 233
Mynde Park, Herefs., 881

Naburn, Yorks., Lock or
    Banqueting Ho., 73
Nackington Ho., Kent, 769
Nailsworth, Glos., Chapel, 278
Nairn, bridge, 157
Nairne, House of, Perths., 154,
    530
Nannau, Merioneths., 142
Nanswhyden, Cornwall, 284
Nanteos, Card., 407
Nantwich, Cheshire, Ch., 966
Narford Hall, Norfolk, 319
Natland, Westmld., Ch., 876

Naworth Castle, Cumb., 810
Nayland, Suffolk
  bridge, 767
  Ch., 418
Nazeing Park, Essex, 518
Neasham Hall, Durham, 267
Nelmes, Essex, 483
Nenthead, Cumb., Ch., 123
Nercwys Hall, Flints., see Nerquis
Nerquis Hall, Flints., 369, 467
Nether Corsock Ho., Kirkcud.,
    588
Nether Hoyland, Yorks., Ch.,
    665, 869
Nether Poppleton, Yorks., railway
    bridge, 363
Nether Witton Hall, Northumb.,
    837
Netheravon Ho., Wilts., 769
Netherby Hall, Cumb., 164
Netherthong, Yorks., Ch., 210
Netherton, Worcs., Ch., 510
Netherurd, Peebles., 158, 533
Netley Fort, Hants., 274
Netley Hall., Salop., 407
Netley Place, Surrey, 244
Nevill Holt, Leics., 618
New Ballaugh, Isle of Man, Ch.,
    878
New Brampton, Derbys., St.
    Thomas's Ch., 441
New Bridge, Denbighs., 631
New Brighton, Cheshire, see
    Wallasey
New Deer, Aberdeens.
  Ch., 761
  School, 761
New Geneva, Ireland, 327
New Hall, Essex, 336, 473, 724
New Hall, Nunton, Wilts., 949
New Hutton, Westmld., Ch., 876
New Mill, Yorks., Ch., 73
New Mills, Derbys., Ch., 210
New Park, Wilts., 262, 307, 947
New River, Herts., 573, 578
New Shoreham, Sussex, Ch., 107
Newark, Notts.
  Assembly Rooms, 191
  Bridge, 933
  Christ Ch., 613
  Library, 321
  School, 321
  Town Hall, 191
Newark Park, Glos., 951
Newbattle, Midlothian
  Abbey, 570, 571
  Ch., 531
Newberries Park, Herts., 95
Newbold Comyn Ho., Warwicks.,
    709, 901
Newbold Revel Hall., Warwicks.,
    752
Newbold-on-Stour, Warwicks.,
    Ch., 861
Newborough, Staffs., Chapel, 839
Newbrough Hall, Northumb., 267
Newburgh, Fife
  Ch., 162
  Town Hall, 772
Newburgh Priory, Yorks., 860
Newburn, Northumb., Ch., 363
Newbury, Berks.
  Bridge, 217
  Chapel, 863
  Ch., gateways, 882
  Dower Ho., 217
  King's Arms, 217
  Town Hall, 217

Newby Hall, Yorks. (W.R.), 53, 107, 300, 365
Newby Park, Yorks. (N.R.), 107, 184, 207, 301, 703–4
Newby Wiske, Yorks., 682; Hall, 940
Newbyth, E. Lothian, 158, 288
Newcastle, Salop., Ch., 406
Newcastle-upon-Tyne, Northumb.
  All Saints Ch., 268, 477, 779, 785
  Amphitheatre (Circus), 779
  Assembly Rooms, 590
  Bank of England, 590
  Black Dene Ho., 267
  Blackett St., 602
  Castle, 264, 462
  Cemetery, 264; mont., 362
  Charlotte Sq., 590
  Clayton Memorial Ch., 266
  Clayton St., 359
  College of Medicine, 264
  Corn Exchange, 362
  Custom Ho., 264, 972
  Dene Ho., 268
  Eldon Sq., 264
  Ellison Place, 268
  Exchange, see Guildhall
  Exchange (Central), 360, 864
  Gaol, 264
  Grainger St., 359, 864
  Grammar School, 590
  Gresham Place, 268
  Grey Column, 362
  Grey St., 264, 359, 864
  Guildhall (Exchange), 264, 590, 779, 837
  Ho. of Correction, 264
  Independent Chapel, 602
  Infirmary, 264
  Jesmond Dene Ho., 267, 268
  Jesmond Grove, 267
  Jesmond Towers, 267
  Jesmond Villa, 267
  Lambton's Bank, 360
  Leazes Crescent, 602
  Leazes Terrace, 602
  Lunatic Asylum, 264, 590
  Lying-in hospital, 264
  Market St., 359, 864
  Markets (New), 264, 360
  Moot Hall, 785
  Museum, Westgate St., 362
  Nelson St., 359
  New Bridge St., 268
  New White Cross, 779
  Northern Academy of Arts, 264
  Northern Counties' Club, 264
  Nun St., 359
  Pandon Dean Bridge, 785
  Picton Place, 268
  Plummer's Flax Mill, 264
  Police Offices, 264
  Public Baths, 239, 264
  Ragged School, 264
  Railway Station (Central), 264
  Railway Station (The Manors), 264
  Riding School, 264
  Royal Arcade, 264, 360
  Royal Jubilee School, 264
  St. Andrew's Ch., 266, 590
  St. Ann's Chapel, 264
  St. James's Presbyterian Chapel, 265
  St. John's Ch., 265
  St. Mary's Place, 264

Newcastle-upon-Tyne—contd.
  St. Nicholas Ch. (Cathedral), 265, 363, 590, 916; library, 333; mont., 226
  St. Nicholas Charity School, 264
  St Paul's Ch., High Elswick, 266
  St. Peter's Ch., 266
  St. Thomas's Ch., 265
  Salem Methodist Chapel, 360
  Sandyford Park, 267
  Scale Cross, 779
  Scotch Ch., 363
  Shakespeare St., 864
  Strawberry Place, 268
  Sunderland and Durham Union Joint Stock Bank, 264
  Surgeons' Hall, 264
  Theatre (Old), 264
  Theatre Royal, Grey St., 360, 362
  Theatre Royal, Mosley St., 779
  toll-houses, 264
  Trinity Presbyterian Ch., 266
  Tyne bridge, 573, 574, 779, 916
  Unitarian Ch., 266
  Victoria Bazaar, 602
  Villa Reale, 267
  Warehouses, 264
  Wesleyan Chapel, 265
  West Jesmond Ho., 267
Newcastle-under-Lyme, Staffs. Ch., 752
  St. George's Ch., 104
Newcastleton, Roxb., Ch., 724
Newchurch-in-Rossendale, Lancs., Ch., 423
Newent, Glos., Ch., 418, 467, 811–12
Newhailes, Midlothian, 239, 757
Newhall, Midlothian, 219, 571
Newhall Ho., E. Lothian, 59
Newhills, Aberdeens., Ch., 761
Newington Hall, Oxon., 912
Newlaithes Hall, Yorks., 527
Newliston Ho., W. Lothian, 54–5, 56, 57
Newmarket, Suffolk
  Jockey Club, 463, 674
  New Rooms, 463
  Palace (King's Ho.), 314, 472, 495, 712; Prince's Lodging, 472
  Stables, 463
Newnham, Herts., Vicarage, 763
Newnham Paddox, Warwicks., 146
Newport, I. of W., Isle of Wight Institution, 581
Newport, Mon.
  Bridge, 286
  St. Mary's Ch. (R.C.), 724
  St. Paul's Ch., 972
Newport, Salop.
  Ch., 970
  Ch. (R.C.), 655
  Market Ho., 606
Newport Pagnell, Bucks., Ch., 721
Newsham, Yorks., bridge, 734
Newstead Abbey, Notts., 729
Newton Don, Roxb., 745
Newton Hall, Northumb., 268
Newton Heath, Lancs., All Saints Ch., 77
Newton Ho., Yorks., 859

Newton Moor, Cheshire, St. Mary's Ch., 408
Newton Park, Som., 509
Newton Stewart, Wigtowns., bridge, 678
Newton Valence, Hants., Ch., 278
Newton-le-Willows, Lancs., Ch., 423
Newtown, Montgom., Ch., 631
Newtownards, Ireland, Market Ho., 788
Niddrie Ho., Midlothian, 58, 162
Nigg, Kinc., Ch., 761
Ninewells Ho., Berwicks., 165
Noak Hill, Essex, St. Thomas's Ch., 754
Nocton Park, Lincs., 731
Nonsuch Park, Surrey, 961
Norbiton, Surrey
  Place, 506
  St. Peter's Parsonage, 696
  School, 696
Norbury, Cheshire, St. John's Ch., 408
Norbury Park, Surrey, 700
Norfolk Lunatic Asylum, 145, 149
Nork Ho., Surrey, 200, 638, 859
Norley, Cheshire
  Ch., 782
  Hall, 218
Norman Court, Hants., 117, 393, 681n.
Normanby Park, Lincs., 321, 745
Normanton, Rutland
  Ch., 227, 236, 246
  farmho., 245
  Park, 236, 477
Norris Castle, I. of W., 950
North Aston Hall, Oxon., 965
North Ballachulish, Inverness., Ch., 821
North Berwick, E. Lothian, villa, 896
North Court, Berks., 174
North Eling, Hants., Ch., 107
North Esk Bridge, Angus, 89
North Leigh, Oxon., Ch., 486
North Mimms, Herts.
  Ch., 71
  Ho. (Park), 71–2, 118, 770
North Runcton, Norfolk, Ch., 105
North Shields, Northumb.
  Baptist Chapel, 266
  Ch. (R.C.), 346
  Holy Trinity Ch., 363
  Market Place, 779
  Preston Villa, 267
  Quay, 779
  St. Columba's Ch., 266
  Scotch Ch., 265
  Town Hall, 265
  Waterville Ho., 266
  Wesleyan Chapel, 266
  West Churton Ho., 267
North Stoke, Lincs., parsonage, 505
North Stoneham Park, Hants., 434
North Sunderland, Northumb., Ch., 971
North Weald Basset, Essex, Vicarage, 225
Northallerton, Yorks.
  Ch., 107
  Court Ho., 191
  High St., no. 84, 192
  Vicarage, 971
Northam, Hants., bridge, 814

Northampton
All Saints Ch., 105, 284, 497, 773
Baths, 897
Congregational Ch., 253
County Gaol, 139
George Hotel, 496
Infirmary, 496, 721
Market Place, ho., 105
Methodist Chapel, Gold St., 458
St. Katharine's Ch., 897
Sessions Ho., 105, 214, 284
Northaw, Herts., Ch., 308
Northerwood, Hants., 244, 585
Northesk, Midlothian, Ch., 162
Northleach, Glos., Ho. of Correction, 114
Northover, Som., Ch., 101
Northwick Park, Worcs. (Glos.), 131, 439, 916
Northwood, Staffs., Holy Trinity Ch., 838, 840
Northwood Ho., I. of W., 585, 970
Norton, Durham, Ch., 143
Norton, Herts, Ch., 869
Norton, Yorks., Ch., 665, 868
Norton Bavant, Wilts., Ch., 861
Norton Canes, Staffs., Ch., 969
Norton Manor, Som., 696
Norton Place, Lincs., 195, 858
Norton Priory, Cheshire, 947
Norton in Hales, Salop., mont., 84, 472
Norton-in-the Moors, Staffs., Ch., 842
Norwich
Arch, triumphal, 150
Artillery barracks, 448
Assembly Rooms, 170, 448
Baptist Meeting Ho., 785
Bishopsgate, ho., 448
Blackfriars Bridge, 767
Bridewell, 273
Carrow Bridge, 150
Carrow Hill, 150
Castle, 137, 767, 785, 893, 971
Castle Meadow, hos., 145
Cathedral, 119, 145 (bis), 150, 411, 639, 681, 682, 785, 893
Chapel (R.C.), 608
Chapelfield, 101
Christ Ch., New Catton, 145
Ch. (R.C.), Willow Lane, 625
Close (The), nos. 10–12, 671
Corn Exchange, 546
Court Ho., 89
Diocesan School, 145
Dove Lane, shop, 137
Exhibition Room, 546
Friends' Meeting Ho., 625
Fye Bridge, 785
Gaol (City), 89, 147
Gaol (County), 767
Great Hospital, ho., 448
King St., no. 31, 448
Lunatic Asylum, 785
Methodist Meeting-ho., 448
Museum (Broad St.), 145
Museum (Exchange St.), 145
New Norfolk Gaol, 896
Norfolk & Norwich Hospital, 448
Norwich Yarn Co.'s Factory, 145

Norwich—contd.
Octagon Chapel, 138, 448, 559, 672
Post Office St., ho., 145
Royal Bazaar, 824
Royal Hotel, 774
St. Andrew's Broad St., ho., 145
St. Andrew's Hall, 672
St. Andrew's Hospital, 785
St Andrew's Place, ho., 150
St. Clement's Ch., 145
St. Giles, no. 94, 672; ho., 137
St. Helen's Ch., 448
St. Helen's Place, 448
St. Mark's Ch., 145
St. Mark's School, 145
St. Matthew's Ch., 145
St. Peter Mancroft Ch., mont., 150
St. Peter's Methodist Chapel, 625
St. Stephen's Ch., mont., 150
Schools, 625
Shirehouse, 137, 138, 895
Subscription Library, 625
Surrey Court, ho., 137
Surrey St., hos., 137, 448, 575, 772
Theatre, 448, 893, 896
Walls, 114
Waterworks, 573
Norwood, Middlx.
Ch., 704
hos., 260, 770
Norwood, South, see South Norwood
Norwood, Upper, see Upper Norwood
Nostell Priory, Yorks., 52, 565, 607, 609, 666, 869; bridge, 354
Nottingham
Assembly Rooms, 191
Baptist Chapel, 777
Barracks, 789
Blackamoor's Head Inn, 933
Castle, 538, 853, 900
Cotton Mill, Huckley, 789
County Hall, 327, 631, 635, 697, 738, 774 (bis)
Exchange (New), 631, 777, 789
Greyhound Yard, 697
Hospital, 738
hos., 789
Independent Chapel, 626
industrial bldngs., 789
Judges' Lodgings, 908
Leen Bridge, 738
Lunatic Asylum, 444
Market Cross, 631
Navigation Inn, 789
New Inn, 789
Park (The), villa, 701
Plumptre Hospital, 777
Race-stand, 191
Rick's Garden, 789
St. James's Ch., 789
St. John's Ch., 899
St. Mary's Ch., 421, 635
St. Paul's Ch., 895
St. Peter's Ch., 789
School, 466
Stoney St., ho., 185
'Ten-Arch Bridge', 789
Town Hall, 789
Workhouse, 631
Nottington Spa, Dorset, 856

Nunburnholme, Yorks., Rectory, 666
Nuneaton, Warwicks., bridge, 592
Nuneham Courtenay, Oxon., Rectory, 302
Nuneham Park, Oxon., 147, 418, 425, 508, 745, 796
Nunnery (The), Isle of Man, 638
Nunnington, Yorks., mont., 345
Nunnykirk, Northumb., 267
Nunwick, Northumb., 122, 333
Nuthall Temple, Notts., 934, 947
Nuthurst, Warwicks., Ch., 390
Nutley, Hants., Ch., 200
Nutwell Court, Devon, 228
Nynehead Court, Som., 510

Oa, Argylls., Ch., 820
Oakamoor, Staffs., Ch., 665
Oakeley Ho., Salop., 408
Oakham, Rutland, Vicarage, 393
Oakland Ho., Cheshire, see Tabley Hall
Oaklands, Devon, 80, 856
Oaklands, Sussex, 173
Oaklands Park, Hants., 167
Oakley, Hants., Ch., 200
Oakley Ho., Beds., 425
Oakley Park, Salop., 142
Oakley Park, Suffolk, 972
Oakly Park, Salop., 83, 225, 407
Oakridge, Glos., Ch., 784
Oak(e)s (The), Derbys., 80, 441, 522
Oaks (The), Surrey, 53–4
Oakwood Ho., Sussex, 292
Oatlands, Surrey
Ho., 132, 200, 426, 493, 882, 933
ho. (Mathews), 656
Palace, 472, 495
Ochtertyre, Perths.
gates, 810
mausoleum, 810
Ockbrook, Derbys., Ch., 540
Ockham Park, Surrey, 404, 405, 825
Oddington, Glos., ho., 605
Oddington, Oxon., Rectory, 626
Offchurch, Warwicks., Vicarage, 211
Offley, Herts.
Ch., 744
Place, 744
Ogston Hall, Derbys., 522, 635, 774
Ogwen Park, Caern., 936
Okeford, Devon, Ch., 651
Okeover Hall, Staffs., 565, 717
Old Dalby, Leics, see Dalby (Old)
Old Swinford, Worcs., Ch., 213, 280
Old Windsor, Berks.
Holly Grove, 714
ho. (Bateman), 109, 566
Vicarage, 547
Oldaport Farm., Devon, 147
Oldcastle, Ireland, School, 224
Oldham, Lancs.,
Blue-Coat School, 502
St. James's Ch., 354
St. Mary's Ch., 502
Town Hall, 176
Oldland, Glos., Ch., 315
Ombersley, Worcs.
Ch., 110, 691
Court, 110, 874

Onchan, Isle of Man, Ch., 878
Onslow Hall, Salop., 406, 576
Openshaw, Lancs., St. Barnabas
    Ch., 75
Orchard Portman, Som., 819
Ordsall, Notts., Rectory, 444
Ore, Sussex
    Ch., 126
    Place, 862
Organ Hall, Herts., 682
Orleton Hall, Salop., 407
Ormerod Ho., Lancs., 876
Ormesby Hall, Yorks., 195
Ormesby Ho., Norfolk, 823
Ormsby Hall, Lincs., 72
Ormiston Hall, E. Lothian, 99
Ornhams Hall, Yorks., 618
Orpington, Kent., mont., 566
Orsett, Essex, Rectory, 763
Orton Ho., Hunts., 755
Orton Ho., Morays., 699
Orwell Park, Suffolk, 166
Osberton, Notts.
    Ch., 657
    Ho., 896
Osborne Ho., I. of W., 244, 653
Oscott College, Warwicks., 655
Osmaston Hall, Derbys., 952
Ospringe Place, Kent, 102
Ossett, Yorks., Ch., 819
Ossington, Notts.
    Ch., 191
    Hall, 521
Osterley Park, Middlx., 52, 534;
    villas, 613
Oswestry, Salop., Holy Trinity
    Ch., 631
Otford Court, Kent, 117
Otmoor, Oxon., 262
Otterbourne, Hants., Ch., 200
Otterburn, Northumb., Ch., 266
Otterden Place, Kent, 637
Ottershaw Park, Surrey, 167, 817,
    950
Ottery St. Mary, Devon, Ch.,
    119
Oughtrington Hall, Cheshire,
    397
Oulton, Suffolk, Workhouse, 145
Oulton, Yorks., Ch., 691
Oulton Hall (Park), Cheshire, 844,
    874, 954
Oulton Hall, Yorks., 215, 745
Oundle, Northants.
    Brewery, 254
    Vicarage, 271
Ousden Hall, Suffolk, 693
Ouseburn railway bridge,
    Northumb., 362
Ouslethwaite Hall, Yorks., 868
Out Rawcliffe, Lancs., Ch., 258
Over Bridge, Glos., 467, 821
Over Peover, Cheshire, Ch., 844
Over Stowey, Som., Ch., 202
Over Tabley, Cheshire, 72
Over Whitacre, Warwicks., Ch.,
    421
Oving, Sussex
    Almshouses, 289
    Cottages, 289
    School, 289
Owston Hall, Yorks., 522, 653
Oxenfoord Castle, Midlothian, 54,
    165
Oxenhope, Yorks., Ch., 123
Oxford
    Adullam Chapel, 308
    All Saints Ch., 63, 405, 834

Oxford—contd.
    All Souls Coll., 64, 216, 403,
        405, 453, 698, 801, 834,
        890; Buttery, 403; Chapel,
        216, 825, 923; Codrington
        Library, 403, 630, 834;
        Hall, 403; Old Library,
        550; Warden's Ho., 216,
        698
    Ashmolean Museum, 224, 369;
        competition for, 557, 648,
        709, 738, 819, 880
    Ashmolean Museum (Old),
        912
    Balliol Coll., 94, 484, 834, 944
    Baptist Chapel, 438
    Baths, 363
    Beaumont St., 262
    Bodleian Library, 62, 85, 449,
        719, 923, 944
    Botanical Garden, 786, 834,
        847, 952
    Botley Rd., bridges, 816
    Brasenose Coll., 405, 449, 767,
        943
    Carfax Conduit, 215
    Cathedral, 601; monts., 217n,
        835
    Cemetery Chapels, 847
    Christ Church; Anatomy
        School, 484; Canterbury
        Quad., 943; Library, 216,
        633, 834; Peckwater Quad.,
        63, 64, 834; Tom Tower,
        449, 486, 923
    Clarendon Building, 216, 403,
        453, 477, 743, 834
    Clarendon Press, 116, 698
    Convocation Ho., 832
    Corpus Christi Coll., 64, 629,
        831, 834, 912
    Divinity School, 178, 923
    Exeter Coll., 241–2, 581, 679,
        832, 834, 847
    Floating Chapel, 648
    Folly Bridge, 632
    Gaol (City), 114
    Gaol (County), 114, 391, 847
    Hertford Coll., 331
    Independent Chapel, 363
    Jesus Coll., 156, 581
    Magdalen Bridge, 373, 410
    Magdalen Coll., 156, 301, 405,
        621, 629, 833; Chapel, 234,
        484, 944, mont., 156;
        Choristers' Hall, 156; New
        Buildings, 216, 397, 835
    Magdalen Hall, 331
    Markets, 373
    Merton Coll., 61, 116, 119, 302,
        391, 629, 923, 944
    Methodist Chapel, 458
    Music School, 943
    New Coll., 629, 834, 943; arch,
        177; Chapel, 943, mont.,
        832; Garden Quad., 178,
        834, 921
    Oriel Coll., 376–7, 698, 834,
        944
    Oseney lock, 391
    Pembroke Coll., 301, 835
    Queen's Coll., 216, 237, 404,
        405, 832, 833, 834, 923;
        Library, 64, 224
    Radcliffe Infirmary, 509, 717
    Radcliffe Library (Camera),
        339, 405, 461, 633, 763,
        831, 835, 837

Oxford—contd.
    Radcliffe Observatory, 262, 438,
        484, 629, 943
    St. Aldate's Ch., 302
    St. Clement's Ch., 698
    St. Ebbe's Ch., 308
    St. Edmund Hall, 177, 629
    St. Giles', no. 62, 629
    St. Giles' Ch., 847; mont., 835
    St. Giles' Ho., 630
    St. Giles' School, 363
    St. John's Ch., Summertown,
        847
    St. John's Coll., 340, 389,
        449, 835; Canterbury
        Quad., 149–50, 789;
        Chapel, 120, 149, 629, 923;
        mont., 832; Holmes
        Bldng., 629; President's
        Lodging, 629; Senior
        Common Room, 629, 698
    St. John's St., 262
    St. Martin's Ch., 648
    St. Mary's Chapel, 912
    St. Mary's Ch., 63, 120, 449,
        648, 787, 832, 912; monts.,
        217n., 832, 835
    St. Mary Magdalen's Ch.,
        119
    St. Michael's Ch., 648
    St. Paul's Ch., 847
    St. Peter-le-Bailey Ch., 835
    St. Peter's-in-the-East Ch., 648
    St. Peter's Hall, 363
    Schools Quadrangle, 62, 215,
        743
    Sheldonian Theatre, 116, 178,
        484, 719, 922
    Shire Hall, 648
    Stone's Almshouses, 630
    Taylorian Institution, 224, 815
    Town Hall, 831–2, 866
    Trinity Coll.; Chapel, 63–4,
        629, 923; Durham Quad.,
        835; Garden Quad., 791,
        835, 923
    University Coll., 92, 149, 216,
        366, 449, 483, 588;
        Radcliffe Quad., 216, 630
    Wadham Coll., 70–1, 116, 119,
        391, 630, 698; Chapel,
        mont., 120
    Warneford Asylum, 444
    Wesleyan Methodist Chapel,
        302
    Wolsey's Almshouses, 847
    Worcester Coll., 216–17, 403,
        484, 629, 835, 943
    Workhouse, 373
Oxney Park, Kent, 527
Oystermouth, Glam., villa, 701

Packington Hall, Warwicks., 124,
    137, 138, 235, 376, 421
Paddock, Yorks., All Saints Ch.,
    600
Padworth Ho., Berks., 423
Page Hall, Yorks., 641
Pagham, Sussex, repairs, 289
Painshill, Surrey, 173, 478
Painswick, Glos.
    Castle Hale, 82
    Churchyard, 155
    Ho., 95, 923
Paisley, Renfrews.
    Coffee Ho., 594
    County Bldngs., 288, 676
    High Ch., 882

Paisley, Renfrews.—contd.
  Hospital, 882
  inn, 780
  Low Ch., 81
  St. George's Ch., 676
  Tolbooth, 882
Palmer's Farm, I. of W., 859
Pangbourne, Berks., mont., 444
Panmure, Angus
  Ho., 154, 570
  tower, 969
Panshanger, Herts., 76, 682, 958
Panton Hall, Lincs., 195, 403,
  511
Paper Mill Bridge, Yorks., St.
  John's Ch., 673n.
Papillon Hall, Leics., 615
Papworth Hall (Hospital),
  Cambs., 177
Parham Ho., Sussex, 683, 971
Parham New Hall, Suffolk, 881
Park End, Glos., Ch., 650
Park Hatch, Surrey, 173
Park Ho., Aberdeens., 737
Park Place, Berks., 426, 550, 639
Park Wood Ho., Devon, 319
Parkhill Ho., Stirlings., 164
Parkhurst, Kent, 730
Parkstone, Dorset, Ch., 843
Parlington Hall (Ho.), Yorks.,
  638, 666n., 868;
  Triumphal Arch, 517
Parnham Hall, Dorset, 584
Partick, Lanarks., Yorkshire Ho!,
  594
Passingford, Essex, bridge, 464
Pathhead Bridge, Midlothian, 821
Patney, Wilts., Rectory, 278
Pateley Bridge, Yorks., Ch., 441
Patshull, Staffs.
  Ch., 340
  Hall (Ho.), 84, 167, 343, 749,
    937, 953
Pattingham, Staffs., ho., 84
Paul, Cornwall, ho., 252
Paulton, Som., Ch., 638
Paultons, Hants., 489, 810
Pavilion, Roxb., 759
Paxton Ho., Berwicks., 676, 701
Peamore Ho., Devon, 679
Peasenhall, Suffolk, Ch., 211
Peasmarsh, Sussex, Rectory (Ho.),
  271
Pebworth, Glos., mont., 915
Peckforton Castle, Cheshire, 507
Peckham, Surrey
  Coburg Rd., villa, 650
  Hanover Ho., 854
Peebles
  Ch., 144
  St. Peter's Episcopal Ch., 162
  Tweed Bridge, 760
Pelham Place, Hants., 278
Pellwall Ho., Staffs., 187–8, 770
Pelsall, Staffs., Ch., 383
Pelton, Durham, Ch., 449
Pemberton, Lancs., St. John's
  Ch., 691
Pembroke Dockyard, 722
Pendarves, Cornwall, 393, 890
Pendleford Hall, Staffs., 664
Pendleton, Lancs.
  Independent Chapel, 502
  St. Thomas's Ch., 354, 502
Penge, Kent
  King William Naval Asylum,
    387–8
  Watermen's Almshouses, 653

Penicuik, Midlothian
  Ho., 99, 100, 220; stables, 220;
    tower, 220
  Kirk, 220
  Valleyfield Mills, mont., 386
Penistone, Yorks., Cloth Hall, 642
Penkridge, Staffs.
  Ch., 655
  School, 655
Penn, Bucks., School, 116
Penn Hall, Staffs., 83
Penninghame, Wigtowns., Ch.,
  162
Pennington, Hants., Ch., 843
Pennsylvania Castle, Dorset, 950
Penquite, Cornwall, 890
Penrhos Hall, Anglesey, 257
Penrhyn, Caern.
  Baths, 936
  Castle, 435, 957
  Port, 936
  Quarries, 936
Penrice Castle, Glam., 481
Penrith, Cumb., Ch., 301, 395
Pensax, Worcs., Ch., 476
Penshaw Hill, Durham, mont.,
  363
Penshurst, Kent
  Ch., 674
  Grove (The), 173
  Harden Cottage, 66
  ho., 618
  Place, 674
Pentillie Castle, Cornwall, 896
Penton Mewsey, Hants., Rectory,
  862
Pentre, Flints., bridge, 844
Pentre, Pembs., 225
Pentwyn Ho., Mon., 534
Penwortham Priory, Lancs., 876
Pen-y-Bont, Radnors., bridge, 907
Penzance, Cornwall
  Baptist Chapel, 711
  Guildhall & Market Ho., 885–6
  St. Mary's Ch., 442
  Town Hall, 218
Peper Harow, Surrey, 207, 226,
  388, 950
Peplow, Salop., farmho., 84
Pepper Arden, Yorks., 166
Perdiswell Park, Worcs., 177
Perridge Ho., Devon, 177
Perry Barr, Staffs., St. John's Ch.,
  797
Perth
  Academy, 675
  Art Gallery, 557
  Bridge, 567, 568
  City Hall, 533
  Council Chamber, 65
  County Bldngs., 676, 743
  County Library, 675
  Exchange Coffee Rooms, 533
  Infirmary, 533
  Marshall Place, 676
  Monument (The), 557
  Murray's Royal Asylum, 161
  Prison, 675
  Railway Station, 829
  St. John's Ch., 357
  St. Leonard's Ch., 533
  St. Paul's Ch., 624
  Tolbooth, 65
  Triumphal Arch (1842), 533
Peterborough
  Bishop's Palace, 526
  Cathedral, 119, 199, 932
  Deanery, 271

Peterborough—contd.
  Gaol & Sessions Ho., 271
  Market Ho., 526
  Prior's Gate, 271
Peterhead, Aberdeens.
  Bank, 736
  Ch. (Old), 500, 554
  Prison, 761
  St. Peter's Ch., 554
  Town Ho., 101
Petersfield, Hants.
  Dolphin Inn, 79
  Masonic Lodge, 523
Petersham, Surrey
  Bute Ho., 577, 883
  Douglas Ho., 644
  Earl of Rochester's ho., 87, 474,
    964
  Lodge, 131, 640, 732, 768
Petworth, Sussex
  Bridewell (Prison), 555, 944
  Ch., 91
  Ho., 137, 722
  ho., 78
Phesdo, Kinc., 761
Pickenham Hall, Norfolk, 270
Pickhill Ho., Denbighs., 841
Pickworth, Rutland, Ch., 654
Piddletrenthide, Dorset, mont.,
  226
Piercefield, Mon., 125, 768
Pierremont Hall, Kent, 228
Pilrig Ho., Midlothian, 163
Pilton, Som., Ch., 860
Pinkhill, Oxon., lock, 391
Pinkie Ho., Midlothian, 163, 624
Pinner, Middlx., mont., 525
Pishiobury Park, Herts., 947–8
Pitcairns, Perths., 163
Pitcaple Castle, Aberdeens., 163
Pitchford, Salop.
  Hall, 759
  Park Farm, 374
Pitfirrane Ho., Fife, 624
Pitfour Castle, Perths., 54, 163
Pitfour Ho., Aberdeens., 762
Pitlour Ho., Fife, 576
Pitlurg Ho., Aberdeens., 737
Pitmilly, Fife, 86
Pitsford Hall, Northants., 463
Pitshill, Sussex, 769
Pittington, Durham, Ch., 123
Pittodrie Ho., Aberdeens., 737
Pitzhanger Manor, Middlx., 251,
  770
Place Ho., Horton, Bucks., 133
Plaistow, Essex
  St. Mary's Ch., 119
  School, 323
Plas Newydd, Anglesey, 232, 655,
  949–50
Platt, Kent, Ch., 882
Platt Hall, Lancs., 521
Plean Hospital, Stirlings., 783
Pleasington, Lancs., Ch. (R.C.),
  614
Plockton, Ross, Ch., 821
Plompton, Yorks., ho., 193
Plymouth
  Assembly Rooms, 319
  Athenaeum, 319
  Athenaeum Terrace, 889
  Athenian Cottage, 319
  Bank of England, 224
  Baptist Ch., George St., 889
  Breakwater, 497
  Cemetery, 889
  Charles Ch., 86

Plymouth—*contd.*
  Christ Ch., 889
  Citadel, 350
  Civil & Military Library, 319
  Congregational Chapel, 889
  Crescent, 442, 889
  Custom Ho., 501
  Devon & Cornwall Female
    Orphanage, 889
  Dockyard, Hamoaze, 430
  Eldad Chapel, 86
  Esplanade, 889
  Exchange, 319
  Freemasons' Hall, 60
  George St., shops, 889
  Guildhall, 302
  Gun Wharf, 456
  Hamoaze Dockyard, 277
  Holy Trinity Ch., 889
  Independent Chapel, 889
  Libraries, 319, 889
  Mechanics' Institute, 890
  Princess Sq., 319
  Royal Hotel, 319
  Royal Union Baths, 433
  St. Andrew's Chapel (St.
    Catherine's Ch.), 319
  St. Andrew's Ch., 319
  St. Charles' Chapel, 211
  St. Luke's Ch., 86
  St. Paul's Chapel, Stonehouse,
    319
  school, 211
  S. Devon & E. Cornwall
    Hospital, 889
  Sussex Place, 889
  Theatre, 319
  Town Hall, 889
Polesden Lacey Ho., Surrey, 244,
  778, 930
Polesworth, Warwicks., Schools,
  655
Pollok Ho., Renfrews., 59
Polmaise, Stirlings., 167
Polstead Hall, Suffolk, 638
Poltalloch Ho., Argylls., 166
Ponsonby Hall, Cumb., 612
Pont-ar-Tawy, Glam., 286
Pontblyddyn, Flints., Christ Ch.,
  522
Pontefract, Yorks.
  All Saints Ch., 210
  Castle, 197
  Court Ho., 868
  Red Lion Inn, 50
  St. Giles' Ch., 731
  Town Hall, 398
Ponteland, Northumb.
  School, 265
  Workhouse, 363
Pontesbury, Salop., Ch., 762, 844;
  mont., 664
Pontloyrig, Carm., bridge, 286
Pont-y-Cysyllte Aqueduct, 738,
  821
Pontypool, Mon.
  Ch. (R.C.), 724
  hos. & shops, 534
Pont-y-Prydd, Glam., bridge, 286
Pool, Yorks., Ch., 210
Pool Park, Denbighs., 369
Poole, Dorset
  ho., 96
  St. James's Ch., 386
  St. Mary's Hospital, 843
  Workhouse, 843
Poole Hall, Cheshire, 874
Poolewe, Ross, Ch., 821

Porkington, Salop., *see* Brogyntyn
Port Eliot, Cornwall, 393, 672,
  770
Port Elphinstone, Aberdeens.,
  322
Port Glasgow, Renfrews.,
  Custom Ho., 160
  Town Bldngs., 381
Port of Menteith, Perths.,
  mausoleum, 783
Portbury, Som., Vicarage, 667
Porters Lodge, Herts., 817
Porthleven, Cornwall, harbour,
  254
Portland, Dorset, St. George's
  Ch., 346
Portmore, Ireland, 440
Portnahaven, Argylls., Ch., 820
Portnockie, Banffs., Ch., 699
Portobello, Midlothian, *see*
  Edinburgh
Portpatrick, Wigtowns., Ch., 162
Portreath, Cornwall, Ch., 890
Portsdown Hill, Hants.
  Nelson Mont., 367
  Obelisk (proposed), 822
Portsea, Hants.
  Baptist Chapel, 604
  Cemetery, 604
  St. George's Ch., 856
  St. John's Chapel, 856
  St. Mary's Ch., 604
  St. Mary's Ch., Kingston, 563
  Workhouse, 604
Portsmouth
  All Saints Ch., 603
  Commissioner's Ho., 957
  Custom Ho., 637
  Dockyard, 60, 277, 722
  fortifications, 308, 350
  Garrison Hospital, 308
  Guildhall, 132
  St. Anne's Dockyard Chapel,
    538
  St. Mary's Ch., 604
  St. Thomas's Ch., 547, 604
  School of Naval Architecture,
    423
  Theatre Royal, 604
  Town Hall, 844
Portswood Ho., Hants., 242, 814
Portumna Castle, Ireland, 822
Poston Court, Herefs., 207
Potarch Bridge, Aberdeens., 821
Potterne, Wilts., Ch., 352
Potters Bar, Middlx., St. John's
  Ch., 119
Poulshot, Wilts, Rectory, 630
Powderhall, Midlothian, 577 (*bis*)
Powderham Castle, Devon, 321,
  334, 565, 949
Powerscourt, Ireland, 167, 698
Powis Castle, Montgom., 83, 664,
  745, 905
Pradoe, Salop., 187, 408
Prees, Salop., mont., 188
Prescot, Lancs., Ch., 726
Preshaw Ho., Hants., 584
Presteign, Radnors., Gaol, 907
Preston, Lancs.
  All Saints Ch., 507
  Christ Ch., 507
  Ch., 422; mont., 693
  County Bridewell, 114
  Court Ho., 506, 691
  Guildhall, 190
  Institution for Diffusion of
    Knowledge, 879

Preston, Lancs.—*contd.*
  Literary & Philosophical Inst.,
    879
  Police Station, 258
  Prison, 258
  St. Ignatius' Ch. (R.C.), 723
  St. Mary's Ch., 507
  St. Paul's Ch., 690
  St. Peter's Ch., 690
  St. Thomas's Ch., 507
  St. Wilfrid's Ch. (R.C.), 724
Preston Bissett, Bucks., Rectory,
  845
Preston Grange, E. Lothian, 647
Preston Hall, Midlothian, 59, 554
Preston Hospital, Salop., 406, 408
Preston-on-Stour, Warwicks.,
  Ch., 915; mont., 797
Prestonpans, E. Lothian, Schaw's
  Hospital, 161
Prestwich, Lancs., All Saints Ch.,
  Stand, 91
Prestwick Lodge, Northumb., 266
Prestwold Hall, Leics., 165, 893
Prestwood, Staffs., farmho., 701
Prickler's Hill, Middlx., 618
Prideaux, Cornwall, 393
Princethorpe, Warwicks., St.
  Mary's Priory, 723, 877n.
Prior Park, Som., 146, 352, 475,
  911; Church (R.C.), 724
Probus, Cornwall, parsonage, 890
Prospect Hill, Berks., 715
Puckaster Cottage, I. of W., 527
Pudsey, Yorks.
  Rectory, 213
  St. Laurence's Ch., 819
Pulham Market, Norfolk,
  Workhouse, 827
Pull Court, Worcs., 117
Pulloxhill, Beds., Ch., 906n.
Pulteneytown, Caithness, 157, 820
Purbrook Ho., Hants., 817
Purley Hall, Berks., 434
Purley Ho., Berks., 950
Pusey Ho., Berks., 716
Putachie, Aberdeens., *see* Castle
  Forbes
Putney, Surrey
  Ch., 506
  cottage (Clarke), 507
  Hill Ho., 745
  hos. & villas, 137 (Fordyce), 231
    (Johnson), 312 (Bruce), 393
    (Larpent), 729 (Leader),
    887 (Hudson), 965
    (Grantham), 965
    (Polwarth)
  obelisk, 252
  Park, 173, 653
Puttenham, Surrey, Rectory, 632
Pye Nest, Yorks., 194
Pylle, Som., Rectory, 860
Pynes, Devon, 657
Pyrgo Park, Essex, 66
Pythouse, Wilts., 107

Quainton, Bucks., mont., 514
Quarff, Shetland, Ch., 821
Quarley, Hants., Ch., 109
Quarrell, Stirlings., 343
Quarry Hill, Kent, 174
Quatford, Salop.
  Castle, 740
  Ch., 606
  village, 740
Queenstown, Ireland, sea-wall,
  etc., 172

Quernmore Park Hall, Lancs., 398, 874
Querns (The), Glos., 701
Quex Park, Kent, 649
Quidenham Hall, Norfolk, 810
Quinton, Warwicks., Ch., 914
Quorndon, Leics., Ch., 622

Raby Castle, Durham, 165, 194, 334, 344, 610
Raby Hall, Cheshire, 291
Racton Tower, Sussex, 484
Radbourne Hall, Derbys., 763
Radcliffe Chapel, Lancs., 954
Radcliffe-on-Trent, Notts., parsonage, 908
Radford, Notts., St. Peter's Ch., 908
Radford Semele Hall, Warwicks., 823
Radlett, Herts., Ch., 762
Radley Hall, Berks., 630, 835
Radstock, Som., Ch., 70
Radway Grange, Warwicks., 549
Radwinter, Essex, Rectory, 445
Raehills, Dumfriess., 164, 781
Raemoir, Aberdeens., 761
Rafford, Morays., Ch., 357
Ragley Hall, Warwicks., 343, 431, 440, 474, 947
Rainhill, Lancs.
    Lunatic Asylum, 291, 563
    St. Bartholomew's Ch. (R.C.), 255
Rainscombe Ho., Wilts., 86
Raith Park, Fife, 644
Ralston Ho., Renfrews., 382
Ramelwell Crags, Lanarks., bridge, 571
Rampton Manor, Notts., 166
Ramsbury Manor, Wilts., 430
Ramsey, Hunts., Abbey Ch., 120
Ramsey Abbey, Hunts., 118, 770
Ramsey, Isle of Man, Courthouse, 780
Ramsgate, Kent
    Clock-house, etc., 729
    d'Este estate, 66
    East Cliffe Ho., 173
    Harbour, 959
    obelisk, 729
    St. George's Ch., 75, 412, 487–8
Ram's Horn Pool, Lanarks., bridge, 571
Randalls, Surrey, 669
Ranton Abbey, Staffs., 83
Rathfarnham Castle, Ireland, 208
Ratho Hall, Midlothian, 163
Rattray, Perths., Ch., 783
Raunds, Northants., Ch., 773
Ravenfield, Yorks.
    Ch., 191
    Hall, 193
Raveningham, Norfolk, milestone, 625
Ravenscourt, Middlx., cottage, 292
Ravensthorpe, Northants., Vicarage, 648
Ravensworth Castle, Durham, 219, 519, 584, 611
Rawcliffe, Yorks., Ch., 442
Rawdon, Yorks., farmho., 216
Rawmarsh, Yorks., Ch., 665
Rawreth, Essex, Ch., 434
Ray Lodge, Essex, 617
Ray Mead, Berks., 870

Ray Mill, Berks., lock-keeper's cottage, 836
Rayne, Essex, Ch., 858
Raynham Hall, Norfolk, 70, 281, 469, 492
Read Hall, Lancs., Ch., 876
Reading, Berks.
    Albion Place, 111
    Baptist Chapel, 232
    Barclays Bank, 140
    bridges, 721
    Butts (The), ho., 111
    Castle St. Chapel, 140
    Cock's Sauce Establishment, 81
    Congregational Chapel, 232
    County Gaol, 139
    Duke St. Bridge, 139
    Holy Trinity Ch., 330
    Horn St., ho., 111
    obelisk, 767
    Queen's Crescent, 232
    Queen's Road, 232
    Royal Berks. Hospital, 140; competition for, 203, 232, 324, 444, 776, 845, 869
    St. Giles' Ch., 111, 293, 330
    St. James's Ch. (R.C.), 970
    St. John's Ch., 279
    St. Lawrence's Ch., 330
    St. Mary's Chapel, 111
    St. Mary's Ch., 111, 324
    Simond's Bank, 140
    Simond's Brewery, 772
    Southampton Place, 111
    Town Hall, 656
Rearsby, Leics., Railway Station, 622
Red Braes, Midlothian, 57
Red Hall, Durham, 955
Redbourne, Lincs.
    Ch., 528
    Hall, 195
Redcar, Yorks., Ch., 123
Redcastle, Ross, 165
Redditch, Worcs., Ch. of Our Lady (R.C.), 691
Redgorton, Perths., Ch., 411
Redgrave, Suffolk
    Ch.; mont., 455
    Hall, 146
Redhill, Hants., St. John's Ch., 604
Redlynch, Som.
    Chapel, 447
    Ho., 312, 447
Rednock Ho., Perths., 148, 530, 671
Redrice Ho., Hants., 165, 439
Redruth, Cornwall
    Ch., 672
    St. Mary's Ch., 442
Reeth, Yorks., bridge, 192
Reigate, Surrey
    Police Station, 506
    Priory, 726
Rempstone, Notts., ho., 789
Rendlesham Hall, Suffolk, 167, 376
Renfrew, Blythswood School, 230
Renishaw Hall, Derbys., 80
Resolis, Ross, Ch., 120
Restalrig, Midlothian, Ch., 162
Revesby, Lincs.
    Ch., 898n.
    Ho., 165
Rheola, Glam., 584
Rhesycae, Flints., Ch., 657
Rhiwlas, Merioneths., 692

Rhos Llanerchrugog, Denbighs., Ch. 632
Rhos-y-Medre, Denbighs., Ch., 878
Rhual, Flints., 467
Rhyl, Flints., Holy Trinity Ch., 476
Rhymney, Mon., St. David's Ch., 387
Ribston Hall, Yorks., 195
Ribton Hall, Cumb., 350
Riccal, Yorks., bridge, 192
Riccarton, Ayrshire, Ch., 688
Riccarton, Midlothian, 162–3
Richmond, Surrey
    Asgill Ho., 484, 817
    Bridge, 236, 609
    Congregational Chapel, 253
    Gardens, 492; Hermitage, 492; Merlin's Cave, 492
    Green, ho., 320
    Hickey's Almshouses, 857
    ho. (Painter), 858
    ho. (Ward), 858
    'lodge' (projected) for George II, 629
    Observatory, 206
    Ormonde Lodge, 474
    Palace (projected), 209
    Park, lodge, 783; Surrey, Hill or Pembroke Lodge, 769
    Pavilion (1768), 206
    Queensberry Villa, 858
    St. John's Ch., 857
    'Star & Garter' Hotel, 479
    Terrace (The), no. 3, 817
    Thatched Ho. Lodge, 770
    Trumpeters' Ho., 964
    White Lodge, 413, 561, 933, 951
    Wick (The), 208, 576
    villas, 523
Richmond, Yorks.
    Bridge, 192
    Culloden Tower, 333
    St. Nicholas' Hospital, 122
Rickmansworth, Herts.
    Ch., 77
    Moat Ho., 770
Riddenwood, Dumfriess., farmho., 588
Riddings, Derbys., Ch., 104
Riddlesworth Hall, Norfolk, 517
Ridge (The), Glos., 679
Ridgebourne, Herefs., 553
Ridgeway, Derbys., Ch., 442
Ridgmont, Horwich, Lancs., 140
Ridley Hall, Northumb., 267
Ridley Hall Bridge, Northumb., 575
Rigmaden, Westmld., 876
Ringley, Lancs., Ch., 91
Ringsend, Ireland, citadel, 350
Ringwood, Hants., parsonage, 151
Ringwould Ho., Kent, 770
Ripley Hospital, Lancs., 247
Ripon, Yorks.
    Bishop's ho., 670
    Deanery, 258
    Holy Trinity Ch., 818
    Minster, 119, 670
    Spring Hill Schools, 670
    Town Hall, 944
Ripple, Worcs., Ch., 897
Rise, Yorks.
    Ch., 210
    Park, 665, 868
Riseholme Hall, Lincs., 670

Rishworth, Yorks., Grammar School, 599
Riverhead, Kent, Ch., 171
Robert Town, Yorks., Ch., 210
Robin Hood's Well, Yorks., 853
Rochdale, Lancs., Ch., 818
Roche Court, Wilts., 809, 961
Rochester, Kent
  Bridge, 65
  Canon's ho., 859
  Cathedral, 234, 454, 575, 739, 858; Close, 65
  Crown Inn, 507
  King's School, 858
  Methodist Chapel, 458
Rochford, Essex, The Lawn, Stroud Green, 464
Rock Hall, Northumb., 268
Rockingham, Northants.
  Castle, 118
  Ch.; mont., 612
Rockingham Ho., Ireland, 584
Rockland All Saints, Norfolk, Workhouse, 827
Rodborough Manor, Glos., 481
Roddam Hall, Northumb., 733
Rode, Wilts., Ch., 685
Rode Hall, Cheshire, 431, 954
Rode Hill, Som., Christ Ch., 352
Roecliffe, Yorks., Ch., 728
Roehampton, Surrey
  Bessborough Ho., 207
  Cedar Court, 770
  Downshire Ho., 140
  Elm Grove, 343, 773
  lodge (Hobart), 671
  Manresa, 207
  Mount Clare, 284
  Parksted, 207
Roehampton Grove, Surrey, 166, 168, 947; mausoleum, 168
Roehampton Ho., 69
Rokeby, Yorks.
  Ch., 191, 703
  Hall, 296, 702–3, 795n., 860, 865
  parsonage, 703
Roker, Durham
  Baths, 265
  terraces, 265
Rolleston Hall, Staffs., 331
Romford, Essex
  Raphael Park, bridge, 948
  Workhouse, 284, 944
Romsey, Hants., Bridge, 574
Rood Ashton Ho., Wilts., 435, 961
Rookesbury, Hants., 810; tower, 810
Rooksnest, Surrey, 729
Roos, Yorks., Ch., 234
Ropsley, Lincs., parsonage, 132
Roscrea, Ireland, Ch., 292
Rose Castle, Cumb., 532, 692, 838
Rose Hill Cottage, Berks., 527
Rose Hill Park, Sussex, 680n., 744
Roseangle, Angus
  hos., 587
  Laing's Hotel, 587
Rosebery, Midlothian, 76
Rosedale, Yorks., Ch., 858
Rosemount, Greyabbey, Ireland, 717
Rosherville, Kent, 488; St. Mark's Ch., 706
Rosneath, Dunb., 125, 577, 586
Ross Priory, Dunb., 358

Ross-dhu Ho., Dunb., 148, 220
Ross-on-Wye, Herefs.
  Ch., 897
  Royal Hotel, 648
Rossie, Angus, ho., 283
Rossie Castle, Angus, 241
Rossie Ho., Fife, 623
Rossie Priory, Perths., 76
Rossington, Yorks.
  Ch., 215
  Rectory, 522
Rostherne, Cheshire
  Ch., 332, 709, 726
  School, 954
Rotherfield Park, Hants., 621
Rotherham, Yorks.
  Brewery, 642
  Charity School, 642
  Clifton Ho., 196
  Crofts (The), ho., 642
  Eastwood Ho., 196
  Ferham estate, 313
  Ferham Ho., 641
  Market Ho., 642
  Market Place, 80
  Ship Hotel, 442
  Westgate, 442, 641
Rotherhithe, Surrey
  Holy Trinity Parsonage, 670
  Howland Great Dock, 778
Rotherwas, Herefs., 343
Rothes, Morays., 699
Rothesay, Bute, Free Ch., 737
Rothwell, Northants., Market Ho., 367
Rothwell, Yorks., Ch., 73
Roughan, Norfolk
  Ch., 597
  Hall, 597
Round Coppice, Bucks., 131
Roundhay, Yorks.
  Park, 215
  St. John's Ch., 819
Roundway Park, Wilts, see New Park
Rousham Ho., Oxon., 493; Townesend's Temple, 835
Rous Lench, Worcs., mont., 70
Routh, Yorks., rectory, 107
Roveries (The), Salop., 408
Rowde, Wilts., Ch., 352
Rowton Castle, Salop., 939
Roxham Drain Bridge, Norfolk, 785
Roydon, Norfolk, Ch., 858
Royston, Herts., Market Ho., 585
Ruabon, Denbighs., Ch., 663
Rudding Park, Yorks., 210
Rufford Abbey, Notts., 972; Bath Summer Ho., 380
Rugby, Warwicks.
  Brookside, 692
  St. Andrew's Ch., 691
  School, 376
Runcton Hall, Norfolk, 971
Runnymede, Surrey, proposed column, 822
Ruperra Castle, Glam, 388, 903
Ruscombe Ho., Berks., 54
Rushbury, Salop., Rectory, 271
Rushock, Worcs., Ch., 304
Russellstown Ho., Ireland, 717
Rutherford Bridge, Yorks., 192
Ruthin, Denbighs., Ch., 844
Ruthven, Inverness., barracks, 457, 705
Rydal, Westmld., Ch., 876

Ryde, I. of W.
  Brigstock Terrace, 715
  Ch., 715
  ho., 167
  Royal Victoria Arcade, 880
  St. James's Ch., 699
  Town Hall, 715
Rye, Sussex, Town Hall, 457
Ryes Lodge (The), Essex, 527
Ryston Hall, Norfolk, 659, 768
Ryton, Durham, ho., 268
Ryton, Salop., Ch., 606

Sacombe Park, Herts., 344, 854
Sadberge, Durham, Ch., 671
Sadborow Ho., Dorset, 463
Saffron Walden, Essex
  Almshouses, 393
  Ch., 139, 418, 691, 704
  Grove (The), 704
  Vicarage, 448
St. Albans, Herts.
  Abbey Ch., 234, 404, 566
  Abbey Gateway, 763
  Christ Ch., 620
  Gaol, 763
  Ivy Ho., 792
  Market Place, ho., 792
  St. Peter's Ch., 211
  Town Hall, 754
St. Andrews, Fife
  Balfour Ho., 86
  Episcopal Ch., 161
  Infant School, 596
  Madras College, 161
  Martyrs' Monument, 596
  St. Leonard's Ch., 238, 623
  St. Mary's Ch., 162
  St. Mary's College, 675
  St. Salvator's Ch., 238
  St. Salvator's College, 272, 757
  Town (Holy Trinity) Ch., 86, 711
  United College, 596, 675
  University Library, 675
  Victory Memorial Hall, 162
St. Asaph, Flints.
  Bishop's Palace, 117
  Cathedral, 476, 844, 954
  Workhouse, 878
St. Boswell's, Roxb.,
  Ch., 760
  school, 760
  shop, 760
St. Briavel's, Glos., Ch., 141
St. Brycedale Ho., Fife, 624
St. Catherine's, Yorks., 215
St. David's, Pemb.
  Cathedral, 581
  'Tomb of Geraldus', 255
St. Day, Cornwall, Ch., 442
St. Dominic, Cornwall, parsonage, 890
St. Edmund's College, Herts., 813
St. Edmund's Hill, Suffolk, 63
St. Erme, Cornwall, Ch., 319
St. Fort, Fife, 163
St. Gluvias, Cornwall, Ch., 285
St. Helen's, Lancs.
  Holy Cross Ch. (R.C.), 724
  Town Hall, 897
St. Helier, Jersey, Town Hall, 109
St. Ives, Cornwall
  almshouses, 912
  parsonage, 890
St. Ives, Hunts., vicarage, 372
St. Ives, Yorks., 611

St. John Lee, Northumb., Ch., 265
St. John's Bridge, Berks., lock, 836
St. Julian's, Kent, 617
St. Kea, Cornwall, Ch., 945
St. Kew, Cornwall, parsonage, 211
St. Leonard's, Middlx., 715
St. Leonard's-on-Sea, Sussex
  Assembly Rooms, 174
  Cottage (The), Maze Hill, 170
  Masonic Hall, 174
  Royal Victoria Hotel, 174
  St. Leonard's Ch., 174
  St. Leonard's Hotel, 174
St. Leonard's Hill, Berks., 614
St. Leonard's Lodge, Sussex, 464
St. Martin's Perths., Ch., 412
St. Michael Penkevil, Cornwall, Ch.; mont. 55
St. Michael's Mount, Cornwall, 82
St. Neot's, Cornwall, Ch., 411, 622
St. Paul's Walden Bury, Herts., 612; temple, 208
St. Peter Port, Guernsey
  Elizabeth Coll., 900
  Fountain St., 900
  Les Arcades, 900
  Market Hall, 900
  Royal Court Ho., 900
  St. James's Ch., 900
  Springfield Ho., 900
  Town Ch., 900
St. Quivox, Ayrshire, mausoleum, 647
Salcombe, Devon, Ch., 86
Salden Ho., Bucks., 392
Salford, Lancs.
  Christ Ch., 934
  Market, 353
  New Bailey Prison, 114
  Richmond Independent Chapel, 502
  St. John's Ch., Higher Broughton, 502
  St. Philip's Ch., 744
  St. Simon's Ch., 502
  Science Museum, 92
  Town Hall, 502
Saline, Fife, Ch., 776
Salisbury, Wilts.
  Bishop's Palace, 659, 817
  Cathedral, 314, 659, 926, 945; mont., 684
  Guildhall, 434, 816
  Hemingsby Ho., 659
  Infirmary, 912
  Matrons' College, 348
  St. Edmund's College, 228
Sallymount, Ireland, 718
Salperton Park, Glos., 605
Salt, Staffs., Ch., 842
Salter Street, Warwicks., Ch., 390
Saltmarshe Hall, Yorks., 666, 868
Saltoun, E. Lothian
  Hall, 159, 162
  Manse, 159
Saltram Ho., Devon, 53, 319, 704
Salwarpe, Worcs., parsonage, 177
Sampford Ho., Essex, 701
Sand Hutton, Yorks.
  Ch., 972
  Park, 196, 972
Sandbeck Ho. (Park), Yorks., 79, 167, 611

Sandford, Oxon.
  lock, 836
  weir, 391
Sandgate, Kent
  Chapel, 679
  cottage, 700
Sandhoe Ho., Northumb., 268
Sandhurst, Berks., Royal Military College, 714
Sandleford Priory, Berks., 947
Sandling Ho., Kent., 125
Sandon, Staffs.
  Ch., 841n., 842, 959
  Hall, 166, 635, 839, 874, 957
Sandridge Park, Devon, 583
Sandwell Park, Staffs., 692, 750
Sandwich, Kent, harbour, 499
Sandy, Beds.
  bridge, 906
  Ch., 906
Sandywell Park, Glos., 752
Sans Souci, Dorset, 963
Sarsden, Oxon.
  Ch., 679
  Ho., 679, 680
Sarsgrove Cottage (Ho.), Oxon., 679
Saughton Ho., Midlothian, 59
Saundby, Notts., Ch., 899
Saunders Hill, Cornwall, 687
Savernake Lodge, Wilts., 769
Sawley, Derbys., parsonage, 908
Saxby, Leics.
  Ch., 687
  Railway Station, 622
Saxlingham, Norfolk, Rectory, 768
Sayes Court, Surrey, 612
Scampston Ho., Yorks., 517; Bridge, 147
Scar Ho., Yorks., 268
Scarborough, Yorks.
  Christ Church, 73
  Methodist Chapel, 735
  Museum, 728
  Spa, 940
  Trinity Ho., 728
  Valley (The), 728
Scarisbrick Hall, Lancs., 689, 692, 739, 970
Scawby, Lincs., Ch., 970
Scawton, Yorks., bridge, 734
Scilly Isles, St. Agnes lighthouse, 959
Scofton-with-Osberton, Notts., Ch., 657
Scone Palace, Perths., 76, 524
Scotney Castle, Kent, 971
Scotston Ho., Aberdeens., 737
Scotstoun, Renfrews., 383
Scotswood, Northumb., bridge, 362
Scrayingham, Yorks., parsonage, 258
Scremerston, Northumb.
  Ch., 123
  parsonage, 123
Scrivelsby, Lincs.
  Court, 197
  Rectory, 681
Scriven Hall, Yorks., 301
Seacliff(e) Ho., E. Lothian, 165, 642
Seacroft, Yorks., The Grange, 375
Seaham Hall, Durham, 955
Seaham Harbour, Durham, 265
  Ch., 666
  Institute, 602

Seaton Carew, Durham
  Ch., 449, 634
  parsonage, 971
Seaton Delaval, Northumb., 266, 301, 853
Sedburgh, Yorks., ho., 361
Sedbury Park, Glos., 745
Sedbury Park, Yorks., 194, 315
Sedge Fen Drain Bridge, Norfolk, 785
Sedgley, Staffs.
  Ch., 510
  Park, R.C. School, 248
Sefton, Lancs., Ch., 140
Seggieden, Perths., 398, 624
Seghill, Northumb.
  Ch., 363
  parsonage, 268
Seighford, Staffs., Ch., 84
Selsdon, Surrey, farmho., 642
Sennowe Hall, Norfolk, 174
Selby, Yorks.
  Abbey Ch., 78
  Audus Almshouses, 78
  Bridge, 192
  Court Ho., 78
  Crescent, 78
  St. James's Ch., 78
  Wesleyan Chapel, 78
Selside, Westmld., Ch., 318
Serlby Hall, Notts., 111, 522, 611, 874
Seton Castle, E. Lothian, 55
Settle, Yorks.
  Ch., 691
  Town Hall, 875
Settrington, Yorks., Rectory, 268
Sevenoaks, Kent
  Almshouses, 132
  chapel, 200
  Ch., 227
  Lady Boswell's School, 223
  Rectory, 173
  School, 132
  Vine (The), 854
Sevenoaks Weald, Kent, Chapel, 881
Severn navigation, 573
Severndroog Castle, Kent, 478
Sewardstone Manor Ho., Essex, 859
Sewerby Hall, Yorks., 466
Sezincote Ho., Glos., 225, 228
Shadforth, Durham, Ch., 449
Shadwell, Salop.
  farmho., 762
  Hall, 187, 762
Shadwell, Yorks., Ch., 210
Shadwell Lodge (Park), Norfolk, 118, 137, 176, 629
Shanbally Castle, Ireland, 585
Shane's Castle, Ireland, 434n., 584
Shardeloes Ho., Bucks., 52, 509, 514, 751, 946
Shareshill, Staffs., parsonage, 383
Sharlston, Yorks., 831
Sharow, Yorks.
  Ch., 497
  Lucan Ho., 497–8
Sharpham Ho., Devon, 817
Shaw Ho., Berks., 732
Shawbury Park, Salop., 664
Shawdon Hall, Northumb., 268
Shay (The), Yorks., 194
Shedfield, Hants., Ch., 59, 107

Sheerness, Kent
  Dockyard, 60, 423, 705, 722, 813
  Holy Trinity Ch., 813
  Market Ho., 705
Sheffield, Yorks.
  Botanical Gardens, 811
  Boys' Charity School, 441
  Carver St. Methodist Chapel, 458
  Cathedral, *see* St. Peter's Ch.
  Cemetery, 313, 917
  Christ Ch., Attercliffe, 819
  Circus & Theatre, 394
  Corn Market, 441
  Cutlers' Hall, 811, 917
  Ecclesall Workhouse, 313
  Grammar School, 441
  Holy Trinity Ch., Wicker, 313
  Infirmary, 672
  King Edward VII Grammar School, 313
  Little Sheffied Moor, hos., 673
  'The Mount', 313
  Music Hall, 441
  National School, 818
  Nether Chapel, 665, 868
  Nether Edge Hospital, 313
  Norfolk, ho. for Duke of, 774
  St. George's Ch., 441
  St. James's Chapel, 80
  St. Mary's Ch., 655
  St. Mary's Ch., Fulwood, 655
  St. Paul's Ch., 640, 843
  St. Peter's Ch. (Cathedral), 74, 191, 522, 655, 868
  St. Philip's Ch., 819
  Savings Bank, 655
  Sessions Ho., 80
  Shrewsbury Almshouses, 441
  Shrewsbury Hospital Chapel, 74
  streets, 74
  Surgeons' Hall, 394, 917
  Tapton Grove, 80
  Town Hall, 442, 678, 868
  Wards End, ho., 80
  Wesleyan School, 313
  Westbourne Ho., 80
  Writing-School, 917
Sheffield Place, Sussex, 507, 947
Shelford, Cambs.
  Ho., 271
  Mausoleum, 893
Shelsley Beauchamp, Worcs., Rectory, 465, 706
Shelton, Staffs., St. Mark's Ch., 600
Shenfield Place, Essex, 431
Shenley, Herts.
  chapel, 776
  Rectory, 71
Shenstone Park, Staffs., 752
Shepton Mallet, Som.
  Ch., 860
  Market Cross, 537
  Police Station, 860
  Workhouse, 860
Sherborne, Dorset
  Abbey Ch., 98, 632
  Castle, 95
  Digby School, 98
  Pinford Bridge, 575
Sherborne, Glos.
  Ho., 492, 791, 954
  Stone Farmho., 605
Sherdley Hall, Lancs., 394
Shere Manor Ho., Surrey, 95

Sheriff Hutton, Yorks.
  Castle, 728
  ho., 261
Sheriff's Court, Kent, 292
Sheringham, Norfolk
  Ch., 145
  Hall, 682
Shernfold Park, Sussex, 102, 859
Sherston, Wilts., Ch., 798
Shibden Hall, Yorks., 391
Shildon, Durham, Ch., 971
Shieldaig, Ross, Ch., 821
Shillinglee Park, Sussex, 778
Shillingthorpe Hall, Lincs., 746
Shincliffe Bridge, Durham, 122
Shinfield Ho., Berks., 700, 901
Shipbourne, Kent, Ch., 340; mont., 345
Shipley, Yorks., St. Paul's Ch., 600
Shipton Hall, Salop, 664
Shipton-on-Cherwell, Oxon., Ch., 845
Shipton-under-Wychwood, Oxon., Vicarage, 605
Shirburn Castle, Oxon., 167, 347, 417
Shirehampton, Glos., Ch., 315
Shireoaks Hall, Notts., 416
Shirley, Hants., Rectory, 679
Shirley, Warwicks., Ch., 279
Shobdon Court, Herefs., 312, 407
Shobrooke Park, Devon, 269
Sholbrook Lodge, Northants., 557
Shooters Hill, Kent
  cottages, 88
  monument (proposed), 187
  Severndroog Castle, 478
Shoreham, Kent, manor-ho., 128
Shoreham, Sussex
  Buckingham Place, 674
  Custom Ho., 972
Shortgrove, Essex, 136, 138
Shotesham Park, Norfolk, 768
Shotover Park, Oxon., 492–3
Shottesbrooke, Berks.
  Ch., 832
  Park, 653
Shotts, Lanarks., Ch., 133, 357
Shrewsbury
  Abbey (The), 663
  Abbey Ch., 188
  Abbey Foregate, 187
  Allatt's Charity School, 408
  Armoury, 944
  Butter & Cheese Market, 304
  Butter Market (New), 406
  Cann Office, 663
  Carline's Fields, 188
  Carriers Inn, shops, 663
  Castle, 820
  Claremont Bldngs., 188
  Coleham Head, bridge, 187
  County Gaol, 407, 820
  Crescent (The), 142
  Drapers' Almshouses, 188
  English Bridge, 83, 187, 373, 410, 662, 758
  Foundling Hospital, 663
  Guildhall, 407
  High Street, nos. 10–11, 663
  Hill's Column, 187, 397, 405
  Holy Trinity Ch., Coleham, 221
  hos., 304, 408
  Infirmary, 83, 743
  Kingsland Bank, 663
  Lancasterian School, 406

Shrewsbury—*contd.*
  Millington's Hospital, 407, 724
  Music Hall, 406
  Raven Inn, 838
  St. Alkmund's Ch., 187, 213, 759; mont., 606
  St. Chad's Ch. (Old), 820; mont., 664
  St. Chad's Ch. (New), 142, 738, 780
  St. Chad's School, 406
  St. George's Ch., Frankwell, 406
  St. Giles' Ch., 188
  St. Julian's Ch., 663
  St. Julians Friars, no. 37, 142
  St. Mary's Ch., 188, 820; mont., 664
  St. Michael's Ch., 188
  Savings Bank, 406
  School, 408; Headmaster's ho., 408
  Schools (parochial), 188
  Shirehall, 407, 743, 759
  Shoplatch, 663
  Swan Hill Court Ho., 663
  Welsh Bridge, 187
Shrigley Hall, Cheshire, 293
Shrivenham, Berks.
  Ch.; mont., 952
  Rectory, 605
Shrubland Hall (Park), Suffolk, 92, 330, 612
Shrubland Hall, Warwicks., 377
Shuckburgh Hall, Warwicks., 487n.
Shugborough, Staffs., 874, 934, 958; garden bldngs., 796, 839, 934
Sibford Gower, Oxon., Ch., 847
Sibson, Leics., Ch., 556, 753
Sidcup, Kent, ho., 838
Sidmouth, Devon
  All Saints Ch., 814
  Fortfield Crescent, 599
Sidway Hall, Staffs., 84, 838
Silk Willoughby, Lincs., Rectory, 411
Silsoe, Beds., Ch., 365–6, 763
Silwood Park, Berks., 554
Silvermere, Surrey, 77
Silverton, Devon, Rectory, 202
Simonburn, Northumb., Ch., 590
Sindlesham, Berks., chapel, 232
Singleton Ho., Glam., 460, 701
Sinnington, Yorks., bridge, 734
Sissinghurst, Kent
  Ch., 459
  Vicarage, 882
Siston Court, Glos., 551
Sithrey, Cornwall, parsonage, 890
Skellingthorpe, Lincs., Ch., 188
Skelton, Yorks.
  Castle, 125, 208
  Ch., 355
Skene, Aberdeens.
  Ch., 221
  Ho., 644, 737–8
Sketty Park, Glam., 460
Skerne Bridge, Durham, 122
Skipton, Yorks., Christ Ch., 210
Skipton on Swale, Yorks., bridge, 192
Skirlaugh, Yorks., Ch., 107
Skutterskelfe Ho., Yorks., 971
Slad (The), Glos., Ch., 82
Slains Castle, Aberdeens., 762
Slalely, Northumb., Ch., 971

Slane Castle, Ireland, 147, 434, 948
Slaughterford, Wilts., Ch., 313
Sleaford, Lincs.
  Carr's Hospital, 488
  Sessions Ho., 488
Sleat, Skye
  Ch.; mont., 179
  Manse, 358
Slebech Hall, Pemb., 180
Sledmere Ho., Yorks., 666, 868
Slimbridge, Glos., Rectory, 455
Slingsby Castle, Yorks., 764
Smethwick, Staffs., Holy Trinity Ch., 970
Snaigow Ho., Perths., 164
Sneaton, Yorks.
  Castle, 441
  Ch., 441
Sneinton, Notts., Ch., 691
Snelston Hall, Derbys., 234
Snizort, Skye, Ch., 500
Soham, Cambs.
  Ch., 123
  Vicarage, 692
Soho, Staffs.
  Ho., 261, 950, 957
  Works, 520, 936
Solihull, Warwicks.
  Ch., 635
  Ch. (R.C.), 970
Somerford Booths Hall, Cheshire, 874
Somerford Hall (Park), Cheshire, 699, 874
Somerhill, Kent, 963, 971
Somerley, Hants., 167–8, 631, 958
Somerleyton, Suffolk, Ch., 290
Somersby Hall, Lincs., 65, 854
Somerville, Ireland, 755
Sompting, Sussex, Ch., 417
Sophia Lodge, Berks., 951
Sopwell Hall, Herts., 538
Soulbury, Bucks.
  Ch., 391; mont., 345
  Lovett School, 392
Souldrop, Beds., Ch., 711
South Brent, Som., Ch., 537
South Crosland, Yorks., Ch., 73
South Dalton Hall, Yorks., 414
South Darenth, Kent, The Towers, 240
South Ferry, Fife, lighthouse, 587
South Hayling, Hants., 218
South Hill Ho., Durham, 267
South Hill Park, Berks., 770
South Kelsey, Lincs., Ch., 653
South Leigh, Devon, Ch., 656
South Molton, Devon
  Ch., 411
  Town Hall, 244
South Norwood, Surrey
  St. Mark's Ch., 307
  villa, 829
South Ormsby Hall, Yorks., 610
South Otterington, Yorks., bridge, 192
South Pool, Devon, Rectory, 520
South Rauceby Hall, Lincs., 165
South Retford, Notts., Grammar School, 171
South Runcton, Norfolk, Ch., 145
South Shields, Durham
  Ch., 838
  glass-works, 265
  Holy Trinity Ch., 971
  Market, 916
  Presbyterian Ch., 266

South Shields, Durham—contd.
  St. Mary's Ch., Tyne Dock, 266
  School, 265
  Workhouse, 362
South Stack, Anglesey, lighthouse, 65
South Stoke, Lincs.
  almshouses, 161
  Ch., 162
  parsonage, 505
South Stoke, Som., Ch., 537
South Weald, Essex, Vicarage, 377
South Wraxhall, Wilts., Ch., 352
Southampton
  Albion Place, 642
  All Saints Ch., 683
  Audit Ho., 242
  Barracks, 642
  Baths, 274
  Beckford Ho., 679
  Brunswick Place, 642
  Castle, 121
  Holy Rood Ch., 200
  ho., 489
  mansion near, 157
  Northam Bridge, 555
  Polygon, 514
  Railway Station, 828
  R.C. Chapel, 321
  St. Michael's Ch., 354
  St. Peter's Ch., 200
Southborough, Kent
  Ch., 171
  Glebe Ho., 696
Southborough Place, Surrey, 584
Southend, Argylls., Ch., 400
Southend, Essex, St. John's Ch., 434
Southend, Kintyre, Ch., 144
Southgate, Middlx.
  Grove, 583
  ho., 769
  Palmer's Green, ho., 769
  St. Paul's Chapel, 253
Southill Ho., Beds., 426, 499, 502
Southminster, Essex, Ch., 434
Southowram, Yorks., St. Anne's Ch., 818
Southport, Lancs., St. Marie's Ch. (R.C.), 970
Southsea, Hants.
  Clifton Terrace, 604
  Dover Court, 604
  Netley Terrace, 604
  Portland Terrace, 604
  Queen's Terrace, 604
  Richmond Terrace, 604
  St. Jude's Ch., 604
  St. Paul's Ch., 353
  Sussex Place, 604
  Sussex Terrace, 604
Southwell, Notts.
  Assembly Rooms, 443
  Grammar School, 444
  Ho. of Correction, 443
  Minster, 443, 893
  Residence Ho., 443, 466, 528
Southwick Ho., Hants., 437
Southwick-on-Wear, Durham, Ch., 449
Southwold, Suffolk, mont., 88
Sowerby, Yorks.
  Ch., 899
  St. George's Ch., Quarry Hill, 878

Sowerby Bridge, Yorks., Christ Ch., 599
Spalding, Lincs.
  High Street, no. 12, 717
  Holland Ho., 718
  Ho. of Correction, 487
  Langton Ho., 718
  Town Hall, 717
  Triumphal Arch (1749), 717
  Welland Terrace, 247
  Westbourne Ho., 718
Sparkford, Som., Ch., 290
Speenhamland, Berks., Ch., 721
Speke Hall, Lancs., 140
Speldhurst, Kent, Hollands, 173
Spelsbury, Oxon., mont., 484
Spetchley Park, Worcs., 177, 807
Spettisbury, Dorset
  Catholic Chapel, 630
  Rectory, 96
Speymouth, Morays., Ch., 600
Spilsby, Lincs., Sessions Ho., 487
Spinningdale, Sutherld., Mill, 120
Spittle Croft, Wilts., 603
Spotland, Lancs., St. Clement's Ch., 857
Spott Ho., E. Lothian, 164
Spottiswoode Ho., Berwicks., 164
Spring Grove, Kent, 173
Spring Hill, Worcs., 147
Spring Park, Glos., see Woodchester Park
Springfield, Essex
  Holy Trinity Ch., 682
  Mount Hill, 656
Springfield, Lanarks., villa, 676
Springwood Park, Roxb.; gates, 358–9; mausoleum, 358–9
Sproatley, Yorks., Ch., 73, 442
Sprotborough Hall, Yorks., 300, 610
Sproughton, Suffolk, Chantry (The), 823, 824
Spurn Head, Yorks., lighthouse, 729
Spye Park, Wilts., 167, 781
Stackpole Court, Pemb., 822
Stafford
  Castle, 461
  Chapel (R.C.), 461
  Christ Ch., 383
  County Gaol, 232
  Fernleigh Hospital, 842
  ho., 842
  Infirmary, 936
  Shire Hall, 399, 959
  St. Chad's Ch., 842
  Workhouse, 842
Stainborough Hall, Yorks., see Wentworth Castle
Staines, Middlx.
  Bridge, 714
  Ch., 869
  Congregational Ch., 417
  Literary & Scientific Institution, 417
  Public Library, 417
Stainton-by-Langworth, Lincs., Ch., 110
Stalbridge Park, Dorset, 256
Stalybridge, Cheshire, ho., 75
  Hough Hill Priory, 75
  St. Paul's Ch., 811
Stamford, Lincs.
  Barn Hill, 457, 654
  Barn Hill Ho., 151
  Bridge, 151
  Browne's Hospital, 864

Stamford, Lincs.—*contd.*
  Byard Ho., 151
  Conservative Club, 151
  Fryer's Almshouses, 94
  Gaol, 637
  George Hotel, 654
  High St., no. 1, 151
  Infirmary, 330
  Institution, 151
  Iron Foundry, 151
  Markets, 511
  Public Library, 511
  Red Lion Square, 151
  St. Mary's Ch., 279, 654, 777
  St. Michael's Ch., 145, 279
  Snowden's Hospital, 637
  Stamford Hotel, 121
  Truesdale's Hospital, 94
  Vale Ho., 511
  Workhouse, 151
Stamford Bridge, Yorks., bridge, 301
Stamfordham, Northumb., Ch., 265
Stanage Park, Radnors., 407, 682
Stanbridge, Dorset, Ch., 302
Stanbrook Abbey, Worcs., 255
Stand, Lancs., *see* Prestwich
Standground, Hunts., ho., 271
Standish, Glos., Vicarage, 455
Standlynch, Wilts., 684, 912
Stanfield Hall, Norfolk, 893
Stanford Hall, Northants., 542, 751, 763
Stanford Hall, Notts., 413
Stanford-on-Teme, Worcs.
  bridge, 581, 706
  Ch., 706
Stanhoe Ho., Norfolk, 105
Stanhope, Durham, Rectory, 122
Stanley (Old Swan), nr.
        Liverpool, St. Anne's Ch., 782
Stanley, Yorks., Ch., 73
Stanley Hall, Salop., 246, 740
Stanmer Park, Sussex, 276, 436
Stanmore, Middlx.
  Aylmore Grove Cottage, 374
  Ho. (Park), 207, 425, 855
  Rectory, 732
  Stanmore Cottage, 715
  Warren Ho., 745
Stannington, Yorks., Ch., 441
Stanstead Ho. (Park), Sussex, 125, 147, 435, 484, 805, 948
Stanton Hall, Derbys., 522
Stanton St. John, Oxon., Rectory, 648
Stanway Ho., Glos., 167
Stanwell Place, Middlx., 343
Stanwick, Yorks.
  Hall (Park), 173–4, 493, 692
  Rectory, 168
Staplefield Place, Essex, 721
Stapleford, Leics.
  Ch., 687, 777
  Hall. 777
Stapleford, Notts.
  parsonage, 626
  school, 626
Staplehurst Place, Kent, 307
Stapleton, Glos.
  Ch., 315
  ho., 682
Stapleton Park, Yorks., 218
Starcross, Devon, Ch., 411
Starston Place, Norfolk, 818
Staunton, Notts., Ch., 899

Staunton Harold, Leics.
  Ch., 732
  Hall, 413, 733
Staunton Park, Herefs., 361
Staveley, Yorks., Ch., 73
Steephill Castle, I. of W., 715
Steeple Ashton, Wilts., Vicarage, 393
Steeple Aston, Oxon, Ch., 648
Steetly Hall, Glam., 460
Stella, Durham, R.C. Ch., 266, 363
Stenhouse, Stirlings., 164
Stenscholl, Skye, Ch., 821
Stenton, E. Lothian, Ch., 162
Stevenage, Herts.
  Ch., 763
  Rectory, 763
Steventon, Berks., Vicarage, 727
Stewartfield Ho., Roxb., 907
Stewarton, Ayrshire, 671
Stirling
  Allan Park, 127
  Athenaeum, 467, 783
  Bank of Scotland, 161
  Castle, 152
  Court Ho. & Gaol, 241
  Cowane's Hospital, 569
  Craigs Ho., 127
  Erskine Ch., 467
  Grammar School, 361
  Holy Rude Ch., 230, 357, 548
  Melville Place (Terrace), 467
  Queen St., 467
  Tolbooth, 531
  Town Ho., 154, 361
Stisted Hall, Essex, 377, 631
Stivichall Hall, Warwicks., 312
Stoak, Cheshire, Ch., 280
Stobars Hall, Westmld., 755
Stobo Castle, Peebles., 288
Stobs Castle, Roxb., 55
Stockeld Park, Yorks., 611
Stockgrove, Bucks., 173
Stockingford, Warwicks., Ch., 709
Stockport, Cheshire
  Ch., 954
  Grammar School, 387
  Green Hill, 350
  ho., 75
  Infirmary, 502
  St. Thomas's Ch., 74, 94
  Unitarian Chapel, 811
  Wesleyan Chapel, 502
Stockport Etchells, Cheshire,
        Lunatic Asylum, 502–3
Stockton-on-Tees, Durham
  Column, 734
  Exchange Bldngs., 673
  Holy Trinity Ch., 363
Stockwell, Surrey, villas, 292
Stoer, Sutherld., Ch., 821
Stoke Bruern Park, Northants., 212, 473
Stoke Damarel, Devon
  Albemarle Villas, 319
  Belmont Ho., 319
  Orphan Asylum, 889
  St. Michael's Terrace, 319
  Travers Ho., 319
Stoke Doyle, Northants., Ch., 279
Stoke Dry, Rutland, Rectory, 151
Stoke Edith, Herefs.
  Ch., 311; monts., 142, 809
  Ho., 809, 893
Stoke Ferry, Norfolk, Ch., 271, 589

Stoke Gifford Ho., Glos., 825, 934
Stoke Green Ho., Warwicks., 971
Stoke Hall, Derbys., 126
Stoke Hall, Notts., 954
Stoke Lane, Som., Ch., 330
Stoke Newington, Middlx.,
        Friends' Meeting Ho., 62
Stoke Park, Wilts., 132, 350, 780
Stoke Poges, Bucks.
  Ch., 730; mont. (Gray), 952
  Park, 509, 585, 949
  Vicarage, 951
Stoke Rochford, Lincs.
  Ch., 162
  Ho., 165
  obelisk, 168
Stoke Talmage, Oxon., parsonage, 391
Stoke-on-Trent, Staffs., St.
        Peter's Ch., 969
Ston Easton, Som., 846
Stone Castle, Kent, 377
Stone, Staffs.
  Ch., 84, 304, 704, 838–9
  Crown Inn, 425
Stonebyres Ho., Lanarks., 82, 383
Stonefield Ho., Argylls., 647
Stonegate Chapel, Sussex, 858
Stonehaven, Kinc.
  County Ho. & Gaol, 761
  Fetteresso Ch., 624
Stonehouse, Devon
  Battery Hill, 211
  Caroline Place, 211
  Naval Hospital, 707
  Valletort Baths, 211
  Valletort Hotel, 211
  Valletort Terrace, 211
  Victualling Yard, 677
Stonelands, Sussex, 680n., *and see* Buckhurst
Stoneleigh Abbey, Warwicks., 98, 166, 520, 746, 750; bridge, 678
Stoney Stanton, Leics.
  Bridge, 622
  Rectory, 542
Stonor Park, Oxon., 61, 541, 827
Stony Middleton, Derbys., Ch., 126
Stony Stratford, Bucks., Ch., 419
Stonyhurst, Lancs.
  Ho., 62, 276
  Observatory, 724
  St. Peter's Ch. (R.C.), 723
  Shireburn Almshouses, 540
Storrs Hall, Westmld., 328, 329
Stourbridge, Worcs.
  Chapel (Presbyterian), 465
  villa, 304
Stourhead, Wilts., 109, 184, 201, 446, 620, 896; Alfred's Tower, 312; cottage, 200; lodges, 683; Temples, 312
Stourport, Worcs.
  bridge, 662
  Lower Mitton Chapel, 706
Stourton Castle, Staffs., 746
Stover Lodge, Devon, 389
Stow Bedon, Norfolk, Ch., 145
Stowe Ho., Bucks., 53, 115, 127, 311, 343, 422, 514, 550, 639, 693, 770, 848, 853; temples and garden bldngs., 115, 127, 145–6, 343, 492, 550, 639, 848, 851, 853

Stowford, Devon, Rectory, 656
Stracathro Ho., Angus, 737
Strangeways, Lancs., Baptist
    Chapel, 503
Stratfieldsaye, Hants.
    Ch., 639
    Ho., 127, 639, 938
    Rectory, 639
    palace (projected), 808
Stratford-on-Avon, Warwicks.
    Ch., 421, 521, 774
    Headmaster's Ho., 749
    Henley St., nos. 16, 17, 18,
        230
    Shakespeare jubilee (1769), 50
    Town Hall, 521
    Vicarage, 749
    White Lion Inn, 230
Stratford Langthorne, Essex, St.
    John's Ch., 119
Strathallan Castle, Perths., 745
Strathconon, Ross, Ch., 821
Strathendry, Fife, 163
Strathblane, Stirlings., Ch., 133
Strathmartine, Angus, cottage,
    587
Strathtyrum Ho., Fife, 86
Strathy, Sutherld., Ch., 821
Stratton Audley Ho., Oxon., 332
Stratton Park, Hants., 252, 716
    (bis)
Strawberry Hill, Middlx., 53, 109,
    213, 261, 299, 566, 639,
    704, 949
Streatham, Surrey
    Ch., 621
    ho. (Coventry), 951
    Leigham Court, 617
    Park Hill, 618
    Rookery (The), 725
    Streatham Ho., 600
    Streatham Place, 370
Streatlam Castle, Durham, 363
Strelley Hall, Notts., 332
Strenshall, Yorks.
    Bridge, 192
    Manor Ho., 300
Strensham Court, Worcs., 534
Strete, Devon, Ch., 520
Stretford, Lancs., St. Matthew's
    Ch., 408
Stretton, Cheshire, Ch., 387
Stretton Hall, Staffs., 842
Stretton-on-Dunsmore,
    Warwicks., Ch., 691
Strichen, Aberdeens.
    Ho., 761
    Town Ho., 761
Strontian, Argylls., Ch., 820
Strood, Kent, Ch., 232, 744
Stroud, Glos.
    Congregational Ch., 82
    Holy Trinity Ch., 315
    St. Paul's Ch., 315
    Subscription Rooms, 94
    Workhouse, 540
Strowan, Perths., 784
Struan, Perths., Ch., 735
Stubton Hall, Lincs., 961
Studley Castle, Warwicks., 103
Studley Royal, Yorks., 185, 560
Stumperlowe Hall, nr. Sheffield,
    655
Sturminster Newton, Dorset
    Ch., 302
    Workhouse, 857
Styche Hall, Salop., 142, 207
Styford, Northumb., 362

Sudborough, Northants.
    Manor, 663–4
    Vicarage, 820
Sudbourne Hall, Suffolk, 948
Sudbrook Ho., Surrey, 343
Sudbrooke, Lincs., Ch., 266
Sudbrooke Holme, Lincs., 268
Sudbury, Derbys.
    Ch.; mont., 797
    Hall, 332, 636, 841, 886, 900
Sudbury, Suffolk
    Corn Exchange, 488
    Workhouse, 145
Sufton Court, Herefs., 949
Sugley, Northumb., Holy
    Saviour Ch., 363
Sulby Hall, Northants., 508, 769
Sulhamstead Park, Berks., 66
Sunbury, Middlx.
    Ch., 478, 933
    ho., 314
    Sunbury Place, 769
    Sunbury Villa, 671
Sunderland, Durham
    Athenaeum, 112
    bridge (iron), 634
    bridge (stone), 734
    Exchange, 785
    lighthouse, 634
    Nicholson House, 363
    port, 499
    St. Bede's Tower, 363
    St. Mary's Ch. (R.C.), 123
    Warehouses, 265
Sundorn Hall, Salop., 576, 838
Sundridge, Kent
    Ch., 200
    Park, 583, 958
Sunningdale, Berks., Holy Trinity
    Ch., 279
Sunninghill Park, Berks., 951
Sunnyside Ho., Midlothian, 54
Surbiton, Surrey
    St. Raphael's Ch. (R.C.), 620
    Southborough Place, 584
Surrenden-Dering, Kent, 166
Sutton, Surrey, Ch., 666, 773
Sutton Bonington, Notts.,
    Rectory, 777
Sutton Coldfield, Warwicks.
    Ch.; mont., 900
    Langley Hall, 901
    Moat Ho., 901
    Rectory, 749
Sutton Ford Bridge, Essex, 464
Sutton Mallet, Som., Ch., 202
Sutton Park, Beds., 518
Sutton Place, Surrey, 125, 143
Sutton Scarsdale, Derbys., 750
Swaffham, Norfolk
    Assembly Rooms, 589
    ho., 150
    Shirehall, 145
    Workhouse, 271
Swaffham Bulbeck, Cambs.,
    Vicarage, 439
Swaffham Prior, Cambs., St.
    Cyriac's Ch., 438
Swainsthorpe, Norfolk,
    Workhouse, 145
Swainston Ho., I. of W., 653
Swalcliffe, Oxon., Ch., 832
Swallowfield Ho. (Park), Berks.,
    76, 454, 805
Swanage, Dorset
    Baths, 863
    Congregational Chapel, 350
Swanbourne Ho., Bucks., 167

Swannington, Leics., Ch., 542
Swansea, Glam.
    Assembly Rooms, 227
    Countess of Huntingdon's
        Chapel, 460
    Ho. of Correction, 230
    Royal Institution of S. Wales,
        524
    St. John's Ch., 460
    St. Mary's Ch., 915
    Town Hall, 230, 460
Swansfield Ho., Northumb., 267
Swarkestone, Derbys.
    Banqueting Ho., 732
    Bridge, 398, 522
Swarland Hall, Northumb., 190
Sweeney Hall, Salop., 408
Swerford, Oxon.
    Ch., 847
    Ho., 329
Swinburne Castle, Northumb.,
    268
Swindown Ho., Wilts., 666
Swinfen Hall, Staffs., 936
Swinford Bridge, Oxon., 816; inn,
    831
Swinstead, Lincs., 854
Swinton, Lancs., Schools, 811
Swinton Park, Yorks., 194, 315,
    527, 826, 949
Swithland Hall, Leics., 970
Swyncombe, Oxon.
    Ho., 393
    parsonage, 391
Swynnerton, Staffs.
    Hall, 83, 752, 839, 840
    ho., 841
    parsonage, 839
Sydenham, Kent
    Chapel, 898
    cottage, 507
    ho., 807
    Rockhill Ho., 858
    St. Bartholomew's Ch., 857
    School, 869
    villas, 305, 898
Sydenham Ho., Devon, 98
Sydney Lodge, Hants., 769
Syon Ho., Middlx., 52, 246, 275,
    710, 873, 949; boat-ho.,
    577; bridge, 611;
    conservatory, 320; dairy,
    174; entrance-screen, 52,
    466; Evidence Room, 389;
    terrace, 174
Syston New Hall, Lincs., 505, 858

Tabley Ho., Cheshire, 193, 397,
    555
Tai-Bach, Glam., Ch., 406
Tain, Ross
    Academy, 759
    Bank, 68
    Ch., 759
    Town Hall, 759
Talacre Hall, Flints., 398, 476
Tamworth, Staffs.
    Lunatic Asylum, 617
    St. John's Ch. (R.C.), 655
Tannadice, Angus, Manse, 106
Tansley, Derbys., Ch., 540
Tanworth, Warwicks., mont., 70
Taplow, Bucks.
    Ch., 503
    Court, 167
    Ho., 95
    hos., 594, 769
    Lodge, 139, 532

Tarbat, Ross
  farm, 707
  Ho., 533
Tarbolton, Ayrshire, Ch., 467
Tardebigge, Worcs.
  Ch., 419
  parsonage, 246
Tarrington, Herefs., Ch., 662
Tarvit Ho., Fife, 220n.
Tatton Park, Cheshire, 229, 377,
  664, 874, 953, 957
Taunton, Som.
  Holy Trinity Ch., 202
  Hospital, 787
  New Market Hall, 157
  Town Hall, 86
Taverham Hall, Norfolk, 768
Tavistock, Devon
  Abbey Gateway, 319
  Bedford Arms Inn, 319
  Corn Market, 320
  Grammar School, 116
Tawstock Court, Devon, 769
Tayfield Ho., Fife, 754
Taymouth Castle, Perths., 56,
  59, 76, 272, 288, 359, 586,
  624
Tealby, Lincs., Ch., 668
Teasses, Fife, 163
Teddesley Hall, Staffs., 84, 354,
  521, 655, 839
Teddington, Middlx.
  Bushey Villa, 933
  Ch., 898
  Teddington Grove, 207
  Udny Ho., 55
Teeton Hall, Northants., 859
Teffont Ewyas, Wilts., Ch., 320
Tehidy Park, Cornwall, 167, 280,
  285
Teigh, Rutland, Ch., 687
Teignmouth, Devon
  Bitton Grove, 95
  Bridge, 433
  Hennons (The), 364
Temple Balsall, Warwicks.
  Hospital, 440, 746, 751
  Ho., 751
Temple Druid, Pemb., 582
Temple Ho., Berks., 957
Temple Newsham Ho., Yorks.,
  300, 301, 333, 466
Tempsford Bridge, Beds., 721
Tenby, Pembs.
  Laston Ho., 227
  Public Baths, 227
  Sion Ho., 582
  villa, 394
  Woofferton Grange, 582
Tendring Hall, Suffolk, 768
Tenterden, Kent, Workhouse,
  721
Terling, Essex
  Ch., 355
  Place, 435, 463
Tern Aqueduct, Salop., 821
Tern Bridge, Salop., 410
Tern Hall, Salop., 576, 663
Terregles Ho., Kirkcud., 74
Terrick Hall, Salop., 84
Tetbury, Glos.
  Ch., 215, 419, 494, 831
  Market Ho., 494
  White Hart Inn, 859
Tettenhall Wood, Staffs., 692
Teviot Bank, Roxb., 158, 164
Teviot Bridge, Roxb., 289
Tewin Water, Herts., 367, 680n.

Tewkesbury, Glos.
  Abbey Ch., 280, 494
  Holy Trinity Ch., 838
  Market Ho., 280
  Mythe Bridge, 821
Thainston, Aberdeens., 737
Thame, Oxon.
  Ch., 437
  French Ho., 308
  Park, 44, 764
  Prebendal Ho., 437
  Workho. (Rycecote Wood
    College), 896
Thames navigation, 573
Thames Ditton, Surrey, Ch., 143
Thaxted, Essex, Ch., 213, 299,
  463
Theale, Berks., Ch., 156, 330
Theale, Som., Ch., 202
Theberton, Suffolk
  Ch., 234
  lodge, 501
Theddingworth, Leics., cottages,
  103
Theobalds, Herts.
  almshouses, 511
  Palace, 472
Thetford, Norfolk
  bridge, 785
  Workhouse, 827
Thicket Priory, Yorks., 118
Thingwall Hall, Lancs., 291
Thirkleby, Yorks.
  Bridge, 192
  Park, 405, 948
Thirlestane Castle, Berwicks.,
  154, 165, 571
Thirsk Hall, Yorks., 195
Thirsk Mill Bridge, Yorks., 192
Thoresby Ho. (Park), Notts., 88,
  194, 214, 311, 417, 539,
  712, 738, 798, 804–5, 893,
  925
Thornbury Castle, Glos., 364
Thorley, Herts., Ch., 858
Thorncroft, Surrey, 817
Thorndon Hall, Essex, 304, 513,
  611, 957
Thornes, Yorks.
  Ho., 195
  St. James's Ch., 728
Thorney, Cambs.
  Abbey Ch., 119
  Abbey Ho., 526
Thorneyburn, Northumb.
  Ch., 727
  parsonage, 727
Thornham Hall, Suffolk, 972
Thornhill Ho., Dorset, 631, 826
Thornhill Manor Farmho., Wilts.,
  835
Thornton Dale, Yorks., Rectory,
  666
Thornton (Curtis) Hall, Lincs.,
  111
Thornville Royal, Yorks., 642
Thorpe Acre, Leics., Ch., 670
Thorpe Constantine, Staffs.
  Ch., 331
  Hall, 332
Thorpe Hall, Essex, 464, 823
Thorpe Hall, Northants., 552
Thorpe Market, Norfolk, Ch., 907
Thorpe Perrow, Yorks., 315
Thrapston, Northants.
  Rectory, 271
  Workhouse, 271
Thrybergh Park, Yorks., 874

Thundercliffe Grange, Yorks., 641
Thurcaston, Leics., Rectory, 777
Thurland Castle, Lancs., 876, 961
Thurlby, Lincs., ho., 932
Thurmaston, Leics., Vicarage, 622
Thurso, Caithness
  Castle, 164
  Ch., 162
  Washington Mont., 532
Tibbermore, Perths., Manse, 784
Tiberton, Herefs.
  Ch., 910
  Court, 910
Ticehurst, Sussex, Workhouse,
  487
Tickencote, Rutland, Ch., 227
Tickton, Yorks.
  Bridge, 107
  Grange, 701
Tidmarsh Ho., Berks., 282
Tilbury, Essex, fort, 350, 902
Tillery Ho., Aberdeens., 737
Tillicoultry, Clack.
  Ch., 783
  Ho., 296
Tillingbourne, Surrey, 451
Tillington, Sussex, Rectory, 488
Tilstock, Salop., Ch., 406
Timsbury, Som., Ch., 846
Tingrith, Beds., Ch., 906n.
Tinsley, Yorks., Ch., 665
Tinwald Ho., Dumfriess., 58, 220,
  241
Tipton, Staffs.
  St. Martin's Ch., 494
  St. Paul's Ch., 279
Tisbury, Wilts., Ch., 107
Tissington Hall, Derbys., 504
Titanbarrow Logia, nr. Bath, 911
Titchwell, Norfolk, Rectory, 271
Titness Park, Berks., 95
Tiverton, Devon
  Ch., 127–8
  Masonic Hall, 128
  St. George's Chapel, 453
Tixall Hall, Staffs., 74, 84, 446
  (bis), 838, 841, 957; R.C.
  Chapel, 446
Tobermory, Argylls.
  Ch., 820
  Custom Ho., 575
Tockholes, Lancs., St. Stephen's
  Ch., 691
Toddington Manor Ho., Glos.,
  102, 836
Todmorden, Yorks., Christ Ch.,
  857
Toft Hall, Cheshire, 696
Tollimore, Herts., 773
Tolmers, Herts., 773
Tolworth Court Ho., Surrey, 614
Tom a Chaistel, Perths., obelisk,
  783
Tomintoul, Banffs., Ch., 821
Tonbridge, Kent
  Bridge, 574
  Ch., 495
  Lower Bridge, 65
Tong, Lancs., St. Michael's Ch.,
  408
Tong Hall, Yorks., 641, 731
Tongland Bridge, Kirkcud., 586,
  821
Tonley Ho., Aberdeens., 761
Tooting, Surrey
  Bedford Cottage, 621
  St. Nicholas Ch., 75
  Schools, 44

Topsham, Devon, Chapel, 147
Tor Point, Cornwall, Chapel, 280
Torksey, Lincs., Ch., 411
Torquay, Devon
  Ballroom, 319
  Hesketh Crescent, 399
  Higher Terrace, 399
  Market, 399
  Park Crescent, 399
  Park Place, 399
  Rockwood, 399
  St. John's Ch., 515
  Torbay Hotel, 399
  Vaughan Parade, 399
Torrance Ho., Lanarks., 59
Torrie Ho., Fife, 717
Torrile's Hall, Essex, 464
Torrington, Devon
  Ch., 221
  Market Ho., 221
Torrisdale Castle, Argylls., 358
Torteval, Guernsey, Ch., 900
Totnes, Devon, Bridge, 320
Tottenham, Middlx.
  Holy Trinity Ch., 72, 721
  School, 67
Tottenham Park, Wilts., 130, 246
  (bis), 310, 348, 963
Totteridge, Herts.
  Ch., 355
  villa, 60
Totterton Hall, Salop., 187
Tough, Aberdeens.
  Ch., 761
  mausoleum (proposed), 179
Tovil, Kent, Ch., 881
Town Hill Park, Hants., 517
Towneley Hall, Lancs., 125, 962
Townley Hall, Ireland, 645
Trafalgar Ho., Wilts., 684, 912
Tranby Park, Yorks., 446
Tranent, E. Lothian, George
    Stiel's Institution, 160
Traquair Ho., Peebles., 758
Trebartha Hall, Cornwall, 962
Trebursey Ho., Cornwall, 962
Tre-Cefel Bridge, Card., 581
Tredegar, Mon., St. George's
    Ch., 458
Tregenna Castle, Cornwall, 890,
    912
Tregothnan Ho., Cornwall, 859,
    896
Tregrehan Ho₁, Cornwall, 890
Trehill, Devon, ho., 78
Trelissick Ho., Cornwall, 701
Trent Place, Middlx., 208
Trentham, Staffs.
  Bridge, 839
  Ch., 91, 838
  Column, 906
  Hall (Park), 92, 147, 311, 425,
    635, 750, 810, 839, 950
  Mausoleum, 810
Treslothan, Cornwall, Ch., 890
Trevalyn Hall, Denbighs., 476
Trevarno, Cornwall, 890
Trevethin, Mon., St. Thomas's
    Ch., 406
Trewarthenick, Cornwall, 393,
    680n.
Trewhitt Ho., Northumb.,
    267
Trewithen, Cornwall, 114, 138,
    284, 344, 817
Tring, Herts.
  Manor Ho. (Park), 343, 925
  Railway Station, 61

Trowbridge, Wilts.
  Ch., 537
  hos., 302
  parsonage, 308
Trowse, Norfolk, School, 145
Trumisgarry, N. Uist, Ch., 821
Trunch, Norfolk, Rectory, 271
Truro, Cornwall
  Assembly Rooms, 280
  Doric Column, 711
  Prince's Ho., 285
  Prince's St., ho., 285
  St. John's Ch., 711
  St. Mary's Ch., 285, 286
Tulliallan, Fife
  Castle, 76
  Ch., 68
Tullibody Ho., Clack., 296, 784
Tullichewan Castle, Dunb., 527
Tunbridge Wells, Kent
  Baston Cottage, 172
  Baths, 367
  Bellevue, 174
  Blackhurst, 173
  Calverley Estate, 172
  Camden Park, 172n.
  Holy Trinity Ch., 171
  Mount Calverley Lodge, 293
  R.C. Church, 446
  Rustall Common, 907
Tunstall, Staffs., Christ Ch., 104
Tusmore Ho., Oxon, 167, 576
Tutbury, Staffs., Castle, 671–2
Tweedmouth, Northumb.,
    Masonic Lodge, 562
Twerton, Som.
  Ch., 536, 638
  Ho., 254
  Vicarage, 537
Twickenham, Middlx.
  Cambridge Ho., 858
  Carpenters' Almshouses, 651
  Copt Hall, 296
  Cross Deep, 343
  Heath Lane Lodge, 554
  Holy Trinity Ch., 94
  ho. (Briscoe), 575
  ho. (Ogle), 343
  Marble Hill, 109, 136, 413, 561
    706, 957
  National Schools, 94
  Orleans Ho., 296n., 343, 454,
    618
  Pope's Villa, 343, 492
  'Pope's Villa', 487
  St. Mary's Ch., 453
  Spencer Grove, 592
  Twickenham Meadows, 592
  Twickenham Park, 523, 618
  Ulleswater Cottage, 270
  villa (Weld), 858
Twizel Castle, Northumb., 595
Twizell Ho., Northumb., 939
Two Waters, Herts., 883
Twyford Ho., Herts., 858
Twyford, Middlx., Ch., 77
Twyford Abbey, Middlx., 76
Tybberton Court, Herefs., 43
Tyldesley, Lancs., St. George's
    Ch., 744
Tyneholme Ho., E. Lothian, 164
Tynemouth, Northumb.
  Christ Ch., 837
  Collingwood Mont., 265
  Holy Saviour Ch., 363
  Ho. of Correction, 265
  Master Mariners' Asylum,
    362

Tynemouth, Northumb.—contd.
  Priory Ch., 266
  Town Hall, 265
Tyninghame Ho., E. Lothian, 163
Tynron, Dumfriess., Ch., 162
Tyringham Hall, Bucks., 769
Tyttenhanger, Herts., 551, 768

Uckfield, Sussex
  Ch., 563
  Workhouse, 488
Udny, Aberdeens., Ch., 761
Uffington, Berks., Ch., 793
Uffington Ho., Lincs., 932
Ufton Nervet, Berks., Ch., 324
Ugbrooke Park, Devon, 52
Ui, I. of Lewis, Ch., 821
Ullapool, Ross, Ch., 821
Ulva, Argylls., Ch., 820
Ulverston, Lancs.
  Holy Trinity Ch., 971
  Savings Bank, 875
Umberslade Hall, Warwicks., 69,
    182, 749
Underley Hall, Westmld., 875,
    876
Unthank Hall, Northumb., 266
Unerigg, Cumb., 60
Upham, Hants., Rectory, 331
Upleadon, Glos., parsonage, 670
Upleatham, Yorks.
  Ch., 123
  Hall, 196, 744
Upnor Castle, Kent, 705
Uppark, Sussex, 459, 680, 682,
    805; Vandalian Tower, 484
Upper Dicker, Sussex, Holy
    Trinity Ch., 271
Upper Gornal, Staffs., Ch., 280
Upper Hopton, Yorks., Ch., 123
Upper Norwood, Surrey
  All Saints Ch., Beulah Hill,
    666, 720
  hotel, 656
Upper Penn, Staffs., Ch., 84
Upton, Cheshire, Ch., 247
Upton, Oxon., Kit's Quarry Ho.,
    486
Upton, Pemb., villa, 822
Upton Hall, Notts., 270
Upton Ho., Dorset, 630
Upton Ho., Glos., 379
Upton Ho., Kent, 634
Upton Manor, Cheshire, 247
Upton-cum-Chalvey, Bucks., Ch.,
    722
Upton-on-Severn, Worcs., Ch.,
    481, 773, 885
Urie Ho., Kinc., 82, 645
Urrard, Perths., 164
Ushaw, Durham, St. Cuthbert's
    College, 813
Usk Bridge, Mon., 286
Usworth, Durham, Holy Trinity
    Ch., 363
Uttoxeter, Staffs.
  Ch., 840
  Conduit, 331
  ho., 331
  St. Mary's Ch. (R.C.), 970
  Workhouse, 842

Vale Royal, Cheshire, 117
Valence, Kent, 425
Vaynor Park, Montgom., 632
Ven Ho., Som., 173, 447
Ventnor, I. of W., St. Catherine's
    Ch., 279

Viewpark Ho., Lanarks., 82
Virginia Water, Berks. & Surrey,
    229, 312, 713, 963; bridge,
    678, 713; Christ Ch., 650;
    'Clock Case' Tower, 649;
    Glenridge, 650; Schools,
    650
Vyne (The), Hants., 109, 214,
    539, 873

Wadenhoe, Northants., parsonage,
    151
Wadley Ho., Berks., 793
Wadsley, Yorks., Ch., 655
Wadworth Hall, Yorks., 610
Wainfleet All Saints, Lincs., Ch.,
    73
Wainfleet St. Mary, Lincs.,
    School, 387
Wakefield, Yorks.
    All Saints (Parish) Ch., 522,
        564, 767, 868
    Asylum, 110
    Bond Terrace, 112
    Corn Exchange, 441 n.
    Court Ho., 398, 868
    Ho. of Correction, 191
    Library (Museum), 665, 868
    Lunatic Asylum, 665, 868
    Market Cross, 731
    Primitive Methodist Chapel,
        777
    Savings Bank, 112, 564
    St. John's Ch., 431, 522, 868
    St. John's North, 823
    School, 112, 502
    Stafford Arms Hotel, 112
    Wesleyan Methodist Chapel,
        777–8
Wakefield Lodge, Northants.,
    136–7, 493
Walberton Ho., Sussex, 745
Walcot Hall (Park), Salop., 142,
    178n., 207
Walden Bury Ho., Herts., see St.
    Paul's Walden Bury
Waldershare Park, Kent, 140,
    804; Belvedere Tower, 130
Walford Manor, Salop., 407
Walkeringham, Notts., Vicarage,
    840
Walkinshaw Ho., Renfrews., 55
Wallasey, Cheshire
    ho., 304
    New Brighton, villas, 291, 898
    Redcliffe, New Brighton, 291
    St. John's Ch., Egremont, 283
Wallingford, Berks.
    Bridge, 836
    St. Peter's Ch., 816
Wallington Hall, Northumb., 144,
    268, 271, 333, 476, 590,
    933; bridge, 609
Wallington, Surrey, cottage, 557
Wallop Ho., Hants., 200
Wallsend, Northumb., Howden
    Docks, 265
Wallwood Ho., Essex, 329
Walmer, Kent, Walmer Cottage,
    293, 770
Walsall, Staffs.
    Ch., 213, 353
    St. Mary's Ch. (R.C.), 446
    St. Paul's Ch., 354
    St. Peter's Ch., 417
Walsall Wood, Staffs., St. John's
    Ch., 417
Waltham, Essex, Abbey Ch., 506

Waltham Cross, Herts.
    Eleanor Cross, 218
    Holy Trinity Ch., 119
Waltham-on-the-Wolds, Leics.,
    Rectory, 277
Walthamstow, Essex
    Bellevue Ho., 374
    Ch., 80, 461, 536, 767
    Clevelands, 768
    ho., 592
    Monox's Almshouse, 345
    Rectory Manor, 768
    St. Peter's Ch., 730
Walton, Som., Ch., 670
Walton, Staffs., Ch., 842
Walton Hall, Warwicks., 376
Walton Ho., Surrey, 92
Walton-on-the-Hill, Lancs., Ch.,
    142; mont., 693
Walton-on-the-Hill, Surrey, Ch.,
    65n.
Walton-on-the-Naze, Essex, 631
    Kent's Hotel, 631
    pier, 631
Walton-on-Thames, Surrey,
    Bridge, 300, 609
Wamphray, Dumfriess., Ch., 531
Wandsworth, Surrey
    Freemasons' School, 388
    ho., 617
    Lunatic Asylum, 563
    St. Anne's Ch., 744
    St. Peter's Hospital, 798
    West Hill, 345
Wanlip Hall, Leics., 596, 859
Wanstead, Essex
    Ch., 389
    Ho., 184, 489
    Grove, 874
    Orphan Asylum, 814
Wantage, Berks.
    Ch.; mont., 831
    Town Hall, 487
Warborough, Oxon., Ch., 648
Warboys, Hunts.
    Ch., 394n.
    Rectory, 393
Warbrooks Ho., Hants., 454
Wardour Castle, Wilts., 85, 86,
    179, 547, 612, 769, 914
Wareham, Dorset
    Congregational Chapel, 350
    Workhouse, 200
Wareside, Herts., Holy Trinity
    Ch., 763
Waresley, Hunts., Ch., 457
Warfield Hall, Berks., 746
Wargrave Hill (Manor), Berks.,
    965
Wark-on-Tyne, Northumb.
    Ch., 727
    parsonage, 727
Warkworth, Northumb., Ch., 266
Warleigh Ho., Devon, 147, 319
Warleigh Ho., Som., 874
Warley Hall, Worcs., 527, 680
Warley Place, Essex, 327
Warmington, Northants., Ch.,
    203
Warminster, Wilts.
    Christ Ch., 508
    Church St., ho., 348
    School, 285
    Town Hall, 116
Warnford, Hants.
    Park, 508
    Rectory, 305
Warnham Court, Sussex, 394

Warrington, Lancs.
    Bank Hall, 341
    Bluecoat School, 431
    bridge, 397
    Ch.; mont., 693
    Holy Trinity Ch., 547, 690
    Library & Museum, 265
    St. James's Ch., 708
    St. Paul's Ch., 119
    Town Hall, 341
Warter Hall, Yorks., 74, 701
Warwick
    Abbotsford, 752
    Castle, 146, 280, 440, 521, 657
    County Gaol, 235, 465, 466
    Court House, 751
    Great Bridge, 280, 574
    Ho. of Correction, 235
    Independent Chapel, 887
    Joyce Pool Ho., 726
    Judges' Ho., 376
    Landor Ho., 440
    Leafield Bridge, 574
    Market Ho., 440
    St. Mary's Ch., 277, 419, 440,
        752, 787, 901, 926–7;
        Beauchamp Chapel, 277,
        520
    St. Nicholas Ch., 231, 464, 465,
        774
    St. Peter's Chapel, 419
    Shire Hall, 231, 420, 440, 466,
        520, 550
Warwick Bridge, Cumb., Ch., 266
Wasing Ho., Berks., 423
Wassand Hall, Yorks., 245
Waterford, Ireland
    bridge, 643
    Cathedral, 378
    Court Ho. & Gaol, 327
    Custom Ho., 814
    Ho. of Correction, 292
Wateringbury, Kent, Ch., 881
Waterloo, Lancs., Christ Ch., 897
Waterlooville, Hants., Ch., 604
Watermouth Castle, Devon, 890
Waternish, Skye, Ch., 821
Waterstock Ho., Oxon., 228, 602
Watford, Herts., National
    Schools, 365
Wath-upon-Dearne, Yorks.,
    Vicarage, 522, 868
Watlington Hall, Norfolk, 270
Watton Wood Hall, Herts., 516
Waverley Abbey, Surrey, 185
Wavertree, Lancs., Holy Trinity
    Ch., 431
Wayford Manor, Dorset, 70
Weald Bridge, Essex, 464
Weald Hall, Essex, 54
Weald Park, Middlx., 621
Wedderburn Castle, Berwicks.,
    53, 595
Weddington Hall, Warwicks.,
    528
Weeford, Staffs., Ch., 945
Weekley, Northants., Ch., 555
Weem, Perths., Manse, 735
Weeting Hall, Norfolk, 533
Welbeck Abbey, Notts., 193–4,
    287, 442, 455, 456, 538–9,
    574, 680, 764, 774, 806
Welburn, Yorks., bridge, 734
Welcombe Ho., Warwicks., 970
Weldon, Northants.
    ho., 367
    quarries, 367
Welford Park, Berks., 435

Wellesbourne, Warwicks., ho., 465
Wellingborough, Northants., Ch., 98
Wellington, Salop.
  Ch., 780
  Christ Ch., 762
Wellington, Som.
  Ch., 202
  Ch. (R.C.), 80
  Holy Trinity Ch., 202
  Popham's Almshouses, 80
Wellington College, Berks., 730
Wellington Monument, Som., 510
Wells, Som.
  Cathedral, 912; mont., 98
  St. Cuthbert's Ch., mont., 447
  Town Hall, 627
  Workhouse, 860
Wells Court, Worcs., 117
Wells Ho., Ireland, 698
Welton-by-Lincoln, Lincs., Ch., 106
Wells-next-the-Sea, Norfolk, harbour, 573, 574
Welton, Lincs., Ch., 197
Welton-le-Wold, Lincs., Vicarage, 196
Welwyn, Herts., Rectory, 518
Wemyss Castle, Fife, 570, 953
Wemyss Hall, Fife, 154–5
Wendron, Cornwall, parsonage, 890
Wentworth Castle, Yorks., 109, 121, 343, 641, 707, 826, 879
Wentworth Hall, Surrey, 488
Wentworth Woodhouse, Yorks., 110, 193, 311, 344, 641, 796, 843; Brampton Lodge, 193; estate buildings, 664; Hoober Stand, 311; Keppel's Column, 193; Lion Gate, 193; North Lodge, 193; Rainborough Lodge, 193; Rockingham Mausoleum, 193; Stables, 193
Wenvoe Castle, Glam., 54
West Bromwich, Staffs.
  All Saints Ch., 598
  Christ Ch., 354
  St. James's Ch., 280
  St. Michael's Ch. (R.C.), 446
West Coker, Som., Ch., 98, 859
West Cowes, I. of W.
  Ch., 581; mausoleum, 581
  Holy Trinity Ch., 133
  villas, 349, 585, 846
West Dean Park, Sussex, 203, 718–19, 951
West Derby, Lancs.
  ho., 670
  St. James's Ch., 878
West Grinstead Park, Sussex, 584
West Heath School, Kent, 95
West Hill, Surrey, villa, 535
West Hyde, Herts., Ch., 763
West Lodge, Dorset, 639
West Malling, Kent, Ch., 370
West Park, Hants., 274
West Rainton, Durham, Ch., 67
West Rasen, Lincs., Ch., 899
West Retford, Notts., Trinity Hospital, 116
West Teignmouth, Devon, St. James's Ch., 625
West Wickham, Kent, Ch., 882

West Wycombe, Bucks.
  Ch., 77, 253, 684
  Mausoleum, 98
  Park, 269–70, 684
Westacre High Ho., Norfolk, 270
Westbourne, Sussex, Ch., 484
Westbury Court, Glos., 735
Westbury-on-Trym, Glos., Westmead Ho., 631
Wester Bogie Ho., Fife, 359
Wester Duddingston, Midlothian, ho., 480
Wester Elchies Ho., Morays., 699
Wester Ogle, Angus, 644
Westerhall, Dumfriess., 820
Westerkirk, Dumfriess., mausoleum, 55
Westerton Hill, Durham, observatory, 934
Westertown Ho., Morays., 359
Westgate Ho., Norfolk, 640
Westley, Suffolk, Ch., 671
Westmarsh, Kent, Ch., 323
Weston, Hants., 683, 769
Weston, Herts.
  Ch., 763
  Vicarage, 763
Weston, Lincs., mont., 718
Weston, Som.
  Ch., 638; mont., 77
  Newton Bridge, 475
  Partis' College, 606
  St. John's Ch., 536
Weston Beggard, Herefs., Ch., 662
Weston-on-the-Green, Oxon., Vicarage, 107
Weston Ho., Warwicks., 117, 839
Weston-under-Lizard, Staffs.
  Ch.; monts., 900
  Weston Hall (Park), 167, 611, 692, 874, 883
Weston (Longville) Ho., Norfolk, 672
Weston-super-Mare, Som.
  Christ Ch., 537
  Emmanuel Ch., 537
Weston-on-Trent, Staffs., Ch., 842
Weston Underwood, Bucks., 344
Weston Underwood, Derbys., Weston Cottage, 907
Westonbirt, Glos.
  Babdown Farmho., 859
  Down Farm, 859
  Elmstree Farm, 859
  Ho., 859
Westport, Ireland, 938, 947; gateway, 426; marine bath, 700
Westwood Hall, Staffs., 292
Westwood Park, Worcs., 387
Wetherby Grange, Yorks., 190, 948
Weybridge, Surrey
  Chapel (R.C.), 813
  Fir Grove, 619
  Rectory, 271
Weymouth, Dorset
  Holy Trinity Ch., 955
  Masonic Hall, 313
  Monument, 383
  St. Mary's Ch., 383
Whaplode, Lincs., Vicarage, 847
Whaplode Drove, Lincs., Ch., 247, 605, 799
Whatton Hall (Ho.), Leics., 464
Wheatley, Oxon., Ch., 833

Whichcotes, Middlx., 769
Whickham, Durham
  Ch., 265
  ho., 266
Whiligh Ho., Sussex, 858
Whim, Peebles., 46
Whips Cross, Essex
  ho., 174
  villa, 649
Whitburn, Durham
  Ch., 265
  Hall, 268
Whitby, Yorks.
  Bridge, 734
  East Terrace, 265
  Harbour pier, 634
  Town Hall, 634
  West Cliff, 265
Whitchurch, Middlx., St. Lawrence's Ch., 453
Whitchurch, Salop.
  Ch., 88, 752
  St. Catherine's Ch., 406
White Knights, Berks., 227, 617
White Windows, Yorks., 193
Whiteadder Bridge, Berwicks., 678
Whitehaugh, Aberdeens., 762
Whitehaven, Cumb.
  Castle, 53
  Markets, 743
  Trustee Savings Bank, 692
Whitehill Ho., Midlothian, 165, 757
Whiteley Wood Hall, Yorks., 963
Whiteshill, Glos., vicarage, 82
Whitfield Hall, Northumb., 591
Whitford, Flints., Ch., 657; mont., 693
Whitley, Warwicks., bridge, 592
Whitley Abbey, Warwicks., 770
Whitley Beaumont, Yorks., 610
Whitley Park, Surrey, 632
Whitmore Hall, Staffs., 84, 839
Whitson Court, Mon., 582
Whitstable, Kent, parsonage, 218
Whittingham, Northumb., Ch., 363
Whittinghame Ho., E. Lothian, 163, 745
Whittington, Salop., Ch., 397
Whittington Hall, Westmld., 875
Whittlebury Lodge, Northants., 167
Whittle-le-Woods, Lancs., Ch., 691
Whitton Place, Middlx., 207, 343, 344, 561, 562
Whixley, Yorks., school, 265
Whorlton, Durham, bridge, 362
Wibtoft, Warwicks., cross, 277
Wick, Caithness
  Bridge, 821
  Ch., 480
  Chapel (R.C.), 526
Wick, Glos., Ch., 278
Wicken, Northants.
  Ch., 666–7, 716
  Ho., 667
Wickersley, Yorks., Ch., 522
Wickham Court, Kent, 167
Wickham Market, Suffolk, Workhouse, 145
Widcombe, Som.
  Ch., 352
  Cold Bath Ho., 364
  Manor, 475

Widdrington Castle, Northumb., 837
Widford, Essex, bridge, 464
Widley, Hants., villa, 613
Widmerpool, Notts., Ch., 907
Widworthy Court, Devon, 679
Wiganthorpe Hall, Yorks., 196
Wigginton, Staffs.
  Ch., 331
  ho., 937
  Lodge, 953
Wigtoft, Lincs., vicarage, 198, 605
Wigton, Cumb., St. Cuthbert's Ch. (R.C.), 123
Wilbury Ho., Wilts., 108
Wilden, Beds., Ch., 669
Wilderness, Kent, 252
Wilford Hall, Notts., 413, 789
Willen, Bucks., Ch., 431
Willersley Castle, Derbys., 118, 332, 823
Willesden, Middlx., Tattersall's stables, 810
Willey, Salop.
  Ch., mont., 304
  Hall, 954
Williamston Ho., Aberdeens., 322
Williamstrip Park, Glos., 605, 769
Willian, Herts., Vicarage, 439
Willington Bridge, Derbys., 840
Willington Dene railway bridge, Northumb., 362
Willow Hall, Yorks., 868
Willowbank, Aberdeens., 762
Wilsden, Yorks., Ch., 600
Wilsford Hall, Lincs., 609
Wilton, Herefs., ho., 750
Wilton, Roxb., Ch., 289
Wilton, Som., Ch., 202
Wilton, Wilts.
  Ch., mont., 952
  Ho., 206, 256, 296, 474, 872, 950–1
  Palladian Bridge, 415, 562
  St. Mary's Hospital, 116
  The Mount, 313
Wilton Castle, Yorks., 292, 744
Wilton Park, Bucks., 478, 809
Wimbledon, Surrey
  Ch., 463
  Ho. (dem. 1717), 473
  Ho. (Janssen), 184, 355
  Ho. (dem. 1785), 415, 561, 751, 797
  Ho. (Cunliffe/Rush), 53, 464
  Lodge, 441
  Park Ho. (Spencer), 426
  villa, 121
Wimborne Minster, Dorset, Ch., 91, 302
Wimborne (St. Giles) Ho., Dorset, 246, 311, 348
Wimpole, Cambs.
  Ch., 311; monts., 797
  Hall, 237, 311, 343, 488, 769; Gothic Castle, 299, 549; Prospect Ho., 797; Stables, 488, 879
Wincanton, Som.
  Balsam Ho., 447
  Ch., 447
  Hillside Ho., 447
  ho. (Cooper), 631
  Ireson Ho., 447
  'The Dogs', 447
  White Horse Inn, 447

Winchester, Hants.
  Cathedral, 119, 156, 300, 330, 473; mont., 178
  College, 313, 331, 636, 679; Chapel, 178, 299
  Corn Exchange, 200, 500
  County Gaol, 555
  Palace, 178, 294, 486, 714, 791, 923
  Public Library, 200
  St. Cross Hospital, 227, 582
  St. John's Hospital, 331
  St. Maurice's Ch., 355
  St. Peter's Chapel (R.C.), 199
  School, 772
  Wolvesey Palace, 308
Winchmore Hill, Middlx., ho., 273
Windermere, Westmld.
  Belle Isle, 642
  Hotel, 875
Windhill Ho., Herts., 859
Windmill Hill, Sussex, 683
Windlesham, Surrey
  Ch., 279
  Rectory, 279
Windlestone Hall, Durham, 123
Windsor, Berks.
  Castle, 99, 118, 294, 405, 460, 545, 722, 923, 950, 963, 965; Burford Lodge, 208; gateway, 786; Lower Lodge, 208; Queen's Lodge, 208; St. George's Chapel, 293, 714, 796, 912, 926, 945
  Ch., 294, 427
  Church Ho., 268
  Court Ho., 308, 924
  Cumberland Lodge, 714
  Fort Belvedere, 963
  Great Lodge, 714
  Great Park, 855
  Holy Trinity Ch., 119
  hos., 697
  hotel, 445
  Pump Ho., 854
  Railway Station, 828
  Royal Lodge, 584, 963
  villa, 175
  Virginia Water, see Virginia Water
Windsor Forest, Berks.
  Chapel, 652
Winford, Som., Ch., 66–7
Wing, Northants., Rectory, 858
Wingate, Durham, Ch., 449
Wingerworth Hall, Derbys., 84, 752
Wingham, Kent, Chapel, 305
Winksley, Yorks., Ch., 600
Winlaton, Durham, Ch., 123
Winnington Hall, Cheshire, 946, 957
Winsley, Wilts., Ch., 651
Winslade, Hants., Ch., 954
Winslow Hall, Bucks., 87, 925, 964
Winstanley Hall, Lancs., 699, 954
Winster, Derbys., Ch., 375
Winston, Durham
  Bridge, 703
  Ch., 266
Winterborne Clenston, Dorset, Ch., 858
Winterborne Stickland, Dorset, Ch., 96
Winteringham, Lincs., Ch., 321

Winterton, Lincs., Gothic Cottage, 321
Winterton, Norfolk, ho., 284
Winton Ho., E. Lothian, 624
Wintoun Castle, E. Lothian, 862
Winwick, Lancs., Rectory, 394
Wirksworth, Derbys., Moot Hall, 635
Wisbech, Cambs.
  bridge, 169, 727–8
  Castle, 546, 552
  Corn Exchange, 546
  Crescent, 546
  Gaol, 94
  Octagon Chapel, 799
  Rectory, 394
  Session Ho., 879
  Workhouse, 271
Wiscombe Park, Devon, 656
Wishaw Ho., Lanarks., 167, 359
Wistaston, Cheshire, Ch., 506
Wiston Hall, Suffolk, 769
Wiston Park, Sussex, 118, 344
Witham, Essex, All Saints Ch., 145
Witham Friary, Som.
  Park, 52, 344, 806
  Priory Ch., 324
Witham-on-the-Hill, Lincs., Ch., 654
Withyham, Sussex, Ch., 847n.
Withington, Lancs., St. Paul's Ch., 408
Witley Court, Worcs., 312, 583; Chapel, 341
Witney, Oxon., Rectory, 259
Wiveliscombe, Som., Ch., 202
Wivenhoe Park, Essex, 435, 685
Woburn, Beds.
  Abbey, 127, 207, 256, 312, 425, 508, 711, 716, 962
  Birchmore Farm, 426
  Ch., 119
  George Inn, 425
  Market Ho., 116
Woburn Farm, Surrey, 131
Wodehouse (Wode House), Staffs., see Woodhouse
Wokefield Park, Berks., 769
Wollaton Hall, Notts., 764, 789, 961
Wolseley, Staffs.
  Bridge, 678, 841
  Hall, 636, 840
Wolston, Warwicks., Ch., 231
Wolterton Hall, Norfolk, 296, 679, 695
Wolverhampton, Staffs.
  Assembly Rooms, 857
  Ch., 279
  Deanery, 663
  Gifford Ho. Chapel (R.C.), 446
  Grammar School, 750
  Mechanics' Institute, 861
  Race-stand, 857
  Red Lion Inn, 663
  St. George's Ch., 557
  St. John's Ch., 84
  St. Mary's Ch., 670
  St. Paul's Ch., 279
Wolverley, Worcs., Sebright School, 497
Wolverton, Bucks., Ch., 376, 496–7
Wombourne, Staffs.
  Ch., 280
  Wood House, 84, 327, 643
Wonersh Ho., Surrey, 280

Wonham Manor, Surrey, 953
Wood Eaton, Staffs., farmho., 84
Wood Green, Middlx.,
    Fishmongers' Almshouses,
    546
Woodbank, Cheshire, 397
Woodbastwick Hall, Norfolk, 454,
    754
Woodbridge, Suffolk
    Bridewell, 324
    Castle (The), 823
    Seckford Hospital, 224
Woodchester Park, Glos., 244,
    682; garden ho., 788
Woodcote, Oxon., Ch., 847
Woodcote Park, Surrey, 133, 867
Woodeaton Manor, Oxon., 769
Woodford, Essex
    Ch., 80; monts., 702, 815n.
    Hall, 80, 516
    ho., 773
    The Rookery, 527
Woodford Hall (Lodge),
    Northants., 80
Woodhall, Yorks., 584
Woodhall Park, Herts., 516
Woodhays, Surrey, 173
Woodhill Park, Wilts., 605
Woodhorn, Northumb., Ch., 363
Woodhouse, Salop., 576
Woodhouse (Wood House,
    Wodehouse), Staffs., 84,
    327, 643
Woodhouse Eaves, Leics., Ch.,
    669
Woodhouse Farm, Salop., 84
Woodhouse Hill, Yorks., Christ
    Ch., 819
Woodhouse Moor, Yorks., St.
    Mark's Ch., 73
Woodhouselee, Midlothian, 486
Woodland Ho., Glam., 460
Woodlands, Devon, 971
Woodley, Berks., cottages, 715
Woodperry Ho., Oxon., 835
Woodsetts, Yorks., Ch., 442
Woodside, nr. Aberdeen
    Chapel, 736
    Ch. of Scotland, 737
Woodstock, Oxon.
    Ch., 78, 209, 833, 965
    Town Hall, 206
Woolaston, Glos., Ch. 141
Woolbeding, Sussex, 125, 883
Woolcombe Hall, Dorset, 242
Woolhampton Ho., Berks., 859
Woolland Ho., Dorset, 270
Woolley, Som., Ch., 912
Woolley Park, Berks., 961
Woolley Park, Yorks., 665, 868,
    874, 962
Woolmer Lodge, Hants., 701
Woolmers, Herts., 225, 518
Woolsington Hall, Northumb.,
    267
Woolton, Lancs.
    'Druid's Cross', 291
    Hall, 54
    Magdalen Asylum, 723
Woolverstone Hall, Suffolk, 435,
    463; obelisk, 577
Woolwich, Kent
    Arsenal, 77, 854; museum, 581
    Barracks, 555
    Dockyard, 573, 722, 871
    Holy Trinity Ch., 433
    Rectory, 617
    River Wall, 813

Woolwich, Kent—contd.
    Royal Artillery Barracks, 944
    Royal Military Academy, 944
Woore, Salop., Ch., 383
Wootton Court, Kent, 642
Worcester
    All Saints Ch., 773, 884–5
    Barbourne Toll Hos., 230
    Bishop's Palace, 509, 885
    Bridge, 373
    Britannia Ho., 885
    Canal, 573
    Carden St., 526
    Cathedral, 178, 215, 368, 453,
        465, 483, 691, 897; mont.,
        55
    City Gaol, 707
    County Gaol, 176, 481, 719
    Depot of Arms, 230
    Edgar's Tower, 884
    Guildhall, 177, 884
    House of Industry, 177
    Infirmary, 142, 481
    Market Hall, 562
    Methodist Chapel, 707
    Nash's Hospital, 562
    St. Andrew's Ch., 897
    St. Clement's Ch., 510
    St. Helen's Ch., 230
    St. Martin's Ch., 481
    St. Mary's Ch. (R.C.), 707
    St. Nicholas Ch., 465
    St. Peter's Ch., 551
    St. Swithin's Ch., 884, 915
    St. Swithin's Vicarage, 707
    Shire Hall, 255
    Triumphal Arch (1748), 885
    Wick Ho., 177, 634
Worcester Park, Surrey, 585
Wordsley, Staffs.
    Holy Trinity Ch., 857
    Rectory, 859
Workington, Cumb.
    Hall, 195
    St. John's Ch., 390
Worksop Manor, Notts., 44, 611,
    764
Worlingham Hall, Suffolk, 718
Wormington Grange, Glos., 377
Wormleybury, Herts., 54, 576
Worsborough Hall, Yorks., 641,
    665
Worsley Hall, Lancs., 118
Worstead Hall, Norfolk, 949
Worsthorne, Lancs., St. John's
    Ch., 857
Worth, Sussex
    Grove (The), 71
    Park, 173
Worthenbury, Flints., Ch., 841
Worthing, Sussex
    Beach Ho., 674
    Casino, 349
    Clock Tower, 107
    Liverpool Terrace, 235
    Park Crescent, 892
    St. Paul's Ch., 417, 674
    Sea Hotel, 674
    Theatre Royal, 417
Worthy Ho., Hants., 745
Wortley, Yorks.
    Ch., 641
    Hall, 72, 80, 136, 167, 514,
        641
Wotton Ho., Bucks., 550, 770,
    903n.
Wotton Ho., Surrey, 284, 303,
    405

Wotton-under-Edge, Glos., Ch.,
    278; mont., 248
Wragby, Lincs., Ch., 970
Wray Castle, Lancs., 520
Wrecclesham, Surrey, Ch., 386
Wressell Castle, Northumb., 105
Wrest Park, Beds., 219, 365, 368,
    514; Cain Hill Ho., 69;
    Cold Bath, 782;
    Hermitage, 147; Pavilion,
    69, 400; Pavilion
    (Chinese), 207; Silsoe
    Lodges, 365, 763; Theatre,
    782
Wretham Hall, Norfolk, 769
Wrexham, Denbighs.
    Ch., 369, 476; mont., 664
    hos., 631
    Theatre, 631
Wricklemarsh, Kent, 454
Wrockwardine, Salop., Ch., 187
Wrockwardine Wood, Salop.,
    Holy Trinity Ch., 762
Wrotham, Kent
    almshouses, 200
    Park, 866
    Rectory (Court Lodge), 958
Wroxham, Norfolk, mausoleum,
    971
Wroxton Abbey, Oxon., 549, 597,
    869
Wuerdle, Lancs., St. John's Ch.,
    857
Wybunbury, Cheshire, Ch., 84,
    840
Wychbree Bridge, Glam., 286
Wyckhill Ho., Glos., 638
Wycombe Abbey, Bucks., 245,
    951
Wyddial Hall, Herts., 244
Wyke Regis, Dorset, Ch., mont.,
    383
Wylye, Wilts., Rectory, 630
Wynnstay, Denbighs., 147, 179,
    225, 327, 369, 663, 751,
    810, 948, 961
Wynyard Park, Durham, 123,
    519, 955; bridge, 362
Wyreside, Lancs., 55
Wytham Abbey, Berks., 245, 246

Yarmouth, I. of W., Ch., 65
Yarmouth, Norfolk, see Great
    Yarmouth
Yarrow Bridge, Selkirks., 760
Yaxham, Norfolk, Rectory, 528
Yazor, Herefs., Ch., 557
Yeading Bridge, Middlx., 617
Yeadon, Yorks., Ch., 673
Yedmandale, Yorks., 700
Yester Ho., E. Lothian, 46, 54,
    58, 148, 530, 650, 758, 963
Yore Bridge, Yorks., 192
York
    All Saints, Pavement, Ch., 107
    Assembly Rooms, 73, 131, 665,
        868
    Assize Courts, 191
    Bar Convent, 74
    Bootham, no. 47, 192; no. 51,
        72
    Bootham Bar, 701
    Bootham Park Hospital, 191
    Castle, 73
    Castle Museum, 73, 191
    Castle Prison, 701, 861
    Castlegate Ho., 193
    Cavalry Barracks, 461

York—contd.
Cemetery Chapel, 665
Centenary Methodist Chapel, 738
City Gaol, 73
City Wall, 634
Concert Room, 73
Council Chamber, 73
Deanery (old), 610
Deanery, 666
Debtors' Prison, 860
Dispensary, 877
Fairfax Ho., 194
Female Prison, 73, 191
Foss Bridge, 73
Friends' Meeting Ho., 665, 868
Friends' Retreat, 110
Garforth Ho., 193
Guildhall, 73
Ho. of Correction, 73
Knavesmire Race-stand, 190, 608

York—contd.
Lady Hewley's Hospital, 665
Layerthorpe Bridge, 73
Lendal Independent Chapel, 664, 868
Lunatic Asylum, 191
Mansion Ho., 110, 301
Methodist Chapel, New St., 673
Micklegate, no. 54, 193
Minster, 191, 405, 493 (bis), 733, 744; mont., 494
Monk Bridge, 72
Museum, 728, 896
New Residence, 73
Ouse Bridge, 73, 673
Petergate, hos., 193, 300
Pikeing Well-house, 190
St. Andrewgate, no. 20, 74
St. Denys Ch., 634
St. Margaret's Ch., 634
St. Martin-cum-Gregory Ch., 300

York—contd.
St. Mary's Abbey, 728
St. Michael-le-Belfry Ch., 107, 301
St. Peter's School, Clifton, 391
St. Peter's School, Minster Yard, 665, 869
St. Saviour's Ch., 728; mont., 728
Salem Chapel, 665
Savings Bank, 665, 869
Skeldergate, ho., 194
Subscription Library, 73
Theatre Royal, 390
Wesleyan Chapels, 634, 738
Workhouse, 74
Yearsley Bridge, 192
Yorkshire Museum, see Museum
Yoxford, Suffolk, Ch., 696
Ysgeiviog, Flints., Ch., 878

Zetland Ho., Stirlings., 46

II OTHER COUNTRIES

AFRICA
Cape Castle (Gold Coast), 147
AUSTRALIA
Campbellfield, N.S.W., 437
Hobart, Tasmania
Customs Ho., 68
Parliament Ho., 68
Sydney, N.S.W.
Government Ho., 364
Governor's Ho., 118
ho., 439
Hyde Park Barracks, 364
Law Courts, 364
Macquarie Tower, 364
St. James's Ch., 364
AUSTRIA
Vienna, bridge, 669
BELGIUM
Bruges, St. Sauveur's Cathedral, 210
Flushing, 95
La Plante, nr. Namur, 297n.
Ostend, 95
Waterloo, mont., 617
BRAZIL
Quinta da Broa Vista, 467
Rio de Janeiro, English Ch., 467
BRITISH GUIANA
Demerara, ho., 724
CANADA
Charlottetown, 642
Halifax, Admiral's Ho., 643
London, St. Paul's Cathedral, 823
Montreal
Ch., 669
Mansion Ho. Hotel, 649
Nelson Column, 554
Quebec
D'Auteuil St., no. 43, 375
Government Ho., 328
Parliament Ho., 963
Toronto
St. Michael's Cathedral (R.C.), 823
EGYPT
Alexandria
mont., 618
railway station, 618

FRANCE
Cannes
Château Ste-Ursule, 762
Protestant Chapel, 762
Chatou, nr. St. Germain, 296
Choisy, 297n.
Mezières, nr. Orléans, 297
Nice
English Hotel, 762
Protestant Chapel, 762
Paris
British Embassy, 171
St. Denis Ch., 87
GERMANY
Bonn, University, 103
Brunswick, ho., 501
Cannstatt, 616
Gleinicke, 681
Hamburg
St. Nicholas Ch., 75
villa, 546
Heligoland, lighthouse, 65
Herrenhausen, water-works, 108
Meiningen, Ducal palace, 963
Memel, ho., 366
Muskau, 681
Neu Hardenburg, 681
Stuttgart, Protestant Chapel, 762
GIBRALTAR
architect at, 128
Ch., 273
Dockyard, 722
GREECE
Athens, English Ch., 224
Corfu
Cadacchio (temple), 723, 887
Maitland's Mont., 886
Palace, 886
HOLLAND
Amsterdam, club-ho., 422
Bergen-op-Zoom, mont., 455
Hague (The), Nieuwe Kerk, 429
Het Loo, 314
Leiden, no. 19 Rapenberg, 952

INDIA
Calcutta, Government Ho., 939
Lucknow, bridge, 678
Madura, Palace, 217
ITALY
Naples
bridge, 678
Protestant Chapel, 762
Rome
Piazza del Popolo, 395
St. Peter's, sacristy, 124, 395
Vatican museum, 395
MALTA
Dockyard, 722
St. Paul's Cathedral, 722
NEWFOUNDLAND
St. John's
Gaol, 743
Town Hall, etc., 364, 444
PALESTINE
Jerusalem, Anglican Ch. or Cathedral, 374, 418, 461
POLAND
mansion, 456
PORTUGAL
Oporto, Hospital, 191
RUSSIA
Aloupka (Crimea), villa, 118
Bakhtchi-Serai (Crimea), palace, 181
Cronstadt
Cathedral, 181
Naval Base, 181
Ekaterinoslav, 400
Kiev, 400
Monrepos, 810
Moscow
Grand Theatre, 533
town-planning, 400
Pavlovsk, palace, 181–2
St. Petersburg
bridges, 400
British Magazine, 140
railway station, 613
Royal Mint, 427
town-planning, 400
Smolensk, 400
Tomsk, 400
Tsarskoe Selo, palace, 181–2, 400, 547

RUSSIA—*contd.*
 Ukraine, proposed palace,
  398
 Vilna, 400
SOUTH AFRICA
 Greenpoint, villa, 899
SPAIN
 Granada, mont., 617
SWEDEN
 Partille Slot, 208
 Stora Sundby, 701
 Svartsjö, 209
TURKEY
 Istanbul, British Embassy,
  92
UNITED STATES OF AMERICA
 Baltimore
  Cathedral, 507
  Exchange, 507

UNITED STATES OF AMERICA—*contd.*
 Boston, villa, 177
 New Harmony, 886
 New York
  Customs Ho., 707
  ho., 965
  Phoenix Bank, 616
  prison, 400
  sugar-house, 517
 Philadelphia
  Bank of Pennsylvania, 507
  Penitentiary, 400
  Third St., ho., 643
 Raleigh, State Capitol, 626
 Rosewell Ho., Virginia, 662
 Savannah
  Owens-Thomas Ho., 455
  Scarbrough Ho., 455
  Telfair Ho., 455

UNITED STATES OF AMERICA—*contd.*
 Washington
  Arlington Ho., 375
  Assembly Rooms, 375
  Capitol, 375, 507
  City Hall, 375
  U.S. Bank, 375
  Van Ness's Mausoleum, 375
 Williamsburg, William & Mary
  Coll., 924–5
WEST INDIES
 Antigua
  Chapel, 650
  Government Ho., 529
 Bermuda, Dockyard, 722
 Jamaica, St. Andrew's Ch.,
  Halfway Tree, mont.,
  71